2012
U.S. Naval Observatory
Nautical Almanac

The U.S. Naval Observatory &
The United Kingdom
Hydrographic Office

Skyhorse Publishing

Skyhorse Publishing books may be purchased in bulk at special discounts for sales promotion, corporate gifts, fund-raising, or educational purposes. Special editions can also be created to specifications. For details, contact the Special Sales Department, Skyhorse Publishing, 307 West 36th Street, 11th Floor, New York, NY 10018 or info@skyhorsepublishing.com.

Skyhorse® and Skyhorse Publishing® are registered trademarks of Skyhorse Publishing, Inc.®, a Delaware corporation.

Visit our website at www.skyhorsepublishing.com.

10 9 8 7 6 5 4 3 2 1

Library of Congress Cataloging-in-Publication Data is available on file.
ISBN: 978-1-61608-574-2

Printed in the United States of America

THE NAUTICAL ALMANAC 2012

LIST OF CONTENTS

A2 ALTITUDE CORRECTION TABLES 10°-90°—SUN,STARS,PLANETS

OCT.—MAR. **SUN** APR.—SEPT.						**STARS AND PLANETS**			**DIP**			
App. Alt.	Lower Limb	Upper Limb	App. Alt.	Lower Limb	Upper Limb	App Alt.	Corr^n	App. Alt.	Additional Corr^n	Ht. of Eye	Corr^n	Ht. of Eye	Corr^n	Ht. of Eye

OCT.—MAR. SUN			APR.—SEPT.			STARS AND PLANETS		ADD'L		DIP			
° ′	′	′	° ′	′	′	° ′	′	° ′	′	m	′	ft.	m ′
9 33	+10·8	−21·5	9 39	+10·6	−21·2	9 55	−5·3	**2012**		2·4	−2·8	8·0	1·0 − 1·8
9 45	+10·9	−21·4	9 50	+10·7	−21·1	10 07	−5·2	**VENUS**		2·6	−2·9	8·6	1·5 − 2·2
9 56	+11·0	−21·3	10 02	+10·8	−21·0	10 20	−5·1	Jan. 1–Feb. 20		2·8	−3·0	9·2	2·0 − 2·5
10 08	+11·1	−21·2	10 14	+10·9	−20·9	10 32	−5·0	Sept. 20–Dec. 31		3·0	−3·1	9·8	2·5 − 2·8
10 20	+11·2	−21·1	10 27	+11·0	−20·8	10 46	−4·9	° ′		3·2	−3·2	10·5	3·0 − 3·0
10 33	+11·3	−21·0	10 40	+11·1	−20·7	10 59	−4·8	60 +0·1		3·4	−3·3	11·2	See table
10 46	+11·4	−20·9	10 53	+11·2	−20·6	11 14	−4·7			3·6	−3·4	11·9	←
11 00	+11·5	−20·8	11 07	+11·3	−20·5	11 29	−4·6	Feb. 21–Apr. 12		3·8	−3·5	12·6	
11 15	+11·6	−20·7	11 22	+11·4	−20·4	11 44	−4·5	July 31–Sept. 19		4·0	−3·6	13·3	m ′
11 30	+11·7	−20·6	11 37	+11·5	−20·3	12 00	−4·4	° ′		4·3	−3·7	14·1	20 − 7·9
11 45	+11·8	−20·5	11 53	+11·6	−20·2	12 17	−4·3	41 +0·2		4·5	−3·8	14·9	22 − 8·3
12 01	+11·9	−20·4	12 10	+11·7	−20·1	12 35	−4·2	76 +0·1		4·7	−3·9	15·7	24 − 8·6
12 18	+12·0	−20·3	12 27	+11·8	−20·0	12 53	−4·1	Apr. 13–May 4		5·0	−4·0	16·5	26 − 9·0
12 36	+12·1	−20·2	12 45	+11·9	−19·9	13 12	−4·0	July 9–July 30		5·2	−4·1	17·4	28 − 9·3
12 54	+12·2	−20·1	13 04	+12·0	−19·8	13 32	−3·9	° ′		5·5	−4·2	18·3	
13 14	+12·3	−20·0	13 24	+12·1	−19·7	13 53	−3·8	34 +0·3		5·8	−4·3	19·1	30 − 9·6
13 34	+12·4	−19·9	13 44	+12·2	−19·6	14 16	−3·7	60 +0·2		6·1	−4·4	20·1	32 − 10·0
13 55	+12·5	−19·8	14 06	+12·3	−19·5	14 39	−3·6	80 +0·1		6·3	−4·5	21·0	34 − 10·3
14 17	+12·6	−19·7	14 29	+12·4	−19·4	15 03	−3·5	May 5–May 21		6·6	−4·6	22·0	36 − 10·6
14 41	+12·7	−19·6	14 53	+12·5	−19·3	15 29	−3·4	June 22–July 8		6·9	−4·7	22·9	38 − 10·8
15 05	+12·8	−19·5	15 18	+12·6	−19·2	15 56	−3·3	° ′		7·2	−4·8	23·9	
15 31	+12·9	−19·4	15 45	+12·7	−19·1	16 25	−3·2	29 +0·4		7·5	−4·9	24·9	40 − 11·1
15 59	+13·0	−19·3	16 13	+12·8	−19·0	16 55	−3·1	51 +0·3		7·9	−5·0	26·0	42 − 11·4
16 27	+13·1	−19·2	16 43	+12·9	−18·9	17 27	−3·0	68 +0·2		8·2	−5·1	27·1	44 − 11·7
16 58	+13·2	−19·1	17 14	+13·0	−18·8	18 01	−2·9	83 +0·1		8·5	−5·2	28·1	46 − 11·9
17 30	+13·3	−19·0	17 47	+13·1	−18·7	18 37	−2·8	May 22–June 21		8·8	−5·3	29·2	48 − 12·2
18 05	+13·4	−18·9	18 23	+13·2	−18·6	19 16	−2·7	° ′		9·2	−5·4	30·4	ft. ′
18 41	+13·5	−18·8	19 00	+13·3	−18·5	19 56	−2·6	26 +0·5		9·5	−5·5	31·5	2 − 1·4
19 20	+13·6	−18·7	19 41	+13·4	−18·4	20 40	−2·5	46 +0·4		9·9	−5·6	32·7	4 − 1·9
20 02	+13·7	−18·6	20 24	+13·5	−18·3	21 27	−2·4	60 +0·3		10·3	−5·7	33·9	6 − 2·4
20 46	+13·8	−18·5	21 10	+13·6	−18·2	22 17	−2·3	73 +0·2		10·6	−5·8	35·1	8 − 2·7
21 34	+13·9	−18·4	21 59	+13·7	−18·1	23 11	−2·2	84 +0·1		11·0	−5·9	36·3	10 − 3·1
22 25	+14·0	−18·3	22 52	+13·8	−18·0	24 09	−2·1	**MARS**		11·4	−6·0	37·6	See table
23 20	+14·1	−18·2	23 49	+13·9	−17·9	25 12	−2·0	Jan. 1–Jan. 8		11·8	−6·1	38·9	←
24 20	+14·2	−18·1	24 51	+14·0	−17·8	26 20	−1·9	May 6–Dec. 31		12·2	−6·2	40·1	ft. ′
25 24	+14·3	−18·0	25 58	+14·1	−17·7	27 34	−1·8	° ′		12·6	−6·3	41·5	70 − 8·1
26 34	+14·4	−17·9	27 11	+14·2	−17·6	28 54	−1·7	60 +0·1		13·0	−6·4	42·8	75 − 8·4
27 50	+14·5	−17·8	28 31	+14·3	−17·5	30 22	−1·6	Jan. 9–May 5		13·4	−6·5	44·2	80 − 8·7
29 13	+14·6	−17·7	29 58	+14·4	−17·4	31 58	−1·5	° ′		13·8	−6·6	45·5	85 − 8·9
30 44	+14·7	−17·6	31 33	+14·5	−17·3	33 43	−1·4	41 +0·2		14·2	−6·7	46·9	90 − 9·2
32 24	+14·8	−17·5	33 18	+14·6	−17·2	35 38	−1·3	76 +0·1		14·7	−6·8	48·4	95 − 9·5
34 15	+14·9	−17·4	35 15	+14·7	−17·1	37 45	−1·2			15·1	−6·9	49·8	
36 17	+15·0	−17·3	37 24	+14·8	−17·0	40 06	−1·1			15·5	−7·0	51·3	100 − 9·7
38 34	+15·1	−17·2	39 48	+14·9	−16·9	42 42	−1·0			16·0	−7·1	52·8	105 − 9·9
41 06	+15·2	−17·1	42 28	+15·0	−16·8	45 34	−0·9			16·5	−7·2	54·3	110 − 10·2
43 56	+15·3	−17·0	45 29	+15·1	−16·7	48 45	−0·8			16·9	−7·3	55·8	115 − 10·4
47 07	+15·4	−16·9	48 52	+15·2	−16·6	52 16	−0·7			17·4	−7·4	57·4	120 − 10·6
50 43	+15·5	−16·8	52 41	+15·3	−16·5	56 09	−0·6			17·9	−7·5	58·9	125 − 10·8
54 46	+15·6	−16·7	56 59	+15·4	−16·4	60 26	−0·5			18·4	−7·6	60·5	
59 21	+15·7	−16·6	61 50	+15·5	−16·3	65 06	−0·4			18·8	−7·7	62·1	130 − 11·1
64 28	+15·8	−16·5	67 15	+15·6	−16·2	70 09	−0·3			19·3	−7·8	63·8	135 − 11·3
70 10	+15·9	−16·4	73 14	+15·7	−16·1	75 32	−0·2			19·8	−7·9	65·4	140 − 11·5
76 24	+16·0	−16·3	79 42	+15·8	−16·0	81 12	−0·1			20·4	−8·0	67·1	145 − 11·7
83 05	+16·1	−16·2	86 31	+15·9	−15·9	87 03	0·0			20·9	−8·1	68·8	150 − 11·9
90 00			90 00			90 00				21·4		70·5	155 − 12·1

App. Alt. = Apparent altitude = Sextant altitude corrected for index error and dip.

ALTITUDE CORRECTION TABLES 0°-10°—SUN,STARS,PLANETS A3

App. Alt.	OCT.–MAR. SUN Lower Limb	Upper Limb	APR.–SEPT. Lower Limb	Upper Limb	STARS PLANETS	App. Alt.	OCT.–MAR. SUN Lower Limb	Upper Limb	APR.–SEPT. Lower Limb	Upper Limb	STARS PLANETS
° ′	′	′	′	′	′	° ′	′	′	′	′	′
0 00	− 17·5	− 49·8	− 17·8	− 49·6	− 33·8	3 30	+ 3·4	− 28·9	+ 3·1	− 28·7	− 12·9
0 03	16·9	49·2	17·2	49·0	33·2	3 35	3·6	28·7	3·3	28·5	12·7
0 06	16·3	48·6	16·6	48·4	32·6	3 40	3·8	28·5	3·6	28·2	12·5
0 09	15·7	48·0	16·0	47·8	32·0	3 45	4·0	28·3	3·8	28·0	12·3
0 12	15·2	47·5	15·4	47·2	31·5	3 50	4·2	28·1	4·0	27·8	12·1
0 15	14·6	46·9	14·8	46·6	30·9	3 55	4·4	27·9	4·1	27·7	11·9
0 18	− 14·1	− 46·4	− 14·3	− 46·1	− 30·4	4 00	+ 4·6	− 27·7	+ 4·3	− 27·5	− 11·7
0 21	13·5	45·8	13·8	45·6	29·8	4 05	4·8	27·5	4·5	27·3	11·5
0 24	13·0	45·3	13·3	45·1	29·3	4 10	4·9	27·4	4·7	27·1	11·4
0 27	12·5	44·8	12·8	44·6	28·8	4 15	5·1	27·2	4·9	26·9	11·2
0 30	12·0	44·3	12·3	44·1	28·3	4 20	5·3	27·0	5·0	26·8	11·0
0 33	11·6	43·9	11·8	43·6	27·9	4 25	5·4	26·9	5·2	26·6	10·9
0 36	− 11·1	− 43·4	− 11·3	− 43·1	− 27·4	4 30	+ 5·6	− 26·7	+ 5·3	− 26·5	− 10·7
0 39	10·6	42·9	10·9	42·7	26·9	4 35	5·7	26·6	5·5	26·3	10·6
0 42	10·2	42·5	10·5	42·3	26·5	4 40	5·9	26·4	5·6	26·2	10·4
0 45	9·8	42·1	10·0	41·8	26·1	4 45	6·0	26·3	5·8	26·0	10·3
0 48	9·4	41·7	9·6	41·4	25·7	4 50	6·2	26·1	5·9	25·9	10·1
0 51	9·0	41·3	9·2	41·0	25·3	4 55	6·3	26·0	6·1	25·7	10·0
0 54	− 8·6	− 40·9	− 8·8	− 40·6	− 24·9	5 00	+ 6·4	− 25·9	+ 6·2	− 25·6	− 9·8
0 57	8·2	40·5	8·4	40·2	24·5	5 05	6·6	25·7	6·3	25·5	9·7
1 00	7·8	40·1	8·0	39·8	24·1	5 10	6·7	25·6	6·5	25·3	9·6
1 03	7·4	39·7	7·7	39·5	23·7	5 15	6·8	25·5	6·6	25·2	9·5
1 06	7·1	39·4	7·3	39·1	23·4	5 20	7·0	25·3	6·7	25·1	9·3
1 09	6·7	39·0	7·0	38·8	23·0	5 25	7·1	25·2	6·8	25·0	9·2
1 12	− 6·4	− 38·7	− 6·6	− 38·4	− 22·7	5 30	+ 7·2	− 25·1	+ 6·9	− 24·9	− 9·1
1 15	6·0	38·3	6·3	38·1	22·3	5 35	7·3	25·0	7·1	24·7	9·0
1 18	5·7	38·0	6·0	37·8	22·0	5 40	7·4	24·9	7·2	24·6	8·9
1 21	5·4	37·7	5·7	37·5	21·7	5 45	7·5	24·8	7·3	24·5	8·8
1 24	5·1	37·4	5·3	37·1	21·4	5 50	7·6	24·7	7·4	24·4	8·7
1 27	4·8	37·1	5·0	36·8	21·1	5 55	7·7	24·6	7·5	24·3	8·6
1 30	− 4·5	− 36·8	− 4·7	− 36·5	− 20·8	6 00	+ 7·8	− 24·5	+ 7·6	− 24·2	− 8·5
1 35	4·0	36·3	4·3	36·1	20·3	6 10	8·0	24·3	7·8	24·0	8·3
1 40	3·6	35·9	3·8	35·6	19·9	6 20	8·2	24·1	8·0	23·8	8·1
1 45	3·1	35·4	3·4	35·2	19·4	6 30	8·4	23·9	8·2	23·6	7·9
1 50	2·7	35·0	2·9	34·7	19·0	6 40	8·6	23·7	8·3	23·5	7·7
1 55	2·3	34·6	2·5	34·3	18·6	6 50	8·7	23·6	8·5	23·3	7·6
2 00	− 1·9	− 34·2	− 2·1	− 33·9	− 18·2	7 00	+ 8·9	− 23·4	+ 8·7	− 23·1	− 7·4
2 05	1·5	33·8	1·7	33·5	17·8	7 10	9·1	23·2	8·8	23·0	7·2
2 10	1·1	33·4	1·4	33·2	17·4	7 20	9·2	23·1	9·0	22·8	7·1
2 15	0·8	33·1	1·0	32·8	17·1	7 30	9·3	23·0	9·1	22·7	6·9
2 20	0·4	32·7	0·7	32·5	16·7	7 40	9·5	22·8	9·2	22·6	6·8
2 25	− 0·1	32·4	− 0·3	32·1	16·4	7 50	9·6	22·7	9·4	22·4	6·7
2 30	+ 0·2	− 32·1	0·0	− 31·8	− 16·1	8 00	+ 9·7	− 22·6	+ 9·5	− 22·3	− 6·6
2 35	0·5	31·8	+ 0·3	31·5	15·8	8 10	9·9	22·4	9·6	22·2	6·4
2 40	0·8	31·5	0·6	31·2	15·4	8 20	10·0	22·3	9·7	22·1	6·3
2 45	1·1	31·2	0·9	30·9	15·2	8 30	10·1	22·2	9·9	21·9	6·2
2 50	1·4	30·9	1·2	30·6	14·9	8 40	10·2	22·1	10·0	21·8	6·1
2 55	1·7	30·6	1·4	30·4	14·6	8 50	10·3	22·0	10·1	21·7	6·0
3 00	+ 2·0	− 30·3	+ 1·7	− 30·1	− 14·3	9 00	+ 10·4	− 21·9	+ 10·2	− 21·6	− 5·9
3 05	2·2	30·1	2·0	29·8	14·1	9 10	10·5	21·8	10·3	21·5	5·8
3 10	2·5	29·8	2·2	29·6	13·8	9 20	10·6	21·7	10·4	21·4	5·7
3 15	2·7	29·6	2·5	29·3	13·6	9 30	10·7	21·6	10·5	21·3	5·6
3 20	2·9	29·4	2·7	29·1	13·4	9 40	10·8	21·5	10·6	21·2	5·5
3 25	3·2	29·1	2·9	28·9	13·1	9 50	10·9	21·4	10·6	21·2	5·4
3 30	+ 3·4	− 28·9	+ 3·1	− 28·7	− 12·9	10 00	+ 11·0	− 21·3	+ 10·7	− 21·1	− 5·3

Additional corrections for temperature and pressure are given on the following page.

For bubble sextant observations ignore dip and use the star corrections for Sun, planets and stars.

ADDITIONAL REFRACTION CORRECTIONS FOR NON-STANDARD CONDITIONS

The graph plotting Temperature in Fahrenheit (top, −20°F to 100°F) and Temperature in Celsius (bottom, −30°C to 40°C) against Pressure in millibars (left, 970 to 1050) and Pressure in inches (right, 29.0 to 31.0). Diagonal zones are labelled A B C D E F G H J K L M N.

App. Alt.	A	B	C	D	E	F	G	H	J	K	L	M	N	P	App. Alt.
° ′	′	′	′	′	′	′	′	′	′	′	′	′	′	′	° ′
00 00	−7·3	−5·9	−4·6	−3·4	−2·2	−1·1	0·0	+1·0	+2·0	+3·0	+4·0	+4·9	+5·9	+6·9	00 00
00 30	5·5	4·5	3·5	2·6	1·7	0·8	0·0	0·8	1·6	2·3	3·1	3·8	4·5	5·3	00 30
01 00	4·4	3·5	2·8	2·0	1·3	0·7	0·0	0·6	1·2	1·8	2·4	3·0	3·6	4·2	01 00
01 30	3·5	2·9	2·2	1·7	1·1	0·5	0·0	0·5	1·0	1·5	2·0	2·5	2·9	3·4	01 30
02 00	2·9	2·4	1·9	1·4	0·9	0·4	0·0	0·4	0·8	1·3	1·7	2·0	2·4	2·8	02 00
02 30	−2·5	−2·0	−1·6	−1·2	−0·8	−0·4	0·0	+0·4	+0·7	+1·1	+1·4	+1·7	+2·1	+2·4	02 30
03 00	2·1	1·7	1·4	1·0	0·7	0·3	0·0	0·3	0·6	0·9	1·2	1·5	1·8	2·1	03 00
03 30	1·9	1·5	1·2	0·9	0·6	0·3	0·0	0·3	0·5	0·8	1·1	1·3	1·6	1·8	03 30
04 00	1·6	1·3	1·1	0·8	0·5	0·3	0·0	0·2	0·5	0·7	0·9	1·2	1·4	1·6	04 00
04 30	1·5	1·2	0·9	0·7	0·5	0·2	0·0	0·2	0·4	0·6	0·8	1·0	1·3	1·5	04 30
05 00	−1·3	−1·1	−0·9	−0·6	−0·4	−0·2	0·0	+0·2	+0·4	+0·6	+0·8	+0·9	+1·1	+1·3	05 00
06	1·1	0·9	0·7	0·5	0·3	0·2	0·0	0·2	0·3	0·5	0·6	0·8	0·9	1·1	06
07	1·0	0·8	0·6	0·5	0·3	0·1	0·0	0·1	0·3	0·4	0·5	0·7	0·8	0·9	07
08	0·8	0·7	0·5	0·4	0·3	0·1	0·0	0·1	0·2	0·4	0·5	0·6	0·7	0·8	08
09	0·7	0·6	0·5	0·4	0·2	0·1	0·0	0·1	0·2	0·3	0·4	0·5	0·6	0·7	09
10 00	−0·7	−0·5	−0·4	−0·3	−0·2	−0·1	0·0	+0·1	+0·2	+0·3	+0·4	+0·5	+0·6	+0·7	10 00
12	0·6	0·5	0·4	0·3	0·2	0·1	0·0	0·1	0·2	0·2	0·3	0·4	0·5	0·5	12
14	0·5	0·4	0·3	0·2	0·1	0·1	0·0	0·1	0·1	0·2	0·3	0·3	0·4	0·5	14
16	0·4	0·3	0·3	0·2	0·1	0·1	0·0	0·1	0·1	0·2	0·2	0·3	0·3	0·4	16
18	0·4	0·3	0·2	0·2	0·1	−0·1	0·0	+0·1	0·1	0·2	0·2	0·3	0·3	0·4	18
20 00	−0·3	−0·3	−0·2	−0·2	−0·1	0·0	0·0	0·0	+0·1	+0·1	+0·2	+0·2	+0·3	+0·3	20 00
25	0·3	0·2	0·2	0·1	0·1	0·0	0·0	0·0	0·1	0·1	0·1	0·2	0·2	0·2	25
30	0·2	0·2	0·1	0·1	0·1	0·0	0·0	0·0	+0·1	0·1	0·1	0·1	0·2	0·2	30
35	0·2	0·1	0·1	0·1	−0·1	0·0	0·0	0·0	0·0	0·1	0·1	0·1	0·1	0·2	35
40	0·1	0·1	0·1	−0·1	0·0	0·0	0·0	0·0	0·0	+0·1	0·1	0·1	0·1	0·1	40
50 00	−0·1	−0·1	−0·1	0·0	0·0	0·0	0·0	0·0	0·0	0·0	+0·1	+0·1	+0·1	+0·1	50 00

The graph is entered with arguments temperature and pressure to find a zone letter; using as arguments this zone letter and apparent altitude (sextant altitude corrected for index error and dip), a correction is taken from the table. This correction is to be applied to the sextant altitude in addition to the corrections for standard conditions (for the Sun, stars and planets from page A2-A3 and for the Moon from pages xxxiv and xxxv).

RELIGIOUS CALENDARS

Epiphany	Jan. 6	Low Sunday	Apr. 15
Septuagesima Sunday	Feb. 5	Rogation Sunday	May 13
Quinquagesima Sunday	Feb. 19	Ascension Day—Holy Thursday	May 17
Ash Wednesday	Feb. 22	Whit Sunday—Pentecost	May 27
Quadragesima Sunday	Feb. 26	Trinity Sunday	June 3
Palm Sunday	Apr. 1	Corpus Christi	June 7
Good Friday	Apr. 6	First Sunday in Advent	Dec. 2
Easter Day	Apr. 8	Christmas Day (Tuesday)	Dec. 25

First Day of Passover (Pesach)	Apr. 7	Day of Atonement (Yom Kippur)	Sept. 26
Feast of Weeks (Shavuot)	May 27	First day of Tabernacles (Succoth)	Oct. 1
Jewish New Year 5773 (Rosh Hashanah)	Sept. 17		

Ramadân, First day of (tabular)	July 20	Islamic New Year (1434)	Nov. 15

The Jewish and Islamic dates above are tabular dates, which begin at sunset on the previous evening and end at sunset on the date tabulated. In practice, the dates of Islamic fasts and festivals are determined by an actual sighting of the appropriate new moon.

CIVIL CALENDAR—UNITED KINGDOM

Accession of Queen Elizabeth II	Feb. 6	The Queen's Official Birthday†	June 9
St David (Wales)	Mar. 1	Birthday of Prince Philip, Duke of	
Commonwealth Day	Mar. 12	Edinburgh	June 10
St Patrick (Ireland)	Mar. 17	Remembrance Sunday	Nov. 11
Birthday of Queen Elizabeth II	Apr. 21	Birthday of the Prince of Wales	Nov. 14
St George (England)	Apr. 23	St Andrew (Scotland)	Nov. 30
Coronation Day	June 2		

PUBLIC HOLIDAYS

England and Wales—Jan. 2†, Apr. 6, Apr. 9, May 7†, Jun. 4, Jun. 5, Aug. 27, Dec. 25, Dec. 26

Northern Ireland—Jan. 2†, Mar. 19†, Apr. 6, Apr. 9, May 7†, Jun. 4, Jun. 5, Jul. 12†, Aug. 27, Dec. 25, Dec. 26

Scotland—Jan. 2, Jan. 3, Apr. 6, May 7, Jun. 4†, Jun. 5†, Aug. 6, Dec. 25, Dec. 26†

CIVIL CALENDAR—UNITED STATES OF AMERICA

New Year's Day	Jan. 1	Labor Day	Sept. 3
Martin Luther King's Birthday	Jan. 16	Columbus Day	Oct. 8
Washington's Birthday	Feb. 20	General Election Day	Nov. 6
Memorial Day	May 28	Veterans Day	Nov. 11
Independence Day	July 4	Thanksgiving Day	Nov. 22

†Dates subject to confirmation

PHASES OF THE MOON

	New Moon				First Quarter				Full Moon				Last Quarter		
	d	h	m		d	h	m		d	h	m		d	h	m
				Jan.	1	06	15	Jan.	9	07	30	Jan.	16	09	08
Jan.	23	07	39	Jan.	31	04	10	Feb.	7	21	54	Feb.	14	17	04
Feb.	21	22	35	Mar.	1	01	21	Mar.	8	09	39	Mar.	15	01	25
Mar.	22	14	37	Mar.	30	19	41	Apr.	6	19	19	Apr.	13	10	50
Apr.	21	07	18	Apr.	29	09	57	May	6	03	35	May	12	21	47
May	20	23	47	May	28	20	16	June	4	11	12	June	11	10	41
June	19	15	02	June	27	03	30	July	3	18	52	July	11	01	48
July	19	04	24	July	26	08	56	Aug.	2	03	27	Aug.	9	18	55
Aug.	17	15	54	Aug.	24	13	54	Aug.	31	13	58	Sept.	8	13	15
Sept.	16	02	11	Sept.	22	19	41	Sept.	30	03	19	Oct.	8	07	33
Oct.	15	12	03	Oct.	22	03	32	Oct.	29	19	49	Nov.	7	00	36
Nov.	13	22	08	Nov.	20	14	31	Nov.	28	14	46	Dec.	6	15	31
Dec.	13	08	42	Dec.	20	05	19	Dec.	28	10	21				

DAYS OF THE WEEK AND DAYS OF THE YEAR

Day	JAN. Wk Yr	FEB. Wk Yr	MAR. Wk Yr	APR. Wk Yr	MAY Wk Yr	JUNE Wk Yr	JULY Wk Yr	AUG. Wk Yr	SEPT. Wk Yr	OCT. Wk Yr	NOV. Wk Yr	DEC. Wk Yr
1	Su. 1	W. 32	Th. 61	Su. 92	Tu. 122	F. 153	Su. 183	W. 214	Sa. 245	M. 275	Th. 306	Sa. 336
2	M. 2	Th. 33	F. 62	M. 93	W. 123	Sa. 154	M. 184	Th. 215	Su. 246	Tu. 276	F. 307	Su. 337
3	Tu. 3	F. 34	Sa. 63	Tu. 94	Th. 124	Su. 155	Tu. 185	F. 216	M. 247	W. 277	Sa. 308	M. 338
4	W. 4	Sa. 35	Su. 64	W. 95	F. 125	M. 156	W. 186	Sa. 217	Tu. 248	Th. 278	Su. 309	Tu. 339
5	Th. 5	Su. 36	M. 65	Th. 96	Sa. 126	Tu. 157	Th. 187	Su. 218	W. 249	F. 279	M. 310	W. 340
6	F. 6	M. 37	Tu. 66	F. 97	Su. 127	W. 158	F. 188	M. 219	Th. 250	Sa. 280	Tu. 311	Th. 341
7	Sa. 7	Tu. 38	W. 67	Sa. 98	M. 128	Th. 159	Sa. 189	Tu. 220	F. 251	Su. 281	W. 312	F. 342
8	Su. 8	W. 39	Th. 68	Su. 99	Tu. 129	F. 160	Su. 190	W. 221	Sa. 252	M. 282	Th. 313	Sa. 343
9	M. 9	Th. 40	F. 69	M. 100	W. 130	Sa. 161	M. 191	Th. 222	Su. 253	Tu. 283	F. 314	Su. 344
10	Tu. 10	F. 41	Sa. 70	Tu. 101	Th. 131	Su. 162	Tu. 192	F. 223	M. 254	W. 284	Sa. 315	M. 345
11	W. 11	Sa. 42	Su. 71	W. 102	F. 132	M. 163	W. 193	Sa. 224	Tu. 255	Th. 285	Su. 316	Tu. 346
12	Th. 12	Su. 43	M. 72	Th. 103	Sa. 133	Tu. 164	Th. 194	Su. 225	W. 256	F. 286	M. 317	W. 347
13	F. 13	M. 44	Tu. 73	F. 104	Su. 134	W. 165	F. 195	M. 226	Th. 257	Sa. 287	Tu. 318	Th. 348
14	Sa. 14	Tu. 45	W. 74	Sa. 105	M. 135	Th. 166	Sa. 196	Tu. 227	F. 258	Su. 288	W. 319	F. 349
15	Su. 15	W. 46	Th. 75	Su. 106	Tu. 136	F. 167	Su. 197	W. 228	Sa. 259	M. 289	Th. 320	Sa. 350
16	M. 16	Th. 47	F. 76	M. 107	W. 137	Sa. 168	M. 198	Th. 229	Su. 260	Tu. 290	F. 321	Su. 351
17	Tu. 17	F. 48	Sa. 77	Tu. 108	Th. 138	Su. 169	Tu. 199	F. 230	M. 261	W. 291	Sa. 322	M. 352
18	W. 18	Sa. 49	Su. 78	W. 109	F. 139	M. 170	W. 200	Sa. 231	Tu. 262	Th. 292	Su. 323	Tu. 353
19	Th. 19	Su. 50	M. 79	Th. 110	Sa. 140	Tu. 171	Th. 201	Su. 232	W. 263	F. 293	M. 324	W. 354
20	F. 20	M. 51	Tu. 80	F. 111	Su. 141	W. 172	F. 202	M. 233	Th. 264	Sa. 294	Tu. 325	Th. 355
21	Sa. 21	Tu. 52	W. 81	Sa. 112	M. 142	Th. 173	Sa. 203	Tu. 234	F. 265	Su. 295	W. 326	F. 356
22	Su. 22	W. 53	Th. 82	Su. 113	Tu. 143	F. 174	Su. 204	W. 235	Sa. 266	M. 296	Th. 327	Sa. 357
23	M. 23	Th. 54	F. 83	M. 114	W. 144	Sa. 175	M. 205	Th. 236	Su. 267	Tu. 297	F. 328	Su. 358
24	Tu. 24	F. 55	Sa. 84	Tu. 115	Th. 145	Su. 176	Tu. 206	F. 237	M. 268	W. 298	Sa. 329	M. 359
25	W. 25	Sa. 56	Su. 85	W. 116	F. 146	M. 177	W. 207	Sa. 238	Tu. 269	Th. 299	Su. 330	Tu. 360
26	Th. 26	Su. 57	M. 86	Th. 117	Sa. 147	Tu. 178	Th. 208	Su. 239	W. 270	F. 300	M. 331	W. 361
27	F. 27	M. 58	Tu. 87	F. 118	Su. 148	W. 179	F. 209	M. 240	Th. 271	Sa. 301	Tu. 332	Th. 362
28	Sa. 28	Tu. 59	W. 88	Sa. 119	M. 149	Th. 180	Sa. 210	Tu. 241	F. 272	Su. 302	W. 333	F. 363
29	Su. 29	W. 60	Th. 89	Su. 120	Tu. 150	F. 181	Su. 211	W. 242	Sa. 273	M. 303	Th. 334	Sa. 364
30	M. 30		F. 90	M. 121	W. 151	Sa. 182	M. 212	Th. 243	Su. 274	Tu. 304	F. 335	Su. 365
31	Tu. 31		Sa. 91		Th. 152		Tu. 213	F. 244		W. 305		M. 366

ECLIPSES

There are two eclipses of the Sun and one of the Moon.

1. *An annular eclipse of the Sun,* May 20-21. See map on page 6. The eclipse begins on May 20 at 20^h 56^m and ends on May 21 at 02^h 49^m; the annular phase begins on May 20 at 22^h 07^m and ends on May 21 at 01^h 38^m. The maximum duration of the annular phase is 5^m 42^s.

2. *A partial eclipse of the Moon,* June 4. The eclipse begins at 09^h 59^m and ends at 12^h 07^m. The time of maximum eclipse is 11^h 03^m when 0·38 of the Moon's diameter is obscured. It is visible from western and central parts of the Americas, the Pacific Ocean, Antarctica, Australasia, Japan and eastern Asia.

3. *A total eclipse of the Sun,* November 13-14. See map on page 7. The eclipse begins on November 13 at 19^h 38^m and ends on November 14 at 00^h 46^m; the total phase begins on November 13 at 20^h 36^m and ends at 23^h 48^m. The maximum duration of totality is 4^m 06^s.

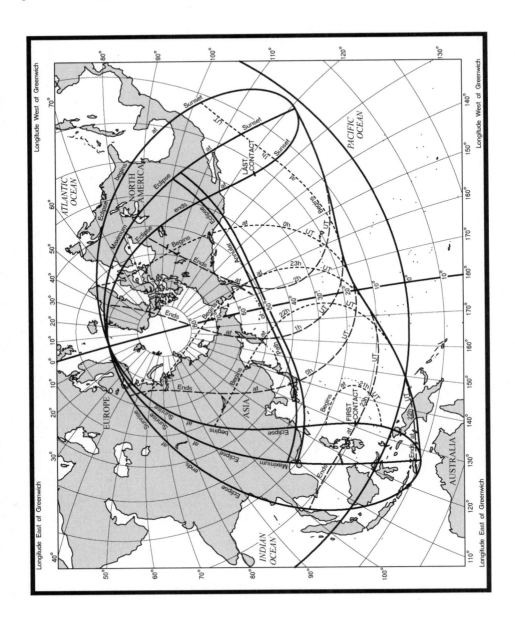

SOLAR ECLIPSE DIAGRAMS

The principal features shown on the above diagrams are: the paths of total and annular eclipses; the northern and southern limits of partial eclipse; the sunrise and sunset curves; dashed lines which show the times of beginning and end of partial eclipse at hourly intervals.

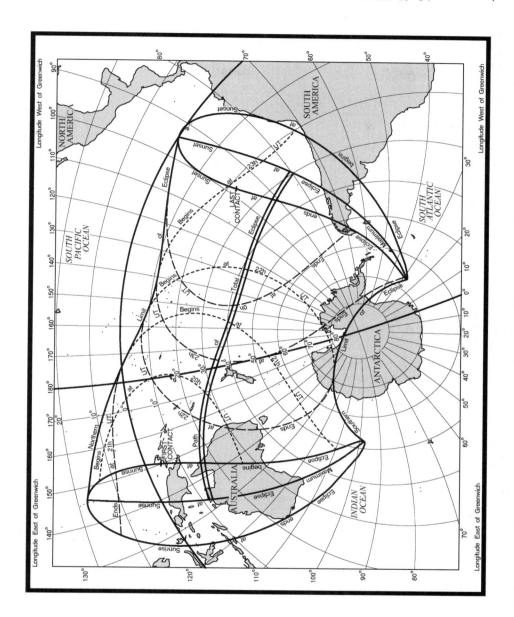

SOLAR ECLIPSE DIAGRAMS

Further details of the paths and times of central eclipse are given in
The Astronomical Almanac.

VISIBILITY OF PLANETS

VENUS is a brilliant object in the evening sky from the beginning of the year until the end of May when it becomes too close to the Sun for observation. From mid-June it reappears in the morning sky where it stays until the end of the year. Venus is in conjunction with Jupiter on March 15 and with Saturn on November 27.

MARS rises shortly before midnight at the beginning of the year in Leo, passing into Virgo in mid-January and into Leo again in early February. It is at opposition on March 3, when it is visible throughout the night as a bright, reddish object. Its eastward elongation gradually decreases and from mid-June until the end of the year it is visible only in the evening sky. In the second half of June it moves again into Virgo (passing 1°.9 N of *Spica* on August 13) until early September, then moving through Libra and into Scorpius from early October and Ophiuchus from mid-October (passing 4° N of *Antares* on October 20). It then continues into Sagittarius from mid-November and into Capricornus in late December. Mars is in conjunction with Saturn on August 17.

JUPITER is in Pisces at the beginning of the year and then moves into Aries during the second week of January. From mid-January it can only be seen in the evening sky until late April when it becomes too close to the Sun for observation. It reappears in the morning sky in Taurus in late May remaining in this constellation for the rest of the year. Its westward elongation gradually increases (passing 5° N of *Aldebaran* on August 3) until it is at opposition on December 3. From early December it continues to be seen for more than half the night (passing 5° N of *Aldebaran* on December 7). Jupiter is in conjunction with Venus on March 15.

SATURN rises shortly after midnight at the beginning of the year in Virgo and remains in this constellation until early December when it moves into Libra for the remainder of the year. Saturn is at opposition on April 15 when it can be seen throughout the night, and from mid-July until early October it is visible only in the evening sky. It then becomes too close to the Sun for observation until mid-November, after which it can be seen in the morning sky for the rest of the year. Saturn is in conjunction with Mars on August 17, with Mercury on October 6 and with Venus on November 27.

MERCURY can only be seen low in the east before sunrise, or low in the west after sunset (about the time of beginning or end of civil twilight). It is visible in the mornings between the following approximate dates: January 1 (−0·4) to January 24 (−0·7), March 29 (+3·0) to May 20 (−1·4), August 6 (+2·6) to September 1 (−1·4) and November 24 (+1·3) to December 31 (−0·6); the planet is brighter at the end of each period. It is visible in the evenings between the following approximate dates: February 19 (−1·3) to March 14 (+1·9), June 4 (−1·4) to July 21 (+3·2) and September 22 (−0·8) to November 12 (+2·0); the planet is brighter at the beginning of each period. The figures in parentheses are the magnitudes.

PLANET DIAGRAM

General Description. The diagram on the opposite page shows, in graphical form for any date during the year, the local mean time of meridian passage of the Sun, of the five planets Mercury, Venus, Mars, Jupiter, and Saturn, and of each 30° of SHA; intermediate lines corresponding to particular stars, may be drawn in by the user if desired. It is intended to provide a general picture of the availability of planets and stars for observation.

On each side of the line marking the time of meridian passage of the Sun a band, 45^m wide, is shaded to indicate that planets and most stars crossing the meridian within 45^m of the Sun are too close to the Sun for observation.

Method of use and interpretation. For any date the diagram provides immediately the local mean times of meridian passage of the Sun, planets and stars, and thus the following information:

(a) whether a planet or star is too close to the Sun for observation;

(b) some indication of its position in the sky, especially during twilight;

(c) the proximity of other planets.

When the meridian passage of an outer planet occurs at midnight the body is in opposition to the Sun and is visible all night; a planet may then be observable during both morning and evening twilights. As the time of meridian passage decreases, the body eventually ceases to be observable in the morning, but its altitude above the eastern horizon at sunset gradually increases; this continues until the body is on the meridian during evening twilight. From then onwards the body is observable above the western horizon and its altitude at sunset gradually decreases; eventually the body becomes too close to the Sun for observation. When the body again becomes visible it is seen low in the east during morning twilight; its altitude at sunrise increases until meridian passage occurs during morning twilight. Then, as the time of meridian passage decreases to 0^h, the body is observable in the west during morning twilight with a gradually decreasing altitude, until it once again reaches opposition.

DO NOT CONFUSE

Venus with Jupiter in mid-March and in late June to early July and with Saturn from late November to early December; on all occasions Venus is the brighter object.

Mars with Saturn in mid-August when Saturn is the brighter object.

Mercury with Saturn in early October when Mercury is the brighter object.

LOCAL MEAN TIME OF MERIDIAN PASSAGE

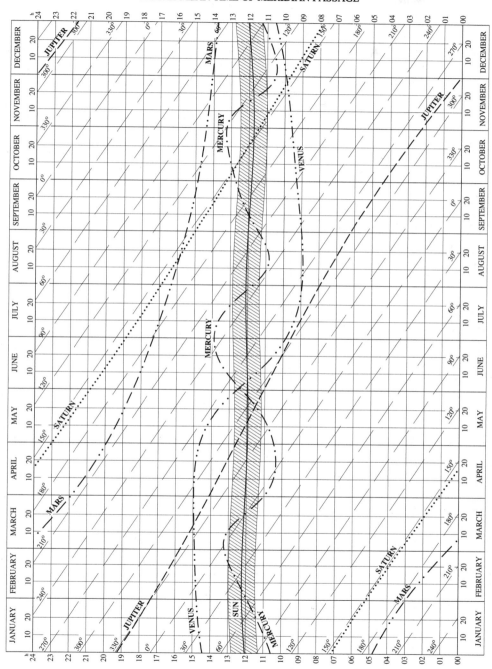

UT	ARIES	VENUS −4.0		MARS +0.2		JUPITER −2.6		SATURN +0.7		STARS		
d h	GHA	GHA	Dec	GHA	Dec	GHA	Dec	GHA	Dec	Name	SHA	Dec
	° ′	° ′	° ′	° ′	° ′	° ′	° ′	° ′	° ′		° ′	° ′
1 00	100 03.9	143 13.3	S18 25.9	287 59.2	N 6 37.2	71 18.3	N10 28.2	252 54.7	S 8 36.2	Acamar	315 18.8	S40 15.6
01	115 06.3	158 12.6	24.9	303 01.1	37.0	86 20.8	28.2	267 57.0	36.2	Achernar	335 27.3	S57 10.8
02	130 08.8	173 12.0	24.0	318 03.0	36.8	101 23.2	28.2	282 59.3	36.3	Acrux	173 10.4	S63 09.7
03	145 11.3	188 11.4	.. 23.1	333 04.9	.. 36.7	116 25.6	.. 28.2	298 01.6	.. 36.3	Adhara	255 12.9	S28 59.4
04	160 13.7	203 10.8	22.2	348 06.8	36.5	131 28.0	28.3	313 03.9	36.4	Aldebaran	290 50.2	N16 32.0
05	175 16.2	218 10.1	21.3	3 08.6	36.3	146 30.4	28.3	328 06.3	36.4			
06	190 18.7	233 09.5	S18 20.4	18 10.5	N 6 36.1	161 32.8	N10 28.3	343 08.6	S 8 36.4	Alioth	166 21.6	N55 53.3
07	205 21.1	248 08.9	19.5	33 12.4	36.0	176 35.3	28.4	358 10.9	36.5	Alkaid	152 59.8	N49 14.9
08	220 23.6	263 08.3	18.6	48 14.3	35.8	191 37.7	28.4	13 13.2	36.5	Al Na'ir	27 45.3	S46 54.2
S 09	235 26.0	278 07.7	.. 17.7	63 16.2	.. 35.6	206 40.1	.. 28.4	28 15.5	.. 36.6	Alnilam	275 47.1	S 1 11.8
U 10	250 28.5	293 07.1	16.7	78 18.1	35.4	221 42.5	28.5	43 17.8	36.6	Alphard	217 56.8	S 8 42.8
N 11	265 31.0	308 06.4	15.8	93 19.9	35.3	236 44.9	28.5	58 20.1	36.7			
D 12	280 33.4	323 05.8	S18 14.9	108 21.8	N 6 35.1	251 47.3	N10 28.5	73 22.4	S 8 36.7	Alphecca	126 12.1	N26 40.3
A 13	295 35.9	338 05.2	14.0	123 23.7	34.9	266 49.8	28.6	88 24.8	36.8	Alpheratz	357 44.6	N29 09.7
Y 14	310 38.4	353 04.6	13.1	138 25.6	34.8	281 52.2	28.6	103 27.1	36.8	Altair	62 09.6	N 8 54.1
15	325 40.8	8 04.0	.. 12.1	153 27.5	.. 34.6	296 54.6	.. 28.6	118 29.4	.. 36.9	Ankaa	353 16.7	S42 14.6
16	340 43.3	23 03.4	11.2	168 29.4	34.4	311 57.0	28.7	133 31.7	36.9	Antares	112 27.8	S26 27.4
17	355 45.8	38 02.7	10.3	183 31.3	34.3	326 59.4	28.7	148 34.0	36.9			
18	10 48.2	53 02.1	S18 09.4	198 33.2	N 6 34.1	342 01.8	N10 28.7	163 36.3	S 8 37.0	Arcturus	145 56.8	N19 07.0
19	25 50.7	68 01.5	08.5	213 35.1	33.9	357 04.2	28.8	178 38.6	37.0	Atria	107 31.1	S69 02.7
20	40 53.2	83 00.9	07.5	228 37.0	33.7	12 06.6	28.8	193 41.0	37.1	Avior	234 17.8	S59 32.9
21	55 55.6	98 00.3	.. 06.6	243 38.9	.. 33.6	27 09.1	.. 28.8	208 43.3	.. 37.1	Bellatrix	278 32.8	N 6 21.5
22	70 58.1	112 59.7	05.7	258 40.8	33.4	42 11.5	28.9	223 45.6	37.2	Betelgeuse	271 02.1	N 7 24.4
23	86 00.5	127 59.1	04.8	273 42.7	33.2	57 13.9	28.9	238 47.9	37.2			
2 00	101 03.0	142 58.5	S18 03.8	288 44.6	N 6 33.1	72 16.3	N10 28.9	253 50.2	S 8 37.3	Canopus	263 56.0	S52 42.3
01	116 05.5	157 57.9	02.9	303 46.5	32.9	87 18.7	29.0	268 52.5	37.3	Capella	280 35.5	N46 00.6
02	131 07.9	172 57.3	02.0	318 48.4	32.7	102 21.1	29.0	283 54.9	37.4	Deneb	49 32.6	N45 19.6
03	146 10.4	187 56.6	.. 01.0	333 50.3	.. 32.6	117 23.5	.. 29.0	298 57.2	.. 37.4	Denebola	182 34.6	N14 30.1
04	161 12.9	202 56.0	18 00.1	348 52.2	32.4	132 25.9	29.1	313 59.5	37.4	Diphda	348 56.9	S17 55.3
05	176 15.3	217 55.4	17 59.2	3 54.1	32.3	147 28.3	29.1	329 01.8	37.5			
06	191 17.8	232 54.8	S17 58.3	18 56.0	N 6 32.1	162 30.7	N10 29.1	344 04.1	S 8 37.5	Dubhe	193 52.6	N61 40.8
07	206 20.3	247 54.2	57.3	33 57.9	31.9	177 33.1	29.2	359 06.4	37.6	Elnath	278 13.5	N28 37.0
08	221 22.7	262 53.6	56.4	48 59.8	31.8	192 35.6	29.2	14 08.7	37.6	Eltanin	90 47.1	N51 29.3
M 09	236 25.2	277 53.0	.. 55.5	64 01.7	.. 31.6	207 38.0	.. 29.2	29 11.1	.. 37.7	Enif	33 48.4	N 9 56.0
O 10	251 27.7	292 52.4	54.5	79 03.6	31.4	222 40.4	29.3	44 13.4	37.7	Fomalhaut	15 25.3	S29 33.6
N 11	266 30.1	307 51.8	53.6	94 05.5	31.3	237 42.8	29.3	59 15.7	37.8			
D 12	281 32.6	322 51.2	S17 52.6	109 07.4	N 6 31.1	252 45.2	N10 29.4	74 18.0	S 8 37.8	Gacrux	172 02.0	S57 10.6
A 13	296 35.0	337 50.6	51.7	124 09.3	30.9	267 47.6	29.4	89 20.3	37.8	Gienah	175 53.3	S17 36.5
Y 14	311 37.5	352 50.0	50.8	139 11.2	30.8	282 50.0	29.4	104 22.6	37.9	Hadar	148 49.6	S60 25.6
15	326 40.0	7 49.4	.. 49.8	154 13.1	.. 30.6	297 52.4	.. 29.4	119 25.0	.. 37.9	Hamal	328 01.8	N23 31.3
16	341 42.4	22 48.8	48.9	169 15.0	30.5	312 54.8	29.5	134 27.3	38.0	Kaus Aust.	83 45.6	S34 22.6
17	356 44.9	37 48.2	47.9	184 16.9	30.3	327 57.2	29.5	149 29.6	38.0			
18	11 47.4	52 47.6	S17 47.0	199 18.9	N 6 30.1	342 59.6	N10 29.6	164 31.9	S 8 38.1	Kochab	137 20.6	N74 06.0
19	26 49.8	67 47.0	46.1	214 20.8	30.0	358 02.0	29.6	179 34.2	38.1	Markab	13 39.5	N15 16.4
20	41 52.3	82 46.4	45.1	229 22.7	29.8	13 04.4	29.6	194 36.6	38.2	Menkar	314 15.9	N 4 08.2
21	56 54.8	97 45.8	.. 44.2	244 24.6	.. 29.7	28 06.8	.. 29.7	209 38.9	.. 38.2	Menkent	148 08.9	S36 25.6
22	71 57.2	112 45.2	43.2	259 26.5	29.5	43 09.2	29.7	224 41.2	38.2	Miaplacidus	221 39.1	S69 45.9
23	86 59.7	127 44.6	42.3	274 28.4	29.3	58 11.6	29.7	239 43.5	38.3			
3 00	102 02.1	142 44.1	S17 41.3	289 30.3	N 6 29.2	73 14.0	N10 29.8	254 45.8	S 8 38.3	Mirfak	308 41.5	N49 54.4
01	117 04.6	157 43.5	40.4	304 32.3	29.0	88 16.4	29.8	269 48.2	38.4	Nunki	75 59.9	S26 16.8
02	132 07.1	172 42.9	39.4	319 34.2	28.9	103 18.8	29.8	284 50.5	38.4	Peacock	53 21.4	S56 41.8
03	147 09.5	187 42.3	.. 38.5	334 36.1	.. 28.7	118 21.2	.. 29.9	299 52.8	.. 38.5	Pollux	243 28.6	N27 59.6
04	162 12.0	202 41.7	37.5	349 38.0	28.6	133 23.6	29.9	314 55.1	38.5	Procyon	245 00.5	N 5 11.5
05	177 14.5	217 41.1	36.6	4 39.9	28.4	148 26.0	30.0	329 57.4	38.5			
06	192 16.9	232 40.5	S17 35.6	19 41.9	N 6 28.3	163 28.4	N10 30.0	344 59.7	S 8 38.6	Rasalhague	96 07.7	N12 33.1
07	207 19.4	247 39.9	34.7	34 43.8	28.1	178 30.8	30.0	0 02.1	38.6	Regulus	207 44.4	N11 54.3
08	222 21.9	262 39.3	33.7	49 45.7	27.9	193 33.2	30.1	15 04.4	38.7	Rigel	281 12.7	S 8 11.4
T 09	237 24.3	277 38.7	.. 32.8	64 47.6	.. 27.8	208 35.6	.. 30.1	30 06.7	.. 38.7	Rigil Kent.	139 53.4	S60 52.8
U 10	252 26.8	292 38.2	31.8	79 49.6	27.6	223 38.0	30.1	45 09.0	38.8	Sabik	102 14.0	S15 44.3
E 11	267 29.3	307 37.6	30.9	94 51.5	27.5	238 40.4	30.2	60 11.3	38.8			
S 12	282 31.7	322 37.0	S17 29.9	109 53.4	N 6 27.3	253 42.8	N10 30.2	75 13.7	S 8 38.8	Schedar	349 41.7	N56 36.6
D 13	297 34.2	337 36.4	28.9	124 55.4	27.2	268 45.2	30.3	90 16.0	38.9	Shaula	96 23.7	S37 06.6
A 14	312 36.6	352 35.8	28.0	139 57.3	27.0	283 47.6	30.3	105 18.3	38.9	Sirius	258 34.2	S16 44.1
Y 15	327 39.1	7 35.2	.. 27.0	154 59.2	.. 26.9	298 50.0	.. 30.3	120 20.6	.. 39.0	Spica	158 32.4	S11 13.5
16	342 41.6	22 34.6	26.1	170 01.1	26.7	313 52.4	30.4	135 23.0	39.0	Suhail	222 52.8	S43 28.9
17	357 44.0	37 34.1	25.1	185 03.1	26.6	328 54.8	30.4	150 25.3	39.1			
18	12 46.5	52 33.5	S17 24.1	200 05.0	N 6 26.4	343 57.2	N10 30.4	165 27.6	S 8 39.1	Vega	80 40.1	N38 47.8
19	27 49.0	67 32.9	23.2	215 06.9	26.3	358 59.6	30.5	180 29.9	39.1	Zuben'ubi	137 06.7	S16 05.5
20	42 51.4	82 32.3	22.2	230 08.9	26.1	14 02.0	30.5	195 32.2	39.2		SHA	Mer. Pass.
21	57 53.9	97 31.7	.. 21.2	245 10.8	.. 26.0	29 04.4	.. 30.6	210 34.5	.. 39.2		° ′	h m
22	72 56.4	112 31.2	20.3	260 12.7	25.8	44 06.8	30.6	225 36.9	39.3	Venus	41 55.5	14 29
23	87 58.8	127 30.6	19.3	275 14.7	25.7	59 09.2	30.6	240 39.2	39.3	Mars	187 41.5	4 44
	h m									Jupiter	331 13.3	19 08
Mer.Pass. 17 13.0		v −0.6 d 0.9		v 1.9 d 0.2		v 2.4 d 0.0		v 2.3 d 0.0		Saturn	152 47.2	7 04

UT	SUN GHA	SUN Dec	MOON GHA	v	MOON Dec	d	HP
d h	° ′	° ′	° ′	′	° ′	′	′
1 00	179 13.7	S23 03.8	95 27.2	15.4	N 7 15.2	10.9	54.5
01	194 13.4	03.6	110 01.6	15.4	7 26.1	10.8	54.5
02	209 13.1	03.4	124 36.0	15.5	7 36.9	10.8	54.5
03	224 12.8	.. 03.2	139 10.5	15.4	7 47.7	10.8	54.5
04	239 12.5	03.0	153 44.9	15.4	7 58.5	10.7	54.4
05	254 12.2	02.8	168 19.3	15.4	8 09.2	10.7	54.4
06	269 11.9	S23 02.6	182 53.7	15.3	N 8 19.9	10.7	54.4
07	284 11.6	02.4	197 28.0	15.4	8 30.6	10.6	54.4
08	299 11.3	02.2	212 02.4	15.3	8 41.2	10.5	54.4
S 09	314 11.0	.. 02.0	226 36.7	15.4	8 51.7	10.6	54.4
U 10	329 10.8	01.8	241 11.1	15.3	9 02.3	10.5	54.4
N 11	344 10.5	01.6	255 45.4	15.3	9 12.8	10.4	54.4
D 12	359 10.2	S23 01.4	270 19.7	15.2	N 9 23.2	10.4	54.4
A 13	14 09.9	01.2	284 53.9	15.3	9 33.6	10.4	54.3
Y 14	29 09.6	01.0	299 28.2	15.2	9 44.0	10.3	54.3
15	44 09.3	.. 00.8	314 02.4	15.2	9 54.3	10.3	54.3
16	59 09.0	00.6	328 36.6	15.2	10 04.6	10.3	54.3
17	74 08.7	00.4	343 10.8	15.2	10 14.9	10.2	54.3
18	89 08.4	S23 00.2	357 45.0	15.1	N10 25.1	10.1	54.3
19	104 08.1	23 00.0	12 19.1	15.2	10 35.2	10.1	54.3
20	119 07.8	22 59.8	26 53.3	15.1	10 45.3	10.1	54.3
21	134 07.5	.. 59.6	41 27.4	15.0	10 55.4	10.0	54.3
22	149 07.2	59.4	56 01.4	15.1	11 05.4	10.0	54.3
23	164 06.9	59.2	70 35.5	15.0	11 15.4	9.9	54.3
2 00	179 06.6	S22 59.0	85 09.5	15.0	N11 25.3	9.9	54.3
01	194 06.3	58.8	99 43.5	15.0	11 35.2	9.8	54.3
02	209 06.0	58.6	114 17.5	14.9	11 45.0	9.8	54.2
03	224 05.7	.. 58.3	128 51.4	14.9	11 54.8	9.8	54.2
04	239 05.4	58.1	143 25.3	14.9	12 04.6	9.6	54.2
05	254 05.2	57.9	157 59.2	14.8	12 14.2	9.7	54.2
06	269 04.9	S22 57.7	172 33.0	14.9	N12 23.9	9.6	54.2
07	284 04.6	57.5	187 06.9	14.7	12 33.5	9.5	54.2
08	299 04.3	57.3	201 40.6	14.8	12 43.0	9.5	54.2
M 09	314 04.0	.. 57.1	216 14.4	14.7	12 52.5	9.4	54.2
O 10	329 03.7	56.8	230 48.1	14.7	13 01.9	9.4	54.2
N 11	344 03.4	56.6	245 21.8	14.6	13 11.3	9.3	54.2
D 12	359 03.1	S22 56.4	259 55.4	14.7	N13 20.6	9.2	54.2
A 13	14 02.8	56.2	274 29.1	14.5	13 29.8	9.3	54.2
Y 14	29 02.5	56.0	289 02.6	14.6	13 39.1	9.1	54.2
15	44 02.2	.. 55.7	303 36.2	14.5	13 48.2	9.1	54.2
16	59 01.9	55.5	318 09.7	14.4	13 57.3	9.0	54.2
17	74 01.6	55.3	332 43.1	14.5	14 06.3	9.0	54.2
18	89 01.4	S22 55.1	347 16.6	14.3	N14 15.3	8.9	54.2
19	104 01.1	54.8	1 49.9	14.4	14 24.2	8.9	54.2
20	119 00.8	54.6	16 23.3	14.3	14 33.1	8.8	54.2
21	134 00.5	.. 54.4	30 56.6	14.3	14 41.9	8.7	54.2
22	149 00.2	54.2	45 29.9	14.2	14 50.6	8.7	54.2
23	163 59.9	53.9	60 03.1	14.2	14 59.3	8.6	54.2
3 00	178 59.6	S22 53.7	74 36.3	14.1	N15 07.9	8.6	54.2
01	193 59.3	53.5	89 09.4	14.1	15 16.5	8.5	54.2
02	208 59.0	53.3	103 42.5	14.1	15 25.0	8.4	54.2
03	223 58.7	.. 53.0	118 15.6	14.0	15 33.4	8.4	54.2
04	238 58.4	52.8	132 48.6	13.9	15 41.8	8.3	54.2
05	253 58.2	52.6	147 21.5	13.9	15 50.1	8.2	54.2
06	268 57.9	S22 52.3	161 54.4	13.9	N15 58.3	8.2	54.2
07	283 57.6	52.1	176 27.3	13.8	16 06.5	8.1	54.2
08	298 57.3	51.9	191 00.1	13.8	16 14.6	8.1	54.2
T 09	313 57.0	.. 51.6	205 32.9	13.8	16 22.7	7.9	54.2
U 10	328 56.7	51.4	220 05.7	13.7	16 30.6	7.9	54.2
E 11	343 56.4	51.2	234 38.4	13.6	16 38.5	7.9	54.2
S 12	358 56.1	S22 50.9	249 11.0	13.6	N16 46.4	7.7	54.2
D 13	13 55.8	50.7	263 43.6	13.5	16 54.1	7.7	54.2
A 14	28 55.6	50.4	278 16.1	13.5	17 01.8	7.7	54.2
Y 15	43 55.3	.. 50.2	292 48.6	13.5	17 09.5	7.5	54.2
16	58 55.0	50.0	307 21.1	13.4	17 17.0	7.5	54.3
17	73 54.7	49.7	321 53.5	13.3	17 24.5	7.4	54.3
18	88 54.5	S22 49.5	336 25.8	13.3	N17 31.9	7.3	54.3
19	103 54.1	49.2	350 58.1	13.3	17 39.2	7.3	54.3
20	118 53.8	49.0	5 30.4	13.2	17 46.5	7.2	54.3
21	133 53.5	.. 48.7	20 02.6	13.1	17 53.7	7.1	54.3
22	148 53.3	48.5	34 34.7	13.1	18 00.8	7.0	54.3
23	163 53.0	48.2	49 06.8	13.0	N18 07.8	7.0	54.3
	SD 16.3	d 0.2	SD 14.8		14.8		14.8

Twilight, Sunrise and Moonrise

Lat.	Twilight Naut.	Twilight Civil	Sunrise	Moonrise 1	2	3	4
°	h m	h m	h m	h m	h m	h m	h m
N 72	08 23	10 41	■	09 59	09 37	09 02	☐
N 70	08 05	09 49	■	10 13	10 00	09 44	09 12
68	07 50	09 16	■	10 24	10 18	10 12	10 05
66	07 37	08 53	10 27	10 33	10 33	10 34	10 38
64	07 26	08 34	09 49	10 40	10 45	10 51	11 02
62	07 17	08 18	09 23	10 47	10 55	11 06	11 21
60	07 09	08 05	09 02	10 52	11 04	11 18	11 37
N 58	07 02	07 54	08 45	10 58	11 11	11 28	11 50
56	06 56	07 44	08 31	11 02	11 18	11 38	12 02
54	06 50	07 35	08 19	11 06	11 24	11 46	12 12
52	06 44	07 28	08 08	11 10	11 30	11 53	12 21
50	06 39	07 20	07 58	11 13	11 35	12 00	12 29
45	06 28	07 05	07 38	11 21	11 46	12 14	12 47
N 40	06 18	06 52	07 22	11 27	11 55	12 26	13 01
35	06 08	06 40	07 08	11 32	12 03	12 36	13 13
30	06 00	06 30	06 56	11 37	12 09	12 45	13 24
20	05 44	06 11	06 35	11 45	12 21	13 00	13 42
N 10	05 28	05 54	06 17	11 52	12 32	13 14	13 58
0	05 11	05 38	06 00	11 59	12 42	13 26	14 13
S 10	04 53	05 20	05 43	12 06	12 52	13 39	14 28
20	04 31	05 00	05 24	12 13	13 03	13 53	14 44
30	04 04	04 35	05 03	12 22	13 15	14 08	15 02
35	03 44	04 20	04 50	12 27	13 22	14 18	15 13
40	03 21	04 03	04 35	12 32	13 30	14 28	15 26
45	02 52	03 41	04 18	12 39	13 40	14 40	15 41
S 50	02 08	03 12	03 56	12 47	13 51	14 56	15 59
52	01 42	02 57	03 45	12 50	13 57	15 03	16 07
54	01 02	02 40	03 33	12 54	14 03	15 11	16 17
56	////	02 19	03 19	12 59	14 09	15 19	16 28
58	////	01 51	03 03	13 04	14 17	15 29	16 40
S 60	////	01 07	02 44	13 10	14 25	15 41	16 55

Sunset, Twilight and Moonset

Lat.	Sunset	Twilight Civil	Twilight Naut.	Moonset 1	2	3	4
°	h m	h m	h m	h m	h m	h m	h m
N 72	■	13 27	15 45	01 14	03 05	05 12	☐
N 70	■	14 19	16 03	01 03	02 44	04 32	06 38
68	■	14 52	16 18	00 54	02 27	04 04	05 46
66	13 41	15 15	16 31	00 46	02 14	03 43	05 14
64	14 19	15 34	16 41	00 40	02 03	03 27	04 50
62	14 45	15 49	16 51	00 35	01 54	03 13	04 32
60	15 06	16 02	16 59	00 30	01 46	03 02	04 16
N 58	15 23	16 14	17 06	00 26	01 39	02 52	04 03
56	15 37	16 24	17 12	00 22	01 33	02 43	03 52
54	15 49	16 32	17 18	00 19	01 27	02 35	03 42
52	16 00	16 40	17 24	00 16	01 22	02 28	03 34
50	16 09	16 47	17 29	00 13	01 18	02 22	03 26
45	16 29	17 03	17 40	00 07	01 08	02 09	03 09
N 40	16 46	17 16	17 50	00 02	01 00	01 58	02 56
35	17 00	17 28	17 59	24 53	00 53	01 49	02 44
30	17 12	17 38	18 08	24 47	00 47	01 41	02 34
20	17 32	17 56	18 24	24 37	00 37	01 27	02 17
N 10	17 50	18 13	18 40	24 28	00 28	01 14	02 02
0	18 08	18 30	18 56	24 20	00 20	01 03	01 48
S 10	18 25	18 48	19 15	24 11	00 11	00 52	01 34
20	18 43	19 08	19 37	24 02	00 02	00 40	01 20
30	19 05	19 32	20 05	23 52	24 26	00 26	01 03
35	19 17	19 47	20 23	23 46	24 18	00 18	00 53
40	19 32	20 05	20 46	23 39	24 09	00 09	00 42
45	19 50	20 27	21 15	23 32	23 58	24 28	00 28
S 50	20 11	20 55	21 59	23 22	23 46	24 12	00 12
52	20 22	21 10	22 25	23 18	23 40	24 05	00 05
54	20 34	21 27	23 03	23 14	23 33	23 57	24 26
56	20 48	21 48	////	23 08	23 26	23 47	24 15
58	21 04	22 16	////	23 03	23 18	23 37	24 02
S 60	21 23	22 58	////	22 56	23 09	23 25	23 47

SUN and MOON

Day	Eqn. of Time 00h	Eqn. of Time 12h	Mer. Pass.	Mer. Pass. Upper	Mer. Pass. Lower	Age	Phase
d	m s	m s	h m	h m	h m	d	%
1	03 05	03 19	12 03	18 09	05 48	08	52
2	03 33	03 47	12 04	18 52	06 31	09	62
3	04 01	04 15	12 04	19 37	07 15	10	71

2012 JANUARY 4, 5, 6 (WED., THURS., FRI.)

UT	ARIES GHA	VENUS −4.0 GHA	Dec	MARS +0.1 GHA	Dec	JUPITER −2.5 GHA	Dec	SATURN +0.7 GHA	Dec	STARS Name	SHA	Dec
4 00	103 01.3	142 30.0	S17 18.3	290 16.6	N 6 25.5	74 11.6	N10 30.7	255 41.5	S 8 39.4	Acamar	315 18.9	S40 15.6
01	118 03.8	157 29.4	17.4	305 18.6	25.4	89 14.0	30.7	270 43.9	39.4	Achernar	335 27.4	S57 10.8
02	133 06.2	172 28.9	16.4	320 20.5	25.2	104 16.4	30.8	285 46.2	39.4	Acrux	173 10.3	S63 09.8
03	148 08.7	187 28.3	.. 15.4	335 22.4	.. 25.1	119 18.8	.. 30.8	300 48.5	.. 39.5	Adhara	255 12.9	S28 59.5
04	163 11.1	202 27.7	14.5	350 24.4	24.9	134 21.1	30.8	315 50.8	39.5	Aldebaran	290 50.2	N16 32.0
05	178 13.6	217 27.1	13.5	5 26.3	24.8	149 23.5	30.9	330 53.1	39.6			
W 06	193 16.1	232 26.6	S17 12.5	20 28.3	N 6 24.6	164 25.9	N10 30.9	345 55.5	S 8 39.6	Alioth	166 21.5	N55 53.3
E 07	208 18.5	247 26.0	11.6	35 30.2	24.5	179 28.3	31.0	0 57.8	39.6	Alkaid	152 59.8	N49 14.9
D 08	223 21.0	262 25.4	10.6	50 32.2	24.3	194 30.7	31.0	16 00.1	39.7	Al Na'ir	27 45.3	S46 54.2
N 09	238 23.5	277 24.8	.. 09.6	65 34.1	.. 24.2	209 33.1	.. 31.0	31 02.4	.. 39.7	Alnilam	275 47.1	S 1 11.8
E 10	253 25.9	292 24.3	08.6	80 36.0	24.0	224 35.5	31.1	46 04.8	39.8	Alphard	217 56.8	S 8 42.8
S 11	268 28.4	307 23.7	07.7	95 38.0	23.9	239 37.9	31.1	61 07.1	39.8			
D 12	283 30.9	322 23.1	S17 06.7	110 39.9	N 6 23.8	254 40.3	N10 31.2	76 09.4	S 8 39.9	Alphecca	126 12.1	N26 40.3
A 13	298 33.3	337 22.5	05.7	125 41.9	23.6	269 42.7	31.2	91 11.7	39.9	Alpheratz	357 44.6	N29 09.6
Y 14	313 35.8	352 22.0	04.7	140 43.8	23.5	284 45.1	31.2	106 14.1	39.9	Altair	62 09.6	N 8 54.1
15	328 38.2	7 21.4	.. 03.8	155 45.8	.. 23.3	299 47.4	.. 31.3	121 16.4	.. 40.0	Ankaa	353 16.7	S42 14.6
16	343 40.7	22 20.8	02.8	170 47.7	23.2	314 49.8	31.3	136 18.7	40.0	Antares	112 27.8	S26 27.4
17	358 43.2	37 20.3	01.8	185 49.7	23.0	329 52.2	31.4	151 21.0	40.1			
18	13 45.6	52 19.7	S17 00.8	200 51.7	N 6 22.9	344 54.6	N10 31.4	166 23.4	S 8 40.1	Arcturus	145 56.8	N19 07.0
19	28 48.1	67 19.1	16 59.8	215 53.6	22.8	359 57.0	31.5	181 25.7	40.1	Atria	107 31.1	S69 02.7
20	43 50.6	82 18.6	58.8	230 55.6	22.6	14 59.4	31.5	196 28.0	40.2	Avior	234 17.8	S59 32.9
21	58 53.0	97 18.0	.. 57.9	245 57.5	.. 22.5	30 01.8	.. 31.5	211 30.3	.. 40.2	Bellatrix	278 32.8	N 6 21.5
22	73 55.5	112 17.4	56.9	260 59.5	22.3	45 04.2	31.6	226 32.7	40.3	Betelgeuse	271 02.1	N 7 24.4
23	88 58.0	127 16.9	55.9	276 01.4	22.2	60 06.5	31.6	241 35.0	40.3			
5 00	104 00.4	142 16.3	S16 54.9	291 03.4	N 6 22.1	75 08.9	N10 31.7	256 37.3	S 8 40.4	Canopus	263 56.0	S52 42.3
01	119 02.9	157 15.8	53.9	306 05.3	21.9	90 11.3	31.7	271 39.6	40.4	Capella	280 35.5	N46 00.6
02	134 05.4	172 15.2	52.9	321 07.3	21.8	105 13.7	31.7	286 42.0	40.4	Deneb	49 32.6	N45 19.6
03	149 07.8	187 14.6	.. 51.9	336 09.3	.. 21.6	120 16.1	.. 31.8	301 44.3	.. 40.5	Denebola	182 34.6	N14 30.1
04	164 10.3	202 14.1	51.0	351 11.2	21.5	135 18.5	31.8	316 46.6	40.5	Diphda	348 56.9	S17 55.3
05	179 12.7	217 13.5	50.0	6 13.2	21.4	150 20.8	31.9	331 48.9	40.6			
T 06	194 15.2	232 13.0	S16 49.0	21 15.2	N 6 21.2	165 23.2	N10 31.9	346 51.3	S 8 40.6	Dubhe	193 52.6	N61 40.8
H 07	209 17.7	247 12.4	48.0	36 17.1	21.1	180 25.6	32.0	1 53.6	40.6	Elnath	278 13.5	N28 37.0
U 08	224 20.1	262 11.8	47.0	51 19.1	21.0	195 28.0	32.0	16 55.9	40.7	Eltanin	90 47.1	N51 29.2
R 09	239 22.6	277 11.3	.. 46.0	66 21.1	.. 20.8	210 30.4	.. 32.0	31 58.3	.. 40.7	Enif	33 48.4	N 9 56.0
S 10	254 25.1	292 10.7	45.0	81 23.0	20.7	225 32.8	32.1	47 00.6	40.8	Fomalhaut	15 25.3	S29 33.6
D 11	269 27.5	307 10.2	44.0	96 25.0	20.5	240 35.1	32.1	62 02.9	40.8			
A 12	284 30.0	322 09.6	S16 43.0	111 27.0	N 6 20.4	255 37.5	N10 32.2	77 05.2	S 8 40.8	Gacrux	172 02.0	S57 10.7
Y 13	299 32.5	337 09.1	42.0	126 28.9	20.3	270 39.9	32.2	92 07.6	40.9	Gienah	175 53.3	S17 36.6
14	314 34.9	352 08.5	41.0	141 30.9	20.1	285 42.3	32.3	107 09.9	40.9	Hadar	148 49.6	S60 25.6
15	329 37.4	7 08.0	.. 40.0	156 32.9	.. 20.0	300 44.7	.. 32.3	122 12.2	.. 41.0	Hamal	328 01.8	N23 31.3
16	344 39.9	22 07.4	39.0	171 34.8	19.9	315 47.1	32.4	137 14.5	41.0	Kaus Aust.	83 45.6	S34 22.6
17	359 42.3	37 06.9	38.0	186 36.8	19.7	330 49.4	32.4	152 16.9	41.0			
18	14 44.8	52 06.3	S16 37.0	201 38.8	N 6 19.6	345 51.8	N10 32.5	167 19.2	S 8 41.1	Kochab	137 20.5	N74 06.0
19	29 47.2	67 05.7	36.0	216 40.8	19.5	0 54.2	32.5	182 21.5	41.1	Markab	13 39.5	N15 16.4
20	44 49.7	82 05.2	35.0	231 42.7	19.3	15 56.6	32.5	197 23.9	41.2	Menkar	314 15.9	N 4 08.2
21	59 52.2	97 04.6	.. 34.0	246 44.7	.. 19.2	30 58.9	.. 32.6	212 26.2	.. 41.2	Menkent	148 08.9	S36 25.6
22	74 54.6	112 04.1	33.0	261 46.7	19.1	46 01.3	32.6	227 28.5	41.2	Miaplacidus	221 39.1	S69 46.0
23	89 57.1	127 03.6	32.0	276 48.7	18.9	61 03.7	32.7	242 30.9	41.3			
6 00	104 59.6	142 03.0	S16 31.0	291 50.7	N 6 18.8	76 06.1	N10 32.7	257 33.2	S 8 41.3	Mirfak	308 41.5	N49 54.4
01	120 02.0	157 02.5	30.0	306 52.6	18.7	91 08.5	32.8	272 35.5	41.4	Nunki	75 59.9	S26 16.8
02	135 04.5	172 01.9	29.0	321 54.6	18.6	106 10.8	32.8	287 37.8	41.4	Peacock	53 21.4	S56 41.8
03	150 07.0	187 01.4	.. 28.0	336 56.6	.. 18.4	121 13.2	.. 32.9	302 40.2	.. 41.4	Pollux	243 28.6	N27 59.6
04	165 09.4	202 00.8	27.0	351 58.6	18.3	136 15.6	32.9	317 42.5	41.5	Procyon	245 00.4	N 5 11.5
05	180 11.9	217 00.3	26.0	7 00.6	18.2	151 18.0	32.9	332 44.8	41.5			
06	195 14.4	231 59.7	S16 25.0	22 02.5	N 6 18.0	166 20.3	N10 33.0	347 47.2	S 8 41.5	Rasalhague	96 07.7	N12 33.1
07	210 16.8	246 59.2	24.0	37 04.5	17.9	181 22.7	33.0	2 49.5	41.6	Regulus	207 44.4	N11 54.3
08	225 19.3	261 58.6	23.0	52 06.5	17.8	196 25.1	33.1	17 51.8	41.6	Rigel	281 12.7	S 8 11.4
F 09	240 21.7	276 58.1	.. 21.9	67 08.5	.. 17.7	211 27.5	.. 33.1	32 54.2	.. 41.7	Rigil Kent.	139 53.4	S60 52.8
R 10	255 24.2	291 57.6	20.9	82 10.5	17.5	226 29.8	33.2	47 56.5	41.7	Sabik	102 14.0	S15 44.3
I 11	270 26.7	306 57.0	19.9	97 12.5	17.4	241 32.2	33.2	62 58.8	41.7			
D 12	285 29.1	321 56.5	S16 18.9	112 14.5	N 6 17.3	256 34.6	N10 33.3	78 01.1	S 8 41.8	Schedar	349 41.7	N56 36.6
A 13	300 31.6	336 55.9	17.9	127 16.5	17.2	271 37.0	33.3	93 03.5	41.8	Shaula	96 23.7	S37 06.6
Y 14	315 34.1	351 55.4	16.9	142 18.5	17.0	286 39.3	33.4	108 05.8	41.9	Sirius	258 34.2	S16 44.1
15	330 36.5	6 54.9	.. 15.9	157 20.4	.. 16.9	301 41.7	.. 33.4	123 08.1	.. 41.9	Spica	158 32.4	S11 13.5
16	345 39.0	21 54.3	14.8	172 22.4	16.8	316 44.1	33.5	138 10.5	41.9	Suhail	222 52.8	S43 28.9
17	0 41.5	36 53.8	13.8	187 24.4	16.7	331 46.5	33.5	153 12.8	42.0			
18	15 43.9	51 53.3	S16 12.8	202 26.4	N 6 16.5	346 48.8	N10 33.6	168 15.1	S 8 42.0	Vega	80 40.1	N38 47.8
19	30 46.4	66 52.7	11.8	217 28.4	16.4	1 51.2	33.6	183 17.5	42.0	Zuben'ubi	137 06.7	S16 05.5
20	45 48.9	81 52.2	10.8	232 30.4	16.3	16 53.6	33.6	198 19.8	42.1		SHA	Mer. Pass.
21	60 51.3	96 51.6	.. 09.8	247 32.4	.. 16.2	31 55.9	.. 33.7	213 22.1	.. 42.1	Venus	38 15.9	14 31
22	75 53.8	111 51.1	08.7	262 34.4	16.0	46 58.3	33.7	228 24.5	42.2	Mars	187 03.0	4 35
23	90 56.2	126 50.6	07.7	277 36.4	15.9	62 00.7	33.8	243 26.8	42.2	Jupiter	331 08.5	18 56
Mer. Pass. 17 01.2		v −0.6	d 1.0	v 2.0	d 0.1	v 2.4	d 0.0	v 2.3	d 0.0	Saturn	152 36.9	6 52

UT	SUN GHA	SUN Dec	MOON GHA	v	Dec	d	HP
d h	° '	° '	° '	'	° '	'	'
4 00	178 52.7	S22 48.0	63 38.8	13.0	N18 14.8	6.8	54.3
01	193 52.4	47.8	78 10.8	13.0	18 21.6	6.8	54.3
02	208 52.1	47.5	92 42.8	12.9	18 28.4	6.8	54.3
03	223 51.8 ..	47.3	107 14.7	12.8	18 35.2	6.6	54.3
04	238 51.5	47.0	121 46.5	12.8	18 41.8	6.6	54.3
05	253 51.3	46.8	136 18.3	12.7	18 48.4	6.5	54.3
06	268 51.0	S22 46.5	150 50.0	12.7	N18 54.9	6.4	54.4
W 07	283 50.7	46.3	165 21.7	12.6	19 01.3	6.3	54.4
E 08	298 50.4	46.0	179 53.3	12.6	19 07.6	6.2	54.4
D 09	313 50.1 ..	45.7	194 24.9	12.5	19 13.8	6.2	54.4
N 10	328 49.8	45.5	208 56.4	12.5	19 20.0	6.0	54.4
E 11	343 49.5	45.2	223 27.9	12.4	19 26.0	6.0	54.4
S 12	358 49.3	S22 45.0	237 59.3	12.4	N19 32.0	5.9	54.4
D 13	13 49.0	44.7	252 30.7	12.3	19 37.9	5.8	54.4
A 14	28 48.7	44.5	267 02.0	12.2	19 43.7	5.7	54.4
Y 15	43 48.4 ..	44.2	281 33.2	12.2	19 49.4	5.7	54.5
16	58 48.1	43.9	296 04.4	12.2	19 55.1	5.5	54.5
17	73 47.8	43.7	310 35.6	12.1	20 00.6	5.5	54.5
18	88 47.6	S22 43.4	325 06.7	12.0	N20 06.1	5.3	54.5
19	103 47.3	43.2	339 37.7	12.0	20 11.4	5.3	54.5
20	118 47.0	42.9	354 08.7	12.0	20 16.7	5.2	54.5
21	133 46.7 ..	42.6	8 39.7	11.8	20 21.9	5.1	54.5
22	148 46.4	42.4	23 10.5	11.9	20 27.0	5.0	54.5
23	163 46.1	42.1	37 41.4	11.7	20 32.0	4.9	54.6
5 00	178 45.9	S22 41.8	52 12.1	11.8	N20 36.9	4.8	54.6
01	193 45.6	41.6	66 42.9	11.7	20 41.7	4.8	54.6
02	208 45.3	41.3	81 13.6	11.6	20 46.5	4.6	54.6
03	223 45.0 ..	41.0	95 44.2	11.5	20 51.1	4.5	54.6
04	238 44.7	40.8	110 14.7	11.6	20 55.6	4.5	54.6
05	253 44.5	40.5	124 45.3	11.4	21 00.1	4.3	54.6
06	268 44.2	S22 40.2	139 15.7	11.4	N21 04.4	4.3	54.7
T 07	283 43.9	40.0	153 46.1	11.4	21 08.7	4.1	54.7
H 08	298 43.6	39.7	168 16.5	11.3	21 12.8	4.0	54.7
U 09	313 43.3 ..	39.4	182 46.8	11.3	21 16.8	4.0	54.7
R 10	328 43.1	39.1	197 17.1	11.2	21 20.8	3.8	54.7
S 11	343 42.8	38.9	211 47.3	11.2	21 24.6	3.8	54.7
D 12	358 42.5	S22 38.6	226 17.5	11.1	N21 28.4	3.6	54.7
A 13	13 42.2	38.3	240 47.6	11.1	21 32.0	3.6	54.8
Y 14	28 41.9	38.0	255 17.7	11.0	21 35.6	3.4	54.8
15	43 41.7 ..	37.8	269 47.7	10.9	21 39.0	3.4	54.8
16	58 41.4	37.5	284 17.6	11.0	21 42.4	3.2	54.8
17	73 41.1	37.2	298 47.6	10.8	21 45.6	3.2	54.8
18	88 40.8	S22 36.9	313 17.4	10.9	N21 48.8	3.0	54.8
19	103 40.5	36.6	327 47.3	10.8	21 51.8	2.9	54.9
20	118 40.3	36.4	342 17.1	10.7	21 54.7	2.8	54.9
21	133 40.0 ..	36.1	356 46.8	10.7	21 57.5	2.8	54.9
22	148 39.7	35.8	11 16.5	10.6	22 00.3	2.6	54.9
23	163 39.4	35.5	25 46.1	10.6	22 02.9	2.5	54.9
6 00	178 39.1	S22 35.2	40 15.7	10.6	N22 05.4	2.4	55.0
01	193 38.9	34.9	54 45.3	10.5	22 07.8	2.2	55.0
02	208 38.6	34.6	69 14.8	10.5	22 10.0	2.2	55.0
03	223 38.3 ..	34.4	83 44.3	10.4	22 12.2	2.1	55.0
04	238 38.0	34.1	98 13.7	10.4	22 14.3	2.0	55.0
05	253 37.8	33.8	112 43.1	10.3	22 16.3	1.8	55.0
06	268 37.5	S22 33.5	127 12.4	10.4	N22 18.1	1.7	55.1
07	283 37.2	33.2	141 41.8	10.2	22 19.8	1.7	55.1
08	298 36.9	32.9	156 11.0	10.3	22 21.5	1.5	55.1
F 09	313 36.7 ..	32.6	170 40.3	10.1	22 23.0	1.4	55.1
R 10	328 36.4	32.3	185 09.4	10.2	22 24.4	1.3	55.1
I 11	343 36.1	32.0	199 38.6	10.1	22 25.7	1.2	55.2
D 12	358 35.8	S22 31.7	214 07.7	10.1	N22 26.9	1.0	55.2
A 13	13 35.6	31.5	228 36.8	10.0	22 27.9	1.0	55.2
Y 14	28 35.3	31.2	243 05.8	10.1	22 28.9	0.8	55.2
15	43 35.0 ..	30.9	257 34.9	9.9	22 29.7	0.7	55.2
16	58 34.7	30.6	272 03.8	10.0	22 30.4	0.6	55.3
17	73 34.5	30.3	286 32.8	9.9	22 31.0	0.5	55.3
18	88 34.2	S22 30.0	301 01.7	9.9	N22 31.5	0.4	55.3
19	103 33.9	29.7	315 30.6	9.8	22 31.9	0.3	55.3
20	118 33.6	29.4	329 59.4	9.9	22 32.2	0.1	55.3
21	133 33.4 ..	29.1	344 28.3	9.8	22 32.3	0.1	55.4
22	148 33.1	28.8	358 57.1	9.7	22 32.4	0.1	55.4
23	163 32.8	28.5	13 25.8	9.8	N22 32.3	0.2	55.4
	SD 16.3 d 0.3		SD 14.8		14.9		15.0

Twilight / Sunrise / Moonrise

Lat.	Naut.	Civil	Sunrise	4	5	6	7
°	h m	h m	h m	h m	h m	h m	h m
N 72	08 20	10 32	■■■	□	□	□	□
N 70	08 02	09 44	■■■	09 12	□	□	□
68	07 47	09 13	11 34	10 05	09 54	□	□
66	07 35	08 50	10 21	10 38	10 48	11 13	□
64	07 25	08 32	09 45	11 02	11 21	11 54	12 07
62	07 16	08 17	09 20	11 21	11 45	12 22	12 48
60	07 08	08 04	09 00	11 37	12 04	12 43	13 16
N 58	07 01	07 53	08 44	11 50	12 20	13 01	13 37
56	06 55	07 44	08 30	12 02	12 34	13 16	13 55
54	06 49	07 35	08 18	12 12	12 46	13 29	14 10
52	06 44	07 27	08 07	12 21	12 56	13 40	14 22
50	06 39	07 20	07 58	12 29	13 06	13 50	14 33
45	06 28	07 05	07 38	12 47	13 25	14 11	14 43
N 40	06 18	06 52	07 22	13 01	13 41	14 28	15 21
35	06 09	06 41	07 08	13 13	13 55	14 42	15 35
30	06 01	06 30	06 57	13 24	14 07	14 55	15 47
20	05 45	06 12	06 36	13 42	14 27	15 16	16 09
N 10	05 29	05 56	06 18	13 58	14 45	15 35	16 27
0	05 13	05 39	06 01	14 13	15 01	15 52	16 44
S 10	04 55	05 22	05 44	14 28	15 18	16 09	17 01
20	04 33	05 02	05 26	14 44	15 36	16 28	17 19
30	04 05	04 38	05 05	15 02	15 56	16 49	17 40
35	03 47	04 23	04 52	15 13	16 08	17 02	17 53
40	03 24	04 05	04 38	15 26	16 22	17 16	18 07
45	02 55	03 44	04 21	15 41	16 39	17 34	18 24
S 50	02 13	03 15	03 59	15 59	16 59	17 55	18 44
52	01 48	03 01	03 49	16 07	17 09	18 05	18 54
54	01 11	02 44	03 37	16 17	17 20	18 17	19 05
56	////	02 24	03 23	16 28	17 32	18 30	19 18
58	////	01 57	03 08	16 40	17 47	18 45	19 32
S 60	////	01 17	02 49	16 55	18 04	19 03	19 50

Sunset / Twilight / Moonset

Lat.	Sunset	Civil	Naut.	4	5	6	7
°	h m	h m	h m	h m	h m	h m	h m
N 72	■■■	13 39	15 51	□	□	□	□
N 70	■■■	14 27	16 09	06 38	□	□	□
68	12 37	14 58	16 23	05 46	07 37	□	□
66	13 50	15 21	16 35	05 14	06 43	08 03	□
64	14 27	15 39	16 46	04 50	06 11	07 22	08 15
62	14 51	15 54	16 54	04 32	05 47	06 54	07 47
60	15 11	16 06	17 02	04 16	05 28	06 32	07 25
N 58	15 27	16 17	17 09	04 03	05 12	06 15	07 08
56	15 41	16 27	17 16	03 52	04 59	06 00	06 53
54	15 53	16 36	17 21	03 42	04 47	05 47	06 40
52	16 03	16 43	17 27	03 34	04 37	05 36	06 29
50	16 13	16 50	17 32	03 26	04 28	05 26	06 19
45	16 32	17 06	17 43	03 09	04 09	05 05	05 58
N 40	16 48	17 19	17 53	02 56	03 53	04 49	05 41
35	17 02	17 30	18 01	02 44	03 40	04 34	05 27
30	17 14	17 40	18 10	02 34	03 28	04 22	05 14
20	17 34	17 58	18 25	02 17	03 09	04 01	04 53
N 10	17 52	18 15	18 41	02 02	02 52	03 43	04 34
0	18 09	18 31	18 57	01 48	02 36	03 25	04 17
S 10	18 26	18 49	19 16	01 34	02 20	03 08	03 59
20	18 44	19 08	19 37	01 20	02 03	02 50	03 41
30	19 05	19 32	20 05	01 03	01 44	02 29	03 19
35	19 18	19 47	20 23	00 53	01 32	02 17	03 07
40	19 32	20 05	20 45	00 42	01 19	02 03	02 52
45	19 49	20 26	21 14	00 28	01 04	01 46	02 35
S 50	20 11	20 54	21 57	00 12	00 45	01 25	02 14
52	20 21	21 08	22 21	00 05	00 36	01 15	02 04
54	20 33	21 25	22 57	24 26	00 26	01 04	01 52
56	20 46	21 45	////	24 15	00 15	00 51	01 39
58	21 02	22 12	////	24 02	00 02	00 37	01 24
S 60	21 21	22 51	////	23 47	24 20	00 20	01 06

SUN / MOON

Day	Eqn. of Time 00ʰ	Eqn. of Time 12ʰ	Mer. Pass.	Mer. Pass. Upper	Mer. Pass. Lower	Age	Phase
d	m s	m s	h m	h m	h m	d	%
4	04 29	04 42	12 05	20 24	08 00	11	79
5	04 56	05 09	12 05	21 13	08 49	12	86
6	05 23	05 36	12 06	22 04	09 39	13	92

14   2012 JANUARY 7, 8, 9 (SAT., SUN., MON.)

UT	ARIES GHA	VENUS −4.0 GHA	Dec	MARS +0.0 GHA	Dec	JUPITER −2.5 GHA	Dec	SATURN +0.7 GHA	Dec	STARS Name	SHA	Dec
SATURDAY 7												
00	105 58.7	141 50.0	S16 06.7	292 38.4	N 6 15.8	77 03.0	N10 33.8	258 29.1	S 8 42.2	Acamar	315 18.9	S40 15.6
01	121 01.2	156 49.5	05.7	307 40.4	15.7	92 05.4	33.9	273 31.5	42.3	Achernar	335 27.4	S57 10.8
02	136 03.6	171 49.0	04.6	322 42.4	15.6	107 07.8	33.9	288 33.8	42.3	Acrux	173 10.3	S63 09.8
03	151 06.1	186 48.5	.. 03.6	337 44.4	.. 15.4	122 10.2	.. 34.0	303 36.1	.. 42.4	Adhara	255 12.9	S28 59.5
04	166 08.6	201 47.9	02.6	352 46.4	15.3	137 12.5	34.0	318 38.5	42.4	Aldebaran	290 50.2	N16 32.0
05	181 11.0	216 47.4	01.6	7 48.4	15.2	152 14.9	34.1	333 40.8	42.4			
06	196 13.5	231 46.9	S16 00.5	22 50.4	N 6 15.1	167 17.3	N10 34.1	348 43.1	S 8 42.5	Alioth	166 21.5	N55 53.3
07	211 16.0	246 46.3	15 59.5	37 52.5	15.0	182 19.6	34.2	3 45.5	42.5	Alkaid	152 59.8	N49 14.9
08	226 18.4	261 45.8	58.5	52 54.5	14.8	197 22.0	34.2	18 47.8	42.5	Al Na'ir	27 45.3	S46 54.2
09	241 20.9	276 45.3	.. 57.5	67 56.5	.. 14.7	212 24.4	.. 34.3	33 50.1	.. 42.6	Alnilam	275 47.1	S 1 11.8
10	256 23.3	291 44.8	56.4	82 58.5	14.6	227 26.7	34.3	48 52.5	42.6	Alphard	217 56.8	S 8 42.8
11	271 25.8	306 44.2	55.4	98 00.5	14.5	242 29.1	34.4	63 54.8	42.7			
12	286 28.3	321 43.7	S15 54.4	113 02.5	N 6 14.4	257 31.5	N10 34.4	78 57.1	S 8 42.7	Alphecca	126 12.1	N26 40.3
13	301 30.7	336 43.2	53.3	128 04.5	14.3	272 33.8	34.5	93 59.5	42.7	Alpheratz	357 44.6	N29 09.6
14	316 33.2	351 42.7	52.3	143 06.5	14.1	287 36.2	34.5	109 01.8	42.8	Altair	62 09.5	N 8 54.1
15	331 35.7	6 42.1	.. 51.3	158 08.5	.. 14.0	302 38.6	.. 34.6	124 04.2	.. 42.8	Ankaa	353 16.7	S42 14.6
16	346 38.1	21 41.6	50.2	173 10.6	13.9	317 40.9	34.6	139 06.5	42.8	Antares	112 27.8	S26 27.4
17	1 40.6	36 41.1	49.2	188 12.6	13.8	332 43.3	34.7	154 08.8	42.9			
18	16 43.1	51 40.6	S15 48.2	203 14.6	N 6 13.7	347 45.6	N10 34.7	169 11.2	S 8 42.9	Arcturus	145 56.7	N19 07.0
19	31 45.5	66 40.0	47.1	218 16.6	13.6	2 48.0	34.8	184 13.5	42.9	Atria	107 31.0	S69 02.7
20	46 48.0	81 39.5	46.1	233 18.6	13.5	17 50.4	34.8	199 15.8	43.0	Avior	234 17.8	S59 32.9
21	61 50.5	96 39.0	.. 45.1	248 20.6	.. 13.4	32 52.7	.. 34.9	214 18.2	.. 43.0	Bellatrix	278 32.8	N 6 21.5
22	76 52.9	111 38.5	44.0	263 22.7	13.2	47 55.1	34.9	229 20.5	43.1	Betelgeuse	271 02.0	N 7 24.4
23	91 55.4	126 38.0	43.0	278 24.7	13.1	62 57.5	35.0	244 22.8	43.1			
SUNDAY 8												
00	106 57.8	141 37.5	S15 41.9	293 26.7	N 6 13.0	77 59.8	N10 35.0	259 25.2	S 8 43.1	Canopus	263 56.0	S52 42.3
01	122 00.3	156 36.9	40.9	308 28.7	12.9	93 02.2	35.1	274 27.5	43.2	Capella	280 35.5	N46 00.6
02	137 02.8	171 36.4	39.9	323 30.8	12.8	108 04.5	35.1	289 29.9	43.2	Deneb	49 32.6	N45 19.6
03	152 05.2	186 35.9	.. 38.8	338 32.8	.. 12.7	123 06.9	.. 35.2	304 32.2	.. 43.2	Denebola	182 34.6	N14 30.1
04	167 07.7	201 35.4	37.8	353 34.8	12.6	138 09.3	35.2	319 34.5	43.3	Diphda	348 56.9	S17 55.3
05	182 10.2	216 34.9	36.7	8 36.8	12.5	153 11.6	35.3	334 36.9	43.3			
06	197 12.6	231 34.4	S15 35.7	23 38.9	N 6 12.4	168 14.0	N10 35.3	349 39.2	S 8 43.3	Dubhe	193 52.5	N61 40.8
07	212 15.1	246 33.8	34.6	38 40.9	12.2	183 16.3	35.4	4 41.5	43.4	Elnath	278 13.5	N28 37.0
08	227 17.6	261 33.3	33.6	53 42.9	12.1	198 18.7	35.4	19 43.9	43.4	Eltanin	90 47.1	N51 29.2
09	242 20.0	276 32.8	.. 32.6	68 45.0	.. 12.0	213 21.1	.. 35.5	34 46.2	.. 43.5	Enif	33 48.4	N 9 56.0
10	257 22.5	291 32.3	31.5	83 47.0	11.9	228 23.4	35.5	49 48.6	43.5	Fomalhaut	15 25.3	S29 33.6
11	272 25.0	306 31.8	30.5	98 49.0	11.8	243 25.8	35.6	64 50.9	43.5			
12	287 27.4	321 31.3	S15 29.4	113 51.1	N 6 11.7	258 28.1	N10 35.7	79 53.2	S 8 43.6	Gacrux	172 01.9	S57 10.7
13	302 29.9	336 30.8	28.4	128 53.1	11.6	273 30.5	35.7	94 55.6	43.6	Gienah	175 53.3	S17 36.6
14	317 32.3	351 30.3	27.3	143 55.1	11.5	288 32.8	35.8	109 57.9	43.6	Hadar	148 49.5	S60 25.6
15	332 34.8	6 29.8	.. 26.3	158 57.2	.. 11.4	303 35.2	.. 35.8	125 00.2	.. 43.7	Hamal	328 01.8	N23 31.3
16	347 37.3	21 29.3	25.2	173 59.2	11.3	318 37.6	35.9	140 02.6	43.7	Kaus Aust.	83 45.5	S34 22.6
17	2 39.7	36 28.7	24.2	189 01.2	11.2	333 39.9	35.9	155 04.9	43.7			
18	17 42.2	51 28.2	S15 23.1	204 03.3	N 6 11.1	348 42.3	N10 36.0	170 07.3	S 8 43.8	Kochab	137 20.5	N74 06.0
19	32 44.7	66 27.7	22.1	219 05.3	11.0	3 44.6	36.0	185 09.6	43.8	Markab	13 39.5	N15 16.4
20	47 47.1	81 27.2	21.0	234 07.4	10.9	18 47.0	36.1	200 11.9	43.8	Menkar	314 15.9	N 4 08.2
21	62 49.6	96 26.7	.. 20.0	249 09.4	.. 10.8	33 49.3	.. 36.1	215 14.3	.. 43.9	Menkent	148 08.9	S36 25.6
22	77 52.1	111 26.2	18.9	264 11.4	10.7	48 51.7	36.2	230 16.6	43.9	Miaplacidus	221 39.1	S69 46.0
23	92 54.5	126 25.7	17.8	279 13.5	10.6	63 54.0	36.2	245 19.0	44.0			
MONDAY 9												
00	107 57.0	141 25.2	S15 16.8	294 15.5	N 6 10.5	78 56.4	N10 36.3	260 21.3	S 8 44.0	Mirfak	308 41.5	N49 54.4
01	122 59.5	156 24.7	15.7	309 17.6	10.4	93 58.8	36.3	275 23.6	44.0	Nunki	75 59.9	S26 16.8
02	138 01.9	171 24.2	14.7	324 19.6	10.3	109 01.1	36.4	290 26.0	44.1	Peacock	53 21.4	S56 41.7
03	153 04.4	186 23.7	.. 13.6	339 21.7	.. 10.2	124 03.5	.. 36.5	305 28.3	.. 44.1	Pollux	243 28.6	N27 59.6
04	168 06.8	201 23.2	12.6	354 23.7	10.1	139 05.8	36.5	320 30.7	44.1	Procyon	245 00.4	N 5 11.5
05	183 09.3	216 22.7	11.5	9 25.8	10.0	154 08.2	36.6	335 33.0	44.2			
06	198 11.8	231 22.2	S15 10.4	24 27.8	N 6 09.9	169 10.5	N10 36.6	350 35.4	S 8 44.2	Rasalhague	96 07.7	N12 33.1
07	213 14.2	246 21.7	09.4	39 29.9	09.8	184 12.9	36.7	5 37.7	44.2	Regulus	207 44.3	N11 54.3
08	228 16.7	261 21.2	08.3	54 31.9	09.7	199 15.2	36.7	20 40.0	44.3	Rigel	281 12.7	S 8 11.4
09	243 19.2	276 20.7	.. 07.3	69 34.0	.. 09.6	214 17.6	.. 36.8	35 42.4	.. 44.3	Rigil Kent.	139 53.4	S60 52.8
10	258 21.6	291 20.2	06.2	84 36.0	09.5	229 19.9	36.8	50 44.7	44.3	Sabik	102 14.0	S15 44.3
11	273 24.1	306 19.7	05.1	99 38.1	09.4	244 22.3	36.9	65 47.1	44.4			
12	288 26.6	321 19.2	S15 04.1	114 40.1	N 6 09.3	259 24.6	N10 36.9	80 49.4	S 8 44.4	Schedar	349 41.7	N56 36.6
13	303 29.0	336 18.7	03.0	129 42.2	09.2	274 27.0	37.0	95 51.7	44.4	Shaula	96 23.7	S37 06.6
14	318 31.5	351 18.2	01.9	144 44.3	09.1	289 29.3	37.1	110 54.1	44.5	Sirius	258 34.2	S16 44.1
15	333 34.0	6 17.7	15 00.9	159 46.3	.. 09.0	304 31.7	.. 37.1	125 56.4	.. 44.5	Spica	158 32.3	S11 13.5
16	348 36.4	21 17.3	14 59.8	174 48.4	08.9	319 34.0	37.2	140 58.8	44.5	Suhail	222 52.8	S43 28.9
17	3 38.9	36 16.8	58.7	189 50.4	08.8	334 36.4	37.2	156 01.1	44.6			
18	18 41.3	51 16.3	S14 57.7	204 52.5	N 6 08.7	349 38.7	N10 37.3	171 03.5	S 8 44.6	Vega	80 40.1	N38 47.7
19	33 43.8	66 15.8	56.6	219 54.6	08.6	4 41.1	37.3	186 05.8	44.6	Zuben'ubi	137 06.7	S16 05.5
20	48 46.3	81 15.3	55.5	234 56.6	08.5	19 43.4	37.4	201 08.1	44.7			
21	63 48.7	96 14.8	.. 54.5	249 58.7	.. 08.4	34 45.8	.. 37.4	216 10.5	.. 44.7		SHA	Mer.Pass.
22	78 51.2	111 14.3	53.4	265 00.7	08.3	49 48.1	37.5	231 12.8	44.7	Venus	34 39.6	14 34
23	93 53.7	126 13.8	52.3	280 02.8	08.2	64 50.4	37.6	246 15.2	44.8	Mars	186 28.9	4 26
Mer.Pass. 16 49.4		v −0.5 d 1.0		v 2.0 d 0.1		v 2.4 d 0.1		v 2.3 d 0.0		Jupiter	331 02.0	18 45
										Saturn	152 27.3	6 41

UT	SUN GHA	Dec	MOON GHA	v	Dec	d	HP
d h	° ′	° ′	° ′	′	° ′	′	′
7 00	178 32.5	S22 28.2	27 54.6	9.7	N22 32.1	0.3	55.4
01	193 32.3	27.9	42 23.3	9.7	22 31.8	0.5	55.5
02	208 32.0	27.6	56 52.0	9.6	22 31.3	0.5	55.5
03	223 31.7 ..	27.2	71 20.6	9.7	22 30.8	0.7	55.5
04	238 31.5	26.9	85 49.3	9.6	22 30.1	0.8	55.5
05	253 31.2	26.6	100 17.9	9.6	22 29.3	0.9	55.5
S 06	268 30.9	S22 26.3	114 46.5	9.5	N22 28.4	1.0	55.6
A 07	283 30.6	26.0	129 15.0	9.5	22 27.4	1.2	55.6
T 08	298 30.4	25.7	143 43.6	9.5	22 26.2	1.3	55.6
U 09	313 30.1 ..	25.4	158 12.1	9.5	22 24.9	1.3	55.6
R 10	328 29.8	25.1	172 40.6	9.5	22 23.6	1.5	55.6
D 11	343 29.6	24.8	187 09.1	9.5	22 22.1	1.7	55.7
A 12	358 29.3	S22 24.5	201 37.6	9.5	N22 20.4	1.7	55.7
Y 13	13 29.0	24.2	216 06.1	9.4	22 18.7	1.9	55.7
14	28 28.8	23.8	230 34.5	9.5	22 16.8	1.9	55.7
15	43 28.5 ..	23.5	245 03.0	9.4	22 14.9	2.1	55.8
16	58 28.2	23.2	259 31.4	9.4	22 12.8	2.3	55.8
17	73 27.9	22.9	273 59.8	9.4	22 10.5	2.3	55.8
18	88 27.7	S22 22.6	288 28.2	9.4	N22 08.2	2.5	55.8
19	103 27.4	22.3	302 56.6	9.4	22 05.7	2.5	55.9
20	118 27.1	21.9	317 25.0	9.3	22 03.2	2.7	55.9
21	133 26.9 ..	21.6	331 53.3	9.4	22 00.5	2.9	55.9
22	148 26.6	21.3	346 21.7	9.4	21 57.6	2.9	55.9
23	163 26.3	21.0	0 50.1	9.3	21 54.7	3.1	55.9
8 00	178 26.1	S22 20.7	15 18.4	9.3	N21 51.6	3.1	56.0
01	193 25.8	20.3	29 46.7	9.4	21 48.5	3.3	56.0
02	208 25.5	20.0	44 15.1	9.3	21 45.2	3.5	56.0
03	223 25.3 ..	19.7	58 43.4	9.4	21 41.7	3.5	56.0
04	238 25.0	19.4	73 11.8	9.3	21 38.2	3.6	56.1
05	253 24.7	19.0	87 40.1	9.3	21 34.6	3.8	56.1
S 06	268 24.5	S22 18.7	102 08.4	9.4	N21 30.8	3.9	56.1
U 07	283 24.2	18.4	116 36.8	9.3	21 26.9	4.0	56.1
N 08	298 23.9	18.1	131 05.1	9.3	21 22.9	4.1	56.2
D 09	313 23.7 ..	17.7	145 33.4	9.4	21 18.8	4.3	56.2
A 10	328 23.4	17.4	160 01.8	9.3	21 14.5	4.4	56.2
Y 11	343 23.1	17.1	174 30.1	9.4	21 10.1	4.4	56.2
12	358 22.9	S22 16.7	188 58.5	9.3	N21 05.7	4.6	56.3
13	13 22.6	16.4	203 26.8	9.4	21 01.1	4.8	56.3
14	28 22.3	16.1	217 55.2	9.4	20 56.3	4.8	56.3
15	43 22.1 ..	15.7	232 23.6	9.3	20 51.5	4.9	56.3
16	58 21.8	15.4	246 51.9	9.4	20 46.6	5.1	56.3
17	73 21.5	15.1	261 20.3	9.4	20 41.5	5.2	56.4
18	88 21.3	S22 14.7	275 48.7	9.4	N20 36.3	5.3	56.4
19	103 21.0	14.4	290 17.1	9.4	20 31.0	5.4	56.4
20	118 20.8	14.1	304 45.5	9.5	20 25.6	5.5	56.4
21	133 20.5 ..	13.7	319 14.0	9.4	20 20.1	5.7	56.5
22	148 20.2	13.4	333 42.4	9.4	20 14.4	5.7	56.5
23	163 20.0	13.1	348 10.8	9.5	20 08.7	5.9	56.5
9 00	178 19.7	S22 12.7	2 39.3	9.5	N20 02.8	6.0	56.5
01	193 19.4	12.4	17 07.8	9.5	19 56.8	6.1	56.5
02	208 19.2	12.0	31 36.3	9.5	19 50.7	6.2	56.6
03	223 18.9 ..	11.7	46 04.8	9.5	19 44.5	6.3	56.6
04	238 18.7	11.3	60 33.3	9.6	19 38.2	6.4	56.6
05	253 18.4	11.0	75 01.9	9.5	19 31.8	6.5	56.6
M 06	268 18.1	S22 10.7	89 30.4	9.6	N19 25.3	6.7	56.7
07	283 17.9	10.3	103 59.0	9.6	19 18.6	6.7	56.7
O 08	298 17.6	10.0	118 27.6	9.6	19 11.9	6.9	56.7
N 09	313 17.4 ..	09.6	132 56.2	9.6	19 05.0	7.0	56.7
D 10	328 17.1	09.3	147 24.8	9.7	18 58.0	7.1	56.8
A 11	343 16.8	08.9	161 53.5	9.7	18 50.9	7.2	56.8
Y 12	358 16.6	S22 08.6	176 22.2	9.7	N18 43.7	7.2	56.8
13	13 16.3	08.2	190 50.9	9.7	18 36.5	7.4	56.8
14	28 16.1	07.9	205 19.6	9.7	18 29.1	7.6	56.8
15	43 15.8 ..	07.5	219 48.3	9.8	18 21.5	7.6	56.9
16	58 15.5	07.2	234 17.1	9.8	18 13.9	7.7	56.9
17	73 15.3	06.8	248 45.9	9.8	18 06.2	7.8	56.9
18	88 15.0	S22 06.5	263 14.7	9.8	N17 58.4	7.9	56.9
19	103 14.8	06.1	277 43.5	9.9	17 50.5	8.0	57.0
20	118 14.5	05.8	292 12.4	9.9	17 42.5	8.2	57.0
21	133 14.3 ..	05.4	306 41.3	9.9	17 34.3	8.2	57.0
22	148 14.0	05.1	321 10.2	9.9	17 26.1	8.3	57.0
23	163 13.7	04.7	335 39.1	10.0	N17 17.8	8.4	57.1
	SD 16.3	d 0.3	SD 15.2		15.3		15.5

Lat.	Twilight Naut.	Twilight Civil	Sunrise	Moonrise 7	8	9	10
°	h m	h m	h m	h m	h m	h m	h m
N 72	08 16	10 21	■	☐	☐	☐	15 38
N 70	07 58	09 37	■	☐	☐	13 55	16 11
68	07 45	09 08	11 12	☐	12 41	14 41	16 35
66	07 33	08 47	10 14	12 07	13 32	15 11	16 53
64	07 23	08 29	09 41	12 48	14 04	15 33	17 08
62	07 14	08 15	09 17	13 16	14 27	15 51	17 20
60	07 07	08 02	08 57	13 37	14 46	16 05	17 31
N 58	07 00	07 52	08 42	13 55	15 01	16 18	17 40
56	06 54	07 42	08 28	14 10	15 15	16 28	17 48
54	06 48	07 34	08 17	14 22	15 26	16 38	17 55
52	06 43	07 26	08 06	14 33	15 36	16 46	18 01
50	06 38	07 19	07 57	14 43	15 45	16 54	18 07
45	06 28	07 04	07 38	15 04	16 04	17 10	18 19
N 40	06 18	06 52	07 22	15 21	16 20	17 23	18 29
35	06 09	06 41	07 09	15 35	16 33	17 34	18 37
30	06 01	06 31	06 57	15 47	16 44	17 44	18 45
20	05 46	06 13	06 37	16 09	17 04	18 00	18 58
N 10	05 30	05 57	06 19	16 27	17 21	18 15	19 09
0	05 14	05 40	06 03	16 44	17 36	18 29	19 20
S 10	04 56	05 23	05 46	17 01	17 52	18 42	19 30
20	04 35	05 04	05 28	17 19	18 09	18 56	19 41
30	04 07	04 40	05 07	17 40	18 28	19 13	19 54
35	03 50	04 26	04 55	17 53	18 40	19 22	20 01
40	03 28	04 08	04 41	18 07	18 53	19 33	20 10
45	02 59	03 47	04 24	18 24	19 08	19 46	20 20
S 50	02 18	03 20	04 03	18 44	19 26	20 02	20 31
52	01 54	03 06	03 53	18 54	19 35	20 09	20 37
54	01 21	02 49	03 41	19 05	19 45	20 17	20 43
56	////	02 29	03 28	19 18	19 56	20 26	20 49
58	////	02 04	03 13	19 32	20 09	20 36	20 57
S 60	////	01 28	02 54	19 50	20 23	20 47	21 05

Lat.	Sunset	Twilight Civil	Twilight Naut.	Moonset 7	8	9	10
°	h m	h m	h m	h m	h m	h m	h m
N 72	■	13 53	15 58	☐	☐	☐	10 54
N 70	■	14 36	16 15	☐	☐	10 47	10 19
68	13 01	15 05	16 29	☐	10 12	10 01	09 54
66	13 59	15 27	16 40	08 56	09 20	09 30	09 34
64	14 33	15 44	16 50	08 15	08 48	09 07	09 19
62	14 57	15 59	16 59	07 47	08 24	08 49	09 06
60	15 16	16 11	17 06	07 25	08 05	08 34	08 54
N 58	15 32	16 22	17 13	07 08	07 49	08 21	08 45
56	15 45	16 31	17 19	06 53	07 36	08 10	08 36
54	15 57	16 39	17 25	06 40	07 24	08 00	08 28
52	16 07	16 47	17 30	06 29	07 14	07 51	08 21
50	16 16	16 54	17 35	06 19	07 04	07 43	08 15
45	16 35	17 09	17 46	05 58	06 45	07 26	08 02
N 40	16 51	17 21	17 55	05 41	06 29	07 12	07 51
35	17 05	17 32	18 04	05 27	06 15	07 00	07 41
30	17 16	17 42	18 12	05 14	06 04	06 50	07 33
20	17 36	18 00	18 27	04 53	05 43	06 32	07 18
N 10	17 54	18 16	18 42	04 34	05 26	06 16	07 05
0	18 10	18 33	18 59	04 17	05 09	06 02	06 53
S 10	18 27	18 50	19 16	03 59	04 53	05 47	06 41
20	18 45	19 09	19 38	03 41	04 35	05 31	06 28
30	19 06	19 33	20 05	03 19	04 14	05 13	06 13
35	19 18	19 47	20 23	03 07	04 02	05 02	06 04
40	19 32	20 04	20 45	02 52	03 48	04 49	05 54
45	19 49	20 25	21 13	02 35	03 32	04 35	05 42
S 50	20 10	20 53	21 54	02 14	03 12	04 17	05 28
52	20 20	21 06	22 17	02 04	03 02	04 09	05 21
54	20 31	21 23	22 50	01 52	02 51	03 59	05 14
56	20 44	21 42	////	01 39	02 39	03 48	05 05
58	20 59	22 07	////	01 24	02 24	03 36	04 56
S 60	21 17	22 43	////	01 06	02 07	03 22	04 45

	SUN			MOON			
Day	Eqn. of Time 00h	12h	Mer. Pass.	Mer. Pass. Upper	Lower	Age	Phase
d	m s	m s	h m	h m	h m	d %	
7	05 49	06 02	12 06	22 57	10 30	14 97	◯
8	06 15	06 28	12 06	23 49	11 23	15 99	
9	06 41	06 53	12 07	24 41	12 15	16 100	

2012 JANUARY 10, 11, 12 (TUES., WED., THURS.)

UT	ARIES GHA	VENUS −4.0 GHA	Dec	MARS +0.0 GHA	Dec	JUPITER −2.5 GHA	Dec	SATURN +0.7 GHA	Dec	STARS Name	SHA	Dec
10 00	108 56.1	141 13.3	S14 51.2	295 04.9	N 6 08.1	79 52.8	N10 37.6	261 17.5	S 8 44.8	Acamar	315 18.9	S40 15.6
01	123 58.6	156 12.8	50.2	310 07.0	08.1	94 55.1	37.7	276 19.9	44.8	Achernar	335 27.4	S57 10.8
02	139 01.1	171 12.4	49.1	325 09.0	08.0	109 57.5	37.7	291 22.2	44.9	Acrux	173 10.3	S63 09.8
03	154 03.5	186 11.9 ..	48.0	340 11.1 ..	07.9	124 59.8 ..	37.8	306 24.6 ..	44.9	Adhara	255 12.9	S28 59.5
04	169 06.0	201 11.4	46.9	355 13.2	07.8	140 02.2	37.8	321 26.9	44.9	Aldebaran	290 50.2	N16 32.0
05	184 08.5	216 10.9	45.9	10 15.2	07.7	155 04.5	37.9	336 29.2	45.0			
06	199 10.9	231 10.4	S14 44.8	25 17.3	N 6 07.6	170 06.9	N10 38.0	351 31.6	S 8 45.0	Alioth	166 21.5	N55 53.3
07	214 13.4	246 09.9	43.7	40 19.4	07.5	185 09.2	38.0	6 33.9	45.0	Alkaid	152 59.7	N49 14.8
T 08	229 15.8	261 09.4	42.6	55 21.5	07.4	200 11.6	38.1	21 36.3	45.1	Al Na'ir	27 45.3	S46 54.2
U 09	244 18.3	276 09.0 ..	41.6	70 23.5 ..	07.3	215 13.9 ..	38.1	36 38.6 ..	45.1	Alnilam	275 47.1	S 1 11.8
E 10	259 20.8	291 08.5	40.5	85 25.6	07.3	230 16.2	38.2	51 41.0	45.1	Alphard	217 56.8	S 8 42.8
S 11	274 23.2	306 08.0	39.4	100 27.7	07.2	245 18.6	38.2	66 43.3	45.2			
D 12	289 25.7	321 07.5	S14 38.3	115 29.8	N 6 07.1	260 20.9	N10 38.3	81 45.7	S 8 45.2	Alphecca	126 12.1	N26 40.3
A 13	304 28.2	336 07.0	37.2	130 31.8	07.0	275 23.3	38.4	96 48.0	45.2	Alpheratz	357 44.6	N29 09.6
Y 14	319 30.6	351 06.6	36.2	145 33.9	06.9	290 25.6	38.4	111 50.4	45.3	Altair	62 09.5	N 8 54.1
15	334 33.1	6 06.1 ..	35.1	160 36.0 ..	06.8	305 27.9 ..	38.5	126 52.7 ..	45.3	Ankaa	353 16.7	S42 14.6
16	349 35.6	21 05.6	34.0	175 38.1	06.7	320 30.3	38.5	141 55.1	45.3	Antares	112 27.8	S26 27.4
17	4 38.0	36 05.1	32.9	190 40.2	06.7	335 32.6	38.6	156 57.4	45.4			
18	19 40.5	51 04.6	S14 31.8	205 42.3	N 6 06.6	350 35.0	N10 38.7	171 59.7	S 8 45.4	Arcturus	145 56.7	N19 07.0
19	34 42.9	66 04.2	30.7	220 44.3	06.5	5 37.3	38.7	187 02.1	45.4	Atria	107 31.0	S69 02.7
20	49 45.4	81 03.7	29.6	235 46.4	06.4	20 39.6	38.8	202 04.4	45.5	Avior	234 17.8	S59 33.0
21	64 47.9	96 03.2 ..	28.6	250 48.5 ..	06.3	35 42.0 ..	38.8	217 06.8 ..	45.5	Bellatrix	278 32.8	N 6 21.5
22	79 50.3	111 02.7	27.5	265 50.6	06.2	50 44.3	38.9	232 09.1	45.5	Betelgeuse	271 02.0	N 7 24.4
23	94 52.8	126 02.3	26.4	280 52.7	06.2	65 46.7	39.0	247 11.5	45.6			
11 00	109 55.3	141 01.8	S14 25.3	295 54.8	N 6 06.1	80 49.0	N10 39.0	262 13.8	S 8 45.6	Canopus	263 56.0	S52 42.3
01	124 57.7	156 01.3	24.2	310 56.9	06.0	95 51.3	39.1	277 16.2	45.6	Capella	280 35.5	N46 00.6
02	140 00.2	171 00.9	23.1	325 59.0	05.9	110 53.7	39.1	292 18.5	45.7	Deneb	49 32.6	N45 19.6
03	155 02.7	186 00.4 ..	22.0	341 01.1 ..	05.8	125 56.0 ..	39.2	307 20.9 ..	45.7	Denebola	182 34.5	N14 30.0
04	170 05.1	200 59.9	20.9	356 03.2	05.8	140 58.4	39.3	322 23.2	45.7	Diphda	348 56.9	S17 55.3
05	185 07.6	215 59.4	19.8	11 05.3	05.7	156 00.7	39.3	337 25.6	45.8			
06	200 10.1	230 59.0	S14 18.8	26 07.3	N 6 05.6	171 03.0	N10 39.4	352 27.9	S 8 45.8	Dubhe	193 52.5	N61 40.8
W 07	215 12.5	245 58.5	17.7	41 09.4	05.5	186 05.4	39.4	7 30.3	45.8	Elnath	278 13.5	N28 37.0
E 08	230 15.0	260 58.0	16.6	56 11.5	05.4	201 07.7	39.5	22 32.6	45.8	Eltanin	90 47.1	N51 29.2
D 09	245 17.4	275 57.6 ..	15.5	71 13.6 ..	05.4	216 10.0 ..	39.6	37 35.0 ..	45.9	Enif	33 48.4	N 9 56.0
N 10	260 19.9	290 57.1	14.4	86 15.7	05.3	231 12.4	39.6	52 37.3	45.9	Fomalhaut	15 25.3	S29 33.6
E 11	275 22.4	305 56.6	13.3	101 17.8	05.2	246 14.7	39.7	67 39.7	45.9			
S 12	290 24.8	320 56.2	S14 12.2	116 19.9	N 6 05.1	261 17.0	N10 39.7	82 42.0	S 8 46.0	Gacrux	172 01.9	S57 10.7
D 13	305 27.3	335 55.7	11.1	131 22.1	05.1	276 19.4	39.8	97 44.4	46.0	Gienah	175 53.2	S17 36.6
A 14	320 29.8	350 55.2	10.0	146 24.2	05.0	291 21.7	39.9	112 46.7	46.0	Hadar	148 49.5	S60 25.6
Y 15	335 32.2	5 54.8 ..	08.9	161 26.3 ..	04.9	306 24.0 ..	39.9	127 49.1 ..	46.1	Hamal	328 01.8	N23 31.3
16	350 34.7	20 54.3	07.8	176 28.4	04.8	321 26.4	40.0	142 51.4	46.1	Kaus Aust.	83 45.5	S34 22.6
17	5 37.2	35 53.8	06.7	191 30.5	04.8	336 28.7	40.0	157 53.8	46.1			
18	20 39.6	50 53.4	S14 05.6	206 32.6	N 6 04.7	351 31.0	N10 40.1	172 56.1	S 8 46.2	Kochab	137 20.4	N74 06.0
19	35 42.1	65 52.9	04.5	221 34.7	04.6	6 33.4	40.2	187 58.5	46.2	Markab	13 39.5	N15 16.4
20	50 44.6	80 52.4	03.4	236 36.8	04.5	21 35.7	40.2	203 00.8	46.2	Menkar	314 15.9	N 4 08.2
21	65 47.0	95 52.0 ..	02.3	251 38.9 ..	04.5	36 38.0 ..	40.3	218 03.2 ..	46.3	Menkent	148 08.8	S36 25.6
22	80 49.5	110 51.5	01.2	266 41.0	04.4	51 40.4	40.3	233 05.5	46.3	Miaplacidus	221 39.1	S69 46.0
23	95 51.9	125 51.1	14 00.1	281 43.1	04.3	66 42.7	40.4	248 07.9	46.3			
12 00	110 54.4	140 50.6	S13 59.0	296 45.3	N 6 04.2	81 45.0	N10 40.5	263 10.2	S 8 46.3	Mirfak	308 41.5	N49 54.4
01	125 56.9	155 50.1	57.9	311 47.4	04.2	96 47.3	40.5	278 12.6	46.4	Nunki	75 59.9	S26 16.8
02	140 59.3	170 49.7	56.8	326 49.5	04.1	111 49.7	40.6	293 14.9	46.4	Peacock	53 21.4	S56 41.7
03	156 01.8	185 49.2 ..	55.7	341 51.6 ..	04.0	126 52.0 ..	40.7	308 17.3 ..	46.4	Pollux	243 28.5	N27 59.6
04	171 04.3	200 48.8	54.6	356 53.7	04.0	141 54.3	40.7	323 19.6	46.5	Procyon	245 00.4	N 5 11.5
05	186 06.7	215 48.3	53.5	11 55.8	03.9	156 56.7	40.8	338 22.0	46.5			
06	201 09.2	230 47.9	S13 52.4	26 58.0	N 6 03.8	171 59.0	N10 40.8	353 24.3	S 8 46.5	Rasalhague	96 07.7	N12 33.1
07	216 11.7	245 47.4	51.3	42 00.1	03.8	187 01.3	40.9	8 26.7	46.6	Regulus	207 44.3	N11 54.3
T 08	231 14.1	260 47.0	50.1	57 02.2	03.7	202 03.7	41.0	23 29.0	46.6	Rigel	281 12.7	S 8 11.4
H 09	246 16.6	275 46.5 ..	49.0	72 04.3 ..	03.6	217 06.0 ..	41.0	38 31.4 ..	46.6	Rigil Kent.	139 53.3	S60 52.8
U 10	261 19.0	290 46.0	47.9	87 06.4	03.6	232 08.3	41.1	53 33.8	46.6	Sabik	102 14.0	S15 44.3
R 11	276 21.5	305 45.6	46.8	102 08.6	03.5	247 10.6	41.2	68 36.1	46.7			
S 12	291 24.0	320 45.1	S13 45.7	117 10.7	N 6 03.4	262 13.0	N10 41.2	83 38.5	S 8 46.7	Schedar	349 41.8	N56 36.5
D 13	306 26.4	335 44.7	44.6	132 12.8	03.4	277 15.3	41.3	98 40.8	46.7	Shaula	96 23.6	S37 06.6
A 14	321 28.9	350 44.2	43.5	147 15.0	03.3	292 17.6	41.4	113 43.2	46.8	Sirius	258 34.2	S16 44.1
Y 15	336 31.4	5 43.8 ..	42.4	162 17.1 ..	03.2	307 19.9 ..	41.4	128 45.5 ..	46.8	Spica	158 32.3	S11 13.5
16	351 33.8	20 43.3	41.3	177 19.2	03.2	322 22.3	41.5	143 47.9	46.8	Suhail	222 52.8	S43 28.9
17	6 36.3	35 42.9	40.1	192 21.3	03.1	337 24.6	41.5	158 50.2	46.9			
18	21 38.8	50 42.4	S13 39.0	207 23.5	N 6 03.0	352 26.9	N10 41.6	173 52.6	S 8 46.9	Vega	80 40.1	N38 47.7
19	36 41.2	65 42.0	37.9	222 25.6	03.0	7 29.2	41.7	188 54.9	46.9	Zuben'ubi	137 06.7	S16 05.5
20	51 43.7	80 41.5	36.8	237 27.7	02.9	22 31.6	41.7	203 57.3	46.9		SHA	Mer.Pass.
21	66 46.2	95 41.1 ..	35.7	252 29.9 ..	02.9	37 33.9 ..	41.8	218 59.7 ..	47.0	Venus	31 06.5	14 36
22	81 48.6	110 40.6	34.6	267 32.0	02.8	52 36.2	41.9	234 02.0	47.0	Mars	185 59.5	4 16
23	96 51.1	125 40.2	33.4	282 34.1	02.7	67 38.5	41.9	249 04.4	47.0	Jupiter	330 53.7	18 34
Mer. Pass. 16 37.6	v −0.5 d 1.1	v 2.1 d 0.1		v 2.3 d 0.1		v 2.3 d 0.0				Saturn	152 18.6	6 30

UT	SUN GHA	SUN Dec	MOON GHA	v	MOON Dec	d	HP
d h	° ′	° ′	° ′	′	° ′	′	′
10 00	178 13.5	S22 04.3	350 08.1	10.0	N17 09.4	8.5	57.1
01	193 13.2	04.0	4 37.1	10.0	17 00.9	8.7	57.1
02	208 13.0	03.6	19 06.1	10.0	16 52.2	8.7	57.1
03	223 12.7 ..	03.3	33 35.1	10.1	16 43.5	8.8	57.1
04	238 12.5	02.9	48 04.2	10.1	16 34.7	8.9	57.2
05	253 12.2	02.5	62 33.3	10.1	16 25.8	9.0	57.2
06	268 11.9	S22 02.2	77 02.4	10.1	N16 16.8	9.1	57.2
07	283 11.7	01.8	91 31.5	10.2	16 07.7	9.2	57.2
08	298 11.4	01.4	106 00.7	10.2	15 58.5	9.2	57.2
09	313 11.2 ..	01.1	120 29.9	10.2	15 49.3	9.4	57.3
10	328 10.9	00.7	134 59.1	10.3	15 39.9	9.5	57.3
11	343 10.7	00.4	149 28.4	10.3	15 30.4	9.5	57.3
12	358 10.4	S22 00.0	163 57.7	10.3	N15 20.9	9.6	57.3
13	13 10.2	21 59.6	178 27.0	10.3	15 11.3	9.8	57.4
14	28 09.9	59.2	192 56.3	10.4	15 01.5	9.8	57.4
15	43 09.7 ..	58.9	207 25.7	10.4	14 51.7	9.9	57.4
16	58 09.4	58.5	221 55.1	10.4	14 41.8	9.9	57.4
17	73 09.2	58.1	236 24.5	10.4	14 31.9	10.1	57.4
18	88 08.9	S21 57.8	250 53.9	10.5	N14 21.8	10.1	57.5
19	103 08.6	57.4	265 23.4	10.5	14 11.7	10.3	57.5
20	118 08.4	57.0	279 52.9	10.5	14 01.4	10.3	57.5
21	133 08.1 ..	56.7	294 22.4	10.6	13 51.1	10.3	57.5
22	148 07.9	56.3	308 52.0	10.6	13 40.8	10.5	57.5
23	163 07.6	55.9	323 21.6	10.6	13 30.3	10.5	57.6
11 00	178 07.4	S21 55.5	337 51.2	10.6	N13 19.8	10.7	57.6
01	193 07.1	55.2	352 20.8	10.7	13 09.1	10.7	57.6
02	208 06.9	54.8	6 50.5	10.8	12 58.4	10.7	57.6
03	223 06.6 ..	54.4	21 20.1	10.8	12 47.7	10.9	57.6
04	238 06.4	54.0	35 49.9	10.7	12 36.8	10.9	57.7
05	253 06.1	53.6	50 19.6	10.8	12 25.9	11.0	57.7
06	268 05.9	S21 53.3	64 49.4	10.8	N12 14.9	11.0	57.7
07	283 05.6	52.9	79 19.2	10.8	12 03.9	11.2	57.7
08	298 05.4	52.5	93 49.0	10.8	11 52.7	11.2	57.7
09	313 05.1 ..	52.1	108 18.8	10.9	11 41.5	11.2	57.8
10	328 04.9	51.7	122 48.7	10.9	11 30.3	11.4	57.8
11	343 04.6	51.3	137 18.6	10.9	11 18.9	11.4	57.8
12	358 04.4	S21 51.0	151 48.5	10.9	N11 07.5	11.4	57.8
13	13 04.2	50.6	166 18.4	11.0	10 56.1	11.5	57.8
14	28 03.9	50.2	180 48.4	11.0	10 44.6	11.6	57.9
15	43 03.7 ..	49.8	195 18.4	11.0	10 33.0	11.7	57.9
16	58 03.4	49.4	209 48.4	11.0	10 21.3	11.7	57.9
17	73 03.2	49.0	224 18.4	11.1	10 09.6	11.8	57.9
18	88 02.9	S21 48.6	238 48.5	11.0	N 9 57.8	11.8	57.9
19	103 02.7	48.2	253 18.5	11.1	9 46.0	11.9	57.9
20	118 02.4	47.9	267 48.6	11.1	9 34.1	11.9	58.0
21	133 02.2 ..	47.5	282 18.7	11.2	9 22.2	12.0	58.0
22	148 01.9	47.1	296 48.9	11.1	9 10.2	12.1	58.0
23	163 01.7	46.7	311 19.0	11.2	8 58.1	12.1	58.0
12 00	178 01.4	S21 46.3	325 49.2	11.2	N 8 46.0	12.1	58.0
01	193 01.2	45.9	340 19.4	11.2	8 33.9	12.2	58.0
02	208 01.0	45.5	354 49.6	11.2	8 21.7	12.3	58.1
03	223 00.7 ..	45.1	9 19.8	11.3	8 09.4	12.3	58.1
04	238 00.5	44.7	23 50.1	11.2	7 57.1	12.3	58.1
05	253 00.2	44.3	38 20.3	11.3	7 44.8	12.4	58.1
06	268 00.0	S21 43.9	52 50.6	11.3	N 7 32.4	12.5	58.1
07	282 59.7	43.5	67 20.9	11.3	7 19.9	12.5	58.1
08	297 59.5	43.1	81 51.2	11.3	7 07.4	12.5	58.2
09	312 59.2 ..	42.7	96 21.5	11.3	6 54.9	12.6	58.2
10	327 59.0	42.3	110 51.8	11.4	6 42.3	12.6	58.2
11	342 58.8	41.9	125 22.2	11.3	6 29.7	12.6	58.2
12	357 58.5	S21 41.5	139 52.5	11.4	N 6 17.1	12.7	58.2
13	12 58.3	41.1	154 22.9	11.3	6 04.4	12.8	58.2
14	27 58.0	40.7	168 53.2	11.4	5 51.6	12.7	58.3
15	42 57.8 ..	40.3	183 23.6	11.4	5 38.9	12.8	58.3
16	57 57.6	39.9	197 54.0	11.4	5 26.1	12.8	58.3
17	72 57.3	39.5	212 24.4	11.4	5 13.3	12.9	58.3
18	87 57.1	S21 39.1	226 54.8	11.4	N 5 00.4	12.9	58.3
19	102 56.8	38.7	241 25.2	11.5	4 47.5	12.9	58.3
20	117 56.6	38.3	255 55.7	11.4	4 34.6	13.0	58.4
21	132 56.4 ..	37.9	270 26.1	11.4	4 21.6	13.0	58.4
22	147 56.1	37.4	284 56.5	11.5	4 08.6	13.0	58.4
23	162 55.9	37.0	299 27.0	11.4	N 3 55.6	13.0	58.4
	SD 16.3 d 0.4		SD 15.6		15.8		15.9

(Rows 06–23 of 10 are **TUESDAY**; 00–23 of 11 are **WEDNESDAY**; 00–23 of 12 are **THURSDAY**.)

Lat.	Twilight Naut.	Twilight Civil	Sunrise	Moonrise 10	Moonrise 11	Moonrise 12	Moonrise 13
°	h m	h m	h m	h m	h m	h m	h m
N 72	08 10	10 10	■	15 38	17 56	20 01	22 04
N 70	07 54	09 30	■	16 11	18 12	20 08	22 02
68	07 41	09 03	10 56	16 35	18 25	20 13	22 00
66	07 30	08 42	10 06	16 53	18 36	20 17	21 59
64	07 20	08 26	09 35	17 08	18 44	20 21	21 58
62	07 12	08 12	09 12	17 20	18 52	20 24	21 57
60	07 05	08 00	08 54	17 31	18 58	20 27	21 56
N 58	06 58	07 49	08 39	17 40	19 04	20 30	21 56
56	06 53	07 40	08 26	17 48	19 09	20 32	21 55
54	06 47	07 32	08 15	17 55	19 14	20 34	21 55
52	06 42	07 25	08 05	18 01	19 18	20 36	21 54
50	06 38	07 18	07 56	18 07	19 21	20 37	21 54
45	06 27	07 04	07 37	18 19	19 29	20 41	21 53
N 40	06 18	06 51	07 21	18 29	19 36	20 44	21 52
35	06 09	06 41	07 08	18 37	19 42	20 46	21 51
30	06 01	06 31	06 57	18 45	19 47	20 48	21 50
20	05 46	06 14	06 37	18 58	19 55	20 52	21 49
N 10	05 32	05 58	06 20	19 09	20 03	20 56	21 49
0	05 16	05 42	06 04	19 20	20 10	20 59	21 48
S 10	04 58	05 25	05 48	19 30	20 17	21 02	21 47
20	04 37	05 06	05 30	19 41	20 24	21 05	21 46
30	04 10	04 43	05 10	19 54	20 33	21 09	21 45
35	03 53	04 28	04 58	20 01	20 37	21 11	21 45
40	03 31	04 12	04 44	20 10	20 43	21 14	21 44
45	03 04	03 51	04 27	20 20	20 49	21 17	21 44
S 50	02 24	03 24	04 07	20 31	20 57	21 20	21 43
52	02 02	03 11	03 57	20 37	21 00	21 22	21 42
54	01 31	02 55	03 46	20 43	21 04	21 24	21 42
56	00 24	02 36	03 33	20 49	21 09	21 26	21 42
58	////	02 12	03 18	20 57	21 13	21 28	21 41
S 60	////	01 39	03 01	21 05	21 19	21 30	21 41

Lat.	Sunset	Twilight Civil	Twilight Naut.	Moonset 10	Moonset 11	Moonset 12	Moonset 13
°	h m	h m	h m	h m	h m	h m	h m
N 72	■	14 06	16 06	10 54	10 21	09 59	09 41
N 70	■	14 46	16 22	10 19	10 03	09 50	09 39
68	13 20	15 13	16 35	09 54	09 48	09 43	09 37
66	14 10	15 34	16 46	09 34	09 36	09 36	09 36
64	14 41	15 50	16 56	09 19	09 26	09 31	09 35
62	15 04	16 04	17 04	09 06	09 17	09 26	09 34
60	15 22	16 16	17 11	08 54	09 10	09 22	09 33
N 58	15 37	16 26	17 17	08 45	09 03	09 18	09 32
56	15 50	16 35	17 23	08 36	08 57	09 15	09 32
54	16 01	16 44	17 29	08 28	08 52	09 12	09 31
52	16 11	16 51	17 34	08 21	08 47	09 09	09 30
50	16 20	16 57	17 38	08 15	08 43	09 07	09 30
45	16 39	17 12	17 49	08 02	08 33	09 02	09 29
N 40	16 54	17 24	17 58	07 51	08 25	08 57	09 28
35	17 07	17 35	18 06	07 41	08 18	08 53	09 27
30	17 19	17 45	18 14	07 33	08 12	08 50	09 26
20	17 38	18 02	18 29	07 18	08 02	08 44	09 25
N 10	17 55	18 18	18 44	07 05	07 52	08 38	09 23
0	18 11	18 34	19 00	06 53	07 44	08 33	09 22
S 10	18 28	18 50	19 17	06 41	07 35	08 28	09 21
20	18 45	19 09	19 38	06 28	07 25	08 22	09 20
30	19 06	19 32	20 05	06 13	07 14	08 16	09 18
35	19 17	19 47	20 22	06 04	07 08	08 12	09 17
40	19 31	20 03	20 43	05 54	07 01	08 08	09 16
45	19 48	20 24	21 11	05 42	06 52	08 03	09 15
S 50	20 08	20 50	21 50	05 28	06 42	07 57	09 13
52	20 18	21 04	22 12	05 21	06 37	07 55	09 13
54	20 29	21 19	22 42	05 14	06 32	07 52	09 12
56	20 41	21 38	23 40	05 05	06 26	07 48	09 11
58	20 56	22 02	////	04 56	06 19	07 45	09 10
S 60	21 13	22 34	////	04 45	06 12	07 40	09 09

Day	SUN Eqn. of Time 00h	SUN Eqn. of Time 12h	SUN Mer. Pass.	MOON Mer. Pass. Upper	MOON Mer. Pass. Lower	Age	Phase
d	m s	m s	h m	h m	h m	d	%
10	07 06	07 18	12 07	00 41	13 06	17	98
11	07 30	07 42	12 08	01 32	13 57	18	94
12	07 54	08 05	12 08	02 21	14 46	19	88

18   2012 JANUARY 13, 14, 15 (FRI., SAT., SUN.)

UT	ARIES GHA	VENUS −4.0 GHA	Dec	MARS −0.1 GHA	Dec	JUPITER −2.5 GHA	Dec	SATURN +0.7 GHA	Dec	STARS Name	SHA	Dec
d h	° ′	° ′	° ′	° ′	° ′	° ′	° ′	° ′	° ′		° ′	° ′
13 00	111 53.5	140 39.8	S13 32.3	297 36.3	N 6 02.7	82 40.9	N10 42.0	264 06.7	S 8 47.1	Acamar	315 18.9	S40 15.6
01	126 56.0	155 39.3	31.2	312 38.4	02.6	97 43.2	42.1	279 09.1	47.1	Achernar	335 27.4	S57 10.8
02	141 58.5	170 38.9	30.1	327 40.6	02.6	112 45.5	42.1	294 11.4	47.1	Acrux	173 10.2	S63 09.8
03	157 00.9	185 38.4 ..	29.0	342 42.7 ..	02.5	127 47.8 ..	42.2	309 13.8 ..	47.1	Adhara	255 12.9	S28 59.5
04	172 03.4	200 38.0	27.9	357 44.8	02.4	142 50.1	42.3	324 16.1	47.2	Aldebaran	290 50.2	N16 32.0
05	187 05.9	215 37.5	26.7	12 47.0	02.4	157 52.5	42.3	339 18.5	47.2			
06	202 08.3	230 37.1	S13 25.6	27 49.1	N 6 02.3	172 54.8	N10 42.4	354 20.9	S 8 47.2	Alioth	166 21.4	N55 53.3
07	217 10.8	245 36.7	24.5	42 51.3	02.3	187 57.1	42.5	9 23.2	47.3	Alkaid	152 59.7	N49 14.8
08	232 13.3	260 36.2	23.4	57 53.4	02.2	202 59.4	42.5	24 25.6	47.3	Al Na'ir	27 45.3	S46 54.2
F 09	247 15.7	275 35.8 ..	22.2	72 55.6 ..	02.2	218 01.7 ..	42.6	39 27.9 ..	47.3	Alnilam	275 47.1	S 1 11.8
R 10	262 18.2	290 35.3	21.1	87 57.7	02.1	233 04.1	42.7	54 30.3	47.3	Alphard	217 56.8	S 8 42.8
I 11	277 20.7	305 34.9	20.0	102 59.9	02.0	248 06.4	42.7	69 32.6	47.4			
D 12	292 23.1	320 34.5	S13 18.9	118 02.0	N 6 02.0	263 08.7	N10 42.8	84 35.0	S 8 47.4	Alphecca	126 12.0	N26 40.3
A 13	307 25.6	335 34.0	17.7	133 04.2	01.9	278 11.0	42.9	99 37.4	47.4	Alpheratz	357 44.7	N29 09.6
Y 14	322 28.0	350 33.6	16.6	148 06.3	01.9	293 13.3	42.9	114 39.7	47.5	Altair	62 09.5	N 8 54.1
15	337 30.5	5 33.1 ..	15.5	163 08.5 ..	01.8	308 15.7 ..	43.0	129 42.1 ..	47.5	Ankaa	353 16.8	S42 14.6
16	352 33.0	20 32.7	14.4	178 10.6	01.8	323 18.0	43.1	144 44.4	47.5	Antares	112 27.7	S26 27.4
17	7 35.4	35 32.3	13.2	193 12.8	01.7	338 20.3	43.1	159 46.8	47.5			
18	22 37.9	50 31.8	S13 12.1	208 14.9	N 6 01.7	353 22.6	N10 43.2	174 49.1	S 8 47.6	Arcturus	145 56.7	N19 07.0
19	37 40.4	65 31.4	11.0	223 17.1	01.6	8 24.9	43.3	189 51.5	47.6	Atria	107 30.9	S69 02.7
20	52 42.8	80 31.0	09.8	238 19.3	01.6	23 27.2	43.3	204 53.9	47.6	Avior	234 17.8	S59 33.0
21	67 45.3	95 30.5 ..	08.7	253 21.4 ..	01.5	38 29.6 ..	43.4	219 56.2 ..	47.6	Bellatrix	278 32.8	N 6 21.5
22	82 47.8	110 30.1	07.6	268 23.6	01.5	53 31.9	43.5	234 58.6	47.7	Betelgeuse	271 02.0	N 7 24.4
23	97 50.2	125 29.7	06.5	283 25.7	01.4	68 34.2	43.5	250 00.9	47.7			
14 00	112 52.7	140 29.2	S13 05.3	298 27.9	N 6 01.4	83 36.5	N10 43.6	265 03.3	S 8 47.7	Canopus	263 56.0	S52 42.3
01	127 55.1	155 28.8	04.2	313 30.1	01.3	98 38.8	43.7	280 05.7	47.8	Capella	280 35.5	N46 00.6
02	142 57.6	170 28.4	03.1	328 32.2	01.3	113 41.1	43.7	295 08.0	47.8	Deneb	49 32.6	N45 19.6
03	158 00.1	185 27.9 ..	01.9	343 34.4 ..	01.2	128 43.4 ..	43.8	310 10.4 ..	47.8	Denebola	182 34.5	N14 30.0
04	173 02.5	200 27.5	13 00.8	358 36.6	01.2	143 45.8	43.9	325 12.7	47.8	Diphda	348 56.9	S17 55.3
05	188 05.0	215 27.1	12 59.7	13 38.7	01.1	158 48.1	43.9	340 15.1	47.9			
06	203 07.5	230 26.7	S12 58.5	28 40.9	N 6 01.1	173 50.4	N10 44.0	355 17.5	S 8 47.9	Dubhe	193 52.4	N61 40.8
07	218 09.9	245 26.2	57.4	43 43.1	01.0	188 52.7	44.1	10 19.8	47.9	Elnath	278 13.5	N28 37.0
S 08	233 12.4	260 25.8	56.2	58 45.2	01.0	203 55.0	44.1	25 22.2	48.0	Eltanin	90 47.1	N51 29.2
A 09	248 14.9	275 25.4 ..	55.1	73 47.4 ..	00.9	218 57.3 ..	44.2	40 24.5 ..	48.0	Enif	33 48.4	N 9 55.9
T 10	263 17.3	290 25.0	54.0	88 49.6	00.9	233 59.6	44.3	55 26.9	48.0	Fomalhaut	15 25.3	S29 33.6
U 11	278 19.8	305 24.5	52.8	103 51.8	00.8	249 01.9	44.3	70 29.3	48.0			
R 12	293 22.3	320 24.1	S12 51.7	118 53.9	N 6 00.8	264 04.3	N10 44.4	85 31.6	S 8 48.1	Gacrux	172 01.9	S57 10.7
D 13	308 24.7	335 23.7	50.6	133 56.1	00.7	279 06.6	44.5	100 34.0	48.1	Gienah	175 53.2	S17 36.6
A 14	323 27.2	350 23.3	49.4	148 58.3	00.7	294 08.9	44.5	115 36.3	48.1	Hadar	148 49.4	S60 25.6
Y 15	338 29.6	5 22.8 ..	48.3	164 00.5 ..	00.7	309 11.2 ..	44.6	130 38.7 ..	48.1	Hamal	328 01.8	N23 31.3
16	353 32.1	20 22.4	47.1	179 02.6	00.6	324 13.5	44.7	145 41.1	48.2	Kaus Aust.	83 45.5	S34 22.6
17	8 34.6	35 22.0	46.0	194 04.8	00.6	339 15.8	44.8	160 43.4	48.2			
18	23 37.0	50 21.6	S12 44.8	209 07.0	N 6 00.5	354 18.1	N10 44.8	175 45.8	S 8 48.2	Kochab	137 20.4	N74 06.0
19	38 39.5	65 21.1	43.7	224 09.2	00.5	9 20.4	44.9	190 48.2	48.2	Markab	13 39.5	N15 16.4
20	53 42.0	80 20.7	42.6	239 11.4	00.5	24 22.7	45.0	205 50.5	48.3	Menkar	314 15.9	N 4 08.2
21	68 44.4	95 20.3 ..	41.4	254 13.6 ..	00.4	39 25.0 ..	45.0	220 52.9 ..	48.3	Menkent	148 08.8	S36 25.6
22	83 46.9	110 19.9	40.3	269 15.7	00.4	54 27.3	45.1	235 55.2	48.3	Miaplacidus	221 39.0	S69 46.0
23	98 49.4	125 19.5	39.1	284 17.9	00.3	69 29.7	45.2	250 57.6	48.3			
15 00	113 51.8	140 19.0	S12 38.0	299 20.1	N 6 00.3	84 32.0	N10 45.2	266 00.0	S 8 48.4	Mirfak	308 41.5	N49 54.4
01	128 54.3	155 18.6	36.8	314 22.3	00.3	99 34.3	45.3	281 02.3	48.4	Nunki	75 59.9	S26 16.8
02	143 56.8	170 18.2	35.7	329 24.5	00.2	114 36.6	45.4	296 04.7	48.4	Peacock	53 21.4	S56 41.7
03	158 59.2	185 17.8 ..	34.5	344 26.7 ..	00.2	129 38.9 ..	45.5	311 07.1 ..	48.5	Pollux	243 28.5	N27 59.6
04	174 01.7	200 17.4	33.4	359 28.9	00.1	144 41.2	45.5	326 09.4	48.5	Procyon	245 00.4	N 5 11.4
05	189 04.1	215 17.0	32.2	14 31.1	00.1	159 43.5	45.6	341 11.8	48.5			
06	204 06.6	230 16.6	S12 31.1	29 33.3	N 6 00.1	174 45.8	N10 45.7	356 14.2	S 8 48.5	Rasalhague	96 07.7	N12 33.1
07	219 09.1	245 16.1	29.9	44 35.5	00.0	189 48.1	45.7	11 16.5	48.6	Regulus	207 44.3	N11 54.3
08	234 11.5	260 15.7	28.8	59 37.7	00.0	204 50.4	45.8	26 18.9	48.6	Rigel	281 12.7	S 8 11.4
S 09	249 14.0	275 15.3 ..	27.6	74 39.9	6 00.0	219 52.7 ..	45.9	41 21.2 ..	48.6	Rigil Kent.	139 53.3	S60 52.8
U 10	264 16.5	290 14.9	26.5	89 42.0	5 59.9	234 55.0	46.0	56 23.6	48.6	Sabik	102 14.0	S15 44.3
N 11	279 18.9	305 14.5	25.3	104 44.2	59.9	249 57.3	46.0	71 26.0	48.7			
D 12	294 21.4	320 14.1	S12 24.2	119 46.4	N 5 59.9	264 59.6	N10 46.1	86 28.3	S 8 48.7	Schedar	349 41.8	N56 36.5
A 13	309 23.9	335 13.7	23.0	134 48.7	59.8	280 01.9	46.2	101 30.7	48.7	Shaula	96 23.6	S37 06.6
Y 14	324 26.3	350 13.3	21.9	149 50.9	59.8	295 04.2	46.2	116 33.1	48.7	Sirius	258 34.2	S16 44.2
15	339 28.8	5 12.8 ..	20.7	164 53.1 ..	59.8	310 06.5 ..	46.3	131 35.4 ..	48.8	Spica	158 32.3	S11 13.5
16	354 31.2	20 12.4	19.6	179 55.3	59.7	325 08.8	46.4	146 37.8	48.8	Suhail	222 52.8	S43 29.0
17	9 33.7	35 12.0	18.4	194 57.5	59.7	340 11.1	46.5	161 40.2	48.8			
18	24 36.2	50 11.6	S12 17.3	209 59.7	N 5 59.7	355 13.4	N10 46.5	176 42.5	S 8 48.8	Vega	80 40.0	N38 47.7
19	39 38.6	65 11.2	16.1	225 01.9	59.6	10 15.7	46.6	191 44.9	48.9	Zuben'ubi	137 06.6	S16 05.5
20	54 41.1	80 10.8	15.0	240 04.1	59.6	25 18.0	46.7	206 47.3	48.9		SHA	Mer.Pass.
21	69 43.6	95 10.4 ..	13.8	255 06.3 ..	59.6	40 20.3 ..	46.7	221 49.6 ..	48.9		° ′	h m
22	84 46.0	110 10.0	12.6	270 08.5	59.6	55 22.6	46.8	236 52.0	48.9	Venus	27 36.6	14 38
23	99 48.5	125 09.6	11.5	285 10.7	59.5	70 24.9	46.9	251 54.4	49.0	Mars	185 35.2	4 06
	h m									Jupiter	330 43.8	18 23
Mer. Pass. 16 25.8		v −0.4	d 1.1	v 2.2	d 0.0	v 2.3	d 0.1	v 2.4	d 0.0	Saturn	152 10.6	6 19

UT	SUN GHA	SUN Dec	MOON GHA	v	MOON Dec	d	HP
d h	° ′	° ′	° ′	′	° ′	′	′
13 00	177 55.6	S21 36.6	313 57.4	11.4	N 3 42.6	13.1	58.4
01	192 55.4	36.2	328 27.8	11.5	3 29.5	13.0	58.4
02	207 55.2	35.8	342 58.3	11.4	3 16.5	13.2	58.4
03	222 54.9	.. 35.4	357 28.7	11.5	3 03.3	13.1	58.5
04	237 54.7	35.0	11 59.2	11.4	2 50.2	13.1	58.5
05	252 54.4	34.6	26 29.6	11.5	2 37.1	13.2	58.5
06	267 54.2	S21 34.1	41 00.1	11.4	N 2 23.9	13.2	58.5
07	282 54.0	33.7	55 30.5	11.4	2 10.7	13.2	58.5
F 08	297 53.7	33.3	70 00.9	11.5	1 57.5	13.2	58.5
R 09	312 53.5	.. 32.9	84 31.4	11.4	1 44.3	13.2	58.5
I 10	327 53.3	32.5	99 01.8	11.4	1 31.1	13.2	58.5
D 11	342 53.0	32.1	113 32.2	11.4	1 17.9	13.3	58.6
A 12	357 52.8	S21 31.6	128 02.6	11.4	N 1 04.6	13.3	58.6
Y 13	12 52.6	31.2	142 33.0	11.4	0 51.3	13.2	58.6
14	27 52.3	30.8	157 03.4	11.4	0 38.1	13.3	58.6
15	42 52.1	.. 30.4	171 33.8	11.4	0 24.8	13.3	58.6
16	57 51.9	30.0	186 04.2	11.4	N 0 11.5	13.3	58.6
17	72 51.6	29.5	200 34.6	11.4	S 0 01.8	13.3	58.6
18	87 51.4	S21 29.1	215 05.0	11.3	S 0 15.1	13.3	58.6
19	102 51.2	28.7	229 35.3	11.3	0 28.4	13.3	58.7
20	117 50.9	28.3	244 05.6	11.4	0 41.7	13.3	58.7
21	132 50.7	.. 27.8	258 36.0	11.3	0 55.0	13.3	58.7
22	147 50.5	27.4	273 06.3	11.3	1 08.3	13.3	58.7
23	162 50.2	27.0	287 36.6	11.2	1 21.6	13.2	58.7
14 00	177 50.0	S21 26.5	302 06.8	11.3	S 1 34.8	13.3	58.7
01	192 49.8	26.1	316 37.1	11.2	1 48.1	13.3	58.7
02	207 49.5	25.7	331 07.3	11.3	2 01.4	13.3	58.8
03	222 49.3	.. 25.3	345 37.6	11.2	2 14.7	13.3	58.8
04	237 49.1	24.8	0 07.8	11.2	2 28.0	13.2	58.8
05	252 48.8	24.4	14 38.0	11.1	2 41.2	13.3	58.8
06	267 48.6	S21 24.0	29 08.1	11.1	S 2 54.5	13.2	58.8
S 07	282 48.4	23.5	43 38.2	11.2	3 07.7	13.2	58.8
A 08	297 48.1	23.1	58 08.4	11.1	3 20.9	13.3	58.8
T 09	312 47.9	.. 22.7	72 38.5	11.0	3 34.2	13.2	58.8
U 10	327 47.7	22.2	87 08.5	11.1	3 47.4	13.1	58.8
R 11	342 47.4	21.8	101 38.6	11.0	4 00.5	13.2	58.8
D 12	357 47.2	S21 21.4	116 08.6	11.0	S 4 13.7	13.1	58.9
A 13	12 47.0	20.9	130 38.6	10.9	4 26.8	13.2	58.9
Y 14	27 46.8	20.5	145 08.5	10.9	4 40.0	13.1	58.9
15	42 46.5	.. 20.0	159 38.4	10.9	4 53.1	13.0	58.9
16	57 46.3	19.6	174 08.3	10.9	5 06.1	13.1	58.9
17	72 46.1	19.2	188 38.2	10.8	5 19.2	13.0	58.9
18	87 45.8	S21 18.7	203 08.0	10.8	S 5 32.2	13.0	58.9
19	102 45.6	18.3	217 37.8	10.8	5 45.2	13.0	58.9
20	117 45.4	17.8	232 07.6	10.7	5 58.2	13.0	58.9
21	132 45.2	.. 17.4	246 37.3	10.7	6 11.2	12.9	58.9
22	147 44.9	16.9	261 07.0	10.7	6 24.1	12.9	58.9
23	162 44.7	16.5	275 36.7	10.6	6 37.0	12.8	59.0
15 00	177 44.5	S21 16.1	290 06.3	10.6	S 6 49.8	12.8	59.0
01	192 44.3	15.6	304 35.9	10.6	7 02.6	12.8	59.0
02	207 44.0	15.2	319 05.5	10.5	7 15.4	12.8	59.0
03	222 43.8	.. 14.7	333 35.0	10.4	7 28.2	12.7	59.0
04	237 43.6	14.3	348 04.4	10.5	7 40.9	12.6	59.0
05	252 43.4	13.8	2 33.9	10.4	7 53.5	12.7	59.0
06	267 43.1	S21 13.4	17 03.3	10.3	S 8 06.2	12.6	59.0
07	282 42.9	12.9	31 32.6	10.3	8 18.8	12.5	59.0
S 08	297 42.7	12.5	46 01.9	10.3	8 31.3	12.5	59.0
U 09	312 42.5	.. 12.0	60 31.2	10.2	8 43.8	12.5	59.0
N 10	327 42.2	11.6	75 00.4	10.2	8 56.3	12.4	59.0
D 11	342 42.0	11.1	89 29.6	10.1	9 08.7	12.3	59.1
A 12	357 41.8	S21 10.6	103 58.7	10.1	S 9 21.0	12.3	59.1
Y 13	12 41.6	10.2	118 27.8	10.0	9 33.3	12.3	59.1
14	27 41.4	09.7	132 56.8	10.0	9 45.6	12.2	59.1
15	42 41.1	.. 09.3	147 25.8	9.9	9 57.8	12.2	59.1
16	57 40.9	08.8	161 54.7	9.9	10 10.0	12.1	59.1
17	72 40.7	08.4	176 23.6	9.8	10 22.1	12.0	59.1
18	87 40.5	S21 07.9	190 52.4	9.8	S10 34.1	12.0	59.1
19	102 40.2	07.5	205 21.2	9.7	10 46.1	11.9	59.1
20	117 40.0	07.0	219 49.9	9.7	10 58.0	11.9	59.1
21	132 39.8	.. 06.5	234 18.6	9.6	11 09.9	11.8	59.1
22	147 39.6	06.1	248 47.2	9.6	11 21.7	11.8	59.1
23	162 39.4	05.6	263 15.8	9.5	S11 33.5	11.7	59.1
	SD 16.3 d 0.4		SD 16.0		16.0		16.1

Twilight / Sunrise / Moonrise

Lat.	Twilight Naut.	Twilight Civil	Sunrise	Moonrise 13	14	15	16
°	h m	h m	h m	h m	h m	h m	h m
N 72	08 04	09 58	■	22 04	24 09	00 09	02 24
N 70	07 49	09 22	■	22 02	23 58	26 00	02 00
68	07 36	08 57	10 40	22 00	23 49	25 43	01 43
66	07 26	08 37	09 58	21 59	23 42	25 28	01 28
64	07 17	08 21	09 29	21 58	23 36	25 17	01 17
62	07 09	08 08	09 07	21 57	23 31	25 07	01 07
60	07 02	07 57	08 50	21 56	23 27	24 58	00 58
N 58	06 56	07 47	08 35	21 56	23 23	24 51	00 51
56	06 51	07 38	08 23	21 55	23 19	24 45	00 45
54	06 45	07 30	08 12	21 55	23 16	24 39	00 39
52	06 41	07 23	08 02	21 54	23 13	24 34	00 34
50	06 36	07 17	07 54	21 54	23 11	24 29	00 29
45	06 26	07 03	07 36	21 53	23 05	24 19	00 19
N 40	06 17	06 51	07 21	21 52	23 01	24 11	00 11
35	06 09	06 40	07 08	21 51	22 57	24 03	00 03
30	06 02	06 31	06 57	21 50	22 53	23 57	25 02
20	05 47	06 14	06 38	21 49	22 47	23 47	24 47
N 10	05 32	05 58	06 21	21 49	22 42	23 37	24 34
0	05 17	05 43	06 05	21 48	22 37	23 29	24 22
S 10	05 00	05 27	05 49	21 47	22 33	23 20	24 10
20	04 39	05 08	05 32	21 46	22 28	23 11	23 57
30	04 13	04 45	05 12	21 45	22 22	23 01	23 43
35	03 56	04 32	05 00	21 45	22 19	22 55	23 34
40	03 35	04 15	04 47	21 44	22 15	22 48	23 25
45	03 08	03 55	04 31	21 44	22 11	22 40	23 13
S 50	02 30	03 29	04 11	21 43	22 06	22 31	23 00
52	02 09	03 16	04 01	21 42	22 04	22 27	22 54
54	01 41	03 01	03 51	21 42	22 01	22 22	22 47
56	00 53	02 43	03 39	21 42	21 58	22 17	22 39
58	////	02 20	03 24	21 41	21 55	22 11	22 31
S 60	////	01 50	03 08	21 41	21 52	22 05	22 21

Sunset / Twilight / Moonset

Lat.	Sunset	Twilight Civil	Twilight Naut.	Moonset 13	14	15	16
°	h m	h m	h m	h m	h m	h m	h m
N 72	■	14 21	16 14	09 41	09 23	09 03	08 36
N 70	■	14 56	16 30	09 39	09 28	09 16	09 01
68	13 38	15 22	16 42	09 37	09 32	09 27	09 21
66	14 18	15 41	16 52	09 36	09 36	09 36	09 36
64	14 49	15 57	17 01	09 35	09 39	09 43	09 49
62	15 11	16 10	17 09	09 34	09 41	09 50	10 00
60	15 28	16 21	17 16	09 33	09 44	09 55	10 10
N 58	15 43	16 31	17 22	09 32	09 46	10 00	10 18
56	15 55	16 40	17 28	09 32	09 48	10 05	10 25
54	16 06	16 48	17 33	09 31	09 49	10 09	10 32
52	16 16	16 55	17 37	09 30	09 51	10 13	10 37
50	16 24	17 01	17 42	09 30	09 52	10 16	10 43
45	16 42	17 15	17 52	09 29	09 55	10 23	10 54
N 40	16 57	17 27	18 01	09 28	09 58	10 29	11 04
35	17 10	17 38	18 09	09 27	10 00	10 35	11 12
30	17 21	17 47	18 16	09 26	10 02	10 39	11 20
20	17 40	18 04	18 31	09 25	10 05	10 48	11 32
N 10	17 57	18 19	18 45	09 23	10 08	10 55	11 43
0	18 13	18 35	19 01	09 22	10 11	11 01	11 54
S 10	18 28	18 51	19 18	09 21	10 14	11 08	12 04
20	18 45	19 10	19 38	09 20	10 17	11 15	12 15
30	19 05	19 32	20 04	09 18	10 20	11 24	12 28
35	19 17	19 46	20 21	09 17	10 22	11 28	12 36
40	19 30	20 02	20 42	09 16	10 25	11 34	12 44
45	19 46	20 22	21 08	09 15	10 27	11 40	12 54
S 50	20 06	20 48	21 46	09 13	10 30	11 48	13 06
52	20 15	21 01	22 07	09 13	10 32	11 51	13 12
54	20 26	21 16	22 34	09 12	10 33	11 55	13 18
56	20 38	21 33	23 19	09 11	10 35	11 59	13 25
58	20 52	21 55	////	09 10	10 37	12 04	13 33
S 60	21 09	22 25	////	09 09	10 39	12 10	13 42

SUN / MOON

Day	SUN Eqn. of Time 00h	SUN Eqn. of Time 12h	SUN Mer. Pass.	MOON Mer. Pass. Upper	MOON Mer. Pass. Lower	Age	Phase
d	m s	m s	h m	h m	h m	d	%
13	08 17	08 28	12 08	03 10	15 35	20	80
14	08 40	08 51	12 09	03 59	16 24	21	71
15	09 02	09 12	12 09	04 49	17 15	22	60

UT	ARIES GHA	VENUS −4.0 GHA	Dec	MARS −0.2 GHA	Dec	JUPITER −2.5 GHA	Dec	SATURN +0.6 GHA	Dec	STARS Name	SHA	Dec
d h	° ′	° ′	° ′	° ′	° ′	° ′	° ′	° ′	° ′		° ′	° ′
16 00	114 51.0	140 09.2	S12 10.3	300 12.9	N 5 59.5	85 27.2	N10 47.0	266 56.7	S 8 49.0	Acamar	315 18.9	S40 15.6
01	129 53.4	155 08.8	09.2	315 15.1	59.5	100 29.5	47.0	281 59.1	49.0	Achernar	335 27.5	S57 10.8
02	144 55.9	170 08.4	08.0	330 17.4	59.4	115 31.8	47.1	297 01.5	49.0	Acrux	173 10.2	S63 09.8
03	159 58.4	185 08.0 ..	06.8	345 19.6 ..	59.4	130 34.1 ..	47.2	312 03.8 ..	49.1	Adhara	255 12.9	S28 59.5
04	175 00.8	200 07.6	05.7	0 21.8	59.4	145 36.4	47.3	327 06.2	49.1	Aldebaran	290 50.3	N16 32.0
05	190 03.3	215 07.2	04.5	15 24.0	59.4	160 38.7	47.3	342 08.6	49.1			
06	205 05.7	230 06.8	S12 03.4	30 26.2	N 5 59.3	175 41.0	N10 47.4	357 10.9	S 8 49.1	Alioth	166 21.4	N55 53.3
07	220 08.2	245 06.4	02.2	45 28.5	59.3	190 43.3	47.5	12 13.3	49.1	Alkaid	152 59.7	N49 14.8
M 08	235 10.7	260 06.0	12 01.0	60 30.7	59.3	205 45.6	47.5	27 15.7	49.2	Al Na'ir	27 45.3	S46 54.2
O 09	250 13.1	275 05.6	11 59.9	75 32.9 ..	59.3	220 47.9 ..	47.6	42 18.0 ..	49.2	Alnilam	275 47.1	S 1 11.8
N 10	265 15.6	290 05.2	58.7	90 35.1	59.2	235 50.2	47.7	57 20.4	49.2	Alphard	217 56.7	S 8 42.8
D 11	280 18.1	305 04.8	57.5	105 37.3	59.2	250 52.5	47.8	72 22.8	49.2			
A 12	295 20.5	320 04.4	S11 56.4	120 39.6	N 5 59.2	265 54.8	N10 47.8	87 25.2	S 8 49.3	Alphecca	126 12.0	N26 40.3
Y 13	310 23.0	335 04.0	55.2	135 41.8	59.2	280 57.1	47.9	102 27.5	49.3	Alpheratz	357 44.7	N29 09.6
14	325 25.5	350 03.6	54.0	150 44.0	59.2	295 59.4	48.0	117 29.9	49.3	Altair	62 09.5	N 8 54.1
15	340 27.9	5 03.2 ..	52.9	165 46.3 ..	59.1	311 01.7 ..	48.1	132 32.3 ..	49.3	Ankaa	353 16.8	S42 14.6
16	355 30.4	20 02.8	51.7	180 48.5	59.1	326 04.0	48.1	147 34.6	49.4	Antares	112 27.7	S26 27.4
17	10 32.9	35 02.4	50.5	195 50.7	59.1	341 06.3	48.2	162 37.0	49.4			
18	25 35.3	50 02.0	S11 49.4	210 53.0	N 5 59.1	356 08.6	N10 48.3	177 39.4	S 8 49.4	Arcturus	145 56.7	N19 07.0
19	40 37.8	65 01.6	48.2	225 55.2	59.1	11 10.9	48.4	192 41.7	49.4	Atria	107 30.9	S69 02.7
20	55 40.2	80 01.2	47.0	240 57.4	59.0	26 13.2	48.4	207 44.1	49.5	Avior	234 17.8	S59 33.0
21	70 42.7	95 00.8 ..	45.9	255 59.7 ..	59.0	41 15.5 ..	48.5	222 46.5 ..	49.5	Bellatrix	278 32.8	N 6 21.5
22	85 45.2	110 00.4	44.7	271 01.9	59.0	56 17.8	48.6	237 48.9	49.5	Betelgeuse	271 02.0	N 7 24.4
23	100 47.6	125 00.0	43.5	286 04.1	59.0	71 20.1	48.7	252 51.2	49.5			
17 00	115 50.1	139 59.6	S11 42.4	301 06.4	N 5 59.0	86 22.3	N10 48.7	267 53.6	S 8 49.5	Canopus	263 56.1	S52 42.3
01	130 52.6	154 59.2	41.2	316 08.6	59.0	101 24.6	48.8	282 56.0	49.6	Capella	280 35.5	N46 00.6
02	145 55.0	169 58.8	40.0	331 10.9	58.9	116 26.9	48.9	297 58.3	49.6	Deneb	49 32.6	N45 19.6
03	160 57.5	184 58.5 ..	38.8	346 13.1 ..	58.9	131 29.2 ..	49.0	313 00.7 ..	49.6	Denebola	182 34.5	N14 30.0
04	176 00.0	199 58.1	37.7	1 15.3	58.9	146 31.5	49.0	328 03.1	49.6	Diphda	348 56.9	S17 55.3
05	191 02.4	214 57.7	36.5	16 17.6	58.9	161 33.8	49.1	343 05.5	49.7			
06	206 04.9	229 57.3	S11 35.3	31 19.8	N 5 58.9	176 36.1	N10 49.2	358 07.8	S 8 49.7	Dubhe	193 52.4	N61 40.8
07	221 07.3	244 56.9	34.1	46 22.1	58.9	191 38.4	49.3	13 10.2	49.7	Elnath	278 13.5	N28 37.0
T 08	236 09.8	259 56.5	33.0	61 24.3	58.9	206 40.7	49.4	28 12.6	49.7	Eltanin	90 47.1	N51 29.2
U 09	251 12.3	274 56.1 ..	31.8	76 26.6 ..	58.8	221 43.0 ..	49.4	43 14.9 ..	49.7	Enif	33 48.4	N 9 55.9
E 10	266 14.7	289 55.7	30.6	91 28.8	58.8	236 45.3	49.5	58 17.3	49.8	Fomalhaut	15 25.3	S29 33.5
S 11	281 17.2	304 55.3	29.4	106 31.1	58.8	251 47.5	49.6	73 19.7	49.8			
D 12	296 19.7	319 55.0	S11 28.3	121 33.3	N 5 58.8	266 49.8	N10 49.7	88 22.1	S 8 49.8	Gacrux	172 01.8	S57 10.7
A 13	311 22.1	334 54.6	27.1	136 35.6	58.8	281 52.1	49.7	103 24.4	49.8	Gienah	175 53.2	S17 36.6
Y 14	326 24.6	349 54.2	25.9	151 37.8	58.8	296 54.4	49.8	118 26.8	49.9	Hadar	148 49.4	S60 25.6
15	341 27.1	4 53.8 ..	24.7	166 40.1 ..	58.8	311 56.7 ..	49.9	133 29.2 ..	49.9	Hamal	328 01.8	N23 31.3
16	356 29.5	19 53.4	23.5	181 42.3	58.8	326 59.0	50.0	148 31.6	49.9	Kaus Aust.	83 45.5	S34 22.6
17	11 32.0	34 53.0	22.4	196 44.6	58.8	342 01.3	50.0	163 33.9	49.9			
18	26 34.5	49 52.7	S11 21.2	211 46.9	N 5 58.8	357 03.6	N10 50.1	178 36.3	S 8 49.9	Kochab	137 20.3	N74 06.0
19	41 36.9	64 52.3	20.0	226 49.1	58.8	12 05.8	50.2	193 38.7	50.0	Markab	13 39.5	N15 16.4
20	56 39.4	79 51.9	18.8	241 51.4	58.7	27 08.1	50.3	208 41.1	50.0	Menkar	314 15.9	N 4 08.2
21	71 41.8	94 51.5 ..	17.6	256 53.6 ..	58.7	42 10.4 ..	50.4	223 43.4 ..	50.0	Menkent	148 08.8	S36 25.6
22	86 44.3	109 51.1	16.5	271 55.9	58.7	57 12.7	50.4	238 45.8	50.0	Miaplacidus	221 39.0	S69 46.0
23	101 46.8	124 50.8	15.3	286 58.2	58.7	72 15.0	50.5	253 48.2	50.1			
18 00	116 49.2	139 50.4	S11 14.1	302 00.4	N 5 58.7	87 17.3	N10 50.6	268 50.6	S 8 50.1	Mirfak	308 41.5	N49 54.4
01	131 51.7	154 50.0	12.9	317 02.7	58.7	102 19.6	50.7	283 52.9	50.1	Nunki	75 59.9	S26 16.8
02	146 54.2	169 49.6	11.7	332 05.0	58.7	117 21.8	50.7	298 55.3	50.1	Peacock	53 21.3	S56 41.7
03	161 56.6	184 49.2 ..	10.5	347 07.2 ..	58.7	132 24.1 ..	50.8	313 57.7 ..	50.1	Pollux	243 28.5	N27 59.6
04	176 59.1	199 48.9	09.4	2 09.5	58.7	147 26.4	50.9	329 00.1	50.2	Procyon	245 00.4	N 5 11.4
05	192 01.6	214 48.5	08.2	17 11.8	58.7	162 28.7	51.0	344 02.4	50.2			
06	207 04.0	229 48.1	S11 07.0	32 14.1	N 5 58.7	177 31.0	N10 51.1	359 04.8	S 8 50.2	Rasalhague	96 07.7	N12 33.1
W 07	222 06.5	244 47.7	05.8	47 16.3	58.7	192 33.3	51.1	14 07.2	50.2	Regulus	207 44.3	N11 54.2
E 08	237 09.0	259 47.4	04.6	62 18.6	58.7	207 35.5	51.2	29 09.6	50.2	Rigel	281 12.7	S 8 11.4
D 09	252 11.4	274 47.0 ..	03.4	77 20.9 ..	58.7	222 37.8 ..	51.3	44 11.9 ..	50.3	Rigil Kent.	139 53.2	S60 52.8
N 10	267 13.9	289 46.6	02.2	92 23.2	58.7	237 40.1	51.4	59 14.3	50.3	Sabik	102 13.9	S15 44.3
E 11	282 16.3	304 46.2	11 01.0	107 25.4	58.7	252 42.4	51.5	74 16.7	50.3			
S 12	297 18.8	319 45.9	S10 59.9	122 27.7	N 5 58.7	267 44.7	N10 51.5	89 19.1	S 8 50.3	Schedar	349 41.8	N56 36.5
D 13	312 21.3	334 45.5	58.7	137 30.0	58.7	282 46.9	51.6	104 21.4	50.3	Shaula	96 23.6	S37 06.6
A 14	327 23.7	349 45.1	57.5	152 32.3	58.7	297 49.2	51.7	119 23.8	50.4	Sirius	258 34.2	S16 44.2
Y 15	342 26.2	4 44.8 ..	56.3	167 34.6 ..	58.7	312 51.5 ..	51.8	134 26.2 ..	50.4	Spica	158 32.3	S11 13.5
16	357 28.7	19 44.4	55.1	182 36.8	58.7	327 53.8	51.9	149 28.6	50.4	Suhail	222 52.7	S43 29.0
17	12 31.1	34 44.0	53.9	197 39.1	58.7	342 56.1	51.9	164 31.0	50.4			
18	27 33.6	49 43.6	S10 52.7	212 41.4	N 5 58.7	357 58.3	N10 52.0	179 33.3	S 8 50.5	Vega	80 40.0	N38 47.7
19	42 36.1	64 43.3	51.5	227 43.7	58.7	13 00.6	52.1	194 35.7	50.5	Zuben'ubi	137 06.6	S16 05.5
20	57 38.5	79 42.9	50.3	242 46.0	58.7	28 02.9	52.2	209 38.1	50.5		SHA	Mer. Pass.
21	72 41.0	94 42.5 ..	49.1	257 48.3 ..	58.7	43 05.2 ..	52.3	224 40.5 ..	50.5		° ′	h m
22	87 43.5	109 42.2	47.9	272 50.6	58.7	58 07.5	52.3	239 42.8	50.5	Venus	24 09.5	14 40
23	102 45.9	124 41.8	46.8	287 52.9	58.7	73 09.7	52.4	254 45.2	50.6	Mars	185 16.3	3 55
	h m									Jupiter	330 32.2	18 12
Mer. Pass. 16 14.0	v −0.4 d 1.2			v 2.3 d 0.0		v 2.3 d 0.1		v 2.4 d 0.0		Saturn	152 03.5	6 07

UT	SUN GHA	SUN Dec	MOON GHA	v	Dec	d	HP
d h	° ′	° ′	° ′	′	° ′	′	′
16 00	177 39.1	S21 05.1	277 44.3	9.5	S11 45.2	11.6	59.1
01	192 38.9	04.7	292 12.8	9.4	11 56.8	11.5	59.1
02	207 38.7	04.2	306 41.2	9.3	12 08.3	11.5	59.2
03	222 38.5	03.8	321 09.5	9.3	12 19.8	11.4	59.2
04	237 38.3	03.3	335 37.8	9.3	12 31.2	11.4	59.2
05	252 38.1	02.8	350 06.1	9.2	12 42.6	11.3	59.2
06	267 37.8	S21 02.4	4 34.3	9.1	S12 53.9	11.2	59.2
M 07	282 37.6	01.9	19 02.4	9.1	13 05.1	11.1	59.2
O 08	297 37.4	01.4	33 30.5	9.0	13 16.2	11.0	59.2
N 09	312 37.2	01.0	47 58.5	8.9	13 27.2	11.0	59.2
D 10	327 37.0	00.5	62 26.4	8.9	13 38.2	10.9	59.2
A 11	342 36.8	21 00.0	76 54.3	8.8	13 49.1	10.8	59.2
Y 12	357 36.5	S20 59.5	91 22.1	8.8	S13 59.9	10.8	59.2
13	12 36.3	59.1	105 49.9	8.7	14 10.7	10.6	59.2
14	27 36.1	58.6	120 17.6	8.7	14 21.3	10.6	59.2
15	42 35.9	58.1	134 45.3	8.6	14 31.9	10.5	59.2
16	57 35.7	57.6	149 12.9	8.5	14 42.4	10.4	59.2
17	72 35.5	57.2	163 40.4	8.5	14 52.8	10.3	59.2
18	87 35.2	S20 56.7	178 07.9	8.4	S15 03.1	10.3	59.2
19	102 35.0	56.2	192 35.3	8.3	15 13.4	10.1	59.2
20	117 34.8	55.7	207 02.6	8.3	15 23.5	10.1	59.2
21	132 34.6	55.3	221 29.9	8.2	15 33.6	9.9	59.2
22	147 34.4	54.8	235 57.1	8.2	15 43.5	9.9	59.2
23	162 34.2	54.3	250 24.3	8.1	15 53.4	9.8	59.2
17 00	177 34.0	S20 53.8	264 51.4	8.0	S16 03.2	9.7	59.2
01	192 33.8	53.4	279 18.4	8.0	16 12.9	9.5	59.3
02	207 33.5	52.9	293 45.4	7.9	16 22.4	9.5	59.3
03	222 33.3	52.4	308 12.3	7.9	16 31.9	9.4	59.3
04	237 33.1	51.9	322 39.2	7.8	16 41.3	9.3	59.3
05	252 32.9	51.4	337 06.0	7.7	16 50.6	9.2	59.3
06	267 32.7	S20 50.9	351 32.7	7.7	S16 59.8	9.1	59.3
T 07	282 32.5	50.5	5 59.4	7.6	17 08.9	8.9	59.3
U 08	297 32.3	50.0	20 26.0	7.5	17 17.8	8.9	59.3
E 09	312 32.1	49.5	34 52.5	7.5	17 26.7	8.8	59.3
S 10	327 31.9	49.0	49 19.0	7.4	17 35.5	8.6	59.3
D 11	342 31.6	48.5	63 45.4	7.4	17 44.1	8.6	59.3
A 12	357 31.4	S20 48.0	78 11.8	7.3	S17 52.7	8.4	59.3
Y 13	12 31.2	47.5	92 38.1	7.2	18 01.1	8.3	59.3
14	27 31.0	47.0	107 04.3	7.2	18 09.4	8.2	59.3
15	42 30.8	46.6	121 30.5	7.1	18 17.6	8.1	59.3
16	57 30.6	46.1	135 56.6	7.1	18 25.7	8.0	59.3
17	72 30.4	45.6	150 22.7	7.0	18 33.7	7.9	59.3
18	87 30.2	S20 45.1	164 48.7	6.9	S18 41.6	7.7	59.3
19	102 30.0	44.6	179 14.6	6.9	18 49.3	7.7	59.3
20	117 29.8	44.1	193 40.5	6.8	18 57.0	7.5	59.3
21	132 29.6	43.6	208 06.3	6.8	19 04.5	7.4	59.3
22	147 29.4	43.1	222 32.1	6.7	19 11.9	7.2	59.3
23	162 29.2	42.6	236 57.8	6.7	19 19.1	7.2	59.3
18 00	177 29.0	S20 42.1	251 23.5	6.6	S19 26.3	7.0	59.3
01	192 28.7	41.6	265 49.1	6.5	19 33.3	6.9	59.3
02	207 28.5	41.1	280 14.6	6.5	19 40.2	6.8	59.3
03	222 28.3	40.6	294 40.1	6.5	19 47.0	6.6	59.3
04	237 28.1	40.1	309 05.6	6.4	19 53.6	6.6	59.3
05	252 27.9	39.6	323 31.0	6.3	20 00.2	6.4	59.3
06	267 27.7	S20 39.1	337 56.3	6.3	S20 06.6	6.2	59.3
W 07	282 27.5	38.6	352 21.6	6.2	20 12.8	6.2	59.3
E 08	297 27.3	38.1	6 46.8	6.2	20 19.0	6.0	59.3
D 09	312 27.1	37.6	21 12.0	6.2	20 25.0	5.8	59.3
N 10	327 26.9	37.1	35 37.2	6.1	20 30.8	5.8	59.3
E 11	342 26.7	36.6	50 02.3	6.1	20 36.6	5.6	59.3
S 12	357 26.5	S20 36.1	64 27.3	6.0	S20 42.2	5.4	59.3
D 13	12 26.3	35.6	78 52.3	6.0	20 47.6	5.4	59.3
A 14	27 26.1	35.1	93 17.3	5.9	20 53.0	5.2	59.3
Y 15	42 25.9	34.6	107 42.2	5.9	20 58.2	5.0	59.3
16	57 25.7	34.1	122 07.1	5.8	21 03.2	5.0	59.3
17	72 25.5	33.6	136 31.9	5.8	21 08.2	4.8	59.3
18	87 25.3	S20 33.1	150 56.7	5.8	S21 12.9	4.7	59.2
19	102 25.1	32.6	165 21.5	5.7	21 17.6	4.5	59.2
20	117 24.9	32.1	179 46.2	5.7	21 22.1	4.3	59.2
21	132 24.7	31.6	194 10.9	5.6	21 26.4	4.3	59.2
22	147 24.5	31.0	208 35.5	5.6	21 30.7	4.0	59.2
23	162 24.3	30.5	223 00.1	5.6	S21 34.7	4.0	59.2
	SD 16.3	d 0.5	SD 16.1		16.2		16.1

Lat.	Twilight Naut.	Twilight Civil	Sunrise	Moonrise 16	17	18	19
°	h m	h m	h m	h m	h m	h m	h m
N 72	07 57	09 46	■■	02 24	05 14	■■	■■
N 70	07 43	09 13	11 56	02 00	04 16	■■	■■
68	07 31	08 50	10 26	01 43	03 42	05 52	■■
66	07 22	08 32	09 49	01 28	03 18	05 09	06 52
64	07 13	08 17	09 22	01 17	02 59	04 40	06 11
62	07 06	08 04	09 02	01 07	02 44	04 18	05 44
60	06 59	07 53	08 45	00 58	02 31	04 01	05 22
N 58	06 54	07 44	08 31	00 51	02 20	03 46	05 05
56	06 48	07 35	08 20	00 45	02 10	03 33	04 50
54	06 43	07 28	08 09	00 39	02 02	03 22	04 37
52	06 39	07 21	08 00	00 34	01 54	03 13	04 26
50	06 35	07 15	07 52	00 29	01 47	03 04	04 16
45	06 25	07 01	07 34	00 19	01 33	02 46	03 55
N 40	06 16	06 50	07 19	00 11	01 21	02 31	03 39
35	06 09	06 40	07 07	00 03	01 11	02 19	03 24
30	06 01	06 31	06 56	25 02	01 02	02 08	03 12
20	05 47	06 14	06 38	24 47	00 47	01 49	02 51
N 10	05 33	05 59	06 22	24 34	00 34	01 33	02 33
0	05 18	05 44	06 06	24 22	00 22	01 18	02 16
S 10	05 02	05 28	05 51	24 10	00 10	01 03	02 00
20	04 42	05 10	05 34	23 57	24 47	00 47	01 42
30	04 16	04 48	05 15	23 43	24 29	00 29	01 21
35	03 59	04 35	05 03	23 34	24 19	00 19	01 09
40	03 39	04 19	04 50	23 25	24 07	00 07	00 55
45	03 13	03 59	04 35	23 13	23 53	24 39	00 39
S 50	02 37	03 34	04 15	23 00	23 35	24 19	00 19
52	02 17	03 22	04 06	22 54	23 27	24 10	00 10
54	01 51	03 07	03 56	22 47	23 18	23 59	24 52
56	01 12	02 50	03 44	22 39	23 08	23 47	24 39
58	////	02 29	03 31	22 31	22 57	23 33	24 24
S 60	////	02 01	03 15	22 21	22 44	23 17	24 06

Lat.	Sunset	Twilight Civil	Twilight Naut.	Moonset 16	17	18	19
°	h m	h m	h m	h m	h m	h m	h m
N 72	■■	14 35	16 24	08 36	07 39	■■	■■
N 70	12 24	15 07	16 38	09 01	08 38	■■	■■
68	13 54	15 31	16 49	09 21	09 13	09 02	■■
66	14 32	15 49	16 59	09 36	09 39	09 46	10 05
64	14 58	16 04	17 07	09 49	09 59	10 15	10 44
62	15 18	16 17	17 15	10 00	10 17	10 37	11 14
60	15 35	16 27	17 21	10 10	10 28	10 55	11 36
N 58	15 49	16 37	17 27	10 18	10 40	11 11	11 53
56	16 01	16 45	17 32	10 25	10 50	11 24	12 08
54	16 11	16 53	17 37	10 32	10 59	11 35	12 21
52	16 20	16 59	17 42	10 37	11 07	11 45	12 32
50	16 29	17 05	17 46	10 43	11 15	11 54	12 43
45	16 46	17 19	17 55	10 54	11 30	12 13	13 04
N 40	17 01	17 30	18 04	11 04	11 43	12 28	13 21
35	17 13	17 40	18 11	11 12	11 54	12 41	13 35
30	17 24	17 49	18 19	11 20	12 04	12 53	13 48
20	17 42	18 06	18 33	11 32	12 20	13 12	14 09
N 10	17 58	18 21	18 47	11 43	12 35	13 30	14 27
0	18 14	18 36	19 01	11 54	12 48	13 46	14 45
S 10	18 29	18 52	19 18	12 04	13 02	14 02	15 02
20	18 46	19 10	19 38	12 15	13 17	14 19	15 20
30	19 05	19 31	20 04	12 28	13 33	14 39	15 42
35	19 16	19 45	20 20	12 36	13 43	14 50	15 54
40	19 29	20 00	20 40	12 44	13 54	15 03	16 09
45	19 44	20 20	21 05	12 54	14 08	15 19	16 26
S 50	20 04	20 45	21 41	13 06	14 24	15 39	16 47
52	20 13	20 57	22 01	13 12	14 31	15 48	16 57
54	20 23	21 11	22 26	13 18	14 40	15 58	17 08
56	20 34	21 28	23 03	13 25	14 49	16 10	17 21
58	20 48	21 49	////	13 33	15 00	16 23	17 36
S 60	21 03	22 16	////	13 42	15 13	16 39	17 53

Day	SUN Eqn. of Time 00ʰ	SUN Eqn. of Time 12ʰ	SUN Mer. Pass.	MOON Mer. Pass. Upper	MOON Mer. Pass. Lower	Age	Phase
d	m s	m s	h m	h m	h m	d	%
16	09 23	09 33	12 10	05 41	18 08	23	49
17	09 44	09 54	12 10	06 35	19 03	24	37
18	10 04	10 14	12 10	07 32	20 01	25	27

UT	ARIES	VENUS −4.0		MARS −0.3		JUPITER −2.4		SATURN +0.6		STARS		
	GHA	GHA	Dec	GHA	Dec	GHA	Dec	GHA	Dec	Name	SHA	Dec
d h	° ′	° ′	° ′	° ′	° ′	° ′	° ′	° ′	° ′		° ′	° ′
19 00	117 48.4	139 41.4	S10 45.6	302 55.2	N 5 58.7	88 12.0	N10 52.5	269 47.6	S 8 50.6	Acamar	315 18.9	S40 15.6
01	132 50.8	154 41.1	44.4	317 57.4	58.7	103 14.3	52.6	284 50.0	50.6	Achernar	335 27.5	S57 10.8
02	147 53.3	169 40.7	43.2	332 59.7	58.8	118 16.6	52.7	299 52.4	50.6	Acrux	173 10.1	S63 09.8
03	162 55.8	184 40.3	. . 42.0	348 02.0	. . 58.8	133 18.8	. . 52.7	314 54.7	. . 50.6	Adhara	255 12.9	S28 59.5
04	177 58.2	199 40.0	40.8	3 04.3	58.8	148 21.1	52.8	329 57.1	50.7	Aldebaran	290 50.3	N16 32.0
05	193 00.7	214 39.6	39.6	18 06.6	58.8	163 23.4	52.9	344 59.5	50.7			
06	208 03.2	229 39.2	S10 38.4	33 08.9	N 5 58.8	178 25.7	N10 53.0	0 01.9	S 8 50.7	Alioth	166 21.4	N55 53.3
07	223 05.6	244 38.9	37.2	48 11.2	58.8	193 27.9	53.1	15 04.3	50.7	Alkaid	152 59.6	N49 14.8
T 08	238 08.1	259 38.5	36.0	63 13.5	58.8	208 30.2	53.1	30 06.6	50.7	Al Na'ir	27 45.3	S46 54.2
H 09	253 10.6	274 38.2	. . 34.8	78 15.8	. . 58.8	223 32.5	. . 53.2	45 09.0	. . 50.7	Alnilam	275 47.1	S 1 11.8
U 10	268 13.0	289 37.8	33.6	93 18.1	58.8	238 34.8	53.3	60 11.4	50.8	Alphard	217 56.7	S 8 42.9
R 11	283 15.5	304 37.4	32.4	108 20.4	58.8	253 37.0	53.4	75 13.8	50.8			
S 12	298 17.9	319 37.1	S10 31.2	123 22.7	N 5 58.9	268 39.3	N10 53.5	90 16.2	S 8 50.8	Alphecca	126 12.0	N26 40.3
D 13	313 20.4	334 36.7	30.0	138 25.1	58.9	283 41.6	53.6	105 18.5	50.8	Alpheratz	357 44.7	N29 09.6
A 14	328 22.9	349 36.3	28.8	153 27.4	58.9	298 43.9	53.6	120 20.9	50.8	Altair	62 09.5	N 8 54.1
Y 15	343 25.3	4 36.0	. . 27.6	168 29.7	. . 58.9	313 46.1	. . 53.7	135 23.3	. . 50.9	Ankaa	353 16.8	S42 14.6
16	358 27.8	19 35.6	26.4	183 32.0	58.9	328 48.4	53.8	150 25.7	50.9	Antares	112 27.7	S26 27.4
17	13 30.3	34 35.3	25.2	198 34.3	58.9	343 50.7	53.9	165 28.1	50.9			
18	28 32.7	49 34.9	S10 24.0	213 36.6	N 5 58.9	358 52.9	N10 54.0	180 30.4	S 8 50.9	Arcturus	145 56.6	N19 07.0
19	43 35.2	64 34.6	22.8	228 38.9	59.0	13 55.2	54.0	195 32.8	50.9	Atria	107 30.8	S69 02.7
20	58 37.7	79 34.2	21.6	243 41.2	59.0	28 57.5	54.1	210 35.2	51.0	Avior	234 17.8	S59 33.0
21	73 40.1	94 33.8	. . 20.4	258 43.6	. . 59.0	43 59.8	. . 54.2	225 37.6	. . 51.0	Bellatrix	278 32.8	N 6 21.5
22	88 42.6	109 33.5	19.2	273 45.9	59.0	59 02.0	54.3	240 40.0	51.0	Betelgeuse	271 02.0	N 7 24.4
23	103 45.1	124 33.1	18.0	288 48.2	59.0	74 04.3	54.4	255 42.4	51.0			
20 00	118 47.5	139 32.8	S10 16.7	303 50.5	N 5 59.0	89 06.6	N10 54.5	270 44.7	S 8 51.0	Canopus	263 56.1	S52 42.4
01	133 50.0	154 32.4	15.5	318 52.8	59.1	104 08.8	54.5	285 47.1	51.0	Capella	280 35.5	N46 00.6
02	148 52.4	169 32.1	14.3	333 55.2	59.1	119 11.1	54.6	300 49.5	51.1	Deneb	49 32.6	N45 19.6
03	163 54.9	184 31.7	. . 13.1	348 57.5	. . 59.1	134 13.4	. . 54.7	315 51.9	. . 51.1	Denebola	182 34.5	N14 30.0
04	178 57.4	199 31.4	11.9	3 59.8	59.1	149 15.6	54.8	330 54.3	51.1	Diphda	348 56.9	S17 55.3
05	193 59.8	214 31.0	10.7	19 02.1	59.1	164 17.9	54.9	345 56.7	51.1			
06	209 02.3	229 30.7	S10 09.5	34 04.5	N 5 59.2	179 20.2	N10 55.0	0 59.0	S 8 51.1	Dubhe	193 52.4	N61 40.8
07	224 04.8	244 30.3	08.3	49 06.8	59.2	194 22.5	55.0	16 01.4	51.2	Elnath	278 13.5	N28 37.0
08	239 07.2	259 30.0	07.1	64 09.1	59.2	209 24.7	55.1	31 03.8	51.2	Eltanin	90 47.1	N51 29.2
F 09	254 09.7	274 29.6	. . 05.9	79 11.4	. . 59.2	224 27.0	. . 55.2	46 06.2	. . 51.2	Enif	33 48.4	N 9 55.9
R 10	269 12.2	289 29.3	04.7	94 13.8	59.2	239 29.3	55.3	61 08.6	51.2	Fomalhaut	15 25.3	S29 33.5
I 11	284 14.6	304 28.9	03.5	109 16.1	59.3	254 31.5	55.4	76 11.0	51.2			
D 12	299 17.1	319 28.6	S10 02.3	124 18.4	N 5 59.3	269 33.8	N10 55.5	91 13.4	S 8 51.2	Gacrux	172 01.8	S57 10.7
A 13	314 19.6	334 28.2	10 01.0	139 20.8	59.3	284 36.1	55.6	106 15.7	51.3	Gienah	175 53.2	S17 36.6
Y 14	329 22.0	349 27.9	9 59.8	154 23.1	59.3	299 38.3	55.6	121 18.1	51.3	Hadar	148 49.3	S60 25.6
15	344 24.5	4 27.5	. . 58.6	169 25.5	. . 59.4	314 40.6	. . 55.7	136 20.5	. . 51.3	Hamal	328 01.8	N23 31.3
16	359 26.9	19 27.2	57.4	184 27.8	59.4	329 42.8	55.8	151 22.9	51.3	Kaus Aust.	83 45.5	S34 22.6
17	14 29.4	34 26.8	56.2	199 30.1	59.4	344 45.1	55.9	166 25.3	51.3			
18	29 31.9	49 26.5	S 9 55.0	214 32.5	N 5 59.4	359 47.4	N10 56.0	181 27.7	S 8 51.4	Kochab	137 20.2	N74 06.0
19	44 34.3	64 26.1	53.8	229 34.8	59.5	14 49.6	56.1	196 30.1	51.4	Markab	13 39.5	N15 16.3
20	59 36.8	79 25.8	52.5	244 37.2	59.5	29 51.9	56.1	211 32.4	51.4	Menkar	314 16.0	N 4 08.2
21	74 39.3	94 25.4	. . 51.3	259 39.5	. . 59.5	44 54.2	. . 56.2	226 34.8	. . 51.4	Menkent	148 08.7	S36 25.6
22	89 41.7	109 25.1	50.1	274 41.8	59.6	59 56.4	56.3	241 37.2	51.4	Miaplacidus	221 39.0	S69 46.1
23	104 44.2	124 24.8	48.9	289 44.2	59.6	74 58.7	56.4	256 39.6	51.4			
21 00	119 46.7	139 24.4	S 9 47.7	304 46.5	N 5 59.6	90 01.0	N10 56.5	271 42.0	S 8 51.5	Mirfak	308 41.5	N49 54.4
01	134 49.1	154 24.1	46.5	319 48.9	59.7	105 03.2	56.6	286 44.4	51.5	Nunki	75 59.9	S26 16.8
02	149 51.6	169 23.7	45.3	334 51.2	59.7	120 05.5	56.7	301 46.8	51.5	Peacock	53 21.3	S56 41.7
03	164 54.1	184 23.4	. . 44.0	349 53.6	. . 59.7	135 07.7	. . 56.7	316 49.1	. . 51.5	Pollux	243 28.5	N27 59.6
04	179 56.5	199 23.0	42.8	4 55.9	59.7	150 10.0	56.8	331 51.5	51.5	Procyon	245 00.4	N 5 11.4
05	194 59.0	214 22.7	41.6	19 58.3	59.8	165 12.3	56.9	346 53.9	51.5			
06	210 01.4	229 22.4	S 9 40.4	35 00.6	N 5 59.8	180 14.5	N10 57.0	1 56.3	S 8 51.6	Rasalhague	96 07.6	N12 33.1
07	225 03.9	244 22.0	39.2	50 03.0	59.8	195 16.8	57.1	16 58.7	51.6	Regulus	207 44.3	N11 54.2
S 08	240 06.4	259 21.7	37.9	65 05.4	59.9	210 19.0	57.2	32 01.1	51.6	Rigel	281 12.7	S 8 11.4
A 09	255 08.8	274 21.4	. . 36.7	80 07.7	. . 59.9	225 21.3	. . 57.3	47 03.5	. . 51.6	Rigil Kent.	139 53.2	S60 52.8
T 10	270 11.3	289 21.0	35.5	95 10.1	5 59.9	240 23.6	57.4	62 05.9	51.6	Sabik	102 13.9	S15 44.3
U 11	285 13.8	304 20.7	34.3	110 12.4	6 00.0	255 25.8	57.4	77 08.3	51.6			
R 12	300 16.2	319 20.3	S 9 33.1	125 14.8	N 6 00.0	270 28.1	N10 57.5	92 10.6	S 8 51.6	Schedar	349 41.8	N56 36.5
D 13	315 18.7	334 20.0	31.8	140 17.2	00.1	285 30.3	57.6	107 13.0	51.7	Shaula	96 23.6	S37 06.6
A 14	330 21.2	349 19.7	30.6	155 19.5	00.1	300 32.6	57.7	122 15.4	51.7	Sirius	258 34.2	S16 44.2
Y 15	345 23.6	4 19.3	. . 29.4	170 21.9	. . 00.1	315 34.9	. . 57.8	137 17.8	. . 51.7	Spica	158 32.2	S11 13.5
16	0 26.1	19 19.0	28.2	185 24.3	00.2	330 37.1	57.9	152 20.2	51.7	Suhail	222 52.7	S43 29.0
17	15 28.6	34 18.7	27.0	200 26.6	00.2	345 39.4	58.0	167 22.6	51.7			
18	30 31.0	49 18.3	S 9 25.7	215 29.0	N 6 00.2	0 41.6	N10 58.1	182 25.0	S 8 51.7	Vega	80 40.0	N38 47.7
19	45 33.5	64 18.0	24.5	230 31.4	00.3	15 43.9	58.1	197 27.4	51.8	Zuben'ubi	137 06.6	S16 05.5
20	60 35.9	79 17.7	23.3	245 33.7	00.3	30 46.1	58.2	212 29.8	51.8			SHA Mer. Pass.
21	75 38.4	94 17.3	. . 22.1	260 36.1	. . 00.4	45 48.4	. . 58.3	227 32.2	. . 51.8		° ′	h m
22	90 40.9	109 17.0	20.8	275 38.5	00.4	60 50.7	58.4	242 34.5	51.8	Venus	20 45.3	14 42
23	105 43.3	124 16.7	19.6	290 40.9	00.4	75 52.9	58.5	257 36.9	51.8	Mars	185 03.0	3 44
	h m									Jupiter	330 19.1	18 01
Mer. Pass. 16 02.2		v −0.3	d 1.2	v 2.3	d 0.0	v 2.3	d 0.1	v 2.4	d 0.0	Saturn	151 57.2	5 56

UT	SUN GHA	SUN Dec	MOON GHA	v	Dec	d	HP
d h	° ′	° ′	° ′	′	° ′	′	′
19 00	177 24.1	S20 30.0	237 24.7	5.6	S21 38.7	3.8	59.2
01	192 23.9	29.5	251 49.3	5.5	21 42.5	3.6	59.2
02	207 23.7	29.0	266 13.8	5.5	21 46.1	3.5	59.2
03	222 23.5	.. 28.5	280 38.3	5.5	21 49.6	3.4	59.2
04	237 23.3	28.0	295 02.8	5.4	21 53.0	3.2	59.2
05	252 23.1	27.4	309 27.2	5.4	21 56.2	3.1	59.2
06	267 22.9	S20 26.9	323 51.6	5.4	S21 59.3	2.9	59.2
T 07	282 22.7	26.4	338 16.0	5.4	22 02.2	2.8	59.2
H 08	297 22.5	25.9	352 40.4	5.4	22 05.0	2.6	59.2
U 09	312 22.3	.. 25.4	7 04.8	5.3	22 07.6	2.5	59.2
R 10	327 22.2	24.9	21 29.1	5.3	22 10.1	2.3	59.2
S 11	342 22.0	24.3	35 53.4	5.3	22 12.4	2.2	59.2
D 12	357 21.8	S20 23.8	50 17.7	5.3	S22 14.6	2.0	59.2
A 13	12 21.6	23.3	64 42.0	5.3	22 16.6	1.9	59.1
Y 14	27 21.4	22.8	79 06.3	5.3	22 18.5	1.8	59.1
15	42 21.2	.. 22.3	93 30.6	5.3	22 20.3	1.5	59.1
16	57 21.0	21.7	107 54.9	5.2	22 21.8	1.5	59.1
17	72 20.8	21.2	122 19.1	5.3	22 23.3	1.3	59.1
18	87 20.6	S20 20.7	136 43.4	5.2	S22 24.6	1.1	59.1
19	102 20.4	20.2	151 07.6	5.3	22 25.7	1.0	59.1
20	117 20.2	19.6	165 31.9	5.2	22 26.7	0.8	59.1
21	132 20.0	.. 19.1	179 56.1	5.3	22 27.5	0.7	59.1
22	147 19.8	18.6	194 20.4	5.2	22 28.2	0.6	59.1
23	162 19.6	18.0	208 44.6	5.3	22 28.8	0.4	59.1
20 00	177 19.5	S20 17.5	223 08.9	5.3	S22 29.2	0.2	59.1
01	192 19.3	17.0	237 33.2	5.2	22 29.4	0.1	59.0
02	207 19.1	16.5	251 57.4	5.3	22 29.5	0.1	59.0
03	222 18.9	.. 15.9	266 21.7	5.3	22 29.4	0.2	59.0
04	237 18.7	15.4	280 46.0	5.3	22 29.2	0.3	59.0
05	252 18.5	14.9	295 10.3	5.3	22 28.9	0.5	59.0
06	267 18.3	S20 14.3	309 34.6	5.4	S22 28.4	0.7	59.0
F 07	282 18.1	13.8	323 59.0	5.3	22 27.7	0.8	59.0
R 08	297 17.9	13.3	338 23.3	5.4	22 26.9	1.0	59.0
I 09	312 17.7	.. 12.7	352 47.7	5.4	22 25.9	1.1	59.0
D 10	327 17.6	12.2	7 12.1	5.4	22 24.8	1.2	59.0
A 11	342 17.4	11.7	21 36.5	5.4	22 23.6	1.4	58.9
Y 12	357 17.2	S20 11.1	36 00.9	5.5	S22 22.2	1.5	58.9
13	12 17.0	10.6	50 25.4	5.5	22 20.7	1.7	58.9
14	27 16.8	10.1	64 49.9	5.5	22 19.0	1.9	58.9
15	42 16.6	.. 09.5	79 14.4	5.6	22 17.1	2.0	58.9
16	57 16.4	09.0	93 39.0	5.6	22 15.1	2.1	58.9
17	72 16.3	08.4	108 03.6	5.6	22 13.0	2.3	58.9
18	87 16.1	S20 07.9	122 28.2	5.6	S22 10.7	2.4	58.8
19	102 15.9	07.4	136 52.8	5.7	22 08.3	2.5	58.8
20	117 15.7	06.8	151 17.5	5.8	22 05.8	2.7	58.8
21	132 15.5	.. 06.3	165 42.3	5.7	22 03.1	2.9	58.8
22	147 15.3	05.7	180 07.0	5.8	22 00.2	3.0	58.8
23	162 15.2	05.2	194 31.8	5.9	21 57.2	3.1	58.8
21 00	177 15.0	S20 04.6	208 56.7	5.9	S21 54.1	3.3	58.8
01	192 14.8	04.1	223 21.6	5.9	21 50.8	3.4	58.8
02	207 14.6	03.6	237 46.5	6.0	21 47.4	3.5	58.7
03	222 14.4	.. 03.0	252 11.5	6.1	21 43.9	3.7	58.7
04	237 14.2	02.5	266 36.6	6.1	21 40.2	3.8	58.7
05	252 14.1	01.9	281 01.7	6.1	21 36.4	4.0	58.7
06	267 13.9	S20 01.4	295 26.8	6.2	S21 32.4	4.1	58.7
S 07	282 13.7	00.8	309 52.0	6.2	21 28.3	4.2	58.7
A 08	297 13.5	20 00.3	324 17.2	6.3	21 24.1	4.4	58.6
T 09	312 13.3	19 59.7	338 42.5	6.4	21 19.7	4.5	58.6
U 10	327 13.2	59.2	353 07.9	6.4	21 15.2	4.6	58.6
R 11	342 13.0	58.6	7 33.3	6.5	21 10.6	4.8	58.6
D 12	357 12.8	S19 58.1	21 58.8	6.5	S21 05.8	4.9	58.6
A 13	12 12.6	57.5	36 24.3	6.6	21 00.9	5.0	58.6
Y 14	27 12.4	57.0	50 49.9	6.7	20 55.9	5.2	58.5
15	42 12.3	.. 56.4	65 15.6	6.7	20 50.7	5.2	58.5
16	57 12.1	55.8	79 41.3	6.8	20 45.5	5.5	58.5
17	72 11.9	55.3	94 07.1	6.8	20 40.0	5.5	58.5
18	87 11.7	S19 54.7	108 32.9	6.9	S20 34.5	5.6	58.5
19	102 11.6	54.2	122 58.8	7.0	20 28.9	5.8	58.5
20	117 11.4	53.6	137 24.8	7.0	20 23.1	5.9	58.4
21	132 11.2	.. 53.1	151 50.8	7.2	20 17.2	6.1	58.4
22	147 11.0	52.5	166 17.0	7.1	20 11.1	6.1	58.4
23	162 10.8	51.9	180 43.1	7.3	S20 05.0	6.3	58.4
	SD 16.3	d 0.5	SD 16.1		16.1		16.0

Lat.	Twilight Naut.	Civil	Sunrise	Moonrise 19	20	21	22
°	h m	h m	h m	h m	h m	h m	h m
N 72	07 49	09 33	■	■	■	■	■
N 70	07 36	09 04	11 10	■	■	■	10 05
68	07 26	08 42	10 12	■	■	09 32	09 15
66	07 17	08 25	09 39	06 52	08 03	08 33	08 43
64	07 09	08 11	09 15	06 11	07 19	07 59	08 20
62	07 02	07 59	08 56	05 44	06 50	07 34	08 01
60	06 56	07 49	08 40	05 22	06 28	07 14	07 46
N 58	06 50	07 40	08 27	05 05	06 09	06 58	07 32
56	06 45	07 32	08 16	04 50	05 54	06 44	07 21
54	06 41	07 25	08 06	04 37	05 41	06 32	07 11
52	06 36	07 18	07 57	04 26	05 30	06 21	07 02
50	06 32	07 12	07 49	04 16	05 19	06 12	06 54
45	06 23	07 00	07 32	03 55	04 58	05 52	06 37
N 40	06 15	06 49	07 18	03 39	04 41	05 36	06 23
35	06 08	06 39	07 06	03 24	04 26	05 22	06 11
30	06 01	06 30	06 56	03 12	04 14	05 10	06 00
20	05 47	06 14	06 38	02 51	03 52	04 49	05 42
N 10	05 34	06 00	06 22	02 33	03 33	04 31	05 26
0	05 20	05 45	06 07	02 16	03 16	04 15	05 12
S 10	05 03	05 30	05 52	02 00	02 58	03 58	04 57
20	04 44	05 12	05 36	01 42	02 40	03 40	04 41
30	04 19	04 51	05 17	01 21	02 18	03 20	04 23
35	04 03	04 38	05 06	01 09	02 06	03 08	04 12
40	03 44	04 22	04 54	00 55	01 51	02 54	04 00
45	03 19	04 04	04 39	00 39	01 34	02 37	03 45
S 50	02 44	03 39	04 20	00 19	01 13	02 17	03 28
52	02 25	03 28	04 11	00 10	01 03	02 07	03 19
54	02 01	03 14	04 02	24 52	00 52	01 56	03 10
56	01 28	02 58	03 50	24 39	00 39	01 44	02 59
58	////	02 38	03 37	24 24	00 24	01 30	02 47
S 60	////	02 12	03 22	24 06	00 06	01 13	02 33

Lat.	Sunset	Twilight Civil	Naut.	Moonset 19	20	21	22
°	h m	h m	h m	h m	h m	h m	h m
N 72	■	14 50	16 33	■	■	■	■
N 70	13 12	15 19	16 46	■	■	■	12 58
68	14 10	15 40	16 57	■	■	11 33	13 46
66	14 43	15 57	17 06	10 05	10 58	12 31	14 17
64	15 08	16 11	17 14	10 46	11 42	13 04	14 40
62	15 27	16 23	17 21	11 14	12 11	13 29	14 58
60	15 42	16 33	17 27	11 36	12 34	13 48	15 13
N 58	15 55	16 42	17 32	11 53	12 52	14 04	15 26
56	16 07	16 50	17 37	12 08	13 07	14 18	15 37
54	16 17	16 57	17 42	12 21	13 20	14 30	15 46
52	16 25	17 04	17 46	12 32	13 31	14 40	15 55
50	16 33	17 10	17 50	12 43	13 42	14 49	16 02
45	16 50	17 23	17 59	13 04	14 03	15 09	16 19
N 40	17 04	17 34	18 07	13 21	14 20	15 25	16 32
35	17 16	17 43	18 14	13 35	14 34	15 38	16 43
30	17 26	17 52	18 21	13 48	14 47	15 50	16 53
20	17 44	18 07	18 34	14 09	15 08	16 09	17 10
N 10	18 00	18 22	18 48	14 27	15 27	16 26	17 24
0	18 14	18 36	19 02	14 45	15 44	16 42	17 38
S 10	18 29	18 52	19 19	15 02	16 01	16 58	17 51
20	18 45	19 09	19 38	15 20	16 20	17 15	18 05
30	19 04	19 30	20 02	15 42	16 41	17 34	18 22
35	19 15	19 43	20 18	15 54	16 53	17 46	18 31
40	19 27	19 59	20 37	16 09	17 07	17 58	18 42
45	19 42	20 17	21 02	16 26	17 24	18 13	18 54
S 50	20 01	20 41	21 36	16 47	17 45	18 32	19 10
52	20 09	20 53	21 55	16 57	17 55	18 41	19 17
54	20 19	21 06	22 18	17 08	18 06	18 50	19 24
56	20 30	21 22	22 50	17 21	18 18	19 01	19 33
58	20 43	21 42	////	17 36	18 33	19 14	19 43
S 60	20 58	22 07	////	17 53	18 50	19 28	19 54

	SUN			MOON			
Day	Eqn. of Time 00h	12h	Mer. Pass.	Mer. Pass. Upper	Lower	Age	Phase
d	m s	m s	h m	h m	h m	d	%
19	10 23	10 33	12 11	08 31	21 00	26	17
20	10 42	10 51	12 11	09 30	22 00	27	10
21	11 00	11 08	12 11	10 29	22 57	28	4

UT	ARIES GHA	VENUS −4.0 GHA	Dec	MARS −0.3 GHA	Dec	JUPITER −2.4 GHA	Dec	SATURN +0.6 GHA	Dec	Name (STARS)	SHA	Dec
22 00	120 45.8	139 16.3	S 9 18.4	305 43.2	N 6 00.5	90 55.2	N10 58.6	272 39.3	S 8 51.8	Acamar	315 18.9	S40 15.6
01	135 48.3	154 16.0	17.2	320 45.6	00.5	105 57.4	58.7	287 41.7	51.9	Achernar	335 27.5	S57 10.8
02	150 50.7	169 15.7	15.9	335 48.0	00.6	120 59.7	58.8	302 44.1	51.9	Acrux	173 10.1	S63 09.8
03	165 53.2	184 15.3	.. 14.7	350 50.4	.. 00.6	136 01.9	.. 58.8	317 46.5	.. 51.9	Adhara	255 12.9	S28 59.5
04	180 55.7	199 15.0	13.5	5 52.8	00.7	151 04.2	58.9	332 48.9	51.9	Aldebaran	290 50.3	N16 32.0
05	195 58.1	214 14.7	12.3	20 55.1	00.7	166 06.4	59.0	347 51.3	51.9			
06	211 00.6	229 14.4	S 9 11.0	35 57.5	N 6 00.7	181 08.7	N10 59.1	2 53.7	S 8 51.9	Alioth	166 21.3	N55 53.3
07	226 03.1	244 14.0	09.8	50 59.9	00.8	196 10.9	59.2	17 56.1	51.9	Alkaid	152 59.6	N49 14.8
S 08	241 05.5	259 13.7	08.6	66 02.3	00.8	211 13.2	59.3	32 58.5	52.0	Al Na'ir	27 45.3	S46 54.2
U 09	256 08.0	274 13.4	.. 07.3	81 04.7	.. 00.9	226 15.5	.. 59.4	48 00.9	.. 52.0	Alnilam	275 47.1	S 1 11.8
N 10	271 10.4	289 13.0	06.1	96 07.1	00.9	241 17.7	59.5	63 03.2	52.0	Alphard	217 56.7	S 8 42.9
D 11	286 12.9	304 12.7	04.9	111 09.4	01.0	256 20.0	59.6	78 05.6	52.0			
A 12	301 15.4	319 12.4	S 9 03.7	126 11.8	N 6 01.0	271 22.2	N10 59.6	93 08.0	S 8 52.0	Alphecca	126 12.0	N26 40.2
Y 13	316 17.8	334 12.1	02.4	141 14.2	01.1	286 24.5	59.7	108 10.4	52.0	Alpheratz	357 44.7	N29 09.6
14	331 20.3	349 11.7	01.2	156 16.6	01.1	301 26.7	59.8	123 12.8	52.0	Altair	62 09.5	N 8 54.1
15	346 22.8	4 11.4	9 00.0	171 19.0	.. 01.2	316 29.0	10 59.9	138 15.2	.. 52.1	Ankaa	353 16.8	S42 14.6
16	1 25.2	19 11.1	8 58.7	186 21.4	01.2	331 31.2	11 00.0	153 17.6	52.1	Antares	112 27.7	S26 27.4
17	16 27.7	34 10.8	57.5	201 23.8	01.3	346 33.5	00.1	168 20.0	52.1			
18	31 30.2	49 10.4	S 8 56.3	216 26.2	N 6 01.3	1 35.7	N11 00.2	183 22.4	S 8 52.1	Arcturus	145 56.6	N19 07.0
19	46 32.6	64 10.1	55.0	231 28.6	01.4	16 38.0	00.3	198 24.8	52.1	Atria	107 30.7	S69 02.7
20	61 35.1	79 09.8	53.8	246 31.0	01.4	31 40.2	00.4	213 27.2	52.1	Avior	234 17.8	S59 33.0
21	76 37.5	94 09.5	.. 52.6	261 33.4	.. 01.5	46 42.5	.. 00.5	228 29.6	.. 52.1	Bellatrix	278 32.8	N 6 21.5
22	91 40.0	109 09.2	51.3	276 35.8	01.5	61 44.7	00.5	243 32.0	52.2	Betelgeuse	271 02.0	N 7 24.4
23	106 42.5	124 08.8	50.1	291 38.2	01.6	76 47.0	00.6	258 34.4	52.2			
23 00	121 44.9	139 08.5	S 8 48.9	306 40.6	N 6 01.6	91 49.2	N11 00.7	273 36.8	S 8 52.2	Canopus	263 56.1	S52 42.4
01	136 47.4	154 08.2	47.6	321 43.0	01.7	106 51.5	00.8	288 39.2	52.2	Capella	280 35.5	N46 00.6
02	151 49.9	169 07.9	46.4	336 45.4	01.7	121 53.7	00.9	303 41.6	52.2	Deneb	49 32.6	N45 19.5
03	166 52.3	184 07.6	.. 45.2	351 47.8	.. 01.8	136 56.0	.. 01.0	318 44.0	.. 52.2	Denebola	182 34.4	N14 30.0
04	181 54.8	199 07.2	43.9	6 50.2	01.9	151 58.2	01.1	333 46.3	52.2	Diphda	348 57.0	S17 55.3
05	196 57.3	214 06.9	42.7	21 52.7	01.9	167 00.4	01.2	348 48.7	52.3			
06	211 59.7	229 06.6	S 8 41.4	36 55.1	N 6 02.0	182 02.7	N11 01.3	3 51.1	S 8 52.3	Dubhe	193 52.3	N61 40.8
07	227 02.2	244 06.3	40.2	51 57.5	02.0	197 04.9	01.4	18 53.5	52.3	Elnath	278 13.5	N28 37.0
M 08	242 04.7	259 06.0	39.0	66 59.9	02.1	212 07.2	01.5	33 55.9	52.3	Eltanin	90 47.0	N51 29.1
O 09	257 07.1	274 05.7	.. 37.7	82 02.3	.. 02.1	227 09.4	.. 01.5	48 58.3	.. 52.3	Enif	33 48.4	N 9 55.9
N 10	272 09.6	289 05.3	36.5	97 04.7	02.2	242 11.7	01.6	64 00.7	52.3	Fomalhaut	15 25.3	S29 33.5
D 11	287 12.0	304 05.0	35.3	112 07.1	02.3	257 13.9	01.7	79 03.1	52.3			
A 12	302 14.5	319 04.7	S 8 34.0	127 09.6	N 6 02.3	272 16.2	N11 01.8	94 05.5	S 8 52.3	Gacrux	172 01.8	S57 10.7
Y 13	317 17.0	334 04.4	32.8	142 12.0	02.4	287 18.4	01.9	109 07.9	52.4	Gienah	175 53.1	S17 36.6
14	332 19.4	349 04.1	31.5	157 14.4	02.4	302 20.7	02.0	124 10.3	52.4	Hadar	148 49.3	S60 25.7
15	347 21.9	4 03.8	.. 30.3	172 16.8	.. 02.5	317 22.9	.. 02.1	139 12.7	.. 52.4	Hamal	328 01.8	N23 31.3
16	2 24.4	19 03.5	29.1	187 19.3	02.6	332 25.1	02.2	154 15.1	52.4	Kaus Aust.	83 45.4	S34 22.6
17	17 26.8	34 03.1	27.8	202 21.7	02.6	347 27.4	02.3	169 17.5	52.4			
18	32 29.3	49 02.8	S 8 26.6	217 24.1	N 6 02.7	2 29.6	N11 02.4	184 19.9	S 8 52.4	Kochab	137 20.2	N74 06.0
19	47 31.8	64 02.5	25.3	232 26.5	02.8	17 31.9	02.5	199 22.3	52.4	Markab	13 39.5	N15 16.3
20	62 34.2	79 02.2	24.1	247 29.0	02.8	32 34.1	02.6	214 24.7	52.4	Menkar	314 16.0	N 4 08.2
21	77 36.7	94 01.9	.. 22.8	262 31.4	.. 02.9	47 36.4	.. 02.7	229 27.1	.. 52.5	Menkent	148 08.7	S36 25.7
22	92 39.2	109 01.6	21.6	277 33.8	02.9	62 38.6	02.7	244 29.5	52.5	Miaplacidus	221 39.0	S69 46.1
23	107 41.6	124 01.3	20.4	292 36.3	03.0	77 40.8	02.8	259 31.9	52.5			
24 00	122 44.1	139 01.0	S 8 19.1	307 38.7	N 6 03.1	92 43.1	N11 02.9	274 34.3	S 8 52.5	Mirfak	308 41.5	N49 54.4
01	137 46.5	154 00.7	17.9	322 41.1	03.1	107 45.3	03.0	289 36.7	52.5	Nunki	75 59.8	S26 16.8
02	152 49.0	169 00.4	16.6	337 43.6	03.2	122 47.6	03.1	304 39.1	52.5	Peacock	53 21.3	S56 41.7
03	167 51.5	184 00.0	.. 15.4	352 46.0	.. 03.3	137 49.8	.. 03.2	319 41.5	.. 52.5	Pollux	243 28.5	N27 59.6
04	182 53.9	198 59.7	14.1	7 48.4	03.3	152 52.0	03.3	334 43.9	52.5	Procyon	245 00.4	N 5 11.4
05	197 56.4	213 59.4	12.9	22 50.9	03.4	167 54.3	03.4	349 46.3	52.6			
06	212 58.9	228 59.1	S 8 11.7	37 53.3	N 6 03.5	182 56.5	N11 03.5	4 48.7	S 8 52.6	Rasalhague	96 07.6	N12 33.0
07	228 01.3	243 58.8	10.4	52 55.8	03.6	197 58.8	03.6	19 51.1	52.6	Regulus	207 44.2	N11 54.2
T 08	243 03.8	258 58.5	09.2	67 58.2	03.6	213 01.0	03.7	34 53.5	52.6	Rigel	281 12.7	S 8 11.4
U 09	258 06.3	273 58.2	.. 07.9	83 00.6	.. 03.7	228 03.2	.. 03.8	49 55.9	.. 52.6	Rigil Kent.	139 53.1	S60 52.8
E 10	273 08.7	288 57.9	06.7	98 03.1	03.8	243 05.5	03.9	64 58.3	52.6	Sabik	102 13.9	S15 44.3
S 11	288 11.2	303 57.6	05.4	113 05.5	03.8	258 07.7	04.0	80 00.7	52.6			
D 12	303 13.7	318 57.3	S 8 04.2	128 08.0	N 6 03.9	273 09.9	N11 04.1	95 03.1	S 8 52.6	Schedar	349 41.8	N56 36.5
A 13	318 16.1	333 57.0	02.9	143 10.4	04.0	288 12.2	04.1	110 05.5	52.6	Shaula	96 23.5	S37 06.6
Y 14	333 18.6	348 56.7	01.7	158 12.9	04.1	303 14.4	04.2	125 07.9	52.7	Sirius	258 34.2	S16 44.2
15	348 21.0	3 56.4	8 00.4	173 15.3	.. 04.1	318 16.7	.. 04.3	140 10.3	.. 52.7	Spica	158 32.2	S11 13.5
16	3 23.5	18 56.1	7 59.2	188 17.8	04.2	333 18.9	04.4	155 12.7	52.7	Suhail	222 52.7	S43 29.0
17	18 26.0	33 55.8	57.9	203 20.2	04.3	348 21.1	04.5	170 15.1	52.7			
18	33 28.4	48 55.5	S 7 56.7	218 22.7	N 6 04.4	3 23.4	N11 04.6	185 17.5	S 8 52.7	Vega	80 40.0	N38 47.7
19	48 30.9	63 55.2	55.4	233 25.2	04.4	18 25.6	04.7	200 19.9	52.7	Zuben'ubi	137 06.6	S16 05.5
20	63 33.4	78 54.9	54.2	248 27.6	04.5	33 27.8	04.8	215 22.3	52.7			
21	78 35.8	93 54.6	.. 52.9	263 30.1	.. 04.6	48 30.1	.. 04.9	230 24.7	.. 52.7			
22	93 38.3	108 54.3	51.7	278 32.5	04.7	63 32.3	05.0	245 27.1	52.7			
23	108 40.8	123 54.0	50.4	293 35.0	04.7	78 34.5	05.1	260 29.5	52.8			
Mer. Pass.	15h 50.4m	v −0.3	d 1.2	v 2.4	d 0.1	v 2.2	d 0.1	v 2.4	d 0.0			

	SHA	Mer. Pass.
Venus	17 23.6	14 44
Mars	184 55.7	3 33
Jupiter	330 04.3	17 50
Saturn	151 51.8	5 45

UT	SUN GHA	SUN Dec	MOON GHA	v	MOON Dec	d	HP
d h	° ′	° ′	° ′	′	° ′	′	′
22 00	177 10.7	S19 51.4	195 09.4	7.3	S19 58.7	6.3	58.4
01	192 10.5	50.8	209 35.7	7.4	19 52.4	6.5	58.3
02	207 10.3	50.3	224 02.1	7.5	19 45.9	6.7	58.3
03	222 10.1 ..	49.7	238 28.6	7.5	19 39.2	6.7	58.3
04	237 10.0	49.1	252 55.1	7.6	19 32.5	6.8	58.3
05	252 09.8	48.6	267 21.7	7.7	19 25.7	7.0	58.3
06	267 09.6	S19 48.0	281 48.4	7.8	S19 18.7	7.1	58.2
07	282 09.5	47.5	296 15.2	7.8	19 11.6	7.1	58.2
08	297 09.3	46.9	310 42.0	7.9	19 04.5	7.3	58.2
S 09	312 09.1 ..	46.3	325 08.9	8.0	18 57.2	7.4	58.2
U 10	327 08.9	45.8	339 35.9	8.1	18 49.8	7.5	58.2
N 11	342 08.8	45.2	354 03.0	8.1	18 42.3	7.6	58.1
D 12	357 08.6	S19 44.6	8 30.1	8.3	S18 34.7	7.7	58.1
A 13	12 08.4	44.1	22 57.4	8.3	18 27.0	7.8	58.1
Y 14	27 08.3	43.5	37 24.7	8.4	18 19.2	7.9	58.1
15	42 08.1 ..	42.9	51 52.1	8.4	18 11.3	8.0	58.0
16	57 07.9	42.3	66 19.5	8.6	18 03.3	8.1	58.0
17	72 07.7	41.8	80 47.1	8.6	17 55.2	8.2	58.0
18	87 07.6	S19 41.2	95 14.7	8.7	S17 47.0	8.3	58.0
19	102 07.4	40.6	109 42.4	8.8	17 38.7	8.4	58.0
20	117 07.2	40.1	124 10.2	8.8	17 30.3	8.5	57.9
21	132 07.1 ..	39.5	138 38.0	9.0	17 21.8	8.6	57.9
22	147 06.9	38.9	153 06.0	9.0	17 13.2	8.7	57.9
23	162 06.7	38.3	167 34.0	9.1	17 04.5	8.7	57.9
23 00	177 06.6	S19 37.8	182 02.1	9.2	S16 55.8	8.9	57.8
01	192 06.4	37.2	196 30.3	9.2	16 46.9	8.9	57.8
02	207 06.2	36.6	210 58.5	9.4	16 38.0	9.0	57.8
03	222 06.1 ..	36.0	225 26.9	9.4	16 29.0	9.1	57.8
04	237 05.9	35.5	239 55.3	9.5	16 19.9	9.2	57.7
05	252 05.7	34.9	254 23.8	9.6	16 10.7	9.3	57.7
06	267 05.6	S19 34.3	268 52.4	9.7	S16 01.4	9.3	57.7
07	282 05.4	33.7	283 21.1	9.7	15 52.1	9.4	57.7
08	297 05.2	33.1	297 49.8	9.9	15 42.7	9.5	57.6
M 09	312 05.1 ..	32.6	312 18.7	9.9	15 33.2	9.6	57.6
O 10	327 04.9	32.0	326 47.6	10.0	15 23.6	9.7	57.6
N 11	342 04.7	31.4	341 16.6	10.1	15 13.9	9.7	57.6
D 12	357 04.6	S19 30.8	355 45.7	10.1	S15 04.2	9.8	57.5
A 13	12 04.4	30.2	10 14.8	10.3	14 54.4	9.9	57.5
Y 14	27 04.3	29.7	24 44.1	10.3	14 44.5	9.9	57.5
15	42 04.1 ..	29.1	39 13.4	10.4	14 34.6	10.0	57.5
16	57 03.9	28.5	53 42.8	10.5	14 24.6	10.1	57.4
17	72 03.8	27.9	68 12.3	10.5	14 14.5	10.1	57.4
18	87 03.6	S19 27.3	82 41.8	10.6	S14 04.4	10.2	57.4
19	102 03.4	26.7	97 11.4	10.7	13 54.2	10.3	57.4
20	117 03.3	26.1	111 41.1	10.8	13 43.9	10.3	57.3
21	132 03.1 ..	25.5	126 10.9	10.9	13 33.6	10.4	57.3
22	147 03.0	25.0	140 40.8	11.0	13 23.2	10.5	57.3
23	162 02.8	24.4	155 10.8	11.0	13 12.7	10.5	57.3
24 00	177 02.6	S19 23.8	169 40.8	11.1	S13 02.2	10.6	57.2
01	192 02.5	23.2	184 10.9	11.1	12 51.6	10.6	57.2
02	207 02.3	22.6	198 41.0	11.3	12 41.0	10.7	57.2
03	222 02.2 ..	22.0	213 11.3	11.3	12 30.3	10.7	57.2
04	237 02.0	21.4	227 41.6	11.4	12 19.6	10.8	57.1
05	252 01.9	20.8	242 12.0	11.5	12 08.8	10.8	57.1
06	267 01.7	S19 20.2	256 42.5	11.5	S11 58.0	10.9	57.1
07	282 01.5	19.6	271 13.0	11.7	11 47.1	10.9	57.1
08	297 01.4	19.0	285 43.7	11.7	11 36.2	11.0	57.0
T 09	312 01.2 ..	18.4	300 14.4	11.7	11 25.2	11.0	57.0
U 10	327 01.1	17.8	314 45.1	11.9	11 14.2	11.1	57.0
E 11	342 00.9	17.2	329 16.0	11.9	11 03.1	11.1	56.9
S 12	357 00.8	S19 16.7	343 46.9	11.9	S10 52.0	11.1	56.9
D 13	12 00.6	16.1	358 17.8	12.1	10 40.9	11.2	56.9
A 14	27 00.5	15.5	12 48.9	12.1	10 29.7	11.3	56.9
Y 15	42 00.3 ..	14.9	27 20.0	12.2	10 18.4	11.2	56.8
16	57 00.1	14.3	41 51.2	12.2	10 07.2	11.3	56.8
17	72 00.0	13.7	56 22.4	12.4	9 55.9	11.4	56.8
18	86 59.8	S19 13.1	70 53.8	12.3	S 9 44.5	11.4	56.8
19	101 59.7	12.5	85 25.1	12.5	9 33.1	11.4	56.7
20	116 59.5	11.8	99 56.6	12.5	9 21.7	11.4	56.7
21	131 59.4 ..	11.2	114 28.1	12.6	9 10.3	11.5	56.7
22	146 59.2	10.6	128 59.7	12.6	8 58.8	11.5	56.6
23	161 59.1	10.0	143 31.3	12.7	S 8 47.3	11.5	56.6
	SD 16.3	d 0.6	SD 15.8		15.7		15.5

Lat.	Twilight Naut.	Twilight Civil	Sunrise	Moonrise 22	Moonrise 23	Moonrise 24	Moonrise 25
°	h m	h m	h m	h m	h m	h m	h m
N 72	07 41	09 20	■■	■■	10 08	09 34	09 13
N 70	07 29	08 54	10 45	10 05	09 32	09 16	09 03
68	07 19	08 34	09 59	09 15	09 07	09 01	08 55
66	07 11	08 18	09 29	08 43	08 47	08 48	08 48
64	07 04	08 05	09 07	08 20	08 31	08 38	08 43
62	06 57	07 54	08 49	08 01	08 18	08 29	08 38
60	06 52	07 44	08 35	07 46	08 07	08 22	08 33
N 58	06 47	07 36	08 22	07 32	07 57	08 15	08 30
56	06 42	07 28	08 11	07 21	07 48	08 09	08 26
54	06 38	07 22	08 02	07 11	07 40	08 04	08 23
52	06 34	07 15	07 53	07 02	07 34	07 59	08 20
50	06 30	07 10	07 46	06 54	07 27	07 54	08 18
45	06 22	06 57	07 30	06 37	07 14	07 45	08 12
N 40	06 14	06 47	07 16	06 23	07 03	07 37	08 07
35	06 07	06 38	07 05	06 11	06 53	07 30	08 03
30	06 00	06 29	06 55	06 00	06 45	07 24	08 00
20	05 47	06 14	06 38	05 42	06 30	07 13	07 53
N 10	05 34	06 00	06 22	05 26	06 17	07 04	07 48
0	05 21	05 46	06 08	05 12	06 05	06 55	07 43
S 10	05 05	05 31	05 54	04 57	05 53	06 47	07 37
20	04 46	05 14	05 38	04 41	05 40	06 37	07 32
30	04 22	04 54	05 20	04 23	05 26	06 27	07 26
35	04 07	04 41	05 09	04 12	05 17	06 21	07 22
40	03 48	04 26	04 57	04 00	05 07	06 13	07 18
45	03 24	04 08	04 43	03 45	04 56	06 05	07 13
S 50	02 51	03 45	04 25	03 28	04 42	05 55	07 07
52	02 33	03 34	04 17	03 19	04 35	05 51	07 04
54	02 12	03 21	04 08	03 10	04 28	05 46	07 02
56	01 42	03 05	03 57	02 59	04 19	05 40	06 58
58	00 48	02 47	03 44	02 47	04 10	05 33	06 55
S 60	////	02 23	03 30	02 33	04 00	05 26	06 51

Lat.	Sunset	Twilight Civil	Twilight Naut.	Moonset 22	Moonset 23	Moonset 24	Moonset 25
°	h m	h m	h m	h m	h m	h m	h m
N 72	■■	15 04	16 44	■■	14 46	17 02	19 01
N 70	13 39	15 30	16 56	12 58	15 20	17 19	19 08
68	14 25	15 50	17 05	13 46	15 44	17 32	19 14
66	14 55	16 06	17 13	14 17	16 03	17 43	19 19
64	15 17	16 19	17 21	14 40	16 18	17 52	19 23
62	15 35	16 30	17 27	14 58	16 30	18 00	19 26
60	15 49	16 40	17 32	15 13	16 41	18 07	19 30
N 58	16 02	16 48	17 37	15 26	16 50	18 12	19 32
56	16 13	16 56	17 42	15 37	16 58	18 17	19 35
54	16 23	17 02	17 46	15 46	17 05	18 22	19 37
52	16 31	17 09	17 50	15 55	17 11	18 26	19 39
50	16 38	17 14	17 54	16 02	17 17	18 30	19 41
45	16 54	17 26	18 02	16 19	17 29	18 38	19 45
N 40	17 08	17 37	18 10	16 32	17 39	18 45	19 48
35	17 19	17 46	18 17	16 43	17 48	18 50	19 51
30	17 29	17 54	18 23	16 53	17 55	18 55	19 53
20	17 46	18 09	18 36	17 10	18 08	19 04	19 57
N 10	18 01	18 23	18 49	17 24	18 19	19 11	20 01
0	18 15	18 37	19 03	17 38	18 30	19 18	20 04
S 10	18 30	18 52	19 18	17 51	18 40	19 25	20 08
20	18 45	19 09	19 37	18 05	18 51	19 33	20 11
30	19 03	19 29	20 01	18 22	19 04	19 41	20 15
35	19 13	19 42	20 16	18 31	19 11	19 46	20 18
40	19 26	19 56	20 35	18 42	19 19	19 51	20 20
45	19 40	20 14	20 58	18 54	19 28	19 57	20 23
S 50	19 57	20 37	21 31	19 10	19 40	20 05	20 27
52	20 06	20 48	21 48	19 17	19 45	20 08	20 28
54	20 15	21 01	22 09	19 24	19 51	20 12	20 30
56	20 25	21 16	22 38	19 33	19 57	20 16	20 32
58	20 37	21 34	23 25	19 43	20 04	20 21	20 34
S 60	20 51	21 57	////	19 54	20 12	20 26	20 37

	SUN			SUN	MOON	MOON		
Day	Eqn. of Time 00h	Eqn. of Time 12h	Mer. Pass.	Mer. Pass. Upper	Mer. Pass. Lower	Age	Phase	
d	m s	m s	h m	h m	h m	d	%	
22	11 17	11 25	12 11	11 25	23 52	29	1	●
23	11 33	11 41	12 12	12 18	24 43	00	0	
24	11 49	11 57	12 12	13 07	00 43	01	2	

UT (d h)	ARIES GHA	VENUS −4.1 GHA	Dec	MARS −0.4 GHA	Dec	JUPITER −2.4 GHA	Dec	SATURN +0.6 GHA	Dec	STARS Name	SHA	Dec
25 00	123 43.2	138 53.7	S 7 49.2	308 37.5	N 6 04.8	93 36.8	N11 05.2	275 31.9	S 8 52.8	Acamar	315 19.0	S40 15.6
01	138 45.7	153 53.4	47.9	323 39.9	04.9	108 39.0	05.3	290 34.3	52.8	Achernar	335 27.5	S57 10.8
02	153 48.1	168 53.1	46.7	338 42.4	05.0	123 41.2	05.4	305 36.7	52.8	Acrux	173 10.0	S63 09.8
03	168 50.6	183 52.8	.. 45.4	353 44.9	.. 05.0	138 43.5	.. 05.5	320 39.1	.. 52.8	Adhara	255 12.9	S28 59.5
04	183 53.1	198 52.5	44.2	8 47.3	05.1	153 45.7	05.6	335 41.6	52.8	Aldebaran	290 50.3	N16 32.0
05	198 55.5	213 52.2	42.9	23 49.8	05.2	168 47.9	05.7	350 44.0	52.8			
W 06	213 58.0	228 51.9	S 7 41.7	38 52.3	N 6 05.3	183 50.2	N11 05.8	5 46.4	S 8 52.8	Alioth	166 21.3	N55 53.3
E 07	229 00.5	243 51.6	40.4	53 54.7	05.4	198 52.4	05.9	20 48.8	52.8	Alkaid	152 59.6	N49 14.8
D 08	244 02.9	258 51.3	39.2	68 57.2	05.5	213 54.6	06.0	35 51.2	52.8	Al Na'ir	27 45.3	S46 54.2
N 09	259 05.4	273 51.0	.. 37.9	83 59.7	.. 05.5	228 56.9	.. 06.1	50 53.6	.. 52.9	Alnilam	275 47.1	S 1 11.8
E 10	274 07.9	288 50.7	36.6	99 02.2	05.6	243 59.1	06.2	65 56.0	52.9	Alphard	217 56.7	S 8 42.9
S 11	289 10.3	303 50.4	35.4	114 04.6	05.7	259 01.3	06.2	80 58.4	52.9			
D 12	304 12.8	318 50.1	S 7 34.1	129 07.1	N 6 05.8	274 03.6	N11 06.3	96 00.8	S 8 52.9	Alphecca	126 11.9	N26 40.2
A 13	319 15.3	333 49.8	32.9	144 09.6	05.9	289 05.8	06.4	111 03.2	52.9	Alpheratz	357 44.7	N29 09.6
Y 14	334 17.7	348 49.6	31.6	159 12.1	06.0	304 08.0	06.5	126 05.6	52.9	Altair	62 09.5	N 8 54.1
15	349 20.2	3 49.3	.. 30.4	174 14.5	.. 06.0	319 10.2	.. 06.6	141 08.0	.. 52.9	Ankaa	353 16.8	S42 14.6
16	4 22.6	18 49.0	29.1	189 17.0	06.1	334 12.5	06.7	156 10.4	52.9	Antares	112 27.6	S26 27.4
17	19 25.1	33 48.7	27.9	204 19.5	06.2	349 14.7	06.8	171 12.8	52.9			
18	34 27.6	48 48.4	S 7 26.6	219 22.0	N 6 06.3	4 16.9	N11 06.9	186 15.2	S 8 52.9	Arcturus	145 56.6	N19 06.9
19	49 30.0	63 48.1	25.3	234 24.5	06.4	19 19.2	07.0	201 17.6	53.0	Atria	107 30.7	S69 02.7
20	64 32.5	78 47.8	24.1	249 27.0	06.5	34 21.4	07.1	216 20.0	53.0	Avior	234 17.8	S59 33.1
21	79 35.0	93 47.5	.. 22.8	264 29.5	.. 06.6	49 23.6	.. 07.2	231 22.4	.. 53.0	Bellatrix	278 32.8	N 6 21.5
22	94 37.4	108 47.2	21.6	279 31.9	06.7	64 25.8	07.3	246 24.9	53.0	Betelgeuse	271 02.0	N 7 24.4
23	109 39.9	123 46.9	20.3	294 34.4	06.7	79 28.1	07.4	261 27.3	53.0			
26 00	124 42.4	138 46.7	S 7 19.0	309 36.9	N 6 06.8	94 30.3	N11 07.5	276 29.7	S 8 53.0	Canopus	263 56.1	S52 42.4
01	139 44.8	153 46.4	17.8	324 39.4	06.9	109 32.5	07.6	291 32.1	53.0	Capella	280 35.5	N46 00.6
02	154 47.3	168 46.1	16.5	339 41.9	07.0	124 34.8	07.7	306 34.5	53.0	Deneb	49 32.6	N45 19.5
03	169 49.7	183 45.8	.. 15.3	354 44.4	.. 07.1	139 37.0	.. 07.8	321 36.9	.. 53.0	Denebola	182 34.4	N14 30.0
04	184 52.2	198 45.5	14.0	9 46.9	07.2	154 39.2	07.9	336 39.3	53.0	Diphda	348 57.0	S17 55.3
05	199 54.7	213 45.2	12.7	24 49.4	07.3	169 41.4	08.0	351 41.7	53.0			
T 06	214 57.1	228 44.9	S 7 11.5	39 51.9	N 6 07.4	184 43.7	N11 08.1	6 44.1	S 8 53.1	Dubhe	193 52.3	N61 40.8
H 07	229 59.6	243 44.7	10.2	54 54.4	07.5	199 45.9	08.2	21 46.5	53.1	Elnath	278 13.5	N28 37.0
U 08	245 02.1	258 44.4	09.0	69 56.9	07.6	214 48.1	08.3	36 48.9	53.1	Eltanin	90 47.0	N51 29.1
R 09	260 04.5	273 44.1	.. 07.7	84 59.4	.. 07.7	229 50.3	.. 08.4	51 51.3	.. 53.1	Enif	33 48.4	N 9 55.9
S 10	275 07.0	288 43.8	06.4	100 01.9	07.8	244 52.6	08.5	66 53.8	53.1	Fomalhaut	15 25.3	S29 33.5
D 11	290 09.5	303 43.5	05.2	115 04.4	07.9	259 54.8	08.6	81 56.2	53.1			
A 12	305 11.9	318 43.2	S 7 03.9	130 06.9	N 6 08.0	274 57.0	N11 08.7	96 58.6	S 8 53.1	Gacrux	172 01.7	S57 10.7
Y 13	320 14.4	333 43.0	02.6	145 09.4	08.0	289 59.2	08.8	112 01.0	53.1	Gienah	175 53.1	S17 36.6
14	335 16.9	348 42.7	01.4	160 12.0	08.1	305 01.4	08.9	127 03.4	53.1	Hadar	148 49.2	S60 25.7
15	350 19.3	3 42.4	7 00.1	175 14.5	.. 08.2	320 03.7	.. 09.0	142 05.8	.. 53.1	Hamal	328 01.8	N23 31.3
16	5 21.8	18 42.1	6 58.9	190 17.0	08.3	335 05.9	09.1	157 08.2	53.1	Kaus Aust.	83 45.4	S34 22.6
17	20 24.2	33 41.8	57.6	205 19.5	08.4	350 08.1	09.2	172 10.6	53.1			
18	35 26.7	48 41.5	S 6 56.3	220 22.0	N 6 08.5	5 10.3	N11 09.3	187 13.0	S 8 53.2	Kochab	137 20.1	N74 06.0
19	50 29.2	63 41.3	55.1	235 24.5	08.6	20 12.6	09.4	202 15.4	53.2	Markab	13 39.5	N15 16.3
20	65 31.6	78 41.0	53.8	250 27.0	08.7	35 14.8	09.5	217 17.9	53.2	Menkar	314 16.0	N 4 08.2
21	80 34.1	93 40.7	.. 52.5	265 29.6	.. 08.8	50 17.0	.. 09.6	232 20.3	.. 53.2	Menkent	148 08.7	S36 25.7
22	95 36.6	108 40.4	51.3	280 32.1	08.9	65 19.2	09.7	247 22.7	53.2	Miaplacidus	221 39.0	S69 46.1
23	110 39.0	123 40.1	50.0	295 34.6	09.0	80 21.4	09.8	262 25.1	53.2			
27 00	125 41.5	138 39.9	S 6 48.7	310 37.1	N 6 09.1	95 23.7	N11 09.9	277 27.5	S 8 53.2	Mirfak	308 41.6	N49 54.4
01	140 44.0	153 39.6	47.5	325 39.6	09.2	110 25.9	10.0	292 29.9	53.2	Nunki	75 59.8	S26 16.8
02	155 46.4	168 39.3	46.2	340 42.2	09.3	125 28.1	10.1	307 32.3	53.2	Peacock	53 21.3	S56 41.7
03	170 48.9	183 39.0	.. 44.9	355 44.7	.. 09.5	140 30.3	.. 10.2	322 34.7	.. 53.2	Pollux	243 28.5	N27 59.6
04	185 51.4	198 38.8	43.7	10 47.2	09.6	155 32.5	10.3	337 37.2	53.2	Procyon	245 00.4	N 5 11.4
05	200 53.8	213 38.5	42.4	25 49.7	09.7	170 34.8	10.4	352 39.6	53.2			
F 06	215 56.3	228 38.2	S 6 41.1	40 52.3	N 6 09.8	185 37.0	N11 10.5	7 42.0	S 8 53.2	Rasalhague	96 07.6	N12 33.0
R 07	230 58.7	243 37.9	39.9	55 54.8	09.9	200 39.2	10.6	22 44.4	53.2	Regulus	207 44.2	N11 54.2
I 08	246 01.2	258 37.7	38.6	70 57.3	10.0	215 41.4	10.7	37 46.8	53.3	Rigel	281 12.7	S 8 11.4
D 09	261 03.7	273 37.4	.. 37.3	85 59.9	.. 10.1	230 43.6	.. 10.8	52 49.2	.. 53.3	Rigil Kent.	139 53.1	S60 52.8
A 10	276 06.1	288 37.1	36.1	101 02.4	10.2	245 45.8	10.9	67 51.6	53.3	Sabik	102 13.9	S15 44.3
Y 11	291 08.6	303 36.8	34.8	116 04.9	10.3	260 48.1	11.0	82 54.0	53.3			
12	306 11.1	318 36.6	S 6 33.5	131 07.5	N 6 10.4	275 50.3	N11 11.1	97 56.5	S 8 53.3	Schedar	349 41.9	N56 36.5
13	321 13.5	333 36.3	32.3	146 10.0	10.5	290 52.5	11.2	112 58.9	53.3	Shaula	96 23.5	S37 06.6
14	336 16.0	348 36.0	31.0	161 12.6	10.6	305 54.7	11.3	128 01.3	53.3	Sirius	258 34.2	S16 44.2
15	351 18.5	3 35.8	.. 29.7	176 15.1	.. 10.7	320 56.9	.. 11.4	143 03.7	.. 53.3	Spica	158 32.2	S11 13.5
16	6 20.9	18 35.5	28.4	191 17.6	10.8	335 59.1	11.5	158 06.1	53.3	Suhail	222 52.7	S43 29.0
17	21 23.4	33 35.2	27.2	206 20.2	11.0	351 01.4	11.6	173 08.5	53.3			
18	36 25.8	48 34.9	S 6 25.9	221 22.7	N 6 11.1	6 03.6	N11 11.7	188 10.9	S 8 53.3	Vega	80 40.0	N38 47.6
19	51 28.3	63 34.7	24.6	236 25.3	11.2	21 05.8	11.8	203 13.4	53.3	Zuben'ubi	137 06.5	S16 05.5
20	66 30.8	78 34.4	23.4	251 27.8	11.3	36 08.0	11.9	218 15.8	53.3		SHA	Mer.Pass.
21	81 33.2	93 34.1	.. 22.1	266 30.4	.. 11.4	51 10.2	.. 12.0	233 18.2	.. 53.3		° ′	h m
22	96 35.7	108 33.9	20.8	281 32.9	11.5	66 12.4	12.1	248 20.6	53.3	Venus	14 04.3	14 45
23	111 38.2	123 33.6	19.5	296 35.5	11.6	81 14.6	12.2	263 23.0	53.4	Mars	184 54.6	3 21
Mer.Pass.	h m 15 38.6	v −0.3	d 1.3	v 2.5	d 0.1	v 2.2	d 0.1	v 2.4	d 0.0	Jupiter	329 47.9	17 39
										Saturn	151 47.3	5 33

UT	SUN GHA	SUN Dec	MOON GHA	v	Dec	d	HP
d h	° ′	° ′	° ′	′	° ′	′	′
25 00	176 58.9	S19 09.4	158 03.0	12.8	S 8 35.8	11.6	56.6
01	191 58.8	08.8	172 34.8	12.8	8 24.2	11.6	56.6
02	206 58.6	08.2	187 06.6	12.9	8 12.6	11.6	56.5
03	221 58.5	.. 07.6	201 38.5	13.0	8 01.0	11.7	56.5
04	236 58.3	07.0	216 10.5	13.0	7 49.3	11.6	56.5
05	251 58.2	06.4	230 42.5	13.1	7 37.7	11.7	56.5
06	266 58.0	S19 05.8	245 14.6	13.1	S 7 26.0	11.8	56.4
W 07	281 57.9	05.2	259 46.7	13.2	7 14.2	11.7	56.4
E 08	296 57.7	04.6	274 18.9	13.2	7 02.5	11.8	56.4
D 09	311 57.6	.. 04.0	288 51.1	13.3	6 50.7	11.7	56.3
N 10	326 57.4	03.4	303 23.4	13.4	6 39.0	11.8	56.3
E 11	341 57.3	02.7	317 55.8	13.4	6 27.2	11.8	56.3
S 12	356 57.1	S19 02.1	332 28.2	13.5	S 6 15.4	11.9	56.3
D 13	11 57.0	01.5	347 00.7	13.5	6 03.5	11.8	56.2
A 14	26 56.8	07.0	1 33.2	13.5	5 51.7	11.9	56.2
Y 15	41 56.7	19 00.3	16 05.7	13.6	5 39.8	11.8	56.2
16	56 56.6	18 59.7	30 38.3	13.7	5 28.0	11.9	56.2
17	71 56.4	59.1	45 11.0	13.7	5 16.1	11.9	56.1
18	86 56.3	S18 58.4	59 43.7	13.8	S 5 04.2	11.9	56.1
19	101 56.1	57.8	74 16.5	13.8	4 52.3	11.9	56.1
20	116 56.0	57.2	88 49.3	13.9	4 40.4	11.9	56.1
21	131 55.8	.. 56.6	103 22.2	13.9	4 28.5	12.0	56.0
22	146 55.7	56.0	117 55.1	13.9	4 16.5	11.9	56.0
23	161 55.5	55.4	132 28.0	14.0	4 04.6	11.9	56.0
26 00	176 55.4	S18 54.7	147 01.0	14.0	S 3 52.7	12.0	56.0
01	191 55.3	54.1	161 34.0	14.1	3 40.7	11.9	55.9
02	206 55.1	53.5	176 07.1	14.1	3 28.8	12.0	55.9
03	221 55.0	.. 52.9	190 40.2	14.2	3 16.8	12.0	55.9
04	236 54.8	52.3	205 13.4	14.2	3 04.9	12.0	55.8
05	251 54.7	51.6	219 46.6	14.2	2 52.9	11.9	55.8
06	266 54.6	S18 51.0	234 19.8	14.3	S 2 41.0	12.0	55.8
T 07	281 54.4	50.4	248 53.1	14.3	2 29.0	11.9	55.8
H 08	296 54.3	49.8	263 26.4	14.4	2 17.1	12.0	55.7
U 09	311 54.1	.. 49.2	277 59.8	14.4	2 05.1	11.9	55.7
R 10	326 54.0	48.5	292 33.2	14.4	1 53.2	12.0	55.7
S 11	341 53.9	47.9	307 06.6	14.5	1 41.2	11.9	55.7
D 12	356 53.7	S18 47.3	321 40.1	14.4	S 1 29.3	12.0	55.6
A 13	11 53.6	46.6	336 13.5	14.6	1 17.3	11.9	55.6
Y 14	26 53.4	46.0	350 47.1	14.5	1 05.4	11.9	55.6
15	41 53.3	.. 45.4	5 20.6	14.6	0 53.5	11.9	55.6
16	56 53.2	44.7	19 54.2	14.6	0 41.6	11.9	55.5
17	71 53.0	44.1	34 27.8	14.7	0 29.7	11.9	55.5
18	86 52.9	S18 43.5	49 01.5	14.7	S 0 17.8	11.9	55.5
19	101 52.8	42.9	63 35.2	14.7	S 0 05.9	11.9	55.5
20	116 52.6	42.2	78 08.9	14.7	N 0 06.0	11.8	55.5
21	131 52.5	.. 41.6	92 42.6	14.7	0 17.8	11.9	55.4
22	146 52.4	41.0	107 16.3	14.8	0 29.7	11.8	55.4
23	161 52.2	40.3	121 50.1	14.8	0 41.5	11.8	55.4
27 00	176 52.1	S18 39.7	136 23.9	14.8	N 0 53.3	11.8	55.4
01	191 52.0	39.1	150 57.7	14.9	1 05.1	11.8	55.3
02	206 51.8	38.4	165 31.6	14.9	1 16.9	11.8	55.3
03	221 51.7	.. 37.8	180 05.5	14.9	1 28.7	11.7	55.3
04	236 51.6	37.2	194 39.4	14.9	1 40.4	11.8	55.3
05	251 51.4	36.5	209 13.3	14.9	1 52.2	11.7	55.2
06	266 51.3	S18 35.9	223 47.2	14.9	N 2 03.9	11.7	55.2
07	281 51.2	35.2	238 21.1	15.0	2 15.6	11.7	55.2
F 08	296 51.0	34.6	252 55.1	15.0	2 27.3	11.6	55.2
R 09	311 50.9	.. 34.0	267 29.1	15.0	2 38.9	11.7	55.2
I 10	326 50.8	33.3	282 03.1	15.0	2 50.6	11.6	55.1
D 11	341 50.6	32.7	296 37.1	15.0	3 02.2	11.6	55.1
A 12	356 50.5	S18 32.0	311 11.1	15.1	N 3 13.8	11.5	55.1
Y 13	11 50.4	31.4	325 45.2	15.0	3 25.4	11.5	55.1
14	26 50.2	30.8	340 19.2	15.1	3 36.9	11.5	55.1
15	41 50.1	.. 30.1	354 53.3	15.0	3 48.4	11.5	55.0
16	56 50.0	29.5	9 27.3	15.1	3 59.9	11.4	55.0
17	71 49.9	28.8	24 01.4	15.1	4 11.4	11.4	55.0
18	86 49.7	S18 28.2	38 35.5	15.1	N 4 22.8	11.5	55.0
19	101 49.6	27.5	53 09.6	15.1	4 34.3	11.4	55.0
20	116 49.5	26.9	67 43.7	15.1	4 45.7	11.3	54.9
21	131 49.3	.. 26.3	82 17.8	15.2	4 57.0	11.3	54.9
22	146 49.2	25.6	96 52.0	15.1	5 08.3	11.3	54.9
23	161 49.1	25.0	111 26.1	15.1	N 5 19.6	11.3	54.9
	SD 16.3	d 0.6	SD 15.3		15.2		15.0

Lat.	Twilight Naut.	Twilight Civil	Sunrise	Moonrise 25	26	27	28
°	h m	h m	h m	h m	h m	h m	h m
N 72	07 32	09 07	11 56	09 13	08 55	08 39	08 22
N 70	07 21	08 44	10 24	09 03	08 52	08 42	08 32
68	07 12	08 26	09 46	08 55	08 50	08 45	08 40
66	07 05	08 11	09 19	08 48	08 48	08 47	08 47
64	06 58	07 59	08 59	08 43	08 46	08 49	08 53
62	06 52	07 48	08 42	08 38	08 45	08 51	08 58
60	06 47	07 39	08 29	08 33	08 43	08 52	09 02
N 58	06 43	07 31	08 17	08 30	08 42	08 54	09 06
56	06 38	07 24	08 07	08 26	08 41	08 55	09 09
54	06 34	07 18	07 58	08 23	08 40	08 56	09 12
52	06 31	07 12	07 50	08 20	08 39	08 57	09 15
50	06 27	07 07	07 42	08 18	08 38	08 58	09 18
45	06 19	06 55	07 27	08 12	08 37	09 00	09 23
N 40	06 12	06 45	07 14	08 07	08 35	09 02	09 28
35	06 06	06 36	07 03	08 03	08 34	09 03	09 32
30	05 59	06 28	06 54	08 00	08 33	09 05	09 36
20	05 47	06 14	06 37	07 53	08 31	09 07	09 42
N 10	05 35	06 00	06 23	07 48	08 29	09 09	09 48
0	05 22	05 47	06 09	07 43	08 27	09 11	09 53
S 10	05 07	05 33	05 55	07 37	08 26	09 13	09 59
20	04 48	05 16	05 40	07 32	08 24	09 15	10 05
30	04 25	04 57	05 23	07 26	08 22	09 17	10 11
35	04 10	04 44	05 13	07 22	08 21	09 19	10 15
40	03 52	04 30	05 01	07 18	08 20	09 20	10 19
45	03 29	04 13	04 47	07 13	08 19	09 22	10 24
S 50	02 58	03 51	04 30	07 07	08 17	09 24	10 31
52	02 42	03 40	04 22	07 04	08 16	09 25	10 33
54	02 22	03 28	04 13	07 02	08 15	09 27	10 37
56	01 56	03 13	04 03	06 58	08 14	09 28	10 40
58	01 15	02 56	03 52	06 55	08 13	09 29	10 44
S 60	////	02 35	03 38	06 51	08 12	09 31	10 48

Lat.	Sunset	Twilight Civil	Twilight Naut.	Moonset 25	26	27	28
°	h m	h m	h m	h m	h m	h m	h m
N 72	12 30	15 19	16 55	19 01	20 51	22 38	24 27
N 70	14 02	15 42	17 05	19 08	20 51	22 31	24 11
68	14 40	16 00	17 14	19 14	20 50	22 24	23 58
66	15 07	16 15	17 21	19 19	20 50	22 19	23 47
64	15 27	16 27	17 28	19 23	20 50	22 15	23 39
62	15 43	16 37	17 33	19 26	20 50	22 11	23 31
60	15 57	16 46	17 38	19 30	20 50	22 08	23 25
N 58	16 09	16 54	17 43	19 32	20 50	22 05	23 19
56	16 19	17 01	17 47	19 35	20 50	22 03	23 14
54	16 28	17 08	17 51	19 37	20 50	22 00	23 10
52	16 36	17 13	17 55	19 39	20 50	21 58	23 06
50	16 43	17 19	17 58	19 41	20 49	21 56	23 02
45	16 58	17 30	18 06	19 45	20 49	21 52	22 54
N 40	17 11	17 40	18 13	19 48	20 49	21 49	22 48
35	17 22	17 49	18 20	19 51	20 49	21 46	22 42
30	17 31	17 57	18 26	19 53	20 49	21 43	22 37
20	17 48	18 11	18 38	19 57	20 49	21 39	22 28
N 10	18 02	18 24	18 50	20 01	20 49	21 35	22 21
0	18 16	18 38	19 03	20 04	20 48	21 31	22 14
S 10	18 30	18 52	19 18	20 08	20 48	21 28	22 07
20	18 45	19 08	19 36	20 11	20 48	21 24	22 00
30	19 02	19 28	19 59	20 15	20 48	21 19	21 51
35	19 12	19 40	20 14	20 18	20 48	21 17	21 46
40	19 23	19 54	20 32	20 20	20 47	21 14	21 41
45	19 37	20 11	20 54	20 23	20 47	21 11	21 34
S 50	19 54	20 33	21 25	20 27	20 47	21 07	21 27
52	20 02	20 44	21 41	20 28	20 47	21 05	21 23
54	20 10	20 56	22 01	20 30	20 47	21 03	21 20
56	20 20	21 10	22 26	20 32	20 47	21 01	21 16
58	20 32	21 27	23 03	20 34	20 46	20 58	21 11
S 60	20 45	21 48	////	20 37	20 46	20 55	21 05

	SUN			MOON			
Day	Eqn. of Time 00h	12h	Mer. Pass.	Mer. Pass. Upper	Lower	Age	Phase
d	m s	m s	h m	h m	h m	d	%
25	12 04	12 11	12 12	13 54	01 31	02	5
26	12 18	12 25	12 12	14 38	02 16	03	11
27	12 31	12 38	12 13	15 21	03 00	04	18

2012 JANUARY 28, 29, 30 (SAT., SUN., MON.)

UT	ARIES GHA	VENUS −4.1 GHA	VENUS Dec	MARS −0.5 GHA	MARS Dec	JUPITER −2.4 GHA	JUPITER Dec	SATURN +0.6 GHA	SATURN Dec	Name	STARS SHA	STARS Dec
d h	° ′	° ′	° ′	° ′	° ′	° ′	° ′	° ′	° ′		° ′	° ′
28 00	126 40.6	138 33.3	S 6 18.3	311 38.0	N 6 11.7	96 16.9	N11 12.3	278 25.4	S 8 53.4	Acamar	315 19.0	S40 15.6
01	141 43.1	153 33.1	17.0	326 40.6	11.9	111 19.1	12.4	293 27.9	53.4	Achernar	335 27.6	S57 10.8
02	156 45.6	168 32.8	15.7	341 43.1	12.0	126 21.3	12.5	308 30.3	53.4	Acrux	173 10.0	S63 09.9
03	171 48.0	183 32.5	. . 14.4	356 45.7	. . 12.1	141 23.5	. . 12.6	323 32.7	. . 53.4	Adhara	255 12.9	S28 59.6
04	186 50.5	198 32.3	13.2	11 48.2	12.2	156 25.7	12.7	338 35.1	53.4	Aldebaran	290 50.3	N16 32.0
05	201 53.0	213 32.0	11.9	26 50.8	12.3	171 27.9	12.8	353 37.5	53.4			
06	216 55.4	228 31.7	S 6 10.6	41 53.4	N 6 12.4	186 30.1	N11 12.9	8 39.9	S 8 53.4	Alioth	166 21.2	N55 53.3
07	231 57.9	243 31.5	09.4	56 55.9	12.6	201 32.3	13.0	23 42.4	53.4	Alkaid	152 59.5	N49 14.8
S 08	247 00.3	258 31.2	08.1	71 58.5	12.7	216 34.6	13.1	38 44.8	53.4	Al Na'ir	27 45.3	S46 54.2
A 09	262 02.8	273 30.9	. . 06.8	87 01.0	. . 12.8	231 36.8	. . 13.2	53 47.2	. . 53.4	Alnilam	275 47.1	S 1 11.8
T 10	277 05.3	288 30.7	05.5	102 03.6	12.9	246 39.0	13.3	68 49.6	53.4	Alphard	217 56.7	S 8 42.9
U 11	292 07.7	303 30.4	04.3	117 06.2	13.0	261 41.2	13.4	83 52.0	53.4			
R 12	307 10.2	318 30.1	S 6 03.0	132 08.7	N 6 13.2	276 43.4	N11 13.5	98 54.4	S 8 53.4	Alphecca	126 11.9	N26 40.2
D 13	322 12.7	333 29.9	01.7	147 11.3	13.3	291 45.6	13.6	113 56.9	53.4	Alpheratz	357 44.7	N29 09.6
A 14	337 15.1	348 29.6	6 00.4	162 13.9	13.4	306 47.8	13.7	128 59.3	53.4	Altair	62 09.5	N 8 54.1
Y 15	352 17.6	3 29.4	5 59.1	177 16.5	. . 13.5	321 50.0	. . 13.9	144 01.7	. . 53.4	Ankaa	353 16.8	S42 14.6
16	7 20.1	18 29.1	57.9	192 19.0	13.6	336 52.2	14.0	159 04.1	53.4	Antares	112 27.6	S26 27.4
17	22 22.5	33 28.8	56.6	207 21.6	13.8	351 54.4	14.1	174 06.5	53.4			
18	37 25.0	48 28.6	S 5 55.3	222 24.2	N 6 13.9	6 56.6	N11 14.2	189 09.0	S 8 53.5	Arcturus	145 56.6	N19 06.9
19	52 27.5	63 28.3	54.0	237 26.7	14.0	21 58.9	14.3	204 11.4	53.5	Atria	107 30.7	S69 02.7
20	67 29.9	78 28.0	52.8	252 29.3	14.1	37 01.1	14.4	219 13.8	53.5	Avior	234 17.8	S59 33.1
21	82 32.4	93 27.8	. . 51.5	267 31.9	. . 14.3	52 03.3	. . 14.5	234 16.2	. . 53.5	Bellatrix	278 32.8	N 6 21.5
22	97 34.8	108 27.5	50.2	282 34.5	14.4	67 05.5	14.6	249 18.6	53.5	Betelgeuse	271 02.1	N 7 24.4
23	112 37.3	123 27.3	48.9	297 37.1	14.5	82 07.7	14.7	264 21.0	53.5			
29 00	127 39.8	138 27.0	S 5 47.7	312 39.6	N 6 14.6	97 09.9	N11 14.8	279 23.5	S 8 53.5	Canopus	263 56.1	S52 42.4
01	142 42.2	153 26.8	46.4	327 42.2	14.8	112 12.1	14.9	294 25.9	53.5	Capella	280 35.5	N46 00.6
02	157 44.7	168 26.5	45.1	342 44.8	14.9	127 14.3	15.0	309 28.3	53.5	Deneb	49 32.6	N45 19.5
03	172 47.2	183 26.2	. . 43.8	357 47.4	. . 15.0	142 16.5	. . 15.1	324 30.7	. . 53.5	Denebola	182 34.4	N14 30.0
04	187 49.6	198 26.0	42.5	12 50.0	15.2	157 18.7	15.2	339 33.2	53.5	Diphda	348 57.0	S17 55.3
05	202 52.1	213 25.7	41.3	27 52.6	15.3	172 20.9	15.3	354 35.6	53.5			
06	217 54.6	228 25.5	S 5 40.0	42 55.2	N 6 15.4	187 23.1	N11 15.4	9 38.0	S 8 53.5	Dubhe	193 52.3	N61 40.8
07	232 57.0	243 25.2	38.7	57 57.8	15.5	202 25.3	15.5	24 40.4	53.5	Elnath	278 13.5	N28 37.0
08	247 59.5	258 25.0	37.4	73 00.4	15.7	217 27.5	15.6	39 42.8	53.5	Eltanin	90 47.0	N51 29.1
S 09	263 01.9	273 24.7	. . 36.1	88 02.9	. . 15.8	232 29.7	. . 15.7	54 45.3	. . 53.5	Enif	33 48.4	N 9 55.9
U 10	278 04.4	288 24.4	34.9	103 05.5	15.9	247 31.9	15.8	69 47.7	53.5	Fomalhaut	15 25.3	S29 33.5
N 11	293 06.9	303 24.2	33.6	118 08.1	16.1	262 34.1	15.9	84 50.1	53.5			
D 12	308 09.3	318 23.9	S 5 32.3	133 10.7	N 6 16.2	277 36.3	N11 16.0	99 52.5	S 8 53.5	Gacrux	172 01.7	S57 10.7
A 13	323 11.8	333 23.7	31.0	148 13.3	16.3	292 38.5	16.2	114 54.9	53.5	Gienah	175 53.1	S17 36.6
Y 14	338 14.3	348 23.4	29.7	163 15.9	16.5	307 40.7	16.3	129 57.4	53.5	Hadar	148 49.2	S60 25.7
15	353 16.7	3 23.2	. . 28.4	178 18.5	. . 16.6	322 43.0	. . 16.4	144 59.8	. . 53.5	Hamal	328 01.9	N23 31.3
16	8 19.2	18 22.9	27.2	193 21.1	16.7	337 45.2	16.5	160 02.2	53.5	Kaus Aust.	83 45.4	S34 22.6
17	23 21.7	33 22.7	25.9	208 23.7	16.9	352 47.4	16.6	175 04.6	53.5			
18	38 24.1	48 22.4	S 5 24.6	223 26.3	N 6 17.0	7 49.6	N11 16.7	190 07.1	S 8 53.5	Kochab	137 20.0	N74 06.0
19	53 26.6	63 22.2	23.3	238 29.0	17.1	22 51.8	16.8	205 09.5	53.5	Markab	13 39.5	N15 16.3
20	68 29.1	78 21.9	22.0	253 31.6	17.3	37 54.0	16.9	220 11.9	53.6	Menkar	314 16.0	N 4 08.2
21	83 31.5	93 21.7	. . 20.7	268 34.2	. . 17.4	52 56.2	. . 17.0	235 14.3	. . 53.6	Menkent	148 08.7	S36 25.7
22	98 34.0	108 21.4	19.5	283 36.8	17.5	67 58.4	17.1	250 16.8	53.6	Miaplacidus	221 39.0	S69 46.1
23	113 36.4	123 21.2	18.2	298 39.4	17.7	83 00.6	17.2	265 19.2	53.6			
30 00	128 38.9	138 20.9	S 5 16.9	313 42.0	N 6 17.8	98 02.8	N11 17.3	280 21.6	S 8 53.6	Mirfak	308 41.6	N49 54.4
01	143 41.4	153 20.7	15.6	328 44.6	18.0	113 05.0	17.4	295 24.0	53.6	Nunki	75 59.8	S26 16.8
02	158 43.8	168 20.4	14.3	343 47.2	18.1	128 07.2	17.5	310 26.5	53.6	Peacock	53 21.3	S56 41.7
03	173 46.3	183 20.2	. . 13.0	358 49.8	. . 18.2	143 09.4	. . 17.6	325 28.9	. . 53.6	Pollux	243 28.5	N27 59.6
04	188 48.8	198 19.9	11.8	13 52.5	18.4	158 11.6	17.7	340 31.3	53.6	Procyon	245 00.4	N 5 11.4
05	203 51.2	213 19.7	10.5	28 55.1	18.5	173 13.8	17.9	355 33.7	53.6			
06	218 53.7	228 19.4	S 5 09.2	43 57.7	N 6 18.7	188 16.0	N11 18.0	10 36.2	S 8 53.6	Rasalhague	96 07.6	N12 33.0
07	233 56.2	243 19.2	07.9	59 00.3	18.8	203 18.1	18.1	25 38.6	53.6	Regulus	207 44.2	N11 54.2
08	248 58.6	258 18.9	06.6	74 03.0	18.9	218 20.3	18.2	40 41.0	53.6	Rigel	281 12.7	S 8 11.5
M 09	264 01.1	273 18.7	. . 05.3	89 05.6	. . 19.1	233 22.5	. . 18.3	55 43.4	. . 53.6	Rigil Kent.	139 53.1	S60 52.8
O 10	279 03.5	288 18.4	04.0	104 08.2	19.2	248 24.7	18.4	70 45.9	53.6	Sabik	102 13.9	S15 44.3
N 11	294 06.0	303 18.2	02.8	119 10.8	19.4	263 26.9	18.5	85 48.3	53.6			
D 12	309 08.5	318 18.0	S 5 01.5	134 13.5	N 6 19.5	278 29.1	N11 18.6	100 50.7	S 8 53.6	Schedar	349 41.9	N56 36.5
A 13	324 10.9	333 17.7	5 00.2	149 16.1	19.7	293 31.3	18.7	115 53.1	53.6	Shaula	96 23.5	S37 06.6
Y 14	339 13.4	348 17.5	4 58.9	164 18.7	19.8	308 33.5	18.8	130 55.6	53.6	Sirius	258 34.2	S16 44.2
15	354 15.9	3 17.2	. . 57.6	179 21.3	. . 20.0	323 35.7	. . 18.9	145 58.0	. . 53.6	Spica	158 32.2	S11 13.6
16	9 18.3	18 17.0	56.3	194 24.0	20.1	338 37.9	19.0	161 00.4	53.6	Suhail	222 52.7	S43 29.0
17	24 20.8	33 16.7	55.0	209 26.6	20.3	353 40.1	19.1	176 02.8	53.6			
18	39 23.3	48 16.5	S 4 53.7	224 29.2	N 6 20.4	8 42.3	N11 19.3	191 05.3	S 8 53.6	Vega	80 40.0	N38 47.6
19	54 25.7	63 16.2	52.5	239 31.9	20.5	23 44.5	19.4	206 07.7	53.6	Zuben'ubi	137 06.5	S16 05.5
20	69 28.2	78 16.0	51.2	254 34.5	20.7	38 46.7	19.5	221 10.1	53.6		SHA	Mer. Pass.
21	84 30.7	93 15.8	. . 49.9	269 37.2	. . 20.8	53 48.9	. . 19.6	236 12.6	. . 53.6		° ′	h m
22	99 33.1	108 15.5	48.6	284 39.8	21.0	68 51.1	19.7	251 15.0	53.6	Venus	10 47.2	14 46
23	114 35.6	123 15.3	47.3	299 42.4	21.1	83 53.3	19.8	266 17.4	53.6	Mars	184 59.9	3 09
	h m									Jupiter	329 30.1	17 29
Mer. Pass. 15 26.8		v −0.3 d 1.3		v 2.6 d 0.1		v 2.2 d 0.1		v 2.4 d 0.0		Saturn	151 43.7	5 22

Main Table — SUN and MOON

UT	SUN GHA	SUN Dec	MOON GHA	v	MOON Dec	d	HP
d h	° ′	° ′	° ′	′	° ′	′	′
28 00	176 49.0	S18 24.3	126 00.2	15.1	N 5 30.9	11.3	54.9
01	191 48.8	23.7	140 34.3	15.2	5 42.2	11.2	54.8
02	206 48.7	23.0	155 08.5	15.1	5 53.4	11.1	54.8
03	221 48.6 . .	22.4	169 42.6	15.1	6 04.5	11.2	54.8
04	236 48.5	21.7	184 16.7	15.2	6 15.7	11.1	54.8
05	251 48.3	21.1	198 50.9	15.1	6 26.8	11.1	54.8
06	266 48.2	S18 20.4	213 25.0	15.1	N 6 37.9	11.0	54.8
S 07	281 48.1	19.8	227 59.1	15.2	6 48.9	11.0	54.7
A 08	296 48.0	19.1	242 33.3	15.1	6 59.9	11.0	54.7
T 09	311 47.9 . .	18.5	257 07.4	15.1	7 10.9	10.9	54.7
U 10	326 47.7	17.8	271 41.5	15.2	7 21.8	10.9	54.7
R 11	341 47.6	17.2	286 15.7	15.1	7 32.7	10.9	54.7
D 12	356 47.5	S18 16.5	300 49.8	15.1	N 7 43.6	10.8	54.7
A 13	11 47.4	15.8	315 23.9	15.1	7 54.4	10.8	54.6
Y 14	26 47.2	15.2	329 58.0	15.1	8 05.2	10.7	54.6
15	41 47.1 . .	14.5	344 32.1	15.1	8 15.9	10.7	54.6
16	56 47.0	13.9	359 06.2	15.0	8 26.6	10.7	54.6
17	71 46.9	13.2	13 40.2	15.1	8 37.3	10.6	54.6
18	86 46.8	S18 12.6	28 14.3	15.1	N 8 47.9	10.6	54.6
19	101 46.7	11.9	42 48.4	15.0	8 58.5	10.5	54.6
20	116 46.5	11.2	57 22.4	15.0	9 09.0	10.5	54.5
21	131 46.4 . .	10.6	71 56.4	15.1	9 19.5	10.5	54.5
22	146 46.3	09.9	86 30.5	15.0	9 30.0	10.4	54.5
23	161 46.2	09.3	101 04.5	14.9	9 40.4	10.4	54.5
29 00	176 46.1	S18 08.6	115 38.4	15.0	N 9 50.8	10.3	54.5
01	191 45.9	07.9	130 12.4	15.0	10 01.1	10.2	54.5
02	206 45.8	07.3	144 46.4	14.9	10 11.3	10.3	54.5
03	221 45.7 . .	06.6	159 20.3	15.0	10 21.6	10.1	54.5
04	236 45.6	06.0	173 54.3	14.9	10 31.7	10.2	54.4
05	251 45.5	05.3	188 28.2	14.9	10 41.9	10.1	54.4
06	266 45.4	S18 04.6	203 02.1	14.8	N10 52.0	10.0	54.4
S 07	281 45.3	04.0	217 35.9	14.9	11 02.0	10.0	54.4
U 08	296 45.1	03.3	232 09.8	14.8	11 12.0	9.9	54.4
N 09	311 45.0 . .	02.6	246 43.6	14.8	11 21.9	9.9	54.4
D 10	326 44.9	02.0	261 17.4	14.8	11 31.8	9.8	54.4
A 11	341 44.8	01.3	275 51.2	14.8	11 41.6	9.8	54.4
Y 12	356 44.7	S18 00.6	290 25.0	14.7	N11 51.4	9.7	54.4
13	11 44.6	18 00.0	304 58.7	14.7	12 01.1	9.7	54.4
14	26 44.5	17 59.3	319 32.4	14.7	12 10.8	9.6	54.3
15	41 44.4 . .	58.6	334 06.1	14.7	12 20.4	9.6	54.3
16	56 44.2	58.0	348 39.8	14.6	12 30.0	9.5	54.3
17	71 44.1	57.3	3 13.4	14.6	12 39.5	9.5	54.3
18	86 44.0	S17 56.6	17 47.0	14.6	N12 49.0	9.4	54.3
19	101 43.9	55.9	32 20.6	14.6	12 58.4	9.3	54.3
20	116 43.8	55.3	46 54.2	14.5	13 07.7	9.3	54.3
21	131 43.7 . .	54.6	61 27.7	14.5	13 17.0	9.3	54.3
22	146 43.6	53.9	76 01.2	14.5	13 26.3	9.1	54.3
23	161 43.5	53.2	90 34.7	14.4	13 35.4	9.2	54.3
30 00	176 43.4	S17 52.6	105 08.1	14.5	N13 44.6	9.0	54.3
01	191 43.3	51.9	119 41.6	14.3	13 53.6	9.0	54.3
02	206 43.1	51.2	134 14.9	14.4	14 02.6	9.0	54.3
03	221 43.0 . .	50.5	148 48.3	14.3	14 11.6	8.8	54.3
04	236 42.9	49.9	163 21.6	14.3	14 20.4	8.9	54.3
05	251 42.8	49.2	177 54.9	14.2	14 29.3	8.7	54.3
06	266 42.7	S17 48.5	192 28.1	14.3	N14 38.0	8.7	54.3
07	281 42.6	47.8	207 01.4	14.1	14 46.7	8.7	54.2
M 08	296 42.5	47.2	221 34.5	14.2	14 55.4	8.5	54.2
O 09	311 42.4 . .	46.5	236 07.7	14.1	15 03.9	8.5	54.2
N 10	326 42.3	45.8	250 40.8	14.1	15 12.4	8.5	54.2
D 11	341 42.2	45.1	265 13.9	14.0	15 20.9	8.3	54.2
A 12	356 42.1	S17 44.4	279 46.9	14.0	N15 29.2	8.4	54.2
Y 13	11 42.0	43.7	294 19.9	14.0	15 37.6	8.2	54.2
14	26 41.9	43.1	308 52.9	13.9	15 45.8	8.2	54.2
15	41 41.8 . .	42.4	323 25.8	13.9	15 54.0	8.1	54.2
16	56 41.7	41.7	337 58.7	13.8	16 02.1	8.0	54.2
17	71 41.6	41.0	352 31.5	13.9	16 10.1	8.0	54.2
18	86 41.5	S17 40.3	7 04.4	13.7	N16 18.1	7.9	54.2
19	101 41.4	39.6	21 37.1	13.8	16 26.0	7.8	54.2
20	116 41.3	39.0	36 09.9	13.6	16 33.8	7.8	54.2
21	131 41.2 . .	38.3	50 42.5	13.7	16 41.6	7.7	54.2
22	146 41.1	37.6	65 15.2	13.6	16 49.3	7.6	54.2
23	161 41.0	36.9	79 47.8	13.6	N16 56.9	7.6	54.2
	SD 16.3	d 0.7	SD 14.9		14.8		14.8

Twilight / Sunrise / Moonrise

Lat.	Twilight Naut.	Twilight Civil	Sunrise	Moonrise 28	29	30	31
°	h m	h m	h m	h m	h m	h m	h m
N 72	07 22	08 54	11 02	08 22	08 03	07 36	06 32
N 70	07 12	08 33	10 06	08 32	08 21	08 07	07 46
68	07 05	08 16	09 33	08 40	08 35	08 30	08 24
66	06 58	08 03	09 09	08 47	08 47	08 48	08 51
64	06 52	07 52	08 50	08 53	08 57	09 03	09 12
62	06 47	07 42	08 35	08 58	09 05	09 15	09 28
60	06 42	07 34	08 22	09 02	09 12	09 25	09 42
N 58	06 38	07 26	08 11	09 06	09 19	09 35	09 54
56	06 34	07 20	08 01	09 09	09 25	09 43	10 05
54	06 31	07 14	07 53	09 12	09 30	09 50	10 14
52	06 27	07 08	07 45	09 15	09 35	09 56	10 22
50	06 24	07 03	07 39	09 18	09 39	10 02	10 30
45	06 17	06 52	07 24	09 23	09 48	10 15	10 46
N 40	06 10	06 43	07 12	09 28	09 56	10 26	10 59
35	06 04	06 35	07 01	09 32	10 03	10 35	11 10
30	05 58	06 27	06 52	09 36	10 08	10 43	11 20
20	05 47	06 13	06 37	09 42	10 19	10 56	11 37
N 10	05 35	06 01	06 23	09 48	10 28	11 09	11 51
0	05 22	05 48	06 09	09 53	10 36	11 20	12 05
S 10	05 08	05 34	05 56	09 59	10 45	11 32	12 19
20	04 51	05 18	05 42	10 05	10 54	11 44	12 34
30	04 28	04 59	05 25	10 11	11 05	11 58	12 52
35	04 14	04 48	05 16	10 15	11 11	12 06	13 02
40	03 57	04 34	05 05	10 19	11 18	12 16	13 13
45	03 35	04 18	04 51	10 24	11 26	12 27	13 27
S 50	03 05	03 57	04 35	10 31	11 36	12 40	13 44
52	02 50	03 46	04 28	10 33	11 40	12 47	13 52
54	02 32	03 35	04 19	10 37	11 46	12 54	14 00
56	02 08	03 21	04 10	10 40	11 51	13 01	14 10
58	01 35	03 05	03 59	10 44	11 58	13 10	14 22
S 60	////	02 46	03 46	10 48	12 05	13 20	14 35

Sunset / Twilight / Moonset

Lat.	Sunset	Twilight Civil	Twilight Naut.	Moonset 28	29	30	31
°	h m	h m	h m	h m	h m	h m	h m
N 72	13 26	15 33	17 06	24 27	00 27	02 24	05 02
N 70	14 21	15 54	17 15	24 11	00 11	01 55	03 49
68	14 54	16 11	17 23	23 58	25 33	01 33	03 12
66	15 18	16 24	17 29	23 47	25 16	01 16	02 46
64	15 37	16 35	17 35	23 39	25 02	01 02	02 26
62	15 52	16 45	17 40	23 31	24 51	00 51	02 09
60	16 05	16 53	17 45	23 25	24 41	00 41	01 56
N 58	16 16	17 01	17 49	23 19	24 32	00 32	01 45
56	16 25	17 07	17 53	23 14	24 25	00 25	01 35
54	16 34	17 13	17 56	23 10	24 18	00 18	01 26
52	16 41	17 18	17 59	23 06	24 12	00 12	01 18
50	16 48	17 23	18 03	23 02	24 07	00 07	01 11
45	17 03	17 34	18 10	22 54	23 55	24 56	00 56
N 40	17 15	17 44	18 16	22 48	23 46	24 44	00 44
35	17 25	17 52	18 22	22 42	23 38	24 33	00 33
30	17 34	17 59	18 28	22 37	23 30	24 24	00 24
20	17 50	18 13	18 39	22 28	23 18	24 08	00 08
N 10	18 04	18 26	18 51	22 21	23 07	23 54	24 43
0	18 17	18 38	19 04	22 14	22 57	23 42	24 28
S 10	18 30	18 52	19 18	22 07	22 47	23 29	24 13
20	18 44	19 07	19 35	22 00	22 36	23 15	23 57
30	19 00	19 26	19 57	21 51	22 24	23 00	23 39
35	19 10	19 38	20 11	21 46	22 17	22 51	23 28
40	19 21	19 51	20 28	21 41	22 09	22 41	23 16
45	19 34	20 07	20 50	21 34	22 00	22 29	23 01
S 50	19 50	20 28	21 19	21 27	21 49	22 14	22 44
52	19 57	20 38	21 34	21 23	21 44	22 07	22 36
54	20 05	20 50	21 52	21 20	21 38	22 00	22 27
56	20 15	21 03	22 15	21 15	21 32	21 52	22 16
58	20 26	21 19	22 46	21 11	21 25	21 42	22 05
S 60	20 38	21 38	23 52	21 05	21 17	21 31	21 51

SUN and MOON (lower right)

Day	SUN Eqn. of Time 00ʰ	SUN Eqn. of Time 12ʰ	SUN Mer. Pass.	MOON Mer. Pass. Upper	MOON Mer. Pass. Lower	Age	Phase
d	m s	m s	h m	h m	h m	d %	
28	12 44	12 50	12 13	16 04	03 42	05 26	
29	12 56	13 01	12 13	16 47	04 25	06 35	
30	13 06	13 11	12 13	17 31	05 09	07 44	

UT	ARIES GHA	VENUS −4.1 GHA	Dec	MARS −0.6 GHA	Dec	JUPITER −2.3 GHA	Dec	SATURN +0.6 GHA	Dec	STARS Name	SHA	Dec
31 00	129 38.0	138 15.0	S 4 46.0	314 45.1	N 6 21.3	98 55.5	N11 19.9	281 19.8	S 8 53.6	Acamar	315 19.0	S40 15.6
01	144 40.5	153 14.8	44.7	329 47.7	21.4	113 57.7	20.0	296 22.3	53.6	Achernar	335 27.6	S57 10.8
02	159 43.0	168 14.6	43.4	344 50.4	21.6	128 59.9	20.1	311 24.7	53.6	Acrux	173 10.0	S63 09.9
03	174 45.4	183 14.3	.. 42.1	359 53.0	.. 21.7	144 02.0	.. 20.2	326 27.1	.. 53.6	Adhara	255 12.9	S28 59.6
04	189 47.9	198 14.1	40.9	14 55.7	21.9	159 04.2	20.3	341 29.6	53.6	Aldebaran	290 50.3	N16 32.0
05	204 50.4	213 13.8	39.6	29 58.3	22.1	174 06.4	20.5	356 32.0	53.6			
T 06	219 52.8	228 13.6	S 4 38.3	45 01.0	N 6 22.2	189 08.6	N11 20.6	11 34.4	S 8 53.6	Alioth	166 21.2	N55 53.3
U 07	234 55.3	243 13.4	37.0	60 03.6	22.4	204 10.8	20.7	26 36.8	53.6	Alkaid	152 59.5	N49 14.8
E 08	249 57.8	258 13.1	35.7	75 06.3	22.5	219 13.0	20.8	41 39.3	53.6	Al Na'ir	27 45.3	S46 54.2
S 09	265 00.2	273 12.9	.. 34.4	90 08.9	.. 22.7	234 15.2	.. 20.9	56 41.7	.. 53.6	Alnilam	275 47.1	S 1 11.8
D 10	280 02.7	288 12.7	33.1	105 11.6	22.8	249 17.4	21.0	71 44.1	53.6	Alphard	217 56.7	S 8 42.9
A 11	295 05.2	303 12.4	31.8	120 14.2	23.0	264 19.6	21.1	86 46.6	53.6			
Y 12	310 07.6	318 12.2	S 4 30.5	135 16.9	N 6 23.1	279 21.8	N11 21.2	101 49.0	S 8 53.6	Alphecca	126 11.9	N26 40.2
13	325 10.1	333 11.9	29.2	150 19.6	23.3	294 24.0	21.3	116 51.4	53.6	Alpheratz	357 44.7	N29 09.6
14	340 12.5	348 11.7	27.9	165 22.2	23.5	309 26.1	21.4	131 53.9	53.6	Altair	62 09.5	N 8 54.1
15	355 15.0	3 11.5	.. 26.7	180 24.9	.. 23.6	324 28.3	.. 21.5	146 56.3	.. 53.6	Ankaa	353 16.8	S42 14.6
16	10 17.5	18 11.2	25.4	195 27.6	23.8	339 30.5	21.7	161 58.7	53.6	Antares	112 27.6	S26 27.4
17	25 19.9	33 11.0	24.1	210 30.2	23.9	354 32.7	21.8	177 01.1	53.6			
18	40 22.4	48 10.8	S 4 22.8	225 32.9	N 6 24.1	9 34.9	N11 21.9	192 03.6	S 8 53.6	Arcturus	145 56.5	N19 06.9
19	55 24.9	63 10.5	21.5	240 35.6	24.2	24 37.1	22.0	207 06.0	53.6	Atria	107 30.6	S69 02.7
20	70 27.3	78 10.3	20.2	255 38.2	24.4	39 39.3	22.1	222 08.4	53.6	Avior	234 17.8	S59 33.1
21	85 29.8	93 10.1	.. 18.9	270 40.9	.. 24.6	54 41.5	.. 22.2	237 10.9	.. 53.6	Bellatrix	278 32.8	N 6 21.5
22	100 32.3	108 09.8	17.6	285 43.6	24.7	69 43.6	22.3	252 13.3	53.6	Betelgeuse	271 02.1	N 7 24.4
23	115 34.7	123 09.6	16.3	300 46.2	24.9	84 45.8	22.4	267 15.7	53.6			
1 00	130 37.2	138 09.4	S 4 15.0	315 48.9	N 6 25.1	99 48.0	N11 22.5	282 18.2	S 8 53.6	Canopus	263 56.1	S52 42.4
01	145 39.6	153 09.1	13.7	330 51.6	25.2	114 50.2	22.7	297 20.6	53.6	Capella	280 35.5	N46 00.6
02	160 42.1	168 08.9	12.4	345 54.3	25.4	129 52.4	22.8	312 23.0	53.6	Deneb	49 32.6	N45 19.5
03	175 44.6	183 08.7	.. 11.1	0 56.9	.. 25.5	144 54.6	.. 22.9	327 25.5	.. 53.6	Denebola	182 34.4	N14 30.0
04	190 47.0	198 08.5	09.8	15 59.6	25.7	159 56.8	23.0	342 27.9	53.6	Diphda	348 57.0	S17 55.3
05	205 49.5	213 08.2	08.6	31 02.3	25.9	174 59.0	23.1	357 30.3	53.6			
W 06	220 52.0	228 08.0	S 4 07.3	46 05.0	N 6 26.0	190 01.1	N11 23.2	12 32.8	S 8 53.6	Dubhe	193 52.2	N61 40.8
E 07	235 54.4	243 07.8	06.0	61 07.7	26.2	205 03.3	23.3	27 35.2	53.6	Elnath	278 13.6	N28 37.0
D 08	250 56.9	258 07.5	04.7	76 10.3	26.4	220 05.5	23.4	42 37.6	53.6	Eltanin	90 47.0	N51 29.1
N 09	265 59.4	273 07.3	.. 03.4	91 13.0	.. 26.5	235 07.7	.. 23.5	57 40.1	.. 53.6	Enif	33 48.4	N 9 55.9
E 10	281 01.8	288 07.1	02.1	106 15.7	26.7	250 09.9	23.7	72 42.5	53.6	Fomalhaut	15 25.3	S29 33.5
S 11	296 04.3	303 06.8	4 00.8	121 18.4	26.9	265 12.1	23.8	87 44.9	53.6			
D 12	311 06.8	318 06.6	S 3 59.5	136 21.1	N 6 27.0	280 14.2	N11 23.9	102 47.4	S 8 53.6	Gacrux	172 01.7	S57 10.8
A 13	326 09.2	333 06.4	58.2	151 23.8	27.2	295 16.4	24.0	117 49.8	53.6	Gienah	175 53.1	S17 36.7
Y 14	341 11.7	348 06.2	56.9	166 26.5	27.4	310 18.6	24.1	132 52.2	53.6	Hadar	148 49.2	S60 25.7
15	356 14.1	3 05.9	.. 55.6	181 29.2	.. 27.6	325 20.8	.. 24.2	147 54.7	.. 53.6	Hamal	328 01.9	N23 31.3
16	11 16.6	18 05.7	54.3	196 31.9	27.7	340 23.0	24.3	162 57.1	53.6	Kaus Aust.	83 45.4	S34 22.6
17	26 19.1	33 05.5	53.0	211 34.6	27.9	355 25.2	24.4	177 59.6	53.6			
18	41 21.5	48 05.3	S 3 51.7	226 37.3	N 6 28.1	10 27.3	N11 24.5	193 02.0	S 8 53.6	Kochab	137 20.0	N74 06.0
19	56 24.0	63 05.0	50.4	241 40.0	28.2	25 29.5	24.7	208 04.4	53.6	Markab	13 39.5	N15 16.3
20	71 26.5	78 04.8	49.1	256 42.7	28.4	40 31.7	24.8	223 06.9	53.6	Menkar	314 16.0	N 4 08.2
21	86 28.9	93 04.6	.. 47.8	271 45.4	.. 28.6	55 33.9	.. 24.9	238 09.3	.. 53.6	Menkent	148 08.6	S36 25.7
22	101 31.4	108 04.4	46.5	286 48.1	28.8	70 36.1	25.0	253 11.7	53.6	Miaplacidus	221 39.0	S69 46.1
23	116 33.9	123 04.1	45.2	301 50.8	28.9	85 38.2	25.1	268 14.2	53.6			
2 00	131 36.3	138 03.9	S 3 43.9	316 53.5	N 6 29.1	100 40.4	N11 25.2	283 16.6	S 8 53.6	Mirfak	308 41.6	N49 54.4
01	146 38.8	153 03.7	42.6	331 56.2	29.3	115 42.6	25.3	298 19.0	53.6	Nunki	75 59.8	S26 16.8
02	161 41.3	168 03.5	41.3	346 58.9	29.5	130 44.8	25.5	313 21.5	53.6	Peacock	53 21.3	S56 41.6
03	176 43.7	183 03.2	.. 40.0	2 01.6	.. 29.6	145 47.0	.. 25.6	328 23.9	.. 53.6	Pollux	243 28.5	N27 59.6
04	191 46.2	198 03.0	38.7	17 04.3	29.8	160 49.1	25.7	343 26.4	53.6	Procyon	245 00.4	N 5 11.4
05	206 48.6	213 02.8	37.4	32 07.0	30.0	175 51.3	25.8	358 28.8	53.6			
T 06	221 51.1	228 02.6	S 3 36.1	47 09.7	N 6 30.2	190 53.5	N11 25.9	13 31.2	S 8 53.6	Rasalhague	96 07.6	N12 33.0
H 07	236 53.6	243 02.4	34.8	62 12.4	30.3	205 55.7	26.0	28 33.7	53.6	Regulus	207 44.2	N11 54.2
U 08	251 56.0	258 02.1	33.5	77 15.2	30.5	220 57.9	26.1	43 36.1	53.6	Rigel	281 12.7	S 8 11.5
R 09	266 58.5	273 01.9	.. 32.2	92 17.9	.. 30.7	236 00.0	.. 26.2	58 38.5	.. 53.6	Rigil Kent.	139 53.0	S60 52.8
S 10	282 01.0	288 01.7	30.9	107 20.6	30.9	251 02.2	26.4	73 41.0	53.6	Sabik	102 13.8	S15 44.3
D 11	297 03.4	303 01.5	29.7	122 23.3	31.1	266 04.4	26.5	88 43.4	53.6			
A 12	312 05.9	318 01.3	S 3 28.4	137 26.0	N 6 31.2	281 06.6	N11 26.6	103 45.9	S 8 53.6	Schedar	349 41.9	N56 36.5
Y 13	327 08.4	333 01.0	27.1	152 28.7	31.4	296 08.7	26.7	118 48.3	53.6	Shaula	96 23.5	S37 06.6
14	342 10.8	348 00.8	25.8	167 31.5	31.6	311 10.9	26.8	133 50.7	53.6	Sirius	258 34.2	S16 44.2
15	357 13.3	3 00.6	.. 24.5	182 34.2	.. 31.8	326 13.1	.. 26.9	148 53.2	.. 53.6	Spica	158 32.1	S11 13.6
16	12 15.8	18 00.4	23.2	197 36.9	32.0	341 15.3	27.0	163 55.6	53.6	Suhail	222 52.7	S43 29.1
17	27 18.2	33 00.2	21.9	212 39.6	32.1	356 17.4	27.2	178 58.1	53.6			
18	42 20.7	47 59.9	S 3 20.6	227 42.4	N 6 32.3	11 19.6	N11 27.3	194 00.5	S 8 53.6	Vega	80 40.0	N38 47.6
19	57 23.1	62 59.7	19.3	242 45.1	32.5	26 21.8	27.4	209 02.9	53.6	Zuben'ubi	137 06.5	S16 05.5
20	72 25.6	77 59.5	18.0	257 47.8	32.7	41 24.0	27.5	224 05.4	53.5		SHA	Mer.Pass.
21	87 28.1	92 59.3	.. 16.7	272 50.6	.. 32.9	56 26.1	.. 27.6	239 07.8	.. 53.5	Venus	° 32.2	h m 14 48
22	102 30.5	107 59.1	15.4	287 53.3	33.1	71 28.3	27.7	254 10.3	53.5	Mars	185 11.7	2 56
23	117 33.0	122 58.9	14.1	302 56.0	33.2	86 30.5	27.8	269 12.7	53.5	Jupiter	329 10.8	17 18
Mer.Pass. 15 15.0		v −0.2	d 1.3	v 2.7	d 0.2	v 2.2	d 0.1	v 2.4	d 0.0	Saturn	151 41.0	5 10

UT	SUN		MOON					Lat.	Twilight		Sunrise	Moonrise			
									Naut.	Civil		31	1	2	3
	GHA	Dec	GHA	v	Dec	d	HP	°	h m	h m	h m	h m	h m	h m	h m
d h	° ′	° ′	° ′	′	° ′	′	′	N 72	07 12	08 41	10 32	06 32	☐	☐	☐
31 00	176 40.9	S17 36.2	94 20.4 13.5		N17 04.5	7.4	54.2	N 70	07 03	08 22	09 49	07 46	☐	☐	☐
01	191 40.8	35.5	108 52.9 13.5		17 11.9	7.4	54.2	68	06 57	08 07	09 20	08 24	08 17		☐
02	206 40.7	34.8	123 25.4 13.4		17 19.3	7.4	54.2	66	06 51	07 55	08 58	09 12	08 51	09 15	☐
03	221 40.6 ..	34.1	137 57.8 13.4		17 26.7	7.2	54.2	64	06 46	07 44	08 41	09 12	09 26	09 52	09 55
04	236 40.5	33.5	152 30.2 13.4		17 33.9	7.2	54.2	62	06 41	07 36	08 27	09 28	09 48	10 18	10 35
05	251 40.4	32.8	167 02.6 13.3		17 41.1	7.1	54.3	60	06 37	07 28	08 15	09 42	10 06	10 39	11 25
06	266 40.3	S17 32.1	181 34.9 13.2		N17 48.2	7.0	54.3	N 58	06 33	07 21	08 05	09 54	10 20	10 56	11 43
07	281 40.2	31.4	196 07.1 13.2		17 55.2	7.0	54.3	56	06 30	07 15	07 56	10 05	10 33	11 10	11 57
T 08	296 40.1	30.7	210 39.3 13.2		18 02.2	6.9	54.3	54	06 27	07 09	07 48	10 14	10 44	11 22	12 10
U 09	311 40.0 ..	30.0	225 11.5 13.2		18 09.1	6.8	54.3	52	06 24	07 04	07 41	10 22	10 54	11 33	12 21
E 10	326 39.9	29.3	239 43.7 13.0		18 15.9	6.7	54.3	50	06 21	07 00	07 34	10 30	11 03	11 43	12 31
S 11	341 39.8	28.6	254 15.7 13.1		18 22.6	6.6	54.3	45	06 14	06 49	07 21	10 46	11 21	12 03	12 52
D 12	356 39.7	S17 27.9	268 47.8 13.0		N18 29.2	6.6	54.3	N 40	06 08	06 40	07 09	10 59	11 36	12 20	13 09
A 13	11 39.6	27.2	283 19.8 12.9		18 35.8	6.5	54.3	35	06 02	06 33	06 59	11 10	11 49	12 34	13 24
Y 14	26 39.5	26.5	297 51.7 12.9		18 42.3	6.4	54.3	30	05 57	06 26	06 51	11 20	12 01	12 46	13 36
15	41 39.4 ..	25.8	312 23.6 12.9		18 48.7	6.3	54.3	20	05 46	06 13	06 36	11 37	12 20	13 07	13 57
16	56 39.3	25.1	326 55.5 12.8		18 55.0	6.2	54.3	N 10	05 35	06 01	06 22	11 51	12 37	13 25	14 16
17	71 39.2	24.4	341 27.3 12.7		19 01.2	6.2	54.3	0	05 23	05 48	06 10	12 05	12 53	13 42	14 33
18	86 39.1	S17 23.7	355 59.0 12.7		N19 07.4	6.0	54.3	S 10	05 09	05 35	05 57	12 19	13 08	13 59	14 50
19	101 39.0	23.0	10 30.7 12.7		19 13.4	6.0	54.3	20	04 53	05 20	05 44	12 34	13 26	14 17	15 08
20	116 38.9	22.3	25 02.4 12.6		19 19.4	5.9	54.3	30	04 31	05 02	05 28	12 52	13 45	14 38	15 30
21	131 38.9 ..	21.6	39 34.0 12.6		19 25.3	5.9	54.3	35	04 18	04 51	05 19	13 02	13 57	14 51	15 42
22	146 38.8	20.9	54 05.6 12.5		19 31.2	5.7	54.4	40	04 01	04 38	05 08	13 13	14 10	15 05	15 56
23	161 38.7	20.2	68 37.1 12.5		19 36.9	5.6	54.4	45	03 40	04 22	04 56	13 27	14 26	15 22	16 13
1 00	176 38.6	S17 19.5	83 08.6 12.4		N19 42.5	5.6	54.4	S 50	03 13	04 02	04 41	13 44	14 45	15 42	16 35
01	191 38.5	18.8	97 40.0 12.4		19 48.1	5.5	54.4	52	02 58	03 53	04 33	13 52	14 54	15 52	16 45
02	206 38.4	18.1	112 11.4 12.4		19 53.6	5.3	54.4	54	02 41	03 42	04 25	14 00	15 04	16 04	16 56
03	221 38.3 ..	17.4	126 42.8 12.2		19 58.9	5.3	54.4	56	02 20	03 29	04 17	14 10	15 16	16 16	17 09
04	236 38.2	16.7	141 14.0 12.3		20 04.2	5.2	54.4	58	01 52	03 14	04 06	14 22	15 30	16 31	17 23
05	251 38.1	16.0	155 45.3 12.2		20 09.4	5.2	54.4	S 60	01 04	02 56	03 55	14 35	15 46	16 49	17 41
06	266 38.0	S17 15.3	170 16.5 12.1		N20 14.6	5.0	54.4								

UT	SUN		MOON					Lat.	Sunset	Twilight		Moonset			
										Civil	Naut.	31	1	2	3
W 07	281 38.0	14.6	184 47.6 12.1		20 19.6	4.9	54.4	°	h m	h m	h m	h m	h m	h m	h m
E 08	296 37.9	13.9	199 18.7 12.0		20 24.5	4.9	54.5	N 72	13 56	15 47	17 17	05 02	☐	☐	☐
D 09	311 37.8 ..	13.2	213 49.7 12.0		20 29.4	4.7	54.5	N 70	14 40	16 06	17 25	03 49	☐	☐	☐
N 10	326 37.7	12.5	228 20.7 12.0		20 34.1	4.7	54.5	68	15 08	16 21	17 32	03 12	04 55	06 52	☐
E 11	341 37.6	11.8	242 51.7 11.9		20 38.8	4.5	54.5	66	15 30	16 33	17 37	02 46	04 15	05 39	06 44
S 12	356 37.5	S17 11.1	257 22.6 11.9		N20 43.3	4.5	54.5	64	15 47	16 44	17 42	02 26	03 47	05 02	06 04
D 13	11 37.4	10.4	271 53.5 11.8		20 47.8	4.4	54.5	62	16 01	16 52	17 47	02 09	03 26	04 36	05 36
A 14	26 37.3	09.7	286 24.3 11.7		20 52.2	4.3	54.5	60	16 13	17 00	17 51	01 56	03 09	04 16	05 14
Y 15	41 37.3 ..	09.0	300 55.0 11.7		20 56.5	4.2	54.5	N 58	16 23	17 07	17 55	01 45	02 54	03 59	04 56
16	56 37.2	08.3	315 25.7 11.7		21 00.7	4.1	54.6	56	16 32	17 13	17 58	01 35	02 42	03 45	04 42
17	71 37.1	07.6	329 56.4 11.6		21 04.8	4.0	54.6	54	16 40	17 18	18 01	01 26	02 31	03 33	04 29
18	86 37.0	S17 06.8	344 27.0 11.6		N21 08.8	3.9	54.6	52	16 47	17 23	18 04	01 18	02 22	03 22	04 18
19	101 36.9	06.1	358 57.6 11.5		21 12.7	3.8	54.6	50	16 53	17 28	18 07	01 11	02 13	03 13	04 08
20	116 36.8	05.4	13 28.1 11.5		21 16.5	3.7	54.6	45	17 07	17 38	18 13	00 56	01 55	02 53	03 47
21	131 36.7 ..	04.7	27 58.6 11.4		21 20.2	3.6	54.6	N 40	17 18	17 47	18 19	00 44	01 41	02 36	03 30
22	146 36.7	04.0	42 29.0 11.4		21 23.8	3.5	54.6	35	17 28	17 55	18 25	00 33	01 28	02 22	03 16
23	161 36.6	03.3	56 59.4 11.4		21 27.3	3.4	54.7	30	17 37	18 02	18 30	00 24	01 17	02 11	03 03
2 00	176 36.5	S17 02.6	71 29.8 11.2		N21 30.7	3.3	54.7	20	17 52	18 15	18 41	00 08	00 59	01 50	02 42
01	191 36.4	01.9	86 00.0 11.3		21 34.0	3.2	54.7	N 10	18 05	18 27	18 52	24 43	00 43	01 33	02 23
02	206 36.3	01.1	100 30.3 11.2		21 37.2	3.1	54.7	0	18 17	18 39	19 04	24 28	00 28	01 16	02 06
03	221 36.3	17 00.4	115 00.5 11.2		21 40.3	3.0	54.7	S 10	18 30	18 52	19 17	24 13	00 13	01 00	01 49
04	236 36.2	16 59.7	129 30.7 11.1		21 43.3	2.9	54.7	20	18 43	19 06	19 34	23 57	24 42	00 42	01 30
05	251 36.1	59.0	144 00.8 11.0		21 46.2	2.8	54.8	30	18 59	19 24	19 55	23 39	24 22	00 22	01 09
06	266 36.0	S16 58.3	158 30.8 11.1		N21 49.0	2.7	54.8	35	19 08	19 35	20 08	23 28	24 10	00 10	00 57
T 07	281 35.9	57.6	173 00.9 10.9		21 51.7	2.6	54.8	40	19 18	19 48	20 25	23 16	23 56	24 42	00 42
H 08	296 35.9	56.9	187 30.8 11.0		21 54.3	2.5	54.8	45	19 30	20 04	20 45	23 01	23 40	24 25	00 25
U 09	311 35.8 ..	56.1	202 00.8 10.9		21 56.8	2.4	54.8	S 50	19 45	20 23	21 13	22 44	23 20	24 04	00 04
R 10	326 35.7	55.4	216 30.7 10.8		21 59.2	2.2	54.9	52	19 52	20 33	21 27	22 36	23 11	23 54	24 47
S 11	341 35.6	54.7	231 00.5 10.9		22 01.4	2.2	54.9	54	20 00	20 44	21 43	22 27	23 00	23 43	24 36
D 12	356 35.5	S16 54.0	245 30.4 10.7		N22 03.6	2.1	54.9	56	20 09	20 56	22 04	22 16	22 48	23 30	24 24
A 13	11 35.5	53.3	260 00.1 10.8		22 05.7	1.9	54.9	58	20 19	21 11	22 31	22 05	22 35	23 15	24 09
Y 14	26 35.4	52.5	274 29.9 10.6		22 07.6	1.9	54.9	S 60	20 31	21 28	23 14	21 51	22 18	22 57	23 51
15	41 35.3 ..	51.8	288 59.5 10.7		22 09.5	1.7	55.0								
16	56 35.2	51.1	303 29.2 10.6		22 11.2	1.7	55.0			SUN				MOON	
17	71 35.2	50.4	317 58.8 10.6		22 12.9	1.5	55.0	Day	Eqn. of Time		Mer.	Mer. Pass.		Age	Phase
18	86 35.1	S16 49.7	332 28.4 10.5		N22 14.4	1.4	55.0		00ʰ	12ʰ	Pass.	Upper	Lower		
19	101 35.0	48.9	346 57.9 10.5		22 15.8	1.3	55.0	d	m s	m s	h m	h m	h m	d %	
20	116 34.9	48.2	1 27.4 10.4		22 17.1	1.2	55.1	31	13 16	13 21	12 13	18 17	05 53	08 53	
21	131 34.9 ..	47.5	15 56.8 10.3		22 18.3	1.1	55.1	1	13 26	13 30	12 13	19 04	06 40	09 63	
22	146 34.8	46.8	30 26.3 10.3		22 19.4	1.0	55.1	2	13 34	13 38	12 14	19 54	07 29	10 72	
23	161 34.7	46.0	44 55.6 10.4		N22 20.4	0.8	55.1								
	SD 16.3	d 0.7	SD 14.8		14.9		15.0									

UT	ARIES GHA	VENUS −4.1 GHA	VENUS Dec	MARS −0.6 GHA	MARS Dec	JUPITER −2.3 GHA	JUPITER Dec	SATURN +0.6 GHA	SATURN Dec	STARS Name	SHA	Dec
3 00	132 35.5	137 58.6	S 3 12.8	317 58.8	N 6 33.4	101 32.7	N11 28.0	284 15.1	S 8 53.5	Acamar	315 19.0	S40 15.6
01	147 37.9	152 58.4	11.5	333 01.5	33.6	116 34.8	28.1	299 17.6	53.5	Achernar	335 27.6	S57 10.8
02	162 40.4	167 58.2	10.2	348 04.2	33.8	131 37.0	28.2	314 20.0	53.5	Acrux	173 09.9	S63 09.9
03	177 42.9	182 58.0	.. 08.8	3 07.0	.. 34.0	146 39.2	.. 28.3	329 22.5	.. 53.5	Adhara	255 12.9	S28 59.6
04	192 45.3	197 57.8	07.5	18 09.7	34.2	161 41.4	28.4	344 24.9	53.5	Aldebaran	290 50.3	N16 31.9
05	207 47.8	212 57.6	06.2	33 12.5	34.4	176 43.5	28.5	359 27.3	53.5			
06	222 50.2	227 57.4	S 3 04.9	48 15.2	N 6 34.6	191 45.7	N11 28.7	14 29.8	S 8 53.5	Alioth	166 21.2	N55 53.3
F 07	237 52.7	242 57.1	03.6	63 18.0	34.7	206 47.9	28.8	29 32.2	53.5	Alkaid	152 59.5	N49 14.8
R 08	252 55.2	257 56.9	02.3	78 20.7	34.9	221 50.0	28.9	44 34.7	53.5	Al Na'ir	27 45.3	S46 54.1
I 09	267 57.6	272 56.7	3 01.0	93 23.4	.. 35.1	236 52.2	.. 29.0	59 37.1	.. 53.5	Alnilam	275 47.1	S 1 11.8
D 10	283 00.1	287 56.5	2 59.7	108 26.2	35.3	251 54.4	29.1	74 39.6	53.5	Alphard	217 56.7	S 8 42.9
A 11	298 02.6	302 56.3	58.4	123 28.9	35.5	266 56.6	29.2	89 42.0	53.5			
Y 12	313 05.0	317 56.1	S 2 57.1	138 31.7	N 6 35.7	281 58.7	N11 29.3	104 44.4	S 8 53.5	Alphecca	126 11.9	N26 40.2
13	328 07.5	332 55.9	55.8	153 34.4	35.9	297 00.9	29.5	119 46.9	53.5	Alpheratz	357 44.7	N29 09.6
14	343 10.0	347 55.7	54.5	168 37.2	36.1	312 03.1	29.6	134 49.3	53.5	Altair	62 09.5	N 8 54.0
15	358 12.4	2 55.4	.. 53.2	183 40.0	.. 36.3	327 05.2	.. 29.7	149 51.8	.. 53.5	Ankaa	353 16.8	S42 14.6
16	13 14.9	17 55.2	51.9	198 42.7	36.5	342 07.4	29.8	164 54.2	53.5	Antares	112 27.6	S26 27.4
17	28 17.4	32 55.0	50.6	213 45.5	36.7	357 09.6	29.9	179 56.7	53.5			
18	43 19.8	47 54.8	S 2 49.3	228 48.2	N 6 36.9	12 11.7	N11 30.0	194 59.1	S 8 53.5	Arcturus	145 56.5	N19 06.9
19	58 22.3	62 54.6	48.0	243 51.0	37.1	27 13.9	30.2	210 01.5	53.5	Atria	107 30.5	S69 02.7
20	73 24.7	77 54.4	46.7	258 53.8	37.3	42 16.1	30.3	225 04.0	53.5	Avior	234 17.8	S59 33.1
21	88 27.2	92 54.2	.. 45.4	273 56.5	.. 37.5	57 18.3	.. 30.4	240 06.4	.. 53.5	Bellatrix	278 32.8	N 6 21.5
22	103 29.7	107 54.0	44.1	288 59.3	37.6	72 20.4	30.5	255 08.9	53.4	Betelgeuse	271 02.1	N 7 24.4
23	118 32.1	122 53.8	42.8	304 02.0	37.8	87 22.6	30.6	270 11.3	53.4			
4 00	133 34.6	137 53.6	S 2 41.5	319 04.8	N 6 38.0	102 24.8	N11 30.7	285 13.8	S 8 53.4	Canopus	263 56.1	S52 42.4
01	148 37.1	152 53.3	40.2	334 07.6	38.2	117 26.9	30.9	300 16.2	53.4	Capella	280 35.5	N46 00.6
02	163 39.5	167 53.1	38.9	349 10.3	38.4	132 29.1	31.0	315 18.7	53.4	Deneb	49 32.6	N45 19.5
03	178 42.0	182 52.9	.. 37.6	4 13.1	.. 38.6	147 31.3	.. 31.1	330 21.1	.. 53.4	Denebola	182 34.4	N14 30.0
04	193 44.5	197 52.7	36.3	19 15.9	38.8	162 33.4	31.2	345 23.6	53.4	Diphda	348 57.0	S17 55.3
05	208 46.9	212 52.5	35.0	34 18.7	39.0	177 35.6	31.3	0 26.0	53.4			
06	223 49.4	227 52.3	S 2 33.7	49 21.4	N 6 39.2	192 37.8	N11 31.4	15 28.4	S 8 53.4	Dubhe	193 52.2	N61 40.8
S 07	238 51.9	242 52.1	32.4	64 24.2	39.4	207 39.9	31.6	30 30.9	53.4	Elnath	278 13.6	N28 37.0
A 08	253 54.3	257 51.9	31.1	79 27.0	39.6	222 42.1	31.7	45 33.3	53.4	Eltanin	90 47.0	N51 29.1
T 09	268 56.8	272 51.7	.. 29.8	94 29.8	.. 39.8	237 44.3	.. 31.8	60 35.8	.. 53.4	Enif	33 48.4	N 9 55.9
U 10	283 59.2	287 51.5	28.5	109 32.5	40.0	252 46.4	31.9	75 38.2	53.4	Fomalhaut	15 25.3	S29 33.5
R 11	299 01.7	302 51.3	27.2	124 35.3	40.2	267 48.6	32.0	90 40.7	53.4			
D 12	314 04.2	317 51.1	S 2 25.8	139 38.1	N 6 40.5	282 50.7	N11 32.2	105 43.1	S 8 53.4	Gacrux	172 01.6	S57 10.8
A 13	329 06.6	332 50.9	24.5	154 40.9	40.7	297 52.9	32.3	120 45.6	53.4	Gienah	175 53.0	S17 36.7
Y 14	344 09.1	347 50.7	23.2	169 43.7	40.9	312 55.1	32.4	135 48.0	53.4	Hadar	148 49.1	S60 25.7
15	359 11.6	2 50.5	.. 21.9	184 46.5	.. 41.1	327 57.2	.. 32.5	150 50.5	.. 53.4	Hamal	328 01.9	N23 31.3
16	14 14.0	17 50.3	20.6	199 49.2	41.3	342 59.4	32.6	165 52.9	53.4	Kaus Aust.	83 45.4	S34 22.6
17	29 16.5	32 50.1	19.3	214 52.0	41.5	358 01.6	32.7	180 55.4	53.3			
18	44 19.0	47 49.9	S 2 18.0	229 54.8	N 6 41.7	13 03.7	N11 32.9	195 57.8	S 8 53.3	Kochab	137 19.9	N74 06.0
19	59 21.4	62 49.7	16.7	244 57.6	41.9	28 05.9	33.0	211 00.3	53.3	Markab	13 39.5	N15 16.3
20	74 23.9	77 49.5	15.4	260 00.4	42.1	43 08.1	33.1	226 02.7	53.3	Menkar	314 16.0	N 4 08.2
21	89 26.4	92 49.3	.. 14.1	275 03.2	.. 42.3	58 10.2	.. 33.2	241 05.2	.. 53.3	Menkent	148 08.6	S36 25.7
22	104 28.8	107 49.1	12.8	290 06.0	42.5	73 12.4	33.3	256 07.6	53.3	Miaplacidus	221 39.0	S69 46.1
23	119 31.3	122 48.9	11.5	305 08.8	42.7	88 14.5	33.5	271 10.1	53.3			
5 00	134 33.7	137 48.7	S 2 10.2	320 11.6	N 6 42.9	103 16.7	N11 33.6	286 12.5	S 8 53.3	Mirfak	308 41.6	N49 54.4
01	149 36.2	152 48.5	08.9	335 14.4	43.1	118 18.9	33.7	301 15.0	53.3	Nunki	75 59.8	S26 16.8
02	164 38.7	167 48.3	07.6	350 17.2	43.4	133 21.0	33.8	316 17.4	53.3	Peacock	53 21.3	S56 41.6
03	179 41.1	182 48.1	.. 06.3	5 20.0	.. 43.6	148 23.2	.. 33.9	331 19.9	.. 53.3	Pollux	243 28.5	N27 59.6
04	194 43.6	197 47.9	05.0	20 22.8	43.8	163 25.3	34.0	346 22.3	53.3	Procyon	245 00.4	N 5 11.4
05	209 46.1	212 47.7	03.7	35 25.6	44.0	178 27.5	34.2	1 24.8	53.3			
06	224 48.5	227 47.5	S 2 02.3	50 28.4	N 6 44.2	193 29.7	N11 34.3	16 27.2	S 8 53.3	Rasalhague	96 07.5	N12 33.0
07	239 51.0	242 47.3	2 01.0	65 31.2	44.4	208 31.8	34.4	31 29.7	53.3	Regulus	207 44.2	N11 54.2
S 08	254 53.5	257 47.1	1 59.7	80 34.0	44.6	223 34.0	34.5	46 32.1	53.2	Rigel	281 12.8	S 8 11.5
U 09	269 55.9	272 46.9	.. 58.4	95 36.8	.. 44.8	238 36.1	.. 34.6	61 34.6	.. 53.2	Rigil Kent.	139 53.0	S60 52.9
N 10	284 58.4	287 46.7	57.1	110 39.6	45.0	253 38.3	34.8	76 37.0	53.2	Sabik	102 13.8	S15 44.3
D 11	300 00.9	302 46.5	55.8	125 42.4	45.3	268 40.5	34.9	91 39.5	53.2			
A 12	315 03.3	317 46.3	S 1 54.5	140 45.3	N 6 45.5	283 42.6	N11 35.0	106 41.9	S 8 53.2	Schedar	349 41.9	N56 36.5
Y 13	330 05.8	332 46.1	53.2	155 48.1	45.7	298 44.8	35.1	121 44.4	53.2	Shaula	96 23.4	S37 06.6
14	345 08.2	347 45.9	51.9	170 50.9	45.9	313 46.9	35.2	136 46.8	53.2	Sirius	258 34.2	S16 44.2
15	0 10.7	2 45.7	.. 50.6	185 53.7	.. 46.1	328 49.1	.. 35.4	151 49.3	.. 53.2	Spica	158 32.1	S11 13.6
16	15 13.2	17 45.5	49.3	200 56.5	46.3	343 51.2	35.5	166 51.7	53.2	Suhail	222 52.7	S43 29.1
17	30 15.6	32 45.3	48.0	215 59.3	46.6	358 53.4	35.6	181 54.2	53.2			
18	45 18.1	47 45.1	S 1 46.7	231 02.2	N 6 46.8	13 55.6	N11 35.7	196 56.6	S 8 53.2	Vega	80 39.9	N38 47.6
19	60 20.6	62 44.9	45.4	246 05.0	47.0	28 57.7	35.8	211 59.1	53.2	Zuben'ubi	137 06.5	S16 05.5
20	75 23.0	77 44.7	44.0	261 07.8	47.2	43 59.9	36.0	227 01.5	53.2		SHA	Mer.Pass.
21	90 25.5	92 44.5	.. 42.7	276 10.6	.. 47.4	59 02.0	.. 36.1	242 04.0	.. 53.2	Venus	4 19.0	14 49
22	105 28.0	107 44.3	41.4	291 13.4	47.7	74 04.2	36.2	257 06.4	53.1	Mars	185 30.2	2 43
23	120 32.2	122 44.1	40.1	306 16.3	47.9	89 06.3	36.3	272 08.9	53.1	Jupiter	328 50.2	17 08
Mer.Pass. 15 03.2		v −0.2	d 1.3	v 2.8	d 0.2	v 2.2	d 0.1	v 2.4	d 0.0	Saturn	151 39.2	4 58

UT	SUN GHA	Dec	MOON GHA	v	Dec	d	HP
d h	° ′	° ′	° ′	′	° ′	′	′
3 00	176 34.6	S16 45.3	59 25.0	10.3	N22 21.2	0.8	55.1
01	191 34.6	44.6	73 54.3	10.3	22 22.0	0.6	55.2
02	206 34.5	43.9	88 23.6	10.2	22 22.6	0.6	55.2
03	221 34.4	.. 43.1	102 52.8	10.2	22 23.2	0.4	55.2
04	236 34.3	42.4	117 22.0	10.2	22 23.6	0.3	55.2
05	251 34.3	41.7	131 51.2	10.1	22 23.9	0.2	55.3
06	266 34.2	S16 40.9	146 20.3	10.1	N22 24.1	0.1	55.3
07	281 34.1	40.2	160 49.4	10.1	22 24.2	0.1	55.3
08	296 34.1	39.5	175 18.5	10.0	22 24.1	0.1	55.3
F 09	311 34.0	.. 38.8	189 47.5	10.1	22 24.0	0.3	55.4
R 10	326 33.9	38.0	204 16.6	9.9	22 23.7	0.4	55.4
I 11	341 33.8	37.3	218 45.5	10.0	22 23.3	0.5	55.4
D 12	356 33.8	S16 36.6	233 14.5	9.9	N22 22.8	0.6	55.4
A 13	11 33.7	35.8	247 43.4	9.9	22 22.2	0.7	55.5
Y 14	26 33.6	35.1	262 12.3	9.9	22 21.5	0.8	55.5
15	41 33.6	.. 34.4	276 41.2	9.8	22 20.7	1.0	55.5
16	56 33.5	33.6	291 10.0	9.9	22 19.7	1.1	55.5
17	71 33.4	32.9	305 38.9	9.7	22 18.6	1.2	55.6
18	86 33.4	S16 32.2	320 07.6	9.8	N22 17.4	1.3	55.6
19	101 33.3	31.4	334 36.4	9.8	22 16.1	1.4	55.6
20	116 33.2	30.7	349 05.2	9.7	22 14.7	1.5	55.6
21	131 33.2	.. 30.0	3 33.9	9.7	22 13.2	1.7	55.7
22	146 33.1	29.2	18 02.6	9.7	22 11.5	1.8	55.7
23	161 33.0	28.5	32 31.3	9.6	22 09.7	1.9	55.7
4 00	176 33.0	S16 27.7	46 59.9	9.7	N22 07.8	2.0	55.7
01	191 32.9	27.0	61 28.6	9.6	22 05.8	2.1	55.8
02	206 32.8	26.3	75 57.2	9.6	22 03.7	2.3	55.8
03	221 32.8	.. 25.5	90 25.8	9.6	22 01.4	2.3	55.8
04	236 32.7	24.8	104 54.4	9.6	21 59.1	2.5	55.8
05	251 32.7	24.0	119 23.0	9.5	21 56.6	2.6	55.9
06	266 32.6	S16 23.3	133 51.5	9.5	N21 54.0	2.7	55.9
S 07	281 32.5	22.6	148 20.0	9.6	21 51.3	2.9	55.9
A 08	296 32.5	21.8	162 48.6	9.5	21 48.4	2.9	56.0
T 09	311 32.4	.. 21.1	177 17.1	9.5	21 45.5	3.1	56.0
U 10	326 32.3	20.3	191 45.6	9.5	21 42.4	3.2	56.0
R 11	341 32.3	19.6	206 14.1	9.4	21 39.2	3.3	56.0
D 12	356 32.2	S16 18.9	220 42.5	9.5	N21 35.9	3.4	56.1
A 13	11 32.2	18.1	235 11.0	9.4	21 32.5	3.6	56.1
Y 14	26 32.1	17.4	249 39.4	9.5	21 28.9	3.7	56.1
15	41 32.0	.. 16.6	264 07.9	9.4	21 25.2	3.8	56.2
16	56 32.0	15.9	278 36.3	9.4	21 21.4	3.9	56.2
17	71 31.9	15.1	293 04.7	9.4	21 17.5	4.0	56.2
18	86 31.9	S16 14.4	307 33.1	9.5	N21 13.5	4.1	56.2
19	101 31.8	13.6	322 01.6	9.4	21 09.4	4.3	56.3
20	116 31.7	12.9	336 30.0	9.4	21 05.1	4.4	56.3
21	131 31.7	.. 12.1	350 58.4	9.3	21 00.7	4.5	56.3
22	146 31.6	11.4	5 26.7	9.4	20 56.2	4.6	56.4
23	161 31.6	10.6	19 55.1	9.4	20 51.6	4.7	56.4
5 00	176 31.5	S16 09.9	34 23.5	9.4	N20 46.9	4.8	56.4
01	191 31.5	09.1	48 51.9	9.4	20 42.1	5.0	56.4
02	206 31.4	08.4	63 20.3	9.4	20 37.1	5.1	56.5
03	221 31.3	.. 07.6	77 48.7	9.4	20 32.0	5.2	56.5
04	236 31.3	06.9	92 17.1	9.3	20 26.8	5.3	56.5
05	251 31.2	06.1	106 45.4	9.4	20 21.5	5.4	56.6
06	266 31.2	S16 05.4	121 13.8	9.4	N20 16.1	5.6	56.6
07	281 31.1	04.6	135 42.2	9.4	20 10.5	5.6	56.6
S 08	296 31.1	03.9	150 10.6	9.4	20 04.9	5.8	56.7
U 09	311 31.0	.. 03.1	164 39.0	9.4	19 59.1	5.9	56.7
N 10	326 31.0	02.4	179 07.4	9.4	19 53.2	6.0	56.7
D 11	341 30.9	01.6	193 35.8	9.4	19 47.2	6.1	56.7
A 12	356 30.9	S16 00.9	208 04.2	9.4	N19 41.1	6.3	56.8
Y 13	11 30.8	16 00.1	222 32.6	9.4	19 34.8	6.3	56.8
14	26 30.8	15 59.4	237 01.0	9.4	19 28.5	6.5	56.8
15	41 30.7	.. 58.6	251 29.4	9.4	19 22.0	6.5	56.9
16	56 30.7	57.8	265 57.8	9.4	19 15.5	6.7	56.9
17	71 30.6	57.1	280 26.2	9.5	19 08.8	6.8	56.9
18	86 30.6	S15 56.3	294 54.7	9.4	N19 02.0	6.9	57.0
19	101 30.5	55.6	309 23.1	9.5	18 55.1	7.0	57.0
20	116 30.5	54.8	323 51.6	9.4	18 48.1	7.2	57.0
21	131 30.4	.. 54.1	338 20.0	9.5	18 40.9	7.2	57.0
22	146 30.4	53.3	352 48.5	9.5	18 33.7	7.3	57.1
23	161 30.3	52.5	7 17.0	9.5	N18 26.4	7.5	57.1
SD	16.3	d 0.7	SD 15.1		15.3		15.5

Lat.	Twilight Naut.	Twilight Civil	Sunrise	Moonrise 3	4	5	6
°	h m	h m	h m	h m	h m	h m	h m
N 72	07 01	08 28	10 08	□	□	□	12 38
N 70	06 54	08 11	09 32	□	□	10 48	13 26
68	06 48	07 57	09 07	□	09 59	12 02	13 57
66	06 43	07 46	08 48	09 55	11 06	12 38	14 20
64	06 39	07 37	08 32	10 35	11 41	13 05	14 38
62	06 35	07 29	08 19	11 03	12 07	13 25	14 52
60	06 31	07 21	08 08	11 25	12 27	13 41	15 05
N 58	06 28	07 15	07 59	11 43	12 43	13 55	15 15
56	06 25	07 10	07 50	11 57	12 57	14 07	15 24
54	06 22	07 04	07 43	12 10	13 09	14 17	15 32
52	06 19	07 00	07 36	12 21	13 20	14 26	15 40
50	06 17	06 55	07 30	12 31	13 29	14 35	15 46
45	06 11	06 46	07 17	12 52	13 49	14 52	16 00
N 40	06 06	06 38	07 06	13 09	14 05	15 06	16 12
35	06 00	06 31	06 57	13 24	14 19	15 18	16 21
30	05 55	06 24	06 49	13 36	14 31	15 29	16 30
20	05 45	06 12	06 35	13 57	14 51	15 47	16 45
N 10	05 35	06 00	06 22	14 16	15 08	16 03	16 57
0	05 24	05 49	06 10	14 33	15 25	16 17	17 09
S 10	05 11	05 36	05 58	14 50	15 41	16 32	17 21
20	04 55	05 22	05 46	15 08	15 59	16 47	17 34
30	04 34	05 05	05 31	15 30	16 19	17 05	17 49
35	04 21	04 55	05 22	15 42	16 31	17 16	17 57
40	04 06	04 42	05 12	15 56	16 44	17 27	18 06
45	03 46	04 27	05 00	16 13	17 00	17 41	18 18
S 50	03 20	04 08	04 46	16 35	17 20	17 58	18 31
52	03 06	03 59	04 39	16 45	17 29	18 06	18 37
54	02 51	03 49	04 32	16 56	17 39	18 15	18 44
56	02 32	03 37	04 23	17 09	17 51	18 25	18 52
58	02 07	03 23	04 13	17 23	18 05	18 36	19 00
S 60	01 30	03 07	04 03	17 41	18 21	18 49	19 10

Lat.	Sunset	Twilight Civil	Twilight Naut.	Moonset 3	4	5	6
°	h m	h m	h m	h m	h m	h m	h m
N 72	14 21	16 02	17 29	□	□	□	09 30
N 70	14 57	16 18	17 35	□	□	09 30	08 40
68	15 22	16 32	17 41	□	08 28	08 15	08 08
66	15 41	16 43	17 46	06 44	07 21	07 38	07 45
64	15 57	16 52	17 50	06 04	06 46	07 11	07 26
62	16 10	17 00	17 54	05 36	06 20	06 50	07 11
60	16 20	17 07	17 57	05 14	06 00	06 33	06 58
N 58	16 30	17 13	18 01	04 56	05 43	06 19	06 47
56	16 38	17 19	18 04	04 42	05 29	06 07	06 37
54	16 46	17 24	18 06	04 29	05 17	05 56	06 28
52	16 52	17 29	18 09	04 18	05 06	05 47	06 20
50	16 58	17 33	18 12	04 08	04 56	05 38	06 13
45	17 11	17 42	18 17	03 47	04 36	05 20	05 58
N 40	17 22	17 50	18 23	03 30	04 20	05 05	05 46
35	17 31	17 58	18 28	03 16	04 06	04 52	05 35
30	17 39	18 04	18 33	03 03	03 54	04 41	05 26
20	17 53	18 16	18 42	02 42	03 33	04 22	05 10
N 10	18 06	18 27	18 53	02 23	03 15	04 06	04 56
0	18 17	18 39	19 04	02 06	02 58	03 50	04 42
S 10	18 29	18 51	19 17	01 49	02 41	03 34	04 29
20	18 42	19 05	19 32	01 30	02 23	03 18	04 15
30	18 57	19 22	19 53	01 09	02 02	02 58	03 58
35	19 05	19 33	20 05	00 57	01 49	02 47	03 48
40	19 15	19 45	20 21	00 42	01 35	02 34	03 37
45	19 27	20 00	20 40	00 25	01 18	02 18	03 24
S 50	19 41	20 18	21 06	00 04	00 57	01 59	03 08
52	19 47	20 27	21 19	24 47	00 47	01 50	03 00
54	19 55	20 37	21 35	24 36	00 36	01 40	02 52
56	20 03	20 49	21 53	24 24	00 24	01 28	02 43
58	20 12	21 02	22 17	24 09	00 09	01 15	02 32
S 60	20 23	21 18	22 51	23 51	25 00	01 00	02 19

Day	SUN Eqn. of Time 00h	12h	Mer. Pass.	MOON Mer. Pass. Upper	Lower	Age	Phase
d	m s	m s	h m	h m	h m	d	%
3	13 41	13 45	12 14	20 45	08 19	11	80
4	13 48	13 51	12 14	21 37	09 11	12	87
5	13 54	13 56	12 14	22 30	10 04	13	93

UT	ARIES GHA	VENUS −4.1 GHA	Dec	MARS −0.7 GHA	Dec	JUPITER −2.3 GHA	Dec	SATURN +0.6 GHA	Dec	STARS Name	SHA	Dec
d h	° ′	° ′	° ′	° ′	° ′	° ′	° ′	° ′	° ′		° ′	° ′
6 00	135 32.9	137 43.9	S 1 38.8	321 19.1	N 6 48.1	104 08.5	N11 36.4	287 11.3	S 8 53.1	Acamar	315 19.0	S40 15.6
01	150 35.3	152 43.7	37.5	336 21.9	48.3	119 10.7	36.6	302 13.8	53.1	Achernar	335 27.6	S57 10.8
02	165 37.8	167 43.5	36.2	351 24.8	48.5	134 12.8	36.7	317 16.3	53.1	Acrux	173 09.9	S63 09.9
03	180 40.3	182 43.3	.. 34.9	6 27.6	.. 48.8	149 15.0	.. 36.8	332 18.7	.. 53.1	Adhara	255 12.9	S28 59.6
04	195 42.7	197 43.1	33.6	21 30.4	49.0	164 17.1	36.9	347 21.2	53.1	Aldebaran	290 50.3	N16 32.0
05	210 45.2	212 43.0	32.3	36 33.3	49.2	179 19.3	37.1	2 23.6	53.1			
06	225 47.7	227 42.8	S 1 31.0	51 36.1	N 6 49.4	194 21.4	N11 37.2	17 26.1	S 8 53.1	Alioth	166 21.1	N55 53.3
07	240 50.1	242 42.6	29.7	66 38.9	49.7	209 23.6	37.3	32 28.5	53.1	Alkaid	152 59.4	N49 14.8
08	255 52.6	257 42.4	28.3	81 41.8	49.9	224 25.7	37.4	47 31.0	53.1	Al Na'ir	27 45.3	S46 54.1
M 09	270 55.1	272 42.2	.. 27.0	96 44.6	.. 50.1	239 27.9	.. 37.5	62 33.4	.. 53.1	Alnilam	275 47.1	S 1 11.8
O 10	285 57.5	287 42.0	25.7	111 47.5	50.3	254 30.0	37.7	77 35.9	53.0	Alphard	217 56.7	S 8 42.9
N 11	301 00.0	302 41.8	24.4	126 50.3	50.6	269 32.2	37.8	92 38.3	53.0			
D 12	316 02.5	317 41.6	S 1 23.1	141 53.1	N 6 50.8	284 34.3	N11 37.9	107 40.8	S 8 53.0	Alphecca	126 11.8	N26 40.2
A 13	331 04.9	332 41.4	21.8	156 56.0	51.0	299 36.5	38.0	122 43.3	53.0	Alpheratz	357 44.7	N29 09.6
Y 14	346 07.4	347 41.2	20.5	171 58.8	51.2	314 38.6	38.1	137 45.7	53.0	Altair	62 09.5	N 8 54.0
15	1 09.8	2 41.0	.. 19.2	187 01.7	.. 51.5	329 40.8	.. 38.3	152 48.2	.. 53.0	Ankaa	353 16.9	S42 14.6
16	16 12.3	17 40.9	17.9	202 04.5	51.7	344 42.9	38.4	167 50.6	53.0	Antares	112 27.5	S26 27.4
17	31 14.8	32 40.7	16.6	217 07.4	51.9	359 45.1	38.5	182 53.1	53.0			
18	46 17.2	47 40.5	S 1 15.3	232 10.2	N 6 52.1	14 47.2	N11 38.6	197 55.5	S 8 53.0	Arcturus	145 56.5	N19 06.9
19	61 19.7	62 40.3	14.0	247 13.1	52.4	29 49.4	38.8	212 58.0	53.0	Atria	107 30.5	S69 02.6
20	76 22.2	77 40.1	12.6	262 15.9	52.6	44 51.5	38.9	228 00.4	53.0	Avior	234 17.8	S59 33.1
21	91 24.6	92 39.9	.. 11.3	277 18.8	.. 52.8	59 53.7	.. 39.0	243 02.9	.. 52.9	Bellatrix	278 32.8	N 6 21.5
22	106 27.1	107 39.7	10.0	292 21.6	53.1	74 55.8	39.1	258 05.4	52.9	Betelgeuse	271 02.1	N 7 24.4
23	121 29.6	122 39.5	08.7	307 24.5	53.3	89 58.0	39.2	273 07.8	52.9			
7 00	136 32.0	137 39.3	S 1 07.4	322 27.4	N 6 53.5	105 00.1	N11 39.4	288 10.3	S 8 52.9	Canopus	263 56.1	S52 42.4
01	151 34.5	152 39.2	06.1	337 30.2	53.8	120 02.3	39.5	303 12.7	52.9	Capella	280 35.6	N46 00.6
02	166 37.0	167 39.0	04.8	352 33.1	54.0	135 04.4	39.6	318 15.2	52.9	Deneb	49 32.6	N45 19.5
03	181 39.4	182 38.8	.. 03.5	7 35.9	.. 54.2	150 06.6	.. 39.7	333 17.7	.. 52.9	Denebola	182 34.3	N14 30.0
04	196 41.9	197 38.6	02.2	22 38.8	54.5	165 08.7	39.9	348 20.1	52.9	Diphda	348 57.0	S17 55.3
05	211 44.3	212 38.4	1 00.9	37 41.7	54.7	180 10.9	40.0	3 22.6	52.9			
06	226 46.8	227 38.2	S 0 59.6	52 44.5	N 6 54.9	195 13.0	N11 40.1	18 25.0	S 8 52.9	Dubhe	193 52.2	N61 40.8
07	241 49.3	242 38.0	58.2	67 47.4	55.2	210 15.2	40.2	33 27.5	52.9	Elnath	278 13.6	N28 37.0
08	256 51.7	257 37.9	56.9	82 50.3	55.4	225 17.3	40.3	48 29.9	52.8	Eltanin	90 46.9	N51 29.1
T 09	271 54.2	272 37.7	.. 55.6	97 53.1	.. 55.6	240 19.5	.. 40.5	63 32.4	.. 52.8	Enif	33 48.4	N 9 55.9
U 10	286 56.7	287 37.5	54.3	112 56.0	55.9	255 21.6	40.6	78 34.9	52.8	Fomalhaut	15 25.3	S29 33.5
E 11	301 59.1	302 37.3	53.0	127 58.9	56.1	270 23.8	40.7	93 37.3	52.8			
S 12	317 01.6	317 37.1	S 0 51.7	143 01.8	N 6 56.3	285 25.9	N11 40.8	108 39.8	S 8 52.8	Gacrux	172 01.6	S57 10.8
D 13	332 04.1	332 36.9	50.4	158 04.6	56.6	300 28.1	41.0	123 42.2	52.8	Gienah	175 53.0	S17 36.7
A 14	347 06.5	347 36.7	49.1	173 07.5	56.8	315 30.2	41.1	138 44.7	52.8	Hadar	148 49.1	S60 25.7
Y 15	2 09.0	2 36.6	.. 47.8	188 10.4	.. 57.1	330 32.4	.. 41.2	153 47.2	.. 52.8	Hamal	328 01.9	N23 31.3
16	17 11.5	17 36.4	46.5	203 13.3	57.3	345 34.5	41.3	168 49.6	52.8	Kaus Aust.	83 45.3	S34 22.6
17	32 13.9	32 36.2	45.1	218 16.1	57.5	0 36.6	41.5	183 52.1	52.8			
18	47 16.4	47 36.0	S 0 43.8	233 19.0	N 6 57.8	15 38.8	N11 41.6	198 54.5	S 8 52.7	Kochab	137 19.9	N74 06.0
19	62 18.8	62 35.8	42.5	248 21.9	58.0	30 40.9	41.7	213 57.0	52.7	Markab	13 39.5	N15 16.3
20	77 21.3	77 35.7	41.2	263 24.8	58.3	45 43.1	41.8	228 59.5	52.7	Menkar	314 16.0	N 4 08.2
21	92 23.8	92 35.5	.. 39.9	278 27.7	.. 58.5	60 45.2	.. 42.0	244 01.9	.. 52.7	Menkent	148 08.6	S36 25.7
22	107 26.2	107 35.3	38.6	293 30.6	58.7	75 47.4	42.1	259 04.4	52.7	Miaplacidus	221 39.0	S69 46.2
23	122 28.7	122 35.1	37.3	308 33.5	59.0	90 49.5	42.2	274 06.9	52.7			
8 00	137 31.2	137 34.9	S 0 36.0	323 36.3	N 6 59.2	105 51.7	N11 42.3	289 09.3	S 8 52.7	Mirfak	308 41.6	N49 54.4
01	152 33.6	152 34.7	34.7	338 39.2	59.5	120 53.8	42.5	304 11.8	52.7	Nunki	75 59.8	S26 16.8
02	167 36.1	167 34.6	33.4	353 42.1	6 59.7	135 55.9	42.6	319 14.2	52.7	Peacock	53 21.3	S56 41.6
03	182 38.6	182 34.4	.. 32.0	8 45.0	7 00.0	150 58.1	.. 42.7	334 16.7	.. 52.6	Pollux	243 28.5	N27 59.6
04	197 41.0	197 34.2	30.7	23 47.9	00.2	166 00.2	42.8	349 19.2	52.6	Procyon	245 00.4	N 5 11.4
05	212 43.5	212 34.0	29.4	38 50.8	00.4	181 02.4	43.0	4 21.6	52.6			
06	227 45.9	227 33.8	S 0 28.1	53 53.7	N 7 00.7	196 04.5	N11 43.1	19 24.1	S 8 52.6	Rasalhague	96 07.5	N12 33.0
W 07	242 48.4	242 33.7	26.8	68 56.6	00.9	211 06.6	43.2	34 26.6	52.6	Regulus	207 44.2	N11 54.2
E 08	257 50.9	257 33.5	25.5	83 59.5	01.2	226 08.8	43.3	49 29.0	52.6	Rigel	281 12.8	S 8 11.5
D 09	272 53.3	272 33.3	.. 24.2	99 02.4	.. 01.4	241 10.9	.. 43.5	64 31.5	.. 52.6	Rigil Kent.	139 52.9	S60 52.9
N 10	287 55.8	287 33.1	22.9	114 05.3	01.7	256 13.1	43.6	79 33.9	52.6	Sabik	102 13.8	S15 44.3
E 11	302 58.3	302 32.9	21.6	129 08.2	01.9	271 15.2	43.7	94 36.4	52.6			
S 12	318 00.7	317 32.8	S 0 20.3	144 11.1	N 7 02.2	286 17.3	N11 43.8	109 38.9	S 8 52.5	Schedar	349 41.9	N56 36.5
D 13	333 03.2	332 32.6	18.9	159 14.0	02.4	301 19.5	44.0	124 41.3	52.5	Shaula	96 23.4	S37 06.6
A 14	348 05.7	347 32.4	17.6	174 16.9	02.7	316 21.6	44.1	139 43.8	52.5	Sirius	258 34.2	S16 44.2
Y 15	3 08.1	2 32.2	.. 16.3	189 19.8	.. 02.9	331 23.8	.. 44.2	154 46.3	.. 52.5	Spica	158 32.1	S11 13.6
16	18 10.6	17 32.1	15.0	204 22.7	03.2	346 25.9	44.3	169 48.7	52.5	Suhail	222 52.7	S43 29.1
17	33 13.1	32 31.9	13.7	219 25.7	03.4	1 28.0	44.5	184 51.2	52.5			
18	48 15.5	47 31.7	S 0 12.4	234 28.6	N 7 03.7	16 30.2	N11 44.6	199 53.7	S 8 52.5	Vega	80 39.9	N38 47.6
19	63 18.0	62 31.5	11.1	249 31.5	03.9	31 32.3	44.7	214 56.1	52.5	Zuben'ubi	137 06.4	S16 05.5
20	78 20.4	77 31.4	09.8	264 34.4	04.2	46 34.5	44.8	229 58.6	52.4		SHA	Mer. Pass.
21	93 22.9	92 31.2	.. 08.5	279 37.3	.. 04.4	61 36.6	.. 45.0	245 01.1	.. 52.4	Venus	1 07.3	14 50
22	108 25.4	107 31.0	07.1	294 40.2	04.7	76 38.7	45.1	260 03.5	52.4	Mars	185 55.3	2 30
23	123 27.8	122 30.8	05.8	309 43.1	04.9	91 40.9	45.2	275 06.0	52.4	Jupiter	328 28.1	16 58
Mer. Pass. 14 51.4		v −0.2	d 1.3	v 2.9	d 0.2	v 2.1	d 0.1	v 2.5	d 0.0	Saturn	151 38.3	4 47

UT	SUN GHA	SUN Dec	MOON GHA	v	MOON Dec	d	HP
d h	° ′	° ′	° ′	′	° ′	′	′
MONDAY							
6 00	176 30.3	S15 51.8	21 45.5	9.5	N18 18.9	7.5	57.1
01	191 30.2	51.0	36 14.0	9.5	18 11.4	7.7	57.2
02	206 30.2	50.3	50 42.5	9.5	18 03.7	7.8	57.2
03	221 30.1	.. 49.5	65 11.0	9.6	17 55.9	7.9	57.2
04	236 30.1	48.7	79 39.6	9.5	17 48.0	8.0	57.3
05	251 30.0	48.0	94 08.1	9.6	17 40.0	8.1	57.3
06	266 30.0	S15 47.2	108 36.7	9.6	N17 31.9	8.2	57.3
07	281 29.9	46.4	123 05.3	9.6	17 23.7	8.3	57.3
08	296 29.9	45.7	137 33.9	9.6	17 15.4	8.4	57.4
09	311 29.8	.. 44.9	152 02.5	9.6	17 07.0	8.5	57.4
10	326 29.8	44.1	166 31.1	9.7	16 58.5	8.6	57.4
11	341 29.8	43.4	180 59.8	9.6	16 49.9	8.7	57.5
12	356 29.7	S15 42.6	195 28.4	9.7	N16 41.2	8.8	57.5
13	11 29.7	41.8	209 57.1	9.7	16 32.4	8.9	57.5
14	26 29.6	41.1	224 25.8	9.7	16 23.5	9.0	57.6
15	41 29.6	.. 40.3	238 54.5	9.7	16 14.5	9.1	57.6
16	56 29.5	39.5	253 23.2	9.7	16 05.4	9.2	57.6
17	71 29.5	38.8	267 51.9	9.8	15 56.2	9.3	57.6
18	86 29.5	S15 38.0	282 20.7	9.7	N15 46.9	9.4	57.7
19	101 29.4	37.2	296 49.4	9.8	15 37.5	9.5	57.7
20	116 29.4	36.5	311 18.2	9.8	15 28.0	9.6	57.7
21	131 29.3	.. 35.7	325 47.0	9.8	15 18.4	9.7	57.8
22	146 29.3	34.9	340 15.8	9.9	15 08.7	9.8	57.8
23	161 29.3	34.1	354 44.7	9.8	14 58.9	9.8	57.8
TUESDAY							
7 00	176 29.2	S15 33.4	9 13.5	9.9	N14 49.1	10.0	57.8
01	191 29.2	32.6	23 42.4	9.9	14 39.1	10.0	57.9
02	206 29.1	31.8	38 11.3	9.9	14 29.1	10.2	57.9
03	221 29.1	.. 31.1	52 40.2	9.9	14 18.9	10.2	57.9
04	236 29.1	30.3	67 09.1	9.9	14 08.7	10.3	58.0
05	251 29.0	29.5	81 38.0	10.0	13 58.4	10.4	58.0
06	266 29.0	S15 28.7	96 07.0	9.9	N13 48.0	10.5	58.0
07	281 29.0	28.0	110 35.9	10.0	13 37.5	10.5	58.0
08	296 28.9	27.2	125 04.9	10.0	13 27.0	10.7	58.1
09	311 28.9	.. 26.4	139 33.9	10.1	13 16.3	10.7	58.1
10	326 28.8	25.6	154 03.0	10.0	13 05.6	10.8	58.1
11	341 28.8	24.9	168 32.0	10.0	12 54.8	10.9	58.1
12	356 28.8	S15 24.1	183 01.0	10.1	N12 43.9	11.0	58.2
13	11 28.7	23.3	197 30.1	10.1	12 32.9	11.1	58.2
14	26 28.7	22.5	211 59.2	10.1	12 21.8	11.1	58.2
15	41 28.7	.. 21.7	226 28.3	10.1	12 10.7	11.2	58.2
16	56 28.6	21.0	240 57.4	10.2	11 59.5	11.3	58.3
17	71 28.6	20.2	255 26.6	10.1	11 48.2	11.3	58.3
18	86 28.6	S15 19.4	269 55.7	10.2	N11 36.9	11.5	58.3
19	101 28.5	18.6	284 24.9	10.2	11 25.4	11.5	58.4
20	116 28.5	17.8	298 54.1	10.2	11 13.9	11.5	58.4
21	131 28.5	.. 17.1	313 23.3	10.2	11 02.4	11.7	58.4
22	146 28.4	16.3	327 52.5	10.3	10 50.7	11.7	58.4
23	161 28.4	15.5	342 21.8	10.2	10 39.0	11.8	58.5
WEDNESDAY							
8 00	176 28.4	S15 14.7	356 51.0	10.3	N10 27.2	11.8	58.5
01	191 28.3	13.9	11 20.3	10.2	10 15.4	11.9	58.5
02	206 28.3	13.1	25 49.5	10.3	10 03.5	12.0	58.5
03	221 28.3	.. 12.4	40 18.8	10.3	9 51.5	12.0	58.5
04	236 28.3	11.6	54 48.1	10.4	9 39.5	12.1	58.6
05	251 28.2	10.8	69 17.5	10.3	9 27.4	12.2	58.6
06	266 28.2	S15 10.0	83 46.8	10.3	N 9 15.2	12.2	58.6
07	281 28.2	09.2	98 16.1	10.4	9 03.0	12.3	58.6
08	296 28.1	08.4	112 45.5	10.4	8 50.7	12.3	58.7
09	311 28.1	.. 07.7	127 14.9	10.3	8 38.4	12.4	58.7
10	326 28.1	06.9	141 44.2	10.4	8 26.0	12.4	58.7
11	341 28.1	06.1	156 13.6	10.4	8 13.6	12.5	58.7
12	356 28.0	S15 05.3	170 43.0	10.4	N 8 01.1	12.6	58.8
13	11 28.0	04.5	185 12.4	10.5	7 48.5	12.6	58.8
14	26 28.0	03.7	199 41.9	10.4	7 35.9	12.7	58.8
15	41 27.9	.. 02.9	214 11.3	10.4	7 23.2	12.7	58.8
16	56 27.9	02.1	228 40.7	10.5	7 10.5	12.7	58.8
17	71 27.9	01.3	243 10.2	10.4	6 57.8	12.8	58.9
18	86 27.9	S15 00.5	257 39.6	10.5	N 6 45.0	12.8	58.9
19	101 27.8	14 59.8	272 09.1	10.5	6 32.2	12.9	58.9
20	116 27.8	59.0	286 38.6	10.4	6 19.3	13.0	58.9
21	131 27.8	.. 58.2	301 08.0	10.5	6 06.3	12.9	58.9
22	146 27.8	57.4	315 37.5	10.5	5 53.4	13.0	59.0
23	161 27.8	56.6	330 07.0	10.5	N 5 40.4	13.1	59.0
	SD 16.2	d 0.8	SD 15.7		15.8		16.0

Lat.	Twilight Naut.	Twilight Civil	Sunrise	Moonrise 6	7	8	9
°	h m	h m	h m	h m	h m	h m	h m
N 72	06 49	08 14	09 47	12 38	15 11	17 23	19 29
N 70	06 44	07 59	09 17	13 26	15 33	17 33	19 31
68	06 39	07 47	08 54	13 57	15 50	17 42	19 32
66	06 35	07 37	08 37	14 20	16 04	17 48	19 33
64	06 31	07 29	08 23	14 38	16 15	17 54	19 34
62	06 28	07 21	08 11	14 52	16 25	17 59	19 34
60	06 25	07 15	08 01	15 05	16 33	18 03	19 35
N 58	06 22	07 09	07 52	15 15	16 40	18 07	19 36
56	06 20	07 04	07 44	15 24	16 46	18 11	19 36
54	06 17	06 59	07 37	15 32	16 52	18 14	19 36
52	06 15	06 55	07 31	15 40	16 57	18 16	19 37
50	06 13	06 51	07 25	15 46	17 02	18 19	19 37
45	06 08	06 42	07 13	16 00	17 11	18 24	19 38
N 40	06 03	06 35	07 03	16 12	17 19	18 29	19 39
35	05 58	06 28	06 54	16 21	17 26	18 32	19 39
30	05 54	06 22	06 47	16 30	17 33	18 36	19 40
20	05 44	06 11	06 33	16 45	17 43	18 42	19 41
N 10	05 35	06 00	06 22	16 57	17 52	18 47	19 41
0	05 24	05 49	06 11	17 09	18 01	18 52	19 42
S 10	05 12	05 37	05 59	17 21	18 09	18 57	19 43
20	04 57	05 24	05 47	17 34	18 19	19 02	19 44
30	04 37	05 08	05 33	17 49	18 29	19 07	19 45
35	04 25	04 58	05 25	17 57	18 35	19 11	19 45
40	04 10	04 46	05 16	18 06	18 42	19 15	19 46
45	03 52	04 32	05 05	18 18	18 50	19 19	19 47
S 50	03 27	04 14	04 51	18 31	18 59	19 24	19 48
52	03 14	04 06	04 45	18 37	19 03	19 27	19 48
54	03 00	03 56	04 38	18 44	19 08	19 29	19 49
56	02 42	03 45	04 30	18 52	19 13	19 32	19 49
58	02 20	03 32	04 21	19 00	19 19	19 35	19 50
S 60	01 50	03 17	04 11	19 10	19 26	19 39	19 50

Lat.	Sunset	Twilight Civil	Twilight Naut.	Moonset 6	7	8	9
°	h m	h m	h m	h m	h m	h m	h m
N 72	14 43	16 16	17 41	09 30	08 46	08 21	08 02
N 70	15 13	16 30	17 46	08 40	08 22	08 08	07 57
68	15 35	16 42	17 50	08 08	08 03	07 58	07 53
66	15 52	16 52	17 54	07 45	07 48	07 49	07 50
64	16 07	17 01	17 58	07 26	07 35	07 42	07 47
62	16 18	17 08	18 01	07 11	07 25	07 36	07 44
60	16 28	17 14	18 04	06 58	07 16	07 30	07 42
N 58	16 37	17 20	18 07	06 47	07 08	07 25	07 40
56	16 45	17 25	18 09	06 37	07 01	07 21	07 38
54	16 52	17 30	18 12	06 28	06 54	07 17	07 37
52	16 58	17 34	18 14	06 20	06 49	07 13	07 35
50	17 03	17 38	18 16	06 13	06 44	07 10	07 34
45	17 16	17 46	18 21	05 58	06 32	07 03	07 31
N 40	17 26	17 54	18 26	05 46	06 23	06 57	07 29
35	17 34	18 00	18 30	05 35	06 15	06 52	07 27
30	17 42	18 07	18 35	05 26	06 08	06 47	07 25
20	17 55	18 18	18 44	05 10	05 55	06 39	07 21
N 10	18 07	18 28	18 53	04 56	05 44	06 32	07 19
0	18 18	18 39	19 04	04 42	05 34	06 25	07 16
S 10	18 29	18 51	19 16	04 29	05 24	06 18	07 13
20	18 41	19 04	19 31	04 15	05 13	06 11	07 10
30	18 55	19 20	19 50	03 58	05 00	06 03	07 06
35	19 03	19 30	20 02	03 48	04 52	05 58	07 04
40	19 12	19 41	20 17	03 37	04 44	05 52	07 02
45	19 23	19 55	20 35	03 24	04 34	05 46	06 59
S 50	19 36	20 13	21 00	03 08	04 21	05 38	06 56
52	19 42	20 21	21 12	03 00	04 16	05 34	06 54
54	19 49	20 31	21 26	02 52	04 10	05 30	06 53
56	19 57	20 41	21 43	02 43	04 03	05 26	06 51
58	20 05	20 54	22 04	02 32	03 55	05 21	06 49
S 60	20 15	21 09	22 33	02 19	03 46	05 15	06 47

Day	Eqn. of Time 00h	Eqn. of Time 12h	Mer. Pass.	Mer. Pass. Upper	Mer. Pass. Lower	Age	Phase
d	m s	m s	h m	h m	h m	d	%
6	13 59	14 01	12 14	23 22	10 56	14	97
7	14 03	14 05	12 14	24 13	11 48	15	100
8	14 06	14 08	12 14	00 13	12 38	16	99

2012 FEBRUARY 9, 10, 11 (THURS., FRI., SAT.)

UT	ARIES GHA	VENUS −4.1 GHA	Dec	MARS −0.8 GHA	Dec	JUPITER −2.3 GHA	Dec	SATURN +0.5 GHA	Dec	STARS Name	SHA	Dec
9 00	138 30.3	137 30.7 S 0 04.5		324 46.1 N 7 05.2		106 43.0 N11 45.3		290 08.5 S 8 52.4		Acamar	315 19.0	S40 15.6
01	153 32.8	152 30.5	03.2	339 49.0	05.4	121 45.1	45.5	305 10.9	52.4	Achernar	335 27.7	S57 10.8
02	168 35.2	167 30.3	01.9	354 51.9	05.7	136 47.3	45.6	320 13.4	52.4	Acrux	173 09.9	S63 09.9
03	183 37.7	182 30.1 S	00.6	9 54.8 ..	05.9	151 49.4 ..	45.7	335 15.9 ..	52.4	Adhara	255 12.9	S28 59.6
04	198 40.2	197 30.0 N	00.7	24 57.8	06.2	166 51.6	45.8	350 18.3	52.3	Aldebaran	290 50.3	N16 31.9
05	213 42.6	212 29.8	02.0	40 00.7	06.5	181 53.7	46.0	5 20.8	52.3			
T 06	228 45.1	227 29.6 N 0 03.3		55 03.6 N 7 06.7		196 55.8 N11 46.1		20 23.3 S 8 52.3		Alioth	166 21.1	N55 53.3
H 07	243 47.5	242 29.4	04.6	70 06.5	07.0	211 58.0	46.2	35 25.7	52.3	Alkaid	152 59.4	N49 14.8
U 08	258 50.0	257 29.3	06.0	85 09.5	07.2	227 00.1	46.3	50 28.2	52.3	Al Na'ir	27 45.3	S46 54.1
R 09	273 52.5	272 29.1 ..	07.3	100 12.4 ..	07.5	242 02.2 ..	46.5	65 30.7 ..	52.3	Alnilam	275 47.1	S 1 11.8
S 10	288 54.9	287 28.9	08.6	115 15.3	07.7	257 04.4	46.6	80 33.1	52.3	Alphard	217 56.7	S 8 42.9
D 11	303 57.4	302 28.7	09.9	130 18.3	08.0	272 06.5	46.7	95 35.6	52.3			
A 12	318 59.9	317 28.6 N 0 11.2		145 21.2 N 7 08.3		287 08.6 N11 46.9		110 38.1 S 8 52.2		Alphecca	126 11.8	N26 40.2
Y 13	334 02.3	332 28.4	12.5	160 24.1	08.5	302 10.8	47.0	125 40.5	52.2	Alpheratz	357 44.7	N29 09.6
14	349 04.8	347 28.2	13.8	175 27.1	08.8	317 12.9	47.1	140 43.0	52.2	Altair	62 09.4	N 8 54.0
15	4 07.3	2 28.1 ..	15.1	190 30.0 ..	09.0	332 15.0 ..	47.2	155 45.5 ..	52.2	Ankaa	353 16.9	S42 14.5
16	19 09.7	17 27.9	16.4	205 33.0	09.3	347 17.2	47.4	170 47.9	52.2	Antares	112 27.5	S26 27.4
17	34 12.2	32 27.7	17.8	220 35.9	09.6	2 19.3	47.5	185 50.4	52.2			
18	49 14.7	47 27.5 N 0 19.1		235 38.8 N 7 09.8		17 21.4 N11 47.6		200 52.9 S 8 52.2		Arcturus	145 56.5	N19 06.9
19	64 17.1	62 27.4	20.4	250 41.8	10.1	32 23.6	47.7	215 55.3	52.1	Atria	107 30.4	S69 02.6
20	79 19.6	77 27.2	21.7	265 44.7	10.3	47 25.7	47.9	230 57.8	52.1	Avior	234 17.8	S59 33.1
21	94 22.0	92 27.0 ..	23.0	280 47.7 ..	10.6	62 27.8 ..	48.0	246 00.3 ..	52.1	Bellatrix	278 32.8	N 6 21.5
22	109 24.5	107 26.9	24.3	295 50.6	10.9	77 30.0	48.1	261 02.7	52.1	Betelgeuse	271 02.1	N 7 24.4
23	124 27.0	122 26.7	25.6	310 53.6	11.1	92 32.1	48.3	276 05.2	52.1			
10 00	139 29.4	137 26.5 N 0 26.9		325 56.5 N 7 11.4		107 34.2 N11 48.4		291 07.7 S 8 52.1		Canopus	263 56.2	S52 42.5
01	154 31.9	152 26.4	28.2	340 59.5	11.7	122 36.4	48.5	306 10.2	52.1	Capella	280 35.6	N46 00.7
02	169 34.4	167 26.2	29.5	356 02.4	11.9	137 38.5	48.6	321 12.6	52.0	Deneb	49 32.6	N45 19.4
03	184 36.8	182 26.0 ..	30.9	11 05.4 ..	12.2	152 40.6 ..	48.8	336 15.1 ..	52.0	Denebola	182 34.3	N14 30.0
04	199 39.3	197 25.8	32.2	26 08.3	12.5	167 42.8	48.9	351 17.6	52.0	Diphda	348 57.0	S17 55.3
05	214 41.8	212 25.7	33.5	41 11.3	12.7	182 44.9	49.0	6 20.0	52.0			
F 06	229 44.2	227 25.5 N 0 34.8		56 14.2 N 7 13.0		197 47.0 N11 49.2		21 22.5 S 8 52.0		Dubhe	193 52.2	N61 40.8
R 07	244 46.7	242 25.3	36.1	71 17.2	13.3	212 49.1	49.3	36 25.0	52.0	Elnath	278 13.6	N28 37.0
I 08	259 49.2	257 25.2	37.4	86 20.2	13.5	227 51.3	49.4	51 27.5	52.0	Eltanin	90 46.9	N51 29.1
D 09	274 51.6	272 25.0 ..	38.7	101 23.1 ..	13.8	242 53.4 ..	49.5	66 29.9 ..	51.9	Enif	33 48.4	N 9 55.9
A 10	289 54.1	287 24.8	40.0	116 26.1	14.1	257 55.5	49.7	81 32.4	51.9	Fomalhaut	15 25.3	S29 33.5
Y 11	304 56.5	302 24.7	41.3	131 29.0	14.3	272 57.7	49.8	96 34.9	51.9			
12	319 59.0	317 24.5 N 0 42.6		146 32.0 N 7 14.6		287 59.8 N11 49.9		111 37.3 S 8 51.9		Gacrux	172 01.6	S57 10.8
13	335 01.5	332 24.3	44.0	161 35.0	14.9	303 01.9	50.1	126 39.8	51.9	Gienah	175 53.0	S17 36.7
14	350 03.9	347 24.2	45.3	176 37.9	15.1	318 04.0	50.2	141 42.3	51.9	Hadar	148 49.0	S60 25.7
15	5 06.4	2 24.0 ..	46.6	191 40.9 ..	15.4	333 06.2 ..	50.3	156 44.8 ..	51.9	Hamal	328 01.9	N23 31.3
16	20 08.9	17 23.8	47.9	206 43.9	15.7	348 08.3	50.4	171 47.2	51.8	Kaus Aust.	83 45.3	S34 22.6
17	35 11.3	32 23.7	49.2	221 46.8	15.9	3 10.4	50.6	186 49.7	51.8			
18	50 13.8	47 23.5 N 0 50.5		236 49.8 N 7 16.2		18 12.6 N11 50.7		201 52.2 S 8 51.8		Kochab	137 19.8	N74 06.0
19	65 16.3	62 23.3	51.8	251 52.8	16.5	33 14.7	50.8	216 54.7	51.8	Markab	13 39.6	N15 16.3
20	80 18.7	77 23.2	53.1	266 55.8	16.8	48 16.8	51.0	231 57.1	51.8	Menkar	314 16.0	N 4 08.2
21	95 21.2	92 23.0 ..	54.4	281 58.7 ..	17.0	63 18.9 ..	51.1	246 59.6 ..	51.8	Menkent	148 08.6	S36 25.7
22	110 23.6	107 22.8	55.7	297 01.7	17.3	78 21.1	51.2	262 02.1	51.8	Miaplacidus	221 39.0	S69 46.2
23	125 26.1	122 22.7	57.1	312 04.7	17.6	93 23.2	51.3	277 04.5	51.7			
11 00	140 28.6	137 22.5 N 0 58.4		327 07.7 N 7 17.9		108 25.3 N11 51.5		292 07.0 S 8 51.7		Mirfak	308 41.7	N49 54.4
01	155 31.0	152 22.4	0 59.7	342 10.7	18.1	123 27.4	51.6	307 09.5	51.7	Nunki	75 59.7	S26 16.8
02	170 33.5	167 22.2	1 01.0	357 13.6	18.4	138 29.6	51.7	322 12.0	51.7	Peacock	53 21.2	S56 41.6
03	185 36.0	182 22.0 ..	02.3	12 16.6 ..	18.7	153 31.7 ..	51.9	337 14.4 ..	51.7	Pollux	243 28.5	N27 59.6
04	200 38.4	197 21.9	03.6	27 19.6	19.0	168 33.8	52.0	352 16.9	51.7	Procyon	245 00.4	N 5 11.4
05	215 40.9	212 21.7	04.9	42 22.6	19.2	183 35.9	52.1	7 19.4	51.6			
S 06	230 43.4	227 21.5 N 1 06.2		57 25.6 N 7 19.5		198 38.1 N11 52.3		22 21.9 S 8 51.6		Rasalhague	96 07.5	N12 33.0
A 07	245 45.8	242 21.4	07.5	72 28.6	19.8	213 40.2	52.4	37 24.3	51.6	Regulus	207 44.2	N11 54.2
T 08	260 48.3	257 21.2	08.8	87 31.6	20.1	228 42.3	52.5	52 26.8	51.6	Rigel	281 12.8	S 8 11.5
U 09	275 50.8	272 21.0 ..	10.2	102 34.6 ..	20.3	243 44.4 ..	52.6	67 29.3 ..	51.6	Rigil Kent.	139 52.9	S60 52.9
R 10	290 53.2	287 20.9	11.5	117 37.5	20.6	258 46.6	52.8	82 31.8	51.6	Sabik	102 13.8	S15 44.3
D 11	305 55.7	302 20.7	12.8	132 40.5	20.9	273 48.7	52.9	97 34.3	51.5			
A 12	320 58.1	317 20.6 N 1 14.1		147 43.5 N 7 21.2		288 50.8 N11 53.0		112 36.7 S 8 51.5		Schedar	349 42.0	N56 36.5
Y 13	336 00.6	332 20.4	15.4	162 46.5	21.5	303 52.9	53.2	127 39.2	51.5	Shaula	96 23.4	S37 06.6
14	351 03.1	347 20.2	16.7	177 49.5	21.7	318 55.0	53.3	142 41.7	51.5	Sirius	258 34.3	S16 44.2
15	6 05.5	2 20.1 ..	18.0	192 52.5 ..	22.0	333 57.2 ..	53.4	157 44.2 ..	51.5	Spica	158 32.1	S11 13.6
16	21 08.0	17 19.9	19.3	207 55.5	22.3	348 59.3	53.6	172 46.6	51.5	Suhail	222 52.7	S43 29.1
17	36 10.5	32 19.8	20.6	222 58.5	22.6	4 01.4	53.7	187 49.1	51.4			
18	51 12.9	47 19.6 N 1 21.9		238 01.5 N 7 22.9		19 03.5 N11 53.8		202 51.6 S 8 51.4		Vega	80 39.9	N38 47.6
19	66 15.4	62 19.4	23.2	253 04.5	23.1	34 05.7	54.0	217 54.1	51.4	Zuben'ubi	137 06.4	S16 05.6
20	81 17.9	77 19.3	24.6	268 07.5	23.4	49 07.8	54.1	232 56.5	51.4		SHA	Mer.Pass.
21	96 20.3	92 19.1 ..	25.9	283 10.5 ..	23.7	64 09.9 ..	54.2	247 59.0 ..	51.4		° ′	h m
22	111 22.8	107 19.0	27.2	298 13.5	24.0	79 12.0	54.3	263 01.5	51.4	Venus	357 57.1	14 50
23	126 25.2	122 18.8	28.5	313 16.5	24.3	94 14.1	54.5	278 04.0	51.3	Mars	186 27.1	2 16
Mer.Pass. 14 39.6		v −0.2 d 1.3		v 3.0 d 0.3		v 2.1 d 0.1		v 2.5 d 0.0		Jupiter	328 04.8	16 47
										Saturn	151 38.2	4 35

UT	SUN GHA	SUN Dec	MOON GHA	v	Dec	d	HP
d h	° ′	° ′	° ′	′	° ′	′	′
9 00	176 27.7	S14 55.8	344 36.5	10.5	N 5 27.3	13.1	59.0
01	191 27.7	55.0	359 06.0	10.5	5 14.2	13.1	59.0
02	206 27.7	54.2	13 35.5	10.5	5 01.1	13.1	59.0
03	221 27.7 ..	53.4	28 05.0	10.5	4 48.0	13.2	59.0
04	236 27.6	52.6	42 34.5	10.5	4 34.8	13.2	59.1
05	251 27.6	51.8	57 04.0	10.5	4 21.6	13.3	59.1
T 06	266 27.6	S14 51.0	71 33.5	10.5	N 4 08.3	13.3	59.1
H 07	281 27.6	50.2	86 03.0	10.6	3 55.0	13.3	59.1
U 08	296 27.6	49.4	100 32.6	10.5	3 41.7	13.3	59.1
R 09	311 27.5 ..	48.6	115 02.1	10.5	3 28.4	13.4	59.1
S 10	326 27.5	47.8	129 31.6	10.5	3 15.0	13.5	59.2
D 11	341 27.5	47.0	144 01.1	10.5	3 01.7	13.5	59.2
A 12	356 27.5	S14 46.2	158 30.6	10.5	N 2 48.2	13.4	59.2
Y 13	11 27.5	45.4	173 00.1	10.5	2 34.8	13.4	59.2
14	26 27.4	44.6	187 29.6	10.5	2 21.4	13.5	59.2
15	41 27.4 ..	43.8	201 59.1	10.5	2 07.9	13.5	59.2
16	56 27.4	43.0	216 28.6	10.5	1 54.4	13.5	59.3
17	71 27.4	42.2	230 58.1	10.5	1 40.9	13.5	59.3
18	86 27.4	S14 41.4	245 27.6	10.4	N 1 27.4	13.5	59.3
19	101 27.4	40.6	259 57.0	10.5	1 13.9	13.5	59.3
20	116 27.3	39.8	274 26.5	10.5	1 00.4	13.6	59.3
21	131 27.3 ..	39.0	288 56.0	10.4	0 46.8	13.6	59.3
22	146 27.3	38.2	303 25.4	10.5	0 33.2	13.5	59.3
23	161 27.3	37.4	317 54.9	10.4	0 19.7	13.6	59.3
10 00	176 27.3	S14 36.6	332 24.3	10.4	N 0 06.1	13.6	59.4
01	191 27.3	35.8	346 53.7	10.4	S 0 07.5	13.5	59.4
02	206 27.2	35.0	1 23.1	10.4	0 21.0	13.6	59.4
03	221 27.2 ..	34.2	15 52.5	10.4	0 34.6	13.6	59.4
04	236 27.2	33.4	30 21.9	10.4	0 48.2	13.6	59.4
05	251 27.2	32.6	44 51.3	10.3	1 01.8	13.6	59.4
F 06	266 27.2	S14 31.8	59 20.6	10.4	S 1 15.4	13.5	59.4
R 07	281 27.2	31.0	73 50.0	10.3	1 28.9	13.6	59.4
I 08	296 27.2	30.2	88 19.3	10.3	1 42.5	13.6	59.4
D 09	311 27.2 ..	29.4	102 48.6	10.3	1 56.1	13.5	59.4
A 10	326 27.1	28.6	117 17.9	10.3	2 09.6	13.6	59.5
Y 11	341 27.1	27.8	131 47.2	10.2	2 23.2	13.5	59.5
12	356 27.1	S14 26.9	146 16.4	10.3	S 2 36.7	13.5	59.5
13	11 27.1	26.1	160 45.7	10.2	2 50.2	13.5	59.5
14	26 27.1	25.3	175 14.9	10.2	3 03.7	13.5	59.5
15	41 27.1 ..	24.5	189 44.1	10.2	3 17.2	13.5	59.5
16	56 27.1	23.7	204 13.3	10.1	3 30.7	13.4	59.5
17	71 27.1	22.9	218 42.4	10.1	3 44.1	13.5	59.5
18	86 27.1	S14 22.1	233 11.5	10.2	S 3 57.6	13.4	59.5
19	101 27.1	21.3	247 40.7	10.0	4 11.0	13.4	59.5
20	116 27.1	20.5	262 09.7	10.1	4 24.4	13.4	59.5
21	131 27.0 ..	19.6	276 38.8	10.0	4 37.8	13.3	59.5
22	146 27.0	18.8	291 07.8	10.1	4 51.1	13.3	59.5
23	161 27.0	18.0	305 36.9	9.9	5 04.4	13.3	59.5
11 00	176 27.0	S14 17.2	320 05.8	10.0	S 5 17.7	13.3	59.6
01	191 27.0	16.4	334 34.8	9.9	5 31.0	13.2	59.6
02	206 27.0	15.6	349 03.7	9.9	5 44.2	13.2	59.6
03	221 27.0 ..	14.8	3 32.6	9.9	5 57.4	13.2	59.6
04	236 27.0	13.9	18 01.5	9.8	6 10.6	13.1	59.6
05	251 27.0	13.1	32 30.3	9.9	6 23.8	13.1	59.6
S 06	266 27.0	S14 12.3	46 59.2	9.7	S 6 36.9	13.0	59.6
A 07	281 27.0	11.5	61 27.9	9.8	6 49.9	13.0	59.6
T 08	296 27.0	10.7	75 56.7	9.7	7 02.9	13.0	59.6
U 09	311 27.0 ..	09.9	90 25.4	9.7	7 15.9	13.0	59.6
R 10	326 27.0	09.0	104 54.1	9.6	7 28.7	12.9	59.6
D 11	341 27.0	08.2	119 22.7	9.7	7 41.8	12.8	59.6
A 12	356 27.0	S14 07.4	133 51.4	9.5	S 7 54.6	12.8	59.6
Y 13	11 27.0	06.6	148 19.9	9.6	8 07.4	12.8	59.6
14	26 27.0	05.8	162 48.5	9.5	8 20.2	12.7	59.6
15	41 27.0 ..	04.9	177 17.0	9.5	8 32.9	12.6	59.6
16	56 27.0	04.1	191 45.5	9.4	8 45.5	12.6	59.6
17	71 27.0	03.3	206 13.9	9.4	8 58.1	12.6	59.6
18	86 27.0	S14 02.5	220 42.3	9.4	S 9 10.7	12.5	59.6
19	101 27.0	01.7	235 10.7	9.3	9 23.2	12.4	59.6
20	116 27.0	00.8	249 39.0	9.3	9 35.6	12.4	59.6
21	131 27.0	14 00.0	264 07.3	9.2	9 48.0	12.4	59.6
22	146 27.0	13 59.2	278 35.5	9.3	10 00.4	12.2	59.6
23	161 27.0	S13 58.4	293 03.8	9.1	S10 12.6	12.2	59.6
	SD 16.2	d 0.8	SD 16.1		16.2		16.2

Lat.	Twilight Naut.	Twilight Civil	Sunrise	Moonrise 9	10	11	12
°	h m	h m	h m	h m	h m	h m	h m
N 72	06 38	08 00	09 27	19 29	21 36	23 49	26 21
N 70	06 33	07 47	09 01	19 31	21 29	23 31	25 42
68	06 30	07 37	08 42	19 32	21 23	23 17	25 15
66	06 27	07 28	08 26	19 33	21 18	23 05	24 55
64	06 24	07 20	08 13	19 34	21 14	22 56	24 39
62	06 21	07 14	08 02	19 34	21 10	22 48	24 25
60	06 19	07 08	07 53	19 35	21 07	22 41	24 14
N 58	06 16	07 03	07 45	19 36	21 05	22 35	24 04
56	06 14	06 58	07 38	19 36	21 02	22 29	23 56
54	06 12	06 54	07 31	19 36	21 00	22 24	23 48
52	06 10	06 50	07 26	19 37	20 58	22 20	23 42
50	06 08	06 47	07 20	19 37	20 56	22 16	23 36
45	06 04	06 39	07 09	19 38	20 53	22 08	23 23
N 40	06 00	06 32	07 00	19 39	20 49	22 01	23 12
35	05 56	06 26	06 52	19 39	20 47	21 55	23 03
30	05 52	06 20	06 45	19 40	20 44	21 49	22 55
20	05 43	06 09	06 32	19 41	20 40	21 40	22 41
N 10	05 34	06 00	06 21	19 41	20 36	21 32	22 30
0	05 25	05 49	06 11	19 42	20 33	21 25	22 19
S 10	05 13	05 38	06 00	19 43	20 30	21 18	22 08
20	04 59	05 26	05 49	19 44	20 26	21 10	21 56
30	04 40	05 10	05 36	19 45	20 22	21 01	21 43
35	04 29	05 01	05 28	19 45	20 20	20 56	21 35
40	04 15	04 50	05 19	19 46	20 18	20 51	21 27
45	03 57	04 37	05 09	19 47	20 15	20 44	21 17
S 50	03 34	04 20	04 56	19 48	20 11	20 37	21 05
52	03 22	04 12	04 51	19 48	20 10	20 33	20 59
54	03 09	04 03	04 44	19 49	20 08	20 29	20 53
56	02 53	03 53	04 37	19 49	20 06	20 25	20 47
58	02 33	03 41	04 29	19 50	20 04	20 20	20 39
S 60	02 07	03 27	04 20	19 50	20 02	20 15	20 30

Lat.	Sunset	Twilight Civil	Twilight Naut.	Moonset 9	10	11	12
°	h m	h m	h m	h m	h m	h m	h m
N 72	15 03	16 30	17 53	08 02	07 44	07 25	07 02
N 70	15 28	16 43	17 57	07 57	07 46	07 35	07 22
68	15 48	16 53	18 00	07 53	07 48	07 43	07 38
66	16 04	17 02	18 03	07 50	07 50	07 50	07 51
64	16 16	17 09	18 06	07 47	07 51	07 56	08 02
62	16 27	17 16	18 09	07 44	07 52	08 01	08 11
60	16 36	17 21	18 11	07 42	07 54	08 05	08 19
N 58	16 44	17 27	18 13	07 40	07 55	08 09	08 26
56	16 51	17 31	18 15	07 38	07 55	08 13	08 33
54	16 58	17 35	18 17	07 37	07 56	08 16	08 38
52	17 03	17 39	18 19	07 35	07 57	08 19	08 43
50	17 09	17 43	18 21	07 34	07 58	08 22	08 48
45	17 20	17 50	18 25	07 31	07 59	08 27	08 58
N 40	17 29	17 57	18 29	07 29	08 00	08 32	09 07
35	17 37	18 03	18 33	07 27	08 01	08 36	09 14
30	17 44	18 09	18 37	07 25	08 02	08 40	09 20
20	17 56	18 19	18 45	07 21	08 04	08 47	09 31
N 10	18 07	18 29	18 54	07 19	08 05	08 52	09 41
0	18 18	18 39	19 04	07 16	08 06	08 58	09 50
S 10	18 28	18 50	19 15	07 13	08 08	09 03	09 59
20	18 39	19 02	19 29	07 10	08 09	09 09	10 09
30	18 52	19 17	19 47	07 06	08 10	09 15	10 21
35	19 00	19 24	19 59	07 04	08 11	09 19	10 28
40	19 08	19 37	20 13	07 02	08 12	09 23	10 35
45	19 19	19 51	20 30	06 59	08 13	09 28	10 43
S 50	19 31	20 07	20 53	06 56	08 15	09 34	10 54
52	19 37	20 15	21 04	06 54	08 15	09 37	10 59
54	19 43	20 24	21 17	06 53	08 16	09 40	11 04
56	19 50	20 34	21 33	06 51	08 17	09 43	11 10
58	19 58	20 45	21 52	06 49	08 18	09 47	11 17
S 60	20 07	20 59	22 16	06 47	08 18	09 51	11 24

Day	SUN Eqn. of Time 00h	SUN Eqn. of Time 12h	SUN Mer. Pass.	MOON Mer. Pass. Upper	MOON Mer. Pass. Lower	Age	Phase
d	m s	m s	h m	h m	h m	d	%
9	14 09	14 10	12 14	01 04	13 29	17	97
10	14 11	14 11	12 14	01 54	14 20	18	91
11	14 12	14 12	12 14	02 45	15 11	19	84

UT	ARIES	VENUS −4.2		MARS −0.9		JUPITER −2.3		SATURN +0.5		STARS		
	GHA	GHA	Dec	GHA	Dec	GHA	Dec	GHA	Dec	Name	SHA	Dec
d h	° ′	° ′	° ′	° ′	° ′	° ′	° ′	° ′	° ′		° ′	° ′
12 00	141 27.7	137 18.6 N 1 29.8		328 19.6 N 7 24.6		109 16.3 N11 54.6		293 06.5 S 8 51.3		Acamar	315 19.1	S40 15.6
01	156 30.2	152 18.5	31.1	343 22.6	24.8	124 18.4	54.7	308 08.9	51.3	Achernar	335 27.7	S57 10.7
02	171 32.6	167 18.3	32.4	358 25.6	25.1	139 20.5	54.9	323 11.4	51.3	Acrux	173 09.8	S63 09.9
03	186 35.1	182 18.2 ..	33.7	13 28.6 ..	25.4	154 22.6 ..	55.0	338 13.9 ..	51.3	Adhara	255 13.0	S28 59.6
04	201 37.6	197 18.0	35.0	28 31.6	25.7	169 24.7	55.1	353 16.4	51.3	Aldebaran	290 50.3	N16 31.9
05	216 40.0	212 17.8	36.3	43 34.6	26.0	184 26.9	55.3	8 18.9	51.2			
06	231 42.5	227 17.7 N 1 37.6		58 37.6 N 7 26.3		199 29.0 N11 55.4		23 21.3 S 8 51.2		Alioth	166 21.1	N55 53.3
07	246 45.0	242 17.5	39.0	73 40.7	26.6	214 31.1	55.5	38 23.8	51.2	Alkaid	152 59.4	N49 14.8
08	261 47.4	257 17.4	40.3	88 43.7	26.8	229 33.2	55.7	53 26.3	51.2	Al Na'ir	27 45.3	S46 54.1
S 09	276 49.9	272 17.2 ..	41.6	103 46.7 ..	27.1	244 35.3 ..	55.8	68 28.8 ..	51.2	Alnilam	275 47.1	S 1 11.9
U 10	291 52.4	287 17.0	42.9	118 49.7	27.4	259 37.4	55.9	83 31.3	51.2	Alphard	217 56.7	S 8 42.9
N 11	306 54.8	302 16.9	44.2	133 52.7	27.7	274 39.6	56.1	98 33.7	51.1			
D 12	321 57.3	317 16.7 N 1 45.5		148 55.8 N 7 28.0		289 41.7 N11 56.2		113 36.2 S 8 51.1		Alphecca	126 11.8	N26 40.2
A 13	336 59.7	332 16.6	46.8	163 58.8	28.3	304 43.8	56.3	128 38.7	51.1	Alpheratz	357 44.7	N29 09.6
Y 14	352 02.2	347 16.4	48.1	179 01.8	28.6	319 45.9	56.5	143 41.2	51.1	Altair	62 09.4	N 8 54.0
15	7 04.7	2 16.3 ..	49.4	194 04.8 ..	28.9	334 48.0 ..	56.6	158 43.7 ..	51.1	Ankaa	353 16.9	S42 14.5
16	22 07.1	17 16.1	50.7	209 07.9	29.1	349 50.1	56.7	173 46.1	51.1	Antares	112 27.5	S26 27.4
17	37 09.6	32 16.0	52.0	224 10.9	29.4	4 52.3	56.9	188 48.6	51.0			
18	52 12.1	47 15.8 N 1 53.3		239 13.9 N 7 29.7		19 54.4 N11 57.0		203 51.1 S 8 51.0		Arcturus	145 56.5	N19 06.9
19	67 14.5	62 15.6	54.7	254 17.0	30.0	34 56.5	57.1	218 53.6	51.0	Atria	107 30.4	S69 02.6
20	82 17.0	77 15.5	56.0	269 20.0	30.3	49 58.6	57.2	233 56.1	51.0	Avior	234 17.8	S59 33.2
21	97 19.5	92 15.3 ..	57.3	284 23.0 ..	30.6	65 00.7 ..	57.4	248 58.5 ..	51.0	Bellatrix	278 32.8	N 6 21.5
22	112 21.9	107 15.2	58.6	299 26.1	30.9	80 02.8	57.5	264 01.0	50.9	Betelgeuse	271 02.1	N 7 24.4
23	127 24.4	122 15.0	1 59.9	314 29.1	31.2	95 05.0	57.6	279 03.5	50.9			
13 00	142 26.9	137 14.9 N 2 01.2		329 32.1 N 7 31.5		110 07.1 N11 57.8		294 06.0 S 8 50.9		Canopus	263 56.2	S52 42.5
01	157 29.3	152 14.7	02.5	344 35.2	31.8	125 09.2	57.9	309 08.5	50.9	Capella	280 35.6	N46 00.7
02	172 31.8	167 14.6	03.8	359 38.2	32.1	140 11.3	58.0	324 11.0	50.9	Deneb	49 32.6	N45 19.4
03	187 34.2	182 14.4 ..	05.1	14 41.3 ..	32.4	155 13.4 ..	58.2	339 13.4 ..	50.9	Denebola	182 34.3	N14 30.0
04	202 36.7	197 14.2	06.4	29 44.3	32.7	170 15.5	58.3	354 15.9	50.8	Diphda	348 57.0	S17 55.3
05	217 39.2	212 14.1	07.7	44 47.4	33.0	185 17.6	58.4	9 18.4	50.8			
06	232 41.6	227 13.9 N 2 09.0		59 50.4 N 7 33.3		200 19.7 N11 58.6		24 20.9 S 8 50.8		Dubhe	193 52.1	N61 40.8
07	247 44.1	242 13.8	10.3	74 53.4	33.5	215 21.9	58.7	39 23.4	50.8	Elnath	278 13.6	N28 37.0
08	262 46.6	257 13.6	11.6	89 56.5	33.8	230 24.0	58.8	54 25.9	50.8	Eltanin	90 46.9	N51 29.0
M 09	277 49.0	272 13.5 ..	13.0	104 59.5 ..	34.1	245 26.1 ..	59.0	69 28.3 ..	50.7	Enif	33 48.4	N 9 55.9
O 10	292 51.5	287 13.3	14.3	120 02.6	34.4	260 28.2	59.1	84 30.8	50.7	Fomalhaut	15 25.3	S29 33.5
N 11	307 54.0	302 13.2	15.6	135 05.6	34.7	275 30.3	59.2	99 33.3	50.7			
D 12	322 56.4	317 13.0 N 2 16.9		150 08.7 N 7 35.0		290 32.4 N11 59.4		114 35.8 S 8 50.7		Gacrux	172 01.5	S57 10.8
A 13	337 58.9	332 12.9	18.2	165 11.7	35.3	305 34.5	59.5	129 38.3	50.7	Gienah	175 53.0	S17 36.7
Y 14	353 01.3	347 12.7	19.5	180 14.8	35.6	320 36.6	59.6	144 40.8	50.6	Hadar	148 49.0	S60 25.7
15	8 03.8	2 12.6 ..	20.8	195 17.9 ..	35.9	335 38.8 ..	59.8	159 43.3 ..	50.6	Hamal	328 01.9	N23 31.2
16	23 06.3	17 12.4	22.1	210 20.9	36.2	350 40.9	11 59.9	174 45.7	50.6	Kaus Aust.	83 45.3	S34 22.6
17	38 08.7	32 12.3	23.4	225 24.0	36.5	5 43.0	12 00.1	189 48.2	50.6			
18	53 11.2	47 12.1 N 2 24.7		240 27.0 N 7 36.8		20 45.1 N12 00.2		204 50.7 S 8 50.6		Kochab	137 19.7	N74 06.0
19	68 13.7	62 12.0	26.0	255 30.1	37.1	35 47.2	00.3	219 53.2	50.5	Markab	13 39.6	N15 16.3
20	83 16.1	77 11.8	27.3	270 33.2	37.4	50 49.3	00.5	234 55.7	50.5	Menkar	314 16.0	N 4 08.2
21	98 18.6	92 11.7 ..	28.6	285 36.2 ..	37.7	65 51.4 ..	00.6	249 58.2 ..	50.5	Menkent	148 08.5	S36 25.7
22	113 21.1	107 11.5	29.9	300 39.3	38.0	80 53.5	00.7	265 00.7	50.5	Miaplacidus	221 39.0	S69 46.2
23	128 23.5	122 11.3	31.2	315 42.4	38.3	95 55.6	00.9	280 03.1	50.5			
14 00	143 26.0	137 11.2 N 2 32.5		330 45.4 N 7 38.6		110 57.7 N12 01.0		295 05.6 S 8 50.4		Mirfak	308 41.7	N49 54.4
01	158 28.5	152 11.0	33.9	345 48.5	38.9	125 59.8	01.1	310 08.1	50.4	Nunki	75 59.7	S26 16.8
02	173 30.9	167 10.9	35.2	0 51.6	39.2	141 02.0	01.3	325 10.6	50.4	Peacock	53 21.2	S56 41.6
03	188 33.4	182 10.7 ..	36.5	15 54.6 ..	39.5	156 04.1 ..	01.4	340 13.1 ..	50.4	Pollux	243 28.5	N27 59.6
04	203 35.8	197 10.6	37.8	30 57.7	39.8	171 06.2	01.5	355 15.6	50.4	Procyon	245 00.4	N 5 11.4
05	218 38.3	212 10.4	39.1	46 00.8	40.2	186 08.3	01.7	10 18.1	50.3			
06	233 40.8	227 10.3 N 2 40.4		61 03.8 N 7 40.5		201 10.4 N12 01.8		25 20.6 S 8 50.3		Rasalhague	96 07.5	N12 33.0
07	248 43.2	242 10.1	41.7	76 06.9	40.8	216 12.5	01.9	40 23.0	50.3	Regulus	207 44.2	N11 54.2
08	263 45.7	257 10.0	43.0	91 10.0	41.1	231 14.6	02.1	55 25.5	50.3	Rigel	281 12.8	S 8 11.5
T 09	278 48.2	272 09.8 ..	44.3	106 13.1 ..	41.4	246 16.7 ..	02.2	70 28.0 ..	50.3	Rigil Kent.	139 52.8	S60 52.9
U 10	293 50.6	287 09.7	45.6	121 16.2	41.7	261 18.8	02.3	85 30.5	50.2	Sabik	102 13.7	S15 44.3
E 11	308 53.1	302 09.6	46.9	136 19.2	42.0	276 20.9	02.5	100 33.0	50.2			
S 12	323 55.6	317 09.4 N 2 48.2		151 22.3 N 7 42.3		291 23.0 N12 02.6		115 35.5 S 8 50.2		Schedar	349 42.0	N56 36.5
D 13	338 58.0	332 09.3	49.5	166 25.4	42.6	306 25.1	02.7	130 38.0	50.2	Shaula	96 23.4	S37 06.6
A 14	354 00.5	347 09.1	50.8	181 28.5	42.9	321 27.2	02.8	145 40.5	50.2	Sirius	258 34.3	S16 44.2
Y 15	9 03.0	2 09.0 ..	52.1	196 31.6 ..	43.2	336 29.3 ..	03.0	160 43.0 ..	50.1	Spica	158 32.1	S11 13.6
16	24 05.4	17 08.8	53.4	211 34.6	43.5	351 31.4	03.1	175 45.4	50.1	Suhail	222 52.7	S43 29.1
17	39 07.9	32 08.7	54.7	226 37.7	43.8	6 33.6	03.3	190 47.9	50.1			
18	54 10.3	47 08.5 N 2 56.0		241 40.8 N 7 44.1		21 35.7 N12 03.4		205 50.4 S 8 50.1		Vega	80 39.9	N38 47.6
19	69 12.8	62 08.4	57.3	256 43.9	44.4	36 37.8	03.6	220 52.9	50.1	Zuben'ubi	137 06.4	S16 05.6
20	84 15.3	77 08.2	58.6	271 47.0	44.8	51 39.9	03.7	235 55.4	50.0		SHA	Mer. Pass.
21	99 17.7	92 08.1	2 59.9	286 50.1 ..	45.1	66 42.0 ..	03.8	250 57.9 ..	50.0		° ′	h m
22	114 20.2	107 07.9	3 01.2	301 53.2	45.4	81 44.1	04.0	266 00.4	50.0	Venus	354 48.0	14 51
23	129 22.7	122 07.8 N 3 02.5		316 56.3	45.7	96 46.2	04.1	281 02.9	50.0	Mars	187 05.3	2 02
	h m									Jupiter	327 40.2	16 37
Mer. Pass. 14 27.8		v −0.2 d 1.3		v 3.1 d 0.3		v 2.1 d 0.1		v 2.5 d 0.0		Saturn	151 39.1	4 23

UT	SUN GHA	Dec	MOON GHA	v	Dec	d	HP
12 00	176 27.0	S13 57.5	307 31.9	9.2	S10 24.8	12.2	59.6
01	191 27.0	56.7	322 00.1	9.0	10 37.0	12.1	59.6
02	206 27.0	55.9	336 28.1	9.1	10 49.1	12.0	59.6
03	221 27.0	.. 55.1	350 56.2	9.0	11 01.1	11.9	59.6
04	236 27.0	54.2	5 24.2	8.9	11 13.0	11.9	59.6
05	251 27.0	53.4	19 52.1	9.0	11 24.9	11.8	59.6
06	266 27.0	S13 52.6	34 20.1	8.8	S11 36.7	11.8	59.6
07	281 27.0	51.8	48 47.9	8.9	11 48.5	11.6	59.6
08	296 27.0	50.9	63 15.8	8.7	12 00.1	11.6	59.6
S 09	311 27.0	.. 50.1	77 43.5	8.8	12 11.7	11.6	59.6
U 10	326 27.0	49.3	92 11.3	8.7	12 23.3	11.4	59.6
N 11	341 27.0	48.5	106 39.0	8.6	12 34.7	11.4	59.6
D 12	356 27.0	S13 47.6	121 06.6	8.6	S12 46.1	11.3	59.6
A 13	11 27.0	46.8	135 34.2	8.6	12 57.4	11.2	59.6
Y 14	26 27.0	46.0	150 01.8	8.5	13 08.6	11.1	59.6
15	41 27.0	.. 45.1	164 29.3	8.5	13 19.7	11.1	59.5
16	56 27.0	44.3	178 56.8	8.4	13 30.8	10.9	59.5
17	71 27.0	43.5	193 24.2	8.4	13 41.7	10.9	59.5
18	86 27.0	S13 42.7	207 51.6	8.3	S13 52.6	10.8	59.5
19	101 27.0	41.8	222 18.9	8.3	14 03.4	10.7	59.5
20	116 27.0	41.0	236 46.2	8.2	14 14.1	10.6	59.5
21	131 27.0	.. 40.2	251 13.4	8.2	14 24.7	10.5	59.5
22	146 27.1	39.3	265 40.6	8.2	14 35.2	10.5	59.5
23	161 27.1	38.5	280 07.8	8.1	14 45.7	10.3	59.5
13 00	176 27.1	S13 37.7	294 34.9	8.0	S14 56.0	10.3	59.5
01	191 27.1	36.8	309 01.9	8.0	15 06.3	10.1	59.5
02	206 27.1	36.0	323 28.9	8.0	15 16.4	10.1	59.5
03	221 27.1	.. 35.2	337 55.9	7.9	15 26.5	9.9	59.5
04	236 27.1	34.3	352 22.8	7.8	15 36.4	9.9	59.5
05	251 27.1	33.5	6 49.6	7.9	15 46.3	9.8	59.5
06	266 27.1	S13 32.6	21 16.5	7.7	S15 56.1	9.6	59.5
07	281 27.1	31.8	35 43.2	7.8	16 05.7	9.6	59.5
M 08	296 27.2	31.0	50 10.0	7.6	16 15.3	9.4	59.4
O 09	311 27.2	.. 30.1	64 36.6	7.7	16 24.7	9.4	59.4
N 10	326 27.2	29.3	79 03.3	7.5	16 34.1	9.2	59.4
11	341 27.2	28.5	93 29.8	7.6	16 43.3	9.2	59.4
D 12	356 27.2	S13 27.6	107 56.4	7.5	S16 52.5	9.0	59.4
A 13	11 27.2	26.8	122 22.9	7.4	17 01.5	8.9	59.4
Y 14	26 27.2	25.9	136 49.3	7.4	17 10.4	8.9	59.4
15	41 27.2	.. 25.1	151 15.7	7.3	17 19.3	8.7	59.4
16	56 27.3	24.3	165 42.0	7.4	17 28.0	8.5	59.4
17	71 27.3	23.4	180 08.4	7.2	17 36.5	8.5	59.4
18	86 27.3	S13 22.6	194 34.6	7.2	S17 45.0	8.4	59.4
19	101 27.3	21.8	209 00.8	7.2	17 53.4	8.2	59.3
20	116 27.3	20.9	223 27.0	7.1	18 01.6	8.2	59.3
21	131 27.3	.. 20.1	237 53.1	7.1	18 09.8	8.0	59.3
22	146 27.4	19.2	252 19.2	7.1	18 17.8	7.9	59.3
23	161 27.4	18.4	266 45.3	7.0	18 25.7	7.8	59.3
14 00	176 27.4	S13 17.5	281 11.3	6.9	S18 33.5	7.6	59.3
01	191 27.4	16.7	295 37.2	7.0	18 41.1	7.6	59.3
02	206 27.4	15.9	310 03.2	6.8	18 48.7	7.4	59.3
03	221 27.4	.. 15.0	324 29.0	6.9	18 56.1	7.3	59.3
04	236 27.4	14.2	338 54.9	6.8	19 03.4	7.2	59.3
05	251 27.5	13.3	353 20.7	6.7	19 10.6	7.0	59.2
06	266 27.5	S13 12.5	7 46.4	6.8	S19 17.6	6.9	59.2
07	281 27.5	11.6	22 12.2	6.7	19 24.5	6.8	59.2
T 08	296 27.5	10.8	36 37.9	6.6	19 31.3	6.7	59.2
U 09	311 27.5	.. 09.9	51 03.5	6.6	19 38.0	6.6	59.2
E 10	326 27.6	09.1	65 29.1	6.6	19 44.6	6.4	59.2
S 11	341 27.6	08.2	79 54.7	6.5	19 51.0	6.3	59.2
D 12	356 27.6	S13 07.4	94 20.2	6.6	S19 57.3	6.1	59.2
A 13	11 27.6	06.6	108 45.8	6.4	20 03.4	6.0	59.2
Y 14	26 27.6	05.7	123 11.2	6.5	20 09.4	5.9	59.1
15	41 27.7	.. 04.9	137 36.7	6.4	20 15.3	5.8	59.1
16	56 27.7	04.0	152 02.1	6.4	20 21.1	5.6	59.1
17	71 27.7	03.2	166 27.5	6.3	20 26.7	5.5	59.1
18	86 27.7	S13 02.3	180 52.8	6.4	S20 32.2	5.4	59.1
19	101 27.7	01.5	195 18.2	6.3	20 37.6	5.2	59.1
20	116 27.8	13 00.6	209 43.5	6.2	20 42.8	5.1	59.1
21	131 27.8	12 59.8	224 08.7	6.3	20 47.9	5.0	59.1
22	146 27.8	58.9	238 34.0	6.2	20 52.9	4.8	59.0
23	161 27.8	58.1	252 59.2	6.2	S20 57.7	4.7	59.0
	SD 16.2	d 0.8	SD 16.2		16.2		16.1

Twilight / Sunrise / Moonrise

Lat.	Naut.	Civil	Sunrise	Moonrise 12	13	14	15
N 72	06 25	07 47	09 09	26 21	02 21	■	■
N 70	06 23	07 35	08 46	25 42	01 42	04 20	■
68	06 20	07 26	08 29	25 15	01 15	03 19	05 37
66	06 18	07 18	08 15	24 55	00 55	02 45	04 30
64	06 16	07 12	08 03	24 39	00 39	02 20	03 55
62	06 14	07 06	07 54	24 25	00 25	02 01	03 29
60	06 12	07 01	07 45	24 14	00 14	01 45	03 09
N 58	06 10	06 56	07 38	24 04	00 04	01 32	02 53
56	06 08	06 52	07 31	23 56	25 10	01 20	02 39
54	06 07	06 48	07 25	23 48	25 10	01 10	02 27
52	06 05	06 45	07 20	23 42	25 01	01 01	02 16
50	06 04	06 42	07 15	23 36	24 53	00 53	02 07
45	06 00	06 35	07 05	23 23	24 36	00 36	01 47
N 40	05 57	06 28	06 56	23 12	24 23	00 23	01 31
35	05 53	06 23	06 49	23 03	24 11	00 11	01 17
30	05 49	06 18	06 42	22 55	24 01	00 01	01 05
20	05 42	06 08	06 31	22 41	23 43	24 45	00 45
N 10	05 34	05 59	06 20	22 30	23 28	24 28	00 28
0	05 25	05 50	06 11	22 19	23 14	24 11	00 11
S 10	05 14	05 39	06 01	22 08	23 00	23 55	24 52
20	05 01	05 28	05 50	21 56	22 45	23 38	24 34
30	04 43	05 13	05 38	21 43	22 28	23 18	24 13
35	04 32	05 04	05 31	21 35	22 19	23 07	24 01
40	04 19	04 54	05 23	21 27	22 07	22 54	23 47
45	04 02	04 42	05 13	21 17	21 54	22 38	23 30
S 50	03 41	04 26	05 02	21 05	21 38	22 19	23 09
52	03 30	04 19	04 56	20 59	21 31	22 10	22 59
54	03 18	04 10	04 50	20 53	21 23	22 00	22 48
56	03 03	04 01	04 44	20 47	21 14	21 49	22 36
58	02 45	03 50	04 36	20 39	21 03	21 36	22 21
S 60	02 23	03 37	04 28	20 30	20 51	21 21	22 04

Sunset / Twilight / Moonset

Lat.	Sunset	Civil	Naut.	Moonset 12	13	14	15
N 72	15 21	16 44	18 05	07 02	06 23	■	■
N 70	15 43	16 55	18 08	07 22	07 04	06 24	■
68	16 01	17 04	18 10	07 38	07 32	07 25	07 08
66	16 15	17 11	18 12	07 51	07 54	08 00	08 15
64	16 26	17 18	18 14	08 02	08 11	08 25	08 51
62	16 36	17 24	18 16	08 11	08 25	08 45	09 17
60	16 44	17 29	18 18	08 19	08 37	09 02	09 37
N 58	16 52	17 33	18 19	08 26	08 47	09 15	09 54
56	16 58	17 37	18 21	08 33	08 57	09 27	10 08
54	17 04	17 41	18 23	08 38	09 05	09 38	10 20
52	17 09	17 44	18 24	08 43	09 12	09 47	10 31
50	17 14	17 47	18 25	08 48	09 19	09 56	10 41
45	17 24	17 54	18 29	08 58	09 33	10 13	11 01
N 40	17 33	18 01	18 32	09 07	09 45	10 28	11 18
35	17 40	18 06	18 36	09 14	09 55	10 40	11 31
30	17 47	18 11	18 39	09 20	10 04	10 51	11 44
20	17 58	18 21	18 47	09 31	10 19	11 10	12 04
N 10	18 08	18 30	18 56	09 41	10 32	11 26	12 22
0	18 18	18 39	19 04	09 50	10 45	11 41	12 39
S 10	18 27	18 49	19 14	09 59	10 57	11 57	12 56
20	18 38	19 01	19 27	10 09	11 11	12 13	13 14
30	18 50	19 15	19 44	10 21	11 26	12 32	13 35
35	18 57	19 23	19 55	10 27	11 35	12 43	13 47
40	19 05	19 34	20 08	10 35	11 46	12 55	14 01
45	19 14	19 46	20 25	10 43	11 58	13 10	14 17
S 50	19 26	20 01	20 46	10 54	12 13	13 28	14 38
52	19 31	20 08	20 56	10 59	12 20	13 37	14 48
54	19 37	20 17	21 09	11 04	12 27	13 47	14 59
56	19 43	20 26	21 23	11 10	12 36	13 58	15 11
58	19 50	20 37	21 40	11 17	12 46	14 10	15 25
S 60	19 59	20 49	22 02	11 24	12 57	14 25	15 42

SUN — MOON

Day	Eqn. of Time 00h	Eqn. of Time 12h	Mer. Pass.	Mer. Pass. Upper	Lower	Age	Phase
d	m s	m s	h m	h m	h m	d	%
12	14 12	14 12	12 14	03 38	16 04	20	74
13	14 12	14 11	12 14	04 32	16 59	21	64
14	14 11	14 10	12 14	05 28	17 56	22	53

UT	ARIES GHA	VENUS −4.2 GHA	Dec	MARS −0.9 GHA	Dec	JUPITER −2.3 GHA	Dec	SATURN +0.5 GHA	Dec	STARS Name	SHA	Dec
15 00	144 25.1	137 07.6	N 3 03.8	331 59.4	N 7 46.0	111 48.3	N12 04.2	296 05.4	S 8 49.9	Acamar	315 19.1	S40 15.6
01	159 27.6	152 07.5	05.2	347 02.5	46.3	126 50.4	04.4	311 07.9	49.9	Achernar	335 27.7	S57 10.7
02	174 30.1	167 07.3	06.5	2 05.6	46.6	141 52.5	04.5	326 10.3	49.9	Acrux	173 09.8	S63 09.9
03	189 32.5	182 07.2	.. 07.8	17 08.7	.. 46.9	156 54.6	.. 04.6	341 12.8	.. 49.9	Adhara	255 13.0	S28 59.6
04	204 35.0	197 07.0	09.1	32 11.8	47.2	171 56.7	04.8	356 15.3	49.9	Aldebaran	290 50.3	N16 31.9
05	219 37.4	212 06.9	10.4	47 14.9	47.6	186 58.8	04.9	11 17.8	49.8			
W 06	234 39.9	227 06.8	N 3 11.7	62 18.0	N 7 47.9	202 00.9	N12 05.1	26 20.3	S 8 49.8	Alioth	166 21.1	N55 53.3
E 07	249 42.4	242 06.6	13.0	77 21.1	48.2	217 03.0	05.2	41 22.8	49.8	Alkaid	152 59.4	N49 14.8
D 08	264 44.8	257 06.5	14.3	92 24.2	48.5	232 05.1	05.3	56 25.3	49.8	Al Na'ir	27 45.3	S46 54.1
N 09	279 47.3	272 06.3	.. 15.6	107 27.3	.. 48.8	247 07.2	.. 05.5	71 27.8	.. 49.8	Alnilam	275 47.1	S 1 11.9
E 10	294 49.8	287 06.2	16.9	122 30.4	49.1	262 09.3	05.6	86 30.3	49.7	Alphard	217 56.7	S 8 42.9
S 11	309 52.2	302 06.0	18.2	137 33.5	49.4	277 11.4	05.7	101 32.8	49.7			
D 12	324 54.7	317 05.9	N 3 19.5	152 36.6	N 7 49.8	292 13.5	N12 05.9	116 35.3	S 8 49.7	Alphecca	126 11.8	N26 40.2
A 13	339 57.2	332 05.7	20.8	167 39.7	50.1	307 15.6	06.0	131 37.8	49.7	Alpheratz	357 44.7	N29 09.6
Y 14	354 59.6	347 05.6	22.1	182 42.8	50.4	322 17.7	06.2	146 40.3	49.6	Altair	62 09.4	N 8 54.0
15	10 02.1	2 05.4	.. 23.4	197 45.9	.. 50.7	337 19.8	.. 06.3	161 42.7	.. 49.6	Ankaa	353 16.9	S42 14.5
16	25 04.6	17 05.3	24.7	212 49.0	51.0	352 21.9	06.4	176 45.2	49.6	Antares	112 27.5	S26 27.4
17	40 07.0	32 05.2	26.0	227 52.2	51.3	7 24.0	06.6	191 47.7	49.6			
18	55 09.5	47 05.0	N 3 27.3	242 55.3	N 7 51.7	22 26.1	N12 06.7	206 50.2	S 8 49.6	Arcturus	145 56.4	N19 06.9
19	70 11.9	62 04.9	28.6	257 58.4	52.0	37 28.2	06.8	221 52.7	49.5	Atria	107 30.3	S69 02.6
20	85 14.4	77 04.7	29.9	273 01.5	52.3	52 30.3	07.0	236 55.2	49.5	Avior	234 17.8	S59 33.2
21	100 16.9	92 04.6	.. 31.2	288 04.6	.. 52.6	67 32.4	.. 07.1	251 57.7	.. 49.5	Bellatrix	278 32.8	N 6 21.5
22	115 19.3	107 04.4	32.5	303 07.8	52.9	82 34.5	07.3	267 00.2	49.5	Betelgeuse	271 02.1	N 7 24.4
23	130 21.8	122 04.3	33.8	318 10.9	53.2	97 36.6	07.4	282 02.7	49.4			
16 00	145 24.3	137 04.2	N 3 35.1	333 14.0	N 7 53.6	112 38.7	N12 07.5	297 05.2	S 8 49.4	Canopus	263 56.2	S52 42.5
01	160 26.7	152 04.0	36.4	348 17.1	53.9	127 40.8	07.7	312 07.7	49.4	Capella	280 35.6	N46 00.7
02	175 29.2	167 03.9	37.7	3 20.2	54.2	142 42.9	07.8	327 10.2	49.4	Deneb	49 32.6	N45 19.4
03	190 31.7	182 03.7	.. 39.0	18 23.4	.. 54.5	157 45.0	.. 07.9	342 12.7	.. 49.3	Denebola	182 34.3	N14 30.0
04	205 34.1	197 03.6	40.3	33 26.5	54.8	172 47.1	08.1	357 15.2	49.3	Diphda	348 57.0	S17 55.3
05	220 36.6	212 03.4	41.6	48 29.6	55.2	187 49.2	08.2	12 17.7	49.3			
06	235 39.1	227 03.3	N 3 42.9	63 32.8	N 7 55.5	202 51.3	N12 08.4	27 20.2	S 8 49.3	Dubhe	193 52.1	N61 40.8
T 07	250 41.5	242 03.2	44.2	78 35.9	55.8	217 53.4	08.5	42 22.7	49.3	Elnath	278 13.6	N28 37.0
H 08	265 44.0	257 03.0	45.5	93 39.0	56.1	232 55.5	08.6	57 25.2	49.2	Eltanin	90 46.9	N51 29.0
U 09	280 46.4	272 02.9	.. 46.8	108 42.1	.. 56.4	247 57.6	.. 08.8	72 27.7	.. 49.2	Enif	33 48.3	N 9 55.9
R 10	295 48.9	287 02.7	48.1	123 45.3	56.8	262 59.7	08.9	87 30.2	49.2	Fomalhaut	15 25.3	S29 33.5
S 11	310 51.4	302 02.6	49.4	138 48.4	57.1	278 01.7	09.0	102 32.7	49.2			
D 12	325 53.8	317 02.4	N 3 50.7	153 51.5	N 7 57.4	293 03.8	N12 09.2	117 35.2	S 8 49.1	Gacrux	172 01.5	S57 10.8
A 13	340 56.3	332 02.3	52.0	168 54.7	57.7	308 05.9	09.3	132 37.6	49.1	Gienah	175 53.0	S17 36.7
Y 14	355 58.8	347 02.2	53.3	183 57.8	58.1	323 08.0	09.5	147 40.1	49.1	Hadar	148 49.0	S60 25.7
15	11 01.2	2 02.0	.. 54.6	199 01.0	.. 58.4	338 10.1	.. 09.6	162 42.6	.. 49.1	Hamal	328 01.9	N23 31.2
16	26 03.7	17 01.9	55.9	214 04.1	58.7	353 12.2	09.7	177 45.1	49.0	Kaus Aust.	83 45.3	S34 22.6
17	41 06.2	32 01.7	57.2	229 07.2	59.0	8 14.3	09.9	192 47.6	49.0			
18	56 08.6	47 01.6	N 3 58.5	244 10.4	N 7 59.4	23 16.4	N12 10.0	207 50.1	S 8 49.0	Kochab	137 19.7	N74 06.0
19	71 11.1	62 01.5	3 59.8	259 13.5	7 59.7	38 18.5	10.2	222 52.6	49.0	Markab	13 39.6	N15 16.3
20	86 13.6	77 01.3	4 01.1	274 16.7	8 00.0	53 20.6	10.3	237 55.1	48.9	Menkar	314 16.0	N 4 08.2
21	101 16.0	92 01.2	.. 02.4	289 19.8	.. 00.3	68 22.7	.. 10.4	252 57.6	.. 48.9	Menkent	148 08.5	S36 25.7
22	116 18.5	107 01.0	03.7	304 23.0	00.7	83 24.8	10.6	268 00.1	48.9	Miaplacidus	221 39.0	S69 46.2
23	131 20.9	122 00.9	05.0	319 26.1	01.0	98 26.9	10.7	283 02.6	48.9			
17 00	146 23.4	137 00.8	N 4 06.3	334 29.3	N 8 01.3	113 29.0	N12 10.8	298 05.1	S 8 48.9	Mirfak	308 41.7	N49 54.4
01	161 25.9	152 00.6	07.5	349 32.4	01.6	128 31.1	11.0	313 07.6	48.8	Nunki	75 59.7	S26 16.8
02	176 28.3	167 00.5	08.8	4 35.6	02.0	143 33.1	11.1	328 10.1	48.8	Peacock	53 21.2	S56 41.6
03	191 30.8	182 00.3	.. 10.1	19 38.7	.. 02.3	158 35.2	.. 11.3	343 12.6	.. 48.8	Pollux	243 28.5	N27 59.6
04	206 33.3	197 00.2	11.4	34 41.9	02.6	173 37.3	11.4	358 15.1	48.8	Procyon	245 00.4	N 5 11.4
05	221 35.7	212 00.1	12.7	49 45.0	03.0	188 39.4	11.5	13 17.6	48.7			
06	236 38.2	226 59.9	N 4 14.0	64 48.2	N 8 03.3	203 41.5	N12 11.7	28 20.1	S 8 48.7	Rasalhague	96 07.5	N12 33.0
07	251 40.7	241 59.8	15.3	79 51.3	03.6	218 43.6	11.8	43 22.6	48.7	Regulus	207 44.1	N11 54.2
08	266 43.1	256 59.6	16.6	94 54.5	03.9	233 45.7	12.0	58 25.1	48.7	Rigel	281 12.8	S 8 11.5
F 09	281 45.6	271 59.5	.. 17.9	109 57.7	.. 04.3	248 47.8	.. 12.1	73 27.6	.. 48.6	Rigil Kent.	139 52.8	S60 52.9
R 10	296 48.1	286 59.4	19.2	125 00.8	04.6	263 49.9	12.2	88 30.1	48.6	Sabik	102 13.7	S15 44.3
I 11	311 50.5	301 59.2	20.5	140 04.0	04.9	278 52.0	12.4	103 32.6	48.6			
D 12	326 53.0	316 59.1	N 4 21.8	155 07.1	N 8 05.3	293 54.1	N12 12.5	118 35.1	S 8 48.6	Schedar	349 42.0	N56 36.5
A 13	341 55.4	331 58.9	23.1	170 10.3	05.6	308 56.1	12.7	133 37.6	48.5	Shaula	96 23.3	S37 06.6
Y 14	356 57.9	346 58.8	24.4	185 13.5	05.9	323 58.2	12.8	148 40.1	48.5	Sirius	258 34.3	S16 44.3
15	12 00.4	1 58.7	.. 25.7	200 16.6	.. 06.2	339 00.3	.. 12.9	163 42.6	.. 48.5	Spica	158 32.0	S11 13.6
16	27 02.8	16 58.5	27.0	215 19.8	06.6	354 02.4	13.1	178 45.1	48.5	Suhail	222 52.7	S43 29.1
17	42 05.3	31 58.4	28.3	230 23.0	06.9	9 04.5	13.2	193 47.6	48.4			
18	57 07.8	46 58.3	N 4 29.6	245 26.1	N 8 07.2	24 06.6	N12 13.4	208 50.1	S 8 48.4	Vega	80 39.9	N38 47.6
19	72 10.2	61 58.1	30.9	260 29.3	07.6	39 08.7	13.5	223 52.6	48.4	Zuben'ubi	137 06.4	S16 05.6
20	87 12.7	76 58.0	32.2	275 32.5	07.9	54 10.8	13.6	238 55.2	48.4		SHA	Mer.Pass.
21	102 15.2	91 57.8	.. 33.5	290 35.6	.. 08.2	69 12.9	.. 13.8	253 57.7	.. 48.3		° ′	h m
22	117 17.6	106 57.7	34.7	305 38.8	08.6	84 14.9	13.9	269 00.2	48.3	Venus	351 39.9	14 52
23	132 20.1	121 57.6	36.0	320 42.0	08.9	99 17.0	14.1	284 02.7	48.3	Mars	187 49.7	1 47
Mer.Pass.	h m 14 16.0	v −0.1	d 1.3	v 3.1	d 0.3	v 2.1	d 0.1	v 2.5	d 0.0	Jupiter	327 14.4	16 27
										Saturn	151 40.9	4 11

SUN / MOON

UT	SUN GHA	SUN Dec	MOON GHA	v	MOON Dec	d	HP
15 00	176 27.9	S12 57.2	267 24.4	6.2	S21 02.4	4.5	59.0
01	191 27.9	56.4	281 49.6	6.1	21 06.9	4.4	59.0
02	206 27.9	55.5	296 14.7	6.2	21 11.3	4.3	59.0
03	221 27.9 ..	54.6	310 39.9	6.1	21 15.6	4.1	59.0
04	236 28.0	53.8	325 05.0	6.1	21 19.7	4.0	59.0
05	251 28.0	52.9	339 30.1	6.1	21 23.7	3.9	59.0
W 06	266 28.0	S12 52.1	353 55.2	6.0	S21 27.6	3.7	58.9
E 07	281 28.0	51.2	8 20.2	6.1	21 31.3	3.6	58.9
D 08	296 28.1	50.4	22 45.3	6.0	21 34.9	3.4	58.9
N 09	311 28.1 ..	49.5	37 10.3	6.0	21 38.3	3.3	58.9
E 10	326 28.1	48.7	51 35.3	6.1	21 41.6	3.1	58.9
S 11	341 28.1	47.8	66 00.4	6.0	21 44.7	3.1	58.9
D 12	356 28.2	S12 47.0	80 25.4	5.9	S21 47.8	2.8	58.9
A 13	11 28.2	46.1	94 50.3	6.0	21 50.6	2.7	58.8
Y 14	26 28.2	45.2	109 15.3	6.0	21 53.3	2.6	58.8
15	41 28.3 ..	44.4	123 40.3	6.0	21 55.9	2.5	58.8
16	56 28.3	43.5	138 05.3	6.0	21 58.4	2.3	58.8
17	71 28.3	42.7	152 30.3	5.9	22 00.7	2.1	58.8
18	86 28.3	S12 41.8	166 55.2	6.0	S22 02.8	2.0	58.8
19	101 28.4	41.0	181 20.2	6.0	22 04.8	1.9	58.8
20	116 28.4	40.1	195 45.2	5.9	22 06.7	1.7	58.7
21	131 28.4 ..	39.2	210 10.1	6.0	22 08.4	1.6	58.7
22	146 28.5	38.4	224 35.1	6.0	22 10.0	1.4	58.7
23	161 28.5	37.5	239 00.1	6.0	22 11.4	1.3	58.7
16 00	176 28.5	S12 36.7	253 25.1	6.0	S22 12.7	1.2	58.7
01	191 28.6	35.8	267 50.1	6.0	22 13.9	1.0	58.7
02	206 28.6	34.9	282 15.1	6.0	22 14.9	0.8	58.7
03	221 28.6 ..	34.1	296 40.1	6.0	22 15.7	0.7	58.6
04	236 28.6	33.2	311 05.1	6.0	22 16.4	0.6	58.6
05	251 28.7	32.4	325 30.1	6.0	22 17.0	0.5	58.6
06	266 28.7	S12 31.5	339 55.1	6.1	S22 17.5	0.2	58.6
T 07	281 28.7	30.6	354 20.2	6.1	22 17.7	0.2	58.6
H 08	296 28.8	29.8	8 45.3	6.1	22 17.9	0.0	58.6
U 09	311 28.8 ..	28.9	23 10.4	6.1	22 17.9	0.1	58.5
R 10	326 28.8	28.0	37 35.5	6.1	22 17.8	0.3	58.5
S 11	341 28.9	27.2	52 00.6	6.1	22 17.5	0.4	58.5
D 12	356 28.9	S12 26.3	66 25.7	6.2	S22 17.1	0.6	58.5
A 13	11 29.0	25.4	80 50.9	6.2	22 16.5	0.7	58.5
Y 14	26 29.0	24.6	95 16.1	6.2	22 15.8	0.9	58.5
15	41 29.0 ..	23.7	109 41.3	6.3	22 14.9	1.0	58.4
16	56 29.1	22.8	124 06.6	6.2	22 13.9	1.1	58.4
17	71 29.1	22.0	138 31.8	6.3	22 12.8	1.2	58.4
18	86 29.1	S12 21.1	152 57.1	6.4	S22 11.6	1.5	58.4
19	101 29.2	20.2	167 22.5	6.3	22 10.1	1.5	58.4
20	116 29.2	19.4	181 47.8	6.4	22 08.6	1.7	58.4
21	131 29.2 ..	18.5	196 13.2	6.5	22 06.9	1.8	58.4
22	146 29.3	17.6	210 38.7	6.4	22 05.1	2.0	58.3
23	161 29.3	16.8	225 04.1	6.5	22 03.1	2.1	58.3
17 00	176 29.4	S12 15.9	239 29.6	6.6	S22 01.0	2.2	58.3
01	191 29.4	15.0	253 55.2	6.5	21 58.8	2.4	58.3
02	206 29.4	14.2	268 20.7	6.7	21 56.4	2.5	58.3
03	221 29.5 ..	13.3	282 46.4	6.6	21 53.9	2.6	58.3
04	236 29.5	12.4	297 12.0	6.7	21 51.3	2.8	58.2
05	251 29.6	11.6	311 37.7	6.8	21 48.5	2.9	58.2
06	266 29.6	S12 10.7	326 03.5	6.7	S21 45.6	3.0	58.2
07	281 29.6	09.8	340 29.2	6.9	21 42.6	3.2	58.2
F 08	296 29.7	08.9	354 55.1	6.8	21 39.4	3.3	58.2
R 09	311 29.7 ..	08.1	9 20.9	7.0	21 36.1	3.5	58.2
I 10	326 29.8	07.2	23 46.9	6.9	21 32.6	3.5	58.1
D 11	341 29.8	06.3	38 12.8	7.1	21 29.1	3.7	58.1
A 12	356 29.8	S12 05.5	52 38.9	7.0	S21 25.4	3.9	58.1
Y 13	11 29.9	04.6	67 04.9	7.2	21 21.5	3.9	58.1
14	26 29.9	03.7	81 31.1	7.1	21 17.6	4.1	58.1
15	41 30.0 ..	02.8	95 57.2	7.3	21 13.5	4.2	58.0
16	56 30.0	02.0	110 23.5	7.2	21 09.3	4.3	58.0
17	71 30.1	01.1	124 49.7	7.4	21 05.0	4.5	58.0
18	86 30.1	S12 00.2	139 16.1	7.4	S21 00.5	4.6	58.0
19	101 30.1	11 59.3	153 42.5	7.4	20 55.9	4.7	58.0
20	116 30.2	58.5	168 08.9	7.5	20 51.2	4.8	57.9
21	131 30.2 ..	57.6	182 35.4	7.6	20 46.4	5.0	57.9
22	146 30.3	56.7	197 02.0	7.6	20 41.4	5.0	57.9
23	161 30.3	55.8	211 28.6	7.7	S20 36.4	5.2	57.9
	SD 16.2	d 0.9	SD 16.0		15.9		15.8

Twilight / Moonrise

Lat.	Naut.	Civil	Sunrise	Moonrise 15	16	17	18
N 72	06 13	07 33	08 51	■	■	■	■
N 70	06 11	07 23	08 32	■	■	■	08 43
68	06 10	07 15	08 16	05 37	■	07 48	07 28
66	06 08	07 08	08 04	04 30	05 52	06 35	06 51
64	06 07	07 03	07 54	03 55	05 10	05 58	06 24
62	06 06	06 58	07 45	03 29	04 41	05 32	06 04
60	06 05	06 53	07 37	03 09	04 19	05 11	05 47
N 58	06 03	06 49	07 30	02 53	04 01	04 54	05 32
56	06 02	06 46	07 24	02 39	03 46	04 40	05 20
54	06 01	06 42	07 19	02 27	03 33	04 27	05 09
52	06 00	06 39	07 14	02 16	03 22	04 16	05 00
50	05 59	06 37	07 10	02 07	03 12	04 07	04 51
45	05 56	06 30	07 00	01 47	02 51	03 46	04 33
N 40	05 53	06 25	06 52	01 31	02 34	03 30	04 18
35	05 50	06 20	06 46	01 17	02 19	03 16	04 06
30	05 47	06 15	06 40	01 05	02 07	03 03	03 55
20	05 41	06 06	06 29	00 45	01 45	02 43	03 36
N 10	05 33	05 58	06 20	00 28	01 27	02 24	03 19
0	05 25	05 49	06 11	00 11	01 10	02 08	03 04
S 10	05 15	05 40	06 02	24 52	00 52	01 51	02 48
20	05 02	05 29	05 52	24 34	00 34	01 32	02 32
30	04 46	05 16	05 41	24 13	00 13	01 12	02 13
35	04 36	05 08	05 34	24 01	00 01	00 59	02 01
40	04 23	04 58	05 27	23 47	24 45	00 45	01 49
45	04 08	04 46	05 18	23 30	24 29	00 29	01 33
S 50	03 48	04 32	05 07	23 09	24 08	00 08	01 15
52	03 38	04 25	05 02	22 59	23 58	25 06	01 06
54	03 26	04 17	04 57	22 48	23 47	24 56	00 56
56	03 13	04 08	04 51	22 36	23 35	24 45	00 45
58	02 57	03 58	04 44	22 21	23 20	24 32	00 32
S 60	02 37	03 47	04 36	22 04	23 03	24 17	00 17

Sunset / Twilight / Moonset

Lat.	Sunset	Civil	Naut.	Moonset 15	16	17	18
N 72	15 39	16 57	18 18	■	■	■	■
N 70	15 58	17 07	18 19	■	■		10 01
68	16 13	17 15	18 20	07 08	■	09 00	11 15
66	16 26	17 21	18 21	08 15	08 55	10 13	11 52
64	16 36	17 27	18 22	08 51	09 37	10 49	12 18
62	16 45	17 32	18 24	09 17	10 06	11 15	12 38
60	16 52	17 36	18 25	09 37	10 28	11 35	12 55
N 58	16 59	17 40	18 26	09 54	10 46	11 52	13 08
56	17 05	17 43	18 27	10 08	11 01	12 06	13 20
54	17 10	17 47	18 28	10 20	11 14	12 18	13 31
52	17 15	17 50	18 29	10 31	11 25	12 29	13 40
50	17 19	17 52	18 30	10 41	11 35	12 39	13 48
45	17 28	17 59	18 33	11 01	11 56	12 59	14 05
N 40	17 36	18 04	18 36	11 18	12 14	13 15	14 19
35	17 43	18 09	18 39	11 31	12 28	13 29	14 31
30	17 49	18 13	18 41	11 44	12 40	13 40	14 42
20	17 59	18 22	18 48	12 04	13 02	14 01	15 00
N 10	18 09	18 30	18 55	12 22	13 20	14 18	15 15
0	18 17	18 39	19 03	12 39	13 37	14 35	15 30
S 10	18 26	18 48	19 13	12 56	13 55	14 51	15 44
20	18 36	18 59	19 25	13 14	14 13	15 08	15 59
30	18 47	19 12	19 41	13 35	14 34	15 28	16 17
35	18 54	19 20	19 52	13 47	14 47	15 40	16 27
40	19 01	19 29	20 04	14 01	15 01	15 53	16 38
45	19 10	19 41	20 19	14 17	15 18	16 09	16 52
S 50	19 20	19 55	20 39	14 38	15 38	16 28	17 08
52	19 25	20 02	20 49	14 48	15 48	16 37	17 16
54	19 30	20 09	21 00	14 59	15 59	16 47	17 24
56	19 36	20 18	21 13	15 11	16 12	16 59	17 34
58	19 43	20 28	21 29	15 25	16 26	17 12	17 45
S 60	19 50	20 39	21 48	15 42	16 44	17 27	17 57

SUN / MOON

Day	Eqn. of Time 00h	Eqn. of Time 12h	Mer. Pass.	Mer. Pass. Upper	Mer. Pass. Lower	Age	Phase
	m s	m s	h m	h m	h m	d	%
15	14 09	14 07	12 14	06 25	18 54	23	41
16	14 06	14 04	12 14	07 24	19 53	24	31
17	14 03	14 01	12 14	08 21	20 49	25	21

UT	ARIES GHA	VENUS −4.2 GHA	VENUS Dec	MARS −1.0 GHA	MARS Dec	JUPITER −2.2 GHA	JUPITER Dec	SATURN +0.5 GHA	SATURN Dec
18 00	147 22.5	136 57.4	N 4 37.3	335 45.2	N 8 09.2	114 19.1	N12 14.2	299 05.2	S 8 48.3
01	162 25.0	151 57.3	38.6	350 48.3	09.6	129 21.2	14.4	314 07.7	48.2
02	177 27.5	166 57.2	39.9	5 51.5	09.9	144 23.3	14.5	329 10.2	48.2
03	192 29.9	181 57.0	.. 41.2	20 54.7	.. 10.2	159 25.4	.. 14.6	344 12.7	.. 48.2
04	207 32.4	196 56.9	42.5	35 57.9	10.6	174 27.5	14.8	359 15.2	48.1
05	222 34.9	211 56.7	43.8	51 01.0	10.9	189 29.5	14.9	14 17.7	48.1
S 06	237 37.3	226 56.6	N 4 45.1	66 04.2	N 8 11.2	204 31.6	N12 15.1	29 20.2	S 8 48.1
A 07	252 39.8	241 56.5	46.4	81 07.4	11.6	219 33.7	15.2	44 22.7	48.1
T 08	267 42.3	256 56.3	47.7	96 10.6	11.9	234 35.8	15.3	59 25.2	48.0
U 09	282 44.7	271 56.2	.. 49.0	111 13.8	.. 12.3	249 37.9	.. 15.5	74 27.7	.. 48.0
R 10	297 47.2	286 56.1	50.3	126 17.0	12.6	264 40.0	15.6	89 30.2	48.0
U 11	312 49.7	301 55.9	51.5	141 20.1	12.9	279 42.1	15.8	104 32.7	48.0
R 12	327 52.1	316 55.8	N 4 52.8	156 23.3	N 8 13.3	294 44.1	N12 15.9	119 35.2	S 8 47.9
D 13	342 54.6	331 55.7	54.1	171 26.5	13.6	309 46.2	16.0	134 37.7	47.9
A 14	357 57.0	346 55.5	55.4	186 29.7	13.9	324 48.3	16.2	149 40.2	47.9
Y 15	12 59.5	1 55.4	.. 56.7	201 32.9	.. 14.3	339 50.4	.. 16.3	164 42.7	.. 47.9
16	28 02.0	16 55.3	58.0	216 36.1	14.6	354 52.5	16.5	179 45.2	47.8
17	43 04.4	31 55.1	4 59.3	231 39.3	15.0	9 54.6	16.6	194 47.7	47.8
18	58 06.9	46 55.0	N 5 00.6	246 42.5	N 8 15.3	24 56.6	N12 16.8	209 50.3	S 8 47.8
19	73 09.4	61 54.9	01.9	261 45.7	15.6	39 58.7	16.9	224 52.8	47.8
20	88 11.8	76 54.7	03.2	276 48.9	16.0	55 00.8	17.0	239 55.3	47.7
21	103 14.3	91 54.6	.. 04.4	291 52.1	.. 16.3	70 02.9	.. 17.2	254 57.8	.. 47.7
22	118 16.8	106 54.4	05.7	306 55.3	16.7	85 05.0	17.3	270 00.3	47.7
23	133 19.2	121 54.3	07.0	321 58.5	17.0	100 07.1	17.5	285 02.8	47.6
19 00	148 21.7	136 54.2	N 5 08.3	337 01.7	N 8 17.3	115 09.1	N12 17.6	300 05.3	S 8 47.6
01	163 24.2	151 54.0	09.6	352 04.9	17.7	130 11.2	17.7	315 07.8	47.6
02	178 26.6	166 53.9	10.9	7 08.1	18.0	145 13.3	17.9	330 10.3	47.6
03	193 29.1	181 53.8	.. 12.2	22 11.3	.. 18.4	160 15.4	.. 18.0	345 12.8	.. 47.5
04	208 31.5	196 53.6	13.5	37 14.5	18.7	175 17.5	18.2	0 15.3	47.5
05	223 34.0	211 53.5	14.8	52 17.7	19.0	190 19.5	18.3	15 17.8	47.5
S 06	238 36.5	226 53.4	N 5 16.0	67 20.9	N 8 19.4	205 21.6	N12 18.5	30 20.3	S 8 47.5
U 07	253 38.9	241 53.2	17.3	82 24.1	19.7	220 23.7	18.6	45 22.8	47.4
N 08	268 41.4	256 53.1	18.6	97 27.3	20.1	235 25.8	18.7	60 25.4	47.4
D 09	283 43.9	271 53.0	.. 19.9	112 30.5	.. 20.4	250 27.9	.. 18.9	75 27.9	.. 47.4
A 10	298 46.3	286 52.8	21.2	127 33.7	20.7	265 29.9	19.0	90 30.4	47.3
Y 11	313 48.8	301 52.7	22.5	142 36.9	21.1	280 32.0	19.2	105 32.9	47.3
12	328 51.3	316 52.6	N 5 23.8	157 40.1	N 8 21.4	295 34.1	N12 19.3	120 35.4	S 8 47.3
13	343 53.7	331 52.4	25.0	172 43.3	21.8	310 36.2	19.5	135 37.9	47.3
14	358 56.2	346 52.3	26.3	187 46.6	22.1	325 38.3	19.6	150 40.4	47.2
15	13 58.7	1 52.2	.. 27.6	202 49.8	.. 22.5	340 40.3	.. 19.7	165 42.9	.. 47.2
16	29 01.1	16 52.0	28.9	217 53.0	22.8	355 42.4	19.9	180 45.4	47.2
17	44 03.6	31 51.9	30.2	232 56.2	23.1	10 44.5	20.0	195 47.9	47.1
18	59 06.0	46 51.8	N 5 31.5	247 59.4	N 8 23.5	25 46.6	N12 20.2	210 50.5	S 8 47.1
19	74 08.5	61 51.6	32.8	263 02.6	23.8	40 48.6	20.3	225 53.0	47.1
20	89 11.0	76 51.5	34.0	278 05.9	24.2	55 50.7	20.5	240 55.5	47.1
21	104 13.4	91 51.4	.. 35.3	293 09.1	.. 24.5	70 52.8	.. 20.6	255 58.0	.. 47.0
22	119 15.9	106 51.3	36.6	308 12.3	24.9	85 54.9	20.7	271 00.5	47.0
23	134 18.4	121 51.1	37.9	323 15.5	25.2	100 57.0	20.9	286 03.0	47.0
20 00	149 20.8	136 51.0	N 5 39.2	338 18.7	N 8 25.6	115 59.0	N12 21.0	301 05.5	S 8 46.9
01	164 23.3	151 50.9	40.5	353 22.0	25.9	131 01.1	21.2	316 08.0	46.9
02	179 25.8	166 50.7	41.7	8 25.2	26.3	146 03.2	21.3	331 10.5	46.9
03	194 28.2	181 50.6	.. 43.0	23 28.4	.. 26.6	161 05.3	.. 21.5	346 13.1	.. 46.9
04	209 30.7	196 50.5	44.3	38 31.6	26.9	176 07.3	21.6	1 15.6	46.8
05	224 33.1	211 50.3	45.6	53 34.9	27.3	191 09.4	21.7	16 18.1	46.8
M 06	239 35.6	226 50.2	N 5 46.9	68 38.1	N 8 27.6	206 11.5	N12 21.9	31 20.6	S 8 46.8
O 07	254 38.1	241 50.1	48.2	83 41.3	28.0	221 13.6	22.0	46 23.1	46.7
N 08	269 40.5	256 49.9	49.4	98 44.6	28.3	236 15.6	22.2	61 25.6	46.7
D 09	284 43.0	271 49.8	.. 50.7	113 47.8	.. 28.7	251 17.7	.. 22.3	76 28.1	.. 46.7
A 10	299 45.5	286 49.7	52.0	128 51.0	29.0	266 19.8	22.5	91 30.6	46.7
Y 11	314 47.9	301 49.5	53.3	143 54.3	29.4	281 21.9	22.6	106 33.2	46.6
12	329 50.4	316 49.4	N 5 54.6	158 57.5	N 8 29.7	296 23.9	N12 22.8	121 35.7	S 8 46.6
13	344 52.9	331 49.3	55.9	174 00.7	30.1	311 26.0	22.9	136 38.2	46.6
14	359 55.3	346 49.2	57.1	189 04.0	30.4	326 28.1	23.0	151 40.7	46.5
15	14 57.8	1 49.0	.. 58.4	204 07.2	.. 30.8	341 30.2	.. 23.2	166 43.2	.. 46.5
16	30 00.3	16 48.9	5 59.7	219 10.4	31.1	356 32.2	23.3	181 45.7	46.5
17	45 02.7	31 48.8	6 01.0	234 13.7	31.5	11 34.3	23.5	196 48.2	46.5
18	60 05.2	46 48.6	N 6 02.3	249 16.9	N 8 31.8	26 36.4	N12 23.6	211 50.8	S 8 46.4
19	75 07.6	61 48.5	03.6	264 20.2	32.2	41 38.4	23.8	226 53.3	46.4
20	90 10.1	76 48.4	04.8	279 23.4	32.5	56 40.5	23.9	241 55.8	46.4
21	105 12.6	91 48.2	.. 06.1	294 26.6	.. 32.9	71 42.6	.. 24.1	256 58.3	.. 46.3
22	120 15.0	106 48.1	07.4	309 29.9	33.2	86 44.7	24.2	272 00.8	46.3
23	135 17.5	121 48.0	08.6	324 33.1	33.6	101 46.7	24.3	287 03.3	46.3
Mer.Pass.	14 04.2	v −0.1	d 1.3	v 3.2	d 0.3	v 2.1	d 0.1	v 2.5	d 0.0

STARS

Name	SHA	Dec
Acamar	315 19.1	S40 15.6
Achernar	335 27.7	S57 10.7
Acrux	173 09.8	S63 10.0
Adhara	255 13.0	S28 59.6
Aldebaran	290 50.3	N16 31.9
Alioth	166 21.0	N55 53.3
Alkaid	152 59.3	N49 14.8
Al Na'ir	27 45.3	S46 54.1
Alnilam	275 47.1	S 1 11.9
Alphard	217 56.7	S 8 42.9
Alphecca	126 11.7	N26 40.2
Alpheratz	357 44.7	N29 09.5
Altair	62 09.4	N 8 54.0
Ankaa	353 16.9	S42 14.5
Antares	112 27.4	S26 27.4
Arcturus	145 56.4	N19 06.9
Atria	107 30.2	S69 02.6
Avior	234 17.8	S59 33.2
Bellatrix	278 32.8	N 6 21.5
Betelgeuse	271 02.1	N 7 24.4
Canopus	263 56.2	S52 42.5
Capella	280 35.6	N46 00.7
Deneb	49 32.5	N45 19.4
Denebola	182 34.3	N14 30.0
Diphda	348 57.0	S17 55.3
Dubhe	193 52.1	N61 40.8
Elnath	278 13.6	N28 37.0
Eltanin	90 46.8	N51 29.0
Enif	33 48.3	N 9 55.9
Fomalhaut	15 25.3	S29 33.5
Gacrux	172 01.5	S57 10.9
Gienah	175 53.0	S17 36.7
Hadar	148 48.9	S60 25.7
Hamal	328 01.9	N23 31.2
Kaus Aust.	83 45.2	S34 22.6
Kochab	137 19.6	N74 06.0
Markab	13 39.5	N15 16.3
Menkar	314 16.1	N 4 08.2
Menkent	148 08.5	S36 25.7
Miaplacidus	221 39.0	S69 46.2
Mirfak	308 41.7	N49 54.4
Nunki	75 59.7	S26 16.8
Peacock	53 21.2	S56 41.6
Pollux	243 28.5	N27 59.6
Procyon	245 00.4	N 5 11.4
Rasalhague	96 07.4	N12 33.0
Regulus	207 44.1	N11 54.2
Rigel	281 12.8	S 8 11.5
Rigil Kent.	139 52.7	S60 52.9
Sabik	102 13.7	S15 44.4
Schedar	349 42.0	N56 36.4
Shaula	96 23.3	S37 06.6
Sirius	258 34.3	S16 44.3
Spica	158 32.0	S11 13.6
Suhail	222 52.7	S43 29.2
Vega	80 39.8	N38 47.6
Zuben'ubi	137 06.3	S16 05.6

	SHA	Mer.Pass.
Venus	348 32.5	14 53
Mars	188 40.0	1 32
Jupiter	326 47.4	16 17
Saturn	151 43.6	3 59

2012 FEBRUARY 18, 19, 20 (SAT., SUN., MON.) 43

UT	SUN GHA	SUN Dec	MOON GHA	v	MOON Dec	d	HP
d h	° '	° '	° '	'	° '	'	'
18 00	176 30.4	S11 55.0	225 55.3	7.7	S20 31.2	5.3	57.9
01	191 30.4	54.1	240 22.0	7.8	20 25.9	5.5	57.9
02	206 30.5	53.2	254 48.8	7.9	20 20.4	5.5	57.9
03	221 30.5	.. 52.3	269 15.7	7.9	20 14.9	5.7	57.8
04	236 30.6	51.4	283 42.6	8.0	20 09.2	5.8	57.8
05	251 30.6	50.6	298 09.6	8.0	20 03.4	5.8	57.8
S 06	266 30.6	S11 49.7	312 36.6	8.2	S19 57.6	6.1	57.8
A 07	281 30.7	48.8	327 03.8	8.1	19 51.5	6.1	57.8
T 08	296 30.7	47.9	341 30.9	8.3	19 45.4	6.2	57.7
U 09	311 30.8	.. 47.1	355 58.2	8.3	19 39.2	6.3	57.7
R 10	326 30.8	46.2	10 25.5	8.4	19 32.9	6.5	57.7
D 11	341 30.9	45.3	24 52.9	8.4	19 26.4	6.5	57.7
A 12	356 30.9	S11 44.4	39 20.3	8.5	S19 19.9	6.7	57.7
Y 13	11 31.0	43.5	53 47.8	8.6	19 13.2	6.8	57.7
14	26 31.0	42.6	68 15.4	8.6	19 06.4	6.8	57.6
15	41 31.1	.. 41.8	82 43.0	8.7	18 59.6	7.0	57.6
16	56 31.1	40.9	97 10.7	8.8	18 52.6	7.1	57.6
17	71 31.2	40.0	111 38.5	8.9	18 45.5	7.2	57.6
18	86 31.2	S11 39.1	126 06.4	8.9	S18 38.3	7.3	57.6
19	101 31.3	38.2	140 34.3	9.0	18 31.0	7.4	57.5
20	116 31.3	37.4	155 02.3	9.0	18 23.6	7.4	57.5
21	131 31.4	.. 36.5	169 30.3	9.2	18 16.2	7.6	57.5
22	146 31.4	35.6	183 58.5	9.2	18 08.6	7.7	57.5
23	161 31.5	34.7	198 26.7	9.2	18 00.9	7.8	57.5
19 00	176 31.5	S11 33.8	212 54.9	9.4	S17 53.1	7.8	57.4
01	191 31.6	32.9	227 23.3	9.4	17 45.3	8.0	57.4
02	206 31.7	32.0	241 51.7	9.5	17 37.3	8.0	57.4
03	221 31.7	.. 31.2	256 20.2	9.5	17 29.3	8.2	57.4
04	236 31.8	30.3	270 48.7	9.6	17 21.1	8.2	57.4
05	251 31.8	29.4	285 17.3	9.7	17 12.9	8.3	57.3
S 06	266 31.9	S11 28.5	299 46.0	9.8	S17 04.6	8.4	57.3
U 07	281 31.9	27.6	314 14.8	9.8	16 56.2	8.5	57.3
N 08	296 32.0	26.7	328 43.6	9.9	16 47.7	8.6	57.3
D 09	311 32.0	.. 25.8	343 12.5	10.0	16 39.1	8.7	57.3
A 10	326 32.1	25.0	357 41.5	10.0	16 30.4	8.7	57.2
Y 11	341 32.1	24.1	12 10.5	10.2	16 21.7	8.8	57.2
12	356 32.2	S11 23.2	26 39.7	10.1	S16 12.9	9.0	57.2
13	11 32.3	22.3	41 08.8	10.3	16 03.9	8.9	57.2
14	26 32.3	21.4	55 38.1	10.3	15 55.0	9.1	57.2
15	41 32.4	.. 20.5	70 07.4	10.4	15 45.9	9.2	57.1
16	56 32.4	19.6	84 36.8	10.5	15 36.7	9.2	57.1
17	71 32.5	18.7	99 06.3	10.5	15 27.5	9.3	57.1
18	86 32.5	S11 17.8	113 35.8	10.6	S15 18.2	9.3	57.1
19	101 32.6	17.0	128 05.4	10.7	15 08.9	9.5	57.1
20	116 32.7	16.1	142 35.1	10.8	14 59.4	9.5	57.0
21	131 32.7	.. 15.2	157 04.9	10.8	14 49.9	9.6	57.0
22	146 32.8	14.3	171 34.7	10.9	14 40.3	9.6	57.0
23	161 32.8	13.4	186 04.6	10.9	14 30.7	9.7	57.0
20 00	176 32.9	S11 12.5	200 34.5	11.0	S14 21.0	9.8	57.0
01	191 33.0	11.6	215 04.5	11.1	14 11.2	9.9	56.9
02	206 33.0	10.7	229 34.6	11.2	14 01.3	9.9	56.9
03	221 33.1	.. 09.8	244 04.8	11.2	13 51.4	10.0	56.9
04	236 33.1	08.9	258 35.0	11.3	13 41.4	10.0	56.9
05	251 33.2	08.0	273 05.3	11.3	13 31.4	10.1	56.9
M 06	266 33.3	S11 07.1	287 35.6	11.5	S13 21.3	10.2	56.8
O 07	281 33.3	06.2	302 06.1	11.5	13 11.1	10.2	56.8
N 08	296 33.4	05.3	316 36.6	11.5	13 00.9	10.3	56.8
D 09	311 33.4	.. 04.5	331 07.1	11.6	12 50.6	10.3	56.8
A 10	326 33.5	03.6	345 37.7	11.7	12 40.3	10.4	56.8
Y 11	341 33.6	02.7	0 08.4	11.8	12 29.9	10.5	56.7
12	356 33.6	S11 01.8	14 39.2	11.8	S12 19.4	10.5	56.7
13	11 33.7	00.9	29 10.0	11.9	12 08.9	10.5	56.7
14	26 33.8	11 00.0	43 40.9	11.9	11 58.4	10.6	56.7
15	41 33.8	10 59.1	58 11.8	12.0	11 47.8	10.7	56.7
16	56 33.9	58.2	72 42.8	12.1	11 37.1	10.7	56.6
17	71 34.0	57.3	87 13.9	12.1	11 26.4	10.7	56.6
18	86 34.0	S10 56.4	101 45.0	12.2	S11 15.7	10.8	56.6
19	101 34.1	55.5	116 16.2	12.2	11 04.9	10.9	56.6
20	116 34.1	54.6	130 47.4	12.3	10 54.0	10.9	56.6
21	131 34.2	.. 53.7	145 18.7	12.4	10 43.1	10.9	56.5
22	146 34.3	52.8	159 50.1	12.4	10 32.2	11.0	56.5
23	161 34.3	51.9	174 21.5	12.5	S10 21.2	11.0	56.5
	SD 16.2	d 0.9	SD 15.7	15.6			15.5

Lat.	Twilight Naut.	Twilight Civil	Sunrise	Moonrise 18	19	20	21
°	h m	h m	h m	h m	h m	h m	h m
N 72	06 00	07 19	08 34	■	08 41	07 57	07 34
N 70	06 00	07 11	08 17	08 43	07 52	07 33	07 21
68	05 59	07 04	08 04	07 28	07 21	07 15	07 10
66	05 59	06 58	07 53	06 51	06 57	07 00	07 01
64	05 58	06 54	07 44	06 24	06 39	06 48	06 53
62	05 58	06 49	07 36	06 04	06 24	06 37	06 47
60	05 57	06 46	07 29	05 47	06 11	06 28	06 41
N 58	05 57	06 42	07 23	05 32	06 00	06 20	06 36
56	05 56	06 39	07 17	05 20	05 50	06 13	06 32
54	05 55	06 36	07 13	05 09	05 42	06 07	06 28
52	05 54	06 34	07 08	05 00	05 34	06 01	06 24
50	05 54	06 31	07 04	04 51	05 27	05 56	06 21
45	05 52	06 26	06 56	04 33	05 12	05 45	06 13
N 40	05 49	06 21	06 49	04 18	05 00	05 36	06 07
35	05 47	06 17	06 42	04 06	04 49	05 28	06 02
30	05 45	06 13	06 37	03 55	04 40	05 21	05 57
20	05 39	06 05	06 27	03 36	04 24	05 09	05 49
N 10	05 32	05 57	06 19	03 19	04 10	04 58	05 42
0	05 25	05 49	06 10	03 04	03 57	04 48	05 35
S 10	05 16	05 41	06 02	02 48	03 44	04 38	05 29
20	05 04	05 31	05 53	02 32	03 30	04 27	05 22
30	04 49	05 18	05 43	02 13	03 14	04 14	05 13
35	04 39	05 11	05 37	02 01	03 05	04 07	05 09
40	04 28	05 02	05 30	01 49	02 54	03 59	05 03
45	04 13	04 51	05 22	01 33	02 41	03 50	04 57
S 50	03 54	04 37	05 12	01 15	02 26	03 38	04 49
52	03 45	04 31	05 08	01 06	02 18	03 33	04 46
54	03 34	04 24	05 03	00 56	02 10	03 27	04 42
56	03 22	04 16	04 57	00 45	02 01	03 20	04 38
58	03 08	04 07	04 51	00 32	01 51	03 12	04 33
S 60	02 50	03 56	04 44	00 17	01 39	03 04	04 28

Lat.	Sunset	Twilight Civil	Twilight Naut.	Moonset 18	19	20	21
°	h m	h m	h m	h m	h m	h m	h m
N 72	15 55	17 11	18 30	■	11 55	14 22	16 24
N 70	16 12	17 19	18 30	10 01	12 42	14 44	16 35
68	16 25	17 25	18 30	11 15	13 12	15 01	16 44
66	16 36	17 31	18 31	11 52	13 35	15 15	16 51
64	16 45	17 35	18 31	12 18	13 52	15 26	16 57
62	16 53	17 40	18 31	12 38	14 07	15 36	17 02
60	17 00	17 43	18 32	12 55	14 19	15 44	17 07
N 58	17 06	17 47	18 32	13 08	14 29	15 51	17 11
56	17 11	17 50	18 33	13 20	14 38	15 57	17 14
54	17 16	17 52	18 34	13 31	14 46	16 03	17 18
52	17 20	17 55	18 34	13 40	14 54	16 08	17 20
50	17 24	17 57	18 35	13 48	15 00	16 12	17 23
45	17 33	18 03	18 37	14 05	15 14	16 22	17 29
N 40	17 40	18 07	18 39	14 19	15 25	16 30	17 34
35	17 46	18 12	18 41	14 31	15 35	16 37	17 38
30	17 51	18 16	18 44	14 42	15 43	16 43	17 41
20	18 01	18 23	18 49	15 00	15 58	16 53	17 47
N 10	18 09	18 31	18 55	15 15	16 10	17 02	17 53
0	18 17	18 38	19 03	15 30	16 22	17 11	17 58
S 10	18 25	18 47	19 12	15 44	16 33	17 19	18 02
20	18 34	18 57	19 23	15 59	16 46	17 28	18 08
30	18 44	19 09	19 38	16 17	17 00	17 38	18 14
35	18 50	19 16	19 48	16 27	17 08	17 44	18 17
40	18 57	19 25	20 01	16 38	17 17	17 51	18 21
45	19 05	19 36	20 14	16 52	17 28	17 58	18 25
S 50	19 14	19 49	20 32	17 08	17 41	18 07	18 30
52	19 19	19 55	20 41	17 16	17 46	18 11	18 33
54	19 24	20 02	20 51	17 24	17 53	18 16	18 35
56	19 29	20 10	21 03	17 34	18 00	18 21	18 38
58	19 35	20 19	21 17	17 45	18 09	18 27	18 41
S 60	19 42	20 29	21 35	17 57	18 18	18 33	18 45

Day	SUN Eqn. of Time 00h	12h	SUN Mer. Pass.	MOON Mer. Pass. Upper	Lower	Age	Phase
d	m s	m s	h m	h m	h m	d	%
18	13 59	13 56	12 14	09 17	21 44	26	13
19	13 54	13 51	12 14	10 10	22 35	27	7
20	13 49	13 46	12 14	10 59	23 23	28	2	●

	UT	ARIES	VENUS −4.2		MARS −1.1		JUPITER −2.2		SATURN +0.5	
		GHA	GHA	Dec	GHA	Dec	GHA	Dec	GHA	Dec
	d h	° ′	° ′	° ′	° ′	° ′	° ′	° ′	° ′	° ′
	21 00	150 20.0	136 47.9	N 6 09.9	339 36.4	N 8 33.9	116 48.8	N12 24.5	302 05.8	S 8 46.2
	01	165 22.4	151 47.7	11.2	354 39.6	34.3	131 50.9	24.6	317 08.4	46.2
	02	180 24.9	166 47.6	12.5	9 42.9	34.6	146 52.9	24.8	332 10.9	46.2
	03	195 27.4	181 47.5	. . 13.8	24 46.1	. . 35.0	161 55.0	. . 24.9	347 13.4	. . 46.2
	04	210 29.8	196 47.3	15.0	39 49.4	35.3	176 57.1	25.1	2 15.9	46.1
	05	225 32.3	211 47.2	16.3	54 52.6	35.7	191 59.2	25.2	17 18.4	46.1
	06	240 34.8	226 47.1	N 6 17.6	69 55.9	N 8 36.0	207 01.2	N12 25.4	32 20.9	S 8 46.1
	07	255 37.2	241 47.0	18.9	84 59.1	36.4	222 03.3	25.5	47 23.5	46.0
T	08	270 39.7	256 46.8	20.1	100 02.4	36.7	237 05.4	25.7	62 26.0	46.0
U	09	285 42.1	271 46.7	. . 21.4	115 05.6	. . 37.1	252 07.4	. . 25.8	77 28.5	. . 46.0
E	10	300 44.6	286 46.6	22.7	130 08.9	37.4	267 09.5	25.9	92 31.0	45.9
	11	315 47.1	301 46.4	24.0	145 12.1	37.8	282 11.6	26.1	107 33.5	45.9
S	12	330 49.5	316 46.3	N 6 25.3	160 15.4	N 8 38.2	297 13.6	N12 26.2	122 36.0	S 8 45.9
D	13	345 52.0	331 46.2	26.5	175 18.6	38.5	312 15.7	26.4	137 38.6	45.8
A	14	0 54.5	346 46.1	27.8	190 21.9	38.9	327 17.8	26.5	152 41.1	45.8
Y	15	15 56.9	1 45.9	. . 29.1	205 25.2	. . 39.2	342 19.8	. . 26.7	167 43.6	. . 45.8
	16	30 59.4	16 45.8	30.4	220 28.4	39.6	357 21.9	26.8	182 46.1	45.8
	17	46 01.9	31 45.7	31.6	235 31.7	39.9	12 24.0	27.0	197 48.6	45.7
	18	61 04.3	46 45.5	N 6 32.9	250 34.9	N 8 40.3	27 26.1	N12 27.1	212 51.1	S 8 45.7
	19	76 06.8	61 45.4	34.2	265 38.2	40.6	42 28.1	27.3	227 53.7	45.7
	20	91 09.2	76 45.3	35.5	280 41.5	41.0	57 30.2	27.4	242 56.2	45.6
	21	106 11.7	91 45.2	. . 36.7	295 44.7	. . 41.3	72 32.3	. . 27.5	257 58.7	. . 45.6
	22	121 14.2	106 45.0	38.0	310 48.0	41.7	87 34.3	27.7	273 01.2	45.6
	23	136 16.6	121 44.9	39.3	325 51.3	42.1	102 36.4	27.8	288 03.7	45.5
	22 00	151 19.1	136 44.8	N 6 40.5	340 54.5	N 8 42.4	117 38.5	N12 28.0	303 06.3	S 8 45.5
	01	166 21.6	151 44.7	41.8	355 57.8	42.8	132 40.5	28.1	318 08.8	45.5
	02	181 24.0	166 44.5	43.1	11 01.1	43.1	147 42.6	28.3	333 11.3	45.4
	03	196 26.5	181 44.4	. . 44.4	26 04.3	. . 43.5	162 44.7	. . 28.4	348 13.8	. . 45.4
	04	211 29.0	196 44.3	45.6	41 07.6	43.8	177 46.7	28.6	3 16.3	45.4
	05	226 31.4	211 44.1	46.9	56 10.9	44.2	192 48.8	28.7	18 18.9	45.3
	06	241 33.9	226 44.0	N 6 48.2	71 14.1	N 8 44.5	207 50.8	N12 28.9	33 21.4	S 8 45.3
W	07	256 36.4	241 43.9	49.4	86 17.4	44.9	222 52.9	29.0	48 23.9	45.3
E	08	271 38.8	256 43.8	50.7	101 20.7	45.3	237 55.0	29.2	63 26.4	45.3
D	09	286 41.3	271 43.6	. . 52.0	116 24.0	. . 45.6	252 57.0	. . 29.3	78 28.9	. . 45.2
N	10	301 43.7	286 43.5	53.3	131 27.2	46.0	267 59.1	29.4	93 31.5	45.2
E	11	316 46.2	301 43.4	54.5	146 30.5	46.3	283 01.2	29.6	108 34.0	45.2
S	12	331 48.7	316 43.3	N 6 55.8	161 33.8	N 8 46.7	298 03.2	N12 29.7	123 36.5	S 8 45.1
D	13	346 51.1	331 43.1	57.1	176 37.1	47.0	313 05.3	29.9	138 39.0	45.1
	14	1 53.6	346 43.0	58.3	191 40.4	47.4	328 07.4	30.0	153 41.6	45.1
A	15	16 56.1	1 42.9	6 59.6	206 43.6	. . 47.8	343 09.4	. . 30.2	168 44.1	. . 45.0
Y	16	31 58.5	16 42.8	7 00.9	221 46.9	48.1	358 11.5	30.3	183 46.6	45.0
	17	47 01.0	31 42.6	02.1	236 50.2	48.5	13 13.5	30.5	198 49.1	45.0
	18	62 03.5	46 42.5	N 7 03.4	251 53.5	N 8 48.8	28 15.6	N12 30.6	213 51.6	S 8 44.9
	19	77 05.9	61 42.4	04.7	266 56.8	49.2	43 17.7	30.8	228 54.2	44.9
	20	92 08.4	76 42.3	05.9	282 00.0	49.5	58 19.7	30.9	243 56.7	44.9
	21	107 10.8	91 42.1	. . 07.2	297 03.3	. . 49.9	73 21.8	. . 31.1	258 59.2	. . 44.8
	22	122 13.3	106 42.0	08.5	312 06.6	50.3	88 23.9	31.2	274 01.7	44.8
	23	137 15.8	121 41.9	09.7	327 09.9	50.6	103 25.9	31.4	289 04.3	44.8
	23 00	152 18.2	136 41.8	N 7 11.0	342 13.2	N 8 51.0	118 28.0	N12 31.5	304 06.8	S 8 44.7
	01	167 20.7	151 41.6	12.3	357 16.5	51.3	133 30.0	31.7	319 09.3	44.7
	02	182 23.2	166 41.5	13.5	12 19.8	51.7	148 32.1	31.8	334 11.8	44.7
	03	197 25.6	181 41.4	. . 14.8	27 23.0	. . 52.1	163 34.2	. . 32.0	349 14.3	. . 44.6
	04	212 28.1	196 41.3	16.1	42 26.3	52.4	178 36.2	32.1	4 16.9	44.6
	05	227 30.6	211 41.1	17.3	57 29.6	52.8	193 38.3	32.2	19 19.4	44.6
	06	242 33.0	226 41.0	N 7 18.6	72 32.9	N 8 53.1	208 40.3	N12 32.4	34 21.9	S 8 44.5
	07	257 35.5	241 40.9	19.9	87 36.2	53.5	223 42.4	32.5	49 24.4	44.5
T	08	272 38.0	256 40.8	21.1	102 39.5	53.9	238 44.5	32.7	64 27.0	44.5
H	09	287 40.4	271 40.6	. . 22.4	117 42.8	. . 54.2	253 46.5	. . 32.8	79 29.5	. . 44.4
U	10	302 42.9	286 40.5	23.7	132 46.1	54.6	268 48.6	33.0	94 32.0	44.4
R	11	317 45.3	301 40.4	24.9	147 49.4	54.9	283 50.6	33.1	109 34.5	44.4
S	12	332 47.8	316 40.3	N 7 26.2	162 52.7	N 8 55.3	298 52.7	N12 33.3	124 37.1	S 8 44.3
D	13	347 50.3	331 40.1	27.5	177 56.0	55.7	313 54.8	33.4	139 39.6	44.3
A	14	2 52.7	346 40.0	28.7	192 59.3	56.0	328 56.8	33.6	154 42.1	44.3
Y	15	17 55.2	1 39.9	. . 30.0	208 02.6	. . 56.4	343 58.9	. . 33.7	169 44.6	. . 44.2
	16	32 57.7	16 39.8	31.2	223 05.9	56.7	359 00.9	33.9	184 47.2	44.2
	17	48 00.1	31 39.6	32.5	238 09.2	57.1	14 03.0	34.0	199 49.7	44.2
	18	63 02.6	46 39.5	N 7 33.8	253 12.5	N 8 57.5	29 05.1	N12 34.2	214 52.2	S 8 44.1
	19	78 05.1	61 39.4	35.0	268 15.8	57.8	44 07.1	34.3	229 54.8	44.1
	20	93 07.5	76 39.3	36.3	283 19.1	58.2	59 09.2	34.5	244 57.3	44.1
	21	108 10.0	91 39.1	. . 37.6	298 22.4	. . 58.6	74 11.2	. . 34.6	259 59.8	. . 44.0
	22	123 12.4	106 39.0	38.8	313 25.7	58.9	89 13.3	34.8	275 02.3	44.0
	23	138 14.9	121 38.9	40.1	328 29.0	59.3	104 15.3	34.9	290 04.9	44.0
	Mer. Pass.	h m 13 52.4	v −0.1	d 1.3	v 3.3	d 0.4	v 2.1	d 0.1	v 2.5	d 0.0

STARS

Name	SHA	Dec
	° ′	° ′
Acamar	315 19.1	S40 15.6
Achernar	335 27.7	S57 10.7
Acrux	173 09.8	S63 10.0
Adhara	255 13.0	S28 59.6
Aldebaran	290 50.4	N16 31.9
Alioth	166 21.0	N55 53.3
Alkaid	152 59.3	N49 14.8
Al Na'ir	27 45.3	S46 54.1
Alnilam	275 47.1	S 1 11.9
Alphard	217 56.7	S 8 43.0
Alphecca	126 11.7	N26 40.2
Alpheratz	357 44.8	N29 09.5
Altair	62 09.4	N 8 54.0
Ankaa	353 16.9	S42 14.5
Antares	112 27.4	S26 27.5
Arcturus	145 56.4	N19 06.9
Atria	107 30.2	S69 02.6
Avior	234 17.8	S59 33.2
Bellatrix	278 32.9	N 6 21.5
Betelgeuse	271 02.1	N 7 24.4
Canopus	263 56.2	S52 42.5
Capella	280 35.6	N46 00.7
Deneb	49 32.5	N45 19.4
Denebola	182 34.3	N14 30.0
Diphda	348 57.0	S17 55.3
Dubhe	193 52.1	N61 40.9
Elnath	278 13.6	N28 37.0
Eltanin	90 46.8	N51 29.0
Enif	33 48.3	N 9 55.9
Fomalhaut	15 25.3	S29 33.5
Gacrux	172 01.5	S57 10.9
Gienah	175 52.9	S17 36.7
Hadar	148 48.9	S60 25.8
Hamal	328 01.9	N23 31.2
Kaus Aust.	83 45.2	S34 22.6
Kochab	137 19.5	N74 06.0
Markab	13 39.5	N15 16.3
Menkar	314 16.1	N 4 08.2
Menkent	148 08.4	S36 25.8
Miaplacidus	221 39.0	S69 46.3
Mirfak	308 41.7	N49 54.4
Nunki	75 59.7	S26 16.8
Peacock	53 21.1	S56 41.6
Pollux	243 28.5	N27 59.6
Procyon	245 00.4	N 5 11.4
Rasalhague	96 07.4	N12 33.0
Regulus	207 44.1	N11 54.2
Rigel	281 12.8	S 8 11.5
Rigil Kent.	139 52.7	S60 52.9
Sabik	102 13.7	S15 44.4
Schedar	349 42.0	N56 36.4
Shaula	96 23.3	S37 06.6
Sirius	258 34.3	S16 44.3
Spica	158 32.0	S11 13.6
Suhail	222 52.7	S43 29.2
Vega	80 39.8	N38 47.5
Zuben'ubi	137 06.3	S16 05.6

	SHA	Mer. Pass.
	° ′	h m
Venus	345 25.7	14 53
Mars	189 35.4	1 16
Jupiter	326 19.3	16 07
Saturn	151 47.2	3 47

UT	SUN GHA	SUN Dec	MOON GHA	v	Dec	d	HP
d h	° ′	° ′	° ′	′	° ′	′	′
21 00	176 34.4	S10 51.0	188 53.0	12.5	S10 10.2	11.0	56.5
01	191 34.5	50.1	203 24.5	12.6	9 59.2	11.1	56.4
02	206 34.5	49.2	217 56.1	12.7	9 48.1	11.1	56.4
03	221 34.6	.. 48.3	232 27.8	12.7	9 37.0	11.2	56.4
04	236 34.7	47.4	246 59.5	12.7	9 25.8	11.2	56.4
05	251 34.7	46.5	261 31.2	12.9	9 14.6	11.3	56.4
06	266 34.8	S10 45.6	276 03.1	12.8	S 9 03.3	11.2	56.3
07	281 34.9	44.7	290 34.9	13.0	8 52.1	11.3	56.3
T 08	296 34.9	43.8	305 06.9	12.9	8 40.8	11.4	56.3
U 09	311 35.0	.. 42.9	319 38.8	13.1	8 29.4	11.3	56.3
E 10	326 35.1	42.0	334 10.9	13.0	8 18.1	11.4	56.3
S 11	341 35.2	41.1	348 42.9	13.2	8 06.7	11.5	56.2
D 12	356 35.2	S10 40.2	3 15.1	13.2	S 7 55.2	11.4	56.2
A 13	11 35.3	39.3	17 47.3	13.2	7 43.8	11.5	56.2
Y 14	26 35.4	38.4	32 19.5	13.3	7 32.3	11.5	56.2
15	41 35.4	.. 37.5	46 51.8	13.3	7 20.8	11.5	56.2
16	56 35.5	36.6	61 24.1	13.4	7 09.3	11.6	56.1
17	71 35.6	35.7	75 56.5	13.4	6 57.7	11.6	56.1
18	86 35.7	S10 34.8	90 28.9	13.5	S 6 46.1	11.6	56.1
19	101 35.7	33.9	105 01.4	13.5	6 34.5	11.6	56.1
20	116 35.8	33.0	119 33.9	13.5	6 22.9	11.6	56.0
21	131 35.9	.. 32.0	134 06.4	13.6	6 11.3	11.7	56.0
22	146 35.9	31.1	148 39.0	13.7	5 59.6	11.6	56.0
23	161 36.0	30.2	163 11.7	13.7	5 48.0	11.7	56.0
22 00	176 36.1	S10 29.3	177 44.4	13.7	S 5 36.3	11.7	56.0
01	191 36.2	28.4	192 17.1	13.8	5 24.6	11.8	55.9
02	206 36.2	27.5	206 49.9	13.8	5 12.8	11.7	55.9
03	221 36.3	.. 26.6	221 22.7	13.9	5 01.1	11.7	55.9
04	236 36.4	25.7	235 55.6	13.8	4 49.4	11.8	55.9
05	251 36.5	24.8	250 28.4	14.0	4 37.6	11.8	55.9
06	266 36.5	S10 23.9	265 01.4	14.0	S 4 25.8	11.8	55.8
W 07	281 36.6	23.0	279 34.4	14.0	4 14.0	11.8	55.8
E 08	296 36.7	22.1	294 07.4	14.0	4 02.2	11.8	55.8
D 09	311 36.8	.. 21.2	308 40.4	14.1	3 50.4	11.8	55.8
N 10	326 36.8	20.3	323 13.5	14.1	3 38.6	11.8	55.8
E 11	341 36.9	19.3	337 46.6	14.1	3 26.8	11.8	55.7
S 12	356 37.0	S10 18.4	352 19.7	14.2	S 3 15.0	11.8	55.7
D 13	11 37.1	17.5	6 52.9	14.2	3 03.2	11.8	55.7
A 14	26 37.1	16.6	21 26.1	14.3	2 51.4	11.9	55.7
Y 15	41 37.2	.. 15.7	35 59.4	14.3	2 39.5	11.8	55.7
16	56 37.3	14.8	50 32.7	14.3	2 27.7	11.8	55.6
17	71 37.4	13.9	65 06.0	14.3	2 15.9	11.9	55.6
18	86 37.4	S10 13.0	79 39.3	14.4	S 2 04.0	11.8	55.6
19	101 37.5	12.1	94 12.7	14.4	1 52.2	11.8	55.6
20	116 37.6	11.2	108 46.1	14.4	1 40.4	11.9	55.6
21	131 37.7	.. 10.2	123 19.5	14.4	1 28.5	11.8	55.5
22	146 37.8	09.3	137 52.9	14.5	1 16.7	11.8	55.5
23	161 37.8	08.4	152 26.4	14.5	1 04.9	11.8	55.5
23 00	176 37.9	S10 07.5	166 59.9	14.5	S 0 53.1	11.9	55.5
01	191 38.0	06.6	181 33.4	14.6	0 41.2	11.8	55.5
02	206 38.1	05.7	196 07.0	14.6	0 29.4	11.8	55.4
03	221 38.2	.. 04.8	210 40.6	14.6	0 17.6	11.8	55.4
04	236 38.2	03.8	225 14.2	14.6	S 0 05.8	11.7	55.4
05	251 38.3	02.9	239 47.8	14.6	N 0 05.9	11.8	55.4
06	266 38.4	S10 02.0	254 21.4	14.7	N 0 17.7	11.8	55.4
T 07	281 38.5	01.1	268 55.1	14.6	0 29.5	11.7	55.3
H 08	296 38.6	10 00.2	283 28.7	14.7	0 41.2	11.8	55.3
U 09	311 38.6	9 59.3	298 02.4	14.8	0 53.0	11.7	55.3
R 10	326 38.7	58.4	312 36.2	14.7	1 04.7	11.7	55.3
S 11	341 38.8	57.4	327 09.9	14.7	1 16.4	11.7	55.3
D 12	356 38.9	S 9 56.5	341 43.6	14.8	N 1 28.1	11.7	55.2
A 13	11 39.0	55.6	356 17.4	14.8	1 39.8	11.7	55.2
Y 14	26 39.1	54.7	10 51.2	14.8	1 51.5	11.6	55.2
15	41 39.1	.. 53.8	25 25.0	14.8	2 03.1	11.6	55.2
16	56 39.2	52.9	39 58.8	14.8	2 14.7	11.7	55.2
17	71 39.3	51.9	54 32.6	14.9	2 26.4	11.5	55.1
18	86 39.4	S 9 51.0	69 06.5	14.8	N 2 37.9	11.6	55.1
19	101 39.5	50.1	83 40.3	14.9	2 49.5	11.6	55.1
20	116 39.6	49.2	98 14.2	14.8	3 01.1	11.5	55.1
21	131 39.7	.. 48.3	112 48.0	14.9	3 12.6	11.5	55.1
22	146 39.7	47.4	127 21.9	14.9	3 24.1	11.5	55.1
23	161 39.8	46.4	141 55.8	14.9	N 3 35.6	11.5	55.0
	SD 16.2	d 0.9	SD 15.3		15.2		15.1

Moonrise

Lat.	Twilight Naut.	Twilight Civil	Sunrise	21	22	23	24
°	h m	h m	h m	h m	h m	h m	h m
N 72	05 46	07 04	08 18	07 34	07 16	07 00	06 44
N 70	05 47	06 58	08 03	07 21	07 10	07 00	06 51
68	05 48	06 53	07 51	07 10	07 05	07 01	06 56
66	05 49	06 48	07 42	07 01	07 01	07 01	07 01
64	05 49	06 44	07 33	06 53	06 58	07 01	07 05
62	05 49	06 41	07 26	06 47	06 55	07 02	07 08
60	05 49	06 38	07 20	06 41	06 52	07 02	07 11
N 58	05 49	06 35	07 15	06 36	06 50	07 02	07 14
56	05 49	06 32	07 10	06 32	06 48	07 02	07 17
54	05 49	06 30	07 06	06 28	06 46	07 02	07 19
52	05 49	06 28	07 02	06 24	06 44	07 03	07 21
50	05 48	06 26	06 59	06 21	06 42	07 03	07 23
45	05 47	06 21	06 51	06 13	06 39	07 03	07 27
N 40	05 46	06 17	06 44	06 07	06 36	07 03	07 30
35	05 44	06 13	06 39	06 02	06 34	07 04	07 33
30	05 42	06 10	06 34	05 57	06 31	07 04	07 36
20	05 37	06 03	06 25	05 49	06 28	07 04	07 40
N 10	05 32	05 56	06 18	05 42	06 24	07 05	07 44
0	05 25	05 49	06 10	05 35	06 21	07 05	07 48
S 10	05 16	05 41	06 03	05 29	06 18	07 05	07 52
20	05 06	05 32	05 55	05 22	06 14	07 06	07 56
30	04 52	05 21	05 45	05 13	06 11	07 06	08 01
35	04 43	05 14	05 40	05 09	06 08	07 06	08 03
40	04 32	05 05	05 34	05 03	06 06	07 07	08 07
45	04 18	04 56	05 26	04 57	06 03	07 07	08 10
S 50	04 01	04 43	05 18	04 49	05 59	07 08	08 15
52	03 52	04 37	05 13	04 46	05 58	07 08	08 17
54	03 42	04 31	05 09	04 42	05 56	07 08	08 19
56	03 31	04 23	05 04	04 38	05 54	07 08	08 21
58	03 18	04 15	04 58	04 33	05 52	07 09	08 24
S 60	03 02	04 05	04 52	04 28	05 49	07 09	08 27

Moonset

Lat.	Sunset	Twilight Civil	Twilight Naut.	21	22	23	24
°	h m	h m	h m	h m	h m	h m	h m
N 72	16 11	17 25	18 43	16 24	18 16	20 03	21 51
N 70	16 26	17 31	18 42	16 35	18 19	19 59	21 39
68	16 37	17 36	18 41	16 44	18 21	19 56	21 29
66	16 47	17 40	18 40	16 51	18 23	19 53	21 21
64	16 55	17 44	18 39	16 57	18 25	19 50	21 15
62	17 02	17 48	18 39	17 02	18 26	19 48	21 09
60	17 08	17 51	18 39	17 07	18 28	19 46	21 04
N 58	17 13	17 53	18 39	17 11	18 29	19 45	21 00
56	17 18	17 56	18 39	17 14	18 30	19 43	20 56
54	17 22	17 58	18 39	17 18	18 31	19 42	20 52
52	17 26	18 00	18 39	17 20	18 32	19 41	20 49
50	17 29	18 02	18 40	17 23	18 32	19 40	20 46
45	17 37	18 07	18 41	17 29	18 34	19 38	20 40
N 40	17 43	18 11	18 42	17 34	18 35	19 36	20 35
35	17 49	18 14	18 44	17 38	18 36	19 34	20 31
30	17 54	18 18	18 46	17 41	18 38	19 33	20 27
20	18 02	18 24	18 50	17 47	18 39	19 30	20 20
N 10	18 10	18 31	18 56	17 53	18 41	19 28	20 14
0	18 17	18 38	19 02	17 58	18 42	19 26	20 09
S 10	18 24	18 46	19 11	18 02	18 44	19 24	20 03
20	18 32	18 55	19 21	18 08	18 45	19 21	19 57
30	18 41	19 06	19 35	18 14	18 47	19 19	19 51
35	18 47	19 13	19 44	18 17	18 48	19 17	19 47
40	18 53	19 21	19 54	18 21	18 49	19 16	19 43
45	19 00	19 31	20 08	18 25	18 50	19 14	19 38
S 50	19 08	19 43	20 25	18 30	18 51	19 11	19 32
52	19 12	19 48	20 33	18 33	18 52	19 10	19 29
54	19 17	19 55	20 43	18 35	18 53	19 09	19 26
56	19 22	20 02	20 54	18 38	18 53	19 08	19 23
58	19 27	20 10	21 07	18 41	18 54	19 06	19 19
S 60	19 33	20 20	21 22	18 45	18 55	19 05	19 15

	SUN			MOON			
Day	Eqn. of Time 00ʰ	12ʰ	Mer. Pass.	Mer. Pass. Upper	Lower	Age	Phase
d	m s	m s	h m	h m	h m	d	%
21	13 42	13 39	12 14	11 47	24 09	29	0
22	13 36	13 32	12 14	12 32	00 09	01	1
23	13 28	13 25	12 13	13 15	00 54	02	3

46   2012 FEBRUARY 24, 25, 26 (FRI., SAT., SUN.)

UT	ARIES GHA	VENUS −4.2 GHA	Dec	MARS −1.1 GHA	Dec	JUPITER −2.2 GHA	Dec	SATURN +0.5 GHA	Dec	Name	SHA	Dec
24 00	153 17.4	136 38.8	N 7 41.3	343 32.3	N 8 59.6	119 17.4	N12 35.1	305 07.4	S 8 43.9	Acamar	315 19.1	S40 15.6
01	168 19.8	151 38.6	42.6	358 35.6	9 00.0	134 19.5	35.2	320 09.9	43.9	Achernar	335 27.8	S57 10.7
02	183 22.3	166 38.5	43.8	13 38.9	00.4	149 21.5	35.4	335 12.4	43.9	Acrux	173 09.7	S63 10.0
03	198 24.8	181 38.4	.. 45.1	28 42.2	.. 00.7	164 23.6	.. 35.5	350 15.0	.. 43.8	Adhara	255 13.0	S28 59.7
04	213 27.2	196 38.3	46.4	43 45.5	01.1	179 25.6	35.7	5 17.5	43.8	Aldebaran	290 50.4	N16 31.9
05	228 29.7	211 38.1	47.6	58 48.8	01.4	194 27.7	35.8	20 20.0	43.8			
06	243 32.2	226 38.0	N 7 48.9	73 52.1	N 9 01.8	209 29.7	N12 36.0	35 22.6	S 8 43.7	Alioth	166 21.0	N55 53.3
07	258 34.6	241 37.9	50.1	88 55.5	02.2	224 31.8	36.1	50 25.1	43.7	Alkaid	152 59.3	N49 14.8
08	273 37.1	256 37.8	51.4	103 58.8	02.5	239 33.8	36.3	65 27.6	43.7	Al Na'ir	27 45.3	S46 54.1
F 09	288 39.6	271 37.7	.. 52.7	119 02.1	.. 02.9	254 35.9	.. 36.4	80 30.1	.. 43.6	Alnilam	275 47.2	S 1 11.9
R 10	303 42.0	286 37.5	53.9	134 05.4	03.3	269 37.9	36.6	95 32.7	43.6	Alphard	217 56.7	S 8 43.0
I 11	318 44.5	301 37.4	55.2	149 08.7	03.6	284 40.0	36.7	110 35.2	43.6			
D 12	333 46.9	316 37.3	N 7 56.4	164 12.0	N 9 04.0	299 42.1	N12 36.8	125 37.7	S 8 43.5	Alphecca	126 11.7	N26 40.2
A 13	348 49.4	331 37.2	57.7	179 15.3	04.4	314 44.1	37.0	140 40.3	43.5	Alpheratz	357 44.8	N29 09.5
Y 14	3 51.9	346 37.0	7 58.9	194 18.6	04.7	329 46.2	37.1	155 42.8	43.4	Altair	62 09.4	N 8 54.0
15	18 54.3	1 36.9	8 00.2	209 22.0	.. 05.1	344 48.2	.. 37.3	170 45.3	.. 43.4	Ankaa	353 16.9	S42 14.5
16	33 56.8	16 36.8	01.4	224 25.3	05.4	359 50.3	37.4	185 47.8	43.4	Antares	112 27.4	S26 27.5
17	48 59.3	31 36.7	02.7	239 28.6	05.8	14 52.3	37.6	200 50.4	43.3			
18	64 01.7	46 36.6	N 8 04.0	254 31.9	N 9 06.2	29 54.4	N12 37.7	215 52.9	S 8 43.3	Arcturus	145 56.4	N19 06.9
19	79 04.2	61 36.4	05.2	269 35.2	06.5	44 56.4	37.9	230 55.4	43.3	Atria	107 30.1	S69 02.6
20	94 06.7	76 36.3	06.5	284 38.6	06.9	59 58.5	38.0	245 58.0	43.2	Avior	234 17.9	S59 33.2
21	109 09.1	91 36.2	.. 07.7	299 41.9	.. 07.3	75 00.5	.. 38.2	261 00.5	.. 43.2	Bellatrix	278 32.9	N 6 21.5
22	124 11.6	106 36.1	09.0	314 45.2	07.6	90 02.6	38.3	276 03.0	43.2	Betelgeuse	271 02.1	N 7 24.4
23	139 14.0	121 35.9	10.2	329 48.5	08.0	105 04.6	38.5	291 05.6	43.1			
25 00	154 16.5	136 35.8	N 8 11.5	344 51.8	N 9 08.4	120 06.7	N12 38.6	306 08.1	S 8 43.1	Canopus	263 56.3	S52 42.5
01	169 19.0	151 35.7	12.7	359 55.2	08.7	135 08.7	38.8	321 10.6	43.1	Capella	280 35.7	N46 00.7
02	184 21.4	166 35.6	14.0	14 58.5	09.1	150 10.8	38.9	336 13.2	43.0	Deneb	49 32.5	N45 19.4
03	199 23.9	181 35.5	.. 15.2	30 01.8	.. 09.4	165 12.8	.. 39.1	351 15.7	.. 43.0	Denebola	182 34.3	N14 30.0
04	214 26.4	196 35.3	16.5	45 05.1	09.8	180 14.9	39.2	6 18.2	43.0	Diphda	348 57.0	S17 55.3
05	229 28.8	211 35.2	17.7	60 08.5	10.2	195 16.9	39.4	21 20.8	42.9			
06	244 31.3	226 35.1	N 8 19.0	75 11.8	N 9 10.5	210 19.0	N12 39.5	36 23.3	S 8 42.9	Dubhe	193 52.1	N61 40.9
S 07	259 33.8	241 35.0	20.2	90 15.1	10.9	225 21.0	39.7	51 25.8	42.8	Elnath	278 13.6	N28 37.0
A 08	274 36.2	256 34.8	21.5	105 18.4	11.3	240 23.1	39.8	66 28.3	42.8	Eltanin	90 46.8	N51 29.0
T 09	289 38.7	271 34.7	.. 22.7	120 21.8	.. 11.6	255 25.1	.. 40.0	81 30.9	.. 42.8	Enif	33 48.3	N 9 55.9
U 10	304 41.2	286 34.6	24.0	135 25.1	12.0	270 27.2	40.1	96 33.4	42.7	Fomalhaut	15 25.3	S29 33.5
R 11	319 43.6	301 34.5	25.2	150 28.4	12.4	285 29.2	40.3	111 35.9	42.7			
D 12	334 46.1	316 34.4	N 8 26.5	165 31.8	N 9 12.7	300 31.3	N12 40.4	126 38.5	S 8 42.7	Gacrux	172 01.5	S57 10.9
A 13	349 48.5	331 34.2	27.7	180 35.1	13.1	315 33.3	40.6	141 41.0	42.6	Gienah	175 52.9	S17 36.7
Y 14	4 51.0	346 34.1	29.0	195 38.4	13.5	330 35.4	40.7	156 43.5	42.6	Hadar	148 48.9	S60 25.8
15	19 53.5	1 34.0	.. 30.2	210 41.8	.. 13.8	345 37.4	.. 40.9	171 46.1	.. 42.6	Hamal	328 02.0	N23 31.2
16	34 55.9	16 33.9	31.5	225 45.1	14.2	0 39.5	41.0	186 48.6	42.5	Kaus Aust.	83 45.2	S34 22.6
17	49 58.4	31 33.8	32.7	240 48.4	14.6	15 41.5	41.2	201 51.1	42.5			
18	65 00.9	46 33.6	N 8 34.0	255 51.8	N 9 14.9	30 43.6	N12 41.3	216 53.7	S 8 42.4	Kochab	137 19.5	N74 06.0
19	80 03.3	61 33.5	35.2	270 55.1	15.3	45 45.6	41.5	231 56.2	42.4	Markab	13 39.6	N15 16.3
20	95 05.8	76 33.4	36.5	285 58.4	15.6	60 47.7	41.7	246 58.8	42.4	Menkar	314 16.1	N 4 08.2
21	110 08.3	91 33.3	.. 37.7	301 01.8	.. 16.0	75 49.7	.. 41.8	262 01.3	.. 42.3	Menkent	148 08.4	S36 25.8
22	125 10.7	106 33.2	39.0	316 05.1	16.4	90 51.8	42.0	277 03.8	42.3	Miaplacidus	221 39.0	S69 46.3
23	140 13.2	121 33.0	40.2	331 08.4	16.7	105 53.8	42.1	292 06.4	42.3			
26 00	155 15.7	136 32.9	N 8 41.4	346 11.8	N 9 17.1	120 55.9	N12 42.3	307 08.9	S 8 42.2	Mirfak	308 41.8	N49 54.4
01	170 18.1	151 32.8	42.7	1 15.1	17.5	135 57.9	42.4	322 11.4	42.2	Nunki	75 59.6	S26 16.8
02	185 20.6	166 32.7	43.9	16 18.4	17.8	151 00.0	42.6	337 14.0	42.2	Peacock	53 21.1	S56 41.5
03	200 23.0	181 32.6	.. 45.2	31 21.8	.. 18.2	166 02.0	.. 42.7	352 16.5	.. 42.1	Pollux	243 28.5	N27 59.6
04	215 25.5	196 32.4	46.4	46 25.1	18.6	181 04.1	42.9	7 19.0	42.1	Procyon	245 00.4	N 5 11.4
05	230 28.0	211 32.3	47.7	61 28.5	18.9	196 06.1	43.0	22 21.6	42.0			
06	245 30.4	226 32.2	N 8 48.9	76 31.8	N 9 19.3	211 08.1	N12 43.2	37 24.1	S 8 42.0	Rasalhague	96 07.4	N12 33.0
07	260 32.9	241 32.1	50.2	91 35.2	19.7	226 10.2	43.3	52 26.6	42.0	Regulus	207 44.1	N11 54.2
08	275 35.4	256 32.0	51.4	106 38.5	20.0	241 12.2	43.5	67 29.2	41.9	Rigel	281 12.8	S 8 11.5
S 09	290 37.8	271 31.8	.. 52.6	121 41.8	.. 20.4	256 14.3	.. 43.6	82 31.7	.. 41.9	Rigil Kent.	139 52.7	S60 52.9
U 10	305 40.3	286 31.7	53.9	136 45.2	20.8	271 16.3	43.8	97 34.2	41.9	Sabik	102 13.6	S15 44.4
N 11	320 42.8	301 31.6	55.1	151 48.5	21.1	286 18.4	43.9	112 36.8	41.8			
D 12	335 45.2	316 31.5	N 8 56.4	166 51.9	N 9 21.5	301 20.4	N12 44.1	127 39.3	S 8 41.8	Schedar	349 42.0	N56 36.4
A 13	350 47.7	331 31.4	57.6	181 55.2	21.9	316 22.5	44.2	142 41.9	41.7	Shaula	96 23.3	S37 06.6
Y 14	5 50.1	346 31.2	8 58.8	196 58.6	22.2	331 24.5	44.4	157 44.4	41.7	Sirius	258 34.3	S16 44.3
15	20 52.6	1 31.1	9 00.1	212 01.9	.. 22.6	346 26.5	.. 44.5	172 46.9	.. 41.7	Spica	158 32.0	S11 13.6
16	35 55.1	16 31.0	01.3	227 05.3	23.0	1 28.6	44.7	187 49.5	41.6	Suhail	222 52.7	S43 29.2
17	50 57.5	31 30.9	02.6	242 08.6	23.3	16 30.6	44.8	202 52.0	41.6			
18	66 00.0	46 30.8	N 9 03.8	257 12.0	N 9 23.7	31 32.7	N12 45.0	217 54.5	S 8 41.6	Vega	80 39.8	N38 47.5
19	81 02.5	61 30.6	05.0	272 15.3	24.1	46 34.7	45.1	232 57.1	41.5	Zuben'ubi	137 06.3	S16 05.6
20	96 04.9	76 30.5	06.3	287 18.7	24.4	61 36.8	45.3	247 59.6	41.5		SHA	Mer.Pass.
21	111 07.4	91 30.4	.. 07.5	302 22.0	.. 24.8	76 38.8	.. 45.4	263 02.2	.. 41.4		° ′	h m
22	126 09.9	106 30.3	08.8	317 25.4	25.2	91 40.9	45.6	278 04.7	41.4	Venus	342 19.3	14 54
23	141 12.3	121 30.2	10.0	332 28.7	25.5	106 42.9	45.7	293 07.2	41.4	Mars	190 35.3	1 00
	h m									Jupiter	325 50.2	15 57
Mer. Pass. 13 40.7		v −0.1	d 1.2	v 3.3	d 0.4	v 2.0	d 0.2	v 2.5	d 0.0	Saturn	151 51.6	3 35

UT	SUN GHA	Dec	MOON GHA	v	Dec	d	HP
24	° ′	° ′	° ′	′	° ′	′	′
00	176 39.9	S 9 45.5	156 29.7	14.9	N 3 47.1	11.4	55.0
01	191 40.0	44.6	171 03.6	14.9	3 58.5	11.4	55.0
02	206 40.1	43.7	185 37.5	14.9	4 09.9	11.4	55.0
03	221 40.2	.. 42.8	200 11.4	14.9	4 21.3	11.4	55.0
04	236 40.3	41.8	214 45.3	14.9	4 32.7	11.3	54.9
05	251 40.3	40.9	229 19.2	15.0	4 44.0	11.3	54.9
06	266 40.4	S 9 40.0	243 53.2	14.9	N 4 55.3	11.3	54.9
07	281 40.5	39.1	258 27.1	14.9	5 06.6	11.3	54.9
08	296 40.6	38.2	273 01.0	15.0	5 17.9	11.2	54.9
09	311 40.7	.. 37.2	287 35.0	14.9	5 29.1	11.2	54.9
10	326 40.8	36.3	302 08.9	15.0	5 40.3	11.2	54.8
11	341 40.9	35.4	316 42.9	14.9	5 51.5	11.1	54.8
12	356 41.0	S 9 34.5	331 16.8	14.9	N 6 02.6	11.1	54.8
13	11 41.1	33.6	345 50.7	15.0	6 13.7	11.1	54.8
14	26 41.1	32.6	0 24.7	14.9	6 24.8	11.0	54.8
15	41 41.2	.. 31.7	14 58.6	14.9	6 35.8	11.0	54.8
16	56 41.3	30.8	29 32.5	15.0	6 46.8	10.9	54.8
17	71 41.4	29.9	44 06.5	14.9	6 57.7	11.0	54.7
18	86 41.5	S 9 29.0	58 40.4	14.9	N 7 08.7	10.9	54.7
19	101 41.6	28.0	73 14.3	14.9	7 19.6	10.8	54.7
20	116 41.7	27.1	87 48.2	14.9	7 30.4	10.8	54.7
21	131 41.8	.. 26.2	102 22.1	14.9	7 41.2	10.8	54.7
22	146 41.9	25.2	116 56.0	14.9	7 52.0	10.7	54.7
23	161 42.0	24.3	131 29.9	14.9	8 02.7	10.7	54.6
25 00	176 42.1	S 9 23.4	146 03.8	14.9	N 8 13.4	10.7	54.6
01	191 42.2	22.5	160 37.7	14.8	8 24.1	10.6	54.6
02	206 42.2	21.5	175 11.5	14.9	8 34.7	10.6	54.6
03	221 42.3	.. 20.6	189 45.4	14.8	8 45.3	10.5	54.6
04	236 42.4	19.7	204 19.2	14.9	8 55.8	10.5	54.6
05	251 42.5	18.8	218 53.1	14.8	9 06.3	10.4	54.6
06	266 42.6	S 9 17.8	233 26.9	14.8	N 9 16.7	10.4	54.6
07	281 42.7	16.9	248 00.7	14.8	9 27.1	10.4	54.5
08	296 42.8	16.0	262 34.5	14.8	9 37.5	10.3	54.5
09	311 42.9	.. 15.1	277 08.3	14.8	9 47.8	10.3	54.5
10	326 43.0	14.1	291 42.1	14.7	9 58.1	10.2	54.5
11	341 43.1	13.2	306 15.8	14.8	10 08.3	10.1	54.5
12	356 43.2	S 9 12.3	320 49.6	14.7	N10 18.4	10.2	54.5
13	11 43.3	11.3	335 23.3	14.7	10 28.6	10.0	54.5
14	26 43.4	10.4	349 57.0	14.7	10 38.6	10.1	54.5
15	41 43.5	.. 09.5	4 30.7	14.7	10 48.7	9.9	54.4
16	56 43.6	08.6	19 04.4	14.6	10 58.6	9.9	54.4
17	71 43.7	07.6	33 38.0	14.7	11 08.5	9.9	54.4
18	86 43.8	S 9 06.7	48 11.7	14.6	N11 18.4	9.8	54.4
19	101 43.9	05.8	62 45.3	14.6	11 28.2	9.8	54.4
20	116 44.0	04.8	77 18.9	14.6	11 38.0	9.7	54.4
21	131 44.1	.. 03.9	91 52.5	14.5	11 47.7	9.7	54.4
22	146 44.2	03.0	106 26.0	14.6	11 57.4	9.6	54.4
23	161 44.3	02.1	120 59.6	14.5	12 07.0	9.5	54.4
26 00	176 44.4	S 9 01.1	135 33.1	14.5	N12 16.5	9.5	54.3
01	191 44.5	9 00.2	150 06.6	14.5	12 26.0	9.5	54.3
02	206 44.6	8 59.3	164 40.1	14.4	12 35.5	9.4	54.3
03	221 44.7	.. 58.3	179 13.5	14.4	12 44.9	9.3	54.3
04	236 44.8	57.4	193 46.9	14.4	12 54.2	9.3	54.3
05	251 44.9	56.5	208 20.3	14.4	13 03.5	9.2	54.3
06	266 45.0	S 8 55.5	222 53.7	14.4	N13 12.7	9.1	54.3
07	281 45.1	54.6	237 27.1	14.3	13 21.8	9.1	54.3
08	296 45.2	53.7	252 00.4	14.3	13 30.9	9.1	54.3
09	311 45.3	.. 52.7	266 33.7	14.3	13 40.0	8.9	54.3
10	326 45.4	51.8	281 07.0	14.2	13 48.9	9.0	54.3
11	341 45.5	50.9	295 40.2	14.2	13 57.9	8.8	54.3
12	356 45.6	S 8 49.9	310 13.4	14.2	N14 06.7	8.8	54.2
13	11 45.7	49.0	324 46.6	14.2	14 15.5	8.7	54.2
14	26 45.8	48.1	339 19.8	14.1	14 24.2	8.7	54.2
15	41 45.9	.. 47.1	353 52.9	14.1	14 32.9	8.6	54.2
16	56 46.0	46.2	8 26.0	14.1	14 41.5	8.5	54.2
17	71 46.1	45.3	22 59.1	14.0	14 50.0	8.5	54.2
18	86 46.2	S 8 44.3	37 32.1	14.0	N14 58.5	8.4	54.2
19	101 46.3	43.4	52 05.1	14.0	15 06.9	8.3	54.2
20	116 46.4	42.5	66 38.1	14.0	15 15.2	8.3	54.2
21	131 46.5	.. 41.5	81 11.1	13.9	15 23.5	8.2	54.2
22	146 46.6	40.6	95 44.0	13.9	15 31.7	8.2	54.2
23	161 46.7	39.7	110 16.9	13.8	N15 39.9	8.0	54.2
	SD 16.2	d 0.9	SD 14.9		14.8		14.8

Vertical day labels (left margin): FRIDAY, SATURDAY, SUNDAY

Lat.	Twilight Naut.	Twilight Civil	Sunrise	Moonrise 24	25	26	27
°	h m	h m	h m	h m	h m	h m	h m
N 72	05 32	06 50	08 01	06 44	06 27	06 05	05 30
N 70	05 35	06 45	07 49	06 51	06 40	06 29	06 14
68	05 37	06 41	07 39	06 56	06 52	06 47	06 43
66	05 39	06 38	07 30	07 01	07 01	07 02	07 05
64	05 40	06 35	07 23	07 05	07 09	07 15	07 23
62	05 41	06 32	07 17	07 08	07 16	07 25	07 37
60	05 42	06 30	07 12	07 11	07 22	07 34	07 50
N 58	05 42	06 27	07 07	07 14	07 27	07 42	08 00
56	05 42	06 25	07 03	07 17	07 32	07 49	08 10
54	05 43	06 23	06 59	07 19	07 36	07 55	08 18
52	05 43	06 22	06 56	07 21	07 40	08 01	08 25
50	05 43	06 20	06 53	07 23	07 43	08 06	08 32
45	05 42	06 16	06 46	07 27	07 51	08 17	08 46
N 40	05 42	06 13	06 40	07 30	07 57	08 26	08 58
35	05 40	06 10	06 35	07 33	08 03	08 34	09 08
30	05 39	06 07	06 31	07 36	08 08	08 41	09 17
20	05 35	06 01	06 23	07 40	08 16	08 54	09 33
N 10	05 31	05 55	06 16	07 44	08 24	09 04	09 46
0	05 25	05 49	06 10	07 48	08 31	09 15	09 59
S 10	05 17	05 42	06 03	07 52	08 38	09 25	10 12
20	05 07	05 33	05 56	07 56	08 46	09 36	10 26
30	04 54	05 23	05 48	08 01	08 55	09 48	10 42
35	04 46	05 17	05 43	08 03	09 00	09 55	10 51
40	04 36	05 09	05 37	08 07	09 05	10 04	11 02
45	04 23	05 00	05 31	08 10	09 12	10 14	11 14
S 50	04 07	04 49	05 23	08 15	09 20	10 25	11 29
52	03 59	04 43	05 19	08 17	09 24	10 31	11 36
54	03 50	04 37	05 15	08 19	09 28	10 37	11 44
56	03 40	04 31	05 11	08 21	09 33	10 44	11 53
58	03 28	04 23	05 06	08 24	09 38	10 51	12 03
S 60	03 13	04 14	05 00	08 27	09 44	11 00	12 15

Lat.	Sunset	Twilight Civil	Twilight Naut.	Moonset 24	25	26	27
°	h m	h m	h m	h m	h m	h m	h m
N 72	16 27	17 38	18 57	21 51	23 43	25 50	01 50
N 70	16 39	17 43	18 54	21 39	23 21	25 08	01 08
68	16 49	17 47	18 51	21 29	23 03	24 40	00 40
66	16 57	17 50	18 49	21 21	22 50	24 18	00 18
64	17 04	17 53	18 48	21 15	22 38	24 02	00 02
62	17 10	17 56	18 47	21 09	22 29	23 48	25 05
60	17 15	17 58	18 46	21 04	22 21	23 36	24 49
N 58	17 20	18 00	18 46	21 00	22 13	23 26	24 36
56	17 24	18 02	18 45	20 56	22 07	23 17	24 25
54	17 28	18 04	18 45	20 52	22 01	23 09	24 16
52	17 31	18 05	18 45	20 49	21 56	23 02	24 07
50	17 34	18 07	18 45	20 46	21 52	22 56	23 59
45	17 41	18 11	18 45	20 40	21 42	22 43	23 43
N 40	17 47	18 14	18 45	20 35	21 34	22 32	23 29
35	17 51	18 17	18 46	20 31	21 27	22 22	23 17
30	17 56	18 20	18 48	20 27	21 20	22 14	23 07
20	18 03	18 26	18 51	20 20	21 10	22 00	22 50
N 10	18 10	18 31	18 56	20 14	21 01	21 48	22 35
0	18 16	18 37	19 02	20 09	20 52	21 36	22 21
S 10	18 23	18 44	19 09	20 03	20 43	21 24	22 07
20	18 30	18 52	19 19	19 57	20 34	21 12	21 53
30	18 38	19 03	19 31	19 51	20 24	20 58	21 36
35	18 43	19 09	19 40	19 47	20 17	20 50	21 26
40	18 48	19 16	19 50	19 43	20 11	20 41	21 14
45	18 55	19 25	20 02	19 38	20 03	20 30	21 01
S 50	19 02	19 36	20 18	19 32	19 53	20 17	20 45
52	19 06	19 42	20 26	19 29	19 49	20 11	20 38
54	19 10	19 47	20 34	19 26	19 44	20 05	20 29
56	19 14	19 54	20 44	19 23	19 39	19 57	20 20
58	19 19	20 01	20 56	19 19	19 33	19 49	20 09
S 60	19 24	20 10	21 10	19 15	19 26	19 40	19 57

Day	SUN Eqn. of Time 00h	12h	Mer. Pass.	MOON Mer. Pass. Upper	Lower	Age	Phase
d	m s	m s	h m	h m	h m	d	%
24	13 21	13 16	12 13	13 58	01 37	03	7
25	13 12	13 07	12 13	14 41	02 20	04	12
26	13 03	12 58	12 13	15 25	03 03	05	19

UT	ARIES	VENUS −4.3		MARS −1.2		JUPITER −2.2		SATURN +0.4		STARS		
	GHA	GHA	Dec	GHA	Dec	GHA	Dec	GHA	Dec	Name	SHA	Dec
d h	° ′	° ′	° ′	° ′	° ′	° ′	° ′	° ′	° ′		° ′	° ′
27 00	156 14.8	136 30.0 N 9 11.2		347 32.1 N 9 25.9		121 44.9 N12 45.9		308 09.8 S 8 41.3		Acamar	315 19.2 S40 15.6	
01	171 17.3	151 29.9	12.5	2 35.4	26.3	136 47.0	46.0	323 12.3	41.3	Achernar	335 27.8 S57 10.7	
02	186 19.7	166 29.8	13.7	17 38.8	26.6	151 49.0	46.2	338 14.9	41.2	Acrux	173 09.7 S63 10.0	
03	201 22.2	181 29.7 . .	14.9	32 42.1 . .	27.0	166 51.1 . .	46.3	353 17.4 . .	41.2	Adhara	255 13.0 S28 59.7	
04	216 24.6	196 29.6	16.2	47 45.5	27.4	181 53.1	46.5	8 19.9	41.2	Aldebaran	290 50.4 N16 31.9	
05	231 27.1	211 29.4	17.4	62 48.8	27.7	196 55.1	46.7	23 22.5	41.1			
06	246 29.6	226 29.3 N 9 18.6		77 52.2 N 9 28.1		211 57.2 N12 46.8		38 25.0 S 8 41.1		Alioth	166 21.0 N55 53.3	
07	261 32.0	241 29.2	19.9	92 55.5	28.5	226 59.2	47.0	53 27.6	41.1	Alkaid	152 59.2 N49 14.8	
08	276 34.5	256 29.1	21.1	107 58.9	28.8	242 01.3	47.1	68 30.1	41.0	Al Na'ir	27 45.3 S46 54.0	
M 09	291 37.0	271 29.0 . .	22.3	123 02.2 . .	29.2	257 03.3 . .	47.3	83 32.6 . .	41.0	Alnilam	275 47.2 S 1 11.9	
O 10	306 39.4	286 28.9	23.6	138 05.6	29.6	272 05.3	47.4	98 35.2	40.9	Alphard	217 56.7 S 8 43.0	
N 11	321 41.9	301 28.7	24.8	153 09.0	29.9	287 07.4	47.6	113 37.7	40.9			
D 12	336 44.4	316 28.6 N 9 26.0		168 12.3 N 9 30.3		302 09.4 N12 47.7		128 40.3 S 8 40.9		Alphecca	126 11.7 N26 40.2	
A 13	351 46.8	331 28.5	27.3	183 15.7	30.7	317 11.5	47.9	143 42.8	40.8	Alpheratz	357 44.8 N29 09.5	
Y 14	6 49.3	346 28.4	28.5	198 19.0	31.0	332 13.5	48.0	158 45.3	40.8	Altair	62 09.4 N 8 54.0	
15	21 51.7	1 28.3 . .	29.7	213 22.4 . .	31.4	347 15.5 . .	48.2	173 47.9 . .	40.7	Ankaa	353 16.9 S42 14.5	
16	36 54.2	16 28.1	31.0	228 25.8	31.8	2 17.6	48.3	188 50.4	40.7	Antares	112 27.4 S26 27.5	
17	51 56.7	31 28.0	32.2	243 29.1	32.1	17 19.6	48.5	203 53.0	40.7			
18	66 59.1	46 27.9 N 9 33.4		258 32.5 N 9 32.5		32 21.7 N12 48.6		218 55.5 S 8 40.6		Arcturus	145 56.3 N19 06.9	
19	82 01.6	61 27.8	34.7	273 35.8	32.9	47 23.7	48.8	233 58.0	40.6	Atria	107 30.1 S69 02.6	
20	97 04.1	76 27.7	35.9	288 39.2	33.2	62 25.7	48.9	249 00.6	40.6	Avior	234 15.9 S59 33.2	
21	112 06.5	91 27.6 . .	37.1	303 42.6 . .	33.6	77 27.8 . .	49.1	264 03.1 . .	40.5	Bellatrix	278 32.9 N 6 21.5	
22	127 09.0	106 27.4	38.4	318 45.9	34.0	92 29.8	49.3	279 05.7	40.5	Betelgeuse	271 02.1 N 7 24.4	
23	142 11.5	121 27.3	39.6	333 49.3	34.3	107 31.9	49.4	294 08.2	40.4			
28 00	157 13.9	136 27.2 N 9 40.8		348 52.7 N 9 34.7		122 33.9 N12 49.6		309 10.8 S 8 40.4		Canopus	263 56.3 S52 42.5	
01	172 16.4	151 27.1	42.0	3 56.0	35.0	137 35.9	49.7	324 13.3	40.4	Capella	280 35.7 N46 00.7	
02	187 18.9	166 27.0	43.3	18 59.4	35.4	152 38.0	49.9	339 15.8	40.3	Deneb	49 32.5 N45 19.4	
03	202 21.3	181 26.8 . .	44.5	34 02.8 . .	35.8	167 40.0 . .	50.0	354 18.4 . .	40.3	Denebola	182 34.3 N14 30.0	
04	217 23.8	196 26.7	45.7	49 06.1	36.1	182 42.0	50.2	9 20.9	40.2	Diphda	348 57.0 S17 55.3	
05	232 26.2	211 26.6	46.9	64 09.5	36.5	197 44.1	50.3	24 23.5	40.2			
06	247 28.7	226 26.5 N 9 48.2		79 12.9 N 9 36.9		212 46.1 N12 50.5		39 26.0 S 8 40.2		Dubhe	193 52.1 N61 40.9	
07	262 31.2	241 26.4	49.4	94 16.2	37.2	227 48.2	50.6	54 28.6	40.1	Elnath	278 13.7 N28 37.0	
08	277 33.6	256 26.3	50.6	109 19.6	37.6	242 50.2	50.8	69 31.1	40.1	Eltanin	90 46.7 N51 29.0	
T 09	292 36.1	271 26.1 . .	51.9	124 23.0 . .	38.0	257 52.2 . .	50.9	84 33.6 . .	40.0	Enif	33 48.3 N 9 55.9	
U 10	307 38.6	286 26.0	53.1	139 26.3	38.3	272 54.3	51.1	99 36.2	40.0	Fomalhaut	15 25.3 S29 33.5	
E 11	322 41.0	301 25.9	54.3	154 29.7	38.7	287 56.3	51.2	114 38.7	40.0			
S 12	337 43.5	316 25.8 N 9 55.5		169 33.1 N 9 39.1		302 58.3 N12 51.4		129 41.3 S 8 39.9		Gacrux	172 01.4 S57 10.9	
D 13	352 46.0	331 25.7	56.7	184 36.4	39.4	318 00.4	51.6	144 43.8	39.9	Gienah	175 52.9 S17 36.7	
A 14	7 48.4	346 25.6	58.0	199 39.8	39.8	333 02.4	51.7	159 46.4	39.8	Hadar	148 48.8 S60 25.5	
Y 15	22 50.9	1 25.4 . . 9	59.2	214 43.2 . .	40.2	348 04.4 . .	51.9	174 48.9 . .	39.8	Hamal	328 02.0 N23 31.2	
16	37 53.4	16 25.3 10 00.4		229 46.5	40.5	3 06.5	52.0	189 51.5	39.8	Kaus Aust.	83 45.2 S34 22.6	
17	52 55.8	31 25.2	01.6	244 49.9	40.9	18 08.5	52.2	204 54.0	39.7			
18	67 58.3	46 25.1 N10 02.9		259 53.3 N 9 41.3		33 10.5 N12 52.3		219 56.6 S 8 39.7		Kochab	137 19.4 N74 06.0	
19	83 00.7	61 25.0	04.1	274 56.7	41.6	48 12.6	52.5	234 59.1	39.6	Markab	13 39.6 N15 16.3	
20	98 03.2	76 24.9	05.3	290 00.0	42.0	63 14.6	52.6	250 01.6	39.6	Menkar	314 16.1 N 4 08.1	
21	113 05.7	91 24.7 . .	06.5	305 03.4 . .	42.4	78 16.6 . .	52.8	265 04.2 . .	39.6	Menkent	148 08.4 S36 25.8	
22	128 08.1	106 24.6	07.7	320 06.8	42.7	93 18.7	52.9	280 06.7	39.5	Miaplacidus	221 39.0 S69 46.3	
23	143 10.6	121 24.5	09.0	335 10.2	43.1	108 20.7	53.1	295 09.3	39.5			
29 00	158 13.1	136 24.4 N10 10.2		350 13.5 N 9 43.5		123 22.7 N12 53.2		310 11.8 S 8 39.4		Mirfak	308 41.8 N49 54.4	
01	173 15.5	151 24.3	11.4	5 16.9	43.8	138 24.8	53.4	325 14.4	39.4	Nunki	75 59.6 S26 16.8	
02	188 18.0	166 24.2	12.6	20 20.3	44.2	153 26.8	53.6	340 16.9	39.4	Peacock	53 21.1 S56 41.5	
03	203 20.5	181 24.0 . .	13.8	35 23.7 . .	44.6	168 28.8 . .	53.7	355 19.5 . .	39.3	Pollux	243 28.5 N27 59.6	
04	218 22.9	196 23.9	15.1	50 27.0	44.9	183 30.9	53.9	10 22.0	39.3	Procyon	245 00.4 N 5 11.4	
05	233 25.4	211 23.8	16.3	65 30.4	45.3	198 32.9	54.0	25 24.6	39.2			
06	248 27.8	226 23.7 N10 17.5		80 33.8 N 9 45.6		213 34.9 N12 54.2		40 27.1 S 8 39.2		Rasalhague	96 07.4 N12 33.0	
W 07	263 30.3	241 23.6	18.7	95 37.2	46.0	228 37.0	54.3	55 29.7	39.1	Regulus	207 44.1 N11 54.2	
E 08	278 32.8	256 23.5	19.9	110 40.5	46.4	243 39.0	54.5	70 32.2	39.1	Rigel	281 12.8 S 8 11.5	
D 09	293 35.2	271 23.3 . .	21.1	125 43.9 . .	46.7	258 41.0 . .	54.6	85 34.8 . .	39.1	Rigil Kent.	139 52.6 S60 52.9	
N 10	308 37.7	286 23.2	22.4	140 47.3	47.1	273 43.1	54.8	100 37.3	39.0	Sabik	102 13.6 S15 44.4	
E 11	323 40.2	301 23.1	23.6	155 50.7	47.5	288 45.1	54.9	115 39.8	39.0			
S 12	338 42.6	316 23.0 N10 24.8		170 54.1 N 9 47.8		303 47.1 N12 55.1		130 42.4 S 8 38.9		Schedar	349 42.1 N56 36.4	
D 13	353 45.1	331 22.9	26.0	185 57.4	48.2	318 49.2	55.3	145 44.9	38.9	Shaula	96 23.2 S37 06.6	
A 14	8 47.6	346 22.8	27.2	201 00.8	48.6	333 51.2	55.4	160 47.5	38.9	Sirius	258 34.3 S16 44.3	
Y 15	23 50.0	1 22.6 . .	28.4	216 04.2 . .	48.9	348 53.2 . .	55.6	175 50.0 . .	38.8	Spica	158 32.0 S11 13.6	
16	38 52.5	16 22.5	29.6	231 07.6	49.3	3 55.2	55.7	190 52.6	38.8	Suhail	222 52.7 S43 29.2	
17	53 55.0	31 22.4	30.9	246 11.0	49.7	18 57.3	55.9	205 55.1	38.7			
18	68 57.4	46 22.3 N10 32.1		261 14.3 N 9 50.0		33 59.3 N12 56.0		220 57.7 S 8 38.7		Vega	80 39.8 N38 47.5	
19	83 59.9	61 22.2	33.3	276 17.7	50.4	49 01.3	56.2	236 00.2	38.7	Zuben'ubi	137 06.3 S16 05.6	
20	99 02.3	76 22.1	34.5	291 21.1	50.8	64 03.4	56.3	251 02.8	38.6		SHA	Mer.Pass.
21	114 04.8	91 22.0 . .	35.7	306 24.5 . .	51.1	79 05.4 . .	56.5	266 05.3 . .	38.6		° ′	h m
22	129 07.3	106 21.8	36.9	321 27.9	51.5	94 07.4	56.7	281 07.9	38.5	Venus	339 13.3	14 54
23	144 09.7	121 21.7	38.1	336 31.3	51.8	109 09.5	56.8	296 10.4	38.5	Mars	191 38.7	0 44
	h m									Jupiter	325 20.0	15 48
Mer.Pass. 13 28.9		v −0.1 d 1.2		v 3.4 d 0.4		v 2.0 d 0.2		v 2.5 d 0.0		Saturn	151 56.8	3 23

UT	SUN		MOON					Lat.	Twilight		Sunrise	Moonrise			
	GHA	Dec	GHA	v	Dec	d	HP		Naut.	Civil		27	28	29	1
d h	° ′	° ′	° ′	′	° ′	′	′	°	h m	h m	h m	h m	h m	h m	h m
27 00	176 46.8	S 8 38.7	124 49.7	13.8	N15 47.9	8.0	54.2	N 72	05 18	06 36	07 45	05 30	▭	▭	▭
01	191 46.9	37.8	139 22.5	13.8	15 55.9	8.0	54.2	N 70	05 22	06 32	07 35	06 14	05 46	▭	▭
02	206 47.0	36.8	153 55.3	13.8	16 03.9	7.8	54.2	68	05 25	06 29	07 26	06 43	06 39	06 34	06 24
03	221 47.1	.. 35.9	168 28.1	13.7	16 11.7	7.8	54.2	66	05 28	06 27	07 19	07 05	07 11	07 24	07 53
04	236 47.2	35.0	183 00.8	13.7	16 19.5	7.7	54.2	64	05 30	06 25	07 13	07 23	07 35	07 56	08 31
05	251 47.3	34.0	197 33.5	13.7	16 27.2	7.7	54.2	62	05 32	06 23	07 08	07 37	07 54	08 20	08 58
06	266 47.4	S 8 33.1	212 06.2	13.6	N16 34.9	7.5	54.2	60	05 33	06 21	07 03	07 50	08 10	08 39	09 18
07	281 47.5	32.2	226 38.8	13.6	16 42.4	7.5	54.2	N 58	05 34	06 20	06 59	08 00	08 24	08 54	09 35
M 08	296 47.6	31.2	241 11.4	13.5	16 49.9	7.5	54.2	56	05 35	06 18	06 56	08 10	08 35	09 08	09 50
O 09	311 47.7	.. 30.3	255 43.9	13.5	16 57.4	7.3	54.2	54	05 36	06 17	06 52	08 18	08 45	09 19	10 02
N 10	326 47.9	29.3	270 16.4	13.5	17 04.7	7.3	54.2	52	05 37	06 15	06 49	08 25	08 54	09 30	10 13
D 11	341 48.0	28.4	284 48.9	13.4	17 12.0	7.2	54.2	50	05 37	06 14	06 47	08 32	09 02	09 39	10 23
A 12	356 48.1	S 8 27.5	299 21.3	13.4	N17 19.2	7.1	54.2	45	05 37	06 11	06 41	08 46	09 20	09 58	10 44
Y 13	11 48.2	26.5	313 53.7	13.4	17 26.3	7.1	54.2	N 40	05 37	06 09	06 36	08 58	09 34	10 14	11 00
14	26 48.3	25.6	328 26.1	13.3	17 33.4	7.0	54.2	35	05 37	06 06	06 32	09 08	09 46	10 28	11 14
15	41 48.4	.. 24.7	342 58.4	13.3	17 40.4	6.9	54.2	30	05 36	06 04	06 28	09 17	09 56	10 39	11 27
16	56 48.5	23.7	357 30.7	13.3	17 47.3	6.8	54.2	20	05 33	05 59	06 21	09 33	10 15	10 59	11 47
17	71 48.6	22.8	12 03.0	13.2	17 54.1	6.7	54.2	N 10	05 29	05 54	06 15	09 46	10 31	11 17	12 06
18	86 48.7	S 8 21.8	26 35.2	13.2	N18 00.8	6.7	54.2	0	05 24	05 48	06 09	09 59	10 45	11 33	12 23
19	101 48.8	20.9	41 07.4	13.1	18 07.5	6.6	54.2	S 10	05 17	05 42	06 03	10 12	11 00	11 50	12 40
20	116 48.9	20.0	55 39.5	13.1	18 14.1	6.5	54.2	20	05 09	05 35	05 57	10 26	11 16	12 07	12 58
21	131 49.0	.. 19.0	70 11.6	13.1	18 20.6	6.4	54.2	30	04 57	05 25	05 50	10 42	11 35	12 28	13 19
22	146 49.2	18.1	84 43.7	13.0	18 27.0	6.4	54.2	35	04 49	05 20	05 45	10 51	11 46	12 40	13 31
23	161 49.3	17.1	99 15.7	13.0	18 33.4	6.2	54.2	40	04 40	05 13	05 41	11 02	11 58	12 53	13 46
28 00	176 49.4	S 8 16.2	113 47.7	13.0	N18 39.6	6.2	54.2	45	04 28	05 04	05 35	11 14	12 13	13 09	14 02
01	191 49.5	15.2	128 19.7	12.9	18 45.8	6.1	54.2	S 50	04 13	04 54	05 28	11 29	12 31	13 29	14 23
02	206 49.6	14.3	142 51.6	12.9	18 51.9	6.0	54.2	52	04 06	04 49	05 25	11 36	12 40	13 39	14 33
03	221 49.7	.. 13.4	157 23.5	12.8	18 57.9	6.0	54.2	54	03 58	04 44	05 21	11 44	12 49	13 50	14 44
04	236 49.8	12.4	171 55.3	12.8	19 03.9	5.8	54.2	56	03 48	04 38	05 17	11 53	13 00	14 02	14 57
05	251 49.9	11.5	186 27.1	12.8	19 09.7	5.8	54.2	S 60	03 37	04 31	05 13	12 03	13 12	14 16	15 12
06	266 50.0	S 8 10.5	200 58.9	12.7	N19 15.5	5.7	54.2			Twilight			Moonset		
07	281 50.2	09.6	215 30.6	12.7	19 21.2	5.6	54.2	Lat.	Sunset			27	28	29	1
08	296 50.3	08.7	230 02.3	12.6	19 26.8	5.5	54.2			Civil	Naut.				
T 09	311 50.4	.. 07.7	244 33.9	12.6	19 32.3	5.4	54.2								
U 10	326 50.5	06.8	259 05.5	12.6	19 37.7	5.3	54.2	°	h m	h m	h m	h m	h m	h m	h m
E 11	341 50.6	05.8	273 37.1	12.5	19 43.0	5.3	54.2	N 72	16 42	17 52	19 10	01 50	▭	▭	▭
S 12	356 50.7	S 8 04.9	288 08.6	12.5	N19 48.3	5.1	54.2	N 70	16 52	17 55	19 06	01 08	03 11	▭	▭
D 13	11 50.8	03.9	302 40.1	12.5	19 53.4	5.1	54.2	68	17 01	17 58	19 02	00 40	02 19	04 02	▭
A 14	26 51.0	03.0	317 11.6	12.4	19 58.5	5.0	54.2	66	17 08	18 00	18 59	00 18	01 47	03 12	05 54
Y 15	41 51.1	.. 02.0	331 43.0	12.3	20 03.5	4.9	54.2	64	17 14	18 02	18 57	00 02	01 23	02 40	04 25
16	56 51.2	01.1	346 14.3	12.4	20 08.4	4.8	54.3	62	17 19	18 04	18 55	25 05	01 05	02 17	03 47
17	71 51.3	8 00.2	0 45.7	12.2	20 13.2	4.7	54.3	60	17 23	18 05	18 53	24 49	00 49	01 58	03 21
18	86 51.4	S 7 59.2	15 16.9	12.3	N20 17.9	4.6	54.3	N 58	17 27	18 07	18 52	24 36	00 36	01 43	03 00
19	101 51.5	58.3	29 48.2	12.2	20 22.5	4.5	54.3	56	17 31	18 08	18 51	24 25	00 25	01 30	02 43
20	116 51.6	57.3	44 19.4	12.2	20 27.0	4.5	54.3	54	17 34	18 09	18 50	24 16	00 16	01 18	02 28
21	131 51.8	.. 56.4	58 50.6	12.1	20 31.5	4.3	54.3	52	17 37	18 11	18 50	24 07	00 07	01 08	02 16
22	146 51.9	55.4	73 21.7	12.1	20 35.8	4.3	54.3	50	17 39	18 12	18 49	23 59	24 59	00 59	02 05
23	161 52.0	54.5	87 52.8	12.0	20 40.1	4.1	54.3	45	17 45	18 15	18 49	23 43	24 40	00 40	01 55
29 00	176 52.1	S 7 53.5	102 23.8	12.1	N20 44.2	4.1	54.3	N 40	17 50	18 17	18 49	23 29	24 25	00 25	01 35
01	191 52.2	52.6	116 54.9	11.9	20 48.3	4.0	54.3	35	17 54	18 20	18 49	23 17	24 12	00 12	01 19
02	206 52.3	51.6	131 25.8	12.0	20 52.3	3.8	54.3	30	17 58	18 22	18 50	23 07	24 00	00 00	01 05
03	221 52.5	.. 50.7	145 56.8	11.9	20 56.1	3.8	54.4	20	18 04	18 27	18 52	22 50	23 41	24 32	00 53
04	236 52.6	49.8	160 27.7	11.8	20 59.9	3.7	54.4	N 10	18 10	18 31	18 56	22 35	23 24	24 14	00 32
05	251 52.7	48.8	174 58.5	11.9	21 03.6	3.6	54.4	0	18 16	18 37	19 01	22 21	23 08	23 57	00 14
06	266 52.8	S 7 47.9	189 29.4	11.7	N21 07.2	3.5	54.4	S 10	18 22	18 43	19 08	22 07	22 53	23 40	24 30
W 07	281 52.9	46.9	204 00.1	11.8	21 10.7	3.4	54.4	20	18 28	18 50	19 16	21 53	22 36	23 22	24 12
E 08	296 53.0	46.0	218 30.9	11.7	21 14.1	3.3	54.4	30	18 35	18 59	19 28	21 36	22 16	23 01	23 51
D 09	311 53.2	.. 45.0	233 01.6	11.7	21 17.4	3.2	54.4	35	18 39	19 05	19 36	21 26	22 05	22 49	23 38
N 10	326 53.3	44.1	247 32.3	11.6	21 20.6	3.1	54.4	40	18 44	19 12	19 45	21 14	21 52	22 35	23 24
E 11	341 53.4	43.1	262 02.9	11.6	21 23.7	3.0	54.5	45	18 50	19 20	19 56	21 01	21 37	22 19	23 07
S 12	356 53.5	S 7 42.2	276 33.5	11.6	N21 26.7	2.9	54.5	S 50	18 56	19 30	20 11	20 45	21 18	21 59	22 47
D 13	11 53.6	41.2	291 04.1	11.5	21 29.6	2.8	54.5	52	18 59	19 35	20 18	20 38	21 10	21 49	22 37
A 14	26 53.8	40.3	305 34.6	11.5	21 32.4	2.7	54.5	54	19 03	19 40	20 26	20 29	21 00	21 38	22 26
Y 15	41 53.9	.. 39.3	320 05.1	11.4	21 35.1	2.6	54.5	56	19 07	19 46	20 35	20 20	20 49	21 26	22 13
16	56 54.0	38.4	334 35.5	11.5	21 37.7	2.5	54.5	58	19 11	19 53	20 46	20 09	20 36	21 11	21 58
17	71 54.1	37.4	349 06.0	11.3	21 40.2	2.4	54.5	S 60	19 16	20 00	20 58	19 57	20 21	20 55	21 41
18	86 54.2	S 7 36.5	3 36.3	11.4	N21 42.6	2.3	54.6			SUN			MOON		
19	101 54.4	35.5	18 06.7	11.3	21 44.9	2.2	54.6								
20	116 54.5	34.6	32 37.0	11.3	21 47.1	2.0	54.6	Day	Eqn. of Time		Mer.	Mer. Pass.		Age	Phase
21	131 54.6	.. 33.6	47 07.3	11.2	21 49.1	2.0	54.6		00ʰ	12ʰ	Pass.	Upper	Lower		
22	146 54.7	32.7	61 37.5	11.2	21 51.1	1.9	54.6	d	m s	m s	h m	h m	h m	d	%
23	161 54.8	31.7	76 07.7	11.2	N21 53.0	1.8	54.6	27	12 53	12 48	12 13	16 10	03 48	06	27
	SD 16.2	d 0.9	SD 14.8		14.8		14.8	28	12 43	12 37	12 13	16 57	04 33	07	36
								29	12 32	12 26	12 12	17 45	05 21	08	45

UT	ARIES GHA	VENUS −4.3 GHA	Dec	MARS −1.2 GHA	Dec	JUPITER −2.2 GHA	Dec	SATURN +0.4 GHA	Dec	STARS Name	SHA	Dec
1 00	159 12.2	136 21.6	N10 39.3	351 34.6	N 9 52.2	124 11.5	N12 57.0	311 13.0	S 8 38.4	Acamar	315 19.2	S40 15.6
01	174 14.7	151 21.5	40.5	6 38.0	52.6	139 13.5	57.1	326 15.5	38.4	Achernar	335 27.8	S57 10.7
02	189 17.1	166 21.4	41.7	21 41.4	52.9	154 15.5	57.3	341 18.1	38.4	Acrux	173 09.7	S63 10.0
03	204 19.6	181 21.3	.. 43.0	36 44.8	.. 53.3	169 17.6	.. 57.4	356 20.6	.. 38.3	Adhara	255 13.0	S28 59.7
04	219 22.1	196 21.1	44.2	51 48.2	53.7	184 19.6	57.6	11 23.2	38.3	Aldebaran	290 50.4	N16 31.9
05	234 24.5	211 21.0	45.4	66 51.6	54.0	199 21.6	57.7	26 25.7	38.2			
06	249 27.0	226 20.9	N10 46.6	81 55.0	N 9 54.4	214 23.6	N12 57.9	41 28.3	S 8 38.2	Alioth	166 20.9	N55 53.3
07	264 29.5	241 20.8	47.8	96 58.3	54.7	229 25.7	58.1	56 30.8	38.1	Alkaid	152 59.2	N49 14.8
T 08	279 31.9	256 20.7	49.0	112 01.7	55.1	244 27.7	58.2	71 33.4	38.1	Al Na'ir	27 45.3	S46 54.0
H 09	294 34.4	271 20.6	.. 50.2	127 05.1	.. 55.5	259 29.7	.. 58.4	86 35.9	.. 38.1	Alnilam	275 47.2	S 1 11.9
U 10	309 36.8	286 20.5	51.4	142 08.5	55.8	274 31.8	58.5	101 38.5	38.0	Alphard	217 56.7	S 8 43.0
R 11	324 39.3	301 20.3	52.6	157 11.9	56.2	289 33.8	58.7	116 41.0	38.0			
S 12	339 41.8	316 20.2	N10 53.8	172 15.3	N 9 56.6	304 35.8	N12 58.8	131 43.6	S 8 37.9	Alphecca	126 11.6	N26 40.2
D 13	354 44.2	331 20.1	55.0	187 18.7	56.9	319 37.8	59.0	146 46.2	37.9	Alpheratz	357 44.8	N29 09.5
A 14	9 46.7	346 20.0	56.2	202 22.1	57.3	334 39.9	59.1	161 48.7	37.9	Altair	62 09.3	N 8 54.0
Y 15	24 49.2	1 19.9	.. 57.4	217 25.4	.. 57.6	349 41.9	.. 59.3	176 51.3	.. 37.8	Ankaa	353 16.9	S42 14.5
16	39 51.6	16 19.8	58.6	232 28.8	58.0	4 43.9	59.5	191 53.8	37.8	Antares	112 27.3	S26 27.5
17	54 54.1	31 19.7	10 59.8	247 32.2	58.4	19 45.9	59.6	206 56.4	37.7			
18	69 56.6	46 19.5	N11 01.0	262 35.6	N 9 58.7	34 48.0	N12 59.8	221 58.9	S 8 37.7	Arcturus	145 56.3	N19 06.9
19	84 59.0	61 19.4	02.2	277 39.0	59.1	49 50.0	12 59.9	237 01.5	37.6	Atria	107 30.0	S69 02.6
20	100 01.5	76 19.3	03.4	292 42.4	59.5	64 52.0	13 00.1	252 04.0	37.6	Avior	234 17.9	S59 33.3
21	115 04.0	91 19.2	.. 04.6	307 45.8	9 59.8	79 54.0	.. 00.2	267 06.6	.. 37.6	Bellatrix	278 32.9	N 6 21.5
22	130 06.4	106 19.1	05.8	322 49.2	10 00.2	94 56.1	00.4	282 09.1	37.5	Betelgeuse	271 02.2	N 7 24.4
23	145 08.9	121 19.0	07.0	337 52.6	00.5	109 58.1	00.5	297 11.7	37.5			
2 00	160 11.3	136 18.9	N11 08.2	352 56.0	N10 00.9	125 00.1	N13 00.7	312 14.2	S 8 37.4	Canopus	263 56.3	S52 42.5
01	175 13.8	151 18.7	09.4	7 59.3	01.3	140 02.1	00.9	327 16.8	37.4	Capella	280 35.7	N46 00.7
02	190 16.3	166 18.6	10.6	23 02.7	01.6	155 04.2	01.0	342 19.3	37.3	Deneb	49 32.5	N45 19.4
03	205 18.7	181 18.5	.. 11.8	38 06.1	.. 02.0	170 06.2	.. 01.2	357 21.9	.. 37.3	Denebola	182 34.2	N14 30.0
04	220 21.2	196 18.4	13.0	53 09.5	02.3	185 08.2	01.3	12 24.4	37.2	Diphda	348 57.1	S17 55.3
05	235 23.7	211 18.3	14.2	68 12.9	02.7	200 10.2	01.5	27 27.0	37.2			
06	250 26.1	226 18.2	N11 15.4	83 16.3	N10 03.1	215 12.3	N13 01.6	42 29.6	S 8 37.2	Dubhe	193 52.1	N61 40.9
07	265 28.6	241 18.1	16.6	98 19.7	03.4	230 14.3	01.8	57 32.1	37.1	Elnath	278 13.7	N28 37.0
F 08	280 31.1	256 17.9	17.8	113 23.1	03.8	245 16.3	02.0	72 34.7	37.1	Eltanin	90 46.7	N51 29.0
R 09	295 33.5	271 17.8	.. 19.0	128 26.5	.. 04.1	260 18.3	.. 02.1	87 37.2	.. 37.0	Enif	33 48.3	N 9 55.9
I 10	310 36.0	286 17.7	20.2	143 29.9	04.5	275 20.3	02.3	102 39.8	37.0	Fomalhaut	15 25.3	S29 33.5
D 11	325 38.4	301 17.6	21.4	158 33.3	04.9	290 22.4	02.4	117 42.3	36.9			
A 12	340 40.9	316 17.5	N11 22.6	173 36.7	N10 05.2	305 24.4	N13 02.6	132 44.9	S 8 36.9	Gacrux	172 01.4	S57 10.9
Y 13	355 43.4	331 17.4	23.8	188 40.1	05.6	320 26.4	02.7	147 47.4	36.9	Gienah	175 52.9	S17 36.8
14	10 45.8	346 17.3	25.0	203 43.5	05.9	335 28.4	02.9	162 50.0	36.8	Hadar	148 48.8	S60 25.8
15	25 48.3	1 17.1	.. 26.2	218 46.9	.. 06.3	350 30.5	.. 03.1	177 52.6	.. 36.8	Hamal	328 02.0	N23 31.2
16	40 50.8	16 17.0	27.4	233 50.2	06.7	5 32.5	03.2	192 55.1	36.7	Kaus Aust.	83 45.1	S34 22.6
17	55 53.2	31 16.9	28.6	248 53.6	07.0	20 34.5	03.4	207 57.7	36.7			
18	70 55.7	46 16.8	N11 29.8	263 57.0	N10 07.4	35 36.5	N13 03.5	223 00.2	S 8 36.6	Kochab	137 19.4	N74 06.0
19	85 58.2	61 16.7	31.0	279 00.4	07.8	50 38.5	03.7	238 02.8	36.6	Markab	13 39.5	N15 16.3
20	101 00.6	76 16.6	32.2	294 03.8	08.1	65 40.6	03.8	253 05.3	36.6	Menkar	314 16.1	N 4 08.1
21	116 03.1	91 16.5	.. 33.3	309 07.2	.. 08.5	80 42.6	.. 04.0	268 07.9	.. 36.5	Menkent	148 08.4	S36 25.8
22	131 05.6	106 16.4	34.5	324 10.6	08.8	95 44.6	04.2	283 10.5	36.5	Miaplacidus	221 39.1	S69 46.3
23	146 08.0	121 16.2	35.7	339 14.0	09.2	110 46.6	04.3	298 13.0	36.4			
3 00	161 10.5	136 16.1	N11 36.9	354 17.4	N10 09.5	125 48.6	N13 04.5	313 15.6	S 8 36.4	Mirfak	308 41.8	N49 54.4
01	176 12.9	151 16.0	38.1	9 20.8	09.9	140 50.7	04.6	328 18.1	36.3	Nunki	75 59.6	S26 16.8
02	191 15.4	166 15.9	39.3	24 24.2	10.3	155 52.7	04.8	343 20.7	36.3	Peacock	53 21.1	S56 41.5
03	206 17.9	181 15.8	.. 40.5	39 27.6	.. 10.6	170 54.7	.. 04.9	358 23.2	.. 36.2	Pollux	243 28.6	N27 59.7
04	221 20.3	196 15.7	41.7	54 31.0	11.0	185 56.7	05.1	13 25.8	36.2	Procyon	245 00.4	N 5 11.4
05	236 22.8	211 15.6	42.9	69 34.4	11.3	200 58.7	05.3	28 28.4	36.2			
06	251 25.3	226 15.4	N11 44.0	84 37.8	N10 11.7	216 00.8	N13 05.4	43 30.9	S 8 36.1	Rasalhague	96 07.3	N12 33.0
07	266 27.7	241 15.3	45.2	99 41.2	12.0	231 02.8	05.6	58 33.5	36.1	Regulus	207 44.1	N11 54.2
S 08	281 30.2	256 15.2	46.4	114 44.6	12.4	246 04.8	05.7	73 36.0	36.0	Rigel	281 12.9	S 8 11.5
A 09	296 32.7	271 15.1	.. 47.6	129 48.0	.. 12.8	261 06.8	.. 05.9	88 38.6	.. 36.0	Rigil Kent.	139 52.6	S60 52.9
T 10	311 35.1	286 15.0	48.8	144 51.4	13.1	276 08.8	06.0	103 41.1	35.9	Sabik	102 13.6	S15 44.4
U 11	326 37.6	301 14.9	50.0	159 54.8	13.5	291 10.9	06.2	118 43.7	35.9			
R 12	341 40.1	316 14.8	N11 51.2	174 58.2	N10 13.8	306 12.9	N13 06.4	133 46.3	S 8 35.8	Schedar	349 42.1	N56 36.4
D 13	356 42.5	331 14.7	52.3	190 01.6	14.2	321 14.9	06.5	148 48.8	35.8	Shaula	96 23.2	S37 06.6
A 14	11 45.0	346 14.5	53.5	205 05.0	14.5	336 16.9	06.7	163 51.4	35.7	Sirius	258 34.3	S16 44.3
Y 15	26 47.4	1 14.4	.. 54.7	220 08.4	.. 14.9	351 18.9	.. 06.8	178 53.9	.. 35.7	Spica	158 31.9	S11 13.6
16	41 49.9	16 14.3	55.9	235 11.8	15.2	6 20.9	07.0	193 56.5	35.7	Suhail	222 52.7	S43 29.2
17	56 52.4	31 14.2	57.1	250 15.2	15.6	21 23.0	07.1	208 59.1	35.6			
18	71 54.8	46 14.1	N11 58.2	265 18.6	N10 16.0	36 25.0	N13 07.3	224 01.6	S 8 35.6	Vega	80 39.8	N38 47.5
19	86 57.3	61 14.0	11 59.4	280 22.0	16.3	51 27.0	07.5	239 04.2	35.5	Zuben'ubi	137 06.2	S16 05.6
20	101 59.8	76 13.9	12 00.6	295 25.4	16.7	66 29.0	07.6	254 06.7	35.5		SHA	Mer.Pass.
21	117 02.2	91 13.8	.. 01.8	310 28.8	.. 17.0	81 31.0	.. 07.8	269 09.3	.. 35.4	Venus	336 07.5	14 55
22	132 04.7	106 13.6	03.0	325 32.2	17.4	96 33.0	07.9	284 11.9	35.4	Mars	192 44.6	0 28
23	147 07.2	121 13.5	04.1	340 35.6	17.7	111 35.1	08.1	299 14.4	35.3	Jupiter	324 48.8	15 38
Mer. Pass.	13 17.1	v −0.1	d 1.2	v 3.4	d 0.4	v 2.0	d 0.2	v 2.6	d 0.0	Saturn	152 02.9	3 11

UT	SUN GHA	SUN Dec	MOON GHA	v	MOON Dec	d	HP
d h	° '	° '	° '	'	° '	'	'
1 00	176 55.0	S 7 30.8	90 37.9	11.1	N21 54.8	1.7	54.6
01	191 55.1	29.8	105 08.0	11.2	21 56.5	1.6	54.7
02	206 55.2	28.9	119 38.2	11.0	21 58.1	1.4	54.7
03	221 55.3	.. 27.9	134 08.2	11.1	21 59.5	1.4	54.7
04	236 55.4	27.0	148 38.3	11.0	22 00.9	1.2	54.7
05	251 55.6	26.0	163 08.3	11.0	22 02.1	1.2	54.7
06	266 55.7	S 7 25.1	177 38.3	10.9	N22 03.3	1.0	54.8
07	281 55.8	24.1	192 08.2	10.9	22 04.3	1.0	54.8
08	296 55.9	23.2	206 38.1	10.9	22 05.3	0.8	54.8
09	311 56.1	.. 22.2	221 08.0	10.9	22 06.1	0.7	54.8
10	326 56.2	21.3	235 37.9	10.8	22 06.8	0.7	54.8
11	341 56.3	20.3	250 07.7	10.8	22 07.5	0.5	54.9
12	356 56.4	S 7 19.4	264 37.5	10.8	N22 08.0	0.4	54.9
13	11 56.6	18.4	279 07.3	10.7	22 08.4	0.3	54.9
14	26 56.7	17.4	293 37.0	10.8	22 08.7	0.2	54.9
15	41 56.8	.. 16.5	308 06.8	10.7	22 08.9	0.0	54.9
16	56 56.9	15.5	322 36.5	10.6	22 08.9	0.0	55.0
17	71 57.1	14.6	337 06.1	10.7	22 08.9	0.1	55.0
18	86 57.2	S 7 13.6	351 35.8	10.6	N22 08.8	0.3	55.0
19	101 57.3	12.7	6 05.4	10.6	22 08.5	0.3	55.0
20	116 57.4	11.7	20 35.0	10.5	22 08.2	0.5	55.0
21	131 57.6	.. 10.8	35 04.5	10.6	22 07.7	0.6	55.1
22	146 57.7	09.8	49 34.1	10.5	22 07.1	0.7	55.1
23	161 57.8	08.9	64 03.6	10.5	22 06.4	0.8	55.1
2 00	176 57.9	S 7 07.9	78 33.1	10.4	N22 05.6	0.9	55.1
01	191 58.1	07.0	93 02.5	10.5	22 04.7	1.0	55.2
02	206 58.2	06.0	107 32.0	10.4	22 03.7	1.2	55.2
03	221 58.3	.. 05.0	122 01.4	10.4	22 02.5	1.2	55.2
04	236 58.5	04.1	136 30.8	10.4	22 01.3	1.4	55.2
05	251 58.6	03.1	151 00.2	10.3	21 59.9	1.4	55.3
06	266 58.7	S 7 02.2	165 29.5	10.4	N21 58.5	1.6	55.3
07	281 58.8	01.2	179 58.9	10.3	21 56.9	1.7	55.3
08	296 59.0	7 00.3	194 28.2	10.3	21 55.2	1.8	55.3
09	311 59.1	6 59.3	208 57.5	10.3	21 53.4	1.9	55.4
10	326 59.2	58.3	223 26.8	10.2	21 51.5	2.1	55.4
11	341 59.4	57.4	237 56.0	10.3	21 49.4	2.1	55.4
12	356 59.5	S 6 56.4	252 25.3	10.2	N21 47.3	2.3	55.4
13	11 59.6	55.5	266 54.5	10.2	21 45.0	2.3	55.5
14	26 59.7	54.5	281 23.7	10.2	21 42.7	2.5	55.5
15	41 59.9	.. 53.6	295 52.9	10.2	21 40.2	2.6	55.5
16	57 00.0	52.6	310 22.1	10.2	21 37.6	2.7	55.6
17	72 00.1	51.6	324 51.3	10.1	21 34.9	2.9	55.6
18	87 00.3	S 6 50.7	339 20.4	10.2	N21 32.0	2.9	55.6
19	102 00.4	49.7	353 49.6	10.1	21 29.1	3.0	55.6
20	117 00.5	48.8	8 18.7	10.1	21 26.1	3.2	55.7
21	132 00.7	.. 47.8	22 47.8	10.1	21 22.9	3.3	55.7
22	147 00.8	46.9	37 16.9	10.1	21 19.6	3.4	55.7
23	162 00.9	45.9	51 46.0	10.1	21 16.2	3.5	55.8
3 00	177 01.1	S 6 44.9	66 15.1	10.0	N21 12.7	3.6	55.8
01	192 01.2	44.0	80 44.1	10.1	21 09.1	3.7	55.8
02	207 01.3	43.0	95 13.2	10.0	21 05.4	3.9	55.8
03	222 01.5	.. 42.1	109 42.2	10.1	21 01.5	3.9	55.9
04	237 01.6	41.1	124 11.3	10.0	20 57.6	4.1	55.9
05	252 01.7	40.1	138 40.3	10.0	20 53.5	4.2	55.9
06	267 01.9	S 6 39.2	153 09.3	10.0	N20 49.3	4.3	56.0
07	282 02.0	38.2	167 38.3	10.0	20 45.0	4.4	56.0
08	297 02.1	37.3	182 07.3	10.0	20 40.6	4.5	56.0
09	312 02.3	.. 36.3	196 36.3	10.0	20 36.1	4.6	56.1
10	327 02.4	35.3	211 05.3	10.0	20 31.5	4.8	56.1
11	342 02.5	34.4	225 34.3	10.0	20 26.7	4.8	56.1
12	357 02.7	S 6 33.4	240 03.3	10.0	N20 21.9	5.0	56.2
13	12 02.8	32.5	254 32.3	9.9	20 16.9	5.1	56.2
14	27 02.9	31.5	269 01.2	10.0	20 11.8	5.2	56.2
15	42 03.1	.. 30.5	283 30.2	9.9	20 06.6	5.3	56.3
16	57 03.2	29.6	297 59.1	10.0	20 01.3	5.4	56.3
17	72 03.3	28.6	312 28.1	10.0	19 55.9	5.5	56.3
18	87 03.5	S 6 27.7	326 57.1	9.9	N19 50.4	5.7	56.4
19	102 03.6	26.7	341 26.0	9.9	19 44.7	5.7	56.4
20	117 03.7	25.7	355 54.9	10.0	19 39.0	5.9	56.4
21	132 03.9	.. 24.8	10 23.9	9.9	19 33.1	5.9	56.5
22	147 04.0	23.8	24 52.8	10.0	19 27.2	6.1	56.5
23	162 04.2	22.8	39 21.8	9.9	N19 21.1	6.2	56.5
	SD 16.2 d 1.0		SD 15.0		15.1		15.3

Day labels: THURSDAY (day 1), FRIDAY (day 2), SATURDAY (day 3)

Twilight / Sunrise / Moonrise

Lat.	Naut.	Civil	Sunrise	Moonrise 1	2	3	4
°	h m	h m	h m	h m	h m	h m	h m
N 72	05 03	06 21	07 29	□	□	□	
N 70	05 09	06 19	07 21	□	□	□	10 36
68	05 13	06 18	07 14	06 24	07 31	09 25	11 17
66	05 17	06 16	07 08	07 53	08 48	10 09	11 45
64	05 20	06 15	07 03	08 31	09 25	10 39	12 06
62	05 23	06 14	06 58	08 58	09 51	11 01	12 23
60	05 25	06 13	06 55	09 18	10 12	11 19	12 37
N 58	05 27	06 12	06 51	09 35	10 29	11 34	12 49
56	05 28	06 11	06 48	09 50	10 43	11 47	12 59
54	05 29	06 10	06 45	10 02	10 55	11 58	13 08
52	05 30	06 09	06 43	10 13	11 06	12 08	13 17
50	05 31	06 08	06 41	10 23	11 16	12 16	13 24
45	05 32	06 06	06 36	10 44	11 36	12 35	13 39
N 40	05 33	06 04	06 31	11 00	11 52	12 50	13 52
35	05 33	06 02	06 28	11 14	12 06	13 03	14 03
30	05 33	06 01	06 25	11 27	12 18	13 14	14 12
20	05 31	05 57	06 19	11 47	12 39	13 33	14 29
N 10	05 28	05 53	06 14	12 06	12 57	13 49	14 43
0	05 24	05 48	06 09	12 23	13 13	14 05	14 56
S 10	05 18	05 43	06 04	12 40	13 30	14 20	15 09
20	05 10	05 36	05 58	12 58	13 48	14 36	15 23
30	04 59	05 28	05 52	13 19	14 08	14 55	15 39
35	04 52	05 22	05 48	13 31	14 20	15 06	15 49
40	04 43	05 16	05 44	13 46	14 34	15 19	15 59
45	04 33	05 09	05 39	14 02	14 51	15 34	16 12
S 50	04 19	05 00	05 33	14 23	15 11	15 52	16 27
52	04 12	04 55	05 30	14 33	15 20	16 00	16 34
54	04 05	04 50	05 27	14 44	15 31	16 10	16 41
56	03 56	04 45	05 24	14 57	15 43	16 20	16 50
58	03 46	04 39	05 20	15 12	15 57	16 33	17 00
S 60	03 35	04 31	05 16	15 29	16 14	16 47	17 11

Sunset / Twilight / Moonset

Lat.	Sunset	Civil	Naut.	Moonset 1	2	3	4
°	h m	h m	h m	h m	h m	h m	h m
N 72	16 57	18 05	19 24	□	□	□	
N 70	17 05	18 07	19 18	□	□	□	07 02
68	17 12	18 08	19 13	05 54	06 32	06 25	06 20
66	17 18	18 10	19 09	04 25	05 14	05 40	05 51
64	17 23	18 11	19 06	03 47	04 37	05 10	05 30
62	17 27	18 12	19 03	03 21	04 11	04 47	05 12
60	17 31	18 13	19 01	03 00	03 50	04 29	04 57
N 58	17 34	18 14	18 59	02 43	03 33	04 14	04 45
56	17 37	18 14	18 57	02 28	03 19	04 01	04 34
54	17 40	18 15	18 56	02 16	03 07	03 49	04 24
52	17 42	18 16	18 55	02 05	02 56	03 39	04 16
50	17 44	18 17	18 54	01 55	02 46	03 30	04 08
45	17 49	18 19	18 53	01 35	02 26	03 11	03 52
N 40	17 53	18 20	18 52	01 19	02 09	02 56	03 38
35	17 57	18 22	18 52	01 05	01 55	02 42	03 27
30	18 00	18 24	18 52	00 53	01 43	02 31	03 16
20	18 06	18 28	18 53	00 32	01 22	02 11	02 59
N 10	18 11	18 32	18 56	00 14	01 04	01 54	02 44
0	18 15	18 36	19 00	24 47	00 47	01 38	02 29
S 10	18 20	18 41	19 06	24 30	00 30	01 22	02 15
20	18 26	18 48	19 14	24 10	00 10	01 04	01 59
30	18 32	18 56	19 24	23 51	24 44	00 44	01 41
35	18 35	19 01	19 31	23 38	24 33	00 33	01 31
40	18 39	19 07	19 40	23 24	24 19	00 19	01 19
45	18 44	19 14	19 50	23 07	24 03	00 03	01 05
S 50	18 50	19 23	20 04	22 47	23 43	24 48	00 48
52	18 53	19 28	20 10	22 37	23 34	24 39	00 39
54	18 56	19 32	20 17	22 26	23 23	24 30	00 30
56	18 59	19 38	20 26	22 13	23 11	24 20	00 20
58	19 03	19 44	20 35	21 58	22 58	24 08	00 08
S 60	19 07	19 51	20 47	21 41	22 41	23 54	25 16

SUN and MOON

Day	Eqn. of Time 00h	Eqn. of Time 12h	Mer. Pass.	Mer. Pass. Upper	Mer. Pass. Lower	Age	Phase
d	m s	m s	h m	h m	h m	d	%
1	12 20	12 14	12 12	18 35	06 10	09	54
2	12 08	12 02	12 12	19 26	07 00	10	64
3	11 56	11 50	12 12	20 17	07 51	11	73

UT	ARIES	VENUS −4.3		MARS −1.2		JUPITER −2.2		SATURN +0.4		STARS		
	GHA	GHA	Dec	GHA	Dec	GHA	Dec	GHA	Dec	Name	SHA	Dec
d h	° ′	° ′	° ′	° ′	° ′	° ′	° ′	° ′	° ′		° ′	° ′
4 00	162 09.6	136 13.4	N12 05.3	355 39.0	N10 18.1	126 37.1	N13 08.3	314 17.0	S 8 35.3	Acamar	315 19.2	S40 15.6
01	177 12.1	151 13.3	06.5	10 42.4	18.4	141 39.1	08.4	329 19.5	35.3	Achernar	335 27.8	S57 10.7
02	192 14.6	166 13.2	07.7	25 45.8	18.8	156 41.1	08.6	344 22.1	35.2	Acrux	173 09.7	S63 10.0
03	207 17.0	181 13.1	.. 08.9	40 49.2	.. 19.1	171 43.1	.. 08.7	359 24.7	.. 35.2	Adhara	255 13.0	S28 59.7
04	222 19.5	196 13.0	10.0	55 52.6	19.5	186 45.1	08.9	14 27.2	35.1	Aldebaran	290 50.4	N16 31.9
05	237 21.9	211 12.9	11.2	70 56.0	19.9	201 47.1	09.0	29 29.8	35.1			
06	252 24.4	226 12.7	N12 12.4	85 59.4	N10 20.2	216 49.2	N13 09.2	44 32.4	S 8 35.0	Alioth	166 20.9	N55 53.3
07	267 26.9	241 12.6	13.6	101 02.8	20.6	231 51.2	09.3	59 34.9	35.0	Alkaid	152 59.2	N49 14.8
08	282 29.3	256 12.5	14.7	116 06.2	20.9	246 53.2	09.5	74 37.5	34.9	Al Na'ir	27 45.3	S46 54.0
S 09	297 31.8	271 12.4	.. 15.9	131 09.6	.. 21.3	261 55.2	.. 09.7	89 40.0	.. 34.9	Alnilam	275 47.2	S 1 11.9
U 10	312 34.3	286 12.3	17.1	146 13.0	21.6	276 57.2	09.8	104 42.6	34.8	Alphard	217 56.7	S 8 43.0
N 11	327 36.7	301 12.2	18.3	161 16.4	22.0	291 59.2	10.0	119 45.2	34.8			
D 12	342 39.2	316 12.1	N12 19.4	176 19.8	N10 22.3	307 01.2	N13 10.2	134 47.7	S 8 34.7	Alphecca	126 11.6	N26 40.2
A 13	357 41.7	331 12.0	20.6	191 23.2	22.7	322 03.3	10.3	149 50.3	34.7	Alpheratz	357 44.8	N29 09.5
Y 14	12 44.1	346 11.9	21.8	206 26.6	23.0	337 05.3	10.5	164 52.8	34.7	Altair	62 09.3	N 8 54.0
15	27 46.6	1 11.7	.. 23.0	221 30.0	.. 23.4	352 07.3	.. 10.6	179 55.4	.. 34.6	Ankaa	353 16.9	S42 14.5
16	42 49.0	16 11.6	24.1	236 33.4	23.7	7 09.3	10.8	194 58.0	34.6	Antares	112 27.3	S26 27.5
17	57 51.5	31 11.5	25.3	251 36.8	24.1	22 11.3	10.9	210 00.5	34.5			
18	72 54.0	46 11.4	N12 26.5	266 40.2	N10 24.4	37 13.3	N13 11.1	225 03.1	S 8 34.5	Arcturus	145 56.3	N19 06.9
19	87 56.4	61 11.3	27.6	281 43.6	24.8	52 15.3	11.3	240 05.7	34.4	Atria	107 29.9	S69 02.6
20	102 58.9	76 11.2	28.8	296 47.0	25.1	67 17.4	11.4	255 08.2	34.4	Avior	234 17.9	S59 33.3
21	118 01.4	91 11.1	.. 30.0	311 50.4	.. 25.5	82 19.4	.. 11.6	270 10.8	.. 34.3	Bellatrix	278 32.9	N 6 21.5
22	133 03.8	106 11.0	31.1	326 53.8	25.8	97 21.4	11.7	285 13.4	34.3	Betelgeuse	271 02.2	N 7 24.4
23	148 06.3	121 10.9	32.3	341 57.2	26.2	112 23.4	11.9	300 15.9	34.2			
5 00	163 08.8	136 10.7	N12 33.5	357 00.6	N10 26.5	127 25.4	N13 12.1	315 18.5	S 8 34.2	Canopus	263 56.3	S52 42.5
01	178 11.2	151 10.6	34.6	12 04.0	26.9	142 27.4	12.2	330 21.0	34.1	Capella	280 35.7	N46 00.7
02	193 13.7	166 10.5	35.8	27 07.4	27.2	157 29.4	12.4	345 23.6	34.1	Deneb	49 32.5	N45 19.3
03	208 16.2	181 10.4	.. 37.0	42 10.8	.. 27.6	172 31.4	.. 12.5	0 26.2	.. 34.1	Denebola	182 34.2	N14 30.0
04	223 18.6	196 10.3	38.1	57 14.2	27.9	187 33.4	12.7	15 28.7	34.0	Diphda	348 57.1	S17 55.3
05	238 21.1	211 10.2	39.3	72 17.6	28.3	202 35.5	12.9	30 31.3	34.0			
06	253 23.5	226 10.1	N12 40.5	87 21.0	N10 28.6	217 37.5	N13 13.0	45 33.9	S 8 33.9	Dubhe	193 52.1	N61 40.9
07	268 26.0	241 10.0	41.6	102 24.4	29.0	232 39.5	13.2	60 36.4	33.9	Elnath	278 13.7	N28 37.0
08	283 28.5	256 09.9	42.8	117 27.8	29.3	247 41.5	13.3	75 39.0	33.8	Eltanin	90 46.7	N51 29.0
M 09	298 30.9	271 09.7	.. 44.0	132 31.2	.. 29.7	262 43.5	.. 13.5	90 41.6	.. 33.8	Enif	33 48.3	N 9 55.9
O 10	313 33.4	286 09.6	45.1	147 34.7	30.0	277 45.5	13.6	105 44.1	33.7	Fomalhaut	15 25.3	S29 33.4
N 11	328 35.9	301 09.5	46.3	162 38.1	30.4	292 47.5	13.8	120 46.7	33.7			
D 12	343 38.3	316 09.4	N12 47.4	177 41.5	N10 30.7	307 49.5	N13 14.0	135 49.3	S 8 33.6	Gacrux	172 01.4	S57 10.9
A 13	358 40.8	331 09.3	48.6	192 44.9	31.1	322 51.5	14.1	150 51.8	33.6	Gienah	175 52.9	S17 36.8
Y 14	13 43.3	346 09.2	49.8	207 48.3	31.4	337 53.5	14.3	165 54.4	33.5	Hadar	148 48.7	S60 25.8
15	28 45.7	1 09.1	.. 50.9	222 51.7	.. 31.7	352 55.6	.. 14.4	180 57.0	.. 33.5	Hamal	328 02.0	N23 31.2
16	43 48.2	16 09.0	52.1	237 55.1	32.1	7 57.6	14.6	195 59.5	33.4	Kaus Aust.	83 45.1	S34 22.6
17	58 50.7	31 08.9	53.2	252 58.5	32.4	22 59.6	14.8	211 02.1	33.4			
18	73 53.1	46 08.8	N12 54.4	268 01.9	N10 32.8	38 01.6	N13 14.9	226 04.7	S 8 33.3	Kochab	137 19.3	N74 06.0
19	88 55.6	61 08.6	55.6	283 05.3	33.1	53 03.6	15.1	241 07.2	33.3	Markab	13 39.5	N15 16.3
20	103 58.0	76 08.5	56.7	298 08.7	33.5	68 05.6	15.2	256 09.8	33.2	Menkar	314 16.1	N 4 08.1
21	119 00.5	91 08.4	.. 57.9	313 12.1	.. 33.8	83 07.6	.. 15.4	271 12.4	.. 33.2	Menkent	148 08.4	S36 25.8
22	134 03.0	106 08.3	12 59.0	328 15.5	34.2	98 09.6	15.6	286 14.9	33.2	Miaplacidus	221 39.1	S69 46.3
23	149 05.4	121 08.2	13 00.2	343 18.9	34.5	113 11.6	15.7	301 17.5	33.1			
6 00	164 07.9	136 08.1	N13 01.3	358 22.3	N10 34.9	128 13.6	N13 15.9	316 20.1	S 8 33.1	Mirfak	308 41.8	N49 54.4
01	179 10.4	151 08.0	02.5	13 25.7	35.2	143 15.6	16.0	331 22.6	33.0	Nunki	75 59.6	S26 16.8
02	194 12.8	166 07.9	03.7	28 29.1	35.5	158 17.6	16.2	346 25.2	33.0	Peacock	53 21.0	S56 41.5
03	209 15.3	181 07.8	.. 04.8	43 32.5	.. 35.9	173 19.7	.. 16.4	1 27.8	.. 32.9	Pollux	243 28.6	N27 59.7
04	224 17.8	196 07.7	06.0	58 35.9	36.2	188 21.7	16.5	16 30.3	32.9	Procyon	245 00.4	N 5 11.4
05	239 20.2	211 07.5	07.1	73 39.3	36.6	203 23.7	16.7	31 32.9	32.8			
06	254 22.7	226 07.4	N13 08.3	88 42.7	N10 36.9	218 25.7	N13 16.8	46 35.5	S 8 32.8	Rasalhague	96 07.3	N12 33.0
07	269 25.1	241 07.3	09.4	103 46.1	37.3	233 27.7	17.0	61 38.0	32.7	Regulus	207 44.1	N11 54.2
08	284 27.6	256 07.2	10.6	118 49.5	37.6	248 29.7	17.2	76 40.6	32.7	Rigel	281 12.9	S 8 11.5
T 09	299 30.1	271 07.1	.. 11.7	133 52.9	.. 37.9	263 31.7	.. 17.3	91 43.2	.. 32.6	Rigil Kent.	139 52.6	S60 53.0
U 10	314 32.5	286 07.0	12.9	148 56.3	38.3	278 33.7	17.5	106 45.8	32.6	Sabik	102 13.6	S15 44.4
E 11	329 35.0	301 06.9	14.0	163 59.7	38.6	293 35.7	17.6	121 48.3	32.5			
S 12	344 37.5	316 06.8	N13 15.2	179 03.1	N10 39.0	308 37.7	N13 17.8	136 50.9	S 8 32.5	Schedar	349 42.1	N56 36.4
D 13	359 39.9	331 06.7	16.3	194 06.5	39.3	323 39.7	18.0	151 53.5	32.4	Shaula	96 23.2	S37 06.6
A 14	14 42.4	346 06.6	17.5	209 09.9	39.7	338 41.7	18.1	166 56.0	32.4	Sirius	258 34.3	S16 44.3
Y 15	29 44.9	1 06.4	.. 18.6	224 13.3	.. 40.0	353 43.7	.. 18.3	181 58.6	.. 32.3	Spica	158 31.9	S11 13.7
16	44 47.3	16 06.3	19.8	239 16.7	40.3	8 45.7	18.4	197 01.2	32.3	Suhail	222 52.7	S43 29.2
17	59 49.8	31 06.2	20.9	254 20.1	40.7	23 47.7	18.6	212 03.7	32.2			
18	74 52.3	46 06.1	N13 22.1	269 23.5	N10 41.0	38 49.7	N13 18.8	227 06.3	S 8 32.2	Vega	80 39.7	N38 47.5
19	89 54.7	61 06.0	23.2	284 26.9	41.4	53 51.7	18.9	242 08.9	32.1	Zuben'ubi	137 06.2	S16 05.6
20	104 57.2	76 05.9	24.4	299 30.3	41.7	68 53.7	19.1	257 11.5	32.1		SHA	Mer.Pass.
21	119 59.6	91 05.8	.. 25.5	314 33.7	.. 42.0	83 55.8	.. 19.2	272 14.0	.. 32.0		° ′	h m
22	135 02.1	106 05.7	26.6	329 37.1	42.4	98 57.8	19.4	287 16.6	32.0	Venus	333 02.0	14 55
23	150 04.6	121 05.6	27.8	344 40.5	42.7	113 59.8	19.6	302 19.2	31.9	Mars	193 51.9	0 12
	h m									Jupiter	324 16.6	15 28
Mer. Pass. 13 05.3		v −0.1	d 1.2	v 3.4	d 0.3	v 2.0	d 0.2	v 2.6	d 0.0	Saturn	152 09.7	2 58

UT	SUN GHA	Dec	MOON GHA	v	Dec	d	HP
d h	° ′	° ′	° ′	′	° ′	′	′
4 00	177 04.3	S 6 21.9	53 50.7	10.0	N19 14.9	6.3	56.6
01	192 04.4	20.9	68 19.7	9.9	19 08.6	6.4	56.6
02	207 04.6	20.0	82 48.6	9.9	19 02.2	6.5	56.6
03	222 04.7	.. 19.0	97 17.5	10.0	18 55.7	6.7	56.7
04	237 04.8	18.0	111 46.5	9.9	18 49.0	6.7	56.7
05	252 05.0	17.1	126 15.4	10.0	18 42.3	6.9	56.7
S 06	267 05.1	S 6 16.1	140 44.4	9.9	N18 35.4	6.9	56.8
U 07	282 05.3	15.1	155 13.3	9.9	18 28.5	7.1	56.8
N 08	297 05.4	14.2	169 42.2	10.0	18 21.4	7.1	56.8
D 09	312 05.5	.. 13.2	184 11.2	9.9	18 14.3	7.3	56.9
A 10	327 05.7	12.2	198 40.1	10.0	18 07.0	7.4	56.9
Y 11	342 05.8	11.3	213 09.1	9.9	17 59.6	7.5	56.9
12	357 06.0	S 6 10.3	227 38.0	10.0	N17 52.1	7.5	57.0
13	12 06.1	09.3	242 07.0	10.0	17 44.6	7.7	57.0
14	27 06.2	08.4	256 36.0	9.9	17 36.9	7.8	57.1
15	42 06.4	.. 07.4	271 04.9	10.0	17 29.1	7.9	57.1
16	57 06.5	06.5	285 33.9	9.9	17 21.2	8.0	57.1
17	72 06.7	05.5	300 02.8	10.0	17 13.2	8.1	57.2
18	87 06.8	S 6 04.5	314 31.8	10.0	N17 05.1	8.3	57.2
19	102 06.9	03.6	329 00.8	10.0	16 56.8	8.3	57.2
20	117 07.1	02.6	343 29.8	10.0	16 48.5	8.4	57.3
21	132 07.2	.. 01.6	357 58.8	9.9	16 40.1	8.5	57.3
22	147 07.4	6 00.7	12 27.7	10.0	16 31.6	8.6	57.3
23	162 07.5	5 59.7	26 56.7	10.0	16 23.0	8.7	57.4
5 00	177 07.6	S 5 58.7	41 25.7	10.0	N16 14.3	8.8	57.4
01	192 07.8	57.8	55 54.7	10.0	16 05.5	8.9	57.5
02	207 07.9	56.8	70 23.7	10.1	15 56.6	9.0	57.5
03	222 08.1	.. 55.8	84 52.8	10.0	15 47.6	9.1	57.5
04	237 08.2	54.9	99 21.8	10.0	15 38.5	9.2	57.6
05	252 08.4	53.9	113 50.8	10.0	15 29.3	9.3	57.6
M 06	267 08.5	S 5 52.9	128 19.8	10.0	N15 20.0	9.4	57.6
O 07	282 08.6	52.0	142 48.8	10.1	15 10.6	9.5	57.7
N 08	297 08.8	51.0	157 17.9	10.0	15 01.1	9.6	57.7
D 09	312 08.9	.. 50.0	171 46.9	10.1	14 51.5	9.7	57.7
A 10	327 09.1	49.1	186 16.0	10.0	14 41.8	9.7	57.8
Y 11	342 09.2	48.1	200 45.0	10.1	14 32.1	9.9	57.8
12	357 09.4	S 5 47.1	215 14.1	10.0	N14 22.2	9.9	57.9
13	12 09.5	46.2	229 43.1	10.1	14 12.3	10.1	57.9
14	27 09.6	45.2	244 12.2	10.0	14 02.2	10.1	57.9
15	42 09.8	.. 44.2	258 41.2	10.1	13 52.1	10.2	58.0
16	57 09.9	43.3	273 10.3	10.1	13 41.9	10.3	58.0
17	72 10.1	42.3	287 39.4	10.1	13 31.6	10.4	58.0
18	87 10.2	S 5 41.3	302 08.5	10.1	N13 21.2	10.5	58.1
19	102 10.4	40.3	316 37.6	10.0	13 10.7	10.6	58.1
20	117 10.5	39.4	331 06.6	10.1	13 00.1	10.6	58.1
21	132 10.7	.. 38.4	345 35.7	10.1	12 49.5	10.7	58.2
22	147 10.8	37.4	0 04.8	10.1	12 38.8	10.8	58.2
23	162 11.0	36.5	14 33.9	10.1	12 28.0	10.9	58.2
6 00	177 11.1	S 5 35.5	29 03.0	10.1	N12 17.1	11.0	58.3
01	192 11.2	34.5	43 32.1	10.2	12 06.1	11.1	58.3
02	207 11.4	33.6	58 01.3	10.1	11 55.0	11.1	58.4
03	222 11.5	.. 32.6	72 30.4	10.1	11 43.9	11.2	58.4
04	237 11.7	31.6	86 59.5	10.1	11 32.7	11.3	58.4
05	252 11.8	30.7	101 28.6	10.1	11 21.4	11.4	58.5
T 06	267 12.0	S 5 29.7	115 57.7	10.1	N11 10.0	11.4	58.5
U 07	282 12.1	28.7	130 26.8	10.1	10 58.6	11.5	58.5
E 08	297 12.3	27.7	144 55.9	10.2	10 47.1	11.6	58.6
S 09	312 12.4	.. 26.8	159 25.1	10.1	10 35.5	11.7	58.6
D 10	327 12.6	25.8	173 54.2	10.1	10 23.8	11.7	58.6
A 11	342 12.7	24.8	188 23.3	10.1	10 12.1	11.8	58.7
Y 12	357 12.9	S 5 23.9	202 52.4	10.2	N10 00.3	11.9	58.7
13	12 13.0	22.9	217 21.6	10.1	9 48.4	12.0	58.7
14	27 13.2	21.9	231 50.7	10.1	9 36.4	12.0	58.8
15	42 13.3	.. 20.9	246 19.8	10.2	9 24.4	12.0	58.8
16	57 13.5	20.0	260 48.9	10.1	9 12.4	12.2	58.8
17	72 13.6	19.0	275 18.0	10.2	9 00.2	12.2	58.9
18	87 13.8	S 5 18.0	289 47.2	10.1	N 8 48.0	12.3	58.9
19	102 13.9	17.1	304 16.3	10.1	8 35.7	12.3	58.9
20	117 14.1	16.1	318 45.4	10.1	8 23.4	12.4	59.0
21	132 14.2	.. 15.1	333 14.5	10.1	8 11.0	12.4	59.0
22	147 14.4	14.1	347 43.6	10.1	7 58.6	12.5	59.0
23	162 14.5	13.2	2 12.7	10.1	N 7 46.1	12.6	59.1
	SD 16.1 d 1.0		SD 15.5		15.8		16.0

Twilight / Sunrise / Moonrise

Lat.	Naut.	Civil	Sunrise	4	5	6	7
°	h m	h m	h m	h m	h m	h m	h m
N 72	04 47	06 06	07 14	☐	12 15	14 32	16 41
N 70	04 55	06 06	07 07	10 36	12 46	14 47	16 46
68	05 01	06 06	07 01	11 17	13 08	15 00	16 51
66	05 06	06 05	06 56	11 45	13 26	15 09	16 54
64	05 10	06 05	06 52	12 06	13 40	15 18	16 58
62	05 13	06 05	06 49	12 23	13 52	15 25	17 00
60	05 16	06 04	06 46	12 37	14 02	15 31	17 03
N 58	05 18	06 04	06 43	12 49	14 11	15 36	17 05
56	05 20	06 03	06 40	12 59	14 18	15 41	17 07
54	05 22	06 03	06 38	13 08	14 25	15 45	17 08
52	05 24	06 03	06 36	13 17	14 31	15 49	17 10
50	05 25	06 02	06 34	13 24	14 37	15 53	17 11
45	05 27	06 01	06 30	13 39	14 48	16 00	17 14
N 40	05 29	06 00	06 27	13 52	14 58	16 07	17 17
35	05 29	05 59	06 24	14 03	15 06	16 12	17 19
30	05 30	05 57	06 21	14 12	15 14	16 17	17 21
20	05 29	05 54	06 16	14 29	15 26	16 25	17 24
N 10	05 27	05 51	06 12	14 43	15 37	16 32	17 27
0	05 23	05 47	06 08	14 56	15 47	16 39	17 30
S 10	05 18	05 43	06 04	15 09	15 58	16 45	17 33
20	05 11	05 37	05 59	15 23	16 09	16 52	17 36
30	05 01	05 30	05 54	15 39	16 21	17 01	17 39
35	04 55	05 25	05 51	15 49	16 28	17 05	17 41
40	04 47	05 20	05 47	15 59	16 36	17 10	17 43
45	04 37	05 13	05 43	16 12	16 46	17 16	17 46
S 50	04 25	05 05	05 38	16 27	16 57	17 24	17 49
52	04 19	05 01	05 36	16 34	17 02	17 27	17 50
54	04 12	04 57	05 33	16 41	17 08	17 31	17 52
56	04 04	04 52	05 30	16 50	17 14	17 35	17 53
58	03 55	04 46	05 27	17 00	17 21	17 39	17 55
S 60	03 45	04 40	05 23	17 11	17 29	17 44	17 57

Sunset / Twilight / Moonset

Lat.	Sunset	Civil	Naut.	4	5	6	7
°	h m	h m	h m	h m	h m	h m	h m
N 72	17 11	18 19	19 38	☐	07 12	06 43	06 22
N 70	17 18	18 19	19 30	07 02	06 39	06 25	06 14
68	17 23	18 19	19 24	06 20	06 16	06 11	06 07
66	17 28	18 19	19 19	05 51	05 57	06 00	06 01
64	17 32	18 19	19 15	05 30	05 42	05 50	05 56
62	17 35	18 20	19 11	05 12	05 29	05 42	05 52
60	17 38	18 20	19 08	04 57	05 18	05 35	05 48
N 58	17 41	18 20	19 06	04 45	05 09	05 28	05 45
56	17 43	18 21	19 04	04 34	05 01	05 23	05 42
54	17 46	18 21	19 02	04 24	04 53	05 18	05 39
52	17 47	18 21	19 00	04 16	04 46	05 13	05 37
50	17 49	18 22	18 59	04 08	04 40	05 09	05 34
45	17 53	18 23	18 57	03 52	04 27	05 00	05 29
N 40	17 57	18 24	18 55	03 38	04 17	04 52	05 25
35	17 59	18 25	18 54	03 27	04 07	04 45	05 22
30	18 02	18 26	18 54	03 16	03 59	04 40	05 18
20	18 07	18 29	18 54	02 59	03 45	04 29	05 13
N 10	18 11	18 32	18 56	02 44	03 32	04 20	05 08
0	18 15	18 35	19 00	02 29	03 21	04 12	05 03
S 10	18 19	18 40	19 04	02 15	03 09	04 03	04 58
20	18 23	18 45	19 11	01 59	02 56	03 54	04 53
30	18 28	18 52	19 21	01 41	02 42	03 44	04 47
35	18 31	18 57	19 27	01 31	02 33	03 37	04 44
40	18 35	19 02	19 35	01 19	02 23	03 30	04 40
45	18 39	19 09	19 44	01 05	02 12	03 22	04 35
S 50	18 44	19 17	19 57	00 48	01 58	03 12	04 30
52	18 46	19 21	20 02	00 39	01 51	03 08	04 27
54	18 49	19 25	20 09	00 30	01 44	03 03	04 24
56	18 51	19 30	20 17	00 20	01 36	02 57	04 21
58	18 54	19 35	20 25	00 08	01 27	02 51	04 18
S 60	18 58	19 41	20 36	25 10	01 16	02 43	04 14

SUN / MOON

Day	Eqn. of Time 00ʰ	Eqn. of Time 12ʰ	Mer. Pass.	Mer. Pass. Upper	Mer. Pass. Lower	Age	Phase
d	m s	m s	h m	h m	h m	d	%
4	11 43	11 36	12 12	21 08	08 43	12	82
5	11 30	11 23	12 11	22 00	09 34	13	89
6	11 16	11 09	12 11	22 51	10 25	14	95

UT	ARIES GHA	VENUS −4.3 GHA	Dec	MARS −1.2 GHA	Dec	JUPITER −2.1 GHA	Dec	SATURN +0.4 GHA	Dec	STARS Name	SHA	Dec
7 00	165 07.0	136 05.5	N13 28.9	359 43.9	N10 43.1	129 01.8	N13 19.7	317 21.7	S 8 31.9	Acamar	315 19.2	S40 15.6
01	180 09.5	151 05.4	. . 30.1	14 47.3	43.4	144 03.8	19.9	332 24.3	31.8	Achernar	335 27.8	S57 10.7
02	195 12.0	166 05.2	31.2	29 50.7	43.7	159 05.8	20.0	347 26.9	31.8	Acrux	173 09.7	S63 10.1
03	210 14.4	181 05.1	. . 32.4	44 54.1	. . 44.1	174 07.8	. . 20.2	2 29.4	. . 31.8	Adhara	255 13.0	S28 59.7
04	225 16.9	196 05.0	33.5	59 57.6	44.4	189 09.8	20.4	17 32.0	31.7	Aldebaran	290 50.4	N16 31.9
05	240 19.4	211 04.9	34.6	75 01.0	44.7	204 11.8	20.5	32 34.6	31.7			
06	255 21.8	226 04.8	N13 35.8	90 04.4	N10 45.1	219 13.8	N13 20.7	47 37.2	S 8 31.6	Alioth	166 20.9	N55 53.3
W 07	270 24.3	241 04.7	36.9	105 07.8	45.4	234 15.8	20.9	62 39.7	31.6	Alkaid	152 59.2	N49 14.8
E 08	285 26.7	256 04.6	38.1	120 11.2	45.8	249 17.8	21.0	77 42.3	31.5	Al Na'ir	27 45.2	S46 54.0
D 09	300 29.2	271 04.5	. . 39.2	135 14.6	. . 46.1	264 19.8	. . 21.2	92 44.9	. . 31.5	Alnilam	275 47.2	S 1 11.9
N 10	315 31.7	286 04.4	40.3	150 18.0	46.4	279 21.8	21.3	107 47.5	31.4	Alphard	217 56.7	S 8 43.0
E 11	330 34.1	301 04.3	41.5	165 21.4	46.8	294 23.8	21.5	122 50.0	31.4			
S 12	345 36.6	316 04.2	N13 42.6	180 24.8	N10 47.1	309 25.8	N13 21.7	137 52.6	S 8 31.3	Alphecca	126 11.6	N26 40.2
D 13	0 39.1	331 04.1	43.8	195 28.2	47.4	324 27.8	21.8	152 55.2	31.3	Alpheratz	357 44.8	N29 09.5
A 14	15 41.5	346 03.9	44.9	210 31.6	47.8	339 29.8	22.0	167 57.7	31.2	Altair	62 09.3	N 8 54.0
Y 15	30 44.0	1 03.8	. . 46.0	225 35.0	. . 48.1	354 31.8	. . 22.1	183 00.3	. . 31.2	Ankaa	353 16.9	S42 14.5
16	45 46.5	16 03.7	47.2	240 38.4	48.4	9 33.8	22.3	198 02.9	31.1	Antares	112 27.3	S26 27.5
17	60 48.9	31 03.6	48.3	255 41.8	48.8	24 35.8	22.5	213 05.5	31.1			
18	75 51.4	46 03.5	N13 49.4	270 45.2	N10 49.1	39 37.8	N13 22.6	228 08.0	S 8 31.0	Arcturus	145 56.3	N19 06.9
19	90 53.9	61 03.4	50.6	285 48.6	49.4	54 39.8	22.8	243 10.6	31.0	Atria	107 29.9	S69 02.7
20	105 56.3	76 03.3	51.7	300 51.9	49.8	69 41.8	22.9	258 13.2	30.9	Avior	234 17.9	S59 33.3
21	120 58.8	91 03.2	. . 52.8	315 55.3	. . 50.1	84 43.8	. . 23.1	273 15.8	. . 30.9	Bellatrix	278 32.9	N 6 21.5
22	136 01.2	106 03.1	54.0	330 58.7	50.4	99 45.8	23.3	288 18.3	30.8	Betelgeuse	271 02.2	N 7 24.4
23	151 03.7	121 03.0	55.1	346 02.1	50.8	114 47.8	23.4	303 20.9	30.8			
8 00	166 06.2	136 02.9	N13 56.2	1 05.5	N10 51.1	129 49.8	N13 23.6	318 23.5	S 8 30.7	Canopus	263 56.4	S52 42.5
01	181 08.6	151 02.8	57.4	16 08.9	51.4	144 51.8	23.8	333 26.1	30.7	Capella	280 35.7	N46 00.7
02	196 11.1	166 02.7	58.5	31 12.3	51.8	159 53.8	23.9	348 28.6	30.6	Deneb	49 32.5	N45 19.3
03	211 13.6	181 02.5	13 59.6	46 15.7	. . 52.1	174 55.8	. . 24.1	3 31.2	. . 30.6	Denebola	182 34.2	N14 30.0
04	226 16.0	196 02.4	14 00.7	61 19.1	52.4	189 57.8	24.2	18 33.8	30.5	Diphda	348 57.1	S17 55.3
05	241 18.5	211 02.3	01.9	76 22.5	52.8	204 59.8	24.4	33 36.4	30.5			
06	256 21.0	226 02.2	N14 03.0	91 25.9	N10 53.1	220 01.8	N13 24.6	48 38.9	S 8 30.4	Dubhe	193 52.0	N61 40.9
T 07	271 23.4	241 02.1	04.1	106 29.3	53.4	235 03.8	24.7	63 41.5	30.4	Elnath	278 13.7	N28 37.0
H 08	286 25.9	256 02.0	05.3	121 32.7	53.7	250 05.8	24.9	78 44.1	30.3	Eltanin	90 46.7	N51 29.0
U 09	301 28.4	271 01.9	. . 06.4	136 36.1	. . 54.1	265 07.8	. . 25.0	93 46.7	. . 30.3	Enif	33 48.3	N 9 55.8
R 10	316 30.8	286 01.8	07.5	151 39.5	54.4	280 09.8	25.2	108 49.2	30.2	Fomalhaut	15 25.3	S29 33.4
S 11	331 33.3	301 01.7	08.6	166 42.9	54.7	295 11.8	25.4	123 51.8	30.2			
D 12	346 35.7	316 01.6	N14 09.8	181 46.3	N10 55.1	310 13.8	N13 25.5	138 54.4	S 8 30.1	Gacrux	172 01.4	S57 11.0
A 13	1 38.2	331 01.5	10.9	196 49.7	55.4	325 15.8	25.7	153 57.0	30.1	Gienah	175 52.9	S17 36.8
Y 14	16 40.7	346 01.4	12.0	211 53.1	55.7	340 17.8	25.9	168 59.5	30.0	Hadar	148 48.7	S60 25.8
15	31 43.1	1 01.3	. . 13.1	226 56.5	. . 56.0	355 19.8	. . 26.0	184 02.1	. . 30.0	Hamal	328 02.0	N23 31.2
16	46 45.6	16 01.1	14.2	241 59.9	56.4	10 21.8	26.2	199 04.7	29.9	Kaus Aust.	83 45.1	S34 22.6
17	61 48.1	31 01.0	15.4	257 03.3	56.7	25 23.8	26.3	214 07.3	29.9			
18	76 50.5	46 00.9	N14 16.5	272 06.7	N10 57.0	40 25.8	N13 26.5	229 09.8	S 8 29.8	Kochab	137 19.3	N74 06.0
19	91 53.0	61 00.8	17.6	287 10.1	57.4	55 27.8	26.7	244 12.4	29.8	Markab	13 39.5	N15 16.3
20	106 55.5	76 00.7	18.7	302 13.5	57.7	70 29.8	26.8	259 15.0	29.7	Menkar	314 16.1	N 4 08.1
21	121 57.9	91 00.6	. . 19.9	317 16.9	. . 58.0	85 31.8	. . 27.0	274 17.6	. . 29.6	Menkent	148 08.3	S36 25.8
22	137 00.4	106 00.5	21.0	332 20.3	58.3	100 33.8	27.2	289 20.1	29.6	Miaplacidus	221 39.1	S69 46.3
23	152 02.8	121 00.4	22.1	347 23.7	58.7	115 35.7	27.3	304 22.7	29.5			
9 00	167 05.3	136 00.3	N14 23.2	2 27.0	N10 59.0	130 37.7	N13 27.5	319 25.3	S 8 29.5	Mirfak	308 41.8	N49 54.4
01	182 07.8	151 00.2	24.3	17 30.4	59.3	145 39.7	27.6	334 27.9	29.4	Nunki	75 59.6	S26 16.8
02	197 10.2	166 00.1	25.4	32 33.8	10 59.6	160 41.7	27.8	349 30.5	29.4	Peacock	53 21.0	S56 41.5
03	212 12.7	181 00.0	. . 26.6	47 37.2	11 00.0	175 43.7	. . 28.0	4 33.0	. . 29.3	Pollux	243 28.6	N27 59.7
04	227 15.2	195 59.9	27.7	62 40.6	00.3	190 45.7	28.1	19 35.6	29.3	Procyon	245 00.5	N 5 11.4
05	242 17.6	210 59.8	28.8	77 44.0	00.6	205 47.7	28.3	34 38.2	29.2			
06	257 20.1	225 59.7	N14 29.9	92 47.4	N11 00.9	220 49.7	N13 28.4	49 40.8	S 8 29.2	Rasalhague	96 07.3	N12 32.9
07	272 22.6	240 59.6	31.0	107 50.8	01.2	235 51.7	28.6	64 43.3	29.1	Regulus	207 44.1	N11 54.2
08	287 25.0	255 59.4	32.1	122 54.2	01.6	250 53.7	28.8	79 45.9	29.1	Rigel	281 12.9	S 8 11.5
F 09	302 27.5	270 59.3	. . 33.2	137 57.6	. . 01.9	265 55.7	. . 28.9	94 48.5	. . 29.0	Rigil Kent.	139 52.5	S60 53.0
R 10	317 30.0	285 59.2	34.4	153 01.0	02.2	280 57.7	29.1	109 51.1	29.0	Sabik	102 13.5	S15 44.4
I 11	332 32.4	300 59.1	35.5	168 04.4	02.5	295 59.7	29.3	124 53.7	28.9			
D 12	347 34.9	315 59.0	N14 36.6	183 07.8	N11 02.9	311 01.7	N13 29.5	139 56.2	S 8 28.9	Schedar	349 42.1	N56 36.4
A 13	2 37.3	330 58.9	37.7	198 11.1	03.2	326 03.7	29.6	154 58.8	28.8	Shaula	96 23.2	S37 06.6
Y 14	17 39.8	345 58.8	38.8	213 14.5	03.5	341 05.7	29.7	170 01.4	28.8	Sirius	258 34.4	S16 44.3
15	32 42.3	0 58.7	. . 39.9	228 17.9	. . 03.8	356 07.7	. . 29.9	185 04.0	. . 28.7	Spica	158 31.9	S11 13.7
16	47 44.7	15 58.6	41.0	243 21.3	04.1	11 09.7	30.1	200 06.6	28.7	Suhail	222 52.7	S43 29.2
17	62 47.2	30 58.5	42.1	258 24.7	04.5	26 11.6	30.2	215 09.1	28.6			
18	77 49.7	45 58.4	N14 43.2	273 28.1	N11 04.8	41 13.6	N13 30.3	230 11.7	S 8 28.6	Vega	80 39.7	N38 47.5
19	92 52.1	60 58.3	44.3	288 31.5	05.1	56 15.6	30.6	245 14.3	28.5	Zuben'ubi	137 06.2	S16 05.6
20	107 54.6	75 58.2	45.5	303 34.9	05.4	71 17.6	30.7	260 16.9	28.5		SHA	Mer.Pass.
21	122 57.1	90 58.1	. . 46.6	318 38.3	. . 05.7	86 19.6	. . 30.9	275 19.5	. . 28.4			
22	137 59.5	105 58.0	47.7	333 41.6	06.1	101 21.6	31.0	290 22.0	28.4	Venus	329 56.7	h m 14 56
23	153 02.0	120 57.9	48.8	348 45.0	06.4	116 23.6	31.2	305 24.6	28.3	Mars	194 59.4	23 50
Mer.Pass. 12 53.5		v −0.1	d 1.1	v 3.4	d 0.3	v 2.0	d 0.2	v 2.6	d 0.1	Jupiter	323 43.6	15 19
										Saturn	152 17.3	2 46

UT	SUN GHA	Dec	MOON GHA	v	Dec	d	HP
d h	° ′	° ′	° ′	′	° ′	′	′
7 00	177 14.7	S 5 12.2	16 41.8	10.1	N 7 33.5	12.6	59.1
01	192 14.8	11.2	31 10.9	10.1	7 20.9	12.7	59.1
02	207 15.0	10.3	45 40.0	10.0	7 08.2	12.7	59.2
03	222 15.1	.. 09.3	60 09.0	10.1	6 55.5	12.8	59.2
04	237 15.3	08.3	74 38.1	10.1	6 42.7	12.8	59.2
05	252 15.4	07.3	89 07.2	10.0	6 29.9	12.9	59.2
06	267 15.6	S 5 06.4	103 36.2	10.1	N 6 17.0	12.9	59.3
07	282 15.7	05.4	118 05.3	10.0	6 04.1	13.0	59.3
W 08	297 15.9	04.4	132 34.3	10.1	5 51.1	13.0	59.3
E 09	312 16.0	.. 03.4	147 03.4	10.0	5 38.1	13.1	59.4
D 10	327 16.2	02.5	161 32.4	10.0	5 25.0	13.1	59.4
N 11	342 16.3	01.5	176 01.4	10.0	5 11.9	13.2	59.4
E 12	357 16.5	S 5 00.5	190 30.4	10.0	N 4 58.7	13.2	59.5
S 13	12 16.6	4 59.5	204 59.4	10.0	4 45.5	13.2	59.5
D 14	27 16.8	58.6	219 28.4	10.0	4 32.3	13.3	59.5
A 15	42 16.9	.. 57.6	233 57.4	9.9	4 19.0	13.3	59.5
Y 16	57 17.1	56.6	248 26.3	10.0	4 05.7	13.3	59.6
17	72 17.3	55.6	262 55.3	9.9	3 52.4	13.4	59.6
18	87 17.4	S 4 54.7	277 24.2	9.9	N 3 39.0	13.4	59.6
19	102 17.6	53.7	291 53.1	9.9	3 25.6	13.5	59.6
20	117 17.7	52.7	306 22.0	9.9	3 12.1	13.4	59.7
21	132 17.9	.. 51.7	320 50.9	9.9	2 58.7	13.5	59.7
22	147 18.0	50.8	335 19.8	9.8	2 45.2	13.6	59.7
23	162 18.2	49.8	349 48.6	9.9	2 31.6	13.5	59.7
8 00	177 18.3	S 4 48.8	4 17.5	9.8	N 2 18.1	13.6	59.8
01	192 18.5	47.8	18 46.3	9.8	2 04.5	13.6	59.8
02	207 18.6	46.9	33 15.1	9.8	1 50.9	13.6	59.8
03	222 18.8	.. 45.9	47 43.9	9.7	1 37.3	13.6	59.8
04	237 19.0	44.9	62 12.6	9.8	1 23.7	13.7	59.9
05	252 19.1	43.9	76 41.4	9.7	1 10.0	13.7	59.9
06	267 19.3	S 4 43.0	91 10.1	9.7	N 0 56.3	13.7	59.9
07	282 19.4	42.0	105 38.8	9.7	0 42.6	13.7	59.9
T 08	297 19.6	41.0	120 07.5	9.7	0 28.9	13.7	60.0
H 09	312 19.7	.. 40.0	134 36.2	9.6	0 15.2	13.7	60.0
U 10	327 19.9	39.1	149 04.8	9.6	N 0 01.5	13.7	60.0
R 11	342 20.0	38.1	163 33.4	9.6	S 0 12.2	13.8	60.0
S 12	357 20.2	S 4 37.1	178 02.0	9.6	S 0 26.0	13.7	60.1
D 13	12 20.4	36.1	192 30.6	9.5	0 39.7	13.8	60.1
A 14	27 20.5	35.2	206 59.1	9.5	0 53.5	13.7	60.1
Y 15	42 20.7	.. 34.2	221 27.6	9.5	1 07.2	13.8	60.1
16	57 20.8	33.2	235 56.1	9.5	1 21.0	13.8	60.1
17	72 21.0	32.2	250 24.6	9.4	1 34.8	13.7	60.1
18	87 21.1	S 4 31.3	264 53.0	9.4	S 1 48.5	13.8	60.2
19	102 21.3	30.3	279 21.4	9.4	2 02.3	13.7	60.2
20	117 21.5	29.3	293 49.8	9.3	2 16.0	13.8	60.2
21	132 21.6	.. 28.3	308 18.1	9.3	2 29.8	13.7	60.2
22	147 21.8	27.3	322 46.4	9.3	2 43.5	13.7	60.2
23	162 21.9	26.4	337 14.7	9.3	2 57.2	13.7	60.2
9 00	177 22.1	S 4 25.4	351 43.0	9.2	S 3 10.9	13.7	60.3
01	192 22.2	24.4	6 11.2	9.2	3 24.6	13.7	60.3
02	207 22.4	23.4	20 39.4	9.2	3 38.3	13.7	60.3
03	222 22.6	.. 22.5	35 07.6	9.1	3 52.0	13.7	60.3
04	237 22.7	21.5	49 35.7	9.1	4 05.7	13.6	60.3
05	252 22.9	20.5	64 03.8	9.0	4 19.3	13.6	60.3
06	267 23.0	S 4 19.5	78 31.8	9.1	S 4 32.9	13.6	60.3
07	282 23.2	18.5	92 59.9	8.9	4 46.5	13.6	60.3
F 08	297 23.4	17.6	107 27.8	9.0	5 00.1	13.5	60.4
R 09	312 23.5	.. 16.6	121 55.8	8.9	5 13.6	13.5	60.4
I 10	327 23.7	15.6	136 23.7	8.9	5 27.1	13.5	60.4
D 11	342 23.8	14.6	150 51.6	8.8	5 40.6	13.4	60.4
A 12	357 24.0	S 4 13.6	165 19.4	8.8	S 5 54.0	13.5	60.4
Y 13	12 24.2	12.7	179 47.2	8.8	6 07.5	13.4	60.4
14	27 24.3	11.7	194 15.0	8.7	6 20.9	13.3	60.4
15	42 24.5	.. 10.7	208 42.7	8.7	6 34.2	13.3	60.4
16	57 24.6	09.7	223 10.4	8.6	6 47.5	13.3	60.4
17	72 24.8	08.8	237 38.0	8.6	7 00.8	13.2	60.4
18	87 25.0	S 4 07.8	252 05.6	8.6	S 7 14.0	13.2	60.5
19	102 25.1	06.8	266 33.2	8.5	7 27.2	13.2	60.5
20	117 25.3	05.8	281 00.7	8.5	7 40.4	13.1	60.5
21	132 25.4	.. 04.8	295 28.2	8.4	7 53.5	13.0	60.5
22	147 25.6	03.9	309 55.6	8.3	8 06.5	13.1	60.5
23	162 25.8	02.9	324 23.0	8.4	S 8 19.6	12.9	60.5
SD 16.1	d 1.0		SD 16.2		16.4		16.5

Twilight — Sunrise — Moonrise

Lat.	Naut.	Civil	Sunrise	Moonrise 7	8	9	10
°	h m	h m	h m	h m	h m	h m	h m
N 72	04 31	05 51	06 58	16 41	18 49	21 02	23 26
N 70	04 41	05 52	06 53	16 46	18 46	20 49	22 59
68	04 48	05 53	06 49	16 51	18 43	20 39	22 38
66	04 54	05 54	06 45	16 54	18 41	20 30	22 22
64	04 59	05 55	06 42	16 58	18 39	20 23	22 09
62	05 04	05 55	06 39	17 00	18 38	20 17	21 58
60	05 07	05 55	06 37	17 03	18 37	20 12	21 49
N 58	05 10	05 56	06 35	17 05	18 35	20 07	21 40
56	05 13	05 56	06 33	17 07	18 34	20 03	21 33
54	05 15	05 56	06 31	17 08	18 33	20 00	21 27
52	05 17	05 56	06 29	17 10	18 33	19 57	21 21
50	05 18	05 56	06 28	17 11	18 32	19 54	21 16
45	05 22	05 56	06 25	17 14	18 30	19 47	21 05
N 40	05 24	05 55	06 22	17 17	18 29	19 42	20 56
35	05 25	05 55	06 20	17 19	18 28	19 37	20 48
30	05 26	05 54	06 18	17 21	18 27	19 33	20 41
20	05 26	05 52	06 14	17 24	18 25	19 27	20 30
N 10	05 25	05 50	06 11	17 27	18 23	19 21	20 19
0	05 23	05 47	06 07	17 30	18 22	19 15	20 10
S 10	05 18	05 43	06 04	17 33	18 21	19 10	20 00
20	05 12	05 38	06 00	17 36	18 19	19 04	19 50
30	05 04	05 32	05 56	17 39	18 18	18 57	19 39
35	04 58	05 28	05 53	17 41	18 17	18 53	19 33
40	04 51	05 23	05 50	17 43	18 16	18 49	19 25
45	04 42	05 17	05 47	17 46	18 14	18 44	19 17
S 50	04 31	05 10	05 43	17 49	18 13	18 39	19 07
52	04 25	05 07	05 41	17 50	18 12	18 36	19 02
54	04 19	05 03	05 39	17 52	18 12	18 33	18 57
56	04 12	04 58	05 37	17 53	18 11	18 30	18 51
58	04 04	04 54	05 34	17 55	18 10	18 26	18 45
S 60	03 54	04 48	05 31	17 57	18 09	18 22	18 38

Sunset — Twilight — Moonset

Lat.	Sunset	Civil	Naut.	Moonset 7	8	9	10
°	h m	h m	h m	h m	h m	h m	h m
N 72	17 25	18 33	19 53	06 22	06 05	05 47	05 27
N 70	17 30	18 31	19 43	06 14	06 04	05 53	05 42
68	17 34	18 30	19 36	06 07	06 03	05 59	05 54
66	17 38	18 29	19 29	06 01	06 02	06 03	06 04
64	17 41	18 28	19 24	05 56	06 02	06 07	06 13
62	17 44	18 28	19 20	05 52	06 01	06 10	06 20
60	17 46	18 27	19 16	05 48	06 01	06 13	06 27
N 58	17 48	18 27	19 13	05 45	06 00	06 16	06 33
56	17 50	18 27	19 10	05 42	06 00	06 18	06 38
54	17 51	18 27	19 08	05 39	05 59	06 20	06 42
52	17 53	18 26	19 06	05 37	05 59	06 22	06 46
50	17 54	18 26	19 04	05 34	05 59	06 23	06 50
45	17 57	18 26	19 01	05 29	05 58	06 27	06 58
N 40	18 00	18 27	18 58	05 25	05 58	06 30	07 05
35	18 02	18 27	18 57	05 22	05 57	06 33	07 11
30	18 04	18 28	18 56	05 18	05 57	06 36	07 16
20	18 08	18 30	18 55	05 13	05 56	06 40	07 25
N 10	18 11	18 32	18 56	05 08	05 55	06 43	07 33
0	18 14	18 35	18 59	05 03	05 54	06 47	07 41
S 10	18 17	18 38	19 03	04 58	05 54	06 50	07 48
20	18 21	18 43	19 09	04 53	05 53	06 54	07 56
30	18 25	18 49	19 17	04 47	05 52	06 58	08 06
35	18 27	18 53	19 23	04 44	05 52	07 01	08 11
40	18 30	18 57	19 30	04 40	05 51	07 03	08 17
45	18 33	19 03	19 38	04 35	05 50	07 07	08 24
S 50	18 37	19 10	19 49	04 30	05 49	07 10	08 33
52	18 39	19 13	19 55	04 27	05 49	07 12	08 37
54	18 41	19 17	20 01	04 24	05 48	07 14	08 41
56	18 43	19 21	20 08	04 21	05 48	07 16	08 46
58	18 46	19 26	20 16	04 18	05 47	07 19	08 51
S 60	18 49	19 32	20 25	04 14	05 47	07 21	08 57

SUN — MOON

Day	Eqn. of Time 00h	12h	Mer. Pass.	Mer. Pass. Upper	Lower	Age	Phase
d	m s	m s	h m	h m	h m	d	%
7	11 02	10 54	12 11	23 42	11 16	15	99
8	10 47	10 40	12 11	24 34	12 08	16	100
9	10 32	10 24	12 10	00 34	13 01	17	98

UT	ARIES GHA	VENUS −4.3 GHA	Dec	MARS −1.2 GHA	Dec	JUPITER −2.1 GHA	Dec	SATURN +0.4 GHA	Dec	STARS Name	SHA	Dec
SAT 10 00	168 04.4	135 57.8	N14 49.9	3 48.4	N11 06.7	131 25.6	N13 31.4	320 27.2	S 8 28.3	Acamar	315 19.2	S40 15.6
01	183 06.9	150 57.6	51.0	18 51.8	07.0	146 27.6	31.5	335 29.8	28.2	Achernar	335 27.9	S57 10.7
02	198 09.4	165 57.5	52.1	33 55.2	07.3	161 29.6	31.7	350 32.4	28.2	Acrux	173 09.6	S63 10.1
03	213 11.8	180 57.4	.. 53.2	48 58.6	.. 07.6	176 31.6	.. 31.9	5 34.9	.. 28.1	Adhara	255 13.1	S28 59.7
04	228 14.3	195 57.3	54.3	64 02.0	08.0	191 33.6	32.0	20 37.5	28.0	Aldebaran	290 50.4	N16 31.9
05	243 16.8	210 57.2	55.4	79 05.3	08.3	206 35.6	32.2	35 40.1	28.0			
S 06	258 19.2	225 57.1	N14 56.5	94 08.7	N11 08.6	221 37.5	N13 32.4	50 42.7	S 8 27.9	Alioth	166 20.9	N55 53.4
A 07	273 21.7	240 57.0	57.6	109 12.1	08.9	236 39.5	32.5	65 45.3	27.9	Alkaid	152 59.2	N49 14.9
T 08	288 24.2	255 56.9	58.7	124 15.5	09.2	251 41.5	32.7	80 47.9	27.8	Al Na'ir	27 45.2	S46 54.0
U 09	303 26.6	270 56.8	14 59.8	139 18.9	.. 09.5	266 43.5	.. 32.8	95 50.4	.. 27.8	Alnilam	275 47.2	S 1 11.9
R 10	318 29.1	285 56.7	15 00.9	154 22.3	09.8	281 45.5	33.0	110 53.0	27.7	Alphard	217 56.7	S 8 43.0
D 11	333 31.6	300 56.6	02.0	169 25.7	10.2	296 47.5	33.2	125 55.6	27.7			
A 12	348 34.0	315 56.5	N15 03.1	184 29.0	N11 10.5	311 49.5	N13 33.3	140 58.2	S 8 27.6	Alphecca	126 11.6	N26 40.2
Y 13	3 36.5	330 56.4	04.2	199 32.4	10.8	326 51.5	33.5	156 00.8	27.6	Alpheratz	357 44.8	N29 09.5
14	18 38.9	345 56.3	05.3	214 35.8	11.1	341 53.5	33.7	171 03.3	27.5	Altair	62 09.3	N 8 54.0
15	33 41.4	0 56.2	.. 06.4	229 39.2	.. 11.4	356 55.5	.. 33.8	186 05.9	.. 27.5	Ankaa	353 16.9	S42 14.4
16	48 43.9	15 56.1	07.5	244 42.6	11.7	11 57.4	34.0	201 08.5	27.4	Antares	112 27.3	S26 27.5
17	63 46.3	30 56.0	08.6	259 45.9	12.0	26 59.4	34.1	216 11.1	27.4			
18	78 48.8	45 55.9	N15 09.7	274 49.3	N11 12.3	42 01.4	N13 34.3	231 13.7	S 8 27.3	Arcturus	145 56.3	N19 06.9
19	93 51.3	60 55.8	10.8	289 52.7	12.7	57 03.4	34.5	246 16.3	27.3	Atria	107 29.8	S69 02.7
20	108 53.7	75 55.7	11.8	304 56.1	13.0	72 05.4	34.6	261 18.8	27.2	Avior	234 18.0	S59 33.3
21	123 56.2	90 55.6	.. 12.9	319 59.5	.. 13.3	87 07.4	.. 34.8	276 21.4	.. 27.2	Bellatrix	278 32.9	N 6 21.5
22	138 58.7	105 55.5	14.0	335 02.9	13.6	102 09.4	35.0	291 24.0	27.1	Betelgeuse	271 02.2	N 7 24.4
23	154 01.1	120 55.3	15.1	350 06.2	13.9	117 11.4	35.1	306 26.6	27.0			
11 00	169 03.6	135 55.2	N15 16.2	5 09.6	N11 14.2	132 13.4	N13 35.3	321 29.2	S 8 27.0	Canopus	263 56.4	S52 42.5
01	184 06.0	150 55.1	17.3	20 13.0	14.5	147 15.3	35.5	336 31.8	26.9	Capella	280 35.8	N46 00.7
02	199 08.5	165 55.0	18.4	35 16.4	14.8	162 17.3	35.6	351 34.3	26.9	Deneb	49 32.4	N45 19.3
03	214 11.0	180 54.9	.. 19.5	50 19.7	.. 15.1	177 19.3	.. 35.8	6 36.9	.. 26.8	Denebola	182 34.2	N14 30.0
04	229 13.4	195 54.8	20.6	65 23.1	15.4	192 21.3	35.9	21 39.5	26.8	Diphda	348 57.1	S17 55.3
05	244 15.9	210 54.7	21.7	80 26.5	15.7	207 23.3	36.1	36 42.1	26.7			
S 06	259 18.4	225 54.6	N15 22.7	95 29.9	N11 16.0	222 25.3	N13 36.3	51 44.7	S 8 26.7	Dubhe	193 52.1	N61 40.9
U 07	274 20.8	240 54.5	23.8	110 33.3	16.4	237 27.3	36.4	66 47.3	26.6	Elnath	278 13.7	N28 37.0
N 08	289 23.3	255 54.4	24.9	125 36.6	16.7	252 29.3	36.6	81 49.9	26.6	Eltanin	90 46.6	N51 29.0
D 09	304 25.8	270 54.3	.. 26.0	140 40.0	.. 17.0	267 31.2	.. 36.8	96 52.4	.. 26.5	Enif	33 48.3	N 9 55.8
A 10	319 28.2	285 54.2	27.1	155 43.4	17.3	282 33.2	36.9	111 55.0	26.5	Fomalhaut	15 25.3	S29 33.4
Y 11	334 30.7	300 54.1	28.2	170 46.8	17.6	297 35.2	37.1	126 57.6	26.4			
12	349 33.2	315 54.0	N15 29.3	185 50.1	N11 17.9	312 37.2	N13 37.3	142 00.2	S 8 26.4	Gacrux	172 01.4	S57 11.0
13	4 35.6	330 53.9	30.3	200 53.5	18.2	327 39.2	37.4	157 02.8	26.3	Gienah	175 52.9	S17 36.8
14	19 38.1	345 53.8	31.4	215 56.9	18.5	342 41.2	37.6	172 05.4	26.2	Hadar	148 48.7	S60 25.8
15	34 40.5	0 53.7	.. 32.5	231 00.3	.. 18.8	357 43.2	.. 37.7	187 08.0	.. 26.2	Hamal	328 02.0	N23 31.2
16	49 43.0	15 53.6	33.6	246 03.6	19.1	12 45.1	37.9	202 10.5	26.1	Kaus Aust.	83 45.1	S34 22.6
17	64 45.5	30 53.5	34.7	261 07.0	19.4	27 47.1	38.1	217 13.1	26.1			
18	79 47.9	45 53.4	N15 35.8	276 10.4	N11 19.7	42 49.1	N13 38.2	232 15.7	S 8 26.0	Kochab	137 19.2	N74 06.0
19	94 50.4	60 53.3	36.8	291 13.7	20.0	57 51.1	38.4	247 18.3	26.0	Markab	13 39.5	N15 16.2
20	109 52.9	75 53.2	37.9	306 17.1	20.3	72 53.1	38.6	262 20.9	25.9	Menkar	314 16.1	N 4 08.1
21	124 55.3	90 53.1	.. 39.0	321 20.5	.. 20.6	87 55.1	.. 38.7	277 23.5	.. 25.9	Menkent	148 08.3	S36 25.8
22	139 57.8	105 53.0	40.1	336 23.9	20.9	102 57.1	38.9	292 26.1	25.8	Miaplacidus	221 39.1	S69 46.4
23	155 00.3	120 52.9	41.1	351 27.2	21.2	117 59.0	39.1	307 28.6	25.8			
12 00	170 02.7	135 52.8	N15 42.2	6 30.6	N11 21.5	133 01.0	N13 39.2	322 31.2	S 8 25.7	Mirfak	308 41.9	N49 54.4
01	185 05.2	150 52.7	43.3	21 34.0	21.8	148 03.0	39.4	337 33.8	25.7	Nunki	75 59.5	S26 16.8
02	200 07.7	165 52.6	44.4	36 37.3	22.1	163 05.0	39.5	352 36.4	25.6	Peacock	53 21.0	S56 41.5
03	215 10.1	180 52.5	.. 45.4	51 40.7	.. 22.4	178 07.0	.. 39.7	7 39.0	.. 25.5	Pollux	243 28.6	N27 59.7
04	230 12.6	195 52.4	46.5	66 44.1	22.7	193 09.0	39.9	22 41.6	25.5	Procyon	245 00.5	N 5 11.4
05	245 15.0	210 52.3	47.6	81 47.4	23.0	208 10.9	40.0	37 44.2	25.4			
M 06	260 17.5	225 52.2	N15 48.7	96 50.8	N11 23.3	223 12.9	N13 40.2	52 46.8	S 8 25.4	Rasalhague	96 07.3	N12 32.9
O 07	275 20.0	240 52.1	49.7	111 54.2	23.6	238 14.9	40.4	67 49.3	25.3	Regulus	207 44.1	N11 54.2
N 08	290 22.4	255 51.9	50.8	126 57.5	23.9	253 16.9	40.5	82 51.9	25.3	Rigel	281 12.9	S 8 11.5
D 09	305 24.9	270 51.8	.. 51.9	142 00.9	.. 24.2	268 18.9	.. 40.7	97 54.5	.. 25.2	Rigil Kent.	139 52.5	S60 53.0
A 10	320 27.4	285 51.7	53.0	157 04.3	24.5	283 20.9	40.9	112 57.1	25.2	Sabik	102 13.5	S15 44.4
Y 11	335 29.8	300 51.6	54.0	172 07.6	24.8	298 22.8	41.0	127 59.7	25.1			
12	350 32.3	315 51.5	N15 55.1	187 11.0	N11 25.1	313 24.8	N13 41.2	143 02.3	S 8 25.1	Schedar	349 42.1	N56 36.4
13	5 34.8	330 51.4	56.2	202 14.4	25.4	328 26.8	41.4	158 04.9	25.0	Shaula	96 23.1	S37 06.6
14	20 37.2	345 51.3	57.2	217 17.7	25.7	343 28.8	41.5	173 07.5	24.9	Sirius	258 34.4	S16 44.3
15	35 39.7	0 51.2	.. 58.3	232 21.1	.. 26.0	358 30.8	.. 41.7	188 10.1	.. 24.9	Spica	158 31.9	S11 13.7
16	50 42.1	15 51.1	15 59.4	247 24.4	26.3	13 32.8	41.8	203 12.6	24.8	Suhail	222 52.7	S43 29.3
17	65 44.6	30 51.0	16 00.4	262 27.8	26.5	28 34.7	42.0	218 15.2	24.8			
18	80 47.1	45 50.9	N16 01.5	277 31.2	N11 26.8	43 36.7	N13 42.2	233 17.8	S 8 24.7	Vega	80 39.7	N38 47.5
19	95 49.5	60 50.8	02.6	292 34.5	27.1	58 38.7	42.3	248 20.4	24.7	Zuben'ubi	137 06.2	S16 05.6
20	110 52.0	75 50.7	03.6	307 37.9	27.4	73 40.7	42.5	263 23.0	24.6		SHA	Mer.Pass.
21	125 54.5	90 50.6	.. 04.7	322 41.2	.. 27.7	88 42.7	.. 42.7	278 25.6	.. 24.6	Venus	326 51.7	14 56
22	140 56.9	105 50.5	05.8	337 44.6	28.0	103 44.6	42.8	293 28.2	24.5	Mars	196 06.0	23 34
23	155 59.4	120 50.4	06.8	352 48.0	28.3	118 46.6	43.0	308 30.8	24.4	Jupiter	323 09.8	15 09
Mer. Pass. 12 41.7		v −0.1	d 1.1	v 3.4	d 0.3	v 2.0	d 0.2	v 2.6	d 0.1	Saturn	152 25.6	2 34

SUN and MOON

UT	SUN GHA	SUN Dec	MOON GHA	v	Dec	d	HP
SATURDAY 10							
00	177 25.9	S 4 01.9	338 50.4	8.3	S 8 32.5	12.9	60.5
01	192 26.1	4 00.9	353 17.7	8.2	8 45.4	12.9	60.5
02	207 26.3	3 59.9	7 44.9	8.3	8 58.3	12.8	60.5
03	222 26.4	.. 59.0	22 12.2	8.1	9 11.1	12.7	60.5
04	237 26.6	58.0	36 39.3	8.2	9 23.8	12.7	60.5
05	252 26.7	57.0	51 06.5	8.1	9 36.5	12.6	60.5
06	267 26.9	S 3 56.0	65 33.6	8.0	S 9 49.1	12.6	60.5
07	282 27.1	55.0	80 00.6	8.0	10 01.7	12.5	60.5
08	297 27.2	54.1	94 27.6	7.9	10 14.2	12.4	60.5
09	312 27.4	.. 53.1	108 54.5	8.0	10 26.6	12.4	60.5
10	327 27.6	52.1	123 21.5	7.8	10 39.0	12.3	60.5
11	342 27.7	51.1	137 48.3	7.8	10 51.3	12.2	60.5
12	357 27.9	S 3 50.1	152 15.1	7.8	S11 03.5	12.2	60.5
13	12 28.0	49.2	166 41.9	7.7	11 15.7	12.0	60.5
14	27 28.2	48.2	181 08.6	7.7	11 27.7	12.1	60.5
15	42 28.4	.. 47.2	195 35.3	7.6	11 39.8	11.9	60.5
16	57 28.5	46.2	210 01.9	7.6	11 51.7	11.8	60.5
17	72 28.7	45.2	224 28.5	7.5	12 03.5	11.8	60.5
18	87 28.9	S 3 44.2	238 55.0	7.5	S12 15.3	11.7	60.5
19	102 29.0	43.3	253 21.5	7.4	12 27.0	11.6	60.5
20	117 29.2	42.3	267 47.9	7.4	12 38.6	11.6	60.5
21	132 29.4	.. 41.3	282 14.3	7.4	12 50.2	11.4	60.5
22	147 29.5	40.3	296 40.7	7.3	13 01.6	11.4	60.5
23	162 29.7	39.3	311 07.0	7.2	13 13.0	11.3	60.5
SUNDAY 11							
00	177 29.9	S 3 38.4	325 33.2	7.2	S13 24.3	11.1	60.5
01	192 30.0	37.4	339 59.4	7.2	13 35.4	11.1	60.5
02	207 30.2	36.4	354 25.6	7.1	13 46.5	11.0	60.5
03	222 30.4	.. 35.4	8 51.7	7.1	13 57.5	10.9	60.4
04	237 30.5	34.4	23 17.8	7.0	14 08.4	10.9	60.4
05	252 30.7	33.4	37 43.8	6.9	14 19.3	10.7	60.4
06	267 30.8	S 3 32.5	52 09.7	7.0	S14 30.0	10.6	60.4
07	282 31.0	31.5	66 35.7	6.8	14 40.6	10.5	60.4
08	297 31.2	30.5	81 01.5	6.9	14 51.1	10.4	60.4
09	312 31.3	.. 29.5	95 27.4	6.8	15 01.5	10.3	60.4
10	327 31.5	28.5	109 53.2	6.7	15 11.8	10.2	60.4
11	342 31.7	27.5	124 18.9	6.7	15 22.0	10.2	60.4
12	357 31.8	S 3 26.6	138 44.6	6.7	S15 32.2	10.0	60.4
13	12 32.0	25.6	153 10.3	6.6	15 42.2	9.8	60.4
14	27 32.2	24.6	167 35.9	6.5	15 52.0	9.8	60.3
15	42 32.3	.. 23.6	182 01.4	6.5	16 01.8	9.7	60.3
16	57 32.5	22.6	196 26.9	6.5	16 11.5	9.6	60.3
17	72 32.7	21.6	210 52.4	6.5	16 21.1	9.4	60.3
18	87 32.8	S 3 20.7	225 17.9	6.4	S16 30.5	9.4	60.3
19	102 33.0	19.7	239 43.3	6.3	16 39.9	9.2	60.3
20	117 33.2	18.7	254 08.6	6.3	16 49.1	9.1	60.3
21	132 33.4	.. 17.7	268 33.9	6.3	16 58.2	9.0	60.3
22	147 33.5	16.7	282 59.2	6.2	17 07.2	8.8	60.2
23	162 33.7	15.7	297 24.4	6.2	17 16.0	8.8	60.2
MONDAY 12							
00	177 33.9	S 3 14.8	311 49.6	6.2	S17 24.8	8.6	60.2
01	192 34.0	13.8	326 14.8	6.1	17 33.4	8.5	60.2
02	207 34.2	12.8	340 39.9	6.1	17 41.9	8.4	60.2
03	222 34.4	.. 11.9	355 05.0	6.0	17 50.3	8.3	60.2
04	237 34.5	10.8	9 30.0	6.0	17 58.6	8.1	60.2
05	252 34.7	09.8	23 55.0	6.0	18 06.7	8.0	60.1
06	267 34.9	S 3 08.9	38 20.0	5.9	S18 14.7	7.9	60.1
07	282 35.0	07.9	52 44.9	5.9	18 22.6	7.8	60.1
08	297 35.2	06.9	67 09.8	5.9	18 30.4	7.6	60.1
09	312 35.4	.. 05.9	81 34.7	5.8	18 38.0	7.5	60.1
10	327 35.5	04.9	95 59.5	5.8	18 45.5	7.4	60.1
11	342 35.7	03.9	110 24.3	5.8	18 52.9	7.2	60.0
12	357 35.9	S 3 03.0	124 49.1	5.8	S19 00.1	7.1	60.0
13	12 36.1	02.0	139 13.9	5.7	19 07.2	7.0	60.0
14	27 36.2	01.0	153 38.6	5.7	19 14.2	6.8	60.0
15	42 36.4	3 00.0	168 03.3	5.7	19 21.0	6.7	60.0
16	57 36.6	2 59.0	182 28.0	5.6	19 27.7	6.6	59.9
17	72 36.7	58.0	196 52.6	5.6	19 34.3	6.4	59.9
18	87 36.9	S 2 57.1	211 17.2	5.6	S19 40.7	6.3	59.9
19	102 37.1	56.1	225 41.8	5.6	19 47.0	6.1	59.9
20	117 37.2	55.1	240 06.4	5.5	19 53.1	6.1	59.9
21	132 37.4	.. 54.1	254 30.9	5.6	19 59.2	5.8	59.8
22	147 37.6	53.1	268 55.5	5.5	20 05.0	5.8	59.8
23	162 37.8	52.1	283 20.0	5.5	S20 10.8	5.6	59.8
	SD 16.1	d 1.0	SD 16.5		16.4		16.4

Twilight and Moonrise

Lat.	Naut.	Civil	Sunrise	Moonrise 10	11	12	13
N 72	04 15	05 36	06 43	23 26	■	■	■
N 70	04 26	05 39	06 39	22 59	25 23	01 23	■
68	04 35	05 41	06 36	22 38	24 43	00 43	02 53
66	04 43	05 43	06 34	22 21	24 15	00 15	02 05
64	04 49	05 44	06 31	22 09	23 54	25 34	01 34
62	04 54	05 45	06 29	21 58	23 38	25 11	01 11
60	04 58	05 46	06 28	21 49	23 24	24 53	00 53
N 58	05 02	05 47	06 26	21 40	23 12	24 38	00 38
56	05 05	05 48	06 25	21 33	23 02	24 25	00 25
54	05 08	05 49	06 24	21 27	22 53	24 13	00 13
52	05 10	05 49	06 23	21 21	22 45	24 03	00 03
50	05 12	05 49	06 22	21 16	22 37	23 54	24 43
45	05 16	05 50	06 19	21 05	22 22	23 36	24 43
N 40	05 19	05 51	06 17	20 56	22 09	23 20	24 26
35	05 21	05 51	06 16	20 48	21 59	23 08	24 12
30	05 23	05 50	06 14	20 41	21 49	22 56	24 00
20	05 24	05 50	06 12	20 30	21 33	22 37	23 39
N 10	05 24	05 48	06 09	20 19	21 20	22 21	23 21
0	05 22	05 46	06 07	20 10	21 07	22 05	23 04
S 10	05 19	05 43	06 04	20 00	20 54	21 50	22 48
20	05 13	05 39	06 01	19 50	20 40	21 33	22 30
30	05 06	05 34	05 58	19 39	20 25	21 15	22 09
35	05 01	05 31	05 56	19 33	20 16	21 04	21 57
40	04 54	05 26	05 54	19 25	20 06	20 52	21 43
45	04 46	05 21	05 51	19 17	19 54	20 37	21 27
S 50	04 36	05 15	05 48	19 07	19 40	20 19	21 07
52	04 31	05 12	05 46	19 02	19 33	20 11	20 58
54	04 25	05 09	05 45	18 57	19 26	20 02	20 47
56	04 19	05 05	05 43	18 51	19 17	19 51	20 35
58	04 12	05 01	05 41	18 45	19 08	19 39	20 21
S 60	04 03	04 56	05 39	18 38	18 58	19 25	20 05

Twilight and Moonset

Lat.	Sunset	Civil	Naut.	Moonset 10	11	12	13
N 72	17 39	18 47	20 09	05 27	04 58	■	■
N 70	17 43	18 43	19 57	05 42	05 28	05 04	■
68	17 45	18 41	19 47	05 54	05 50	05 45	05 38
66	17 48	18 39	19 40	06 04	06 07	06 13	06 27
64	17 50	18 37	19 33	06 13	06 22	06 35	06 58
62	17 52	18 36	19 28	06 20	06 34	06 52	07 21
60	17 53	18 35	19 23	06 27	06 44	07 07	07 40
N 58	17 55	18 34	19 20	06 33	06 53	07 19	07 55
56	17 56	18 33	19 16	06 38	07 01	07 30	08 09
54	17 57	18 32	19 13	06 42	07 08	07 40	08 20
52	17 58	18 32	19 11	06 46	07 14	07 48	08 30
50	17 59	18 31	19 09	06 50	07 20	07 56	08 40
45	18 01	18 30	19 04	06 58	07 33	08 12	08 59
N 40	18 03	18 30	19 01	07 05	07 43	08 26	09 15
35	18 05	18 30	18 59	07 11	07 52	08 37	09 28
30	18 06	18 30	18 58	07 16	08 00	08 48	09 40
20	18 08	18 31	18 56	07 25	08 13	09 05	10 00
N 10	18 11	18 32	18 56	07 33	08 25	09 20	10 17
0	18 13	18 34	18 58	07 41	08 37	09 34	10 33
S 10	18 16	18 37	19 01	07 48	08 48	09 49	10 50
20	18 18	18 40	19 06	07 56	09 00	10 04	11 07
30	18 21	18 45	19 13	08 06	09 14	10 21	11 27
35	18 23	18 49	19 18	08 11	09 22	10 32	11 39
40	18 25	18 53	19 25	08 17	09 31	10 43	11 52
45	18 28	18 57	19 32	08 24	09 42	10 57	12 08
S 50	18 31	19 04	19 42	08 33	09 55	11 14	12 28
52	18 32	19 06	19 47	08 37	10 01	11 22	12 37
54	18 34	19 10	19 53	08 41	10 07	11 31	12 48
56	18 36	19 13	19 59	08 46	10 15	11 41	12 59
58	18 38	19 17	20 06	08 51	10 24	11 53	13 13
S 60	18 40	19 22	20 14	08 57	10 33	12 06	13 29

SUN and MOON notes

Day	Eqn. of Time 00h	12h	Mer. Pass.	Mer. Pass. Upper	Lower	Age	Phase %
10	10 17	10 09	12 10	01 28	13 55	18	94
11	10 01	09 53	12 10	02 23	14 52	19	87
12	09 45	09 37	12 10	03 20	15 50	20	78

UT	ARIES GHA	VENUS −4.4 GHA	VENUS Dec	MARS −1.1 GHA	MARS Dec	JUPITER −2.1 GHA	JUPITER Dec	SATURN +0.4 GHA	SATURN Dec	STARS Name	SHA	Dec
13 00	171 01.9	135 50.3	N16 07.9	7 51.3	N11 28.6	133 48.6	N13 43.2	323 33.4	S 8 24.4	Acamar	315 19.2	S40 15.6
01	186 04.3	150 50.2	08.9	22 54.7	28.9	148 50.6	43.3	338 36.0	24.3	Achernar	335 27.9	S57 10.6
02	201 06.8	165 50.1	10.0	37 58.0	29.2	163 52.6	43.5	353 38.5	24.3	Acrux	173 09.6	S63 10.1
03	216 09.3	180 50.0	.. 11.1	53 01.4	.. 29.5	178 54.5	.. 43.7	8 41.1	.. 24.2	Adhara	255 13.1	S28 59.7
04	231 11.7	195 49.9	12.1	68 04.7	29.8	193 56.5	43.8	23 43.7	24.2	Aldebaran	290 50.5	N16 31.9
05	246 14.2	210 49.8	13.2	83 08.1	30.0	208 58.5	44.0	38 46.3	24.1			
T 06	261 16.6	225 49.7	N16 14.2	98 11.5	N11 30.3	224 00.5	N13 44.2	53 48.9	S 8 24.1	Alioth	166 20.9	N55 53.4
U 07	276 19.1	240 49.6	15.3	113 14.8	30.6	239 02.5	44.3	68 51.5	24.0	Alkaid	152 59.1	N49 14.9
E 08	291 21.6	255 49.5	16.4	128 18.2	30.9	254 04.4	44.5	83 54.1	24.0	Al Na'ir	27 45.2	S46 54.0
S 09	306 24.0	270 49.4	.. 17.4	143 21.5	.. 31.2	269 06.4	.. 44.7	98 56.7	.. 23.9	Alnilam	275 47.2	S 1 11.9
D 10	321 26.5	285 49.3	18.5	158 24.9	31.5	284 08.4	44.8	113 59.3	23.8	Alphard	217 56.7	S 8 43.0
A 11	336 29.0	300 49.2	19.5	173 28.2	31.8	299 10.4	45.0	129 01.9	23.8			
Y 12	351 31.4	315 49.1	N16 20.6	188 31.6	N11 32.1	314 12.4	N13 45.1	144 04.4	S 8 23.7	Alphecca	126 11.6	N26 40.2
13	6 33.9	330 49.0	21.6	203 34.9	32.3	329 14.3	45.3	159 07.0	23.7	Alpheratz	357 44.8	N29 09.5
14	21 36.4	345 48.9	22.7	218 38.3	32.6	344 16.3	45.5	174 09.6	23.6	Altair	62 09.3	N 8 54.0
15	36 38.8	0 48.8	.. 23.7	233 41.6	.. 32.9	359 18.3	.. 45.6	189 12.2	.. 23.6	Ankaa	353 16.9	S42 14.4
16	51 41.3	15 48.7	24.8	248 45.0	33.2	14 20.3	45.8	204 14.8	23.5	Antares	112 27.2	S26 27.5
17	66 43.8	30 48.6	25.8	263 48.3	33.5	29 22.3	46.0	219 17.4	23.5			
18	81 46.2	45 48.5	N16 26.9	278 51.7	N11 33.8	44 24.2	N13 46.1	234 20.0	S 8 23.4	Arcturus	145 56.3	N19 06.9
19	96 48.7	60 48.4	28.0	293 55.0	34.0	59 26.2	46.3	249 22.6	23.3	Atria	107 29.8	S69 02.7
20	111 51.1	75 48.3	29.0	308 58.4	34.3	74 28.2	46.5	264 25.2	23.3	Avior	234 18.0	S59 33.3
21	126 53.6	90 48.2	.. 30.1	324 01.7	.. 34.6	89 30.2	.. 46.6	279 27.8	.. 23.2	Bellatrix	278 32.9	N 6 21.5
22	141 56.1	105 48.1	31.1	339 05.1	34.9	104 32.1	46.8	294 30.4	23.2	Betelgeuse	271 02.2	N 7 24.4
23	156 58.5	120 48.0	32.1	354 08.4	35.2	119 34.1	47.0	309 33.0	23.1			
14 00	172 01.0	135 47.9	N16 33.2	9 11.8	N11 35.5	134 36.1	N13 47.1	324 35.6	S 8 23.1	Canopus	263 56.4	S52 42.5
01	187 03.5	150 47.8	34.2	24 15.1	35.7	149 38.1	47.3	339 38.2	23.0	Capella	280 35.8	N46 00.7
02	202 05.9	165 47.7	35.3	39 18.4	36.0	164 40.0	47.5	354 40.7	22.9	Deneb	49 32.4	N45 19.3
03	217 08.4	180 47.6	.. 36.3	54 21.8	.. 36.3	179 42.0	.. 47.6	9 43.3	.. 22.9	Denebola	182 34.2	N14 30.0
04	232 10.9	195 47.5	37.4	69 25.1	36.6	194 44.0	47.8	24 45.9	22.8	Diphda	348 57.1	S17 55.2
05	247 13.3	210 47.4	38.4	84 28.5	36.9	209 46.0	48.0	39 48.5	22.8			
W 06	262 15.8	225 47.3	N16 39.5	99 31.8	N11 37.1	224 48.0	N13 48.1	54 51.1	S 8 22.7	Dubhe	193 52.1	N61 41.0
E 07	277 18.3	240 47.2	40.5	114 35.2	37.4	239 49.9	48.3	69 53.7	22.7	Elnath	278 13.7	N28 37.0
D 08	292 20.7	255 47.1	41.6	129 38.5	37.7	254 51.9	48.5	84 56.3	22.6	Eltanin	90 46.6	N51 29.0
N 09	307 23.2	270 47.0	.. 42.6	144 41.8	.. 38.0	269 53.9	.. 48.6	99 58.9	.. 22.6	Enif	33 48.3	N 9 55.8
E 10	322 25.6	285 46.9	43.6	159 45.2	38.2	284 55.9	48.8	115 01.5	22.5	Fomalhaut	15 25.3	S29 33.4
S 11	337 28.1	300 46.8	44.7	174 48.5	38.5	299 57.8	48.9	130 04.1	22.4			
D 12	352 30.6	315 46.7	N16 45.7	189 51.9	N11 38.8	314 59.8	N13 49.1	145 06.7	S 8 22.4	Gacrux	172 01.3	S57 11.0
A 13	7 33.0	330 46.6	46.8	204 55.2	39.1	330 01.8	49.3	160 09.3	22.3	Gienah	175 52.9	S17 36.8
Y 14	22 35.5	345 46.5	47.8	219 58.5	39.3	345 03.8	49.4	175 11.9	22.3	Hadar	148 48.7	S60 25.8
15	37 38.0	0 46.4	.. 48.8	235 01.9	.. 39.6	0 05.7	.. 49.6	190 14.5	.. 22.2	Hamal	328 02.0	N23 31.2
16	52 40.4	15 46.3	49.9	250 05.2	39.9	15 07.7	49.8	205 17.1	22.2	Kaus Aust.	83 45.0	S34 22.5
17	67 42.9	30 46.2	50.9	265 08.5	40.2	30 09.7	49.9	220 19.7	22.1			
18	82 45.4	45 46.1	N16 51.9	280 11.9	N11 40.4	45 11.7	N13 50.1	235 22.3	S 8 22.0	Kochab	137 19.2	N74 06.0
19	97 47.8	60 46.1	53.0	295 15.2	40.7	60 13.6	50.3	250 24.8	22.0	Markab	13 39.5	N15 16.2
20	112 50.3	75 46.0	54.0	310 18.5	41.0	75 15.6	50.4	265 27.4	21.9	Menkar	314 16.2	N 4 08.1
21	127 52.7	90 45.9	.. 55.0	325 21.9	.. 41.3	90 17.6	.. 50.6	280 30.0	.. 21.9	Menkent	148 08.3	S36 25.8
22	142 55.2	105 45.8	56.1	340 25.2	41.5	105 19.6	50.8	295 32.6	21.8	Miaplacidus	221 39.2	S69 46.4
23	157 57.7	120 45.7	57.1	355 28.5	41.8	120 21.5	50.9	310 35.2	21.8			
15 00	173 00.1	135 45.6	N16 58.1	10 31.9	N11 42.1	135 23.5	N13 51.1	325 37.8	S 8 21.7	Mirfak	308 41.9	N49 54.4
01	188 02.6	150 45.5	16 59.2	25 35.2	42.3	150 25.5	51.3	340 40.4	21.6	Nunki	75 59.5	S26 16.8
02	203 05.1	165 45.4	17 00.2	40 38.5	42.6	165 27.4	51.4	355 43.0	21.6	Peacock	53 21.0	S56 41.5
03	218 07.5	180 45.3	.. 01.2	55 41.9	.. 42.9	180 29.4	.. 51.6	10 45.6	.. 21.5	Pollux	243 28.6	N27 59.7
04	233 10.0	195 45.2	02.3	70 45.2	43.1	195 31.4	51.8	25 48.2	21.5	Procyon	245 00.5	N 5 11.4
05	248 12.5	210 45.1	03.3	85 48.5	43.4	210 33.4	51.9	40 50.8	21.4			
T 06	263 14.9	225 45.0	N17 04.3	100 51.8	N11 43.7	225 35.3	N13 52.1	55 53.4	S 8 21.4	Rasalhague	96 07.3	N12 32.9
H 07	278 17.4	240 44.9	05.4	115 55.2	44.0	240 37.3	52.3	70 56.0	21.3	Regulus	207 44.1	N11 54.2
U 08	293 19.9	255 44.8	06.4	130 58.5	44.2	255 39.3	52.4	85 58.6	21.2	Rigel	281 12.9	S 8 11.5
R 09	308 22.3	270 44.7	.. 07.4	146 01.8	.. 44.5	270 41.3	.. 52.6	101 01.2	.. 21.2	Rigil Kent.	139 52.5	S60 53.0
S 10	323 24.8	285 44.6	08.4	161 05.1	44.8	285 43.2	52.8	116 03.8	21.1	Sabik	102 13.5	S15 44.4
D 11	338 27.2	300 44.5	09.5	176 08.5	45.0	300 45.2	52.9	131 06.4	21.1			
A 12	353 29.7	315 44.4	N17 10.5	191 11.8	N11 45.3	315 47.2	N13 53.1	146 09.0	S 8 21.0	Schedar	349 42.1	N56 36.3
Y 13	8 32.2	330 44.3	11.5	206 15.1	45.5	330 49.1	53.3	161 11.6	21.0	Shaula	96 23.1	S37 06.6
14	23 34.6	345 44.2	12.5	221 18.4	45.8	345 51.1	53.4	176 14.2	20.9	Sirius	258 34.4	S16 44.3
15	38 37.1	0 44.1	.. 13.5	236 21.8	.. 46.1	0 53.1	.. 53.6	191 16.8	.. 20.8	Spica	158 31.9	S11 13.7
16	53 39.6	15 44.0	14.6	251 25.1	46.3	15 55.1	53.8	206 19.4	20.8	Suhail	222 52.8	S43 29.3
17	68 42.0	30 43.9	15.6	266 28.4	46.6	30 57.0	53.9	221 22.0	20.7			
18	83 44.5	45 43.8	N17 16.6	281 31.7	N11 46.9	45 59.0	N13 54.1	236 24.6	S 8 20.7	Vega	80 39.7	N38 47.5
19	98 47.0	60 43.7	17.6	296 35.0	47.1	61 01.0	54.3	251 27.2	20.6	Zuben'ubi	137 06.2	S16 05.6
20	113 49.4	75 43.6	18.7	311 38.3	47.4	76 02.9	54.4	266 29.8	20.6		SHA	Mer. Pass.
21	128 51.9	90 43.5	.. 19.7	326 41.7	.. 47.7	91 04.9	.. 54.6	281 32.4	.. 20.5			h m
22	143 54.4	105 43.4	20.7	341 45.0	47.9	106 06.9	54.8	296 35.0	20.4	Venus	323 46.9	14 57
23	158 56.8	120 43.3	21.7	356 48.3	48.2	121 08.9	54.9	311 37.6	20.4	Mars	197 10.8	23 18
Mer. Pass.	h m 12 29.9	v −0.1	d 1.0	v 3.3	d 0.3	v 2.0	d 0.2	v 2.6	d 0.1	Jupiter	322 35.1	15 00
										Saturn	152 34.6	2 21

SUN and MOON

UT (d h)	SUN GHA	SUN Dec	MOON GHA	v	MOON Dec	d	HP
13 00	177 37.9	S 2 51.1	297 44.5	5.5	S20 16.4	5.4	59.8
01	192 38.1	50.2	312 09.0	5.4	20 21.8	5.3	59.8
02	207 38.3	49.2	326 33.4	5.5	20 27.1	5.2	59.7
03	222 38.4	.. 48.2	340 57.9	5.4	20 32.3	5.1	59.7
04	237 38.6	47.2	355 22.3	5.5	20 37.4	4.8	59.7
05	252 38.8	46.2	9 46.8	5.4	20 42.2	4.8	59.7
T 06	267 39.0	S 2 45.2	24 11.2	5.4	S20 47.0	4.6	59.7
U 07	282 39.1	44.2	38 35.6	5.4	20 51.6	4.5	59.6
E 08	297 39.3	43.3	53 00.0	5.4	20 56.1	4.3	59.6
S 09	312 39.5	.. 42.3	67 24.4	5.4	21 00.4	4.1	59.6
D 10	327 39.6	41.3	81 48.8	5.4	21 04.5	4.1	59.6
A 11	342 39.8	40.3	96 13.2	5.3	21 08.6	3.8	59.5
Y 12	357 40.0	S 2 39.3	110 37.5	5.4	S21 12.4	3.8	59.5
13	12 40.2	38.3	125 01.9	5.4	21 16.2	3.6	59.5
14	27 40.3	37.3	139 26.3	5.4	21 19.8	3.4	59.5
15	42 40.5	.. 36.4	153 50.7	5.4	21 23.2	3.3	59.5
16	57 40.7	35.4	168 15.1	5.4	21 26.5	3.1	59.4
17	72 40.8	34.4	182 39.5	5.4	21 29.6	3.0	59.4
18	87 41.0	S 2 33.4	197 03.9	5.4	S21 32.6	2.9	59.4
19	102 41.2	32.4	211 28.3	5.4	21 35.5	2.7	59.4
20	117 41.4	31.4	225 52.7	5.4	21 38.2	2.6	59.3
21	132 41.5	.. 30.4	240 17.1	5.4	21 40.8	2.4	59.3
22	147 41.7	29.4	254 41.5	5.5	21 43.2	2.3	59.3
23	162 41.9	28.5	269 06.0	5.4	21 45.5	2.1	59.3
14 00	177 42.1	S 2 27.5	283 30.4	5.5	S21 47.6	2.0	59.2
01	192 42.2	26.5	297 54.9	5.5	21 49.6	1.8	59.2
02	207 42.4	25.5	312 19.4	5.5	21 51.4	1.7	59.2
03	222 42.6	.. 24.5	326 43.9	5.5	21 53.1	1.5	59.2
04	237 42.7	23.5	341 08.4	5.5	21 54.6	1.4	59.1
05	252 42.9	22.5	355 32.9	5.6	21 56.0	1.2	59.1
W 06	267 43.1	S 2 21.6	9 57.5	5.6	S21 57.2	1.1	59.1
E 07	282 43.3	20.6	24 22.1	5.6	21 58.3	1.0	59.1
D 08	297 43.4	19.6	38 46.7	5.6	21 59.3	0.8	59.0
N 09	312 43.6	.. 18.6	53 11.3	5.7	22 00.1	0.7	59.0
E 10	327 43.8	17.6	67 36.0	5.7	22 00.8	0.5	59.0
S 11	342 44.0	16.6	82 00.7	5.7	22 01.3	0.3	59.0
D 12	357 44.1	S 2 15.6	96 25.4	5.8	S22 01.6	0.3	58.9
A 13	12 44.3	14.6	110 50.2	5.8	22 01.9	0.1	58.9
Y 14	27 44.5	13.7	125 15.0	5.8	22 02.0	0.1	58.9
15	42 44.7	.. 12.7	139 39.8	5.9	22 01.9	0.2	58.9
16	57 44.8	11.7	154 04.7	5.8	22 01.7	0.4	58.8
17	72 45.0	10.7	168 29.5	6.0	22 01.3	0.4	58.8
18	87 45.2	S 2 09.7	182 54.5	5.9	S22 00.9	0.7	58.8
19	102 45.3	08.7	197 19.4	6.0	22 00.2	0.7	58.8
20	117 45.5	07.7	211 44.4	6.1	21 59.5	1.0	58.7
21	132 45.7	.. 06.7	226 09.5	6.1	21 58.5	1.0	58.7
22	147 45.9	05.8	240 34.6	6.1	21 57.5	1.2	58.7
23	162 46.1	04.8	254 59.7	6.2	21 56.3	1.3	58.6
15 00	177 46.2	S 2 03.8	269 24.9	6.2	S21 55.0	1.5	58.6
01	192 46.4	02.8	283 50.1	6.3	21 53.5	1.6	58.6
02	207 46.6	01.8	298 15.4	6.3	21 51.9	1.7	58.6
03	222 46.8	2 00.8	312 40.7	6.4	21 50.2	1.9	58.5
04	237 46.9	1 59.8	327 06.1	6.4	21 48.3	2.0	58.5
05	252 47.1	58.8	341 31.5	6.5	21 46.3	2.2	58.5
T 06	267 47.3	S 1 57.9	355 57.0	6.5	S21 44.1	2.3	58.5
H 07	282 47.5	56.9	10 22.5	6.6	21 41.8	2.4	58.4
U 08	297 47.7	55.9	24 48.1	6.6	21 39.4	2.6	58.4
R 09	312 47.8	.. 54.9	39 13.7	6.7	21 36.8	2.7	58.4
S 10	327 48.0	53.9	53 39.4	6.7	21 34.1	2.8	58.4
D 11	342 48.2	52.9	68 05.1	6.8	21 31.3	2.9	58.3
A 12	357 48.4	S 1 51.9	82 30.9	6.9	S21 28.4	3.1	58.3
Y 13	12 48.5	50.9	96 56.8	6.9	21 25.3	3.2	58.3
14	27 48.7	50.0	111 22.7	7.0	21 22.1	3.4	58.2
15	42 48.9	.. 49.0	125 48.7	7.0	21 18.7	3.4	58.2
16	57 49.1	48.0	140 14.7	7.1	21 15.3	3.6	58.2
17	72 49.2	47.0	154 40.8	7.2	21 11.7	3.7	58.2
18	87 49.4	S 1 46.0	169 07.0	7.2	S21 08.0	3.9	58.1
19	102 49.6	45.0	183 33.2	7.3	21 04.1	4.0	58.1
20	117 49.8	44.0	197 59.5	7.3	21 00.1	4.0	58.1
21	132 50.0	.. 43.0	212 25.8	7.4	20 56.1	4.3	58.1
22	147 50.1	42.1	226 52.2	7.5	20 51.8	4.3	58.0
23	162 50.3	41.1	241 18.7	7.6	S20 47.5	4.5	58.0
	SD 16.1	d 1.0	SD 16.2		16.1		15.9

Twilight, Sunrise and Moonrise

Lat.	Naut.	Civil	Sunrise	Moonrise 13	14	15	16
N 72	03 57	05 20	06 27	■	■	■	■
N 70	04 11	05 25	06 25	■	■	05 51	05 37
68	04 22	05 28	06 24	02 53	■	04 32	04 56
66	04 30	05 31	06 22	02 05	03 36	04 32	04 56
64	04 37	05 34	06 21	01 34	02 57	03 54	04 27
62	04 44	05 36	06 20	01 11	02 30	03 28	04 05
60	04 49	05 37	06 19	00 53	02 09	03 07	03 47
N 58	04 53	05 39	06 18	00 38	01 52	02 50	03 33
56	04 57	05 40	06 17	00 25	01 37	02 36	03 20
54	05 00	05 41	06 16	00 13	01 25	02 23	03 09
52	05 03	05 42	06 16	00 03	01 14	02 12	02 59
50	05 05	05 43	06 15	25 04	01 04	02 02	02 50
45	05 11	05 45	06 14	24 26	00 43	01 42	02 31
N 40	05 14	05 46	06 13	24 26	00 26	01 25	02 16
35	05 17	05 46	06 12	24 12	00 12	01 11	02 03
30	05 19	05 47	06 11	24 00	00 00	00 59	01 52
20	05 21	05 47	06 09	23 39	24 38	00 38	01 32
N 10	05 21	05 46	06 07	23 04	24 20	00 20	01 16
0	05 21	05 45	06 06	23 04	24 03	00 03	01 00
S 10	05 19	05 43	06 04	22 48	23 46	24 44	00 44
20	05 14	05 40	06 02	22 30	23 28	24 27	00 27
30	05 08	05 36	06 00	22 09	23 07	24 08	00 08
35	05 03	05 33	05 58	21 57	22 55	23 56	24 58
40	04 58	05 30	05 57	21 43	22 41	23 43	24 47
45	04 51	05 25	05 55	21 27	22 25	23 28	24 34
S 50	04 41	05 20	05 53	21 08	22 04	23 09	24 18
52	04 37	05 18	05 52	20 58	21 54	23 00	24 10
54	04 32	05 15	05 50	20 47	21 43	22 49	24 01
56	04 26	05 12	05 49	20 35	21 31	22 38	23 41
58	04 20	05 08	05 48	20 21	21 17	22 25	23 41
S 60	04 12	05 04	05 46	20 05	21 00	22 09	23 28

Sunset, Twilight and Moonset

Lat.	Sunset	Civil	Naut.	Moonset 13	14	15	16
N 72	17 53	19 01	20 25	■	■	■	■
N 70	17 55	18 56	20 11	■	■	■	■
68	17 56	18 52	19 59	05 38	■	06 46	08 57
66	17 58	18 49	19 50	06 27	06 59	08 05	09 38
64	17 59	18 46	19 43	06 58	07 38	08 43	10 06
62	18 00	18 44	19 37	07 21	08 05	09 09	10 28
60	18 01	18 42	19 31	07 40	08 27	09 29	10 45
N 58	18 01	18 41	19 27	07 55	08 44	09 46	10 59
56	18 02	18 39	19 23	08 09	08 59	10 01	11 12
54	18 03	18 38	19 19	08 20	09 11	10 13	11 23
52	18 03	18 37	19 16	08 30	09 22	10 24	11 32
50	18 04	18 36	19 14	08 40	09 32	10 33	11 41
45	18 05	18 34	19 09	08 59	09 53	10 54	11 59
N 40	18 06	18 33	19 05	09 15	10 10	11 10	12 13
35	18 07	18 32	19 02	09 28	10 24	11 24	12 26
30	18 08	18 32	18 59	09 40	10 36	11 36	12 37
20	18 09	18 31	18 57	10 00	10 57	11 56	12 55
N 10	18 11	18 32	18 56	10 17	11 16	12 14	13 11
0	18 12	18 33	18 57	10 33	11 33	12 30	13 26
S 10	18 14	18 35	18 59	10 50	11 50	12 47	13 41
20	18 16	18 38	19 03	11 07	12 08	13 05	13 57
30	18 18	18 42	19 10	11 27	12 29	13 25	14 15
35	18 19	18 44	19 14	11 39	12 41	13 37	14 25
40	18 21	18 48	19 20	11 52	12 55	13 50	14 37
45	18 22	18 52	19 26	12 08	13 12	14 06	14 51
S 50	18 24	18 57	19 35	12 28	13 32	14 25	15 08
52	18 25	18 59	19 40	12 37	13 42	14 35	15 16
54	18 27	19 02	19 45	12 48	13 53	14 45	15 25
56	18 28	19 05	19 50	12 59	14 05	14 57	15 35
58	18 29	19 09	19 56	13 13	14 20	15 10	15 47
S 60	18 31	19 13	20 04	13 31	14 37	15 26	16 00

SUN and MOON

Day	Eqn. of Time 00h	Eqn. of Time 12h	Mer. Pass.	Mer. Pass. Upper	Mer. Pass. Lower	Age	Phase
	m s	m s	h m	h m	h m	d	%
13	09 29	09 20	12 09	04 19	16 49	21	67
14	09 12	09 04	12 09	05 19	17 48	22	56
15	08 55	08 47	12 09	06 17	18 45	23	45

UT	ARIES GHA	VENUS −4.4 GHA	VENUS Dec	MARS −1.0 GHA	MARS Dec	JUPITER −2.1 GHA	JUPITER Dec	SATURN +0.4 GHA	SATURN Dec	Name	SHA	Dec
16 00	173 59.3	135 43.3	N17 22.7	11 51.6	N11 48.4	136 10.8	N13 55.1	326 40.2	S 8 20.3	Acamar	315 19.2	S40 15.6
01	189 01.7	150 43.2	23.7	26 54.9	48.7	151 12.8	55.3	341 42.8	20.3	Achernar	335 27.9	S57 10.6
02	204 04.2	165 43.1	24.8	41 58.2	49.0	166 14.8	55.4	356 45.4	20.2	Acrux	173 09.6	S63 10.1
03	219 06.7	180 43.0	.. 25.8	57 01.6	.. 49.2	181 16.7	.. 55.6	11 48.0	.. 20.1	Adhara	255 13.1	S28 59.7
04	234 09.1	195 42.9	26.8	72 04.9	49.5	196 18.7	55.8	26 50.6	20.1	Aldebaran	290 50.5	N16 31.9
05	249 11.6	210 42.8	27.8	87 08.2	49.7	211 20.7	55.9	41 53.2	20.0			
F 06	264 14.1	225 42.7	N17 28.8	102 11.5	N11 50.0	226 22.6	N13 56.1	56 55.8	S 8 20.0	Alioth	166 20.9	N55 53.4
R 07	279 16.5	240 42.6	29.8	117 14.8	50.2	241 24.6	56.3	71 58.4	19.9	Alkaid	152 59.1	N49 14.9
I 08	294 19.0	255 42.5	30.8	132 18.1	50.5	256 26.6	56.4	87 01.0	19.9	Al Na'ir	27 45.2	S46 54.0
D 09	309 21.5	270 42.4	.. 31.8	147 21.4	.. 50.8	271 28.5	.. 56.6	102 03.6	.. 19.8	Alnilam	275 47.3	S 1 11.9
A 10	324 23.9	285 42.3	32.8	162 24.7	51.0	286 30.5	56.8	117 06.2	19.7	Alphard	217 56.7	S 8 43.0
Y 11	339 26.4	300 42.2	33.9	177 28.0	51.3	301 32.5	56.9	132 08.8	19.7			
12	354 28.9	315 42.1	N17 34.9	192 31.3	N11 51.5	316 34.5	N13 57.1	147 11.4	S 8 19.6	Alphecca	126 11.5	N26 40.2
13	9 31.3	330 42.0	35.9	207 34.6	51.8	331 36.4	57.3	162 14.0	19.6	Alpheratz	357 44.8	N29 09.5
14	24 33.8	345 41.9	36.9	222 37.9	52.0	346 38.4	57.4	177 16.6	19.5	Altair	62 09.2	N 8 54.0
15	39 36.2	0 41.8	.. 37.9	237 41.3	.. 52.3	1 40.4	.. 57.6	192 19.2	.. 19.5	Ankaa	353 16.9	S42 14.4
16	54 38.7	15 41.7	38.9	252 44.6	52.5	16 42.3	57.8	207 21.8	19.4	Antares	112 27.2	S26 27.5
17	69 41.2	30 41.6	39.9	267 47.9	52.8	31 44.3	57.9	222 24.4	19.3			
18	84 43.6	45 41.6	N17 40.9	282 51.2	N11 53.0	46 46.3	N13 58.1	237 27.0	S 8 19.3	Arcturus	145 56.2	N19 06.9
19	99 46.1	60 41.5	41.9	297 54.5	53.3	61 48.2	58.3	252 29.6	19.2	Atria	107 29.7	S69 02.7
20	114 48.6	75 41.4	42.9	312 57.8	53.5	76 50.2	58.4	267 32.2	19.2	Avior	234 18.0	S59 33.3
21	129 51.0	90 41.3	.. 43.9	328 01.1	.. 53.8	91 52.2	.. 58.6	282 34.8	.. 19.1	Bellatrix	278 33.0	N 6 21.5
22	144 53.5	105 41.2	44.9	343 04.4	54.0	106 54.1	58.8	297 37.4	19.0	Betelgeuse	271 02.2	N 7 24.4
23	159 56.0	120 41.1	45.9	358 07.7	54.3	121 56.1	58.9	312 40.0	19.0			
17 00	174 58.4	135 41.0	N17 46.9	13 11.0	N11 54.5	136 58.1	N13 59.1	327 42.6	S 8 18.9	Canopus	263 56.4	S52 42.5
01	190 00.9	150 40.9	47.9	28 14.3	54.8	152 00.0	59.3	342 45.2	18.9	Capella	280 35.8	N46 00.7
02	205 03.3	165 40.8	48.9	43 17.5	55.0	167 02.0	59.4	357 47.8	18.8	Deneb	49 32.4	N45 19.3
03	220 05.8	180 40.7	.. 49.9	58 20.8	.. 55.3	182 04.0	.. 59.6	12 50.4	.. 18.7	Denebola	182 34.2	N14 30.0
04	235 08.3	195 40.6	50.9	73 24.1	55.5	197 05.9	59.8	27 53.0	18.7	Diphda	348 57.1	S17 55.2
05	250 10.7	210 40.5	51.9	88 27.4	55.8	212 07.9	13 59.9	42 55.6	18.6			
S 06	265 13.2	225 40.4	N17 52.9	103 30.7	N11 56.0	227 09.9	N14 00.1	57 58.2	S 8 18.6	Dubhe	193 52.0	N61 41.0
A 07	280 15.7	240 40.3	53.9	118 34.0	56.3	242 11.8	00.3	73 00.8	18.5	Elnath	278 13.7	N28 37.0
T 08	295 18.1	255 40.3	54.9	133 37.3	56.5	257 13.8	00.4	88 03.4	18.5	Eltanin	90 46.6	N51 29.0
U 09	310 20.6	270 40.2	.. 55.9	148 40.6	.. 56.8	272 15.8	.. 00.6	103 06.0	.. 18.4	Enif	33 48.2	N 9 55.8
R 10	325 23.1	285 40.1	56.9	163 43.9	57.0	287 17.7	00.8	118 08.6	18.3	Fomalhaut	15 25.3	S29 33.4
D 11	340 25.5	300 40.0	57.9	178 47.2	57.2	302 19.7	00.9	133 11.2	18.3			
A 12	355 28.0	315 39.9	N17 58.9	193 50.5	N11 57.5	317 21.6	N14 01.1	148 13.8	S 8 18.2	Gacrux	172 01.3	S57 11.0
Y 13	10 30.5	330 39.8	17 59.9	208 53.8	57.7	332 23.6	01.3	163 16.4	18.2	Gienah	175 52.9	S17 36.8
14	25 32.9	345 39.7	18 00.9	223 57.0	58.0	347 25.6	01.4	178 19.0	18.1	Hadar	148 48.6	S60 25.9
15	40 35.4	0 39.6	.. 01.8	239 00.3	.. 58.2	2 27.5	.. 01.6	193 21.6	.. 18.0	Hamal	328 02.0	N23 31.2
16	55 37.8	15 39.5	02.8	254 03.6	58.4	17 29.5	01.8	208 24.2	18.0	Kaus Aust.	83 45.0	S34 22.5
17	70 40.3	30 39.4	03.8	269 06.9	58.7	32 31.5	01.9	223 26.8	17.9			
18	85 42.8	45 39.3	N18 04.8	284 10.2	N11 58.9	47 33.4	N14 02.1	238 29.4	S 8 17.9	Kochab	137 19.1	N74 06.0
19	100 45.2	60 39.3	05.8	299 13.5	59.2	62 35.4	02.3	253 32.0	17.8	Markab	13 39.5	N15 16.2
20	115 47.7	75 39.2	06.8	314 16.7	59.4	77 37.4	02.4	268 34.6	17.7	Menkar	314 16.2	N 4 08.1
21	130 50.2	90 39.1	.. 07.8	329 20.0	.. 59.6	92 39.3	.. 02.6	283 37.2	.. 17.7	Menkent	148 08.3	S36 25.8
22	145 52.6	105 39.0	08.8	344 23.3	11 59.9	107 41.3	02.8	298 39.8	17.6	Miaplacidus	221 39.2	S69 46.4
23	160 55.1	120 38.9	09.7	359 26.6	12 00.1	122 43.3	02.9	313 42.4	17.6			
18 00	175 57.6	135 38.8	N18 10.7	14 29.9	N12 00.4	137 45.2	N14 03.1	328 45.0	S 8 17.5	Mirfak	308 41.9	N49 54.4
01	191 00.0	150 38.7	11.7	29 33.1	00.6	152 47.2	03.3	343 47.6	17.4	Nunki	75 59.5	S26 16.8
02	206 02.5	165 38.6	12.7	44 36.4	00.8	167 49.1	03.4	358 50.2	17.4	Peacock	53 20.9	S56 41.5
03	221 05.0	180 38.5	.. 13.7	59 39.7	.. 01.1	182 51.1	.. 03.6	13 52.9	.. 17.3	Pollux	243 28.6	N27 59.7
04	236 07.4	195 38.4	14.7	74 43.0	01.3	197 53.1	03.8	28 55.5	17.3	Procyon	245 00.5	N 5 11.4
05	251 09.9	210 38.4	15.6	89 46.2	01.5	212 55.0	03.9	43 58.1	17.2			
S 06	266 12.3	225 38.3	N18 16.6	104 49.5	N12 01.8	227 57.0	N14 04.1	59 00.7	S 8 17.1	Rasalhague	96 07.2	N12 32.9
U 07	281 14.8	240 38.2	17.6	119 52.8	02.0	242 59.0	04.3	74 03.3	17.1	Regulus	207 44.1	N11 54.2
N 08	296 17.3	255 38.1	18.6	134 56.1	02.2	258 00.9	04.4	89 05.9	17.0	Rigel	281 12.9	S 8 11.5
D 09	311 19.7	270 38.0	.. 19.6	149 59.3	.. 02.5	273 02.9	.. 04.6	104 08.5	.. 17.0	Rigil Kent.	139 52.4	S60 53.0
A 10	326 22.2	285 37.9	20.5	165 02.6	02.7	288 04.8	04.8	119 11.1	16.9	Sabik	102 13.5	S15 44.4
Y 11	341 24.7	300 37.8	21.5	180 05.9	02.9	303 06.8	04.9	134 13.7	16.8			
12	356 27.1	315 37.7	N18 22.5	195 09.1	N12 03.2	318 08.8	N14 05.1	149 16.3	S 8 16.8	Schedar	349 42.1	N56 36.3
13	11 29.6	330 37.6	23.5	210 12.4	03.4	333 10.7	05.3	164 18.9	16.7	Shaula	96 23.1	S37 06.6
14	26 32.1	345 37.6	24.4	225 15.7	03.6	348 12.7	05.5	179 21.5	16.7	Sirius	258 34.4	S16 44.3
15	41 34.5	0 37.5	.. 25.4	240 18.9	.. 03.9	3 14.6	.. 05.6	194 24.1	.. 16.6	Spica	158 31.9	S11 13.7
16	56 37.0	15 37.4	26.4	255 22.2	04.1	18 16.6	05.8	209 26.7	16.5	Suhail	222 52.8	S43 29.3
17	71 39.4	30 37.3	27.3	270 25.5	04.3	33 18.6	06.0	224 29.3	16.5			
18	86 41.9	45 37.2	N18 28.3	285 28.7	N12 04.6	48 20.5	N14 06.1	239 31.9	S 8 16.4	Vega	80 39.6	N38 47.5
19	101 44.4	60 37.1	29.3	300 32.0	04.8	63 22.5	06.3	254 34.5	16.4	Zuben'ubi	137 06.1	S16 05.6
20	116 46.8	75 37.0	30.3	315 35.3	05.0	78 24.4	06.5	269 37.1	16.3		SHA	Mer.Pass.
21	131 49.3	90 36.9	.. 31.2	330 38.5	.. 05.2	93 26.4	.. 06.6	284 39.8	.. 16.2	Venus	320 42.6	14 57
22	146 51.8	105 36.8	32.2	345 41.8	05.5	108 28.4	06.8	299 42.4	16.2	Mars	198 12.5	23 02
23	161 54.2	120 36.8	33.2	0 45.0	05.7	123 30.3	07.0	314 45.0	16.1	Jupiter	321 59.6	14 50
Mer. Pass. 12 18.1		v −0.1	d 1.0	v 3.3	d 0.2	v 2.0	d 0.2	v 2.6	d 0.1	Saturn	152 44.1	2 09

SUN and MOON

UT	SUN GHA	SUN Dec	MOON GHA	v	MOON Dec	d	HP
16 00	177 50.5	S 1 40.1	255 45.3	7.6	S20 43.0	4.5	58.0
01	192 50.7	39.1	270 11.9	7.6	20 38.5	4.7	58.0
02	207 50.8	38.1	284 38.5	7.8	20 33.8	4.9	57.9
03	222 51.0 ..	37.1	299 05.3	7.8	20 28.9	4.9	57.9
04	237 51.2	36.1	313 32.1	7.9	20 24.0	5.0	57.9
05	252 51.4	35.1	327 59.0	8.0	20 19.0	5.2	57.9
06	267 51.6	S 1 34.1	342 26.0	8.0	S20 13.8	5.3	57.8
F 07	282 51.7	33.2	356 53.0	8.1	20 08.5	5.4	57.8
R 08	297 51.9	32.2	11 20.1	8.1	20 03.1	5.5	57.8
I 09	312 52.1 ..	31.2	25 47.2	8.3	19 57.6	5.6	57.8
D 10	327 52.3	30.2	40 14.5	8.3	19 52.0	5.7	57.7
A 11	342 52.4	29.2	54 41.8	8.4	19 46.3	5.8	57.7
Y 12	357 52.6	S 1 28.2	69 09.2	8.4	S19 40.5	6.0	57.7
13	12 52.8	27.2	83 36.6	8.6	19 34.5	6.0	57.7
14	27 53.0	26.2	98 04.2	8.6	19 28.5	6.2	57.6
15	42 53.2 ..	25.3	112 31.8	8.6	19 22.3	6.3	57.6
16	57 53.3	24.3	126 59.4	8.8	19 16.0	6.3	57.6
17	72 53.5	23.3	141 27.2	8.8	19 09.7	6.5	57.5
18	87 53.7	S 1 22.3	155 55.0	8.9	S19 03.2	6.6	57.5
19	102 53.9	21.3	170 22.9	9.0	18 56.6	6.6	57.5
20	117 54.1	20.3	184 50.9	9.0	18 50.0	6.8	57.5
21	132 54.2 ..	19.3	199 18.9	9.1	18 43.2	6.9	57.4
22	147 54.4	18.3	213 47.0	9.2	18 36.3	6.9	57.4
23	162 54.6	17.3	228 15.2	9.3	18 29.4	7.1	57.4
17 00	177 54.8	S 1 16.4	242 43.5	9.3	S18 22.3	7.2	57.4
01	192 55.0	15.4	257 11.8	9.5	18 15.1	7.2	57.3
02	207 55.1	14.4	271 40.3	9.5	18 07.9	7.4	57.3
03	222 55.3 ..	13.4	286 08.8	9.5	18 00.5	7.4	57.3
04	237 55.5	12.4	300 37.3	9.7	17 53.1	7.5	57.3
05	252 55.7	11.4	315 06.0	9.7	17 45.6	7.6	57.2
06	267 55.9	S 1 10.4	329 34.7	9.8	S17 38.0	7.7	57.2
S 07	282 56.0	09.4	344 03.5	9.8	17 30.3	7.8	57.2
A 08	297 56.2	08.4	358 32.3	10.0	17 22.5	7.9	57.2
T 09	312 56.4 ..	07.5	13 01.3	10.0	17 14.6	8.0	57.1
U 10	327 56.6	06.5	27 30.3	10.1	17 06.6	8.1	57.1
R 11	342 56.8	05.5	41 59.4	10.1	16 58.5	8.1	57.1
D 12	357 56.9	S 1 04.5	56 28.5	10.3	S16 50.4	8.2	57.1
A 13	12 57.1	03.5	70 57.8	10.3	16 42.2	8.3	57.0
Y 14	27 57.3	02.5	85 27.1	10.4	16 33.9	8.4	57.0
15	42 57.5 ..	01.5	99 56.5	10.4	16 25.5	8.5	57.0
16	57 57.7	1 00.5	114 25.9	10.6	16 17.0	8.5	57.0
17	72 57.8	0 59.5	128 55.5	10.6	16 08.5	8.6	57.0
18	87 58.0	S 0 58.6	143 25.1	10.6	S15 59.9	8.7	56.9
19	102 58.2	57.6	157 54.7	10.8	15 51.2	8.8	56.9
20	117 58.4	56.6	172 24.5	10.8	15 42.4	8.8	56.9
21	132 58.6 ..	55.6	186 54.3	10.9	15 33.6	9.0	56.9
22	147 58.7	54.6	201 24.2	10.9	15 24.6	8.9	56.8
23	162 58.9	53.6	215 54.1	11.1	15 15.7	9.1	56.8
18 00	177 59.1	S 0 52.6	230 24.2	11.1	S15 06.6	9.1	56.8
01	192 59.3	51.6	244 54.3	11.1	14 57.5	9.2	56.8
02	207 59.5	50.6	259 24.4	11.3	14 48.3	9.3	56.7
03	222 59.6 ..	49.7	273 54.7	11.3	14 39.0	9.3	56.7
04	237 59.8	48.7	288 25.0	11.4	14 29.7	9.4	56.7
05	253 00.0	47.7	302 55.4	11.4	14 20.3	9.5	56.7
06	268 00.2	S 0 46.7	317 25.8	11.5	S14 10.8	9.5	56.6
S 07	283 00.4	45.7	331 56.3	11.6	14 01.3	9.6	56.6
U 08	298 00.6	44.7	346 26.9	11.7	13 51.7	9.7	56.6
N 09	313 00.7 ..	43.7	0 57.6	11.7	13 42.0	9.7	56.6
D 10	328 00.9	42.7	15 28.3	11.8	13 32.3	9.7	56.6
A 11	343 01.1	41.7	29 59.1	11.8	13 22.6	9.9	56.5
Y 12	358 01.3	S 0 40.8	44 29.9	11.9	S13 12.7	9.9	56.5
13	13 01.5	39.8	59 00.8	12.0	13 02.8	9.9	56.5
14	28 01.6	38.8	73 31.8	12.0	12 52.9	10.0	56.5
15	43 01.8 ..	37.8	88 02.8	12.1	12 42.9	10.0	56.4
16	58 02.0	36.8	102 33.9	12.2	12 32.9	10.2	56.4
17	73 02.2	35.8	117 05.1	12.2	12 22.7	10.1	56.4
18	88 02.4	S 0 34.8	131 36.3	12.3	S12 12.6	10.2	56.4
19	103 02.6	33.8	146 07.6	12.4	12 02.4	10.3	56.4
20	118 02.7	32.8	160 39.0	12.4	11 52.1	10.3	56.3
21	133 02.9 ..	31.9	175 10.4	12.5	11 41.8	10.3	56.3
22	148 03.1	30.9	189 41.9	12.5	11 31.5	10.4	56.3
23	163 03.3	29.9	204 13.4	12.6	S11 21.1	10.5	56.3
SD	16.1	d 1.0	SD 15.7		15.6		15.4

Twilight, Sunrise and Moonrise

Lat.	Naut.	Civil	Sunrise	Moonrise 16	17	18	19
N 72	03 39	05 05	06 12	■■■	07 14	06 17	05 51
N 70	03 55	05 11	06 11	■■	06 08	05 48	05 35
68	04 07	05 16	06 11	05 37	05 32	05 27	05 23
66	04 18	05 20	06 11	04 56	05 06	05 10	05 12
64	04 26	05 23	06 10	04 27	04 45	04 56	05 03
62	04 33	05 26	06 10	04 05	04 29	04 44	04 55
60	04 39	05 28	06 10	03 47	04 15	04 34	04 49
N 58	04 44	05 30	06 09	03 33	04 03	04 25	04 43
56	04 49	05 32	06 09	03 20	03 53	04 18	04 37
54	04 52	05 34	06 09	03 09	03 44	04 11	04 33
52	04 56	05 35	06 09	02 59	03 36	04 05	04 28
50	04 59	05 37	06 09	02 50	03 28	03 59	04 25
45	05 05	05 39	06 08	02 31	03 12	03 47	04 16
N 40	05 09	05 41	06 08	02 16	02 59	03 37	04 09
35	05 13	05 42	06 07	02 03	02 48	03 28	04 03
30	05 16	05 43	06 07	01 52	02 39	03 20	03 58
20	05 19	05 44	06 06	01 32	02 22	03 07	03 48
N 10	05 20	05 45	06 06	01 16	02 07	02 55	03 40
0	05 20	05 44	06 05	01 00	01 54	02 44	03 32
S 10	05 19	05 43	06 04	00 44	01 40	02 33	03 24
20	05 15	05 41	06 03	00 27	01 25	02 22	03 16
30	05 10	05 38	06 02	00 08	01 08	02 08	03 07
35	05 06	05 36	06 01	24 58	00 58	02 00	03 01
40	05 01	05 33	06 00	24 47	00 47	01 51	02 55
45	04 55	05 29	05 59	24 34	00 34	01 41	02 47
S 50	04 47	05 25	05 57	24 18	00 18	01 28	02 39
52	04 43	05 23	05 57	24 10	00 10	01 22	02 35
54	04 38	05 21	05 56	24 01	00 01	01 16	02 30
56	04 33	05 18	05 55	23 52	25 08	01 08	02 25
58	04 27	05 15	05 54	23 41	25 00	01 00	02 19
S 60	04 21	05 12	05 53	23 28	24 51	00 51	02 13

Sunset, Twilight and Moonset

Lat.	Sunset	Civil	Naut.	Moonset 16	17	18	19
N 72	18 07	19 15	20 42	■■■	09 13	11 54	13 57
N 70	18 07	19 08	20 25	■■	10 18	12 21	14 11
68	18 07	19 03	20 12	08 57	10 53	12 41	14 23
66	18 08	18 59	20 01	09 38	11 18	12 57	14 32
64	18 08	18 55	19 53	10 06	11 38	13 10	14 39
62	18 08	18 52	19 45	10 28	11 54	13 21	14 46
60	18 08	18 50	19 39	10 45	12 07	13 30	14 52
N 58	18 08	18 47	19 34	10 59	12 18	13 38	14 57
56	18 08	18 45	19 29	11 12	12 28	13 45	15 01
54	18 08	18 44	19 25	11 23	12 36	13 51	15 05
52	18 09	18 42	19 22	11 32	12 44	13 57	15 09
50	18 09	18 41	19 19	11 41	12 51	14 02	15 12
45	18 09	18 38	19 13	11 59	13 06	14 13	15 19
N 40	18 09	18 36	19 08	12 13	13 18	14 22	15 25
35	18 09	18 35	19 04	12 26	13 28	14 30	15 30
30	18 10	18 34	19 01	12 37	13 37	14 36	15 34
20	18 10	18 32	18 58	12 55	13 52	14 48	15 42
N 10	18 11	18 32	18 56	13 11	14 06	14 58	15 48
0	18 11	18 32	18 57	13 26	14 18	15 08	15 54
S 10	18 12	18 33	18 58	13 41	14 31	15 17	16 00
20	18 13	18 35	19 01	13 57	14 44	15 27	16 07
30	18 14	18 38	19 06	14 15	14 59	15 38	16 14
35	18 15	18 40	19 10	14 25	15 07	15 45	16 18
40	18 16	18 43	19 14	14 37	15 17	15 52	16 23
45	18 17	18 46	19 21	14 51	15 29	16 00	16 28
S 50	18 18	18 50	19 28	15 08	15 43	16 11	16 35
52	18 19	18 52	19 32	15 16	15 49	16 15	16 38
54	18 19	18 54	19 37	15 25	15 56	16 21	16 41
56	18 20	18 57	19 42	15 35	16 04	16 26	16 44
58	18 21	19 00	19 47	15 47	16 13	16 33	16 48
S 60	18 22	19 03	19 54	16 00	16 23	16 40	16 53

SUN and MOON

Day	Eqn. of Time 00h	12h	Mer. Pass.	Mer. Pass. Upper	Lower	Age	Phase
16	08 38	08 30	12 08	07 13	19 40	24	35
17	08 21	08 13	12 08	08 06	20 31	25	25
18	08 04	07 55	12 08	08 56	21 20	26	16

UT	ARIES GHA	VENUS −4.4 GHA	Dec	MARS −1.0 GHA	Dec	JUPITER −2.1 GHA	Dec	SATURN +0.3 GHA	Dec	STARS Name	SHA	Dec
19 00	176 56.7	135 36.7	N18 34.1	15 48.3	N12 05.9	138 32.3	N14 07.1	329 47.6	S 8 16.1	Acamar	315 19.3	S40 15.6
01	191 59.2	150 36.6	35.1	30 51.6	06.1	153 34.2	07.3	344 50.2	16.0	Achernar	335 27.9	S57 10.6
02	207 01.6	165 36.5	36.1	45 54.8	06.4	168 36.2	07.5	359 52.8	15.9	Acrux	173 09.6	S63 10.1
03	222 04.1	180 36.4	.. 37.0	60 58.1	.. 06.6	183 38.2	.. 07.6	14 55.4	.. 15.9	Adhara	255 13.1	S28 59.7
04	237 06.6	195 36.3	38.0	76 01.3	06.8	198 40.1	07.8	29 58.0	15.8	Aldebaran	290 50.5	N16 31.9
05	252 09.0	210 36.2	39.0	91 04.6	07.0	213 42.1	08.0	45 00.6	15.8			
M 06	267 11.5	225 36.2	N18 39.9	106 07.8	N12 07.3	228 44.0	N14 08.1	60 03.2	S 8 15.7	Alioth	166 20.9	N55 53.4
O 07	282 13.9	240 36.1	40.9	121 11.1	07.5	243 46.0	08.3	75 05.8	15.6	Alkaid	152 59.1	N49 14.9
N 08	297 16.4	255 36.0	41.8	136 14.3	07.7	258 48.0	08.5	90 08.4	15.6	Al Na'ir	27 45.2	S46 54.0
D 09	312 18.9	270 35.9	.. 42.8	151 17.6	.. 07.9	273 49.9	.. 08.6	105 11.0	.. 15.5	Alnilam	275 47.3	S 1 11.9
A 10	327 21.3	285 35.8	43.8	166 20.8	08.1	288 51.9	08.8	120 13.6	15.5	Alphard	217 56.7	S 8 43.0
Y 11	342 23.8	300 35.7	44.7	181 24.1	08.4	303 53.8	09.0	135 16.3	15.4			
12	357 26.3	315 35.6	N18 45.7	196 27.3	N12 08.6	318 55.8	N14 09.1	150 18.9	S 8 15.3	Alphecca	126 11.5	N26 40.2
13	12 28.7	330 35.6	46.6	211 30.6	08.8	333 57.8	09.3	165 21.5	15.3	Alpheratz	357 44.8	N29 09.5
14	27 31.2	345 35.5	47.6	226 33.8	09.0	348 59.7	09.5	180 24.1	15.2	Altair	62 09.2	N 8 54.0
15	42 33.7	0 35.4	.. 48.5	241 37.1	.. 09.2	4 01.7	.. 09.6	195 26.7	.. 15.2	Ankaa	353 16.9	S42 14.4
16	57 36.1	15 35.3	49.5	256 40.3	09.5	19 03.6	09.8	210 29.3	15.1	Antares	112 27.2	S26 27.5
17	72 38.6	30 35.2	50.5	271 43.6	09.7	34 05.6	10.0	225 31.9	15.0			
18	87 41.0	45 35.1	N18 51.4	286 46.8	N12 09.9	49 07.5	N14 10.2	240 34.5	S 8 15.0	Arcturus	145 56.2	N19 06.9
19	102 43.5	60 35.0	52.4	301 50.0	10.1	64 09.5	10.3	255 37.1	14.9	Atria	107 29.7	S69 02.7
20	117 46.0	75 35.0	53.3	316 53.3	10.3	79 11.5	10.5	270 39.7	14.8	Avior	234 18.0	S59 33.3
21	132 48.4	90 34.9	.. 54.3	331 56.5	.. 10.5	94 13.4	.. 10.7	285 42.3	.. 14.8	Bellatrix	278 33.0	N 6 21.5
22	147 50.9	105 34.8	55.2	346 59.8	10.7	109 15.4	10.8	300 45.0	14.7	Betelgeuse	271 02.2	N 7 24.4
23	162 53.4	120 34.7	56.2	2 03.0	11.0	124 17.3	11.0	315 47.6	14.7			
20 00	177 55.8	135 34.6	N18 57.1	17 06.2	N12 11.2	139 19.3	N14 11.2	330 50.2	S 8 14.6	Canopus	263 56.5	S52 42.5
01	192 58.3	150 34.5	58.1	32 09.5	11.4	154 21.2	11.3	345 52.8	14.5	Capella	280 35.8	N46 00.7
02	208 00.8	165 34.5	18 59.0	47 12.7	11.6	169 23.2	11.5	0 55.4	14.5	Deneb	49 32.4	N45 19.3
03	223 03.2	180 34.4	19 00.0	62 15.9	.. 11.8	184 25.2	.. 11.7	15 58.0	.. 14.4	Denebola	182 34.2	N14 30.0
04	238 05.7	195 34.3	00.9	77 19.2	12.0	199 27.1	11.8	31 00.6	14.4	Diphda	348 57.1	S17 55.2
05	253 08.2	210 34.2	01.9	92 22.4	12.2	214 29.1	12.0	46 03.2	14.3			
T 06	268 10.6	225 34.1	N19 02.8	107 25.6	N12 12.4	229 31.0	N14 12.2	61 05.8	S 8 14.2	Dubhe	193 52.1	N61 41.0
U 07	283 13.1	240 34.0	03.8	122 28.9	12.7	244 33.0	12.3	76 08.4	14.2	Elnath	278 13.8	N28 37.0
E 08	298 15.5	255 34.0	04.7	137 32.1	12.9	259 34.9	12.5	91 11.1	14.1	Eltanin	90 46.5	N51 29.0
S 09	313 18.0	270 33.9	.. 05.7	152 35.3	.. 13.1	274 36.9	.. 12.7	106 13.7	.. 14.1	Enif	33 48.2	N 9 55.8
D 10	328 20.5	285 33.8	06.6	167 38.6	13.3	289 38.8	12.8	121 16.3	14.0	Fomalhaut	15 25.3	S29 33.4
A 11	343 22.9	300 33.7	07.5	182 41.8	13.5	304 40.8	13.0	136 18.9	13.9			
Y 12	358 25.4	315 33.6	N19 08.5	197 45.0	N12 13.7	319 42.8	N14 13.2	151 21.5	S 8 13.9	Gacrux	172 01.3	S57 11.0
13	13 27.9	330 33.6	09.4	212 48.2	13.9	334 44.7	13.3	166 24.1	13.8	Gienah	175 52.9	S17 36.8
14	28 30.3	345 33.5	10.4	227 51.5	14.1	349 46.7	13.5	181 26.7	13.7	Hadar	148 48.6	S60 25.9
15	43 32.8	0 33.4	.. 11.3	242 54.7	.. 14.3	4 48.6	.. 13.7	196 29.3	.. 13.7	Hamal	328 02.0	N23 31.2
16	58 35.3	15 33.3	12.2	257 57.9	14.5	19 50.6	13.9	211 31.9	13.6	Kaus Aust.	83 45.0	S34 22.5
17	73 37.7	30 33.2	13.2	273 01.1	14.7	34 52.5	14.0	226 34.5	13.6			
18	88 40.2	45 33.2	N19 14.1	288 04.3	N12 14.9	49 54.5	N14 14.2	241 37.2	S 8 13.5	Kochab	137 19.1	N74 06.0
19	103 42.7	60 33.1	15.1	303 07.6	15.1	64 56.4	14.4	256 39.8	13.4	Markab	13 39.5	N15 16.2
20	118 45.1	75 33.0	16.0	318 10.8	15.3	79 58.4	14.5	271 42.4	13.4	Menkar	314 16.2	N 4 08.1
21	133 47.6	90 32.9	.. 16.9	333 14.0	.. 15.5	95 00.3	.. 14.7	286 45.0	.. 13.3	Menkent	148 08.3	S36 25.9
22	148 50.0	105 32.8	17.9	348 17.2	15.7	110 02.3	14.9	301 47.6	13.2	Miaplacidus	221 39.2	S69 46.4
23	163 52.5	120 32.8	18.8	3 20.4	15.9	125 04.2	15.0	316 50.2	13.2			
21 00	178 55.0	135 32.7	N19 19.7	18 23.6	N12 16.1	140 06.2	N14 15.2	331 52.8	S 8 13.1	Mirfak	308 41.9	N49 54.4
01	193 57.4	150 32.6	20.7	33 26.9	16.3	155 08.2	15.4	346 55.4	13.1	Nunki	75 59.5	S26 16.8
02	208 59.9	165 32.5	21.6	48 30.1	16.5	170 10.1	15.5	1 58.1	13.0	Peacock	53 20.9	S56 41.5
03	224 02.4	180 32.4	.. 22.5	63 33.3	.. 16.7	185 12.1	.. 15.7	17 00.7	.. 12.9	Pollux	243 28.6	N27 59.7
04	239 04.8	195 32.4	23.5	78 36.5	16.9	200 14.0	15.9	32 03.3	12.9	Procyon	245 00.5	N 5 11.4
05	254 07.3	210 32.3	24.4	93 39.7	17.1	215 16.0	16.0	47 05.9	12.8			
W 06	269 09.8	225 32.2	N19 25.3	108 42.9	N12 17.3	230 17.9	N14 16.2	62 08.5	S 8 12.8	Rasalhague	96 07.2	N12 32.9
E 07	284 12.2	240 32.1	26.2	123 46.1	17.5	245 19.9	16.4	77 11.1	12.7	Regulus	207 44.1	N11 54.2
D 08	299 14.7	255 32.0	27.2	138 49.3	17.7	260 21.8	16.6	92 13.7	12.6	Rigel	281 12.9	S 8 11.5
N 09	314 17.1	270 32.0	.. 28.1	153 52.5	.. 17.9	275 23.8	.. 16.7	107 16.3	.. 12.6	Rigil Kent.	139 52.4	S60 53.0
E 10	329 19.6	285 31.9	29.0	168 55.7	18.1	290 25.7	16.9	122 19.0	12.5	Sabik	102 13.5	S15 44.4
S 11	344 22.1	300 31.8	29.9	183 58.9	18.3	305 27.7	17.1	137 21.6	12.4			
D 12	359 24.5	315 31.7	N19 30.9	199 02.1	N12 18.5	320 29.6	N14 17.2	152 24.2	S 8 12.4	Schedar	349 42.1	N56 36.3
A 13	14 27.0	330 31.7	31.8	214 05.3	18.7	335 31.6	17.4	167 26.8	12.3	Shaula	96 23.0	S37 06.6
Y 14	29 29.5	345 31.6	32.7	229 08.5	18.9	350 33.5	17.6	182 29.4	12.3	Sirius	258 34.4	S16 44.3
15	44 31.9	0 31.5	.. 33.6	244 11.7	.. 19.1	5 35.5	.. 17.7	197 32.0	.. 12.2	Spica	158 31.9	S11 13.7
16	59 34.4	15 31.4	34.6	259 14.9	19.3	20 37.4	17.9	212 34.6	12.1	Suhail	222 52.8	S43 29.3
17	74 36.9	30 31.3	35.5	274 18.1	19.5	35 39.4	18.1	227 37.2	12.1			
18	89 39.3	45 31.3	N19 36.4	289 21.3	N12 19.7	50 41.3	N14 18.2	242 39.9	S 8 12.0	Vega	80 39.6	N38 47.5
19	104 41.8	60 31.2	37.3	304 24.5	19.9	65 43.3	18.4	257 42.5	11.9	Zuben'ubi	137 06.1	S16 05.6
20	119 44.3	75 31.1	38.2	319 27.7	20.0	80 45.2	18.6	272 45.1	11.9		SHA	Mer.Pass.
21	134 46.7	90 31.0	.. 39.1	334 30.9	.. 20.2	95 47.2	.. 18.7	287 47.7	.. 11.8		° ′	h m
22	149 49.2	105 31.0	40.1	349 34.1	20.4	110 49.1	18.9	302 50.3	11.8	Venus	317 38.8	14 58
23	164 51.6	120 30.9	41.0	4 37.3	20.6	125 51.1	19.1	317 52.9	11.7	Mars	199 10.4	22 47
Mer.Pass.	h m 12 06.3	v −0.1	d 0.9	v 3.2	d 0.2	v 2.0	d 0.2	v 2.6	d 0.1	Jupiter	321 23.5	14 41
										Saturn	152 54.3	1 56

2012 MARCH 19, 20, 21 (MON., TUES., WED.) 63

SUN / MOON

UT (d h)	SUN GHA	SUN Dec	MOON GHA	v	MOON Dec	d	HP
19 00	178 03.5	S 0 28.9	218 45.0	12.6	S11 10.6	10.5	56.2
01	193 03.7	27.9	233 16.6	12.7	11 00.1	10.5	56.2
02	208 03.8	26.9	247 48.3	12.8	10 49.6	10.6	56.2
03	223 04.0	.. 25.9	262 20.1	12.8	10 39.0	10.6	56.2
04	238 04.2	24.9	276 51.9	12.9	10 28.4	10.7	56.2
05	253 04.4	24.0	291 23.8	12.9	10 17.7	10.7	56.1
06	268 04.6	S 0 23.0	305 55.7	13.0	S10 07.0	10.7	56.1
07	283 04.8	22.0	320 27.7	13.0	9 56.3	10.8	56.1
M 08	298 04.9	21.0	334 59.7	13.1	9 45.5	10.9	56.1
O 09	313 05.1	.. 20.0	349 31.8	13.1	9 34.6	10.8	56.1
N 10	328 05.3	19.0	4 03.9	13.2	9 23.8	10.9	56.0
D 11	343 05.5	18.0	18 36.1	13.3	9 12.9	10.9	56.0
A 12	358 05.7	S 0 17.0	33 08.4	13.2	S 9 02.0	11.0	56.0
Y 13	13 05.9	16.0	47 40.6	13.4	8 51.0	11.0	56.0
14	28 06.0	15.1	62 13.0	13.4	8 40.0	11.0	56.0
15	43 06.2	.. 14.1	76 45.4	13.4	8 29.0	11.1	55.9
16	58 06.4	13.1	91 17.8	13.5	8 17.9	11.1	55.9
17	73 06.6	12.1	105 50.3	13.5	8 06.8	11.1	55.9
18	88 06.8	S 0 11.1	120 22.8	13.6	S 7 55.7	11.1	55.9
19	103 07.0	10.1	134 55.4	13.6	7 44.6	11.2	55.9
20	118 07.1	09.1	149 28.0	13.7	7 33.4	11.2	55.8
21	133 07.3	.. 08.1	164 00.7	13.7	7 22.2	11.2	55.8
22	148 07.5	07.1	178 33.4	13.8	7 11.0	11.3	55.8
23	163 07.7	06.2	193 06.2	13.8	6 59.7	11.2	55.8
20 00	178 07.9	S 0 05.2	207 39.0	13.8	S 6 48.5	11.3	55.8
01	193 08.1	04.2	222 11.8	13.9	6 37.2	11.3	55.7
02	208 08.2	03.2	236 44.7	13.9	6 25.9	11.4	55.7
03	223 08.4	.. 02.2	251 17.6	13.9	6 14.5	11.3	55.7
04	238 08.6	01.2	265 50.5	14.0	6 03.2	11.4	55.7
05	253 08.8	S 00.2	280 23.5	14.1	5 51.8	11.4	55.7
06	268 09.0	N 0 00.8	294 56.6	14.1	S 5 40.4	11.4	55.6
07	283 09.2	01.7	309 29.7	14.1	5 29.0	11.4	55.6
T 08	298 09.4	02.7	324 02.8	14.1	5 17.6	11.5	55.6
U 09	313 09.5	.. 03.7	338 35.9	14.2	5 06.1	11.4	55.6
E 10	328 09.7	04.7	353 09.1	14.2	4 54.7	11.5	55.6
S 11	343 09.9	05.7	7 42.3	14.2	4 43.2	11.5	55.5
D 12	358 10.1	N 0 06.7	22 15.5	14.3	S 4 31.7	11.5	55.5
A 13	13 10.3	07.7	36 48.8	14.3	4 20.2	11.5	55.5
Y 14	28 10.5	08.7	51 22.1	14.4	4 08.7	11.5	55.5
15	43 10.6	.. 09.7	65 55.5	14.4	3 57.2	11.5	55.5
16	58 10.8	10.6	80 28.9	14.4	3 45.7	11.6	55.5
17	73 11.0	11.6	95 02.3	14.4	3 34.1	11.5	55.4
18	88 11.2	N 0 12.6	109 35.7	14.5	S 3 22.6	11.6	55.4
19	103 11.4	13.6	124 09.2	14.4	3 11.0	11.6	55.4
20	118 11.6	14.6	138 42.6	14.6	2 59.5	11.6	55.4
21	133 11.8	.. 15.6	153 16.2	14.5	2 47.9	11.6	55.4
22	148 11.9	16.6	167 49.7	14.6	2 36.3	11.6	55.4
23	163 12.1	17.6	182 23.3	14.6	2 24.7	11.5	55.3
21 00	178 12.3	N 0 18.5	196 56.9	14.6	S 2 13.2	11.6	55.3
01	193 12.5	19.5	211 30.5	14.6	2 01.6	11.6	55.3
02	208 12.7	20.5	226 04.1	14.7	1 50.0	11.6	55.3
03	223 12.9	.. 21.5	240 37.8	14.7	1 38.4	11.6	55.3
04	238 13.1	22.5	255 11.5	14.7	1 26.8	11.5	55.2
05	253 13.2	23.5	269 45.2	14.7	1 15.3	11.6	55.2
06	268 13.4	N 0 24.5	284 18.9	14.8	S 1 03.7	11.6	55.2
07	283 13.6	25.5	298 52.7	14.7	0 52.1	11.6	55.2
W 08	298 13.8	26.4	313 26.4	14.8	0 40.5	11.5	55.2
E 09	313 14.0	.. 27.4	328 00.2	14.8	0 29.0	11.6	55.2
D 10	328 14.2	28.4	342 34.0	14.8	0 17.4	11.6	55.1
N 11	343 14.4	29.4	357 07.8	14.9	S 0 05.8	11.5	55.1
E 12	358 14.5	N 0 30.4	11 41.7	14.8	N 0 05.7	11.5	55.1
S 13	13 14.7	31.4	26 15.5	14.9	0 17.2	11.5	55.1
D 14	28 14.9	32.4	40 49.4	14.9	0 28.8	11.5	55.1
A 15	43 15.1	.. 33.4	55 23.3	14.8	0 40.3	11.5	55.1
Y 16	58 15.3	34.3	69 57.1	14.9	0 51.8	11.5	55.0
17	73 15.5	35.3	84 31.0	15.0	1 03.3	11.5	55.0
18	88 15.7	N 0 36.3	99 05.0	14.9	N 1 14.8	11.5	55.0
19	103 15.8	37.3	113 38.9	14.9	1 26.3	11.5	55.0
20	118 16.0	38.3	128 12.8	15.0	1 37.8	11.5	55.0
21	133 16.2	.. 39.3	142 46.8	14.9	1 49.3	11.4	55.0
22	148 16.4	40.3	157 20.7	15.0	2 00.7	11.4	55.0
23	163 16.6	41.3	171 54.7	15.0	N 2 12.1	11.4	54.9
SD	16.1	d 1.0	SD 15.3		15.1		15.0

Twilight / Sunrise / Moonrise

Lat.	Naut.	Civil	Sunrise	Moonrise 19	20	21	22
N 72	03 19	04 48	05 56	05 51	05 33	05 18	05 03
N 70	03 38	04 56	05 58	05 35	05 25	05 16	05 07
68	03 53	05 03	05 58	05 23	05 18	05 14	05 11
66	04 05	05 08	05 59	05 12	05 13	05 13	05 14
64	04 14	05 12	06 00	05 03	05 08	05 12	05 16
62	04 22	05 16	06 00	04 55	05 04	05 11	05 18
60	04 29	05 19	06 01	04 49	05 00	05 11	05 20
N 58	04 35	05 22	06 01	04 43	04 57	05 10	05 22
56	04 40	05 24	06 01	04 37	04 54	05 09	05 24
54	04 45	05 26	06 02	04 33	04 52	05 09	05 25
52	04 49	05 28	06 02	04 28	04 49	05 08	05 27
50	04 52	05 30	06 02	04 25	04 47	05 08	05 28
45	04 59	05 33	06 03	04 16	04 42	05 07	05 30
N 40	05 04	05 36	06 03	04 09	04 38	05 06	05 33
35	05 09	05 38	06 03	04 03	04 35	05 05	05 35
30	05 12	05 40	06 04	03 58	04 32	05 04	05 36
20	05 16	05 42	06 04	03 48	04 27	05 03	05 39
N 10	05 19	05 43	06 04	03 40	04 22	05 02	05 42
0	05 19	05 43	06 04	03 32	04 18	05 01	05 44
S 10	05 19	05 43	06 04	03 24	04 13	05 01	05 47
20	05 16	05 42	06 04	03 16	04 09	05 00	05 50
30	05 12	05 40	06 04	03 07	04 03	04 59	05 53
35	05 09	05 38	06 03	03 01	04 00	04 58	05 55
40	05 04	05 36	06 03	02 55	03 57	04 57	05 57
45	04 59	05 33	06 03	02 47	03 53	04 56	05 59
S 50	04 52	05 30	06 02	02 39	03 48	04 55	06 02
52	04 48	05 28	06 02	02 35	03 45	04 55	06 03
54	04 45	05 26	06 02	02 30	03 43	04 54	06 05
56	04 40	05 24	06 02	02 25	03 40	04 54	06 06
58	04 35	05 22	06 01	02 19	03 37	04 53	06 08
S 60	04 29	05 19	06 01	02 13	03 34	04 53	06 10

Sunset / Twilight / Moonset

Lat.	Sunset	Civil	Naut.	Moonset 19	20	21	22
N 72	18 21	19 29	21 01	13 57	15 49	17 36	19 22
N 70	18 19	19 21	20 41	14 11	15 55	17 35	19 13
68	18 18	19 14	20 25	14 23	15 59	17 33	19 06
66	18 17	19 09	20 13	14 32	16 03	17 32	19 00
64	18 17	19 04	20 03	14 39	16 06	17 31	18 55
62	18 16	19 00	19 54	14 46	16 09	17 31	18 51
60	18 15	18 57	19 47	14 52	16 12	17 30	18 47
N 58	18 15	18 54	19 41	14 57	16 14	17 29	18 44
56	18 14	18 52	19 36	15 01	16 16	17 29	18 41
54	18 14	18 49	19 31	15 05	16 17	17 28	18 38
52	18 14	18 48	19 27	15 09	16 19	17 28	18 36
50	18 13	18 46	19 24	15 12	16 20	17 28	18 34
45	18 13	18 42	19 17	15 19	16 23	17 27	18 29
N 40	18 12	18 39	19 11	15 25	16 26	17 26	18 25
35	18 12	18 37	19 07	15 30	16 28	17 25	18 22
30	18 12	18 35	19 03	15 34	16 30	17 25	18 19
20	18 11	18 33	18 59	15 42	16 33	17 24	18 14
N 10	18 11	18 32	18 56	15 48	16 36	17 23	18 09
0	18 11	18 31	18 55	15 54	16 39	17 22	18 05
S 10	18 10	18 31	18 56	16 00	16 41	17 21	18 01
20	18 10	18 32	18 58	16 07	16 44	17 20	17 56
30	18 10	18 34	19 02	16 14	16 47	17 19	17 51
35	18 10	18 36	19 05	16 18	16 49	17 19	17 48
40	18 11	18 38	19 09	16 23	16 51	17 18	17 45
45	18 11	18 40	19 15	16 28	16 53	17 17	17 41
S 50	18 11	18 44	19 22	16 35	16 56	17 17	17 37
52	18 12	18 45	19 25	16 38	16 57	17 16	17 35
54	18 12	18 47	19 29	16 41	16 59	17 16	17 32
56	18 12	18 49	19 33	16 44	17 00	17 15	17 29
58	18 12	18 51	19 38	16 48	17 02	17 15	17 27
S 60	18 12	18 54	19 44	16 53	17 04	17 14	17 24

SUN / MOON

Day	Eqn. of Time 00h	12h	Mer. Pass.	Mer. Pass. Upper	Lower	Age	Phase
d	m s	m s	h m	h m	h m	d	%
19	07 46	07 38	12 08	09 43	22 06	27	10
20	07 29	07 20	12 07	10 28	22 50	28	5
21	07 11	07 02	12 07	11 12	23 33	29	1

● (new moon)

2012 MARCH 22, 23, 24 (THURS., FRI., SAT.)

UT	ARIES GHA	VENUS −4.4 GHA	Dec	MARS −0.9 GHA	Dec	JUPITER −2.1 GHA	Dec	SATURN +0.3 GHA	Dec	STARS Name	SHA	Dec
d h	° ′	° ′	° ′	° ′	° ′	° ′	° ′	° ′	° ′		° ′	° ′
22 00	179 54.1	135 30.8	N19 41.9	19 40.5	N12 20.8	140 53.0	N14 19.3	332 55.5	S 8 11.6	Acamar	315 19.3	S40 15.6
01	194 56.6	150 30.7	42.8	34 43.7	21.0	155 55.0	19.4	347 58.2	11.6	Achernar	335 27.9	S57 10.6
02	209 59.0	165 30.7	43.7	49 46.9	21.2	170 56.9	19.6	3 00.8	11.5	Acrux	173 09.6	S63 10.2
03	225 01.5	180 30.6	.. 44.6	64 50.0	.. 21.4	185 58.9	.. 19.8	18 03.4	.. 11.4	Adhara	255 13.1	S28 59.7
04	240 04.0	195 30.5	45.5	79 53.2	21.6	201 00.8	19.9	33 06.0	11.4	Aldebaran	290 50.5	N16 31.9
05	255 06.4	210 30.4	46.5	94 56.4	21.7	216 02.8	20.1	48 08.6	11.3			
06	270 08.9	225 30.4	N19 47.4	109 59.6	N12 21.9	231 04.7	N14 20.3	63 11.2	S 8 11.3	Alioth	166 20.8	N55 53.4
07	285 11.4	240 30.3	48.3	125 02.8	22.1	246 06.7	20.4	78 13.8	11.2	Alkaid	152 59.1	N49 14.9
T 08	300 13.8	255 30.2	49.2	140 06.0	22.3	261 08.6	20.6	93 16.5	11.1	Al Na'ir	27 45.2	S46 53.9
H 09	315 16.3	270 30.2	.. 50.1	155 09.1	.. 22.5	276 10.6	.. 20.8	108 19.1	.. 11.1	Alnilam	275 47.3	S 1 11.9
U 10	330 18.7	285 30.1	51.0	170 12.3	22.7	291 12.5	20.9	123 21.7	11.0	Alphard	217 56.7	S 8 43.0
R 11	345 21.2	300 30.0	51.9	185 15.5	22.8	306 14.5	21.1	138 24.3	10.9			
S 12	0 23.7	315 29.9	N19 52.8	200 18.7	N12 23.0	321 16.4	N14 21.3	153 26.9	S 8 10.9	Alphecca	126 11.5	N26 40.2
D 13	15 26.1	330 29.9	53.7	215 21.9	23.2	336 18.4	21.4	168 29.5	10.8	Alpheratz	357 44.8	N29 09.5
A 14	30 28.6	345 29.8	54.6	230 25.0	23.4	351 20.3	21.6	183 32.2	10.7	Altair	62 09.2	N 8 54.0
Y 15	45 31.1	0 29.7	.. 55.5	245 28.2	.. 23.6	6 22.3	.. 21.8	198 34.8	.. 10.7	Ankaa	353 16.9	S42 14.4
16	60 33.5	15 29.6	56.4	260 31.4	23.7	21 24.2	22.0	213 37.4	10.6	Antares	112 27.2	S26 27.5
17	75 36.0	30 29.6	57.3	275 34.6	23.9	36 26.2	22.1	228 40.0	10.6			
18	90 38.5	45 29.5	N19 58.2	290 37.7	N12 24.1	51 28.1	N14 22.3	243 42.6	S 8 10.5	Arcturus	145 56.2	N19 06.9
19	105 40.9	60 29.4	19 59.1	305 40.9	24.3	66 30.1	22.5	258 45.2	10.4	Atria	107 29.6	S69 02.7
20	120 43.4	75 29.4	20 00.0	320 44.1	24.5	81 32.0	22.6	273 47.8	10.4	Avior	234 18.1	S59 33.3
21	135 45.9	90 29.3	.. 00.9	335 47.2	.. 24.6	96 34.0	.. 22.8	288 50.5	.. 10.3	Bellatrix	278 33.0	N 6 21.5
22	150 48.3	105 29.2	01.8	350 50.4	24.8	111 35.9	23.0	303 53.1	10.2	Betelgeuse	271 02.2	N 7 24.4
23	165 50.8	120 29.1	02.7	5 53.6	25.0	126 37.9	23.1	318 55.7	10.2			
23 00	180 53.2	135 29.1	N20 03.6	20 56.7	N12 25.2	141 39.8	N14 23.3	333 58.3	S 8 10.1	Canopus	263 56.5	S52 42.6
01	195 55.7	150 29.0	04.5	35 59.9	25.3	156 41.8	23.5	349 00.9	10.1	Capella	280 35.8	N46 00.7
02	210 58.2	165 28.9	05.4	51 03.1	25.5	171 43.7	23.6	4 03.5	10.0	Deneb	49 32.3	N45 19.3
03	226 00.6	180 28.9	.. 06.3	66 06.2	.. 25.7	186 45.7	.. 23.8	19 06.2	.. 09.9	Denebola	182 34.2	N14 30.0
04	241 03.1	195 28.8	07.2	81 09.4	25.9	201 47.6	24.0	34 08.8	09.9	Diphda	348 57.1	S17 55.2
05	256 05.6	210 28.7	08.1	96 12.5	26.0	216 49.5	24.2	49 11.4	09.8			
06	271 08.0	225 28.7	N20 09.0	111 15.7	N12 26.2	231 51.5	N14 24.3	64 14.0	S 8 09.7	Dubhe	193 52.1	N61 41.0
07	286 10.5	240 28.6	09.9	126 18.9	26.4	246 53.4	24.5	79 16.6	09.7	Elnath	278 13.8	N28 37.0
F 08	301 13.0	255 28.5	10.8	141 22.0	26.6	261 55.4	24.7	94 19.3	09.6	Eltanin	90 46.5	N51 29.0
R 09	316 15.4	270 28.5	.. 11.7	156 25.2	.. 26.7	276 57.3	.. 24.8	109 21.9	.. 09.5	Enif	33 48.2	N 9 55.8
I 10	331 17.9	285 28.4	12.6	171 28.3	26.9	291 59.3	25.0	124 24.5	09.5	Fomalhaut	15 25.2	S29 33.4
D 11	346 20.3	300 28.3	13.4	186 31.5	27.1	307 01.2	25.2	139 27.1	09.4			
A 12	1 22.8	315 28.3	N20 14.3	201 34.6	N12 27.2	322 03.2	N14 25.3	154 29.7	S 8 09.4	Gacrux	172 01.3	S57 11.0
Y 13	16 25.3	330 28.2	15.2	216 37.8	27.4	337 05.1	25.5	169 32.3	09.3	Gienah	175 52.9	S17 36.8
14	31 27.7	345 28.1	16.1	231 40.9	27.6	352 07.1	25.7	184 35.0	09.2	Hadar	148 48.6	S60 25.9
15	46 30.2	0 28.1	.. 17.0	246 44.1	.. 27.7	7 09.0	.. 25.8	199 37.6	.. 09.2	Hamal	328 02.0	N23 31.2
16	61 32.7	15 28.0	17.9	261 47.2	27.9	22 10.9	26.0	214 40.2	09.1	Kaus Aust.	83 45.0	S34 22.5
17	76 35.1	30 27.9	18.8	276 50.4	28.1	37 12.9	26.2	229 42.8	09.0			
18	91 37.6	45 27.9	N20 19.6	291 53.5	N12 28.2	52 14.8	N14 26.4	244 45.4	S 8 09.0	Kochab	137 19.0	N74 06.1
19	106 40.1	60 27.8	20.5	306 56.7	28.4	67 16.8	26.5	259 48.0	08.9	Markab	13 39.5	N15 16.2
20	121 42.5	75 27.7	21.4	321 59.8	28.6	82 18.7	26.7	274 50.7	08.8	Menkar	314 16.2	N 4 08.1
21	136 45.0	90 27.7	.. 22.3	337 03.0	.. 28.7	97 20.7	.. 26.9	289 53.3	.. 08.8	Menkent	148 08.3	S36 25.9
22	151 47.5	105 27.6	23.2	352 06.1	28.9	112 22.6	27.0	304 55.9	08.7	Miaplacidus	221 39.3	S69 46.4
23	166 49.9	120 27.5	24.0	7 09.2	29.1	127 24.6	27.2	319 58.5	08.7			
24 00	181 52.4	135 27.5	N20 24.9	22 12.4	N12 29.2	142 26.5	N14 27.4	335 01.1	S 8 08.6	Mirfak	308 41.9	N49 54.3
01	196 54.8	150 27.4	25.8	37 15.5	29.4	157 28.4	27.5	350 03.8	08.5	Nunki	75 59.4	S26 16.7
02	211 57.3	165 27.3	26.7	52 18.7	29.5	172 30.4	27.7	5 06.4	08.5	Peacock	53 20.9	S56 41.5
03	226 59.8	180 27.3	.. 27.6	67 21.8	.. 29.7	187 32.3	.. 27.9	20 09.0	.. 08.4	Pollux	243 28.6	N27 59.7
04	242 02.2	195 27.2	28.4	82 24.9	29.9	202 34.3	28.0	35 11.6	08.3	Procyon	245 00.5	N 5 11.4
05	257 04.7	210 27.1	29.3	97 28.1	30.0	217 36.2	28.2	50 14.2	08.3			
06	272 07.2	225 27.1	N20 30.2	112 31.2	N12 30.2	232 38.2	N14 28.4	65 16.9	S 8 08.2	Rasalhague	96 07.2	N12 32.9
07	287 09.6	240 27.0	31.0	127 34.3	30.3	247 40.1	28.6	80 19.5	08.1	Regulus	207 44.1	N11 54.2
S 08	302 12.1	255 27.0	31.9	142 37.5	30.5	262 42.1	28.7	95 22.1	08.1	Rigel	281 13.0	S 8 11.5
A 09	317 14.6	270 26.9	.. 32.8	157 40.6	.. 30.7	277 44.0	.. 28.9	110 24.7	.. 08.0	Rigil Kent.	139 52.4	S60 53.0
T 10	332 17.0	285 26.8	33.7	172 43.7	30.8	292 45.9	29.1	125 27.3	07.9	Sabik	102 13.4	S15 44.4
U 11	347 19.5	300 26.8	34.5	187 46.8	31.0	307 47.9	29.2	140 30.0	07.9			
R 12	2 21.9	315 26.7	N20 35.4	202 50.0	N12 31.1	322 49.8	N14 29.4	155 32.6	S 8 07.8	Schedar	349 42.1	N56 36.3
D 13	17 24.4	330 26.7	36.3	217 53.1	31.3	337 51.8	29.6	170 35.2	07.8	Shaula	96 23.0	S37 06.6
A 14	32 26.9	345 26.6	37.1	232 56.2	31.4	352 53.7	29.7	185 37.8	07.7	Sirius	258 34.4	S16 44.3
Y 15	47 29.3	0 26.5	.. 38.0	247 59.3	.. 31.6	7 55.7	.. 29.9	200 40.4	.. 07.6	Spica	158 31.9	S11 13.7
16	62 31.8	15 26.5	38.9	263 02.5	31.7	22 57.6	30.1	215 43.1	07.6	Suhail	222 52.8	S43 29.3
17	77 34.3	30 26.4	39.7	278 05.6	31.9	37 59.5	30.3	230 45.7	07.5			
18	92 36.7	45 26.4	N20 40.6	293 08.7	N12 32.1	53 01.5	N14 30.4	245 48.3	S 8 07.4	Vega	80 39.6	N38 47.5
19	107 39.2	60 26.3	41.5	308 11.8	32.2	68 03.4	30.6	260 50.9	07.4	Zuben'ubi	137 06.1	S16 05.6
20	122 41.7	75 26.2	42.3	323 14.9	32.4	83 05.4	30.8	275 53.5	07.3			
21	137 44.1	90 26.2	.. 43.2	338 18.0	.. 32.5	98 07.3	.. 30.9	290 56.2	.. 07.2			
22	152 46.6	105 26.1	44.1	353 21.2	32.7	113 09.2	31.1	305 58.8	07.2			
23	167 49.1	120 26.1	44.9	8 24.3	32.8	128 11.2	31.3	321 01.4	07.1			

	SHA	Mer. Pass.
	° ′	h m
Venus	314 35.8	14 58
Mars	200 03.5	22 31
Jupiter	320 46.6	14 31
Saturn	153 05.1	1 44

	h m							
Mer. Pass. 11 54.5		*v* −0.1	*d* 0.9	*v* 3.2	*d* 0.2	*v* 1.9	*d* 0.2	*v* 2.6 *d* 0.1

UT	SUN GHA	SUN Dec	MOON GHA	v	MOON Dec	d	HP
d h	° ′	° ′	° ′	′	° ′	′	′
22 00	178 16.8	N 0 42.2	186 28.7	15.0	N 2 23.5	11.4	54.9
01	193 17.0	43.2	201 02.7	14.9	2 34.9	11.4	54.9
02	208 17.1	44.2	215 36.6	15.0	2 46.3	11.4	54.9
03	223 17.3	.. 45.2	230 10.6	15.0	2 57.7	11.3	54.9
04	238 17.5	46.2	244 44.6	15.0	3 09.0	11.4	54.9
05	253 17.7	47.2	259 18.6	15.1	3 20.4	11.3	54.8
06	268 17.9	N 0 48.2	273 52.7	15.0	N 3 31.7	11.2	54.8
T 07	283 18.1	49.1	288 26.7	15.0	3 42.9	11.3	54.8
H 08	298 18.3	50.1	303 00.7	15.0	3 54.2	11.2	54.8
U 09	313 18.4	.. 51.1	317 34.7	15.0	4 05.4	11.3	54.8
R 10	328 18.6	52.1	332 08.7	15.0	4 16.7	11.2	54.8
S 11	343 18.8	53.1	346 42.7	15.0	4 27.9	11.1	54.8
D 12	358 19.0	N 0 54.1	1 16.7	15.1	N 4 39.0	11.2	54.7
A 13	13 19.2	55.1	15 50.8	15.0	4 50.2	11.1	54.7
Y 14	28 19.4	56.1	30 24.8	15.0	5 01.3	11.1	54.7
15	43 19.6	.. 57.0	44 58.8	15.0	5 12.4	11.1	54.7
16	58 19.8	58.0	59 32.8	15.0	5 23.5	11.0	54.7
17	73 19.9	0 59.0	74 06.8	15.0	5 34.5	11.0	54.7
18	88 20.1	N 1 00.0	88 40.8	15.0	N 5 45.5	11.0	54.7
19	103 20.3	01.0	103 14.8	15.0	5 56.5	10.9	54.7
20	118 20.5	02.0	117 48.8	15.0	6 07.4	10.9	54.6
21	133 20.7	.. 03.0	132 22.8	15.0	6 18.3	10.9	54.6
22	148 20.9	03.9	146 56.8	14.9	6 29.2	10.9	54.6
23	163 21.1	04.9	161 30.7	15.0	6 40.1	10.8	54.6
23 00	178 21.2	N 1 05.9	176 04.7	15.0	N 6 50.9	10.8	54.6
01	193 21.4	06.9	190 38.7	14.9	7 01.7	10.8	54.6
02	208 21.6	07.9	205 12.6	15.0	7 12.5	10.7	54.6
03	223 21.8	.. 08.9	219 46.6	14.9	7 23.2	10.7	54.5
04	238 22.0	09.9	234 20.5	14.9	7 33.9	10.6	54.5
05	253 22.2	10.8	248 54.4	14.9	7 44.5	10.6	54.5
06	268 22.4	N 1 11.8	263 28.3	14.9	N 7 55.1	10.6	54.5
07	283 22.6	12.8	278 02.2	14.9	8 05.7	10.5	54.5
F 08	298 22.7	13.8	292 36.1	14.9	8 16.2	10.5	54.5
R 09	313 22.9	.. 14.8	307 10.0	14.8	8 26.7	10.5	54.5
I 10	328 23.1	15.8	321 43.8	14.9	8 37.2	10.4	54.5
D 11	343 23.3	16.8	336 17.7	14.8	8 47.6	10.4	54.5
A 12	358 23.5	N 1 17.7	350 51.5	14.8	N 8 58.0	10.3	54.4
Y 13	13 23.7	18.7	5 25.3	14.8	9 08.3	10.3	54.4
14	28 23.9	19.7	19 59.1	14.8	9 18.6	10.2	54.4
15	43 24.1	.. 20.7	34 32.9	14.8	9 28.8	10.2	54.4
16	58 24.2	21.7	49 06.7	14.8	9 39.0	10.2	54.4
17	73 24.4	22.7	63 40.5	14.7	9 49.2	10.1	54.4
18	88 24.6	N 1 23.6	78 14.2	14.7	N 9 59.3	10.1	54.4
19	103 24.8	24.6	92 47.9	14.7	10 09.4	10.0	54.4
20	118 25.0	25.6	107 21.6	14.7	10 19.4	10.0	54.4
21	133 25.2	.. 26.6	121 55.3	14.7	10 29.4	9.9	54.3
22	148 25.4	27.6	136 29.0	14.6	10 39.3	9.9	54.3
23	163 25.6	28.6	151 02.6	14.6	10 49.2	9.8	54.3
24 00	178 25.7	N 1 29.6	165 36.2	14.6	N10 59.0	9.8	54.3
01	193 25.9	30.5	180 09.8	14.6	11 08.8	9.7	54.3
02	208 26.1	31.5	194 43.4	14.6	11 18.5	9.7	54.3
03	223 26.3	.. 32.5	209 17.0	14.5	11 28.2	9.6	54.3
04	238 26.5	33.5	223 50.5	14.5	11 37.8	9.6	54.3
05	253 26.7	34.5	238 24.0	14.5	11 47.4	9.5	54.3
06	268 26.9	N 1 35.5	252 57.5	14.5	N11 56.9	9.5	54.3
S 07	283 27.1	36.4	267 31.0	14.5	12 06.4	9.4	54.3
A 08	298 27.3	37.4	282 04.5	14.4	12 15.8	9.4	54.2
T 09	313 27.4	.. 38.4	296 37.9	14.4	12 25.2	9.3	54.2
U 10	328 27.6	39.4	311 11.3	14.4	12 34.5	9.2	54.2
R 11	343 27.8	40.4	325 44.7	14.3	12 43.7	9.2	54.2
D 12	358 28.0	N 1 41.4	340 18.0	14.3	N12 52.9	9.2	54.2
A 13	13 28.2	42.3	354 51.3	14.3	13 02.1	9.0	54.2
Y 14	28 28.4	43.3	9 24.6	14.3	13 11.1	9.1	54.2
15	43 28.6	.. 44.3	23 57.9	14.2	13 20.2	8.9	54.2
16	58 28.7	45.3	38 31.1	14.2	13 29.1	8.9	54.2
17	73 28.9	46.3	53 04.4	14.2	13 38.0	8.9	54.2
18	88 29.1	N 1 47.3	67 37.6	14.1	N13 46.9	8.7	54.2
19	103 29.3	48.2	82 10.7	14.2	13 55.6	8.8	54.2
20	118 29.5	49.2	96 43.9	14.1	14 04.4	8.6	54.2
21	133 29.7	.. 50.2	111 17.0	14.0	14 13.0	8.6	54.1
22	148 29.9	51.2	125 50.0	14.1	14 21.6	8.5	54.1
23	163 30.1	52.2	140 23.1	14.0	N14 30.1	8.5	54.1
	SD 16.1	d 1.0	SD 14.9		14.8		14.8

Lat.	Twilight Naut.	Civil	Sunrise	Moonrise 22	23	24	25
°	h m	h m	h m	h m	h m	h m	h m
N 72	02 57	04 32	05 41	05 03	04 47	04 29	04 03
N 70	03 20	04 42	05 44	05 07	04 58	04 48	04 36
68	03 38	04 49	05 46	05 11	05 07	05 03	05 00
66	03 51	04 56	05 48	05 14	05 14	05 16	05 18
64	04 02	05 01	05 49	05 16	05 21	05 26	05 34
62	04 11	05 06	05 50	05 18	05 26	05 35	05 46
60	04 19	05 10	05 52	05 20	05 31	05 43	05 57
N 58	04 26	05 13	05 53	05 22	05 35	05 50	06 07
56	04 32	05 16	05 53	05 24	05 39	05 56	06 15
54	04 37	05 19	05 54	05 25	05 42	06 01	06 23
52	04 41	05 21	05 55	05 27	05 46	06 06	06 29
50	04 45	05 23	05 56	05 28	05 48	06 10	06 35
45	04 53	05 28	05 57	05 30	05 55	06 20	06 48
N 40	04 59	05 31	05 58	05 33	06 00	06 28	06 59
35	05 04	05 34	05 59	05 35	06 04	06 35	07 08
30	05 08	05 36	06 00	05 36	06 08	06 41	07 17
20	05 14	05 39	06 01	05 39	06 15	06 52	07 31
N 10	05 17	05 41	06 02	05 42	06 21	07 02	07 43
0	05 19	05 43	06 03	05 44	06 27	07 11	07 55
S 10	05 19	05 43	06 04	05 47	06 33	07 20	08 07
20	05 17	05 43	06 05	05 50	06 39	07 29	08 19
30	05 14	05 42	06 05	05 53	06 47	07 40	08 34
35	05 11	05 41	06 06	05 55	06 51	07 47	08 42
40	05 08	05 39	06 06	05 57	06 56	07 54	08 52
45	05 03	05 37	06 07	05 59	07 01	08 03	09 03
S 50	04 57	05 35	06 07	06 02	07 08	08 13	09 17
52	04 54	05 34	06 07	06 03	07 11	08 18	09 24
54	04 51	05 32	06 07	06 05	07 14	08 23	09 31
56	04 47	05 31	06 08	06 06	07 18	08 29	09 39
58	04 42	05 29	06 08	06 08	07 22	08 36	09 48
S 60	04 37	05 27	06 08	06 10	07 27	08 43	09 58

Lat.	Sunset	Twilight Civil	Naut.	Moonset 22	23	24	25
°	h m	h m	h m	h m	h m	h m	h m
N 72	18 35	19 44	21 21	19 22	21 11	23 08	25 53
N 70	18 32	19 34	20 57	19 13	20 53	22 36	24 29
68	18 29	19 26	20 39	19 06	20 39	22 14	23 50
66	18 27	19 19	20 25	19 00	20 28	21 56	23 24
64	18 25	19 14	20 13	18 55	20 18	21 41	23 03
62	18 24	19 09	20 04	18 51	20 10	21 29	22 47
60	18 23	19 05	19 56	18 47	20 03	21 19	22 33
N 58	18 22	19 01	19 49	18 44	19 57	21 10	22 21
56	18 21	18 58	19 43	18 41	19 52	21 03	22 11
54	18 20	18 55	19 38	18 38	19 47	20 56	22 02
52	18 19	18 53	19 33	18 36	19 43	20 49	21 54
50	18 18	18 51	19 29	18 34	19 39	20 44	21 47
45	18 17	18 46	19 21	18 29	19 31	20 32	21 32
N 40	18 15	18 43	19 14	18 25	19 24	20 22	21 20
35	18 14	18 40	19 09	18 22	19 18	20 14	21 09
30	18 13	18 37	19 05	18 19	19 13	20 06	21 00
20	18 12	18 34	19 00	18 14	19 03	19 53	20 44
N 10	18 11	18 32	18 56	18 09	18 56	19 42	20 30
0	18 10	18 30	18 54	18 05	18 48	19 32	20 17
S 10	18 09	18 30	18 54	18 01	18 41	19 21	20 04
20	18 08	18 30	18 55	17 56	18 33	19 10	19 50
30	18 07	18 31	18 59	17 51	18 24	18 58	19 34
35	18 07	18 32	19 01	17 48	18 19	18 51	19 25
40	18 06	18 34	19 04	17 45	18 13	18 42	19 15
45	18 05	18 35	19 09	17 41	18 06	18 33	19 03
S 50	18 05	18 37	19 15	17 37	17 58	18 21	18 48
52	18 05	18 38	19 18	17 35	17 54	18 16	18 41
54	18 04	18 40	19 21	17 32	17 50	18 10	18 33
56	18 04	18 41	19 25	17 30	17 46	18 04	18 25
58	18 04	18 43	19 29	17 27	17 41	17 56	18 15
S 60	18 03	18 45	19 34	17 24	17 35	17 48	18 04

	SUN		MOON			
Day	Eqn. of Time 00^h	12^h	Mer. Pass.	Mer. Pass. Upper	Lower	Age	Phase
d	m s	m s	h m	h m	h m	d	%
22	06 53	06 44	12 07	11 55	24 16	30	0
23	06 35	06 26	12 06	12 38	00 16	01	1
24	06 17	06 08	12 06	13 21	00 59	02	3

● (New Moon)

2012 MARCH 25, 26, 27 (SUN., MON., TUES.)

UT	ARIES GHA	VENUS −4.5 GHA	Dec	MARS −0.9 GHA	Dec	JUPITER −2.1 GHA	Dec	SATURN +0.3 GHA	Dec	STARS Name	SHA	Dec
25 00	182 51.5	135 26.0	N20 45.8	23 27.4	N12 33.0	143 13.1	N14 31.4	336 04.0	S 8 07.0	Acamar	315 19.3	S40 15.6
01	197 54.0	150 25.9	46.6	38 30.5	33.1	158 15.1	31.6	351 06.6	07.0	Achernar	335 27.9	S57 10.6
02	212 56.4	165 25.9	47.5	53 33.6	33.3	173 17.0	31.8	6 09.3	06.9	Acrux	173 09.6	S63 10.2
03	227 58.9	180 25.8 ..	48.3	68 36.7 ..	33.4	188 18.9 ..	32.0	21 11.9 ..	06.9	Adhara	255 13.1	S28 59.7
04	243 01.4	195 25.8	49.2	83 39.8	33.5	203 20.9	32.1	36 14.5	06.8	Aldebaran	290 50.5	N16 31.9
05	258 03.8	210 25.7	50.1	98 42.9	33.7	218 22.8	32.3	51 17.1	06.7			
06	273 06.3	225 25.7	N20 50.9	113 46.0	N12 33.8	233 24.8	N14 32.5	66 19.7	S 8 06.7	Alioth	166 20.8	N55 53.4
07	288 08.8	240 25.6	51.8	128 49.1	34.0	248 26.7	32.6	81 22.4	06.6	Alkaid	152 59.1	N49 14.9
08	303 11.2	255 25.5	52.6	143 52.2	34.1	263 28.6	32.8	96 25.0	06.5	Al Na'ir	27 45.2	S46 53.9
S 09	318 13.7	270 25.5 ..	53.5	158 55.3 ..	34.3	278 30.6 ..	33.0	111 27.6 ..	06.5	Alnilam	275 47.3	S 1 11.9
U 10	333 16.2	285 25.4	54.3	173 58.4	34.4	293 32.5	33.1	126 30.2	06.4	Alphard	217 56.7	S 8 43.0
N 11	348 18.6	300 25.4	55.2	189 01.5	34.6	308 34.5	33.3	141 32.9	06.3			
D 12	3 21.1	315 25.3	N20 56.0	204 04.6	N12 34.7	323 36.4	N14 33.5	156 35.5	S 8 06.3	Alphecca	126 11.5	N26 40.2
A 13	18 23.6	330 25.3	56.9	219 07.7	34.9	338 38.3	33.6	171 38.1	06.2	Alpheratz	357 44.8	N29 09.5
Y 14	33 26.0	345 25.2	57.7	234 10.8	35.0	353 40.3	33.8	186 40.7	06.1	Altair	62 09.2	N 8 54.0
15	48 28.5	0 25.2 ..	58.6	249 13.9 ..	35.1	8 42.2 ..	34.0	201 43.3 ..	06.1	Ankaa	353 16.9	S42 14.4
16	63 30.9	15 25.1	20 59.4	264 17.0	35.3	23 44.2	34.2	216 46.0	06.0	Antares	112 27.1	S26 27.5
17	78 33.4	30 25.1	21 00.3	279 20.1	35.4	38 46.1	34.3	231 48.6	05.9			
18	93 35.9	45 25.0	N21 01.1	294 23.2	N12 35.6	53 48.0	N14 34.5	246 51.2	S 8 05.9	Arcturus	145 56.2	N19 06.9
19	108 38.3	60 24.9	02.0	309 26.3	35.7	68 50.0	34.7	261 53.8	05.8	Atria	107 29.6	S69 02.7
20	123 40.8	75 24.9	02.8	324 29.4	35.8	83 51.9	34.8	276 56.5	05.7	Avior	234 18.1	S59 33.3
21	138 43.3	90 24.8 ..	03.6	339 32.5 ..	36.0	98 53.9 ..	35.0	291 59.1 ..	05.7	Bellatrix	278 33.0	N 6 21.5
22	153 45.7	105 24.8	04.5	354 35.6	36.1	113 55.8	35.2	307 01.7	05.6	Betelgeuse	271 02.3	N 7 24.4
23	168 48.2	120 24.7	05.3	9 38.7	36.2	128 57.7	35.3	322 04.3	05.6			
26 00	183 50.7	135 24.7	N21 06.2	24 41.7	N12 36.4	143 59.7	N14 35.5	337 06.9	S 8 05.5	Canopus	263 56.5	S52 42.6
01	198 53.1	150 24.6	07.0	39 44.8	36.5	159 01.6	35.7	352 09.6	05.4	Capella	280 35.8	N46 00.6
02	213 55.6	165 24.6	07.8	54 47.9	36.7	174 03.6	35.9	7 12.2	05.4	Deneb	49 32.3	N45 19.3
03	228 58.0	180 24.5 ..	08.7	69 51.0 ..	36.8	189 05.5 ..	36.0	22 14.8 ..	05.3	Denebola	182 34.2	N14 30.0
04	244 00.5	195 24.5	09.5	84 54.1	36.9	204 07.4	36.2	37 17.4	05.2	Diphda	348 57.1	S17 55.2
05	259 03.0	210 24.4	10.4	99 57.1	37.1	219 09.4	36.4	52 20.1	05.2			
06	274 05.4	225 24.4	N21 11.2	115 00.2	N12 37.2	234 11.3	N14 36.5	67 22.7	S 8 05.1	Dubhe	193 52.1	N61 41.0
07	289 07.9	240 24.3	12.0	130 03.3	37.3	249 13.2	36.7	82 25.3	05.0	Elnath	278 13.8	N28 37.0
08	304 10.4	255 24.3	12.9	145 06.4	37.5	264 15.2	36.9	97 27.9	05.0	Eltanin	90 46.5	N51 29.0
M 09	319 12.8	270 24.2 ..	13.7	160 09.4 ..	37.6	279 17.1 ..	37.0	112 30.6 ..	04.9	Enif	33 48.2	N 9 55.8
O 10	334 15.3	285 24.2	14.5	175 12.5	37.7	294 19.1	37.2	127 33.2	04.8	Fomalhaut	15 25.2	S29 33.4
N 11	349 17.8	300 24.1	15.4	190 15.6	37.8	309 21.0	37.4	142 35.8	04.8			
D 12	4 20.2	315 24.1	N21 16.2	205 18.7	N12 38.0	324 22.9	N14 37.6	157 38.4	S 8 04.7	Gacrux	172 01.3	S57 11.1
A 13	19 22.7	330 24.1	17.0	220 21.7	38.1	339 24.9	37.7	172 41.1	04.6	Gienah	175 52.9	S17 36.8
Y 14	34 25.2	345 24.0	17.9	235 24.8	38.2	354 26.8	37.9	187 43.7	04.6	Hadar	148 48.6	S60 25.9
15	49 27.6	0 24.0 ..	18.7	250 27.9 ..	38.4	9 28.7 ..	38.1	202 46.3 ..	04.5	Hamal	328 02.0	N23 31.2
16	64 30.1	15 23.9	19.5	265 30.9	38.5	24 30.7	38.2	217 48.9	04.4	Kaus Aust.	83 44.9	S34 22.5
17	79 32.5	30 23.9	20.3	280 34.0	38.6	39 32.6	38.4	232 51.5	04.4			
18	94 35.0	45 23.8	N21 21.2	295 37.1	N12 38.7	54 34.5	N14 38.6	247 54.2	S 8 04.3	Kochab	137 19.0	N74 06.1
19	109 37.5	60 23.8	22.0	310 40.1	38.9	69 36.5	38.7	262 56.8	04.2	Markab	13 39.5	N15 16.2
20	124 39.9	75 23.7	22.8	325 43.2	39.0	84 38.4	38.9	277 59.4	04.2	Menkar	314 16.2	N 4 08.1
21	139 42.4	90 23.7 ..	23.6	340 46.2 ..	39.1	99 40.4 ..	39.1	293 02.0 ..	04.1	Menkent	148 08.2	S36 25.9
22	154 44.9	105 23.6	24.5	355 49.3	39.2	114 42.3	39.3	308 04.7	04.0	Miaplacidus	221 39.3	S69 46.4
23	169 47.3	120 23.6	25.3	10 52.4	39.4	129 44.2	39.4	323 07.3	04.0			
27 00	184 49.8	135 23.6	N21 26.1	25 55.4	N12 39.5	144 46.2	N14 39.6	338 09.9	S 8 03.9	Mirfak	308 41.9	N49 54.3
01	199 52.3	150 23.5	26.9	40 58.5	39.6	159 48.1	39.8	353 12.5	03.9	Nunki	75 59.4	S26 16.7
02	214 54.7	165 23.5	27.7	56 01.5	39.7	174 50.0	39.9	8 15.2	03.8	Peacock	53 20.8	S56 41.4
03	229 57.2	180 23.4 ..	28.6	71 04.6 ..	39.9	189 52.0 ..	40.1	23 17.8 ..	03.7	Pollux	243 28.7	N27 59.7
04	244 59.7	195 23.4	29.4	86 07.6	40.0	204 53.9	40.3	38 20.4	03.7	Procyon	245 00.5	N 5 11.4
05	260 02.1	210 23.3	30.2	101 10.7	40.1	219 55.8	40.4	53 23.0	03.6			
06	275 04.6	225 23.3	N21 31.0	116 13.7	N12 40.2	234 57.8	N14 40.6	68 25.7	S 8 03.5	Rasalhague	96 07.2	N12 33.0
07	290 07.0	240 23.3	31.8	131 16.8	40.3	249 59.7	40.8	83 28.3	03.5	Regulus	207 44.2	N11 54.2
08	305 09.5	255 23.2	32.6	146 19.8	40.5	265 01.6	41.0	98 30.9	03.4	Rigel	281 13.0	S 8 11.5
T 09	320 12.0	270 23.2 ..	33.5	161 22.9 ..	40.6	280 03.6 ..	41.1	113 33.5 ..	03.3	Rigil Kent.	139 52.4	S60 53.0
U 10	335 14.4	285 23.1	34.3	176 25.9	40.7	295 05.5	41.3	128 36.2	03.3	Sabik	102 13.4	S15 44.4
E 11	350 16.9	300 23.1	35.1	191 29.0	40.8	310 07.4	41.5	143 38.8	03.2			
S 12	5 19.4	315 23.1	N21 35.9	206 32.0	N12 40.9	325 09.4	N14 41.6	158 41.4	S 8 03.1	Schedar	349 42.1	N56 36.3
D 13	20 21.8	330 23.0	36.7	221 35.0	41.0	340 11.3	41.8	173 44.1	03.1	Shaula	96 23.0	S37 06.6
A 14	35 24.3	345 23.0	37.5	236 38.1	41.0	355 13.2	42.0	188 46.7	03.0	Sirius	258 34.4	S16 44.3
Y 15	50 26.8	0 23.0 ..	38.3	251 41.1 ..	41.3	10 15.2 ..	42.1	203 49.3 ..	02.9	Spica	158 31.8	S11 13.7
16	65 29.2	15 22.9	39.1	266 44.2	41.4	25 17.1	42.3	218 51.9	02.9	Suhail	222 52.8	S43 29.3
17	80 31.7	30 22.9	39.9	281 47.2	41.5	40 19.0	42.5	233 54.6	02.8			
18	95 34.1	45 22.8	N21 40.8	296 50.2	N12 41.6	55 21.0	N14 42.7	248 57.2	S 8 02.7	Vega	80 39.6	N38 47.5
19	110 36.6	60 22.8	41.6	311 53.3	41.7	70 22.9	42.8	263 59.8	02.7	Zuben'ubi	137 06.1	S16 05.6
20	125 39.1	75 22.8	42.4	326 56.3	41.8	85 24.8	43.0	279 02.4	02.6		SHA	Mer.Pass.
21	140 41.5	90 22.7 ..	43.2	341 59.3 ..	41.9	100 26.8 ..	43.2	294 05.1 ..	02.5	Venus	311 34.0	14 58
22	155 44.0	105 22.7	44.0	357 02.4	42.1	115 28.7	43.3	309 07.7	02.5	Mars	200 51.1	22 17
23	170 46.5	120 22.7	44.8	12 05.4	42.2	130 30.6	43.5	324 10.3	02.4	Jupiter	320 09.0	14 22
Mer.Pass. 11 42.7		v 0.0 d 0.8		v 3.1 d 0.1		v 1.9 d 0.2		v 2.6 d 0.1		Saturn	153 16.3	1 31

UT	SUN GHA	SUN Dec	MOON GHA	v	MOON Dec	d	HP
d h	° ′	° ′	° ′	′	° ′	′	′
25 00	178 30.2	N 1 53.2	154 56.1	14.0	N14 38.6	8.4	54.1
01	193 30.4	54.1	169 29.1	14.0	14 47.0	8.3	54.1
02	208 30.6	55.1	184 02.1	13.9	14 55.3	8.3	54.1
03	223 30.8	.. 56.1	198 35.0	13.9	15 03.6	8.2	54.1
04	238 31.0	57.1	213 07.9	13.9	15 11.8	8.2	54.1
05	253 31.2	58.1	227 40.8	13.8	15 20.0	8.0	54.1
06	268 31.4	N 1 59.1	242 13.6	13.8	N15 28.0	8.0	54.1
07	283 31.6	2 00.0	256 46.4	13.8	15 36.0	8.0	54.1
S 08	298 31.8	01.0	271 19.2	13.7	15 44.0	7.8	54.1
U 09	313 31.9	.. 02.0	285 51.9	13.8	15 51.8	7.8	54.1
N 10	328 32.1	03.0	300 24.7	13.6	15 59.6	7.7	54.1
D 11	343 32.3	04.0	314 57.3	13.7	16 07.3	7.7	54.1
A 12	358 32.5	N 2 04.9	329 30.0	13.6	N16 15.0	7.6	54.1
Y 13	13 32.7	05.9	344 02.6	13.6	16 22.6	7.5	54.1
14	28 32.9	06.9	358 35.2	13.6	16 30.1	7.4	54.1
15	43 33.1	.. 07.9	13 07.8	13.5	16 37.5	7.4	54.1
16	58 33.3	08.9	27 40.3	13.5	16 44.9	7.3	54.1
17	73 33.4	09.9	42 12.8	13.4	16 52.2	7.2	54.1
18	88 33.6	N 2 10.8	56 45.2	13.4	N16 59.4	7.1	54.1
19	103 33.8	11.8	71 17.6	13.4	17 06.5	7.1	54.1
20	118 34.0	12.8	85 50.0	13.4	17 13.6	7.0	54.0
21	133 34.2	.. 13.8	100 22.4	13.3	17 20.6	6.9	54.1
22	148 34.4	14.8	114 54.7	13.3	17 27.5	6.8	54.1
23	163 34.6	15.7	129 27.0	13.3	17 34.3	6.8	54.1
26 00	178 34.8	N 2 16.7	143 59.3	13.2	N17 41.1	6.7	54.0
01	193 35.0	17.7	158 31.5	13.2	17 47.8	6.6	54.0
02	208 35.1	18.7	173 03.7	13.1	17 54.4	6.5	54.0
03	223 35.3	.. 19.7	187 35.8	13.1	18 00.9	6.4	54.0
04	238 35.5	20.6	202 07.9	13.1	18 07.3	6.4	54.0
05	253 35.7	21.6	216 40.0	13.1	18 13.7	6.3	54.0
06	268 35.9	N 2 22.6	231 12.1	13.0	N18 20.0	6.2	54.0
07	283 36.1	23.6	245 44.1	13.0	18 26.2	6.1	54.0
08	298 36.3	24.6	260 16.1	12.9	18 32.3	6.0	54.0
M 09	313 36.5	.. 25.5	274 48.0	13.0	18 38.3	6.0	54.0
O 10	328 36.6	26.5	289 20.0	12.8	18 44.3	5.9	54.0
N 11	343 36.8	27.5	303 51.8	12.9	18 50.2	5.7	54.0
D 12	358 37.0	N 2 28.5	318 23.7	12.8	N18 55.9	5.7	54.0
A 13	13 37.2	29.5	332 55.5	12.8	19 01.6	5.7	54.0
Y 14	28 37.4	30.4	347 27.3	12.7	19 07.3	5.5	54.0
15	43 37.6	.. 31.4	1 59.0	12.7	19 12.8	5.4	54.0
16	58 37.8	32.4	16 30.7	12.7	19 18.2	5.4	54.0
17	73 38.0	33.4	31 02.4	12.7	19 23.6	5.3	54.1
18	88 38.2	N 2 34.4	45 34.1	12.6	N19 28.9	5.2	54.1
19	103 38.3	35.3	60 05.7	12.6	19 34.1	5.1	54.1
20	118 38.5	36.3	74 37.3	12.5	19 39.2	5.0	54.1
21	133 38.7	.. 37.3	89 08.8	12.5	19 44.2	4.9	54.1
22	148 38.9	38.3	103 40.3	12.5	19 49.1	4.8	54.1
23	163 39.1	39.3	118 11.8	12.4	19 53.9	4.8	54.1
27 00	178 39.3	N 2 40.2	132 43.2	12.5	N19 58.7	4.6	54.1
01	193 39.5	41.2	147 14.7	12.3	20 03.3	4.6	54.1
02	208 39.7	42.2	161 46.0	12.4	20 07.9	4.5	54.1
03	223 39.9	.. 43.2	176 17.4	12.3	20 12.4	4.3	54.1
04	238 40.0	44.1	190 48.7	12.3	20 16.7	4.3	54.1
05	253 40.2	45.1	205 20.0	12.2	20 21.0	4.2	54.1
06	268 40.4	N 2 46.1	219 51.2	12.3	N20 25.2	4.1	54.1
07	283 40.6	47.1	234 22.5	12.2	20 29.3	4.0	54.1
T 08	298 40.8	48.1	248 53.7	12.1	20 33.3	4.0	54.1
U 09	313 41.0	.. 49.0	263 24.8	12.1	20 37.3	3.8	54.1
E 10	328 41.2	50.0	277 55.9	12.1	20 41.1	3.7	54.1
S 11	343 41.4	51.0	292 27.0	12.1	20 44.8	3.6	54.1
D 12	358 41.5	N 2 52.0	306 58.1	12.0	N20 48.4	3.6	54.1
A 13	13 41.7	52.9	321 29.1	12.0	20 52.0	3.4	54.1
Y 14	28 41.9	53.9	336 00.1	12.0	20 55.4	3.4	54.2
15	43 42.1	.. 54.9	350 31.1	12.0	20 58.8	3.2	54.2
16	58 42.3	55.9	5 02.1	11.9	21 02.0	3.2	54.2
17	73 42.5	56.9	19 33.0	11.9	21 05.2	3.0	54.2
18	88 42.7	N 2 57.8	34 03.9	11.8	N21 08.2	3.0	54.2
19	103 42.9	58.8	48 34.7	11.9	21 11.2	2.9	54.2
20	118 43.1	2 59.8	63 05.6	11.8	21 14.1	2.7	54.2
21	133 43.2	3 00.8	77 36.4	11.7	21 16.8	2.7	54.2
22	148 43.4	01.7	92 07.1	11.8	21 19.5	2.6	54.2
23	163 43.6	02.7	106 37.9	11.7	N21 22.1	2.5	54.2
	SD 16.1	d 1.0	SD 14.7		14.7		14.8

Lat.	Twilight Naut.	Twilight Civil	Sunrise	Moonrise 25	26	27	28
°	h m	h m	h m	h m	h m	h m	h m
N 72	02 34	04 15	05 25	04 03	02 53	□	□
N 70	03 01	04 27	05 30	04 36	04 17	□	□
68	03 22	04 36	05 33	05 00	04 57	04 55	04 57
66	03 37	04 44	05 36	05 18	05 24	05 35	05 58
64	03 50	04 50	05 38	05 34	05 45	06 03	06 32
62	04 00	04 56	05 41	05 46	06 02	06 24	06 57
60	04 09	05 00	05 42	05 57	06 16	06 42	07 17
N 58	04 17	05 05	05 44	06 07	06 28	06 56	07 33
56	04 23	05 08	05 46	06 15	06 39	07 09	07 47
54	04 29	05 11	05 47	06 23	06 48	07 20	07 59
52	04 34	05 14	05 48	06 29	06 57	07 30	08 10
50	04 38	05 17	05 49	06 35	07 04	07 38	08 19
45	04 47	05 22	05 51	06 48	07 20	07 57	08 39
N 40	04 54	05 26	05 53	06 59	07 33	08 12	08 55
35	05 00	05 30	05 55	07 08	07 45	08 25	09 09
30	05 04	05 32	05 56	07 17	07 55	08 36	09 21
20	05 11	05 37	05 59	07 31	08 12	08 55	09 42
N 10	05 15	05 40	06 01	07 43	08 27	09 12	09 59
0	05 18	05 42	06 02	07 55	08 41	09 28	10 16
S 10	05 19	05 43	06 04	08 07	08 55	09 43	10 33
20	05 18	05 44	06 06	08 19	09 10	10 00	10 51
30	05 16	05 43	06 07	08 34	09 27	10 20	11 11
35	05 14	05 43	06 08	08 42	09 37	10 31	11 23
40	05 11	05 42	06 09	08 52	09 49	10 44	11 37
45	05 07	05 41	06 10	09 03	10 03	11 00	11 54
S 50	05 02	05 40	06 12	09 17	10 19	11 19	12 14
52	04 59	05 39	06 12	09 24	10 27	11 28	12 24
54	04 56	05 38	06 13	09 31	10 36	11 38	12 34
56	04 53	05 37	06 14	09 39	10 46	11 50	12 47
58	04 49	05 35	06 15	09 48	10 58	12 03	13 01
S 60	04 45	05 34	06 15	09 58	11 11	12 19	13 18

Lat.	Sunset	Twilight Civil	Twilight Naut.	Moonset 25	26	27	28
°	h m	h m	h m	h m	h m	h m	h m
N 72	18 48	20 00	21 44	25 53	01 53	□	□
N 70	18 44	19 48	21 14	24 29	00 29	□	□
68	18 40	19 38	20 53	23 50	25 29	01 29	03 07
66	18 37	19 30	20 37	23 24	24 49	00 49	02 06
64	18 34	19 23	20 24	23 03	24 22	00 22	01 32
62	18 32	19 17	20 13	22 47	24 01	00 01	01 07
60	18 30	19 12	20 04	22 33	23 43	24 47	00 47
N 58	18 28	19 08	19 56	22 21	23 29	24 31	00 31
56	18 27	19 04	19 50	22 11	23 17	24 17	00 17
54	18 25	19 01	19 44	22 02	23 06	24 05	00 05
52	18 24	18 58	19 39	21 54	22 57	23 55	24 47
50	18 23	18 55	19 34	21 47	22 48	23 46	24 38
45	18 21	18 50	19 25	21 32	22 30	23 26	24 17
N 40	18 18	18 46	19 18	21 20	22 16	23 10	24 01
35	18 17	18 42	19 12	21 09	22 03	22 56	23 47
30	18 15	18 39	19 07	21 00	21 53	22 45	23 35
20	18 13	18 35	19 01	20 44	21 34	22 25	23 14
N 10	18 11	18 32	18 56	20 30	21 18	22 07	22 56
0	18 09	18 29	18 54	20 17	21 03	21 51	22 40
S 10	18 07	18 28	18 52	20 04	20 48	21 35	22 23
20	18 05	18 27	18 53	19 50	20 32	21 17	22 05
30	18 03	18 27	18 55	19 34	20 14	20 57	21 44
35	18 02	18 28	18 57	19 25	20 03	20 45	21 32
40	18 01	18 28	19 00	19 15	19 51	20 32	21 18
45	18 00	18 29	19 03	19 03	19 37	20 16	21 01
S 50	17 58	18 31	19 08	18 48	19 19	19 57	20 41
52	17 58	18 31	19 11	18 41	19 11	19 47	20 31
54	17 57	18 32	19 13	18 33	19 02	19 37	20 20
56	17 56	18 33	19 16	18 25	18 51	19 25	20 08
58	17 55	18 34	19 20	18 15	18 40	19 12	19 54
S 60	17 54	18 36	19 24	18 04	18 26	18 56	19 37

Day	SUN Eqn. of Time 00h	12h	SUN Mer. Pass.	MOON Mer. Pass. Upper	Lower	Age	Phase
d	m s	m s	h m	h m	h m	d	%
25	05 59	05 50	12 06	14 06	01 43	03	8
26	05 41	05 32	12 06	14 52	02 29	04	13
27	05 23	05 14	12 05	15 39	03 15	05	20

UT	ARIES GHA	VENUS −4.5 GHA	Dec	MARS −0.8 GHA	Dec	JUPITER −2.1 GHA	Dec	SATURN +0.3 GHA	Dec	STARS Name	SHA	Dec
28 00	185 48.9	135 22.6	N21 45.6	27 08.4	N12 42.3	145 32.6	N14 43.7	339 12.9	S 8 02.3	Acamar	315 19.3	S40 15.5
01	200 51.4	150 22.6	46.4	42 11.4	42.4	160 34.5	43.9	354 15.6	02.3	Achernar	335 27.9	S57 10.6
02	215 53.9	165 22.6	47.2	57 14.5	42.5	175 36.4	44.0	9 18.2	02.2	Acrux	173 09.6	S63 10.2
03	230 56.3	180 22.5	.. 48.0	72 17.5	.. 42.6	190 38.4	.. 44.2	24 20.8	... 02.1	Adhara	255 13.2	S28 59.7
04	245 58.8	195 22.5	48.8	87 20.5	42.7	205 40.3	44.4	39 23.4	02.1	Aldebaran	290 50.5	N16 31.9
05	261 01.3	210 22.5	49.6	102 23.5	42.8	220 42.2	44.5	54 26.1	02.0			
06	276 03.7	225 22.4	N21 50.4	117 26.5	N12 42.9	235 44.2	N14 44.7	69 28.7	S 8 01.9	Alioth	166 20.8	N55 53.4
W 07	291 06.2	240 22.4	51.2	132 29.6	43.0	250 46.1	44.9	84 31.3	01.9	Alkaid	152 59.1	N49 14.9
E 08	306 08.6	255 22.4	52.0	147 32.6	43.1	265 48.0	45.0	99 34.0	01.8	Al Na'ir	27 45.1	S46 53.9
D 09	321 11.1	270 22.3	.. 52.8	162 35.6	.. 43.2	280 50.0	.. 45.2	114 36.6	.. 01.7	Alnilam	275 47.3	S 1 11.9
N 10	336 13.6	285 22.3	53.6	177 38.6	43.4	295 51.9	45.4	129 39.2	01.7	Alphard	217 56.7	S 8 43.0
E 11	351 16.0	300 22.3	54.3	192 41.6	43.5	310 53.8	45.6	144 41.8	01.6			
S 12	6 18.5	315 22.2	N21 55.1	207 44.6	N12 43.6	325 55.8	N14 45.7	159 44.5	S 8 01.5	Alphecca	126 11.5	N26 40.2
D 13	21 21.0	330 22.2	55.9	222 47.7	43.7	340 57.7	45.9	174 47.1	01.5	Alpheratz	357 44.7	N29 09.4
A 14	36 23.4	345 22.2	56.7	237 50.7	43.8	355 59.6	46.1	189 49.7	01.4	Altair	62 09.2	N 8 54.0
Y 15	51 25.9	0 22.2	.. 57.5	252 53.7	.. 43.9	11 01.6	.. 46.2	204 52.4	.. 01.3	Ankaa	353 16.9	S42 14.4
16	66 28.4	15 22.1	58.3	267 56.7	44.0	26 03.5	46.4	219 55.0	01.3	Antares	112 27.1	S26 27.5
17	81 30.8	30 22.1	59.1	282 59.7	44.1	41 05.4	46.6	234 57.6	01.2			
18	96 33.3	45 22.1	N21 59.9	298 02.7	N14 44.2	56 07.3	N14 46.7	250 00.2	S 8 01.1	Arcturus	145 56.2	N19 06.9
19	111 35.8	60 22.0	22 00.7	313 05.7	44.3	71 09.3	46.9	265 02.9	01.1	Atria	107 29.5	S69 02.7
20	126 38.2	75 22.0	01.4	328 08.7	44.4	86 11.2	47.1	280 05.5	01.0	Avior	234 18.1	S59 33.4
21	141 40.7	90 22.0	.. 02.2	343 11.7	.. 44.5	101 13.1	.. 47.3	295 08.1	.. 00.9	Bellatrix	278 33.0	N 6 21.5
22	156 43.1	105 22.0	03.0	358 14.7	44.6	116 15.1	47.4	310 10.7	00.9	Betelgeuse	271 02.3	N 7 24.4
23	171 45.6	120 21.9	03.8	13 17.7	44.7	131 17.0	47.6	325 13.4	00.8			
29 00	186 48.1	135 21.9	N22 04.6	28 20.7	N14 44.8	146 18.9	N14 47.8	340 16.0	S 8 00.7	Canopus	263 56.6	S52 42.6
01	201 50.5	150 21.9	05.4	43 23.7	44.9	161 20.9	47.9	355 18.6	00.7	Capella	280 35.9	N46 00.6
02	216 53.0	165 21.9	06.1	58 26.7	44.9	176 22.8	48.1	10 21.3	00.6	Deneb	49 32.3	N45 19.3
03	231 55.5	180 21.8	.. 06.9	73 29.7	.. 45.0	191 24.7	.. 48.3	25 23.9	.. 00.5	Denebola	182 34.2	N14 30.0
04	246 57.9	195 21.8	07.7	88 32.7	45.1	206 26.6	48.4	40 26.5	00.5	Diphda	348 57.1	S17 55.2
05	262 00.4	210 21.8	08.5	103 35.7	45.2	221 28.6	48.6	55 29.2	00.4			
06	277 02.9	225 21.8	N22 09.2	118 38.7	N12 45.3	236 30.5	N14 48.8	70 31.8	S 8 00.3	Dubhe	193 52.1	N61 41.0
T 07	292 05.3	240 21.7	10.0	133 41.6	45.4	251 32.4	49.0	85 34.4	00.3	Elnath	278 13.8	N28 37.0
H 08	307 07.8	255 21.7	10.8	148 44.6	45.5	266 34.4	49.1	100 37.0	00.2	Eltanin	90 46.4	N51 29.0
U 09	322 10.2	270 21.7	.. 11.6	163 47.6	.. 45.6	281 36.3	.. 49.3	115 39.7	.. 00.1	Enif	33 48.2	N 9 55.8
R 10	337 12.7	285 21.7	12.3	178 50.6	45.7	296 38.2	49.5	130 42.3	00.1	Fomalhaut	15 25.2	S29 33.4
S 11	352 15.2	300 21.7	13.1	193 53.6	45.8	311 40.1	49.6	145 44.9	8 00.0			
D 12	7 17.6	315 21.6	N22 13.9	208 56.6	N12 45.9	326 42.1	N14 49.8	160 47.6	S 7 59.9	Gacrux	172 01.3	S57 11.1
A 13	22 20.1	330 21.6	14.7	223 59.6	46.0	341 44.0	50.0	175 50.2	59.9	Gienah	175 52.9	S17 36.8
Y 14	37 22.6	345 21.6	15.4	239 02.5	46.1	356 45.9	50.2	190 52.8	59.8	Hadar	148 48.5	S60 25.9
15	52 25.0	0 21.6	.. 16.2	254 05.5	.. 46.1	11 47.9	.. 50.3	205 55.4	.. 59.7	Hamal	328 02.0	N23 31.2
16	67 27.5	15 21.6	17.0	269 08.5	46.2	26 49.8	50.5	220 58.1	59.7	Kaus Aust.	83 44.9	S34 22.5
17	82 30.0	30 21.5	17.7	284 11.5	46.3	41 51.7	50.7	236 00.7	59.6			
18	97 32.4	45 21.5	N22 18.5	299 14.4	N12 46.4	56 53.6	N14 50.8	251 03.3	S 7 59.5	Kochab	137 19.0	N74 06.1
19	112 34.9	60 21.5	19.3	314 17.4	46.5	71 55.6	51.0	266 06.0	59.5	Markab	13 39.5	N15 16.2
20	127 37.4	75 21.5	20.0	329 20.4	46.6	86 57.5	51.2	281 08.6	59.4	Menkar	314 16.2	N 4 08.1
21	142 39.8	90 21.5	.. 20.8	344 23.4	.. 46.7	101 59.4	.. 51.3	296 11.2	.. 59.3	Menkent	148 08.2	S36 25.9
22	157 42.3	105 21.5	21.6	359 26.3	46.8	117 01.4	51.5	311 13.9	59.3	Miaplacidus	221 39.3	S69 46.4
23	172 44.7	120 21.4	22.3	14 29.3	46.8	132 03.3	51.7	326 16.5	59.2			
30 00	187 47.2	135 21.4	N22 23.1	29 32.3	N12 46.9	147 05.2	N14 51.9	341 19.1	S 7 59.1	Mirfak	308 41.9	N49 54.3
01	202 49.7	150 21.4	23.9	44 35.2	47.0	162 07.1	52.0	356 21.7	59.1	Nunki	75 59.4	S26 16.7
02	217 52.1	165 21.4	24.6	59 38.2	47.1	177 09.1	52.2	11 24.4	59.0	Peacock	53 20.8	S56 41.4
03	232 54.6	180 21.4	.. 25.4	74 41.2	.. 47.2	192 11.0	.. 52.4	26 27.0	.. 58.9	Pollux	243 28.7	N27 59.7
04	247 57.1	195 21.4	26.1	89 44.1	47.2	207 12.9	52.5	41 29.6	58.9	Procyon	245 00.5	N 5 11.4
05	262 59.5	210 21.4	26.9	104 47.1	47.3	222 14.8	52.7	56 32.3	58.8			
06	278 02.0	225 21.3	N22 27.6	119 50.1	N12 47.4	237 16.8	N14 52.9	71 34.9	S 7 58.7	Rasalhague	96 07.2	N12 33.0
07	293 04.5	240 21.3	28.4	134 53.0	47.5	252 18.7	53.1	86 37.5	58.7	Regulus	207 44.2	N11 54.2
08	308 06.9	255 21.3	29.2	149 56.0	47.6	267 20.6	53.2	101 40.2	58.6	Rigel	281 13.0	S 8 11.5
F 09	323 09.4	270 21.3	.. 29.9	164 58.9	.. 47.6	282 22.6	.. 53.4	116 42.8	.. 58.5	Rigil Kent.	139 52.3	S60 53.1
R 10	338 11.9	285 21.3	30.7	180 01.9	47.7	297 24.5	53.6	131 45.4	58.5	Sabik	102 13.4	S15 44.4
I 11	353 14.3	300 21.3	31.4	195 04.8	47.8	312 26.4	53.7	146 48.0	58.4			
D 12	8 16.8	315 21.3	N22 32.2	210 07.8	N12 47.9	327 28.3	N14 53.9	161 50.7	S 7 58.3	Schedar	349 42.1	N56 36.3
A 13	23 19.2	330 21.3	32.9	225 10.7	48.0	342 30.3	54.1	176 53.3	58.3	Shaula	96 23.0	S37 06.6
Y 14	38 21.7	345 21.3	33.7	240 13.7	48.0	357 32.2	54.2	191 55.9	58.2	Sirius	258 34.5	S16 44.3
15	53 24.2	0 21.3	.. 34.4	255 16.6	.. 48.1	12 34.1	.. 54.4	206 58.6	.. 58.1	Spica	158 31.8	S11 13.7
16	68 26.6	15 21.3	35.2	270 19.6	48.2	27 36.0	54.6	222 01.2	58.1	Suhail	222 52.8	S43 29.3
17	83 29.1	30 21.2	35.9	285 22.5	48.3	42 38.0	54.8	237 03.8	58.0			
18	98 31.6	45 21.2	N22 36.7	300 25.5	N12 48.3	57 39.9	N14 54.9	252 06.5	S 7 57.9	Vega	80 39.5	N38 47.5
19	113 34.0	60 21.2	37.4	315 28.4	48.4	72 41.8	55.1	267 09.1	57.9	Zuben'ubi	137 06.1	S16 05.6
20	128 36.5	75 21.2	38.2	330 31.4	48.5	87 43.7	55.3	282 11.7	57.8		SHA	Mer. Pass.
21	143 39.0	90 21.2	.. 38.9	345 34.3	.. 48.6	102 45.7	.. 55.4	297 14.4	.. 57.7		° ′	h m
22	158 41.4	105 21.2	39.6	0 37.2	48.6	117 47.6	55.6	312 17.0	57.7	Venus	308 33.8	14 59
23	173 43.9	120 21.2	40.4	15 40.2	48.7	132 49.5	55.8	327 19.6	57.6	Mars	201 32.6	22 02
	h m									Jupiter	319 30.9	14 13
Mer. Pass. 11 30.9	v 0.0	d 0.8		v 3.0	d 0.1	v 1.9	d 0.2	v 2.6	d 0.1	Saturn	153 27.9	1 19

UT	SUN GHA	SUN Dec	MOON GHA	v	MOON Dec	d	HP
d h	° ′	° ′	° ′	′	° ′	′	′
28 00	178 43.8	N 3 03.7	121 08.6	11.7	N21 24.6	2.3	54.2
01	193 44.0	04.7	135 39.3	11.6	21 26.9	2.3	54.3
02	208 44.2	05.6	150 09.9	11.6	21 29.2	2.2	54.3
03	223 44.4 ..	06.6	164 40.6	11.6	21 31.4	2.0	54.3
04	238 44.6	07.6	179 11.2	11.6	21 33.4	2.0	54.3
05	253 44.7	08.6	193 41.8	11.5	21 35.4	1.9	54.3
06	268 44.9	N 3 09.5	208 12.3	11.6	N21 37.3	1.8	54.3
W 07	283 45.1	10.5	222 42.9	11.5	21 39.1	1.6	54.3
E 08	298 45.3	11.5	237 13.4	11.5	21 40.7	1.6	54.3
D 09	313 45.5 ..	12.5	251 43.9	11.5	21 42.3	1.5	54.3
N 10	328 45.7	13.4	266 14.4	11.4	21 43.8	1.3	54.4
E 11	343 45.9	14.4	280 44.8	11.4	21 45.1	1.3	54.4
S 12	358 46.1	N 3 15.4	295 15.2	11.4	N21 46.4	1.1	54.4
D 13	13 46.2	16.4	309 45.6	11.4	21 47.5	1.1	54.4
A 14	28 46.4	17.3	324 16.0	11.3	21 48.6	1.0	54.4
Y 15	43 46.6 ..	18.3	338 46.3	11.4	21 49.6	0.8	54.4
16	58 46.8	19.3	353 16.7	11.3	21 50.4	0.8	54.4
17	73 47.0	20.3	7 47.0	11.3	21 51.2	0.6	54.5
18	88 47.2	N 3 21.2	22 17.3	11.2	N21 51.8	0.5	54.5
19	103 47.4	22.2	36 47.5	11.3	21 52.3	0.5	54.5
20	118 47.6	23.2	51 17.8	11.2	21 52.8	0.3	54.5
21	133 47.8 ..	24.2	65 48.0	11.2	21 53.1	0.2	54.5
22	148 47.9	25.1	80 18.2	11.2	21 53.3	0.1	54.5
23	163 48.1	26.1	94 48.4	11.2	21 53.4	0.1	54.5
29 00	178 48.3	N 3 27.1	109 18.6	11.2	N21 53.5	0.1	54.6
01	193 48.5	28.1	123 48.8	11.1	21 53.4	0.2	54.6
02	208 48.7	29.0	138 18.9	11.1	21 53.2	0.3	54.6
03	223 48.9 ..	30.0	152 49.0	11.1	21 52.9	0.4	54.6
04	238 49.1	31.0	167 19.1	11.1	21 52.5	0.5	54.6
05	253 49.3	32.0	181 49.2	11.1	21 52.0	0.7	54.7
06	268 49.4	N 3 32.9	196 19.3	11.1	N21 51.3	0.7	54.7
T 07	283 49.6	33.9	210 49.4	11.0	21 50.6	0.8	54.7
H 08	298 49.8	34.9	225 19.4	11.0	21 49.8	1.0	54.7
U 09	313 50.0 ..	35.8	239 49.4	11.1	21 48.8	1.0	54.7
R 10	328 50.2	36.8	254 19.5	11.0	21 47.8	1.1	54.7
S 11	343 50.4	37.8	268 49.5	11.0	21 46.7	1.3	54.8
D 12	358 50.6	N 3 38.8	283 19.5	10.9	N21 45.4	1.4	54.8
A 13	13 50.8	39.7	297 49.4	11.0	21 44.0	1.4	54.8
Y 14	28 50.9	40.7	312 19.4	11.0	21 42.6	1.6	54.8
15	43 51.1 ..	41.7	326 49.4	11.0	21 41.0	1.7	54.8
16	58 51.3	42.6	341 19.3	10.9	21 39.3	1.8	54.9
17	73 51.5	43.6	355 49.2	11.0	21 37.5	1.9	54.9
18	88 51.7	N 3 44.6	10 19.2	10.9	N21 35.6	2.0	54.9
19	103 51.9	45.6	24 49.1	10.9	21 33.6	2.1	54.9
20	118 52.1	46.5	39 19.0	10.9	21 31.5	2.2	55.0
21	133 52.3 ..	47.5	53 48.9	10.9	21 29.3	2.3	55.0
22	148 52.4	48.5	68 18.8	10.8	21 27.0	2.5	55.0
23	163 52.6	49.4	82 48.6	10.9	21 24.5	2.5	55.0
30 00	178 52.8	N 3 50.4	97 18.5	10.9	N21 22.0	2.6	55.0
01	193 53.0	51.4	111 48.4	10.8	21 19.4	2.8	55.1
02	208 53.2	52.4	126 18.2	10.9	21 16.6	2.9	55.1
03	223 53.4 ..	53.3	140 48.1	10.8	21 13.7	2.9	55.1
04	238 53.6	54.3	155 17.9	10.9	21 10.8	3.1	55.1
05	253 53.8	55.3	169 47.8	10.8	21 07.7	3.2	55.2
06	268 53.9	N 3 56.2	184 17.6	10.8	N21 04.5	3.3	55.2
07	283 54.1	57.2	198 47.4	10.8	21 01.2	3.4	55.2
F 08	298 54.3	58.2	213 17.2	10.9	20 57.8	3.5	55.2
R 09	313 54.5	3 59.1	227 47.1	10.8	20 54.3	3.6	55.3
I 10	328 54.7	4 00.1	242 16.9	10.8	20 50.7	3.7	55.3
D 11	343 54.9	01.1	256 46.7	10.8	20 47.0	3.8	55.3
A 12	358 55.1	N 4 02.1	271 16.5	10.8	N20 43.2	3.9	55.3
Y 13	13 55.3	03.0	285 46.3	10.8	20 39.3	4.1	55.4
14	28 55.4	04.0	300 16.1	10.8	20 35.2	4.1	55.4
15	43 55.6 ..	05.0	314 45.9	10.8	20 31.1	4.3	55.4
16	58 55.8	05.9	329 15.7	10.8	20 26.8	4.3	55.5
17	73 56.0	06.9	343 45.5	10.8	20 22.5	4.5	55.5
18	88 56.2	N 4 07.9	358 15.3	10.8	N20 18.0	4.5	55.5
19	103 56.4	08.8	12 45.1	10.7	20 13.5	4.7	55.5
20	118 56.6	09.8	27 14.8	10.8	20 08.8	4.8	55.6
21	133 56.8 ..	10.8	41 44.6	10.8	20 04.0	4.8	55.6
22	148 56.9	11.7	56 14.4	10.8	19 59.2	5.0	55.6
23	163 57.1	12.7	70 44.2	10.8	N19 54.2	5.1	55.7
	SD 16.0	d 1.0	SD 14.8		14.9		15.1

Lat.	Twilight Naut.	Twilight Civil	Sunrise	Moonrise 28	29	30	31
°	h m	h m	h m	h m	h m	h m	h m
N 72	02 07	03 57	05 10	□	□	□	□
N 70	02 41	04 11	05 16	□	□	□	07 51
68	03 05	04 22	05 20	04 57	05 29	07 01	08 45
66	03 23	04 31	05 24	05 58	06 42	07 51	09 18
64	03 37	04 39	05 28	06 32	07 18	08 22	09 42
62	03 49	04 45	05 31	06 57	07 44	08 46	10 00
60	03 59	04 51	05 33	07 17	08 04	09 05	10 16
N 58	04 07	04 56	05 36	07 33	08 21	09 20	10 29
56	04 14	05 00	05 38	07 47	08 35	09 33	10 40
54	04 21	05 04	05 39	07 59	08 47	09 45	10 50
52	04 26	05 07	05 41	08 10	08 58	09 55	10 59
50	04 31	05 10	05 43	08 19	09 08	10 04	11 07
45	04 41	05 16	05 46	08 39	09 28	10 23	11 23
N 40	04 49	05 21	05 48	08 55	09 44	10 38	11 37
35	04 54	05 25	05 51	09 09	09 58	10 51	11 49
30	04 58	05 29	05 53	09 21	10 10	11 03	11 59
20	05 02	05 34	05 56	09 42	10 31	11 22	12 16
N 10	05 08	05 38	05 59	09 59	10 49	11 39	12 31
0	05 13	05 41	06 01	10 16	11 05	11 55	12 45
S 10	05 17	05 43	06 04	10 33	11 22	12 11	12 59
20	05 18	05 44	06 06	10 51	11 40	12 28	13 14
30	05 17	05 45	06 09	11 11	12 01	12 47	13 31
35	05 16	05 45	06 11	11 23	12 13	12 59	13 41
40	05 14	05 45	06 12	11 37	12 26	13 12	13 53
45	05 11	05 45	06 14	11 54	12 43	13 27	14 06
S 50	05 07	05 44	06 16	12 14	13 03	13 46	14 22
52	05 05	05 44	06 18	12 24	13 13	13 55	14 30
54	05 02	05 43	06 19	12 34	13 23	14 04	14 38
56	04 59	05 43	06 20	12 47	13 36	14 16	14 48
58	04 56	05 42	06 21	13 01	13 50	14 28	14 58
S 60	04 53	05 41	06 23	13 18	14 06	14 43	15 11

Lat.	Sunset	Twilight Civil	Twilight Naut.	Moonset 28	29	30	31
°	h m	h m	h m	h m	h m	h m	h m
N 72	19 02	20 16	22 11	□	□	□	□
N 70	18 56	20 01	21 34	□	□	□	05 23
68	18 51	19 50	21 09	03 07	04 17	04 29	04 29
66	18 47	19 40	20 50	02 06	03 04	03 38	03 55
64	18 43	19 32	20 35	01 32	02 28	03 06	03 31
62	18 40	19 26	20 23	01 07	02 02	02 43	03 12
60	18 37	19 20	20 13	00 47	01 41	02 24	02 56
N 58	18 35	19 15	20 04	00 31	01 25	02 08	02 42
56	18 33	19 11	19 57	00 17	01 10	01 55	02 31
54	18 31	19 07	19 50	00 05	00 58	01 43	02 20
52	18 29	19 03	19 45	24 47	00 47	01 33	02 11
50	18 28	19 00	19 40	24 38	00 38	01 24	02 03
45	18 24	18 54	19 29	24 17	00 17	01 04	01 46
N 40	18 22	18 49	19 21	24 01	00 01	00 48	01 31
35	18 19	18 45	19 14	23 47	24 35	00 35	01 19
30	18 17	18 41	19 09	23 35	24 23	00 23	01 09
20	18 14	18 36	19 01	23 14	24 03	00 03	00 50
N 10	18 11	18 32	18 56	22 56	23 46	24 34	00 34
0	18 08	18 29	18 53	22 40	23 29	24 19	00 19
S 10	18 05	18 27	18 51	22 23	23 13	24 04	00 04
20	18 03	18 25	18 50	22 05	22 55	23 48	24 42
30	18 00	18 23	18 51	21 44	22 35	23 29	24 24
35	17 58	18 23	18 53	21 32	22 23	23 18	24 17
40	17 56	18 23	18 55	21 18	22 09	23 06	24 07
45	17 54	18 23	18 57	21 01	21 53	22 51	23 54
S 50	17 52	18 24	19 01	20 41	21 33	22 33	23 39
52	17 51	18 24	19 03	20 31	21 24	22 24	23 31
54	17 50	18 25	19 06	20 20	21 13	22 15	23 23
56	17 48	18 25	19 08	20 08	21 01	22 04	23 14
58	17 47	18 26	19 11	19 54	20 47	21 51	23 04
S 60	17 45	18 27	19 15	19 37	20 30	21 37	22 52

SUN			MOON				
Day	Eqn. of Time 00h	Eqn. of Time 12h	Mer. Pass.	Mer. Pass. Upper	Lower	Age	Phase
d	m s	m s	h m	h m	h m	d	%
28	05 05	04 56	12 05	16 28	04 03	06	28
29	04 47	04 38	12 05	17 17	04 52	07	37
30	04 29	04 20	12 04	18 07	05 42	08	47

2012 MAR. 31, APR. 1, 2 (SAT., SUN., MON.)

UT	ARIES GHA	VENUS −4.5 GHA	Dec	MARS −0.7 GHA	Dec	JUPITER −2.1 GHA	Dec	SATURN +0.3 GHA	Dec	Star Name	SHA	Dec
31 00	188 46.4	135 21.2	N22 41.1	30 43.1	N12 48.8	147 51.4	N14 56.0	342 22.3	S 7 57.5	Acamar	315 19.3	S40 15.5
01	203 48.8	150 21.2	41.9	45 46.1	48.8	162 53.4	56.1	357 24.9	57.5	Achernar	335 27.9	S57 10.5
02	218 51.3	165 21.2	42.6	60 49.0	48.9	177 55.3	56.3	12 27.5	57.4	Acrux	173 09.6	S63 10.2
03	233 53.7	180 21.2	.. 43.3	75 51.9	.. 49.0	192 57.2	.. 56.5	27 30.2	.. 57.3	Adhara	255 13.2	S28 59.7
04	248 56.2	195 21.2	44.1	90 54.9	49.0	207 59.1	56.6	42 32.8	57.2	Aldebaran	290 50.5	N16 31.9
05	263 58.7	210 21.2	44.8	105 57.8	49.1	223 01.1	56.8	57 35.4	57.2			
06	279 01.1	225 21.2	N22 45.6	121 00.7	N12 49.2	238 03.0	N14 57.0	72 38.0	S 7 57.1	Alioth	166 20.8	N55 53.4
07	294 03.6	240 21.2	46.3	136 03.6	49.2	253 04.9	57.1	87 40.7	57.0	Alkaid	152 59.1	N49 14.9
S 08	309 06.1	255 21.2	47.0	151 06.6	49.3	268 06.8	57.3	102 43.3	57.0	Al Na'ir	27 45.1	S46 53.9
A 09	324 08.5	270 21.2	.. 47.8	166 09.5	.. 49.4	283 08.8	.. 57.5	117 45.9	.. 56.9	Alnilam	275 47.3	S 1 11.9
T 10	339 11.0	285 21.2	48.5	181 12.4	49.4	298 10.7	57.7	132 48.6	56.8	Alphard	217 56.7	S 8 43.0
U 11	354 13.5	300 21.2	49.2	196 15.3	49.5	313 12.6	57.8	147 51.2	56.8			
R 12	9 15.9	315 21.2	N22 50.0	211 18.3	N12 49.6	328 14.5	N14 58.0	162 53.8	S 7 56.7	Alphecca	126 11.4	N26 40.2
D 13	24 18.4	330 21.2	50.7	226 21.2	49.6	343 16.4	58.2	177 56.5	56.6	Alpheratz	357 44.7	N29 09.4
A 14	39 20.8	345 21.2	51.4	241 24.1	49.7	358 18.4	58.3	192 59.1	56.6	Altair	62 09.1	N 8 54.0
Y 15	54 23.3	0 21.2	.. 52.2	256 27.0	.. 49.8	13 20.3	.. 58.5	208 01.7	.. 56.5	Ankaa	353 16.9	S42 14.3
16	69 25.8	15 21.2	52.9	271 29.9	49.8	28 22.2	58.7	223 04.4	56.4	Antares	112 27.1	S26 27.5
17	84 28.2	30 21.2	53.6	286 32.9	49.9	43 24.1	58.8	238 07.0	56.4			
18	99 30.7	45 21.2	N22 54.3	301 35.8	N12 49.9	58 26.1	N14 59.0	253 09.6	S 7 56.3	Arcturus	145 56.2	N19 06.9
19	114 33.2	60 21.2	55.1	316 38.7	50.0	73 28.0	59.2	268 12.3	56.2	Atria	107 29.4	S69 02.7
20	129 35.6	75 21.2	55.8	331 41.6	50.1	88 29.9	59.4	283 14.9	56.2	Avior	234 18.1	S59 33.4
21	144 38.1	90 21.2	.. 56.5	346 44.5	.. 50.1	103 31.8	.. 59.5	298 17.5	.. 56.1	Bellatrix	278 33.0	N 6 21.5
22	159 40.6	105 21.3	57.2	1 47.4	50.2	118 33.8	59.7	313 20.2	56.0	Betelgeuse	271 02.3	N 7 24.4
23	174 43.0	120 21.3	58.0	16 50.3	50.2	133 35.7	14 59.9	328 22.8	56.0			
1 00	189 45.5	135 21.3	N22 58.7	31 53.2	N12 50.3	148 37.6	N15 00.0	343 25.4	S 7 55.9	Canopus	263 56.6	S52 42.6
01	204 48.0	150 21.3	22 59.4	46 56.1	50.4	163 39.5	00.2	358 28.1	55.8	Capella	280 35.9	N46 00.6
02	219 50.4	165 21.3	23 00.1	61 59.0	50.4	178 41.4	00.4	13 30.7	55.8	Deneb	49 32.3	N45 19.3
03	234 52.9	180 21.3	.. 00.8	77 02.0	.. 50.5	193 43.4	.. 00.6	28 33.3	.. 55.7	Denebola	182 34.2	N14 30.0
04	249 55.3	195 21.3	01.5	92 04.9	50.5	208 45.3	00.7	43 36.0	55.6	Diphda	348 57.1	S17 55.2
05	264 57.8	210 21.3	02.3	107 07.8	50.6	223 47.2	00.9	58 38.6	55.6			
06	280 00.3	225 21.3	N23 03.0	122 10.7	N12 50.6	238 49.1	N15 01.1	73 41.2	S 7 55.5	Dubhe	193 52.1	N61 41.0
07	295 02.7	240 21.3	03.7	137 13.5	50.7	253 51.1	01.2	88 43.9	55.4	Elnath	278 13.8	N28 37.0
S 08	310 05.2	255 21.4	04.4	152 16.4	50.7	268 53.0	01.4	103 46.5	55.4	Eltanin	90 46.4	N51 29.0
U 09	325 07.7	270 21.4	.. 05.1	167 19.3	.. 50.8	283 54.9	.. 01.6	118 49.1	.. 55.3	Enif	33 48.2	N 9 55.8
N 10	340 10.1	285 21.4	05.8	182 22.2	50.9	298 56.8	01.7	133 51.8	55.2	Fomalhaut	15 25.2	S29 33.4
D 11	355 12.6	300 21.4	06.5	197 25.1	50.9	313 58.7	01.9	148 54.4	55.1			
A 12	10 15.1	315 21.4	N23 07.3	212 28.0	N12 51.0	329 00.7	N15 02.1	163 57.0	S 7 55.1	Gacrux	172 01.3	S57 11.1
Y 13	25 17.5	330 21.4	08.0	227 30.9	51.0	344 02.6	02.3	178 59.7	55.0	Gienah	175 52.8	S17 36.8
14	40 20.0	345 21.5	08.7	242 33.8	51.1	359 04.5	02.4	194 02.3	54.9	Hadar	148 48.5	S60 25.9
15	55 22.5	0 21.5	.. 09.4	257 36.7	.. 51.1	14 06.4	.. 02.6	209 04.9	.. 54.9	Hamal	328 02.0	N23 31.2
16	70 24.9	15 21.5	10.1	272 39.6	51.2	29 08.3	02.8	224 07.6	54.8	Kaus Aust.	83 44.9	S34 22.5
17	85 27.4	30 21.5	10.8	287 42.5	51.2	44 10.3	02.9	239 10.2	54.7			
18	100 29.8	45 21.5	N23 11.5	302 45.3	N12 51.3	59 12.2	N15 03.1	254 12.8	S 7 54.7	Kochab	137 18.9	N74 06.1
19	115 32.3	60 21.5	12.2	317 48.2	51.3	74 14.1	03.3	269 15.5	54.6	Markab	13 39.5	N15 16.2
20	130 34.8	75 21.6	12.9	332 51.1	51.3	89 16.0	03.5	284 18.1	54.5	Menkar	314 16.2	N 4 08.1
21	145 37.2	90 21.6	.. 13.6	347 54.0	.. 51.4	104 17.9	.. 03.6	299 20.8	.. 54.5	Menkent	148 08.2	S36 25.9
22	160 39.7	105 21.6	14.3	2 56.9	51.4	119 19.9	03.8	314 23.4	54.4	Miaplacidus	221 39.4	S69 46.5
23	175 42.2	120 21.6	15.0	17 59.7	51.5	134 21.8	04.0	329 26.0	54.3			
2 00	190 44.6	135 21.6	N23 15.7	33 02.6	N12 51.5	149 23.7	N15 04.1	344 28.7	S 7 54.3	Mirfak	308 42.0	N49 54.3
01	205 47.1	150 21.7	16.4	48 05.5	51.6	164 25.6	04.3	359 31.3	54.2	Nunki	75 59.4	S26 16.7
02	220 49.6	165 21.7	17.1	63 08.4	51.6	179 27.5	04.5	14 33.9	54.1	Peacock	53 20.8	S56 41.4
03	235 52.0	180 21.7	.. 17.8	78 11.2	.. 51.7	194 29.5	.. 04.6	29 36.6	.. 54.1	Pollux	243 28.7	N27 59.7
04	250 54.5	195 21.7	18.5	93 14.1	51.7	209 31.4	04.8	44 39.2	54.0	Procyon	245 00.5	N 5 11.4
05	265 56.9	210 21.8	19.2	108 17.0	51.7	224 33.3	05.0	59 41.8	53.9			
06	280 59.4	225 21.8	N23 19.9	123 19.8	N12 51.8	239 35.2	N15 05.2	74 44.5	S 7 53.9	Rasalhague	96 07.1	N12 33.0
07	296 01.9	240 21.8	20.6	138 22.7	51.8	254 37.1	05.3	89 47.1	53.8	Regulus	207 44.2	N11 54.2
M 08	311 04.3	255 21.8	21.3	153 25.6	51.9	269 39.1	05.5	104 49.7	53.7	Rigel	281 13.0	S 8 11.5
O 09	326 06.8	270 21.9	.. 22.0	168 28.4	.. 51.9	284 41.0	.. 05.7	119 52.4	.. 53.6	Rigil Kent.	139 52.3	S60 53.1
N 10	341 09.3	285 21.9	22.7	183 31.3	52.0	299 42.9	05.8	134 55.0	53.6	Sabik	102 13.4	S15 44.4
D 11	356 11.7	300 21.9	23.4	198 34.2	52.0	314 44.8	06.0	149 57.6	53.5			
A 12	11 14.2	315 22.0	N23 24.1	213 37.0	N12 52.0	329 46.7	N15 06.2	165 00.3	S 7 53.4	Schedar	349 42.1	N56 36.3
Y 13	26 16.7	330 22.0	24.7	228 39.9	52.1	344 48.7	06.4	180 02.9	53.4	Shaula	96 22.9	S37 06.6
14	41 19.1	345 22.0	25.4	243 42.7	52.1	359 50.6	06.5	195 05.5	53.3	Sirius	258 34.5	S16 44.3
15	56 21.6	0 22.0	.. 26.1	258 45.6	.. 52.1	14 52.5	.. 06.7	210 08.2	.. 53.2	Spica	158 31.8	S11 13.7
16	71 24.1	15 22.1	26.8	273 48.5	52.2	29 54.4	06.9	225 10.8	53.2	Suhail	222 52.8	S43 29.3
17	86 26.5	30 22.1	27.5	288 51.3	52.2	44 56.3	07.0	240 13.5	53.1			
18	101 29.0	45 22.1	N23 28.2	303 54.2	N12 52.3	59 58.2	N15 07.2	255 16.1	S 7 53.0	Vega	80 39.5	N38 47.5
19	116 31.4	60 22.2	28.9	318 57.0	52.3	75 00.2	07.4	270 18.7	53.0	Zuben'ubi	137 06.1	S16 05.7
20	131 33.9	75 22.2	29.5	333 59.9	52.3	90 02.1	07.5	285 21.4	52.9			
21	146 36.4	90 22.2	.. 30.2	349 02.7	.. 52.4	105 04.0	.. 07.7	300 24.0	.. 52.8		SHA	Mer. Pass.
22	161 38.8	105 22.3	30.9	4 05.6	52.4	120 05.9	07.9	315 26.6	52.8	Venus	305 35.8	14 59
23	176 41.3	120 22.3	31.6	19 08.4	52.4	135 07.8	08.1	330 29.3	52.7	Mars	202 07.7	21 48
Mer. Pass. 11 19.1		v 0.0	d 0.7	v 2.9	d 0.1	v 1.9	d 0.2	v 2.6	d 0.1	Jupiter	318 52.1	14 04
										Saturn	153 39.9	1 06

UT	SUN GHA	Dec	MOON GHA	v	Dec	d	HP
d h	° ′	° ′	° ′	′	° ′	′	′
31 00	178 57.3	N 4 13.7	85 14.0	10.8	N19 49.1	5.2	55.7
01	193 57.5	14.6	99 43.8	10.8	19 43.9	5.3	55.7
02	208 57.7	15.6	114 13.6	10.7	19 38.6	5.4	55.7
03	223 57.9	.. 16.6	128 43.3	10.8	19 33.2	5.5	55.8
04	238 58.1	17.5	143 13.1	10.8	19 27.7	5.6	55.8
05	253 58.2	18.5	157 42.9	10.8	19 22.1	5.7	55.8
S 06	268 58.4	N 4 19.5	172 12.7	10.8	N19 16.4	5.9	55.9
A 07	283 58.6	20.4	186 42.5	10.8	19 10.5	5.9	55.9
T 08	298 58.8	21.4	201 12.3	10.8	19 04.6	6.0	55.9
U 09	313 59.0	.. 22.4	215 42.1	10.8	18 58.6	6.1	56.0
R 10	328 59.2	23.3	230 11.9	10.8	18 52.5	6.2	56.0
D 11	343 59.4	24.3	244 41.7	10.8	18 46.3	6.4	56.0
A 12	358 59.5	N 4 25.3	259 11.5	10.8	N18 39.9	6.4	56.1
Y 13	13 59.7	26.2	273 41.3	10.8	18 33.5	6.5	56.1
14	28 59.9	27.2	288 11.1	10.8	18 27.0	6.7	56.1
15	44 00.1	.. 28.2	302 40.9	10.8	18 20.3	6.7	56.2
16	59 00.3	29.1	317 10.7	10.8	18 13.6	6.8	56.2
17	74 00.5	30.1	331 40.5	10.8	18 06.8	7.0	56.2
18	89 00.7	N 4 31.1	346 10.3	10.8	N17 59.8	7.0	56.3
19	104 00.9	32.0	0 40.1	10.9	17 52.8	7.1	56.3
20	119 01.0	33.0	15 10.0	10.8	17 45.7	7.3	56.3
21	134 01.2	.. 34.0	29 39.8	10.8	17 38.4	7.3	56.4
22	149 01.4	34.9	44 09.6	10.8	17 31.1	7.4	56.4
23	164 01.6	35.9	58 39.4	10.7	17 23.7	7.6	56.4
1 00	179 01.8	N 4 36.9	73 09.3	10.8	N17 16.1	7.6	56.5
01	194 02.0	37.8	87 39.1	10.8	17 08.5	7.7	56.5
02	209 02.2	38.8	102 08.9	10.9	17 00.8	7.8	56.5
03	224 02.3	.. 39.7	116 38.8	10.8	16 53.0	7.9	56.6
04	239 02.5	40.7	131 08.6	10.9	16 45.1	8.0	56.6
05	254 02.7	41.7	145 38.5	10.8	16 37.1	8.1	56.6
06	269 02.9	N 4 42.6	160 08.3	10.9	N16 29.0	8.2	56.7
07	284 03.1	43.6	174 38.2	10.8	16 20.8	8.3	56.7
S 08	299 03.3	44.6	189 08.0	10.9	16 12.5	8.4	56.8
U 09	314 03.5	.. 45.5	203 37.9	10.9	16 04.1	8.5	56.8
N 10	329 03.6	46.5	218 07.7	10.9	15 55.6	8.6	56.8
D 11	344 03.8	47.4	232 37.6	10.8	15 47.0	8.6	56.9
A 12	359 04.0	N 4 48.4	247 07.4	10.9	N15 38.4	8.8	56.9
Y 13	14 04.2	49.4	261 37.3	10.9	15 29.6	8.9	56.9
14	29 04.4	50.3	276 07.2	10.8	15 20.7	8.9	57.0
15	44 04.6	.. 51.3	290 37.0	10.9	15 11.8	9.0	57.0
16	59 04.7	52.3	305 06.9	10.9	15 02.8	9.1	57.0
17	74 04.9	53.2	319 36.8	10.8	14 53.7	9.3	57.1
18	89 05.1	N 4 54.2	334 06.6	10.9	N14 44.4	9.3	57.1
19	104 05.3	55.1	348 36.5	10.9	14 35.1	9.3	57.2
20	119 05.5	56.1	3 06.4	10.8	14 25.8	9.5	57.2
21	134 05.7	.. 57.1	17 36.2	10.9	14 16.3	9.6	57.2
22	149 05.9	58.0	32 06.1	10.9	14 06.7	9.6	57.3
23	164 06.0	59.0	46 36.0	10.9	13 57.1	9.8	57.3
2 00	179 06.2	N 4 59.9	61 05.9	10.8	N13 47.3	9.8	57.4
01	194 06.4	5 00.9	75 35.7	10.9	13 37.5	9.9	57.4
02	209 06.6	01.9	90 05.6	10.9	13 27.6	10.0	57.4
03	224 06.8	.. 02.8	104 35.5	10.8	13 17.6	10.1	57.5
04	239 07.0	03.8	119 05.3	10.9	13 07.5	10.1	57.5
05	254 07.2	04.7	133 35.2	10.8	12 57.4	10.3	57.6
06	269 07.3	N 5 05.7	148 05.0	10.9	N12 47.1	10.3	57.6
07	284 07.5	06.7	162 34.9	10.9	12 36.8	10.4	57.6
M 08	299 07.7	07.6	177 04.8	10.8	12 26.4	10.4	57.7
O 09	314 07.9	.. 08.6	191 34.6	10.9	12 16.0	10.6	57.7
N 10	329 08.1	09.5	206 04.5	10.8	12 05.4	10.6	57.8
D 11	344 08.3	10.5	220 34.3	10.8	11 54.8	10.8	57.8
A 12	359 08.4	N 5 11.5	235 04.1	10.9	N11 44.0	10.7	57.8
Y 13	14 08.6	12.4	249 34.0	10.8	11 33.3	10.9	57.9
14	29 08.8	13.4	264 03.8	10.8	11 22.4	11.0	57.9
15	44 09.0	.. 14.3	278 33.6	10.8	11 11.4	11.0	57.9
16	59 09.2	15.3	293 03.4	10.9	11 00.4	11.1	58.0
17	74 09.4	16.3	307 33.3	10.8	10 49.3	11.1	58.0
18	89 09.5	N 5 17.2	322 03.1	10.8	N10 38.2	11.3	58.1
19	104 09.7	18.2	336 32.9	10.7	10 26.9	11.3	58.1
20	119 09.9	19.1	351 02.6	10.8	10 15.6	11.4	58.1
21	134 10.1	.. 20.1	5 32.4	10.8	10 04.2	11.4	58.2
22	149 10.3	21.0	20 02.2	10.8	9 52.8	11.5	58.2
23	164 10.5	22.0	34 32.0	10.7	N 9 41.3	11.6	58.3
	SD 16.0 d 1.0		SD 15.3		15.5		15.8

Lat.	Twilight Naut.	Civil	Sunrise	Moonrise 31	1	2	3
°	h m	h m	h m	h m	h m	h m	h m
N 72	01 33	03 39	04 54	▭	09 21	11 42	13 49
N 70	02 18	03 55	05 02	07 51	10 04	12 03	13 59
68	02 47	04 08	05 08	08 45	10 32	12 19	14 07
66	03 07	04 19	05 13	09 18	10 53	12 32	14 14
64	03 24	04 28	05 17	09 42	11 10	12 43	14 19
62	03 37	04 35	05 21	10 00	11 24	12 52	14 24
60	03 48	04 41	05 24	10 16	11 35	13 00	14 28
N 58	03 57	04 47	05 27	10 29	11 45	13 07	14 32
56	04 05	04 52	05 30	10 40	11 54	13 13	14 35
54	04 12	04 56	05 32	10 50	12 02	13 18	14 38
52	04 18	05 00	05 34	10 59	12 09	13 23	14 41
50	04 24	05 03	05 36	11 07	12 15	13 28	14 43
45	04 35	05 11	05 40	11 23	12 28	13 37	14 48
N 40	04 44	05 16	05 44	11 37	12 40	13 45	14 53
35	04 51	05 21	05 47	11 49	12 49	13 52	14 57
30	04 57	05 25	05 49	11 59	12 57	13 58	15 00
20	05 05	05 31	05 53	12 16	13 11	14 08	15 06
N 10	05 12	05 36	05 57	12 31	13 24	14 17	15 11
0	05 16	05 41	06 00	12 45	13 35	14 25	15 15
S 10	05 18	05 43	06 04	12 59	13 47	14 33	15 20
20	05 20	05 45	06 07	13 14	13 59	14 42	15 25
30	05 19	05 47	06 11	13 31	14 13	14 52	15 31
35	05 18	05 48	06 13	13 41	14 21	14 58	15 34
40	05 17	05 48	06 15	13 53	14 30	15 05	15 38
45	05 15	05 49	06 18	14 06	14 41	15 12	15 42
S 50	05 11	05 49	06 21	14 22	14 54	15 22	15 47
52	05 10	05 49	06 23	14 30	15 00	15 26	15 49
54	05 08	05 49	06 24	14 38	15 06	15 30	15 52
56	05 06	05 49	06 26	14 48	15 14	15 36	15 55
58	05 03	05 49	06 28	14 58	15 22	15 41	15 58
S 60	05 00	05 48	06 30	15 11	15 31	15 48	16 01

Lat.	Sunset	Twilight Civil	Naut.	Moonset 31	1	2	3
°	h m	h m	h m	h m	h m	h m	h m
N 72	19 16	20 33	22 46	▭	05 39	05 03	04 42
N 70	19 09	20 16	21 56	05 23	04 55	04 41	04 29
68	19 02	20 02	21 26	04 29	04 26	04 23	04 19
66	18 57	19 51	21 04	03 55	04 04	04 08	04 11
64	18 52	19 42	20 47	03 31	03 46	03 56	04 04
62	18 48	19 34	20 33	03 12	03 32	03 46	03 58
60	18 45	19 28	20 22	02 56	03 19	03 37	03 52
N 58	18 42	19 22	20 12	02 42	03 09	03 30	03 47
56	18 39	19 17	20 04	02 31	02 59	03 23	03 43
54	18 37	19 13	19 57	02 20	02 51	03 17	03 39
52	18 34	19 09	19 50	02 11	02 44	03 11	03 36
50	18 32	19 05	19 45	02 03	02 37	03 06	03 33
45	18 28	18 58	19 33	01 46	02 22	02 55	03 26
N 40	18 25	18 52	19 24	01 31	02 11	02 46	03 20
35	18 22	18 47	19 17	01 19	02 00	02 39	03 15
30	18 19	18 43	19 11	01 09	01 51	02 32	03 10
20	18 14	18 37	19 02	00 50	01 36	02 20	03 02
N 10	18 11	18 32	18 56	00 34	01 22	02 09	02 56
0	18 07	18 28	18 52	00 19	01 09	01 59	02 49
S 10	18 04	18 25	18 49	00 04	00 56	01 49	02 42
20	18 00	18 22	18 48	24 42	00 42	01 38	02 35
30	17 56	18 20	18 48	24 26	00 26	01 26	02 27
35	17 54	18 19	18 49	24 17	00 17	01 19	02 22
40	17 52	18 19	18 50	24 07	00 07	01 10	02 17
45	17 49	18 18	18 52	23 54	25 01	01 01	02 11
S 50	17 45	18 18	18 55	23 39	24 49	00 49	02 03
52	17 44	18 18	18 57	23 31	24 44	00 44	02 00
54	17 42	18 17	18 58	23 23	24 38	00 38	01 56
56	17 40	18 17	19 01	23 14	24 31	00 31	01 51
58	17 39	18 18	19 03	23 04	24 23	00 23	01 47
S 60	17 36	18 18	19 06	22 52	24 15	00 15	01 41

Day	SUN Eqn. of Time 00h	12h	Mer. Pass.	MOON Mer. Pass. Upper	Lower	Age	Phase
d	m s	m s	h m	h m	h m	d	%
31	04 11	04 02	12 04	18 57	06 32	09	57
1	03 53	03 44	12 04	19 47	07 22	10	67
2	03 35	03 27	12 03	20 37	08 12	11	76

UT	ARIES GHA	VENUS −4.6 GHA	Dec	MARS −0.6 GHA	Dec	JUPITER −2.0 GHA	Dec	SATURN +0.3 GHA	Dec
d h	° ′	° ′	° ′	° ′	° ′	° ′	° ′	° ′	° ′
3 00	191 43.8	135 22.4 N23 32.3		34 11.3 N12 52.5		150 09.7 N15 08.2		345 31.9 S 7 52.6	
01	206 46.2	150 22.4	33.0	49 14.1	52.5	165 11.7	08.4	0 34.5	52.6
02	221 48.7	165 22.4	33.6	64 16.9	52.5	180 13.6	08.6	15 37.2	52.5
03	236 51.2	180 22.5 . .	34.3	79 19.8 . .	52.5	195 15.5 . .	08.7	30 39.8 . .	52.4
04	251 53.6	195 22.5	35.0	94 22.6	52.6	210 17.4	08.9	45 42.4	52.3
05	266 56.1	210 22.5	35.7	109 25.5	52.6	225 19.3	09.1	60 45.1	52.3
06	281 58.6	225 22.6 N23 36.3		124 28.3 N12 52.6		240 21.3 N15 09.3		75 47.7 S 7 52.2	
07	297 01.0	240 22.6	37.0	139 31.1	52.7	255 23.2	09.4	90 50.4	52.1
T 08	312 03.5	255 22.7	37.7	154 34.0	52.7	270 25.1	09.6	105 53.0	52.1
U 09	327 05.9	270 22.7 . .	38.3	169 36.8 . .	52.7	285 27.0 . .	09.8	120 55.6 . .	52.0
E 10	342 08.4	285 22.8	39.0	184 39.6	52.7	300 28.9	09.9	135 58.3	51.9
S 11	357 10.9	300 22.8	39.7	199 42.5	52.8	315 30.8	10.1	151 00.9	51.9
D 12	12 13.3	315 22.8 N23 40.4		214 45.3 N12 52.8		330 32.7 N15 10.3		166 03.5 S 7 51.8	
A 13	27 15.8	330 22.9	41.0	229 48.1	52.8	345 34.7	10.4	181 06.2	51.7
Y 14	42 18.3	345 22.9	41.7	244 50.9	52.9	0 36.6	10.6	196 08.8	51.7
15	57 20.7	0 23.0 . .	42.4	259 53.8 . .	52.9	15 38.5 . .	10.8	211 11.4 . .	51.6
16	72 23.2	15 23.0	43.0	274 56.6	52.9	30 40.4	11.0	226 14.1	51.5
17	87 25.7	30 23.1	43.7	289 59.4	52.9	45 42.3	11.1	241 16.7	51.5
18	102 28.1	45 23.1 N23 44.4		305 02.2 N12 52.9		60 44.2 N15 11.3		256 19.4 S 7 51.4	
19	117 30.6	60 23.2	45.0	320 05.1	53.0	75 46.2	11.5	271 22.0	51.3
20	132 33.0	75 23.2	45.7	335 07.9	53.0	90 48.1	11.6	286 24.6	51.2
21	147 35.5	90 23.3 . .	46.3	350 10.7 . .	53.0	105 50.0 . .	11.8	301 27.3 . .	51.2
22	162 38.0	105 23.3	47.0	5 13.5	53.0	120 51.9	12.0	316 29.9	51.1
23	177 40.4	120 23.4	47.7	20 16.3	53.1	135 53.8	12.2	331 32.5	51.0
4 00	192 42.9	135 23.4 N23 48.3		35 19.1 N12 53.1		150 55.7 N15 12.3		346 35.2 S 7 51.0	
01	207 45.4	150 23.5	49.0	50 22.0	53.1	165 57.7	12.5	1 37.8	50.9
02	222 47.8	165 23.5	49.6	65 24.8	53.1	180 59.6	12.7	16 40.5	50.8
03	237 50.3	180 23.6 . .	50.3	80 27.6 . .	53.1	196 01.5 . .	12.8	31 43.1 . .	50.8
04	252 52.8	195 23.6	50.9	95 30.4	53.1	211 03.4	13.0	46 45.7	50.7
05	267 55.2	210 23.7	51.6	110 33.2	53.2	226 05.3	13.2	61 48.4	50.6
06	282 57.7	225 23.7 N23 52.3		125 36.0 N12 53.2		241 07.2 N15 13.3		76 51.0 S 7 50.6	
W 07	298 00.2	240 23.8	52.9	140 38.8	53.2	256 09.1	13.5	91 53.6	50.5
E 08	313 02.6	255 23.9	53.6	155 41.6	53.2	271 11.1	13.7	106 56.3	50.4
D 09	328 05.1	270 23.9 . .	54.2	170 44.4 . .	53.2	286 13.0 . .	13.9	121 58.9 . .	50.4
N 10	343 07.5	285 24.0	54.9	185 47.2	53.2	301 14.9	14.0	137 01.6	50.3
E 11	358 10.0	300 24.0	55.5	200 50.0	53.3	316 16.8	14.2	152 04.2	50.2
S 12	13 12.5	315 24.1 N23 56.2		215 52.8 N12 53.3		331 18.7 N15 14.4		167 06.8 S 7 50.1	
D 13	28 14.9	330 24.2	56.8	230 55.6	53.3	346 20.6	14.5	182 09.5	50.1
A 14	43 17.4	345 24.2	57.4	245 58.4	53.3	1 22.5	14.7	197 12.1	50.0
Y 15	58 19.9	0 24.3 . .	58.1	261 01.2 . .	53.3	16 24.5 . .	14.9	212 14.7 . .	49.9
16	73 22.3	15 24.3	58.7	276 04.0	53.3	31 26.4	15.1	227 17.4	49.9
17	88 24.8	30 24.4 23 59.4		291 06.8	53.3	46 28.3	15.2	242 20.0	49.8
18	103 27.3	45 24.5 N24 00.0		306 09.6 N12 53.3		61 30.2 N15 15.4		257 22.7 S 7 49.7	
19	118 29.7	60 24.5	00.7	321 12.4	53.4	76 32.1	15.6	272 25.3	49.7
20	133 32.2	75 24.6	01.3	336 15.1	53.4	91 34.0	15.7	287 27.9	49.6
21	148 34.6	90 24.7 . .	01.9	351 17.9 . .	53.4	106 35.9 . .	15.9	302 30.6 . .	49.5
22	163 37.1	105 24.7	02.6	6 20.7	53.4	121 37.8	16.1	317 33.2	49.5
23	178 39.6	120 24.8	03.2	21 23.5	53.4	136 39.8	16.2	332 35.8	49.4
5 00	193 42.0	135 24.9 N24 03.9		36 26.3 N12 53.4		151 41.7 N15 16.4		347 38.5 S 7 49.3	
01	208 44.5	150 24.9	04.5	51 29.1	53.4	166 43.6	16.6	2 41.1	49.3
02	223 47.0	165 25.0	05.1	66 31.8	53.4	181 45.5	16.8	17 43.8	49.2
03	238 49.4	180 25.1 . .	05.8	81 34.6 . .	53.4	196 47.4 . .	16.9	32 46.4 . .	49.1
04	253 51.9	195 25.2	06.4	96 37.4	53.4	211 49.3	17.1	47 49.0	49.0
05	268 54.4	210 25.2	07.0	111 40.2	53.4	226 51.2	17.3	62 51.7	49.0
06	283 56.8	225 25.3 N24 07.7		126 43.0 N12 53.4		241 53.1 N15 17.4		77 54.3 S 7 48.9	
07	298 59.3	240 25.4	08.3	141 45.7	53.4	256 55.1	17.6	92 57.0	48.8
T 08	314 01.8	255 25.5	08.9	156 48.5	53.4	271 57.0	17.8	107 59.6	48.8
H 09	329 04.2	270 25.5 . .	09.6	171 51.3 . .	53.4	286 58.9 . .	17.9	123 02.2 . .	48.7
U 10	344 06.7	285 25.6	10.2	186 54.0	53.4	302 00.8	18.1	138 04.9	48.6
R 11	359 09.1	300 25.7	10.8	201 56.8	53.4	317 02.7	18.3	153 07.5	48.6
S 12	14 11.6	315 25.8 N24 11.4		216 59.6 N12 53.4		332 04.6 N15 18.5		168 10.2 S 7 48.5	
D 13	29 14.1	330 25.8	12.1	232 02.3	53.4	347 06.5	18.6	183 12.8	48.4
A 14	44 16.5	345 25.9	12.7	247 05.1	53.4	2 08.4	18.8	198 15.4	48.4
Y 15	59 19.0	0 26.0 . .	13.3	262 07.9 . .	53.4	17 10.4 . .	19.0	213 18.1 . .	48.3
16	74 21.5	15 26.1	13.9	277 10.6	53.4	32 12.3	19.1	228 20.7	48.2
17	89 23.9	30 26.2	14.6	292 13.4	53.4	47 14.2	19.3	243 23.3	48.1
18	104 26.4	45 26.2 N24 15.2		307 16.2 N12 53.4		62 16.1 N15 19.5		258 26.0 S 7 48.1	
19	119 28.9	60 26.3	15.8	322 18.9	53.4	77 18.0	19.7	273 28.6	48.0
20	134 31.3	75 26.4	16.4	337 21.7	53.4	92 19.9	19.8	288 31.3	47.9
21	149 33.8	90 26.5 . .	17.0	352 24.4 . .	53.4	107 21.8 . .	20.0	303 33.9 . .	47.9
22	164 36.2	105 26.6	17.6	7 27.2	53.4	122 23.7	20.2	318 36.5	47.8
23	179 38.7	120 26.7	18.3	22 29.9	53.4	137 25.6	20.3	333 39.2	47.7
Mer. Pass. 11 07.3		v 0.1 d 0.6		v 2.8 d 0.0		v 1.9 d 0.2		v 2.6 d 0.1	

STARS

Name	SHA	Dec
Acamar	315 19.3	S40 15.5
Achernar	335 27.9	S57 10.5
Acrux	173 09.6	S63 10.2
Adhara	255 13.2	S28 59.7
Aldebaran	290 50.5	N16 31.9
Alioth	166 20.8	N55 53.5
Alkaid	152 59.1	N49 14.9
Al Na'ir	27 45.1	S46 53.9
Alnilam	275 47.3	S 1 11.9
Alphard	217 56.7	S 8 43.0
Alphecca	126 11.4	N26 40.2
Alpheratz	357 44.7	N29 09.4
Altair	62 09.1	N 8 54.0
Ankaa	353 16.9	S42 14.3
Antares	112 27.1	S26 27.5
Arcturus	145 56.2	N19 06.9
Atria	107 29.4	S69 02.7
Avior	234 18.2	S59 33.4
Bellatrix	278 33.0	N 6 21.5
Betelgeuse	271 02.3	N 7 24.4
Canopus	263 56.6	S52 42.5
Capella	280 35.9	N46 00.6
Deneb	49 32.2	N45 19.3
Denebola	182 34.2	N14 30.0
Diphda	348 57.0	S17 55.2
Dubhe	193 52.1	N61 41.0
Elnath	278 13.8	N28 37.0
Eltanin	90 46.4	N51 29.0
Enif	33 48.2	N 9 55.8
Fomalhaut	15 25.2	S29 33.3
Gacrux	172 01.3	S57 11.1
Gienah	175 52.8	S17 36.8
Hadar	148 48.5	S60 25.9
Hamal	328 02.0	N23 31.2
Kaus Aust.	83 44.9	S34 22.5
Kochab	137 18.9	N74 06.1
Markab	13 39.5	N15 16.2
Menkar	314 16.2	N 4 08.1
Menkent	148 08.2	S36 25.9
Miaplacidus	221 39.4	S69 46.5
Mirfak	308 42.0	N49 54.3
Nunki	75 59.3	S26 16.7
Peacock	53 20.7	S56 41.4
Pollux	243 28.7	N27 59.7
Procyon	245 00.6	N 5 11.4
Rasalhague	96 07.1	N12 33.0
Regulus	207 44.2	N11 54.2
Rigel	281 13.0	S 8 11.5
Rigil Kent.	139 52.3	S60 53.1
Sabik	102 13.3	S15 44.4
Schedar	349 42.1	N56 36.3
Shaula	96 22.9	S37 06.6
Sirius	258 34.5	S16 44.3
Spica	158 31.8	S11 13.7
Suhail	222 52.9	S43 29.3
Vega	80 39.5	N38 47.5
Zuben'ubi	137 06.1	S16 05.7

	SHA	Mer. Pass.
	° ′	h m
Venus	302 40.5	14 58
Mars	202 36.2	21 35
Jupiter	318 12.8	13 55
Saturn	153 52.3	0 53

SUN and MOON

d h	SUN GHA	SUN Dec	MOON GHA	v	Dec	d	HP
3 00	179 10.6	N 5 22.9	49 01.7	10.8	N 9 29.7	11.7	58.3
01	194 10.8	23.9	63 31.5	10.7	9 18.0	11.7	58.4
02	209 11.0	24.9	78 01.2	10.7	9 06.3	11.8	58.4
03	224 11.2	.. 25.8	92 30.9	10.7	8 54.5	11.8	58.4
04	239 11.4	26.8	107 00.6	10.7	8 42.7	11.9	58.5
05	254 11.6	27.7	121 30.3	10.7	8 30.8	12.0	58.5
T 06	269 11.7	N 5 28.7	136 00.0	10.6	N 8 18.8	12.1	58.5
U 07	284 11.9	29.6	150 29.6	10.7	8 06.7	12.1	58.6
E 08	299 12.1	30.6	164 59.3	10.6	7 54.6	12.1	58.6
S 09	314 12.3	.. 31.6	179 28.9	10.7	7 42.5	12.2	58.7
D 10	329 12.5	32.5	193 58.6	10.6	7 30.3	12.3	58.7
A 11	344 12.7	33.5	208 28.2	10.6	7 18.0	12.3	58.7
Y 12	359 12.8	N 5 34.4	222 57.8	10.5	N 7 05.7	12.4	58.8
13	14 13.0	35.4	237 27.3	10.6	6 53.3	12.5	58.8
14	29 13.2	36.3	251 56.9	10.5	6 40.8	12.5	58.9
15	44 13.4	.. 37.3	266 26.4	10.5	6 28.3	12.5	58.9
16	59 13.6	38.2	280 55.9	10.5	6 15.8	12.6	58.9
17	74 13.8	39.2	295 25.4	10.5	6 03.2	12.7	59.0
18	89 13.9	N 5 40.1	309 54.9	10.5	N 5 50.5	12.7	59.0
19	104 14.1	41.1	324 24.4	10.4	5 37.8	12.7	59.1
20	119 14.3	42.0	338 53.8	10.4	5 25.1	12.8	59.1
21	134 14.5	.. 43.0	353 23.2	10.4	5 12.3	12.9	59.1
22	149 14.7	44.0	7 52.6	10.4	4 59.4	12.8	59.2
23	164 14.9	44.9	22 22.0	10.3	4 46.6	13.0	59.2
4 00	179 15.0	N 5 45.9	36 51.3	10.4	N 4 33.6	12.9	59.3
01	194 15.2	46.8	51 20.7	10.2	4 20.7	13.1	59.3
02	209 15.4	47.8	65 49.9	10.3	4 07.6	13.0	59.3
03	224 15.6	.. 48.7	80 19.2	10.3	3 54.6	13.1	59.4
04	239 15.8	49.7	94 48.5	10.2	3 41.5	13.1	59.4
05	254 15.9	50.6	109 17.7	10.2	3 28.4	13.2	59.4
W 06	269 16.1	N 5 51.6	123 46.9	10.1	N 3 15.2	13.2	59.5
E 07	284 16.3	52.5	138 16.0	10.1	3 02.0	13.2	59.5
D 08	299 16.5	53.5	152 45.1	10.1	2 48.8	13.3	59.5
N 09	314 16.7	.. 54.4	167 14.2	10.1	2 35.5	13.3	59.6
E 10	329 16.8	55.4	181 43.3	10.0	2 22.2	13.3	59.6
S 11	344 17.0	56.3	196 12.3	10.0	2 08.9	13.4	59.7
D 12	359 17.2	N 5 57.3	210 41.3	10.0	N 1 55.5	13.4	59.7
A 13	14 17.4	58.2	225 10.3	9.9	1 42.1	13.4	59.7
Y 14	29 17.6	5 59.2	239 39.2	9.9	1 28.7	13.4	59.8
15	44 17.8	6 00.1	254 08.1	9.9	1 15.3	13.5	59.8
16	59 17.9	01.1	268 37.0	9.8	1 01.8	13.5	59.8
17	74 18.1	02.0	283 05.8	9.8	0 48.3	13.5	59.9
18	89 18.3	N 6 03.0	297 34.6	9.8	N 0 34.8	13.5	59.9
19	104 18.5	03.9	312 03.4	9.7	0 21.3	13.5	59.9
20	119 18.7	04.9	326 32.1	9.7	N 0 07.8	13.6	60.0
21	134 18.8	.. 05.8	341 00.8	9.6	S 0 05.8	13.5	60.0
22	149 19.0	06.8	355 29.4	9.6	0 19.3	13.6	60.0
23	164 19.2	07.7	9 58.0	9.6	0 32.9	13.6	60.1
5 00	179 19.4	N 6 08.7	24 26.6	9.5	S 0 46.5	13.6	60.1
01	194 19.6	09.6	38 55.1	9.5	1 00.1	13.6	60.1
02	209 19.7	10.6	53 23.6	9.4	1 13.7	13.7	60.2
03	224 19.9	.. 11.5	67 52.0	9.4	1 27.4	13.6	60.2
04	239 20.1	12.5	82 20.4	9.4	1 41.0	13.6	60.2
05	254 20.3	13.4	96 48.8	9.3	1 54.6	13.6	60.2
T 06	269 20.5	N 6 14.3	111 17.1	9.2	S 2 08.2	13.7	60.3
H 07	284 20.6	15.3	125 45.3	9.2	2 21.9	13.6	60.3
U 08	299 20.8	16.2	140 13.5	9.2	2 35.5	13.6	60.3
R 09	314 21.0	.. 17.2	154 41.7	9.1	2 49.1	13.7	60.4
S 10	329 21.2	18.1	169 09.8	9.1	3 02.8	13.6	60.4
D 11	344 21.4	19.1	183 37.9	9.0	3 16.4	13.6	60.4
A 12	359 21.5	N 6 20.0	198 05.9	9.0	S 3 30.0	13.6	60.4
Y 13	14 21.7	21.0	212 33.9	8.9	3 43.6	13.6	60.5
14	29 21.9	21.9	227 01.8	8.9	3 57.2	13.6	60.5
15	44 22.1	.. 22.9	241 29.7	8.8	4 10.8	13.5	60.5
16	59 22.3	23.8	255 57.5	8.7	4 24.3	13.5	60.5
17	74 22.4	24.8	270 25.2	8.8	4 37.9	13.5	60.6
18	89 22.6	N 6 25.7	284 53.0	8.6	S 4 51.4	13.6	60.6
19	104 22.8	26.6	299 20.6	8.6	5 05.0	13.6	60.6
20	119 23.0	27.6	313 48.2	8.6	5 18.5	13.4	60.6
21	134 23.1	.. 28.5	328 15.8	8.5	5 31.9	13.5	60.7
22	149 23.3	29.5	342 43.3	8.4	5 45.4	13.4	60.7
23	164 23.5	30.4	357 10.7	8.4	S 5 58.8	13.4	60.7
	SD 16.0	d 1.0	SD 16.0		16.3		16.5

Twilight / Sunrise / Moonrise

Lat.	Naut.	Civil	Sunrise	Moonrise 3	4	5	6
N 72	00 39	03 20	04 38	13 49	15 54	18 04	20 22
N 70	01 52	03 39	04 47	13 59	15 56	17 56	20 03
68	02 27	03 54	04 55	14 07	15 57	17 50	19 49
66	02 51	04 06	05 01	14 14	15 58	17 45	19 37
64	03 10	04 16	05 07	14 19	15 58	17 41	19 27
62	03 25	04 25	05 11	14 24	15 59	17 37	19 18
60	03 37	04 32	05 15	14 28	16 00	17 34	19 11
N 58	03 47	04 38	05 19	14 32	16 00	17 31	19 05
56	03 56	04 44	05 22	14 35	16 01	17 29	18 59
54	04 04	04 48	05 25	14 38	16 01	17 27	18 54
52	04 11	04 53	05 27	14 41	16 01	17 25	18 50
50	04 17	04 57	05 30	14 43	16 02	17 23	18 46
45	04 29	05 05	05 35	14 48	16 02	17 19	18 37
N 40	04 39	05 11	05 39	14 53	16 03	17 16	18 30
35	04 47	05 17	05 42	14 57	16 04	17 13	18 24
30	04 53	05 21	05 45	15 00	16 04	17 10	18 19
20	05 03	05 29	05 51	15 06	16 05	17 06	18 09
N 10	05 10	05 34	05 55	15 11	16 06	17 02	18 01
0	05 15	05 39	06 00	15 15	16 06	16 59	17 54
S 10	05 18	05 43	06 04	15 20	16 07	16 56	17 46
20	05 20	05 46	06 08	15 25	16 08	16 52	17 38
30	05 21	05 49	06 13	15 31	16 09	16 48	17 30
35	05 21	05 50	06 15	15 34	16 09	16 46	17 24
40	05 20	05 51	06 18	15 38	16 10	16 43	17 19
45	05 18	05 52	06 22	15 42	16 11	16 40	17 12
S 50	05 16	05 53	06 26	15 47	16 12	16 37	17 04
52	05 15	05 54	06 28	15 49	16 12	16 35	17 01
54	05 13	05 54	06 30	15 52	16 12	16 33	16 57
56	05 12	05 55	06 32	15 55	16 13	16 32	16 52
58	05 10	05 55	06 34	15 58	16 13	16 29	16 47
S 60	05 07	05 55	06 37	16 01	16 14	16 27	16 42

Sunset / Twilight / Moonset

Lat.	Sunset	Civil	Naut.	Moonset 3	4	5	6
N 72	19 31	20 51	////	04 42	04 24	04 08	03 50
N 70	19 21	20 30	22 23	04 29	04 20	04 12	04 00
68	19 13	20 15	21 44	04 19	04 16	04 12	04 08
66	19 07	20 02	21 19	04 11	04 13	04 14	04 16
64	19 01	19 52	20 59	04 04	04 10	04 15	04 22
62	18 56	19 43	20 44	03 58	04 07	04 17	04 27
60	18 52	19 36	20 31	03 52	04 05	04 18	04 31
N 58	18 48	19 29	20 20	03 47	04 03	04 19	04 35
56	18 45	19 24	20 11	03 43	04 02	04 20	04 39
54	18 42	19 19	20 03	03 39	04 00	04 21	04 42
52	18 40	19 14	19 56	03 36	03 59	04 21	04 45
50	18 37	19 10	19 50	03 33	03 57	04 22	04 48
45	18 32	19 02	19 38	03 26	03 55	04 23	04 54
N 40	18 28	18 55	19 28	03 20	03 52	04 25	05 00
35	18 24	18 50	19 20	03 15	03 50	04 26	05 03
30	18 21	18 45	19 13	03 10	03 48	04 27	05 07
20	18 15	18 37	19 03	03 02	03 45	04 28	05 13
N 10	18 10	18 32	18 56	02 56	03 42	04 30	05 19
0	18 06	18 27	18 51	02 49	03 39	04 31	05 25
S 10	18 02	18 23	18 47	02 42	03 37	04 32	05 30
20	17 58	18 21	18 45	02 35	03 34	04 34	05 36
30	17 53	18 17	18 44	02 27	03 30	04 35	05 43
35	17 50	18 15	18 44	02 22	03 28	04 36	05 46
40	17 47	18 14	18 45	02 17	03 26	04 37	05 51
45	17 43	18 13	18 46	02 11	03 23	04 38	05 56
S 50	17 39	18 11	18 49	02 03	03 20	04 40	06 02
52	17 37	18 11	18 50	02 00	03 19	04 40	06 05
54	17 35	18 10	18 51	01 56	03 17	04 41	06 08
56	17 33	18 10	18 53	01 51	03 15	04 42	06 11
58	17 30	18 09	18 55	01 47	03 13	04 43	06 15
S 60	17 27	18 09	18 57	01 41	03 11	04 44	06 19

SUN and MOON

Day	Eqn. of Time 00h	Eqn. of Time 12h	Mer. Pass.	Mer. Pass. Upper	Mer. Pass. Lower	Age	Phase
d	m s	m s	h m	h m	h m	d	%
3	03 18	03 09	12 03	21 27	09 02	12	85
4	03 00	02 52	12 03	22 19	09 53	13	92
5	02 43	02 34	12 03	23 12	10 45	14	97

UT	ARIES GHA	VENUS −4.6 GHA	VENUS Dec	MARS −0.6 GHA	MARS Dec	JUPITER −2.0 GHA	JUPITER Dec	SATURN +0.3 GHA	SATURN Dec	STARS Name	SHA	Dec
6 00	194 41.2	135 26.8	N24 18.9	37 32.7	N12 53.4	152 27.5	N15 20.5	348 41.8	S 7 47.7	Acamar	315 19.3	S40 15.5
01	209 43.6	150 26.8	19.5	52 35.4	53.4	167 29.5	20.7	3 44.5	47.6	Achernar	335 27.9	S57 10.5
02	224 46.1	165 26.9	20.1	67 38.2	53.4	182 31.4	20.8	18 47.1	47.5	Acrux	173 09.6	S63 10.2
03	239 48.6	180 27.0	.. 20.7	82 40.9	.. 53.4	197 33.3	.. 21.0	33 49.7	.. 47.5	Adhara	255 13.2	S28 59.7
04	254 51.0	195 27.1	21.3	97 43.7	53.4	212 35.2	21.2	48 52.4	47.4	Aldebaran	290 50.6	N16 31.9
05	269 53.5	210 27.2	21.9	112 46.4	53.4	227 37.1	21.4	63 55.0	47.3			
06	284 56.0	225 27.3	N24 22.6	127 49.2	N12 53.4	242 39.0	N15 21.5	78 57.7	S 7 47.2	Alioth	166 20.8	N55 53.5
07	299 58.4	240 27.4	23.2	142 51.9	53.4	257 40.9	21.7	94 00.3	47.2	Alkaid	152 59.0	N49 15.0
F 08	315 00.9	255 27.5	23.8	157 54.7	53.4	272 42.8	21.9	109 02.9	47.1	Al Na'ir	27 45.1	S46 53.9
R 09	330 03.4	270 27.6	.. 24.4	172 57.4	.. 53.4	287 44.7	.. 22.0	124 05.6	.. 47.0	Alnilam	275 47.4	S 1 11.9
I 10	345 05.8	285 27.7	25.0	188 00.1	53.3	302 46.6	22.2	139 08.2	47.0	Alphard	217 56.7	S 8 43.0
D 11	0 08.3	300 27.8	25.6	203 02.9	53.3	317 48.6	22.4	154 10.9	46.9			
A 12	15 10.7	315 27.9	N24 26.2	218 05.6	N12 53.3	332 50.5	N15 22.5	169 13.5	S 7 46.8	Alphecca	126 11.4	N26 40.2
Y 13	30 13.2	330 28.0	26.8	233 08.3	53.3	347 52.4	22.7	184 16.1	46.8	Alpheratz	357 44.7	N29 09.4
14	45 15.7	345 28.1	27.4	248 11.1	53.3	2 54.3	22.9	199 18.8	46.7	Altair	62 09.1	N 8 54.0
15	60 18.1	0 28.1	.. 28.0	263 13.8	.. 53.3	17 56.2	.. 23.1	214 21.4	.. 46.6	Ankaa	353 16.9	S42 14.3
16	75 20.6	15 28.2	28.6	278 16.5	53.3	32 58.1	23.2	229 24.1	46.6	Antares	112 27.1	S26 27.5
17	90 23.1	30 28.3	29.2	293 19.3	53.3	48 00.0	23.4	244 26.7	46.5			
18	105 25.5	45 28.5	N24 29.8	308 22.0	N12 53.2	63 01.9	N15 23.6	259 29.3	S 7 46.4	Arcturus	145 56.2	N19 06.9
19	120 28.0	60 28.6	30.4	323 24.7	53.2	78 03.8	23.7	274 32.0	46.3	Atria	107 29.4	S69 02.7
20	135 30.5	75 28.7	31.0	338 27.4	53.2	93 05.7	23.9	289 34.6	46.3	Avior	234 18.2	S59 33.4
21	150 32.9	90 28.8	.. 31.6	353 30.2	.. 53.2	108 07.6	.. 24.1	304 37.3	.. 46.2	Bellatrix	278 33.1	N 6 21.5
22	165 35.4	105 28.9	32.2	8 32.9	53.2	123 09.6	24.2	319 39.9	46.1	Betelgeuse	271 02.3	N 7 24.4
23	180 37.8	120 29.0	32.8	23 35.6	53.2	138 11.5	24.4	334 42.5	46.1			
7 00	195 40.3	135 29.1	N24 33.4	38 38.3	N12 53.2	153 13.4	N15 24.6	349 45.2	S 7 46.0	Canopus	263 56.6	S52 42.5
01	210 42.8	150 29.2	34.0	53 41.1	53.1	168 15.3	24.8	4 47.8	45.9	Capella	280 35.9	N46 00.6
02	225 45.2	165 29.3	34.6	68 43.8	53.1	183 17.2	24.9	19 50.5	45.9	Deneb	49 32.2	N45 19.3
03	240 47.7	180 29.4	.. 35.2	83 46.5	.. 53.1	198 19.1	.. 25.1	34 53.1	.. 45.8	Denebola	182 34.2	N14 30.0
04	255 50.2	195 29.5	35.8	98 49.2	53.1	213 21.0	25.3	49 55.7	45.7	Diphda	348 57.0	S17 55.2
05	270 52.6	210 29.6	36.4	113 51.9	53.1	228 22.9	25.4	64 58.4	45.7			
06	285 55.1	225 29.7	N24 36.9	128 54.6	N12 53.0	243 24.8	N15 25.6	80 01.0	S 7 46.6	Dubhe	193 52.1	N61 41.1
07	300 57.6	240 29.8	37.5	143 57.3	53.0	258 26.7	25.8	95 03.7	45.5	Elnath	278 13.8	N28 37.0
S 08	316 00.0	255 30.0	38.1	159 00.1	53.0	273 28.6	26.0	110 06.3	45.4	Eltanin	90 46.4	N51 29.0
A 09	331 02.5	270 30.1	.. 38.7	174 02.8	.. 53.0	288 30.5	.. 26.1	125 08.9	.. 45.4	Enif	33 48.1	N 9 55.8
T 10	346 05.0	285 30.2	39.3	189 05.5	53.0	303 32.5	26.3	140 11.6	45.3	Fomalhaut	15 25.2	S29 33.3
U 11	1 07.4	300 30.3	39.9	204 08.2	52.9	318 34.4	26.5	155 14.2	45.2			
R 12	16 09.9	315 30.4	N24 40.5	219 10.9	N12 52.9	333 36.3	N15 26.6	170 16.9	S 7 45.2	Gacrux	172 01.3	S57 11.1
D 13	31 12.3	330 30.5	41.0	234 13.6	52.9	348 38.2	26.8	185 19.5	45.1	Gienah	175 52.9	S17 36.8
A 14	46 14.8	345 30.6	41.6	249 16.3	52.9	3 40.1	27.0	200 22.1	45.0	Hadar	148 48.5	S60 26.0
Y 15	61 17.3	0 30.8	.. 42.2	264 19.0	.. 52.8	18 42.0	.. 27.1	215 24.8	.. 45.0	Hamal	328 02.0	N23 31.2
16	76 19.7	15 30.9	42.8	279 21.7	52.8	33 43.9	27.3	230 27.4	44.9	Kaus Aust.	83 44.8	S34 22.5
17	91 22.2	30 31.0	43.4	294 24.4	52.8	48 45.8	27.5	245 30.1	44.8			
18	106 24.7	45 31.1	N24 43.9	309 27.1	N12 52.8	63 47.7	N15 27.7	260 32.7	S 7 44.8	Kochab	137 18.9	N74 06.1
19	121 27.1	60 31.3	44.5	324 29.8	52.7	78 49.6	27.8	275 35.3	44.7	Markab	13 39.4	N15 16.2
20	136 29.6	75 31.4	45.1	339 32.5	52.7	93 51.5	28.0	290 38.0	44.6	Menkar	314 16.2	N 4 08.1
21	151 32.1	90 31.5	.. 45.7	354 35.2	.. 52.7	108 53.4	.. 28.2	305 40.6	.. 44.5	Menkent	148 08.2	S36 25.9
22	166 34.5	105 31.6	46.2	9 37.9	52.7	123 55.3	28.3	320 43.3	44.5	Miaplacidus	221 39.5	S69 46.5
23	181 37.0	120 31.7	46.8	24 40.6	52.6	138 57.2	28.5	335 45.9	44.4			
8 00	196 39.5	135 31.9	N24 47.4	39 43.3	N12 52.6	153 59.1	N15 28.7	350 48.6	S 7 44.3	Mirfak	308 42.0	N49 54.3
01	211 41.9	150 32.0	48.0	54 45.9	52.6	169 01.1	28.8	5 51.2	44.3	Nunki	75 59.3	S26 16.7
02	226 44.4	165 32.1	48.5	69 48.6	52.5	184 03.0	29.0	20 53.8	44.2	Peacock	53 20.7	S56 41.4
03	241 46.8	180 32.3	.. 49.1	84 51.3	.. 52.5	199 04.9	.. 29.2	35 56.5	.. 44.1	Pollux	243 28.7	N27 59.7
04	256 49.3	195 32.4	49.7	99 54.0	52.5	214 06.8	29.4	50 59.1	44.1	Procyon	245 00.6	N 5 11.4
05	271 51.8	210 32.5	50.2	114 56.7	52.5	229 08.7	29.5	66 01.8	44.0			
06	286 54.2	225 32.7	N24 50.8	129 59.4	N12 52.4	244 10.6	N15 29.7	81 04.4	S 7 43.9	Rasalhague	96 07.1	N12 33.0
07	301 56.7	240 32.8	51.4	145 02.1	52.4	259 12.5	29.9	96 07.0	43.8	Regulus	207 44.2	N11 54.2
08	316 59.2	255 32.9	51.9	160 04.7	52.4	274 14.4	30.0	111 09.7	43.8	Rigel	281 13.0	S 8 11.5
S 09	332 01.6	270 33.1	.. 52.5	175 07.4	.. 52.3	289 16.3	.. 30.2	126 12.3	.. 43.7	Rigil Kent.	139 52.3	S60 53.1
U 10	347 04.1	285 33.2	53.1	190 10.1	52.3	304 18.2	30.4	141 15.0	43.6	Sabik	102 13.3	S15 44.4
N 11	2 06.6	300 33.3	53.6	205 12.8	52.3	319 20.1	30.5	156 17.6	43.6			
D 12	17 09.0	315 33.5	N24 54.2	220 15.4	N12 52.2	334 22.0	N15 30.7	171 20.2	S 7 43.5	Schedar	349 42.1	N56 36.2
A 13	32 11.5	330 33.6	54.8	235 18.1	52.2	349 23.9	30.9	186 22.9	43.4	Shaula	96 22.9	S37 06.6
Y 14	47 13.9	345 33.7	55.3	250 20.8	52.1	4 25.8	31.1	201 25.5	43.4	Sirius	258 34.5	S16 44.3
15	62 16.4	0 33.9	.. 55.9	265 23.5	.. 52.1	19 27.7	.. 31.2	216 28.2	.. 43.3	Spica	158 31.8	S11 13.7
16	77 18.9	15 34.0	56.4	280 26.1	52.1	34 29.6	31.4	231 30.8	43.2	Suhail	222 52.9	S43 29.3
17	92 21.3	30 34.2	57.0	295 28.8	52.0	49 31.5	31.6	246 33.5	43.2			
18	107 23.8	45 34.3	N24 57.5	310 31.5	N12 52.0	64 33.4	N15 31.7	261 36.1	S 7 43.1	Vega	80 39.5	N38 47.5
19	122 26.3	60 34.5	58.1	325 34.1	52.0	79 35.3	31.9	276 38.7	43.0	Zuben'ubi	137 06.1	S16 05.7
20	137 28.7	75 34.6	58.7	340 36.8	51.9	94 37.3	32.1	291 41.4	42.9		SHA	Mer. Pass.
21	152 31.2	90 34.7	.. 59.2	355 39.5	.. 51.9	109 39.2	.. 32.2	306 44.0	.. 42.9	Venus	299 48.8	14 58
22	167 33.7	105 34.9	24 59.8	10 42.1	51.8	124 41.1	32.4	321 46.7	42.8	Mars	202 58.0	21 22
23	182 36.1	120 35.0	N25 00.3	25 44.8	51.8	139 43.0	32.6	336 49.3	42.7	Jupiter	317 33.1	13 45
Mer. Pass.	10 55.5	v 0.1	d 0.6	v 2.7	d 0.0	v 1.9	d 0.2	v 2.6	d 0.1	Saturn	154 04.9	0 41

UT	SUN GHA	SUN Dec	MOON GHA	v	MOON Dec	d	HP
d h	° ′	° ′	° ′	′	° ′	′	′
6 00	179 23.7	N 6 31.4	11 38.1	8.4	S 6 12.2	13.4	60.7
01	194 23.9	32.3	26 05.5	8.2	6 25.6	13.3	60.8
02	209 24.0	33.2	40 32.7	8.3	6 38.9	13.3	60.8
03	224 24.2	.. 34.2	55 00.0	8.1	6 52.2	13.3	60.8
04	239 24.4	35.1	69 27.1	8.1	7 05.5	13.3	60.8
05	254 24.6	36.1	83 54.2	8.1	7 18.8	13.2	60.8
F 06	269 24.7	N 6 37.0	98 21.3	8.0	S 7 32.0	13.1	60.9
R 07	284 24.9	38.0	112 48.3	7.9	7 45.1	13.1	60.9
I 08	299 25.1	38.9	127 15.2	7.9	7 58.2	13.1	60.9
D 09	314 25.3	.. 39.8	141 42.1	7.8	8 11.3	13.1	60.9
A 10	329 25.5	40.8	156 08.9	7.7	8 24.4	12.9	60.9
Y 11	344 25.6	41.7	170 35.6	7.7	8 37.3	13.0	60.9
12	359 25.8	N 6 42.7	185 02.3	7.6	S 8 50.3	12.9	61.0
13	14 26.0	43.6	199 28.9	7.6	9 03.2	12.8	61.0
14	29 26.2	44.6	213 55.5	7.5	9 16.0	12.8	61.0
15	44 26.3	.. 45.5	228 22.0	7.5	9 28.8	12.7	61.0
16	59 26.5	46.4	242 48.5	7.3	9 41.5	12.7	61.0
17	74 26.7	47.4	257 14.8	7.4	9 54.2	12.6	61.0
18	89 26.9	N 6 48.3	271 41.2	7.2	S10 06.8	12.6	61.0
19	104 27.1	49.3	286 07.4	7.2	10 19.4	12.4	61.1
20	119 27.2	50.2	300 33.6	7.1	10 31.8	12.5	61.1
21	134 27.4	.. 51.1	314 59.7	7.1	10 44.3	12.3	61.1
22	149 27.6	52.1	329 25.8	7.0	10 56.6	12.3	61.1
23	164 27.8	53.0	343 51.8	7.0	11 08.9	12.2	61.1
7 00	179 27.9	N 6 53.9	358 17.8	6.8	S11 21.1	12.2	61.1
01	194 28.1	54.9	12 43.6	6.9	11 33.3	12.1	61.1
02	209 28.3	55.8	27 09.5	6.7	11 45.4	12.0	61.1
03	224 28.5	.. 56.8	41 35.2	6.7	11 57.4	11.9	61.1
04	239 28.6	57.7	56 00.9	6.6	12 09.3	11.8	61.1
05	254 28.8	58.6	70 26.5	6.6	12 21.1	11.8	61.2
S 06	269 29.0	N 6 59.6	84 52.1	6.5	S12 32.9	11.7	61.2
A 07	284 29.2	7 00.5	99 17.6	6.4	12 44.6	11.6	61.2
T 08	299 29.3	01.5	113 43.0	6.4	12 56.2	11.5	61.2
U 09	314 29.5	.. 02.4	128 08.4	6.3	13 07.7	11.4	61.2
R 10	329 29.7	03.3	142 33.7	6.3	13 19.1	11.3	61.2
D 11	344 29.9	04.3	156 59.0	6.1	13 30.4	11.3	61.2
A 12	359 30.0	N 7 05.2	171 24.1	6.2	S13 41.7	11.1	61.2
Y 13	14 30.2	06.1	185 49.3	6.0	13 52.8	11.1	61.2
14	29 30.4	07.1	200 14.3	6.0	14 03.9	10.9	61.2
15	44 30.6	.. 08.0	214 39.3	6.0	14 14.8	10.9	61.2
16	59 30.7	08.9	229 04.3	5.9	14 25.7	10.8	61.2
17	74 30.9	09.9	243 29.2	5.8	14 36.5	10.6	61.2
18	89 31.1	N 7 10.8	257 54.0	5.7	S14 47.1	10.6	61.2
19	104 31.3	11.7	272 18.7	5.7	14 57.7	10.4	61.2
20	119 31.4	12.7	286 43.4	5.7	15 08.1	10.4	61.2
21	134 31.6	.. 13.6	301 08.1	5.6	15 18.5	10.2	61.2
22	149 31.8	14.6	315 32.7	5.5	15 28.7	10.1	61.2
23	164 32.0	15.5	329 57.2	5.5	15 38.8	10.0	61.2
8 00	179 32.1	N 7 16.4	344 21.7	5.4	S15 48.9	9.9	61.2
01	194 32.3	17.4	358 46.1	5.3	15 58.8	9.8	61.2
02	209 32.5	18.3	13 10.4	5.3	16 08.6	9.6	61.2
03	224 32.6	.. 19.2	27 34.7	5.3	16 18.2	9.6	61.2
04	239 32.8	20.2	41 59.0	5.2	16 27.8	9.5	61.2
05	254 33.0	21.1	56 23.2	5.1	16 37.3	9.3	61.2
S 06	269 33.2	N 7 22.0	70 47.3	5.1	S16 46.6	9.2	61.1
U 07	284 33.3	23.0	85 11.4	5.1	16 55.8	9.1	61.1
N 08	299 33.5	23.9	99 35.5	5.0	17 04.9	8.9	61.1
D 09	314 33.7	.. 24.8	113 59.5	4.9	17 13.8	8.9	61.1
A 10	329 33.9	25.7	128 23.4	4.9	17 22.7	8.7	61.1
Y 11	344 34.0	26.7	142 47.3	4.8	17 31.4	8.5	61.1
12	359 34.2	N 7 27.6	157 11.1	4.8	S17 39.9	8.5	61.1
13	14 34.4	28.5	171 34.9	4.8	17 48.4	8.3	61.1
14	29 34.5	29.5	185 58.7	4.7	17 56.7	8.2	61.1
15	44 34.7	.. 30.4	200 22.4	4.7	18 04.9	8.0	61.1
16	59 34.9	31.3	214 46.1	4.6	18 12.9	8.0	61.1
17	74 35.1	32.3	229 09.7	4.6	18 20.9	7.7	61.0
18	89 35.2	N 7 33.2	243 33.3	4.5	S18 28.6	7.7	61.0
19	104 35.4	34.1	257 56.8	4.5	18 36.3	7.5	61.0
20	119 35.6	35.1	272 20.3	4.5	18 43.8	7.4	61.0
21	134 35.7	.. 36.0	286 43.8	4.5	18 51.2	7.2	61.0
22	149 35.9	36.9	301 07.3	4.4	18 58.4	7.1	61.0
23	164 36.1	37.8	315 30.7	4.3	S19 05.5	7.0	61.0
	SD 16.0	d 0.9	SD 16.6		16.7		16.6

Lat.	Twilight Naut.	Twilight Civil	Sunrise	Moonrise 6	7	8	9
°	h m	h m	h m	h m	h m	h m	h m
N 72	////	02 59	04 22	20 22	23 03	■	
N 70	01 18	03 22	04 33	20 03	22 21	25 11	01 11
68	02 05	03 39	04 42	19 49	21 53	24 03	00 03
66	02 34	03 53	04 50	19 37	21 32	23 27	25 11
64	02 55	04 05	04 56	19 27	21 15	23 01	24 36
62	03 12	04 14	05 01	19 18	21 01	22 41	24 10
60	03 26	04 22	05 06	19 11	20 50	22 25	23 50
N 58	03 37	04 29	05 10	19 05	20 40	22 11	23 34
56	03 47	04 35	05 14	18 59	20 31	22 00	23 20
54	03 56	04 41	05 17	18 54	20 23	21 49	23 08
52	04 03	04 46	05 20	18 50	20 16	21 40	22 57
50	04 10	04 50	05 23	18 46	20 10	21 32	22 48
45	04 23	04 59	05 29	18 37	19 57	21 15	22 28
N 40	04 34	05 06	05 34	18 30	19 46	21 01	22 12
35	04 42	05 13	05 38	18 24	19 37	20 49	21 58
30	04 49	05 18	05 42	18 19	19 28	20 38	21 46
20	05 00	05 26	05 48	18 09	19 14	20 21	21 26
N 10	05 08	05 33	05 54	18 01	19 02	20 05	21 09
0	05 14	05 38	05 59	17 54	18 51	19 51	20 52
S 10	05 18	05 42	06 04	17 46	18 40	19 37	20 36
20	05 21	05 47	06 09	17 38	18 28	19 22	20 19
30	05 23	05 50	06 14	17 30	18 15	19 04	19 59
35	05 23	05 52	06 18	17 24	18 07	18 54	19 48
40	05 23	05 54	06 21	17 19	17 58	18 43	19 34
45	05 22	05 56	06 25	17 12	17 48	18 30	19 19
S 50	05 21	05 58	06 30	17 04	17 36	18 14	19 00
52	05 20	05 59	06 33	17 01	17 30	18 06	18 51
54	05 19	06 00	06 35	16 57	17 24	17 58	18 41
56	05 18	06 01	06 38	16 52	17 17	17 48	18 29
58	05 16	06 02	06 41	16 47	17 09	17 38	18 16
S 60	05 14	06 02	06 44	16 42	17 00	17 25	18 01

Lat.	Sunset	Twilight Civil	Twilight Naut.	Moonset 6	7	8	9
°	h m	h m	h m	h m	h m	h m	h m
N 72	19 45	21 10	////	03 50	03 27	02 48	■
N 70	19 34	20 46	22 59	04 00	03 48	03 32	02 49
68	19 24	20 28	22 06	04 08	04 05	04 01	03 58
66	19 17	20 14	21 35	04 16	04 18	04 23	04 34
64	19 10	20 02	21 12	04 22	04 29	04 41	05 01
62	19 04	19 52	20 55	04 27	04 39	04 56	05 21
60	18 59	19 44	20 41	04 31	04 47	05 08	05 38
N 58	18 55	19 37	20 29	04 35	04 55	05 19	05 52
56	18 51	19 30	20 19	04 39	05 01	05 29	06 04
54	18 48	19 25	20 10	04 42	05 07	05 37	06 15
52	18 45	19 20	20 03	04 45	05 12	05 44	06 24
50	18 42	19 15	19 56	04 48	05 17	05 51	06 33
45	18 36	19 06	19 42	04 54	05 27	06 06	06 51
N 40	18 31	18 58	19 31	04 59	05 36	06 18	07 06
35	18 26	18 52	19 22	05 03	05 43	06 28	07 18
30	18 23	18 47	19 15	05 07	05 50	06 37	07 29
20	18 16	18 38	19 04	05 13	06 01	06 53	07 48
N 10	18 10	18 32	18 56	05 19	06 11	07 06	08 05
0	18 05	18 26	18 50	05 25	06 21	07 19	08 20
S 10	18 00	18 21	18 46	05 30	06 30	07 32	08 36
20	17 55	18 17	18 43	05 36	06 40	07 46	08 52
30	17 49	18 13	18 41	05 43	06 52	08 02	09 11
35	17 46	18 11	18 40	05 46	06 58	08 11	09 22
40	17 42	18 09	18 41	05 51	07 06	08 21	09 35
45	17 38	18 07	18 41	05 56	07 15	08 34	09 50
S 50	17 33	18 05	18 42	06 02	07 26	08 49	10 08
52	17 30	18 04	18 43	06 05	07 31	08 56	10 17
54	17 28	18 03	18 44	06 08	07 36	09 04	10 27
56	17 25	18 02	18 45	06 11	07 42	09 13	10 38
58	17 22	18 01	18 47	06 15	07 49	09 23	10 51
S 60	17 18	18 00	18 48	06 19	07 57	09 34	11 05

Day	SUN Eqn. of Time 00ʰ	12ʰ	Mer. Pass.	MOON Mer. Pass. Upper	Lower	Age	Phase
d	m s	m s	h m	h m	h m	d	%
6	02 26	02 17	12 02	24 07	11 39	15	100
7	02 09	02 00	12 02	00 07	12 36	16	99
8	01 52	01 44	12 02	01 05	13 35	17	96

UT	ARIES	VENUS −4.6		MARS −0.5		JUPITER −2.0		SATURN +0.2		STARS		
	GHA	GHA	Dec	GHA	Dec	GHA	Dec	GHA	Dec	Name	SHA	Dec
d h	° ′	° ′	° ′	° ′	° ′	° ′	° ′	° ′	° ′		° ′	° ′
9 00	197 38.6	135 35.2	N25 00.9	40 47.4	N12 51.8	154 44.9	N15 32.8	351 52.0	S 7 42.7	Acamar	315 19.3	S40 15.5
01	212 41.1	150 35.3	01.4	55 50.1	51.7	169 46.8	32.9	6 54.6	42.6	Achernar	335 27.9	S57 10.5
02	227 43.5	165 35.5	02.0	70 52.7	51.7	184 48.7	33.1	21 57.2	42.5	Acrux	173 09.6	S63 10.3
03	242 46.0	180 35.6 . .	02.5	85 55.4 . .	51.6	199 50.6 . .	33.3	36 59.9 . .	42.5	Adhara	255 13.2	S28 59.7
04	257 48.4	195 35.8	03.1	100 58.1	51.6	214 52.5	33.4	52 02.5	42.4	Aldebaran	290 50.6	N16 31.9
05	272 50.9	210 35.9	03.6	116 00.7	51.6	229 54.4	33.6	67 05.2	42.3			
06	287 53.4	225 36.1	N25 04.2	131 03.4	N12 51.5	244 56.3	N15 33.8	82 07.8	S 7 42.2	Alioth	166 20.8	N55 53.5
07	302 55.8	240 36.3	04.7	146 06.0	51.5	259 58.2	33.9	97 10.4	42.2	Alkaid	152 59.0	N49 15.0
08	317 58.3	255 36.4	05.2	161 08.7	51.4	275 00.1	34.1	112 13.1	42.1	Al Na'ir	27 45.0	S46 53.9
M 09	333 00.8	270 36.6 . .	05.8	176 11.3 . .	51.4	290 02.0 . .	34.3	127 15.7 . .	42.0	Alnilam	275 47.4	S 1 11.9
O 10	348 03.2	285 36.7	06.3	191 14.0	51.3	305 03.9	34.4	142 18.4	42.0	Alphard	217 56.8	S 8 43.0
N 11	3 05.7	300 36.9	06.9	206 16.6	51.3	320 05.8	34.6	157 21.0	41.9			
D 12	18 08.2	315 37.0	N25 07.4	221 19.2	N12 51.2	335 07.7	N15 34.8	172 23.7	S 7 41.8	Alphecca	126 11.4	N26 40.2
A 13	33 10.6	330 37.2	08.0	236 21.9	51.2	350 09.6	35.0	187 26.3	41.8	Alpheratz	357 44.7	N29 09.4
Y 14	48 13.1	345 37.4	08.5	251 24.5	51.2	5 11.5	35.1	202 28.9	41.7	Altair	62 09.1	N 8 54.0
15	63 15.6	0 37.5 . .	09.0	266 27.2 . .	51.1	20 13.4 . .	35.3	217 31.6 . .	41.6	Ankaa	353 16.9	S42 14.3
16	78 18.0	15 37.7	09.6	281 29.8	51.1	35 15.3	35.5	232 34.2	41.6	Antares	112 27.0	S26 27.5
17	93 20.5	30 37.9	10.1	296 32.5	51.0	50 17.2	35.6	247 36.9	41.5			
18	108 22.9	45 38.0	N25 10.6	311 35.1	N12 51.0	65 19.1	N15 35.8	262 39.5	S 7 41.4	Arcturus	145 56.2	N19 06.9
19	123 25.4	60 38.2	11.2	326 37.7	50.9	80 21.0	36.0	277 42.2	41.3	Atria	107 29.3	S69 02.7
20	138 27.9	75 38.4	11.7	341 40.4	50.9	95 22.9	36.1	292 44.8	41.3	Avior	234 18.2	S59 33.4
21	153 30.3	90 38.5 . .	12.2	356 43.0 . .	50.8	110 24.8 . .	36.3	307 47.4 . .	41.2	Bellatrix	278 33.1	N 6 21.5
22	168 32.8	105 38.7	12.8	11 45.6	50.8	125 26.7	36.5	322 50.1	41.1	Betelgeuse	271 02.3	N 7 24.4
23	183 35.3	120 38.9	13.3	26 48.3	50.7	140 28.6	36.7	337 52.7	41.1			
10 00	198 37.7	135 39.0	N25 13.8	41 50.9	N12 50.7	155 30.5	N15 36.8	352 55.4	S 7 41.0	Canopus	263 56.7	S52 42.5
01	213 40.2	150 39.2	14.4	56 53.5	50.6	170 32.4	37.0	7 58.0	40.9	Capella	280 35.9	N46 00.6
02	228 42.7	165 39.4	14.9	71 56.1	50.5	185 34.3	37.2	23 00.6	40.9	Deneb	49 32.2	N45 19.3
03	243 45.1	180 39.6 . .	15.4	86 58.8 . .	50.5	200 36.2 . .	37.3	38 03.3 . .	40.8	Denebola	182 34.2	N14 30.0
04	258 47.6	195 39.7	15.9	102 01.4	50.4	215 38.2	37.5	53 05.9	40.7	Diphda	348 57.0	S17 55.2
05	273 50.1	210 39.9	16.5	117 04.0	50.4	230 40.1	37.7	68 08.6	40.6			
06	288 52.5	225 40.1	N25 17.0	132 06.6	N12 50.3	245 42.0	N15 37.8	83 11.2	S 7 40.6	Dubhe	193 52.1	N61 41.1
07	303 55.0	240 40.3	17.5	147 09.2	50.3	260 43.9	38.0	98 13.9	40.5	Elnath	278 13.9	N28 37.0
T 08	318 57.4	255 40.4	18.0	162 11.9	50.2	275 45.8	38.2	113 16.5	40.4	Eltanin	90 46.3	N51 29.0
U 09	333 59.9	270 40.6 . .	18.5	177 14.5 . .	50.2	290 47.7 . .	38.4	128 19.1 . .	40.4	Enif	33 48.1	N 9 55.8
E 10	349 02.4	285 40.8	19.1	192 17.1	50.1	305 49.6	38.5	143 21.8	40.3	Fomalhaut	15 25.2	S29 33.3
S 11	4 04.8	300 41.0	19.6	207 19.7	50.1	320 51.5	38.7	158 24.4	40.2			
D 12	19 07.3	315 41.2	N25 20.1	222 22.3	N12 50.0	335 53.4	N15 38.9	173 27.1	S 7 40.2	Gacrux	172 01.3	S57 11.1
A 13	34 09.8	330 41.4	20.6	237 24.9	49.9	350 55.3	39.0	188 29.7	40.1	Gienah	175 52.8	S17 36.8
Y 14	49 12.2	345 41.5	21.1	252 27.6	49.9	5 57.2	39.2	203 32.4	40.0	Hadar	148 48.5	S60 26.0
15	64 14.7	0 41.7 . .	21.7	267 30.2 . .	49.8	20 59.1 . .	39.4	218 35.0 . .	40.0	Hamal	328 02.0	N23 31.2
16	79 17.2	15 41.9	22.2	282 32.8	49.8	36 01.0	39.5	233 37.6	39.9	Kaus Aust.	83 44.8	S34 22.5
17	94 19.6	30 42.1	22.7	297 35.4	49.7	51 02.9	39.7	248 40.3	39.8			
18	109 22.1	45 42.3	N25 23.2	312 38.0	N12 49.6	66 04.8	N15 39.9	263 42.9	S 7 39.7	Kochab	137 18.8	N74 06.1
19	124 24.5	60 42.5	23.7	327 40.6	49.6	81 06.7	40.1	278 45.6	39.7	Markab	13 39.4	N15 16.2
20	139 27.0	75 42.7	24.2	342 43.2	49.5	96 08.6	40.2	293 48.2	39.6	Menkar	314 16.2	N 4 08.1
21	154 29.5	90 42.9 . .	24.7	357 45.8 . .	49.5	111 10.5 . .	40.4	308 50.9 . .	39.5	Menkent	148 08.2	S36 25.9
22	169 31.9	105 43.1	25.2	12 48.4	49.4	126 12.4	40.6	323 53.5	39.5	Miaplacidus	221 39.5	S69 46.5
23	184 34.4	120 43.3	25.8	27 51.0	49.3	141 14.3	40.7	338 56.2	39.4			
11 00	199 36.9	135 43.5	N25 26.3	42 53.6	N12 49.3	156 16.2	N15 40.9	353 58.8	S 7 39.3	Mirfak	308 42.0	N49 54.3
01	214 39.3	150 43.7	26.8	57 56.2	49.2	171 18.1	41.1	9 01.4	39.3	Nunki	75 59.3	S26 16.7
02	229 41.8	165 43.9	27.3	72 58.8	49.1	186 20.0	41.2	24 04.1	39.2	Peacock	53 20.7	S56 41.4
03	244 44.3	180 44.1 . .	27.8	88 01.4 . .	49.1	201 21.9 . .	41.4	39 06.7 . .	39.1	Pollux	243 28.7	N27 59.7
04	259 46.7	195 44.3	28.3	103 04.0	49.0	216 23.8	41.6	54 09.4	39.0	Procyon	245 00.6	N 5 11.4
05	274 49.2	210 44.5	28.8	118 06.6	48.9	231 25.7	41.7	69 12.0	39.0			
06	289 51.7	225 44.7	N25 29.3	133 09.2	N12 48.9	246 27.6	N15 41.9	84 14.7	S 7 38.9	Rasalhague	96 07.1	N12 33.0
W 07	304 54.1	240 44.9	29.8	148 11.8	48.8	261 29.5	42.1	99 17.3	38.8	Regulus	207 44.2	N11 54.2
E 08	319 56.6	255 45.1	30.3	163 14.3	48.7	276 31.4	42.3	114 19.9	38.8	Rigel	281 13.0	S 8 11.5
D 09	334 59.0	270 45.3 . .	30.8	178 16.9 . .	48.7	291 33.3 . .	42.4	129 22.6 . .	38.7	Rigil Kent.	139 52.2	S60 53.1
N 10	350 01.5	285 45.5	31.3	193 19.5	48.6	306 35.2	42.6	144 25.2	38.6	Sabik	102 13.3	S15 44.4
E 11	5 04.0	300 45.7	31.8	208 22.1	48.5	321 37.1	42.8	159 27.9	38.6			
S 12	20 06.4	315 45.9	N25 32.3	223 24.7	N12 48.5	336 39.0	N15 42.9	174 30.5	S 7 38.5	Schedar	349 42.1	N56 36.2
D 13	35 08.9	330 46.1	32.8	238 27.3	48.4	351 40.9	43.1	189 33.2	38.4	Shaula	96 22.9	S37 06.6
A 14	50 11.4	345 46.3	33.3	253 29.8	48.3	6 42.8	43.3	204 35.8	38.4	Sirius	258 34.5	S16 44.3
Y 15	65 13.8	0 46.5 . .	33.8	268 32.4 . .	48.3	21 44.7 . .	43.4	219 38.4 . .	38.3	Spica	158 31.8	S11 13.7
16	80 16.3	15 46.8	34.3	283 35.0	48.2	36 46.6	43.6	234 41.1	38.2	Suhail	222 52.9	S43 29.4
17	95 18.8	30 47.0	34.8	298 37.6	48.1	51 48.5	43.8	249 43.7	38.1			
18	110 21.2	45 47.2	N25 35.2	313 40.2	N12 48.0	66 50.4	N15 43.9	264 46.4	S 7 38.1	Vega	80 39.4	N38 47.5
19	125 23.7	60 47.4	35.7	328 42.7	48.0	81 52.3	44.1	279 49.0	38.0	Zuben'ubi	137 06.0	S16 05.7
20	140 26.2	75 47.6	36.2	343 45.3	47.9	96 54.1	44.3	294 51.7	37.9		SHA	Mer. Pass.
21	155 28.6	90 47.8 . .	36.7	358 47.9 . .	47.8	111 56.0 . .	44.5	309 54.3 . .	37.9		° ′	h m
22	170 31.1	105 48.1	37.2	13 50.5	47.8	126 57.9	44.6	324 57.0	37.8	Venus	297 01.3	14 57
23	185 33.5	120 48.3	37.7	28 53.0	47.7	141 59.8	44.8	339 59.6	37.7	Mars	203 13.2	21 09
	h m									Jupiter	316 52.8	13 36
Mer. Pass. 10 43.7		v 0.2	d 0.5	v 2.6	d 0.1	v 1.9	d 0.2	v 2.6	d 0.1	Saturn	154 17.6	0 28

UT	SUN GHA	SUN Dec	MOON GHA	v	Dec	d	HP
d h	° '	° '	° '	'	° '	'	'
9 00	179 36.3	N 7 38.8	329 54.0	4.4	S19 12.5	6.8	60.9
01	194 36.4	39.7	344 17.4	4.3	19 19.3	6.6	60.9
02	209 36.6	40.6	358 40.7	4.3	19 25.9	6.5	60.9
03	224 36.8	.. 41.6	13 04.0	4.2	19 32.4	6.4	60.9
04	239 36.9	42.5	27 27.2	4.2	19 38.8	6.2	60.9
05	254 37.1	43.4	41 50.4	4.2	19 45.0	6.1	60.9
M 06	269 37.3	N 7 44.3	56 13.6	4.2	S19 51.1	6.0	60.8
O 07	284 37.5	45.3	70 36.8	4.2	19 57.1	5.7	60.8
N 08	299 37.6	46.2	85 00.0	4.1	20 02.8	5.7	60.8
D 09	314 37.8	.. 47.1	99 23.1	4.1	20 08.5	5.5	60.8
A 10	329 38.0	48.0	113 46.2	4.1	20 14.0	5.3	60.8
Y 11	344 38.1	49.0	128 09.3	4.1	20 19.3	5.2	60.7
12	359 38.3	N 7 49.9	142 32.4	4.1	S20 24.5	5.0	60.7
13	14 38.5	50.8	156 55.5	4.1	20 29.5	4.9	60.7
14	29 38.6	51.7	171 18.6	4.0	20 34.4	4.7	60.7
15	44 38.8	.. 52.7	185 41.6	4.1	20 39.1	4.6	60.6
16	59 39.0	53.6	200 04.7	4.0	20 43.7	4.4	60.6
17	74 39.2	54.5	214 27.7	4.1	20 48.1	4.3	60.6
18	89 39.3	N 7 55.4	228 50.8	4.0	S20 52.4	4.1	60.6
19	104 39.5	56.4	243 13.8	4.0	20 56.5	4.0	60.6
20	119 39.7	57.3	257 36.8	4.1	21 00.5	3.8	60.5
21	134 39.8	.. 58.2	271 59.9	4.0	21 04.3	3.6	60.5
22	149 40.0	7 59.1	286 22.9	4.0	21 07.9	3.5	60.5
23	164 40.2	8 00.0	300 45.9	4.1	21 11.4	3.3	60.5
10 00	179 40.3	N 8 01.0	315 09.0	4.0	S21 14.7	3.2	60.4
01	194 40.5	01.9	329 32.0	4.1	21 17.9	3.0	60.4
02	209 40.7	02.8	343 55.1	4.1	21 20.9	2.9	60.4
03	224 40.8	.. 03.8	358 18.2	4.0	21 23.8	2.7	60.3
04	239 41.0	04.7	12 41.2	4.1	21 26.5	2.6	60.3
05	254 41.2	05.6	27 04.3	4.2	21 29.1	2.4	60.3
T 06	269 41.3	N 8 06.5	41 27.5	4.1	S21 31.5	2.2	60.3
U 07	284 41.5	07.4	55 50.6	4.1	21 33.7	2.1	60.2
E 08	299 41.7	08.4	70 13.7	4.2	21 35.8	1.9	60.2
S 09	314 41.8	.. 09.3	84 36.9	4.2	21 37.7	1.8	60.2
D 10	329 42.0	10.2	99 00.1	4.2	21 39.5	1.6	60.2
A 11	344 42.2	11.1	113 23.3	4.3	21 41.1	1.5	60.1
Y 12	359 42.3	N 8 12.1	127 46.6	4.3	S21 42.6	1.3	60.1
13	14 42.5	13.0	142 09.9	4.3	21 43.9	1.2	60.1
14	29 42.7	13.9	156 33.2	4.3	21 45.1	1.0	60.0
15	44 42.8	.. 14.8	170 56.5	4.4	21 46.1	0.8	60.0
16	59 43.0	15.7	185 19.9	4.4	21 46.9	0.7	60.0
17	74 43.2	16.6	199 43.3	4.4	21 47.6	0.5	59.9
18	89 43.3	N 8 17.6	214 06.7	4.5	S21 48.1	0.4	59.9
19	104 43.5	18.5	228 30.2	4.6	21 48.5	0.3	59.9
20	119 43.7	19.4	242 53.8	4.5	21 48.8	0.0	59.9
21	134 43.8	.. 20.3	257 17.3	4.6	21 48.8	0.0	59.8
22	149 44.0	21.2	271 40.9	4.7	21 48.8	0.3	59.8
23	164 44.2	22.2	286 04.6	4.7	21 48.5	0.3	59.8
11 00	179 44.3	N 8 23.1	300 28.3	4.7	S21 48.2	0.6	59.7
01	194 44.5	24.0	314 52.0	4.8	21 47.6	0.6	59.7
02	209 44.7	24.9	329 15.8	4.9	21 47.0	0.9	59.7
03	224 44.8	.. 25.8	343 39.7	4.9	21 46.1	0.9	59.6
04	239 45.0	26.7	358 03.6	5.0	21 45.2	1.2	59.6
05	254 45.1	27.6	12 27.6	5.0	21 44.0	1.2	59.6
W 06	269 45.3	N 8 28.6	26 51.6	5.0	S21 42.8	1.4	59.5
E 07	284 45.5	29.5	41 15.6	5.2	21 41.4	1.6	59.5
D 08	299 45.6	30.4	55 39.8	5.2	21 39.8	1.7	59.5
N 09	314 45.8	.. 31.3	70 04.0	5.3	21 38.1	1.8	59.4
E 10	329 46.0	32.2	84 28.2	5.3	21 36.3	2.0	59.4
S 11	344 46.1	33.2	98 52.5	5.4	21 34.3	2.2	59.4
D 12	359 46.3	N 8 34.1	113 16.9	5.4	S21 32.1	2.2	59.3
A 13	14 46.5	35.0	127 41.3	5.5	21 29.9	2.4	59.3
Y 14	29 46.6	35.9	142 05.8	5.6	21 27.5	2.6	59.3
15	44 46.8	.. 36.8	156 30.4	5.7	21 24.9	2.7	59.2
16	59 46.9	37.7	170 55.1	5.7	21 22.2	2.8	59.2
17	74 47.1	38.6	185 19.8	5.8	21 19.4	3.0	59.2
18	89 47.3	N 8 39.6	199 44.6	5.8	S21 16.4	3.1	59.1
19	104 47.4	40.5	214 09.4	5.9	21 13.3	3.2	59.1
20	119 47.6	41.4	228 34.3	6.0	21 10.1	3.4	59.1
21	134 47.8	.. 42.3	242 59.3	6.1	21 06.7	3.5	59.0
22	149 47.9	43.2	257 24.4	6.2	21 03.2	3.6	59.0
23	164 48.1	44.1	271 49.6	6.2	S20 59.6	3.8	59.0
	SD 16.0	d 0.9	SD 16.5		16.4		16.2

Moonrise

Lat.	Twilight Naut.	Civil	Sunrise	Moonrise 9	10	11	12
°	h m	h m	h m	h m	h m	h m	h m
N 72	////	02 37	04 05	■	■	■	■
N 70	////	03 04	04 19	■	■	■	■
68	01 39	03 24	04 29	01 11	02 15	03 46	03 45
66	02 15	03 40	04 38	00 03	01 11	02 23	02 58
64	02 40	03 53	04 45	24 36	00 36	01 45	02 27
62	02 59	04 03	04 52	24 10	00 10	01 18	02 04
60	03 14	04 12	04 57	23 50	24 58	00 58	01 45
N 58	03 27	04 20	05 02	23 34	24 41	00 41	01 30
56	03 38	04 27	05 06	23 20	24 26	00 26	01 17
54	03 47	04 33	05 10	23 08	24 14	00 14	01 05
52	03 55	04 38	05 14	22 57	24 03	00 03	00 55
50	04 05	04 43	05 17	22 48	23 53	24 46	00 46
45	04 17	04 53	05 24	22 28	23 32	24 27	00 27
N 40	04 29	05 02	05 29	22 12	23 16	24 11	00 11
35	04 38	05 08	05 34	21 58	23 02	23 58	24 46
30	04 46	05 14	05 38	21 46	22 50	23 46	24 36
20	04 57	05 23	05 46	21 26	22 29	23 26	24 19
N 10	05 06	05 31	05 52	21 09	22 11	23 09	24 03
0	05 13	05 37	05 58	20 52	21 54	22 53	23 49
S 10	05 18	05 42	06 04	20 36	21 37	22 37	23 35
20	05 22	05 47	06 10	20 19	21 19	22 20	23 20
30	05 24	05 52	06 16	19 59	20 58	22 00	23 02
35	05 25	05 55	06 20	19 48	20 46	21 48	22 52
40	05 26	05 57	06 24	19 34	20 32	21 35	22 40
45	05 26	06 00	06 29	19 19	20 16	21 19	22 25
S 50	05 25	06 03	06 35	19 00	19 55	21 00	22 09
52	05 25	06 04	06 38	18 51	19 46	20 50	22 01
54	05 24	06 05	06 41	18 41	19 35	20 40	21 52
56	05 23	06 06	06 45	18 29	19 23	20 28	21 42
58	05 22	06 08	06 48	18 16	19 09	20 15	21 30
S 60	05 21	06 09	06 52	18 01	18 52	19 59	21 17

Moonset

Lat.	Sunset	Twilight Civil	Naut.	Moonset 9	10	11	12
°	h m	h m	h m	h m	h m	h m	h m
N 72	20 01	21 31	////	■	■	■	■
N 70	19 47	21 03	////	02 49	■	■	■
68	19 36	20 42	22 32	03 58	03 55	04 32	06 36
66	19 27	20 25	21 52	04 34	04 59	05 55	07 23
64	19 19	20 12	21 26	05 01	05 35	06 33	07 53
62	19 12	20 01	21 06	05 21	06 06	06 59	08 15
60	19 07	19 52	20 51	05 38	06 21	07 20	08 34
N 58	19 02	19 44	20 38	05 52	06 37	07 37	08 49
56	18 57	19 37	20 27	06 04	06 51	07 51	09 02
54	18 53	19 31	20 17	06 15	07 04	08 04	09 13
52	18 50	19 25	20 09	06 24	07 14	08 15	09 23
50	18 47	19 20	20 01	06 33	07 24	08 24	09 32
45	18 39	19 10	19 46	06 51	07 44	08 45	09 50
N 40	18 34	19 01	19 35	07 06	08 01	09 01	10 05
35	18 29	18 55	19 25	07 18	08 14	09 15	10 18
30	18 24	18 49	19 17	07 29	08 26	09 27	10 29
20	18 17	18 39	19 05	07 48	08 47	09 48	10 48
N 10	18 10	18 32	18 56	08 05	09 05	10 06	11 05
0	18 04	18 25	18 50	08 20	09 22	10 22	11 20
S 10	17 59	18 20	18 44	08 36	09 38	10 39	11 36
20	17 53	18 15	18 40	08 52	09 56	10 57	11 52
30	17 46	18 10	18 38	09 11	10 17	11 17	12 11
35	17 42	18 07	18 37	09 22	10 29	11 29	12 21
40	17 37	18 05	18 36	09 35	10 43	11 43	12 34
45	17 32	18 02	18 36	09 50	10 59	11 59	12 48
S 50	17 26	17 59	18 36	10 08	11 19	12 19	13 06
52	17 24	17 58	18 37	10 17	11 29	12 28	13 15
54	17 21	17 56	18 37	10 27	11 40	12 38	13 24
56	17 17	17 55	18 38	10 38	11 52	12 50	13 34
58	17 14	17 53	18 39	10 51	12 06	13 04	13 46
S 60	17 10	17 52	18 41	11 05	12 22	13 20	14 00

Day	SUN Eqn. of Time 00h	12h	Mer. Pass.	MOON Mer. Pass. Upper	Lower	Age	Phase
d	m s	m s	h m	h m	h m	d	%
9	01 35	01 27	12 01	02 06	14 36	18	89
10	01 19	01 11	12 01	03 07	15 38	19	81
11	01 03	00 55	12 01	04 08	16 38	20	71

2012 APRIL 12, 13, 14 (THURS., FRI., SAT.)

UT	ARIES GHA	VENUS −4.6 GHA	Dec	MARS −0.4 GHA	Dec	JUPITER −2.0 GHA	Dec	SATURN +0.2 GHA	Dec	Name	SHA	Dec
12 00	200 36.0	135 48.5	N25 38.2	43 55.6	N12 47.6	157 01.7	N15 45.0	355 02.2	S 7 37.7	Acamar	315 19.3	S40 15.5
01	215 38.5	150 48.7	38.7	58 58.2	47.5	172 03.6	45.1	10 04.9	37.6	Achernar	335 27.9	S57 10.5
02	230 40.9	165 48.9	39.1	74 00.7	47.5	187 05.5	45.3	25 07.5	37.5	Acrux	173 09.6	S63 10.3
03	245 43.4	180 49.2	.. 39.6	89 03.3	.. 47.4	202 07.4	.. 45.5	40 10.2	.. 37.4	Adhara	255 13.2	S28 59.7
04	260 45.9	195 49.4	40.1	104 05.9	47.3	217 09.3	45.6	55 12.8	37.4	Aldebaran	290 50.6	N16 31.9
05	275 48.3	210 49.6	40.6	119 08.4	47.2	232 11.2	45.8	70 15.5	37.3			
06	290 50.8	225 49.9	N25 41.1	134 11.0	N12 47.1	247 13.1	N15 46.0	85 18.1	S 7 37.2	Alioth	166 20.8	N55 53.5
T 07	305 53.3	240 50.1	41.5	149 13.5	47.1	262 15.0	46.1	100 20.7	37.2	Alkaid	152 59.0	N49 15.0
H 08	320 55.7	255 50.3	42.0	164 16.1	47.0	277 16.9	46.3	115 23.4	37.1	Al Na'ir	27 45.0	S46 53.8
U 09	335 58.2	270 50.6	.. 42.5	179 18.7	.. 46.9	292 18.8	.. 46.5	130 26.0	.. 37.0	Alnilam	275 47.4	S 1 11.9
R 10	351 00.7	285 50.8	43.0	194 21.2	46.8	307 20.7	46.7	145 28.7	37.0	Alphard	217 56.8	S 8 43.0
S 11	6 03.1	300 51.0	43.5	209 23.8	46.8	322 22.6	46.8	160 31.3	36.9			
D 12	21 05.6	315 51.3	N25 43.9	224 26.3	N12 46.7	337 24.5	N15 47.0	175 34.0	S 7 36.8	Alphecca	126 11.4	N26 40.2
A 13	36 08.0	330 51.5	44.4	239 28.9	46.6	352 26.4	47.2	190 36.6	36.8	Alpheratz	357 44.7	N29 09.4
Y 14	51 10.5	345 51.7	44.9	254 31.4	46.5	7 28.3	47.3	205 39.3	36.7	Altair	62 09.1	N 8 54.0
15	66 13.0	0 52.0	.. 45.4	269 34.0	.. 46.4	22 30.2	.. 47.5	220 41.9	.. 36.6	Ankaa	353 16.9	S42 14.3
16	81 15.4	15 52.2	45.8	284 36.5	46.4	37 32.1	47.7	235 44.5	36.5	Antares	112 27.0	S26 27.5
17	96 17.9	30 52.5	46.3	299 39.1	46.3	52 34.0	47.8	250 47.2	36.5			
18	111 20.4	45 52.7	N25 46.8	314 41.6	N12 46.2	67 35.9	N15 48.0	265 49.8	S 7 36.4	Arcturus	145 56.1	N19 06.9
19	126 22.8	60 52.9	47.2	329 44.2	46.1	82 37.8	48.2	280 52.5	36.3	Atria	107 29.2	S69 02.7
20	141 25.3	75 53.2	47.7	344 46.7	46.0	97 39.7	48.3	295 55.1	36.3	Avior	234 18.3	S59 33.4
21	156 27.8	90 53.4	.. 48.2	359 49.2	.. 45.9	112 41.6	.. 48.5	310 57.8	.. 36.2	Bellatrix	278 33.1	N 6 21.5
22	171 30.2	105 53.7	48.6	14 51.8	45.8	127 43.5	48.7	326 00.4	36.1	Betelgeuse	271 02.3	N 7 24.4
23	186 32.7	120 53.9	49.1	29 54.3	45.8	142 45.4	48.9	341 03.0	36.1			
13 00	201 35.1	135 54.2	N25 49.6	44 56.9	N12 45.7	157 47.3	N15 49.0	356 05.7	S 7 36.0	Canopus	263 56.7	S52 42.5
01	216 37.6	150 54.4	50.0	59 59.4	45.6	172 49.2	49.2	11 08.3	35.9	Capella	280 35.9	N46 00.6
02	231 40.1	165 54.7	50.5	75 01.9	45.5	187 51.1	49.4	26 11.0	35.9	Deneb	49 32.2	N45 19.3
03	246 42.5	180 54.9	.. 50.9	90 04.5	.. 45.4	202 53.0	.. 49.5	41 13.6	.. 35.8	Denebola	182 34.2	N14 30.0
04	261 45.0	195 55.2	51.4	105 07.0	45.3	217 54.9	49.7	56 16.3	35.7	Diphda	348 57.0	S17 55.2
05	276 47.5	210 55.5	51.9	120 09.5	45.2	232 56.7	49.9	71 18.9	35.6			
06	291 49.9	225 55.7	N25 52.3	135 12.1	N12 45.2	247 58.6	N15 50.0	86 21.6	S 7 35.6	Dubhe	193 52.1	N61 41.1
07	306 52.4	240 56.0	52.8	150 14.6	45.1	263 00.5	50.2	101 24.2	35.5	Elnath	278 13.9	N28 37.0
08	321 54.9	255 56.2	53.2	165 17.1	45.0	278 02.4	50.4	116 26.8	35.4	Eltanin	90 46.3	N51 29.0
F 09	336 57.3	270 56.5	.. 53.7	180 19.7	.. 44.9	293 04.3	.. 50.5	131 29.5	.. 35.4	Enif	33 48.1	N 9 55.9
R 10	351 59.8	285 56.8	54.2	195 22.2	44.8	308 06.2	50.7	146 32.1	35.3	Fomalhaut	15 25.1	S29 33.3
I 11	7 02.3	300 57.0	54.6	210 24.7	44.7	323 08.1	50.9	161 34.8	35.2			
D 12	22 04.7	315 57.3	N25 55.1	225 27.2	N12 44.6	338 10.0	N15 51.1	176 37.4	S 7 35.2	Gacrux	172 01.3	S57 11.2
A 13	37 07.2	330 57.5	55.5	240 29.8	44.5	353 11.9	51.2	191 40.1	35.1	Gienah	175 52.8	S17 36.9
Y 14	52 09.6	345 57.8	56.0	255 32.3	44.4	8 13.8	51.4	206 42.7	35.0	Hadar	148 48.4	S60 26.0
15	67 12.1	0 58.1	.. 56.4	270 34.8	.. 44.3	23 15.7	.. 51.6	221 45.4	.. 34.9	Hamal	328 02.0	N23 31.2
16	82 14.6	15 58.4	56.9	285 37.3	44.2	38 17.6	51.7	236 48.0	34.9	Kaus Aust.	83 44.8	S34 22.5
17	97 17.0	30 58.6	57.3	300 39.8	44.2	53 19.5	51.9	251 50.6	34.8			
18	112 19.5	45 58.9	N25 57.8	315 42.3	N12 44.1	68 21.4	N15 52.1	266 53.3	S 7 34.7	Kochab	137 18.8	N74 06.1
19	127 22.0	60 59.2	58.2	330 44.9	44.0	83 23.3	52.2	281 55.9	34.7	Markab	13 39.4	N15 16.2
20	142 24.4	75 59.4	58.6	345 47.4	43.9	98 25.2	52.4	296 58.6	34.6	Menkar	314 16.2	N 4 08.2
21	157 26.9	90 59.7	.. 59.1	0 49.9	.. 43.8	113 27.1	.. 52.5	312 01.2	.. 34.5	Menkent	148 08.2	S36 25.9
22	172 29.4	106 00.0	25 59.5	15 52.4	43.7	128 29.0	52.7	327 03.9	34.5	Miaplacidus	221 39.5	S69 46.5
23	187 31.8	121 00.3	26 00.0	30 54.9	43.6	143 30.9	52.9	342 06.5	34.4			
14 00	202 34.3	136 00.6	N26 00.4	45 57.4	N12 43.5	158 32.8	N15 53.1	357 09.2	S 7 34.3	Mirfak	308 42.0	N49 54.3
01	217 36.8	151 00.8	00.9	60 59.9	43.4	173 34.6	53.2	12 11.8	34.3	Nunki	75 59.3	S26 16.7
02	232 39.2	166 01.1	01.3	76 02.4	43.3	188 36.5	53.4	27 14.4	34.2	Peacock	53 20.6	S56 41.4
03	247 41.7	181 01.4	.. 01.7	91 04.9	.. 43.2	203 38.4	.. 53.6	42 17.1	.. 34.1	Pollux	243 28.7	N27 59.7
04	262 44.1	196 01.7	02.2	106 07.4	43.1	218 40.3	53.8	57 19.7	34.0	Procyon	245 00.6	N 5 11.4
05	277 46.6	211 02.0	02.6	121 09.9	43.0	233 42.2	53.9	72 22.4	34.0			
06	292 49.1	226 02.3	N26 03.1	136 12.4	N12 42.9	248 44.1	N15 54.1	87 25.0	S 7 33.9	Rasalhague	96 07.0	N12 33.0
07	307 51.5	241 02.5	03.5	151 15.0	42.8	263 46.0	54.3	102 27.7	33.8	Regulus	207 44.2	N11 54.2
S 08	322 54.0	256 02.8	03.9	166 17.4	42.7	278 47.9	54.4	117 30.3	33.8	Rigel	281 13.0	S 8 11.5
A 09	337 56.5	271 03.1	.. 04.4	181 19.9	.. 42.6	293 49.8	.. 54.6	132 33.0	.. 33.7	Rigil Kent.	139 52.2	S60 53.1
T 10	352 58.9	286 03.4	04.8	196 22.4	42.5	308 51.7	54.8	147 35.6	33.6	Sabik	102 13.3	S15 44.4
U 11	8 01.4	301 03.7	05.2	211 24.9	42.4	323 53.6	54.9	162 38.2	33.6			
R 12	23 03.9	316 04.0	N26 05.7	226 27.4	N12 42.3	338 55.5	N15 55.1	177 40.9	S 7 33.5	Schedar	349 42.0	N56 36.2
D 13	38 06.3	331 04.3	06.1	241 29.9	42.2	353 57.4	55.3	192 43.5	33.4	Shaula	96 22.8	S37 06.6
A 14	53 08.8	346 04.6	06.5	256 32.4	42.1	8 59.3	55.4	207 46.2	33.4	Sirius	258 34.5	S16 44.3
Y 15	68 11.3	1 04.9	.. 06.9	271 34.9	.. 42.0	24 01.2	.. 55.6	222 48.8	.. 33.3	Spica	158 31.8	S11 13.7
16	83 13.7	16 05.2	07.4	286 37.4	41.9	39 03.0	55.8	237 51.5	33.2	Suhail	222 52.9	S43 29.4
17	98 16.2	31 05.5	07.8	301 39.9	41.8	54 04.9	55.9	252 54.1	33.1			
18	113 18.6	46 05.8	N26 08.2	316 42.4	N12 41.7	69 06.8	N15 56.1	267 56.8	S 7 33.1	Vega	80 39.4	N38 47.5
19	128 21.1	61 06.1	08.7	331 44.9	41.6	84 08.7	56.3	282 59.4	33.0	Zuben'ubi	137 06.0	S16 05.7
20	143 23.6	76 06.4	09.1	346 47.3	41.5	99 10.6	56.5	298 02.0	32.9		SHA	Mer.Pass.
21	158 26.0	91 06.7	.. 09.5	1 49.8	.. 41.4	114 12.5	.. 56.6	313 04.7	.. 32.9	Venus	294 19.0	14 56
22	173 28.5	106 07.0	09.9	16 52.3	41.3	129 14.4	56.8	328 07.3	32.8	Mars	203 21.7	20 57
23	188 31.0	121 07.3	10.3	31 54.8	41.1	144 16.3	57.0	343 10.0	32.7	Jupiter	316 12.1	13 27
Mer.Pass. 10 31.9		v 0.3	d 0.5	v 2.5	d 0.1	v 1.9	d 0.2	v 2.6	d 0.1	Saturn	154 30.5	0 16

UT	SUN GHA	Dec	MOON GHA	v	Dec	d	HP
12 00	179 48.2	N 8 45.0	286 14.8	6.3	S20 55.8	3.9	58.9
01	194 48.4	45.9	300 40.1	6.4	20 51.9	4.0	58.9
02	209 48.6	46.9	315 05.5	6.5	20 47.9	4.2	58.8
03	224 48.7	.. 47.8	329 31.0	6.5	20 43.7	4.3	58.8
04	239 48.9	48.7	343 56.5	6.6	20 39.4	4.4	58.8
05	254 49.0	49.6	358 22.1	6.7	20 35.0	4.5	58.7
06	269 49.2	N 8 50.5	12 47.8	6.8	S20 30.5	4.6	58.7
07	284 49.4	51.4	27 13.6	6.9	20 25.9	4.8	58.7
T 08	299 49.5	52.3	41 39.5	6.9	20 21.1	4.9	58.6
H 09	314 49.7	.. 53.2	56 05.4	7.1	20 16.2	5.0	58.6
U 10	329 49.8	54.1	70 31.5	7.1	20 11.2	5.1	58.6
R 11	344 50.0	55.0	84 57.6	7.2	20 06.1	5.3	58.5
S 12	359 50.2	N 8 55.9	99 23.8	7.3	S20 00.8	5.4	58.5
D 13	14 50.3	56.9	113 50.1	7.4	19 55.4	5.4	58.5
A 14	29 50.5	57.8	128 16.5	7.5	19 50.0	5.6	58.4
Y 15	44 50.6	.. 58.7	142 43.0	7.5	19 44.4	5.7	58.4
16	59 50.8	8 59.6	157 09.5	7.6	19 38.7	5.9	58.4
17	74 51.0	9 00.5	171 36.1	7.8	19 32.8	5.9	58.3
18	89 51.1	N 9 01.4	186 02.9	7.8	S19 26.9	6.0	58.3
19	104 51.3	02.3	200 29.7	7.9	19 20.9	6.2	58.2
20	119 51.4	03.2	214 56.6	8.0	19 14.7	6.2	58.2
21	134 51.6	.. 04.1	229 23.6	8.1	19 08.5	6.4	58.2
22	149 51.8	05.0	243 50.7	8.1	19 02.1	6.4	58.1
23	164 51.9	05.9	258 17.8	8.3	18 55.7	6.6	58.1
13 00	179 52.1	N 9 06.8	272 45.1	8.3	S18 49.1	6.7	58.1
01	194 52.2	07.7	287 12.4	8.5	18 42.4	6.7	58.0
02	209 52.4	08.6	301 39.9	8.5	18 35.7	6.9	58.0
03	224 52.5	.. 09.5	316 07.4	8.6	18 28.8	7.0	58.0
04	239 52.7	10.5	330 35.0	8.7	18 21.8	7.0	57.9
05	254 52.9	11.4	345 02.7	8.8	18 14.8	7.2	57.9
06	269 53.0	N 9 12.3	359 30.5	8.9	S18 07.6	7.3	57.9
07	284 53.2	13.2	13 58.4	8.9	18 00.3	7.3	57.8
F 08	299 53.3	14.1	28 26.3	9.1	17 53.0	7.4	57.8
R 09	314 53.5	.. 15.0	42 54.4	9.1	17 45.6	7.6	57.8
I 10	329 53.6	15.9	57 22.5	9.3	17 38.0	7.6	57.7
D 11	344 53.8	16.8	71 50.8	9.3	17 30.4	7.7	57.7
A 12	359 54.0	N 9 17.7	86 19.1	9.4	S17 22.7	7.8	57.7
Y 13	14 54.1	18.6	100 47.5	9.5	17 14.9	7.9	57.6
14	29 54.3	19.5	115 16.0	9.6	17 07.0	7.9	57.6
15	44 54.4	.. 20.4	129 44.6	9.6	16 59.1	8.1	57.6
16	59 54.6	21.3	144 13.2	9.8	16 51.0	8.1	57.5
17	74 54.7	22.2	158 42.0	9.9	16 42.9	8.2	57.5
18	89 54.9	N 9 23.1	173 10.9	9.9	S16 34.7	8.3	57.5
19	104 55.1	24.0	187 39.8	10.0	16 26.4	8.4	57.4
20	119 55.2	24.9	202 08.8	10.1	16 18.0	8.4	57.4
21	134 55.4	.. 25.8	216 37.9	10.2	16 09.6	8.6	57.4
22	149 55.5	26.7	231 07.1	10.3	16 01.0	8.6	57.3
23	164 55.7	27.6	245 36.4	10.3	15 52.4	8.6	57.3
14 00	179 55.8	N 9 28.5	260 05.7	10.5	S15 43.8	8.8	57.3
01	194 56.0	29.4	274 35.2	10.5	15 35.0	8.8	57.2
02	209 56.1	30.3	289 04.7	10.6	15 26.2	8.9	57.2
03	224 56.3	.. 31.2	303 34.3	10.7	15 17.3	9.0	57.2
04	239 56.4	32.1	318 04.0	10.8	15 08.3	9.0	57.1
05	254 56.6	33.0	332 33.8	10.9	14 59.3	9.1	57.1
06	269 56.7	N 9 33.9	347 03.7	10.9	S14 50.2	9.2	57.1
07	284 56.9	34.8	1 33.6	11.0	14 41.0	9.2	57.0
S 08	299 57.1	35.7	16 03.6	11.1	14 31.8	9.3	57.0
A 09	314 57.2	.. 36.6	30 33.7	11.2	14 22.5	9.3	57.0
T 10	329 57.4	37.5	45 03.9	11.3	14 13.2	9.4	56.9
U 11	344 57.5	38.4	59 34.2	11.3	14 03.8	9.5	56.9
R 12	359 57.7	N 9 39.3	74 04.5	11.4	S13 54.3	9.6	56.9
D 13	14 57.8	40.2	88 34.9	11.5	13 44.7	9.6	56.8
A 14	29 58.0	41.0	103 05.4	11.6	13 35.1	9.6	56.8
Y 15	44 58.1	.. 41.9	117 36.0	11.7	13 25.5	9.7	56.8
16	59 58.3	42.8	132 06.7	11.7	13 15.8	9.8	56.8
17	74 58.4	43.7	146 37.4	11.8	13 06.0	9.8	56.7
18	89 58.6	N 9 44.6	161 08.2	11.8	S12 56.2	9.9	56.7
19	104 58.7	45.5	175 39.0	12.0	12 46.3	9.9	56.7
20	119 58.9	46.4	190 10.0	12.0	12 36.4	10.0	56.6
21	134 59.0	.. 47.3	204 41.0	12.1	12 26.4	10.0	56.6
22	149 59.2	48.2	219 12.1	12.2	12 16.4	10.1	56.6
23	164 59.3	49.1	233 43.3	12.2	S12 06.3	10.1	56.5
	SD 16.0	d 0.9	SD 15.9		15.7		15.5

Twilight — Moonrise

Lat.	Naut.	Civil	Sunrise	Moonrise 12	13	14	15
N 72	////	02 13	03 49	■	■	04 35	04 08
N 70	////	02 45	04 04	■	04 24	04 02	03 49
68	01 06	03 09	04 16	03 45	03 41	03 38	03 34
66	01 54	03 26	04 26	02 58	03 12	03 19	03 22
64	02 24	03 41	04 35	02 27	02 50	03 04	03 12
62	02 46	03 53	04 42	02 04	02 32	02 51	03 03
60	03 03	04 03	04 48	01 45	02 18	02 40	02 56
N 58	03 17	04 11	04 54	01 30	02 05	02 30	02 49
56	03 28	04 19	04 59	01 17	01 54	02 22	02 43
54	03 39	04 26	05 04	01 05	01 44	02 14	02 38
52	03 47	04 31	05 07	00 55	01 36	02 08	02 33
50	03 55	04 37	05 11	00 46	01 28	02 01	02 29
45	04 11	04 48	05 18	00 27	01 12	01 48	02 19
N 40	04 24	04 57	05 25	00 11	00 58	01 37	02 11
35	04 34	05 04	05 30	24 46	00 46	01 28	02 05
30	04 42	05 11	05 35	24 36	00 36	01 20	01 59
20	04 55	05 21	05 43	24 19	00 19	01 06	01 48
N 10	05 04	05 29	05 50	24 03	00 03	00 51	01 39
0	05 11	05 36	05 57	23 49	24 42	00 42	01 30
S 10	05 18	05 42	06 04	23 35	24 30	00 30	01 22
20	05 22	05 48	06 10	23 20	24 17	00 17	01 13
30	05 26	05 54	06 18	23 02	24 03	00 03	01 02
35	05 27	05 57	06 22	22 52	23 55	24 56	00 56
40	05 28	06 00	06 27	22 40	23 45	24 49	00 49
45	05 29	06 03	06 33	22 26	23 34	24 41	00 41
S 50	05 30	06 07	06 40	22 09	23 20	24 31	00 31
52	05 29	06 09	06 43	22 01	23 14	24 26	00 26
54	05 29	06 10	06 46	21 52	23 07	24 21	00 21
56	05 29	06 12	06 50	21 42	22 59	24 16	00 16
58	05 29	06 14	06 54	21 30	22 50	24 09	00 09
S 60	05 28	06 16	06 59	21 17	22 40	24 02	00 02

Twilight — Moonset

Lat.	Sunset	Civil	Naut.	Moonset 12	13	14	15
N 72	20 16	21 55	////	■	■	09 29	11 37
N 70	20 00	21 20	////	■	07 52	10 01	11 54
68	19 47	20 56	23 09	06 36	08 34	10 24	12 07
66	19 37	20 37	22 13	07 23	09 03	10 42	12 18
64	19 28	20 23	21 41	07 53	09 24	10 57	12 27
62	19 21	20 10	21 19	08 15	09 41	11 09	12 34
60	19 14	20 00	21 01	08 34	09 55	11 19	12 41
N 58	19 08	19 51	20 47	08 49	10 07	11 28	12 47
56	19 03	19 44	20 34	09 02	10 18	11 35	12 52
54	18 59	19 37	20 24	09 13	10 27	11 42	12 56
52	18 55	19 31	20 15	09 23	10 35	11 48	13 00
50	18 51	19 25	20 07	09 32	10 43	11 54	13 04
45	18 43	19 14	19 51	09 50	10 58	12 06	13 12
N 40	18 37	19 05	19 38	10 05	11 11	12 16	13 19
35	18 31	18 57	19 28	10 18	11 22	12 24	13 25
30	18 26	18 51	19 20	10 29	11 31	12 31	13 30
20	18 18	18 40	19 06	10 48	11 47	12 44	13 38
N 10	18 10	18 32	18 57	11 05	12 02	12 55	13 46
0	18 04	18 25	18 49	11 20	12 15	13 05	13 53
S 10	17 57	18 18	18 43	11 36	12 28	13 16	14 00
20	17 50	18 12	18 38	11 52	12 42	13 26	14 07
30	17 42	18 07	18 34	12 11	12 57	13 39	14 15
35	17 38	18 03	18 33	12 21	13 07	13 46	14 20
40	17 33	18 00	18 32	12 34	13 17	13 54	14 26
45	17 27	17 57	18 31	12 48	13 29	14 03	14 32
S 50	17 20	17 53	18 30	13 06	13 44	14 14	14 39
52	17 17	17 51	18 30	13 15	13 51	14 19	14 43
54	17 14	17 50	18 30	13 24	13 58	14 25	14 47
56	17 10	17 48	18 31	13 34	14 07	14 31	14 51
58	17 06	17 46	18 31	13 46	14 16	14 38	14 55
S 60	17 01	17 43	18 31	14 00	14 27	14 46	15 00

SUN — MOON

Day	Eqn. of Time 00h	12h	Mer. Pass.	Mer. Pass. Upper	Lower	Age	Phase
d	m s	m s	h m	h m	h m	d	%
12	00 47	00 40	12 01	05 07	17 35	21	60
13	00 32	00 24	12 00	06 02	18 28	22	50
14	00 17	00 10	12 00	06 54	19 18	23	39

2012 APRIL 15, 16, 17 (SUN., MON., TUES.)

UT	ARIES GHA	VENUS −4.7 GHA	Dec	MARS −0.4 GHA	Dec	JUPITER −2.0 GHA	Dec	SATURN +0.2 GHA	Dec	STARS Name	SHA	Dec
d h	° ′	° ′	° ′	° ′	° ′	° ′	° ′	° ′	° ′		° ′	° ′
15 00	203 33.4	136 07.6	N26 10.8	46 57.3	N12 41.0	159 18.2	N15 57.1	358 12.6	S 7 32.7	Acamar	315 19.3	S40 15.5
01	218 35.9	151 08.0	11.2	61 59.8	40.9	174 20.1	57.3	13 15.3	32.6	Achernar	335 27.9	S57 10.5
02	233 38.4	166 08.3	11.6	77 02.2	40.8	189 22.0	57.5	28 17.9	32.5	Acrux	173 09.6	S63 10.3
03	248 40.8	181 08.6 · ·	12.0	92 04.7 · ·	40.7	204 23.9 · ·	57.6	43 20.6 · ·	32.4	Adhara	255 13.3	S28 59.7
04	263 43.3	196 08.9	12.4	107 07.2	40.6	219 25.8	57.8	58 23.2	32.4	Aldebaran	290 50.6	N16 31.9
05	278 45.7	211 09.2	12.9	122 09.7	40.5	234 27.7	58.0	73 25.8	32.3			
06	293 48.2	226 09.5	N26 13.3	137 12.1	N12 40.4	249 29.5	N15 58.1	88 28.5	S 7 32.2	Alioth	166 20.8	N55 53.5
07	308 50.7	241 09.9	13.7	152 14.6	40.3	264 31.4	58.3	103 31.1	32.2	Alkaid	152 59.0	N49 15.0
08	323 53.1	256 10.2	14.1	167 17.1	40.2	279 33.3	58.5	118 33.8	32.1	Al Na'ir	27 45.0	S46 53.8
S 09	338 55.6	271 10.5 · ·	14.5	182 19.5 · ·	40.1	294 35.2 · ·	58.6	133 36.4 · ·	32.0	Alnilam	275 47.4	S 1 11.9
U 10	353 58.1	286 10.8	14.9	197 22.0	39.9	309 37.1	58.8	148 39.1	32.0	Alphard	217 56.8	S 8 43.0
N 11	9 00.5	301 11.2	15.3	212 24.5	39.8	324 39.0	59.0	163 41.7	31.9			
D 12	24 03.0	316 11.5	N26 15.7	227 26.9	N12 39.7	339 40.9	N15 59.1	178 44.4	S 7 31.8	Alphecca	126 11.4	N26 40.2
A 13	39 05.5	331 11.8	16.1	242 29.4	39.6	354 42.8	59.3	193 47.0	31.8	Alpheratz	357 44.7	N29 09.4
Y 14	54 07.9	346 12.1	16.6	257 31.9	39.5	9 44.7	59.5	208 49.6	31.7	Altair	62 09.0	N 8 54.0
15	69 10.4	1 12.5 · ·	17.0	272 34.3 · ·	39.4	24 46.6 · ·	59.7	223 52.3 · ·	31.6	Ankaa	353 16.9	S42 14.3
16	84 12.9	16 12.8	17.4	287 36.8	39.3	39 48.5	15 59.8	238 54.9	31.5	Antares	112 27.0	S26 27.5
17	99 15.3	31 13.1	17.8	302 39.2	39.2	54 50.3	16 00.0	253 57.6	31.5			
18	114 17.8	46 13.5	N26 18.2	317 41.7	N12 39.0	69 52.2	N16 00.2	269 00.2	S 7 31.4	Arcturus	145 56.1	N19 07.0
19	129 20.2	61 13.8	18.6	332 44.2	38.9	84 54.1	00.3	284 02.9	31.3	Atria	107 29.2	S69 02.7
20	144 22.7	76 14.1	19.0	347 46.6	38.8	99 56.0	00.5	299 05.5	31.3	Avior	234 18.3	S59 33.4
21	159 25.2	91 14.5 · ·	19.4	2 49.1 · ·	38.7	114 57.9 · ·	00.7	314 08.2 · ·	31.2	Bellatrix	278 33.1	N 6 21.5
22	174 27.6	106 14.8	19.8	17 51.5	38.6	129 59.8	00.8	329 10.8	31.1	Betelgeuse	271 02.3	N 7 24.4
23	189 30.1	121 15.2	20.2	32 54.0	38.5	145 01.7	01.0	344 13.5	31.1			
16 00	204 32.6	136 15.5	N26 20.6	47 56.4	N12 38.3	160 03.6	N16 01.2	359 16.1	S 7 31.0	Canopus	263 56.7	S52 42.5
01	219 35.0	151 15.9	21.0	62 58.9	38.2	175 05.5	01.3	14 18.7	30.9	Capella	280 36.0	N46 00.6
02	234 37.5	166 16.2	21.4	78 01.3	38.1	190 07.4	01.5	29 21.4	30.9	Deneb	49 32.1	N45 19.3
03	249 40.0	181 16.5 · ·	21.8	93 03.8 · ·	38.0	205 09.3 · ·	01.7	44 24.0 · ·	30.8	Denebola	182 34.2	N14 30.0
04	264 42.4	196 16.9	22.2	108 06.2	37.9	220 11.1	01.8	59 26.7	30.7	Diphda	348 57.0	S17 55.2
05	279 44.9	211 17.2	22.6	123 08.7	37.7	235 13.0	02.0	74 29.3	30.7			
06	294 47.3	226 17.6	N26 23.0	138 11.1	N12 37.6	250 14.9	N16 02.2	89 32.0	S 7 30.6	Dubhe	193 52.2	N61 41.1
07	309 49.8	241 18.0	23.3	153 13.5	37.5	265 16.8	02.3	104 34.6	30.5	Elnath	278 13.9	N28 37.0
08	324 52.3	256 18.3	23.7	168 16.0	37.4	280 18.7	02.5	119 37.3	30.4	Eltanin	90 46.3	N51 29.0
M 09	339 54.7	271 18.7 · ·	24.1	183 18.4 · ·	37.3	295 20.6 · ·	02.7	134 39.9 · ·	30.4	Enif	33 48.1	N 9 55.9
O 10	354 57.2	286 19.0	24.5	198 20.9	37.1	310 22.5	02.8	149 42.5	30.3	Fomalhaut	15 25.1	S29 33.3
N 11	9 59.7	301 19.4	24.9	213 23.3	37.0	325 24.4	03.0	164 45.2	30.2			
D 12	25 02.1	316 19.7	N26 25.3	228 25.7	N12 36.9	340 26.3	N16 03.2	179 47.8	S 7 30.2	Gacrux	172 01.3	S57 11.2
A 13	40 04.6	331 20.1	25.7	243 28.2	36.8	355 28.2	03.4	194 50.5	30.1	Gienah	175 52.8	S17 36.9
Y 14	55 07.1	346 20.5	26.1	258 30.6	36.6	10 30.0	03.5	209 53.1	30.0	Hadar	148 48.4	S60 26.0
15	70 09.5	1 20.8 · ·	26.4	273 33.0 · ·	36.5	25 31.9 · ·	03.7	224 55.8 · ·	30.0	Hamal	328 02.0	N23 31.2
16	85 12.0	16 21.2	26.8	288 35.5	36.4	40 33.8	03.9	239 58.4	29.9	Kaus Aust.	83 44.7	S34 22.5
17	100 14.5	31 21.6	27.2	303 37.9	36.3	55 35.7	04.0	255 01.1	29.8			
18	115 16.9	46 21.9	N26 27.6	318 40.3	N12 36.1	70 37.6	N16 04.2	270 03.7	S 7 29.8	Kochab	137 18.8	N74 06.2
19	130 19.4	61 22.3	28.0	333 42.8	36.0	85 39.5	04.4	285 06.3	29.7	Markab	13 39.4	N15 16.2
20	145 21.8	76 22.7	28.4	348 45.2	35.9	100 41.4	04.5	300 09.0	29.6	Menkar	314 16.2	N 4 08.2
21	160 24.3	91 23.0 · ·	28.7	3 47.6 · ·	35.8	115 43.3 · ·	04.7	315 11.6 · ·	29.5	Menkent	148 08.2	S36 25.9
22	175 26.8	106 23.4	29.1	18 50.0	35.6	130 45.2	04.9	330 14.3	29.5	Miaplacidus	221 39.6	S69 46.5
23	190 29.2	121 23.8	29.5	33 52.5	35.5	145 47.0	05.0	345 16.9	29.4			
17 00	205 31.7	136 24.2	N26 29.9	48 54.9	N12 35.4	160 48.9	N16 05.2	0 19.6	S 7 29.3	Mirfak	308 42.0	N49 54.3
01	220 34.2	151 24.6	30.2	63 57.3	35.3	175 50.8	05.4	15 22.2	29.3	Nunki	75 59.2	S26 16.7
02	235 36.6	166 24.9	30.6	78 59.7	35.1	190 52.7	05.5	30 24.9	29.2	Peacock	53 20.6	S56 41.4
03	250 39.1	181 25.3 · ·	31.0	94 02.1 · ·	35.0	205 54.6 · ·	05.7	45 27.5 · ·	29.1	Pollux	243 28.7	N27 59.7
04	265 41.6	196 25.7	31.4	109 04.6	34.9	220 56.5	05.9	60 30.1	29.1	Procyon	245 00.6	N 5 11.4
05	280 44.0	211 26.1	31.7	124 07.0	34.7	235 58.4	06.0	75 32.8	29.0			
06	295 46.5	226 26.5	N26 32.1	139 09.4	N12 34.6	251 00.3	N16 06.2	90 35.4	S 7 28.9	Rasalhague	96 07.0	N12 33.0
07	310 49.0	241 26.9	32.5	154 11.8	34.5	266 02.2	06.4	105 38.1	28.9	Regulus	207 44.2	N11 54.2
08	325 51.4	256 27.3	32.9	169 14.2	34.3	281 04.0	06.5	120 40.7	28.8	Rigel	281 13.0	S 8 11.5
T 09	340 53.9	271 27.7 · ·	33.2	184 16.6 · ·	34.2	296 05.9 · ·	06.7	135 43.4 · ·	28.7	Rigil Kent.	139 52.2	S60 53.1
U 10	355 56.3	286 28.0	33.6	199 19.0	34.1	311 07.8	06.9	150 46.0	28.7	Sabik	102 13.3	S15 44.4
E 11	10 58.8	301 28.4	34.0	214 21.4	33.9	326 09.7	07.0	165 48.7	28.6			
S 12	26 01.3	316 28.8	N26 34.3	229 23.8	N12 33.8	341 11.6	N16 07.2	180 51.3	S 7 28.5	Schedar	349 42.0	N56 36.2
D 13	41 03.7	331 29.2	34.7	244 26.3	33.7	356 13.5	07.4	195 54.0	28.4	Shaula	96 22.8	S37 06.6
A 14	56 06.2	346 29.6	35.1	259 28.7	33.5	11 15.4	07.5	210 56.6	28.4	Sirius	258 34.5	S16 44.3
Y 15	71 08.7	1 30.0 · ·	35.4	274 31.1 · ·	33.4	26 17.3 · ·	07.7	225 59.2 · ·	28.3	Spica	158 31.8	S11 13.7
16	86 11.1	16 30.4	35.8	289 33.5	33.3	41 19.1	07.9	241 01.9	28.2	Suhail	222 52.9	S43 29.4
17	101 13.6	31 30.8	36.1	304 35.9	33.1	56 21.0	08.0	256 04.5	28.2			
18	116 16.1	46 31.2	N26 36.5	319 38.3	N12 33.0	71 22.9	N16 08.2	271 07.2	S 7 28.1	Vega	80 39.4	N38 47.5
19	131 18.5	61 31.7	36.9	334 40.7	32.9	86 24.8	08.4	286 09.8	28.0	Zuben'ubi	137 06.0	S16 05.7
20	146 21.0	76 32.1	37.2	349 43.1	32.7	101 26.7	08.5	301 12.5	28.0		SHA	Mer.Pass.
21	161 23.4	91 32.5 · ·	37.6	4 45.5 · ·	32.6	116 28.6 · ·	08.7	316 15.1 · ·	27.9		° ′	h m
22	176 25.9	106 32.9	37.9	19 47.9	32.5	131 30.5	08.9	331 17.8	27.8	Venus	291 42.9	14 55
23	191 28.4	121 33.3	38.3	34 50.2	32.3	146 32.4	09.1	346 20.4	27.8	Mars	203 23.9	20 45
	h m									Jupiter	315 31.0	13 18
Mer.Pass. 10 20.1	v 0.4	d 0.4		v 2.4	d 0.1	v 1.9	d 0.2	v 2.6	d 0.1	Saturn	154 43.5	0 03

UT	SUN GHA	SUN Dec	MOON GHA	v	Dec	d	HP
d h	° ′	° ′	° ′	′	° ′	′	′
15 00	179 59.5	N 9 50.0	248 14.5	12.3	S11 56.2	10.2	56.5
01	194 59.6	50.9	262 45.8	12.4	11 46.0	10.2	56.5
02	209 59.8	51.8	277 17.2	12.4	11 35.8	10.3	56.5
03	224 59.9	.. 52.7	291 48.6	12.5	11 25.5	10.3	56.4
04	240 00.1	53.6	306 20.1	12.6	11 15.2	10.4	56.4
05	255 00.2	54.4	320 51.7	12.6	11 04.8	10.5	56.4
06	270 00.4	N 9 55.3	335 23.3	12.7	S10 54.5	10.5	56.3
07	285 00.5	56.2	349 55.0	12.8	10 44.0	10.5	56.3
S 08	300 00.7	57.1	4 26.8	12.8	10 33.5	10.5	56.3
U 09	315 00.8	.. 58.0	18 58.6	12.9	10 23.0	10.5	56.3
N 10	330 01.0	58.9	33 30.5	12.9	10 12.5	10.6	56.2
D 11	345 01.1	9 59.8	48 02.4	13.1	10 01.9	10.6	56.2
A 12	0 01.3	N10 00.7	62 34.5	13.0	S 9 51.3	10.7	56.2
Y 13	15 01.4	01.6	77 06.5	13.2	9 40.6	10.7	56.2
14	30 01.6	02.5	91 38.7	13.2	9 29.9	10.7	56.1
15	45 01.7	.. 03.3	106 10.9	13.2	9 19.2	10.8	56.1
16	60 01.9	04.2	120 43.1	13.3	9 08.4	10.8	56.1
17	75 02.0	05.1	135 15.4	13.4	8 57.6	10.8	56.0
18	90 02.2	N10 06.0	149 47.8	13.4	S 8 46.8	10.9	56.0
19	105 02.3	06.9	164 20.2	13.5	8 35.9	10.9	56.0
20	120 02.5	07.8	178 52.7	13.5	8 25.0	10.9	56.0
21	135 02.6	.. 08.7	193 25.2	13.6	8 14.1	10.9	55.9
22	150 02.8	09.6	207 57.8	13.6	8 03.2	11.0	55.9
23	165 02.9	10.4	222 30.4	13.7	7 52.2	11.0	55.9
16 00	180 03.1	N10 11.3	237 03.1	13.7	S 7 41.2	11.0	55.9
01	195 03.2	12.2	251 35.8	13.8	7 30.2	11.1	55.8
02	210 03.3	13.0	266 08.6	13.8	7 19.1	11.0	55.8
03	225 03.5	.. 14.0	280 41.4	13.9	7 08.1	11.1	55.8
04	240 03.6	14.9	295 14.3	13.9	6 57.0	11.1	55.8
05	255 03.8	15.7	309 47.2	14.0	6 45.9	11.2	55.7
06	270 03.9	N10 16.6	324 20.2	14.0	S 6 34.7	11.1	55.7
07	285 04.1	17.5	338 53.2	14.1	6 23.6	11.2	55.7
M 08	300 04.2	18.4	353 26.3	14.1	6 12.4	11.2	55.7
O 09	315 04.4	.. 19.3	7 59.4	14.1	6 01.2	11.2	55.6
N 10	330 04.5	20.2	22 32.5	14.2	5 50.0	11.2	55.6
D 11	345 04.7	21.0	37 05.7	14.2	5 38.8	11.3	55.6
A 12	0 04.8	N10 21.9	51 38.9	14.3	S 5 27.5	11.2	55.6
Y 13	15 04.9	22.8	66 12.2	14.3	5 16.3	11.3	55.6
14	30 05.1	23.7	80 45.5	14.4	5 05.0	11.3	55.5
15	45 05.2	.. 24.6	95 18.9	14.4	4 53.7	11.3	55.5
16	60 05.4	25.5	109 52.3	14.4	4 42.4	11.3	55.5
17	75 05.5	26.3	124 25.7	14.4	4 31.1	11.3	55.5
18	90 05.7	N10 27.2	138 59.1	14.5	S 4 19.8	11.3	55.4
19	105 05.8	28.1	153 32.6	14.5	4 08.5	11.3	55.4
20	120 05.9	29.0	168 06.1	14.6	3 57.2	11.4	55.4
21	135 06.1	.. 29.9	182 39.7	14.6	3 45.8	11.3	55.4
22	150 06.2	30.7	197 13.3	14.6	3 34.5	11.4	55.4
23	165 06.4	31.6	211 46.9	14.7	3 23.1	11.4	55.3
17 00	180 06.5	N10 32.5	226 20.6	14.7	S 3 11.7	11.3	55.3
01	195 06.7	33.4	240 54.3	14.7	3 00.4	11.4	55.3
02	210 06.8	34.3	255 28.0	14.7	2 49.0	11.4	55.3
03	225 06.9	.. 35.1	270 01.7	14.8	2 37.6	11.4	55.3
04	240 07.1	36.0	284 35.5	14.8	2 26.2	11.4	55.2
05	255 07.2	36.9	299 09.3	14.8	2 14.8	11.4	55.2
06	270 07.4	N10 37.8	313 43.1	14.8	S 2 03.4	11.4	55.2
07	285 07.5	38.6	328 16.9	14.9	1 52.0	11.4	55.2
T 08	300 07.7	39.5	342 50.8	14.9	1 40.6	11.3	55.2
U 09	315 07.8	.. 40.4	357 24.7	14.9	1 29.3	11.4	55.1
E 10	330 07.9	41.3	11 58.6	14.9	1 17.9	11.4	55.1
S 11	345 08.1	42.1	26 32.5	15.0	1 06.5	11.4	55.1
D 12	0 08.2	N10 43.0	41 06.5	15.0	S 0 55.1	11.4	55.1
A 13	15 08.4	43.9	55 40.5	15.0	0 43.7	11.4	55.1
Y 14	30 08.5	44.8	70 14.5	15.0	0 32.3	11.3	55.0
15	45 08.6	.. 45.6	84 48.5	15.0	0 21.0	11.4	55.0
16	60 08.8	46.5	99 22.5	15.0	S 0 09.6	11.4	55.0
17	75 08.9	47.4	113 56.5	15.1	N 0 01.8	11.3	55.0
18	90 09.1	N10 48.3	128 30.6	15.1	N 0 13.1	11.4	55.0
19	105 09.2	49.1	143 04.7	15.1	0 24.5	11.3	54.9
20	120 09.3	50.0	157 38.8	15.1	0 35.8	11.4	54.9
21	135 09.5	.. 50.9	172 12.9	15.1	0 47.2	11.3	54.9
22	150 09.6	51.7	186 47.0	15.1	0 58.5	11.3	54.9
23	165 09.8	52.6	201 21.1	15.2	N 1 09.8	11.3	54.9
	SD 16.0	d 0.9	SD 15.3		15.1		15.0

Twilight / Sunrise / Moonrise

Lat.	Twilight Naut.	Twilight Civil	Sunrise	Moonrise 15	16	17	18
°	h m	h m	h m	h m	h m	h m	h m
N 72	////	01 44	03 31	04 08	03 49	03 33	03 19
N 70	////	02 25	03 49	03 49	03 39	03 30	03 21
68	////	02 52	04 03	03 34	03 31	03 27	03 23
66	01 30	03 13	04 15	03 22	03 24	03 25	03 25
64	02 06	03 29	04 24	03 12	03 18	03 22	03 27
62	02 31	03 42	04 32	03 03	03 13	03 21	03 28
60	02 50	03 53	04 40	02 56	03 08	03 19	03 29
N 58	03 06	04 02	04 46	02 49	03 04	03 18	03 30
56	03 19	04 11	04 51	02 43	03 01	03 16	03 31
54	03 30	04 18	04 56	02 38	02 58	03 15	03 32
52	03 40	04 24	05 00	02 33	02 55	03 14	03 33
50	03 48	04 30	05 04	02 29	02 52	03 13	03 33
45	04 05	04 42	05 13	02 19	02 46	03 11	03 35
N 40	04 19	04 52	05 20	02 11	02 42	03 09	03 36
35	04 30	05 00	05 26	02 05	02 37	03 08	03 37
30	04 38	05 07	05 32	01 59	02 34	03 07	03 38
20	04 52	05 19	05 41	01 48	02 27	03 04	03 40
N 10	05 03	05 28	05 49	01 39	02 22	03 02	03 42
0	05 11	05 35	05 56	01 30	02 16	03 00	03 43
S 10	05 18	05 42	06 04	01 22	02 11	02 58	03 45
20	05 23	05 49	06 11	01 13	02 05	02 56	03 46
30	05 28	05 56	06 20	01 02	01 59	02 54	03 48
35	05 30	05 59	06 25	00 56	01 55	02 53	03 49
40	05 31	06 03	06 30	00 49	01 51	02 51	03 50
45	05 33	06 07	06 37	00 41	01 46	02 50	03 52
S 50	05 34	06 11	06 44	00 31	01 40	02 47	03 54
52	05 34	06 13	06 48	00 26	01 37	02 46	03 54
54	05 34	06 16	06 52	00 21	01 34	02 45	03 55
56	05 35	06 18	06 56	00 16	01 31	02 44	03 56
58	05 35	06 20	07 01	00 09	01 27	02 43	03 57
S 60	05 35	06 23	07 06	00 02	01 23	02 42	03 59

Sunset / Twilight / Moonset

Lat.	Sunset	Twilight Civil	Twilight Naut.	Moonset 15	16	17	18
°	h m	h m	h m	h m	h m	h m	h m
N 72	20 32	22 25	////	11 37	13 30	15 16	17 01
N 70	20 14	21 40	////	11 54	13 38	15 17	16 54
68	19 59	21 11	////	12 07	13 44	15 17	16 49
66	19 47	20 50	22 38	12 18	13 49	15 18	16 45
64	19 37	20 34	21 58	12 27	13 54	15 18	16 41
62	19 29	20 21	21 32	12 34	13 57	15 18	16 38
60	19 22	20 08	21 12	12 41	14 01	15 18	16 35
N 58	19 15	19 59	20 56	12 47	14 04	15 19	16 33
56	19 10	19 50	20 43	12 52	14 06	15 19	16 30
54	19 05	19 43	20 31	12 56	14 08	15 19	16 28
52	19 00	19 36	20 22	13 00	14 11	15 19	16 27
50	18 56	19 30	20 13	13 04	14 13	15 19	16 25
45	18 47	19 18	19 55	13 12	14 17	15 20	16 22
N 40	18 40	19 08	19 42	13 19	14 20	15 20	16 19
35	18 34	19 00	19 31	13 25	14 23	15 20	16 16
30	18 28	18 53	19 22	13 30	14 26	15 20	16 14
20	18 19	18 41	19 08	13 38	14 30	15 21	16 10
N 10	18 11	18 32	18 57	13 46	14 34	15 21	16 07
0	18 03	18 24	18 48	13 53	14 38	15 21	16 04
S 10	17 56	18 17	18 42	14 00	14 41	15 21	16 00
20	17 48	18 10	18 36	14 07	14 45	15 21	15 57
30	17 39	18 03	18 31	14 15	14 49	15 22	15 53
35	17 34	18 00	18 29	14 20	14 52	15 22	15 51
40	17 29	17 56	18 27	14 26	14 55	15 22	15 49
45	17 22	17 52	18 26	14 32	14 58	15 22	15 46
S 50	17 14	17 47	18 25	14 39	15 02	15 22	15 42
52	17 11	17 45	18 24	14 43	15 03	15 22	15 41
54	17 07	17 43	18 24	14 47	15 05	15 23	15 39
56	17 03	17 41	18 24	14 51	15 07	15 22	15 37
58	16 58	17 38	18 23	14 55	15 10	15 23	15 35
S 60	16 52	17 35	18 23	15 00	15 12	15 23	15 33

SUN / MOON

Day	SUN Eqn. of Time 00ʰ	SUN Eqn. of Time 12ʰ	SUN Mer. Pass.	MOON Mer. Pass. Upper	MOON Mer. Pass. Lower	Age	Phase
d	m s	m s	h m	h m	h m	d	%
15	00 02	00 05	12 00	07 42	20 05	24	29
16	00 12	00 19	12 00	08 27	20 49	25	21
17	00 26	00 33	11 59	09 11	21 32	26	13

UT	ARIES	VENUS −4.7		MARS −0.3		JUPITER −2.0		SATURN +0.2	
d h	GHA	GHA	Dec	GHA	Dec	GHA	Dec	GHA	Dec
18 00	206 30.8	136 33.7	N26 38.6	49 52.6	N12 32.2	161 34.2	N16 09.2	1 23.0	S 7 27.7
01	221 33.3	151 34.1	39.0	64 55.0	32.0	176 36.1	09.4	16 25.7	27.6
02	236 35.8	166 34.5	39.3	79 57.4	31.9	191 38.0	09.6	31 28.3	27.6
03	251 38.2	181 35.0	.. 39.7	94 59.8	.. 31.8	206 39.9	.. 09.7	46 31.0	.. 27.5
04	266 40.7	196 35.4	40.1	110 02.2	31.6	221 41.8	09.9	61 33.6	27.4
05	281 43.2	211 35.8	40.4	125 04.6	31.5	236 43.7	10.1	76 36.3	27.3
06	296 45.6	226 36.2	N26 40.8	140 07.0	N12 31.3	251 45.6	N16 10.2	91 38.9	S 7 27.3
07	311 48.1	241 36.7	41.1	155 09.4	31.2	266 47.5	10.4	106 41.6	27.2
08	326 50.6	256 37.1	41.4	170 11.7	31.1	281 49.3	10.6	121 44.2	27.1
09	341 53.0	271 37.5	.. 41.8	185 14.1	.. 30.9	296 51.2	.. 10.7	136 46.8	.. 27.1
10	356 55.5	286 37.9	42.1	200 16.5	30.8	311 53.1	10.9	151 49.5	27.0
11	11 57.9	301 38.4	42.5	215 18.9	30.6	326 55.0	11.1	166 52.1	26.9
12	27 00.4	316 38.8	N26 42.8	230 21.3	N12 30.5	341 56.9	N16 11.2	181 54.8	S 7 26.9
13	42 02.9	331 39.3	43.2	245 23.6	30.3	356 58.8	11.4	196 57.4	26.8
14	57 05.3	346 39.7	43.5	260 26.0	30.2	12 00.7	11.6	212 00.1	26.7
15	72 07.8	1 40.1	.. 43.9	275 28.4	.. 30.0	27 02.5	.. 11.7	227 02.7	.. 26.7
16	87 10.3	16 40.6	44.2	290 30.8	29.9	42 04.4	11.9	242 05.4	26.6
17	102 12.7	31 41.0	44.5	305 33.1	29.8	57 06.3	12.1	257 08.0	26.5
18	117 15.2	46 41.5	N26 44.9	320 35.5	N12 29.6	72 08.2	N16 12.2	272 10.6	S 7 26.5
19	132 17.7	61 41.9	45.2	335 37.9	29.5	87 10.1	12.4	287 13.3	26.4
20	147 20.1	76 42.3	45.6	350 40.3	29.3	102 12.0	12.6	302 15.9	26.3
21	162 22.6	91 42.8	.. 45.9	5 42.6	.. 29.2	117 13.9	.. 12.7	317 18.6	.. 26.2
22	177 25.0	106 43.2	46.2	20 45.0	29.0	132 15.7	12.9	332 21.2	26.2
23	192 27.5	121 43.7	46.6	35 47.4	28.9	147 17.6	13.1	347 23.9	26.1
19 00	207 30.0	136 44.2	N26 46.9	50 49.7	N12 28.7	162 19.5	N16 13.2	2 26.5	S 7 26.0
01	222 32.4	151 44.6	47.2	65 52.1	28.6	177 21.4	13.4	17 29.2	26.0
02	237 34.9	166 45.1	47.6	80 54.5	28.4	192 23.3	13.6	32 31.8	25.9
03	252 37.4	181 45.5	.. 47.9	95 56.8	.. 28.3	207 25.2	.. 13.7	47 34.4	.. 25.8
04	267 39.8	196 46.0	48.2	110 59.2	28.1	222 27.1	13.9	62 37.1	25.8
05	282 42.3	211 46.4	48.5	126 01.5	28.0	237 28.9	14.1	77 39.7	25.7
06	297 44.8	226 46.9	N26 48.9	141 03.9	N12 27.8	252 30.8	N16 14.2	92 42.4	S 7 25.6
07	312 47.2	241 47.4	49.2	156 06.3	27.7	267 32.7	14.4	107 45.0	25.6
08	327 49.7	256 47.8	49.5	171 08.6	27.5	282 34.6	14.6	122 47.7	25.5
09	342 52.2	271 48.3	.. 49.8	186 11.0	.. 27.4	297 36.5	.. 14.7	137 50.3	.. 25.4
10	357 54.6	286 48.8	50.2	201 13.3	27.2	312 38.4	14.9	152 53.0	25.4
11	12 57.1	301 49.3	50.5	216 15.7	27.1	327 40.3	15.1	167 55.6	25.3
12	27 59.5	316 49.7	N26 50.8	231 18.0	N12 26.9	342 42.1	N16 15.2	182 58.2	S 7 25.2
13	43 02.0	331 50.2	51.1	246 20.4	26.8	357 44.0	15.4	198 00.9	25.2
14	58 04.5	346 50.7	51.5	261 22.7	26.6	12 45.9	15.6	213 03.5	25.1
15	73 06.9	1 51.2	.. 51.8	276 25.1	.. 26.4	27 47.8	.. 15.7	228 06.2	.. 25.0
16	88 09.4	16 51.6	52.1	291 27.4	26.3	42 49.7	15.9	243 08.8	24.9
17	103 11.9	31 52.1	52.4	306 29.8	26.1	57 51.6	16.1	258 11.5	24.9
18	118 14.3	46 52.6	N26 52.7	321 32.1	N12 26.0	72 53.4	N16 16.2	273 14.1	S 7 24.8
19	133 16.8	61 53.1	53.0	336 34.4	25.8	87 55.3	16.4	288 16.8	24.7
20	148 19.3	76 53.6	53.4	351 36.8	25.7	102 57.2	16.6	303 19.4	24.7
21	163 21.7	91 54.1	.. 53.7	6 39.1	.. 25.5	117 59.1	.. 16.7	318 22.0	.. 24.6
22	178 24.2	106 54.6	54.0	21 41.5	25.4	133 01.0	16.9	333 24.7	24.5
23	193 26.6	121 55.1	54.3	36 43.8	25.2	148 02.9	17.1	348 27.3	24.5
20 00	208 29.1	136 55.5	N26 54.6	51 46.1	N12 25.0	163 04.8	N16 17.2	3 30.0	S 7 24.4
01	223 31.6	151 56.0	54.9	66 48.5	24.9	178 06.6	17.4	18 32.6	24.3
02	238 34.0	166 56.5	55.2	81 50.8	24.7	193 08.5	17.6	33 35.3	24.3
03	253 36.5	181 57.0	.. 55.5	96 53.2	.. 24.6	208 10.4	.. 17.7	48 37.9	.. 24.2
04	268 39.0	196 57.5	55.9	111 55.5	24.4	223 12.3	17.9	63 40.6	24.1
05	283 41.4	211 58.0	56.2	126 57.8	24.2	238 14.2	18.1	78 43.2	24.1
06	298 43.9	226 58.6	N26 56.5	142 00.1	N12 24.1	253 16.1	N16 18.2	93 45.8	S 7 24.0
07	313 46.4	241 59.1	56.8	157 02.5	23.9	268 17.9	18.4	108 48.5	23.9
08	328 48.8	256 59.6	57.1	172 04.8	23.8	283 19.8	18.6	123 51.1	23.9
09	343 51.3	272 00.1	.. 57.4	187 07.1	.. 23.6	298 21.7	.. 18.7	138 53.8	.. 23.8
10	358 53.8	287 00.6	57.7	202 09.5	23.4	313 23.6	18.9	153 56.4	23.7
11	13 56.2	302 01.1	58.0	217 11.8	23.3	328 25.5	19.1	168 59.1	23.7
12	28 58.7	317 01.6	N26 58.3	232 14.1	N12 23.1	343 27.4	N16 19.2	184 01.7	S 7 23.6
13	44 01.1	332 02.1	58.6	247 16.4	22.9	358 29.2	19.4	199 04.4	23.5
14	59 03.6	347 02.7	58.9	262 18.8	22.8	13 31.1	19.6	214 07.0	23.5
15	74 06.1	2 03.2	.. 59.2	277 21.1	.. 22.6	28 33.0	.. 19.7	229 09.6	.. 23.4
16	89 08.5	17 03.7	59.5	292 23.4	22.4	43 34.9	19.9	244 12.3	23.3
17	104 11.0	32 04.2	26 59.8	307 25.7	22.3	58 36.8	20.1	259 14.9	23.2
18	119 13.5	47 04.8	N27 00.1	322 28.0	N12 22.1	73 38.7	N16 20.2	274 17.6	S 7 23.2
19	134 15.9	62 05.3	00.4	337 30.3	21.9	88 40.5	20.4	289 20.2	23.1
20	149 18.4	77 05.8	00.7	352 32.7	21.8	103 42.4	20.6	304 22.9	23.0
21	164 20.9	92 06.3	.. 01.0	7 35.0	.. 21.6	118 44.3	.. 20.7	319 25.5	.. 23.0
22	179 23.3	107 06.9	01.2	22 37.3	21.4	133 46.2	20.9	334 28.1	22.9
23	194 25.8	122 07.4	01.5	37 39.6	21.3	148 48.1	21.1	349 30.8	22.8
h m									
Mer.Pass. 10 08.3		v 0.5	d 0.3	v 2.4	d 0.2	v 1.9	d 0.2	v 2.6	d 0.1

STARS

Name	SHA	Dec
Acamar	315 19.4	S40 15.5
Achernar	335 27.9	S57 10.4
Acrux	173 09.6	S63 10.3
Adhara	255 13.3	S28 59.7
Aldebaran	290 50.6	N16 31.9
Alioth	166 20.8	N55 53.5
Alkaid	152 59.0	N49 15.0
Al Na'ir	27 45.0	S46 53.8
Alnilam	275 47.4	S 1 11.9
Alphard	217 56.8	S 8 43.0
Alphecca	126 11.4	N26 40.3
Alpheratz	357 44.7	N29 09.4
Altair	62 09.0	N 8 54.0
Ankaa	353 16.9	S42 14.3
Antares	112 27.0	S26 27.5
Arcturus	145 56.1	N19 07.0
Atria	107 29.2	S69 02.7
Avior	234 18.3	S59 33.4
Bellatrix	278 33.1	N 6 21.5
Betelgeuse	271 02.4	N 7 24.4
Canopus	263 56.7	S52 42.5
Capella	280 36.0	N46 00.6
Deneb	49 32.1	N45 19.3
Denebola	182 34.2	N14 30.0
Diphda	348 57.0	S17 55.1
Dubhe	193 52.2	N61 41.1
Elnath	278 13.9	N28 37.0
Eltanin	90 46.2	N51 29.0
Enif	33 48.1	N 9 55.9
Fomalhaut	15 25.1	S29 33.3
Gacrux	172 01.3	S57 11.2
Gienah	175 52.9	S17 36.9
Hadar	148 48.4	S60 26.0
Hamal	328 02.0	N23 31.2
Kaus Aust.	83 44.7	S34 22.5
Kochab	137 18.8	N74 06.2
Markab	13 39.4	N15 16.2
Menkar	314 16.2	N 4 08.2
Menkent	148 08.1	S36 25.9
Miaplacidus	221 39.6	S69 46.5
Mirfak	308 42.0	N49 54.3
Nunki	75 59.2	S26 16.7
Peacock	53 20.6	S56 41.4
Pollux	243 28.8	N27 59.7
Procyon	245 00.6	N 5 11.4
Rasalhague	96 07.0	N12 33.0
Regulus	207 44.2	N11 54.2
Rigel	281 13.1	S 8 11.5
Rigil Kent.	139 52.2	S60 53.2
Sabik	102 13.2	S15 44.4
Schedar	349 42.0	N56 36.2
Shaula	96 22.8	S37 06.6
Sirius	258 34.6	S16 44.3
Spica	158 31.8	S11 13.7
Suhail	222 52.9	S43 29.4
Vega	80 39.4	N38 47.5
Zuben'ubi	137 06.0	S16 05.7

	SHA	Mer.Pass.
		h m
Venus	289 14.2	14 53
Mars	203 19.8	20 33
Jupiter	314 49.5	13 09
Saturn	154 56.5	23 46

UT	SUN GHA	SUN Dec	MOON GHA	v	MOON Dec	d	HP
d h	° '	° '	° '	'	° '	'	'
18 00	180 09.9	N10 53.5	215 55.3	15.1	N 1 21.1	11.3	54.9
01	195 10.0	54.4	230 29.4	15.2	1 32.4	11.3	54.8
02	210 10.2	55.2	245 03.6	15.2	1 43.7	11.2	54.8
03	225 10.3	.. 56.1	259 37.8	15.1	1 54.9	11.3	54.8
04	240 10.4	57.0	274 11.9	15.2	2 06.2	11.2	54.8
05	255 10.6	57.8	288 46.1	15.2	2 17.4	11.2	54.8
06	270 10.7	N10 58.7	303 20.3	15.2	N 2 28.6	11.2	54.8
W 07	285 10.9	10 59.6	317 54.5	15.2	2 39.8	11.2	54.8
E 08	300 11.0	11 00.4	332 28.7	15.2	2 51.0	11.2	54.7
D 09	315 11.1	.. 01.3	347 02.9	15.3	3 02.2	11.1	54.7
N 10	330 11.3	02.2	1 37.2	15.2	3 13.3	11.2	54.7
E 11	345 11.4	03.1	16 11.4	15.2	3 24.5	11.1	54.7
S 12	0 11.5	N11 03.9	30 45.6	15.2	N 3 35.6	11.1	54.7
D 13	15 11.7	04.8	45 19.8	15.2	3 46.7	11.1	54.7
A 14	30 11.8	05.7	59 54.0	15.2	3 57.8	11.0	54.6
Y 15	45 11.9	.. 06.5	74 28.2	15.3	4 08.8	11.0	54.6
16	60 12.1	07.4	89 02.5	15.2	4 19.8	11.1	54.6
17	75 12.2	08.3	103 36.7	15.2	4 30.9	10.9	54.6
18	90 12.4	N11 09.1	118 10.9	15.2	N 4 41.8	11.0	54.6
19	105 12.5	10.0	132 45.1	15.2	4 52.8	10.9	54.6
20	120 12.6	10.9	147 19.3	15.2	5 03.7	10.9	54.6
21	135 12.8	.. 11.7	161 53.5	15.2	5 14.6	10.9	54.5
22	150 12.9	12.6	176 27.7	15.2	5 25.5	10.9	54.5
23	165 13.0	13.4	191 01.9	15.2	5 36.4	10.8	54.5
19 00	180 13.2	N11 14.3	205 36.1	15.2	N 5 47.2	10.8	54.5
01	195 13.3	15.2	220 10.3	15.2	5 58.0	10.8	54.5
02	210 13.4	16.0	234 44.5	15.2	6 08.8	10.8	54.5
03	225 13.6	.. 16.9	249 18.7	15.1	6 19.6	10.7	54.5
04	240 13.7	17.8	263 52.8	15.2	6 30.3	10.7	54.5
05	255 13.8	18.6	278 27.0	15.1	6 41.0	10.6	54.5
06	270 14.0	N11 19.5	293 01.1	15.1	N 6 51.6	10.6	54.4
T 07	285 14.1	20.3	307 35.2	15.2	7 02.2	10.6	54.4
H 08	300 14.2	21.2	322 09.4	15.1	7 12.8	10.6	54.4
U 09	315 14.4	.. 22.1	336 43.5	15.1	7 23.4	10.5	54.4
R 10	330 14.5	22.9	351 17.6	15.0	7 33.9	10.5	54.4
S 11	345 14.6	23.8	5 51.6	15.1	7 44.4	10.4	54.4
D 12	0 14.8	N11 24.6	20 25.7	15.1	N 7 54.8	10.5	54.4
A 13	15 14.9	25.5	34 59.8	15.0	8 05.3	10.3	54.4
Y 14	30 15.0	26.4	49 33.8	15.0	8 15.6	10.4	54.3
15	45 15.1	.. 27.2	64 07.8	15.0	8 26.0	10.3	54.3
16	60 15.3	28.1	78 41.8	15.0	8 36.3	10.2	54.3
17	75 15.4	28.9	93 15.8	15.0	8 46.5	10.3	54.3
18	90 15.5	N11 29.8	107 49.8	15.0	N 8 56.8	10.1	54.3
19	105 15.7	30.7	122 23.8	14.9	9 07.0	10.1	54.3
20	120 15.8	31.5	136 57.7	14.9	9 17.1	10.1	54.3
21	135 15.9	.. 32.4	151 31.6	14.9	9 27.2	10.1	54.3
22	150 16.1	33.2	166 05.5	14.9	9 37.3	10.0	54.3
23	165 16.2	34.1	180 39.4	14.9	9 47.3	10.0	54.3
20 00	180 16.3	N11 34.9	195 13.3	14.8	N 9 57.3	9.9	54.2
01	195 16.4	35.8	209 47.1	14.8	10 07.2	9.9	54.2
02	210 16.6	36.6	224 20.9	14.8	10 17.1	9.9	54.2
03	225 16.7	.. 37.5	238 54.7	14.8	10 27.0	9.8	54.2
04	240 16.8	38.4	253 28.5	14.8	10 36.8	9.7	54.2
05	255 17.0	39.2	268 02.3	14.7	10 46.5	9.7	54.2
06	270 17.1	N11 40.1	282 36.0	14.7	N10 56.2	9.7	54.2
07	285 17.2	40.9	297 09.7	14.7	11 05.9	9.6	54.2
08	300 17.4	41.8	311 43.4	14.7	11 15.5	9.5	54.2
F 09	315 17.5	.. 42.6	326 17.1	14.6	11 25.0	9.6	54.2
R 10	330 17.6	43.5	340 50.7	14.6	11 34.6	9.4	54.2
I 11	345 17.7	44.3	355 24.3	14.6	11 44.0	9.4	54.1
D 12	0 17.9	N11 45.2	9 57.9	14.6	N11 53.4	9.4	54.1
A 13	15 18.0	46.0	24 31.5	14.5	12 02.8	9.3	54.1
Y 14	30 18.1	46.9	39 05.0	14.5	12 12.1	9.2	54.1
15	45 18.2	.. 47.7	53 38.5	14.5	12 21.3	9.2	54.1
16	60 18.4	48.6	68 12.0	14.4	12 30.5	9.2	54.1
17	75 18.5	49.4	82 45.4	14.4	12 39.7	9.1	54.1
18	90 18.6	N11 50.3	97 18.8	14.4	N12 48.8	9.0	54.1
19	105 18.7	51.1	111 52.2	14.4	12 57.8	9.0	54.1
20	120 18.9	52.0	126 25.6	14.3	13 06.8	8.9	54.1
21	135 19.0	.. 52.8	140 58.9	14.3	13 15.7	8.9	54.1
22	150 19.1	53.7	155 32.2	14.3	13 24.6	8.8	54.1
23	165 19.2	54.5	170 05.5	14.3	N13 33.4	8.7	54.1
	SD 15.9	d 0.9	SD 14.9		14.8		14.8

Twilight / Moonrise

Lat.	Naut.	Civil	Sunrise	Moonrise 18	19	20	21
°	h m	h m	h m	h m	h m	h m	h m
N 72	////	01 06	03 13	03 19	03 04	02 48	02 26
N 70	////	02 02	03 34	03 21	03 13	03 04	02 53
68	////	02 35	03 50	03 23	03 20	03 17	03 14
66	00 57	02 58	04 03	03 25	03 26	03 27	03 30
64	01 47	03 16	04 14	03 27	03 31	03 37	03 44
62	02 16	03 31	04 23	03 28	03 36	03 44	03 55
60	02 38	03 43	04 31	03 29	03 40	03 51	04 05
N 58	02 55	03 54	04 38	03 30	03 43	03 57	04 13
56	03 09	04 03	04 44	03 31	03 46	04 02	04 21
54	03 21	04 10	04 49	03 32	03 49	04 07	04 28
52	03 32	04 17	04 54	03 33	03 51	04 11	04 34
50	03 41	04 24	04 58	03 33	03 54	04 15	04 39
45	03 59	04 37	05 08	03 35	03 59	04 24	04 51
N 40	04 14	04 48	05 16	03 36	04 03	04 31	05 01
35	04 25	04 56	05 23	03 37	04 07	04 37	05 10
30	04 35	05 04	05 29	03 38	04 10	04 43	05 17
20	04 50	05 16	05 39	03 40	04 16	04 52	05 30
N 10	05 01	05 26	05 48	03 42	04 21	05 01	05 42
0	05 10	05 35	05 56	03 43	04 26	05 08	05 52
S 10	05 18	05 42	06 04	03 45	04 30	05 16	06 03
20	05 24	05 50	06 12	03 46	04 36	05 25	06 15
30	05 29	05 57	06 22	03 48	04 41	05 35	06 28
35	05 32	06 01	06 27	03 49	04 45	05 40	06 36
40	05 34	06 06	06 33	03 50	04 49	05 47	06 45
45	05 36	06 10	06 40	03 52	04 53	05 54	06 55
S 50	05 38	06 16	06 49	03 54	04 59	06 04	07 08
52	05 39	06 18	06 53	03 54	05 01	06 08	07 14
54	05 40	06 21	06 57	03 55	05 04	06 13	07 20
56	05 40	06 24	07 02	03 56	05 07	06 18	07 27
58	05 41	06 27	07 07	03 57	05 11	06 24	07 36
S 60	05 41	06 30	07 13	03 59	05 15	06 30	07 45

Sunset / Twilight / Moonset

Lat.	Sunset	Civil	Naut.	Moonset 18	19	20	21
°	h m	h m	h m	h m	h m	h m	h m
N 72	20 49	23 08	////	17 01	18 46	20 39	22 51
N 70	20 28	22 02	////	16 54	18 32	20 13	22 00
68	20 11	21 28	////	16 49	18 21	19 54	21 29
66	19 57	21 03	23 15	16 45	18 11	19 38	21 06
64	19 46	20 45	22 17	16 41	18 03	19 26	20 47
62	19 37	20 30	21 46	16 38	17 57	19 15	20 33
60	19 29	20 17	21 23	16 35	17 51	19 06	20 20
N 58	19 22	20 06	21 06	16 33	17 46	18 58	20 10
56	19 16	19 57	20 51	16 30	17 41	18 51	20 00
54	19 10	19 49	20 39	16 28	17 37	18 45	19 52
52	19 05	19 42	20 28	16 27	17 33	18 40	19 45
50	19 01	19 35	20 19	16 25	17 30	18 35	19 38
45	18 51	19 22	20 00	16 22	17 23	18 24	19 24
N 40	18 43	19 11	19 45	16 19	17 17	18 15	19 12
35	18 36	19 02	19 34	16 16	17 12	18 07	19 03
30	18 30	18 55	19 24	16 14	17 07	18 01	18 54
20	18 20	18 42	19 09	16 10	16 59	17 49	18 39
N 10	18 11	18 32	18 57	16 07	16 53	17 39	18 26
0	18 02	18 23	18 48	16 04	16 46	17 29	18 14
S 10	17 54	18 16	18 40	16 00	16 40	17 20	18 02
20	17 46	18 08	18 34	15 57	16 33	17 10	17 49
30	17 36	18 00	18 28	15 53	16 25	16 59	17 34
35	17 30	17 56	18 26	15 51	16 21	16 52	17 26
40	17 24	17 52	18 23	15 49	16 16	16 45	17 16
45	17 17	17 47	18 21	15 46	16 10	16 36	17 05
S 50	17 08	17 41	18 19	15 42	16 03	16 26	16 51
52	17 04	17 39	18 18	15 41	16 00	16 21	16 45
54	17 00	17 36	18 18	15 39	15 56	16 16	16 38
56	16 55	17 34	18 17	15 37	15 53	16 10	16 30
58	16 50	17 30	18 16	15 35	15 48	16 03	16 21
S 60	16 44	17 27	18 15	15 33	15 44	15 56	16 11

SUN / MOON

Day	Eqn. of Time 00h	12h	Mer. Pass.	Mer. Pass. Upper	Lower	Age	Phase
d	m s	m s	h m	h m	h m	d	%
18	00 39	00 46	11 59	09 53	22 15	27	7
19	00 52	00 59	11 59	10 36	22 57	28	3
20	01 05	01 11	11 59	11 19	23 41	29	1

UT	ARIES GHA	VENUS −4.7 GHA	VENUS Dec	MARS −0.2 GHA	MARS Dec	JUPITER −2.0 GHA	JUPITER Dec	SATURN +0.3 GHA	SATURN Dec	Name	SHA	Dec
21 00	209 28.3	137 08.0	N27 01.8	52 41.9	N12 21.1	163 50.0	N16 21.2	4 33.4	S 7 22.8	Acamar	315 19.4	S40 15.4
01	224 30.7	152 08.5	02.1	67 44.2	20.9	178 51.8	21.4	19 36.1	22.7	Achernar	335 27.9	S57 10.4
02	239 33.2	167 09.0	02.4	82 46.5	20.8	193 53.7	21.6	34 38.7	22.6	Acrux	173 09.6	S63 10.3
03	254 35.6	182 09.6	.. 02.7	97 48.8	.. 20.6	208 55.6	.. 21.7	49 41.4	.. 22.6	Adhara	255 13.3	S28 59.7
04	269 38.1	197 10.1	03.0	112 51.1	20.4	223 57.5	21.9	64 44.0	22.5	Aldebaran	290 50.6	N16 31.9
05	284 40.6	212 10.7	03.3	127 53.4	20.3	238 59.4	22.1	79 46.7	22.4			
06	299 43.0	227 11.2	N27 03.5	142 55.7	N12 20.1	254 01.2	N16 22.2	94 49.3	S 7 22.4	Alioth	166 20.8	N55 53.5
07	314 45.5	242 11.8	03.8	157 58.0	19.9	269 03.1	22.4	109 51.9	22.3	Alkaid	152 59.0	N49 15.0
S 08	329 48.0	257 12.3	04.1	173 00.3	19.8	284 05.0	22.6	124 54.6	22.2	Al Na'ir	27 44.9	S46 53.8
A 09	344 50.4	272 12.9	.. 04.4	188 02.6	.. 19.6	299 06.9	.. 22.7	139 57.2	.. 22.2	Alnilam	275 47.4	S 1 11.9
T 10	359 52.9	287 13.4	04.7	203 04.9	19.4	314 08.8	22.9	154 59.9	22.1	Alphard	217 56.8	S 8 43.0
U 11	14 55.4	302 14.0	05.0	218 07.2	19.2	329 10.7	23.1	170 02.5	22.0			
R 12	29 57.8	317 14.6	N27 05.2	233 09.5	N12 19.1	344 12.5	N16 23.2	185 05.2	S 7 22.0	Alphecca	126 11.4	N26 40.3
D 13	45 00.3	332 15.1	05.5	248 11.8	18.9	359 14.4	23.4	200 07.8	21.9	Alpheratz	357 44.7	N29 09.4
A 14	60 02.7	347 15.7	05.8	263 14.1	18.7	14 16.3	23.6	215 10.4	21.8	Altair	62 09.0	N 8 54.0
Y 15	75 05.2	2 16.2	.. 06.1	278 16.4	.. 18.5	29 18.2	.. 23.7	230 13.1	.. 21.8	Ankaa	353 16.9	S42 14.2
16	90 07.7	17 16.8	06.3	293 18.7	18.4	44 20.1	23.9	245 15.7	21.7	Antares	112 27.0	S26 27.5
17	105 10.1	32 17.4	06.6	308 21.0	18.2	59 21.9	24.1	260 18.4	21.6			
18	120 12.6	47 18.0	N27 06.9	323 23.3	N12 18.0	74 23.8	N16 24.2	275 21.0	S 7 21.6	Arcturus	145 56.1	N19 07.0
19	135 15.1	62 18.5	07.2	338 25.6	17.8	89 25.7	24.4	290 23.7	21.5	Atria	107 29.1	S69 02.7
20	150 17.5	77 19.1	07.4	353 27.9	17.7	104 27.6	24.5	305 26.3	21.4	Avior	234 18.4	S59 33.4
21	165 20.0	92 19.7	.. 07.7	8 30.2	.. 17.5	119 29.5	.. 24.7	320 29.0	.. 21.4	Bellatrix	278 33.1	N 6 21.5
22	180 22.5	107 20.3	08.0	23 32.4	17.3	134 31.4	24.9	335 31.6	21.3	Betelgeuse	271 02.4	N 7 24.4
23	195 24.9	122 20.8	08.3	38 34.7	17.1	149 33.2	25.0	350 34.2	21.2			
22 00	210 27.4	137 21.4	N27 08.5	53 37.0	N12 17.0	164 35.1	N16 25.2	5 36.9	S 7 21.2	Canopus	263 56.8	S52 42.5
01	225 29.9	152 22.0	08.8	68 39.3	16.8	179 37.0	25.4	20 39.5	21.1	Capella	280 36.0	N46 00.6
02	240 32.3	167 22.6	09.1	83 41.6	16.6	194 38.9	25.5	35 42.2	21.0	Deneb	49 32.1	N45 19.3
03	255 34.8	182 23.2	.. 09.3	98 43.9	.. 16.4	209 40.8	.. 25.7	50 44.8	.. 21.0	Denebola	182 34.2	N14 30.0
04	270 37.2	197 23.8	09.6	113 46.1	16.2	224 42.6	25.9	65 47.5	20.9	Diphda	348 57.0	S17 55.1
05	285 39.7	212 24.4	09.8	128 48.4	16.1	239 44.5	26.0	80 50.1	20.8			
06	300 42.2	227 25.0	N27 10.1	143 50.7	N12 15.9	254 46.4	N16 26.2	95 52.7	S 7 20.8	Dubhe	193 52.2	N61 41.1
07	315 44.6	242 25.6	10.4	158 53.0	15.7	269 48.3	26.4	110 55.4	20.7	Elnath	278 13.9	N28 37.0
S 08	330 47.1	257 26.2	10.6	173 55.2	15.5	284 50.2	26.5	125 58.0	20.6	Eltanin	90 46.2	N51 29.0
U 09	345 49.6	272 26.8	.. 10.9	188 57.5	.. 15.3	299 52.0	.. 26.7	141 00.7	.. 20.5	Enif	33 48.0	N 9 55.9
N 10	0 52.0	287 27.4	11.2	203 59.8	15.2	314 53.9	26.9	156 03.3	20.5	Fomalhaut	15 25.1	S29 33.3
D 11	15 54.5	302 28.0	11.4	219 02.0	15.0	329 55.8	27.0	171 06.0	20.4			
A 12	30 57.0	317 28.6	N27 11.7	234 04.3	N12 14.8	344 57.7	N16 27.2	186 08.6	S 7 20.3	Gacrux	172 01.3	S57 11.2
Y 13	45 59.4	332 29.2	11.9	249 06.6	14.6	359 59.6	27.4	201 11.2	20.3	Gienah	175 52.9	S17 36.9
14	61 01.9	347 29.8	12.2	264 08.9	14.4	15 01.4	27.5	216 13.9	20.2	Hadar	148 48.4	S60 26.0
15	76 04.3	2 30.4	.. 12.4	279 11.1	.. 14.2	30 03.3	.. 27.7	231 16.5	.. 20.1	Hamal	328 02.0	N23 31.1
16	91 06.8	17 31.0	12.7	294 13.4	14.1	45 05.2	27.9	246 19.2	20.1	Kaus Aust.	83 44.7	S34 22.5
17	106 09.3	32 31.6	12.9	309 15.7	13.9	60 07.1	28.0	261 21.8	20.0			
18	121 11.7	47 32.3	N27 13.2	324 17.9	N12 13.7	75 09.0	N16 28.2	276 24.5	S 7 19.9	Kochab	137 18.8	N74 06.2
19	136 14.2	62 32.9	13.5	339 20.2	13.5	90 10.8	28.4	291 27.1	19.9	Markab	13 39.4	N15 16.2
20	151 16.7	77 33.5	13.7	354 22.4	13.3	105 12.7	28.5	306 29.7	19.8	Menkar	314 16.2	N 4 08.2
21	166 19.1	92 34.1	.. 14.0	9 24.7	.. 13.1	120 14.6	.. 28.7	321 32.4	.. 19.7	Menkent	148 08.1	S36 26.0
22	181 21.6	107 34.8	14.2	24 27.0	12.9	135 16.5	28.9	336 35.0	19.7	Miaplacidus	221 39.7	S69 46.5
23	196 24.1	122 35.4	14.4	39 29.2	12.8	150 18.4	29.0	351 37.7	19.6			
23 00	211 26.5	137 36.0	N27 14.7	54 31.5	N12 12.6	165 20.2	N16 29.2	6 40.3	S 7 19.5	Mirfak	308 42.0	N49 54.3
01	226 29.0	152 36.6	14.9	69 33.7	12.4	180 22.1	29.3	21 43.0	19.5	Nunki	75 59.2	S26 16.7
02	241 31.5	167 37.3	15.2	84 36.0	12.2	195 24.0	29.5	36 45.6	19.4	Peacock	53 20.5	S56 41.4
03	256 33.9	182 37.9	.. 15.4	99 38.2	.. 12.0	210 25.9	.. 29.7	51 48.2	.. 19.3	Pollux	243 28.8	N27 59.7
04	271 36.4	197 38.6	15.7	114 40.5	11.8	225 27.8	29.8	66 50.9	19.3	Procyon	245 00.6	N 5 11.4
05	286 38.8	212 39.2	15.9	129 42.7	11.6	240 29.6	30.0	81 53.5	19.2			
06	301 41.3	227 39.8	N27 16.2	144 45.0	N12 11.4	255 31.5	N16 30.2	96 56.2	S 7 19.1	Rasalhague	96 07.0	N12 33.0
07	316 43.8	242 40.5	16.4	159 47.2	11.2	270 33.4	30.3	111 58.8	19.1	Regulus	207 44.2	N11 54.2
M 08	331 46.2	257 41.1	16.6	174 49.5	11.1	285 35.3	30.5	127 01.5	19.0	Rigel	281 13.1	S 8 11.5
O 09	346 48.7	272 41.8	.. 16.9	189 51.7	.. 10.9	300 37.2	.. 30.7	142 04.1	.. 18.9	Rigil Kent.	139 52.2	S60 53.2
N 10	1 51.2	287 42.4	17.1	204 54.0	10.7	315 39.0	30.8	157 06.7	18.9	Sabik	102 13.2	S15 44.4
D 11	16 53.6	302 43.1	17.4	219 56.2	10.5	330 40.9	31.0	172 09.4	18.8			
A 12	31 56.1	317 43.7	N27 17.7	234 58.5	N12 10.3	345 42.8	N16 31.2	187 12.0	S 7 18.7	Schedar	349 42.0	N56 36.2
Y 13	46 58.6	332 44.4	17.8	250 00.7	10.1	0 44.7	31.3	202 14.7	18.7	Shaula	96 22.8	S37 06.6
14	62 01.0	347 45.1	18.1	265 02.9	09.9	15 46.5	31.5	217 17.3	18.6	Sirius	258 34.6	S16 44.3
15	77 03.5	2 45.7	.. 18.3	280 05.2	.. 09.7	30 48.4	.. 31.7	232 20.0	.. 18.5	Spica	158 31.8	S11 13.7
16	92 06.0	17 46.4	18.5	295 07.4	09.5	45 50.3	31.8	247 22.6	18.5	Suhail	222 53.0	S43 29.4
17	107 08.4	32 47.1	18.8	310 09.7	09.3	60 52.2	32.0	262 25.2	18.4			
18	122 10.9	47 47.7	N27 19.0	325 11.9	N12 09.1	75 54.1	N16 32.2	277 27.9	S 7 18.3	Vega	80 39.3	N38 47.5
19	137 13.3	62 48.4	19.2	340 14.1	08.9	90 55.9	32.3	292 30.5	18.3	Zuben'ubi	137 06.0	S16 05.7
20	152 15.8	77 49.1	19.5	355 16.4	08.7	105 57.8	32.5	307 33.2	18.2		SHA	Mer.Pass.
21	167 18.3	92 49.7	.. 19.7	10 18.6	.. 08.5	120 59.7	.. 32.6	322 35.8	.. 18.1	Venus	286 54.0	14 50
22	182 20.7	107 50.4	19.9	25 20.8	08.4	136 01.6	32.8	337 38.4	18.1	Mars	203 09.6	20 22
23	197 23.2	122 51.1	20.1	40 23.1	08.2	151 03.5	33.0	352 41.1	18.0	Jupiter	314 07.7	13 00
Mer.Pass.	h m 9 56.5	v 0.6	d 0.3	v 2.3	d 0.2	v 1.9	d 0.2	v 2.6	d 0.1	Saturn	155 09.5	23 33

UT	SUN GHA	SUN Dec	MOON GHA	v	Dec	d	HP
d h	° ′	° ′	° ′	′	° ′	′	′
21 00	180 19.4	N11 55.4	184 38.8	14.2	N13 42.1	8.7	54.1
01	195 19.5	56.2	199 12.0	14.2	13 50.8	8.7	54.1
02	210 19.6	57.1	213 45.2	14.1	13 59.5	8.5	54.1
03	225 19.7	.. 57.9	228 18.3	14.1	14 08.0	8.5	54.0
04	240 19.9	58.8	242 51.4	14.1	14 16.5	8.5	54.0
05	255 20.0	11 59.6	257 24.5	14.1	14 25.0	8.4	54.0
S 06	270 20.1	N12 00.5	271 57.6	14.0	N14 33.4	8.3	54.0
A 07	285 20.2	01.3	286 30.6	14.0	14 41.7	8.3	54.0
T 08	300 20.4	02.2	301 03.6	14.0	14 50.0	8.1	54.0
U 09	315 20.5	.. 03.0	315 36.6	13.9	14 58.1	8.2	54.0
R 10	330 20.6	03.8	330 09.5	13.9	15 06.3	8.0	54.0
D 11	345 20.7	04.7	344 42.4	13.9	15 14.3	8.0	54.0
A 12	0 20.9	N12 05.5	359 15.3	13.8	N15 22.3	8.0	54.0
Y 13	15 21.0	06.4	13 48.1	13.8	15 30.3	7.8	54.0
14	30 21.1	07.2	28 20.9	13.8	15 38.1	7.8	54.0
15	45 21.2	.. 08.1	42 53.7	13.7	15 45.9	7.8	54.0
16	60 21.3	08.9	57 26.4	13.7	15 53.7	7.6	54.0
17	75 21.5	09.7	71 59.1	13.7	16 01.3	7.6	54.0
18	90 21.6	N12 10.6	86 31.8	13.6	N16 08.9	7.5	54.0
19	105 21.7	11.4	101 04.4	13.6	16 16.4	7.5	54.0
20	120 21.8	12.3	115 37.0	13.6	16 23.9	7.3	54.0
21	135 22.0	.. 13.1	130 09.6	13.5	16 31.2	7.3	54.0
22	150 22.1	13.9	144 42.1	13.5	16 38.5	7.3	54.0
23	165 22.2	14.8	159 14.6	13.4	16 45.8	7.1	54.0
22 00	180 22.3	N12 15.6	173 47.0	13.5	N16 52.9	7.1	54.0
01	195 22.4	16.5	188 19.5	13.3	17 00.0	7.0	54.0
02	210 22.6	17.3	202 51.8	13.4	17 07.0	7.0	54.0
03	225 22.7	.. 18.1	217 24.2	13.3	17 14.0	6.8	54.0
04	240 22.8	19.0	231 56.5	13.3	17 20.8	6.8	54.0
05	255 22.9	19.8	246 28.8	13.2	17 27.6	6.7	54.0
S 06	270 23.0	N12 20.7	261 01.0	13.3	N17 34.3	6.6	54.0
U 07	285 23.2	21.5	275 33.3	13.1	17 40.9	6.6	54.0
N 08	300 23.3	22.3	290 05.4	13.2	17 47.5	6.5	54.0
D 09	315 23.4	.. 23.2	304 37.6	13.1	17 54.0	6.4	54.0
A 10	330 23.5	24.0	319 09.7	13.1	18 00.4	6.3	54.0
Y 11	345 23.6	24.8	333 41.8	13.0	18 06.7	6.2	54.0
12	0 23.7	N12 25.7	348 13.8	13.0	N18 12.9	6.2	54.0
13	15 23.9	26.5	2 45.8	13.0	18 19.1	6.0	54.0
14	30 24.0	27.3	17 17.8	12.9	18 25.1	6.0	54.0
15	45 24.1	.. 28.2	31 49.7	12.9	18 31.1	5.9	54.0
16	60 24.3	29.0	46 21.6	12.9	18 37.0	5.8	54.0
17	75 24.3	29.8	60 53.5	12.8	18 42.8	5.8	54.0
18	90 24.5	N12 30.7	75 25.3	12.8	N18 48.6	5.6	54.0
19	105 24.6	31.5	89 57.1	12.8	18 54.2	5.6	54.0
20	120 24.7	32.3	104 28.9	12.7	18 59.8	5.5	54.0
21	135 24.8	.. 33.2	119 00.6	12.7	19 05.3	5.4	54.0
22	150 24.9	34.0	133 32.3	12.7	19 10.7	5.3	54.0
23	165 25.0	34.8	148 04.0	12.6	19 16.0	5.3	54.0
23 00	180 25.1	N12 35.7	162 35.6	12.6	N19 21.3	5.1	54.0
01	195 25.3	36.5	177 07.2	12.5	19 26.4	5.1	54.0
02	210 25.4	37.3	191 38.7	12.6	19 31.5	4.9	54.0
03	225 25.5	.. 38.2	206 10.3	12.5	19 36.4	4.9	54.0
04	240 25.6	39.0	220 41.8	12.4	19 41.3	4.8	54.0
05	255 25.7	39.8	235 13.2	12.5	19 46.1	4.7	54.0
M 06	270 25.8	N12 40.6	249 44.7	12.4	N19 50.8	4.6	54.0
O 07	285 25.9	41.5	264 16.1	12.4	19 55.4	4.6	54.0
N 08	300 26.1	42.3	278 47.5	12.3	20 00.0	4.4	54.0
D 09	315 26.2	.. 43.1	293 18.8	12.3	20 04.4	4.3	54.0
A 10	330 26.3	44.0	307 50.1	12.3	20 08.7	4.3	54.0
Y 11	345 26.4	44.8	322 21.4	12.2	20 13.0	4.2	54.0
12	0 26.5	N12 45.6	336 52.6	12.3	N20 17.2	4.0	54.0
13	15 26.6	46.4	351 23.9	12.1	20 21.2	4.0	54.0
14	30 26.7	47.3	5 55.0	12.2	20 25.2	3.9	54.0
15	45 26.9	.. 48.1	20 26.2	12.1	20 29.1	3.8	54.0
16	60 27.0	48.9	34 57.3	12.1	20 32.9	3.7	54.0
17	75 27.1	49.7	49 28.4	12.1	20 36.6	3.6	54.0
18	90 27.2	N12 50.6	63 59.5	12.1	N20 40.2	3.5	54.0
19	105 27.3	51.4	78 30.6	12.0	20 43.7	3.4	54.0
20	120 27.4	52.2	93 01.6	12.0	20 47.1	3.3	54.0
21	135 27.5	.. 53.0	107 32.6	11.9	20 50.4	3.2	54.0
22	150 27.6	53.9	122 03.5	12.0	20 53.6	3.1	54.0
23	165 27.8	54.7	136 34.5	11.9	N20 56.7	3.1	54.0
	SD 15.9	d 0.8	SD 14.7		14.7		14.7

Lat.	Twilight Naut.	Twilight Civil	Sunrise	Moonrise 21	22	23	24
°	h m	h m	h m	h m	h m	h m	h m
N 72	////	////	02 55	02 26	01 47	▭	▭
N 70	////	01 36	03 18	02 53	02 39	02 10	▭
68	////	02 16	03 37	03 14	03 11	03 10	▭
66	////	02 43	03 51	03 30	03 35	03 45	04 03
64	01 24	03 04	04 03	03 44	03 54	04 10	04 35
62	02 00	03 20	04 13	03 55	04 09	04 30	04 59
60	02 25	03 33	04 22	04 05	04 22	04 46	05 18
N 58	02 44	03 45	04 30	04 13	04 34	05 00	05 33
56	03 00	03 54	04 36	04 21	04 43	05 11	05 47
54	03 13	04 03	04 42	04 28	04 52	05 22	05 58
52	03 24	04 11	04 48	04 34	05 00	05 31	06 09
50	03 34	04 17	04 53	04 39	05 07	05 39	06 18
45	03 53	04 32	05 03	04 51	05 22	05 57	06 37
N 40	04 09	04 43	05 12	05 01	05 34	06 11	06 53
35	04 21	04 53	05 19	05 10	05 45	06 24	07 07
30	04 31	05 01	05 25	05 17	05 54	06 34	07 18
20	04 47	05 14	05 37	05 30	06 10	06 53	07 38
N 10	04 59	05 25	05 46	05 42	06 24	07 09	07 56
0	05 09	05 34	05 55	05 52	06 37	07 24	08 12
S 10	05 18	05 42	06 04	06 03	06 51	07 39	08 28
20	05 25	05 51	06 13	06 15	07 05	07 56	08 46
30	05 31	05 59	06 24	06 28	07 21	08 14	09 06
35	05 34	06 04	06 30	06 36	07 31	08 25	09 18
40	05 37	06 09	06 36	06 45	07 42	08 38	09 32
45	05 40	06 14	06 44	06 55	07 55	08 53	09 48
S 50	05 42	06 20	06 54	07 08	08 11	09 11	10 08
52	05 43	06 23	06 58	07 14	08 18	09 20	10 17
54	05 44	06 26	07 03	07 20	08 26	09 29	10 28
56	05 46	06 29	07 08	07 27	08 36	09 40	10 40
58	05 47	06 33	07 14	07 36	08 46	09 53	10 54
S 60	05 48	06 37	07 20	07 45	08 58	10 08	11 10

Lat.	Sunset	Twilight Civil	Naut.	Moonset 21	22	23	24
°	h m	h m	h m	h m	h m	h m	h m
N 72	21 07	////	////	22 51	▭	▭	▭
N 70	20 42	22 30	////	22 00	24 05	00 05	▭
68	20 23	21 46	////	21 29	23 06	24 42	00 42
66	20 08	21 17	////	21 06	22 32	23 52	24 56
64	19 56	20 56	22 41	20 47	22 07	23 20	24 21
62	19 45	20 40	22 02	20 33	21 48	22 57	23 55
60	19 36	20 26	21 35	20 20	21 32	22 38	23 35
N 58	19 29	20 14	21 16	20 10	21 18	22 22	23 19
56	19 22	20 04	21 00	20 00	21 07	22 09	23 05
54	19 16	19 55	20 46	19 52	20 57	21 58	22 52
52	19 11	19 48	20 35	19 45	20 48	21 48	22 42
50	19 05	19 41	20 25	19 38	20 40	21 39	22 32
45	18 55	19 26	20 05	19 24	20 23	21 19	22 12
N 40	18 46	19 15	19 49	19 12	20 09	21 04	21 56
35	18 38	19 05	19 37	19 03	19 57	20 51	21 42
30	18 32	18 57	19 29	18 54	19 47	20 39	21 30
20	18 21	18 43	19 10	18 39	19 29	20 20	21 10
N 10	18 11	18 32	18 58	18 26	19 14	20 03	20 52
0	18 02	18 23	18 48	18 14	19 00	19 47	20 36
S 10	17 53	18 14	18 39	18 02	18 46	19 31	20 19
20	17 43	18 06	18 32	17 49	18 30	19 14	20 01
30	17 33	17 57	18 25	17 34	18 13	18 55	19 41
35	17 27	17 53	18 22	17 26	18 03	18 44	19 29
40	17 20	17 48	18 19	17 16	17 51	18 31	19 15
45	17 12	17 42	18 17	17 05	17 38	18 15	18 59
S 50	17 03	17 36	18 14	16 51	17 21	17 56	18 39
52	16 58	17 33	18 13	16 45	17 13	17 48	18 29
54	16 53	17 30	18 11	16 38	17 05	17 38	18 18
56	16 48	17 27	18 10	16 30	16 55	17 26	18 06
58	16 42	17 23	18 09	16 21	16 44	17 14	17 52
S 60	16 35	17 19	18 08	16 11	16 31	16 59	17 36

Day	SUN Eqn. of Time 00h	12h	Mer. Pass.	MOON Mer. Pass. Upper	Lower	Age	Phase
d	m s	m s	h m	h m	h m	d	%
21	01 17	01 23	11 59	12 03	24 26	00	0
22	01 29	01 35	11 58	12 49	00 26	01	1
23	01 40	01 46	11 58	13 36	01 12	02	4 ●

UT	ARIES GHA	VENUS −4.7 GHA	Dec	MARS −0.1 GHA	Dec	JUPITER −2.0 GHA	Dec	SATURN +0.3 GHA	Dec	STARS Name	SHA	Dec
24 00	212 25.7	137 51.8	N27 20.4	55 25.3	N12 08.0	166 05.3	N16 33.1	7 43.7	S 7 17.9	Acamar	315 19.4	S40 15.4
01	227 28.1	152 52.5	20.6	70 27.5	07.8	181 07.2	33.3	22 46.4	17.9	Achernar	335 27.9	S57 10.4
02	242 30.6	167 53.2	20.8	85 29.8	07.6	196 09.1	33.5	37 49.0	17.8	Acrux	173 09.6	S63 10.3
03	257 33.1	182 53.8	.. 21.0	100 32.0	.. 07.4	211 11.0	.. 33.6	52 51.7	.. 17.7	Adhara	255 13.3	S28 59.7
04	272 35.5	197 54.5	21.3	115 34.2	07.2	226 12.8	33.8	67 54.3	17.7	Aldebaran	290 50.6	N16 31.9
05	287 38.0	212 55.2	21.5	130 36.4	07.0	241 14.7	34.0	82 56.9	17.6			
T 06	302 40.5	227 55.9	N27 21.7	145 38.7	N12 06.8	256 16.6	N16 34.1	97 59.6	S 7 17.5	Alioth	166 20.8	N55 53.6
U 07	317 42.9	242 56.6	21.9	160 40.9	06.6	271 18.5	34.3	113 02.2	17.5	Alkaid	152 59.0	N49 15.0
E 08	332 45.4	257 57.3	22.1	175 43.1	06.4	286 20.4	34.5	128 04.9	17.4	Al Na'ir	27 44.9	S46 53.8
S 09	347 47.8	272 58.0	.. 22.4	190 45.3	.. 06.2	301 22.2	.. 34.6	143 07.5	.. 17.3	Alnilam	275 47.4	S 1 11.9
D 10	2 50.3	287 58.7	22.6	205 47.5	06.0	316 24.1	34.8	158 10.2	17.3	Alphard	217 56.8	S 8 43.0
A 11	17 52.8	302 59.4	22.8	220 49.8	05.8	331 26.0	35.0	173 12.8	17.2			
Y 12	32 55.2	318 00.1	N27 23.0	235 52.0	N12 05.6	346 27.9	N16 35.1	188 15.4	S 7 17.1	Alphecca	126 11.3	N26 40.3
13	47 57.7	333 00.8	23.2	250 54.2	05.4	1 29.7	35.3	203 18.1	17.1	Alpheratz	357 44.6	N29 09.4
14	63 00.2	348 01.6	23.4	265 56.4	05.2	16 31.6	35.4	218 20.7	17.0	Altair	62 09.0	N 8 54.0
15	78 02.6	3 02.3	.. 23.6	280 58.6	.. 05.0	31 33.5	.. 35.6	233 23.4	.. 17.0	Ankaa	353 16.8	S42 14.2
16	93 05.1	18 03.0	23.9	296 00.8	04.8	46 35.4	35.8	248 26.0	16.9	Antares	112 26.9	S26 27.5
17	108 07.6	33 03.7	24.1	311 03.1	04.6	61 37.3	35.9	263 28.6	16.8			
18	123 10.0	48 04.4	N27 24.3	326 05.3	N12 04.4	76 39.1	N16 36.1	278 31.3	S 7 16.8	Arcturus	145 56.1	N19 07.0
19	138 12.5	63 05.1	24.5	341 07.5	04.2	91 41.0	36.3	293 33.9	16.7	Atria	107 29.1	S69 02.8
20	153 14.9	78 05.9	24.7	356 09.7	04.0	106 42.9	36.4	308 36.6	16.6	Avior	234 18.4	S59 33.4
21	168 17.4	93 06.6	.. 24.9	11 11.9	.. 03.7	121 44.8	.. 36.6	323 39.2	.. 16.6	Bellatrix	278 33.1	N 6 21.5
22	183 19.9	108 07.3	25.1	26 14.1	03.5	136 46.6	36.8	338 41.9	16.5	Betelgeuse	271 02.4	N 7 24.4
23	198 22.3	123 08.1	25.3	41 16.3	03.3	151 48.5	36.9	353 44.5	16.4			
25 00	213 24.8	138 08.8	N27 25.5	56 18.5	N12 03.1	166 50.4	N16 37.1	8 47.1	S 7 16.4	Canopus	263 56.8	S52 42.5
01	228 27.3	153 09.5	25.7	71 20.7	02.9	181 52.3	37.3	23 49.8	16.3	Capella	280 36.0	N46 00.6
02	243 29.7	168 10.3	25.9	86 22.9	02.7	196 54.2	37.4	38 52.4	16.2	Deneb	49 32.1	N45 19.3
03	258 32.2	183 11.0	.. 26.1	101 25.1	.. 02.5	211 56.0	.. 37.6	53 55.1	.. 16.2	Denebola	182 34.2	N14 30.0
04	273 34.7	198 11.8	26.3	116 27.3	02.3	226 57.9	37.7	68 57.7	16.1	Diphda	348 57.0	S17 55.1
05	288 37.1	213 12.5	26.5	131 29.5	02.1	241 59.8	37.9	84 00.3	16.0			
W 06	303 39.6	228 13.2	N27 26.7	146 31.7	N12 01.9	257 01.7	N16 38.1	99 03.0	S 7 16.0	Dubhe	193 52.2	N61 41.1
E 07	318 42.1	243 14.0	26.9	161 33.9	01.7	272 03.5	38.2	114 05.6	15.9	Elnath	278 13.9	N28 37.0
D 08	333 44.5	258 14.8	27.1	176 36.1	01.5	287 05.4	38.4	129 08.3	15.8	Eltanin	90 46.2	N51 29.1
N 09	348 47.0	273 15.5	.. 27.3	191 38.3	.. 01.3	302 07.3	.. 38.6	144 10.9	.. 15.8	Enif	33 48.0	N 9 55.9
E 10	3 49.4	288 16.3	27.5	206 40.5	01.1	317 09.2	38.7	159 13.5	15.7	Fomalhaut	15 25.1	S29 33.3
S 11	18 51.9	303 17.0	27.7	221 42.7	00.8	332 11.0	38.9	174 16.2	15.6			
D 12	33 54.4	318 17.8	N27 27.9	236 44.9	N12 00.6	347 12.9	N16 39.1	189 18.8	S 7 15.6	Gacrux	172 01.3	S57 11.2
A 13	48 56.8	333 18.5	28.1	251 47.1	00.4	2 14.8	39.2	204 21.5	15.5	Gienah	175 52.9	S17 36.9
Y 14	63 59.3	348 19.3	28.3	266 49.3	00.2	17 16.7	39.4	219 24.1	15.4	Hadar	148 48.4	S60 26.0
15	79 01.8	3 20.1	.. 28.5	281 51.5	12 00.0	32 18.5	.. 39.5	234 26.7	.. 15.4	Hamal	328 02.0	N23 31.1
16	94 04.2	18 20.9	28.7	296 53.6	11 59.8	47 20.4	39.7	249 29.4	15.3	Kaus Aust.	83 44.7	S34 22.5
17	109 06.7	33 21.6	28.9	311 55.8	59.6	62 22.3	39.9	264 32.0	15.2			
18	124 09.2	48 22.4	N27 29.1	326 58.0	N11 59.4	77 24.2	N16 40.0	279 34.7	S 7 15.2	Kochab	137 18.8	N74 06.2
19	139 11.6	63 23.2	29.2	342 00.2	59.2	92 26.1	40.2	294 37.3	15.1	Markab	13 39.3	N15 16.2
20	154 14.1	78 24.0	29.4	357 02.4	58.9	107 27.9	40.4	309 40.0	15.0	Menkar	314 16.2	N 4 08.2
21	169 16.6	93 24.7	.. 29.6	12 04.6	.. 58.7	122 29.8	.. 40.5	324 42.6	.. 15.0	Menkent	148 08.1	S36 26.0
22	184 19.0	108 25.5	29.8	27 06.8	58.5	137 31.7	40.7	339 45.2	14.9	Miaplacidus	221 39.7	S69 46.5
23	199 21.5	123 26.3	30.0	42 08.9	58.3	152 33.6	40.9	354 47.9	14.8			
26 00	214 23.9	138 27.1	N27 30.2	57 11.1	N11 58.1	167 35.4	N16 41.0	9 50.5	S 7 14.8	Mirfak	308 42.0	N49 54.2
01	229 26.4	153 27.9	30.3	72 13.3	57.9	182 37.3	41.2	24 53.2	14.7	Nunki	75 59.2	S26 16.7
02	244 28.9	168 28.7	30.5	87 15.5	57.7	197 39.2	41.4	39 55.8	14.7	Peacock	53 20.5	S56 41.4
03	259 31.3	183 29.5	.. 30.7	102 17.6	.. 57.4	212 41.1	.. 41.5	54 58.4	.. 14.6	Pollux	243 28.8	N27 59.7
04	274 33.8	198 30.3	30.9	117 19.8	57.2	227 42.9	41.7	70 01.1	14.5	Procyon	245 00.7	N 5 11.4
05	289 36.3	213 31.1	31.1	132 22.0	57.0	242 44.8	41.8	85 03.7	14.5			
T 06	304 38.7	228 31.9	N27 31.2	147 24.2	N11 56.8	257 46.7	N16 42.0	100 06.4	S 7 14.4	Rasalhague	96 07.0	N12 33.0
H 07	319 41.2	243 32.7	31.4	162 26.3	56.6	272 48.6	42.2	115 09.0	14.3	Regulus	207 44.2	N11 54.2
U 08	334 43.7	258 33.5	31.6	177 28.5	56.4	287 50.4	42.3	130 11.6	14.3	Rigel	281 13.1	S 8 11.5
R 09	349 46.1	273 34.3	.. 31.8	192 30.7	.. 56.1	302 52.3	.. 42.5	145 14.3	.. 14.2	Rigil Kent.	139 52.2	S60 53.2
S 10	4 48.6	288 35.1	32.0	207 32.9	55.9	317 54.2	42.7	160 16.9	14.1	Sabik	102 13.2	S15 44.4
D 11	19 51.1	303 36.0	32.1	222 35.0	55.7	332 56.1	42.8	175 19.6	14.1			
A 12	34 53.5	318 36.8	N27 32.3	237 37.2	N11 55.5	347 57.9	N16 43.0	190 22.2	S 7 14.0	Schedar	349 42.0	N56 36.2
Y 13	49 56.0	333 37.6	32.5	252 39.4	55.3	2 59.8	43.1	205 24.8	13.9	Shaula	96 22.7	S37 06.6
14	64 58.4	348 38.4	32.6	267 41.5	55.0	18 01.7	43.3	220 27.5	13.9	Sirius	258 34.6	S16 44.3
15	80 00.9	3 39.2	.. 32.8	282 43.7	.. 54.8	33 03.6	.. 43.5	235 30.1	.. 13.8	Spica	158 31.8	S11 13.7
16	95 03.4	18 40.1	33.0	297 45.9	54.6	48 05.4	43.6	250 32.8	13.7	Suhail	222 53.0	S43 29.4
17	110 05.8	33 40.9	33.2	312 48.0	54.4	63 07.3	43.8	265 35.4	13.7			
18	125 08.3	48 41.7	N27 33.3	327 50.2	N11 54.2	78 09.2	N16 44.0	280 38.0	S 7 13.6	Vega	80 39.3	N38 47.6
19	140 10.8	63 42.6	33.5	342 52.3	53.9	93 11.1	44.1	295 40.7	13.5	Zuben'ubi	137 06.0	S16 05.7
20	155 13.2	78 43.4	33.7	357 54.5	53.7	108 12.9	44.3	310 43.3	13.5			
21	170 15.7	93 44.3	.. 33.8	12 56.7	.. 53.5	123 14.8	.. 44.5	325 46.0	.. 13.4		SHA	Mer.Pass.
22	185 18.2	108 45.1	34.0	27 58.8	53.3	138 16.7	44.6	340 48.6	13.4	Venus	284 45.0	14 47
23	200 20.6	123 45.9	34.1	43 01.0	53.1	153 18.6	44.8	355 51.2	13.3	Mars	202 53.7	20 12
Mer. Pass.	9 44.7	v 0.8	d 0.2	v 2.2	d 0.2	v 1.9	d 0.2	v 2.6	d 0.1	Jupiter	313 25.6	12 51
										Saturn	155 22.3	23 21

2012 APRIL 24, 25, 26 (TUES., WED., THURS.)

UT	SUN GHA	SUN Dec	MOON GHA	MOON v	MOON Dec	MOON d	MOON HP
d h	° ′	° ′	° ′	′	° ′	′	′
24 00	180 27.9	N12 55.5	151 05.4	11.9	N20 59.8	2.9	54.1
01	195 28.0	56.3	165 36.3	11.8	21 02.7	2.8	54.1
02	210 28.1	57.1	180 07.1	11.9	21 05.5	2.8	54.1
03	225 28.2	.. 58.0	194 38.0	11.8	21 08.3	2.6	54.1
04	240 28.3	58.8	209 08.8	11.8	21 10.9	2.6	54.1
05	255 28.4	12 59.6	223 39.6	11.7	21 13.5	2.4	54.1
06	270 28.5	N13 00.4	238 10.3	11.8	N21 15.9	2.3	54.1
07	285 28.6	01.2	252 41.1	11.7	21 18.2	2.3	54.1
T 08	300 28.7	02.1	267 11.8	11.7	21 20.5	2.1	54.1
U 09	315 28.9	.. 02.9	281 42.5	11.7	21 22.6	2.1	54.1
E 10	330 29.0	03.7	296 13.2	11.6	21 24.7	1.9	54.1
S 11	345 29.1	04.5	310 43.8	11.7	21 26.6	1.9	54.1
D 12	0 29.2	N13 05.3	325 14.5	11.6	N21 28.5	1.7	54.1
A 13	15 29.3	06.2	339 45.1	11.6	21 30.2	1.7	54.1
Y 14	30 29.4	07.0	354 15.7	11.5	21 31.9	1.5	54.2
15	45 29.5	.. 07.8	8 46.2	11.6	21 33.4	1.5	54.2
16	60 29.6	08.6	23 16.8	11.5	21 34.9	1.3	54.2
17	75 29.7	09.4	37 47.3	11.6	21 36.2	1.2	54.2
18	90 29.8	N13 10.2	52 17.9	11.5	N21 37.4	1.2	54.2
19	105 29.9	11.1	66 48.4	11.4	21 38.6	1.0	54.2
20	120 30.0	11.9	81 18.8	11.5	21 39.6	1.0	54.2
21	135 30.1	.. 12.7	95 49.3	11.5	21 40.6	0.8	54.2
22	150 30.3	13.5	110 19.8	11.4	21 41.4	0.7	54.2
23	165 30.4	14.3	124 50.2	11.4	21 42.1	0.7	54.2
25 00	180 30.5	N13 15.1	139 20.6	11.4	N21 42.8	0.5	54.3
01	195 30.6	15.9	153 51.0	11.4	21 43.3	0.4	54.3
02	210 30.7	16.7	168 21.4	11.4	21 43.7	0.3	54.3
03	225 30.8	.. 17.6	182 51.8	11.4	21 44.0	0.2	54.3
04	240 30.9	18.4	197 22.2	11.4	21 44.2	0.2	54.3
05	255 31.0	19.2	211 52.6	11.3	21 44.4	0.0	54.3
06	270 31.1	N13 20.0	226 22.9	11.3	N21 44.4	0.1	54.3
W 07	285 31.2	20.8	240 53.2	11.4	21 44.3	0.2	54.3
E 08	300 31.3	21.6	255 23.6	11.3	21 44.1	0.3	54.3
D 09	315 31.4	.. 22.4	269 53.9	11.3	21 43.8	0.4	54.4
N 10	330 31.5	23.2	284 24.2	11.3	21 43.4	0.5	54.4
E 11	345 31.6	24.0	298 54.5	11.3	21 42.9	0.6	54.4
S 12	0 31.7	N13 24.9	313 24.8	11.3	N21 42.3	0.8	54.4
D 13	15 31.8	25.7	327 55.1	11.2	21 41.5	0.8	54.4
A 14	30 31.9	26.5	342 25.3	11.3	21 40.7	0.9	54.4
Y 15	45 32.0	.. 27.3	356 55.6	11.3	21 39.8	1.0	54.4
16	60 32.1	28.1	11 25.9	11.2	21 38.8	1.2	54.4
17	75 32.2	28.9	25 56.1	11.3	21 37.6	1.2	54.5
18	90 32.3	N13 29.7	40 26.4	11.2	N21 36.4	1.3	54.5
19	105 32.4	30.5	54 56.6	11.2	21 35.1	1.5	54.5
20	120 32.5	31.3	69 26.8	11.3	21 33.6	1.5	54.5
21	135 32.6	.. 32.1	83 57.1	11.2	21 32.1	1.7	54.5
22	150 32.7	32.9	98 27.3	11.2	21 30.4	1.7	54.5
23	165 32.8	33.7	112 57.5	11.3	21 28.7	1.9	54.6
26 00	180 32.9	N13 34.5	127 27.8	11.2	N21 26.8	2.0	54.6
01	195 33.0	35.3	141 58.0	11.2	21 24.8	2.0	54.6
02	210 33.2	36.1	156 28.2	11.2	21 22.8	2.2	54.6
03	225 33.3	.. 36.9	170 58.4	11.3	21 20.6	2.3	54.6
04	240 33.4	37.7	185 28.7	11.2	21 18.3	2.3	54.6
05	255 33.5	38.5	199 58.9	11.2	21 16.0	2.5	54.7
06	270 33.6	N13 39.3	214 29.1	11.2	N21 13.5	2.6	54.7
07	285 33.7	40.1	228 59.3	11.2	21 10.9	2.7	54.7
T 08	300 33.7	40.9	243 29.5	11.3	21 08.2	2.8	54.7
H 09	315 33.8	.. 41.7	257 59.8	11.2	21 05.4	2.9	54.7
U 10	330 33.9	42.5	272 30.0	11.2	21 02.5	3.0	54.7
R 11	345 34.0	43.3	287 00.2	11.3	20 59.5	3.1	54.8
S 12	0 34.1	N13 44.1	301 30.5	11.2	N20 56.4	3.2	54.8
D 13	15 34.2	44.9	316 00.7	11.2	20 53.2	3.3	54.8
A 14	30 34.3	45.7	330 30.9	11.3	20 49.9	3.4	54.8
Y 15	45 34.4	.. 46.5	345 01.2	11.2	20 46.5	3.5	54.8
16	60 34.5	47.3	359 31.4	11.3	20 43.0	3.6	54.9
17	75 34.6	48.1	14 01.7	11.2	20 39.4	3.8	54.9
18	90 34.7	N13 48.9	28 31.9	11.3	N20 35.6	3.8	54.9
19	105 34.8	49.7	43 02.2	11.3	20 31.8	3.9	54.9
20	120 34.9	50.5	57 32.5	11.2	20 27.9	4.0	54.9
21	135 35.0	.. 51.3	72 02.7	11.3	20 23.9	4.2	55.0
22	150 35.1	52.1	86 33.0	11.3	20 19.7	4.2	55.0
23	165 35.2	52.9	101 03.3	11.3	N20 15.5	4.3	55.0
	SD 15.9 d 0.8		SD 14.8		14.8		14.9

Lat.	Naut.	Civil	Sunrise	Moonrise 24	25	26	27
°	h m	h m	h m	h m	h m	h m	h m
N 72	////	////	02 35	□	□	□	□
N 70	////	01 02	03 03	□	□	□	05 10
68	////	01 56	03 23	03 12	03 33	04 45	06 24
66	////	02 28	03 40	04 03	04 40	05 40	07 00
64	00 54	02 51	03 53	04 35	05 15	06 13	07 26
62	01 42	03 09	04 04	04 59	05 41	06 37	07 47
60	02 11	03 23	04 14	05 18	06 01	06 56	08 03
N 58	02 33	03 36	04 22	05 33	06 17	07 12	08 17
56	02 50	03 46	04 29	05 47	06 31	07 26	08 29
54	03 04	03 56	04 36	05 58	06 44	07 37	08 39
52	03 16	04 04	04 42	06 09	06 54	07 48	08 48
50	03 26	04 11	04 47	06 18	07 04	07 57	08 57
45	03 48	04 26	04 58	06 37	07 24	08 16	09 14
N 40	04 04	04 39	05 08	06 53	07 40	08 32	09 28
35	04 17	04 49	05 16	07 07	07 54	08 45	09 40
30	04 28	04 57	05 22	07 18	08 06	08 57	09 51
20	04 45	05 12	05 34	07 38	08 26	09 17	10 09
N 10	04 58	05 23	05 45	07 56	08 44	09 34	10 25
0	05 09	05 33	05 55	08 12	09 01	09 50	10 39
S 10	05 18	05 42	06 04	08 28	09 18	10 06	10 54
20	05 25	05 51	06 14	08 46	09 35	10 23	11 10
30	05 33	06 01	06 25	09 06	09 56	10 43	11 27
35	05 36	06 06	06 32	09 18	10 08	10 55	11 38
40	05 40	06 11	06 39	09 32	10 22	11 08	11 50
45	05 43	06 17	06 48	09 48	10 38	11 24	12 04
S 50	05 46	06 24	06 58	10 08	10 58	11 43	12 21
52	05 48	06 28	07 03	10 17	11 08	11 52	12 29
54	05 49	06 31	07 08	10 28	11 19	12 02	12 38
56	05 51	06 35	07 14	10 40	11 31	12 13	12 48
58	05 52	06 39	07 20	10 54	11 45	12 27	12 59
S 60	05 54	06 43	07 28	11 10	12 02	12 42	13 12

Lat.	Sunset	Civil	Naut.	Moonset 24	25	26	27
°	h m	h m	h m	h m	h m	h m	h m
N 72	21 26	////	////	□	□	□	□
N 70	20 57	23 09	////	□	□	□	03 51
68	20 36	22 06	////		00 42	02 03	02 37
66	20 19	21 32	////	24 56	00 56	01 38	02 00
64	20 05	21 08	23 15	24 21	00 21	01 05	01 33
62	19 54	20 50	22 19	23 55	24 40	00 40	01 13
60	19 44	20 35	21 49	23 35	24 21	00 21	00 56
N 58	19 35	20 22	21 26	23 19	24 05	00 05	00 42
56	19 28	20 11	21 09	23 05	23 51	24 30	00 30
54	19 21	20 02	20 54	22 52	23 40	24 19	00 19
52	19 15	19 53	20 42	22 42	23 29	24 09	00 09
50	19 10	19 46	20 31	22 32	23 20	24 01	00 01
45	18 58	19 30	20 09	22 12	23 00	23 43	24 21
N 40	18 49	19 18	19 53	21 56	22 44	23 28	24 08
35	18 41	19 08	19 40	21 42	22 31	23 16	23 57
30	18 34	18 59	19 29	21 30	22 19	23 05	23 47
20	18 22	18 44	19 11	21 10	21 59	22 46	23 31
N 10	18 11	18 33	18 58	20 52	21 41	22 29	23 16
0	18 01	18 23	18 47	20 36	21 25	22 14	23 03
S 10	17 52	18 13	18 38	20 19	21 08	21 58	22 49
20	17 41	18 04	18 30	20 01	20 50	21 42	22 34
30	17 30	17 55	18 23	19 41	20 30	21 23	22 18
35	17 23	17 49	18 19	19 29	20 18	21 11	22 08
40	17 16	17 44	18 16	19 15	20 04	20 58	21 56
45	17 07	17 38	18 12	18 59	19 48	20 43	21 43
S 50	16 57	17 31	18 09	18 39	19 28	20 24	21 27
52	16 52	17 27	18 07	18 29	19 18	20 16	21 19
54	16 47	17 24	18 06	18 18	19 08	20 06	21 11
56	16 41	17 20	18 04	18 06	18 56	19 54	21 01
58	16 35	17 16	18 02	17 52	18 41	19 44	20 50
S 60	16 27	17 12	18 01	17 36	18 25	19 26	20 37

Day	SUN Eqn. of Time 00h	SUN Eqn. of Time 12h	SUN Mer. Pass.	MOON Mer. Pass. Upper	MOON Mer. Pass. Lower	Age	Phase
d	m s	m s	h m	h m	h m	d	%
24	01 51	01 57	11 58	14 24	02 00	03	9
25	02 02	02 07	11 58	15 13	02 48	04	15
26	02 12	02 16	11 58	16 02	03 37	05	23

UT	ARIES GHA	VENUS −4.7 GHA	Dec	MARS −0.1 GHA	Dec	JUPITER −2.0 GHA	Dec	SATURN +0.3 GHA	Dec	STARS Name	SHA	Dec
27 00	215 23.1	138 46.8	N27 34.3	58 03.1	N11 52.8	168 20.4	N16 44.9	10 53.9	S 7 13.2	Acamar	315 19.4	S40 15.4
01	230 25.5	153 47.6	34.5	73 05.3	52.6	183 22.3	45.1	25 56.5	13.2	Achernar	335 27.9	S57 10.4
02	245 28.0	168 48.5	34.6	88 07.4	52.4	198 24.2	45.3	40 59.2	13.1	Acrux	173 09.6	S63 10.3
03	260 30.5	183 49.3	.. 34.8	103 09.6	.. 52.2	213 26.1	.. 45.4	56 01.8	.. 13.0	Adhara	255 13.3	S28 59.7
04	275 32.9	198 50.2	34.9	118 11.7	51.9	228 27.9	45.6	71 04.4	13.0	Aldebaran	290 50.6	N16 31.9
05	290 35.4	213 51.1	35.1	133 13.9	51.7	243 29.8	45.8	86 07.1	12.9			
06	305 37.9	228 51.9	N27 35.3	148 16.0	N11 51.5	258 31.7	N16 45.9	101 09.7	S 7 12.8	Alioth	166 20.9	N55 53.6
07	320 40.3	243 52.8	35.4	163 18.2	51.3	273 33.6	46.1	116 12.3	12.8	Alkaid	152 59.0	N49 15.0
F 08	335 42.8	258 53.7	35.6	178 20.3	51.0	288 35.4	46.2	131 15.0	12.7	Al Na'ir	27 44.9	S46 53.8
R 09	350 45.3	273 54.5	.. 35.7	193 22.5	.. 50.8	303 37.3	.. 46.4	146 17.6	.. 12.6	Alnilam	275 47.4	S 1 11.9
I 10	5 47.7	288 55.4	35.9	208 24.6	50.6	318 39.2	46.6	161 20.3	12.6	Alphard	217 56.8	S 8 43.0
D 11	20 50.2	303 56.3	36.0	223 26.8	50.4	333 41.1	46.7	176 22.9	12.5			
A 12	35 52.7	318 57.2	N27 36.2	238 28.9	N11 50.1	348 42.9	N16 46.9	191 25.5	S 7 12.4	Alphecca	126 11.3	N26 40.3
Y 13	50 55.1	333 58.0	36.3	253 31.0	49.9	3 44.8	47.1	206 28.2	12.4	Alpheratz	357 44.6	N29 09.4
14	65 57.6	348 58.9	36.5	268 33.2	49.7	18 46.7	47.2	221 30.8	12.3	Altair	62 08.9	N 8 54.0
15	81 00.0	3 59.8	.. 36.6	283 35.3	.. 49.4	33 48.6	.. 47.4	236 33.5	.. 12.3	Ankaa	353 16.8	S42 14.2
16	96 02.5	19 00.7	36.8	298 37.5	49.2	48 50.4	47.6	251 36.1	12.2	Antares	112 26.9	S26 27.5
17	111 05.0	34 01.6	36.9	313 39.6	49.0	63 52.3	47.7	266 38.7	12.1			
18	126 07.4	49 02.5	N27 37.1	328 41.7	N11 48.8	78 54.2	N16 47.9	281 41.4	S 7 12.1	Arcturus	145 56.1	N19 07.0
19	141 09.9	64 03.4	37.2	343 43.9	48.5	93 56.0	48.0	296 44.0	12.0	Atria	107 29.0	S69 02.8
20	156 12.4	79 04.3	37.4	358 46.0	48.3	108 57.9	48.2	311 46.7	11.9	Avior	234 18.4	S59 33.4
21	171 14.8	94 05.2	.. 37.5	13 48.1	.. 48.1	123 59.8	.. 48.4	326 49.3	.. 11.9	Bellatrix	278 33.1	N 6 21.5
22	186 17.3	109 06.1	37.7	28 50.3	47.8	139 01.7	48.5	341 51.9	11.8	Betelgeuse	271 02.4	N 7 24.4
23	201 19.8	124 07.0	37.8	43 52.4	47.6	154 03.5	48.7	356 54.6	11.7			
28 00	216 22.2	139 07.9	N27 37.9	58 54.5	N11 47.4	169 05.4	N16 48.9	11 57.2	S 7 11.7	Canopus	263 56.8	S52 42.5
01	231 24.7	154 08.8	38.1	73 56.7	47.1	184 07.3	49.0	26 59.8	11.6	Capella	280 36.0	N46 00.6
02	246 27.2	169 09.7	38.2	88 58.8	46.9	199 09.2	49.2	42 02.5	11.5	Deneb	49 32.0	N45 19.3
03	261 29.6	184 10.6	.. 38.4	104 00.9	.. 46.7	214 11.0	.. 49.3	57 05.1	.. 11.5	Denebola	182 34.2	N14 30.0
04	276 32.1	199 11.6	38.5	119 03.1	46.4	229 12.9	49.5	72 07.8	11.4	Diphda	348 57.0	S17 55.1
05	291 34.5	214 12.5	38.6	134 05.2	46.2	244 14.8	49.7	87 10.4	11.4			
06	306 37.0	229 13.4	N27 38.8	149 07.3	N11 46.0	259 16.7	N16 49.8	102 13.0	S 7 11.3	Dubhe	193 52.3	N61 41.1
07	321 39.5	244 14.3	38.9	164 09.4	45.7	274 18.5	50.0	117 15.7	11.2	Elnath	278 13.9	N28 37.0
S 08	336 41.9	259 15.3	39.0	179 11.5	45.5	289 20.4	50.2	132 18.3	11.2	Eltanin	90 46.2	N51 29.1
A 09	351 44.4	274 16.2	.. 39.2	194 13.7	.. 45.3	304 22.3	.. 50.3	147 21.0	.. 11.1	Enif	33 48.0	N 9 55.9
T 10	6 46.9	289 17.1	39.3	209 15.8	45.0	319 24.1	50.5	162 23.6	11.0	Fomalhaut	15 25.1	S29 33.3
U 11	21 49.3	304 18.1	39.4	224 17.9	44.8	334 26.0	50.6	177 26.2	11.0			
R 12	36 51.8	319 19.0	N27 39.6	239 20.0	N11 44.6	349 27.9	N16 50.8	192 28.9	S 7 10.9	Gacrux	172 01.3	S57 11.2
D 13	51 54.3	334 20.0	39.7	254 22.1	44.3	4 29.8	51.0	207 31.5	10.8	Gienah	175 52.9	S17 36.9
A 14	66 56.7	349 20.9	39.8	269 24.3	44.1	19 31.6	51.1	222 34.1	10.8	Hadar	148 48.4	S60 26.1
Y 15	81 59.2	4 21.9	.. 40.0	284 26.4	.. 43.9	34 33.5	.. 51.3	237 36.8	.. 10.7	Hamal	328 02.0	N23 31.1
16	97 01.6	19 22.8	40.1	299 28.5	43.6	49 35.4	51.4	252 39.4	10.7	Kaus Aust.	83 44.6	S34 22.5
17	112 04.1	34 23.8	40.2	314 30.6	43.4	64 37.3	51.6	267 42.1	10.6			
18	127 06.6	49 24.7	N27 40.3	329 32.7	N11 43.1	79 39.1	N16 51.8	282 44.7	S 7 10.5	Kochab	137 18.8	N74 06.2
19	142 09.0	64 25.7	40.5	344 34.8	42.9	94 41.0	51.9	297 47.3	10.5	Markab	13 39.3	N15 16.2
20	157 11.5	79 26.6	40.6	359 36.9	42.7	109 42.9	52.1	312 50.0	10.4	Menkar	314 16.2	N 4 08.2
21	172 14.0	94 27.6	.. 40.7	14 39.1	.. 42.4	124 44.7	.. 52.3	327 52.6	.. 10.3	Menkent	148 08.1	S36 26.0
22	187 16.4	109 28.6	40.8	29 41.2	42.2	139 46.6	52.4	342 55.2	10.3	Miaplacidus	221 39.7	S69 46.5
23	202 18.9	124 29.5	41.0	44 43.3	41.9	154 48.5	52.6	357 57.9	10.2			
29 00	217 21.4	139 30.5	N27 41.1	59 45.4	N11 41.7	169 50.4	N16 52.7	13 00.5	S 7 10.1	Mirfak	308 42.0	N49 54.2
01	232 23.8	154 31.5	41.2	74 47.5	41.5	184 52.2	52.9	28 03.2	10.1	Nunki	75 59.1	S26 16.7
02	247 26.3	169 32.5	41.3	89 49.6	41.2	199 54.1	53.1	43 05.8	10.0	Peacock	53 20.4	S56 41.4
03	262 28.8	184 33.4	.. 41.4	104 51.7	.. 41.0	214 56.0	.. 53.2	58 08.4	.. 10.0	Pollux	243 28.8	N27 59.7
04	277 31.2	199 34.4	41.6	119 53.8	40.7	229 57.9	53.4	73 11.1	09.9	Procyon	245 00.7	N 5 11.4
05	292 33.7	214 35.4	41.7	134 55.9	40.5	244 59.7	53.6	88 13.7	09.8			
06	307 36.1	229 36.4	N27 41.8	149 58.0	N11 40.3	260 01.6	N16 53.7	103 16.3	S 7 09.8	Rasalhague	96 07.0	N12 33.0
07	322 38.6	244 37.4	41.9	165 00.1	40.0	275 03.5	53.9	118 19.0	09.7	Regulus	207 44.2	N11 54.2
S 08	337 41.1	259 38.4	42.0	180 02.2	39.8	290 05.3	54.0	133 21.6	09.6	Rigel	281 13.1	S 8 11.5
U 09	352 43.5	274 39.4	.. 42.1	195 04.3	.. 39.5	305 07.2	.. 54.2	148 24.2	.. 09.6	Rigil Kent.	139 52.2	S60 53.2
N 10	7 46.0	289 40.4	42.2	210 06.4	39.3	320 09.1	54.4	163 26.9	09.5	Sabik	102 13.2	S15 44.4
D 11	22 48.5	304 41.4	42.4	225 08.5	39.0	335 11.0	54.5	178 29.5	09.4			
A 12	37 50.9	319 42.4	N27 42.5	240 10.6	N11 38.8	350 12.8	N16 54.7	193 32.2	S 7 09.4	Schedar	349 42.0	N56 36.2
Y 13	52 53.4	334 43.4	42.6	255 12.7	38.6	5 14.7	54.8	208 34.8	09.3	Shaula	96 22.7	S37 06.6
14	67 55.9	349 44.4	42.7	270 14.8	38.3	20 16.6	55.0	223 37.4	09.3	Sirius	258 34.6	S16 44.3
15	82 58.3	4 45.4	.. 42.8	285 16.9	.. 38.1	35 18.4	.. 55.2	238 40.1	.. 09.2	Spica	158 31.8	S11 13.7
16	98 00.8	19 46.5	42.9	300 19.0	37.8	50 20.3	55.3	253 42.7	09.1	Suhail	222 53.0	S43 29.4
17	113 03.3	34 47.5	43.0	315 21.1	37.6	65 22.2	55.5	268 45.3	09.1			
18	128 05.7	49 48.5	N27 43.1	330 23.1	N11 37.3	80 24.1	N16 55.7	283 48.0	S 7 09.0	Vega	80 39.3	N38 47.6
19	143 08.2	64 49.5	43.2	345 25.2	37.1	95 25.9	55.8	298 50.6	08.9	Zuben'ubi	137 06.0	S16 05.7
20	158 10.6	79 50.6	43.3	0 27.3	36.8	110 27.8	56.0	313 53.3	08.9		SHA	Mer. Pass.
21	173 13.1	94 51.6	.. 43.4	15 29.4	.. 36.6	125 29.7	.. 56.1	328 55.9	.. 08.8			h m
22	188 15.6	109 52.6	43.5	30 31.5	36.3	140 31.5	56.3	343 58.5	08.8	Venus	282 45.7	14 43
23	203 18.0	124 53.7	43.6	45 33.6	36.1	155 33.4	56.5	359 01.2	08.7	Mars	202 32.3	20 02
	h m									Jupiter	312 43.2	12 42
Mer. Pass.	9 32.9	v 0.9	d 0.1	v 2.1	d 0.2	v 1.9	d 0.2	v 2.6	d 0.1	Saturn	155 35.0	23 08

SUN / MOON

UT	SUN GHA	SUN Dec	MOON GHA	v	Dec	d	HP
d h	° ′	° ′	° ′	′	° ′	′	′
27 00	180 35.3	N13 53.7	115 33.6	11.3	N20 11.2	4.4	55.0
01	195 35.4	54.5	130 03.9	11.3	20 06.8	4.6	55.0
02	210 35.5	55.3	144 34.2	11.3	20 02.2	4.6	55.1
03	225 35.6	.. 56.1	159 04.5	11.3	19 57.6	4.7	55.1
04	240 35.7	56.9	173 34.8	11.4	19 52.9	4.8	55.1
05	255 35.8	57.7	188 05.2	11.3	19 48.1	5.0	55.1
06	270 35.9	N13 58.5	202 35.5	11.4	N19 43.1	5.0	55.2
07	285 36.0	13 59.3	217 05.9	11.3	19 38.1	5.1	55.2
08	300 36.1	14 00.0	231 36.2	11.4	19 33.0	5.2	55.2
09	315 36.2	.. 00.8	246 06.6	11.4	19 27.8	5.4	55.2
10	330 36.3	01.6	260 37.0	11.3	19 22.4	5.4	55.2
11	345 36.4	02.4	275 07.3	11.4	19 17.0	5.5	55.3
12	0 36.4	N14 03.2	289 37.7	11.4	N19 11.5	5.6	55.3
13	15 36.5	04.0	304 08.1	11.5	19 05.9	5.7	55.3
14	30 36.6	04.8	318 38.6	11.4	19 00.2	5.8	55.3
15	45 36.7	.. 05.6	333 09.0	11.4	18 54.4	5.9	55.4
16	60 36.8	06.4	347 39.4	11.5	18 48.5	6.1	55.4
17	75 36.9	07.1	2 09.9	11.4	18 42.4	6.1	55.4
18	90 37.0	N14 07.9	16 40.3	11.5	N18 36.3	6.1	55.4
19	105 37.1	08.7	31 10.8	11.5	18 30.2	6.3	55.5
20	120 37.2	09.5	45 41.3	11.4	18 23.9	6.4	55.5
21	135 37.3	.. 10.3	60 11.7	11.5	18 17.5	6.5	55.5
22	150 37.4	11.1	74 42.2	11.5	18 11.0	6.6	55.6
23	165 37.5	11.9	89 12.7	11.6	18 04.4	6.6	55.6
28 00	180 37.5	N14 12.7	103 43.3	11.5	N17 57.8	6.8	55.6
01	195 37.6	13.4	118 13.8	11.5	17 51.0	6.9	55.6
02	210 37.7	14.2	132 44.3	11.6	17 44.1	6.9	55.7
03	225 37.8	.. 15.0	147 14.9	11.5	17 37.2	7.0	55.7
04	240 37.9	15.8	161 45.4	11.6	17 30.2	7.2	55.7
05	255 38.0	16.6	176 16.0	11.6	17 23.0	7.2	55.7
06	270 38.1	N14 17.4	190 46.6	11.6	N17 15.8	7.3	55.8
07	285 38.2	18.1	205 17.2	11.6	17 08.5	7.4	55.8
08	300 38.3	18.9	219 47.8	11.6	17 01.1	7.5	55.8
09	315 38.4	.. 19.7	234 18.4	11.6	16 53.6	7.6	55.9
10	330 38.4	20.5	248 49.0	11.6	16 46.0	7.6	55.9
11	345 38.5	21.3	263 19.6	11.7	16 38.4	7.8	55.9
12	0 38.6	N14 22.0	277 50.3	11.6	N16 30.6	7.9	55.9
13	15 38.7	22.8	292 20.9	11.7	16 22.7	7.9	56.0
14	30 38.8	23.6	306 51.6	11.7	16 14.8	8.0	56.0
15	45 38.9	.. 24.4	321 22.3	11.7	16 06.8	8.1	56.0
16	60 39.0	25.2	335 53.0	11.6	15 58.7	8.2	56.1
17	75 39.1	25.9	350 23.6	11.7	15 50.5	8.3	56.1
18	90 39.1	N14 26.7	4 54.3	11.7	N15 42.2	8.4	56.1
19	105 39.2	27.5	19 25.0	11.6	15 33.8	8.4	56.2
20	120 39.3	28.3	33 55.8	11.7	15 25.4	8.6	56.2
21	135 39.4	.. 29.0	48 26.5	11.7	15 16.8	8.6	56.2
22	150 39.5	29.8	62 57.2	11.7	15 08.2	8.7	56.3
23	165 39.6	30.6	77 27.9	11.8	14 59.5	8.8	56.3
29 00	180 39.7	N14 31.4	91 58.7	11.7	N14 50.7	8.9	56.3
01	195 39.7	32.1	106 29.4	11.8	14 41.8	8.9	56.4
02	210 39.8	32.9	121 00.2	11.8	14 32.9	9.1	56.4
03	225 39.9	.. 33.7	135 31.0	11.7	14 23.8	9.1	56.4
04	240 40.0	34.5	150 01.7	11.8	14 14.7	9.2	56.5
05	255 40.1	35.2	164 32.5	11.8	14 05.5	9.3	56.5
06	270 40.2	N14 36.0	179 03.3	11.8	N13 56.2	9.3	56.5
07	285 40.3	36.8	193 34.1	11.8	13 46.9	9.5	56.6
08	300 40.3	37.5	208 04.9	11.8	13 37.4	9.5	56.6
09	315 40.4	.. 38.3	222 35.7	11.7	13 27.9	9.6	56.6
10	330 40.5	39.1	237 06.4	11.8	13 18.3	9.6	56.7
11	345 40.6	39.9	251 37.2	11.9	13 08.7	9.8	56.7
12	0 40.7	N14 40.6	266 08.1	11.8	N12 58.9	9.8	56.7
13	15 40.8	41.4	280 38.9	11.8	12 49.1	9.9	56.8
14	30 40.8	42.2	295 09.7	11.8	12 39.2	10.0	56.8
15	45 40.9	.. 42.9	309 40.5	11.8	12 29.2	10.0	56.8
16	60 41.0	43.7	324 11.3	11.8	12 19.2	10.1	56.9
17	75 41.1	44.5	338 42.1	11.8	12 09.1	10.2	56.9
18	90 41.2	N14 45.2	353 12.9	11.8	N11 58.9	10.3	56.9
19	105 41.2	46.0	7 43.7	11.8	11 48.6	10.3	57.0
20	120 41.3	46.8	22 14.5	11.8	11 38.3	10.4	57.0
21	135 41.4	.. 47.5	36 45.3	11.8	11 27.9	10.5	57.1
22	150 41.5	48.3	51 16.1	11.9	11 17.4	10.6	57.1
23	165 41.6	49.1	65 47.0	11.8	N11 06.8	10.6	57.1
	SD 15.9	d 0.8	SD 15.1		15.2		15.5

Day labels (vertical): 27 = FRIDAY, 28 = SATURDAY, 29 = SUNDAY

Twilight / Sunrise / Moonrise

Lat.	Naut.	Civil	Sunrise	27	28	29	30
°	h m	h m	h m	h m	h m	h m	h m
N 72	////	////	02 13	▭	06 34	09 02	11 07
N 70	////	////	02 46	05 10	07 32	09 29	11 21
68	////	01 32	03 10	06 24	08 06	09 49	11 33
66	////	02 11	03 28	07 00	08 31	10 05	11 42
64	////	02 37	03 43	07 26	08 49	10 18	11 49
62	01 21	02 57	03 55	07 47	09 05	10 29	11 56
60	01 56	03 14	04 05	08 03	09 18	10 38	12 02
N 58	02 21	03 27	04 14	08 17	09 29	10 46	12 07
56	02 40	03 39	04 22	08 29	09 39	10 53	12 11
54	02 55	03 49	04 29	08 39	09 47	10 59	12 15
52	03 08	03 57	04 36	08 48	09 55	11 05	12 19
50	03 19	04 05	04 41	08 57	10 01	11 10	12 22
45	03 42	04 21	04 53	09 14	10 16	11 21	12 29
N 40	03 59	04 34	05 04	09 28	10 28	11 30	12 35
35	04 13	04 45	05 12	09 40	10 38	11 38	12 40
30	04 25	04 54	05 20	09 51	10 47	11 45	12 44
20	04 43	05 10	05 33	10 09	11 02	11 57	12 52
N 10	04 57	05 22	05 44	10 25	11 16	12 07	12 59
0	05 08	05 33	05 54	10 39	11 28	12 16	13 05
S 10	05 18	05 43	06 04	10 54	11 41	12 26	13 11
20	05 26	05 52	06 15	11 10	11 54	12 36	13 18
30	05 34	06 03	06 27	11 27	12 09	12 48	13 25
35	05 38	06 08	06 34	11 38	12 18	12 55	13 30
40	05 42	06 14	06 42	11 50	12 28	13 02	13 35
45	05 46	06 21	06 52	12 04	12 39	13 11	13 40
S 50	05 51	06 29	07 03	12 21	12 53	13 22	13 47
52	05 52	06 32	07 08	12 29	13 00	13 26	13 50
54	05 54	06 36	07 13	12 38	13 07	13 32	13 54
56	05 56	06 40	07 20	12 48	13 15	13 38	13 57
58	05 58	06 45	07 27	12 59	13 24	13 44	14 01
S 60	06 00	06 50	07 35	13 12	13 35	13 52	14 06

Sunset / Twilight / Moonset

Lat.	Sunset	Civil	Naut.	27	28	29	30
°	h m	h m	h m	h m	h m	h m	h m
N 72	21 48	////	////	▭	04 11	03 24	03 00
N 70	21 13	////	////	03 51	03 11	02 55	02 44
68	20 49	22 30	////	02 37	02 36	02 34	02 31
66	20 30	21 49	////	02 00	02 11	02 17	02 21
64	20 15	21 21	////	01 33	01 51	02 03	02 12
62	20 02	21 00	22 40	01 13	01 35	01 52	02 04
60	19 51	20 44	22 03	00 56	01 22	01 42	01 57
N 58	19 42	20 30	21 37	00 42	01 10	01 33	01 51
56	19 34	20 18	21 18	00 30	01 00	01 25	01 46
54	19 27	20 08	21 02	00 19	00 51	01 18	01 41
52	19 20	19 59	20 49	00 09	00 43	01 12	01 37
50	19 15	19 51	20 37	00 01	00 36	01 06	01 33
45	19 02	19 34	20 14	24 21	00 21	00 54	01 24
N 40	18 52	19 21	19 57	24 08	00 08	00 44	01 17
35	18 43	19 10	19 43	23 57	24 35	00 35	01 11
30	18 36	19 01	19 31	23 47	24 27	00 27	01 05
20	18 23	18 46	19 13	23 31	24 14	00 14	00 56
N 10	18 11	18 33	18 58	23 16	24 02	00 02	00 48
0	18 01	18 22	18 47	23 03	23 51	24 40	00 40
S 10	17 50	18 12	18 37	22 49	23 40	24 32	00 32
20	17 40	18 02	18 28	22 34	23 28	24 23	00 23
30	17 27	17 52	18 20	22 18	23 15	24 13	00 13
35	17 20	17 46	18 16	22 08	23 07	24 07	00 07
40	17 12	17 40	18 12	21 56	22 57	24 01	00 01
45	17 03	17 33	18 08	21 43	22 47	23 53	25 02
S 50	16 52	17 25	18 04	21 27	22 34	23 44	24 57
52	16 46	17 22	18 02	21 19	22 28	23 40	24 55
54	16 41	17 18	18 00	21 11	22 21	23 35	24 53
56	16 34	17 14	17 58	21 01	22 13	23 30	24 49
58	16 27	17 09	17 56	20 50	22 05	23 24	24 46
S 60	16 19	17 04	17 54	20 37	21 55	23 17	24 42

SUN / MOON

Day	Eqn. of Time 00h	Eqn. of Time 12h	Mer. Pass.	Mer. Pass. Upper	Mer. Pass. Lower	Age	Phase
d	m s	m s	h m	h m	h m	d	%
27	02 21	02 26	11 58	16 51	04 27	06	31
28	02 30	02 34	11 57	17 40	05 15	07	41
29	02 38	02 43	11 57	18 28	06 04	08	51

UT	ARIES GHA	VENUS −4.7 GHA	Dec	MARS +0.0 GHA	Dec	JUPITER −2.0 GHA	Dec	SATURN +0.3 GHA	Dec	Name	SHA	Dec
30 00	218 20.5	139 54.7	N27 43.7	60 35.7	N11 35.8	170 35.3	N16 56.6	14 03.8	S 7 08.6	Acamar	315 19.4	S40 15.4
01	233 23.0	154 55.7	43.8	75 37.7	35.6	185 37.2	56.8	29 06.4	08.6	Achernar	335 27.9	S57 10.4
02	248 25.4	169 56.8	43.9	90 39.8	35.3	200 39.0	56.9	44 09.1	08.5	Acrux	173 09.6	S63 10.4
03	263 27.9	184 57.8	. . 44.0	105 41.9	. . 35.1	215 40.9	. . 57.1	59 11.7	. . 08.4	Adhara	255 13.3	S28 59.7
04	278 30.4	199 58.9	44.1	120 44.0	34.8	230 42.8	57.3	74 14.3	08.4	Aldebaran	290 50.6	N16 31.9
05	293 32.8	214 59.9	44.2	135 46.1	34.6	245 44.6	57.4	89 17.0	08.3			
06	308 35.3	230 01.0	N27 44.3	150 48.1	N11 34.3	260 46.5	N16 57.6	104 19.6	S 7 08.3	Alioth	166 20.9	N55 53.6
07	323 37.7	245 02.1	44.4	165 50.2	34.1	275 48.4	57.8	119 22.2	08.2	Alkaid	152 59.0	N49 15.1
08	338 40.2	260 03.1	44.5	180 52.3	33.8	290 50.3	57.9	134 24.9	08.1	Al Na'ir	27 44.9	S46 53.8
M 09	353 42.7	275 04.2	. . 44.6	195 54.4	. . 33.6	305 52.1	. . 58.1	149 27.5	. . 08.1	Alnilam	275 47.4	S 1 11.8
O 10	8 45.1	290 05.3	44.7	210 56.4	33.3	320 54.0	58.2	164 30.2	08.0	Alphard	217 56.8	S 8 43.0
N 11	23 47.6	305 06.3	44.8	225 58.5	33.1	335 55.9	58.4	179 32.8	07.9			
D 12	38 50.1	320 07.4	N27 44.8	241 00.6	N11 32.8	350 57.7	N16 58.6	194 35.4	S 7 07.9	Alphecca	126 11.3	N26 40.3
A 13	53 52.5	335 08.5	44.9	256 02.7	32.6	5 59.6	58.7	209 38.1	07.8	Alpheratz	357 44.6	N29 09.4
Y 14	68 55.0	350 09.6	45.0	271 04.7	32.3	21 01.5	58.9	224 40.7	07.8	Altair	62 08.9	N 8 54.0
15	83 57.5	5 10.6	. . 45.1	286 06.8	. . 32.1	36 03.4	. . 59.0	239 43.3	. . 07.7	Ankaa	353 16.8	S42 14.2
16	98 59.9	20 11.7	45.2	301 08.9	31.8	51 05.2	59.2	254 46.0	07.6	Antares	112 26.9	S26 27.5
17	114 02.4	35 12.8	45.3	316 10.9	31.6	66 07.1	59.4	269 48.6	07.6			
18	129 04.9	50 13.9	N27 45.4	331 13.0	N11 31.3	81 09.0	N16 59.5	284 51.2	S 7 07.5	Arcturus	145 56.1	N19 07.0
19	144 07.3	65 15.0	45.4	346 15.1	31.1	96 10.8	59.7	299 53.9	07.4	Atria	107 29.0	S69 02.8
20	159 09.8	80 16.1	45.5	1 17.1	30.8	111 12.7	16 59.8	314 56.5	07.4	Avior	234 18.4	S59 33.4
21	174 12.2	95 17.2	. . 45.6	16 19.2	. . 30.6	126 14.6	17 00.0	329 59.1	. . 07.3	Bellatrix	278 33.1	N 6 21.5
22	189 14.7	110 18.3	45.7	31 21.3	30.3	141 16.5	00.2	345 01.8	07.3	Betelgeuse	271 02.4	N 7 24.4
23	204 17.2	125 19.4	45.8	46 23.3	30.0	156 18.3	00.3	0 04.4	07.2			
1 00	219 19.6	140 20.5	N27 45.9	61 25.4	N11 29.8	171 20.2	N17 00.5	15 07.0	S 7 07.1	Canopus	263 56.8	S52 42.5
01	234 22.1	155 21.6	45.9	76 27.5	29.5	186 22.1	00.6	30 09.7	07.1	Capella	280 36.0	N46 00.6
02	249 24.6	170 22.7	46.0	91 29.5	29.3	201 23.9	00.8	45 12.3	07.0	Deneb	49 32.0	N45 19.3
03	264 27.0	185 23.9	. . 46.1	106 31.6	. . 29.0	216 25.8	. . 01.0	60 14.9	. . 06.9	Denebola	182 34.2	N14 30.0
04	279 29.5	200 25.0	46.2	121 33.6	28.8	231 27.7	01.1	75 17.6	06.9	Diphda	348 57.0	S17 55.1
05	294 32.0	215 26.1	46.2	136 35.7	28.5	246 29.5	01.3	90 20.2	06.8			
06	309 34.4	230 27.2	N27 46.3	151 37.7	N11 28.2	261 31.4	N17 01.5	105 22.9	S 7 06.8	Dubhe	193 52.3	N61 41.1
07	324 36.9	245 28.4	46.4	166 39.8	28.0	276 33.3	01.6	120 25.5	06.7	Elnath	278 13.9	N28 37.0
08	339 39.4	260 29.5	46.5	181 41.8	27.7	291 35.2	01.8	135 28.1	06.6	Eltanin	90 46.1	N51 29.1
T 09	354 41.8	275 30.6	. . 46.5	196 43.9	. . 27.5	306 37.0	. . 01.9	150 30.8	. . 06.6	Enif	33 48.0	N 9 55.9
U 10	9 44.3	290 31.8	46.6	211 46.0	27.2	321 38.9	02.1	165 33.4	06.5	Fomalhaut	15 25.0	S29 33.2
E 11	24 46.7	305 32.9	46.7	226 48.0	27.0	336 40.8	02.3	180 36.0	06.4			
S 12	39 49.2	320 34.1	N27 46.7	241 50.1	N11 26.7	351 42.6	N17 02.4	195 38.7	S 7 06.4	Gacrux	172 01.3	S57 11.2
D 13	54 51.7	335 35.2	46.8	256 52.1	26.4	6 44.5	02.6	210 41.3	06.3	Gienah	175 52.9	S17 36.9
A 14	69 54.1	350 36.4	46.9	271 54.1	26.2	21 46.4	02.7	225 43.9	06.3	Hadar	148 48.4	S60 26.1
Y 15	84 56.6	5 37.5	. . 46.9	286 56.2	. . 25.9	36 48.2	. . 02.9	240 46.6	. . 06.2	Hamal	328 02.0	N23 31.1
16	99 59.1	20 38.7	47.0	301 58.2	25.6	51 50.1	03.1	255 49.2	06.1	Kaus Aust.	83 44.6	S34 22.5
17	115 01.5	35 39.8	47.1	317 00.3	25.4	66 52.0	03.2	270 51.8	06.1			
18	130 04.0	50 41.0	N27 47.1	332 02.3	N11 25.1	81 53.9	N17 03.4	285 54.5	S 7 06.0	Kochab	137 18.8	N74 06.2
19	145 06.5	65 42.2	47.2	347 04.4	24.9	96 55.7	03.5	300 57.1	06.0	Markab	13 39.3	N15 16.2
20	160 08.9	80 43.3	47.3	2 06.4	24.6	111 57.6	03.7	315 59.7	05.9	Menkar	314 16.2	N 4 08.2
21	175 11.4	95 44.5	. . 47.3	17 08.5	. . 24.3	126 59.5	. . 03.9	331 02.4	. . 05.8	Menkent	148 08.1	S36 26.0
22	190 13.8	110 45.7	47.4	32 10.5	24.1	142 01.3	04.0	346 05.0	05.8	Miaplacidus	221 39.8	S69 46.5
23	205 16.3	125 46.9	47.4	47 12.5	23.8	157 03.2	04.2	1 07.6	05.7			
2 00	220 18.8	140 48.1	N27 47.5	62 14.6	N11 23.5	172 05.1	N17 04.3	16 10.3	S 7 05.6	Mirfak	308 42.0	N49 54.2
01	235 21.2	155 49.2	47.5	77 16.6	23.3	187 06.9	04.5	31 12.9	05.6	Nunki	75 59.1	S26 16.7
02	250 23.7	170 50.4	47.6	92 18.7	23.0	202 08.8	04.7	46 15.5	05.5	Peacock	53 20.4	S56 41.4
03	265 26.2	185 51.6	. . 47.7	107 20.7	. . 22.7	217 10.7	. . 04.8	61 18.2	. . 05.5	Pollux	243 28.8	N27 59.7
04	280 28.6	200 52.8	47.7	122 22.7	22.5	232 12.6	05.0	76 20.8	05.4	Procyon	245 00.7	N 5 11.4
05	295 31.1	215 54.0	47.8	137 24.8	22.2	247 14.4	05.1	91 23.4	05.3			
06	310 33.6	230 55.2	N27 47.8	152 26.8	N11 21.9	262 16.3	N17 05.3	106 26.1	S 7 05.3	Rasalhague	96 06.9	N12 33.0
W 07	325 36.0	245 56.4	47.9	167 28.8	21.7	277 18.2	05.5	121 28.7	05.2	Regulus	207 44.3	N11 54.2
E 08	340 38.5	260 57.6	47.9	182 30.9	21.4	292 20.0	05.6	136 31.3	05.2	Rigel	281 13.1	S 8 11.5
D 09	355 41.0	275 58.8	. . 48.0	197 32.9	. . 21.1	307 21.9	. . 05.8	151 34.0	. . 05.1	Rigil Kent.	139 52.2	S60 53.2
N 10	10 43.4	291 00.0	48.0	212 34.9	20.9	322 23.8	05.9	166 36.6	05.0	Sabik	102 13.2	S15 44.4
E 11	25 45.9	306 01.3	48.1	227 37.0	20.6	337 25.6	06.1	181 39.2	05.0			
S 12	40 48.3	321 02.5	N27 48.1	242 39.0	N11 20.3	352 27.5	N17 06.3	196 41.9	S 7 04.9	Schedar	349 41.9	N56 36.2
D 13	55 50.8	336 03.7	48.2	257 41.0	20.1	7 29.4	06.4	211 44.5	04.9	Shaula	96 22.7	S37 06.6
A 14	70 53.3	351 04.9	48.2	272 43.0	19.8	22 31.2	06.6	226 47.1	04.8	Sirius	258 34.6	S16 44.3
Y 15	85 55.7	6 06.2	. . 48.3	287 45.1	. . 19.5	37 33.1	. . 06.7	241 49.8	. . 04.7	Spica	158 31.8	S11 13.7
16	100 58.2	21 07.4	48.3	302 47.1	19.3	52 35.0	06.9	256 52.4	04.7	Suhail	222 53.0	S43 29.4
17	116 00.7	36 08.6	48.3	317 49.1	19.0	67 36.9	07.0	271 55.0	04.6			
18	131 03.1	51 09.9	N27 48.4	332 51.1	N11 18.7	82 38.7	N17 07.2	286 57.6	S 7 04.5	Vega	80 39.3	N38 47.6
19	146 05.6	66 11.1	48.4	347 53.2	18.5	97 40.6	07.4	302 00.3	04.5	Zuben'ubi	137 06.0	S16 05.7
20	161 08.1	81 12.4	48.5	2 55.2	18.2	112 42.5	07.5	317 02.9	04.4		SHA	Mer.Pass.
21	176 10.5	96 13.6	. . 48.5	17 57.2	. . 17.9	127 44.3	. . 07.7	332 05.5	. . 04.4			
22	191 13.0	111 14.9	48.5	32 59.2	17.6	142 46.2	07.8	347 08.2	04.3	Venus	281 00.9	14 38
23	206 15.4	126 16.1	48.6	48 01.2	17.4	157 48.1	08.0	2 10.8	04.2	Mars	202 05.8	19 52
Mer. Pass.	9 21.2	v 1.1	d 0.1	v 2.0	d 0.3	v 1.9	d 0.2	v 2.6	d 0.1	Jupiter	312 00.6	12 33
										Saturn	155 47.4	22 56

UT	SUN GHA	SUN Dec	MOON GHA	v	Dec	d	HP
d h	° ′	° ′	° ′	′	° ′	′	′
30 00	180 41.7	N14 49.8	80 17.8	11.8	N10 56.2	10.7	57.2
01	195 41.7	50.6	94 48.6	11.7	10 45.5	10.7	57.2
02	210 41.8	51.4	109 19.3	11.8	10 34.8	10.8	57.2
03	225 41.9 ..	52.1	123 50.1	11.8	10 24.0	10.9	57.3
04	240 42.0	52.9	138 20.9	11.8	10 13.1	11.0	57.3
05	255 42.1	53.7	152 51.7	11.8	10 02.1	11.0	57.3
M 06	270 42.1	N14 54.4	167 22.5	11.7	N 9 51.1	11.1	57.4
O 07	285 42.2	55.2	181 53.2	11.8	9 40.0	11.1	57.4
N 08	300 42.3	55.9	196 24.0	11.7	9 28.9	11.2	57.5
D 09	315 42.4 ..	56.7	210 54.7	11.8	9 17.7	11.3	57.5
A 10	330 42.4	57.5	225 25.5	11.7	9 06.4	11.3	57.5
Y 11	345 42.5	58.2	239 56.2	11.7	8 55.1	11.4	57.6
12	0 42.6	N14 59.0	254 26.9	11.7	N 8 43.7	11.4	57.6
13	15 42.7	14 59.7	268 57.6	11.7	8 32.3	11.5	57.7
14	30 42.8	15 00.5	283 28.3	11.7	8 20.8	11.6	57.7
15	45 42.8 ..	01.3	297 59.0	11.7	8 09.2	11.6	57.7
16	60 42.9	02.0	312 29.7	11.6	7 57.6	11.7	57.8
17	75 43.0	02.8	327 00.3	11.7	7 45.9	11.7	57.8
18	90 43.1	N15 03.6	341 31.0	11.6	N 7 34.2	11.8	57.8
19	105 43.1	04.3	356 01.6	11.6	7 22.4	11.9	57.9
20	120 43.2	05.0	10 32.2	11.6	7 10.5	11.9	57.9
21	135 43.3 ..	05.8	25 02.8	11.6	6 58.6	11.9	58.0
22	150 43.4	06.6	39 33.4	11.5	6 46.7	12.0	58.0
23	165 43.4	07.3	54 03.9	11.6	6 34.7	12.1	58.0
1 00	180 43.5	N15 08.1	68 34.5	11.5	N 6 22.6	12.1	58.1
01	195 43.6	08.8	83 05.0	11.5	6 10.5	12.1	58.1
02	210 43.7	09.6	97 35.5	11.5	5 58.4	12.2	58.2
03	225 43.7 ..	10.3	112 06.0	11.4	5 46.2	12.3	58.2
04	240 43.8	11.1	126 36.4	11.4	5 33.9	12.2	58.2
05	255 43.9	11.8	141 06.8	11.5	5 21.7	12.4	58.3
T 06	270 44.0	N15 12.6	155 37.3	11.3	N 5 09.3	12.4	58.3
U 07	285 44.0	13.3	170 07.6	11.4	4 56.9	12.4	58.4
E 08	300 44.1	14.1	184 38.0	11.3	4 44.5	12.4	58.4
S 09	315 44.2 ..	14.8	199 08.3	11.3	4 32.1	12.5	58.4
D 10	330 44.3	15.6	213 38.6	11.3	4 19.6	12.6	58.5
A 11	345 44.3	16.3	228 08.9	11.3	4 07.0	12.6	58.5
Y 12	0 44.4	N15 17.1	242 39.2	11.2	N 3 54.4	12.6	58.6
13	15 44.5	17.8	257 09.4	11.2	3 41.8	12.7	58.6
14	30 44.5	18.6	271 39.6	11.1	3 29.1	12.7	58.6
15	45 44.6 ..	19.3	286 09.7	11.2	3 16.4	12.7	58.7
16	60 44.7	20.1	300 39.9	11.0	3 03.7	12.8	58.7
17	75 44.8	20.8	315 09.9	11.1	2 50.9	12.8	58.8
18	90 44.8	N15 21.6	329 40.0	11.0	N 2 38.1	12.8	58.8
19	105 44.9	22.3	344 10.0	11.0	2 25.3	12.8	58.8
20	120 45.0	23.1	358 40.0	11.0	2 12.5	12.9	58.9
21	135 45.0 ..	23.8	13 10.0	10.9	1 59.6	13.0	58.9
22	150 45.1	24.5	27 39.9	10.9	1 46.6	12.9	59.0
23	165 45.2	25.2	42 09.8	10.8	1 33.7	13.0	59.0
2 00	180 45.2	N15 26.0	56 39.6	10.8	N 1 20.7	13.0	59.0
01	195 45.3	26.8	71 09.4	10.8	1 07.7	13.0	59.1
02	210 45.4	27.5	85 39.2	10.7	0 54.7	13.0	59.1
03	225 45.5 ..	28.3	100 08.9	10.7	0 41.7	13.1	59.1
04	240 45.5	29.0	114 38.6	10.6	0 28.6	13.1	59.2
05	255 45.6	29.7	129 08.2	10.7	0 15.5	13.1	59.2
W 06	270 45.7	N15 30.5	143 37.8	10.5	N 0 02.4	13.1	59.3
E 07	285 45.8	31.2	158 07.3	10.5	S 0 10.7	13.2	59.3
D 08	300 45.8	32.0	172 36.8	10.5	0 23.9	13.1	59.3
N 09	315 45.9 ..	32.7	187 06.3	10.4	0 37.0	13.2	59.4
E 10	330 45.9	33.4	201 35.7	10.4	0 50.2	13.2	59.4
S 11	345 46.0	34.2	216 05.1	10.3	1 03.4	13.2	59.5
D 12	0 46.1	N15 34.9	230 34.4	10.2	S 1 16.6	13.2	59.5
A 13	15 46.1	35.7	245 03.6	10.2	1 29.8	13.2	59.5
Y 14	30 46.2	36.4	259 32.8	10.2	1 43.0	13.2	59.6
15	45 46.3 ..	37.1	274 02.0	10.1	1 56.2	13.3	59.6
16	60 46.3	37.9	288 31.1	10.0	2 09.5	13.2	59.6
17	75 46.4	38.6	303 00.1	10.0	2 22.7	13.2	59.7
18	90 46.5	N15 39.3	317 29.1	10.0	S 2 35.9	13.3	59.7
19	105 46.5	40.1	331 58.1	9.9	2 49.2	13.2	59.7
20	120 46.6	40.8	346 27.0	9.8	3 02.4	13.3	59.8
21	135 46.7 ..	41.6	0 55.8	9.8	3 15.7	13.2	59.8
22	150 46.7	42.3	15 24.6	9.7	3 28.9	13.2	59.9
23	165 46.8	43.0	29 53.3	9.6	S 3 42.1	13.3	59.9
	SD 15.9	d 0.7	SD 15.7		16.0		16.2

Twilight / Sunrise / Moonrise

Lat.	Naut.	Civil	Sunrise	Moonrise 30	1	2	3
°	h m	h m	h m	h m	h m	h m	h m
N 72	////	////	01 49	11 07	13 08	15 11	17 20
N 70	////	////	02 29	11 21	13 13	15 08	17 08
68	////	01 03	02 56	11 33	13 17	15 05	16 58
66	////	01 53	03 16	11 42	13 21	15 03	16 50
64	////	02 24	03 32	11 49	13 24	15 01	16 43
62	00 55	02 46	03 46	11 56	13 26	15 00	16 37
60	01 40	03 04	03 57	12 02	13 28	14 58	16 32
N 58	02 08	03 18	04 07	12 07	13 30	14 57	16 28
56	02 29	03 31	04 15	12 11	13 32	14 56	16 24
54	02 46	03 41	04 23	12 15	13 34	14 55	16 20
52	03 00	03 51	04 30	12 19	13 35	14 55	16 17
50	03 12	03 59	04 36	12 22	13 36	14 54	16 14
45	03 36	04 17	04 49	12 29	13 39	14 52	16 08
N 40	03 55	04 30	05 00	12 35	13 42	14 51	16 03
35	04 09	04 42	05 09	12 40	13 44	14 50	15 58
30	04 21	04 52	05 17	12 44	13 45	14 49	15 54
20	04 40	05 08	05 31	12 52	13 48	14 47	15 48
N 10	04 55	05 21	05 43	12 59	13 51	14 45	15 42
0	05 07	05 32	05 54	13 05	13 54	14 44	15 36
S 10	05 18	05 43	06 05	13 11	13 56	14 43	15 31
20	05 27	05 53	06 16	13 18	13 59	14 41	15 25
30	05 36	06 04	06 29	13 25	14 02	14 40	15 19
35	05 40	06 10	06 37	13 30	14 04	14 39	15 15
40	05 45	06 17	06 45	13 35	14 06	14 38	15 11
45	05 50	06 24	06 55	13 40	14 08	14 37	15 06
S 50	05 55	06 33	07 07	13 47	14 11	14 35	15 01
52	05 57	06 37	07 13	13 50	14 12	14 35	14 58
54	05 59	06 41	07 19	13 54	14 14	14 34	14 55
56	06 01	06 45	07 26	13 57	14 15	14 33	14 52
58	06 04	06 50	07 33	14 01	14 17	14 32	14 49
S 60	06 06	06 56	07 42	14 06	14 19	14 31	14 45

Sunset / Twilight / Moonset

Lat.	Sunset	Civil	Naut.	Moonset 30	1	2	3
°	h m	h m	h m	h m	h m	h m	h m
N 72	22 12	////	////	03 00	02 42	02 26	02 10
N 70	21 30	////	////	02 44	02 35	02 25	02 16
68	21 02	23 03	////	02 31	02 28	02 25	02 21
66	20 41	22 06	////	02 21	02 23	02 24	02 26
64	20 24	21 34	////	02 12	02 18	02 24	02 29
62	20 10	21 11	23 09	02 04	02 14	02 23	02 33
60	19 59	20 53	22 18	01 57	02 10	02 23	02 35
N 58	19 49	20 38	21 49	01 51	02 07	02 22	02 38
56	19 40	20 25	21 27	01 46	02 04	02 22	02 40
54	19 32	20 14	21 10	01 41	02 02	02 22	02 42
52	19 25	20 05	20 56	01 37	01 59	02 21	02 44
50	19 19	19 56	20 43	01 33	01 57	02 21	02 46
45	19 06	19 38	20 19	01 24	01 53	02 21	02 49
N 40	18 55	19 24	20 00	01 17	01 49	02 20	02 52
35	18 46	19 13	19 45	01 11	01 45	02 20	02 55
30	18 38	19 03	19 33	01 05	01 42	02 19	02 57
20	18 24	18 47	19 14	00 56	01 37	02 19	03 01
N 10	18 12	18 33	18 59	00 48	01 32	02 18	03 05
0	18 00	18 22	18 47	00 40	01 28	02 17	03 08
S 10	17 49	18 11	18 36	00 32	01 24	02 17	03 12
20	17 38	18 01	18 27	00 23	01 19	02 16	03 15
30	17 25	17 49	18 18	00 13	01 13	02 15	03 20
35	17 17	17 43	18 13	00 07	01 10	02 15	03 22
40	17 08	17 37	18 09	00 01	01 06	02 14	03 25
45	16 58	17 29	18 04	25 02	01 02	02 14	03 28
S 50	16 46	17 21	17 59	24 57	00 57	02 13	03 31
52	16 41	17 17	17 57	24 55	00 55	02 12	03 33
54	16 35	17 12	17 54	24 52	00 52	02 12	03 35
56	16 28	17 08	17 52	24 49	00 49	02 12	03 37
58	16 20	17 03	17 50	24 46	00 46	02 11	03 39
S 60	16 11	16 57	17 47	24 42	00 42	02 10	03 42

SUN / MOON

Day	Eqn. of Time 00ʰ	12ʰ	Mer. Pass.	Mer. Pass. Upper	Lower	Age	Phase
d	m s	m s	h m	h m	h m	d	%
30	02 46	02 50	11 57	19 16	06 52	09	62
1	02 54	02 57	11 57	20 06	07 41	10	72
2	03 01	03 04	11 57	20 56	08 31	11	81

92 2012 MAY 3, 4, 5 (THURS., FRI., SAT.)

UT	ARIES GHA	VENUS −4.7 GHA	Dec	MARS +0.0 GHA	Dec	JUPITER −2.0 GHA	Dec	SATURN +0.3 GHA	Dec	STARS Name	SHA	Dec
d h	° ′	° ′	° ′	° ′	° ′	° ′	° ′	° ′	° ′		° ′	° ′
3 00	221 17.9	141 17.4	N27 48.6	63 03.2	N11 17.1	172 49.9	N17 08.2	17 13.4	S 7 04.2	Acamar	315 19.4	S40 15.4
01	236 20.4	156 18.6	48.7	78 05.3	16.8	187 51.8	08.3	32 16.1	04.1	Achernar	335 27.9	S57 10.4
02	251 22.8	171 19.9	48.7	93 07.3	16.6	202 53.7	08.5	47 18.7	04.1	Acrux	173 09.6	S63 10.4
03	266 25.3	186 21.2 ..	48.7	108 09.3 ..	16.3	217 55.5 ..	08.6	62 21.3 ..	04.0	Adhara	255 13.3	S28 59.7
04	281 27.8	201 22.4	48.8	123 11.3	16.0	232 57.4	08.8	77 24.0	03.9	Aldebaran	290 50.6	N16 31.9
05	296 30.2	216 23.7	48.8	138 13.3	15.7	247 59.3	09.0	92 26.6	03.9			
06	311 32.7	231 25.0	N27 48.8	153 15.3	N11 15.5	263 01.2	N17 09.1	107 29.2	S 7 03.8	Alioth	166 20.9	N55 53.6
07	326 35.2	246 26.3	48.9	168 17.3	15.2	278 03.0	09.3	122 31.9	03.8	Alkaid	152 59.0	N49 15.1
T 08	341 37.6	261 27.6	48.9	183 19.4	14.9	293 04.9	09.4	137 34.5	03.7	Al Na'ir	27 44.8	S46 53.8
H 09	356 40.1	276 28.8 ..	48.9	198 21.4 ..	14.6	308 06.8 ..	09.6	152 37.1 ..	03.6	Alnilam	275 47.4	S 1 11.8
U 10	11 42.6	291 30.1	49.0	213 23.4	14.4	323 08.6	09.8	167 39.8	03.6	Alphard	217 56.8	S 8 43.0
R 11	26 45.0	306 31.4	49.0	228 25.4	14.1	338 10.5	09.9	182 42.4	03.5			
S 12	41 47.5	321 32.7	N27 49.0	243 27.4	N11 13.8	353 12.4	N17 10.1	197 45.0	S 7 03.5	Alphecca	126 11.3	N26 40.3
D 13	56 49.9	336 34.0	49.0	258 29.4	13.5	8 14.2	10.2	212 47.6	03.4	Alpheratz	357 44.6	N29 09.4
A 14	71 52.4	351 35.3	49.1	273 31.4	13.3	23 16.1	10.4	227 50.3	03.3	Altair	62 08.9	N 8 54.1
Y 15	86 54.9	6 36.6 ..	49.1	288 33.4 ..	13.0	38 18.0 ..	10.6	242 52.9 ..	03.3	Ankaa	353 16.8	S42 14.2
16	101 57.3	21 37.9	49.1	303 35.4	12.7	53 19.8	10.7	257 55.5	03.2	Antares	112 26.9	S26 27.5
17	116 59.8	36 39.3	49.1	318 37.4	12.4	68 21.7	10.9	272 58.2	03.2			
18	132 02.3	51 40.6	N27 49.1	333 39.4	N11 12.2	83 23.6	N17 11.0	288 00.8	S 7 03.1	Arcturus	145 56.1	N19 07.0
19	147 04.7	66 41.9	49.2	348 41.4	11.9	98 25.4	11.2	303 03.4	03.0	Atria	107 29.0	S69 02.8
20	162 07.2	81 43.2	49.2	3 43.4	11.6	113 27.3	11.3	318 06.1	03.0	Avior	234 18.5	S59 33.4
21	177 09.7	96 44.5 ..	49.2	18 45.4 ..	11.3	128 29.2 ..	11.5	333 08.7 ..	02.9	Bellatrix	278 33.1	N 6 21.5
22	192 12.1	111 45.9	49.2	33 47.4	11.0	143 31.0	11.7	348 11.3	02.9	Betelgeuse	271 02.4	N 7 24.4
23	207 14.6	126 47.2	49.2	48 49.4	10.8	158 32.9	11.8	3 14.0	02.8			
4 00	222 17.1	141 48.5	N27 49.3	63 51.4	N11 10.5	173 34.8	N17 12.0	18 16.6	S 7 02.7	Canopus	263 56.8	S52 42.5
01	237 19.5	156 49.9	49.3	78 53.4	10.2	188 36.6	12.1	33 19.2	02.7	Capella	280 36.0	N46 00.6
02	252 22.0	171 51.2	49.3	93 55.4	09.9	203 38.5	12.3	48 21.8	02.6	Deneb	49 32.0	N45 19.3
03	267 24.4	186 52.6 ..	49.3	108 57.4 ..	09.6	218 40.4 ..	12.5	63 24.5 ..	02.6	Denebola	182 34.2	N14 30.1
04	282 26.9	201 53.9	49.3	123 59.4	09.4	233 42.3	12.6	78 27.1	02.5	Diphda	348 57.0	S17 55.1
05	297 29.4	216 55.3	49.3	139 01.4	09.1	248 44.1	12.8	93 29.7	02.4			
06	312 31.8	231 56.6	N27 49.3	154 03.4	N11 08.8	263 46.0	N17 12.9	108 32.4	S 7 02.4	Dubhe	193 52.3	N61 41.1
07	327 34.3	246 58.0	49.4	169 05.4	08.5	278 47.9	13.1	123 35.0	02.3	Elnath	278 13.9	N28 37.0
08	342 36.8	261 59.4	49.4	184 07.3	08.2	293 49.7	13.2	138 37.6	02.3	Eltanin	90 46.1	N51 29.1
F 09	357 39.2	277 00.7 ..	49.4	199 09.3 ..	08.0	308 51.6 ..	13.4	153 40.3 ..	02.2	Enif	33 48.0	N 9 55.9
R 10	12 41.7	292 02.1	49.4	214 11.3	07.7	323 53.5	13.6	168 42.9	02.1	Fomalhaut	15 25.0	S29 33.2
I 11	27 44.2	307 03.5	49.4	229 13.3	07.4	338 55.3	13.7	183 45.5	02.1			
D 12	42 46.6	322 04.9	N27 49.4	244 15.3	N11 07.1	353 57.2	N17 13.9	198 48.1	S 7 02.0	Gacrux	172 01.3	S57 11.2
A 13	57 49.1	337 06.2	49.4	259 17.3	06.8	8 59.1	14.0	213 50.8	02.0	Gienah	175 52.9	S17 36.9
Y 14	72 51.5	352 07.6	49.4	274 19.3	06.5	24 00.9	14.2	228 53.4	01.9	Hadar	148 48.4	S60 26.1
15	87 54.0	7 09.0 ..	49.4	289 21.2 ..	06.3	39 02.8 ..	14.4	243 56.0 ..	01.8	Hamal	328 02.0	N23 31.1
16	102 56.5	22 10.4	49.4	304 23.2	06.0	54 04.7	14.5	258 58.7	01.8	Kaus Aust.	83 44.6	S34 22.5
17	117 58.9	37 11.8	49.4	319 25.2	05.7	69 06.5	14.7	274 01.3	01.7			
18	133 01.4	52 13.2	N27 49.4	334 27.2	N11 05.4	84 08.4	N17 14.8	289 03.9	S 7 01.7	Kochab	137 18.8	N74 06.3
19	148 03.9	67 14.6	49.4	349 29.2	05.1	99 10.3	15.0	304 06.5	01.6	Markab	13 39.3	N15 16.3
20	163 06.3	82 16.0	49.4	4 31.1	04.8	114 12.1	15.1	319 09.2	01.5	Menkar	314 16.2	N 4 08.2
21	178 08.8	97 17.4 ..	49.4	19 33.1 ..	04.5	129 14.0 ..	15.3	334 11.8 ..	01.5	Menkent	148 08.1	S36 26.0
22	193 11.3	112 18.8	49.4	34 35.1	04.3	144 15.9	15.5	349 14.4	01.4	Miaplacidus	221 39.8	S69 46.5
23	208 13.7	127 20.2	49.4	49 37.1	04.0	159 17.7	15.6	4 17.1	01.4			
5 00	223 16.2	142 21.6	N27 49.4	64 39.1	N11 03.7	174 19.6	N17 15.8	19 19.7	S 7 01.3	Mirfak	308 42.0	N49 54.2
01	238 18.7	157 23.1	49.3	79 41.0	03.4	189 21.5	15.9	34 22.3	01.3	Nunki	75 59.1	S26 16.7
02	253 21.1	172 24.5	49.3	94 43.0	03.1	204 23.3	16.1	49 24.9	01.2	Peacock	53 20.4	S56 41.4
03	268 23.6	187 25.9 ..	49.3	109 45.0 ..	02.8	219 25.2 ..	16.2	64 27.6 ..	01.1	Pollux	243 28.8	N27 59.7
04	283 26.0	202 27.4	49.3	124 46.9	02.5	234 27.1	16.4	79 30.2	01.1	Procyon	245 00.7	N 5 11.4
05	298 28.5	217 28.8	49.3	139 48.9	02.2	249 28.9	16.6	94 32.8	01.0			
06	313 31.0	232 30.2	N27 49.4	154 50.9	N11 02.0	264 30.8	N17 16.7	109 35.5	S 7 01.0	Rasalhague	96 06.9	N12 33.0
07	328 33.4	247 31.7	49.3	169 52.9	01.7	279 32.7	16.9	124 38.1	00.9	Regulus	207 44.3	N11 54.2
S 08	343 35.9	262 33.1	49.3	184 54.8	01.4	294 34.5	17.0	139 40.7	00.8	Rigel	281 13.1	S 8 11.5
A 09	358 38.4	277 34.6 ..	49.3	199 56.8 ..	01.1	309 36.4 ..	17.2	154 43.3 ..	00.8	Rigil Kent.	139 52.2	S60 53.2
T 10	13 40.8	292 36.0	49.3	214 58.8	00.8	324 38.3	17.4	169 46.0	00.7	Sabik	102 13.2	S15 44.4
U 11	28 43.3	307 37.5	49.3	230 00.7	00.5	339 40.1	17.5	184 48.6	00.7			
R 12	43 45.8	322 38.9	N27 49.3	245 02.7	N11 00.2	354 42.0	N17 17.7	199 51.2	S 7 00.6	Schedar	349 41.9	N56 36.2
D 13	58 48.2	337 40.4	49.3	260 04.7	10 59.9	9 43.9	17.8	214 53.9	00.5	Shaula	96 22.7	S37 06.6
A 14	73 50.7	352 41.9	49.2	275 06.6	59.6	24 45.7	18.0	229 56.5	00.5	Sirius	258 34.6	S16 44.3
Y 15	88 53.2	7 43.3 ..	49.2	290 08.6 ..	59.4	39 47.6 ..	18.1	244 59.1 ..	00.4	Spica	158 31.8	S11 13.7
16	103 55.6	22 44.8	49.2	305 10.5	59.1	54 49.5	18.3	260 01.7	00.4	Suhail	222 53.0	S43 29.4
17	118 58.1	37 46.3	49.2	320 12.5	58.8	69 51.3	18.5	275 04.4	00.3			
18	134 00.5	52 47.8	N27 49.2	335 14.5	N10 58.5	84 53.2	N17 18.6	290 07.0	S 7 00.3	Vega	80 39.2	N38 48.4
19	149 03.0	67 49.3	49.1	350 16.4	58.2	99 55.1	18.8	305 09.6	00.2	Zuben'ubi	137 06.0	S16 05.7
20	164 05.5	82 50.8	49.1	5 18.4	57.9	114 56.9	18.9	320 12.2	00.1		SHA	Mer.Pass.
21	179 07.9	97 52.3 ..	49.1	20 20.3 ..	57.6	129 58.8 ..	19.1	335 14.9 ..	00.1		° ′	h m
22	194 10.4	112 53.7	49.1	35 22.3	57.3	145 00.7	19.2	350 17.5	00.0	Venus	279 31.5	14 31
23	209 12.9	127 55.2	49.1	50 24.3	57.0	160 02.5	19.4	5 20.1	00.0	Mars	201 34.4	19 42
	h m									Jupiter	311 17.7	12 24
Mer.Pass. 9 09.4		v 1.4	d 0.0	v 2.0	d 0.3	v 1.9	d 0.2	v 2.6	d 0.1	Saturn	155 59.5	22 43

UT	SUN GHA	SUN Dec	MOON GHA	v	MOON Dec	d	HP
d h	° ′	° ′	° ′	′	° ′	′	′
THURSDAY							
3 00	180 46.8	N15 43.8	44 21.9	9.6	S 3 55.4	13.2	59.9
01	195 46.9	44.5	58 50.5	9.6	4 08.6	13.2	60.0
02	210 47.0	45.2	73 19.1	9.4	4 21.8	13.2	60.0
03	225 47.0	.. 45.9	87 47.5	9.4	4 35.0	13.2	60.0
04	240 47.1	46.7	102 15.9	9.4	4 48.2	13.2	60.1
05	255 47.2	47.4	116 44.3	9.3	5 01.4	13.2	60.1
06	270 47.2	N15 48.1	131 12.6	9.2	S 5 14.6	13.1	60.1
07	285 47.3	48.9	145 40.8	9.1	5 27.7	13.1	60.2
08	300 47.4	49.6	160 08.9	9.1	5 40.8	13.2	60.2
09	315 47.4	.. 50.3	174 37.0	9.0	5 54.0	13.1	60.2
10	330 47.5	51.1	189 05.0	9.0	6 07.1	13.0	60.3
11	345 47.5	51.8	203 33.0	8.9	6 20.1	13.1	60.3
12	0 47.6	N15 52.5	218 00.9	8.8	S 6 33.2	13.0	60.3
13	15 47.7	53.2	232 28.7	8.7	6 46.2	13.0	60.4
14	30 47.7	54.0	246 56.4	8.7	6 59.2	13.0	60.4
15	45 47.8	.. 54.7	261 24.1	8.6	7 12.2	12.9	60.4
16	60 47.8	55.4	275 51.7	8.5	7 25.1	12.9	60.5
17	75 47.9	56.1	290 19.2	8.5	7 38.0	12.9	60.5
18	90 48.0	N15 56.9	304 46.7	8.4	S 7 50.9	12.9	60.5
19	105 48.0	57.6	319 14.1	8.3	8 03.8	12.8	60.5
20	120 48.1	58.3	333 41.4	8.3	8 16.6	12.7	60.6
21	135 48.1	.. 59.0	348 08.6	8.2	8 29.3	12.8	60.6
22	150 48.2	15 59.8	2 35.8	8.1	8 42.1	12.7	60.6
23	165 48.3	16 00.5	17 02.9	8.0	8 54.8	12.7	60.7
FRIDAY							
4 00	180 48.3	N16 01.2	31 29.9	7.9	S 9 07.4	12.6	60.7
01	195 48.4	01.9	45 56.8	7.9	9 20.0	12.5	60.7
02	210 48.4	02.7	60 23.7	7.8	9 32.5	12.5	60.7
03	225 48.5	.. 03.4	74 50.5	7.7	9 45.0	12.5	60.8
04	240 48.5	04.1	89 17.2	7.6	9 57.5	12.4	60.8
05	255 48.6	04.8	103 43.8	7.6	10 09.9	12.3	60.8
06	270 48.7	N16 05.5	118 10.4	7.4	S10 22.2	12.3	60.8
07	285 48.7	06.2	132 36.8	7.4	10 34.5	12.2	60.9
08	300 48.8	07.0	147 03.2	7.4	10 46.7	12.2	60.9
09	315 48.8	.. 07.7	161 29.6	7.2	10 58.9	12.1	60.9
10	330 48.9	08.4	175 55.8	7.1	11 11.0	12.1	60.9
11	345 48.9	09.1	190 21.9	7.1	11 23.1	11.9	61.0
12	0 49.0	N16 09.8	204 48.0	7.0	S11 35.0	12.0	61.0
13	15 49.1	10.6	219 14.0	6.9	11 47.0	11.8	61.0
14	30 49.1	11.3	233 39.9	6.9	11 58.8	11.8	61.0
15	45 49.2	.. 12.0	248 05.8	6.7	12 10.6	11.7	61.0
16	60 49.2	12.7	262 31.5	6.7	12 22.3	11.6	61.1
17	75 49.3	13.4	276 57.2	6.6	12 33.9	11.6	61.1
18	90 49.3	N16 14.1	291 22.8	6.5	S12 45.5	11.4	61.1
19	105 49.4	14.8	305 48.3	6.5	12 56.9	11.4	61.1
20	120 49.4	15.6	320 13.8	6.3	13 08.3	11.3	61.1
21	135 49.5	.. 16.3	334 39.1	6.3	13 19.6	11.3	61.2
22	150 49.5	17.0	349 04.4	6.2	13 30.9	11.1	61.2
23	165 49.6	17.7	3 29.6	6.1	13 42.0	11.1	61.2
SATURDAY							
5 00	180 49.6	N16 18.4	17 54.7	6.0	S13 53.1	10.9	61.2
01	195 49.7	19.1	32 19.7	6.0	14 04.0	10.9	61.2
02	210 49.7	19.8	46 44.7	5.8	14 14.9	10.8	61.2
03	225 49.8	.. 20.5	61 09.5	5.8	14 25.7	10.7	61.3
04	240 49.9	21.2	75 34.3	5.8	14 36.4	10.6	61.3
05	255 49.9	21.9	89 59.1	5.6	14 47.0	10.5	61.3
06	270 50.0	N16 22.7	104 23.7	5.6	S14 57.5	10.4	61.3
07	285 50.0	23.4	118 48.3	5.4	15 07.9	10.3	61.3
08	300 50.1	24.1	133 12.7	5.4	15 18.2	10.2	61.3
09	315 50.1	.. 24.8	147 37.1	5.4	15 28.4	10.1	61.3
10	330 50.2	25.5	162 01.5	5.2	15 38.5	9.9	61.3
11	345 50.2	26.2	176 25.7	5.2	15 48.4	9.9	61.3
12	0 50.3	N16 26.9	190 49.9	5.1	S15 58.3	9.8	61.4
13	15 50.3	27.6	205 14.0	5.0	16 08.1	9.6	61.4
14	30 50.4	28.3	219 38.0	5.0	16 17.7	9.6	61.4
15	45 50.4	.. 29.0	234 02.0	4.9	16 27.3	9.4	61.4
16	60 50.5	29.7	248 25.9	4.8	16 36.7	9.3	61.4
17	75 50.5	30.4	262 49.7	4.7	16 46.0	9.2	61.4
18	90 50.6	N16 31.1	277 13.4	4.7	S16 55.2	9.0	61.4
19	105 50.6	31.8	291 37.1	4.6	17 04.2	9.0	61.4
20	120 50.6	32.5	306 00.7	4.5	17 13.2	8.8	61.4
21	135 50.7	.. 33.2	320 24.2	4.4	17 22.0	8.7	61.4
22	150 50.7	33.9	334 47.6	4.4	17 30.7	8.6	61.4
23	165 50.8	34.6	349 11.0	4.4	S17 39.3	8.4	61.4
	SD 15.9	d 0.7	SD 16.4		16.6		16.7

Lat.	Twilight Naut.	Twilight Civil	Sunrise	Moonrise 3	4	5	6
°	h m	h m	h m	h m	h m	h m	h m
N 72	////	////	01 21	17 20	19 45	23 15	■
N 70	////	////	02 11	17 08	19 18	21 44	■
68	////	////	02 42	16 58	18 58	21 05	23 17
66	////	01 33	03 04	16 50	18 42	20 38	22 31
64	////	02 09	03 22	16 43	18 29	20 17	22 00
62	////	02 34	03 37	16 37	18 18	20 01	21 38
60	01 23	02 54	03 49	16 32	18 09	19 47	21 19
N 58	01 56	03 10	04 00	16 28	18 01	19 35	21 04
56	02 19	03 23	04 09	16 24	17 54	19 25	20 51
54	02 37	03 35	04 17	16 20	17 48	19 16	20 40
52	02 53	03 45	04 24	16 17	17 42	19 08	20 30
50	03 06	03 53	04 31	16 14	17 37	19 01	20 21
45	03 31	04 12	04 45	16 08	17 26	18 45	20 03
N 40	03 50	04 26	04 56	16 03	17 17	18 33	19 47
35	04 06	04 39	05 06	15 58	17 09	18 22	19 35
30	04 18	04 49	05 14	15 54	17 03	18 13	19 23
20	04 38	05 06	05 29	15 48	16 51	17 57	19 04
N 10	04 54	05 20	05 42	15 42	16 41	17 43	18 48
0	05 07	05 32	05 53	15 36	16 32	17 31	18 32
S 10	05 18	05 43	06 05	15 31	16 23	17 18	18 17
20	05 28	05 54	06 17	15 25	16 13	17 04	18 01
30	05 38	06 06	06 31	15 19	16 02	16 49	17 42
35	05 42	06 13	06 39	15 15	15 55	16 40	17 31
40	05 47	06 20	06 48	15 11	15 48	16 30	17 19
45	05 53	06 28	06 59	15 06	15 40	16 18	17 05
S 50	05 58	06 37	07 12	15 01	15 30	16 04	16 47
52	06 01	06 41	07 17	14 58	15 25	15 58	16 39
54	06 03	06 46	07 24	14 55	15 20	15 50	16 29
56	06 06	06 51	07 31	14 52	15 15	15 42	16 19
58	06 09	06 56	07 40	14 49	15 08	15 33	16 07
S 60	06 12	07 02	07 49	14 45	15 01	15 23	15 53

Lat.	Sunset	Twilight Civil	Twilight Naut.	Moonset 3	4	5	6
°	h m	h m	h m	h m	h m	h m	h m
N 72	22 43	////	////	02 10	01 51	{01 24 / 23 59}	■
N 70	21 48	////	////	02 16	02 06	01 53	01 31
68	21 16	////	////	02 21	02 18	02 15	02 12
66	20 52	22 27	////	02 26	02 28	02 32	02 40
64	20 34	21 48	////	02 29	02 36	02 46	03 01
62	20 19	21 22	////	02 33	02 43	02 58	03 19
60	20 06	21 02	22 36	02 35	02 50	03 08	03 33
N 58	19 55	20 46	22 01	02 38	02 55	03 17	03 45
56	19 46	20 32	21 37	02 40	03 00	03 25	03 56
54	19 38	20 20	21 18	02 42	03 05	03 32	04 06
52	19 30	20 10	21 03	02 44	03 09	03 38	04 14
50	19 24	20 01	20 50	02 46	03 12	03 44	04 22
45	19 10	19 43	20 24	02 49	03 21	03 56	04 38
N 40	18 58	19 28	20 04	02 52	03 27	04 06	04 52
35	18 48	19 15	19 48	02 55	03 33	04 15	05 03
30	18 40	19 05	19 36	02 57	03 38	04 23	05 13
20	18 25	18 48	19 15	03 01	03 47	04 36	05 30
N 10	18 12	18 34	19 00	03 05	03 55	04 48	05 46
0	18 00	18 22	18 47	03 08	04 02	04 59	06 00
S 10	17 48	18 10	18 36	03 12	04 10	05 10	06 14
20	17 36	17 59	18 25	03 15	04 18	05 22	06 29
30	17 22	17 47	18 16	03 20	04 27	05 36	06 47
35	17 14	17 40	18 11	03 22	04 32	05 44	06 57
40	17 05	17 33	18 05	03 25	04 38	05 53	07 08
45	16 54	17 25	18 00	03 28	04 45	06 04	07 22
S 50	16 41	17 16	17 54	03 31	04 53	06 16	07 39
52	16 35	17 12	17 52	03 33	04 57	06 22	07 47
54	16 29	17 07	17 49	03 35	05 01	06 29	07 56
56	16 21	17 02	17 47	03 37	05 06	06 37	08 06
58	16 13	16 56	17 44	03 39	05 11	06 45	08 17
S 60	16 04	16 50	17 40	03 42	05 17	06 55	08 30

	SUN			MOON			
Day	Eqn. of Time 00h	Eqn. of Time 12h	Mer. Pass.	Mer. Pass. Upper	Mer. Pass. Lower	Age	Phase
d	m s	m s	h m	h m	h m	d	%
3	03 07	03 10	11 57	21 49	09 22	12	90
4	03 13	03 16	11 57	22 45	10 17	13	96
5	03 18	03 21	11 57	23 45	11 15	14	99

UT	ARIES GHA	VENUS −4.7 GHA	Dec	MARS +0.1 GHA	Dec	JUPITER −2.0 GHA	Dec	SATURN +0.4 GHA	Dec	STARS Name	SHA	Dec
6 00	224 15.3	142 56.7	N27 49.0	65 26.2	N10 56.7	175 04.4	N17 19.6	20 22.8	S 6 59.9	Acamar	315 19.4	S40 15.4
01	239 17.8	157 58.3	. . 49.0	80 28.2	56.4	190 06.3	19.7	35 25.4	59.8	Achernar	335 27.9	S57 10.3
02	254 20.3	172 59.8	49.0	95 30.1	56.1	205 08.1	19.9	50 28.0	59.8	Acrux	173 09.6	S63 10.4
03	269 22.7	188 01.3	. . 48.9	110 32.1	. . 55.8	220 10.0	. . 20.0	65 30.6	. . 59.7	Adhara	255 13.4	S28 59.7
04	284 25.2	203 02.8	48.9	125 34.0	55.5	235 11.9	20.2	80 33.3	59.7	Aldebaran	290 50.6	N16 31.9
05	299 27.6	218 04.3	48.9	140 36.0	55.2	250 13.7	20.3	95 35.9	59.6			
06	314 30.1	233 05.8	N27 48.9	155 37.9	N10 54.9	265 15.6	N17 20.5	110 38.5	S 6 59.6	Alioth	166 20.9	N55 53.6
07	329 32.6	248 07.4	48.8	170 39.9	54.6	280 17.5	20.7	125 41.1	59.5	Alkaid	152 59.0	N49 15.1
08	344 35.0	263 08.9	48.8	185 41.8	54.4	295 19.3	20.8	140 43.8	59.4	Al Na'ir	27 44.8	S46 53.8
S 09	359 37.5	278 10.4	. . 48.8	200 43.8	. . 54.1	310 21.2	. . 21.0	155 46.4	. . 59.4	Alnilam	275 47.4	S 1 11.8
U 10	14 40.0	293 12.0	48.7	215 45.7	53.8	325 23.1	21.1	170 49.0	59.3	Alphard	217 56.8	S 8 43.0
N 11	29 42.4	308 13.5	48.7	230 47.7	53.5	340 24.9	21.3	185 51.6	59.3			
D 12	44 44.9	323 15.1	N27 48.7	245 49.6	N10 53.2	355 26.8	N17 21.4	200 54.3	S 6 59.2	Alphecca	126 11.3	N26 40.3
A 13	59 47.4	338 16.6	48.6	260 51.6	52.9	10 28.7	21.6	215 56.9	59.2	Alpheratz	357 44.6	N29 09.4
Y 14	74 49.8	353 18.2	48.6	275 53.5	52.6	25 30.5	21.8	230 59.5	59.1	Altair	62 08.9	N 8 54.1
15	89 52.3	8 19.7	. . 48.5	290 55.4	. . 52.3	40 32.4	. . 21.9	246 02.1	. . 59.0	Ankaa	353 16.8	S42 14.2
16	104 54.8	23 21.3	48.5	305 57.4	52.0	55 34.3	22.1	261 04.8	59.0	Antares	112 26.9	S26 27.5
17	119 57.2	38 22.9	48.5	320 59.3	51.7	70 36.1	22.2	276 07.4	58.9			
18	134 59.7	53 24.4	N27 48.4	336 01.3	N10 51.4	85 38.0	N17 22.4	291 10.0	S 6 58.9	Arcturus	145 56.1	N19 07.0
19	150 02.1	68 26.0	48.4	351 03.2	51.1	100 39.9	22.5	306 12.7	58.8	Atria	107 28.9	S69 02.8
20	165 04.6	83 27.6	48.3	6 05.2	50.8	115 41.7	22.7	321 15.3	58.8	Avior	234 18.5	S59 33.4
21	180 07.1	98 29.2	. . 48.3	21 07.1	. . 50.5	130 43.6	. . 22.8	336 17.9	. . 58.7	Bellatrix	278 33.1	N 6 21.5
22	195 09.5	113 30.7	48.2	36 09.0	50.2	145 45.5	23.0	351 20.5	58.6	Betelgeuse	271 02.4	N 7 24.4
23	210 12.0	128 32.3	48.2	51 11.0	49.9	160 47.3	23.2	6 23.2	58.6			
7 00	225 14.5	143 33.9	N27 48.2	66 12.9	N10 49.6	175 49.2	N17 23.3	21 25.8	S 6 58.5	Canopus	263 56.9	S52 42.5
01	240 16.9	158 35.5	48.1	81 14.8	49.3	190 51.1	23.5	36 28.4	58.5	Capella	280 36.0	N46 00.6
02	255 19.4	173 37.1	48.1	96 16.8	49.0	205 52.9	23.6	51 31.0	58.4	Deneb	49 31.9	N45 19.3
03	270 21.9	188 38.7	. . 48.0	111 18.7	. . 48.7	220 54.8	. . 23.8	66 33.7	. . 58.3	Denebola	182 34.3	N14 30.1
04	285 24.3	203 40.3	48.0	126 20.6	48.4	235 56.7	23.9	81 36.3	58.3	Diphda	348 56.9	S17 55.1
05	300 26.8	218 41.9	47.9	141 22.6	48.1	250 58.5	24.1	96 38.9	58.2			
06	315 29.3	233 43.5	N27 47.9	156 24.5	N10 47.8	266 00.4	N17 24.3	111 41.5	S 6 58.2	Dubhe	193 52.3	N61 41.2
07	330 31.7	248 45.2	47.8	171 26.4	47.4	281 02.2	24.4	126 44.2	58.1	Elnath	278 13.9	N28 37.0
08	345 34.2	263 46.8	47.8	186 28.4	47.1	296 04.1	24.6	141 46.8	58.1	Eltanin	90 46.1	N51 29.1
M 09	0 36.6	278 48.4	. . 47.7	201 30.3	. . 46.8	311 06.0	. . 24.7	156 49.4	. . 58.0	Enif	33 47.9	N 9 55.9
O 10	15 39.1	293 50.0	47.6	216 32.2	46.5	326 07.8	24.9	171 52.0	58.0	Fomalhaut	15 25.0	S29 33.2
N 11	30 41.6	308 51.7	47.6	231 34.1	46.2	341 09.7	25.0	186 54.6	57.9			
D 12	45 44.0	323 53.3	N27 47.5	246 36.1	N10 45.9	356 11.6	N17 25.2	201 57.3	S 6 57.8	Gacrux	172 01.3	S57 11.2
A 13	60 46.5	338 54.9	47.5	261 38.0	45.6	11 13.4	25.3	216 59.9	57.8	Gienah	175 52.9	S17 36.9
Y 14	75 49.0	353 56.6	47.4	276 39.9	45.3	26 15.3	25.5	232 02.5	57.7	Hadar	148 48.4	S60 26.1
15	90 51.4	8 58.2	. . 47.4	291 41.8	. . 45.0	41 17.2	. . 25.7	247 05.1	. . 57.7	Hamal	328 02.0	N23 31.1
16	105 53.9	23 59.9	47.3	306 43.8	44.7	56 19.0	25.8	262 07.8	57.6	Kaus Aust.	83 44.6	S34 22.5
17	120 56.4	39 01.5	47.2	321 45.7	44.4	71 20.9	26.0	277 10.4	57.6			
18	135 58.8	54 03.2	N27 47.2	336 47.6	N10 44.1	86 22.8	N17 26.1	292 13.0	S 6 57.5	Kochab	137 18.8	N74 06.3
19	151 01.3	69 04.9	47.1	351 49.5	43.8	101 24.6	26.3	307 15.6	57.4	Markab	13 39.3	N15 16.3
20	166 03.8	84 06.5	47.0	6 51.4	43.5	116 26.5	26.4	322 18.3	57.4	Menkar	314 16.2	N 4 08.2
21	181 06.2	99 08.2	. . 47.0	21 53.4	. . 43.2	131 28.4	. . 26.6	337 20.9	. . 57.3	Menkent	148 08.1	S36 26.0
22	196 08.7	114 09.9	46.9	36 55.3	42.9	146 30.2	26.8	352 23.5	57.3	Miaplacidus	221 39.9	S69 46.5
23	211 11.1	129 11.5	46.8	51 57.2	42.6	161 32.1	26.9	7 26.1	57.2			
8 00	226 13.6	144 13.2	N27 46.8	66 59.1	N10 42.2	176 34.0	N17 27.1	22 28.8	S 6 57.2	Mirfak	308 42.0	N49 54.2
01	241 16.1	159 14.9	46.7	82 01.0	41.9	191 35.8	27.2	37 31.4	57.1	Nunki	75 59.1	S26 16.7
02	256 18.5	174 16.6	46.6	97 02.9	41.6	206 37.7	27.4	52 34.0	57.0	Peacock	53 20.3	S56 41.3
03	271 21.0	189 18.3	. . 46.6	112 04.9	. . 41.3	221 39.6	. . 27.5	67 36.6	. . 57.0	Pollux	243 28.8	N27 59.7
04	286 23.5	204 20.0	46.5	127 06.8	41.0	236 41.4	27.7	82 39.2	56.9	Procyon	245 00.7	N 5 11.4
05	301 25.9	219 21.7	46.4	142 08.7	40.7	251 43.3	27.8	97 41.9	56.9			
06	316 28.4	234 23.4	N27 46.3	157 10.6	N10 40.4	266 45.1	N17 28.0	112 44.5	S 6 56.8	Rasalhague	96 06.9	N12 33.0
07	331 30.9	249 25.1	46.3	172 12.5	40.1	281 47.0	28.2	127 47.1	56.8	Regulus	207 44.3	N11 54.2
T 08	346 33.3	264 26.8	46.2	187 14.4	39.8	296 48.9	28.3	142 49.7	56.7	Rigel	281 13.1	S 8 11.4
U 09	1 35.8	279 28.5	. . 46.1	202 16.3	. . 39.5	311 50.7	. . 28.5	157 52.4	. . 56.7	Rigil Kent.	139 52.1	S60 53.2
E 10	16 38.2	294 30.3	46.0	217 18.2	39.1	326 52.6	28.6	172 55.0	56.6	Sabik	102 13.1	S15 44.4
S 11	31 40.7	309 32.0	46.0	232 20.1	38.8	341 54.5	28.8	187 57.6	56.5			
D 12	46 43.2	324 33.7	N27 45.9	247 22.1	N10 38.5	356 56.3	N17 28.9	203 00.2	S 6 56.5	Schedar	349 41.9	N56 36.2
A 13	61 45.6	339 35.4	45.8	262 24.0	38.2	11 58.2	29.1	218 02.9	56.4	Shaula	96 22.6	S37 06.6
Y 14	76 48.1	354 37.2	45.7	277 25.9	37.9	27 00.1	29.2	233 05.5	56.4	Sirius	258 34.6	S16 44.3
15	91 50.6	9 38.9	. . 45.6	292 27.8	. . 37.6	42 01.9	. . 29.4	248 08.1	. . 56.3	Spica	158 31.8	S11 13.7
16	106 53.0	24 40.7	45.6	307 29.7	37.3	57 03.8	29.6	263 10.7	56.3	Suhail	222 53.0	S43 29.4
17	121 55.5	39 42.4	45.5	322 31.6	37.0	72 05.7	29.7	278 13.3	56.2			
18	136 58.0	54 44.1	N27 45.4	337 33.5	N10 36.6	87 07.5	N17 29.9	293 16.0	S 6 56.2	Vega	80 39.2	N38 47.6
19	152 00.4	69 45.9	45.3	352 35.4	36.3	102 09.4	30.0	308 18.6	56.1	Zuben'ubi	137 06.0	S16 05.7
20	167 02.9	84 47.7	45.2	7 37.3	36.0	117 11.3	30.2	323 21.2	56.0		SHA	Mer.Pass.
21	182 05.4	99 49.4	. . 45.1	22 39.2	. . 35.7	132 13.1	. . 30.3	338 23.8	. . 56.0	Venus	278 19.5	14 24
22	197 07.8	114 51.2	45.1	37 41.1	35.4	147 15.0	30.5	353 26.4	55.9	Mars	200 58.4	19 59
23	212 10.3	129 53.0	45.0	52 43.0	35.1	162 16.8	30.6	8 29.1	55.9	Jupiter	310 34.7	12 15
Mer. Pass.	8 57.6	v 1.6	d 0.1	v 1.9	d 0.3	v 1.9	d 0.2	v 2.6	d 0.1	Saturn	156 11.3	22 30

UT	SUN GHA	SUN Dec	MOON GHA	v	Dec	d	HP
d h	° ′	° ′	° ′	′	° ′	′	′
6 00	180 50.8	N16 35.3	3 34.4	4.2	S17 47.7	8.3	61.4
01	195 50.9	36.0	17 57.6	4.2	17 56.0	8.2	61.4
02	210 50.9	36.7	32 20.8	4.2	18 04.2	8.1	61.4
03	225 51.0	.. 37.4	46 44.0	4.1	18 12.3	7.9	61.4
04	240 51.0	38.1	61 07.1	4.0	18 20.2	7.8	61.4
05	255 51.1	38.8	75 30.1	3.9	18 28.0	7.6	61.4
06	270 51.1	N16 39.5	89 53.0	3.9	S18 35.6	7.5	61.4
07	285 51.2	40.2	104 15.9	3.9	18 43.1	7.4	61.4
08	300 51.2	40.9	118 38.8	3.8	18 50.5	7.2	61.4
S 09	315 51.2	.. 41.6	133 01.6	3.7	18 57.7	7.1	61.4
U 10	330 51.3	42.3	147 24.3	3.7	19 04.8	6.9	61.4
N 11	345 51.3	43.0	161 47.0	3.7	19 11.7	6.8	61.4
D 12	0 51.4	N16 43.7	176 09.7	3.6	S19 18.5	6.7	61.4
A 13	15 51.4	44.4	190 32.3	3.5	19 25.2	6.5	61.4
Y 14	30 51.5	45.1	204 54.8	3.5	19 31.7	6.4	61.4
15	45 51.5	.. 45.8	219 17.3	3.5	19 38.1	6.2	61.4
16	60 51.6	46.4	233 39.8	3.4	19 44.3	6.0	61.4
17	75 51.6	47.1	248 02.2	3.4	19 50.3	5.9	61.4
18	90 51.6	N16 47.8	262 24.6	3.3	S19 56.2	5.8	61.4
19	105 51.7	48.5	276 46.9	3.3	20 02.0	5.6	61.4
20	120 51.7	49.2	291 09.2	3.3	20 07.6	5.5	61.3
21	135 51.8	.. 49.9	305 31.5	3.3	20 13.1	5.3	61.3
22	150 51.8	50.6	319 53.8	3.2	20 18.4	5.1	61.3
23	165 51.8	51.3	334 16.0	3.2	20 23.5	5.0	61.3
7 00	180 51.9	N16 52.0	348 38.2	3.1	S20 28.5	4.8	61.3
01	195 51.9	52.6	3 00.3	3.2	20 33.3	4.7	61.3
02	210 52.0	53.3	17 22.5	3.1	20 38.0	4.5	61.3
03	225 52.0	.. 54.0	31 44.6	3.1	20 42.5	4.3	61.3
04	240 52.0	54.7	46 06.7	3.0	20 46.8	4.2	61.3
05	255 52.1	55.4	60 28.7	3.1	20 51.0	4.1	61.2
06	270 52.1	N16 56.1	74 50.8	3.0	S20 55.1	3.8	61.2
07	285 52.2	56.8	89 12.8	3.1	20 58.9	3.8	61.2
08	300 52.2	57.4	103 34.9	3.0	21 02.7	3.5	61.2
M 09	315 52.2	.. 58.1	117 56.9	3.0	21 06.2	3.4	61.2
O 10	330 52.3	58.8	132 18.9	3.0	21 09.6	3.2	61.2
N 11	345 52.3	16 59.5	146 40.9	3.0	21 12.8	3.1	61.1
D 12	0 52.4	N17 00.2	161 02.9	3.0	S21 15.9	2.9	61.1
A 13	15 52.4	00.9	175 24.9	3.0	21 18.8	2.7	61.1
Y 14	30 52.4	01.5	189 46.9	3.0	21 21.5	2.6	61.1
15	45 52.5	.. 02.2	204 08.9	3.0	21 24.1	2.4	61.1
16	60 52.5	02.9	218 30.9	3.1	21 26.5	2.3	61.0
17	75 52.5	03.6	232 53.0	3.0	21 28.8	2.0	61.0
18	90 52.6	N17 04.3	247 15.0	3.0	S21 30.8	2.0	61.0
19	105 52.6	04.9	261 37.0	3.1	21 32.8	1.7	61.0
20	120 52.7	05.6	275 59.1	3.1	21 34.5	1.6	61.0
21	135 52.7	.. 06.3	290 21.2	3.1	21 36.1	1.4	60.9
22	150 52.7	07.0	304 43.3	3.1	21 37.5	1.3	60.9
23	165 52.8	07.7	319 05.4	3.1	21 38.8	1.1	60.9
8 00	180 52.8	N17 08.3	333 27.5	3.2	S21 39.9	0.9	60.9
01	195 52.8	09.0	347 49.7	3.2	21 40.8	0.8	60.8
02	210 52.9	09.7	2 11.9	3.2	21 41.6	0.6	60.8
03	225 52.9	.. 10.4	16 34.1	3.2	21 42.2	0.5	60.8
04	240 52.9	11.0	30 56.3	3.3	21 42.7	0.2	60.8
05	255 53.0	11.7	45 18.6	3.3	21 42.9	0.2	60.7
06	270 53.0	N17 12.4	59 40.9	3.4	S21 43.1	0.1	60.7
07	285 53.0	13.0	74 03.3	3.4	21 43.0	0.2	60.7
08	300 53.1	13.7	88 25.7	3.4	21 42.8	0.3	60.7
T 09	315 53.1	.. 14.4	102 48.1	3.5	21 42.5	0.5	60.6
U 10	330 53.1	15.1	117 10.6	3.5	21 42.0	0.7	60.6
E 11	345 53.2	15.7	131 33.1	3.6	21 41.3	0.8	60.6
S 12	0 53.2	N17 16.4	145 55.7	3.6	S21 40.5	1.0	60.5
D 13	15 53.2	17.1	160 18.3	3.6	21 39.5	1.2	60.5
A 14	30 53.3	17.7	174 40.9	3.8	21 38.3	1.3	60.5
Y 15	45 53.3	.. 18.4	189 03.7	3.7	21 37.0	1.5	60.5
16	60 53.3	19.1	203 26.4	3.9	21 35.5	1.6	60.4
17	75 53.4	19.7	217 49.3	3.9	21 33.9	1.7	60.4
18	90 53.4	N17 20.4	232 12.2	3.9	S21 32.2	2.0	60.4
19	105 53.4	21.1	246 35.1	4.0	21 30.2	2.0	60.3
20	120 53.4	21.7	260 58.1	4.1	21 28.2	2.3	60.3
21	135 53.5	.. 22.4	275 21.2	4.2	21 25.9	2.4	60.3
22	150 53.5	23.1	289 44.4	4.2	21 23.5	2.5	60.2
23	165 53.5	23.7	304 07.6	4.3	S21 21.0	2.7	60.2
SD	15.9	d 0.7	SD 16.7		16.7		16.5

Twilight / Moonrise

Lat.	Naut.	Civil	Sunrise	6	7	8	9
°	h m	h m	h m	h m	h m	h m	h m
N 72	////	////	00 39	■	■	■	■
N 70	////	////	01 51	■	■	■	■
68	////	////	02 27	23 17	25 22	01 22	01 53
66	////	01 09	02 52	22 31	24 03	00 03	00 55
64	////	01 54	03 12	22 00	23 26	24 22	00 22
62	////	02 23	03 28	21 38	22 59	23 57	24 33
60	01 02	02 44	03 41	21 19	22 38	23 37	24 17
N 58	01 42	03 01	03 52	21 04	22 21	23 21	24 03
56	02 09	03 16	04 02	20 51	22 07	23 07	23 51
54	02 29	03 28	04 11	20 40	21 55	22 55	23 41
52	02 45	03 39	04 19	20 30	21 44	22 44	23 32
50	02 59	03 48	04 26	20 21	21 34	22 35	23 23
45	03 26	04 07	04 40	20 03	21 14	22 15	23 06
N 40	03 46	04 23	04 53	19 47	20 57	21 59	22 51
35	04 02	04 35	05 03	19 35	20 43	21 45	22 39
30	04 16	04 46	05 12	19 23	20 31	21 33	22 28
20	04 37	05 04	05 27	19 04	20 10	21 13	22 09
N 10	04 53	05 19	05 41	18 48	19 52	20 55	21 53
0	05 06	05 31	05 53	18 32	19 36	20 38	21 38
S 10	05 18	05 43	06 05	18 17	19 19	20 22	21 23
20	05 29	05 55	06 18	18 01	19 01	20 04	21 07
30	05 39	06 08	06 33	17 42	18 41	19 44	20 48
35	05 45	06 15	06 41	17 31	18 29	19 32	20 37
40	05 50	06 22	06 51	17 19	18 15	19 18	20 25
45	05 56	06 31	07 02	17 05	17 59	19 02	20 10
S 50	06 02	06 41	07 16	16 47	17 39	18 42	19 52
52	06 05	06 46	07 22	16 39	17 30	18 33	19 44
54	06 08	06 51	07 29	16 29	17 20	18 22	19 34
56	06 11	06 56	07 37	16 19	17 08	18 10	19 23
58	06 14	07 02	07 46	16 07	16 54	17 56	19 11
S 60	06 18	07 09	07 56	15 53	16 38	17 40	18 56

Sunset / Twilight / Moonset

Lat.	Sunset	Civil	Naut.	6	7	8	9
°	h m	h m	h m	h m	h m	h m	h m
N 72	23 43	////	////	■	■	■	■
N 70	22 08	////	////	01 31	■	■	■
68	21 30	////	////	02 12	02 10	02 19	■
66	21 04	22 52	////	02 40	02 57	03 38	03 58
64	20 43	22 03	////	03 01	03 28	04 15	04 55
62	20 27	21 34	////	03 19	03 51	04 42	05 29
60	20 14	21 11	22 59	03 33	04 09	05 02	05 53
N 58	20 02	20 54	22 15	03 45	04 25	05 19	06 13
56	19 52	20 39	21 47	03 56	04 38	05 34	06 29
54	19 43	20 27	21 27	04 06	04 50	05 46	06 42
52	19 35	20 16	21 10	04 14	05 00	05 57	06 54
50	19 28	20 06	20 56	04 22	05 09	06 07	07 05
45	19 13	19 47	20 28	04 38	05 28	06 27	07 14
N 40	19 01	19 31	20 08	04 52	05 44	06 44	07 49
35	18 51	19 18	19 51	05 03	05 57	06 58	08 03
30	18 41	19 07	19 38	05 13	06 09	07 10	08 14
20	18 26	18 49	19 17	05 30	06 29	07 31	08 34
N 10	18 12	18 35	19 00	05 46	06 46	07 49	08 51
0	18 00	18 22	18 47	06 00	07 03	08 06	09 07
S 10	17 48	18 10	18 35	06 14	07 19	08 23	09 23
20	17 35	17 58	18 24	06 29	07 36	08 41	09 40
30	17 20	17 45	18 13	06 47	07 56	09 01	10 00
35	17 11	17 38	18 08	06 57	08 08	09 13	10 11
40	17 02	17 30	18 03	07 08	08 21	09 27	10 24
45	16 50	17 21	17 57	07 22	08 37	09 43	10 39
S 50	16 37	17 11	17 50	07 39	08 56	10 03	10 58
52	16 30	17 07	17 47	07 47	09 05	10 13	11 07
54	16 23	17 02	17 44	07 56	09 16	10 24	11 17
56	16 15	16 56	17 41	08 06	09 28	10 36	11 28
58	16 06	16 50	17 37	08 17	09 41	10 50	11 41
S 60	15 56	16 44	17 34	08 30	09 57	11 06	11 55

SUN and MOON

Day	Eqn. of Time 00h	Eqn. of Time 12h	Mer. Pass.	Mer. Pass. Upper	Mer. Pass. Lower	Age	Phase
d	m s	m s	h m	h m	h m	d %	
6	03 23	03 25	11 57	24 47	12 16	15 100	◯
7	03 27	03 29	11 57	00 47	13 19	16 97	
8	03 31	03 33	11 56	01 51	14 22	17 92	

2012 MAY 9, 10, 11 (WED., THURS., FRI.)

UT	ARIES GHA	VENUS −4.7 GHA	Dec	MARS +0.2 GHA	Dec	JUPITER −2.0 GHA	Dec	SATURN +0.4 GHA	Dec	STARS Name	SHA	Dec
d h												
9 00	227 12.7	144 54.7	N27 44.9	67 44.9	N10 34.8	177 18.7	N17 30.8	23 31.7	S 6 55.8	Acamar	315 19.3	S40 15.4
01	242 15.2	159 56.5	44.8	82 46.8	34.4	192 20.6	30.9	38 34.3	55.8	Achernar	335 27.9	S57 10.3
02	257 17.7	174 58.3	44.7	97 48.7	34.1	207 22.4	31.1	53 36.9	55.7	Acrux	173 09.6	S63 10.4
03	272 20.1	190 00.1	.. 44.6	112 50.6	.. 33.8	222 24.3	.. 31.3	68 39.6	.. 55.7	Adhara	255 13.4	S28 59.7
04	287 22.6	205 01.9	44.5	127 52.5	33.5	237 26.2	31.4	83 42.2	55.6	Aldebaran	290 50.6	N16 31.9
05	302 25.1	220 03.7	44.4	142 54.4	33.2	252 28.0	31.6	98 44.8	55.5			
W 06	317 27.5	235 05.5	N27 44.3	157 56.2	N10 32.9	267 29.9	N17 31.7	113 47.4	S 6 55.5	Alioth	166 20.9	N55 53.6
E 07	332 30.0	250 07.3	44.2	172 58.1	32.5	282 31.8	31.9	128 50.0	55.4	Alkaid	152 59.0	N49 15.1
D 08	347 32.5	265 09.1	44.1	188 00.0	32.2	297 33.6	32.0	143 52.7	55.4	Al Na'ir	27 44.8	S46 53.7
N 09	2 34.9	280 10.9	.. 44.0	203 01.9	.. 31.9	312 35.5	.. 32.2	158 55.3	.. 55.3	Alnilam	275 47.4	S 1 11.8
E 10	17 37.4	295 12.7	43.9	218 03.8	31.6	327 37.4	32.3	173 57.9	55.3	Alphard	217 56.9	S 8 43.0
S 11	32 39.9	310 14.5	43.8	233 05.7	31.3	342 39.2	32.5	189 00.5	55.2			
D 12	47 42.3	325 16.3	N27 43.7	248 07.6	N10 31.0	357 41.1	N17 32.6	204 03.1	S 6 55.2	Alphecca	126 11.3	N26 40.3
A 13	62 44.8	340 18.2	43.6	263 09.5	30.6	12 43.0	32.8	219 05.8	55.1	Alpheratz	357 44.5	N29 09.4
Y 14	77 47.2	355 20.0	43.5	278 11.4	30.3	27 44.8	33.0	234 08.4	55.0	Altair	62 08.9	N 8 54.1
15	92 49.7	10 21.8	.. 43.4	293 13.3	.. 30.0	42 46.7	.. 33.1	249 11.0	.. 55.0	Ankaa	353 16.8	S42 14.2
16	107 52.2	25 23.7	43.3	308 15.1	29.7	57 48.5	33.3	264 13.6	54.9	Antares	112 26.9	S26 27.5
17	122 54.6	40 25.5	43.2	323 17.0	29.4	72 50.4	33.4	279 16.2	54.9			
18	137 57.1	55 27.4	N27 43.1	338 18.9	N10 29.0	87 52.3	N17 33.6	294 18.9	S 6 54.8	Arcturus	145 56.1	N19 07.0
19	152 59.6	70 29.2	43.0	353 20.8	28.7	102 54.1	33.7	309 21.5	54.8	Atria	107 28.9	S69 02.8
20	168 02.0	85 31.1	42.9	8 22.7	28.4	117 56.0	33.9	324 24.1	54.7	Avior	234 18.5	S59 33.4
21	183 04.5	100 32.9	.. 42.8	23 24.6	.. 28.1	132 57.9	.. 34.0	339 26.7	.. 54.7	Bellatrix	278 33.1	N 6 21.5
22	198 07.0	115 34.8	42.7	38 26.4	27.8	147 59.7	34.2	354 29.3	54.6	Betelgeuse	271 02.4	N 7 24.4
23	213 09.4	130 36.6	42.6	53 28.3	27.4	163 01.6	34.3	9 32.0	54.6			
10 00	228 11.9	145 38.5	N27 42.5	68 30.2	N10 27.1	178 03.5	N17 34.5	24 34.6	S 6 54.5	Canopus	263 56.9	S52 42.5
01	243 14.4	160 40.4	42.3	83 32.1	26.8	193 05.3	34.7	39 37.2	54.4	Capella	280 36.0	N46 00.6
02	258 16.8	175 42.3	42.2	98 33.9	26.5	208 07.2	34.8	54 39.8	54.4	Deneb	49 31.9	N45 19.3
03	273 19.3	190 44.1	.. 42.1	113 35.8	.. 26.1	223 09.0	.. 35.0	69 42.4	.. 54.3	Denebola	182 34.3	N14 30.1
04	288 21.7	205 46.0	42.0	128 37.7	25.8	238 10.9	35.1	84 45.1	54.3	Diphda	348 56.9	S17 55.1
05	303 24.2	220 47.9	41.9	143 39.6	25.5	253 12.8	35.3	99 47.7	54.2			
T 06	318 26.7	235 49.8	N27 41.8	158 41.4	N10 25.2	268 14.6	N17 35.4	114 50.3	S 6 54.2	Dubhe	193 52.4	N61 41.2
H 07	333 29.1	250 51.7	41.6	173 43.3	24.9	283 16.5	35.6	129 52.9	54.1	Elnath	278 13.9	N28 37.0
U 08	348 31.6	265 53.6	41.5	188 45.2	24.5	298 18.4	35.7	144 55.5	54.1	Eltanin	90 46.1	N51 29.1
R 09	3 34.1	280 55.5	.. 41.4	203 47.1	.. 24.2	313 20.2	.. 35.9	159 58.1	.. 54.0	Enif	33 47.9	N 9 55.9
S 10	18 36.5	295 57.4	41.3	218 48.9	23.9	328 22.1	36.0	175 00.8	54.0	Fomalhaut	15 25.0	S29 33.2
D 11	33 39.0	310 59.4	41.2	233 50.8	23.6	343 24.0	36.2	190 03.4	53.9			
A 12	48 41.5	326 01.3	N27 41.0	248 52.7	N10 23.3	358 25.8	N17 36.3	205 06.0	S 6 53.9	Gacrux	172 01.3	S57 11.3
Y 13	63 43.9	341 03.2	40.9	263 54.6	22.9	13 27.7	36.5	220 08.6	53.8	Gienah	175 52.9	S17 36.9
14	78 46.4	356 05.1	40.8	278 56.4	22.6	28 29.5	36.7	235 11.2	53.7	Hadar	148 48.4	S60 26.1
15	93 48.9	11 07.1	.. 40.7	293 58.3	.. 22.2	43 31.4	.. 36.8	250 13.9	.. 53.7	Hamal	328 02.0	N23 31.1
16	108 51.3	26 09.0	40.5	309 00.2	21.9	58 33.3	37.0	265 16.5	53.6	Kaus Aust.	83 44.5	S34 22.5
17	123 53.8	41 10.9	40.4	324 02.0	21.6	73 35.1	37.1	280 19.1	53.6			
18	138 56.2	56 12.9	N27 40.2	339 03.9	N10 21.3	88 37.0	N17 37.3	295 21.7	S 6 53.5	Kochab	137 18.8	N74 06.3
19	153 58.7	71 14.8	40.2	354 05.8	20.9	103 38.9	37.4	310 24.3	53.5	Markab	13 39.2	N15 16.3
20	169 01.2	86 16.8	40.0	9 07.6	20.6	118 40.7	37.6	325 26.9	53.4	Menkar	314 16.2	N 4 08.2
21	184 03.6	101 18.7	.. 39.9	24 09.5	.. 20.3	133 42.6	.. 37.7	340 29.6	.. 53.4	Menkent	148 08.1	S36 26.0
22	199 06.1	116 20.7	39.8	39 11.3	20.0	148 44.5	37.9	355 32.2	53.3	Miaplacidus	221 39.9	S69 46.5
23	214 08.6	131 22.6	39.6	54 13.2	19.6	163 46.3	38.0	10 34.8	53.3			
11 00	229 11.0	146 24.6	N27 39.5	69 15.1	N10 19.3	178 48.2	N17 38.2	25 37.4	S 6 53.2	Mirfak	308 42.0	N49 54.2
01	244 13.5	161 26.6	39.4	84 16.9	19.0	193 50.0	38.3	40 40.0	53.2	Nunki	75 59.0	S26 16.7
02	259 16.0	176 28.6	39.2	99 18.8	18.6	208 51.9	38.5	55 42.6	53.1	Peacock	53 20.3	S56 41.3
03	274 18.4	191 30.5	.. 39.1	114 20.6	.. 18.3	223 53.8	.. 38.7	70 45.3	.. 53.1	Pollux	243 28.8	N27 59.7
04	289 20.9	206 32.5	39.0	129 22.5	18.0	238 55.6	38.8	85 47.9	53.0	Procyon	245 00.7	N 5 11.4
05	304 23.4	221 34.5	38.8	144 24.4	17.7	253 57.5	39.0	100 50.5	52.9			
06	319 25.8	236 36.5	N27 38.7	159 26.2	N10 17.3	268 59.4	N17 39.1	115 53.1	S 6 52.9	Rasalhague	96 06.9	N12 33.0
07	334 28.3	251 38.5	38.5	174 28.1	17.0	284 01.2	39.3	130 55.7	52.8	Regulus	207 44.3	N11 54.2
08	349 30.7	266 40.5	38.4	189 29.9	16.7	299 03.1	39.4	145 58.3	52.8	Rigel	281 13.1	S 8 11.4
F 09	4 33.2	281 42.5	.. 38.3	204 31.8	.. 16.3	314 05.0	.. 39.6	161 01.0	.. 52.7	Rigil Kent.	139 52.1	S60 53.2
R 10	19 35.7	296 44.5	38.1	219 33.6	16.0	329 06.8	39.7	176 03.6	52.7	Sabik	102 13.1	S15 44.4
I 11	34 38.1	311 46.5	38.0	234 35.5	15.7	344 08.7	39.9	191 06.2	52.6			
D 12	49 40.6	326 48.6	N27 37.8	249 37.3	N10 15.3	359 10.5	N17 40.0	206 08.8	S 6 52.6	Schedar	349 41.9	N56 36.2
A 13	64 43.1	341 50.6	37.7	264 39.2	15.0	14 12.4	40.2	221 11.4	52.5	Shaula	96 22.6	S37 06.6
Y 14	79 45.5	356 52.6	37.5	279 41.0	14.7	29 14.3	40.3	236 14.0	52.5	Sirius	258 34.6	S16 44.3
15	94 48.0	11 54.6	.. 37.4	294 42.9	.. 14.3	44 16.1	.. 40.5	251 16.7	.. 52.4	Spica	158 31.8	S11 13.7
16	109 50.5	26 56.7	37.2	309 44.7	14.0	59 18.0	40.6	266 19.3	52.4	Suhail	222 53.1	S43 29.4
17	124 52.9	41 58.7	37.1	324 46.6	13.7	74 19.9	40.8	281 21.9	52.3			
18	139 55.4	57 00.8	N27 36.9	339 48.4	N10 13.3	89 21.7	N17 40.9	296 24.5	S 6 52.3	Vega	80 39.2	N38 47.6
19	154 57.8	72 02.8	36.8	354 50.3	13.0	104 23.6	41.1	311 27.1	52.2	Zuben'ubi	137 05.9	S16 05.7
20	170 00.3	87 04.9	36.6	9 52.1	12.7	119 25.4	41.2	326 29.7	52.2		SHA	Mer.Pass.
21	185 02.8	102 06.9	.. 36.5	24 54.0	.. 12.3	134 27.3	.. 41.4	341 32.4	.. 52.1		° ′	h m
22	200 05.2	117 09.0	36.3	39 55.8	12.0	149 29.2	41.6	356 35.0	52.0	Venus	277 26.6	14 16
23	215 07.7	132 11.0	36.2	54 57.7	11.7	164 31.0	41.7	11 37.6	52.0	Mars	200 18.3	19 24
	h m									Jupiter	309 51.6	12 06
Mer.Pass.	8 45.8	*v* 1.9	*d* 0.1	*v* 1.9	*d* 0.3	*v* 1.9	*d* 0.2	*v* 2.6	*d* 0.1	Saturn	156 22.7	22 18

UT	SUN GHA	Dec	MOON GHA	v	Dec	d	HP
d h	° ′	° ′	° ′	′	° ′	′	′
9 00	180 53.6	N17 24.4	318 30.9	4.3	S21 18.3	2.8	60.2
01	195 53.6	25.1	332 54.2	4.4	21 15.5	3.0	60.1
02	210 53.6	25.7	347 17.6	4.5	21 12.5	3.1	60.1
03	225 53.6 ..	26.4	1 41.1	4.6	21 09.4	3.2	60.1
04	240 53.7	27.1	16 04.7	4.7	21 06.2	3.4	60.0
05	255 53.7	27.7	30 28.4	4.7	21 02.8	3.6	60.0
06	270 53.7	N17 28.4	44 52.1	4.8	S20 59.2	3.7	60.0
W 07	285 53.8	29.0	59 15.9	4.9	20 55.5	3.8	59.9
E 08	300 53.8	29.7	73 39.8	5.0	20 51.7	4.0	59.9
D 09	315 53.8 ..	30.4	88 03.8	5.0	20 47.7	4.1	59.9
N 10	330 53.8	31.0	102 27.8	5.1	20 43.6	4.2	59.8
E 11	345 53.9	31.7	116 51.9	5.3	20 39.4	4.4	59.8
S 12	0 53.9	N17 32.3	131 16.2	5.3	S20 35.0	4.5	59.8
D 13	15 53.9	33.0	145 40.5	5.4	20 30.5	4.7	59.7
A 14	30 53.9	33.6	160 04.9	5.4	20 25.8	4.7	59.7
Y 15	45 54.0 ..	34.3	174 29.3	5.6	20 21.1	5.0	59.6
16	60 54.0	35.0	188 53.9	5.7	20 16.1	5.0	59.6
17	75 54.0	35.6	203 18.6	5.7	20 11.1	5.2	59.6
18	90 54.0	N17 36.3	217 43.3	5.9	S20 05.9	5.2	59.5
19	105 54.1	36.9	232 08.2	5.9	20 00.7	5.5	59.5
20	120 54.1	37.6	246 33.1	6.0	19 55.2	5.5	59.5
21	135 54.1 ..	38.2	260 58.1	6.2	19 49.7	5.7	59.4
22	150 54.1	38.9	275 23.3	6.2	19 44.0	5.7	59.4
23	165 54.2	39.5	289 48.5	6.3	19 38.3	5.9	59.3
10 00	180 54.2	N17 40.2	304 13.8	6.4	S19 32.4	6.1	59.3
01	195 54.2	40.8	318 39.2	6.5	19 26.3	6.1	59.3
02	210 54.2	41.5	333 04.7	6.6	19 20.2	6.2	59.2
03	225 54.2 ..	42.1	347 30.3	6.7	19 14.0	6.4	59.2
04	240 54.3	42.8	1 56.0	6.8	19 07.6	6.5	59.1
05	255 54.3	43.4	16 21.8	6.9	19 01.1	6.6	59.1
06	270 54.3	N17 44.1	30 47.7	7.0	S18 54.5	6.7	59.1
T 07	285 54.3	44.7	45 13.7	7.1	18 47.8	6.8	59.0
H 08	300 54.3	45.4	59 39.8	7.2	18 41.0	6.9	59.0
U 09	315 54.4 ..	46.0	74 06.0	7.3	18 34.1	7.0	59.0
R 10	330 54.4	46.7	88 32.3	7.4	18 27.1	7.1	58.9
S 11	345 54.4	47.3	102 58.7	7.5	18 20.0	7.3	58.9
D 12	0 54.4	N17 48.0	117 25.2	7.6	S18 12.7	7.3	58.8
A 13	15 54.4	48.6	131 51.8	7.7	18 05.4	7.4	58.8
Y 14	30 54.5	49.3	146 18.5	7.8	17 58.0	7.6	58.8
15	45 54.5 ..	49.9	160 45.3	7.9	17 50.4	7.6	58.7
16	60 54.5	50.6	175 12.2	8.0	17 42.8	7.7	58.7
17	75 54.5	51.2	189 39.2	8.1	17 35.1	7.8	58.6
18	90 54.5	N17 51.8	204 06.3	8.2	S17 27.3	7.9	58.6
19	105 54.6	52.5	218 33.5	8.4	17 19.4	8.0	58.6
20	120 54.6	53.1	233 00.9	8.4	17 11.4	8.1	58.5
21	135 54.6 ..	53.8	247 28.3	8.5	17 03.3	8.2	58.5
22	150 54.6	54.4	261 55.8	8.6	16 55.1	8.2	58.4
23	165 54.6	55.0	276 23.4	8.7	16 46.9	8.4	58.4
11 00	180 54.6	N17 55.7	290 51.1	8.8	S16 38.5	8.4	58.4
01	195 54.7	56.3	305 18.9	8.9	16 30.1	8.5	58.3
02	210 54.7	57.0	319 46.8	9.0	16 21.6	8.6	58.3
03	225 54.7 ..	57.6	334 14.8	9.1	16 13.0	8.7	58.2
04	240 54.7	58.2	348 42.9	9.2	16 04.3	8.8	58.2
05	255 54.7	58.9	3 11.1	9.3	15 55.5	8.8	58.2
06	270 54.7	N17 59.5	17 39.4	9.4	S15 46.7	8.9	58.1
F 07	285 54.8	18 00.1	32 07.8	9.5	15 37.8	9.0	58.1
R 08	300 54.8	00.8	46 36.3	9.6	15 28.8	9.0	58.0
I 09	315 54.8 ..	01.4	61 04.9	9.7	15 19.8	9.2	58.0
D 10	330 54.8	02.1	75 33.6	9.7	15 10.6	9.2	58.0
A 11	345 54.8	02.7	90 02.3	9.9	15 01.4	9.2	57.9
Y 12	0 54.8	N18 03.3	104 31.2	10.0	S14 52.2	9.4	57.9
13	15 54.8	04.0	119 00.2	10.1	14 42.8	9.4	57.8
14	30 54.9	04.6	133 29.3	10.1	14 33.4	9.5	57.8
15	45 54.9 ..	05.2	147 58.4	10.3	14 23.9	9.5	57.8
16	60 54.9	05.8	162 27.7	10.3	14 14.4	9.6	57.7
17	75 54.9	06.5	176 57.0	10.5	14 04.8	9.7	57.7
18	90 54.9	N18 07.1	191 26.5	10.5	S13 55.1	9.7	57.7
19	105 54.9	07.7	205 56.0	10.6	13 45.4	9.8	57.6
20	120 54.9	08.4	220 25.6	10.8	13 35.6	9.8	57.6
21	135 54.9 ..	09.0	234 55.4	10.8	13 25.8	9.7	57.5
22	150 54.9	09.6	249 25.2	10.8	13 15.9	9.9	57.5
23	165 55.0	10.3	263 55.0	11.0	S13 06.0	10.0	57.5
	SD 15.9	d 0.6	SD 16.3		16.0		15.8

Moonrise

Lat.	Twilight Naut.	Civil	Sunrise	Moonrise 9	10	11	12
°	h m	h m	h m	h m	h m	h m	h m
N 72	▢	▢	▢	▮	▮	03 01	02 26
N 70	////	////	01 28	▮	02 51	02 19	02 04
68	////	////	02 12	01 53	01 52	01 50	01 46
66	////	00 35	02 41	00 55	01 18	01 28	01 32
64	////	01 38	03 02	00 22	00 53	01 10	01 21
62	////	02 10	03 19	24 33	00 33	00 56	01 11
60	00 31	02 34	03 34	24 17	00 17	00 43	01 02
N 58	01 27	02 53	03 46	24 03	00 03	00 33	00 54
56	01 58	03 08	03 56	23 51	24 23	00 23	00 48
54	02 20	03 21	04 05	23 41	24 15	00 15	00 42
52	02 37	03 33	04 14	23 32	24 08	00 08	00 36
50	02 52	03 43	04 21	23 23	24 01	00 01	00 31
45	03 21	04 03	04 37	23 06	23 47	24 21	00 21
N 40	03 42	04 19	04 49	22 51	23 35	24 12	00 12
35	03 59	04 33	05 00	22 39	23 25	24 04	00 04
30	04 13	04 44	05 10	22 28	23 16	23 57	24 34
20	04 35	05 02	05 26	22 09	23 00	23 46	24 27
N 10	04 52	05 18	05 40	21 53	22 47	23 35	24 20
0	05 06	05 31	05 53	21 38	22 34	23 26	24 14
S 10	05 18	05 44	06 06	21 23	22 21	23 16	24 07
20	05 30	05 56	06 19	21 07	22 08	23 06	24 00
30	05 41	06 10	06 35	20 48	21 52	22 54	23 53
35	05 47	06 17	06 44	20 37	21 43	22 47	23 48
40	05 53	06 25	06 54	20 25	21 33	22 39	23 43
45	05 59	06 34	07 06	20 10	21 20	22 30	23 37
S 50	06 06	06 45	07 20	19 52	21 06	22 19	23 30
52	06 09	06 50	07 27	19 44	20 59	22 14	23 27
54	06 12	06 55	07 34	19 34	20 51	22 08	23 23
56	06 16	07 01	07 43	19 23	20 42	22 02	23 19
58	06 19	07 07	07 52	19 11	20 32	21 54	23 15
S 60	06 23	07 15	08 03	18 56	20 21	21 46	23 09

Moonset

Lat.	Sunset	Twilight Civil	Naut.	Moonset 9	10	11	12
°	h m	h m	h m	h m	h m	h m	h m
N 72	▢	▢	▢	▮	▮	06 49	09 09
N 70	22 32	////	////	▮	05 04	07 30	09 30
68	21 45	////	////	03 58	06 02	07 58	09 46
66	21 15	23 37	////	04 55	06 36	08 19	09 59
64	20 53	22 20	////	05 29	07 00	08 36	10 09
62	20 35	21 46	////	05 53	07 19	08 50	10 18
60	20 21	21 21	23 39	06 13	07 35	09 01	10 26
N 58	20 09	21 02	22 30	06 29	07 48	09 11	10 33
56	19 58	20 46	21 58	06 42	08 00	09 20	10 39
54	19 49	20 33	21 35	06 54	08 10	09 27	10 44
52	19 40	20 21	21 17	07 05	08 19	09 34	10 49
50	19 33	20 11	21 02	07 14	08 27	09 40	10 53
45	19 17	19 51	20 33	07 34	08 43	09 54	11 02
N 40	19 04	19 34	20 11	07 49	08 57	10 05	11 10
35	18 53	19 21	19 54	08 03	09 09	10 14	11 17
30	18 43	19 09	19 40	08 14	09 19	10 22	11 22
20	18 27	18 51	19 18	08 34	09 36	10 36	11 32
N 10	18 13	18 35	19 01	08 51	09 51	10 48	11 41
0	18 00	18 22	18 47	09 07	10 05	10 59	11 49
S 10	17 47	18 09	18 34	09 23	10 19	11 10	11 57
20	17 33	17 56	18 23	09 40	10 34	11 22	12 06
30	17 18	17 43	18 12	10 00	10 51	11 36	12 15
35	17 09	17 34	18 06	10 11	11 01	11 44	12 21
40	16 58	17 27	18 00	10 24	11 12	11 52	12 27
45	16 46	17 18	17 53	10 39	11 25	12 03	12 34
S 50	16 32	17 07	17 46	10 58	11 41	12 15	12 43
52	16 25	17 02	17 43	11 07	11 49	12 21	12 47
54	16 18	16 57	17 40	11 17	11 57	12 27	12 51
56	16 09	16 51	17 36	11 28	12 06	12 34	12 56
58	16 00	16 45	17 33	11 41	12 16	12 42	13 01
S 60	15 49	16 37	17 29	11 55	12 28	12 51	13 07

Day	SUN Eqn. of Time 00h	12h	Mer. Pass.	MOON Mer. Pass. Upper	Lower	Age	Phase
d	m s	m s	h m	h m	h m	d	%
9	03 34	03 35	11 56	02 53	15 23	18	84
10	03 37	03 38	11 56	03 52	16 20	19	75
11	03 39	03 39	11 56	04 47	17 13	20	65

UT	ARIES GHA	VENUS −4.7 GHA	Dec	MARS +0.2 GHA	Dec	JUPITER −2.0 GHA	Dec	SATURN +0.4 GHA	Dec	STARS Name	SHA	Dec
12 00	230 10.2	147 13.1	N27 36.0	69 59.5	N10 11.3	179 32.9	N17 41.9	26 40.2	S 6 51.9	Acamar	315 19.3	S40 15.3
01	245 12.6	162 15.2	35.9	85 01.4	11.0	194 34.8	42.0	41 42.8	51.9	Achernar	335 27.9	S57 10.3
02	260 15.1	177 17.3	35.7	100 03.2	10.7	209 36.6	42.2	56 45.4	51.8	Acrux	173 09.7	S63 10.4
03	275 17.6	192 19.3	.. 35.5	115 05.0	.. 10.3	224 38.5	.. 42.3	71 48.0	.. 51.8	Adhara	255 13.4	S28 59.7
04	290 20.0	207 21.4	35.4	130 06.9	10.0	239 40.3	42.5	86 50.7	51.7	Aldebaran	290 50.6	N16 31.9
05	305 22.5	222 23.5	35.2	145 08.7	09.6	254 42.2	42.6	101 53.3	51.7			
06	320 25.0	237 25.6	N27 35.1	160 10.6	N10 09.3	269 44.1	N17 42.8	116 55.9	S 6 51.6	Alioth	166 20.9	N55 53.6
07	335 27.4	252 27.7	34.9	175 12.4	09.0	284 45.9	42.9	131 58.5	51.6	Alkaid	152 59.0	N49 15.1
S 08	350 29.9	267 29.8	34.7	190 14.2	08.6	299 47.8	43.1	147 01.1	51.5	Al Na'ir	27 44.7	S46 53.7
A 09	5 32.3	282 31.9	.. 34.6	205 16.1	.. 08.3	314 49.7	.. 43.2	162 03.7	.. 51.5	Alnilam	275 47.4	S 1 11.8
T 10	20 34.8	297 34.0	34.4	220 17.9	08.0	329 51.5	43.4	177 06.3	51.4	Alphard	217 56.9	S 8 43.0
U 11	35 37.3	312 36.2	34.2	235 19.7	07.6	344 53.4	43.5	192 09.0	51.4			
R 12	50 39.7	327 38.3	N27 34.1	250 21.6	N10 07.3	359 55.2	N17 43.7	207 11.6	S 6 51.3	Alphecca	126 11.3	N26 40.3
D 13	65 42.2	342 40.4	33.9	265 23.4	06.9	14 57.1	43.8	222 14.2	51.3	Alpheratz	357 44.5	N29 09.4
A 14	80 44.7	357 42.5	33.7	280 25.2	06.6	29 59.0	44.0	237 16.8	51.2	Altair	62 08.8	N 8 54.1
Y 15	95 47.1	12 44.7	.. 33.6	295 27.1	.. 06.3	45 00.8	.. 44.1	252 19.4	.. 51.2	Ankaa	353 16.7	S42 14.1
16	110 49.6	27 46.8	33.4	310 28.9	05.9	60 02.7	44.3	267 22.0	51.1	Antares	112 26.8	S26 27.5
17	125 52.1	42 48.9	33.2	325 30.7	05.6	75 04.6	44.4	282 24.6	51.1			
18	140 54.5	57 51.1	N27 33.0	340 32.6	N10 05.2	90 06.4	N17 44.6	297 27.3	S 6 51.0	Arcturus	145 56.1	N19 07.0
19	155 57.0	72 53.2	32.9	355 34.4	04.9	105 08.3	44.7	312 29.9	51.0	Atria	107 28.8	S69 02.8
20	170 59.5	87 55.4	32.7	10 36.2	04.6	120 10.1	44.9	327 32.5	50.9	Avior	234 18.6	S59 33.4
21	186 01.9	102 57.5	.. 32.5	25 38.0	.. 04.2	135 12.0	.. 45.1	342 35.1	.. 50.9	Bellatrix	278 33.1	N 6 21.5
22	201 04.4	117 59.7	32.3	40 39.9	03.9	150 13.9	45.2	357 37.7	50.8	Betelgeuse	271 02.4	N 7 24.4
23	216 06.8	133 01.9	32.2	55 41.7	03.5	165 15.7	45.4	12 40.3	50.7			
13 00	231 09.3	148 04.1	N27 32.0	70 43.5	N10 03.2	180 17.6	N17 45.5	27 42.9	S 6 50.7	Canopus	263 56.9	S52 42.5
01	246 11.8	163 06.2	31.8	85 45.4	02.9	195 19.5	45.7	42 45.5	50.6	Capella	280 36.0	N46 00.6
02	261 14.2	178 08.4	31.6	100 47.2	02.5	210 21.3	45.8	57 48.2	50.6	Deneb	49 31.9	N45 19.3
03	276 16.7	193 10.6	.. 31.4	115 49.0	.. 02.2	225 23.2	.. 46.0	72 50.8	.. 50.5	Denebola	182 34.3	N14 30.1
04	291 19.2	208 12.8	31.3	130 50.8	01.8	240 25.0	46.1	87 53.4	50.5	Diphda	348 56.9	S17 55.1
05	306 21.6	223 15.0	31.1	145 52.6	01.5	255 26.9	46.3	102 56.0	50.4			
06	321 24.1	238 17.2	N27 30.9	160 54.5	N10 01.1	270 28.8	N17 46.4	117 58.6	S 6 50.4	Dubhe	193 52.4	N61 41.2
07	336 26.6	253 19.4	30.7	175 56.3	00.8	285 30.6	46.6	133 01.2	50.3	Elnath	278 13.9	N28 37.0
08	351 29.0	268 21.6	30.5	190 58.1	00.5	300 32.5	46.7	148 03.8	50.3	Eltanin	90 46.1	N51 29.1
S 09	6 31.5	283 23.8	.. 30.3	205 59.9	10 00.1	315 34.4	.. 46.9	163 06.4	.. 50.2	Enif	33 47.9	N 9 55.9
U 10	21 33.9	298 26.0	30.1	221 01.7	9 59.8	330 36.2	47.0	178 09.1	50.2	Fomalhaut	15 24.9	S29 33.2
N 11	36 36.4	313 28.2	30.0	236 03.6	59.4	345 38.1	47.2	193 11.7	50.1			
D 12	51 38.9	328 30.5	N27 29.8	251 05.4	N 9 59.1	0 40.0	N17 47.3	208 14.3	S 6 50.1	Gacrux	172 01.4	S57 11.3
A 13	66 41.3	343 32.7	29.6	266 07.2	58.7	15 41.8	47.5	223 16.9	50.0	Gienah	175 52.9	S17 36.9
Y 14	81 43.8	358 34.9	29.4	281 09.0	58.4	30 43.7	47.6	238 19.5	50.0	Hadar	148 48.4	S60 26.1
15	96 46.3	13 37.2	.. 29.2	296 10.8	.. 58.0	45 45.5	.. 47.8	253 22.1	.. 49.9	Hamal	328 02.0	N23 31.1
16	111 48.7	28 39.4	29.0	311 12.6	57.7	60 47.4	47.9	268 24.7	49.9	Kaus Aust.	83 44.5	S34 22.5
17	126 51.2	43 41.6	28.8	326 14.5	57.3	75 49.3	48.1	283 27.3	49.8			
18	141 53.7	58 43.9	N27 28.6	341 16.3	N 9 57.0	90 51.1	N17 48.2	298 29.9	S 6 49.8	Kochab	137 18.8	N74 06.3
19	156 56.1	73 46.1	28.4	356 18.1	56.7	105 53.0	48.4	313 32.6	49.7	Markab	13 39.2	N15 16.3
20	171 58.6	88 48.4	28.2	11 19.9	56.3	120 54.9	48.5	328 35.2	49.7	Menkar	314 16.2	N 4 08.2
21	187 01.1	103 50.7	.. 28.0	26 21.7	.. 56.0	135 56.7	.. 48.7	343 37.8	.. 49.6	Menkent	148 08.1	S36 26.0
22	202 03.5	118 52.9	27.8	41 23.5	55.6	150 58.6	48.8	358 40.4	49.6	Miaplacidus	221 40.0	S69 46.5
23	217 06.0	133 55.2	27.6	56 25.3	55.3	166 00.4	49.0	13 43.0	49.5			
14 00	232 08.4	148 57.5	N27 27.4	71 27.1	N 9 54.9	181 02.3	N17 49.1	28 45.6	S 6 49.5	Mirfak	308 42.0	N49 54.2
01	247 10.9	163 59.8	27.2	86 28.9	54.6	196 04.2	49.3	43 48.2	49.4	Nunki	75 59.0	S26 16.7
02	262 13.4	179 02.1	27.0	101 30.8	54.2	211 06.0	49.4	58 50.8	49.4	Peacock	53 20.2	S56 41.3
03	277 15.8	194 04.3	.. 26.8	116 32.6	.. 53.9	226 07.9	.. 49.6	73 53.4	.. 49.3	Pollux	243 28.9	N27 59.7
04	292 18.3	209 06.6	26.6	131 34.4	53.5	241 09.7	49.7	88 56.1	49.3	Procyon	245 00.7	N 5 11.4
05	307 20.8	224 08.9	26.4	146 36.2	53.2	256 11.6	49.9	103 58.7	49.2			
06	322 23.2	239 11.2	N27 26.2	161 38.0	N 9 52.8	271 13.5	N17 50.0	119 01.3	S 6 49.2	Rasalhague	96 06.9	N12 33.0
07	337 25.7	254 13.6	26.0	176 39.8	52.5	286 15.3	50.2	134 03.9	49.1	Regulus	207 44.3	N11 54.3
08	352 28.2	269 15.9	25.7	191 41.6	52.1	301 17.2	50.3	149 06.5	49.1	Rigel	281 13.1	S 8 11.4
M 09	7 30.6	284 18.2	.. 25.5	206 43.4	.. 51.8	316 19.1	.. 50.5	164 09.1	.. 49.0	Rigil Kent.	139 52.1	S60 53.3
O 10	22 33.1	299 20.5	25.3	221 45.2	51.4	331 20.9	50.6	179 11.7	49.0	Sabik	102 13.1	S15 44.4
N 11	37 35.5	314 22.8	25.1	236 47.0	51.1	346 22.8	50.8	194 14.3	48.9			
D 12	52 38.0	329 25.2	N27 24.9	251 48.8	N 9 50.7	1 24.6	N17 50.9	209 16.9	S 6 48.9	Schedar	349 41.8	N56 36.1
A 13	67 40.5	344 27.5	24.7	266 50.6	50.4	16 26.5	51.1	224 19.5	48.8	Shaula	96 22.6	S37 06.6
Y 14	82 42.9	359 29.8	24.5	281 52.4	50.0	31 28.4	51.2	239 22.1	48.8	Sirius	258 34.6	S16 44.3
15	97 45.4	14 32.2	.. 24.2	296 54.2	.. 49.7	46 30.2	.. 51.4	254 24.8	.. 48.7	Spica	158 31.8	S11 13.7
16	112 47.9	29 34.5	24.0	311 56.0	49.3	61 32.1	51.5	269 27.4	48.7	Suhail	222 53.1	S43 29.4
17	127 50.3	44 36.9	23.8	326 57.8	48.9	76 34.0	51.7	284 30.0	48.6			
18	142 52.8	59 39.2	N27 23.6	341 59.6	N 9 48.6	91 35.8	N17 51.8	299 32.6	S 6 48.6	Vega	80 39.2	N38 47.6
19	157 55.3	74 41.6	23.4	357 01.4	48.2	106 37.7	52.0	314 35.2	48.5	Zuben'ubi	137 05.9	S16 05.7
20	172 57.7	89 44.0	23.1	12 03.2	47.9	121 39.5	52.1	329 37.8	48.5		SHA	Mer.Pass.
21	188 00.2	104 46.3	.. 22.9	27 05.0	.. 47.5	136 41.4	.. 52.3	344 40.4	.. 48.4	Venus	276 54.7	14 06
22	203 02.7	119 48.7	22.7	42 06.8	47.2	151 43.3	52.4	359 43.0	48.4	Mars	199 34.2	19 15
23	218 05.1	134 51.1	22.5	57 08.6	46.8	166 45.1	52.6	14 45.6	48.3	Jupiter	309 08.3	11 57
Mer.Pass. 8 34.0		v 2.2	d 0.2	v 1.8	d 0.3	v 1.9	d 0.2	v 2.6	d 0.1	Saturn	156 33.6	22 05

UT	SUN GHA	SUN Dec	MOON GHA	v	Dec	d	HP
d h	° ′	° ′	° ′	′	° ′	′	′
12 00	180 55.0	N18 10.9	278 25.0	11.1	S12 56.0	10.1	57.4
01	195 55.0	11.5	292 55.1	11.1	12 45.9	10.1	57.4
02	210 55.0	12.1	307 25.2	11.3	12 35.8	10.2	57.3
03	225 55.0	.. 12.8	321 55.5	11.3	12 25.6	10.2	57.3
04	240 55.0	13.4	336 25.8	11.4	12 15.4	10.2	57.3
05	255 55.0	14.0	350 56.2	11.5	12 05.2	10.3	57.2
06	270 55.0	N18 14.6	5 26.7	11.6	S11 54.9	10.4	57.2
07	285 55.0	15.3	19 57.3	11.6	11 44.5	10.4	57.2
S 08	300 55.0	15.9	34 27.9	11.8	11 34.1	10.4	57.1
A 09	315 55.1	.. 16.5	48 58.7	11.8	11 23.7	10.5	57.1
T 10	330 55.1	17.1	63 29.5	11.9	11 13.2	10.6	57.0
U 11	345 55.1	17.7	78 00.4	12.0	11 02.6	10.5	57.0
R 12	0 55.1	N18 18.4	92 31.4	12.0	S10 52.1	10.6	57.0
D 13	15 55.1	19.0	107 02.4	12.2	10 41.5	10.7	56.9
A 14	30 55.1	19.6	121 33.6	12.2	10 30.8	10.7	56.9
Y 15	45 55.1	.. 20.2	136 04.8	12.3	10 20.1	10.7	56.9
16	60 55.1	20.8	150 36.1	12.3	10 09.4	10.7	56.8
17	75 55.1	21.5	165 07.4	12.4	9 58.7	10.8	56.8
18	90 55.1	N18 22.1	179 38.8	12.5	S 9 47.9	10.8	56.8
19	105 55.1	22.7	194 10.3	12.6	9 37.1	10.9	56.7
20	120 55.1	23.3	208 41.9	12.7	9 26.2	10.9	56.7
21	135 55.1	.. 23.9	223 13.6	12.7	9 15.3	10.9	56.7
22	150 55.1	24.5	237 45.3	12.7	9 04.4	11.0	56.6
23	165 55.1	25.2	252 17.0	12.9	8 53.4	10.9	56.6
13 00	180 55.1	N18 25.8	266 48.9	12.9	S 8 42.5	11.0	56.6
01	195 55.1	26.4	281 20.8	13.0	8 31.5	11.1	56.5
02	210 55.2	27.0	295 52.8	13.0	8 20.4	11.0	56.5
03	225 55.2	.. 27.6	310 24.8	13.1	8 09.4	11.1	56.5
04	240 55.2	28.2	324 56.9	13.2	7 58.3	11.1	56.4
05	255 55.2	28.8	339 29.1	13.3	7 47.2	11.1	56.4
06	270 55.2	N18 29.4	354 01.4	13.3	S 7 36.1	11.2	56.4
07	285 55.2	30.0	8 33.7	13.3	7 24.9	11.1	56.3
S 08	300 55.2	30.7	23 06.0	13.4	7 13.8	11.2	56.3
U 09	315 55.2	.. 31.3	37 38.4	13.5	7 02.6	11.2	56.3
N 10	330 55.2	31.9	52 10.9	13.5	6 51.4	11.3	56.2
D 11	345 55.2	32.5	66 43.4	13.6	6 40.1	11.2	56.2
A 12	0 55.2	N18 33.1	81 16.0	13.7	S 6 28.9	11.3	56.2
Y 13	15 55.2	33.7	95 48.7	13.7	6 17.6	11.2	56.1
14	30 55.2	34.3	110 21.4	13.7	6 06.4	11.3	56.1
15	45 55.2	.. 34.9	124 54.1	13.8	5 55.1	11.3	56.1
16	60 55.2	35.5	139 26.9	13.9	5 43.8	11.4	56.0
17	75 55.2	36.1	153 59.8	13.9	5 32.4	11.3	56.0
18	90 55.2	N18 36.7	168 32.7	13.9	S 5 21.1	11.3	56.0
19	105 55.2	37.3	183 05.6	14.0	5 09.8	11.4	55.9
20	120 55.2	37.9	197 38.6	14.1	4 58.4	11.4	55.9
21	135 55.2	.. 38.5	212 11.7	14.1	4 47.0	11.3	55.9
22	150 55.2	39.1	226 44.8	14.1	4 35.7	11.4	55.9
23	165 55.2	39.7	241 17.9	14.2	4 24.3	11.4	55.8
14 00	180 55.2	N18 40.3	255 51.1	14.2	S 4 12.9	11.4	55.8
01	195 55.2	40.9	270 24.3	14.3	4 01.5	11.4	55.8
02	210 55.2	41.5	284 57.6	14.3	3 50.1	11.4	55.7
03	225 55.2	.. 42.1	299 30.9	14.4	3 38.7	11.4	55.7
04	240 55.2	42.7	314 04.3	14.4	3 27.3	11.4	55.7
05	255 55.2	43.3	328 37.7	14.4	3 15.9	11.4	55.7
06	270 55.2	N18 43.9	343 11.1	14.5	S 3 04.5	11.5	55.6
07	285 55.1	44.5	357 44.6	14.5	2 53.0	11.4	55.6
M 08	300 55.1	45.1	12 18.1	14.5	2 41.6	11.4	55.6
O 09	315 55.1	.. 45.7	26 51.6	14.6	2 30.2	11.4	55.5
N 10	330 55.1	46.3	41 25.2	14.6	2 18.8	11.4	55.5
D 11	345 55.1	46.9	55 58.8	14.7	2 07.4	11.5	55.5
A 12	0 55.1	N18 47.5	70 32.5	14.6	S 1 55.9	11.4	55.5
Y 13	15 55.1	48.1	85 06.1	14.7	1 44.5	11.4	55.4
14	30 55.1	48.7	99 39.8	14.8	1 33.1	11.4	55.4
15	45 55.1	.. 49.3	114 13.6	14.8	1 21.7	11.4	55.4
16	60 55.1	49.9	128 47.4	14.8	1 10.3	11.4	55.4
17	75 55.1	50.5	143 21.2	14.8	0 58.9	11.4	55.3
18	90 55.1	N18 51.1	157 55.0	14.8	S 0 47.5	11.4	55.3
19	105 55.1	51.7	172 28.8	14.9	0 36.1	11.4	55.3
20	120 55.1	52.3	187 02.7	14.9	0 24.7	11.4	55.3
21	135 55.1	.. 52.8	201 36.6	14.9	0 13.3	11.3	55.2
22	150 55.1	53.4	216 10.5	15.0	S 0 02.0	11.4	55.2
23	165 55.1	54.0	230 44.5	15.0	N 0 09.4	11.3	55.2
	SD 15.9	d 0.6	SD 15.5		15.3		15.1

Lat.	Twilight Naut.	Twilight Civil	Sunrise	Moonrise 12	13	14	15
°	h m	h m	h m	h m	h m	h m	h m
N 72	▭	▭	▭	02 26	02 05	01 49	01 35
N 70	////	////	01 01	02 04	01 53	01 44	01 36
68	////	////	01 56	01 46	01 43	01 40	01 36
66	////	////	02 29	01 32	01 35	01 36	01 37
64	////	01 19	02 52	01 21	01 27	01 33	01 37
62	////	01 58	03 11	01 11	01 21	01 30	01 38
60	////	02 24	03 26	01 02	01 16	01 27	01 38
N 58	01 11	02 45	03 39	00 54	01 11	01 25	01 38
56	01 47	03 01	03 50	00 48	01 07	01 23	01 38
54	02 11	03 15	04 00	00 42	01 03	01 22	01 39
52	02 30	03 27	04 09	00 36	01 00	01 20	01 39
50	02 46	03 37	04 16	00 31	00 56	01 19	01 39
45	03 16	03 59	04 33	00 21	00 50	01 15	01 40
N 40	03 38	04 16	04 46	00 12	00 44	01 13	01 40
35	03 56	04 30	04 58	00 04	00 39	01 10	01 40
30	04 10	04 42	05 08	24 34	00 34	01 08	01 41
20	04 33	05 01	05 25	24 27	00 27	01 05	01 41
N 10	04 51	05 17	05 39	24 20	00 20	01 02	01 42
0	05 06	05 31	05 53	24 14	00 14	00 59	01 42
S 10	05 19	05 44	06 06	24 07	00 07	00 56	01 43
20	05 31	05 57	06 21	24 00	00 00	00 53	01 43
30	05 43	06 11	06 37	23 53	24 49	00 49	01 44
35	05 49	06 19	06 46	23 48	24 47	00 47	01 44
40	05 55	06 28	06 57	23 43	24 45	00 45	01 45
45	06 02	06 37	07 09	23 37	24 42	00 42	01 45
S 50	06 10	06 49	07 24	23 30	24 39	00 39	01 46
52	06 13	06 54	07 32	23 27	24 37	00 37	01 46
54	06 16	07 00	07 39	23 23	24 36	00 36	01 46
56	06 20	07 06	07 48	23 19	24 34	00 34	01 47
58	06 24	07 13	07 58	23 15	24 32	00 32	01 47
S 60	06 29	07 21	08 10	23 09	24 30	00 30	01 47

Lat.	Sunset	Twilight Civil	Twilight Naut.	Moonset 12	13	14	15
°	h m	h m	h m	h m	h m	h m	h m
N 72	▭	▭	▭	09 09	11 08	12 56	14 41
N 70	23 03	////	////	09 30	11 18	12 59	14 37
68	22 01	////	////	09 46	11 26	13 01	14 33
66	21 27	////	////	09 59	11 33	13 03	14 30
64	21 03	22 39	////	10 09	11 39	13 05	14 28
62	20 44	21 58	////	10 18	11 44	13 06	14 26
60	20 28	21 31	////	10 26	11 48	13 07	14 24
N 58	20 15	21 10	22 47	10 33	11 52	13 08	14 22
56	20 04	20 53	22 09	10 39	11 55	13 09	14 21
54	19 54	20 39	21 44	10 44	11 58	13 10	14 20
52	19 45	20 27	21 24	10 49	12 01	13 10	14 18
50	19 37	20 16	21 08	10 53	12 03	13 11	14 17
45	19 20	19 55	20 38	11 02	12 09	13 13	14 15
N 40	19 07	19 37	20 15	11 10	12 13	13 14	14 13
35	18 55	19 23	19 57	11 17	12 17	13 15	14 11
30	18 45	19 11	19 43	11 22	12 20	13 16	14 10
20	18 28	18 52	19 20	11 32	12 26	13 17	14 07
N 10	18 14	18 36	19 02	11 41	12 31	13 19	14 05
0	18 00	18 22	18 47	11 49	12 36	13 20	14 03
S 10	17 46	18 08	18 34	11 57	12 40	13 21	14 00
20	17 32	17 55	18 22	12 06	12 45	13 22	13 58
30	17 16	17 41	18 10	12 15	12 51	13 24	13 56
35	17 06	17 33	18 04	12 21	12 54	13 24	13 54
40	16 55	17 24	17 57	12 27	12 57	13 25	13 52
45	16 43	17 15	17 50	12 34	13 01	13 26	13 50
S 50	16 28	17 03	17 43	12 43	13 06	13 28	13 48
52	16 21	16 58	17 39	12 47	13 09	13 28	13 47
54	16 13	16 52	17 36	12 51	13 11	13 29	13 46
56	16 04	16 46	17 32	12 56	13 14	13 29	13 44
58	15 54	16 39	17 28	13 01	13 17	13 30	13 43
S 60	15 42	16 31	17 23	13 07	13 20	13 31	13 41

	SUN			MOON			
Day	Eqn. of Time 00h	12h	Mer. Pass.	Mer. Pass. Upper	Lower	Age	Phase
d	m s	m s	h m	h m	h m	d	%
12	03 40	03 40	11 56	05 37	18 01	21	54
13	03 41	03 41	11 56	06 25	18 47	22	44
14	03 41	03 41	11 56	07 09	19 31	23	34

UT	ARIES GHA	VENUS −4.6 GHA	Dec	MARS +0.3 GHA	Dec	JUPITER −2.0 GHA	Dec	SATURN +0.4 GHA	Dec	STARS Name	SHA	Dec
15 00	233 07.6	149 53.5	N27 22.2	72 10.3	N 9 46.5	181 47.0	N17 52.7	29 48.2	S 6 48.3	Acamar	315 19.3	S40 15.3
01	248 10.0	164 55.9	22.0	87 12.1	46.1	196 48.8	52.9	44 50.8	48.2	Achernar	335 27.8	S57 10.3
02	263 12.5	179 58.2	21.8	102 13.9	45.8	211 50.7	53.0	59 53.4	48.2	Acrux	173 09.7	S63 10.4
03	278 15.0	195 00.6 ..	21.6	117 15.7 ..	45.4	226 52.6 ..	53.2	74 56.1 ..	48.1	Adhara	255 13.4	S28 59.6
04	293 17.4	210 03.0	21.3	132 17.5	45.1	241 54.4	53.3	89 58.7	48.1	Aldebaran	290 50.6	N16 31.9
05	308 19.9	225 05.5	21.1	147 19.3	44.7	256 56.3	53.5	105 01.3	48.0			
06	323 22.4	240 07.9	N27 20.9	162 21.1	N 9 44.3	271 58.2	N17 53.6	120 03.9	S 6 48.0	Alioth	166 20.9	N55 53.6
T 07	338 24.8	255 10.3	20.6	177 22.9	44.0	287 00.0	53.8	135 06.5	47.9	Alkaid	152 59.1	N49 15.1
U 08	353 27.3	270 12.7	20.4	192 24.7	43.6	302 01.9	53.9	150 09.1	47.9	Al Na'ir	27 44.7	S46 53.7
E 09	8 29.8	285 15.1 ..	20.2	207 26.4 ..	43.3	317 03.7 ..	54.1	165 11.7 ..	47.8	Alnilam	275 47.4	S 1 11.8
S 10	23 32.2	300 17.6	19.9	222 28.2	42.9	332 05.6	54.2	180 14.3	47.8	Alphard	217 56.9	S 8 43.0
D 11	38 34.7	315 20.0	19.7	237 30.0	42.6	347 07.5	54.4	195 16.9	47.7			
A 12	53 37.2	330 22.4	N27 19.4	252 31.8	N 9 42.2	2 09.3	N17 54.5	210 19.5	S 6 47.7	Alphecca	126 11.3	N26 40.4
Y 13	68 39.6	345 24.9	19.2	267 33.6	41.8	17 11.2	54.7	225 22.1	47.6	Alpheratz	357 44.5	N29 09.4
14	83 42.1	0 27.3	19.0	282 35.4	41.5	32 13.1	54.8	240 24.7	47.6	Altair	62 08.8	N 8 54.1
15	98 44.5	15 29.8 ..	18.7	297 37.1 ..	41.1	47 14.9 ..	55.0	255 27.3 ..	47.6	Ankaa	353 16.7	S42 14.1
16	113 47.0	30 32.2	18.5	312 38.9	40.8	62 16.8	55.1	270 29.9	47.5	Antares	112 26.8	S26 27.5
17	128 49.5	45 34.7	18.2	327 40.7	40.4	77 18.6	55.3	285 32.6	47.5			
18	143 51.9	60 37.1	N27 18.0	342 42.5	N 9 40.0	92 20.5	N17 55.4	300 35.2	S 6 47.4	Arcturus	145 56.1	N19 07.0
19	158 54.4	75 39.6	17.7	357 44.3	39.7	107 22.4	55.6	315 37.8	47.4	Atria	107 28.8	S69 02.8
20	173 56.9	90 42.1	17.5	12 46.0	39.3	122 24.2	55.7	330 40.4	47.3	Avior	234 18.6	S59 33.4
21	188 59.3	105 44.6 ..	17.2	27 47.8 ..	39.0	137 26.1 ..	55.9	345 43.0 ..	47.3	Bellatrix	278 33.1	N 6 21.5
22	204 01.8	120 47.1	17.0	42 49.6	38.6	152 27.9	56.0	0 45.6	47.2	Betelgeuse	271 02.4	N 7 24.4
23	219 04.3	135 49.5	16.8	57 51.4	38.2	167 29.8	56.2	15 48.2	47.2			
16 00	234 06.7	150 52.0	N27 16.5	72 53.1	N 9 37.9	182 31.7	N17 56.3	30 50.8	S 6 47.1	Canopus	263 56.9	S52 42.5
01	249 09.2	165 54.5	16.2	87 54.9	37.5	197 33.5	56.5	45 53.4	47.1	Capella	280 36.0	N46 00.5
02	264 11.6	180 57.0	16.0	102 56.7	37.2	212 35.4	56.6	60 56.0	47.0	Deneb	49 31.9	N45 19.3
03	279 14.1	195 59.5 ..	15.7	117 58.5 ..	36.8	227 37.3 ..	56.8	75 58.6 ..	47.0	Denebola	182 34.3	N14 30.1
04	294 16.6	211 02.0	15.5	133 00.2	36.4	242 39.1	56.9	91 01.2	46.9	Diphda	348 56.9	S17 55.0
05	309 19.0	226 04.6	15.2	148 02.0	36.1	257 41.0	57.1	106 03.8	46.9			
06	324 21.5	241 07.1	N27 15.0	163 03.8	N 9 35.7	272 42.8	N17 57.2	121 06.4	S 6 46.8	Dubhe	193 52.4	N61 41.2
W 07	339 24.0	256 09.6	14.7	178 05.6	35.3	287 44.7	57.4	136 09.0	46.8	Elnath	278 13.9	N28 37.0
E 08	354 26.4	271 12.1	14.5	193 07.3	35.0	302 46.6	57.5	151 11.6	46.7	Eltanin	90 46.0	N51 29.2
D 09	9 28.9	286 14.7 ..	14.2	208 09.1 ..	34.6	317 48.4 ..	57.7	166 14.2 ..	46.7	Enif	33 47.9	N 9 55.9
N 10	24 31.4	301 17.2	13.9	223 10.9	34.3	332 50.3	57.8	181 16.8	46.6	Fomalhaut	15 24.9	S29 33.2
E 11	39 33.8	316 19.7	13.7	238 12.6	33.9	347 52.1	58.0	196 19.5	46.6			
S 12	54 36.3	331 22.3	N27 13.4	253 14.4	N 9 33.5	2 54.0	N17 58.1	211 22.1	S 6 46.5	Gacrux	172 01.4	S57 11.3
D 13	69 38.8	346 24.8	13.1	268 16.2	33.2	17 55.9	58.3	226 24.7	46.5	Gienah	175 52.9	S17 36.9
A 14	84 41.2	1 27.4	12.9	283 17.9	32.8	32 57.7	58.4	241 27.3	46.5	Hadar	148 48.4	S60 26.1
Y 15	99 43.7	16 30.0 ..	12.6	298 19.7 ..	32.4	47 59.6 ..	58.6	256 29.9 ..	46.4	Hamal	328 01.9	N23 31.1
16	114 46.1	31 32.5	12.3	313 21.5	32.1	63 01.4	58.7	271 32.5	46.4	Kaus Aust.	83 44.5	S34 22.5
17	129 48.6	46 35.1	12.1	328 23.2	31.7	78 03.3	58.9	286 35.1	46.3			
18	144 51.1	61 37.7	N27 11.8	343 25.0	N 9 31.3	93 05.2	N17 59.0	301 37.7	S 6 46.3	Kochab	137 18.8	N74 06.3
19	159 53.5	76 40.3	11.5	358 26.8	31.0	108 07.0	59.2	316 40.3	46.2	Markab	13 39.2	N15 16.3
20	174 56.0	91 42.8	11.3	13 28.5	30.6	123 08.9	59.3	331 42.9	46.2	Menkar	314 16.2	N 4 08.2
21	189 58.5	106 45.4 ..	11.0	28 30.3 ..	30.2	138 10.8 ..	59.5	346 45.5 ..	46.1	Menkent	148 08.1	S36 26.0
22	205 00.9	121 48.0	10.7	43 32.0	29.9	153 12.6	59.6	1 48.1	46.1	Miaplacidus	221 40.0	S69 46.5
23	220 03.4	136 50.6	10.4	58 33.8	29.5	168 14.5	59.8	16 50.7	46.0			
17 00	235 05.9	151 53.2	N27 10.2	73 35.6	N 9 29.1	183 16.3	N17 59.9	31 53.3	S 6 46.0	Mirfak	308 42.0	N49 54.2
01	250 08.3	166 55.8	09.9	88 37.3	28.8	198 18.2	18 00.1	46 55.9	45.9	Nunki	75 59.0	S26 16.7
02	265 10.8	181 58.4	09.6	103 39.1	28.4	213 20.1	00.2	61 58.5	45.9	Peacock	53 20.2	S56 41.3
03	280 13.2	197 01.0 ..	09.3	118 40.8 ..	28.0	228 21.9 ..	00.4	77 01.1 ..	45.8	Pollux	243 28.9	N27 59.7
04	295 15.7	212 03.7	09.1	133 42.6	27.7	243 23.8	00.5	92 03.7	45.8	Procyon	245 00.7	N 5 11.4
05	310 18.2	227 06.3	08.8	148 44.4	27.3	258 25.6	00.6	107 06.3	45.7			
06	325 20.6	242 08.9	N27 08.5	163 46.1	N 9 26.9	273 27.5	N18 00.8	122 08.9	S 6 45.7	Rasalhague	96 06.9	N12 33.1
T 07	340 23.1	257 11.6	08.2	178 47.9	26.6	288 29.4	00.9	137 11.5	45.7	Regulus	207 44.3	N11 54.3
H 08	355 25.6	272 14.2	07.9	193 49.6	26.2	303 31.2	01.1	152 14.1	45.6	Rigel	281 13.1	S 8 11.4
U 09	10 28.0	287 16.8 ..	07.6	208 51.4 ..	25.8	318 33.1 ..	01.2	167 16.7 ..	45.6	Rigil Kent.	139 52.1	S60 53.3
R 10	25 30.5	302 19.5	07.4	223 53.1	25.5	333 34.9	01.4	182 19.3	45.5	Sabik	102 13.1	S15 44.4
S 11	40 33.0	317 22.1	07.1	238 54.9	25.1	348 36.8	01.5	197 21.9	45.5			
D 12	55 35.4	332 24.8	N27 06.8	253 56.6	N 9 24.7	3 38.7	N18 01.7	212 24.5	S 6 45.4	Schedar	349 41.8	N56 36.1
A 13	70 37.9	347 27.5	06.5	268 58.4	24.3	18 40.5	01.8	227 27.1	45.4	Shaula	96 22.6	S37 06.6
Y 14	85 40.4	2 30.1	06.2	284 00.1	24.0	33 42.4	02.0	242 29.7	45.3	Sirius	258 34.6	S16 44.3
15	100 42.8	17 32.8 ..	05.9	299 01.9 ..	23.6	48 44.3 ..	02.1	257 32.3 ..	45.3	Spica	158 31.8	S11 13.7
16	115 45.3	32 35.5	05.6	314 03.6	23.2	63 46.1	02.3	272 34.9	45.2	Suhail	222 53.1	S43 29.4
17	130 47.7	47 38.1	05.3	329 05.4	22.9	78 48.0	02.4	287 37.5	45.2			
18	145 50.2	62 40.8	N27 05.0	344 07.1	N 9 22.5	93 49.8	N18 02.6	302 40.1	S 6 45.1	Vega	80 39.2	N38 47.6
19	160 52.7	77 43.5	04.7	359 08.9	22.1	108 51.7	02.7	317 42.7	45.1	Zuben'ubi	137 05.9	S16 05.7
20	175 55.1	92 46.2	04.4	14 10.6	21.7	123 53.6	02.9	332 45.3	45.1		SHA	Mer.Pass.
21	190 57.6	107 48.9 ..	04.1	29 12.4 ..	21.4	138 55.4 ..	03.0	347 47.9 ..	45.0			h m
22	206 00.1	122 51.6	03.8	44 14.1	21.0	153 57.3	03.2	2 50.5	45.0	Venus	276 45.3	13 54
23	221 02.5	137 54.3	03.5	59 15.9	20.6	168 59.1	03.3	17 53.1	44.9	Mars	198 46.4	19 06
	h m									Jupiter	308 24.9	11 48
Mer. Pass. 8 22.2	v 2.5 d 0.3	v 1.8	d 0.4	v 1.9	d 0.1	v 2.6	d 0.0			Saturn	156 44.1	21 53

UT	SUN GHA	SUN Dec	MOON GHA	v	MOON Dec	d	HP
d h	° ′	° ′	° ′	′	° ′	′	′
15 00	180 55.0	N18 54.6	245 18.5	15.0	N 0 20.7	11.4	55.2
01	195 55.0	55.2	259 52.5	15.0	0 32.1	11.3	55.1
02	210 55.0	55.8	274 26.5	15.0	0 43.4	11.3	55.1
03	225 55.0	.. 56.4	289 00.5	15.1	0 54.7	11.3	55.1
04	240 55.0	57.0	303 34.6	15.0	1 06.0	11.3	55.1
05	255 55.0	57.5	318 08.6	15.1	1 17.3	11.3	55.1
T 06	270 55.0	N18 58.1	332 42.7	15.1	N 1 28.6	11.3	55.0
U 07	285 55.0	58.7	347 16.8	15.1	1 39.9	11.2	55.0
E 08	300 55.0	59.3	1 50.9	15.2	1 51.1	11.2	55.0
S 09	315 55.0	18 59.9	16 25.1	15.1	2 02.3	11.3	55.0
D 10	330 55.0	19 00.5	30 59.2	15.2	2 13.6	11.2	54.9
A 11	345 54.9	01.0	45 33.4	15.1	2 24.8	11.1	54.9
Y 12	0 54.9	N19 01.6	60 07.5	15.2	N 2 35.9	11.2	54.9
13	15 54.9	02.2	74 41.7	15.2	2 47.1	11.1	54.9
14	30 54.9	02.8	89 15.9	15.2	2 58.2	11.2	54.9
15	45 54.9	.. 03.4	103 50.1	15.2	3 09.4	11.1	54.8
16	60 54.9	03.9	118 24.3	15.2	3 20.5	11.1	54.8
17	75 54.9	04.5	132 58.5	15.2	3 31.6	11.0	54.8
18	90 54.9	N19 05.1	147 32.7	15.2	N 3 42.6	11.1	54.8
19	105 54.9	05.7	162 06.9	15.3	3 53.7	11.0	54.8
20	120 54.8	06.2	176 41.2	15.2	4 04.7	11.0	54.7
21	135 54.8	.. 06.8	191 15.4	15.2	4 15.7	11.0	54.7
22	150 54.8	07.4	205 49.6	15.3	4 26.7	10.9	54.7
23	165 54.8	08.0	220 23.9	15.2	4 37.6	10.9	54.7
16 00	180 54.8	N19 08.5	234 58.1	15.3	N 4 48.5	10.9	54.7
01	195 54.8	09.1	249 32.4	15.2	4 59.4	10.9	54.7
02	210 54.8	09.7	264 06.6	15.2	5 10.3	10.9	54.6
03	225 54.7	.. 10.3	278 40.8	15.3	5 21.2	10.8	54.6
04	240 54.7	10.8	293 15.1	15.2	5 32.0	10.8	54.6
05	255 54.7	11.4	307 49.3	15.2	5 42.8	10.7	54.6
W 06	270 54.7	N19 12.0	322 23.5	15.3	N 5 53.5	10.8	54.6
E 07	285 54.7	12.6	336 57.8	15.2	6 04.3	10.7	54.6
D 08	300 54.7	13.1	351 32.0	15.2	6 15.0	10.6	54.5
N 09	315 54.6	.. 13.7	6 06.2	15.2	6 25.6	10.7	54.5
E 10	330 54.6	14.3	20 40.4	15.2	6 36.3	10.6	54.5
S 11	345 54.6	14.8	35 14.6	15.2	6 46.9	10.6	54.5
D 12	0 54.6	N19 15.4	49 48.8	15.2	N 6 57.5	10.5	54.5
A 13	15 54.6	16.0	64 23.0	15.2	7 08.0	10.5	54.5
Y 14	30 54.6	16.5	78 57.2	15.2	7 18.5	10.5	54.5
15	45 54.5	.. 17.1	93 31.4	15.1	7 29.0	10.4	54.4
16	60 54.5	17.7	108 05.5	15.2	7 39.4	10.4	54.4
17	75 54.5	18.2	122 39.7	15.1	7 49.8	10.4	54.4
18	90 54.5	N19 18.8	137 13.8	15.2	N 8 00.2	10.3	54.4
19	105 54.5	19.4	151 48.0	15.1	8 10.5	10.3	54.4
20	120 54.5	19.9	166 22.1	15.1	8 20.8	10.3	54.4
21	135 54.4	.. 20.5	180 56.2	15.1	8 31.1	10.2	54.4
22	150 54.4	21.0	195 30.3	15.0	8 41.3	10.2	54.3
23	165 54.4	21.6	210 04.3	15.1	8 51.5	10.1	54.3
17 00	180 54.4	N19 22.2	224 38.4	15.0	N 9 01.6	10.1	54.3
01	195 54.4	22.7	239 12.4	15.0	9 11.7	10.1	54.3
02	210 54.3	23.3	253 46.4	15.1	9 21.8	10.0	54.3
03	225 54.3	.. 23.8	268 20.5	14.9	9 31.8	10.0	54.3
04	240 54.3	24.4	282 54.4	15.0	9 41.8	9.9	54.3
05	255 54.3	25.0	297 28.4	15.0	9 51.7	9.9	54.3
T 06	270 54.2	N19 25.5	312 02.4	14.9	N10 01.6	9.9	54.3
H 07	285 54.2	26.1	326 36.3	14.9	10 11.5	9.8	54.2
U 08	300 54.2	26.6	341 10.2	14.9	10 21.3	9.7	54.2
R 09	315 54.2	.. 27.2	355 44.1	14.8	10 31.0	9.8	54.2
S 10	330 54.2	27.7	10 17.9	14.9	10 40.8	9.6	54.2
D 11	345 54.1	28.3	24 51.8	14.8	10 50.4	9.7	54.2
A 12	0 54.1	N19 28.9	39 25.6	14.8	N11 00.1	9.5	54.2
Y 13	15 54.1	29.4	53 59.4	14.8	11 09.6	9.6	54.2
14	30 54.1	30.0	68 33.2	14.7	11 19.2	9.4	54.2
15	45 54.0	.. 30.5	83 06.9	14.7	11 28.6	9.5	54.2
16	60 54.0	31.1	97 40.6	14.7	11 38.1	9.3	54.2
17	75 54.0	31.6	112 14.3	14.7	11 47.4	9.4	54.1
18	90 54.0	N19 32.2	126 48.0	14.6	N11 56.8	9.2	54.1
19	105 53.9	32.7	141 21.6	14.7	12 06.0	9.3	54.1
20	120 53.9	33.3	155 55.3	14.6	12 15.3	9.1	54.1
21	135 53.9	.. 33.8	170 28.9	14.5	12 24.4	9.2	54.1
22	150 53.9	34.4	185 02.4	14.6	12 33.6	9.0	54.1
23	165 53.8	34.9	199 36.0	14.5	N12 42.6	9.0	54.1
	SD 15.8	d 0.6	SD 15.0		14.8		14.8

Lat.	Twilight Naut.	Twilight Civil	Sunrise	Moonrise 15	16	17	18
°	h m	h m	h m	h m	h m	h m	h m
N 72	▭	▭	▭	01 35	01 21	01 05	00 46
N 70	////	////	00 08	01 36	01 27	01 19	01 09
68	////	////	01 39	01 36	01 33	01 30	01 27
66	////	////	02 17	01 37	01 38	01 39	01 41
64	////	00 58	02 43	01 37	01 42	01 47	01 53
62	////	01 45	03 03	01 38	01 45	01 53	02 03
60	////	02 15	03 19	01 38	01 48	01 59	02 12
N 58	00 52	02 37	03 33	01 38	01 51	02 04	02 20
56	01 35	02 54	03 45	01 38	01 53	02 09	02 27
54	02 02	03 09	03 55	01 39	01 56	02 13	02 33
52	02 23	03 22	04 04	01 39	01 58	02 17	02 38
50	02 40	03 33	04 12	01 39	01 59	02 20	02 44
45	03 11	03 55	04 30	01 40	02 03	02 28	02 54
N 40	03 35	04 13	04 44	01 40	02 07	02 34	03 03
35	03 53	04 27	04 55	01 40	02 10	02 40	03 11
30	04 08	04 40	05 06	01 41	02 12	02 44	03 18
20	04 32	05 00	05 23	01 41	02 17	02 53	03 30
N 10	04 50	05 16	05 39	01 42	02 21	03 00	03 41
0	05 05	05 31	05 53	01 42	02 25	03 07	03 51
S 10	05 19	05 45	06 07	01 43	02 28	03 14	04 01
20	05 32	05 58	06 22	01 43	02 33	03 22	04 11
30	05 44	06 13	06 39	01 44	02 37	03 30	04 23
35	05 51	06 21	06 48	01 44	02 40	03 35	04 31
40	05 57	06 30	07 00	01 45	02 43	03 41	04 39
45	06 05	06 41	07 13	01 45	02 47	03 48	04 48
S 50	06 13	06 53	07 29	01 46	02 51	03 56	05 00
52	06 17	06 58	07 36	01 46	02 53	04 00	05 05
54	06 20	07 04	07 44	01 46	02 55	04 04	05 11
56	06 25	07 11	07 54	01 47	02 58	04 08	05 18
58	06 29	07 18	08 04	01 47	03 01	04 13	05 25
S 60	06 34	07 26	08 16	01 47	03 04	04 19	05 34

Lat.	Sunset	Twilight Civil	Twilight Naut.	Moonset 15	16	17	18
°	h m	h m	h m	h m	h m	h m	h m
N 72	▭	▭	▭	14 41	16 26	18 15	20 17
N 70	▭	▭	▭	14 37	16 14	17 53	19 37
68	22 19	////	////	14 33	16 05	17 37	19 10
66	21 39	////	////	14 30	15 57	17 23	18 50
64	21 12	23 03	////	14 28	15 50	17 12	18 34
62	20 52	22 11	////	14 26	15 45	17 03	18 20
60	20 35	21 41	////	14 24	15 40	16 55	18 09
N 58	20 21	21 18	23 08	14 22	15 35	16 48	17 59
56	20 09	21 00	22 21	14 21	15 32	16 42	17 51
54	19 59	20 45	21 53	14 20	15 28	16 36	17 43
52	19 50	20 32	21 32	14 18	15 25	16 31	17 36
50	19 41	20 21	21 15	14 17	15 22	16 27	17 30
45	19 24	19 58	20 42	14 15	15 16	16 17	17 17
N 40	19 10	19 41	20 19	14 13	15 11	16 09	17 06
35	18 58	19 26	20 00	14 11	15 07	16 02	16 57
30	18 47	19 14	19 45	14 10	15 03	15 56	16 49
20	18 29	18 53	19 21	14 07	14 56	15 46	16 35
N 10	18 14	18 37	19 03	14 05	14 51	15 37	16 23
0	18 00	18 22	18 47	14 03	14 45	15 28	16 12
S 10	17 46	18 08	18 34	14 00	14 40	15 19	16 01
20	17 31	17 54	18 21	13 58	14 34	15 10	15 49
30	17 14	17 39	18 08	13 56	14 27	15 00	15 35
35	17 04	17 31	18 02	13 54	14 24	14 54	15 27
40	16 53	17 22	17 55	13 52	14 19	14 48	15 18
45	16 40	17 12	17 47	13 50	14 14	14 40	15 08
S 50	16 24	17 00	17 39	13 48	14 09	14 30	14 55
52	16 16	16 54	17 36	13 47	14 06	14 26	14 49
54	16 08	16 48	17 32	13 46	14 03	14 21	14 43
56	15 59	16 41	17 28	13 44	14 00	14 16	14 35
58	15 48	16 34	17 23	13 43	13 56	14 10	14 27
S 60	15 36	16 26	17 18	13 41	13 52	14 04	14 18

	SUN			MOON			
Day	Eqn. of Time 00ʰ	12ʰ	Mer. Pass.	Mer. Pass. Upper	Lower	Age	Phase
d	m s	m s	h m	h m	h m	d	%
15	03 40	03 40	11 56	07 52	20 14	24	25
16	03 39	03 38	11 56	08 35	20 56	25	17
17	03 38	03 37	11 56	09 18	21 39	26	11

UT	ARIES GHA	VENUS −4.5 GHA	Dec	MARS +0.3 GHA	Dec	JUPITER −2.0 GHA	Dec	SATURN +0.4 GHA	Dec	STARS Name	SHA	Dec
18 00	236 05.0	152 57.0	N27 03.2	74 17.6	N 9 20.3	184 01.0	N18 03.5	32 55.7	S 6 44.9	Acamar	315 19.3	S40 15.3
01	251 07.5	167 59.8	02.9	89 19.3	19.9	199 02.9	03.6	47 58.3	44.8	Achernar	335 27.8	S57 10.3
02	266 09.9	183 02.5	02.6	104 21.1	19.5	214 04.7	03.7	63 00.9	44.8	Acrux	173 09.7	S63 10.4
03	281 12.4	198 05.2	.. 02.3	119 22.8	.. 19.1	229 06.6	.. 03.9	78 03.5	.. 44.7	Adhara	255 13.4	S28 59.6
04	296 14.9	213 07.9	02.0	134 24.6	18.8	244 08.4	04.0	93 06.1	44.7	Aldebaran	290 50.6	N16 31.9
05	311 17.3	228 10.7	01.7	149 26.3	18.4	259 10.3	04.2	108 08.7	44.6			
06	326 19.8	243 13.4	N27 01.4	164 28.1	N 9 18.0	274 12.2	N18 04.3	123 11.3	S 6 44.6	Alioth	166 20.9	N55 53.6
07	341 22.2	258 16.2	01.1	179 29.8	17.6	289 14.0	04.5	138 13.9	44.5	Alkaid	152 59.1	N49 15.1
F 08	356 24.7	273 18.9	00.8	194 31.5	17.3	304 15.9	04.6	153 16.5	44.5	Al Na'ir	27 44.7	S46 53.7
R 09	11 27.2	288 21.7	.. 00.5	209 33.3	.. 16.9	319 17.8	.. 04.8	168 19.1	.. 44.5	Alnilam	275 47.4	S 1 11.8
I 10	26 29.6	303 24.4	27 00.2	224 35.0	16.5	334 19.6	04.9	183 21.7	44.4	Alphard	217 56.9	S 8 43.0
D 11	41 32.1	318 27.2	26 59.8	239 36.7	16.1	349 21.5	05.1	198 24.3	44.4			
A 12	56 34.6	333 29.9	N26 59.5	254 38.5	N 9 15.8	4 23.3	N18 05.2	213 26.9	S 6 44.3	Alphecca	126 11.3	N26 40.4
Y 13	71 37.0	348 32.7	59.2	269 40.2	15.4	19 25.2	05.4	228 29.5	44.3	Alpheratz	357 44.5	N29 09.4
14	86 39.5	3 35.5	58.9	284 42.0	15.0	34 27.1	05.5	243 32.1	44.2	Altair	62 08.8	N 8 54.1
15	101 42.0	18 38.3	.. 58.6	299 43.7	.. 14.6	49 28.9	.. 05.7	258 34.7	.. 44.2	Ankaa	353 16.7	S42 14.1
16	116 44.4	33 41.1	58.3	314 45.4	14.2	64 30.8	05.8	273 37.3	44.1	Antares	112 26.8	S26 27.5
17	131 46.9	48 43.9	57.9	329 47.2	13.9	79 32.6	06.0	288 39.9	44.1			
18	146 49.3	63 46.6	N26 57.6	344 48.9	N 9 13.5	94 34.5	N18 06.1	303 42.5	S 6 44.1	Arcturus	145 56.1	N19 07.0
19	161 51.8	78 49.4	57.3	359 50.6	13.1	109 36.4	06.2	318 45.1	44.0	Atria	107 28.8	S69 02.9
20	176 54.3	93 52.3	57.0	14 52.4	12.7	124 38.2	06.4	333 47.7	44.0	Avior	234 18.6	S59 33.4
21	191 56.7	108 55.1	.. 56.6	29 54.1	.. 12.4	139 40.1	.. 06.5	348 50.3	.. 43.9	Bellatrix	278 33.1	N 6 21.5
22	206 59.2	123 57.9	56.3	44 55.8	12.0	154 41.9	06.7	3 52.9	43.9	Betelgeuse	271 02.4	N 7 24.4
23	222 01.7	139 00.7	56.0	59 57.5	11.6	169 43.8	06.8	18 55.5	43.8			
19 00	237 04.1	154 03.5	N26 55.7	74 59.3	N 9 11.2	184 45.7	N18 07.0	33 58.1	S 6 43.8	Canopus	263 56.9	S52 42.4
01	252 06.6	169 06.3	55.3	90 01.0	10.8	199 47.5	07.1	49 00.7	43.7	Capella	280 36.0	N46 00.5
02	267 09.1	184 09.2	55.0	105 02.7	10.5	214 49.4	07.3	64 03.3	43.7	Deneb	49 31.8	N45 19.3
03	282 11.5	199 12.0	.. 54.7	120 04.5	.. 10.1	229 51.3	.. 07.4	79 05.9	.. 43.7	Denebola	182 34.3	N14 30.1
04	297 14.0	214 14.9	54.3	135 06.2	09.7	244 53.1	07.6	94 08.5	43.6	Diphda	348 56.9	S17 55.0
05	312 16.5	229 17.7	54.0	150 07.9	09.3	259 55.0	07.7	109 11.1	43.6			
06	327 18.9	244 20.6	N26 53.7	165 09.6	N 9 08.9	274 56.8	N18 07.9	124 13.7	S 6 43.5	Dubhe	193 52.4	N61 41.2
07	342 21.4	259 23.4	53.3	180 11.4	08.6	289 58.7	08.0	139 16.3	43.5	Elnath	278 13.9	N28 37.0
S 08	357 23.8	274 26.3	53.0	195 13.1	08.2	305 00.6	08.1	154 18.9	43.4	Eltanin	90 46.0	N51 29.2
A 09	12 26.3	289 29.1	.. 52.7	210 14.8	.. 07.8	320 02.4	.. 08.3	169 21.5	.. 43.4	Enif	33 47.8	N 9 55.9
T 10	27 28.8	304 32.0	52.3	225 16.5	07.4	335 04.3	08.4	184 24.1	43.3	Fomalhaut	15 24.9	S29 33.2
U 11	42 31.2	319 34.9	52.0	240 18.2	07.0	350 06.1	08.6	199 26.7	43.3			
R 12	57 33.7	334 37.8	N26 51.7	255 20.0	N 9 06.6	5 08.0	N18 08.7	214 29.3	S 6 43.3	Gacrux	172 01.4	S57 11.3
D 13	72 36.2	349 40.6	51.3	270 21.7	06.3	20 09.9	08.9	229 31.9	43.2	Gienah	175 52.9	S17 36.9
A 14	87 38.6	4 43.5	51.0	285 23.4	05.9	35 11.7	09.0	244 34.5	43.2	Hadar	148 48.4	S60 26.2
Y 15	102 41.1	19 46.4	.. 50.6	300 25.1	.. 05.5	50 13.6	.. 09.2	259 37.1	.. 43.1	Hamal	328 01.9	N23 31.1
16	117 43.6	34 49.3	50.3	315 26.8	05.1	65 15.4	09.3	274 39.7	43.1	Kaus Aust.	83 44.5	S34 22.5
17	132 46.0	49 52.2	49.9	330 28.6	04.7	80 17.3	09.5	289 42.3	43.0			
18	147 48.5	64 55.1	N26 49.6	345 30.3	N 9 04.3	95 19.2	N18 09.6	304 44.9	S 6 43.0	Kochab	137 18.8	N74 06.3
19	162 51.0	79 58.0	49.2	0 32.0	04.0	110 21.0	09.8	319 47.5	43.0	Markab	13 39.2	N15 16.3
20	177 53.4	95 00.9	48.9	15 33.7	03.6	125 22.9	09.9	334 50.1	42.9	Menkar	314 16.2	N 4 08.2
21	192 55.9	110 03.9	.. 48.5	30 35.4	.. 03.2	140 24.7	.. 10.0	349 52.6	.. 42.9	Menkent	148 08.1	S36 26.0
22	207 58.3	125 06.8	48.2	45 37.1	02.8	155 26.6	10.2	4 55.2	42.8	Miaplacidus	221 40.0	S69 46.5
23	223 00.8	140 09.7	47.8	60 38.9	02.4	170 28.5	10.3	19 57.8	42.8			
20 00	238 03.3	155 12.7	N26 47.5	75 40.6	N 9 02.0	185 30.3	N18 10.5	35 00.4	S 6 42.7	Mirfak	308 42.0	N49 54.2
01	253 05.7	170 15.6	47.1	90 42.3	01.7	200 32.2	10.6	50 03.0	42.7	Nunki	75 59.0	S26 16.7
02	268 08.2	185 18.5	46.8	105 44.0	01.3	215 34.1	10.8	65 05.6	42.6	Peacock	53 20.2	S56 41.3
03	283 10.7	200 21.5	.. 46.4	120 45.7	.. 00.9	230 35.9	.. 10.9	80 08.2	.. 42.6	Pollux	243 28.9	N27 59.7
04	298 13.1	215 24.4	46.0	135 47.4	00.5	245 37.8	11.1	95 10.8	42.6	Procyon	245 00.7	N 5 11.4
05	313 15.6	230 27.4	45.7	150 49.1	9 00.1	260 39.6	11.2	110 13.4	42.5			
06	328 18.1	245 30.4	N26 45.3	165 50.8	N 8 59.7	275 41.5	N18 11.4	125 16.0	S 6 42.5	Rasalhague	96 06.8	N12 33.1
07	343 20.5	260 33.3	45.0	180 52.5	59.3	290 43.4	11.5	140 18.6	42.4	Regulus	207 44.3	N11 54.3
S 08	358 23.0	275 36.3	44.6	195 54.3	58.9	305 45.2	11.6	155 21.2	42.4	Rigel	281 13.1	S 8 11.4
U 09	13 25.5	290 39.3	.. 44.2	210 56.0	.. 58.6	320 47.1	.. 11.8	170 23.8	.. 42.3	Rigil Kent.	139 52.1	S60 53.3
N 10	28 27.9	305 42.2	43.9	225 57.7	58.2	335 48.9	11.9	185 26.4	42.3	Sabik	102 13.1	S15 44.4
D 11	43 30.4	320 45.2	43.5	240 59.4	57.8	350 50.8	12.1	200 29.0	42.3			
A 12	58 32.8	335 48.2	N26 43.1	256 01.1	N 8 57.4	5 52.7	N18 12.2	215 31.6	S 6 42.2	Schedar	349 41.8	N56 36.1
Y 13	73 35.3	350 51.2	42.8	271 02.8	57.0	20 54.5	12.4	230 34.2	42.2	Shaula	96 22.6	S37 06.6
14	88 37.8	5 54.2	42.4	286 04.5	56.6	35 56.4	12.5	245 36.8	42.1	Sirius	258 34.7	S16 44.2
15	103 40.2	20 57.2	.. 42.0	301 06.2	.. 56.2	50 58.2	.. 12.7	260 39.3	.. 42.1	Spica	158 31.8	S11 13.7
16	118 42.7	36 00.2	41.7	316 07.9	55.8	66 00.1	12.8	275 41.9	42.0	Suhail	222 53.1	S43 29.4
17	133 45.2	51 03.2	41.3	331 09.6	55.5	81 02.0	12.9	290 44.5	42.0			
18	148 47.6	66 06.2	N26 40.9	346 11.3	N 8 55.1	96 03.8	N18 13.1	305 47.1	S 6 42.0	Vega	80 39.1	N38 47.6
19	163 50.1	81 09.3	40.5	1 13.0	54.7	111 05.7	13.2	320 49.7	41.9	Zuben'ubi	137 05.9	S16 05.7
20	178 52.6	96 12.3	40.2	16 14.7	54.3	126 07.5	13.4	335 52.3	41.9		SHA	Mer.Pass.
21	193 55.0	111 15.3	.. 39.8	31 16.4	.. 53.9	141 09.4	.. 13.5	350 54.9	.. 41.8		° ′	h m
22	208 57.5	126 18.4	39.4	46 18.1	53.5	156 11.3	13.7	5 57.5	41.8	Venus	276 59.4	13 41
23	223 59.9	141 21.4	39.0	61 19.8	53.1	171 13.1	13.8	21 00.1	41.8	Mars	197 55.1	18 58
	h m									Jupiter	307 41.5	11 40
Mer.Pass. 8 10.4		v 2.9	d 0.3	v 1.7	d 0.4	v 1.9	d 0.1	v 2.6	d 0.0	Saturn	156 54.0	21 40

2012 MAY 18, 19, 20 (FRI., SAT., SUN.)

UT	SUN GHA	Dec	MOON GHA	v	Dec	d	HP
d h	° ′	° ′	° ′	′	° ′	′	′
18 00	180 53.8	N19 35.5	214 09.5	14.4	N12 51.6	9.0	54.1
01	195 53.8	36.0	228 42.9	14.5	13 00.6	8.9	54.1
02	210 53.8	36.6	243 16.4	14.4	13 09.5	8.8	54.1
03	225 53.7	.. 37.1	257 49.8	14.4	13 18.3	8.8	54.1
04	240 53.7	37.6	272 23.2	14.3	13 27.1	8.8	54.1
05	255 53.7	38.2	286 56.5	14.4	13 35.9	8.6	54.1
06	270 53.7	N19 38.7	301 29.9	14.3	N13 44.5	8.7	54.0
F 07	285 53.6	39.3	316 03.2	14.2	13 53.2	8.5	54.0
R 08	300 53.6	39.8	330 36.4	14.3	14 01.7	8.5	54.0
I 09	315 53.6	.. 40.4	345 09.7	14.1	14 10.2	8.5	54.0
D 10	330 53.5	40.9	359 42.8	14.2	14 18.7	8.3	54.0
A 11	345 53.5	41.4	14 16.0	14.1	14 27.0	8.3	54.0
Y 12	0 53.5	N19 42.0	28 49.1	14.1	N14 35.3	8.3	54.0
13	15 53.5	42.5	43 22.2	14.1	14 43.6	8.2	54.0
14	30 53.4	43.1	57 55.3	14.0	14 51.8	8.1	54.0
15	45 53.4	.. 43.6	72 28.3	14.0	14 59.9	8.1	54.0
16	60 53.4	44.1	87 01.3	14.0	15 08.0	8.0	54.0
17	75 53.3	44.7	101 34.3	13.9	15 16.0	7.9	54.0
18	90 53.3	N19 45.2	116 07.2	13.9	N15 23.9	7.9	54.0
19	105 53.3	45.7	130 40.1	13.8	15 31.8	7.8	54.0
20	120 53.3	46.3	145 12.9	13.9	15 39.6	7.7	54.0
21	135 53.2	.. 46.8	159 45.8	13.7	15 47.3	7.7	54.0
22	150 53.2	47.3	174 18.5	13.8	15 55.0	7.6	54.0
23	165 53.2	47.9	188 51.3	13.7	16 02.6	7.5	54.0
19 00	180 53.1	N19 48.4	203 24.0	13.7	N16 10.1	7.5	54.0
01	195 53.1	48.9	217 56.7	13.6	16 17.6	7.4	54.0
02	210 53.1	49.5	232 29.3	13.6	16 25.0	7.3	54.0
03	225 53.0	.. 50.0	247 01.9	13.6	16 32.3	7.2	54.0
04	240 53.0	50.5	261 34.5	13.5	16 39.5	7.2	54.0
05	255 53.0	51.1	276 07.0	13.5	16 46.7	7.1	54.0
06	270 52.9	N19 51.6	290 39.5	13.4	N16 53.8	7.1	54.0
S 07	285 52.9	52.1	305 11.9	13.5	17 00.9	6.9	54.0
A 08	300 52.9	52.7	319 44.4	13.3	17 07.8	6.9	54.0
T 09	315 52.8	.. 53.2	334 16.7	13.4	17 14.7	6.8	54.0
U 10	330 52.8	53.7	348 49.1	13.3	17 21.5	6.7	54.0
R 11	345 52.8	54.2	3 21.4	13.2	17 28.2	6.7	54.0
D 12	0 52.7	N19 54.8	17 53.6	13.3	N17 34.9	6.6	54.0
A 13	15 52.7	55.3	32 25.9	13.2	17 41.5	6.5	53.9
Y 14	30 52.7	55.8	46 58.1	13.1	17 48.0	6.4	53.9
15	45 52.6	.. 56.3	61 30.2	13.1	17 54.4	6.4	53.9
16	60 52.6	56.9	76 02.3	13.1	18 00.8	6.2	53.9
17	75 52.6	57.4	90 34.4	13.1	18 07.0	6.2	53.9
18	90 52.5	N19 58.0	105 06.5	13.0	N18 13.2	6.2	53.9
19	105 52.5	58.4	119 38.5	12.9	18 19.4	6.0	53.9
20	120 52.4	59.0	134 10.4	12.9	18 25.4	5.9	53.9
21	135 52.4	19 59.5	148 42.3	12.9	18 31.3	5.9	54.0
22	150 52.4	20 00.0	163 14.2	12.9	18 37.2	5.8	54.0
23	165 52.3	00.5	177 46.1	12.8	18 43.0	5.7	54.0
20 00	180 52.3	N20 01.0	192 17.9	12.8	N18 48.7	5.6	54.0
01	195 52.3	01.6	206 49.7	12.7	18 54.3	5.6	54.0
02	210 52.2	02.1	221 21.4	12.7	18 59.9	5.4	54.0
03	225 52.2	.. 02.6	235 53.1	12.7	19 05.3	5.4	54.0
04	240 52.1	03.1	250 24.8	12.6	19 10.7	5.3	54.0
05	255 52.1	03.6	264 56.4	12.6	19 16.0	5.2	54.0
06	270 52.1	N20 04.1	279 28.0	12.6	N19 21.2	5.1	54.0
07	285 52.0	04.7	293 59.6	12.5	19 26.3	5.0	54.0
08	300 52.0	05.2	308 31.1	12.5	19 31.3	4.9	54.0
S 09	315 51.9	.. 05.7	323 02.6	12.5	19 36.2	4.9	54.0
U 10	330 51.9	06.2	337 34.1	12.4	19 41.1	4.8	54.0
N 11	345 51.9	06.7	352 05.5	12.4	19 45.9	4.6	54.0
D 12	0 51.8	N20 07.2	6 36.9	12.3	N19 50.5	4.6	54.0
A 13	15 51.8	07.7	21 08.2	12.4	19 55.1	4.5	54.0
Y 14	30 51.7	08.2	35 39.6	12.2	19 59.6	4.4	54.0
15	45 51.7	.. 08.7	50 10.8	12.3	20 04.0	4.3	54.0
16	60 51.7	09.3	64 42.1	12.2	20 08.3	4.3	54.0
17	75 51.6	09.8	79 13.3	12.2	N20 12.6	4.1	54.0
18	90 51.6	N20 10.3					
19	105 51.5	10.8					
20	120 51.5	11.3	*An annular eclipse of*				
21	135 51.5	.. 11.8	*the Sun occurs on this*				
22	150 51.4	12.3	*date. See page 5.*				
23	165 51.4	12.8					
	SD 15.8 d 0.5		SD 14.7		14.7		14.7

Lat.	Twilight Naut.	Civil	Sunrise	Moonrise 18	19	20	21
°	h m	h m	h m	h m	h m	h m	h m
N 72	☐	☐	☐	00 46	00 16	☐	☐
N 70	////	////	////	01 09	00 56	00 36	☐
68	////	////	01 21	01 27	01 24	01 23	01 24
66	////	////	02 05	01 41	01 45	01 53	02 09
64	////	00 25	02 33	01 53	02 02	02 16	02 38
62	////	01 32	02 55	02 03	02 17	02 35	03 01
60	////	02 05	03 13	02 12	02 29	02 50	03 19
N 58	00 23	02 29	03 27	02 20	02 39	03 03	03 34
56	01 23	02 48	03 40	02 27	02 48	03 14	03 47
54	01 54	03 03	03 50	02 33	02 56	03 24	03 58
52	02 16	03 17	04 00	02 38	03 03	03 33	04 08
50	02 34	03 28	04 08	02 44	03 10	03 41	04 17
45	03 07	03 52	04 26	02 54	03 24	03 57	04 36
N 40	03 31	04 10	04 41	03 03	03 35	04 11	04 52
35	03 50	04 25	04 53	03 11	03 45	04 23	05 05
30	04 06	04 38	05 04	03 18	03 54	04 33	05 16
20	04 30	04 59	05 22	03 30	04 09	04 51	05 36
N 10	04 49	05 16	05 38	03 41	04 23	05 07	05 53
0	05 05	05 31	05 53	03 51	04 35	05 21	06 09
S 10	05 19	05 45	06 07	04 01	04 48	05 36	06 25
20	05 33	05 59	06 23	04 11	05 01	05 52	06 42
30	05 46	06 15	06 40	04 23	05 17	06 10	07 02
35	05 53	06 23	06 51	04 31	05 26	06 20	07 14
40	06 00	06 33	07 02	04 39	05 36	06 32	07 27
45	06 08	06 44	07 16	04 48	05 48	06 47	07 43
S 50	06 16	06 56	07 32	05 00	06 03	07 04	08 02
52	06 20	07 02	07 40	05 05	06 10	07 13	08 12
54	06 24	07 08	07 49	05 11	06 18	07 22	08 22
56	06 29	07 15	07 59	05 18	06 26	07 32	08 34
58	06 34	07 23	08 10	05 25	06 36	07 44	08 47
S 60	06 39	07 32	08 23	05 34	06 48	07 58	09 03

Lat.	Sunset	Twilight Civil	Naut.	Moonset 18	19	20	21
°	h m	h m	h m	h m	h m	h m	h m
N 72	☐	☐	☐	20 17	☐	☐	☐
N 70	☐	☐	☐	19 37	21 33	☐	☐
68	22 38	////	////	19 10	20 47	22 24	23 52
66	21 52	////	////	18 50	20 17	21 39	22 50
64	21 22	////	////	18 34	19 54	21 10	22 15
62	21 00	22 25	////	18 20	19 36	20 48	21 50
60	20 42	21 51	////	18 09	19 22	20 30	21 30
N 58	20 27	21 26	////	17 59	19 09	20 15	21 14
56	20 15	21 07	22 34	17 51	18 58	20 02	21 00
54	20 04	20 51	22 02	17 43	18 49	19 51	20 48
52	19 54	20 38	21 39	17 36	18 40	19 41	20 37
50	19 45	20 26	21 21	17 30	18 33	19 32	20 28
45	19 27	20 02	20 47	17 17	18 17	19 14	20 08
N 40	19 12	19 44	20 23	17 06	18 03	18 59	19 52
35	19 00	19 28	20 03	16 57	17 52	18 46	19 39
30	18 49	19 16	19 47	16 49	17 42	18 35	19 27
20	18 31	18 55	19 23	16 35	17 26	18 16	19 06
N 10	18 15	18 37	19 04	16 23	17 11	18 00	18 49
0	18 00	18 22	18 48	16 12	16 57	17 44	18 32
S 10	17 45	18 08	18 33	16 01	16 44	17 29	18 16
20	17 30	17 53	18 20	15 49	16 29	17 12	17 58
30	17 12	17 38	18 07	15 35	16 12	16 53	17 38
35	17 02	17 29	18 00	15 27	16 03	16 42	17 26
40	16 50	17 17	17 53	15 18	15 52	16 30	17 13
45	16 37	17 09	17 45	15 08	15 39	16 15	16 57
S 50	16 20	16 56	17 36	14 55	15 23	15 57	16 37
52	16 12	16 50	17 32	14 49	15 16	15 48	16 27
54	16 04	16 44	17 28	14 43	15 08	15 39	16 17
56	15 54	16 37	17 24	14 35	14 59	15 28	16 05
58	15 43	16 29	17 19	14 27	14 48	15 16	15 51
S 60	15 30	16 21	17 13	14 18	14 37	15 01	15 35

Day	SUN Eqn. of Time 00ʰ	12ʰ	Mer. Pass.	MOON Mer. Pass. Upper	Lower	Age	Phase
d	m s	m s	h m	h m	h m	d	%
18	03 35	03 34	11 56	10 01	22 23	27	6
19	03 33	03 31	11 56	10 46	23 09	28	2
20	03 29	03 27	11 57	11 33	23 56	29	0

UT	ARIES GHA	VENUS −4.4 GHA	Dec	MARS +0.4 GHA	Dec	JUPITER −2.0 GHA	Dec	SATURN +0.5 GHA	Dec
21 00	239 02.4	156 24.4	N26 38.6	76 21.5	N 8 52.7	186 15.0	N18 14.0	36 02.7	S 6 41.7
01	254 04.9	171 27.5	38.2	91 23.2	52.3	201 16.9	14.1	51 05.3	41.7
02	269 07.3	186 30.5	37.9	106 24.9	51.9	216 18.7	14.2	66 07.9	41.6
03	284 09.8	201 33.6 ..	37.5	121 26.6 ..	51.5	231 20.6 ..	14.4	81 10.5 ..	41.6
04	299 12.3	216 36.7	37.1	136 28.3	51.2	246 22.4	14.5	96 13.0	41.5
05	314 14.7	231 39.7	36.7	151 30.0	50.8	261 24.3	14.7	111 15.6	41.5
06	329 17.2	246 42.8	N26 36.3	166 31.7	N 8 50.4	276 26.2	N18 14.8	126 18.2	S 6 41.5
07	344 19.7	261 45.9	35.9	181 33.4	50.0	291 28.0	15.0	141 20.8	41.4
08	359 22.1	276 48.9	35.5	196 35.1	49.6	306 29.9	15.1	156 23.4	41.4
09	14 24.6	291 52.0 ..	35.1	211 36.8 ..	49.2	321 31.7 ..	15.3	171 26.0 ..	41.3
10	29 27.1	306 55.1	34.8	226 38.5	48.8	336 33.6	15.4	186 28.6	41.3
11	44 29.5	321 58.2	34.4	241 40.2	48.4	351 35.5	15.5	201 31.2	41.3
12	59 32.0	337 01.3	N26 34.0	256 41.8	N 8 48.0	6 37.3	N18 15.7	216 33.8	S 6 41.2
13	74 34.4	352 04.4	33.6	271 43.5	47.6	21 39.2	15.8	231 36.4	41.2
14	89 36.9	7 07.5	33.2	286 45.2	47.2	36 41.0	16.0	246 39.0	41.1
15	104 39.4	22 10.6 ..	32.8	301 46.9 ..	46.8	51 42.9 ..	16.1	261 41.6 ..	41.1
16	119 41.8	37 13.7	32.4	316 48.6	46.4	66 44.8	16.3	276 44.1	41.0
17	134 44.3	52 16.9	32.0	331 50.3	46.0	81 46.6	16.4	291 46.7	41.0
18	149 46.8	67 20.0	N26 31.6	346 52.0	N 8 45.6	96 48.5	N18 16.6	306 49.3	S 6 41.0
19	164 49.2	82 23.1	31.2	1 53.7	45.2	111 50.3	16.7	321 51.9	40.9
20	179 51.7	97 26.3	30.8	16 55.4	44.8	126 52.2	16.8	336 54.5	40.9
21	194 54.2	112 29.4 ..	30.4	31 57.0 ..	44.5	141 54.1 ..	17.0	351 57.1 ..	40.8
22	209 56.6	127 32.5	29.9	46 58.7	44.1	156 55.9	17.1	6 59.7	40.8
23	224 59.1	142 35.7	29.5	62 00.4	43.7	171 57.8	17.3	22 02.3	40.8
22 00	240 01.6	157 38.8	N26 29.1	77 02.1	N 8 43.3	186 59.7	N18 17.4	37 04.9	S 6 40.7
01	255 04.0	172 42.0	28.7	92 03.8	42.9	202 01.5	17.6	52 07.5	40.7
02	270 06.5	187 45.2	28.3	107 05.5	42.5	217 03.4	17.7	67 10.0	40.6
03	285 08.9	202 48.3 ..	27.9	122 07.1 ..	42.1	232 05.2 ..	17.8	82 12.6 ..	40.6
04	300 11.4	217 51.5	27.5	137 08.8	41.7	247 07.1	18.0	97 15.2	40.6
05	315 13.9	232 54.7	27.1	152 10.5	41.3	262 09.0	18.1	112 17.8	40.5
06	330 16.3	247 57.8	N26 26.6	167 12.2	N 8 40.9	277 10.8	N18 18.3	127 20.4	S 6 40.5
07	345 18.8	263 01.0	26.2	182 13.9	40.5	292 12.7	18.4	142 23.0	40.4
08	0 21.3	278 04.2	25.8	197 15.6	40.1	307 14.5	18.6	157 25.6	40.4
09	15 23.7	293 07.4 ..	25.4	212 17.2 ..	39.7	322 16.4 ..	18.7	172 28.2 ..	40.4
10	30 26.2	308 10.6	25.0	227 18.9	39.3	337 18.3	18.8	187 30.7	40.3
11	45 28.7	323 13.8	24.6	242 20.6	38.9	352 20.1	19.0	202 33.3	40.3
12	60 31.1	338 17.0	N26 24.1	257 22.3	N 8 38.5	7 22.0	N18 19.1	217 35.9	S 6 40.2
13	75 33.6	353 20.2	23.7	272 23.9	38.1	22 23.8	19.3	232 38.5	40.2
14	90 36.1	8 23.4	23.3	287 25.6	37.7	37 25.7	19.4	247 41.1	40.2
15	105 38.5	23 26.7 ..	22.9	302 27.3 ..	37.3	52 27.6 ..	19.6	262 43.7 ..	40.1
16	120 41.0	38 29.9	22.4	317 29.0	36.9	67 29.4	19.7	277 46.3	40.1
17	135 43.4	53 33.1	22.0	332 30.6	36.5	82 31.3	19.9	292 48.9	40.0
18	150 45.9	68 36.3	N26 21.6	347 32.3	N 8 36.1	97 33.2	N18 20.0	307 51.5	S 6 40.0
19	165 48.4	83 39.6	21.1	2 34.0	35.7	112 35.0	20.1	322 54.0	40.0
20	180 50.8	98 42.8	20.7	17 35.7	35.3	127 36.9	20.3	337 56.6	39.9
21	195 53.3	113 46.1 ..	20.3	32 37.3 ..	34.9	142 38.7 ..	20.4	352 59.2 ..	39.9
22	210 55.8	128 49.3	19.8	47 39.0	34.5	157 40.6	20.6	8 01.8	39.8
23	225 58.2	143 52.6	19.4	62 40.7	34.1	172 42.5	20.7	23 04.4	39.8
23 00	241 00.7	158 55.8	N26 19.0	77 42.3	N 8 33.7	187 44.3	N18 20.9	38 07.0	S 6 39.8
01	256 03.2	173 59.1	18.5	92 44.0	33.3	202 46.2	21.0	53 09.6	39.7
02	271 05.6	189 02.4	18.1	107 45.7	32.9	217 48.0	21.1	68 12.1	39.7
03	286 08.1	204 05.6 ..	17.6	122 47.4 ..	32.5	232 49.9 ..	21.3	83 14.7 ..	39.6
04	301 10.5	219 08.9	17.2	137 49.0	32.1	247 51.8	21.4	98 17.3	39.6
05	316 13.0	234 12.2	16.8	152 50.7	31.7	262 53.6	21.6	113 19.9	39.6
06	331 15.5	249 15.5	N26 16.3	167 52.4	N 8 31.3	277 55.5	N18 21.7	128 22.5	S 6 39.5
07	346 17.9	264 18.8	15.9	182 54.0	30.8	292 57.3	21.8	143 25.1	39.5
08	1 20.4	279 22.1	15.4	197 55.7	30.4	307 59.2	22.0	158 27.7	39.4
09	16 22.9	294 25.3 ..	15.0	212 57.4 ..	30.0	323 01.1 ..	22.1	173 30.2 ..	39.4
10	31 25.3	309 28.7	14.5	227 59.0	29.6	338 02.9	22.3	188 32.8	39.4
11	46 27.8	324 32.0	14.1	243 00.7	29.2	353 04.8	22.4	203 35.4	39.3
12	61 30.3	339 35.3	N26 13.6	258 02.3	N 8 28.8	8 06.7	N18 22.6	218 38.0	S 6 39.3
13	76 32.7	354 38.6	13.2	273 04.0	28.4	23 08.5	22.7	233 40.6	39.3
14	91 35.2	9 41.9	12.7	288 05.7	28.0	38 10.4	22.8	248 43.2	39.2
15	106 37.7	24 45.2 ..	12.3	303 07.3 ..	27.6	53 12.2 ..	23.0	263 45.8 ..	39.2
16	121 40.1	39 48.6	11.8	318 09.0	27.2	68 14.1	23.1	278 48.3	39.1
17	136 42.6	54 51.9	11.3	333 10.7	26.8	83 16.0	23.3	293 50.9	39.1
18	151 45.0	69 55.2	N26 10.9	348 12.3	N 8 26.4	98 17.8	N18 23.4	308 53.5	S 6 39.1
19	166 47.5	84 58.6	10.4	3 14.0	26.0	113 19.7	23.5	323 56.1	39.0
20	181 50.0	100 01.9	10.0	18 15.6	25.6	128 21.5	23.7	338 58.7	39.0
21	196 52.4	115 05.3 ..	09.5	33 17.3 ..	25.2	143 23.4 ..	23.8	354 01.3 ..	38.9
22	211 54.9	130 08.6	09.0	48 18.9	24.8	158 25.3	24.0	9 03.8	38.9
23	226 57.4	145 12.0	08.6	63 20.6	24.4	173 27.1	24.1	24 06.4	38.9
Mer. Pass.	7 58.6	*v* 3.2	*d* 0.4	*v* 1.7	*d* 0.4	*v* 1.9	*d* 0.1	*v* 2.6	*d* 0.0

Vertical day labels: M O N D A Y (21), T U E S D A Y (22), W E D N E S D A Y (23)

STARS

Name	SHA	Dec
Acamar	315 19.3	S40 15.3
Achernar	335 27.8	S57 10.2
Acrux	173 09.7	S63 10.4
Adhara	255 13.4	S28 59.6
Aldebaran	290 50.6	N16 31.9
Alioth	166 21.0	N55 53.7
Alkaid	152 59.1	N49 15.2
Al Na'ir	27 44.7	S46 53.7
Alnilam	275 47.4	S 1 11.8
Alphard	217 56.9	S 8 43.0
Alphecca	126 11.3	N26 40.4
Alpheratz	357 44.5	N29 09.4
Altair	62 08.8	N 8 54.1
Ankaa	353 16.7	S42 14.1
Antares	112 26.8	S26 27.5
Arcturus	145 56.1	N19 07.1
Atria	107 28.8	S69 02.9
Avior	234 18.6	S59 33.4
Bellatrix	278 33.1	N 6 21.5
Betelgeuse	271 02.4	N 7 24.4
Canopus	263 56.9	S52 42.4
Capella	280 36.0	N46 00.5
Deneb	49 31.8	N45 19.4
Denebola	182 34.3	N14 30.1
Diphda	348 56.9	S17 55.0
Dubhe	193 52.5	N61 41.2
Elnath	278 13.9	N28 36.9
Eltanin	90 46.0	N51 29.2
Enif	33 47.8	N 9 55.9
Fomalhaut	15 24.9	S29 33.2
Gacrux	172 01.4	S57 11.3
Gienah	175 52.9	S17 36.9
Hadar	148 48.4	S60 26.2
Hamal	328 01.9	N23 31.1
Kaus Aust.	83 44.5	S34 22.5
Kochab	137 18.8	N74 06.4
Markab	13 39.2	N15 16.3
Menkar	314 16.2	N 4 08.2
Menkent	148 08.1	S36 26.0
Miaplacidus	221 40.1	S69 46.5
Mirfak	308 41.9	N49 54.2
Nunki	75 59.0	S26 16.7
Peacock	53 20.1	S56 41.3
Pollux	243 28.9	N27 59.7
Procyon	245 00.7	N 5 11.4
Rasalhague	96 06.8	N12 33.1
Regulus	207 44.3	N11 54.3
Rigel	281 13.1	S 8 11.4
Rigil Kent.	139 52.1	S60 53.3
Sabik	102 13.1	S15 44.3
Schedar	349 41.7	N56 36.1
Shaula	96 22.5	S37 06.6
Sirius	258 34.7	S16 44.2
Spica	158 31.8	S11 13.7
Suhail	222 53.1	S43 29.4
Vega	80 39.1	N38 47.7
Zuben'ubi	137 05.9	S16 05.7

	SHA	Mer. Pass.
Venus	277 37.3	13 27
Mars	197 00.5	18 50
Jupiter	306 58.1	11 31
Saturn	157 03.3	21 28

UT	SUN GHA	SUN Dec	MOON GHA	v	Dec	d	HP
d h	° ′	° ′	° ′	′	° ′	′	′
21 00	180 51.3	N20 13.3	180 50.9	12.0	N20 39.5	3.5	54.0
01	195 51.3	13.8	195 21.9	11.9	20 43.0	3.4	54.0
02	210 51.2	14.3	209 52.8	12.0	20 46.4	3.3	54.0
03	225 51.2 ..	14.8	224 23.8	11.8	20 49.7	3.2	54.0
04	240 51.2	15.3	238 54.6	11.9	20 52.9	3.1	54.0
05	255 51.1	15.8	253 25.5	11.8	20 56.0	3.0	54.1
06	270 51.1	N20 16.3	267 56.3	11.8	N20 59.0	2.9	54.1
07	285 51.0	16.8	282 27.1	11.8	21 01.9	2.8	54.1
08	300 51.0	17.3	296 57.9	11.7	21 04.7	2.7	54.1
M 09	315 50.9 ..	17.8	311 28.6	11.7	21 07.4	2.6	54.1
O 10	330 50.9	18.3	325 59.3	11.7	21 10.0	2.5	54.1
N 11	345 50.8	18.8	340 30.0	11.7	21 12.5	2.4	54.1
D 12	0 50.8	N20 19.3	355 00.7	11.6	N21 14.9	2.3	54.1
A 13	15 50.7	19.8	9 31.3	11.6	21 17.2	2.2	54.1
Y 14	30 50.7	20.3	24 01.9	11.6	21 19.4	2.2	54.1
15	45 50.7 ..	20.8	38 32.5	11.6	21 21.6	2.0	54.1
16	60 50.6	21.3	53 03.1	11.5	21 23.6	1.9	54.1
17	75 50.6	21.8	67 33.6	11.5	21 25.5	1.8	54.1
18	90 50.5	N20 22.3	82 04.2	11.5	N21 27.3	1.7	54.1
19	105 50.5	22.8	96 34.7	11.5	21 29.0	1.6	54.1
20	120 50.4	23.3	111 05.2	11.4	21 30.6	1.5	54.2
21	135 50.4 ..	23.8	125 35.6	11.5	21 32.1	1.5	54.2
22	150 50.3	24.3	140 06.1	11.4	21 33.6	1.3	54.2
23	165 50.3	24.8	154 36.5	11.4	21 34.9	1.2	54.2
22 00	180 50.2	N20 25.2	169 06.9	11.4	N21 36.1	1.1	54.2
01	195 50.2	25.7	183 37.3	11.4	21 37.2	1.0	54.2
02	210 50.1	26.2	198 07.7	11.3	21 38.2	0.9	54.2
03	225 50.1 ..	26.7	212 38.0	11.4	21 39.1	0.8	54.2
04	240 50.0	27.2	227 08.4	11.3	21 39.9	0.7	54.2
05	255 50.0	27.7	241 38.7	11.3	21 40.6	0.6	54.2
06	270 49.9	N20 28.2	256 09.0	11.3	N21 41.2	0.5	54.2
07	285 49.9	28.7	270 39.3	11.3	21 41.7	0.3	54.3
T 08	300 49.8	29.1	285 09.6	11.3	21 42.0	0.3	54.3
U 09	315 49.8 ..	29.6	299 39.9	11.2	21 42.3	0.2	54.3
E 10	330 49.7	30.1	314 10.1	11.3	21 42.5	0.1	54.3
S 11	345 49.7	30.6	328 40.4	11.2	21 42.6	0.0	54.3
D 12	0 49.6	N20 31.1	343 10.6	11.3	N21 42.6	0.2	54.3
A 13	15 49.6	31.6	357 40.9	11.2	21 42.4	0.2	54.3
Y 14	30 49.5	32.0	12 11.1	11.2	21 42.2	0.4	54.3
15	45 49.5 ..	32.5	26 41.3	11.2	21 41.8	0.4	54.3
16	60 49.4	33.0	41 11.5	11.2	21 41.4	0.5	54.3
17	75 49.4	33.5	55 41.7	11.2	21 40.9	0.7	54.4
18	90 49.3	N20 34.0	70 11.9	11.2	N21 40.2	0.8	54.4
19	105 49.3	34.4	84 42.1	11.1	21 39.4	0.8	54.4
20	120 49.2	34.9	99 12.2	11.2	21 38.6	1.0	54.4
21	135 49.2 ..	35.4	113 42.4	11.2	21 37.6	1.1	54.4
22	150 49.1	35.9	128 12.6	11.1	21 36.5	1.1	54.4
23	165 49.1	36.3	142 42.7	11.2	21 35.4	1.3	54.4
23 00	180 49.0	N20 36.8	157 12.9	11.1	N21 34.1	1.4	54.4
01	195 48.9	37.3	171 43.0	11.2	21 32.7	1.5	54.4
02	210 48.9	37.8	186 13.2	11.2	21 31.2	1.6	54.5
03	225 48.8 ..	38.2	200 43.4	11.1	21 29.6	1.7	54.5
04	240 48.8	38.7	215 13.5	11.2	21 27.9	1.8	54.5
05	255 48.7	39.2	229 43.7	11.1	21 26.1	1.9	54.5
06	270 48.7	N20 39.7	244 13.8	11.2	N21 24.2	2.0	54.5
W 07	285 48.6	40.1	258 44.0	11.1	21 22.2	2.1	54.5
E 08	300 48.6	40.6	273 14.1	11.2	21 20.1	2.2	54.5
D 09	315 48.5 ..	41.1	287 44.3	11.1	21 17.9	2.3	54.6
N 10	330 48.4	41.5	302 14.4	11.2	21 15.6	2.5	54.6
E 11	345 48.4	42.0	316 44.6	11.2	21 13.1	2.5	54.6
S 12	0 48.3	N20 42.5	331 14.8	11.1	N21 10.6	2.6	54.6
D 13	15 48.3	43.0	345 44.9	11.2	21 08.0	2.8	54.6
A 14	30 48.2	43.4	0 15.1	11.2	21 05.2	2.8	54.6
Y 15	45 48.2 ..	43.9	14 45.3	11.2	21 02.4	2.9	54.6
16	60 48.1	44.3	29 15.5	11.2	20 59.5	3.1	54.6
17	75 48.0	44.8	43 45.7	11.2	20 56.4	3.1	54.7
18	90 48.0	N20 45.3	58 15.9	11.2	N20 53.3	3.3	54.7
19	105 47.9	45.7	72 46.1	11.2	20 50.0	3.3	54.7
20	120 47.9	46.2	87 16.3	11.3	20 46.7	3.5	54.7
21	135 47.8 ..	46.7	101 46.6	11.2	20 43.2	3.5	54.7
22	150 47.8	47.1	116 16.8	11.2	20 39.7	3.7	54.7
23	165 47.7	47.6	130 47.0	11.3	N20 36.0	3.7	54.8
	SD 15.8	d 0.5	SD 14.7		14.8		14.9

Lat.	Twilight Naut.	Twilight Civil	Sunrise	Moonrise 21	Moonrise 22	Moonrise 23	Moonrise 24
°	h m	h m	h m	h m	h m	h m	h m
N 72	▭	▭	▭	▭	▭	▭	▭
N 70	▭	▭	▭	▭	▭	▭	▭
68	////	////	00 59	01 24	01 36	02 32	04 06
66	////	////	01 52	02 09	02 39	03 32	04 47
64	////	////	02 24	02 38	03 13	04 06	05 15
62	////	01 18	02 48	03 01	03 39	04 31	05 37
60	////	01 56	03 06	03 19	03 59	04 50	05 54
N 58	////	02 21	03 22	03 34	04 15	05 07	06 08
56	01 10	02 42	03 35	03 47	04 29	05 20	06 21
54	01 45	02 58	03 46	03 58	04 41	05 32	06 32
52	02 09	03 12	03 56	04 08	04 52	05 43	06 41
50	02 28	03 24	04 05	04 17	05 01	05 52	06 50
45	03 03	03 48	04 24	04 36	05 21	06 12	07 08
N 40	03 28	04 07	04 39	04 52	05 37	06 28	07 23
35	03 48	04 23	04 52	05 05	05 51	06 41	07 35
30	04 04	04 36	05 03	05 16	06 03	06 53	07 46
20	04 29	04 58	05 22	05 36	06 23	07 13	08 05
N 10	04 49	05 15	05 38	05 53	06 41	07 31	08 21
0	05 05	05 31	05 53	06 09	06 58	07 47	08 36
S 10	05 20	05 46	06 08	06 25	07 14	08 03	08 51
20	05 34	06 01	06 24	06 42	07 32	08 21	09 08
30	05 47	06 17	06 42	07 02	07 53	08 41	09 26
35	05 54	06 25	06 53	07 14	08 05	08 53	09 37
40	06 02	06 35	07 05	07 27	08 19	09 06	09 49
45	06 10	06 46	07 19	07 43	08 35	09 22	10 04
S 50	06 20	07 00	07 36	08 02	08 55	09 42	10 22
52	06 24	07 06	07 44	08 12	09 05	09 51	10 30
54	06 28	07 12	07 53	08 22	09 16	10 01	10 39
56	06 33	07 20	08 04	08 34	09 28	10 13	10 50
58	06 38	07 28	08 15	08 47	09 42	10 27	11 02
S 60	06 43	07 37	08 29	09 03	09 59	10 43	11 16

Lat.	Sunset	Twilight Civil	Twilight Naut.	Moonset 21	Moonset 22	Moonset 23	Moonset 24
°	h m	h m	h m	h m	h m	h m	h m
N 72	▭	▭	▭	▭	▭	▭	▭
N 70	▭	▭	▭	▭	▭	▭	▭
68	23 02	////	////	23 52	24 39	00 39	00 48
66	22 04	////	////	22 50	23 39	24 06	00 06
64	21 31	////	////	22 15	23 05	23 38	23 59
62	21 08	22 40	////	21 50	22 40	23 16	23 41
60	20 49	22 01	////	21 30	22 20	22 58	23 27
N 58	20 33	21 34	////	21 14	22 04	22 43	23 14
56	20 20	21 13	22 47	21 00	21 50	22 31	23 03
54	20 08	20 57	22 12	20 48	21 38	22 20	22 54
52	19 58	20 43	21 46	20 37	21 27	22 10	22 45
50	19 49	20 30	21 27	20 28	21 18	22 01	22 38
45	19 30	20 06	20 51	20 08	20 58	21 42	22 21
N 40	19 15	19 46	20 26	19 52	20 42	21 27	22 08
35	19 02	19 31	20 06	19 39	20 28	21 14	21 57
30	18 51	19 18	19 50	19 27	20 16	21 03	21 47
20	18 32	18 56	19 24	19 06	19 56	20 44	21 29
N 10	18 16	18 38	19 05	18 49	19 38	20 27	21 14
0	18 00	18 22	18 48	18 32	19 22	20 11	21 00
S 10	17 45	18 08	18 33	18 16	19 05	19 55	20 45
20	17 29	17 53	18 20	17 58	18 47	19 38	20 30
30	17 11	17 37	18 06	17 38	18 27	19 18	20 13
35	17 00	17 28	17 59	17 26	18 15	19 07	20 02
40	16 48	17 18	17 51	17 13	18 01	18 54	19 50
45	16 34	17 07	17 43	16 57	17 44	18 38	19 36
S 50	16 17	16 53	17 33	16 37	17 23	18 19	19 19
52	16 09	16 47	17 29	16 27	17 15	18 10	19 11
54	15 59	16 41	17 25	16 17	17 04	17 59	19 02
56	15 49	16 33	17 20	16 05	16 52	17 48	18 52
58	15 38	16 25	17 15	15 51	16 37	17 34	18 40
S 60	15 24	16 16	17 09	15 35	16 21	17 19	18 27

	SUN			MOON	
Day	Eqn. of Time 00ʰ	Eqn. of Time 12ʰ	Mer. Pass.	Mer. Pass. Upper	Mer. Pass. Lower	Age	Phase
d	m s	m s	h m	h m	h m	d	%
21	03 25	03 23	11 57	12 21	24 45	01	0
22	03 21	03 19	11 57	13 10	00 45	02	2
23	03 16	03 13	11 57	13 59	01 34	03	6

UT	ARIES	VENUS −4.3		MARS +0.4		JUPITER −2.0		SATURN +0.5		STARS		
	GHA	GHA	Dec	GHA	Dec	GHA	Dec	GHA	Dec	Name	SHA	Dec
d h	° ′	° ′	° ′	° ′	° ′	° ′	° ′	° ′	° ′		° ′	° ′
24 00	241 59.8	160 15.3	N26 08.1	78 22.3	N 8 23.9	188 29.0	N18 24.3	39 09.0	S 6 38.8	Acamar	315 19.3	S40 15.3
01	257 02.3	175 18.7	07.6	93 23.9	23.5	203 30.8	24.4	54 11.6	38.8	Achernar	335 27.8	S57 10.2
02	272 04.8	190 22.1	07.2	108 25.6	23.1	218 32.7	24.5	69 14.2	38.8	Acrux	173 09.7	S63 10.4
03	287 07.2	205 25.4	.. 06.7	123 27.2	.. 22.7	233 34.6	.. 24.7	84 16.8	.. 38.7	Adhara	255 13.4	S28 59.6
04	302 09.7	220 28.8	06.2	138 28.9	22.3	248 36.4	24.8	99 19.3	38.7	Aldebaran	290 50.6	N16 31.9
05	317 12.2	235 32.2	05.8	153 30.5	21.9	263 38.3	25.0	114 21.9	38.6			
06	332 14.6	250 35.6	N26 05.3	168 32.2	N 8 21.5	278 40.2	N18 25.1	129 24.5	S 6 38.6	Alioth	166 21.0	N55 53.7
07	347 17.1	265 39.0	04.8	183 33.8	21.1	293 42.0	25.3	144 27.1	38.6	Alkaid	152 59.1	N49 15.2
T 08	2 19.5	280 42.4	04.3	198 35.5	20.7	308 43.9	25.4	159 29.7	38.5	Al Na'ir	27 44.6	S46 53.7
H 09	17 22.0	295 45.8	.. 03.9	213 37.1	.. 20.3	323 45.7	.. 25.5	174 32.3	.. 38.5	Alnilam	275 47.4	S 1 11.8
U 10	32 24.5	310 49.2	03.4	228 38.8	19.9	338 47.6	25.7	189 34.8	38.5	Alphard	217 56.9	S 8 43.0
R 11	47 26.9	325 52.6	02.9	243 40.4	19.4	353 49.5	25.8	204 37.4	38.4			
S 12	62 29.4	340 56.0	N26 02.4	258 42.1	N 8 19.0	8 51.3	N18 26.0	219 40.0	S 6 38.4	Alphecca	126 11.3	N26 40.4
D 13	77 31.9	355 59.4	01.9	273 43.7	18.6	23 53.2	26.1	234 42.6	38.3	Alpheratz	357 44.4	N29 09.4
A 14	92 34.3	11 02.8	01.5	288 45.4	18.2	38 55.0	26.2	249 45.2	38.3	Altair	62 08.8	N 8 54.1
Y 15	107 36.8	26 06.3	.. 01.0	303 47.0	.. 17.8	53 56.9	.. 26.4	264 47.7	.. 38.3	Ankaa	353 16.7	S42 14.1
16	122 39.3	41 09.7	00.5	318 48.7	17.4	68 58.8	26.5	279 50.3	38.2	Antares	112 26.8	S26 27.5
17	137 41.7	56 13.1	26 00.0	333 50.3	17.0	84 00.6	26.7	294 52.9	38.2			
18	152 44.2	71 16.6	N25 59.5	348 52.0	N 8 16.6	99 02.5	N18 26.8	309 55.5	S 6 38.2	Arcturus	145 56.1	N19 07.1
19	167 46.7	86 20.0	59.0	3 53.6	16.1	114 04.3	26.9	324 58.1	38.1	Atria	107 28.7	S69 02.9
20	182 49.1	101 23.5	58.5	18 55.3	15.7	129 06.2	27.1	340 00.7	38.1	Avior	234 18.7	S59 33.4
21	197 51.6	116 26.9	.. 58.1	33 56.9	.. 15.3	144 08.1	.. 27.2	355 03.2	.. 38.0	Bellatrix	278 33.1	N 6 21.5
22	212 54.0	131 30.4	57.6	48 58.6	14.9	159 09.9	27.4	10 05.8	38.0	Betelgeuse	271 02.4	N 7 24.4
23	227 56.5	146 33.8	57.1	64 00.2	14.5	174 11.8	27.5	25 08.4	38.0			
25 00	242 59.0	161 37.3	N25 56.6	79 01.8	N 8 14.1	189 13.7	N18 27.6	40 11.0	S 6 37.9	Canopus	263 57.0	S52 42.4
01	258 01.4	176 40.8	56.1	94 03.5	13.7	204 15.5	27.8	55 13.6	37.9	Capella	280 36.0	N46 00.5
02	273 03.9	191 44.2	55.6	109 05.1	13.3	219 17.4	27.9	70 16.1	37.9	Deneb	49 31.8	N45 19.4
03	288 06.4	206 47.7	.. 55.1	124 06.8	.. 12.8	234 19.2	.. 28.1	85 18.7	.. 37.8	Denebola	182 34.3	N14 30.1
04	303 08.8	221 51.2	54.6	139 08.4	12.4	249 21.1	28.2	100 21.3	37.8	Diphda	348 56.8	S17 55.0
05	318 11.3	236 54.7	54.1	154 10.1	12.0	264 23.0	28.4	115 23.9	37.8			
06	333 13.8	251 58.1	N25 53.6	169 11.7	N 8 11.6	279 24.8	N18 28.5	130 26.5	S 6 37.7	Dubhe	193 52.5	N61 41.2
07	348 16.2	267 01.6	53.1	184 13.3	11.2	294 26.7	28.6	145 29.0	37.7	Elnath	278 13.9	N28 36.9
F 08	3 18.7	282 05.1	52.6	199 15.0	10.8	309 28.5	28.8	160 31.6	37.6	Eltanin	90 46.0	N51 29.2
R 09	18 21.2	297 08.6	.. 52.1	214 16.6	.. 10.4	324 30.4	.. 28.9	175 34.2	.. 37.6	Enif	33 47.8	N 9 55.9
I 10	33 23.6	312 12.1	51.6	229 18.2	09.9	339 32.3	29.1	190 36.8	37.6	Fomalhaut	15 24.9	S29 33.2
11	48 26.1	327 15.6	51.1	244 19.9	09.5	354 34.1	29.2	205 39.4	37.5			
D 12	63 28.5	342 19.2	N25 50.6	259 21.5	N 8 09.1	9 36.0	N18 29.3	220 41.9	S 6 37.5	Gacrux	172 01.4	S57 11.3
A 13	78 31.0	357 22.7	50.0	274 23.2	08.7	24 37.9	29.5	235 44.5	37.5	Gienah	175 52.9	S17 36.9
Y 14	93 33.5	12 26.2	49.5	289 24.8	08.3	39 39.7	29.6	250 47.1	37.4	Hadar	148 48.4	S60 26.2
15	108 35.9	27 29.7	.. 49.0	304 26.4	.. 07.9	54 41.6	.. 29.8	265 49.7	.. 37.4	Hamal	328 01.9	N23 31.2
16	123 38.4	42 33.2	48.5	319 28.1	07.4	69 43.4	29.9	280 52.2	37.4	Kaus Aust.	83 44.4	S34 22.5
17	138 40.9	57 36.8	48.0	334 29.7	07.0	84 45.3	30.0	295 54.8	37.3			
18	153 43.3	72 40.3	N24 47.5	349 31.3	N 8 06.6	99 47.2	N18 30.2	310 57.4	S 6 37.3	Kochab	137 18.9	N74 06.4
19	168 45.8	87 43.8	47.0	4 33.0	06.2	114 49.0	30.3	326 00.0	37.2	Markab	13 39.1	N15 16.3
20	183 48.3	102 47.4	46.4	19 34.6	05.8	129 50.9	30.5	341 02.6	37.2	Menkar	314 16.1	N 4 08.2
21	198 50.7	117 50.9	.. 45.9	34 36.2	.. 05.4	144 52.7	.. 30.6	356 05.1	.. 37.2	Menkent	148 08.1	S36 26.0
22	213 53.2	132 54.5	45.4	49 37.9	04.9	159 54.6	30.7	11 07.7	37.1	Miaplacidus	221 40.1	S69 46.5
23	228 55.6	147 58.0	44.9	64 39.5	04.5	174 56.5	30.9	26 10.3	37.1			
26 00	243 58.1	163 01.6	N25 44.4	79 41.1	N 8 04.1	189 58.3	N18 31.0	41 12.9	S 6 37.1	Mirfak	308 41.9	N49 54.2
01	259 00.6	178 05.2	43.8	94 42.7	03.7	205 00.2	31.2	56 15.4	37.0	Nunki	75 58.9	S26 16.7
02	274 03.0	193 08.7	43.3	109 44.4	03.3	220 02.1	31.3	71 18.0	37.0	Peacock	53 20.1	S56 41.3
03	289 05.5	208 12.3	.. 42.8	124 46.0	.. 02.8	235 03.9	.. 31.4	86 20.6	.. 37.0	Pollux	243 28.9	N27 59.7
04	304 08.0	223 15.9	42.3	139 47.6	02.4	250 05.8	31.6	101 23.2	36.9	Procyon	245 00.7	N 5 11.4
05	319 10.4	238 19.4	41.7	154 49.3	02.0	265 07.6	31.7	116 25.8	36.9			
06	334 12.9	253 23.0	N25 41.2	169 50.9	N 8 01.6	280 09.5	N18 31.8	131 28.3	S 6 36.9	Rasalhague	96 06.8	N12 33.1
07	349 15.4	268 26.6	40.7	184 52.5	01.2	295 11.4	32.0	146 30.9	36.8	Regulus	207 44.3	N11 54.3
S 08	4 17.8	283 30.2	40.1	199 54.1	00.7	310 13.2	32.1	161 33.5	36.8	Rigel	281 13.1	S 8 11.4
A 09	19 20.3	298 33.8	.. 39.6	214 55.8	8 00.3	325 15.1	.. 32.3	176 36.1	.. 36.8	Rigil Kent.	139 52.1	S60 53.3
T 10	34 22.8	313 37.4	39.1	229 57.4	7 59.9	340 17.0	32.4	191 38.6	36.7	Sabik	102 13.1	S15 44.3
U 11	49 25.2	328 41.0	38.5	244 59.0	59.5	355 18.8	32.5	206 41.2	36.7			
R 12	64 27.7	343 44.6	N25 38.0	260 00.6	N 7 59.1	10 20.7	N18 32.7	221 43.8	S 6 36.6	Schedar	349 41.7	N56 36.1
D 13	79 30.1	358 48.2	37.5	275 02.3	58.6	25 22.5	32.8	236 46.4	36.6	Shaula	96 22.5	S37 06.6
A 14	94 32.6	13 51.8	36.9	290 03.9	58.2	40 24.4	33.0	251 48.9	36.6	Sirius	258 34.7	S16 44.2
Y 15	109 35.1	28 55.4	.. 36.4	305 05.5	.. 57.8	55 26.3	.. 33.1	266 51.5	.. 36.5	Spica	158 31.8	S11 13.7
16	124 37.5	43 59.0	35.8	320 07.1	57.4	70 28.1	33.2	281 54.1	36.5	Suhail	222 53.1	S43 29.4
17	139 40.0	59 02.7	35.3	335 08.7	56.9	85 30.0	33.4	296 56.7	36.5			
18	154 42.5	74 06.3	N25 34.7	350 10.4	N 7 56.5	100 31.8	N18 33.5	311 59.2	S 6 36.4	Vega	80 39.1	N38 47.7
19	169 44.9	89 09.9	34.2	5 12.0	56.1	115 33.7	33.7	327 01.8	36.4	Zuben'ubi	137 05.9	S16 05.7
20	184 47.4	104 13.6	33.7	20 13.6	55.7	130 35.6	33.8	342 04.4	36.4		SHA	Mer.Pass.
21	199 49.9	119 17.2	.. 33.1	35 15.2	.. 55.5	145 37.4	.. 33.9	357 07.0	.. 36.3		° ′	h m
22	214 52.3	134 20.8	32.6	50 16.8	54.8	160 39.3	34.1	12 09.5	36.3	Venus	278 38.3	13 10
23	229 54.8	149 24.5	32.0	65 18.5	54.4	175 41.2	34.2	27 12.1	36.3	Mars	196 02.9	18 42
Mer. Pass.	h m 7 46.8	v 3.5	d 0.5	v 1.6	d 0.4	v 1.9	d 0.1	v 2.6	d 0.0	Jupiter	306 14.7	11 22
										Saturn	157 12.0	21 16

UT	SUN GHA	SUN Dec	MOON GHA	v	MOON Dec	d	HP
24 00	180 47.6	N20 48.1	145 17.3	11.3	N20 32.3	3.9	54.8
01	195 47.6	48.5	159 47.6	11.3	20 28.4	3.9	54.8
02	210 47.5	49.0	174 17.9	11.2	20 24.5	4.1	54.8
03	225 47.5	.. 49.4	188 48.1	11.3	20 20.4	4.2	54.8
04	240 47.4	49.9	203 18.4	11.4	20 16.2	4.2	54.8
05	255 47.3	50.3	217 48.8	11.3	20 12.0	4.4	54.9
T 06	270 47.3	N20 50.8	232 19.1	11.3	N20 07.6	4.4	54.9
H 07	285 47.2	51.3	246 49.4	11.4	20 03.2	4.6	54.9
U 08	300 47.2	51.7	261 19.8	11.3	19 58.6	4.6	54.9
R 09	315 47.1	.. 52.2	275 50.1	11.4	19 54.0	4.8	54.9
S 10	330 47.0	52.6	290 20.5	11.4	19 49.2	4.8	54.9
D 11	345 47.0	53.1	304 50.9	11.4	19 44.4	5.0	55.0
A 12	0 46.9	N20 53.5	319 21.3	11.5	N19 39.4	5.0	55.0
Y 13	15 46.9	54.0	333 51.8	11.4	19 34.4	5.2	55.0
14	30 46.8	54.4	348 22.2	11.5	19 29.2	5.2	55.0
15	45 46.7	.. 54.9	2 52.7	11.4	19 24.0	5.4	55.0
16	60 46.7	55.3	17 23.1	11.5	19 18.6	5.4	55.0
17	75 46.6	55.8	31 53.6	11.5	19 13.2	5.5	55.1
18	90 46.5	N20 56.2	46 24.1	11.6	N19 07.7	5.6	55.1
19	105 46.5	56.7	60 54.7	11.5	19 02.1	5.8	55.1
20	120 46.4	57.1	75 25.2	11.5	18 56.3	5.8	55.1
21	135 46.4	.. 57.6	89 55.7	11.6	18 50.5	5.9	55.1
22	150 46.3	58.0	104 26.3	11.6	18 44.6	6.0	55.2
23	165 46.2	58.5	118 56.9	11.6	18 38.6	6.1	55.2
25 00	180 46.2	N20 58.9	133 27.5	11.7	N18 32.5	6.2	55.2
01	195 46.1	59.4	147 58.2	11.6	18 26.3	6.3	55.2
02	210 46.0	20 59.8	162 28.8	11.7	18 20.0	6.3	55.2
03	225 46.0	21 00.3	176 59.5	11.6	18 13.7	6.5	55.3
04	240 45.9	00.7	191 30.1	11.7	18 07.2	6.5	55.3
05	255 45.8	01.1	206 00.8	11.8	18 00.7	6.7	55.3
F 06	270 45.8	N21 01.6	220 31.6	11.7	N17 54.0	6.7	55.3
R 07	285 45.7	02.0	235 02.3	11.8	17 47.3	6.9	55.3
I 08	300 45.6	02.5	249 33.1	11.7	17 40.4	6.9	55.4
D 09	315 45.6	.. 02.9	264 03.8	11.8	17 33.5	7.0	55.4
A 10	330 45.5	03.3	278 34.6	11.8	17 26.5	7.1	55.4
Y 11	345 45.4	03.8	293 05.4	11.9	17 19.4	7.1	55.4
12	0 45.4	N21 04.2	307 36.3	11.8	17 12.3	7.3	55.5
13	15 45.3	04.7	322 07.1	11.9	17 05.0	7.4	55.5
14	30 45.2	05.1	336 38.0	11.9	16 57.6	7.4	55.5
15	45 45.2	.. 05.5	351 08.9	11.9	16 50.2	7.5	55.5
16	60 45.1	06.0	5 39.8	11.9	16 42.7	7.6	55.5
17	75 45.0	06.4	20 10.7	11.9	16 35.1	7.7	55.6
18	90 45.0	N21 06.8	34 41.6	12.0	N16 27.4	7.8	55.6
19	105 44.9	07.3	49 12.6	12.0	16 19.6	7.9	55.6
20	120 44.8	07.7	63 43.6	12.0	16 11.7	7.9	55.6
21	135 44.8	.. 08.1	78 14.6	12.0	16 03.8	8.1	55.7
22	150 44.7	08.6	92 45.6	12.0	15 55.7	8.1	55.7
23	165 44.6	09.0	107 16.6	12.1	15 47.6	8.2	55.7
26 00	180 44.6	N21 09.4	121 47.7	12.0	N15 39.4	8.2	55.7
01	195 44.5	09.9	136 18.7	12.1	15 31.2	8.4	55.7
02	210 44.4	10.3	150 49.8	12.1	15 22.8	8.4	55.8
03	225 44.4	.. 10.7	165 20.9	12.2	15 14.4	8.5	55.8
04	240 44.3	11.1	179 52.1	12.1	15 05.9	8.6	55.8
05	255 44.2	11.6	194 23.2	12.1	14 57.3	8.7	55.8
S 06	270 44.1	N21 12.0	208 54.3	12.2	N14 48.6	8.7	55.9
A 07	285 44.0	12.4	223 25.5	12.2	14 39.9	8.9	55.9
T 08	300 44.0	12.8	237 56.7	12.2	14 31.0	8.9	55.9
U 09	315 43.9	.. 13.3	252 27.9	12.2	14 22.1	9.0	55.9
R 10	330 43.9	13.7	266 59.1	12.2	14 13.1	9.0	56.0
D 11	345 43.8	14.1	281 30.3	12.3	14 04.1	9.1	56.0
A 12	0 43.7	N21 14.5	296 01.6	12.2	N13 55.0	9.2	56.0
Y 13	15 43.6	15.0	310 32.8	12.3	13 45.8	9.3	56.1
14	30 43.6	15.4	325 04.1	12.3	13 36.5	9.4	56.1
15	45 43.5	.. 15.8	339 35.4	12.3	13 27.1	9.4	56.1
16	60 43.4	16.2	354 06.7	12.3	13 17.7	9.5	56.1
17	75 43.4	16.6	8 38.0	12.3	13 08.2	9.5	56.2
18	90 43.3	N21 17.1	23 09.3	12.4	N12 58.7	9.7	56.2
19	105 43.2	17.5	37 40.7	12.3	12 49.0	9.7	56.2
20	120 43.1	17.9	52 12.0	12.4	12 39.3	9.7	56.2
21	135 43.1	.. 18.3	66 43.4	12.3	12 29.6	9.9	56.3
22	150 43.0	18.7	81 14.7	12.4	12 19.7	9.9	56.3
23	165 42.9	19.2	95 46.1	12.4	N12 09.8	10.0	56.3
	SD 15.8	d 0.4	SD 15.0		15.1		15.3

Twilight / Moonrise

Lat.	Naut.	Civil	Sunrise	24	25	26	27
N 72	☐	☐	☐	☐		06 32	08 38
N 70	☐	☐	☐	☐	05 06	07 05	08 56
68	////	////	00 28	04 06	05 47	07 28	09 09
66	////	////	01 40	04 47	06 14	07 47	09 21
64	////	////	02 16	05 15	06 35	08 01	09 30
62	////	01 02	02 41	05 37	06 52	08 14	09 38
60	////	01 46	03 00	05 54	07 06	08 24	09 45
N 58	////	02 14	03 17	06 08	07 18	08 33	09 51
56	00 56	02 36	03 30	06 21	07 28	08 41	09 56
54	01 37	02 53	03 42	06 32	07 38	08 48	10 01
52	02 03	03 08	03 52	06 41	07 46	08 54	10 05
50	02 23	03 20	04 02	06 50	07 53	09 00	10 09
45	03 00	03 46	04 21	07 08	08 08	09 12	10 18
N 40	03 26	04 05	04 37	07 23	08 21	09 22	10 25
35	03 46	04 21	04 50	07 35	08 32	09 31	10 31
30	04 02	04 35	05 01	07 46	08 41	09 38	10 36
20	04 28	04 57	05 21	08 05	08 58	09 51	10 45
N 10	04 49	05 15	05 38	08 21	09 12	10 02	10 53
0	05 05	05 31	05 53	08 36	09 25	10 13	11 00
S 10	05 20	05 46	06 09	08 51	09 38	10 23	11 08
20	05 35	06 02	06 25	09 08	09 52	10 35	11 16
30	05 49	06 18	06 44	09 26	10 08	10 47	11 25
35	05 56	06 27	06 55	09 37	10 18	10 55	11 30
40	06 04	06 38	07 07	09 49	10 28	11 03	11 36
45	06 13	06 49	07 22	10 04	10 41	11 13	11 42
S 50	06 23	07 03	07 40	10 22	10 56	11 25	11 50
52	06 27	07 09	07 48	10 30	11 03	11 30	11 54
54	06 32	07 16	07 58	10 39	11 10	11 36	11 58
56	06 36	07 24	08 08	10 50	11 19	11 43	12 03
58	06 42	07 32	08 21	11 02	11 29	11 50	12 08
S 60	06 48	07 42	08 35	11 16	11 40	11 59	12 13

Sunset / Twilight / Moonset

Lat.	Sunset	Civil	Naut.	24	25	26	27
N 72	☐	☐	☐	☐		01 46	01 19
N 70	☐	☐	☐	☐	01 30	01 11	01 00
68	23 50	////	////	00 48	00 49	00 47	00 44
66	22 17	////	////	00 06	00 20	00 28	00 32
64	21 41	////	////	23 59	24 12	00 12	00 21
62	21 15	22 57	////	23 41	23 59	24 12	00 12
60	20 55	22 11	////	23 27	23 48	24 04	00 04
N 58	20 39	21 42	////	23 14	23 38	23 57	24 14
56	20 25	21 20	23 03	23 03	23 30	23 51	24 10
54	20 13	21 02	22 20	22 54	23 22	23 46	24 07
52	20 02	20 47	21 53	22 45	23 15	23 41	24 04
50	19 53	20 35	21 32	22 38	23 09	23 36	24 01
45	19 33	20 09	20 55	22 21	22 56	23 27	23 55
N 40	19 18	19 49	20 29	22 08	22 45	23 18	23 50
35	19 04	19 33	20 08	21 57	22 35	23 10	23 45
30	18 53	19 20	19 52	21 47	22 27	23 05	23 41
20	18 33	18 57	19 26	21 29	22 13	22 54	23 35
N 10	18 16	18 39	19 06	21 14	22 00	22 45	23 29
0	18 01	18 23	18 49	21 00	21 48	22 36	23 23
S 10	17 45	18 07	18 33	20 46	21 36	22 27	23 17
20	17 29	17 52	18 19	20 30	21 23	22 17	23 11
30	17 10	17 36	18 05	20 13	21 09	22 06	23 04
35	16 59	17 26	17 57	20 02	21 00	21 59	23 00
40	16 46	17 16	17 49	19 50	20 50	21 52	22 55
45	16 32	17 04	17 41	19 36	20 39	21 43	22 50
S 50	16 14	16 51	17 31	19 19	20 24	21 33	22 43
52	16 05	16 44	17 27	19 11	20 18	21 28	22 40
54	15 56	16 37	17 22	19 02	20 10	21 22	22 37
56	15 45	16 30	17 17	18 52	20 02	21 16	22 33
58	15 33	16 21	17 12	18 40	19 53	21 10	22 29
S 60	15 19	16 11	17 05	18 27	19 42	21 02	22 24

SUN / MOON

Day	Eqn. of Time 00h	Eqn. of Time 12h	Mer. Pass.	Mer. Pass. Upper	Mer. Pass. Lower	Age	Phase
d	m s	m s	h m	h m	h m	d	%
24	03 11	03 08	11 57	14 48	02 24	04	11
25	03 05	03 02	11 57	15 37	03 12	05	18
26	02 58	02 55	11 57	16 24	04 01	06	26

UT	ARIES GHA	VENUS −4.1 GHA	Dec	MARS +0.5 GHA	Dec	JUPITER −2.0 GHA	Dec	SATURN +0.5 GHA	Dec	STARS Name	SHA	Dec
27 00	244 57.3	164 28.1	N25 31.5	80 20.1	N 7 54.0	190 43.0	N18 34.3	42 14.7	S 6 36.2	Acamar	315 19.3	S40 15.3
01	259 59.7	179 31.8	30.9	95 21.7	53.6	205 44.9	34.5	57 17.3	36.2	Achernar	335 27.8	S57 10.2
02	275 02.2	194 35.4	30.4	110 23.3	53.1	220 46.7	34.6	72 19.8	36.2	Acrux	173 09.8	S63 10.4
03	290 04.6	209 39.1 ..	29.8	125 24.9 ..	52.7	235 48.6 ..	34.8	87 22.4 ..	36.1	Adhara	255 13.4	S28 59.6
04	305 07.1	224 42.8	29.2	140 26.5	52.3	250 50.5	34.9	102 25.0	36.1	Aldebaran	290 50.6	N16 31.9
05	320 09.6	239 46.4	28.7	155 28.1	51.9	265 52.3	35.0	117 27.6	36.1			
06	335 12.0	254 50.1	N25 28.1	170 29.8	N 7 51.4	280 54.2	N18 35.2	132 30.1	S 6 36.0	Alioth	166 21.0	N55 53.7
07	350 14.5	269 53.8	27.6	185 31.4	51.0	295 56.1	35.3	147 32.7	36.0	Alkaid	152 59.1	N49 15.2
08	5 17.0	284 57.4	27.0	200 33.0	50.6	310 57.9	35.5	162 35.3	36.0	Al Na'ir	27 44.6	S46 53.7
S 09	20 19.4	300 01.1 ..	26.4	215 34.6 ..	50.2	325 59.8 ..	35.6	177 37.9 ..	35.9	Alnilam	275 47.4	S 1 11.8
U 10	35 21.9	315 04.8	25.9	230 36.2	49.7	341 01.6	35.7	192 40.4	35.9	Alphard	217 56.9	S 8 43.0
N 11	50 24.4	330 08.5	25.3	245 37.8	49.3	356 03.5	35.9	207 43.0	35.9			
D 12	65 26.8	345 12.2	N25 24.8	260 39.4	N 7 48.9	11 05.4	N18 36.0	222 45.6	S 6 35.8	Alphecca	126 11.3	N26 40.4
A 13	80 29.3	0 15.9	24.2	275 41.0	48.5	26 07.2	36.1	237 48.1	35.8	Alpheratz	357 44.4	N29 09.4
Y 14	95 31.7	15 19.6	23.6	290 42.7	48.0	41 09.1	36.3	252 50.7	35.8	Altair	62 08.7	N 8 54.1
15	110 34.2	30 23.3 ..	23.1	305 44.3 ..	47.6	56 11.0 ..	36.4	267 53.3 ..	35.7	Ankaa	353 16.6	S42 14.1
16	125 36.7	45 27.0	22.5	320 45.9	47.2	71 12.8	36.6	282 55.9	35.7	Antares	112 26.8	S26 27.5
17	140 39.1	60 30.7	21.9	335 47.5	46.7	86 14.7	36.7	297 58.4	35.7			
18	155 41.6	75 34.4	N25 21.3	350 49.1	N 7 46.3	101 16.5	N18 36.8	313 01.0	S 6 35.6	Arcturus	145 56.1	N19 07.1
19	170 44.1	90 38.1	20.8	5 50.7	45.9	116 18.4	37.0	328 03.6	35.6	Atria	107 28.7	S69 02.9
20	185 46.5	105 41.8	20.2	20 52.3	45.5	131 20.3	37.1	343 06.1	35.6	Avior	234 18.7	S59 33.4
21	200 49.0	120 45.6 ..	19.6	35 53.9 ..	45.0	146 22.1 ..	37.3	358 08.7 ..	35.5	Bellatrix	278 33.1	N 6 21.5
22	215 51.5	135 49.3	19.0	50 55.5	44.6	161 24.0	37.4	13 11.3	35.5	Betelgeuse	271 02.4	N 7 24.4
23	230 53.9	150 53.0	18.5	65 57.1	44.2	176 25.9	37.5	28 13.9	35.5			
28 00	245 56.4	165 56.8	N25 17.9	80 58.7	N 7 43.7	191 27.7	N18 37.7	43 16.4	S 6 35.4	Canopus	263 57.0	S52 42.4
01	260 58.9	181 00.5	17.3	96 00.3	43.3	206 29.6	37.8	58 19.0	35.4	Capella	280 36.0	N46 00.5
02	276 01.3	196 04.2	16.7	111 01.9	42.9	221 31.4	37.9	73 21.6	35.4	Deneb	49 31.8	N45 19.4
03	291 03.8	211 08.0 ..	16.1	126 03.5 ..	42.5	236 33.3 ..	38.1	88 24.1 ..	35.3	Denebola	182 34.3	N14 30.1
04	306 06.2	226 11.7	15.6	141 05.1	42.0	251 35.2	38.2	103 26.7	35.3	Diphda	348 56.8	S17 55.0
05	321 08.7	241 15.5	15.0	156 06.7	41.6	266 37.0	38.4	118 29.3	35.3			
06	336 11.2	256 19.2	N25 14.4	171 08.3	N 7 41.2	281 38.9	N18 38.5	133 31.9	S 6 35.2	Dubhe	193 52.5	N61 41.2
07	351 13.6	271 23.0	13.8	186 09.9	40.7	296 40.8	38.6	148 34.4	35.2	Elnath	278 13.9	N28 36.9
08	6 16.1	286 26.7	13.2	201 11.5	40.3	311 42.6	38.8	163 37.0	35.2	Eltanin	90 46.0	N51 29.2
M 09	21 18.6	301 30.5 ..	12.6	216 13.1 ..	39.9	326 44.5 ..	38.9	178 39.6 ..	35.1	Enif	33 47.8	N 9 56.0
O 10	36 21.0	316 34.3	12.0	231 14.7	39.4	341 46.3	39.0	193 42.1	35.1	Fomalhaut	15 24.8	S29 33.1
N 11	51 23.5	331 38.0	11.4	246 16.3	39.0	356 48.2	39.2	208 44.7	35.1			
D 12	66 26.0	346 41.8	N25 10.9	261 17.9	N 7 38.6	11 50.1	N18 39.3	223 47.3	S 6 35.0	Gacrux	172 01.4	S57 11.3
A 13	81 28.4	1 45.6	10.3	276 19.5	38.1	26 51.9	39.4	238 49.8	35.0	Gienah	175 52.9	S17 36.9
Y 14	96 30.9	16 49.4	09.7	291 21.1	37.7	41 53.8	39.6	253 52.4	35.0	Hadar	148 48.4	S60 26.2
15	111 33.4	31 53.2 ..	09.1	306 22.7 ..	37.3	56 55.7 ..	39.7	268 55.0 ..	35.0	Hamal	328 01.9	N23 31.2
16	126 35.8	46 56.9	08.5	321 24.3	36.8	71 57.5	39.9	283 57.6	34.9	Kaus Aust.	83 44.4	S34 22.5
17	141 38.3	62 00.7	07.9	336 25.9	36.4	86 59.4	40.0	299 00.1	34.9			
18	156 40.7	77 04.5	N25 07.3	351 27.5	N 7 36.0	102 01.2	N18 40.1	314 02.7	S 6 34.9	Kochab	137 18.9	N74 06.4
19	171 43.2	92 08.3	06.7	6 29.1	35.5	117 03.1	40.3	329 05.3	34.8	Markab	13 39.1	N15 16.3
20	186 45.7	107 12.1	06.1	21 30.7	35.1	132 05.0	40.4	344 07.8	34.8	Menkar	314 16.1	N 4 08.2
21	201 48.1	122 15.9 ..	05.5	36 32.3 ..	34.7	147 06.8 ..	40.5	359 10.4 ..	34.8	Menkent	148 08.1	S36 26.0
22	216 50.6	137 19.7	04.9	51 33.9	34.2	162 08.7	40.7	14 13.0	34.7	Miaplacidus	221 46.2	S69 46.5
23	231 53.1	152 23.5	04.3	66 35.5	33.8	177 10.6	40.8	29 15.5	34.7			
29 00	246 55.5	167 27.3	N25 03.7	81 37.1	N 7 33.4	192 12.4	N18 41.0	44 18.1	S 6 34.7	Mirfak	308 41.9	N49 54.2
01	261 58.0	182 31.1	03.1	96 38.7	32.9	207 14.3	41.1	59 20.7	34.6	Nunki	75 58.9	S26 16.7
02	277 00.5	197 35.0	02.4	111 40.3	32.5	222 16.1	41.2	74 23.2	34.6	Peacock	53 20.1	S56 41.3
03	292 02.9	212 38.8 ..	01.8	126 41.8 ..	32.1	237 18.0 ..	41.4	89 25.8 ..	34.6	Pollux	243 28.9	N27 59.7
04	307 05.4	227 42.6	01.2	141 43.4	31.6	252 19.9	41.5	104 28.4	34.5	Procyon	245 00.7	N 5 11.4
05	322 07.8	242 46.4	00.6	156 45.0	31.2	267 21.7	41.6	119 30.9	34.5			
06	337 10.3	257 50.3	N25 00.0	171 46.6	N 7 30.8	282 23.6	N18 41.8	134 33.5	S 6 34.5	Rasalhague	96 06.8	N12 33.1
07	352 12.8	272 54.1	24 59.4	186 48.2	30.3	297 25.5	41.9	149 36.1	34.5	Regulus	207 44.3	N11 54.3
08	7 15.2	287 57.9	58.8	201 49.8	29.9	312 27.3	42.0	164 38.6	34.4	Rigel	281 13.1	S 8 11.4
T 09	22 17.7	303 01.8 ..	58.2	216 51.4 ..	29.5	327 29.2 ..	42.2	179 41.2 ..	34.4	Rigil Kent.	139 52.1	S60 53.3
U 10	37 20.2	318 05.6	57.5	231 53.0	29.0	342 31.1	42.3	194 43.8	34.4	Sabik	102 13.0	S15 44.3
E 11	52 22.6	333 09.4	56.9	246 54.5	28.6	357 32.9	42.5	209 46.3	34.3			
S 12	67 25.1	348 13.3	N24 56.3	261 56.1	N 7 28.2	12 34.8	N18 42.6	224 48.9	S 6 34.3	Schedar	349 41.7	N56 36.1
D 13	82 27.6	3 17.1	55.7	276 57.7	27.7	27 36.6	42.7	239 51.5	34.3	Shaula	96 22.5	S37 06.6
A 14	97 30.0	18 21.0	55.1	291 59.3	27.3	42 38.5	42.9	254 54.0	34.2	Sirius	258 34.7	S16 44.2
Y 15	112 32.5	33 24.9 ..	54.4	307 00.9 ..	26.8	57 40.4 ..	43.0	269 56.6 ..	34.2	Spica	158 31.8	S11 13.7
16	127 35.0	48 28.7	53.8	322 02.5	26.4	72 42.2	43.1	284 59.2	34.2	Suhail	222 53.2	S43 29.4
17	142 37.4	63 32.6	53.2	337 04.1	26.0	87 44.1	43.3	300 01.7	34.1			
18	157 39.9	78 36.4	N24 52.6	352 05.6	N 7 25.5	102 46.0	N18 43.4	315 04.3	S 6 34.1	Vega	80 39.1	N38 47.7
19	172 42.3	93 40.3	51.9	7 07.2	25.1	117 47.8	43.5	330 06.9	34.1	Zuben'ubi	137 05.9	S16 05.7
20	187 44.8	108 44.2	51.3	22 08.8	24.7	132 49.7	43.7	345 09.4	34.1		SHA	Mer.Pass.
21	202 47.3	123 48.0 ..	50.7	37 10.4 ..	24.2	147 51.5 ..	43.8	0 12.0 ..	34.0	Venus	280 00.4	12 53
22	217 49.7	138 51.9	50.1	52 12.0	23.8	162 53.4	43.9	15 14.6	34.0	Mars	195 02.3	18 34
23	232 52.2	153 55.8	49.4	67 13.5	23.3	177 55.3	44.1	30 17.1	34.0	Jupiter	305 31.3	11 13
Mer.Pass.	7 35.0	v 3.8	d 0.6	v 1.6	d 0.4	v 1.9	d 0.1	v 2.6	d 0.0	Saturn	157 20.0	21 03

UT	SUN		MOON					Lat.	Twilight		Sunrise	Moonrise			
									Naut.	Civil		27	28	29	30
	GHA	Dec	GHA	v	Dec	d	HP								
d h	° ′	° ′	° ′	′	° ′	′	′	°	h m	h m	h m	h m	h m	h m	h m
27 00	180 42.8	N21 19.6	110 17.5	12.4	N11 59.8	10.0	56.4	N 72	☐	☐	☐	08 38	10 36	12 33	14 34
01	195 42.8	20.0	124 48.9	12.4	11 49.8	10.1	56.4	N 70	☐	☐	☐	08 56	10 44	12 33	14 26
02	210 42.7	20.4	139 20.3	12.4	11 39.7	10.2	56.4	68	////	////	☐	09 09	10 51	12 33	14 20
03	225 42.6	.. 20.8	153 51.7	12.5	11 29.5	10.2	56.4	66	////	////	01 28	09 21	10 56	12 33	14 14
04	240 42.6	21.2	168 23.2	12.4	11 19.3	10.3	56.5	64	////	////	02 07	09 30	11 01	12 34	14 10
05	255 42.5	21.6	182 54.6	12.4	11 09.0	10.4	56.5	62	////	00 43	02 34	09 38	11 05	12 34	14 06
06	270 42.4	N21 22.0	197 26.0	12.5	N10 58.6	10.4	56.5	60	////	01 37	02 55	09 45	11 08	12 34	14 02
07	285 42.3	22.5	211 57.5	12.4	10 48.2	10.5	56.6	N 58	////	02 08	03 12	09 51	11 11	12 34	13 59
08	300 42.3	22.9	226 28.9	12.5	10 37.7	10.6	56.6	56	00 39	02 30	03 26	09 56	11 14	12 34	13 57
S 09	315 42.2	.. 23.3	241 00.4	12.4	10 27.1	10.6	56.6	54	01 28	02 49	03 39	10 01	11 16	12 34	13 54
U 10	330 42.1	23.7	255 31.8	12.5	10 16.5	10.6	56.6	52	01 57	03 04	03 49	10 05	11 19	12 34	13 52
N 11	345 42.0	24.1	270 03.3	12.5	10 05.9	10.8	56.7	50	02 18	03 17	03 59	10 09	11 21	12 34	13 50
D 12	0 41.9	N21 24.5	284 34.8	12.4	N 9 55.1	10.8	56.7	45	02 56	03 43	04 19	10 18	11 25	12 34	13 46
A 13	15 41.9	24.9	299 06.2	12.5	9 44.3	10.8	56.7	N 40	03 23	04 03	04 35	10 25	11 29	12 35	13 43
Y 14	30 41.8	25.3	313 37.7	12.5	9 33.5	10.9	56.8	35	03 44	04 20	04 49	10 31	11 32	12 35	13 40
15	45 41.7	.. 25.7	328 09.2	12.4	9 22.6	11.0	56.8	30	04 01	04 34	05 00	10 36	11 35	12 35	13 37
16	60 41.6	26.1	342 40.6	12.5	9 11.6	11.0	56.8	20	04 28	04 56	05 20	10 45	11 39	12 35	13 33
17	75 41.6	26.5	357 12.1	12.5	9 00.6	11.1	56.9	N 10	04 48	05 15	05 38	10 53	11 44	12 35	13 29
18	90 41.5	N21 26.9	11 43.6	12.4	N 8 49.5	11.1	56.9	0	05 06	05 31	05 54	11 00	11 48	12 35	13 25
19	105 41.4	27.3	26 15.0	12.5	8 38.4	11.2	56.9	S 10	05 21	05 47	06 10	11 08	11 51	12 36	13 21
20	120 41.3	27.7	40 46.5	12.5	8 27.2	11.2	56.9	20	05 36	06 03	06 26	11 16	11 56	12 36	13 17
21	135 41.3	.. 28.1	55 18.0	12.4	8 16.0	11.3	57.0	30	05 50	06 20	06 46	11 25	12 00	12 36	13 13
22	150 41.2	28.5	69 49.4	12.5	8 04.7	11.3	57.0	35	05 58	06 29	06 57	11 30	12 03	12 36	13 11
23	165 41.1	28.9	84 20.9	12.4	7 53.4	11.4	57.0	40	06 06	06 40	07 10	11 36	12 06	12 37	13 08
								45	06 15	06 52	07 25	11 42	12 10	12 37	13 05
28 00	180 41.0	N21 29.3	98 52.3	12.5	N 7 42.0	11.4	57.1	S 50	06 25	07 06	07 43	11 50	12 14	12 37	13 01
01	195 40.9	29.7	113 23.8	12.4	7 30.6	11.5	57.1	52	06 30	07 13	07 52	11 54	12 16	12 37	12 59
02	210 40.9	30.1	127 55.2	12.4	7 19.1	11.5	57.1	54	06 35	07 20	08 02	11 58	12 18	12 38	12 57
03	225 40.8	.. 30.5	142 26.6	12.5	7 07.6	11.6	57.2	56	06 40	07 28	08 13	12 03	12 21	12 38	12 55
04	240 40.7	30.9	156 58.1	12.4	6 56.0	11.6	57.2	58	06 46	07 37	08 25	12 08	12 23	12 38	12 53
05	255 40.6	31.3	171 29.5	12.4	6 44.4	11.7	57.2	S 60	06 52	07 47	08 40	12 13	12 26	12 38	12 51
06	270 40.5	N21 31.7	186 00.9	12.4	N 6 32.7	11.7	57.3	Lat.	Sunset	Twilight		Moonset			
07	285 40.5	32.1	200 32.3	12.4	6 21.0	11.8	57.3			Civil	Naut.	27	28	29	30
08	300 40.4	32.5	215 03.7	12.3	6 09.2	11.8	57.3								
M 09	315 40.3	.. 32.9	229 35.0	12.4	5 57.4	11.8	57.4								
O 10	330 40.2	33.3	244 06.4	12.3	5 45.6	11.9	57.4	°	h m	h m	h m	h m	h m	h m	h m
N 11	345 40.1	33.7	258 37.7	12.4	5 33.7	11.9	57.4	N 72	☐	☐	☐	01 19	01 00	00 44	00 29
D 12	0 40.1	N21 34.1	273 09.1	12.3	N 5 21.8	12.0	57.5	N 70	☐	☐	☐	01 00	00 50	00 41	00 32
A 13	15 40.0	34.5	287 40.4	12.3	5 09.8	12.0	57.5	68	☐	☐	☐	00 44	00 41	00 38	00 35
Y 14	30 39.9	34.9	302 11.7	12.3	4 57.8	12.0	57.5	66	22 31	////	////	00 32	00 34	00 36	00 37
15	45 39.8	.. 35.3	316 43.0	12.2	4 45.8	12.1	57.6	64	21 50	////	////	00 21	00 28	00 33	00 39
16	60 39.7	35.6	331 14.2	12.3	4 33.7	12.1	57.6	62	21 22	23 19	////	00 12	00 22	00 32	00 40
17	75 39.7	36.0	345 45.5	12.2	4 21.6	12.2	57.6	60	21 01	22 20	////	00 04	00 18	00 30	00 42
18	90 39.6	N21 36.4	0 16.7	12.2	N 4 09.4	12.1	57.7	N 58	20 44	21 49	////	24 14	00 14	00 28	00 43
19	105 39.5	36.8	14 47.9	12.2	3 57.3	12.3	57.7	56	20 29	21 26	23 22	24 10	00 10	00 27	00 44
20	120 39.4	37.2	29 19.1	12.1	3 45.0	12.2	57.7	54	20 17	21 07	22 29	24 07	00 07	00 26	00 45
21	135 39.3	.. 37.6	43 50.2	12.2	3 32.8	12.3	57.8	52	20 06	20 52	22 00	24 04	00 04	00 25	00 46
22	150 39.3	38.0	58 21.4	12.1	3 20.5	12.3	57.8	50	19 56	20 39	21 38	24 01	00 01	00 24	00 47
23	165 39.2	38.4	72 52.5	12.1	3 08.2	12.4	57.8	45	19 36	20 12	20 59	23 55	24 22	00 22	00 49
29 00	180 39.1	N21 38.7	87 23.6	12.1	N 2 55.8	12.3	57.9	N 40	19 20	19 52	20 32	23 50	24 20	00 20	00 51
01	195 39.0	39.1	101 54.7	12.0	2 43.5	12.4	57.9	35	19 06	19 35	20 11	23 45	24 18	00 18	00 52
02	210 38.9	39.5	116 25.7	12.0	2 31.1	12.5	57.9	30	18 55	19 21	19 54	23 41	24 17	00 17	00 53
03	225 38.8	.. 39.9	130 56.7	12.0	2 18.6	12.4	58.0	20	18 34	18 59	19 27	23 35	24 15	00 15	00 55
04	240 38.8	40.3	145 27.7	11.9	2 06.2	12.5	58.0	N 10	18 17	18 40	19 06	23 29	24 12	00 12	00 57
05	255 38.7	40.7	159 58.6	12.0	1 53.7	12.5	58.0	0	18 01	18 23	18 49	23 23	24 10	00 10	00 59
06	270 38.6	N21 41.0	174 29.6	11.9	N 1 41.2	12.5	58.1	S 10	17 45	18 08	18 34	23 17	24 08	00 08	01 00
07	285 38.5	41.4	189 00.5	11.8	1 28.7	12.6	58.1	20	17 28	17 52	18 19	23 11	24 06	00 06	01 02
08	300 38.4	41.8	203 31.3	11.8	1 16.1	12.6	58.1	30	17 09	17 35	18 04	23 04	24 03	00 03	01 04
T 09	315 38.3	.. 42.2	218 02.1	11.8	1 03.5	12.6	58.2	35	16 58	17 25	17 56	23 00	24 02	00 02	01 05
U 10	330 38.2	42.5	232 32.9	11.8	0 50.9	12.6	58.2	40	16 45	17 15	17 48	22 55	24 00	00 00	01 07
E 11	345 38.2	42.9	247 03.7	11.7	0 38.3	12.6	58.2	45	16 30	17 03	17 39	22 50	23 58	25 08	01 08
S 12	0 38.1	N21 43.3	261 34.4	11.7	N 0 25.7	12.7	58.3	S 50	16 11	16 48	17 29	22 43	23 55	25 10	01 10
D 13	15 38.0	43.7	276 05.1	11.6	0 13.0	12.6	58.3	52	16 02	16 42	17 24	22 40	23 54	25 11	01 11
A 14	30 37.9	44.0	290 35.7	11.6	N 0 00.4	12.7	58.3	54	15 53	16 35	17 19	22 37	23 53	25 12	01 12
Y 15	45 37.8	.. 44.4	305 06.3	11.6	S 0 12.3	12.7	58.4	56	15 41	16 27	17 14	22 33	23 52	25 13	01 13
16	60 37.7	44.8	319 36.9	11.5	0 25.0	12.7	58.4	58	15 29	16 18	17 08	22 29	23 50	25 14	01 14
17	75 37.7	45.2	334 07.4	11.5	0 37.7	12.8	58.5	S 60	15 14	16 08	17 02	22 24	23 48	25 15	01 15
18	90 37.6	N21 45.5	348 37.9	11.5	S 0 50.5	12.7	58.5			SUN		MOON			
19	105 37.5	45.9	3 08.4	11.4	1 03.2	12.7	58.5	Day	Eqn. of Time		Mer.	Mer. Pass.		Age	Phase
20	120 37.4	46.3	17 38.8	11.3	1 15.9	12.8	58.6		00ʰ	12ʰ	Pass.	Upper	Lower		
21	135 37.3	.. 46.7	32 09.1	11.3	1 28.7	12.8	58.6	d	m s	m s	h m	h m	h m	d	%
22	150 37.2	47.0	46 39.4	11.3	1 41.4	12.8	58.6	27	02 52	02 48	11 57	17 12	04 48	07	36
23	165 37.1	47.4	61 09.7	11.2	S 1 54.2	12.8	58.7	28	02 44	02 40	11 57	17 59	05 35	08	46
	SD 15.8	d 0.4	SD 15.4		15.7		15.9	29	02 37	02 32	11 57	18 47	06 23	09	57

110 2012 MAY 30, 31, JUNE 1 (WED., THURS., FRI.)

UT	ARIES GHA	VENUS −4.1 GHA	Dec	MARS +0.5 GHA	Dec	JUPITER −2.0 GHA	Dec	SATURN +0.5 GHA	Dec	STARS Name	SHA	Dec
30 00	247 54.7	168 59.7	N24 48.8	82 15.1	N 7 22.9	192 57.1	N18 44.2	45 19.7	S 6 33.9	Acamar	315 19.3	S40 15.2
01	262 57.1	184 03.6	48.2	97 16.7	22.5	207 59.0	44.4	60 22.3	33.9	Achernar	335 27.7	S57 10.2
02	277 59.6	199 07.4	47.5	112 18.3	22.0	223 00.9	44.5	75 24.8	33.9	Acrux	173 09.8	S63 10.5
03	293 02.1	214 11.3	.. 46.9	127 19.9	.. 21.6	238 02.7	.. 44.6	90 27.4	.. 33.8	Adhara	255 13.4	S28 59.6
04	308 04.5	229 15.2	46.3	142 21.4	21.1	253 04.6	44.8	105 29.9	33.8	Aldebaran	290 50.6	N16 31.9
05	323 07.0	244 19.1	45.6	157 23.0	20.7	268 06.5	44.9	120 32.5	33.8			
W 06	338 09.5	259 23.0	N24 45.0	172 24.6	N 7 20.3	283 08.3	N18 45.0	135 35.1	S 6 33.8	Alioth	166 21.0	N55 53.7
E 07	353 11.9	274 26.9	44.3	187 26.2	19.8	298 10.2	45.2	150 37.6	33.7	Alkaid	152 59.1	N49 15.2
D 08	8 14.4	289 30.8	43.7	202 27.8	19.4	313 12.0	45.3	165 40.2	33.7	Al Na'ir	27 44.6	S46 53.7
N 09	23 16.8	304 34.7	.. 43.1	217 29.3	.. 18.9	328 13.9	.. 45.4	180 42.8	.. 33.7	Alnilam	275 47.4	S 1 11.8
E 10	38 19.3	319 38.6	42.4	232 30.9	18.5	343 15.8	45.6	195 45.3	33.6	Alphard	217 56.9	S 8 43.0
S 11	53 21.8	334 42.5	41.8	247 32.5	18.1	358 17.6	45.7	210 47.9	33.6			
D 12	68 24.2	349 46.4	N24 41.1	262 34.1	N 7 17.6	13 19.5	N18 45.8	225 50.5	S 6 33.6	Alphecca	126 11.3	N26 40.4
A 13	83 26.7	4 50.4	40.5	277 35.6	17.2	28 21.4	46.0	240 53.0	33.6	Alpheratz	357 44.4	N29 09.4
Y 14	98 29.2	19 54.3	39.8	292 37.2	16.7	43 23.2	46.1	255 55.6	33.5	Altair	62 08.7	N 8 54.1
15	113 31.6	34 58.2	.. 39.2	307 38.8	.. 16.3	58 25.1	.. 46.2	270 58.1	.. 33.5	Ankaa	353 16.6	S42 14.1
16	128 34.1	50 02.1	38.5	322 40.3	15.8	73 27.0	46.4	286 00.7	33.5	Antares	112 26.8	S26 27.5
17	143 36.6	65 06.0	37.9	337 41.9	15.4	88 28.8	46.5	301 03.3	33.4			
18	158 39.0	80 10.0	N24 37.2	352 43.5	N 7 15.0	103 30.7	N18 46.6	316 05.8	S 6 33.4	Arcturus	145 56.1	N19 07.1
19	173 41.5	95 13.9	36.6	7 45.1	14.5	118 32.5	46.8	331 08.4	33.4	Atria	107 28.7	S69 02.9
20	188 43.9	110 17.8	35.9	22 46.6	14.1	133 34.4	46.9	346 11.0	33.3	Avior	234 18.7	S59 33.4
21	203 46.4	125 21.8	.. 35.3	37 48.2	.. 13.6	148 36.3	.. 47.1	1 13.5	.. 33.3	Bellatrix	278 33.1	N 6 21.5
22	218 48.9	140 25.7	34.6	52 49.8	13.2	163 38.1	47.2	16 16.1	33.3	Betelgeuse	271 02.4	N 7 24.4
23	233 51.3	155 29.6	34.0	67 51.3	12.7	178 40.0	47.3	31 18.6	33.3			
31 00	248 53.8	170 33.6	N24 33.3	82 52.9	N 7 12.3	193 41.9	N18 47.5	46 21.2	S 6 33.2	Canopus	263 57.0	S52 42.4
01	263 56.3	185 37.5	32.7	97 54.5	11.9	208 43.7	47.6	61 23.8	33.2	Capella	280 36.0	N46 00.5
02	278 58.7	200 41.5	32.0	112 56.0	11.4	223 45.6	47.7	76 26.3	33.2	Deneb	49 31.7	N45 19.4
03	294 01.2	215 45.4	.. 31.4	127 57.6	.. 11.0	238 47.5	.. 47.9	91 28.9	.. 33.1	Denebola	182 34.3	N14 30.1
04	309 03.7	230 49.4	30.7	142 59.2	10.5	253 49.3	48.0	106 31.4	33.1	Diphda	348 56.8	S17 55.0
05	324 06.1	245 53.3	30.0	158 00.7	10.1	268 51.2	48.1	121 34.0	33.1			
T 06	339 08.6	260 57.3	N24 29.4	173 02.3	N 7 09.6	283 53.1	N18 48.3	136 36.6	S 6 33.1	Dubhe	193 52.5	N61 41.2
H 07	354 11.1	276 01.2	28.7	188 03.9	09.2	298 54.9	48.4	151 39.1	33.0	Elnath	278 13.9	N28 36.9
U 08	9 13.5	291 05.2	28.0	203 05.4	08.7	313 56.8	48.5	166 41.7	33.0	Eltanin	90 46.0	N51 29.2
R 09	24 16.0	306 09.2	.. 27.4	218 07.0	.. 08.3	328 58.6	.. 48.7	181 44.2	.. 33.0	Enif	33 47.7	N 9 56.0
S 10	39 18.4	321 13.1	26.7	233 08.6	07.8	344 00.5	48.8	196 46.8	33.0	Fomalhaut	15 24.8	S29 33.1
D 11	54 20.9	336 17.1	26.0	248 10.1	07.4	359 02.4	48.9	211 49.4	32.9			
A 12	69 23.4	351 21.0	N24 25.4	263 11.7	N 7 07.0	14 04.2	N18 49.1	226 51.9	S 6 32.9	Gacrux	172 01.4	S57 11.3
Y 13	84 25.8	6 25.0	24.7	278 13.3	06.5	29 06.1	49.2	241 54.5	32.9	Gienah	175 52.9	S17 36.9
14	99 28.3	21 29.0	24.0	293 14.8	06.1	44 08.0	49.3	256 57.0	32.8	Hadar	148 48.4	S60 26.2
15	114 30.8	36 33.0	.. 23.4	308 16.4	.. 05.6	59 09.8	.. 49.5	271 59.6	.. 32.8	Hamal	328 01.9	N23 31.2
16	129 33.2	51 36.9	22.7	323 17.9	05.2	74 11.7	49.6	287 02.2	32.8	Kaus Aust.	83 44.4	S34 22.5
17	144 35.7	66 40.9	22.0	338 19.5	04.7	89 13.6	49.7	302 04.7	32.8			
18	159 38.2	81 44.9	N24 21.3	353 21.1	N 7 04.3	104 15.4	N18 49.9	317 07.3	S 6 32.7	Kochab	137 18.9	N74 06.4
19	174 40.6	96 48.9	20.7	8 22.6	03.8	119 17.3	50.0	332 09.8	32.7	Markab	13 39.1	N15 16.3
20	189 43.1	111 52.9	20.0	23 24.2	03.4	134 19.2	50.1	347 12.4	32.7	Menkar	314 16.1	N 4 08.2
21	204 45.5	126 56.9	.. 19.3	38 25.7	.. 02.9	149 21.0	.. 50.3	2 15.0	.. 32.6	Menkent	148 08.1	S36 26.0
22	219 48.0	142 00.8	18.6	53 27.3	02.5	164 22.9	50.4	17 17.5	32.6	Miaplacidus	221 40.2	S69 46.5
23	234 50.5	157 04.8	18.0	68 28.9	02.0	179 24.7	50.5	32 20.1	32.6			
1 00	249 52.9	172 08.8	N24 17.3	83 30.4	N 7 01.6	194 26.6	N18 50.7	47 22.6	S 6 32.6	Mirfak	308 41.9	N49 54.2
01	264 55.4	187 12.8	16.6	98 32.0	01.1	209 28.5	50.8	62 25.2	32.5	Nunki	75 58.9	S26 16.7
02	279 57.9	202 16.8	15.9	113 33.5	00.7	224 30.3	50.9	77 27.7	32.5	Peacock	53 20.0	S56 41.3
03	295 00.3	217 20.8	.. 15.2	128 35.1	7 00.2	239 32.2	.. 51.1	92 30.3	.. 32.5	Pollux	243 28.9	N27 59.7
04	310 02.8	232 24.8	14.6	143 36.6	6 59.8	254 34.1	51.2	107 32.9	32.5	Procyon	245 00.7	N 5 11.4
05	325 05.3	247 28.8	13.9	158 38.2	59.3	269 35.9	51.3	122 35.4	32.4			
F 06	340 07.7	262 32.8	N24 12.3	173 39.7	N 6 58.9	284 37.8	N18 51.5	137 38.0	S 6 32.4	Rasalhague	96 06.8	N12 33.1
R 07	355 10.2	277 36.8	12.5	188 41.3	58.4	299 39.7	51.6	152 40.5	32.4	Regulus	207 44.4	N11 54.3
I 08	10 12.7	292 40.8	11.8	203 42.8	58.0	314 41.5	51.7	167 43.1	32.4	Rigel	281 13.1	S 8 11.4
D 09	25 15.1	307 44.9	.. 11.1	218 44.4	.. 57.5	329 43.4	.. 51.9	182 45.6	.. 32.3	Rigil Kent.	139 52.1	S60 53.3
A 10	40 17.6	322 48.9	10.4	233 46.0	57.1	344 45.3	52.0	197 48.2	32.3	Sabik	102 13.0	S15 44.3
Y 11	55 20.0	337 52.9	09.8	248 47.5	56.6	359 47.1	52.1	212 50.8	32.3			
12	70 22.5	352 56.9	N24 09.1	263 49.1	N 6 56.2	14 49.0	N18 52.3	227 53.3	S 6 32.2	Schedar	349 41.6	N56 36.1
13	85 25.0	8 00.9	08.4	278 50.6	55.7	29 50.8	52.4	242 55.9	32.2	Shaula	96 22.5	S37 06.6
14	100 27.4	23 04.9	07.7	293 52.2	55.3	44 52.7	52.5	257 58.4	32.2	Sirius	258 34.7	S16 44.2
15	115 29.9	38 08.9	.. 07.0	308 53.7	.. 54.8	59 54.6	.. 52.7	273 01.0	.. 32.2	Spica	158 31.8	S11 13.7
16	130 32.4	53 13.0	06.3	323 55.3	54.4	74 56.4	52.8	288 03.5	32.1	Suhail	222 53.2	S43 29.3
17	145 34.8	68 17.0	05.6	338 56.8	53.9	89 58.3	52.9	303 06.1	32.1			
18	160 37.3	83 21.0	N24 04.9	353 58.4	N 6 53.5	105 00.2	N18 53.1	318 08.6	S 6 32.1	Vega	80 39.1	N38 47.7
19	175 39.8	98 25.0	04.2	8 59.9	53.0	120 02.0	53.2	333 11.2	32.1	Zuben'ubi	137 05.9	S16 05.7
20	190 42.2	113 29.1	03.5	24 01.5	52.6	135 03.9	53.3	348 13.8	32.0		SHA	Mer.Pass.
21	205 44.7	128 33.1	.. 02.8	39 03.0	.. 52.1	150 05.8	.. 53.5	3 16.3	.. 32.0		° ′	h m
22	220 47.2	143 37.1	02.1	54 04.5	51.7	165 07.6	53.6	18 18.9	32.0	Venus	281 39.8	12 34
23	235 49.6	158 41.2	01.4	69 06.1	51.2	180 09.5	53.7	33 21.4	32.0	Mars	193 59.1	18 27
										Jupiter	304 48.1	11 04
Mer. Pass.	h m 7 23.2	v 4.0	d 0.7	v 1.6	d 0.4	v 1.9	d 0.1	v 2.6	d 0.0	Saturn	157 27.4	20 51

UT	SUN GHA	SUN Dec	MOON GHA	v	MOON Dec	d	HP
d h	° ′	° ′	° ′	′	° ′	′	′
30 00	180 37.0	N21 47.8	75 39.9	11.2	S 2 07.0	12.8	58.7
01	195 37.0	48.1	90 10.1	11.1	2 19.8	12.8	58.7
02	210 36.9	48.5	104 40.2	11.1	2 32.6	12.7	58.8
03	225 36.8	.. 48.9	119 10.3	11.0	2 45.3	12.8	58.8
04	240 36.7	49.2	133 40.3	10.9	2 58.1	12.8	58.8
05	255 36.6	49.6	148 10.2	11.0	3 10.9	12.8	58.9
06	270 36.5	N21 50.0	162 40.2	10.8	S 3 23.7	12.8	58.9
W 07	285 36.4	50.3	177 10.0	10.8	3 36.5	12.7	58.9
E 08	300 36.3	50.7	191 39.8	10.8	3 49.2	12.8	59.0
D 09	315 36.3	.. 51.0	206 09.6	10.7	4 02.0	12.8	59.0
N 10	330 36.2	51.4	220 39.3	10.6	4 14.8	12.7	59.0
E 11	345 36.1	51.8	235 08.9	10.6	4 27.5	12.8	59.1
S 12	0 36.0	N21 52.1	249 38.5	10.5	S 4 40.3	12.7	59.1
D 13	15 35.9	52.5	264 08.0	10.4	4 53.0	12.8	59.1
A 14	30 35.8	52.9	278 37.4	10.4	5 05.8	12.7	59.2
Y 15	45 35.7	.. 53.2	293 06.8	10.3	5 18.5	12.7	59.2
16	60 35.6	53.6	307 36.1	10.3	5 31.2	12.6	59.2
17	75 35.5	53.9	322 05.4	10.2	5 43.8	12.7	59.3
18	90 35.4	N21 54.3	336 34.6	10.2	S 5 56.5	12.7	59.3
19	105 35.4	54.6	351 03.8	10.0	6 09.2	12.6	59.3
20	120 35.3	55.0	5 32.8	10.0	6 21.8	12.6	59.4
21	135 35.2	.. 55.3	20 01.8	10.0	6 34.4	12.6	59.4
22	150 35.1	55.7	34 30.8	9.8	6 47.0	12.6	59.4
23	165 35.0	56.1	48 59.6	9.8	6 59.6	12.5	59.5
31 00	180 34.9	N21 56.4	63 28.4	9.8	S 7 12.1	12.5	59.5
01	195 34.8	56.8	77 57.2	9.6	7 24.6	12.5	59.5
02	210 34.7	57.1	92 25.8	9.6	7 37.1	12.4	59.6
03	225 34.6	.. 57.5	106 54.4	9.5	7 49.5	12.5	59.6
04	240 34.5	57.8	121 22.9	9.5	8 02.0	12.4	59.6
05	255 34.4	58.2	135 51.4	9.3	8 14.4	12.3	59.7
06	270 34.4	N21 58.5	150 19.7	9.3	S 8 26.7	12.3	59.7
T 07	285 34.3	58.9	164 48.0	9.2	8 39.0	12.3	59.7
H 08	300 34.2	59.2	179 16.2	9.2	8 51.3	12.3	59.8
U 09	315 34.1	.. 59.5	193 44.4	9.0	9 03.6	12.2	59.8
R 10	330 34.0	21 59.9	208 12.4	9.0	9 15.8	12.1	59.8
S 11	345 33.9	22 00.2	222 40.4	8.9	9 27.9	12.2	59.9
D 12	0 33.8	N22 00.6	237 08.3	8.9	S 9 40.1	12.0	59.9
A 13	15 33.7	00.9	251 36.2	8.7	9 52.1	12.1	59.9
Y 14	30 33.6	01.3	266 03.9	8.7	10 04.2	11.9	60.0
15	45 33.5	.. 01.6	280 31.6	8.6	10 16.1	11.9	60.0
16	60 33.4	02.0	294 59.2	8.5	10 28.1	11.9	60.0
17	75 33.3	02.3	309 26.7	8.4	10 40.0	11.8	60.0
18	90 33.2	N22 02.6	323 54.1	8.3	S10 51.8	11.8	60.1
19	105 33.1	03.0	338 21.4	8.3	11 03.6	11.7	60.1
20	120 33.0	03.3	352 48.7	8.2	11 15.3	11.7	60.1
21	135 33.0	.. 03.7	7 15.9	8.0	11 27.0	11.6	60.2
22	150 32.9	04.0	21 42.9	8.0	11 38.6	11.5	60.2
23	165 32.8	04.3	36 09.9	8.0	11 50.1	11.5	60.2
1 00	180 32.7	N22 04.7	50 36.9	7.8	S12 01.6	11.4	60.2
01	195 32.6	05.0	65 03.7	7.8	12 13.0	11.4	60.3
02	210 32.5	05.3	79 30.5	7.6	12 24.4	11.3	60.3
03	225 32.4	.. 05.7	93 57.1	7.6	12 35.7	11.2	60.3
04	240 32.3	06.0	108 23.7	7.5	12 46.9	11.1	60.4
05	255 32.2	06.3	122 50.2	7.4	12 58.0	11.1	60.4
06	270 32.1	N22 06.7	137 16.6	7.3	S13 09.1	11.0	60.4
F 07	285 32.0	07.0	151 42.9	7.2	13 20.1	10.9	60.4
R 08	300 31.9	07.3	166 09.1	7.2	13 31.0	10.9	60.5
I 09	315 31.8	.. 07.7	180 35.3	7.0	13 41.9	10.7	60.5
D 10	330 31.7	08.0	195 01.3	7.0	13 52.6	10.7	60.5
A 11	345 31.6	08.3	209 27.3	6.9	14 03.3	10.6	60.5
Y 12	0 31.5	N22 08.7	223 53.2	6.8	S14 13.9	10.6	60.6
13	15 31.4	09.0	238 19.0	6.7	14 24.5	10.4	60.6
14	30 31.3	09.3	252 44.7	6.6	14 34.9	10.3	60.6
15	45 31.2	.. 09.6	267 10.3	6.5	14 45.2	10.3	60.6
16	60 31.1	10.0	281 35.8	6.4	14 55.5	10.2	60.6
17	75 31.0	10.3	296 01.2	6.4	15 05.7	10.0	60.7
18	90 30.9	N22 10.6	310 26.6	6.2	S15 15.7	10.0	60.7
19	105 30.8	10.9	324 51.8	6.2	15 25.7	9.9	60.7
20	120 30.7	11.3	339 17.0	6.1	15 35.6	9.8	60.7
21	135 30.6	.. 11.6	353 42.1	6.0	15 45.4	9.7	60.7
22	150 30.5	11.9	8 07.1	5.9	15 55.1	9.6	60.8
23	165 30.4	12.2	22 32.0	5.8	S16 04.7	9.5	60.8
SD 15.8	d 0.3		SD 16.1		16.3		16.5

Lat.	Naut.	Civil	Sunrise	Moonrise 30	31	1	2
°	h m	h m	h m	h m	h m	h m	h m
N 72	☐	☐	☐	14 34	16 45	19 20	■
N 70	☐	☐	☐	14 26	16 26	18 39	21 22
68	☐	☐	☐	14 20	16 12	18 12	20 19
66	////	////	01 15	14 14	16 00	17 51	19 45
64	////	////	01 59	14 10	15 50	17 34	19 19
62	////	00 13	02 28	14 06	15 42	17 21	19 00
60	////	01 28	02 50	14 02	15 35	17 09	18 44
N 58	////	02 01	03 08	13 59	15 28	17 00	18 30
56	00 12	02 25	03 23	13 57	15 23	16 51	18 19
54	01 20	02 44	03 35	13 54	15 18	16 43	18 09
52	01 51	03 00	03 47	13 52	15 13	16 37	18 00
50	02 14	03 14	03 56	13 50	15 09	16 30	17 52
45	02 53	03 41	04 17	13 46	15 01	16 17	17 35
N 40	03 21	04 02	04 34	13 43	14 53	16 07	17 21
35	03 43	04 18	04 47	13 40	14 47	15 57	17 09
30	04 00	04 33	05 00	13 37	14 42	15 49	16 59
20	04 27	04 56	05 20	13 33	14 33	15 36	16 41
N 10	04 48	05 15	05 38	13 29	14 25	15 24	16 26
0	05 06	05 32	05 54	13 25	14 17	15 12	16 12
S 10	05 22	05 48	06 10	13 21	14 10	15 01	15 58
20	05 37	06 04	06 28	13 17	14 02	14 50	15 43
30	05 52	06 21	06 47	13 13	13 53	14 36	15 26
35	06 00	06 31	06 59	13 11	13 48	14 29	15 16
40	06 08	06 42	07 12	13 08	13 42	14 20	15 04
45	06 18	06 54	07 27	13 05	13 35	14 10	14 51
S 50	06 28	07 09	07 46	13 01	13 27	13 58	14 35
52	06 33	07 16	07 55	12 59	13 24	13 52	14 28
54	06 38	07 23	08 05	12 57	13 20	13 46	14 20
56	06 43	07 31	08 17	12 55	13 15	13 39	14 10
58	06 49	07 40	08 30	12 53	13 10	13 32	14 00
S 60	06 56	07 51	08 45	12 51	13 05	13 23	13 48

Lat.	Sunset	Civil	Naut.	Moonset 30	31	1	2
°	h m	h m	h m	h m	h m	h m	h m
N 72	☐	☐	☐	00 29	{00 12 / 23 51}	23 14	■
N 70	☐	☐	☐	00 32	00 23	{00 12 / 23 56}	23 19
68	☐	☐	☐	00 35	00 31	00 28	00 25
66	22 44	////	////	00 37	00 39	00 41	00 47
64	21 58	////	////	00 39	00 45	00 53	01 04
62	21 29	////	////	00 40	00 50	01 02	01 19
60	21 06	22 30	////	00 42	00 55	01 10	01 31
N 58	20 49	21 56	////	00 43	00 59	01 18	01 41
56	20 34	21 31	////	00 44	01 03	01 24	01 51
54	20 21	21 12	22 38	00 45	01 06	01 30	01 59
52	20 10	20 56	22 06	00 46	01 09	01 35	02 06
50	20 00	20 43	21 43	00 47	01 12	01 40	02 13
45	19 39	20 15	21 03	00 49	01 18	01 50	02 27
N 40	19 22	19 54	20 35	00 51	01 23	01 58	02 39
35	19 08	19 37	20 13	00 52	01 27	02 06	02 50
30	18 56	19 23	19 56	00 53	01 31	02 12	02 58
20	18 36	19 00	19 29	00 55	01 38	02 24	03 14
N 10	18 18	18 41	19 07	00 57	01 44	02 34	03 27
0	18 01	18 24	18 50	00 59	01 49	02 43	03 40
S 10	17 45	18 08	18 34	01 00	01 55	02 52	03 53
20	17 28	17 52	18 19	01 02	02 01	03 02	04 06
30	17 08	17 34	18 04	01 04	02 08	03 14	04 22
35	16 56	17 24	17 56	01 05	02 12	03 20	04 31
40	16 43	17 13	17 47	01 07	02 16	03 28	04 42
45	16 28	17 01	17 38	01 08	02 21	03 37	04 54
S 50	16 09	16 46	17 27	01 10	02 27	03 47	05 09
52	16 00	16 40	17 22	01 11	02 30	03 52	05 16
54	15 50	16 32	17 17	01 12	02 33	03 58	05 24
56	15 38	16 24	17 12	01 13	02 37	04 04	05 32
58	15 25	16 15	17 06	01 14	02 41	04 11	05 42
S 60	15 10	16 04	16 59	01 15	02 45	04 19	05 54

	SUN		MOON			
Day	Eqn. of Time 00h	12h	Mer. Pass.	Mer. Pass. Upper	Lower	Age	Phase
d	m s	m s	h m	h m	h m	d %	
30	02 28	02 24	11 58	19 37	07 12	10 68	
31	02 20	02 15	11 58	20 30	08 03	11 78	
1	02 11	02 06	11 58	21 26	08 58	12 87	◖

UT	ARIES GHA	VENUS −4.2 GHA	Dec	MARS +0.5 GHA	Dec	JUPITER −2.0 GHA	Dec	SATURN +0.5 GHA	Dec
2 00	250 52.1	173 45.2	N24 00.7	84 07.6	N 6 50.8	195 11.4	N18 53.9	48 24.0	S 6 31.9
01	265 54.5	188 49.2	24 00.0	99 09.2	50.3	210 13.2	54.0	63 26.5	31.9
02	280 57.0	203 53.3	23 59.3	114 10.7	49.8	225 15.1	54.1	78 29.1	31.9
03	295 59.5	218 57.3	.. 58.6	129 12.3	.. 49.4	240 17.0	.. 54.2	93 31.6	.. 31.9
04	311 01.9	234 01.4	57.9	144 13.8	48.9	255 18.8	54.4	108 34.2	31.8
05	326 04.4	249 05.4	57.2	159 15.4	48.5	270 20.7	54.5	123 36.7	31.8
06	341 06.9	264 09.4	N23 56.5	174 16.9	N 6 48.0	285 22.6	N18 54.6	138 39.3	S 6 31.8
07	356 09.3	279 13.5	55.8	189 18.5	47.6	300 24.4	54.8	153 41.9	31.8
08	11 11.8	294 17.5	55.1	204 20.0	47.1	315 26.3	54.9	168 44.4	31.7
09	26 14.3	309 21.6	.. 54.4	219 21.5	.. 46.7	330 28.2	.. 55.0	183 47.0	.. 31.7
10	41 16.7	324 25.6	53.7	234 23.1	46.2	345 30.0	55.2	198 49.5	31.7
11	56 19.2	339 29.7	53.0	249 24.6	45.8	0 31.9	55.3	213 52.1	31.7
12	71 21.7	354 33.7	N23 52.3	264 26.2	N 6 45.3	15 33.7	N18 55.4	228 54.6	S 6 31.6
13	86 24.1	9 37.8	51.6	279 27.7	44.8	30 35.6	55.6	243 57.2	31.6
14	101 26.6	24 41.8	50.8	294 29.2	44.4	45 37.5	55.7	258 59.7	31.6
15	116 29.0	39 45.9	.. 50.1	309 30.8	.. 43.9	60 39.3	.. 55.8	274 02.3	.. 31.6
16	131 31.5	54 50.0	49.4	324 32.3	43.5	75 41.2	56.0	289 04.8	31.5
17	146 34.0	69 54.0	48.7	339 33.9	43.0	90 43.1	56.1	304 07.4	31.5
18	161 36.4	84 58.1	N23 48.0	354 35.4	N 6 42.6	105 44.9	N18 56.2	319 09.9	S 6 31.5
19	176 38.9	100 02.1	47.3	9 36.9	42.1	120 46.8	56.4	334 12.5	31.5
20	191 41.4	115 06.2	46.6	24 38.5	41.6	135 48.7	56.5	349 15.0	31.4
21	206 43.8	130 10.3	.. 45.9	39 40.0	.. 41.2	150 50.5	.. 56.6	4 17.6	.. 31.4
22	221 46.3	145 14.3	45.1	54 41.5	40.7	165 52.4	56.7	19 20.1	31.4
23	236 48.8	160 18.4	44.4	69 43.1	40.3	180 54.3	56.9	34 22.7	31.4
3 00	251 51.2	175 22.5	N23 43.7	84 44.6	N 6 39.8	195 56.1	N18 57.0	49 25.2	S 6 31.3
01	266 53.7	190 26.5	43.0	99 46.1	39.4	210 58.0	57.1	64 27.8	31.3
02	281 56.1	205 30.6	42.3	114 47.7	38.9	225 59.9	57.3	79 30.3	31.3
03	296 58.6	220 34.7	.. 41.5	129 49.2	.. 38.4	241 01.7	.. 57.4	94 32.9	.. 31.3
04	312 01.1	235 38.7	40.8	144 50.7	38.0	256 03.6	57.5	109 35.4	31.2
05	327 03.5	250 42.8	40.1	159 52.3	37.5	271 05.5	57.7	124 38.0	31.2
06	342 06.0	265 46.9	N23 39.3	174 53.8	N 6 37.1	286 07.3	N18 57.8	139 40.5	S 6 31.2
07	357 08.5	280 50.9	38.7	189 55.3	36.6	301 09.2	57.9	154 43.1	31.2
08	12 10.9	295 55.0	37.9	204 56.9	36.1	316 11.1	58.1	169 45.6	31.2
09	27 13.4	310 59.1	.. 37.2	219 58.4	.. 35.7	331 12.9	.. 58.2	184 48.2	.. 31.1
10	42 15.9	326 03.2	36.5	234 59.9	35.2	346 14.8	58.3	199 50.7	31.1
11	57 18.3	341 07.2	35.8	250 01.5	34.8	1 16.7	58.5	214 53.3	31.1
12	72 20.8	356 11.3	N23 35.0	265 03.0	N 6 34.3	16 18.5	N18 58.6	229 55.8	S 6 31.1
13	87 23.3	11 15.4	34.3	280 04.5	33.8	31 20.4	58.7	244 58.4	31.0
14	102 25.7	26 19.5	33.6	295 06.1	33.4	46 22.3	58.8	260 00.9	31.0
15	117 28.2	41 23.6	.. 32.8	310 07.6	.. 32.9	61 24.1	.. 59.0	275 03.5	.. 31.0
16	132 30.6	56 27.6	32.1	325 09.1	32.5	76 26.0	59.1	290 06.0	31.0
17	147 33.1	71 31.7	31.4	340 10.6	32.0	91 27.9	59.2	305 08.6	30.9
18	162 35.6	86 35.8	N23 30.7	355 12.2	N 6 31.5	106 29.7	N18 59.4	320 11.1	S 6 30.9
19	177 38.0	101 39.9	29.9	10 13.7	31.1	121 31.6	59.5	335 13.7	30.9
20	192 40.5	116 44.0	29.2	25 15.2	30.6	136 33.5	59.6	350 16.2	30.9
21	207 43.0	131 48.1	.. 28.5	40 16.7	.. 30.1	151 35.3	.. 59.8	5 18.8	.. 30.8
22	222 45.4	146 52.1	27.7	55 18.3	29.7	166 37.2	18 59.9	20 21.3	30.8
23	237 47.9	161 56.2	27.0	70 19.8	29.2	181 39.1	19 00.0	35 23.9	30.8
4 00	252 50.4	177 00.3	N23 26.3	85 21.3	N 6 28.8	196 40.9	N19 00.1	50 26.4	S 6 30.8
01	267 52.8	192 04.4	25.5	100 22.8	28.3	211 42.8	00.3	65 29.0	30.8
02	282 55.3	207 08.5	24.8	115 24.4	27.8	226 44.7	00.4	80 31.5	30.7
03	297 57.8	222 12.6	.. 24.1	130 25.9	.. 27.4	241 46.5	.. 00.5	95 34.1	.. 30.7
04	313 00.2	237 16.7	23.3	145 27.4	26.9	256 48.4	00.7	110 36.6	30.7
05	328 02.7	252 20.8	22.6	160 28.9	26.4	271 50.3	00.8	125 39.2	30.7
06	343 05.1	267 24.9	N23 21.8	175 30.5	N 6 26.0	286 52.1	N19 00.9	140 41.7	S 6 30.6
07	358 07.6	282 28.9	21.1	190 32.0	25.5	301 54.0	01.1	155 44.3	30.6
08	13 10.1	297 33.0	20.4	205 33.5	25.1	316 55.9	01.2	170 46.8	30.6
09	28 12.5	312 37.1	.. 19.6	220 35.0	.. 24.6	331 57.7	.. 01.3	185 49.3	.. 30.6
10	43 15.0	327 41.2	18.9	235 36.5	24.1	346 59.6	01.4	200 51.9	30.6
11	58 17.5	342 45.3	18.2	250 38.1	23.7	2 01.5	01.6	215 54.4	30.5
12	73 19.9	357 49.4	N23 17.4	265 39.6	N 6 23.2	17 03.3	N19 01.7	230 57.0	S 6 30.5
13	88 22.4	12 53.5	16.7	280 41.1	22.7	32 05.2	01.8	245 59.5	30.5
14	103 24.9	27 57.6	15.9	295 42.6	22.3	47 07.1	02.0	261 02.1	30.5
15	118 27.3	43 01.7	.. 15.2	310 44.1	.. 21.8	62 08.9	.. 02.1	276 04.6	.. 30.4
16	133 29.8	58 05.8	14.4	325 45.7	21.3	77 10.8	02.2	291 07.2	30.4
17	148 32.3	73 09.9	13.7	340 47.2	20.9	92 12.7	02.4	306 09.7	30.4
18	163 34.7	88 14.0	N23 13.0	355 48.7	N 6 20.4	107 14.5	N19 02.5	321 12.3	S 6 30.4
19	178 37.2	103 18.1	12.2	10 50.2	19.9	122 16.4	02.6	336 14.8	30.4
20	193 39.6	118 22.2	11.5	25 51.7	19.5	137 18.3	02.7	351 17.3	30.3
21	208 42.1	133 26.2	.. 10.7	40 53.2	.. 19.0	152 20.1	.. 02.9	6 19.9	.. 30.3
22	223 44.6	148 30.3	10.0	55 54.8	18.5	167 22.0	03.0	21 22.4	30.3
23	238 47.0	163 34.4	09.2	70 56.3	18.1	182 23.9	03.1	36 25.0	30.3
h m Mer. Pass. 7 11.4		v 4.1	d 0.7	v 1.5	d 0.5	v 1.9	d 0.1	v 2.5	d 0.0

Day labels (left margin): **S A T U R D A Y** (June 2), **S U N D A Y** (June 3), **M O N D A Y** (June 4)

STARS

Name	SHA	Dec
Acamar	315 19.3	S40 15.2
Achernar	335 27.7	S57 10.2
Acrux	173 09.8	S63 10.5
Adhara	255 13.4	S28 59.6
Aldebaran	290 50.6	N16 31.9
Alioth	166 21.0	N55 53.7
Alkaid	152 59.1	N49 15.2
Al Na'ir	27 44.5	S46 53.7
Alnilam	275 47.4	S 1 11.8
Alphard	217 56.9	S 8 43.0
Alphecca	126 11.3	N26 40.4
Alpheratz	357 44.4	N29 09.4
Altair	62 08.7	N 8 54.2
Ankaa	353 16.6	S42 14.0
Antares	112 26.8	S26 27.5
Arcturus	145 56.1	N19 07.1
Atria	107 28.7	S69 02.9
Avior	234 18.7	S59 33.3
Bellatrix	278 33.1	N 6 21.5
Betelgeuse	271 02.4	N 7 24.4
Canopus	263 57.0	S52 42.4
Capella	280 36.0	N46 00.5
Deneb	49 31.7	N45 19.4
Denebola	182 34.3	N14 30.1
Diphda	348 56.8	S17 55.0
Dubhe	193 52.6	N61 41.2
Elnath	278 13.9	N28 36.9
Eltanin	90 46.0	N51 29.3
Enif	33 47.7	N 9 56.0
Fomalhaut	15 24.8	S29 33.1
Gacrux	172 01.5	S57 11.3
Gienah	175 52.9	S17 36.9
Hadar	148 48.4	S60 26.2
Hamal	328 01.8	N23 31.2
Kaus Aust.	83 44.4	S34 22.5
Kochab	137 18.9	N74 06.4
Markab	13 39.1	N15 16.3
Menkar	314 16.1	N 4 08.2
Menkent	148 08.1	S36 26.0
Miaplacidus	221 40.3	S69 46.5
Mirfak	308 41.9	N49 54.1
Nunki	75 58.9	S26 16.7
Peacock	53 20.0	S56 41.3
Pollux	243 28.9	N27 59.7
Procyon	245 00.8	N 5 11.4
Rasalhague	96 06.8	N12 33.1
Regulus	207 44.4	N11 54.3
Rigel	281 13.1	S 8 11.4
Rigil Kent.	139 52.1	S60 53.3
Sabik	102 13.0	S15 44.3
Schedar	349 41.6	N56 36.1
Shaula	96 22.5	S37 06.6
Sirius	258 34.7	S16 44.2
Spica	158 31.8	S11 13.7
Suhail	222 53.2	S43 29.3
Vega	80 39.1	N38 47.7
Zuben'ubi	137 05.9	S16 05.7

	SHA	Mer. Pass.
	° ′	h m
Venus	283 31.2	12 15
Mars	192 53.4	18 19
Jupiter	304 04.9	10 55
Saturn	157 34.0	20 39

UT	SUN GHA	SUN Dec	MOON GHA	v	MOON Dec	d	HP
d h	° ′	° ′	° ′	′	° ′	′	′
2 00	180 30.3	N22 12.5	36 56.8	5.8	S16 14.2	9.3	60.8
01	195 30.2	12.9	51 21.6	5.6	16 23.5	9.3	60.8
02	210 30.1	13.2	65 46.2	5.6	16 32.8	9.2	60.8
03	225 30.0	.. 13.5	80 10.8	5.5	16 42.0	9.0	60.9
04	240 29.9	13.8	94 35.3	5.4	16 51.0	9.0	60.9
05	255 29.8	14.1	108 59.7	5.3	17 00.0	8.8	60.9
06	270 29.7	N22 14.5	123 24.0	5.3	S17 08.8	8.7	60.9
S 07	285 29.6	14.8	137 48.3	5.1	17 17.5	8.6	60.9
A 08	300 29.5	15.1	152 12.4	5.1	17 26.1	8.5	60.9
T 09	315 29.4	.. 15.4	166 36.5	5.0	17 34.6	8.4	61.0
U 10	330 29.3	15.7	181 00.5	4.9	17 43.0	8.2	61.0
R 11	345 29.2	16.0	195 24.4	4.8	17 51.2	8.2	61.0
D 12	0 29.1	N22 16.3	209 48.2	4.8	S17 59.4	8.0	61.0
A 13	15 29.0	16.6	224 12.0	4.7	18 07.4	7.8	61.0
Y 14	30 28.9	17.0	238 35.7	4.6	18 15.2	7.8	61.0
15	45 28.8	.. 17.3	252 59.3	4.5	18 23.0	7.6	61.0
16	60 28.7	17.6	267 22.8	4.5	18 30.6	7.5	61.0
17	75 28.6	17.9	281 46.3	4.4	18 38.1	7.4	61.1
18	90 28.5	N22 18.2	296 09.7	4.3	S18 45.5	7.2	61.1
19	105 28.4	18.5	310 33.0	4.2	18 52.7	7.1	61.1
20	120 28.3	18.8	324 56.2	4.2	18 59.8	6.9	61.1
21	135 28.2	.. 19.1	339 19.4	4.1	19 06.7	6.9	61.1
22	150 28.1	19.4	353 42.5	4.0	19 13.6	6.6	61.1
23	165 28.0	19.7	8 05.5	4.0	19 20.2	6.6	61.1
3 00	180 27.9	N22 20.0	22 28.5	3.9	S19 26.8	6.4	61.1
01	195 27.8	20.3	36 51.4	3.9	19 33.2	6.2	61.1
02	210 27.7	20.6	51 14.3	3.8	19 39.4	6.2	61.1
03	225 27.6	.. 20.9	65 37.1	3.7	19 45.6	5.9	61.1
04	240 27.5	21.2	79 59.8	3.7	19 51.5	5.9	61.1
05	255 27.4	21.5	94 22.5	3.6	19 57.4	5.6	61.1
06	270 27.3	N22 21.8	108 45.1	3.5	S20 03.0	5.6	61.2
S 07	285 27.2	22.1	123 07.6	3.5	20 08.6	5.4	61.2
U 08	300 27.1	22.4	137 30.1	3.5	20 14.0	5.2	61.2
N 09	315 27.0	.. 22.7	151 52.6	3.4	20 19.2	5.1	61.2
D 10	330 26.9	23.0	166 15.0	3.4	20 24.3	4.9	61.2
A 11	345 26.8	23.3	180 37.4	3.3	20 29.2	4.8	61.2
Y 12	0 26.7	N22 23.6	194 59.7	3.3	S20 34.0	4.6	61.2
13	15 26.6	23.9	209 22.0	3.2	20 38.6	4.5	61.2
14	30 26.5	24.2	223 44.2	3.2	20 43.1	4.3	61.2
15	45 26.4	.. 24.5	238 06.4	3.2	20 47.4	4.1	61.2
16	60 26.2	24.8	252 28.6	3.1	20 51.5	4.0	61.2
17	75 26.1	25.1	266 50.7	3.1	20 55.5	3.9	61.2
18	90 26.0	N22 25.4	281 12.8	3.0	S20 59.4	3.6	61.2
19	105 25.9	25.7	295 34.8	3.1	21 03.0	3.6	61.2
20	120 25.8	26.0	309 56.9	3.0	21 06.6	3.3	61.2
21	135 25.7	.. 26.3	324 18.9	2.9	21 09.9	3.2	61.2
22	150 25.6	26.6	338 40.8	3.0	21 13.1	3.1	61.1
23	165 25.5	26.8	353 02.8	2.9	21 16.2	2.8	61.1
4 00	180 25.4	N22 27.1	7 24.7	2.9	S21 19.0	2.8	61.1
01	195 25.3	27.4	21 46.6	2.9	21 21.8	2.5	61.1
02	210 25.2	27.7	36 08.5	2.9	21 24.3	2.4	61.1
03	225 25.1	.. 28.0	50 30.4	2.9	21 26.7	2.2	61.1
04	240 25.0	28.3	64 52.3	2.8	21 28.9	2.1	61.1
05	255 24.9	28.6	79 14.1	2.9	21 31.0	1.9	61.1
06	270 24.8	N22 28.8	93 36.0	2.8	S21 32.9	1.7	61.1
M 07	285 24.7	29.1	107 57.8	2.9	21 34.6	1.6	61.1
O 08	300 24.5	29.4	122 19.7	2.8	21 36.2	1.4	61.1
N 09	315 24.4	.. 29.7	136 41.5	2.9	21 37.6	1.2	61.1
D 10	330 24.3	30.0	151 03.4	2.8	21 38.8	1.1	61.0
A 11	345 24.2	30.3	165 25.2	2.9	21 39.9	0.9	61.0
Y 12	0 24.1	N22 30.5	179 47.1	2.9	S21 40.8	0.7	61.0
13	15 24.0	30.8	194 09.0	2.8	21 41.5	0.6	61.0
14	30 23.9	31.1	208 30.8	2.9	21 42.1	0.4	61.0
15	45 23.8	.. 31.4	222 52.7	2.9	21 42.5	0.3	61.0
16	60 23.7	31.6	237 14.6	2.9	21 42.8	0.1	61.0
17	75 23.6	31.9	251 36.6	2.9	21 42.9	0.1	61.0
18	90 23.5	N22 32.2	265 58.5	3.0	S21 42.8	0.3	60.9
19	105 23.4	32.5	280 20.5	3.0	21 42.5	0.4	60.9
20	120 23.2	32.7	294 42.5	3.0	21 42.1	0.5	60.9
21	135 23.1	.. 33.0	309 04.5	3.0	21 41.6	0.8	60.9
22	150 23.0	33.3	323 26.5	3.1	21 40.8	0.9	60.9
23	165 22.9	33.6	337 48.6	3.1	S21 39.9	1.0	60.9
	SD 15.8	d 0.3	SD 16.6		16.7		16.6

Lat.	Twilight Naut.	Twilight Civil	Sunrise	Moonrise 2	Moonrise 3	Moonrise 4	Moonrise 5
°	h m	h m	h m	h m	h m	h m	h m
N 72	□	□	□	■	■	■	
N 70	□	□	□	21 22	■	■	■
68	□	□	□	20 19	22 31	24 00	00 00
66	////	////	01 02	19 45	21 30	22 45	23 21
64	////	////	01 52	19 19	20 55	22 08	22 51
62	////	////	02 23	19 00	20 30	21 41	22 29
60	////	01 19	02 46	18 44	20 11	21 21	22 11
N 58	////	01 56	03 04	18 30	19 54	21 04	21 55
56	////	02 21	03 20	18 19	19 40	20 49	21 42
54	01 12	02 41	03 33	18 09	19 29	20 37	21 31
52	01 46	02 57	03 44	18 00	19 18	20 26	21 21
50	02 10	03 11	03 54	17 52	19 09	20 16	21 12
45	02 51	03 39	04 15	17 35	18 49	19 56	20 53
N 40	03 19	04 00	04 32	17 21	18 33	19 39	20 38
35	03 41	04 17	04 47	17 09	18 19	19 25	20 24
30	03 59	04 32	04 59	16 59	18 08	19 13	20 13
20	04 27	04 56	05 20	16 41	17 47	18 52	19 53
N 10	04 48	05 15	05 38	16 26	17 30	18 34	19 36
0	05 06	05 32	05 55	16 12	17 14	18 18	19 20
S 10	05 22	05 48	06 11	15 58	16 58	18 01	19 04
20	05 38	06 05	06 29	15 43	16 41	17 43	18 47
30	05 53	06 23	06 49	15 26	16 21	17 22	18 27
35	06 01	06 33	07 01	15 16	16 10	17 10	18 16
40	06 10	06 44	07 14	15 04	15 56	16 56	18 03
45	06 20	06 56	07 30	14 51	15 41	16 40	17 47
S 50	06 31	07 12	07 49	14 35	15 22	16 20	17 28
52	06 35	07 18	07 59	14 28	15 13	16 10	17 19
54	06 41	07 26	08 09	14 20	15 03	16 00	17 08
56	06 46	07 35	08 21	14 10	14 52	15 47	16 57
58	06 52	07 44	08 34	14 00	14 39	15 33	16 43
S 60	06 59	07 55	08 50	13 48	14 24	15 17	16 28

Lat.	Sunset	Twilight Civil	Twilight Naut.	Moonset 2	Moonset 3	Moonset 4	Moonset 5
°	h m	h m	h m	h m	h m	h m	h m
N 72	□	□	□	■	■	■	
N 70	□	□	□	23 19	■	■	■
68	□	□	□	00 25	00 22	00 22	01 07
66	22 59	////	////	00 47	00 58	01 24	02 22
64	22 06	////	////	01 04	01 24	01 59	02 59
62	21 35	////	////	01 19	01 44	02 24	03 26
60	21 12	22 40	////	01 31	02 00	02 44	03 46
N 58	20 53	22 02	////	01 41	02 14	03 00	04 03
56	20 38	21 36	////	01 51	02 26	03 14	04 17
54	20 24	21 16	22 46	01 59	02 37	03 27	04 30
52	20 13	21 00	22 12	02 06	02 46	03 37	04 40
50	20 03	20 46	21 48	02 13	02 55	03 47	04 50
45	19 41	20 18	21 06	02 27	03 13	04 07	05 10
N 40	19 24	19 57	20 37	02 39	03 27	04 23	05 27
35	19 10	19 39	20 16	02 50	03 40	04 37	05 41
30	18 58	19 25	19 58	02 58	03 51	04 49	05 53
20	18 37	19 01	19 30	03 14	04 09	05 10	06 13
N 10	18 19	18 42	19 08	03 27	04 26	05 28	06 31
0	18 02	18 24	18 50	03 40	04 41	05 44	06 48
S 10	17 45	18 08	18 34	03 53	04 56	06 01	07 04
20	17 28	17 51	18 19	04 06	05 13	06 19	07 22
30	17 07	17 34	18 03	04 22	05 31	06 39	07 42
35	16 56	17 24	17 55	04 31	05 42	06 51	07 54
40	16 42	17 12	17 46	04 42	05 55	07 05	08 08
45	16 26	17 00	17 37	04 54	06 10	07 21	08 24
S 50	16 07	16 45	17 26	05 09	06 28	07 41	08 43
52	15 58	16 38	17 21	05 16	06 37	07 51	08 52
54	15 47	16 30	17 16	05 24	06 47	08 01	09 03
56	15 36	16 22	17 10	05 32	06 58	08 13	09 15
58	15 22	16 12	17 04	05 42	07 10	08 27	09 28
S 60	15 06	16 01	16 57	05 54	07 25	08 44	09 44

Day	SUN Eqn. of Time 00h	SUN Eqn. of Time 12h	SUN Mer. Pass.	MOON Mer. Pass. Upper	MOON Mer. Pass. Lower	Age	Phase
d	m s	m s	h m	h m	h m	d	%
2	02 02	01 57	11 58	22 26	09 56	13	94
3	01 52	01 47	11 58	23 29	10 57	14	99
4	01 42	01 37	11 58	24 33	12 01	15	100

114 2012 JUNE 5, 6, 7 (TUES., WED., THURS.)

UT	ARIES GHA	VENUS −4.2 GHA	Dec	MARS +0.6 GHA	Dec	JUPITER −2.0 GHA	Dec	SATURN +0.6 GHA	Dec	STARS Name	SHA	Dec
d h 5 00	253 49.5	178 38.5	N23 08.5	85 57.8	N 6 17.6	197 25.7	N19 03.3	51 27.5	S 6 30.3	Acamar	315 19.3	S40 15.2
01	268 52.0	193 42.6	07.7	100 59.3	17.1	212 27.6	03.4	66 30.1	30.2	Achernar	335 27.7	S57 10.2
02	283 54.4	208 46.7	07.0	116 00.8	16.7	227 29.5	03.5	81 32.6	30.2	Acrux	173 09.8	S63 10.5
03	298 56.9	223 50.8 ..	06.2	131 02.3 ..	16.2	242 31.3 ..	03.6	96 35.2 ..	30.2	Adhara	255 13.4	S28 59.6
04	313 59.4	238 54.9	05.5	146 03.8	15.7	257 33.2	03.8	111 37.7	30.2	Aldebaran	290 50.5	N16 31.9
05	329 01.8	253 59.0	04.7	161 05.3	15.3	272 35.1	03.9	126 40.2	30.2			
T 06	344 04.3	269 03.1	N23 04.0	176 06.9	N 6 14.8	287 36.9	N19 04.0	141 42.8	S 6 30.1	Alioth	166 21.0	N55 53.7
U 07	359 06.8	284 07.2	03.2	191 08.4	14.3	302 38.8	04.2	156 45.3	30.1	Alkaid	152 59.1	N49 15.2
E 08	14 09.2	299 11.3	02.5	206 09.9	13.9	317 40.7	04.3	171 47.9	30.1	Al Na'ir	27 44.5	S46 53.7
S 09	29 11.7	314 15.4 ..	01.7	221 11.4 ..	13.4	332 42.5 ..	04.4	186 50.4 ..	30.1	Alnilam	275 47.4	S 1 11.8
D 10	44 14.1	329 19.5	01.0	236 12.9	12.9	347 44.4	04.5	201 53.0	30.0	Alphard	217 56.9	S 8 43.0
A 11	59 16.6	344 23.6	23 00.2	251 14.4	12.5	2 46.3	04.7	216 55.5	30.0			
Y 12	74 19.1	359 27.7	N22 59.5	266 15.9	N 6 12.0	17 48.1	N19 04.8	231 58.0	S 6 30.0	Alphecca	126 11.3	N26 40.4
13	89 21.5	14 31.8	58.7	281 17.4	11.5	32 50.0	04.9	247 00.6	30.0	Alpheratz	357 44.3	N29 09.5
14	104 24.0	29 35.9	58.0	296 18.9	11.0	47 51.9	05.1	262 03.1	30.0	Altair	62 08.7	N 8 54.2
15	119 26.5	44 40.0 ..	57.2	311 20.4 ..	10.6	62 53.7 ..	05.2	277 05.7 ..	29.9	Ankaa	353 16.5	S42 14.0
16	134 28.9	59 44.1	56.4	326 22.0	10.1	77 55.6	05.3	292 08.2	29.9	Antares	112 26.8	S26 27.5
17	149 31.4	74 48.1	55.7	341 23.5	09.6	92 57.5	05.4	307 10.8	29.9			
18	164 33.9	89 52.2	N22 54.9	356 25.0	N 6 09.2	107 59.4	N19 05.6	322 13.3	S 6 29.9	Arcturus	145 56.1	N19 07.1
19	179 36.3	104 56.3	54.1	11 26.5	08.7	123 01.2	05.7	337 15.8	29.9	Atria	107 28.7	S69 02.9
20	194 38.8	120 00.4	53.4	26 28.0	08.2	138 03.1	05.8	352 18.4	29.8	Avior	234 18.7	S59 33.3
21	209 41.3	135 04.5 ..	52.6	41 29.5 ..	07.8	153 05.0 ..	06.0	7 20.9 ..	29.8	Bellatrix	278 33.1	N 6 21.5
22	224 43.7	150 08.5	51.8	56 31.0	07.3	168 06.8	06.1	22 23.5	29.8	Betelgeuse	271 02.4	N 7 24.4
23	239 46.2	165 12.6	51.0	71 32.5	06.8	183 08.7	06.2	37 26.0	29.8			
6 00	254 48.6	180 16.6	N22 50.2	86 34.0	N 6 06.3	198 10.6	N19 06.3	52 28.5	S 6 29.8	Canopus	263 57.0	S52 42.4
01	269 51.1	195 20.5	49.4	101 35.5	05.9	213 12.4	06.5	67 31.1	29.7	Capella	280 36.0	N46 00.5
02	284 53.6	210 24.4	48.7	116 37.0	05.4	228 14.3	06.6	82 33.6	29.7	Deneb	49 31.7	N45 19.4
03	299 56.0	225 28.4 ..	48.1	131 38.5	04.9	243 16.2 ..	06.7	97 36.2 ..	29.7	Denebola	182 34.3	N14 30.1
04	314 58.5	240 32.4	47.4	146 40.0	04.5	258 18.0	06.8	112 38.7	29.7	Diphda	348 56.7	S17 55.0
05	330 01.0	255 36.5	46.7	161 41.5	04.0	273 19.9	07.0	127 41.2	29.7			
W 06	345 03.4	270 40.6	N22 46.0	176 43.0	N 6 03.5	288 21.8	N19 07.1	142 43.8	S 6 29.7	Dubhe	193 52.6	N61 41.2
E 07	0 05.9	285 44.6	45.2	191 44.5	03.0	303 23.6	07.2	157 46.3	29.6	Elnath	278 13.9	N28 36.9
D 08	15 08.4	300 48.7	44.5	206 46.0	02.6	318 25.5	07.4	172 48.9	29.6	Eltanin	90 45.9	N51 29.3
N 09	30 10.8	315 52.8 ..	43.8	221 47.5 ..	02.1	333 27.4 ..	07.5	187 51.4 ..	29.6	Enif	33 47.7	N 9 56.0
E 10	45 13.3	330 56.9	43.0	236 49.0	01.6	348 29.2	07.6	202 53.9	29.6	Fomalhaut	15 24.7	S29 33.1
S 11	60 15.8	346 01.0	42.3	251 50.5	01.1	3 31.1	07.7	217 56.5	29.6			
D 12	75 18.2	1 05.1	N22 41.5	266 52.0	N 6 00.7	18 33.0	N19 07.9	232 59.0	S 6 29.5	Gacrux	172 01.5	S57 11.3
A 13	90 20.7	16 09.2	40.8	281 53.5	6 00.2	33 34.8	08.0	248 01.6	29.5	Gienah	175 52.9	S17 36.9
Y 14	105 23.1	31 13.3	40.0	296 55.0	5 59.7	48 36.7	08.1	263 04.1	29.5	Hadar	148 48.4	S60 26.2
15	120 25.6	46 17.4 ..	39.3	311 56.5 ..	59.2	63 38.6 ..	08.3	278 06.6 ..	29.5	Hamal	328 01.8	N23 31.2
16	135 28.1	61 21.4	38.5	326 58.0	58.8	78 40.5	08.4	293 09.2	29.5	Kaus Aust.	83 44.4	S34 22.5
17	150 30.5	76 25.5	37.8	341 59.5	58.3	93 42.3	08.5	308 11.7	29.4			
18	165 33.0	91 29.6	N22 37.0	357 01.0	N 5 57.8	108 44.2	N19 08.6	323 14.3	S 6 29.4	Kochab	137 19.0	N74 06.4
19	180 35.5	106 33.7	36.3	12 02.5	57.3	123 46.1	08.8	338 16.8	29.4	Markab	13 39.0	N15 16.3
20	195 37.9	121 37.8	35.5	27 04.0	56.9	138 47.9	08.9	353 19.3	29.4	Menkar	314 16.1	N 4 08.2
21	210 40.4	136 41.9 ..	34.7	42 05.5 ..	56.4	153 49.8 ..	09.0	8 21.9 ..	29.4	Menkent	148 08.1	S36 26.0
22	225 42.9	151 46.0	34.0	57 07.0	55.9	168 51.7	09.1	23 24.4	29.4	Miaplacidus	221 40.3	S69 46.5
23	240 45.3	166 50.0	33.2	72 08.5	55.4	183 53.5	09.3	38 26.9	29.3			
7 00	255 47.8	181 54.1	N22 32.5	87 10.0	N 5 55.0	198 55.4	N19 09.4	53 29.5	S 6 29.3	Mirfak	308 41.8	N49 54.1
01	270 50.2	196 58.2	31.7	102 11.5	54.5	213 57.3	09.5	68 32.0	29.3	Nunki	75 58.9	S26 16.7
02	285 52.7	212 02.3	30.9	117 13.0	54.0	228 59.1	09.6	83 34.6	29.3	Peacock	53 20.0	S56 41.3
03	300 55.2	227 06.4 ..	30.2	132 14.4 ..	53.5	244 01.0 ..	09.8	98 37.1 ..	29.3	Pollux	243 28.9	N27 59.7
04	315 57.6	242 10.4	29.4	147 15.9	53.1	259 02.9	09.9	113 39.6	29.2	Procyon	245 00.7	N 5 11.4
05	331 00.1	257 14.5	28.7	162 17.4	52.6	274 04.8	10.0	128 42.2	29.2			
T 06	346 02.6	272 18.6	N22 27.9	177 18.9	N 5 52.1	289 06.6	N19 10.2	143 44.7	S 6 29.2	Rasalhague	96 06.8	N12 33.1
H 07	1 05.0	287 22.7	27.1	192 20.4	51.6	304 08.5	10.3	158 47.2	29.2	Regulus	207 44.4	N11 54.3
U 08	16 07.5	302 26.8	26.4	207 21.9	51.2	319 10.4	10.4	173 49.8	29.2	Rigel	281 13.1	S 8 11.4
R 09	31 10.0	317 30.8 ..	25.6	222 23.4 ..	50.7	334 12.2 ..	10.5	188 52.3 ..	29.2	Rigil Kent.	139 52.1	S60 53.3
S 10	46 12.4	332 34.9	24.9	237 24.9	50.2	349 14.1	10.7	203 54.8	29.1	Sabik	102 13.0	S15 44.3
D 11	61 14.9	347 39.0	24.1	252 26.4	49.7	4 16.0	10.8	218 57.4	29.1			
A 12	76 17.4	2 43.0	N22 23.3	267 27.9	N 5 49.2	19 17.8	N19 10.9	233 59.9	S 6 29.1	Schedar	349 41.6	N56 36.1
Y 13	91 19.8	17 47.1	22.6	282 29.4	48.8	34 19.7	11.0	249 02.4	29.1	Shaula	96 22.5	S37 06.6
14	106 22.3	32 51.2	21.8	297 30.8	48.3	49 21.6	11.2	264 05.0	29.1	Sirius	258 34.7	S16 44.2
15	121 24.7	47 55.3 ..	21.1	312 32.3 ..	47.8	64 23.4 ..	11.3	279 07.5 ..	29.0	Spica	158 31.8	S11 13.7
16	136 27.2	62 59.3	20.3	327 33.8	47.3	79 25.3	11.4	294 10.1	29.0	Suhail	222 53.2	S43 29.3
17	151 29.7	78 03.4	19.5	342 35.3	46.9	94 27.2	11.5	309 12.6	29.0			
18	166 32.1	93 07.5	N22 18.8	357 36.8	N 5 46.4	109 29.1	N19 11.7	324 15.1	S 6 29.0	Vega	80 39.0	N38 47.7
19	181 34.6	108 11.5	18.0	12 38.3	45.9	124 30.9	11.8	339 17.7	29.0	Zuben'ubi	137 05.9	S16 05.7
20	196 37.1	123 15.6	17.2	27 39.8	45.4	139 32.8	11.9	354 20.2	29.0		SHA	Mer. Pass.
21	211 39.5	138 19.6 ..	16.5	42 41.3 ..	44.9	154 34.7 ..	12.0	9 22.7 ..	28.9			h m
22	226 42.0	153 23.7	15.7	57 42.7	44.5	169 36.5	12.2	24 25.3	28.9	Venus	285 27.9	11 56
23	241 44.5	168 27.8	15.0	72 44.2	44.0	184 38.4	12.3	39 27.8	28.9	Mars	191 45.4	18 12
	h m									Jupiter	303 21.9	10 46
Mer. Pass. 6 59.6	v 4.1 d 0.7		v 1.5 d 0.5		v 1.9 d 0.1		v 2.5 d 0.0		Saturn	157 39.9	20 27

SUN / MOON

UT	SUN GHA	Dec	MOON GHA	v	Dec	d	HP
d h	° ′	° ′	° ′	′	° ′	′	′
5 00	180 22.8	N22 33.8	352 10.7	3.2	S21 38.9	1.2	60.8
01	195 22.7	34.1	6 32.9	3.2	21 37.7	1.4	60.8
02	210 22.6	34.4	20 55.1	3.2	21 36.3	1.6	60.8
03	225 22.5 ..	34.6	35 17.3	3.3	21 34.7	1.7	60.8
04	240 22.4	34.9	49 39.6	3.3	21 33.0	1.8	60.8
05	255 22.3	35.2	64 01.9	3.3	21 31.2	2.0	60.7
06	270 22.1	N22 35.5	78 24.2	3.5	S21 29.2	2.2	60.7
07	285 22.0	35.7	92 46.7	3.4	21 27.0	2.3	60.7
T 08	300 21.9	36.0	107 09.1	3.5	21 24.7	2.5	60.7
U 09	315 21.8 ..	36.2	121 31.6	3.6	21 22.2	2.7	60.7
E 10	330 21.7	36.5	135 54.2	3.6	21 19.5	2.8	60.6
S 11	345 21.6	36.8	150 16.8	3.7	21 16.7	2.9	60.6
D 12	0 21.5	N22 37.0	164 39.5	3.7	S21 13.8	3.1	60.6
A 13	15 21.4	37.3	179 02.2	3.9	21 10.7	3.3	60.6
Y 14	30 21.3	37.6	193 25.1	3.8	21 07.4	3.4	60.5
15	45 21.1 ..	37.8	207 47.9	4.0	21 04.0	3.5	60.5
16	60 21.0	38.1	222 10.9	4.0	21 00.5	3.7	60.5
17	75 20.9	38.3	236 33.9	4.0	20 56.8	3.9	60.5
18	90 20.8	N22 38.6	250 56.9	4.2	S20 52.9	4.0	60.4
19	105 20.7	38.9	265 20.1	4.2	20 48.9	4.1	60.4
20	120 20.6	39.1	279 43.3	4.3	20 44.8	4.3	60.4
21	135 20.5 ..	39.4	294 06.6	4.3	20 40.5	4.5	60.3
22	150 20.4	39.6	308 29.9	4.5	20 36.0	4.5	60.3
23	165 20.2	39.9	322 53.4	4.5	20 31.5	4.7	60.3
6 00	180 20.1	N22 40.1	337 16.9	4.6	S20 26.8	4.9	60.3
01	195 20.0	40.4	351 40.5	4.7	20 21.9	5.0	60.2
02	210 19.9	40.7	6 04.2	4.7	20 16.9	5.1	60.2
03	225 19.8 ..	40.9	20 27.9	4.9	20 11.8	5.3	60.2
04	240 19.7	41.2	34 51.8	4.9	20 06.5	5.4	60.1
05	255 19.6	41.4	49 15.7	5.0	20 01.1	5.5	60.1
06	270 19.4	N22 41.7	63 39.7	5.1	S19 55.6	5.6	60.1
07	285 19.3	41.9	78 03.8	5.2	19 50.0	5.8	60.1
W 08	300 19.2	42.2	92 28.0	5.3	19 44.2	6.0	60.0
E 09	315 19.1 ..	42.4	106 52.3	5.3	19 38.2	6.0	60.0
D 10	330 19.0	42.7	121 16.6	5.5	19 32.2	6.2	60.0
N 11	345 18.9	42.9	135 41.1	5.6	19 26.0	6.3	59.9
E 12	0 18.8	N22 43.2	150 05.7	5.6	S19 19.7	6.4	59.9
S 13	15 18.6	43.4	164 30.3	5.7	19 13.3	6.5	59.9
D 14	30 18.5	43.6	178 55.0	5.9	19 06.8	6.7	59.8
A 15	45 18.4 ..	43.9	193 19.9	5.9	19 00.1	6.8	59.8
Y 16	60 18.3	44.1	207 44.8	6.0	18 53.3	6.8	59.8
17	75 18.2	44.4	222 09.8	6.1	18 46.5	7.1	59.7
18	90 18.1	N22 44.6	236 34.9	6.3	S18 39.4	7.1	59.7
19	105 18.0	44.9	251 00.2	6.3	18 32.3	7.2	59.7
20	120 17.8	45.1	265 25.5	6.4	18 25.1	7.4	59.6
21	135 17.7 ..	45.3	279 50.9	6.5	18 17.7	7.4	59.6
22	150 17.6	45.6	294 16.4	6.6	18 10.3	7.6	59.5
23	165 17.5	45.8	308 42.0	6.7	18 02.7	7.7	59.5
7 00	180 17.4	N22 46.1	323 07.7	6.9	S17 55.0	7.7	59.5
01	195 17.3	46.3	337 33.6	6.9	17 47.3	7.9	59.4
02	210 17.1	46.6	351 59.5	7.0	17 39.4	8.0	59.4
03	225 17.0 ..	46.8	6 25.5	7.1	17 31.4	8.1	59.4
04	240 16.9	47.0	20 51.6	7.2	17 23.3	8.1	59.3
05	255 16.8	47.2	35 17.8	7.3	17 15.2	8.3	59.3
06	270 16.7	N22 47.5	49 44.1	7.5	S17 06.9	8.4	59.3
07	285 16.6	47.7	64 10.6	7.5	16 58.5	8.5	59.2
T 08	300 16.4	47.9	78 37.1	7.6	16 50.0	8.5	59.2
H 09	315 16.3 ..	48.2	93 03.7	7.7	16 41.5	8.7	59.1
U 10	330 16.2	48.4	107 30.4	7.9	16 32.8	8.7	59.1
R 11	345 16.1	48.6	121 57.3	7.9	16 24.1	8.8	59.1
S 12	0 16.0	N22 48.9	136 24.2	8.0	S16 15.3	8.9	59.0
D 13	15 15.9	49.1	150 51.2	8.2	16 06.4	9.0	59.0
A 14	30 15.7	49.3	165 18.4	8.2	15 57.4	9.1	59.0
Y 15	45 15.6 ..	49.5	179 45.6	8.3	15 48.3	9.2	58.9
16	60 15.5	49.8	194 12.9	8.5	15 39.1	9.2	58.9
17	75 15.4	50.0	208 40.4	8.5	15 29.9	9.3	58.8
18	90 15.3	N22 50.2	223 07.9	8.7	S15 20.6	9.4	58.8
19	105 15.1	50.5	237 35.6	8.7	15 11.2	9.5	58.8
20	120 15.0	50.7	252 03.3	8.8	15 01.7	9.5	58.7
21	135 14.9 ..	50.9	266 31.1	9.0	14 52.2	9.7	58.7
22	150 14.8	51.1	280 59.1	9.0	14 42.5	9.7	58.6
23	165 14.7	51.4	295 27.1	9.2	S14 32.8	9.7	58.6
	SD 15.8	d 0.2	SD 16.5		16.3		16.1

Twilight / Moonrise

Lat.	Twilight Naut.	Twilight Civil	Sunrise	Moonrise 5	6	7	8
°	h m	h m	h m	h m	h m	h m	h m
N 72	▭	▭	▭	■■	■■	01 58	00 51
N 70	▭	▭	▭	■■	■■	00 41	00 22
68	▭	▭	▭	00 00	00 05	00 03	00 09 / 23 59
66	////	////	00 48	23 21	23 36	23 43	23 46
64	////	////	01 46	22 51	23 15	23 29	23 37
62	////	////	02 19	22 29	22 58	23 17	23 29
60	////	01 11	02 42	22 11	22 44	23 06	23 23
N 58	////	01 51	03 01	21 55	22 32	22 58	23 17
56	////	02 17	03 17	21 42	22 21	22 50	23 12
54	01 05	02 38	03 31	21 31	22 12	22 43	23 07
52	01 42	02 55	03 42	21 21	22 04	22 36	23 03
50	02 06	03 09	03 53	21 12	21 56	22 31	22 59
45	02 49	03 37	04 14	20 53	21 40	22 18	22 50
N 40	03 18	03 59	04 31	20 38	21 27	22 08	22 43
35	03 40	04 17	04 46	20 24	21 15	21 59	22 37
30	03 58	04 31	04 59	20 13	21 06	21 51	22 32
20	04 26	04 55	05 20	19 53	20 49	21 38	22 22
N 10	04 48	05 14	05 38	19 36	20 34	21 26	22 14
0	05 07	05 33	05 55	19 20	20 20	21 15	22 06
S 10	05 23	05 49	06 12	19 04	20 06	21 04	21 58
20	05 39	06 07	06 30	18 47	19 51	20 52	21 50
30	05 54	06 24	06 50	18 27	19 34	20 38	21 41
35	06 03	06 34	07 02	18 16	19 24	20 31	21 35
40	06 12	06 46	07 16	18 03	19 12	20 21	21 29
45	06 22	06 59	07 32	17 47	18 59	20 11	21 21
S 50	06 33	07 14	07 52	17 28	18 42	19 58	21 13
52	06 38	07 21	08 01	17 19	18 34	19 52	21 09
54	06 43	07 29	08 12	17 08	18 25	19 45	21 04
56	06 49	07 37	08 24	16 57	18 16	19 38	20 59
58	06 55	07 47	08 38	16 43	18 05	19 30	20 53
S 60	07 02	07 58	08 54	16 28	17 52	19 20	20 47

Sunset / Moonset

Lat.	Sunset	Twilight Civil	Twilight Naut.	Moonset 5	6	7	8
°	h m	h m	h m	h m	h m	h m	h m
N 72	▭	▭	▭	■■	■■	03 24	06 24
N 70	▭	▭	▭	■■	■■	04 39	06 51
68	▭	▭	▭	01 07	03 12	05 17	07 12
66	23 14	////	////	02 22	03 56	05 43	07 28
64	22 13	////	////	02 59	04 25	06 03	07 41
62	21 40	////	////	03 26	04 47	06 19	07 52
60	21 18	22 49	////	03 46	05 05	06 33	08 01
N 58	20 57	22 08	////	04 03	05 20	06 44	08 09
56	20 41	21 41	////	04 17	05 32	06 54	08 17
54	20 27	21 20	22 55	04 30	05 43	07 03	08 23
52	20 16	21 03	22 17	04 40	05 53	07 11	08 29
50	20 05	20 49	21 52	04 50	06 02	07 18	08 34
45	19 44	20 21	21 09	05 10	06 20	07 33	08 45
N 40	19 26	19 59	20 40	05 27	06 35	07 45	08 54
35	19 12	19 41	20 18	05 41	06 48	07 56	09 02
30	18 59	19 26	19 59	05 53	06 59	08 05	09 09
20	18 38	19 02	19 31	06 13	07 18	08 20	09 20
N 10	18 19	18 42	19 09	06 31	07 34	08 34	09 30
0	18 02	18 25	18 51	06 48	07 49	08 47	09 40
S 10	17 46	18 08	18 34	07 04	08 04	08 59	09 49
20	17 28	17 51	18 19	07 22	08 20	09 13	09 59
30	17 07	17 33	18 03	07 42	08 39	09 28	10 11
35	16 55	17 23	17 55	07 54	08 49	09 37	10 17
40	16 41	17 12	17 46	08 08	09 01	09 46	10 25
45	16 25	16 59	17 36	08 24	09 16	09 58	10 33
S 50	16 05	16 43	17 25	08 43	09 33	10 12	10 43
52	15 56	16 36	17 20	08 52	09 41	10 19	10 48
54	15 45	16 28	17 14	09 03	09 50	10 26	10 53
56	15 33	16 20	17 08	09 15	10 00	10 34	10 59
58	15 19	16 10	17 02	09 28	10 12	10 43	11 05
S 60	15 03	15 59	16 55	09 44	10 25	10 53	11 13

SUN / MOON

Day	Eqn. of Time 00h	Eqn. of Time 12h	Mer. Pass.	Mer. Pass. Upper	Mer. Pass. Lower	Age	Phase
d	m s	m s	h m	h m	h m	d	%
5	01 31	01 26	11 59	00 33	13 04	16	98
6	01 21	01 15	11 59	01 35	14 05	17	94
7	01 10	01 04	11 59	02 33	15 01	18	87

UT	ARIES GHA	VENUS −4.2 GHA	Dec	MARS +0.6 GHA	Dec	JUPITER −2.0 GHA	Dec	SATURN +0.6 GHA	Dec	STARS Name	SHA	Dec
8 00	256 46.9	183 31.8	N22 14.2	87 45.7	N 5 43.5	199 40.3	N19 12.4	54 30.3	S 6 28.9	Acamar	315 19.2	S40 15.2
01	271 49.4	198 35.9	13.4	102 47.2	43.0	214 42.1	12.6	69 32.9	28.9	Achernar	335 27.7	S57 10.2
02	286 51.9	213 39.9	12.7	117 48.7	42.5	229 44.0	12.7	84 35.4	28.9	Acrux	173 09.8	S63 10.5
03	301 54.3	228 44.0	.. 11.9	132 50.2	.. 42.1	244 45.9	.. 12.8	99 37.9	.. 28.8	Adhara	255 13.4	S28 59.6
04	316 56.8	243 48.1	11.1	147 51.6	41.6	259 47.8	12.9	114 40.5	28.8	Aldebaran	290 50.5	N16 31.9
05	331 59.2	258 52.1	10.4	162 53.1	41.1	274 49.6	13.1	129 43.0	28.8			
06	347 01.7	273 56.2	N22 09.6	177 54.6	N 5 40.6	289 51.5	N19 13.2	144 45.5	S 6 28.8	Alioth	166 21.1	N55 53.7
F 07	2 04.2	289 00.2	08.9	192 56.1	40.1	304 53.4	13.3	159 48.1	28.8	Alkaid	152 59.1	N49 15.2
R 08	17 06.6	304 04.3	08.1	207 57.6	39.7	319 55.2	13.4	174 50.6	28.8	Al Na'ir	27 44.5	S46 53.7
I 09	32 09.1	319 08.3	.. 07.3	222 59.0	.. 39.2	334 57.1	.. 13.6	189 53.1	.. 28.7	Alnilam	275 47.4	S 1 11.8
D 10	47 11.6	334 12.3	06.6	238 00.5	38.7	349 59.0	13.7	204 55.7	28.7	Alphard	217 56.9	S 8 43.0
A 11	62 14.0	349 16.4	05.8	253 02.0	38.2	5 00.8	13.8	219 58.2	28.7			
Y 12	77 16.5	4 20.4	N22 05.1	268 03.5	N 5 37.7	20 02.7	N19 13.9	235 00.7	S 6 28.7	Alphecca	126 11.3	N26 40.4
13	92 19.0	19 24.5	04.3	283 05.0	37.2	35 04.6	14.1	250 03.3	28.7	Alpheratz	357 44.3	N29 09.5
14	107 21.4	34 28.5	03.5	298 06.4	36.8	50 06.5	14.2	265 05.8	28.7	Altair	62 08.7	N 8 54.2
15	122 23.9	49 32.6	.. 02.8	313 07.9	.. 36.3	65 08.3	.. 14.3	280 08.3	.. 28.7	Ankaa	353 16.5	S42 14.0
16	137 26.4	64 36.6	02.0	328 09.4	35.8	80 10.2	14.4	295 10.8	28.6	Antares	112 26.8	S26 27.5
17	152 28.8	79 40.6	01.2	343 10.9	35.3	95 12.1	14.6	310 13.4	28.6			
18	167 31.3	94 44.7	N22 00.3	358 12.4	N 5 34.8	110 13.9	N19 14.7	325 15.9	S 6 28.6	Arcturus	145 56.1	N19 07.1
19	182 33.7	109 48.7	21 59.7	13 13.8	34.3	125 15.8	14.8	340 18.4	28.6	Atria	107 28.6	S69 02.9
20	197 36.2	124 52.7	59.0	28 15.3	33.9	140 17.7	14.9	355 21.0	28.6	Avior	234 18.8	S59 33.3
21	212 38.7	139 56.8	.. 58.2	43 16.8	.. 33.4	155 19.5	.. 15.1	10 23.5	.. 28.6	Bellatrix	278 33.1	N 6 21.5
22	227 41.1	155 00.8	57.4	58 18.3	32.9	170 21.4	15.2	25 26.0	28.5	Betelgeuse	271 02.4	N 7 24.4
23	242 43.6	170 04.8	56.7	73 19.7	32.4	185 23.3	15.3	40 28.6	28.5			
9 00	257 46.1	185 08.8	N21 55.9	88 21.2	N 5 31.9	200 25.2	N19 15.4	55 31.1	S 6 28.5	Canopus	263 57.0	S52 42.3
01	272 48.5	200 12.9	55.2	103 22.7	31.4	215 27.0	15.6	70 33.6	28.5	Capella	280 36.0	N46 00.5
02	287 51.0	215 16.9	54.4	118 24.2	31.0	230 28.9	15.7	85 36.1	28.5	Deneb	49 31.6	N45 19.4
03	302 53.5	230 20.9	.. 53.6	133 25.6	.. 30.5	245 30.8	.. 15.8	100 38.7	.. 28.5	Denebola	182 34.3	N14 30.1
04	317 55.9	245 24.9	52.9	148 27.1	30.0	260 32.6	15.9	115 41.2	28.5	Diphda	348 56.7	S17 55.0
05	332 58.4	260 28.9	52.1	163 28.6	29.5	275 34.5	16.0	130 43.7	28.4			
06	348 00.8	275 33.0	N21 51.4	178 30.0	N 5 29.0	290 36.4	N19 16.2	145 46.3	S 6 28.4	Dubhe	193 52.6	N61 41.2
S 07	3 03.3	290 37.0	50.6	193 31.5	28.5	305 38.3	16.3	160 48.8	28.4	Elnath	278 13.9	N28 36.9
A 08	18 05.8	305 41.0	49.8	208 33.0	28.0	320 40.1	16.4	175 51.3	28.4	Eltanin	90 45.9	N51 29.3
T 09	33 08.2	320 45.0	.. 49.1	223 34.5	.. 27.6	335 42.0	.. 16.5	190 53.9	.. 28.4	Enif	33 47.7	N 9 56.0
U 10	48 10.7	335 49.0	48.3	238 35.9	27.1	350 43.9	16.7	205 56.4	28.4	Fomalhaut	15 24.7	S29 33.1
R 11	63 13.2	350 53.0	47.6	253 37.4	26.6	5 45.7	16.8	220 58.9	28.4			
D 12	78 15.6	5 57.0	N21 46.8	268 38.9	N 5 26.1	20 47.6	N19 16.9	236 01.4	S 6 28.3	Gacrux	172 01.5	S57 11.3
A 13	93 18.1	21 01.0	46.0	283 40.3	25.6	35 49.5	17.0	251 04.0	28.3	Gienah	175 52.9	S17 36.9
Y 14	108 20.6	36 05.0	45.3	298 41.8	25.1	50 51.4	17.2	266 06.5	28.3	Hadar	148 48.4	S60 26.2
15	123 23.0	51 09.0	.. 44.5	313 43.3	.. 24.6	65 53.2	.. 17.3	281 09.0	.. 28.3	Hamal	328 01.8	N23 31.2
16	138 25.5	66 13.0	43.8	328 44.7	24.2	80 55.1	17.4	296 11.6	28.3	Kaus Aust.	83 44.4	S34 22.5
17	153 28.0	81 17.0	43.0	343 46.2	23.7	95 57.0	17.5	311 14.1	28.3			
18	168 30.4	96 21.0	N21 42.3	358 47.7	N 5 23.2	110 58.8	N19 17.7	326 16.6	S 6 28.3	Kochab	137 19.0	N74 06.4
19	183 32.9	111 25.0	41.5	13 49.1	22.7	126 00.7	17.8	341 19.1	28.2	Markab	13 39.0	N15 16.3
20	198 35.3	126 29.0	40.7	28 50.6	22.2	141 02.6	17.9	356 21.7	28.2	Menkar	314 16.1	N 4 08.3
21	213 37.8	141 33.0	.. 40.0	43 52.1	.. 21.7	156 04.5	.. 18.0	11 24.2	.. 28.2	Menkent	148 08.1	S36 26.1
22	228 40.3	156 37.0	39.2	58 53.5	21.2	171 06.3	18.2	26 26.7	28.2	Miaplacidus	221 40.3	S69 46.5
23	243 42.7	171 40.9	38.5	73 55.0	20.7	186 08.2	18.3	41 29.2	28.2			
10 00	258 45.2	186 44.9	N21 37.7	88 56.5	N 5 20.3	201 10.1	N19 18.4	56 31.8	S 6 28.2	Mirfak	308 41.8	N49 54.1
01	273 47.7	201 48.9	37.0	103 57.9	19.8	216 11.9	18.5	71 34.3	28.2	Nunki	75 58.8	S26 16.7
02	288 50.1	216 52.9	36.2	118 59.4	19.3	231 13.8	18.6	86 36.8	28.1	Peacock	53 19.9	S56 41.3
03	303 52.6	231 56.9	.. 35.5	134 00.9	.. 18.8	246 15.7	.. 18.8	101 39.3	.. 28.1	Pollux	243 28.9	N27 59.7
04	318 55.1	247 00.8	34.7	149 02.3	18.3	261 17.6	18.9	116 41.9	28.1	Procyon	245 00.7	N 5 11.4
05	333 57.5	262 04.8	33.9	164 03.8	17.8	276 19.4	19.0	131 44.4	28.1			
06	349 00.0	277 08.8	N21 33.2	179 05.3	N 5 17.3	291 21.3	N19 19.1	146 46.9	S 6 28.1	Rasalhague	96 06.8	N12 33.1
07	4 02.5	292 12.7	32.4	194 06.7	16.8	306 23.2	19.3	161 49.4	28.1	Regulus	207 44.4	N11 54.3
S 08	19 04.9	307 16.7	31.7	209 08.2	16.3	321 25.1	19.4	176 52.0	28.1	Rigel	281 13.1	S 8 11.4
U 09	34 07.4	322 20.7	.. 30.9	224 09.6	.. 15.9	336 26.9	.. 19.5	191 54.5	.. 28.0	Rigil Kent.	139 52.2	S60 53.4
N 10	49 09.8	337 24.6	30.2	239 11.1	15.4	351 28.8	19.6	206 57.0	28.0	Sabik	102 13.0	S15 44.3
D 11	64 12.3	352 28.6	29.4	254 12.6	14.9	6 30.7	19.8	221 59.5	28.0			
A 12	79 14.8	7 32.6	N21 28.7	269 14.0	N 5 14.4	21 32.5	N19 19.9	237 02.1	S 6 28.0	Schedar	349 41.5	N56 36.1
Y 13	94 17.2	22 36.5	27.9	284 15.5	13.9	36 34.4	20.0	252 04.6	28.0	Shaula	96 22.4	S37 06.7
14	109 19.7	37 40.5	27.2	299 16.9	13.4	51 36.3	20.1	267 07.1	28.0	Sirius	258 34.7	S16 44.2
15	124 22.2	52 44.4	.. 26.4	314 18.4	.. 12.9	66 38.2	.. 20.2	282 09.6	.. 28.0	Spica	158 31.8	S11 13.7
16	139 24.6	67 48.4	25.7	329 19.9	12.4	81 40.0	20.4	297 12.2	28.0	Suhail	222 53.2	S43 29.3
17	154 27.1	82 52.3	24.9	344 21.3	11.9	96 41.9	20.5	312 14.7	27.9			
18	169 29.6	97 56.3	N21 24.2	359 22.8	N 5 11.4	111 43.8	N19 20.6	327 17.2	S 6 27.9	Vega	80 39.0	N38 47.8
19	184 32.0	113 00.2	23.4	14 24.2	10.9	126 45.6	20.7	342 19.7	27.9	Zuben'ubi	137 05.9	S16 05.7
20	199 34.5	128 04.1	22.7	29 25.7	10.5	141 47.5	20.9	357 22.3	27.9			
21	214 36.9	143 08.1	.. 21.9	44 27.1	.. 10.0	156 49.4	.. 21.0	12 24.8	.. 27.9		SHA	Mer.Pass.
22	229 39.4	158 12.0	21.2	59 28.6	09.5	171 51.3	21.1	27 27.3	27.9	Venus	287 22.8	11 36
23	244 41.9	173 15.9	20.4	74 30.1	09.0	186 53.1	21.2	42 29.8	27.9	Mars	190 35.1	18 05
Mer.Pass.	6 47.8	v 4.0	d 0.8	v 1.5	d 0.5	v 1.9	d 0.1	v 2.5	d 0.0	Jupiter	302 39.1	10 37
										Saturn	157 45.0	20 15

SUN / MOON

UT (d h)	SUN GHA	SUN Dec	MOON GHA	v	Dec	d	HP
8 00	180 14.5	N22 51.6	309 55.3	9.2	S14 23.1	9.8	58.6
01	195 14.4	51.8	324 23.5	9.3	14 13.3	9.9	58.5
02	210 14.3	52.0	338 51.8	9.5	14 03.4	10.0	58.5
03	225 14.2 ..	52.2	353 20.3	9.5	13 53.4	10.0	58.4
04	240 14.1	52.5	7 48.8	9.6	13 43.4	10.1	58.4
05	255 14.0	52.7	22 17.4	9.8	13 33.3	10.2	58.4
06	270 13.8	N22 52.9	36 46.2	9.8	S13 23.1	10.2	58.3
07	285 13.7	53.1	51 15.0	9.9	13 12.9	10.2	58.3
08	300 13.6	53.3	65 43.9	10.0	13 02.7	10.4	58.2
09	315 13.5 ..	53.5	80 12.9	10.1	12 52.3	10.3	58.2
10	330 13.4	53.8	94 42.0	10.2	12 42.0	10.5	58.2
11	345 13.2	54.0	109 11.2	10.3	12 31.5	10.5	58.1
12	0 13.1	N22 54.2	123 40.5	10.4	S12 21.0	10.5	58.1
13	15 13.0	54.4	138 09.9	10.4	12 10.5	10.6	58.0
14	30 12.9	54.6	152 39.3	10.6	11 59.9	10.6	58.0
15	45 12.7 ..	54.8	167 08.9	10.7	11 49.3	10.7	58.0
16	60 12.6	55.0	181 38.6	10.7	11 38.6	10.7	57.9
17	75 12.5	55.2	196 08.3	10.8	11 27.9	10.8	57.9
18	90 12.4	N22 55.4	210 38.1	11.0	S11 17.1	10.8	57.8
19	105 12.3	55.7	225 08.1	11.0	11 06.3	10.9	57.8
20	120 12.1	55.9	239 38.1	11.0	10 55.4	10.9	57.8
21	135 12.0 ..	56.1	254 08.1	11.2	10 44.5	10.9	57.7
22	150 11.9	56.3	268 38.3	11.3	10 33.6	11.0	57.7
23	165 11.8	56.5	283 08.6	11.3	10 22.6	11.0	57.7
9 00	180 11.7	N22 56.7	297 38.9	11.5	S10 11.6	11.1	57.6
01	195 11.5	56.9	312 09.4	11.5	10 00.5	11.1	57.6
02	210 11.4	57.1	326 39.9	11.6	9 49.4	11.1	57.5
03	225 11.3 ..	57.3	341 10.5	11.6	9 38.3	11.2	57.5
04	240 11.2	57.5	355 41.1	11.8	9 27.1	11.2	57.5
05	255 11.0	57.7	10 11.9	11.8	9 15.9	11.2	57.4
06	270 10.9	N22 57.9	24 42.7	11.9	S 9 04.7	11.2	57.4
07	285 10.8	58.1	39 13.6	12.0	8 53.5	11.3	57.3
08	300 10.7	58.3	53 44.6	12.0	8 42.2	11.3	57.3
09	315 10.5 ..	58.5	68 15.6	12.2	8 30.9	11.3	57.3
10	330 10.4	58.7	82 46.8	12.2	8 19.6	11.4	57.2
11	345 10.3	58.9	97 18.0	12.3	8 08.2	11.4	57.2
12	0 10.2	N22 59.1	111 49.3	12.3	S 7 56.8	11.4	57.1
13	15 10.1	59.3	126 20.6	12.4	7 45.4	11.4	57.1
14	30 09.9	59.5	140 52.0	12.5	7 34.0	11.5	57.1
15	45 09.8 ..	59.7	155 23.5	12.6	7 22.5	11.4	57.0
16	60 09.7	22 59.9	169 55.1	12.6	7 11.1	11.5	57.0
17	75 09.6	23 00.1	184 26.7	12.7	6 59.6	11.5	57.0
18	90 09.4	N23 00.3	198 58.4	12.8	S 6 48.1	11.5	56.9
19	105 09.3	00.4	213 30.2	12.8	6 36.6	11.6	56.9
20	120 09.2	00.6	228 02.0	12.9	6 25.0	11.5	56.9
21	135 09.1 ..	00.8	242 33.9	12.9	6 13.5	11.6	56.8
22	150 08.9	01.0	257 05.8	13.0	6 01.9	11.5	56.8
23	165 08.8	01.2	271 37.8	13.1	5 50.4	11.6	56.7
10 00	180 08.7	N23 01.4	286 09.9	13.2	S 5 38.8	11.6	56.7
01	195 08.6	01.6	300 42.1	13.2	5 27.2	11.6	56.7
02	210 08.4	01.8	315 14.3	13.2	5 15.6	11.6	56.6
03	225 08.3 ..	02.0	329 46.5	13.3	5 04.0	11.7	56.6
04	240 08.2	02.1	344 18.8	13.4	4 52.3	11.6	56.6
05	255 08.1	02.3	358 51.2	13.4	4 40.7	11.6	56.5
06	270 07.9	N23 02.5	13 23.6	13.5	S 4 29.1	11.7	56.5
07	285 07.8	02.7	27 56.1	13.5	4 17.4	11.6	56.5
08	300 07.7	02.9	42 28.6	13.6	4 05.8	11.7	56.4
09	315 07.6 ..	03.1	57 01.2	13.6	3 54.1	11.6	56.4
10	330 07.4	03.2	71 33.8	13.7	3 42.5	11.7	56.3
11	345 07.3	03.4	86 06.5	13.8	3 30.8	11.7	56.3
12	0 07.2	N23 03.6	100 39.3	13.7	S 3 19.1	11.6	56.3
13	15 07.1	03.8	115 12.0	13.9	3 07.5	11.7	56.2
14	30 06.9	04.0	129 44.9	13.9	2 55.8	11.6	56.2
15	45 06.8 ..	04.1	144 17.8	13.9	2 44.2	11.7	56.2
16	60 06.7	04.3	158 50.7	13.9	2 32.5	11.7	56.1
17	75 06.6	04.5	173 23.6	14.1	2 20.8	11.6	56.1
18	90 06.4	N23 04.7	187 56.7	14.0	S 2 09.2	11.6	56.1
19	105 06.3	04.8	202 29.7	14.1	1 57.6	11.7	56.1
20	120 06.2	05.0	217 02.8	14.1	1 45.9	11.6	56.0
21	135 06.0 ..	05.2	231 35.9	14.2	1 34.3	11.6	56.0
22	150 05.9	05.4	246 09.1	14.2	1 22.7	11.7	56.0
23	165 05.8	05.5	260 42.3	14.3	S 1 11.0	11.6	55.9
	SD 15.8	d 0.2	SD 15.8		15.6		15.3

(Day labels: 8 = FRIDAY, 9 = SATURDAY, 10 = SUNDAY)

Twilight / Sunrise / Moonrise

Lat.	Naut.	Civil	Sunrise	Moonrise 8	9	10	11
N 72	□	□	□			(00 08 / 23 53)	23 38
N 70	□	□	□	00 22	00 10	(00 00 / 23 51)	23 43
68	////	////	□	(00 00 / 23 57)	23 53	23 50	23 47
66	////	////	00 32	23 46	23 48	23 49	23 50
64	////	////	01 40	23 37	23 43	23 48	23 53
62	////	////	02 15	23 29	23 39	23 47	23 55
60	////	01 04	02 40	23 23	23 36	23 47	23 57
N 58	////	01 47	02 59	23 17	23 32	23 46	23 59
56	////	02 14	03 15	23 12	23 30	23 45	24 01
54	00 58	02 36	03 29	23 07	23 27	23 45	24 02
52	01 38	02 53	03 41	23 03	23 25	23 45	24 04
50	02 04	03 07	03 51	22 59	23 23	23 44	24 05
45	02 47	03 36	04 13	22 50	23 18	23 43	24 08
N 40	03 17	03 58	04 31	22 43	23 14	23 43	24 10
35	03 40	04 16	04 46	22 37	23 11	23 42	24 12
30	03 58	04 31	04 58	22 32	23 08	23 41	24 14
20	04 26	04 55	05 20	22 22	23 03	23 40	24 17
N 10	04 48	05 15	05 38	22 14	22 58	23 40	24 22
0	05 07	05 33	05 56	22 06	22 54	23 39	24 22
S 10	05 24	05 50	06 13	21 58	22 49	23 38	24 25
20	05 40	06 07	06 31	21 50	22 45	23 37	24 28
30	05 56	06 25	06 52	21 41	22 40	23 36	24 31
35	06 04	06 36	07 04	21 35	22 37	23 36	24 33
40	06 13	06 47	07 18	21 29	22 33	23 35	24 35
45	06 23	07 00	07 34	21 21	22 29	23 35	24 38
S 50	06 35	07 16	07 54	21 13	22 25	23 34	24 41
52	06 40	07 23	08 04	21 09	22 22	23 33	24 42
54	06 45	07 31	08 15	21 04	22 20	23 33	24 44
56	06 51	07 40	08 27	20 59	22 17	23 33	24 45
58	06 58	07 50	08 41	20 53	22 14	23 32	24 47
S 60	07 05	08 01	08 58	20 47	22 11	23 32	24 49

Sunset / Twilight / Moonset

Lat.	Sunset	Civil	Naut.	Moonset 8	9	10	11
N 72	□	□	□	06 24	08 33	10 28	12 16
N 70	□	□	□	06 51	08 47	10 34	12 14
68	□	□	□	07 12	08 58	10 38	12 13
66	23 33	////	////	07 28	09 07	10 42	12 12
64	22 20	////	////	07 41	09 15	10 45	12 11
62	21 45	////	////	07 52	09 22	10 47	12 10
60	21 20	22 57	////	08 01	09 27	10 50	12 09
N 58	21 00	22 13	////	08 09	09 32	10 52	12 08
56	20 44	21 45	////	08 17	09 37	10 54	12 08
54	20 30	21 24	23 02	08 23	09 41	10 55	12 07
52	20 18	21 06	22 22	08 29	09 44	10 57	12 07
50	20 08	20 52	21 56	08 34	09 47	10 58	12 06
45	19 46	20 23	21 12	08 45	09 54	11 01	12 05
N 40	19 28	20 01	20 42	08 54	10 00	11 03	12 04
35	19 13	19 43	20 19	09 02	10 05	11 05	12 03
30	19 00	19 28	20 01	09 09	10 09	11 07	12 03
20	18 39	19 03	19 32	09 20	10 17	11 10	12 02
N 10	18 20	18 43	19 10	09 30	10 23	11 13	12 01
0	18 03	18 25	18 52	09 40	10 29	11 16	12 00
S 10	17 46	18 09	18 35	09 49	10 35	11 18	11 59
20	17 28	17 52	18 19	09 59	10 42	11 21	11 58
30	17 07	17 33	18 03	10 11	10 49	11 24	11 57
35	16 55	17 23	17 54	10 17	10 53	11 25	11 56
40	16 41	17 11	17 45	10 25	10 58	11 27	11 55
45	16 25	16 58	17 35	10 33	11 03	11 29	11 54
S 50	16 04	16 42	17 24	10 43	11 09	11 32	11 53
52	15 55	16 35	17 19	10 48	11 13	11 33	11 53
54	15 44	16 27	17 13	10 53	11 16	11 35	11 52
56	15 32	16 18	17 07	10 59	11 19	11 36	11 52
58	15 17	16 09	17 01	11 05	11 23	11 38	11 51
S 60	15 01	15 57	16 53	11 13	11 27	11 39	11 50

SUN / MOON

Day	Eqn. of Time 00h	Eqn. of Time 12h	Mer. Pass.	Mer. Pass. Upper	Mer. Pass. Lower	Age	Phase
d	m s	m s	h m	h m	h m	d	%
8	00 58	00 53	11 59	03 28	15 53	19	79
9	00 47	00 41	11 59	04 18	16 42	20	70
10	00 35	00 29	12 00	05 05	17 27	21	60

2012 JUNE 11, 12, 13 (MON., TUES., WED.)

UT	ARIES GHA	VENUS −4.1 GHA	Dec	MARS +0.7 GHA	Dec	JUPITER −2.0 GHA	Dec	SATURN +0.6 GHA	Dec
11 00	259 44.3	188 19.9	N21 19.7	89 31.5	N 5 08.5	201 55.0	N19 21.3	57 32.4	S 6 27.9
01	274 46.8	203 23.8	19.0	104 33.0	08.0	216 56.9	21.5	72 34.9	27.8
02	289 49.3	218 27.7	18.2	119 34.4	07.5	231 58.8	21.6	87 37.4	27.8
03	304 51.7	233 31.6 ..	17.5	134 35.9 ..	07.0	247 00.6 ..	21.7	102 39.9 ..	27.8
04	319 54.2	248 35.6	16.7	149 37.3	06.5	262 02.5	21.8	117 42.4	27.8
05	334 56.7	263 39.5	16.0	164 38.8	06.0	277 04.4	22.0	132 45.0	27.8
06	349 59.1	278 43.4	N21 15.2	179 40.2	N 5 05.5	292 06.2	N19 22.1	147 47.5	S 6 27.8
07	5 01.6	293 47.3	14.5	194 41.7	05.0	307 08.1	22.2	162 50.0	27.8
M 08	20 04.1	308 51.2	13.8	209 43.1	04.5	322 10.0	22.3	177 52.5	27.8
O 09	35 06.5	323 55.1 ..	13.0	224 44.6 ..	04.0	337 11.9 ..	22.4	192 55.1 ..	27.8
N 10	50 09.0	338 59.0	12.3	239 46.1	03.5	352 13.7	22.6	207 57.6	27.7
D 11	65 11.4	354 02.9	11.5	254 47.5	03.1	7 15.6	22.7	223 00.1	27.7
A 12	80 13.9	9 06.8	N21 10.8	269 49.0	N 5 02.6	22 17.5	N19 22.8	238 02.6	S 6 27.7
Y 13	95 16.4	24 10.7	10.0	284 50.4	02.1	37 19.4	22.9	253 05.1	27.7
14	110 18.8	39 14.6	09.3	299 51.9	01.6	52 21.2	23.1	268 07.7	27.7
15	125 21.3	54 18.5 ..	08.6	314 53.3 ..	01.1	67 23.1 ..	23.2	283 10.2 ..	27.7
16	140 23.8	69 22.4	07.8	329 54.8	00.6	82 25.0	23.3	298 12.7	27.7
17	155 26.2	84 26.3	07.1	344 56.2	5 00.1	97 26.9	23.4	313 15.2	27.7
18	170 28.7	99 30.2	N21 06.4	359 57.7	N 4 59.6	112 28.7	N19 23.5	328 17.7	S 6 27.6
19	185 31.2	114 34.1	05.6	14 59.1	59.1	127 30.6	23.7	343 20.3	27.6
20	200 33.6	129 37.9	04.9	30 00.5	58.6	142 32.5	23.8	358 22.8	27.6
21	215 36.1	144 41.8 ..	04.2	45 02.0 ..	58.1	157 34.4 ..	23.9	13 25.3 ..	27.6
22	230 38.6	159 45.7	03.4	60 03.4	57.6	172 36.2	24.0	28 27.8	27.6
23	245 41.0	174 49.6	02.7	75 04.9	57.1	187 38.1	24.1	43 30.3	27.6
12 00	260 43.5	189 53.4	N21 02.0	90 06.3	N 4 56.6	202 40.0	N19 24.3	58 32.9	S 6 27.6
01	275 45.9	204 57.3	01.2	105 07.8	56.1	217 41.8	24.4	73 35.4	27.6
02	290 48.4	220 01.2	21 00.5	120 09.2	55.6	232 43.7	24.5	88 37.9	27.6
03	305 50.9	235 05.0	20 59.8	135 10.7 ..	55.1	247 45.6 ..	24.6	103 40.4 ..	27.6
04	320 53.3	250 08.9	59.0	150 12.1	54.6	262 47.5	24.8	118 42.9	27.5
05	335 55.8	265 12.7	58.3	165 13.6	54.1	277 49.3	24.9	133 45.4	27.5
06	350 58.3	280 16.6	N20 57.6	180 15.0	N 4 53.6	292 51.2	N19 25.0	148 48.0	S 6 27.5
07	6 00.7	295 20.4	56.8	195 16.5	53.1	307 53.1	25.1	163 50.5	27.5
T 08	21 03.2	310 24.3	56.1	210 17.9	52.6	322 55.0	25.2	178 53.0	27.5
U 09	36 05.7	325 28.1 ..	55.4	225 19.3 ..	52.1	337 56.8 ..	25.4	193 55.5 ..	27.5
E 10	51 08.1	340 32.0	54.7	240 20.8	51.6	352 58.7	25.5	208 58.0	27.5
S 11	66 10.6	355 35.8	53.9	255 22.2	51.1	8 00.6	25.6	224 00.6	27.5
D 12	81 13.0	10 39.7	N20 53.2	270 23.7	N 4 50.6	23 02.5	N19 25.7	239 03.1	S 6 27.5
A 13	96 15.5	25 43.5	52.5	285 25.1	50.1	38 04.3	25.8	254 05.6	27.5
Y 14	111 18.0	40 47.3	51.8	300 26.5	49.6	53 06.2	26.0	269 08.1	27.4
15	126 20.4	55 51.1 ..	51.0	315 28.0 ..	49.1	68 08.1 ..	26.1	284 10.6 ..	27.4
16	141 22.9	70 55.0	50.3	330 29.4	48.6	83 10.0	26.2	299 13.1	27.4
17	156 25.4	85 58.8	49.6	345 30.9	48.1	98 11.8	26.3	314 15.7	27.4
18	171 27.8	101 02.6	N20 48.9	0 32.3	N 4 47.6	113 13.7	N19 26.4	329 18.2	S 6 27.4
19	186 30.3	116 06.4	48.1	15 33.7	47.1	128 15.6	26.6	344 20.7	27.4
20	201 32.8	131 10.2	47.4	30 35.2	46.6	143 17.5	26.7	359 23.2	27.4
21	216 35.2	146 14.1 ..	46.7	45 36.6 ..	46.1	158 19.3 ..	26.8	14 25.7 ..	27.4
22	231 37.7	161 17.9	46.0	60 38.1	45.6	173 21.2	26.9	29 28.2	27.4
23	246 40.2	176 21.7	45.3	75 39.5	45.1	188 23.1	27.0	44 30.8	27.4
13 00	261 42.6	191 25.5	N20 44.6	90 40.9	N 4 44.6	203 25.0	N19 27.2	59 33.3	S 6 27.3
01	276 45.1	206 29.3	43.8	105 42.4	44.1	218 26.8	27.3	74 35.8	27.3
02	291 47.5	221 33.1	43.1	120 43.8	43.6	233 28.7	27.4	89 38.3	27.3
03	306 50.0	236 36.9 ..	42.4	135 45.2 ..	43.1	248 30.6 ..	27.5	104 40.8 ..	27.3
04	321 52.5	251 40.6	41.7	150 46.7	42.6	263 32.5	27.6	119 43.3	27.3
05	336 54.9	266 44.4	41.0	165 48.1	42.1	278 34.3	27.8	134 45.8	27.3
06	351 57.4	281 48.2	N20 40.3	180 49.6	N 4 41.6	293 36.2	N19 27.9	149 48.4	S 6 27.3
W 07	6 59.9	296 52.0	39.6	195 51.0	41.1	308 38.1	28.0	164 50.9	27.3
E 08	22 02.3	311 55.8	38.8	210 52.4	40.6	323 40.0	28.1	179 53.4	27.3
D 09	37 04.8	326 59.5 ..	38.1	225 53.9 ..	40.1	338 41.8 ..	28.2	194 55.9 ..	27.3
N 10	52 07.3	342 03.3	37.4	240 55.3	39.6	353 43.7	28.4	209 58.4	27.3
E 11	67 09.7	357 07.1	36.7	255 56.7	39.1	8 45.6	28.5	225 00.9	27.3
S 12	82 12.2	12 10.8	N20 36.0	270 58.2	N 4 38.6	23 47.5	N19 28.6	240 03.4	S 6 27.2
D 13	97 14.6	27 14.6	35.3	285 59.6	38.1	38 49.3	28.7	255 06.0	27.2
A 14	112 17.1	42 18.4	34.6	301 01.0	37.6	53 51.2	28.8	270 08.5	27.2
Y 15	127 19.6	57 22.1 ..	33.9	316 02.5 ..	37.1	68 53.1 ..	29.0	285 11.0 ..	27.2
16	142 22.0	72 25.9	33.2	331 03.9	36.6	83 55.0	29.1	300 13.5	27.2
17	157 24.5	87 29.6	32.5	346 05.3	36.1	98 56.9	29.2	315 16.0	27.2
18	172 27.0	102 33.4	N20 31.8	1 06.7	N 4 35.6	113 58.7	N19 29.3	330 18.5	S 6 27.2
19	187 29.4	117 37.1	31.1	16 08.2	35.1	129 00.6	29.4	345 21.0	27.2
20	202 31.9	132 40.8	30.4	31 09.6	34.6	144 02.5	29.5	0 23.5	27.2
21	217 34.4	147 44.6 ..	29.7	46 11.0 ..	34.1	159 04.4 ..	29.7	15 26.1 ..	27.2
22	232 36.8	162 48.3	29.0	61 12.5	33.6	174 06.2	29.8	30 28.6	27.2
23	247 39.3	177 52.0	28.3	76 13.9	33.1	189 08.1	29.9	45 31.1	27.2
Mer.Pass.	h m 6 36.0	v 3.8	d 0.7	v 1.4	d 0.5	v 1.9	d 0.1	v 2.5	d 0.0

STARS

Name	SHA	Dec
Acamar	315 19.2	S40 15.2
Achernar	335 27.6	S57 10.1
Acrux	173 09.9	S63 10.5
Adhara	255 13.4	S28 59.6
Aldebaran	290 50.5	N16 31.9
Alioth	166 21.1	N55 53.7
Alkaid	152 59.2	N49 15.2
Al Na'ir	27 44.4	S46 53.7
Alnilam	275 47.4	S 1 11.8
Alphard	217 57.0	S 8 43.0
Alphecca	126 11.3	N26 40.5
Alpheratz	357 44.3	N29 09.5
Altair	62 08.6	N 8 54.2
Ankaa	353 16.5	S42 14.0
Antares	112 26.8	S26 27.5
Arcturus	145 56.1	N19 07.1
Atria	107 28.6	S69 03.0
Avior	234 18.8	S59 33.3
Bellatrix	278 33.1	N 6 21.5
Betelgeuse	271 02.4	N 7 24.4
Canopus	263 57.0	S52 42.3
Capella	280 36.0	N46 00.5
Deneb	49 31.6	N45 19.4
Denebola	182 34.3	N14 30.1
Diphda	348 56.7	S17 54.9
Dubhe	193 52.6	N61 41.2
Elnath	278 13.9	N28 36.9
Eltanin	90 45.9	N51 29.3
Enif	33 47.7	N 9 56.0
Fomalhaut	15 24.7	S29 33.1
Gacrux	172 01.5	S57 11.3
Gienah	175 52.9	S17 36.9
Hadar	148 48.5	S60 26.2
Hamal	328 01.8	N23 31.2
Kaus Aust.	83 44.3	S34 22.5
Kochab	137 19.0	N74 06.5
Markab	13 39.0	N15 16.4
Menkar	314 16.1	N 4 08.3
Menkent	148 08.1	S36 26.1
Miaplacidus	221 40.4	S69 46.5
Mirfak	308 41.8	N49 54.1
Nunki	75 58.8	S26 16.7
Peacock	53 19.9	S56 41.3
Pollux	243 28.9	N27 59.7
Procyon	245 00.8	N 5 11.4
Rasalhague	96 06.8	N12 33.1
Regulus	207 44.4	N11 54.3
Rigel	281 13.1	S 8 11.4
Rigil Kent.	139 52.2	S60 53.4
Sabik	102 13.0	S15 44.3
Schedar	349 41.5	N56 36.1
Shaula	96 22.4	S37 06.7
Sirius	258 34.7	S16 44.2
Spica	158 31.8	S11 13.7
Suhail	222 53.2	S43 29.3
Vega	80 39.0	N38 47.8
Zuben'ubi	137 05.9	S16 05.7

	SHA	Mer.Pass.
	° ′	h m
Venus	289 10.0	11 18
Mars	189 22.9	17 58
Jupiter	301 56.5	10 20
Saturn	157 49.4	20 02

UT	SUN GHA	SUN Dec	MOON GHA	v	MOON Dec	d	HP
11 00	180 05.7	N23 05.7	275 15.6	14.3	S 0 59.4	11.6	55.9
01	195 05.5	05.9	289 48.9	14.3	0 47.8	11.6	55.9
02	210 05.4	06.0	304 22.2	14.3	0 36.2	11.6	55.8
03	225 05.3	.. 06.2	318 55.5	14.4	0 24.6	11.5	55.8
04	240 05.2	06.4	333 28.9	14.4	0 13.1	11.6	55.8
05	255 05.0	06.5	348 02.3	14.5	S 0 01.5	11.5	55.7
M 06	270 04.9	N23 06.7	2 35.8	14.5	N 0 10.0	11.6	55.7
O 07	285 04.8	06.9	17 09.3	14.5	0 21.6	11.5	55.7
N 08	300 04.6	07.0	31 42.8	14.5	0 33.1	11.5	55.7
D 09	315 04.5	.. 07.2	46 16.3	14.6	0 44.6	11.5	55.6
A 10	330 04.4	07.4	60 49.9	14.6	0 56.1	11.5	55.6
Y 11	345 04.3	07.5	75 23.5	14.6	1 07.6	11.4	55.6
12	0 04.1	N23 07.7	89 57.1	14.7	N 1 19.0	11.5	55.5
13	15 04.0	07.9	104 30.8	14.6	1 30.5	11.4	55.5
14	30 03.9	08.0	119 04.4	14.7	1 41.9	11.4	55.5
15	45 03.8	.. 08.2	133 38.1	14.8	1 53.3	11.4	55.5
16	60 03.6	08.3	148 11.9	14.7	2 04.7	11.4	55.4
17	75 03.5	08.5	162 45.6	14.8	2 16.1	11.3	55.4
18	90 03.4	N23 08.7	177 19.4	14.7	N 2 27.4	11.3	55.4
19	105 03.2	08.8	191 53.1	14.8	2 38.7	11.3	55.4
20	120 03.1	09.0	206 26.9	14.8	2 50.0	11.3	55.3
21	135 03.0	.. 09.1	221 00.7	14.9	3 01.3	11.3	55.3
22	150 02.8	09.3	235 34.6	14.8	3 12.6	11.2	55.3
23	165 02.7	09.4	250 08.4	14.9	3 23.8	11.2	55.2
12 00	180 02.6	N23 09.6	264 42.3	14.8	N 3 35.0	11.2	55.2
01	195 02.5	09.8	279 16.1	14.9	3 46.2	11.2	55.2
02	210 02.3	09.9	293 50.0	14.9	3 57.4	11.1	55.2
03	225 02.2	.. 10.1	308 23.9	14.9	4 08.5	11.1	55.1
04	240 02.1	10.2	322 57.8	15.0	4 19.6	11.1	55.1
05	255 01.9	10.4	337 31.8	14.9	4 30.7	11.0	55.1
T 06	270 01.8	N23 10.5	352 05.7	14.9	N 4 41.7	11.1	55.1
U 07	285 01.7	10.7	6 39.6	15.0	4 52.8	10.9	55.0
E 08	300 01.5	10.8	21 13.6	14.9	5 03.7	11.0	55.0
S 09	315 01.4	.. 11.0	35 47.5	15.0	5 14.7	10.9	55.0
D 10	330 01.3	11.1	50 21.5	15.0	5 25.6	11.0	55.0
A 11	345 01.2	11.2	64 55.5	14.9	5 36.6	10.8	55.0
Y 12	0 01.0	N23 11.4	79 29.4	15.0	N 5 47.4	10.9	54.9
13	15 00.9	11.5	94 03.4	15.0	5 58.3	10.8	54.9
14	30 00.8	11.7	108 37.4	15.0	6 09.1	10.7	54.9
15	45 00.6	.. 11.8	123 11.4	14.9	6 19.8	10.8	54.9
16	60 00.5	12.0	137 45.3	15.0	6 30.6	10.7	54.8
17	75 00.4	12.1	152 19.3	15.0	6 41.3	10.7	54.8
18	90 00.3	N23 12.3	166 53.3	15.0	N 6 52.0	10.6	54.8
19	105 00.1	12.4	181 27.3	14.9	7 02.6	10.6	54.8
20	120 00.0	12.5	196 01.2	15.0	7 13.2	10.6	54.8
21	134 59.9	.. 12.7	210 35.2	15.0	7 23.8	10.5	54.7
22	149 59.7	12.8	225 09.2	14.9	7 34.3	10.5	54.7
23	164 59.6	12.9	239 43.1	15.0	7 44.8	10.4	54.7
13 00	179 59.5	N23 13.1	254 17.1	14.9	N 7 55.2	10.5	54.7
01	194 59.3	13.2	268 51.0	15.0	8 05.7	10.3	54.7
02	209 59.2	13.4	283 25.0	14.9	8 16.0	10.4	54.7
03	224 59.1	.. 13.5	297 58.9	15.0	8 26.4	10.2	54.6
04	239 58.9	13.6	312 32.9	14.9	8 36.6	10.3	54.6
05	254 58.8	13.8	327 06.8	14.9	8 46.9	10.2	54.6
W 06	269 58.7	N23 13.9	341 40.7	14.9	N 8 57.1	10.2	54.6
E 07	284 58.5	14.0	356 14.6	14.9	9 07.3	10.1	54.6
D 08	299 58.4	14.2	10 48.5	14.8	9 17.4	10.1	54.5
N 09	314 58.3	.. 14.3	25 22.3	14.9	9 27.5	10.0	54.5
E 10	329 58.2	14.4	39 56.2	14.9	9 37.5	10.0	54.5
S 11	344 58.0	14.5	54 30.1	14.8	9 47.5	10.0	54.5
D 12	359 57.9	N23 14.7	69 03.9	14.8	N 9 57.5	9.9	54.5
A 13	14 57.8	14.8	83 37.7	14.8	10 07.4	9.8	54.5
Y 14	29 57.6	14.9	98 11.5	14.8	10 17.2	9.8	54.5
15	44 57.5	.. 15.1	112 45.3	14.8	10 27.0	9.8	54.4
16	59 57.4	15.2	127 19.1	14.7	10 36.8	9.7	54.4
17	74 57.2	15.3	141 52.8	14.8	10 46.5	9.7	54.4
18	89 57.1	N23 15.4	156 26.6	14.7	N10 56.2	9.6	54.4
19	104 57.0	15.6	171 00.3	14.7	11 05.8	9.6	54.4
20	119 56.8	15.7	185 34.0	14.7	11 15.4	9.5	54.4
21	134 56.7	.. 15.8	200 07.7	14.6	11 24.9	9.4	54.4
22	149 56.6	15.9	214 41.3	14.7	11 34.4	9.4	54.3
23	164 56.4	16.0	229 15.0	14.6	N11 43.8	9.3	54.3
	SD 15.8	d 0.1	SD 15.1		15.0		14.8

Lat.	Twilight Naut.	Civil	Sunrise	Moonrise 11	12	13	14
N 72	▢	▢	▢	23 38	23 23	23 06	22 41
N 70	▢	▢	▢	23 43	23 34	23 25	23 14
68	▢	▢	▢	23 47	23 43	23 40	23 38
66	////	////	00 05	23 50	23 51	23 53	23 56
64	////	////	01 36	23 53	23 57	24 03	00 03
62	////	////	02 12	23 55	24 03	00 03	00 12
60	////	00 58	02 37	23 57	24 08	00 08	00 20
N 58	////	01 44	02 57	23 59	24 12	00 12	00 27
56	////	02 12	03 14	24 01	00 01	00 16	00 33
54	00 53	02 34	03 28	24 02	00 02	00 20	00 39
52	01 35	02 51	03 40	24 03	00 03	00 23	00 44
50	02 02	03 06	03 51	24 04	00 04	00 26	00 48
45	02 46	03 36	04 13	24 08	00 08	00 32	00 58
N 40	03 16	03 58	04 31	24 10	00 10	00 37	01 06
35	03 39	04 16	04 45	24 12	00 12	00 42	01 13
30	03 58	04 31	04 58	24 14	00 14	00 46	01 19
20	04 26	04 56	05 20	24 17	00 17	00 53	01 30
N 10	04 49	05 16	05 39	24 20	00 20	00 59	01 39
0	05 08	05 34	05 56	24 22	00 22	01 05	01 48
S 10	05 24	05 51	06 14	24 25	00 25	01 11	01 57
20	05 40	06 08	06 32	24 28	00 28	01 17	02 07
30	05 57	06 26	06 53	24 31	00 31	01 25	02 18
35	06 05	06 37	07 05	24 33	00 33	01 29	02 24
40	06 15	06 49	07 19	24 35	00 35	01 34	02 32
45	06 25	07 02	07 36	24 38	00 38	01 39	02 40
S 50	06 36	07 18	07 56	24 41	00 41	01 46	02 51
52	06 42	07 25	08 06	24 42	00 42	01 49	02 56
54	06 47	07 33	08 17	24 44	00 44	01 53	03 01
56	06 53	07 42	08 29	24 45	00 45	01 57	03 07
58	07 00	07 52	08 44	24 47	00 47	02 01	03 13
S 60	07 07	08 04	09 01	24 49	00 49	02 06	03 21

Lat.	Sunset	Twilight Civil	Naut.	Moonset 11	12	13	14
N 72	▢	▢	▢	12 16	14 02	15 49	17 45
N 70	▢	▢	▢	12 14	13 53	15 32	17 14
68	▢	▢	▢	12 13	13 45	15 18	16 51
66	▢	▢	▢	12 12	13 39	15 06	16 33
64	22 25	////	////	12 11	13 34	14 57	16 19
62	21 49	////	////	12 10	13 30	14 49	16 07
60	21 23	23 04	////	12 09	13 26	14 42	15 57
N 58	21 03	22 17	////	12 08	13 23	14 36	15 48
56	20 46	21 48	////	12 08	13 20	14 30	15 40
54	20 32	21 26	23 09	12 07	13 17	14 26	15 33
52	20 20	21 09	22 26	12 07	13 15	14 21	15 27
50	20 10	20 54	21 59	12 06	13 12	14 17	15 21
45	19 47	20 25	21 14	12 05	13 08	14 09	15 09
N 40	19 29	20 02	20 44	12 04	13 04	14 02	15 00
35	19 15	19 44	20 21	12 03	13 00	13 56	14 51
30	19 02	19 29	20 02	12 03	12 57	13 51	14 44
20	18 40	19 04	19 34	12 02	12 52	13 41	14 31
N 10	18 21	18 44	19 11	12 01	12 47	13 33	14 20
0	18 04	18 26	18 52	12 00	12 43	13 26	14 09
S 10	17 46	18 09	18 35	11 59	12 39	13 18	13 59
20	17 28	17 52	18 19	11 58	12 34	13 10	13 48
30	17 07	17 33	18 03	11 57	12 29	13 01	13 35
35	16 55	17 23	17 54	11 56	12 26	12 56	13 28
40	16 41	17 11	17 45	11 55	12 22	12 50	13 20
45	16 24	16 58	17 35	11 54	12 18	12 44	13 10
S 50	16 04	16 42	17 23	11 53	12 14	12 35	12 59
52	15 54	16 35	17 18	11 53	12 12	12 32	12 54
54	15 43	16 27	17 13	11 52	12 09	12 27	12 48
56	15 30	16 18	17 07	11 52	12 07	12 23	12 41
58	15 16	16 07	17 00	11 51	12 04	12 18	12 34
S 60	14 59	15 56	16 53	11 50	12 01	12 12	12 26

Day	SUN Eqn. of Time 00h	12h	Mer. Pass.	MOON Mer. Pass. Upper	Lower	Age	Phase
d	m s	m s	h m	h m	h m	d	%
11	00 23	00 17	12 00	05 49	18 11	22	50
12	00 11	00 04	12 00	06 33	18 54	23	40
13	00 02	00 08	12 00	07 15	19 37	24	31

2012 JUNE 14, 15, 16 (THURS., FRI., SAT.)

UT	ARIES GHA	VENUS −4.1 GHA	Dec	MARS +0.7 GHA	Dec	JUPITER −2.0 GHA	Dec	SATURN +0.6 GHA	Dec
14 00	262 41.8	192 55.8	N20 27.6	91 15.3	N 4 32.6	204 10.0	N19 30.0	60 33.6	S 6 27.1
01	277 44.2	207 59.5	26.9	106 16.7	32.1	219 11.9	30.1	75 36.1	27.1
02	292 46.7	223 03.2	26.2	121 18.2	31.6	234 13.7	30.3	90 38.6	27.1
03	307 49.1	238 06.9 ..	25.5	136 19.6 ..	31.1	249 15.6 ..	30.4	105 41.1 ..	27.1
04	322 51.6	253 10.6	24.8	151 21.0	30.6	264 17.5	30.5	120 43.6	27.1
05	337 54.1	268 14.4	24.1	166 22.5	30.1	279 19.4	30.6	135 46.1	27.1
06	352 56.5	283 18.1	N20 23.4	181 23.9	N 4 29.6	294 21.2	N19 30.7	150 48.7	S 6 27.1
07	7 59.0	298 21.8	22.7	196 25.3	29.0	309 23.1	30.9	165 51.2	27.1
T 08	23 01.5	313 25.5	22.0	211 26.7	28.5	324 25.0	31.0	180 53.7	27.1
H 09	38 03.9	328 29.2 ..	21.4	226 28.2 ..	28.0	339 26.9 ..	31.1	195 56.2 ..	27.1
U 10	53 06.4	343 32.9	20.7	241 29.6	27.5	354 28.8	31.2	210 58.7	27.1
R 11	68 08.9	358 36.5	20.0	256 31.0	27.0	9 30.6	31.3	226 01.2	27.1
S 12	83 11.3	13 40.2	N20 19.3	271 32.4	N 4 26.5	24 32.5	N19 31.4	241 03.7	S 6 27.1
D 13	98 13.8	28 43.9	18.6	286 33.9	26.0	39 34.4	31.6	256 06.2	27.1
A 14	113 16.3	43 47.6	17.9	301 35.3	25.5	54 36.3	31.7	271 08.7	27.0
Y 15	128 18.7	58 51.3 ..	17.2	316 36.7 ..	25.0	69 38.1 ..	31.8	286 11.2 ..	27.0
16	143 21.2	73 54.9	16.6	331 38.1	24.5	84 40.0	31.9	301 13.8	27.0
17	158 23.6	88 58.6	15.9	346 39.5	24.0	99 41.9	32.0	316 16.3	27.0
18	173 26.1	104 02.3	N20 15.2	1 41.0	N 4 23.5	114 43.8	N19 32.2	331 18.8	S 6 27.0
19	188 28.6	119 05.9	14.5	16 42.4	23.0	129 45.6	32.3	346 21.3	27.0
20	203 31.0	134 09.6	13.8	31 43.8	22.5	144 47.5	32.4	1 23.8	27.0
21	218 33.5	149 13.3 ..	13.2	46 45.2 ..	22.0	159 49.4 ..	32.5	16 26.3 ..	27.0
22	233 36.0	164 16.9	12.5	61 46.6	21.4	174 51.3	32.6	31 28.8	27.0
23	248 38.4	179 20.6	11.8	76 48.1	20.9	189 53.2	32.7	46 31.3	27.0
15 00	263 40.9	194 24.2	N20 11.1	91 49.5	N 4 20.4	204 55.0	N19 32.9	61 33.8	S 6 27.0
01	278 43.4	209 27.8	10.5	106 50.9	19.9	219 56.9	33.0	76 36.3	27.0
02	293 45.8	224 31.5	09.8	121 52.3	19.4	234 58.8	33.1	91 38.8	27.0
03	308 48.3	239 35.1 ..	09.1	136 53.7 ..	18.9	250 00.7 ..	33.2	106 41.3 ..	27.0
04	323 50.7	254 38.7	08.5	151 55.2	18.4	265 02.5	33.3	121 43.9	27.0
05	338 53.2	269 42.4	07.8	166 56.6	17.9	280 04.4	33.4	136 46.4	27.0
06	353 55.7	284 46.0	N20 07.1	181 58.0	N 4 17.4	295 06.3	N19 33.6	151 48.9	S 6 27.0
07	8 58.1	299 49.6	06.4	196 59.4	16.9	310 08.2	33.7	166 51.4	26.9
F 08	24 00.6	314 53.2	05.8	212 00.8	16.4	325 10.1	33.8	181 53.9	26.9
R 09	39 03.1	329 56.9 ..	05.1	227 02.2 ..	15.8	340 11.9 ..	33.9	196 56.4 ..	26.9
I 10	54 05.5	345 00.5	04.5	242 03.7	15.3	355 13.8	34.0	211 58.9	26.9
D 11	69 08.0	0 04.1	03.8	257 05.1	14.8	10 15.7	34.1	227 01.4	26.9
A 12	84 10.5	15 07.7	N20 03.1	272 06.5	N 4 14.3	25 17.6	N19 34.3	242 03.9	S 6 26.9
Y 13	99 12.9	30 11.3	02.5	287 07.9	13.8	40 19.4	34.4	257 06.4	26.9
14	114 15.4	45 14.9	01.8	302 09.3	13.3	55 21.3	34.5	272 08.9	26.9
15	129 17.9	60 18.5 ..	01.2	317 10.7 ..	12.8	70 23.2 ..	34.6	287 11.4 ..	26.9
16	144 20.3	75 22.1	20 00.5	332 12.1	12.3	85 25.1	34.7	302 13.9	26.9
17	159 22.8	90 25.6	19 59.8	347 13.6	11.8	100 27.0	34.9	317 16.4	26.9
18	174 25.2	105 29.2	N19 59.2	2 15.0	N 4 11.3	115 28.8	N19 35.0	332 18.9	S 6 26.9
19	189 27.7	120 32.8	58.5	17 16.4	10.7	130 30.7	35.1	347 21.4	26.9
20	204 30.2	135 36.4	57.9	32 17.8	10.2	145 32.6	35.2	2 24.0	26.9
21	219 32.6	150 39.9 ..	57.2	47 19.2 ..	09.7	160 34.5 ..	35.3	17 26.5 ..	26.9
22	234 35.1	165 43.5	56.6	62 20.6	09.2	175 36.4	35.4	32 29.0	26.9
23	249 37.6	180 47.1	55.9	77 22.0	08.7	190 38.2	35.5	47 31.5	26.9
16 00	264 40.0	195 50.6	N19 55.3	92 23.4	N 4 08.2	205 40.1	N19 35.7	62 34.0	S 6 26.9
01	279 42.5	210 54.2	54.6	107 24.9	07.7	220 42.0	35.8	77 36.5	26.9
02	294 45.0	225 57.7	54.0	122 26.3	07.2	235 43.9	35.9	92 39.0	26.9
03	309 47.4	241 01.3 ..	53.3	137 27.7 ..	06.6	250 45.8 ..	36.0	107 41.5 ..	26.8
04	324 49.9	256 04.8	52.7	152 29.1	06.1	265 47.6	36.1	122 44.0	26.8
05	339 52.4	271 08.4	52.0	167 30.5	05.6	280 49.5	36.2	137 46.5	26.8
06	354 54.8	286 11.9	N19 51.4	182 31.9	N 4 05.1	295 51.4	N19 36.4	152 49.0	S 6 26.8
07	9 57.3	301 15.4	50.8	197 33.3	04.6	310 53.3	36.5	167 51.5	26.8
S 08	24 59.7	316 19.0	50.1	212 34.7	04.1	325 55.1	36.6	182 54.0	26.8
A 09	40 02.2	331 22.5 ..	49.5	227 36.1 ..	03.6	340 57.0 ..	36.7	197 56.5 ..	26.8
T 10	55 04.7	346 26.0	48.8	242 37.5	03.1	355 58.9	36.8	212 59.0	26.8
U 11	70 07.1	1 29.5	48.2	257 38.9	02.5	11 00.8	36.9	228 01.5	26.8
R 12	85 09.6	16 33.1	N19 47.6	272 40.3	N 4 02.0	26 02.7	N19 37.1	243 04.0	S 6 26.8
D 13	100 12.1	31 36.6	46.9	287 41.7	01.5	41 04.5	37.2	258 06.5	26.8
A 14	115 14.5	46 40.1	46.3	302 43.2	01.0	56 06.4	37.3	273 09.0	26.8
Y 15	130 17.0	61 43.6 ..	45.7	317 44.6 ..	00.5	71 08.3 ..	37.4	288 11.5 ..	26.8
16	145 19.5	76 47.1	45.0	332 46.0	4 00.0	86 10.2	37.5	303 14.0	26.8
17	160 21.9	91 50.6	44.4	347 47.4	3 59.5	101 12.1	37.6	318 16.5	26.8
18	175 24.4	106 54.1	N19 43.8	2 48.8	N 3 58.9	116 13.9	N19 37.8	333 19.0	S 6 26.8
19	190 26.9	121 57.6	43.2	17 50.2	58.4	131 15.8	37.9	348 21.5	26.8
20	205 29.3	137 01.0	42.5	32 51.6	57.9	146 17.7	38.0	3 24.0	26.8
21	220 31.8	152 04.5 ..	41.9	47 53.0 ..	57.4	161 19.6 ..	38.1	18 26.5 ..	26.8
22	235 34.2	167 08.0	41.3	62 54.4	56.9	176 21.5	38.2	33 29.0	26.8
23	250 36.7	182 11.5	40.7	77 55.8	56.4	191 23.3	38.3	48 31.5	26.8
Mer. Pass.	6 24.2	v 3.6	d 0.7	v 1.4	d 0.5	v 1.9	d 0.1	v 2.5	d 0.0

STARS

Name	SHA	Dec
Acamar	315 19.2	S40 15.2
Achernar	335 27.6	S57 10.1
Acrux	173 09.9	S63 10.5
Adhara	255 13.4	S28 59.5
Aldebaran	290 50.5	N16 31.9
Alioth	166 21.1	N55 53.7
Alkaid	152 59.2	N49 15.2
Al Na'ir	27 44.4	S46 53.7
Alnilam	275 47.4	S 1 11.8
Alphard	217 57.0	S 8 43.0
Alphecca	126 11.3	N26 40.5
Alpheratz	357 44.3	N29 09.5
Altair	62 08.6	N 8 54.2
Ankaa	353 16.5	S42 14.0
Antares	112 26.7	S26 27.5
Arcturus	145 56.1	N19 07.1
Atria	107 28.6	S69 03.0
Avior	234 18.8	S59 33.3
Bellatrix	278 33.1	N 6 21.5
Betelgeuse	271 02.4	N 7 24.4
Canopus	263 57.0	S52 42.3
Capella	280 36.0	N46 00.5
Deneb	49 31.6	N45 19.5
Denebola	182 34.4	N14 30.1
Diphda	348 56.7	S17 54.9
Dubhe	193 52.7	N61 41.2
Elnath	278 13.9	N28 36.9
Eltanin	90 45.9	N51 29.3
Enif	33 47.6	N 9 56.0
Fomalhaut	15 24.7	S29 33.1
Gacrux	172 01.5	S57 11.3
Gienah	175 53.0	S17 36.9
Hadar	148 48.5	S60 26.2
Hamal	328 01.8	N23 31.2
Kaus Aust.	83 44.3	S34 22.5
Kochab	137 19.1	N74 06.5
Markab	13 39.0	N15 16.4
Menkar	314 16.0	N 4 08.3
Menkent	148 08.1	S36 26.1
Miaplacidus	221 40.4	S69 46.5
Mirfak	308 41.8	N49 54.1
Nunki	75 58.8	S26 16.7
Peacock	53 19.9	S56 41.3
Pollux	243 28.9	N27 59.7
Procyon	245 00.8	N 5 11.4
Rasalhague	96 06.8	N12 33.2
Regulus	207 44.4	N11 54.3
Rigel	281 13.1	S 8 11.3
Rigil Kent.	139 52.2	S60 53.4
Sabik	102 13.0	S15 44.3
Schedar	349 41.5	N56 36.1
Shaula	96 22.4	S37 06.7
Sirius	258 34.7	S16 44.2
Spica	158 31.8	S11 13.7
Suhail	222 53.2	S43 29.3
Vega	80 39.0	N38 47.8
Zuben'ubi	137 05.9	S16 05.7

	SHA	Mer. Pass.
Venus	290 43.3	11 00
Mars	188 08.6	17 51
Jupiter	301 14.1	10 29
Saturn	157 52.9	19 50

UT	SUN GHA	SUN Dec	MOON GHA	v	Dec	d	HP
d h	° ′	° ′	° ′	′	° ′	′	′
14 00	179 56.3	N23 16.2	243 48.6	14.6	N11 53.1	9.3	54.3
01	194 56.2	16.3	258 22.2	14.6	12 02.4	9.3	54.3
02	209 56.0	16.4	272 55.8	14.5	12 11.7	9.2	54.3
03	224 55.9	.. 16.5	287 29.3	14.5	12 20.9	9.2	54.3
04	239 55.8	16.6	302 02.8	14.5	12 30.1	9.1	54.3
05	254 55.6	16.8	316 36.3	14.5	12 39.2	9.0	54.3
T 06	269 55.5	N23 16.9	331 09.8	14.5	N12 48.2	9.0	54.3
H 07	284 55.4	17.0	345 43.3	14.4	12 57.2	8.9	54.2
U 08	299 55.2	17.1	0 16.7	14.4	13 06.1	8.9	54.2
R 09	314 55.1	.. 17.2	14 50.1	14.4	13 15.0	8.8	54.2
S 10	329 55.0	17.3	29 23.5	14.3	13 23.8	8.8	54.2
D 11	344 54.8	17.4	43 56.8	14.3	13 32.6	8.7	54.2
A 12	359 54.7	N23 17.5	58 30.1	14.3	N13 41.3	8.6	54.2
Y 13	14 54.6	17.7	73 03.4	14.3	13 49.9	8.6	54.2
14	29 54.4	17.8	87 36.7	14.2	13 58.5	8.5	54.2
15	44 54.3	.. 17.9	102 09.9	14.2	14 07.0	8.5	54.2
16	59 54.2	18.0	116 43.1	14.1	14 15.5	8.4	54.2
17	74 54.0	18.1	131 16.2	14.2	14 23.9	8.3	54.2
18	89 53.9	N23 18.2	145 49.4	14.1	N14 32.2	8.3	54.1
19	104 53.8	18.3	160 22.5	14.1	14 40.5	8.2	54.1
20	119 53.6	18.4	174 55.6	14.0	14 48.7	8.2	54.1
21	134 53.5	.. 18.5	189 28.6	14.0	14 56.9	8.1	54.1
22	149 53.4	18.6	204 01.6	14.0	15 05.0	8.0	54.1
23	164 53.2	18.7	218 34.6	13.9	15 13.0	7.9	54.1
15 00	179 53.1	N23 18.8	233 07.5	13.9	N15 20.9	7.9	54.1
01	194 53.0	18.9	247 40.4	13.9	15 28.8	7.9	54.1
02	209 52.8	19.0	262 13.3	13.9	15 36.7	7.7	54.1
03	224 52.7	.. 19.1	276 46.2	13.8	15 44.4	7.7	54.1
04	239 52.6	19.2	291 19.0	13.7	15 52.1	7.6	54.1
05	254 52.4	19.3	305 51.7	13.8	15 59.7	7.6	54.1
06	269 52.3	N23 19.4	320 24.5	13.7	N16 07.3	7.5	54.1
F 07	284 52.2	19.5	334 57.2	13.6	16 14.8	7.4	54.1
R 08	299 52.0	19.6	349 29.8	13.7	16 22.2	7.3	54.1
I 09	314 51.9	.. 19.7	4 02.5	13.6	16 29.5	7.3	54.1
D 10	329 51.7	19.8	18 35.1	13.5	16 36.8	7.2	54.1
A 11	344 51.6	19.9	33 07.6	13.5	16 44.0	7.1	54.1
Y 12	359 51.5	N23 20.0	47 40.1	13.5	N16 51.1	7.1	54.1
13	14 51.3	20.1	62 12.6	13.5	16 58.2	7.0	54.1
14	29 51.2	20.2	76 45.1	13.4	17 05.2	6.9	54.1
15	44 51.1	.. 20.3	91 17.5	13.4	17 12.1	6.8	54.0
16	59 50.9	20.4	105 49.9	13.3	17 18.9	6.8	54.0
17	74 50.8	20.5	120 22.2	13.3	17 25.7	6.7	54.0
18	89 50.7	N23 20.6	134 54.5	13.3	N17 32.4	6.6	54.0
19	104 50.5	20.6	149 26.8	13.2	17 39.0	6.5	54.0
20	119 50.4	20.7	163 59.0	13.2	17 45.5	6.5	54.0
21	134 50.3	.. 20.8	178 31.2	13.1	17 52.0	6.4	54.0
22	149 50.1	20.9	193 03.3	13.1	17 58.4	6.3	54.0
23	164 50.0	21.0	207 35.4	13.1	18 04.7	6.2	54.0
16 00	179 49.9	N23 21.1	222 07.5	13.0	N18 10.9	6.1	54.0
01	194 49.7	21.2	236 39.5	13.0	18 17.0	6.1	54.0
02	209 49.6	21.3	251 11.5	13.0	18 23.1	6.0	54.0
03	224 49.4	.. 21.3	265 43.5	12.9	18 29.1	5.9	54.0
04	239 49.3	21.4	280 15.4	12.9	18 35.0	5.8	54.0
05	254 49.2	21.5	294 47.3	12.8	18 40.8	5.7	54.0
06	269 49.0	N23 21.6	309 19.1	12.8	N18 46.5	5.7	54.0
S 07	284 48.9	21.7	323 50.9	12.8	18 52.2	5.6	54.0
A 08	299 48.8	21.7	338 22.7	12.7	18 57.8	5.5	54.0
T 09	314 48.6	.. 21.8	352 54.4	12.7	19 03.3	5.4	54.0
U 10	329 48.5	21.9	7 26.1	12.7	19 08.7	5.3	54.0
R 11	344 48.4	22.0	21 57.8	12.6	19 14.0	5.2	54.0
D 12	359 48.2	N23 22.1	36 29.4	12.6	N19 19.2	5.2	54.1
A 13	14 48.1	22.1	51 01.0	12.5	19 24.4	5.1	54.1
Y 14	29 48.0	22.2	65 32.5	12.5	19 29.5	4.9	54.1
15	44 47.8	.. 22.3	80 04.0	12.5	19 34.4	4.9	54.1
16	59 47.7	22.4	94 35.5	12.4	19 39.3	4.8	54.1
17	74 47.5	22.4	109 06.9	12.4	19 44.1	4.7	54.1
18	89 47.4	N23 22.5	123 38.3	12.4	N19 48.8	4.5	54.1
19	104 47.3	22.6	138 09.7	12.3	19 53.5	4.5	54.1
20	119 47.1	22.7	152 41.0	12.3	19 58.0	4.5	54.1
21	134 47.0	.. 22.7	167 12.3	12.2	20 02.5	4.3	54.1
22	149 46.9	22.8	181 43.5	12.2	20 06.8	4.3	54.1
23	164 46.7	22.9	196 14.7	12.2	N20 11.1	4.2	54.1
	SD 15.8	d 0.1	SD 14.8		14.7		14.7

Moonrise / Twilight / Sunrise

Lat.	Naut.	Civil	Sunrise	14	15	16	17
°	h m	h m	h m	h m	h m	h m	h m
N 72				22 41	21 38		
N 70				23 14	22 57		
68				23 38	23 36	23 36	23 42
66				23 56	24 03	00 03	00 15
64	////	////	01 33	00 03	00 12	00 24	00 42
62	////	////	02 10	00 12	00 24	00 40	01 03
60	////	00 53	02 36	00 20	00 35	00 55	01 21
N 58	////	01 41	02 56	00 27	00 45	01 07	01 35
56	////	02 11	03 13	00 33	00 53	01 17	01 48
54	00 48	02 33	03 27	00 39	01 00	01 26	01 58
52	01 33	02 51	03 39	00 44	01 07	01 35	02 08
50	02 01	03 06	03 50	00 48	01 13	01 42	02 17
45	02 46	03 35	04 13	00 58	01 26	01 58	02 35
N 40	03 16	03 58	04 31	01 06	01 37	02 11	02 50
35	03 39	04 16	04 46	01 13	01 46	02 22	03 03
30	03 58	04 31	04 59	01 19	01 54	02 32	03 14
20	04 27	04 56	05 20	01 30	02 08	02 49	03 33
N 10	04 49	05 16	05 39	01 39	02 21	03 04	03 50
0	05 08	05 34	05 57	01 48	02 32	03 18	04 05
S 10	05 25	05 51	06 14	01 57	02 44	03 32	04 21
20	05 41	06 09	06 33	02 07	02 57	03 47	04 38
30	05 58	06 28	06 54	02 18	03 11	04 04	04 57
35	06 06	06 38	07 06	02 24	03 20	04 14	05 08
40	06 16	06 50	07 20	02 32	03 29	04 26	05 21
45	06 26	07 03	07 37	02 40	03 41	04 40	05 37
S 50	06 38	07 19	07 58	02 51	03 54	04 56	05 56
52	06 43	07 27	08 08	02 56	04 01	05 04	06 05
54	06 49	07 35	08 19	03 01	04 08	05 13	06 15
56	06 55	07 44	08 31	03 07	04 16	05 23	06 26
58	07 01	07 54	08 46	03 13	04 25	05 34	06 39
S 60	07 09	08 06	09 03	03 21	04 35	05 47	06 55

Moonset / Sunset / Twilight

Lat.	Sunset	Civil	Naut.	14	15	16	17
°	h m	h m	h m	h m	h m	h m	h m
N 72				17 45	20 22		
N 70				17 14	19 04		
68				16 51	18 26	20 03	21 37
66				16 33	18 00	19 24	20 41
64	22 29	////	////	16 19	17 40	18 57	20 07
62	21 52	////	////	16 07	17 23	18 37	19 43
60	21 25	23 10	////	15 57	17 10	18 20	19 23
N 58	21 05	22 20	////	15 48	16 58	18 06	19 07
56	20 48	21 51	////	15 40	16 48	17 54	18 54
54	20 34	21 29	23 14	15 33	16 39	17 43	18 42
52	20 22	21 11	22 29	15 27	16 31	17 34	18 32
50	20 11	20 56	22 01	15 21	16 24	17 25	18 22
45	19 49	20 26	21 16	15 09	16 09	17 07	18 03
N 40	19 31	20 04	20 45	15 00	15 57	16 53	17 47
35	19 16	19 45	20 22	14 51	15 46	16 41	17 34
30	19 03	19 30	20 03	14 44	15 37	16 30	17 22
20	18 41	19 05	19 34	14 31	15 21	16 11	17 02
N 10	18 22	18 45	19 12	14 20	15 07	15 56	16 45
0	18 04	18 27	18 53	14 09	14 54	15 41	16 29
S 10	17 47	18 10	18 36	13 59	14 41	15 26	16 12
20	17 28	17 52	18 20	13 48	14 28	15 10	15 55
30	17 07	17 34	18 03	13 35	14 12	14 52	15 35
35	16 55	17 24	17 55	13 28	14 03	14 41	15 24
40	16 41	17 11	17 45	13 20	13 53	14 29	15 10
45	16 24	16 58	17 35	13 10	13 40	14 15	14 54
S 50	16 03	16 42	17 23	12 59	13 26	13 57	14 35
52	15 54	16 34	17 18	12 54	13 19	13 49	14 26
54	15 42	16 26	17 12	12 48	13 11	13 40	14 16
56	15 30	16 17	17 06	12 41	13 03	13 30	14 04
58	15 15	16 07	17 00	12 34	12 53	13 18	13 51
S 60	14 58	15 55	16 52	12 26	12 42	13 05	13 35

SUN / MOON

Day	SUN Eqn. of Time 00h	SUN Eqn. of Time 12h	SUN Mer. Pass.	MOON Mer. Pass. Upper	MOON Mer. Pass. Lower	Age	Phase
d	m s	m s	h m	h m	h m	d	%
14	00 15	00 21	12 00	07 59	20 21	25	22
15	00 27	00 34	12 01	08 43	21 06	26	15
16	00 40	00 47	12 01	09 29	21 53	27	9

2012 JUNE 17, 18, 19 (SUN., MON., TUES.)

UT	ARIES	VENUS −4.3		MARS +0.7		JUPITER −2.0		SATURN +0.6		STARS		
	GHA	GHA	Dec	GHA	Dec	GHA	Dec	GHA	Dec	Name	SHA	Dec
d h	° ′	° ′	° ′	° ′	° ′	° ′	° ′	° ′	° ′		° ′	° ′
17 00	265 39.2	197 14.9	N19 40.0	92 57.2	N 3 55.8	206 25.2	N19 38.4	63 34.0	S 6 26.8	Acamar	315 19.2	S40 15.2
01	280 41.6	212 18.4	39.4	107 58.6	55.3	221 27.1	38.6	78 36.5	26.8	Achernar	335 27.6	S57 10.1
02	295 44.1	227 21.9	38.8	123 00.0	54.8	236 29.0	38.7	93 39.0	26.8	Acrux	173 09.9	S63 10.5
03	310 46.6	242 25.3 ..	38.2	138 01.4 ..	54.3	251 30.9 ..	38.8	108 41.5 ..	26.8	Adhara	255 13.4	S28 59.5
04	325 49.0	257 28.8	37.6	153 02.8	53.8	266 32.8	38.9	123 44.0	26.8	Aldebaran	290 50.5	N16 31.9
05	340 51.5	272 32.2	37.0	168 04.2	53.3	281 34.6	39.0	138 46.5	26.8			
06	355 54.0	287 35.7	N19 36.3	183 05.6	N 3 52.7	296 36.5	N19 39.1	153 49.0	S 6 26.8	Alioth	166 21.1	N55 53.7
07	10 56.4	302 39.1	35.7	198 07.0	52.2	311 38.4	39.3	168 51.5	26.8	Alkaid	152 59.2	N49 15.2
08	25 58.9	317 42.6	35.1	213 08.4	51.7	326 40.3	39.4	183 54.0	26.8	Al Na'ir	27 44.4	S46 53.7
S 09	41 01.3	332 46.0 ..	34.5	228 09.8 ..	51.2	341 42.2 ..	39.5	198 56.5 ..	26.8	Alnilam	275 47.4	S 1 11.8
U 10	56 03.8	347 49.4	33.9	243 11.2	50.7	356 44.0	39.6	213 59.0	26.7	Alphard	217 57.0	S 8 43.0
N 11	71 06.3	2 52.9	33.3	258 12.6	50.2	11 45.9	39.7	229 01.5	26.7			
D 12	86 08.7	17 56.3	N19 32.7	273 14.0	N 3 49.6	26 47.8	N19 39.8	244 04.0	S 6 26.7	Alphecca	126 11.3	N26 40.5
A 13	101 11.2	32 59.7	32.1	288 15.4	49.1	41 49.7	39.9	259 06.5	26.7	Alpheratz	357 44.2	N29 09.5
Y 14	116 13.7	48 03.1	31.5	303 16.8	48.6	56 51.6	40.1	274 09.0	26.7	Altair	62 08.6	N 8 54.2
15	131 16.1	63 06.5 ..	30.9	318 18.2 ..	48.1	71 53.4 ..	40.2	289 11.5 ..	26.7	Ankaa	353 16.4	S42 14.0
16	146 18.6	78 09.9	30.3	333 19.6	47.6	86 55.3	40.3	304 14.0	26.7	Antares	112 26.7	S26 27.5
17	161 21.1	93 13.3	29.7	348 21.0	47.1	101 57.2	40.4	319 16.5	26.7			
18	176 23.5	108 16.7	N19 29.1	3 22.4	N 3 46.5	116 59.1	N19 40.5	334 19.0	S 6 26.7	Arcturus	145 56.1	N19 07.1
19	191 26.0	123 20.1	28.5	18 23.8	46.0	132 01.0	40.6	349 21.5	26.7	Atria	107 28.6	S69 03.0
20	206 28.5	138 23.5	27.9	33 25.2	45.5	147 02.9	40.7	4 24.0	26.7	Avior	234 18.8	S59 33.3
21	221 30.9	153 26.9 ..	27.3	48 26.6 ..	45.0	162 04.7 ..	40.9	19 26.5 ..	26.7	Bellatrix	278 33.1	N 6 21.5
22	236 33.4	168 30.3	26.7	63 27.9	44.5	177 06.6	41.0	34 29.0	26.7	Betelgeuse	271 02.4	N 7 24.4
23	251 35.8	183 33.7	26.1	78 29.3	43.9	192 08.5	41.1	49 31.5	26.7			
18 00	266 38.3	198 37.1	N19 25.5	93 30.7	N 3 43.4	207 10.4	N19 41.2	64 34.0	S 6 26.7	Canopus	263 57.0	S52 42.3
01	281 40.8	213 40.4	24.9	108 32.1	42.9	222 12.3	41.3	79 36.5	26.7	Capella	280 35.9	N46 00.5
02	296 43.2	228 43.8	24.3	123 33.5	42.4	237 14.1	41.4	94 39.0	26.7	Deneb	49 31.6	N45 19.5
03	311 45.7	243 47.2 ..	23.7	138 34.9 ..	41.9	252 16.0 ..	41.5	109 41.5 ..	26.7	Denebola	182 34.4	N14 30.1
04	326 48.2	258 50.5	23.2	153 36.3	41.3	267 17.9	41.7	124 44.0	26.7	Diphda	348 56.7	S17 54.9
05	341 50.6	273 53.9	22.6	168 37.7	40.8	282 19.8	41.8	139 46.5	26.7			
06	356 53.1	288 57.2	N19 22.0	183 39.1	N 3 40.3	297 21.7	N19 41.9	154 49.0	S 6 26.7	Dubhe	193 52.7	N61 41.2
07	11 55.6	304 00.6	21.4	198 40.5	39.8	312 23.6	42.0	169 51.5	26.7	Elnath	278 13.9	N28 36.9
08	26 58.0	319 03.9	20.8	213 41.9	39.3	327 25.4	42.1	184 53.9	26.7	Eltanin	90 45.9	N51 29.3
M 09	42 00.5	334 07.3 ..	20.3	228 43.3 ..	38.7	342 27.3 ..	42.2	199 56.4 ..	26.7	Enif	33 47.6	N 9 56.0
O 10	57 03.0	349 10.6	19.7	243 44.7	38.2	357 29.2	42.3	214 58.9	26.7	Fomalhaut	15 24.6	S29 33.1
N 11	72 05.4	4 13.9	19.1	258 46.0	37.7	12 31.1	42.4	230 01.4	26.7			
D 12	87 07.9	19 17.3	N19 18.5	273 47.4	N 3 37.2	27 33.0	N19 42.6	245 03.9	S 6 26.7	Gacrux	172 01.5	S57 11.3
A 13	102 10.3	34 20.6	17.9	288 48.8	36.7	42 34.8	42.7	260 06.4	26.7	Gienah	175 53.0	S17 36.9
Y 14	117 12.8	49 23.9	17.4	303 50.2	36.1	57 36.7	42.8	275 08.9	26.7	Hadar	148 48.5	S60 26.2
15	132 15.3	64 27.2 ..	16.8	318 51.6 ..	35.6	72 38.6 ..	42.9	290 11.4 ..	26.7	Hamal	328 01.7	N23 31.2
16	147 17.7	79 30.5	16.2	333 53.0	35.1	87 40.5	43.0	305 13.9	26.7	Kaus Aust.	83 44.3	S34 22.5
17	162 20.2	94 33.8	15.7	348 54.4	34.6	102 42.4	43.1	320 16.4	26.7			
18	177 22.7	109 37.1	N19 15.1	3 55.8	N 3 34.0	117 44.3	N19 43.2	335 18.9	S 6 26.7	Kochab	137 19.1	N74 06.5
19	192 25.1	124 40.4	14.5	18 57.1	33.5	132 46.1	43.4	350 21.4	26.7	Markab	13 38.9	N15 16.4
20	207 27.6	139 43.7	14.0	33 58.5	33.0	147 48.0	43.5	5 23.9	26.7	Menkar	314 16.0	N 4 08.3
21	222 30.1	154 47.0 ..	13.4	48 59.9 ..	32.5	162 49.9 ..	43.6	20 26.4 ..	26.7	Menkent	148 08.1	S36 26.1
22	237 32.5	169 50.3	12.8	64 01.3	32.0	177 51.8	43.7	35 28.9	26.7	Miaplacidus	221 40.4	S69 46.5
23	252 35.0	184 53.6	12.3	79 02.7	31.4	192 53.7	43.8	50 31.4	26.7			
19 00	267 37.5	199 56.9	N19 11.7	94 04.1	N 3 30.9	207 55.6	N19 43.9	65 33.9	S 6 26.7	Mirfak	308 41.8	N49 54.1
01	282 39.9	215 00.2	11.2	109 05.5	30.4	222 57.4	44.0	80 36.3	26.7	Nunki	75 58.8	S26 16.7
02	297 42.4	230 03.4	10.6	124 06.8	29.9	237 59.3	44.1	95 38.8	26.7	Peacock	53 19.8	S56 41.3
03	312 44.8	245 06.7 ..	10.1	139 08.2 ..	29.3	253 01.2 ..	44.3	110 41.3 ..	26.7	Pollux	243 28.9	N27 59.7
04	327 47.3	260 10.0	09.5	154 09.6	28.8	268 03.1	44.4	125 43.8	26.7	Procyon	245 00.8	N 5 11.4
05	342 49.8	275 13.2	09.0	169 11.0	28.3	283 05.0	44.5	140 46.3	26.7			
06	357 52.2	290 16.5	N19 08.4	184 12.4	N 3 27.8	298 06.9	N19 44.6	155 48.8	S 6 26.7	Rasalhague	96 06.7	N12 33.2
07	12 54.7	305 19.7	07.8	199 13.8	27.2	313 08.8	44.7	170 51.3	26.7	Regulus	207 44.4	N11 54.3
T 08	27 57.2	320 23.0	07.3	214 15.1	26.7	328 10.6	44.8	185 53.8	26.7	Rigel	281 13.1	S 8 11.3
U 09	42 59.6	335 26.2 ..	06.8	229 16.5 ..	26.2	343 12.5 ..	44.9	200 56.3 ..	26.7	Rigil Kent.	139 52.2	S60 53.4
E 10	58 02.1	350 29.5	06.2	244 17.9	25.7	358 14.4	45.0	215 58.8	26.7	Sabik	102 13.0	S15 44.3
S 11	73 04.6	5 32.7	05.7	259 19.3	25.1	13 16.3	45.2	231 01.3	26.7			
D 12	88 07.0	20 35.9	N19 05.1	274 20.7	N 3 24.6	28 18.2	N19 45.3	246 03.8	S 6 26.7	Schedar	349 41.4	N56 36.1
A 13	103 09.5	35 39.1	04.6	289 22.1	24.1	43 20.1	45.4	261 06.2	26.7	Shaula	96 22.4	S37 06.7
Y 14	118 12.0	50 42.4	04.0	304 23.4	23.6	58 21.9	45.5	276 08.7	26.7	Sirius	258 34.7	S16 44.2
15	133 14.4	65 45.6 ..	03.5	319 24.8 ..	23.0	73 23.8 ..	45.7	291 11.2 ..	26.7	Spica	158 31.8	S11 13.7
16	148 16.9	80 48.8	03.0	334 26.2	22.5	88 25.7	45.7	306 13.7	26.7	Suhail	222 53.3	S43 29.3
17	163 19.3	95 52.0	02.4	349 27.6	22.0	103 27.6	45.8	321 16.2	26.7			
18	178 21.8	110 55.2	N19 01.9	4 29.0	N 3 21.5	118 29.5	N19 45.9	336 18.7	S 6 26.7	Vega	80 39.0	N38 47.8
19	193 24.3	125 58.4	01.4	19 30.3	20.9	133 31.4	46.1	351 21.2	26.7	Zuben'ubi	137 05.9	S16 05.7
20	208 26.7	141 01.6	00.8	34 31.7	20.4	148 33.2	46.2	6 23.7	26.7		SHA	Mer. Pass.
21	223 29.2	156 04.8	19 00.3	49 33.1 ..	19.9	163 35.1 ..	46.3	21 26.2 ..	26.7		° ′	h m
22	238 31.7	171 08.0	18 59.8	64 34.5	19.4	178 37.0	46.4	36 28.7	26.7	Venus	291 58.7	10 43
23	253 34.1	186 11.2	N18 59.2	79 35.8	18.8	193 38.9	46.5	51 31.1	26.7	Mars	186 52.4	17 44
	h m									Jupiter	300 32.1	10 10
Mer. Pass.	6 12.4	v 3.3	d 0.6	v 1.4	d 0.5	v 1.9	d 0.1	v 2.5	d 0.0	Saturn	157 55.7	19 38

SUN and MOON

UT (d h)	SUN GHA	SUN Dec	MOON GHA	v	MOON Dec	d	HP
17 00	179 46.6	N23 22.9	210 45.9	12.1	N20 15.3	4.1	54.1
01	194 46.5	23.0	225 17.0	12.1	20 19.4	4.0	54.1
02	209 46.3	23.1	239 48.1	12.1	20 23.4	3.9	54.1
03	224 46.2	.. 23.1	254 19.2	12.0	20 27.3	3.8	54.1
04	239 46.1	23.2	268 50.2	12.0	20 31.1	3.7	54.1
05	254 45.9	23.3	283 21.2	12.0	20 34.8	3.6	54.1
06	269 45.8	N23 23.3	297 52.2	11.9	N20 38.4	3.5	54.1
07	284 45.6	23.4	312 23.1	12.0	20 41.9	3.5	54.1
08	299 45.5	23.5	326 54.1	11.8	20 45.4	3.3	54.1
S 09	314 45.4	.. 23.5	341 24.9	11.9	20 48.7	3.2	54.1
U 10	329 45.2	23.6	355 55.8	11.8	20 51.9	3.2	54.1
N 11	344 45.1	23.6	10 26.6	11.7	20 55.1	3.0	54.1
D 12	359 45.0	N23 23.7	24 57.3	11.8	N20 58.1	3.0	54.2
A 13	14 44.8	23.8	39 28.1	11.7	21 01.1	2.9	54.2
Y 14	29 44.7	23.8	53 58.8	11.7	21 04.0	2.7	54.2
15	44 44.5	.. 23.9	68 29.5	11.6	21 06.7	2.7	54.2
16	59 44.4	23.9	83 00.1	11.6	21 09.4	2.5	54.2
17	74 44.3	24.0	97 30.7	11.6	21 11.9	2.5	54.2
18	89 44.1	N24 24.0	112 01.3	11.6	N21 14.4	2.4	54.2
19	104 44.0	24.1	126 31.9	11.5	21 16.8	2.2	54.2
20	119 43.9	24.1	141 02.4	11.6	21 19.0	2.2	54.2
21	134 43.7	.. 24.2	155 33.0	11.4	21 21.2	2.1	54.2
22	149 43.6	24.3	170 03.4	11.5	21 23.3	1.9	54.2
23	164 43.5	24.3	184 33.9	11.4	21 25.2	1.9	54.2
18 00	179 43.3	N23 24.4	199 04.3	11.4	N21 27.1	1.8	54.2
01	194 43.2	24.4	213 34.7	11.4	21 28.9	1.6	54.3
02	209 43.0	24.5	228 05.1	11.4	21 30.5	1.6	54.3
03	224 42.9	.. 24.5	242 35.5	11.3	21 32.1	1.5	54.3
04	239 42.8	24.6	257 05.8	11.3	21 33.6	1.3	54.3
05	254 42.6	24.6	271 36.1	11.3	21 34.9	1.3	54.3
06	269 42.5	N23 24.7	286 06.4	11.3	N21 36.2	1.1	54.3
07	284 42.4	24.7	300 36.7	11.2	21 37.3	1.1	54.3
08	299 42.2	24.7	315 06.9	11.3	21 38.4	1.0	54.3
M 09	314 42.1	.. 24.8	329 37.2	11.2	21 39.4	0.8	54.3
O 10	329 41.9	24.8	344 07.4	11.2	21 40.2	0.7	54.3
N 11	344 41.8	24.9	358 37.6	11.1	21 40.9	0.7	54.4
D 12	359 41.7	N23 24.9	13 07.7	11.2	N21 41.6	0.5	54.4
A 13	14 41.5	25.0	27 37.9	11.1	21 42.1	0.4	54.4
Y 14	29 41.4	25.0	42 08.0	11.1	21 42.5	0.4	54.4
15	44 41.3	.. 25.0	56 38.1	11.2	21 42.9	0.2	54.4
16	59 41.1	25.1	71 08.3	11.0	21 43.1	0.1	54.4
17	74 41.0	25.1	85 38.3	11.1	21 43.2	0.1	54.4
18	89 40.9	N23 25.2	100 08.4	11.1	N21 43.2	0.1	54.4
19	104 40.7	25.2	114 38.5	11.0	21 43.1	0.2	54.4
20	119 40.6	25.2	129 08.5	11.1	21 42.9	0.3	54.4
21	134 40.4	.. 25.3	143 38.6	11.0	21 42.6	0.4	54.5
22	149 40.3	25.3	158 08.6	11.0	21 42.2	0.5	54.5
23	164 40.2	25.3	172 38.6	11.0	21 41.7	0.6	54.5
19 00	179 40.0	N23 25.4	187 08.6	11.0	N21 41.1	0.8	54.5
01	194 39.9	25.4	201 38.6	11.0	21 40.4	0.8	54.5
02	209 39.8	25.5	216 08.6	10.9	21 39.6	1.0	54.5
03	224 39.6	.. 25.5	230 38.5	11.0	21 38.6	1.0	54.5
04	239 39.5	25.5	245 08.5	10.9	21 37.6	1.2	54.5
05	254 39.3	25.5	259 38.4	11.0	21 36.4	1.2	54.6
06	269 39.2	N23 25.6	274 08.4	10.9	N21 35.2	1.4	54.6
07	284 39.1	25.6	288 38.3	11.0	21 33.8	1.4	54.6
T 08	299 38.9	25.6	303 08.3	10.9	21 32.4	1.6	54.6
U 09	314 38.8	.. 25.7	317 38.2	11.0	21 30.8	1.7	54.6
E 10	329 38.7	25.7	332 08.2	10.9	21 29.1	1.7	54.6
S 11	344 38.5	25.7	346 38.1	10.9	21 27.4	1.9	54.6
D 12	359 38.4	N23 25.7	1 08.0	10.9	N21 25.5	2.0	54.6
A 13	14 38.2	25.8	15 37.9	11.0	21 23.5	2.1	54.7
Y 14	29 38.1	25.8	30 07.9	10.9	21 21.4	2.2	54.7
15	44 38.0	.. 25.8	44 37.8	10.9	21 19.2	2.3	54.7
16	59 37.8	25.8	59 07.7	10.9	21 16.9	2.4	54.7
17	74 37.7	25.8	73 37.6	10.9	21 14.5	2.5	54.7
18	89 37.6	N23 25.9	88 07.5	11.0	N21 12.0	2.7	54.7
19	104 37.4	25.9	102 37.5	10.9	21 09.3	2.7	54.7
20	119 37.3	25.9	117 07.4	10.9	21 06.6	2.8	54.8
21	134 37.1	.. 25.9	131 37.3	11.0	21 03.8	2.9	54.8
22	149 37.0	25.9	146 07.3	10.9	21 00.9	3.1	54.8
23	164 36.9	26.0	160 37.2	11.0	N20 57.8	3.1	54.8
	SD 15.8	d 0.0	SD 14.8	14.8			14.9

Moonrise

Lat.	Twilight Naut.	Twilight Civil	Sunrise	17	18	19	20
N 72	□	□	□	□	□	□	□
N 70	□	□	□	□	□	□	□
68	□	□	□	23 42	24 19	00 19	01 45
66	□	□	□	00 15	00 39	01 24	02 33
64	////	////	01 31	00 42	01 12	01 59	03 03
62	////	////	02 09	01 03	01 37	02 24	03 26
60	////	00 50	02 36	01 21	01 56	02 44	03 45
N 58	////	01 40	02 56	01 35	02 13	03 01	04 00
56	////	02 10	03 13	01 48	02 26	03 15	04 13
54	00 46	02 33	03 27	01 58	02 38	03 27	04 24
52	01 32	02 51	03 39	02 08	02 49	03 37	04 34
50	02 00	03 06	03 50	02 17	02 58	03 47	04 43
45	02 46	03 35	04 13	02 35	03 18	04 07	05 02
N 40	03 16	03 58	04 31	02 50	03 34	04 23	05 17
35	03 39	04 16	04 46	03 03	03 47	04 37	05 30
30	03 58	04 31	04 59	03 14	03 59	04 49	05 41
20	04 27	04 56	05 21	03 33	04 20	05 09	06 01
N 10	04 50	05 17	05 40	03 50	04 37	05 27	06 17
0	05 09	05 35	05 58	04 05	04 54	05 43	06 33
S 10	05 26	05 52	06 15	04 21	05 10	06 00	06 49
20	05 42	06 10	06 34	04 38	05 28	06 18	07 05
30	05 58	06 28	06 55	04 57	05 49	06 38	07 25
35	06 07	06 39	07 07	05 08	06 00	06 50	07 36
40	06 17	06 51	07 21	05 21	06 14	07 04	07 49
45	06 27	07 04	07 38	05 37	06 31	07 20	08 04
S 50	06 39	07 20	07 59	05 56	06 51	07 40	08 22
52	06 44	07 28	08 09	06 05	07 00	07 49	08 31
54	06 50	07 36	08 20	06 15	07 11	08 00	08 41
56	06 56	07 45	08 33	06 26	07 23	08 12	08 52
58	07 03	07 55	08 47	06 39	07 37	08 26	09 04
S 60	07 10	08 07	09 05	06 55	07 54	08 42	09 19

Moonset

Lat.	Sunset	Twilight Civil	Twilight Naut.	17	18	19	20
N 72	□	□	□	□	□	□	23 53
N 70	□	□	□	□	21 37	22 43	23 00
68	□	□	□	20 41	21 38	22 12	22 06
66	□	□	□	20 07	21 03	21 41	21 47
64	22 32	////	////	19 43	20 37	21 18	21 31
62	21 53	////	////	19 23	20 17	21 00	21 31
60	21 27	23 13	////	19 07	20 01	20 44	21 18
N 58	21 07	22 22	////	19 07	20 01	20 44	21 18
56	20 50	21 52	////	18 54	19 47	20 31	21 07
54	20 35	21 30	23 17	18 42	19 35	20 20	20 57
52	20 23	21 12	22 30	18 32	19 24	20 09	20 48
50	20 12	20 57	22 03	18 22	19 15	20 00	20 40
45	19 50	20 27	21 17	18 03	18 55	19 41	20 22
N 40	19 32	20 05	20 46	17 47	18 38	19 25	20 08
35	19 17	19 46	20 23	17 34	18 25	19 12	19 56
30	19 04	19 31	20 04	17 22	18 13	19 01	19 46
20	18 41	19 06	19 35	17 02	17 52	18 41	19 28
N 10	18 25	18 46	19 13	16 45	17 34	18 24	19 12
0	18 05	18 27	18 54	16 29	17 18	18 07	18 57
S 10	17 47	18 10	18 37	16 12	17 01	17 51	18 42
20	17 29	17 53	18 20	15 55	16 43	17 34	18 26
30	17 08	17 34	18 04	15 35	16 23	17 14	18 08
35	16 55	17 23	17 55	15 24	16 11	17 02	17 57
40	16 41	17 12	17 46	15 10	15 57	16 48	17 44
45	16 24	16 58	17 35	14 54	15 40	16 32	17 30
S 50	16 03	16 42	17 24	14 35	15 20	16 13	17 12
52	15 54	16 35	17 18	14 26	15 10	16 03	17 03
54	15 42	16 26	17 13	14 16	15 00	15 53	16 54
56	15 30	16 17	17 06	14 04	14 47	15 41	16 43
58	15 15	16 07	17 00	13 51	14 33	15 27	16 31
S 60	14 58	15 55	16 52	13 35	14 16	15 11	16 16

SUN / MOON

Day	SUN Eqn. of Time 00h	12h	Mer. Pass.	MOON Mer. Pass. Upper	Lower	Age	Phase
d	m s	m s	h m	h m	h m	d	%
17	00 53	01 00	12 01	10 17	22 41	28	4
18	01 06	01 13	12 01	11 06	23 30	29	1
19	01 20	01 26	12 01	11 55	24 20	30	0

Phase: ● (New Moon)

UT	ARIES GHA	VENUS −4.4 GHA	Dec	MARS +0.8 GHA	Dec	JUPITER −2.0 GHA	Dec	SATURN +0.6 GHA	Dec	STARS Name	SHA	Dec
20 00	268 36.6	201 14.4	N18 58.7	94 37.2	N 3 18.3	208 40.8	N19 46.6	66 33.6	S 6 26.7	Acamar	315 19.2	S40 15.1
01	283 39.1	216 17.5	58.2	109 38.6	17.8	223 42.7	46.7	81 36.1	26.7	Achernar	335 27.5	S57 10.1
02	298 41.5	231 20.7	57.7	124 40.0	17.3	238 44.6	46.8	96 38.6	26.7	Acrux	173 09.9	S63 10.5
03	313 44.0	246 23.9 ..	57.2	139 41.4 ..	16.7	253 46.4 ..	46.9	111 41.1 ..	26.7	Adhara	255 13.4	S28 59.5
04	328 46.4	261 27.1	56.6	154 42.7	16.2	268 48.3	47.1	126 43.6	26.7	Aldebaran	290 50.5	N16 31.9
05	343 48.9	276 30.2	56.1	169 44.1	15.7	283 50.2	47.2	141 46.1	26.7			
W 06	358 51.4	291 33.4	N18 55.6	184 45.5	N 3 15.1	298 52.1	N19 47.3	156 48.6	S 6 26.8	Alioth	166 21.1	N55 53.7
E 07	13 53.8	306 36.5	55.1	199 46.9	14.6	313 54.0	47.4	171 51.0	26.8	Alkaid	152 59.2	N49 15.2
D 08	28 56.3	321 39.7	54.6	214 48.2	14.1	328 55.9	47.5	186 53.5	26.8	Al Na'ir	27 44.3	S46 53.7
N 09	43 58.8	336 42.8 ..	54.1	229 49.6 ..	13.6	343 57.8 ..	47.6	201 56.0 ..	26.8	Alnilam	275 47.4	S 1 11.8
E 10	59 01.2	351 46.0	53.5	244 51.0	13.0	358 59.6	47.7	216 58.5	26.8	Alphard	217 57.0	S 8 43.0
S 11	74 03.7	6 49.1	53.0	259 52.3	12.5	14 01.5	47.8	232 01.0	26.8			
D 12	89 06.2	21 52.2	N18 52.5	274 53.7	N 3 12.0	29 03.4	N19 47.9	247 03.5	S 6 26.8	Alphecca	126 11.3	N26 40.5
A 13	104 08.6	36 55.4	52.0	289 55.1	11.5	44 05.3	48.1	262 06.0	26.8	Alpheratz	357 44.2	N29 09.5
Y 14	119 11.1	51 58.5	51.5	304 56.5	10.9	59 07.2	48.2	277 08.5	26.8	Altair	62 08.6	N 8 54.2
15	134 13.6	67 01.6 ..	51.0	319 57.8 ..	10.4	74 09.1 ..	48.3	292 10.9 ..	26.8	Ankaa	353 16.4	S42 14.0
16	149 16.0	82 04.7	50.5	334 59.2	09.9	89 11.0	48.4	307 13.4	26.8	Antares	112 26.7	S26 27.5
17	164 18.5	97 07.8	50.0	350 00.6	09.3	104 12.8	48.5	322 15.9	26.8			
18	179 20.9	112 10.9	N18 49.5	5 02.0	N 3 08.8	119 14.7	N19 48.6	337 18.4	S 6 26.8	Arcturus	145 56.1	N19 07.1
19	194 23.4	127 14.0	49.0	20 03.3	08.3	134 16.6	48.7	352 20.9	26.8	Atria	107 28.6	S69 03.0
20	209 25.9	142 17.1	48.5	35 04.7	07.8	149 18.5	48.8	7 23.4	26.8	Avior	234 18.8	S59 33.3
21	224 28.3	157 20.2 ..	48.0	50 06.1 ..	07.2	164 20.4 ..	48.9	22 25.9 ..	26.8	Bellatrix	278 33.1	N 6 21.5
22	239 30.8	172 23.3	47.5	65 07.4	06.7	179 22.3	49.1	37 28.3	26.8	Betelgeuse	271 02.4	N 7 24.4
23	254 33.3	187 26.4	47.0	80 08.8	06.2	194 24.2	49.2	52 30.8	26.8			
21 00	269 35.7	202 29.5	N18 46.5	95 10.2	N 3 05.6	209 26.1	N19 49.3	67 33.3	S 6 26.8	Canopus	263 57.0	S52 42.3
01	284 38.2	217 32.6	46.0	110 11.5	05.1	224 27.9	49.4	82 35.8	26.8	Capella	280 35.9	N46 00.5
02	299 40.7	232 35.6	45.6	125 12.9	04.6	239 29.8	49.5	97 38.3	26.8	Deneb	49 31.6	N45 19.5
03	314 43.1	247 38.7 ..	45.1	140 14.3 ..	04.0	254 31.7 ..	49.6	112 40.8 ..	26.8	Denebola	182 34.4	N14 30.1
04	329 45.6	262 41.8	44.6	155 15.6	03.5	269 33.6	49.7	127 43.3	26.8	Diphda	348 56.6	S17 54.9
05	344 48.1	277 44.8	44.1	170 17.0	03.0	284 35.5	49.8	142 45.7	26.8			
T 06	359 50.5	292 47.9	N18 43.6	185 18.4	N 3 02.4	299 37.4	N19 49.9	157 48.2	S 6 26.8	Dubhe	193 52.7	N61 41.2
H 07	14 53.0	307 50.9	43.1	200 19.7	01.9	314 39.3	50.0	172 50.7	26.8	Elnath	278 13.9	N28 36.9
U 08	29 55.4	322 54.0	42.7	215 21.1	01.4	329 41.1	50.2	187 53.2	26.8	Eltanin	90 45.9	N51 29.4
R 09	44 57.9	337 57.0 ..	42.2	230 22.5 ..	00.9	344 43.0 ..	50.3	202 55.7 ..	26.8	Enif	33 47.6	N 9 56.0
S 10	60 00.4	353 00.1	41.7	245 23.8	3 00.3	359 44.9	50.4	217 58.2	26.8	Fomalhaut	15 24.6	S29 33.1
D 11	75 02.8	8 03.1	41.2	260 25.2	2 59.8	14 46.8	50.5	233 00.6	26.8			
A 12	90 05.3	23 06.1	N18 40.7	275 26.6	N 2 59.3	29 48.7	N19 50.6	248 03.1	S 6 26.9	Gacrux	172 01.6	S57 11.3
Y 13	105 07.8	38 09.2	40.3	290 27.9	58.7	44 50.6	50.7	263 05.6	26.9	Gienah	175 53.0	S17 36.9
14	120 10.2	53 12.2	39.8	305 29.3	58.2	59 52.5	50.8	278 08.1	26.9	Hadar	148 48.5	S60 26.3
15	135 12.7	68 15.2 ..	39.3	320 30.7 ..	57.7	74 54.4 ..	50.9	293 10.6 ..	26.9	Hamal	328 01.7	N23 31.2
16	150 15.2	83 18.2	38.9	335 32.0	57.1	89 56.3	51.0	308 13.1	26.9	Kaus Aust.	83 44.3	S34 22.5
17	165 17.6	98 21.2	38.4	350 33.4	56.6	104 58.1	51.1	323 15.5	26.9			
18	180 20.1	113 24.2	N18 37.9	5 34.8	N 2 56.1	120 00.0	N19 51.3	338 18.0	S 6 26.9	Kochab	137 19.2	N74 06.5
19	195 22.6	128 27.2	37.5	20 36.1	55.5	135 01.9	51.4	353 20.5	26.9	Markab	13 38.9	N15 16.4
20	210 25.0	143 30.2	37.0	35 37.5	55.0	150 03.8	51.5	8 23.0	26.9	Menkar	314 16.0	N 4 08.3
21	225 27.5	158 33.2 ..	36.6	50 38.8 ..	54.5	165 05.7 ..	51.6	23 25.5 ..	26.9	Menkent	148 08.1	S36 26.1
22	240 29.9	173 36.2	36.1	65 40.2	53.9	180 07.6	51.7	38 27.9	26.9	Miaplacidus	221 40.5	S69 46.5
23	255 32.4	188 39.2	35.6	80 41.6	53.4	195 09.5	51.8	53 30.4	26.9			
22 00	270 34.9	203 42.2	N18 35.2	95 42.9	N 2 52.9	210 11.4	N19 51.9	68 32.9	S 6 26.9	Mirfak	308 41.7	N49 54.1
01	285 37.3	218 45.2	34.7	110 44.3	52.3	225 13.2	52.0	83 35.4	26.9	Nunki	75 58.8	S26 16.7
02	300 39.8	233 48.1	34.3	125 45.6	51.8	240 15.1	52.1	98 37.9	26.9	Peacock	53 19.8	S56 41.4
03	315 42.3	248 51.1 ..	33.8	140 47.0 ..	51.3	255 17.0 ..	52.2	113 40.3 ..	26.9	Pollux	243 28.9	N27 59.7
04	330 44.7	263 54.1	33.4	155 48.4	50.7	270 18.9	52.4	128 42.8	26.9	Procyon	245 00.8	N 5 11.4
05	345 47.2	278 57.0	32.9	170 49.7	50.2	285 20.8	52.5	143 45.3	26.9			
F 06	0 49.7	294 00.0	N18 32.5	185 51.1	N 2 49.7	300 22.7	N19 52.6	158 47.8	S 6 26.9	Rasalhague	96 06.7	N12 33.2
R 07	15 52.1	309 02.9	32.0	200 52.4	49.1	315 24.6	52.7	173 50.3	26.9	Regulus	207 44.4	N11 54.3
I 08	30 54.6	324 05.9	31.6	215 53.8	48.6	330 26.5	52.8	188 52.8	26.9	Rigel	281 13.0	S 8 11.3
D 09	45 57.1	339 08.8 ..	31.1	230 55.2 ..	48.1	345 28.4 ..	52.9	203 55.2 ..	27.0	Rigil Kent.	139 52.2	S60 53.4
A 10	60 59.5	354 11.8	30.7	245 56.5	47.5	0 30.2	53.0	218 57.7	27.0	Sabik	102 13.0	S15 44.3
Y 11	76 02.0	9 14.7	30.3	260 57.9	47.0	15 32.1	53.1	234 00.2	27.0			
12	91 04.4	24 17.6	N18 29.8	275 59.2	N 2 46.5	30 34.0	N19 53.2	249 02.7	S 6 27.0	Schedar	349 41.4	N56 36.1
13	106 06.9	39 20.6	29.4	291 00.6	45.9	45 35.9	53.3	264 05.1	27.0	Shaula	96 22.4	S37 06.7
14	121 09.4	54 23.5	28.9	306 01.9	45.4	60 37.8	53.4	279 07.6	27.0	Sirius	258 34.7	S16 44.2
15	136 11.8	69 26.4 ..	28.5	321 03.3 ..	44.9	75 39.7 ..	53.5	294 10.1 ..	27.0	Spica	158 31.8	S11 13.7
16	151 14.3	84 29.3	28.1	336 04.7	44.3	90 41.6	53.7	309 12.6	27.0	Suhail	222 53.3	S43 29.3
17	166 16.8	99 32.2	27.7	351 06.0	43.8	105 43.5	53.8	324 15.1	27.0			
18	181 19.2	114 35.1	N18 27.2	6 07.4	N 2 43.2	120 45.4	N19 53.9	339 17.5	S 6 27.0	Vega	80 39.0	N38 47.8
19	196 21.7	129 38.0	26.8	21 08.7	42.7	135 47.3	54.0	354 20.0	27.0	Zuben'ubi	137 05.9	S16 05.7
20	211 24.2	144 40.9	26.4	36 10.1	42.2	150 49.1	54.1	9 22.5	27.0		SHA	Mer.Pass.
21	226 26.6	159 43.8 ..	25.9	51 11.4 ..	41.6	165 51.0 ..	54.2	24 25.0 ..	27.0	Venus	292 53.7	10 28
22	241 29.1	174 46.7	25.5	66 12.8	41.1	180 52.9	54.3	39 27.5	27.0	Mars	185 34.4	17 38
23	256 31.5	189 49.6	25.1	81 14.1	40.6	195 54.8	54.4	54 29.9	27.0	Jupiter	299 50.3	10 01
Mer.Pass. 6 00.6		v 3.0	d 0.5	v 1.4	d 0.5	v 1.9	d 0.1	v 2.5	d 0.0	Saturn	157 57.6	19 27

2012 JUNE 20, 21, 22 (WED., THURS., FRI.)

UT	SUN GHA	SUN Dec	MOON GHA	v	Dec	d	HP
d h	° ′	° ′	° ′	′	° ′	′	′
20 00	179 36.7	N23 26.0	175 07.2	10.9	N20 54.7	3.3	54.8
01	194 36.6	26.0	189 37.1	11.0	20 51.4	3.3	54.8
02	209 36.5	26.0	204 07.1	11.0	20 48.1	3.5	54.8
03	224 36.3 ..	26.0	218 37.0	11.0	20 44.6	3.5	54.9
04	239 36.2	26.0	233 07.0	11.0	20 41.1	3.7	54.9
05	254 36.0	26.1	247 37.0	11.0	20 37.4	3.8	54.9
06	269 35.9	N23 26.1	262 07.0	11.0	N20 33.6	3.8	54.9
W 07	284 35.8	26.1	276 37.0	11.0	20 29.8	4.0	54.9
E 08	299 35.6	26.1	291 07.0	11.0	20 25.8	4.1	54.9
D 09	314 35.5 ..	26.1	305 37.0	11.1	20 21.7	4.1	55.0
N 10	329 35.4	26.1	320 07.1	11.0	20 17.6	4.3	55.0
E 11	344 35.2	26.1	334 37.1	11.1	20 13.3	4.4	55.0
S 12	359 35.1	N23 26.1	349 07.2	11.0	N20 08.9	4.5	55.0
D 13	14 35.0	26.1	3 37.2	11.1	20 04.4	4.5	55.0
A 14	29 34.8	26.1	18 07.3	11.1	19 59.9	4.7	55.0
Y 15	44 34.7 ..	26.1	32 37.4	11.1	19 55.2	4.8	55.1
16	59 34.5	26.2	47 07.5	11.1	19 50.4	4.9	55.1
17	74 34.4	26.2	61 37.6	11.2	19 45.5	5.0	55.1
18	89 34.3	N23 26.2	76 07.8	11.1	N19 40.5	5.0	55.1
19	104 34.1	26.2	90 37.9	11.2	19 35.5	5.2	55.1
20	119 34.0	26.2	105 08.1	11.2	19 30.3	5.3	55.1
21	134 33.9 ..	26.2	119 38.3	11.2	19 25.0	5.4	55.2
22	149 33.7	26.2	134 08.5	11.2	19 19.6	5.4	55.2
23	164 33.6	26.2	148 38.7	11.3	19 14.2	5.6	55.2
21 00	179 33.4	N23 26.2	163 09.0	11.2	N19 08.6	5.7	55.2
01	194 33.3	26.2	177 39.2	11.3	19 02.9	5.7	55.2
02	209 33.2	26.2	192 09.5	11.3	18 57.2	5.9	55.2
03	224 33.0 ..	26.2	206 39.8	11.3	18 51.3	5.9	55.3
04	239 32.9	26.2	221 10.1	11.3	18 45.4	6.1	55.3
05	254 32.8	26.2	235 40.4	11.4	18 39.3	6.1	55.3
06	269 32.6	N23 26.2	250 10.8	11.3	N18 33.2	6.2	55.3
T 07	284 32.5	26.1	264 41.1	11.4	18 27.0	6.4	55.3
H 08	299 32.4	26.1	279 11.5	11.4	18 20.6	6.4	55.3
U 09	314 32.2 ..	26.1	293 41.9	11.5	18 14.2	6.5	55.4
R 10	329 32.1	26.1	308 12.4	11.4	18 07.7	6.6	55.4
S 11	344 31.9	26.1	322 42.8	11.5	18 01.1	6.7	55.4
D 12	359 31.8	N23 26.1	337 13.3	11.5	N17 54.4	6.8	55.4
A 13	14 31.7	26.1	351 43.8	11.5	17 47.6	6.8	55.4
Y 14	29 31.5	26.1	6 14.3	11.5	17 40.8	7.0	55.5
15	44 31.4 ..	26.1	20 44.8	11.6	17 33.8	7.1	55.5
16	59 31.3	26.1	35 15.4	11.6	17 26.7	7.1	55.5
17	74 31.1	26.1	49 46.0	11.6	17 19.6	7.2	55.5
18	89 31.0	N23 26.0	64 16.6	11.6	N17 12.4	7.4	55.5
19	104 30.8	26.0	78 47.2	11.6	17 05.0	7.4	55.5
20	119 30.7	26.0	93 17.8	11.7	16 57.6	7.5	55.6
21	134 30.6 ..	26.0	107 48.5	11.7	16 50.1	7.6	55.6
22	149 30.4	26.0	122 19.2	11.7	16 42.5	7.6	55.6
23	164 30.3	26.0	136 49.9	11.7	16 34.9	7.8	55.6
22 00	179 30.2	N23 25.9	151 20.6	11.8	N16 27.1	7.8	55.6
01	194 30.0	25.9	165 51.4	11.8	16 19.3	7.9	55.7
02	209 29.9	25.9	180 22.2	11.8	16 11.4	8.0	55.7
03	224 29.8 ..	25.9	194 53.0	11.8	16 03.4	8.1	55.7
04	239 29.6	25.9	209 23.8	11.8	15 55.3	8.2	55.7
05	254 29.5	25.8	223 54.6	11.9	15 47.1	8.2	55.7
06	269 29.3	N23 25.8	238 25.5	11.9	N15 38.9	8.3	55.8
07	284 29.2	25.8	252 56.4	11.9	15 30.6	8.5	55.8
F 08	299 29.1	25.8	267 27.3	11.9	15 22.1	8.4	55.8
R 09	314 28.9 ..	25.8	281 58.2	12.0	15 13.7	8.6	55.8
I 10	329 28.8	25.7	296 29.2	12.0	15 05.1	8.6	55.8
11	344 28.7	25.7	311 00.2	12.0	14 56.5	8.8	55.9
D 12	359 28.5	N23 25.7	325 31.2	12.0	N14 47.7	8.8	55.9
A 13	14 28.4	25.7	340 02.2	12.0	14 38.9	8.8	55.9
Y 14	29 28.3	25.6	354 33.2	12.1	14 30.1	9.0	55.9
15	44 28.1 ..	25.6	9 04.3	12.1	14 21.1	9.0	55.9
16	59 28.0	25.6	23 35.4	12.1	14 12.1	9.1	56.0
17	74 27.9	25.5	38 06.5	12.1	14 03.0	9.2	56.0
18	89 27.7	N23 25.5	52 37.6	12.2	N13 53.8	9.2	56.0
19	104 27.6	25.5	67 08.8	12.1	13 44.6	9.3	56.0
20	119 27.4	25.4	81 39.9	12.2	13 35.3	9.4	56.0
21	134 27.3 ..	25.4	96 11.1	12.2	13 25.9	9.5	56.1
22	149 27.2	25.4	110 42.3	12.3	13 16.4	9.5	56.1
23	164 27.0	25.3	125 13.6	12.2	N13 06.9	9.6	56.1
	SD 15.8	d 0.0	SD 15.0		15.1		15.2

Moonrise

Lat.	Twilight Naut.	Twilight Civil	Sunrise	Moonrise 20	21	22	23
°	h m	h m	h m	h m	h m	h m	h m
N 72						04 00	06 13
N 70					02 36	04 41	06 34
68				01 45	03 26	05 09	06 51
66				02 33	03 58	05 30	07 04
64	////	////	01 31	03 03	04 21	05 47	07 15
62	////	////	02 09	03 26	04 40	06 00	07 24
60	////	00 49	02 36	03 45	04 55	06 12	07 32
N 58	////	01 40	02 56	04 00	05 08	06 22	07 39
56	////	02 10	03 13	04 13	05 19	06 31	07 45
54	00 45	02 33	03 27	04 24	05 29	06 38	07 51
52	01 32	02 51	03 40	04 34	05 37	06 45	07 56
50	02 00	03 06	03 51	04 43	05 45	06 51	08 00
45	02 46	03 36	04 13	05 02	06 02	07 05	08 10
N 40	03 17	03 58	04 31	05 17	06 15	07 16	08 18
35	03 40	04 17	04 46	05 30	06 26	07 25	08 25
30	03 59	04 32	04 59	05 41	06 36	07 33	08 31
20	04 28	04 57	05 22	06 01	06 54	07 47	08 41
N 10	04 50	05 18	05 41	06 17	07 09	08 00	08 50
0	05 09	05 36	05 58	06 33	07 22	08 11	08 59
S 10	05 26	05 53	06 16	06 49	07 36	08 22	09 07
20	05 43	06 10	06 34	07 05	07 51	08 35	09 16
30	06 00	06 29	06 55	07 25	08 08	08 49	09 26
35	06 08	06 40	07 08	07 36	08 18	08 57	09 32
40	06 17	06 51	07 22	07 49	08 29	09 06	09 39
45	06 28	07 05	07 39	08 04	08 42	09 16	09 47
S 50	06 40	07 21	08 00	08 22	08 58	09 29	09 56
52	06 45	07 29	08 10	08 31	09 06	09 35	10 00
54	06 51	07 37	08 21	08 41	09 14	09 42	10 05
56	06 57	07 46	08 33	08 52	09 24	09 49	10 10
58	07 04	07 56	08 48	09 04	09 34	09 57	10 16
S 60	07 11	08 08	09 06	09 19	09 46	10 06	10 22

Moonset

Lat.	Sunset	Twilight Civil	Twilight Naut.	Moonset 20	21	22	23
°	h m	h m	h m	h m	h m	h m	h m
N 72						{00 23 / 12 10}	23 19
N 70				23 53	23 30	23 16	23 06
68				23 02	23 01	22 58	22 56
66				22 30	22 39	22 44	22 47
64	22 33	////	////	22 06	22 22	22 32	22 39
62	21 54	////	////	21 47	22 07	22 22	22 33
60	21 28	23 14	////	21 31	21 55	22 13	22 27
N 58	21 07	22 23	////	21 18	21 44	22 05	22 22
56	20 51	21 53	////	21 07	21 35	21 58	22 18
54	20 36	21 31	23 19	20 57	21 27	21 52	22 14
52	20 24	21 13	22 31	20 48	21 20	21 46	22 10
50	20 13	20 58	22 03	20 40	21 13	21 41	22 07
45	19 50	20 28	21 18	20 22	20 59	21 30	21 59
N 40	19 32	20 05	20 47	20 08	20 47	21 21	21 53
35	19 17	19 47	20 24	19 56	20 37	21 14	21 48
30	19 04	19 32	20 05	19 46	20 28	21 07	21 43
20	18 42	19 07	19 36	19 28	20 12	20 55	21 35
N 10	18 23	18 46	19 13	19 12	19 59	20 44	21 28
0	18 06	18 28	18 54	18 57	19 46	20 34	21 21
S 10	17 48	18 11	18 37	18 42	19 33	20 24	21 14
20	17 30	17 54	18 21	18 26	19 19	20 13	21 07
30	17 08	17 35	18 05	18 08	19 04	20 01	20 59
35	16 56	17 24	17 56	17 57	18 54	19 54	20 54
40	16 42	17 12	17 46	17 44	18 44	19 45	20 48
45	16 25	16 59	17 36	17 30	18 31	19 36	20 42
S 50	16 04	16 43	17 24	17 12	18 16	19 24	20 34
52	15 54	16 35	17 19	17 03	18 09	19 19	20 30
54	15 43	16 27	17 13	16 54	18 01	19 12	20 26
56	15 30	16 18	17 07	16 43	17 52	19 06	20 21
58	15 16	16 08	17 00	16 31	17 42	18 58	20 17
S 60	14 58	15 56	16 53	16 16	17 31	18 50	20 11

SUN / MOON

Day	SUN Eqn. of Time 00h	SUN Eqn. of Time 12h	SUN Mer. Pass.	MOON Mer. Pass. Upper	MOON Mer. Pass. Lower	Age	Phase
d	m s	m s	h m	h m	h m	d	%
20	01 33	01 39	12 02	12 45	00 20	01	1
21	01 46	01 53	12 02	13 34	01 10	02	4
22	01 59	02 06	12 02	14 23	01 58	03	8

UT	ARIES GHA	VENUS −4.5 GHA	Dec	MARS +0.8 GHA	Dec	JUPITER −2.0 GHA	Dec	SATURN +0.7 GHA	Dec	Name	SHA	Dec
d h	° ′	° ′	° ′	° ′	° ′	° ′	° ′	° ′	° ′		° ′	° ′
23 00	271 34.0	204 52.5	N18 24.7	96 15.5	N 2 40.0	210 56.7	N19 54.5	69 32.4	S 6 27.0	Acamar	315 19.1	S40 15.1
01	286 36.5	219 55.4	24.3	111 16.8	39.5	225 58.6	54.6	84 34.9	27.0	Achernar	335 27.5	S57 10.1
02	301 38.9	234 58.2	23.8	126 18.2	39.0	241 00.5	54.7	99 37.4	27.1	Acrux	173 10.0	S63 10.5
03	316 41.4	250 01.1	.. 23.4	141 19.5	.. 38.4	256 02.4	.. 54.8	114 39.8	.. 27.1	Adhara	255 13.4	S28 59.5
04	331 43.9	265 04.0	23.0	156 20.9	37.9	271 04.3	55.0	129 42.3	27.1	Aldebaran	290 50.5	N16 31.9
05	346 46.3	280 06.8	22.6	171 22.2	37.3	286 06.2	55.1	144 44.8	27.1			
06	1 48.8	295 09.7	N18 22.2	186 23.6	N 2 36.8	301 08.0	N19 55.2	159 47.3	S 6 27.1	Alioth	166 21.2	N55 53.7
S 07	16 51.3	310 12.5	21.8	201 24.9	36.3	316 09.9	55.3	174 49.7	27.1	Alkaid	152 59.2	N49 15.3
A 08	31 53.7	325 15.4	21.4	216 26.3	35.7	331 11.8	55.4	189 52.2	27.1	Al Na'ir	27 44.3	S46 53.7
T 09	46 56.2	340 18.2	.. 21.0	231 27.7	.. 35.2	346 13.7	.. 55.5	204 54.7	.. 27.1	Alnilam	275 47.4	S 1 11.7
U 10	61 58.7	355 21.1	20.6	246 29.0	34.7	1 15.6	55.6	219 57.2	27.1	Alphard	217 57.0	S 8 43.0
R 11	77 01.1	10 23.9	20.2	261 30.3	34.1	16 17.5	55.7	234 59.6	27.1			
D 12	92 03.6	25 26.7	N18 19.8	276 31.7	N 2 33.6	31 19.4	N19 55.8	250 02.1	S 6 27.1	Alphecca	126 11.3	N26 40.5
A 13	107 06.0	40 29.6	19.4	291 33.0	33.0	46 21.3	55.9	265 04.6	27.1	Alpheratz	357 44.2	N29 09.5
Y 14	122 08.5	55 32.4	19.0	306 34.4	32.5	61 23.2	56.0	280 07.1	27.1	Altair	62 08.6	N 8 54.2
15	137 11.0	70 35.2	.. 18.6	321 35.7	.. 32.0	76 25.1	.. 56.1	295 09.5	.. 27.1	Ankaa	353 16.4	S42 14.0
16	152 13.4	85 38.0	18.2	336 37.1	31.4	91 27.0	56.2	310 12.0	27.2	Antares	112 26.7	S26 27.6
17	167 15.9	100 40.8	17.8	351 38.4	30.9	106 28.9	56.4	325 14.5	27.2			
18	182 18.4	115 43.6	N18 17.4	6 39.8	N 2 30.3	121 30.7	N19 56.5	340 17.0	S 6 27.2	Arcturus	145 56.2	N19 07.1
19	197 20.8	130 46.4	17.0	21 41.1	29.8	136 32.6	56.6	355 19.4	27.2	Atria	107 28.6	S69 03.0
20	212 23.3	145 49.2	16.6	36 42.5	29.3	151 34.5	56.7	10 21.9	27.2	Avior	234 18.8	S59 33.3
21	227 25.8	160 52.0	.. 16.2	51 43.8	.. 28.7	166 36.4	.. 56.8	25 24.4	.. 27.2	Bellatrix	278 33.1	N 6 21.5
22	242 28.2	175 54.8	15.8	66 45.2	28.2	181 38.3	56.9	40 26.9	27.2	Betelgeuse	271 02.4	N 7 24.4
23	257 30.7	190 57.6	15.4	81 46.5	27.6	196 40.2	57.0	55 29.3	27.2			
24 00	272 33.2	206 00.4	N18 15.0	96 47.9	N 2 27.1	211 42.1	N19 57.1	70 31.8	S 6 27.2	Canopus	263 57.0	S52 42.3
01	287 35.6	221 03.2	14.7	111 49.2	26.6	226 44.0	57.2	85 34.3	27.2	Capella	280 35.9	N46 00.5
02	302 38.1	236 05.9	14.3	126 50.6	26.0	241 45.9	57.3	100 36.8	27.2	Deneb	49 31.5	N45 19.5
03	317 40.5	251 08.7	.. 13.9	141 51.9	.. 25.5	256 47.8	.. 57.4	115 39.2	.. 27.2	Denebola	182 34.4	N14 30.1
04	332 43.0	266 11.5	13.5	156 53.2	24.9	271 49.7	57.5	130 41.7	27.3	Diphda	348 56.6	S17 54.9
05	347 45.5	281 14.2	13.1	171 54.6	24.4	286 51.6	57.6	145 44.2	27.3			
06	2 47.9	296 17.0	N18 12.8	186 55.9	N 2 23.9	301 53.5	N19 57.7	160 46.7	S 6 27.3	Dubhe	193 52.7	N61 41.2
07	17 50.4	311 19.7	12.4	201 57.3	23.3	316 55.3	57.8	175 49.1	27.3	Elnath	278 13.8	N28 36.9
08	32 52.9	326 22.5	12.0	216 58.6	22.8	331 57.2	58.0	190 51.6	27.3	Eltanin	90 45.9	N51 29.4
S 09	47 55.3	341 25.2	.. 11.7	232 00.0	.. 22.2	346 59.1	.. 58.1	205 54.1	.. 27.3	Enif	33 47.6	N 9 56.1
U 10	62 57.8	356 28.0	11.3	247 01.3	21.7	2 01.0	58.2	220 56.5	27.3	Fomalhaut	15 24.6	S29 33.1
N 11	78 00.3	11 30.7	10.9	262 02.6	21.2	17 02.9	58.3	235 59.0	27.3			
D 12	93 02.7	26 33.4	N18 10.5	277 04.0	N 2 20.6	32 04.8	N19 58.4	251 01.5	S 6 27.3	Gacrux	172 01.6	S57 11.3
A 13	108 05.2	41 36.1	10.2	292 05.3	20.1	47 06.7	58.5	266 04.0	27.3	Gienah	175 53.0	S17 36.9
Y 14	123 07.6	56 38.9	09.8	307 06.7	19.5	62 08.6	58.6	281 06.4	27.3	Hadar	148 48.5	S60 26.3
15	138 10.1	71 41.6	.. 09.5	322 08.0	.. 19.0	77 10.5	.. 58.7	296 08.9	.. 27.3	Hamal	328 01.7	N23 31.2
16	153 12.6	86 44.3	09.1	337 09.3	18.5	92 12.4	58.8	311 11.4	27.4	Kaus Aust.	83 44.3	S34 22.6
17	168 15.0	101 47.0	08.7	352 10.7	17.9	107 14.3	58.9	326 13.8	27.4			
18	183 17.5	116 49.7	N18 08.4	7 12.0	N 2 17.4	122 16.2	N19 59.0	341 16.3	S 6 27.4	Kochab	137 19.2	N74 06.5
19	198 20.0	131 52.4	08.0	22 13.4	16.8	137 18.1	59.1	356 18.8	27.4	Markab	13 38.9	N15 16.4
20	213 22.4	146 55.1	07.7	37 14.7	16.3	152 20.0	59.2	11 21.2	27.4	Menkar	314 16.0	N 4 08.3
21	228 24.9	161 57.8	.. 07.3	52 16.0	.. 15.7	167 21.9	.. 59.3	26 23.7	.. 27.4	Menkent	148 08.2	S36 26.1
22	243 27.4	177 00.5	07.0	67 17.4	15.2	182 23.7	59.4	41 26.2	27.4	Miaplacidus	221 40.5	S69 46.5
23	258 29.8	192 03.2	06.6	82 18.7	14.7	197 25.6	59.5	56 28.7	27.4			
25 00	273 32.3	207 05.9	N18 06.3	97 20.1	N 2 14.1	212 27.5	N19 59.6	71 31.1	S 6 27.4	Mirfak	308 41.7	N49 54.1
01	288 34.8	222 08.5	05.9	112 21.4	13.6	227 29.4	59.8	86 33.6	27.4	Nunki	75 58.8	S26 16.7
02	303 37.2	237 11.2	05.6	127 22.7	13.0	242 31.3	19 59.9	101 36.1	27.5	Peacock	53 19.8	S56 41.4
03	318 39.7	252 13.9	.. 05.2	142 24.1	.. 12.5	257 33.2	20 00.0	116 38.5	.. 27.5	Pollux	243 28.9	N27 59.7
04	333 42.1	267 16.5	04.9	157 25.4	11.9	272 35.1	00.1	131 41.0	27.5	Procyon	245 00.7	N 5 11.4
05	348 44.6	282 19.2	04.6	172 26.7	11.4	287 37.0	00.2	146 43.5	27.5			
06	3 47.1	297 21.9	N18 04.2	187 28.1	N 2 10.9	302 38.9	N20 00.3	161 45.9	S 6 27.5	Rasalhague	96 06.7	N12 33.2
07	18 49.5	312 24.5	03.9	202 29.4	10.3	317 40.8	00.4	176 48.4	27.5	Regulus	207 44.4	N11 54.3
08	33 52.0	327 27.2	03.5	217 30.7	09.8	332 42.7	00.5	191 50.9	27.5	Rigel	281 13.0	S 8 11.3
M 09	48 54.5	342 29.8	.. 03.2	232 32.1	.. 09.2	347 44.6	.. 00.6	206 53.3	.. 27.5	Rigil Kent.	139 52.2	S60 53.4
O 10	63 56.9	357 32.4	02.9	247 33.4	08.7	2 46.5	00.7	221 55.8	27.5	Sabik	102 13.0	S15 44.3
N 11	78 59.4	12 35.1	02.5	262 34.8	08.1	17 48.4	00.8	236 58.3	27.5			
D 12	94 01.9	27 37.7	N18 02.2	277 36.1	N 2 07.6	32 50.3	N20 00.9	252 00.7	S 6 27.6	Schedar	349 41.4	N56 36.2
A 13	109 04.3	42 40.3	01.9	292 37.4	07.0	47 52.2	01.0	267 03.2	27.6	Shaula	96 22.4	S37 06.7
Y 14	124 06.8	57 43.0	01.5	307 38.8	06.5	62 54.1	01.1	282 05.7	27.6	Sirius	258 34.7	S16 44.1
15	139 09.3	72 45.6	.. 01.2	322 40.1	.. 06.0	77 56.0	.. 01.2	297 08.2	.. 27.6	Spica	158 31.8	S11 13.7
16	154 11.7	87 48.2	00.9	337 41.4	05.4	92 57.9	01.3	312 10.6	27.6	Suhail	222 53.3	S43 29.3
17	169 14.2	102 50.8	00.6	352 42.8	04.9	107 59.7	01.4	327 13.1	27.6			
18	184 16.6	117 53.4	N18 00.3	7 44.1	N 2 04.3	123 01.6	N20 01.5	342 15.6	S 6 27.6	Vega	80 39.0	N38 47.8
19	199 19.1	132 56.0	17 59.9	22 45.4	03.8	138 03.5	01.6	357 18.0	27.6	Zuben'ubi	137 05.9	S16 05.7
20	214 21.6	147 58.6	59.6	37 46.7	03.2	153 05.4	01.7	12 20.5	27.6		SHA	Mer. Pass.
21	229 24.0	163 01.2	.. 59.3	52 48.1	.. 02.7	168 07.3	.. 01.9	27 22.9	.. 27.6		° ′	h m
22	244 26.5	178 03.8	59.0	67 49.4	02.1	183 09.2	02.0	42 25.4	27.7	Venus	293 27.2	10 14
23	259 29.0	193 06.4	58.7	82 50.7	01.6	198 11.1	02.1	57 27.9	27.7	Mars	184 14.7	17 31
Mer. Pass.	h m 5 48.8	v 2.7	d 0.4	v 1.3	d 0.5	v 1.9	d 0.1	v 2.5	d 0.0	Jupiter	299 08.9	9 52
										Saturn	157 58.7	19 15

SUN and MOON

UT	SUN GHA	SUN Dec	MOON GHA	v	MOON Dec	d	HP
23 00	179 26.9	N23 25.3	139 44.8	12.3	N12 57.3	9.7	56.1
01	194 26.8	25.3	154 16.1	12.3	12 47.6	9.7	56.2
02	209 26.6	25.2	168 47.4	12.3	12 37.9	9.8	56.2
03	224 26.5	.. 25.2	183 18.7	12.3	12 28.1	9.9	56.2
04	239 26.4	25.2	197 50.0	12.3	12 18.2	9.9	56.2
05	254 26.2	25.1	212 21.3	12.4	12 08.3	10.0	56.2
S 06	269 26.1	N23 25.1	226 52.7	12.3	N11 58.3	10.0	56.3
A 07	284 26.0	25.0	241 24.0	12.4	11 48.3	10.2	56.3
T 08	299 25.8	25.0	255 55.4	12.4	11 38.1	10.1	56.3
U 09	314 25.7	.. 25.0	270 26.8	12.4	11 28.0	10.3	56.3
R 10	329 25.5	24.9	284 58.2	12.5	11 17.7	10.3	56.4
D 11	344 25.4	24.9	299 29.7	12.4	11 07.4	10.4	56.4
A 12	359 25.3	N23 24.8	314 01.1	12.5	N10 57.0	10.4	56.4
Y 13	14 25.1	24.8	328 32.6	12.4	10 46.6	10.5	56.4
14	29 25.0	24.8	343 04.0	12.5	10 36.1	10.5	56.4
15	44 24.9	.. 24.7	357 35.5	12.5	10 25.6	10.6	56.4
16	59 24.7	24.7	12 07.0	12.5	10 15.0	10.7	56.5
17	74 24.6	24.6	26 38.5	12.5	10 04.3	10.7	56.5
18	89 24.5	N23 24.6	41 10.0	12.6	N 9 53.6	10.8	56.5
19	104 24.3	24.5	55 41.6	12.5	9 42.8	10.8	56.6
20	119 24.2	24.5	70 13.1	12.6	9 32.0	10.9	56.6
21	134 24.1	.. 24.4	84 44.7	12.5	9 21.1	10.9	56.6
22	149 23.9	24.4	99 16.2	12.6	9 10.2	11.0	56.6
23	164 23.8	24.3	113 47.8	12.6	8 59.2	11.0	56.7
24 00	179 23.7	N23 24.3	128 19.4	12.6	N 8 48.2	11.1	56.7
01	194 23.5	24.2	142 51.0	12.6	8 37.1	11.1	56.7
02	209 23.4	24.2	157 22.6	12.6	8 26.0	11.2	56.7
03	224 23.3	.. 24.1	171 54.2	12.6	8 14.8	11.2	56.7
04	239 23.1	24.0	186 25.8	12.6	8 03.6	11.3	56.8
05	254 23.0	24.0	200 57.4	12.6	7 52.3	11.3	56.8
S 06	269 22.9	N23 23.9	215 29.0	12.6	N 7 41.0	11.4	56.8
U 07	284 22.7	23.9	230 00.6	12.6	7 29.6	11.4	56.8
N 08	299 22.6	23.8	244 32.2	12.7	7 18.2	11.4	56.9
D 09	314 22.5	.. 23.8	259 03.9	12.6	7 06.8	11.5	56.9
A 10	329 22.3	23.7	273 35.5	12.6	6 55.3	11.6	56.9
Y 11	344 22.2	23.6	288 07.1	12.6	6 43.7	11.6	56.9
12	359 22.1	N23 23.6	302 38.7	12.7	N 6 32.1	11.6	57.0
13	14 21.9	23.5	317 10.4	12.6	6 20.5	11.6	57.0
14	29 21.8	23.5	331 42.0	12.6	6 08.9	11.7	57.0
15	44 21.7	.. 23.4	346 13.6	12.6	5 57.2	11.8	57.0
16	59 21.5	23.3	0 45.2	12.6	5 45.4	11.7	57.1
17	74 21.4	23.3	15 16.8	12.7	5 33.7	11.8	57.1
18	89 21.3	N23 23.2	29 48.5	12.6	5 21.9	11.9	57.1
19	104 21.1	23.1	44 20.1	12.6	5 10.0	11.9	57.1
20	119 21.0	23.1	58 51.7	12.6	4 58.1	11.9	57.2
21	134 20.9	.. 23.0	73 23.3	12.6	4 46.2	11.9	57.2
22	149 20.7	22.9	87 54.9	12.5	4 34.3	12.0	57.2
23	164 20.6	22.9	102 26.4	12.6	4 22.3	12.0	57.2
25 00	179 20.5	N23 22.8	116 58.0	12.6	N 4 10.3	12.0	57.3
01	194 20.3	22.7	131 29.6	12.5	3 58.3	12.1	57.3
02	209 20.2	22.7	146 01.1	12.6	3 46.2	12.1	57.3
03	224 20.1	.. 22.6	160 32.7	12.5	3 34.1	12.1	57.3
04	239 19.9	22.5	175 04.2	12.5	3 22.0	12.1	57.4
05	254 19.8	22.4	189 35.7	12.5	3 09.9	12.2	57.4
M 06	269 19.7	N23 22.4	204 07.2	12.5	N 2 57.7	12.2	57.4
O 07	284 19.5	22.3	218 38.7	12.5	2 45.5	12.2	57.4
N 08	299 19.4	22.2	233 10.2	12.4	2 33.3	12.3	57.5
D 09	314 19.3	.. 22.2	247 41.6	12.5	2 21.0	12.3	57.5
A 10	329 19.1	22.1	262 13.1	12.4	2 08.8	12.3	57.5
Y 11	344 19.0	22.0	276 44.5	12.4	1 56.5	12.3	57.5
12	359 18.9	N23 21.9	291 15.9	12.4	N 1 44.2	12.3	57.6
13	14 18.7	21.8	305 47.3	12.3	1 31.9	12.4	57.6
14	29 18.6	21.8	320 18.6	12.4	1 19.5	12.3	57.6
15	44 18.5	.. 21.7	334 50.0	12.3	1 07.2	12.4	57.6
16	59 18.3	21.6	349 21.3	12.3	0 54.8	12.4	57.7
17	74 18.2	21.5	3 52.6	12.3	0 42.4	12.4	57.7
18	89 18.1	N23 21.4	18 23.9	12.2	N 0 30.0	12.4	57.7
19	104 17.9	21.4	32 55.1	12.2	0 17.6	12.5	57.7
20	119 17.8	21.3	47 26.3	12.2	N 0 05.1	12.4	57.8
21	134 17.7	.. 21.2	61 57.5	12.2	S 0 07.3	12.4	57.8
22	149 17.5	21.1	76 28.7	12.1	0 19.7	12.4	57.8
23	164 17.4	21.0	90 59.8	12.1	S 0 32.2	12.5	57.9
SD	15.8	d 0.1	SD 15.4		15.5		15.7

Twilight, Sunrise and Moonrise

Lat.	Naut.	Civil	Sunrise	23	24	25	26
N 72	▭	▭	▭	06 13	08 12	10 07	12 03
N 70	▭	▭	▭	06 34	08 22	10 10	11 59
68	▭	▭	▭	06 51	08 31	10 12	11 55
66	▭	▭	▭	07 04	08 39	10 14	11 51
64	////	////	01 33	07 15	08 45	10 16	11 48
62	////	////	02 11	07 24	08 50	10 17	11 46
60	////	00 51	02 37	07 32	08 55	10 18	11 44
N 58	////	01 42	02 57	07 39	08 59	10 19	11 42
56	////	02 12	03 14	07 45	09 02	10 20	11 40
54	00 47	02 34	03 28	07 51	09 05	10 21	11 39
52	01 34	02 52	03 41	07 56	09 08	10 22	11 38
50	02 01	03 07	03 52	08 00	09 11	10 23	11 36
45	02 47	03 37	04 14	08 10	09 17	10 24	11 34
N 40	03 18	03 59	04 32	08 18	09 21	10 26	11 32
35	03 41	04 18	04 47	08 25	09 25	10 27	11 30
30	03 59	04 33	05 00	08 31	09 29	10 28	11 28
20	04 28	04 58	05 22	08 41	09 35	10 30	11 25
N 10	04 51	05 18	05 41	08 50	09 41	10 31	11 23
0	05 10	05 36	05 59	08 59	09 46	10 33	11 20
S 10	05 27	05 53	06 16	09 07	09 51	10 34	11 18
20	05 43	06 11	06 35	09 16	09 56	10 36	11 16
30	06 00	06 30	06 56	09 26	10 02	10 38	11 13
35	06 09	06 40	07 08	09 32	10 06	10 39	11 12
40	06 18	06 52	07 23	09 39	10 10	10 40	11 10
45	06 28	07 06	07 39	09 47	10 14	10 41	11 08
S 50	06 40	07 22	08 00	09 56	10 20	10 43	11 06
52	06 45	07 29	08 10	10 00	10 23	10 44	11 05
54	06 51	07 37	08 21	10 05	10 25	10 44	11 04
56	06 57	07 46	08 34	10 10	10 28	10 45	11 02
58	07 04	07 57	08 48	10 16	10 32	10 46	11 01
S 60	07 11	08 08	09 06	10 22	10 35	10 47	10 59

Sunset, Twilight and Moonset

Lat.	Sunset	Civil	Naut.	23	24	25	26
N 72	▭	▭	▭	23 19	23 03	22 48	22 32
N 70	▭	▭	▭	23 06	22 57	22 49	22 40
68	▭	▭	▭	22 56	22 53	22 49	22 46
66	▭	▭	▭	22 47	22 49	22 50	22 51
64	22 32	////	////	22 39	22 45	22 50	22 56
62	21 54	////	////	22 33	22 42	22 51	23 00
60	21 28	23 13	////	22 27	22 39	22 51	23 03
N 58	21 07	22 23	////	22 22	22 37	22 51	23 06
56	20 51	21 53	////	22 18	22 35	22 52	23 09
54	20 36	21 31	23 17	22 14	22 33	22 52	23 12
52	20 24	21 13	22 31	22 10	22 31	22 52	23 14
50	20 13	20 58	22 03	22 07	22 30	22 53	23 16
45	19 51	20 28	21 18	21 59	22 26	22 53	23 20
N 40	19 33	20 06	20 47	21 53	22 24	22 53	23 24
35	19 18	19 47	20 24	21 48	22 21	22 54	23 27
30	19 05	19 32	20 06	21 43	22 19	22 54	23 30
20	18 43	19 07	19 37	21 35	22 15	22 55	23 35
N 10	18 24	18 47	19 14	21 28	22 11	22 55	23 40
0	18 06	18 29	18 55	21 21	22 08	22 55	23 44
S 10	17 49	18 12	18 38	21 14	22 05	22 56	23 48
20	17 30	17 54	18 22	21 07	22 01	22 56	23 52
30	17 09	17 35	18 05	20 59	21 57	22 56	23 57
35	16 57	17 25	17 57	20 54	21 55	22 57	24 00
40	16 43	17 13	17 47	20 48	21 52	22 57	24 04
45	16 26	17 00	17 37	20 42	21 49	22 57	24 07
S 50	16 05	16 43	17 25	20 34	21 45	22 58	24 12
52	15 55	16 36	17 20	20 30	21 43	22 58	24 14
54	15 44	16 28	17 14	20 26	21 41	22 58	24 17
56	15 32	16 20	17 08	20 22	21 39	22 58	24 19
58	15 17	16 09	17 01	20 17	21 37	22 58	24 22
S 60	14 59	15 57	16 54	20 11	21 34	22 59	24 25

SUN and MOON data

Day	SUN Eqn. of Time 00h	SUN Eqn. of Time 12h	Mer. Pass.	MOON Mer. Pass. Upper	MOON Mer. Pass. Lower	Age	Phase
d	m s	m s	h m	h m	h m	d	%
23	02 12	02 19	12 02	15 10	02 46	04	15
24	02 25	02 32	12 03	15 57	03 33	05	23
25	02 38	02 44	12 03	16 44	04 20	06	32

2012 JUNE 26, 27, 28 (TUES., WED., THURS.)

UT	ARIES GHA	VENUS −4.6 GHA	Dec	MARS +0.8 GHA	Dec	JUPITER −2.0 GHA	Dec	SATURN +0.7 GHA	Dec
26 00	274 31.4	208 09.0	N17 58.4	97 52.1	N 2 01.0	213 13.0	N20 02.2	72 30.3	S 6 27.7
01	289 33.9	223 11.5	58.1	112 53.4	00.5	228 14.9	02.3	87 32.8	27.7
02	304 36.4	238 14.1	57.7	127 54.7	2 00.0	243 16.8	02.4	102 35.3	27.7
03	319 38.8	253 16.7 ..	57.4	142 56.1	1 59.4	258 18.7 ..	02.5	117 37.7 ..	27.7
04	334 41.3	268 19.2	57.1	157 57.4	58.9	273 20.6	02.6	132 40.2	27.7
05	349 43.7	283 21.8	56.8	172 58.7	58.3	288 22.5	02.7	147 42.7	27.7
06	4 46.2	298 24.4	N17 56.5	188 00.0	N 1 57.8	303 24.4	N20 02.8	162 45.1	S 6 27.8
07	19 48.7	313 26.9	56.2	203 01.4	57.2	318 26.3	02.9	177 47.6	27.8
T 08	34 51.1	328 29.5	55.9	218 02.7	56.7	333 28.2	03.0	192 50.1	27.8
U 09	49 53.6	343 32.0 ..	55.6	233 04.0 ..	56.1	348 30.1 ..	03.1	207 52.5 ..	27.8
E 10	64 56.1	358 34.5	55.3	248 05.4	55.6	3 32.0	03.2	222 55.0	27.8
S 11	79 58.5	13 37.1	55.0	263 06.7	55.0	18 33.9	03.3	237 57.5	27.8
D 12	95 01.0	28 39.6	N17 54.7	278 08.0	N 1 54.5	33 35.8	N20 03.4	252 59.9	S 6 27.8
A 13	110 03.5	43 42.1	54.4	293 09.3	53.9	48 37.7	03.5	268 02.4	27.8
Y 14	125 05.9	58 44.7	54.1	308 10.7	53.4	63 39.6	03.6	283 04.8	27.8
15	140 08.4	73 47.2 ..	53.9	323 12.0 ..	52.8	78 41.5 ..	03.7	298 07.3 ..	27.9
16	155 10.9	88 49.7	53.6	338 13.3	52.3	93 43.4	03.8	313 09.8	27.9
17	170 13.3	103 52.2	53.3	353 14.6	51.7	108 45.3	03.9	328 12.2	27.9
18	185 15.8	118 54.7	N17 53.0	8 16.0	N 1 51.2	123 47.2	N20 04.0	343 14.7	S 6 27.9
19	200 18.2	133 57.2	52.7	23 17.3	50.6	138 49.1	04.1	358 17.2	27.9
20	215 20.7	148 59.7	52.4	38 18.6	50.1	153 51.0	04.2	13 19.6	27.9
21	230 23.2	164 02.2 ..	52.1	53 19.9 ..	49.5	168 52.9 ..	04.3	28 22.1 ..	27.9
22	245 25.6	179 04.7	51.9	68 21.3	49.0	183 54.8	04.4	43 24.5	27.9
23	260 28.1	194 07.2	51.6	83 22.6	48.5	198 56.7	04.6	58 27.0	28.0
27 00	275 30.6	209 09.7	N17 51.3	98 23.9	N 1 47.9	213 58.6	N20 04.7	73 29.5	S 6 28.0
01	290 33.0	224 12.2	51.0	113 25.2	47.4	229 00.4	04.8	88 31.9	28.0
02	305 35.5	239 14.6	50.8	128 26.5	46.8	244 02.3	04.9	103 34.4	28.0
03	320 38.0	254 17.1 ..	50.5	143 27.9 ..	46.3	259 04.2 ..	05.0	118 36.9 ..	28.0
04	335 40.4	269 19.6	50.2	158 29.2	45.7	274 06.1	05.1	133 39.3	28.0
05	350 42.9	284 22.1	49.9	173 30.5	45.2	289 08.0	05.2	148 41.8	28.0
06	5 45.4	299 24.5	N17 49.7	188 31.8	N 1 44.6	304 09.9	N20 05.3	163 44.2	S 6 28.0
W 07	20 47.8	314 27.0	49.4	203 33.2	44.1	319 11.8	05.4	178 46.7	28.1
E 08	35 50.3	329 29.4	49.1	218 34.5	43.5	334 13.7	05.5	193 49.2	28.1
D 09	50 52.7	344 31.9 ..	48.9	233 35.8 ..	43.0	349 15.6 ..	05.6	208 51.6 ..	28.1
N 10	65 55.2	359 34.3	48.6	248 37.1	42.4	4 17.5	05.7	223 54.1	28.1
E 11	80 57.7	14 36.7	48.4	263 38.4	41.9	19 19.4	05.8	238 56.5	28.1
S 12	96 00.1	29 39.2	N17 48.1	278 39.8	N 1 41.3	34 21.3	N20 05.9	253 59.0	S 6 28.1
D 13	111 02.6	44 41.6	47.8	293 41.1	40.8	49 23.2	06.0	269 01.5	28.1
A 14	126 05.1	59 44.0	47.6	308 42.4	40.2	64 25.1	06.1	284 03.9	28.2
Y 15	141 07.5	74 46.5 ..	47.3	323 43.7 ..	39.7	79 27.0 ..	06.2	299 06.4 ..	28.2
16	156 10.0	89 48.9	47.1	338 45.0	39.1	94 28.9	06.3	314 08.8	28.2
17	171 12.5	104 51.3	46.8	353 46.3	38.6	109 30.8	06.4	329 11.3	28.2
18	186 14.9	119 53.7	N17 46.6	8 47.7	N 1 38.0	124 32.7	N20 06.5	344 13.8	S 6 28.2
19	201 17.4	134 56.1	46.3	23 49.0	37.4	139 34.6	06.6	359 16.2	28.2
20	216 19.8	149 58.5	46.1	38 50.3	36.9	154 36.5	06.7	14 18.7	28.3
21	231 22.3	165 00.9 ..	45.8	53 51.6 ..	36.3	169 38.4 ..	06.8	29 21.1 ..	28.3
22	246 24.8	180 03.3	45.6	68 52.9	35.8	184 40.3	06.9	44 23.6	28.3
23	261 27.2	195 05.7	45.3	83 54.2	35.2	199 42.2	07.0	59 26.0	28.3
28 00	276 29.7	210 08.1	N17 45.1	98 55.6	N 1 34.7	214 44.1	N20 07.1	74 28.5	S 6 28.3
01	291 32.2	225 10.5	44.9	113 56.9	34.1	229 46.0	07.2	89 31.0	28.3
02	306 34.6	240 12.9	44.6	128 58.2	33.6	244 47.9	07.3	104 33.4	28.3
03	321 37.1	255 15.2 ..	44.4	143 59.5 ..	33.0	259 49.8 ..	07.4	119 35.9 ..	28.3
04	336 39.6	270 17.6	44.1	159 00.8	32.5	274 51.7	07.5	134 38.3	28.4
05	351 42.0	285 20.0	43.9	174 02.1	31.9	289 53.6	07.6	149 40.8	28.4
06	6 44.5	300 22.3	N17 43.7	189 03.5	N 1 31.4	304 55.5	N20 07.7	164 43.3	S 6 28.4
07	21 47.0	315 24.7	43.4	204 04.8	30.8	319 57.4	07.8	179 45.7	28.4
T 08	36 49.4	330 27.1	43.2	219 06.1	30.3	334 59.3	07.9	194 48.2	28.4
H 09	51 51.9	345 29.4 ..	43.0	234 07.4 ..	29.7	350 01.2 ..	08.0	209 50.6 ..	28.4
U 10	66 54.3	0 31.8	42.8	249 08.7	29.2	5 03.1	08.1	224 53.1	28.4
R 11	81 56.8	15 34.1	42.5	264 10.0	28.6	20 05.0	08.2	239 55.5	28.5
S 12	96 59.3	30 36.4	N17 42.3	279 11.3	N 1 28.1	35 06.9	N20 08.3	254 58.0	S 6 28.5
D 13	112 01.7	45 38.8	42.1	294 12.6	27.5	50 08.8	08.4	270 00.4	28.5
A 14	127 04.2	60 41.1	41.9	309 14.0	27.0	65 10.7	08.5	285 02.9	28.5
Y 15	142 06.7	75 43.4 ..	41.6	324 15.3 ..	26.4	80 12.6 ..	08.6	300 05.4 ..	28.5
16	157 09.1	90 45.8	41.4	339 16.6	25.8	95 14.6	08.7	315 07.8	28.5
17	172 11.6	105 48.1	41.2	354 17.9	25.3	110 16.5	08.8	330 10.3	28.5
18	187 14.1	120 50.4	N17 41.0	9 19.2	N 1 24.7	125 18.4	N20 08.9	345 12.7	S 6 28.6
19	202 16.5	135 52.7	40.8	24 20.5	24.2	140 20.3	09.0	0 15.2	28.6
20	217 19.0	150 55.0	40.6	39 21.8	23.6	155 22.2	09.1	15 17.6	28.6
21	232 21.5	165 57.3 ..	40.3	54 23.1 ..	23.1	170 24.1 ..	09.2	30 20.1 ..	28.6
22	247 23.9	180 59.6	40.1	69 24.4	22.5	185 26.0	09.3	45 22.5	28.6
23	262 26.4	196 01.9	39.9	84 25.7	22.0	200 27.9	09.4	60 25.0	28.6
Mer.Pass. 5 37.0		v 2.4	d 0.3	v 1.3	d 0.6	v 1.9	d 0.1	v 2.5	d 0.0

STARS

Name	SHA	Dec
Acamar	315 19.1	S40 15.1
Achernar	335 27.5	S57 10.1
Acrux	173 10.0	S63 10.5
Adhara	255 13.4	S28 59.5
Aldebaran	290 50.5	N16 31.9
Alioth	166 21.2	N55 53.7
Alkaid	152 59.2	N49 15.3
Al Na'ir	27 44.3	S46 53.7
Alnilam	275 47.4	S 1 11.7
Alphard	217 57.0	S 8 42.9
Alphecca	126 11.3	N26 40.5
Alpheratz	357 44.2	N29 09.5
Altair	62 08.6	N 8 54.2
Ankaa	353 16.4	S42 14.0
Antares	112 26.7	S26 27.6
Arcturus	145 56.2	N19 07.1
Atria	107 28.6	S69 03.0
Avior	234 18.9	S59 33.3
Bellatrix	278 33.1	N 6 21.6
Betelgeuse	271 02.4	N 7 24.4
Canopus	263 57.0	S52 42.3
Capella	280 35.9	N46 00.5
Deneb	49 31.5	N45 19.5
Denebola	182 34.4	N14 30.1
Diphda	348 56.6	S17 54.9
Dubhe	193 52.8	N61 41.2
Elnath	278 13.8	N28 36.9
Eltanin	90 45.9	N51 29.4
Enif	33 47.6	N 9 56.1
Fomalhaut	15 24.6	S29 33.1
Gacrux	172 01.6	S57 11.3
Gienah	175 53.0	S17 36.9
Hadar	148 48.5	S60 26.3
Hamal	328 01.7	N23 31.2
Kaus Aust.	83 44.3	S34 22.6
Kochab	137 19.3	N74 06.5
Markab	13 38.9	N15 16.4
Menkar	314 16.0	N 4 08.3
Menkent	148 08.2	S36 26.1
Miaplacidus	221 40.5	S69 46.5
Mirfak	308 41.7	N49 54.1
Nunki	75 58.8	S26 16.7
Peacock	53 19.8	S56 41.4
Pollux	243 28.9	N27 59.7
Procyon	245 00.7	N 5 11.4
Rasalhague	96 06.7	N12 33.2
Regulus	207 44.4	N11 54.3
Rigel	281 13.0	S 8 11.3
Rigil Kent.	139 52.2	S60 53.4
Sabik	102 13.0	S15 44.3
Schedar	349 41.3	N56 36.2
Shaula	96 22.4	S37 06.7
Sirius	258 34.7	S16 44.1
Spica	158 31.9	S11 13.7
Suhail	222 53.3	S43 29.3
Vega	80 39.0	N38 47.8
Zuben'ubi	137 05.9	S16 05.7

	SHA	Mer.Pass.
	° '	h m
Venus	293 39.1	10 02
Mars	182 53.3	17 25
Jupiter	298 28.0	9 47
Saturn	157 58.9	19 03

	UT	SUN GHA	SUN Dec	MOON GHA	v	MOON Dec	d	HP
	d h	° ′	° ′	° ′	′	° ′	′	′
	26 00	179 17.3	N23 20.9	105 30.9	12.1	S 0 44.7	12.4	57.9
	01	194 17.1	20.8	120 02.0	12.1	0 57.1	12.5	57.9
	02	209 17.0	20.8	134 33.1	12.0	1 09.6	12.5	57.9
	03	224 16.9	. . 20.7	149 04.1	12.0	1 22.1	12.5	58.0
	04	239 16.8	20.6	163 35.1	11.9	1 34.6	12.5	58.0
	05	254 16.6	20.5	178 06.0	11.9	1 47.1	12.5	58.0
	06	269 16.5	N23 20.4	192 36.9	11.9	S 1 59.6	12.5	58.0
	07	284 16.4	20.3	207 07.8	11.8	2 12.1	12.5	58.1
TUESDAY	08	299 16.2	20.2	221 38.6	11.8	2 24.6	12.5	58.1
	09	314 16.1	. . 20.1	236 09.4	11.8	2 37.1	12.5	58.1
	10	329 16.0	20.0	250 40.2	11.7	2 49.6	12.5	58.1
	11	344 15.8	19.9	265 10.9	11.7	3 02.1	12.4	58.2
	12	359 15.7	N23 19.8	279 41.6	11.7	S 3 14.5	12.5	58.2
	13	14 15.6	19.7	294 12.3	11.5	3 27.0	12.5	58.2
	14	29 15.4	19.7	308 42.8	11.6	3 39.5	12.5	58.2
	15	44 15.3	. . 19.6	323 13.4	11.5	3 52.0	12.4	58.3
	16	59 15.2	19.5	337 43.9	11.5	4 04.4	12.5	58.3
	17	74 15.1	19.4	352 14.4	11.4	4 16.9	12.4	58.3
	18	89 14.9	N23 19.3	6 44.8	11.4	S 4 29.3	12.4	58.4
	19	104 14.8	19.2	21 15.2	11.3	4 41.7	12.4	58.4
	20	119 14.7	19.1	35 45.5	11.3	4 54.1	12.4	58.4
	21	134 14.5	. . 19.0	50 15.8	11.2	5 06.5	12.4	58.4
	22	149 14.4	18.9	64 46.0	11.2	5 18.9	12.4	58.5
	23	164 14.3	18.8	79 16.2	11.1	5 31.3	12.3	58.5
	27 00	179 14.1	N23 18.7	93 46.3	11.1	S 5 43.6	12.3	58.5
	01	194 14.0	18.5	108 16.4	11.0	5 55.9	12.3	58.5
	02	209 13.9	18.4	122 46.4	10.9	6 08.2	12.3	58.6
	03	224 13.8	. . 18.3	137 16.3	10.9	6 20.5	12.3	58.6
	04	239 13.6	18.2	151 46.2	10.9	6 32.8	12.2	58.6
	05	254 13.5	18.1	166 16.1	10.8	6 45.0	12.2	58.6
	06	269 13.4	N23 18.0	180 45.9	10.7	S 6 57.2	12.2	58.7
WEDNESDAY	07	284 13.2	17.9	195 15.6	10.7	7 09.4	12.2	58.7
	08	299 13.1	17.8	209 45.3	10.6	7 21.6	12.1	58.7
	09	314 13.0	. . 17.7	224 14.9	10.6	7 33.7	12.1	58.8
	10	329 12.9	17.6	238 44.5	10.5	7 45.8	12.1	58.8
	11	344 12.7	17.5	253 14.0	10.4	7 57.9	12.0	58.8
	12	359 12.6	N23 17.4	267 43.4	10.4	S 8 09.9	12.0	58.8
	13	14 12.5	17.2	282 12.8	10.3	8 21.9	12.0	58.9
	14	29 12.3	17.1	296 42.1	10.2	8 33.9	11.9	58.9
	15	44 12.2	. . 17.0	311 11.3	10.2	8 45.8	11.9	58.9
	16	59 12.1	16.9	325 40.5	10.1	8 57.7	11.8	58.9
	17	74 12.0	16.8	340 09.6	10.1	9 09.5	11.8	59.0
	18	89 11.8	N23 16.7	354 38.7	9.9	S 9 21.3	11.8	59.0
	19	104 11.7	16.6	9 07.6	10.0	9 33.1	11.7	59.0
	20	119 11.6	16.4	23 36.6	9.8	9 44.8	11.7	59.0
	21	134 11.4	. . 16.3	38 05.4	9.8	9 56.5	11.7	59.1
	22	149 11.3	16.2	52 34.2	9.7	10 08.2	11.6	59.1
	23	164 11.2	16.1	67 02.9	9.6	10 19.8	11.5	59.1
	28 00	179 11.1	N23 16.0	81 31.5	9.6	S10 31.3	11.5	59.1
	01	194 10.9	15.8	96 00.1	9.4	10 42.8	11.4	59.2
	02	209 10.8	15.7	110 28.5	9.4	10 54.2	11.4	59.2
	03	224 10.7	. . 15.6	124 56.9	9.4	11 05.6	11.4	59.2
	04	239 10.6	15.5	139 25.3	9.2	11 17.0	11.2	59.2
	05	254 10.4	15.4	153 53.5	9.2	11 28.2	11.3	59.3
	06	269 10.3	N23 15.2	168 21.7	9.1	S11 39.5	11.1	59.3
THURSDAY	07	284 10.2	15.1	182 49.8	9.1	11 50.6	11.1	59.3
	08	299 10.1	15.0	197 17.9	8.9	12 01.7	11.1	59.3
	09	314 09.9	. . 14.8	211 45.8	8.9	12 12.8	11.0	59.4
	10	329 09.8	14.7	226 13.7	8.8	12 23.8	10.9	59.4
	11	344 09.7	14.6	240 41.5	8.7	12 34.7	10.8	59.4
	12	359 09.5	N23 14.5	255 09.2	8.7	S12 45.5	10.8	59.4
	13	14 09.4	14.3	269 36.9	8.6	12 56.3	10.7	59.5
	14	29 09.3	14.2	284 04.5	8.5	13 07.0	10.7	59.5
	15	44 09.2	. . 14.1	298 32.0	8.4	13 17.7	10.6	59.5
	16	59 09.0	13.9	312 59.4	8.3	13 28.3	10.5	59.5
	17	74 08.9	13.8	327 26.7	8.2	13 38.8	10.4	59.6
	18	89 08.8	N23 13.7	341 53.9	8.2	S13 49.2	10.4	59.6
	19	104 08.7	13.5	356 21.1	8.1	13 59.6	10.2	59.6
	20	119 08.5	13.4	10 48.2	8.0	14 09.8	10.2	59.6
	21	134 08.4	. . 13.3	25 15.2	7.9	14 20.0	10.2	59.6
	22	149 08.3	13.1	39 42.1	7.8	14 30.2	10.0	59.7
	23	164 08.2	13.0	54 08.9	7.8	S14 40.2	10.0	59.7
		SD 15.8	*d* 0.1	SD 15.9		16.0		16.2

Lat.	Twilight Naut.	Twilight Civil	Sunrise	Moonrise 26	Moonrise 27	Moonrise 28	Moonrise 29
°	h m	h m	h m	h m	h m	h m	h m
N 72	□	□	□	12 03	14 06	16 23	■
N 70	□	□	□	11 59	13 52	15 55	18 13
68	□	□	□	11 55	13 41	15 34	17 33
66	□	□	□	11 51	13 32	15 17	17 06
64	////	////	01 36	11 48	13 24	15 04	16 45
62	////	////	02 13	11 46	13 18	14 52	16 29
60	////	00 56	02 39	11 44	13 12	14 43	16 15
N 58	////	01 44	02 59	11 42	13 07	14 35	16 03
56	////	02 14	03 16	11 40	13 03	14 27	15 53
54	00 51	02 36	03 30	11 39	12 59	14 21	15 44
52	01 36	02 53	03 42	11 38	12 55	14 15	15 36
50	02 03	03 08	03 53	11 36	12 52	14 10	15 28
45	02 48	03 38	04 15	11 34	12 45	13 58	15 13
N 40	03 19	04 00	04 33	11 32	12 39	13 49	15 00
35	03 42	04 19	04 48	11 30	12 34	13 41	14 50
30	04 00	04 34	05 01	11 28	12 30	13 34	14 40
20	04 29	04 59	05 23	11 25	12 23	13 22	14 25
N 10	04 52	05 19	05 42	11 23	12 16	13 12	14 11
0	05 11	05 37	05 59	11 20	12 10	13 02	13 58
S 10	05 28	05 54	06 17	11 18	12 04	12 53	13 45
20	05 44	06 11	06 35	11 16	11 58	12 42	13 31
30	06 00	06 30	06 56	11 13	11 51	12 31	13 16
35	06 09	06 41	07 09	11 12	11 46	12 24	13 07
40	06 18	06 52	07 23	11 10	11 42	12 17	12 57
45	06 28	07 06	07 39	11 08	11 36	12 08	12 45
S 50	06 40	07 22	08 00	11 06	11 30	11 58	12 31
52	06 45	07 29	08 10	11 05	11 27	11 53	12 24
54	06 51	07 37	08 21	11 04	11 24	11 48	12 17
56	06 57	07 46	08 33	11 02	11 21	11 42	12 08
58	07 04	07 56	08 48	11 01	11 17	11 35	11 59
S 60	07 11	08 08	09 05	10 59	11 12	11 28	11 49

Lat.	Sunset	Twilight Civil	Twilight Naut.	Moonset 26	Moonset 27	Moonset 28	Moonset 29
°	h m	h m	h m	h m	h m	h m	h m
N 72	□	□	□	22 32	22 14	21 47	■
N 70	□	□	□	22 40	22 30	22 17	21 56
68	□	□	□	22 46	22 43	22 40	22 37
66	□	□	□	22 51	22 54	22 57	23 05
64	22 30	////	////	22 56	23 03	23 12	23 27
62	21 53	////	////	23 00	23 10	23 24	23 44
60	21 27	23 09	////	23 03	23 17	23 35	23 59
N 58	21 07	22 21	////	23 06	23 23	23 44	24 11
56	20 50	21 52	////	23 09	23 28	23 52	24 22
54	20 36	21 30	23 14	23 12	23 33	23 59	24 31
52	20 24	21 13	22 30	23 14	23 37	24 05	00 05
50	20 13	20 58	22 03	23 16	23 41	24 11	00 11
45	19 51	20 28	21 18	23 20	23 50	24 24	00 24
N 40	19 33	20 06	20 47	23 24	23 57	24 34	00 34
35	19 18	19 48	20 24	23 27	24 03	00 03	00 43
30	19 05	19 32	20 06	23 30	24 09	00 09	00 51
20	18 43	19 08	19 37	23 35	24 18	00 18	01 05
N 10	18 24	18 47	19 14	23 40	24 27	00 27	01 17
0	18 07	18 29	18 56	23 44	24 34	00 34	01 28
S 10	17 49	18 12	18 39	23 48	24 42	00 42	01 40
20	17 31	17 55	18 23	23 52	24 51	00 51	01 52
30	17 10	17 36	18 06	23 57	25 00	01 00	02 06
35	16 58	17 26	17 57	24 00	00 00	01 06	02 14
40	16 44	17 14	17 48	24 04	00 04	01 12	02 23
45	16 27	17 01	17 38	24 07	00 07	01 20	02 34
S 50	16 06	16 45	17 26	24 12	00 12	01 29	02 47
52	15 57	16 37	17 21	24 14	00 14	01 33	02 53
54	15 45	16 29	17 15	24 17	00 17	01 37	03 00
56	15 33	16 20	17 09	24 19	00 19	01 42	03 07
58	15 18	16 10	17 03	24 22	00 22	01 48	03 16
S 60	15 01	15 58	16 55	24 25	00 25	01 54	03 26

Day	SUN Eqn. of Time 00^h	SUN Eqn. of Time 12^h	SUN Mer. Pass.	MOON Mer. Pass. Upper	MOON Mer. Pass. Lower	MOON Age	MOON Phase
d	m s	m s	h m	h m	h m	d %	
26	02 51	02 57	12 03	17 32	05 08	07 43	
27	03 03	03 09	12 03	18 22	05 57	08 54	◐
28	03 15	03 22	12 03	19 15	06 48	09 65	

UT	ARIES	VENUS −4.6		MARS +0.9		JUPITER −2.0		SATURN +0.7		STARS		
	GHA	GHA	Dec	GHA	Dec	GHA	Dec	GHA	Dec	Name	SHA	Dec
d h	° ′	° ′	° ′	° ′	° ′	° ′	° ′	° ′	° ′		° ′	° ′
29 00	277 28.8	211 04.2 N17 39.7		99 27.1 N 1 21.4		215 29.8 N20 09.5		75 27.4 S 6 28.7		Acamar	315 19.1 S40 15.1	
01	292 31.3	226 06.5	39.5	114 28.4	20.9	230 31.7	09.6	90 29.9	28.7	Achernar	335 27.4 S57 10.1	
02	307 33.8	241 08.8	39.3	129 29.7	20.3	245 33.6	09.7	105 32.4	28.7	Acrux	173 10.0 S63 10.5	
03	322 36.2	256 11.1 . .	39.1	144 31.0 . .	19.7	260 35.5 . .	09.8	120 34.8 . .	28.7	Adhara	255 13.4 S28 59.5	
04	337 38.7	271 13.4	38.9	159 32.3	19.2	275 37.4	09.9	135 37.3	28.7	Aldebaran	290 50.4 N16 31.9	
05	352 41.2	286 15.6	38.7	174 33.6	18.6	290 39.3	10.0	150 39.7	28.7			
06	7 43.6	301 17.9 N17 38.5		189 34.9 N 1 18.1		305 41.2 N20 10.1		165 42.2 S 6 28.8		Alioth	166 21.2 N55 53.7	
07	22 46.1	316 20.2	38.3	204 36.2	17.5	320 43.1	10.2	180 44.6	28.8	Alkaid	152 59.3 N49 15.3	
08	37 48.6	331 22.4	38.1	219 37.5	17.0	335 45.0	10.3	195 47.1	28.8	Al Na'ir	27 44.3 S46 53.7	
F 09	52 51.0	346 24.7 . .	37.9	234 38.8 . .	16.4	350 46.9 . .	10.4	210 49.5 . .	28.8	Alnilam	275 47.4 S 1 11.7	
R 10	67 53.5	1 26.9	37.7	249 40.1	15.9	5 48.8	10.5	225 52.0	28.8	Alphard	217 57.0 S 8 42.9	
I 11	82 55.9	16 29.2	37.5	264 41.4	15.3	20 50.7	10.6	240 54.4	28.8			
D 12	97 58.4	31 31.4 N17 37.3		279 42.7 N 1 14.7		35 52.6 N20 10.7		255 56.9 S 6 28.9		Alphecca	126 11.3 N26 40.5	
A 13	113 00.9	46 33.7	37.1	294 44.0	14.2	50 54.5	10.8	270 59.3	28.9	Alpheratz	357 44.1 N29 09.5	
Y 14	128 03.3	61 35.9	36.9	309 45.3	13.6	65 56.4	10.9	286 01.8	28.9	Altair	62 08.6 N 8 54.2	
15	143 05.8	76 38.1 . .	36.8	324 46.6 . .	13.1	80 58.3 . .	11.0	301 04.2 . .	28.9	Ankaa	353 16.3 S42 14.0	
16	158 08.3	91 40.4	36.6	339 47.9	12.5	96 00.2	11.1	316 06.7	28.9	Antares	112 26.5 S26 27.6	
17	173 10.7	106 42.6	36.4	354 49.3	12.0	111 02.1	11.2	331 09.1	28.9			
18	188 13.2	121 44.8 N17 36.2		9 50.6 N 1 11.4		126 04.0 N20 11.3		346 11.6 S 6 29.0		Arcturus	145 56.2 N19 07.1	
19	203 15.7	136 47.0	36.0	24 51.9	10.9	141 05.9	11.4	1 14.0	29.0	Atria	107 28.6 S69 03.0	
20	218 18.1	151 49.3	35.8	39 53.2	10.3	156 07.8	11.5	16 16.5	29.0	Avior	234 18.9 S59 33.2	
21	233 20.6	166 51.5 . .	35.7	54 54.5 . .	09.7	171 09.7 . .	11.6	31 18.9 . .	29.0	Bellatrix	278 33.0 N 6 21.6	
22	248 23.1	181 53.7	35.5	69 55.8	09.2	186 11.6	11.7	46 21.4	29.0	Betelgeuse	271 02.3 N 7 24.4	
23	263 25.5	196 55.9	35.3	84 57.1	08.6	201 13.6	11.8	61 23.8	29.0			
30 00	278 28.0	211 58.1 N17 35.1		99 58.4 N 1 08.1		216 15.5 N20 11.9		76 26.3 S 6 29.1		Canopus	263 57.0 S52 42.2	
01	293 30.4	227 00.3	35.0	114 59.7	07.5	231 17.4	12.0	91 28.7	29.1	Capella	280 35.9 N46 00.4	
02	308 32.9	242 02.5	34.8	130 01.0	06.9	246 19.3	12.1	106 31.2	29.1	Deneb	49 31.5 N45 19.5	
03	323 35.4	257 04.7 . .	34.6	145 02.3 . .	06.4	261 21.2 . .	12.2	121 33.6 . .	29.1	Denebola	182 34.4 N14 30.1	
04	338 37.8	272 06.9	34.4	160 03.6	05.8	276 23.1	12.3	136 36.1	29.1	Diphda	348 56.6 S17 54.9	
05	353 40.3	287 09.0	34.3	175 04.9	05.3	291 25.0	12.4	151 38.5	29.1			
06	8 42.8	302 11.2 N17 34.1		190 06.2 N 1 04.7		306 26.9 N20 12.5		166 41.0 S 6 29.2		Dubhe	193 52.8 N61 41.2	
07	23 45.2	317 13.4	33.9	205 07.5	04.2	321 28.8	12.6	181 43.4	29.2	Elnath	278 13.8 N28 36.9	
S 08	38 47.7	332 15.6	33.8	220 08.8	03.6	336 30.7	12.7	196 45.9	29.2	Eltanin	90 45.9 N51 29.4	
A 09	53 50.2	347 17.7 . .	33.6	235 10.1 . .	03.0	351 32.6 . .	12.8	211 48.3 . .	29.2	Enif	33 47.5 N 9 56.1	
T 10	68 52.6	2 19.9	33.5	250 11.4	02.5	6 34.5	12.9	226 50.8	29.2	Fomalhaut	15 24.5 S29 33.1	
U 11	83 55.1	17 22.0	33.3	265 12.7	01.9	21 36.4	13.0	241 53.2	29.3			
R 12	98 57.6	32 24.2 N17 33.1		280 14.0 N 1 01.4		36 38.3 N20 13.1		256 55.7 S 6 29.3		Gacrux	172 01.6 S57 11.3	
D 13	114 00.0	47 26.3	33.0	295 15.3	00.8	51 40.2	13.2	271 58.1	29.3	Gienah	175 53.0 S17 36.9	
A 14	129 02.5	62 28.5	32.8	310 16.6	1 00.2	66 42.1	13.3	287 00.6	29.3	Hadar	148 48.5 S60 26.3	
Y 15	144 04.9	77 30.6 . .	32.7	325 17.9	0 59.7	81 44.0 . .	13.4	302 03.0 . .	29.3	Hamal	328 01.6 N23 31.2	
16	159 07.4	92 32.8	32.5	340 19.2	59.1	96 45.9	13.5	317 05.5	29.3	Kaus Aust.	83 44.3 S34 22.6	
17	174 09.9	107 34.9	32.4	355 20.5	58.6	111 47.8	13.6	332 07.9	29.4			
18	189 12.3	122 37.0 N17 32.2		10 21.7 N 0 58.0		126 49.8 N20 13.7		347 10.4 S 6 29.4		Kochab	137 19.3 N74 06.5	
19	204 14.8	137 39.2	32.1	25 23.0	57.5	141 51.7	13.8	2 12.8	29.4	Markab	13 38.9 N15 16.4	
20	219 17.3	152 41.3	31.9	40 24.3	56.9	156 53.6	13.9	17 15.3	29.4	Menkar	314 15.9 N 4 08.3	
21	234 19.7	167 43.4 . .	31.8	55 25.6 . .	56.3	171 55.5 . .	14.0	32 17.7 . .	29.4	Menkent	148 08.2 S36 26.1	
22	249 22.2	182 45.5	31.6	70 26.9	55.8	186 57.4	14.1	47 20.2	29.5	Miaplacidus	221 40.5 S69 46.5	
23	264 24.7	197 47.6	31.5	85 28.2	55.2	201 59.3	14.2	62 22.6	29.5			
1 00	279 27.1	212 49.8 N17 31.3		100 29.5 N 0 54.7		217 01.2 N20 14.3		77 25.1 S 6 29.5		Mirfak	308 41.6 N49 54.1	
01	294 29.6	227 51.9	31.2	115 30.8	54.1	232 03.1	14.4	92 27.5	29.5	Nunki	75 58.8 S26 16.7	
02	309 32.1	242 54.0	31.1	130 32.1	53.5	247 05.0	14.5	107 29.9	29.5	Peacock	53 19.7 S56 41.4	
03	324 34.5	257 56.1 . .	30.9	145 33.4 . .	53.0	262 06.9 . .	14.6	122 32.4 . .	29.5	Pollux	243 28.9 N27 59.7	
04	339 37.0	272 58.2	30.8	160 34.7	52.4	277 08.8	14.7	137 34.8	29.6	Procyon	245 00.7 N 5 11.4	
05	354 39.4	288 00.2	30.6	175 36.0	51.9	292 10.7	14.8	152 37.3	29.6			
06	9 41.9	303 02.3 N17 30.5		190 37.3 N 0 51.3		307 12.6 N20 14.9		167 39.7 S 6 29.6		Rasalhague	96 06.7 N12 33.2	
07	24 44.4	318 04.4	30.4	205 38.6	50.7	322 14.5	15.0	182 42.2	29.6	Regulus	207 44.4 N11 54.3	
08	39 46.8	333 06.5	30.2	220 39.9	50.2	337 16.5	15.1	197 44.6	29.6	Rigel	281 13.0 S 8 11.3	
S 09	54 49.3	348 08.6 . .	30.1	235 41.2 . .	49.6	352 18.4 . .	15.2	212 47.1 . .	29.7	Rigil Kent.	139 52.3 S60 53.4	
U 10	69 51.8	3 10.6	30.0	250 42.5	49.0	7 20.3	15.3	227 49.5	29.7	Sabik	102 13.0 S15 44.3	
N 11	84 54.2	18 12.7	29.9	265 43.7	48.5	22 22.2	15.4	242 51.9	29.7			
D 12	99 56.7	33 14.8 N17 29.7		280 45.0 N 0 47.9		37 24.1 N20 15.5		257 54.4 S 6 29.7		Schedar	349 41.3 N56 36.2	
A 13	114 59.2	48 16.8	29.6	295 46.3	47.4	52 26.0	15.6	272 56.8	29.7	Shaula	96 22.4 S37 06.7	
Y 14	130 01.6	63 18.9	29.4	310 47.6	46.8	67 27.9	15.7	287 59.3	29.8	Sirius	258 34.6 S16 44.1	
15	145 04.1	78 20.9 . .	29.4	325 48.9 . .	46.2	82 29.8 . .	15.8	303 01.7 . .	29.8	Spica	158 31.9 S11 13.7	
16	160 06.5	93 23.0	29.2	340 50.2	45.7	97 31.7	15.9	318 04.2	29.8	Suhail	222 53.3 S43 29.3	
17	175 09.0	108 25.0	29.1	355 51.5	45.1	112 33.6	16.0	333 06.6	29.8			
18	190 11.5	123 27.1 N17 29.0		10 52.8 N 0 44.6		127 35.5 N20 16.1		348 09.1 S 6 29.8		Vega	80 39.0 N38 47.9	
19	205 13.9	138 29.1	28.9	25 54.1	44.0	142 37.4	16.2	3 11.5	29.9	Zuben'ubi	137 05.9 S16 05.7	
20	220 16.4	153 31.2	28.8	40 55.4	43.4	157 39.4	16.3	18 13.9	29.9		SHA	Mer. Pass.
21	235 18.9	168 33.2 . .	28.6	55 56.6 . .	42.9	172 41.3 . .	16.4	33 16.4 . .	29.9		° ′	h m
22	250 21.3	183 35.2	28.5	70 57.9	42.3	187 43.2	16.5	48 18.8	29.9	Venus	293 30.1	9 51
23	265 23.8	198 37.2	28.4	85 59.2	41.7	202 45.1	16.6	63 21.3	29.9	Mars	181 30.4	17 19
	h m									Jupiter	297 47.5	9 34
Mer. Pass.	5 25.2	v 2.2	d 0.2	v 1.3	d 0.6	v 1.9	d 0.1	v 2.4	d 0.0	Saturn	157 58.3	18 51

UT	SUN GHA	Dec	MOON GHA	v	Dec	d	HP
d h	° ′	° ′	° ′	′	° ′	′	′
29 00	179 08.0	N23 12.9	68 35.7	7.7	S14 50.2	9.8	59.7
01	194 07.9	12.7	83 02.4	7.6	15 00.0	9.8	59.7
02	209 07.8	12.6	97 29.0	7.5	15 09.8	9.7	59.8
03	224 07.7	.. 12.4	111 55.5	7.4	15 19.5	9.6	59.8
04	239 07.5	12.3	126 21.9	7.3	15 29.1	9.6	59.8
05	254 07.4	12.2	140 48.2	7.3	15 38.7	9.4	59.8
06	269 07.3	N23 12.0	155 14.5	7.2	S15 48.1	9.3	59.8
07	284 07.2	11.9	169 40.7	7.1	15 57.4	9.3	59.9
F 08	299 07.0	11.7	184 06.8	7.0	16 06.7	9.1	59.9
R 09	314 06.9	.. 11.6	198 32.8	6.9	16 15.8	9.1	59.9
I 10	329 06.8	11.5	212 58.7	6.9	16 24.9	8.9	59.9
11	344 06.7	11.3	227 24.6	6.7	16 33.8	8.9	59.9
D 12	359 06.5	N23 11.2	241 50.3	6.7	S16 42.7	8.7	60.0
A 13	14 06.4	11.0	256 16.0	6.6	16 51.4	8.6	60.0
Y 14	29 06.3	10.9	270 41.6	6.5	17 00.0	8.6	60.0
15	44 06.2	.. 10.7	285 07.1	6.5	17 08.6	8.4	60.0
16	59 06.1	10.6	299 32.6	6.3	17 17.0	8.3	60.0
17	74 05.9	10.4	313 57.9	6.3	17 25.3	8.3	60.0
18	89 05.8	N23 10.3	328 23.2	6.2	S17 33.6	8.1	60.1
19	104 05.7	10.1	342 48.4	6.1	17 41.7	8.0	60.1
20	119 05.6	10.0	357 13.5	6.1	17 49.7	7.8	60.1
21	134 05.4	.. 09.8	11 38.6	5.9	17 57.5	7.8	60.1
22	149 05.3	09.7	26 03.5	5.9	18 05.3	7.7	60.1
23	164 05.2	09.5	40 28.4	5.8	18 13.0	7.5	60.1
30 00	179 05.1	N23 09.4	54 53.2	5.7	S18 20.5	7.4	60.2
01	194 04.9	09.2	69 17.9	5.7	18 27.9	7.3	60.2
02	209 04.8	09.1	83 42.6	5.6	18 35.2	7.2	60.2
03	224 04.7	.. 08.9	98 07.2	5.5	18 42.4	7.0	60.2
04	239 04.6	08.7	112 31.7	5.4	18 49.4	6.9	60.2
05	254 04.5	08.6	126 56.1	5.4	18 56.3	6.8	60.2
06	269 04.3	N23 08.4	141 20.5	5.3	S19 03.1	6.7	60.3
07	284 04.2	08.3	155 44.8	5.2	19 09.8	6.6	60.3
S 08	299 04.1	08.1	170 09.0	5.1	19 16.4	6.4	60.3
A 09	314 04.0	.. 07.9	184 33.1	5.1	19 22.8	6.3	60.3
T 10	329 03.9	07.8	198 57.2	5.0	19 29.1	6.1	60.3
U 11	344 03.7	07.6	213 21.2	5.0	19 35.2	6.0	60.3
R 12	359 03.6	N23 07.5	227 45.2	4.8	S19 41.2	5.9	60.3
D 13	14 03.5	07.3	242 09.0	4.8	19 47.1	5.8	60.3
A 14	29 03.4	07.1	256 32.8	4.8	19 52.9	5.6	60.4
Y 15	44 03.2	.. 07.0	270 56.6	4.7	19 58.5	5.4	60.4
16	59 03.1	06.8	285 20.3	4.6	20 03.9	5.4	60.4
17	74 03.0	06.6	299 43.9	4.6	20 09.3	5.2	60.4
18	89 02.9	N23 06.5	314 07.5	4.5	S20 14.5	5.0	60.4
19	104 02.8	06.3	328 31.0	4.4	20 19.5	5.0	60.4
20	119 02.6	06.1	342 54.4	4.4	20 24.5	4.7	60.4
21	134 02.5	.. 06.0	357 17.8	4.4	20 29.2	4.6	60.4
22	149 02.4	05.8	11 41.2	4.3	20 33.8	4.5	60.4
23	164 02.3	05.6	26 04.5	4.2	20 38.3	4.4	60.4
1 00	179 02.2	N23 05.5	40 27.7	4.2	S20 42.7	4.2	60.4
01	194 02.0	05.3	54 50.9	4.2	20 46.9	4.0	60.5
02	209 01.9	05.1	69 14.1	4.1	20 50.9	3.9	60.5
03	224 01.8	.. 04.9	83 37.2	4.0	20 54.8	3.7	60.5
04	239 01.7	04.8	98 00.2	4.0	20 58.5	3.6	60.5
05	254 01.6	04.6	112 23.2	4.0	21 02.1	3.5	60.5
06	269 01.5	N23 04.4	126 46.2	3.9	S21 05.6	3.3	60.5
07	284 01.3	04.2	141 09.1	3.9	21 08.9	3.1	60.5
S 08	299 01.2	04.1	155 32.0	3.9	21 12.0	3.0	60.5
U 09	314 01.1	.. 03.9	169 54.9	3.8	21 15.0	2.8	60.5
N 10	329 01.0	03.7	184 17.7	3.8	21 17.8	2.7	60.5
D 11	344 00.9	03.5	198 40.5	3.8	21 20.5	2.5	60.5
A 12	359 00.7	N23 03.3	213 03.3	3.7	S21 23.0	2.4	60.5
Y 13	14 00.6	03.2	227 26.0	3.7	21 25.4	2.2	60.5
14	29 00.5	03.0	241 48.7	3.7	21 27.6	2.1	60.5
15	44 00.4	.. 02.8	256 11.4	3.7	21 29.7	1.9	60.5
16	59 00.3	02.6	270 34.1	3.6	21 31.6	1.7	60.5
17	74 00.2	02.4	284 56.7	3.7	21 33.3	1.6	60.5
18	89 00.0	N23 02.3	299 19.4	3.6	S21 34.9	1.4	60.5
19	103 59.9	02.1	313 42.0	3.6	21 36.3	1.3	60.5
20	118 59.8	01.9	328 04.6	3.6	21 37.6	1.1	60.5
21	133 59.7	.. 01.7	342 27.2	3.6	21 38.7	1.0	60.5
22	148 59.6	01.5	356 49.8	3.5	21 39.7	0.8	60.5
23	163 59.5	01.3	11 12.3	3.6	S21 40.5	0.6	60.5
	SD 15.8	d 0.2	SD 16.3		16.4		16.5

Twilight / Sunrise / Moonrise

Lat.	Naut.	Civil	Sunrise	Moonrise 29	30	1	2
°	h m	h m	h m	h m	h m	h m	h m
N 72	□	□	□	■	■	■	■
N 70	□	□	□	■	■	■	■
68	□	□	□	18 13	■	■	■
66	////	////	00 11	17 33	19 40	21 41	22 17
64	////	////	01 40	17 06	18 54	20 25	21 19
62	////	////	02 16	16 45	18 24	19 47	20 44
60	////	01 02	02 41	16 29	18 01	19 21	20 20
N 58	////	01 48	03 01	16 03	17 28	18 44	19 43
56	////	02 16	03 18	15 53	17 15	18 29	19 30
54	00 57	02 38	03 32	15 44	17 04	18 17	19 18
52	01 39	02 56	03 44	15 36	16 54	18 06	19 07
50	02 06	03 10	03 55	15 28	16 45	17 56	18 57
45	02 50	03 40	04 17	15 13	16 27	17 36	18 37
N 40	03 20	04 02	04 35	15 00	16 12	17 19	18 21
35	03 43	04 20	04 49	14 50	15 59	17 06	18 07
30	04 02	04 35	05 02	14 40	15 48	16 54	17 56
20	04 30	04 59	05 24	14 25	15 29	16 33	17 35
N 10	04 53	05 20	05 43	14 11	15 12	16 15	17 17
0	05 11	05 38	06 00	13 58	14 57	15 58	17 01
S 10	05 28	05 55	06 17	13 45	14 42	15 42	16 44
20	05 44	06 12	06 36	13 31	14 25	15 24	16 26
30	06 00	06 30	06 57	13 16	14 07	15 04	16 06
35	06 09	06 41	07 09	13 07	13 56	14 52	15 54
40	06 18	06 52	07 23	12 57	13 44	14 38	15 40
45	06 28	07 06	07 39	12 45	13 29	14 22	15 24
S 50	06 40	07 21	08 00	12 31	13 11	14 02	15 04
52	06 45	07 29	08 09	12 24	13 03	13 53	14 55
54	06 51	07 37	08 20	12 17	12 54	13 43	14 44
56	06 57	07 46	08 33	12 08	12 44	13 31	14 32
58	07 03	07 56	08 47	11 59	12 32	13 17	14 18
S 60	07 11	08 07	09 04	11 49	12 18	13 01	14 02

Sunset / Twilight / Moonset

Lat.	Sunset	Civil	Naut.	Moonset 29	30	1	2
°	h m	h m	h m	h m	h m	h m	h m
N 72	□	□	□	■	■	■	■
N 70	□	□	□	21 56	■	■	■
68	□	□	□	22 37	22 35	22 44	24 19
66	23 45	////	////	23 05	23 22	24 01	00 01
64	22 26	////	////	23 27	23 52	24 38	00 38
62	21 51	////	////	23 44	24 15	00 15	01 04
60	21 25	23 04	////	23 59	24 34	00 34	01 25
N 58	21 06	22 19	////	24 11	00 11	00 49	01 42
56	20 49	21 51	////	24 22	00 22	01 02	01 56
54	20 35	21 29	23 09	24 31	00 31	01 14	02 09
52	20 23	21 12	22 28	00 05	00 40	01 24	02 20
50	20 13	20 57	22 01	00 11	00 47	01 33	02 29
45	19 51	20 28	21 17	00 24	01 04	01 52	02 50
N 40	19 33	20 05	20 47	00 34	01 17	02 08	03 06
35	19 18	19 48	20 24	00 43	01 29	02 21	03 20
30	19 05	19 33	20 06	00 51	01 39	02 33	03 33
20	18 43	19 08	19 37	01 05	01 56	02 52	03 53
N 10	18 25	18 48	19 15	01 17	02 11	03 10	04 11
0	18 07	18 30	18 56	01 28	02 25	03 26	04 28
S 10	17 50	18 13	18 39	01 40	02 40	03 42	04 45
20	17 32	17 56	18 23	01 52	02 55	03 59	05 03
30	17 11	17 37	18 07	02 06	03 12	04 19	05 23
35	16 59	17 27	17 59	02 14	03 23	04 31	05 35
40	16 45	17 15	17 49	02 23	03 34	04 44	05 49
45	16 28	17 02	17 39	02 34	03 48	05 00	06 06
S 50	16 08	16 46	17 28	02 47	04 05	05 19	06 26
52	15 58	16 39	17 23	02 53	04 13	05 28	06 35
54	15 47	16 31	17 17	03 00	04 22	05 39	06 46
56	15 35	16 22	17 11	03 07	04 32	05 50	06 58
58	15 21	16 12	17 04	03 16	04 43	06 04	07 12
S 60	15 04	16 01	16 57	03 26	04 56	06 20	07 28

SUN / MOON

Day	Eqn. of Time 00ʰ	12ʰ	Mer. Pass.	MOON Mer. Pass. Upper	Lower	Age	Phase
d	m s	m s	h m	h m	h m	d	%
29	03 28	03 34	12 04	20 12	07 43	10	76
30	03 39	03 45	12 04	21 11	08 41	11	85
1	03 51	03 57	12 04	22 13	09 42	12	93

UT	ARIES	VENUS −4.7		MARS +0.9		JUPITER −2.1		SATURN +0.7		STARS		
	GHA	GHA	Dec	GHA	Dec	GHA	Dec	GHA	Dec	Name	SHA	Dec
d h	° ′	° ′	° ′	° ′	° ′	° ′	° ′	° ′	° ′		° ′	° ′
2 00	280 26.3	213 39.3	N17 28.3	101 00.5	N 0 41.2	217 47.0	N20 16.7	78 23.7	S 6 30.0	Acamar	315 19.1	S40 15.1
01	295 28.7	228 41.3	28.2	116 01.8	40.6	232 48.9	16.8	93 26.2	30.0	Achernar	335 27.4	S57 10.1
02	310 31.2	243 43.3	28.1	131 03.1	40.1	247 50.8	16.9	108 28.6	30.0	Acrux	173 10.0	S63 10.5
03	325 33.7	258 45.3	.. 28.0	146 04.4	.. 39.5	262 52.7	.. 16.9	123 31.0	.. 30.0	Adhara	255 13.4	S28 59.5
04	340 36.1	273 47.3	27.9	161 05.7	38.9	277 54.6	17.0	138 33.5	30.0	Aldebaran	290 50.4	N16 32.0
05	355 38.6	288 49.3	27.8	176 06.9	38.4	292 56.5	17.1	153 35.9	30.1			
06	10 41.0	303 51.3	N17 27.7	191 08.2	N 0 37.8	307 58.4	N20 17.2	168 38.4	S 6 30.1	Alioth	166 21.2	N55 53.7
07	25 43.5	318 53.3	27.6	206 09.5	37.2	323 00.4	17.3	183 40.8	30.1	Alkaid	152 59.3	N49 15.3
08	40 46.0	333 55.3	27.5	221 10.8	36.7	338 02.3	17.4	198 43.2	30.1	Al Na'ir	27 44.2	S46 53.7
M 09	55 48.4	348 57.3	.. 27.4	236 12.1	.. 36.1	353 04.2	.. 17.5	213 45.7	.. 30.2	Alnilam	275 47.3	S 1 11.7
O 10	70 50.9	3 59.3	27.3	251 13.4	35.5	8 06.1	17.6	228 48.1	30.2	Alphard	217 57.0	S 8 42.9
N 11	85 53.4	19 01.2	27.2	266 14.7	35.0	23 08.0	17.7	243 50.6	30.2			
D 12	100 55.8	34 03.2	N17 27.1	281 15.9	N 0 34.4	38 09.9	N20 17.8	258 53.0	S 6 30.2	Alphecca	126 11.3	N26 40.5
A 13	115 58.3	49 05.2	27.0	296 17.2	33.9	53 11.8	17.9	273 55.5	30.2	Alpheratz	357 44.1	N29 09.5
Y 14	131 00.8	64 07.2	26.9	311 18.5	33.3	68 13.7	18.0	288 57.9	30.3	Altair	62 08.5	N 8 54.3
15	146 03.2	79 09.1	.. 26.8	326 19.8	.. 32.7	83 15.6	.. 18.1	304 00.3	.. 30.3	Ankaa	353 16.3	S42 13.9
16	161 05.7	94 11.1	26.7	341 21.1	32.2	98 17.6	18.2	319 02.8	30.3	Antares	112 26.7	S26 27.6
17	176 08.2	109 13.0	26.6	356 22.4	31.6	113 19.5	18.3	334 05.2	30.3			
18	191 10.6	124 15.0	N17 26.5	11 23.6	N 0 31.0	128 21.4	N20 18.4	349 07.7	S 6 30.3	Arcturus	145 56.2	N19 07.1
19	206 13.1	139 17.0	26.4	26 24.9	30.5	143 23.3	18.5	4 10.1	30.4	Atria	107 28.6	S69 03.0
20	221 15.5	154 18.9	26.3	41 26.2	29.9	158 25.2	18.6	19 12.5	30.4	Avior	234 18.9	S59 33.2
21	236 18.0	169 20.8	.. 26.2	56 27.5	.. 29.3	173 27.1	.. 18.7	34 15.0	.. 30.4	Bellatrix	278 33.0	N 6 21.6
22	251 20.5	184 22.8	26.2	71 28.8	28.8	188 29.0	18.8	49 17.4	30.4	Betelgeuse	271 02.3	N 7 24.4
23	266 22.9	199 24.7	26.1	86 30.1	28.2	203 30.9	18.9	64 19.8	30.5			
3 00	281 25.4	214 26.7	N17 26.0	101 31.3	N 0 27.6	218 32.8	N20 19.0	79 22.3	S 6 30.5	Canopus	263 57.0	S52 42.2
01	296 27.9	229 28.6	25.9	116 32.6	27.1	233 34.8	19.1	94 24.7	30.5	Capella	280 35.9	N46 00.4
02	311 30.3	244 30.5	25.8	131 33.9	26.5	248 36.7	19.2	109 27.2	30.5	Deneb	49 31.5	N45 19.6
03	326 32.8	259 32.4	.. 25.8	146 35.2	.. 26.0	263 38.6	.. 19.3	124 29.6	.. 30.5	Denebola	182 34.4	N14 30.1
04	341 35.3	274 34.4	25.7	161 36.5	25.4	278 40.5	19.4	139 32.0	30.6	Diphda	348 56.5	S17 54.9
05	356 37.7	289 36.3	25.6	176 37.7	24.8	293 42.4	19.4	154 34.5	30.6			
06	11 40.2	304 38.2	N17 25.5	191 39.0	N 0 24.3	308 44.3	N20 19.5	169 36.9	S 6 30.6	Dubhe	193 52.8	N61 41.2
07	26 42.7	319 40.1	25.5	206 40.3	23.7	323 46.2	19.6	184 39.4	30.6	Elnath	278 13.8	N28 36.9
08	41 45.1	334 42.0	25.4	221 41.6	23.1	338 48.1	19.7	199 41.8	30.7	Eltanin	90 45.9	N51 29.4
T 09	56 47.6	349 43.9	.. 25.3	236 42.9	.. 22.6	353 50.1	.. 19.8	214 44.2	.. 30.7	Enif	33 47.5	N 9 56.1
U 10	71 50.0	4 45.8	25.2	251 44.1	22.0	8 52.0	19.9	229 46.7	30.7	Fomalhaut	15 24.5	S29 33.0
E 11	86 52.5	19 47.7	25.2	266 45.4	21.4	23 53.9	20.0	244 49.1	30.7			
S 12	101 55.0	34 49.6	N17 25.1	281 46.7	N 0 20.9	38 55.8	N20 20.1	259 51.5	S 6 30.7	Gacrux	172 01.6	S57 11.3
D 13	116 57.4	49 51.5	25.0	296 48.0	20.3	53 57.7	20.2	274 54.0	30.8	Gienah	175 53.0	S17 36.9
A 14	131 59.9	64 53.4	25.0	311 49.2	19.7	68 59.6	20.3	289 56.4	30.8	Hadar	148 48.6	S60 26.3
Y 15	147 02.4	79 55.2	.. 24.9	326 50.5	.. 19.2	84 01.5	.. 20.4	304 58.8	.. 30.8	Hamal	328 01.6	N23 31.2
16	162 04.8	94 57.1	24.8	341 51.8	18.6	99 03.4	20.5	320 01.3	30.8	Kaus Aust.	83 44.3	S34 22.6
17	177 07.3	109 59.0	24.8	356 53.1	18.0	114 05.4	20.6	335 03.7	30.9			
18	192 09.8	125 00.9	N17 24.7	11 54.3	N 0 17.5	129 07.3	N20 20.7	350 06.2	S 6 30.9	Kochab	137 19.4	N74 06.5
19	207 12.2	140 02.7	24.7	26 55.6	16.9	144 09.2	20.8	5 08.6	30.9	Markab	13 38.8	N15 16.4
20	222 14.7	155 04.6	24.6	41 56.9	16.3	159 11.1	20.9	20 11.0	30.9	Menkar	314 15.9	N 4 08.3
21	237 17.2	170 06.4	.. 24.5	56 58.2	.. 15.8	174 13.0	.. 21.0	35 13.5	.. 31.0	Menkent	148 08.2	S36 26.1
22	252 19.6	185 08.3	24.5	71 59.4	15.2	189 14.9	21.1	50 15.9	31.0	Miaplacidus	221 40.6	S69 46.4
23	267 22.1	200 10.2	24.4	87 00.7	14.6	204 16.8	21.2	65 18.3	31.0			
4 00	282 24.5	215 12.0	N17 24.4	102 02.0	N 0 14.1	219 18.8	N20 21.3	80 20.8	S 6 31.0	Mirfak	308 41.6	N49 54.1
01	297 27.0	230 13.8	24.3	117 03.3	13.5	234 20.7	21.3	95 23.2	31.0	Nunki	75 58.7	S26 16.7
02	312 29.5	245 15.7	24.3	132 04.5	12.9	249 22.6	21.4	110 25.6	31.1	Peacock	53 19.7	S56 41.4
03	327 31.9	260 17.5	.. 24.2	147 05.8	.. 12.3	264 24.5	.. 21.5	125 28.1	.. 31.1	Pollux	243 28.9	N27 59.7
04	342 34.4	275 19.4	24.2	162 07.1	11.8	279 26.4	21.6	140 30.5	31.1	Procyon	245 00.7	N 5 11.4
05	357 36.9	290 21.2	24.1	177 08.4	11.2	294 28.3	21.7	155 32.9	31.1			
06	12 39.3	305 23.0	N17 24.1	192 09.6	N 0 10.6	309 30.2	N20 21.8	170 35.4	S 6 31.2	Rasalhague	96 06.7	N12 33.2
W 07	27 41.8	320 24.8	24.0	207 10.9	10.1	324 32.2	21.9	185 37.8	31.2	Regulus	207 44.4	N11 54.3
E 08	42 44.3	335 26.7	24.0	222 12.2	09.5	339 34.1	22.0	200 40.2	31.2	Rigel	281 13.0	S 8 11.3
D 09	57 46.7	350 28.5	.. 24.0	237 13.5	.. 08.9	354 36.0	.. 22.1	215 42.7	.. 31.2	Rigil Kent.	139 52.3	S60 53.4
N 10	72 49.2	5 30.3	23.9	252 14.7	08.4	9 37.9	22.2	230 45.1	31.3	Sabik	102 13.0	S15 44.3
E 11	87 51.7	20 32.1	23.9	267 16.0	07.8	24 39.8	22.3	245 47.5	31.3			
S 12	102 54.1	35 33.9	N17 23.8	282 17.3	N 0 07.2	39 41.7	N20 22.4	260 50.0	S 6 31.3	Schedar	349 41.2	N56 36.2
D 13	117 56.6	50 35.7	23.8	297 18.5	06.7	54 43.6	22.5	275 52.4	31.3	Shaula	96 22.4	S37 06.7
A 14	132 59.0	65 37.5	23.8	312 19.8	06.1	69 45.6	22.6	290 54.8	31.4	Sirius	258 34.6	S16 44.1
Y 15	148 01.5	80 39.3	.. 23.7	327 21.1	.. 05.5	84 47.5	.. 22.7	305 57.3	.. 31.4	Spica	158 31.9	S11 13.7
16	163 04.0	95 41.1	23.7	342 22.4	05.0	99 49.4	22.8	320 59.7	31.4	Suhail	222 53.3	S43 29.3
17	178 06.4	110 42.9	23.6	357 23.6	04.4	114 51.3	22.9	336 02.1	31.4			
18	193 08.9	125 44.7	N17 23.6	12 24.9	N 0 03.8	129 53.2	N20 22.9	351 04.6	S 6 31.5	Vega	80 39.0	N38 47.9
19	208 11.4	140 46.5	23.6	27 26.2	03.3	144 55.1	23.0	6 07.0	31.5	Zuben'ubi	137 05.9	S16 05.7
20	223 13.8	155 48.3	23.6	42 27.4	02.7	159 57.1	23.1	21 09.4	31.5		SHA	Mer.Pass.
21	238 16.3	170 50.0	.. 23.5	57 28.7	.. 02.1	174 59.0	.. 23.2	36 11.9	.. 31.5		° ′	h m
22	253 18.8	185 51.8	23.5	72 30.0	01.5	190 00.9	23.3	51 14.3	31.6	Venus	293 01.3	9 41
23	268 21.2	200 53.6	23.5	87 31.2	01.0	205 02.8	23.4	66 16.7	31.6	Mars	180 05.9	17 12
	h m									Jupiter	297 07.4	9 25
Mer. Pass. 5 13.4		v 1.9	d 0.1	v 1.3	d 0.6	v 1.9	d 0.1	v 2.4	d 0.0	Saturn	157 56.9	18 39

SUN / MOON

UT	SUN GHA	SUN Dec	MOON GHA	v	Dec	d	HP
d h	° '	° '	° '	'	° '	'	'
2 00	178 59.3	N23 01.1	25 34.9	3.5	S21 41.1	0.5	60.5
01	193 59.2	01.0	39 57.4	3.6	21 41.6	0.3	60.5
02	208 59.1	00.8	54 20.0	3.6	21 41.9	0.2	60.5
03	223 59.0	.. 00.6	68 42.6	3.5	21 42.1	0.0	60.5
04	238 58.9	00.4	83 05.1	3.6	21 42.1	0.2	60.5
05	253 58.8	00.2	97 27.7	3.6	21 41.9	0.3	60.5
M 06	268 58.6	N23 00.0	111 50.3	3.5	S21 41.6	0.5	60.5
O 07	283 58.5	22 59.8	126 12.8	3.6	21 41.1	0.6	60.5
N 08	298 58.4	59.6	140 35.4	3.6	21 40.5	0.8	60.5
D 09	313 58.3	.. 59.4	154 58.0	3.6	21 39.7	0.9	60.5
A 10	328 58.2	59.2	169 20.6	3.7	21 38.8	1.2	60.4
Y 11	343 58.1	59.0	183 43.3	3.6	21 37.6	1.2	60.4
12	358 57.9	N22 58.8	198 05.9	3.7	S21 36.4	1.4	60.4
13	13 57.8	58.6	212 28.6	3.7	21 35.0	1.6	60.4
14	28 57.7	58.4	226 51.3	3.7	21 33.4	1.7	60.4
15	43 57.6	.. 58.2	241 14.0	3.8	21 31.7	1.9	60.4
16	58 57.5	58.0	255 36.8	3.8	21 29.8	2.1	60.4
17	73 57.4	57.8	269 59.6	3.8	21 27.7	2.2	60.4
18	88 57.3	N22 57.6	284 22.4	3.8	S21 25.5	2.3	60.4
19	103 57.1	57.4	298 45.2	3.9	21 23.2	2.6	60.4
20	118 57.0	57.2	313 08.1	3.9	21 20.6	2.6	60.4
21	133 56.9	.. 57.0	327 31.0	4.0	21 18.0	2.8	60.4
22	148 56.8	56.8	341 54.0	4.0	21 15.2	3.0	60.3
23	163 56.7	56.6	356 17.0	4.0	21 12.2	3.1	60.3
3 00	178 56.6	N22 56.4	10 40.0	4.1	S21 09.1	3.3	60.3
01	193 56.5	56.2	25 03.1	4.1	21 05.8	3.4	60.3
02	208 56.3	56.0	39 26.2	4.2	21 02.4	3.6	60.3
03	223 56.2	.. 55.8	53 49.4	4.2	20 58.8	3.7	60.3
04	238 56.1	55.6	68 12.6	4.3	20 55.1	3.8	60.3
05	253 56.0	55.4	82 35.9	4.3	20 51.3	4.1	60.2
T 06	268 55.9	N22 55.2	96 59.2	4.4	S20 47.2	4.1	60.2
U 07	283 55.8	55.0	111 22.6	4.5	20 43.1	4.3	60.2
E 08	298 55.7	54.8	125 46.1	4.5	20 38.8	4.4	60.2
S 09	313 55.6	.. 54.6	140 09.6	4.5	20 34.4	4.6	60.2
D 10	328 55.4	54.3	154 33.1	4.7	20 29.8	4.8	60.2
A 11	343 55.3	54.1	168 56.8	4.7	20 25.0	4.8	60.1
Y 12	358 55.2	N22 53.9	183 20.5	4.7	S20 20.2	5.0	60.1
13	13 55.1	53.7	197 44.2	4.8	20 15.2	5.2	60.1
14	28 55.0	53.5	212 08.0	4.9	20 10.0	5.2	60.1
15	43 54.9	.. 53.3	226 31.9	4.9	20 04.8	5.5	60.1
16	58 54.8	53.1	240 55.8	5.1	19 59.3	5.5	60.1
17	73 54.7	52.8	255 19.9	5.1	19 53.8	5.7	60.0
18	88 54.6	N22 52.6	269 44.0	5.1	S19 48.1	5.8	60.0
19	103 54.4	52.4	284 08.1	5.3	19 42.3	5.9	60.0
20	118 54.3	52.2	298 32.4	5.3	19 36.4	6.1	60.0
21	133 54.2	.. 52.0	312 56.7	5.4	19 30.3	6.2	59.9
22	148 54.1	51.8	327 21.1	5.4	19 24.1	6.4	59.9
23	163 54.0	51.5	341 45.5	5.6	19 17.7	6.4	59.9
4 00	178 53.9	N22 51.3	356 10.1	5.6	S19 11.3	6.6	59.9
01	193 53.8	51.1	10 34.7	5.7	19 04.7	6.7	59.9
02	208 53.7	50.9	24 59.4	5.8	18 58.0	6.8	59.8
03	223 53.6	.. 50.6	39 24.2	5.8	18 51.2	7.0	59.8
04	238 53.5	50.4	53 49.0	6.0	18 44.2	7.0	59.8
05	253 53.3	50.2	68 14.0	6.0	18 37.2	7.2	59.8
W 06	268 53.2	N22 50.0	82 39.0	6.1	S18 30.0	7.3	59.7
E 07	283 53.1	49.8	97 04.1	6.2	18 22.7	7.4	59.7
D 08	298 53.0	49.5	111 29.3	6.3	18 15.3	7.5	59.7
N 09	313 52.9	.. 49.3	125 54.6	6.4	18 07.8	7.7	59.7
E 10	328 52.8	49.1	140 20.0	6.4	18 00.1	7.7	59.6
S 11	343 52.7	48.8	154 45.4	6.6	17 52.4	7.9	59.6
D 12	358 52.6	N22 48.6	169 11.0	6.6	S17 44.5	7.9	59.6
A 13	13 52.5	48.4	183 36.6	6.7	17 36.6	8.1	59.6
Y 14	28 52.4	48.2	198 02.3	6.9	17 28.5	8.2	59.5
15	43 52.3	.. 47.9	212 28.2	6.9	17 20.3	8.3	59.5
16	58 52.1	47.7	226 54.1	7.0	17 12.0	8.3	59.5
17	73 52.0	47.5	241 20.1	7.0	17 03.7	8.5	59.4
18	88 51.9	N22 47.2	255 46.1	7.2	S16 55.2	8.6	59.4
19	103 51.8	47.0	270 12.3	7.3	16 46.6	8.7	59.4
20	118 51.7	46.8	284 38.6	7.3	16 37.9	8.7	59.4
21	133 51.6	.. 46.5	299 04.9	7.5	16 29.2	8.9	59.3
22	148 51.5	46.3	313 31.4	7.5	16 20.3	8.9	59.3
23	163 51.4	46.0	327 57.9	7.6	S16 11.4	9.1	59.3
	SD 15.8	d 0.2	SD 16.5		16.4		16.2

Twilight / Sunrise / Moonrise

Lat.	Twilight Naut.	Twilight Civil	Sunrise	Moonrise 2	3	4	5
°	h m	h m	h m	h m	h m	h m	h m
N 72	▭	▭	▭	■	■	23 25	22 50
N 70	▭	▭	▭	■	23 16	22 43	22 28
68	▭	▭	▭	22 17	22 17	22 14	22 11
66	////	////	00 38	21 19	21 42	21 53	21 58
64	////	////	01 46	20 44	21 17	21 35	21 46
62	////	////	02 20	20 20	20 57	21 21	21 37
60	////	01 09	02 45	20 00	20 41	21 09	21 28
N 58	////	01 52	03 04	19 43	20 27	20 58	21 21
56	////	02 20	03 20	19 30	20 15	20 49	21 14
54	01 04	02 41	03 34	19 18	20 05	20 41	21 08
52	01 43	02 58	03 46	19 07	19 55	20 33	21 03
50	02 09	03 13	03 57	18 57	19 47	20 27	20 58
45	02 53	03 41	04 18	18 37	19 29	20 12	20 48
N 40	03 22	04 03	04 36	18 21	19 15	20 00	20 39
35	03 45	04 21	04 51	18 07	19 02	19 50	20 32
30	04 03	04 36	05 03	17 56	18 52	19 41	20 25
20	04 31	05 00	05 25	17 35	18 33	19 26	20 14
N 10	04 54	05 20	05 43	17 17	18 17	19 12	20 03
0	05 12	05 38	06 01	17 01	18 02	19 00	19 54
S 10	05 29	05 55	06 18	16 44	17 47	18 47	19 44
20	05 44	06 12	06 36	16 26	17 30	18 34	19 34
30	06 00	06 30	06 56	16 06	17 12	18 18	19 23
35	06 09	06 41	07 09	15 54	17 01	18 09	19 16
40	06 18	06 52	07 22	15 40	16 48	17 59	19 08
45	06 28	07 05	07 39	15 24	16 34	17 46	18 59
S 50	06 39	07 21	07 59	15 04	16 15	17 32	18 48
52	06 44	07 28	08 08	14 55	16 07	17 25	18 43
54	06 50	07 36	08 19	14 44	15 57	17 17	18 38
56	06 56	07 45	08 31	14 32	15 46	17 08	18 31
58	07 02	07 54	08 45	14 18	15 34	16 58	18 24
S 60	07 09	08 06	09 02	14 02	15 20	16 47	18 17

Sunset / Twilight / Moonset

Lat.	Sunset	Twilight Civil	Twilight Naut.	Moonset 2	3	4	5
°	h m	h m	h m	h m	h m	h m	h m
N 72	▭	▭	▭	■	■	■	03 19
N 70	▭	▭	▭	■	■	01 27	03 59
68	▭	▭	▭	24 19	00 19	02 26	04 47
66	23 25	////	////	00 01	01 17	02 59	04 47
64	22 21	////	////	00 38	01 51	03 24	05 04
62	21 47	////	////	01 04	02 16	03 43	05 17
60	21 23	22 57	////	01 25	02 35	03 59	05 29
N 58	21 04	22 15	////	01 42	02 51	04 12	05 39
56	20 48	21 48	////	01 56	03 05	04 24	05 47
54	20 34	21 27	23 03	02 09	03 17	04 34	05 55
52	20 22	21 10	22 24	02 20	03 27	04 43	06 02
50	20 12	20 55	21 59	02 29	03 36	04 51	06 08
45	19 50	20 27	21 16	02 50	03 56	05 08	06 21
N 40	19 32	20 05	20 46	03 06	04 12	05 21	06 32
35	19 18	19 47	20 24	03 20	04 25	05 33	06 41
30	19 05	19 32	20 05	03 33	04 37	05 43	06 49
20	18 44	19 08	19 37	03 53	04 57	06 01	07 03
N 10	18 25	18 48	19 15	04 11	05 14	06 16	07 15
0	18 08	18 30	18 57	04 28	05 30	06 30	07 26
S 10	17 51	18 14	18 40	04 45	05 46	06 44	07 37
20	17 33	17 57	18 24	05 03	06 03	06 59	07 49
30	17 12	17 38	18 08	05 23	06 23	07 16	08 02
35	17 00	17 28	18 00	05 35	06 34	07 26	08 10
40	16 46	17 17	17 51	05 49	06 47	07 38	08 19
45	16 30	17 04	17 41	06 06	07 02	07 50	08 29
S 50	16 10	16 48	17 29	06 26	07 21	08 06	08 41
52	16 00	16 41	17 24	06 35	07 30	08 13	08 47
54	15 50	16 33	17 19	06 46	07 40	08 21	08 53
56	15 38	16 24	17 13	06 58	07 51	08 30	09 00
58	15 23	16 14	17 07	07 12	08 04	08 41	09 08
S 60	15 07	16 03	16 59	07 28	08 19	08 53	09 16

SUN / MOON

	SUN Eqn. of Time 00h	SUN Eqn. of Time 12h	SUN Mer. Pass.	MOON Mer. Pass. Upper	MOON Mer. Pass. Lower	Age	Phase
Day	m s	m s	h m	h m	h m	d	%
2	04 02	04 08	12 04	23 16	10 44	13	98
3	04 13	04 19	12 04	24 16	11 46	14	100
4	04 24	04 29	12 04	00 16	12 45	15	99

2012 JULY 5, 6, 7 (THURS., FRI., SAT.)

UT	ARIES GHA	VENUS −4.7 GHA	Dec	MARS +0.9 GHA	Dec	JUPITER −2.1 GHA	Dec	SATURN +0.7 GHA	Dec	Name	SHA	Dec
THURS. 5 00	283 23.7	215 55.3	N17 23.4	102 32.5	N 0 00.4	220 04.7	N20 23.5	81 19.2	S 6 31.6	Acamar	315 19.1	S40 15.1
01	298 26.2	230 57.1	23.4	117 33.8	S 00.2	235 06.6	23.6	96 21.6	31.6	Achernar	335 27.4	S57 10.0
02	313 28.6	245 58.9	23.4	132 35.0	00.7	250 08.6	23.7	111 24.0	31.7	Acrux	173 10.1	S63 10.5
03	328 31.1	261 00.6	. . 23.4	147 36.3	. . 01.3	265 10.5	. . 23.8	126 26.4	. . 31.7	Adhara	255 13.4	S28 59.5
04	343 33.5	276 02.4	23.3	162 37.6	01.9	280 12.4	23.9	141 28.9	31.7	Aldebaran	290 50.4	N16 32.0
05	358 36.0	291 04.1	23.3	177 38.8	02.4	295 14.3	24.0	156 31.3	31.7			
06	13 38.5	306 05.9	N17 23.3	192 40.1	S 0 03.0	310 16.2	N20 24.1	171 33.7	S 6 31.8	Alioth	166 21.3	N55 53.7
07	28 40.9	321 07.6	23.3	207 41.4	03.6	325 18.1	24.2	186 36.2	31.8	Alkaid	153 59.3	N49 15.3
T 08	43 43.4	336 09.4	23.3	222 42.6	04.2	340 20.1	24.3	201 38.6	31.8	Al Na'ir	27 44.2	S46 53.7
H 09	58 45.9	351 11.1	. . 23.2	237 43.9	. . 04.7	355 22.0	. . 24.3	216 41.0	. . 31.8	Alnilam	275 47.3	S 1 11.7
U 10	73 48.3	6 12.8	23.2	252 45.2	05.3	10 23.9	24.4	231 43.5	31.9	Alphard	217 57.0	S 8 42.9
R 11	88 50.8	21 14.5	23.2	267 46.4	05.9	25 25.8	24.5	246 45.9	31.9			
S 12	103 53.3	36 16.3	N17 23.2	282 47.7	S 0 06.4	40 27.7	N20 24.6	261 48.3	S 6 31.9	Alphecca	126 11.3	N26 40.5
D 13	118 55.7	51 18.0	23.2	297 49.0	07.0	55 29.6	24.7	276 50.7	31.9	Alpheratz	357 44.1	N29 09.5
A 14	133 58.2	66 19.7	23.2	312 50.2	07.6	70 31.6	24.8	291 53.2	32.0	Altair	62 08.5	N 8 54.3
Y 15	149 00.6	81 21.4	. . 23.2	327 51.5	. . 08.2	85 33.5	. . 24.9	306 55.6	. . 32.0	Ankaa	353 16.3	S42 13.9
16	164 03.1	96 23.1	23.2	342 52.8	08.7	100 35.4	25.0	321 58.0	32.0	Antares	112 26.7	S26 27.6
17	179 05.6	111 24.9	23.2	357 54.0	09.3	115 37.3	25.1	337 00.5	32.0			
18	194 08.0	126 26.6	N17 23.1	12 55.3	S 0 09.9	130 39.2	N20 25.2	352 02.9	S 6 32.1	Arcturus	145 56.2	N19 07.2
19	209 10.5	141 28.3	23.1	27 56.5	10.4	145 41.2	25.3	7 05.3	32.1	Atria	107 28.6	S69 03.0
20	224 13.0	156 30.0	23.1	42 57.8	11.0	160 43.1	25.4	22 07.7	32.1	Avior	234 18.9	S59 33.2
21	239 15.4	171 31.7	. . 23.1	57 59.1	. . 11.6	175 45.0	. . 25.5	37 10.2	. . 32.1	Bellatrix	278 33.0	N 6 21.6
22	254 17.9	186 33.4	23.1	73 00.3	12.2	190 46.9	25.5	52 12.6	32.2	Betelgeuse	271 02.3	N 7 24.5
23	269 20.4	201 35.0	23.1	88 01.6	12.7	205 48.8	25.6	67 15.0	32.2			
6 00	284 22.8	216 36.7	N17 23.1	103 02.9	S 0 13.3	220 50.8	N20 25.7	82 17.4	S 6 32.2	Canopus	263 57.0	S52 42.2
01	299 25.3	231 38.4	23.1	118 04.1	13.9	235 52.7	25.8	97 19.9	32.2	Capella	280 35.8	N46 00.4
02	314 27.8	246 40.1	23.1	133 05.4	14.4	250 54.6	25.9	112 22.3	32.3	Deneb	49 31.5	N45 19.6
03	329 30.2	261 41.8	. . 23.1	148 06.6	. . 15.0	265 56.5	. . 26.0	127 24.7	. . 32.3	Denebola	182 34.4	N14 30.1
04	344 32.7	276 43.4	23.1	163 07.9	15.6	280 58.4	26.1	142 27.2	32.3	Diphda	348 56.5	S17 54.9
05	359 35.1	291 45.1	23.1	178 09.2	16.2	296 00.3	26.2	157 29.6	32.4			
06	14 37.6	306 46.8	N17 23.1	193 10.4	S 0 16.7	311 02.3	N20 26.3	172 32.0	S 6 32.4	Dubhe	193 52.8	N61 41.2
07	29 40.1	321 48.4	23.2	208 11.7	17.3	326 04.2	26.4	187 34.4	32.4	Elnath	278 13.8	N28 36.9
F 08	44 42.5	336 50.1	23.2	223 12.9	17.9	341 06.1	26.5	202 36.9	32.4	Eltanin	90 45.9	N51 29.4
R 09	59 45.0	351 51.8	. . 23.2	238 14.2	. . 18.5	356 08.0	. . 26.6	217 39.3	. . 32.5	Enif	33 47.5	N 9 56.1
I 10	74 47.5	6 53.4	23.2	253 15.4	19.0	11 09.9	26.6	232 41.7	32.5	Fomalhaut	15 24.5	S29 33.0
D 11	89 49.9	21 55.1	23.2	268 16.7	19.6	26 11.9	26.6	247 44.1	32.5			
A 12	104 52.4	36 56.7	N17 23.2	283 18.0	S 0 20.2	41 13.8	N20 26.8	262 46.6	S 6 32.5	Gacrux	172 01.7	S57 11.3
Y 13	119 54.9	51 58.4	23.2	298 19.2	20.8	56 15.7	26.9	277 49.0	32.6	Gienah	175 53.0	S17 36.6
14	134 57.3	67 00.0	23.2	313 20.5	21.3	71 17.6	27.0	292 51.4	32.6	Hadar	148 48.6	S60 26.3
15	149 59.8	82 01.6	. . 23.2	328 21.7	. . 21.9	86 19.6	. . 27.1	307 53.8	. . 32.6	Hamal	328 01.6	N23 31.2
16	165 02.3	97 03.3	23.3	343 23.0	22.5	101 21.5	27.2	322 56.3	32.7	Kaus Aust.	83 44.2	S34 22.6
17	180 04.7	112 04.9	23.3	358 24.2	23.0	116 23.4	27.3	337 58.7	32.7			
18	195 07.2	127 06.5	N17 23.3	13 25.5	S 0 23.6	131 25.3	N20 27.4	353 01.1	S 6 32.7	Kochab	137 19.4	N74 06.5
19	210 09.6	142 08.2	23.3	28 26.8	24.2	146 27.2	27.5	8 03.5	32.7	Markab	13 38.8	N15 16.4
20	225 12.1	157 09.8	23.3	43 28.0	24.8	161 29.2	27.6	23 06.0	32.8	Menkar	314 15.9	N 4 08.3
21	240 14.6	172 11.4	. . 23.4	58 29.3	. . 25.3	176 31.1	. . 27.7	38 08.4	. . 32.8	Menkent	148 08.2	S36 26.1
22	255 17.0	187 13.0	23.4	73 30.5	25.9	191 33.0	27.7	53 10.8	32.8	Miaplacidus	221 40.6	S69 46.4
23	270 19.5	202 14.6	23.4	88 31.8	26.5	206 34.9	27.8	68 13.2	32.8			
7 00	285 22.0	217 16.2	N17 23.4	103 33.0	S 0 27.1	221 36.8	N20 27.9	83 15.7	S 6 32.9	Mirfak	308 41.6	N49 54.1
01	300 24.4	232 17.8	23.4	118 34.3	27.6	236 38.8	28.0	98 18.1	32.9	Nunki	75 58.7	S26 16.7
02	315 26.9	247 19.4	23.5	133 35.5	28.2	251 40.7	28.1	113 20.5	32.9	Peacock	53 19.7	S56 41.4
03	330 29.4	262 21.0	. . 23.5	148 36.8	. . 28.8	266 42.6	. . 28.2	128 22.9	. . 33.0	Pollux	243 28.9	N27 59.7
04	345 31.8	277 22.6	23.5	163 38.1	29.4	281 44.5	28.3	143 25.3	33.0	Procyon	245 00.7	N 5 11.4
05	0 34.3	292 24.2	23.6	178 39.3	29.9	296 46.5	28.4	158 27.8	33.0			
06	15 36.7	307 25.8	N17 23.6	193 40.6	S 0 30.5	311 48.4	N20 28.5	173 30.2	S 6 33.0	Rasalhague	96 06.7	N12 33.2
07	30 39.2	322 27.4	23.6	208 41.8	31.1	326 50.3	28.6	188 32.6	33.1	Regulus	207 44.4	N11 54.3
S 08	45 41.7	337 29.0	23.6	223 43.1	31.7	341 52.2	28.6	203 35.0	33.1	Rigel	281 13.0	S 8 11.3
A 09	60 44.1	352 30.6	. . 23.7	238 44.3	. . 32.2	356 54.1	. . 28.7	218 37.5	. . 33.1	Rigil Kent.	139 52.3	S60 53.4
T 10	75 46.6	7 32.1	23.7	253 45.6	32.8	11 56.1	28.8	233 39.9	33.2	Sabik	102 13.0	S15 44.3
U 11	90 49.1	22 33.7	23.7	268 46.8	33.4	26 58.0	28.9	248 42.3	33.2			
R 12	105 51.5	37 35.3	N17 23.8	283 48.1	S 0 34.0	41 59.9	N20 29.0	263 44.7	S 6 33.2	Schedar	349 41.2	N56 36.2
D 13	120 54.0	52 36.9	23.8	298 49.3	34.5	57 01.8	29.1	278 47.1	33.2	Shaula	96 22.4	S37 06.7
A 14	135 56.5	67 38.4	23.9	313 50.6	35.1	72 03.8	29.2	293 49.6	33.3	Sirius	258 34.6	S16 44.1
Y 15	150 58.9	82 40.0	. . 23.9	328 51.8	. . 35.7	87 05.7	. . 29.3	308 52.0	. . 33.3	Spica	158 31.9	S11 13.7
16	166 01.4	97 41.5	23.9	343 53.1	36.3	102 07.6	29.4	323 54.4	33.3	Suhail	222 53.3	S43 29.2
17	181 03.9	112 43.1	24.0	358 54.3	36.8	117 09.5	29.5	338 56.8	33.4			
18	196 06.3	127 44.6	N17 24.0	13 55.6	S 0 37.4	132 11.5	N20 29.6	353 59.2	S 6 33.4	Vega	80 39.0	N38 47.9
19	211 08.8	142 46.2	24.1	28 56.8	38.0	147 13.4	29.6	9 01.7	33.4	Zuben'ubi	137 06.0	S16 05.7
20	226 11.2	157 47.7	24.1	43 58.1	38.6	162 15.3	29.7	24 04.1	33.4		SHA	Mer.Pass.
21	241 13.7	172 49.3	. . 24.1	58 59.3	. . 39.1	177 17.2	. . 29.8	39 06.5	. . 33.5	Venus	292 13.9	9 32
22	256 16.2	187 50.8	24.2	74 00.6	39.7	192 19.1	29.9	54 08.9	33.5	Mars	178 40.0	17 06
23	271 18.6	202 52.4	24.2	89 01.8	40.3	207 21.1	30.0	69 11.3	33.5	Jupiter	296 27.9	9 15
Mer. Pass.	5 01.7	v 1.6 d 0.0		v 1.3 d 0.6		v 1.9 d 0.1		v 2.4 d 0.0		Saturn	157 54.6	18 28

UT	SUN GHA	SUN Dec	MOON GHA	v	MOON Dec	d	HP
d h	° ′	° ′	° ′	′	° ′	′	′
5 00	178 51.3	N22 45.8	342 24.5	7.8	S16 02.3	9.1	59.2
01	193 51.2	45.6	356 51.3	7.8	15 53.2	9.2	59.2
02	208 51.1	45.3	11 18.1	7.9	15 44.0	9.3	59.2
03	223 51.0	.. 45.1	25 45.0	8.0	15 34.7	9.4	59.2
04	238 50.9	44.9	40 12.0	8.1	15 25.3	9.5	59.1
05	253 50.8	44.6	54 39.1	8.2	15 15.8	9.5	59.1
06	268 50.7	N22 44.4	69 06.3	8.3	S15 06.3	9.7	59.1
07	283 50.5	44.1	83 33.6	8.3	14 56.6	9.7	59.0
T 08	298 50.4	43.9	98 00.9	8.5	14 46.9	9.8	59.0
H 09	313 50.3	.. 43.6	112 28.4	8.5	14 37.1	9.8	59.0
U 10	328 50.2	43.4	126 55.9	8.7	14 27.3	10.0	58.9
R 11	343 50.1	43.2	141 23.6	8.7	14 17.3	10.0	58.9
S 12	358 50.0	N22 42.9	155 51.3	8.9	S14 07.3	10.1	58.9
D 13	13 49.9	42.7	170 19.2	8.9	13 57.2	10.1	58.8
A 14	28 49.8	42.4	184 47.1	9.0	13 47.1	10.2	58.8
Y 15	43 49.7	.. 42.2	199 15.1	9.1	13 36.9	10.3	58.8
16	58 49.6	41.9	213 43.2	9.2	13 26.6	10.4	58.7
17	73 49.5	41.7	228 11.4	9.3	13 16.2	10.4	58.7
18	88 49.4	N22 41.4	242 39.7	9.3	S13 05.8	10.5	58.7
19	103 49.3	41.2	257 08.0	9.5	12 55.3	10.5	58.6
20	118 49.2	40.9	271 36.5	9.5	12 44.8	10.6	58.6
21	133 49.1	.. 40.7	286 05.0	9.7	12 34.2	10.6	58.6
22	148 49.0	40.4	300 33.7	9.7	12 23.6	10.7	58.5
23	163 48.9	40.2	315 02.4	9.8	12 12.9	10.8	58.5
6 00	178 48.8	N22 39.9	329 31.2	9.9	S12 02.1	10.8	58.5
01	193 48.7	39.6	344 00.1	10.0	11 51.3	10.9	58.4
02	208 48.6	39.4	358 29.1	10.1	11 40.4	10.9	58.4
03	223 48.5	.. 39.1	12 58.2	10.1	11 29.5	11.0	58.4
04	238 48.4	38.9	27 27.3	10.3	11 18.5	11.0	58.3
05	253 48.3	38.6	41 56.6	10.3	11 07.5	11.1	58.3
06	268 48.2	N22 38.4	56 25.9	10.4	S10 56.4	11.1	58.2
07	283 48.1	38.1	70 55.3	10.5	10 45.3	11.2	58.2
F 08	298 48.0	37.8	85 24.8	10.6	10 34.2	11.2	58.2
R 09	313 47.8	.. 37.6	99 54.4	10.6	10 23.0	11.2	58.1
I 10	328 47.7	37.3	114 24.0	10.8	10 11.8	11.3	58.1
D 11	343 47.6	37.1	128 53.8	10.8	10 00.5	11.3	58.1
A 12	358 47.5	N22 36.8	143 23.6	10.9	S 9 49.2	11.4	58.0
Y 13	13 47.4	36.5	157 53.5	11.0	9 37.8	11.3	58.0
14	28 47.3	36.3	172 23.5	11.0	9 26.5	11.5	58.0
15	43 47.2	.. 36.0	186 53.5	11.2	9 15.0	11.4	57.9
16	58 47.1	35.7	201 23.7	11.2	9 03.6	11.5	57.9
17	73 47.0	35.5	215 53.9	11.3	8 52.1	11.5	57.9
18	88 46.9	N22 35.2	230 24.2	11.3	S 8 40.6	11.6	57.8
19	103 46.8	34.9	244 54.5	11.5	8 29.0	11.5	57.8
20	118 46.7	34.7	259 25.0	11.5	8 17.5	11.6	57.7
21	133 46.6	.. 34.4	273 55.5	11.5	8 05.9	11.7	57.7
22	148 46.5	34.1	288 26.0	11.7	7 54.2	11.6	57.7
23	163 46.4	33.9	302 56.7	11.7	7 42.6	11.7	57.6
7 00	178 46.3	N22 33.6	317 27.4	11.8	S 7 30.9	11.7	57.6
01	193 46.2	33.3	331 58.2	11.9	7 19.2	11.7	57.6
02	208 46.1	33.1	346 29.1	11.9	7 07.5	11.7	57.5
03	223 46.0	.. 32.8	1 00.0	12.0	6 55.8	11.8	57.5
04	238 45.9	32.5	15 31.0	12.1	6 44.0	11.7	57.5
05	253 45.8	32.2	30 02.1	12.1	6 32.3	11.8	57.4
06	268 45.7	N22 32.0	44 33.2	12.2	S 6 20.5	11.8	57.4
07	283 45.6	31.7	59 04.4	12.3	6 08.7	11.8	57.3
S 08	298 45.6	31.4	73 35.7	12.3	5 56.9	11.9	57.3
A 09	313 45.5	.. 31.1	88 07.0	12.4	5 45.0	11.8	57.3
T 10	328 45.4	30.9	102 38.4	12.4	5 33.2	11.9	57.2
U 11	343 45.3	30.6	117 09.8	12.6	5 21.3	11.9	57.2
R 12	358 45.2	N22 30.3	131 41.4	12.5	S 5 09.5	11.9	57.2
D 13	13 45.1	30.0	146 12.9	12.7	4 57.6	11.9	57.1
A 14	28 45.0	29.7	160 44.6	12.7	4 45.7	11.9	57.1
Y 15	43 44.9	.. 29.5	175 16.3	12.7	4 33.8	11.9	57.1
16	58 44.8	29.2	189 48.0	12.8	4 21.9	11.9	57.0
17	73 44.7	28.9	204 19.8	12.9	4 10.0	11.9	57.0
18	88 44.6	N22 28.6	218 51.7	12.9	S 3 58.1	11.9	57.0
19	103 44.5	28.3	233 23.6	13.0	3 46.2	11.9	56.9
20	118 44.4	28.1	247 55.6	13.0	3 34.3	11.9	56.9
21	133 44.3	.. 27.8	262 27.6	13.0	3 22.4	11.9	56.9
22	148 44.2	27.5	276 59.6	13.2	3 10.5	11.9	56.8
23	163 44.1	27.2	291 31.8	13.1	S 2 58.6	11.9	56.8
	SD 15.8	d 0.3	SD 16.0		15.8		15.6

Twilight / Moonrise

Lat.	Naut.	Civil	Sunrise	Moonrise 5	6	7	8
°	h m	h m	h m	h m	h m	h m	h m
N 72	▭	▭	▭	22 50	22 29	22 13	21 58
N 70	▭	▭	▭	22 28	22 18	22 09	22 00
68	▭	▭	▭	22 11	22 08	22 05	22 02
66	////	////	00 55	21 58	22 00	22 02	22 03
64	////	////	01 52	21 46	21 54	21 59	22 04
62	////	////	02 25	21 37	21 48	21 57	22 05
60	////	01 18	02 49	21 28	21 43	21 55	22 06
N 58	////	01 57	03 08	21 21	21 38	21 53	22 07
56	////	02 24	03 24	21 14	21 34	21 52	22 08
54	01 11	02 44	03 37	21 08	21 31	21 50	22 08
52	01 48	03 01	03 49	21 03	21 28	21 49	22 09
50	02 13	03 15	03 59	20 58	21 25	21 48	22 09
45	02 55	03 44	04 20	20 48	21 18	21 45	22 10
N 40	03 24	04 05	04 38	20 39	21 13	21 43	22 11
35	03 47	04 23	04 52	20 32	21 08	21 41	22 12
30	04 05	04 38	05 05	20 25	21 04	21 39	22 13
20	04 33	05 02	05 26	20 14	20 57	21 37	22 14
N 10	04 54	05 21	05 44	20 03	20 50	21 34	22 16
0	05 13	05 39	06 01	19 54	20 44	21 32	22 17
S 10	05 29	05 55	06 18	19 44	20 38	21 29	22 18
20	05 45	06 12	06 36	19 34	20 32	21 27	22 19
30	06 00	06 30	06 56	19 23	20 25	21 24	22 21
35	06 09	06 40	07 08	19 16	20 20	21 22	22 22
40	06 18	06 51	07 22	19 08	20 16	21 20	22 23
45	06 27	07 04	07 38	18 59	20 10	21 18	22 24
S 50	06 38	07 20	07 58	18 48	20 03	21 16	22 25
52	06 43	07 27	08 07	18 43	20 00	21 14	22 26
54	06 49	07 34	08 17	18 38	19 57	21 13	22 26
56	06 55	07 43	08 29	18 31	19 53	21 12	22 27
58	07 01	07 53	08 43	18 24	19 49	21 10	22 28
S 60	07 08	08 04	08 59	18 17	19 44	21 08	22 29

Sunset / Twilight / Moonset

Lat.	Sunset	Civil	Naut.	Moonset 5	6	7	8
°	h m	h m	h m	h m	h m	h m	h m
N 72	▭	▭	▭	03 19	05 45	07 48	09 41
N 70	▭	▭	▭	03 59	06 04	07 57	09 43
68	▭	▭	▭	04 27	06 20	08 05	09 44
66	23 11	////	////	04 47	06 32	08 11	09 45
64	22 15	////	////	05 04	06 42	08 16	09 46
62	21 43	////	////	05 17	06 51	08 20	09 46
60	21 20	22 49	////	05 29	06 58	08 24	09 47
N 58	21 01	22 11	////	05 39	07 05	08 28	09 47
56	20 45	21 45	////	05 47	07 10	08 31	09 48
54	20 32	21 24	22 56	05 55	07 16	08 33	09 48
52	20 20	21 08	22 20	06 02	07 20	08 36	09 49
50	20 10	20 54	21 56	06 08	07 24	08 38	09 49
45	19 49	20 26	21 14	06 21	07 33	08 43	09 50
N 40	19 32	20 04	20 45	06 32	07 41	08 47	09 50
35	19 17	19 47	20 23	06 41	07 47	08 50	09 51
30	19 05	19 32	20 05	06 49	07 53	08 53	09 51
20	18 44	19 08	19 37	07 03	08 02	08 59	09 52
N 10	18 25	18 48	19 15	07 15	08 11	09 03	09 53
0	18 08	18 31	18 57	07 26	08 18	09 07	09 53
S 10	17 52	18 14	18 41	07 37	08 26	09 11	09 54
20	17 34	17 58	18 25	07 49	08 34	09 16	09 55
30	17 14	17 40	18 09	08 02	08 44	09 21	09 56
35	17 02	17 30	18 01	08 10	08 49	09 24	09 56
40	16 48	17 18	17 52	08 19	08 55	09 27	09 56
45	16 32	17 06	17 42	08 29	09 02	09 30	09 57
S 50	16 12	16 50	17 31	08 41	09 10	09 35	09 57
52	16 03	16 43	17 26	08 47	09 14	09 37	09 57
54	15 52	16 35	17 21	08 53	09 18	09 39	09 58
56	15 41	16 27	17 15	09 00	09 23	09 41	09 58
58	15 27	16 17	17 09	09 08	09 28	09 44	09 58
S 60	15 11	16 06	17 02	09 16	09 34	09 47	09 59

SUN and MOON

Day	Eqn. of Time 00ʰ	Eqn. of Time 12ʰ	Mer. Pass.	Mer. Pass. Upper	Mer. Pass. Lower	Age	Phase
d	m s	m s	h m	h m	h m	d	%
5	04 35	04 40	12 05	01 13	13 40	16	96
6	04 45	04 50	12 05	02 06	14 31	17	90
7	04 54	04 59	12 05	02 56	15 20	18	83

UT	ARIES GHA	VENUS −4.7 GHA	Dec	MARS +0.9 GHA	Dec	JUPITER −2.1 GHA	Dec	SATURN +0.7 GHA	Dec	STARS Name	SHA	Dec
d h	° ′	° ′	° ′	° ′	° ′	° ′	° ′	° ′	° ′		° ′	° ′
8 00	286 21.1	217 53.9	N17 24.3	104 03.1	S 0 40.9	222 23.0	N20 30.1	84 13.8	S 6 33.6	Acamar	315 19.0	S40 15.1
01	301 23.6	232 55.4	24.3	119 04.3	41.5	237 24.9	30.2	99 16.2	33.6	Achernar	335 27.3	S57 10.0
02	316 26.0	247 57.0	24.4	134 05.6	42.0	252 26.8	30.3	114 18.6	33.6	Acrux	173 10.1	S63 10.5
03	331 28.5	262 58.5	.. 24.4	149 06.8	.. 42.6	267 28.8	.. 30.4	129 21.0	.. 33.7	Adhara	255 13.4	S28 59.4
04	346 31.0	278 00.0	24.5	164 08.1	43.2	282 30.7	30.4	144 23.4	33.7	Aldebaran	290 50.4	N16 32.0
05	1 33.4	293 01.5	24.5	179 09.3	43.8	297 32.6	30.5	159 25.9	33.7			
06	16 35.9	308 03.0	N17 24.6	194 10.6	S 0 44.3	312 34.5	N20 30.6	174 28.3	S 6 33.7	Alioth	166 21.3	N55 53.7
07	31 38.4	323 04.5	24.6	209 11.8	44.9	327 36.5	30.7	189 30.7	33.8	Alkaid	152 59.3	N49 15.3
S 08	46 40.8	338 06.0	24.7	224 13.0	45.5	342 38.4	30.8	204 33.1	33.8	Al Na'ir	27 44.2	S46 53.7
U 09	61 43.3	353 07.6	.. 24.7	239 14.3	.. 46.1	357 40.3	.. 30.9	219 35.5	.. 33.8	Alnilam	275 47.3	S 1 11.7
N 10	76 45.7	8 09.1	24.8	254 15.5	46.7	12 42.2	31.0	234 38.0	33.9	Alphard	217 57.0	S 8 42.9
11	91 48.2	23 10.6	24.8	269 16.8	47.2	27 44.2	31.1	249 40.4	33.9			
D 12	106 50.7	38 12.1	N17 24.9	284 18.0	S 0 47.8	42 46.1	N20 31.2	264 42.8	S 6 33.9	Alphecca	126 11.3	N26 40.5
A 13	121 53.1	53 13.5	25.0	299 19.3	48.4	57 48.0	31.2	279 45.2	34.0	Alpheratz	357 44.1	N29 09.6
Y 14	136 55.6	68 15.0	25.0	314 20.5	49.0	72 50.0	31.3	294 47.6	34.0	Altair	62 08.5	N 8 54.3
15	151 58.1	83 16.5	.. 25.1	329 21.8	.. 49.5	87 51.9	.. 31.4	309 50.0	.. 34.0	Ankaa	353 16.2	S42 13.9
16	167 00.5	98 18.0	25.1	344 23.0	50.1	102 53.8	31.5	324 52.5	34.0	Antares	112 26.7	S26 27.6
17	182 03.0	113 19.5	25.2	359 24.2	50.7	117 55.7	31.6	339 54.9	34.1			
18	197 05.5	128 21.0	N17 25.3	14 25.5	S 0 51.3	132 57.7	N20 31.7	354 57.3	S 6 34.1	Arcturus	145 56.2	N19 07.2
19	212 07.9	143 22.4	25.3	29 26.7	51.9	147 59.6	31.8	9 59.7	34.1	Atria	107 28.6	S69 03.1
20	227 10.4	158 23.9	25.4	44 28.0	52.4	163 01.5	31.9	25 02.1	34.2	Avior	234 18.9	S59 33.2
21	242 12.8	173 25.4	.. 25.5	59 29.2	.. 53.0	178 03.4	.. 32.0	40 04.5	.. 34.2	Bellatrix	278 33.0	N 6 21.6
22	257 15.3	188 26.9	25.5	74 30.5	53.6	193 05.4	32.0	55 07.0	34.2	Betelgeuse	271 02.3	N 7 24.5
23	272 17.8	203 28.3	25.6	89 31.7	54.2	208 07.3	32.1	70 09.4	34.3			
9 00	287 20.2	218 29.8	N17 25.7	104 32.9	S 0 54.7	223 09.2	N20 32.2	85 11.8	S 6 34.3	Canopus	263 57.0	S52 42.2
01	302 22.7	233 31.2	25.7	119 34.2	55.3	238 11.1	32.3	100 14.2	34.3	Capella	280 35.8	N46 00.4
02	317 25.2	248 32.7	25.8	134 35.4	55.9	253 13.1	32.4	115 16.6	34.3	Deneb	49 31.5	N45 19.6
03	332 27.6	263 34.1	.. 25.9	149 36.7	.. 56.5	268 15.0	.. 32.5	130 19.0	.. 34.4	Denebola	182 34.4	N14 30.1
04	347 30.1	278 35.6	25.9	164 37.9	57.1	283 16.9	32.6	145 21.4	34.4	Diphda	348 56.5	S17 54.9
05	2 32.6	293 37.0	26.0	179 39.1	57.6	298 18.9	32.7	160 23.9	34.4			
06	17 35.0	308 38.5	N17 26.1	194 40.4	S 0 58.2	313 20.8	N20 32.8	175 26.3	S 6 34.5	Dubhe	193 52.8	N61 41.1
07	32 37.5	323 39.9	26.2	209 41.6	58.8	328 22.7	32.8	190 28.7	34.5	Elnath	278 13.8	N28 36.9
M 08	47 40.0	338 41.4	26.2	224 42.9	0 59.4	343 24.6	32.9	205 31.1	34.5	Eltanin	90 45.9	N51 29.4
O 09	62 42.4	353 42.8	.. 26.3	239 44.1	1 00.0	358 26.6	.. 33.0	220 33.5	.. 34.6	Enif	33 47.5	N 9 56.1
N 10	77 44.9	8 44.2	26.4	254 45.3	00.5	13 28.5	33.1	235 35.9	34.6	Fomalhaut	15 24.5	S29 33.0
11	92 47.3	23 45.6	26.5	269 46.6	01.1	28 30.4	33.2	250 38.3	34.6			
D 12	107 49.8	38 47.1	N17 26.5	284 47.8	S 1 01.7	43 32.4	N20 33.3	265 40.8	S 6 34.7	Gacrux	172 01.7	S57 11.3
A 13	122 52.3	53 48.5	26.6	299 49.1	02.3	58 34.3	33.4	280 43.2	34.7	Gienah	175 53.0	S17 36.8
Y 14	137 54.7	68 49.9	26.7	314 50.3	02.9	73 36.2	33.5	295 45.6	34.7	Hadar	148 48.6	S60 26.3
15	152 57.2	83 51.3	.. 26.8	329 51.5	.. 03.4	88 38.1	.. 33.5	310 48.0	.. 34.8	Hamal	328 01.6	N23 31.2
16	167 59.7	98 52.7	26.9	344 52.8	04.0	103 40.1	33.6	325 50.4	34.8	Kaus Aust.	83 44.2	S34 22.6
17	183 02.1	113 54.1	26.9	359 54.0	04.6	118 42.0	33.7	340 52.8	34.8			
18	198 04.6	128 55.6	N17 27.0	14 55.2	S 1 05.2	133 43.9	N20 33.8	355 55.2	S 6 34.9	Kochab	137 19.5	N74 06.5
19	213 07.1	143 57.0	27.1	29 56.5	05.8	148 45.9	33.9	10 57.7	34.9	Markab	13 38.8	N15 16.5
20	228 09.5	158 58.4	27.2	44 57.7	06.3	163 47.8	34.0	26 00.1	34.9	Menkar	314 15.9	N 4 08.3
21	243 12.0	173 59.8	.. 27.3	59 59.0	.. 06.9	178 49.7	.. 34.1	41 02.5	.. 34.9	Menkent	148 08.2	S36 26.1
22	258 14.5	189 01.2	27.4	75 00.2	07.5	193 51.6	34.2	56 04.9	35.0	Miaplacidus	221 40.6	S69 46.4
23	273 16.9	204 02.5	27.5	90 01.4	08.1	208 53.6	34.2	71 07.3	35.0			
10 00	288 19.4	219 03.9	N17 27.5	105 02.7	S 1 08.7	223 55.5	N20 34.3	86 09.7	S 6 35.0	Mirfak	308 41.5	N49 54.1
01	303 21.8	234 05.3	27.6	120 03.9	09.2	238 57.4	34.4	101 12.1	35.1	Nunki	75 58.7	S26 16.7
02	318 24.3	249 06.7	27.7	135 05.1	09.8	253 59.4	34.5	116 14.5	35.1	Peacock	53 19.7	S56 41.4
03	333 26.8	264 08.1	.. 27.8	150 06.4	.. 10.4	269 01.3	.. 34.6	131 17.0	.. 35.1	Pollux	243 28.9	N27 59.6
04	348 29.2	279 09.5	27.9	165 07.6	11.0	284 03.2	34.7	146 19.4	35.2	Procyon	245 00.7	N 5 11.5
05	3 31.7	294 10.8	28.0	180 08.8	11.6	299 05.2	34.8	161 21.8	35.2			
06	18 34.2	309 12.2	N17 28.1	195 10.1	S 1 12.1	314 07.1	N20 34.8	176 24.2	S 6 35.2	Rasalhague	96 06.7	N12 33.2
07	33 36.6	324 13.6	28.2	210 11.3	12.7	329 09.0	34.9	191 26.6	35.3	Regulus	207 44.4	N11 54.3
T 08	48 39.1	339 15.0	28.3	225 12.5	13.3	344 10.9	35.0	206 29.0	35.3	Rigel	281 13.0	S 8 11.3
U 09	63 41.6	354 16.3	.. 28.4	240 13.8	.. 13.9	359 12.9	.. 35.1	221 31.4	.. 35.3	Rigil Kent.	139 52.3	S60 53.4
E 10	78 44.0	9 17.7	28.5	255 15.0	14.5	14 14.8	35.2	236 33.8	35.4	Sabik	102 13.0	S15 44.3
S 11	93 46.5	24 19.0	28.6	270 16.2	15.1	29 16.7	35.3	251 36.2	35.4			
D 12	108 48.9	39 20.4	N17 28.7	285 17.5	S 1 15.6	44 18.7	N20 35.4	266 38.6	S 6 35.4	Schedar	349 41.2	N56 36.2
A 13	123 51.4	54 21.7	28.8	300 18.7	16.2	59 20.6	35.5	281 41.1	35.5	Shaula	96 22.4	S37 06.7
Y 14	138 53.9	69 23.1	28.9	315 19.9	16.8	74 22.5	35.5	296 43.5	35.5	Sirius	258 34.6	S16 44.1
15	153 56.3	84 24.4	.. 29.0	330 21.2	.. 17.4	89 24.5	.. 35.6	311 45.9	.. 35.5	Spica	158 31.9	S11 13.7
16	168 58.8	99 25.8	29.1	345 22.4	18.0	104 26.4	35.7	326 48.3	35.6	Suhail	222 53.3	S43 29.2
17	184 01.3	114 27.1	29.2	0 23.6	18.5	119 28.3	35.8	341 50.7	35.6			
18	199 03.7	129 28.5	N17 29.3	15 24.8	S 1 19.1	134 30.3	N20 35.9	356 53.1	S 6 35.6	Vega	80 39.0	N38 47.9
19	214 06.2	144 29.8	29.4	30 26.1	19.7	149 32.2	36.0	11 55.5	35.7	Zuben'ubi	137 06.0	S16 05.7
20	229 08.7	159 31.1	29.5	45 27.3	20.3	164 34.1	36.1	26 57.9	35.7			
21	244 11.1	174 32.5	.. 29.6	60 28.5	.. 20.9	179 36.1	.. 36.1	42 00.3	.. 35.7		SHA	Mer. Pass.
22	259 13.6	189 33.8	29.7	75 29.8	21.5	194 38.0	36.2	57 02.7	35.8	Venus	° ′ 291 09.5	h m 9 25
23	274 16.1	204 35.1	29.8	90 31.0	22.0	209 39.9	36.3	72 05.1	35.8	Mars	177 12.7	17 00
Mer. Pass.	h m 4 49.9	v 1.4	d 0.1	v 1.2	d 0.6	v 1.9	d 0.1	v 2.4	d 0.0	Jupiter	295 49.0	9 06
										Saturn	157 51.5	18 16

UT	SUN GHA	SUN Dec	MOON GHA	v	MOON Dec	d	HP
d h	° ′	° ′	° ′	′	° ′	′	′
8 00	178 44.0	N22 26.9	306 03.9	13.3	S 2 46.7	11.9	56.7
01	193 43.9	26.6	320 36.2	13.2	2 34.8	11.9	56.7
02	208 43.8	26.3	335 08.4	13.4	2 22.9	11.9	56.7
03	223 43.7 ..	26.1	349 40.8	13.3	2 11.0	11.9	56.6
04	238 43.6	25.8	4 13.1	13.4	1 59.1	11.9	56.6
05	253 43.5	25.5	18 45.5	13.5	1 47.2	11.9	56.6
06	268 43.4	N22 25.2	33 18.0	13.5	S 1 35.3	11.9	56.5
07	283 43.3	24.9	47 50.5	13.5	1 23.4	11.8	56.5
08	298 43.2	24.6	62 23.0	13.6	1 11.6	11.9	56.5
09	313 43.2 ..	24.3	76 55.6	13.6	0 59.7	11.8	56.4
10	328 43.1	24.0	91 28.2	13.7	0 47.9	11.8	56.4
11	343 43.0	23.7	106 00.9	13.7	0 36.1	11.9	56.4
12	358 42.9	N22 23.4	120 33.6	13.7	S 0 24.2	11.8	56.3
13	13 42.8	23.1	135 06.3	13.8	0 12.4	11.7	56.3
14	28 42.7	22.8	149 39.1	13.8	S 0 00.7	11.8	56.3
15	43 42.6 ..	22.5	164 11.9	13.9	N 0 11.1	11.8	56.2
16	58 42.5	22.2	178 44.8	13.9	0 22.9	11.7	56.2
17	73 42.4	21.9	193 17.7	13.9	0 34.6	11.8	56.2
18	88 42.3	N22 21.6	207 50.6	13.9	N 0 46.4	11.7	56.2
19	103 42.2	21.3	222 23.5	14.0	0 58.1	11.7	56.1
20	118 42.1	21.0	236 56.5	14.0	1 09.8	11.6	56.1
21	133 42.0 ..	20.7	251 29.5	14.1	1 21.4	11.7	56.1
22	148 41.9	20.4	266 02.6	14.0	1 33.1	11.6	56.0
23	163 41.9	20.1	280 35.6	14.1	1 44.7	11.6	56.0
9 00	178 41.8	N22 19.8	295 08.7	14.2	N 1 56.3	11.6	56.0
01	193 41.7	19.5	309 41.9	14.1	2 07.9	11.6	55.9
02	208 41.6	19.2	324 15.0	14.2	2 19.5	11.5	55.9
03	223 41.5 ..	18.9	338 48.2	14.2	2 31.0	11.6	55.9
04	238 41.4	18.6	353 21.4	14.2	2 42.6	11.5	55.8
05	253 41.3	18.3	7 54.6	14.3	2 54.1	11.4	55.8
06	268 41.2	N22 18.0	22 27.9	14.3	N 3 05.5	11.5	55.8
07	283 41.1	17.7	37 01.2	14.2	3 17.0	11.4	55.8
08	298 41.0	17.4	51 34.4	14.4	3 28.4	11.4	55.7
09	313 40.9 ..	17.1	66 07.8	14.3	3 39.8	11.3	55.7
10	328 40.9	16.8	80 41.1	14.3	3 51.1	11.4	55.7
11	343 40.8	16.5	95 14.4	14.4	4 02.5	11.3	55.6
12	358 40.7	N22 16.2	109 47.8	14.4	N 4 13.8	11.2	55.6
13	13 40.6	15.8	124 21.2	14.4	4 25.0	11.3	55.6
14	28 40.5	15.5	138 54.6	14.4	4 36.3	11.2	55.6
15	43 40.4 ..	15.2	153 28.0	14.4	4 47.5	11.2	55.5
16	58 40.3	14.9	168 01.4	14.5	4 58.7	11.1	55.5
17	73 40.2	14.6	182 34.9	14.5	5 09.8	11.1	55.5
18	88 40.1	N22 14.3	197 08.3	14.5	N 5 20.9	11.1	55.4
19	103 40.1	14.0	211 41.8	14.4	5 32.0	11.1	55.4
20	118 40.0	13.6	226 15.2	14.5	5 43.1	11.0	55.4
21	133 39.9 ..	13.3	240 48.7	14.5	5 54.1	10.9	55.4
22	148 39.8	13.0	255 22.2	14.5	6 05.0	11.0	55.3
23	163 39.7	12.7	269 55.7	14.6	6 16.0	10.9	55.3
10 00	178 39.6	N22 12.4	284 29.2	14.6	N 6 26.9	10.8	55.3
01	193 39.5	12.1	299 02.8	14.5	6 37.7	10.9	55.3
02	208 39.4	11.7	313 36.3	14.5	6 48.6	10.7	55.2
03	223 39.4 ..	11.4	328 09.8	14.5	6 59.3	10.8	55.2
04	238 39.3	11.1	342 43.3	14.6	7 10.1	10.7	55.2
05	253 39.2	10.8	357 16.9	14.5	7 20.8	10.7	55.2
06	268 39.1	N22 10.4	11 50.4	14.5	N 7 31.5	10.6	55.1
07	283 39.0	10.1	26 23.9	14.6	7 42.1	10.6	55.1
08	298 38.9	09.8	40 57.5	14.5	7 52.7	10.5	55.1
09	313 38.8 ..	09.5	55 31.0	14.5	8 03.2	10.5	55.1
10	328 38.8	09.1	70 04.5	14.6	8 13.7	10.5	55.1
11	343 38.7	08.8	84 38.1	14.5	8 24.2	10.4	55.0
12	358 38.6	N22 08.5	99 11.6	14.6	N 8 34.6	10.4	55.0
13	13 38.5	08.2	113 45.2	14.5	8 45.0	10.3	55.0
14	28 38.4	07.8	128 18.7	14.5	8 55.3	10.3	55.0
15	43 38.3 ..	07.5	142 52.2	14.5	9 05.6	10.2	54.9
16	58 38.2	07.2	157 25.7	14.5	9 15.8	10.2	54.9
17	73 38.2	06.9	171 59.2	14.5	9 26.0	10.1	54.9
18	88 38.1	N22 06.5	186 32.7	14.5	N 9 36.1	10.1	54.9
19	103 38.0	06.2	201 06.2	14.5	9 46.2	10.0	54.9
20	118 37.9	05.9	215 39.7	14.5	9 56.2	10.0	54.8
21	133 37.8 ..	05.5	230 13.2	14.5	10 06.2	10.0	54.8
22	148 37.7	05.2	244 46.7	14.5	10 16.2	9.9	54.8
23	163 37.7	04.9	259 20.2	14.4	N10 26.1	9.8	54.8
	SD 15.8	d 0.3	SD 15.4		15.2		15.0

(Left margin labels: SUNDAY, MONDAY, TUESDAY)

Lat.	Twilight Naut.	Twilight Civil	Sunrise	Moonrise 8	9	10	11
°	h m	h m	h m	h m	h m	h m	h m
N 72	▭	▭	▭	21 58	21 44	21 27	21 07
N 70	▭	▭	▭	22 00	21 52	21 43	21 33
68	▭	▭	▭	22 02	21 59	21 56	21 53
66	////	////	01 09	22 03	22 04	22 06	22 09
64	////	////	02 00	22 04	22 09	22 15	22 22
62	////	////	02 31	22 05	22 13	22 22	22 33
60	////	01 27	02 53	22 06	22 17	22 29	22 43
N 58	////	02 03	03 12	22 07	22 20	22 35	22 51
56	////	02 29	03 27	22 08	22 23	22 40	22 59
54	01 20	02 48	03 40	22 08	22 26	22 44	23 05
52	01 53	03 05	03 52	22 09	22 28	22 49	23 11
50	02 17	03 19	04 02	22 09	22 30	22 52	23 17
45	02 58	03 46	04 23	22 10	22 35	23 01	23 28
N 40	03 27	04 07	04 40	22 11	22 39	23 08	23 38
35	03 49	04 25	04 54	22 12	22 43	23 14	23 46
30	04 06	04 39	05 06	22 13	22 46	23 19	23 54
20	04 34	05 03	05 27	22 14	22 51	23 28	24 07
N 10	04 55	05 22	05 45	22 16	22 56	23 37	24 20
0	05 13	05 39	06 02	22 17	23 01	23 44	24 28
S 10	05 29	05 56	06 18	22 18	23 05	23 52	24 39
20	05 45	06 12	06 36	22 19	23 10	24 00	00 00
30	06 00	06 30	06 56	22 21	23 16	24 10	00 10
35	06 08	06 40	07 07	22 22	23 19	24 16	00 16
40	06 17	06 51	07 21	22 23	23 23	24 22	00 22
45	06 26	07 03	07 37	22 24	23 27	24 29	00 29
S 50	06 37	07 18	07 56	22 25	23 32	24 38	00 38
52	06 42	07 25	08 05	22 26	23 35	24 42	00 42
54	06 47	07 33	08 15	22 26	23 38	24 47	00 47
56	06 53	07 41	08 27	22 27	23 40	24 52	00 52
58	06 59	07 50	08 40	22 28	23 44	24 58	00 58
S 60	07 06	08 01	08 56	22 29	23 47	25 04	01 04

Lat.	Sunset	Twilight Civil	Twilight Naut.	Moonset 8	9	10	11
°	h m	h m	h m	h m	h m	h m	h m
N 72	▭	▭	▭	09 41	11 30	13 18	15 10
N 70	▭	▭	▭	09 43	11 24	13 04	14 45
68	▭	▭	▭	09 44	11 19	12 53	14 27
66	22 57	////	////	09 45	11 15	12 44	14 12
64	22 09	////	////	09 46	11 12	12 36	13 59
62	21 39	////	////	09 46	11 09	12 30	13 49
60	21 16	22 41	////	09 47	11 07	12 24	13 40
N 58	20 58	22 06	////	09 47	11 04	12 19	13 32
56	20 43	21 41	////	09 48	11 02	12 15	13 26
54	20 30	21 21	22 48	09 48	11 01	12 11	13 20
52	20 18	21 05	22 16	09 49	10 59	12 07	13 14
50	20 08	20 51	21 52	09 49	10 58	12 04	13 09
45	19 47	20 24	21 12	09 50	10 54	11 57	12 59
N 40	19 31	20 03	20 43	09 50	10 52	11 51	12 50
35	19 16	19 46	20 22	09 51	10 49	11 46	12 43
30	19 04	19 31	20 04	09 51	10 47	11 42	12 36
20	18 43	19 08	19 37	09 52	10 44	11 35	12 25
N 10	18 26	18 48	19 15	09 53	10 41	11 28	12 15
0	18 09	18 31	18 57	09 53	10 38	11 22	12 06
S 10	17 52	18 15	18 41	09 54	10 35	11 15	11 56
20	17 35	17 59	18 26	09 55	10 32	11 09	11 46
30	17 15	17 41	18 11	09 55	10 28	11 01	11 35
35	17 03	17 31	18 03	09 56	10 26	10 57	11 29
40	16 50	17 20	17 54	09 56	10 24	10 52	11 22
45	16 34	17 08	17 44	09 57	10 22	10 47	11 13
S 50	16 15	16 53	17 34	09 57	10 18	10 40	11 03
52	16 06	16 46	17 29	09 57	10 17	10 37	10 58
54	15 56	16 38	17 24	09 58	10 15	10 33	10 53
56	15 44	16 30	17 18	09 58	10 14	10 30	10 47
58	15 31	16 21	17 12	09 58	10 12	10 26	10 41
S 60	15 15	16 10	17 05	09 59	10 10	10 21	10 34

Day	SUN Eqn. of Time 00h	SUN Eqn. of Time 12h	SUN Mer. Pass.	MOON Mer. Pass. Upper	MOON Mer. Pass. Lower	Age	Phase
d	m s	m s	h m	h m	h m	d	%
8	05 04	05 08	12 05	03 43	16 05	19	75
9	05 13	05 17	12 05	04 27	16 49	20	65
10	05 21	05 25	12 05	05 11	17 33	21	56

2012 JULY 11, 12, 13 (WED., THURS., FRI.)

UT	ARIES GHA	VENUS −4.7 GHA	Dec	MARS +1.0 GHA	Dec	JUPITER −2.1 GHA	Dec	SATURN +0.7 GHA	Dec	STARS Name	SHA	Dec
11 00	289 18.5	219 36.4	N17 29.9	105 32.2	S 1 22.6	224 41.9	N20 36.4	87 07.6	S 6 35.8	Acamar	315 19.0	S40 15.0
01	304 21.0	234 37.8	30.0	120 33.5	23.2	239 43.8	36.5	102 10.0	35.9	Achernar	335 27.3	S57 10.0
02	319 23.4	249 39.1	30.1	135 34.7	23.8	254 45.7	36.6	117 12.4	35.9	Acrux	173 10.1	S63 10.5
03	334 25.9	264 40.4	.. 30.2	150 35.9	.. 24.4	269 47.7	.. 36.7	132 14.8	.. 35.9	Adhara	255 13.4	S28 59.4
04	349 28.4	279 41.7	30.3	165 37.1	25.0	284 49.6	36.7	147 17.2	36.0	Aldebaran	290 50.4	N16 32.0
05	4 30.8	294 43.0	30.4	180 38.4	25.5	299 51.5	36.8	162 19.6	36.0			
W 06	19 33.3	309 44.3	N17 30.5	195 39.6	S 1 26.1	314 53.5	N20 36.9	177 22.0	S 6 36.0	Alioth	166 21.3	N55 53.7
E 07	34 35.8	324 45.6	30.7	210 40.8	26.7	329 55.4	37.0	192 24.4	36.1	Alkaid	152 59.3	N49 15.3
D 08	49 38.2	339 46.9	30.8	225 42.0	27.3	344 57.3	37.1	207 26.8	36.1	Al Na'ir	27 44.2	S46 53.7
N 09	64 40.7	354 48.2	.. 30.9	240 43.3	.. 27.9	359 59.3	.. 37.2	222 29.2	.. 36.1	Alnilam	275 47.3	S 1 11.7
E 10	79 43.2	9 49.5	31.0	255 44.5	28.5	15 01.2	37.2	237 31.6	36.2	Alphard	217 57.0	S 8 42.9
S 11	94 45.6	24 50.8	31.1	270 45.7	29.0	30 03.1	37.3	252 34.0	36.2			
D 12	109 48.1	39 52.1	N17 31.2	285 46.9	S 1 29.6	45 05.1	N20 37.4	267 36.4	S 6 36.3	Alphecca	126 11.3	N26 40.6
A 13	124 50.5	54 53.4	31.3	300 48.2	30.2	60 07.0	37.5	282 38.8	36.3	Alpheratz	357 44.0	N29 09.6
Y 14	139 53.0	69 54.6	31.5	315 49.4	30.8	75 08.9	37.6	297 41.3	36.3	Altair	62 08.5	N 8 54.3
15	154 55.5	84 55.9	.. 31.6	330 50.6	.. 31.4	90 10.9	.. 37.7	312 43.7	.. 36.4	Ankaa	353 16.2	S42 13.9
16	169 57.9	99 57.2	31.7	345 51.8	32.0	105 12.8	37.8	327 46.1	36.4	Antares	112 26.7	S26 27.6
17	185 00.4	114 58.5	31.8	0 53.1	32.5	120 14.7	37.9	342 48.5	36.4			
18	200 02.9	129 59.7	N17 31.9	15 54.3	S 1 33.1	135 16.7	N20 37.9	357 50.9	S 6 36.5	Arcturus	145 56.2	N19 07.2
19	215 05.3	145 01.0	32.0	30 55.5	33.7	150 18.6	38.0	12 53.3	36.5	Atria	107 28.7	S69 03.1
20	230 07.8	160 02.3	32.2	45 56.7	34.3	165 20.5	38.1	27 55.7	36.5	Avior	234 18.9	S59 33.2
21	245 10.3	175 03.5	.. 32.3	60 58.0	.. 34.9	180 22.5	.. 38.2	42 58.1	.. 36.6	Bellatrix	278 33.0	N 6 21.6
22	260 12.7	190 04.8	32.4	75 59.2	35.5	195 24.4	38.3	58 00.5	36.6	Betelgeuse	271 02.3	N 7 24.5
23	275 15.2	205 06.1	32.5	91 00.4	36.1	210 26.3	38.4	73 02.9	36.6			
12 00	290 17.7	220 07.3	N17 32.7	106 01.6	S 1 36.6	225 28.3	N20 38.4	88 05.3	S 6 36.7	Canopus	263 57.0	S52 42.2
01	305 20.1	235 08.6	32.8	121 02.9	37.2	240 30.2	38.5	103 07.7	36.7	Capella	280 35.8	N46 00.4
02	320 22.6	250 09.8	32.9	136 04.1	37.8	255 32.2	38.6	118 10.1	36.7	Deneb	49 31.5	N45 19.6
03	335 25.0	265 11.1	.. 33.0	151 05.3	.. 38.4	270 34.1	.. 38.7	133 12.5	.. 36.8	Denebola	182 34.4	N14 30.1
04	350 27.5	280 12.3	33.2	166 06.5	39.0	285 36.0	38.8	148 14.9	36.8	Diphda	348 56.5	S17 54.8
05	5 30.0	295 13.6	33.3	181 07.7	39.6	300 38.0	38.9	163 17.3	36.8			
T 06	20 32.4	310 14.8	N17 33.4	196 09.0	S 1 40.2	315 39.9	N20 39.0	178 19.7	S 6 36.9	Dubhe	193 52.9	N61 41.1
H 07	35 34.9	325 16.0	33.5	211 10.2	40.7	330 41.8	39.0	193 22.1	36.9	Elnath	278 13.8	N28 36.9
U 08	50 37.4	340 17.3	33.7	226 11.4	41.3	345 43.8	39.1	208 24.5	37.0	Eltanin	90 45.9	N51 29.5
R 09	65 39.8	355 18.5	.. 33.8	241 12.6	.. 41.9	0 45.7	.. 39.2	223 26.9	.. 37.0	Enif	33 47.5	N 9 56.1
S 10	80 42.3	10 19.7	33.9	256 13.8	42.5	15 47.6	39.3	238 29.3	37.0	Fomalhaut	15 24.5	S29 33.0
D 11	95 44.8	25 20.9	34.1	271 15.1	43.1	30 49.6	39.4	253 31.7	37.1			
A 12	110 47.2	40 22.2	N17 34.2	286 16.3	S 1 43.7	45 51.5	N20 39.5	268 34.1	S 6 37.1	Gacrux	172 01.7	S57 11.3
Y 13	125 49.7	55 23.4	34.3	301 17.5	44.2	60 53.5	39.5	283 36.5	37.1	Gienah	175 53.0	S17 36.8
14	140 52.2	70 24.6	34.5	316 18.7	44.8	75 55.4	39.6	298 38.9	37.2	Hadar	148 48.6	S60 26.3
15	155 54.6	85 25.8	.. 34.6	331 19.9	.. 45.4	90 57.3	.. 39.7	313 41.4	.. 37.2	Hamal	328 01.5	N23 31.2
16	170 57.1	100 27.0	34.7	346 21.1	46.0	105 59.3	39.8	328 43.8	37.2	Kaus Aust.	83 44.2	S34 22.6
17	185 59.5	115 28.2	34.9	1 22.4	46.6	121 01.2	39.9	343 46.2	37.3			
18	201 02.0	130 29.5	N17 35.0	16 23.6	S 1 47.2	136 03.1	N20 40.0	358 48.6	S 6 37.3	Kochab	137 19.5	N74 06.5
19	216 04.5	145 30.7	35.1	31 24.8	47.8	151 05.1	40.0	13 51.0	37.4	Markab	13 38.8	N15 16.5
20	231 06.9	160 31.9	35.3	46 26.0	48.4	166 07.0	40.1	28 53.4	37.4	Menkar	314 15.9	N 4 08.3
21	246 09.4	175 33.1	.. 35.4	61 27.2	.. 48.9	181 09.0	.. 40.2	43 55.8	.. 37.4	Menkent	148 08.2	S36 26.1
22	261 11.9	190 34.3	35.5	76 28.4	49.5	196 10.9	40.3	58 58.2	37.5	Miaplacidus	221 40.6	S69 46.4
23	276 14.3	205 35.4	35.7	91 29.7	50.1	211 12.8	40.4	74 00.6	37.5			
13 00	291 16.8	220 36.6	N17 35.8	106 30.9	S 1 50.7	226 14.8	N20 40.5	89 03.0	S 6 37.5	Mirfak	308 41.5	N49 54.1
01	306 19.3	235 37.8	36.0	121 32.1	51.3	241 16.7	40.5	104 05.4	37.6	Nunki	75 58.7	S26 16.7
02	321 21.7	250 39.0	36.1	136 33.3	51.9	256 18.7	40.6	119 07.8	37.6	Peacock	53 19.6	S56 41.4
03	336 24.2	265 40.2	.. 36.2	151 34.5	.. 52.5	271 20.6	.. 40.7	134 10.2	.. 37.6	Pollux	243 28.9	N27 59.6
04	351 26.7	280 41.4	36.4	166 35.7	53.0	286 22.5	40.8	149 12.6	37.7	Procyon	245 00.7	N 5 11.5
05	6 29.1	295 42.6	36.5	181 37.0	53.6	301 24.5	40.9	164 15.0	37.7			
06	21 31.6	310 43.7	N17 36.7	196 38.2	S 1 54.2	316 26.4	N20 41.0	179 17.4	S 6 37.8	Rasalhague	96 06.7	N12 33.2
07	36 34.0	325 44.9	36.8	211 39.4	54.8	331 28.4	41.0	194 19.8	37.8	Regulus	207 44.4	N11 54.3
08	51 36.5	340 46.1	37.0	226 40.6	55.4	346 30.3	41.1	209 22.2	37.8	Rigel	281 13.0	S 8 11.3
F 09	66 39.0	355 47.2	.. 37.1	241 41.8	.. 56.0	1 32.2	.. 41.2	224 24.6	.. 37.9	Rigil Kent.	139 52.3	S60 53.4
R 10	81 41.4	10 48.4	37.3	256 43.0	56.6	16 34.2	41.3	239 27.0	37.9	Sabik	102 13.0	S15 44.3
I 11	96 43.9	25 49.6	37.4	271 44.2	57.2	31 36.1	41.4	254 29.4	37.9			
D 12	111 46.4	40 50.7	N17 37.5	286 45.4	S 1 57.7	46 38.1	N20 41.5	269 31.8	S 6 38.0	Schedar	349 41.1	N56 36.2
A 13	126 48.8	55 51.9	37.7	301 46.7	58.3	61 40.0	41.5	284 34.2	38.0	Shaula	96 22.4	S37 06.7
Y 14	141 51.3	70 53.0	37.8	316 47.9	58.9	76 41.9	41.6	299 36.6	38.1	Sirius	258 34.6	S16 44.1
15	156 53.8	85 54.2	.. 38.0	331 49.1	1 59.5	91 43.9	.. 41.7	314 39.0	.. 38.1	Spica	158 31.9	S11 13.7
16	171 56.2	100 55.3	38.1	346 50.3	2 00.1	106 45.8	41.8	329 41.4	38.1	Suhail	222 53.3	S43 29.2
17	186 58.7	115 56.5	38.3	1 51.5	00.7	121 47.8	41.9	344 43.7	38.2			
18	202 01.1	130 57.6	N17 38.4	16 52.7	S 2 01.3	136 49.7	N20 42.0	359 46.1	S 6 38.2	Vega	80 39.0	N38 47.9
19	217 03.6	145 58.8	38.6	31 53.9	01.9	151 51.6	42.0	14 48.5	38.2	Zuben'ubi	137 06.0	S16 05.7
20	232 06.1	160 59.9	38.7	46 55.1	02.4	166 53.6	42.1	29 50.9	38.3			
21	247 08.5	176 01.1	.. 38.9	61 56.3	.. 03.0	181 55.5	.. 42.2	44 53.3	.. 38.3		SHA	Mer.Pass.
22	262 11.0	191 02.2	39.0	76 57.6	03.6	196 57.5	42.3	59 55.7	38.4	Venus	289 49.7	9 19
23	277 13.5	206 03.3	39.2	91 58.8	04.2	211 59.4	42.4	74 58.1	38.4	Mars	175 44.0	16 55
Mer.Pass.	h m 4 38.1	v 1.2	d 0.1	v 1.2	d 0.6	v 1.9	d 0.1	v 2.4	d 0.0	Jupiter	295 10.6	8 57
										Saturn	157 47.6	18 05

SUN / MOON

UT	SUN GHA	SUN Dec	MOON GHA	v	MOON Dec	d	HP
d h	° ′	° ′	° ′	′	° ′	′	′
11 00	178 37.6	N22 04.5	273 53.6	14.5	N10 35.9	9.8	54.8
01	193 37.5	04.2	288 27.1	14.4	10 45.7	9.7	54.7
02	208 37.4	03.9	303 00.5	14.4	10 55.4	9.7	54.7
03	223 37.3	.. 03.5	317 33.9	14.4	11 05.1	9.7	54.7
04	238 37.3	03.2	332 07.3	14.4	11 14.8	9.5	54.7
05	253 37.2	02.8	346 40.7	14.4	11 24.3	9.6	54.7
06	268 37.1	N22 02.5	1 14.1	14.3	N11 33.9	9.4	54.7
W 07	283 37.0	02.2	15 47.4	14.4	11 43.3	9.5	54.6
E 08	298 36.9	01.8	30 20.8	14.3	11 52.8	9.3	54.6
D 09	313 36.8	.. 01.5	44 54.1	14.3	12 02.1	9.3	54.6
N 10	328 36.8	01.1	59 27.4	14.3	12 11.4	9.3	54.6
E 11	343 36.7	00.8	74 00.7	14.3	12 20.7	9.2	54.6
S 12	358 36.6	N22 00.5	88 34.0	14.3	N12 29.9	9.1	54.6
D 13	13 36.5	22 00.1	103 07.3	14.2	12 39.0	9.1	54.5
A 14	28 36.4	21 59.8	117 40.5	14.2	12 48.1	9.0	54.5
Y 15	43 36.4	.. 59.4	132 13.7	14.2	12 57.1	9.0	54.5
16	58 36.3	59.1	146 46.9	14.2	13 06.1	8.9	54.5
17	73 36.2	58.7	161 20.1	14.2	13 15.0	8.8	54.5
18	88 36.1	N21 58.4	175 53.3	14.1	N13 23.8	8.8	54.5
19	103 36.0	58.0	190 26.4	14.1	13 32.6	8.7	54.5
20	118 36.0	57.7	204 59.5	14.1	13 41.3	8.7	54.5
21	133 35.9	.. 57.3	219 32.6	14.0	13 50.0	8.6	54.4
22	148 35.8	57.0	234 05.6	14.1	13 58.6	8.5	54.4
23	163 35.7	56.6	248 38.7	14.0	14 07.1	8.5	54.4
12 00	178 35.6	N21 56.3	263 11.7	14.0	N14 15.6	8.4	54.4
01	193 35.6	55.9	277 44.7	14.0	14 24.0	8.4	54.4
02	208 35.5	55.6	292 17.7	13.9	14 32.4	8.3	54.4
03	223 35.4	.. 55.2	306 50.6	13.9	14 40.7	8.2	54.4
04	238 35.3	54.9	321 23.5	13.9	14 48.9	8.1	54.4
05	253 35.3	54.5	335 56.4	13.9	14 57.0	8.1	54.3
06	268 35.2	N21 54.2	350 29.3	13.8	N15 05.1	8.0	54.3
T 07	283 35.1	53.8	5 02.1	13.8	15 13.1	8.0	54.3
H 08	298 35.0	53.5	19 34.9	13.8	15 21.1	7.9	54.3
U 09	313 35.0	.. 53.1	34 07.7	13.7	15 29.0	7.8	54.3
R 10	328 34.9	52.8	48 40.4	13.7	15 36.8	7.7	54.3
S 11	343 34.8	52.4	63 13.1	13.7	15 44.5	7.7	54.3
D 12	358 34.7	N21 52.0	77 45.8	13.7	N15 52.2	7.6	54.3
A 13	13 34.6	51.7	92 18.5	13.6	15 59.8	7.5	54.3
Y 14	28 34.6	51.3	106 51.1	13.6	16 07.3	7.5	54.3
15	43 34.5	.. 51.0	121 23.7	13.6	16 14.8	7.4	54.3
16	58 34.4	50.6	135 56.3	13.5	16 22.2	7.3	54.3
17	73 34.3	50.2	150 28.8	13.5	16 29.5	7.3	54.2
18	88 34.3	N21 49.9	165 01.3	13.5	N16 36.8	7.1	54.2
19	103 34.2	49.5	179 33.8	13.4	16 43.9	7.2	54.2
20	118 34.1	49.2	194 06.2	13.4	16 51.1	7.0	54.2
21	133 34.1	.. 48.8	208 38.6	13.4	16 58.1	6.9	54.2
22	148 34.0	48.4	223 11.0	13.3	17 05.0	6.9	54.2
23	163 33.9	48.1	237 43.3	13.3	17 11.9	6.8	54.2
13 00	178 33.8	N21 47.7	252 15.6	13.3	N17 18.7	6.8	54.2
01	193 33.8	47.3	266 47.9	13.2	17 25.5	6.6	54.2
02	208 33.7	47.0	281 20.1	13.2	17 32.1	6.6	54.2
03	223 33.6	.. 46.6	295 52.3	13.2	17 38.7	6.5	54.2
04	238 33.5	46.2	310 24.5	13.1	17 45.2	6.4	54.2
05	253 33.5	45.9	324 56.6	13.1	17 51.6	6.3	54.2
06	268 33.4	N21 45.5	339 28.7	13.1	N17 57.9	6.3	54.2
07	283 33.3	45.1	354 00.8	13.0	18 04.2	6.2	54.2
F 08	298 33.2	44.7	8 32.8	13.0	18 10.4	6.1	54.2
R 09	313 33.2	.. 44.4	23 04.8	13.0	18 16.5	6.0	54.2
I 10	328 33.1	44.0	37 36.8	12.9	18 22.5	6.0	54.2
11	343 33.0	43.6	52 08.7	12.9	18 28.5	5.8	54.2
D 12	358 32.9	N21 43.2	66 40.6	12.8	N18 34.3	5.8	54.2
A 13	13 32.9	42.9	81 12.4	12.9	18 40.1	5.7	54.2
Y 14	28 32.8	42.5	95 44.3	12.7	18 45.8	5.6	54.2
15	43 32.8	.. 42.1	110 16.0	12.8	18 51.4	5.5	54.2
16	58 32.7	41.7	124 47.8	12.7	18 56.9	5.5	54.2
17	73 32.6	41.4	139 19.5	12.7	19 02.4	5.4	54.2
18	88 32.5	N21 41.0	153 51.2	12.6	N19 07.8	5.2	54.2
19	103 32.5	40.6	168 22.8	12.6	19 13.0	5.2	54.2
20	118 32.4	40.2	182 54.4	12.6	19 18.2	5.1	54.2
21	133 32.3	.. 39.9	197 26.0	12.5	19 23.3	5.1	54.2
22	148 32.3	39.5	211 57.5	12.5	19 28.4	4.9	54.2
23	163 32.2	39.1	226 29.0	12.5	N19 33.3	4.8	54.2
	SD 15.8	d 0.4	SD 14.9	14.8			14.8

Twilight / Sunrise / Moonrise

Lat.	Naut.	Civil	Sunrise	Moonrise 11	12	13	14
°	h m	h m	h m	h m	h m	h m	h m
N 72	□	□	□	21 07	20 31	□	□
N 70	□	□	□	21 33	21 19	20 54	□
68	□	□	□	21 53	21 51	21 50	21 53
66	////	////	01 24	22 09	22 14	22 24	22 42
64	////	////	02 08	22 22	22 32	22 48	23 13
62	////	00 22	02 37	22 33	22 48	23 08	23 37
60	////	01 36	02 59	22 43	23 00	23 24	23 55
N 58	////	02 10	03 16	22 51	23 11	23 37	24 11
56	00 20	02 34	03 31	22 59	23 21	23 49	24 24
54	01 28	02 53	03 44	23 05	23 30	23 59	24 36
52	01 59	03 09	03 55	23 11	23 37	24 08	00 08
50	02 22	03 22	04 05	23 17	23 44	24 16	00 16
45	03 02	03 49	04 25	23 28	23 59	24 34	00 34
N 40	03 29	04 10	04 42	23 38	24 11	00 11	00 48
35	03 51	04 27	04 56	23 46	24 22	00 22	01 00
30	04 08	04 41	05 08	23 54	24 31	00 31	01 11
20	04 35	05 04	05 28	24 07	00 07	00 47	01 29
N 10	04 56	05 23	05 46	24 18	00 18	01 01	01 45
0	05 14	05 40	06 02	24 28	00 28	01 14	02 00
S 10	05 30	05 56	06 18	24 39	00 39	01 27	02 15
20	05 45	06 12	06 35	00 00	00 51	01 41	02 31
30	06 00	06 29	06 55	00 10	01 04	01 57	02 50
35	06 07	06 39	07 06	00 16	01 11	02 07	03 01
40	06 16	06 50	07 20	00 22	01 20	02 17	03 13
45	06 25	07 02	07 35	00 29	01 30	02 30	03 28
S 50	06 36	07 16	07 54	00 38	01 43	02 46	03 46
52	06 40	07 23	08 03	00 42	01 49	02 53	03 55
54	06 45	07 30	08 13	00 47	01 55	03 01	04 04
56	06 51	07 39	08 24	00 52	02 02	03 10	04 15
58	06 57	07 48	08 38	00 58	02 10	03 21	04 28
S 60	07 03	07 58	08 52	01 04	02 19	03 33	04 42

Sunset / Twilight / Moonset

Lat.	Sunset	Civil	Naut.	Moonset 11	12	13	14
°	h m	h m	h m	h m	h m	h m	h m
N 72	□	□	□	15 10	17 20	□	□
N 70	□	□	□	14 45	16 32	18 33	□
68	□	□	□	14 27	16 01	17 38	19 13
66	22 44	////	////	14 12	15 39	17 05	18 25
64	22 01	////	////	13 59	15 21	16 41	17 54
62	21 33	23 37	////	13 49	15 07	16 22	17 31
60	21 11	22 32	////	13 40	14 55	16 06	17 12
N 58	20 54	22 00	////	13 32	14 44	15 53	16 57
56	20 39	21 36	23 39	13 26	14 35	15 42	16 44
54	20 27	21 17	22 40	13 20	14 27	15 32	16 33
52	20 16	21 02	22 10	13 14	14 20	15 23	16 23
50	20 06	20 49	21 48	13 09	14 13	15 15	16 14
45	19 46	20 22	21 09	12 59	13 59	14 58	15 55
N 40	19 29	20 01	20 41	12 50	13 48	14 44	15 39
35	19 15	19 45	20 20	12 43	13 38	14 33	15 26
30	19 03	19 30	20 03	12 36	13 29	14 23	15 15
20	18 43	19 07	19 36	12 25	13 15	14 05	14 56
N 10	18 26	18 48	19 15	12 15	13 02	13 50	14 39
0	18 09	18 32	18 57	12 06	12 50	13 36	14 23
S 10	17 53	18 16	18 42	11 56	12 38	13 22	14 07
20	17 36	18 00	18 27	11 46	12 25	13 07	13 51
30	17 16	17 42	18 12	11 35	12 11	12 49	13 31
35	17 05	17 33	18 04	11 29	12 03	12 39	13 20
40	16 52	17 22	17 56	11 22	11 53	12 28	13 07
45	16 37	17 10	17 46	11 13	11 42	12 15	12 52
S 50	16 18	16 55	17 36	11 03	11 29	11 58	12 33
52	16 09	16 49	17 31	10 58	11 22	11 51	12 25
54	15 59	16 41	17 26	10 53	11 15	11 42	12 15
56	15 48	16 33	17 21	10 47	11 08	11 32	12 04
58	15 35	16 24	17 15	10 41	10 59	11 22	11 51
S 60	15 20	16 14	17 09	10 34	10 49	11 09	11 36

SUN / MOON

Day	SUN Eqn. of Time 00ʰ	12ʰ	SUN Mer. Pass.	MOON Mer. Pass. Upper	Lower	Age	Phase
d	m s	m s	h m	h m	h m	d	%
11	05 30	05 33	12 06	05 55	18 17	22	46
12	05 37	05 41	12 06	06 39	19 02	23	37
13	05 45	05 48	12 06	07 25	19 48	24	28

UT	ARIES	VENUS −4.7		MARS +1.0		JUPITER −2.1		SATURN +0.7		STARS		
	GHA	GHA	Dec	GHA	Dec	GHA	Dec	GHA	Dec	Name	SHA	Dec
d h	° ′	° ′	° ′	° ′	° ′	° ′	° ′	° ′	° ′		° ′	° ′
14 00	292 15.9	221 04.5	N17 39.4	107 00.0	S 2 04.8	227 01.3	N20 42.4	90 00.5	S 6 38.4	Acamar	315 19.0	S40 15.0
01	307 18.4	236 05.6	39.5	122 01.2	05.4	242 03.3	42.5	105 02.9	38.5	Achernar	335 27.3	S57 10.0
02	322 20.9	251 06.7	39.7	137 02.4	06.0	257 05.2	42.6	120 05.3	38.5	Acrux	173 10.1	S63 10.5
03	337 23.3	266 07.8 . .	39.8	152 03.6 . .	06.6	272 07.2 . .	42.7	135 07.7 . .	38.5	Adhara	255 13.4	S28 59.4
04	352 25.8	281 08.9	40.0	167 04.8	07.2	287 09.1	42.8	150 10.1	38.6	Aldebaran	290 50.3	N16 32.0
05	7 28.3	296 10.1	40.1	182 06.0	07.7	302 11.1	42.9	165 12.5	38.6			
06	22 30.7	311 11.2	N17 40.3	197 07.2	S 2 08.3	317 13.0	N20 42.9	180 14.9	S 6 38.7	Alioth	166 21.3	N55 53.7
07	37 33.2	326 12.3	40.4	212 08.4	08.9	332 14.9	43.0	195 17.3	38.7	Alkaid	152 59.3	N49 15.3
S 08	52 35.6	341 13.4	40.6	227 09.6	09.5	347 16.9	43.1	210 19.7	38.7	Al Na'ir	27 44.1	S46 53.7
A 09	67 38.1	356 14.5 . .	40.8	242 10.8 . .	10.1	2 18.8 . .	43.2	225 22.1 . .	38.8	Alnilam	275 47.3	S 1 11.7
T 10	82 40.6	11 15.6	40.9	257 12.1	10.7	17 20.8	43.3	240 24.5	38.8	Alphard	217 57.0	S 8 42.9
U 11	97 43.0	26 16.7	41.1	272 13.3	11.3	32 22.7	43.3	255 26.9	38.9			
R 12	112 45.5	41 17.8	N17 41.2	287 14.5	S 2 11.9	47 24.7	N20 43.4	270 29.3	S 6 38.9	Alphecca	126 11.3	N26 40.6
D 13	127 48.0	56 18.9	41.4	302 15.7	12.5	62 26.6	43.5	285 31.7	38.9	Alpheratz	357 44.0	N29 09.6
A 14	142 50.4	71 20.0	41.6	317 16.9	13.0	77 28.5	43.6	300 34.1	39.0	Altair	62 08.5	N 8 54.3
Y 15	157 52.9	86 21.1 . .	41.7	332 18.1 . .	13.6	92 30.5 . .	43.7	315 36.5 . .	39.0	Ankaa	353 16.2	S42 13.9
16	172 55.4	101 22.2	41.9	347 19.3	14.2	107 32.4	43.8	330 38.9	39.1	Antares	112 26.7	S26 27.6
17	187 57.8	116 23.3	42.1	2 20.5	14.8	122 34.4	43.8	345 41.3	39.1			
18	203 00.3	131 24.4	N17 42.2	17 21.7	S 2 15.4	137 36.3	N20 43.9	0 43.6	S 6 39.1	Arcturus	145 56.2	N19 07.2
19	218 02.8	146 25.4	42.4	32 22.9	16.0	152 38.3	44.0	15 46.0	39.2	Atria	107 28.7	S69 03.1
20	233 05.2	161 26.5	42.5	47 24.1	16.6	167 40.2	44.1	30 48.4	39.2	Avior	234 18.9	S59 33.2
21	248 07.7	176 27.6 . .	42.7	62 25.3 . .	17.2	182 42.2 . .	44.2	45 50.8 . .	39.2	Bellatrix	278 33.0	N 6 21.6
22	263 10.1	191 28.7	42.9	77 26.5	17.8	197 44.1	44.2	60 53.2	39.3	Betelgeuse	271 02.3	N 7 24.5
23	278 12.6	206 29.7	43.0	92 27.7	18.4	212 46.0	44.3	75 55.6	39.3			
15 00	293 15.1	221 30.8	N17 43.2	107 28.9	S 2 18.9	227 48.0	N20 44.4	90 58.0	S 6 39.4	Canopus	263 57.0	S52 42.2
01	308 17.5	236 31.9	43.4	122 30.1	19.5	242 49.9	44.5	106 00.4	39.4	Capella	280 35.8	N46 00.4
02	323 20.0	251 32.9	43.5	137 31.3	20.1	257 51.9	44.6	121 02.8	39.4	Deneb	49 31.4	N45 19.6
03	338 22.5	266 34.0 . .	43.7	152 32.5 . .	20.7	272 53.8 . .	44.6	136 05.2 . .	39.5	Denebola	182 34.4	N14 30.1
04	353 24.9	281 35.1	43.9	167 33.7	21.3	287 55.8	44.7	151 07.6	39.5	Diphda	348 56.4	S17 54.8
05	8 27.4	296 36.1	44.0	182 34.9	21.9	302 57.7	44.8	166 10.0	39.6			
06	23 29.9	311 37.2	N17 44.2	197 36.1	S 2 22.5	317 59.7	N20 44.9	181 12.4	S 6 39.6	Dubhe	193 52.9	N61 41.1
07	38 32.3	326 38.2	44.4	212 37.3	23.1	333 01.6	45.0	196 14.8	39.6	Elnath	278 13.7	N28 36.9
08	53 34.8	341 39.3	44.6	227 38.5	23.7	348 03.6	45.1	211 17.1	39.7	Eltanin	90 45.9	N51 29.5
S 09	68 37.3	356 40.3 . .	44.7	242 39.7 . .	24.3	3 05.5 . .	45.1	226 19.5 . .	39.7	Enif	33 47.4	N 9 56.1
U 10	83 39.7	11 41.4	44.9	257 40.9	24.9	18 07.4	45.2	241 21.9	39.8	Fomalhaut	15 24.4	S29 33.0
N 11	98 42.2	26 42.4	45.1	272 42.1	25.4	33 09.4	45.3	256 24.3	39.8			
D 12	113 44.6	41 43.5	N17 45.2	287 43.3	S 2 26.0	48 11.3	N20 45.4	271 26.7	S 6 39.8	Gacrux	172 01.7	S57 11.3
A 13	128 47.1	56 44.5	45.4	302 44.5	26.6	63 13.3	45.5	286 29.1	39.9	Gienah	175 53.0	S17 36.8
Y 14	143 49.6	71 45.5	45.6	317 45.7	27.2	78 15.2	45.5	301 31.5	39.9	Hadar	148 48.6	S60 26.3
15	158 52.0	86 46.6 . .	45.8	332 46.9 . .	27.8	93 17.2 . .	45.6	316 33.9 . .	40.0	Hamal	328 01.5	N23 31.2
16	173 54.5	101 47.6	45.9	347 48.1	28.4	108 19.1	45.7	331 36.3	40.0	Kaus Aust.	83 44.2	S34 22.6
17	188 57.0	116 48.6	46.1	2 49.3	29.0	123 21.1	45.8	346 38.7	40.1			
18	203 59.4	131 49.7	N17 46.3	17 50.5	S 2 29.6	138 23.0	N20 45.8	1 41.1	S 6 40.1	Kochab	137 19.6	N74 06.5
19	219 01.9	146 50.7	46.5	32 51.7	30.2	153 25.0	45.9	16 43.4	40.1	Markab	13 38.7	N15 16.5
20	234 04.4	161 51.7	46.6	47 52.9	30.8	168 26.9	46.0	31 45.8	40.2	Menkar	314 15.8	N 4 08.3
21	249 06.8	176 52.7 . .	46.8	62 54.1 . .	31.4	183 28.9 . .	46.1	46 48.2 . .	40.2	Menkent	148 08.2	S36 26.1
22	264 09.3	191 53.7	47.0	77 55.3	32.0	198 30.8	46.2	61 50.6	40.3	Miaplacidus	221 40.7	S69 46.4
23	279 11.7	206 54.8	47.2	92 56.5	32.5	213 32.8	46.3	76 53.0	40.3			
16 00	294 14.2	221 55.8	N17 47.4	107 57.7	S 2 33.1	228 34.7	N20 46.3	91 55.4	S 6 40.3	Mirfak	308 41.5	N49 54.1
01	309 16.7	236 56.8	47.5	122 58.9	33.7	243 36.7	46.4	106 57.8	40.4	Nunki	75 58.7	S26 16.7
02	324 19.1	251 57.8	47.7	138 00.1	34.3	258 38.6	46.5	122 00.2	40.4	Peacock	53 19.6	S56 41.4
03	339 21.6	266 58.8 . .	47.9	153 01.3 . .	34.9	273 40.6 . .	46.6	137 02.6 . .	40.5	Pollux	243 28.9	N27 59.6
04	354 24.1	281 59.8	48.1	168 02.5	35.5	288 42.5	46.7	152 05.0	40.5	Procyon	245 00.7	N 5 11.5
05	9 26.5	297 00.8	48.3	183 03.7	36.1	303 44.5	46.7	167 07.3	40.5			
06	24 29.0	312 01.8	N17 48.4	198 04.9	S 2 36.7	318 46.4	N20 46.8	182 09.7	S 6 40.6	Rasalhague	96 06.7	N12 33.3
07	39 31.5	327 02.8	48.6	213 06.1	37.3	333 48.4	46.9	197 12.1	40.6	Regulus	207 44.4	N11 54.3
08	54 33.9	342 03.8	48.8	228 07.3	37.9	348 50.3	47.0	212 14.5	40.7	Rigel	281 12.9	S 8 11.3
M 09	69 36.4	357 04.8 . .	49.0	243 08.5 . .	38.5	3 52.2 . .	47.0	227 16.9 . .	40.7	Rigil Kent.	139 52.4	S60 53.4
O 10	84 38.9	12 05.8	49.2	258 09.6	39.1	18 54.2	47.1	242 19.3	40.7	Sabik	102 13.0	S15 44.3
N 11	99 41.3	27 06.7	49.3	273 10.8	39.7	33 56.1	47.2	257 21.7	40.8			
D 12	114 43.8	42 07.7	N17 49.5	288 12.0	S 2 40.2	48 58.1	N20 47.3	272 24.1	S 6 40.8	Schedar	349 44.1	N56 36.2
A 13	129 46.2	57 08.7	49.7	303 13.2	40.8	64 00.0	47.4	287 26.4	40.9	Shaula	96 22.4	S37 06.7
Y 14	144 48.7	72 09.7	49.9	318 14.4	41.4	79 02.0	47.4	302 28.8	40.9	Sirius	258 34.6	S16 44.1
15	159 51.2	87 10.7 . .	50.1	333 15.6 . .	42.0	94 03.9 . .	47.5	317 31.2 . .	41.0	Spica	158 31.9	S11 13.7
16	174 53.6	102 11.6	50.3	348 16.8	42.6	109 05.9	47.6	332 33.6	41.0	Suhail	222 53.3	S43 29.2
17	189 56.1	117 12.6	50.5	3 18.0	43.2	124 07.9	47.7	347 36.0	41.0			
18	204 58.6	132 13.6	N17 50.7	18 19.2	S 2 43.8	139 09.8	N20 47.7	2 38.4	S 6 41.1	Vega	80 39.0	N38 47.9
19	220 01.0	147 14.6	50.8	33 20.4	44.4	154 11.8	47.8	17 40.8	41.1	Zuben'ubi	137 06.0	S16 05.7
20	235 03.5	162 15.5	51.0	48 21.6	45.0	169 13.7	47.9	32 43.2	41.2		SHA	Mer.Pass.
21	250 06.0	177 16.5 . .	51.2	63 22.8 . .	45.6	184 15.7 . .	48.0	47 45.5 . .	41.2		° ′	h m
22	265 08.4	192 17.4	51.4	78 24.0	46.2	199 17.6	48.1	62 47.9	41.3	Venus	288 15.7	9 13
23	280 10.9	207 18.4	51.6	93 25.1	46.8	214 19.6	48.2	77 50.3	41.3	Mars	174 13.8	16 49
	h m									Jupiter	294 32.9	8 48
Mer.Pass.	4 26.3	v 1.0	d 0.2	v 1.2	d 0.6	v 1.9	d 0.1	v 2.4	d 0.0	Saturn	157 42.9	17 53

UT	SUN GHA	SUN Dec	MOON GHA	v	MOON Dec	d	HP
14 00	178 32.1	N21 38.7	241 00.5	12.4	N19 38.1	4.8	54.2
01	193 32.1	38.3	255 31.9	12.4	19 42.9	4.7	54.2
02	208 32.0	37.9	270 03.3	12.4	19 47.6	4.5	54.2
03	223 31.9	.. 37.6	284 34.7	12.3	19 52.1	4.5	54.2
04	238 31.9	37.2	299 06.0	12.3	19 56.6	4.4	54.2
05	253 31.8	36.8	313 37.3	12.2	20 01.0	4.4	54.2
06	268 31.7	N21 36.4	328 08.5	12.2	N20 05.4	4.2	54.2
07	283 31.7	36.0	342 39.7	12.2	20 09.6	4.1	54.2
S 08	298 31.6	35.6	357 10.9	12.2	20 13.7	4.0	54.2
A 09	313 31.5	.. 35.3	11 42.1	12.1	20 17.7	4.0	54.2
T 10	328 31.5	34.9	26 13.2	12.1	20 21.7	3.9	54.2
U 11	343 31.4	34.5	40 44.3	12.0	20 25.6	3.7	54.2
R 12	358 31.3	N21 34.1	55 15.3	12.0	N20 29.3	3.7	54.2
D 13	13 31.3	33.7	69 46.3	12.0	20 33.0	3.6	54.2
A 14	28 31.2	33.3	84 17.3	12.0	20 36.6	3.4	54.2
Y 15	43 31.1	.. 32.9	98 48.3	11.9	20 40.0	3.4	54.2
16	58 31.1	32.5	113 19.2	11.8	20 43.4	3.3	54.2
17	73 31.0	32.1	127 50.0	11.9	20 46.7	3.2	54.2
18	88 30.9	N21 31.7	142 20.9	11.8	N20 49.9	3.1	54.3
19	103 30.9	31.3	156 51.7	11.8	20 53.0	3.0	54.3
20	118 30.8	30.9	171 22.5	11.7	20 56.0	3.0	54.3
21	133 30.7	.. 30.6	185 53.2	11.8	20 59.0	2.8	54.3
22	148 30.7	30.2	200 24.0	11.7	21 01.8	2.7	54.3
23	163 30.6	29.8	214 54.7	11.6	21 04.5	2.6	54.3
15 00	178 30.5	N21 29.4	229 25.3	11.6	N21 07.1	2.5	54.3
01	193 30.5	29.0	243 55.9	11.6	21 09.6	2.4	54.3
02	208 30.4	28.6	258 26.5	11.6	21 12.0	2.4	54.3
03	223 30.4	.. 28.2	272 57.1	11.6	21 14.4	2.2	54.3
04	238 30.3	27.8	287 27.7	11.5	21 16.6	2.1	54.3
05	253 30.2	27.4	301 58.2	11.5	21 18.7	2.1	54.3
06	268 30.2	N21 27.0	316 28.7	11.4	N21 20.8	1.9	54.3
07	283 30.1	26.6	330 59.1	11.4	21 22.7	1.8	54.4
S 08	298 30.0	26.2	345 29.5	11.4	21 24.5	1.7	54.4
U 09	313 30.0	.. 25.8	359 59.9	11.4	21 26.2	1.7	54.4
N 10	328 29.9	25.4	14 30.3	11.4	21 27.9	1.5	54.4
D 11	343 29.9	25.0	29 00.7	11.3	21 29.4	1.4	54.4
A 12	358 29.8	N21 24.6	43 31.0	11.3	N21 30.8	1.3	54.4
Y 13	13 29.7	24.1	58 01.3	11.3	21 32.1	1.3	54.4
14	28 29.7	23.7	72 31.6	11.2	21 33.4	1.1	54.4
15	43 29.6	.. 23.3	87 01.8	11.3	21 34.5	1.0	54.4
16	58 29.6	22.9	101 32.1	11.2	21 35.5	0.9	54.4
17	73 29.5	22.5	116 02.3	11.1	21 36.4	0.8	54.5
18	88 29.4	N21 22.1	130 32.4	11.2	N21 37.2	0.7	54.5
19	103 29.4	21.7	145 02.6	11.1	21 37.9	0.6	54.5
20	118 29.3	21.3	159 32.7	11.2	21 38.5	0.5	54.5
21	133 29.3	.. 20.9	174 02.9	11.1	21 39.0	0.4	54.5
22	148 29.2	20.5	188 33.0	11.0	21 39.4	0.3	54.5
23	163 29.1	20.1	203 03.0	11.1	21 39.7	0.2	54.5
16 00	178 29.1	N21 19.7	217 33.1	11.0	N21 39.9	0.1	54.5
01	193 29.0	19.2	232 03.1	11.1	21 40.0	0.0	54.6
02	208 29.0	18.8	246 33.2	11.0	21 40.0	0.2	54.6
03	223 28.9	.. 18.4	261 03.2	11.0	21 39.8	0.2	54.6
04	238 28.8	18.0	275 33.2	11.0	21 39.6	0.3	54.6
05	253 28.8	17.6	290 03.1	11.0	21 39.3	0.5	54.6
06	268 28.7	N21 17.2	304 33.1	10.9	N21 38.8	0.7	54.6
07	283 28.7	16.7	319 03.0	10.9	21 38.3	0.7	54.6
M 08	298 28.6	16.3	333 32.9	11.0	21 37.6	0.7	54.6
O 09	313 28.6	.. 15.9	348 02.9	10.9	21 36.9	0.9	54.7
N 10	328 28.5	15.5	2 32.8	10.8	21 36.0	1.0	54.7
D 11	343 28.5	15.1	17 02.6	10.9	21 35.0	1.0	54.7
A 12	358 28.4	N21 14.7	31 32.5	10.9	N21 34.0	1.2	54.7
Y 13	13 28.3	14.2	46 02.4	10.8	21 32.8	1.3	54.7
14	28 28.3	13.8	60 32.2	10.9	21 31.5	1.4	54.7
15	43 28.2	.. 13.4	75 02.1	10.8	21 30.1	1.5	54.8
16	58 28.2	13.0	89 31.9	10.8	21 28.6	1.6	54.8
17	73 28.1	12.6	104 01.7	10.9	21 27.0	1.7	54.8
18	88 28.1	N21 12.1	118 31.6	10.8	N21 25.3	1.9	54.8
19	103 28.0	11.7	133 01.4	10.8	21 23.4	1.9	54.8
20	118 28.0	11.3	147 31.2	10.8	21 21.5	2.0	54.8
21	133 27.9	.. 10.9	162 01.0	10.8	21 19.5	2.2	54.8
22	148 27.9	10.4	176 30.8	10.7	21 17.3	2.2	54.9
23	163 27.8	10.0	191 00.5	10.8	N21 15.1	2.4	54.9
	SD 15.8	d 0.4	SD 14.8		14.8		14.9

Twilight / Sunrise / Moonrise

Lat.	Naut.	Civil	Sunrise	14	15	16	17
N 72	▭	▭	▭	▭	▭	▭	▭
N 70	▭	▭	▭	▭	▭	▭	23 50
68	▭	▭	▭	21 53	22 14	23 24	25 02
66	////	////	01 37	22 42	23 18	24 18	00 18
64	////	////	02 16	23 13	23 53	24 51	00 51
62	////	00 52	02 43	23 37	24 18	00 18	01 15
60	////	01 46	03 04	23 55	24 38	00 38	01 34
N 58	////	02 17	03 21	24 11	00 11	00 55	01 50
56	00 48	02 39	03 35	24 24	00 24	01 09	02 03
54	01 37	02 58	03 48	24 36	00 36	01 21	02 15
52	02 06	03 13	03 58	00 08	00 46	01 31	02 25
50	02 27	03 26	04 08	00 16	00 55	01 41	02 34
45	03 05	03 52	04 28	00 34	01 14	02 01	02 54
N 40	03 32	04 12	04 44	00 48	01 30	02 17	03 09
35	03 53	04 29	04 58	01 00	01 43	02 31	03 23
30	04 10	04 42	05 09	01 11	01 55	02 43	03 34
20	04 36	05 05	05 29	01 29	02 15	03 03	03 54
N 10	04 57	05 24	05 46	01 45	02 32	03 21	04 11
0	05 14	05 40	06 02	02 00	02 48	03 37	04 27
S 10	05 30	05 56	06 18	02 15	03 04	03 54	04 43
20	05 44	06 11	06 35	02 31	03 22	04 12	05 01
30	05 59	06 28	06 54	02 50	03 42	04 32	05 20
35	06 07	06 38	07 05	03 01	03 54	04 44	05 32
40	06 15	06 48	07 18	03 13	04 07	04 58	05 45
45	06 24	07 00	07 33	03 28	04 23	05 14	06 01
S 50	06 34	07 14	07 51	03 46	04 43	05 35	06 20
52	06 38	07 21	08 00	03 55	04 52	05 44	06 29
54	06 43	07 28	08 10	04 04	05 03	05 55	06 39
56	06 48	07 36	08 21	04 15	05 15	06 07	06 51
58	06 54	07 44	08 33	04 28	05 29	06 21	07 04
S 60	07 00	07 54	08 48	04 42	05 45	06 38	07 19

Sunset / Twilight / Moonset

Lat.	Sunset	Civil	Naut.	14	15	16	17
N 72	▭	▭	▭	▭	▭	▭	▭
N 70	▭	▭	▭	▭	▭	▭	22 27
68	▭	▭	▭	19 13	20 34	21 08	21 14
66	22 31	////	////	18 25	19 31	20 14	20 37
64	21 53	////	////	17 54	18 56	19 41	20 11
62	21 27	23 13	////	17 31	18 30	19 17	19 50
60	21 06	22 23	////	17 12	18 10	18 58	19 34
N 58	20 50	21 53	////	16 57	17 54	18 42	19 19
56	20 36	21 31	23 18	16 44	17 40	18 28	19 07
54	20 24	21 13	22 32	16 33	17 28	18 16	18 57
52	20 13	20 58	22 05	16 23	17 18	18 06	18 47
50	20 03	20 45	21 44	16 14	17 08	17 57	18 39
45	19 44	20 19	21 06	15 55	16 48	17 37	18 21
N 40	19 28	19 59	20 39	15 39	16 32	17 21	18 06
35	19 14	19 43	20 18	15 26	16 18	17 07	17 53
30	19 02	19 29	20 02	15 15	16 06	16 56	17 42
20	18 43	19 07	19 35	14 56	15 46	16 36	17 23
N 10	18 26	18 48	19 15	14 39	15 28	16 18	17 07
0	18 10	18 32	18 58	14 23	15 12	16 01	16 52
S 10	17 54	18 16	18 42	14 07	14 55	15 45	16 36
20	17 37	18 01	18 28	13 51	14 38	15 27	16 19
30	17 17	17 44	18 13	13 31	14 17	15 07	16 00
35	17 07	17 35	18 06	13 20	14 05	14 55	15 49
40	16 54	17 24	17 58	13 07	13 52	14 41	15 36
45	16 39	17 12	17 49	12 52	13 35	14 25	15 21
S 50	16 21	16 58	17 39	12 33	13 15	14 05	15 02
52	16 12	16 52	17 34	12 25	13 06	13 56	14 53
54	16 03	16 45	17 29	12 15	12 55	13 45	14 43
56	15 52	16 37	17 24	12 04	12 43	13 33	14 32
58	15 39	16 28	17 19	11 51	12 29	13 19	14 19
S 60	15 25	16 18	17 13	11 36	12 13	13 02	14 04

SUN / MOON

Day	Eqn. of Time 00h	Eqn. of Time 12h	Mer. Pass.	Mer. Pass. Upper	Mer. Pass. Lower	Age	Phase
	m s	m s	h m	h m	h m	d	%
14	05 51	05 55	12 06	08 12	20 36	25	20
15	05 58	06 01	12 06	09 00	21 25	26	13
16	06 04	06 06	12 06	09 49	22 14	27	7

2012 JULY 17, 18, 19 (TUES., WED., THURS.)

UT	ARIES GHA	VENUS −4.7 GHA	Dec	MARS +1.0 GHA	Dec	JUPITER −2.1 GHA	Dec	SATURN +0.8 GHA	Dec	STARS Name	SHA	Dec
d h	° ′	° ′	° ′	° ′	° ′	° ′	° ′	° ′	° ′		° ′	° ′
17 00	295 13.4	222 19.4	N17 51.8	108 26.3	S 2 47.4	229 21.5	N20 48.2	92 52.7	S 6 41.3	Acamar	315 19.0	S40 15.0
01	310 15.8	237 20.3	52.0	123 27.5	48.0	244 23.5	48.3	107 55.1	41.4	Achernar	335 27.2	S57 10.0
02	325 18.3	252 21.3	52.1	138 28.7	48.5	259 25.4	48.4	122 57.5	41.4	Acrux	173 10.2	S63 10.5
03	340 20.7	267 22.2	.. 52.3	153 29.9	.. 49.1	274 27.4	.. 48.5	137 59.9	.. 41.5	Adhara	255 13.4	S28 59.4
04	355 23.2	282 23.2	52.5	168 31.1	49.7	289 29.3	48.5	153 02.2	41.5	Aldebaran	290 50.3	N16 32.0
05	10 25.7	297 24.1	52.7	183 32.3	50.3	304 31.3	48.6	168 04.6	41.6			
06	25 28.1	312 25.1	N17 52.9	198 33.5	S 2 50.9	319 33.2	N20 48.7	183 07.0	S 6 41.6	Alioth	166 21.3	N55 53.7
07	40 30.6	327 26.0	53.1	213 34.7	51.5	334 35.2	48.8	198 09.4	41.6	Alkaid	152 59.4	N49 15.3
08	55 33.1	342 26.9	53.3	228 35.8	52.1	349 37.1	48.9	213 11.8	41.7	Al Na'ir	27 44.1	S46 53.7
09	70 35.5	357 27.9	.. 53.5	243 37.0	.. 52.7	4 39.1	.. 48.9	228 14.2	.. 41.7	Alnilam	275 47.3	S 1 11.7
10	85 38.0	12 28.8	53.7	258 38.2	53.3	19 41.0	49.0	243 16.5	41.8	Alphard	217 57.0	S 8 42.9
11	100 40.5	27 29.7	53.9	273 39.4	53.9	34 43.0	49.1	258 18.9	41.8			
12	115 42.9	42 30.7	N17 54.1	288 40.6	S 2 54.5	49 44.9	N20 49.2	273 21.3	S 6 41.9	Alphecca	126 11.3	N26 40.6
13	130 45.4	57 31.6	54.3	303 41.8	55.1	64 46.9	49.2	288 23.7	41.9	Alpheratz	357 44.0	N29 09.6
14	145 47.9	72 32.5	54.5	318 43.0	55.7	79 48.8	49.3	303 26.1	41.9	Altair	62 08.5	N 8 54.3
15	160 50.3	87 33.4	.. 54.6	333 44.1	.. 56.3	94 50.8	.. 49.4	318 28.5	.. 42.0	Ankaa	353 16.2	S42 13.9
16	175 52.8	102 34.4	54.8	348 45.3	56.9	109 52.8	49.5	333 30.8	42.0	Antares	112 26.7	S26 27.6
17	190 55.2	117 35.3	55.0	3 46.5	57.5	124 54.7	49.6	348 33.2	42.1			
18	205 57.7	132 36.2	N17 55.2	18 47.7	S 2 58.1	139 56.7	N20 49.6	3 35.6	S 6 42.1	Arcturus	145 56.2	N19 07.2
19	221 00.2	147 37.1	55.4	33 48.9	58.7	154 58.6	49.7	18 38.0	42.2	Atria	107 28.7	S69 03.1
20	236 02.6	162 38.0	55.6	48 50.1	59.2	170 00.6	49.8	33 40.4	42.2	Avior	234 18.9	S59 33.2
21	251 05.1	177 38.9	.. 55.8	63 51.3	2 59.8	185 02.5	.. 49.9	48 42.8	.. 42.2	Bellatrix	278 32.9	N 6 21.6
22	266 07.6	192 39.8	56.0	78 52.4	3 00.4	200 04.5	49.9	63 45.1	42.3	Betelgeuse	271 02.3	N 7 24.5
23	281 10.0	207 40.7	56.2	93 53.6	01.0	215 06.4	50.0	78 47.5	42.3			
18 00	296 12.5	222 41.6	N17 56.4	108 54.8	S 3 01.6	230 08.4	N20 50.1	93 49.9	S 6 42.4	Canopus	263 56.9	S52 42.1
01	311 15.0	237 42.5	56.6	123 56.0	02.2	245 10.3	50.2	108 52.3	42.4	Capella	280 35.7	N46 00.4
02	326 17.4	252 43.4	56.8	138 57.2	02.8	260 12.3	50.3	123 54.7	42.5	Deneb	49 31.4	N45 19.6
03	341 19.9	267 44.3	.. 57.0	153 58.4	.. 03.4	275 14.3	.. 50.3	138 57.1	.. 42.5	Denebola	182 34.4	N14 30.1
04	356 22.4	282 45.2	57.2	168 59.5	04.0	290 16.2	50.4	153 59.4	42.6	Diphda	348 56.4	S17 54.8
05	11 24.8	297 46.1	57.4	184 00.7	04.6	305 18.2	50.5	169 01.8	42.6			
06	26 27.3	312 47.0	N17 57.6	199 01.9	S 3 05.2	320 20.1	N20 50.6	184 04.2	S 6 42.6	Dubhe	193 52.9	N61 41.1
07	41 29.7	327 47.9	57.8	214 03.1	05.8	335 22.1	50.6	199 06.6	42.7	Elnath	278 13.7	N28 36.9
08	56 32.2	342 48.8	58.0	229 04.3	06.4	350 24.0	50.7	214 09.0	42.7	Eltanin	90 45.9	N51 29.5
09	71 34.7	357 49.7	.. 58.2	244 05.4	.. 07.0	5 26.0	.. 50.8	229 11.3	.. 42.8	Enif	33 47.4	N 9 56.1
10	86 37.1	12 50.5	58.4	259 06.6	07.6	20 27.9	50.9	244 13.7	42.8	Fomalhaut	15 24.4	S29 33.0
11	101 39.6	27 51.4	58.6	274 07.8	08.2	35 29.9	50.9	259 16.1	42.9			
12	116 42.1	42 52.3	N17 58.8	289 09.0	S 3 08.8	50 31.9	N20 51.0	274 18.5	S 6 42.9	Gacrux	172 01.7	S57 11.3
13	131 44.5	57 53.2	59.0	304 10.2	09.4	65 33.8	51.1	289 20.9	43.0	Gienah	175 53.0	S17 36.8
14	146 47.0	72 54.1	59.2	319 11.3	10.0	80 35.8	51.2	304 23.2	43.0	Hadar	148 48.7	S60 26.3
15	161 49.5	87 54.9	.. 59.4	334 12.5	.. 10.6	95 37.7	.. 51.3	319 25.6	.. 43.0	Hamal	328 01.5	N23 31.2
16	176 51.9	102 55.8	59.6	349 13.7	11.2	110 39.7	51.3	334 28.0	43.1	Kaus Aust.	83 44.2	S34 22.6
17	191 54.4	117 56.7	17 59.8	4 14.9	11.8	125 41.6	51.4	349 30.4	43.1			
18	206 56.8	132 57.5	N18 00.0	19 16.1	S 3 12.3	140 43.6	N20 51.5	4 32.8	S 6 43.2	Kochab	137 19.6	N74 06.5
19	221 59.3	147 58.4	00.2	34 17.2	12.9	155 45.6	51.6	19 35.1	43.2	Markab	13 38.7	N15 16.5
20	237 01.8	162 59.2	00.4	49 18.4	13.5	170 47.5	51.6	34 37.5	43.3	Menkar	314 15.8	N 4 08.4
21	252 04.2	178 00.1	.. 00.6	64 19.6	.. 14.1	185 49.5	.. 51.7	49 39.9	.. 43.3	Menkent	148 08.2	S36 26.1
22	267 06.7	193 01.0	00.9	79 20.8	14.7	200 51.4	51.8	64 42.3	43.4	Miaplacidus	221 40.7	S69 46.4
23	282 09.2	208 01.8	01.1	94 22.0	15.3	215 53.4	51.9	79 44.7	43.4			
19 00	297 11.6	223 02.7	N18 01.3	109 23.1	S 3 15.9	230 55.4	N20 51.9	94 47.0	S 6 43.4	Mirfak	308 41.5	N49 54.1
01	312 14.1	238 03.5	01.5	124 24.3	16.5	245 57.3	52.0	109 49.4	43.5	Nunki	75 58.7	S26 16.7
02	327 16.6	253 04.3	01.7	139 25.5	17.1	260 59.3	52.1	124 51.8	43.5	Peacock	53 19.6	S56 41.4
03	342 19.0	268 05.2	.. 01.9	154 26.7	.. 17.7	276 01.2	.. 52.2	139 54.2	.. 43.6	Pollux	243 28.9	N27 59.6
04	357 21.5	283 06.0	02.1	169 27.8	18.3	291 03.2	52.2	154 56.5	43.6	Procyon	245 00.7	N 5 11.5
05	12 24.0	298 06.9	02.3	184 29.0	18.9	306 05.1	52.3	169 58.9	43.7			
06	27 26.4	313 07.7	N18 02.5	199 30.2	S 3 19.5	321 07.1	N20 52.4	185 01.3	S 6 43.7	Rasalhague	96 06.7	N12 33.3
07	42 28.9	328 08.5	02.7	214 31.4	20.1	336 09.1	52.5	200 03.7	43.8	Regulus	207 44.4	N11 54.3
08	57 31.3	343 09.4	02.9	229 32.5	20.7	351 11.0	52.5	215 06.1	43.8	Rigel	281 12.9	S 8 11.2
09	72 33.8	358 10.2	.. 03.1	244 33.7	.. 21.3	6 13.0	.. 52.6	230 08.4	.. 43.9	Rigil Kent.	139 52.4	S60 53.4
10	87 36.3	13 11.0	03.3	259 34.9	21.9	21 14.9	52.7	245 10.8	43.9	Sabik	102 13.0	S15 44.3
11	102 38.7	28 11.9	03.5	274 36.1	22.5	36 16.9	52.8	260 13.2	43.9			
12	117 41.2	43 12.7	N18 03.8	289 37.2	S 3 23.1	51 18.9	N20 52.8	275 15.6	S 6 44.0	Schedar	349 41.1	N56 36.2
13	132 43.7	58 13.5	04.0	304 38.4	23.7	66 20.8	52.9	290 17.9	44.0	Shaula	96 22.4	S37 06.7
14	147 46.1	73 14.3	04.2	319 39.6	24.3	81 22.8	53.0	305 20.3	44.1	Sirius	258 34.6	S16 44.1
15	162 48.6	88 15.2	.. 04.4	334 40.8	.. 24.9	96 24.7	.. 53.1	320 22.7	.. 44.1	Spica	158 31.9	S11 13.7
16	177 51.1	103 16.0	04.6	349 41.9	25.5	111 26.7	53.1	335 25.1	44.2	Suhail	222 53.3	S43 29.2
17	192 53.5	118 16.8	04.8	4 43.1	26.1	126 28.7	53.2	350 27.4	44.2			
18	207 56.0	133 17.6	N18 05.0	19 44.3	S 3 26.7	141 30.6	N20 53.3	5 29.8	S 6 44.3	Vega	80 39.0	N38 48.0
19	222 58.5	148 18.4	05.2	34 45.4	27.3	156 32.6	53.4	20 32.2	44.3	Zuben'ubi	137 06.0	S16 05.7
20	238 00.9	163 19.2	05.4	49 46.6	27.9	171 34.6	53.4	35 34.6	44.4		SHA	Mer.Pass.
21	253 03.4	178 20.0	.. 05.7	64 47.8	.. 28.5	186 36.5	.. 53.5	50 36.9	.. 44.4	Venus	286 29.1	9 09
22	268 05.9	193 20.8	05.9	79 49.0	29.1	201 38.5	53.6	65 39.3	44.5	Mars	172 42.3	16 43
23	283 08.3	208 21.6	06.1	94 50.1	29.7	216 40.4	53.7	80 41.7	44.5	Jupiter	293 55.9	8 38
Mer. Pass. 4 14.5		v 0.9	d 0.2	v 1.2	d 0.6	v 2.0	d 0.1	v 2.4	d 0.0	Saturn	157 37.4	17 42

UT	SUN GHA	Dec	MOON GHA	v	Dec	d	HP
d h	° ′	° ′	° ′	′	° ′	′	′
17 00	178 27.7	N21 09.6	205 30.3	10.8	N21 12.7	2.4	54.9
01	193 27.7	09.1	220 00.1	10.8	21 10.3	2.6	54.9
02	208 27.6	08.7	234 29.9	10.7	21 07.7	2.6	54.9
03	223 27.6	.. 08.3	248 59.6	10.8	21 05.1	2.8	54.9
04	238 27.5	07.9	263 29.4	10.8	21 02.3	2.9	55.0
05	253 27.5	07.4	277 59.2	10.7	20 59.4	3.0	55.0
T 06	268 27.4	N21 07.0	292 28.9	10.8	N20 56.4	3.1	55.0
U 07	283 27.4	06.6	306 58.7	10.8	20 53.3	3.2	55.0
E 08	298 27.3	06.1	321 28.5	10.7	20 50.1	3.3	55.0
S 09	313 27.3	.. 05.7	335 58.2	10.8	20 46.8	3.4	55.0
D 10	328 27.2	05.3	350 28.0	10.8	20 43.4	3.5	55.1
A 11	343 27.2	04.8	4 57.8	10.7	20 39.9	3.6	55.1
Y 12	358 27.1	N21 04.4	19 27.5	10.8	N20 36.3	3.7	55.1
13	13 27.1	04.0	33 57.3	10.8	20 32.6	3.9	55.1
14	28 27.0	03.5	48 27.1	10.8	20 28.7	3.9	55.1
15	43 27.0	.. 03.1	62 56.9	10.8	20 24.8	4.0	55.2
16	58 26.9	02.7	77 26.7	10.8	20 20.8	4.2	55.2
17	73 26.9	02.2	91 56.5	10.8	20 16.6	4.2	55.2
18	88 26.8	N21 01.8	106 26.3	10.8	N20 12.4	4.4	55.2
19	103 26.8	01.3	120 56.1	10.8	20 08.0	4.4	55.2
20	118 26.7	00.9	135 25.9	10.8	20 03.6	4.6	55.2
21	133 26.7	.. 00.5	149 55.7	10.8	19 59.0	4.6	55.3
22	148 26.6	21 00.0	164 25.5	10.9	19 54.4	4.8	55.3
23	163 26.6	20 59.6	178 55.4	10.9	19 49.6	4.8	55.3
18 00	178 26.5	N20 59.1	193 25.2	10.9	N19 44.8	5.0	55.3
01	193 26.5	58.7	207 55.1	10.9	19 39.8	5.0	55.3
02	208 26.4	58.3	222 25.0	10.8	19 34.8	5.2	55.4
03	223 26.4	.. 57.8	236 54.8	10.9	19 29.6	5.3	55.4
04	238 26.4	57.4	251 24.7	10.9	19 24.3	5.3	55.4
05	253 26.3	56.9	265 54.6	10.9	19 19.0	5.5	55.4
W 06	268 26.3	N20 56.5	280 24.5	11.0	N19 13.5	5.6	55.4
E 07	283 26.2	56.0	294 54.5	10.9	19 07.9	5.6	55.5
D 08	298 26.2	55.6	309 24.4	11.0	19 02.3	5.8	55.5
N 09	313 26.1	.. 55.1	323 54.4	10.9	18 56.5	5.8	55.5
E 10	328 26.1	54.7	338 24.3	11.0	18 50.7	6.0	55.5
S 11	343 26.0	54.2	352 54.3	11.0	18 44.7	6.0	55.5
D 12	358 26.0	N20 53.8	7 24.3	11.0	N18 38.7	6.2	55.6
A 13	13 25.9	53.3	21 54.3	11.0	18 32.5	6.2	55.6
Y 14	28 25.9	52.9	36 24.3	11.1	18 26.3	6.4	55.6
15	43 25.9	.. 52.4	50 54.4	11.0	18 19.9	6.4	55.6
16	58 25.8	52.0	65 24.4	11.1	18 13.5	6.6	55.7
17	73 25.8	51.5	79 54.5	11.1	18 06.9	6.6	55.7
18	88 25.7	N20 51.1	94 24.6	11.1	N18 00.3	6.7	55.7
19	103 25.7	50.6	108 54.7	11.1	17 53.6	6.8	55.7
20	118 25.6	50.2	123 24.8	11.2	17 46.8	6.9	55.7
21	133 25.6	.. 49.7	137 55.0	11.1	17 39.9	7.0	55.7
22	148 25.5	49.3	152 25.1	11.2	17 32.9	7.1	55.8
23	163 25.5	48.8	166 55.3	11.2	17 25.8	7.2	55.8
19 00	178 25.5	N20 48.4	181 25.5	11.2	N17 18.6	7.3	55.8
01	193 25.4	47.9	195 55.7	11.2	17 11.3	7.4	55.8
02	208 25.4	47.4	210 25.9	11.3	17 03.9	7.4	55.8
03	223 25.3	.. 47.0	224 56.2	11.2	16 56.5	7.6	55.9
04	238 25.3	46.5	239 26.4	11.3	16 48.9	7.6	55.9
05	253 25.3	46.0	253 56.7	11.3	16 41.3	7.7	55.9
T 06	268 25.2	N20 45.6	268 27.0	11.3	N16 33.6	7.8	55.9
H 07	283 25.2	45.1	282 57.3	11.4	16 25.8	7.9	55.9
U 08	298 25.1	44.7	297 27.7	11.3	16 17.9	8.0	56.0
R 09	313 25.1	.. 44.2	311 58.0	11.4	16 09.9	8.1	56.0
S 10	328 25.1	43.8	326 28.4	11.4	16 01.8	8.2	56.0
D 11	343 25.0	43.3	340 58.8	11.4	15 53.6	8.2	56.0
A 12	358 25.0	N20 42.8	355 29.2	11.5	N15 45.4	8.3	56.1
Y 13	13 25.0	42.4	9 59.7	11.4	15 37.1	8.4	56.1
14	28 24.9	41.9	24 30.1	11.5	15 28.7	8.5	56.1
15	43 24.9	.. 41.4	39 00.6	11.5	15 20.2	8.6	56.1
16	58 24.8	41.0	53 31.1	11.5	15 11.6	8.6	56.1
17	73 24.8	40.5	68 01.6	11.6	15 03.0	8.8	56.2
18	88 24.8	N20 40.0	82 32.2	11.5	N14 54.2	8.8	56.2
19	103 24.7	39.6	97 02.7	11.6	14 45.4	8.9	56.2
20	118 24.7	39.1	111 33.3	11.6	14 36.5	9.0	56.2
21	133 24.7	.. 38.6	126 03.9	11.6	14 27.5	9.0	56.2
22	148 24.6	38.2	140 34.5	11.7	14 18.5	9.1	56.3
23	163 24.6	37.7	155 05.2	11.6	N14 09.4	9.2	56.3
	SD 15.8	d 0.4	SD 15.0		15.1		15.3

Twilight / Sunrise / Moonrise

Lat.	Naut.	Civil	Sunrise	Moonrise 17	18	19	20
°	h m	h m	h m	h m	h m	h m	h m
N 72	▭	▭	▭	▭	▭	01 14	03 42
N 70	////	////	▭	23 50	26 12	02 12	04 09
68	////	////	00 37	25 02	01 02	02 45	04 29
66	////	////	01 50	00 18	01 39	03 10	04 44
64	////	////	02 25	00 51	02 05	03 29	04 57
62	////	01 12	02 51	01 15	02 25	03 44	05 08
60	////	01 56	03 10	01 34	02 41	03 57	05 17
N 58	////	02 24	03 26	01 50	02 55	04 08	05 25
56	01 06	02 45	03 40	02 03	03 07	04 18	05 32
54	01 46	03 03	03 52	02 15	03 17	04 26	05 39
52	02 12	03 17	04 02	02 25	03 27	04 34	05 44
50	02 33	03 30	04 11	02 34	03 35	04 40	05 49
45	03 09	03 55	04 31	02 54	03 52	04 55	06 00
N 40	03 35	04 15	04 46	03 09	04 06	05 07	06 09
35	03 56	04 31	05 00	03 23	04 19	05 17	06 17
30	04 12	04 44	05 11	03 34	04 29	05 26	06 24
20	04 38	05 06	05 30	03 54	04 47	05 41	06 36
N 10	04 58	05 25	05 47	04 11	05 03	05 54	06 46
0	05 15	05 41	06 03	04 27	05 17	06 07	06 56
S 10	05 30	05 56	06 18	04 43	05 32	06 19	07 05
20	05 44	06 11	06 34	05 01	05 48	06 33	07 15
30	05 58	06 27	06 53	05 20	06 06	06 48	07 27
35	06 05	06 36	07 04	05 32	06 16	06 56	07 34
40	06 13	06 47	07 16	05 45	06 28	07 06	07 41
45	06 22	06 58	07 31	06 01	06 42	07 18	07 50
S 50	06 31	07 12	07 49	06 20	06 59	07 32	08 00
52	06 36	07 18	07 57	06 29	07 07	07 38	08 05
54	06 40	07 25	08 06	06 39	07 16	07 46	08 11
56	06 45	07 32	08 17	06 51	07 26	07 54	08 17
58	06 51	07 41	08 29	07 04	07 37	08 03	08 23
S 60	06 56	07 50	08 43	07 19	07 50	08 13	08 31

Sunset / Twilight / Moonset

Lat.	Sunset	Civil	Naut.	Moonset 17	18	19	20
°	h m	h m	h m	h m	h m	h m	h m
N 72	▭	▭	▭	▭	22 48	22 02	21 39
N 70	▭	▭	▭	22 27	21 49	21 34	21 23
68	23 23	////	////	22 14	21 14	21 13	21 10
66	22 19	////	////	20 37	20 49	20 56	21 00
64	21 45	////	////	20 11	20 30	20 42	20 51
62	21 20	22 56	////	19 50	20 14	20 30	20 43
60	21 01	22 14	////	19 34	20 00	20 20	20 36
N 58	20 45	21 47	////	19 19	19 49	20 12	20 30
56	20 31	21 26	23 02	19 07	19 39	20 04	20 25
54	20 20	21 08	22 24	18 57	19 30	19 57	20 20
52	20 10	20 54	21 58	18 47	19 22	19 51	20 16
50	20 00	20 42	21 39	18 39	19 14	19 45	20 12
45	19 41	20 17	21 02	18 21	18 59	19 33	20 03
N 40	19 26	19 57	20 37	18 06	18 46	19 23	19 56
35	19 13	19 41	20 16	17 53	18 35	19 14	19 50
30	19 01	19 28	20 00	17 42	18 26	19 06	19 45
20	18 42	19 06	19 34	17 23	18 09	18 53	19 35
N 10	18 25	18 48	19 14	17 07	17 55	18 41	19 27
0	18 10	18 32	18 58	16 52	17 41	18 30	19 19
S 10	17 55	18 17	18 43	16 36	17 28	18 19	19 11
20	17 38	18 02	18 29	16 19	17 13	18 07	19 02
30	17 20	17 45	18 15	16 00	16 56	17 54	18 52
35	17 09	17 36	18 07	15 49	16 46	17 46	18 46
40	16 57	17 26	18 00	15 36	16 35	17 37	18 40
45	16 42	17 15	17 51	15 21	16 22	17 26	18 32
S 50	16 24	17 01	17 42	15 02	16 05	17 13	18 23
52	16 16	16 55	17 37	14 53	15 58	17 07	18 19
54	16 08	16 48	17 33	14 43	15 49	17 00	18 14
56	15 56	16 41	17 28	14 32	15 40	16 53	18 09
58	15 44	16 32	17 23	14 19	15 29	16 44	18 03
S 60	15 30	16 23	17 17	14 04	15 16	16 34	17 56

SUN / MOON

Day	Eqn. of Time 00ʰ	12ʰ	Mer. Pass.	Mer. Pass. Upper	Lower	Age	Phase
d	m s	m s	h m	h m	h m	d	%
17	06 09	06 11	12 06	10 39	23 04	28	3
18	06 14	06 16	12 06	11 29	23 54	29	1
19	06 18	06 20	12 06	12 19	24 43	00	0 ●

2012 JULY 20, 21, 22 (FRI., SAT., SUN.)

UT	ARIES GHA	VENUS −4.6 GHA	VENUS Dec	MARS +1.0 GHA	MARS Dec	JUPITER −2.1 GHA	JUPITER Dec	SATURN +0.8 GHA	SATURN Dec	STARS Name	SHA	Dec
20 00	298 10.8	223 22.4	N18 06.3	109 51.3	S 3 30.3	231 42.4	N20 53.7	95 44.1	S 6 44.5	Acamar	315 18.9	S40 15.0
01	313 13.2	238 23.2	06.5	124 52.5	30.9	246 44.4	53.8	110 46.4	44.6	Achernar	335 27.2	S57 10.0
02	328 15.7	253 24.0	06.7	139 53.6	31.5	261 46.3	53.9	125 48.8	44.6	Acrux	173 10.2	S63 10.5
03	343 18.2	268 24.8 ..	06.9	154 54.8 ..	32.1	276 48.3 ..	54.0	140 51.2 ..	44.7	Adhara	255 13.4	S28 59.4
04	358 20.6	283 25.6	07.1	169 56.0	32.6	291 50.3	54.0	155 53.6	44.7	Aldebaran	290 50.3	N16 32.0
05	13 23.1	298 26.4	07.4	184 57.2	33.2	306 52.2	54.1	170 55.9	44.8			
06	28 25.6	313 27.2	N18 07.6	199 58.3	S 3 33.8	321 54.2	N20 54.2	185 58.3	S 6 44.8	Alioth	166 21.4	N55 53.7
07	43 28.0	328 28.0	07.8	214 59.5	34.4	336 56.1	54.3	201 00.7	44.9	Alkaid	152 59.4	N49 15.3
08	58 30.5	343 28.8	08.0	230 00.7	35.0	351 58.1	54.3	216 03.1	44.9	Al Na'ir	27 44.1	S46 53.7
F 09	73 33.0	358 29.5 ..	08.2	245 01.8 ..	35.6	7 00.1 ..	54.4	231 05.4 ..	45.0	Alnilam	275 47.3	S 1 11.7
R 10	88 35.4	13 30.3	08.4	260 03.0	36.2	22 02.0	54.5	246 07.8	45.0	Alphard	217 57.0	S 8 42.9
I 11	103 37.9	28 31.1	08.6	275 04.2	36.8	37 04.0	54.6	261 10.2	45.1			
D 12	118 40.3	43 31.9	N18 08.9	290 05.3	S 3 37.4	52 06.0	N20 54.6	276 12.6	S 6 45.1	Alphecca	126 11.4	N26 40.6
A 13	133 42.8	58 32.7	09.1	305 06.5	38.0	67 07.9	54.7	291 14.9	45.2	Alpheratz	357 44.0	N29 09.6
Y 14	148 45.3	73 33.4	09.3	320 07.7	38.6	82 09.9	54.8	306 17.3	45.2	Altair	62 08.5	N 8 54.3
15	163 47.7	88 34.2 ..	09.5	335 08.8 ..	39.2	97 11.9 ..	54.9	321 19.7 ..	45.3	Ankaa	353 16.1	S42 13.9
16	178 50.2	103 35.0	09.7	350 10.0	39.8	112 13.8	54.9	336 22.0	45.3	Antares	112 26.8	S26 27.6
17	193 52.7	118 35.7	09.9	5 11.2	40.4	127 15.8	55.0	351 24.4	45.3			
18	208 55.1	133 36.5	N18 10.2	20 12.3	S 3 41.0	142 17.7	N20 55.1	6 26.8	S 6 45.4	Arcturus	145 56.2	N19 07.2
19	223 57.6	148 37.3	10.4	35 13.5	41.6	157 19.7	55.2	21 29.2	45.4	Atria	107 28.7	S69 03.1
20	239 00.1	163 38.0	10.6	50 14.7	42.2	172 21.7	55.2	36 31.5	45.5	Avior	234 18.9	S59 33.1
21	254 02.5	178 38.8 ..	10.8	65 15.8 ..	42.8	187 23.6 ..	55.3	51 33.9 ..	45.5	Bellatrix	278 32.9	N 6 21.6
22	269 05.0	193 39.5	11.0	80 17.0	43.4	202 25.6	55.4	66 36.3	45.6	Betelgeuse	271 02.2	N 7 24.5
23	284 07.4	208 40.3	11.2	95 18.2	44.0	217 27.6	55.5	81 38.6	45.6			
21 00	299 09.9	223 41.0	N18 11.5	110 19.3	S 3 44.6	232 29.5	N20 55.6	96 41.0	S 6 45.7	Canopus	263 56.9	S52 42.1
01	314 12.4	238 41.8	11.7	125 20.5	45.2	247 31.5	55.6	111 43.4	45.7	Capella	280 35.7	N46 00.4
02	329 14.8	253 42.5	11.9	140 21.6	45.8	262 33.5	55.7	126 45.8	45.8	Deneb	49 31.4	N45 19.7
03	344 17.3	268 43.3 ..	12.1	155 22.8 ..	46.4	277 35.4 ..	55.7	141 48.1 ..	45.8	Denebola	182 34.4	N14 30.1
04	359 19.8	283 44.0	12.3	170 24.0	47.0	292 37.4	55.8	156 50.5	45.9	Diphda	348 56.4	S17 54.8
05	14 22.2	298 44.8	12.5	185 25.1	47.6	307 39.4	55.9	171 52.9	45.9			
06	29 24.7	313 45.5	N18 12.8	200 26.3	S 3 48.2	322 41.3	N20 56.0	186 55.2	S 6 46.0	Dubhe	193 52.9	N61 41.1
07	44 27.2	328 46.2	13.0	215 27.5	48.8	337 43.3	56.0	201 57.6	46.0	Elnath	278 13.7	N28 36.9
08	59 29.6	343 47.0	13.2	230 28.6	49.4	352 45.3	56.1	217 00.0	46.1	Eltanin	90 45.9	N51 29.5
S 09	74 32.1	358 47.7 ..	13.4	245 29.8 ..	50.0	7 47.2 ..	56.2	232 02.3 ..	46.1	Enif	33 47.4	N 9 56.2
A 10	89 34.6	13 48.4	13.6	260 31.0	50.6	22 49.2	56.3	247 04.7	46.2	Fomalhaut	15 24.4	S29 33.0
T 11	104 37.0	28 49.2	13.9	275 32.1	51.2	37 51.2	56.3	262 07.1	46.2			
U 12	119 39.5	43 49.9	N18 14.1	290 33.3	S 3 51.8	52 53.1	N20 56.4	277 09.5	S 6 46.3	Gacrux	172 01.8	S57 11.3
R 13	134 41.9	58 50.6	14.3	305 34.4	52.4	67 55.1	56.5	292 11.8	46.3	Gienah	175 53.1	S17 36.8
D 14	149 44.4	73 51.4	14.5	320 35.6	53.0	82 57.1	56.6	307 14.2	46.4	Hadar	148 48.7	S60 26.3
A 15	164 46.9	88 52.1 ..	14.7	335 36.8 ..	53.6	97 59.0 ..	56.6	322 16.6 ..	46.4	Hamal	328 01.5	N23 31.3
Y 16	179 49.3	103 52.8	15.0	350 37.9	54.2	113 01.0	56.7	337 18.9	46.5	Kaus Aust.	83 44.2	S34 22.6
17	194 51.8	118 53.5	15.2	5 39.1	54.8	128 03.0	56.8	352 21.3	46.5			
18	209 54.3	133 54.2	N18 15.4	20 40.2	S 3 55.4	143 04.9	N20 56.8	7 23.7	S 6 46.6	Kochab	137 19.7	N74 06.5
19	224 56.7	148 54.9	15.6	35 41.4	56.0	158 06.9	56.9	22 26.0	46.6	Markab	13 38.7	N15 16.5
20	239 59.2	163 55.7	15.9	50 42.6	56.6	173 08.9	57.0	37 28.4	46.7	Menkar	314 15.8	N 4 08.4
21	255 01.7	178 56.4 ..	16.1	65 43.7 ..	57.2	188 10.9 ..	57.1	52 30.8 ..	46.7	Menkent	148 08.2	S36 26.1
22	270 04.1	193 57.1	16.3	80 44.9	57.8	203 12.8	57.1	67 33.1	46.8	Miaplacidus	221 40.7	S69 46.4
23	285 06.6	208 57.8	16.5	95 46.1	58.4	218 14.8	57.2	82 35.5	46.8			
22 00	300 09.1	223 58.5	N18 16.7	110 47.2	S 3 59.0	233 16.8	N20 57.3	97 37.9	S 6 46.9	Mirfak	308 41.4	N49 54.1
01	315 11.5	238 59.2	17.0	125 48.3	3 59.6	248 18.7	57.4	112 40.2	46.9	Nunki	75 58.7	S26 16.7
02	330 14.0	253 59.9	17.2	140 49.5	4 00.2	263 20.7	57.4	127 42.6	46.9	Peacock	53 19.6	S56 41.4
03	345 16.4	269 00.6 ..	17.4	155 50.7 ..	00.8	278 22.7 ..	57.5	142 45.0 ..	47.0	Pollux	243 28.8	N27 59.6
04	0 18.9	284 01.3	17.6	170 51.8	01.4	293 24.6	57.6	157 47.3	47.0	Procyon	245 00.7	N 5 11.5
05	15 21.4	299 02.0	17.9	185 53.0	02.0	308 26.6	57.6	172 49.7	47.1			
06	30 23.8	314 02.7	N18 18.1	200 54.1	S 4 02.6	323 28.6	N20 57.7	187 52.1	S 6 47.1	Rasalhague	96 06.7	N12 33.3
07	45 26.3	329 03.4	18.3	215 55.3	03.2	338 30.6	57.8	202 54.4	47.2	Regulus	207 44.4	N11 54.3
08	60 28.8	344 04.1	18.5	230 56.4	03.8	353 32.5	57.9	217 56.8	47.2	Rigel	281 12.9	S 8 11.2
S 09	75 31.2	359 04.7 ..	18.7	245 57.6 ..	04.4	8 34.5 ..	57.9	232 59.2 ..	47.3	Rigil Kent.	139 52.4	S60 53.4
U 10	90 33.7	14 05.4	19.0	260 58.8	05.0	23 36.5	58.0	248 01.5	47.3	Sabik	102 13.0	S15 44.3
N 11	105 36.2	29 06.1	19.2	275 59.9	05.6	38 38.4	58.1	263 03.9	47.4			
D 12	120 38.6	44 06.8	N18 19.4	291 01.1	S 4 06.2	53 40.4	N20 58.1	278 06.3	S 6 47.4	Schedar	349 41.0	N56 36.2
A 13	135 41.1	59 07.5	19.6	306 02.2	06.8	68 42.4	58.2	293 08.6	47.5	Shaula	96 22.4	S37 06.7
Y 14	150 43.5	74 08.1	19.9	321 03.4	07.4	83 44.4	58.3	308 11.0	47.5	Sirius	258 34.6	S16 44.1
15	165 46.0	89 08.8 ..	20.1	336 04.5 ..	08.0	98 46.3 ..	58.4	323 13.4 ..	47.6	Spica	158 31.9	S11 13.7
16	180 48.5	104 09.5	20.3	351 05.7	08.6	113 48.3	58.4	338 15.7	47.6	Suhail	222 53.3	S43 29.2
17	195 50.9	119 10.2	20.5	6 06.8	09.2	128 50.3	58.5	353 18.1	47.7			
18	210 53.4	134 10.8	N18 20.8	21 08.0	S 4 09.8	143 52.2	N20 58.6	8 20.5	S 6 47.7	Vega	80 39.0	N38 48.0
19	225 55.9	149 11.5	21.0	36 09.1	10.4	158 54.2	58.6	23 22.8	47.8	Zuben'ubi	137 06.0	S16 05.7
20	240 58.3	164 12.2	21.2	51 10.3	11.0	173 56.2	58.7	38 25.2	47.8		SHA	Mer. Pass.
21	256 00.8	179 12.8 ..	21.4	66 11.4 ..	11.6	188 58.2 ..	58.8	53 27.6 ..	47.9	Venus	284 31.1	9 05
22	271 03.3	194 13.5	21.7	81 12.6	12.2	204 00.1	58.9	68 29.9	47.9	Mars	171 09.4	16 37
23	286 05.7	209 14.2	21.9	96 13.7	12.8	219 02.1	58.9	83 32.3	48.0	Jupiter	293 19.6	8 29
Mer. Pass.	4 02.7	v 0.7	d 0.2	v 1.2	d 0.6	v 2.0	d 0.1	v 2.4	d 0.0	Saturn	157 31.1	17 30

SUN and MOON

UT	SUN GHA	SUN Dec	MOON GHA	v	MOON Dec	d	HP
20 00	178 24.5	N20 37.2	169 35.8	11.7	N14 00.2	9.3	56.3
01	193 24.5	36.7	184 06.5	11.7	13 50.9	9.4	56.3
02	208 24.5	36.3	198 37.2	11.7	13 41.5	9.4	56.3
03	223 24.4	.. 35.8	213 07.9	11.8	13 32.1	9.5	56.4
04	238 24.4	35.3	227 38.7	11.7	13 22.6	9.5	56.4
05	253 24.4	34.8	242 09.4	11.8	13 13.1	9.7	56.4
F 06	268 24.3	N20 34.4	256 40.2	11.8	N13 03.4	9.7	56.4
R 07	283 24.3	33.9	271 11.0	11.8	12 53.7	9.8	56.5
I 08	298 24.3	33.4	285 41.8	11.8	12 43.9	9.8	56.5
D 09	313 24.2	.. 32.9	300 12.6	11.9	12 34.1	10.0	56.5
A 10	328 24.2	32.5	314 43.5	11.8	12 24.1	9.9	56.5
Y 11	343 24.2	32.0	329 14.3	11.9	12 14.2	10.1	56.5
12	358 24.1	N20 31.5	343 45.2	11.9	N12 04.1	10.1	56.6
13	13 24.1	31.0	358 16.1	11.9	11 54.0	10.2	56.6
14	28 24.1	30.6	12 47.0	11.9	11 43.8	10.3	56.6
15	43 24.0	.. 30.1	27 17.9	12.0	11 33.5	10.3	56.6
16	58 24.0	29.6	41 48.9	12.0	11 23.2	10.4	56.6
17	73 24.0	29.1	56 19.9	11.9	11 12.8	10.4	56.7
18	88 23.9	N20 28.6	70 50.8	12.0	N11 02.4	10.5	56.7
19	103 23.9	28.1	85 21.8	12.0	10 51.9	10.6	56.7
20	118 23.9	27.7	99 52.8	12.1	10 41.3	10.6	56.7
21	133 23.8	.. 27.2	114 23.9	12.0	10 30.7	10.7	56.7
22	148 23.8	26.7	128 54.9	12.0	10 20.0	10.7	56.8
23	163 23.8	26.2	143 25.9	12.1	10 09.3	10.8	56.8
21 00	178 23.8	N20 25.7	157 57.0	12.1	N 9 58.5	10.8	56.8
01	193 23.7	25.2	172 28.1	12.1	9 47.7	10.9	56.8
02	208 23.7	24.8	186 59.2	12.1	9 36.8	11.0	56.9
03	223 23.7	.. 24.3	201 30.3	12.1	9 25.8	11.0	56.9
04	238 23.6	23.8	216 01.4	12.1	9 14.8	11.1	56.9
05	253 23.6	23.3	230 32.5	12.2	9 03.7	11.1	56.9
S 06	268 23.6	N20 22.8	245 03.7	12.1	N 8 52.6	11.2	56.9
A 07	283 23.5	22.3	259 34.8	12.2	8 41.4	11.2	57.0
T 08	298 23.5	21.8	274 06.0	12.1	8 30.2	11.2	57.0
U 09	313 23.5	.. 21.3	288 37.1	12.2	8 19.0	11.4	57.0
R 10	328 23.4	20.8	303 08.3	12.2	8 07.6	11.3	57.0
D 11	343 23.4	20.3	317 39.5	12.2	7 56.3	11.4	57.0
A 12	358 23.4	N20 19.9	332 10.7	12.2	N 7 44.9	11.5	57.1
Y 13	13 23.4	19.4	346 41.9	12.2	7 33.4	11.5	57.1
14	28 23.4	18.9	1 13.1	12.2	7 21.9	11.5	57.1
15	43 23.3	.. 18.4	15 44.3	12.2	7 10.4	11.6	57.1
16	58 23.3	17.9	30 15.5	12.2	6 58.8	11.6	57.1
17	73 23.3	17.4	44 46.7	12.3	6 47.2	11.7	57.2
18	88 23.3	N20 16.9	59 18.0	12.2	N 6 35.5	11.7	57.2
19	103 23.2	16.4	73 49.2	12.2	6 23.8	11.7	57.2
20	118 23.2	15.9	88 20.4	12.3	6 12.1	11.8	57.2
21	133 23.2	.. 15.4	102 51.7	12.2	6 00.3	11.8	57.2
22	148 23.2	14.9	117 22.9	12.3	5 48.5	11.9	57.3
23	163 23.1	14.4	131 54.2	12.2	5 36.6	11.9	57.3
22 00	178 23.1	N20 13.9	146 25.4	12.3	N 5 24.7	11.9	57.3
01	193 23.1	13.4	160 56.7	12.3	5 12.8	12.0	57.3
02	208 23.1	12.9	175 27.9	12.2	5 00.8	12.0	57.4
03	223 23.0	.. 12.4	189 59.1	12.3	4 48.8	12.0	57.4
04	238 23.0	11.9	204 30.4	12.2	4 36.8	12.0	57.4
05	253 23.0	11.4	219 01.6	12.3	4 24.8	12.1	57.4
S 06	268 23.0	N20 10.9	233 32.9	12.2	N 4 12.7	12.1	57.4
U 07	283 22.9	10.4	248 04.1	12.2	4 00.6	12.1	57.5
N 08	298 22.9	09.9	262 35.3	12.2	3 48.5	12.2	57.5
D 09	313 22.9	.. 09.4	277 06.5	12.3	3 36.3	12.2	57.5
A 10	328 22.9	08.9	291 37.8	12.2	3 24.1	12.2	57.5
Y 11	343 22.9	08.4	306 09.0	12.2	3 11.9	12.2	57.5
12	358 22.8	N20 07.9	320 40.2	12.2	N 2 59.7	12.3	57.6
13	13 22.8	07.3	335 11.4	12.2	2 47.4	12.3	57.6
14	28 22.8	06.8	349 42.6	12.1	2 35.1	12.3	57.6
15	43 22.8	.. 06.3	4 13.7	12.2	2 22.8	12.3	57.6
16	58 22.8	05.8	18 44.9	12.2	2 10.5	12.3	57.6
17	73 22.7	05.3	33 16.1	12.1	1 58.2	12.4	57.7
18	88 22.7	N20 04.8	47 47.2	12.2	N 1 45.8	12.3	57.7
19	103 22.7	04.3	62 18.4	12.1	1 33.5	12.4	57.7
20	118 22.7	03.8	76 49.5	12.1	1 21.1	12.4	57.7
21	133 22.7	.. 03.3	91 20.6	12.1	1 08.7	12.4	57.7
22	148 22.6	02.8	105 51.7	12.1	0 56.3	12.4	57.7
23	163 22.6	02.2	120 22.8	12.0	N 0 43.9	12.5	57.8
	SD 15.8	d 0.5	SD 15.4		15.5		15.7

Twilight, Sunrise and Moonrise

Lat.	Naut.	Civil	Sunrise	Moonrise 20	21	22	23
N 72	□	□	□	03 42	05 46	07 43	09 39
N 70	□	□	□	04 09	06 00	07 48	09 37
68	////	////	01 09	04 29	06 11	07 53	09 35
66	////	////	02 03	04 44	06 20	07 56	09 33
64	////	////	02 35	04 57	06 28	07 59	09 32
62	////	01 28	02 58	05 08	06 35	08 02	09 31
60	////	02 06	03 17	05 17	06 40	08 04	09 30
N 58	////	02 32	03 32	05 25	06 45	08 07	09 29
56	01 20	02 52	03 45	05 32	06 50	08 08	09 28
54	01 55	03 08	03 56	05 39	06 54	08 10	09 28
52	02 19	03 22	04 06	05 44	06 57	08 12	09 27
50	02 38	03 34	04 15	05 49	07 01	08 13	09 26
45	03 13	03 59	04 34	06 00	07 08	08 16	09 25
N 40	03 38	04 18	04 49	06 09	07 13	08 19	09 24
35	03 58	04 33	05 02	06 17	07 18	08 20	09 23
30	04 14	04 46	05 13	06 24	07 23	08 22	09 22
20	04 39	05 08	05 32	06 36	07 31	08 26	09 21
N 10	04 59	05 25	05 48	06 46	07 37	08 28	09 20
0	05 15	05 41	06 03	06 56	07 44	08 31	09 19
S 10	05 30	05 56	06 18	07 05	07 50	08 34	09 18
20	05 43	06 10	06 34	07 15	07 57	08 37	09 17
30	05 57	06 26	06 52	07 27	08 04	08 40	09 16
35	06 04	06 35	07 02	07 34	08 08	08 42	09 15
40	06 12	06 45	07 14	07 41	08 13	08 44	09 14
45	06 20	06 56	07 28	07 50	08 19	08 46	09 13
S 50	06 29	07 09	07 45	08 00	08 26	08 49	09 12
52	06 33	07 15	07 53	08 05	08 29	08 51	09 12
54	06 37	07 21	08 02	08 11	08 32	08 52	09 11
56	06 42	07 29	08 12	08 17	08 36	08 54	09 11
58	06 47	07 37	08 24	08 23	08 40	08 56	09 11
S 60	06 52	07 46	08 37	08 31	08 45	08 58	09 10

Sunset, Twilight and Moonset

Lat.	Sunset	Civil	Naut.	Moonset 20	21	22	23
N 72	□	□	□	21 39	21 22	21 07	20 52
N 70	□	□	□	21 23	21 14	21 06	20 57
68	22 57	////	////	21 10	21 08	21 05	21 02
66	22 07	////	////	21 00	21 02	21 04	21 05
64	21 36	////	////	20 51	20 57	21 03	21 08
62	21 13	22 41	////	20 43	20 53	21 02	21 11
60	20 55	22 05	////	20 36	20 49	21 02	21 14
N 58	20 40	21 39	////	20 30	20 46	21 01	21 16
56	20 27	21 20	22 49	20 25	20 43	21 00	21 18
54	20 16	21 03	22 15	20 20	20 41	21 00	21 19
52	20 06	20 50	21 52	20 16	20 38	21 00	21 21
50	19 57	20 38	21 33	20 12	20 36	20 59	21 22
45	19 39	20 14	20 59	20 03	20 31	20 58	21 26
N 40	19 24	19 55	20 34	19 56	20 27	20 58	21 28
35	19 11	19 39	20 14	19 50	20 24	20 57	21 31
30	19 00	19 26	19 58	19 45	20 21	20 57	21 33
20	18 41	19 05	19 33	19 35	20 16	20 56	21 36
N 10	18 25	18 48	19 14	19 27	20 11	20 55	21 39
0	18 10	18 32	18 58	19 19	20 06	20 54	21 42
S 10	17 55	18 17	18 43	19 11	20 02	20 53	21 45
20	17 39	18 03	18 30	19 02	19 57	20 52	21 48
30	17 21	17 47	18 16	18 52	19 51	20 51	21 52
35	17 11	17 38	18 09	18 46	19 48	20 50	21 54
40	16 59	17 29	18 02	18 40	19 44	20 50	21 56
45	16 45	17 17	17 54	18 32	19 40	20 49	21 59
S 50	16 28	17 04	17 45	18 23	19 35	20 48	22 02
52	16 20	16 58	17 40	18 19	19 32	20 47	22 03
54	16 11	16 52	17 36	18 14	19 30	20 47	22 05
56	16 01	16 45	17 32	18 09	19 27	20 46	22 07
58	15 49	16 37	17 27	18 03	19 24	20 46	22 09
S 60	15 36	16 28	17 21	17 56	19 20	20 45	22 11

SUN and MOON

Day	SUN Eqn. of Time 00h	12h	Mer. Pass.	MOON Mer. Pass. Upper	Lower	Age	Phase
20	06 22	06 23	12 06	13 07	00 43	01	2
21	06 25	06 26	12 06	13 55	01 31	02	6
22	06 28	06 29	12 06	14 43	02 19	03	12

UT	ARIES GHA	VENUS GHA	VENUS Dec	MARS GHA	MARS Dec	JUPITER GHA	JUPITER Dec	SATURN GHA	SATURN Dec	Name	SHA	Dec
23 00	301 08.2	224 14.8	N18 22.1	111 14.9	S 4 13.4	234 04.1	N20 59.0	98 34.6	S 6 48.0	Acamar	315 18.9	S40 15.0
01	316 10.7	239 15.5	22.3	126 16.1	14.0	249 06.0	59.1	113 37.0	48.1	Achernar	335 27.2	S57 10.0
02	331 13.1	254 16.1	22.6	141 17.2	14.6	264 08.0	59.1	128 39.4	48.2	Acrux	173 10.2	S63 10.5
03	346 15.6	269 16.8	.. 22.8	156 18.4	.. 15.2	279 10.0	.. 59.2	143 41.7	.. 48.2	Adhara	255 13.4	S28 59.4
04	1 18.0	284 17.4	23.0	171 19.5	15.8	294 12.0	59.3	158 44.1	48.3	Aldebaran	290 50.3	N16 32.0
05	16 20.5	299 18.1	23.2	186 20.7	16.4	309 13.9	59.4	173 46.5	48.3			
06	31 23.0	314 18.7	N18 23.5	201 21.8	S 4 17.0	324 15.9	N20 59.4	188 48.8	S 6 48.4	Alioth	166 21.4	N55 53.7
07	46 25.4	329 19.4	23.7	216 23.0	17.6	339 17.9	59.5	203 51.2	48.4	Alkaid	152 59.4	N49 15.3
M 08	61 27.9	344 20.0	23.9	231 24.1	18.2	354 19.9	59.6	218 53.6	48.5	Al Na'ir	27 44.1	S46 53.7
O 09	76 30.4	359 20.7	.. 24.2	246 25.3	.. 18.8	9 21.8	.. 59.6	233 55.9	.. 48.5	Alnilam	275 47.2	S 1 11.7
N 10	91 32.8	14 21.3	24.4	261 26.4	19.4	24 23.8	59.7	248 58.3	48.6	Alphard	217 57.0	S 8 42.9
D 11	106 35.3	29 22.0	24.6	276 27.6	20.1	39 25.8	59.8	264 00.6	48.6			
A 12	121 37.8	44 22.6	N18 24.8	291 28.7	S 4 20.7	54 27.8	N20 59.9	279 03.0	S 6 48.7	Alphecca	126 11.4	N26 40.6
Y 13	136 40.2	59 23.2	25.1	306 29.9	21.3	69 29.7	20 59.9	294 05.4	48.7	Alpheratz	357 43.9	N29 09.6
14	151 42.7	74 23.9	25.3	321 31.0	21.9	84 31.7	21 00.0	309 07.7	48.8	Altair	62 08.5	N 8 54.3
15	166 45.1	89 24.5	.. 25.5	336 32.1	.. 22.5	99 33.7	.. 00.1	324 10.1	.. 48.8	Ankaa	353 16.1	S42 13.9
16	181 47.6	104 25.1	25.7	351 33.3	23.1	114 35.7	00.1	339 12.4	48.9	Antares	112 26.8	S26 27.6
17	196 50.1	119 25.7	26.0	6 34.4	23.7	129 37.6	00.2	354 14.8	48.9			
18	211 52.5	134 26.4	N18 26.2	21 35.6	S 4 24.3	144 39.6	N21 00.3	9 17.2	S 6 49.0	Arcturus	145 56.3	N19 07.2
19	226 55.0	149 27.0	26.4	36 36.7	24.9	159 41.6	00.3	24 19.5	49.0	Atria	107 28.7	S69 03.1
20	241 57.5	164 27.6	26.6	51 37.9	25.5	174 43.6	00.4	39 21.9	49.1	Avior	234 18.9	S59 33.1
21	256 59.9	179 28.2	.. 26.9	66 39.0	.. 26.1	189 45.6	.. 00.5	54 24.3	.. 49.1	Bellatrix	278 32.9	N 6 21.6
22	272 02.4	194 28.9	27.1	81 40.2	26.7	204 47.5	00.6	69 26.6	49.2	Betelgeuse	271 02.2	N 7 24.5
23	287 04.9	209 29.5	27.3	96 41.3	27.3	219 49.5	00.6	84 29.0	49.2			
24 00	302 07.3	224 30.1	N18 27.6	111 42.5	S 4 27.9	234 51.5	N21 00.7	99 31.3	S 6 49.3	Canopus	263 56.9	S52 42.1
01	317 09.8	239 30.7	27.8	126 43.6	28.5	249 53.5	00.8	114 33.7	49.3	Capella	280 35.7	N46 00.4
02	332 12.3	254 31.3	28.0	141 44.8	29.1	264 55.4	00.8	129 36.1	49.4	Deneb	49 31.4	N45 19.7
03	347 14.7	269 31.9	.. 28.2	156 45.9	.. 29.7	279 57.4	.. 00.9	144 38.4	.. 49.4	Denebola	182 34.5	N14 30.1
04	2 17.2	284 32.5	28.5	171 47.0	30.3	294 59.4	01.0	159 40.8	49.5	Diphda	348 56.4	S17 54.8
05	17 19.6	299 33.1	28.7	186 48.2	30.9	310 01.4	01.0	174 43.1	49.5			
06	32 22.1	314 33.7	N18 28.9	201 49.3	S 4 31.5	325 03.3	N21 01.1	189 45.5	S 6 49.6	Dubhe	193 52.9	N61 41.1
07	47 24.6	329 34.3	29.1	216 50.5	32.1	340 05.3	01.2	204 47.9	49.6	Elnath	278 13.7	N28 36.9
T 08	62 27.0	344 34.9	29.4	231 51.6	32.7	355 07.3	01.3	219 50.2	49.7	Eltanin	90 46.0	N51 29.5
U 09	77 29.5	359 35.5	.. 29.6	246 52.8	.. 33.3	10 09.3	.. 01.3	234 52.6	.. 49.8	Enif	33 47.4	N 9 56.2
E 10	92 32.0	14 36.1	29.8	261 53.9	33.9	25 11.3	01.4	249 54.9	49.8	Fomalhaut	15 24.4	S29 33.0
S 11	107 34.4	29 36.7	30.1	276 55.0	34.5	40 13.2	01.5	264 57.3	49.9			
D 12	122 36.9	44 37.3	N18 30.3	291 56.2	S 4 35.1	55 15.2	N21 01.5	279 59.6	S 6 49.9	Gacrux	172 01.8	S57 11.3
A 13	137 39.4	59 37.9	30.5	306 57.3	35.7	70 17.2	01.6	295 02.0	50.0	Gienah	175 53.1	S17 36.8
Y 14	152 41.8	74 38.5	30.7	321 58.5	36.3	85 19.2	01.7	310 04.4	50.0	Hadar	148 48.7	S60 26.3
15	167 44.3	89 39.1	.. 31.0	336 59.6	.. 36.9	100 21.2	.. 01.7	325 06.7	.. 50.1	Hamal	328 01.4	N23 31.3
16	182 46.8	104 39.7	31.2	352 00.8	37.5	115 23.1	01.8	340 09.1	50.1	Kaus Aust.	83 44.2	S34 22.6
17	197 49.2	119 40.3	31.4	7 01.9	38.1	130 25.1	01.9	355 11.4	50.2			
18	212 51.7	134 40.9	N18 31.7	22 03.0	S 4 38.7	145 27.1	N21 01.9	10 13.8	S 6 50.2	Kochab	137 19.7	N74 06.5
19	227 54.1	149 41.4	31.9	37 04.2	39.3	160 29.1	02.0	25 16.2	50.3	Markab	13 38.7	N15 16.5
20	242 56.6	164 42.0	32.1	52 05.3	39.9	175 31.1	02.1	40 18.5	50.3	Menkar	314 15.8	N 4 08.4
21	257 59.1	179 42.6	.. 32.3	67 06.5	.. 40.5	190 33.0	.. 02.2	55 20.9	.. 50.4	Menkent	148 08.3	S36 26.1
22	273 01.5	194 43.2	32.6	82 07.6	41.1	205 35.0	02.2	70 23.2	50.4	Miaplacidus	221 40.7	S69 46.3
23	288 04.0	209 43.7	32.8	97 08.7	41.7	220 37.0	02.3	85 25.6	50.5			
25 00	303 06.5	224 44.3	N18 33.0	112 09.9	S 4 42.3	235 39.0	N21 02.4	100 27.9	S 6 50.5	Mirfak	308 41.4	N49 54.1
01	318 08.9	239 44.9	33.3	127 11.0	42.9	250 41.0	02.4	115 30.3	50.6	Nunki	75 58.7	S26 16.7
02	333 11.4	254 45.5	33.5	142 12.2	43.6	265 42.9	02.5	130 32.7	50.6	Peacock	53 19.6	S56 41.4
03	348 13.9	269 46.0	.. 33.7	157 13.3	.. 44.2	280 44.9	.. 02.6	145 35.0	.. 50.7	Pollux	243 28.8	N27 59.6
04	3 16.3	284 46.6	33.9	172 14.4	44.8	295 46.9	02.6	160 37.4	50.8	Procyon	245 00.7	N 5 11.5
05	18 18.8	299 47.2	34.1	187 15.6	45.4	310 48.9	02.7	175 39.7	50.8			
06	33 21.2	314 47.7	N18 34.4	202 16.7	S 4 46.0	325 50.9	N21 02.8	190 42.1	S 6 50.9	Rasalhague	96 06.7	N12 33.3
W 07	48 23.7	329 48.3	34.6	217 17.8	46.6	340 52.9	02.8	205 44.4	50.9	Regulus	207 44.4	N11 54.3
E 08	63 26.2	344 48.8	34.9	232 19.0	47.2	355 54.8	02.9	220 46.8	51.0	Rigel	281 12.9	S 8 11.2
D 09	78 28.6	359 49.4	.. 35.1	247 20.1	.. 47.8	10 56.8	.. 03.0	235 49.1	.. 51.0	Rigil Kent.	139 52.4	S60 53.4
N 10	93 31.1	14 49.9	35.3	262 21.3	48.4	25 58.8	03.0	250 51.5	51.1	Sabik	102 13.0	S15 44.3
E 11	108 33.6	29 50.5	35.5	277 22.4	49.0	41 00.8	03.1	265 53.9	51.1			
S 12	123 36.0	44 51.1	N18 35.7	292 23.5	S 4 49.6	56 02.8	N21 03.2	280 56.2	S 6 51.2	Schedar	349 41.0	N56 36.2
D 13	138 38.5	59 51.6	36.0	307 24.7	50.2	71 04.8	03.2	295 58.6	51.2	Shaula	96 22.4	S37 06.7
A 14	153 41.0	74 52.1	36.2	322 25.8	50.8	86 06.7	03.3	311 00.9	51.3	Sirius	258 34.6	S16 44.0
Y 15	168 43.4	89 52.7	.. 36.5	337 26.9	.. 51.4	101 08.7	.. 03.4	326 03.3	.. 51.3	Spica	158 31.9	S11 13.7
16	183 45.9	104 53.2	36.7	352 28.1	52.0	116 10.7	03.4	341 05.6	51.4	Suhail	222 53.3	S43 29.2
17	198 48.4	119 53.8	36.9	7 29.2	52.6	131 12.7	03.5	356 08.0	51.5			
18	213 50.8	134 54.3	N18 37.1	22 30.3	S 4 53.2	146 14.7	N21 03.6	11 10.3	S 6 51.5	Vega	80 39.0	N38 48.0
19	228 53.3	149 54.9	37.4	37 31.5	53.8	161 16.7	03.7	26 12.7	51.6	Zuben'ubi	137 06.0	S16 05.6
20	243 55.7	164 55.4	37.6	52 32.6	54.4	176 18.6	03.7	41 15.0	51.6		SHA	Mer.Pass.
21	258 58.2	179 55.9	.. 37.8	67 33.7	.. 55.0	191 20.6	.. 03.8	56 17.4	.. 51.7	Venus	282 22.8	9 02
22	274 00.7	194 56.5	38.1	82 34.9	55.6	206 22.6	03.9	71 19.7	51.7	Mars	169 35.1	16 32
23	289 03.1	209 57.0	38.3	97 36.0	56.2	221 24.6	03.9	86 22.1	51.8	Jupiter	292 44.2	8 19
Mer.Pass. 3 50.9		v 0.6	d 0.2	v 1.1	d 0.6	v 2.0	d 0.1	v 2.4	d 0.1	Saturn	157 24.0	17 19

SUN and MOON

UT	SUN GHA	SUN Dec	MOON GHA	v	MOON Dec	d	HP
23 MONDAY							
00	178 22.6	N20 01.7	134 53.8	12.1	N 0 31.4	12.4	57.8
01	193 22.6	01.2	149 24.9	12.0	0 19.0	12.4	57.8
02	208 22.6	00.7	163 55.9	12.0	N 0 06.6	12.5	57.8
03	223 22.6	20 00.2	178 26.9	12.0	S 0 05.9	12.5	57.8
04	238 22.5	19 59.7	192 57.9	12.0	0 18.4	12.4	57.9
05	253 22.5	59.2	207 28.9	11.9	0 30.8	12.5	57.9
06	268 22.5	N19 58.6	221 59.8	11.9	S 0 43.3	12.5	57.9
07	283 22.5	58.1	236 30.7	12.0	0 55.8	12.5	57.9
08	298 22.5	57.6	251 01.7	11.8	1 08.3	12.4	57.9
09	313 22.5 ..	57.1	265 32.5	11.9	1 20.7	12.5	58.0
10	328 22.4	56.6	280 03.4	11.8	1 33.2	12.5	58.0
11	343 22.4	56.0	294 34.2	11.8	1 45.7	12.5	58.0
12	358 22.4	N19 55.5	309 05.0	11.8	S 1 58.2	12.5	58.0
13	13 22.4	55.0	323 35.8	11.8	2 10.7	12.4	58.0
14	28 22.4	54.5	338 06.6	11.7	2 23.1	12.5	58.1
15	43 22.4 ..	54.0	352 37.3	11.7	2 35.6	12.4	58.1
16	58 22.4	53.4	7 08.0	11.7	2 48.0	12.5	58.1
17	73 22.3	52.9	21 38.7	11.6	3 00.5	12.4	58.1
18	88 22.3	N19 52.4	36 09.3	11.6	S 3 12.9	12.5	58.1
19	103 22.3	51.9	50 39.9	11.6	3 25.4	12.4	58.1
20	118 22.3	51.3	65 10.5	11.6	3 37.8	12.4	58.2
21	133 22.3 ..	50.8	79 41.1	11.5	3 50.2	12.4	58.2
22	148 22.3	50.3	94 11.6	11.5	4 02.6	12.4	58.2
23	163 22.3	49.8	108 42.1	11.4	4 15.0	12.4	58.2
24 TUESDAY							
00	178 22.3	N19 49.2	123 12.5	11.4	S 4 27.4	12.3	58.2
01	193 22.2	48.7	137 42.9	11.4	4 39.7	12.3	58.3
02	208 22.2	48.2	152 13.3	11.3	4 52.0	12.4	58.3
03	223 22.2 ..	47.6	166 43.6	11.3	5 04.4	12.3	58.3
04	238 22.2	47.1	181 13.9	11.3	5 16.7	12.2	58.3
05	253 22.2	46.6	195 44.2	11.2	5 28.9	12.3	58.3
06	268 22.2	N19 46.1	210 14.4	11.1	S 5 41.2	12.2	58.3
07	283 22.2	45.5	224 44.5	11.2	5 53.4	12.2	58.4
08	298 22.2	45.0	239 14.7	11.1	6 05.6	12.2	58.4
09	313 22.2 ..	44.5	253 44.8	11.0	6 17.8	12.1	58.4
10	328 22.2	43.9	268 14.8	11.0	6 29.9	12.2	58.4
11	343 22.1	43.4	282 44.8	11.0	6 42.1	12.1	58.4
12	358 22.1	N19 42.9	297 14.8	10.9	S 6 54.2	12.0	58.4
13	13 22.1	42.3	311 44.7	10.9	7 06.2	12.1	58.5
14	28 22.1	41.8	326 14.6	10.8	7 18.3	12.0	58.5
15	43 22.1 ..	41.3	340 44.4	10.8	7 30.3	11.9	58.5
16	58 22.1	40.7	355 14.2	10.7	7 42.2	12.0	58.5
17	73 22.1	40.2	9 43.9	10.7	7 54.2	11.9	58.5
18	88 22.1	N19 39.6	24 13.6	10.6	S 8 06.1	11.8	58.6
19	103 22.1	39.1	38 43.2	10.6	8 17.9	11.8	58.6
20	118 22.1	38.6	53 12.8	10.5	8 29.7	11.8	58.6
21	133 22.1 ..	38.0	67 42.3	10.5	8 41.5	11.7	58.6
22	148 22.1	37.5	82 11.8	10.4	8 53.2	11.7	58.6
23	163 22.1	36.9	96 41.2	10.4	9 04.9	11.7	58.6
25 WEDNESDAY							
00	178 22.1	N19 36.4	111 10.6	10.3	S 9 16.6	11.6	58.7
01	193 22.0	35.9	125 39.9	10.2	9 28.2	11.6	58.7
02	208 22.0	35.3	140 09.1	10.2	9 39.8	11.5	58.7
03	223 22.0 ..	34.8	154 38.3	10.2	9 51.3	11.4	58.7
04	238 22.0	34.2	169 07.5	10.1	10 02.7	11.5	58.7
05	253 22.0	33.7	183 36.6	10.0	10 14.2	11.3	58.7
06	268 22.0	N19 33.1	198 05.6	10.0	S10 25.5	11.3	58.8
07	283 22.0	32.6	212 34.6	9.9	10 36.8	11.3	58.8
08	298 22.0	32.1	227 03.5	9.9	10 48.1	11.2	58.8
09	313 22.0 ..	31.5	241 32.4	9.8	10 59.3	11.1	58.8
10	328 22.0	31.0	256 01.2	9.7	11 10.4	11.1	58.8
11	343 22.0	30.4	270 29.9	9.7	11 21.5	11.1	58.8
12	358 22.0	N19 29.9	284 58.6	9.6	S11 32.6	10.9	58.8
13	13 22.0	29.3	299 27.2	9.6	11 43.5	10.9	58.9
14	28 22.0	28.8	313 55.8	9.5	11 54.4	10.9	58.9
15	43 22.0 ..	28.2	328 24.3	9.4	12 05.3	10.8	58.9
16	58 22.0	27.7	342 52.7	9.4	12 16.1	10.7	58.9
17	73 22.0	27.1	357 21.1	9.3	12 26.8	10.7	58.9
18	88 22.0	N19 26.6	11 49.4	9.2	S12 37.5	10.5	58.9
19	103 22.0	26.0	26 17.6	9.2	12 48.0	10.6	59.0
20	118 22.0	25.5	40 45.8	9.1	12 58.6	10.4	59.0
21	133 22.0 ..	24.9	55 13.9	9.0	13 09.0	10.4	59.0
22	148 22.0	24.4	69 41.9	9.0	13 19.4	10.3	59.0
23	163 22.0	23.8	84 09.9	8.9	S13 29.7	10.2	59.0
	SD 15.8	d 0.5	SD 15.8		15.9		16.0

Twilight, Sunrise and Moonrise

Lat.	Naut.	Civil	Sunrise	Moonrise 23	24	25	26
N 72	□	□	□	09 39	11 39	13 48	16 21
N 70	////	////	01 31	09 37	11 28	13 25	15 33
68	////	////	02 15	09 35	11 20	13 08	15 02
66	////	////	02 44	09 33	11 12	12 55	14 40
64	////	00 35	03 06	09 32	11 07	12 43	14 22
62	////	01 42	03 06	09 31	11 01	12 34	14 08
60	////	02 15	03 23	09 30	10 57	12 26	13 55
N 58	00 32	02 39	03 38	09 29	10 53	12 19	13 45
56	01 33	02 58	03 50	09 28	10 50	12 12	13 36
54	02 04	03 14	04 01	09 28	10 47	12 07	13 28
52	02 26	03 27	04 10	09 27	10 44	12 02	13 21
50	02 44	03 39	04 19	09 26	10 41	11 57	13 14
45	03 18	04 02	04 37	09 25	10 36	11 47	13 00
N 40	03 42	04 20	04 51	09 24	10 31	11 39	12 49
35	04 01	04 35	05 04	09 23	10 27	11 33	12 39
30	04 16	04 48	05 14	09 22	10 24	11 26	12 31
20	04 41	05 09	05 33	09 21	10 18	11 16	12 16
N 10	05 00	05 26	05 48	09 20	10 13	11 07	12 04
0	05 15	05 41	06 03	09 19	10 08	10 59	11 52
S 10	05 29	05 55	06 17	09 18	10 03	10 50	11 40
20	05 43	06 09	06 33	09 17	09 58	10 41	11 28
30	05 56	06 25	06 50	09 16	09 52	10 31	11 14
35	06 02	06 33	07 00	09 15	09 49	10 26	11 06
40	06 10	06 43	07 12	09 14	09 45	10 19	10 56
45	06 19	06 53	07 25	09 13	09 41	10 11	10 46
S 50	06 26	07 06	07 42	09 12	09 36	10 02	10 33
52	06 30	07 11	07 50	09 12	09 34	09 58	10 27
54	06 34	07 18	07 58	09 11	09 31	09 54	10 20
56	06 38	07 25	08 08	09 11	09 29	09 49	10 13
58	06 43	07 32	08 19	09 10	09 26	09 43	10 05
S 60	06 48	07 41	08 31	09 10	09 22	09 37	09 55

Sunset, Twilight and Moonset

Lat.	Sunset	Civil	Naut.	Moonset 23	24	25	26
N 72	□	□	□	20 52	20 35	20 13	19 32
N 70	□	□	□	20 57	20 48	20 37	20 22
68	22 36	////	////	21 02	20 59	20 56	20 53
66	21 55	////	////	21 05	21 07	21 11	21 17
64	21 25	23 25	////	21 08	21 15	21 23	21 36
62	21 05	22 27	////	21 11	21 21	21 34	21 51
60	20 48	21 55	////	21 14	21 27	21 43	22 04
N 58	20 34	21 32	23 29	21 16	21 32	21 51	22 15
56	20 22	21 13	22 36	21 18	21 36	21 58	22 25
54	20 11	20 58	22 07	21 19	21 40	22 04	22 33
52	20 02	20 45	21 45	21 21	21 44	22 10	22 41
50	19 53	20 33	21 27	21 22	21 47	22 15	22 48
45	19 36	20 10	20 54	21 24	21 54	22 26	23 03
N 40	19 21	19 52	20 30	21 28	22 00	22 35	23 15
35	19 09	19 37	20 12	21 31	22 05	22 43	23 26
30	18 58	19 25	19 56	21 33	22 10	22 50	23 35
20	18 40	19 04	19 32	21 36	22 18	23 03	23 51
N 10	18 25	18 47	19 13	21 39	22 25	23 13	24 05
0	18 11	18 32	18 58	21 42	22 32	23 24	24 18
S 10	17 56	18 18	18 44	21 45	22 38	23 34	24 31
20	17 40	18 04	18 31	21 48	22 45	23 45	24 45
30	17 23	17 49	18 18	21 52	22 53	23 57	25 02
35	17 13	17 40	18 11	21 54	22 58	24 04	00 04
40	17 02	17 31	18 04	21 56	23 03	24 12	00 12
45	16 48	17 20	17 56	21 59	23 10	24 22	00 22
S 50	16 32	17 08	17 48	22 02	23 17	24 34	00 34
52	16 24	17 02	17 44	22 03	23 21	24 39	00 39
54	16 15	16 56	17 40	22 05	23 24	24 45	00 45
56	16 06	16 49	17 36	22 07	23 29	24 52	00 52
58	15 55	16 41	17 31	22 09	23 33	24 59	00 59
S 60	15 42	16 33	17 26	22 11	23 39	25 08	01 08

SUN and MOON

Day	SUN Eqn. of Time 00h	12h	Mer. Pass.	MOON Mer. Pass. Upper	Lower	Age	Phase
23	06 30	06 30	12 07	15 31	03 06	04	20
24	06 31	06 31	12 07	16 20	03 55	05	30
25	06 32	06 32	12 07	17 11	04 45	06	40

UT	ARIES	VENUS −4.6		MARS +1.1		JUPITER −2.1		SATURN +0.8		STARS		
d h	GHA	GHA	Dec	GHA	Dec	GHA	Dec	GHA	Dec	Name	SHA	Dec
26 00	304 05.6	224 57.5	N18 38.5	112 37.1	S 4 56.8	236 26.6	N21 04.0	101 24.5	S 6 51.8	Acamar	315 18.9	S40 15.0
01	319 08.1	239 58.1	38.7	127 38.3	57.4	251 28.6	04.1	116 26.8	51.9	Achernar	335 27.1	S57 10.0
02	334 10.5	254 58.6	39.0	142 39.4	58.0	266 30.5	04.1	131 29.2	51.9	Acrux	173 10.3	S63 10.5
03	349 13.0	269 59.1	.. 39.2	157 40.5	.. 58.6	281 32.5	.. 04.2	146 31.5	.. 52.0	Adhara	255 13.4	S28 59.4
04	4 15.5	284 59.6	39.4	172 41.7	59.3	296 34.5	04.3	161 33.9	52.1	Aldebaran	290 50.3	N16 32.0
05	19 17.9	300 00.2	39.7	187 42.8	4 59.9	311 36.5	04.3	176 36.2	52.1			
06	34 20.4	315 00.7	N18 39.9	202 43.9	S 5 00.5	326 38.5	N21 04.4	191 38.6	S 6 52.2	Alioth	166 21.4	N55 53.7
07	49 22.8	330 01.2	40.1	217 45.1	01.1	341 40.5	04.5	206 40.9	52.2	Alkaid	152 59.4	N49 15.3
T 08	64 25.3	345 01.7	40.3	232 46.2	01.7	356 42.5	04.5	221 43.3	52.3	Al Na'ir	27 44.1	S46 53.7
H 09	79 27.8	0 02.2	.. 40.6	247 47.3	.. 02.3	11 44.5	.. 04.6	236 45.6	.. 52.3	Alnilam	275 47.2	S 1 11.7
U 10	94 30.2	15 02.8	40.8	262 48.5	02.9	26 46.4	04.7	251 48.0	52.4	Alphard	217 57.0	S 8 42.9
R 11	109 32.7	30 03.3	41.0	277 49.6	03.5	41 48.4	04.7	266 50.3	52.4			
S 12	124 35.2	45 03.8	N18 41.3	292 50.7	S 5 04.1	56 50.4	N21 04.8	281 52.7	S 6 52.5	Alphecca	126 11.4	N26 40.6
D 13	139 37.6	60 04.3	41.5	307 51.9	04.7	71 52.4	04.9	296 55.0	52.6	Alpheratz	357 43.9	N29 09.6
A 14	154 40.1	75 04.8	41.7	322 53.0	05.3	86 54.4	04.9	311 57.4	52.6	Altair	62 08.5	N 8 54.3
Y 15	169 42.6	90 05.3	.. 41.9	337 54.1	.. 05.9	101 56.4	.. 05.0	326 59.7	.. 52.7	Ankaa	353 16.1	S42 13.9
16	184 45.0	105 05.8	42.2	352 55.2	06.5	116 58.4	05.1	342 02.1	52.7	Antares	112 26.8	S26 27.6
17	199 47.5	120 06.3	42.4	7 56.4	07.1	132 00.4	05.1	357 04.4	52.8			
18	214 50.0	135 06.8	N18 42.6	22 57.5	S 5 07.7	147 02.3	N21 05.2	12 06.8	S 6 52.9	Arcturus	145 56.3	N19 07.2
19	229 52.4	150 07.3	42.9	37 58.6	08.3	162 04.3	05.3	27 09.1	52.9	Atria	107 28.8	S69 03.1
20	244 54.9	165 07.8	43.1	52 59.8	08.9	177 06.3	05.3	42 11.5	52.9	Avior	234 18.9	S59 33.1
21	259 57.3	180 08.3	.. 43.3	68 00.9	.. 09.5	192 08.3	.. 05.4	57 13.8	.. 53.0	Bellatrix	278 32.9	N 6 21.6
22	274 59.8	195 08.8	43.5	83 02.0	10.1	207 10.3	05.5	72 16.2	53.0	Betelgeuse	271 02.2	N 7 24.5
23	290 02.3	210 09.3	43.8	98 03.1	10.7	222 12.3	05.5	87 18.5	53.1			
27 00	305 04.7	225 09.8	N18 44.0	113 04.3	S 5 11.3	237 14.3	N21 05.6	102 20.9	S 6 53.2	Canopus	263 56.9	S52 42.1
01	320 07.2	240 10.3	44.2	128 05.4	11.9	252 16.3	05.7	117 23.2	53.2	Capella	280 35.7	N46 00.4
02	335 09.7	255 10.8	44.5	143 06.5	12.6	267 18.2	05.7	132 25.6	53.3	Deneb	49 31.4	N45 19.7
03	350 12.1	270 11.2	.. 44.7	158 07.6	.. 13.2	282 20.2	.. 05.8	147 27.9	.. 53.3	Denebola	182 34.5	N14 30.1
04	5 14.6	285 11.7	44.9	173 08.8	13.8	297 22.2	05.9	162 30.3	53.4	Diphda	348 56.4	S17 54.8
05	20 17.1	300 12.2	45.1	188 09.9	14.4	312 24.2	05.9	177 32.6	53.4			
06	35 19.5	315 12.7	N18 45.4	203 11.0	S 5 15.0	327 26.2	N21 06.0	192 35.0	S 6 53.5	Dubhe	193 52.9	N61 41.1
07	50 22.0	330 13.2	45.6	218 12.1	15.6	342 28.2	06.1	207 37.3	53.6	Elnath	278 13.7	N28 36.9
F 08	65 24.5	345 13.6	45.8	233 13.3	16.2	357 30.2	06.1	222 39.7	53.6	Eltanin	90 46.0	N51 29.5
R 09	80 26.9	0 14.1	.. 46.0	248 14.4	.. 16.8	12 32.2	.. 06.2	237 42.0	.. 53.7	Enif	33 47.4	N 9 56.2
I 10	95 29.4	15 14.6	46.3	263 15.5	17.4	27 34.2	06.3	252 44.4	53.7	Fomalhaut	15 24.4	S29 33.0
11	110 31.8	30 15.1	46.5	278 16.6	18.0	42 36.2	06.3	267 46.7	53.8			
D 12	125 34.3	45 15.5	N18 46.7	293 17.8	S 5 18.6	57 38.2	N21 06.4	282 49.1	S 6 53.8	Gacrux	172 01.8	S57 11.3
A 13	140 36.8	60 16.0	47.0	308 18.9	19.2	72 40.1	06.5	297 51.4	53.9	Gienah	175 53.1	S17 36.8
Y 14	155 39.2	75 16.5	47.2	323 20.0	19.8	87 42.1	06.5	312 53.8	53.9	Hadar	148 48.7	S60 26.3
15	170 41.7	90 16.9	.. 47.4	338 21.1	.. 20.4	102 44.1	.. 06.6	327 56.1	.. 54.0	Hamal	328 01.4	N23 31.3
16	185 44.2	105 17.4	47.6	353 22.3	21.0	117 46.1	06.6	342 58.5	54.1	Kaus Aust.	83 44.2	S34 22.6
17	200 46.6	120 17.9	47.9	8 23.4	21.6	132 48.1	06.7	358 00.8	54.1			
18	215 49.1	135 18.3	N18 48.1	23 24.5	S 5 22.2	147 50.1	N21 06.8	13 03.2	S 6 54.2	Kochab	137 19.8	N74 06.5
19	230 51.6	150 18.8	48.3	38 25.6	22.8	162 52.1	06.8	28 05.5	54.2	Markab	13 38.7	N15 16.5
20	245 54.0	165 19.2	48.5	53 26.7	23.4	177 54.1	06.9	43 07.9	54.3	Menkar	314 15.7	N 4 08.4
21	260 56.5	180 19.7	.. 48.8	68 27.9	.. 24.1	192 56.1	.. 07.0	58 10.2	.. 54.3	Menkent	148 08.3	S36 26.1
22	275 59.0	195 20.2	49.0	83 29.0	24.7	207 58.1	07.0	73 12.5	54.4	Miaplacidus	221 40.7	S69 46.3
23	291 01.4	210 20.6	49.2	98 30.1	25.3	223 00.1	07.1	88 14.9	54.5			
28 00	306 03.9	225 21.1	N18 49.4	113 31.2	S 5 25.9	238 02.1	N21 07.2	103 17.2	S 6 54.5	Mirfak	308 41.4	N49 54.1
01	321 06.3	240 21.5	49.7	128 32.4	26.5	253 04.1	07.2	118 19.6	54.6	Nunki	75 58.7	S26 16.7
02	336 08.8	255 22.0	49.9	143 33.5	27.1	268 06.0	07.3	133 21.9	54.6	Peacock	53 19.6	S56 41.4
03	351 11.3	270 22.4	.. 50.1	158 34.6	.. 27.7	283 08.0	.. 07.4	148 24.3	.. 54.7	Pollux	243 28.8	N27 59.6
04	6 13.7	285 22.9	50.3	173 35.7	28.3	298 10.0	07.4	163 26.6	54.7	Procyon	245 00.7	N 5 11.5
05	21 16.2	300 23.3	50.6	188 36.8	28.9	313 12.0	07.5	178 29.0	54.8			
06	36 18.7	315 23.7	N18 50.8	203 37.9	S 5 29.5	328 14.0	N21 07.6	193 31.3	S 6 54.9	Rasalhague	96 06.7	N12 33.3
07	51 21.1	330 24.2	51.0	218 39.1	30.1	343 16.0	07.6	208 33.7	54.9	Regulus	207 44.4	N11 54.3
S 08	66 23.6	345 24.6	51.2	233 40.2	30.7	358 18.0	07.7	223 36.0	55.0	Rigel	281 12.9	S 8 11.2
A 09	81 26.1	0 25.1	.. 51.5	248 41.3	.. 31.3	13 20.0	.. 07.8	238 38.4	.. 55.0	Rigil Kent.	139 52.5	S60 53.4
T 10	96 28.5	15 25.5	51.7	263 42.4	31.9	28 22.0	07.8	253 40.7	55.1	Sabik	102 13.0	S15 44.3
U 11	111 31.0	30 25.9	51.9	278 43.5	32.5	43 24.0	07.9	268 43.0	55.1			
R 12	126 33.4	45 26.4	N18 52.1	293 44.7	S 5 33.1	58 26.0	N21 07.9	283 45.4	S 6 55.2	Schedar	349 41.0	N56 36.2
D 13	141 35.9	60 26.8	52.4	308 45.8	33.7	73 28.0	08.0	298 47.7	55.3	Shaula	96 22.4	S37 06.7
A 14	156 38.4	75 27.2	52.6	323 46.9	34.3	88 30.0	08.1	313 50.1	55.3	Sirius	258 34.6	S16 44.0
Y 15	171 40.8	90 27.6	.. 52.8	338 48.0	.. 35.0	103 32.0	.. 08.1	328 52.4	.. 55.4	Spica	158 31.9	S11 13.7
16	186 43.3	105 28.1	53.0	353 49.1	35.6	118 34.0	08.2	343 54.8	55.4	Suhail	222 53.3	S43 29.2
17	201 45.8	120 28.5	53.3	8 50.2	36.2	133 36.0	08.3	358 57.1	55.5			
18	216 48.2	135 28.9	N18 53.5	23 51.4	S 5 36.8	148 38.0	N21 08.3	13 59.5	S 6 55.6	Vega	80 39.0	N38 48.0
19	231 50.7	150 29.3	53.7	38 52.5	37.4	163 40.0	08.4	29 01.8	55.6	Zuben'ubi	137 06.0	S16 05.6
20	246 53.2	165 29.8	53.9	53 53.6	38.0	178 42.0	08.5	44 04.1	55.7		SHA	Mer.Pass.
21	261 55.6	180 30.2	.. 54.2	68 54.7	.. 38.6	193 44.0	.. 08.5	59 06.5	.. 55.7	Venus	280 05.0	8 59
22	276 58.1	195 30.6	54.4	83 55.8	39.2	208 46.0	08.6	74 08.8	55.8	Mars	167 59.5	16 26
23	292 00.6	210 31.0	54.6	98 56.9	39.8	223 48.0	08.7	89 11.2	55.8	Jupiter	292 09.5	8 10
Mer. Pass. 3 39.1		v 0.5	d 0.2	v 1.1	d 0.6	v 2.0	d 0.1	v 2.3	d 0.1	Saturn	157 16.2	17 08

UT	SUN GHA	SUN Dec	MOON GHA	v	Dec	d	HP
d h	° ′	° ′	° ′	′	° ′	′	′
26 00	178 22.0	N19 23.3	98 37.8	8.9	S13 39.9	10.2	59.0
01	193 22.0	22.7	113 05.7	8.8	13 50.1	10.1	59.0
02	208 22.0	22.1	127 33.5	8.7	14 00.2	10.0	59.1
03	223 22.0	.. 21.6	142 01.2	8.6	14 10.2	9.9	59.1
04	238 22.0	21.0	156 28.8	8.6	14 20.1	9.8	59.1
05	253 22.0	20.5	170 56.4	8.5	14 29.9	9.8	59.1
T 06	268 22.0	N19 19.9	185 23.9	8.5	S14 39.7	9.7	59.1
H 07	283 22.0	19.4	199 51.4	8.3	14 49.4	9.6	59.1
U 08	298 22.0	18.8	214 18.7	8.4	14 59.0	9.5	59.1
R 09	313 22.0	.. 18.2	228 46.1	8.2	15 08.5	9.4	59.2
S 10	328 22.0	17.7	243 13.3	8.2	15 17.9	9.3	59.2
D 11	343 22.0	17.1	257 40.5	8.1	15 27.2	9.3	59.2
A 12	358 22.0	N19 16.6	272 07.6	8.0	S15 36.5	9.1	59.2
Y 13	13 22.0	16.0	286 34.6	8.0	15 45.6	9.1	59.2
14	28 22.1	15.4	301 01.6	7.9	15 54.7	9.0	59.2
15	43 22.1	.. 14.9	315 28.5	7.8	16 03.7	8.8	59.2
16	58 22.1	14.3	329 55.3	7.7	16 12.5	8.8	59.2
17	73 22.1	13.7	344 22.0	7.7	16 21.3	8.7	59.3
18	88 22.1	N19 13.2	358 48.7	7.6	S16 30.0	8.6	59.3
19	103 22.1	12.6	13 15.3	7.6	16 38.6	8.5	59.3
20	118 22.1	12.1	27 41.9	7.5	16 47.1	8.4	59.3
21	133 22.1	.. 11.5	42 08.4	7.4	16 55.5	8.3	59.3
22	148 22.1	10.9	56 34.8	7.3	17 03.8	8.2	59.3
23	163 22.1	10.4	71 01.1	7.3	17 12.0	8.0	59.3
27 00	178 22.1	N19 09.8	85 27.4	7.2	S17 20.0	8.0	59.3
01	193 22.1	09.2	99 53.6	7.2	17 28.0	7.9	59.4
02	208 22.1	08.6	114 19.8	7.1	17 35.9	7.7	59.4
03	223 22.1	.. 08.1	128 45.9	7.0	17 43.6	7.7	59.4
04	238 22.2	07.5	143 11.9	6.9	17 51.3	7.5	59.4
05	253 22.2	06.9	157 37.8	6.9	17 58.8	7.5	59.4
F 06	268 22.2	N19 06.4	172 03.7	6.8	S18 06.3	7.3	59.4
R 07	283 22.2	05.8	186 29.5	6.8	18 13.6	7.2	59.4
I 08	298 22.2	05.2	200 55.3	6.6	18 20.8	7.1	59.4
D 09	313 22.2	.. 04.7	215 20.9	6.7	18 27.9	7.0	59.4
A 10	328 22.2	04.1	229 46.6	6.5	18 34.9	6.8	59.4
Y 11	343 22.2	03.5	244 12.1	6.5	18 41.7	6.8	59.5
12	358 22.2	N19 02.9	258 37.6	6.4	S18 48.5	6.6	59.5
13	13 22.2	02.4	273 03.0	6.4	18 55.1	6.5	59.5
14	28 22.3	01.8	287 28.4	6.3	19 01.6	6.4	59.5
15	43 22.3	.. 01.2	301 53.7	6.3	19 08.0	6.2	59.5
16	58 22.3	00.6	316 19.0	6.2	19 14.2	6.1	59.5
17	73 22.3	19 00.1	330 44.2	6.1	19 20.3	6.1	59.5
18	88 22.3	N18 59.5	345 09.3	6.1	S19 26.4	5.8	59.5
19	103 22.3	58.9	359 34.4	6.0	19 32.2	5.8	59.5
20	118 22.3	58.3	13 59.4	5.9	19 38.0	5.6	59.5
21	133 22.3	.. 57.7	28 24.3	5.9	19 43.6	5.5	59.5
22	148 22.4	57.2	42 49.2	5.9	19 49.1	5.4	59.6
23	163 22.4	56.6	57 14.1	5.8	19 54.5	5.2	59.6
28 00	178 22.4	N18 56.0	71 38.9	5.7	S19 59.7	5.2	59.6
01	193 22.4	55.4	86 03.6	5.7	20 04.9	4.9	59.6
02	208 22.4	54.8	100 28.3	5.7	20 09.8	4.9	59.6
03	223 22.4	.. 54.3	114 53.0	5.5	20 14.7	4.7	59.6
04	238 22.4	53.7	129 17.5	5.6	20 19.4	4.6	59.6
05	253 22.5	53.1	143 42.1	5.5	20 24.0	4.4	59.6
S 06	268 22.5	N18 52.5	158 06.6	5.4	S20 28.4	4.3	59.6
A 07	283 22.5	51.9	172 31.0	5.4	20 32.7	4.2	59.6
T 08	298 22.5	51.3	186 55.4	5.4	20 36.9	4.0	59.6
U 09	313 22.5	.. 50.7	201 19.8	5.3	20 40.9	3.9	59.6
R 10	328 22.6	50.2	215 44.1	5.3	20 44.8	3.8	59.6
D 11	343 22.6	49.6	230 08.4	5.2	20 48.6	3.6	59.6
A 12	358 22.6	N18 49.0	244 32.6	5.2	S20 52.2	3.5	59.6
Y 13	13 22.6	48.4	258 56.8	5.2	20 55.7	3.3	59.6
14	28 22.6	47.8	273 21.0	5.1	20 59.0	3.2	59.7
15	43 22.6	.. 47.2	287 45.1	5.1	21 02.2	3.0	59.7
16	58 22.6	46.6	302 09.2	5.1	21 05.2	2.9	59.7
17	73 22.7	46.0	316 33.3	5.0	21 08.1	2.8	59.7
18	88 22.7	N18 45.5	330 57.3	5.0	S21 10.9	2.6	59.7
19	103 22.7	44.9	345 21.3	5.0	21 13.5	2.5	59.7
20	118 22.7	44.3	359 45.3	4.9	21 16.0	2.3	59.7
21	133 22.7	.. 43.7	14 09.2	4.9	21 18.3	2.2	59.7
22	148 22.7	43.1	28 33.1	4.9	21 20.5	2.0	59.7
23	163 22.8	42.5	42 57.0	4.9	S21 22.5	1.9	59.7
	SD 15.8	d 0.6	SD 16.1		16.2		16.3

Lat.	Twilight Naut.	Twilight Civil	Sunrise	Moonrise 26	27	28	29
°	h m	h m	h m	h m	h m	h m	h m
N 72	□	□	□	16 21	■	■	■
N 70	////	////	00 12	15 33	18 13	■	■
68	////	////	01 50	15 02	17 02	19 02	20 18
66	////	////	02 27	14 40	16 25	18 02	19 10
64	////	01 08	02 53	14 22	16 00	17 27	18 34
62	////	01 56	03 14	14 08	15 39	17 03	18 08
60	////	02 25	03 30	13 55	15 23	16 43	17 48
N 58	01 02	02 47	03 44	13 45	15 09	16 27	17 31
56	01 45	03 05	03 55	13 36	14 57	16 13	17 17
54	02 13	03 20	04 06	13 28	14 47	16 01	17 05
52	02 33	03 32	04 15	13 21	14 38	15 50	16 54
50	02 50	03 43	04 23	13 14	14 30	15 41	16 45
45	03 22	04 06	04 40	13 00	14 12	15 21	16 24
N 40	03 45	04 23	04 54	12 49	13 58	15 05	16 08
35	04 03	04 38	05 06	12 39	13 46	14 52	15 54
30	04 18	04 50	05 16	12 31	13 36	14 40	15 42
20	04 42	05 10	05 34	12 16	13 18	14 20	15 22
N 10	05 00	05 27	05 49	12 04	13 02	14 03	15 04
0	05 15	05 41	06 03	11 52	12 48	13 47	14 47
S 10	05 29	05 55	06 17	11 40	12 34	13 31	14 30
20	05 42	06 08	06 32	11 28	12 18	13 13	14 13
30	05 54	06 23	06 48	11 14	12 01	12 54	13 52
35	06 01	06 31	06 58	11 06	11 51	12 42	13 40
40	06 07	06 40	07 09	10 56	11 39	12 29	13 26
45	06 15	06 50	07 22	10 46	11 26	12 14	13 10
S 50	06 23	07 02	07 38	10 33	11 09	11 55	12 50
52	06 26	07 08	07 45	10 27	11 02	11 46	12 41
54	06 30	07 14	07 54	10 20	10 53	11 36	12 30
56	06 34	07 20	08 03	10 13	10 44	11 24	12 18
58	06 38	07 27	08 13	10 05	10 33	11 12	12 04
S 60	06 43	07 35	08 25	09 55	10 20	10 56	11 48

Lat.	Sunset	Twilight Civil	Twilight Naut.	Moonset 26	27	28	29
°	h m	h m	h m	h m	h m	h m	h m
N 72	□	□	□	19 32	■	■	■
N 70	00 02	////	////	20 22	19 41	■	■
68	22 18	////	////	20 53	20 52	20 57	21 47
66	21 43	////	////	21 17	21 29	21 57	22 55
64	21 17	22 58	////	21 36	21 56	22 31	23 30
62	20 58	22 14	////	21 51	22 16	22 56	23 56
60	20 42	21 45	////	22 04	22 33	23 16	24 16
N 58	20 28	21 24	23 05	22 15	22 48	23 33	24 33
56	20 16	21 06	22 24	22 25	23 00	23 46	24 47
54	20 06	20 52	21 58	22 33	23 10	23 59	24 59
52	19 57	20 40	21 38	22 41	23 20	24 09	00 09
50	19 49	20 29	21 21	22 48	23 29	24 19	00 19
45	19 32	20 07	20 50	23 03	23 47	24 39	00 39
N 40	19 18	19 49	20 27	23 15	24 01	00 01	00 55
35	19 07	19 35	20 09	23 26	24 14	00 14	01 09
30	18 56	19 23	19 54	23 35	24 25	00 25	01 21
20	18 39	19 03	19 31	23 51	24 44	00 44	01 41
N 10	18 24	18 46	19 12	24 05	00 05	01 00	01 59
0	18 10	18 32	18 57	24 18	00 18	01 16	02 15
S 10	17 56	18 18	18 44	24 31	00 31	01 31	02 32
20	17 42	18 05	18 31	24 45	00 45	01 48	02 50
30	17 25	17 50	18 19	25 02	01 02	02 07	03 10
35	17 15	17 42	18 13	00 04	01 11	02 18	03 22
40	17 04	17 33	18 06	00 12	01 22	02 30	03 36
45	16 51	17 23	17 59	00 22	01 34	02 45	03 52
S 50	16 36	17 11	17 51	00 34	01 50	03 04	04 12
52	16 28	17 06	17 47	00 39	01 57	03 13	04 21
54	16 20	17 00	17 44	00 45	02 05	03 22	04 32
56	16 11	16 54	17 40	00 52	02 14	03 33	04 44
58	16 01	16 46	17 35	00 59	02 25	03 46	04 58
S 60	15 49	16 38	17 31	01 08	02 37	04 01	05 14

Day	SUN Eqn. of Time 00h	SUN Eqn. of Time 12h	SUN Mer. Pass.	MOON Mer. Pass. Upper	MOON Mer. Pass. Lower	Age	Phase
d	m s	m s	h m	h m	h m	d	%
26	06 32	06 32	12 07	18 05	05 38	07	52
27	06 32	06 31	12 07	19 02	06 33	08	63
28	06 30	06 30	12 06	20 01	07 31	09	74

UT	ARIES	VENUS −4.6		MARS +1.1		JUPITER −2.2		SATURN +0.8		STARS		
	GHA	GHA	Dec	GHA	Dec	GHA	Dec	GHA	Dec	Name	SHA	Dec
d h	° ′	° ′	° ′	° ′	° ′	° ′	° ′	° ′	° ′		° ′	° ′
29 00	307 03.0	225 31.4	N18 54.8	113 58.1	S 5 40.4	238 50.0	N21 08.7	104 13.5	S 6 55.9	Acamar	315 18.9	S40 15.0
01	322 05.5	240 31.8	55.0	128 59.2	41.0	253 52.0	08.8	119 15.9	56.0	Achernar	335 27.1	S57 10.0
02	337 07.9	255 32.3	55.3	144 00.3	41.6	268 53.9	08.8	134 18.2	56.0	Acrux	173 10.3	S63 10.4
03	352 10.4	270 32.7	.. 55.5	159 01.4	.. 42.2	283 55.9	.. 08.9	149 20.5	.. 56.1	Adhara	255 13.3	S28 59.4
04	7 12.9	285 33.1	55.7	174 02.5	42.8	298 57.9	09.0	164 22.9	56.1	Aldebaran	290 50.2	N16 32.0
05	22 15.3	300 33.5	55.9	189 03.6	43.4	313 59.9	09.0	179 25.2	56.2			
06	37 17.8	315 33.9	N18 56.2	204 04.7	S 5 44.0	329 01.9	N21 09.1	194 27.6	S 6 56.3	Alioth	166 21.4	N55 53.7
07	52 20.3	330 34.3	56.4	219 05.8	44.7	344 03.9	09.2	209 29.9	56.3	Alkaid	152 59.4	N49 15.3
08	67 22.7	345 34.7	56.6	234 07.0	45.3	359 05.9	09.2	224 32.2	56.4	Al Na'ir	27 44.0	S46 53.7
S 09	82 25.2	0 35.1	.. 56.8	249 08.1	.. 45.9	14 07.9	.. 09.3	239 34.6	.. 56.4	Alnilam	275 47.2	S 1 11.7
U 10	97 27.7	15 35.5	57.0	264 09.2	46.5	29 09.9	09.4	254 36.9	56.5	Alphard	217 57.0	S 8 42.9
N 11	112 30.1	30 35.9	57.3	279 10.3	47.1	44 11.9	09.4	269 39.3	56.5			
D 12	127 32.6	45 36.3	N18 57.5	294 11.4	S 5 47.7	59 13.9	N21 09.5	284 41.6	S 6 56.6	Alphecca	126 11.4	N26 40.6
A 13	142 35.1	60 36.7	57.7	309 12.5	48.3	74 15.9	09.6	299 44.0	56.7	Alpheratz	357 43.9	N29 09.6
Y 14	157 37.5	75 37.1	57.9	324 13.6	48.9	89 17.9	09.6	314 46.3	56.7	Altair	62 08.5	N 8 54.3
15	172 40.0	90 37.5	.. 58.2	339 14.7	.. 49.5	104 19.9	.. 09.7	329 48.6	.. 56.8	Ankaa	353 16.1	S42 13.9
16	187 42.4	105 37.8	58.4	354 15.9	50.1	119 21.9	09.7	344 51.0	56.8	Antares	112 26.8	S26 27.6
17	202 44.9	120 38.2	58.6	9 17.0	50.7	134 23.9	09.8	359 53.3	56.9			
18	217 47.4	135 38.6	N18 58.8	24 18.1	S 5 51.3	149 25.9	N21 09.9	14 55.7	S 6 57.0	Arcturus	145 56.3	N19 07.2
19	232 49.8	150 39.0	59.0	39 19.2	51.9	164 27.9	09.9	29 58.0	57.0	Atria	107 28.8	S69 03.1
20	247 52.3	165 39.4	59.3	54 20.3	52.5	179 29.9	10.0	45 00.3	57.1	Avior	234 18.9	S59 33.1
21	262 54.8	180 39.8	.. 59.5	69 21.4	.. 53.1	194 31.9	.. 10.1	60 02.7	.. 57.1	Bellatrix	278 32.9	N 6 21.6
22	277 57.2	195 40.1	59.7	84 22.5	53.7	209 33.9	10.1	75 05.0	57.2	Betelgeuse	271 02.2	N 7 24.5
23	292 59.7	210 40.5	18 59.9	99 23.6	54.4	224 35.9	10.2	90 07.4	57.3			
30 00	308 02.2	225 40.9	N19 00.1	114 24.7	S 5 55.0	239 37.9	N21 10.2	105 09.7	S 6 57.3	Canopus	263 56.9	S52 42.1
01	323 04.6	240 41.3	00.3	129 25.8	55.6	254 39.9	10.3	120 12.0	57.4	Capella	280 35.6	N46 00.4
02	338 07.1	255 41.7	00.6	144 26.9	56.2	269 41.9	10.4	135 14.4	57.4	Deneb	49 31.4	N45 19.7
03	353 09.6	270 42.0	.. 00.8	159 28.1	.. 56.8	284 44.0	.. 10.4	150 16.7	.. 57.5	Denebola	182 34.5	N14 30.1
04	8 12.0	285 42.4	01.0	174 29.2	57.4	299 46.0	10.5	165 19.1	57.6	Diphda	348 56.3	S17 54.8
05	23 14.5	300 42.8	01.2	189 30.3	58.0	314 48.0	10.6	180 21.4	57.6			
06	38 16.9	315 43.1	N19 01.4	204 31.4	S 5 58.6	329 50.0	N21 10.6	195 23.7	S 6 57.7	Dubhe	193 52.9	N61 41.1
07	53 19.4	330 43.5	01.7	219 32.5	59.2	344 52.0	10.7	210 26.1	57.7	Elnath	278 13.6	N28 36.9
08	68 21.9	345 43.9	01.9	234 33.6	5 59.8	359 54.0	10.7	225 28.4	57.8	Eltanin	90 46.0	N51 29.5
M 09	83 24.3	0 44.2	.. 02.1	249 34.7	6 00.4	14 56.0	.. 10.8	240 30.7	.. 57.9	Enif	33 47.4	N 9 56.2
O 10	98 26.8	15 44.6	02.3	264 35.8	01.0	29 58.0	10.9	255 33.1	57.9	Fomalhaut	15 24.3	S29 33.0
N 11	113 29.3	30 45.0	02.5	279 36.9	01.6	45 00.0	10.9	270 35.4	58.0			
D 12	128 31.7	45 45.3	N19 02.7	294 38.0	S 6 02.2	60 02.0	N21 11.0	285 37.8	S 6 58.0	Gacrux	172 01.8	S57 11.3
A 13	143 34.2	60 45.7	03.0	309 39.1	02.8	75 04.0	11.1	300 40.1	58.1	Gienah	175 53.1	S17 36.8
Y 14	158 36.7	75 46.0	03.2	324 40.2	03.5	90 06.0	11.1	315 42.4	58.2	Hadar	148 48.8	S60 26.3
15	173 39.1	90 46.4	.. 03.4	339 41.3	.. 04.1	105 08.0	.. 11.2	330 44.8	.. 58.2	Hamal	328 01.4	N23 31.3
16	188 41.6	105 46.7	03.6	354 42.4	04.7	120 10.0	11.2	345 47.1	58.3	Kaus Aust.	83 44.2	S34 22.6
17	203 44.1	120 47.1	03.8	9 43.5	05.3	135 12.0	11.3	0 49.4	58.3			
18	218 46.5	135 47.4	N19 04.0	24 44.6	S 6 05.9	150 14.0	N21 11.4	15 51.8	S 6 58.4	Kochab	137 19.9	N74 06.5
19	233 49.0	150 47.8	04.3	39 45.7	06.5	165 16.0	11.4	30 54.1	58.5	Markab	13 38.7	N15 16.5
20	248 51.4	165 48.1	04.5	54 46.8	07.1	180 18.0	11.5	45 56.5	58.5	Menkar	314 15.7	N 4 08.4
21	263 53.9	180 48.5	.. 04.7	69 47.9	.. 07.7	195 20.0	.. 11.5	60 58.8	.. 58.6	Menkent	148 08.3	S36 26.1
22	278 56.4	195 48.8	04.9	84 49.0	08.3	210 22.0	11.6	76 01.1	58.6	Miaplacidus	221 40.7	S69 46.3
23	293 58.8	210 49.2	05.1	99 50.2	08.9	225 24.0	11.7	91 03.5	58.7			
31 00	309 01.3	225 49.5	N19 05.3	114 51.3	S 6 09.5	240 26.0	N21 11.7	106 05.8	S 6 58.8	Mirfak	308 41.3	N49 54.1
01	324 03.8	240 49.8	05.5	129 52.4	10.1	255 28.0	11.8	121 08.1	58.8	Nunki	75 58.7	S26 16.7
02	339 06.2	255 50.2	05.8	144 53.5	10.7	270 30.1	11.9	136 10.5	58.9	Peacock	53 19.6	S56 41.4
03	354 08.7	270 50.5	.. 06.0	159 54.6	.. 11.3	285 32.1	.. 11.9	151 12.8	.. 58.9	Pollux	243 28.8	N27 59.6
04	9 11.2	285 50.9	06.2	174 55.7	11.9	300 34.1	12.0	166 15.1	59.0	Procyon	245 00.7	N 5 11.5
05	24 13.6	300 51.2	06.4	189 56.8	12.6	315 36.1	12.0	181 17.5	59.1			
06	39 16.1	315 51.5	N19 06.6	204 57.9	S 6 13.2	330 38.1	N21 12.1	196 19.8	S 6 59.1	Rasalhague	96 06.7	N12 33.3
07	54 18.6	330 51.9	06.8	219 59.0	13.8	345 40.1	12.2	211 22.2	59.2	Regulus	207 44.4	N11 54.3
08	69 21.0	345 52.2	07.0	235 00.1	14.4	0 42.1	12.2	226 24.5	59.3	Rigel	281 12.8	S 8 11.2
T 09	84 23.5	0 52.5	.. 07.3	250 01.2	.. 15.0	15 44.1	.. 12.3	241 26.8	.. 59.3	Rigil Kent.	139 52.5	S60 53.4
U 10	99 25.9	15 52.8	07.5	265 02.3	15.6	30 46.1	12.3	256 29.2	59.4	Sabik	102 13.0	S15 44.3
E 11	114 28.4	30 53.2	07.7	280 03.4	16.2	45 48.1	12.4	271 31.5	59.4			
S 12	129 30.9	45 53.5	N19 07.9	295 04.5	S 6 16.8	60 50.1	N21 12.5	286 33.8	S 6 59.5	Schedar	349 40.9	N56 36.3
D 13	144 33.3	60 53.8	08.1	310 05.6	17.4	75 52.1	12.5	301 36.2	59.6	Shaula	96 22.4	S37 06.7
A 14	159 35.8	75 54.1	08.3	325 06.7	18.0	90 54.1	12.6	316 38.5	59.6	Sirius	258 34.5	S16 44.0
Y 15	174 38.3	90 54.5	.. 08.5	340 07.8	.. 18.6	105 56.2	.. 12.7	331 40.8	.. 59.7	Spica	158 31.9	S11 13.7
16	189 40.7	105 54.8	08.7	355 08.9	19.2	120 58.2	12.7	346 43.2	59.7	Suhail	222 53.3	S43 29.1
17	204 43.2	120 55.1	08.9	10 10.0	19.8	136 00.2	12.8	1 45.5	59.8			
18	219 45.7	135 55.4	N19 09.2	25 11.1	S 6 20.4	151 02.2	N21 12.8	16 47.8	S 6 59.9	Vega	80 39.0	N38 48.0
19	234 48.1	150 55.7	09.4	40 12.2	21.1	166 04.2	12.9	31 50.2	6 59.9	Zuben'ubi	137 06.0	S16 05.6
20	249 50.6	165 56.0	09.6	55 13.2	21.7	181 06.2	13.0	46 52.5	7 00.0		SHA	Mer.Pass.
21	264 53.0	180 56.3	.. 09.8	70 14.3	.. 22.3	196 08.2	.. 13.0	61 54.8	.. 00.1		° ′	h m
22	279 55.5	195 56.6	10.0	85 15.4	22.9	211 10.2	13.1	76 57.2	00.1	Venus	277 38.7	8 57
23	294 58.0	210 57.0	10.2	100 16.5	23.5	226 12.2	13.1	91 59.5	00.2	Mars	166 22.6	16 21
	h m									Jupiter	291 35.8	8 00
Mer.Pass. 3 27.3		v 0.4	d 0.2	v 1.1	d 0.6	v 2.0	d 0.1	v 2.3	d 0.1	Saturn	157 07.5	16 57

SUN and MOON

UT	SUN GHA	SUN Dec	MOON GHA	v	MOON Dec	d	HP
29 00	178 22.8	N18 41.9	57 20.9	4.8	S21 24.4	1.8	59.7
01	193 22.8	41.3	71 44.7	4.8	21 26.2	1.6	59.7
02	208 22.8	40.7	86 08.5	4.8	21 27.8	1.4	59.7
03	223 22.9	.. 40.1	100 32.3	4.8	21 29.2	1.3	59.7
04	238 22.9	39.5	114 56.1	4.8	21 30.5	1.2	59.7
05	253 22.9	38.9	129 19.9	4.8	21 31.7	1.0	59.7
S 06	268 22.9	N18 38.3	143 43.7	4.7	S21 32.7	0.8	59.7
U 07	283 23.0	37.7	158 07.4	4.8	21 33.5	0.7	59.7
N 08	298 23.0	37.1	172 31.2	4.7	21 34.2	0.6	59.7
D 09	313 23.0	.. 36.5	186 54.9	4.7	21 34.8	0.4	59.7
A 10	328 23.0	35.9	201 18.6	4.7	21 35.2	0.2	59.7
Y 11	343 23.0	35.3	215 42.3	4.8	21 35.4	0.2	59.7
12	358 23.1	N18 34.7	230 06.1	4.7	S21 35.6	0.1	59.7
13	13 23.1	34.1	244 29.8	4.7	21 35.6	0.1	59.7
14	28 23.1	33.5	258 53.5	4.7	21 35.3	0.3	59.7
15	43 23.1	.. 32.9	273 17.2	4.7	21 35.0	0.5	59.7
16	58 23.2	32.3	287 40.9	4.8	21 34.5	0.6	59.7
17	73 23.2	31.7	302 04.7	4.7	21 33.9	0.8	59.7
18	88 23.2	N18 31.1	316 28.4	4.7	S21 33.1	1.0	59.7
19	103 23.2	30.5	330 52.1	4.8	21 32.1	1.0	59.7
20	118 23.3	29.9	345 15.9	4.7	21 31.1	1.3	59.7
21	133 23.3	.. 29.3	359 39.6	4.8	21 29.8	1.3	59.7
22	148 23.3	28.7	14 03.4	4.8	21 28.5	1.6	59.7
23	163 23.4	28.1	28 27.2	4.8	21 26.9	1.6	59.7
30 00	178 23.4	N18 27.5	42 51.0	4.8	S21 25.3	1.9	59.7
01	193 23.4	26.9	57 14.8	4.9	21 23.4	1.9	59.7
02	208 23.4	26.3	71 38.7	4.8	21 21.5	2.1	59.7
03	223 23.5	.. 25.7	86 02.5	4.9	21 19.4	2.3	59.7
04	238 23.5	25.1	100 26.4	4.9	21 17.1	2.4	59.6
05	253 23.5	24.5	114 50.3	5.0	21 14.7	2.6	59.6
M 06	268 23.5	N18 23.9	129 14.3	5.0	S21 12.1	2.7	59.6
O 07	283 23.6	23.2	143 38.3	4.9	21 09.4	2.8	59.6
N 08	298 23.6	22.6	158 02.2	5.1	21 06.6	3.0	59.6
D 09	313 23.6	.. 22.0	172 26.3	5.0	21 03.6	3.1	59.6
A 10	328 23.7	21.4	186 50.3	5.1	21 00.5	3.3	59.6
Y 11	343 23.7	20.8	201 14.4	5.2	20 57.2	3.4	59.6
12	358 23.7	N18 20.2	215 38.6	5.1	S20 53.8	3.6	59.6
13	13 23.8	19.6	230 02.7	5.2	20 50.2	3.7	59.6
14	28 23.8	19.0	244 26.9	5.3	20 46.5	3.8	59.6
15	43 23.8	.. 18.3	258 51.2	5.3	20 42.7	4.0	59.6
16	58 23.9	17.7	273 15.5	5.3	20 38.7	4.1	59.6
17	73 23.9	17.1	287 39.8	5.4	20 34.6	4.2	59.6
18	88 23.9	N18 16.5	302 04.2	5.4	S20 30.4	4.4	59.5
19	103 23.9	15.9	316 28.6	5.5	20 26.0	4.5	59.5
20	118 24.0	15.3	330 53.1	5.5	20 21.5	4.7	59.5
21	133 24.0	.. 14.6	345 17.6	5.5	20 16.8	4.8	59.5
22	148 24.0	14.0	359 42.1	5.7	20 12.0	4.9	59.5
23	163 24.1	13.4	14 06.8	5.6	20 07.1	5.1	59.5
31 00	178 24.1	N18 12.8	28 31.4	5.7	S20 02.0	5.2	59.5
01	193 24.1	12.2	42 56.1	5.8	19 56.8	5.3	59.5
02	208 24.2	11.6	57 20.9	5.8	19 51.5	5.4	59.5
03	223 24.2	.. 10.9	71 45.7	5.9	19 46.1	5.6	59.4
04	238 24.2	10.3	86 10.6	6.0	19 40.5	5.7	59.4
05	253 24.3	09.7	100 35.6	6.0	19 34.8	5.9	59.4
T 06	268 24.3	N18 09.1	115 00.6	6.0	S19 28.9	5.9	59.4
U 07	283 24.4	08.5	129 25.6	6.2	19 23.0	6.1	59.4
E 08	298 24.4	07.8	143 50.8	6.1	19 16.9	6.2	59.4
S 09	313 24.4	.. 07.2	158 15.9	6.3	19 10.7	6.3	59.4
D 10	328 24.5	06.6	172 41.2	6.3	19 04.4	6.5	59.4
A 11	343 24.5	06.0	187 06.5	6.4	18 57.9	6.5	59.3
Y 12	358 24.5	N18 05.3	201 31.9	6.4	S18 51.4	6.7	59.3
13	13 24.6	04.7	215 57.3	6.5	18 44.7	6.8	59.3
14	28 24.6	04.1	230 22.8	6.6	18 37.9	7.0	59.3
15	43 24.6	.. 03.4	244 48.4	6.7	18 30.9	7.0	59.3
16	58 24.7	02.8	259 14.1	6.7	18 23.9	7.2	59.3
17	73 24.7	02.2	273 39.8	6.7	18 16.7	7.2	59.2
18	88 24.8	N18 01.6	288 05.5	6.9	S18 09.5	7.4	59.2
19	103 24.8	00.9	302 31.4	6.9	18 02.1	7.5	59.2
20	118 24.8	18 00.3	316 57.3	7.0	17 54.6	7.6	59.2
21	133 24.9	17 59.7	331 23.3	7.1	17 47.0	7.7	59.2
22	148 24.9	59.1	345 49.4	7.1	17 39.3	7.8	59.2
23	163 25.0	58.4	0 15.5	7.2	S17 31.5	7.9	59.1
SD	15.8	d 0.6	SD 16.3		16.2		16.2

Twilight and Moonrise

Lat.	Naut.	Civil	Sunrise	Moonrise 29	30	31	1
N 72	////	////	01 10	■	■	22 19	21 16
N 70	////	////	02 06	■	■	21 06	20 47
68	////	////	02 39	■	20 18	20 28	20 25
66	////	////	03 03	19 10	19 45	20 01	20 08
64	////	01 29	03 21	18 34	19 16	19 40	19 54
62	////	02 08	03 37	18 08	18 54	19 23	19 42
60	////	02 35	03 44	17 48	18 36	19 09	19 32
N 58	01 21	02 55	03 50	17 31	18 21	18 57	19 23
56	01 57	03 12	04 01	17 17	18 08	18 46	19 15
54	02 21	03 25	04 11	17 05	17 57	18 37	19 08
52	02 40	03 37	04 19	16 54	17 47	18 29	19 02
50	02 56	03 48	04 27	16 45	17 38	18 21	18 56
45	03 26	04 09	04 43	16 24	17 19	18 05	18 44
N 40	03 49	04 26	04 57	16 08	17 04	17 52	18 34
35	04 06	04 40	05 08	15 54	16 51	17 41	18 25
30	04 21	04 52	05 18	15 42	16 39	17 31	18 17
20	04 43	05 11	05 35	15 22	16 20	17 14	18 04
N 10	05 01	05 27	05 49	15 04	16 03	16 59	17 52
0	05 16	05 41	06 03	14 47	15 47	16 45	17 41
S 10	05 29	05 54	06 16	14 30	15 31	16 32	17 30
20	05 41	06 07	06 30	14 13	15 14	16 17	17 18
30	05 52	06 21	06 47	13 52	14 55	15 59	17 04
35	05 59	06 29	06 56	13 40	14 43	15 50	16 56
40	06 05	06 38	07 06	13 26	14 30	15 38	16 47
45	06 12	06 47	07 19	13 10	14 15	15 25	16 37
S 50	06 19	06 58	07 34	12 50	13 56	15 08	16 24
52	06 22	07 04	07 41	12 41	13 47	15 00	16 18
54	06 26	07 09	07 49	12 30	13 36	14 52	16 11
56	06 30	07 15	07 57	12 18	13 25	14 42	16 04
58	06 34	07 22	08 07	12 04	13 12	14 31	15 56
S 60	06 38	07 30	08 18	11 48	13 00	14 18	15 46

Sunset, Twilight and Moonset

Lat.	Sunset	Civil	Naut.	Moonset 29	30	31	1
N 72	22 53	////	////	■	■	23 54	26 51
N 70	22 02	////	////	■	■	■	01 06
68	21 47	////	////	21 47	23 42	25 43	01 43
66	21 31	////	////	22 55	24 25	00 25	02 09
64	21 08	22 38	////	23 30	24 45	00 53	02 29
62	20 49	22 01	////	23 56	25 15	01 15	02 45
60	20 34	21 35	////	24 16	00 16	01 33	02 59
N 58	20 22	21 16	22 47	24 33	00 33	01 47	03 10
56	20 11	21 00	22 13	24 47	00 47	02 00	03 20
54	20 01	20 46	21 49	24 59	00 59	02 11	03 29
52	19 53	20 34	21 30	00 09	01 10	02 20	03 37
50	19 45	20 24	21 15	00 19	01 19	02 29	03 44
45	19 29	20 03	20 45	00 39	01 39	02 47	03 59
N 40	19 15	19 46	20 23	00 55	01 56	03 02	04 11
35	19 04	19 32	20 06	01 09	02 09	03 14	04 21
30	18 54	19 20	19 52	01 21	02 21	03 25	04 30
20	18 38	19 01	19 29	01 41	02 42	03 44	04 46
N 10	18 23	18 46	19 12	01 59	02 59	04 00	05 00
0	18 10	18 32	18 57	02 15	03 16	04 15	05 12
S 10	17 57	18 19	18 44	02 32	03 32	04 30	05 25
20	17 43	18 06	18 32	02 50	03 50	04 46	05 38
30	17 27	17 52	18 21	03 10	04 10	05 04	05 53
35	17 17	17 44	18 15	03 22	04 22	05 15	06 02
40	17 07	17 36	18 08	03 36	04 35	05 27	06 12
45	16 54	17 26	18 02	03 52	04 51	05 41	06 24
S 50	16 40	17 15	17 54	04 12	05 10	05 59	06 38
52	16 33	17 10	17 51	04 21	05 19	06 07	06 44
54	16 25	17 04	17 48	04 32	05 30	06 16	06 51
56	16 16	16 58	17 44	04 44	05 41	06 26	06 59
58	16 06	16 51	17 40	04 58	05 55	06 37	07 08
S 60	15 55	16 44	17 36	05 14	06 10	06 51	07 18

SUN and MOON

Day	Eqn. of Time 00h	12h	Mer. Pass.	Mer. Pass. Upper	Lower	Age	Phase
29	06 29	06 28	12 06	21 01	08 31	10	83
30	06 27	06 25	12 06	22 01	09 32	11	91
31	06 24	06 22	12 06	22 59	10 30	12	96

UT	ARIES GHA	VENUS −4.6 GHA	Dec	MARS +1.1 GHA	Dec	JUPITER −2.2 GHA	Dec	SATURN +0.8 GHA	Dec	Name	SHA	Dec
d h	° ′	° ′	° ′	° ′	° ′	° ′	° ′	° ′	° ′		° ′	° ′
1 00	310 00.4	225 57.3	N19 10.4	115 17.6	S 6 24.1	241 14.2	N21 13.2	107 01.8	S 7 00.2	Acamar	315 18.8	S40 15.0
01	325 02.9	240 57.6	.. 10.6	130 18.7	24.7	256 16.3	13.3	122 04.2	00.3	Achernar	335 27.1	S57 10.0
02	340 05.4	255 57.9	10.8	145 19.8	25.3	271 18.3	13.3	137 06.5	00.4	Acrux	173 10.3	S63 10.4
03	355 07.8	270 58.2	.. 11.0	160 20.9	.. 25.9	286 20.3	.. 13.4	152 08.8	.. 00.4	Adhara	255 13.3	S28 59.4
04	10 10.3	285 58.5	11.2	175 22.0	26.5	301 22.3	13.4	167 11.2	00.5	Aldebaran	290 50.2	N16 32.0
05	25 12.8	300 58.8	11.5	190 23.1	27.1	316 24.3	13.5	182 13.5	00.5			
W 06	40 15.2	315 59.1	N19 11.7	205 24.2	S 6 27.7	331 26.3	N21 13.6	197 15.8	S 7 00.6	Alioth	166 21.4	N55 53.7
E 07	55 17.7	330 59.4	11.9	220 25.3	28.3	346 28.3	13.6	212 18.2	00.7	Alkaid	152 59.4	N49 15.3
D 08	70 20.2	345 59.7	12.1	235 26.4	29.0	1 30.3	13.7	227 20.5	00.7	Al Na'ir	27 44.0	S46 53.7
N 09	85 22.6	1 00.0	.. 12.3	250 27.5	.. 29.6	16 32.3	.. 13.7	242 22.8	.. 00.8	Alnilam	275 47.2	S 1 11.7
E 10	100 25.1	16 00.3	12.5	265 28.6	30.2	31 34.4	13.8	257 25.2	00.9	Alphard	217 57.0	S 8 42.9
S 11	115 27.5	31 00.5	12.7	280 29.7	30.8	46 36.4	13.9	272 27.5	00.9			
D 12	130 30.0	46 00.8	N19 12.9	295 30.8	S 6 31.4	61 38.4	N21 13.9	287 29.8	S 7 01.0	Alphecca	126 11.4	N26 40.6
A 13	145 32.5	61 01.1	13.1	310 31.9	32.0	76 40.4	14.0	302 32.1	01.0	Alpheratz	357 43.9	N29 09.7
Y 14	160 34.9	76 01.4	13.3	325 33.0	32.6	91 42.4	14.0	317 34.5	01.1	Altair	62 08.5	N 8 54.4
15	175 37.4	91 01.7	.. 13.5	340 34.1	.. 33.2	106 44.4	.. 14.1	332 36.8	.. 01.2	Ankaa	353 16.0	S42 13.9
16	190 39.9	106 02.0	13.7	355 35.1	33.8	121 46.4	14.2	347 39.1	01.2	Antares	112 26.8	S26 27.6
17	205 42.3	121 02.3	13.9	10 36.2	34.4	136 48.5	14.2	2 41.5	01.3			
18	220 44.8	136 02.5	N19 14.1	25 37.3	S 6 35.0	151 50.5	N21 14.3	17 43.8	S 7 01.4	Arcturus	145 56.3	N19 07.2
19	235 47.3	151 02.8	14.3	40 38.4	35.6	166 52.5	14.3	32 46.1	01.4	Atria	107 28.8	S69 03.1
20	250 49.7	166 03.1	14.5	55 39.5	36.2	181 54.5	14.4	47 48.5	01.5	Avior	234 18.9	S59 33.1
21	265 52.2	181 03.4	.. 14.7	70 40.6	.. 36.8	196 56.5	.. 14.5	62 50.8	.. 01.6	Bellatrix	278 32.8	N 6 21.6
22	280 54.7	196 03.7	14.9	85 41.7	37.5	211 58.5	14.5	77 53.1	01.6	Betelgeuse	271 02.2	N 7 24.5
23	295 57.1	211 03.9	15.1	100 42.8	38.1	227 00.5	14.6	92 55.4	01.7			
2 00	310 59.6	226 04.2	N19 15.4	115 43.9	S 6 38.7	242 02.6	N21 14.6	107 57.8	S 7 01.7	Canopus	263 56.9	S52 42.1
01	326 02.0	241 04.5	15.6	130 45.0	39.3	257 04.6	14.7	123 00.1	01.8	Capella	280 35.6	N46 00.4
02	341 04.5	256 04.7	15.8	145 46.1	39.9	272 06.6	14.8	138 02.4	01.9	Deneb	49 31.4	N45 19.7
03	356 07.0	271 05.0	.. 16.2	160 47.1	.. 40.5	287 08.6	.. 14.8	153 04.8	.. 01.9	Denebola	182 34.5	N14 30.1
04	11 09.4	286 05.3	16.2	175 48.2	41.1	302 10.6	14.9	168 07.1	02.0	Diphda	348 56.3	S17 54.8
05	26 11.9	301 05.5	16.4	190 49.3	41.7	317 12.6	14.9	183 09.4	02.1			
T 06	41 14.4	316 05.8	N19 16.6	205 50.4	S 6 42.3	332 14.6	N21 15.0	198 11.8	S 7 02.1	Dubhe	193 53.0	N61 41.1
H 07	56 16.8	331 06.1	16.8	220 51.5	42.9	347 16.7	15.0	213 14.1	02.2	Elnath	278 13.6	N28 36.9
U 08	71 19.3	346 06.3	17.0	235 52.6	43.5	2 18.7	15.1	228 16.4	02.2	Eltanin	90 46.0	N51 29.6
R 09	86 21.8	1 06.6	.. 17.2	250 53.7	.. 44.1	17 20.7	.. 15.2	243 18.7	.. 02.3	Enif	33 47.4	N 9 56.2
S 10	101 24.2	16 06.9	17.4	265 54.8	44.7	32 22.7	15.2	258 21.1	02.4	Fomalhaut	15 24.3	S29 33.0
D 11	116 26.7	31 07.1	17.6	280 55.8	45.4	47 24.7	15.3	273 23.4	02.4			
A 12	131 29.2	46 07.4	N19 17.8	295 56.9	S 6 46.0	62 26.7	N21 15.3	288 25.7	S 7 02.5	Gacrux	172 01.8	S57 11.3
Y 13	146 31.6	61 07.6	18.0	310 58.0	46.6	77 28.8	15.4	303 28.0	02.6	Gienah	175 53.1	S17 36.8
14	161 34.1	76 07.9	18.2	325 59.1	47.2	92 30.8	15.5	318 30.4	02.6	Hadar	148 48.8	S60 26.3
15	176 36.5	91 08.1	.. 18.4	341 00.2	.. 47.8	107 32.8	.. 15.5	333 32.7	.. 02.7	Hamal	328 01.4	N23 31.3
16	191 39.0	106 08.4	18.6	356 01.3	48.4	122 34.8	15.6	348 35.0	02.8	Kaus Aust.	83 44.2	S34 22.6
17	206 41.5	121 08.6	18.7	11 02.4	49.0	137 36.8	15.6	3 37.4	02.8			
18	221 43.9	136 08.9	N19 18.9	26 03.5	S 6 49.6	152 38.9	N21 15.7	18 39.7	S 7 02.9	Kochab	137 19.9	N74 06.5
19	236 46.4	151 09.1	19.1	41 04.5	50.2	167 40.9	15.8	33 42.0	03.0	Markab	13 38.6	N15 16.5
20	251 48.9	166 09.4	19.3	56 05.6	50.8	182 42.9	15.8	48 44.3	03.0	Menkar	314 15.7	N 4 08.4
21	266 51.3	181 09.6	.. 19.5	71 06.7	.. 51.4	197 44.9	.. 15.9	63 46.7	.. 03.1	Menkent	148 08.3	S36 26.1
22	281 53.8	196 09.9	19.7	86 07.8	52.0	212 46.9	15.9	78 49.0	03.1	Miaplacidus	221 40.7	S69 46.3
23	296 56.3	211 10.1	19.9	101 08.9	52.6	227 48.9	16.0	93 51.3	03.2			
3 00	311 58.7	226 10.3	N19 20.1	116 10.0	S 6 53.3	242 51.0	N21 16.0	108 53.6	S 7 03.3	Mirfak	308 41.3	N49 54.1
01	327 01.2	241 10.6	20.3	131 11.0	53.9	257 53.0	16.1	123 56.0	03.3	Nunki	75 58.7	S26 16.7
02	342 03.6	256 10.8	20.5	146 12.1	54.5	272 55.0	16.2	138 58.3	03.4	Peacock	53 19.5	S56 41.5
03	357 06.1	271 11.1	.. 20.7	161 13.2	.. 55.1	287 57.0	.. 16.2	154 00.6	.. 03.5	Pollux	243 28.8	N27 59.6
04	12 08.6	286 11.3	20.9	176 14.3	55.7	302 59.0	16.3	169 02.9	03.5	Procyon	245 00.7	N 5 11.5
05	27 11.0	301 11.5	21.1	191 15.4	56.3	318 01.1	16.3	184 05.3	03.6			
F 06	42 13.5	316 11.8	N19 21.3	206 16.5	S 6 56.9	333 03.1	N21 16.4	199 07.6	S 7 03.7	Rasalhague	96 06.7	N12 33.3
R 07	57 16.0	331 12.0	21.5	221 17.5	57.5	348 05.1	16.4	214 09.9	03.7	Regulus	207 44.4	N11 54.3
I 08	72 18.4	346 12.2	21.7	236 18.6	58.1	3 07.1	16.5	229 12.3	03.8	Rigel	281 12.8	S 8 11.2
D 09	87 20.9	1 12.4	.. 21.9	251 19.7	.. 58.7	18 09.2	.. 16.6	244 14.6	.. 03.9	Rigil Kent.	139 52.5	S60 53.4
A 10	102 23.4	16 12.7	22.1	266 20.8	59.3	33 11.2	16.6	259 16.9	03.9	Sabik	102 13.0	S15 44.3
Y 11	117 25.8	31 12.9	22.3	281 21.9	6 59.9	48 13.2	16.7	274 19.2	04.0			
12	132 28.3	46 13.1	N19 22.4	296 22.9	S 7 00.5	63 15.2	N21 16.7	289 21.6	S 7 04.0	Schedar	349 40.9	N56 36.3
13	147 30.8	61 13.3	22.6	311 24.0	01.1	78 17.2	16.8	304 23.9	04.1	Shaula	96 22.4	S37 06.7
14	162 33.2	76 13.6	22.8	326 25.1	01.8	93 19.3	16.9	319 26.2	04.2	Sirius	258 34.5	S16 44.0
15	177 35.7	91 13.8	.. 23.0	341 26.2	.. 02.4	108 21.3	.. 16.9	334 28.5	.. 04.2	Spica	158 32.0	S11 13.7
16	192 38.1	106 14.0	23.2	356 27.3	03.0	123 23.3	17.0	349 30.8	04.3	Suhail	222 53.3	S43 29.1
17	207 40.6	121 14.2	23.4	11 28.3	03.6	138 25.3	17.0	4 33.2	04.4			
18	222 43.1	136 14.4	N19 23.6	26 29.4	S 7 04.2	153 27.4	N21 17.1	19 35.5	S 7 04.4	Vega	80 39.0	N38 48.0
19	237 45.5	151 14.7	23.8	41 30.5	04.8	168 29.4	17.1	34 37.8	04.5	Zuben'ubi	137 06.0	S16 05.6
20	252 48.0	166 14.9	24.0	56 31.6	05.4	183 31.4	17.2	49 40.1	04.6		SHA	Mer.Pass.
21	267 50.5	181 15.1	.. 24.1	71 32.7	06.0	198 33.4	.. 17.3	64 42.5	.. 04.6		° ′	h m
22	282 52.9	196 15.3	24.3	86 33.7	06.6	213 35.4	17.3	79 44.8	04.7	Venus	275 04.6	8 56
23	297 55.4	211 15.5	24.5	101 34.8	07.2	228 37.5	17.4	94 47.1	04.8	Mars	164 44.3	16 16
	h m									Jupiter	291 03.0	7 51
Mer. Pass.	3 15.5	v 0.3	d 0.2	v 1.1	d 0.6	v 2.0	d 0.1	v 2.3	d 0.1	Saturn	156 58.2	16 46

UT	SUN GHA	SUN Dec	MOON GHA	v	MOON Dec	d	HP
d h	° ′	° ′	° ′	′	° ′	′	′
1 00	178 25.0	N17 57.8	14 41.7	7.3	S17 23.6	8.0	59.1
01	193 25.0	57.2	29 08.0	7.4	17 15.6	8.1	59.1
02	208 25.1	56.5	43 34.4	7.4	17 07.5	8.3	59.1
03	223 25.1 ..	55.9	58 00.8	7.5	16 59.2	8.3	59.1
04	238 25.2	55.3	72 27.3	7.6	16 50.9	8.4	59.0
05	253 25.2	54.6	86 53.9	7.6	16 42.5	8.5	59.0
W 06	268 25.3	N17 54.0	101 20.5	7.8	S16 34.0	8.6	59.0
E 07	283 25.3	53.4	115 47.3	7.8	16 25.4	8.7	59.0
D 08	298 25.3	52.7	130 14.1	7.9	16 16.7	8.8	59.0
N 09	313 25.4 ..	52.1	144 41.0	7.9	16 07.9	8.9	58.9
E 10	328 25.4	51.5	159 07.9	8.1	15 59.0	9.0	58.9
S 11	343 25.5	50.8	173 35.0	8.1	15 50.0	9.1	58.9
D 12	358 25.5	N17 50.2	188 02.1	8.2	S15 40.9	9.2	58.9
A 13	13 25.5	49.5	202 29.3	8.3	15 31.7	9.2	58.9
Y 14	28 25.6	48.9	216 56.6	8.3	15 22.5	9.3	58.8
15	43 25.6 ..	48.3	231 23.9	8.4	15 13.2	9.4	58.8
16	58 25.7	47.6	245 51.3	8.5	15 03.8	9.5	58.8
17	73 25.7	47.0	260 18.8	8.6	14 54.3	9.6	58.8
18	88 25.8	N17 46.4	274 46.4	8.7	S14 44.7	9.7	58.8
19	103 25.8	45.7	289 14.1	8.7	14 35.0	9.7	58.7
20	118 25.9	45.1	303 41.8	8.8	14 25.3	9.8	58.7
21	133 25.9 ..	44.4	318 09.6	8.9	14 15.5	9.9	58.7
22	148 25.9	43.8	332 37.5	9.0	14 05.6	10.0	58.7
23	163 26.0	43.1	347 05.5	9.0	13 55.6	10.0	58.6
2 00	178 26.0	N17 42.5	1 33.5	9.2	S13 45.6	10.1	58.6
01	193 26.1	41.9	16 01.7	9.2	13 35.5	10.2	58.6
02	208 26.1	41.2	30 29.9	9.3	13 25.3	10.2	58.6
03	223 26.2 ..	40.6	44 58.2	9.3	13 15.1	10.3	58.5
04	238 26.2	39.9	59 26.5	9.4	13 04.8	10.4	58.5
05	253 26.3	39.3	73 54.9	9.6	12 54.4	10.4	58.5
T 06	268 26.3	N17 38.6	88 23.5	9.5	S12 44.0	10.5	58.5
H 07	283 26.4	38.0	102 52.0	9.7	12 33.5	10.6	58.4
U 08	298 26.4	37.3	117 20.7	9.7	12 22.9	10.6	58.4
R 09	313 26.5 ..	36.7	131 49.4	9.9	12 12.3	10.7	58.4
S 10	328 26.5	36.0	146 18.3	9.8	12 01.6	10.7	58.4
D 11	343 26.6	35.4	160 47.1	10.0	11 50.9	10.8	58.3
A 12	358 26.6	N17 34.7	175 16.1	10.0	S11 40.1	10.8	58.3
Y 13	13 26.7	34.1	189 45.1	10.1	11 29.3	10.9	58.3
14	28 26.7	33.4	204 14.2	10.2	11 18.4	11.0	58.3
15	43 26.8 ..	32.8	218 43.4	10.3	11 07.4	11.0	58.2
16	58 26.8	32.1	233 12.7	10.3	10 56.4	11.0	58.2
17	73 26.9	31.5	247 42.0	10.4	10 45.4	11.1	58.2
18	88 26.9	N17 30.8	262 11.4	10.5	S10 34.3	11.1	58.1
19	103 27.0	30.2	276 40.9	10.5	10 23.2	11.2	58.1
20	118 27.0	29.5	291 10.4	10.6	10 12.0	11.3	58.1
21	133 27.1 ..	28.9	305 40.0	10.7	10 00.7	11.3	58.1
22	148 27.1	28.2	320 09.7	10.8	9 49.4	11.3	58.0
23	163 27.2	27.6	334 39.5	10.8	9 38.2	11.4	58.0
3 00	178 27.2	N17 26.9	349 09.3	10.9	S 9 26.8	11.4	58.0
01	193 27.3	26.3	3 39.2	10.9	9 15.4	11.4	58.0
02	208 27.3	25.6	18 09.1	11.1	9 04.0	11.5	57.9
03	223 27.4 ..	25.0	32 39.2	11.1	8 52.5	11.5	57.9
04	238 27.4	24.3	47 09.3	11.1	8 41.0	11.5	57.9
05	253 27.5	23.6	61 39.4	11.2	8 29.5	11.5	57.8
F 06	268 27.6	N17 23.0	76 09.6	11.3	S 8 18.0	11.6	57.8
07	283 27.6	22.3	90 39.9	11.4	8 06.4	11.7	57.8
08	298 27.7	21.7	105 10.3	11.4	7 54.7	11.6	57.8
R 09	313 27.7 ..	21.0	119 40.7	11.5	7 43.1	11.7	57.7
I 10	328 27.8	20.3	134 11.2	11.5	7 31.4	11.7	57.7
11	343 27.8	19.7	148 41.7	11.6	7 19.7	11.7	57.7
D 12	358 27.9	N17 19.0	163 12.3	11.7	S 7 08.0	11.8	57.6
A 13	13 27.9	18.4	177 43.0	11.7	6 56.2	11.7	57.6
Y 14	28 28.0	17.7	192 13.7	11.8	6 44.5	11.8	57.6
15	43 28.1 ..	17.0	206 44.5	11.8	6 32.7	11.8	57.5
16	58 28.1	16.4	221 15.3	11.9	6 20.9	11.9	57.5
17	73 28.2	15.7	235 46.2	12.0	6 09.0	11.8	57.5
18	88 28.2	N17 15.1	250 17.2	12.0	S 5 57.2	11.9	57.5
19	103 28.3	14.4	264 48.2	12.1	5 45.3	11.9	57.4
20	118 28.3	13.7	279 19.3	12.1	5 33.4	11.9	57.4
21	133 28.4 ..	13.1	293 50.4	12.2	5 21.5	11.9	57.4
22	148 28.5	12.4	308 21.6	12.2	5 09.6	11.9	57.3
23	163 28.5	11.7	322 52.8	12.3	S 4 57.7	11.9	57.3
	SD 15.8	d 0.6	SD 16.0		15.9		15.7

Lat.	Twilight Naut.	Twilight Civil	Sunrise	Moonrise 1	2	3	4
°	h m	h m	h m	h m	h m	h m	h m
N 72	☐	☐	☐	21 16	20 51	20 34	20 19
N 70	////	////	01 38	20 47	20 35	20 26	20 18
68	////	////	02 22	20 25	20 23	20 20	20 17
66	////	00 44	02 51	20 08	20 12	20 15	20 16
64	////	01 47	03 12	19 54	20 03	20 10	20 16
62	////	02 20	03 30	19 42	19 56	20 06	20 15
60	00 40	02 44	03 44	19 32	19 49	20 03	20 14
N 58	01 37	03 03	03 56	19 23	19 43	20 00	20 14
56	02 08	03 18	04 06	19 15	19 38	19 57	20 14
54	02 30	03 31	04 16	19 08	19 33	19 54	20 13
52	02 48	03 43	04 24	19 02	19 29	19 52	20 13
50	03 02	03 53	04 31	18 56	19 25	19 50	20 13
45	03 31	04 13	04 47	18 44	19 17	19 46	20 12
N 40	03 52	04 29	05 00	18 34	19 10	19 42	20 11
35	04 09	04 43	05 10	18 25	19 04	19 38	20 11
30	04 23	04 54	05 20	18 17	18 58	19 36	20 11
20	04 45	05 12	05 36	18 04	18 49	19 31	20 10
N 10	05 02	05 28	05 50	17 52	18 41	19 26	20 09
0	05 16	05 41	06 03	17 41	18 33	19 22	20 09
S 10	05 28	05 54	06 16	17 30	18 25	19 18	20 08
20	05 40	06 06	06 29	17 18	18 17	19 13	20 08
30	05 51	06 19	06 44	17 04	18 07	19 08	20 07
35	05 56	06 27	06 53	16 56	18 02	19 05	20 07
40	06 02	06 35	07 03	16 47	17 56	19 02	20 06
45	06 08	06 44	07 15	16 37	17 48	18 58	20 06
S 50	06 15	06 54	07 29	16 24	17 40	18 54	20 05
52	06 18	06 59	07 36	16 18	17 36	18 52	20 05
54	06 21	07 04	07 43	16 11	17 31	18 49	20 05
56	06 25	07 10	07 52	16 04	17 26	18 47	20 04
58	06 29	07 16	08 01	15 56	17 21	18 44	20 04
S 60	06 33	07 24	08 11	15 46	17 14	18 41	20 04

Lat.	Sunset	Twilight Civil	Twilight Naut.	Moonset 1	2	3	4
°	h m	h m	h m	h m	h m	h m	h m
N 72	☐	☐	☐	26 51	02 51	05 02	07 00
N 70	22 28	////	////	01 06	03 18	05 16	07 05
68	21 46	////	////	01 43	03 38	05 27	07 09
66	21 19	23 16	////	02 09	03 54	05 36	07 13
64	20 58	22 20	////	02 29	04 07	05 43	07 16
62	20 41	21 49	////	02 45	04 18	05 50	07 20
60	20 27	21 26	23 21	02 59	04 28	05 55	07 20
N 58	20 15	21 07	22 31	03 10	04 36	06 00	07 22
56	20 05	20 52	22 02	03 20	04 43	06 05	07 24
54	19 56	20 39	21 40	03 29	04 49	06 09	07 26
52	19 48	20 28	21 23	03 37	04 55	06 12	07 27
50	19 40	20 19	21 09	03 44	05 00	06 15	07 28
45	19 25	19 58	20 40	03 59	05 11	06 22	07 31
N 40	19 12	19 42	20 19	04 11	05 20	06 28	07 33
35	19 02	19 29	20 03	04 21	05 28	06 33	07 35
30	18 52	19 18	19 49	04 30	05 35	06 37	07 37
20	18 36	19 00	19 27	04 46	05 46	06 44	07 40
N 10	18 23	18 45	19 11	05 00	05 57	06 51	07 42
0	18 10	18 31	18 57	05 12	06 06	06 57	07 45
S 10	17 57	18 19	18 44	05 25	06 15	07 03	07 47
20	17 44	18 07	18 33	05 38	06 25	07 09	07 49
30	17 28	17 53	18 22	05 53	06 37	07 16	07 52
35	17 19	17 46	18 17	06 02	06 43	07 20	07 54
40	17 09	17 38	18 11	06 12	06 51	07 25	07 55
45	16 58	17 29	18 05	06 24	06 59	07 30	07 58
S 50	16 44	17 19	17 58	06 38	07 09	07 36	08 00
52	16 37	17 14	17 55	06 44	07 14	07 39	08 01
54	16 30	17 09	17 52	06 51	07 19	07 42	08 02
56	16 22	17 03	17 48	06 59	07 25	07 46	08 04
58	16 12	16 57	17 45	07 08	07 31	07 50	08 05
S 60	16 02	16 50	17 41	07 18	07 38	07 54	08 07

	SUN			MOON			
Day	Eqn. of Time 00h	Eqn. of Time 12h	Mer. Pass.	Mer. Pass. Upper	Mer. Pass. Lower	Age	Phase
d	m s	m s	h m	h m	h m	d	%
1	06 20	06 18	12 06	23 54	11 27	13	99
2	06 16	06 14	12 06	24 45	12 20	14	100
3	06 11	06 09	12 06	00 45	13 09	15	98

UT	ARIES GHA	VENUS −4.5 GHA	Dec	MARS +1.1 GHA	Dec	JUPITER −2.2 GHA	Dec	SATURN +0.8 GHA	Dec	STARS Name	SHA	Dec
4 00	312 57.9	226 15.7	N19 24.7	116 35.9	S 7 07.8	243 39.5	N21 17.4	109 49.4	S 7 04.8	Acamar	315 18.8	S40 15.0
01	328 00.3	241 15.9	24.9	131 37.0	08.4	258 41.5	17.5	124 51.8	04.9	Achernar	335 27.0	S57 10.0
02	343 02.8	256 16.1	25.1	146 38.1	09.0	273 43.5	17.5	139 54.1	05.0	Acrux	173 10.3	S63 10.4
03	358 05.2	271 16.3	.. 25.3	161 39.1	.. 09.7	288 45.6	.. 17.6	154 56.4	.. 05.0	Adhara	255 13.3	S28 59.3
04	13 07.7	286 16.5	25.5	176 40.2	10.3	303 47.6	17.6	169 58.7	05.1	Aldebaran	290 50.2	N16 32.0
05	28 10.2	301 16.7	25.6	191 41.3	10.9	318 49.6	17.7	185 01.0	05.2			
S 06	43 12.6	316 16.9	N19 25.8	206 42.4	S 7 11.5	333 51.6	N21 17.8	200 03.4	S 7 05.2	Alioth	166 21.5	N55 53.7
A 07	58 15.1	331 17.1	26.0	221 43.4	12.1	348 53.7	17.8	215 05.7	05.3	Alkaid	153 00.9	N49 15.3
T 08	73 17.6	346 17.3	26.2	236 44.5	12.7	3 55.7	17.9	230 08.0	05.4	Al Na'ir	27 44.0	S46 53.7
U 09	88 20.0	1 17.5	.. 26.4	251 45.6	.. 13.3	18 57.7	.. 17.9	245 10.3	.. 05.4	Alnilam	275 47.2	S 1 11.6
R 10	103 22.5	16 17.7	26.6	266 46.7	13.9	33 59.7	18.0	260 12.7	05.5	Alphard	217 57.0	S 8 42.9
D 11	118 25.0	31 17.9	26.7	281 47.7	14.5	49 01.8	18.0	275 15.0	05.6			
A 12	133 27.4	46 18.1	N19 26.9	296 48.8	S 7 15.1	64 03.8	N21 18.1	290 17.3	S 7 05.6	Alphecca	126 11.4	N26 40.6
Y 13	148 29.9	61 18.3	27.1	311 49.9	15.7	79 05.8	18.2	305 19.6	05.7	Alpheratz	357 43.9	N29 09.7
14	163 32.4	76 18.5	27.3	326 51.0	16.3	94 07.9	18.2	320 21.9	05.8	Altair	62 08.5	N 8 54.4
15	178 34.8	91 18.7	.. 27.5	341 52.0	.. 16.9	109 09.9	.. 18.3	335 24.3	.. 05.8	Ankaa	353 16.0	S42 13.9
16	193 37.3	106 18.9	27.7	356 53.1	17.6	124 11.9	18.3	350 26.6	05.9	Antares	112 26.8	S26 27.6
17	208 39.7	121 19.1	27.8	11 54.2	18.2	139 13.9	18.4	5 28.9	05.9			
18	223 42.2	136 19.3	N19 28.0	26 55.3	S 7 18.8	154 16.0	N21 18.4	20 31.2	S 7 06.0	Arcturus	145 56.3	N19 07.2
19	238 44.7	151 19.4	28.2	41 56.3	19.4	169 18.0	18.5	35 33.5	06.1	Atria	107 28.8	S69 03.1
20	253 47.1	166 19.6	28.4	56 57.4	20.0	184 20.0	18.6	50 35.9	06.1	Avior	234 18.9	S59 33.1
21	268 49.6	181 19.8	.. 28.6	71 58.5	.. 20.6	199 22.0	.. 18.6	65 38.2	.. 06.2	Bellatrix	278 32.8	N 6 21.6
22	283 52.1	196 20.0	28.7	86 59.5	21.2	214 24.1	18.7	80 40.5	06.3	Betelgeuse	271 02.2	N 7 24.5
23	298 54.5	211 20.2	28.9	102 00.6	21.8	229 26.1	18.7	95 42.8	06.3			
5 00	313 57.0	226 20.4	N19 29.1	117 01.7	S 7 22.4	244 28.1	N21 18.8	110 45.1	S 7 06.4	Canopus	263 56.8	S52 42.1
01	328 59.5	241 20.5	29.3	132 02.8	23.0	259 30.2	18.8	125 47.5	06.5	Capella	280 35.6	N46 00.4
02	344 01.9	256 20.7	29.5	147 03.8	23.6	274 32.2	18.9	140 49.8	06.5	Deneb	49 31.4	N45 19.7
03	359 04.4	271 20.9	.. 29.6	162 04.9	.. 24.2	289 34.2	.. 18.9	155 52.1	.. 06.6	Denebola	182 34.5	N14 30.1
04	14 06.9	286 21.0	29.8	177 06.0	24.8	304 36.3	19.0	170 54.4	06.7	Diphda	348 56.3	S17 54.8
05	29 09.3	301 21.2	30.0	192 07.0	25.5	319 38.3	19.1	185 56.7	06.7			
S 06	44 11.8	316 21.4	N19 30.2	207 08.1	S 7 26.1	334 40.3	N21 19.1	200 59.1	S 7 06.8	Dubhe	193 53.0	N61 41.1
U 07	59 14.2	331 21.5	30.3	222 09.2	26.7	349 42.3	19.2	216 01.4	06.9	Elnath	278 13.6	N28 36.9
N 08	74 16.7	346 21.7	30.5	237 10.2	27.3	4 44.4	19.2	231 03.7	06.9	Eltanin	90 46.0	N51 29.6
D 09	89 19.2	1 21.9	.. 30.7	252 11.3	.. 27.9	19 46.4	.. 19.3	246 06.0	.. 07.0	Enif	33 47.4	N 9 56.2
A 10	104 21.6	16 22.0	30.9	267 12.4	28.5	34 48.4	19.3	261 08.3	07.1	Fomalhaut	15 24.3	S29 33.0
Y 11	119 24.1	31 22.2	31.0	282 13.5	29.1	49 50.5	19.4	276 10.7	07.2			
12	134 26.6	46 22.4	N19 31.2	297 14.5	S 7 29.7	64 52.5	N21 19.4	291 13.0	S 7 07.2	Gacrux	172 01.9	S57 11.3
13	149 29.0	61 22.5	31.4	312 15.6	30.3	79 54.5	19.5	306 15.3	07.3	Gienah	175 53.1	S17 36.8
14	164 31.5	76 22.7	31.6	327 16.7	30.9	94 56.6	19.6	321 17.6	07.4	Hadar	148 48.8	S60 26.3
15	179 34.0	91 22.9	.. 31.7	342 17.7	.. 31.5	109 58.6	.. 19.6	336 19.9	.. 07.4	Hamal	328 01.3	N23 31.3
16	194 36.4	106 23.0	31.9	357 18.8	32.1	125 00.6	19.7	351 22.2	07.5	Kaus Aust.	83 44.2	S34 22.6
17	209 38.9	121 23.2	32.1	12 19.9	32.7	140 02.7	19.7	6 24.6	07.6			
18	224 41.3	136 23.3	N19 32.2	27 20.9	S 7 33.4	155 04.7	N21 19.8	21 26.9	S 7 07.6	Kochab	137 20.0	N74 06.5
19	239 43.8	151 23.5	32.4	42 22.0	34.0	170 06.7	19.8	36 29.2	07.7	Markab	13 38.6	N15 16.6
20	254 46.3	166 23.6	32.6	57 23.1	34.6	185 08.8	19.9	51 31.5	07.8	Menkar	314 15.7	N 4 08.4
21	269 48.7	181 23.8	.. 32.8	72 24.1	.. 35.2	200 10.8	.. 19.9	66 33.8	.. 07.8	Menkent	148 08.3	S36 26.1
22	284 51.2	196 23.9	32.9	87 25.2	35.8	215 12.8	20.0	81 36.1	07.9	Miaplacidus	221 40.7	S69 46.3
23	299 53.7	211 24.1	33.1	102 26.3	36.4	230 14.9	20.0	96 38.5	08.0			
6 00	314 56.1	226 24.2	N19 33.3	117 27.3	S 7 37.0	245 16.9	N21 20.1	111 40.8	S 7 08.0	Mirfak	308 41.3	N49 54.1
01	329 58.6	241 24.4	33.4	132 28.4	37.6	260 18.9	20.2	126 43.1	08.1	Nunki	75 58.7	S26 16.7
02	345 01.1	256 24.5	33.6	147 29.5	38.2	275 21.0	20.2	141 45.4	08.2	Peacock	53 19.5	S56 41.5
03	0 03.5	271 24.7	.. 33.8	162 30.5	.. 38.8	290 23.0	.. 20.3	156 47.7	.. 08.2	Pollux	243 28.8	N27 59.6
04	15 06.0	286 24.8	33.9	177 31.6	39.4	305 25.0	20.3	171 50.0	08.3	Procyon	245 00.6	N 5 11.5
05	30 08.5	301 25.0	34.1	192 32.6	40.0	320 27.1	20.4	186 52.4	08.4			
M 06	45 10.9	316 25.1	N19 34.3	207 33.7	S 7 40.6	335 29.1	N21 20.4	201 54.7	S 7 08.4	Rasalhague	96 06.8	N12 33.3
O 07	60 13.4	331 25.2	34.4	222 34.8	41.3	350 31.1	20.5	216 57.0	08.5	Regulus	207 44.4	N11 54.3
N 08	75 15.8	346 25.4	34.6	237 35.8	41.9	5 33.2	20.5	231 59.3	08.6	Rigel	281 12.8	S 8 11.2
D 09	90 18.3	1 25.5	.. 34.8	252 36.9	.. 42.5	20 35.2	.. 20.6	247 01.6	.. 08.6	Rigil Kent.	139 52.5	S60 53.4
A 10	105 20.8	16 25.7	34.9	267 38.0	43.1	35 37.2	20.6	262 03.9	08.7	Sabik	102 13.0	S15 44.3
Y 11	120 23.2	31 25.8	35.1	282 39.0	43.7	50 39.3	20.7	277 06.3	08.8			
12	135 25.7	46 25.9	N19 35.3	297 40.1	S 7 44.3	65 41.3	N21 20.8	292 08.6	S 7 08.8	Schedar	349 40.9	N56 36.3
13	150 28.2	61 26.1	35.4	312 41.1	44.9	80 43.3	20.8	307 10.9	08.9	Shaula	96 22.4	S37 06.7
14	165 30.6	76 26.2	35.6	327 42.2	45.5	95 45.4	20.9	322 13.2	09.0	Sirius	258 34.5	S16 44.0
15	180 33.1	91 26.3	.. 35.7	342 43.3	.. 46.1	110 47.4	.. 20.9	337 15.5	.. 09.0	Spica	158 32.0	S11 13.6
16	195 35.6	106 26.4	35.9	357 44.3	46.7	125 49.5	21.0	352 17.8	09.1	Suhail	222 53.3	S43 29.1
17	210 38.0	121 26.6	36.1	12 45.4	47.3	140 51.5	21.0	7 20.1	09.2			
18	225 40.5	136 26.7	N19 36.2	27 46.5	S 7 47.9	155 53.5	N21 21.1	22 22.5	S 7 09.3	Vega	80 39.0	N38 48.0
19	240 42.9	151 26.8	36.4	42 47.5	48.5	170 55.6	21.1	37 24.8	09.3	Zuben'ubi	137 06.0	S16 05.6
20	255 45.4	166 26.9	36.6	57 48.6	49.2	185 57.6	21.2	52 27.1	09.4		SHA	Mer.Pass.
21	270 47.9	181 27.1	.. 36.7	72 49.6	.. 49.8	200 59.6	.. 21.2	67 29.4	.. 09.5	Venus	272 23.3	8 55
22	285 50.3	196 27.2	36.9	87 50.7	50.4	216 01.7	21.3	82 31.7	09.5	Mars	163 04.7	16 11
23	300 52.8	211 27.3	37.0	102 51.8	51.0	231 03.7	21.3	97 34.0	09.6	Jupiter	290 31.1	7 41
Mer. Pass.	h m 3 03.7	v 0.2	d 0.2	v 1.1	d 0.6	v 2.0	d 0.1	v 2.3	d 0.1	Saturn	156 48.2	16 34

SUN and MOON

UT	SUN GHA	SUN Dec	MOON GHA	v	MOON Dec	d	HP
4 00	178 28.6	N17 11.1	337 24.1	12.4	S 4 45.8	12.0	57.3
01	193 28.6	10.4	351 55.5	12.4	4 33.8	11.9	57.2
02	208 28.7	09.7	6 26.9	12.4	4 21.9	12.0	57.2
03	223 28.7	.. 09.1	20 58.3	12.5	4 09.9	11.9	57.2
04	238 28.8	08.4	35 29.8	12.6	3 58.0	12.0	57.2
05	253 28.9	07.7	50 01.4	12.6	3 46.0	12.0	57.1
06	268 28.9	N17 07.0	64 33.0	12.6	S 3 34.0	12.0	57.1
S 07	283 29.0	06.4	79 04.6	12.7	3 22.0	11.9	57.1
A 08	298 29.1	05.7	93 36.3	12.7	3 10.1	12.0	57.0
T 09	313 29.1	.. 05.0	108 08.0	12.8	2 58.1	12.0	57.0
U 10	328 29.2	04.4	122 39.8	12.8	2 46.1	12.0	57.0
R 11	343 29.2	03.7	137 11.6	12.9	2 34.1	12.0	56.9
D 12	358 29.3	N17 03.0	151 43.5	12.9	S 2 22.1	11.9	56.9
A 13	13 29.4	02.3	166 15.4	13.0	2 10.2	12.0	56.9
Y 14	28 29.4	01.7	180 47.4	13.0	1 58.2	12.0	56.8
15	43 29.5	.. 01.0	195 19.4	13.0	1 46.2	11.9	56.8
16	58 29.5	17 00.3	209 51.4	13.1	1 34.3	12.0	56.8
17	73 29.6	16 59.7	224 23.5	13.1	1 22.3	11.9	56.8
18	88 29.7	N16 59.0	238 55.6	13.2	S 1 10.4	12.0	56.7
19	103 29.7	58.3	253 27.8	13.2	0 58.4	11.9	56.7
20	118 29.8	57.6	268 00.0	13.2	0 46.5	11.9	56.7
21	133 29.9	.. 56.9	282 32.2	13.3	0 34.6	11.9	56.6
22	148 29.9	56.3	297 04.5	13.3	0 22.7	11.9	56.6
23	163 30.0	55.6	311 36.8	13.3	S 0 10.8	11.9	56.6
5 00	178 30.1	N16 54.9	326 09.1	13.4	N 0 01.1	11.9	56.5
01	193 30.1	54.2	340 41.5	13.4	0 13.0	11.9	56.5
02	208 30.2	53.6	355 13.9	13.4	0 24.9	11.8	56.5
03	223 30.3	.. 52.9	9 46.3	13.5	0 36.7	11.8	56.5
04	238 30.3	52.2	24 18.8	13.5	0 48.5	11.8	56.4
05	253 30.4	51.5	38 51.3	13.5	1 00.3	11.8	56.4
06	268 30.5	N16 50.8	53 23.8	13.6	N 1 12.1	11.8	56.4
S 07	283 30.5	50.2	67 56.4	13.6	1 23.9	11.7	56.3
U 08	298 30.6	49.5	82 29.0	13.6	1 35.6	11.8	56.3
N 09	313 30.7	.. 48.8	97 01.6	13.6	1 47.4	11.7	56.3
D 10	328 30.7	48.1	111 34.2	13.7	1 59.1	11.7	56.3
A 11	343 30.8	47.4	126 06.9	13.7	2 10.8	11.6	56.2
Y 12	358 30.9	N16 46.7	140 39.6	13.7	N 2 22.4	11.7	56.2
13	13 30.9	46.1	155 12.3	13.7	2 34.1	11.6	56.2
14	28 31.0	45.4	169 45.0	13.8	2 45.7	11.6	56.1
15	43 31.1	.. 44.7	184 17.8	13.8	2 57.3	11.5	56.1
16	58 31.1	44.0	198 50.6	13.8	3 08.8	11.6	56.1
17	73 31.2	43.3	213 23.4	13.8	3 20.4	11.5	56.1
18	88 31.3	N16 42.6	227 56.2	13.9	N 3 31.9	11.4	56.0
19	103 31.3	41.9	242 29.1	13.8	3 43.3	11.5	56.0
20	118 31.4	41.3	257 01.9	13.9	3 54.8	11.4	56.0
21	133 31.5	.. 40.6	271 34.8	13.9	4 06.2	11.4	55.9
22	148 31.6	39.9	286 07.7	13.9	4 17.6	11.3	55.9
23	163 31.6	39.2	300 40.6	14.0	4 29.0	11.3	55.9
6 00	178 31.7	N16 38.5	315 13.6	13.9	N 4 40.3	11.3	55.9
01	193 31.8	37.8	329 46.5	14.0	4 51.6	11.2	55.8
02	208 31.8	37.1	344 19.5	13.9	5 02.8	11.3	55.8
03	223 31.9	.. 36.4	358 52.4	14.0	5 14.1	11.2	55.8
04	238 32.0	35.7	13 25.4	14.0	5 25.3	11.1	55.7
05	253 32.1	35.0	27 58.4	14.0	5 36.4	11.1	55.7
06	268 32.1	N16 34.4	42 31.4	14.1	N 5 47.5	11.1	55.7
M 07	283 32.2	33.7	57 04.5	14.0	5 58.6	11.1	55.7
O 08	298 32.3	33.0	71 37.5	14.1	6 09.7	11.0	55.6
N 09	313 32.4	.. 32.3	86 10.6	14.0	6 20.7	10.9	55.6
D 10	328 32.4	31.6	100 43.6	14.1	6 31.6	11.0	55.6
A 11	343 32.5	30.9	115 16.7	14.0	6 42.6	10.8	55.6
Y 12	358 32.6	N16 30.2	129 49.7	14.1	N 6 53.4	10.9	55.5
13	13 32.6	29.5	144 22.8	14.1	7 04.3	10.8	55.5
14	28 32.7	28.8	158 55.9	14.1	7 15.1	10.8	55.5
15	43 32.8	.. 28.1	173 29.0	14.1	7 25.9	10.7	55.5
16	58 32.9	27.4	188 02.1	14.0	7 36.6	10.7	55.4
17	73 32.9	26.7	202 35.2	14.0	7 47.3	10.6	55.4
18	88 33.0	N16 26.0	217 08.2	14.1	N 7 57.9	10.6	55.4
19	103 33.1	25.3	231 41.3	14.1	8 08.5	10.5	55.4
20	118 33.2	24.6	246 14.4	14.1	8 19.0	10.5	55.3
21	133 33.3	.. 23.9	260 47.5	14.1	8 29.5	10.5	55.3
22	148 33.3	23.2	275 20.6	14.1	8 40.0	10.4	55.3
23	163 33.4	22.5	289 53.7	14.1	N 8 50.4	10.3	55.3
SD	15.8	d 0.7	SD 15.5		15.3		15.1

Twilight and Moonrise

Lat.	Twilight Naut.	Twilight Civil	Sunrise	Moonrise 4	5	6	7
N 72	////	////	00 46	20 19	20 05	19 50	19 32
N 70	////	////	02 00	20 18	20 10	20 02	19 53
68	////	////	02 37	20 17	20 14	20 11	20 09
66	////	01 18	03 02	20 16	20 18	20 20	20 22
64	////	02 03	03 22	20 16	20 21	20 26	20 33
62	////	02 32	03 38	20 15	20 23	20 32	20 43
60	01 10	02 54	03 51	20 14	20 26	20 38	20 51
N 58	01 51	03 11	04 02	20 14	20 28	20 42	20 58
56	02 18	03 25	04 12	20 14	20 30	20 46	21 04
54	02 38	03 38	04 21	20 13	20 31	20 50	21 10
52	02 55	03 48	04 28	20 13	20 33	20 53	21 15
50	03 08	03 58	04 35	20 13	20 34	20 56	21 20
45	03 35	04 17	04 50	20 12	20 37	21 03	21 30
N 40	03 56	04 32	05 02	20 11	20 40	21 09	21 39
35	04 12	04 45	05 13	20 11	20 42	21 14	21 46
30	04 25	04 56	05 22	20 11	20 44	21 18	21 52
20	04 46	05 14	05 37	20 10	20 48	21 25	22 04
N 10	05 02	05 28	05 50	20 09	20 51	21 32	22 14
0	05 16	05 41	06 02	20 09	20 54	21 38	22 23
S 10	05 27	05 53	06 15	20 08	20 57	21 45	22 32
20	05 38	06 05	06 28	20 08	21 00	21 52	22 42
30	05 49	06 17	06 42	20 07	21 04	21 59	22 54
35	05 54	06 24	06 51	20 07	21 06	22 04	23 01
40	05 59	06 32	07 00	20 06	21 08	22 09	23 08
45	06 05	06 40	07 11	20 06	21 11	22 15	23 17
S 50	06 11	06 50	07 25	20 05	21 15	22 22	23 28
52	06 14	06 54	07 31	20 05	21 16	22 25	23 33
54	06 17	06 59	07 38	20 05	21 18	22 29	23 39
56	06 20	07 05	07 46	20 04	21 20	22 33	23 45
58	06 23	07 11	07 54	20 04	21 22	22 38	23 52
S 60	06 27	07 17	08 04	20 04	21 24	22 43	24 00

Sunset and Moonset

Lat.	Sunset	Twilight Civil	Twilight Naut.	Moonset 4	5	6	7
N 72	23 09	////	////	07 00	08 52	10 41	12 32
N 70	22 06	////	////	07 05	08 50	10 31	12 13
68	21 32	////	////	07 09	08 48	10 23	11 58
66	21 07	22 46	////	07 13	08 46	10 17	11 46
64	20 48	22 04	////	07 16	08 45	10 11	11 35
62	20 32	21 37	////	07 18	08 43	10 06	11 27
60	20 19	21 16	22 55	07 20	08 42	10 02	11 20
N 58	20 08	20 59	22 17	07 22	08 42	09 58	11 13
56	19 58	20 45	21 51	07 24	08 41	09 55	11 08
54	19 50	20 33	21 31	07 26	08 40	09 52	11 03
52	19 42	20 22	21 15	07 27	08 39	09 50	10 58
50	19 35	20 13	21 02	07 28	08 39	09 47	10 54
45	19 21	19 54	20 35	07 31	08 37	09 42	10 45
N 40	19 09	19 39	20 15	07 33	08 36	09 38	10 38
35	18 59	19 26	19 59	07 35	08 35	09 34	10 31
30	18 50	19 16	19 46	07 37	08 35	09 31	10 26
20	18 35	18 58	19 25	07 40	08 33	09 25	10 16
N 10	18 22	18 44	19 09	07 42	08 32	09 20	10 08
0	18 09	18 31	18 56	07 45	08 31	09 15	10 00
S 10	17 57	18 19	18 44	07 47	08 29	09 11	09 52
20	17 45	18 07	18 34	07 49	08 28	09 06	09 44
30	17 30	17 55	18 24	07 52	08 26	09 00	09 34
35	17 22	17 48	18 18	07 54	08 26	08 57	09 29
40	17 12	17 41	18 13	07 55	08 25	08 53	09 22
45	17 01	17 32	18 07	07 58	08 23	08 49	09 15
S 50	16 48	17 23	18 01	08 00	08 22	08 44	09 07
52	16 42	17 18	17 59	08 01	08 21	08 42	09 03
54	16 35	17 13	17 56	08 02	08 21	08 39	08 58
56	16 27	17 08	17 53	08 04	08 20	08 36	08 53
58	16 18	17 02	17 50	08 05	08 19	08 33	08 48
S 60	16 08	16 56	17 46	08 07	08 18	08 30	08 42

SUN and MOON

Day	Eqn. of Time 00h	Eqn. of Time 12h	Mer. Pass.	Mer. Pass. Upper	Mer. Pass. Lower	Age	Phase
4	06 06	06 03	12 06	01 33	13 57	16	93
5	06 00	05 57	12 06	02 20	14 42	17	87
6	05 53	05 50	12 06	03 05	15 27	18	80

2012 AUGUST 7, 8, 9 (TUES., WED., THURS.)

UT	ARIES GHA	VENUS −4.5 GHA	Dec	MARS +1.1 GHA	Dec	JUPITER −2.2 GHA	Dec	SATURN +0.8 GHA	Dec
7 00	315 55.3	226 27.4	N19 37.2	117 52.8	S 7 51.6	246 05.8	N21 21.4	112 36.3	S 7 09.7
01	330 57.7	241 27.6	37.4	132 53.9	52.2	261 07.8	21.5	127 38.7	09.7
02	346 00.2	256 27.7	37.5	147 54.9	52.8	276 09.8	21.5	142 41.0	09.8
03	1 02.7	271 27.8 ..	37.7	162 56.0 ..	53.4	291 11.9 ..	21.6	157 43.3 ..	09.9
04	16 05.1	286 27.9	37.8	177 57.0	54.0	306 13.9	21.6	172 45.6	09.9
05	31 07.6	301 28.0	38.0	192 58.1	54.6	321 16.0	21.7	187 47.9	10.0
T 06	46 10.1	316 28.1	N19 38.1	207 59.2	S 7 55.2	336 18.0	N21 21.7	202 50.2	S 7 10.1
U 07	61 12.5	331 28.2	38.3	223 00.2	55.8	351 20.0	21.8	217 52.5	10.2
E 08	76 15.0	346 28.3	38.4	238 01.3	56.4	6 22.1	21.8	232 54.8	10.2
S 09	91 17.4	1 28.5 ..	38.6	253 02.3 ..	57.0	21 24.1 ..	21.9	247 57.2 ..	10.3
D 10	106 19.9	16 28.6	38.8	268 03.4	57.7	36 26.2	21.9	262 59.5	10.4
A 11	121 22.4	31 28.7	38.9	283 04.4	58.3	51 28.2	22.0	278 01.8	10.4
Y 12	136 24.8	46 28.8	N19 39.1	298 05.5	S 7 58.9	66 30.2	N21 22.0	293 04.1	S 7 10.5
13	151 27.3	61 28.9	39.2	313 06.6	7 59.5	81 32.3	22.1	308 06.4	10.6
14	166 29.8	76 29.0	39.4	328 07.6	8 00.1	96 34.3	22.1	323 08.7	10.6
15	181 32.2	91 29.1 ..	39.5	343 08.7 ..	00.7	111 36.4 ..	22.2	338 11.0 ..	10.7
16	196 34.7	106 29.2	39.7	358 09.7	01.3	126 38.4	22.2	353 13.3	10.8
17	211 37.2	121 29.3	39.8	13 10.8	01.9	141 40.4	22.3	8 15.6	10.8
18	226 39.6	136 29.4	N19 40.0	28 11.8	S 8 02.5	156 42.5	N21 22.4	23 18.0	S 7 10.9
19	241 42.1	151 29.5	40.1	43 12.9	03.1	171 44.5	22.4	38 20.3	11.0
20	256 44.6	166 29.6	40.3	58 13.9	03.7	186 46.6	22.5	53 22.6	11.1
21	271 47.0	181 29.7 ..	40.4	73 15.0 ..	04.3	201 48.6 ..	22.5	68 24.9 ..	11.1
22	286 49.5	196 29.8	40.6	88 16.0	04.9	216 50.7	22.6	83 27.2	11.2
23	301 51.9	211 29.9	40.7	103 17.1	05.5	231 52.7	22.6	98 29.5	11.3
8 00	316 54.4	226 30.0	N19 40.9	118 18.1	S 8 06.2	246 54.7	N21 22.7	113 31.8	S 7 11.3
01	331 56.9	241 30.0	41.0	133 19.2	06.8	261 56.8	22.7	128 34.1	11.4
02	346 59.3	256 30.1	41.2	148 20.3	07.4	276 58.8	22.8	143 36.4	11.5
03	2 01.8	271 30.2 ..	41.3	163 21.3 ..	08.0	292 00.9 ..	22.8	158 38.8 ..	11.5
04	17 04.3	286 30.3	41.5	178 22.4	08.6	307 02.9	22.9	173 41.1	11.6
05	32 06.7	301 30.4	41.6	193 23.4	09.2	322 05.0	22.9	188 43.4	11.7
W 06	47 09.2	316 30.5	N19 41.7	208 24.5	S 8 09.8	337 07.0	N21 23.0	203 45.7	S 7 11.8
E 07	62 11.7	331 30.6	41.9	223 25.5	10.4	352 09.1	23.0	218 48.0	11.8
D 08	77 14.1	346 30.7	42.0	238 26.6	11.0	7 11.1	23.1	233 50.3	11.9
N 09	92 16.6	1 30.7 ..	42.2	253 27.6 ..	11.6	22 13.1 ..	23.1	248 52.6 ..	12.0
E 10	107 19.0	16 30.8	42.3	268 28.7	12.2	37 15.2	23.2	263 54.9	12.0
S 11	122 21.5	31 30.9	42.5	283 29.7	12.8	52 17.2	23.2	278 57.2	12.1
D 12	137 24.0	46 31.0	N19 42.6	298 30.8	S 8 13.4	67 19.3	N21 23.3	293 59.5	S 7 12.2
A 13	152 26.4	61 31.0	42.8	313 31.8	14.0	82 21.3	23.3	309 01.8	12.2
Y 14	167 28.9	76 31.1	42.9	328 32.9	14.7	97 23.4	23.4	324 04.2	12.3
15	182 31.4	91 31.2 ..	43.0	343 33.9 ..	15.3	112 25.4 ..	23.4	339 06.5 ..	12.4
16	197 33.8	106 31.3	43.2	358 35.0	15.9	127 27.5	23.5	354 08.8	12.5
17	212 36.3	121 31.3	43.3	13 36.0	16.5	142 29.5	23.5	9 11.1	12.5
18	227 38.8	136 31.4	N19 43.4	28 37.0	S 8 17.1	157 31.6	N21 23.6	24 13.4	S 7 12.6
19	242 41.2	151 31.5	43.6	43 38.1	17.7	172 33.6	23.7	39 15.7	12.7
20	257 43.7	166 31.6	43.7	58 39.1	18.3	187 35.7	23.7	54 18.0	12.7
21	272 46.2	181 31.6 ..	43.9	73 40.2 ..	18.9	202 37.7 ..	23.8	69 20.3 ..	12.8
22	287 48.6	196 31.7	44.0	88 41.2	19.5	217 39.8	23.8	84 22.6	12.9
23	302 51.1	211 31.8	44.1	103 42.3	20.1	232 41.8	23.9	99 24.9	13.0
9 00	317 53.5	226 31.8	N19 44.3	118 43.3	S 8 20.7	247 43.9	N21 23.9	114 27.2	S 7 13.0
01	332 56.0	241 31.9	44.4	133 44.4	21.3	262 45.9	24.0	129 29.5	13.1
02	347 58.5	256 32.0	44.5	148 45.4	21.9	277 47.9	24.0	144 31.8	13.2
03	3 00.9	271 32.0 ..	44.7	163 46.5 ..	22.5	292 50.0 ..	24.1	159 34.2 ..	13.2
04	18 03.4	286 32.1	44.8	178 47.5	23.2	307 52.0	24.1	174 36.5	13.3
05	33 05.9	301 32.1	44.9	193 48.6	23.8	322 54.1	24.2	189 38.8	13.4
T 06	48 08.3	316 32.2	N19 45.1	208 49.6	S 8 24.4	337 56.1	N21 24.2	204 41.1	S 7 13.5
H 07	63 10.8	331 32.2	45.2	223 50.6	25.0	352 58.2	24.3	219 43.4	13.5
U 08	78 13.3	346 32.3	45.3	238 51.7	25.6	8 00.2	24.3	234 45.7	13.6
R 09	93 15.7	1 32.4 ..	45.5	253 52.7 ..	26.2	23 02.3 ..	24.4	249 48.0 ..	13.7
S 10	108 18.2	16 32.4	45.6	268 53.8	26.8	38 04.3	24.4	264 50.3	13.7
D 11	123 20.7	31 32.5	45.7	283 54.8	27.4	53 06.4	24.5	279 52.6	13.8
A 12	138 23.1	46 32.5	N19 45.9	298 55.9	S 8 28.0	68 08.5	N21 24.5	294 54.9	S 7 13.9
Y 13	153 25.6	61 32.6	46.0	313 56.9	28.6	83 10.5	24.6	309 57.2	14.0
14	168 28.0	76 32.6	46.1	328 57.9	29.2	98 12.6	24.6	324 59.5	14.0
15	183 30.5	91 32.7 ..	46.3	343 59.0 ..	29.8	113 14.6 ..	24.7	340 01.8 ..	14.1
16	198 33.0	106 32.7	46.4	359 00.0	30.4	128 16.7	24.7	355 04.1	14.2
17	213 35.4	121 32.8	46.5	14 01.1	31.0	143 18.7	24.8	10 06.4	14.2
18	228 37.9	136 32.8	N19 46.6	29 02.1	S 8 31.6	158 20.8	N21 24.8	25 08.7	S 7 14.3
19	243 40.4	151 32.9	46.8	44 03.2	32.2	173 22.8	24.9	40 11.0	14.4
20	258 42.8	166 32.9	46.9	59 04.2	32.9	188 24.9	24.9	55 13.3	14.5
21	273 45.3	181 32.9 ..	47.0	74 05.2 ..	33.5	203 26.9 ..	25.0	70 15.7 ..	14.5
22	288 47.8	196 33.0	47.1	89 06.3	34.1	218 29.0	25.0	85 18.0	14.6
23	303 50.2	211 33.0	47.3	104 07.3	34.7	233 31.0	25.1	100 20.3	14.7
Mer.Pass.	2 51.9	v 0.1	d 0.1	v 1.0	d 0.6	v 2.0	d 0.1	v 2.3	d 0.1

STARS

Name	SHA	Dec
Acamar	315 18.8	S40 15.0
Achernar	335 27.0	S57 10.0
Acrux	173 10.3	S63 10.4
Adhara	255 13.3	S28 59.3
Aldebaran	290 50.2	N16 32.0
Alioth	166 21.5	N55 53.7
Alkaid	152 59.5	N49 15.3
Al Na'ir	27 44.0	S46 53.7
Alnilam	275 47.2	S 1 11.6
Alphard	217 57.0	S 8 42.9
Alphecca	126 11.4	N26 40.6
Alpheratz	357 43.8	N29 09.7
Altair	62 08.5	N 8 54.4
Ankaa	353 16.0	S42 13.9
Antares	112 26.8	S26 27.6
Arcturus	145 56.3	N19 07.2
Atria	107 28.9	S69 03.1
Avior	234 18.9	S59 33.0
Bellatrix	278 32.8	N 6 21.6
Betelgeuse	271 02.1	N 7 24.5
Canopus	263 56.8	S52 42.0
Capella	280 35.6	N46 00.4
Deneb	49 31.4	N45 19.8
Denebola	182 34.5	N14 30.1
Diphda	348 56.3	S17 54.8
Dubhe	193 53.0	N61 41.0
Elnath	278 13.6	N28 36.9
Eltanin	90 46.0	N51 29.6
Enif	33 47.4	N 9 56.2
Fomalhaut	15 24.3	S29 33.0
Gacrux	172 01.9	S57 11.3
Gienah	175 53.1	S17 36.8
Hadar	148 48.8	S60 26.3
Hamal	328 01.3	N23 31.3
Kaus Aust.	83 44.3	S34 22.6
Kochab	137 20.0	N74 06.5
Markab	13 38.6	N15 16.6
Menkar	314 15.7	N 4 08.4
Menkent	148 08.3	S36 26.0
Miaplacidus	221 46.7	S69 46.3
Mirfak	308 41.2	N49 54.1
Nunki	75 58.7	S26 16.7
Peacock	53 19.5	S56 41.5
Pollux	243 28.8	N27 59.6
Procyon	245 00.6	N 5 11.5
Rasalhague	96 06.8	N12 33.3
Regulus	207 44.4	N11 54.3
Rigel	281 12.8	S 8 11.2
Rigil Kent.	139 52.6	S60 53.4
Sabik	102 13.0	S15 44.3
Schedar	349 40.8	N56 36.3
Shaula	96 22.4	S37 06.7
Sirius	258 34.5	S16 44.0
Spica	158 32.0	S11 13.6
Suhail	222 53.3	S43 29.1
Vega	80 39.0	N38 48.0
Zuben'ubi	137 06.1	S16 05.6

	SHA	Mer.Pass.
Venus	269 35.5	8 54
Mars	161 23.7	16 06
Jupiter	290 00.3	7 31
Saturn	156 37.4	16 23

UT	SUN GHA	Dec	MOON GHA	v	Dec	d	HP
d h	° ′	° ′	° ′	′	° ′	′	′
7 00	178 33.5	N16 21.8	304 26.8	14.1	N 9 00.7	10.3	55.3
01	193 33.6	21.1	318 59.9	14.1	9 11.0	10.3	55.2
02	208 33.6	20.4	333 33.0	14.1	9 21.3	10.2	55.2
03	223 33.7	.. 19.7	348 06.1	14.1	9 31.5	10.2	55.2
04	238 33.8	19.0	2 39.2	14.1	9 41.7	10.1	55.2
05	253 33.9	18.3	17 12.3	14.1	9 51.8	10.0	55.1
06	268 34.0	N16 17.6	31 45.4	14.1	N10 01.8	10.0	55.1
T 07	283 34.0	16.9	46 18.5	14.0	10 11.8	10.0	55.1
U 08	298 34.1	16.2	60 51.5	14.1	10 21.8	9.9	55.1
E 09	313 34.2	.. 15.5	75 24.6	14.1	10 31.7	9.8	55.1
S 10	328 34.3	14.8	89 57.7	14.0	10 41.5	9.8	55.0
D 11	343 34.3	14.1	104 30.7	14.0	10 51.3	9.7	55.0
A 12	358 34.4	N16 13.4	119 03.7	14.1	N11 01.0	9.7	55.0
Y 13	13 34.5	12.7	133 36.8	14.0	11 10.7	9.7	55.0
14	28 34.6	12.0	148 09.8	14.0	11 20.4	9.5	55.0
15	43 34.7	.. 11.2	162 42.8	14.0	11 29.9	9.5	54.9
16	58 34.8	10.5	177 15.8	14.0	11 39.4	9.5	54.9
17	73 34.8	09.8	191 48.8	14.0	11 48.9	9.4	54.9
18	88 34.9	N16 09.1	206 21.8	13.9	N11 58.3	9.3	54.9
19	103 35.0	08.4	220 54.7	14.0	12 07.6	9.3	54.9
20	118 35.1	07.7	235 27.7	13.9	12 16.9	9.2	54.8
21	133 35.2	.. 07.0	250 00.6	13.9	12 26.1	9.2	54.8
22	148 35.2	06.3	264 33.5	13.9	12 35.3	9.1	54.8
23	163 35.3	05.6	279 06.4	13.9	12 44.4	9.0	54.8
8 00	178 35.4	N16 04.9	293 39.3	13.9	N12 53.4	9.0	54.8
01	193 35.5	04.1	308 12.2	13.9	13 02.4	8.9	54.8
02	208 35.6	03.4	322 45.1	13.8	13 11.3	8.9	54.7
03	223 35.7	.. 02.7	337 17.9	13.9	13 20.2	8.8	54.7
04	238 35.7	02.0	351 50.8	13.8	13 29.0	8.7	54.7
05	253 35.8	01.3	6 23.6	13.8	13 37.7	8.7	54.7
06	268 35.9	N16 00.6	20 56.4	13.7	N13 46.4	8.6	54.7
W 07	283 36.0	15 59.9	35 29.1	13.8	13 55.0	8.5	54.7
E 08	298 36.1	59.2	50 01.9	13.7	14 03.5	8.5	54.6
D 09	313 36.2	.. 58.4	64 34.6	13.7	14 12.0	8.4	54.6
N 10	328 36.3	57.7	79 07.3	13.7	14 20.4	8.3	54.6
E 11	343 36.3	57.0	93 40.0	13.7	14 28.7	8.3	54.6
S 12	358 36.4	N15 56.3	108 12.7	13.7	N14 37.0	8.2	54.6
D 13	13 36.5	55.6	122 45.4	13.6	14 45.2	8.1	54.6
A 14	28 36.6	54.8	137 18.0	13.6	14 53.3	8.1	54.6
Y 15	43 36.7	.. 54.1	151 50.6	13.6	15 01.4	8.0	54.5
16	58 36.8	53.4	166 23.2	13.6	15 09.4	7.9	54.5
17	73 36.9	52.7	180 55.8	13.5	15 17.3	7.8	54.5
18	88 36.9	N15 52.0	195 28.3	13.5	N15 25.1	7.8	54.5
19	103 37.0	51.3	210 00.8	13.5	15 32.9	7.7	54.5
20	118 37.1	50.5	224 33.3	13.5	15 40.6	7.7	54.5
21	133 37.2	.. 49.8	239 05.8	13.5	15 48.3	7.5	54.5
22	148 37.3	49.1	253 38.3	13.4	15 55.8	7.5	54.5
23	163 37.4	48.4	268 10.7	13.4	16 03.3	7.5	54.5
9 00	178 37.5	N15 47.6	282 43.1	13.4	N16 10.8	7.3	54.4
01	193 37.6	46.9	297 15.5	13.3	16 18.1	7.3	54.4
02	208 37.7	46.2	311 47.8	13.3	16 25.4	7.2	54.4
03	223 37.7	.. 45.5	326 20.1	13.3	16 32.6	7.1	54.4
04	238 37.8	44.8	340 52.4	13.3	16 39.7	7.1	54.4
05	253 37.9	44.0	355 24.7	13.2	16 46.8	6.9	54.4
06	268 38.0	N15 43.3	9 56.9	13.3	N16 53.7	6.9	54.4
T 07	283 38.1	42.6	24 29.2	13.1	17 00.6	6.8	54.4
H 08	298 38.2	41.9	39 01.3	13.2	17 07.4	6.8	54.4
U 09	313 38.3	.. 41.2	53 33.5	13.1	17 14.2	6.7	54.4
R 10	328 38.4	40.4	68 05.6	13.1	17 20.9	6.5	54.3
S 11	343 38.5	39.7	82 37.7	13.1	17 27.4	6.6	54.3
D 12	358 38.6	N15 38.9	97 09.8	13.1	N17 34.0	6.4	54.3
A 13	13 38.7	38.2	111 41.9	13.0	17 40.4	6.3	54.3
Y 14	28 38.7	37.5	126 13.9	13.0	17 46.7	6.3	54.3
15	43 38.8	.. 36.8	140 45.9	13.0	17 53.0	6.2	54.3
16	58 38.9	36.0	155 17.9	12.9	17 59.2	6.1	54.3
17	73 39.0	35.3	169 49.8	12.9	18 05.3	6.0	54.3
18	88 39.1	N15 34.6	184 21.7	12.9	N18 11.3	6.0	54.3
19	103 39.2	33.8	198 53.6	12.8	18 17.3	5.9	54.3
20	118 39.3	33.1	213 25.4	12.8	18 23.2	5.7	54.3
21	133 39.4	.. 32.4	227 57.2	12.8	18 28.9	5.7	54.3
22	148 39.5	31.6	242 29.0	12.8	18 34.6	5.7	54.3
23	163 39.6	30.9	257 00.8	12.7	N18 40.3	5.5	54.3
	SD 15.8	d 0.7	SD 15.0		14.9		14.8

Twilight — Sunrise — Moonrise

Lat.	Twilight Naut.	Twilight Civil	Sunrise	Moonrise 7	8	9	10
°	h m	h m	h m	h m	h m	h m	h m
N 72	////	////	01 29	19 32	19 07	▭	▭
N 70	////	////	02 19	19 53	19 42	19 26	▭
68	////	////	02 50	20 09	20 07	20 07	20 09
66	////	01 41	03 13	20 22	20 27	20 35	20 50
64	////	02 18	03 31	20 33	20 43	20 56	21 17
62	////	02 43	03 46	20 43	20 56	21 14	21 39
60	01 31	03 03	03 58	20 51	21 07	21 28	21 56
N 58	02 04	03 19	04 09	20 58	21 17	21 40	22 11
56	02 28	03 32	04 18	21 04	21 26	21 51	22 23
54	02 46	03 44	04 26	21 10	21 33	22 01	22 34
52	03 02	03 54	04 33	21 15	21 40	22 09	22 44
50	03 14	04 03	04 40	21 20	21 46	22 17	22 52
45	03 40	04 21	04 54	21 30	22 00	22 33	23 11
N 40	03 59	04 36	05 05	21 39	22 11	22 46	23 26
35	04 15	04 48	05 15	21 46	22 20	22 58	23 39
30	04 27	04 58	05 23	21 52	22 29	23 08	23 50
20	04 47	05 15	05 38	22 04	22 43	23 25	24 09
N 10	05 03	05 29	05 50	22 14	22 56	23 40	24 26
0	05 16	05 41	06 02	22 23	23 08	23 54	24 41
S 10	05 27	05 52	06 14	22 32	23 20	24 08	00 08
20	05 37	06 03	06 26	22 42	23 33	24 23	00 23
30	05 46	06 15	06 40	22 54	23 48	24 41	00 41
35	05 51	06 21	06 48	23 01	23 56	24 51	00 51
40	05 57	06 28	06 57	23 08	24 06	00 06	01 03
45	06 01	06 36	07 07	23 17	24 18	00 18	01 17
S 50	06 07	06 45	07 20	23 28	24 32	00 32	01 34
52	06 09	06 50	07 26	23 33	24 39	00 39	01 42
54	06 12	06 54	07 32	23 39	24 46	00 46	01 51
56	06 14	06 59	07 39	23 45	24 54	00 54	02 01
58	06 17	07 04	07 47	23 52	25 04	01 04	02 12
S 60	06 20	07 10	07 57	24 00	00 00	01 14	02 26

Sunset — Twilight — Moonset

Lat.	Sunset	Twilight Civil	Twilight Naut.	Moonset 7	8	9	10
°	h m	h m	h m	h m	h m	h m	h m
N 72	22 33	////	////	12 32	14 31	▭	▭
N 70	21 47	////	////	12 13	13 57	15 48	▭
68	21 17	23 34	////	11 58	13 32	15 08	16 43
66	20 55	22 24	////	11 46	13 14	14 40	16 03
64	20 38	21 49	////	11 35	12 59	14 19	15 34
62	20 23	21 25	23 37	11 27	12 46	14 03	15 14
60	20 11	21 06	22 35	11 20	12 35	13 49	14 57
N 58	20 01	20 50	22 03	11 13	12 26	13 37	14 43
56	19 52	20 37	21 41	11 08	12 18	13 26	14 31
54	19 44	20 26	21 23	11 03	12 11	13 17	14 20
52	19 37	20 16	21 08	10 58	12 05	13 09	14 11
50	19 30	20 07	20 55	10 54	11 59	13 02	14 02
45	19 17	19 49	20 30	10 45	11 46	12 46	13 44
N 40	19 05	19 35	20 11	10 38	11 36	12 34	13 30
35	18 56	19 23	19 56	10 31	11 28	12 23	13 17
30	18 47	19 13	19 43	10 26	11 20	12 13	13 06
20	18 33	18 56	19 23	10 16	11 07	11 57	12 48
N 10	18 21	18 42	19 08	10 08	10 55	11 43	12 32
0	18 09	18 30	18 55	10 00	10 44	11 30	12 17
S 10	17 58	18 19	18 45	09 52	10 34	11 17	12 02
20	17 45	18 08	18 35	09 44	10 22	11 03	11 46
30	17 32	17 57	18 25	09 34	10 09	10 47	11 27
35	17 24	17 50	18 20	09 29	10 02	10 38	11 17
40	17 15	17 43	18 16	09 22	09 53	10 27	11 04
45	17 05	17 36	18 10	09 15	09 43	10 15	10 50
S 50	16 52	17 26	18 05	09 07	09 31	10 00	10 32
52	16 46	17 22	18 03	09 03	09 26	09 53	10 24
54	16 40	17 18	18 00	08 58	09 20	09 45	10 15
56	16 33	17 13	17 58	08 54	09 13	09 36	10 05
58	16 24	17 08	17 55	08 48	09 05	09 26	09 53
S 60	16 15	17 02	17 52	08 42	08 57	09 15	09 39

SUN — MOON

Day	SUN Eqn. of Time 00h	SUN Eqn. of Time 12h	Mer. Pass.	MOON Mer. Pass. Upper	Lower	Age	Phase
d	m s	m s	h m	h m	h m	d	%
7	05 46	05 42	12 06	03 49	16 11	19	71
8	05 39	05 34	12 06	04 34	16 56	20	62
9	05 30	05 26	12 05	05 19	17 42	21	53

UT	ARIES GHA	VENUS −4.5 GHA	Dec	MARS +1.1 GHA	Dec	JUPITER −2.2 GHA	Dec	SATURN +0.8 GHA	Dec	STARS Name	SHA	Dec
10 00	318 52.7	226 33.1	N19 47.4	119 08.4	S 8 35.3	248 33.1	N21 25.1	115 22.6	S 7 14.7	Acamar	315 18.7	S40 15.0
01	333 55.1	241 33.1	47.5	134 09.4	35.9	263 35.1	25.2	130 24.9	14.8	Achernar	335 27.0	S57 10.0
02	348 57.6	256 33.1	47.6	149 10.4	36.5	278 37.2	25.2	145 27.2	14.9	Acrux	173 10.4	S63 10.4
03	4 00.1	271 33.2	.. 47.8	164 11.5	.. 37.1	293 39.2	.. 25.3	160 29.5	.. 15.0	Adhara	255 13.3	S28 59.3
04	19 02.5	286 33.2	47.9	179 12.5	37.7	308 41.3	25.3	175 31.8	15.0	Aldebaran	290 50.2	N16 32.0
05	34 05.0	301 33.2	48.0	194 13.5	38.3	323 43.4	25.4	190 34.1	15.1			
06	49 07.5	316 33.3	N19 48.1	209 14.6	S 8 38.9	338 45.4	N21 25.4	205 36.4	S 7 15.2	Alioth	166 21.5	N55 53.7
07	64 09.9	331 33.3	48.2	224 15.6	39.5	353 47.5	25.5	220 38.7	15.3	Alkaid	152 59.5	N49 15.3
08	79 12.4	346 33.3	48.4	239 16.7	40.1	8 49.5	25.5	235 41.0	15.3	Al Na'ir	27 44.0	S46 53.7
F 09	94 14.9	1 33.4	.. 48.5	254 17.7	.. 40.7	23 51.6	.. 25.6	250 43.3	.. 15.4	Alnilam	275 47.1	S 1 11.6
R 10	109 17.3	16 33.4	48.6	269 18.7	41.3	38 53.6	25.6	265 45.6	15.5	Alphard	217 57.0	S 8 42.9
I 11	124 19.8	31 33.4	48.7	284 19.8	42.0	53 55.7	25.7	280 47.9	15.5			
D 12	139 22.3	46 33.4	N19 48.8	299 20.8	S 8 42.6	68 57.7	N21 25.7	295 50.2	S 7 15.6	Alphecca	126 11.4	N26 40.6
A 13	154 24.7	61 33.5	49.0	314 21.8	43.2	83 59.8	25.8	310 52.5	15.7	Alpheratz	357 43.8	N29 09.7
Y 14	169 27.2	76 33.5	49.1	329 22.9	43.8	99 01.9	25.8	325 54.8	15.8	Altair	62 08.5	N 8 54.4
15	184 29.6	91 33.5	.. 49.2	344 23.9	.. 44.4	114 03.9	.. 25.9	340 57.1	.. 15.8	Ankaa	353 16.0	S42 13.9
16	199 32.1	106 33.5	49.3	359 25.0	45.0	129 06.0	25.9	355 59.4	15.9	Antares	112 26.8	S26 27.6
17	214 34.6	121 33.6	49.4	14 26.0	45.6	144 08.0	26.0	11 01.7	16.0			
18	229 37.0	136 33.6	N19 49.5	29 27.0	S 8 46.2	159 10.1	N21 26.0	26 04.0	S 7 16.1	Arcturus	145 56.3	N19 07.2
19	244 39.5	151 33.6	49.6	44 28.1	46.8	174 12.1	26.1	41 06.3	16.1	Atria	107 28.9	S69 03.1
20	259 42.0	166 33.6	49.8	59 29.1	47.4	189 14.2	26.1	56 08.6	16.2	Avior	234 18.9	S59 33.0
21	274 44.4	181 33.6	.. 49.9	74 30.1	.. 48.0	204 16.3	.. 26.2	71 10.9	.. 16.3	Bellatrix	278 32.8	N 6 21.6
22	289 46.9	196 33.7	50.0	89 31.2	48.6	219 18.3	26.2	86 13.2	16.3	Betelgeuse	271 02.1	N 7 24.5
23	304 49.4	211 33.7	50.1	104 32.2	49.2	234 20.4	26.3	101 15.5	16.4			
11 00	319 51.8	226 33.7	N19 50.2	119 33.2	S 8 49.8	249 22.4	N21 26.3	116 17.8	S 7 16.5	Canopus	263 56.8	S52 42.0
01	334 54.3	241 33.7	50.3	134 34.3	50.4	264 24.5	26.4	131 20.1	16.6	Capella	280 35.5	N46 00.4
02	349 56.8	256 33.7	50.4	149 35.3	51.0	279 26.6	26.4	146 22.4	16.6	Deneb	49 31.4	N45 19.8
03	4 59.2	271 33.7	.. 50.5	164 36.3	.. 51.6	294 28.6	.. 26.5	161 24.7	.. 16.7	Denebola	182 34.5	N14 30.1
04	20 01.7	286 33.7	50.6	179 37.4	52.3	309 30.7	26.5	176 27.0	16.8	Diphda	348 56.3	S17 54.8
05	35 04.1	301 33.7	50.8	194 38.4	52.9	324 32.7	26.6	191 29.3	16.9			
06	50 06.6	316 33.8	N19 50.9	209 39.4	S 8 53.5	339 34.8	N21 26.6	206 31.6	S 7 16.9	Dubhe	193 53.0	N61 41.0
S 07	65 09.1	331 33.8	51.0	224 40.4	54.1	354 36.9	26.7	221 33.9	17.0	Elnath	278 13.5	N28 36.9
A 08	80 11.5	346 33.8	51.1	239 41.5	54.7	9 38.9	26.7	236 36.2	17.1	Eltanin	90 46.1	N51 29.6
T 09	95 14.0	1 33.8	.. 51.2	254 42.5	.. 55.3	24 41.0	.. 26.8	251 38.5	.. 17.2	Enif	33 47.3	N 9 56.2
U 10	110 16.5	16 33.8	51.3	269 43.5	55.9	39 43.0	26.8	266 40.8	17.2	Fomalhaut	15 24.3	S29 33.0
R 11	125 18.9	31 33.8	51.4	284 44.6	56.5	54 45.1	26.8	281 43.1	17.3			
D 12	140 21.4	46 33.8	N19 51.5	299 45.6	S 8 57.1	69 47.2	N21 26.9	296 45.4	S 7 17.4	Gacrux	172 01.9	S57 11.3
A 13	155 23.9	61 33.8	51.6	314 46.6	57.7	84 49.2	26.9	311 47.7	17.4	Gienah	175 53.1	S17 36.8
Y 14	170 26.3	76 33.8	51.7	329 47.7	58.3	99 51.3	27.0	326 50.0	17.5	Hadar	148 48.9	S60 26.3
15	185 28.8	91 33.8	.. 51.8	344 48.7	.. 58.9	114 53.3	.. 27.0	341 52.3	.. 17.6	Hamal	328 01.3	N23 31.3
16	200 31.2	106 33.8	51.9	359 49.7	8 59.5	129 55.4	27.1	356 54.6	17.7	Kaus Aust.	83 44.3	S34 22.6
17	215 33.7	121 33.8	52.0	14 50.7	9 00.1	144 57.5	27.1	11 56.9	17.7			
18	230 36.2	136 33.8	N19 52.1	29 51.8	S 9 00.7	159 59.5	N21 27.2	26 59.2	S 7 17.8	Kochab	137 20.1	N74 06.5
19	245 38.6	151 33.8	52.2	44 52.8	01.3	175 01.6	27.2	42 01.5	17.9	Markab	13 38.6	N15 16.6
20	260 41.1	166 33.8	52.3	59 53.8	01.9	190 03.7	27.3	57 03.8	18.0	Menkar	314 15.6	N 4 08.4
21	275 43.6	181 33.8	.. 52.4	74 54.9	.. 02.6	205 05.7	.. 27.3	72 06.1	.. 18.0	Menkent	148 08.3	S36 26.0
22	290 46.0	196 33.7	52.5	89 55.9	03.2	220 07.8	27.4	87 08.4	18.1	Miaplacidus	221 40.7	S69 46.3
23	305 48.5	211 33.7	52.6	104 56.9	03.8	235 09.8	27.4	102 10.7	18.2			
12 00	320 51.0	226 33.7	N19 52.7	119 57.9	S 9 04.4	250 11.9	N21 27.5	117 13.0	S 7 18.3	Mirfak	308 41.2	N49 54.1
01	335 53.4	241 33.7	52.8	134 59.0	05.0	265 14.0	27.5	132 15.3	18.3	Nunki	75 58.7	S26 16.7
02	350 55.9	256 33.7	52.9	150 00.0	05.6	280 16.0	27.6	147 17.6	18.4	Peacock	53 19.5	S56 41.5
03	5 58.4	271 33.7	.. 53.0	165 01.0	.. 06.2	295 18.1	.. 27.6	162 19.9	.. 18.5	Pollux	243 28.8	N27 59.6
04	21 00.8	286 33.7	53.1	180 02.0	06.8	310 20.2	27.7	177 22.2	18.6	Procyon	245 00.6	N 5 11.5
05	36 03.3	301 33.7	53.2	195 03.1	07.4	325 22.2	27.7	192 24.5	18.6			
06	51 05.7	316 33.7	N19 53.3	210 04.1	S 9 08.0	340 24.3	N21 27.8	207 26.8	S 7 18.7	Rasalhague	96 06.8	N12 33.3
07	66 08.2	331 33.6	53.4	225 05.1	08.6	355 26.4	27.8	222 29.1	18.8	Regulus	207 44.4	N11 54.3
08	81 10.7	346 33.6	53.5	240 06.1	09.2	10 28.4	27.9	237 31.4	18.9	Rigel	281 12.8	S 8 11.2
S 09	96 13.1	1 33.6	.. 53.6	255 07.2	.. 09.8	25 30.5	.. 27.9	252 33.7	.. 18.9	Rigil Kent.	139 52.6	S60 53.4
U 10	111 15.6	16 33.6	53.7	270 08.2	10.4	40 32.6	28.0	267 36.0	19.0	Sabik	102 13.0	S15 44.3
N 11	126 18.1	31 33.6	53.7	285 09.2	11.0	55 34.6	28.0	282 38.3	19.1			
D 12	141 20.5	46 33.5	N19 53.8	300 10.2	S 9 11.6	70 36.7	N21 28.0	297 40.6	S 7 19.2	Schedar	349 40.8	N56 36.3
A 13	156 23.0	61 33.5	53.9	315 11.3	12.2	85 38.8	28.1	312 42.9	19.2	Shaula	96 22.4	S37 06.7
Y 14	171 25.5	76 33.5	54.0	330 12.3	12.8	100 40.8	28.1	327 45.2	19.3	Sirius	258 34.5	S16 44.0
15	186 27.9	91 33.5	.. 54.1	345 13.3	.. 13.4	115 42.9	.. 28.2	342 47.5	.. 19.4	Spica	158 32.0	S11 13.6
16	201 30.4	106 33.4	54.2	0 14.3	14.0	130 45.0	28.2	357 49.8	19.5	Suhail	222 53.3	S43 29.1
17	216 32.9	121 33.4	54.3	15 15.3	14.7	145 47.0	28.3	12 52.1	19.5			
18	231 35.3	136 33.4	N19 54.4	30 16.4	S 9 15.3	160 49.1	N21 28.3	27 54.4	S 7 19.6	Vega	80 39.0	N38 48.1
19	246 37.8	151 33.4	54.5	45 17.4	15.9	175 51.2	28.4	42 56.6	19.7	Zuben'ubi	137 06.1	S16 05.6
20	261 40.2	166 33.3	54.5	60 18.4	16.5	190 53.2	28.4	57 58.9	19.8		SHA	Mer.Pass.
21	276 42.7	181 33.3	.. 54.6	75 19.4	.. 17.1	205 55.3	.. 28.5	73 01.2	.. 19.8			
22	291 45.2	196 33.3	54.7	90 20.5	17.7	220 57.4	28.5	88 03.5	19.9	Venus	266 41.9	h m 8 54
23	306 47.6	211 33.2	54.8	105 21.5	18.3	235 59.5	28.6	103 05.8	20.0	Mars	159 41.4	16 01
Mer.Pass.	2 40.1	v 0.0	d 0.1	v 1.0	d 0.6	v 2.1	d 0.0	v 2.3	d 0.1	Jupiter	289 30.6	7 21
										Saturn	156 26.0	16 12

UT	SUN GHA	SUN Dec	MOON GHA	v	MOON Dec	d	HP
10 FRIDAY							
00	178 39.7	N15 30.2	271 32.5	12.7	N18 45.8	5.4	54.3
01	193 39.8	29.4	286 04.2	12.7	18 51.2	5.4	54.3
02	208 39.9	28.7	300 35.9	12.6	18 56.6	5.3	54.3
03	223 40.0	.. 28.0	315 07.5	12.6	19 01.9	5.2	54.3
04	238 40.1	27.2	329 39.1	12.6	19 07.1	5.1	54.3
05	253 40.2	26.5	344 10.7	12.6	19 12.2	5.0	54.3
06	268 40.3	N15 25.8	358 42.3	12.5	N19 17.2	4.9	54.3
07	283 40.4	25.0	13 13.8	12.5	19 22.1	4.9	54.3
08	298 40.5	24.3	27 45.3	12.4	19 27.0	4.7	54.3
09	313 40.6	.. 23.6	42 16.7	12.4	19 31.7	4.7	54.3
10	328 40.6	22.8	56 48.1	12.4	19 36.4	4.6	54.3
11	343 40.7	22.1	71 19.5	12.4	19 41.0	4.5	54.3
12	358 40.8	N15 21.4	85 50.9	12.4	N19 45.5	4.4	54.3
13	13 40.9	20.6	100 22.3	12.3	19 49.9	4.3	54.3
14	28 41.0	19.9	114 53.6	12.2	19 54.2	4.2	54.3
15	43 41.1	.. 19.1	129 24.8	12.3	19 58.4	4.1	54.3
16	58 41.2	18.4	143 56.1	12.2	20 02.5	4.1	54.3
17	73 41.3	17.7	158 27.3	12.2	20 06.6	3.9	54.3
18	88 41.4	N15 16.9	172 58.5	12.2	N20 10.5	3.9	54.3
19	103 41.5	16.2	187 29.7	12.1	20 14.4	3.7	54.3
20	118 41.6	15.4	202 00.8	12.1	20 18.1	3.7	54.3
21	133 41.7	.. 14.7	216 31.9	12.1	20 21.8	3.6	54.3
22	148 41.8	14.0	231 03.0	12.0	20 25.4	3.5	54.3
23	163 41.9	13.2	245 34.0	12.0	20 28.9	3.4	54.3
11 SATURDAY							
00	178 42.0	N15 12.5	260 05.0	12.0	N20 32.3	3.3	54.3
01	193 42.1	11.7	274 36.0	12.0	20 35.6	3.2	54.3
02	208 42.2	11.0	289 07.0	11.9	20 38.8	3.1	54.3
03	223 42.3	.. 10.2	303 37.9	11.9	20 41.9	3.0	54.3
04	238 42.4	09.5	318 08.8	11.9	20 44.9	2.9	54.3
05	253 42.5	08.7	332 39.7	11.8	20 47.8	2.9	54.3
06	268 42.6	N15 08.0	347 10.5	11.8	N20 50.7	2.7	54.3
07	283 42.7	07.3	1 41.3	11.8	20 53.4	2.6	54.3
08	298 42.8	06.5	16 12.1	11.8	20 56.0	2.6	54.3
09	313 42.9	.. 05.8	30 42.9	11.7	20 58.6	2.4	54.3
10	328 43.1	05.0	45 13.6	11.7	21 01.0	2.3	54.3
11	343 43.2	04.3	59 44.3	11.7	21 03.3	2.3	54.3
12	358 43.3	N15 03.5	74 15.0	11.7	N21 05.6	2.1	54.4
13	13 43.4	02.8	88 45.7	11.6	21 07.7	2.1	54.4
14	28 43.5	02.0	103 16.3	11.6	21 09.8	1.9	54.4
15	43 43.6	.. 01.2	117 46.9	11.6	21 11.7	1.9	54.4
16	58 43.7	15 00.5	132 17.5	11.6	21 13.6	1.7	54.4
17	73 43.8	14 59.7	146 48.1	11.5	21 15.3	1.7	54.4
18	88 43.9	N14 59.0	161 18.6	11.5	N21 17.0	1.5	54.4
19	103 44.0	58.3	175 49.1	11.5	21 18.5	1.5	54.4
20	118 44.1	57.5	190 19.6	11.4	21 20.0	1.3	54.4
21	133 44.2	.. 56.8	204 50.0	11.5	21 21.3	1.3	54.4
22	148 44.3	56.0	219 20.5	11.4	21 22.6	1.1	54.4
23	163 44.4	55.3	233 50.9	11.4	21 23.7	1.1	54.4
12 SUNDAY							
00	178 44.5	N14 54.5	248 21.3	11.4	N21 24.8	0.9	54.5
01	193 44.6	53.8	262 51.7	11.3	21 25.7	0.9	54.5
02	208 44.7	53.0	277 22.0	11.4	21 26.6	0.7	54.5
03	223 44.8	.. 52.2	291 52.4	11.3	21 27.3	0.7	54.5
04	238 44.9	51.5	306 22.7	11.3	21 28.0	0.5	54.5
05	253 45.1	50.7	320 53.0	11.2	21 28.5	0.5	54.5
06	268 45.2	N14 50.0	335 23.2	11.3	N21 29.0	0.3	54.5
07	283 45.3	49.2	349 53.5	11.2	21 29.3	0.2	54.5
08	298 45.4	48.5	4 23.7	11.2	21 29.5	0.0	54.6
09	313 45.5	.. 47.7	18 53.9	11.2	21 29.5	0.0	54.6
10	328 45.6	47.0	33 24.1	11.2	21 29.7	0.1	54.6
11	343 45.7	46.2	47 54.3	11.2	21 29.6	0.1	54.6
12	358 45.8	N14 45.4	62 24.5	11.1	N21 29.5	0.3	54.6
13	13 45.9	44.7	76 54.6	11.1	21 29.2	0.4	54.6
14	28 46.0	43.9	91 24.7	11.1	21 28.8	0.5	54.6
15	43 46.1	.. 43.2	105 54.8	11.1	21 28.3	0.6	54.6
16	58 46.2	42.4	120 24.9	11.1	21 27.7	0.7	54.7
17	73 46.4	41.6	134 55.0	11.1	21 27.0	0.8	54.7
18	88 46.5	N14 40.9	149 25.1	11.0	N21 26.2	0.9	54.7
19	103 46.6	40.1	163 55.1	11.1	21 25.3	1.0	54.7
20	118 46.7	39.4	178 25.2	11.0	21 24.3	1.1	54.7
21	133 46.8	.. 38.6	192 55.2	11.0	21 23.2	1.2	54.7
22	148 46.9	37.8	207 25.2	11.0	21 22.0	1.3	54.8
23	163 47.0	37.1	221 55.2	11.0	N21 20.7	1.5	54.8
	SD 15.8　d 0.7		SD 14.8		14.8		14.9

Twilight / Sunrise / Moonrise

Lat.	Naut.	Civil	Sunrise	Moonrise 10	11	12	13
N 72	////	////	01 57	□	□	□	□
N 70	////	////	02 37	□	□	□	□
68	////	01 09	03 04	20 09	20 22	21 10	22 37
66	////	02 01	03 24	20 50	21 17	22 07	23 19
64	////	02 31	03 41	21 17	21 50	22 40	23 47
62	01 02	02 54	03 54	21 39	22 15	23 05	24 09
60	01 48	03 12	04 05	21 56	22 34	23 24	24 26
N 58	02 16	03 27	04 15	22 11	22 50	23 40	24 41
56	02 37	03 39	04 24	22 23	23 04	23 54	24 53
54	02 54	03 50	04 31	22 34	23 15	24 05	00 05
52	03 08	03 59	04 38	22 44	23 26	24 16	00 16
50	03 21	04 07	04 44	22 52	23 35	24 25	00 25
45	03 45	04 25	04 57	23 11	23 55	24 45	00 45
N 40	04 03	04 39	05 08	23 26	24 11	00 11	01 01
35	04 18	04 50	05 17	23 39	24 24	00 24	01 14
30	04 30	05 00	05 25	23 50	24 36	00 36	01 26
20	04 49	05 16	05 39	24 09	00 09	00 56	01 46
N 10	05 03	05 29	05 51	24 26	00 26	01 14	02 03
0	05 15	05 40	06 02	24 41	00 41	01 30	02 19
S 10	05 26	05 51	06 13	00 08	00 57	01 46	02 36
20	05 35	06 01	06 24	00 23	01 14	02 04	02 53
30	05 44	06 12	06 37	00 41	01 33	02 24	03 13
35	05 48	06 18	06 45	00 51	01 45	02 36	03 25
40	05 53	06 25	06 53	01 03	01 58	02 50	03 38
45	05 57	06 32	07 03	01 17	02 13	03 06	03 54
S 50	06 02	06 41	07 15	01 34	02 32	03 26	04 14
52	06 04	06 44	07 20	01 42	02 41	03 35	04 23
54	06 06	06 48	07 26	01 51	02 51	03 46	04 33
56	06 09	06 53	07 33	02 01	03 03	03 58	04 45
58	06 11	06 58	07 40	02 12	03 16	04 12	04 59
S 60	06 14	07 03	07 49	02 26	03 31	04 28	05 14

Sunset / Twilight / Moonset

Lat.	Sunset	Civil	Naut.	Moonset 10	11	12	13
N 72	22 07	////	////	□	□	□	□
N 70	21 29	////	////	□	□	□	□
68	21 03	22 51	////	16 43	18 10	19 05	19 22
66	20 43	22 05	////	16 03	17 15	18 08	18 39
64	20 27	21 35	////	15 35	16 42	17 34	18 11
62	20 14	21 13	23 00	15 14	16 18	17 10	17 49
60	20 03	20 56	22 18	14 57	15 59	16 50	17 31
N 58	19 54	20 42	21 51	14 43	15 43	16 34	17 16
56	19 45	20 30	21 30	14 31	15 29	16 21	17 03
54	19 38	20 19	21 14	14 20	15 18	16 09	16 52
52	19 31	20 10	21 00	14 11	15 07	15 58	16 42
50	19 25	20 02	20 48	14 02	14 58	15 49	16 34
45	19 12	19 44	20 24	13 44	14 39	15 29	16 15
N 40	19 02	19 31	20 06	13 30	14 23	15 13	16 00
35	18 53	19 20	19 52	13 17	14 10	15 00	15 47
30	18 45	19 10	19 40	13 06	13 58	14 48	15 36
20	18 31	18 54	19 21	12 48	13 38	14 28	15 16
N 10	18 19	18 41	19 07	12 32	13 21	14 10	14 59
0	18 09	18 30	18 55	12 17	13 05	13 54	14 43
S 10	17 58	18 19	18 45	12 02	12 49	13 37	14 28
20	17 46	18 09	18 35	11 46	12 31	13 20	14 10
30	17 34	17 58	18 27	11 27	12 11	12 59	13 51
35	17 26	17 52	18 22	11 17	12 00	12 47	13 39
40	17 17	17 46	18 18	11 04	11 47	12 34	13 26
45	17 08	17 39	18 14	10 50	11 31	12 18	13 11
S 50	16 56	17 30	18 09	10 32	11 11	11 58	12 51
52	16 51	17 27	18 07	10 24	11 02	11 48	12 42
54	16 45	17 23	18 05	10 15	10 52	11 38	12 32
56	16 38	17 18	18 02	10 05	10 40	11 25	12 20
58	16 31	17 13	18 00	09 53	10 27	11 12	12 07
S 60	16 22	17 08	17 57	09 39	10 11	10 55	11 51

SUN and MOON

Day	SUN Eqn. of Time 00h	12h	Mer. Pass.	MOON Mer. Pass. Upper	Lower	Age	Phase
10	05 21	05 17	12 05	06 05	18 29	22	43
11	05 12	05 07	12 05	06 53	19 17	23	34
12	05 02	04 57	12 05	07 42	20 07	24	25

2012 AUGUST 13, 14, 15 (MON., TUES., WED.)

UT	ARIES	VENUS −4.4		MARS +1.1		JUPITER −2.2		SATURN +0.8		STARS		
	GHA	GHA	Dec	GHA	Dec	GHA	Dec	GHA	Dec	Name	SHA	Dec
d h	° ′	° ′	° ′	° ′	° ′	° ′	° ′	° ′	° ′		° ′	° ′
13 00	321 50.1	226 33.2	N19 54.9	120 22.5	S 9 18.9	251 01.5	N21 28.6	118 08.1	S 7 20.1	Acamar	315 18.7	S40 15.0
01	336 52.6	241 33.2	55.0	135 23.5	19.5	266 03.6	28.7	133 10.4	20.1	Achernar	335 26.9	S57 10.0
02	351 55.0	256 33.1	55.0	150 24.5	20.1	281 05.7	28.7	148 12.7	20.2	Acrux	173 10.4	S63 10.4
03	6 57.5	271 33.1	.. 55.1	165 25.6	.. 20.7	296 07.7	.. 28.8	163 15.0	.. 20.3	Adhara	255 13.3	S28 59.3
04	22 00.0	286 33.1	55.2	180 26.6	21.3	311 09.8	28.8	178 17.3	20.4	Aldebaran	290 50.1	N16 32.0
05	37 02.4	301 33.0	55.3	195 27.6	21.9	326 11.9	28.8	193 19.6	20.4			
06	52 04.9	316 33.0	N19 55.4	210 28.6	S 9 22.5	341 13.9	N21 28.9	208 21.9	S 7 20.5	Alioth	166 21.5	N55 53.7
07	67 07.4	331 33.0	55.4	225 29.6	23.1	356 16.0	28.9	223 24.2	20.6	Alkaid	152 59.5	N49 15.3
08	82 09.8	346 32.9	55.5	240 30.6	23.7	11 18.1	29.0	238 26.5	20.7	Al Na'ir	27 44.0	S46 53.7
M 09	97 12.3	1 32.9	.. 55.6	255 31.7	.. 24.3	26 20.2	.. 29.0	253 28.8	.. 20.7	Alnilam	275 47.1	S 1 11.6
O 10	112 14.7	16 32.8	55.7	270 32.7	24.9	41 22.2	29.1	268 31.1	20.8	Alphard	217 57.0	S 8 42.9
N 11	127 17.2	31 32.8	55.8	285 33.7	25.5	56 24.3	29.1	283 33.4	20.9			
D 12	142 19.7	46 32.7	N19 55.8	300 34.7	S 9 26.1	71 26.4	N21 29.2	298 35.7	S 7 21.0	Alphecca	126 11.5	N26 40.6
A 13	157 22.1	61 32.7	55.9	315 35.7	26.7	86 28.4	29.2	313 37.9	21.0	Alpheratz	357 43.8	N29 09.7
Y 14	172 24.6	76 32.6	56.0	330 36.7	27.3	101 30.5	29.3	328 40.2	21.1	Altair	62 08.5	N 8 54.4
15	187 27.1	91 32.6	.. 56.1	345 37.8	.. 28.0	116 32.6	.. 29.3	343 42.5	.. 21.2	Ankaa	353 15.9	S42 13.9
16	202 29.5	106 32.6	56.1	0 38.8	28.6	131 34.7	29.4	358 44.8	21.3	Antares	112 26.8	S26 27.6
17	217 32.0	121 32.5	56.2	15 39.8	29.2	146 36.7	29.4	13 47.1	21.3			
18	232 34.5	136 32.5	N19 56.3	30 40.8	S 9 29.8	161 38.8	N21 29.4	28 49.4	S 7 21.4	Arcturus	145 56.3	N19 07.2
19	247 36.9	151 32.4	56.4	45 41.8	30.4	176 40.9	29.5	43 51.7	21.5	Atria	107 28.9	S69 03.2
20	262 39.4	166 32.4	56.4	60 42.8	31.0	191 43.0	29.5	58 54.0	21.6	Avior	234 18.9	S59 33.0
21	277 41.8	181 32.3	.. 56.5	75 43.8	.. 31.6	206 45.0	.. 29.6	73 56.3	.. 21.6	Bellatrix	278 32.8	N 6 21.6
22	292 44.3	196 32.2	56.6	90 44.9	32.2	221 47.1	29.6	88 58.6	21.7	Betelgeuse	271 02.1	N 7 24.5
23	307 46.8	211 32.2	56.6	105 45.9	32.8	236 49.2	29.7	104 00.9	21.8			
14 00	322 49.2	226 32.1	N19 56.7	120 46.9	S 9 33.4	251 51.3	N21 29.7	119 03.2	S 7 21.9	Canopus	263 56.8	S52 42.0
01	337 51.7	241 32.1	56.8	135 47.9	34.0	266 53.3	29.8	134 05.5	22.0	Capella	280 35.5	N46 00.4
02	352 54.2	256 32.0	56.8	150 48.9	34.6	281 55.4	29.8	149 07.7	22.0	Deneb	49 31.4	N45 19.8
03	7 56.6	271 32.0	.. 56.9	165 49.9	.. 35.2	296 57.5	.. 29.9	164 10.0	.. 22.1	Denebola	182 34.5	N14 30.1
04	22 59.1	286 31.9	57.0	180 50.9	35.8	311 59.6	29.9	179 12.3	22.2	Diphda	348 56.2	S17 54.8
05	38 01.6	301 31.9	57.0	195 52.0	36.4	327 01.6	30.0	194 14.6	22.3			
06	53 04.0	316 31.8	N19 57.1	210 53.0	S 9 37.0	342 03.7	N21 30.0	209 16.9	S 7 22.3	Dubhe	193 53.0	N61 41.0
07	68 06.5	331 31.7	57.2	225 54.0	37.6	357 05.8	30.0	224 19.2	22.4	Elnath	278 13.5	N28 36.9
T 08	83 09.0	346 31.7	57.2	240 55.0	38.2	12 07.9	30.1	239 21.5	22.5	Eltanin	90 46.1	N51 29.6
U 09	98 11.4	1 31.6	.. 57.3	255 56.0	.. 38.8	27 09.9	.. 30.1	254 23.8	.. 22.6	Enif	33 47.3	N 9 56.2
E 10	113 13.9	16 31.5	57.4	270 57.0	39.4	42 12.0	30.2	269 26.1	22.6	Fomalhaut	15 24.3	S29 33.0
S 11	128 16.3	31 31.5	57.4	285 58.0	40.0	57 14.1	30.2	284 28.4	22.7			
D 12	143 18.8	46 31.4	N19 57.5	300 59.0	S 9 40.6	72 16.2	N21 30.3	299 30.7	S 7 22.8	Gacrux	172 01.9	S57 11.3
A 13	158 21.3	61 31.3	57.6	316 00.0	41.2	87 18.3	30.3	314 32.9	22.9	Gienah	175 53.1	S17 36.8
Y 14	173 23.7	76 31.3	57.6	331 01.0	41.8	102 20.3	30.4	329 35.2	23.0	Hadar	148 48.9	S60 26.3
15	188 26.2	91 31.2	.. 57.7	346 02.1	.. 42.4	117 22.4	.. 30.4	344 37.5	.. 23.0	Hamal	328 01.3	N23 31.3
16	203 28.7	106 31.1	57.7	1 03.1	43.0	132 24.5	30.4	359 39.8	23.1	Kaus Aust.	83 44.3	S34 22.6
17	218 31.1	121 31.1	57.8	16 04.1	43.7	147 26.6	30.5	14 42.1	23.2			
18	233 33.6	136 31.0	N19 57.8	31 05.1	S 9 44.3	162 28.7	N21 30.5	29 44.4	S 7 23.3	Kochab	137 20.1	N74 06.5
19	248 36.1	151 30.9	57.9	46 06.1	44.9	177 30.7	30.6	44 46.7	23.3	Markab	13 38.6	N15 16.6
20	263 38.5	166 30.9	58.0	61 07.1	45.5	192 32.8	30.6	59 49.0	23.4	Menkar	314 15.6	N 4 08.4
21	278 41.0	181 30.8	.. 58.0	76 08.1	.. 46.1	207 34.9	.. 30.7	74 51.3	.. 23.5	Menkent	148 08.3	S36 26.0
22	293 43.5	196 30.7	58.1	91 09.1	46.7	222 37.0	30.7	89 53.6	23.6	Miaplacidus	221 40.7	S69 46.2
23	308 45.9	211 30.6	58.1	106 10.1	47.3	237 39.1	30.8	104 55.8	23.6			
15 00	323 48.4	226 30.6	N19 58.2	121 11.1	S 9 47.9	252 41.1	N21 30.8	119 58.1	S 7 23.7	Mirfak	308 41.2	N49 54.1
01	338 50.8	241 30.5	58.2	136 12.1	48.5	267 43.2	30.9	135 00.4	23.8	Nunki	75 58.7	S26 16.7
02	353 53.3	256 30.4	58.3	151 13.1	49.1	282 45.3	30.9	150 02.7	23.9	Peacock	53 19.5	S56 41.5
03	8 55.8	271 30.3	.. 58.3	166 14.1	.. 49.7	297 47.4	.. 30.9	165 05.0	.. 24.0	Pollux	243 28.7	N27 59.6
04	23 58.2	286 30.2	58.4	181 15.2	50.3	312 49.5	31.0	180 07.3	24.0	Procyon	245 00.6	N 5 11.5
05	39 00.7	301 30.2	58.4	196 16.2	50.9	327 51.5	31.0	195 09.6	24.1			
06	54 03.2	316 30.1	N19 58.5	211 17.2	S 9 51.5	342 53.6	N21 31.1	210 11.9	S 7 24.2	Rasalhague	96 06.8	N12 33.3
W 07	69 05.6	331 30.0	58.5	226 18.2	52.1	357 55.7	31.1	225 14.2	24.3	Regulus	207 44.4	N11 54.3
E 08	84 08.1	346 29.9	58.6	241 19.2	52.7	12 57.8	31.2	240 16.4	24.3	Rigel	281 12.7	S 8 11.2
D 09	99 10.6	1 29.8	.. 58.6	256 20.2	.. 53.3	27 59.9	.. 31.2	255 18.7	.. 24.4	Rigil Kent.	139 52.6	S60 53.4
N 10	114 13.0	16 29.7	58.7	271 21.2	53.9	43 02.0	31.3	270 21.0	24.5	Sabik	102 13.0	S15 44.3
E 11	129 15.5	31 29.7	58.7	286 22.2	54.5	58 04.0	31.3	285 23.3	24.6			
S 12	144 18.0	46 29.6	N19 58.8	301 23.2	S 9 55.1	73 06.1	N21 31.3	300 25.6	S 7 24.7	Schedar	349 40.8	N56 36.3
D 13	159 20.4	61 29.5	58.8	316 24.2	55.7	88 08.2	31.4	315 27.9	24.7	Shaula	96 22.4	S37 06.7
A 14	174 22.9	76 29.4	58.9	331 25.2	56.3	103 10.3	31.4	330 30.2	24.8	Sirius	258 34.5	S16 44.0
Y 15	189 25.3	91 29.3	.. 58.9	346 26.2	.. 56.9	118 12.4	.. 31.5	345 32.5	.. 24.9	Spica	158 32.0	S11 13.6
16	204 27.8	106 29.2	59.0	1 27.2	57.5	133 14.5	31.5	0 34.7	25.0	Suhail	222 53.3	S43 29.1
17	219 30.3	121 29.1	59.0	16 28.2	58.1	148 16.5	31.6	15 37.0	25.0			
18	234 32.7	136 29.0	N19 59.1	31 29.2	S 9 58.7	163 18.6	N21 31.6	30 39.3	S 7 25.1	Vega	80 39.0	N38 48.1
19	249 35.2	151 28.9	59.1	46 30.2	59.3	178 20.7	31.6	45 41.6	25.2	Zuben'ubi	137 06.1	S16 05.6
20	264 37.7	166 28.8	59.1	61 31.2	9 59.9	193 22.8	31.7	60 43.9	25.3		SHA	Mer.Pass.
21	279 40.1	181 28.8	.. 59.2	76 32.2	10 00.5	208 24.9	.. 31.7	75 46.2	.. 25.4		° ′	h m
22	294 42.6	196 28.7	59.2	91 33.2	01.1	223 27.0	31.8	90 48.5	25.4	Venus	263 42.9	8 54
23	309 45.5	211 28.6	59.3	106 34.2	01.7	238 29.1	31.8	105 50.7	25.5	Mars	157 57.6	15 56
	h m									Jupiter	289 02.0	7 12
Mer.Pass. 2 28.3	v −0.1 d 0.1			v 1.0 d 0.6		v 2.1 d 0.0		v 2.3 d 0.1		Saturn	156 13.9	16 01

UT	SUN GHA	SUN Dec	MOON GHA	MOON v	MOON Dec	MOON d	MOON HP
d h	° ′	° ′	° ′	′	° ′	′	′
13 00	178 47.1	N14 36.3	236 25.2	11.0	N21 19.2	1.5	54.8
01	193 47.3	35.5	250 55.2	10.9	21 17.7	1.6	54.8
02	208 47.4	34.8	265 25.1	11.0	21 16.1	1.8	54.8
03	223 47.5	.. 34.0	279 55.1	10.9	21 14.3	1.8	54.8
04	238 47.6	33.3	294 25.0	11.0	21 12.5	2.0	54.9
05	253 47.7	32.5	308 55.0	10.9	21 10.5	2.0	54.9
M 06	268 47.8	N14 31.7	323 24.9	10.9	N21 08.5	2.2	54.9
O 07	283 47.9	31.0	337 54.8	10.9	21 06.3	2.2	54.9
N 08	298 48.0	30.2	352 24.7	10.9	21 04.1	2.4	54.9
D 09	313 48.2	.. 29.4	6 54.6	10.9	21 01.7	2.5	54.9
A 10	328 48.3	28.7	21 24.5	10.9	20 59.2	2.6	55.0
Y 11	343 48.4	27.9	35 54.4	10.9	20 56.6	2.6	55.0
12	358 48.5	N14 27.1	50 24.3	10.9	N20 54.0	2.8	55.0
13	13 48.6	26.4	64 54.2	10.9	20 51.2	2.9	55.0
14	28 48.7	25.6	79 24.1	10.8	20 48.3	3.0	55.0
15	43 48.8	.. 24.8	93 53.9	10.9	20 45.3	3.1	55.1
16	58 49.0	24.0	108 23.8	10.9	20 42.2	3.2	55.1
17	73 49.1	23.3	122 53.7	10.8	20 39.0	3.3	55.1
18	88 49.2	N14 22.5	137 23.5	10.9	N20 35.7	3.4	55.1
19	103 49.3	21.7	151 53.4	10.8	20 32.3	3.6	55.1
20	118 49.4	21.0	166 23.2	10.9	20 28.7	3.6	55.2
21	133 49.5	.. 20.2	180 53.1	10.8	20 25.1	3.7	55.2
22	148 49.7	19.4	195 22.9	10.9	20 21.4	3.8	55.2
23	163 49.8	18.6	209 52.8	10.8	20 17.6	4.0	55.2
14 00	178 49.9	N14 17.9	224 22.6	10.9	N20 13.6	4.0	55.2
01	193 50.0	17.1	238 52.5	10.8	20 09.6	4.2	55.3
02	208 50.1	16.3	253 22.3	10.9	20 05.4	4.2	55.3
03	223 50.2	.. 15.6	267 52.2	10.8	20 01.2	4.4	55.3
04	238 50.4	14.8	282 22.0	10.9	19 56.8	4.4	55.3
05	253 50.5	14.0	296 51.9	10.9	19 52.4	4.6	55.4
T 06	268 50.6	N14 13.2	311 21.8	10.8	N19 47.8	4.6	55.4
U 07	283 50.7	12.5	325 51.6	10.9	19 43.2	4.8	55.4
E 08	298 50.8	11.7	340 21.5	10.8	19 38.4	4.8	55.4
S 09	313 51.0	.. 10.9	354 51.3	10.9	19 33.6	5.0	55.4
D 10	328 51.1	10.1	9 21.2	10.9	19 28.6	5.0	55.5
A 11	343 51.2	09.4	23 51.1	10.9	19 23.6	5.2	55.5
Y 12	358 51.3	N14 08.6	38 21.0	10.8	N19 18.4	5.3	55.5
13	13 51.4	07.8	52 50.8	10.9	19 13.1	5.3	55.5
14	28 51.6	07.0	67 20.7	10.9	19 07.8	5.5	55.6
15	43 51.7	.. 06.2	81 50.6	10.9	19 02.3	5.6	55.6
16	58 51.8	05.5	96 20.5	10.9	18 56.7	5.6	55.6
17	73 51.9	04.7	110 50.4	10.9	18 51.1	5.8	55.6
18	88 52.0	N14 03.9	125 20.3	11.0	N18 45.3	5.9	55.7
19	103 52.1	03.1	139 50.3	10.9	18 39.4	5.9	55.7
20	118 52.3	02.3	154 20.2	10.9	18 33.5	6.1	55.7
21	133 52.4	.. 01.6	168 50.1	11.0	18 27.4	6.1	55.7
22	148 52.5	00.8	183 20.1	10.9	18 21.3	6.3	55.7
23	163 52.7	14 00.0	197 50.0	11.0	18 15.0	6.3	55.8
15 00	178 52.8	N13 59.2	212 20.0	10.9	N18 08.7	6.5	55.8
01	193 52.9	58.4	226 49.9	11.0	18 02.2	6.5	55.8
02	208 53.0	57.6	241 19.9	11.0	17 55.7	6.7	55.8
03	223 53.1	.. 56.9	255 49.9	11.0	17 49.0	6.7	55.9
04	238 53.3	56.1	270 19.9	11.0	17 42.3	6.8	55.9
05	253 53.4	55.3	284 49.9	11.0	17 35.5	7.0	55.9
W 06	268 53.5	N13 54.5	299 19.9	11.0	N17 28.5	7.0	55.9
E 07	283 53.6	53.7	313 49.9	11.1	17 21.5	7.1	56.0
D 08	298 53.8	52.9	328 20.0	11.0	17 14.4	7.2	56.0
N 09	313 53.9	.. 52.2	342 50.0	11.1	17 07.2	7.3	56.0
E 10	328 54.0	51.4	357 20.1	11.0	16 59.9	7.4	56.0
S 11	343 54.1	50.6	11 50.1	11.1	16 52.5	7.5	56.1
D 12	358 54.3	N13 49.8	26 20.2	11.1	N16 45.0	7.5	56.1
A 13	13 54.4	49.0	40 50.3	11.1	16 37.5	7.7	56.1
Y 14	28 54.5	48.2	55 20.4	11.1	16 29.8	7.8	56.1
15	43 54.6	.. 47.4	69 50.5	11.1	16 22.0	7.8	56.2
16	58 54.8	46.7	84 20.6	11.2	16 14.2	7.9	56.2
17	73 54.9	45.9	98 50.8	11.1	16 06.3	8.0	56.2
18	88 55.0	N13 45.1	113 20.9	11.2	N15 58.3	8.2	56.3
19	103 55.2	44.3	127 51.1	11.1	15 50.1	8.1	56.3
20	118 55.3	43.5	142 21.2	11.2	15 42.0	8.3	56.3
21	133 55.4	.. 42.7	156 51.4	11.2	15 33.7	8.4	56.3
22	148 55.5	41.9	171 21.6	11.2	15 25.3	8.5	56.4
23	163 55.7	41.1	185 51.8	11.2	N15 16.8	8.5	56.4
	SD 15.8	d 0.8	SD 15.0		15.1		15.3

Twilight / Sunrise / Moonrise

Lat.	Twilight Naut.	Twilight Civil	Sunrise	Moonrise 13	14	15	16
°	h m	h m	h m	h m	h m	h m	h m
N 72	////	////	02 20	▭	▭		01 01
N 70	////	////	02 53	▭	23 35	25 36	01 36
68	////	01 38	03 17	22 37	24 17	00 17	02 00
66	////	02 18	03 35	23 19	24 45	00 45	02 19
64	////	02 44	03 50	23 47	25 07	01 07	02 34
62	01 27	03 04	04 02	24 09	00 09	01 24	02 47
60	02 03	03 21	04 13	24 26	00 26	01 38	02 57
N 58	02 28	03 34	04 22	24 41	00 41	01 51	03 07
56	02 47	03 46	04 30	24 53	00 53	02 01	03 15
54	03 02	03 56	04 37	00 05	01 04	02 10	03 22
52	03 15	04 05	04 43	00 16	01 14	02 18	03 28
50	03 27	04 12	04 49	00 25	01 22	02 26	03 34
45	03 49	04 29	05 01	00 45	01 41	02 42	03 46
N 40	04 06	04 42	05 11	01 01	01 55	02 55	03 57
35	04 20	04 53	05 19	01 14	02 08	03 05	04 05
30	04 32	05 02	05 27	01 26	02 19	03 15	04 13
20	04 50	05 17	05 40	01 46	02 38	03 31	04 26
N 10	05 04	05 29	05 51	02 03	02 54	03 46	04 38
0	05 15	05 40	06 01	02 19	03 09	03 59	04 49
S 10	05 25	05 50	06 11	02 36	03 25	04 12	04 59
20	05 33	05 59	06 22	02 53	03 41	04 27	05 11
30	05 41	06 10	06 34	03 13	03 59	04 43	05 24
35	05 45	06 15	06 41	03 25	04 10	04 52	05 31
40	05 49	06 21	06 49	03 38	04 23	05 03	05 40
45	05 53	06 28	06 58	03 54	04 37	05 16	05 50
S 50	05 57	06 35	07 09	04 14	04 55	05 31	06 02
52	05 59	06 39	07 14	04 23	05 04	05 38	06 07
54	06 01	06 43	07 20	04 33	05 13	05 46	06 13
56	06 03	06 47	07 26	04 45	05 24	05 55	06 20
58	06 05	06 51	07 33	04 59	05 36	06 05	06 28
S 60	06 07	06 56	07 41	05 14	05 50	06 16	06 36

Sunset / Twilight / Moonset

Lat.	Sunset	Twilight Civil	Twilight Naut.	Moonset 13	14	15	16
°	h m	h m	h m	h m	h m	h m	h m
N 72	21 44	////	////	▭	▭	20 26	20 00
N 70	21 12	23 56	////	▭	20 08	19 51	19 40
68	20 49	22 24	////	19 22	19 25	19 25	19 24
66	20 31	21 47	////	18 39	18 56	19 05	19 11
64	20 17	21 22	23 57	18 11	18 34	18 49	19 00
62	20 05	21 02	22 35	17 49	18 16	18 36	18 51
60	19 55	20 46	22 02	17 31	18 02	18 25	18 43
N 58	19 46	20 33	21 39	17 16	17 49	18 15	18 36
56	19 38	20 22	21 20	17 03	17 38	18 06	18 29
54	19 31	20 12	21 05	16 52	17 29	17 58	18 24
52	19 25	20 03	20 52	16 42	17 20	17 52	18 19
50	19 20	19 56	20 41	16 34	17 12	17 45	18 14
45	19 08	19 39	20 19	16 15	16 56	17 32	18 04
N 40	18 58	19 27	20 02	16 00	16 42	17 21	17 56
35	18 49	19 16	19 48	15 47	16 31	17 11	17 49
30	18 42	19 07	19 37	15 36	16 20	17 03	17 42
20	18 29	18 52	19 19	15 16	16 03	16 48	17 31
N 10	18 18	18 40	19 05	14 59	15 48	16 35	17 21
0	18 08	18 29	18 54	14 43	15 33	16 23	17 12
S 10	17 58	18 19	18 44	14 28	15 19	16 11	17 03
20	17 47	18 10	18 36	14 10	15 03	15 58	16 53
30	17 35	18 00	18 30	13 51	14 46	15 43	16 41
35	17 28	17 54	18 24	13 39	14 35	15 34	16 35
40	17 21	17 49	18 21	13 26	14 23	15 24	16 27
45	17 11	17 42	18 17	13 11	14 09	15 12	16 18
S 50	17 01	17 34	18 13	12 51	13 52	14 58	16 08
52	16 56	17 31	18 11	12 42	13 44	14 51	16 03
54	16 50	17 27	18 09	12 32	13 35	14 44	15 57
56	16 44	17 23	18 07	12 20	13 24	14 35	15 51
58	16 37	17 19	18 05	12 07	13 13	14 26	15 44
S 60	16 29	17 14	18 03	11 51	12 59	14 15	15 36

SUN / MOON

Day	Eqn. of Time 00ʰ	Eqn. of Time 12ʰ	Mer. Pass.	Mer. Pass. Upper	Mer. Pass. Lower	Age	Phase
d	m s	m s	h m	h m	h m	d	%
13	04 52	04 46	12 05	08 31	20 56	25	18
14	04 41	04 35	12 05	09 21	21 46	26	11
15	04 29	04 23	12 04	10 11	22 36	27	5

UT	ARIES GHA	VENUS −4.4 GHA	Dec	MARS +1.1 GHA	Dec	JUPITER −2.2 GHA	Dec	SATURN +0.8 GHA	Dec	STARS Name	SHA	Dec
16 00	324 47.5	226 28.5	N19 59.3	121 35.2	S10 02.3	253 31.1	N21 31.9	120 53.0	S 7 25.6	Acamar	315 18.7	S40 15.0
01	339 50.0	241 28.4	59.3	136 36.2	02.9	268 33.2	31.9	135 55.3	25.7	Achernar	335 26.9	S57 10.0
02	354 52.4	256 28.3	59.4	151 37.2	03.5	283 35.3	32.0	150 57.6	25.7	Acrux	173 10.4	S63 10.4
03	9 54.9	271 28.2	.. 59.4	166 38.2	.. 04.1	298 37.4	.. 32.0	165 59.9	.. 25.8	Adhara	255 13.2	S28 59.3
04	24 57.4	286 28.1	59.4	181 39.2	04.7	313 39.5	32.0	181 02.2	25.9	Aldebaran	290 50.1	N16 32.0
05	39 59.8	301 28.0	59.5	196 40.2	05.3	328 41.6	32.1	196 04.5	26.0			
06	55 02.3	316 27.9	N19 59.5	211 41.2	S10 05.9	343 43.7	N21 32.1	211 06.7	S 7 26.1	Alioth	166 21.5	N55 53.7
07	70 04.8	331 27.8	59.5	226 42.2	06.5	358 45.8	32.2	226 09.0	26.1	Alkaid	152 59.5	N49 15.3
T 08	85 07.2	346 27.7	59.6	241 43.2	07.2	13 47.8	32.2	241 11.3	26.2	Al Na'ir	27 43.9	S46 53.7
H 09	100 09.7	1 27.6	.. 59.6	256 44.2	.. 07.8	28 49.9	.. 32.3	256 13.6	.. 26.3	Alnilam	275 47.1	S 1 11.6
U 10	115 12.2	16 27.5	59.6	271 45.2	08.4	43 52.0	32.3	271 15.9	26.4	Alphard	217 57.0	S 8 42.9
R 11	130 14.6	31 27.3	59.7	286 46.2	09.0	58 54.1	32.3	286 18.2	26.5			
S 12	145 17.1	46 27.2	N19 59.7	301 47.2	S10 09.6	73 56.2	N21 32.4	301 20.5	S 7 26.5	Alphecca	126 11.5	N26 40.6
D 13	160 19.6	61 27.1	59.7	316 48.2	10.2	88 58.3	32.4	316 22.7	26.6	Alpheratz	357 43.8	N29 09.7
A 14	175 22.0	76 27.0	59.8	331 49.2	10.8	104 00.4	32.5	331 25.0	26.7	Altair	62 08.5	N 8 54.4
Y 15	190 24.5	91 26.9	.. 59.8	346 50.2	.. 11.4	119 02.5	.. 32.5	346 27.3	.. 26.8	Ankaa	353 15.9	S42 13.9
16	205 26.9	106 26.8	59.8	1 51.2	12.0	134 04.6	32.6	1 29.6	26.8	Antares	112 26.8	S26 27.6
17	220 29.4	121 26.7	59.9	16 52.2	12.6	149 06.6	32.6	16 31.9	26.9			
18	235 31.9	136 26.6	N19 59.9	31 53.2	S10 13.2	164 08.7	N21 32.6	31 34.2	S 7 27.0	Arcturus	145 56.3	N19 07.2
19	250 34.3	151 26.5	59.9	46 54.2	13.8	179 10.8	32.7	46 36.4	27.1	Atria	107 28.9	S69 03.2
20	265 36.8	166 26.4	19 59.9	61 55.1	14.4	194 12.9	32.7	61 38.7	27.2	Avior	234 18.8	S59 33.0
21	280 39.3	181 26.2	20 00.0	76 56.1	.. 15.0	209 15.0	.. 32.8	76 41.0	.. 27.2	Bellatrix	278 32.8	N 6 21.6
22	295 41.7	196 26.1	00.0	91 57.1	15.6	224 17.1	32.8	91 43.3	27.3	Betelgeuse	271 02.1	N 7 24.5
23	310 44.2	211 26.0	00.0	106 58.1	16.2	239 19.2	32.9	106 45.6	27.4			
17 00	325 46.7	226 25.9	N20 00.0	121 59.1	S10 16.8	254 21.3	N21 32.9	121 47.9	S 7 27.5	Canopus	263 56.8	S52 42.0
01	340 49.1	241 25.8	00.0	137 00.1	17.4	269 23.4	32.9	136 50.1	27.6	Capella	280 35.5	N46 00.4
02	355 51.6	256 25.7	00.1	152 01.1	18.0	284 25.5	33.0	151 52.4	27.6	Deneb	49 31.4	N45 19.8
03	10 54.1	271 25.5	.. 00.1	167 02.1	.. 18.6	299 27.6	.. 33.0	166 54.7	.. 27.7	Denebola	182 34.5	N14 30.1
04	25 56.5	286 25.4	00.1	182 03.1	19.2	314 29.7	33.1	181 57.0	27.8	Diphda	348 56.2	S17 54.8
05	40 59.0	301 25.3	00.1	197 04.1	19.8	329 31.8	33.1	196 59.3	27.9			
06	56 01.4	316 25.2	N20 00.1	212 05.1	S10 20.4	344 33.8	N21 33.2	212 01.6	S 7 28.0	Dubhe	193 53.0	N61 41.0
07	71 03.9	331 25.1	00.2	227 06.1	21.0	359 35.9	33.2	227 03.8	28.0	Elnath	278 13.5	N28 36.9
08	86 06.4	346 24.9	00.2	242 07.1	21.6	14 38.0	33.2	242 06.1	28.1	Eltanin	90 46.1	N51 29.6
F 09	101 08.8	1 24.8	.. 00.2	257 08.0	.. 22.2	29 40.1	.. 33.3	257 08.4	.. 28.2	Enif	33 47.3	N 9 56.2
R 10	116 11.3	16 24.7	00.2	272 09.0	22.8	44 42.2	33.3	272 10.7	28.3	Fomalhaut	15 24.2	S29 33.0
I 11	131 13.8	31 24.6	00.2	287 10.0	23.4	59 44.3	33.4	287 13.0	28.4			
D 12	146 16.2	46 24.4	N20 00.2	302 11.0	S10 24.0	74 46.4	N21 33.4	302 15.3	S 7 28.4	Gacrux	172 01.9	S57 11.3
A 13	161 18.7	61 24.3	00.3	317 12.0	24.6	89 48.5	33.4	317 17.5	28.5	Gienah	175 53.1	S17 36.8
Y 14	176 21.2	76 24.2	00.3	332 13.0	25.2	104 50.6	33.5	332 19.8	28.6	Hadar	148 48.9	S60 26.3
15	191 23.6	91 24.1	.. 00.3	347 14.0	.. 25.8	119 52.7	.. 33.5	347 22.1	.. 28.7	Hamal	328 01.2	N23 31.3
16	206 26.1	106 23.9	00.3	2 15.0	26.4	134 54.8	33.6	2 24.4	28.8	Kaus Aust.	83 44.3	S34 22.6
17	221 28.5	121 23.8	00.3	17 16.0	27.0	149 56.9	33.6	17 26.7	28.8			
18	236 31.0	136 23.7	N20 00.3	32 17.0	S10 27.6	164 59.0	N21 33.7	32 28.9	S 7 28.9	Kochab	137 20.2	N74 06.5
19	251 33.5	151 23.5	00.3	47 17.9	28.2	180 01.1	33.7	47 31.2	29.0	Markab	13 38.6	N15 16.6
20	266 35.9	166 23.4	00.3	62 18.9	28.8	195 03.2	33.7	62 33.5	29.1	Menkar	314 15.6	N 4 08.4
21	281 38.4	181 23.3	.. 00.3	77 19.9	.. 29.4	210 05.3	.. 33.8	77 35.8	.. 29.2	Menkent	148 08.4	S36 26.0
22	296 40.9	196 23.1	00.4	92 20.9	30.0	225 07.4	33.8	92 38.1	29.2	Miaplacidus	221 40.7	S69 46.2
23	311 43.3	211 23.0	00.4	107 21.9	30.6	240 09.5	33.9	107 40.3	29.3			
18 00	326 45.8	226 22.9	N20 00.4	122 22.9	S10 31.2	255 11.6	N21 33.9	122 42.6	S 7 29.4	Mirfak	308 41.1	N49 54.1
01	341 48.3	241 22.7	00.4	137 23.9	31.8	270 13.7	33.9	137 44.9	29.5	Nunki	75 58.7	S26 16.7
02	356 50.7	256 22.6	00.4	152 24.8	32.4	285 15.8	34.0	152 47.2	29.6	Peacock	53 19.5	S56 41.5
03	11 53.2	271 22.5	.. 00.4	167 25.8	.. 33.0	300 17.9	.. 34.0	167 49.5	.. 29.6	Pollux	243 28.7	N27 59.6
04	26 55.7	286 22.3	00.4	182 26.8	33.6	315 20.0	34.1	182 51.7	29.7	Procyon	245 00.6	N 5 11.5
05	41 58.1	301 22.2	00.4	197 27.8	34.2	330 22.1	34.1	197 54.0	29.8			
06	57 00.6	316 22.0	N20 00.4	212 28.8	S10 34.8	345 24.2	N21 34.2	212 56.3	S 7 29.9	Rasalhague	96 06.8	N12 33.3
S 07	72 03.0	331 21.9	00.4	227 29.8	35.4	0 26.3	34.2	227 58.6	30.0	Regulus	207 44.4	N11 54.3
A 08	87 05.5	346 21.8	00.4	242 30.8	36.0	15 28.4	34.2	243 00.9	30.0	Rigel	281 12.7	S 8 11.2
T 09	102 08.0	1 21.6	.. 00.4	257 31.7	.. 36.6	30 30.5	.. 34.3	258 03.1	.. 30.1	Rigil Kent.	139 52.6	S60 53.4
U 10	117 10.4	16 21.5	00.4	272 32.7	37.2	45 32.6	34.3	273 05.4	30.2	Sabik	102 13.0	S15 44.3
R 11	132 12.9	31 21.3	00.4	287 33.7	37.8	60 34.7	34.4	288 07.7	30.3			
D 12	147 15.4	46 21.2	N20 00.4	302 34.7	S10 38.4	75 36.8	N21 34.4	303 10.0	S 7 30.4	Schedar	349 40.7	N56 36.3
A 13	162 17.8	61 21.0	00.4	317 35.7	39.0	90 38.9	34.4	318 12.3	30.4	Shaula	96 22.5	S37 06.7
Y 14	177 20.3	76 20.9	00.4	332 36.7	39.6	105 41.0	34.5	333 14.5	30.5	Sirius	258 34.4	S16 44.0
15	192 22.8	91 20.8	.. 00.4	347 37.6	.. 40.2	120 43.1	.. 34.5	348 16.8	.. 30.6	Spica	158 32.0	S11 13.6
16	207 25.2	106 20.6	00.4	2 38.6	40.8	135 45.2	34.6	3 19.1	30.7	Suhail	222 53.3	S43 29.1
17	222 27.7	121 20.5	00.4	17 39.6	41.4	150 47.3	34.6	18 21.4	30.8			
18	237 30.1	136 20.3	N20 00.4	32 40.6	S10 42.0	165 49.4	N21 34.6	33 23.6	S 7 30.8	Vega	80 39.0	N38 48.1
19	252 32.6	151 20.2	00.4	47 41.6	42.6	180 51.5	34.7	48 25.9	30.9	Zuben'ubi	137 06.1	S16 05.6
20	267 35.1	166 20.0	00.4	62 42.5	43.2	195 53.6	34.7	63 28.2	31.0		SHA	Mer. Pass.
21	282 37.5	181 19.9	.. 00.3	77 43.5	.. 43.8	210 55.7	.. 34.8	78 30.5	.. 31.1	Venus	260 39.2	h m 15
22	297 40.0	196 19.7	00.3	92 44.5	44.4	225 57.8	34.8	93 32.8	31.2	Mars	156 12.5	15 51
23	312 42.5	211 19.6	00.3	107 45.5	45.0	240 59.9	34.8	108 35.0	31.2	Jupiter	288 34.6	7 02
Mer. Pass.	h m 2 16.5	v −0.1	d 0.0	v 1.0	d 0.6	v 2.1	d 0.0	v 2.3	d 0.1	Saturn	156 01.2	15 50

UT	SUN GHA	SUN Dec	MOON GHA	v	MOON Dec	d	HP
d h	° ′	° ′	° ′	′	° ′	′	′
16 00	178 55.8	N13 40.3	200 22.0	11.3	N15 08.3	8.6	56.4
01	193 55.9	39.5	214 52.3	11.2	14 59.7	8.7	56.4
02	208 56.0	38.7	229 22.5	11.2	14 51.0	8.8	56.5
03	223 56.2	.. 38.0	243 52.7	11.3	14 42.2	8.9	56.5
04	238 56.3	37.2	258 23.0	11.3	14 33.3	8.9	56.5
05	253 56.4	36.4	272 53.3	11.3	14 24.4	9.1	56.5
T 06	268 56.6	N13 35.6	287 23.6	11.3	N14 15.3	9.1	56.6
H 07	283 56.7	34.8	301 53.9	11.3	14 06.2	9.2	56.6
U 08	298 56.8	34.0	316 24.2	11.3	13 57.0	9.2	56.6
R 09	313 57.0	.. 33.2	330 54.5	11.4	13 47.8	9.4	56.6
S 10	328 57.1	32.4	345 24.9	11.3	13 38.4	9.4	56.7
D 11	343 57.2	31.6	359 55.2	11.4	13 29.0	9.5	56.7
A 12	358 57.3	N13 30.8	14 25.6	11.3	N13 19.5	9.6	56.7
Y 13	13 57.5	30.0	28 55.9	11.4	13 09.9	9.7	56.7
14	28 57.6	29.2	43 26.3	11.4	13 00.2	9.7	56.8
15	43 57.7	.. 28.4	57 56.7	11.4	12 50.5	9.8	56.8
16	58 57.9	27.6	72 27.1	11.4	12 40.7	9.9	56.8
17	73 58.0	26.8	86 57.5	11.4	12 30.8	9.9	56.9
18	88 58.1	N13 26.0	101 27.9	11.5	N12 20.9	10.0	56.9
19	103 58.3	25.2	115 58.4	11.4	12 10.9	10.1	56.9
20	118 58.4	24.4	130 28.8	11.5	12 00.8	10.2	56.9
21	133 58.5	.. 23.6	144 59.3	11.4	11 50.6	10.2	57.0
22	148 58.7	22.8	159 29.7	11.5	11 40.4	10.3	57.0
23	163 58.8	22.0	174 00.2	11.5	11 30.1	10.4	57.0
17 00	178 58.9	N13 21.2	188 30.7	11.5	N11 19.7	10.4	57.0
01	193 59.1	20.4	203 01.2	11.5	11 09.3	10.5	57.1
02	208 59.2	19.6	217 31.7	11.5	10 58.8	10.6	57.1
03	223 59.3	.. 18.8	232 02.2	11.5	10 48.2	10.6	57.1
04	238 59.5	18.0	246 32.7	11.5	10 37.6	10.7	57.1
05	253 59.6	17.2	261 03.2	11.6	10 26.9	10.7	57.2
06	268 59.7	N13 16.4	275 33.8	11.5	N10 16.2	10.9	57.2
F 07	283 59.9	15.6	290 04.3	11.6	10 05.3	10.8	57.2
R 08	299 00.0	14.8	304 34.9	11.5	9 54.5	11.0	57.2
I 09	314 00.1	.. 14.0	319 05.4	11.6	9 43.5	10.9	57.3
D 10	329 00.3	13.2	333 36.0	11.6	9 32.6	11.1	57.3
A 11	344 00.4	12.4	348 06.6	11.5	9 21.5	11.1	57.3
Y 12	359 00.6	N13 11.6	2 37.1	11.6	N 9 10.4	11.2	57.3
13	14 00.7	10.8	17 07.7	11.6	8 59.2	11.2	57.4
14	29 00.8	10.0	31 38.3	11.6	8 48.0	11.2	57.4
15	44 01.0	.. 09.2	46 08.9	11.6	8 36.8	11.4	57.4
16	59 01.1	08.4	60 39.5	11.6	8 25.4	11.3	57.4
17	74 01.2	07.6	75 10.1	11.6	8 14.1	11.5	57.5
18	89 01.4	N13 06.8	89 40.7	11.6	N 8 02.6	11.5	57.5
19	104 01.5	06.0	104 11.3	11.6	7 51.1	11.5	57.5
20	119 01.7	05.2	118 41.9	11.6	7 39.6	11.6	57.5
21	134 01.8	.. 04.3	133 12.5	11.6	7 28.0	11.6	57.6
22	149 01.9	03.5	147 43.1	11.6	7 16.4	11.6	57.6
23	164 02.1	02.7	162 13.7	11.6	7 04.8	11.8	57.6
18 00	179 02.2	N13 01.9	176 44.3	11.6	N 6 53.0	11.7	57.6
01	194 02.3	01.1	191 14.9	11.6	6 41.3	11.8	57.7
02	209 02.5	13 00.3	205 45.5	11.6	6 29.5	11.9	57.7
03	224 02.6	12 59.5	220 16.1	11.6	6 17.6	11.8	57.7
04	239 02.8	58.7	234 46.7	11.6	6 05.8	12.0	57.7
05	254 02.9	57.9	249 17.3	11.6	5 53.8	11.9	57.7
S 06	269 03.0	N12 57.1	263 47.9	11.6	N 5 41.9	12.0	57.8
A 07	284 03.2	56.3	278 18.5	11.6	5 29.9	12.1	57.8
T 08	299 03.3	55.4	292 49.1	11.6	5 17.8	12.0	57.8
U 09	314 03.5	.. 54.6	307 19.7	11.6	5 05.8	12.1	57.8
R 10	329 03.6	53.8	321 50.3	11.6	4 53.7	12.2	57.9
D 11	344 03.7	53.0	336 20.9	11.6	4 41.5	12.2	57.9
A 12	359 03.9	N12 52.2	350 51.5	11.6	N 4 29.3	12.2	57.9
Y 13	14 04.0	51.4	5 22.1	11.5	4 17.1	12.2	57.9
14	29 04.2	50.6	19 52.6	11.6	4 04.9	12.3	57.9
15	44 04.3	.. 49.7	34 23.2	11.5	3 52.6	12.3	58.0
16	59 04.5	48.9	48 53.7	11.6	3 40.3	12.3	58.0
17	74 04.6	48.1	63 24.3	11.5	3 28.0	12.4	58.0
18	89 04.7	N12 47.3	77 54.8	11.5	N 3 15.6	12.3	58.0
19	104 04.9	46.5	92 25.3	11.6	3 03.3	12.4	58.1
20	119 05.0	45.7	106 55.9	11.5	2 50.9	12.4	58.1
21	134 05.2	.. 44.9	121 26.4	11.4	2 38.5	12.5	58.1
22	149 05.3	44.0	135 56.8	11.5	2 26.0	12.5	58.1
23	164 05.5	43.2	150 27.3	11.5	N 2 13.5	12.4	58.1
	SD 15.8	d 0.8	SD 15.5		15.6		15.8

Lat.	Twilight Naut.	Civil	Sunrise	Moonrise 16	17	18	19
°	h m	h m	h m	h m	h m	h m	h m
N 72	////	////	02 40	01 01	03 11	05 11	07 10
N 70	////	01 04	03 08	01 36	03 29	05 20	07 10
68	////	02 01	03 29	02 00	03 44	05 27	07 11
66	////	02 33	03 46	02 19	03 55	05 33	07 11
64	00 57	02 56	03 59	02 34	04 05	05 37	07 11
62	01 47	03 15	04 10	02 47	04 13	05 42	07 12
60	02 17	03 29	04 20	02 57	04 20	05 45	07 12
N 58	02 38	03 42	04 28	03 07	04 26	05 48	07 12
56	02 56	03 53	04 35	03 15	04 32	05 51	07 12
54	03 10	04 02	04 42	03 22	04 37	05 54	07 13
52	03 22	04 10	04 48	03 28	04 41	05 56	07 13
50	03 32	04 17	04 53	03 34	04 45	05 58	07 13
45	03 54	04 33	05 04	03 46	04 54	06 03	07 13
N 40	04 10	04 45	05 14	03 57	05 01	06 07	07 13
35	04 23	04 55	05 22	04 05	05 07	06 10	07 14
30	04 34	05 04	05 29	04 13	05 12	06 13	07 14
20	04 51	05 18	05 41	04 26	05 22	06 18	07 14
N 10	05 04	05 29	05 51	04 38	05 30	06 22	07 14
0	05 15	05 39	06 01	04 49	05 38	06 26	07 15
S 10	05 24	05 49	06 10	04 59	05 45	06 30	07 15
20	05 32	05 58	06 20	05 11	05 53	06 35	07 16
30	05 39	06 07	06 31	05 24	06 02	06 40	07 16
35	05 42	06 12	06 38	05 31	06 08	06 42	07 17
40	05 45	06 17	06 45	05 40	06 14	06 46	07 17
45	05 49	06 23	06 54	05 50	06 21	06 49	07 17
S 50	05 52	06 30	07 04	06 02	06 29	06 54	07 18
52	05 54	06 33	07 08	06 07	06 33	06 56	07 18
54	05 55	06 37	07 14	06 13	06 37	06 58	07 18
56	05 57	06 40	07 19	06 20	06 42	07 01	07 18
58	05 58	06 44	07 26	06 28	06 47	07 03	07 19
S 60	06 00	06 49	07 33	06 36	06 53	07 06	07 19

Lat.	Sunset	Twilight Civil	Naut.	Moonset 16	17	18	19
°	h m	h m	h m	h m	h m	h m	h m
N 72	21 23	////	////	20 00	19 41	19 26	19 11
N 70	20 56	22 51	////	19 40	19 30	19 22	19 14
68	20 36	22 00	////	19 24	19 22	19 19	19 17
66	20 20	21 31	////	19 11	19 14	19 17	19 19
64	20 07	21 08	23 00	19 00	19 08	19 14	19 20
62	19 56	20 51	22 16	18 51	19 02	19 12	19 22
60	19 47	20 36	21 48	18 43	18 57	19 11	19 23
N 58	19 38	20 24	21 27	18 36	18 53	19 09	19 24
56	19 31	20 14	21 10	18 29	18 49	19 08	19 25
54	19 25	20 05	20 56	18 24	18 46	19 06	19 26
52	19 19	19 57	20 44	18 19	18 43	19 05	19 27
50	19 14	19 49	20 34	18 14	18 40	19 04	19 28
45	19 03	19 34	20 13	18 04	18 34	19 02	19 30
N 40	18 54	19 22	19 57	17 56	18 28	19 00	19 31
35	18 46	19 12	19 44	17 49	18 24	18 58	19 32
30	18 39	19 04	19 33	17 42	18 20	18 57	19 33
20	18 27	18 50	19 17	17 31	18 13	18 54	19 35
N 10	18 17	18 38	19 04	17 21	18 07	18 52	19 37
0	18 07	18 29	18 53	17 12	18 01	18 49	19 38
S 10	17 58	18 19	18 44	17 03	17 55	18 47	19 40
20	17 48	18 11	18 37	16 53	17 49	18 45	19 42
30	17 37	18 01	18 30	16 41	17 41	18 42	19 43
35	17 31	17 57	18 26	16 35	17 37	18 40	19 45
40	17 23	17 51	18 23	16 27	17 32	18 38	19 46
45	17 15	17 45	18 20	16 18	17 27	18 36	19 47
S 50	17 05	17 38	18 16	16 08	17 20	18 34	19 49
52	17 00	17 35	18 15	16 03	17 17	18 32	19 49
54	16 55	17 32	18 14	15 57	17 13	18 31	19 50
56	16 49	17 29	18 12	15 51	17 09	18 30	19 51
58	16 43	17 25	18 11	15 44	17 05	18 28	19 52
S 60	16 36	17 20	18 09	15 36	17 00	18 26	19 53

	SUN			MOON			
Day	Eqn. of Time 00h	12h	Mer. Pass.	Mer. Pass. Upper	Lower	Age	Phase
d	m s	m s	h m	h m	h m	d	%
16	04 17	04 11	12 04	11 00	23 25	28	2
17	04 05	03 58	12 04	11 49	24 13	29	0
18	03 51	03 45	12 04	12 38	00 13	01	1

UT	ARIES GHA	VENUS −4.4 GHA	Dec	MARS +1.2 GHA	Dec	JUPITER −2.3 GHA	Dec	SATURN +0.8 GHA	Dec	STARS Name	SHA	Dec
d h	° ′	° ′	° ′	° ′	° ′	° ′	° ′	° ′	° ′		° ′	° ′
19 00	327 44.9	226 19.4	N20 00.3	122 46.5	S10 45.6	256 02.0	N21 34.9	123 37.3	S 7 31.3	Acamar	315 18.7	S40 15.0
01	342 47.4	241 19.2	.. 00.3	137 47.4	46.2	271 04.1	34.9	138 39.6	31.4	Achernar	335 26.9	S57 10.0
02	357 49.9	256 19.1	00.3	152 48.4	46.8	286 06.2	35.0	153 41.9	31.5	Acrux	173 10.4	S63 10.4
03	12 52.3	271 18.9	.. 00.3	167 49.4	.. 47.4	301 08.3	.. 35.0	168 44.1	.. 31.6	Adhara	255 13.2	S28 59.3
04	27 54.8	286 18.8	00.3	182 50.4	48.0	316 10.4	35.0	183 46.4	31.7	Aldebaran	290 50.1	N16 32.0
05	42 57.3	301 18.6	00.3	197 51.4	48.6	331 12.5	35.1	198 48.7	31.7			
06	57 59.7	316 18.5	N20 00.2	212 52.3	S10 49.2	346 14.6	N21 35.1	213 51.0	S 7 31.8	Alioth	166 21.5	N55 53.7
07	73 02.2	331 18.3	00.2	227 53.3	49.8	1 16.7	35.2	228 53.3	31.9	Alkaid	152 59.6	N49 15.3
08	88 04.6	346 18.2	00.2	242 54.3	50.4	16 18.8	35.2	243 55.5	32.0	Al Na'ir	27 43.9	S46 53.7
S 09	103 07.1	1 18.0	.. 00.2	257 55.3	.. 50.9	31 20.9	.. 35.2	258 57.8	.. 32.1	Alnilam	275 47.1	S 1 11.6
U 10	118 09.6	16 17.8	00.2	272 56.2	51.5	46 23.1	35.2	274 00.1	32.1	Alphard	217 57.0	S 8 42.8
N 11	133 12.0	31 17.7	00.2	287 57.2	52.1	61 25.2	35.3	289 02.4	32.2			
D 12	148 14.5	46 17.5	N20 00.1	302 58.2	S10 52.7	76 27.3	N21 35.4	304 04.6	S 7 32.3	Alphecca	126 11.5	N26 40.6
A 13	163 17.0	61 17.3	00.1	317 59.2	53.3	91 29.4	35.4	319 06.9	32.4	Alpheratz	357 43.8	N29 09.7
Y 14	178 19.4	76 17.2	00.1	333 00.2	53.9	106 31.5	35.4	334 09.2	32.5	Altair	62 08.5	N 8 54.4
15	193 21.9	91 17.0	.. 00.1	348 01.1	.. 54.5	121 33.6	.. 35.5	349 11.5	.. 32.6	Ankaa	353 15.9	S42 13.9
16	208 24.4	106 16.9	00.1	3 02.1	55.1	136 35.7	35.5	4 13.7	32.6	Antares	112 26.9	S26 27.6
17	223 26.8	121 16.7	00.0	18 03.1	55.7	151 37.8	35.6	19 16.0	32.7			
18	238 29.3	136 16.5	N20 00.0	33 04.1	S10 56.3	166 39.9	N21 35.6	34 18.3	S 7 32.8	Arcturus	145 56.4	N19 07.2
19	253 31.8	151 16.4	00.0	48 05.0	56.9	181 42.0	35.6	49 20.6	32.9	Atria	107 29.0	S69 03.2
20	268 34.2	166 16.2	20 00.0	63 06.0	57.5	196 44.1	35.7	64 22.8	33.0	Avior	234 18.8	S59 33.0
21	283 36.7	181 16.0	19 59.9	78 07.0	.. 58.1	211 46.2	.. 35.7	79 25.1	.. 33.0	Bellatrix	278 32.7	N 6 21.6
22	298 39.1	196 15.9	59.9	93 07.9	58.7	226 48.4	35.8	94 27.4	33.1	Betelgeuse	271 02.1	N 7 24.5
23	313 41.6	211 15.7	59.9	108 08.9	59.3	241 50.5	35.8	109 29.7	33.2			
20 00	328 44.1	226 15.5	N19 59.9	123 09.9	S10 59.9	256 52.6	N21 35.8	124 31.9	S 7 33.3	Canopus	263 56.7	S52 42.0
01	343 46.5	241 15.3	59.8	138 10.9	11 00.5	271 54.7	35.9	139 34.2	33.4	Capella	280 35.4	N46 00.4
02	358 49.0	256 15.2	59.8	153 11.8	01.1	286 56.8	35.9	154 36.5	33.5	Deneb	49 31.4	N45 19.8
03	13 51.5	271 15.0	.. 59.8	168 12.8	.. 01.7	301 58.9	.. 36.0	169 38.8	.. 33.5	Denebola	182 34.5	N14 30.1
04	28 53.9	286 14.8	59.7	183 13.8	02.3	317 01.0	36.0	184 41.0	33.6	Diphda	348 56.2	S17 54.8
05	43 56.4	301 14.7	59.7	198 14.8	02.9	332 03.1	36.0	199 43.3	33.7			
06	58 58.9	316 14.5	N19 59.7	213 15.7	S11 03.5	347 05.2	N21 36.1	214 45.6	S 7 33.8	Dubhe	193 53.0	N61 41.0
07	74 01.3	331 14.3	59.6	228 16.7	04.1	2 07.3	36.1	229 47.9	33.9	Elnath	278 13.5	N28 36.9
08	89 03.8	346 14.1	59.6	243 17.7	04.7	17 09.5	36.2	244 50.1	33.9	Eltanin	90 46.1	N51 29.6
M 09	104 06.2	1 14.0	.. 59.6	258 18.6	.. 05.3	32 11.6	.. 36.2	259 52.4	.. 34.0	Enif	33 47.3	N 9 56.2
O 10	119 08.7	16 13.8	59.5	273 19.6	05.9	47 13.7	36.2	274 54.7	34.1	Fomalhaut	15 24.2	S29 33.0
N 11	134 11.2	31 13.6	59.5	288 20.6	06.5	62 15.8	36.3	289 57.0	34.2			
D 12	149 13.6	46 13.4	N19 59.5	303 21.5	S11 07.1	77 17.9	N21 36.3	304 59.2	S 7 34.3	Gacrux	172 02.0	S57 11.2
A 13	164 16.1	61 13.2	59.4	318 22.5	07.7	92 20.0	36.3	320 01.5	34.4	Gienah	175 53.1	S17 36.8
Y 14	179 18.6	76 13.1	59.4	333 23.5	08.3	107 22.1	36.4	335 03.8	34.4	Hadar	148 48.9	S60 26.3
15	194 21.0	91 12.9	.. 59.3	348 24.5	.. 08.9	122 24.3	.. 36.4	350 06.0	.. 34.5	Hamal	328 01.2	N23 31.3
16	209 23.5	106 12.7	59.3	3 25.4	09.5	137 26.4	36.5	5 08.3	34.6	Kaus Aust.	83 44.3	S34 22.6
17	224 26.0	121 12.5	59.3	18 26.4	10.1	152 28.5	36.5	20 10.6	34.7			
18	239 28.4	136 12.3	N19 59.2	33 27.4	S11 10.7	167 30.6	N21 36.6	35 12.9	S 7 34.8	Kochab	137 20.3	N74 06.5
19	254 30.9	151 12.2	59.2	48 28.3	11.2	182 32.7	36.6	50 15.1	34.9	Markab	13 38.6	N15 16.6
20	269 33.4	166 12.0	59.1	63 29.3	11.8	197 34.8	36.6	65 17.4	34.9	Menkar	314 15.6	N 4 08.4
21	284 35.8	181 11.8	.. 59.1	78 30.3	.. 12.4	212 36.9	.. 36.7	80 19.7	.. 35.0	Menkent	148 08.4	S36 26.0
22	299 38.3	196 11.6	59.1	93 31.2	13.0	227 39.1	36.7	95 22.0	35.1	Miaplacidus	221 40.7	S69 46.2
23	314 40.7	211 11.4	59.0	108 32.2	13.6	242 41.2	36.7	110 24.2	35.2			
21 00	329 43.2	226 11.2	N19 59.0	123 33.2	S11 14.2	257 43.3	N21 36.8	125 26.5	S 7 35.3	Mirfak	308 41.1	N49 54.2
01	344 45.7	241 11.0	58.9	138 34.1	14.8	272 45.4	36.8	140 28.8	35.4	Nunki	75 58.7	S26 16.7
02	359 48.1	256 10.9	58.9	153 35.1	15.4	287 47.5	36.8	155 31.0	35.4	Peacock	53 19.5	S56 41.5
03	14 50.6	271 10.7	.. 58.8	168 36.1	.. 16.0	302 49.6	.. 36.9	170 33.3	.. 35.5	Pollux	243 28.7	N27 59.6
04	29 53.1	286 10.5	58.8	183 37.0	16.6	317 51.8	36.9	185 35.6	35.6	Procyon	245 00.6	N 5 11.5
05	44 55.5	301 10.3	58.7	198 38.0	17.2	332 53.9	37.0	200 37.9	35.7			
06	59 58.0	316 10.1	N19 58.7	213 39.0	S11 17.8	347 56.0	N21 37.0	215 40.1	S 7 35.8	Rasalhague	96 06.8	N12 33.3
07	75 00.5	331 09.9	58.6	228 39.9	18.4	2 58.1	37.0	230 42.4	35.8	Regulus	207 44.4	N11 54.3
08	90 02.9	346 09.7	58.6	243 40.9	19.0	18 00.2	37.1	245 44.7	35.9	Rigel	281 12.7	S 8 11.2
T 09	105 05.4	1 09.5	.. 58.5	258 41.8	.. 19.6	33 02.3	.. 37.1	260 46.9	.. 36.0	Rigil Kent.	139 52.7	S60 53.4
U 10	120 07.8	16 09.3	58.5	273 42.8	20.2	48 04.5	37.1	275 49.2	36.1	Sabik	102 13.0	S15 44.3
E 11	135 10.3	31 09.1	58.4	288 43.8	20.8	63 06.6	37.2	290 51.5	36.2			
S 12	150 12.8	46 08.9	N19 58.4	303 44.7	S11 21.4	78 08.7	N21 37.2	305 53.8	S 7 36.3	Schedar	349 40.7	N56 36.4
D 13	165 15.2	61 08.7	58.3	318 45.7	22.0	93 10.8	37.3	320 56.0	36.3	Shaula	96 22.5	S37 06.7
A 14	180 17.7	76 08.5	58.3	333 46.7	22.6	108 12.9	37.3	335 58.3	36.4	Sirius	258 34.4	S16 44.0
Y 15	195 20.2	91 08.3	.. 58.2	348 47.6	.. 23.2	123 15.1	.. 37.3	351 00.6	.. 36.5	Spica	158 32.0	S11 13.6
16	210 22.6	106 08.2	58.1	3 48.6	23.7	138 17.2	37.4	6 02.8	36.6	Suhail	222 53.3	S43 29.0
17	225 25.1	121 08.0	58.1	18 49.5	24.3	153 19.3	37.4	21 05.1	36.7			
18	240 27.6	136 07.8	N19 58.0	33 50.5	S11 24.9	168 21.4	N21 37.4	36 07.4	S 7 36.8	Vega	80 39.0	N38 48.1
19	255 30.0	151 07.6	58.0	48 51.5	25.5	183 23.5	37.5	51 09.6	36.8	Zuben'ubi	137 06.1	S16 05.6
20	270 32.5	166 07.4	57.9	63 52.4	26.1	198 25.7	37.5	66 11.9	36.9		SHA	Mer.Pass.
21	285 35.0	181 07.2	.. 57.8	78 53.4	.. 26.7	213 27.8	.. 37.0	81 14.2	.. 37.0		° ′	h m
22	300 37.4	196 07.0	57.8	93 54.3	27.3	228 29.9	37.6	96 16.5	37.1	Venus	257 31.4	8 55
23	315 39.9	211 06.8	57.7	108 55.3	27.9	243 32.0	37.6	111 18.7	37.2	Mars	154 25.8	15 25
Mer. Pass. 2 04.7		v −0.2	d 0.0	v 1.0	d 0.6	v 2.1	d 0.0	v 2.3	d 0.1	Jupiter	288 08.5	6 52
										Saturn	155 47.9	15 39

UT	SUN GHA	SUN Dec	MOON GHA	v	Dec	d	HP
d h	° ′	° ′	° ′	′	° ′	′	′
19 00	179 05.6	N12 42.4	164 57.8 11.5	N 2 01.1	12.5	58.2	
01	194 05.7	41.6	179 28.3 11.4	1 48.6	12.6	58.2	
02	209 05.9	40.8	193 58.7 11.4	1 36.0	12.5	58.2	
03	224 06.0 . .	40.0	208 29.1 11.4	1 23.5	12.5	58.2	
04	239 06.2	39.1	222 59.5 11.4	1 11.0	12.6	58.2	
05	254 06.3	38.3	237 29.9 11.4	0 58.4	12.6	58.3	
06	269 06.5	N12 37.5	252 00.3 11.4	N 0 45.8	12.6	58.3	
07	284 06.6	36.7	266 30.7 11.3	0 33.2	12.6	58.3	
08	299 06.8	35.9	281 01.0 11.3	0 20.6	12.6	58.3	
S 09	314 06.9 . .	35.0	295 31.3 11.4	N 0 08.0	12.6	58.3	
U 10	329 07.1	34.2	310 01.7 11.2	S 0 04.6	12.6	58.4	
N 11	344 07.2	33.4	324 31.9 11.3	0 17.2	12.6	58.4	
D 12	359 07.3	N12 32.6	339 02.2 11.3	S 0 29.8	12.7	58.4	
A 13	14 07.5	31.8	353 32.5 11.2	0 42.5	12.6	58.4	
Y 14	29 07.6	30.9	8 02.7 11.2	0 55.1	12.6	58.4	
15	44 07.8 . .	30.1	22 32.9 11.2	1 07.7	12.7	58.4	
16	59 07.9	29.3	37 03.1 11.1	1 20.4	12.6	58.5	
17	74 08.1	28.5	51 33.2 11.1	1 33.0	12.6	58.5	
18	89 08.2	N12 27.6	66 03.4 11.1	S 1 45.6	12.7	58.5	
19	104 08.4	26.8	80 33.5 11.1	1 58.3	12.6	58.5	
20	119 08.5	26.0	95 03.6 11.0	2 10.9	12.6	58.5	
21	134 08.7 . .	25.2	109 33.6 11.1	2 23.5	12.6	58.6	
22	149 08.8	24.3	124 03.7 11.0	2 36.1	12.6	58.6	
23	164 09.0	23.5	138 33.7 10.9	2 48.7	12.6	58.6	
20 00	179 09.1	N12 22.7	153 03.6 11.0	S 3 01.3	12.6	58.6	
01	194 09.3	21.9	167 33.6 10.9	3 13.9	12.6	58.6	
02	209 09.4	21.0	182 03.5 10.9	3 26.5	12.6	58.6	
03	224 09.6 . .	20.2	196 33.4 10.9	3 39.1	12.5	58.6	
04	239 09.7	19.4	211 03.3 10.8	3 51.6	12.6	58.7	
05	254 09.9	18.6	225 33.1 10.8	4 04.2	12.5	58.7	
06	269 10.0	N12 17.7	240 02.9 10.8	S 4 16.7	12.5	58.7	
07	284 10.2	16.9	254 32.7 10.7	4 29.2	12.4	58.7	
08	299 10.3	16.1	269 02.4 10.7	4 41.6	12.3	58.7	
M 09	314 10.5 . .	15.2	283 32.1 10.6	4 54.1	12.4	58.7	
O 10	329 10.6	14.4	298 01.7 10.7	5 06.5	12.5	58.8	
N 11	344 10.8	13.6	312 31.4 10.6	5 19.0	12.4	58.8	
D 12	359 10.9	N12 12.8	327 01.0 10.5	S 5 31.4	12.3	58.8	
A 13	14 11.1	11.9	341 30.5 10.5	5 43.7	12.4	58.8	
Y 14	29 11.2	11.1	356 00.0 10.5	5 56.1	12.3	58.8	
15	44 11.4 . .	10.3	10 29.5 10.5	6 08.4	12.2	58.8	
16	59 11.5	09.4	24 59.0 10.4	6 20.6	12.3	58.8	
17	74 11.7	08.6	39 28.4 10.3	6 32.9	12.2	58.8	
18	89 11.8	N12 07.8	53 57.7 10.4	S 6 45.1	12.2	58.9	
19	104 12.0	06.9	68 27.1 10.2	6 57.3	12.2	58.9	
20	119 12.1	06.1	82 56.3 10.3	7 09.5	12.1	58.9	
21	134 12.3 . .	05.3	97 25.6 10.2	7 21.6	12.0	58.9	
22	149 12.4	04.4	111 54.8 10.1	7 33.6	12.1	58.9	
23	164 12.6	03.6	126 23.9 10.2	7 45.7	12.0	58.9	
21 00	179 12.8	N12 02.8	140 53.1 10.0	S 7 57.7	11.9	58.9	
01	194 12.9	01.9	155 22.1 10.1	8 09.6	12.0	58.9	
02	209 13.1	01.1	169 51.2 10.0	8 21.6	11.8	59.0	
03	224 13.2	12 00.3	184 20.2 9.9	8 33.4	11.9	59.0	
04	239 13.4	11 59.4	198 49.1 9.9	8 45.3	11.7	59.0	
05	254 13.5	58.6	213 18.0 9.8	8 57.0	11.8	59.0	
06	269 13.7	N11 57.8	227 46.8 9.8	S 9 08.8	11.7	59.0	
07	284 13.8	56.9	242 15.6 9.8	9 20.5	11.6	59.0	
08	299 14.0	56.1	256 44.4 9.7	9 32.1	11.6	59.0	
T 09	314 14.2 . .	55.3	271 13.1 9.7	9 43.7	11.5	59.0	
U 10	329 14.3	54.4	285 41.8 9.6	9 55.2	11.5	59.0	
E 11	344 14.5	53.6	300 10.4 9.5	10 06.7	11.4	59.1	
S 12	359 14.6	N11 52.8	314 38.9 9.5	S10 18.1	11.4	59.1	
D 13	14 14.8	51.9	329 07.4 9.5	10 29.5	11.3	59.1	
A 14	29 14.9	51.1	343 35.9 9.4	10 40.8	11.3	59.1	
Y 15	44 15.1 . .	50.2	358 04.3 9.4	10 52.1	11.1	59.1	
16	59 15.2	49.4	12 32.7 9.3	11 03.2	11.2	59.1	
17	74 15.4	48.6	27 01.0 9.3	11 14.4	11.0	59.1	
18	89 15.6	N11 47.7	41 29.3 9.2	S11 25.4	11.0	59.1	
19	104 15.7	46.9	55 57.5 9.1	11 36.4	11.0	59.1	
20	119 15.9	46.0	70 25.6 9.1	11 47.4	10.8	59.1	
21	134 16.0 . .	45.2	84 53.7 9.1	11 58.2	10.8	59.1	
22	149 16.2	44.4	99 21.8 9.0	12 09.1	10.7	59.1	
23	164 16.4	43.5	113 49.8 8.9	S12 19.8	10.6	59.2	
	SD 15.8 d 0.8		SD 15.9	16.0			16.1

Lat.	Twilight Naut.	Twilight Civil	Sunrise	Moonrise 19	Moonrise 20	Moonrise 21	Moonrise 22
°	h m	h m	h m	h m	h m	h m	h m
N 72	////	////	02 59	07 10	09 10	11 16	13 37
N 70	////	01 39	03 23	07 10	09 02	10 59	13 02
68	////	02 20	03 41	07 11	08 56	10 45	12 37
66	////	02 47	03 56	07 11	08 51	10 34	12 18
64	01 27	03 08	04 08	07 11	08 47	10 24	12 03
62	02 04	03 24	04 18	07 12	08 43	10 16	11 50
60	02 29	03 38	04 27	07 12	08 40	10 10	11 40
N 58	02 48	03 49	04 35	07 12	08 37	10 04	11 30
56	03 04	03 59	04 41	07 12	08 35	09 58	11 22
54	03 17	04 08	04 47	07 13	08 33	09 54	11 15
52	03 28	04 16	04 53	07 13	08 31	09 49	11 09
50	03 38	04 22	04 58	07 13	08 29	09 46	11 03
45	03 58	04 37	05 08	07 13	08 25	09 37	10 50
N 40	04 14	04 48	05 17	07 13	08 21	09 30	10 40
35	04 26	04 57	05 24	07 14	08 19	09 25	10 31
30	04 36	05 06	05 30	07 14	08 16	09 19	10 24
20	04 52	05 19	05 41	07 14	08 12	09 10	10 11
N 10	05 04	05 30	05 51	07 15	08 08	09 03	09 59
0	05 14	05 39	06 00	07 15	08 05	08 56	09 49
S 10	05 22	05 47	06 09	07 15	08 01	08 48	09 38
20	05 30	05 55	06 18	07 16	07 58	08 41	09 27
30	05 36	06 04	06 28	07 16	07 53	08 32	09 14
35	05 39	06 08	06 34	07 17	07 51	08 27	09 07
40	05 42	06 13	06 41	07 17	07 49	08 22	08 59
45	05 44	06 19	06 49	07 17	07 46	08 16	08 49
S 50	05 47	06 25	06 58	07 18	07 42	08 08	08 37
52	05 48	06 27	07 02	07 18	07 40	08 04	08 32
54	05 49	06 30	07 07	07 18	07 39	08 01	08 26
56	05 50	06 34	07 12	07 19	07 37	07 56	08 20
58	05 51	06 37	07 18	07 19	07 34	07 52	08 12
S 60	05 52	06 41	07 25	07 19	07 32	07 46	08 04

Lat.	Sunset	Twilight Civil	Twilight Naut.	Moonset 19	Moonset 20	Moonset 21	Moonset 22
°	h m	h m	h m	h m	h m	h m	h m
N 72	21 03	////	////	19 11	18 56	18 37	18 08
N 70	20 40	22 20	////	19 14	19 06	18 57	18 44
68	20 22	21 42	////	19 17	19 14	19 12	19 10
66	20 08	21 15	////	19 19	19 21	19 25	19 31
64	19 56	20 55	22 33	19 20	19 27	19 35	19 47
62	19 46	20 40	21 58	19 22	19 32	19 44	20 00
60	19 38	20 26	21 34	19 23	19 37	19 52	20 12
N 58	19 30	20 15	21 15	19 24	19 41	19 59	20 22
56	19 24	20 06	21 00	19 25	19 44	20 05	20 31
54	19 18	19 57	20 47	19 26	19 47	20 11	20 38
52	19 13	19 50	20 36	19 27	19 50	20 16	20 45
50	19 08	19 43	20 27	19 28	19 53	20 20	20 52
45	18 58	19 29	20 07	19 30	19 59	20 30	21 05
N 40	18 49	19 18	19 52	19 31	20 03	20 38	21 17
35	18 42	19 08	19 40	19 32	20 08	20 45	21 26
30	18 36	19 00	19 30	19 33	20 11	20 51	21 35
20	18 25	18 47	19 14	19 35	20 18	21 02	21 50
N 10	18 16	18 37	19 02	19 37	20 23	21 12	22 03
0	18 07	18 28	18 52	19 38	20 29	21 21	22 15
S 10	17 58	18 19	18 44	19 40	20 34	21 29	22 27
20	17 49	18 11	18 37	19 42	20 40	21 39	22 40
30	17 39	18 03	18 31	19 43	20 46	21 50	22 55
35	17 33	17 59	18 28	19 45	20 50	21 56	23 03
40	17 26	17 54	18 26	19 46	20 54	22 04	23 13
45	17 18	17 49	18 23	19 47	20 59	22 12	23 25
S 50	17 09	17 43	18 20	19 49	21 05	22 22	23 39
52	17 05	17 40	18 19	19 49	21 08	22 27	23 46
54	17 00	17 37	18 18	19 50	21 11	22 32	23 53
56	16 55	17 34	18 17	19 51	21 14	22 38	24 01
58	16 49	17 30	18 16	19 52	21 18	22 44	24 11
S 60	16 43	17 27	18 15	19 53	21 22	22 52	24 21

	SUN				MOON			
Day	Eqn. of Time 00h	Eqn. of Time 12h	Mer. Pass.		Mer. Pass. Upper	Mer. Pass. Lower	Age	Phase
d	m s	m s	h m		h m	h m	d	%
19	03 38	03 31	12 04		13 27	01 02	02	4
20	03 24	03 17	12 03		14 17	01 51	03	10
21	03 09	03 02	12 03		15 08	02 42	04	18

UT	ARIES GHA	VENUS −4.4 GHA	Dec	MARS +1.2 GHA	Dec	JUPITER −2.3 GHA	Dec	SATURN +0.8 GHA	Dec
22 00	330 42.3	226 06.6	N19 57.7	123 56.3	S11 28.5	258 34.2	N21 37.7	126 21.0	S 7 37.3
01	345 44.8	241 06.4	57.6	138 57.2	29.1	273 36.3	37.7	141 23.3	37.4
02	0 47.3	256 06.1	57.5	153 58.2	29.7	288 38.4	37.7	156 25.5	37.4
03	15 49.7	271 05.9 ..	57.5	168 59.1 ..	30.3	303 40.5 ..	37.8	171 27.8 ..	37.5
04	30 52.2	286 05.7	57.4	184 00.1	30.9	318 42.6	37.8	186 30.1	37.6
05	45 54.7	301 05.5	57.3	199 01.1	31.5	333 44.8	37.9	201 32.3	37.7
W 06	60 57.1	316 05.3	N19 57.3	214 02.0	S11 32.1	348 46.9	N21 37.9	216 34.6	S 7 37.8
E 07	75 59.6	331 05.1	57.2	229 03.0	32.7	3 49.0	37.9	231 36.9	37.9
D 08	91 02.1	346 04.9	57.1	244 03.9	33.3	18 51.1	38.0	246 39.1	37.9
N 09	106 04.5	1 04.7 ..	57.1	259 04.9 ..	33.8	33 53.3 ..	38.0	261 41.4 ..	38.0
E 10	121 07.0	16 04.5	57.0	274 05.8	34.4	48 55.4	38.0	276 43.7	38.1
S 11	136 09.5	31 04.3	56.9	289 06.8	35.0	63 57.5	38.1	291 45.9	38.2
D 12	151 11.9	46 04.1	N19 56.8	304 07.8	S11 35.6	78 59.6	N21 38.1	306 48.2	S 7 38.3
A 13	166 14.4	61 03.9	56.8	319 08.7	36.2	94 01.8	38.2	321 50.5	38.4
Y 14	181 16.8	76 03.7	56.7	334 09.7	36.8	109 03.9	38.2	336 52.8	38.4
15	196 19.3	91 03.4 ..	56.6	349 10.6 ..	37.4	124 06.0 ..	38.2	351 55.0 ..	38.5
16	211 21.8	106 03.2	56.5	4 11.6	38.0	139 08.1	38.3	6 57.3	38.6
17	226 24.2	121 03.0	56.5	19 12.5	38.6	154 10.3	38.3	21 59.6	38.7
18	241 26.7	136 02.8	N19 56.4	34 13.5	S11 39.2	169 12.4	N21 38.3	37 01.8	S 7 38.8
19	256 29.2	151 02.6	56.3	49 14.4	39.8	184 14.5	38.4	52 04.1	38.9
20	271 31.6	166 02.4	56.2	64 15.4	40.4	199 16.7	38.4	67 06.4	39.0
21	286 34.1	181 02.2 ..	56.2	79 16.3 ..	41.0	214 18.8 ..	38.4	82 08.6 ..	39.0
22	301 36.6	196 01.9	56.1	94 17.3	41.6	229 20.9	38.5	97 10.9	39.1
23	316 39.0	211 01.7	56.0	109 18.2	42.2	244 23.0	38.5	112 13.2	39.2
23 00	331 41.5	226 01.5	N19 55.9	124 19.2	S11 42.7	259 25.2	N21 38.6	127 15.4	S 7 39.3
01	346 43.9	241 01.3	55.8	139 20.2	43.3	274 27.3	38.6	142 17.7	39.4
02	1 46.4	256 01.1	55.8	154 21.1	43.9	289 29.4	38.6	157 20.0	39.5
03	16 48.9	271 00.9 ..	55.7	169 22.1 ..	44.5	304 31.6 ..	38.7	172 22.2 ..	39.5
04	31 51.3	286 00.6	55.6	184 23.0	45.1	319 33.7	38.7	187 24.5	39.6
05	46 53.8	301 00.4	55.5	199 24.0	45.7	334 35.8	38.7	202 26.8	39.7
T 06	61 56.3	316 00.2	N19 55.4	214 24.9	S11 46.3	349 37.9	N21 38.8	217 29.0	S 7 39.8
H 07	76 58.7	331 00.0	55.3	229 25.9	46.9	4 40.1	38.8	232 31.3	39.9
U 08	92 01.2	345 59.8	55.2	244 26.8	47.5	19 42.2	38.8	247 33.6	40.0
R 09	107 03.7	0 59.5 ..	55.1	259 27.8 ..	48.1	34 44.3 ..	38.9	262 35.8 ..	40.1
S 10	122 06.1	15 59.3	55.1	274 28.7	48.7	49 46.5	38.9	277 38.1	40.1
D 11	137 08.6	30 59.1	55.0	289 29.7	49.3	64 48.6	38.9	292 40.3	40.2
A 12	152 11.1	45 58.9	N19 54.9	304 30.6	S11 49.8	79 50.7	N21 39.0	307 42.6	S 7 40.3
Y 13	167 13.5	60 58.6	54.8	319 31.6	50.4	94 52.9	39.0	322 44.9	40.4
14	182 16.0	75 58.4	54.7	334 32.5	51.0	109 55.0	39.1	337 47.1	40.5
15	197 18.4	90 58.2 ..	54.6	349 33.5 ..	51.6	124 57.1 ..	39.1	352 49.4 ..	40.6
16	212 20.9	105 58.0	54.5	4 34.4	52.2	139 59.3	39.1	7 51.7	40.6
17	227 23.4	120 57.7	54.4	19 35.4	52.8	155 01.4	39.2	22 53.9	40.7
18	242 25.8	135 57.5	N19 54.3	34 36.3	S11 53.4	170 03.5	N21 39.2	37 56.2	S 7 40.8
19	257 28.3	150 57.3	54.2	49 37.2	54.0	185 05.7	39.2	52 58.5	40.9
20	272 30.8	165 57.1	54.1	64 38.2	54.6	200 07.8	39.3	68 00.7	41.0
21	287 33.2	180 56.8 ..	54.0	79 39.1 ..	55.2	215 09.9 ..	39.3	83 03.0 ..	41.1
22	302 35.7	195 56.6	53.9	94 40.1	55.8	230 12.1	39.3	98 05.3	41.2
23	317 38.2	210 56.4	53.8	109 41.0	56.3	245 14.2	39.4	113 07.5	41.2
24 00	332 40.6	225 56.1	N19 53.7	124 42.0	S11 56.9	260 16.3	N21 39.4	128 09.8	S 7 41.3
01	347 43.1	240 55.9	53.6	139 42.9	57.5	275 18.5	39.4	143 12.1	41.4
02	2 45.6	255 55.7	53.5	154 43.9	58.1	290 20.6	39.5	158 14.3	41.5
03	17 48.0	270 55.4 ..	53.4	169 44.8 ..	58.7	305 22.7 ..	39.5	173 16.6 ..	41.6
04	32 50.5	285 55.2	53.3	184 45.8	59.3	320 24.9	39.5	188 18.8	41.7
05	47 52.9	300 55.0	53.2	199 46.7	11 59.9	335 27.0	39.6	203 21.1	41.8
F 06	62 55.4	315 54.7	N19 53.1	214 47.6	S12 00.5	350 29.1	N21 39.6	218 23.4	S 7 41.8
R 07	77 57.9	330 54.5	53.0	229 48.6	01.1	5 31.3	39.7	233 25.6	41.9
I 08	93 00.3	345 54.3	52.9	244 49.5	01.7	20 33.4	39.7	248 27.9	42.0
D 09	108 02.8	0 54.0 ..	52.8	259 50.5 ..	02.3	35 35.6 ..	39.7	263 30.2 ..	42.1
A 10	123 05.3	15 53.8	52.7	274 51.4	02.8	50 37.7	39.8	278 32.4	42.2
Y 11	138 07.7	30 53.5	52.6	289 52.4	03.4	65 39.8	39.8	293 34.7	42.3
12	153 10.2	45 53.3	N19 52.5	304 53.3	S12 04.0	80 42.0	N21 39.8	308 36.9	S 7 42.4
13	168 12.7	60 53.1	52.4	319 54.2	04.6	95 44.1	39.9	323 39.2	42.4
14	183 15.1	75 52.8	52.2	334 55.2	05.2	110 46.3	39.9	338 41.5	42.5
15	198 17.6	90 52.6 ..	52.1	349 56.1 ..	05.8	125 48.4 ..	39.9	353 43.7 ..	42.6
16	213 20.0	105 52.4	52.0	4 57.1	06.4	140 50.5	40.0	8 46.0	42.7
17	228 22.5	120 52.1	51.9	19 58.0	07.0	155 52.7	40.0	23 48.3	42.8
18	243 25.0	135 51.9	N19 51.8	34 59.0	S12 07.6	170 54.8	N21 40.0	38 50.5	S 7 42.9
19	258 27.4	150 51.6	51.7	49 59.9	08.1	185 56.9	40.1	53 52.8	43.0
20	273 29.9	165 51.4	51.6	65 00.8	08.7	200 59.1	40.1	68 55.0	43.0
21	288 32.4	180 51.1 ..	51.4	80 01.8 ..	09.3	216 01.2 ..	40.1	83 57.3 ..	43.1
22	303 34.8	195 50.9	51.3	95 02.7	09.9	231 03.4	40.2	98 59.6	43.2
23	318 37.3	210 50.7	51.2	110 03.7	10.5	246 05.5	40.2	114 01.8	43.3
Mer.Pass.	h m 1 52.9	v −0.2	d 0.1	v 0.9	d 0.6	v 2.1	d 0.0	v 2.3	d 0.1

STARS

Name	SHA	Dec
Acamar	315 18.6	S40 15.0
Achernar	335 26.8	S57 10.0
Acrux	173 10.4	S63 10.4
Adhara	255 13.2	S28 59.3
Aldebaran	290 50.1	N16 32.0
Alioth	166 21.6	N55 53.6
Alkaid	152 59.6	N49 15.2
Al Na'ir	27 43.9	S46 53.7
Alnilam	275 47.1	S 1 11.6
Alphard	217 56.9	S 8 42.8
Alphecca	126 11.5	N26 40.6
Alpheratz	357 43.8	N29 09.7
Altair	62 08.5	N 8 54.4
Ankaa	353 15.9	S42 13.9
Antares	112 26.9	S26 27.6
Arcturus	145 56.4	N19 07.2
Atria	107 29.0	S69 03.2
Avior	234 18.8	S59 33.0
Bellatrix	278 32.7	N 6 21.6
Betelgeuse	271 02.0	N 7 24.5
Canopus	263 56.7	S52 42.0
Capella	280 35.4	N46 00.4
Deneb	49 31.4	N45 19.8
Denebola	182 34.5	N14 30.1
Diphda	348 56.2	S17 54.8
Dubhe	193 53.0	N61 41.0
Elnath	278 13.4	N28 36.9
Eltanin	90 46.1	N51 29.6
Enif	33 47.3	N 9 56.3
Fomalhaut	15 24.2	S29 33.0
Gacrux	172 02.0	S57 11.2
Gienah	175 53.1	S17 36.8
Hadar	148 49.0	S60 26.2
Hamal	328 01.2	N23 31.3
Kaus Aust.	83 44.3	S34 22.6
Kochab	137 20.3	N74 06.5
Markab	13 38.6	N15 16.6
Menkar	314 15.5	N 4 08.4
Menkent	148 08.4	S36 26.0
Miaplacidus	221 40.7	S69 46.2
Mirfak	308 41.1	N49 54.2
Nunki	75 58.7	S26 16.7
Peacock	53 19.6	S56 41.5
Pollux	243 28.7	N27 59.6
Procyon	245 00.6	N 5 11.5
Rasalhague	96 06.8	N12 33.3
Regulus	207 44.4	N11 54.3
Rigel	281 12.7	S 8 11.2
Rigil Kent.	139 52.7	S60 53.4
Sabik	102 13.1	S15 44.3
Schedar	349 40.7	N56 36.4
Shaula	96 22.5	S37 06.7
Sirius	258 34.4	S16 44.0
Spica	158 32.0	S11 13.6
Suhail	222 53.3	S43 29.0
Vega	80 39.1	N38 48.1
Zuben'ubi	137 06.1	S16 05.6

	SHA	Mer. Pass.
		h m
Venus	254 20.0	8 56
Mars	152 37.7	15 42
Jupiter	287 43.7	6 47
Saturn	155 33.9	15 29

UT	SUN GHA	SUN Dec	MOON GHA	v	Dec	d	HP
22 00	179 16.5	N11 42.7	128 17.7	8.9	S12 30.4	10.6	59.2
01	194 16.7	41.8	142 45.6	8.9	12 41.0	10.6	59.2
02	209 16.8	41.0	157 13.5	8.8	12 51.6	10.4	59.2
03	224 17.0	.. 40.2	171 41.3	8.7	13 02.0	10.4	59.2
04	239 17.2	39.3	186 09.0	8.7	13 12.4	10.3	59.2
05	254 17.3	38.5	200 36.7	8.6	13 22.7	10.2	59.2
06	269 17.5	N11 37.6	215 04.3	8.6	S13 32.9	10.1	59.2
W 07	284 17.6	36.8	229 31.9	8.5	13 43.0	10.1	59.2
E 08	299 17.8	35.9	243 59.4	8.4	13 53.1	9.9	59.2
D 09	314 18.0	.. 35.1	258 26.8	8.4	14 03.0	9.9	59.2
N 10	329 18.1	34.2	272 54.2	8.4	14 12.9	9.8	59.2
E 11	344 18.3	33.4	287 21.6	8.3	14 22.7	9.7	59.2
S 12	359 18.4	N11 32.6	301 48.9	8.2	S14 32.4	9.7	59.2
D 13	14 18.6	31.7	316 16.1	8.2	14 42.1	9.5	59.2
A 14	29 18.8	30.9	330 43.3	8.1	14 51.6	9.5	59.2
Y 15	44 18.9	.. 30.0	345 10.4	8.1	15 01.1	9.3	59.2
16	59 19.1	29.2	359 37.5	8.0	15 10.4	9.3	59.2
17	74 19.2	28.3	14 04.5	8.0	15 19.7	9.2	59.3
18	89 19.4	N11 27.5	28 31.5	7.9	S15 28.9	9.1	59.3
19	104 19.6	26.6	42 58.4	7.8	15 38.0	9.0	59.3
20	119 19.7	25.8	57 25.2	7.8	15 47.0	8.9	59.3
21	134 19.9	.. 24.9	71 52.0	7.8	15 55.9	8.7	59.3
22	149 20.1	24.1	86 18.8	7.6	16 04.6	8.7	59.3
23	164 20.2	23.2	100 45.4	7.7	16 13.3	8.6	59.3
23 00	179 20.4	N11 22.4	115 12.1	7.5	S16 21.9	8.5	59.3
01	194 20.5	21.5	129 38.6	7.6	16 30.4	8.4	59.3
02	209 20.7	20.7	144 05.2	7.4	16 38.8	8.3	59.3
03	224 20.9	.. 19.8	158 31.6	7.5	16 47.1	8.2	59.3
04	239 21.0	19.0	172 58.1	7.3	16 55.3	8.1	59.3
05	254 21.2	18.1	187 24.4	7.3	17 03.4	8.0	59.3
06	269 21.4	N11 17.3	201 50.7	7.3	S17 11.4	7.9	59.3
T 07	284 21.5	16.4	216 17.0	7.2	17 19.3	7.7	59.3
H 08	299 21.7	15.6	230 43.2	7.1	17 27.0	7.7	59.3
U 09	314 21.9	.. 14.7	245 09.3	7.1	17 34.7	7.5	59.3
R 10	329 22.0	13.9	259 35.4	7.1	17 42.2	7.4	59.3
S 11	344 22.2	13.0	274 01.5	7.0	17 49.6	7.4	59.3
D 12	359 22.4	N11 12.2	288 27.5	6.9	S17 57.0	7.2	59.3
A 13	14 22.5	11.3	302 53.4	6.9	18 04.2	7.0	59.3
Y 14	29 22.7	10.5	317 19.3	6.9	18 11.2	7.0	59.3
15	44 22.9	.. 09.6	331 45.2	6.8	18 18.2	6.9	59.3
16	59 23.0	08.8	346 11.0	6.7	18 25.1	6.7	59.3
17	74 23.2	07.9	0 36.7	6.7	18 31.8	6.6	59.3
18	89 23.4	N11 07.1	15 02.4	6.7	S18 38.4	6.5	59.3
19	104 23.5	06.2	29 28.1	6.6	18 44.9	6.4	59.3
20	119 23.7	05.4	43 53.7	6.6	18 51.3	6.3	59.3
21	134 23.9	.. 04.5	58 19.3	6.5	18 57.6	6.1	59.3
22	149 24.0	03.6	72 44.8	6.5	19 03.7	6.0	59.3
23	164 24.2	02.8	87 10.3	6.4	19 09.7	5.9	59.3
24 00	179 24.4	N11 01.9	101 35.7	6.4	S19 15.6	5.8	59.3
01	194 24.5	01.1	116 01.1	6.4	19 21.4	5.6	59.3
02	209 24.7	11 00.2	130 26.5	6.3	19 27.0	5.5	59.3
03	224 24.9	10 59.4	144 51.8	6.3	19 32.5	5.4	59.3
04	239 25.0	58.5	159 17.1	6.2	19 37.9	5.3	59.3
05	254 25.2	57.6	173 42.3	6.2	19 43.2	5.1	59.3
06	269 25.4	N10 56.8	188 07.5	6.2	S19 48.3	5.0	59.3
07	284 25.6	55.9	202 32.7	6.1	19 53.3	4.9	59.3
08	299 25.7	55.1	216 57.8	6.1	19 58.2	4.7	59.3
F 09	314 25.9	.. 54.2	231 22.9	6.0	20 02.9	4.6	59.3
R 10	329 26.1	53.4	245 47.9	6.0	20 07.5	4.5	59.3
I 11	344 26.2	52.5	260 12.9	6.0	20 12.0	4.4	59.3
D 12	359 26.4	N10 51.6	274 37.9	6.0	S20 16.4	4.2	59.3
A 13	14 26.6	50.8	289 02.9	5.9	20 20.6	4.1	59.3
Y 14	29 26.7	49.9	303 27.8	5.9	20 24.7	3.9	59.3
15	44 26.9	.. 49.1	317 52.7	5.9	20 28.6	3.8	59.3
16	59 27.1	48.2	332 17.6	5.8	20 32.4	3.7	59.3
17	74 27.3	47.3	346 42.4	5.8	20 36.1	3.5	59.3
18	89 27.4	N10 46.5	1 07.2	5.8	S20 39.6	3.4	59.3
19	104 27.6	45.6	15 32.0	5.8	20 43.0	3.3	59.3
20	119 27.8	44.7	29 56.8	5.7	20 46.3	3.1	59.3
21	134 27.9	.. 43.9	44 21.5	5.7	20 49.4	3.0	59.3
22	149 28.1	43.0	58 46.2	5.7	20 52.4	2.8	59.3
23	164 28.3	42.2	73 10.9	5.7	S20 55.2	2.8	59.3
	SD 15.8	d 0.9	SD 16.1		16.2		16.2

Twilight and Moonrise

Lat.	Naut.	Civil	Sunrise	Moonrise 22	23	24	25
N 72	////	01 05	03 16	13 37	■	■	■
N 70	////	02 04	03 37	13 02	15 21	■	■
68	////	02 37	03 53	12 37	14 34	16 30	18 02
66	00 56	03 01	04 06	12 18	14 03	15 42	16 59
64	01 48	03 19	04 17	12 03	13 41	15 11	16 24
62	02 19	03 34	04 26	11 50	13 23	14 48	15 59
60	02 41	03 46	04 34	11 40	13 08	14 30	15 39
N 58	02 58	03 57	04 41	11 30	12 56	14 15	15 23
56	03 12	04 06	04 47	11 22	12 45	14 02	15 09
54	03 25	04 14	04 53	11 15	12 35	13 50	14 56
52	03 35	04 21	04 58	11 09	12 27	13 40	14 46
50	03 44	04 27	05 02	11 03	12 19	13 31	14 36
45	04 03	04 40	05 12	10 50	12 03	13 12	14 16
N 40	04 17	04 51	05 19	10 40	11 50	12 57	14 00
35	04 29	05 00	05 26	10 31	11 38	12 44	13 47
30	04 38	05 07	05 32	10 24	11 29	12 33	13 35
20	04 53	05 20	05 42	10 11	11 12	12 14	13 14
N 10	05 05	05 30	05 51	09 59	10 57	11 57	12 57
0	05 14	05 38	05 59	09 49	10 44	11 41	12 40
S 10	05 21	05 46	06 07	09 38	10 30	11 26	12 24
20	05 27	05 53	06 16	09 27	10 16	11 09	12 06
30	05 33	06 01	06 25	09 14	10 00	10 51	11 46
35	05 35	06 05	06 31	09 07	09 50	10 40	11 34
40	05 38	06 09	06 37	08 59	09 40	10 27	11 21
45	05 40	06 14	06 44	08 49	09 27	10 12	11 05
S 50	05 42	06 19	06 52	08 37	09 12	09 54	10 45
52	05 42	06 21	06 56	08 32	09 05	09 46	10 36
54	05 43	06 24	07 00	08 26	08 57	09 36	10 26
56	05 44	06 27	07 05	08 20	08 48	09 26	10 14
58	05 44	06 30	07 10	08 12	08 38	09 13	10 00
S 60	05 45	06 33	07 16	08 04	08 27	08 59	09 45

Sunset, Twilight and Moonset

Lat.	Sunset	Civil	Naut.	Moonset 22	23	24	25
N 72	20 45	22 46	////	18 08	■	■	■
N 70	20 25	21 55	////	18 44	18 22	■	■
68	20 09	21 23	////	19 10	19 10	19 15	19 46
66	19 56	21 01	22 57	19 31	19 41	20 04	20 49
64	19 46	20 43	22 11	19 47	20 05	20 35	21 24
62	19 37	20 29	21 42	20 00	20 23	20 58	21 50
60	19 29	20 17	21 21	20 12	20 39	21 17	22 10
N 58	19 22	20 06	21 04	20 22	20 52	21 32	22 26
56	19 16	19 57	20 50	20 31	21 03	21 45	22 40
54	19 11	19 50	20 39	20 38	21 13	21 57	22 52
52	19 06	19 43	20 28	20 45	21 22	22 07	23 03
50	19 02	19 37	20 19	20 52	21 30	22 16	23 12
45	18 53	19 24	20 01	21 07	21 47	22 36	23 32
N 40	18 45	19 13	19 47	21 17	22 01	22 51	23 48
35	18 38	19 04	19 36	21 26	22 13	23 05	24 02
30	18 32	18 57	19 26	21 35	22 23	23 16	24 14
20	18 22	18 45	19 12	21 50	22 41	23 36	24 34
N 10	18 14	18 35	19 00	22 03	22 56	23 53	24 52
0	18 06	18 27	18 51	22 15	23 11	24 09	00 09
S 10	17 58	18 19	18 44	22 27	23 26	24 25	00 25
20	17 50	18 12	18 38	22 40	23 41	24 43	00 43
30	17 40	18 05	18 33	22 55	23 59	25 03	01 03
35	17 35	18 01	18 30	23 03	24 10	00 10	01 14
40	17 29	17 57	18 28	23 13	24 22	00 22	01 27
45	17 22	17 52	18 26	23 25	24 36	00 36	01 43
S 50	17 14	17 47	18 24	23 39	24 54	00 54	02 03
52	17 10	17 44	18 24	23 46	25 02	01 02	02 12
54	17 06	17 42	18 23	23 53	25 11	01 11	02 22
56	17 01	17 39	18 23	24 01	00 01	01 21	02 34
58	16 56	17 36	18 22	24 11	00 11	01 33	02 47
S 60	16 50	17 33	18 22	24 21	00 21	01 47	03 03

SUN and MOON

Day	Eqn. of Time 00h	12h	Mer. Pass.	Mer. Pass. Upper	Lower	Age	Phase
d	m s	m s	h m	h m	h m	d	%
22	02 54	02 47	12 03	16 02	03 34	05	27
23	02 39	02 31	12 03	16 57	04 29	06	38
24	02 23	02 15	12 02	17 55	05 26	07	49

2012 AUGUST 25, 26, 27 (SAT., SUN., MON.)

UT	ARIES GHA	VENUS −4.3 GHA	Dec	MARS +1.2 GHA	Dec	JUPITER −2.3 GHA	Dec	SATURN +0.8 GHA	Dec
25 00	333 39.8	225 50.4	N19 51.1	125 04.6	S12 11.1	261 07.7	N21 40.2	129 04.1	S 7 43.4
01	348 42.2	240 50.2	51.0	140 05.5	11.7	276 09.8	40.3	144 06.4	43.5
02	3 44.7	255 49.9	50.9	155 06.5	12.3	291 11.9	40.3	159 08.6	43.6
03	18 47.2	270 49.7 ..	50.7	170 07.4 ..	12.9	306 14.1 ..	40.3	174 10.9 ..	43.7
04	33 49.6	285 49.4	50.6	185 08.3	13.4	321 16.2	40.4	189 13.1	43.7
05	48 52.1	300 49.2	50.5	200 09.3	14.0	336 18.4	40.4	204 15.4	43.8
S 06	63 54.5	315 48.9	N19 50.4	215 10.2	S12 14.6	351 20.5	N21 40.4	219 17.7	S 7 43.9
A 07	78 57.0	330 48.7	50.2	230 11.2	15.2	6 22.6	40.5	234 19.9	44.0
T 08	93 59.5	345 48.4	50.1	245 12.1	15.8	21 24.8	40.5	249 22.2	44.1
U 09	109 01.9	0 48.2 ..	50.0	260 13.0 ..	16.4	36 26.9 ..	40.5	264 24.4 ..	44.2
R 10	124 04.4	15 47.9	49.9	275 14.0	17.0	51 29.1	40.6	279 26.7	44.3
D 11	139 06.9	30 47.7	49.7	290 14.9	17.6	66 31.2	40.6	294 29.0	44.3
A 12	154 09.3	45 47.4	N19 49.6	305 15.8	S12 18.1	81 33.4	N21 40.6	309 31.2	S 7 44.4
Y 13	169 11.8	60 47.2	49.5	320 16.8	18.7	96 35.5	40.7	324 33.5	44.5
14	184 14.3	75 46.9	49.3	335 17.7	19.3	111 37.7	40.7	339 35.7	44.6
15	199 16.7	90 46.7 ..	49.2	350 18.6 ..	19.9	126 39.8 ..	40.7	354 38.0 ..	44.7
16	214 19.2	105 46.4	49.1	5 19.6	20.5	141 42.0	40.8	9 40.3	44.8
17	229 21.7	120 46.2	48.9	20 20.5	21.1	156 44.1	40.8	24 42.5	44.9
18	244 24.1	135 45.9	N19 48.8	35 21.4	S12 21.7	171 46.2	N21 40.8	39 44.8	S 7 45.0
19	259 26.6	150 45.7	48.7	50 22.4	22.3	186 48.4	40.9	54 47.0	45.0
20	274 29.0	165 45.4	48.5	65 23.3	22.8	201 50.5	40.9	69 49.3	45.1
21	289 31.5	180 45.1 ..	48.4	80 24.2 ..	23.4	216 52.7 ..	40.9	84 51.6 ..	45.2
22	304 34.0	195 44.9	48.3	95 25.2	24.0	231 54.8	41.0	99 53.8	45.3
23	319 36.4	210 44.6	48.1	110 26.1	24.6	246 57.0	41.0	114 56.1	45.4
26 00	334 38.9	225 44.4	N19 48.0	125 27.0	S12 25.2	261 59.1	N21 41.0	129 58.3	S 7 45.5
01	349 41.4	240 44.1	47.9	140 28.0	25.8	277 01.3	41.1	145 00.6	45.6
02	4 43.8	255 43.9	47.7	155 28.9	26.4	292 03.4	41.1	160 02.9	45.6
03	19 46.3	270 43.6 ..	47.6	170 29.8 ..	27.0	307 05.6 ..	41.1	175 05.1 ..	45.7
04	34 48.8	285 43.3	47.4	185 30.8	27.5	322 07.7	41.2	190 07.4	45.8
05	49 51.2	300 43.1	47.3	200 31.7	28.1	337 09.9	41.2	205 09.6	45.9
S 06	64 53.7	315 42.8	N19 47.2	215 32.6	S12 28.7	352 12.0	N21 41.2	220 11.9	S 7 46.0
U 07	79 56.2	330 42.6	47.0	230 33.6	29.3	7 14.2	41.3	235 14.1	46.1
N 08	94 58.6	345 42.3	46.9	245 34.5	29.9	22 16.3	41.3	250 16.4	46.2
D 09	110 01.1	0 42.0 ..	46.7	260 35.4 ..	30.5	37 18.5 ..	41.3	265 18.7 ..	46.3
A 10	125 03.5	15 41.8	46.6	275 36.3	31.1	52 20.6	41.4	280 20.9	46.3
Y 11	140 06.0	30 41.5	46.4	290 37.3	31.6	67 22.8	41.4	295 23.2	46.4
12	155 08.5	45 41.2	N19 46.3	305 38.2	S12 32.2	82 24.9	N21 41.4	310 25.4	S 7 46.5
13	170 10.9	60 41.0	46.1	320 39.1	32.8	97 27.1	41.5	325 27.7	46.6
14	185 13.4	75 40.7	46.0	335 40.1	33.4	112 29.2	41.5	340 29.9	46.7
15	200 15.9	90 40.4 ..	45.8	350 41.0 ..	34.0	127 31.4 ..	41.5	355 32.2 ..	46.8
16	215 18.3	105 40.2	45.7	5 41.9	34.6	142 33.5	41.6	10 34.5	46.9
17	230 20.8	120 39.9	45.5	20 42.8	35.2	157 35.7	41.6	25 36.7	47.0
18	245 23.3	135 39.6	N19 45.4	35 43.8	S12 35.7	172 37.8	N21 41.6	40 39.0	S 7 47.0
19	260 25.7	150 39.4	45.2	50 44.7	36.3	187 40.0	41.7	55 41.2	47.1
20	275 28.2	165 39.1	45.1	65 45.6	36.9	202 42.1	41.7	70 43.5	47.2
21	290 30.6	180 38.8 ..	44.9	80 46.5 ..	37.5	217 44.3 ..	41.7	85 45.7 ..	47.3
22	305 33.1	195 38.6	44.8	95 47.5	38.1	232 46.4	41.8	100 48.0	47.4
23	320 35.6	210 38.3	44.6	110 48.4	38.7	247 48.6	41.8	115 50.3	47.5
27 00	335 38.0	225 38.0	N19 44.4	125 49.3	S12 39.2	262 50.8	N21 41.8	130 52.5	S 7 47.6
01	350 40.5	240 37.8	44.3	140 50.2	39.8	277 52.9	41.9	145 54.8	47.7
02	5 43.0	255 37.5	44.1	155 51.2	40.4	292 55.1	41.9	160 57.0	47.8
03	20 45.4	270 37.2 ..	44.0	170 52.1 ..	41.0	307 57.2 ..	41.9	175 59.3 ..	47.8
04	35 47.9	285 37.0	43.8	185 53.0	41.6	322 59.4	42.0	191 01.5	47.9
05	50 50.4	300 36.7	43.6	200 53.9	42.2	338 01.5	42.0	206 03.8	48.0
M 06	65 52.8	315 36.4	N19 43.5	215 54.9	S12 42.8	353 03.7	N21 42.0	221 06.1	S 7 48.1
O 07	80 55.3	330 36.1	43.3	230 55.8	43.3	8 05.8	42.0	236 08.3	48.2
N 08	95 57.8	345 35.9	43.2	245 56.7	43.9	23 08.0	42.1	251 10.6	48.3
D 09	111 00.2	0 35.6 ..	43.0	260 57.6 ..	44.5	38 10.2 ..	42.1	266 12.8 ..	48.4
A 10	126 02.7	15 35.3	42.8	275 58.6	45.1	53 12.3	42.1	281 15.1	48.5
Y 11	141 05.1	30 35.0	42.7	290 59.5	45.7	68 14.5	42.2	296 17.3	48.5
12	156 07.6	45 34.8	N19 42.5	306 00.4	S12 46.3	83 16.6	N21 42.2	311 19.6	S 7 48.6
13	171 10.1	60 34.5	42.3	321 01.3	46.8	98 18.8	42.2	326 21.8	48.7
14	186 12.5	75 34.2	42.2	336 02.2	47.4	113 20.9	42.3	341 24.1	48.8
15	201 15.0	90 33.9 ..	42.0	351 03.2 ..	48.0	128 23.1 ..	42.3	356 26.3 ..	48.9
16	216 17.5	105 33.7	41.8	6 04.1	48.6	143 25.3	42.3	11 28.6	49.0
17	231 19.9	120 33.4	41.6	21 05.0	49.2	158 27.4	42.4	26 30.9	49.1
18	246 22.4	135 33.1	N19 41.5	36 05.9	S12 49.8	173 29.6	N21 42.4	41 33.1	S 7 49.2
19	261 24.9	150 32.8	41.3	51 06.8	50.3	188 31.7	42.4	56 35.4	49.3
20	276 27.3	165 32.5	41.1	66 07.8	50.9	203 33.9	42.5	71 37.6	49.3
21	291 29.8	180 32.3 ..	40.9	81 08.7 ..	51.5	218 36.1 ..	42.5	86 39.9 ..	49.4
22	306 32.3	195 32.0	40.8	96 09.6	52.1	233 38.2	42.5	101 42.1	49.5
23	321 34.7	210 31.7	40.6	111 10.5	52.7	248 40.4	42.6	116 44.4	49.6
Mer. Pass.	h m 1 41.1	v −0.3	d 0.1	v 0.9	d 0.6	v 2.2	d 0.0	v 2.3	d 0.1

STARS

Name	SHA	Dec
Acamar	315 18.6	S40 15.0
Achernar	335 26.8	S57 10.0
Acrux	173 10.5	S63 10.4
Adhara	255 13.2	S28 59.3
Aldebaran	290 50.0	N16 32.0
Alioth	166 21.6	N55 53.6
Alkaid	152 59.6	N49 15.2
Al Na'ir	27 43.9	S46 53.7
Alnilam	275 47.0	S 1 11.6
Alphard	217 56.9	S 8 42.8
Alphecca	126 11.5	N26 40.6
Alpheratz	357 43.7	N29 09.7
Altair	62 08.5	N 8 54.4
Ankaa	353 15.9	S42 13.9
Antares	112 26.9	S26 27.6
Arcturus	145 56.4	N19 07.2
Atria	107 29.1	S69 03.2
Avior	234 18.8	S59 33.0
Bellatrix	278 32.7	N 6 21.6
Betelgeuse	271 02.0	N 7 24.5
Canopus	263 56.7	S52 42.0
Capella	280 35.4	N46 00.4
Deneb	49 31.4	N45 19.9
Denebola	182 34.5	N14 30.1
Diphda	348 56.2	S17 54.8
Dubhe	193 53.0	N61 41.0
Elnath	278 13.4	N28 36.9
Eltanin	90 46.2	N51 29.6
Enif	33 47.3	N 9 56.3
Fomalhaut	15 24.2	S29 33.0
Gacrux	172 02.0	S57 11.2
Gienah	175 53.1	S17 36.8
Hadar	148 49.0	S60 26.2
Hamal	328 01.2	N23 31.4
Kaus Aust.	83 44.3	S34 22.6
Kochab	137 20.4	N74 06.5
Markab	13 38.5	N15 16.6
Menkar	314 15.5	N 4 08.4
Menkent	148 08.4	S36 26.0
Miaplacidus	221 40.7	S69 46.2
Mirfak	308 41.0	N49 54.2
Nunki	75 58.7	S26 16.7
Peacock	53 19.6	S56 41.5
Pollux	243 28.7	N27 59.6
Procyon	245 00.5	N 5 11.5
Rasalhague	96 06.8	N12 33.3
Regulus	207 44.4	N11 54.3
Rigel	281 12.7	S 8 11.2
Rigil Kent.	139 52.7	S60 53.4
Sabik	102 13.1	S15 44.3
Schedar	349 40.7	N56 36.4
Shaula	96 22.5	S37 06.7
Sirius	258 34.4	S16 44.0
Spica	158 32.0	S11 13.6
Suhail	222 53.3	S43 29.0
Vega	80 39.1	N38 48.1
Zuben'ubi	137 06.1	S16 05.6

	SHA	Mer. Pass.
	° ′	h m
Venus	251 05.5	8 57
Mars	150 48.1	15 37
Jupiter	287 20.2	6 24
Saturn	155 19.4	15 18

UT	SUN GHA	SUN Dec	MOON GHA	v	MOON Dec	d	HP
d h	° ′	° ′	° ′	′	° ′	′	′
25 00	179 28.5	N10 41.3	87 35.6	5.7	S20 58.0	2.5	59.2
01	194 28.6	40.4	102 00.3	5.6	21 00.5	2.5	59.2
02	209 28.8	39.6	116 24.9	5.7	21 03.0	2.3	59.2
03	224 29.0	.. 38.7	130 49.6	5.6	21 05.3	2.1	59.2
04	239 29.2	37.8	145 14.2	5.6	21 07.4	2.0	59.2
05	254 29.3	37.0	159 38.8	5.6	21 09.4	1.9	59.2
S 06	269 29.5	N10 36.1	174 03.4	5.6	S21 11.3	1.7	59.2
A 07	284 29.7	35.2	188 28.0	5.5	21 13.0	1.6	59.2
T 08	299 29.9	34.4	202 52.5	5.6	21 14.6	1.5	59.2
U 09	314 30.0	.. 33.5	217 17.1	5.6	21 16.1	1.3	59.2
R 10	329 30.2	32.6	231 41.7	5.5	21 17.4	1.1	59.2
D 11	344 30.4	31.8	246 06.2	5.6	21 18.5	1.1	59.2
A 12	359 30.6	N10 30.9	260 30.8	5.5	S21 19.6	0.8	59.2
Y 13	14 30.7	30.0	274 55.3	5.6	21 20.4	0.8	59.2
14	29 30.9	29.2	289 19.9	5.5	21 21.2	0.6	59.2
15	44 31.1	.. 28.3	303 44.4	5.6	21 21.8	0.4	59.2
16	59 31.3	27.4	318 09.0	5.6	21 22.2	0.4	59.2
17	74 31.4	26.6	332 33.6	5.5	21 22.6	0.1	59.2
18	89 31.6	N10 25.7	346 58.1	5.6	S21 22.7	0.1	59.1
19	104 31.8	24.8	1 22.7	5.6	21 22.8	0.2	59.1
20	119 32.0	24.0	15 47.3	5.6	21 22.6	0.2	59.1
21	134 32.1	.. 23.1	30 11.9	5.5	21 22.4	0.4	59.1
22	149 32.3	22.2	44 36.4	5.7	21 22.0	0.5	59.1
23	164 32.5	21.4	59 01.1	5.6	21 21.5	0.7	59.1
26 00	179 32.7	N10 20.5	73 25.7	5.6	S21 20.8	0.8	59.1
01	194 32.8	19.6	87 50.3	5.7	21 20.0	1.0	59.1
02	209 33.0	18.8	102 15.0	5.6	21 19.0	1.1	59.1
03	224 33.2	.. 17.9	116 39.6	5.7	21 17.9	1.2	59.1
04	239 33.4	17.0	131 04.3	5.7	21 16.7	1.4	59.1
05	254 33.6	16.1	145 29.0	5.6	21 15.3	1.5	59.1
S 06	269 33.7	N10 15.3	159 53.7	5.8	S21 13.8	1.7	59.1
U 07	284 33.9	14.4	174 18.5	5.7	21 12.1	1.8	59.1
N 08	299 34.1	13.5	188 43.2	5.8	21 10.3	1.9	59.1
D 09	314 34.3	.. 12.6	203 08.0	5.9	21 08.4	2.1	59.0
A 10	329 34.5	11.8	217 32.9	5.8	21 06.3	2.2	59.0
Y 11	344 34.6	10.9	231 57.7	5.9	21 04.1	2.3	59.0
12	359 34.8	N10 10.0	246 22.6	5.9	S21 01.8	2.5	59.0
13	14 35.0	09.2	260 47.5	5.9	20 59.3	2.6	59.0
14	29 35.2	08.3	275 12.4	6.0	20 56.7	2.8	59.0
15	44 35.3	.. 07.4	289 37.4	6.0	20 53.9	2.9	59.0
16	59 35.5	06.5	304 02.4	6.0	20 51.0	3.0	59.0
17	74 35.7	05.7	318 27.4	6.1	20 48.0	3.2	59.0
18	89 35.9	N10 04.8	332 52.5	6.1	S20 44.8	3.2	59.0
19	104 36.1	03.9	347 17.6	6.1	20 41.6	3.5	58.9
20	119 36.3	03.0	1 42.7	6.2	20 38.1	3.5	58.9
21	134 36.4	.. 02.2	16 07.9	6.2	20 34.6	3.7	58.9
22	149 36.6	01.3	30 33.1	6.3	20 30.9	3.8	58.9
23	164 36.8	10 00.4	44 58.4	6.3	20 27.1	4.0	58.9
27 00	179 37.0	N 9 59.5	59 23.7	6.4	S20 23.1	4.1	58.9
01	194 37.2	58.6	73 49.1	6.4	20 19.0	4.2	58.9
02	209 37.3	57.8	88 14.5	6.4	20 14.8	4.3	58.9
03	224 37.5	.. 56.9	102 39.9	6.5	20 10.5	4.5	58.9
04	239 37.7	56.0	117 05.4	6.5	20 06.0	4.6	58.9
05	254 37.9	55.1	131 30.9	6.6	20 01.4	4.7	58.8
M 06	269 38.1	N 9 54.3	145 56.5	6.6	S19 56.7	4.8	58.8
O 07	284 38.2	53.4	160 22.1	6.7	19 51.9	5.0	58.8
N 08	299 38.4	52.5	174 47.8	6.7	19 46.9	5.1	58.8
D 09	314 38.6	.. 51.6	189 13.5	6.8	19 41.8	5.2	58.8
A 10	329 38.8	50.7	203 39.3	6.9	19 36.6	5.3	58.8
Y 11	344 39.0	49.8	218 05.2	6.8	19 31.3	5.5	58.8
12	359 39.2	N 9 49.0	232 31.0	7.0	S19 25.8	5.6	58.8
13	14 39.3	48.1	246 57.0	7.0	19 20.2	5.6	58.7
14	29 39.5	47.2	261 23.0	7.0	19 14.6	5.9	58.7
15	44 39.7	.. 46.3	275 49.0	7.1	19 08.7	5.9	58.7
16	59 39.9	45.5	290 15.1	7.2	19 02.8	6.0	58.7
17	74 40.1	44.6	304 41.3	7.2	18 56.8	6.2	58.7
18	89 40.3	N 9 43.7	319 07.5	7.3	S18 50.6	6.3	58.7
19	104 40.5	42.8	333 33.8	7.4	18 44.3	6.3	58.7
20	119 40.6	41.9	348 00.2	7.4	18 38.0	6.5	58.6
21	134 40.8	.. 41.1	2 26.6	7.4	18 31.5	6.6	58.6
22	149 41.0	40.2	16 53.0	7.5	18 24.9	6.8	58.6
23	164 41.2	39.3	31 19.5	7.6	S18 18.1	6.8	58.6
SD 15.9	d 0.9		SD 16.1		16.1		16.0

Lat.	Twilight Naut.	Twilight Civil	Sunrise	Moonrise 25	26	27	28
°	h m	h m	h m	h m	h m	h m	h m
N 72	////	01 43	03 32	■	■	■	19 41
N 70	////	02 25	03 51	■	■	19 25	19 04
68	////	02 53	04 05	■	■	18 37	18 37
66	01 29	03 14	04 16	18 02	18 32	18 06	18 17
64	02 07	03 30	04 26	16 59	17 44	17 43	18 00
62	02 32	03 43	04 34	16 24	17 13	17 24	17 47
60	02 52	03 55	04 41	15 59	16 50	17 09	17 35
N 58	03 07	04 04	04 48	15 39	16 32	16 56	17 25
56	03 20	04 13	04 53	15 23	16 16	16 45	17 08
54	03 32	04 20	04 58	15 09	16 03	16 35	17 01
52	03 41	04 26	05 02	14 56	15 51	16 26	17 01
50	03 50	04 32	05 06	14 46	15 41	16 18	16 55
45	04 07	04 44	05 15	14 36	15 32	16 01	16 41
N 40	04 20	04 54	05 22	14 16	15 13	15 47	16 30
35	04 31	05 02	05 28	14 00	14 57	15 35	16 20
30	04 40	05 09	05 34	13 47	14 44	15 25	16 11
20	04 54	05 21	05 43	13 35	14 32	15 07	15 57
N 10	05 05	05 30	05 51	13 14	14 12	14 51	15 44
0	05 13	05 37	05 58	12 57	13 55	14 36	15 32
S 10	05 20	05 44	06 06	12 40	13 39	14 22	15 19
20	05 25	05 51	06 13	12 24	13 23	14 06	15 06
30	05 30	05 58	06 22	12 06	13 06	13 48	14 51
35	05 32	06 01	06 27	11 46	12 46	13 38	14 43
40	05 33	06 05	06 32	11 34	12 34	13 26	14 33
45	05 35	06 09	06 39	11 21	12 21	13 11	14 21
S 50	05 36	06 13	06 46	11 05	12 05	12 54	14 07
52	05 36	06 15	06 50	10 45	11 46	12 46	14 00
54	05 36	06 17	06 53	10 36	11 37	12 37	13 53
56	05 37	06 20	06 58	10 26	11 27	12 26	13 44
58	05 37	06 22	07 02	10 14	11 15	12 15	13 35
S 60	05 37	06 25	07 08	10 00	11 02	12 01	13 24

Lat.	Sunset	Twilight Civil	Twilight Naut.	Moonset 25	26	27	28
°	h m	h m	h m	h m	h m	h m	h m
N 72	20 27	22 12	////	■	■	■	■
N 70	20 10	21 33	////	■	■	22 26	24 41
68	19 56	21 06	23 56	19 46	21 19	23 13	25 06
66	19 45	20 46	22 27	20 49	22 07	23 43	25 25
64	19 35	20 31	21 52	21 24	22 37	24 06	00 06
62	19 27	20 18	21 27	21 50	23 00	24 24	00 24
60	19 20	20 07	21 09	22 10	23 18	24 39	00 39
N 58	19 14	19 57	20 53	22 26	23 34	24 51	00 51
56	19 09	19 49	20 41	22 40	23 47	25 02	01 02
54	19 04	19 42	20 30	22 52	23 58	25 12	01 12
52	19 00	19 36	20 21	23 03	24 08	00 08	01 20
50	18 56	19 30	20 12	23 12	24 17	00 17	01 28
45	18 47	19 18	19 55	23 32	24 36	00 36	01 44
N 40	18 40	19 08	19 42	23 48	24 51	00 51	01 57
35	18 34	19 00	19 31	24 02	00 02	01 04	02 09
30	18 29	18 54	19 23	24 14	00 14	01 15	02 18
20	18 20	18 43	19 09	24 34	00 34	01 34	02 35
N 10	18 12	18 34	18 58	24 52	00 52	01 51	02 50
0	18 05	18 26	18 50	00 09	01 08	02 07	03 03
S 10	17 58	18 19	18 44	00 25	01 25	02 22	03 17
20	17 50	18 13	18 38	00 43	01 42	02 39	03 31
30	17 42	18 06	18 34	01 03	02 01	02 58	03 47
35	17 37	18 03	18 32	01 14	02 14	03 08	03 57
40	17 32	17 59	18 31	01 27	02 28	03 21	04 07
45	17 25	17 55	18 29	01 43	02 44	03 36	04 20
S 50	17 18	17 51	18 28	02 03	03 03	03 54	04 34
52	17 15	17 49	18 28	02 12	03 12	04 02	04 42
54	17 11	17 47	18 28	02 22	03 23	04 12	04 50
56	17 07	17 45	18 28	02 34	03 34	04 22	04 59
58	17 02	17 42	18 28	02 47	03 48	04 35	05 09
S 60	16 57	17 40	18 28	03 03	04 04	04 49	05 20

Day	SUN Eqn. of Time 00ʰ	SUN Eqn. of Time 12ʰ	SUN Mer. Pass.	MOON Mer. Pass. Upper	MOON Mer. Pass. Lower	Age	Phase
d	m s	m s	h m	h m	h m	d	%
25	02 06	01 58	12 02	12 02	06 25	08	61
26	01 50	01 41	12 02	19 53	07 24	09	71
27	01 32	01 24	12 01	20 50	08 22	10	81

2012 AUGUST 28, 29, 30 (TUES., WED., THURS.)

UT	ARIES GHA	VENUS −4.3 GHA	Dec	MARS +1.2 GHA	Dec	JUPITER −2.3 GHA	Dec	SATURN +0.8 GHA	Dec	STARS Name	SHA	Dec
28 00	336 37.2	225 31.4	N19 40.4	126 11.4	S12 53.3	263 42.5	N21 42.6	131 46.6	S 7 49.7	Acamar	315 18.6	S40 15.0
01	351 39.6	240 31.1	40.2	141 12.4	53.8	278 44.7	42.6	146 48.9	49.8	Achernar	335 26.8	S57 10.0
02	6 42.1	255 30.8	40.1	156 13.3	54.4	293 46.9	42.6	161 51.1	49.9	Acrux	173 10.5	S63 10.3
03	21 44.6	270 30.6	.. 39.9	171 14.2	.. 55.0	308 49.0	.. 42.7	176 53.4	.. 50.0	Adhara	255 13.2	S28 59.3
04	36 47.0	285 30.3	39.7	186 15.1	55.6	323 51.2	42.7	191 55.7	50.1	Aldebaran	290 50.0	N16 32.0
05	51 49.5	300 30.0	39.5	201 16.0	56.2	338 53.4	42.7	206 57.9	50.1			
06	66 52.0	315 29.7	N19 39.3	216 16.9	S12 56.7	353 55.5	N21 42.8	222 00.2	S 7 50.2	Alioth	166 21.6	N55 53.6
07	81 54.4	330 29.4	39.2	231 17.9	57.3	8 57.7	42.8	237 02.4	50.3	Alkaid	152 59.6	N49 15.2
08	96 56.9	345 29.1	39.0	246 18.8	57.9	23 59.8	42.8	252 04.7	50.4	Al Na'ir	27 43.9	S46 53.8
T 09	111 59.4	0 28.9	.. 38.8	261 19.7	.. 58.5	39 02.0	.. 42.9	267 06.9	.. 50.5	Alnilam	275 47.0	S 1 11.6
U 10	127 01.8	15 28.6	38.6	276 20.6	59.1	54 04.2	42.9	282 09.2	50.6	Alphard	217 56.9	S 8 42.8
E 11	142 04.3	30 28.3	38.4	291 21.5	12 59.7	69 06.3	42.9	297 11.4	50.7			
S 12	157 06.8	45 28.0	N19 38.2	306 22.4	S13 00.2	84 08.5	N21 43.0	312 13.7	S 7 50.8	Alphecca	126 11.5	N26 40.6
D 13	172 09.2	60 27.7	38.0	321 23.4	00.8	99 10.7	43.0	327 15.9	50.9	Alpheratz	357 43.7	N29 09.8
A 14	187 11.7	75 27.4	37.9	336 24.3	01.4	114 12.8	43.0	342 18.2	50.9	Altair	62 08.5	N 8 54.4
Y 15	202 14.1	90 27.1	.. 37.7	351 25.2	.. 02.0	129 15.0	.. 43.0	357 20.4	.. 51.0	Ankaa	353 15.8	S42 13.9
16	217 16.6	105 26.8	37.5	6 26.1	02.6	144 17.2	43.1	12 22.7	51.1	Antares	112 26.9	S26 27.6
17	232 19.1	120 26.6	37.3	21 27.0	03.1	159 19.3	43.1	27 24.9	51.2			
18	247 21.5	135 26.3	N19 37.1	36 27.9	S13 03.7	174 21.5	N21 43.1	42 27.2	S 7 51.3	Arcturus	145 56.4	N19 07.2
19	262 24.0	150 26.0	36.9	51 28.8	04.3	189 23.7	43.2	57 29.4	51.4	Atria	107 29.1	S69 03.2
20	277 26.5	165 25.7	36.7	66 29.7	04.9	204 25.8	43.2	72 31.7	51.5	Avior	234 18.8	S59 33.0
21	292 28.9	180 25.4	.. 36.5	81 30.7	.. 05.5	219 28.0	.. 43.2	87 33.9	.. 51.6	Bellatrix	278 32.7	N 6 21.7
22	307 31.4	195 25.1	36.3	96 31.6	06.0	234 30.2	43.3	102 36.2	51.7	Betelgeuse	271 02.0	N 7 24.5
23	322 33.9	210 24.8	36.1	111 32.5	06.6	249 32.3	43.3	117 38.4	51.7			
29 00	337 36.3	225 24.5	N19 35.9	126 33.4	S13 07.2	264 34.5	N21 43.3	132 40.7	S 7 51.8	Canopus	263 56.6	S52 42.0
01	352 38.8	240 24.2	35.7	141 34.3	07.8	279 36.7	43.3	147 43.0	51.9	Capella	280 35.3	N46 00.4
02	7 41.2	255 23.9	35.5	156 35.2	08.4	294 38.8	43.4	162 45.2	52.0	Deneb	49 31.4	N45 19.9
03	22 43.7	270 23.6	.. 35.3	171 36.1	.. 08.9	309 41.0	.. 43.4	177 47.5	.. 52.1	Denebola	182 34.5	N14 30.1
04	37 46.2	285 23.3	35.1	186 37.0	09.5	324 43.2	43.4	192 49.7	52.2	Diphda	348 56.1	S17 54.8
05	52 48.6	300 23.0	34.9	201 37.9	10.1	339 45.3	43.5	207 52.0	52.3			
06	67 51.1	315 22.8	N19 34.7	216 38.9	S13 10.7	354 47.5	N21 43.5	222 54.2	S 7 52.4	Dubhe	193 53.0	N61 40.9
W 07	82 53.6	330 22.5	34.5	231 39.8	11.3	9 49.7	43.5	237 56.5	52.5	Elnath	278 13.4	N28 36.9
E 08	97 56.0	345 22.2	34.3	246 40.7	11.8	24 51.9	43.6	252 58.7	52.6	Eltanin	90 46.2	N51 29.6
D 09	112 58.5	0 21.9	.. 34.1	261 41.6	.. 12.4	39 54.0	.. 43.6	268 01.0	.. 52.6	Enif	33 47.3	N 9 56.3
N 10	128 01.0	15 21.6	33.9	276 42.5	13.0	54 56.2	43.6	283 03.2	52.7	Fomalhaut	15 24.2	S29 33.0
E 11	143 03.4	30 21.3	33.7	291 43.4	13.6	69 58.4	43.6	298 05.5	52.8			
S 12	158 05.9	45 21.0	N19 33.5	306 44.3	S13 14.1	85 00.5	N21 43.7	313 07.7	S 7 52.9	Gacrux	172 02.0	S57 11.2
D 13	173 08.4	60 20.7	33.3	321 45.2	14.7	100 02.7	43.7	328 10.0	53.0	Gienah	175 53.1	S17 36.8
A 14	188 10.8	75 20.4	33.1	336 46.1	15.3	115 04.9	43.7	343 12.2	53.1	Hadar	148 49.0	S60 26.2
Y 15	203 13.3	90 20.1	.. 32.9	351 47.0	.. 15.9	130 07.0	.. 43.8	358 14.5	.. 53.2	Hamal	328 01.2	N23 31.4
16	218 15.7	105 19.8	32.7	6 47.9	16.5	145 09.2	43.8	13 16.7	53.3	Kaus Aust.	83 44.3	S34 22.6
17	233 18.2	120 19.5	32.4	21 48.8	17.0	160 11.4	43.8	28 19.0	53.4			
18	248 20.7	135 19.2	N19 32.2	36 49.8	S13 17.6	175 13.6	N21 43.9	43 21.2	S 7 53.4	Kochab	137 20.4	N74 06.5
19	263 23.1	150 18.9	32.0	51 50.7	18.2	190 15.7	43.9	58 23.5	53.5	Markab	13 38.5	N15 16.6
20	278 25.6	165 18.6	31.8	66 51.6	18.8	205 17.9	43.9	73 25.7	53.6	Menkar	314 15.5	N 4 08.5
21	293 28.1	180 18.3	.. 31.6	81 52.5	.. 19.4	220 20.1	.. 43.9	88 28.0	.. 53.7	Menkent	148 08.4	S36 26.0
22	308 30.5	195 18.0	31.4	96 53.4	19.9	235 22.3	44.0	103 30.2	53.8	Miaplacidus	221 40.7	S69 46.2
23	323 33.0	210 17.7	31.2	111 54.3	20.5	250 24.4	44.0	118 32.5	53.9			
30 00	338 35.5	225 17.4	N19 30.9	126 55.2	S13 21.1	265 26.6	N21 44.0	133 34.7	S 7 54.0	Mirfak	308 41.0	N49 54.2
01	353 37.9	240 17.1	30.7	141 56.1	21.7	280 28.8	44.1	148 37.0	54.1	Nunki	75 58.7	S26 16.7
02	8 40.4	255 16.8	30.5	156 57.0	22.2	295 31.0	44.1	163 39.2	54.2	Peacock	53 19.6	S56 41.5
03	23 42.9	270 16.5	.. 30.3	171 57.9	.. 22.8	310 33.1	.. 44.1	178 41.5	.. 54.3	Pollux	243 28.7	N27 59.6
04	38 45.3	285 16.2	30.1	186 58.8	23.4	325 35.3	44.1	193 43.7	54.3	Procyon	245 00.5	N 5 11.5
05	53 47.8	300 15.8	29.8	201 59.7	24.0	340 37.5	44.2	208 45.9	54.4			
06	68 50.2	315 15.5	N19 29.6	217 00.6	S13 24.5	355 39.7	N21 44.2	223 48.2	S 7 54.5	Rasalhague	96 06.8	N12 33.3
07	83 52.7	330 15.2	29.4	232 01.5	25.1	10 41.8	44.2	238 50.4	54.6	Regulus	207 44.4	N11 54.3
T 08	98 55.2	345 14.9	29.2	247 02.4	25.7	25 44.0	44.3	253 52.7	54.7	Rigel	281 12.6	S 8 11.2
H 09	113 57.6	0 14.6	.. 28.9	262 03.3	.. 26.3	40 46.2	.. 44.3	268 54.9	.. 54.8	Rigil Kent.	139 52.7	S60 53.4
U 10	129 00.1	15 14.3	28.7	277 04.2	26.9	55 48.4	44.3	283 57.2	54.9	Sabik	102 13.1	S15 44.3
R 11	144 02.6	30 14.0	28.5	292 05.1	27.4	70 50.6	44.3	298 59.4	55.0			
S 12	159 05.0	45 13.7	N19 28.3	307 06.0	S13 28.0	85 52.7	N21 44.4	314 01.7	S 7 55.1	Schedar	349 40.7	N56 36.4
D 13	174 07.5	60 13.4	28.0	322 06.9	28.6	100 54.9	44.4	329 03.9	55.2	Shaula	96 22.5	S37 06.7
A 14	189 10.0	75 13.1	27.8	337 07.8	29.2	115 57.1	44.4	344 06.2	55.3	Sirius	258 34.4	S16 44.0
Y 15	204 12.4	90 12.8	.. 27.6	352 08.7	.. 29.7	130 59.3	.. 44.5	359 08.4	.. 55.3	Spica	158 32.0	S11 13.6
16	219 14.9	105 12.5	27.4	7 09.6	30.3	146 01.4	44.5	14 10.7	55.4	Suhail	222 53.2	S43 29.0
17	234 17.3	120 12.2	27.1	22 10.5	30.9	161 03.6	44.5	29 12.9	55.5			
18	249 19.8	135 11.8	N19 26.9	37 11.4	S13 31.5	176 05.8	N21 44.5	44 15.2	S 7 55.6	Vega	80 39.1	N38 48.1
19	264 22.3	150 11.5	26.7	52 12.3	32.0	191 08.0	44.6	59 17.4	55.7	Zuben'ubi	137 06.1	S16 05.6
20	279 24.7	165 11.2	26.4	67 13.2	32.6	206 10.2	44.6	74 19.7	55.8		SHA	Mer.Pass.
21	294 27.2	180 10.9	.. 26.2	82 14.1	.. 33.2	221 12.3	.. 44.6	89 21.9	.. 55.9	Venus	247 48.2	8 59
22	309 29.7	195 10.6	26.0	97 15.0	33.8	236 14.5	44.7	104 24.2	56.0	Mars	148 57.1	15 33
23	324 32.1	210 10.3	25.7	112 15.9	34.3	251 16.7	44.7	119 26.4	56.1	Jupiter	286 58.2	6 21
Mer. Pass.	1 29.3	v −0.3	d 0.2	v 0.9	d 0.6	v 2.2	d 0.0	v 2.3	d 0.1	Saturn	155 04.4	15 07

UT	SUN GHA	SUN Dec	MOON GHA	v	MOON Dec	d	HP
d h	° '	° '	° '	'	° '	'	'
28 00	179 41.4	N 9 38.4	45 46.1	7.7	S18 11.3	6.9	58.6
01	194 41.6	37.5	60 12.8	7.7	18 04.4	7.1	58.6
02	209 41.7	36.6	74 39.5	7.7	17 57.3	7.1	58.6
03	224 41.9	.. 35.8	89 06.2	7.9	17 50.2	7.3	58.6
04	239 42.1	34.9	103 33.1	7.9	17 42.9	7.3	58.5
05	254 42.3	34.0	118 00.0	7.9	17 35.6	7.5	58.5
06	269 42.5	N 9 33.1	132 26.9	8.0	S17 28.1	7.5	58.5
07	284 42.7	32.2	146 53.9	8.1	17 20.6	7.7	58.5
08	299 42.9	31.3	161 21.0	8.2	17 12.9	7.7	58.5
09	314 43.1	.. 30.4	175 48.2	8.2	17 05.2	7.9	58.5
10	329 43.2	29.6	190 15.4	8.3	16 57.3	8.0	58.5
11	344 43.4	28.7	204 42.7	8.3	16 49.3	8.0	58.4
12	359 43.6	N 9 27.8	219 10.0	8.4	S16 41.3	8.1	58.4
13	14 43.8	26.9	233 37.4	8.5	16 33.2	8.3	58.4
14	29 44.0	26.0	248 04.9	8.6	16 24.9	8.3	58.4
15	44 44.2	.. 25.1	262 32.5	8.6	16 16.6	8.4	58.4
16	59 44.4	24.2	277 00.1	8.7	16 08.2	8.5	58.4
17	74 44.6	23.3	291 27.8	8.7	15 59.7	8.6	58.3
18	89 44.7	N 9 22.5	305 55.5	8.8	S15 51.1	8.7	58.3
19	104 44.9	21.6	320 23.3	8.9	15 42.4	8.8	58.3
20	119 45.1	20.7	334 51.2	9.0	15 33.6	8.8	58.3
21	134 45.3	.. 19.8	349 19.2	9.0	15 24.8	9.0	58.3
22	149 45.5	18.9	3 47.2	9.1	15 15.8	9.0	58.3
23	164 45.7	18.0	18 15.3	9.1	15 06.8	9.1	58.2
29 00	179 45.9	N 9 17.1	32 43.4	9.2	S14 57.7	9.2	58.2
01	194 46.1	16.2	47 11.6	9.3	14 48.5	9.2	58.2
02	209 46.3	15.4	61 39.9	9.3	14 39.3	9.4	58.2
03	224 46.4	.. 14.5	76 08.2	9.5	14 29.9	9.4	58.2
04	239 46.6	13.6	90 36.7	9.4	14 20.5	9.5	58.2
05	254 46.8	12.7	105 05.1	9.6	14 11.0	9.5	58.1
06	269 47.0	N 9 11.8	119 33.7	9.6	S14 01.5	9.7	58.1
07	284 47.2	10.9	134 02.3	9.7	13 51.8	9.7	58.1
08	299 47.4	10.0	148 31.0	9.7	13 42.1	9.7	58.1
09	314 47.6	.. 09.1	162 59.7	9.8	13 32.4	9.9	58.1
10	329 47.8	08.2	177 28.5	9.9	13 22.5	9.9	58.0
11	344 48.0	07.3	191 57.4	10.0	13 12.6	10.0	58.0
12	359 48.2	N 9 06.4	206 26.4	10.0	S13 02.6	10.0	58.0
13	14 48.3	05.5	220 55.4	10.1	12 52.6	10.1	58.0
14	29 48.5	04.7	235 24.5	10.1	12 42.5	10.2	58.0
15	44 48.7	.. 03.8	249 53.6	10.2	12 32.3	10.2	57.9
16	59 48.9	02.9	264 22.8	10.3	12 22.1	10.3	57.9
17	74 49.1	02.0	278 52.1	10.3	12 11.8	10.4	57.9
18	89 49.3	N 9 01.1	293 21.4	10.4	S12 01.4	10.4	57.9
19	104 49.5	9 00.2	307 50.8	10.4	11 51.0	10.5	57.9
20	119 49.7	8 59.3	322 20.2	10.6	11 40.5	10.5	57.8
21	134 49.9	.. 58.4	336 49.8	10.6	11 30.0	10.6	57.8
22	149 50.1	57.5	351 19.4	10.6	11 19.4	10.6	57.8
23	164 50.3	56.6	5 49.0	10.7	11 08.8	10.7	57.8
30 00	179 50.5	N 8 55.7	20 18.7	10.8	S10 58.1	10.7	57.8
01	194 50.7	54.8	34 48.5	10.8	10 47.4	10.8	57.7
02	209 50.8	53.9	49 18.3	10.9	10 36.6	10.8	57.7
03	224 51.0	.. 53.0	63 48.2	10.9	10 25.8	10.9	57.7
04	239 51.2	52.1	78 18.1	11.0	10 14.9	10.9	57.7
05	254 51.4	51.2	92 48.1	11.1	10 04.0	11.0	57.7
06	269 51.6	N 8 50.3	107 18.2	11.1	S 9 53.0	11.0	57.6
07	284 51.8	49.4	121 48.3	11.2	9 42.0	11.1	57.6
08	299 52.0	48.5	136 18.5	11.3	9 30.9	11.1	57.6
09	314 52.2	.. 47.6	150 48.8	11.3	9 19.8	11.1	57.6
10	329 52.4	46.7	165 19.1	11.3	9 08.7	11.2	57.6
11	344 52.6	45.8	179 49.4	11.4	8 57.5	11.2	57.5
12	359 52.8	N 8 44.9	194 19.8	11.5	S 8 46.3	11.3	57.5
13	14 53.0	44.0	208 50.3	11.5	8 35.0	11.2	57.5
14	29 53.2	43.1	223 20.8	11.6	8 23.8	11.4	57.5
15	44 53.4	.. 42.2	237 51.4	11.6	8 12.4	11.3	57.4
16	59 53.6	41.3	252 22.0	11.7	8 01.1	11.4	57.4
17	74 53.8	40.4	266 52.7	11.7	7 49.7	11.4	57.4
18	89 54.0	N 8 39.6	281 23.4	11.8	S 7 38.3	11.5	57.4
19	104 54.1	38.7	295 54.2	11.8	7 26.8	11.4	57.4
20	119 54.3	37.7	310 25.0	11.9	7 15.4	11.5	57.3
21	134 54.5	.. 36.8	324 55.9	12.0	7 03.9	11.5	57.3
22	149 54.7	35.9	339 26.9	12.0	6 52.4	11.6	57.3
23	164 54.9	35.0	353 57.9	12.0	S 6 40.8	11.6	57.3
	SD 15.9	d 0.9	SD 15.9		15.8		15.7

Column indicator for days: T U E S D A Y (28); W E D N E S D A Y (29); T H U R S D A Y (30).

Lat.	Twilight Naut.	Twilight Civil	Sunrise	Moonrise 28	29	30	31
°	h m	h m	h m	h m	h m	h m	h m
N 72	////	02 11	03 48	19 41	19 12	18 53	18 38
N 70	////	02 44	04 04	19 04	18 52	18 42	18 34
68	01 01	03 08	04 16	18 37	18 36	18 33	18 31
66	01 52	03 26	04 26	18 17	18 23	18 26	18 28
64	02 23	03 41	04 35	18 00	18 12	18 20	18 26
62	02 45	03 53	04 42	17 47	18 02	18 14	18 24
60	03 02	04 03	04 49	17 35	17 54	18 09	18 22
N 58	03 16	04 11	04 54	17 25	17 47	18 05	18 21
56	03 28	04 19	04 59	17 16	17 41	18 01	18 19
54	03 39	04 26	05 03	17 08	17 35	17 58	18 18
52	03 47	04 32	05 07	17 01	17 30	17 55	18 17
50	03 55	04 37	05 11	16 55	17 26	17 52	18 16
45	04 11	04 48	05 19	16 41	17 16	17 46	18 13
N 40	04 24	04 57	05 25	16 30	17 07	17 41	18 11
35	04 34	05 05	05 31	16 20	17 00	17 36	18 09
30	04 42	05 11	05 35	16 11	16 54	17 32	18 08
20	04 55	05 21	05 44	15 57	16 43	17 25	18 05
N 10	05 05	05 30	05 51	15 44	16 33	17 19	18 03
0	05 12	05 37	05 57	15 32	16 24	17 13	18 01
S 10	05 18	05 43	06 04	15 19	16 15	17 08	17 59
20	05 23	05 49	06 11	15 06	16 05	17 02	17 56
30	05 26	05 54	06 18	14 51	15 54	16 55	17 54
35	05 28	05 57	06 23	14 43	15 47	16 51	17 52
40	05 29	06 00	06 28	14 33	15 40	16 46	17 51
45	05 30	06 04	06 33	14 21	15 31	16 41	17 49
S 50	05 30	06 07	06 40	14 07	15 21	16 34	17 46
52	05 30	06 09	06 43	14 00	15 16	16 31	17 45
54	05 30	06 11	06 46	13 53	15 11	16 28	17 44
56	05 30	06 12	06 50	13 44	15 05	16 25	17 43
58	05 30	06 14	06 54	13 35	14 58	16 21	17 41
S 60	05 29	06 17	06 59	13 24	14 50	16 16	17 40

Lat.	Sunset	Twilight Civil	Twilight Naut.	Moonset 28	29	30	31
°	h m	h m	h m	h m	h m	h m	h m
N 72	20 10	21 44	////	■	00 05	02 22	04 22
N 70	19 55	21 13	////	24 41	00 41	02 40	04 31
68	19 43	20 50	22 49	25 06	01 06	02 54	04 38
66	19 33	20 33	22 03	25 25	01 25	03 06	04 43
64	19 25	20 18	21 35	00 06	01 41	03 16	04 48
62	19 18	20 07	21 13	00 24	01 54	03 24	04 52
60	19 11	19 57	20 57	00 39	02 05	03 31	04 56
N 58	19 06	19 48	20 43	00 51	02 14	03 37	04 59
56	19 01	19 41	20 31	01 02	02 22	03 43	05 02
54	18 57	19 34	20 21	01 12	02 29	03 48	05 04
52	18 53	19 29	20 13	01 20	02 36	03 52	05 07
50	18 50	19 23	20 05	01 28	02 42	03 56	05 09
45	18 42	19 12	19 49	01 44	02 54	04 05	05 13
N 40	18 36	19 04	19 37	01 57	03 05	04 12	05 17
35	18 30	18 56	19 27	02 09	03 14	04 18	05 20
30	18 26	18 50	19 19	02 18	03 21	04 23	05 23
20	18 18	18 40	19 06	02 35	03 35	04 32	05 28
N 10	18 11	18 32	18 57	02 50	03 46	04 40	05 32
0	18 04	18 25	18 49	03 03	03 57	04 48	05 36
S 10	17 58	18 19	18 44	03 17	04 08	04 55	05 40
20	17 51	18 13	18 39	03 31	04 19	05 03	05 44
30	17 44	18 08	18 36	03 47	04 32	05 12	05 49
35	17 39	18 05	18 34	03 57	04 39	05 17	05 52
40	17 35	18 02	18 33	04 07	04 48	05 23	05 55
45	17 29	17 59	18 33	04 20	04 57	05 30	05 58
S 50	17 22	17 55	18 33	04 35	05 09	05 37	06 02
52	17 19	17 54	18 33	04 42	05 14	05 41	06 04
54	17 16	17 52	18 33	04 50	05 20	05 45	06 06
56	17 12	17 50	18 33	04 59	05 27	05 50	06 09
58	17 08	17 48	18 34	05 09	05 34	05 54	06 11
S 60	17 04	17 46	18 34	05 20	05 43	06 00	06 14

Day	SUN Eqn. of Time 00h	12h	SUN Mer. Pass.	MOON Mer. Pass. Upper	Lower	Age	Phase
d	m s	m s	h m	h m	h m	d	%
28	01 15	01 06	12 01	21 44	09 17	11	89
29	00 57	00 48	12 01	22 36	10 10	12	95
30	00 39	00 29	12 00	23 25	11 01	13	98

Phase: ◯

2012 AUG. 31, SEPT. 1, 2 (FRI., SAT., SUN.)

UT	ARIES	VENUS −4.3		MARS +1.2		JUPITER −2.3		SATURN +0.8		STARS		
	GHA	GHA	Dec	GHA	Dec	GHA	Dec	GHA	Dec	Name	SHA	Dec
d h	° ′	° ′	° ′	° ′	° ′	° ′	° ′	° ′	° ′		° ′	° ′
31 00	339 34.6	225 10.0	N19 25.5	127 16.8	S13 34.9	266 18.9	N21 44.7	134 28.7	S 7 56.2	Acamar	315 18.6	S40 15.0
01	354 37.1	240 09.7	25.2	142 17.7	35.5	281 21.1	44.7	149 30.9	56.3	Achernar	335 26.8	S57 10.0
02	9 39.5	255 09.3	25.0	157 18.6	36.1	296 23.3	44.8	164 33.1	56.3	Acrux	173 10.5	S63 10.3
03	24 42.0	270 09.0	.. 24.8	172 19.5	.. 36.6	311 25.4	.. 44.8	179 35.4	.. 56.4	Adhara	255 13.2	S28 59.3
04	39 44.5	285 08.7	24.5	187 20.4	37.2	326 27.6	44.8	194 37.6	56.5	Aldebaran	290 50.0	N16 32.0
05	54 46.9	300 08.4	24.3	202 21.3	37.8	341 29.8	44.9	209 39.9	56.6			
06	69 49.4	315 08.1	N19 24.0	217 22.2	S13 38.4	356 32.0	N21 44.9	224 42.1	S 7 56.7	Alioth	166 21.6	N55 53.6
07	84 51.8	330 07.8	23.8	232 23.1	38.9	11 34.2	44.9	239 44.4	56.8	Alkaid	152 59.6	N49 15.2
08	99 54.3	345 07.5	23.5	247 24.0	39.5	26 36.4	44.9	254 46.6	56.9	Al Na'ir	27 43.9	S46 53.8
F 09	114 56.8	0 07.1	.. 23.3	262 24.9	.. 40.1	41 38.5	.. 45.0	269 48.9	.. 57.0	Alnilam	275 47.0	S 1 11.6
R 10	129 59.2	15 06.8	23.1	277 25.8	40.7	56 40.7	45.0	284 51.1	57.1	Alphard	217 56.9	S 8 42.8
I 11	145 01.7	30 06.5	22.8	292 26.7	41.2	71 42.9	45.0	299 53.4	57.2			
D 12	160 04.2	45 06.2	N19 22.6	307 27.6	S13 41.8	86 45.1	N21 45.1	314 55.6	S 7 57.3	Alphecca	126 11.5	N26 40.6
A 13	175 06.6	60 05.9	22.3	322 28.4	42.4	101 47.3	45.1	329 57.9	57.3	Alpheratz	357 43.7	N29 09.8
Y 14	190 09.1	75 05.6	22.1	337 29.3	43.0	116 49.5	45.1	345 00.1	57.4	Altair	62 08.5	N 8 54.4
15	205 11.6	90 05.2	.. 21.8	352 30.2	.. 43.5	131 51.6	.. 45.1	0 02.3	.. 57.5	Ankaa	353 15.8	S42 13.9
16	220 14.0	105 04.9	21.6	7 31.1	44.1	146 53.8	45.2	15 04.6	57.6	Antares	112 26.9	S26 27.6
17	235 16.5	120 04.6	21.3	22 32.0	44.7	161 56.0	45.2	30 06.8	57.7			
18	250 18.9	135 04.3	N19 21.1	37 32.9	S13 45.2	176 58.2	N21 45.2	45 09.1	S 7 57.8	Arcturus	145 56.4	N19 07.2
19	265 21.4	150 04.0	20.8	52 33.8	45.8	192 00.4	45.2	60 11.3	57.9	Atria	107 29.1	S69 03.2
20	280 23.9	165 03.6	20.6	67 34.7	46.4	207 02.6	45.3	75 13.6	58.0	Avior	234 18.8	S59 32.9
21	295 26.3	180 03.3	.. 20.3	82 35.6	.. 47.0	222 04.8	.. 45.3	90 15.8	.. 58.1	Bellatrix	278 32.6	N 6 21.7
22	310 28.8	195 03.0	20.0	97 36.5	47.5	237 07.0	45.3	105 18.1	58.2	Betelgeuse	271 02.0	N 7 24.5
23	325 31.3	210 02.7	19.8	112 37.4	48.1	252 09.1	45.4	120 20.3	58.3			
1 00	340 33.7	225 02.4	N19 19.5	127 38.3	S13 48.7	267 11.3	N21 45.4	135 22.5	S 7 58.3	Canopus	263 56.6	S52 42.0
01	355 36.2	240 02.0	19.3	142 39.1	49.2	282 13.5	45.4	150 24.8	58.4	Capella	280 35.3	N46 00.4
02	10 38.7	255 01.7	19.0	157 40.0	49.8	297 15.7	45.4	165 27.0	58.5	Deneb	49 31.4	N45 19.9
03	25 41.1	270 01.4	.. 18.7	172 40.9	.. 50.4	312 17.9	.. 45.5	180 29.3	.. 58.6	Denebola	182 34.5	N14 30.1
04	40 43.6	285 01.1	18.5	187 41.8	51.0	327 20.1	45.5	195 31.5	58.7	Diphda	348 56.1	S17 54.8
05	55 46.1	300 00.7	18.2	202 42.7	51.5	342 22.3	45.5	210 33.8	58.8			
06	70 48.5	315 00.4	N19 18.0	217 43.6	S13 52.1	357 24.5	N21 45.5	225 36.0	S 7 58.9	Dubhe	193 53.0	N61 40.9
07	85 51.0	330 00.1	17.7	232 44.5	52.7	12 26.7	45.6	240 38.3	59.0	Elnath	278 13.4	N28 36.9
S 08	100 53.4	344 59.8	17.4	247 45.4	53.3	27 28.8	45.6	255 40.5	59.1	Eltanin	90 46.2	N51 29.6
A 09	115 55.9	359 59.4	.. 17.2	262 46.3	.. 53.8	42 31.0	.. 45.6	270 42.7	.. 59.2	Enif	33 47.3	N 9 56.3
T 10	130 58.4	14 59.1	16.9	277 47.1	54.4	57 33.2	45.7	285 45.0	59.3	Fomalhaut	15 24.2	S29 33.0
U 11	146 00.8	29 58.8	16.6	292 48.0	55.0	72 35.4	45.7	300 47.2	59.4			
R 12	161 03.3	44 58.5	N19 16.4	307 48.9	S13 55.5	87 37.6	N21 45.7	315 49.5	S 7 59.5	Gacrux	172 02.0	S57 11.2
D 13	176 05.8	59 58.1	16.1	322 49.8	56.1	102 39.8	45.7	330 51.7	59.5	Gienah	175 53.1	S17 36.8
A 14	191 08.2	74 57.8	15.8	337 50.7	56.7	117 42.0	45.8	345 54.0	59.6	Hadar	148 49.0	S60 26.2
Y 15	206 10.7	89 57.5	.. 15.6	352 51.6	.. 57.2	132 44.2	.. 45.8	0 56.2	.. 59.7	Hamal	328 01.1	N23 31.4
16	221 13.2	104 57.2	15.3	7 52.5	57.8	147 46.4	45.8	15 58.4	59.8	Kaus Aust.	83 44.3	S34 22.6
17	236 15.6	119 56.8	15.0	22 53.4	58.4	162 48.6	45.8	31 00.7	7 59.9			
18	251 18.1	134 56.5	N19 14.7	37 54.2	S13 59.0	177 50.8	N21 45.9	46 02.9	S 8 00.0	Kochab	137 20.5	N74 06.5
19	266 20.6	149 56.2	14.5	52 55.1	13 59.5	192 53.0	45.9	61 05.2	00.1	Markab	13 38.5	N15 16.6
20	281 23.0	164 55.8	14.2	67 56.0	14 00.1	207 55.2	45.9	76 07.4	00.2	Menkar	314 15.5	N 4 08.5
21	296 25.5	179 55.5	.. 13.9	82 56.9	.. 00.7	222 57.4	.. 45.9	91 09.7	.. 00.3	Menkent	148 08.4	S36 26.0
22	311 27.9	194 55.2	13.6	97 57.8	01.2	237 59.6	46.0	106 11.9	00.4	Miaplacidus	221 40.6	S69 46.1
23	326 30.4	209 54.9	13.4	112 58.7	01.8	253 01.7	46.0	121 14.1	00.5			
2 00	341 32.9	224 54.5	N19 13.1	127 59.5	S14 02.4	268 03.9	N21 46.0	136 16.4	S 8 00.6	Mirfak	308 41.0	N49 54.2
01	356 35.3	239 54.2	12.8	143 00.4	02.9	283 06.1	46.1	151 18.6	00.6	Nunki	75 58.8	S26 16.7
02	11 37.8	254 53.9	12.5	158 01.3	03.5	298 08.3	46.1	166 20.9	00.7	Peacock	53 19.6	S56 41.6
03	26 40.3	269 53.5	.. 12.2	173 02.2	.. 04.1	313 10.5	.. 46.1	181 23.1	.. 00.8	Pollux	243 28.6	N27 59.6
04	41 42.7	284 53.2	12.0	188 03.1	04.7	328 12.7	46.1	196 25.3	00.9	Procyon	245 00.5	N 5 11.5
05	56 45.2	299 52.9	11.7	203 04.0	05.2	343 14.9	46.2	211 27.6	01.0			
06	71 47.7	314 52.5	N19 11.4	218 04.8	S14 05.8	358 17.1	N21 46.2	226 29.8	S 8 01.1	Rasalhague	96 06.9	N12 33.3
07	86 50.1	329 52.2	11.1	233 05.7	06.4	13 19.3	46.2	241 32.1	01.2	Regulus	207 44.4	N11 54.3
08	101 52.6	344 51.9	10.8	248 06.6	06.9	28 21.5	46.2	256 34.3	01.3	Rigel	281 12.6	S 8 11.1
S 09	116 55.0	359 51.5	.. 10.5	263 07.5	.. 07.5	43 23.7	.. 46.3	271 36.6	.. 01.4	Rigil Kent.	139 52.8	S60 53.4
U 10	131 57.5	14 51.2	10.3	278 08.4	08.1	58 25.9	46.3	286 38.8	01.5	Sabik	102 13.1	S15 44.3
N 11	147 00.0	29 50.9	10.0	293 09.2	08.6	73 28.1	46.3	301 41.0	01.6			
D 12	162 02.4	44 50.5	N19 09.7	308 10.1	S14 09.2	88 30.3	N21 46.3	316 43.3	S 8 01.7	Schedar	349 40.6	N56 36.4
A 13	177 04.9	59 50.2	09.4	323 11.0	09.8	103 32.5	46.3	331 45.5	01.8	Shaula	96 22.5	S37 06.7
Y 14	192 07.4	74 49.9	09.1	338 11.9	10.3	118 34.7	46.4	346 47.8	01.8	Sirius	258 34.4	S16 43.9
15	207 09.8	89 49.5	.. 08.8	353 12.8	.. 10.9	133 36.9	.. 46.4	1 50.0	.. 01.9	Spica	158 32.0	S11 13.6
16	222 12.3	104 49.2	08.5	8 13.6	11.5	148 39.1	46.4	16 52.2	02.0	Suhail	222 53.2	S43 29.0
17	237 14.8	119 48.9	08.2	23 14.5	12.0	163 41.3	46.5	31 54.5	02.1			
18	252 17.2	134 48.5	N19 07.9	38 15.4	S14 12.6	178 43.5	N21 46.5	46 56.7	S 8 02.2	Vega	80 39.1	N38 48.1
19	267 19.7	149 48.2	07.6	53 16.3	13.2	193 45.7	46.5	61 59.0	02.3	Zuben'ubi	137 06.1	S16 05.6
20	282 22.2	164 47.8	07.3	68 17.1	13.7	208 47.9	46.5	77 01.2	02.4		SHA	Mer. Pass.
21	297 24.6	179 47.5	.. 07.0	83 18.0	.. 14.3	223 50.1	.. 46.6	92 03.4	.. 02.5		° ′	h m
22	312 27.1	194 47.2	06.7	98 18.9	14.9	238 52.3	46.6	107 05.7	02.6	Venus	244 28.6	9 00
23	327 29.9	209 46.8	06.4	113 19.8	15.4	253 54.5	46.6	122 07.9	02.7	Mars	147 04.5	15 29
	h m									Jupiter	286 37.6	6 10
Mer. Pass. 1 17.5	v −0.3 d 0.3	v 0.9 d 0.6				v 2.2 d 0.0		v 2.2 d 0.1		Saturn	154 48.8	14 56

UT	SUN GHA	SUN Dec	MOON GHA	v	MOON Dec	d	HP
d h	° ′	° ′	° ′	′	° ′	′	′
31 00	179 55.1	N 8 34.1	8 28.9	12.1	S 6 29.2	11.6	57.2
01	194 55.3	33.2	23 00.0	12.1	6 17.6	11.6	57.2
02	209 55.5	32.3	37 31.1	12.2	6 06.0	11.6	57.2
03	224 55.7	.. 31.4	52 02.3	12.2	5 54.4	11.7	57.2
04	239 55.9	30.5	66 33.5	12.3	5 42.7	11.7	57.1
05	254 56.1	29.6	81 04.8	12.3	5 31.0	11.7	57.1
06	269 56.3	N 8 28.7	95 36.1	12.4	S 5 19.3	11.7	57.1
07	284 56.5	27.8	110 07.5	12.4	5 07.6	11.7	57.1
08	299 56.7	26.9	124 38.9	12.4	4 55.9	11.7	57.1
F 09	314 56.9	.. 26.0	139 10.3	12.5	4 44.2	11.8	57.0
R 10	329 57.1	25.1	153 41.8	12.6	4 32.4	11.7	57.0
I 11	344 57.3	24.2	168 13.4	12.6	4 20.7	11.8	57.0
D 12	359 57.5	N 8 23.3	182 45.0	12.6	S 4 08.9	11.8	57.0
A 13	14 57.7	22.4	197 16.6	12.6	3 57.1	11.8	56.9
Y 14	29 57.9	21.5	211 48.2	12.7	3 45.3	11.8	56.9
15	44 58.1	.. 20.6	226 19.9	12.8	3 33.5	11.8	56.9
16	59 58.3	19.7	240 51.7	12.7	3 21.7	11.8	56.9
17	74 58.5	18.8	255 23.4	12.9	3 09.9	11.8	56.8
18	89 58.7	N 8 17.9	269 55.3	12.8	S 2 58.1	11.9	56.8
19	104 58.9	17.0	284 27.1	12.9	2 46.2	11.8	56.8
20	119 59.1	16.1	298 59.0	12.9	2 34.4	11.8	56.8
21	134 59.3	.. 15.2	313 30.9	13.0	2 22.6	11.8	56.7
22	149 59.5	14.3	328 02.9	13.0	2 10.8	11.9	56.7
23	164 59.7	13.4	342 34.9	13.0	1 58.9	11.8	56.7
1 00	179 59.9	N 8 12.4	357 06.9	13.0	S 1 47.1	11.8	56.7
01	195 00.1	11.5	11 38.9	13.1	1 35.3	11.8	56.6
02	210 00.3	10.6	26 11.0	13.1	1 23.5	11.8	56.6
03	225 00.5	.. 09.7	40 43.1	13.2	1 11.7	11.8	56.6
04	240 00.7	08.8	55 15.3	13.2	0 59.9	11.8	56.6
05	255 00.9	07.9	69 47.5	13.2	0 48.1	11.8	56.6
06	270 01.1	N 8 07.0	84 19.7	13.2	S 0 36.3	11.8	56.5
S 07	285 01.3	06.1	98 51.9	13.3	0 24.5	11.8	56.5
A 08	300 01.5	05.2	113 24.2	13.3	S 0 12.7	11.8	56.5
T 09	315 01.7	.. 04.3	127 56.5	13.3	S 0 00.9	11.7	56.5
U 10	330 01.9	03.4	142 28.8	13.3	N 0 10.8	11.8	56.4
R 11	345 02.1	02.5	157 01.1	13.4	0 22.6	11.7	56.4
D 12	0 02.3	N 8 01.5	171 33.5	13.4	N 0 34.3	11.7	56.4
A 13	15 02.5	8 00.6	186 05.9	13.4	0 46.0	11.8	56.4
Y 14	30 02.7	7 59.7	200 38.3	13.5	0 57.8	11.6	56.3
15	45 02.9	.. 58.8	215 10.8	13.4	1 09.4	11.7	56.3
16	60 03.1	57.9	229 43.2	13.5	1 21.1	11.7	56.3
17	75 03.3	57.0	244 15.7	13.5	1 32.8	11.6	56.3
18	90 03.5	N 7 56.1	258 48.2	13.6	N 1 44.4	11.6	56.2
19	105 03.7	55.2	273 20.8	13.5	1 56.0	11.6	56.2
20	120 03.9	54.3	287 53.3	13.6	2 07.6	11.6	56.2
21	135 04.1	.. 53.3	302 25.9	13.6	2 19.2	11.6	56.2
22	150 04.3	52.4	316 58.5	13.6	2 30.8	11.5	56.1
23	165 04.5	51.5	331 31.1	13.6	2 42.3	11.5	56.1
2 00	180 04.7	N 7 50.6	346 03.7	13.6	N 2 53.8	11.5	56.1
01	195 04.9	49.7	0 36.3	13.7	3 05.3	11.5	56.1
02	210 05.1	48.8	15 09.0	13.7	3 16.8	11.4	56.0
03	225 05.3	.. 47.9	29 41.7	13.6	3 28.2	11.5	56.0
04	240 05.5	47.0	44 14.3	13.7	3 39.7	11.4	56.0
05	255 05.7	46.0	58 47.0	13.7	3 51.1	11.3	56.0
06	270 05.9	N 7 45.1	73 19.7	13.8	N 4 02.4	11.3	55.9
07	285 06.1	44.2	87 52.5	13.7	4 13.7	11.3	55.9
08	300 06.3	43.3	102 25.2	13.8	4 25.0	11.3	55.9
S 09	315 06.5	.. 42.4	116 58.0	13.7	4 36.3	11.3	55.9
U 10	330 06.7	41.5	131 30.7	13.8	4 47.6	11.2	55.8
N 11	345 06.9	40.6	146 03.5	13.8	4 58.8	11.1	55.8
D 12	0 07.1	N 7 39.6	160 36.3	13.7	N 5 09.9	11.2	55.8
A 13	15 07.3	38.7	175 09.0	13.8	5 21.1	11.1	55.8
Y 14	30 07.5	37.8	189 41.8	13.8	5 32.2	11.1	55.7
15	45 07.7	.. 36.9	204 14.6	13.9	5 43.3	11.0	55.7
16	60 07.9	36.0	218 47.5	13.8	5 54.3	11.0	55.7
17	75 08.2	35.1	233 20.3	13.8	6 05.3	11.0	55.7
18	90 08.4	N 7 34.2	247 53.1	13.8	N 6 16.3	10.9	55.7
19	105 08.6	33.2	262 25.9	13.8	6 27.2	10.9	55.6
20	120 08.8	32.3	276 58.7	13.9	6 38.1	10.9	55.6
21	135 09.0	.. 31.4	291 31.6	13.8	6 49.0	10.8	55.6
22	150 09.2	30.5	306 04.4	13.9	6 59.8	10.7	55.6
23	165 09.4	29.6	320 37.3	13.8	N 7 10.5	10.8	55.6
	SD 15.9	d 0.9	SD 15.5		15.4		15.2

Lat.	Twilight Naut.	Twilight Civil	Sunrise	Moonrise 31	Moonrise 1	Moonrise 2	Moonrise 3
°	h m	h m	h m	h m	h m	h m	h m
N 72	////	02 34	04 03	18 38	18 25	18 11	17 55
N 70	////	03 01	04 17	18 34	18 27	18 19	18 12
68	01 34	03 22	04 27	18 31	18 29	18 27	18 25
66	02 12	03 38	04 36	18 28	18 30	18 32	18 35
64	02 37	03 51	04 44	18 26	18 32	18 38	18 44
62	02 57	04 02	04 50	18 24	18 33	18 42	18 52
60	03 12	04 11	04 56	18 22	18 34	18 46	18 59
N 58	03 25	04 19	05 01	18 21	18 35	18 49	19 05
56	03 36	04 25	05 05	18 19	18 36	18 52	19 10
54	03 45	04 31	05 09	18 18	18 36	18 55	19 15
52	03 53	04 37	05 12	18 17	18 37	18 58	19 19
50	04 01	04 42	05 15	18 16	18 38	19 00	19 23
45	04 16	04 52	05 22	18 13	18 39	19 05	19 32
N 40	04 27	05 00	05 28	18 11	18 40	19 09	19 39
35	04 36	05 07	05 33	18 09	18 41	19 13	19 45
30	04 44	05 13	05 37	18 08	18 42	19 16	19 51
20	04 56	05 22	05 44	18 05	18 44	19 22	20 00
N 10	05 05	05 30	05 51	18 03	18 45	19 27	20 09
0	05 11	05 36	05 57	18 01	18 47	19 32	20 16
S 10	05 17	05 41	06 02	17 59	18 48	19 36	20 24
20	05 22	05 46	06 08	17 56	18 50	19 42	20 33
30	05 23	05 51	06 15	17 54	18 51	19 48	20 43
35	05 24	05 53	06 19	17 52	18 52	19 51	20 49
40	05 24	05 56	06 23	17 51	18 53	19 55	20 55
45	05 24	05 58	06 28	17 49	18 55	19 59	21 03
S 50	05 24	06 01	06 34	17 46	18 56	20 05	21 12
52	05 23	06 02	06 36	17 45	18 57	20 07	21 16
54	05 23	06 04	06 39	17 44	18 58	20 10	21 21
56	05 22	06 05	06 43	17 43	18 59	20 13	21 26
58	05 21	06 07	06 46	17 41	19 00	20 17	21 32
S 60	05 20	06 08	06 50	17 40	19 01	20 21	21 38

Lat.	Sunset	Twilight Civil	Twilight Naut.	Moonset 31	Moonset 1	Moonset 2	Moonset 3
°	h m	h m	h m	h m	h m	h m	h m
N 72	19 53	21 20	////	04 22	06 15	08 04	09 54
N 70	19 40	20 54	23 32	04 31	06 16	07 58	09 39
68	19 30	20 34	22 18	04 38	06 16	07 53	09 28
66	19 21	20 19	21 43	04 43	06 17	07 49	09 18
64	19 14	20 07	21 19	04 48	06 18	07 45	09 10
62	19 08	19 56	21 00	04 52	06 18	07 42	09 04
60	19 02	19 47	20 45	04 56	06 19	07 39	08 58
N 58	18 58	19 39	20 32	04 59	06 19	07 37	08 53
56	18 54	19 33	20 22	05 02	06 19	07 35	08 48
54	18 50	19 27	20 13	05 04	06 20	07 33	08 44
52	18 46	19 22	20 05	05 07	06 20	07 31	08 40
50	18 43	19 17	19 58	05 09	06 20	07 29	08 37
45	18 37	19 07	19 43	05 13	06 21	07 26	08 30
N 40	18 31	18 59	19 32	05 17	06 21	07 23	08 24
35	18 26	18 52	19 23	05 20	06 21	07 21	08 19
30	18 22	18 46	19 15	05 23	06 22	07 18	08 14
20	18 15	18 37	19 03	05 28	06 22	07 15	08 06
N 10	18 09	18 30	18 55	05 32	06 23	07 11	08 00
0	18 03	18 24	18 48	05 36	06 23	07 08	07 53
S 10	17 58	18 19	18 43	05 40	06 23	07 05	07 47
20	17 52	18 14	18 40	05 44	06 24	07 02	07 40
30	17 45	18 09	18 37	05 49	06 24	06 58	07 32
35	17 41	18 07	18 36	05 52	06 25	06 56	07 28
40	17 37	18 05	18 36	05 55	06 25	06 54	07 23
45	17 33	18 02	18 36	05 58	06 25	06 51	07 17
S 50	17 27	17 59	18 37	06 02	06 25	06 47	07 10
52	17 24	17 58	18 37	06 04	06 25	06 46	07 07
54	17 21	17 57	18 38	06 06	06 26	06 44	07 03
56	17 18	17 56	18 39	06 09	06 26	06 42	06 59
58	17 15	17 54	18 40	06 11	06 26	06 40	06 55
S 60	17 11	17 53	18 41	06 14	06 26	06 38	06 50

	SUN Eqn. of Time 00ʰ	SUN Eqn. of Time 12ʰ	SUN Mer. Pass.	MOON Mer. Pass. Upper	MOON Mer. Pass. Lower	Age	Phase
Day	m s	m s	h m	h m	h m	d	%
31	00 20	00 10	12 00	24 12	11 49	14	100
1	00 01	00 09	12 00	00 12	12 35	15	99
2	00 18	00 28	12 00	00 58	13 20	16	96

UT	ARIES GHA	VENUS −4.3 GHA	Dec	MARS +1.2 GHA	Dec	JUPITER −2.4 GHA	Dec	SATURN +0.8 GHA	Dec	STARS Name	SHA	Dec
3 00	342 32.0	224 46.5	N19 06.1	128 20.7	S14 16.0	268 56.7	N21 46.6	137 10.2	S 8 02.8	Acamar	315 18.5	S40 15.0
01	357 34.5	239 46.2	05.8	143 21.5	16.6	283 58.9	46.7	152 12.4	02.9	Achernar	335 26.7	S57 10.0
02	12 36.9	254 45.8	05.5	158 22.4	17.1	299 01.1	46.7	167 14.6	03.0	Acrux	173 10.5	S63 10.3
03	27 39.4	269 45.5 ..	05.2	173 23.3 ..	17.7	314 03.3 ..	46.7	182 16.9 ..	03.1	Adhara	255 13.1	S28 59.3
04	42 41.9	284 45.1	04.9	188 24.2	18.3	329 05.5	46.7	197 19.1	03.1	Aldebaran	290 50.0	N16 32.0
05	57 44.3	299 44.8	04.6	203 25.0	18.8	344 07.7	46.8	212 21.4	03.2			
06	72 46.8	314 44.5	N19 04.3	218 25.9	S14 19.4	359 09.9	N21 46.8	227 23.6	S 8 03.3	Alioth	166 21.6	N55 53.6
07	87 49.3	329 44.1	04.0	233 26.8	20.0	14 12.1	46.8	242 25.8	03.4	Alkaid	153 59.6	N49 15.2
08	102 51.7	344 43.8	03.7	248 27.7	20.5	29 14.4	46.8	257 28.1	03.5	Al Na'ir	27 43.9	S46 53.8
M 09	117 54.2	359 43.4 ..	03.4	263 28.5 ..	21.1	44 16.6 ..	46.9	272 30.3 ..	03.6	Alnilam	275 47.0	S 1 11.6
O 10	132 56.6	14 43.1	03.1	278 29.4	21.7	59 18.8	46.9	287 32.6	03.7	Alphard	217 56.9	S 8 42.8
N 11	147 59.1	29 42.7	02.8	293 30.3	22.2	74 21.0	46.9	302 34.8	03.8			
D 12	163 01.6	44 42.4	N19 02.5	308 31.1	S14 22.8	89 23.2	N21 46.9	317 37.0	S 8 03.9	Alphecca	126 11.6	N26 40.6
A 13	178 04.0	59 42.1	02.2	323 32.0	23.4	104 25.4	47.0	332 39.3	04.0	Alpheratz	357 43.7	N29 09.8
Y 14	193 06.5	74 41.7	01.9	338 32.9	23.9	119 27.6	47.0	347 41.5	04.1	Altair	62 08.5	N 8 54.4
15	208 09.0	89 41.4 ..	01.6	353 33.8 ..	24.5	134 29.8 ..	47.0	2 43.7 ..	04.2	Ankaa	353 15.8	S42 13.9
16	223 11.4	104 41.0	01.2	8 34.6	25.1	149 32.0	47.0	17 46.0	04.3	Antares	112 26.9	S26 27.5
17	238 13.9	119 40.7	00.9	23 35.5	25.6	164 34.2	47.1	32 48.2	04.4			
18	253 16.4	134 40.3	N19 00.6	38 36.4	S14 26.2	179 36.4	N21 47.1	47 50.5	S 8 04.5	Arcturus	145 56.4	N19 07.2
19	268 18.8	149 40.0	00.3	53 37.2	26.7	194 38.6	47.1	62 52.7	04.5	Atria	107 29.2	S69 03.2
20	283 21.3	164 39.7	19 00.0	68 38.1	27.3	209 40.8	47.1	77 54.9	04.6	Avior	234 18.7	S59 32.9
21	298 23.8	179 39.3	18 59.7	83 39.0 ..	27.9	224 43.0 ..	47.2	92 57.2 ..	04.7	Bellatrix	278 32.6	N 6 21.7
22	313 26.2	194 39.0	59.3	98 39.9	28.4	239 45.3	47.2	107 59.4	04.8	Betelgeuse	271 02.0	N 7 24.5
23	328 28.7	209 38.6	59.0	113 40.7	29.0	254 47.5	47.2	123 01.7	04.9			
4 00	343 31.1	224 38.3	N18 58.7	128 41.6	S14 29.6	269 49.7	N21 47.2	138 03.9	S 8 05.0	Canopus	263 56.6	S52 42.0
01	358 33.6	239 37.9	58.4	143 42.5	30.1	284 51.9	47.3	153 06.1	05.1	Capella	280 35.3	N46 00.4
02	13 36.1	254 37.6	58.1	158 43.3	30.7	299 54.1	47.3	168 08.4	05.2	Deneb	49 31.5	N45 19.9
03	28 38.5	269 37.2 ..	57.7	173 44.2 ..	31.3	314 56.3 ..	47.3	183 10.6 ..	05.3	Denebola	182 34.5	N14 30.1
04	43 41.0	284 36.9	57.4	188 45.1	31.8	329 58.5	47.3	198 12.8	05.4	Diphda	348 56.1	S17 54.8
05	58 43.5	299 36.5	57.1	203 45.9	32.4	345 00.7	47.4	213 15.1	05.5			
06	73 45.9	314 36.2	N18 56.8	218 46.8	S14 32.9	0 02.9	N21 47.4	228 17.3	S 8 05.6	Dubhe	193 53.0	N61 40.9
07	88 48.4	329 35.8	56.4	233 47.7	33.5	15 05.2	47.4	243 19.6	05.7	Elnath	278 13.3	N28 36.9
08	103 50.9	344 35.5	56.1	248 48.5	34.1	30 07.4	47.4	258 21.8	05.8	Eltanin	90 46.2	N51 29.6
T 09	118 53.3	359 35.1 ..	55.8	263 49.4 ..	34.6	45 09.6 ..	47.5	273 24.0 ..	05.9	Enif	33 47.3	N 9 56.3
U 10	133 55.8	14 34.8	55.5	278 50.3	35.2	60 11.8	47.5	288 26.3	06.0	Fomalhaut	15 24.2	S29 33.1
E 11	148 58.2	29 34.5	55.1	293 51.1	35.8	75 14.0	47.5	303 28.5	06.0			
S 12	164 00.7	44 34.1	N18 54.8	308 52.0	S14 36.3	90 16.2	N21 47.5	318 30.7	S 8 06.1	Gacrux	172 02.0	S57 11.2
D 13	179 03.2	59 33.8	54.5	323 52.9	36.9	105 18.4	47.6	333 33.0	06.2	Gienah	175 53.1	S17 36.7
A 14	194 05.6	74 33.4	54.1	338 53.7	37.4	120 20.6	47.6	348 35.2	06.3	Hadar	148 49.1	S60 26.2
Y 15	209 08.1	89 33.1 ..	53.8	353 54.6 ..	38.0	135 22.9 ..	47.6	3 37.4 ..	06.4	Hamal	328 01.1	N23 31.4
16	224 10.6	104 32.7	53.5	8 55.5	38.6	150 25.1	47.6	18 39.7	06.5	Kaus Aust.	83 44.3	S34 22.6
17	239 13.0	119 32.4	53.1	23 56.3	39.1	165 27.3	47.6	33 41.9	06.6			
18	254 15.5	134 32.0	N18 52.8	38 57.2	S14 39.7	180 29.5	N21 47.7	48 44.2	S 8 06.7	Kochab	137 20.5	N74 06.5
19	269 18.0	149 31.6	52.5	53 58.1	40.3	195 31.7	47.7	63 46.4	06.8	Markab	13 38.5	N15 16.7
20	284 20.4	164 31.3	52.1	68 58.9	40.8	210 33.9	47.7	78 48.6	06.9	Menkar	314 15.5	N 4 08.5
21	299 22.9	179 30.9 ..	51.8	83 59.8 ..	41.4	225 36.1 ..	47.7	93 50.9 ..	07.0	Menkent	148 08.4	S36 26.0
22	314 25.4	194 30.6	51.5	99 00.6	41.9	240 38.4	47.8	108 53.1	07.1	Miaplacidus	221 40.6	S69 46.1
23	329 27.8	209 30.2	51.1	114 01.5	42.5	255 40.6	47.8	123 55.3	07.2			
5 00	344 30.3	224 29.9	N18 50.8	129 02.4	S14 43.1	270 42.8	N21 47.8	138 57.6	S 8 07.3	Mirfak	308 40.9	N49 54.2
01	359 32.7	239 29.5	50.4	144 03.2	43.6	285 45.0	47.8	153 59.8	07.4	Nunki	75 58.8	S26 16.7
02	14 35.2	254 29.2	50.1	159 04.1	44.2	300 47.2	47.9	169 02.0	07.5	Peacock	53 19.6	S56 41.6
03	29 37.7	269 28.8 ..	49.7	174 04.9 ..	44.7	315 49.5 ..	47.9	184 04.3 ..	07.5	Pollux	243 28.6	N27 59.6
04	44 40.1	284 28.5	49.4	189 05.8	45.3	330 51.7	47.9	199 06.5	07.6	Procyon	245 00.5	N 5 11.5
05	59 42.6	299 28.1	49.1	204 06.7	45.9	345 53.9	47.9	214 08.7	07.7			
06	74 45.1	314 27.8	N18 48.7	219 07.5	S14 46.4	0 56.1	N21 48.0	229 11.0	S 8 07.8	Rasalhague	96 06.9	N12 33.3
W 07	89 47.5	329 27.4	48.4	234 08.4	47.0	15 58.3	48.0	244 13.2	07.9	Regulus	207 44.4	N11 54.3
E 08	104 50.0	344 27.1	48.0	249 09.2	47.5	31 00.5	48.0	259 15.4	08.0	Rigel	281 12.6	S 8 11.1
D 09	119 52.5	359 26.7 ..	47.7	264 10.1 ..	48.1	46 02.8 ..	48.0	274 17.7 ..	08.1	Rigil Kent.	139 52.8	S60 53.4
N 10	134 54.9	14 26.3	47.3	279 11.0	48.7	61 05.0	48.0	289 19.9	08.2	Sabik	102 13.1	S15 44.3
E 11	149 57.4	29 26.0	47.0	294 11.8	49.2	76 07.2	48.1	304 22.1	08.3			
S 12	164 59.9	44 25.6	N18 46.6	309 12.7	S14 49.8	91 09.4	N21 48.1	319 24.4	S 8 08.4	Schedar	349 40.6	N56 36.4
D 13	180 02.3	59 25.3	46.3	324 13.5	50.3	106 11.6	48.1	334 26.6	08.5	Shaula	96 22.5	S37 06.7
A 14	195 04.8	74 24.9	45.9	339 14.4	50.9	121 13.9	48.1	349 28.9	08.6	Sirius	258 34.3	S16 43.9
Y 15	210 07.2	89 24.6 ..	45.6	354 15.3 ..	51.4	136 16.1 ..	48.2	4 31.1 ..	08.7	Spica	158 32.1	S11 13.6
16	225 09.7	104 24.2	45.2	9 16.1	52.0	151 18.3	48.2	19 33.3	08.8	Suhail	222 53.2	S43 29.0
17	240 12.2	119 23.9	44.9	24 17.0	52.6	166 20.5	48.2	34 35.6	08.9			
18	255 14.6	134 23.5	N18 44.5	39 17.8	S14 53.1	181 22.8	N21 48.2	49 37.8	S 8 09.0	Vega	80 39.1	N38 48.1
19	270 17.1	149 23.1	44.1	54 18.7	53.7	196 25.0	48.3	64 40.0	09.1	Zuben'ubi	137 06.2	S16 05.6
20	285 19.6	164 22.8	43.8	69 19.5	54.2	211 27.2	48.3	79 42.3	09.2		SHA	Mer.Pass.
21	300 22.0	179 22.4 ..	43.4	84 20.4 ..	54.8	226 29.4 ..	48.3	94 44.5 ..	09.2		° '	h m
22	315 24.5	194 22.1	43.1	99 21.3	55.4	241 31.7	48.3	109 46.7	09.3	Venus	241 07.1	9 02
23	330 27.0	209 21.7	42.7	114 22.1	55.9	256 33.9	48.3	124 49.0	09.4	Mars	145 10.5	15 24
Mer. Pass.	1 05.7	v −0.3	d 0.3	v 0.9	d 0.6	v 2.2	d 0.0	v 2.2	d 0.1	Jupiter	286 18.5	6 00
										Saturn	154 32.7	14 46

SUN / MOON

UT	SUN GHA	SUN Dec	MOON GHA	v	MOON Dec	d	HP
d h	° ′	° ′	° ′	′	° ′	′	′
3 00	180 09.6	N 7 28.7	335 10.1	13.9	N 7 21.3	10.6	55.5
01	195 09.8	27.7	349 43.0	13.8	7 31.9	10.7	55.5
02	210 10.0	26.8	4 15.8	13.9	7 42.6	10.6	55.5
03	225 10.2	.. 25.9	18 48.7	13.8	7 53.2	10.5	55.5
04	240 10.4	25.0	33 21.5	13.9	8 03.7	10.6	55.4
05	255 10.6	24.1	47 54.4	13.8	8 14.3	10.4	55.4
06	270 10.8	N 7 23.1	62 27.2	13.8	N 8 24.7	10.4	55.4
07	285 11.0	22.2	77 00.0	13.9	8 35.1	10.4	55.4
08	300 11.2	21.3	91 32.9	13.8	8 45.5	10.3	55.3
09	315 11.4	.. 20.4	106 05.7	13.9	8 55.8	10.3	55.3
10	330 11.6	19.5	120 38.6	13.8	9 06.1	10.2	55.3
11	345 11.8	18.5	135 11.4	13.8	9 16.3	10.2	55.3
12	0 12.1	N 7 17.6	149 44.2	13.9	N 9 26.5	10.2	55.3
13	15 12.3	16.7	164 17.1	13.8	9 36.7	10.0	55.3
14	30 12.5	15.8	178 49.9	13.8	9 46.7	10.1	55.2
15	45 12.7	.. 14.9	193 22.7	13.8	9 56.8	9.9	55.2
16	60 12.9	13.9	207 55.5	13.8	10 06.7	10.0	55.2
17	75 13.1	13.0	222 28.3	13.8	10 16.7	9.8	55.2
18	90 13.3	N 7 12.1	237 01.1	13.8	N10 26.5	9.8	55.2
19	105 13.5	11.2	251 33.9	13.8	10 36.3	9.8	55.1
20	120 13.7	10.3	266 06.7	13.7	10 46.1	9.7	55.1
21	135 13.9	.. 09.3	280 39.4	13.8	10 55.8	9.7	55.1
22	150 14.1	08.4	295 12.2	13.7	11 05.5	9.5	55.1
23	165 14.3	07.5	309 44.9	13.8	11 15.0	9.6	55.1
4 00	180 14.5	N 7 06.6	324 17.7	13.7	N11 24.6	9.5	55.0
01	195 14.7	05.6	338 50.4	13.7	11 34.1	9.4	55.0
02	210 15.0	04.7	353 23.1	13.7	11 43.5	9.3	55.0
03	225 15.2	.. 03.8	7 55.8	13.7	11 52.8	9.4	55.0
04	240 15.4	02.9	22 28.5	13.7	12 02.2	9.2	55.0
05	255 15.6	02.0	37 01.2	13.7	12 11.4	9.2	54.9
06	270 15.8	N 7 01.0	51 33.9	13.7	N12 20.6	9.1	54.9
07	285 16.0	7 00.1	66 06.6	13.6	12 29.7	9.1	54.9
08	300 16.2	6 59.2	80 39.2	13.6	12 38.8	9.0	54.9
09	315 16.4	.. 58.3	95 11.8	13.7	12 47.8	8.9	54.9
10	330 16.6	57.3	109 44.5	13.6	12 56.7	8.9	54.9
11	345 16.8	56.4	124 17.1	13.5	13 05.6	8.8	54.8
12	0 17.0	N 6 55.5	138 49.6	13.6	N13 14.4	8.7	54.8
13	15 17.2	54.6	153 22.2	13.6	13 23.1	8.7	54.8
14	30 17.5	53.6	167 54.8	13.5	13 31.8	8.6	54.8
15	45 17.7	.. 52.7	182 27.3	13.5	13 40.4	8.6	54.8
16	60 17.9	51.8	196 59.8	13.5	13 49.0	8.4	54.8
17	75 18.1	50.9	211 32.3	13.5	13 57.4	8.5	54.8
18	90 18.3	N 6 49.9	226 04.8	13.5	N14 05.9	8.3	54.7
19	105 18.5	49.0	240 37.3	13.5	14 14.2	8.3	54.7
20	120 18.7	48.1	255 09.8	13.4	14 22.5	8.2	54.7
21	135 18.9	.. 47.2	269 42.2	13.4	14 30.7	8.1	54.7
22	150 19.1	46.2	284 14.6	13.4	14 38.8	8.1	54.7
23	165 19.3	45.3	298 47.0	13.4	14 46.9	8.0	54.7
5 00	180 19.5	N 6 44.4	313 19.4	13.4	N14 54.9	7.9	54.6
01	195 19.8	43.4	327 51.8	13.3	15 02.8	7.9	54.6
02	210 20.0	42.5	342 24.1	13.4	15 10.7	7.8	54.6
03	225 20.2	.. 41.6	356 56.5	13.3	15 18.5	7.7	54.6
04	240 20.4	40.7	11 28.8	13.2	15 26.2	7.7	54.6
05	255 20.6	39.7	26 01.0	13.3	15 33.9	7.5	54.6
06	270 20.8	N 6 38.8	40 33.3	13.3	N15 41.4	7.5	54.6
07	285 21.0	37.9	55 05.6	13.2	15 48.9	7.4	54.5
08	300 21.2	36.9	69 37.8	13.2	15 56.3	7.4	54.5
09	315 21.4	.. 36.0	84 10.0	13.2	16 03.7	7.3	54.5
10	330 21.6	35.1	98 42.2	13.1	16 11.0	7.2	54.5
11	345 21.9	34.2	113 14.3	13.2	16 18.2	7.1	54.5
12	0 22.1	N 6 33.2	127 46.5	13.1	N16 25.3	7.0	54.5
13	15 22.3	32.3	142 18.6	13.1	16 32.3	7.0	54.5
14	30 22.5	31.4	156 50.7	13.0	16 39.3	6.9	54.5
15	45 22.7	.. 30.5	171 22.7	13.1	16 46.2	6.8	54.5
16	60 22.9	29.5	185 54.8	13.0	16 53.0	6.8	54.4
17	75 23.1	28.6	200 26.8	13.0	16 59.8	6.6	54.4
18	90 23.3	N 6 27.6	214 58.8	13.0	N17 06.4	6.6	54.4
19	105 23.5	26.7	229 30.8	13.0	17 13.0	6.5	54.4
20	120 23.8	25.8	244 02.8	12.9	17 19.5	6.4	54.4
21	135 24.0	.. 24.9	258 34.7	12.9	17 25.9	6.3	54.4
22	150 24.2	23.9	273 06.6	12.9	17 32.2	6.3	54.4
23	165 24.4	23.0	287 38.5	12.9	N17 38.5	6.2	54.4
	SD 15.9	d 0.9	SD 15.1		14.9		14.8

Day labels: MONDAY (3 hours), TUESDAY (4 hours), WEDNESDAY (5 hours).

Twilight / Sunrise / Moonrise

Lat.	Twilight Naut.	Twilight Civil	Sunrise	Moonrise 3	4	5	6
°	h m	h m	h m	h m	h m	h m	h m
N 72	////	02 54	04 18	17 55	17 36	17 01	▭
N 70	01 08	03 17	04 29	18 12	18 03	17 51	17 31
68	01 59	03 35	04 38	18 25	18 23	18 23	18 26
66	02 29	03 49	04 46	18 35	18 40	18 47	18 59
64	02 51	04 01	04 52	18 44	18 53	19 05	19 24
62	03 08	04 10	04 58	18 52	19 05	19 21	19 43
60	03 22	04 18	05 03	18 59	19 14	19 34	19 59
N 58	03 33	04 26	05 07	19 05	19 23	19 45	20 12
56	03 43	04 32	05 11	19 10	19 30	19 54	20 24
54	03 52	04 37	05 14	19 15	19 37	20 03	20 34
52	03 59	04 42	05 17	19 19	19 43	20 11	20 43
50	04 06	04 47	05 20	19 23	19 49	20 18	20 51
45	04 20	04 56	05 26	19 32	20 01	20 32	21 09
N 40	04 30	05 03	05 31	19 39	20 10	20 45	21 23
35	04 39	05 09	05 35	19 45	20 19	20 55	21 35
30	04 46	05 15	05 39	19 51	20 26	21 04	21 45
20	04 57	05 23	05 45	20 00	20 39	21 20	22 04
N 10	05 05	05 29	05 51	20 09	20 51	21 34	22 20
0	05 11	05 35	05 56	20 16	21 02	21 48	22 34
S 10	05 15	05 39	06 01	20 24	21 12	22 01	22 49
20	05 18	05 44	06 06	20 33	21 24	22 15	23 05
30	05 20	05 47	06 11	20 43	21 37	22 31	23 24
35	05 20	05 49	06 15	20 49	21 45	22 41	23 35
40	05 20	05 51	06 18	20 55	21 54	22 52	23 47
45	05 19	05 53	06 22	21 03	22 04	23 04	24 02
S 50	05 18	05 55	06 27	21 12	22 17	23 20	24 20
52	05 17	05 56	06 30	21 16	22 23	23 27	24 28
54	05 16	05 57	06 32	21 21	22 29	23 36	24 38
56	05 15	05 58	06 35	21 26	22 37	23 45	24 49
58	05 13	05 59	06 38	21 32	22 45	23 55	25 01
S 60	05 12	06 00	06 41	21 38	22 54	24 07	00 07

Sunset / Twilight / Moonset

Lat.	Sunset	Twilight Civil	Twilight Naut.	Moonset 3	4	5	6
°	h m	h m	h m	h m	h m	h m	h m
N 72	19 37	20 59	////	09 54	11 47	13 57	▭
N 70	19 26	20 36	22 38	09 39	11 22	13 08	15 06
68	19 17	20 19	21 53	09 28	11 02	12 37	14 11
66	19 10	20 06	21 24	09 18	10 47	12 14	13 38
64	19 03	19 55	21 03	09 10	10 34	11 56	13 14
62	18 58	19 45	20 47	09 04	10 24	11 42	12 56
60	18 53	19 37	20 34	08 58	10 15	11 29	12 40
N 58	18 49	19 31	20 22	08 53	10 07	11 19	12 27
56	18 46	19 24	20 13	08 48	10 00	11 09	12 16
54	18 42	19 19	20 04	08 44	09 54	11 01	12 06
52	18 40	19 14	19 57	08 40	09 48	10 54	11 57
50	18 37	19 10	19 50	08 37	09 43	10 47	11 49
45	18 31	19 01	19 37	08 30	09 32	10 33	11 32
N 40	18 26	18 54	19 27	08 24	09 24	10 22	11 19
35	18 22	18 48	19 18	08 19	09 16	10 12	11 07
30	18 19	18 43	19 11	08 14	09 09	10 03	10 57
20	18 12	18 35	19 01	08 06	08 58	09 49	10 39
N 10	18 07	18 28	18 53	08 00	08 48	09 36	10 24
0	18 02	18 23	18 47	07 53	08 38	09 24	10 10
S 10	17 57	18 18	18 43	07 47	08 29	09 12	09 56
20	17 52	18 14	18 40	07 40	08 19	08 59	09 41
30	17 47	18 11	18 39	07 32	08 07	08 44	09 24
35	17 44	18 09	18 38	07 28	08 01	08 36	09 14
40	17 40	18 07	18 39	07 23	07 53	08 26	09 02
45	17 36	18 05	18 39	07 17	07 45	08 15	08 49
S 50	17 31	18 04	18 41	07 10	07 34	08 01	08 32
52	17 29	18 03	18 42	07 07	07 29	07 55	08 25
54	17 27	18 02	18 43	07 03	07 24	07 48	08 16
56	17 24	18 01	18 44	06 59	07 18	07 40	08 07
58	17 21	18 00	18 46	06 55	07 12	07 31	07 56
S 60	17 18	17 59	18 48	06 50	07 04	07 21	07 43

SUN and MOON

Day	SUN Eqn. of Time 00h	12h	SUN Mer. Pass.	MOON Mer. Pass. Upper	Lower	Age	Phase
d	m s	m s	h m	h m	h m	d	%
3	00 38	00 48	11 59	01 42	14 05	17	91
4	00 58	01 08	11 59	02 27	14 50	18	85
5	01 18	01 28	11 59	03 13	15 36	19	77

UT	ARIES GHA	VENUS −4.3 GHA	Dec	MARS +1.2 GHA	Dec	JUPITER −2.4 GHA	Dec	SATURN +0.8 GHA	Dec	Name	SHA	Dec
d h	° ′	° ′	° ′	° ′	° ′	° ′	° ′	° ′	° ′		° ′	° ′
6 00	345 29.4	224 21.3	N18 42.3	129 23.0	S14 56.5	271 36.1	N21 48.4	139 51.2	S 8 09.5	Acamar	315 18.5	S40 15.0
01	0 31.9	239 21.0	42.0	144 23.8	57.0	286 38.3	48.4	154 53.4	09.6	Achernar	335 26.7	S57 10.1
02	15 34.3	254 20.6	41.6	159 24.7	57.6	301 40.6	48.4	169 55.7	09.7	Acrux	173 10.5	S63 10.3
03	30 36.8	269 20.3	.. 41.3	174 25.5	.. 58.1	316 42.8	.. 48.4	184 57.9	.. 09.8	Adhara	255 13.1	S28 59.2
04	45 39.3	284 19.9	40.9	189 26.4	58.7	331 45.0	48.5	200 00.1	09.9	Aldebaran	290 49.9	N16 32.0
05	60 41.7	299 19.5	40.5	204 27.2	59.3	346 47.2	48.5	215 02.4	10.0			
06	75 44.2	314 19.2	N18 40.2	219 28.1	S14 59.8	1 49.5	N21 48.5	230 04.6	S 8 10.1	Alioth	166 21.6	N55 53.6
07	90 46.7	329 18.8	39.8	234 28.9	15 00.4	16 51.7	48.5	245 06.8	10.2	Alkaid	152 59.7	N49 15.2
T 08	105 49.1	344 18.5	39.4	249 29.8	00.9	31 53.9	48.5	260 09.0	10.3	Al Na'ir	27 43.9	S46 53.8
H 09	120 51.6	359 18.1	.. 39.1	264 30.6	.. 01.5	46 56.1	.. 48.6	275 11.3	.. 10.4	Alnilam	275 47.0	S 1 11.6
U 10	135 54.1	14 17.7	38.7	279 31.5	02.0	61 58.4	48.6	290 13.5	10.5	Alphard	217 56.9	S 8 42.8
R 11	150 56.5	29 17.4	38.3	294 32.3	02.6	77 00.6	48.6	305 15.7	10.6			
S 12	165 59.0	44 17.0	N18 37.9	309 33.2	S15 03.1	92 02.8	N21 48.6	320 18.0	S 8 10.7	Alphecca	126 11.6	N26 40.6
D 13	181 01.5	59 16.7	37.6	324 34.0	03.7	107 05.0	48.7	335 20.2	10.8	Alpheratz	357 43.7	N29 09.8
A 14	196 03.9	74 16.3	37.2	339 34.9	04.3	122 07.3	48.7	350 22.4	10.9	Altair	62 08.5	N 8 54.4
Y 15	211 06.4	89 15.9	.. 36.8	354 35.7	.. 04.8	137 09.5	.. 48.7	5 24.7	.. 11.0	Ankaa	353 15.8	S42 14.0
16	226 08.8	104 15.6	36.4	9 36.6	05.4	152 11.7	48.7	20 26.9	11.1	Antares	112 26.9	S26 27.5
17	241 11.3	119 15.2	36.1	24 37.4	05.9	167 14.0	48.7	35 29.1	11.1			
18	256 13.8	134 14.8	N18 35.7	39 38.3	S15 06.5	182 16.2	N21 48.8	50 31.4	S 8 11.2	Arcturus	145 56.4	N19 07.2
19	271 16.2	149 14.5	35.3	54 39.1	07.0	197 18.4	48.8	65 33.6	11.3	Atria	107 29.2	S69 03.2
20	286 18.7	164 14.1	34.9	69 40.0	07.6	212 20.7	48.8	80 35.8	11.4	Avior	234 18.7	S59 32.9
21	301 21.2	179 13.8	.. 34.6	84 40.8	.. 08.1	227 22.9	.. 48.8	95 38.1	.. 11.5	Bellatrix	278 32.6	N 6 21.7
22	316 23.6	194 13.4	34.2	99 41.7	08.7	242 25.1	48.8	110 40.3	11.6	Betelgeuse	271 01.9	N 7 24.5
23	331 26.1	209 13.0	33.8	114 42.5	09.2	257 27.3	48.9	125 42.5	11.7			
7 00	346 28.6	224 12.7	N18 33.4	129 43.4	S15 09.8	272 29.6	N21 48.9	140 44.8	S 8 11.8	Canopus	263 56.6	S52 41.9
01	1 31.0	239 12.3	33.0	144 44.2	10.4	287 31.8	48.9	155 47.0	11.9	Capella	280 35.3	N46 00.4
02	16 33.5	254 11.9	32.6	159 45.1	10.9	302 34.0	48.9	170 49.2	12.0	Deneb	49 31.5	N45 19.9
03	31 36.0	269 11.6	.. 32.3	174 45.9	.. 11.5	317 36.3	.. 49.0	185 51.4	.. 12.1	Denebola	182 34.5	N14 30.1
04	46 38.4	284 11.2	31.9	189 46.8	12.0	332 38.5	49.0	200 53.7	12.2	Diphda	348 56.1	S17 54.8
05	61 40.9	299 10.8	31.5	204 47.6	12.6	347 40.7	49.0	215 55.9	12.3			
06	76 43.3	314 10.5	N18 31.1	219 48.5	S15 13.1	2 43.0	N21 49.0	230 58.1	S 8 12.4	Dubhe	193 53.0	N61 40.9
07	91 45.8	329 10.1	30.7	234 49.3	13.7	17 45.2	49.0	246 00.4	12.5	Elnath	278 13.3	N28 36.9
F 08	106 48.3	344 09.7	30.3	249 50.1	14.2	32 47.4	49.1	261 02.6	12.6	Eltanin	90 46.3	N51 29.7
R 09	121 50.7	359 09.4	.. 29.9	264 51.0	.. 14.8	47 49.7	.. 49.1	276 04.8	.. 12.7	Enif	33 47.3	N 9 56.3
I 10	136 53.2	14 09.0	29.2	279 51.8	15.3	62 51.9	49.1	291 07.1	12.8	Fomalhaut	15 24.2	S29 33.1
D 11	151 55.7	29 08.6	29.2	294 52.7	15.9	77 54.2	49.1	306 09.3	12.9			
A 12	166 58.1	44 08.3	N18 28.8	309 53.5	S15 16.4	92 56.4	N21 49.1	321 11.5	S 8 13.0	Gacrux	172 02.0	S57 11.2
Y 13	182 00.6	59 07.9	28.4	324 54.4	17.0	107 58.6	49.2	336 13.8	13.1	Gienah	175 53.1	S17 36.7
14	197 03.1	74 07.5	28.0	339 55.2	17.5	123 00.9	49.2	351 16.0	13.2	Hadar	148 49.1	S60 26.2
15	212 05.5	89 07.2	.. 27.6	354 56.0	.. 18.1	138 03.1	.. 49.2	6 18.2	.. 13.3	Hamal	328 01.1	N23 31.4
16	227 08.0	104 06.8	27.2	9 56.9	18.6	153 05.3	49.2	21 20.4	13.3	Kaus Aust.	83 44.4	S34 22.6
17	242 10.4	119 06.4	26.8	24 57.7	19.2	168 07.6	49.3	36 22.7	13.4			
18	257 12.9	134 06.1	N18 26.4	39 58.6	S15 19.7	183 09.8	N21 49.3	51 24.9	S 8 13.5	Kochab	137 20.6	N74 06.5
19	272 15.4	149 05.7	26.0	54 59.4	20.3	198 12.0	49.3	66 27.1	13.6	Markab	13 38.5	N15 16.7
20	287 17.8	164 05.3	25.6	70 00.3	20.9	213 14.3	49.3	81 29.4	13.7	Menkar	314 15.4	N 4 08.5
21	302 20.3	179 05.0	.. 25.2	85 01.1	.. 21.4	228 16.5	.. 49.3	96 31.6	.. 13.8	Menkent	148 08.5	S36 26.0
22	317 22.8	194 04.6	24.8	100 01.9	22.0	243 18.8	49.4	111 33.8	13.9	Miaplacidus	221 40.6	S69 46.1
23	332 25.2	209 04.2	24.4	115 02.8	22.5	258 21.0	49.4	126 36.0	14.0			
8 00	347 27.7	224 03.9	N18 24.0	130 03.6	S15 23.1	273 23.2	N21 49.4	141 38.3	S 8 14.1	Mirfak	308 40.9	N49 54.2
01	2 30.2	239 03.5	23.6	145 04.5	23.6	288 25.5	49.4	156 40.5	14.2	Nunki	75 58.8	S26 16.7
02	17 32.6	254 03.1	23.2	160 05.3	24.2	303 27.7	49.4	171 42.7	14.3	Peacock	53 19.6	S56 41.6
03	32 35.1	269 02.7	.. 22.8	175 06.1	.. 24.7	318 30.0	.. 49.5	186 45.0	.. 14.4	Pollux	243 28.6	N27 59.6
04	47 37.6	284 02.4	22.4	190 07.0	25.3	333 32.2	49.5	201 47.2	14.5	Procyon	245 00.5	N 5 11.5
05	62 40.0	299 02.0	22.0	205 07.8	25.8	348 34.4	49.5	216 49.4	14.6			
06	77 42.5	314 01.6	N18 21.5	220 08.7	S15 26.4	3 36.7	N21 49.5	231 51.6	S 8 14.7	Rasalhague	96 06.9	N12 33.4
07	92 44.9	329 01.3	21.1	235 09.5	26.9	18 38.9	49.5	246 53.9	14.8	Regulus	207 44.4	N11 54.3
S 08	107 47.4	344 00.9	20.7	250 10.3	27.5	33 41.2	49.6	261 56.1	14.9	Rigel	281 12.6	S 8 11.1
A 09	122 49.9	359 00.5	.. 20.3	265 11.2	.. 28.0	48 43.4	.. 49.6	276 58.3	.. 15.0	Rigil Kent.	139 52.8	S60 53.4
T 10	137 52.3	14 00.1	19.9	280 12.0	28.6	63 45.7	49.6	292 00.6	15.1	Sabik	102 13.1	S15 44.3
U 11	152 54.8	28 59.8	19.5	295 12.8	29.1	78 47.9	49.6	307 02.8	15.2			
R 12	167 57.3	43 59.4	N18 19.1	310 13.7	S15 29.6	93 50.1	N21 49.6	322 05.0	S 8 15.3	Schedar	349 40.6	N56 36.5
D 13	182 59.7	58 59.0	18.7	325 14.5	30.2	108 52.4	49.7	337 07.2	15.4	Shaula	96 22.6	S37 06.7
A 14	198 02.2	73 58.7	18.2	340 15.3	30.7	123 54.6	49.7	352 09.5	15.5	Sirius	258 34.3	S16 43.9
Y 15	213 04.7	88 58.3	.. 17.8	355 16.2	.. 31.3	138 56.9	.. 49.7	7 11.7	.. 15.6	Spica	158 32.1	S11 13.6
16	228 07.1	103 57.9	17.4	10 17.0	31.8	153 59.1	49.7	22 13.9	15.7	Suhail	222 53.2	S43 29.0
17	243 09.6	118 57.5	17.0	25 17.8	32.4	169 01.4	49.7	37 16.2	15.7			
18	258 12.1	133 57.2	N18 16.6	40 18.7	S15 32.9	184 03.6	N21 49.8	52 18.4	S 8 15.8	Vega	80 39.1	N38 48.1
19	273 14.5	148 56.8	16.2	55 19.5	33.5	199 05.9	49.8	67 20.6	15.9	Zuben'ubi	137 06.2	S16 05.6
20	288 17.0	163 56.4	15.7	70 20.4	34.0	214 08.1	49.8	82 22.8	16.0		SHA	Mer. Pass.
21	303 19.4	178 56.0	.. 15.3	85 21.2	.. 34.6	229 10.3	.. 49.8	97 25.1	.. 16.1		° ′	h m
22	318 21.9	193 55.7	14.9	100 22.0	35.1	244 12.6	49.8	112 27.3	16.2	Venus	237 44.1	9 03
23	333 24.4	208 55.3	14.5	115 22.9	35.7	259 14.8	49.9	127 29.5	16.3	Mars	143 14.8	15 20
	h m									Jupiter	286 01.0	5 49
Mer. Pass.	0 53.9	v −0.4	d 0.4	v 0.8	d 0.6	v 2.2	d 0.0	v 2.2	d 0.1	Saturn	154 16.2	14 35

UT	SUN GHA	SUN Dec	MOON GHA	MOON v	MOON Dec	MOON d	MOON HP
d h	° ′	° ′	° ′	′	° ′	′	′
THURSDAY							
6 00	180 24.6	N 6 22.1	302 10.4	12.8	N17 44.7	6.1	54.4
01	195 24.8	21.1	316 42.2	12.8	17 50.8	6.0	54.4
02	210 25.0	20.2	331 14.0	12.8	17 56.8	5.9	54.3
03	225 25.2	.. 19.3	345 45.8	12.8	18 02.7	5.9	54.3
04	240 25.5	18.3	0 17.6	12.8	18 08.6	5.7	54.3
05	255 25.7	17.4	14 49.4	12.7	18 14.3	5.7	54.3
06	270 25.9	N 6 16.5	29 21.1	12.7	N18 20.0	5.6	54.3
07	285 26.1	15.5	43 52.8	12.7	18 25.6	5.5	54.3
08	300 26.3	14.6	58 24.5	12.6	18 31.1	5.5	54.3
09	315 26.5	.. 13.7	72 56.1	12.6	18 36.6	5.3	54.3
10	330 26.7	12.7	87 27.7	12.7	18 41.9	5.3	54.3
11	345 26.9	11.8	101 59.4	12.5	18 47.2	5.1	54.3
12	0 27.2	N 6 10.9	116 30.9	12.6	N18 52.3	5.1	54.3
13	15 27.4	09.9	131 02.5	12.5	18 57.4	5.0	54.3
14	30 27.6	09.0	145 34.0	12.5	19 02.4	4.9	54.3
15	45 27.8	.. 08.1	160 05.5	12.5	19 07.3	4.8	54.3
16	60 28.0	07.1	174 37.0	12.5	19 12.1	4.8	54.3
17	75 28.2	06.2	189 08.5	12.4	19 16.9	4.6	54.3
18	90 28.4	N 6 05.3	203 39.9	12.3	N19 21.5	4.6	54.3
19	105 28.7	04.3	218 11.4	12.3	19 26.1	4.4	54.3
20	120 28.9	03.4	232 42.7	12.4	19 30.5	4.4	54.3
21	135 29.1	.. 02.5	247 14.1	12.4	19 34.9	4.3	54.2
22	150 29.3	01.5	261 45.5	12.3	19 39.2	4.2	54.2
23	165 29.5	6 00.6	276 16.8	12.3	19 43.4	4.1	54.2
FRIDAY							
7 00	180 29.7	N 5 59.6	290 48.1	12.3	N19 47.5	4.0	54.2
01	195 29.9	58.7	305 19.4	12.2	19 51.5	4.0	54.2
02	210 30.1	57.8	319 50.6	12.3	19 55.5	3.8	54.2
03	225 30.4	.. 56.8	334 21.9	12.2	19 59.3	3.8	54.2
04	240 30.6	55.9	348 53.1	12.2	20 03.1	3.6	54.2
05	255 30.8	55.0	3 24.3	12.1	20 06.7	3.6	54.2
06	270 31.0	N 5 54.0	17 55.4	12.2	N20 10.3	3.4	54.2
07	285 31.2	53.1	32 26.6	12.1	20 13.7	3.4	54.2
08	300 31.4	52.1	46 57.7	12.1	20 17.1	3.3	54.2
09	315 31.6	.. 51.2	61 28.8	12.1	20 20.4	3.2	54.2
10	330 31.9	50.3	75 59.9	12.0	20 23.6	3.1	54.2
11	345 32.1	49.3	90 30.9	12.0	20 26.7	3.0	54.2
12	0 32.3	N 5 48.4	105 01.9	12.1	N20 29.7	2.9	54.2
13	15 32.5	47.5	119 33.0	11.9	20 32.6	2.8	54.2
14	30 32.7	46.5	134 03.9	12.0	20 35.4	2.7	54.2
15	45 32.9	.. 45.6	148 34.9	12.0	20 38.1	2.6	54.2
16	60 33.1	44.6	163 05.9	11.9	20 40.7	2.6	54.3
17	75 33.4	43.7	177 36.8	11.9	20 43.3	2.4	54.3
18	90 33.6	N 5 42.8	192 07.7	11.9	N20 45.7	2.3	54.3
19	105 33.8	41.8	206 38.6	11.9	20 48.0	2.3	54.3
20	120 34.0	40.9	221 09.5	11.8	20 50.3	2.1	54.3
21	135 34.2	.. 39.9	235 40.3	11.8	20 52.4	2.1	54.3
22	150 34.4	39.0	250 11.1	11.9	20 54.5	1.9	54.3
23	165 34.7	38.1	264 42.0	11.7	20 56.4	1.9	54.3
SATURDAY							
8 00	180 34.9	N 5 37.1	279 12.7	11.8	N20 58.3	1.7	54.3
01	195 35.1	36.2	293 43.5	11.8	21 00.0	1.7	54.3
02	210 35.3	35.3	308 14.3	11.7	21 01.7	1.5	54.3
03	225 35.5	.. 34.3	322 45.0	11.7	21 03.2	1.5	54.3
04	240 35.7	33.4	337 15.7	11.7	21 04.7	1.4	54.3
05	255 36.0	32.4	351 46.4	11.7	21 06.1	1.2	54.3
06	270 36.2	N 5 31.5	6 17.1	11.7	N21 07.3	1.2	54.3
07	285 36.4	30.5	20 47.8	11.7	21 08.5	1.1	54.3
08	300 36.6	29.6	35 18.5	11.6	21 09.6	0.9	54.3
09	315 36.8	.. 28.7	49 49.1	11.6	21 10.5	0.9	54.3
10	330 37.0	27.7	64 19.7	11.6	21 11.4	0.8	54.4
11	345 37.2	26.8	78 50.3	11.6	21 12.2	0.6	54.4
12	0 37.5	N 5 25.8	93 20.9	11.6	N21 12.8	0.6	54.4
13	15 37.7	24.9	107 51.5	11.6	21 13.4	0.5	54.4
14	30 37.9	23.9	122 22.1	11.5	21 13.9	0.4	54.4
15	45 38.1	.. 23.0	136 52.6	11.5	21 14.3	0.2	54.4
16	60 38.3	22.1	151 23.1	11.6	21 14.5	0.2	54.4
17	75 38.5	21.1	165 53.7	11.5	21 14.7	0.1	54.4
18	90 38.8	N 5 20.2	180 24.2	11.5	N21 14.8	0.1	54.4
19	105 39.0	19.2	194 54.7	11.4	21 14.7	0.0	54.4
20	120 39.2	18.3	209 25.1	11.5	21 14.6	0.2	54.5
21	135 39.4	.. 17.3	223 55.6	11.5	21 14.4	0.3	54.5
22	150 39.6	16.4	238 26.1	11.4	21 14.1	0.5	54.5
23	165 39.8	15.5	252 56.5	11.4	N21 13.6	0.5	54.5
	SD 15.9	d 0.9	SD 14.8		14.8		14.8

Twilight / Sunrise / Moonrise

Lat.	Twilight Naut.	Twilight Civil	Sunrise	Moonrise 6	7	8	9
°	h m	h m	h m	h m	h m	h m	h m
N 72	00 04	03 13	04 32	□	□	□	□
N 70	01 42	03 32	04 41	17 31	□	□	□
68	02 19	03 48	04 49	18 26	18 36	19 08	20 17
66	02 44	04 00	04 56	18 59	19 21	20 01	21 03
64	03 03	04 10	05 01	19 24	19 51	20 34	21 32
62	03 19	04 19	05 06	19 43	20 14	20 58	21 55
60	03 31	04 26	05 10	19 59	20 32	21 17	22 13
N 58	03 42	04 32	05 13	20 12	20 47	21 33	22 28
56	03 51	04 38	05 17	20 24	21 00	21 46	22 41
54	03 58	04 43	05 17	20 34	21 12	21 58	22 52
52	04 05	04 47	05 22	20 43	21 22	22 08	23 02
50	04 11	04 51	05 24	20 51	21 31	22 17	23 11
45	04 24	05 00	05 29	21 09	21 50	22 37	23 29
N 40	04 34	05 06	05 34	21 23	22 05	22 52	23 45
35	04 41	05 12	05 37	21 35	22 18	23 06	23 57
30	04 48	05 16	05 40	21 45	22 30	23 17	24 09
20	04 58	05 24	05 46	22 04	22 49	23 37	24 28
N 10	05 05	05 29	05 50	22 20	23 06	23 55	24 44
0	05 10	05 34	05 55	22 34	23 22	24 11	00 11
S 10	05 13	05 38	05 59	22 49	23 38	24 27	00 27
20	05 15	05 41	06 03	23 05	23 55	24 45	00 45
30	05 16	05 44	06 08	23 24	24 15	00 15	01 05
35	05 16	05 45	06 10	23 35	24 27	00 27	01 16
40	05 15	05 46	06 13	23 47	24 40	00 40	01 30
45	05 14	05 48	06 17	24 02	00 02	00 56	01 46
S 50	05 11	05 49	06 21	24 20	00 20	01 15	02 05
52	05 10	05 49	06 23	24 28	00 28	01 24	02 14
54	05 09	05 50	06 25	24 38	00 38	01 35	02 25
56	05 07	05 50	06 27	24 49	00 49	01 46	02 37
58	05 05	05 50	06 30	25 01	01 01	02 00	02 50
S 60	05 03	05 51	06 32	00 07	01 15	02 16	03 06

Sunset / Twilight / Moonset

Lat.	Sunset	Twilight Civil	Twilight Naut.	Moonset 6	7	8	9
°	h m	h m	h m	h m	h m	h m	h m
N 72	19 21	20 39	23 11	□	□	□	□
N 70	19 12	20 20	22 06	15 06	□	□	□
68	19 04	20 05	21 31	14 11	15 40	16 49	17 22
66	18 58	19 53	21 07	13 38	14 55	15 56	16 36
64	18 53	19 43	20 49	13 14	14 25	15 23	16 06
62	18 48	19 35	20 34	12 56	14 02	14 59	15 43
60	18 44	19 28	20 22	12 40	13 44	14 40	15 25
N 58	18 41	19 22	20 12	12 27	13 29	14 24	15 10
56	18 38	19 16	20 03	12 16	13 17	14 11	14 57
54	18 35	19 11	19 56	12 06	13 05	13 59	14 45
52	18 33	19 07	19 49	11 57	12 56	13 49	14 35
50	18 30	19 03	19 43	11 49	12 47	13 39	14 26
45	18 25	18 55	19 31	11 32	12 28	13 20	14 07
N 40	18 21	18 49	19 21	11 19	12 13	13 04	13 52
35	18 18	18 43	19 14	11 07	12 00	12 51	13 39
30	18 15	18 39	19 07	10 57	11 49	12 39	13 27
20	18 10	18 32	18 58	10 39	11 30	12 19	13 08
N 10	18 05	18 26	18 51	10 24	11 13	12 02	12 51
0	18 01	18 22	18 46	10 10	10 57	11 46	12 35
S 10	17 57	18 18	18 43	09 56	10 42	11 30	12 19
20	17 53	18 15	18 41	09 41	10 25	11 12	12 01
30	17 48	18 12	18 40	09 24	10 06	10 52	11 42
35	17 46	18 11	18 40	09 14	09 55	10 40	11 30
40	17 43	18 10	18 41	09 02	09 42	10 27	11 17
45	17 40	18 09	18 43	08 49	09 27	10 11	11 01
S 50	17 36	18 08	18 45	08 32	09 09	09 52	10 42
52	17 34	18 08	18 47	08 25	09 00	09 42	10 32
54	17 32	18 07	18 48	08 16	08 50	09 32	10 22
56	17 30	18 07	18 50	08 07	08 39	09 20	10 10
58	17 27	18 07	18 52	07 56	08 27	09 07	09 57
S 60	17 25	18 06	18 54	07 43	08 12	08 51	09 41

SUN and MOON

Day	SUN Eqn. of Time 00h	SUN Eqn. of Time 12h	SUN Mer. Pass.	MOON Mer. Pass. Upper	MOON Mer. Pass. Lower	Age	Phase
d	m s	m s	h m	h m	h m	d	%
6	01 38	01 48	11 58	03 59	16 22	20	69
7	01 58	02 09	11 58	04 46	17 10	21	60
8	02 19	02 29	11 58	05 34	17 58	22	51

2012 SEPTEMBER 9, 10, 11 (SUN., MON., TUES.)

UT	ARIES GHA	VENUS −4.2 GHA	Dec	MARS +1.2 GHA	Dec	JUPITER −2.4 GHA	Dec	SATURN +0.8 GHA	Dec
9 00	348 26.8	223 54.9	N18 14.0	130 23.7	S15 36.2	274 17.1	N21 49.9	142 31.7	S 8 16.4
01	3 29.3	238 54.6	13.6	145 24.5	36.8	289 19.3	49.9	157 34.0	16.5
02	18 31.8	253 54.2	13.2	160 25.3	37.3	304 21.6	49.9	172 36.2	16.6
03	33 34.2	268 53.8 ..	12.8	175 26.2 ..	37.9	319 23.8 ..	49.9	187 38.4 ..	16.7
04	48 36.7	283 53.4	12.3	190 27.0	38.4	334 26.1	50.0	202 40.7	16.8
05	63 39.2	298 53.1	11.9	205 27.8	39.0	349 28.3	50.0	217 42.9	16.9
S 06	78 41.6	313 52.7	N18 11.5	220 28.7	S15 39.5	4 30.6	N21 50.0	232 45.1	S 8 17.0
U 07	93 44.1	328 52.3	11.1	235 29.5	40.0	19 32.8	50.0	247 47.3	17.1
N 08	108 46.5	343 51.9	10.6	250 30.3	40.6	34 35.1	50.0	262 49.6	17.2
D 09	123 49.0	358 51.6 ..	10.2	265 31.2 ..	41.1	49 37.3 ..	50.1	277 51.8 ..	17.3
A 10	138 51.5	13 51.2	09.8	280 32.0	41.7	64 39.6	50.1	292 54.0	17.4
Y 11	153 53.9	28 50.8	09.3	295 32.8	42.2	79 41.8	50.1	307 56.2	17.5
12	168 56.4	43 50.4	N18 08.9	310 33.6	S15 42.8	94 44.1	N21 50.1	322 58.5	S 8 17.6
13	183 58.9	58 50.0	08.5	325 34.5	43.3	109 46.3	50.1	338 00.7	17.7
14	199 01.3	73 49.7	08.0	340 35.3	43.9	124 48.6	50.2	353 02.9	17.8
15	214 03.8	88 49.3 ..	07.6	355 36.1 ..	44.4	139 50.8 ..	50.2	8 05.1 ..	17.9
16	229 06.3	103 48.9	07.1	10 37.0	45.0	154 53.1	50.2	23 07.4	18.0
17	244 08.7	118 48.5	06.7	25 37.8	45.5	169 55.3	50.2	38 09.6	18.1
18	259 11.2	133 48.2	N18 06.3	40 38.6	S15 46.0	184 57.6	N21 50.2	53 11.8	S 8 18.2
19	274 13.7	148 47.8	05.8	55 39.4	46.6	199 59.8	50.3	68 14.0	18.3
20	289 16.1	163 47.4	05.4	70 40.3	47.1	215 02.1	50.3	83 16.3	18.4
21	304 18.6	178 47.0 ..	04.9	85 41.1 ..	47.7	230 04.3 ..	50.3	98 18.5 ..	18.5
22	319 21.0	193 46.7	04.5	100 41.9	48.2	245 06.6	50.3	113 20.7	18.6
23	334 23.5	208 46.3	04.1	115 42.7	48.8	260 08.9	50.3	128 22.9	18.7
10 00	349 26.0	223 45.9	N18 03.6	130 43.6	S15 49.3	275 11.1	N21 50.3	143 25.2	S 8 18.7
01	4 28.4	238 45.5	03.2	145 44.4	49.8	290 13.4	50.4	158 27.4	18.8
02	19 30.9	253 45.1	02.7	160 45.2	50.4	305 15.6	50.4	173 29.6	18.9
03	34 33.4	268 44.8 ..	02.3	175 46.0 ..	50.9	320 17.9 ..	50.4	188 31.8 ..	19.0
04	49 35.8	283 44.4	01.8	190 46.9	51.5	335 20.1	50.4	203 34.1	19.1
05	64 38.3	298 44.0	01.4	205 47.7	52.0	350 22.4	50.4	218 36.3	19.2
M 06	79 40.8	313 43.6	N18 00.9	220 48.5	S15 52.6	5 24.6	N21 50.5	233 38.5	S 8 19.3
O 07	94 43.2	328 43.2	00.5	235 49.3	53.1	20 26.9	50.5	248 40.7	19.4
N 08	109 45.7	343 42.9	18 00.0	250 50.2	53.6	35 29.2	50.5	263 43.0	19.5
D 09	124 48.2	358 42.5	17 59.6	265 51.0 ..	54.2	50 31.4 ..	50.5	278 45.2 ..	19.6
A 10	139 50.6	13 42.1	59.1	280 51.8	54.7	65 33.7	50.5	293 47.4	19.7
Y 11	154 53.1	28 41.7	58.7	295 52.6	55.3	80 35.9	50.6	308 49.6	19.8
12	169 55.5	43 41.3	N17 58.2	310 53.4	S15 55.8	95 38.2	N21 50.6	323 51.9	S 8 19.9
13	184 58.0	58 41.0	57.8	325 54.3	56.4	110 40.5	50.6	338 54.1	20.0
14	200 00.5	73 40.6	57.3	340 55.1	56.9	125 42.7	50.6	353 56.3	20.1
15	215 02.9	88 40.2 ..	56.8	355 55.9 ..	57.4	140 45.0 ..	50.6	8 58.5 ..	20.2
16	230 05.4	103 39.8	56.4	10 56.7	58.0	155 47.2	50.6	24 00.8	20.3
17	245 07.9	118 39.4	55.9	25 57.5	58.5	170 49.5	50.7	39 03.0	20.4
18	260 10.3	133 39.1	N17 55.5	40 58.4	S15 59.1	185 51.8	N21 50.7	54 05.2	S 8 20.5
19	275 12.8	148 38.7	55.0	55 59.2	15 59.6	200 54.0	50.7	69 07.4	20.6
20	290 15.3	163 38.3	54.5	71 00.0	16 00.1	215 56.3	50.7	84 09.6	20.7
21	305 17.7	178 37.9 ..	54.1	86 00.8 ..	00.7	230 58.5 ..	50.7	99 11.9 ..	20.8
22	320 20.2	193 37.5	53.6	101 01.6	01.2	246 00.8	50.8	114 14.1	20.9
23	335 22.7	208 37.2	53.2	116 02.5	01.8	261 03.1	50.8	129 16.3	21.0
11 00	350 25.1	223 36.8	N17 52.7	131 03.3	S16 02.3	276 05.3	N21 50.8	144 18.5	S 8 21.1
01	5 27.6	238 36.4	52.2	146 04.1	02.8	291 07.6	50.8	159 20.8	21.2
02	20 30.0	253 36.0	51.8	161 04.9	03.4	306 09.9	50.8	174 23.0	21.3
03	35 32.5	268 35.6 ..	51.3	176 05.7 ..	03.9	321 12.1 ..	50.8	189 25.2 ..	21.4
04	50 35.0	283 35.3	50.8	191 06.5	04.5	336 14.4	50.9	204 27.4	21.5
05	65 37.4	298 34.9	50.3	206 07.4	05.0	351 16.6	50.9	219 29.7	21.6
T 06	80 39.9	313 34.5	N17 49.9	221 08.2	S16 05.5	6 18.9	N21 50.9	234 31.9	S 8 21.7
U 07	95 42.4	328 34.1	49.4	236 09.0	06.1	21 21.2	50.9	249 34.1	21.8
E 08	110 44.8	343 33.7	48.9	251 09.8	06.6	36 23.4	50.9	264 36.3	21.9
S 09	125 47.3	358 33.3 ..	48.5	266 10.6 ..	07.1	51 25.7 ..	50.9	279 38.5 ..	22.0
D 10	140 49.8	13 33.0	48.0	281 11.4	07.7	66 28.0	51.0	294 40.8	22.1
A 11	155 52.2	28 32.6	47.5	296 12.2	08.2	81 30.2	51.0	309 43.0	22.2
Y 12	170 54.7	43 32.2	N17 47.0	311 13.1	S16 08.8	96 32.5	N21 51.0	324 45.2	S 8 22.3
13	185 57.1	58 31.8	46.6	326 13.9	09.3	111 34.8	51.0	339 47.4	22.4
14	200 59.6	73 31.4	46.1	341 14.7	09.8	126 37.0	51.0	354 49.6	22.5
15	216 02.1	88 31.0 ..	45.6	356 15.5 ..	10.4	141 39.3 ..	51.1	9 51.9 ..	22.6
16	231 04.5	103 30.7	45.1	11 16.3	10.9	156 41.6	51.1	24 54.1	22.7
17	246 07.0	118 30.3	44.6	26 17.1	11.4	171 43.8	51.1	39 56.3	22.8
18	261 09.5	133 29.9	N17 44.2	41 17.9	S16 12.0	186 46.1	N21 51.1	54 58.5	S 8 22.8
19	276 11.9	148 29.5	43.7	56 18.7	12.5	201 48.4	51.1	70 00.8	22.9
20	291 14.4	163 29.1	43.2	71 19.6	13.1	216 50.6	51.1	85 03.0	23.0
21	306 16.9	178 28.7 ..	42.7	86 20.4 ..	13.6	231 52.9 ..	51.2	100 05.2 ..	23.1
22	321 19.3	193 28.4	42.2	101 21.2	14.1	246 55.2	51.2	115 07.4	23.2
23	336 21.8	208 28.0	41.7	116 22.0	14.7	261 57.5	51.2	130 09.6	23.3
Mer.Pass. 0 42.2		v −0.4	d 0.5	v 0.8	d 0.5	v 2.3	d 0.0	v 2.2	d 0.1

STARS

Name	SHA	Dec
Acamar	315 18.5	S40 15.0
Achernar	335 26.7	S57 10.1
Acrux	173 10.5	S63 10.3
Adhara	255 13.1	S28 59.2
Aldebaran	290 49.9	N16 32.0
Alioth	166 21.6	N55 53.6
Alkaid	152 59.7	N49 15.2
Al Na'ir	27 43.9	S46 53.8
Alnilam	275 46.9	S 1 11.6
Alphard	217 56.9	S 8 42.8
Alphecca	126 11.6	N26 40.6
Alpheratz	357 43.7	N29 09.8
Altair	62 08.5	N 8 54.4
Ankaa	353 15.8	S42 14.0
Antares	112 26.9	S26 27.5
Arcturus	145 56.4	N19 07.2
Atria	107 29.3	S69 03.2
Avior	234 18.7	S59 32.9
Bellatrix	278 32.6	N 6 21.7
Betelgeuse	271 01.9	N 7 24.5
Canopus	263 56.5	S52 41.9
Capella	280 35.2	N46 00.4
Deneb	49 31.5	N45 19.9
Denebola	182 34.5	N14 30.1
Diphda	348 56.1	S17 54.8
Dubhe	193 53.0	N61 40.9
Elnath	278 13.3	N28 36.9
Eltanin	90 46.3	N51 29.7
Enif	33 47.3	N 9 56.3
Fomalhaut	15 24.2	S29 33.1
Gacrux	172 02.0	S57 11.2
Gienah	175 53.1	S17 36.7
Hadar	148 49.1	S60 26.2
Hamal	328 01.1	N23 31.4
Kaus Aust.	83 44.4	S34 22.6
Kochab	137 20.6	N74 06.5
Markab	13 38.5	N15 16.7
Menkar	314 15.4	N 4 08.5
Menkent	148 08.5	S36 26.0
Miaplacidus	221 40.6	S69 46.1
Mirfak	308 40.9	N49 54.2
Nunki	75 58.8	S26 16.7
Peacock	53 19.6	S56 41.6
Pollux	243 28.6	N27 59.6
Procyon	245 00.5	N 5 11.5
Rasalhague	96 06.9	N12 33.4
Regulus	207 44.4	N11 54.3
Rigel	281 12.6	S 8 11.1
Rigil Kent.	139 52.8	S60 53.4
Sabik	102 13.1	S15 44.3
Schedar	349 40.6	N56 36.5
Shaula	96 22.6	S37 06.7
Sirius	258 34.3	S16 43.9
Spica	158 32.1	S11 13.6
Suhail	222 53.2	S43 29.0
Vega	80 39.2	N38 48.1
Zuben'ubi	137 06.2	S16 05.6

	SHA	Mer.Pass.
Venus	234 16.9	9 05
Mars	141 17.6	15 16
Jupiter	285 45.1	5 38
Saturn	153 59.2	14 24

UT	SUN GHA	SUN Dec	MOON GHA	v	Dec	d	HP
d h	° ′	° ′	° ′	′	° ′	′	′
9 00	180 40.1	N 5 14.5	267 26.9	11.5	N21 13.1	0.6	54.5
01	195 40.3	13.6	281 57.4	11.4	21 12.5	0.8	54.5
02	210 40.5	12.6	296 27.8	11.4	21 11.7	0.8	54.5
03	225 40.7	.. 11.7	310 58.2	11.4	21 10.9	0.9	54.5
04	240 40.9	10.7	325 28.6	11.4	21 10.0	1.1	54.6
05	255 41.1	09.8	339 59.0	11.3	21 08.9	1.1	54.6
06	270 41.4	N 5 08.8	354 29.3	11.4	N21 07.8	1.2	54.6
07	285 41.6	07.9	8 59.7	11.3	21 06.6	1.4	54.6
S 08	300 41.8	07.0	23 30.0	11.4	21 05.2	1.4	54.6
U 09	315 42.0	.. 06.0	38 00.4	11.3	21 03.8	1.6	54.6
N 10	330 42.2	05.1	52 30.7	11.4	21 02.2	1.6	54.6
D 11	345 42.5	04.1	67 01.1	11.3	21 00.6	1.8	54.7
A 12	0 42.7	N 5 03.2	81 31.4	11.3	N20 58.8	1.8	54.7
Y 13	15 42.9	02.2	96 01.7	11.3	20 57.0	2.0	54.7
14	30 43.1	01.3	110 32.0	11.3	20 55.0	2.0	54.7
15	45 43.3	5 00.3	125 02.3	11.3	20 53.0	2.2	54.7
16	60 43.5	4 59.4	139 32.6	11.3	20 50.8	2.2	54.7
17	75 43.8	58.4	154 02.9	11.3	20 48.6	2.4	54.8
18	90 44.0	N 4 57.5	168 33.2	11.3	N20 46.2	2.4	54.8
19	105 44.2	56.5	183 03.5	11.3	20 43.8	2.6	54.8
20	120 44.4	55.6	197 33.8	11.2	20 41.2	2.7	54.8
21	135 44.6	.. 54.6	212 04.0	11.3	20 38.5	2.7	54.8
22	150 44.9	53.7	226 34.3	11.3	20 35.8	2.9	54.8
23	165 45.1	52.8	241 04.6	11.2	20 32.9	2.9	54.9
10 00	180 45.3	N 4 51.8	255 34.8	11.3	N20 30.0	3.1	54.9
01	195 45.5	50.9	270 05.1	11.3	20 26.9	3.2	54.9
02	210 45.7	49.9	284 35.4	11.2	20 23.7	3.2	54.9
03	225 45.9	.. 49.0	299 05.6	11.3	20 20.5	3.4	54.9
04	240 46.2	48.0	313 35.9	11.2	20 17.1	3.5	55.0
05	255 46.4	47.1	328 06.1	11.3	20 13.6	3.5	55.0
06	270 46.6	N 4 46.1	342 36.4	11.2	N20 10.1	3.7	55.0
07	285 46.8	45.2	357 06.6	11.3	20 06.4	3.8	55.0
M 08	300 47.0	44.2	11 36.9	11.2	20 02.6	3.8	55.0
O 09	315 47.3	.. 43.3	26 07.1	11.3	19 58.8	4.0	55.1
N 10	330 47.5	42.3	40 37.4	11.2	19 54.8	4.1	55.1
D 11	345 47.7	41.4	55 07.6	11.3	19 50.7	4.2	55.1
A 12	0 47.9	N 4 40.4	69 37.9	11.2	N19 46.5	4.2	55.1
Y 13	15 48.1	39.5	84 08.1	11.2	19 42.3	4.4	55.2
14	30 48.4	38.5	98 38.3	11.3	19 37.9	4.5	55.2
15	45 48.6	.. 37.6	113 08.6	11.2	19 33.4	4.5	55.2
16	60 48.8	36.6	127 38.8	11.3	19 28.9	4.7	55.2
17	75 49.0	35.7	142 09.1	11.3	19 24.2	4.8	55.2
18	90 49.2	N 4 34.7	156 39.4	11.2	N19 19.4	4.8	55.3
19	105 49.4	33.8	171 09.6	11.3	19 14.6	5.0	55.3
20	120 49.7	32.8	185 39.9	11.2	19 09.6	5.0	55.3
21	135 49.9	.. 31.9	200 10.1	11.3	19 04.6	5.2	55.3
22	150 50.1	30.9	214 40.4	11.2	18 59.4	5.3	55.4
23	165 50.3	30.0	229 10.6	11.3	18 54.1	5.3	55.4
11 00	180 50.5	N 4 29.0	243 40.9	11.3	N18 48.8	5.5	55.4
01	195 50.8	28.1	258 11.2	11.3	18 43.3	5.5	55.4
02	210 51.0	27.1	272 41.5	11.2	18 37.8	5.6	55.5
03	225 51.2	.. 26.2	287 11.7	11.3	18 32.2	5.8	55.5
04	240 51.4	25.2	301 42.0	11.3	18 26.4	5.8	55.5
05	255 51.6	24.3	316 12.3	11.3	18 20.6	6.0	55.5
06	270 51.9	N 4 23.3	330 42.6	11.3	N18 14.6	6.0	55.6
07	285 52.1	22.4	345 12.9	11.3	18 08.6	6.1	55.6
T 08	300 52.3	21.4	359 43.2	11.3	18 02.5	6.2	55.6
U 09	315 52.5	.. 20.5	14 13.5	11.3	17 56.3	6.3	55.7
E 10	330 52.7	19.5	28 43.8	11.3	17 50.0	6.4	55.7
S 11	345 53.0	18.5	43 14.1	11.3	17 43.6	6.5	55.7
D 12	0 53.2	N 4 17.6	57 44.4	11.3	N17 37.1	6.6	55.7
A 13	15 53.4	16.6	72 14.7	11.3	17 30.5	6.7	55.8
Y 14	30 53.6	15.7	86 45.0	11.4	17 23.8	6.8	55.8
15	45 53.8	.. 14.7	101 15.4	11.3	17 17.0	6.9	55.8
16	60 54.1	13.8	115 45.7	11.3	17 10.1	6.9	55.8
17	75 54.3	12.8	130 16.0	11.4	17 03.2	7.1	55.9
18	90 54.5	N 4 11.9	144 46.4	11.3	N16 56.1	7.1	55.9
19	105 54.7	10.9	159 16.7	11.4	16 49.0	7.3	55.9
20	120 54.9	10.0	173 47.1	11.3	16 41.7	7.3	56.0
21	135 55.2	.. 09.0	188 17.4	11.4	16 34.4	7.4	56.0
22	150 55.4	08.1	202 47.8	11.3	16 27.0	7.5	56.0
23	165 55.6	07.1	217 18.1	11.4	N16 19.5	7.6	56.1
SD	15.9	d 0.9	SD 14.9		15.0		15.2

Twilight / Sunrise / Moonrise

Lat.	Naut.	Civil	Sunrise	Moonrise 9	10	11	12
°	h m	h m	h m	h m	h m	h m	h m
N 72	01 19	03 30	04 46	☐	☐	22 12	24 28
N 70	02 07	03 47	04 54	☐	20 56	22 59	24 52
68	02 37	04 00	05 00	20 17	21 49	23 29	25 10
66	02 59	04 11	05 05	21 03	22 22	23 51	25 25
64	03 15	04 20	05 10	21 32	22 46	24 08	00 08
62	03 29	04 27	05 13	21 55	23 04	24 23	00 23
60	03 40	04 34	05 17	22 13	23 20	24 35	00 35
N 58	03 49	04 39	05 20	22 28	23 33	24 45	00 45
56	03 58	04 44	05 22	22 41	23 44	24 54	00 54
54	04 05	04 49	05 25	22 52	23 54	25 02	01 02
52	04 11	04 52	05 27	23 02	24 03	00 03	01 09
50	04 16	04 56	05 29	23 11	24 11	00 11	01 16
45	04 28	05 03	05 33	23 29	24 27	00 27	01 30
N 40	04 37	05 09	05 36	23 45	24 41	00 41	01 41
35	04 44	05 14	05 39	23 57	24 53	00 53	01 51
30	04 50	05 18	05 42	24 09	00 09	01 03	01 59
20	04 58	05 24	05 46	24 28	00 28	01 20	02 14
N 10	05 05	05 29	05 50	24 44	00 44	01 35	02 27
0	05 09	05 33	05 54	00 11	01 00	01 49	02 38
S 10	05 11	05 36	05 57	00 27	01 16	02 03	02 50
20	05 13	05 38	06 00	00 45	01 32	02 18	03 03
30	05 12	05 40	06 04	01 05	01 51	02 36	03 17
35	05 12	05 41	06 06	01 16	02 03	02 46	03 26
40	05 10	05 42	06 09	01 30	02 15	02 57	03 35
45	05 08	05 42	06 11	01 46	02 30	03 11	03 46
S 50	05 05	05 42	06 14	02 05	02 49	03 27	04 00
52	05 03	05 42	06 16	02 14	02 58	03 34	04 06
54	05 01	05 42	06 18	02 25	03 07	03 43	04 13
56	04 59	05 42	06 19	02 37	03 18	03 52	04 20
58	04 57	05 42	06 21	02 50	03 31	04 03	04 29
S 60	04 54	05 42	06 23	03 06	03 46	04 16	04 39

Sunset / Twilight / Moonset

Lat.	Sunset	Civil	Naut.	Moonset 9	10	11	12
°	h m	h m	h m	h m	h m	h m	h m
N 72	19 05	20 20	22 23	☐	☐	18 53	18 20
N 70	18 57	20 03	21 40	☐	18 26	18 06	17 54
68	18 51	19 51	21 12	17 22	17 32	17 35	17 35
66	18 46	19 40	20 51	16 36	16 59	17 12	17 19
64	18 42	19 32	20 35	16 06	16 34	16 53	17 06
62	18 39	19 24	20 22	15 43	16 15	16 38	16 55
60	18 35	19 18	20 11	15 25	15 59	16 26	16 46
N 58	18 32	19 13	20 02	15 10	15 46	16 15	16 38
56	18 30	19 08	19 54	14 57	15 34	16 05	16 30
54	18 28	19 04	19 47	14 45	15 24	15 57	16 24
52	18 26	19 00	19 41	14 35	15 15	15 49	16 18
50	18 24	18 57	19 36	14 26	15 07	15 42	16 13
45	18 20	18 49	19 25	14 07	14 50	15 27	16 01
N 40	18 16	18 44	19 16	13 52	14 36	15 15	15 52
35	18 14	18 39	19 09	13 39	14 23	15 05	15 43
30	18 11	18 35	19 03	13 27	14 13	14 56	15 36
20	18 07	18 29	18 55	13 08	13 55	14 40	15 24
N 10	18 03	18 24	18 49	12 51	13 39	14 26	15 12
0	18 00	18 21	18 45	12 35	13 24	14 13	15 02
S 10	17 57	18 18	18 42	12 19	13 09	14 00	14 51
20	17 54	18 16	18 41	12 01	12 53	13 46	14 40
30	17 50	18 14	18 42	11 42	12 34	13 30	14 27
35	17 48	18 13	18 43	11 30	12 23	13 20	14 20
40	17 46	18 13	18 44	11 17	12 11	13 09	14 11
45	17 43	18 12	18 46	11 01	11 56	12 57	14 01
S 50	17 40	18 12	18 50	10 42	11 38	12 41	13 48
52	17 39	18 12	18 51	10 32	11 30	12 34	13 43
54	17 37	18 12	18 53	10 22	11 20	12 26	13 36
56	17 35	18 13	18 56	10 10	11 10	12 17	13 29
58	17 34	18 13	18 58	09 57	10 57	12 06	13 21
S 60	17 32	18 13	19 01	09 41	10 43	11 54	13 12

SUN / MOON

Day	Eqn. of Time 00ʰ	Eqn. of Time 12ʰ	Mer. Pass.	Mer. Pass. Upper	Mer. Pass. Lower	Age	Phase
d	m s	m s	h m	h m	h m	d	%
9	02 40	02 50	11 57	06 23	18 47	23	41
10	03 01	03 11	11 57	07 12	19 37	24	32
11	03 22	03 32	11 56	08 01	20 26	25	23

UT	ARIES GHA	VENUS −4.2 GHA	Dec	MARS +1.2 GHA	Dec	JUPITER −2.4 GHA	Dec	SATURN +0.8 GHA	Dec	STARS Name	SHA	Dec
12 00	351 24.3	223 27.6	N17 41.3	131 22.8	S16 15.2	276 59.7	N21 51.2	145 11.9	S 8 23.4	Acamar	315 18.5	S40 15.0
01	6 26.7	238 27.2	40.8	146 23.6	15.7	292 02.0	51.2	160 14.1	23.5	Achernar	335 26.7	S57 10.1
02	21 29.2	253 26.8	40.3	161 24.4	16.3	307 04.3	51.2	175 16.3	23.6	Acrux	173 10.5	S63 10.3
03	36 31.6	268 26.4	.. 39.8	176 25.2	.. 16.8	322 06.5	.. 51.3	190 18.5	.. 23.7	Adhara	255 13.1	S28 59.2
04	51 34.1	283 26.0	39.3	191 26.0	17.3	337 08.8	51.3	205 20.7	23.8	Aldebaran	290 49.9	N16 32.0
05	66 36.6	298 25.7	38.8	206 26.8	17.9	352 11.1	51.3	220 23.0	23.9			
W 06	81 39.0	313 25.3	N17 38.3	221 27.6	S16 18.4	7 13.4	N21 51.3	235 25.2	S 8 24.0	Alioth	166 21.6	N55 53.6
E 07	96 41.5	328 24.9	37.8	236 28.5	18.9	22 15.6	51.3	250 27.4	24.1	Alkaid	152 59.7	N49 15.2
D 08	111 44.0	343 24.5	37.3	251 29.3	19.5	37 17.9	51.3	265 29.6	24.2	Al Na'ir	27 43.9	S46 53.8
N 09	126 46.4	358 24.1	.. 36.8	266 30.1	.. 20.0	52 20.2	.. 51.4	280 31.8	.. 24.3	Alnilam	275 46.9	S 1 11.6
E 10	141 48.9	13 23.7	36.4	281 30.9	20.6	67 22.5	51.4	295 34.1	24.4	Alphard	217 56.9	S 8 42.8
S 11	156 51.4	28 23.3	35.9	296 31.7	21.1	82 24.7	51.4	310 36.3	24.5			
D 12	171 53.8	43 23.0	N17 35.4	311 32.5	S16 21.6	97 27.0	N21 51.4	325 38.5	S 8 24.6	Alphecca	126 11.6	N26 40.6
A 13	186 56.3	58 22.6	34.9	326 33.3	22.2	112 29.3	51.4	340 40.7	24.7	Alpheratz	357 43.7	N29 09.8
Y 14	201 58.8	73 22.2	34.4	341 34.1	22.7	127 31.6	51.4	355 42.9	24.8	Altair	62 08.5	N 8 54.3
15	217 01.2	88 21.8	.. 33.9	356 34.9	.. 23.2	142 33.8	.. 51.5	10 45.2	.. 24.9	Ankaa	353 15.8	S42 14.0
16	232 03.7	103 21.4	33.4	11 35.7	23.8	157 36.1	51.5	25 47.4	25.0	Antares	112 27.0	S26 27.5
17	247 06.1	118 21.0	32.9	26 36.5	24.3	172 38.4	51.5	40 49.6	25.1			
18	262 08.6	133 20.6	N17 32.4	41 37.3	S16 24.8	187 40.7	N21 51.5	55 51.8	S 8 25.2	Arcturus	145 56.4	N19 07.2
19	277 11.1	148 20.3	31.9	56 38.1	25.3	202 42.9	51.5	70 54.0	25.3	Atria	107 29.3	S69 03.2
20	292 13.5	163 19.9	31.4	71 38.9	25.9	217 45.2	51.5	85 56.3	25.4	Avior	234 18.7	S59 32.9
21	307 16.0	178 19.5	.. 30.9	86 39.7	.. 26.4	232 47.5	.. 51.6	100 58.5	.. 25.5	Bellatrix	278 32.6	N 6 21.7
22	322 18.5	193 19.1	30.4	101 40.5	26.9	247 49.8	51.6	116 00.7	25.6	Betelgeuse	271 01.9	N 7 24.5
23	337 20.9	208 18.7	29.9	116 41.3	27.5	262 52.0	51.6	131 02.9	25.7			
13 00	352 23.4	223 18.3	N17 29.3	131 42.1	S16 28.0	277 54.3	N21 51.6	146 05.1	S 8 25.8	Canopus	263 56.5	S52 41.9
01	7 25.9	238 17.9	28.8	146 42.9	28.5	292 56.6	51.6	161 07.4	25.9	Capella	280 35.2	N46 00.4
02	22 28.3	253 17.6	28.3	161 43.7	29.1	307 58.9	51.6	176 09.6	26.0	Deneb	49 31.5	N45 19.9
03	37 30.8	268 17.2	.. 27.8	176 44.5	.. 29.6	323 01.2	.. 51.7	191 11.8	.. 26.1	Denebola	182 34.5	N14 30.1
04	52 33.2	283 16.8	27.3	191 45.3	30.1	338 03.4	51.7	206 14.0	26.2	Diphda	348 56.1	S17 54.8
05	67 35.7	298 16.4	26.8	206 46.1	30.7	353 05.7	51.7	221 16.2	26.3			
T 06	82 38.2	313 16.0	N17 26.3	221 46.9	S16 31.2	8 08.0	N21 51.7	236 18.5	S 8 26.4	Dubhe	193 53.0	N61 40.9
H 07	97 40.6	328 15.6	25.8	236 47.7	31.7	23 10.3	51.7	251 20.7	26.5	Elnath	278 13.3	N28 36.9
U 08	112 43.1	343 15.2	25.3	251 48.5	32.3	38 12.6	51.7	266 22.9	26.6	Eltanin	90 46.3	N51 29.7
R 09	127 45.6	358 14.8	.. 24.8	266 49.3	.. 32.8	53 14.8	.. 51.8	281 25.1	.. 26.7	Enif	33 47.3	N 9 56.3
S 10	142 48.0	13 14.4	24.2	281 50.1	33.3	68 17.1	51.8	296 27.3	26.8	Fomalhaut	15 24.2	S29 33.1
D 11	157 50.5	28 14.1	23.7	296 50.9	33.8	83 19.4	51.8	311 29.5	26.9			
A 12	172 53.0	43 13.7	N17 23.2	311 51.7	S16 34.4	98 21.7	N21 51.8	326 31.8	S 8 27.0	Gacrux	172 02.0	S57 11.1
Y 13	187 55.4	58 13.3	22.7	326 52.5	34.9	113 24.0	51.8	341 34.0	27.1	Gienah	175 53.1	S17 36.7
14	202 57.9	73 12.9	22.2	341 53.3	35.4	128 26.3	51.8	356 36.2	27.2	Hadar	148 49.1	S60 26.2
15	218 00.4	88 12.5	.. 21.6	356 54.1	.. 36.0	143 28.5	.. 51.8	11 38.4	.. 27.3	Hamal	328 01.1	N23 31.4
16	233 02.8	103 12.1	21.1	11 54.9	36.5	158 30.8	51.9	26 40.6	27.4	Kaus Aust.	83 44.4	S34 22.6
17	248 05.3	118 11.7	20.6	26 55.7	37.0	173 33.1	51.9	41 42.9	27.5			
18	263 07.7	133 11.3	N17 20.1	41 56.5	S16 37.6	188 35.4	N21 51.9	56 45.1	S 8 27.6	Kochab	137 20.7	N74 06.5
19	278 10.2	148 11.0	19.6	56 57.3	38.1	203 37.7	51.9	71 47.3	27.7	Markab	13 38.5	N15 16.7
20	293 12.7	163 10.6	19.0	71 58.1	38.6	218 40.0	51.9	86 49.5	27.8	Menkar	314 15.4	N 4 08.5
21	308 15.1	178 10.2	.. 18.5	86 58.9	.. 39.1	233 42.2	.. 51.9	101 51.7	.. 27.9	Menkent	148 08.5	S36 26.0
22	323 17.6	193 09.8	18.0	101 59.7	39.7	248 44.5	52.0	116 53.9	28.0	Miaplacidus	221 40.6	S69 46.1
23	338 20.1	208 09.4	17.5	117 00.5	40.2	263 46.8	52.0	131 56.2	28.1			
14 00	353 22.5	223 09.0	N17 16.9	132 01.3	S16 40.7	278 49.1	N21 52.0	146 58.4	S 8 28.2	Mirfak	308 40.8	N49 54.2
01	8 25.0	238 08.6	16.4	147 02.1	41.2	293 51.4	52.0	162 00.6	28.3	Nunki	75 58.8	S26 16.7
02	23 27.5	253 08.2	15.9	162 02.9	41.8	308 53.7	52.0	177 02.8	28.4	Peacock	53 19.6	S56 41.6
03	38 29.9	268 07.8	.. 15.4	177 03.7	.. 42.3	323 56.0	.. 52.0	192 05.0	.. 28.5	Pollux	243 28.6	N27 59.6
04	53 32.4	283 07.5	14.8	192 04.5	42.8	338 58.3	52.0	207 07.2	28.6	Procyon	245 00.4	N 5 11.5
05	68 34.8	298 07.1	14.3	207 05.3	43.4	354 00.5	52.1	222 09.5	28.7			
06	83 37.3	313 06.7	N17 13.8	222 06.1	S16 43.9	9 02.8	N21 52.1	237 11.7	S 8 28.8	Rasalhague	96 06.9	N12 33.4
07	98 39.8	328 06.3	13.2	237 06.8	44.4	24 05.1	52.1	252 13.9	28.9	Regulus	207 44.4	N11 54.3
08	113 42.2	343 05.9	12.7	252 07.6	44.9	39 07.4	52.1	267 16.1	29.0	Rigel	281 12.5	S 8 11.1
F 09	128 44.7	358 05.5	.. 12.2	267 08.4	.. 45.5	54 09.7	.. 52.1	282 18.3	.. 29.1	Rigil Kent.	139 52.9	S60 53.4
R 10	143 47.2	13 05.1	11.6	282 09.2	46.0	69 12.0	52.1	297 20.5	29.2	Sabik	102 13.1	S15 44.3
I 11	158 49.6	28 04.7	11.1	297 10.0	46.5	84 14.3	52.2	312 22.8	29.3			
D 12	173 52.1	43 04.3	N17 10.6	312 10.8	S16 47.0	99 16.6	N21 52.2	327 25.0	S 8 29.4	Schedar	349 40.6	N56 36.5
A 13	188 54.6	58 03.9	10.0	327 11.6	47.6	114 18.9	52.2	342 27.2	29.5	Shaula	96 22.6	S37 06.7
Y 14	203 57.0	73 03.6	09.5	342 12.4	48.1	129 21.2	52.2	357 29.4	29.6	Sirius	258 34.3	S16 43.9
15	218 59.5	88 03.2	.. 08.9	357 13.2	.. 48.6	144 23.4	.. 52.2	12 31.6	.. 29.7	Spica	158 32.1	S11 13.6
16	234 02.0	103 02.8	08.4	12 14.0	49.1	159 25.7	52.2	27 33.8	29.8	Suhail	222 53.2	S43 29.0
17	249 04.4	118 02.4	07.9	27 14.8	49.7	174 28.0	52.2	42 36.1	29.9			
18	264 06.9	133 02.0	N17 07.3	42 15.5	S16 50.2	189 30.3	N21 52.3	57 38.3	S 8 30.0	Vega	80 39.2	N38 48.1
19	279 09.3	148 01.6	06.8	57 16.3	50.7	204 32.6	52.3	72 40.5	30.1	Zuben'ubi	137 06.2	S16 05.6
20	294 11.8	163 01.2	06.2	72 17.1	51.2	219 34.9	52.3	87 42.7	30.2		SHA	Mer.Pass.
21	309 14.3	178 00.8	.. 05.7	87 17.9	.. 51.8	234 37.2	.. 52.3	102 44.9	.. 30.3			h m
22	324 16.7	193 00.4	05.1	102 18.7	52.3	249 39.5	52.3	117 47.1	30.4	Venus	230 54.9	9 07
23	339 19.2	208 00.0	04.6	117 19.5	52.8	264 41.8	52.3	132 49.3	30.5	Mars	139 18.7	15 12
Mer.Pass.	h m 0 30.4	v −0.4	d 0.5	v 0.8	d 0.5	v 2.3	d 0.0	v 2.2	d 0.1	Jupiter	285 30.9	5 28
										Saturn	153 41.7	14 14

UT	SUN GHA	SUN Dec	MOON GHA	v	Dec	d	HP
d h	° ′	° ′	° ′	′	° ′	′	′
12 00	180 55.8	N 4 06.1	231 48.5	11.4	N16 11.9	7.7	56.1
01	195 56.0	05.2	246 18.9	11.4	16 04.2	7.8	56.1
02	210 56.3	04.2	260 49.3	11.3	15 56.4	7.8	56.1
03	225 56.5	.. 03.3	275 19.6	11.4	15 48.6	8.0	56.2
04	240 56.7	02.3	289 50.0	11.4	15 40.6	8.0	56.2
05	255 56.9	01.4	304 20.4	11.4	15 32.6	8.1	56.2
W 06	270 57.1	N 4 00.4	318 50.8	11.4	N15 24.5	8.2	56.3
E 07	285 57.4	3 59.5	333 21.2	11.4	15 16.3	8.3	56.3
D 08	300 57.6	58.5	347 51.6	11.4	15 08.0	8.4	56.3
N 09	315 57.8	.. 57.6	2 22.0	11.4	14 59.6	8.5	56.4
E 10	330 58.0	56.6	16 52.4	11.5	14 51.1	8.5	56.4
S 11	345 58.2	55.6	31 22.9	11.4	14 42.6	8.6	56.4
D 12	0 58.5	N 3 54.7	45 53.3	11.4	N14 34.0	8.8	56.4
A 13	15 58.7	53.7	60 23.7	11.5	14 25.2	8.7	56.5
Y 14	30 58.9	52.8	74 54.2	11.4	14 16.5	8.9	56.5
15	45 59.1	.. 51.8	89 24.6	11.4	14 07.6	9.0	56.5
16	60 59.3	50.9	103 55.0	11.5	13 58.6	9.0	56.6
17	75 59.6	49.9	118 25.5	11.4	13 49.6	9.1	56.6
18	90 59.8	N 3 49.0	132 55.9	11.5	N13 40.5	9.2	56.6
19	106 00.0	48.0	147 26.4	11.4	13 31.3	9.3	56.7
20	121 00.2	47.0	161 56.8	11.5	13 22.0	9.3	56.7
21	136 00.5	.. 46.1	176 27.3	11.4	13 12.7	9.5	56.7
22	151 00.7	45.1	190 57.7	11.5	13 03.2	9.5	56.8
23	166 00.9	44.2	205 28.2	11.4	12 53.7	9.6	56.8
13 00	181 01.1	N 3 43.2	219 58.6	11.5	N12 44.1	9.6	56.8
01	196 01.3	42.3	234 29.1	11.5	12 34.5	9.7	56.9
02	211 01.6	41.3	248 59.6	11.4	12 24.8	9.9	56.9
03	226 01.8	.. 40.3	263 30.0	11.5	12 14.9	9.8	56.9
04	241 02.0	39.4	278 00.5	11.4	12 05.1	10.0	57.0
05	256 02.2	38.4	292 30.9	11.5	11 55.1	10.0	57.0
T 06	271 02.4	N 3 37.5	307 01.4	11.5	N11 45.1	10.1	57.0
H 07	286 02.7	36.5	321 31.9	11.4	11 35.0	10.2	57.1
U 08	301 02.9	35.5	336 02.3	11.5	11 24.8	10.2	57.1
R 09	316 03.1	.. 34.6	350 32.8	11.5	11 14.6	10.3	57.1
S 10	331 03.3	33.6	5 03.3	11.4	11 04.3	10.4	57.2
D 11	346 03.6	32.7	19 33.7	11.5	10 53.9	10.4	57.2
A 12	1 03.8	N 3 31.7	34 04.2	11.5	N10 43.5	10.5	57.2
Y 13	16 04.0	30.8	48 34.7	11.4	10 33.0	10.6	57.2
14	31 04.2	29.8	63 05.1	11.5	10 22.4	10.6	57.3
15	46 04.4	.. 28.8	77 35.6	11.4	10 11.8	10.7	57.3
16	61 04.7	27.9	92 06.0	11.5	10 01.1	10.8	57.3
17	76 04.9	26.9	106 36.5	11.4	9 50.3	10.8	57.4
18	91 05.1	N 3 26.0	121 06.9	11.5	N 9 39.5	10.9	57.4
19	106 05.3	25.0	135 37.4	11.4	9 28.6	11.0	57.4
20	121 05.5	24.0	150 07.8	11.4	9 17.6	11.0	57.5
21	136 05.8	.. 23.1	164 38.2	11.4	9 06.6	11.1	57.5
22	151 06.0	22.1	179 08.6	11.5	8 55.5	11.1	57.5
23	166 06.2	21.2	193 39.1	11.4	8 44.4	11.2	57.6
14 00	181 06.4	N 3 20.2	208 09.5	11.4	N 8 33.2	11.2	57.6
01	196 06.7	19.2	222 39.9	11.4	8 22.0	11.3	57.6
02	211 06.9	18.3	237 10.3	11.4	8 10.7	11.4	57.7
03	226 07.1	.. 17.3	251 40.7	11.4	7 59.3	11.4	57.7
04	241 07.3	16.4	266 11.1	11.3	7 47.9	11.5	57.7
05	256 07.5	15.4	280 41.4	11.4	7 36.4	11.5	57.8
F 06	271 07.8	N 3 14.4	295 11.8	11.4	N 7 24.9	11.5	57.8
R 07	286 08.0	13.5	309 42.2	11.3	7 13.4	11.7	57.8
I 08	301 08.2	12.5	324 12.5	11.4	7 01.7	11.6	57.9
09	316 08.4	.. 11.5	338 42.9	11.3	6 50.1	11.7	57.9
D 10	331 08.6	10.6	353 13.2	11.3	6 38.4	11.8	57.9
A 11	346 08.9	09.6	7 43.5	11.3	6 26.6	11.8	58.0
Y 12	1 09.1	N 3 08.7	22 13.8	11.3	N 6 14.8	11.9	58.0
13	16 09.3	07.7	36 44.1	11.3	6 02.9	11.9	58.0
14	31 09.5	06.8	51 14.4	11.3	5 51.0	11.9	58.0
15	46 09.8	.. 05.8	65 44.7	11.2	5 39.1	12.0	58.1
16	61 10.0	04.8	80 14.9	11.2	5 27.1	12.0	58.1
17	76 10.2	03.9	94 45.1	11.3	5 15.1	12.1	58.1
18	91 10.4	N 3 02.9	109 15.4	11.2	N 5 03.0	12.1	58.2
19	106 10.6	01.9	123 45.6	11.2	4 50.9	12.2	58.2
20	121 11.0	01.0	138 15.8	11.1	4 38.7	12.1	58.2
21	136 11.1	3 00.0	152 45.9	11.2	4 26.6	12.3	58.3
22	151 11.3	2 59.1	167 16.1	11.1	4 14.3	12.3	58.3
23	166 11.5	N 2 58.1	181 46.2	11.2	N 4 02.1	12.3	58.3
SD	15.9	d 1.0	SD 15.4		15.6		15.8

Twilight / Sunrise / Moonrise

Lat.	Naut.	Civil	Sunrise	12	13	14	15
°	h m	h m	h m	h m	h m	h m	h m
N 72	01 53	03 46	05 00	24 28	00 28	02 31	04 30
N 70	02 29	04 01	05 06	24 52	00 52	02 43	04 34
68	02 53	04 12	05 11	25 10	01 10	02 53	04 37
66	03 12	04 21	05 15	25 25	01 25	03 01	04 40
64	03 27	04 29	05 18	00 08	01 37	03 08	04 42
62	03 39	04 36	05 21	00 23	01 47	03 14	04 44
60	03 49	04 41	05 24	00 35	01 55	03 19	04 46
N 58	03 57	04 46	05 26	00 45	02 03	03 24	04 47
56	04 04	04 50	05 28	00 54	02 09	03 28	04 49
54	04 11	04 54	05 30	01 02	02 15	03 31	04 50
52	04 17	04 58	05 32	01 09	02 20	03 35	04 51
50	04 22	05 01	05 33	01 16	02 25	03 37	04 52
45	04 32	05 07	05 37	01 30	02 35	03 44	04 54
N 40	04 40	05 12	05 39	01 41	02 44	03 49	04 56
35	04 46	05 16	05 42	01 51	02 51	03 54	04 58
30	04 51	05 20	05 44	01 59	02 58	03 58	04 59
20	04 59	05 25	05 47	02 14	03 09	04 05	05 01
N 10	05 04	05 29	05 50	02 27	03 18	04 11	05 04
0	05 08	05 32	05 53	02 38	03 27	04 16	05 06
S 10	05 10	05 34	05 55	02 50	03 36	04 22	05 08
20	05 10	05 36	05 58	03 03	03 46	04 28	05 10
30	05 09	05 37	06 00	03 17	03 57	04 35	05 12
35	05 07	05 37	06 02	03 26	04 03	04 39	05 14
40	05 05	05 37	06 04	03 35	04 10	04 43	05 15
45	05 02	05 36	06 06	03 46	04 19	04 48	05 17
S 50	04 58	05 36	06 08	04 00	04 28	04 55	05 19
52	04 56	05 35	06 09	04 06	04 33	04 57	05 20
54	04 54	05 35	06 10	04 13	04 38	05 01	05 22
56	04 51	05 34	06 11	04 20	04 44	05 04	05 23
58	04 48	05 34	06 13	04 29	04 50	05 08	05 24
S 60	04 45	05 33	06 14	04 39	04 57	05 12	05 26

Sunset / Twilight / Moonset

Lat.	Sunset	Civil	Naut.	12	13	14	15
°	h m	h m	h m	h m	h m	h m	h m
N 72	18 49	20 01	21 51	18 20	18 00	17 44	17 30
N 70	18 43	19 48	21 17	17 54	17 45	17 38	17 30
68	18 39	19 37	20 54	17 35	17 34	17 32	17 30
66	18 35	19 28	20 36	17 19	17 24	17 27	17 30
64	18 32	19 20	20 22	17 06	17 16	17 23	17 30
62	18 29	19 14	20 11	16 55	17 09	17 20	17 30
60	18 26	19 09	20 01	16 46	17 02	17 17	17 30
N 58	18 24	19 04	19 53	16 38	16 57	17 14	17 30
56	18 22	19 00	19 45	16 30	16 52	17 11	17 30
54	18 20	18 56	19 39	16 24	16 48	17 09	17 30
52	18 19	18 53	19 34	16 18	16 44	17 07	17 30
50	18 17	18 50	19 29	16 13	16 40	17 05	17 30
45	18 14	18 44	19 19	16 01	16 32	17 01	17 30
N 40	18 12	18 39	19 11	15 52	16 26	16 58	17 30
35	18 09	18 35	19 05	15 43	16 20	16 55	17 30
30	18 07	18 31	18 59	15 36	16 15	16 52	17 30
20	18 04	18 26	18 52	15 24	16 06	16 48	17 30
N 10	18 01	18 23	18 47	15 12	15 58	16 44	17 30
0	17 59	18 20	18 44	15 02	15 51	16 40	17 29
S 10	17 57	18 18	18 42	14 51	15 43	16 36	17 29
20	17 54	18 16	18 42	14 40	15 35	16 32	17 29
30	17 52	18 15	18 43	14 27	15 26	16 27	17 29
35	17 50	18 15	18 45	14 20	15 21	16 24	17 29
40	17 48	18 15	18 47	14 11	15 15	16 21	17 29
45	17 47	18 16	18 50	14 01	15 08	16 17	17 28
S 50	17 44	18 17	18 54	13 48	14 59	16 13	17 28
52	17 43	18 17	18 56	13 43	14 55	16 11	17 28
54	17 42	18 18	18 59	13 36	14 51	16 08	17 28
56	17 41	18 18	19 02	13 29	14 46	16 06	17 28
58	17 40	18 19	19 05	13 21	14 41	16 03	17 28
S 60	17 38	18 20	19 09	13 12	14 35	16 00	17 27

SUN / MOON

Day	Eqn. of Time 00h	12h	Mer. Pass.	Mer. Pass. Upper	Lower	Age	Phase
d	m s	m s	h m	h m	h m	d	%
12	03 43	03 53	11 56	08 50	21 15	26	15
13	04 04	04 15	11 56	09 39	22 04	27	8
14	04 25	04 36	11 55	10 28	22 53	28	3

UT	ARIES	VENUS −4.2		MARS +1.2		JUPITER −2.4		SATURN +0.8		STARS		
	GHA	GHA	Dec	GHA	Dec	GHA	Dec	GHA	Dec	Name	SHA	Dec
d h	° ′	° ′	° ′	° ′	° ′	° ′	° ′	° ′	° ′		° ′	° ′
15 00	354 21.7	222 59.7	N17 04.0	132 20.3	S16 53.3	279 44.1	N21 52.3	147 51.6	S 8 30.6	Acamar	315 18.5	S40 15.0
01	9 24.1	237 59.3	03.5	147 21.1	53.8	294 46.4	52.4	162 53.8	30.7	Achernar	335 26.6	S57 10.1
02	24 26.6	252 58.9	02.9	162 21.8	54.4	309 48.7	52.4	177 56.0	30.8	Acrux	173 10.5	S63 10.3
03	39 29.1	267 58.5	. . 02.4	177 22.6	. . 54.9	324 51.0	. . 52.4	192 58.2	. . 30.9	Adhara	255 13.1	S28 59.2
04	54 31.5	282 58.1	01.8	192 23.4	55.4	339 53.3	52.4	208 00.4	31.0	Aldebaran	290 49.9	N16 32.1
05	69 34.0	297 57.7	01.3	207 24.2	55.9	354 55.6	52.4	223 02.6	31.1			
06	84 36.5	312 57.3	N17 00.7	222 25.0	S16 56.5	9 57.9	N21 52.4	238 04.9	S 8 31.2	Alioth	166 21.7	N55 53.5
07	99 38.9	327 56.9	17 00.2	237 25.8	57.0	25 00.2	52.4	253 07.1	31.3	Alkaid	152 59.7	N49 15.2
S 08	114 41.4	342 56.5	16 59.6	252 26.6	57.5	40 02.5	52.5	268 09.3	31.4	Al Na'ir	27 43.9	S46 53.8
A 09	129 43.8	357 56.1	. . 59.1	267 27.3	. . 58.0	55 04.8	. . 52.5	283 11.5	. . 31.5	Alnilam	275 46.9	S 1 11.6
T 10	144 46.3	12 55.7	58.5	282 28.1	58.5	70 07.1	52.5	298 13.7	31.6	Alphard	217 56.9	S 8 42.8
U 11	159 48.8	27 55.4	58.0	297 28.9	59.1	85 09.4	52.5	313 15.9	31.7			
R 12	174 51.2	42 55.0	N16 57.4	312 29.7	S16 59.6	100 11.6	N21 52.5	328 18.1	S 8 31.8	Alphecca	126 11.6	N26 40.6
D 13	189 53.7	57 54.6	56.9	327 30.5	17 00.1	115 13.9	52.5	343 20.4	31.9	Alpheratz	357 43.7	N29 09.8
A 14	204 56.2	72 54.2	56.3	342 31.3	00.6	130 16.2	52.5	358 22.6	32.0	Altair	62 08.6	N 8 54.4
Y 15	219 58.6	87 53.8	. . 55.7	357 32.0	. . 01.2	145 18.5	. . 52.6	13 24.8	. . 32.1	Ankaa	353 15.8	S42 14.0
16	235 01.1	102 53.4	55.2	12 32.8	01.7	160 20.8	52.6	28 27.0	32.2	Antares	112 27.0	S26 27.5
17	250 03.6	117 53.0	54.6	27 33.6	02.2	175 23.1	52.6	43 29.2	32.3			
18	265 06.0	132 52.6	N16 54.1	42 34.4	S17 02.7	190 25.4	N21 52.6	58 31.4	S 8 32.4	Arcturus	145 56.4	N19 07.1
19	280 08.5	147 52.2	53.5	57 35.2	03.2	205 27.8	52.6	73 33.6	32.5	Atria	107 29.3	S69 03.2
20	295 10.9	162 51.8	53.0	72 35.9	03.8	220 30.1	52.6	88 35.9	32.6	Avior	234 18.6	S59 32.9
21	310 13.4	177 51.4	. . 52.4	87 36.7	. . 04.3	235 32.4	. . 52.6	103 38.1	. . 32.7	Bellatrix	278 32.5	N 6 21.7
22	325 15.9	192 51.1	51.8	102 37.5	04.8	250 34.7	52.7	118 40.3	32.8	Betelgeuse	271 01.9	N 7 24.5
23	340 18.3	207 50.7	51.2	117 38.3	05.3	265 37.0	52.7	133 42.5	32.9			
16 00	355 20.8	222 50.3	N16 50.7	132 39.1	S17 05.8	280 39.3	N21 52.7	148 44.7	S 8 33.0	Canopus	263 56.5	S52 41.9
01	10 23.3	237 49.9	50.1	147 39.8	06.3	295 41.6	52.7	163 46.9	33.1	Capella	280 35.2	N46 00.4
02	25 25.7	252 49.5	49.5	162 40.6	06.9	310 43.9	52.7	178 49.1	33.2	Deneb	49 31.5	N45 19.9
03	40 28.2	267 49.1	. . 49.0	177 41.4	. . 07.4	325 46.2	. . 52.7	193 51.3	. . 33.3	Denebola	182 34.5	N14 30.1
04	55 30.7	282 48.7	48.4	192 42.2	07.9	340 48.5	52.7	208 53.6	33.4	Diphda	348 56.1	S17 54.8
05	70 33.1	297 48.3	47.8	207 43.0	08.4	355 50.8	52.7	223 55.8	33.5			
06	85 35.6	312 47.9	N16 47.2	222 43.7	S17 08.9	10 53.1	N21 52.8	238 58.0	S 8 33.6	Dubhe	193 53.0	N61 40.8
07	100 38.1	327 47.5	46.7	237 44.5	09.5	25 55.4	52.8	254 00.2	33.7	Elnath	278 13.2	N28 36.9
08	115 40.5	342 47.1	46.1	252 45.3	10.0	40 57.7	52.8	269 02.4	33.8	Eltanin	90 46.3	N51 29.7
S 09	130 43.0	357 46.7	. . 45.5	267 46.1	. . 10.5	56 00.0	. . 52.8	284 04.6	. . 33.9	Enif	33 47.3	N 9 56.3
U 10	145 45.4	12 46.4	44.9	282 46.8	11.0	71 02.3	52.8	299 06.8	34.0	Fomalhaut	15 24.2	S29 33.1
N 11	160 47.9	27 46.0	44.4	297 47.6	11.5	86 04.6	52.8	314 09.0	34.1			
D 12	175 50.4	42 45.6	N16 43.8	312 48.4	S17 12.0	101 06.9	N21 52.9	329 11.3	S 8 34.2	Gacrux	172 02.0	S57 11.1
A 13	190 52.8	57 45.2	43.2	327 49.2	12.6	116 09.2	52.9	344 13.5	34.3	Gienah	175 53.1	S17 36.7
Y 14	205 55.3	72 44.8	42.6	342 49.9	13.1	131 11.5	52.9	359 15.7	34.4	Hadar	148 49.1	S60 26.2
15	220 57.8	87 44.4	. . 42.1	357 50.7	. . 13.6	146 13.8	. . 52.9	14 17.9	. . 34.5	Hamal	328 01.1	N23 31.4
16	236 00.2	102 44.0	41.5	12 51.5	14.1	161 16.2	52.9	29 20.1	34.6	Kaus Aust.	83 44.4	S34 22.6
17	251 02.7	117 43.6	40.9	27 52.3	14.6	176 18.5	52.9	44 22.3	34.7			
18	266 05.2	132 43.2	N16 40.3	42 53.0	S17 15.1	191 20.8	N21 52.9	59 24.5	S 8 34.8	Kochab	137 20.7	N74 06.4
19	281 07.6	147 42.8	39.7	57 53.8	15.7	206 23.1	52.9	74 26.7	34.9	Markab	13 38.5	N15 16.7
20	296 10.1	162 42.4	39.1	72 54.6	16.2	221 25.4	52.9	89 29.0	35.0	Menkar	314 15.4	N 4 08.5
21	311 12.5	177 42.0	. . 38.6	87 55.4	. . 16.7	236 27.7	. . 53.0	104 31.2	. . 35.1	Menkent	148 08.5	S36 26.0
22	326 15.0	192 41.6	38.0	102 56.1	17.2	251 30.0	53.0	119 33.4	35.2	Miaplacidus	221 40.5	S69 46.1
23	341 17.5	207 41.3	37.4	117 56.9	17.7	266 32.3	53.0	134 35.6	35.3			
17 00	356 19.9	222 40.9	N16 36.8	132 57.7	S17 18.2	281 34.6	N21 53.0	149 37.8	S 8 35.4	Mirfak	308 40.8	N49 54.2
01	11 22.4	237 40.5	36.2	147 58.4	18.7	296 36.9	53.0	164 40.0	35.5	Nunki	75 58.8	S26 16.7
02	26 24.9	252 40.1	35.6	162 59.2	19.3	311 39.3	53.0	179 42.2	35.6	Peacock	53 19.6	S56 41.6
03	41 27.3	267 39.7	. . 35.0	178 00.0	. . 19.8	326 41.6	. . 53.0	194 44.4	. . 35.7	Pollux	243 28.5	N27 59.6
04	56 29.8	282 39.3	34.4	193 00.8	20.3	341 43.9	53.0	209 46.7	35.8	Procyon	245 00.4	N 5 11.5
05	71 32.3	297 38.9	33.9	208 01.5	20.8	356 46.2	53.1	224 48.9	35.9			
06	86 34.7	312 38.5	N16 33.3	223 02.3	S17 21.3	11 48.5	N21 53.1	239 51.1	S 8 36.0	Rasalhague	96 06.9	N12 33.4
07	101 37.2	327 38.1	32.7	238 03.1	21.8	26 50.8	53.1	254 53.3	36.1	Regulus	207 44.4	N11 54.3
08	116 39.7	342 37.7	32.1	253 03.8	22.3	41 53.1	53.1	269 55.5	36.2	Rigel	281 12.5	S 8 11.1
M 09	131 42.1	357 37.3	. . 31.5	268 04.6	. . 22.8	56 55.5	. . 53.1	284 57.7	. . 36.3	Rigil Kent.	139 52.9	S60 53.3
O 10	146 44.6	12 36.9	30.9	283 05.4	23.4	71 57.8	53.1	299 59.9	36.4	Sabik	102 13.2	S15 44.3
N 11	161 47.0	27 36.5	30.3	298 06.1	23.9	87 00.1	53.1	315 02.1	36.5			
D 12	176 49.5	42 36.2	N16 29.7	313 06.9	S17 24.4	102 02.4	N21 53.1	330 04.3	S 8 36.6	Schedar	349 40.6	N56 36.5
A 13	191 52.0	57 35.8	29.1	328 07.7	24.9	117 04.7	53.2	345 06.6	36.7	Shaula	96 22.6	S37 06.7
Y 14	206 54.4	72 35.4	28.5	343 08.4	25.4	132 07.0	53.2	0 08.8	36.8	Sirius	258 34.3	S16 43.9
15	221 56.9	87 35.0	. . 27.9	358 09.2	. . 25.9	147 09.3	. . 53.2	15 11.0	. . 36.9	Spica	158 32.1	S11 13.6
16	236 59.4	102 34.6	27.3	13 10.0	26.4	162 11.7	53.2	30 13.2	37.0	Suhail	222 53.2	S43 29.0
17	252 01.8	117 34.2	26.7	28 10.7	26.9	177 14.0	53.2	45 15.4	37.1			
18	267 04.3	132 33.8	N16 26.1	43 11.5	S17 27.5	192 16.3	N21 53.2	60 17.6	S 8 37.2	Vega	80 39.2	N38 48.1
19	282 06.8	147 33.4	25.5	58 12.3	28.0	207 18.6	53.2	75 19.8	37.3	Zuben'ubi	137 06.2	S16 05.6
20	297 09.2	162 33.0	24.9	73 13.0	28.5	222 20.9	53.2	90 22.0	37.4		SHA	Mer.Pass.
21	312 11.7	177 32.6	. . 24.3	88 13.8	. . 29.0	237 23.3	. . 53.3	105 24.2	. . 37.5		° ′	h m
22	327 14.1	192 32.2	23.7	103 14.6	29.5	252 25.6	53.3	120 26.4	37.6	Venus	227 29.5	9 09
23	342 16.6	207 31.8	23.1	118 15.3	30.0	267 27.9	53.3	135 28.7	37.7	Mars	137 18.3	15 09
	h m									Jupiter	285 18.5	5 17
Mer. Pass. 0 18.6		v −0.4	d 0.6	v 0.8	d 0.5	v 2.3	d 0.0	v 2.2	d 0.1	Saturn	153 23.9	14 03

UT	SUN GHA	Dec	MOON GHA	v	Dec	d	HP
d h	° ′	° ′	° ′	′	° ′	′	′
15 00	181 11.8	N 2 57.1	196 16.4	11.1	N 3 49.8	12.3	58.4
01	196 12.0	56.2	210 46.5	11.1	3 37.5	12.4	58.4
02	211 12.2	55.2	225 16.6	11.0	3 25.1	12.4	58.4
03	226 12.4	.. 54.2	239 46.6	11.1	3 12.7	12.4	58.4
04	241 12.6	53.3	254 16.7	11.0	3 00.3	12.4	58.5
05	256 12.9	52.3	268 46.7	11.0	2 47.9	12.5	58.5
S 06	271 13.1	N 2 51.4	283 16.7	11.0	N 2 35.4	12.5	58.5
A 07	286 13.3	50.4	297 46.7	10.9	2 22.9	12.5	58.6
T 08	301 13.5	49.4	312 16.6	11.0	2 10.4	12.5	58.6
U 09	316 13.8	.. 48.5	326 46.6	10.9	1 57.9	12.6	58.6
R 10	331 14.0	47.5	341 16.5	10.9	1 45.3	12.6	58.6
D 11	346 14.2	46.5	355 46.4	10.8	1 32.7	12.6	58.7
A 12	1 14.4	N 2 45.6	10 16.2	10.9	N 1 20.1	12.6	58.7
Y 13	16 14.6	44.6	24 46.1	10.8	1 07.5	12.7	58.7
14	31 14.9	43.6	39 15.9	10.8	0 54.8	12.6	58.7
15	46 15.1	.. 42.7	53 45.7	10.7	0 42.2	12.7	58.8
16	61 15.3	41.7	68 15.4	10.8	0 29.5	12.7	58.8
17	76 15.5	40.8	82 45.2	10.7	0 16.8	12.7	58.8
18	91 15.8	N 2 39.8	97 14.9	10.6	N 0 04.1	12.7	58.9
19	106 16.0	38.8	111 44.5	10.7	S 0 08.6	12.7	58.9
20	121 16.2	37.9	126 14.2	10.6	0 21.3	12.7	58.9
21	136 16.4	.. 36.9	140 43.8	10.6	0 34.0	12.8	58.9
22	151 16.6	35.9	155 13.4	10.5	0 46.8	12.7	59.0
23	166 16.9	35.0	169 42.9	10.5	0 59.5	12.8	59.0
16 00	181 17.1	N 2 34.0	184 12.4	10.5	S 1 12.3	12.7	59.0
01	196 17.3	33.0	198 41.9	10.4	1 25.0	12.8	59.0
02	211 17.5	32.1	213 11.3	10.5	1 37.8	12.7	59.1
03	226 17.8	.. 31.1	227 40.8	10.3	1 50.5	12.8	59.1
04	241 18.0	30.1	242 10.1	10.4	2 03.3	12.7	59.1
05	256 18.2	29.2	256 39.5	10.3	2 16.0	12.8	59.1
S 06	271 18.4	N 2 28.2	271 08.8	10.3	S 2 28.8	12.7	59.1
U 07	286 18.6	27.3	285 38.1	10.2	2 41.5	12.8	59.2
N 08	301 18.9	26.3	300 07.3	10.2	2 54.3	12.7	59.2
D 09	316 19.1	.. 25.3	314 36.5	10.2	3 07.0	12.7	59.2
A 10	331 19.3	24.4	329 05.7	10.1	3 19.7	12.8	59.2
Y 11	346 19.5	23.4	343 34.8	10.1	3 32.5	12.7	59.3
12	1 19.8	N 2 22.4	358 03.9	10.0	S 3 45.2	12.7	59.3
13	16 20.0	21.5	12 32.9	10.0	3 57.9	12.6	59.3
14	31 20.2	20.5	27 01.9	10.0	4 10.5	12.7	59.3
15	46 20.4	.. 19.5	41 30.9	9.9	4 23.2	12.6	59.3
16	61 20.6	18.6	55 59.8	9.9	4 35.8	12.7	59.4
17	76 20.9	17.6	70 28.7	9.8	4 48.5	12.6	59.4
18	91 21.1	N 2 16.6	84 57.5	9.8	S 5 01.1	12.6	59.4
19	106 21.3	15.7	99 26.3	9.8	5 13.7	12.5	59.4
20	121 21.5	14.7	113 55.1	9.7	5 26.2	12.6	59.5
21	136 21.8	.. 13.7	128 23.8	9.6	5 38.8	12.5	59.5
22	151 22.0	12.8	142 52.4	9.7	5 51.3	12.5	59.5
23	166 22.2	11.8	157 21.1	9.5	6 03.8	12.4	59.5
17 00	181 22.4	N 2 10.8	171 49.6	9.6	S 6 16.2	12.4	59.5
01	196 22.6	09.9	186 18.2	9.4	6 28.6	12.4	59.5
02	211 22.9	08.9	200 46.6	9.5	6 41.0	12.4	59.6
03	226 23.1	.. 07.9	215 15.1	9.4	6 53.4	12.3	59.6
04	241 23.3	07.0	229 43.5	9.3	7 05.7	12.3	59.6
05	256 23.5	06.0	244 11.8	9.3	7 18.0	12.3	59.6
M 06	271 23.8	N 2 05.0	258 40.1	9.2	S 7 30.3	12.2	59.6
O 07	286 24.0	04.1	273 08.3	9.2	7 42.5	12.2	59.6
N 08	301 24.2	03.1	287 36.5	9.2	7 54.7	12.1	59.6
D 09	316 24.4	.. 02.1	302 04.7	9.1	8 06.8	12.1	59.7
A 10	331 24.6	01.2	316 32.8	9.0	8 18.9	12.1	59.7
Y 11	346 24.9	2 00.2	331 00.8	9.0	8 31.0	12.0	59.7
12	1 25.1	N 1 59.2	345 28.8	8.9	S 8 43.0	11.9	59.7
13	16 25.3	58.3	359 56.7	8.9	8 54.9	11.9	59.7
14	31 25.5	57.3	14 24.6	8.9	9 06.8	11.9	59.7
15	46 25.8	.. 56.3	28 52.5	8.8	9 18.7	11.8	59.7
16	61 26.0	55.4	43 20.3	8.7	9 30.5	11.8	59.7
17	76 26.2	54.4	57 48.0	8.7	9 42.3	11.6	59.8
18	91 26.4	N 1 53.4	72 15.7	8.6	S 9 53.9	11.7	59.8
19	106 26.6	52.5	86 43.3	8.6	10 05.6	11.6	59.8
20	121 26.9	51.5	101 10.9	8.5	10 17.2	11.5	59.8
21	136 27.1	.. 50.5	115 38.4	8.5	10 28.7	11.5	59.8
22	151 27.3	49.5	130 05.9	8.4	10 40.2	11.4	59.8
23	166 27.5	48.6	144 33.3	8.4	S10 51.6	11.3	59.8
	SD 15.9	d 1.0	SD 16.0		16.2		16.3

Lat.	Twilight Naut.	Civil	Sunrise	Moonrise 15	16	17	18
°	h m	h m	h m	h m	h m	h m	h m
N 72	02 19	04 02	05 13	04 30	06 30	08 36	10 53
N 70	02 47	04 14	05 18	04 34	06 26	08 23	10 26
68	03 08	04 24	05 21	04 37	06 23	08 13	10 06
66	03 24	04 32	05 24	04 40	06 21	08 04	09 51
64	03 37	04 38	05 27	04 42	06 18	07 57	09 38
62	03 48	04 44	05 29	04 44	06 16	07 51	09 27
60	03 57	04 49	05 31	04 46	06 15	07 46	09 18
N 58	04 05	04 53	05 33	04 47	06 13	07 41	09 10
56	04 11	04 57	05 34	04 49	06 12	07 37	09 03
54	04 17	05 00	05 35	04 50	06 11	07 33	08 57
52	04 22	05 03	05 37	04 51	06 10	07 30	08 51
50	04 27	05 05	05 38	04 52	06 09	07 27	08 46
45	04 36	05 11	05 40	04 54	06 07	07 20	08 36
N 40	04 43	05 15	05 42	04 56	06 05	07 15	08 27
35	04 49	05 18	05 44	04 58	06 03	07 10	08 19
30	04 53	05 21	05 45	04 59	06 02	07 06	08 12
20	05 00	05 26	05 48	05 01	06 00	06 59	08 01
N 10	05 04	05 29	05 50	05 04	05 58	06 53	07 51
0	05 07	05 31	05 51	05 06	05 56	06 48	07 41
S 10	05 08	05 32	05 53	05 08	05 54	06 42	07 32
20	05 07	05 33	05 55	05 10	05 52	06 36	07 22
30	05 05	05 33	05 57	05 12	05 50	06 29	07 11
35	05 03	05 32	05 58	05 14	05 49	06 26	07 05
40	05 00	05 32	05 59	05 15	05 48	06 21	06 58
45	04 57	05 31	06 00	05 17	05 46	06 16	06 49
S 50	04 52	05 29	06 01	05 19	05 44	06 10	06 39
52	04 49	05 28	06 02	05 20	05 43	06 08	06 35
54	04 46	05 28	06 03	05 22	05 42	06 05	06 30
56	04 43	05 27	06 03	05 23	05 41	06 01	06 24
58	04 39	05 25	06 04	05 24	05 40	05 58	06 18
S 60	04 35	05 24	06 05	05 26	05 39	05 54	06 11

Lat.	Sunset	Twilight Civil	Naut.	Moonset 15	16	17	18
°	h m	h m	h m	h m	h m	h m	h m
N 72	18 34	19 44	21 24	17 30	17 16	16 59	16 37
N 70	18 29	19 32	20 57	17 30	17 23	17 15	17 05
68	18 26	19 23	20 37	17 30	17 28	17 27	17 26
66	18 23	19 15	20 22	17 30	17 33	17 37	17 43
64	18 21	19 09	20 09	17 30	17 37	17 45	17 57
62	18 19	19 04	19 59	17 30	17 41	17 53	18 08
60	18 17	18 59	19 50	17 30	17 44	17 59	18 18
N 58	18 15	18 55	19 43	17 30	17 47	18 05	18 27
56	18 14	18 51	19 37	17 30	17 49	18 10	18 35
54	18 13	18 48	19 31	17 30	17 51	18 15	18 42
52	18 12	18 46	19 26	17 30	17 53	18 19	18 48
50	18 11	18 43	19 22	17 30	17 55	18 22	18 53
45	18 08	18 38	19 13	17 30	17 59	18 31	19 06
N 40	18 07	18 34	19 06	17 30	18 03	18 37	19 16
35	18 05	18 30	19 00	17 30	18 05	18 43	19 24
30	18 04	18 28	18 56	17 30	18 08	18 48	19 32
20	18 01	18 23	18 49	17 30	18 13	18 57	19 47
N 10	18 00	18 21	18 45	17 30	18 17	19 05	19 57
0	17 58	18 19	18 43	17 29	18 20	19 13	20 08
S 10	17 56	18 17	18 42	17 29	18 24	19 20	20 19
20	17 55	18 17	18 42	17 29	18 28	19 28	20 31
30	17 53	18 17	18 45	17 29	18 32	19 38	20 44
35	17 52	18 18	18 47	17 29	18 35	19 43	20 52
40	17 51	18 18	18 50	17 29	18 38	19 49	21 01
45	17 50	18 19	18 54	17 28	18 41	19 56	21 11
S 50	17 49	18 21	18 59	17 28	18 46	20 04	21 24
52	17 48	18 22	19 01	17 28	18 47	20 08	21 30
54	17 48	18 23	19 04	17 28	18 50	20 13	21 36
56	17 47	18 24	19 08	17 28	18 52	20 17	21 43
58	17 46	18 25	19 12	17 28	18 54	20 23	21 52
S 60	17 45	18 27	19 16	17 27	18 57	20 29	22 01

Day	SUN Eqn. of Time 00ʰ	12ʰ	Mer. Pass.	MOON Mer. Pass. Upper	Lower	Age	Phase
d	m s	m s	h m	h m	h m	d	%
15	04 47	04 57	11 55	11 17	23 43	29	1
16	05 08	05 19	11 55	12 08	24 34	00	0
17	05 29	05 40	11 54	13 00	00 34	01	3

UT	ARIES	VENUS −4.2		MARS +1.2		JUPITER −2.5		SATURN +0.7		STARS		
d h	GHA	GHA	Dec	GHA	Dec	GHA	Dec	GHA	Dec	Name	SHA	Dec
18 00	357 19.1	222 31.4	N16 22.5	133 16.1	S17 30.5	282 30.2	N21 53.3	150 30.9	S 8 37.8	Acamar	315 18.4	S40 15.0
01	12 21.5	237 31.0	21.9	148 16.9	31.0	297 32.5	53.3	165 33.1	37.9	Achernar	335 26.6	S57 10.1
02	27 24.0	252 30.7	21.3	163 17.6	31.5	312 34.8	53.3	180 35.3	38.0	Acrux	173 10.5	S63 10.2
03	42 26.5	267 30.3 ..	20.6	178 18.4 ..	32.0	327 37.2 ..	53.3	195 37.5 ..	38.1	Adhara	255 13.0	S28 59.2
04	57 28.9	282 29.9	20.0	193 19.1	32.5	342 39.5	53.3	210 39.7	38.2	Aldebaran	290 49.9	N16 32.1
05	72 31.4	297 29.5	19.4	208 19.9	33.1	357 41.8	53.3	225 41.9	38.3			
06	87 33.9	312 29.1	N16 18.8	223 20.7	S17 33.6	12 44.1	N21 53.4	240 44.1	S 8 38.4	Alioth	166 21.7	N55 53.5
07	102 36.3	327 28.7	18.2	238 21.4	34.1	27 46.5	53.4	255 46.3	38.5	Alkaid	152 59.7	N49 15.2
08	117 38.8	342 28.3	17.6	253 22.2	34.6	42 48.8	53.4	270 48.5	38.6	Al Na'ir	27 43.9	S46 53.8
09	132 41.3	357 27.9 ..	17.0	268 23.0 ..	35.1	57 51.1 ..	53.4	285 50.8 ..	38.7	Alnilam	275 46.9	S 1 11.6
10	147 43.7	12 27.5	16.4	283 23.7	35.6	72 53.4	53.4	300 53.0	38.8	Alphard	217 56.8	S 8 42.8
11	162 46.2	27 27.1	15.7	298 24.5	36.1	87 55.7	53.4	315 55.2	38.9			
12	177 48.6	42 26.7	N16 15.1	313 25.2	S17 36.6	102 58.1	N21 53.4	330 57.4	S 8 39.0	Alphecca	126 11.6	N26 40.6
13	192 51.1	57 26.3	14.5	328 26.0	37.1	118 00.4	53.4	345 59.6	39.1	Alpheratz	357 43.7	N29 09.8
14	207 53.6	72 25.9	13.9	343 26.8	37.6	133 02.7	53.5	1 01.8	39.2	Altair	62 08.6	N 8 54.4
15	222 56.0	87 25.6 ..	13.3	358 27.5 ..	38.1	148 05.0 ..	53.5	16 04.0 ..	39.3	Ankaa	353 15.8	S42 14.0
16	237 58.5	102 25.2	12.6	13 28.3	38.6	163 07.4	53.5	31 06.2	39.4	Antares	112 27.0	S26 27.5
17	253 01.0	117 24.8	12.0	28 29.0	39.1	178 09.7	53.5	46 08.4	39.5			
18	268 03.4	132 24.4	N16 11.4	43 29.8	S17 39.7	193 12.0	N21 53.5	61 10.6	S 8 39.6	Arcturus	145 56.5	N19 07.1
19	283 05.9	147 24.0	10.8	58 30.6	40.2	208 14.3	53.5	76 12.8	39.7	Atria	107 29.4	S69 03.2
20	298 08.4	162 23.6	10.2	73 31.3	40.7	223 16.7	53.5	91 15.1	39.8	Avior	234 18.6	S59 32.9
21	313 10.8	177 23.2 ..	09.5	88 32.1 ..	41.2	238 19.0 ..	53.5	106 17.3 ..	39.9	Bellatrix	278 32.5	N 6 21.7
22	328 13.3	192 22.8	08.9	103 32.8	41.7	253 21.3	53.5	121 19.5	40.0	Betelgeuse	271 01.9	N 7 24.5
23	343 15.7	207 22.4	08.3	118 33.6	42.2	268 23.7	53.6	136 21.7	40.1			
19 00	358 18.2	222 22.0	N16 07.7	133 34.3	S17 42.7	283 26.0	N21 53.6	151 23.9	S 8 40.2	Canopus	263 56.5	S52 41.9
01	13 20.7	237 21.6	07.0	148 35.1	43.2	298 28.3	53.6	166 26.1	40.3	Capella	280 35.1	N46 00.4
02	28 23.1	252 21.2	06.4	163 35.8	43.7	313 30.6	53.6	181 28.3	40.4	Deneb	49 31.5	N45 19.9
03	43 25.6	267 20.8 ..	05.8	178 36.6 ..	44.2	328 33.0 ..	53.6	196 30.5 ..	40.5	Denebola	182 34.5	N14 30.1
04	58 28.1	282 20.5	05.1	193 37.4	44.7	343 35.3	53.6	211 32.7	40.6	Diphda	348 56.1	S17 54.8
05	73 30.5	297 20.1	04.5	208 38.1	45.2	358 37.6	53.6	226 34.9	40.7			
06	88 33.0	312 19.7	N16 03.9	223 38.9	S17 45.7	13 40.0	N21 53.6	241 37.1	S 8 40.8	Dubhe	193 53.0	N61 40.8
07	103 35.5	327 19.3	03.3	238 39.6	46.2	28 42.3	53.6	256 39.3	40.9	Elnath	278 13.2	N28 36.9
08	118 37.9	342 18.9	02.6	253 40.4	46.7	43 44.6	53.6	271 41.6	41.0	Eltanin	90 46.4	N51 29.7
09	133 40.4	357 18.5 ..	02.0	268 41.1 ..	47.2	58 47.0 ..	53.7	286 43.8 ..	41.1	Enif	33 47.3	N 9 56.3
10	148 42.9	12 18.1	01.3	283 41.9	47.7	73 49.3	53.7	301 46.0	41.2	Fomalhaut	15 24.2	S29 33.1
11	163 45.3	27 17.7	00.7	298 42.6	48.2	88 51.6	53.7	316 48.2	41.3			
12	178 47.8	42 17.3	N16 00.1	313 43.4	S17 48.7	103 53.9	N21 53.7	331 50.4	S 8 41.4	Gacrux	172 02.0	S57 11.1
13	193 50.2	57 16.9	15 59.4	328 44.1	49.2	118 56.3	53.7	346 52.6	41.5	Gienah	175 53.1	S17 36.7
14	208 52.7	72 16.5	58.8	343 44.9	49.7	133 58.6	53.7	1 54.8	41.6	Hadar	148 49.1	S60 26.2
15	223 55.2	87 16.1 ..	58.2	358 45.6 ..	50.2	149 00.9 ..	53.7	16 57.0 ..	41.7	Hamal	328 01.0	N23 31.4
16	238 57.6	102 15.7	57.5	13 46.4	50.7	164 03.3	53.7	31 59.2	41.8	Kaus Aust.	83 44.4	S34 22.6
17	254 00.1	117 15.3	56.9	28 47.1	51.2	179 05.6	53.7	47 01.4	41.9			
18	269 02.6	132 15.0	N15 56.2	43 47.9	S17 51.7	194 07.9	N21 53.8	62 03.6	S 8 42.0	Kochab	137 20.8	N74 06.4
19	284 05.0	147 14.6	55.6	58 48.6	52.2	209 10.3	53.8	77 05.8	42.1	Markab	13 38.5	N15 16.7
20	299 07.5	162 14.2	55.0	73 49.4	52.7	224 12.6	53.8	92 08.0	42.2	Menkar	314 15.4	N 4 08.5
21	314 10.0	177 13.8 ..	54.3	88 50.1 ..	53.2	239 15.0 ..	53.8	107 10.2 ..	42.3	Menkent	148 08.5	S36 26.0
22	329 12.4	192 13.4	53.7	103 50.9	53.7	254 17.3	53.8	122 12.5	42.4	Miaplacidus	221 40.5	S69 46.1
23	344 14.9	207 13.0	53.0	118 51.6	54.2	269 19.6	53.8	137 14.7	42.5			
20 00	359 17.4	222 12.6	N15 52.4	133 52.4	S17 54.7	284 22.0	N21 53.8	152 16.9	S 8 42.6	Mirfak	308 40.8	N49 54.2
01	14 19.8	237 12.2	51.7	148 53.1	55.2	299 24.3	53.8	167 19.1	42.7	Nunki	75 58.8	S26 16.7
02	29 22.3	252 11.8	51.1	163 53.9	55.7	314 26.6	53.8	182 21.3	42.8	Peacock	53 19.7	S56 41.6
03	44 24.7	267 11.4 ..	50.4	178 54.6 ..	56.2	329 29.0 ..	53.8	197 23.5 ..	42.9	Pollux	243 28.5	N27 59.6
04	59 27.2	282 11.0	49.8	193 55.4	56.7	344 31.3	53.9	212 25.7	43.0	Procyon	245 00.4	N 5 11.5
05	74 29.7	297 10.6	49.1	208 56.1	57.2	359 33.6	53.9	227 27.9	43.1			
06	89 32.1	312 10.3	N15 48.5	223 56.9	S17 57.7	14 36.0	N21 53.9	242 30.1	S 8 43.2	Rasalhague	96 06.9	N12 33.4
07	104 34.6	327 09.9	47.8	238 57.6	58.2	29 38.3	53.9	257 32.3	43.3	Regulus	207 44.3	N11 54.3
08	119 37.1	342 09.5	47.2	253 58.4	58.7	44 40.7	53.9	272 34.5	43.4	Rigel	281 12.5	S 8 11.1
09	134 39.5	357 09.1 ..	46.5	268 59.1 ..	59.2	59 43.0 ..	53.9	287 36.7 ..	43.6	Rigil Kent.	139 52.9	S60 53.3
10	149 42.0	12 08.7	45.9	283 59.9	17 59.7	74 45.3	53.9	302 38.9	43.7	Sabik	102 13.2	S15 44.3
11	164 44.5	27 08.3	45.2	299 00.6	18 00.2	89 47.7	53.9	317 41.1	43.8			
12	179 46.9	42 07.9	N15 44.6	314 01.4	S18 00.2	104 50.0	N21 53.9	332 43.3	S 8 43.9	Schedar	349 40.5	N56 36.5
13	194 49.4	57 07.5	43.9	329 02.1	01.2	119 52.4	53.9	347 45.5	44.0	Shaula	96 22.6	S37 06.7
14	209 51.8	72 07.1	43.3	344 02.8	01.7	134 54.7	54.0	2 47.8	44.1	Sirius	258 34.2	S16 43.9
15	224 54.3	87 06.7 ..	42.6	359 03.6 ..	02.2	149 57.0 ..	54.0	17 50.0 ..	44.2	Spica	158 32.1	S11 13.6
16	239 56.8	102 06.3	41.9	14 04.3	02.7	164 59.4	54.0	32 52.2	44.3	Suhail	222 53.1	S43 28.9
17	254 59.2	117 05.9	41.3	29 05.1	03.2	180 01.7	54.0	47 54.4	44.4			
18	270 01.7	132 05.5	N15 40.6	44 05.8	S18 03.7	195 04.1	N21 54.0	62 56.6	S 8 44.5	Vega	80 39.2	N38 48.1
19	285 04.2	147 05.2	40.0	59 06.6	04.2	210 06.4	54.0	77 58.8	44.6	Zuben'ubi	137 06.2	S16 05.6
20	300 06.6	162 04.8	39.3	74 07.3	04.7	225 08.8	54.0	93 01.0	44.7		SHA	Mer.Pass.
21	315 09.1	177 04.4 ..	38.6	89 08.0 ..	05.2	240 11.1 ..	54.0	108 03.2 ..	44.8	Venus	224 03.8	9 11
22	330 11.6	192 04.0	38.0	104 08.8	05.7	255 13.4	54.0	123 05.4	44.9	Mars	135 16.1	15 05
23	345 14.0	207 03.6	37.3	119 09.5	06.2	270 15.8	54.0	138 07.6	45.0	Jupiter	285 07.8	5 05
Mer.Pass. 0 06.8		v −0.4 d 0.6		v 0.8 d 0.5		v 2.3 d 0.0		v 2.2 d 0.1		Saturn	153 05.7	13 52

UT	SUN GHA	SUN Dec	MOON GHA	v	MOON Dec	d	HP
d h	° ′	° ′	° ′	′	° ′	′	′
18 00	181 27.8	N 1 47.6	159 00.7	8.3	S11 02.9	11.3	59.8
01	196 28.0	46.6	173 28.0	8.2	11 14.2	11.2	59.8
02	211 28.2	45.7	187 55.2	8.2	11 25.4	11.1	59.8
03	226 28.4	.. 44.7	202 22.4	8.2	11 36.5	11.1	59.9
04	241 28.6	43.7	216 49.6	8.1	11 47.6	11.0	59.9
05	256 28.9	42.8	231 16.7	8.0	11 58.6	10.9	59.9
06	271 29.1	N 1 41.8	245 43.7	8.0	S12 09.5	10.9	59.9
T 07	286 29.3	40.8	260 10.7	7.9	12 20.4	10.7	59.9
U 08	301 29.5	39.9	274 37.6	7.9	12 31.1	10.7	59.9
E 09	316 29.7	.. 38.9	289 04.5	7.8	12 41.8	10.7	59.9
S 10	331 30.0	37.9	303 31.3	7.8	12 52.5	10.5	59.9
D 11	346 30.2	37.0	317 58.1	7.7	13 03.0	10.5	59.9
A 12	1 30.4	N 1 36.0	332 24.8	7.6	S13 13.5	10.3	59.9
Y 13	16 30.6	35.0	346 51.4	7.6	13 23.8	10.3	59.9
14	31 30.9	34.1	1 18.0	7.6	13 34.1	10.3	59.9
15	46 31.1	.. 33.1	15 44.6	7.4	13 44.4	10.1	59.9
16	61 31.3	32.1	30 11.0	7.5	13 54.5	10.0	59.9
17	76 31.5	31.1	44 37.5	7.4	14 04.5	10.0	59.9
18	91 31.7	N 1 30.2	59 03.9	7.3	S14 14.5	9.8	59.9
19	106 32.0	29.2	73 30.2	7.3	14 24.3	9.8	59.9
20	121 32.2	28.2	87 56.5	7.2	14 34.1	9.7	59.9
21	136 32.4	.. 27.3	102 22.7	7.2	14 43.8	9.5	59.9
22	151 32.6	26.3	116 48.9	7.1	14 53.3	9.5	59.9
23	166 32.9	25.3	131 15.0	7.0	15 02.8	9.4	59.9
19 00	181 33.1	N 1 24.4	145 41.0	7.0	S15 12.2	9.3	60.0
01	196 33.3	23.4	160 07.0	7.0	15 21.5	9.2	60.0
02	211 33.5	22.4	174 33.0	6.9	15 30.7	9.1	60.0
03	226 33.7	.. 21.4	188 58.9	6.9	15 39.8	9.0	60.0
04	241 34.0	20.5	203 24.8	6.8	15 48.8	8.8	60.0
05	256 34.2	19.5	217 50.6	6.7	15 57.6	8.8	60.0
06	271 34.4	N 1 18.5	232 16.3	6.7	S16 06.4	8.7	60.0
W 07	286 34.6	17.6	246 42.0	6.7	16 15.1	8.5	59.9
E 08	301 34.9	16.6	261 07.7	6.6	16 23.6	8.5	59.9
D 09	316 35.1	.. 15.6	275 33.3	6.5	16 32.1	8.3	59.9
N 10	331 35.3	14.7	289 58.8	6.5	16 40.4	8.3	59.9
E 11	346 35.5	13.7	304 24.3	6.5	16 48.7	8.1	59.9
S 12	1 35.7	N 1 12.7	318 49.8	6.4	S16 56.8	8.0	59.9
D 13	16 36.0	11.7	333 15.2	6.4	17 04.8	7.9	59.9
A 14	31 36.2	10.8	347 40.6	6.3	17 12.7	7.8	59.9
Y 15	46 36.4	.. 09.8	2 05.9	6.3	17 20.5	7.7	59.9
16	61 36.6	08.8	16 31.2	6.2	17 28.2	7.5	59.9
17	76 36.8	07.9	30 56.4	6.2	17 35.7	7.4	59.9
18	91 37.1	N 1 06.9	45 21.6	6.1	S17 43.1	7.3	59.9
19	106 37.3	05.9	59 46.7	6.1	17 50.4	7.2	59.9
20	121 37.5	05.0	74 11.8	6.1	17 57.6	7.1	59.9
21	136 37.7	.. 04.0	88 36.9	6.0	18 04.7	7.0	59.9
22	151 38.0	03.0	103 01.9	6.0	18 11.7	6.8	59.9
23	166 38.2	02.0	117 26.9	5.9	18 18.5	6.7	59.9
20 00	181 38.4	N 1 01.1	131 51.8	6.0	S18 25.2	6.6	59.9
01	196 38.6	1 00.1	146 16.8	5.8	18 31.8	6.4	59.9
02	211 38.8	0 59.1	160 41.6	5.9	18 38.2	6.3	59.9
03	226 39.1	.. 58.2	175 06.5	5.8	18 44.5	6.2	59.9
04	241 39.3	57.2	189 31.3	5.7	18 50.7	6.1	59.9
05	256 39.5	56.2	203 56.0	5.8	18 56.8	5.9	59.8
06	271 39.7	N 0 55.2	218 20.8	5.7	S19 02.7	5.8	59.8
T 07	286 39.9	54.3	232 45.5	5.6	19 08.5	5.7	59.8
H 08	301 40.2	53.3	247 10.1	5.7	19 14.2	5.5	59.8
U 09	316 40.4	.. 52.3	261 34.8	5.6	19 19.7	5.5	59.8
R 10	331 40.6	51.4	275 59.4	5.6	19 25.2	5.2	59.8
S 11	346 40.8	50.4	290 24.0	5.5	19 30.4	5.2	59.8
D 12	1 41.1	N 0 49.4	304 48.5	5.5	S19 35.6	5.0	59.8
A 13	16 41.3	48.4	319 13.0	5.5	19 40.6	4.9	59.8
Y 14	31 41.5	47.5	333 37.5	5.5	19 45.5	4.7	59.8
15	46 41.7	.. 46.5	348 02.0	5.5	19 50.2	4.6	59.8
16	61 41.9	45.5	2 26.5	5.4	19 54.8	4.5	59.7
17	76 42.2	44.6	16 50.9	5.5	19 59.3	4.3	59.7
18	91 42.4	N 0 43.6	31 15.4	5.4	S20 03.6	4.2	59.7
19	106 42.6	42.6	45 39.8	5.3	20 07.8	4.1	59.7
20	121 42.8	41.6	60 04.1	5.3	20 11.9	3.9	59.7
21	136 43.0	.. 40.7	74 28.5	5.4	20 15.8	3.8	59.7
22	151 43.3	39.7	88 52.9	5.3	20 19.6	3.6	59.7
23	166 43.5	38.7	103 17.2	5.3	S20 23.2	3.5	59.7
	SD 15.9	d 1.0	SD 16.3		16.3		16.3

Moonrise

Lat.	Twilight Naut.	Twilight Civil	Sunrise	18	19	20	21
°	h m	h m	h m	h m	h m	h m	h m
N 72	02 41	04 17	05 27	10 53	13 44	■■	■■
N 70	03 05	04 27	05 29	10 26	12 39	■■	■■
68	03 22	04 35	05 32	10 06	12 04	14 01	15 42
66	03 36	04 42	05 34	09 51	11 38	13 21	14 47
64	03 48	04 47	05 35	09 38	11 19	12 54	14 13
62	03 57	04 52	05 37	09 27	11 03	12 33	13 49
60	04 05	04 56	05 38	09 18	10 50	12 16	13 30
N 58	04 12	05 00	05 39	09 10	10 38	12 01	13 14
56	04 18	05 03	05 40	09 03	10 28	11 49	13 00
54	04 23	05 05	05 41	08 57	10 20	11 38	12 49
52	04 27	05 08	05 42	08 51	10 12	11 29	12 38
50	04 31	05 10	05 42	08 46	10 05	11 20	12 29
45	04 40	05 14	05 44	08 36	09 50	11 03	12 09
N 40	04 46	05 18	05 45	08 27	09 38	10 48	11 53
35	04 51	05 21	05 46	08 19	09 28	10 36	11 40
30	04 55	05 23	05 47	08 12	09 19	10 25	11 28
20	05 01	05 26	05 48	08 01	09 03	10 07	11 08
N 10	05 04	05 28	05 49	07 51	08 50	09 51	10 51
0	05 06	05 30	05 50	07 41	08 38	09 36	10 35
S 10	05 06	05 30	05 51	07 32	08 25	09 21	10 19
20	05 05	05 30	05 52	07 22	08 12	09 05	10 02
30	05 01	05 29	05 53	07 11	07 57	08 47	09 42
35	04 59	05 28	05 53	07 05	07 48	08 37	09 31
40	04 55	05 27	05 54	06 58	07 39	08 25	09 18
45	04 51	05 25	05 54	06 49	07 27	08 11	09 02
S 50	04 45	05 23	05 55	06 39	07 13	07 54	08 43
52	04 42	05 21	05 55	06 35	07 07	07 46	08 34
54	04 39	05 20	05 55	06 30	07 00	07 37	08 24
56	04 35	05 19	05 56	06 24	06 52	07 27	08 13
58	04 31	05 17	05 56	06 18	06 43	07 16	08 00
S 60	04 25	05 15	05 56	06 11	06 33	07 03	07 45

Moonset

Lat.	Sunset	Twilight Civil	Twilight Naut.	18	19	20	21
°	h m	h m	h m	h m	h m	h m	h m
N 72	18 18	19 27	21 01	16 37	15 44	■■	■■
N 70	18 16	19 17	20 39	17 05	16 50	■■	■■
68	18 13	19 10	20 21	17 26	17 27	17 32	17 55
66	18 12	19 03	20 08	17 43	17 53	18 12	18 50
64	18 10	18 58	19 57	17 57	18 13	18 40	19 21
62	18 09	18 54	19 48	18 08	18 30	19 01	19 48
60	18 08	18 50	19 40	18 18	18 43	19 18	20 07
N 58	18 07	18 46	19 34	18 27	18 55	19 33	20 23
56	18 06	18 43	19 28	18 35	19 06	19 46	20 37
54	18 05	18 41	19 23	18 42	19 15	19 57	20 49
52	18 05	18 38	19 18	18 48	19 23	20 06	20 59
50	18 04	18 36	19 15	18 53	19 30	20 15	21 09
45	18 03	18 32	19 07	19 06	19 46	20 34	21 28
N 40	18 02	18 29	19 00	19 16	19 59	20 49	21 44
35	18 01	18 26	18 56	19 24	20 10	21 01	21 58
30	18 00	18 24	18 52	19 32	20 20	21 13	22 10
20	17 59	18 21	18 46	19 45	20 37	21 32	22 30
N 10	17 58	18 19	18 43	19 57	20 51	21 48	22 47
0	17 57	18 18	18 42	20 08	21 05	22 04	23 03
S 10	17 56	18 17	18 41	20 19	21 19	22 20	23 20
20	17 55	18 17	18 43	20 31	21 34	22 36	23 37
30	17 55	18 19	18 46	20 44	21 50	22 55	23 57
35	17 54	18 20	18 49	20 52	22 00	23 07	24 09
40	17 54	18 21	18 53	21 01	22 12	23 19	24 22
45	17 54	18 23	18 57	21 11	22 25	23 35	24 38
S 50	17 53	18 26	19 04	21 24	22 41	23 53	24 57
52	17 53	18 27	19 07	21 30	22 49	24 02	00 02
54	17 53	18 28	19 10	21 36	22 57	24 12	00 12
56	17 53	18 30	19 14	21 43	23 07	24 23	00 23
58	17 53	18 32	19 18	21 52	23 18	24 36	00 36
S 60	17 52	18 34	19 24	22 01	23 30	24 51	00 51

	SUN Eqn. of Time 00h	SUN Eqn. of Time 12h	SUN Mer. Pass.	MOON Mer. Pass. Upper	MOON Mer. Pass. Lower	MOON Age	MOON Phase
Day							
d	m s	m s	h m	h m	h m	d %	
18	05 51	06 01	11 54	13 55	01 27	02 8	
19	06 12	06 23	11 54	14 51	02 23	03 15	
20	06 33	06 44	11 53	15 50	03 20	04 25	

2012 SEPTEMBER 21, 22, 23 (FRI., SAT., SUN.)

UT	ARIES GHA	VENUS −4.2 GHA	Dec	MARS +1.2 GHA	Dec	JUPITER −2.5 GHA	Dec	SATURN +0.7 GHA	Dec	STARS Name	SHA	Dec
21 00	0 16.5	222 03.2	N15 36.6	134 10.3	S18 06.7	285 18.1	N21 54.0	153 09.8	S 8 45.1	Acamar	315 18.4	S40 15.0
01	15 19.0	237 02.8	36.0	149 11.0	07.2	300 20.5	54.1	168 12.0	45.2	Achernar	335 26.6	S57 10.1
02	30 21.4	252 02.4	35.3	164 11.8	07.7	315 22.8	54.1	183 14.2	45.3	Acrux	173 10.5	S63 10.2
03	45 23.9	267 02.0 ..	34.6	179 12.5 ..	08.2	330 25.2 ..	54.1	198 16.4 ..	45.4	Adhara	255 13.0	S28 59.2
04	60 26.3	282 01.6	34.0	194 13.2	08.7	345 27.5	54.1	213 18.6	45.5	Aldebaran	290 49.8	N16 32.1
05	75 28.8	297 01.2	33.3	209 14.0	09.2	0 29.9	54.1	228 20.8	45.6			
06	90 31.3	312 00.9	N15 32.6	224 14.7	S18 09.6	15 32.2	N21 54.1	243 23.0	S 8 45.7	Alioth	166 21.7	N55 53.5
07	105 33.7	327 00.5	32.0	239 15.4	10.1	30 34.6	54.1	258 25.2	45.8	Alkaid	152 59.7	N49 15.1
08	120 36.2	342 00.1	31.3	254 16.2	10.6	45 36.9	54.1	273 27.4	45.9	Al Na'ir	27 43.9	S46 53.8
F 09	135 38.7	356 59.7 ..	30.6	269 16.9 ..	11.1	60 39.3 ..	54.1	288 29.7 ..	46.0	Alnilam	275 46.8	S 1 11.6
R 10	150 41.1	11 59.3	30.0	284 17.7	11.6	75 41.6	54.1	303 31.9	46.1	Alphard	217 56.8	S 8 42.8
I 11	165 43.6	26 58.9	29.3	299 18.4	12.1	90 44.0	54.1	318 34.1	46.2			
D 12	180 46.1	41 58.5	N15 28.6	314 19.1	S18 12.6	105 46.3	N21 54.2	333 36.3	S 8 46.3	Alphecca	126 11.6	N26 40.6
A 13	195 48.5	56 58.1	27.9	329 19.9	13.1	120 48.7	54.2	348 38.5	46.4	Alpheratz	357 43.7	N29 09.8
Y 14	210 51.0	71 57.7	27.3	344 20.6	13.6	135 51.0	54.2	3 40.7	46.5	Altair	62 08.6	N 8 54.4
15	225 53.5	86 57.3 ..	26.6	359 21.3 ..	14.1	150 53.4 ..	54.2	18 42.9 ..	46.6	Ankaa	353 15.8	S42 14.0
16	240 55.9	101 56.9	25.9	14 22.1	14.6	165 55.7	54.2	33 45.1	46.7	Antares	112 27.0	S26 27.5
17	255 58.4	116 56.5	25.2	29 22.8	15.1	180 58.1	54.2	48 47.3	46.8			
18	271 00.8	131 56.2	N15 24.5	44 23.6	S18 15.6	196 00.4	N21 54.2	63 49.5	S 8 46.9	Arcturus	145 56.5	N19 07.1
19	286 03.3	146 55.8	23.9	59 24.3	16.0	211 02.8	54.2	78 51.7	47.0	Atria	107 29.4	S69 03.1
20	301 05.8	161 55.4	23.2	74 25.0	16.5	226 05.1	54.2	93 53.9	47.1	Avior	234 18.6	S59 32.9
21	316 08.2	176 55.0 ..	22.5	89 25.8 ..	17.0	241 07.5 ..	54.2	108 56.1 ..	47.2	Bellatrix	278 32.5	N 6 21.7
22	331 10.7	191 54.6	21.8	104 26.5	17.5	256 09.8	54.2	123 58.3	47.3	Betelgeuse	271 01.8	N 7 24.5
23	346 13.2	206 54.2	21.1	119 27.2	18.0	271 12.2	54.3	139 00.5	47.4			
22 00	1 15.6	221 53.8	N15 20.4	134 28.0	S18 18.5	286 14.5	N21 54.3	154 02.7	S 8 47.5	Canopus	263 56.4	S52 41.9
01	16 18.1	236 53.4	19.8	149 28.7	19.0	301 16.9	54.3	169 04.9	47.6	Capella	280 35.1	N46 00.4
02	31 20.6	251 53.0	19.1	164 29.4	19.5	316 19.2	54.3	184 07.1	47.7	Deneb	49 31.5	N45 20.0
03	46 23.0	266 52.6 ..	18.4	179 30.2 ..	20.0	331 21.6 ..	54.3	199 09.3 ..	47.8	Denebola	182 34.5	N14 30.1
04	61 25.5	281 52.3	17.7	194 30.9	20.5	346 23.9	54.3	214 11.5	47.9	Diphda	348 56.1	S17 54.8
05	76 28.0	296 51.9	17.0	209 31.6	20.9	1 26.3	54.3	229 13.7	48.0			
06	91 30.4	311 51.5	N15 16.3	224 32.4	S18 21.4	16 28.6	N21 54.3	244 15.9	S 8 48.1	Dubhe	193 52.9	N61 40.8
07	106 32.9	326 51.1	15.6	239 33.1	21.9	31 31.0	54.3	259 18.1	48.2	Elnath	278 13.2	N28 36.9
S 08	121 35.3	341 50.7	15.0	254 33.8	22.4	46 33.4	54.3	274 20.3	48.4	Eltanin	90 46.4	N51 29.7
A 09	136 37.8	356 50.3 ..	14.3	269 34.5 ..	22.9	61 35.7 ..	54.3	289 22.5 ..	48.5	Enif	33 47.3	N 9 56.3
T 10	151 40.3	11 49.9	13.6	284 35.3	23.4	76 38.1	54.4	304 24.7	48.6	Fomalhaut	15 24.2	S29 33.1
U 11	166 42.7	26 49.5	12.9	299 36.0	23.9	91 40.4	54.4	319 26.9	48.7			
R 12	181 45.2	41 49.1	N15 12.2	314 36.7	S18 24.4	106 42.8	N21 54.4	334 29.1	S 8 48.8	Gacrux	172 02.0	S57 11.1
D 13	196 47.7	56 48.7	11.5	329 37.5	24.8	121 45.1	54.4	349 31.4	48.9	Gienah	175 53.1	S17 36.7
A 14	211 50.1	71 48.3	10.8	344 38.2	25.3	136 47.5	54.4	4 33.6	49.0	Hadar	148 49.1	S60 26.1
Y 15	226 52.6	86 48.0 ..	10.1	359 38.9 ..	25.8	151 49.9 ..	54.4	19 35.8 ..	49.1	Hamal	328 01.0	N23 31.4
16	241 55.1	101 47.6	09.4	14 39.7	26.3	166 52.2	54.4	34 38.0	49.2	Kaus Aust.	83 44.4	S34 22.6
17	256 57.5	116 47.2	08.7	29 40.4	26.8	181 54.6	54.4	49 40.2	49.3			
18	272 00.0	131 46.8	N15 08.0	44 41.1	S18 27.3	196 56.9	N21 54.4	64 42.4	S 8 49.4	Kochab	137 20.8	N74 06.4
19	287 02.5	146 46.4	07.3	59 41.8	27.8	211 59.3	54.4	79 44.6	49.5	Markab	13 38.5	N15 16.7
20	302 04.9	161 46.0	06.6	74 42.6	28.2	227 01.7	54.4	94 46.8	49.6	Menkar	314 15.4	N 4 08.5
21	317 07.4	176 45.6 ..	05.9	89 43.3 ..	28.7	242 04.0 ..	54.4	109 49.0 ..	49.7	Menkent	148 08.5	S36 26.0
22	332 09.8	191 45.2	05.2	104 44.0	29.2	257 06.4	54.4	124 51.2	49.8	Miaplacidus	221 40.5	S69 46.1
23	347 12.3	206 44.8	04.5	119 44.7	29.7	272 08.7	54.4	139 53.4	49.9			
23 00	2 14.8	221 44.5	N15 03.8	134 45.5	S18 30.2	287 11.1	N21 54.5	154 55.6	S 8 50.0	Mirfak	308 40.8	N49 54.2
01	17 17.2	236 44.1	03.1	149 46.2	30.7	302 13.5	54.5	169 57.8	50.1	Nunki	75 58.9	S26 16.7
02	32 19.7	251 43.7	02.4	164 46.9	31.2	317 15.8	54.5	185 00.0	50.2	Peacock	53 19.7	S56 41.6
03	47 22.2	266 43.3 ..	01.7	179 47.6 ..	31.6	332 18.2 ..	54.5	200 02.2 ..	50.3	Pollux	243 28.5	N27 59.6
04	62 24.6	281 42.9	01.0	194 48.4	32.1	347 20.6	54.5	215 04.4	50.4	Procyon	245 00.4	N 5 11.5
05	77 27.1	296 42.5	15 00.3	209 49.1	32.6	2 22.9	54.5	230 06.6	50.5			
06	92 29.6	311 42.1	N14 59.6	224 49.8	S18 33.1	17 25.3	N21 54.5	245 08.8	S 8 50.6	Rasalhague	96 07.0	N12 33.4
07	107 32.0	326 41.7	58.9	239 50.5	33.6	32 27.7	54.5	260 11.0	50.7	Regulus	207 44.3	N11 54.3
08	122 34.5	341 41.3	58.2	254 51.3	34.1	47 30.0	54.5	275 13.2	50.8	Rigel	281 12.5	S 8 11.1
S 09	137 36.9	356 40.9 ..	57.4	269 52.0 ..	34.5	62 32.4 ..	54.5	290 15.4 ..	50.9	Rigil Kent.	139 52.9	S60 53.3
U 10	152 39.4	11 40.6	56.7	284 52.7	35.0	77 34.7	54.5	305 17.6	51.0	Sabik	102 13.2	S15 44.3
N 11	167 41.9	26 40.2	56.0	299 53.4	35.5	92 37.1	54.5	320 19.8	51.1			
D 12	182 44.3	41 39.8	N14 55.3	314 54.2	S18 36.0	107 39.5	N21 54.5	335 22.0	S 8 51.2	Schedar	349 40.5	N56 36.5
A 13	197 46.8	56 39.4	54.6	329 54.9	36.5	122 41.8	54.6	350 24.2	51.3	Shaula	96 22.6	S37 06.7
Y 14	212 49.3	71 39.0	53.9	344 55.6	37.0	137 44.2	54.6	5 26.4	51.4	Sirius	258 34.2	S16 43.9
15	227 51.7	86 38.6 ..	53.2	359 56.3 ..	37.4	152 46.6 ..	54.6	20 28.6 ..	51.5	Spica	158 32.1	S11 13.6
16	242 54.2	101 38.2	52.5	14 57.0	37.9	167 49.0	54.6	35 30.8	51.6	Suhail	222 53.1	S43 28.9
17	257 56.7	116 37.8	51.7	29 57.8	38.4	182 51.3	54.6	50 33.0	51.7			
18	272 59.1	131 37.5	N14 51.0	44 58.5	S18 38.9	197 53.7	N21 54.6	65 35.2	S 8 51.8	Vega	80 39.2	N38 48.2
19	288 01.6	146 37.1	50.3	59 59.2	39.4	212 56.1	54.6	80 37.4	51.9	Zuben'ubi	137 06.2	S16 05.6
20	303 04.1	161 36.7	49.6	74 59.9	39.8	227 58.4	54.6	95 39.6	52.0		SHA	Mer.Pass.
21	318 06.5	176 36.3 ..	48.9	90 00.6 ..	40.3	243 00.8 ..	54.6	110 41.8 ..	52.1		° '	h m
22	333 09.0	191 35.9	48.2	105 01.4	40.8	258 03.2	54.6	125 44.0	52.3	Venus	220 38.2	9 13
23	348 11.4	206 35.5	47.4	120 02.1	41.3	273 05.5	54.6	140 46.2	52.4	Mars	133 12.3	15 01
	h m									Jupiter	284 58.9	4 54
Mer.Pass. 23 51.0	v −0.4 d 0.7			v 0.7 d 0.5		v 2.4 d 0.0		v 2.2 d 0.1		Saturn	152 47.1	13 42

UT	SUN GHA	SUN Dec	MOON GHA	v	MOON Dec	d	HP
d h	° ′	° ′	° ′	′	° ′	′	′
21 00	181 43.7	N 0 37.8	117 41.5	5.3	S20 26.7	3.4	59.7
01	196 43.9	36.8	132 05.8	5.4	20 30.1	3.2	59.6
02	211 44.1	35.8	146 30.2	5.3	20 33.3	3.1	59.6
03	226 44.4	.. 34.8	160 54.5	5.3	20 36.4	2.9	59.6
04	241 44.6	33.9	175 18.8	5.2	20 39.3	2.8	59.6
05	256 44.8	32.9	189 43.0	5.3	20 42.1	2.6	59.6
06	271 45.0	N 0 31.9	204 07.3	5.3	S20 44.7	2.5	59.6
07	286 45.3	30.9	218 31.6	5.3	20 47.2	2.4	59.6
08	301 45.5	30.0	232 55.9	5.3	20 49.6	2.2	59.6
F 09	316 45.7	.. 29.0	247 20.2	5.2	20 51.8	2.1	59.5
R 10	331 45.9	28.0	261 44.4	5.3	20 53.9	2.0	59.5
I 11	346 46.1	27.1	276 08.7	5.3	20 55.9	1.8	59.5
D 12	1 46.4	N 0 26.1	290 33.0	5.3	S20 57.7	1.6	59.5
A 13	16 46.6	25.1	304 57.3	5.3	20 59.3	1.5	59.5
Y 14	31 46.8	24.1	319 21.6	5.3	21 00.8	1.4	59.5
15	46 47.0	.. 23.2	333 45.9	5.3	21 02.2	1.2	59.5
16	61 47.2	22.2	348 10.2	5.3	21 03.4	1.1	59.4
17	76 47.5	21.2	2 34.5	5.4	21 04.5	1.0	59.4
18	91 47.7	N 0 20.3	16 58.9	5.3	S21 05.5	0.8	59.4
19	106 47.9	19.3	31 23.2	5.4	21 06.3	0.6	59.4
20	121 48.1	18.3	45 47.6	5.4	21 06.9	0.5	59.4
21	136 48.3	.. 17.3	60 12.0	5.4	21 07.4	0.4	59.4
22	151 48.6	16.4	74 36.4	5.4	21 07.8	0.2	59.3
23	166 48.8	15.4	89 00.8	5.5	21 08.0	0.1	59.3
22 00	181 49.0	N 0 14.4	103 25.3	5.4	S21 08.1	0.0	59.3
01	196 49.2	13.4	117 49.7	5.5	21 08.1	0.2	59.3
02	211 49.4	12.5	132 14.2	5.5	21 07.9	0.4	59.3
03	226 49.7	.. 11.5	146 38.7	5.5	21 07.5	0.4	59.3
04	241 49.9	10.5	161 03.2	5.6	21 07.1	0.6	59.2
05	256 50.1	09.6	175 27.8	5.6	21 06.5	0.8	59.2
06	271 50.3	N 0 08.6	189 52.4	5.6	S21 05.7	0.9	59.2
S 07	286 50.5	07.6	204 17.0	5.7	21 04.8	1.0	59.2
A 08	301 50.8	06.6	218 41.7	5.6	21 03.8	1.2	59.2
T 09	316 51.0	.. 05.7	233 06.3	5.8	21 02.6	1.3	59.2
U 10	331 51.2	04.7	247 31.1	5.7	21 01.3	1.5	59.1
R 11	346 51.4	03.7	261 55.8	5.8	20 59.8	1.5	59.1
D 12	1 51.6	N 0 02.7	276 20.6	5.8	S20 58.3	1.8	59.1
A 13	16 51.9	01.8	290 45.4	5.9	20 56.5	1.8	59.1
Y 14	31 52.1	N 00.8	305 10.3	5.9	20 54.7	2.0	59.1
15	46 52.3	S 00.2	319 35.2	5.9	20 52.7	2.1	59.1
16	61 52.5	01.2	334 00.1	6.0	20 50.6	2.3	59.0
17	76 52.7	02.2	348 25.1	6.0	20 48.3	2.4	59.0
18	91 52.9	S 0 03.1	2 50.1	6.1	S20 45.9	2.5	59.0
19	106 53.2	04.1	17 15.2	6.1	20 43.4	2.7	59.0
20	121 53.4	05.0	31 40.3	6.1	20 40.7	2.8	59.0
21	136 53.6	.. 06.0	46 05.4	6.2	20 37.9	2.9	59.0
22	151 53.8	07.0	60 30.6	6.3	20 35.0	3.1	58.9
23	166 54.0	08.0	74 55.9	6.3	20 31.9	3.2	58.9
23 00	181 54.3	S 0 08.9	89 21.2	6.3	S20 28.7	3.3	58.9
01	196 54.5	09.9	103 46.5	6.4	20 25.4	3.5	58.9
02	211 54.7	10.9	118 11.9	6.5	20 21.9	3.5	58.9
03	226 54.9	.. 11.9	132 37.4	6.5	20 18.4	3.7	58.8
04	241 55.1	12.8	147 02.9	6.5	20 14.7	3.9	58.8
05	256 55.4	13.8	161 28.4	6.6	20 10.8	3.9	58.8
06	271 55.6	S 0 14.8	175 54.0	6.7	S20 06.9	4.1	58.8
07	286 55.8	15.7	190 19.7	6.7	20 02.8	4.2	58.8
08	301 56.0	16.7	204 45.4	6.8	19 58.6	4.3	58.7
S 09	316 56.2	.. 17.7	219 11.2	6.8	19 54.3	4.5	58.7
U 10	331 56.4	18.7	233 37.0	6.9	19 49.8	4.6	58.7
N 11	346 56.7	19.6	248 02.9	7.0	19 45.2	4.6	58.7
D 12	1 56.9	S 0 20.6	262 28.9	7.0	S19 40.6	4.9	58.7
A 13	16 57.1	21.6	276 54.9	7.0	19 35.7	4.9	58.6
Y 14	31 57.3	22.6	291 20.9	7.2	19 30.8	5.0	58.6
15	46 57.5	.. 23.5	305 47.1	7.2	19 25.8	5.2	58.6
16	61 57.8	24.5	320 13.3	7.2	19 20.6	5.3	58.6
17	76 58.0	25.5	334 39.5	7.3	19 15.3	5.4	58.6
18	91 58.2	S 0 26.5	349 05.8	7.4	S19 09.9	5.5	58.5
19	106 58.4	27.4	3 32.2	7.4	19 04.4	5.6	58.5
20	121 58.6	28.4	17 58.6	7.6	18 58.8	5.7	58.5
21	136 58.8	.. 29.4	32 25.2	7.5	18 53.1	5.9	58.5
22	151 59.1	30.3	46 51.7	7.7	18 47.2	6.0	58.5
23	166 59.3	31.3	61 18.4	7.7	S18 41.2	6.0	58.4
	SD 16.0	d 1.0	SD 16.2		16.1		16.0

Lat.	Twilight Naut.	Civil	Sunrise	Moonrise 21	22	23	24
°	h m	h m	h m	h m	h m	h m	h m
N 72	03 00	04 31	05 40	■	■	■	18 03
N 70	03 20	04 40	05 41	■	■	17 41	17 17
68	03 36	04 46	05 42	15 42	16 32	16 44	16 47
66	03 48	04 52	05 43	14 47	15 42	16 10	16 24
64	03 58	04 56	05 44	14 13	15 10	15 45	16 06
62	04 06	05 00	05 44	13 49	14 47	15 25	15 51
60	04 13	05 03	05 45	13 30	14 28	15 09	15 38
N 58	04 19	05 06	05 45	13 14	14 12	14 56	15 28
56	04 24	05 09	05 46	13 00	13 59	14 44	15 18
54	04 29	05 11	05 46	12 49	13 47	14 34	15 10
52	04 33	05 13	05 46	12 38	13 37	14 24	15 02
50	04 36	05 14	05 47	12 29	13 28	14 16	14 55
45	04 44	05 18	05 47	12 09	13 08	13 59	14 41
N 40	04 49	05 21	05 48	11 53	12 53	13 44	14 29
35	04 53	05 23	05 48	11 40	12 39	13 32	14 18
30	04 57	05 25	05 48	11 28	12 28	13 21	14 09
20	05 01	05 27	05 49	11 08	12 08	13 03	13 54
N 10	05 04	05 28	05 49	10 51	11 50	12 47	13 40
0	05 05	05 29	05 49	10 35	11 34	12 32	13 27
S 10	05 04	05 28	05 49	10 19	11 18	12 17	13 14
20	05 02	05 27	05 49	10 02	11 01	12 01	13 00
30	04 57	05 25	05 49	09 42	10 41	11 42	12 45
35	04 54	05 24	05 49	09 31	10 30	11 32	12 35
40	04 50	05 22	05 49	09 18	10 16	11 19	12 25
45	04 45	05 19	05 49	09 02	10 01	11 05	12 12
S 50	04 38	05 16	05 48	08 43	09 41	10 47	11 57
52	04 35	05 14	05 48	08 34	09 32	10 38	11 50
54	04 31	05 13	05 48	08 24	09 22	10 29	11 42
56	04 26	05 11	05 48	08 13	09 10	10 18	11 34
58	04 21	05 08	05 48	08 00	08 57	10 06	11 24
S 60	04 16	05 06	05 47	07 45	08 41	09 52	11 12

Lat.	Sunset	Twilight Civil	Naut.	Moonset 21	22	23	24
°	h m	h m	h m	h m	h m	h m	h m
N 72	18 03	19 11	20 40	■	■	■	21 32
N 70	18 02	19 03	20 21	■	■	19 59	22 17
68	18 01	18 57	20 06	17 55	19 09	20 56	22 46
66	18 00	18 51	19 55	18 50	19 58	21 29	23 08
64	18 00	18 47	19 45	19 24	20 30	21 53	23 25
62	17 59	18 43	19 37	19 48	20 53	22 12	23 39
60	17 59	18 40	19 30	20 07	21 12	22 28	23 51
N 58	17 58	18 38	19 24	20 23	21 27	22 41	24 01
56	17 58	18 35	19 19	20 37	21 40	22 53	24 10
54	17 58	18 33	19 15	20 49	21 52	23 03	24 18
52	17 58	18 31	19 11	20 59	22 02	23 12	24 25
50	17 57	18 30	19 08	21 09	22 11	23 20	24 31
45	17 57	18 26	19 01	21 28	22 30	23 36	24 45
N 40	17 57	18 24	18 55	21 44	22 46	23 50	24 56
35	17 56	18 22	18 51	21 58	22 59	24 02	00 02
30	17 56	18 20	18 48	22 10	23 10	24 12	00 12
20	17 56	18 18	18 44	22 30	23 29	24 29	00 29
N 10	17 56	18 17	18 41	22 47	23 46	24 44	00 44
0	17 56	18 16	18 40	23 03	24 02	00 02	00 59
S 10	17 56	18 17	18 41	23 20	24 18	00 18	01 13
20	17 56	18 18	18 44	23 37	24 34	00 34	01 27
30	17 56	18 20	18 48	23 57	24 54	00 54	01 44
35	17 57	18 22	18 51	24 09	00 09	01 05	01 54
40	17 57	18 24	18 56	24 22	00 22	01 17	02 06
45	17 57	18 27	19 01	24 38	00 38	01 32	02 19
S 50	17 58	18 30	19 08	24 57	00 57	01 51	02 35
52	17 58	18 32	19 12	00 02	01 06	02 00	02 42
54	17 58	18 34	19 16	00 12	01 17	02 09	02 50
56	17 59	18 36	19 20	00 23	01 28	02 20	03 00
58	17 59	18 38	19 25	00 36	01 42	02 32	03 10
S 60	18 00	18 41	19 31	00 51	01 57	02 47	03 22

Day	SUN Eqn. of Time 00h	12h	Mer. Pass.	MOON Mer. Pass. Upper	Lower	Age	Phase
d	m s	m s	h m	h m	h m	d	%
21	06 54	07 05	11 53	16 49	04 20	05	35
22	07 16	07 26	11 53	17 48	05 19	06	46
23	07 37	07 47	11 52	18 45	06 17	07	58

UT	ARIES GHA	VENUS −4.1 GHA	Dec	MARS +1.2 GHA	Dec	JUPITER −2.5 GHA	Dec	SATURN +0.7 GHA	Dec
24 00	3 13.9	221 35.1	N14 46.7	135 02.8	S18 41.8	288 07.9	N21 54.6	155 48.4	S 8 52.5
01	18 16.4	236 34.7	46.0	150 03.5	42.2	303 10.3	54.6	170 50.6	52.6
02	33 18.8	251 34.3	45.3	165 04.2	42.7	318 12.6	54.6	185 52.8	52.7
03	48 21.3	266 34.0 ..	44.5	180 05.0 ..	43.2	333 15.0 ..	54.6	200 55.0 ..	52.8
04	63 23.8	281 33.6	43.8	195 05.7	43.7	348 17.4	54.7	215 57.2	52.9
05	78 26.2	296 33.2	43.1	210 06.4	44.1	3 19.8	54.7	230 59.4	53.0
06	93 28.7	311 32.8	N14 42.4	225 07.1	S18 44.6	18 22.1	N21 54.7	246 01.6	S 8 53.1
07	108 31.2	326 32.4	41.6	240 07.8	45.1	33 24.5	54.7	261 03.8	53.2
08	123 33.6	341 32.0	40.9	255 08.5	45.6	48 26.9	54.7	276 06.0	53.3
M 09	138 36.1	356 31.6 ..	40.2	270 09.3 ..	46.1	63 29.3 ..	54.7	291 08.2 ..	53.4
O 10	153 38.6	11 31.2	39.5	285 10.0	46.5	78 31.6	54.7	306 10.4	53.5
N 11	168 41.0	26 30.9	38.7	300 10.7	47.0	93 34.0	54.7	321 12.6	53.6
D 12	183 43.5	41 30.5	N14 38.0	315 11.4	S18 47.5	108 36.4	N21 54.7	336 14.8	S 8 53.7
A 13	198 45.9	56 30.1	37.3	330 12.1	48.0	123 38.8	54.7	351 17.0	53.8
Y 14	213 48.4	71 29.7	36.5	345 12.8	48.4	138 41.1	54.7	6 19.2	53.9
15	228 50.9	86 29.3 ..	35.8	0 13.5 ..	48.9	153 43.5 ..	54.7	21 21.4 ..	54.0
16	243 53.3	101 28.9	35.1	15 14.3	49.4	168 45.9	54.7	36 23.6	54.1
17	258 55.8	116 28.5	34.3	30 15.0	49.9	183 48.3	54.7	51 25.8	54.2
18	273 58.3	131 28.1	N14 33.6	45 15.7	S18 50.3	198 50.6	N21 54.8	66 28.0	S 8 54.3
19	289 00.7	146 27.8	32.9	60 16.4	50.8	213 53.0	54.8	81 30.2	54.4
20	304 03.2	161 27.4	32.1	75 17.1	51.3	228 55.4	54.8	96 32.4	54.5
21	319 05.7	176 27.0 ..	31.4	90 17.8 ..	51.8	243 57.8 ..	54.8	111 34.6 ..	54.6
22	334 08.1	191 26.6	30.7	105 18.5	52.2	259 00.1	54.8	126 36.8	54.7
23	349 10.6	206 26.2	29.9	120 19.2	52.7	274 02.5	54.8	141 39.0	54.8
25 00	4 13.0	221 25.8	N14 29.2	135 20.0	S18 53.2	289 04.9	N21 54.8	156 41.2	S 8 54.9
01	19 15.5	236 25.4	28.4	150 20.7	53.7	304 07.3	54.8	171 43.4	55.0
02	34 18.0	251 25.1	27.7	165 21.4	54.1	319 09.7	54.8	186 45.6	55.1
03	49 20.4	266 24.7 ..	27.0	180 22.1 ..	54.6	334 12.0 ..	54.8	201 47.8 ..	55.2
04	64 22.9	281 24.3	26.2	195 22.8	55.1	349 14.4	54.8	216 50.0	55.3
05	79 25.4	296 23.9	25.5	210 23.5	55.5	4 16.8	54.8	231 52.2	55.4
06	94 27.8	311 23.5	N14 24.7	225 24.2	S18 56.0	19 19.2	N21 54.8	246 54.4	S 8 55.6
07	109 30.3	326 23.1	24.0	240 24.9	56.5	34 21.6	54.8	261 56.6	55.7
T 08	124 32.8	341 22.7	23.2	255 25.6	57.0	49 24.0	54.8	276 58.8	55.8
U 09	139 35.2	356 22.3 ..	22.5	270 26.3 ..	57.4	64 26.3 ..	54.8	292 01.0 ..	55.9
E 10	154 37.7	11 22.0	21.7	285 27.0	57.9	79 28.7	54.8	307 03.2	56.0
S 11	169 40.2	26 21.6	21.0	300 27.8	58.4	94 31.1	54.8	322 05.4	56.1
D 12	184 42.6	41 21.2	N14 20.3	315 28.5	S18 58.8	109 33.5	N21 54.9	337 07.6	S 8 56.2
A 13	199 45.1	56 20.8	19.5	330 29.2	59.3	124 35.9	54.9	352 09.8	56.3
Y 14	214 47.5	71 20.4	18.8	345 29.9	18 59.8	139 38.3	54.9	7 12.0	56.4
15	229 50.0	86 20.0 ..	18.0	0 30.6	19 00.3	154 40.6 ..	54.9	22 14.2 ..	56.5
16	244 52.5	101 19.6	17.3	15 31.3	00.7	169 43.0	54.9	37 16.4	56.6
17	259 54.9	116 19.3	16.5	30 32.0	01.2	184 45.4	54.9	52 18.6	56.7
18	274 57.4	131 18.9	N14 15.7	45 32.7	S19 01.7	199 47.8	N21 54.9	67 20.8	S 8 56.8
19	289 59.9	146 18.5	15.0	60 33.4	02.1	214 50.2	54.9	82 23.0	56.9
20	305 02.3	161 18.1	14.2	75 34.1	02.6	229 52.6	54.9	97 25.2	57.0
21	320 04.8	176 17.7 ..	13.5	90 34.8 ..	03.1	244 55.0 ..	54.9	112 27.4 ..	57.1
22	335 07.3	191 17.3	12.7	105 35.5	03.5	259 57.3	54.9	127 29.6	57.2
23	350 09.7	206 17.0	12.0	120 36.2	04.0	274 59.7	54.9	142 31.8	57.3
26 00	5 12.2	221 16.6	N14 11.2	135 36.9	S19 04.5	290 02.1	N21 55.0	157 34.0	S 8 57.4
01	20 14.7	236 16.2	10.5	150 37.6	04.9	305 04.5	54.9	172 36.2	57.5
02	35 17.1	251 15.8	09.7	165 38.3	05.4	320 06.9	54.9	187 38.4	57.6
03	50 19.6	266 15.4 ..	08.9	180 39.0 ..	05.9	335 09.3 ..	54.9	202 40.6 ..	57.7
04	65 22.0	281 15.0	08.2	195 39.7	06.3	350 11.7	54.9	217 42.8	57.8
05	80 24.5	296 14.6	07.4	210 40.4	06.8	5 14.1	54.9	232 45.0	57.9
06	95 27.0	311 14.3	N14 06.7	225 41.1	S19 07.3	20 16.5	N21 54.9	247 47.2	S 8 58.0
W 07	110 29.4	326 13.9	05.9	240 41.8	07.7	35 18.8	55.0	262 49.4	58.1
E 08	125 31.9	341 13.5	05.1	255 42.5	08.2	50 21.2	55.0	277 51.6	58.2
D 09	140 34.4	356 13.1 ..	04.4	270 43.2 ..	08.7	65 23.6 ..	55.0	292 53.8 ..	58.3
N 10	155 36.8	11 12.7	03.6	285 43.9	09.1	80 26.0	55.0	307 56.0	58.4
E 11	170 39.3	26 12.3	02.8	300 44.6	09.6	95 28.4	55.0	322 58.1	58.6
S 12	185 41.8	41 12.0	N14 02.1	315 45.3	S19 10.1	110 30.8	N21 55.0	338 00.3	S 8 58.7
D 13	200 44.2	56 11.6	01.3	330 46.0	10.5	125 33.2	55.0	353 02.5	58.8
A 14	215 46.7	71 11.2	14 00.5	345 46.7	11.0	140 35.6	55.0	8 04.7	58.9
Y 15	230 49.1	86 10.8	13 59.8	0 47.4 ..	11.5	155 38.0 ..	55.0	23 06.9 ..	59.0
16	245 51.6	101 10.4	59.0	15 48.1	11.9	170 40.4	55.0	38 09.1	59.1
17	260 54.1	116 10.0	58.2	30 48.8	12.4	185 42.8	55.0	53 11.3	59.2
18	275 56.5	131 09.6	N13 57.5	45 49.5	S19 12.9	200 45.2	N21 55.0	68 13.5	S 8 59.3
19	290 59.0	146 09.3	56.7	60 50.2	13.3	215 47.6	55.0	83 15.7	59.4
20	306 01.5	161 08.9	55.9	75 50.9	13.8	230 50.0	55.0	98 17.9	59.5
21	321 03.9	176 08.5 ..	55.1	90 51.6 ..	14.3	245 52.3 ..	55.0	113 20.1 ..	59.6
22	336 06.4	191 08.1	54.4	105 52.3	14.7	260 54.7	55.0	128 22.3	59.7
23	351 08.9	206 07.7	53.6	120 53.0	15.2	275 57.1	55.0	143 24.5	59.8
h m Mer.Pass. 23 39.2		v −0.4	d 0.7	v 0.7	d 0.5	v 2.4	d 0.0	v 2.2	d 0.1

STARS

Name	SHA	Dec
Acamar	315 18.4	S40 15.0
Achernar	335 26.6	S57 10.1
Acrux	173 10.5	S63 10.2
Adhara	255 13.0	S28 59.2
Aldebaran	290 49.8	N16 32.1
Alioth	166 21.7	N55 53.5
Alkaid	152 59.7	N49 15.1
Al Na'ir	27 44.0	S46 53.8
Alnilam	275 46.8	S 1 11.6
Alphard	217 56.8	S 8 42.8
Alphecca	126 11.6	N26 40.6
Alpheratz	357 43.6	N29 09.9
Altair	62 08.6	N 8 54.4
Ankaa	353 15.8	S42 14.0
Antares	112 27.0	S26 27.5
Arcturus	145 56.5	N19 07.1
Atria	107 29.4	S69 03.1
Avior	234 18.5	S59 32.9
Bellatrix	278 32.5	N 6 21.7
Betelgeuse	271 01.8	N 7 24.5
Canopus	263 56.4	S52 41.9
Capella	280 35.1	N46 00.4
Deneb	49 31.5	N45 20.0
Denebola	182 34.5	N14 30.1
Diphda	348 56.1	S17 54.8
Dubhe	193 52.9	N61 40.8
Elnath	278 13.2	N28 36.9
Eltanin	90 46.4	N51 29.7
Enif	33 47.4	N 9 56.3
Fomalhaut	15 24.2	S29 33.1
Gacrux	172 02.0	S57 11.1
Gienah	175 53.1	S17 36.7
Hadar	148 49.2	S60 26.1
Hamal	328 01.0	N23 31.4
Kaus Aust.	83 44.4	S34 22.6
Kochab	137 20.9	N74 06.4
Markab	13 38.5	N15 16.7
Menkar	314 15.3	N 4 08.5
Menkent	148 08.5	S36 25.9
Miaplacidus	221 40.4	S69 46.0
Mirfak	308 40.7	N49 54.2
Nunki	75 58.9	S26 16.7
Peacock	53 19.7	S56 41.6
Pollux	243 28.5	N27 59.5
Procyon	245 00.4	N 5 11.5
Rasalhague	96 07.0	N12 33.4
Regulus	207 44.3	N11 54.3
Rigel	281 12.4	S 8 11.1
Rigil Kent.	139 52.9	S60 53.3
Sabik	102 13.2	S15 44.3
Schedar	349 40.5	N56 36.5
Shaula	96 22.7	S37 06.7
Sirius	258 34.2	S16 43.9
Spica	158 32.1	S11 13.6
Suhail	222 53.1	S43 28.9
Vega	80 39.3	N38 48.2
Zuben'ubi	137 06.2	S16 05.6

	SHA	Mer.Pass.
		h m
Venus	217 12.8	9 15
Mars	131 06.9	14 58
Jupiter	284 51.9	4 43
Saturn	152 28.2	13 31

2012 SEPTEMBER 24, 25, 26 (MON., TUES., WED.)

UT	SUN GHA	SUN Dec	MOON GHA	v	Dec	d	HP
d h	° ′	° ′	° ′	′	° ′	′	′
24 00	181 59.5	S 0 32.3	75 45.1	7.7	S18 35.2	6.2	58.4
01	196 59.7	33.3	90 11.8	7.9	18 29.0	6.3	58.4
02	211 59.9	34.2	104 38.7	7.9	18 22.7	6.4	58.4
03	227 00.2	. . 35.2	119 05.6	7.9	18 16.3	6.5	58.4
04	242 00.4	36.2	133 32.5	8.1	18 09.8	6.5	58.3
05	257 00.6	37.2	147 59.6	8.1	18 03.3	6.7	58.3
06	272 00.8	S 0 38.1	162 26.7	8.1	S17 56.6	6.9	58.3
07	287 01.0	39.1	176 53.8	8.3	17 49.7	6.9	58.3
08	302 01.2	40.1	191 21.1	8.3	17 42.8	7.0	58.3
M 09	317 01.5	. . 41.1	205 48.4	8.4	17 35.8	7.1	58.2
O 10	332 01.7	42.0	220 15.8	8.4	17 28.7	7.2	58.2
N 11	347 01.9	43.0	234 43.2	8.5	17 21.5	7.2	58.2
D 12	2 02.1	S 0 44.0	249 10.7	8.6	S17 14.3	7.4	58.2
A 13	17 02.3	44.9	263 38.3	8.6	17 06.9	7.5	58.2
Y 14	32 02.5	45.9	278 05.9	8.8	16 59.4	7.6	58.1
15	47 02.8	. . 46.9	292 33.7	8.7	16 51.8	7.7	58.1
16	62 03.0	47.9	307 01.4	8.9	16 44.1	7.7	58.1
17	77 03.2	48.8	321 29.3	8.9	16 36.4	7.9	58.1
18	92 03.4	S 0 49.8	335 57.2	9.0	S16 28.5	7.9	58.1
19	107 03.6	50.8	350 25.2	9.1	16 20.6	8.1	58.0
20	122 03.8	51.8	4 53.3	9.1	16 12.5	8.1	58.0
21	137 04.1	. . 52.7	19 21.4	9.2	16 04.4	8.2	58.0
22	152 04.3	53.7	33 49.6	9.3	15 56.2	8.3	58.0
23	167 04.5	54.7	48 17.9	9.3	15 47.9	8.3	58.0
25 00	182 04.7	S 0 55.7	62 46.2	9.4	S15 39.6	8.5	57.9
01	197 04.9	56.6	77 14.6	9.5	15 31.1	8.5	57.9
02	212 05.1	57.6	91 43.1	9.6	15 22.6	8.6	57.9
03	227 05.4	. . 58.6	106 11.7	9.5	15 14.0	8.7	57.9
04	242 05.6	0 59.6	120 40.3	9.7	15 05.3	8.8	57.9
05	257 05.8	1 00.5	135 09.0	9.7	14 56.5	8.8	57.8
06	272 06.0	S 1 01.5	149 37.7	9.8	S14 47.7	8.9	57.8
07	287 06.2	02.5	164 06.5	9.9	14 38.8	9.0	57.8
08	302 06.4	03.4	178 35.4	10.0	14 29.8	9.1	57.8
T 09	317 06.7	. . 04.4	193 04.4	10.0	14 20.7	9.1	57.8
U 10	332 06.9	05.4	207 33.4	10.1	14 11.6	9.3	57.7
E 11	347 07.1	06.4	222 02.5	10.1	14 02.3	9.2	57.7
S 12	2 07.3	S 1 07.3	236 31.6	10.2	S13 53.1	9.4	57.7
D 13	17 07.5	08.3	251 00.8	10.3	13 43.7	9.4	57.7
A 14	32 07.7	09.3	265 30.1	10.4	13 34.3	9.5	57.7
Y 15	47 07.9	. . 10.3	279 59.5	10.4	13 24.8	9.5	57.6
16	62 08.2	11.2	294 28.9	10.5	13 15.3	9.7	57.6
17	77 08.4	12.2	308 58.4	10.5	13 05.6	9.6	57.6
18	92 08.6	S 1 13.2	323 27.9	10.6	S12 56.0	9.8	57.6
19	107 08.8	14.2	337 57.5	10.7	12 46.2	9.8	57.5
20	122 09.0	15.1	352 27.2	10.7	12 36.4	9.8	57.5
21	137 09.2	. . 16.1	6 56.9	10.8	12 26.6	9.9	57.5
22	152 09.4	17.1	21 26.7	10.9	12 16.7	10.0	57.5
23	167 09.7	18.0	35 56.6	10.9	12 06.7	10.1	57.5
26 00	182 09.9	S 1 19.0	50 26.5	11.0	S11 56.6	10.0	57.4
01	197 10.1	20.0	64 56.5	11.0	11 46.6	10.2	57.4
02	212 10.3	21.0	79 26.5	11.1	11 36.4	10.2	57.4
03	227 10.5	. . 21.9	93 56.6	11.2	11 26.2	10.2	57.4
04	242 10.7	22.9	108 26.8	11.2	11 16.0	10.3	57.4
05	257 11.0	23.9	122 57.0	11.3	11 05.7	10.4	57.3
06	272 11.2	S 1 24.9	137 27.3	11.3	S10 55.3	10.4	57.3
W 07	287 11.4	25.8	151 57.6	11.4	10 44.9	10.4	57.3
E 08	302 11.6	26.8	166 28.0	11.5	10 34.5	10.5	57.3
D 09	317 11.8	. . 27.8	180 58.5	11.5	10 24.0	10.6	57.3
N 10	332 12.0	28.8	195 29.0	11.5	10 13.4	10.6	57.2
E 11	347 12.2	29.7	209 59.5	11.7	10 02.8	10.6	57.2
S 12	2 12.4	S 1 30.7	224 30.2	11.6	S 9 52.2	10.7	57.2
D 13	17 12.7	31.7	239 00.8	11.8	9 41.5	10.7	57.2
A 14	32 12.9	32.6	253 31.6	11.7	9 30.8	10.7	57.2
Y 15	47 13.1	. . 33.6	268 02.3	11.9	9 20.1	10.8	57.1
16	62 13.3	34.6	282 33.2	11.9	9 09.3	10.8	57.1
17	77 13.5	35.6	297 04.1	11.9	8 58.5	10.9	57.1
18	92 13.7	S 1 36.5	311 35.0	12.0	S 8 47.6	10.9	57.1
19	107 13.9	37.5	326 06.0	12.0	8 36.7	11.0	57.0
20	122 14.2	38.5	340 37.0	12.1	8 25.7	10.9	57.0
21	137 14.4	. . 39.5	355 08.1	12.2	8 14.8	11.0	57.0
22	152 14.6	40.4	9 39.3	12.2	8 03.8	11.1	57.0
23	167 14.8	41.4	24 10.5	12.2	S 7 52.7	11.0	57.0
	SD 16.0	d 1.0	SD 15.9		15.7		15.6

Lat.	Twilight Naut.	Twilight Civil	Sunrise	Moonrise 24	25	26	27
°	h m	h m	h m	h m	h m	h m	h m
N 72	03 18	04 46	05 53	18 03	17 29	17 10	16 55
N 70	03 35	04 52	05 53	17 17	17 05	16 56	16 49
68	03 48	04 57	05 53	16 47	16 47	16 45	16 44
66	03 59	05 01	05 53	16 24	16 32	16 36	16 39
64	04 08	05 05	05 52	16 06	16 19	16 28	16 35
62	04 15	05 08	05 52	15 51	16 09	16 22	16 32
60	04 21	05 10	05 52	15 38	16 00	16 16	16 29
N 58	04 26	05 13	05 52	15 28	15 52	16 11	16 27
56	04 31	05 15	05 52	15 18	15 45	16 06	16 25
54	04 35	05 16	05 52	15 10	15 38	16 02	16 23
52	04 38	05 18	05 51	15 02	15 33	15 58	16 21
50	04 41	05 19	05 51	14 55	15 28	15 55	16 19
45	04 47	05 22	05 51	14 41	15 16	15 47	16 15
N 40	04 52	05 24	05 51	14 29	15 07	15 41	16 12
35	04 56	05 25	05 50	14 18	14 59	15 36	16 09
30	04 58	05 26	05 50	14 09	14 52	15 31	16 07
20	05 02	05 28	05 50	13 54	14 40	15 23	16 03
N 10	05 04	05 28	05 49	13 40	14 29	15 15	15 59
0	05 04	05 28	05 48	13 27	14 19	15 09	15 56
S 10	05 02	05 27	05 48	13 14	14 09	15 02	15 52
20	04 59	05 25	05 47	13 00	13 58	14 54	15 49
30	04 54	05 22	05 45	12 45	13 46	14 46	15 45
35	04 50	05 19	05 45	12 35	13 39	14 41	15 42
40	04 45	05 17	05 44	12 25	13 31	14 36	15 39
45	04 39	05 14	05 43	12 12	13 21	14 29	15 36
S 50	04 31	05 09	05 42	11 57	13 10	14 22	15 33
52	04 27	05 07	05 41	11 50	13 04	14 18	15 31
54	04 23	05 05	05 40	11 42	12 58	14 14	15 29
56	04 18	05 02	05 40	11 34	12 52	14 10	15 27
58	04 12	05 00	05 39	11 24	12 44	14 05	15 24
S 60	04 06	04 56	05 38	11 12	12 36	13 59	15 22

Lat.	Sunset	Twilight Civil	Twilight Naut.	Moonset 24	25	26	27
°	h m	h m	h m	h m	h m	h m	h m
N 72	17 47	18 55	20 20	21 32	23 53	25 54	01 54
N 70	17 48	18 49	20 04	22 17	24 15	00 15	02 05
68	17 48	18 44	19 52	22 46	24 32	00 32	02 14
66	17 49	18 40	19 42	23 08	24 46	00 46	02 22
64	17 49	18 36	19 33	23 25	24 58	00 58	02 28
62	17 49	18 33	19 26	23 39	25 07	01 07	02 34
60	17 50	18 31	19 20	23 51	25 15	01 15	02 39
N 58	17 50	18 29	19 15	24 01	00 01	01 22	02 43
56	17 50	18 27	19 11	24 10	00 10	01 29	02 47
54	17 50	18 26	19 07	24 18	00 18	01 34	02 50
52	17 51	18 24	19 04	24 25	00 25	01 39	02 53
50	17 51	18 23	19 01	24 31	00 31	01 44	02 56
45	17 51	18 20	18 55	24 45	00 45	01 54	03 02
N 40	17 52	18 19	18 50	24 56	00 56	02 02	03 06
35	17 52	18 17	18 47	00 02	01 06	02 09	03 11
30	17 52	18 16	18 44	00 12	01 14	02 15	03 14
20	17 53	18 15	18 41	00 29	01 28	02 25	03 21
N 10	17 54	18 15	18 39	00 44	01 41	02 35	03 26
0	17 55	18 15	18 39	00 59	01 52	02 43	03 31
S 10	17 56	18 17	18 41	01 13	02 04	02 52	03 37
20	17 57	18 19	18 44	01 27	02 16	03 01	03 42
30	17 58	18 22	18 50	01 44	02 30	03 11	03 48
35	17 59	18 24	18 54	01 54	02 38	03 17	03 52
40	18 00	18 27	18 59	02 06	02 47	03 23	03 56
45	18 01	18 30	19 05	02 19	02 58	03 31	04 00
S 50	18 02	18 35	19 13	02 35	03 10	03 40	04 06
52	18 03	18 37	19 17	02 42	03 16	03 44	04 08
54	18 04	18 39	19 22	02 50	03 23	03 49	04 11
56	18 05	18 42	19 27	03 00	03 30	03 54	04 14
58	18 06	18 45	19 33	03 10	03 38	04 00	04 17
S 60	18 07	18 48	19 39	03 22	03 47	04 06	04 21

	SUN			MOON			
Day	Eqn. of Time 00ʰ	Eqn. of Time 12ʰ	Mer. Pass.	Mer. Pass. Upper	Mer. Pass. Lower	Age	Phase
d	m s	m s	h m	h m	h m	d	%
24	07 58	08 08	11 52	19 40	07 13	08	68
25	08 18	08 29	11 52	20 31	08 06	09	78
26	08 39	08 49	11 51	21 20	08 56	10	86

UT	ARIES GHA	VENUS −4.1 GHA	Dec	MARS +1.2 GHA	Dec	JUPITER −2.5 GHA	Dec	SATURN +0.7 GHA	Dec	STARS Name	SHA	Dec
27 00	6 11.3	221 07.3	N13 52.8	135 53.7	S19 15.6	290 59.5	N21 55.0	158 26.7	S 8 59.9	Acamar	315 18.4	S40 15.0
01	21 13.8	236 07.0	. . 52.0	150 54.4	. . 16.1	306 01.9	. . 55.0	173 28.9	. . 9 00.0	Achernar	335 26.6	S57 10.1
02	36 16.3	251 06.6	. . 51.3	165 55.1	. . 16.6	321 04.3	. . 55.0	188 31.1	. . 00.1	Acrux	173 10.5	S63 10.2
03	51 18.7	266 06.2	. . 50.5	180 55.8	. . 17.0	336 06.7	. . 55.0	203 33.3	. . 00.2	Adhara	255 13.0	S28 59.2
04	66 21.2	281 05.8	. . 49.7	195 56.5	. . 17.5	351 09.1	. . 55.0	218 35.5	. . 00.3	Aldebaran	290 49.8	N16 32.1
05	81 23.6	296 05.4	. . 48.9	210 57.2	. . 17.9	6 11.5	. . 55.1	233 37.7	. . 00.4			
06	96 26.1	311 05.1	N13 48.2	225 57.9	S19 18.4	21 13.9	N21 55.1	248 39.9	S 9 00.5	Alioth	166 21.7	N55 53.5
07	111 28.6	326 04.7	. . 47.4	240 58.6	. . 18.9	36 16.3	. . 55.1	263 42.1	. . 00.6	Alkaid	152 59.7	N49 15.1
T 08	126 31.0	341 04.3	. . 46.6	255 59.3	. . 19.3	51 18.7	. . 55.1	278 44.3	. . 00.7	Al Na'ir	27 44.0	S46 53.8
H 09	141 33.5	356 03.9	. . 45.8	271 00.0	. . 19.8	66 21.1	. . 55.1	293 46.5	. . 00.8	Alnilam	275 46.8	S 1 11.6
U 10	156 36.0	11 03.5	. . 45.0	286 00.7	. . 20.2	81 23.5	. . 55.1	308 48.7	. . 00.9	Alphard	217 56.8	S 8 42.8
R 11	171 38.4	26 03.1	. . 44.3	301 01.3	. . 20.7	96 25.9	. . 55.1	323 50.9	. . 01.0			
S 12	186 40.9	41 02.8	N13 43.5	316 02.0	S19 21.2	111 28.3	N21 55.1	338 53.1	S 9 01.1	Alphecca	126 11.7	N26 40.6
D 13	201 43.4	56 02.4	. . 42.7	331 02.7	. . 21.6	126 30.7	. . 55.1	353 55.3	. . 01.2	Alpheratz	357 43.6	N29 09.9
A 14	216 45.8	71 02.0	. . 41.9	346 03.4	. . 22.1	141 33.1	. . 55.1	8 57.5	. . 01.4	Altair	62 08.6	N 8 54.4
Y 15	231 48.3	86 01.6	. . 41.1	1 04.1	. . 22.5	156 35.5	. . 55.1	23 59.6	. . 01.5	Ankaa	353 15.7	S42 14.0
16	246 50.7	101 01.2	. . 40.3	16 04.8	. . 23.0	171 37.9	. . 55.1	39 01.8	. . 01.6	Antares	112 27.0	S26 27.5
17	261 53.2	116 00.8	. . 39.5	31 05.5	. . 23.5	186 40.3	. . 55.1	54 04.0	. . 01.7			
18	276 55.7	131 00.5	N13 38.8	46 06.2	S19 23.9	201 42.7	N21 55.1	69 06.2	S 9 01.8	Arcturus	145 56.5	N19 07.1
19	291 58.1	146 00.1	. . 38.0	61 06.9	. . 24.4	216 45.1	. . 55.1	84 08.4	. . 01.9	Atria	107 29.5	S69 03.1
20	307 00.6	160 59.7	. . 37.2	76 07.6	. . 24.8	231 47.5	. . 55.1	99 10.6	. . 02.0	Avior	234 18.5	S59 32.9
21	322 03.1	175 59.3	. . 36.4	91 08.3	. . 25.3	246 50.0	. . 55.1	114 12.8	. . 02.1	Bellatrix	278 32.5	N 6 21.7
22	337 05.5	190 58.9	. . 35.6	106 08.9	. . 25.7	261 52.4	. . 55.1	129 15.0	. . 02.2	Betelgeuse	271 01.8	N 7 24.5
23	352 08.0	205 58.6	. . 34.8	121 09.6	. . 26.2	276 54.8	. . 55.1	144 17.2	. . 02.3			
28 00	7 10.5	220 58.2	N13 34.0	136 10.3	S19 26.7	291 57.2	N21 55.1	159 19.4	S 9 02.4	Canopus	263 56.4	S52 41.9
01	22 12.9	235 57.8	. . 33.2	151 11.0	. . 27.1	306 59.6	. . 55.1	174 21.6	. . 02.5	Capella	280 35.0	N46 00.4
02	37 15.4	250 57.4	. . 32.4	166 11.7	. . 27.6	322 02.0	. . 55.1	189 23.8	. . 02.6	Deneb	49 31.6	N45 20.0
03	52 17.9	265 57.0	. . 31.6	181 12.4	. . 28.0	337 04.4	. . 55.1	204 26.0	. . 02.7	Denebola	182 34.5	N14 30.1
04	67 20.3	280 56.7	. . 30.8	196 13.1	. . 28.5	352 06.8	. . 55.1	219 28.2	. . 02.8	Diphda	348 56.0	S17 54.8
05	82 22.8	295 56.3	. . 30.0	211 13.8	. . 28.9	7 09.2	. . 55.1	234 30.4	. . 02.9			
06	97 25.2	310 55.9	N13 29.2	226 14.4	S19 29.4	22 11.6	N21 55.1	249 32.6	S 9 03.0	Dubhe	193 52.9	N61 40.8
07	112 27.7	325 55.5	. . 28.4	241 15.1	. . 29.8	37 14.0	. . 55.1	264 34.8	. . 03.1	Elnath	278 13.1	N28 36.9
F 08	127 30.2	340 55.1	. . 27.6	256 15.8	. . 30.3	52 16.4	. . 55.2	279 37.0	. . 03.2	Eltanin	90 46.4	N51 29.7
R 09	142 32.6	355 54.7	. . 26.9	271 16.5	. . 30.7	67 18.8	. . 55.2	294 39.2	. . 03.3	Enif	33 47.4	N 9 56.3
I 10	157 35.1	10 54.4	. . 26.1	286 17.2	. . 31.2	82 21.2	. . 55.2	309 41.4	. . 03.4	Fomalhaut	15 24.2	S29 33.1
D 11	172 37.6	25 54.0	. . 25.3	301 17.9	. . 31.7	97 23.7	. . 55.2	324 43.6	. . 03.5			
A 12	187 40.0	40 53.6	N13 24.5	316 18.6	S19 32.1	112 26.1	N21 55.2	339 45.7	S 9 03.6	Gacrux	172 02.0	S57 11.1
Y 13	202 42.5	55 53.2	. . 23.6	331 19.2	. . 32.6	127 28.5	. . 55.2	354 47.9	. . 03.7	Gienah	175 53.1	S17 36.7
14	217 45.0	70 52.8	. . 22.8	346 19.9	. . 33.0	142 30.9	. . 55.2	9 50.1	. . 03.8	Hadar	148 49.2	S60 26.1
15	232 47.4	85 52.5	. . 22.0	1 20.6	. . 33.5	157 33.3	. . 55.2	24 52.3	. . 03.9	Hamal	328 01.0	N23 31.4
16	247 49.9	100 52.1	. . 21.2	16 21.3	. . 33.9	172 35.7	. . 55.2	39 54.5	. . 04.1	Kaus Aust.	83 44.5	S34 22.6
17	262 52.4	115 51.7	. . 20.4	31 22.0	. . 34.4	187 38.1	. . 55.2	54 56.7	. . 04.2			
18	277 54.8	130 51.3	N13 19.6	46 22.7	S19 34.8	202 40.5	N21 55.2	69 58.9	S 9 04.3	Kochab	137 20.9	N74 06.4
19	292 57.3	145 50.9	. . 18.8	61 23.3	. . 35.3	217 42.9	. . 55.2	85 01.1	. . 04.4	Markab	13 38.5	N15 16.7
20	307 59.7	160 50.6	. . 18.0	76 24.0	. . 35.7	232 45.4	. . 55.2	100 03.3	. . 04.5	Menkar	314 15.3	N 4 08.5
21	323 02.2	175 50.2	. . 17.2	91 24.7	. . 36.2	247 47.8	. . 55.2	115 05.5	. . 04.6	Menkent	148 08.5	S36 25.9
22	338 04.7	190 49.8	. . 16.4	106 25.4	. . 36.6	262 50.2	. . 55.2	130 07.7	. . 04.7	Miaplacidus	221 40.4	S69 46.0
23	353 07.1	205 49.4	. . 15.6	121 26.1	. . 37.1	277 52.6	. . 55.2	145 09.9	. . 04.8			
29 00	8 09.6	220 49.1	N13 14.8	136 26.7	S19 37.5	292 55.0	N21 55.2	160 12.1	S 9 04.9	Mirfak	308 40.7	N49 54.3
01	23 12.1	235 48.7	. . 14.0	151 27.4	. . 38.0	307 57.4	. . 55.2	175 14.3	. . 05.0	Nunki	75 58.9	S26 16.7
02	38 14.5	250 48.3	. . 13.2	166 28.1	. . 38.4	322 59.8	. . 55.2	190 16.5	. . 05.1	Peacock	53 19.7	S56 41.6
03	53 17.0	265 47.9	. . 12.4	181 28.8	. . 38.9	338 02.3	. . 55.2	205 18.7	. . 05.2	Pollux	243 28.5	N27 59.5
04	68 19.5	280 47.5	. . 11.5	196 29.5	. . 39.3	353 04.7	. . 55.2	220 20.9	. . 05.3	Procyon	245 00.3	N 5 11.5
05	83 21.9	295 47.2	. . 10.7	211 30.1	. . 39.8	8 07.1	. . 55.2	235 23.0	. . 05.4			
06	98 24.4	310 46.8	N13 09.9	226 30.8	S19 40.2	23 09.5	N21 55.2	250 25.2	S 9 05.5	Rasalhague	96 07.0	N12 33.4
07	113 26.8	325 46.4	. . 09.1	241 31.5	. . 40.7	38 11.9	. . 55.2	265 27.4	. . 05.6	Regulus	207 44.3	N11 54.2
S 08	128 29.3	340 46.0	. . 08.3	256 32.2	. . 41.1	53 14.3	. . 55.2	280 29.6	. . 05.7	Rigel	281 12.4	S 8 11.1
A 09	143 31.8	355 45.6	. . 07.5	271 32.9	. . 41.6	68 16.8	. . 55.2	295 31.8	. . 05.8	Rigil Kent.	139 52.9	S60 53.3
T 10	158 34.2	10 45.3	. . 06.7	286 33.5	. . 42.0	83 19.2	. . 55.2	310 34.0	. . 05.9	Sabik	102 13.2	S15 44.3
U 11	173 36.7	25 44.9	. . 05.8	301 34.2	. . 42.5	98 21.6	. . 55.2	325 36.2	. . 06.0			
R 12	188 39.2	40 44.5	N13 05.0	316 34.9	S19 42.9	113 24.0	N21 55.2	340 38.4	S 9 06.1	Schedar	349 40.5	N56 36.6
D 13	203 41.6	55 44.1	. . 04.2	331 35.6	. . 43.4	128 26.4	. . 55.2	355 40.6	. . 06.2	Shaula	96 22.7	S37 06.7
A 14	218 44.1	70 43.8	. . 03.4	346 36.2	. . 43.8	143 28.8	. . 55.2	10 42.8	. . 06.3	Sirius	258 34.2	S16 43.9
Y 15	233 46.6	85 43.4	. . 02.6	1 36.9	. . 44.2	158 31.3	. . 55.2	25 45.0	. . 06.4	Spica	158 32.1	S11 13.6
16	248 49.0	100 43.0	. . 01.7	16 37.6	. . 44.7	173 33.7	. . 55.2	40 47.2	. . 06.6	Suhail	222 53.1	S43 28.9
17	263 51.5	115 42.6	. . 00.9	31 38.3	. . 45.1	188 36.1	. . 55.2	55 49.4	. . 06.7			
18	278 54.0	130 42.2	N13 00.1	46 38.9	S19 45.6	203 38.5	N21 55.2	70 51.6	S 9 06.8	Vega	80 39.3	N38 48.2
19	293 56.4	145 41.9	12 59.3	61 39.6	. . 46.0	218 40.9	. . 55.2	85 53.8	. . 06.9	Zuben'ubi	137 06.2	S16 05.6
20	308 58.9	160 41.5	. . 58.5	76 40.3	. . 46.5	233 43.4	. . 55.2	100 55.9	. . 07.0		SHA	Mer.Pass.
21	324 01.3	175 41.1	. . 57.6	91 41.0	. . 46.9	248 45.8	. . 55.2	115 58.1	. . 07.1	Venus	213 47.7	9 16
22	339 03.8	190 40.7	. . 56.8	106 41.6	. . 47.4	263 48.2	. . 55.3	131 00.3	. . 07.2	Mars	128 59.9	14 55
23	354 06.3	205 40.4	. . 56.0	121 42.3	. . 47.8	278 50.6	. . 55.3	146 02.5	. . 07.3	Jupiter	284 46.7	4 31
Mer.Pass. 23 27.4	*v* −0.4 *d* 0.8			*v* 0.7 *d* 0.5		*v* 2.4 *d* 0.0		*v* 2.2 *d* 0.1		Saturn	152 08.9	13 21

SUN / MOON

UT	SUN GHA	SUN Dec	MOON GHA	v	MOON Dec	d	HP
d h	° ′	° ′	° ′	′	° ′	′	′
27 00	182 15.0	S 1 42.4	38 41.7	12.3	S 7 41.7	11.1	56.9
01	197 15.2	43.3	53 13.0	12.3	7 30.6	11.2	56.9
02	212 15.4	44.3	67 44.3	12.4	7 19.4	11.1	56.9
03	227 15.6	.. 45.3	82 15.7	12.4	7 08.3	11.2	56.9
04	242 15.9	46.3	96 47.1	12.5	6 57.1	11.2	56.9
05	257 16.1	47.2	111 18.6	12.5	6 45.9	11.3	56.8
06	272 16.3	S 1 48.2	125 50.1	12.6	S 6 34.6	11.2	56.8
07	287 16.5	49.2	140 21.7	12.6	6 23.4	11.3	56.8
T 08	302 16.7	50.2	154 53.3	12.6	6 12.1	11.3	56.8
H 09	317 16.9	.. 51.1	169 24.9	12.7	6 00.8	11.3	56.8
U 10	332 17.1	52.1	183 56.6	12.7	5 49.5	11.4	56.7
R 11	347 17.3	53.1	198 28.3	12.8	5 38.1	11.3	56.7
S 12	2 17.5	S 1 54.0	213 00.1	12.8	S 5 26.8	11.4	56.7
D 13	17 17.8	55.0	227 31.9	12.8	5 15.4	11.4	56.7
A 14	32 18.0	56.0	242 03.7	12.9	5 04.0	11.4	56.7
Y 15	47 18.2	.. 57.0	256 35.6	12.9	4 52.6	11.5	56.6
16	62 18.4	57.9	271 07.5	13.0	4 41.1	11.4	56.6
17	77 18.6	58.9	285 39.5	13.0	4 29.7	11.5	56.6
18	92 18.8	S 1 59.9	300 11.5	13.0	S 4 18.2	11.5	56.6
19	107 19.0	2 00.9	314 43.5	13.0	4 06.7	11.4	56.6
20	122 19.2	01.8	329 15.5	13.1	3 55.3	11.5	56.5
21	137 19.4	.. 02.8	343 47.6	13.2	3 43.8	11.5	56.5
22	152 19.7	03.8	358 19.8	13.1	3 32.3	11.5	56.5
23	167 19.9	04.7	12 51.9	13.2	3 20.8	11.6	56.5
28 00	182 20.1	S 2 05.7	27 24.1	13.2	S 3 09.2	11.5	56.5
01	197 20.3	06.7	41 56.3	13.3	2 57.7	11.5	56.4
02	212 20.5	07.7	56 28.6	13.3	2 46.2	11.6	56.4
03	227 20.7	.. 08.6	71 00.9	13.3	2 34.6	11.5	56.4
04	242 20.9	09.6	85 33.2	13.3	2 23.1	11.5	56.4
05	257 21.1	10.6	100 05.5	13.4	2 11.6	11.6	56.3
06	272 21.3	S 2 11.5	114 37.9	13.4	S 2 00.0	11.5	56.3
07	287 21.5	12.5	129 10.3	13.4	1 48.5	11.6	56.3
F 08	302 21.8	13.5	143 42.7	13.4	1 36.9	11.5	56.3
R 09	317 22.0	.. 14.5	158 15.1	13.5	1 25.4	11.6	56.3
I 10	332 22.2	15.4	172 47.6	13.5	1 13.8	11.5	56.2
D 11	347 22.4	16.4	187 20.1	13.5	1 02.3	11.5	56.2
A 12	2 22.6	S 2 17.4	201 52.6	13.6	S 0 50.8	11.6	56.2
Y 13	17 22.8	18.3	216 25.2	13.6	0 39.2	11.5	56.2
14	32 23.0	19.3	230 57.7	13.6	0 27.7	11.5	56.2
15	47 23.2	.. 20.3	245 30.3	13.6	0 16.2	11.5	56.1
16	62 23.4	21.3	260 02.9	13.6	0 04.7	11.6	56.1
17	77 23.6	22.2	274 35.5	13.7	N 0 06.9	11.5	56.1
18	92 23.8	S 2 23.2	289 08.2	13.6	N 0 18.4	11.4	56.1
19	107 24.1	24.2	303 40.8	13.7	0 29.8	11.5	56.1
20	122 24.3	25.1	318 13.5	13.7	0 41.3	11.5	56.0
21	137 24.5	.. 26.1	332 46.2	13.7	0 52.8	11.5	56.0
22	152 24.7	27.1	347 18.9	13.8	1 04.3	11.4	56.0
23	167 24.9	28.1	1 51.7	13.7	1 15.7	11.4	56.0
29 00	182 25.1	S 2 29.0	16 24.4	13.8	N 1 27.1	11.4	56.0
01	197 25.3	30.0	30 57.2	13.8	1 38.5	11.4	55.9
02	212 25.5	31.0	45 30.0	13.8	1 49.9	11.4	55.9
03	227 25.7	.. 31.9	60 02.8	13.8	2 01.3	11.4	55.9
04	242 25.9	32.9	74 35.6	13.8	2 12.7	11.3	55.9
05	257 26.1	33.9	89 08.4	13.8	2 24.0	11.4	55.9
06	272 26.3	S 2 34.9	103 41.2	13.8	N 2 35.4	11.3	55.8
07	287 26.6	35.8	118 14.0	13.9	2 46.7	11.3	55.8
S 08	302 26.8	36.8	132 46.9	13.9	2 58.0	11.3	55.8
A 09	317 27.0	.. 37.8	147 19.8	13.8	3 09.3	11.2	55.8
T 10	332 27.2	38.7	161 52.6	13.9	3 20.5	11.2	55.8
U 11	347 27.4	39.7	176 25.5	13.9	3 31.7	11.2	55.7
R 12	2 27.6	S 2 40.7	190 58.4	13.9	N 3 42.9	11.2	55.7
D 13	17 27.8	41.7	205 31.3	13.9	3 54.1	11.2	55.7
A 14	32 28.0	42.6	220 04.2	13.9	4 05.3	11.1	55.7
Y 15	47 28.2	.. 43.6	234 37.1	13.9	4 16.4	11.1	55.7
16	62 28.4	44.6	249 10.0	13.9	4 27.5	11.1	55.7
17	77 28.6	45.5	263 42.9	13.9	4 38.6	11.0	55.6
18	92 28.8	S 2 46.5	278 15.8	14.0	N 4 49.6	11.0	55.6
19	107 29.0	47.5	292 48.8	13.9	5 00.6	11.0	55.6
20	122 29.2	48.5	307 21.7	13.9	5 11.6	11.0	55.6
21	137 29.4	.. 49.4	321 54.6	13.9	5 22.6	10.9	55.6
22	152 29.6	50.4	336 27.5	14.0	5 33.5	10.9	55.5
23	167 29.9	51.4	351 00.5	13.9	N 5 44.4	10.8	55.5
	SD 16.0	d 1.0	SD 15.4		15.3		15.2

Twilight / Moonrise

Lat.	Naut.	Civil	Sunrise	Moonrise 27	28	29	30
°	h m	h m	h m	h m	h m	h m	h m
N 72	03 35	04 59	06 07	16 55	16 42	16 29	16 15
N 70	03 49	05 04	06 05	16 49	16 42	16 35	16 28
68	04 01	05 08	06 03	16 44	16 42	16 40	16 38
66	04 10	05 11	06 02	16 39	16 42	16 44	16 47
64	04 17	05 14	06 01	16 35	16 42	16 48	16 55
62	04 23	05 16	06 00	16 32	16 42	16 51	17 01
60	04 29	05 18	05 59	16 29	16 42	16 54	17 06
N 58	04 33	05 19	05 58	16 27	16 42	16 56	17 11
56	04 37	05 21	05 58	16 25	16 42	16 58	17 16
54	04 40	05 22	05 57	16 23	16 42	17 00	17 20
52	04 43	05 23	05 56	16 21	16 42	17 02	17 23
50	04 46	05 24	05 56	16 19	16 42	17 04	17 27
45	04 51	05 25	05 55	16 15	16 42	17 07	17 34
N 40	04 55	05 27	05 54	16 12	16 41	17 10	17 40
35	04 58	05 27	05 53	16 09	16 41	17 13	17 45
30	05 00	05 28	05 52	16 07	16 41	17 15	17 49
20	05 03	05 28	05 50	16 03	16 41	17 19	17 57
N 10	05 03	05 28	05 49	15 59	16 41	17 23	18 04
0	05 03	05 27	05 47	15 56	16 42	17 26	18 11
S 10	05 00	05 25	05 46	15 52	16 42	17 30	18 18
20	04 56	05 22	05 44	15 49	16 42	17 34	18 25
30	04 50	05 18	05 42	15 45	16 42	17 38	18 33
35	04 45	05 15	05 40	15 42	16 42	17 40	18 38
40	04 40	05 12	05 39	15 39	16 42	17 43	18 43
45	04 33	05 08	05 37	15 36	16 42	17 46	18 50
S 50	04 24	05 03	05 35	15 33	16 42	17 50	18 57
52	04 20	05 00	05 34	15 31	16 42	17 52	19 01
54	04 15	04 57	05 33	15 29	16 42	17 54	19 05
56	04 09	04 54	05 32	15 27	16 42	17 56	19 09
58	04 03	04 51	05 30	15 24	16 42	17 59	19 14
S 60	03 56	04 47	05 29	15 22	16 42	18 02	19 19

Twilight / Moonset

Lat.	Sunset	Civil	Naut.	Moonset 27	28	29	30
°	h m	h m	h m	h m	h m	h m	h m
N 72	17 32	18 39	20 02	01 54	03 46	05 34	07 22
N 70	17 34	18 34	19 48	02 05	03 49	05 31	07 11
68	17 36	18 31	19 38	02 14	03 52	05 28	07 02
66	17 37	18 28	19 29	02 22	03 55	05 25	06 55
64	17 38	18 26	19 22	02 28	03 57	05 23	06 49
62	17 40	18 24	19 16	02 34	03 59	05 22	06 43
60	17 41	18 22	19 11	02 39	04 00	05 20	06 39
N 58	17 41	18 20	19 06	02 43	04 02	05 19	06 35
56	17 42	18 19	19 03	02 47	04 03	05 18	06 31
54	17 43	18 18	18 59	02 50	04 04	05 17	06 28
52	17 44	18 17	18 56	02 53	04 05	05 16	06 25
50	17 44	18 16	18 54	02 56	04 06	05 15	06 23
45	17 46	18 15	18 49	03 02	04 08	05 13	06 17
N 40	17 47	18 14	18 45	03 06	04 10	05 11	06 12
35	17 48	18 13	18 42	03 11	04 11	05 10	06 08
30	17 49	18 13	18 40	03 14	04 12	05 09	06 05
20	17 50	18 12	18 38	03 21	04 14	05 07	05 58
N 10	17 52	18 13	18 37	03 26	04 16	05 05	05 53
0	17 54	18 14	18 38	03 31	04 18	05 03	05 48
S 10	17 55	18 17	18 41	03 37	04 20	05 01	05 43
20	17 57	18 19	18 45	03 42	04 21	04 59	05 37
30	18 00	18 24	18 52	03 48	04 23	04 57	05 31
35	18 01	18 27	18 56	03 52	04 24	04 56	05 28
40	18 03	18 30	19 02	03 56	04 26	04 55	05 24
45	18 05	18 34	19 09	04 00	04 27	04 53	05 19
S 50	18 07	18 40	19 18	04 06	04 29	04 51	05 14
52	18 08	18 42	19 23	04 08	04 30	04 50	05 11
54	18 09	18 45	19 28	04 11	04 31	04 49	05 08
56	18 11	18 48	19 33	04 14	04 31	04 48	05 05
58	18 12	18 52	19 40	04 17	04 33	04 47	05 02
S 60	18 14	18 56	19 48	04 21	04 34	04 46	04 58

SUN / MOON

Day	Eqn. of Time 00ʰ	12ʰ	Mer. Pass.	Mer. Pass. Upper	Lower	Age	Phase
d	m s	m s	h m	h m	h m	d	%
27	09 00	09 10	11 51	22 07	09 44	11	93
28	09 20	09 30	11 51	22 52	10 30	12	97
29	09 40	09 50	11 50	23 37	11 15	13	99

UT	ARIES GHA	VENUS −4.1 GHA	VENUS Dec	MARS +1.2 GHA	MARS Dec	JUPITER −2.5 GHA	JUPITER Dec	SATURN +0.7 GHA	SATURN Dec
30 00	9 08.7	220 40.0	N12 55.2	136 43.0	S19 48.3	293 53.1	N21 55.3	161 04.7	S 9 07.4
01	24 11.2	235 39.6	54.3	151 43.7	48.7	308 55.5	55.3	176 06.9	07.5
02	39 13.7	250 39.2	53.5	166 44.3	49.1	323 57.9	55.3	191 09.1	07.6
03	54 16.1	265 38.8 ..	52.7	181 45.0 ..	49.6	339 00.3 ..	55.3	206 11.3 ..	07.7
04	69 18.6	280 38.5	51.8	196 45.7	50.0	354 02.8	55.3	221 13.5	07.8
05	84 21.1	295 38.1	51.0	211 46.4	50.5	9 05.2	55.3	236 15.7	07.9
06	99 23.5	310 37.7	N12 50.2	226 47.0	S19 50.9	24 07.6	N21 55.3	251 17.9	S 9 08.0
07	114 26.0	325 37.3	49.4	241 47.7	51.4	39 10.0	55.3	266 20.1	08.1
08	129 28.4	340 37.0	48.5	256 48.4	51.8	54 12.5	55.3	281 22.3	08.2
S 09	144 30.9	355 36.6 ..	47.7	271 49.0 ..	52.2	69 14.9 ..	55.3	296 24.5 ..	08.3
U 10	159 33.4	10 36.2	46.9	286 49.7	52.7	84 17.3	55.3	311 26.6	08.4
N 11	174 35.8	25 35.8	46.0	301 50.4	53.1	99 19.7	55.3	326 28.8	08.5
D 12	189 38.3	40 35.5	N12 45.2	316 51.0	S19 53.6	114 22.2	N21 55.3	341 31.0	S 9 08.6
A 13	204 40.8	55 35.1	44.4	331 51.7	54.0	129 24.6	55.3	356 33.2	08.7
Y 14	219 43.2	70 34.7	43.5	346 52.4	54.4	144 27.0	55.3	11 35.4	08.8
15	234 45.7	85 34.3 ..	42.7	1 53.1 ..	54.8	159 29.4 ..	55.3	26 37.6 ..	09.0
16	249 48.2	100 34.0	41.8	16 53.7	55.3	174 31.9	55.3	41 39.8	09.1
17	264 50.6	115 33.6	41.0	31 54.4	55.8	189 34.3	55.3	56 42.0	09.2
18	279 53.1	130 33.2	N12 40.2	46 55.1	S19 56.2	204 36.7	N21 55.3	71 44.2	S 9 09.3
19	294 55.6	145 32.8	39.3	61 55.7	56.6	219 39.2	55.3	86 46.4	09.4
20	309 58.0	160 32.5	38.5	76 56.4	57.1	234 41.6	55.3	101 48.6	09.5
21	325 00.5	175 32.1 ..	37.6	91 57.1 ..	57.5	249 44.0 ..	55.3	116 50.8 ..	09.6
22	340 02.9	190 31.7	36.8	106 57.7	58.0	264 46.5	55.3	131 52.9	09.7
23	355 05.4	205 31.3	36.0	121 58.4	58.4	279 48.9	55.3	146 55.1	09.8
1 00	10 07.9	220 31.0	N12 35.1	136 59.1	S19 58.8	294 51.3	N21 55.3	161 57.3	S 9 09.9
01	25 10.3	235 30.6	34.3	151 59.7	59.3	309 53.8	55.3	176 59.5	10.0
02	40 12.8	250 30.2	33.4	167 00.4	19 59.7	324 56.2	55.3	192 01.7	10.1
03	55 15.3	265 29.8 ..	32.6	182 01.1	20 00.1	339 58.6 ..	55.3	207 03.9 ..	10.2
04	70 17.7	280 29.5	31.7	197 01.7	00.6	355 01.1	55.3	222 06.1	10.3
05	85 20.2	295 29.1	30.9	212 02.4	01.0	10 03.5	55.3	237 08.3	10.4
06	100 22.7	310 28.7	N12 30.1	227 03.0	S20 01.4	25 05.9	N21 55.3	252 10.5	S 9 10.5
07	115 25.1	325 28.3	29.2	242 03.7	01.9	40 08.4	55.3	267 12.7	10.6
08	130 27.6	340 28.0	28.4	257 04.4	02.3	55 10.8	55.3	282 14.9	10.7
M 09	145 30.0	355 27.6 ..	27.5	272 05.0 ..	02.8	70 13.2 ..	55.3	297 17.1 ..	10.8
O 10	160 32.5	10 27.2	26.7	287 05.7	03.2	85 15.7	55.3	312 19.2	10.9
N 11	175 35.0	25 26.8	25.8	302 06.4	03.6	100 18.1	55.3	327 21.4	11.0
D 12	190 37.4	40 26.5	N12 25.0	317 07.0	S20 04.1	115 20.5	N21 55.3	342 23.6	S 9 11.1
A 13	205 39.9	55 26.1	24.1	332 07.7	04.5	130 23.0	55.3	357 25.8	11.2
Y 14	220 42.4	70 25.7	23.3	347 08.3	04.9	145 25.4	55.3	12 28.0	11.4
15	235 44.8	85 25.3 ..	22.4	2 09.0 ..	05.4	160 27.8 ..	55.3	27 30.2 ..	11.5
16	250 47.3	100 25.0	21.6	17 09.7	05.8	175 30.3	55.3	42 32.4	11.6
17	265 49.8	115 24.6	20.7	32 10.3	06.2	190 32.7	55.3	57 34.6	11.7
18	280 52.2	130 24.2	N12 19.8	47 11.0	S20 06.7	205 35.2	N21 55.3	72 36.8	S 9 11.8
19	295 54.7	145 23.8	19.0	62 11.6	07.1	220 37.6	55.3	87 39.0	11.9
20	310 57.2	160 23.5	18.1	77 12.3	07.5	235 40.0	55.3	102 41.2	12.0
21	325 59.6	175 23.1 ..	17.3	92 13.0 ..	08.0	250 42.5 ..	55.3	117 43.3 ..	12.1
22	341 02.1	190 22.7	16.4	107 13.6	08.4	265 44.9	55.3	132 45.5	12.2
23	356 04.5	205 22.4	15.6	122 14.3	08.8	280 47.4	55.3	147 47.7	12.3
2 00	11 07.0	220 22.0	N12 14.7	137 14.9	S20 09.2	295 49.8	N21 55.3	162 49.9	S 9 12.4
01	26 09.5	235 21.6	13.8	152 15.6	09.7	310 52.2	55.3	177 52.1	12.5
02	41 11.9	250 21.2	13.0	167 16.3	10.1	325 54.7	55.3	192 54.3	12.6
03	56 14.4	265 20.9 ..	12.1	182 16.9 ..	10.5	340 57.1 ..	55.3	207 56.5 ..	12.7
04	71 16.9	280 20.5	11.3	197 17.6	11.0	355 59.6	55.3	222 58.7	12.8
05	86 19.3	295 20.1	10.4	212 18.2	11.4	11 02.0	55.3	238 00.9	12.9
06	101 21.8	310 19.7	N12 09.5	227 18.9	S20 11.8	26 04.5	N21 55.3	253 03.1	S 9 13.0
07	116 24.3	325 19.4	08.7	242 19.5	12.3	41 06.9	55.3	268 05.2	13.1
T 08	131 26.7	340 19.0	07.8	257 20.2	12.7	56 09.3	55.3	283 07.4	13.2
U 09	146 29.2	355 18.6 ..	06.9	272 20.8 ..	13.1	71 11.8 ..	55.3	298 09.6 ..	13.3
E 10	161 31.6	10 18.3	06.1	287 21.5	13.5	86 14.2	55.3	313 11.8	13.4
S 11	176 34.1	25 17.9	05.2	302 22.2	14.0	101 16.7	55.3	328 14.0	13.6
D 12	191 36.6	40 17.5	N12 04.3	317 22.8	S20 14.4	116 19.1	N21 55.3	343 16.2	S 9 13.7
A 13	206 39.0	55 17.1	03.5	332 23.5	14.8	131 21.6	55.3	358 18.4	13.8
Y 14	221 41.5	70 16.8	02.6	347 24.1	15.3	146 24.0	55.3	13 20.6	13.9
15	236 44.0	85 16.4 ..	01.7	2 24.8 ..	15.7	161 26.5 ..	55.3	28 22.8 ..	14.0
16	251 46.4	100 16.0	00.9	17 25.4	16.1	176 28.9	55.3	43 25.0	14.1
17	266 48.9	115 15.7	12 00.0	32 26.1	16.5	191 31.4	55.3	58 27.1	14.2
18	281 51.4	130 15.3	N11 59.1	47 26.7	S20 17.0	206 33.8	N21 55.3	73 29.3	S 9 14.3
19	296 53.8	145 14.9	58.3	62 27.4	17.4	221 36.2	55.3	88 31.5	14.4
20	311 56.3	160 14.5	57.4	77 28.0	17.8	236 38.7	55.3	103 33.7	14.5
21	326 58.8	175 14.2 ..	56.5	92 28.7 ..	18.2	251 41.1 ..	55.3	118 35.9 ..	14.6
22	342 01.2	190 13.8	55.6	107 29.3	18.7	266 43.6	55.3	133 38.1	14.7
23	357 03.7	205 13.4	54.8	122 30.0	19.1	281 46.0	55.3	148 40.3	14.8
h m Mer.Pass. 23 15.7		v −0.4 d 0.9		v 0.7 d 0.4		v 2.4 d 0.0		v 2.2 d 0.1	

STARS

Name	SHA	Dec
Acamar	315 18.4	S40 15.0
Achernar	335 26.6	S57 10.1
Acrux	173 10.5	S63 10.2
Adhara	255 12.9	S28 59.2
Aldebaran	290 49.8	N16 32.1
Alioth	166 21.7	N55 53.5
Alkaid	152 59.7	N49 15.1
Al Na'ir	27 44.0	S46 53.9
Alnilam	275 46.8	S 1 11.6
Alphard	217 56.8	S 8 42.8
Alphecca	126 11.7	N26 40.6
Alpheratz	357 43.6	N29 09.9
Altair	62 08.6	N 8 54.4
Ankaa	353 15.8	S42 14.0
Antares	112 27.0	S26 27.5
Arcturus	145 56.5	N19 07.1
Atria	107 29.5	S69 03.1
Avior	234 18.5	S59 32.8
Bellatrix	278 32.4	N 6 21.7
Betelgeuse	271 01.8	N 7 24.5
Canopus	263 56.3	S52 41.9
Capella	280 35.0	N46 00.4
Deneb	49 31.6	N45 20.0
Denebola	182 34.5	N14 30.1
Diphda	348 56.0	S17 54.8
Dubhe	193 52.9	N61 40.8
Elnath	278 13.1	N28 36.9
Eltanin	90 46.5	N51 29.7
Enif	33 47.4	N 9 56.3
Fomalhaut	15 24.2	S29 33.1
Gacrux	172 02.0	S57 11.1
Gienah	175 53.1	S17 36.7
Hadar	148 49.2	S60 26.1
Hamal	328 01.0	N23 31.5
Kaus Aust.	83 44.5	S34 22.6
Kochab	137 21.0	N74 06.4
Markab	13 38.5	N15 16.7
Menkar	314 15.3	N 4 08.5
Menkent	148 08.5	S36 25.9
Miaplacidus	221 40.3	S69 46.0
Mirfak	308 40.7	N49 54.3
Nunki	75 58.9	S26 16.7
Peacock	53 19.8	S56 41.6
Pollux	243 28.4	N27 59.5
Procyon	245 00.3	N 5 11.5
Rasalhague	96 07.0	N12 33.4
Regulus	207 44.3	N11 54.2
Rigel	281 12.4	S 8 11.1
Rigil Kent.	139 53.0	S60 53.3
Sabik	102 13.2	S15 44.3
Schedar	349 40.5	N56 36.6
Shaula	96 22.7	S37 06.7
Sirius	258 34.2	S16 43.9
Spica	158 32.1	S11 13.6
Suhail	222 53.1	S43 28.9
Vega	80 39.3	N38 48.2
Zuben'ubi	137 06.2	S16 05.6

	SHA	Mer.Pass.
	° ′	h m
Venus	210 23.1	9 18
Mars	126 51.2	14 51
Jupiter	284 43.5	4 20
Saturn	151 49.5	13 10

UT	SUN GHA	SUN Dec	MOON GHA	MOON v	MOON Dec	MOON d	MOON HP
d h	° ′	° ′	° ′	′	° ′	′	′
30 00	182 30.1	S 2 52.3	5 33.4	13.9	N 5 55.2	10.9	55.5
01	197 30.3	53.3	20 06.3	14.0	6 06.1	10.7	55.5
02	212 30.5	54.3	34 39.3	13.9	6 16.8	10.8	55.5
03	227 30.7	.. 55.2	49 12.2	13.9	6 27.6	10.7	55.4
04	242 30.9	56.2	63 45.1	14.0	6 38.3	10.7	55.4
05	257 31.1	57.2	78 18.1	13.9	6 49.0	10.6	55.4
06	272 31.3	S 2 58.2	92 51.0	13.9	N 6 59.6	10.7	55.4
07	287 31.5	2 59.1	107 23.9	14.0	7 10.3	10.5	55.4
08	302 31.7	3 00.1	121 56.9	13.9	7 20.8	10.6	55.4
09	317 31.9	.. 01.1	136 29.8	13.9	7 31.4	10.4	55.3
10	332 32.1	02.0	151 02.7	13.9	7 41.8	10.5	55.3
11	347 32.3	03.0	165 35.6	13.9	7 52.3	10.4	55.3
12	2 32.5	S 3 04.0	180 08.5	13.9	N 8 02.7	10.4	55.3
13	17 32.7	04.9	194 41.4	13.9	8 13.1	10.3	55.3
14	32 32.9	05.9	209 14.3	13.9	8 23.4	10.3	55.2
15	47 33.1	.. 06.9	223 47.2	13.9	8 33.7	10.2	55.2
16	62 33.3	07.8	238 20.1	13.8	8 43.9	10.2	55.2
17	77 33.5	08.8	252 52.9	13.9	8 54.1	10.1	55.2
18	92 33.7	S 3 09.8	267 25.8	13.8	N 9 04.2	10.1	55.2
19	107 33.9	10.8	281 58.6	13.9	9 14.3	10.1	55.2
20	122 34.1	11.7	296 31.5	13.8	9 24.4	9.9	55.1
21	137 34.3	.. 12.7	311 04.3	13.8	9 34.3	10.0	55.1
22	152 34.5	13.7	325 37.1	13.9	9 44.3	9.9	55.1
23	167 34.7	14.6	340 10.0	13.8	9 54.2	9.8	55.1
1 00	182 34.9	S 3 15.6	354 42.8	13.8	N10 04.0	9.8	55.1
01	197 35.2	16.6	9 15.6	13.7	10 13.8	9.8	55.1
02	212 35.4	17.5	23 48.3	13.8	10 23.6	9.7	55.0
03	227 35.6	.. 18.5	38 21.1	13.8	10 33.3	9.6	55.0
04	242 35.8	19.5	52 53.9	13.7	10 42.9	9.6	55.0
05	257 36.0	20.4	67 26.6	13.7	10 52.5	9.6	55.0
06	272 36.2	S 3 21.4	81 59.3	13.8	N11 02.1	9.4	55.0
07	287 36.4	22.4	96 32.1	13.7	11 11.5	9.5	55.0
08	302 36.6	23.3	111 04.8	13.7	11 21.0	9.3	54.9
09	317 36.8	.. 24.3	125 37.5	13.6	11 30.3	9.4	54.9
10	332 37.0	25.3	140 10.1	13.7	11 39.7	9.2	54.9
11	347 37.2	26.3	154 42.8	13.6	11 48.9	9.2	54.9
2 00	182 39.8	S 3 38.8	343 45.9	13.4	N13 43.8	8.3	54.7
12	2 37.4	S 3 27.2	169 15.4	13.7	N11 58.1	9.1	54.9
13	17 37.6	28.2	183 48.1	13.6	12 07.2	9.1	54.9
14	32 37.8	29.2	198 20.7	13.6	12 16.3	9.1	54.8
15	47 38.0	.. 30.1	212 53.3	13.6	12 25.4	8.9	54.8
16	62 38.2	31.1	227 25.9	13.5	12 34.3	8.9	54.8
17	77 38.4	32.1	241 58.4	13.6	12 43.2	8.9	54.8
18	92 38.6	S 3 33.0	256 31.0	13.5	N12 52.1	8.7	54.8
19	107 38.8	34.0	271 03.5	13.5	13 00.8	8.7	54.8
20	122 39.0	35.0	285 36.0	13.5	13 09.5	8.7	54.8
21	137 39.2	.. 35.9	300 08.5	13.5	13 18.2	8.6	54.7
22	152 39.4	36.9	314 41.0	13.4	13 26.8	8.5	54.7
23	167 39.6	37.9	329 13.5	13.4	13 35.3	8.5	54.7
2 00	182 39.8	S 3 38.8	343 45.9	13.4	N13 43.8	8.3	54.7
01	197 40.0	39.8	358 18.3	13.5	13 52.1	8.4	54.7
02	212 40.2	40.8	12 50.8	13.3	14 00.5	8.2	54.7
03	227 40.4	.. 41.7	27 23.1	13.4	14 08.7	8.2	54.6
04	242 40.6	42.7	41 55.5	13.4	14 16.9	8.1	54.6
05	257 40.8	43.7	56 27.9	13.3	14 25.0	8.1	54.6
06	272 41.0	S 3 44.6	71 00.2	13.3	N14 33.1	8.0	54.6
07	287 41.2	45.6	85 32.5	13.3	14 41.1	7.9	54.6
08	302 41.4	46.6	100 04.8	13.2	14 49.0	7.8	54.6
09	317 41.6	.. 47.5	114 37.0	13.3	14 56.8	7.8	54.5
10	332 41.7	48.5	129 09.3	13.2	15 04.6	7.7	54.6
11	347 41.9	49.5	143 41.5	13.2	15 12.3	7.7	54.5
12	2 42.1	S 3 50.4	158 13.7	13.2	N15 20.0	7.5	54.5
13	17 42.3	51.4	172 45.9	13.2	15 27.5	7.5	54.5
14	32 42.5	52.4	187 18.1	13.1	15 35.0	7.4	54.5
15	47 42.7	.. 53.3	201 50.2	13.1	15 42.4	7.4	54.5
16	62 42.9	54.3	216 22.3	13.1	15 49.8	7.2	54.5
17	77 43.1	55.3	230 54.4	13.1	15 57.0	7.2	54.5
18	92 43.3	S 3 56.2	245 26.5	13.1	N16 04.2	7.1	54.5
19	107 43.5	57.2	259 58.6	13.0	16 11.3	7.1	54.4
20	122 43.7	58.2	274 30.6	13.0	16 18.4	6.9	54.4
21	137 43.9	3 59.1	289 02.6	13.0	16 25.3	6.9	54.4
22	152 44.1	4 00.1	303 34.6	13.0	16 32.2	6.8	54.4
23	167 44.3	S 4 01.1	318 06.6	12.9	N16 39.0	6.7	54.4
	SD 16.0	d 1.0	SD 15.1		15.0		14.9

Lat.	Twilight Naut.	Twilight Civil	Sunrise	Moonrise 30	Moonrise 1	Moonrise 2	Moonrise 3
°	h m	h m	h m	h m	h m	h m	h m
N 72	03 51	05 13	06 20	16 15	15 59	15 35	▭
N 70	04 03	05 16	06 17	16 28	16 21	16 12	15 59
68	04 12	05 19	06 14	16 38	16 38	16 38	16 40
66	04 20	05 21	06 12	16 47	16 51	16 58	17 09
64	04 26	05 22	06 10	16 55	17 03	17 14	17 30
62	04 32	05 24	06 08	17 01	17 13	17 28	17 48
60	04 36	05 25	06 06	17 06	17 21	17 39	18 02
N 58	04 40	05 26	06 05	17 11	17 29	17 49	18 15
56	04 43	05 27	06 04	17 16	17 35	17 58	18 25
54	04 46	05 27	06 02	17 20	17 41	18 06	18 35
52	04 48	05 28	06 01	17 23	17 46	18 13	18 43
50	04 51	05 28	06 00	17 27	17 51	18 19	18 51
45	04 55	05 29	05 58	17 34	18 02	18 33	19 07
N 40	04 58	05 30	05 57	17 40	18 10	18 44	19 21
35	05 00	05 30	05 55	17 45	18 18	18 54	19 32
30	05 02	05 30	05 53	17 49	18 25	19 02	19 42
20	05 03	05 29	05 51	17 57	18 36	19 17	19 59
N 10	05 03	05 28	05 49	18 04	18 46	19 30	20 14
0	05 02	05 26	05 46	18 11	18 56	19 42	20 28
S 10	04 58	05 23	05 44	18 18	19 06	19 54	20 43
20	04 53	05 19	05 41	18 25	19 16	20 07	20 58
30	04 46	05 14	05 38	18 33	19 28	20 22	21 15
35	04 41	05 11	05 36	18 38	19 35	20 31	21 26
40	04 35	05 07	05 34	18 43	19 43	20 41	21 37
45	04 27	05 02	05 31	18 50	19 52	20 53	21 51
S 50	04 17	04 56	05 28	18 57	20 03	21 07	22 08
52	04 12	04 53	05 27	19 01	20 08	21 14	22 16
54	04 07	04 50	05 25	19 05	20 14	21 21	22 25
56	04 00	04 46	05 24	19 09	20 20	21 30	22 35
58	03 53	04 42	05 22	19 14	20 28	21 39	22 47
S 60	03 45	04 37	05 20	19 19	20 36	21 50	23 00

Lat.	Sunset	Twilight Civil	Twilight Naut.	Moonset 30	Moonset 1	Moonset 2	Moonset 3
°	h m	h m	h m	h m	h m	h m	h m
N 72	17 17	18 23	19 45	07 22	09 12	11 11	▭
N 70	17 20	18 21	19 33	07 11	08 52	10 35	12 24
68	17 23	18 18	19 24	07 02	08 36	10 10	11 43
66	17 26	18 17	19 17	06 55	08 23	09 51	11 16
64	17 28	18 15	19 11	06 49	08 13	09 35	10 55
62	17 30	18 14	19 06	06 43	08 04	09 22	10 38
60	17 32	18 13	19 01	06 39	07 56	09 11	10 24
N 58	17 33	18 12	18 58	06 35	07 49	09 02	10 12
56	17 34	18 11	18 55	06 31	07 43	08 54	10 01
54	17 36	18 11	18 52	06 28	07 38	08 46	09 52
52	17 37	18 10	18 49	06 25	07 33	08 40	09 44
50	17 38	18 10	18 47	06 23	07 29	08 34	09 37
45	17 40	18 09	18 43	06 17	07 20	08 21	09 21
N 40	17 42	18 09	18 40	06 12	07 12	08 11	09 08
35	17 44	18 09	18 38	06 08	07 05	08 02	08 57
30	17 45	18 09	18 37	06 05	07 00	07 54	08 48
20	17 48	18 10	18 35	05 58	06 50	07 41	08 32
N 10	17 50	18 11	18 36	05 53	06 41	07 29	08 17
0	17 53	18 13	18 38	05 48	06 33	07 18	08 04
S 10	17 55	18 16	18 41	05 43	06 24	07 07	07 51
20	17 58	18 20	18 46	05 37	06 16	06 55	07 37
30	18 02	18 26	18 54	05 31	06 06	06 42	07 21
35	18 03	18 29	18 59	05 28	06 00	06 34	07 11
40	18 06	18 33	19 05	05 24	05 54	06 26	07 01
45	18 08	18 38	19 13	05 19	05 46	06 16	06 48
S 50	18 12	18 44	19 23	05 14	05 37	06 03	06 33
52	18 13	18 47	19 28	05 11	05 33	05 58	06 26
54	18 15	18 51	19 34	05 08	05 29	05 51	06 18
56	18 17	18 54	19 40	05 05	05 24	05 44	06 09
58	18 19	18 59	19 48	05 02	05 18	05 37	05 59
S 60	18 21	19 03	19 56	04 58	05 12	05 28	05 48

	SUN			MOON			
Day	Eqn. of Time 00h	Eqn. of Time 12h	Mer. Pass.	Mer. Pass. Upper	Mer. Pass. Lower	Age	Phase
d	m s	m s	h m	h m	h m	d	%
30	10 00	10 10	11 50	24 22	11 59	14	100
1	10 19	10 29	11 50	00 22	12 44	15	98
2	10 39	10 48	11 49	01 07	13 30	16	95

UT	ARIES GHA	VENUS −4.1 GHA	Dec	MARS +1.2 GHA	Dec	JUPITER −2.6 GHA	Dec	SATURN +0.7 GHA	Dec	STARS Name	SHA	Dec
3 00	12 06.1	220 13.1	N11 53.9	137 30.6	S20 19.5	296 48.5	N21 55.3	163 42.5	S 9 14.9	Acamar	315 18.4	S40 15.0
01	27 08.6	235 12.7	53.0	152 31.3	19.9	311 50.9	55.3	178 44.7	15.0	Achernar	335 26.6	S57 10.2
02	42 11.1	250 12.3	52.1	167 31.9	20.4	326 53.4	55.3	193 46.9	15.1	Acrux	173 10.5	S63 10.2
03	57 13.5	265 12.0 ..	51.3	182 32.6 ..	20.8	341 55.8 ..	55.3	208 49.0 ..	15.2	Adhara	255 12.9	S28 59.2
04	72 16.0	280 11.6	50.4	197 33.2	21.2	356 58.3	55.3	223 51.2	15.3	Aldebaran	290 49.8	N16 32.1
05	87 18.5	295 11.2	49.5	212 33.9	21.6	12 00.7	55.3	238 53.4	15.4			
06	102 20.9	310 10.8	N11 48.6	227 34.5	S20 22.1	27 03.2	N21 55.3	253 55.6	S 9 15.5	Alioth	166 21.7	N55 53.4
W 07	117 23.4	325 10.5	47.8	242 35.2	22.5	42 05.7	55.3	268 57.8	15.6	Alkaid	152 59.7	N49 15.1
E 08	132 25.9	340 10.1	46.9	257 35.8	22.9	57 08.1	55.3	284 00.0	15.8	Al Na'ir	27 44.0	S46 53.9
D 09	147 28.3	355 09.7 ..	46.0	272 36.5 ..	23.3	72 10.6 ..	55.3	299 02.2 ..	15.9	Alnilam	275 46.8	S 1 11.6
N 10	162 30.8	10 09.4	45.1	287 37.1	23.7	87 13.0	55.3	314 04.4	16.0	Alphard	217 56.8	S 8 42.8
E 11	177 33.3	25 09.0	44.2	302 37.8	24.2	102 15.5	55.3	329 06.6	16.1			
S 12	192 35.7	40 08.6	N11 43.4	317 38.4	S20 24.6	117 17.9	N21 55.3	344 08.7	S 9 16.2	Alphecca	126 11.7	N26 40.6
D 13	207 38.2	55 08.3	42.5	332 39.1	25.0	132 20.4	55.3	359 10.9	16.3	Alpheratz	357 43.6	N29 09.9
A 14	222 40.6	70 07.9	41.6	347 39.7	25.4	147 22.8	55.3	14 13.1	16.4	Altair	62 08.6	N 8 54.5
Y 15	237 43.1	85 07.5 ..	40.7	2 40.4 ..	25.8	162 25.3 ..	55.3	29 15.3 ..	16.5	Ankaa	353 15.8	S42 14.0
16	252 45.6	100 07.2	39.8	17 41.0	26.3	177 27.7	55.3	44 17.5	16.6	Antares	112 27.1	S26 27.5
17	267 48.0	115 06.8	38.9	32 41.7	26.7	192 30.2	55.3	59 19.7	16.7			
18	282 50.5	130 06.4	N11 38.1	47 42.3	S20 27.1	207 32.7	N21 55.3	74 21.9	S 9 16.8	Arcturus	145 56.5	N19 07.1
19	297 53.0	145 06.0	37.2	62 42.9	27.5	222 35.1	55.3	89 24.1	16.9	Atria	107 29.6	S69 03.1
20	312 55.4	160 05.7	36.3	77 43.6	27.9	237 37.6	55.3	104 26.2	17.0	Avior	234 18.5	S59 32.8
21	327 57.9	175 05.3 ..	35.4	92 44.2 ..	28.4	252 40.0 ..	55.3	119 28.4 ..	17.1	Bellatrix	278 32.4	N 6 21.7
22	343 00.4	190 04.9	34.5	107 44.9	28.8	267 42.5	55.3	134 30.6	17.2	Betelgeuse	271 01.7	N 7 24.5
23	358 02.8	205 04.6	33.6	122 45.5	29.2	282 44.9	55.3	149 32.8	17.3			
4 00	13 05.3	220 04.2	N11 32.7	137 46.2	S20 29.6	297 47.4	N21 55.3	164 35.0	S 9 17.4	Canopus	263 56.3	S52 41.9
01	28 07.7	235 03.8	31.8	152 46.8	30.0	312 49.9	55.3	179 37.2	17.5	Capella	280 35.0	N46 00.4
02	43 10.2	250 03.5	30.9	167 47.5	30.5	327 52.3	55.3	194 39.4	17.6	Deneb	49 31.6	N45 20.0
03	58 12.7	265 03.1 ..	30.0	182 48.1 ..	30.9	342 54.8 ..	55.3	209 41.6 ..	17.7	Denebola	182 34.5	N14 30.1
04	73 15.1	280 02.7	29.2	197 48.7	31.3	357 57.2	55.3	224 43.8	17.8	Diphda	348 56.0	S17 54.8
05	88 17.6	295 02.4	28.3	212 49.4	31.7	12 59.7	55.3	239 45.9	18.0			
06	103 20.1	310 02.0	N11 27.4	227 50.0	S20 32.1	28 02.2	N21 55.3	254 48.1	S 9 18.1	Dubhe	193 52.9	N61 40.7
T 07	118 22.5	325 01.6	26.5	242 50.7	32.5	43 04.6	55.3	269 50.3	18.2	Elnath	278 13.1	N28 36.9
H 08	133 25.0	340 01.3	25.6	257 51.3	33.0	58 07.1	55.3	284 52.5	18.3	Eltanin	90 46.5	N51 29.7
U 09	148 27.5	355 00.9 ..	24.7	272 51.9 ..	33.4	73 09.5 ..	55.3	299 54.7 ..	18.4	Enif	33 47.4	N 9 56.3
R 10	163 29.9	10 00.5	23.8	287 52.6	33.8	88 12.0	55.3	314 56.9	18.5	Fomalhaut	15 24.2	S29 33.1
S 11	178 32.4	25 00.2	22.9	302 53.2	34.2	103 14.5	55.3	329 59.1	18.6			
D 12	193 34.9	39 59.8	N11 22.0	317 53.9	S20 34.6	118 16.9	N21 55.3	345 01.3	S 9 18.7	Gacrux	172 02.0	S57 11.1
A 13	208 37.3	54 59.4	21.1	332 54.5	35.0	133 19.4	55.3	0 03.4	18.8	Gienah	175 53.1	S17 36.7
Y 14	223 39.8	69 59.1	20.2	347 55.1	35.4	148 21.9	55.3	15 05.6	18.9	Hadar	148 49.2	S60 26.1
15	238 42.2	84 58.7 ..	19.3	2 55.8 ..	35.9	163 24.3 ..	55.3	30 07.8 ..	19.0	Hamal	328 01.0	N23 31.5
16	253 44.7	99 58.3	18.4	17 56.4	36.3	178 26.8	55.3	45 10.0	19.1	Kaus Aust.	83 44.5	S34 22.6
17	268 47.2	114 58.0	17.5	32 57.1	36.7	193 29.3	55.3	60 12.2	19.2			
18	283 49.6	129 57.6	N11 16.6	47 57.7	S20 37.1	208 31.7	N21 55.3	75 14.4	S 9 19.3	Kochab	137 21.0	N74 06.4
19	298 52.1	144 57.2	15.7	62 58.3	37.5	223 34.2	55.2	90 16.6	19.4	Markab	13 38.5	N15 16.7
20	313 54.6	159 56.9	14.8	77 59.0	37.9	238 36.7	55.2	105 18.8	19.5	Menkar	314 15.3	N 4 08.5
21	328 57.0	174 56.5 ..	13.9	92 59.6 ..	38.3	253 39.1 ..	55.2	120 20.9 ..	19.6	Menkent	148 08.5	S36 25.9
22	343 59.5	189 56.1	13.0	108 00.2	38.7	268 41.6	55.2	135 23.1	19.7	Miaplacidus	221 40.3	S69 46.0
23	359 02.0	204 55.8	12.1	123 00.9	39.2	283 44.1	55.2	150 25.3	19.8			
5 00	14 04.4	219 55.4	N11 11.2	138 01.5	S20 39.6	298 46.5	N21 55.2	165 27.5	S 9 19.9	Mirfak	308 40.7	N49 54.3
01	29 06.9	234 55.0	10.3	153 02.1	40.0	313 49.0	55.2	180 29.7	20.1	Nunki	75 58.9	S26 16.7
02	44 09.4	249 54.7	09.4	168 02.8	40.4	328 51.5	55.2	195 31.9	20.2	Peacock	53 19.8	S56 41.6
03	59 11.8	264 54.3 ..	08.5	183 03.4 ..	40.8	343 53.9 ..	55.2	210 34.1 ..	20.3	Pollux	243 28.4	N27 59.5
04	74 14.3	279 53.9	07.6	198 04.0	41.2	358 56.4	55.2	225 36.3	20.4	Procyon	245 00.3	N 5 11.5
05	89 16.7	294 53.6	06.6	213 04.7	41.6	13 58.9	55.2	240 38.4	20.5			
06	104 19.2	309 53.2	N11 05.7	228 05.3	S20 42.0	29 01.3	N21 55.2	255 40.6	S 9 20.6	Rasalhague	96 07.0	N12 33.4
07	119 21.7	324 52.8	04.8	243 06.0	42.4	44 03.8	55.2	270 42.8	20.7	Regulus	207 44.3	N11 54.2
08	134 24.1	339 52.5	03.9	258 06.6	42.8	59 06.3	55.2	285 45.0	20.8	Rigel	281 12.4	S 8 11.1
F 09	149 26.6	354 52.1 ..	03.0	273 07.2 ..	43.3	74 08.7 ..	55.2	300 47.2 ..	20.9	Rigil Kent.	139 53.0	S60 53.3
R 10	164 29.1	9 51.8	02.1	288 07.8	43.7	89 11.2	55.2	315 49.4	21.0	Sabik	102 13.2	S15 44.3
I 11	179 31.5	24 51.4	01.2	303 08.5	44.1	104 13.7	55.2	330 51.6	21.1			
D 12	194 34.0	39 51.0	N11 00.3	318 09.1	S20 44.5	119 16.2	N21 55.2	345 53.8	S 9 21.2	Schedar	349 40.5	N56 36.6
A 13	209 36.5	54 50.7	10 59.4	333 09.7	44.9	134 18.6	55.2	0 55.9	21.3	Shaula	96 22.7	S37 06.7
Y 14	224 38.9	69 50.3	58.4	348 10.4	45.3	149 21.1	55.2	15 58.1	21.4	Sirius	258 34.1	S16 43.3
15	239 41.4	84 49.9 ..	57.5	3 11.0 ..	45.7	164 23.6 ..	55.2	31 00.3 ..	21.5	Spica	158 32.1	S11 13.6
16	254 43.8	99 49.6	56.6	18 11.6	46.1	179 26.1	55.2	46 02.5	21.6	Suhail	222 53.0	S43 28.9
17	269 46.3	114 49.2	55.7	33 12.3	46.5	194 28.5	55.2	61 04.7	21.7			
18	284 48.8	129 48.8	N10 54.8	48 12.9	S20 46.9	209 31.0	N21 55.2	76 06.9	S 9 21.8	Vega	80 39.3	N38 48.2
19	299 51.2	144 48.5	53.9	63 13.5	47.3	224 33.5	55.2	91 09.1	21.9	Zuben'ubi	137 06.2	S16 05.6
20	314 53.7	159 48.1	53.0	78 14.2	47.7	239 36.0	55.2	106 11.2	22.0		SHA	Mer.Pass.
21	329 56.2	174 47.7 ..	52.0	93 14.8 ..	48.1	254 38.4 ..	55.2	121 13.4 ..	22.2	Venus	206 58.9	9 20
22	344 58.6	189 47.4	51.1	108 15.4	48.5	269 40.9	55.2	136 15.6	22.3	Mars	124 40.9	14 48
23	0 01.1	204 47.0	50.2	123 16.0	48.9	284 43.4	55.2	151 17.8	22.4	Jupiter	284 42.1	4 08
Mer.Pass. 23 03.9		v −0.4	d 0.9	v 0.6	d 0.4	v 2.5	d 0.0	v 2.2	d 0.1	Saturn	151 29.7	13 00

UT	SUN GHA	SUN Dec	MOON GHA	v	Dec	d	HP
d h	° ′	° ′	° ′	′	° ′	′	′
3 00	182 44.5	S 4 02.0	332 38.5	13.0	N16 45.7	6.7	54.4
01	197 44.7	03.0	347 10.5	12.9	16 52.4	6.6	54.4
02	212 44.9	04.0	1 42.4	12.9	16 59.0	6.5	54.4
03	227 45.1	.. 04.9	16 14.3	12.8	17 05.5	6.4	54.4
04	242 45.3	05.9	30 46.1	12.9	17 11.9	6.3	54.4
05	257 45.5	06.9	45 18.0	12.8	17 18.2	6.3	54.3
W 06	272 45.7	S 4 07.8	59 49.8	12.8	N17 24.5	6.1	54.3
E 07	287 45.9	08.8	74 21.6	12.8	17 30.6	6.1	54.3
D 08	302 46.1	09.8	88 53.4	12.7	17 36.7	6.0	54.3
N 09	317 46.3	.. 10.7	103 25.1	12.8	17 42.7	6.0	54.3
E 10	332 46.5	11.7	117 56.9	12.7	17 48.7	5.8	54.3
S 11	347 46.6	12.6	132 28.6	12.7	17 54.5	5.8	54.3
D 12	2 46.8	S 4 13.6	147 00.3	12.6	N18 00.3	5.7	54.3
A 13	17 47.0	14.6	161 31.9	12.7	18 06.0	5.6	54.3
Y 14	32 47.2	15.5	176 03.6	12.6	18 11.6	5.5	54.3
15	47 47.4	.. 16.5	190 35.2	12.6	18 17.1	5.4	54.3
16	62 47.6	17.5	205 06.8	12.6	18 22.5	5.3	54.2
17	77 47.8	18.4	219 38.4	12.6	18 27.8	5.3	54.2
18	92 48.0	S 4 19.4	234 10.0	12.5	N18 33.1	5.2	54.2
19	107 48.2	20.4	248 41.5	12.5	18 38.3	5.0	54.2
20	122 48.4	21.3	263 13.0	12.6	18 43.3	5.0	54.2
21	137 48.6	.. 22.3	277 44.6	12.4	18 48.3	4.9	54.2
22	152 48.8	23.2	292 16.0	12.5	18 53.2	4.9	54.2
23	167 49.0	24.2	306 47.5	12.4	18 58.1	4.7	54.2
4 00	182 49.2	S 4 25.2	321 18.9	12.5	N19 02.8	4.6	54.2
01	197 49.3	26.1	335 50.4	12.4	19 07.4	4.6	54.2
02	212 49.5	27.1	350 21.8	12.4	19 12.0	4.5	54.2
03	227 49.7	.. 28.1	4 53.2	12.3	19 16.5	4.4	54.2
04	242 49.9	29.0	19 24.5	12.4	19 20.9	4.2	54.2
05	257 50.1	30.0	33 55.9	12.3	19 25.1	4.2	54.2
T 06	272 50.3	S 4 31.0	48 27.2	12.3	N19 29.3	4.2	54.2
H 07	287 50.5	31.9	62 58.5	12.3	19 33.5	4.0	54.2
U 08	302 50.7	32.9	77 29.8	12.3	19 37.5	3.9	54.2
R 09	317 50.9	.. 33.8	92 01.1	12.2	19 41.4	3.8	54.2
S 10	332 51.1	34.8	106 32.3	12.2	19 45.2	3.8	54.1
D 11	347 51.3	35.8	121 03.5	12.3	19 49.0	3.6	54.1
A 12	2 51.4	S 4 36.7	135 34.8	12.2	N19 52.6	3.6	54.1
Y 13	17 51.6	37.7	150 06.0	12.1	19 56.2	3.5	54.1
14	32 51.8	38.7	164 37.1	12.2	19 59.7	3.4	54.1
15	47 52.0	.. 39.6	179 08.3	12.2	20 03.1	3.2	54.1
16	62 52.2	40.6	193 39.5	12.1	20 06.3	3.2	54.1
17	77 52.4	41.5	208 10.6	12.1	20 09.5	3.1	54.1
18	92 52.6	S 4 42.5	222 41.7	12.1	N20 12.6	3.1	54.1
19	107 52.8	43.5	237 12.8	12.1	20 15.7	2.9	54.1
20	122 53.0	44.4	251 43.9	12.1	20 18.6	2.8	54.1
21	137 53.1	.. 45.4	266 15.0	12.1	20 21.4	2.7	54.1
22	152 53.3	46.4	280 46.0	12.1	20 24.1	2.6	54.1
23	167 53.5	47.3	295 17.1	12.0	20 26.7	2.6	54.1
5 00	182 53.7	S 4 48.3	309 48.1	12.0	N20 29.3	2.4	54.1
01	197 53.9	49.2	324 19.1	12.0	20 31.7	2.4	54.1
02	212 54.1	50.2	338 50.1	12.0	20 34.1	2.2	54.1
03	227 54.3	.. 51.2	353 21.1	11.9	20 36.3	2.2	54.1
04	242 54.5	52.1	7 52.0	12.0	20 38.5	2.0	54.1
05	257 54.7	53.1	22 23.0	12.0	20 40.5	2.0	54.1
F 06	272 54.8	S 4 54.0	36 54.0	11.9	N20 42.5	1.9	54.1
R 07	287 55.0	55.0	51 24.9	11.9	20 44.4	1.8	54.1
I 08	302 55.2	56.0	65 55.8	11.9	20 46.2	1.6	54.1
D 09	317 55.4	.. 56.9	80 26.7	11.9	20 47.8	1.6	54.1
A 10	332 55.6	57.9	94 57.6	11.9	20 49.4	1.5	54.1
Y 11	347 55.8	58.8	109 28.5	11.9	20 50.9	1.4	54.1
12	2 56.0	S 4 59.8	123 59.4	11.8	N20 52.3	1.3	54.1
13	17 56.1	S 5 00.8	138 30.2	11.9	20 53.6	1.2	54.1
14	32 56.3	01.7	153 01.1	11.8	20 54.8	1.1	54.1
15	47 56.5	.. 02.7	167 31.9	11.9	20 55.9	1.0	54.1
16	62 56.7	03.6	182 02.8	11.8	20 56.9	0.9	54.2
17	77 56.9	04.6	196 33.6	11.8	20 57.8	0.8	54.2
18	92 57.1	S 5 05.6	211 04.4	11.8	N20 58.6	0.7	54.2
19	107 57.3	06.5	225 35.2	11.8	20 59.3	0.6	54.2
20	122 57.4	07.5	240 06.0	11.8	20 59.9	0.5	54.2
21	137 57.6	.. 08.4	254 36.8	11.8	21 00.4	0.4	54.2
22	152 57.8	09.4	269 07.6	11.8	21 00.8	0.3	54.2
23	167 58.0	10.4	283 38.4	11.8	N21 01.1	0.3	54.2
	SD 16.0	d 1.0	SD 14.8		14.8		14.8

Lat.	Twilight Naut.	Twilight Civil	Sunrise	Moonrise 3	4	5	6
°	h m	h m	h m	h m	h m	h m	h m
N 72	04 06	05 26	06 34	☐	☐	☐	☐
N 70	04 16	05 28	06 29	15 59	15 16	☐	☐
68	04 24	05 29	06 25	16 40	16 48	17 11	☐
66	04 30	05 30	06 21	17 09	17 27	18 00	18 52
64	04 35	05 31	06 18	17 30	17 54	18 31	19 22
62	04 40	05 31	06 16	17 48	18 15	18 54	19 45
60	04 43	05 32	06 13	18 02	18 33	19 13	20 04
N 58	04 47	05 32	06 11	18 15	18 47	19 28	20 19
56	04 49	05 32	06 10	18 25	18 59	19 41	20 32
54	04 52	05 33	06 08	18 35	19 10	19 53	20 43
52	04 54	05 33	06 06	18 43	19 20	20 03	20 53
50	04 55	05 33	06 05	18 51	19 28	20 12	21 02
45	04 59	05 33	06 02	19 07	19 46	20 31	21 21
N 40	05 01	05 32	05 59	19 21	20 01	20 46	21 36
35	05 03	05 32	05 57	19 32	20 14	21 00	21 49
30	05 04	05 31	05 55	19 42	20 25	21 11	22 00
20	05 04	05 30	05 52	19 59	20 44	21 31	22 20
N 10	05 03	05 27	05 48	20 14	21 00	21 48	22 37
0	05 01	05 25	05 45	20 28	21 16	22 04	22 52
S 10	04 57	05 21	05 42	20 43	21 31	22 20	23 08
20	04 51	05 16	05 39	20 58	21 48	22 37	23 25
30	04 42	05 10	05 34	21 15	22 07	22 57	23 44
35	04 37	05 06	05 32	21 26	22 18	23 09	23 56
40	04 30	05 02	05 29	21 37	22 31	23 22	24 09
45	04 21	04 56	05 26	21 51	22 47	23 38	24 24
S 50	04 10	04 49	05 22	22 08	23 05	23 57	24 43
52	04 04	04 46	05 20	22 16	23 14	24 06	00 06
54	03 58	04 42	05 18	22 25	23 24	24 16	00 16
56	03 52	04 38	05 16	22 35	23 35	24 28	00 28
58	03 44	04 33	05 13	22 47	23 48	24 41	00 41
S 60	03 34	04 28	05 11	23 00	24 03	00 03	00 57

Lat.	Sunset	Twilight Civil	Twilight Naut.	Moonset 3	4	5	6
°	h m	h m	h m	h m	h m	h m	h m
N 72	17 01	18 08	19 28	☐	☐	☐	☐
N 70	17 06	18 07	19 18	12 24	14 46	☐	☐
68	17 11	18 06	19 11	11 43	13 14	14 30	15 17
66	17 14	18 05	19 05	11 16	12 35	13 42	14 30
64	17 17	18 05	19 00	10 55	12 08	13 11	13 59
62	17 20	18 04	18 56	10 38	11 47	12 48	13 36
60	17 23	18 04	18 52	10 24	11 31	12 29	13 18
N 58	17 25	18 04	18 49	10 12	11 16	12 14	13 03
56	17 27	18 03	18 47	10 01	11 04	12 01	12 50
54	17 28	18 03	18 44	09 52	10 54	11 50	12 38
52	17 30	18 03	18 42	09 44	10 44	11 39	12 28
50	17 31	18 03	18 41	09 37	10 36	11 30	12 19
45	17 34	18 04	18 38	09 21	10 18	11 11	12 00
N 40	17 37	18 05	18 35	09 08	10 04	10 56	11 45
35	17 39	18 05	18 34	08 57	09 51	10 43	11 32
30	17 41	18 05	18 33	08 48	09 41	10 31	11 20
20	17 45	18 07	18 33	08 32	09 22	10 12	11 00
N 10	17 49	18 10	18 34	08 17	09 06	09 55	10 43
0	17 52	18 13	18 37	08 04	08 51	09 39	10 27
S 10	17 56	18 16	18 41	07 51	08 36	09 23	10 11
20	17 59	18 21	18 47	07 37	08 20	09 06	09 54
30	18 03	18 27	18 56	07 21	08 02	08 47	09 34
35	18 06	18 31	19 01	07 11	07 51	08 35	09 23
40	18 09	18 36	19 08	07 01	07 39	08 22	09 10
45	18 12	18 42	19 17	06 48	07 25	08 07	08 54
S 50	18 16	18 49	19 29	06 33	07 07	07 48	08 35
52	18 18	18 53	19 34	06 26	06 59	07 39	08 25
54	18 20	18 56	19 40	06 18	06 50	07 29	08 15
56	18 23	19 01	19 47	06 09	06 40	07 17	08 04
58	18 25	19 06	19 56	05 59	06 28	07 04	07 50
S 60	18 28	19 11	20 05	05 48	06 14	06 49	07 34

Day	SUN Eqn. of Time 00^h	SUN Eqn. of Time 12^h	SUN Mer. Pass.	MOON Mer. Pass. Upper	MOON Mer. Pass. Lower	Age	Phase
d	m s	m s	h m	h m	h m	d	%
3	10 58	11 07	11 49	01 53	14 16	17	90
4	11 16	11 25	11 49	02 40	15 04	18	83
5	11 34	11 43	11 48	03 27	15 52	19	76

UT	ARIES GHA	VENUS −4.1 GHA	Dec	MARS +1.2 GHA	Dec	JUPITER −2.6 GHA	Dec	SATURN +0.7 GHA	Dec	Name	SHA	Dec
6 00	15 03.6	219 46.7	N10 49.3	138 16.7	S20 49.3	299 45.9	N21 55.2	166 20.0	S 9 22.5	Acamar	315 18.3	S40 15.0
01	30 06.0	234 46.3	48.4	153 17.3	49.8	314 48.3	55.2	181 22.2	22.6	Achernar	335 26.6	S57 10.2
02	45 08.5	249 45.9	.. 47.4	168 17.9	50.2	329 50.8	55.2	196 24.4	22.7	Acrux	173 10.5	S63 10.2
03	60 11.0	264 45.6	.. 46.5	183 18.6	.. 50.6	344 53.3	.. 55.2	211 26.5	.. 22.8	Adhara	255 12.9	S28 59.2
04	75 13.4	279 45.2	45.6	198 19.2	51.0	359 55.8	55.2	226 28.7	22.9	Aldebaran	290 49.7	N16 32.1
05	90 15.9	294 44.8	44.7	213 19.8	51.4	14 58.3	55.2	241 30.9	23.0			
S 06	105 18.3	309 44.5	N10 43.8	228 20.4	S20 51.8	30 00.7	N21 55.2	256 33.1	S 9 23.1	Alioth	166 21.7	N55 53.4
A 07	120 20.8	324 44.1	42.8	243 21.1	52.2	45 03.2	55.2	271 35.3	23.2	Alkaid	152 59.7	N49 15.1
T 08	135 23.3	339 43.8	41.9	258 21.7	52.6	60 05.7	55.2	286 37.5	23.3	Al Na'ir	27 44.0	S46 53.9
U 09	150 25.7	354 43.4	.. 41.0	273 22.3	.. 53.0	75 08.2	.. 55.1	301 39.7	.. 23.4	Alnilam	275 46.7	S 1 11.6
R 10	165 28.2	9 43.0	40.1	288 22.9	53.4	90 10.6	55.1	316 41.8	23.5	Alphard	217 56.7	S 8 42.8
D 11	180 30.7	24 42.7	39.1	303 23.6	53.8	105 13.1	55.1	331 44.0	23.6			
A 12	195 33.1	39 42.3	N10 38.2	318 24.2	S20 54.2	120 15.6	N21 55.1	346 46.2	S 9 23.7	Alphecca	126 11.7	N26 40.5
Y 13	210 35.6	54 41.9	37.3	333 24.8	54.6	135 18.1	55.1	1 48.4	23.8	Alpheratz	357 43.6	N29 09.9
14	225 38.1	69 41.6	36.3	348 25.4	55.0	150 20.6	55.1	16 50.6	23.9	Altair	62 08.6	N 8 54.5
15	240 40.5	84 41.2	.. 35.4	3 26.1	.. 55.4	165 23.1	.. 55.1	31 52.8	.. 24.0	Ankaa	353 15.7	S42 14.1
16	255 43.0	99 40.9	34.5	18 26.7	55.8	180 25.5	55.1	46 55.0	24.2	Antares	112 27.1	S26 27.5
17	270 45.5	114 40.5	33.6	33 27.3	56.2	195 28.0	55.1	61 57.1	24.3			
18	285 47.9	129 40.1	N10 32.6	48 27.9	S20 56.6	210 30.5	N21 55.1	76 59.3	S 9 24.4	Arcturus	145 56.5	N19 07.1
19	300 50.4	144 39.8	31.7	63 28.5	57.0	225 33.0	55.1	92 01.5	24.5	Atria	107 29.6	S69 03.1
20	315 52.8	159 39.4	30.8	78 29.2	57.4	240 35.5	55.1	107 03.7	24.6	Avior	234 18.4	S59 32.8
21	330 55.3	174 39.0	.. 29.8	93 29.8	.. 57.8	255 38.0	.. 55.1	122 05.9	.. 24.7	Bellatrix	278 32.4	N 6 21.7
22	345 57.8	189 38.7	28.9	108 30.4	58.2	270 40.4	55.1	137 08.1	24.8	Betelgeuse	271 01.7	N 7 24.5
23	1 00.2	204 38.3	28.0	123 31.0	58.6	285 42.9	55.1	152 10.3	24.9			
7 00	16 02.7	219 38.0	N10 27.0	138 31.7	S20 59.0	300 45.4	N21 55.1	167 12.4	S 9 25.0	Canopus	263 56.3	S52 41.9
01	31 05.2	234 37.6	26.1	153 32.3	59.4	315 47.9	55.1	182 14.6	25.1	Capella	280 34.9	N46 00.4
02	46 07.6	249 37.2	25.2	168 32.9	20 59.8	330 50.4	55.1	197 16.8	25.2	Deneb	49 31.6	N45 20.0
03	61 10.1	264 36.9	.. 24.2	183 33.5	21 00.1	345 52.9	.. 55.1	212 19.0	.. 25.3	Denebola	182 34.5	N14 30.0
04	76 12.6	279 36.5	23.3	198 34.1	00.5	0 55.4	55.1	227 21.2	25.4	Diphda	348 56.0	S17 54.8
05	91 15.0	294 36.2	22.4	213 34.8	00.9	15 57.9	55.1	242 23.4	25.5			
S 06	106 17.5	309 35.8	N10 21.4	228 35.4	S21 01.3	31 00.3	N21 55.1	257 25.6	S 9 25.6	Dubhe	193 52.9	N61 40.7
U 07	121 20.0	324 35.4	20.5	243 36.0	01.7	46 02.8	55.1	272 27.7	25.7	Elnath	278 13.1	N28 36.9
N 08	136 22.4	339 35.1	19.5	258 36.6	02.1	61 05.3	55.1	287 29.9	25.8	Eltanin	90 46.5	N51 29.7
D 09	151 24.9	354 34.7	.. 18.6	273 37.2	.. 02.5	76 07.8	.. 55.1	302 32.1	.. 25.9	Enif	33 47.4	N 9 56.3
A 10	166 27.3	9 34.4	17.7	288 37.8	02.9	91 10.3	55.1	317 34.3	26.0	Fomalhaut	15 24.2	S29 33.1
Y 11	181 29.8	24 34.0	16.7	303 38.5	03.3	106 12.8	55.1	332 36.5	26.2			
12	196 32.3	39 33.6	N10 15.8	318 39.1	S21 03.7	121 15.3	N21 55.1	347 38.7	S 9 26.3	Gacrux	172 02.0	S57 11.0
13	211 34.7	54 33.3	14.8	333 39.7	04.1	136 17.8	55.0	2 40.9	26.4	Gienah	175 53.1	S17 36.7
14	226 37.2	69 32.9	13.9	348 40.3	04.5	151 20.3	55.0	17 43.0	26.5	Hadar	148 49.2	S60 26.1
15	241 39.7	84 32.6	.. 13.0	3 40.9	.. 04.9	166 22.7	.. 55.0	32 45.2	.. 26.6	Hamal	328 01.0	N23 31.5
16	256 42.1	99 32.2	12.0	18 41.5	05.3	181 25.2	55.0	47 47.4	26.7	Kaus Aust.	83 44.5	S34 22.6
17	271 44.6	114 31.8	11.1	33 42.2	05.7	196 27.7	55.0	62 49.6	26.8			
18	286 47.1	129 31.5	N10 10.1	48 42.8	S21 06.1	211 30.2	N21 55.0	77 51.8	S 9 26.9	Kochab	137 21.0	N74 06.3
19	301 49.5	144 31.1	09.2	63 43.4	06.4	226 32.7	55.0	92 54.0	27.0	Markab	13 38.5	N15 16.7
20	316 52.0	159 30.8	08.2	78 44.0	06.8	241 35.2	55.0	107 56.1	27.1	Menkar	314 15.3	N 4 08.5
21	331 54.4	174 30.4	.. 07.3	93 44.6	.. 07.2	256 37.7	.. 55.0	122 58.3	.. 27.2	Menkent	148 08.5	S36 25.9
22	346 56.9	189 30.0	06.3	108 45.2	07.6	271 40.2	55.0	138 00.5	27.3	Miaplacidus	221 46.3	S69 46.0
23	1 59.4	204 29.7	05.4	123 45.8	08.0	286 42.7	55.0	153 02.7	27.4			
8 00	17 01.8	219 29.3	N10 04.5	138 46.5	S21 08.4	301 45.2	N21 55.0	168 04.9	S 9 27.5	Mirfak	308 40.6	N49 54.3
01	32 04.3	234 29.0	03.5	153 47.1	08.8	316 47.7	55.0	183 07.1	27.6	Nunki	75 58.9	S26 16.7
02	47 06.8	249 28.6	02.6	168 47.7	09.2	331 50.2	55.0	198 09.3	27.7	Peacock	53 19.8	S56 41.6
03	62 09.2	264 28.3	.. 01.6	183 48.3	.. 09.6	346 52.7	.. 55.0	213 11.4	.. 27.8	Pollux	243 28.4	N27 59.5
04	77 11.7	279 27.9	10 00.7	198 48.9	10.0	1 55.2	55.0	228 13.6	27.9	Procyon	245 00.3	N 5 11.5
05	92 14.2	294 27.5	9 59.7	213 49.5	10.3	16 57.7	55.0	243 15.8	28.0			
M 06	107 16.6	309 27.2	N 9 58.8	228 50.1	S21 10.7	32 00.2	N21 55.0	258 18.0	S 9 28.2	Rasalhague	96 07.0	N12 33.3
O 07	122 19.1	324 26.8	57.8	243 50.7	11.1	47 02.7	55.0	273 20.2	28.3	Regulus	207 44.3	N11 54.2
N 08	137 21.6	339 26.5	56.9	258 51.4	11.5	62 05.2	55.0	288 22.4	28.4	Rigel	281 12.4	S 8 11.1
D 09	152 24.0	354 26.1	.. 55.9	273 52.0	.. 11.9	77 07.7	.. 55.0	303 24.5	.. 28.5	Rigil Kent.	139 53.0	S60 53.3
A 10	167 26.5	9 25.7	54.9	288 52.6	12.3	92 10.2	55.0	318 26.7	28.6	Sabik	102 13.2	S15 44.3
Y 11	182 28.9	24 25.4	54.0	303 53.2	12.7	107 12.7	54.9	333 28.9	28.7			
12	197 31.4	39 25.0	N 9 53.0	318 53.8	S21 13.1	122 15.2	N21 54.9	348 31.1	S 9 28.8	Schedar	349 40.5	N56 36.6
13	212 33.9	54 24.7	52.1	333 54.4	13.4	137 17.7	54.9	3 33.3	28.9	Shaula	96 22.7	S37 06.7
14	227 36.3	69 24.3	51.1	348 55.0	13.8	152 20.2	54.9	18 35.5	29.0	Sirius	258 34.1	S16 43.9
15	242 38.8	84 24.0	.. 50.2	3 55.6	.. 14.2	167 22.7	.. 54.9	33 37.6	.. 29.1	Spica	158 32.1	S11 13.6
16	257 41.3	99 23.6	49.2	18 56.2	14.6	182 25.2	54.9	48 39.8	29.2	Suhail	222 53.0	S43 28.9
17	272 43.7	114 23.2	48.3	33 56.8	15.0	197 27.7	54.9	63 42.0	29.3			
18	287 46.2	129 22.9	N 9 47.3	48 57.4	S21 15.4	212 30.2	N21 54.9	78 44.2	S 9 29.4	Vega	80 39.3	N38 48.2
19	302 48.7	144 22.5	46.3	63 58.0	15.8	227 32.7	54.9	93 46.4	29.5	Zuben'ubi	137 06.2	S16 05.6
20	317 51.1	159 22.2	45.4	78 58.7	16.1	242 35.2	54.9	108 48.6	29.6			
21	332 53.6	174 21.8	.. 44.4	93 59.3	.. 16.5	257 37.7	.. 54.9	123 50.7	.. 29.7		SHA	Mer. Pass.
22	347 56.1	189 21.5	43.5	108 59.9	16.9	272 40.2	54.9	138 52.9	29.8	Venus	203 55.3	
23	2 58.5	204 21.1	42.5	124 00.5	17.3	287 42.7	54.9	153 55.1	29.9	Mars	122 29.0	14 45
Mer. Pass.	22 52.1	v −0.4	d 0.9	v 0.6	d 0.4	v 2.5	d 0.0	v 2.2	d 0.1	Jupiter	284 42.7	3 56
										Saturn	151 09.7	12 49

SUN and MOON

UT	SUN GHA	SUN Dec	MOON GHA	v	MOON Dec	d	HP
d h	° ′	° ′	° ′	′	° ′	′	′
6 00	182 58.2	S 5 11.3	298 09.2	11.8	N21 01.4	0.1	54.2
01	197 58.4	12.3	312 40.0	11.7	21 01.5	0.0	54.2
02	212 58.5	13.2	327 10.7	11.8	21 01.5	0.1	54.2
03	227 58.7	.. 14.2	341 41.5	11.7	21 01.4	0.1	54.2
04	242 58.9	15.1	356 12.2	11.8	21 01.3	0.3	54.2
05	257 59.1	16.1	10 43.0	11.7	21 01.0	0.4	54.2
S 06	272 59.3	S 5 17.1	25 13.7	11.7	N21 00.6	0.5	54.2
A 07	287 59.5	18.0	39 44.4	11.8	21 00.1	0.5	54.2
T 08	302 59.6	19.0	54 15.2	11.7	20 59.6	0.7	54.2
U 09	317 59.8	.. 19.9	68 45.9	11.7	20 58.9	0.7	54.3
R 10	333 00.0	20.9	83 16.6	11.8	20 58.2	0.9	54.3
D 11	348 00.2	21.9	97 47.4	11.7	20 57.3	1.0	54.3
A 12	3 00.4	S 5 22.8	112 18.1	11.7	N20 56.3	1.0	54.3
Y 13	18 00.6	23.8	126 48.8	11.7	20 55.3	1.2	54.3
14	33 00.7	24.7	141 19.5	11.7	20 54.1	1.2	54.3
15	48 00.9	.. 25.7	155 50.2	11.7	20 52.9	1.4	54.3
16	63 01.1	26.6	170 20.9	11.8	20 51.5	1.4	54.3
17	78 01.3	27.6	184 51.7	11.7	20 50.1	1.6	54.3
18	93 01.5	S 5 28.5	199 22.4	11.7	N20 48.5	1.6	54.3
19	108 01.6	29.5	213 53.1	11.7	20 46.9	1.8	54.4
20	123 01.8	30.5	228 23.8	11.7	20 45.1	1.8	54.4
21	138 02.0	.. 31.4	242 54.5	11.7	20 43.3	1.9	54.4
22	153 02.2	32.4	257 25.2	11.7	20 41.4	2.1	54.4
23	168 02.4	33.3	271 55.9	11.7	20 39.3	2.1	54.4
7 00	183 02.5	S 5 34.3	286 26.6	11.8	N20 37.2	2.3	54.4
01	198 02.7	35.2	300 57.4	11.7	20 34.9	2.3	54.4
02	213 02.9	36.2	315 28.1	11.7	20 32.6	2.4	54.4
03	228 03.1	.. 37.2	329 58.8	11.7	20 30.2	2.5	54.5
04	243 03.3	38.1	344 29.5	11.7	20 27.7	2.7	54.5
05	258 03.4	39.1	359 00.2	11.8	20 25.0	2.7	54.5
S 06	273 03.6	S 5 40.0	13 31.0	11.7	N20 22.3	2.8	54.5
U 07	288 03.8	41.0	28 01.7	11.7	20 19.5	2.9	54.5
N 08	303 04.0	41.9	42 32.4	11.8	20 16.6	3.0	54.5
D 09	318 04.2	.. 42.9	57 03.2	11.7	20 13.6	3.1	54.6
A 10	333 04.3	43.8	71 33.9	11.7	20 10.5	3.2	54.6
Y 11	348 04.5	44.8	86 04.6	11.8	20 07.3	3.3	54.6
12	3 04.7	S 5 45.7	100 35.4	11.7	N20 04.0	3.4	54.6
13	18 04.9	46.7	115 06.1	11.8	20 00.6	3.5	54.6
14	33 05.0	47.7	129 36.9	11.8	19 57.1	3.6	54.6
15	48 05.2	.. 48.6	144 07.7	11.7	19 53.5	3.7	54.7
16	63 05.4	49.6	158 38.4	11.8	19 49.8	3.8	54.7
17	78 05.6	50.5	173 09.2	11.8	19 46.0	3.9	54.7
18	93 05.7	S 5 51.5	187 40.0	11.7	N19 42.1	3.9	54.7
19	108 05.9	52.4	202 10.7	11.8	19 38.2	4.1	54.7
20	123 06.1	53.4	216 41.5	11.8	19 34.1	4.1	54.7
21	138 06.3	.. 54.3	231 12.3	11.8	19 30.0	4.3	54.8
22	153 06.4	55.3	245 43.1	11.8	19 25.7	4.4	54.8
23	168 06.6	56.2	260 13.9	11.8	19 21.3	4.4	54.8
8 00	183 06.8	S 5 57.2	274 44.7	11.8	N19 16.9	4.5	54.8
01	198 07.0	58.1	289 15.5	11.9	19 12.4	4.7	54.8
02	213 07.1	59.1	303 46.4	11.8	19 07.7	4.7	54.9
03	228 07.3	6 00.0	318 17.2	11.8	19 03.0	4.8	54.9
04	243 07.5	01.0	332 48.0	11.9	18 58.2	4.9	54.9
05	258 07.7	02.0	347 18.9	11.8	18 53.3	5.0	54.9
M 06	273 07.8	S 6 02.9	1 49.7	11.9	N18 48.3	5.1	54.9
O 07	288 08.0	03.9	16 20.6	11.8	18 43.2	5.2	55.0
N 08	303 08.2	04.8	30 51.4	11.9	18 38.0	5.3	55.0
D 09	318 08.4	.. 05.8	45 22.3	11.9	18 32.7	5.4	55.0
A 10	333 08.5	06.7	59 53.2	11.8	18 27.3	5.5	55.0
Y 11	348 08.7	07.7	74 24.0	11.9	18 21.8	5.5	55.1
12	3 08.9	S 6 08.6	88 54.9	11.9	N18 16.3	5.7	55.1
13	18 09.1	09.6	103 25.8	11.9	18 10.6	5.7	55.1
14	33 09.2	10.5	117 56.7	11.9	18 04.9	5.8	55.1
15	48 09.4	.. 11.5	132 27.6	11.9	17 59.1	6.0	55.2
16	63 09.6	12.4	146 58.5	12.0	17 53.1	6.0	55.2
17	78 09.7	13.4	161 29.5	11.9	17 47.1	6.1	55.2
18	93 09.9	S 6 14.3	176 00.4	11.9	N17 41.0	6.2	55.2
19	108 10.1	15.3	190 31.3	12.0	17 34.8	6.2	55.3
20	123 10.3	16.2	205 02.3	11.9	17 28.6	6.4	55.3
21	138 10.4	.. 17.2	219 33.2	12.0	17 22.2	6.5	55.3
22	153 10.6	18.1	234 04.2	11.9	17 15.7	6.5	55.3
23	168 10.8	19.1	248 35.1	12.0	N17 09.2	6.6	55.4
	SD 16.0	d 1.0	SD 14.8		14.9		15.0

Moonrise

Lat.	Twilight Naut.	Twilight Civil	Sunrise	Moonrise 6	7	8	9
°	h m	h m	h m	h m	h m	h m	h m
N 72	04 20	05 40	06 48	▨	▨	19 17	21 46
N 70	04 28	05 40	06 41	▨	18 19	20 25	22 16
68	04 35	05 40	06 36	18 05	19 27	21 01	22 38
66	04 40	05 40	06 31	18 52	20 03	21 26	22 56
64	04 44	05 39	06 27	19 22	20 29	21 46	23 10
62	04 48	05 39	06 24	19 45	20 49	22 02	23 21
60	04 51	05 39	06 21	20 04	21 05	22 15	23 31
N 58	04 53	05 39	06 18	20 19	21 19	22 27	23 40
56	04 55	05 38	06 16	20 32	21 31	22 37	23 48
54	04 57	05 38	06 13	20 43	21 41	22 45	23 54
52	04 59	05 38	06 11	20 53	21 50	22 53	24 01
50	05 00	05 37	06 10	21 02	21 58	23 00	24 06
45	05 02	05 36	06 06	21 21	22 16	23 15	24 18
N 40	05 04	05 35	06 02	21 36	22 30	23 27	24 28
35	05 05	05 34	06 00	21 49	22 42	23 38	24 36
30	05 05	05 33	05 57	22 00	22 52	23 47	24 43
20	05 05	05 30	05 52	22 20	23 10	24 03	00 03
N 10	05 03	05 27	05 48	22 37	23 26	24 16	00 16
0	05 00	05 24	05 44	22 52	23 41	24 29	00 29
S 10	04 55	05 19	05 40	23 08	23 55	24 42	00 42
20	04 48	05 14	05 36	23 25	24 11	00 11	00 55
30	04 38	05 07	05 31	23 44	24 29	00 29	01 11
35	04 32	05 02	05 28	23 56	24 39	00 39	01 20
40	04 24	04 57	05 24	24 09	00 09	00 51	01 30
45	04 15	04 50	05 20	24 24	00 24	01 05	01 42
S 50	04 03	04 42	05 15	24 43	00 43	01 22	01 57
52	03 57	04 39	05 13	00 06	00 52	01 30	02 03
54	03 50	04 34	05 11	00 16	01 02	01 39	02 11
56	03 43	04 30	05 08	00 28	01 13	01 49	02 19
58	03 34	04 24	05 05	00 41	01 26	02 01	02 29
S 60	03 24	04 18	05 01	00 57	01 41	02 14	02 39

Moonset

Lat.	Sunset	Twilight Civil	Twilight Naut.	Moonset 6	7	8	9
°	h m	h m	h m	h m	h m	h m	h m
N 72	16 46	17 53	19 12	▨	▨	17 27	16 39
N 70	16 52	17 53	19 04	▨	16 45	16 19	16 08
68	16 58	17 54	18 58	15 17	15 36	15 42	15 44
66	17 03	17 54	18 53	14 30	14 59	15 16	15 26
64	17 07	17 54	18 49	13 59	14 33	14 56	15 11
62	17 10	17 55	18 46	13 36	14 13	14 39	14 58
60	17 14	17 55	18 43	13 18	13 56	14 25	14 48
N 58	17 16	17 55	18 41	13 03	13 42	14 14	14 38
56	17 19	17 56	18 39	12 50	13 30	14 03	14 30
54	17 21	17 56	18 37	12 38	13 20	13 54	14 23
52	17 23	17 57	18 36	12 28	13 10	13 46	14 16
50	17 25	17 57	18 34	12 19	13 02	13 39	14 10
45	17 29	17 58	18 32	12 00	12 44	13 23	13 58
N 40	17 32	17 59	18 31	11 45	12 29	13 10	13 47
35	17 35	18 01	18 30	11 32	12 17	12 59	13 38
30	17 38	18 02	18 30	11 20	12 06	12 49	13 30
20	17 43	18 05	18 30	11 00	11 47	12 32	13 16
N 10	17 47	18 08	18 32	10 43	11 31	12 18	13 04
0	17 51	18 12	18 36	10 27	11 16	12 04	12 52
S 10	17 55	18 16	18 41	10 11	11 00	11 50	12 40
20	18 00	18 22	18 48	09 54	10 44	11 35	12 28
30	18 05	18 29	18 58	09 34	10 25	11 18	12 14
35	18 08	18 34	19 04	09 23	10 14	11 08	12 05
40	18 12	18 39	19 12	09 10	10 01	10 57	11 56
45	18 16	18 46	19 22	08 54	09 46	10 44	11 45
S 50	18 21	18 54	19 34	08 35	09 28	10 27	11 31
52	18 23	18 58	19 40	08 25	09 19	10 19	11 25
54	18 26	19 02	19 47	08 15	09 09	10 11	11 18
56	18 29	19 07	19 55	08 04	08 58	10 01	11 10
58	18 32	19 13	20 04	07 50	08 46	09 50	11 01
S 60	18 35	19 19	20 14	07 34	08 31	09 37	10 51

SUN / MOON

Day	Eqn. of Time 00h	Eqn. of Time 12h	Mer. Pass.	Mer. Pass. Upper	Mer. Pass. Lower	Age	Phase
d	m s	m s	h m	h m	h m	d	%
6	11 52	12 01	11 48	04 16	16 40	20	67
7	12 10	12 18	11 48	05 04	17 28	21	58
8	12 27	12 35	11 47	05 52	18 17	22	48

UT	ARIES GHA	VENUS −4.1 GHA	Dec	MARS +1.2 GHA	Dec	JUPITER −2.6 GHA	Dec	SATURN +0.7 GHA	Dec	STARS Name	SHA	Dec
9 00	18 01.0	219 20.8	N 9 41.5	139 01.1	S21 17.7	302 45.2	N21 54.9	168 57.3	S 9 30.0	Acamar	315 18.3	S40 15.0
01	33 03.4	234 20.4	40.6	154 01.7	18.0	317 47.7	54.9	183 59.5	30.2	Achernar	335 26.5	S57 10.2
02	48 05.9	249 20.0	39.6	169 02.3	18.4	332 50.2	54.9	199 01.7	30.3	Acrux	173 10.5	S63 10.2
03	63 08.4	264 19.7	.. 38.7	184 02.9	.. 18.8	347 52.7	.. 54.9	214 03.8	.. 30.4	Adhara	255 12.9	S28 59.2
04	78 10.8	279 19.3	37.7	199 03.5	19.2	2 55.2	54.9	229 06.0	30.5	Aldebaran	290 49.7	N16 32.1
05	93 13.3	294 19.0	36.7	214 04.1	19.6	17 57.7	54.9	244 08.2	30.6			
06	108 15.8	309 18.6	N 9 35.8	229 04.7	S21 20.0	33 00.2	N21 54.8	259 10.4	S 9 30.7	Alioth	166 21.7	N55 53.4
07	123 18.2	324 18.3	34.8	244 05.3	20.3	48 02.7	54.8	274 12.6	30.8	Alkaid	152 59.7	N49 15.1
T 08	138 20.7	339 17.9	33.8	259 05.9	20.7	63 05.2	54.8	289 14.8	30.9	Al Na'ir	27 44.0	S46 53.9
U 09	153 23.2	354 17.5	.. 32.9	274 06.5	.. 21.1	78 07.7	.. 54.8	304 16.9	.. 31.0	Alnilam	275 46.7	S 1 11.6
E 10	168 25.6	9 17.2	31.9	289 07.1	21.5	93 10.2	54.8	319 19.1	31.1	Alphard	217 56.7	S 8 42.8
S 11	183 28.1	24 16.8	30.9	304 07.7	21.9	108 12.7	54.8	334 21.3	31.2			
D 12	198 30.5	39 16.5	N 9 30.0	319 08.3	S21 22.2	123 15.3	N21 54.8	349 23.5	S 9 31.3	Alphecca	126 11.7	N26 40.5
A 13	213 33.0	54 16.1	29.0	334 08.9	22.6	138 17.8	54.8	4 25.7	31.4	Alpheratz	357 43.6	N29 09.9
Y 14	228 35.5	69 15.8	28.0	349 09.5	23.0	153 20.3	54.8	19 27.9	31.5	Altair	62 08.7	N 8 54.5
15	243 37.9	84 15.4	.. 27.1	4 10.1	.. 23.4	168 22.8	.. 54.8	34 30.0	.. 31.6	Ankaa	353 15.7	S42 14.1
16	258 40.4	99 15.1	26.1	19 10.7	23.7	183 25.3	54.8	49 32.2	31.7	Antares	112 27.1	S26 27.5
17	273 42.9	114 14.7	25.1	34 11.3	24.1	198 27.8	54.8	64 34.4	31.8			
18	288 45.3	129 14.4	N 9 24.1	49 11.9	S21 24.5	213 30.3	N21 54.8	79 36.6	S 9 31.9	Arcturus	145 56.5	N19 07.1
19	303 47.8	144 14.0	23.2	64 12.5	24.9	228 32.8	54.8	94 38.8	32.0	Atria	107 29.6	S69 03.1
20	318 50.3	159 13.6	22.2	79 13.1	25.3	243 35.3	54.8	109 41.0	32.2	Avior	234 18.4	S59 32.8
21	333 52.7	174 13.3	.. 21.2	94 13.7	.. 25.6	258 37.8	.. 54.8	124 43.1	.. 32.3	Bellatrix	278 32.4	N 6 21.7
22	348 55.2	189 12.9	20.3	109 14.3	26.0	273 40.4	54.8	139 45.3	32.4	Betelgeuse	271 01.7	N 7 24.5
23	3 57.7	204 12.6	19.3	124 14.9	26.4	288 42.9	54.8	154 47.5	32.5			
10 00	19 00.1	219 12.2	N 9 18.3	139 15.5	S21 26.8	303 45.4	N21 54.7	169 49.7	S 9 32.6	Canopus	263 56.2	S52 41.9
01	34 02.6	234 11.9	17.3	154 16.1	27.1	318 47.9	54.7	184 51.9	32.7	Capella	280 34.9	N46 00.4
02	49 05.0	249 11.5	16.4	169 16.7	27.5	333 50.4	54.7	199 54.1	32.8	Deneb	49 31.6	N45 20.0
03	64 07.5	264 11.2	.. 15.4	184 17.3	.. 27.9	348 52.9	.. 54.7	214 56.2	.. 32.9	Denebola	182 34.4	N14 30.0
04	79 10.0	279 10.8	14.4	199 17.9	28.3	3 55.4	54.7	229 58.4	33.0	Diphda	348 56.0	S17 54.8
05	94 12.4	294 10.5	13.4	214 18.5	28.6	18 58.0	54.7	245 00.6	33.1			
06	109 14.9	309 10.1	N 9 12.5	229 19.1	S21 29.0	34 00.5	N21 54.7	260 02.8	S 9 33.2	Dubhe	193 52.8	N61 40.7
W 07	124 17.4	324 09.8	11.5	244 19.7	29.4	49 03.0	54.7	275 05.0	33.3	Elnath	278 13.1	N28 36.9
E 08	139 19.8	339 09.4	10.5	259 20.3	29.7	64 05.5	54.7	290 07.1	33.4	Eltanin	90 46.5	N51 29.7
D 09	154 22.3	354 09.0	.. 09.5	274 20.9	.. 30.1	79 08.0	.. 54.7	305 09.3	.. 33.5	Enif	33 47.4	N 9 56.3
N 10	169 24.8	9 08.7	08.5	289 21.5	30.5	94 10.5	54.7	320 11.5	33.6	Fomalhaut	15 24.2	S29 33.1
E 11	184 27.2	24 08.3	07.6	304 22.1	30.9	109 13.1	54.7	335 13.7	33.7			
S 12	199 29.7	39 08.0	N 9 06.6	319 22.7	S21 31.2	124 15.6	N21 54.7	350 15.9	S 9 33.8	Gacrux	172 02.0	S57 11.0
D 13	214 32.2	54 07.6	05.6	334 23.3	31.6	139 18.1	54.7	5 18.1	33.9	Gienah	175 53.1	S17 36.7
A 14	229 34.6	69 07.3	04.6	349 23.9	32.0	154 20.6	54.7	20 20.2	34.1	Hadar	148 49.2	S60 26.1
Y 15	244 37.1	84 06.9	.. 03.6	4 24.5	.. 32.3	169 23.1	.. 54.6	35 22.4	.. 34.2	Hamal	328 01.0	N23 31.5
16	259 39.5	99 06.6	02.7	19 25.1	32.7	184 25.6	54.6	50 24.6	34.3	Kaus Aust.	83 44.5	S34 22.6
17	274 42.0	114 06.2	01.7	34 25.7	33.1	199 28.2	54.6	65 26.8	34.4			
18	289 44.5	129 05.9	N 9 00.7	49 26.2	S21 33.5	214 30.7	N21 54.6	80 29.0	S 9 34.5	Kochab	137 21.1	N74 06.3
19	304 46.9	144 05.5	8 59.7	64 26.8	33.8	229 33.2	54.6	95 31.2	34.6	Markab	13 38.5	N15 16.7
20	319 49.4	159 05.2	58.7	79 27.4	34.2	244 35.7	54.6	110 33.3	34.7	Menkar	314 15.3	N 4 08.5
21	334 51.9	174 04.8	.. 57.7	94 28.0	.. 34.6	259 38.2	.. 54.6	125 35.5	.. 34.8	Menkent	148 08.5	S36 25.9
22	349 54.3	189 04.5	56.7	109 28.6	34.9	274 40.8	54.6	140 37.7	34.9	Miaplacidus	221 40.2	S69 46.0
23	4 56.8	204 04.1	55.8	124 29.2	35.3	289 43.3	54.6	155 39.9	35.0			
11 00	19 59.3	219 03.8	N 8 54.8	139 29.8	S21 35.7	304 45.8	N21 54.6	170 42.1	S 9 35.1	Mirfak	308 40.6	N49 54.3
01	35 01.7	234 03.4	53.8	154 30.4	36.0	319 48.3	54.6	185 44.2	35.2	Nunki	75 58.9	S26 16.7
02	50 04.2	249 03.1	52.8	169 31.0	36.4	334 50.9	54.6	200 46.4	35.3	Peacock	53 19.8	S56 41.7
03	65 06.6	264 02.7	.. 51.8	184 31.6	.. 36.8	349 53.4	.. 54.6	215 48.6	.. 35.4	Pollux	243 28.4	N27 59.5
04	80 09.1	279 02.3	50.8	199 32.2	37.1	4 55.9	54.6	230 50.8	35.5	Procyon	245 00.3	N 5 11.5
05	95 11.6	294 02.0	49.8	214 32.7	37.5	19 58.4	54.6	245 53.0	35.6			
06	110 14.0	309 01.6	N 8 48.8	229 33.3	S21 37.9	35 00.9	N21 54.5	260 55.2	S 9 35.7	Rasalhague	96 07.0	N12 33.3
07	125 16.5	324 01.3	47.9	244 33.9	38.2	50 03.5	54.5	275 57.3	35.8	Regulus	207 44.2	N11 54.2
T 08	140 19.0	339 00.9	46.9	259 34.5	38.6	65 06.0	54.5	290 59.5	35.9	Rigel	281 12.3	S 8 11.2
H 09	155 21.4	354 00.6	.. 45.9	274 35.1	.. 39.0	80 08.5	.. 54.5	306 01.7	.. 36.1	Rigil Kent.	139 53.0	S60 53.3
U 10	170 23.9	9 00.2	44.9	289 35.7	39.3	95 11.1	54.5	321 03.9	36.2	Sabik	102 13.3	S15 44.3
R 11	185 26.4	23 59.9	43.9	304 36.3	39.7	110 13.6	54.5	336 06.1	36.3			
S 12	200 28.8	38 59.5	N 8 42.9	319 36.9	S21 40.1	125 16.1	N21 54.5	351 08.2	S 9 36.4	Schedar	349 40.5	N56 36.6
D 13	215 31.3	53 59.2	41.9	334 37.4	40.4	140 18.6	54.5	6 10.4	36.5	Shaula	96 22.7	S37 06.7
A 14	230 33.8	68 58.8	40.9	349 38.0	40.8	155 21.2	54.5	21 12.6	36.6	Sirius	258 34.1	S16 43.9
Y 15	245 36.2	83 58.5	.. 39.9	4 38.6	.. 41.1	170 23.7	.. 54.5	36 14.8	.. 36.7	Spica	158 32.1	S11 13.6
16	260 38.7	98 58.1	38.9	19 39.2	41.5	185 26.2	54.5	51 17.0	36.8	Suhail	222 53.0	S43 28.9
17	275 41.1	113 57.8	37.9	34 39.8	41.9	200 28.7	54.5	66 19.1	36.9			
18	290 43.6	128 57.4	N 8 36.9	49 40.4	S21 42.2	215 31.3	N21 54.5	81 21.3	S 9 37.0	Vega	80 39.4	N38 48.2
19	305 46.1	143 57.1	35.9	64 41.0	42.6	230 33.8	54.5	96 23.5	37.1	Zuben'ubi	137 06.2	S16 05.6
20	320 48.5	158 56.7	34.9	79 41.6	42.9	245 36.3	54.4	111 25.7	37.2		SHA	Mer.Pass.
21	335 51.0	173 56.4	.. 33.9	94 42.1	.. 43.3	260 38.9	.. 54.4	126 27.9	.. 37.3		° '	h m
22	350 53.5	188 56.0	32.9	109 42.7	43.7	275 41.4	54.4	141 30.1	37.4	Venus	200 12.1	9 23
23	5 55.9	203 55.7	31.9	124 43.3	44.0	290 43.9	54.4	156 32.2	37.5	Mars	120 15.4	14 42
Mer.Pass.	h m 22 40.3	v −0.4	d 1.0	v 0.6	d 0.4	v 2.5	d 0.0	v 2.2	d 0.1	Jupiter	284 45.3	3 44
										Saturn	150 49.6	12 39

UT	SUN GHA	SUN Dec	MOON GHA	v	MOON Dec	d	HP
d h	° ′	° ′	° ′	′	° ′	′	′
9 00	183 10.9	S 6 20.0	263 06.1	12.0	N17 02.6	6.8	55.4
01	198 11.1	21.0	277 37.1	12.0	16 55.8	6.8	55.4
02	213 11.3	21.9	292 08.1	11.9	16 49.0	6.9	55.4
03	228 11.5	.. 22.9	306 39.0	12.0	16 42.1	6.9	55.5
04	243 11.6	23.8	321 10.0	12.0	16 35.2	7.1	55.5
05	258 11.8	24.8	335 41.0	12.0	16 28.1	7.2	55.5
06	273 12.0	S 6 25.7	350 12.0	12.0	N16 20.9	7.2	55.5
07	288 12.1	26.7	4 43.0	12.1	16 13.7	7.3	55.6
08	303 12.3	27.6	19 14.1	12.0	16 06.4	7.4	55.6
09	318 12.5	.. 28.6	33 45.1	12.0	15 59.0	7.5	55.6
10	333 12.6	29.5	48 16.1	12.0	15 51.5	7.6	55.7
11	348 12.8	30.5	62 47.1	12.1	15 43.9	7.6	55.7
12	3 13.0	S 6 31.4	77 18.2	12.0	N15 36.3	7.8	55.7
13	18 13.1	32.4	91 49.2	12.1	15 28.5	7.8	55.8
14	33 13.3	33.3	106 20.3	12.0	15 20.7	7.9	55.8
15	48 13.5	.. 34.2	120 51.3	12.1	15 12.8	8.0	55.8
16	63 13.6	35.2	135 22.4	12.0	15 04.8	8.1	55.8
17	78 13.8	36.1	149 53.4	12.1	14 56.7	8.1	55.9
18	93 14.0	S 6 37.1	164 24.5	12.0	N14 48.6	8.2	55.9
19	108 14.1	38.0	178 55.5	12.1	14 40.4	8.3	55.9
20	123 14.3	39.0	193 26.6	12.1	14 32.1	8.4	56.0
21	138 14.5	.. 39.9	207 57.7	12.0	14 23.7	8.5	56.0
22	153 14.6	40.9	222 28.7	12.1	14 15.2	8.5	56.0
23	168 14.8	41.8	236 59.8	12.1	14 06.7	8.7	56.1
10 00	183 15.0	S 6 42.8	251 30.9	12.1	N13 58.0	8.7	56.1
01	198 15.1	43.7	266 02.0	12.0	13 49.3	8.7	56.1
02	213 15.3	44.7	280 33.0	12.1	13 40.6	8.9	56.2
03	228 15.5	.. 45.6	295 04.1	12.0	13 31.7	8.9	56.2
04	243 15.6	46.6	309 35.2	12.1	13 22.8	9.0	56.2
05	258 15.8	47.5	324 06.3	12.1	13 13.8	9.1	56.3
06	273 16.0	S 6 48.4	338 37.4	12.0	N13 04.7	9.2	56.3
07	288 16.1	49.4	353 08.4	12.1	12 55.5	9.2	56.3
08	303 16.3	50.3	7 39.5	12.1	12 46.3	9.3	56.4
09	318 16.4	.. 51.3	22 10.6	12.1	12 37.0	9.4	56.4
10	333 16.6	52.2	36 41.7	12.0	12 27.6	9.4	56.4
11	348 16.8	53.2	51 12.7	12.1	12 18.2	9.5	56.5
12	3 16.9	S 6 54.1	65 43.8	12.1	N12 08.7	9.6	56.5
13	18 17.1	55.1	80 14.9	12.0	11 59.1	9.7	56.5
14	33 17.3	56.0	94 45.9	12.1	11 49.4	9.7	56.6
15	48 17.4	.. 56.9	109 17.0	12.0	11 39.7	9.8	56.6
16	63 17.6	57.9	123 48.0	12.1	11 29.9	9.9	56.6
17	78 17.7	58.8	138 19.1	12.0	11 20.0	9.9	56.7
18	93 17.9	S 6 59.8	152 50.1	12.1	N11 10.1	10.0	56.7
19	108 18.1	7 00.7	167 21.2	12.0	11 00.1	10.1	56.7
20	123 18.2	01.7	181 52.2	12.0	10 50.0	10.1	56.8
21	138 18.4	.. 02.6	196 23.2	12.0	10 39.9	10.2	56.8
22	153 18.6	03.5	210 54.2	12.0	10 29.7	10.3	56.9
23	168 18.7	04.5	225 25.2	12.0	10 19.4	10.3	56.9
11 00	183 18.9	S 7 05.4	239 56.2	12.0	N10 09.1	10.4	56.9
01	198 19.0	06.4	254 27.2	12.0	9 58.7	10.5	57.0
02	213 19.2	07.3	268 58.2	12.0	9 48.2	10.5	57.0
03	228 19.4	.. 08.3	283 29.2	12.0	9 37.7	10.6	57.0
04	243 19.5	09.2	298 00.2	11.9	9 27.1	10.7	57.1
05	258 19.7	10.1	312 31.1	11.9	9 16.4	10.7	57.1
06	273 19.8	S 7 11.1	327 02.0	12.0	N 9 05.7	10.7	57.1
07	288 20.0	12.0	341 33.0	11.9	8 55.0	10.9	57.2
08	303 20.1	13.0	356 03.9	11.9	8 44.1	10.8	57.2
09	318 20.3	.. 13.9	10 34.8	11.9	8 33.3	11.0	57.3
10	333 20.5	14.8	25 05.7	11.9	8 22.3	11.0	57.3
11	348 20.6	15.8	39 36.6	11.8	8 11.3	11.0	57.3
12	3 20.8	S 7 16.7	54 07.4	11.9	N 8 00.3	11.1	57.4
13	18 20.9	17.7	68 38.3	11.8	7 49.2	11.2	57.4
14	33 21.1	18.6	83 09.1	11.8	7 38.0	11.2	57.4
15	48 21.2	.. 19.5	97 39.9	11.8	7 26.8	11.3	57.5
16	63 21.4	20.5	112 10.7	11.8	7 15.5	11.3	57.5
17	78 21.6	21.4	126 41.5	11.8	7 04.2	11.4	57.6
18	93 21.7	S 7 22.4	141 12.3	11.7	N 6 52.8	11.4	57.6
19	108 21.9	23.3	155 43.0	11.7	6 41.4	11.5	57.6
20	123 22.0	24.2	170 13.7	11.7	6 29.9	11.5	57.7
21	138 22.2	.. 25.2	184 44.4	11.7	6 18.4	11.6	57.7
22	153 22.3	26.1	199 15.1	11.7	6 06.8	11.6	57.8
23	168 22.5	27.1	213 45.8	11.6	N 5 55.2	11.7	57.8
	SD 16.0	d 0.9	SD 15.2		15.4		15.6

Row labels at left: TUESDAY (09), WEDNESDAY (10), THURSDAY (11)

Twilight / Sunrise / Moonrise

Lat.	Naut.	Civil	Sunrise	Moonrise 9	10	11	12
°	h m	h m	h m	h m	h m	h m	h m
N 72	04 34	05 53	07 02	21 46	23 47	25 45	01 45
N 70	04 41	05 52	06 53	22 16	24 04	00 04	01 52
68	04 46	05 50	06 46	22 38	24 18	00 18	01 59
66	04 50	05 49	06 41	22 56	24 29	00 29	02 04
64	04 53	05 48	06 36	23 10	24 38	00 38	02 08
62	04 56	05 47	06 32	23 21	24 45	00 45	02 12
60	04 58	05 46	06 28	23 31	24 52	00 52	02 16
N 58	05 00	05 45	06 25	23 40	24 58	00 58	02 18
56	05 01	05 44	06 22	23 48	25 03	01 03	02 21
54	05 03	05 44	06 19	23 54	25 07	01 07	02 23
52	05 04	05 43	06 17	24 01	00 01	01 12	02 26
50	05 05	05 42	06 14	24 06	00 06	01 15	02 27
45	05 06	05 40	06 10	24 18	00 18	01 23	02 32
N 40	05 07	05 38	06 06	24 28	00 28	01 30	02 35
35	05 07	05 37	06 02	24 36	00 36	01 36	02 38
30	05 07	05 35	05 59	24 43	00 43	01 41	02 41
20	05 06	05 31	05 53	00 03	00 56	01 50	02 45
N 10	05 03	05 27	05 48	00 16	01 07	01 58	02 49
0	04 59	05 23	05 44	00 29	01 17	02 05	02 53
S 10	04 53	05 18	05 39	00 42	01 27	02 12	02 57
20	04 45	05 11	05 33	00 55	01 38	02 20	03 01
30	04 35	05 03	05 27	01 11	01 50	02 28	03 05
35	04 28	04 58	05 24	01 20	01 58	02 33	03 08
40	04 19	04 52	05 20	01 30	02 06	02 39	03 11
45	04 09	04 45	05 15	01 42	02 15	02 46	03 14
S 50	03 56	04 36	05 09	01 57	02 26	02 53	03 19
52	03 49	04 32	05 06	02 03	02 32	02 57	03 20
54	03 42	04 27	05 03	02 11	02 38	03 01	03 22
56	03 33	04 21	05 00	02 19	02 44	03 05	03 25
58	03 24	04 15	04 57	02 29	02 51	03 10	03 27
S 60	03 12	04 09	04 52	02 39	02 59	03 16	03 30

Sunset / Twilight / Moonset

Lat.	Sunset	Civil	Naut.	Moonset 9	10	11	12
°	h m	h m	h m	h m	h m	h m	h m
N 72	16 30	17 38	18 56	16 39	16 18	16 02	15 48
N 70	16 39	17 40	18 51	16 08	15 59	15 52	15 45
68	16 46	17 42	18 46	15 44	15 44	15 43	15 42
66	16 52	17 43	18 42	15 26	15 32	15 36	15 40
64	16 57	17 44	18 39	15 11	15 22	15 30	15 38
62	17 01	17 45	18 36	14 58	15 13	15 25	15 35
60	17 05	17 46	18 34	14 48	15 06	15 21	15 35
N 58	17 08	17 47	18 33	14 38	14 59	15 17	15 33
56	17 11	17 48	18 31	14 30	14 53	15 13	15 32
54	17 14	17 49	18 30	14 23	14 48	15 10	15 31
52	17 16	17 50	18 29	14 16	14 43	15 07	15 30
50	17 19	17 51	18 28	14 10	14 39	15 04	15 29
45	17 23	17 53	18 27	13 58	14 29	14 59	15 27
N 40	17 28	17 55	18 26	13 47	14 21	14 54	15 25
35	17 31	17 57	18 26	13 38	14 14	14 49	15 24
30	17 34	17 58	18 26	13 30	14 08	14 46	15 23
20	17 40	18 02	18 28	13 16	13 58	14 39	15 20
N 10	17 45	18 06	18 31	13 04	13 49	14 33	15 18
0	17 50	18 11	18 35	12 52	13 40	14 28	15 16
S 10	17 55	18 16	18 41	12 40	13 31	14 22	15 14
20	18 01	18 23	18 49	12 28	13 22	14 16	15 12
30	18 07	18 31	19 00	12 14	13 11	14 09	15 10
35	18 11	18 36	19 07	12 05	13 04	14 05	15 09
40	18 15	18 42	19 15	11 56	12 57	14 01	15 07
45	18 20	18 50	19 26	11 45	12 49	13 56	15 05
S 50	18 26	18 59	19 40	11 31	12 39	13 49	15 03
52	18 29	19 04	19 46	11 25	12 34	13 46	15 02
54	18 32	19 08	19 54	11 18	12 29	13 43	15 00
56	18 35	19 14	20 02	11 10	12 23	13 40	14 59
58	18 39	19 20	20 12	11 01	12 16	13 36	14 58
S 60	18 43	19 27	20 24	10 51	12 09	13 31	14 56

SUN / MOON

Day	Eqn. of Time 00h	Eqn. of Time 12h	Mer. Pass.	Mer. Pass. Upper	Mer. Pass. Lower	Age	Phase
d	m s	m s	h m	h m	h m	d	%
9	12 43	12 52	11 47	06 41	19 04	23	39
10	13 00	13 07	11 47	07 28	19 52	24	29
11	13 15	13 23	11 47	08 16	20 40	25	20

2012 OCTOBER 12, 13, 14 (FRI., SAT., SUN.)

UT	ARIES	VENUS −4.1		MARS +1.2		JUPITER −2.6		SATURN +0.7		STARS		
	GHA	GHA	Dec	GHA	Dec	GHA	Dec	GHA	Dec	Name	SHA	Dec
d h	° ′	° ′	° ′	° ′	° ′	° ′	° ′	° ′	° ′		° ′	° ′
12 00	20 58.4	218 55.3	N 8 30.9	139 43.9	S21 44.4	305 46.5	N21 54.4	171 34.4	S 9 37.6	Acamar	315 18.3	S40 15.1
01	36 00.9	233 55.0	29.9	154 44.5	44.8	320 49.0	54.4	186 36.6	37.7	Achernar	335 26.5	S57 10.2
02	51 03.3	248 54.6	28.9	169 45.1	45.1	335 51.5	54.4	201 38.8	37.8	Acrux	173 10.5	S63 10.1
03	66 05.8	263 54.3	.. 27.9	184 45.6	.. 45.5	350 54.0	.. 54.4	216 41.0	.. 37.9	Adhara	255 12.8	S28 59.2
04	81 08.3	278 53.9	26.9	199 46.2	45.8	5 56.6	54.4	231 43.1	38.1	Aldebaran	290 49.7	N16 32.1
05	96 10.7	293 53.6	25.9	214 46.8	46.2	20 59.1	54.4	246 45.3	38.2			
06	111 13.2	308 53.2	N 8 24.9	229 47.4	S21 46.5	36 01.6	N21 54.4	261 47.5	S 9 38.3	Alioth	166 21.7	N55 53.4
07	126 15.6	323 52.9	23.9	244 48.0	46.9	51 04.2	54.4	276 49.7	38.4	Alkaid	152 59.8	N49 15.0
08	141 18.1	338 52.5	22.9	259 48.5	47.3	66 06.7	54.4	291 51.9	38.5	Al Na'ir	27 44.0	S46 53.9
F 09	156 20.6	353 52.2	.. 21.9	274 49.1	.. 47.6	81 09.2	.. 54.3	306 54.0	.. 38.6	Alnilam	275 46.7	S 1 11.6
R 10	171 23.0	8 51.8	20.9	289 49.7	48.0	96 11.8	54.3	321 56.2	38.7	Alphard	217 56.7	S 8 42.8
I 11	186 25.5	23 51.5	19.9	304 50.3	48.3	111 14.3	54.3	336 58.4	38.8			
D 12	201 28.0	38 51.1	N 8 18.9	319 50.9	S21 48.7	126 16.9	N21 54.3	352 00.6	S 9 38.9	Alphecca	126 11.7	N26 40.5
A 13	216 30.4	53 50.8	17.9	334 51.4	49.0	141 19.4	54.3	7 02.8	39.0	Alpheratz	357 43.6	N29 09.9
Y 14	231 32.9	68 50.5	16.9	349 52.0	49.4	156 21.9	54.3	22 05.0	39.1	Altair	62 08.7	N 8 54.5
15	246 35.4	83 50.1	.. 15.9	4 52.6	.. 49.7	171 24.5	.. 54.3	37 07.1	.. 39.2	Ankaa	353 15.7	S42 14.1
16	261 37.8	98 49.8	14.9	19 53.2	50.1	186 27.0	54.3	52 09.3	39.3	Antares	112 27.1	S26 27.5
17	276 40.3	113 49.4	13.9	34 53.8	50.5	201 29.5	54.3	67 11.5	39.4			
18	291 42.7	128 49.1	N 8 12.9	49 54.3	S21 50.8	216 32.1	N21 54.3	82 13.7	S 9 39.5	Arcturus	145 56.5	N19 07.1
19	306 45.2	143 48.7	11.9	64 54.9	51.2	231 34.6	54.3	97 15.9	39.6	Atria	107 29.7	S69 03.1
20	321 47.7	158 48.4	10.9	79 55.5	51.5	246 37.2	54.3	112 18.0	39.7	Avior	234 18.4	S59 32.8
21	336 50.1	173 48.0	.. 09.8	94 56.1	.. 51.9	261 39.7	.. 54.2	127 20.2	.. 39.8	Bellatrix	278 32.4	N 6 21.7
22	351 52.6	188 47.7	08.8	109 56.6	52.2	276 42.2	54.2	142 22.4	39.9	Betelgeuse	271 01.7	N 7 24.5
23	6 55.1	203 47.3	07.8	124 57.2	52.6	291 44.8	54.2	157 24.6	40.1			
13 00	21 57.5	218 47.0	N 8 06.8	139 57.8	S21 52.9	306 47.3	N21 54.2	172 26.8	S 9 40.2	Canopus	263 56.2	S52 41.9
01	37 00.0	233 46.6	05.8	154 58.4	53.3	321 49.9	54.2	187 28.9	40.3	Capella	280 34.9	N46 00.4
02	52 02.5	248 46.3	04.8	169 59.0	53.6	336 52.4	54.2	202 31.1	40.4	Deneb	49 31.7	N45 20.0
03	67 04.9	263 45.9	.. 03.8	184 59.5	.. 54.0	351 54.9	.. 54.2	217 33.3	.. 40.5	Denebola	182 34.4	N14 30.0
04	82 07.4	278 45.6	02.8	200 00.1	54.3	6 57.5	54.2	232 35.5	40.6	Diphda	348 56.0	S17 54.8
05	97 09.9	293 45.2	01.8	215 00.7	54.7	22 00.0	54.2	247 37.7	40.7			
06	112 12.3	308 44.9	N 8 00.7	230 01.3	S21 55.0	37 02.6	N21 54.2	262 39.8	S 9 40.8	Dubhe	193 52.8	N61 40.7
07	127 14.8	323 44.5	7 59.7	245 01.8	55.4	52 05.1	54.2	277 42.0	40.9	Elnath	278 13.0	N28 37.0
08	142 17.2	338 44.2	58.7	260 02.4	55.7	67 07.6	54.1	292 44.2	41.0	Eltanin	90 46.6	N51 29.6
S 09	157 19.7	353 43.8	.. 57.7	275 03.0	.. 56.1	82 10.2	.. 54.1	307 46.4	.. 41.1	Enif	33 47.4	N 9 56.3
A 10	172 22.2	8 43.5	56.7	290 03.5	56.4	97 12.7	54.1	322 48.6	41.2	Fomalhaut	15 24.2	S29 33.1
T 11	187 24.6	23 43.2	55.7	305 04.1	56.8	112 15.3	54.1	337 50.7	41.3			
U 12	202 27.1	38 42.8	N 7 54.7	320 04.7	S21 57.1	127 17.8	N21 54.1	352 52.9	S 9 41.4	Gacrux	172 02.0	S57 11.0
R 13	217 29.6	53 42.5	53.6	335 05.3	57.5	142 20.4	54.1	7 55.1	41.5	Gienah	175 53.1	S17 36.7
D 14	232 32.0	68 42.1	52.6	350 05.8	57.8	157 22.9	54.1	22 57.3	41.6	Hadar	148 49.2	S60 26.1
A 15	247 34.5	83 41.8	.. 51.6	5 06.4	.. 58.2	172 25.5	.. 54.1	37 59.5	.. 41.7	Hamal	328 00.9	N23 31.5
Y 16	262 37.0	98 41.4	50.6	20 07.0	58.5	187 28.0	54.1	53 01.6	41.8	Kaus Aust.	83 44.5	S34 22.6
17	277 39.4	113 41.1	49.6	35 07.6	58.9	202 30.6	54.1	68 03.8	41.9			
18	292 41.9	128 40.7	N 7 48.5	50 08.1	S21 59.2	217 33.1	N21 54.1	83 06.0	S 9 42.1	Kochab	137 21.1	N74 06.3
19	307 44.3	143 40.4	47.5	65 08.7	59.6	232 35.6	54.1	98 08.2	42.2	Markab	13 38.5	N15 16.7
20	322 46.8	158 40.0	46.5	80 09.3	21 59.9	247 38.2	54.0	113 10.4	42.3	Menkar	314 15.3	N 4 08.5
21	337 49.3	173 39.7	.. 45.5	95 09.9	22 00.2	262 40.7	.. 54.0	128 12.5	.. 42.4	Menkent	148 08.5	S36 25.9
22	352 51.7	188 39.3	44.5	110 10.4	00.6	277 43.3	54.0	143 14.7	42.5	Miaplacidus	221 40.2	S69 46.0
23	7 54.2	203 39.0	43.4	125 11.0	00.9	292 45.8	54.0	158 16.9	42.6			
14 00	22 56.7	218 38.7	N 7 42.4	140 11.5	S22 01.3	307 48.4	N21 54.0	173 19.1	S 9 42.7	Mirfak	308 40.6	N49 54.3
01	37 59.1	233 38.3	41.4	155 12.1	01.6	322 50.9	54.0	188 21.3	42.8	Nunki	75 59.0	S26 16.7
02	53 01.6	248 38.0	40.4	170 12.7	02.0	337 53.5	54.0	203 23.4	42.9	Peacock	53 19.8	S56 41.7
03	68 04.1	263 37.6	.. 39.3	185 13.2	.. 02.3	352 56.0	.. 54.0	218 25.6	.. 43.0	Pollux	243 28.3	N27 58.5
04	83 06.5	278 37.3	38.3	200 13.8	02.7	7 58.6	54.0	233 27.8	43.1	Procyon	245 00.2	N 5 11.5
05	98 09.0	293 36.9	37.3	215 14.4	03.0	23 01.1	54.0	248 30.0	43.2			
06	113 11.5	308 36.6	N 7 36.3	230 15.0	S22 03.3	38 03.7	N21 53.9	263 32.2	S 9 43.3	Rasalhague	96 07.1	N12 33.3
07	128 13.9	323 36.2	35.2	245 15.5	03.7	53 06.2	53.9	278 34.3	43.4	Regulus	207 44.2	N11 54.2
08	143 16.4	338 35.9	34.2	260 16.1	04.0	68 08.8	53.9	293 36.5	43.5	Rigel	281 12.3	S 8 11.2
S 09	158 18.8	353 35.5	.. 33.2	275 16.7	.. 04.4	83 11.3	.. 53.9	308 38.7	.. 43.6	Rigil Kent.	139 53.0	S60 53.2
U 10	173 21.3	8 35.2	32.2	290 17.2	04.7	98 13.9	53.9	323 40.9	43.7	Sabik	102 13.3	S15 44.3
N 11	188 23.8	23 34.9	31.1	305 17.8	05.0	113 16.5	53.9	338 43.1	43.8			
D 12	203 26.2	38 34.5	N 7 30.1	320 18.3	S22 05.4	128 19.0	N21 53.9	353 45.2	S 9 43.9	Schedar	349 40.5	N56 36.6
A 13	218 28.7	53 34.2	29.1	335 18.9	05.7	143 21.6	53.9	8 47.4	44.1	Shaula	96 22.8	S37 06.7
Y 14	233 31.2	68 33.8	28.1	350 19.5	06.1	158 24.1	53.9	23 49.6	44.2	Sirius	258 34.1	S16 43.9
15	248 33.6	83 33.5	.. 27.0	5 20.0	.. 06.4	173 26.7	.. 53.9	38 51.8	.. 44.3	Spica	158 32.1	S11 13.6
16	263 36.1	98 33.1	26.0	20 20.6	06.7	188 29.2	53.9	53 53.9	44.4	Suhail	222 53.0	S43 28.9
17	278 38.6	113 32.8	25.0	35 21.2	07.1	203 31.8	53.8	68 56.1	44.5			
18	293 41.0	128 32.4	N 7 23.9	50 21.7	S22 07.4	218 34.3	N21 53.8	83 58.3	S 9 44.6	Vega	80 39.4	N38 48.1
19	308 43.5	143 32.1	22.9	65 22.3	07.8	233 36.9	53.8	99 00.5	44.7	Zuben'ubi	137 06.3	S16 05.6
20	323 45.9	158 31.8	21.9	80 22.9	08.1	248 39.4	53.8	114 02.7	44.8		SHA	Mer.Pass.
21	338 48.4	173 31.4	.. 20.8	95 23.4	.. 08.4	263 42.0	.. 53.8	129 04.8	.. 44.9		° ′	h m
22	353 50.9	188 31.1	19.8	110 24.0	08.8	278 44.6	53.8	144 07.0	45.0	Venus	196 49.4	9 25
23	8 53.3	203 30.7	18.8	125 24.5	09.1	293 47.1	53.8	159 09.2	45.1	Mars	118 00.3	14 40
	h m									Jupiter	284 49.8	3 32
Mer.Pass. 22 28.5	v −0.3 d 1.0		v 0.6 d 0.3		v 2.5 d 0.0		v 2.2 d 0.1		Saturn	150 29.2	12 28

UT	SUN GHA	SUN Dec	MOON GHA	v	MOON Dec	d	HP
12 00	183 22.7	S 7 28.0	228 16.4	11.6	N 5 43.5	11.7	57.8
01	198 22.8	28.9	242 47.0	11.6	5 31.8	11.7	57.9
02	213 23.0	29.9	257 17.6	11.6	5 20.1	11.8	57.9
03	228 23.1	.. 30.8	271 48.2	11.5	5 08.3	11.9	57.9
04	243 23.3	31.7	286 18.7	11.5	4 56.4	11.9	58.0
05	258 23.4	32.7	300 49.2	11.5	4 44.5	11.9	58.0
06	273 23.6	S 7 33.6	315 19.7	11.5	N 4 32.6	12.0	58.1
07	288 23.7	34.6	329 50.2	11.4	4 20.6	12.0	58.1
F 08	303 23.9	35.5	344 20.6	11.4	4 08.6	12.0	58.1
R 09	318 24.0	.. 36.4	358 51.0	11.3	3 56.6	12.1	58.2
I 10	333 24.2	37.4	13 21.4	11.4	3 44.5	12.1	58.2
D 11	348 24.3	38.3	27 51.8	11.3	3 32.4	12.1	58.2
A 12	3 24.5	S 7 39.2	42 22.1	11.3	N 3 20.3	12.2	58.3
Y 13	18 24.6	40.2	56 52.4	11.2	3 08.1	12.2	58.3
14	33 24.8	41.1	71 22.6	11.3	2 55.9	12.3	58.4
15	48 24.9	.. 42.0	85 52.9	11.2	2 43.6	12.3	58.4
16	63 25.1	43.0	100 23.1	11.1	2 31.3	12.3	58.4
17	78 25.2	43.9	114 53.2	11.1	2 19.0	12.3	58.5
18	93 25.4	S 7 44.8	129 23.3	11.1	N 2 06.7	12.4	58.5
19	108 25.5	45.8	143 53.4	11.1	1 54.3	12.4	58.5
20	123 25.7	46.7	158 23.5	11.0	1 41.9	12.4	58.6
21	138 25.8	.. 47.6	172 53.5	11.0	1 29.5	12.4	58.6
22	153 26.0	48.6	187 23.5	10.9	1 17.1	12.5	58.7
23	168 26.1	49.5	201 53.4	10.9	1 04.6	12.5	58.7
13 00	183 26.3	S 7 50.5	216 23.3	10.9	N 0 52.1	12.5	58.7
01	198 26.4	51.4	230 53.2	10.8	0 39.6	12.5	58.8
02	213 26.6	52.3	245 23.0	10.8	0 27.1	12.5	58.8
03	228 26.7	.. 53.3	259 52.8	10.7	0 14.6	12.6	58.8
04	243 26.9	54.2	274 22.5	10.7	N 0 02.0	12.6	58.9
05	258 27.0	55.1	288 52.2	10.7	S 0 10.6	12.6	58.9
06	273 27.2	S 7 56.0	303 21.9	10.6	S 0 23.2	12.6	58.9
07	288 27.3	57.0	317 51.5	10.6	0 35.8	12.6	59.0
S 08	303 27.5	57.9	332 21.1	10.5	0 48.4	12.6	59.0
A 09	318 27.6	.. 58.8	346 50.6	10.5	1 01.0	12.7	59.1
T 10	333 27.8	7 59.8	1 20.1	10.4	1 13.7	12.6	59.1
U 11	348 27.9	8 00.7	15 49.5	10.4	1 26.3	12.7	59.1
R 12	3 28.1	S 8 01.6	30 18.9	10.3	S 1 39.0	12.6	59.2
D 13	18 28.2	02.6	44 48.2	10.3	1 51.6	12.7	59.2
A 14	33 28.4	03.5	59 17.5	10.3	2 04.3	12.7	59.2
Y 15	48 28.5	.. 04.4	73 46.8	10.1	2 17.0	12.7	59.3
16	63 28.7	05.4	88 15.9	10.2	2 29.7	12.6	59.3
17	78 28.8	06.3	102 45.1	10.1	2 42.3	12.7	59.3
18	93 28.9	S 8 07.2	117 14.2	10.0	S 2 55.0	12.7	59.4
19	108 29.1	08.2	131 43.2	10.0	3 07.7	12.6	59.4
20	123 29.2	09.1	146 12.2	9.9	3 20.3	12.7	59.4
21	138 29.4	.. 10.0	160 41.1	9.9	3 33.0	12.7	59.5
22	153 29.5	10.9	175 10.0	9.8	3 45.7	12.6	59.5
23	168 29.7	11.9	189 38.8	9.8	3 58.3	12.7	59.5
14 00	183 29.8	S 8 12.8	204 07.6	9.7	S 4 11.0	12.6	59.6
01	198 30.0	13.7	218 36.3	9.7	4 23.6	12.6	59.6
02	213 30.1	14.7	233 05.0	9.6	4 36.2	12.6	59.6
03	228 30.2	.. 15.6	247 33.6	9.5	4 48.8	12.6	59.6
04	243 30.4	16.5	262 02.1	9.5	5 01.4	12.6	59.7
05	258 30.5	17.4	276 30.6	9.4	5 14.0	12.5	59.7
06	273 30.7	S 8 18.4	290 59.0	9.4	S 5 26.5	12.6	59.7
07	288 30.8	19.3	305 27.4	9.3	5 39.1	12.5	59.8
S 08	303 31.0	20.2	319 55.7	9.2	5 51.6	12.5	59.8
U 09	318 31.1	.. 21.2	334 23.9	9.2	6 04.1	12.5	59.8
N 10	333 31.2	22.1	348 52.1	9.1	6 16.6	12.4	59.9
D 11	348 31.4	23.0	3 20.2	9.1	6 29.0	12.3	59.9
A 12	3 31.5	S 8 23.9	17 48.3	9.0	S 6 41.4	12.4	59.9
Y 13	18 31.7	24.9	32 16.3	9.0	6 53.8	12.4	59.9
14	33 31.8	25.8	46 44.3	8.8	7 06.2	12.3	60.0
15	48 31.9	.. 26.7	61 12.1	8.8	7 18.5	12.3	60.0
16	63 32.1	27.6	75 39.9	8.8	7 30.8	12.3	60.0
17	78 32.2	28.6	90 07.7	8.7	7 43.1	12.2	60.0
18	93 32.4	S 8 29.5	104 35.4	8.6	S 7 55.3	12.2	60.1
19	108 32.5	30.4	119 03.0	8.5	8 07.5	12.1	60.1
20	123 32.6	31.3	133 30.5	8.5	8 19.6	12.1	60.1
21	138 32.8	.. 32.3	147 58.0	8.4	8 31.7	12.1	60.1
22	153 32.9	33.2	162 25.4	8.3	8 43.8	12.0	60.2
23	168 33.0	34.1	176 52.8	8.3	S 8 55.8	12.0	60.2
	SD 16.1	d 0.9	SD 15.9		16.1		16.3

Twilight / Moonrise

Lat.	Naut.	Civil	Sunrise	Moonrise 12	13	14	15
N 72	04 48	06 06	07 16	01 45	03 43	05 45	07 57
N 70	04 53	06 03	07 06	01 52	03 43	05 37	07 38
68	04 56	06 01	06 58	01 59	03 43	05 30	07 23
66	04 59	05 58	06 51	02 04	03 43	05 25	07 11
64	05 02	05 57	06 45	02 08	03 42	05 20	07 01
62	05 03	05 55	06 40	02 12	03 42	05 16	06 53
60	05 05	05 53	06 35	02 16	03 42	05 13	06 46
N 58	05 06	05 52	06 31	02 18	03 42	05 09	06 39
56	05 07	05 50	06 28	02 21	03 42	05 07	06 34
54	05 08	05 49	06 25	02 23	03 42	05 04	06 29
52	05 09	05 48	06 22	02 26	03 42	05 02	06 24
50	05 09	05 47	06 19	02 27	03 42	05 00	06 20
45	05 10	05 44	06 13	02 32	03 42	04 56	06 11
N 40	05 10	05 41	06 09	02 35	03 42	04 52	06 04
35	05 10	05 39	06 04	02 38	03 42	04 49	05 58
30	05 09	05 37	06 01	02 41	03 42	04 46	05 52
20	05 06	05 32	05 54	02 45	03 42	04 42	05 43
N 10	05 03	05 27	05 48	02 49	03 42	04 37	05 35
0	04 58	05 22	05 43	02 53	03 42	04 34	05 27
S 10	04 51	05 16	05 37	02 57	03 43	04 30	05 20
20	04 43	05 09	05 31	03 01	03 43	04 26	05 12
30	04 31	05 00	05 24	03 05	03 43	04 22	05 03
35	04 23	04 54	05 20	03 08	03 43	04 19	04 58
40	04 14	04 47	05 15	03 11	03 43	04 16	04 52
45	04 03	04 39	05 09	03 14	03 43	04 13	04 45
S 50	03 48	04 29	05 03	03 19	03 43	04 09	04 37
52	03 41	04 24	05 00	03 20	03 43	04 07	04 33
54	03 33	04 19	04 56	03 22	03 43	04 05	04 29
56	03 24	04 13	04 52	03 25	03 44	04 03	04 25
58	03 14	04 07	04 48	03 27	03 44	04 01	04 20
S 60	03 01	03 59	04 44	03 30	03 44	03 58	04 14

Sunset / Twilight / Moonset

Lat.	Sunset	Civil	Naut.	Moonset 12	13	14	15
N 72	16 14	17 24	18 42	15 48	15 34	15 20	15 01
N 70	16 25	17 27	18 37	15 45	15 38	15 30	15 22
68	16 33	17 30	18 34	15 42	15 41	15 39	15 39
66	16 40	17 32	18 31	15 40	15 43	15 47	15 52
64	16 46	17 34	18 29	15 38	15 45	15 53	16 03
62	16 51	17 36	18 27	15 36	15 47	15 58	16 13
60	16 56	17 38	18 26	15 35	15 48	16 03	16 21
N 58	17 00	17 39	18 25	15 33	15 50	16 07	16 28
56	17 03	17 41	18 24	15 32	15 51	16 11	16 35
54	17 07	17 42	18 23	15 31	15 52	16 15	16 41
52	17 10	17 44	18 23	15 30	15 53	16 18	16 46
50	17 12	17 45	18 22	15 29	15 54	16 21	16 50
45	17 18	17 48	18 22	15 27	15 56	16 27	17 01
N 40	17 23	17 50	18 22	15 25	15 58	16 32	17 09
35	17 27	17 53	18 22	15 24	15 59	16 36	17 17
30	17 31	17 55	18 23	15 23	16 00	16 40	17 23
20	17 38	18 00	18 26	15 20	16 03	16 47	17 35
N 10	17 44	18 05	18 29	15 18	16 05	16 53	17 44
0	17 49	18 10	18 35	15 16	16 07	16 59	17 54
S 10	17 55	18 17	18 41	15 14	16 08	17 04	18 03
20	18 02	18 24	18 50	15 12	16 10	17 11	18 13
30	18 09	18 33	19 02	15 10	16 13	17 17	18 25
35	18 13	18 39	19 10	15 09	16 14	17 21	18 31
40	18 18	18 46	19 19	15 07	16 15	17 26	18 39
45	18 24	18 54	19 31	15 05	16 17	17 31	18 48
S 50	18 31	19 04	19 45	15 03	16 19	17 38	18 58
52	18 34	19 09	19 53	15 02	16 20	17 41	19 03
54	18 37	19 15	20 01	15 00	16 21	17 44	19 09
56	18 41	19 21	20 10	14 59	16 22	17 47	19 15
58	18 45	19 27	20 21	14 58	16 23	17 51	19 22
S 60	18 50	19 35	20 34	14 56	16 24	17 56	19 29

SUN / MOON

Day	Eqn. of Time 00h	12h	Mer. Pass.	Mer. Pass. Upper	Lower	Age	Phase
d	m s	m s	h m	h m	h m	d	%
12	13 30	13 38	11 46	09 05	21 29	26	12
13	13 45	13 52	11 46	09 54	22 20	27	6
14	13 59	14 06	11 46	10 46	23 13	28	2

UT	ARIES	VENUS −4.0		MARS +1.2		JUPITER −2.6		SATURN +0.6		STARS		
	GHA	GHA	Dec	GHA	Dec	GHA	Dec	GHA	Dec	Name	SHA	Dec
d h	° ′	° ′	° ′	° ′	° ′	° ′	° ′	° ′	° ′		° ′	° ′
15 00	23 55.8	218 30.4	N 7 17.8	140 25.1	S22 09.4	308 49.7	N21 53.8	174 11.4	S 9 45.2	Acamar	315 18.3	S40 15.1
01	38 58.3	233 30.0	16.7	155 25.7	09.8	323 52.2	53.8	189 13.6	45.3	Achernar	335 26.5	S57 10.2
02	54 00.7	248 29.7	15.7	170 26.2	10.1	338 54.8	53.8	204 15.7	45.4	Acrux	173 10.5	S63 10.1
03	69 03.2	263 29.3 . .	14.6	185 26.8 . .	10.4	353 57.4 . .	53.7	219 17.9 . .	45.5	Adhara	255 12.8	S28 59.2
04	84 05.7	278 29.0	13.6	200 27.4	10.8	8 59.9	53.7	234 20.1	45.6	Aldebaran	290 49.7	N16 32.1
05	99 08.1	293 28.7	12.6	215 27.9	11.1	24 02.5	53.7	249 22.3	45.7			
06	114 10.6	308 28.3	N 7 11.5	230 28.5	S22 11.4	39 05.0	N21 53.7	264 24.5	S 9 45.8	Alioth	166 21.7	N55 53.4
07	129 13.1	323 28.0	10.5	245 29.0	11.8	54 07.6	53.7	279 26.6	45.9	Alkaid	152 59.8	N49 15.0
M 08	144 15.5	338 27.6	09.5	260 29.6	12.1	69 10.2	53.7	294 28.8	46.1	Al Na'ir	27 44.0	S46 53.9
O 09	159 18.0	353 27.3 . .	08.4	275 30.2 . .	12.4	84 12.7 . .	53.7	309 31.0 . .	46.2	Alnilam	275 46.7	S 1 11.6
N 10	174 20.4	8 26.9	07.4	290 30.7	12.8	99 15.3	53.7	324 33.2	46.3	Alphard	217 56.7	S 8 42.8
D 11	189 22.9	23 26.6	06.4	305 31.3	13.1	114 17.8	53.7	339 35.4	46.4			
A 12	204 25.4	38 26.3	N 7 05.3	320 31.8	S22 13.4	129 20.4	N21 53.6	354 37.5	S 9 46.5	Alphecca	126 11.7	N26 40.5
Y 13	219 27.8	53 25.9	04.3	335 32.4	13.8	144 23.0	53.6	9 39.7	46.6	Alpheratz	357 43.6	N29 09.9
14	234 30.3	68 25.6	03.2	350 32.9	14.1	159 25.5	53.6	24 41.9	46.7	Altair	62 08.7	N 8 54.5
15	249 32.8	83 25.2 . .	02.2	5 33.5 . .	14.4	174 28.1 . .	53.6	39 44.1 . .	46.8	Ankaa	353 15.8	S42 14.1
16	264 35.2	98 24.9	01.2	20 34.1	14.8	189 30.7	53.6	54 46.2	46.9	Antares	112 27.1	S26 27.5
17	279 37.7	113 24.5	7 00.1	35 34.6	15.1	204 33.2	53.6	69 48.4	47.0			
18	294 40.2	128 24.2	N 6 59.1	50 35.2	S22 15.4	219 35.8	N21 53.6	84 50.6	S 9 47.1	Arcturus	145 56.5	N19 07.1
19	309 42.6	143 23.9	58.0	65 35.7	15.8	234 38.4	53.6	99 52.8	47.2	Atria	107 29.7	S69 03.1
20	324 45.1	158 23.5	57.0	80 36.3	16.1	249 40.9	53.6	114 55.0	47.3	Avior	234 18.3	S59 32.8
21	339 47.5	173 23.2 . .	56.0	95 36.8 . .	16.4	264 43.5 . .	53.6	129 57.1 . .	47.4	Bellatrix	278 32.3	N 6 21.7
22	354 50.0	188 22.8	54.9	110 37.4	16.7	279 46.1	53.5	144 59.3	47.5	Betelgeuse	271 01.7	N 7 24.5
23	9 52.5	203 22.5	53.9	125 38.0	17.1	294 48.6	53.5	160 01.5	47.6			
16 00	24 54.9	218 22.2	N 6 52.8	140 38.5	S22 17.4	309 51.2	N21 53.5	175 03.7	S 9 47.7	Canopus	263 56.2	S52 42.0
01	39 57.4	233 21.8	51.8	155 39.1	17.7	324 53.8	53.5	190 05.9	47.8	Capella	280 34.9	N46 00.4
02	54 59.9	248 21.5	50.7	170 39.6	18.0	339 56.3	53.5	205 08.0	47.9	Deneb	49 31.7	N45 20.0
03	70 02.3	263 21.1 . .	49.7	185 40.2 . .	18.4	354 58.9 . .	53.5	220 10.2 . .	48.0	Denebola	182 34.4	N14 30.0
04	85 04.8	278 20.8	48.6	200 40.7	18.7	10 01.5	53.5	235 12.4	48.2	Diphda	348 56.0	S17 54.8
05	100 07.3	293 20.4	47.6	215 41.3	19.0	25 04.0	53.5	250 14.6	48.3			
06	115 09.7	308 20.1	N 6 46.6	230 41.8	S22 19.4	40 06.6	N21 53.5	265 16.7	S 9 48.4	Dubhe	193 52.8	N61 40.7
07	130 12.2	323 19.8	45.5	245 42.4	19.7	55 09.2	53.4	280 18.9	48.5	Elnath	278 13.0	N28 37.0
T 08	145 14.7	338 19.4	44.5	260 42.9	20.0	70 11.7	53.4	295 21.1	48.6	Eltanin	90 46.6	N51 29.6
U 09	160 17.1	353 19.1 . .	43.4	275 43.5 . .	20.3	85 14.3 . .	53.4	310 23.3 . .	48.7	Enif	33 47.4	N 9 56.3
E 10	175 19.6	8 18.7	42.4	290 44.0	20.7	100 16.9	53.4	325 25.5	48.8	Fomalhaut	15 24.2	S29 33.1
S 11	190 22.0	23 18.4	41.3	305 44.6	21.0	115 19.4	53.4	340 27.6	48.9			
D 12	205 24.5	38 18.1	N 6 40.3	320 45.1	S22 21.3	130 22.0	N21 53.4	355 29.8	S 9 49.0	Gacrux	172 02.0	S57 11.0
A 13	220 27.0	53 17.7	39.2	335 45.7	21.6	145 24.6	53.4	10 32.0	49.1	Gienah	175 53.1	S17 36.7
Y 14	235 29.4	68 17.4	38.2	350 46.2	21.9	160 27.2	53.4	25 34.2	49.2	Hadar	148 49.2	S60 26.0
15	250 31.9	83 17.0 . .	37.1	5 46.8 . .	22.3	175 29.7 . .	53.4	40 36.3 . .	49.3	Hamal	328 00.9	N23 31.5
16	265 34.4	98 16.7	36.1	20 47.3	22.6	190 32.3	53.3	55 38.5	49.4	Kaus Aust.	83 44.6	S34 22.6
17	280 36.8	113 16.3	35.0	35 47.9	22.9	205 34.9	53.3	70 40.7	49.5			
18	295 39.3	128 16.0	N 6 34.0	50 48.4	S22 23.2	220 37.5	N21 53.3	85 42.9	S 9 49.6	Kochab	137 21.1	N74 06.3
19	310 41.8	143 15.7	32.9	65 49.0	23.6	235 40.0	53.3	100 45.1	49.7	Markab	13 38.5	N15 16.7
20	325 44.2	158 15.3	31.9	80 49.5	23.9	250 42.6	53.3	115 47.2	49.8	Menkar	314 15.2	N 4 08.5
21	340 46.7	173 15.0 . .	30.8	95 50.1 . .	24.2	265 45.2 . .	53.3	130 49.4 . .	49.9	Menkent	148 40.1	S36 25.9
22	355 49.2	188 14.6	29.8	110 50.6	24.5	280 47.8	53.3	145 51.6	50.0	Miaplacidus	221 40.1	S69 46.0
23	10 51.6	203 14.3	28.7	125 51.2	24.8	295 50.3	53.3	160 53.8	50.2			
17 00	25 54.1	218 14.0	N 6 27.7	140 51.7	S22 25.2	310 52.9	N21 53.2	175 56.0	S 9 50.3	Mirfak	308 40.6	N49 54.3
01	40 56.5	233 13.6	26.6	155 52.3	25.5	325 55.5	53.2	190 58.1	50.4	Nunki	75 59.0	S26 16.7
02	55 59.0	248 13.3	25.6	170 52.8	25.8	340 58.1	53.2	206 00.3	50.5	Peacock	53 19.9	S56 41.7
03	71 01.5	263 12.9 . .	24.5	185 53.4 . .	26.1	356 00.6 . .	53.2	221 02.5 . .	50.6	Pollux	243 28.3	N27 59.5
04	86 03.9	278 12.6	23.4	200 53.9	26.4	11 03.2	53.2	236 04.7	50.7	Procyon	245 00.2	N 5 11.5
05	101 06.4	293 12.3	22.4	215 54.5	26.7	26 05.8	53.2	251 06.8	50.8			
06	116 08.9	308 11.9	N 6 21.3	230 55.0	S22 27.1	41 08.4	N21 53.2	266 09.0	S 9 50.9	Rasalhague	96 07.1	N12 33.3
07	131 11.3	323 11.6	20.3	245 55.6	27.4	56 10.9	53.2	281 11.2	51.0	Regulus	207 44.2	N11 54.2
W 08	146 13.8	338 11.2	19.2	260 56.1	27.7	71 13.5	53.2	296 13.4	51.1	Rigel	281 12.3	S 8 11.2
E 09	161 16.3	353 10.9 . .	18.2	275 56.7 . .	28.0	86 16.1 . .	53.1	311 15.6 . .	51.2	Rigil Kent.	139 53.0	S60 53.2
D 10	176 18.7	8 10.6	17.1	290 57.2	28.3	101 18.7	53.1	326 17.7	51.3	Sabik	102 13.3	S15 44.3
N 11	191 21.2	23 10.2	16.0	305 57.7	28.6	116 21.3	53.1	341 19.9	51.4			
E 12	206 23.6	38 09.9	N 6 15.0	320 58.3	S22 29.0	131 23.8	N21 53.1	356 22.1	S 9 51.5	Schedar	349 40.5	N56 36.7
S 13	221 26.1	53 09.5	13.9	335 58.8	29.3	146 26.4	53.1	11 24.3	51.6	Shaula	96 22.8	S37 06.7
D 14	236 28.6	68 09.2	12.9	350 59.4	29.6	161 29.0	53.1	26 26.4	51.7	Sirius	258 34.0	S16 44.0
A 15	251 31.0	83 08.9 . .	11.8	5 59.9 . .	29.9	176 31.6 . .	53.1	41 28.6 . .	51.8	Spica	158 32.1	S11 13.6
Y 16	266 33.5	98 08.5	10.7	21 00.5	30.2	191 34.2	53.1	56 30.8	51.9	Suhail	222 52.9	S43 28.9
17	281 36.0	113 08.2	09.7	36 01.0	30.5	206 36.8	53.0	71 33.0	52.0			
18	296 38.4	128 07.8	N 6 08.6	51 01.6	S22 30.8	221 39.3	N21 53.0	86 35.2	S 9 52.1	Vega	80 39.4	N38 48.1
19	311 40.9	143 07.5	07.6	66 02.1	31.2	236 41.9	53.0	101 37.3	52.3	Zuben'ubi	137 06.3	S16 05.6
20	326 43.4	158 07.2	06.5	81 02.6	31.5	251 44.5	53.0	116 39.5	52.4			
21	341 45.8	173 06.8 . .	05.4	96 03.2 . .	31.8	266 47.1 . .	53.0	131 41.7 . .	52.5		SHA	Mer. Pass.
22	356 48.3	188 06.5	04.4	111 03.7	32.1	281 49.7	53.0	146 43.9	52.6	Venus	° ′	h m
23	11 50.8	203 06.2	03.3	126 04.3	32.4	296 52.3	53.0	161 46.0	52.7	Venus	193 27.2	9 27
	h m									Mars	115 43.6	14 37
Mer. Pass. 22 16.7		v −0.3	d 1.0	v 0.6	d 0.3	v 2.6	d 0.0	v 2.2	d 0.1	Jupiter	284 56.2	3 20
										Saturn	150 08.7	12 18

UT	SUN GHA	SUN Dec	MOON GHA	v	MOON Dec	d	HP
d h	° ′	° ′	° ′	′	° ′	′	′
15 00	183 33.2	S 8 35.0	191 20.1	8.2	S 9 07.8	11.9	60.2
01	198 33.3	36.0	205 47.3	8.2	9 19.7	11.9	60.2
02	213 33.5	36.9	220 14.5	8.0	9 31.6	11.8	60.3
03	228 33.6	.. 37.8	234 41.5	8.1	9 43.4	11.8	60.3
04	243 33.7	38.7	249 08.6	7.9	9 55.2	11.8	60.3
05	258 33.9	39.7	263 35.5	7.9	10 07.0	11.6	60.3
06	273 34.0	S 8 40.6	278 02.4	7.8	S10 18.6	11.6	60.3
07	288 34.1	41.5	292 29.2	7.8	10 30.2	11.6	60.4
M 08	303 34.3	42.4	306 56.0	7.6	10 41.8	11.5	60.4
O 09	318 34.4	.. 43.4	321 22.6	7.6	10 53.3	11.4	60.4
N 10	333 34.5	44.3	335 49.2	7.6	11 04.7	11.4	60.4
D 11	348 34.7	45.2	350 15.8	7.4	11 16.1	11.3	60.4
A 12	3 34.8	S 8 46.1	4 42.2	7.4	S11 27.4	11.2	60.5
Y 13	18 35.0	47.0	19 08.6	7.4	11 38.6	11.2	60.5
14	33 35.1	48.0	33 35.0	7.2	11 49.8	11.1	60.5
15	48 35.2	.. 48.9	48 01.2	7.2	12 00.9	11.0	60.5
16	63 35.4	49.8	62 27.4	7.1	12 11.9	10.9	60.5
17	78 35.5	50.7	76 53.5	7.1	12 22.8	10.9	60.5
18	93 35.6	S 8 51.6	91 19.6	7.0	S12 33.7	10.8	60.6
19	108 35.8	52.6	105 45.6	6.9	12 44.5	10.7	60.6
20	123 35.9	53.5	120 11.5	6.8	12 55.2	10.7	60.6
21	138 36.0	.. 54.4	134 37.3	6.8	13 05.9	10.5	60.6
22	153 36.2	55.3	149 03.1	6.7	13 16.4	10.5	60.6
23	168 36.3	56.2	163 28.8	6.6	13 26.9	10.4	60.6
16 00	183 36.4	S 8 57.2	177 54.4	6.6	S13 37.3	10.3	60.6
01	198 36.6	58.1	192 20.0	6.5	13 47.6	10.2	60.7
02	213 36.7	59.0	206 45.5	6.4	13 57.8	10.1	60.7
03	228 36.8	8 59.9	221 10.9	6.4	14 07.9	10.0	60.7
04	243 36.9	9 00.8	235 36.3	6.3	14 17.9	10.0	60.7
05	258 37.1	01.8	250 01.6	6.2	14 27.9	9.8	60.7
06	273 37.2	S 9 02.7	264 26.8	6.2	S14 37.7	9.8	60.7
07	288 37.3	03.6	278 52.0	6.1	14 47.5	9.6	60.7
T 08	303 37.5	04.5	293 17.1	6.0	14 57.1	9.6	60.7
U 09	318 37.6	.. 05.4	307 42.1	6.0	15 06.7	9.4	60.7
E 10	333 37.7	06.3	322 07.1	5.9	15 16.1	9.4	60.7
S 11	348 37.9	07.3	336 32.0	5.9	15 25.5	9.2	60.7
D 12	3 38.0	S 9 08.2	350 56.9	5.8	S15 34.7	9.1	60.8
A 13	18 38.1	09.1	5 21.7	5.7	15 43.8	9.1	60.8
Y 14	33 38.2	10.0	19 46.4	5.6	15 52.9	8.9	60.8
15	48 38.4	.. 10.9	34 11.0	5.6	16 01.8	8.8	60.8
16	63 38.5	11.8	48 35.6	5.6	16 10.6	8.7	60.8
17	78 38.6	12.7	63 00.2	5.4	16 19.3	8.6	60.8
18	93 38.7	S 9 13.7	77 24.6	5.5	S16 27.9	8.5	60.8
19	108 38.9	14.6	91 49.1	5.3	16 36.4	8.3	60.8
20	123 39.0	15.5	106 13.4	5.3	16 44.7	8.3	60.8
21	138 39.1	.. 16.4	120 37.7	5.3	16 53.0	8.1	60.8
22	153 39.3	17.3	135 02.0	5.2	17 01.1	8.0	60.8
23	168 39.4	18.2	149 26.2	5.1	17 09.1	7.9	60.8
17 00	183 39.5	S 9 19.1	163 50.3	5.1	S17 17.0	7.8	60.8
01	198 39.6	20.1	178 14.4	5.0	17 24.8	7.6	60.8
02	213 39.8	21.0	192 38.4	5.0	17 32.4	7.5	60.8
03	228 39.9	.. 21.9	207 02.4	4.9	17 39.9	7.4	60.8
04	243 40.0	22.8	221 26.3	4.9	17 47.3	7.3	60.8
05	258 40.1	23.7	235 50.2	4.9	17 54.6	7.1	60.8
06	273 40.3	S 9 24.6	250 14.1	4.7	S18 01.7	7.0	60.8
W 07	288 40.4	25.5	264 37.8	4.8	18 08.7	6.9	60.8
E 08	303 40.5	26.5	279 01.6	4.7	18 15.6	6.7	60.8
D 09	318 40.6	.. 27.4	293 25.3	4.6	18 22.3	6.6	60.8
N 10	333 40.8	28.3	307 48.9	4.7	18 28.9	6.5	60.8
E 11	348 40.9	29.2	322 12.6	4.5	18 35.4	6.4	60.8
S 12	3 41.0	S 9 30.1	336 36.1	4.6	S18 41.8	6.2	60.8
D 13	18 41.1	31.0	350 59.7	4.5	18 48.0	6.1	60.8
A 14	33 41.2	31.9	5 23.2	4.4	18 54.1	5.9	60.8
Y 15	48 41.4	.. 32.8	19 46.6	4.4	19 00.0	5.8	60.7
16	63 41.5	33.7	34 10.0	4.4	19 05.8	5.6	60.7
17	78 41.6	34.6	48 33.4	4.4	19 11.4	5.6	60.7
18	93 41.7	S 9 35.6	62 56.8	4.3	S19 17.0	5.3	60.7
19	108 41.8	36.5	77 20.1	4.3	19 22.3	5.3	60.7
20	123 42.0	37.4	91 43.4	4.3	19 27.6	5.1	60.7
21	138 42.1	.. 38.3	106 06.7	4.2	19 32.7	4.9	60.7
22	153 42.2	39.2	120 29.9	4.3	19 37.6	4.8	60.7
23	168 42.3	40.1	134 53.2	4.2	S19 42.4	4.7	60.7
	SD 16.1	d 0.9	SD 16.5		16.6		16.6

Moonrise

Lat.	Twilight Naut.	Twilight Civil	Sunrise	Moonrise 15	16	17	18
°	h m	h m	h m	h m	h m	h m	h m
N 72	05 01	06 19	07 31	07 57	10 27	■	■
N 70	05 04	06 15	07 19	07 38	09 48	12 15	■
68	05 07	06 11	07 09	07 23	09 21	11 22	13 14
66	05 09	06 08	07 01	07 11	09 01	10 49	12 26
64	05 10	06 05	06 54	07 01	08 45	10 26	11 55
62	05 11	06 02	06 48	06 53	08 31	10 07	11 32
60	05 12	06 00	06 43	06 46	08 20	09 52	11 14
N 58	05 13	05 58	06 38	06 39	08 10	09 39	10 58
56	05 13	05 56	06 34	06 34	08 02	09 27	10 45
54	05 13	05 54	06 30	06 29	07 54	09 17	10 34
52	05 14	05 53	06 27	06 24	07 47	09 09	10 24
50	05 14	05 51	06 24	06 20	07 41	09 01	10 15
45	05 14	05 48	06 17	06 11	07 28	08 44	09 56
N 40	05 13	05 44	06 12	06 04	07 18	08 31	09 40
35	05 12	05 41	06 07	05 58	07 08	08 19	09 27
30	05 11	05 39	06 03	05 52	07 00	08 09	09 16
20	05 07	05 33	05 55	05 43	06 47	07 52	08 57
N 10	05 03	05 27	05 49	05 35	06 35	07 37	08 40
0	04 57	05 21	05 42	05 27	06 24	07 23	08 24
S 10	04 50	05 14	05 36	05 20	06 13	07 09	08 09
20	04 40	05 06	05 29	05 12	06 01	06 55	07 52
30	04 27	04 56	05 21	05 03	05 48	06 38	07 33
35	04 19	04 50	05 16	04 58	05 40	06 28	07 22
40	04 09	04 43	05 10	04 52	05 32	06 17	07 09
45	03 57	04 34	05 04	04 45	05 22	06 04	06 54
S 50	03 41	04 23	04 57	04 37	05 10	05 49	06 36
52	03 33	04 17	04 53	04 33	05 04	05 41	06 28
54	03 25	04 12	04 49	04 29	04 58	05 33	06 18
56	03 15	04 05	04 45	04 25	04 51	05 24	06 07
58	03 03	03 58	04 40	04 20	04 43	05 14	05 55
S 60	02 49	03 49	04 35	04 14	04 35	05 02	05 41

Moonset

Lat.	Sunset	Twilight Civil	Naut.	Moonset 15	16	17	18
°	h m	h m	h m	h m	h m	h m	h m
N 72	15 58	17 09	18 27	15 01	14 31	■	■
N 70	16 11	17 14	18 24	15 22	15 11	14 50	■
68	16 21	17 18	18 22	15 39	15 39	15 44	16 00
66	16 29	17 22	18 21	15 52	16 01	16 17	16 48
64	16 36	17 24	18 19	16 03	16 18	16 41	17 19
62	16 42	17 27	18 18	16 13	16 32	17 00	17 43
60	16 47	17 30	18 18	16 21	16 44	17 16	18 01
N 58	16 52	17 32	18 17	16 28	16 55	17 30	18 17
56	16 56	17 34	18 17	16 35	17 04	17 41	18 30
54	17 00	17 35	18 16	16 41	17 12	17 51	18 42
52	17 03	17 37	18 16	16 46	17 19	18 01	18 52
50	17 06	17 39	18 16	16 50	17 26	18 09	19 01
45	17 13	17 43	18 17	17 01	17 40	18 26	19 20
N 40	17 19	17 46	18 17	17 09	17 52	18 40	19 36
35	17 23	17 49	18 18	17 17	18 02	18 52	19 49
30	17 28	17 52	18 20	17 23	18 11	19 03	20 01
20	17 35	17 58	18 23	17 35	18 26	19 21	20 20
N 10	17 42	18 04	18 28	17 44	18 39	19 37	20 38
0	17 49	18 10	18 34	17 54	18 52	19 52	20 54
S 10	17 55	18 17	18 42	18 03	19 04	20 07	21 10
20	18 03	18 25	18 51	18 13	19 18	20 23	21 27
30	18 11	18 35	19 04	18 25	19 33	20 41	21 46
35	18 16	18 42	19 13	18 31	19 42	20 52	21 58
40	18 21	18 49	19 23	18 39	19 52	21 04	22 11
45	18 28	18 58	19 35	18 48	20 04	21 19	22 27
S 50	18 35	19 10	19 51	18 58	20 19	21 36	22 46
52	18 39	19 15	19 59	19 03	20 26	21 45	22 55
54	18 43	19 21	20 08	19 09	20 33	21 54	23 05
56	18 47	19 27	20 18	19 15	20 42	22 04	23 17
58	18 52	19 35	20 30	19 22	20 52	22 14	23 30
S 60	18 58	19 44	20 44	19 29	21 03	22 30	23 45

SUN / MOON

Day	Eqn. of Time 00h	Eqn. of Time 12h	Mer. Pass.	Mer. Pass. Upper	Mer. Pass. Lower	Age	Phase
d	m s	m s	h m	h m	h m	d	%
15	14 12	14 19	11 46	11 40	24 09	29	0
16	14 25	14 32	11 45	12 38	00 09	01	1
17	14 38	14 44	11 45	13 38	01 07	02	6

UT	ARIES GHA	VENUS −4.0 GHA	Dec	MARS +1.2 GHA	Dec	JUPITER −2.7 GHA	Dec	SATURN +0.6 GHA	Dec	Name	SHA	Dec
18 00	26 53.2	218 05.8 N 6	02.3	141 04.8 S22	32.7	311 54.8 N21	53.0	176 48.2 S 9	52.8	Acamar	315 18.3	S40 15.1
01	41 55.7	233 05.5	01.2	156 05.3	33.0	326 57.4	52.9	191 50.4	52.9	Achernar	335 26.5	S57 10.2
02	56 58.1	248 05.1 6	00.1	171 05.9	33.3	342 00.0	52.9	206 52.6	53.0	Acrux	173 10.4	S63 10.1
03	72 00.6	263 04.8 5	59.1	186 06.4 ..	33.6	357 02.6 ..	52.9	221 54.8 ..	53.1	Adhara	255 12.8	S28 59.3
04	87 03.1	278 04.5	58.0	201 07.0	34.0	12 05.2	52.9	236 56.9	53.2	Aldebaran	290 49.7	N16 32.1
05	102 05.5	293 04.1	56.9	216 07.5	34.3	27 07.8	52.9	251 59.1	53.3			
06	117 08.0	308 03.8 N 5	55.9	231 08.0 S22	34.6	42 10.4 N21	52.9	267 01.3 S 9	53.4	Alioth	166 21.7	N55 53.4
07	132 10.5	323 03.4	54.8	246 08.6	34.9	57 12.9	52.9	282 03.5	53.5	Alkaid	152 59.8	N49 15.0
T 08	147 12.9	338 03.1	53.7	261 09.1	35.2	72 15.5	52.9	297 05.6	53.6	Al Na'ir	27 44.1	S46 53.9
H 09	162 15.4	353 02.8 ..	52.7	276 09.7 ..	35.5	87 18.1 ..	52.8	312 07.8 ..	53.7	Alnilam	275 46.7	S 1 11.6
U 10	177 17.9	8 02.4	51.6	291 10.2	35.8	102 20.7	52.8	327 10.0	53.8	Alphard	217 56.7	S 8 42.8
R 11	192 20.3	23 02.1	50.5	306 10.7	36.1	117 23.3	52.8	342 12.2	53.9			
S 12	207 22.8	38 01.8 N 5	49.5	321 11.3 S22	36.4	132 25.9 N21	52.8	357 14.3 S 9	54.0	Alphecca	126 11.7	N26 40.5
D 13	222 25.3	53 01.4	48.4	336 11.8	36.7	147 28.5	52.8	12 16.5	54.1	Alpheratz	357 43.6	N29 09.9
A 14	237 27.7	68 01.1	47.3	351 12.3	37.0	162 31.1	52.8	27 18.7	54.2	Altair	62 08.7	N 8 54.5
Y 15	252 30.2	83 00.7 ..	46.3	6 12.9 ..	37.3	177 33.7 ..	52.8	42 20.9 ..	54.3	Ankaa	353 15.8	S42 14.1
16	267 32.6	98 00.4	45.2	21 13.4	37.6	192 36.2	52.8	57 23.1	54.4	Antares	112 27.1	S26 27.5
17	282 35.1	113 00.1	44.1	36 14.0	38.0	207 38.8	52.7	72 25.2	54.6			
18	297 37.6	127 59.7 N 5	43.1	51 14.5 S22	38.3	222 41.4 N21	52.7	87 27.4 S 9	54.7	Arcturus	145 56.5	N19 07.1
19	312 40.0	142 59.4	42.0	66 15.0	38.6	237 44.0	52.7	102 29.6	54.8	Atria	107 29.7	S69 03.1
20	327 42.5	157 59.0	40.9	81 15.6	38.9	252 46.6	52.7	117 31.8	54.9	Avior	234 18.3	S59 32.8
21	342 45.0	172 58.7 ..	39.8	96 16.1 ..	39.2	267 49.2 ..	52.7	132 33.9 ..	55.0	Bellatrix	278 32.3	N 6 21.6
22	357 47.4	187 58.4	38.8	111 16.6	39.5	282 51.8	52.7	147 36.1	55.1	Betelgeuse	271 01.6	N 7 24.5
23	12 49.9	202 58.0	37.7	126 17.2	39.8	297 54.4	52.7	162 38.3	55.2			
19 00	27 52.4	217 57.7 N 5	36.6	141 17.7 S22	40.1	312 57.0 N21	52.6	177 40.5 S 9	55.3	Canopus	263 56.1	S52 42.0
01	42 54.8	232 57.4	35.6	156 18.2	40.4	327 59.6	52.6	192 42.7	55.4	Capella	280 34.8	N46 00.4
02	57 57.3	247 57.0	34.5	171 18.8	40.7	343 02.2	52.6	207 44.8	55.5	Deneb	49 31.7	N45 20.0
03	72 59.8	262 56.7 ..	33.4	186 19.3 ..	41.0	358 04.8 ..	52.6	222 47.0 ..	55.6	Denebola	182 34.4	N14 30.0
04	88 02.2	277 56.3	32.3	201 19.8	41.3	13 07.4	52.6	237 49.2	55.7	Diphda	348 56.0	S17 54.8
05	103 04.7	292 56.0	31.3	216 20.4	41.6	28 10.0	52.6	252 51.4	55.8			
06	118 07.1	307 55.7 N 5	30.2	231 20.9 S22	41.9	43 12.6 N21	52.6	267 53.5 S 9	55.9	Dubhe	193 52.8	N61 40.7
07	133 09.6	322 55.3	29.1	246 21.4	42.2	58 15.1	52.6	282 55.7	56.0	Elnath	278 13.0	N28 36.9
08	148 12.1	337 55.0	28.0	261 22.0	42.5	73 17.7	52.5	297 57.9	56.1	Eltanin	90 46.6	N51 29.6
F 09	163 14.5	352 54.7 ..	27.0	276 22.5 ..	42.8	88 20.3 ..	52.5	313 00.1 ..	56.2	Enif	33 47.4	N 9 56.3
R 10	178 17.0	7 54.3	25.9	291 23.0	43.1	103 22.9	52.5	328 02.2	56.3	Fomalhaut	15 24.2	S29 33.2
I 11	193 19.5	22 54.0	24.8	306 23.6	43.4	118 25.5	52.5	343 04.4	56.4			
D 12	208 21.9	37 53.7 N 5	23.7	321 24.1 S22	43.7	133 28.1 N21	52.5	358 06.6 S 9	56.5	Gacrux	172 02.0	S57 11.0
A 13	223 24.4	52 53.3	22.7	336 24.6	44.0	148 30.7	52.5	13 08.8	56.7	Gienah	175 53.1	S17 36.7
Y 14	238 26.9	67 53.0	21.6	351 25.1	44.3	163 33.3	52.5	28 11.0	56.8	Hadar	148 49.2	S60 26.0
15	253 29.3	82 52.6 ..	20.5	6 25.7 ..	44.6	178 35.9 ..	52.4	43 13.1 ..	56.9	Hamal	328 00.9	N23 31.5
16	268 31.8	97 52.3	19.4	21 26.2	44.9	193 38.5	52.4	58 15.3	57.0	Kaus Aust.	83 44.6	S34 22.6
17	283 34.3	112 52.0	18.3	36 26.7	45.2	208 41.1	52.4	73 17.5	57.1			
18	298 36.7	127 51.6 N 5	17.3	51 27.3 S22	45.5	223 43.7 N21	52.4	88 19.7 S 9	57.2	Kochab	137 21.1	N74 06.3
19	313 39.2	142 51.3	16.2	66 27.8	45.8	238 46.3	52.4	103 21.8	57.3	Markab	13 38.5	N15 16.7
20	328 41.6	157 51.0	15.1	81 28.3	46.0	253 48.9	52.4	118 24.0	57.4	Menkar	314 15.2	N 4 08.5
21	343 44.1	172 50.6 ..	14.0	96 28.9 ..	46.3	268 51.5 ..	52.4	133 26.2 ..	57.5	Menkent	148 08.5	S36 25.9
22	358 46.6	187 50.3	12.9	111 29.4	46.6	283 54.1	52.3	148 28.4	57.6	Miaplacidus	221 40.1	S69 46.0
23	13 49.0	202 49.9	11.9	126 29.9	46.9	298 56.7	52.3	163 30.5	57.7			
20 00	28 51.5	217 49.6 N 5	10.8	141 30.4 S22	47.2	313 59.3 N21	52.3	178 32.7 S 9	57.8	Mirfak	308 40.5	N49 54.3
01	43 54.0	232 49.3	09.7	156 31.0	47.5	329 01.9	52.3	193 34.9	57.9	Nunki	75 59.0	S26 16.7
02	58 56.4	247 48.9	08.6	171 31.5	47.8	344 04.5	52.3	208 37.1	58.0	Peacock	53 19.9	S56 41.7
03	73 58.9	262 48.6 ..	07.5	186 32.0 ..	48.1	359 07.1 ..	52.3	223 39.3 ..	58.1	Pollux	243 28.3	N27 59.5
04	89 01.4	277 48.3	06.5	201 32.5	48.4	14 09.8	52.3	238 41.4	58.2	Procyon	245 00.2	N 5 11.5
05	104 03.8	292 47.9	05.4	216 33.1	48.7	29 12.4	52.2	253 43.6	58.3			
06	119 06.3	307 47.6 N 5	04.3	231 33.6 S22	49.0	44 15.0 N21	52.2	268 45.8 S 9	58.4	Rasalhague	96 07.1	N12 33.3
07	134 08.7	322 47.3	03.2	246 34.1	49.3	59 17.6	52.2	283 48.0	58.5	Regulus	207 44.2	N11 54.2
S 08	149 11.2	337 46.9	02.1	261 34.6	49.6	74 20.2	52.2	298 50.1	58.6	Rigel	281 12.3	S 8 11.2
A 09	164 13.7	352 46.6 ..	01.0	276 35.2 ..	49.9	89 22.8 ..	52.2	313 52.3 ..	58.7	Rigil Kent.	139 53.0	S60 53.2
T 10	179 16.1	7 46.2 5	00.0	291 35.7	50.1	104 25.4	52.2	328 54.5	58.9	Sabik	102 13.3	S15 44.3
U 11	194 18.6	22 45.9 4	58.9	306 36.2	50.4	119 28.0	52.2	343 56.7	59.0			
R 12	209 21.1	37 45.6 N 4	57.8	321 36.7 S22	50.7	134 30.6 N21	52.1	358 58.8 S 9	59.1	Schedar	349 40.5	N56 36.7
D 13	224 23.5	52 45.2	56.7	336 37.3	51.0	149 33.2	52.1	14 01.0	59.2	Shaula	96 22.8	S37 06.7
A 14	239 26.0	67 44.9	55.6	351 37.8	51.3	164 35.8	52.1	29 03.2	59.3	Sirius	258 34.0	S16 44.0
Y 15	254 28.5	82 44.6 ..	54.5	6 38.3 ..	51.6	179 38.4 ..	52.1	44 05.4 ..	59.4	Spica	158 32.1	S11 13.6
16	269 30.9	97 44.2	53.4	21 38.8	51.9	194 41.0	52.1	59 07.5	59.5	Suhail	222 52.9	S43 28.9
17	284 33.4	112 43.9	52.4	36 39.4	52.2	209 43.6	52.1	74 09.7	59.6			
18	299 35.9	127 43.6 N 4	51.3	51 39.9 S22	52.5	224 46.2 N21	52.1	89 11.9 S 9	59.7	Vega	80 39.4	N38 48.1
19	314 38.3	142 43.2	50.2	66 40.4	52.7	239 48.8	52.0	104 14.1	59.8	Zuben'ubi	137 06.3	S16 05.6
20	329 40.8	157 42.9	49.1	81 40.9	53.0	254 51.5	52.0	119 16.3 9	59.9		SHA	Mer.Pass.
21	344 43.2	172 42.6 ..	48.0	96 41.5 ..	53.3	269 54.1 ..	52.0	134 18.4 10	00.0		° ′	h m
22	359 45.7	187 42.2	46.9	111 42.0	53.6	284 56.7	52.0	149 20.6	00.1	Venus	190 05.3	9 28
23	14 48.2	202 41.9	45.8	126 42.5	53.9	299 59.3	52.0	164 22.8	00.2	Mars	113 25.3	14 34
Mer.Pass. 22 04.9		v −0.3 d 1.1		v 0.5 d 0.3		v 2.6 d 0.0		v 2.2 d 0.1		Jupiter	285 04.6	3 08
										Saturn	149 48.1	12 08

UT	SUN GHA	SUN Dec	MOON GHA	v	Dec	d	HP
d h	° ′	° ′	° ′	′	° ′	′	′
18 00	183 42.4	S 9 41.0	149 16.4	4.1	S19 47.1	4.5	60.7
01	198 42.6	41.9	163 39.5	4.1	19 51.6	4.4	60.7
02	213 42.7	42.8	178 02.7	4.1	19 56.0	4.2	60.6
03	228 42.8	.. 43.7	192 25.8	4.2	20 00.2	4.1	60.6
04	243 42.9	44.6	206 49.0	4.1	20 04.3	3.9	60.6
05	258 43.0	45.5	221 12.1	4.1	20 08.2	3.8	60.6
06	273 43.2	S 9 46.4	235 35.2	4.1	S20 12.0	3.6	60.6
T 07	288 43.3	47.4	249 58.3	4.0	20 15.6	3.5	60.6
H 08	303 43.4	48.3	264 21.3	4.1	20 19.1	3.4	60.6
U 09	318 43.5	.. 49.2	278 44.4	4.1	20 22.5	3.2	60.5
R 10	333 43.6	50.1	293 07.5	4.0	20 25.7	3.0	60.5
S 11	348 43.7	51.0	307 30.5	4.1	20 28.7	2.9	60.5
D 12	3 43.9	S 9 51.9	321 53.6	4.0	S20 31.6	2.7	60.5
A 13	18 44.0	52.8	336 16.6	4.1	20 34.3	2.6	60.5
Y 14	33 44.1	53.7	350 39.7	4.0	20 36.9	2.5	60.5
15	48 44.2	.. 54.6	5 02.7	4.1	20 39.4	2.2	60.5
16	63 44.3	55.5	19 25.8	4.0	20 41.6	2.2	60.4
17	78 44.4	56.4	33 48.8	4.1	20 43.8	2.0	60.4
18	93 44.6	S 9 57.3	48 11.9	4.1	S20 45.8	1.8	60.4
19	108 44.7	58.2	62 35.0	4.1	20 47.6	1.7	60.4
20	123 44.8	9 59.1	76 58.1	4.1	20 49.3	1.5	60.4
21	138 44.9	10 00.0	91 21.2	4.1	20 50.8	1.4	60.4
22	153 45.0	00.9	105 44.3	4.1	20 52.2	1.2	60.3
23	168 45.1	01.8	120 07.4	4.2	20 53.4	1.1	60.3
19 00	183 45.2	S10 02.7	134 30.6	4.2	S20 54.5	0.9	60.3
01	198 45.4	03.6	148 53.8	4.2	20 55.4	0.8	60.3
02	213 45.5	04.5	163 17.0	4.2	20 56.2	0.7	60.3
03	228 45.6	.. 05.4	177 40.2	4.2	20 56.9	0.4	60.2
04	243 45.7	06.3	192 03.4	4.3	20 57.3	0.4	60.2
05	258 45.8	07.2	206 26.7	4.3	20 57.7	0.1	60.2
06	273 45.9	S10 08.1	220 50.0	4.3	S20 57.8	0.1	60.2
F 07	288 46.0	09.0	235 13.3	4.4	20 57.9	0.2	60.2
R 08	303 46.1	09.9	249 36.7	4.4	20 57.7	0.2	60.1
I 09	318 46.2	.. 10.8	264 00.1	4.4	20 57.5	0.4	60.1
D 10	333 46.4	11.7	278 23.5	4.5	20 57.1	0.6	60.1
A 11	348 46.5	12.6	292 47.0	4.5	20 56.5	0.7	60.1
Y 12	3 46.6	S10 13.5	307 10.5	4.5	S20 55.8	0.9	60.0
13	18 46.7	14.4	321 34.0	4.6	20 54.9	1.0	60.0
14	33 46.8	15.3	335 57.6	4.6	20 53.9	1.1	60.0
15	48 46.9	.. 16.2	350 21.2	4.7	20 52.8	1.3	60.0
16	63 47.0	17.1	4 44.9	4.7	20 51.5	1.4	59.9
17	78 47.1	18.0	19 08.6	4.7	20 50.1	1.6	59.9
18	93 47.2	S10 18.9	33 32.3	4.9	S20 48.5	1.8	59.9
19	108 47.3	19.8	47 56.2	4.8	20 46.7	1.8	59.9
20	123 47.4	20.7	62 20.0	4.9	20 44.9	2.0	59.9
21	138 47.6	.. 21.6	76 43.9	5.0	20 42.9	2.2	59.8
22	153 47.7	22.5	91 07.9	5.0	20 40.7	2.3	59.8
23	168 47.8	23.4	105 31.9	5.1	20 38.4	2.4	59.8
20 00	183 47.9	S10 24.3	119 56.0	5.1	S20 36.0	2.6	59.7
01	198 48.0	25.2	134 20.1	5.2	20 33.4	2.7	59.7
02	213 48.1	26.1	148 44.3	5.2	20 30.7	2.8	59.7
03	228 48.2	.. 27.0	163 08.5	5.3	20 27.9	3.0	59.7
04	243 48.3	27.9	177 32.8	5.4	20 24.9	3.1	59.6
05	258 48.4	28.8	191 57.2	5.4	20 21.8	3.3	59.6
06	273 48.5	S10 29.7	206 21.6	5.5	S20 18.5	3.4	59.6
S 07	288 48.6	30.5	220 46.1	5.6	20 15.1	3.5	59.6
A 08	303 48.7	31.4	235 10.7	5.6	20 11.6	3.6	59.5
T 09	318 48.8	.. 32.3	249 35.3	5.7	20 08.0	3.8	59.5
U 10	333 48.9	33.2	264 00.0	5.8	20 04.2	3.9	59.5
R 11	348 49.0	34.1	278 24.8	5.8	20 00.3	4.1	59.5
D 12	3 49.1	S10 35.0	292 49.6	5.9	S19 56.2	4.1	59.4
A 13	18 49.2	35.9	307 14.5	6.0	19 52.1	4.3	59.4
Y 14	33 49.3	36.8	321 39.5	6.0	19 47.8	4.4	59.4
15	48 49.4	.. 37.7	336 04.5	6.1	19 43.4	4.6	59.3
16	63 49.5	38.6	350 29.6	6.2	19 38.8	4.6	59.3
17	78 49.6	39.5	4 54.8	6.3	19 34.2	4.8	59.3
18	93 49.8	S10 40.4	19 20.1	6.3	S19 29.4	4.9	59.3
19	108 49.9	41.2	33 45.4	6.4	19 24.5	5.1	59.2
20	123 50.0	42.1	48 10.8	6.5	19 19.4	5.1	59.2
21	138 50.1	.. 43.0	62 36.3	6.6	19 14.3	5.2	59.2
22	153 50.2	43.9	77 01.9	6.6	19 09.0	5.4	59.1
23	168 50.3	44.8	91 27.5	6.7	S19 03.6	5.5	59.1
	SD 16.1	d 0.9	SD 16.5		16.4		16.2

Lat.	Twilight Naut.	Twilight Civil	Sunrise	Moonrise 18	19	20	21
°	h m	h m	h m	h m	h m	h m	h m
N 72	05 14	06 33	07 46	■	■		16 29
N 70	05 16	06 27	07 32	■	■	16 04	15 30
68	05 17	06 22	07 20	13 14	14 26	14 50	14 56
66	05 18	06 17	07 11	12 26	13 35	14 12	14 31
64	05 18	06 14	07 03	11 55	13 03	13 46	14 11
62	05 19	06 10	06 56	11 32	12 39	13 25	13 55
60	05 19	06 07	06 50	11 14	12 20	13 08	13 41
N 58	05 19	06 05	06 45	10 58	12 04	12 54	13 30
56	05 19	06 02	06 40	10 45	11 51	12 41	13 20
54	05 19	06 00	06 36	10 34	11 39	12 31	13 11
52	05 19	05 58	06 32	10 24	11 29	12 21	13 03
50	05 18	05 56	06 29	10 15	11 19	12 13	12 55
45	05 17	05 51	06 21	09 56	11 00	11 55	12 40
N 40	05 16	05 48	06 15	09 40	10 44	11 40	12 27
35	05 14	05 44	06 10	09 27	10 31	11 27	12 16
30	05 13	05 40	06 05	09 16	10 19	11 16	12 07
20	05 08	05 34	05 56	08 57	09 59	10 57	11 51
N 10	05 03	05 27	05 49	08 40	09 42	10 41	11 36
0	04 56	05 21	05 42	08 24	09 26	10 26	11 23
S 10	04 48	05 13	05 34	08 09	09 10	10 10	11 09
20	04 38	05 04	05 26	07 52	08 52	09 54	10 55
30	04 24	04 53	05 17	07 33	08 33	09 35	10 38
35	04 15	04 46	05 12	07 22	08 21	09 24	10 29
40	04 04	04 38	05 06	07 09	08 08	09 11	10 18
45	03 51	04 28	04 59	06 54	07 52	08 56	10 05
S 50	03 34	04 16	04 50	06 36	07 33	08 38	09 49
52	03 26	04 10	04 46	06 28	07 24	08 30	09 41
54	03 16	04 04	04 42	06 18	07 14	08 20	09 33
56	03 05	03 57	04 37	06 07	07 02	08 09	09 24
58	02 53	03 49	04 32	05 55	06 49	07 56	09 13
S 60	02 37	03 39	04 26	05 41	06 34	07 42	09 01

Lat.	Sunset	Twilight Civil	Twilight Naut.	Moonset 18	19	20	21
°	h m	h m	h m	h m	h m	h m	h m
N 72	15 42	16 55	18 13	■	■		18 56
N 70	15 57	17 01	18 12	■	■	17 23	19 54
68	16 08	17 07	18 11	16 00	16 56	18 37	20 28
66	16 18	17 11	18 10	16 48	17 48	19 14	20 52
64	16 26	17 15	18 10	17 19	18 20	19 40	21 11
62	16 33	17 18	18 10	17 43	18 43	20 00	21 26
60	16 39	17 21	18 10	18 01	19 02	20 17	21 39
N 58	16 44	17 24	18 10	18 17	19 18	20 31	21 50
56	16 49	17 27	18 10	18 30	19 31	20 43	22 00
54	16 53	17 29	18 10	18 42	19 43	20 53	22 08
52	16 57	17 31	18 10	18 52	19 53	21 02	22 16
50	17 00	17 33	18 11	19 01	20 02	21 11	22 23
45	17 08	17 38	18 12	19 20	20 21	21 28	22 37
N 40	17 14	17 42	18 13	19 36	20 37	21 42	22 49
35	17 20	17 45	18 15	19 49	20 50	21 55	22 59
30	17 25	17 49	18 17	20 01	21 02	22 05	23 08
20	17 33	17 56	18 21	20 20	21 22	22 23	23 23
N 10	17 41	18 02	18 27	20 38	21 39	22 39	23 36
0	17 48	18 09	18 34	20 54	21 55	22 53	23 49
S 10	17 56	18 17	18 42	21 10	22 10	23 08	24 01
20	18 04	18 26	18 53	21 27	22 27	23 23	24 14
30	18 13	18 38	19 07	21 46	22 47	23 41	24 29
35	18 18	18 44	19 16	21 58	22 58	23 51	24 37
40	18 24	18 53	19 26	22 11	23 11	24 03	00 03
45	18 32	19 03	19 40	22 27	23 26	24 16	00 16
S 50	18 40	19 15	19 57	22 46	23 45	24 33	00 33
52	18 44	19 21	20 06	22 55	23 54	24 40	00 41
54	18 49	19 27	20 15	23 05	24 04	00 04	00 50
56	18 54	19 35	20 27	23 17	24 15	00 15	00 59
58	18 59	19 43	20 40	23 30	24 28	00 28	01 10
S 60	19 06	19 52	20 56	23 45	24 42	00 42	01 23

Day	SUN Eqn. of Time 00h	12h	Mer. Pass.	MOON Mer. Pass. Upper	Lower	Age	Phase
d	m s	m s	h m	h m	h m	d %	
18	14 50	14 55	11 45	14 39	02 08	03 13	
19	15 01	15 06	11 45	15 40	03 10	04 22	
20	15 11	15 16	11 45	16 40	04 10	05 32	

UT	ARIES GHA	VENUS −4.0 GHA	Dec	MARS +1.2 GHA	Dec	JUPITER −2.7 GHA	Dec	SATURN +0.6 GHA	Dec	Name	SHA	Dec
21 00	29 50.6	217 41.5	N 4 44.7	141 43.0	S22 54.2	315 01.9	N21 52.0	179 25.0	S10 00.3	Acamar	315 18.3	S40 15.1
01	44 53.1	232 41.2	43.7	156 43.5	54.5	330 04.5	52.0	194 27.1	00.4	Achernar	335 26.5	S57 10.2
02	59 55.6	247 40.9	42.6	171 44.1	54.7	345 07.1	51.9	209 29.3	00.5	Acrux	173 10.4	S63 10.1
03	74 58.0	262 40.5	.. 41.5	186 44.6	.. 55.0	0 09.7	.. 51.9	224 31.5	.. 00.6	Adhara	255 12.8	S28 59.3
04	90 00.5	277 40.2	40.4	201 45.1	55.3	15 12.3	51.9	239 33.7	00.7	Aldebaran	290 49.6	N16 32.1
05	105 03.0	292 39.9	39.3	216 45.6	55.6	30 15.0	51.9	254 35.8	00.8			
06	120 05.4	307 39.5	N 4 38.2	231 46.1	S22 55.9	45 17.6	N21 51.9	269 38.0	S10 00.9	Alioth	166 21.6	N55 53.3
07	135 07.9	322 39.2	37.1	246 46.7	56.2	60 20.2	51.9	284 40.2	01.0	Alkaid	152 59.7	N49 15.0
08	150 10.4	337 38.9	36.0	261 47.2	56.4	75 22.8	51.8	299 42.4	01.1	Al Na'ir	27 44.1	S46 53.9
S 09	165 12.8	352 38.5	.. 34.9	276 47.7	.. 56.7	90 25.4	.. 51.8	314 44.5	.. 01.3	Alnilam	275 46.6	S 1 11.6
U 10	180 15.3	7 38.2	33.8	291 48.2	57.0	105 28.0	51.8	329 46.7	01.4	Alphard	217 56.6	S 8 42.8
N 11	195 17.7	22 37.9	32.7	306 48.7	57.3	120 30.6	51.8	344 48.9	01.5			
D 12	210 20.2	37 37.5	N 4 31.7	321 49.2	S22 57.6	135 33.3	N21 51.8	359 51.1	S10 01.6	Alphecca	126 11.7	N26 40.5
A 13	225 22.7	52 37.2	30.6	336 49.8	57.8	150 35.9	51.8	14 53.3	01.7	Alpheratz	357 43.6	N29 09.9
Y 14	240 25.1	67 36.9	29.5	351 50.3	58.1	165 38.5	51.8	29 55.4	01.8	Altair	62 08.7	N 8 54.5
15	255 27.6	82 36.5	.. 28.4	6 50.8	.. 58.4	180 41.1	.. 51.7	44 57.6	.. 01.9	Ankaa	353 15.8	S42 14.1
16	270 30.1	97 36.2	27.3	21 51.3	58.7	195 43.7	51.7	59 59.8	02.0	Antares	112 27.1	S26 27.5
17	285 32.5	112 35.8	26.2	36 51.8	59.0	210 46.3	51.7	75 02.0	02.1			
18	300 35.0	127 35.5	N 4 25.1	51 52.3	S22 59.2	225 49.0	N21 51.7	90 04.1	S10 02.2	Arcturus	145 56.5	N19 07.1
19	315 37.5	142 35.2	24.0	66 52.9	59.5	240 51.6	51.7	105 06.3	02.3	Atria	107 29.7	S69 03.1
20	330 39.9	157 34.8	22.9	81 53.4	22 59.8	255 54.2	51.7	120 08.5	02.4	Avior	234 18.2	S59 32.8
21	345 42.4	172 34.5	.. 21.8	96 53.9	23 00.1	270 56.8	.. 51.6	135 10.7	.. 02.5	Bellatrix	278 32.3	N 6 21.6
22	0 44.9	187 34.2	20.7	111 54.4	00.3	285 59.4	51.6	150 12.8	02.6	Betelgeuse	271 01.6	N 7 24.5
23	15 47.3	202 33.8	19.6	126 54.9	00.6	301 02.0	51.6	165 15.0	02.7			
22 00	30 49.8	217 33.5	N 4 18.5	141 55.4	S23 00.9	316 04.7	N21 51.6	180 17.2	S10 02.8	Canopus	263 56.1	S52 42.0
01	45 52.2	232 33.2	17.4	156 56.0	01.2	331 07.3	51.6	195 19.4	02.9	Capella	280 34.8	N46 00.4
02	60 54.7	247 32.8	16.3	171 56.5	01.4	346 09.9	51.6	210 21.5	03.0	Deneb	49 31.7	N45 20.0
03	75 57.2	262 32.5	.. 15.2	186 57.0	.. 01.7	1 12.5	.. 51.6	225 23.7	.. 03.1	Denebola	182 34.4	N14 30.0
04	90 59.6	277 32.2	14.1	201 57.5	02.0	16 15.1	51.5	240 25.9	03.2	Diphda	348 56.0	S17 54.8
05	106 02.1	292 31.8	13.0	216 58.0	02.3	31 17.8	51.5	255 28.1	03.3			
06	121 04.6	307 31.5	N 4 11.9	231 58.5	S23 02.5	46 20.4	N21 51.5	270 30.2	S10 03.4	Dubhe	193 52.7	N61 40.6
07	136 07.0	322 31.2	10.8	246 59.0	02.8	61 23.0	51.5	285 32.4	03.5	Elnath	278 13.0	N28 37.0
08	151 09.5	337 30.8	09.7	261 59.5	03.1	76 25.6	51.5	300 34.6	03.7	Eltanin	90 46.6	N51 29.6
M 09	166 12.0	352 30.5	.. 08.6	277 00.1	.. 03.4	91 28.3	.. 51.5	315 36.8	.. 03.8	Enif	33 47.4	N 9 56.3
O 10	181 14.4	7 30.2	07.5	292 00.6	03.6	106 30.9	51.4	330 39.0	03.9	Fomalhaut	15 24.2	S29 33.2
N 11	196 16.9	22 29.8	06.4	307 01.1	03.9	121 33.5	51.4	345 41.1	04.0			
D 12	211 19.3	37 29.5	N 4 05.3	322 01.6	S23 04.2	136 36.1	N21 51.4	0 43.3	S10 04.1	Gacrux	172 01.9	S57 11.0
A 13	226 21.8	52 29.1	04.2	337 02.1	04.4	151 38.7	51.4	15 45.5	04.2	Gienah	175 53.1	S17 36.7
Y 14	241 24.3	67 28.8	03.1	352 02.6	04.7	166 41.4	51.4	30 47.7	04.3	Hadar	148 49.2	S60 26.0
15	256 26.7	82 28.5	.. 02.0	7 03.1	.. 05.0	181 44.0	.. 51.4	45 49.8	.. 04.4	Hamal	328 00.9	N23 31.5
16	271 29.2	97 28.1	4 00.9	22 03.6	05.3	196 46.6	51.3	60 52.0	04.5	Kaus Aust.	83 44.6	S34 22.6
17	286 31.7	112 27.8	3 59.8	37 04.1	05.5	211 49.2	51.3	75 54.2	04.6			
18	301 34.1	127 27.5	N 3 58.7	52 04.7	S23 05.8	226 51.9	N21 51.3	90 56.4	S10 04.7	Kochab	137 21.2	N74 06.3
19	316 36.6	142 27.1	57.6	67 05.2	06.1	241 54.5	51.3	105 58.5	04.8	Markab	13 38.5	N15 16.7
20	331 39.1	157 26.8	56.5	82 05.7	06.3	256 57.1	51.3	121 00.7	04.9	Menkar	314 15.2	N 4 08.5
21	346 41.5	172 26.5	.. 55.4	97 06.2	.. 06.6	271 59.8	.. 51.3	136 02.9	.. 05.0	Menkent	148 08.5	S36 25.9
22	1 44.0	187 26.1	54.3	112 06.7	06.9	287 02.4	51.3	151 05.1	05.1	Miaplacidus	221 40.0	S69 46.0
23	16 46.5	202 25.8	53.2	127 07.2	07.1	302 05.0	51.2	166 07.2	05.2			
23 00	31 48.9	217 25.5	N 3 52.1	142 07.7	S23 07.4	317 07.6	N21 51.2	181 09.4	S10 05.3	Mirfak	308 40.5	N49 54.3
01	46 51.4	232 25.1	51.0	157 08.2	07.7	332 10.3	51.2	196 11.6	05.4	Nunki	75 59.0	S26 16.7
02	61 53.8	247 24.8	49.9	172 08.7	07.9	347 12.9	51.2	211 13.8	05.5	Peacock	53 19.9	S56 41.7
03	76 56.3	262 24.5	.. 48.8	187 09.2	.. 08.2	2 15.5	.. 51.2	226 15.9	.. 05.6	Pollux	243 28.3	N27 59.5
04	91 58.8	277 24.1	47.7	202 09.7	08.5	17 18.1	51.2	241 18.1	05.7	Procyon	245 00.2	N 5 11.5
05	107 01.2	292 23.8	46.6	217 10.2	08.7	32 20.8	51.1	256 20.3	05.8			
06	122 03.7	307 23.5	N 3 45.5	232 10.8	S23 09.0	47 23.4	N21 51.1	271 22.5	S10 05.9	Rasalhague	96 07.1	N12 33.3
07	137 06.2	322 23.1	44.4	247 11.3	09.3	62 26.0	51.1	286 24.6	06.0	Regulus	207 44.2	N11 54.2
T 08	152 08.6	337 22.8	43.3	262 11.8	09.5	77 28.7	51.1	301 26.8	06.2	Rigel	281 12.3	S 8 11.2
U 09	167 11.1	352 22.5	.. 42.1	277 12.3	.. 09.8	92 31.3	.. 51.1	316 29.0	.. 06.3	Rigil Kent.	139 53.0	S60 53.2
E 10	182 13.6	7 22.1	41.0	292 12.8	10.1	107 33.9	51.1	331 31.2	06.4	Sabik	102 13.3	S15 44.3
S 11	197 16.0	22 21.8	39.9	307 13.3	10.3	122 36.6	51.0	346 33.3	06.5			
D 12	212 18.5	37 21.5	N 3 38.8	322 13.8	S23 10.6	137 39.2	N21 51.0	1 35.5	S10 06.6	Schedar	349 40.5	N56 36.7
A 13	227 21.0	52 21.1	37.7	337 14.3	10.8	152 41.8	51.0	16 37.7	06.7	Shaula	96 22.8	S37 06.7
Y 14	242 23.4	67 20.8	36.6	352 14.8	11.1	167 44.5	51.0	31 39.9	06.8	Sirius	258 34.0	S16 44.0
15	257 25.9	82 20.5	.. 35.5	7 15.3	.. 11.4	182 47.1	.. 51.0	46 42.1	.. 06.9	Spica	158 32.1	S11 13.6
16	272 28.3	97 20.1	34.4	22 15.8	11.6	197 49.7	51.0	61 44.2	07.0	Suhail	222 52.9	S43 28.9
17	287 30.8	112 19.8	33.3	37 16.3	11.9	212 52.4	50.9	76 46.4	07.1			
18	302 33.3	127 19.4	N 3 32.2	52 16.8	S23 12.1	227 55.0	N21 50.9	91 48.6	S10 07.2	Vega	80 39.4	N38 48.1
19	317 35.7	142 19.1	31.1	67 17.3	12.4	242 57.6	50.9	106 50.8	07.3	Zuben'ubi	137 06.2	S16 05.6
20	332 38.2	157 18.8	30.0	82 17.8	12.7	258 00.3	50.9	121 52.9	07.4		SHA	Mer.Pass.
21	347 40.7	172 18.4	.. 28.8	97 18.3	.. 12.9	273 02.9	.. 50.9	136 55.1	.. 07.5	Venus	186 43.7	h m 9 30
22	2 43.1	187 18.1	27.7	112 18.8	13.2	288 05.5	50.8	151 57.3	07.6	Mars	111 05.7	14 32
23	17 45.6	202 17.8	26.6	127 19.3	13.4	303 08.2	50.8	166 59.5	07.7	Jupiter	285 14.9	2 55
h m Mer.Pass. 21 53.1		v −0.3	d 1.1	v 0.5	d 0.3	v 2.6	d 0.0	v 2.2	d 0.1	Saturn	149 27.4	11 57

UT	SUN GHA	SUN Dec	MOON GHA	v	MOON Dec	d	HP
d h	° ′	° ′	° ′	′	° ′	′	′
21 00	183 50.4	S10 45.7	105 53.2	6.8	S18 58.1	5.6	59.1
01	198 50.5	46.6	120 19.0	6.9	18 52.5	5.7	59.1
02	213 50.6	47.5	134 44.9	7.0	18 46.8	5.9	59.0
03	228 50.7 ..	48.4	149 10.9	7.0	18 40.9	5.9	59.0
04	243 50.8	49.3	163 36.9	7.1	18 35.0	6.1	59.0
05	258 50.9	50.1	178 03.0	7.2	18 28.9	6.2	58.9
06	273 51.0	S10 51.0	192 29.2	7.3	S18 22.7	6.3	58.9
S 07	288 51.0	51.9	206 55.5	7.3	18 16.4	6.3	58.9
U 08	303 51.1	52.8	221 21.8	7.5	18 10.1	6.5	58.8
N 09	318 51.2 ..	53.7	235 48.3	7.5	18 03.6	6.6	58.8
D 10	333 51.3	54.6	250 14.8	7.6	17 57.0	6.7	58.8
A 11	348 51.4	55.5	264 41.4	7.7	17 50.3	6.8	58.8
Y 12	3 51.5	S10 56.3	279 08.1	7.8	S17 43.5	6.9	58.7
13	18 51.6	57.2	293 34.9	7.8	17 36.6	7.0	58.7
14	33 51.7	58.1	308 01.7	8.0	17 29.6	7.1	58.7
15	48 51.8 ..	59.0	322 28.7	8.0	17 22.5	7.2	58.6
16	63 51.9	10 59.9	336 55.7	8.1	17 15.3	7.3	58.6
17	78 52.0	11 00.8	351 22.8	8.2	17 08.0	7.4	58.6
18	93 52.1	S11 01.7	5 50.0	8.2	S17 00.6	7.5	58.5
19	108 52.2	02.5	20 17.2	8.4	16 53.1	7.6	58.5
20	123 52.3	03.4	34 44.6	8.4	16 45.5	7.6	58.5
21	138 52.4 ..	04.3	49 12.0	8.5	16 37.9	7.8	58.5
22	153 52.5	05.2	63 39.5	8.6	16 30.1	7.8	58.4
23	168 52.6	06.1	78 07.1	8.7	16 22.3	8.0	58.4
22 00	183 52.7	S11 06.9	92 34.8	8.8	S16 14.3	8.0	58.4
01	198 52.8	07.8	107 02.6	8.8	16 06.3	8.1	58.3
02	213 52.9	08.7	121 30.4	9.0	15 58.2	8.2	58.3
03	228 53.0 ..	09.6	135 58.4	9.0	15 50.0	8.2	58.3
04	243 53.0	10.5	150 26.4	9.1	15 41.8	8.4	58.2
05	258 53.1	11.4	164 54.5	9.2	15 33.4	8.4	58.2
06	273 53.2	S11 12.2	179 22.7	9.2	S15 25.0	8.5	58.2
M 07	288 53.3	13.1	193 50.9	9.4	15 16.5	8.6	58.2
O 08	303 53.4	14.0	208 19.3	9.4	15 07.9	8.7	58.1
N 09	318 53.5 ..	14.9	222 47.7	9.5	14 59.2	8.7	58.1
D 10	333 53.6	15.8	237 16.2	9.6	14 50.5	8.8	58.1
A 11	348 53.7	16.6	251 44.8	9.6	14 41.7	8.9	58.0
Y 12	3 53.8	S11 17.5	266 13.4	9.8	S14 32.8	9.0	58.0
13	18 53.9	18.4	280 42.2	9.8	14 23.8	9.0	58.0
14	33 54.0	19.3	295 11.0	9.9	14 14.8	9.1	57.9
15	48 54.0 ..	20.1	309 39.9	10.0	14 05.7	9.1	57.9
16	63 54.1	21.0	324 08.9	10.0	13 56.6	9.3	57.9
17	78 54.2	21.9	338 37.9	10.2	13 47.3	9.3	57.9
18	93 54.3	S11 22.8	353 07.1	10.2	S13 38.0	9.3	57.8
19	108 54.4	23.7	7 36.3	10.3	13 28.7	9.4	57.8
20	123 54.5	24.5	22 05.6	10.3	13 19.3	9.5	57.8
21	138 54.6 ..	25.4	36 34.9	10.5	13 09.8	9.6	57.7
22	153 54.7	26.3	51 04.4	10.5	13 00.2	9.6	57.7
23	168 54.7	27.2	65 33.9	10.6	12 50.6	9.6	57.7
23 00	183 54.8	S11 28.0	80 03.5	10.6	S12 41.0	9.8	57.7
01	198 54.9	28.9	94 33.1	10.8	12 31.2	9.7	57.6
02	213 55.0	29.8	109 02.9	10.8	12 21.5	9.9	57.6
03	228 55.1 ..	30.7	123 32.7	10.9	12 11.6	9.9	57.6
04	243 55.2	31.5	138 02.6	10.9	12 01.7	9.9	57.5
05	258 55.3	32.4	152 32.5	11.0	11 51.8	10.0	57.5
06	273 55.4	S11 33.3	167 02.5	11.1	S11 41.8	10.1	57.5
T 07	288 55.4	34.1	181 32.6	11.2	11 31.7	10.0	57.5
U 08	303 55.5	35.0	196 02.8	11.2	11 21.7	10.2	57.4
E 09	318 55.6 ..	35.9	210 33.0	11.3	11 11.5	10.2	57.4
S 10	333 55.7	36.8	225 03.3	11.4	11 01.3	10.2	57.4
D 11	348 55.7	37.6	239 33.7	11.4	10 51.1	10.3	57.3
A 12	3 55.8	S11 38.5	254 04.1	11.5	S10 40.8	10.3	57.3
Y 13	18 55.9	39.4	268 34.6	11.6	10 30.5	10.4	57.3
14	33 56.0	40.2	283 05.2	11.6	10 20.1	10.4	57.2
15	48 56.1 ..	41.1	297 35.8	11.7	10 09.7	10.5	57.2
16	63 56.2	42.0	312 06.5	11.7	9 59.2	10.5	57.2
17	78 56.3	42.9	326 37.2	11.8	9 48.7	10.5	57.2
18	93 56.3	S11 43.7	341 08.0	11.9	S 9 38.2	10.6	57.1
19	108 56.4	44.6	355 38.9	12.0	9 27.6	10.6	57.1
20	123 56.5	45.5	10 09.9	12.0	9 17.0	10.6	57.1
21	138 56.6 ..	46.3	24 40.9	12.0	9 06.4	10.7	57.1
22	153 56.7	47.2	39 11.9	12.1	8 55.7	10.7	57.0
23	168 56.7	48.1	53 43.0	12.2	S 8 45.0	10.8	57.0
SD 16.1	d 0.9		SD 16.0		15.8		15.6

Lat.	Twilight Naut.	Twilight Civil	Sunrise	Moonrise 21	22	23	24
°	h m	h m	h m	h m	h m	h m	h m
N 72	05 27	06 46	08 02	16 29	15 46	15 25	15 10
N 70	05 27	06 38	07 45	15 30	15 18	15 09	15 02
68	05 27	06 32	07 32	14 56	14 57	14 57	14 55
66	05 27	06 27	07 21	14 31	14 40	14 46	14 50
64	05 27	06 22	07 12	14 11	14 27	14 37	14 45
62	05 26	06 18	07 04	13 55	14 15	14 29	14 41
60	05 26	06 14	06 58	13 41	14 05	14 23	14 37
N 58	05 25	06 11	06 52	13 30	13 56	14 17	14 34
56	05 25	06 08	06 47	13 20	13 49	14 12	14 31
54	05 24	06 05	06 42	13 11	13 42	14 07	14 28
52	05 24	06 03	06 38	13 03	13 36	14 03	14 26
50	05 23	06 01	06 34	12 55	13 30	13 59	14 24
45	05 21	05 55	06 25	12 40	13 18	13 50	14 19
N 40	05 19	05 51	06 18	12 27	13 08	13 43	14 15
35	05 17	05 46	06 12	12 16	12 59	13 37	14 11
30	05 14	05 42	06 07	12 07	12 52	13 32	14 08
20	05 09	05 35	05 57	11 51	12 39	13 22	14 03
N 10	05 03	05 28	05 49	11 36	12 27	13 14	13 58
0	04 56	05 20	05 41	11 23	12 16	13 06	13 54
S 10	04 47	05 12	05 33	11 09	12 05	12 59	13 49
20	04 35	05 02	05 24	10 55	11 54	12 50	13 45
30	04 20	04 50	05 14	10 38	11 41	12 41	13 39
35	04 11	04 42	05 08	10 29	11 33	12 35	13 36
40	03 59	04 33	05 02	10 18	11 24	12 29	13 33
45	03 45	04 23	04 54	10 05	11 14	12 22	13 29
S 50	03 27	04 10	04 44	09 49	11 01	12 13	13 24
52	03 18	04 04	04 40	09 41	10 55	12 09	13 22
54	03 08	03 57	04 35	09 33	10 49	12 05	13 19
56	02 56	03 49	04 30	09 24	10 42	12 00	13 16
58	02 42	03 40	04 24	09 13	10 34	11 54	13 13
S 60	02 25	03 30	04 17	09 01	10 24	11 48	13 10

Lat.	Sunset	Twilight Civil	Twilight Naut.	Moonset 21	22	23	24
°	h m	h m	h m	h m	h m	h m	h m
N 72	15 26	16 41	18 00	18 56	21 29	23 33	25 25
N 70	15 42	16 49	18 00	19 54	21 56	23 47	25 31
68	15 56	16 55	18 00	20 28	22 16	23 58	25 36
66	16 06	17 01	18 00	20 52	22 31	24 07	00 07
64	16 16	17 05	18 01	21 11	22 44	24 15	00 15
62	16 23	17 10	18 01	21 26	22 55	24 21	00 21
60	16 30	17 13	18 02	21 39	23 04	24 27	00 27
N 58	16 36	17 17	18 02	21 50	23 12	24 32	00 32
56	16 41	17 20	18 03	22 00	23 19	24 36	00 36
54	16 46	17 22	18 04	22 08	23 25	24 40	00 40
52	16 50	17 25	18 04	22 16	23 30	24 44	00 44
50	16 54	17 27	18 05	22 23	23 35	24 47	00 47
45	17 03	17 33	18 07	22 37	23 46	24 54	00 54
N 40	17 10	17 38	18 09	22 49	23 55	25 00	01 00
35	17 16	17 42	18 11	22 59	24 03	00 03	01 05
30	17 22	17 46	18 14	23 08	24 10	00 10	01 09
20	17 31	17 54	18 19	23 23	24 21	00 21	01 17
N 10	17 40	18 01	18 26	23 36	24 31	00 31	01 23
0	17 48	18 09	18 33	23 49	24 41	00 41	01 29
S 10	17 56	18 17	18 42	24 01	00 01	00 50	01 35
20	18 05	18 27	18 54	24 14	00 14	01 00	01 42
30	18 15	18 40	19 09	24 29	00 29	01 11	01 49
35	18 21	18 47	19 19	24 37	00 37	01 17	01 53
40	18 28	18 56	19 33	00 03	00 47	01 25	01 58
45	18 36	19 07	19 45	00 16	00 58	01 33	02 03
S 50	18 45	19 20	20 04	00 33	01 12	01 43	02 10
52	18 50	19 27	20 13	00 41	01 18	01 48	02 13
54	18 55	19 34	20 23	00 50	01 25	01 53	02 16
56	19 00	19 42	20 35	00 59	01 33	01 59	02 20
58	19 06	19 51	20 50	01 10	01 41	02 05	02 24
S 60	19 13	20 01	21 07	01 23	01 51	02 12	02 28

Day	SUN Eqn. of Time 00h	12h	Mer. Pass.	MOON Mer. Pass. Upper	Lower	Age	Phase
d	m s	m s	h m	h m	h m	d	%
21	15 21	15 26	11 45	17 36	05 08	06	43
22	15 31	15 35	11 44	18 29	06 03	07	54
23	15 39	15 43	11 44	19 18	06 54	08	65

UT	ARIES GHA	VENUS −4.0 GHA	Dec	MARS +1.2 GHA	Dec	JUPITER −2.7 GHA	Dec	SATURN +0.6 GHA	Dec	STARS Name	SHA	Dec
d h 24 00	32 48.1	217 17.4	N 3 25.5	142 19.8	S23 13.7	318 10.8	N21 50.8	182 01.6	S10 07.8	Acamar	315 18.3	S40 15.1
01	47 50.5	232 17.1	24.4	157 20.3	14.0	333 13.4	50.8	197 03.8	07.9	Achernar	335 26.5	S57 10.3
02	62 53.0	247 16.8	23.3	172 20.8	14.2	348 16.1	50.8	212 06.0	08.0	Acrux	173 10.4	S63 10.1
03	77 55.4	262 16.4	. . 22.2	187 21.3	. . 14.5	3 18.7	. . 50.8	227 08.2	. . 08.1	Adhara	255 12.8	S28 59.3
04	92 57.9	277 16.1	21.1	202 21.8	14.7	18 21.4	50.7	242 10.3	08.2	Aldebaran	290 49.6	N16 32.1
05	108 00.4	292 15.8	20.0	217 22.3	15.0	33 24.0	50.7	257 12.5	08.3			
06	123 02.8	307 15.4	N 3 18.8	232 22.8	S23 15.2	48 26.6	N21 50.7	272 14.7	S10 08.4	Alioth	166 21.6	N55 53.3
W 07	138 05.3	322 15.1	17.7	247 23.3	15.5	63 29.3	50.7	287 16.9	08.5	Alkaid	152 59.7	N49 15.0
E 08	153 07.8	337 14.8	16.6	262 23.8	15.7	78 31.9	50.7	302 19.0	08.6	Al Na'ir	27 44.1	S46 53.9
D 09	168 10.2	352 14.4	. . 15.5	277 24.3	. . 16.0	93 34.5	. . 50.7	317 21.2	. . 08.7	Alnilam	275 46.6	S 1 11.6
N 10	183 12.7	7 14.1	14.4	292 24.8	16.3	108 37.2	50.6	332 23.4	08.8	Alphard	217 56.6	S 8 42.8
E 11	198 15.2	22 13.8	13.3	307 25.3	16.5	123 39.8	50.6	347 25.6	09.0			
S 12	213 17.6	37 13.4	N 3 12.2	322 25.8	S23 16.8	138 42.5	N21 50.6	2 27.7	S10 09.1	Alphecca	126 11.7	N26 40.5
D 13	228 20.1	52 13.1	11.0	337 26.3	17.0	153 45.1	50.6	17 29.9	09.2	Alpheratz	357 43.6	N29 09.9
A 14	243 22.6	67 12.8	09.9	352 26.8	17.3	168 47.7	50.6	32 32.1	09.3	Altair	62 08.7	N 8 54.4
Y 15	258 25.0	82 12.4	. . 08.8	7 27.3	. . 17.5	183 50.4	. . 50.6	47 34.3	. . 09.4	Ankaa	353 15.8	S42 14.1
16	273 27.5	97 12.1	07.7	22 27.8	17.8	198 53.0	50.5	62 36.4	09.5	Antares	112 27.1	S26 27.5
17	288 29.9	112 11.8	06.6	37 28.3	18.0	213 55.7	50.5	77 38.6	09.6			
18	303 32.4	127 11.4	N 3 05.5	52 28.8	S23 18.3	228 58.3	N21 50.5	92 40.8	S10 09.7	Arcturus	145 56.5	N19 07.0
19	318 34.9	142 11.1	04.4	67 29.3	18.5	244 01.0	50.5	107 43.0	09.8	Atria	107 29.8	S69 03.1
20	333 37.3	157 10.8	03.2	82 29.8	18.8	259 03.6	50.5	122 45.1	09.9	Avior	234 18.2	S59 32.8
21	348 39.8	172 10.4	. . 02.1	97 30.3	. . 19.0	274 06.2	. . 50.4	137 47.3	. . 10.0	Bellatrix	278 32.3	N 6 21.6
22	3 42.3	187 10.1	3 01.0	112 30.8	19.3	289 08.9	50.4	152 49.5	10.1	Betelgeuse	271 01.6	N 7 24.5
23	18 44.7	202 09.7	2 59.9	127 31.3	19.5	304 11.5	50.4	167 51.7	10.2			
25 00	33 47.2	217 09.4	N 2 58.8	142 31.8	S23 19.8	319 14.2	N21 50.4	182 53.9	S10 10.3	Canopus	263 56.1	S52 42.0
01	48 49.7	232 09.1	57.7	157 32.3	20.0	334 16.8	50.4	197 56.0	10.4	Capella	280 34.8	N46 00.4
02	63 52.1	247 08.7	56.5	172 32.8	20.3	349 19.5	50.4	212 58.2	10.5	Deneb	49 31.7	N45 20.0
03	78 54.6	262 08.4	. . 55.4	187 33.3	. . 20.5	4 22.1	. . 50.3	228 00.4	. . 10.6	Denebola	182 34.4	N14 30.0
04	93 57.0	277 08.1	54.3	202 33.8	20.8	19 24.8	50.3	243 02.6	10.7	Diphda	348 56.0	S17 54.8
05	108 59.5	292 07.7	53.2	217 34.3	21.0	34 27.4	50.3	258 04.7	10.8			
06	124 02.0	307 07.4	N 2 52.1	232 34.8	S23 21.3	49 30.0	N21 50.3	273 06.9	S10 10.9	Dubhe	193 52.7	N61 40.6
T 07	139 04.4	322 07.1	50.9	247 35.3	21.5	64 32.7	50.3	288 09.1	11.0	Elnath	278 12.9	N28 37.0
H 08	154 06.9	337 06.7	49.8	262 35.8	21.7	79 35.3	50.2	303 11.3	11.1	Eltanin	90 46.7	N51 29.6
U 09	169 09.4	352 06.4	. . 48.7	277 36.3	. . 22.0	94 38.0	. . 50.2	318 13.4	. . 11.2	Enif	33 47.4	N 9 56.3
R 10	184 11.8	7 06.1	47.6	292 36.8	22.2	109 40.6	50.2	333 15.6	11.3	Fomalhaut	15 24.2	S29 33.2
S 11	199 14.3	22 05.7	46.5	307 37.2	22.5	124 43.3	50.2	348 17.8	11.4			
D 12	214 16.8	37 05.4	N 2 45.3	322 37.7	S23 22.7	139 45.9	N21 50.2	3 20.0	S10 11.5	Gacrux	172 01.9	S57 11.0
A 13	229 19.2	52 05.1	44.2	337 38.2	23.0	154 48.6	50.2	18 22.1	11.6	Gienah	175 53.1	S17 36.7
Y 14	244 21.7	67 04.7	43.1	352 38.7	23.2	169 51.2	50.1	33 24.3	11.7	Hadar	148 49.2	S60 26.0
15	259 24.2	82 04.4	. . 42.0	7 39.2	. . 23.5	184 53.9	. . 50.1	48 26.5	. . 11.9	Hamal	328 00.9	N23 31.5
16	274 26.6	97 04.1	40.9	22 39.7	23.7	199 56.5	50.1	63 28.7	12.0	Kaus Aust.	83 44.6	S34 22.6
17	289 29.1	112 03.7	39.7	37 40.2	23.9	214 59.2	50.1	78 30.8	12.1			
18	304 31.5	127 03.4	N 2 38.6	52 40.7	S23 24.2	230 01.8	N21 50.1	93 33.0	S10 12.2	Kochab	137 21.2	N74 06.2
19	319 34.0	142 03.1	37.5	67 41.2	24.4	245 04.5	50.0	108 35.2	12.3	Markab	13 38.6	N15 16.7
20	334 36.5	157 02.7	36.4	82 41.7	24.7	260 07.1	50.0	123 37.4	12.4	Menkar	314 15.2	N 4 08.5
21	349 38.9	172 02.4	. . 35.2	97 42.2	. . 24.9	275 09.8	. . 50.0	138 39.5	. . 12.5	Menkent	148 08.5	S36 25.9
22	4 41.4	187 02.0	34.1	112 42.7	25.1	290 12.4	50.0	153 41.7	12.6	Miaplacidus	221 40.0	S69 46.0
23	19 43.9	202 01.7	33.0	127 43.1	25.4	305 15.1	50.0	168 43.9	12.7			
26 00	34 46.3	217 01.4	N 2 31.9	142 43.6	S23 25.6	320 17.7	N21 49.9	183 46.1	S10 12.8	Mirfak	308 40.5	N49 54.3
01	49 48.8	232 01.0	30.8	157 44.1	25.9	335 20.4	49.9	198 48.2	12.9	Nunki	75 59.0	S26 16.7
02	64 51.3	247 00.7	29.6	172 44.6	26.1	350 23.0	49.9	213 50.4	13.0	Peacock	53 19.9	S56 41.7
03	79 53.7	262 00.4	. . 28.5	187 45.1	. . 26.3	5 25.7	. . 49.9	228 52.6	. . 13.1	Pollux	243 28.2	N27 59.5
04	94 56.2	277 00.0	27.4	202 45.6	26.6	20 28.3	49.9	243 54.8	13.2	Procyon	245 00.1	N 5 11.5
05	109 58.7	291 59.7	26.3	217 46.1	26.8	35 31.0	49.9	258 56.9	13.3			
06	125 01.1	306 59.4	N 2 25.1	232 46.6	S23 27.0	50 33.7	N21 49.8	273 59.1	S10 13.4	Rasalhague	96 07.1	N12 33.3
07	140 03.6	321 59.0	24.0	247 47.1	27.3	65 36.3	49.8	289 01.3	13.5	Regulus	207 44.2	N11 54.2
08	155 06.0	336 58.7	22.9	262 47.5	27.5	80 39.0	49.8	304 03.5	13.6	Rigel	281 12.3	S 8 11.2
F 09	170 08.5	351 58.4	. . 21.8	277 48.0	. . 27.8	95 41.6	. . 49.8	319 05.6	. . 13.7	Rigil Kent.	139 53.0	S60 53.2
R 10	185 11.0	6 58.0	20.6	292 48.5	28.0	110 44.3	49.8	334 07.8	13.8	Sabik	102 13.3	S15 44.3
I 11	200 13.4	21 57.7	19.5	307 49.0	28.2	125 46.9	49.7	349 10.0	13.9			
D 12	215 15.9	36 57.4	N 2 18.4	322 49.5	S23 28.5	140 49.6	N21 49.7	4 12.2	S10 14.0	Schedar	349 40.5	N56 36.7
A 13	230 18.4	51 57.0	17.3	337 50.0	28.7	155 52.2	49.7	19 14.3	14.1	Shaula	96 22.8	S37 06.7
Y 14	245 20.8	66 56.7	16.1	352 50.5	28.9	170 54.9	49.7	34 16.5	14.2	Sirius	258 34.0	S16 44.0
15	260 23.3	81 56.3	. . 15.0	7 51.0	. . 29.2	185 57.6	. . 49.7	49 18.7	. . 14.3	Spica	158 32.0	S11 13.6
16	275 25.8	96 56.0	13.9	22 51.4	29.4	201 00.2	49.6	64 20.9	14.4	Suhail	222 52.9	S43 28.9
17	290 28.2	111 55.7	12.7	37 51.9	29.6	216 02.9	49.6	79 23.0	14.5			
18	305 30.7	126 55.3	N 2 11.6	52 52.4	S23 29.9	231 05.5	N21 49.6	94 25.2	S10 14.6	Vega	80 39.4	N38 48.1
19	320 33.1	141 55.0	10.5	67 52.9	30.1	246 08.2	49.6	109 27.4	14.7	Zuben'ubi	137 06.2	S16 05.6
20	335 35.6	156 54.7	09.4	82 53.4	30.3	261 10.9	49.6	124 29.6	14.8		SHA	Mer.Pass.
21	350 38.1	171 54.3	. . 08.2	97 53.9	. . 30.5	276 13.5	. . 49.5	139 31.7	. . 15.0			h m
22	5 40.5	186 54.0	07.1	112 54.4	30.8	291 16.2	49.5	154 33.9	15.1	Venus	183 22.2	9 32
23	20 43.0	201 53.7	06.0	127 54.8	31.0	306 18.8	49.5	169 36.1	15.2	Mars	108 44.6	14 29
	h m									Jupiter	285 27.0	2 43
Mer.Pass. 21 41.3		v −0.3	d 1.1	v 0.5	d 0.2	v 2.6	d 0.0	v 2.2	d 0.1	Saturn	149 06.7	11 47

UT	SUN GHA	SUN Dec	MOON GHA	v	Dec	d	HP
d h	° ′	° ′	° ′	′	° ′	′	′
24 00	183 56.8	S11 48.9	68 14.2	12.2	S 8 34.2	10.8	57.0
01	198 56.9	49.8	82 45.4	12.3	8 23.4	10.8	57.0
02	213 57.0	50.7	97 16.7	12.4	8 12.6	10.8	56.9
03	228 57.1	.. 51.5	111 48.1	12.4	8 01.8	10.9	56.9
04	243 57.1	52.4	126 19.5	12.4	7 50.9	10.9	56.9
05	258 57.2	53.3	140 50.9	12.5	7 40.0	10.9	56.9
06	273 57.3	S11 54.1	155 22.4	12.6	S 7 29.1	11.0	56.8
W 07	288 57.4	55.0	169 54.0	12.6	7 18.1	11.0	56.8
E 08	303 57.4	55.9	184 25.6	12.7	7 07.1	11.0	56.8
D 09	318 57.5	.. 56.7	198 57.3	12.7	6 56.1	11.0	56.7
N 10	333 57.6	57.6	213 29.0	12.7	6 45.1	11.1	56.7
E 11	348 57.7	58.5	228 00.7	12.8	6 34.0	11.1	56.7
S 12	3 57.7	S11 59.3	242 32.5	12.9	S 6 22.9	11.1	56.7
D 13	18 57.8	12 00.2	257 04.4	12.9	6 11.8	11.1	56.6
A 14	33 57.9	01.0	271 36.3	12.9	6 00.7	11.1	56.6
Y 15	48 58.0	.. 01.9	286 08.2	13.0	5 49.6	11.2	56.6
16	63 58.0	02.8	300 40.2	13.1	5 38.4	11.1	56.6
17	78 58.1	03.6	315 12.3	13.0	5 27.3	11.2	56.5
18	93 58.2	S12 04.5	329 44.3	13.2	S 5 16.1	11.2	56.5
19	108 58.3	05.4	344 16.5	13.1	5 04.9	11.2	56.5
20	123 58.3	06.2	358 48.6	13.2	4 53.7	11.3	56.5
21	138 58.4	.. 07.1	13 20.8	13.3	4 42.4	11.2	56.4
22	153 58.5	07.9	27 53.1	13.3	4 31.2	11.3	56.4
23	168 58.6	08.8	42 25.4	13.3	4 19.9	11.2	56.4
25 00	183 58.6	S12 09.7	56 57.7	13.3	S 4 08.7	11.3	56.4
01	198 58.7	10.5	71 30.0	13.4	3 57.4	11.3	56.4
02	213 58.8	11.4	86 02.4	13.5	3 46.1	11.3	56.3
03	228 58.8	.. 12.2	100 34.9	13.4	3 34.8	11.3	56.3
04	243 58.9	13.1	115 07.3	13.5	3 23.5	11.3	56.3
05	258 59.0	14.0	129 39.8	13.6	3 12.2	11.3	56.3
06	273 59.1	S12 14.8	144 12.4	13.5	S 3 00.9	11.3	56.2
T 07	288 59.1	15.7	158 44.9	13.6	2 49.6	11.3	56.2
H 08	303 59.2	16.5	173 17.5	13.7	2 38.3	11.4	56.2
U 09	318 59.3	.. 17.4	187 50.2	13.6	2 26.9	11.3	56.2
R 10	333 59.3	18.2	202 22.8	13.7	2 15.6	11.3	56.1
S 11	348 59.4	19.1	216 55.5	13.7	2 04.3	11.4	56.1
D 12	3 59.5	S12 20.0	231 28.2	13.8	S 1 52.9	11.3	56.1
A 13	18 59.5	20.8	246 01.0	13.8	1 41.6	11.3	56.1
Y 14	33 59.6	21.7	260 33.8	13.8	1 30.3	11.4	56.0
15	48 59.7	.. 22.5	275 06.6	13.8	1 18.9	11.3	56.0
16	63 59.7	23.4	289 39.4	13.8	1 07.6	11.3	56.0
17	78 59.8	24.2	304 12.2	13.9	0 56.3	11.3	56.0
18	93 59.9	S12 25.1	318 45.1	13.9	S 0 45.0	11.4	56.0
19	108 59.9	25.9	333 18.0	13.9	0 33.6	11.3	55.9
20	124 00.0	26.8	347 50.9	14.0	0 22.3	11.3	55.9
21	139 00.1	.. 27.6	2 23.9	13.9	S 0 11.0	11.3	55.9
22	154 00.1	28.5	16 56.8	14.0	N 0 00.3	11.3	55.9
23	169 00.2	29.4	31 29.8	14.0	0 11.6	11.2	55.9
26 00	184 00.3	S12 30.2	46 02.8	14.0	N 0 22.8	11.3	55.8
01	199 00.3	31.1	60 35.8	14.1	0 34.1	11.3	55.8
02	214 00.4	31.9	75 08.9	14.0	0 45.4	11.2	55.8
03	229 00.5	.. 32.8	89 41.9	14.1	0 56.6	11.3	55.8
04	244 00.5	33.6	104 15.0	14.1	1 07.9	11.2	55.7
05	259 00.6	34.5	118 48.1	14.1	1 19.1	11.2	55.7
06	274 00.7	S12 35.3	133 21.2	14.1	N 1 30.3	11.2	55.7
07	289 00.7	36.2	147 54.3	14.1	1 41.5	11.2	55.7
F 08	304 00.8	37.0	162 27.4	14.2	1 52.7	11.2	55.7
R 09	319 00.8	.. 37.9	177 00.6	14.1	2 03.9	11.1	55.6
I 10	334 00.9	38.7	191 33.7	14.2	2 15.0	11.1	55.6
D 11	349 01.0	39.6	206 06.9	14.2	2 26.1	11.2	55.6
A 12	4 01.0	S12 40.4	220 40.1	14.2	N 2 37.3	11.1	55.6
Y 13	19 01.1	41.2	235 13.3	14.2	2 48.4	11.0	55.6
14	34 01.1	42.1	249 46.5	14.2	2 59.4	11.1	55.5
15	49 01.2	.. 42.9	264 19.7	14.2	3 10.5	11.0	55.5
16	64 01.3	43.8	278 52.9	14.2	3 21.5	11.1	55.5
17	79 01.3	44.6	293 26.1	14.2	3 32.6	11.0	55.5
18	94 01.4	S12 45.5	307 59.3	14.2	N 3 43.6	10.9	55.5
19	109 01.4	46.3	322 32.5	14.3	3 54.5	11.0	55.5
20	124 01.5	47.2	337 05.8	14.2	4 05.5	10.9	55.4
21	139 01.5	.. 48.0	351 39.0	14.2	4 16.4	10.9	55.4
22	154 01.6	48.9	6 12.2	14.3	4 27.3	10.9	55.4
23	169 01.7	49.7	20 45.5	14.2	N 4 38.2	10.8	55.4
	SD 16.1	d 0.9	SD 15.4		15.3		15.1

Lat.	Twilight Naut.	Twilight Civil	Sunrise	Moonrise 24	25	26	27
°	h m	h m	h m	h m	h m	h m	h m
N 72	05 39	06 59	08 18	15 10	14 57	14 45	14 32
N 70	05 38	06 50	07 59	15 02	14 55	14 49	14 42
68	05 37	06 42	07 44	14 55	14 54	14 52	14 51
66	05 36	06 36	07 32	14 50	14 52	14 55	14 58
64	05 35	06 31	07 21	14 45	14 51	14 58	15 04
62	05 34	06 26	07 13	14 41	14 50	15 00	15 09
60	05 33	06 21	07 05	14 37	14 50	15 02	15 14
N 58	05 32	06 18	06 59	14 34	14 49	15 03	15 18
56	05 31	06 14	06 53	14 31	14 48	15 05	15 22
54	05 30	06 11	06 48	14 28	14 47	15 06	15 25
52	05 28	06 08	06 43	14 26	14 47	15 07	15 28
50	05 27	06 05	06 39	14 24	14 46	15 08	15 31
45	05 25	05 59	06 29	14 19	14 45	15 11	15 37
N 40	05 22	05 54	06 22	14 15	14 44	15 13	15 42
35	05 19	05 49	06 15	14 11	14 43	15 15	15 46
30	05 16	05 44	06 09	14 08	14 43	15 16	15 50
20	05 10	05 36	05 59	14 03	14 41	15 19	15 56
N 10	05 03	05 28	05 49	13 58	14 40	15 21	16 02
0	04 55	05 20	05 41	13 54	14 39	15 24	16 08
S 10	04 45	05 10	05 32	13 49	14 38	15 26	16 14
20	04 33	05 00	05 22	13 45	14 37	15 29	16 20
30	04 17	04 46	05 11	13 39	14 36	15 32	16 27
35	04 07	04 38	05 05	13 36	14 35	15 33	16 31
40	03 55	04 29	04 58	13 33	14 35	15 35	16 35
45	03 39	04 18	04 49	13 29	14 34	15 38	16 40
S 50	03 20	04 04	04 39	13 24	14 33	15 40	16 47
52	03 10	03 57	04 34	13 22	14 32	15 42	16 50
54	02 59	03 49	04 29	13 19	14 32	15 43	16 53
56	02 46	03 41	04 23	13 16	14 31	15 44	16 57
58	02 31	03 31	04 16	13 13	14 31	15 46	17 01
S 60	02 12	03 20	04 09	13 10	14 30	15 48	17 05

Lat.	Sunset	Twilight Civil	Twilight Naut.	Moonset 24	25	26	27
°	h m	h m	h m	h m	h m	h m	h m
N 72	15 09	16 27	17 47	25 25	01 25	03 12	04 58
N 70	15 28	16 36	17 48	25 31	01 31	03 11	04 50
68	15 43	16 44	17 49	25 36	01 36	03 10	04 43
66	15 55	16 51	17 51	00 07	01 39	03 09	04 37
64	16 06	16 56	17 52	00 15	01 43	03 08	04 33
62	16 14	17 01	17 53	00 21	01 46	03 08	04 28
60	16 22	17 06	17 54	00 27	01 48	03 07	04 25
N 58	16 28	17 09	17 55	00 32	01 50	03 07	04 22
56	16 34	17 13	17 56	00 36	01 52	03 06	04 19
54	16 40	17 16	17 58	00 40	01 54	03 06	04 17
52	16 44	17 19	17 59	00 44	01 56	03 06	04 14
50	16 49	17 22	18 00	00 47	01 57	03 05	04 12
45	16 58	17 28	18 03	00 54	02 00	03 05	04 08
N 40	17 06	17 34	18 05	01 00	02 03	03 04	04 04
35	17 13	17 39	18 08	01 05	02 05	03 03	04 01
30	17 19	17 43	18 11	01 09	02 07	03 03	03 58
20	17 29	17 52	18 18	01 17	02 10	03 02	03 53
N 10	17 39	18 00	18 25	01 23	02 13	03 01	03 49
0	17 47	18 09	18 33	01 29	02 16	03 01	03 45
S 10	17 56	18 18	18 43	01 35	02 19	03 00	03 41
20	18 06	18 29	18 55	01 42	02 21	02 59	03 37
30	18 17	18 42	19 12	01 49	02 25	02 58	03 32
35	18 23	18 50	19 22	01 53	02 26	02 58	03 29
40	18 31	19 00	19 34	01 58	02 28	02 57	03 26
45	18 40	19 11	19 50	02 03	02 31	02 57	03 22
S 50	18 50	19 26	20 10	02 10	02 34	02 56	03 18
52	18 55	19 33	20 20	02 13	02 35	02 56	03 16
54	19 01	19 40	20 31	02 16	02 36	02 55	03 14
56	19 07	19 49	20 44	02 20	02 38	02 55	03 11
58	19 14	19 59	21 00	02 24	02 40	02 54	03 09
S 60	19 21	20 10	21 20	02 28	02 41	02 54	03 06

Day	SUN Eqn. of Time 00h	12h	Mer. Pass.	MOON Mer. Pass. Upper	Lower	Age	Phase
d	m s	m s	h m	h m	h m	d	%
24	15 47	15 51	11 44	20 05	07 42	09	74
25	15 54	15 58	11 44	20 50	08 28	10	83
26	16 01	16 04	11 44	21 34	09 12	11	90

UT	ARIES	VENUS −4.0		MARS +1.2		JUPITER −2.7		SATURN +0.6		STARS		
	GHA	GHA	Dec	GHA	Dec	GHA	Dec	GHA	Dec	Name	SHA	Dec
d h	° ′	° ′	° ′	° ′	° ′	° ′	° ′	° ′	° ′		° ′	° ′
27 00	35 45.5	216 53.3 N 2 04.9		142 55.3 S23 31.2		321 21.5 N21 49.5		184 38.3 S10 15.3		Acamar	315 18.3	S40 15.1
01	50 47.9	231 53.0	03.7	157 55.8	31.5	336 24.2	49.5	199 40.5	15.4	Achernar	335 26.5	S57 10.3
02	65 50.4	246 52.7	02.6	172 56.3	31.7	351 26.8	49.4	214 42.6	15.5	Acrux	173 10.4	S63 10.1
03	80 52.9	261 52.3 . .	01.5	187 56.8 . .	31.9	6 29.5 . .	49.4	229 44.8 . .	15.6	Adhara	255 12.7	S28 59.3
04	95 55.3	276 52.0	2 00.3	202 57.3	32.2	21 32.1	49.4	244 47.0	15.7	Aldebaran	290 49.6	N16 32.1
05	110 57.8	291 51.6	1 59.2	217 57.7	32.4	36 34.8	49.4	259 49.2	15.8			
06	126 00.3	306 51.3 N 1 58.1		232 58.2 S23 32.6		51 37.5 N21 49.4		274 51.3 S10 15.9		Alioth	166 21.6	N55 53.3
07	141 02.7	321 51.0	56.9	247 58.7	32.8	66 40.1	49.3	289 53.5	16.0	Alkaid	152 59.7	N49 15.0
S 08	156 05.2	336 50.6	55.8	262 59.2	33.1	81 42.8	49.3	304 55.7	16.1	Al Na'ir	27 44.1	S46 53.9
A 09	171 07.6	351 50.3 . .	54.7	277 59.7 . .	33.3	96 45.5 . .	49.3	319 57.9 . .	16.2	Alnilam	275 46.6	S 1 11.6
T 10	186 10.1	6 50.0	53.6	293 00.2	33.5	111 48.1	49.3	335 00.0	16.3	Alphard	217 56.6	S 8 42.8
U 11	201 12.6	21 49.6	52.4	308 00.6	33.7	126 50.8	49.3	350 02.2	16.4			
R 12	216 15.0	36 49.3 N 1 51.3		323 01.1 S23 34.0		141 53.4 N21 49.2		5 04.4 S10 16.5		Alphecca	126 11.7	N26 40.5
D 13	231 17.5	51 49.0	50.2	338 01.6	34.2	156 56.1	49.2	20 06.6	16.6	Alpheratz	357 43.7	N29 09.9
A 14	246 20.0	66 48.6	49.0	353 02.1	34.4	171 58.8	49.2	35 08.7	16.7	Altair	62 08.7	N 8 54.4
Y 15	261 22.4	81 48.3 . .	47.9	8 02.6 . .	34.6	187 01.4 . .	49.2	50 10.9 . .	16.8	Ankaa	353 15.8	S42 14.1
16	276 24.9	96 47.9	46.8	23 03.0	34.9	202 04.1	49.2	65 13.1	16.9	Antares	112 27.1	S26 27.5
17	291 27.4	111 47.6	45.6	38 03.5	35.1	217 06.8	49.1	80 15.3	17.0			
18	306 29.8	126 47.3 N 1 44.5		53 04.0 S23 35.3		232 09.4 N21 49.1		95 17.4 S10 17.1		Arcturus	145 56.5	N19 07.0
19	321 32.3	141 46.9	43.4	68 04.5	35.5	247 12.1	49.1	110 19.6	17.2	Atria	107 29.8	S69 03.0
20	336 34.7	156 46.6	42.2	83 05.0	35.7	262 14.8	49.1	125 21.8	17.3	Avior	234 18.2	S59 32.8
21	351 37.2	171 46.3 . .	41.1	98 05.4 . .	36.0	277 17.4 . .	49.1	140 24.0 . .	17.4	Bellatrix	278 32.3	N 6 21.6
22	6 39.7	186 45.9	40.0	113 05.9	36.2	292 20.1	49.0	155 26.1	17.5	Betelgeuse	271 01.6	N 7 24.5
23	21 42.1	201 45.6	38.8	128 06.4	36.4	307 22.8	49.0	170 28.3	17.6			
28 00	36 44.6	216 45.3 N 1 37.7		143 06.9 S23 36.6		322 25.4 N21 49.0		185 30.5 S10 17.7		Canopus	263 56.1	S52 42.0
01	51 47.1	231 44.9	36.6	158 07.3	36.9	337 28.1	49.0	200 32.7	17.8	Capella	280 34.8	N46 00.4
02	66 49.5	246 44.6	35.4	173 07.8	37.1	352 30.8	49.0	215 34.8	17.9	Deneb	49 31.8	N45 20.0
03	81 52.0	261 44.2 . .	34.3	188 08.3 . .	37.3	7 33.5 . .	48.9	230 37.0 . .	18.0	Denebola	182 34.4	N14 30.0
04	96 54.5	276 43.9	33.2	203 08.8	37.5	22 36.1	48.9	245 39.2	18.1	Diphda	348 56.0	S17 54.9
05	111 56.9	291 43.6	32.0	218 09.3	37.7	37 38.8	48.9	260 41.4	18.2			
06	126 59.4	306 43.2 N 1 30.9		233 09.7 S23 37.9		52 41.5 N21 48.9		275 43.5 S10 18.3		Dubhe	193 52.7	N61 40.6
07	142 01.9	321 42.9	29.8	248 10.2	38.2	67 44.1	48.9	290 45.7	18.4	Elnath	278 12.9	N28 37.0
08	157 04.3	336 42.6	28.6	263 10.7	38.4	82 46.8	48.8	305 47.9	18.6	Eltanin	90 46.7	N51 29.6
S 09	172 06.8	351 42.2 . .	27.5	278 11.2 . .	38.6	97 49.5 . .	48.8	320 50.1 . .	18.7	Enif	33 47.5	N 9 56.3
U 10	187 09.2	6 41.9	26.3	293 11.6	38.8	112 52.1	48.8	335 52.2	18.8	Fomalhaut	15 24.3	S29 33.2
N 11	202 11.7	21 41.5	25.2	308 12.1	39.0	127 54.8	48.8	350 54.4	18.9			
D 12	217 14.2	36 41.2 N 1 24.1		323 12.6 S23 39.2		142 57.5 N21 48.8		5 56.6 S10 19.0		Gacrux	172 01.9	S57 11.0
A 13	232 16.6	51 40.9	22.9	338 13.1	39.5	158 00.2	48.7	20 58.8	19.1	Gienah	175 53.0	S17 36.7
Y 14	247 19.1	66 40.5	21.8	353 13.5	39.7	173 02.8	48.7	36 00.9	19.2	Hadar	148 49.2	S60 26.0
15	262 21.6	81 40.2 . .	20.7	8 14.0 . .	39.9	188 05.5 . .	48.7	51 03.1 . .	19.3	Hamal	328 00.9	N23 31.5
16	277 24.0	96 39.9	19.5	23 14.5	40.1	203 08.2	48.7	66 05.3	19.4	Kaus Aust.	83 44.6	S34 22.6
17	292 26.5	111 39.5	18.4	38 15.0	40.3	218 10.9	48.7	81 07.5	19.5			
18	307 29.0	126 39.2 N 1 17.3		53 15.4 S23 40.5		233 13.5 N21 48.6		96 09.6 S10 19.6		Kochab	137 21.2	N74 06.2
19	322 31.4	141 38.8	16.1	68 15.9	40.7	248 16.2	48.6	111 11.8	19.7	Markab	13 38.6	N15 16.7
20	337 33.9	156 38.5	15.0	83 16.4	40.9	263 18.9	48.6	126 14.0	19.8	Menkar	314 15.2	N 4 08.5
21	352 36.3	171 38.2 . .	13.8	98 16.9 . .	41.2	278 21.6 . .	48.6	141 16.2 . .	19.9	Menkent	148 08.5	S36 25.9
22	7 38.8	186 37.8	12.7	113 17.3	41.4	293 24.2	48.5	156 18.3	20.0	Miaplacidus	221 39.9	S69 46.0
23	22 41.3	201 37.5	11.6	128 17.8	41.6	308 26.9	48.5	171 20.5	20.1			
29 00	37 43.7	216 37.2 N 1 10.4		143 18.3 S23 41.8		323 29.6 N21 48.5		186 22.7 S10 20.2		Mirfak	308 40.5	N49 54.4
01	52 46.2	231 36.8	09.3	158 18.8	42.0	338 32.3	48.5	201 24.9	20.3	Nunki	75 59.0	S26 16.7
02	67 48.7	246 36.5	08.2	173 19.2	42.2	353 34.9	48.5	216 27.0	20.4	Peacock	53 20.0	S56 41.7
03	82 51.1	261 36.1 . .	07.0	188 19.7 . .	42.4	8 37.6 . .	48.4	231 29.2 . .	20.5	Pollux	243 28.2	N27 59.5
04	97 53.6	276 35.8	05.9	203 20.2	42.6	23 40.3	48.4	246 31.4	20.6	Procyon	245 00.1	N 5 11.4
05	112 56.1	291 35.5	04.7	218 20.6	42.8	38 43.0	48.4	261 33.6	20.7			
06	127 58.5	306 35.1 N 1 03.6		233 21.1 S23 43.0		53 45.6 N21 48.4		276 35.7 S10 20.8		Rasalhague	96 07.1	N12 33.3
07	143 01.0	321 34.8	02.5	248 21.6	43.3	68 48.3	48.4	291 37.9	20.9	Regulus	207 44.1	N11 52.5
08	158 03.5	336 34.4	01.3	263 22.1	43.5	83 51.0	48.3	306 40.1	21.0	Rigel	281 12.2	S 8 11.2
M 09	173 05.9	351 34.1	1 00.2	278 22.5 . .	43.7	98 53.7 . .	48.3	321 42.3 . .	21.1	Rigil Kent.	139 53.0	S60 53.2
O 10	188 08.4	6 33.8	0 59.0	293 23.0	43.9	113 56.4	48.3	336 44.4	21.2	Sabik	102 13.3	S15 44.3
N 11	203 10.8	21 33.4	57.9	308 23.5	44.1	128 59.0	48.3	351 46.6	21.3			
D 12	218 13.3	36 33.1 N 0 56.8		323 23.9 S23 44.3		144 01.7 N21 48.2		6 48.8 S10 21.4		Schedar	349 40.5	N56 36.7
A 13	233 15.8	51 32.8	55.6	338 24.4	44.5	159 04.4	48.2	21 51.0	21.5	Shaula	96 22.8	S37 06.7
Y 14	248 18.2	66 32.4	54.5	353 24.9	44.7	174 07.1	48.2	36 53.1	21.6	Sirius	258 34.0	S16 44.0
15	263 20.7	81 32.1 . .	53.3	8 25.3 . .	44.9	189 09.8 . .	48.2	51 55.3 . .	21.7	Spica	158 32.0	S11 13.6
16	278 23.2	96 31.7	52.2	23 25.8	45.1	204 12.4	48.2	66 57.5	21.8	Suhail	222 52.8	S43 28.9
17	293 25.6	111 31.4	51.1	38 26.3	45.3	219 15.1	48.1	81 59.7	21.9			
18	308 28.1	126 31.1 N 0 49.9		53 26.7 S23 45.5		234 17.8 N21 48.1		97 01.9 S10 22.0		Vega	80 39.5	N38 48.1
19	323 30.6	141 30.7	48.8	68 27.2	45.7	249 20.5	48.1	112 04.0	22.1	Zuben'ubi	137 06.3	S16 05.6
20	338 33.0	156 30.4	47.6	83 27.7	45.9	264 23.2	48.1	127 06.2	22.2		SHA	Mer.Pass.
21	353 35.5	171 30.0 . .	46.5	98 28.1 . .	46.1	279 25.9 . .	48.1	142 08.4 . .	22.3		° ′	h m
22	8 38.0	186 29.7	45.3	113 28.6	46.3	294 28.5	48.0	157 10.6	22.4	Venus	180 00.7	9 33
23	23 40.4	201 29.4	44.2	128 29.1	46.5	309 31.2	48.0	172 12.7	22.5	Mars	106 22.3	14 27
	h m									Jupiter	285 40.8	2 30
Mer.Pass. 21 29.5		v −0.3	d 1.1	v 0.5	d 0.2	v 2.7	d 0.0	v 2.2	d 0.1	Saturn	148 45.9	11 36

SUN / MOON

UT	SUN GHA	SUN Dec	MOON GHA	v	MOON Dec	d	HP
27 00	184 01.7	S12 50.5	35 18.7	14.3	N 4 49.0	10.8	55.4
01	199 01.8	51.4	49 52.0	14.2	4 59.8	10.8	55.3
02	214 01.8	52.2	64 25.2	14.3	5 10.6	10.8	55.3
03	229 01.9	.. 53.1	78 58.5	14.2	5 21.4	10.7	55.3
04	244 02.0	53.9	93 31.7	14.3	5 32.1	10.7	55.3
05	259 02.0	54.8	108 05.0	14.2	5 42.8	10.7	55.3
06	274 02.1	S12 55.6	122 38.2	14.3	N 5 53.5	10.6	55.3
07	289 02.1	56.4	137 11.5	14.2	6 04.1	10.7	55.2
S 08	304 02.2	57.3	151 44.7	14.2	6 14.8	10.5	55.2
A 09	319 02.2	.. 58.1	166 17.9	14.3	6 25.3	10.6	55.2
T 10	334 02.3	59.0	180 51.2	14.2	6 35.9	10.5	55.2
U 11	349 02.3	12 59.8	195 24.4	14.2	6 46.4	10.5	55.2
R 12	4 02.4	S13 00.6	209 57.6	14.2	N 6 56.9	10.4	55.1
D 13	19 02.4	01.5	224 30.8	14.2	7 07.3	10.4	55.1
A 14	34 02.5	02.3	239 04.0	14.3	7 17.7	10.4	55.1
Y 15	49 02.5	.. 03.2	253 37.3	14.1	7 28.1	10.3	55.1
16	64 02.6	04.0	268 10.4	14.2	7 38.4	10.3	55.1
17	79 02.7	04.8	282 43.6	14.2	7 48.7	10.2	55.1
18	94 02.7	S13 05.7	297 16.8	14.2	N 7 58.9	10.2	55.0
19	109 02.8	06.5	311 50.0	14.1	8 09.1	10.2	55.0
20	124 02.8	07.4	326 23.1	14.2	8 19.3	10.1	55.0
21	139 02.9	.. 08.2	340 56.3	14.1	8 29.4	10.1	55.0
22	154 02.9	09.0	355 29.4	14.2	8 39.5	10.1	55.0
23	169 03.0	09.9	10 02.6	14.1	8 49.6	10.0	55.0
28 00	184 03.0	S13 10.7	24 35.7	14.1	N 8 59.6	9.9	55.0
01	199 03.1	11.5	39 08.8	14.1	9 09.5	9.9	54.9
02	214 03.1	12.4	53 41.9	14.1	9 19.4	9.9	54.9
03	229 03.2	.. 13.2	68 15.0	14.0	9 29.3	9.8	54.9
04	244 03.2	14.0	82 48.0	14.1	9 39.1	9.8	54.9
05	259 03.2	14.9	97 21.1	14.0	9 48.9	9.7	54.9
06	274 03.3	S13 15.7	111 54.1	14.0	N 9 58.6	9.7	54.9
07	289 03.3	16.5	126 27.1	14.1	10 08.3	9.6	54.8
S 08	304 03.4	17.4	141 00.2	13.9	10 17.9	9.6	54.8
U 09	319 03.4	.. 18.2	155 33.1	14.0	10 27.5	9.5	54.8
N 10	334 03.5	19.0	170 06.1	14.0	10 37.0	9.5	54.8
D 11	349 03.5	19.9	184 39.1	13.9	10 46.5	9.4	54.8
A 12	4 03.6	S13 20.7	199 12.0	14.0	N10 55.9	9.4	54.8
Y 13	19 03.6	21.5	213 45.0	13.9	11 05.3	9.3	54.8
14	34 03.7	22.4	228 17.9	13.9	11 14.6	9.3	54.7
15	49 03.7	.. 23.2	242 50.8	13.8	11 23.9	9.2	54.7
16	64 03.8	24.0	257 23.6	13.9	11 33.1	9.2	54.7
17	79 03.8	24.8	271 56.5	13.8	11 42.3	9.1	54.7
18	94 03.8	S13 25.7	286 29.3	13.8	N11 51.4	9.0	54.7
19	109 03.9	26.5	301 02.1	13.8	12 00.4	9.0	54.7
20	124 03.9	27.3	315 34.9	13.8	12 09.4	9.0	54.7
21	139 04.0	.. 28.2	330 07.7	13.8	12 18.4	8.8	54.6
22	154 04.0	29.0	344 40.5	13.7	12 27.2	8.9	54.6
23	169 04.1	29.8	359 13.2	13.7	12 36.1	8.7	54.6
29 00	184 04.1	S13 30.6	13 45.9	13.7	N12 44.8	8.7	54.6
01	199 04.1	31.5	28 18.6	13.7	12 53.5	8.7	54.6
02	214 04.2	32.3	42 51.3	13.6	13 02.2	8.6	54.6
03	229 04.2	.. 33.1	57 23.9	13.6	13 10.8	8.5	54.6
04	244 04.3	33.9	71 56.5	13.6	13 19.3	8.4	54.6
05	259 04.3	34.8	86 29.1	13.6	13 27.7	8.4	54.5
06	274 04.3	S13 35.6	101 01.7	13.6	N13 36.1	8.4	54.5
07	289 04.4	36.4	115 34.3	13.5	13 44.5	8.2	54.5
M 08	304 04.4	37.2	130 06.8	13.5	13 52.7	8.3	54.5
O 09	319 04.4	.. 38.1	144 39.3	13.5	14 01.0	8.1	54.5
N 10	334 04.5	38.9	159 11.8	13.5	14 09.1	8.1	54.5
D 11	349 04.5	39.7	173 44.3	13.5	14 17.2	8.0	54.5
A 12	4 04.6	S13 40.5	188 16.8	13.4	N14 25.2	7.9	54.5
Y 13	19 04.6	41.3	202 49.2	13.4	14 33.1	7.9	54.5
14	34 04.6	42.2	217 21.6	13.3	14 41.0	7.8	54.4
15	49 04.7	.. 43.0	231 53.9	13.4	14 48.8	7.8	54.4
16	64 04.7	43.8	246 26.3	13.3	14 56.6	7.6	54.4
17	79 04.7	44.6	260 58.6	13.3	15 04.2	7.6	54.4
18	94 04.8	S13 45.5	275 30.9	13.3	N15 11.8	7.6	54.4
19	109 04.8	46.3	290 03.2	13.2	15 19.4	7.4	54.4
20	124 04.9	47.1	304 35.4	13.3	15 26.8	7.4	54.4
21	139 04.9	.. 47.9	319 07.7	13.2	15 34.2	7.3	54.4
22	154 04.9	48.7	333 39.9	13.2	15 41.5	7.3	54.4
23	169 05.0	49.5	348 12.1	13.1	N15 48.8	7.1	54.3
	SD 16.1 d 0.8		SD 15.0		14.9		14.8

Twilight / Sunrise / Moonrise

Lat.	Naut.	Civil	Sunrise	Moonrise 27	28	29	30
°	h m	h m	h m	h m	h m	h m	h m
N 72	05 52	07 13	08 35	14 32	14 17	13 58	13 19
N 70	05 49	07 02	08 13	14 42	14 36	14 28	14 18
68	05 47	06 53	07 56	14 51	14 51	14 50	14 52
66	05 45	06 45	07 42	14 58	15 02	15 08	15 17
64	05 43	06 39	07 31	15 04	15 12	15 22	15 37
62	05 41	06 33	07 21	15 09	15 21	15 34	15 53
60	05 39	06 28	07 13	15 14	15 28	15 45	16 06
N 58	05 38	06 24	07 06	15 18	15 35	15 54	16 18
56	05 36	06 20	06 59	15 22	15 40	16 02	16 28
54	05 35	06 16	06 53	15 25	15 46	16 09	16 36
52	05 33	06 13	06 48	15 28	15 50	16 15	16 44
50	05 32	06 10	06 44	15 31	15 55	16 21	16 52
45	05 29	06 03	06 33	15 37	16 04	16 34	17 07
N 40	05 25	05 57	06 25	15 42	16 12	16 44	17 19
35	05 22	05 52	06 18	15 46	16 18	16 53	17 30
30	05 18	05 47	06 11	15 50	16 24	17 01	17 40
20	05 11	05 37	06 00	15 56	16 35	17 14	17 56
N 10	05 03	05 28	05 50	16 02	16 44	17 26	18 10
0	04 54	05 19	05 40	16 08	16 52	17 38	18 24
S 10	04 44	05 09	05 31	16 14	17 01	17 49	18 37
20	04 31	04 58	05 20	16 20	17 10	18 01	18 52
30	04 14	04 44	05 09	16 27	17 21	18 15	19 09
35	04 03	04 35	05 02	16 31	17 27	18 23	19 18
40	03 50	04 25	04 54	16 35	17 34	18 32	19 29
45	03 34	04 13	04 44	16 40	17 42	18 43	19 43
S 50	03 13	03 58	04 33	16 47	17 52	18 57	19 59
52	03 02	03 50	04 28	16 50	17 57	19 03	20 06
54	02 50	03 42	04 22	16 53	18 02	19 10	20 14
56	02 36	03 33	04 16	16 57	18 08	19 17	20 24
58	02 19	03 22	04 08	17 01	18 14	19 26	20 35
S 60	01 58	03 10	04 00	17 05	18 21	19 36	20 47

Sunset / Twilight / Moonset

Lat.	Sunset	Civil	Naut.	Moonset 27	28	29	30
°	h m	h m	h m	h m	h m	h m	h m
N 72	14 51	16 13	17 34	04 58	06 45	08 39	10 53
N 70	15 13	16 24	17 37	04 50	06 29	08 10	09 55
68	15 30	16 33	17 39	04 43	06 15	07 48	09 22
66	15 44	16 41	17 41	04 37	06 05	07 32	08 57
64	15 56	16 47	17 43	04 33	05 56	07 18	08 38
62	16 05	16 53	17 45	04 28	05 48	07 07	08 23
60	16 14	16 58	17 47	04 25	05 42	06 57	08 10
N 58	16 21	17 03	17 49	04 22	05 36	06 49	07 59
56	16 27	17 07	17 50	04 19	05 31	06 41	07 49
54	16 33	17 10	17 52	04 17	05 26	06 35	07 41
52	16 39	17 14	17 53	04 14	05 22	06 29	07 33
50	16 43	17 17	17 55	04 12	05 18	06 23	07 27
45	16 54	17 24	17 58	04 08	05 10	06 12	07 12
N 40	17 02	17 30	18 02	04 04	05 04	06 02	07 00
35	17 10	17 36	18 05	04 01	04 58	05 54	06 50
30	17 16	17 41	18 09	03 58	04 53	05 47	06 41
20	17 27	17 50	18 16	03 53	04 44	05 35	06 26
N 10	17 38	17 59	18 24	03 49	04 36	05 24	06 12
0	17 47	18 08	18 33	03 45	04 29	05 14	06 00
S 10	17 57	18 19	18 44	03 41	04 22	05 04	05 47
20	18 07	18 30	18 57	03 37	04 15	04 53	05 34
30	18 19	18 45	19 14	03 32	04 06	04 41	05 19
35	18 27	18 53	19 25	03 29	04 01	04 34	05 10
40	18 35	19 03	19 38	03 26	03 55	04 26	05 00
45	18 44	19 16	19 55	03 22	03 49	04 17	04 49
S 50	18 56	19 31	20 16	03 18	03 41	04 06	04 34
52	19 01	19 39	20 27	03 16	03 37	04 01	04 28
54	19 07	19 47	20 39	03 14	03 34	03 55	04 21
56	19 13	19 56	20 54	03 12	03 29	03 49	04 12
58	19 21	20 07	21 11	03 09	03 24	03 42	04 03
S 60	19 29	20 20	21 33	03 06	03 19	03 34	03 53

SUN / MOON

Day	Eqn. of Time 00h	12h	Mer. Pass.	Mer. Pass. Upper	Lower	Age	Phase
d	m s	m s	h m	h m	h m	d	%
27	16 07	16 12	11 44	22 19	09 56	12	95
28	16 12	16 14	11 44	23 03	10 41	13	98
29	16 16	16 18	11 44	23 49	11 26	14	100

2012 OCT. 30, 31, NOV. 1 (TUES., WED., THURS.)

UT	ARIES GHA	VENUS −4.0 GHA	Dec	MARS +1.2 GHA	Dec	JUPITER −2.7 GHA	Dec	SATURN +0.6 GHA	Dec	STARS Name	SHA	Dec
30 00	38 42.9	216 29.0	N 0 43.1	143 29.6	S23 46.7	324 33.9	N21 48.0	187 14.9	S10 22.6	Acamar	315 18.3	S40 15.1
01	53 45.3	231 28.7	41.9	158 30.0	46.9	339 36.6	48.0	202 17.1	22.8	Achernar	335 26.5	S57 10.3
02	68 47.8	246 28.3	40.8	173 30.5	47.1	354 39.3	47.9	217 19.3	22.9	Acrux	173 10.3	S63 10.1
03	83 50.3	261 28.0	.. 39.6	188 31.0	.. 47.3	9 42.0	.. 47.9	232 21.4	.. 23.0	Adhara	255 12.7	S28 59.3
04	98 52.7	276 27.7	38.5	203 31.4	47.5	24 44.6	47.9	247 23.6	23.1	Aldebaran	290 49.6	N16 32.1
05	113 55.2	291 27.3	37.3	218 31.9	47.7	39 47.3	47.9	262 25.8	23.2			
06	128 57.7	306 27.0	N 0 36.2	233 32.3	S23 47.9	54 50.0	N21 47.9	277 28.0	S10 23.3	Alioth	166 21.6	N55 53.3
07	144 00.1	321 26.6	35.1	248 32.8	48.1	69 52.7	47.8	292 30.1	23.4	Alkaid	152 59.7	N49 14.9
T 08	159 02.6	336 26.3	33.9	263 33.3	48.3	84 55.4	47.8	307 32.3	23.5	Al Na'ir	27 44.1	S46 53.9
U 09	174 05.1	351 26.0	.. 32.8	278 33.7	.. 48.5	99 58.1	.. 47.8	322 34.5	.. 23.6	Alnilam	275 46.6	S 1 11.6
E 10	189 07.5	6 25.6	31.6	293 34.2	48.7	115 00.8	47.8	337 36.7	23.7	Alphard	217 56.6	S 8 42.9
S 11	204 10.0	21 25.3	30.5	308 34.7	48.9	130 03.5	47.7	352 38.8	23.8			
D 12	219 12.4	36 24.9	N 0 29.3	323 35.1	S23 49.1	145 06.1	N21 47.7	7 41.0	S10 23.9	Alphecca	126 11.7	N26 40.5
A 13	234 14.9	51 24.6	28.2	338 35.6	49.3	160 08.8	47.7	22 43.2	24.0	Alpheratz	357 43.7	N29 10.0
Y 14	249 17.4	66 24.2	27.0	353 36.1	49.5	175 11.5	47.7	37 45.4	24.1	Altair	62 08.8	N 8 54.4
15	264 19.8	81 23.9	.. 25.9	8 36.5	.. 49.7	190 14.2	.. 47.7	52 47.5	.. 24.2	Ankaa	353 15.8	S42 14.1
16	279 22.3	96 23.6	24.8	23 37.0	49.9	205 16.9	47.6	67 49.7	24.3	Antares	112 27.1	S26 27.5
17	294 24.8	111 23.2	23.6	38 37.5	50.1	220 19.6	47.6	82 51.9	24.4			
18	309 27.2	126 22.9	N 0 22.5	53 37.9	S23 50.3	235 22.3	N21 47.6	97 54.1	S10 24.5	Arcturus	145 56.5	N19 07.0
19	324 29.7	141 22.5	21.3	68 38.4	50.5	250 25.0	47.6	112 56.2	24.6	Atria	107 29.8	S69 03.0
20	339 32.2	156 22.2	20.2	83 38.8	50.6	265 27.7	47.5	127 58.4	24.7	Avior	234 18.1	S59 32.8
21	354 34.6	171 21.9	.. 19.0	98 39.3	.. 50.8	280 30.3	.. 47.5	143 00.6	.. 24.8	Bellatrix	278 32.2	N 6 21.6
22	9 37.1	186 21.5	17.9	113 39.8	51.0	295 33.0	47.5	158 02.8	24.9	Betelgeuse	271 01.6	N 7 24.5
23	24 39.6	201 21.2	16.7	128 40.2	51.2	310 35.7	47.5	173 04.9	25.0			
31 00	39 42.0	216 20.8	N 0 15.6	143 40.7	S23 51.4	325 38.4	N21 47.4	188 07.1	S10 25.1	Canopus	263 56.0	S52 42.0
01	54 44.5	231 20.5	14.5	158 41.2	51.6	340 41.1	47.4	203 09.3	25.2	Capella	280 34.7	N46 00.4
02	69 46.9	246 20.1	13.3	173 41.6	51.8	355 43.8	47.4	218 11.5	25.3	Deneb	49 31.8	N45 20.0
03	84 49.4	261 19.8	.. 12.2	188 42.1	.. 52.0	10 46.5	.. 47.4	233 13.6	.. 25.4	Denebola	182 34.4	N14 30.0
04	99 51.9	276 19.5	11.0	203 42.5	52.2	25 49.2	47.4	248 15.8	25.5	Diphda	348 56.0	S17 54.9
05	114 54.3	291 19.1	09.9	218 43.0	52.4	40 51.9	47.3	263 18.0	25.6			
06	129 56.8	306 18.8	N 0 08.7	233 43.5	S23 52.5	55 54.6	N21 47.3	278 20.2	S10 25.7	Dubhe	193 52.7	N61 40.6
07	144 59.3	321 18.4	07.6	248 43.9	52.7	70 57.3	47.3	293 22.3	25.8	Elnath	278 12.9	N28 37.0
W 08	160 01.7	336 18.1	06.4	263 44.4	52.9	86 00.0	47.3	308 24.5	25.9	Eltanin	90 46.7	N51 29.6
E 09	175 04.2	351 17.8	.. 05.3	278 44.8	.. 53.1	101 02.7	.. 47.2	323 26.7	.. 26.0	Enif	33 47.5	N 9 56.3
D 10	190 06.7	6 17.4	04.1	293 45.3	53.3	116 05.3	47.2	338 28.9	26.1	Fomalhaut	15 24.3	S29 33.2
N 11	205 09.1	21 17.1	03.0	308 45.8	53.5	131 08.0	47.2	353 31.0	26.2			
E 12	220 11.6	36 16.7	N 0 01.8	323 46.2	S23 53.7	146 10.7	N21 47.2	8 33.2	S10 26.3	Gacrux	172 01.9	S57 11.0
S 13	235 14.1	51 16.4	N 00.7	338 46.7	53.9	161 13.4	47.1	23 35.4	26.4	Gienah	175 53.0	S17 36.7
D 14	250 16.5	66 16.0	S 00.5	353 47.1	54.0	176 16.1	47.1	38 37.6	26.5	Hadar	148 49.2	S60 26.0
A 15	265 19.0	81 15.7	.. 01.6	8 47.6	.. 54.2	191 18.8	.. 47.1	53 39.7	.. 26.6	Hamal	328 00.9	N23 31.5
Y 16	280 21.4	96 15.3	02.8	23 48.0	54.4	206 21.5	47.1	68 41.9	26.7	Kaus Aust.	83 44.6	S34 22.6
17	295 23.9	111 15.0	03.9	38 48.5	54.6	221 24.2	47.1	83 44.1	26.8			
18	310 26.4	126 14.7	S 0 05.1	53 49.0	S23 54.8	236 26.9	N21 47.0	98 46.3	S10 26.9	Kochab	137 21.2	N74 06.2
19	325 28.8	141 14.3	06.2	68 49.4	55.0	251 29.6	47.0	113 48.4	27.0	Markab	13 38.6	N15 16.7
20	340 31.3	156 14.0	07.4	83 49.9	55.1	266 32.3	47.0	128 50.6	27.1	Menkar	314 15.2	N 4 08.5
21	355 33.8	171 13.6	.. 08.5	98 50.3	.. 55.3	281 35.0	.. 47.0	143 52.8	.. 27.2	Menkent	148 08.5	S36 25.9
22	10 36.2	186 13.3	09.6	113 50.8	55.5	296 37.7	46.9	158 55.0	27.3	Miaplacidus	221 39.9	S69 46.0
23	25 38.7	201 12.9	10.8	128 51.2	55.7	311 40.4	46.9	173 57.2	27.4			
1 00	40 41.2	216 12.6	S 0 11.9	143 51.7	S23 55.9	326 43.1	N21 46.9	188 59.3	S10 27.5	Mirfak	308 40.5	N49 54.4
01	55 43.6	231 12.3	13.1	158 52.2	56.0	341 45.8	46.9	204 01.5	27.6	Nunki	75 59.0	S26 16.7
02	70 46.1	246 11.9	14.2	173 52.6	56.2	356 48.5	46.8	219 03.7	27.7	Peacock	53 20.0	S56 41.7
03	85 48.6	261 11.6	.. 15.4	188 53.1	.. 56.4	11 51.2	.. 46.8	234 05.9	.. 27.8	Pollux	243 28.2	N27 59.5
04	100 51.0	276 11.2	16.5	203 53.5	56.6	26 53.9	46.8	249 08.0	27.9	Procyon	245 00.1	N 5 11.4
05	115 53.5	291 10.9	17.7	218 54.0	56.8	41 56.6	46.8	264 10.2	28.0			
06	130 55.9	306 10.5	S 0 18.8	233 54.4	S23 56.9	56 59.3	N21 46.8	279 12.4	S10 28.1	Rasalhague	96 07.1	N12 33.3
07	145 58.4	321 10.2	20.0	248 54.9	57.1	72 02.0	46.7	294 14.6	28.2	Regulus	207 44.1	N11 54.2
T 08	161 00.9	336 09.8	21.1	263 55.3	57.3	87 04.7	46.7	309 16.7	28.4	Rigel	281 12.2	S 8 11.2
H 09	176 03.3	351 09.5	.. 22.3	278 55.8	.. 57.5	102 07.4	.. 46.7	324 18.9	.. 28.5	Rigil Kent.	139 53.0	S60 53.2
U 10	191 05.8	6 09.2	23.4	293 56.3	57.6	117 10.1	46.7	339 21.1	28.6	Sabik	102 13.3	S15 44.3
R 11	206 08.3	21 08.8	24.6	308 56.7	57.8	132 12.8	46.6	354 23.3	28.7			
S 12	221 10.7	36 08.5	S 0 25.7	323 57.2	S23 58.0	147 15.5	N21 46.6	9 25.4	S10 28.8	Schedar	349 40.5	N56 36.7
D 13	236 13.2	51 08.1	26.9	338 57.6	58.2	162 18.2	46.6	24 27.6	28.9	Shaula	96 22.8	S37 06.7
A 14	251 15.7	66 07.8	28.0	353 58.1	58.3	177 20.9	46.6	39 29.8	29.0	Sirius	258 33.9	S16 44.0
Y 15	266 18.1	81 07.4	.. 29.2	8 58.5	.. 58.5	192 23.6	.. 46.5	54 32.0	.. 29.1	Spica	158 32.0	S11 13.6
16	281 20.6	96 07.1	30.3	23 59.0	58.7	207 26.3	46.5	69 34.1	29.2	Suhail	222 52.8	S43 28.9
17	296 23.0	111 06.7	31.5	38 59.4	58.9	222 29.0	46.5	84 36.3	29.3			
18	311 25.5	126 06.4	S 0 32.6	53 59.9	S23 59.0	237 31.7	N21 46.5	99 38.5	S10 29.4	Vega	80 39.5	N38 48.1
19	326 28.0	141 06.0	33.8	69 00.3	59.2	252 34.4	46.4	114 40.7	29.5	Zuben'ubi	137 06.2	S16 05.6
20	341 30.4	156 05.7	34.9	84 00.8	59.4	267 37.1	46.4	129 42.8	29.6		SHA	Mer.Pass.
21	356 32.9	171 05.3	.. 36.1	99 01.2	.. 59.6	282 39.8	.. 46.4	144 45.0	.. 29.7	Venus	176 38.8	9 35
22	11 35.4	186 05.0	37.3	114 01.7	59.7	297 42.6	46.4	159 47.2	29.8	Mars	103 58.7	14 25
23	26 37.8	201 04.7	38.4	129 02.1	59.9	312 45.3	46.3	174 49.4	29.9	Jupiter	285 56.4	2 17
Mer.Pass. 21 17.7		v −0.3	d 1.1	v 0.5	d 0.2	v 2.7	d 0.0	v 2.2	d 0.1	Saturn	148 25.1	11 26

UT d h	SUN GHA ° ′	SUN Dec ° ′	MOON GHA ° ′	v ′	MOON Dec ° ′	d ′	HP ′
30 00 (TUESDAY)	184 05.0	S13 50.4	2 44.2	13.1	N15 55.9	7.1	54.3
01	199 05.0	51.2	17 16.3	13.1	16 03.0	7.1	54.3
02	214 05.1	52.0	31 48.4	13.1	16 10.1	6.9	54.3
03	229 05.1	. . 52.8	46 20.5	13.1	16 17.0	6.9	54.3
04	244 05.1	53.6	60 52.6	13.0	16 23.9	6.8	54.3
05	259 05.1	54.4	75 24.6	13.0	16 30.7	6.7	54.3
06	274 05.2	S13 55.3	89 56.6	13.0	N16 37.4	6.7	54.3
07	289 05.2	56.1	104 28.6	12.9	16 44.1	6.5	54.3
08	304 05.2	56.9	119 00.5	13.0	16 50.6	6.5	54.3
09	319 05.3	. . 57.7	133 32.5	12.9	16 57.1	6.4	54.3
10	334 05.3	58.5	148 04.4	12.9	17 03.5	6.4	54.2
11	349 05.3	13 59.3	162 36.3	12.8	17 09.9	6.2	54.2
12	4 05.4	S14 00.1	177 08.1	12.9	N17 16.1	6.2	54.2
13	19 05.4	01.0	191 40.0	12.8	17 22.3	6.1	54.2
14	34 05.4	01.8	206 11.8	12.7	17 28.4	6.0	54.2
15	49 05.4	. . 02.6	220 43.5	12.8	17 34.4	6.0	54.2
16	64 05.5	03.4	235 15.3	12.7	17 40.4	5.8	54.2
17	79 05.5	04.2	249 47.0	12.8	17 46.2	5.8	54.2
18	94 05.5	S14 05.0	264 18.8	12.6	N17 52.0	5.7	54.2
19	109 05.6	05.8	278 50.4	12.7	17 57.7	5.6	54.2
20	124 05.6	06.6	293 22.1	12.7	18 03.3	5.5	54.2
21	139 05.6	. . 07.4	307 53.8	12.6	18 08.8	5.5	54.2
22	154 05.6	08.3	322 25.4	12.6	18 14.3	5.3	54.2
23	169 05.7	09.1	336 57.0	12.5	18 19.6	5.3	54.1
31 00 (WEDNESDAY)	184 05.7	S14 09.9	351 28.5	12.6	N18 24.9	5.2	54.1
01	199 05.7	10.7	6 00.1	12.5	18 30.1	5.1	54.1
02	214 05.7	11.5	20 31.6	12.5	18 35.2	5.0	54.1
03	229 05.8	. . 12.3	35 03.1	12.5	18 40.2	4.9	54.1
04	244 05.8	13.1	49 34.6	12.5	18 45.1	4.9	54.1
05	259 05.8	13.9	64 06.1	12.4	18 50.0	4.7	54.1
06	274 05.8	S14 14.7	78 37.5	12.4	N18 54.7	4.7	54.1
07	289 05.9	15.5	93 08.9	12.4	18 59.4	4.6	54.1
08	304 05.9	16.3	107 40.3	12.4	19 04.0	4.5	54.1
09	319 05.9	. . 17.1	122 11.7	12.4	19 08.5	4.4	54.1
10	334 05.9	17.9	136 43.1	12.3	19 12.9	4.3	54.1
11	349 05.9	18.7	151 14.4	12.3	19 17.2	4.2	54.1
12	4 06.0	S14 19.5	165 45.7	12.3	N19 21.4	4.2	54.1
13	19 06.0	20.3	180 17.0	12.3	19 25.6	4.0	54.1
14	34 06.0	21.1	194 48.3	12.3	19 29.6	4.0	54.1
15	49 06.0	. . 21.9	209 19.6	12.2	19 33.6	3.8	54.1
16	64 06.0	22.7	223 50.8	12.2	19 37.4	3.8	54.1
17	79 06.1	23.6	238 22.0	12.2	19 41.2	3.7	54.0
18	94 06.1	S14 24.4	252 53.2	12.2	N19 44.9	3.6	54.0
19	109 06.1	25.2	267 24.4	12.2	19 48.5	3.5	54.0
20	124 06.1	26.0	281 55.6	12.1	19 52.0	3.4	54.0
21	139 06.1	. . 26.8	296 26.7	12.2	19 55.4	3.3	54.0
22	154 06.2	27.6	310 57.9	12.1	19 58.7	3.3	54.0
23	169 06.2	28.4	325 29.0	12.1	20 02.0	3.1	54.0
1 00 (THURSDAY)	184 06.2	S14 29.2	340 00.1	12.1	N20 05.1	3.0	54.0
01	199 06.2	30.0	354 31.2	12.1	20 08.1	3.0	54.0
02	214 06.2	30.7	9 02.3	12.0	20 11.1	2.8	54.0
03	229 06.2	. . 31.5	23 33.3	12.1	20 13.9	2.8	54.0
04	244 06.3	32.3	38 04.4	12.0	20 16.7	2.7	54.0
05	259 06.3	33.1	52 35.4	12.0	20 19.4	2.6	54.0
06	274 06.3	S14 33.9	67 06.4	12.1	N20 22.0	2.4	54.0
07	289 06.3	34.7	81 37.5	12.0	20 24.4	2.4	54.0
08	304 06.3	35.5	96 08.5	11.9	20 26.8	2.3	54.0
09	319 06.3	. . 36.3	110 39.4	12.0	20 29.1	2.2	54.0
10	334 06.3	37.1	125 10.4	12.0	20 31.3	2.1	54.0
11	349 06.4	37.9	139 41.4	11.9	20 33.4	2.0	54.0
12	4 06.4	S14 38.7	154 12.3	12.0	N20 35.4	1.9	54.0
13	19 06.4	39.5	168 43.3	11.9	20 37.3	1.8	54.0
14	34 06.4	40.3	183 14.2	11.9	20 39.1	1.7	54.0
15	49 06.4	. . 41.1	197 45.1	11.9	20 40.8	1.7	54.0
16	64 06.4	41.9	212 16.0	11.9	20 42.5	1.5	54.0
17	79 06.4	42.7	226 46.9	11.9	20 44.0	1.4	54.0
18	94 06.4	S14 43.5	241 17.8	11.9	N20 45.4	1.4	54.0
19	109 06.4	44.3	255 48.7	11.9	20 46.8	1.2	54.0
20	124 06.5	45.0	270 19.6	11.9	20 48.0	1.1	54.0
21	139 06.5	. . 45.8	284 50.5	11.8	20 49.1	1.1	54.0
22	154 06.5	46.6	299 21.3	11.9	20 50.2	0.9	54.0
23	169 06.5	47.4	313 52.2	11.8	N20 51.1	0.9	54.0
	SD 16.1	*d* 0.8	SD 14.8		14.7		14.7

Lat. °	Twilight Naut. h m	Twilight Civil h m	Sunrise h m	Moonrise 30 h m	Moonrise 31 h m	Moonrise 1 h m	Moonrise 2 h m
N 72	06 04	07 26	08 53	13 19	□	□	□
N 70	06 00	07 14	08 27	14 18	13 59	□	□
68	05 56	07 03	08 08	14 52	14 59	15 16	15 58
66	05 53	06 55	07 53	15 17	15 33	16 00	16 45
64	05 51	06 47	07 40	15 37	15 58	16 30	17 16
62	05 48	06 41	07 30	15 53	16 18	16 52	17 39
60	05 46	06 35	07 21	16 06	16 34	17 10	17 57
N 58	05 44	06 30	07 13	16 18	16 47	17 25	18 13
56	05 42	06 26	07 06	16 28	16 59	17 38	18 26
54	05 40	06 22	06 59	16 36	17 09	17 49	18 37
52	05 38	06 18	06 54	16 44	17 19	17 59	18 47
50	05 36	06 15	06 49	16 52	17 27	18 08	18 56
45	05 32	06 07	06 37	17 07	17 44	18 27	19 15
N 40	05 28	06 00	06 28	17 19	17 59	18 42	19 30
35	05 24	05 54	06 20	17 30	18 11	18 55	19 44
30	05 20	05 49	06 13	17 40	18 22	19 07	19 55
20	05 12	05 38	06 01	17 56	18 40	19 26	20 14
N 10	05 04	05 29	05 50	18 10	18 56	19 43	20 31
0	04 54	05 19	05 40	18 24	19 11	19 59	20 47
S 10	04 43	05 08	05 30	18 37	19 26	20 15	21 03
20	04 29	04 56	05 19	18 52	19 42	20 32	21 20
30	04 11	04 41	05 06	19 09	20 01	20 52	21 40
35	03 59	04 32	04 58	19 18	20 12	21 03	21 51
40	03 46	04 21	04 50	19 29	20 24	21 16	22 04
45	03 28	04 08	04 40	19 43	20 39	21 32	22 20
S 50	03 06	03 52	04 28	19 59	20 57	21 51	22 39
52	02 55	03 44	04 22	20 06	21 06	22 00	22 48
54	02 42	03 35	04 16	20 14	21 15	22 10	22 58
56	02 26	03 25	04 09	20 24	21 26	22 22	23 09
58	02 07	03 14	04 01	20 35	21 38	22 35	23 22
S 60	01 43	03 00	03 52	20 47	21 53	22 50	23 37

Lat. °	Sunset h m	Twilight Civil h m	Twilight Naut. h m	Moonset 30 h m	Moonset 31 h m	Moonset 1 h m	Moonset 2 h m
N 72	14 33	15 59	17 22	10 53	□	□	□
N 70	14 58	16 12	17 26	09 55	11 52	□	□
68	15 18	16 22	17 29	09 22	10 53	12 15	13 13
66	15 33	16 31	17 32	08 57	10 19	11 30	12 25
64	15 46	16 39	17 35	08 38	09 54	11 01	11 55
62	15 57	16 45	17 38	08 23	09 35	10 39	11 31
60	16 06	16 51	17 40	08 10	09 19	10 21	11 13
N 58	16 14	16 56	17 42	07 59	09 06	10 06	10 58
56	16 21	17 00	17 44	07 49	08 54	09 53	10 45
54	16 27	17 05	17 46	07 41	08 44	09 42	10 33
52	16 33	17 08	17 48	07 33	08 35	09 32	10 23
50	16 38	17 12	17 50	07 27	08 27	09 23	10 14
45	16 49	17 20	17 54	07 12	08 10	09 05	09 55
N 40	16 58	17 26	17 58	07 00	07 56	08 50	09 40
35	17 06	17 33	18 02	06 50	07 44	08 37	09 26
30	17 14	17 38	18 06	06 41	07 34	08 26	09 15
20	17 26	17 48	18 15	06 26	07 16	08 06	08 55
N 10	17 37	17 58	18 23	06 12	07 01	07 50	08 38
0	17 47	18 08	18 33	06 00	06 47	07 34	08 22
S 10	17 57	18 19	18 45	05 47	06 32	07 19	08 06
20	18 09	18 32	18 59	05 34	06 17	07 02	07 49
30	18 22	18 47	19 17	05 19	05 59	06 43	07 30
35	18 29	18 56	19 29	05 10	05 49	06 32	07 18
40	18 38	19 07	19 43	05 00	05 38	06 19	07 05
45	18 48	19 20	20 00	04 49	05 24	06 04	06 49
S 50	19 01	19 37	20 23	04 34	05 07	05 45	06 30
52	19 06	19 45	20 34	04 28	04 59	05 37	06 21
54	19 13	19 54	20 48	04 21	04 51	05 27	06 11
56	19 20	20 04	21 04	04 12	04 41	05 16	05 59
58	19 28	20 16	21 23	04 03	04 30	05 03	05 46
S 60	19 37	20 29	21 48	03 53	04 17	04 49	05 30

Day d	SUN Eqn. of Time 00^h m s	SUN Eqn. of Time 12^h m s	SUN Mer. Pass. h m	MOON Mer. Pass. Upper h m	MOON Mer. Pass. Lower h m	MOON Age d	MOON Phase %
30	16 20	16 21	11 44	24 35	12 12	15	100
31	16 23	16 24	11 44	00 35	12 59	16	97
1	16 25	16 25	11 44	01 23	13 47	17	94

UT	ARIES GHA	VENUS −4.0 GHA	Dec	MARS +1.2 GHA	Dec	JUPITER −2.7 GHA	Dec	SATURN +0.6 GHA	Dec
2 00	41 40.3	216 04.3	S 0 39.6	144 02.6	S24 00.1	327 48.0	N21 46.3	189 51.5	S10 30.0
01	56 42.8	231 04.0	40.7	159 03.0	00.2	342 50.7	46.3	204 53.7	30.1
02	71 45.2	246 03.6	41.9	174 03.5	00.4	357 53.4	46.3	219 55.9	30.2
03	86 47.7	261 03.3	.. 43.0	189 03.9	.. 00.6	12 56.1	.. 46.2	234 58.1	.. 30.3
04	101 50.2	276 02.9	44.2	204 04.4	00.8	27 58.8	46.2	250 00.2	30.4
05	116 52.6	291 02.6	45.3	219 04.8	00.9	43 01.5	46.2	265 02.4	30.5
F 06	131 55.1	306 02.2	S 0 46.5	234 05.3	S24 01.1	58 04.2	N21 46.2	280 04.6	S10 30.6
R 07	146 57.5	321 01.9	47.6	249 05.7	01.3	73 06.9	46.1	295 06.8	30.7
I 08	162 00.0	336 01.5	48.8	264 06.2	01.4	88 09.6	46.1	310 09.0	30.8
D 09	177 02.5	351 01.2	.. 49.9	279 06.6	.. 01.6	103 12.3	.. 46.1	325 11.1	.. 30.9
A 10	192 04.9	6 00.8	51.1	294 07.1	01.8	118 15.0	46.1	340 13.3	31.0
Y 11	207 07.4	21 00.5	52.2	309 07.5	01.9	133 17.8	46.0	355 15.5	31.1
12	222 09.9	36 00.1	S 0 53.4	324 08.0	S24 02.1	148 20.5	N21 46.0	10 17.7	S10 31.2
13	237 12.3	50 59.8	54.5	339 08.4	02.3	163 23.2	46.0	25 19.8	31.3
14	252 14.8	65 59.4	55.7	354 08.9	02.4	178 25.9	46.0	40 22.0	31.4
15	267 17.3	80 59.1	.. 56.8	9 09.3	.. 02.6	193 28.6	.. 45.9	55 24.2	.. 31.5
16	282 19.7	95 58.7	58.0	24 09.8	02.7	208 31.3	45.9	70 26.4	31.6
17	297 22.2	110 58.4	0 59.1	39 10.2	02.9	223 34.0	45.9	85 28.5	31.7
18	312 24.7	125 58.0	S 1 00.3	54 10.7	S24 03.1	238 36.7	N21 45.9	100 30.7	S10 31.8
19	327 27.1	140 57.7	01.5	69 11.1	03.2	253 39.4	45.9	115 32.9	31.9
20	342 29.6	155 57.3	02.6	84 11.6	03.4	268 42.2	45.8	130 35.1	32.0
21	357 32.0	170 57.0	.. 03.8	99 12.0	.. 03.6	283 44.9	.. 45.8	145 37.2	.. 32.1
22	12 34.5	185 56.6	04.9	114 12.5	03.7	298 47.6	45.8	160 39.4	32.2
23	27 37.0	200 56.3	06.1	129 12.9	03.9	313 50.3	45.8	175 41.6	32.3
3 00	42 39.4	215 55.9	S 1 07.2	144 13.3	S24 04.0	328 53.0	N21 45.7	190 43.8	S10 32.4
01	57 41.9	230 55.6	08.4	159 13.8	04.2	343 55.7	45.7	205 45.9	32.5
02	72 44.4	245 55.2	09.5	174 14.2	04.4	358 58.4	45.7	220 48.1	32.6
03	87 46.8	260 54.9	.. 10.7	189 14.7	.. 04.5	14 01.1	.. 45.7	235 50.3	.. 32.7
04	102 49.3	275 54.5	11.8	204 15.1	04.7	29 03.9	45.6	250 52.5	32.8
05	117 51.8	290 54.2	13.0	219 15.6	04.8	44 06.6	45.6	265 54.6	32.9
S 06	132 54.2	305 53.8	S 1 14.1	234 16.0	S24 05.0	59 09.3	N21 45.6	280 56.8	S10 33.0
A 07	147 56.7	320 53.5	15.3	249 16.5	05.2	74 12.0	45.5	295 59.0	33.1
T 08	162 59.1	335 53.1	16.5	264 16.9	05.3	89 14.7	45.5	311 01.2	33.2
U 09	178 01.6	350 52.8	.. 17.6	279 17.4	.. 05.5	104 17.4	.. 45.5	326 03.4	.. 33.3
R 10	193 04.1	5 52.4	18.8	294 17.8	05.6	119 20.2	45.5	341 05.5	33.4
D 11	208 06.5	20 52.1	19.9	309 18.2	05.8	134 22.9	45.4	356 07.7	33.5
A 12	223 09.0	35 51.7	S 1 21.1	324 18.7	S24 05.9	149 25.6	N21 45.4	11 09.9	S10 33.6
Y 13	238 11.5	50 51.4	22.2	339 19.1	06.1	164 28.3	45.4	26 12.1	33.7
14	253 13.9	65 51.0	23.4	354 19.6	06.2	179 31.0	45.4	41 14.2	33.8
15	268 16.4	80 50.7	.. 24.5	9 20.0	.. 06.4	194 33.7	.. 45.3	56 16.4	.. 33.9
16	283 18.9	95 50.3	25.7	24 20.5	06.6	209 36.5	45.3	71 18.6	34.0
17	298 21.3	110 50.0	26.8	39 20.9	06.7	224 39.2	45.3	86 20.8	34.1
18	313 23.8	125 49.6	S 1 28.0	54 21.3	S24 06.9	239 41.9	N21 45.3	101 22.9	S10 34.2
19	328 26.3	140 49.3	29.2	69 21.8	07.0	254 44.6	45.2	116 25.1	34.3
20	343 28.7	155 48.9	30.3	84 22.2	07.2	269 47.3	45.2	131 27.3	34.4
21	358 31.2	170 48.6	.. 31.5	99 22.7	.. 07.3	284 50.1	.. 45.2	146 29.5	.. 34.5
22	13 33.6	185 48.2	32.6	114 23.1	07.5	299 52.8	45.2	161 31.6	34.6
23	28 36.1	200 47.9	33.8	129 23.5	07.6	314 55.5	45.1	176 33.8	34.7
4 00	43 38.6	215 47.5	S 1 34.9	144 24.0	S24 07.8	329 58.2	N21 45.1	191 36.0	S10 34.8
01	58 41.0	230 47.2	36.1	159 24.4	07.9	345 00.9	45.1	206 38.2	34.9
02	73 43.5	245 46.8	37.2	174 24.9	08.1	0 03.7	45.1	221 40.3	35.0
03	88 46.0	260 46.4	.. 38.4	189 25.3	.. 08.2	15 06.4	.. 45.0	236 42.5	.. 35.1
04	103 48.4	275 46.1	39.6	204 25.8	08.4	30 09.1	45.0	251 44.7	35.2
05	118 50.9	290 45.7	40.7	219 26.2	08.5	45 11.8	45.0	266 46.9	35.3
S 06	133 53.4	305 45.4	S 1 41.9	234 26.6	S24 08.7	60 14.5	N21 45.0	281 49.1	S10 35.4
U 07	148 55.8	320 45.0	43.0	249 27.1	08.8	75 17.3	44.9	296 51.2	35.5
N 08	163 58.3	335 44.7	44.2	264 27.5	09.0	90 20.0	44.9	311 53.4	35.6
D 09	179 00.8	350 44.3	.. 45.3	279 27.9	.. 09.1	105 22.7	.. 44.9	326 55.6	.. 35.7
A 10	194 03.2	5 44.0	46.5	294 28.4	09.2	120 25.4	44.9	341 57.8	35.8
Y 11	209 05.7	20 43.6	47.6	309 28.8	09.4	135 28.2	44.8	356 59.9	35.9
12	224 08.1	35 43.3	S 1 48.8	324 29.3	S24 09.5	150 30.9	N21 44.8	12 02.1	S10 36.0
13	239 10.6	50 42.9	50.0	339 29.7	09.7	165 33.6	44.8	27 04.3	36.1
14	254 13.1	65 42.5	51.1	354 30.1	09.8	180 36.3	44.8	42 06.5	36.2
15	269 15.5	80 42.2	.. 52.3	9 30.6	.. 10.0	195 39.1	.. 44.7	57 08.6	.. 36.3
16	284 18.0	95 41.8	53.4	24 31.0	10.1	210 41.8	44.7	72 10.8	36.4
17	299 20.5	110 41.5	54.6	39 31.5	10.3	225 44.5	44.7	87 13.0	36.5
18	314 22.9	125 41.1	S 1 55.7	54 31.9	S24 10.4	240 47.2	N21 44.6	102 15.2	S10 36.6
19	329 25.4	140 40.8	56.9	69 32.3	10.5	255 50.0	44.6	117 17.3	36.7
20	344 27.9	155 40.4	58.0	84 32.8	10.7	270 52.7	44.6	132 19.5	36.8
21	359 30.3	170 40.1	1 59.2	99 33.2	.. 10.8	285 55.4	.. 44.6	147 21.7	.. 36.9
22	14 32.8	185 39.7	2 00.4	114 33.6	11.0	300 58.1	44.5	162 23.9	37.0
23	29 35.3	200 39.3	S 2 01.5	129 34.1	11.1	316 00.9	44.5	177 26.1	37.1
Mer. Pass.	21 05.9 h m	v −0.4	d 1.2	v 0.4	d 0.2	v 2.7	d 0.0	v 2.2	d 0.1

STARS

Name	SHA	Dec
Acamar	315 18.2	S40 15.1
Achernar	335 26.5	S57 10.3
Acrux	173 10.3	S63 10.1
Adhara	255 12.7	S28 59.3
Aldebaran	290 49.6	N16 32.1
Alioth	166 21.6	N55 53.3
Alkaid	152 59.7	N49 14.9
Al Na'ir	27 44.1	S46 53.9
Alnilam	275 46.6	S 1 11.6
Alphard	217 56.6	S 8 42.9
Alphecca	126 11.7	N26 40.5
Alpheratz	357 43.7	N29 10.0
Altair	62 08.8	N 8 54.4
Ankaa	353 15.8	S42 14.2
Antares	112 27.1	S26 27.5
Arcturus	145 56.5	N19 07.0
Atria	107 29.8	S69 03.0
Avior	234 18.1	S59 32.9
Bellatrix	278 32.2	N 6 21.6
Betelgeuse	271 01.5	N 7 24.5
Canopus	263 56.0	S52 42.0
Capella	280 34.7	N46 00.5
Deneb	49 31.8	N45 20.0
Denebola	182 34.3	N14 30.0
Diphda	348 56.0	S17 54.9
Dubhe	193 52.6	N61 40.6
Elnath	278 12.9	N28 37.0
Eltanin	90 46.7	N51 29.6
Enif	33 47.5	N 9 56.3
Fomalhaut	15 24.3	S29 33.2
Gacrux	172 01.9	S57 11.0
Gienah	175 53.0	S17 36.7
Hadar	148 49.1	S60 28.0
Hamal	328 00.9	N23 31.5
Kaus Aust.	83 44.6	S34 22.6
Kochab	137 21.2	N74 06.2
Markab	13 38.6	N15 16.7
Menkar	314 15.2	N 4 08.5
Menkent	148 08.5	S36 25.9
Miaplacidus	221 39.8	S69 46.0
Mirfak	308 40.5	N49 54.4
Nunki	75 59.0	S26 16.7
Peacock	53 20.0	S56 41.7
Pollux	243 28.2	N27 59.5
Procyon	245 00.1	N 5 11.4
Rasalhague	96 07.1	N12 33.3
Regulus	207 44.1	N11 54.2
Rigel	281 12.2	S 8 11.2
Rigil Kent.	139 53.0	S60 53.2
Sabik	102 13.3	S15 44.3
Schedar	349 40.5	N56 36.7
Shaula	96 22.8	S37 06.7
Sirius	258 33.9	S16 44.0
Spica	158 32.0	S11 13.6
Suhail	222 52.8	S43 28.9
Vega	80 39.5	N38 48.1
Zuben'ubi	137 06.2	S16 05.6

	SHA	Mer. Pass.
Venus	173 16.5	9 36 h m
Mars	101 33.9	14 23
Jupiter	286 13.6	2 04
Saturn	148 04.3	11 15

UT	SUN GHA	SUN Dec	MOON GHA	v	Dec	d	HP
d h	° ′	° ′	° ′	′	° ′	′	′
2 00	184 06.5	S14 48.2	328 23.0	11.9	N20 52.0	0.7	54.0
01	199 06.5	49.0	342 53.9	11.8	20 52.7	0.7	54.0
02	214 06.5	49.8	357 24.7	11.9	20 53.4	0.5	54.0
03	229 06.5	.. 50.6	11 55.6	11.8	20 53.9	0.5	54.0
04	244 06.5	51.4	26 26.4	11.9	20 54.4	0.4	54.0
05	259 06.5	52.1	40 57.3	11.8	20 54.8	0.2	54.0
06	274 06.5	S14 52.9	55 28.1	11.8	N20 55.0	0.2	54.0
07	289 06.5	53.7	69 58.9	11.9	20 55.2	0.1	54.0
08	304 06.5	54.5	84 29.8	11.8	20 55.3	0.0	54.0
F 09	319 06.5	.. 55.3	99 00.6	11.8	20 55.3	0.2	54.0
R 10	334 06.6	56.1	113 31.4	11.8	20 55.1	0.2	54.0
I 11	349 06.6	56.9	128 02.2	11.9	20 54.9	0.3	54.0
D 12	4 06.6	S14 57.6	142 33.1	11.8	N20 54.6	0.4	54.0
A 13	19 06.6	58.4	157 03.9	11.8	20 54.2	0.5	54.0
Y 14	34 06.6	14 59.2	171 34.7	11.9	20 53.7	0.6	54.1
15	49 06.6	15 00.0	186 05.6	11.8	20 53.1	0.7	54.1
16	64 06.6	00.8	200 36.4	11.8	20 52.4	0.8	54.1
17	79 06.6	01.6	215 07.2	11.9	20 51.6	0.9	54.1
18	94 06.6	S15 02.3	229 38.1	11.8	N20 50.7	1.0	54.1
19	109 06.6	03.1	244 08.9	11.8	20 49.7	1.1	54.1
20	124 06.6	03.8	258 39.7	11.9	20 48.6	1.2	54.1
21	139 06.6	.. 04.7	273 10.6	11.8	20 47.4	1.3	54.1
22	154 06.6	05.5	287 41.4	11.9	20 46.1	1.4	54.1
23	169 06.6	06.2	302 12.3	11.9	20 44.7	1.4	54.1
3 00	184 06.6	S15 07.0	316 43.2	11.8	N20 43.3	1.6	54.1
01	199 06.6	07.8	331 14.0	11.9	20 41.7	1.7	54.1
02	214 06.6	08.6	345 44.9	11.9	20 40.0	1.7	54.1
03	229 06.6	.. 09.3	0 15.8	11.9	20 38.3	1.9	54.1
04	244 06.6	10.1	14 46.7	11.9	20 36.4	2.0	54.1
05	259 06.6	10.9	29 17.6	11.9	20 34.4	2.0	54.1
06	274 06.6	S15 11.7	43 48.5	11.9	N20 32.4	2.2	54.2
S 07	289 06.6	12.5	58 19.4	11.9	20 30.2	2.2	54.2
A 08	304 06.6	13.2	72 50.3	11.9	20 28.0	2.4	54.2
T 09	319 06.6	.. 14.0	87 21.2	12.0	20 25.6	2.4	54.2
U 10	334 06.6	14.8	101 52.2	11.9	20 23.2	2.5	54.2
R 11	349 06.6	15.6	116 23.1	11.9	20 20.7	2.7	54.2
D 12	4 06.5	S15 16.3	130 54.0	12.0	N20 18.0	2.7	54.2
A 13	19 06.5	17.1	145 25.0	12.0	20 15.3	2.8	54.2
Y 14	34 06.5	17.9	159 56.0	11.9	20 12.5	2.9	54.2
15	49 06.5	.. 18.6	174 27.0	12.0	20 09.6	3.0	54.2
16	64 06.5	19.4	188 58.0	12.0	20 06.6	3.1	54.2
17	79 06.5	20.2	203 29.0	12.0	20 03.5	3.2	54.3
18	94 06.5	S15 21.0	218 00.0	12.0	N20 00.3	3.3	54.3
19	109 06.5	21.7	232 31.0	12.0	19 57.0	3.4	54.3
20	124 06.5	22.5	247 02.0	12.1	19 53.6	3.5	54.3
21	139 06.5	.. 23.3	261 33.1	12.0	19 50.1	3.5	54.3
22	154 06.5	24.0	276 04.2	12.0	19 46.6	3.7	54.3
23	169 06.5	24.8	290 35.2	12.1	19 42.9	3.7	54.3
4 00	184 06.5	S15 25.6	305 06.3	12.1	N19 39.2	3.9	54.3
01	199 06.5	26.3	319 37.4	12.1	19 35.3	3.9	54.4
02	214 06.5	27.1	334 08.5	12.2	19 31.4	4.0	54.4
03	229 06.4	.. 27.9	348 39.7	12.1	19 27.4	4.1	54.4
04	244 06.4	28.6	3 10.8	12.1	19 23.3	4.3	54.4
05	259 06.4	29.4	17 41.9	12.2	19 19.0	4.3	54.4
06	274 06.4	S15 30.2	32 13.1	12.2	N19 14.7	4.3	54.4
07	289 06.4	30.9	46 44.3	12.2	19 10.4	4.5	54.4
S 08	304 06.4	31.7	61 15.5	12.2	19 05.9	4.6	54.5
U 09	319 06.4	.. 32.5	75 46.7	12.2	19 01.3	4.7	54.5
N 10	334 06.4	33.2	90 17.9	12.3	18 56.6	4.7	54.5
D 11	349 06.4	34.0	104 49.2	12.2	18 51.9	4.9	54.5
A 12	4 06.3	S15 34.8	119 20.4	12.3	N18 47.0	4.9	54.5
Y 13	19 06.3	35.5	133 51.7	12.3	18 42.1	5.0	54.5
14	34 06.3	36.3	148 23.0	12.2	18 37.1	5.1	54.5
15	49 06.3	.. 37.1	162 54.2	12.4	18 32.0	5.2	54.6
16	64 06.3	37.8	177 25.6	12.3	18 26.8	5.3	54.6
17	79 06.3	38.6	191 56.9	12.3	18 21.5	5.3	54.6
18	94 06.3	S15 39.3	206 28.2	12.4	N18 16.2	5.5	54.6
19	109 06.2	40.1	220 59.6	12.3	18 10.7	5.5	54.6
20	124 06.2	40.9	235 30.9	12.4	18 05.2	5.7	54.6
21	139 06.2	.. 41.6	250 02.3	12.4	17 59.5	5.7	54.7
22	154 06.2	42.4	264 33.7	12.4	17 53.8	5.8	54.7
23	169 06.2	43.1	279 05.1	12.5	N17 48.0	5.9	54.7
	SD 16.2	d 0.8	SD 14.7		14.8		14.9

Twilight / Sunrise / Moonrise

Lat.	Naut.	Civil	Sunrise	Moonrise 2	3	4	5
°	h m	h m	h m	h m	h m	h m	h m
N 72	06 15	07 40	09 12	□	□	□	19 09
N 70	06 10	07 26	08 43	□	□	17 56	19 47
68	06 06	07 14	08 21	15 58	17 10	18 39	20 13
66	06 02	07 04	08 04	16 45	17 50	19 08	20 33
64	05 59	06 56	07 50	17 16	18 17	19 29	20 49
62	05 55	06 49	07 38	17 39	18 38	19 47	21 02
60	05 53	06 42	07 28	17 57	18 55	20 01	21 14
N 58	05 50	06 37	07 20	18 13	19 09	20 13	21 23
56	05 48	06 32	07 12	18 26	19 21	20 24	21 32
54	05 45	06 27	07 05	18 37	19 32	20 33	21 39
52	05 43	06 23	06 59	18 47	19 41	20 42	21 46
50	05 41	06 19	06 54	18 56	19 50	20 49	21 52
45	05 36	06 11	06 42	19 15	20 08	21 05	22 05
N 40	05 31	06 03	06 32	19 30	20 22	21 18	22 16
35	05 27	05 57	06 23	19 44	20 35	21 29	22 25
30	05 22	05 51	06 16	19 55	20 46	21 38	22 33
20	05 14	05 40	06 03	20 14	21 04	21 55	22 47
N 10	05 04	05 29	05 51	20 31	21 20	22 09	22 59
0	04 54	05 19	05 40	20 47	21 35	22 23	23 10
S 10	04 42	05 07	05 29	21 03	21 50	22 36	23 21
20	04 27	04 54	05 17	21 20	22 06	22 51	23 33
30	04 08	04 38	05 03	21 40	22 25	23 07	23 47
35	03 56	04 28	04 55	21 51	22 36	23 17	23 56
40	03 41	04 17	04 46	22 04	22 48	23 27	24 03
45	03 23	04 03	04 36	22 20	23 02	23 40	24 14
S 50	02 59	03 46	04 22	22 39	23 20	23 56	24 26
52	02 47	03 37	04 16	22 48	23 28	24 03	00 03
54	02 33	03 28	04 10	22 58	23 38	24 11	00 11
56	02 16	03 17	04 02	23 09	23 48	24 20	00 20
58	01 55	03 05	03 53	23 22	24 00	00 00	00 30
S 60	01 27	02 50	03 44	23 37	24 14	00 14	00 41

Sunset / Twilight / Moonset

Lat.	Sunset	Civil	Naut.	Moonset 2	3	4	5
°	h m	h m	h m	h m	h m	h m	h m
N 72	14 14	15 46	17 10	□	□	□	15 01
N 70	14 43	16 00	17 15	□	□	14 34	14 21
68	15 05	16 12	17 20	13 13	13 40	13 50	13 54
66	15 22	16 22	17 24	12 25	13 01	13 21	13 33
64	15 36	16 30	17 27	11 55	12 33	12 59	13 17
62	15 48	16 37	17 31	11 31	12 12	12 41	13 03
60	15 58	16 44	17 33	11 13	11 55	12 27	12 51
N 58	16 07	16 49	17 36	10 58	11 40	12 14	12 41
56	16 14	16 54	17 39	10 45	11 28	12 03	12 32
54	16 21	16 59	17 41	10 33	11 17	11 53	12 24
52	16 27	17 03	17 43	10 23	11 07	11 45	12 17
50	16 33	17 07	17 45	10 14	10 59	11 37	12 10
45	16 45	17 16	17 51	09 55	10 40	11 21	11 56
N 40	16 55	17 23	17 55	09 40	10 25	11 07	11 45
35	17 04	17 30	18 00	09 26	10 13	10 55	11 35
30	17 11	17 36	18 04	09 15	10 02	10 45	11 26
20	17 24	17 47	18 13	08 55	09 43	10 28	11 11
N 10	17 36	17 58	18 23	08 38	09 26	10 13	10 58
0	17 47	18 08	18 33	08 22	09 11	09 58	10 46
S 10	17 58	18 20	18 46	08 06	08 55	09 44	10 33
20	18 10	18 33	19 01	07 49	08 38	09 29	10 20
30	18 24	18 50	19 20	07 30	08 19	09 11	10 04
35	18 32	18 59	19 32	07 18	08 08	09 01	09 56
40	18 42	19 11	19 47	07 05	07 55	08 49	09 45
45	18 52	19 25	20 05	06 49	07 40	08 35	09 33
S 50	19 06	19 43	20 30	06 30	07 21	08 18	09 19
52	19 12	19 51	20 42	06 21	07 12	08 09	09 12
54	19 19	20 01	20 56	06 11	07 02	08 00	09 04
56	19 27	20 12	21 14	05 59	06 51	07 50	08 56
58	19 35	20 24	21 35	05 46	06 38	07 38	08 46
S 60	19 45	20 39	22 05	05 30	06 23	07 25	08 35

SUN / MOON

Day	Eqn. of Time 00h	Eqn. of Time 12h	Mer. Pass.	Mer. Pass. Upper	Mer. Pass. Lower	Age	Phase
d	m s	m s	h m	h m	h m	d	%
2	16 26	16 26	11 44	02 11	14 35	18	88
3	16 26	16 26	11 44	02 59	15 23	19	82
4	16 26	16 25	11 44	03 47	16 11	20	74

UT	ARIES GHA	VENUS −4.0 GHA	Dec	MARS +1.2 GHA	Dec	JUPITER −2.8 GHA	Dec	SATURN +0.6 GHA	Dec	Name	SHA	Dec
5 00	44 37.7	215 39.0	S 2 02.7	144 34.5	S24 11.2	331 03.6	N21 44.5	192 28.2	S10 37.2	Acamar	315 18.2	S40 15.2
01	59 40.2	230 38.6	03.8	159 34.9	11.4	346 06.3	44.5	207 30.4	37.3	Achernar	335 26.5	S57 10.3
02	74 42.6	245 38.3	05.0	174 35.4	11.5	1 09.0	44.5	222 32.6	37.4	Acrux	173 10.3	S63 10.1
03	89 45.1	260 37.9	.. 06.1	189 35.8	.. 11.7	16 11.8	.. 44.4	237 34.8	.. 37.5	Adhara	255 12.7	S28 59.3
04	104 47.6	275 37.6	07.3	204 36.3	11.8	31 14.5	44.4	252 36.9	37.6	Aldebaran	290 49.6	N16 32.1
05	119 50.0	290 37.2	08.5	219 36.7	11.9	46 17.2	44.4	267 39.1	37.7			
06	134 52.5	305 36.8	S 2 09.6	234 37.1	S24 12.1	61 20.0	N21 44.3	282 41.3	S10 37.8	Alioth	166 21.6	N55 53.3
07	149 55.0	320 36.5	10.8	249 37.6	12.2	76 22.7	44.3	297 43.5	37.9	Alkaid	152 59.7	N49 14.9
08	164 57.4	335 36.1	11.9	264 38.0	12.3	91 25.4	44.3	312 45.6	38.0	Al Na'ir	27 44.2	S46 53.9
M 09	179 59.9	350 35.8	.. 13.1	279 38.4	.. 12.5	106 28.1	.. 44.2	327 47.8	.. 38.1	Alnilam	275 46.5	S 1 11.7
O 10	195 02.4	5 35.4	14.2	294 38.9	12.6	121 30.9	44.2	342 50.0	38.2	Alphard	217 56.5	S 8 42.9
N 11	210 04.8	20 35.1	15.4	309 39.3	12.8	136 33.6	44.2	357 52.2	38.3			
D 12	225 07.3	35 34.7	S 2 16.5	324 39.7	S24 12.9	151 36.3	N21 44.2	12 54.4	S10 38.4	Alphecca	126 11.7	N26 40.4
A 13	240 09.7	50 34.3	17.7	339 40.2	13.0	166 39.1	44.1	27 56.5	38.5	Alpheratz	357 43.7	N29 10.0
Y 14	255 12.2	65 34.0	18.9	354 40.6	13.2	181 41.8	44.1	42 58.7	38.6	Altair	62 08.8	N 8 54.4
15	270 14.7	80 33.6	.. 20.0	9 41.0	.. 13.3	196 44.5	.. 44.1	58 00.9	.. 38.7	Ankaa	353 15.8	S42 14.2
16	285 17.1	95 33.3	21.2	24 41.5	13.4	211 47.3	44.1	73 03.1	38.8	Antares	112 27.1	S26 27.5
17	300 19.6	110 32.9	22.3	39 41.9	13.6	226 50.0	44.0	88 05.2	38.9			
18	315 22.1	125 32.5	S 2 23.5	54 42.3	S24 13.7	241 52.7	N21 44.0	103 07.4	S10 39.0	Arcturus	145 56.5	N19 07.0
19	330 24.5	140 32.2	24.6	69 42.8	13.8	256 55.5	44.0	118 09.6	39.1	Atria	107 29.8	S69 03.0
20	345 27.0	155 31.8	25.8	84 43.2	14.0	271 58.2	43.9	133 11.8	39.2	Avior	234 18.1	S59 32.9
21	0 29.5	170 31.5	.. 27.0	99 43.6	.. 14.1	287 00.9	.. 43.9	148 13.9	.. 39.3	Bellatrix	278 32.2	N 6 21.6
22	15 31.9	185 31.1	28.1	114 44.1	14.2	302 03.7	43.9	163 16.1	39.4	Betelgeuse	271 01.5	N 7 24.5
23	30 34.4	200 30.7	29.3	129 44.5	14.3	317 06.4	43.9	178 18.3	39.5			
6 00	45 36.9	215 30.4	S 2 30.4	144 44.9	S24 14.5	332 09.1	N21 43.8	193 20.5	S10 39.6	Canopus	263 56.0	S52 42.0
01	60 39.3	230 30.0	31.6	159 45.3	14.6	347 11.9	43.8	208 22.7	39.7	Capella	280 34.7	N46 00.5
02	75 41.8	245 29.7	32.7	174 45.8	14.7	2 14.6	43.8	223 24.8	39.8	Deneb	49 31.8	N45 20.0
03	90 44.2	260 29.3	.. 33.9	189 46.2	.. 14.9	17 17.3	.. 43.8	238 27.0	.. 39.9	Denebola	182 34.3	N14 30.0
04	105 46.7	275 28.9	35.1	204 46.6	15.0	32 20.1	43.7	253 29.2	40.0	Diphda	348 56.0	S17 54.9
05	120 49.2	290 28.6	36.2	219 47.1	15.1	47 22.8	43.7	268 31.4	40.1			
06	135 51.6	305 28.2	S 2 37.4	234 47.5	S24 15.2	62 25.5	N21 43.7	283 33.5	S10 40.2	Dubhe	193 52.6	N61 40.6
07	150 54.1	320 27.9	38.5	249 47.9	15.4	77 28.3	43.6	298 35.7	40.3	Elnath	278 12.9	N28 37.0
T 08	165 56.6	335 27.5	39.7	264 48.4	15.5	92 31.0	43.6	313 37.9	40.4	Eltanin	90 46.7	N51 29.6
U 09	180 59.0	350 27.1	.. 40.8	279 48.8	.. 15.6	107 33.7	.. 43.6	328 40.1	.. 40.5	Enif	33 47.5	N 9 56.3
E 10	196 01.5	5 26.8	42.0	294 49.2	15.7	122 36.5	43.6	343 42.2	40.6	Fomalhaut	15 24.3	S29 33.2
S 11	211 04.0	20 26.4	43.2	309 49.6	15.9	137 39.2	43.5	358 44.4	40.7			
D 12	226 06.4	35 26.0	S 2 44.3	324 50.1	S24 16.0	152 42.0	N21 43.5	13 46.6	S10 40.8	Gacrux	172 01.8	S57 10.9
A 13	241 08.9	50 25.7	45.5	339 50.5	16.1	167 44.7	43.5	28 48.8	40.9	Gienah	175 53.0	S17 36.7
Y 14	256 11.4	65 25.3	46.6	354 50.9	16.2	182 47.4	43.5	43 51.0	41.0	Hadar	148 49.1	S60 26.0
15	271 13.8	80 25.0	.. 47.8	9 51.4	.. 16.4	197 50.2	.. 43.4	58 53.1	.. 41.1	Hamal	328 00.9	N23 31.5
16	286 16.3	95 24.6	48.9	24 51.8	16.5	212 52.9	43.4	73 55.3	41.2	Kaus Aust.	83 44.6	S34 22.6
17	301 18.7	110 24.2	50.1	39 52.2	16.6	227 55.6	43.4	88 57.5	41.3			
18	316 21.2	125 23.9	S 2 51.3	54 52.6	S24 16.7	242 58.4	N21 43.3	103 59.7	S10 41.4	Kochab	137 21.2	N74 06.2
19	331 23.7	140 23.5	52.4	69 53.1	16.9	258 01.1	43.3	119 01.8	41.5	Markab	13 38.6	N15 16.7
20	346 26.1	155 23.1	53.6	84 53.5	17.0	273 03.9	43.3	134 04.0	41.6	Menkar	314 15.2	N 4 08.5
21	1 28.6	170 22.8	.. 54.7	99 53.9	.. 17.1	288 06.6	.. 43.3	149 06.2	.. 41.7	Menkent	148 08.5	S36 25.9
22	16 31.1	185 22.4	55.9	114 54.4	17.2	303 09.3	43.2	164 08.4	41.8	Miaplacidus	221 39.8	S69 46.0
23	31 33.5	200 22.0	57.0	129 54.8	17.3	318 12.1	43.2	179 10.5	41.9			
7 00	46 36.0	215 21.7	S 2 58.2	144 55.2	S24 17.5	333 14.8	N21 43.2	194 12.7	S10 42.0	Mirfak	308 40.4	N49 54.4
01	61 38.5	230 21.3	2 59.4	159 55.6	17.6	348 17.6	43.1	209 14.9	42.1	Nunki	75 59.1	S26 16.7
02	76 40.9	245 20.9	3 00.5	174 56.1	17.7	3 20.3	43.1	224 17.1	42.2	Peacock	53 20.0	S56 41.7
03	91 43.4	260 20.6	.. 01.7	189 56.5	.. 17.8	18 23.0	.. 43.1	239 19.3	.. 42.3	Pollux	243 28.1	N27 59.5
04	106 45.9	275 20.2	02.8	204 56.9	17.9	33 25.8	43.1	254 21.4	42.4	Procyon	245 00.1	N 5 11.4
05	121 48.3	290 19.8	04.0	219 57.3	18.0	48 28.5	43.0	269 23.6	42.5			
06	136 50.8	305 19.5	S 3 05.1	234 57.8	S24 18.2	63 31.3	N21 43.0	284 25.8	S10 42.6	Rasalhague	96 07.1	N12 33.3
W 07	151 53.2	320 19.1	06.3	249 58.2	18.3	78 34.0	43.0	299 28.0	42.7	Regulus	207 44.1	N11 54.1
E 08	166 55.7	335 18.7	07.5	264 58.6	18.4	93 36.8	43.0	314 30.1	42.8	Rigel	281 12.2	S 8 11.2
D 09	181 58.2	350 18.4	.. 08.6	279 59.0	.. 18.5	108 39.5	.. 42.9	329 32.3	.. 42.9	Rigil Kent.	139 53.0	S60 53.1
N 10	197 00.6	5 18.0	09.8	294 59.5	18.6	123 42.2	42.9	344 34.5	43.0	Sabik	102 13.3	S15 44.3
E 11	212 03.1	20 17.6	10.9	309 59.9	18.7	138 45.0	42.9	359 36.7	43.1			
S 12	227 05.6	35 17.3	S 3 12.1	325 00.3	S24 18.8	153 47.7	N21 42.8	14 38.9	S10 43.2	Schedar	349 40.5	N56 36.7
D 13	242 08.0	50 16.9	13.2	340 00.7	19.0	168 50.5	42.8	29 41.0	43.3	Shaula	96 22.8	S37 06.7
A 14	257 10.5	65 16.5	14.4	355 01.2	19.1	183 53.2	42.8	44 43.2	43.4	Sirius	258 33.9	S16 44.0
Y 15	272 13.0	80 16.2	.. 15.6	10 01.6	.. 19.2	198 56.0	.. 42.8	59 45.4	.. 43.5	Spica	158 32.0	S11 13.6
16	287 15.4	95 15.8	16.7	25 02.0	19.3	213 58.7	42.7	74 47.6	43.6	Suhail	222 52.8	S43 28.9
17	302 17.9	110 15.4	17.9	40 02.4	19.4	229 01.4	42.7	89 49.7	43.7			
18	317 20.3	125 15.1	S 3 19.0	55 02.9	S24 19.5	244 04.2	N21 42.7	104 51.9	S10 43.8	Vega	80 39.5	N38 48.1
19	332 22.8	140 14.7	20.2	70 03.3	19.6	259 06.9	42.6	119 54.1	43.9	Zuben'ubi	137 06.2	S16 05.6
20	347 25.3	155 14.3	21.3	85 03.7	19.7	274 09.7	42.6	134 56.3	44.0		SHA	Mer.Pass.
21	2 27.7	170 14.0	.. 22.5	100 04.1	.. 19.8	289 12.4	.. 42.6	149 58.5	.. 44.1		° ′	h m
22	17 30.2	185 13.6	23.6	115 04.6	20.0	304 15.2	42.6	165 00.6	44.2	Venus	169 55.5	9 38
23	32 32.7	200 13.2	24.8	130 05.0	20.1	319 17.9	42.5	180 02.8	44.3	Mars	99 08.1	14 21
	h m									Jupiter	286 32.3	1 51
Mer.Pass.	20 54.1	v −0.4	d 1.2	v 0.4	d 0.1	v 2.7	d 0.0	v 2.2	d 0.1	Saturn	147 43.6	11 05

UT	SUN GHA	SUN Dec	MOON GHA	v	MOON Dec	d	HP
MONDAY							
d h 5 00	184 06.2	S15 43.9	293 36.6	12.4	N17 42.1	5.9	54.7
01	199 06.1	44.6	308 08.0	12.5	17 36.2	6.1	54.7
02	214 06.1	45.4	322 39.5	12.4	17 30.1	6.1	54.8
03	229 06.1 ..	46.2	337 10.9	12.5	17 24.0	6.3	54.8
04	244 06.1	46.9	351 42.4	12.5	17 17.7	6.3	54.8
05	259 06.1	47.7	6 13.9	12.5	17 11.4	6.3	54.8
06	274 06.0	S15 48.4	20 45.4	12.6	N17 05.1	6.5	54.9
07	289 06.0	49.2	35 17.0	12.5	16 58.6	6.6	54.9
08	304 06.0	49.9	49 48.5	12.6	16 52.0	6.6	54.9
09	319 06.0 ..	50.7	64 20.1	12.5	16 45.4	6.7	54.9
10	334 06.0	51.4	78 51.6	12.6	16 38.7	6.8	54.9
11	349 05.9	52.2	93 23.2	12.6	16 31.9	6.9	54.9
12	4 05.9	S15 52.9	107 54.8	12.6	N16 25.0	7.0	55.0
13	19 05.9	53.7	122 26.4	12.7	16 18.0	7.0	55.0
14	34 05.9	54.5	136 58.1	12.6	16 11.0	7.1	55.0
15	49 05.8 ..	55.2	151 29.7	12.6	16 03.9	7.2	55.0
16	64 05.8	56.0	166 01.3	12.7	15 56.7	7.3	55.1
17	79 05.8	56.7	180 33.0	12.7	15 49.4	7.3	55.1
18	94 05.8	S15 57.5	195 04.7	12.7	N15 42.1	7.5	55.1
19	109 05.7	58.2	209 36.4	12.7	15 34.6	7.5	55.1
20	124 05.7	59.0	224 08.1	12.7	15 27.1	7.6	55.2
21	139 05.7	15 59.7	238 39.8	12.7	15 19.5	7.6	55.2
22	154 05.7	16 00.4	253 11.5	12.7	15 11.9	7.8	55.2
23	169 05.6	01.2	267 43.2	12.8	15 04.1	7.8	55.2
TUESDAY							
6 00	184 05.6	S16 01.9	282 15.0	12.7	N14 56.3	7.9	55.3
01	199 05.6	02.7	296 46.7	12.8	14 48.4	8.0	55.3
02	214 05.6	03.4	311 18.5	12.8	14 40.4	8.0	55.3
03	229 05.5 ..	04.2	325 50.3	12.7	14 32.4	8.1	55.3
04	244 05.5	04.9	340 22.0	12.8	14 24.3	8.2	55.4
05	259 05.5	05.7	354 53.8	12.8	14 16.1	8.3	55.4
06	274 05.5	S16 06.4	9 25.6	12.8	N14 07.8	8.3	55.4
07	289 05.4	07.2	23 57.4	12.9	13 59.5	8.4	55.4
08	304 05.4	07.9	38 29.3	12.8	13 51.1	8.5	55.5
09	319 05.4 ..	08.6	53 01.1	12.8	13 42.6	8.5	55.5
10	334 05.3	09.4	67 32.9	12.9	13 34.1	8.6	55.5
11	349 05.3	10.1	82 04.8	12.8	13 25.5	8.7	55.5
12	4 05.3	S16 10.9	96 36.6	12.8	N13 16.8	8.8	55.6
13	19 05.2	11.6	111 08.4	12.9	13 08.0	8.8	55.6
14	34 05.2	12.4	125 40.3	12.9	12 59.2	8.9	55.6
15	49 05.2 ..	13.1	140 12.2	12.8	12 50.3	9.0	55.7
16	64 05.1	13.8	154 44.0	12.9	12 41.3	9.0	55.7
17	79 05.1	14.6	169 15.9	12.9	12 32.3	9.1	55.7
18	94 05.1	S16 15.3	183 47.8	12.8	N12 23.2	9.2	55.8
19	109 05.0	16.0	198 19.6	12.9	12 14.0	9.2	55.8
20	124 05.0	16.8	212 51.5	12.9	12 04.8	9.3	55.8
21	139 05.0 ..	17.5	227 23.4	12.9	11 55.5	9.4	55.8
22	154 04.9	18.3	241 55.3	12.9	11 46.1	9.4	55.9
23	169 04.9	19.0	256 27.2	12.8	11 36.7	9.5	55.9
WEDNESDAY							
7 00	184 04.9	S16 19.7	270 59.0	12.9	N11 27.2	9.6	55.9
01	199 04.8	20.5	285 30.9	12.9	11 17.6	9.6	56.0
02	214 04.8	21.2	300 02.8	12.9	11 08.0	9.7	56.0
03	229 04.8 ..	21.9	314 34.7	12.9	10 58.3	9.7	56.0
04	244 04.7	22.7	329 06.6	12.8	10 48.6	9.8	56.1
05	259 04.7	23.4	343 38.4	12.9	10 38.8	9.9	56.1
06	274 04.7	S16 24.1	358 10.3	12.9	N10 28.9	9.9	56.1
07	289 04.6	24.9	12 42.2	12.9	10 19.0	10.0	56.2
08	304 04.6	25.6	27 14.1	12.8	10 09.0	10.1	56.2
09	319 04.5 ..	26.3	41 45.9	12.9	9 58.9	10.1	56.2
10	334 04.5	27.1	56 17.8	12.8	9 48.8	10.1	56.3
11	349 04.5	27.8	70 49.6	12.9	9 38.7	10.2	56.3
12	4 04.4	S16 28.5	85 21.5	12.8	N 9 28.5	10.3	56.3
13	19 04.4	29.3	99 53.3	12.8	9 18.2	10.4	56.4
14	34 04.3	30.0	114 25.1	12.9	9 07.8	10.3	56.4
15	49 04.3 ..	30.7	128 57.0	12.8	8 57.5	10.5	56.4
16	64 04.3	31.4	143 28.8	12.8	8 47.0	10.5	56.5
17	79 04.2	32.2	158 00.6	12.8	8 36.5	10.5	56.5
18	94 04.2	S16 32.9	172 32.4	12.7	N 8 26.0	10.7	56.5
19	109 04.1	33.6	187 04.1	12.8	8 15.3	10.6	56.6
20	124 04.1	34.3	201 35.9	12.8	8 04.7	10.7	56.6
21	139 04.0 ..	35.1	216 07.7	12.7	7 54.0	10.8	56.6
22	154 04.0	35.8	230 39.4	12.7	7 43.2	10.8	56.7
23	169 04.0	36.5	245 11.1	12.7	N 7 32.4	10.9	56.7
	SD 16.2	d 0.7	SD 15.0		15.1		15.3

Twilight / Sunrise / Moonrise

Lat.	Naut.	Civil	Sunrise	Moonrise 5	6	7	8
°	h m	h m	h m	h m	h m	h m	h m
N 72	06 27	07 54	09 33	19 09	21 11	23 05	24 58
N 70	06 21	07 37	08 58	19 47	21 32	23 17	25 02
68	06 15	07 24	08 34	20 13	21 49	23 26	25 05
66	06 10	07 13	08 15	20 33	22 02	23 33	25 07
64	06 06	07 04	07 59	20 49	22 13	23 40	25 09
62	06 02	06 56	07 47	21 02	22 22	23 45	25 11
60	05 59	06 49	07 36	21 14	22 30	23 50	25 13
N 58	05 56	06 43	07 27	21 23	22 37	23 54	25 14
56	05 53	06 38	07 18	21 32	22 43	23 58	25 15
54	05 50	06 33	07 11	21 39	22 49	24 01	00 01
52	05 48	06 28	07 04	21 46	22 54	24 04	00 04
50	05 45	06 24	06 58	21 52	22 58	24 07	00 07
45	05 40	06 15	06 46	22 05	23 08	24 13	00 13
N 40	05 34	06 07	06 35	22 16	23 16	24 18	00 18
35	05 29	06 00	06 26	22 25	23 23	24 22	00 22
30	05 25	05 53	06 18	22 33	23 29	24 26	00 26
20	05 15	05 41	06 04	22 47	23 39	24 32	00 32
N 10	05 05	05 30	05 52	22 59	23 48	24 38	00 38
0	04 54	05 19	05 40	23 10	23 56	24 43	00 43
S 10	04 41	05 06	05 28	23 21	24 05	00 05	00 48
20	04 25	04 53	05 16	23 33	24 14	00 14	00 54
30	04 05	04 36	05 01	23 47	24 24	00 24	01 00
35	03 53	04 25	04 53	23 54	24 30	00 30	01 04
40	03 37	04 13	04 43	24 04	00 03	00 37	01 08
45	03 18	03 59	04 31	24 14	00 14	00 44	01 13
S 50	02 52	03 40	04 17	24 26	00 26	00 54	01 19
52	02 39	03 31	04 11	00 03	00 32	00 58	01 21
54	02 24	03 21	04 04	00 11	00 39	01 03	01 24
56	02 06	03 10	03 56	00 20	00 46	01 08	01 27
58	01 42	02 57	03 46	00 30	00 54	01 14	01 31
S 60	01 09	02 41	03 36	00 41	01 03	01 20	01 35

Sunset / Twilight / Moonset

Lat.	Sunset	Civil	Naut.	Moonset 5	6	7	8
°	h m	h m	h m	h m	h m	h m	h m
N 72	13 53	15 32	16 58	15 01	14 36	14 19	14 05
N 70	14 28	15 49	17 05	14 21	14 13	14 06	13 59
68	14 52	16 02	17 11	13 54	13 55	13 55	13 54
66	15 12	16 13	17 16	13 33	13 41	13 46	13 49
64	15 27	16 22	17 20	13 17	13 29	13 38	13 46
62	15 40	16 30	17 24	13 03	13 19	13 31	13 42
60	15 51	16 37	17 27	12 51	13 10	13 26	13 39
N 58	16 00	16 43	17 30	12 41	13 02	13 21	13 37
56	16 08	16 49	17 33	12 32	12 55	13 16	13 35
54	16 16	16 54	17 36	12 24	12 49	13 12	13 33
52	16 22	16 58	17 39	12 17	12 44	13 08	13 31
50	16 28	17 03	17 41	12 10	12 39	13 05	13 29
45	16 41	17 12	17 47	11 56	12 28	12 57	13 25
N 40	16 52	17 20	17 52	11 45	12 19	12 51	13 22
35	17 01	17 27	17 57	11 35	12 11	12 46	13 19
30	17 09	17 34	18 02	11 26	12 04	12 41	13 17
20	17 23	17 46	18 12	11 11	11 53	12 33	13 13
N 10	17 35	17 57	18 22	10 58	11 42	12 26	13 09
0	17 47	18 09	18 34	10 46	11 32	12 19	13 05
S 10	17 59	18 21	18 47	10 33	11 22	12 12	13 02
20	18 12	18 35	19 02	10 20	11 12	12 04	12 58
30	18 27	18 52	19 23	10 04	10 59	11 56	12 53
35	18 35	19 03	19 35	09 56	10 52	11 51	12 51
40	18 45	19 15	19 51	09 45	10 44	11 45	12 48
45	18 57	19 30	20 11	09 33	10 35	11 39	12 45
S 50	19 11	19 48	20 37	09 19	10 23	11 31	12 40
52	19 18	19 57	20 50	09 12	10 18	11 27	12 39
54	19 25	20 08	21 05	09 04	10 12	11 23	12 36
56	19 33	20 19	21 24	08 56	10 05	11 18	12 34
58	19 43	20 33	21 49	08 46	09 58	11 13	12 32
S 60	19 53	20 49	22 24	08 35	09 49	11 08	12 29

Day	SUN Eqn. of Time 00h	12h	Mer. Pass.	MOON Mer. Pass. Upper	Lower	Age	Phase
d	m s	m s	h m	h m	h m	d	%
5	16 25	16 21	11 44	04 34	16 58	21	65
6	16 23	16 21	11 44	05 21	17 44	22	55
7	16 20	16 18	11 44	06 08	18 31	23	45

UT	ARIES GHA	VENUS −4.0 GHA	Dec	MARS +1.2 GHA	Dec	JUPITER −2.8 GHA	Dec	SATURN +0.6 GHA	Dec	Name	SHA	Dec
8 00	47 35.1	215 12.9	S 3 26.0	145 05.4	S24 20.2	334 20.7	N21 42.5	195 05.0	S10 44.4	Acamar	315 18.2	S40 15.2
01	62 37.6	230 12.5	27.1	160 05.8	20.3	349 23.4	42.5	210 07.2	44.5	Achernar	335 26.6	S57 10.3
02	77 40.1	245 12.1	28.3	175 06.2	20.4	4 26.2	42.4	225 09.3	44.6	Acrux	173 10.3	S63 10.1
03	92 42.5	260 11.8	.. 29.4	190 06.7	.. 20.5	19 28.9	.. 42.4	240 11.5	.. 44.7	Adhara	255 12.6	S28 59.3
04	107 45.0	275 11.4	30.6	205 07.1	20.6	34 31.7	42.4	255 13.7	44.8	Aldebaran	290 49.5	N16 32.1
05	122 47.5	290 11.0	31.7	220 07.5	20.7	49 34.4	42.4	270 15.9	44.9			
06	137 49.9	305 10.6	S 3 32.9	235 07.9	S24 20.8	64 37.2	N21 42.3	285 18.1	S10 45.0	Alioth	166 21.6	N55 53.2
07	152 52.4	320 10.3	34.1	250 08.3	20.9	79 39.9	42.3	300 20.2	45.1	Alkaid	152 59.7	N49 14.9
T 08	167 54.8	335 09.9	35.2	265 08.8	21.0	94 42.7	42.3	315 22.4	45.2	Al Na'ir	27 44.2	S46 54.0
H 09	182 57.3	350 09.5	.. 36.4	280 09.2	.. 21.1	109 45.4	.. 42.2	330 24.6	.. 45.3	Alnilam	275 46.5	S 1 11.7
U 10	197 59.8	5 09.2	37.5	295 09.6	21.2	124 48.1	42.2	345 26.8	45.4	Alphard	217 56.5	S 8 42.9
R 11	213 02.2	20 08.8	38.7	310 10.0	21.3	139 50.9	42.2	0 28.9	45.5			
S 12	228 04.7	35 08.4	S 3 39.8	325 10.4	S24 21.4	154 53.6	N21 42.1	15 31.1	S10 45.6	Alphecca	126 11.7	N26 40.4
D 13	243 07.2	50 08.0	41.0	340 10.9	21.5	169 56.4	42.1	30 33.3	45.7	Alpheratz	357 43.7	N29 10.0
A 14	258 09.6	65 07.7	42.1	355 11.3	21.6	184 59.1	42.1	45 35.5	45.7	Altair	62 08.8	N 8 54.4
Y 15	273 12.1	80 07.3	.. 43.3	10 11.7	.. 21.7	200 01.9	.. 42.1	60 37.7	.. 45.8	Ankaa	353 15.8	S42 14.2
16	288 14.6	95 06.9	44.5	25 12.1	21.8	215 04.7	42.0	75 39.8	45.9	Antares	112 27.1	S26 27.5
17	303 17.0	110 06.5	45.6	40 12.5	21.9	230 07.4	42.0	90 42.0	46.0			
18	318 19.5	125 06.2	S 3 46.8	55 13.0	S24 22.0	245 10.2	N21 42.0	105 44.2	S10 46.1	Arcturus	145 56.5	N19 07.0
19	333 21.9	140 05.8	47.9	70 13.4	22.1	260 12.9	41.9	120 46.4	46.2	Atria	107 29.8	S69 03.0
20	348 24.4	155 05.4	49.1	85 13.8	22.2	275 15.7	41.9	135 48.5	46.3	Avior	234 18.0	S59 32.9
21	3 26.9	170 05.1	.. 50.2	100 14.2	.. 22.3	290 18.4	.. 41.9	150 50.7	.. 46.4	Bellatrix	278 32.2	N 6 21.6
22	18 29.3	185 04.7	51.4	115 14.6	22.4	305 21.2	41.9	165 52.9	46.5	Betelgeuse	271 01.5	N 7 24.5
23	33 31.8	200 04.3	52.5	130 15.1	22.5	320 23.9	41.8	180 55.1	46.6			
9 00	48 34.3	215 03.9	S 3 53.7	145 15.5	S24 22.6	335 26.7	N21 41.8	195 57.3	S10 46.7	Canopus	263 56.0	S52 42.0
01	63 36.7	230 03.6	54.9	160 15.9	22.7	350 29.4	41.8	210 59.4	46.8	Capella	280 34.7	N46 00.5
02	78 39.2	245 03.2	56.0	175 16.3	22.8	5 32.2	41.7	226 01.6	46.9	Deneb	49 31.8	N45 20.0
03	93 41.7	260 02.8	.. 57.2	190 16.7	.. 22.9	20 34.9	.. 41.7	241 03.8	.. 47.0	Denebola	182 34.3	N14 29.9
04	108 44.1	275 02.4	58.3	205 17.1	23.0	35 37.7	41.7	256 06.0	47.1	Diphda	348 56.0	S17 54.9
05	123 46.6	290 02.1	3 59.5	220 17.6	23.1	50 40.4	41.6	271 08.2	47.2			
06	138 49.1	305 01.7	S 4 00.6	235 18.0	S24 23.2	65 43.2	N21 41.6	286 10.3	S10 47.3	Dubhe	193 52.5	N61 40.6
07	153 51.5	320 01.3	01.8	250 18.4	23.3	80 45.9	41.6	301 12.5	47.4	Elnath	278 12.8	N28 37.0
08	168 54.0	335 00.9	02.9	265 18.8	23.4	95 48.7	41.6	316 14.7	47.5	Eltanin	90 46.8	N51 29.6
F 09	183 56.4	350 00.6	.. 04.1	280 19.2	.. 23.5	110 51.5	.. 41.5	331 16.9	.. 47.6	Enif	33 47.5	N 9 56.3
R 10	198 58.9	5 00.2	05.3	295 19.6	23.6	125 54.2	41.5	346 19.0	47.7	Fomalhaut	15 24.3	S29 33.2
I 11	214 01.4	19 59.8	06.4	310 20.1	23.7	140 57.0	41.5	1 21.2	47.8			
D 12	229 03.8	34 59.4	S 4 07.6	325 20.5	S24 23.8	155 59.7	N21 41.4	16 23.4	S10 47.9	Gacrux	172 01.8	S57 10.9
A 13	244 06.3	49 59.0	08.7	340 20.9	23.9	171 02.5	41.4	31 25.6	48.0	Gienah	175 53.0	S17 36.7
Y 14	259 08.8	64 58.7	09.9	355 21.3	24.0	186 05.2	41.4	46 27.8	48.1	Hadar	148 49.1	S60 26.0
15	274 11.2	79 58.3	.. 11.0	10 21.7	.. 24.1	201 08.0	.. 41.4	61 29.9	.. 48.2	Hamal	328 00.9	N23 31.5
16	289 13.7	94 57.9	12.2	25 22.1	24.1	216 10.7	41.3	76 32.1	48.3	Kaus Aust.	83 44.7	S34 22.6
17	304 16.2	109 57.5	13.3	40 22.6	24.2	231 13.5	41.3	91 34.3	48.4			
18	319 18.6	124 57.2	S 4 14.5	55 23.0	S24 24.3	246 16.3	N21 41.3	106 36.5	S10 48.5	Kochab	137 21.2	N74 06.1
19	334 21.1	139 56.8	15.6	70 23.4	24.4	261 19.0	41.2	121 38.7	48.6	Markab	13 38.6	N15 16.7
20	349 23.6	154 56.4	16.8	85 23.8	24.5	276 21.8	41.2	136 40.8	48.7	Menkar	314 15.2	N 4 08.5
21	4 26.0	169 56.0	.. 18.0	100 24.2	.. 24.6	291 24.5	.. 41.2	151 43.0	.. 48.8	Menkent	148 08.5	S36 25.9
22	19 28.5	184 55.6	19.1	115 24.6	24.7	306 27.3	41.1	166 45.2	48.9	Miaplacidus	221 39.7	S69 46.0
23	34 30.9	199 55.3	20.3	130 25.0	24.8	321 30.1	41.1	181 47.4	49.0			
10 00	49 33.4	214 54.9	S 4 21.4	145 25.5	S24 24.9	336 32.8	N21 41.0	196 49.5	S10 49.1	Mirfak	308 40.4	N49 54.4
01	64 35.9	229 54.5	22.6	160 25.9	24.9	351 35.6	41.0	211 51.7	49.2	Nunki	75 59.1	S26 16.7
02	79 38.3	244 54.1	23.7	175 26.3	25.0	6 38.3	41.0	226 53.9	49.3	Peacock	53 20.1	S56 41.7
03	94 40.8	259 53.7	.. 24.9	190 26.7	.. 25.1	21 41.1	.. 41.0	241 56.1	.. 49.4	Pollux	243 28.1	N27 59.5
04	109 43.3	274 53.4	26.0	205 27.1	25.2	36 43.9	41.0	256 58.3	49.5	Procyon	245 00.0	N 5 11.4
05	124 45.7	289 53.0	27.2	220 27.5	25.3	51 46.6	40.9	272 00.4	49.6			
06	139 48.2	304 52.6	S 4 28.3	235 27.9	S24 25.4	66 49.4	N21 40.9	287 02.6	S10 49.7	Rasalhague	96 07.1	N12 33.3
07	154 50.7	319 52.2	29.5	250 28.3	25.5	81 52.1	40.9	302 04.8	49.8	Regulus	207 44.0	N11 54.1
S 08	169 53.1	334 51.8	30.6	265 28.8	25.5	96 54.9	40.8	317 07.0	49.9	Rigel	281 12.2	S 8 11.2
A 09	184 55.6	349 51.5	.. 31.8	280 29.2	.. 25.6	111 57.7	.. 40.8	332 09.2	.. 50.0	Rigil Kent.	139 53.0	S60 53.1
T 10	199 58.0	4 51.1	33.0	295 29.6	25.7	127 00.4	40.8	347 11.3	50.1	Sabik	102 13.3	S15 44.3
U 11	215 00.5	19 50.7	34.1	310 30.0	25.8	142 03.2	40.7	2 13.5	50.2			
R 12	230 03.0	34 50.3	S 4 35.3	325 30.4	S24 25.9	157 05.9	N21 40.7	17 15.7	S10 50.3	Schedar	349 40.5	N56 36.8
D 13	245 05.4	49 49.9	36.4	340 30.8	25.9	172 08.7	40.7	32 17.9	50.4	Shaula	96 22.8	S37 06.7
A 14	260 07.9	64 49.6	37.6	355 31.2	26.0	187 11.5	40.7	47 20.1	50.4	Sirius	258 33.9	S16 44.0
Y 15	275 10.4	79 49.2	.. 38.7	10 31.6	.. 26.1	202 14.2	.. 40.6	62 22.2	.. 50.5	Spica	158 32.0	S11 13.6
16	290 12.8	94 48.8	39.9	25 32.1	26.2	217 17.0	40.6	77 24.4	50.6	Suhail	222 52.7	S43 28.9
17	305 15.3	109 48.4	41.0	40 32.5	26.3	232 19.8	40.6	92 26.6	50.7			
18	320 17.8	124 48.0	S 4 42.2	55 32.9	S24 26.3	247 22.5	N21 40.5	107 28.8	S10 50.8	Vega	80 39.5	N38 48.1
19	335 20.2	139 47.6	43.3	70 33.3	26.4	262 25.3	40.5	122 31.0	50.9	Zuben'ubi	137 06.2	S16 05.6
20	350 22.7	154 47.3	44.5	85 33.7	26.5	277 28.0	40.5	137 33.1	51.0		SHA	Mer. Pass.
21	5 25.2	169 46.9	.. 45.6	100 34.1	.. 26.6	292 30.8	.. 40.4	152 35.3	.. 51.1			
22	20 27.6	184 46.5	46.8	115 34.5	26.7	307 33.6	40.4	167 37.5	51.2	Venus	166 29.7	9 40
23	35 30.1	199 46.1	47.9	130 34.9	26.7	322 36.3	40.4	182 39.7	51.3	Mars	96 41.2	14 19
Mer. Pass. 20 42.3		v −0.4	d 1.2	v 0.4	d 0.1	v 2.8	d 0.0	v 2.2	d 0.1	Jupiter	286 52.4	1 38
										Saturn	147 23.0	10 55

UT	SUN GHA	SUN Dec	MOON GHA	v	MOON Dec	d	HP
d h	° ′	° ′	° ′	′	° ′	′	′
8 00	184 03.9	S16 37.2	259 42.8	12.7	N 7 21.5	10.9	56.8
01	199 03.9	38.0	274 14.5	12.7	7 10.6	10.9	56.8
02	214 03.8	38.7	288 46.2	12.7	6 59.7	11.0	56.8
03	229 03.8	.. 39.4	303 17.9	12.6	6 48.7	11.1	56.9
04	244 03.7	40.1	317 49.5	12.7	6 37.6	11.1	56.9
05	259 03.7	40.9	332 21.2	12.6	6 26.5	11.2	56.9
06	274 03.6	S16 41.6	346 52.8	12.6	N 6 15.3	11.2	57.0
T 07	289 03.6	42.3	1 24.4	12.5	6 04.1	11.2	57.0
H 08	304 03.5	43.0	15 55.9	12.6	5 52.9	11.3	57.1
U 09	319 03.5	.. 43.8	30 27.5	12.5	5 41.6	11.3	57.1
R 10	334 03.4	44.5	44 59.0	12.5	5 30.3	11.4	57.1
S 11	349 03.4	45.2	59 30.5	12.5	5 18.9	11.4	57.2
D 12	4 03.3	S16 45.9	74 02.0	12.4	N 5 07.5	11.4	57.2
A 13	19 03.3	46.6	88 33.4	12.4	4 56.1	11.5	57.2
Y 14	34 03.2	47.3	103 04.8	12.4	4 44.6	11.5	57.3
15	49 03.2	.. 48.0	117 36.2	12.4	4 33.1	11.6	57.3
16	64 03.1	48.8	132 07.6	12.4	4 21.5	11.6	57.4
17	79 03.1	49.5	146 39.0	12.3	4 09.9	11.7	57.4
18	94 03.0	S16 50.2	161 10.3	12.3	N 3 58.2	11.6	57.4
19	109 03.0	50.9	175 41.6	12.2	3 46.6	11.8	57.5
20	124 02.9	51.6	190 12.8	12.2	3 34.8	11.7	57.5
21	139 02.9	.. 52.3	204 44.0	12.2	3 23.1	11.8	57.6
22	154 02.8	53.1	219 15.2	12.2	3 11.3	11.8	57.6
23	169 02.8	53.8	233 46.4	12.1	2 59.5	11.8	57.6
9 00	184 02.7	S16 54.5	248 17.5	12.1	N 2 47.7	11.9	57.7
01	199 02.7	55.2	262 48.6	12.1	2 35.8	11.9	57.7
02	214 02.6	55.9	277 19.7	12.0	2 23.9	12.0	57.8
03	229 02.6	.. 56.6	291 50.7	12.0	2 11.9	11.9	57.8
04	244 02.5	57.3	306 21.7	11.9	2 00.0	12.0	57.8
05	259 02.5	58.0	320 52.6	11.9	1 48.0	12.0	57.9
06	274 02.4	S16 58.7	335 23.5	11.9	N 1 36.0	12.1	57.9
07	289 02.3	16 59.5	349 54.4	11.8	1 23.9	12.1	58.0
F 08	304 02.3	17 00.2	4 25.2	11.8	1 11.8	12.1	58.0
R 09	319 02.2	.. 00.9	18 56.0	11.7	0 59.7	12.1	58.0
I 10	334 02.2	01.6	33 26.7	11.7	0 47.6	12.1	58.1
D 11	349 02.1	02.3	47 57.4	11.7	0 35.5	12.2	58.1
A 12	4 02.1	S17 03.0	62 28.1	11.6	N 0 23.3	12.1	58.2
Y 13	19 02.0	03.7	76 58.7	11.5	N 0 11.2	12.2	58.2
14	34 01.9	04.4	91 29.2	11.5	S 0 01.0	12.3	58.2
15	49 01.9	.. 05.1	105 59.7	11.5	0 13.3	12.2	58.3
16	64 01.8	05.8	120 30.2	11.4	0 25.5	12.2	58.3
17	79 01.8	06.5	135 00.6	11.4	0 37.7	12.3	58.4
18	94 01.7	S17 07.2	149 31.0	11.3	S 0 50.0	12.3	58.4
19	109 01.6	07.9	164 01.3	11.3	1 02.3	12.3	58.4
20	124 01.6	08.6	178 31.6	11.2	1 14.6	12.3	58.5
21	139 01.5	.. 09.3	193 01.8	11.2	1 26.9	12.3	58.5
22	154 01.5	10.0	207 32.0	11.1	1 39.2	12.3	58.6
23	169 01.4	10.7	222 02.1	11.0	1 51.5	12.3	58.6
10 00	184 01.3	S17 11.4	236 32.1	11.0	S 2 03.8	12.4	58.6
01	199 01.3	12.1	251 02.1	10.9	2 16.2	12.3	58.7
02	214 01.2	12.8	265 32.0	10.9	2 28.5	12.3	58.7
03	229 01.1	.. 13.5	280 01.9	10.9	2 40.8	12.4	58.8
04	244 01.1	14.2	294 31.8	10.7	2 53.2	12.3	58.8
05	259 01.0	14.9	309 01.5	10.7	3 05.5	12.4	58.9
06	274 01.0	S17 15.6	323 31.2	10.7	S 3 17.9	12.3	58.9
S 07	289 00.9	16.3	338 00.9	10.6	3 30.2	12.4	58.9
A 08	304 00.8	17.0	352 30.5	10.5	3 42.6	12.3	59.0
T 09	319 00.8	.. 17.7	7 00.0	10.4	3 54.9	12.4	59.0
U 10	334 00.7	18.4	21 29.4	10.4	4 07.3	12.3	59.1
R 11	349 00.6	19.1	35 58.8	10.4	4 19.6	12.3	59.1
D 12	4 00.6	S17 19.8	50 28.2	10.2	S 4 31.9	12.4	59.1
A 13	19 00.5	20.5	64 57.4	10.2	4 44.3	12.3	59.2
Y 14	34 00.4	21.2	79 26.6	10.1	4 56.6	12.3	59.2
15	49 00.4	.. 21.9	93 55.7	10.1	5 08.9	12.3	59.2
16	64 00.3	22.6	108 24.8	10.0	5 21.2	12.3	59.3
17	79 00.2	23.3	122 53.8	9.9	5 33.4	12.3	59.3
18	94 00.2	S17 23.9	137 22.7	9.9	S 5 45.7	12.3	59.4
19	109 00.1	24.6	151 51.6	9.8	5 58.0	12.2	59.4
20	124 00.0	25.3	166 20.4	9.7	6 10.2	12.2	59.4
21	138 59.9	.. 26.0	180 49.1	9.6	6 22.4	12.2	59.5
22	153 59.9	26.7	195 17.7	9.6	6 34.6	12.2	59.5
23	168 59.8	27.4	209 46.3	9.5	S 6 46.8	12.1	59.6
	SD 16.2	d 0.7	SD 15.6		15.8		16.1

Twilight / Sunrise / Moonrise

Lat.	Naut.	Civil	Sunrise	8	9	10	11
°	h m	h m	h m	h m	h m	h m	h m
N 72	06 39	08 08	09 57	24 58	00 58	02 55	04 58
N 70	06 31	07 49	09 15	25 02	01 02	02 50	04 45
68	06 24	07 35	08 47	25 05	01 05	02 47	04 35
66	06 19	07 23	08 26	25 07	01 07	02 44	04 26
64	06 14	07 12	08 09	25 09	01 09	02 42	04 19
62	06 09	07 04	07 55	25 11	01 11	02 40	04 13
60	06 05	06 56	07 44	25 13	01 13	02 38	04 08
N 58	06 02	06 50	07 34	25 14	01 14	02 37	04 03
56	05 58	06 44	07 25	25 15	01 15	02 36	03 59
54	05 55	06 38	07 17	00 01	01 15	02 34	03 56
52	05 52	06 33	07 10	00 04	01 17	02 33	03 52
50	05 50	06 29	07 03	00 07	01 18	02 32	03 49
45	05 43	06 19	06 50	00 13	01 20	02 30	03 43
N 40	05 38	06 10	06 39	00 18	01 22	02 28	03 38
35	05 32	06 02	06 29	00 22	01 23	02 27	03 33
30	05 27	05 55	06 20	00 26	01 24	02 25	03 29
20	05 16	05 43	06 06	00 32	01 27	02 23	03 22
N 10	05 05	05 31	05 53	00 38	01 28	02 21	03 16
0	04 54	05 19	05 40	00 43	01 30	02 19	03 10
S 10	04 40	05 06	05 28	00 48	01 32	02 17	03 05
20	04 24	04 51	05 15	00 54	01 34	02 15	02 59
30	04 03	04 33	04 59	01 00	01 36	02 13	02 52
35	03 49	04 23	04 50	01 04	01 38	02 12	02 48
40	03 33	04 10	04 40	01 08	01 39	02 11	02 44
45	03 13	03 54	04 28	01 13	01 41	02 09	02 39
S 50	02 46	03 35	04 13	01 19	01 43	02 07	02 33
52	02 32	03 26	04 06	01 21	01 44	02 06	02 31
54	02 16	03 15	03 58	01 24	01 45	02 05	02 28
56	01 55	03 03	03 49	01 27	01 46	02 04	02 24
58	01 29	02 48	03 39	01 31	01 47	02 03	02 21
S 60	00 48	02 31	03 28	01 35	01 48	02 02	02 17

Sunset / Twilight / Moonset

Lat.	Sunset	Civil	Naut.	8	9	10	11
°	h m	h m	h m	h m	h m	h m	h m
N 72	13 29	15 19	16 48	14 05	13 52	13 39	13 23
N 70	14 12	15 37	16 55	13 59	13 52	13 45	13 38
68	14 40	15 52	17 02	13 54	13 52	13 51	13 50
66	15 01	16 04	17 08	13 49	13 53	13 56	14 00
64	15 18	16 14	17 13	13 46	13 53	14 00	14 09
62	15 32	16 23	17 17	13 42	13 53	14 04	14 16
60	15 43	16 31	17 21	13 40	13 53	14 07	14 23
N 58	15 53	16 37	17 25	13 37	13 53	14 09	14 28
56	16 02	16 43	17 28	13 35	13 53	14 12	14 33
54	16 10	16 49	17 32	13 33	13 53	14 14	14 38
52	16 17	16 54	17 35	13 31	13 53	14 16	14 42
50	16 24	16 59	17 37	13 29	13 53	14 18	14 46
45	16 37	17 09	17 44	13 25	13 53	14 22	14 54
N 40	16 49	17 17	17 50	13 22	13 53	14 25	15 00
35	16 58	17 25	17 55	13 19	13 53	14 28	15 06
30	17 07	17 32	18 01	13 17	13 53	14 31	15 11
20	17 22	17 45	18 11	13 13	13 53	14 35	15 20
N 10	17 35	17 57	18 22	13 09	13 53	14 39	15 28
0	17 47	18 09	18 34	13 05	13 53	14 43	15 36
S 10	18 00	18 22	18 48	13 02	13 53	14 47	15 43
20	18 13	18 37	19 04	12 58	13 53	14 51	15 51
30	18 29	18 55	19 26	12 53	13 53	14 55	16 00
35	18 38	19 06	19 39	12 51	13 53	14 58	16 06
40	18 49	19 19	19 55	12 48	13 53	15 01	16 12
45	19 01	19 34	20 16	12 45	13 53	15 04	16 19
S 50	19 16	19 54	20 44	12 40	13 53	15 08	16 27
52	19 23	20 04	20 58	12 39	13 53	15 10	16 31
54	19 31	20 14	21 15	12 36	13 53	15 12	16 35
56	19 40	20 27	21 35	12 34	13 53	15 15	16 40
58	19 50	20 42	22 03	12 32	13 53	15 17	16 45
S 60	20 01	20 59	22 48	12 29	13 53	15 20	16 51

SUN / MOON

Day	SUN Eqn. of Time 00ʰ	SUN Eqn. of Time 12ʰ	Mer. Pass.	MOON Mer. Pass. Upper	MOON Mer. Pass. Lower	Age	Phase
d	m s	m s	h m	h m	h m	d	%
8	16 16	16 13	11 44	06 54	19 18	24	35
9	16 11	16 08	11 44	07 42	20 06	25	25
10	16 05	16 02	11 44	08 31	20 57	26	16

UT	ARIES GHA	VENUS −3.9 GHA	Dec	MARS +1.2 GHA	Dec	JUPITER −2.8 GHA	Dec	SATURN +0.6 GHA	Dec	Name	SHA	Dec
11 00	50 32.5	214 45.7	S 4 49.1	145 35.3	S24 26.8	337 39.1	N21 40.3	197 41.8	S10 51.4	Acamar	315 18.2	S40 15.2
01	65 35.0	229 45.3	50.2	160 35.7	26.9	352 41.9	40.3	212 44.0	51.5	Achernar	335 26.6	S57 10.4
02	80 37.5	244 44.9	51.4	175 36.2	27.0	7 44.6	40.3	227 46.2	51.6	Acrux	173 10.2	S63 10.0
03	95 39.9	259 44.6 ..	52.5	190 36.6 ..	27.0	22 47.4 ..	40.3	242 48.4 ..	51.7	Adhara	255 12.6	S28 59.3
04	110 42.4	274 44.2	53.7	205 37.0	27.1	37 50.2	40.2	257 50.6	51.8	Aldebaran	290 49.5	N16 32.1
05	125 44.9	289 43.8	54.8	220 37.4	27.2	52 52.9	40.2	272 52.7	51.9			
06	140 47.3	304 43.4	S 4 56.0	235 37.8	S24 27.3	67 55.7	N21 40.2	287 54.9	S10 52.0	Alioth	166 21.5	N55 53.2
07	155 49.8	319 43.0	57.1	250 38.2	27.3	82 58.5	40.1	302 57.1	52.1	Alkaid	152 59.7	N49 14.9
08	170 52.3	334 42.6	58.3	265 38.6	27.4	98 01.2	40.1	317 59.3	52.2	Al Na'ir	27 44.2	S46 54.0
S 09	185 54.7	349 42.2	4 59.4	280 39.0 ..	27.5	113 04.0 ..	40.1	333 01.5 ..	52.3	Alnilam	275 46.5	S 1 11.7
U 10	200 57.2	4 41.8	5 00.6	295 39.4	27.5	128 06.8	40.0	348 03.6	52.4	Alphard	217 56.5	S 8 42.9
N 11	215 59.6	19 41.5	01.8	310 39.8	27.6	143 09.5	40.0	3 05.8	52.5			
D 12	231 02.1	34 41.1	S 5 02.9	325 40.2	S24 27.7	158 12.3	N21 40.0	18 08.0	S10 52.6	Alphecca	126 11.7	N26 40.4
A 13	246 04.6	49 40.7	04.1	340 40.6	27.8	173 15.1	39.9	33 10.2	52.7	Alpheratz	357 43.7	N29 10.0
Y 14	261 07.0	64 40.3	05.2	355 41.1	27.8	188 17.8	39.9	48 12.4	52.8	Altair	62 08.8	N 8 54.4
15	276 09.5	79 39.9 ..	06.4	10 41.5 ..	27.9	203 20.6 ..	39.9	63 14.5 ..	52.9	Ankaa	353 15.8	S42 14.2
16	291 12.0	94 39.5	07.5	25 41.9	28.0	218 23.4	39.8	78 16.7	53.0	Antares	112 27.1	S26 27.5
17	306 14.4	109 39.1	08.7	40 42.3	28.0	233 26.1	39.8	93 18.9	53.1			
18	321 16.9	124 38.7	S 5 09.8	55 42.7	S24 28.1	248 28.9	N21 39.8	108 21.1	S10 53.2	Arcturus	145 56.5	N19 07.0
19	336 19.4	139 38.4	11.0	70 43.1	28.2	263 31.7	39.8	123 23.3	53.3	Atria	107 29.8	S69 03.0
20	351 21.8	154 38.0	12.1	85 43.5	28.2	278 34.4	39.7	138 25.4	53.4	Avior	234 18.0	S59 32.9
21	6 24.3	169 37.6 ..	13.3	100 43.9 ..	28.3	293 37.2 ..	39.7	153 27.6 ..	53.5	Bellatrix	278 32.2	N 6 21.6
22	21 26.8	184 37.2	14.4	115 44.3	28.4	308 40.0	39.7	168 29.8	53.6	Betelgeuse	271 01.5	N 7 24.5
23	36 29.2	199 36.8	15.6	130 44.7	28.4	323 42.7	39.6	183 32.0	53.7			
12 00	51 31.7	214 36.4	S 5 16.7	145 45.1	S24 28.5	338 45.5	N21 39.6	198 34.2	S10 53.7	Canopus	263 55.9	S52 42.0
01	66 34.1	229 36.0	17.8	160 45.5	28.6	353 48.3	39.6	213 36.3	53.8	Capella	280 34.6	N46 00.5
02	81 36.6	244 35.6	19.0	175 45.9	28.6	8 51.1	39.5	228 38.5	53.9	Deneb	49 31.9	N45 20.0
03	96 39.1	259 35.2 ..	20.1	190 46.3 ..	28.7	23 53.8 ..	39.5	243 40.7 ..	54.0	Denebola	182 34.3	N14 29.9
04	111 41.5	274 34.8	21.3	205 46.7	28.8	38 56.6	39.5	258 42.9	54.1	Diphda	348 56.1	S17 54.9
05	126 44.0	289 34.4	22.4	220 47.1	28.8	53 59.4	39.4	273 45.1	54.2			
06	141 46.5	304 34.1	S 5 23.6	235 47.6	S24 28.9	69 02.1	N21 39.4	288 47.2	S10 54.3	Dubhe	193 52.5	N61 40.6
07	156 48.9	319 33.7	24.7	250 48.0	28.9	84 04.9	39.4	303 49.4	54.4	Elnath	278 12.8	N28 37.0
08	171 51.4	334 33.3	25.9	265 48.4	29.0	99 07.7	39.3	318 51.6	54.5	Eltanin	90 46.8	N51 29.6
M 09	186 53.9	349 32.9 ..	27.0	280 48.8 ..	29.1	114 10.5 ..	39.3	333 53.8 ..	54.6	Enif	33 47.5	N 9 56.3
O 10	201 56.3	4 32.5	28.2	295 49.2	29.1	129 13.2	39.3	348 56.0	54.7	Fomalhaut	15 24.3	S29 33.2
N 11	216 58.8	19 32.1	29.3	310 49.6	29.2	144 16.0	39.2	3 58.1	54.8			
D 12	232 01.3	34 31.7	S 5 30.5	325 50.0	S24 29.2	159 18.8	N21 39.2	19 00.3	S10 54.9	Gacrux	172 01.8	S57 10.9
A 13	247 03.7	49 31.3	31.6	340 50.4	29.3	174 21.6	39.2	34 02.5	55.0	Gienah	175 53.0	S17 36.7
Y 14	262 06.2	64 30.9	32.8	355 50.8	29.4	189 24.3	39.1	49 04.7	55.1	Hadar	148 49.1	S60 25.9
15	277 08.6	79 30.5 ..	33.9	10 51.2 ..	29.4	204 27.1 ..	39.1	64 06.9 ..	55.2	Hamal	328 00.9	N23 31.5
16	292 11.1	94 30.1	35.1	25 51.6	29.5	219 29.9	39.1	79 09.0	55.3	Kaus Aust.	83 44.7	S34 22.6
17	307 13.6	109 29.7	36.2	40 52.0	29.5	234 32.6	39.1	94 11.2	55.4			
18	322 16.0	124 29.3	S 5 37.4	55 52.4	S24 29.6	249 35.4	N21 39.0	109 13.4	S10 55.5	Kochab	137 21.2	N74 06.1
19	337 18.5	139 28.9	38.5	70 52.8	29.7	264 38.2	39.0	124 15.6	55.6	Markab	13 38.6	N15 16.7
20	352 21.0	154 28.5	39.7	85 53.2	29.7	279 41.0	39.0	139 17.8	55.7	Menkar	314 15.2	N 4 08.5
21	7 23.4	169 28.1 ..	40.8	100 53.6 ..	29.8	294 43.7 ..	38.9	154 19.9 ..	55.8	Menkent	148 08.4	S36 25.8
22	22 25.9	184 27.7	42.0	115 54.0	29.8	309 46.5	38.9	169 22.1	55.9	Miaplacidus	221 39.6	S69 46.0
23	37 28.4	199 27.3	43.1	130 54.4	29.9	324 49.3	38.9	184 24.3	56.0			
13 00	52 30.8	214 26.9	S 5 44.2	145 54.8	S24 29.9	339 52.1	N21 38.8	199 26.5	S10 56.1	Mirfak	308 40.4	N49 54.4
01	67 33.3	229 26.6	45.4	160 55.2	30.0	354 54.8	38.8	214 28.7	56.2	Nunki	75 59.1	S26 16.7
02	82 35.7	244 26.2	46.5	175 55.6	30.0	9 57.6	38.8	229 30.9	56.3	Peacock	53 20.1	S56 41.7
03	97 38.2	259 25.8 ..	47.7	190 56.0 ..	30.1	25 00.4 ..	38.7	244 33.0 ..	56.4	Pollux	243 28.1	N27 59.5
04	112 40.7	274 25.4	48.8	205 56.4	30.1	40 03.2	38.7	259 35.2	56.4	Procyon	245 00.0	N 5 11.4
05	127 43.1	289 25.0	50.0	220 56.8	30.2	55 06.0	38.7	274 37.4	56.5			
06	142 45.6	304 24.6	S 5 51.1	235 57.2	S24 30.2	70 08.7	N21 38.6	289 39.6	S10 56.6	Rasalhague	96 07.1	N12 33.3
07	157 48.1	319 24.2	52.3	250 57.6	30.3	85 11.5	38.6	304 41.8	56.7	Regulus	207 44.0	N11 54.1
08	172 50.5	334 23.8	53.4	265 58.0	30.3	100 14.3	38.6	319 43.9	56.8	Rigel	281 12.2	S 8 11.2
T 09	187 53.0	349 23.4 ..	54.6	280 58.4 ..	30.4	115 17.1 ..	38.5	334 46.1 ..	56.9	Rigil Kent.	139 52.9	S60 53.1
U 10	202 55.5	4 23.0	55.7	295 58.8	30.4	130 19.8	38.5	349 48.3	57.0	Sabik	102 13.3	S15 44.3
E 11	217 57.9	19 22.6	56.8	310 59.2	30.5	145 22.6	38.5	4 50.5	57.1			
S 12	233 00.4	34 22.2	S 5 58.0	325 59.6	S24 30.5	160 25.4	N21 38.4	19 52.7	S10 57.2	Schedar	349 40.5	N56 36.8
D 13	248 02.9	49 21.8	5 59.1	341 00.0	30.6	175 28.2	38.4	34 54.8	57.3	Shaula	96 22.8	S37 06.7
A 14	263 05.3	64 21.4	6 00.3	356 00.4	30.6	190 30.9	38.4	49 57.0	57.4	Sirius	258 33.9	S16 44.0
Y 15	278 07.8	79 21.0 ..	01.4	11 00.8 ..	30.7	205 33.7 ..	38.3	64 59.2 ..	57.5	Spica	158 32.0	S11 13.6
16	293 10.2	94 20.6	02.6	26 01.2	30.7	220 36.5	38.3	80 01.4	57.6	Suhail	222 52.7	S43 28.9
17	308 12.7	109 20.2	03.7	41 01.6	30.8	235 39.3	38.3	95 03.6	57.7			
18	323 15.2	124 19.8	S 6 04.9	56 02.0	S24 30.8	250 42.1	N21 38.2	110 05.7	S10 57.8	Vega	80 39.5	N38 48.1
19	338 17.6	139 19.4	06.0	71 02.4	30.9	265 44.8	38.2	125 07.9	57.9	Zuben'ubi	137 06.2	S16 05.6
20	353 20.1	154 19.0	07.1	86 02.8	30.9	280 47.6	38.2	140 10.1	58.0		SHA	Mer.Pass.
21	8 22.6	169 18.6 ..	08.3	101 03.2 ..	31.0	295 50.4 ..	38.1	155 12.3 ..	58.1		° ′	h m
22	23 25.0	184 18.2	09.4	116 03.6	31.0	310 53.2	38.1	170 14.5	58.2	Venus	163 04.7	9 42
23	38 27.5	199 17.7	10.6	131 04.0	31.1	325 56.0	38.1	185 16.7	58.3	Mars	94 13.4	14 17
Mer.Pass. 20 30.5		v −0.4	d 1.1	v 0.4	d 0.1	v 2.8	d 0.0	v 2.2	d 0.1	Jupiter	287 13.8	1 25
										Saturn	147 02.5	10 44

UT	SUN GHA	SUN Dec	MOON GHA	v	Dec	d	HP
d h	° '	° '	° '	'	° '	'	'
11 00	183 59.7	S17 28.1	224 14.8	9.4	S 6 58.9	12.1	59.6
01	198 59.7	28.8	238 43.2	9.3	7 11.0	12.1	59.6
02	213 59.6	29.5	253 11.5	9.3	7 23.1	12.1	59.7
03	228 59.5 ..	30.1	267 39.8	9.2	7 35.2	12.0	59.7
04	243 59.4	30.8	282 08.0	9.1	7 47.2	12.0	59.7
05	258 59.4	31.5	296 36.1	9.0	7 59.2	12.0	59.8
06	273 59.3	S17 32.2	311 04.1	9.0	S 8 11.2	12.0	59.8
07	288 59.2	32.9	325 32.1	8.8	8 23.2	11.9	59.8
08	303 59.1	33.6	339 59.9	8.8	8 35.1	11.8	59.9
S 09	318 59.1 ..	34.2	354 27.7	8.7	8 46.9	11.9	59.9
U 10	333 59.0	34.9	8 55.4	8.7	8 58.8	11.8	60.0
N 11	348 58.9	35.6	23 23.1	8.5	9 10.6	11.7	60.0
D 12	3 58.8	S17 36.3	37 50.6	8.5	S 9 22.3	11.7	60.0
A 13	18 58.8	37.0	52 18.1	8.4	9 34.0	11.7	60.1
Y 14	33 58.7	37.7	66 45.5	8.3	9 45.7	11.6	60.1
15	48 58.6 ..	38.3	81 12.8	8.2	9 57.3	11.6	60.1
16	63 58.5	39.0	95 40.0	8.2	10 08.9	11.5	60.2
17	78 58.5	39.7	110 07.2	8.0	10 20.4	11.5	60.2
18	93 58.4	S17 40.4	124 34.2	8.0	S10 31.9	11.4	60.2
19	108 58.3	41.1	139 01.2	7.9	10 43.3	11.4	60.3
20	123 58.2	41.7	153 28.1	7.8	10 54.7	11.3	60.3
21	138 58.1 ..	42.4	167 54.9	7.7	11 06.0	11.2	60.3
22	153 58.1	43.1	182 21.6	7.6	11 17.2	11.2	60.4
23	168 58.0	43.8	196 48.2	7.5	11 28.4	11.1	60.4
12 00	183 57.9	S17 44.4	211 14.7	7.5	S11 39.5	11.1	60.4
01	198 57.8	45.1	225 41.2	7.4	11 50.6	11.0	60.4
02	213 57.7	45.8	240 07.6	7.3	12 01.6	11.0	60.5
03	228 57.7 ..	46.5	254 33.9	7.2	12 12.6	10.8	60.5
04	243 57.6	47.1	269 00.1	7.1	12 23.4	10.8	60.5
05	258 57.5	47.8	283 26.2	7.0	12 34.2	10.8	60.6
06	273 57.4	S17 48.5	297 52.2	6.9	S12 45.0	10.6	60.6
07	288 57.3	49.1	312 18.1	6.9	12 55.6	10.6	60.6
08	303 57.2	49.8	326 44.0	6.7	13 06.2	10.5	60.6
M 09	318 57.2 ..	50.5	341 09.7	6.7	13 16.7	10.4	60.7
O 10	333 57.1	51.2	355 35.4	6.6	13 27.1	10.4	60.7
N 11	348 57.0	51.8	10 01.0	6.5	13 37.5	10.2	60.7
D 12	3 56.9	S17 52.5	24 26.5	6.4	S13 47.7	10.2	60.7
A 13	18 56.8	53.2	38 51.9	6.3	13 57.9	10.1	60.8
Y 14	33 56.7	53.8	53 17.2	6.3	14 08.0	10.0	60.8
15	48 56.7 ..	54.5	67 42.5	6.1	14 18.0	9.9	60.8
16	63 56.6	55.2	82 07.6	6.1	14 27.9	9.9	60.8
17	78 56.5	55.8	96 32.7	6.0	14 37.8	9.7	60.9
18	93 56.4	S17 56.5	110 57.7	5.9	S14 47.5	9.7	60.9
19	108 56.3	57.2	125 22.6	5.8	14 57.2	9.5	60.9
20	123 56.2	57.8	139 47.4	5.7	15 06.7	9.5	60.9
21	138 56.1 ..	58.5	154 12.1	5.7	15 16.2	9.3	61.0
22	153 56.0	59.2	168 36.8	5.5	15 25.5	9.3	61.0
23	168 55.9	17 59.8	183 01.3	5.5	15 34.8	9.1	61.0
13 00	183 55.9	S18 00.5	197 25.8	5.4	S15 43.9	9.1	61.0
01	198 55.8	01.1	211 50.2	5.3	15 53.0	8.9	61.0
02	213 55.7	01.8	226 14.5	5.3	16 01.9	8.9	61.1
03	228 55.6 ..	02.5	240 38.8	5.1	16 10.8	8.7	61.1
04	243 55.5	03.1	255 02.9	5.1	16 19.5	8.6	61.1
05	258 55.4	03.8	269 27.0	5.0	16 28.1	8.5	61.1
06	273 55.3	S18 04.4	283 51.0	4.9	S16 36.6	8.4	61.1
07	288 55.2	05.1	298 14.9	4.9	16 45.0	8.3	61.1
08	303 55.1	05.8	312 38.8	4.7	16 53.3	8.1	61.2
T 09	318 55.0 ..	06.4	327 02.5	4.7	17 01.4	8.1	61.2
U 10	333 54.9	07.1	341 26.2	4.6	17 09.5	7.9	61.2
E 11	348 54.9	07.7	355 49.8	4.6	17 17.4	7.8	61.2
S 12	3 54.8	S18 08.4	10 13.4	4.4	S17 25.2	7.7	61.2
D 13	18 54.7	09.0	24 36.8	4.4	17 32.9	7.5	61.2
A 14	33 54.6	09.7	39 00.2	4.4	17 40.4	7.5	61.2
Y 15	48 54.5 ..	10.4	53 23.6	4.2	17 47.9	7.3	61.2
16	63 54.4	11.0	67 46.8	4.2	17 55.2	7.1	61.3
17	78 54.3	11.7	82 10.0	4.1	S18 02.3	7.1	61.3
18	93 54.2	S18 12.3					
19	108 54.1	13.0					
20	123 54.0	13.6		A total eclipse of			
21	138 53.9 ..	14.3		the Sun occurs on this			
22	153 53.8	14.9		date. See page 5.			
23	168 53.7	15.6					
	SD 16.2	d 0.7	SD 16.4		16.6		16.7

Lat.	Twilight Naut.	Twilight Civil	Sunrise	Moonrise 11	Moonrise 12	Moonrise 13	Moonrise 14
°	h m	h m	h m	h m	h m	h m	h m
N 72	06 50	08 22	10 26	04 58	07 15	10 11	■■
N 70	06 41	08 01	09 33	04 45	06 49	09 05	■■
68	06 33	07 45	09 01	04 35	06 29	08 30	10 31
66	06 27	07 32	08 37	04 26	06 14	08 04	09 51
64	06 21	07 21	08 19	04 19	06 01	07 45	09 23
62	06 16	07 11	08 04	04 13	05 50	07 29	09 02
60	06 12	07 03	07 51	04 08	05 41	07 15	08 45
N 58	06 08	06 56	07 40	04 03	05 33	07 04	08 31
56	06 04	06 49	07 31	03 59	05 26	06 54	08 18
54	06 00	06 43	07 23	03 56	05 20	06 45	08 08
52	05 57	06 38	07 15	03 52	05 15	06 38	07 58
50	05 54	06 33	07 08	03 49	05 10	06 31	07 50
45	05 47	06 22	06 54	03 43	04 59	06 16	07 32
N 40	05 41	06 13	06 42	03 38	04 50	06 04	07 17
35	05 35	06 05	06 32	03 33	04 42	05 53	07 05
30	05 29	05 58	06 23	03 29	04 36	05 44	06 54
20	05 18	05 44	06 07	03 22	04 24	05 29	06 35
N 10	05 06	05 32	05 54	03 16	04 14	05 16	06 19
0	04 54	05 19	05 41	03 10	04 05	05 03	06 05
S 10	04 40	05 05	05 28	03 05	03 56	04 51	05 50
20	04 22	04 50	05 14	02 59	03 46	04 37	05 34
30	04 00	04 31	04 57	02 52	03 35	04 22	05 16
35	03 46	04 20	04 48	02 48	03 29	04 14	05 05
40	03 30	04 07	04 37	02 44	03 21	04 04	04 54
45	03 08	03 50	04 24	02 39	03 13	03 53	04 40
S 50	02 39	03 30	04 08	02 33	03 03	03 39	04 22
52	02 25	03 20	04 01	02 31	02 59	03 32	04 14
54	02 07	03 09	03 53	02 28	02 54	03 25	04 06
56	01 44	02 55	03 43	02 24	02 48	03 17	03 56
58	01 14	02 40	03 33	02 21	02 42	03 08	03 44
S 60	00 15	02 21	03 21	02 17	02 35	02 58	03 31

Lat.	Sunset	Twilight Civil	Twilight Naut.	Moonset 11	Moonset 12	Moonset 13	Moonset 14
°	h m	h m	h m	h m	h m	h m	h m
N 72	13 01	15 05	16 37	13 23	13 01	12 09	■■
N 70	13 55	15 26	16 46	13 38	13 29	13 16	■■
68	14 27	15 42	16 54	13 50	13 50	13 53	14 01
66	14 50	15 56	17 01	14 00	14 07	14 19	14 42
64	15 09	16 07	17 06	14 09	14 21	14 39	15 10
62	15 24	16 16	17 11	14 16	14 33	14 56	15 31
60	15 36	16 25	17 16	14 23	14 43	15 10	15 49
N 58	15 47	16 32	17 20	14 28	14 51	15 22	16 03
56	15 57	16 38	17 24	14 33	14 59	15 32	16 16
54	16 05	16 44	17 27	14 38	15 06	15 41	16 27
52	16 13	16 50	17 31	14 42	15 12	15 49	16 37
50	16 19	16 55	17 34	14 46	15 18	15 57	16 45
45	16 34	17 05	17 41	14 54	15 30	16 13	17 04
N 40	16 46	17 15	17 47	15 00	15 40	16 26	17 19
35	16 56	17 23	17 53	15 06	15 49	16 37	17 32
30	17 05	17 30	17 59	15 11	15 56	16 47	17 43
20	17 21	17 44	18 11	15 20	16 10	17 03	18 02
N 10	17 35	17 57	18 22	15 28	16 21	17 18	18 19
0	17 48	18 09	18 35	15 36	16 32	17 32	18 35
S 10	18 01	18 23	18 49	15 43	16 43	17 46	18 50
20	18 15	18 39	19 06	15 51	16 55	18 00	19 07
30	18 31	18 57	19 29	16 00	17 08	18 17	19 26
35	18 41	19 09	19 43	16 06	17 16	18 27	19 37
40	18 52	19 22	20 00	16 12	17 25	18 39	19 50
45	19 05	19 39	20 21	16 19	17 35	18 52	20 05
S 50	19 21	20 00	20 51	16 27	17 48	19 08	20 24
52	19 29	20 10	21 06	16 31	17 54	19 16	20 33
54	19 37	20 21	21 24	16 35	18 00	19 24	20 43
56	19 46	20 35	21 47	16 40	18 07	19 34	20 54
58	19 57	20 51	22 19	16 45	18 16	19 45	21 06
S 60	20 10	21 10	////	16 51	18 25	19 57	21 21

Day	SUN Eqn. of Time 00h	SUN Eqn. of Time 12h	SUN Mer. Pass.	MOON Mer. Pass. Upper	MOON Mer. Pass. Lower	Age	Phase
d	m s	m s	h m	h m	h m	d	%
11	15 59	15 56	11 44	09 23	21 50	27	9
12	15 52	15 48	11 44	10 18	22 47	28	3
13	15 44	15 39	11 44	11 17	23 48	29	0

2012 NOVEMBER 14, 15, 16 (WED., THURS., FRI.)

UT	ARIES GHA	VENUS −3.9 GHA	VENUS Dec	MARS +1.2 GHA	MARS Dec	JUPITER −2.8 GHA	JUPITER Dec	SATURN +0.6 GHA	SATURN Dec
14 00	53 30.0	214 17.3	S 6 11.7	146 04.4	S24 31.1	340 58.7	N21 38.0	200 18.8	S10 58.4
01	68 32.4	229 16.9	12.9	161 04.8	31.1	356 01.5	38.0	215 21.0	58.5
02	83 34.9	244 16.5	14.0	176 05.2	31.2	11 04.3	38.0	230 23.2	58.6
03	98 37.4	259 16.1	15.1	191 05.6	31.2	26 07.1	37.9	245 25.4	58.7
04	113 39.8	274 15.7	16.3	206 06.0	31.3	41 09.9	37.9	260 27.6	58.7
05	128 42.3	289 15.3	17.4	221 06.4	31.3	56 12.7	37.9	275 29.7	58.8
W 06	143 44.7	304 14.9	S 6 18.6	236 06.8	S24 31.3	71 15.4	N21 37.8	290 31.9	S10 58.9
E 07	158 47.2	319 14.5	19.7	251 07.2	31.4	86 18.2	37.8	305 34.1	59.0
D 08	173 49.7	334 14.1	20.8	266 07.6	31.4	101 21.0	37.8	320 36.3	59.1
N 09	188 52.1	349 13.7	22.0	281 08.0	31.5	116 23.8	37.7	335 38.5	59.2
E 10	203 54.6	4 13.3	23.1	296 08.4	31.5	131 26.6	37.7	350 40.7	59.3
S 11	218 57.1	19 12.9	24.3	311 08.8	31.5	146 29.3	37.7	5 42.8	59.4
D 12	233 59.5	34 12.5	S 6 25.4	326 09.2	S24 31.6	161 32.1	N21 37.6	20 45.0	S10 59.5
A 13	249 02.0	49 12.1	26.5	341 09.6	31.6	176 34.9	37.6	35 47.2	59.6
Y 14	264 04.5	64 11.7	27.7	356 10.0	31.7	191 37.7	37.6	50 49.4	59.7
15	279 06.9	79 11.3	28.8	11 10.4	31.7	206 40.5	37.5	65 51.6	59.8
16	294 09.4	94 10.9	30.0	26 10.8	31.7	221 43.3	37.5	80 53.7	10 59.9
17	309 11.9	109 10.4	31.1	41 11.2	31.8	236 46.0	37.5	95 55.9	11 00.0
18	324 14.3	124 10.0	S 6 32.2	56 11.6	S24 31.8	251 48.8	N21 37.4	110 58.1	S11 00.1
19	339 16.8	139 09.6	33.4	71 12.0	31.8	266 51.6	37.4	126 00.3	00.2
20	354 19.2	154 09.2	34.5	86 12.4	31.9	281 54.4	37.4	141 02.5	00.3
21	9 21.7	169 08.8	35.7	101 12.8	31.9	296 57.2	37.3	156 04.7	00.4
22	24 24.2	184 08.4	36.8	116 13.2	31.9	312 00.0	37.3	171 06.8	00.5
23	39 26.6	199 08.0	37.9	131 13.6	32.0	327 02.8	37.3	186 09.0	00.6
15 00	54 29.1	214 07.6	S 6 39.1	146 13.9	S24 32.0	342 05.5	N21 37.2	201 11.2	S11 00.7
01	69 31.6	229 07.2	40.2	161 14.3	32.0	357 08.3	37.2	216 13.4	00.7
02	84 34.0	244 06.8	41.4	176 14.7	32.1	12 11.1	37.2	231 15.6	00.8
03	99 36.5	259 06.4	42.5	191 15.1	32.1	27 13.9	37.1	246 17.8	00.9
04	114 39.0	274 05.9	43.6	206 15.5	32.1	42 16.7	37.1	261 19.9	01.0
05	129 41.4	289 05.5	44.8	221 15.9	32.2	57 19.5	37.1	276 22.1	01.1
T 06	144 43.9	304 05.1	S 6 45.9	236 16.3	S24 32.2	72 22.3	N21 37.0	291 24.3	S11 01.2
H 07	159 46.3	319 04.7	47.0	251 16.7	32.2	87 25.0	37.0	306 26.5	01.3
U 08	174 48.8	334 04.3	48.2	266 17.1	32.2	102 27.8	37.0	321 28.7	01.4
R 09	189 51.3	349 03.9	49.3	281 17.5	32.3	117 30.6	36.9	336 30.8	01.5
S 10	204 53.7	4 03.5	50.5	296 17.9	32.3	132 33.4	36.9	351 33.0	01.6
D 11	219 56.2	19 03.1	51.6	311 18.3	32.3	147 36.2	36.9	6 35.2	01.7
A 12	234 58.7	34 02.6	S 6 52.7	326 18.7	S24 32.4	162 39.0	N21 36.8	21 37.4	S11 01.8
Y 13	250 01.1	49 02.2	53.9	341 19.1	32.4	177 41.8	36.8	36 39.6	01.9
14	265 03.6	64 01.8	55.0	356 19.5	32.4	192 44.6	36.8	51 41.8	02.0
15	280 06.1	79 01.4	56.1	11 19.9	32.4	207 47.3	36.7	66 43.9	02.1
16	295 08.5	94 01.0	57.3	26 20.3	32.5	222 50.1	36.7	81 46.1	02.2
17	310 11.0	109 00.6	58.4	41 20.7	32.5	237 52.9	36.7	96 48.3	02.3
18	325 13.5	124 00.2	S 6 59.5	56 21.0	S24 32.5	252 55.7	N21 36.6	111 50.5	S11 02.4
19	340 15.9	138 59.7	7 00.7	71 21.4	32.5	267 58.5	36.6	126 52.7	02.5
20	355 18.4	153 59.3	01.8	86 21.8	32.5	283 01.3	36.6	141 54.9	02.6
21	10 20.8	168 58.9	02.9	101 22.2	32.6	298 04.1	36.5	156 57.0	02.6
22	25 23.3	183 58.5	04.1	116 22.6	32.6	313 06.9	36.5	171 59.2	02.7
23	40 25.8	198 58.1	05.2	131 23.0	32.6	328 09.7	36.5	187 01.4	02.8
16 00	55 28.2	213 57.7	S 7 06.3	146 23.4	S24 32.6	343 12.4	N21 36.4	202 03.6	S11 02.9
01	70 30.7	228 57.2	07.5	161 23.8	32.7	358 15.2	36.4	217 05.8	03.0
02	85 33.2	243 56.8	08.6	176 24.2	32.7	13 18.0	36.4	232 08.0	03.1
03	100 35.6	258 56.4	09.7	191 24.6	32.7	28 20.8	36.3	247 10.1	03.2
04	115 38.1	273 56.0	10.9	206 25.0	32.7	43 23.6	36.3	262 12.3	03.3
05	130 40.6	288 55.6	12.0	221 25.4	32.7	58 26.4	36.3	277 14.5	03.4
F 06	145 43.0	303 55.2	S 7 13.1	236 25.8	S24 32.8	73 29.2	N21 36.2	292 16.7	S11 03.5
R 07	160 45.5	318 54.7	14.3	251 26.1	32.8	88 32.0	36.2	307 18.9	03.6
I 08	175 48.0	333 54.3	15.4	266 26.5	32.8	103 34.8	36.2	322 21.1	03.7
D 09	190 50.4	348 53.9	16.5	281 26.9	32.8	118 37.6	36.1	337 23.2	03.8
A 10	205 52.9	3 53.5	17.7	296 27.3	32.8	133 40.4	36.1	352 25.4	03.9
Y 11	220 55.3	18 53.1	18.8	311 27.7	32.8	148 43.1	36.1	7 27.6	04.0
12	235 57.8	33 52.6	S 7 19.9	326 28.1	S24 32.9	163 45.9	N21 36.0	22 29.8	S11 04.1
13	251 00.3	48 52.2	21.1	341 28.5	32.9	178 48.7	36.0	37 32.0	04.2
14	266 02.7	63 51.8	22.2	356 28.9	32.9	193 51.5	36.0	52 34.2	04.3
15	281 05.2	78 51.4	23.3	11 29.3	32.9	208 54.3	35.9	67 36.3	04.3
16	296 07.7	93 51.0	24.5	26 29.7	32.9	223 57.1	35.9	82 38.5	04.4
17	311 10.1	108 50.5	25.6	41 30.1	32.9	238 59.9	35.8	97 40.7	04.5
18	326 12.6	123 50.1	S 7 26.7	56 30.4	S24 32.9	254 02.7	N21 35.8	112 42.9	S11 04.6
19	341 15.1	138 49.7	27.8	71 30.8	33.0	269 05.5	35.8	127 45.1	04.7
20	356 17.5	153 49.3	29.0	86 31.2	33.0	284 08.3	35.7	142 47.3	04.8
21	11 20.0	168 48.8	30.1	101 31.6	33.0	299 11.1	35.7	157 49.4	04.9
22	26 22.5	183 48.4	31.2	116 32.0	33.0	314 13.9	35.7	172 51.6	05.0
23	41 24.9	198 48.0	32.4	131 32.4	33.0	329 16.7	35.6	187 53.8	05.1
Mer. Pass.	20 18.7	v −0.4	d 1.1	v 0.4	d 0.0	v 2.8	d 0.0	v 2.2	d 0.1

STARS

Name	SHA	Dec
Acamar	315 18.2	S40 15.2
Achernar	335 26.6	S57 10.4
Acrux	173 10.2	S63 10.0
Adhara	255 12.6	S28 59.3
Aldebaran	290 49.5	N16 32.1
Alioth	166 21.5	N55 53.2
Alkaid	152 59.7	N49 14.9
Al Na'ir	27 44.2	S46 54.0
Alnilam	275 46.5	S 1 11.7
Alphard	217 56.5	S 8 42.9
Alphecca	126 11.7	N26 40.4
Alpheratz	357 43.7	N29 10.0
Altair	62 08.8	N 8 54.4
Ankaa	353 15.8	S42 14.2
Antares	112 27.1	S26 27.5
Arcturus	145 56.4	N19 07.0
Atria	107 29.8	S69 03.0
Avior	234 17.9	S59 32.9
Bellatrix	278 32.1	N 6 21.6
Betelgeuse	271 01.5	N 7 24.5
Canopus	263 55.9	S52 42.1
Capella	280 34.6	N46 00.5
Deneb	49 31.9	N45 20.0
Denebola	182 34.3	N14 29.9
Diphda	348 56.1	S17 54.9
Dubhe	193 52.5	N61 40.5
Elnath	278 12.8	N28 37.0
Eltanin	90 46.8	N51 29.5
Enif	33 47.5	N 9 56.3
Fomalhaut	15 24.3	S29 33.2
Gacrux	172 01.7	S57 10.9
Gienah	175 52.9	S17 36.7
Hadar	148 49.1	S60 25.9
Hamal	328 00.9	N23 31.5
Kaus Aust.	83 44.7	S34 22.6
Kochab	137 21.2	N74 06.1
Markab	13 38.6	N15 16.7
Menkar	314 15.2	N 4 08.5
Menkent	148 08.4	S36 25.8
Miaplacidus	221 39.6	S69 46.0
Mirfak	308 40.4	N49 54.4
Nunki	75 59.1	S26 16.7
Peacock	53 20.1	S56 41.7
Pollux	243 28.1	N27 59.5
Procyon	245 00.0	N 5 11.4
Rasalhague	96 07.1	N12 33.3
Regulus	207 44.0	N11 54.1
Rigel	281 12.1	S 8 11.2
Rigil Kent.	139 52.9	S60 53.1
Sabik	102 13.3	S15 44.3
Schedar	349 40.5	N56 36.8
Shaula	96 22.8	S37 06.7
Sirius	258 33.8	S16 44.0
Spica	158 32.0	S11 13.6
Suhail	222 52.7	S43 28.9
Vega	80 39.6	N38 48.1
Zuben'ubi	137 06.2	S16 05.6

	SHA	Mer. Pass.
Venus	159 38.5	9 44
Mars	91 44.8	14 15
Jupiter	287 36.4	1 11
Saturn	146 42.1	10 34

UT	SUN GHA	Dec	MOON GHA	v	Dec	d	HP
d h	° ′	° ′	° ′	′	° ′	′	′
14 00	183 53.6	S18 16.2	182 50.6	3.7	S18 48.8	6.1	61.3
01	198 53.5	16.9	197 13.3	3.6	18 54.9	6.0	61.3
02	213 53.4	17.5	211 35.9	3.6	19 00.9	5.8	61.3
03	228 53.3	.. 18.2	225 58.5	3.6	19 06.7	5.7	61.3
04	243 53.2	18.8	240 21.1	3.5	19 12.4	5.5	61.3
05	258 53.1	19.5	254 43.6	3.4	19 17.9	5.4	61.4
06	273 53.0	S18 20.1	269 06.0	3.4	S19 23.3	5.2	61.4
W 07	288 52.9	20.7	283 28.4	3.4	19 28.5	5.1	61.4
E 08	303 52.8	21.4	297 50.8	3.3	19 33.6	5.0	61.4
D 09	318 52.7	.. 22.0	312 13.1	3.2	19 38.6	4.8	61.4
N 10	333 52.6	22.7	326 35.3	3.3	19 43.4	4.6	61.4
E 11	348 52.5	23.3	340 57.6	3.2	19 48.0	4.5	61.4
S 12	3 52.4	S18 24.0	355 19.8	3.1	S19 52.5	4.3	61.4
D 13	18 52.3	24.6	9 41.9	3.1	19 56.8	4.2	61.4
A 14	33 52.2	25.2	24 04.0	3.1	20 01.0	4.1	61.4
Y 15	48 52.1	.. 25.9	38 26.1	3.1	20 05.1	3.9	61.4
16	63 52.0	26.5	52 48.2	3.0	20 09.0	3.7	61.4
17	78 51.9	27.2	67 10.2	3.0	20 12.7	3.6	61.3
18	93 51.8	S18 27.8	81 32.2	3.0	S20 16.3	3.4	61.3
19	108 51.7	28.4	95 54.2	3.0	20 19.7	3.3	61.3
20	123 51.6	29.1	110 16.2	2.9	20 23.0	3.1	61.3
21	138 51.5	.. 29.7	124 38.1	3.0	20 26.1	2.9	61.3
22	153 51.4	30.4	139 00.1	2.9	20 29.0	2.8	61.3
23	168 51.2	31.0	153 22.0	2.9	20 31.8	2.7	61.3
15 00	183 51.1	S18 31.6	167 43.9	2.9	S20 34.5	2.4	61.3
01	198 51.0	32.3	182 05.8	2.9	20 36.9	2.3	61.3
02	213 50.9	32.9	196 27.7	2.8	20 39.2	2.2	61.3
03	228 50.8	.. 33.5	210 49.5	2.9	20 41.4	2.0	61.3
04	243 50.7	34.2	225 11.4	2.9	20 43.4	1.9	61.3
05	258 50.6	34.8	239 33.3	2.8	20 45.3	1.6	61.3
06	273 50.5	S18 35.4	253 55.1	2.9	S20 46.9	1.6	61.2
T 07	288 50.4	36.1	268 17.0	2.9	20 48.5	1.3	61.2
H 08	303 50.3	36.7	282 38.9	2.9	20 49.8	1.2	61.2
U 09	318 50.2	.. 37.3	297 00.8	2.9	20 51.0	1.1	61.2
R 10	333 50.0	38.0	311 22.7	2.9	20 52.1	0.9	61.2
S 11	348 49.9	38.6	325 44.6	2.9	20 53.0	0.7	61.2
D 12	3 49.8	S18 39.2	340 06.5	2.9	S20 53.7	0.5	61.2
A 13	18 49.7	39.8	354 28.4	3.0	20 54.2	0.4	61.2
Y 14	33 49.6	40.5	8 50.4	2.9	20 54.6	0.3	61.1
15	48 49.5	.. 41.1	23 12.3	3.0	20 54.9	0.1	61.1
16	63 49.4	41.7	37 34.3	3.0	20 55.0	0.1	61.1
17	78 49.3	42.3	51 56.3	3.1	20 54.9	0.2	61.1
18	93 49.1	S18 43.0	66 18.4	3.0	S20 54.7	0.4	61.1
19	108 49.0	43.6	80 40.4	3.1	20 54.3	0.6	61.1
20	123 48.9	44.2	95 02.5	3.2	20 53.7	0.7	61.0
21	138 48.8	.. 44.8	109 24.7	3.2	20 53.0	0.8	61.0
22	153 48.7	45.5	123 46.9	3.2	20 52.2	1.0	61.0
23	168 48.6	46.1	138 09.1	3.2	20 51.2	1.2	61.0
16 00	183 48.5	S18 46.7	152 31.3	3.3	S20 50.0	1.4	61.0
01	198 48.3	47.3	166 53.6	3.3	20 48.6	1.4	60.9
02	213 48.2	48.0	181 15.9	3.4	20 47.2	1.7	60.9
03	228 48.1	.. 48.6	195 38.3	3.4	20 45.5	1.8	60.9
04	243 48.0	49.2	210 00.7	3.5	20 43.7	1.9	60.9
05	258 47.9	49.8	224 23.2	3.5	20 41.8	2.1	60.9
06	273 47.8	S18 50.4	238 45.7	3.5	S20 39.7	2.3	60.8
07	288 47.6	51.1	253 08.2	3.7	20 37.4	2.4	60.8
F 08	303 47.5	51.7	267 30.9	3.6	20 35.0	2.5	60.8
R 09	318 47.4	.. 52.3	281 53.5	3.8	20 32.5	2.7	60.8
I 10	333 47.3	52.9	296 16.3	3.8	20 29.8	2.8	60.7
D 11	348 47.2	53.5	310 39.1	3.8	20 27.0	3.0	60.7
A 12	3 47.0	S18 54.1	325 01.9	4.0	S20 24.0	3.2	60.7
Y 13	18 46.9	54.7	339 24.9	3.9	20 20.8	3.3	60.7
14	33 46.8	55.4	353 47.8	4.1	20 17.5	3.4	60.6
15	48 46.7	.. 56.0	8 10.9	4.1	20 14.1	3.5	60.6
16	63 46.6	56.6	22 34.0	4.2	20 10.6	3.8	60.6
17	78 46.4	57.2	36 57.2	4.2	20 06.8	3.8	60.5
18	93 46.3	S18 57.8	51 20.4	4.4	S20 03.0	4.0	60.5
19	108 46.2	58.4	65 43.8	4.4	19 59.0	4.1	60.5
20	123 46.1	59.0	80 07.2	4.4	19 54.9	4.3	60.5
21	138 45.9	18 59.6	94 30.6	4.5	19 50.6	4.4	60.4
22	153 45.8	19 00.3	108 54.2	4.6	19 46.2	4.5	60.4
23	168 45.7	S19 00.9	123 17.8	4.7	S19 41.7	4.7	60.4
	SD 16.2	d 0.6	SD 16.7		16.7		16.5

Lat.	Twilight Naut.	Civil	Sunrise	Moonrise 14	15	16	17
°	h m	h m	h m	h m	h m	h m	h m
N 72	07 01	08 36	11 10	▬	▬	▬	▬
N 70	06 50	08 13	09 52	▬	▬	▬	13 49
68	06 42	07 55	09 15	10 31	12 10	12 54	13 05
66	06 35	07 41	08 49	09 51	11 17	12 10	12 36
64	06 28	07 29	08 29	09 23	10 45	11 41	12 14
62	06 23	07 18	08 12	09 02	10 21	11 18	11 56
60	06 18	07 10	07 59	08 45	10 02	11 00	11 41
N 58	06 13	07 02	07 47	08 31	09 46	10 45	11 28
56	06 09	06 55	07 37	08 18	09 33	10 32	11 17
54	06 05	06 49	07 28	08 08	09 21	10 21	11 07
52	06 02	06 43	07 20	07 58	09 11	10 11	10 59
50	05 58	06 38	07 13	07 50	09 01	10 02	10 51
45	05 51	06 26	06 58	07 32	08 42	09 43	10 34
N 40	05 44	06 16	06 45	07 17	08 26	09 28	10 21
35	05 37	06 08	06 35	07 05	08 13	09 15	10 09
30	05 31	06 00	06 25	06 54	08 01	09 03	09 59
20	05 19	05 46	06 09	06 35	07 41	08 44	09 42
N 10	05 05	05 33	05 55	06 19	07 24	08 27	09 26
0	04 54	05 19	05 41	06 05	07 08	08 11	09 12
S 10	04 39	05 05	05 27	05 50	06 52	07 55	08 58
20	04 21	04 49	05 13	05 34	06 35	07 38	08 42
30	03 58	04 30	04 56	05 16	06 15	07 19	08 25
35	03 44	04 18	04 46	05 05	06 04	07 08	08 14
40	03 26	04 04	04 34	04 54	05 51	06 55	08 03
45	03 04	03 47	04 21	04 40	05 35	06 39	07 49
S 50	02 33	03 25	04 04	04 22	05 16	06 20	07 32
52	02 17	03 15	03 56	04 14	05 07	06 11	07 24
54	01 58	03 03	03 48	04 06	04 57	06 01	07 15
56	01 33	02 49	03 38	03 56	04 46	05 50	07 05
58	00 57	02 32	03 27	03 44	04 33	05 37	06 53
S 60	////	02 11	03 14	03 31	04 18	05 22	06 40

Lat.	Sunset	Twilight Civil	Naut.	Moonset 14	15	16	17
°	h m	h m	h m	h m	h m	h m	h m
N 72	12 18	14 52	16 27	▬	▬	▬	
N 70	13 36	15 15	16 38	▬	▬	▬	17 14
68	14 14	15 33	16 46	14 01	14 36	16 04	17 57
66	14 40	15 48	16 54	14 42	15 28	16 47	18 26
64	15 00	16 00	17 00	15 10	16 01	17 16	18 47
62	15 16	16 10	17 06	15 31	16 25	17 38	19 05
60	15 30	16 19	17 11	15 49	16 44	17 56	19 19
N 58	15 41	16 27	17 15	16 03	17 00	18 11	19 31
56	15 51	16 34	17 20	16 16	17 13	18 23	19 42
54	16 00	16 40	17 23	16 27	17 25	18 34	19 51
52	16 08	16 46	17 27	16 37	17 35	18 44	19 59
50	16 16	16 51	17 30	16 45	17 44	18 53	20 07
45	16 31	17 03	17 38	17 04	18 04	19 11	20 22
N 40	16 43	17 13	17 45	17 19	18 20	19 26	20 35
35	16 54	17 21	17 52	17 32	18 33	19 39	20 46
30	17 04	17 29	17 58	17 43	18 45	19 50	20 56
20	17 20	17 43	18 10	18 02	19 05	20 09	21 12
N 10	17 35	17 57	18 22	18 19	19 22	20 25	21 26
0	17 48	18 10	18 35	18 35	19 38	20 40	21 40
S 10	18 02	18 24	18 50	18 50	19 54	20 56	21 53
20	18 17	18 40	19 08	19 07	20 11	21 12	22 07
30	18 34	19 00	19 32	19 26	20 31	21 30	22 23
35	18 44	19 12	19 46	19 37	20 43	21 41	22 32
40	18 56	19 26	20 04	19 50	20 56	21 53	22 42
45	19 09	19 43	20 27	20 05	21 11	22 08	22 55
S 50	19 26	20 05	20 58	20 24	21 30	22 25	23 09
52	19 34	20 16	21 14	20 33	21 39	22 34	23 16
54	19 43	20 28	21 34	20 43	21 50	22 43	23 24
56	19 53	20 43	21 59	20 54	22 01	22 53	23 32
58	20 04	21 00	22 38	21 06	22 14	23 05	23 42
S 60	20 18	21 21	////	21 21	22 29	23 19	23 53

	SUN			MOON			
Day	Eqn. of Time 00h	12h	Mer. Pass.	Mer. Pass. Upper	Lower	Age	Phase
d	m s	m s	h m	h m	h m	d	%
14	15 35	15 30	11 45	12 20	24 51	01	1
15	15 25	15 20	11 45	13 23	00 51	02	4
16	15 14	15 08	11 45	14 26	01 55	03	10

UT	ARIES GHA	VENUS −3.9 GHA	Dec	MARS +1.2 GHA	Dec	JUPITER −2.8 GHA	Dec	SATURN +0.6 GHA	Dec
17 00	56 27.4	213 47.6	S 7 33.5	146 32.8	S24 33.0	344 19.5	N21 35.6	202 56.0	S11 05.2
01	71 29.8	228 47.1	34.6	161 33.2	33.0	359 22.3	35.6	217 58.2	05.3
02	86 32.3	243 46.7	35.7	176 33.6	33.0	14 25.1	35.5	233 00.4	05.4
03	101 34.8	258 46.3	.. 36.9	191 33.9	.. 33.0	29 27.8	.. 35.5	248 02.5	.. 05.5
04	116 37.2	273 45.9	38.0	206 34.3	33.0	44 30.6	35.5	263 04.7	05.6
05	131 39.7	288 45.4	39.1	221 34.7	33.1	59 33.4	35.4	278 06.9	05.7
S 06	146 42.2	303 45.0	S 7 40.3	236 35.1	S24 33.1	74 36.2	N21 35.4	293 09.1	S11 05.8
A 07	161 44.6	318 44.6	41.4	251 35.5	33.1	89 39.0	35.4	308 11.3	05.8
T 08	176 47.1	333 44.2	42.5	266 35.9	33.1	104 41.8	35.3	323 13.5	05.9
U 09	191 49.6	348 43.7	.. 43.6	281 36.3	.. 33.1	119 44.6	.. 35.3	338 15.7	.. 06.0
R 10	206 52.0	3 43.3	44.8	296 36.7	33.1	134 47.4	35.3	353 17.8	06.1
D 11	221 54.5	18 42.9	45.9	311 37.1	33.1	149 50.2	35.2	8 20.0	06.2
A 12	236 57.0	33 42.5	S 7 47.0	326 37.4	S24 33.1	164 53.0	N21 35.2	23 22.2	S11 06.3
Y 13	251 59.4	48 42.0	48.1	341 37.8	33.1	179 55.8	35.2	38 24.4	06.4
14	267 01.9	63 41.6	49.3	356 38.2	33.1	194 58.6	35.1	53 26.6	06.5
15	282 04.3	78 41.2	.. 50.4	11 38.6	.. 33.1	210 01.4	.. 35.1	68 28.8	.. 06.6
16	297 06.8	93 40.7	51.5	26 39.0	33.1	225 04.2	35.0	83 30.9	06.7
17	312 09.3	108 40.3	52.6	41 39.4	33.1	240 07.0	35.0	98 33.1	06.8
18	327 11.7	123 39.9	S 7 53.8	56 39.8	S24 33.1	255 09.8	N21 35.0	113 35.3	S11 06.9
19	342 14.2	138 39.5	54.9	71 40.2	33.1	270 12.6	34.9	128 37.5	07.0
20	357 16.7	153 39.0	56.0	86 40.5	33.1	285 15.4	34.9	143 39.7	07.1
21	12 19.1	168 38.6	.. 57.1	101 40.9	.. 33.1	300 18.2	.. 34.9	158 41.9	.. 07.2
22	27 21.6	183 38.2	58.2	116 41.3	33.1	315 21.0	34.8	173 44.1	07.3
23	42 24.1	198 37.7	7 59.4	131 41.7	33.1	330 23.8	34.8	188 46.2	07.3
18 00	57 26.5	213 37.3	S 8 00.5	146 42.1	S24 33.1	345 26.6	N21 34.8	203 48.4	S11 07.4
01	72 29.0	228 36.9	01.6	161 42.5	33.1	0 29.4	34.7	218 50.6	07.5
02	87 31.5	243 36.4	02.7	176 42.9	33.1	15 32.2	34.7	233 52.8	07.6
03	102 33.9	258 36.0	.. 03.9	191 43.3	.. 33.1	30 35.0	.. 34.7	248 55.0	.. 07.7
04	117 36.4	273 35.6	05.0	206 43.6	33.1	45 37.8	34.6	263 57.2	07.8
05	132 38.8	288 35.1	06.1	221 44.0	33.1	60 40.6	34.6	278 59.3	07.9
S 06	147 41.3	303 34.7	S 8 07.2	236 44.4	S24 33.1	75 43.4	N21 34.6	294 01.5	S11 08.0
U 07	162 43.8	318 34.3	08.3	251 44.8	33.1	90 46.2	34.5	309 03.7	08.1
N 08	177 46.2	333 33.8	09.5	266 45.2	33.1	105 49.0	34.5	324 05.9	08.2
D 09	192 48.7	348 33.4	.. 10.6	281 45.6	.. 33.1	120 51.8	.. 34.4	339 08.1	.. 08.3
A 10	207 51.2	3 33.0	11.7	296 46.0	33.1	135 54.6	34.4	354 10.3	08.4
Y 11	222 53.6	18 32.5	12.8	311 46.3	33.1	150 57.4	34.4	9 12.5	08.5
12	237 56.1	33 32.1	S 8 13.9	326 46.7	S24 33.1	166 00.2	N21 34.3	24 14.6	S11 08.6
13	252 58.6	48 31.7	15.1	341 47.1	33.1	181 03.0	34.3	39 16.8	08.6
14	268 01.0	63 31.2	16.2	356 47.5	33.1	196 05.8	34.3	54 19.0	08.7
15	283 03.5	78 30.8	.. 17.3	11 47.9	.. 33.0	211 08.6	.. 34.2	69 21.2	.. 08.8
16	298 05.9	93 30.3	18.4	26 48.3	33.0	226 11.4	34.2	84 23.4	08.9
17	313 08.4	108 29.9	19.5	41 48.7	33.0	241 14.2	34.2	99 25.6	09.0
18	328 10.9	123 29.5	S 8 20.7	56 49.0	S24 33.0	256 17.0	N21 34.1	114 27.8	S11 09.1
19	343 13.3	138 29.0	21.8	71 49.4	33.0	271 19.8	34.1	129 29.9	09.2
20	358 15.8	153 28.6	22.9	86 49.8	33.0	286 22.6	34.1	144 32.1	09.3
21	13 18.3	168 28.2	.. 24.0	101 50.2	.. 33.0	301 25.4	.. 34.0	159 34.3	.. 09.4
22	28 20.7	183 27.7	25.1	116 50.6	33.0	316 28.2	34.0	174 36.5	09.5
23	43 23.2	198 27.3	26.2	131 51.0	33.0	331 31.0	33.9	189 38.7	09.6
19 00	58 25.7	213 26.8	S 8 27.4	146 51.3	S24 32.9	346 33.8	N21 33.9	204 40.9	S11 09.7
01	73 28.1	228 26.4	28.5	161 51.7	32.9	1 36.6	33.9	219 43.1	09.8
02	88 30.6	243 26.0	29.6	176 52.1	32.9	16 39.4	33.8	234 45.2	09.9
03	103 33.1	258 25.5	.. 30.7	191 52.5	.. 32.9	31 42.2	.. 33.8	249 47.4	.. 09.9
04	118 35.5	273 25.1	31.8	206 52.9	32.9	46 45.0	33.8	264 49.6	10.0
05	133 38.0	288 24.6	32.9	221 53.3	32.9	61 47.8	33.7	279 51.8	10.1
M 06	148 40.4	303 24.2	S 8 34.1	236 53.7	S24 32.9	76 50.6	N21 33.7	294 54.0	S11 10.2
O 07	163 42.9	318 23.8	35.2	251 54.0	32.9	91 53.4	33.7	309 56.2	10.3
N 08	178 45.4	333 23.3	36.3	266 54.4	32.8	106 56.2	33.6	324 58.4	10.4
D 09	193 47.8	348 22.9	.. 37.4	281 54.8	.. 32.8	121 59.0	.. 33.6	340 00.6	.. 10.5
A 10	208 50.3	3 22.4	38.5	296 55.2	32.8	137 01.8	33.5	355 02.7	10.6
Y 11	223 52.8	18 22.0	39.6	311 55.6	32.8	152 04.6	33.5	10 04.9	10.7
12	238 55.2	33 21.5	S 8 40.7	326 56.0	S24 32.8	167 07.4	N21 33.5	25 07.1	S11 10.8
13	253 57.7	48 21.1	41.8	341 56.3	32.7	182 10.2	33.4	40 09.3	10.9
14	269 00.2	63 20.7	43.0	356 56.7	32.7	197 13.0	33.4	55 11.5	11.0
15	284 02.6	78 20.2	.. 44.1	11 57.1	.. 32.7	212 15.8	.. 33.4	70 13.7	.. 11.1
16	299 05.1	93 19.8	45.2	26 57.5	32.7	227 18.6	33.3	85 15.9	11.1
17	314 07.6	108 19.3	46.3	41 57.9	32.7	242 21.4	33.3	100 18.0	11.2
18	329 10.0	123 18.9	S 8 47.4	56 58.2	S24 32.6	257 24.2	N21 33.3	115 20.2	S11 11.3
19	344 12.5	138 18.4	48.5	71 58.6	32.6	272 27.1	33.2	130 22.4	11.4
20	359 14.9	153 18.0	49.6	86 59.0	32.6	287 29.9	33.2	145 24.6	11.5
21	14 17.4	168 17.5	.. 50.7	101 59.4	.. 32.6	302 32.7	.. 33.1	160 26.8	.. 11.6
22	29 19.9	183 17.1	51.8	116 59.8	32.6	317 35.5	33.1	175 29.0	11.7
23	44 22.3	198 16.6	53.0	132 00.2	32.5	332 38.3	33.1	190 31.2	11.8
Mer. Pass.	20 06.9	v −0.4	d 1.1	v 0.4	d 0.0	v 2.8	d 0.0	v 2.2	d 0.1

STARS

Name	SHA	Dec
Acamar	315 18.2	S40 15.2
Achernar	335 26.6	S57 10.4
Acrux	173 10.1	S63 10.0
Adhara	255 12.6	S28 59.3
Aldebaran	290 49.5	N16 32.1
Alioth	166 21.5	N55 53.2
Alkaid	152 59.7	N49 14.8
Al Na'ir	27 44.2	S46 54.0
Alnilam	275 46.5	S 1 11.7
Alphard	217 56.4	S 8 42.9
Alphecca	126 11.7	N26 40.4
Alpheratz	357 43.7	N29 10.0
Altair	62 08.8	N 8 54.4
Ankaa	353 15.8	S42 14.2
Antares	112 27.1	S26 27.5
Arcturus	145 56.4	N19 06.9
Atria	107 29.8	S69 03.0
Avior	234 17.9	S59 32.9
Bellatrix	278 32.1	N 6 21.6
Betelgeuse	271 01.4	N 7 24.5
Canopus	263 55.9	S52 42.1
Capella	280 34.6	N46 00.5
Deneb	49 31.9	N45 20.0
Denebola	182 34.2	N14 29.9
Diphda	348 56.1	S17 54.9
Dubhe	193 52.4	N61 40.5
Elnath	278 12.8	N28 37.0
Eltanin	90 46.8	N51 29.5
Enif	33 47.5	N 9 56.3
Fomalhaut	15 24.3	S29 33.2
Gacrux	172 01.7	S57 10.9
Gienah	175 52.9	S17 36.7
Hadar	148 49.0	S60 25.9
Hamal	328 00.9	N23 31.5
Kaus Aust.	83 44.7	S34 22.6
Kochab	137 21.2	N74 06.1
Markab	13 38.6	N15 16.8
Menkar	314 15.1	N 4 08.5
Menkent	148 08.4	S36 25.8
Miaplacidus	221 39.5	S69 46.0
Mirfak	308 40.4	N49 54.4
Nunki	75 59.1	S26 16.7
Peacock	53 20.1	S56 41.7
Pollux	243 28.0	N27 59.5
Procyon	245 00.0	N 5 11.4
Rasalhague	96 07.1	N12 33.3
Regulus	207 44.0	N11 54.1
Rigel	281 12.1	S 8 11.2
Rigil Kent.	139 52.9	S60 53.1
Sabik	102 13.3	S15 44.3
Schedar	349 40.5	N56 36.8
Shaula	96 22.8	S37 06.7
Sirius	258 33.8	S16 44.0
Spica	158 31.9	S11 13.6
Suhail	222 52.6	S43 28.9
Vega	80 39.6	N38 48.1
Zuben'ubi	137 06.2	S16 05.6

	SHA	Mer.Pass.
Venus	156 10.8	h m 9 46
Mars	89 15.6	14 13
Jupiter	288 00.1	0 58
Saturn	146 21.9	10 23

2012 NOVEMBER 17, 18, 19 (SAT., SUN., MON.)

UT	SUN GHA	SUN Dec	MOON GHA	v	MOON Dec	d	HP
d h	° ′	° ′	° ′	′	° ′	′	′
17 00	183 45.6	S19 01.5	137 41.5	4.8	S19 37.0	4.8	60.3
01	198 45.5	02.1	152 05.3	4.9	19 32.2	5.0	60.3
02	213 45.3	02.7	166 29.2	4.9	19 27.2	5.0	60.3
03	228 45.2	.. 03.3	180 53.1	5.0	19 22.2	5.2	60.3
04	243 45.1	03.9	195 17.1	5.2	19 17.0	5.4	60.2
05	258 45.0	04.5	209 41.3	5.2	19 11.6	5.4	60.2
06	273 44.8	S19 05.1	224 05.5	5.2	S19 06.2	5.6	60.2
S 07	288 44.7	05.7	238 29.7	5.4	19 00.6	5.7	60.1
A 08	303 44.6	06.3	252 54.1	5.5	18 54.9	5.8	60.1
T 09	318 44.4	.. 06.9	267 18.6	5.5	18 49.1	6.0	60.1
U 10	333 44.3	07.5	281 43.1	5.6	18 43.1	6.0	60.0
R 11	348 44.2	08.1	296 07.7	5.8	18 37.1	6.2	60.0
D 12	3 44.1	S19 08.7	310 32.5	5.8	S18 30.9	6.3	60.0
A 13	18 43.9	09.3	324 57.3	5.9	18 24.6	6.4	59.9
Y 14	33 43.8	09.9	339 22.2	6.0	18 18.2	6.6	59.9
15	48 43.7	.. 10.5	353 47.2	6.1	18 11.6	6.6	59.9
16	63 43.5	11.1	8 12.3	6.2	18 05.0	6.8	59.8
17	78 43.4	11.7	22 37.5	6.2	17 58.2	6.8	59.8
18	93 43.3	S19 12.3	37 02.7	6.4	S17 51.4	7.0	59.8
19	108 43.1	12.9	51 28.1	6.5	17 44.4	7.1	59.7
20	123 43.0	13.5	65 53.6	6.5	17 37.3	7.2	59.7
21	138 42.9	.. 14.1	80 19.1	6.7	17 30.1	7.3	59.7
22	153 42.8	14.7	94 44.8	6.7	17 22.8	7.4	59.6
23	168 42.6	15.3	109 10.5	6.9	17 15.4	7.5	59.6
18 00	183 42.5	S19 15.9	123 36.4	6.9	S17 07.9	7.5	59.6
01	198 42.4	16.5	138 02.3	7.1	17 00.4	7.7	59.5
02	213 42.2	17.1	152 28.4	7.1	16 52.7	7.8	59.5
03	228 42.1	.. 17.7	166 54.5	7.2	16 44.9	7.9	59.4
04	243 42.0	18.2	181 20.7	7.4	16 37.0	8.0	59.4
05	258 41.8	18.8	195 47.1	7.4	16 29.0	8.1	59.4
06	273 41.7	S19 19.4	210 13.5	7.5	S16 20.9	8.1	59.3
S 07	288 41.6	20.0	224 40.0	7.6	16 12.8	8.3	59.3
U 08	303 41.4	20.6	239 06.6	7.7	16 04.5	8.3	59.3
N 09	318 41.3	.. 21.2	253 33.3	7.8	15 56.2	8.5	59.2
D 10	333 41.1	21.8	268 00.1	7.9	15 47.7	8.5	59.2
A 11	348 41.0	22.4	282 27.0	8.0	15 39.2	8.6	59.2
Y 12	3 40.9	S19 23.0	296 54.0	8.1	S15 30.6	8.7	59.1
13	18 40.7	23.5	311 21.1	8.2	15 21.9	8.7	59.1
14	33 40.6	24.1	325 48.3	8.3	15 13.2	8.9	59.0
15	48 40.5	.. 24.7	340 15.6	8.4	15 04.3	8.9	59.0
16	63 40.3	25.3	354 43.0	8.5	14 55.4	9.0	59.0
17	78 40.2	25.9	9 10.5	8.6	14 46.4	9.1	58.9
18	93 40.0	S19 26.5	23 38.1	8.6	S14 37.3	9.1	58.9
19	108 39.9	27.0	38 05.7	8.8	14 28.2	9.2	58.9
20	123 39.8	27.6	52 33.5	8.9	14 19.0	9.3	58.8
21	138 39.6	.. 28.2	67 01.4	8.9	14 09.7	9.4	58.8
22	153 39.5	28.8	81 29.3	9.1	14 00.3	9.4	58.7
23	168 39.3	29.4	95 57.4	9.1	13 50.9	9.5	58.7
19 00	183 39.2	S19 29.9	110 25.5	9.2	S13 41.4	9.6	58.7
01	198 39.1	30.5	124 53.7	9.3	13 31.8	9.6	58.6
02	213 38.9	31.1	139 22.0	9.5	13 22.2	9.7	58.6
03	228 38.8	.. 31.7	153 50.5	9.5	13 12.5	9.7	58.6
04	243 38.6	32.3	168 19.0	9.5	13 02.8	9.9	58.5
05	258 38.5	32.8	182 47.5	9.7	12 52.9	9.8	58.5
06	273 38.3	S19 33.4	197 16.2	9.8	S12 43.1	10.0	58.4
M 07	288 38.2	34.0	211 45.0	9.9	12 33.1	9.9	58.4
O 08	303 38.1	34.6	226 13.9	9.9	12 23.2	10.1	58.4
N 09	318 37.9	.. 35.1	240 42.8	10.0	12 13.1	10.1	58.3
D 10	333 37.8	35.7	255 11.8	10.2	12 03.0	10.1	58.3
A 11	348 37.6	36.3	269 41.0	10.2	11 52.9	10.2	58.2
Y 12	3 37.5	S19 36.8	284 10.2	10.3	S11 42.7	10.3	58.2
13	18 37.3	37.4	298 39.5	10.3	11 32.4	10.3	58.2
14	33 37.2	38.0	313 08.8	10.5	11 22.1	10.3	58.1
15	48 37.0	.. 38.6	327 38.3	10.5	11 11.8	10.4	58.1
16	63 36.9	39.1	342 07.8	10.6	11 01.4	10.5	58.1
17	78 36.7	39.7	356 37.4	10.8	10 50.9	10.4	58.0
18	93 36.6	S19 40.3	11 07.2	10.7	S10 40.5	10.6	58.0
19	108 36.5	40.8	25 36.9	10.9	10 29.9	10.5	58.0
20	123 36.3	41.4	40 06.8	10.9	10 19.4	10.7	57.9
21	138 36.2	.. 42.0	54 36.7	11.1	10 08.7	10.6	57.9
22	153 36.0	42.5	69 06.8	11.1	9 58.1	10.7	57.8
23	168 35.9	43.1	83 36.9	11.1	S 9 47.4	10.7	57.8
	SD 16.2	d 0.6	SD 16.3		16.1		15.9

Twilight / Moonrise

Lat.	Naut.	Civil	Sunrise	Moonrise 17	18	19	20
°	h m	h m	h m	h m	h m	h m	h m
N 72	07 11	08 50	■	■	14 08	13 43	13 27
N 70	07 00	08 25	10 13	13 49	13 33	13 24	13 16
68	06 50	08 05	09 29	13 05	13 08	13 09	13 08
66	06 42	07 49	09 00	12 36	12 49	12 56	13 01
64	06 35	07 37	08 38	12 14	12 33	12 46	12 55
62	06 29	07 26	08 21	11 56	12 20	12 37	12 49
60	06 24	07 16	08 06	11 41	12 09	12 29	12 45
N 58	06 19	07 08	07 54	11 28	11 59	12 22	12 41
56	06 14	07 00	07 43	11 17	11 51	12 16	12 37
54	06 10	06 54	07 34	11 07	11 43	12 11	12 34
52	06 06	06 48	07 26	10 59	11 36	12 06	12 31
50	06 02	06 42	07 18	10 51	11 30	12 01	12 28
45	05 54	06 30	07 02	10 34	11 17	11 52	12 22
N 40	05 47	06 20	06 49	10 21	11 06	11 44	12 17
35	05 40	06 11	06 38	10 09	10 56	11 37	12 13
30	05 33	06 02	06 28	09 59	10 48	11 31	12 09
20	05 21	05 47	06 11	09 42	10 33	11 20	12 03
N 10	05 08	05 34	05 56	09 26	10 21	11 11	11 57
0	04 54	05 20	05 42	09 12	10 09	11 02	11 51
S 10	04 39	05 05	05 27	08 58	09 57	10 53	11 46
20	04 20	04 48	05 12	08 42	09 44	10 43	11 40
30	03 57	04 28	04 54	08 25	09 30	10 33	11 33
35	03 41	04 16	04 44	08 14	09 21	10 27	11 29
40	03 23	04 01	04 32	08 03	09 12	10 20	11 25
45	02 59	03 43	04 18	07 49	09 00	10 11	11 20
S 50	02 27	03 21	04 00	07 32	08 47	10 01	11 14
52	02 10	03 10	03 52	07 24	08 40	09 57	11 11
54	01 50	02 57	03 43	07 15	08 33	09 51	11 08
56	01 22	02 42	03 33	07 05	08 25	09 46	11 05
58	00 36	02 24	03 21	06 53	08 16	09 39	11 01
S 60	////	02 02	03 07	06 40	08 06	09 32	10 56

Sunset / Twilight / Moonset

Lat.	Sunset	Civil	Naut.	Moonset 17	18	19	20
°	h m	h m	h m	h m	h m	h m	h m
N 72	■	14 39	16 18	■	18 53	21 06	23 03
N 70	13 16	15 05	16 30	17 14	19 27	21 24	23 11
68	14 01	15 24	16 39	17 57	19 50	21 37	23 18
66	14 30	15 40	16 47	18 26	20 09	21 48	23 23
64	14 52	15 53	16 54	18 47	20 23	21 58	23 28
62	15 09	16 04	17 01	19 05	20 36	22 05	23 32
60	15 24	16 14	17 06	19 19	20 46	22 12	23 35
N 58	15 36	16 22	17 11	19 31	20 55	22 18	23 38
56	15 47	16 30	17 16	19 42	21 03	22 23	23 41
54	15 56	16 36	17 20	19 51	21 10	22 28	23 44
52	16 04	16 42	17 24	19 59	21 16	22 32	23 46
50	16 12	16 48	17 28	20 07	21 22	22 36	23 48
45	16 28	17 00	17 36	20 22	21 34	22 44	23 52
N 40	16 41	17 10	17 43	20 35	21 44	22 51	23 56
35	16 53	17 20	17 50	20 46	21 53	22 57	23 59
30	17 02	17 28	17 57	20 56	22 00	23 02	24 01
20	17 20	17 43	18 10	21 12	22 13	23 11	24 06
N 10	17 35	17 57	18 23	21 26	22 24	23 19	24 10
0	17 49	18 11	18 36	21 40	22 35	23 26	24 14
S 10	18 03	18 26	18 52	21 53	22 45	23 33	24 18
20	18 19	18 42	19 11	22 07	22 56	23 41	24 21
30	18 37	19 03	19 35	22 23	23 08	23 49	24 26
35	18 47	19 15	19 50	22 32	23 16	23 54	24 28
40	18 59	19 30	20 08	22 42	23 24	23 59	24 31
45	19 13	19 48	20 32	22 55	23 33	24 06	00 06
S 50	19 31	20 11	21 05	23 09	23 45	24 13	00 13
52	19 39	20 22	21 22	23 16	23 50	24 17	00 17
54	19 49	20 35	21 44	23 24	23 55	24 21	00 21
56	19 59	20 50	22 12	23 32	24 02	00 02	00 25
58	20 11	21 09	23 03	23 42	24 09	00 09	00 30
S 60	20 25	21 32	////	23 53	24 17	00 17	00 35

SUN / MOON

Day	Eqn. of Time 00h	12h	Mer. Pass.	MOON Mer. Pass. Upper	Lower	Age	Phase
d	m s	m s	h m	h m	h m	d	%
17	15 03	14 56	11 45	15 26	02 56	04	18
18	14 50	14 44	11 45	16 22	03 54	05	28
19	14 37	14 30	11 45	17 14	04 48	06	38

UT	ARIES GHA	VENUS −3.9 GHA	Dec	MARS +1.2 GHA	Dec	JUPITER −2.8 GHA	Dec	SATURN +0.6 GHA	Dec
20 00	59 24.8	213 16.2	S 8 54.1	147 00.5	S24 32.5	347 41.1	N21 33.0	205 33.4	S11 11.9
01	74 27.3	228 15.7	55.2	162 00.9	32.5	2 43.9	33.0	220 35.5	12.0
02	89 29.7	243 15.3	56.3	177 01.3	32.5	17 46.7	33.0	235 37.7	12.1
03	104 32.2	258 14.8	. . 57.4	192 01.7	. . 32.4	32 49.5	. . 32.9	250 39.9	. . 12.2
04	119 34.7	273 14.4	58.5	207 02.1	32.4	47 52.3	32.9	265 42.1	12.3
05	134 37.1	288 13.9	8 59.6	222 02.5	32.4	62 55.1	32.9	280 44.3	12.3
06	149 39.6	303 13.5	S 9 00.7	237 02.8	S24 32.4	77 57.9	N21 32.8	295 46.5	S11 12.4
07	164 42.1	318 13.0	01.8	252 03.2	32.3	93 00.7	32.8	310 48.7	12.5
T 08	179 44.5	333 12.6	02.9	267 03.6	32.3	108 03.5	32.7	325 50.9	12.6
U 09	194 47.0	348 12.1	. . 04.0	282 04.0	. . 32.3	123 06.3	. . 32.7	340 53.0	. . 12.7
E 10	209 49.4	3 11.7	05.1	297 04.4	32.3	138 09.1	32.7	355 55.2	12.8
S 11	224 51.9	18 11.2	06.2	312 04.7	32.2	153 12.0	32.6	10 57.4	12.9
D 12	239 54.4	33 10.8	S 9 07.4	327 05.1	S24 32.2	168 14.8	N21 32.6	25 59.6	S11 13.0
A 13	254 56.8	48 10.3	08.5	342 05.5	32.2	183 17.6	32.6	41 01.8	13.1
Y 14	269 59.3	63 09.9	09.6	357 05.9	32.1	198 20.4	32.5	56 04.0	13.2
15	285 01.8	78 09.4	. . 10.7	12 06.3	. . 32.1	213 23.2	. . 32.5	71 06.2	. . 13.3
16	300 04.2	93 09.0	11.8	27 06.6	32.1	228 26.0	32.5	86 08.4	13.4
17	315 06.7	108 08.5	12.9	42 07.0	32.0	243 28.8	32.4	101 10.5	13.4
18	330 09.2	123 08.1	S 9 14.0	57 07.4	S24 32.0	258 31.6	N21 32.4	116 12.7	S11 13.5
19	345 11.6	138 07.6	15.1	72 07.8	32.0	273 34.4	32.3	131 14.9	13.6
20	0 14.1	153 07.2	16.2	87 08.2	31.9	288 37.2	32.3	146 17.1	13.7
21	15 16.5	168 06.7	. . 17.3	102 08.5	. . 31.9	303 40.0	. . 32.3	161 19.3	. . 13.8
22	30 19.0	183 06.3	18.4	117 08.9	31.9	318 42.8	32.2	176 21.5	13.9
23	45 21.5	198 05.8	19.5	132 09.3	31.8	333 45.7	32.2	191 23.7	14.0
21 00	60 23.9	213 05.3	S 9 20.6	147 09.7	S24 31.8	348 48.5	N21 32.2	206 25.9	S11 14.1
01	75 26.4	228 04.9	21.7	162 10.1	31.8	3 51.3	32.1	221 28.0	14.2
02	90 28.9	243 04.4	22.8	177 10.4	31.7	18 54.1	32.1	236 30.2	14.3
03	105 31.3	258 04.0	. . 23.9	192 10.8	. . 31.7	33 56.9	. . 32.0	251 32.4	. . 14.4
04	120 33.8	273 03.5	25.0	207 11.2	31.7	48 59.7	32.0	266 34.6	14.4
05	135 36.3	288 03.1	26.1	222 11.6	31.6	64 02.5	32.0	281 36.8	14.5
06	150 38.7	303 02.6	S 9 27.2	237 12.0	S24 31.6	79 05.3	N21 31.9	296 39.0	S11 14.6
07	165 41.2	318 02.1	28.3	252 12.3	31.6	94 08.1	31.9	311 41.2	14.7
W 08	180 43.7	333 01.7	29.4	267 12.7	31.5	109 10.9	31.9	326 43.4	14.8
E 09	195 46.1	348 01.2	. . 30.5	282 13.1	. . 31.5	124 13.7	. . 31.8	341 45.6	. . 14.9
D 10	210 48.6	3 00.8	31.6	297 13.5	31.4	139 16.6	31.8	356 47.7	15.0
N 11	225 51.0	18 00.3	32.7	312 13.9	31.4	154 19.4	31.7	11 49.9	15.1
E 12	240 53.5	32 59.8	S 9 33.8	327 14.2	S24 31.4	169 22.2	N21 31.7	26 52.1	S11 15.2
S 13	255 56.0	47 59.4	34.9	342 14.6	31.3	184 25.0	31.7	41 54.3	15.3
D 14	270 58.4	62 58.9	36.0	357 15.0	31.3	199 27.8	31.6	56 56.5	15.4
A 15	286 00.9	77 58.5	. . 37.1	12 15.4	. . 31.2	214 30.6	. . 31.6	71 58.7	. . 15.5
Y 16	301 03.4	92 58.0	38.2	27 15.8	31.2	229 33.4	31.6	87 00.9	15.5
17	316 05.8	107 57.5	39.3	42 16.1	31.1	244 36.2	31.5	102 03.1	15.6
18	331 08.3	122 57.1	S 9 40.4	57 16.5	S24 31.1	259 39.0	N21 31.5	117 05.3	S11 15.7
19	346 10.8	137 56.6	41.5	72 16.9	31.1	274 41.9	31.4	132 07.4	15.8
20	1 13.2	152 56.1	42.6	87 17.3	31.0	289 44.7	31.4	147 09.6	15.9
21	16 15.7	167 55.7	. . 43.7	102 17.6	. . 31.0	304 47.5	. . 31.4	162 11.8	. . 16.0
22	31 18.1	182 55.2	44.8	117 18.0	30.9	319 50.3	31.3	177 14.0	16.1
23	46 20.6	197 54.7	45.8	132 18.4	30.9	334 53.1	31.3	192 16.2	16.2
22 00	61 23.1	212 54.3	S 9 46.9	147 18.8	S24 30.8	349 55.9	N21 31.3	207 18.4	S11 16.3
01	76 25.5	227 53.8	48.0	162 19.2	30.8	4 58.7	31.2	222 20.6	16.4
02	91 28.0	242 53.3	49.1	177 19.5	30.7	20 01.5	31.2	237 22.8	16.4
03	106 30.5	257 52.9	. . 50.2	192 19.9	. . 30.7	35 04.3	. . 31.1	252 25.0	. . 16.5
04	121 32.9	272 52.4	51.3	207 20.3	30.6	50 07.2	31.1	267 27.1	16.6
05	136 35.4	287 51.9	52.4	222 20.7	30.6	65 10.0	31.1	282 29.3	16.7
06	151 37.9	302 51.5	S 9 53.5	237 21.1	S24 30.6	80 12.8	N21 31.0	297 31.5	S11 16.8
07	166 40.3	317 51.0	54.6	252 21.4	30.5	95 15.6	31.0	312 33.7	16.9
T 08	181 42.8	332 50.5	55.7	267 21.8	30.5	110 18.4	31.0	327 35.9	17.0
H 09	196 45.3	347 50.1	. . 56.8	282 22.2	. . 30.4	125 21.2	. . 30.9	342 38.1	. . 17.1
U 10	211 47.7	2 49.6	57.9	297 22.6	30.4	140 24.0	30.9	357 40.3	17.2
R 11	226 50.2	17 49.1	9 59.0	312 22.9	30.3	155 26.9	30.8	12 42.5	17.3
S 12	241 52.6	32 48.7	S10 00.0	327 23.3	S24 30.2	170 29.7	N21 30.8	27 44.7	S11 17.4
D 13	256 55.1	47 48.2	01.1	342 23.7	30.2	185 32.5	30.8	42 46.9	17.4
A 14	271 57.6	62 47.7	02.2	357 24.1	30.1	200 35.3	30.7	57 49.0	17.5
Y 15	287 00.0	77 47.3	. . 03.3	12 24.4	. . 30.1	215 38.1	. . 30.7	72 51.2	. . 17.6
16	302 02.5	92 46.8	04.4	27 24.8	30.0	230 40.9	30.7	87 53.4	17.7
17	317 05.0	107 46.3	05.5	42 25.2	30.0	245 43.7	30.6	102 55.6	17.8
18	332 07.4	122 45.8	S10 06.6	57 25.6	S24 29.9	260 46.5	N21 30.6	117 57.8	S11 17.9
19	347 09.9	137 45.4	07.7	72 26.0	29.9	275 49.4	30.5	133 00.0	18.0
20	2 12.4	152 44.9	08.8	87 26.3	29.8	290 52.2	30.5	148 02.2	18.1
21	17 14.8	167 44.4	. . 09.8	102 26.7	. . 29.8	305 55.0	. . 30.5	163 04.4	. . 18.2
22	32 17.3	182 44.0	10.9	117 27.1	29.7	320 57.8	30.4	178 06.6	18.3
23	47 19.8	197 43.5	12.0	132 27.5	29.6	336 00.6	30.4	193 08.8	18.3
Mer. Pass.	h m 19 55.1	v −0.5	d 1.1	v 0.4	d 0.0	v 2.8	d 0.0	v 2.2	d 0.1

STARS

Name	SHA	Dec
Acamar	315 18.2	S40 15.2
Achernar	335 26.6	S57 10.4
Acrux	173 10.1	S63 10.0
Adhara	255 12.6	S28 59.4
Aldebaran	290 49.5	N16 32.1
Alioth	166 21.5	N55 53.2
Alkaid	152 59.6	N49 14.8
Al Na'ir	27 44.2	S46 54.0
Alnilam	275 46.5	S 1 11.7
Alphard	217 56.4	S 8 42.9
Alphecca	126 11.7	N26 40.4
Alpheratz	357 43.7	N29 10.0
Altair	62 08.8	N 8 54.4
Ankaa	353 15.8	S42 14.2
Antares	112 27.1	S26 27.5
Arcturus	145 56.4	N19 06.9
Atria	107 29.8	S69 02.9
Avior	234 17.9	S59 32.9
Bellatrix	278 32.1	N 6 21.6
Betelgeuse	271 01.4	N 7 24.5
Canopus	263 55.9	S52 42.1
Capella	280 34.6	N46 00.5
Deneb	49 31.9	N45 20.0
Denebola	182 34.2	N14 29.9
Diphda	348 56.1	S17 54.9
Dubhe	193 52.4	N61 40.5
Elnath	278 12.8	N28 37.0
Eltanin	90 46.8	N51 29.5
Enif	33 47.5	N 9 56.3
Fomalhaut	15 24.3	S29 33.2
Gacrux	172 01.7	S57 10.9
Gienah	175 52.9	S17 36.7
Hadar	148 49.0	S60 25.9
Hamal	328 00.9	N23 31.5
Kaus Aust.	83 44.7	S34 22.6
Kochab	137 21.2	N74 06.1
Markab	13 38.6	N15 16.7
Menkar	314 15.1	N 4 08.4
Menkent	148 08.4	S36 25.8
Miaplacidus	221 39.5	S69 46.0
Mirfak	308 40.4	N49 54.4
Nunki	75 59.1	S26 16.7
Peacock	53 20.1	S56 41.7
Pollux	243 28.0	N27 59.5
Procyon	244 59.9	N 5 11.4
Rasalhague	96 07.1	N12 33.3
Regulus	207 43.9	N11 54.1
Rigel	281 12.1	S 8 11.2
Rigil Kent.	139 52.9	S60 53.1
Sabik	102 13.3	S15 44.3
Schedar	349 40.6	N56 36.8
Shaula	96 22.8	S37 06.7
Sirius	258 33.8	S16 44.1
Spica	158 31.9	S11 13.6
Suhail	222 52.6	S43 29.0
Vega	80 39.6	N38 48.1
Zuben'ubi	137 06.2	S16 05.6

	SHA	Mer. Pass.
	° ′	h m
Venus	152 41.4	9 48
Mars	86 45.7	14 11
Jupiter	288 24.5	0 45
Saturn	146 01.9	10 13

UT	SUN GHA	SUN Dec	MOON GHA	v	Dec	d	HP
d h	° ′	° ′	° ′	′	° ′	′	′
20 00	183 35.7	S19 43.7	98 07.0	11.3	S 9 36.7	10.8	57.8
01	198 35.6	44.2	112 37.3	11.3	9 25.9	10.8	57.7
02	213 35.4	44.8	127 07.6	11.4	9 15.1	10.8	57.7
03	228 35.3	.. 45.4	141 38.0	11.5	9 04.3	10.9	57.7
04	243 35.1	45.9	156 08.5	11.5	8 53.4	10.8	57.6
05	258 35.0	46.5	170 39.0	11.7	8 42.6	11.0	57.6
06	273 34.8	S19 47.0	185 09.7	11.6	S 8 31.6	10.9	57.5
07	288 34.7	47.6	199 40.3	11.8	8 20.7	11.0	57.5
T 08	303 34.5	48.2	214 11.1	11.8	8 09.7	11.0	57.5
U 09	318 34.4	.. 48.7	228 41.9	11.9	7 58.7	11.0	57.4
E 10	333 34.2	49.3	243 12.8	12.0	7 47.7	11.1	57.4
S 11	348 34.0	49.8	257 43.8	12.0	7 36.6	11.1	57.4
D 12	3 33.9	S19 50.4	272 14.8	12.1	S 7 25.5	11.1	57.3
A 13	18 33.7	50.9	286 45.9	12.2	7 14.4	11.1	57.3
Y 14	33 33.6	51.5	301 17.1	12.2	7 03.3	11.2	57.3
15	48 33.4	.. 52.1	315 48.3	12.3	6 52.1	11.1	57.2
16	63 33.3	52.6	330 19.6	12.3	6 41.0	11.2	57.2
17	78 33.1	53.2	344 50.9	12.4	6 29.8	11.2	57.2
18	93 33.0	S19 53.7	359 22.3	12.5	S 6 18.6	11.2	57.1
19	108 32.8	54.3	13 53.8	12.5	6 07.4	11.3	57.1
20	123 32.7	54.8	28 25.3	12.6	5 56.1	11.2	57.1
21	138 32.5	.. 55.4	42 56.9	12.6	5 44.9	11.3	57.0
22	153 32.3	55.9	57 28.5	12.7	5 33.6	11.3	57.0
23	168 32.2	56.5	72 00.2	12.8	5 22.3	11.3	57.0
21 00	183 32.0	S19 57.0	86 32.0	12.8	S 5 11.0	11.3	56.9
01	198 31.9	57.6	101 03.8	12.8	4 59.7	11.3	56.9
02	213 31.7	58.1	115 35.6	12.9	4 48.4	11.3	56.9
03	228 31.5	.. 58.7	130 07.5	13.0	4 37.1	11.4	56.8
04	243 31.4	59.2	144 39.5	13.0	4 25.7	11.3	56.8
05	258 31.2	19 59.8	159 11.5	13.1	4 14.4	11.4	56.8
06	273 31.1	S20 00.3	173 43.6	13.1	S 4 03.0	11.3	56.7
W 07	288 30.9	00.8	188 15.7	13.1	3 51.7	11.4	56.7
E 08	303 30.8	01.4	202 47.8	13.2	3 40.3	11.4	56.7
D 09	318 30.6	.. 01.9	217 20.0	13.3	3 28.9	11.3	56.6
N 10	333 30.4	02.5	231 52.3	13.3	3 17.6	11.4	56.6
E 11	348 30.3	03.0	246 24.6	13.3	3 06.2	11.4	56.6
S 12	3 30.1	S20 03.6	260 56.9	13.4	S 2 54.8	11.3	56.5
D 13	18 29.9	04.1	275 29.3	13.4	2 43.5	11.4	56.5
A 14	33 29.8	04.6	290 01.7	13.4	2 32.1	11.4	56.5
Y 15	48 29.6	.. 05.2	304 34.1	13.5	2 20.7	11.4	56.4
16	63 29.5	05.7	319 06.6	13.6	2 09.3	11.3	56.4
17	78 29.3	06.3	333 39.2	13.6	1 58.0	11.4	56.4
18	93 29.1	S20 06.8	348 11.8	13.6	S 1 46.6	11.4	56.3
19	108 29.0	07.3	2 44.4	13.6	1 35.2	11.3	56.3
20	123 28.8	07.9	17 17.0	13.7	1 23.9	11.4	56.3
21	138 28.6	.. 08.4	31 49.7	13.7	1 12.5	11.3	56.3
22	153 28.5	08.9	46 22.4	13.8	1 01.2	11.4	56.2
23	168 28.3	09.5	60 55.2	13.8	0 49.8	11.3	56.2
22 00	183 28.1	S20 10.0	75 28.0	13.8	S 0 38.5	11.3	56.2
01	198 28.0	10.5	90 00.8	13.8	0 27.2	11.4	56.1
02	213 27.8	11.1	104 33.6	13.9	0 15.8	11.3	56.1
03	228 27.6	.. 11.6	119 06.5	13.9	S 0 04.5	11.3	56.1
04	243 27.5	12.1	133 39.4	13.9	N 0 06.8	11.2	56.1
05	258 27.3	12.7	148 12.3	14.0	0 18.0	11.3	56.0
06	273 27.1	S20 13.2	162 45.3	14.0	N 0 29.3	11.3	56.0
07	288 27.0	13.7	177 18.3	14.0	0 40.6	11.2	56.0
T 08	303 26.8	14.3	191 51.3	14.0	0 51.8	11.3	55.9
H 09	318 26.6	.. 14.8	206 24.3	14.1	1 03.1	11.2	55.9
U 10	333 26.5	15.3	220 57.4	14.1	1 14.3	11.2	55.9
R 11	348 26.3	15.8	235 30.5	14.1	1 25.5	11.2	55.9
S 12	3 26.1	S20 16.4	250 03.6	14.1	N 1 36.7	11.1	55.8
D 13	18 26.0	16.9	264 36.7	14.2	1 47.8	11.2	55.8
A 14	33 25.8	17.4	279 09.9	14.1	1 59.0	11.1	55.8
Y 15	48 25.6	.. 17.9	293 43.0	14.2	2 10.1	11.1	55.8
16	63 25.4	18.5	308 16.2	14.2	2 21.2	11.1	55.7
17	78 25.3	19.0	322 49.4	14.2	2 32.3	11.1	55.7
18	93 25.1	S20 19.5	337 22.6	14.3	N 2 43.4	11.1	55.7
19	108 24.9	20.0	351 55.9	14.2	2 54.5	11.0	55.6
20	123 24.8	20.5	6 29.1	14.3	3 05.5	11.0	55.6
21	138 24.6	.. 21.1	21 02.4	14.2	3 16.5	11.0	55.6
22	153 24.4	21.6	35 35.6	14.3	3 27.5	10.9	55.6
23	168 24.2	22.1	50 08.9	14.3	N 3 38.4	11.0	55.5
	SD 16.2	d 0.5	SD 15.6		15.4		15.2

Twilight / Sunrise / Moonrise

Lat.	Naut.	Civil	Sunrise	Moonrise 20	21	22	23
°	h m	h m	h m	h m	h m	h m	h m
N 72	07 22	09 05	■	13 27	13 13	13 01	12 48
N 70	07 09	08 36	10 39	13 16	13 09	13 03	12 57
68	06 58	08 15	09 44	13 08	13 06	13 05	13 04
66	06 50	07 58	09 11	13 01	13 04	13 06	13 09
64	06 42	07 44	08 48	12 55	13 02	13 08	13 14
62	06 35	07 32	08 29	12 49	13 00	13 09	13 19
60	06 29	07 22	08 14	12 45	12 58	13 10	13 22
N 58	06 24	07 14	08 01	12 41	12 56	13 11	13 26
56	06 19	07 06	07 49	12 37	12 55	13 12	13 29
54	06 15	06 59	07 39	12 34	12 54	13 13	13 31
52	06 10	06 52	07 31	12 31	12 53	13 13	13 34
50	06 07	06 46	07 23	12 28	12 52	13 14	13 36
45	05 58	06 34	07 06	12 22	12 49	13 15	13 41
N 40	05 50	06 23	06 52	12 17	12 48	13 16	13 45
35	05 42	06 13	06 41	12 13	12 46	13 17	13 49
30	05 36	06 05	06 30	12 09	12 45	13 18	13 52
20	05 22	05 49	06 13	12 03	12 42	13 20	13 57
N 10	05 09	05 35	05 57	11 57	12 40	13 21	14 02
0	04 55	05 20	05 42	11 51	12 38	13 23	14 07
S 10	04 39	05 05	05 28	11 46	12 36	13 24	14 11
20	04 20	04 48	05 12	11 40	12 34	13 26	14 16
30	03 55	04 27	04 53	11 33	12 31	13 27	14 22
35	03 39	04 14	04 42	11 29	12 30	13 28	14 25
40	03 20	03 59	04 30	11 25	12 28	13 29	14 29
45	02 56	03 40	04 16	11 20	12 26	13 31	14 33
S 50	02 22	03 17	03 57	11 14	12 24	13 32	14 39
52	02 04	03 05	03 48	11 11	12 23	13 33	14 41
54	01 41	02 52	03 39	11 08	12 22	13 34	14 44
56	01 10	02 36	03 28	11 05	12 21	13 35	14 47
58	////	02 17	03 15	11 01	12 19	13 36	14 50
S 60	////	01 52	03 01	10 56	12 18	13 37	14 54

Sunset / Twilight / Moonset

Lat.	Sunset	Civil	Naut.	Moonset 20	21	22	23
°	h m	h m	h m	h m	h m	h m	h m
N 72	■	14 26	16 09	23 03	24 52	00 52	02 38
N 70	12 52	14 55	16 22	23 11	24 53	00 53	02 32
68	13 47	15 16	16 33	23 18	24 54	00 54	02 27
66	14 20	15 33	16 42	23 23	24 54	00 54	02 23
64	14 44	15 47	16 49	23 28	24 55	00 54	02 19
62	15 02	15 59	16 56	23 32	24 55	00 55	02 15
60	15 18	16 09	17 02	23 35	24 56	00 56	02 14
N 58	15 31	16 18	17 07	23 38	24 56	00 56	02 11
56	15 42	16 26	17 12	23 41	24 56	00 56	02 09
54	15 52	16 33	17 17	23 44	24 57	00 57	02 07
52	16 01	16 39	17 21	23 46	24 57	00 57	02 06
50	16 09	16 45	17 25	23 48	24 57	00 57	02 04
45	16 26	16 58	17 34	23 52	24 58	00 58	02 01
N 40	16 39	17 09	17 42	23 56	24 58	00 58	01 58
35	16 51	17 18	17 49	23 59	24 58	00 58	01 56
30	17 01	17 27	17 56	24 01	00 01	00 58	01 54
20	17 19	17 43	18 10	24 06	00 06	00 59	01 50
N 10	17 35	17 57	18 23	24 10	00 10	00 59	01 47
0	17 50	18 12	18 37	24 14	00 14	00 59	01 44
S 10	18 04	18 27	18 53	24 18	00 18	01 00	01 41
20	18 21	18 44	19 13	24 21	00 21	01 00	01 38
30	18 39	19 06	19 38	24 26	00 26	01 00	01 34
35	18 50	19 19	19 53	24 28	00 28	01 01	01 32
40	19 03	19 34	20 13	24 31	00 31	01 01	01 30
45	19 17	19 52	20 37	00 06	00 35	01 01	01 27
S 50	19 36	20 16	21 12	00 13	00 39	01 01	01 24
52	19 45	20 28	21 30	00 17	00 40	01 02	01 22
54	19 54	20 42	21 54	00 21	00 42	01 02	01 20
56	20 05	20 58	22 26	00 25	00 44	01 02	01 19
58	20 18	21 18	////	00 30	00 47	01 02	01 17
S 60	20 33	21 43	////	00 35	00 49	01 02	01 15

SUN / MOON

Day	SUN Eqn. of Time 00h	12h	Mer. Pass.	MOON Mer. Pass. Upper	Lower	Age	Phase
d	m s	m s	h m	h m	h m	d	%
20	14 23	14 16	11 46	18 03	05 39	07	49
21	14 08	14 01	11 46	18 49	06 26	08	59
22	13 53	13 45	11 46	19 33	07 11	09	69

2012 NOVEMBER 23, 24, 25 (FRI., SAT., SUN.)

UT	ARIES	VENUS −3.9		MARS +1.2		JUPITER −2.8		SATURN +0.6		STARS		
	GHA	GHA	Dec	GHA	Dec	GHA	Dec	GHA	Dec	Name	SHA	Dec
23 **00**	62 22.2	212 43.0	S10 13.1	147 27.8	S24 29.6	351 03.4	N21 30.4	208 10.9	S11 18.4	Acamar	315 18.2	S40 15.2
01	77 24.7	227 42.5	14.2	162 28.2	29.5	6 06.3	30.3	223 13.1	18.5	Achernar	335 26.6	S57 10.4
02	92 27.1	242 42.1	15.3	177 28.6	29.5	21 09.1	30.3	238 15.3	18.6	Acrux	173 10.1	S63 10.0
03	107 29.6	257 41.6	.. 16.3	192 29.0	.. 29.4	36 11.9	.. 30.2	253 17.5	.. 18.7	Adhara	255 12.5	S28 59.4
04	122 32.1	272 41.1	17.4	207 29.3	29.4	51 14.7	30.2	268 19.7	18.8	Aldebaran	290 49.5	N16 32.1
05	137 34.5	287 40.6	18.5	222 29.7	29.3	66 17.5	30.2	283 21.9	18.9			
06	152 37.0	302 40.1	S10 19.6	237 30.1	S24 29.2	81 20.3	N21 30.1	298 24.1	S11 19.0	Alioth	166 21.4	N55 53.2
F 07	167 39.5	317 39.7	20.7	252 30.5	29.2	96 23.1	30.1	313 26.3	19.1	Alkaid	152 59.6	N49 14.8
R 08	182 41.9	332 39.2	21.8	267 30.8	29.1	111 26.0	30.0	328 28.5	19.2	Al Na'ir	27 44.3	S46 54.0
I 09	197 44.4	347 38.7	.. 22.8	282 31.2	.. 29.1	126 28.8	.. 30.0	343 30.7	.. 19.2	Alnilam	275 46.5	S 1 11.7
D 10	212 46.9	2 38.2	23.9	297 31.6	29.0	141 31.6	30.0	358 32.9	19.3	Alphard	217 56.4	S 8 42.9
11	227 49.3	17 37.8	25.0	312 32.0	28.9	156 34.4	29.9	13 35.0	19.4			
A 12	242 51.8	32 37.3	S10 26.1	327 32.3	S24 28.9	171 37.2	N21 29.9	28 37.2	S11 19.5	Alphecca	126 11.7	N26 40.4
Y 13	257 54.2	47 36.8	27.2	342 32.7	28.8	186 40.0	29.9	43 39.4	19.6	Alpheratz	357 43.7	N29 10.0
14	272 56.7	62 36.3	28.3	357 33.1	28.7	201 42.9	29.8	58 41.6	19.7	Altair	62 08.8	N 8 54.4
15	287 59.2	77 35.8	.. 29.3	12 33.5	.. 28.7	216 45.7	.. 29.8	73 43.8	.. 19.8	Ankaa	353 15.9	S42 14.2
16	303 01.6	92 35.4	30.4	27 33.9	28.6	231 48.5	29.7	88 46.0	19.9	Antares	112 27.1	S26 27.5
17	318 04.1	107 34.9	31.5	42 34.2	28.5	246 51.3	29.7	103 48.2	20.0			
18	333 06.6	122 34.4	S10 32.6	57 34.6	S24 28.5	261 54.1	N21 29.6	118 50.4	S11 20.0	Arcturus	145 56.4	N19 06.9
19	348 09.0	137 33.9	33.6	72 35.0	28.4	276 56.9	29.6	133 52.6	20.1	Atria	107 29.8	S69 02.9
20	3 11.5	152 33.4	34.7	87 35.4	28.3	291 59.8	29.6	148 54.8	20.2	Avior	234 17.8	S59 32.9
21	18 14.0	167 33.0	.. 35.8	102 35.7	.. 28.3	307 02.6	.. 29.5	163 57.0	.. 20.3	Bellatrix	278 32.1	N 6 21.6
22	33 16.4	182 32.5	36.9	117 36.1	28.2	322 05.4	29.5	178 59.1	20.4	Betelgeuse	271 01.4	N 7 24.5
23	48 18.9	197 32.0	38.0	132 36.5	28.1	337 08.2	29.5	194 01.3	20.5			
24 **00**	63 21.4	212 31.5	S10 39.0	147 36.9	S24 28.1	352 11.0	N21 29.4	209 03.5	S11 20.6	Canopus	263 55.8	S52 42.1
01	78 23.8	227 31.0	40.1	162 37.2	28.0	7 13.8	29.4	224 05.7	20.7	Capella	280 34.6	N46 00.5
02	93 26.3	242 30.5	41.2	177 37.6	27.9	22 16.7	29.4	239 07.9	20.8	Deneb	49 31.9	N45 20.0
03	108 28.7	257 30.0	.. 42.3	192 38.0	.. 27.9	37 19.5	.. 29.3	254 10.1	.. 20.9	Denebola	182 34.2	N14 29.9
04	123 31.2	272 29.6	43.3	207 38.4	27.8	52 22.3	29.3	269 12.3	20.9	Diphda	348 56.1	S17 54.9
05	138 33.7	287 29.1	44.4	222 38.7	27.7	67 25.1	29.2	284 14.5	21.0			
06	153 36.1	302 28.6	S10 45.5	237 39.1	S24 27.6	82 27.9	N21 29.2	299 16.7	S11 21.1	Dubhe	193 52.4	N61 40.5
S 07	168 38.6	317 28.1	46.6	252 39.5	27.6	97 30.7	29.2	314 18.9	21.2	Elnath	278 12.7	N28 37.0
A 08	183 41.1	332 27.6	47.6	267 39.9	27.5	112 33.6	29.1	329 21.1	21.3	Eltanin	90 46.8	N51 29.5
T 09	198 43.5	347 27.1	.. 48.7	282 40.2	.. 27.4	127 36.4	.. 29.1	344 23.3	.. 21.4	Enif	33 47.6	N 9 56.3
U 10	213 46.0	2 26.6	49.8	297 40.6	27.4	142 39.2	29.0	359 25.4	21.5	Fomalhaut	15 24.4	S29 33.2
R 11	228 48.5	17 26.2	50.9	312 41.0	27.3	157 42.0	29.0	14 27.6	21.6			
D 12	243 50.9	32 25.7	S10 52.0	327 41.3	S24 27.2	172 44.8	N21 29.0	29 29.8	S11 21.7	Gacrux	172 01.6	S57 10.9
A 13	258 53.4	47 25.2	53.0	342 41.7	27.1	187 47.7	28.9	44 32.0	21.7	Gienah	175 52.9	S17 36.7
Y 14	273 55.9	62 24.7	54.1	357 42.1	27.1	202 50.5	28.9	59 34.2	21.8	Hadar	148 49.0	S60 25.9
15	288 58.3	77 24.2	.. 55.1	12 42.5	.. 27.0	217 53.3	.. 28.9	74 36.4	.. 21.9	Hamal	328 00.9	N23 31.5
16	304 00.8	92 23.7	56.2	27 42.8	26.9	232 56.1	28.8	89 38.6	22.0	Kaus Aust.	83 44.7	S34 22.6
17	319 03.2	107 23.2	57.3	42 43.2	26.8	247 58.9	28.8	104 40.8	22.1			
18	334 05.7	122 22.7	S10 58.3	57 43.6	S24 26.8	263 01.7	N21 28.7	119 43.0	S11 22.2	Kochab	137 21.2	N74 06.1
19	349 08.2	137 22.2	10 59.4	72 44.0	26.7	278 04.6	28.7	134 45.2	22.3	Markab	13 38.6	N15 16.7
20	4 10.6	152 21.7	11 00.5	87 44.3	26.6	293 07.4	28.7	149 47.4	22.4	Menkar	314 15.1	N 4 08.4
21	19 13.1	167 21.3	.. 01.6	102 44.7	.. 26.5	308 10.2	.. 28.6	164 49.6	.. 22.5	Menkent	148 08.4	S36 25.8
22	34 15.6	182 20.8	02.6	117 45.1	26.4	323 13.0	28.6	179 51.8	22.5	Miaplacidus	221 39.4	S69 46.0
23	49 18.0	197 20.3	03.7	132 45.5	26.4	338 15.8	28.5	194 54.0	22.6			
25 **00**	64 20.5	212 19.8	S11 04.8	147 45.8	S24 26.3	353 18.7	N21 28.5	209 56.1	S11 22.7	Mirfak	308 40.4	N49 54.5
01	79 23.0	227 19.3	05.8	162 46.2	26.2	8 21.5	28.5	224 58.3	22.8	Nunki	75 59.1	S26 16.7
02	94 25.4	242 18.8	06.9	177 46.6	26.1	23 24.3	28.4	240 00.5	22.9	Peacock	53 20.2	S56 41.7
03	109 27.9	257 18.3	.. 08.0	192 47.0	.. 26.0	38 27.1	.. 28.4	255 02.7	.. 23.0	Pollux	243 28.0	N27 59.5
04	124 30.3	272 17.8	09.0	207 47.3	26.0	53 29.9	28.4	270 04.9	23.1	Procyon	244 59.9	N 5 11.4
05	139 32.8	287 17.3	10.1	222 47.7	25.9	68 32.8	28.3	285 07.1	23.2			
06	154 35.3	302 16.8	S11 11.1	237 48.1	S24 25.8	83 35.6	N21 28.3	300 09.3	S11 23.2	Rasalhague	96 07.1	N12 33.3
07	169 37.7	317 16.3	12.2	252 48.4	25.7	98 38.4	28.2	315 11.5	23.3	Regulus	207 43.9	N11 54.1
08	184 40.2	332 15.8	13.3	267 48.8	25.6	113 41.2	28.2	330 13.7	23.4	Rigel	281 12.1	S 8 11.3
S 09	199 42.7	347 15.3	.. 14.3	282 49.2	.. 25.5	128 44.0	.. 28.2	345 15.9	.. 23.5	Rigil Kent.	139 52.9	S60 53.1
U 10	214 45.1	2 14.8	15.4	297 49.6	25.4	143 46.9	28.1	0 18.1	23.6	Sabik	102 13.3	S15 44.3
N 11	229 47.6	17 14.3	16.5	312 49.9	25.4	158 49.7	28.1	15 20.3	23.7			
D 12	244 50.1	32 13.8	S11 17.5	327 50.3	S24 25.3	173 52.5	N21 28.0	30 22.5	S11 23.8	Schedar	349 40.6	N56 36.8
A 13	259 52.5	47 13.3	18.6	342 50.7	25.2	188 55.3	28.0	45 24.7	23.9	Shaula	96 22.9	S37 06.7
Y 14	274 55.0	62 12.8	19.6	357 51.1	25.1	203 58.1	27.9	60 26.9	24.0	Sirius	258 33.8	S16 44.1
15	289 57.5	77 12.3	.. 20.7	12 51.4	.. 25.0	219 01.0	.. 27.9	75 29.0	.. 24.0	Spica	158 31.9	S11 13.6
16	304 59.9	92 11.8	21.8	27 51.8	24.9	234 03.8	27.9	90 31.2	24.1	Suhail	222 52.6	S43 29.0
17	320 02.4	107 11.3	22.8	42 52.2	24.8	249 06.6	27.8	105 33.4	24.2			
18	335 04.8	122 10.8	S11 23.9	57 52.5	S24 24.8	264 09.4	N21 27.8	120 35.6	S11 24.3	Vega	80 39.6	N38 48.0
19	350 07.3	137 10.3	24.9	72 52.9	24.7	279 12.2	27.8	135 37.8	24.4	Zuben'ubi	137 06.2	S16 05.6
20	5 09.8	152 09.8	26.0	87 53.3	24.6	294 15.1	27.7	150 40.0	24.5		SHA	Mer.Pass.
21	20 12.2	167 09.3	.. 27.1	102 53.7	.. 24.5	309 17.9	.. 27.7	165 42.2	.. 24.6		° ′	h m
22	35 14.7	182 08.8	28.1	117 54.0	24.4	324 20.7	27.6	180 44.4	24.7	Venus	149 10.1	9 50
23	50 17.2	197 08.3	29.2	132 54.4	24.3	339 23.5	27.6	195 46.6	24.7	Mars	84 15.5	14 09
Mer.Pass. 19 43.3		v −0.5	d 1.1	v 0.4	d 0.1	v 2.8	d 0.0	v 2.2	d 0.1	Jupiter	288 49.7	0 31
										Saturn	145 42.2	10 02

UT	SUN GHA	SUN Dec	MOON GHA	v	Dec	d	HP
d h	° ′	° ′	° ′	′	° ′	′	′
23 00	183 24.1	S20 22.6	64 42.2	14.3	N 3 49.4	10.9	55.5
01	198 23.9	23.1	79 15.5	14.4	4 00.3	10.9	55.5
02	213 23.7	23.7	93 48.9	14.3	4 11.2	10.8	55.5
03	228 23.5 · ·	24.2	108 22.2	14.3	4 22.0	10.9	55.5
04	243 23.4	24.7	122 55.5	14.4	4 32.9	10.8	55.4
05	258 23.2	25.2	137 28.9	14.3	4 43.7	10.7	55.4
06	273 23.0	S20 25.7	152 02.2	14.4	N 4 54.4	10.8	55.4
07	288 22.8	26.2	166 35.6	14.4	5 05.2	10.7	55.4
F 08	303 22.7	26.7	181 09.0	14.3	5 15.9	10.7	55.3
R 09	318 22.5 · ·	27.3	195 42.3	14.4	5 26.6	10.7	55.3
I 10	333 22.3	27.8	210 15.7	14.4	5 37.3	10.6	55.3
11	348 22.1	28.3	224 49.1	14.4	5 47.9	10.6	55.3
D 12	3 22.0	S20 28.8	239 22.5	14.4	N 5 58.5	10.5	55.3
A 13	18 21.8	29.3	253 55.9	14.3	6 09.0	10.6	55.2
Y 14	33 21.6	29.8	268 29.2	14.4	6 19.6	10.4	55.2
15	48 21.4 · ·	30.3	283 02.6	14.4	6 30.0	10.5	55.2
16	63 21.2	30.8	297 36.0	14.4	6 40.5	10.4	55.2
17	78 21.1	31.3	312 09.4	14.4	6 50.9	10.4	55.1
18	93 20.9	S20 31.8	326 42.8	14.3	N 7 01.3	10.4	55.1
19	108 20.7	32.3	341 16.1	14.4	7 11.7	10.3	55.1
20	123 20.5	32.9	355 49.5	14.4	7 22.0	10.2	55.1
21	138 20.3 · ·	33.4	10 22.9	14.3	7 32.2	10.3	55.1
22	153 20.2	33.9	24 56.2	14.4	7 42.5	10.2	55.0
23	168 20.0	34.4	39 29.6	14.4	7 52.7	10.1	55.0
24 00	183 19.8	S20 34.9	54 03.0	14.3	N 8 02.8	10.1	55.0
01	198 19.6	35.4	68 36.3	14.4	8 12.9	10.1	55.0
02	213 19.4	35.9	83 09.7	14.3	8 23.0	10.0	55.0
03	228 19.3 · ·	36.4	97 43.0	14.3	8 33.0	10.0	54.9
04	243 19.1	36.9	112 16.3	14.3	8 43.0	10.0	54.9
05	258 18.9	37.4	126 49.6	14.3	8 53.0	9.9	54.9
06	273 18.7	S20 37.9	141 22.9	14.3	N 9 02.9	9.9	54.9
07	288 18.5	38.4	155 56.2	14.3	9 12.8	9.8	54.9
S 08	303 18.3	38.9	170 29.5	14.3	9 22.6	9.7	54.9
A 09	318 18.2 · ·	39.4	185 02.8	14.3	9 32.3	9.8	54.8
T 10	333 18.0	39.9	199 36.1	14.2	9 42.1	9.6	54.8
U 11	348 17.8	40.4	214 09.3	14.3	9 51.7	9.7	54.8
R 12	3 17.6	S20 40.8	228 42.6	14.2	N10 01.4	9.6	54.8
D 13	18 17.4	41.3	243 15.8	14.2	10 11.0	9.5	54.8
A 14	33 17.2	41.8	257 49.0	14.2	10 20.5	9.5	54.8
Y 15	48 17.0 · ·	42.3	272 22.2	14.2	10 30.0	9.4	54.7
16	63 16.9	42.8	286 55.4	14.1	10 39.4	9.4	54.7
17	78 16.7	43.3	301 28.5	14.2	10 48.8	9.3	54.7
18	93 16.5	S20 43.8	316 01.7	14.1	N10 58.1	9.3	54.7
19	108 16.3	44.3	330 34.8	14.1	11 07.4	9.3	54.7
20	123 16.1	44.8	345 07.9	14.1	11 16.7	9.1	54.7
21	138 15.9 · ·	45.3	359 41.0	14.1	11 25.8	9.2	54.6
22	153 15.7	45.8	14 14.1	14.1	11 35.0	9.0	54.6
23	168 15.5	46.2	28 47.2	14.0	11 44.0	9.1	54.6
25 00	183 15.3	S20 46.7	43 20.2	14.0	N11 53.1	8.9	54.6
01	198 15.2	47.2	57 53.2	14.0	12 02.0	8.9	54.6
02	213 15.0	47.7	72 26.2	14.0	12 10.9	8.9	54.6
03	228 14.8 · ·	48.2	86 59.2	14.0	12 19.8	8.8	54.5
04	243 14.6	48.7	101 32.2	13.9	12 28.6	8.7	54.5
05	258 14.4	49.2	116 05.1	13.9	12 37.3	8.7	54.5
06	273 14.2	S20 49.6	130 38.0	13.9	N12 46.0	8.6	54.5
07	288 14.0	50.1	145 10.9	13.9	12 54.6	8.6	54.5
S 08	303 13.8	50.6	159 43.8	13.9	13 03.2	8.5	54.5
U 09	318 13.6 · ·	51.1	174 16.7	13.8	13 11.7	8.5	54.5
N 10	333 13.4	51.6	188 49.5	13.8	13 20.2	8.4	54.5
D 11	348 13.2	52.0	203 22.3	13.8	13 28.6	8.3	54.4
A 12	3 13.1	S20 52.5	217 55.1	13.8	N13 36.9	8.2	54.4
Y 13	18 12.9	53.0	232 27.9	13.7	13 45.1	8.2	54.4
14	33 12.7	53.5	247 00.6	13.7	13 53.3	8.2	54.4
15	48 12.5 · ·	53.9	261 33.3	13.7	14 01.5	8.1	54.4
16	63 12.3	54.4	276 06.0	13.7	14 09.6	8.0	54.4
17	78 12.1	54.9	290 38.7	13.6	14 17.6	7.9	54.4
18	93 11.9	S20 55.4	305 11.3	13.6	N14 25.5	7.9	54.4
19	108 11.7	55.8	319 43.9	13.6	14 33.4	7.8	54.4
20	123 11.5	56.3	334 16.5	13.6	14 41.2	7.8	54.3
21	138 11.3 · ·	56.8	348 49.1	13.5	14 49.0	7.6	54.3
22	153 11.1	57.3	3 21.6	13.5	14 56.6	7.7	54.3
23	168 10.9	57.7	17 54.1	13.5	N15 04.3	7.5	54.3
	SD 16.2 d 0.5		SD 15.1		14.9		14.8

Lat.	Twilight Naut.	Twilight Civil	Sunrise	Moonrise 23	Moonrise 24	Moonrise 25	Moonrise 26
°	h m	h m	h m	h m	h m	h m	h m
N 72	07 31	09 19	■	12 48	12 35	12 17	11 49
N 70	07 17	08 47	11 17	12 57	12 50	12 43	12 34
68	07 06	08 24	09 59	13 04	13 03	13 02	13 04
66	06 57	08 06	09 23	13 09	13 13	13 18	13 26
64	06 48	07 51	08 57	13 14	13 22	13 31	13 44
62	06 41	07 39	08 37	13 19	13 29	13 42	13 58
60	06 35	07 28	08 21	13 22	13 36	13 51	14 11
N 58	06 29	07 19	08 07	13 26	13 41	14 00	14 21
56	06 24	07 11	07 55	13 29	13 47	14 07	14 31
54	06 19	07 03	07 45	13 31	13 51	14 13	14 39
52	06 15	06 57	07 36	13 34	13 55	14 19	14 47
50	06 10	06 51	07 27	13 36	13 59	14 24	14 53
45	06 01	06 37	07 10	13 41	14 07	14 36	15 08
N 40	05 53	06 26	06 56	13 45	14 14	14 46	15 20
35	05 45	06 16	06 43	13 49	14 20	14 54	15 30
30	05 38	06 07	06 33	13 52	14 26	15 01	15 39
20	05 24	05 51	06 14	13 57	14 35	15 14	15 54
N 10	05 10	05 36	05 58	14 02	14 43	15 25	16 08
0	04 55	05 21	05 43	14 07	14 51	15 35	16 21
S 10	04 39	05 05	05 28	14 11	14 58	15 46	16 34
20	04 19	04 47	05 11	14 16	15 07	15 57	16 47
30	03 54	04 26	04 52	14 22	15 16	16 10	17 03
35	03 37	04 12	04 41	14 25	15 22	16 17	17 13
40	03 18	03 57	04 28	14 29	15 28	16 26	17 23
45	02 52	03 38	04 13	14 33	15 35	16 36	17 36
S 50	02 17	03 13	03 54	14 39	15 44	16 48	17 51
52	01 57	03 01	03 45	14 41	15 48	16 54	17 58
54	01 33	02 47	03 35	14 44	15 53	17 00	18 06
56	00 56	02 30	03 23	14 47	15 58	17 07	18 15
58	////	02 09	03 10	14 50	16 03	17 15	18 25
S 60	////	01 43	02 55	14 54	16 10	17 24	18 36

Lat.	Sunset	Twilight Civil	Twilight Naut.	Moonset 23	Moonset 24	Moonset 25	Moonset 26
°	h m	h m	h m	h m	h m	h m	h m
N 72	■	14 14	16 01	02 38	04 24	06 14	08 16
N 70	12 16	14 45	16 15	02 32	04 10	05 49	07 32
68	13 34	15 09	16 27	02 27	03 59	05 31	07 03
66	14 10	15 27	16 36	02 23	03 50	05 16	06 42
64	14 36	15 41	16 45	02 19	03 42	05 04	06 25
62	14 56	15 54	16 52	02 16	03 36	04 54	06 11
60	15 13	16 05	16 58	02 14	03 30	04 45	05 59
N 58	15 26	16 14	17 04	02 11	03 25	04 38	05 49
56	15 38	16 22	17 09	02 09	03 21	04 31	05 40
54	15 48	16 30	17 14	02 07	03 17	04 25	05 32
52	15 58	16 36	17 19	02 06	03 13	04 20	05 25
50	16 06	16 43	17 23	02 04	03 10	04 15	05 18
45	16 23	16 56	17 32	02 01	03 03	04 05	05 05
N 40	16 38	17 07	17 41	01 58	02 57	03 56	04 54
35	16 50	17 17	17 48	01 56	02 53	03 49	04 44
30	17 01	17 26	17 56	01 54	02 48	03 42	04 36
20	17 19	17 43	18 10	01 50	02 41	03 31	04 20
N 10	17 35	17 58	18 23	01 47	02 34	03 21	04 09
0	17 50	18 13	18 38	01 44	02 28	03 12	03 57
S 10	18 06	18 28	18 55	01 41	02 22	03 03	03 45
20	18 22	18 46	19 15	01 38	02 15	02 53	03 33
30	18 42	19 08	19 40	01 34	02 08	02 42	03 19
35	18 53	19 22	19 57	01 32	02 03	02 36	03 11
40	19 06	19 37	20 17	01 30	01 58	02 29	03 01
45	19 21	19 57	20 43	01 27	01 53	02 20	02 50
S 50	19 40	20 22	21 19	01 24	01 46	02 10	02 37
52	19 49	20 34	21 38	01 22	01 43	02 06	02 31
54	20 00	20 48	22 04	01 20	01 40	02 01	02 24
56	20 11	21 05	22 42	01 19	01 36	01 55	02 17
58	20 25	21 26	////	01 17	01 32	01 48	02 08
S 60	20 41	21 54	////	01 14	01 27	01 41	01 59

	SUN			MOON			
Day	Eqn. of Time 00ʰ	Eqn. of Time 12ʰ	Mer. Pass.	Mer. Pass. Upper	Mer. Pass. Lower	Age	Phase
d	m s	m s	h m	h m	h m	d	%
23	13 37	13 28	11 47	20 17	07 55	10	78
24	13 20	13 11	11 47	21 01	08 39	11	85
25	13 02	12 53	11 47	21 46	09 24	12	92

230

2012 NOVEMBER 26, 27, 28 (MON., TUES., WED.)

UT	ARIES	VENUS −3.9		MARS +1.2		JUPITER −2.8		SATURN +0.7		STARS		
	GHA	GHA	Dec	GHA	Dec	GHA	Dec	GHA	Dec	Name	SHA	Dec
d h	° ′	° ′	° ′	° ′	° ′	° ′	° ′	° ′	° ′		° ′	° ′
26 00	65 19.6	212 07.8	S11 30.2	147 54.8	S24 24.2	354 26.4	N21 27.6	210 48.8	S11 24.8	Acamar	315 18.2	S40 15.3
01	80 22.1	227 07.3	31.3	162 55.2	24.1	9 29.2	27.5	225 51.0	24.9	Achernar	335 26.6	S57 10.4
02	95 24.6	242 06.8	32.3	177 55.5	24.0	24 32.0	27.5	240 53.2	25.0	Acrux	173 10.0	S63 10.0
03	110 27.0	257 06.3 . .	33.4	192 55.9 . .	23.9	39 34.8 . .	27.4	255 55.4 . .	25.1	Adhara	255 12.5	S28 59.4
04	125 29.5	272 05.8	34.5	207 56.3	23.8	54 37.6	27.4	270 57.6	25.2	Aldebaran	290 49.5	N16 32.1
05	140 32.0	287 05.3	35.5	222 56.6	23.7	69 40.5	27.4	285 59.8	25.3			
06	155 34.4	302 04.8	S11 36.6	237 57.0	S24 23.7	84 43.3	N21 27.3	301 02.0	S11 25.4	Alioth	166 21.4	N55 53.1
07	170 36.9	317 04.3	37.6	252 57.4	23.6	99 46.1	27.3	316 04.2	25.4	Alkaid	152 59.6	N49 14.8
08	185 39.3	332 03.8	38.7	267 57.8	23.5	114 48.9	27.3	331 06.3	25.5	Al Na'ir	27 44.3	S46 54.0
M 09	200 41.8	347 03.3 . .	39.7	282 58.1 . .	23.4	129 51.8 . .	27.2	346 08.5 . .	25.6	Alnilam	275 46.4	S 1 11.7
O 10	215 44.3	2 02.7	40.8	297 58.5	23.3	144 54.6	27.2	1 10.7	25.7	Alphard	217 56.4	S 8 42.9
N 11	230 46.7	17 02.2	41.8	312 58.9	23.2	159 57.4	27.1	16 12.9	25.8			
D 12	245 49.2	32 01.7	S11 42.9	327 59.2	S24 23.1	175 00.2	N21 27.1	31 15.1	S11 25.9	Alphecca	126 11.7	N26 40.3
A 13	260 51.7	47 01.2	43.9	342 59.6	23.0	190 03.0	27.1	46 17.3	26.0	Alpheratz	357 43.7	N29 10.0
Y 14	275 54.1	62 00.7	45.0	358 00.0	22.9	205 05.9	27.0	61 19.5	26.1	Altair	62 08.8	N 8 54.4
15	290 56.6	77 00.2 . .	46.0	13 00.4 . .	22.8	220 08.7 . .	27.0	76 21.7 . .	26.1	Ankaa	353 15.9	S42 14.2
16	305 59.1	91 59.7	47.1	28 00.7	22.7	235 11.5	26.9	91 23.9	26.2	Antares	112 27.1	S26 27.5
17	321 01.5	106 59.2	48.1	43 01.1	22.6	250 14.3	26.9	106 26.1	26.3			
18	336 04.0	121 58.7	S11 49.2	58 01.5	S24 22.5	265 17.2	N21 26.9	121 28.3	S11 26.4	Arcturus	145 56.4	N19 06.9
19	351 06.4	136 58.2	50.2	73 01.9	22.4	280 20.0	26.8	136 30.5	26.5	Atria	107 29.8	S69 02.9
20	6 08.9	151 57.6	51.3	88 02.2	22.3	295 22.8	26.8	151 32.7	26.6	Avior	234 17.8	S59 32.9
21	21 11.4	166 57.1 . .	52.3	103 02.6 . .	22.2	310 25.6 . .	26.7	166 34.9 . .	26.7	Bellatrix	278 32.1	N 6 21.6
22	36 13.8	181 56.6	53.4	118 03.0	22.1	325 28.4	26.7	181 37.1	26.8	Betelgeuse	271 01.4	N 7 24.5
23	51 16.3	196 56.1	54.4	133 03.3	22.0	340 31.3	26.7	196 39.3	26.8			
27 00	66 18.8	211 55.6	S11 55.5	148 03.7	S24 21.9	355 34.1	N21 26.6	211 41.5	S11 26.9	Canopus	263 55.8	S52 42.1
01	81 21.2	226 55.1	56.5	163 04.1	21.8	10 36.9	26.6	226 43.7	27.0	Capella	280 34.5	N46 00.5
02	96 23.7	241 54.6	57.6	178 04.5	21.7	25 39.7	26.5	241 45.9	27.1	Deneb	49 31.9	N45 20.0
03	111 26.2	256 54.0 . .	58.6	193 04.8 . .	21.6	40 42.6 . .	26.5	256 48.1 . .	27.2	Denebola	182 34.2	N14 29.9
04	126 28.6	271 53.5	11 59.6	208 05.2	21.5	55 45.4	26.5	271 50.3	27.3	Diphda	348 56.1	S17 54.9
05	141 31.1	286 53.0	12 00.7	223 05.6	21.4	70 48.2	26.4	286 52.5	27.4			
06	156 33.6	301 52.5	S12 01.7	238 05.9	S24 21.2	85 51.0	N21 26.4	301 54.6	S11 27.5	Dubhe	193 52.3	N61 40.5
07	171 36.0	316 52.0	02.8	253 06.3	21.1	100 53.9	26.3	316 56.8	27.5	Elnath	278 12.7	N28 37.0
08	186 38.5	331 51.5	03.8	268 06.7	21.0	115 56.7	26.3	331 59.0	27.6	Eltanin	90 46.8	N51 29.5
T 09	201 40.9	346 50.9 . .	04.9	283 07.1 . .	20.9	130 59.5 . .	26.3	347 01.2 . .	27.7	Enif	33 47.6	N 9 56.3
U 10	216 43.4	1 50.4	05.9	298 07.4	20.8	146 02.3	26.2	2 03.4	27.8	Fomalhaut	15 24.4	S29 33.2
E 11	231 45.9	16 49.9	06.9	313 07.8	20.7	161 05.1	26.2	17 05.6	27.9			
S 12	246 48.3	31 49.4	S12 08.0	328 08.2	S24 20.6	176 08.0	N21 26.1	32 07.8	S11 28.0	Gacrux	172 01.6	S57 10.9
D 13	261 50.8	46 48.9	09.0	343 08.5	20.5	191 10.8	26.1	47 10.0	28.1	Gienah	175 52.9	S17 36.7
A 14	276 53.3	61 48.3	10.1	358 08.9	20.4	206 13.6	26.1	62 12.2	28.2	Hadar	148 49.0	S60 25.9
Y 15	291 55.7	76 47.8 . .	11.1	13 09.3 . .	20.3	221 16.4 . .	26.0	77 14.4 . .	28.2	Hamal	328 00.9	N23 31.5
16	306 58.2	91 47.3	12.1	28 09.6	20.2	236 19.3	26.0	92 16.6	28.3	Kaus Aust.	83 44.7	S34 22.6
17	322 00.7	106 46.8	13.2	43 10.0	20.1	251 22.1	25.9	107 18.8	28.4			
18	337 03.1	121 46.3	S12 14.2	58 10.4	S24 19.9	266 24.9	N21 25.9	122 21.0	S11 28.5	Kochab	137 21.2	N74 06.0
19	352 05.6	136 45.7	15.3	73 10.8	19.8	281 27.7	25.9	137 23.2	28.6	Markab	13 38.7	N15 16.7
20	7 08.1	151 45.2	16.3	88 11.1	19.7	296 30.6	25.8	152 25.4	28.7	Menkar	314 15.1	N 4 08.4
21	22 10.5	166 44.7 . .	17.3	103 11.5 . .	19.6	311 33.4 . .	25.8	167 27.6 . .	28.8	Menkent	148 08.4	S36 25.8
22	37 13.0	181 44.2	18.4	118 11.9	19.5	326 36.2	25.7	182 29.8	28.8	Miaplacidus	221 39.4	S69 46.0
23	52 15.4	196 43.6	19.4	133 12.2	19.4	341 39.0	25.7	197 32.0	28.9			
28 00	67 17.9	211 43.1	S12 20.4	148 12.6	S24 19.3	356 41.9	N21 25.7	212 34.2	S11 29.0	Mirfak	308 40.4	N49 54.5
01	82 20.4	226 42.6	21.5	163 13.0	19.1	11 44.7	25.6	227 36.4	29.1	Nunki	75 59.1	S26 16.7
02	97 22.8	241 42.1	22.5	178 13.4	19.0	26 47.5	25.6	242 38.6	29.2	Peacock	53 20.2	S56 41.6
03	112 25.3	256 41.5 . .	23.5	193 13.7 . .	18.9	41 50.3 . .	25.5	257 40.8 . .	29.3	Pollux	243 28.0	N27 59.4
04	127 27.8	271 41.0	24.6	208 14.1	18.8	56 53.2	25.5	272 43.0	29.4	Procyon	244 59.9	N 5 11.4
05	142 30.2	286 40.5	25.6	223 14.5	18.7	71 56.0	25.5	287 45.2	29.4			
06	157 32.7	301 40.0	S12 26.6	238 14.8	S24 18.6	86 58.8	N21 25.4	302 47.4	S11 29.5	Rasalhague	96 07.1	N12 33.2
W 07	172 35.2	316 39.4	27.7	253 15.2	18.4	102 01.6	25.4	317 49.6	29.6	Regulus	207 43.9	N11 54.1
E 08	187 37.6	331 38.9	28.7	268 15.6	18.3	117 04.5	25.3	332 51.8	29.7	Rigel	281 12.1	S 8 11.3
D 09	202 40.1	346 38.4 . .	29.7	283 15.9 . .	18.2	132 07.3 . .	25.3	347 54.0 . .	29.8	Rigil Kent.	139 52.8	S60 53.1
N 10	217 42.5	1 37.9	30.8	298 16.3	18.1	147 10.1	25.3	2 56.2	29.9	Sabik	102 13.3	S15 44.3
E 11	232 45.0	16 37.3	31.8	313 16.7	18.0	162 12.9	25.2	17 58.4	30.0			
S 12	247 47.5	31 36.8	S12 32.8	328 17.1	S24 17.9	177 15.8	N21 25.2	33 00.6	S11 30.0	Schedar	349 46.6	N56 36.8
D 13	262 49.9	46 36.3	33.8	343 17.4	17.7	192 18.6	25.1	48 02.8	30.1	Shaula	96 22.8	S37 06.7
A 14	277 52.4	61 35.7	34.9	358 17.8	17.6	207 21.4	25.1	63 04.9	30.2	Sirius	258 33.8	S16 44.1
Y 15	292 54.9	76 35.2 . .	35.9	13 18.2 . .	17.5	222 24.2 . .	25.1	78 07.1 . .	30.3	Spica	158 31.9	S11 13.6
16	307 57.3	91 34.7	36.9	28 18.5	17.4	237 27.1	25.0	93 09.3	30.4	Suhail	222 52.6	S43 29.0
17	322 59.8	106 34.1	38.0	43 18.9	17.2	252 29.9	25.0	108 11.5	30.5			
18	338 02.3	121 33.6	S12 39.0	58 19.3	S24 17.1	267 32.7	N21 24.9	123 13.7	S11 30.6	Vega	80 39.6	N38 48.0
19	353 04.7	136 33.1	40.0	73 19.6	17.0	282 35.5	24.9	138 15.9	30.7	Zuben'ubi	137 06.2	S16 05.6
20	8 07.2	151 32.5	41.0	88 20.0	16.9	297 38.4	24.9	153 18.1	30.7		SHA	Mer.Pass.
21	23 09.7	166 32.0 . .	42.1	103 20.4 . .	16.7	312 41.2 . .	24.8	168 20.3 . .	30.8		° ′	h m
22	38 12.1	181 31.5	43.1	118 20.8	16.6	327 44.0	24.8	183 22.5	30.9	Venus	145 36.8	9 53
23	53 14.6	196 30.9	44.1	133 21.1	16.5	342 46.8	24.7	198 24.7	31.0	Mars	81 44.9	14 07
	h m									Jupiter	289 15.3	0 18
Mer.Pass. 19 31.5		v −0.5	d 1.0	v 0.4	d 0.1	v 2.8	d 0.0	v 2.2	d 0.1	Saturn	145 22.7	9 52

UT	SUN GHA	SUN Dec	MOON GHA	v	MOON Dec	d	HP
d h	° ′	° ′	° ′	′	° ′	′	′
26 00	183 10.7	S20 58.2	32 26.6	13.5	N15 11.8	7.5	54.3
01	198 10.5	58.7	46 59.1	13.4	15 19.3	7.4	54.3
02	213 10.3	59.1	61 31.5	13.4	15 26.7	7.3	54.3
03	228 10.1	20 59.6	76 03.9	13.4	15 34.0	7.3	54.3
04	243 09.9	21 00.1	90 36.3	13.3	15 41.3	7.2	54.3
05	258 09.7	00.5	105 08.6	13.4	15 48.5	7.1	54.3
06	273 09.5	S21 01.0	119 41.0	13.3	N15 55.6	7.1	54.2
07	288 09.3	01.5	134 13.3	13.2	16 02.7	7.0	54.2
M 08	303 09.1	02.0	148 45.5	13.3	16 09.7	6.9	54.2
O 09	318 08.9	02.4	163 17.8	13.2	16 16.6	6.8	54.2
N 10	333 08.7	02.9	177 50.0	13.2	16 23.4	6.8	54.2
D 11	348 08.5	03.3	192 22.2	13.1	16 30.2	6.7	54.2
A 12	3 08.3	S21 03.8	206 54.3	13.2	N16 36.9	6.6	54.2
Y 13	18 08.1	04.3	221 26.5	13.1	16 43.5	6.6	54.2
14	33 07.9	04.7	235 58.6	13.1	16 50.1	6.4	54.2
15	48 07.7	05.2	250 30.7	13.0	16 56.5	6.4	54.2
16	63 07.5	05.6	265 02.7	13.0	17 02.9	6.3	54.2
17	78 07.3	06.1	279 34.7	13.0	17 09.2	6.3	54.1
18	93 07.1	S21 06.6	294 06.7	13.0	N17 15.5	6.1	54.1
19	108 06.9	07.0	308 38.7	12.9	17 21.6	6.1	54.1
20	123 06.7	07.5	323 10.6	12.9	17 27.7	6.0	54.1
21	138 06.5	07.9	337 42.5	12.9	17 33.7	5.9	54.1
22	153 06.3	08.4	352 14.4	12.9	17 39.6	5.9	54.1
23	168 06.1	08.8	6 46.3	12.8	17 45.5	5.7	54.1
27 00	183 05.9	S21 09.3	21 18.1	12.8	N17 51.2	5.7	54.1
01	198 05.7	09.7	35 49.9	12.8	17 56.9	5.6	54.1
02	213 05.5	10.2	50 21.7	12.7	18 02.5	5.5	54.1
03	228 05.3	10.6	64 53.4	12.7	18 08.0	5.4	54.1
04	243 05.1	11.1	79 25.1	12.7	18 13.4	5.4	54.1
05	258 04.9	11.5	93 56.8	12.7	18 18.8	5.3	54.1
06	273 04.7	S21 12.0	108 28.5	12.6	N18 24.1	5.1	54.1
07	288 04.4	12.4	123 00.1	12.7	18 29.2	5.2	54.1
T 08	303 04.2	12.9	137 31.8	12.5	18 34.4	5.0	54.1
U 09	318 04.0	13.3	152 03.3	12.6	18 39.4	4.9	54.0
E 10	333 03.8	13.8	166 34.9	12.6	18 44.3	4.8	54.0
S 11	348 03.6	14.2	181 06.5	12.5	18 49.1	4.8	54.0
D 12	3 03.4	S21 14.7	195 38.0	12.5	N18 53.9	4.7	54.0
A 13	18 03.2	15.1	210 09.5	12.4	18 58.6	4.6	54.0
Y 14	33 03.0	15.6	224 40.9	12.5	19 03.2	4.5	54.0
15	48 02.8	16.0	239 12.4	12.4	19 07.7	4.4	54.0
16	63 02.6	16.5	253 43.8	12.4	19 12.1	4.3	54.0
17	78 02.4	16.9	268 15.2	12.3	19 16.4	4.3	54.0
18	93 02.2	S21 17.3	282 46.5	12.4	N19 20.7	4.1	54.0
19	108 01.9	17.8	297 17.9	12.3	19 24.8	4.1	54.0
20	123 01.7	18.2	311 49.2	12.3	19 28.9	4.0	54.0
21	138 01.5	18.7	326 20.5	12.3	19 32.9	3.8	54.0
22	153 01.3	19.1	340 51.8	12.2	19 36.7	3.8	54.0
23	168 01.1	19.5	355 23.0	12.3	19 40.5	3.7	54.0
28 00	183 00.9	S21 20.0	9 54.3	12.2	N19 44.2	3.7	54.0
01	198 00.7	20.4	24 25.5	12.2	19 47.9	3.5	54.0
02	213 00.5	20.8	38 56.7	12.1	19 51.4	3.4	54.0
03	228 00.3	21.3	53 27.8	12.2	19 54.8	3.3	54.0
04	243 00.0	21.7	67 59.0	12.1	19 58.1	3.3	54.0
05	257 59.8	22.1	82 30.1	12.1	20 01.4	3.2	54.0
06	272 59.6	S21 22.6	97 01.2	12.1	N20 04.6	3.0	54.0
07	287 59.4	23.0	111 32.3	12.1	20 07.6	3.0	54.0
W 08	302 59.2	23.4	126 03.4	12.0	20 10.6	2.9	54.0
E 09	317 59.0	23.9	140 34.4	12.1	20 13.5	2.8	54.0
D 10	332 58.8	24.3	155 05.5	12.0	20 16.3	2.6	54.0
N 11	347 58.5	24.7	169 36.5	12.0	20 18.9	2.6	54.0
E 12	2 58.3	S21 25.2	184 07.5	12.0	N20 21.5	2.5	54.0
S 13	17 58.1	25.6	198 38.5	12.0	20 24.0	2.5	54.0
D 14	32 57.9	26.0	213 09.5	11.9	20 26.5	2.3	54.0
A 15	47 57.7	26.4	227 40.4	12.0	20 28.8	2.2	54.0
Y 16	62 57.5	26.9	242 11.4	11.9	20 31.0	2.1	54.0
17	77 57.2	27.3	256 42.3	11.9	20 33.1	2.1	54.0
18	92 57.0	S21 27.7	271 13.2	11.9	N20 35.2	1.9	54.0
19	107 56.8	28.1	285 44.1	11.9	20 37.1	1.8	54.0
20	122 56.6	28.6	300 15.0	11.9	20 38.9	1.8	54.0
21	137 56.4	29.0	314 45.9	11.8	20 40.7	1.6	54.0
22	152 56.2	29.4	329 16.7	11.9	20 42.3	1.6	54.0
23	167 55.9	29.8	343 47.6	11.8	N20 43.9	1.4	54.0
	SD 16.2	d 0.4	SD 14.8		14.7		14.7

Lat.	Naut.	Civil	Sunrise	Moonrise 26	27	28	29
°	h m	h m	h m	h m	h m	h m	h m
N 72	07 41	09 33	■■■	11 49	☐	☐	☐
N 70	07 26	08 58	■■■	12 34	12 20	☐	☐
68	07 13	08 33	10 15	13 04	13 08	13 20	13 52
66	07 03	08 14	09 34	13 26	13 39	14 02	14 40
64	06 54	07 58	09 06	13 44	14 02	14 30	15 11
62	06 47	07 45	08 44	13 58	14 21	14 52	15 34
60	06 40	07 34	08 27	14 11	14 36	15 09	15 53
N 58	06 34	07 24	08 13	14 21	14 49	15 24	16 08
56	06 28	07 16	08 01	14 31	15 00	15 37	16 21
54	06 23	07 08	07 50	14 39	15 10	15 48	16 33
52	06 19	07 01	07 40	14 47	15 19	15 57	16 43
50	06 14	06 55	07 32	14 53	15 27	16 06	16 52
45	06 04	06 41	07 14	15 08	15 44	16 25	17 11
N 40	05 56	06 29	06 59	15 20	15 58	16 40	17 26
35	05 48	06 19	06 46	15 30	16 09	16 53	17 40
30	05 40	06 09	06 35	15 39	16 20	17 04	17 51
20	05 26	05 53	06 16	15 54	16 37	17 23	18 11
N 10	05 11	05 37	06 00	16 08	16 53	17 40	18 28
0	04 56	05 22	05 44	16 21	17 08	17 55	18 44
S 10	04 39	05 06	05 28	16 34	17 22	18 11	19 00
20	04 19	04 47	05 11	16 47	17 38	18 28	19 17
30	03 53	04 25	04 52	17 03	17 56	18 47	19 36
35	03 36	04 11	04 40	17 13	18 07	18 59	19 48
40	03 15	03 55	04 27	17 23	18 19	19 12	20 01
45	02 49	03 35	04 11	17 36	18 33	19 27	20 17
S 50	02 12	03 10	03 51	17 51	18 50	19 46	20 36
52	01 51	02 57	03 42	17 58	18 59	19 55	20 45
54	01 24	02 42	03 31	18 06	19 08	20 05	20 55
56	00 41	02 25	03 19	18 15	19 18	20 16	21 07
58	////	02 03	03 06	18 25	19 30	20 29	21 20
S 60	////	01 34	02 49	18 36	19 44	20 45	21 35

Lat.	Sunset	Civil	Naut.	Moonset 26	27	28	29
°	h m	h m	h m	h m	h m	h m	h m
N 72	■■■	14 02	15 54	08 16	☐	☐	☐
N 70	■■■	14 36	16 09	07 32	09 23	☐	☐
68	13 19	15 01	16 21	07 03	08 35	10 02	11 10
66	14 01	15 21	16 32	06 42	08 05	09 20	10 22
64	14 29	15 36	16 41	06 25	07 42	08 52	09 51
62	14 51	15 50	16 48	06 11	07 24	08 31	09 28
60	15 08	16 01	16 55	05 59	07 09	08 13	09 09
N 58	15 22	16 11	17 01	05 49	06 56	07 59	08 54
56	15 35	16 19	17 07	05 40	06 45	07 46	08 41
54	15 45	16 27	17 12	05 32	06 36	07 36	08 29
52	15 55	16 34	17 17	05 25	06 27	07 26	08 19
50	16 03	16 40	17 21	05 18	06 20	07 17	08 10
45	16 22	16 54	17 31	05 05	06 03	06 59	07 51
N 40	16 36	17 06	17 40	04 54	05 50	06 44	07 36
35	16 49	17 17	17 48	04 44	05 39	06 32	07 23
30	17 00	17 26	17 55	04 36	05 29	06 21	07 11
20	17 19	17 43	18 10	04 21	05 12	06 02	06 52
N 10	17 36	17 58	18 24	04 09	04 57	05 46	06 35
0	17 51	18 14	18 39	03 57	04 43	05 31	06 19
S 10	18 07	18 30	18 57	03 45	04 30	05 15	06 03
20	18 24	18 48	19 17	03 33	04 15	04 59	05 46
30	18 44	19 11	19 43	03 19	03 58	04 40	05 26
35	18 56	19 25	20 00	03 11	03 48	04 29	05 15
40	19 09	19 41	20 21	03 01	03 37	04 17	05 01
45	19 25	20 01	20 47	02 50	03 24	04 02	04 46
S 50	19 45	20 27	21 25	02 37	03 08	03 44	04 27
52	19 54	20 40	21 46	02 31	03 01	03 36	04 18
54	20 05	20 55	22 14	02 24	02 52	03 26	04 08
56	20 17	21 13	23 00	02 17	02 43	03 16	03 56
58	20 31	21 35	////	02 08	02 33	03 04	03 43
S 60	20 48	22 05	////	01 59	02 21	02 49	03 28

	SUN Eqn. of Time 00h	12h	SUN Mer. Pass.	MOON Mer. Pass. Upper	Lower	Age	Phase
Day	m s	m s	h m	h m	h m	d	%
26	12 43	12 34	11 47	22 32	10 09	13	96
27	12 24	12 14	11 48	23 19	10 55	14	99
28	12 04	11 54	11 48	24 07	11 43	15	100

UT	ARIES GHA	VENUS −3.9 GHA	Dec	MARS +1.2 GHA	Dec	JUPITER −2.8 GHA	Dec	SATURN +0.7 GHA	Dec	STARS Name	SHA	Dec
29 00	68 17.0	211 30.4	S12 45.1	148 21.5	S24 16.4	357 49.7	N21 24.7	213 26.9	S11 31.1	Acamar	315 18.2	S40 15.3
01	83 19.5	226 29.9	46.2	163 21.9	16.2	12 52.5	24.7	228 29.1	31.2	Achernar	335 26.7	S57 10.4
02	98 22.0	241 29.3	47.2	178 22.2	16.1	27 55.3	24.6	243 31.3	31.2	Acrux	173 10.0	S63 10.0
03	113 24.4	256 28.8	.. 48.2	193 22.6	.. 16.0	42 58.1	.. 24.6	258 33.5	.. 31.3	Adhara	255 12.5	S28 59.4
04	128 26.9	271 28.3	49.2	208 23.0	15.9	58 01.0	24.5	273 35.7	31.4	Aldebaran	290 49.5	N16 32.0
05	143 29.4	286 27.7	50.2	223 23.3	15.7	73 03.8	24.5	288 37.9	31.5			
06	158 31.8	301 27.2	S12 51.3	238 23.7	S24 15.6	88 06.6	N21 24.5	303 40.1	S11 31.6	Alioth	166 21.4	N55 53.1
07	173 34.3	316 26.6	52.3	253 24.1	15.5	103 09.4	24.4	318 42.3	31.7	Alkaid	152 59.6	N49 14.8
T 08	188 36.8	331 26.1	53.3	268 24.5	15.4	118 12.3	24.4	333 44.5	31.8	Al Na'ir	27 44.3	S46 54.0
H 09	203 39.2	346 25.6	.. 54.3	283 24.8	.. 15.2	133 15.1	.. 24.3	348 46.7	.. 31.8	Alnilam	275 46.4	S 1 11.7
U 10	218 41.7	1 25.0	55.3	298 25.2	15.1	148 17.9	24.3	3 48.9	31.9	Alphard	217 56.4	S 8 42.9
R 11	233 44.2	16 24.5	56.4	313 25.6	15.0	163 20.8	24.3	18 51.1	32.0			
S 12	248 46.6	31 23.9	S12 57.4	328 25.9	S24 14.8	178 23.6	N21 24.2	33 53.3	S11 32.1	Alphecca	126 11.7	N26 40.3
D 13	263 49.1	46 23.4	58.4	343 26.3	14.7	193 26.4	24.2	48 55.5	32.2	Alpheratz	357 43.7	N29 10.0
A 14	278 51.5	61 22.9	12 59.4	358 26.7	14.6	208 29.2	24.1	63 57.7	32.3	Altair	62 08.8	N 8 54.4
Y 15	293 54.0	76 22.3	13 00.4	13 27.0	.. 14.4	223 32.1	.. 24.1	78 59.9	.. 32.4	Ankaa	353 15.9	S42 14.2
16	308 56.5	91 21.8	01.4	28 27.4	14.3	238 34.9	24.1	94 02.1	32.4	Antares	112 27.1	S26 27.5
17	323 58.9	106 21.2	02.4	43 27.8	14.2	253 37.7	24.0	109 04.3	32.5			
18	339 01.4	121 20.7	S13 03.5	58 28.2	S24 14.0	268 40.5	N21 24.0	124 06.5	S11 32.6	Arcturus	145 56.4	N19 06.9
19	354 03.9	136 20.1	04.5	73 28.5	13.9	283 43.4	23.9	139 08.7	32.7	Atria	107 29.8	S69 02.9
20	9 06.3	151 19.6	05.5	88 28.9	13.8	298 46.2	23.9	154 10.9	32.8	Avior	234 17.8	S59 32.9
21	24 08.8	166 19.1	.. 06.5	103 29.3	.. 13.6	313 49.0	.. 23.8	169 13.1	.. 32.9	Bellatrix	278 32.1	N 6 21.6
22	39 11.3	181 18.5	07.5	118 29.6	13.5	328 51.8	23.8	184 15.3	33.0	Betelgeuse	271 01.4	N 7 24.5
23	54 13.7	196 18.0	08.5	133 30.0	13.4	343 54.7	23.8	199 17.5	33.0			
30 00	69 16.2	211 17.4	S13 09.5	148 30.4	S24 13.2	358 57.5	N21 23.7	214 19.7	S11 33.1	Canopus	263 55.8	S52 42.1
01	84 18.7	226 16.9	10.5	163 30.7	13.1	14 00.3	23.7	229 21.9	33.2	Capella	280 34.5	N46 00.5
02	99 21.1	241 16.3	11.6	178 31.1	12.9	29 03.1	23.6	244 24.1	33.3	Deneb	49 32.0	N45 20.0
03	114 23.6	256 15.8	.. 12.6	193 31.5	.. 12.8	44 06.0	.. 23.6	259 26.3	.. 33.4	Denebola	182 34.2	N14 29.9
04	129 26.0	271 15.2	13.6	208 31.8	12.7	59 08.8	23.6	274 28.5	33.5	Diphda	348 56.1	S17 54.9
05	144 28.5	286 14.7	14.6	223 32.2	12.5	74 11.6	23.5	289 30.7	33.5			
06	159 31.0	301 14.1	S13 15.6	238 32.6	S24 12.4	89 14.5	N21 23.5	304 32.9	S11 33.6	Dubhe	193 52.3	N61 40.5
07	174 33.4	316 13.6	16.6	253 33.0	12.2	104 17.3	23.4	319 35.1	33.7	Elnath	278 12.7	N28 37.0
F 08	189 35.9	331 13.0	17.6	268 33.3	12.1	119 20.1	23.4	334 37.3	33.8	Eltanin	90 46.8	N51 29.5
R 09	204 38.4	346 12.5	.. 18.6	283 33.7	.. 12.0	134 22.9	.. 23.4	349 39.5	.. 33.9	Enif	33 47.6	N 9 56.3
I 10	219 40.8	1 11.9	19.6	298 34.1	11.8	149 25.8	23.3	4 41.7	34.0	Fomalhaut	15 24.4	S29 33.2
D 11	234 43.3	16 11.4	20.6	313 34.4	11.7	164 28.6	23.3	19 43.9	34.1			
A 12	249 45.8	31 10.8	S13 21.6	328 34.8	S24 11.5	179 31.4	N21 23.2	34 46.1	S11 34.1	Gacrux	172 01.6	S57 10.9
Y 13	264 48.2	46 10.3	22.6	343 35.2	11.4	194 34.2	23.2	49 48.3	34.2	Gienah	175 52.8	S17 36.8
14	279 50.7	61 09.7	23.6	358 35.5	11.2	209 37.1	23.2	64 50.5	34.3	Hadar	148 48.9	S60 25.9
15	294 53.2	76 09.2	.. 24.6	13 35.9	.. 11.1	224 39.9	.. 23.1	79 52.7	.. 34.4	Hamal	328 00.9	N23 31.5
16	309 55.6	91 08.6	25.6	28 36.3	11.0	239 42.7	23.1	94 54.9	34.5	Kaus Aust.	83 44.7	S34 22.6
17	324 58.1	106 08.1	26.6	43 36.6	10.8	254 45.5	23.0	109 57.1	34.6			
18	340 00.5	121 07.5	S13 27.6	58 37.0	S24 10.7	269 48.4	N21 23.0	124 59.3	S11 34.6	Kochab	137 21.2	N74 06.0
19	355 03.0	136 06.9	28.6	73 37.4	10.5	284 51.2	23.0	140 01.5	34.7	Markab	13 38.7	N15 16.7
20	10 05.5	151 06.4	29.6	88 37.8	10.4	299 54.0	22.9	155 03.7	34.8	Menkar	314 15.1	N 4 08.4
21	25 07.9	166 05.8	.. 30.6	103 38.1	.. 10.2	314 56.9	.. 22.9	170 05.9	.. 34.9	Menkent	148 08.8	S36 25.8
22	40 10.4	181 05.3	31.6	118 38.5	10.1	329 59.7	22.8	185 08.1	35.0	Miaplacidus	221 39.3	S69 46.0
23	55 12.9	196 04.7	32.6	133 38.9	09.9	345 02.5	22.8	200 10.3	35.1			
1 00	70 15.3	211 04.2	S13 33.6	148 39.2	S24 09.8	0 05.3	N21 22.8	215 12.5	S11 35.2	Mirfak	308 40.4	N49 54.5
01	85 17.8	226 03.6	34.6	163 39.6	09.6	15 08.2	22.7	230 14.7	35.2	Nunki	75 59.1	S26 16.7
02	100 20.3	241 03.0	35.6	178 40.0	09.5	30 11.0	22.7	245 16.9	35.3	Peacock	53 20.2	S56 41.6
03	115 22.7	256 02.5	.. 36.6	193 40.3	.. 09.3	45 13.8	.. 22.6	260 19.1	.. 35.4	Pollux	243 27.9	N27 59.4
04	130 25.2	271 01.9	37.6	208 40.7	09.2	60 16.6	22.6	275 21.3	35.5	Procyon	244 59.9	N 5 11.4
05	145 27.6	286 01.4	38.6	223 41.1	09.0	75 19.5	22.5	290 23.5	35.6			
06	160 30.1	301 00.8	S13 39.6	238 41.4	S24 08.9	90 22.3	N21 22.5	305 25.7	S11 35.7	Rasalhague	96 07.1	N12 33.2
07	175 32.6	316 00.2	40.6	253 41.8	08.7	105 25.1	22.5	320 27.9	35.7	Regulus	207 43.9	N11 54.1
S 08	190 35.0	330 59.7	41.6	268 42.2	08.6	120 28.0	22.4	335 30.1	35.8	Rigel	281 12.1	S 8 11.3
A 09	205 37.5	345 59.1	.. 42.6	283 42.6	.. 08.4	135 30.8	.. 22.4	350 32.3	.. 35.9	Rigil Kent.	139 52.8	S60 53.1
T 10	220 40.0	0 58.6	43.6	298 42.9	08.3	150 33.6	22.3	5 34.6	36.0	Sabik	102 13.3	S15 44.3
U 11	235 42.4	15 58.0	44.6	313 43.3	08.1	165 36.4	22.3	20 36.8	36.1			
R 12	250 44.9	30 57.4	S13 45.6	328 43.7	S24 08.0	180 39.3	N21 22.3	35 39.0	S11 36.2	Schedar	349 40.6	N56 36.8
D 13	265 47.4	45 56.9	46.6	343 44.0	07.8	195 42.1	22.2	50 41.2	36.2	Shaula	96 22.8	S37 06.6
A 14	280 49.8	60 56.3	47.6	358 44.4	07.7	210 44.9	22.2	65 43.4	36.3	Sirius	258 33.7	S16 44.1
Y 15	295 52.3	75 55.7	.. 48.5	13 44.8	.. 07.5	225 47.7	.. 22.1	80 45.6	.. 36.4	Spica	158 31.9	S11 13.7
16	310 54.8	90 55.2	49.5	28 45.1	07.3	240 50.6	22.1	95 47.8	36.5	Suhail	222 52.5	S43 29.0
17	325 57.2	105 54.6	50.5	43 45.5	07.2	255 53.4	22.1	110 50.0	36.6			
18	340 59.7	120 54.0	S13 51.5	58 45.9	S24 07.0	270 56.2	N21 22.0	125 52.2	S11 36.7	Vega	80 39.6	N38 48.0
19	356 02.1	135 53.5	52.5	73 46.2	06.9	285 59.1	22.0	140 54.4	36.7	Zuben'ubi	137 06.1	S16 05.6
20	11 04.6	150 52.9	53.5	88 46.6	06.7	301 01.9	21.9	155 56.6	36.8		SHA	Mer.Pass.
21	26 07.1	165 52.3	.. 54.5	103 47.0	.. 06.6	316 04.7	.. 21.9	170 58.8	.. 36.9	Venus	142 01.2	9 55
22	41 09.5	180 51.8	55.5	118 47.3	06.4	331 07.5	21.9	186 01.0	37.0	Mars	79 14.2	14 06
23	56 12.0	195 51.2	56.4	133 47.7	06.2	346 10.4	21.8	201 03.2	37.1	Jupiter	289 41.3	0 04
Mer.Pass. 19 19.7		v −0.6	d 1.0	v 0.4	d 0.1	v 2.8	d 0.0	v 2.2	d 0.1	Saturn	145 03.5	9 41

SUN and MOON — GHA / Dec

UT	SUN GHA	SUN Dec	MOON GHA	v	MOON Dec	d	HP
29 00	182 55.7	S21 30.3	358 18.4	11.9	N20 45.3	1.4	54.0
01	197 55.5	30.7	12 49.3	11.8	20 46.7	1.3	54.0
02	212 55.3	31.1	27 20.1	11.8	20 48.0	1.1	54.0
03	227 55.1 ..	31.5	41 50.9	11.8	20 49.1	1.1	54.0
04	242 54.8	31.9	56 21.7	11.8	20 50.2	1.0	54.0
05	257 54.6	32.3	70 52.5	11.8	20 51.2	0.9	54.0
06	272 54.4	S21 32.8	85 23.3	11.8	N20 52.1	0.7	54.0
T 07	287 54.2	33.2	99 54.1	11.8	20 52.8	0.7	54.0
H 08	302 54.0	33.6	114 24.9	11.7	20 53.5	0.6	54.0
U 09	317 53.7 ..	34.0	128 55.6	11.8	20 54.1	0.5	54.0
R 10	332 53.5	34.4	143 26.4	11.8	20 54.6	0.4	54.0
S 11	347 53.3	34.8	157 57.2	11.7	20 55.0	0.3	54.0
D 12	2 53.1	S21 35.2	172 27.9	11.8	N20 55.3	0.2	54.0
A 13	17 52.8	35.7	186 58.7	11.7	20 55.5	0.1	54.0
Y 14	32 52.6	36.1	201 29.4	11.8	20 55.6	0.0	54.0
15	47 52.4 ..	36.5	216 00.2	11.7	20 55.6	0.1	54.0
16	62 52.2	36.9	230 30.9	11.8	20 55.5	0.2	54.0
17	77 51.9	37.3	245 01.7	11.7	20 55.3	0.3	54.0
18	92 51.7	S21 37.7	259 32.4	11.8	N20 55.0	0.4	54.0
19	107 51.5	38.1	274 03.2	11.7	20 54.6	0.5	54.0
20	122 51.3	38.5	288 33.9	11.8	20 54.1	0.6	54.0
21	137 51.1 ..	38.9	303 04.7	11.7	20 53.5	0.6	54.0
22	152 50.8	39.3	317 35.4	11.7	20 52.9	0.8	54.0
23	167 50.6	39.7	332 06.1	11.8	20 52.1	0.9	54.0
30 00	182 50.4	S21 40.1	346 36.9	11.8	N20 51.2	1.0	54.0
01	197 50.1	40.5	1 07.7	11.7	20 50.2	1.0	54.0
02	212 49.9	40.9	15 38.4	11.8	20 49.2	1.2	54.0
03	227 49.7 ..	41.3	30 09.2	11.7	20 48.0	1.3	54.0
04	242 49.5	41.7	44 39.9	11.8	20 46.7	1.3	54.0
05	257 49.2	42.1	59 10.7	11.8	20 45.4	1.5	54.0
06	272 49.0	S21 42.5	73 41.5	11.8	N20 43.9	1.5	54.0
F 07	287 48.8	42.9	88 12.3	11.8	20 42.4	1.7	54.1
R 08	302 48.6	43.3	102 43.1	11.8	20 40.7	1.7	54.1
I 09	317 48.3 ..	43.7	117 13.9	11.8	20 39.0	1.9	54.1
D 10	332 48.1	44.1	131 44.7	11.8	20 37.1	1.9	54.1
A 11	347 47.9	44.5	146 15.5	11.8	20 35.2	2.1	54.1
Y 12	2 47.6	S21 44.9	160 46.3	11.8	N20 33.1	2.1	54.1
13	17 47.4	45.3	175 17.1	11.9	20 31.0	2.2	54.1
14	32 47.2	45.7	189 48.0	11.8	20 28.8	2.4	54.1
15	47 46.9 ..	46.1	204 18.8	11.9	20 26.4	2.4	54.1
16	62 46.7	46.5	218 49.7	11.8	20 24.0	2.5	54.1
17	77 46.5	46.9	233 20.5	11.9	20 21.5	2.6	54.1
18	92 46.3	S21 47.3	247 51.4	11.9	N20 18.9	2.7	54.1
19	107 46.0	47.6	262 22.3	11.9	20 16.2	2.8	54.1
20	122 45.8	48.0	276 53.2	12.0	20 13.4	2.9	54.1
21	137 45.6 ..	48.4	291 24.2	11.9	20 10.5	3.0	54.1
22	152 45.3	48.8	305 55.1	11.9	20 07.5	3.1	54.2
23	167 45.1	49.2	320 26.0	12.0	20 04.4	3.2	54.2
1 00	182 44.9	S21 49.6	334 57.0	12.0	N20 01.2	3.2	54.2
01	197 44.6	50.0	349 28.0	12.0	19 58.0	3.4	54.2
02	212 44.4	50.4	3 59.0	12.0	19 54.6	3.4	54.2
03	227 44.2 ..	50.7	18 30.0	12.0	19 51.2	3.6	54.2
04	242 43.9	51.1	33 01.0	12.0	19 47.6	3.6	54.2
05	257 43.7	51.5	47 32.0	12.1	19 44.0	3.8	54.2
06	272 43.5	S21 51.9	62 03.1	12.0	N19 40.2	3.8	54.2
S 07	287 43.2	52.3	76 34.1	12.1	19 36.4	3.9	54.2
A 08	302 43.0	52.6	91 05.2	12.1	19 32.5	4.0	54.2
T 09	317 42.8 ..	53.0	105 36.3	12.1	19 28.5	4.1	54.2
U 10	332 42.5	53.4	120 07.4	12.2	19 24.4	4.2	54.3
R 11	347 42.3	53.8	134 38.6	12.1	19 20.2	4.3	54.3
D 12	2 42.0	S21 54.2	149 09.7	12.2	N19 15.9	4.3	54.3
A 13	17 41.8	54.5	163 40.9	12.2	19 11.6	4.5	54.3
Y 14	32 41.6	54.9	178 12.1	12.2	19 07.1	4.5	54.3
15	47 41.3 ..	55.3	192 43.3	12.3	19 02.6	4.7	54.3
16	62 41.1	55.7	207 14.6	12.2	18 57.9	4.7	54.3
17	77 40.9	56.0	221 45.8	12.3	18 53.2	4.8	54.3
18	92 40.6	S21 56.4	236 17.1	12.3	N18 48.4	4.9	54.3
19	107 40.4	56.8	250 48.4	12.3	18 43.5	5.0	54.4
20	122 40.1	57.2	265 19.7	12.3	18 38.5	5.1	54.4
21	137 39.9 ..	57.5	279 51.0	12.3	18 33.4	5.2	54.4
22	152 39.7	57.9	294 22.3	12.4	18 28.2	5.2	54.4
23	167 39.4	58.3	308 53.7	12.4	N18 23.0	5.3	54.4
	SD 16.2	d 0.4	SD 14.7		14.7		14.8

Twilight, Sunrise and Moonrise

Lat.	Naut.	Civil	Sunrise	Moonrise 29	30	1	2
N 72	07 49	09 47	■■■■		□		16 34
N 70	07 33	09 09	■■■■	□	□	15 29	17 23
68	07 20	08 42	10 33	□	□	16 21	17 54
66	07 09	08 22	09 45	13 52	14 56	16 53	18 16
64	07 00	08 05	09 14	14 40	15 39	17 17	18 34
62	06 52	07 51	08 52	15 11	16 08	17 35	18 49
60	06 45	07 40	08 34	15 34	16 29	17 51	19 01
N 58	06 38	07 29	08 19	15 53	16 47	18 04	19 12
56	06 33	07 20	08 06	16 08	17 02	18 15	19 21
54	06 27	07 12	07 55	16 21	17 14	18 25	19 29
52	06 22	07 05	07 45	16 33	17 25	18 34	19 36
50	06 18	06 58	07 36	16 43	17 35	18 41	19 43
45	06 07	06 44	07 17	17 11	18 02	18 58	19 57
N 40	05 58	06 32	07 02	17 26	18 17	19 12	20 09
35	05 45	06 21	06 49	17 40	18 30	19 23	20 18
30	05 42	06 12	06 38	17 51	18 41	19 33	20 27
20	05 27	05 54	06 18	18 11	19 00	19 51	20 42
N 10	05 13	05 39	06 01	18 28	19 17	20 06	20 55
0	04 57	05 23	05 45	18 44	19 32	20 20	21 07
S 10	04 40	05 06	05 29	19 00	19 47	20 34	21 19
20	04 19	04 47	05 12	19 17	20 04	20 49	21 32
30	03 52	04 24	04 51	19 36	20 23	21 06	21 46
35	03 35	04 10	04 39	19 48	20 34	21 16	21 55
40	03 14	03 54	04 26	20 01	20 46	21 27	22 04
45	02 46	03 33	04 09	20 17	21 01	21 41	22 15
S 50	02 08	03 07	03 49	20 36	21 19	21 57	22 29
52	01 46	02 54	03 39	20 45	21 28	22 05	22 35
54	01 16	02 38	03 29	20 55	21 38	22 13	22 42
56	00 22	02 20	03 16	21 07	21 48	22 23	22 50
58	////	01 56	03 02	21 20	22 01	22 33	22 59
S 60	////	01 25	02 44	21 35	22 15	22 46	23 09

Sunset, Twilight and Moonset

Lat.	Sunset	Civil	Naut.	Moonset 29	30	1	2
N 72	■■■■	13 50	15 48	□	□	□	13 28
N 70	■■■■	14 28	16 04	□	□	12 54	12 38
68	13 05	14 55	16 17	11 10	11 46	12 01	12 06
66	13 52	15 16	16 28	10 22	11 03	11 28	11 43
64	14 23	15 32	16 37	09 51	10 34	11 04	11 24
62	14 45	15 46	16 45	09 28	10 12	10 45	11 09
60	15 04	15 58	16 52	09 09	09 55	10 30	10 56
N 58	15 19	16 08	16 59	08 54	09 40	10 16	10 45
56	15 32	16 17	17 05	08 41	09 27	10 05	10 35
54	15 43	16 25	17 10	08 29	09 16	09 55	10 27
52	15 53	16 32	17 15	08 19	09 06	09 46	10 19
50	16 01	16 39	17 19	08 10	08 57	09 38	10 12
45	16 20	16 53	17 30	07 51	08 38	09 20	09 57
N 40	16 35	17 05	17 39	07 36	08 23	09 06	09 45
35	16 48	17 16	17 47	07 23	08 10	08 54	09 35
30	17 00	17 26	17 55	07 11	07 59	08 44	09 25
20	17 19	17 43	18 10	06 52	07 40	08 26	09 10
N 10	17 36	17 59	18 25	06 35	07 23	08 10	08 56
0	17 52	18 15	18 41	06 19	07 07	07 55	08 42
S 10	18 09	18 32	18 58	06 03	06 51	07 40	08 29
20	18 26	18 50	19 19	05 46	06 34	07 24	08 15
30	18 47	19 14	19 46	05 26	06 15	07 06	07 59
35	18 59	19 28	20 03	05 15	06 03	06 55	07 50
40	19 12	19 44	20 25	05 01	05 50	06 43	07 39
45	19 29	20 05	20 52	04 46	05 35	06 28	07 26
S 50	19 49	20 32	21 31	04 27	05 16	06 11	07 10
52	19 59	20 45	21 54	04 18	05 07	06 02	07 03
54	20 10	21 01	22 24	04 08	04 57	05 53	06 55
56	20 23	21 19	23 24	03 56	04 45	05 42	06 46
58	20 37	21 43	////	03 43	04 32	05 30	06 35
S 60	20 55	22 16	////	03 28	04 17	05 16	06 23

SUN / MOON

Day	Eqn. of Time 00h	Eqn. of Time 12h	Mer. Pass.	Mer. Pass. Upper	Mer. Pass. Lower	Age	Phase
	m s	m s	h m	h m	h m	d	%
29	11 43	11 33	11 48	00 07	12 31	16	99
30	11 22	11 11	11 49	00 55	13 19	17	97
1	11 00	10 49	11 49	01 44	14 07	18	93

UT	ARIES	VENUS −3.9		MARS +1.2		JUPITER −2.8		SATURN +0.7		STARS		
	GHA	GHA	Dec	GHA	Dec	GHA	Dec	GHA	Dec	Name	SHA	Dec
d h	° ′	° ′	° ′	° ′	° ′	° ′	° ′	° ′	° ′		° ′	° ′
2 00	71 14.5	210 50.6	S13 57.4	148 48.1	S24 06.1	1 13.2	N21 21.8	216 05.4	S11 37.2	Acamar	315 18.2	S40 15.3
01	86 16.9	225 50.1	58.4	163 48.5	05.9	16 16.0	21.7	231 07.6	37.2	Achernar	335 26.7	S57 10.4
02	101 19.4	240 49.5	13 59.4	178 48.8	05.8	31 18.9	21.7	246 09.8	37.3	Acrux	173 09.9	S63 10.0
03	116 21.9	255 48.9	14 00.4	193 49.2	. . 05.6	46 21.7	. . 21.6	261 12.0	. . 37.4	Adhara	255 12.5	S28 59.4
04	131 24.3	270 48.4	01.4	208 49.6	05.4	61 24.5	21.6	276 14.2	37.5	Aldebaran	290 49.4	N16 32.0
05	146 26.8	285 47.8	02.3	223 49.9	05.3	76 27.3	21.6	291 16.4	37.6			
06	161 29.3	300 47.2	S14 03.3	238 50.3	S24 05.1	91 30.2	N21 21.5	306 18.6	S11 37.7	Alioth	166 21.4	N55 53.1
07	176 31.7	315 46.6	04.3	253 50.7	04.9	106 33.0	21.5	321 20.8	37.7	Alkaid	152 59.6	N49 14.7
08	191 34.2	330 46.1	05.3	268 51.0	04.8	121 35.8	21.4	336 23.0	37.8	Al Na'ir	27 44.3	S46 54.0
S 09	206 36.6	345 45.5	. . 06.3	283 51.4	. . 04.6	136 38.6	. . 21.4	351 25.2	. . 37.9	Alnilam	275 46.4	S 1 11.7
U 10	221 39.1	0 44.9	07.2	298 51.8	04.5	151 41.5	21.4	6 27.4	38.0	Alphard	217 56.3	S 8 42.9
N 11	236 41.6	15 44.3	08.2	313 52.1	04.3	166 44.3	21.3	21 29.6	38.1			
D 12	251 44.0	30 43.8	S14 09.2	328 52.5	S24 04.1	181 47.1	N21 21.3	36 31.8	S11 38.2	Alphecca	126 11.7	N26 40.3
A 13	266 46.5	45 43.2	10.2	343 52.9	04.0	196 50.0	21.2	51 34.0	38.2	Alpheratz	357 43.7	N29 10.0
Y 14	281 49.0	60 42.6	11.1	358 53.2	03.8	211 52.8	21.2	66 36.2	38.3	Altair	62 08.8	N 8 54.4
15	296 51.4	75 42.0	. . 12.1	13 53.6	. . 03.6	226 55.6	. . 21.2	81 38.4	. . 38.4	Ankaa	353 15.9	S42 14.3
16	311 53.9	90 41.5	13.1	28 54.0	03.5	241 58.4	21.1	96 40.6	38.5	Antares	112 27.1	S26 27.5
17	326 56.4	105 40.9	14.1	43 54.4	03.3	257 01.3	21.1	111 42.9	38.6			
18	341 58.8	120 40.3	S14 15.0	58 54.7	S24 03.1	272 04.1	N21 21.0	126 45.1	S11 38.7	Arcturus	145 56.4	N19 06.9
19	357 01.3	135 39.7	16.0	73 55.1	02.9	287 06.9	21.0	141 47.3	38.7	Atria	107 29.8	S69 02.9
20	12 03.8	150 39.2	17.0	88 55.5	02.8	302 09.7	20.9	156 49.5	38.8	Avior	234 17.7	S59 33.0
21	27 06.2	165 38.6	. . 18.0	103 55.8	. . 02.6	317 12.6	. . 20.9	171 51.7	. . 38.9	Bellatrix	278 32.1	N 6 21.6
22	42 08.7	180 38.0	18.9	118 56.2	02.4	332 15.4	20.9	186 53.9	39.0	Betelgeuse	271 01.4	N 7 24.4
23	57 11.1	195 37.4	19.9	133 56.6	02.3	347 18.2	20.8	201 56.1	39.1			
3 00	72 13.6	210 36.8	S14 20.9	148 56.9	S24 02.1	2 21.1	N21 20.8	216 58.3	S11 39.1	Canopus	263 55.8	S52 42.2
01	87 16.1	225 36.2	21.9	163 57.3	01.9	17 23.9	20.7	232 00.5	39.2	Capella	280 34.5	N46 00.5
02	102 18.5	240 35.7	22.8	178 57.7	01.8	32 26.7	20.7	247 02.7	39.3	Deneb	49 32.0	N45 20.0
03	117 21.0	255 35.1	. . 23.8	193 58.0	. . 01.6	47 29.5	. . 20.7	262 04.9	. . 39.4	Denebola	182 34.1	N14 29.9
04	132 23.5	270 34.5	24.8	208 58.4	01.4	62 32.4	20.6	277 07.1	39.5	Diphda	348 56.1	S17 54.9
05	147 25.9	285 33.9	25.7	223 58.8	01.2	77 35.2	20.6	292 09.3	39.6			
06	162 28.4	300 33.3	S14 26.7	238 59.2	S24 01.1	92 38.0	N21 20.5	307 11.5	S11 39.6	Dubhe	193 52.2	N61 40.5
07	177 30.9	315 32.8	27.7	253 59.5	00.9	107 40.9	20.5	322 13.7	39.7	Elnath	278 12.7	N28 37.0
08	192 33.3	330 32.2	28.6	268 59.9	00.7	122 43.7	20.5	337 15.9	39.8	Eltanin	90 46.8	N51 29.5
M 09	207 35.8	345 31.6	. . 29.6	284 00.3	. . 00.5	137 46.5	. . 20.4	352 18.1	. . 39.9	Enif	33 47.6	N 9 56.3
O 10	222 38.3	0 31.0	30.6	299 00.6	00.4	152 49.3	20.4	7 20.3	40.0	Fomalhaut	15 24.4	S29 33.2
N 11	237 40.7	15 30.4	31.5	314 01.0	00.2	167 52.2	20.3	22 22.5	40.1			
D 12	252 43.2	30 29.8	S14 32.5	329 01.4	S24 00.0	182 55.0	N21 20.3	37 24.7	S11 40.1	Gacrux	172 01.5	S57 10.9
A 13	267 45.6	45 29.2	33.4	344 01.7	23 59.8	197 57.8	20.2	52 27.0	40.2	Gienah	175 52.8	S17 36.8
Y 14	282 48.1	60 28.6	34.4	359 02.1	59.6	213 00.6	20.2	67 29.2	40.3	Hadar	148 48.9	S60 25.9
15	297 50.6	75 28.1	. . 35.4	14 02.5	. . 59.5	228 03.5	. . 20.2	82 31.4	. . 40.4	Hamal	328 00.9	N23 31.5
16	312 53.0	90 27.5	36.3	29 02.8	59.3	243 06.3	20.1	97 33.6	40.5	Kaus Aust.	83 44.7	S34 22.6
17	327 55.5	105 26.9	37.3	44 03.2	59.1	258 09.1	20.1	112 35.8	40.5			
18	342 58.0	120 26.3	S14 38.3	59 03.6	S23 58.9	273 12.0	N21 20.0	127 38.0	S11 40.6	Kochab	137 21.1	N74 06.0
19	358 00.4	135 25.7	39.2	74 03.9	58.8	288 14.8	20.0	142 40.2	40.7	Markab	13 38.7	N15 16.7
20	13 02.9	150 25.1	40.2	89 04.3	58.6	303 17.6	20.0	157 42.4	40.8	Menkar	314 15.1	N 4 08.4
21	28 05.4	165 24.5	. . 41.1	104 04.7	. . 58.4	318 20.4	. . 19.9	172 44.6	. . 40.9	Menkent	148 08.3	S36 25.8
22	43 07.8	180 23.9	42.1	119 05.1	58.2	333 23.3	19.9	187 46.8	41.0	Miaplacidus	221 39.3	S69 46.1
23	58 10.3	195 23.3	43.0	134 05.4	58.0	348 26.1	19.8	202 49.0	41.0			
4 00	73 12.7	210 22.7	S14 44.0	149 05.8	S23 57.8	3 28.9	N21 19.8	217 51.2	S11 41.1	Mirfak	308 40.4	N49 54.5
01	88 15.2	225 22.1	45.0	164 06.2	57.7	18 31.7	19.7	232 53.4	41.2	Nunki	75 59.1	S26 16.7
02	103 17.7	240 21.6	45.9	179 06.5	57.5	33 34.6	19.7	247 55.6	41.3	Peacock	53 20.2	S56 41.6
03	118 20.1	255 21.0	. . 46.9	194 06.9	. . 57.3	48 37.4	. . 19.7	262 57.8	. . 41.4	Pollux	243 27.9	N27 59.4
04	133 22.6	270 20.4	47.8	209 07.3	57.1	63 40.2	19.6	278 00.0	41.4	Procyon	244 59.9	N 5 11.4
05	148 25.1	285 19.8	48.8	224 07.6	56.9	78 43.1	19.6	293 02.3	41.5			
06	163 27.5	300 19.2	S14 49.7	239 08.0	S23 56.7	93 45.9	N21 19.5	308 04.5	S11 41.6	Rasalhague	96 07.1	N12 33.2
07	178 30.0	315 18.6	50.7	254 08.4	56.6	108 48.7	19.5	323 06.7	41.7	Regulus	207 43.8	N11 54.1
08	193 32.5	330 18.0	51.6	269 08.7	56.4	123 51.5	19.5	338 08.9	41.8	Rigel	281 12.1	S 8 11.3
T 09	208 34.9	345 17.4	. . 52.6	284 09.1	. . 56.2	138 54.4	. . 19.4	353 11.1	. . 41.8	Rigil Kent.	139 52.8	S60 53.1
U 10	223 37.4	0 16.8	53.5	299 09.5	56.0	153 57.2	19.4	8 13.3	41.9	Sabik	102 13.3	S15 44.3
E 11	238 39.9	15 16.2	54.5	314 09.9	55.8	169 00.0	19.3	23 15.5	42.0			
S 12	253 42.3	30 15.6	S14 55.4	329 10.2	S23 55.6	184 02.8	N21 19.3	38 17.7	S11 42.1	Schedar	349 40.6	N56 36.8
D 13	268 44.8	45 15.0	56.4	344 10.6	55.4	199 05.7	19.3	53 19.9	42.2	Shaula	96 22.8	S37 06.6
A 14	283 47.2	60 14.4	57.3	359 11.0	55.2	214 08.5	19.2	68 22.1	42.3	Sirius	258 33.7	S16 44.1
Y 15	298 49.7	75 13.8	. . 58.3	14 11.3	. . 55.0	229 11.3	. . 19.2	83 24.3	. . 42.3	Spica	158 31.9	S11 13.7
16	313 52.2	90 13.2	14 59.2	29 11.7	54.9	244 14.2	19.1	98 26.5	42.4	Suhail	222 52.5	S43 29.0
17	328 54.6	105 12.6	15 00.2	44 12.1	54.7	259 17.0	19.1	113 28.7	42.5			
18	343 57.1	120 12.0	S15 01.1	59 12.4	S23 54.5	274 19.8	N21 19.0	128 30.9	S11 42.6	Vega	80 39.6	N38 48.0
19	358 59.6	135 11.4	02.0	74 12.8	54.3	289 22.6	19.0	143 33.2	42.7	Zuben'ubi	137 06.1	S16 05.6
20	14 02.0	150 10.8	03.0	89 13.2	54.1	304 25.5	19.0	158 35.4	42.7		SHA	Mer.Pass.
21	29 04.5	165 10.2	. . 03.9	104 13.5	. . 53.9	319 28.3	. . 18.9	173 37.6	. . 42.8		° ′	h m
22	44 07.0	180 09.6	04.9	119 13.9	53.7	334 31.1	18.9	188 39.8	42.9	Venus	138 23.2	9 58
23	59 09.4	195 09.0	05.8	134 14.3	53.5	349 33.9	18.8	203 42.0	43.0	Mars	76 43.3	14 04
	h m									Jupiter	290 07.4	23 46
Mer. Pass. 19 07.9		v −0.6	d 1.0	v 0.4	d 0.2	v 2.8	d 0.0	v 2.2	d 0.1	Saturn	144 44.7	9 31

UT	SUN GHA	SUN Dec	MOON GHA	v	MOON Dec	d	HP
d h	° ′	° ′	° ′	′	° ′	′	′
2 00	182 39.2	S21 58.6	323 25.1	12.4	N18 17.7	5.5	54.4
01	197 38.9	59.0	337 56.5	12.5	18 12.2	5.5	54.4
02	212 38.7	59.4	352 28.0	12.4	18 06.7	5.6	54.4
03	227 38.5	21 59.7	6 59.4	12.5	18 01.1	5.6	54.5
04	242 38.2	22 00.1	21 30.9	12.5	17 55.5	5.8	54.5
05	257 38.0	00.5	36 02.4	12.5	17 49.7	5.8	54.5
06	272 37.7	S22 00.8	50 33.9	12.5	N17 43.9	6.0	54.5
07	287 37.5	01.2	65 05.4	12.6	17 37.9	6.0	54.5
08	302 37.3	01.5	79 37.0	12.6	17 31.9	6.0	54.5
S 09	317 37.0	01.9	94 08.6	12.6	17 25.9	6.2	54.5
U 10	332 36.8	02.3	108 40.2	12.6	17 19.7	6.3	54.5
N 11	347 36.5	02.6	123 11.8	12.6	17 13.4	6.3	54.6
D 12	2 36.3	S22 03.0	137 43.4	12.7	N17 07.1	6.4	54.6
A 13	17 36.0	03.4	152 15.1	12.7	17 00.7	6.5	54.6
Y 14	32 35.8	03.7	166 46.8	12.7	16 54.2	6.6	54.6
15	47 35.6	04.1	181 18.5	12.7	16 47.6	6.6	54.6
16	62 35.3	04.4	195 50.2	12.8	16 41.0	6.8	54.6
17	77 35.1	04.8	210 22.0	12.7	16 34.2	6.8	54.7
18	92 34.8	S22 05.1	224 53.7	12.8	N16 27.4	6.9	54.7
19	107 34.6	05.5	239 25.5	12.8	16 20.5	6.9	54.7
20	122 34.3	05.8	253 57.3	12.9	16 13.6	7.1	54.7
21	137 34.1	06.2	268 29.2	12.8	16 06.5	7.1	54.7
22	152 33.8	06.5	283 01.0	12.9	15 59.4	7.2	54.7
23	167 33.6	06.9	297 32.9	12.9	15 52.2	7.3	54.7
3 00	182 33.4	S22 07.2	312 04.8	12.9	N15 44.9	7.3	54.8
01	197 33.1	07.6	326 36.7	13.0	15 37.6	7.4	54.8
02	212 32.9	07.9	341 08.7	12.9	15 30.2	7.5	54.8
03	227 32.6	08.3	355 40.6	13.0	15 22.7	7.6	54.8
04	242 32.4	08.6	10 12.6	13.0	15 15.1	7.6	54.8
05	257 32.1	09.0	24 44.6	13.0	15 07.5	7.7	54.9
06	272 31.9	S22 09.3	39 16.6	13.0	N14 59.8	7.8	54.9
07	287 31.6	09.7	53 48.6	13.1	14 52.0	7.9	54.9
08	302 31.4	10.0	68 20.7	13.0	14 44.1	7.9	54.9
M 09	317 31.1	10.4	82 52.7	13.1	14 36.2	8.0	54.9
O 10	332 30.9	10.7	97 24.8	13.1	14 28.2	8.0	54.9
N 11	347 30.6	11.1	111 56.9	13.2	14 20.2	8.2	55.0
D 12	2 30.4	S22 11.4	126 29.1	13.1	N14 12.0	8.2	55.0
A 13	17 30.1	11.7	141 01.2	13.2	14 03.8	8.2	55.0
Y 14	32 29.9	12.1	155 33.4	13.1	13 55.6	8.4	55.0
15	47 29.6	12.4	170 05.5	13.2	13 47.2	8.4	55.0
16	62 29.4	12.8	184 37.7	13.2	13 38.8	8.5	55.1
17	77 29.1	13.1	199 09.9	13.3	13 30.3	8.5	55.1
18	92 28.9	S22 13.4	213 42.2	13.2	N13 21.8	8.6	55.1
19	107 28.6	13.8	228 14.4	13.3	13 13.2	8.7	55.1
20	122 28.4	14.1	242 46.7	13.2	13 04.5	8.7	55.2
21	137 28.1	14.4	257 18.9	13.3	12 55.8	8.8	55.2
22	152 27.9	14.8	271 51.2	13.3	12 47.0	8.8	55.2
23	167 27.6	15.1	286 23.5	13.3	12 38.2	9.0	55.2
4 00	182 27.4	S22 15.4	300 55.8	13.3	N12 29.2	9.0	55.2
01	197 27.1	15.8	315 28.1	13.4	12 20.2	9.0	55.3
02	212 26.9	16.1	330 00.5	13.3	12 11.2	9.1	55.3
03	227 26.6	16.4	344 32.8	13.4	12 02.1	9.2	55.3
04	242 26.4	16.8	359 05.2	13.3	11 52.9	9.2	55.3
05	257 26.1	17.1	13 37.5	13.4	11 43.7	9.3	55.4
06	272 25.9	S22 17.4	28 09.9	13.4	N11 34.4	9.3	55.4
07	287 25.6	17.8	42 42.3	13.4	11 25.1	9.4	55.4
T 08	302 25.3	18.1	57 14.7	13.4	11 15.7	9.5	55.4
U 09	317 25.1	18.4	71 47.1	13.4	11 06.2	9.5	55.4
E 10	332 24.8	18.7	86 19.5	13.4	10 56.7	9.6	55.5
S 11	347 24.6	19.1	100 51.9	13.5	10 47.1	9.6	55.5
D 12	2 24.3	S22 19.4	115 24.4	13.4	N10 37.5	9.7	55.5
A 13	17 24.1	19.7	129 56.8	13.4	10 27.8	9.8	55.5
Y 14	32 23.8	20.0	144 29.2	13.5	10 18.0	9.8	55.6
15	47 23.6	20.3	159 01.7	13.5	10 08.2	9.8	55.6
16	62 23.3	20.7	173 34.2	13.4	9 58.4	9.9	55.6
17	77 23.0	21.0	188 06.6	13.5	9 48.5	10.0	55.7
18	92 22.8	S22 21.3	202 39.1	13.4	N 9 38.5	10.0	55.7
19	107 22.5	21.6	217 11.5	13.5	9 28.5	10.0	55.7
20	122 22.3	21.9	231 44.0	13.5	9 18.5	10.2	55.7
21	137 22.0	22.3	246 16.5	13.4	9 08.3	10.1	55.8
22	152 21.8	22.6	260 48.9	13.5	8 58.2	10.3	55.8
23	167 21.5	22.9	275 21.4	13.5	N 8 48.0	10.3	55.8
	SD 16.3	d 0.3	SD 14.9		15.0		15.1

Lat.	Twilight Naut.	Twilight Civil	Sunrise	Moonrise 2	3	4	5
°	h m	h m	h m	h m	h m	h m	h m
N 72	07 57	10 01	■	16 34	18 42	20 36	22 26
N 70	07 40	09 19	■	17 23	19 08	20 51	22 32
68	07 26	08 50	10 51	17 54	19 28	21 02	22 38
66	07 15	08 28	09 55	18 16	19 43	21 12	22 42
64	07 05	08 11	09 22	18 34	19 56	21 20	22 46
62	06 57	07 57	08 58	18 49	20 07	21 27	22 49
60	06 49	07 45	08 40	19 01	20 16	21 33	22 52
N 58	06 43	07 34	08 24	19 12	20 24	21 38	22 54
56	06 37	07 25	08 11	19 21	20 31	21 43	22 57
54	06 31	07 16	07 59	19 29	20 37	21 47	22 59
52	06 26	07 09	07 49	19 36	20 42	21 50	23 00
50	06 21	07 02	07 40	19 43	20 47	21 54	23 02
45	06 10	06 47	07 20	19 57	20 58	22 01	23 06
N 40	06 01	06 35	07 05	20 09	21 07	22 07	23 09
35	05 52	06 24	06 52	20 18	21 15	22 12	23 11
30	05 44	06 14	06 40	20 27	21 22	22 17	23 13
20	05 29	05 56	06 20	20 42	21 33	22 25	23 17
N 10	05 14	05 40	06 03	20 55	21 43	22 32	23 21
0	04 58	05 24	05 46	21 07	21 53	22 38	23 24
S 10	04 40	05 07	05 30	21 19	22 02	22 45	23 27
20	04 19	04 48	05 12	21 32	22 12	22 52	23 31
30	03 51	04 24	04 51	21 46	22 24	23 00	23 34
35	03 34	04 10	04 39	21 55	22 30	23 04	23 37
40	03 12	03 53	04 25	22 04	22 38	23 09	23 39
45	02 44	03 32	04 08	22 15	22 47	23 15	23 42
S 50	02 04	03 04	03 47	22 29	22 57	23 22	23 46
52	01 41	02 51	03 37	22 35	23 02	23 25	23 47
54	01 09	02 35	03 26	22 42	23 07	23 29	23 49
56	////	02 15	03 13	22 50	23 13	23 33	23 51
58	////	01 51	02 58	22 59	23 20	23 37	23 53
S 60	////	01 16	02 40	23 09	23 27	23 42	23 55

Lat.	Sunset	Twilight Civil	Twilight Naut.	Moonset 2	3	4	5
°	h m	h m	h m	h m	h m	h m	h m
N 72	■	13 38	15 42	13 28	12 56	12 37	12 23
N 70	■	14 21	15 59	12 38	12 28	12 21	12 14
68	12 48	14 49	16 13	12 06	12 08	12 08	12 07
66	13 44	15 11	16 24	11 43	11 51	11 57	12 01
64	14 17	15 28	16 34	11 24	11 38	11 48	11 56
62	14 41	15 43	16 43	11 09	11 26	11 40	11 51
60	15 00	15 55	16 50	10 56	11 17	11 33	11 47
N 58	15 16	16 06	16 57	10 45	11 08	11 27	11 44
56	15 29	16 15	17 03	10 35	11 00	11 22	11 40
54	15 41	16 23	17 09	10 27	10 54	11 17	11 38
52	15 51	16 31	17 14	10 19	10 48	11 12	11 35
50	16 00	16 38	17 18	10 12	10 42	11 08	11 33
45	16 19	16 52	17 29	09 57	10 30	11 00	11 27
N 40	16 35	17 05	17 39	09 45	10 20	10 53	11 23
35	16 48	17 16	17 47	09 35	10 12	10 46	11 19
30	17 00	17 26	17 55	09 25	10 04	10 41	11 16
20	17 20	17 44	18 11	09 10	09 51	10 31	11 10
N 10	17 37	18 00	18 24	08 56	09 40	10 23	11 05
0	17 54	18 16	18 42	08 42	09 29	10 15	11 00
S 10	18 10	18 33	19 00	08 29	09 18	10 07	10 55
20	18 28	18 52	19 21	08 15	09 07	09 58	10 50
30	18 49	19 16	19 49	07 59	08 53	09 48	10 44
35	19 01	19 30	20 06	07 50	08 45	09 42	10 40
40	19 15	19 48	20 28	07 39	08 37	09 36	10 36
45	19 32	20 09	20 57	07 26	08 26	09 28	10 32
S 50	19 53	20 36	21 37	07 10	08 13	09 19	10 26
52	20 03	20 50	22 01	07 03	08 08	09 15	10 24
54	20 15	21 06	22 34	06 55	08 01	09 10	10 21
56	20 28	21 26	////	06 46	07 54	09 05	10 18
58	20 43	21 51	////	06 35	07 46	08 59	10 14
S 60	21 01	22 27	////	06 23	07 36	08 52	10 10

Day	Eqn. of Time 00h	Eqn. of Time 12h	Mer. Pass.	Mer. Pass. Upper	Mer. Pass. Lower	Age	Phase
d	m s	m s	h m	h m	h m	d	%
2	10 37	10 26	11 50	02 31	14 55	19	87
3	10 14	10 02	11 50	03 18	15 41	20	80
4	09 50	09 38	11 50	04 04	16 27	21	71

UT	ARIES	VENUS −3.9		MARS +1.2		JUPITER −2.8		SATURN +0.7		STARS		
	GHA	GHA	Dec	GHA	Dec	GHA	Dec	GHA	Dec	Name	SHA	Dec
5 00	74 11.9	210 08.4	S15 06.8	149 14.7	S23 53.3	4 36.8	N21 18.8	218 44.2	S11 43.1	Acamar	315 18.2	S40 15.3
01	89 14.4	225 07.8	07.7	164 15.0	53.1	19 39.6	18.8	233 46.4	43.1	Achernar	335 26.7	S57 10.5
02	104 16.8	240 07.2	08.6	179 15.4	52.9	34 42.4	18.7	248 48.6	43.2	Acrux	173 09.9	S63 10.0
03	119 19.3	255 06.5 . .	09.6	194 15.8 . .	52.7	49 45.2 . .	18.7	263 50.8 . .	43.3	Adhara	255 12.5	S28 59.4
04	134 21.7	270 05.9	10.5	209 16.1	52.5	64 48.1	18.6	278 53.0	43.4	Aldebaran	290 49.4	N16 32.0
05	149 24.2	285 05.3	11.5	224 16.5	52.3	79 50.9	18.6	293 55.2	43.5			
06	164 26.7	300 04.7	S15 12.4	239 16.9	S23 52.1	94 53.7	N21 18.5	308 57.4	S11 43.5	Alioth	166 21.3	N55 53.1
W 07	179 29.1	315 04.1	13.3	254 17.2	51.9	109 56.6	18.5	323 59.7	43.6	Alkaid	152 59.5	N49 14.7
E 08	194 31.6	330 03.5	14.3	269 17.6	51.7	124 59.4	18.5	339 01.9	43.7	Al Na'ir	27 44.3	S46 54.0
D 09	209 34.1	345 02.9 . .	15.2	284 18.0 . .	51.6	140 02.2 . .	18.4	354 04.1 . .	43.8	Alnilam	275 46.4	S 1 11.7
N 10	224 36.5	0 02.3	16.1	299 18.3	51.4	155 05.0	18.4	9 06.3	43.9	Alphard	217 56.3	S 8 43.0
E 11	239 39.0	15 01.7	17.1	314 18.7	51.2	170 07.9	18.3	24 08.5	43.9			
S 12	254 41.5	30 01.1	S15 18.0	329 19.1	S23 51.0	185 10.7	N21 18.3	39 10.7	S11 44.0	Alphecca	126 11.7	N26 40.3
D 13	269 43.9	45 00.5	18.9	344 19.5	50.8	200 13.5	18.3	54 12.9	44.1	Alpheratz	357 43.8	N29 10.0
A 14	284 46.4	59 59.8	19.9	359 19.8	50.6	215 16.3	18.2	69 15.1	44.2	Altair	62 08.9	N 8 54.4
Y 15	299 48.8	74 59.2 . .	20.8	14 20.2 . .	50.4	230 19.2 . .	18.2	84 17.3 . .	44.3	Ankaa	353 15.9	S42 14.3
16	314 51.3	89 58.6	21.7	29 20.6	50.2	245 22.0	18.1	99 19.5	44.3	Antares	112 27.1	S26 27.5
17	329 53.8	104 58.0	22.7	44 20.9	49.9	260 24.8	18.1	114 21.7	44.4			
18	344 56.2	119 57.4	S15 23.6	59 21.3	S23 49.7	275 27.6	N21 18.0	129 24.0	S11 44.5	Arcturus	145 56.3	N19 06.9
19	359 58.7	134 56.8	24.5	74 21.7	49.5	290 30.5	18.0	144 26.2	44.6	Atria	107 29.8	S69 02.9
20	15 01.2	149 56.2	25.4	89 22.0	49.3	305 33.3	18.0	159 28.4	44.7	Avior	234 17.7	S59 33.0
21	30 03.6	164 55.5 . .	26.4	104 22.4 . .	49.1	320 36.1 . .	17.9	174 30.6 . .	44.7	Bellatrix	278 32.1	N 6 21.6
22	45 06.1	179 54.9	27.3	119 22.8	48.9	335 39.0	17.9	189 32.8	44.8	Betelgeuse	271 01.4	N 7 24.4
23	60 08.6	194 54.3	28.2	134 23.2	48.7	350 41.8	17.8	204 35.0	44.9			
6 00	75 11.0	209 53.7	S15 29.1	149 23.5	S23 48.5	5 44.6	N21 17.8	219 37.2	S11 45.0	Canopus	263 55.8	S52 42.2
01	90 13.5	224 53.1	30.1	164 23.9	48.3	20 47.4	17.8	234 39.4	45.1	Capella	280 34.5	N46 00.5
02	105 16.0	239 52.5	31.0	179 24.3	48.1	35 50.3	17.7	249 41.6	45.1	Deneb	49 32.0	N45 20.0
03	120 18.4	254 51.8 . .	31.9	194 24.6 . .	47.9	50 53.1 . .	17.7	264 43.8 . .	45.2	Denebola	182 34.1	N14 29.8
04	135 20.9	269 51.2	32.8	209 25.0	47.7	65 55.9	17.6	279 46.1	45.3	Diphda	348 56.1	S17 54.9
05	150 23.3	284 50.6	33.8	224 25.4	47.5	80 58.7	17.6	294 48.3	45.4			
06	165 25.8	299 50.0	S15 34.7	239 25.7	S23 47.3	96 01.6	N21 17.6	309 50.5	S11 45.5	Dubhe	193 52.2	N61 40.5
T 07	180 28.3	314 49.4	35.6	254 26.1	47.1	111 04.4	17.5	324 52.7	45.5	Elnath	278 12.7	N28 37.0
H 08	195 30.7	329 48.7	36.5	269 26.5	46.9	126 07.2	17.5	339 54.9	45.6	Eltanin	90 46.8	N51 29.4
U 09	210 33.2	344 48.1 . .	37.4	284 26.9 . .	46.7	141 10.0 . .	17.4	354 57.1 . .	45.7	Enif	33 47.6	N 9 56.3
R 10	225 35.7	359 47.5	38.4	299 27.2	46.4	156 12.9	17.4	9 59.3	45.8	Fomalhaut	15 24.4	S29 33.2
S 11	240 38.1	14 46.9	39.3	314 27.6	46.2	171 15.7	17.3	25 01.5	45.9			
D 12	255 40.6	29 46.3	S15 40.2	329 28.0	S23 46.0	186 18.5	N21 17.3	40 03.7	S11 45.9	Gacrux	172 01.5	S57 10.9
A 13	270 43.1	44 45.6	41.1	344 28.3	45.8	201 21.3	17.3	55 05.9	46.0	Gienah	175 52.8	S17 36.8
Y 14	285 45.5	59 45.0	42.0	359 28.7	45.6	216 24.2	17.2	70 08.2	46.1	Hadar	148 48.9	S60 25.9
15	300 48.0	74 44.4 . .	42.9	14 29.1 . .	45.4	231 27.0 . .	17.2	85 10.4 . .	46.2	Hamal	328 00.9	N23 31.5
16	315 50.5	89 43.8	43.9	29 29.4	45.2	246 29.8	17.1	100 12.6	46.3	Kaus Aust.	83 44.7	S34 22.6
17	330 52.9	104 43.1	44.8	44 29.8	45.0	261 32.6	17.1	115 14.8	46.3			
18	345 55.4	119 42.5	S15 45.7	59 30.2	S23 44.7	276 35.5	N21 17.1	130 17.0	S11 46.4	Kochab	137 21.1	N74 06.0
19	0 57.8	134 41.9	46.6	74 30.6	44.5	291 38.3	17.0	145 19.2	46.5	Markab	13 38.7	N15 16.7
20	16 00.3	149 41.3	47.5	89 30.9	44.3	306 41.1	17.0	160 21.4	46.6	Menkar	314 15.1	N 4 08.4
21	31 02.8	164 40.6 . .	48.4	104 31.3 . .	44.1	321 43.9 . .	16.9	175 23.6 . .	46.7	Menkent	148 08.3	S36 25.8
22	46 05.2	179 40.0	49.3	119 31.7	43.9	336 46.8	16.9	190 25.8	46.7	Miaplacidus	221 39.2	S69 46.1
23	61 07.7	194 39.4	50.2	134 32.0	43.7	351 49.6	16.8	205 28.1	46.8			
7 00	76 10.2	209 38.7	S15 51.2	149 32.4	S23 43.5	6 52.4	N21 16.8	220 30.3	S11 46.9	Mirfak	308 40.4	N49 54.5
01	91 12.6	224 38.1	52.1	164 32.8	43.2	21 55.2	16.8	235 32.5	47.0	Nunki	75 59.1	S26 16.7
02	106 15.1	239 37.5	53.0	179 33.1	43.0	36 58.1	16.7	250 34.7	47.1	Peacock	53 20.2	S56 41.6
03	121 17.6	254 36.9 . .	53.9	194 33.5 . .	42.8	52 00.9 . .	16.7	265 36.9 . .	47.1	Pollux	243 27.9	N27 59.4
04	136 20.0	269 36.2	54.8	209 33.9	42.6	67 03.7	16.6	280 39.1	47.2	Procyon	244 59.8	N 5 11.3
05	151 22.5	284 35.6	55.7	224 34.3	42.4	82 06.5	16.6	295 41.3	47.3			
06	166 24.9	299 35.0	S15 56.6	239 34.6	S23 42.1	97 09.4	N21 16.6	310 43.5	S11 47.4	Rasalhague	96 07.1	N12 33.2
07	181 27.4	314 34.3	57.5	254 35.0	41.9	112 12.2	16.5	325 45.8	47.4	Regulus	207 43.8	N11 54.1
08	196 29.9	329 33.7	58.4	269 35.4	41.7	127 15.0	16.5	340 48.0	47.5	Rigel	281 12.1	S 8 11.3
F 09	211 32.3	344 33.1	15 59.3	284 35.7 . .	41.5	142 17.8 . .	16.4	355 50.2 . .	47.6	Rigil Kent.	139 52.7	S60 53.1
R 10	226 34.8	359 32.4	16 00.2	299 36.1	41.3	157 20.7	16.4	10 52.4	47.7	Sabik	102 13.3	S15 44.3
I 11	241 37.3	14 31.8	01.1	314 36.5	41.0	172 23.5	16.3	25 54.6	47.8			
D 12	256 39.7	29 31.2	S16 02.0	329 36.9	S23 40.8	187 26.3	N21 16.3	40 56.8	S11 47.8	Schedar	349 40.6	N56 36.8
A 13	271 42.2	44 30.5	02.9	344 37.2	40.6	202 29.1	16.3	55 59.0	47.9	Shaula	96 22.8	S37 06.6
Y 14	286 44.7	59 29.9	03.8	359 37.6	40.4	217 32.0	16.2	71 01.2	48.0	Sirius	258 33.7	S16 44.1
15	301 47.1	74 29.2 . .	04.7	14 38.0 . .	40.1	232 34.8 . .	16.2	86 03.5 . .	48.1	Spica	158 31.8	S11 13.7
16	316 49.6	89 28.6	05.6	29 38.3	39.9	247 37.6	16.1	101 05.7	48.2	Suhail	222 52.5	S43 29.0
17	331 52.1	104 28.0	06.5	44 38.7	39.7	262 40.4	16.1	116 07.9	48.2			
18	346 54.5	119 27.3	S16 07.4	59 39.1	S23 39.5	277 43.3	N21 16.1	131 10.1	S11 48.3	Vega	80 39.6	N38 48.0
19	1 57.0	134 26.7	08.3	74 39.5	39.2	292 46.1	16.0	146 12.3	48.4	Zuben'ubi	137 06.1	S16 05.6
20	16 59.4	149 26.1	09.2	89 39.8	39.0	307 48.9	16.0	161 14.5	48.5		SHA	Mer.Pass.
21	32 01.9	164 25.4 . .	10.1	104 40.2 . .	38.8	322 51.7 . .	15.9	176 16.7 . .	48.5		° ′	h m
22	47 04.4	179 24.8	11.0	119 40.6	38.6	337 54.6	15.9	191 19.0	48.6	Venus	134 42.7	10 01
23	62 06.8	194 24.1	11.9	134 40.9	38.3	352 57.4	15.8	206 21.2	48.7	Mars	74 12.5	14 02
Mer. Pass. 18 56.2		v −0.6	d 0.9	v 0.4	d 0.2	v 2.8	d 0.0	v 2.2	d 0.1	Jupiter	290 33.6	23 33
										Saturn	144 26.2	9 20

SUN and MOON — UT

UT	SUN GHA	SUN Dec	MOON GHA	v	MOON Dec	d	HP
d h	° ′	° ′	° ′	′	° ′	′	′
5 00	182 21.2	S22 23.2	289 53.9	13.5	N 8 37.7	10.3	55.8
01	197 21.0	23.5	304 26.4	13.4	8 27.4	10.4	55.9
02	212 20.7	23.8	318 58.8	13.5	8 17.0	10.4	55.9
03	227 20.5	.. 24.1	333 31.3	13.5	8 06.6	10.4	55.9
04	242 20.2	24.5	348 03.8	13.4	7 56.2	10.5	55.9
05	257 19.9	24.8	2 36.2	13.5	7 45.7	10.5	56.0
06	272 19.7	S22 25.1	17 08.7	13.4	N 7 35.2	10.6	56.0
07	287 19.4	25.4	31 41.1	13.5	7 24.6	10.7	56.0
08	302 19.2	25.7	46 13.6	13.4	7 13.9	10.6	56.1
09	317 18.9	.. 26.0	60 46.0	13.5	7 03.3	10.7	56.1
10	332 18.6	26.3	75 18.5	13.4	6 52.6	10.8	56.1
11	347 18.4	26.6	89 50.9	13.4	6 41.8	10.8	56.2
12	2 18.1	S22 26.9	104 23.3	13.4	N 6 31.0	10.8	56.2
13	17 17.9	27.2	118 55.7	13.4	6 20.2	10.9	56.2
14	32 17.6	27.5	133 28.1	13.4	6 09.3	10.9	56.2
15	47 17.3	.. 27.8	148 00.5	13.4	5 58.4	11.0	56.3
16	62 17.1	28.1	162 32.9	13.3	5 47.4	11.0	56.3
17	77 16.8	28.4	177 05.2	13.4	5 36.4	11.0	56.3
18	92 16.6	S22 28.7	191 37.6	13.3	N 5 25.4	11.1	56.4
19	107 16.3	29.0	206 09.9	13.3	5 14.3	11.1	56.4
20	122 16.0	29.3	220 42.2	13.3	5 03.2	11.1	56.4
21	137 15.8	.. 29.6	235 14.5	13.3	4 52.1	11.2	56.5
22	152 15.5	29.9	249 46.8	13.3	4 40.9	11.2	56.5
23	167 15.2	30.2	264 19.1	13.2	4 29.7	11.3	56.5
6 00	182 15.0	S22 30.5	278 51.3	13.3	N 4 18.4	11.2	56.6
01	197 14.7	30.8	293 23.6	13.2	4 07.2	11.3	56.6
02	212 14.4	31.1	307 55.8	13.2	3 55.9	11.4	56.6
03	227 14.2	.. 31.4	322 28.0	13.2	3 44.5	11.3	56.7
04	242 13.9	31.7	337 00.2	13.1	3 33.2	11.4	56.7
05	257 13.6	32.0	351 32.3	13.1	3 21.8	11.5	56.7
06	272 13.4	S22 32.3	6 04.4	13.1	N 3 10.3	11.4	56.8
07	287 13.1	32.6	20 36.5	13.1	2 58.9	11.5	56.8
08	302 12.8	32.9	35 08.6	13.1	2 47.4	11.5	56.8
09	317 12.6	.. 33.2	49 40.7	13.0	2 35.9	11.6	56.9
10	332 12.3	33.5	64 12.7	13.0	2 24.3	11.5	56.9
11	347 12.0	33.7	78 44.7	12.9	2 12.8	11.6	56.9
12	2 11.8	S22 34.0	93 16.6	13.0	N 2 01.2	11.6	57.0
13	17 11.5	34.3	107 48.6	12.9	1 49.6	11.6	57.0
14	32 11.2	34.6	122 20.5	12.9	1 38.0	11.7	57.0
15	47 11.0	.. 34.9	136 52.4	12.8	1 26.3	11.7	57.1
16	62 10.7	35.2	151 24.2	12.8	1 14.6	11.7	57.1
17	77 10.4	35.5	165 56.0	12.8	1 02.9	11.7	57.1
18	92 10.2	S22 35.7	180 27.8	12.7	N 0 51.2	11.7	57.2
19	107 09.9	36.0	194 59.5	12.7	0 39.5	11.8	57.2
20	122 09.6	36.3	209 31.2	12.7	0 27.7	11.7	57.2
21	137 09.4	.. 36.6	224 02.9	12.6	0 16.0	11.8	57.3
22	152 09.1	36.9	238 34.5	12.6	N 0 04.2	11.8	57.3
23	167 08.8	37.1	253 06.1	12.6	S 0 07.6	11.8	57.3
7 00	182 08.6	S22 37.4	267 37.7	12.5	S 0 19.4	11.8	57.4
01	197 08.3	37.7	282 09.2	12.5	0 31.2	11.9	57.4
02	212 08.0	38.0	296 40.7	12.4	0 43.1	11.8	57.5
03	227 07.7	.. 38.3	311 12.1	12.4	0 54.9	11.9	57.5
04	242 07.5	38.5	325 43.5	12.3	1 06.8	11.9	57.5
05	257 07.2	38.8	340 14.8	12.3	1 18.7	11.8	57.6
06	272 06.9	S22 39.1	354 46.1	12.2	S 1 30.5	11.9	57.6
07	287 06.7	39.4	9 17.3	12.2	1 42.4	11.9	57.6
08	302 06.4	39.6	23 48.5	12.2	1 54.3	11.9	57.7
09	317 06.1	.. 39.9	38 19.7	12.1	2 06.2	11.9	57.7
10	332 05.9	40.2	52 50.8	12.0	2 18.1	11.9	57.8
11	347 05.6	40.4	67 21.8	12.0	2 30.0	12.0	57.8
12	2 05.3	S22 40.7	81 52.8	12.0	S 2 42.0	11.9	57.8
13	17 05.0	41.0	96 23.8	11.9	2 53.9	11.9	57.9
14	32 04.8	41.2	110 54.7	11.8	3 05.8	11.9	57.9
15	47 04.5	.. 41.5	125 25.5	11.8	3 17.7	11.9	57.9
16	62 04.2	41.8	139 56.3	11.7	3 29.6	12.0	58.0
17	77 03.9	42.0	154 27.0	11.7	3 41.6	11.9	58.0
18	92 03.7	S22 42.3	168 57.7	11.6	S 3 53.5	11.9	58.1
19	107 03.4	42.6	183 28.3	11.6	4 05.4	11.9	58.1
20	122 03.1	42.8	197 58.9	11.5	4 17.3	11.9	58.1
21	137 02.8	.. 43.1	212 29.4	11.4	4 29.2	11.9	58.2
22	152 02.6	43.4	226 59.8	11.4	4 41.1	11.9	58.2
23	167 02.3	43.6	241 30.2	11.3	S 4 53.0	11.8	58.2
	SD 16.3	d 0.3	SD 15.3		15.5		15.8

Day labels (left margin): WEDNESDAY, THURSDAY, FRIDAY

Twilight, Sunrise and Moonrise

Lat.	Naut.	Civil	Sunrise	Moonrise 5	6	7	8
°	h m	h m	h m	h m	h m	h m	h m
N 72	08 04	10 14	■■	22 26	24 16	00 16	02 11
N 70	07 47	09 28		22 32	24 16	00 16	02 03
68	07 32	08 57	11 13	22 38	24 15	00 15	01 56
66	07 20	08 35	10 05	22 42	24 15	00 15	01 51
64	07 10	08 17	09 30	22 46	24 14	00 14	01 46
62	07 01	08 02	09 05	22 49	24 14	00 14	01 42
60	06 53	07 49	08 45	22 52	24 13	00 13	01 38
N 58	06 47	07 38	08 29	22 54	24 13	00 13	01 35
56	06 40	07 29	08 15	22 57	24 13	00 13	01 32
54	06 35	07 20	08 03	22 59	24 13	00 13	01 30
52	06 29	07 12	07 53	23 00	24 13	00 13	01 27
50	06 24	07 05	07 43	23 02	24 12	00 12	01 25
45	06 13	06 50	07 24	23 06	24 12	00 12	01 21
N 40	06 04	06 37	07 08	23 09	24 12	00 12	01 17
35	05 55	06 26	06 54	23 11	24 11	00 11	01 14
30	05 46	06 16	06 42	23 13	24 11	00 11	01 11
20	05 31	05 58	06 22	23 17	24 11	00 11	01 07
N 10	05 15	05 42	06 04	23 21	24 11	00 11	01 02
0	04 59	05 25	05 47	23 24	24 10	00 10	00 58
S 10	04 41	05 08	05 31	23 27	24 10	00 10	00 55
20	04 19	04 48	05 12	23 31	24 10	00 10	00 51
30	03 51	04 24	04 51	23 34	24 10	00 10	00 46
35	03 33	04 10	04 39	23 37	24 09	00 09	00 43
40	03 11	03 52	04 25	23 39	24 09	00 09	00 40
45	02 42	03 31	04 07	23 42	24 09	00 09	00 37
S 50	02 01	03 03	03 46	23 46	24 09	00 09	00 33
52	01 36	02 49	03 36	23 47	24 09	00 09	00 31
54	01 01	02 32	03 24	23 49	24 09	00 09	00 29
56	////	02 12	03 11	23 51	24 09	00 09	00 27
58	////	01 46	02 55	23 53	24 08	00 08	00 25
S 60	////	01 08	02 37	23 55	24 08	00 08	00 22

Sunset, Twilight and Moonset

Lat.	Sunset	Civil	Naut.	Moonset 5	6	7	8
°	h m	h m	h m	h m	h m	h m	h m
N 72	■■	13 27	15 37	12 23	12 10	11 57	11 43
N 70	■■	14 14	15 55	12 14	12 08	12 01	11 54
68	12 29	14 45	16 10	12 07	12 06	12 04	12 03
66	13 37	15 07	16 22	12 01	12 04	12 07	12 10
64	14 12	15 25	16 32	11 56	12 02	12 09	12 16
62	14 37	15 40	16 41	11 51	12 01	12 11	12 22
60	14 57	15 53	16 49	11 47	12 00	12 13	12 27
N 58	15 13	16 04	16 56	11 44	11 59	12 14	12 31
56	15 27	16 13	17 02	11 40	11 58	12 16	12 35
54	15 39	16 22	17 08	11 38	11 57	12 17	12 38
52	15 49	16 30	17 13	11 35	11 56	12 18	12 41
50	15 59	16 37	17 18	11 33	11 56	12 19	12 44
45	16 19	16 52	17 29	11 27	11 54	12 21	12 50
N 40	16 35	17 05	17 39	11 23	11 53	12 23	12 55
35	16 48	17 16	17 48	11 19	11 52	12 25	13 00
30	17 00	17 26	17 56	11 16	11 51	12 26	13 04
20	17 20	17 44	18 12	11 10	11 49	12 29	13 11
N 10	17 38	18 01	18 27	11 05	11 47	12 31	13 17
0	17 55	18 17	18 43	11 00	11 46	12 33	13 22
S 10	18 12	18 35	19 02	10 55	11 44	12 35	13 28
20	18 30	18 54	19 23	10 50	11 43	12 37	13 34
30	18 51	19 18	19 51	10 44	11 41	12 40	13 41
35	19 04	19 33	20 09	10 40	11 40	12 41	13 45
40	19 18	19 51	20 32	10 36	11 39	12 43	13 49
45	19 35	20 12	21 01	10 32	11 37	12 45	13 55
S 50	19 57	20 40	21 43	10 26	11 35	12 47	14 01
52	20 07	20 55	22 08	10 24	11 35	12 48	14 04
54	20 19	21 11	22 44	10 21	11 34	12 49	14 07
56	20 32	21 32	////	10 18	11 33	12 50	14 11
58	20 48	21 58	////	10 14	11 32	12 52	14 15
S 60	21 07	22 37	////	10 10	11 30	12 53	14 19

SUN and MOON

Day	SUN Eqn. of Time 00h	12h	Mer. Pass.	MOON Mer. Pass. Upper	Lower	Age	Phase
d	m s	m s	h m	h m	h m	d	%
5	09 25	09 13	11 51	04 49	17 12	22	62
6	09 00	08 48	11 51	05 35	17 58	23	52
7	08 35	08 22	11 52	06 22	18 46	24	41

UT	ARIES	VENUS −3.9		MARS +1.2		JUPITER −2.8		SATURN +0.7	
	GHA	GHA	Dec	GHA	Dec	GHA	Dec	GHA	Dec
d h	° ′	° ′	° ′	° ′	° ′	° ′	° ′	° ′	° ′
8 00	77 09.3	209 23.5	S16 12.8	149 41.3	S23 38.1	8 00.2	N21 15.8	221 23.4	S11 48.8
01	92 11.8	224 22.8	13.7	164 41.7	37.9	23 03.0	15.8	236 25.6	48.9
02	107 14.2	239 22.2	14.6	179 42.0	37.7	38 05.9	15.7	251 27.8	48.9
03	122 16.7	254 21.6	.. 15.4	194 42.4	.. 37.4	53 08.7	.. 15.7	266 30.0	.. 49.0
04	137 19.2	269 20.9	16.3	209 42.8	37.2	68 11.5	15.6	281 32.2	49.1
05	152 21.6	284 20.3	17.2	224 43.2	37.0	83 14.3	15.6	296 34.4	49.2
S 06	167 24.1	299 19.6	S16 18.1	239 43.5	S23 36.7	98 17.1	N21 15.6	311 36.7	S11 49.2
A 07	182 26.5	314 19.0	19.0	254 43.9	36.5	113 20.0	15.5	326 38.9	49.3
T 08	197 29.0	329 18.3	19.9	269 44.3	36.3	128 22.8	15.5	341 41.1	49.4
U 09	212 31.5	344 17.7	.. 20.8	284 44.6	.. 36.0	143 25.6	.. 15.4	356 43.3	.. 49.5
R 10	227 33.9	359 17.0	21.7	299 45.0	35.8	158 28.4	15.4	11 45.5	49.6
D 11	242 36.4	14 16.4	22.5	314 45.4	35.6	173 31.3	15.3	26 47.7	49.6
A 12	257 38.9	29 15.8	S16 23.4	329 45.8	S23 35.3	188 34.1	N21 15.3	41 49.9	S11 49.7
Y 13	272 41.3	44 15.1	24.3	344 46.1	35.1	203 36.9	15.3	56 52.2	49.8
14	287 43.8	59 14.5	25.2	359 46.5	34.9	218 39.7	15.2	71 54.4	49.9
15	302 46.3	74 13.8	.. 26.1	14 46.9	.. 34.6	233 42.6	.. 15.2	86 56.6	.. 49.9
16	317 48.7	89 13.2	27.0	29 47.3	34.4	248 45.4	15.1	101 58.8	50.0
17	332 51.2	104 12.5	27.8	44 47.6	34.2	263 48.2	15.1	117 01.0	50.1
18	347 53.7	119 11.9	S16 28.7	59 48.0	S23 33.9	278 51.0	N21 15.1	132 03.2	S11 50.2
19	2 56.1	134 11.2	29.6	74 48.4	33.7	293 53.8	15.0	147 05.5	50.3
20	17 58.6	149 10.6	30.5	89 48.7	33.5	308 56.7	15.0	162 07.7	50.3
21	33 01.0	164 09.9	.. 31.3	104 49.1	.. 33.2	323 59.5	.. 14.9	177 09.9	.. 50.4
22	48 03.5	179 09.2	32.2	119 49.5	33.0	339 02.3	14.9	192 12.1	50.5
23	63 06.0	194 08.6	33.1	134 49.9	32.7	354 05.1	14.8	207 14.3	50.6
9 00	78 08.4	209 07.9	S16 34.0	149 50.2	S23 32.5	9 08.0	N21 14.8	222 16.5	S11 50.6
01	93 10.9	224 07.3	34.8	164 50.6	32.3	24 10.8	14.8	237 18.7	50.7
02	108 13.4	239 06.6	35.7	179 51.0	32.0	39 13.6	14.7	252 21.0	50.8
03	123 15.8	254 06.0	.. 36.6	194 51.3	.. 31.8	54 16.4	.. 14.7	267 23.2	.. 50.9
04	138 18.3	269 05.3	37.5	209 51.7	31.5	69 19.2	14.6	282 25.4	51.0
05	153 20.8	284 04.7	38.3	224 52.1	31.3	84 22.1	14.6	297 27.6	51.0
S 06	168 23.2	299 04.0	S16 39.2	239 52.5	S23 31.1	99 24.9	N21 14.6	312 29.8	S11 51.1
U 07	183 25.7	314 03.3	40.1	254 52.8	30.8	114 27.7	14.5	327 32.0	51.2
N 08	198 28.2	329 02.7	40.9	269 53.2	30.6	129 30.5	14.5	342 34.3	51.3
D 09	213 30.6	344 02.0	.. 41.8	284 53.6	.. 30.3	144 33.4	.. 14.4	357 36.5	.. 51.3
A 10	228 33.1	359 01.4	42.7	299 53.9	30.1	159 36.2	14.4	12 38.7	51.4
Y 11	243 35.5	14 00.7	43.6	314 54.3	29.8	174 39.0	14.3	27 40.9	51.5
12	258 38.0	29 00.1	S16 44.4	329 54.7	S23 29.6	189 41.8	N21 14.3	42 43.1	S11 51.6
13	273 40.5	43 59.4	45.3	344 55.1	29.4	204 44.6	14.3	57 45.3	51.6
14	288 42.9	58 58.7	46.1	359 55.4	29.1	219 47.5	14.2	72 47.5	51.7
15	303 45.4	73 58.1	.. 47.0	14 55.8	.. 28.9	234 50.3	.. 14.2	87 49.8	.. 51.8
16	318 47.9	88 57.4	47.9	29 56.2	28.6	249 53.1	14.1	102 52.0	51.9
17	333 50.3	103 56.7	48.7	44 56.6	28.4	264 55.9	14.1	117 54.2	51.9
18	348 52.8	118 56.1	S16 49.6	59 56.9	S23 28.1	279 58.7	N21 14.1	132 56.4	S11 52.0
19	3 55.3	133 55.4	50.5	74 57.3	27.9	295 01.6	14.0	147 58.6	52.1
20	18 57.7	148 54.8	51.3	89 57.7	27.6	310 04.4	14.0	163 00.9	52.2
21	34 00.2	163 54.1	.. 52.2	104 58.1	.. 27.4	325 07.2	.. 13.9	178 03.1	.. 52.3
22	49 02.6	178 53.4	53.0	119 58.4	27.1	340 10.0	13.9	193 05.3	52.3
23	64 05.1	193 52.8	53.9	134 58.8	26.9	355 12.8	13.9	208 07.5	52.4
10 00	79 07.6	208 52.1	S16 54.8	149 59.2	S23 26.6	10 15.7	N21 13.8	223 09.7	S11 52.5
01	94 10.0	223 51.4	55.6	164 59.5	26.4	25 18.5	13.8	238 11.9	52.6
02	109 12.5	238 50.8	56.5	179 59.9	26.1	40 21.3	13.7	253 14.2	52.6
03	124 15.0	253 50.1	.. 57.3	195 00.3	.. 25.9	55 24.1	.. 13.7	268 16.4	.. 52.7
04	139 17.4	268 49.4	58.2	210 00.7	25.6	70 26.9	13.6	283 18.6	52.8
05	154 19.9	283 48.8	59.0	225 01.0	25.4	85 29.8	13.6	298 20.8	52.9
M 06	169 22.4	298 48.1	S16 59.9	240 01.4	S23 25.1	100 32.6	N21 13.5	313 23.0	S11 52.9
O 07	184 24.8	313 47.4	17 00.7	255 01.8	24.9	115 35.4	13.5	328 25.3	53.0
N 08	199 27.3	328 46.7	01.6	270 02.2	24.6	130 38.2	13.5	343 27.5	53.1
D 09	214 29.8	343 46.1	.. 02.4	285 02.5	.. 24.4	145 41.0	.. 13.4	358 29.7	.. 53.2
A 10	229 32.2	358 45.4	03.3	300 02.9	24.1	160 43.9	13.4	13 31.9	53.2
Y 11	244 34.7	13 44.7	04.1	315 03.3	23.8	175 46.7	13.4	28 34.1	53.3
12	259 37.1	28 44.1	S17 05.0	330 03.7	S23 23.6	190 49.5	N21 13.3	43 36.3	S11 53.4
13	274 39.6	43 43.4	05.8	345 04.0	23.3	205 52.3	13.3	58 38.6	53.5
14	289 42.1	58 42.7	06.7	0 04.4	23.1	220 55.1	13.2	73 40.8	53.5
15	304 44.5	73 42.0	.. 07.5	15 04.8	.. 22.8	235 58.0	.. 13.2	88 43.0	.. 53.6
16	319 47.0	88 41.4	08.4	30 05.1	22.6	251 00.8	13.1	103 45.2	53.7
17	334 49.5	103 40.7	09.2	45 05.5	22.3	266 03.6	13.1	118 47.4	53.8
18	349 51.9	118 40.0	S17 10.1	60 05.9	S23 22.0	281 06.4	N21 13.0	133 49.7	S11 53.9
19	4 54.4	133 39.3	10.9	75 06.3	21.8	296 09.2	13.0	148 51.9	53.9
20	19 56.9	148 38.7	11.7	90 06.6	21.5	311 12.1	13.0	163 54.1	54.0
21	34 59.3	163 38.0	.. 12.6	105 07.0	.. 21.3	326 14.9	.. 12.9	178 56.3	.. 54.1
22	50 01.8	178 37.3	13.4	120 07.4	21.0	341 17.7	12.9	193 58.5	54.2
23	65 04.3	193 36.6	14.3	135 07.8	20.7	356 20.5	12.9	209 00.8	54.2
Mer. Pass.	h m 18 44.4	v −0.7	d 0.9	v 0.4	d 0.2	v 2.8	d 0.0	v 2.2	d 0.1

STARS

Name	SHA	Dec
Acamar	315 18.3	S40 15.3
Achernar	335 26.7	S57 10.5
Acrux	173 09.9	S63 10.0
Adhara	255 12.5	S28 59.4
Aldebaran	290 49.4	N16 32.0
Alioth	166 21.3	N55 53.1
Alkaid	152 59.5	N49 14.7
Al Na'ir	27 44.3	S46 54.0
Alnilam	275 46.4	S 1 11.7
Alphard	217 56.3	S 8 43.0
Alphecca	126 11.7	N26 40.3
Alpheratz	357 43.8	N29 10.0
Altair	62 08.9	N 8 54.4
Ankaa	353 15.9	S42 14.3
Antares	112 27.1	S26 27.5
Arcturus	145 56.3	N19 06.9
Atria	107 29.8	S69 02.9
Avior	234 17.7	S59 33.0
Bellatrix	278 32.1	N 6 21.6
Betelgeuse	271 01.3	N 7 24.4
Canopus	263 55.8	S52 42.2
Capella	280 34.5	N46 00.5
Deneb	49 32.0	N45 20.0
Denebola	182 34.1	N14 29.8
Diphda	348 56.1	S17 55.0
Dubhe	193 52.1	N61 40.5
Elnath	278 12.7	N28 37.0
Eltanin	90 46.8	N51 29.4
Enif	33 47.6	N 9 56.3
Fomalhaut	15 24.4	S29 33.2
Gacrux	172 01.5	S57 10.9
Gienah	175 52.8	S17 36.8
Hadar	148 48.8	S60 25.9
Hamal	328 00.9	N23 31.5
Kaus Aust.	83 44.7	S34 22.6
Kochab	137 21.1	N74 06.0
Markab	13 38.7	N15 16.7
Menkar	314 15.1	N 4 08.4
Menkent	148 08.3	S36 25.8
Miaplacidus	221 39.2	S69 46.1
Mirfak	308 40.4	N49 54.5
Nunki	75 59.1	S26 16.7
Peacock	53 20.2	S56 44.0
Pollux	243 27.9	N27 59.4
Procyon	244 59.8	N 5 11.3
Rasalhague	96 07.1	N12 33.2
Regulus	207 43.8	N11 54.0
Rigel	281 12.1	S 8 11.3
Rigil Kent.	139 52.7	S60 53.0
Sabik	102 13.3	S15 44.3
Schedar	349 40.7	N56 36.8
Shaula	96 22.8	S37 06.6
Sirius	258 33.7	S16 44.1
Spica	158 31.8	S11 13.7
Suhail	222 52.4	S43 29.0
Vega	80 39.6	N38 48.0
Zuben'ubi	137 06.1	S16 05.6

	SHA	Mer. Pass.
	° ′	h m
Venus	130 59.5	10 04
Mars	71 41.8	14 00
Jupiter	290 59.5	23 19
Saturn	144 08.1	9 10

SUN and MOON

UT		SUN GHA	SUN Dec	MOON GHA	v	MOON Dec	d	HP
d h		° '	° '	° '	'	° '	'	'
SATURDAY 8 00		182 02.0	S22 43.9	256 00.5	11.2	S 5 04.8	11.9	58.3
01		197 01.7	44.1	270 30.7	11.2	5 16.7	11.8	58.3
02		212 01.5	44.4	285 00.9	11.1	5 28.5	11.9	58.4
03		227 01.2	.. 44.6	299 31.0	11.1	5 40.4	11.8	58.4
04		242 00.9	44.9	314 01.1	11.0	5 52.2	11.8	58.4
05		257 00.6	45.2	328 31.1	10.9	6 04.0	11.8	58.5
06		272 00.4	S22 45.4	343 01.0	10.8	S 6 15.8	11.8	58.5
07		287 00.1	45.7	357 30.8	10.8	6 27.6	11.8	58.6
08		301 59.8	45.9	12 00.6	10.7	6 39.4	11.7	58.6
09		316 59.5	.. 46.2	26 30.3	10.6	6 51.1	11.7	58.6
10		331 59.3	46.4	40 59.9	10.6	7 02.8	11.7	58.7
11		346 59.0	46.7	55 29.5	10.5	7 14.5	11.7	58.7
12		1 58.7	S22 46.9	69 59.0	10.4	S 7 26.2	11.6	58.7
13		16 58.4	47.2	84 28.4	10.3	7 37.8	11.7	58.8
14		31 58.2	47.4	98 57.7	10.3	7 49.5	11.5	58.8
15		46 57.9	.. 47.7	113 27.0	10.2	8 01.0	11.6	58.8
16		61 57.6	47.9	127 56.2	10.1	8 12.6	11.5	58.9
17		76 57.3	48.2	142 25.3	10.0	8 24.1	11.6	58.9
18		91 57.0	S22 48.4	156 54.3	10.0	S 8 35.7	11.4	59.0
19		106 56.8	48.7	171 23.3	9.8	8 47.1	11.5	59.0
20		121 56.5	48.9	185 52.1	9.8	8 58.6	11.4	59.1
21		136 56.2	.. 49.1	200 20.9	9.7	9 10.0	11.3	59.1
22		151 55.9	49.4	214 49.6	9.7	9 21.3	11.4	59.1
23		166 55.6	49.6	229 18.3	9.5	9 32.7	11.3	59.2
SUNDAY 9 00		181 55.4	S22 49.9	243 46.8	9.5	S 9 44.0	11.2	59.2
01		196 55.1	50.1	258 15.3	9.3	9 55.2	11.2	59.2
02		211 54.8	50.3	272 43.6	9.3	10 06.4	11.2	59.3
03		226 54.5	.. 50.6	287 11.9	9.2	10 17.6	11.1	59.3
04		241 54.2	50.8	301 40.1	9.1	10 28.7	11.1	59.4
05		256 54.0	51.1	316 08.2	9.1	10 39.8	11.0	59.4
06		271 53.7	S22 51.3	330 36.3	8.9	S10 50.8	11.0	59.4
07		286 53.4	51.5	345 04.2	8.9	11 01.8	10.9	59.5
08		301 53.1	51.8	359 32.1	8.7	11 12.7	10.9	59.5
09		316 52.8	.. 52.0	13 59.8	8.7	11 23.6	10.8	59.5
10		331 52.6	52.2	28 27.5	8.6	11 34.4	10.7	59.6
11		346 52.3	52.5	42 55.1	8.5	11 45.1	10.6	59.6
12		1 52.0	S22 52.7	57 22.6	8.4	S11 55.9	10.6	59.7
13		16 51.7	52.9	71 50.0	8.3	12 06.5	10.6	59.7
14		31 51.4	53.2	86 17.3	8.2	12 17.1	10.5	59.7
15		46 51.1	.. 53.4	100 44.5	8.2	12 27.6	10.5	59.8
16		61 50.9	53.6	115 11.7	8.0	12 38.1	10.4	59.8
17		76 50.6	53.8	129 38.7	7.9	12 48.5	10.3	59.8
18		91 50.3	S22 54.1	144 05.6	7.9	S12 58.8	10.3	59.9
19		106 50.0	54.3	158 32.5	7.7	13 09.1	10.2	59.9
20		121 49.7	54.5	172 59.2	7.7	13 19.3	10.1	59.9
21		136 49.4	.. 54.8	187 25.9	7.6	13 29.4	10.1	60.0
22		151 49.2	55.0	201 52.5	7.5	13 39.5	9.9	60.0
23		166 48.9	55.2	216 19.0	7.3	13 49.4	9.9	60.0
MONDAY 10 00		181 48.6	S22 55.4	230 45.3	7.3	S13 59.3	9.9	60.1
01		196 48.3	55.6	245 11.6	7.2	14 09.2	9.7	60.1
02		211 48.0	55.9	259 37.8	7.1	14 18.9	9.7	60.1
03		226 47.7	.. 56.1	274 03.9	7.0	14 28.6	9.6	60.2
04		241 47.4	56.3	288 29.9	6.9	14 38.2	9.5	60.2
05		256 47.2	56.5	302 55.8	6.8	14 47.7	9.4	60.2
06		271 46.9	S22 56.7	317 21.6	6.8	S14 57.1	9.3	60.3
07		286 46.6	57.0	331 47.4	6.5	15 06.4	9.2	60.3
08		301 46.3	57.2	346 13.0	6.5	15 15.6	9.2	60.3
09		316 46.0	.. 57.4	0 38.5	6.4	15 24.8	9.1	60.4
10		331 45.7	57.6	15 03.9	6.4	15 33.9	8.9	60.4
11		346 45.4	57.8	29 29.3	6.2	15 42.8	8.9	60.4
12		1 45.2	S22 58.0	43 54.5	6.2	S15 51.7	8.8	60.4
13		16 44.9	58.2	58 19.7	6.0	16 00.5	8.6	60.5
14		31 44.6	58.4	72 44.7	6.0	16 09.1	8.6	60.5
15		46 44.3	.. 58.7	87 09.7	5.9	16 17.7	8.5	60.5
16		61 44.0	58.9	101 34.6	5.7	16 26.2	8.4	60.6
17		76 43.7	59.1	115 59.3	5.7	16 34.6	8.2	60.6
18		91 43.4	S22 59.3	130 24.0	5.6	S16 42.8	8.2	60.6
19		106 43.1	59.5	144 48.6	5.5	16 51.0	8.0	60.6
20		121 42.9	59.7	159 13.1	5.4	16 59.0	8.0	60.7
21		136 42.6	22 59.9	173 37.5	5.4	17 07.0	7.8	60.7
22		151 42.3	23 00.1	188 01.9	5.2	17 14.8	7.7	60.7
23		166 42.0	S23 00.3	202 26.1	5.2	S17 22.5	7.6	60.8
	SD	16.3	d 0.2	SD 16.0		16.3		16.5

Twilight / Sunrise / Moonrise

Lat.	Naut.	Civil	Sunrise	Moonrise 8	9	10	11
°	h m	h m	h m	h m	h m	h m	h m
N 72	08 11	10 27	■	02 11	04 16	06 40	■
N 70	07 52	09 36	■	02 03	03 57	06 03	08 26
68	07 37	09 04	■	01 56	03 43	05 37	07 36
66	07 25	08 40	10 14	01 51	03 31	05 17	07 05
64	07 14	08 22	09 36	01 46	03 22	05 01	06 42
62	07 05	08 06	09 10	01 42	03 13	04 48	06 24
60	06 57	07 53	08 50	01 38	03 06	04 37	06 08
N 58	06 50	07 42	08 33	01 35	03 00	04 28	05 56
56	06 44	07 32	08 19	01 32	02 55	04 20	05 45
54	06 38	07 24	08 07	01 30	02 50	04 12	05 35
52	06 32	07 16	07 56	01 27	02 45	04 06	05 26
50	06 27	07 09	07 47	01 25	02 41	04 00	05 19
45	06 16	06 53	07 27	01 21	02 33	03 47	05 02
N 40	06 06	06 40	07 10	01 17	02 25	03 36	04 49
35	05 57	06 28	06 56	01 14	02 19	03 28	04 38
30	05 48	06 18	06 44	01 11	02 14	03 20	04 28
20	05 33	06 00	06 24	01 07	02 05	03 06	04 11
N 10	05 17	05 43	06 06	01 02	01 57	02 55	03 56
0	05 00	05 26	05 49	00 58	01 49	02 44	03 42
S 10	04 42	05 09	05 32	00 55	01 42	02 33	03 29
20	04 20	04 49	05 13	00 51	01 34	02 22	03 14
30	03 51	04 24	04 52	00 46	01 25	02 09	02 58
35	03 33	04 10	04 39	00 43	01 20	02 01	02 48
40	03 11	03 52	04 24	00 40	01 14	01 53	02 37
45	02 41	03 30	04 07	00 37	01 08	01 43	02 25
S 50	01 58	03 01	03 45	00 33	01 00	01 31	02 09
52	01 33	02 47	03 35	00 31	00 56	01 26	02 02
54	00 55	02 30	03 23	00 29	00 52	01 20	01 54
56	////	02 09	03 09	00 27	00 48	01 13	01 45
58	////	01 42	02 53	00 25	00 43	01 05	01 35
S 60	////	01 00	02 34	00 22	00 37	00 57	01 24

Sunset / Twilight / Moonset

Lat.	Sunset	Civil	Naut.	Moonset 8	9	10	11
°	h m	h m	h m	h m	h m	h m	h m
N 72	■	13 18	15 34	11 43	11 26	10 58	■
N 70	■	14 09	15 53	11 54	11 46	11 36	11 17
68	■	14 41	16 07	12 03	12 02	12 03	12 07
66	13 31	15 05	16 20	12 10	12 15	12 24	12 39
64	14 08	15 23	16 30	12 17	12 26	12 40	13 03
62	14 35	15 38	16 40	12 22	12 36	12 54	13 22
60	14 55	15 51	16 48	12 27	12 44	13 06	13 37
N 58	15 12	16 03	16 55	12 31	12 51	13 16	13 50
56	15 26	16 12	17 01	12 35	12 57	13 25	14 02
54	15 38	16 21	17 07	12 38	13 03	13 33	14 12
52	15 49	16 29	17 13	12 41	13 08	13 40	14 21
50	15 58	16 36	17 18	12 44	13 13	13 47	14 29
45	16 18	16 52	17 29	12 50	13 23	14 01	14 46
N 40	16 35	17 05	17 39	12 55	13 31	14 12	15 00
35	16 48	17 16	17 48	13 00	13 38	14 22	15 12
30	17 00	17 27	17 56	13 04	13 45	14 31	15 23
20	17 21	17 45	18 12	13 11	13 56	14 46	15 41
N 10	17 39	18 02	18 28	13 17	14 06	14 59	15 57
0	17 56	18 19	18 45	13 22	14 15	15 11	16 11
S 10	18 13	18 36	19 03	13 28	14 24	15 23	16 26
20	18 32	18 56	19 25	13 34	14 34	15 37	16 42
30	18 53	19 21	19 54	13 41	14 45	15 52	17 00
35	19 06	19 36	20 12	13 45	14 51	16 01	17 11
40	19 21	19 53	20 35	13 49	14 59	16 11	17 23
45	19 38	20 15	21 04	13 55	15 08	16 22	17 37
S 50	20 00	20 44	21 48	14 01	15 18	16 37	17 54
52	20 11	20 59	22 14	14 04	15 23	16 43	18 03
54	20 23	21 16	22 53	14 08	15 28	16 51	18 12
56	20 36	21 37	////	14 11	15 34	16 59	18 22
58	20 52	22 05	////	14 15	15 41	17 09	18 34
S 60	21 12	22 47	////	14 19	15 49	17 20	18 48

SUN and MOON

Day	Eqn. of Time 00h	12h	Mer. Pass.	Mer. Pass. Upper	Lower	Age	Phase
d	m s	m s	h m	h m	h m	d	%
8	08 09	07 55	11 52	07 10	19 36	25	30
9	07 42	07 29	11 53	08 02	20 29	26	21
10	07 15	07 01	11 53	08 57	21 27	27	12

UT	ARIES GHA	VENUS −3.9 GHA	Dec	MARS +1.2 GHA	Dec	JUPITER −2.8 GHA	Dec	SATURN +0.7 GHA	Dec	STARS Name	SHA	Dec
11 00	80 06.7	208 36.0	S17 15.1	150 08.1	S23 20.5	11 23.3	N21 12.8	224 03.0	S11 54.3	Acamar	315 18.3	S40 15.3
01	95 09.2	223 35.3	15.9	165 08.5	20.2	26 26.1	12.8	239 05.2	54.4	Achernar	335 26.7	S57 10.5
02	110 11.6	238 34.6	16.8	180 08.9	20.0	41 29.0	12.7	254 07.4	54.5	Acrux	173 09.8	S63 10.0
03	125 14.1	253 33.9	.. 17.6	195 09.3	.. 19.7	56 31.8	.. 12.7	269 09.6	.. 54.5	Adhara	255 12.4	S28 59.5
04	140 16.6	268 33.2	18.4	210 09.6	19.4	71 34.6	12.6	284 11.9	54.6	Aldebaran	290 49.4	N16 32.0
05	155 19.0	283 32.5	19.3	225 10.0	19.2	86 37.4	12.6	299 14.1	54.7			
06	170 21.5	298 31.9	S17 20.1	240 10.4	S23 18.9	101 40.2	N21 12.6	314 16.3	S11 54.8	Alioth	166 21.3	N55 53.1
T 07	185 24.0	313 31.2	21.0	255 10.8	18.6	116 43.1	12.5	329 18.5	54.8	Alkaid	152 59.5	N49 14.7
U 08	200 26.4	328 30.5	21.8	270 11.1	18.4	131 45.9	12.5	344 20.7	54.9	Al Na'ir	27 44.4	S46 54.0
E 09	215 28.9	343 29.8	.. 22.6	285 11.5	.. 18.1	146 48.7	.. 12.4	359 23.0	.. 55.0	Alnilam	275 46.4	S 1 11.7
S 10	230 31.4	358 29.1	23.4	300 11.9	17.8	161 51.5	12.4	14 25.2	55.1	Alphard	217 56.3	S 8 43.0
D 11	245 33.8	13 28.5	24.3	315 12.3	17.6	176 54.3	12.4	29 27.4	55.1			
A 12	260 36.3	28 27.8	S17 25.1	330 12.6	S23 17.3	191 57.1	N21 12.3	44 29.6	S11 55.2	Alphecca	126 11.7	N26 40.3
Y 13	275 38.8	43 27.1	25.9	345 13.0	17.0	207 00.0	12.3	59 31.8	55.3	Alpheratz	357 43.8	N29 10.0
14	290 41.2	58 26.4	26.8	0 13.4	16.8	222 02.8	12.2	74 34.1	55.4	Altair	62 08.9	N 8 54.4
15	305 43.7	73 25.7	.. 27.6	15 13.8	.. 16.5	237 05.6	.. 12.2	89 36.3	.. 55.4	Ankaa	353 15.9	S42 14.3
16	320 46.1	88 25.0	28.4	30 14.1	16.2	252 08.4	12.2	104 38.5	55.5	Antares	112 27.1	S26 27.5
17	335 48.6	103 24.3	29.2	45 14.5	16.0	267 11.2	12.1	119 40.7	55.6			
18	350 51.1	118 23.6	S17 30.1	60 14.9	S23 15.7	282 14.0	N21 12.1	134 42.9	S11 55.7	Arcturus	145 56.3	N19 06.8
19	5 53.5	133 23.0	30.9	75 15.3	15.4	297 16.9	12.0	149 45.2	55.7	Atria	107 29.8	S69 02.9
20	20 56.0	148 22.3	31.7	90 15.6	15.2	312 19.7	12.0	164 47.4	55.8	Avior	234 17.6	S59 33.0
21	35 58.5	163 21.6	.. 32.5	105 16.0	.. 14.9	327 22.5	.. 11.9	179 49.6	.. 55.9	Bellatrix	278 32.0	N 6 21.6
22	51 00.9	178 20.9	33.4	120 16.4	14.6	342 25.3	11.9	194 51.8	56.0	Betelgeuse	271 01.3	N 7 24.4
23	66 03.4	193 20.2	34.2	135 16.8	14.3	357 28.1	11.9	209 54.0	56.0			
12 00	81 05.9	208 19.5	S17 35.0	150 17.1	S23 14.1	12 30.9	N21 11.8	224 56.3	S11 56.1	Canopus	263 55.7	S52 42.2
01	96 08.3	223 18.8	35.8	165 17.5	13.8	27 33.7	11.8	239 58.5	56.2	Capella	280 34.5	N46 00.5
02	111 10.8	238 18.1	36.6	180 17.9	13.5	42 36.6	11.7	255 00.7	56.3	Deneb	49 32.0	N45 20.0
03	126 13.3	253 17.4	.. 37.5	195 18.3	.. 13.2	57 39.4	.. 11.7	270 02.9	.. 56.3	Denebola	182 34.1	N14 29.8
04	141 15.7	268 16.7	38.3	210 18.7	13.0	72 42.2	11.7	285 05.2	56.4	Diphda	348 56.1	S17 55.0
05	156 18.2	283 16.0	39.1	225 19.0	12.7	87 45.0	11.6	300 07.4	56.5			
06	171 20.6	298 15.4	S17 39.9	240 19.4	S23 12.4	102 47.8	N21 11.6	315 09.6	S11 56.5	Dubhe	193 52.1	N61 40.5
W 07	186 23.1	313 14.7	40.7	255 19.8	12.1	117 50.6	11.5	330 11.8	56.6	Elnath	278 12.7	N28 37.0
E 08	201 25.6	328 14.0	41.5	270 20.2	11.9	132 53.5	11.5	345 14.0	56.7	Eltanin	90 46.8	N51 29.4
D 09	216 28.0	343 13.3	.. 42.3	285 20.5	.. 11.6	147 56.3	.. 11.5	0 16.3	.. 56.8	Enif	33 47.6	N 9 56.3
N 10	231 30.5	358 12.6	43.2	300 20.9	11.3	162 59.1	11.4	15 18.5	56.8	Fomalhaut	15 24.4	S29 33.2
E 11	246 33.0	13 11.9	44.0	315 21.3	11.0	178 01.9	11.4	30 20.7	56.9			
S 12	261 35.4	28 11.2	S17 44.8	330 21.7	S23 10.8	193 04.7	N21 11.3	45 22.9	S11 57.0	Gacrux	172 01.4	S57 10.9
D 13	276 37.9	43 10.5	45.6	345 22.0	10.5	208 07.5	11.3	60 25.2	57.1	Gienah	175 52.7	S17 36.8
A 14	291 40.4	58 09.8	46.4	0 22.4	10.2	223 10.3	11.2	75 27.4	57.1	Hadar	148 48.8	S60 25.9
Y 15	306 42.8	73 09.1	.. 47.2	15 22.8	.. 09.9	238 13.2	.. 11.2	90 29.6	.. 57.2	Hamal	328 00.9	N23 31.5
16	321 45.3	88 08.4	48.0	30 23.2	09.6	253 16.0	11.2	105 31.8	57.3	Kaus Aust.	83 44.7	S34 22.6
17	336 47.7	103 07.7	48.8	45 23.5	09.4	268 18.8	11.1	120 34.0	57.4			
18	351 50.2	118 07.0	S17 49.6	60 23.9	S23 09.1	283 21.6	N21 11.1	135 36.3	S11 57.4	Kochab	137 21.0	N74 05.9
19	6 52.7	133 06.3	50.4	75 24.3	08.8	298 24.4	11.0	150 38.5	57.5	Markab	13 38.7	N15 16.7
20	21 55.1	148 05.6	51.2	90 24.7	08.5	313 27.2	11.0	165 40.7	57.6	Menkar	314 15.1	N 4 08.4
21	36 57.6	163 04.9	.. 52.0	105 25.1	.. 08.2	328 30.0	.. 11.0	180 42.9	.. 57.7	Menkent	148 08.2	S36 25.8
22	52 00.1	178 04.2	52.8	120 25.4	08.0	343 32.8	10.9	195 45.2	57.7	Miaplacidus	221 39.1	S69 46.1
23	67 02.5	193 03.5	53.6	135 25.8	07.7	358 35.7	10.9	210 47.4	57.8			
13 00	82 05.0	208 02.8	S17 54.4	150 26.2	S23 07.4	13 38.5	N21 10.8	225 49.6	S11 57.9	Mirfak	308 40.4	N49 54.5
01	97 07.5	223 02.1	55.2	165 26.6	07.1	28 41.3	10.8	240 51.8	58.0	Nunki	75 59.1	S26 16.7
02	112 09.9	238 01.4	56.0	180 26.9	06.8	43 44.1	10.8	255 54.1	58.0	Peacock	53 20.3	S56 41.6
03	127 12.4	253 00.7	.. 56.8	195 27.3	.. 06.5	58 46.9	.. 10.7	270 56.3	.. 58.1	Pollux	243 27.9	N27 59.4
04	142 14.9	268 00.0	57.6	210 27.7	06.2	73 49.7	10.7	285 58.5	58.2	Procyon	244 59.8	N 5 11.3
05	157 17.3	282 59.2	58.4	225 28.1	06.0	88 52.5	10.6	301 00.7	58.2			
06	172 19.8	297 58.5	S17 59.2	240 28.5	S23 05.7	103 55.3	N21 10.6	316 03.0	S11 58.3	Rasalhague	96 07.1	N12 33.2
07	187 22.2	312 57.8	18 00.0	255 28.8	05.4	118 58.2	10.6	331 05.2	58.4	Regulus	207 43.8	N11 54.0
T 08	202 24.7	327 57.1	00.8	270 29.2	05.1	134 01.0	10.5	346 07.4	58.5	Rigel	281 12.0	S 8 11.3
H 09	217 27.2	342 56.4	.. 01.6	285 29.6	.. 04.8	149 03.8	.. 10.5	1 09.6	.. 58.5	Rigil Kent.	139 52.7	S60 53.0
U 10	232 29.6	357 55.7	02.4	300 30.0	04.5	164 06.6	10.4	16 11.9	58.6	Sabik	102 13.3	S15 44.3
R 11	247 32.1	12 55.0	03.2	315 30.3	04.2	179 09.4	10.4	31 14.1	58.7			
S 12	262 34.6	27 54.3	S18 04.0	330 30.7	S23 04.0	194 12.2	N21 10.3	46 16.3	S11 58.8	Schedar	349 40.7	N56 36.8
D 13	277 37.0	42 53.6	04.8	345 31.1	03.7	209 15.0	10.3	61 18.5	58.8	Shaula	96 22.8	S37 06.6
A 14	292 39.5	57 52.9	05.6	0 31.5	03.4	224 17.8	10.3	76 20.8	58.9	Sirius	258 33.7	S16 44.1
Y 15	307 42.0	72 52.2	.. 06.3	15 31.9	.. 03.1	239 20.7	.. 10.2	91 23.0	.. 59.0	Spica	158 31.8	S11 13.7
16	322 44.4	87 51.4	07.1	30 32.2	02.8	254 23.5	10.2	106 25.2	59.0	Suhail	222 52.4	S43 29.0
17	337 46.9	102 50.7	07.9	45 32.6	02.5	269 26.3	10.1	121 27.4	59.1			
18	352 49.4	117 50.0	S18 08.7	60 33.0	S23 02.3	284 29.1	N21 10.1	136 29.7	S11 59.2	Vega	80 39.6	N38 48.0
19	7 51.8	132 49.3	09.5	75 33.4	01.9	299 31.9	10.1	151 31.9	59.3	Zuben'ubi	137 06.1	S16 05.6
20	22 54.3	147 48.6	10.3	90 33.8	01.6	314 34.7	10.0	166 34.1	59.3		SHA	Mer.Pass.
21	37 56.7	162 47.9	.. 11.1	105 34.1	.. 01.3	329 37.5	.. 10.0	181 36.3	.. 59.4	Venus	127 13.7	10 07
22	52 59.2	177 47.2	11.8	120 34.5	01.0	344 40.3	09.9	196 38.6	59.5	Mars	69 11.3	13 59
23	68 01.7	192 46.5	12.6	135 34.9	00.7	359 43.1	09.9	211 40.8	59.6	Jupiter	291 25.1	23 06
Mer. Pass. 18 32.6		v −0.7	d 0.8	v 0.4	d 0.3	v 2.8	d 0.0	v 2.2	d 0.1	Saturn	143 50.4	8 59

SUN and MOON

UT (d h)	SUN GHA	SUN Dec	MOON GHA	v	MOON Dec	d	HP
11 00	181 41.7	S23 00.5	216 50.3	5.0	S17 30.1	7.5	60.8
01	196 41.4	00.7	231 14.3	5.0	17 37.6	7.4	60.8
02	211 41.1	00.9	245 38.3	4.9	17 45.0	7.2	60.8
03	226 40.8	.. 01.1	260 02.2	4.8	17 52.2	7.2	60.9
04	241 40.5	01.3	274 26.0	4.7	17 59.4	7.0	60.9
05	256 40.3	01.5	288 49.7	4.6	18 06.4	6.9	60.9
T 06	271 40.0	S23 01.7	303 13.3	4.6	S18 13.3	6.7	60.9
U 07	286 39.7	01.9	317 36.9	4.5	18 20.0	6.7	60.9
E 08	301 39.4	02.1	332 00.4	4.4	18 26.7	6.5	61.0
S 09	316 39.1	.. 02.3	346 23.8	4.3	18 33.2	6.3	61.0
D 10	331 38.8	02.5	0 47.1	4.2	18 39.5	6.3	61.0
A 11	346 38.5	02.7	15 10.3	4.2	18 45.8	6.1	61.0
Y 12	1 38.2	S23 02.9	29 33.5	4.1	S18 51.9	6.0	61.1
13	16 37.9	03.1	43 56.6	4.0	18 57.9	5.8	61.1
14	31 37.6	03.3	58 19.6	3.9	19 03.7	5.7	61.1
15	46 37.4	.. 03.5	72 42.5	3.9	19 09.4	5.6	61.1
16	61 37.1	03.7	87 05.4	3.8	19 15.0	5.4	61.1
17	76 36.8	03.9	101 28.2	3.7	19 20.4	5.3	61.1
18	91 36.5	S23 04.0	115 50.9	3.7	S19 25.7	5.2	61.2
19	106 36.2	04.2	130 13.6	3.6	19 30.9	5.0	61.2
20	121 35.9	04.4	144 36.2	3.5	19 35.9	4.9	61.2
21	136 35.6	.. 04.6	158 58.7	3.5	19 40.8	4.7	61.2
22	151 35.3	04.8	173 21.2	3.4	19 45.5	4.6	61.2
23	166 35.0	05.0	187 43.6	3.4	19 50.1	4.4	61.2
12 00	181 34.7	S23 05.2	202 06.0	3.3	S19 54.5	4.3	61.3
01	196 34.4	05.3	216 28.3	3.2	19 58.8	4.1	61.3
02	211 34.1	05.5	230 50.5	3.2	20 02.9	4.0	61.3
03	226 33.8	.. 05.7	245 12.7	3.1	20 06.9	3.9	61.3
04	241 33.6	05.9	259 34.8	3.1	20 10.8	3.6	61.3
05	256 33.3	06.1	273 56.9	3.1	20 14.4	3.6	61.3
W 06	271 33.0	S23 06.2	288 19.0	3.0	S20 18.0	3.3	61.3
E 07	286 32.7	06.4	302 41.0	2.9	20 21.3	3.3	61.3
D 08	301 32.4	06.6	317 02.9	3.0	20 24.6	3.0	61.3
N 09	316 32.1	.. 06.8	331 24.9	2.8	20 27.6	3.0	61.3
E 10	331 31.8	07.0	345 46.7	2.9	20 30.6	2.7	61.4
S 11	346 31.5	07.1	0 08.6	2.8	20 33.3	2.6	61.4
D 12	1 31.2	S23 07.3	14 30.4	2.8	S20 35.9	2.5	61.4
A 13	16 30.9	07.5	28 52.2	2.7	20 38.4	2.2	61.4
Y 14	31 30.6	07.7	43 13.9	2.7	20 40.6	2.2	61.4
15	46 30.3	.. 07.8	57 35.6	2.7	20 42.8	1.9	61.4
16	61 30.0	08.0	71 57.3	2.7	20 44.7	1.8	61.4
17	76 29.7	08.2	86 19.0	2.6	20 46.5	1.7	61.4
18	91 29.4	S23 08.3	100 40.6	2.7	S20 48.2	1.5	61.4
19	106 29.1	08.5	115 02.3	2.6	20 49.7	1.3	61.4
20	121 28.8	08.7	129 23.9	2.6	20 51.0	1.2	61.4
21	136 28.5	.. 08.8	143 45.5	2.6	20 52.2	1.0	61.4
22	151 28.2	09.0	158 07.1	2.5	20 53.2	0.8	61.4
23	166 28.0	09.2	172 28.6	2.6	20 54.0	0.7	61.4
13 00	181 27.7	S23 09.3	186 50.2	2.6	S20 54.7	0.5	61.4
01	196 27.4	09.5	201 11.8	2.5	20 55.2	0.3	61.4
02	211 27.1	09.7	215 33.3	2.6	20 55.5	0.2	61.4
03	226 26.8	.. 09.8	229 54.9	2.5	20 55.7	0.1	61.4
04	241 26.5	10.0	244 16.4	2.6	20 55.8	0.2	61.4
05	256 26.2	10.2	258 38.0	2.6	20 55.6	0.3	61.4
T 06	271 25.9	S23 10.3	272 59.6	2.5	S20 55.3	0.4	61.4
H 07	286 25.6	10.5	287 21.1	2.6	20 54.9	0.6	61.4
U 08	301 25.3	10.6	301 42.7	2.6	20 54.3	0.8	61.4
R 09	316 25.0	.. 10.8	316 04.3	2.7	20 53.5	1.0	61.4
S 10	331 24.7	10.9	330 26.0	2.6	20 52.5	1.1	61.4
D 11	346 24.4	11.1	344 47.6	2.6	20 51.4	1.2	61.4
A 12	1 24.1	S23 11.3	359 09.2	2.7	S20 50.2	1.4	61.4
Y 13	16 23.8	11.4	13 30.9	2.7	20 48.8	1.6	61.4
14	31 23.5	11.6	27 52.6	2.8	20 47.2	1.8	61.3
15	46 23.2	.. 11.7	42 14.4	2.7	20 45.4	1.9	61.3
16	61 22.9	11.9	56 36.1	2.8	20 43.5	2.0	61.3
17	76 22.6	12.0	70 57.9	2.8	20 41.5	2.2	61.3
18	91 22.3	S23 12.2	85 19.7	2.9	S20 39.3	2.4	61.3
19	106 22.0	12.3	99 41.6	2.9	20 36.9	2.6	61.3
20	121 21.7	12.5	114 03.5	2.9	20 34.3	2.6	61.3
21	136 21.4	.. 12.6	128 25.4	3.0	20 31.7	2.9	61.3
22	151 21.1	12.8	142 47.4	3.0	20 28.8	3.0	61.3
23	166 20.8	12.9	157 09.4	3.1	S20 25.8	3.1	61.2
	SD 16.3	d 0.2	SD 16.6		16.7		16.7

Twilight and Moonrise

Lat.	Naut.	Civil	Sunrise	Moonrise 11	12	13	14
N 72	08 16	10 38	■	■	■	■	■
N 70	07 57	09 43	■	08 26	■	■	12 23
68	07 42	09 09	■	07 36	09 32	10 49	11 14
66	07 29	08 45	10 22	07 05	08 45	09 58	10 37
64	07 18	08 26	09 42	06 42	08 14	09 25	10 11
62	07 09	08 10	09 15	06 24	07 51	09 02	09 50
60	07 01	07 57	08 54	06 08	07 33	08 43	09 34
N 58	06 53	07 46	08 37	05 56	07 18	08 27	09 19
56	06 47	07 36	08 23	05 45	07 05	08 13	09 07
54	06 41	07 27	08 10	05 35	06 53	08 02	08 57
52	06 35	07 19	07 59	05 26	06 43	07 51	08 47
50	06 30	07 11	07 50	05 19	06 34	07 42	08 39
45	06 18	06 56	07 29	05 02	06 15	07 23	08 21
N 40	06 08	06 42	07 13	04 49	06 00	07 07	08 06
35	05 59	06 31	06 59	04 38	05 47	06 53	07 53
30	05 50	06 20	06 47	04 28	05 36	06 42	07 42
20	05 34	06 02	06 26	04 11	05 17	06 22	07 24
N 10	05 18	05 45	06 07	03 56	05 00	06 04	07 07
0	05 02	05 28	05 50	03 42	04 44	05 48	06 52
S 10	04 43	05 10	05 33	03 29	04 29	05 32	06 37
20	04 21	04 50	05 14	03 14	04 12	05 15	06 20
30	03 52	04 25	04 52	02 58	03 53	04 55	06 01
35	03 33	04 10	04 40	02 48	03 42	04 44	05 50
40	03 11	03 52	04 25	02 37	03 30	04 30	05 38
45	02 41	03 30	04 07	02 25	03 15	04 15	05 23
S 50	01 57	03 01	03 45	02 09	02 57	03 56	05 05
52	01 30	02 46	03 34	02 02	02 48	03 47	04 56
54	00 49	02 29	03 22	01 54	02 39	03 36	04 46
56	////	02 07	03 08	01 45	02 28	03 25	04 36
58	////	01 39	02 52	01 35	02 16	03 12	04 23
S 60	////	00 54	02 32	01 24	02 02	02 56	04 09

Sunset, Twilight and Moonset

Lat.	Sunset	Civil	Naut.	Moonset 11	12	13	14
N 72	■	13 09	15 31	■	■	■	■
N 70	■	14 05	15 51	11 17	■	■	13 59
68	■	14 38	16 06	12 07	12 23	13 20	15 08
66	13 26	15 03	16 19	12 39	13 10	14 14	15 44
64	14 06	15 22	16 30	13 03	13 41	14 43	16 10
62	14 33	15 38	16 39	13 22	14 04	15 07	16 30
60	14 54	15 51	16 47	13 37	14 23	15 26	16 46
N 58	15 11	16 02	16 54	13 50	14 38	15 42	17 00
56	15 25	16 12	17 01	14 02	14 51	15 55	17 12
54	15 37	16 21	17 07	14 12	15 03	16 07	17 22
52	15 48	16 29	17 13	14 21	15 13	16 17	17 31
50	15 58	16 36	17 18	14 29	15 22	16 26	17 39
45	16 18	16 52	17 29	14 46	15 41	16 46	17 57
N 40	16 35	17 09	17 39	15 00	15 57	17 01	18 11
35	16 49	17 17	17 49	15 12	16 10	17 14	18 23
30	17 01	17 27	17 57	15 23	16 22	17 26	18 33
20	17 22	17 46	18 14	15 41	16 41	17 46	18 51
N 10	17 40	18 03	18 30	15 57	16 59	18 03	19 07
0	17 58	18 20	18 46	16 11	17 15	18 19	19 21
S 10	18 16	18 38	19 04	16 26	17 31	18 35	19 36
20	18 34	18 58	19 27	16 42	17 48	18 52	19 51
30	18 56	19 23	19 56	17 00	18 07	19 11	20 08
35	19 08	19 38	20 15	17 11	18 19	19 22	20 19
40	19 23	19 56	20 37	17 23	18 32	19 35	20 30
45	19 41	20 18	21 08	17 37	18 48	19 50	20 44
S 50	20 03	20 47	21 52	17 54	19 07	20 09	21 00
52	20 14	21 02	22 19	18 03	19 16	20 18	21 08
54	20 26	21 20	23 01	18 12	19 26	20 28	21 16
56	20 40	21 41	////	18 22	19 37	20 39	21 26
58	20 56	22 10	////	18 34	19 50	20 51	21 37
S 60	21 16	22 56	////	18 48	20 06	21 06	21 49

SUN and MOON

Day	Eqn. of Time 00h	Eqn. of Time 12h	Mer. Pass.	Mer. Pass. Upper	Mer. Pass. Lower	Age	Phase %
11	06 47	06 33	11 53	09 57	22 28	28	5
12	06 19	06 05	11 54	10 59	23 31	29	1
13	05 51	05 37	11 54	12 04	24 35	00	0

Phase: ● (New Moon)

UT	ARIES GHA	VENUS −3.9 GHA	Dec	MARS +1.2 GHA	Dec	JUPITER −2.8 GHA	Dec	SATURN +0.7 GHA	Dec
d h									
14 00	83 04.1	207 45.7	S18 13.4	150 35.3	S23 00.4	14 45.9	N21 09.9	226 43.0	S11 59.6
01	98 06.6	222 45.0	14.2	165 35.6	23 00.2	29 48.8	09.8	241 45.2	59.7
02	113 09.1	237 44.3	15.0	180 36.0	22 59.9	44 51.6	09.8	256 47.5	59.8
03	128 11.5	252 43.6 ..	15.7	195 36.4 ..	59.6	59 54.4 ..	09.7	271 49.7 ..	59.8
04	143 14.0	267 42.9	16.5	210 36.8	59.3	74 57.2	09.7	286 51.9	11 59.9
05	158 16.5	282 42.2	17.3	225 37.2	59.0	90 00.0	09.7	301 54.1	12 00.0
06	173 18.9	297 41.4	S18 18.1	240 37.5	S22 58.7	105 02.8	N21 09.6	316 56.4	S12 00.1
F 07	188 21.4	312 40.7	18.8	255 37.9	58.4	120 05.6	09.6	331 58.6	00.1
R 08	203 23.9	327 40.0	19.6	270 38.3	58.1	135 08.4	09.5	347 00.8	00.2
I 09	218 26.3	342 39.3 ..	20.4	285 38.7 ..	57.8	150 11.2 ..	09.5	2 03.1 ..	00.3
D 10	233 28.8	357 38.6	21.2	300 39.1	57.5	165 14.0	09.5	17 05.3	00.4
A 11	248 31.2	12 37.8	21.9	315 39.4	57.2	180 16.8	09.4	32 07.5	00.4
Y 12	263 33.7	27 37.1	S18 22.7	330 39.8	S22 56.9	195 19.7	N21 09.4	47 09.7	S12 00.5
13	278 36.2	42 36.4	23.5	345 40.2	56.6	210 22.5	09.3	62 12.0	00.6
14	293 38.6	57 35.7	24.2	0 40.6	56.3	225 25.3	09.3	77 14.2	00.6
15	308 41.1	72 34.9 ..	25.0	15 41.0 ..	56.0	240 28.1 ..	09.3	92 16.4 ..	00.7
16	323 43.6	87 34.2	25.8	30 41.3	55.7	255 30.9	09.2	107 18.6	00.8
17	338 46.0	102 33.5	26.5	45 41.7	55.4	270 33.7	09.2	122 20.9	00.9
18	353 48.5	117 32.8	S18 27.3	60 42.1	S22 55.1	285 36.5	N21 09.1	137 23.1	S12 00.9
19	8 51.0	132 32.0	28.1	75 42.5	54.8	300 39.3	09.1	152 25.3	01.0
20	23 53.4	147 31.3	28.8	90 42.9	54.5	315 42.1	09.0	167 27.6	01.1
21	38 55.9	162 30.6 ..	29.6	105 43.2 ..	54.2	330 44.9 ..	09.0	182 29.8 ..	01.1
22	53 58.4	177 29.9	30.4	120 43.6	53.9	345 47.7	09.0	197 32.0	01.2
23	69 00.8	192 29.1	31.1	135 44.0	53.6	0 50.5	08.9	212 34.2	01.3
15 00	84 03.3	207 28.4	S18 31.9	150 44.4	S22 53.2	15 53.3	N21 08.9	227 36.5	S12 01.4
01	99 05.7	222 27.7	32.6	165 44.8	52.9	30 56.1	08.8	242 38.7	01.4
02	114 08.2	237 27.0	33.4	180 45.2	52.6	45 59.0	08.8	257 40.9	01.5
03	129 10.7	252 26.2 ..	34.2	195 45.5 ..	52.3	61 01.8 ..	08.8	272 43.2 ..	01.6
04	144 13.1	267 25.5	34.9	210 45.9	52.0	76 04.6	08.7	287 45.4	01.6
05	159 15.6	282 24.8	35.7	225 46.3	51.7	91 07.4	08.7	302 47.6	01.7
06	174 18.1	297 24.0	S18 36.4	240 46.7	S22 51.4	106 10.2	N21 08.6	317 49.8	S12 01.8
S 07	189 20.5	312 23.3	37.2	255 47.1	51.1	121 13.0	08.6	332 52.1	01.9
A 08	204 23.0	327 22.6	37.9	270 47.4	50.8	136 15.8	08.6	347 54.3	01.9
T 09	219 25.5	342 21.8 ..	38.7	285 47.8 ..	50.5	151 18.6 ..	08.5	2 56.5 ..	02.0
U 10	234 27.9	357 21.1	39.4	300 48.2	50.2	166 21.4	08.5	17 58.8	02.1
R 11	249 30.4	12 20.4	40.2	315 48.6	49.9	181 24.2	08.4	33 01.0	02.1
D 12	264 32.9	27 19.6	S18 40.9	330 49.0	S22 49.5	196 27.0	N21 08.4	48 03.2	S12 02.2
A 13	279 35.3	42 18.9	41.7	345 49.4	49.2	211 29.8	08.4	63 05.4	02.3
Y 14	294 37.8	57 18.2	42.4	0 49.7	48.9	226 32.6	08.3	78 07.7	02.4
15	309 40.2	72 17.4 ..	43.2	15 50.1 ..	48.6	241 35.4 ..	08.3	93 09.9 ..	02.4
16	324 42.7	87 16.7	43.9	30 50.5	48.3	256 38.2	08.2	108 12.1	02.5
17	339 45.2	102 16.0	44.7	45 50.9	48.0	271 41.0	08.2	123 14.4	02.6
18	354 47.6	117 15.2	S18 45.4	60 51.3	S22 47.7	286 43.8	N21 08.2	138 16.6	S12 02.6
19	9 50.1	132 14.5	46.2	75 51.7	47.4	301 46.6	08.1	153 18.8	02.7
20	24 52.6	147 13.8	46.9	90 52.0	47.0	316 49.4	08.1	168 21.1	02.8
21	39 55.0	162 13.0 ..	47.6	105 52.4 ..	46.7	331 52.2 ..	08.1	183 23.3 ..	02.9
22	54 57.5	177 12.3	48.4	120 52.8	46.4	346 55.0	08.0	198 25.5	02.9
23	70 00.0	192 11.5	49.1	135 53.2	46.1	1 57.9	08.0	213 27.7	03.0
16 00	85 02.4	207 10.8	S18 49.9	150 53.6	S22 45.8	17 00.7	N21 07.9	228 30.0	S12 03.1
01	100 04.9	222 10.1	50.6	165 53.9	45.5	32 03.5	07.9	243 32.2	03.1
02	115 07.4	237 09.3	51.3	180 54.3	45.1	47 06.3	07.8	258 34.4	03.2
03	130 09.8	252 08.6 ..	52.1	195 54.7 ..	44.8	62 09.1 ..	07.8	273 36.7 ..	03.3
04	145 12.3	267 07.8	52.8	210 55.1	44.5	77 11.9	07.8	288 38.9	03.3
05	160 14.7	282 07.1	53.5	225 55.5	44.2	92 14.7	07.7	303 41.1	03.4
06	175 17.2	297 06.4	S18 54.3	240 55.9	S22 43.9	107 17.5	N21 07.6	318 43.4	S12 03.5
S 07	190 19.7	312 05.6	55.0	255 56.3	43.6	122 20.3	07.6	333 45.6	03.6
U 08	205 22.1	327 04.9	55.7	270 56.6	43.2	137 23.1	07.6	348 47.8	03.6
N 09	220 24.6	342 04.1 ..	56.5	285 57.0 ..	42.9	152 25.9 ..	07.5	3 50.1 ..	03.7
D 10	235 27.1	357 03.4	57.2	300 57.4	42.6	167 28.7	07.5	18 52.3	03.8
A 11	250 29.5	12 02.6	57.9	315 57.8	42.3	182 31.5	07.5	33 54.5	03.8
Y 12	265 32.0	27 01.9	S18 58.7	330 58.2	S22 42.0	197 34.3	N21 07.4	48 56.7	S12 03.9
13	280 34.5	42 01.1	18 59.4	345 58.6	41.6	212 37.1	07.4	63 59.0	04.0
14	295 36.9	57 00.4	19 00.1	0 58.9	41.3	227 39.9	07.4	79 01.2	04.0
15	310 39.4	71 59.6 ..	00.8	15 59.3 ..	41.0	242 42.7 ..	07.3	94 03.4 ..	04.1
16	325 41.8	86 58.9	01.6	30 59.7	40.7	257 45.5	07.3	109 05.7	04.2
17	340 44.3	101 58.2	02.3	46 00.1	40.3	272 48.3	07.2	124 07.9	04.3
18	355 46.8	116 57.4	S19 03.0	61 00.5	S22 40.0	287 51.1	N21 07.2	139 10.1	S12 04.3
19	10 49.2	131 56.7	03.7	76 00.9	39.7	302 53.9	07.2	154 12.4	04.4
20	25 51.7	146 55.9	04.5	91 01.3	39.4	317 56.7	07.1	169 14.6	04.5
21	40 54.2	161 55.2 ..	05.2	106 01.6 ..	39.0	332 59.5 ..	07.1	184 16.8 ..	04.5
22	55 56.6	176 54.4	05.9	121 02.0	38.7	348 02.3	07.0	199 19.1	04.6
23	70 59.1	191 53.7	06.6	136 02.4	38.4	3 05.1	07.0	214 21.3	04.7
Mer.Pass. 18 20.8	v −0.7 d 0.7	v 0.4	d 0.3	v 2.8	d 0.0	v 2.2	d 0.1		

STARS

Name	SHA	Dec
Acamar	315 18.3	S40 15.3
Achernar	335 26.7	S57 10.5
Acrux	173 09.8	S63 10.0
Adhara	255 12.4	S28 59.5
Aldebaran	290 49.4	N16 32.0
Alioth	166 21.3	N55 53.0
Alkaid	152 59.5	N49 14.7
Al Na'ir	27 44.4	S46 54.0
Alnilam	275 46.4	S 1 11.7
Alphard	217 56.2	S 8 43.0
Alphecca	126 11.6	N26 40.3
Alpheratz	357 43.8	N29 10.0
Altair	62 08.9	N 8 54.4
Ankaa	353 16.0	S42 14.3
Antares	112 27.0	S26 27.5
Arcturus	145 56.3	N19 06.8
Atria	107 29.7	S69 02.8
Avior	234 17.6	S59 33.0
Bellatrix	278 32.0	N 6 21.6
Betelgeuse	271 01.3	N 7 24.4
Canopus	263 55.7	S52 42.2
Capella	280 34.4	N46 00.5
Deneb	49 32.0	N45 19.9
Denebola	182 34.0	N14 29.8
Diphda	348 56.1	S17 55.0
Dubhe	193 52.1	N61 40.4
Elnath	278 12.7	N28 37.0
Eltanin	90 46.8	N51 29.4
Enif	33 47.6	N 9 56.3
Fomalhaut	15 24.4	S29 33.2
Gacrux	172 01.4	S57 10.9
Gienah	175 52.7	S17 36.8
Hadar	148 48.7	S60 25.9
Hamal	328 00.9	N23 31.5
Kaus Aust.	83 44.7	S34 22.6
Kochab	137 21.0	N74 05.9
Markab	13 38.7	N15 16.7
Menkar	314 15.1	N 4 08.4
Menkent	148 08.2	S36 25.8
Miaplacidus	221 39.1	S69 46.1
Mirfak	308 40.4	N49 54.5
Nunki	75 59.1	S26 16.7
Peacock	53 20.3	S56 41.6
Pollux	243 27.8	N27 59.4
Procyon	244 59.8	N 5 11.3
Rasalhague	96 07.1	N12 33.2
Regulus	207 43.7	N11 54.0
Rigel	281 12.0	S 8 11.3
Rigil Kent.	139 52.6	S60 53.0
Sabik	102 13.3	S15 44.3
Schedar	349 40.7	N56 36.9
Shaula	96 22.8	S37 06.6
Sirius	258 33.7	S16 44.2
Spica	158 31.8	S11 13.7
Suhail	222 52.4	S43 29.1
Vega	80 39.6	N38 48.0
Zuben'ubi	137 06.1	S16 05.6

	SHA	Mer.Pass.
Venus	123 25.1	10 11
Mars	66 41.1	13 57
Jupiter	291 50.1	22 52
Saturn	143 33.2	8 48

UT	SUN GHA	Dec	MOON GHA	v	Dec	d	HP
d h	° ′	° ′	° ′	′	° ′	′	′
14 00	181 20.5	S23 13.1	171 31.5	3.1	S20 22.7	3.3	61.2
01	196 20.2	13.2	185 53.6	3.2	20 19.4	3.5	61.2
02	211 19.9	13.4	200 15.8	3.2	20 15.9	3.6	61.2
03	226 19.6	.. 13.5	214 38.0	3.3	20 12.3	3.8	61.2
04	241 19.3	13.6	229 00.3	3.3	20 08.5	3.9	61.2
05	256 19.0	13.8	243 22.6	3.4	20 04.6	4.0	61.1
06	271 18.7	S23 13.9	257 45.0	3.5	S20 00.6	4.2	61.1
07	286 18.4	14.1	272 07.5	3.5	19 56.4	4.4	61.1
F 08	301 18.1	14.1	286 30.0	3.5	19 52.0	4.5	61.1
R 09	316 17.8	.. 14.3	300 52.5	3.7	19 47.5	4.6	61.1
I 10	331 17.5	14.5	315 15.2	3.7	19 42.9	4.8	61.1
D 11	346 17.2	14.6	329 37.9	3.8	19 38.1	4.9	61.0
A 12	1 16.9	S23 14.8	344 00.7	3.8	S19 33.2	5.1	61.0
Y 13	16 16.6	14.9	358 23.5	3.9	19 28.1	5.2	61.0
14	31 16.3	15.0	12 46.4	4.0	19 22.9	5.3	61.0
15	46 16.0	.. 15.2	27 09.4	4.1	19 17.6	5.5	60.9
16	61 15.7	15.3	41 32.5	4.1	19 12.1	5.6	60.9
17	76 15.4	15.4	55 55.6	4.2	19 06.5	5.8	60.9
18	91 15.1	S23 15.6	70 18.8	4.3	S19 00.7	5.8	60.9
19	106 14.8	15.7	84 42.1	4.4	18 54.9	6.0	60.9
20	121 14.5	15.8	99 05.5	4.4	18 48.9	6.2	60.8
21	136 14.2	.. 15.9	113 28.9	4.6	18 42.7	6.3	60.8
22	151 13.9	16.1	127 52.5	4.6	18 36.4	6.3	60.8
23	166 13.6	16.2	142 16.1	4.7	18 30.1	6.6	60.8
15 00	181 13.3	S23 16.4	156 39.8	4.8	S18 23.5	6.6	60.7
01	196 13.0	16.5	171 03.6	4.9	18 16.9	6.8	60.7
02	211 12.7	16.6	185 27.5	4.9	18 10.1	6.9	60.7
03	226 12.4	.. 16.7	199 51.4	5.1	18 03.2	7.0	60.6
04	241 12.1	16.8	214 15.5	5.1	17 56.2	7.1	60.6
05	256 11.8	16.9	228 39.6	5.2	17 49.1	7.3	60.6
06	271 11.5	S23 17.1	243 03.8	5.4	S17 41.8	7.3	60.6
07	286 11.2	17.2	257 28.2	5.4	17 34.5	7.5	60.5
S 08	301 10.9	17.3	271 52.6	5.5	17 27.0	7.6	60.5
A 09	316 10.6	.. 17.4	286 17.1	5.6	17 19.4	7.7	60.5
T 10	331 10.3	17.5	300 41.7	5.7	17 11.7	7.8	60.4
U 11	346 10.0	17.7	315 06.4	5.7	17 03.9	7.9	60.4
R 12	1 09.7	S23 17.8	329 31.1	5.9	S16 56.0	8.0	60.4
D 13	16 09.4	17.9	343 56.0	6.0	16 48.0	8.1	60.3
A 14	31 09.0	18.0	358 21.0	6.1	16 39.9	8.2	60.3
Y 15	46 08.7	.. 18.1	12 46.1	6.1	16 31.7	8.4	60.3
16	61 08.4	18.2	27 11.2	6.3	16 23.3	8.4	60.2
17	76 08.1	18.4	41 36.5	6.4	16 14.9	8.5	60.2
18	91 07.8	S23 18.5	56 01.9	6.4	S16 06.4	8.6	60.2
19	106 07.5	18.6	70 27.3	6.6	15 57.8	8.7	60.1
20	121 07.2	18.7	84 52.9	6.6	15 49.1	8.9	60.1
21	136 06.9	.. 18.8	99 18.5	6.8	15 40.2	8.9	60.1
22	151 06.6	18.9	113 44.3	6.8	15 31.3	8.9	60.0
23	166 06.3	19.0	128 10.1	7.0	15 22.4	9.1	60.0
16 00	181 06.0	S23 19.1	142 36.1	7.0	S15 13.3	9.2	60.0
01	196 05.7	19.2	157 02.1	7.2	15 04.1	9.2	59.9
02	211 05.4	19.3	171 28.3	7.2	14 54.9	9.3	59.9
03	226 05.1	.. 19.4	185 54.5	7.3	14 45.6	9.5	59.9
04	241 04.8	19.5	200 20.8	7.5	14 36.1	9.5	59.8
05	256 04.5	19.6	214 47.3	7.5	14 26.6	9.5	59.8
06	271 04.2	S23 19.8	229 13.8	7.6	S14 17.1	9.7	59.8
07	286 03.9	19.9	243 40.4	7.8	14 07.4	9.7	59.7
S 08	301 03.6	20.0	258 07.2	7.8	13 57.7	9.8	59.7
U 09	316 03.3	.. 20.1	272 34.0	7.9	13 47.9	9.8	59.6
N 10	331 03.0	20.2	287 00.9	8.1	13 38.1	10.0	59.6
D 11	346 02.7	20.3	301 28.0	8.1	13 28.1	10.0	59.6
A 12	1 02.3	S23 20.3	315 55.1	8.2	S13 18.1	10.1	59.5
Y 13	16 02.0	20.4	330 22.3	8.3	13 08.0	10.1	59.5
14	31 01.7	20.5	344 49.6	8.4	12 57.9	10.2	59.5
15	46 01.4	.. 20.6	359 17.0	8.5	12 47.7	10.3	59.4
16	61 01.1	20.7	13 44.5	8.6	12 37.4	10.3	59.4
17	76 00.8	20.8	28 12.1	8.7	12 27.1	10.4	59.3
18	91 00.5	S23 20.9	42 39.8	8.8	S12 16.7	10.4	59.3
19	106 00.2	21.0	57 07.6	8.9	12 06.3	10.5	59.3
20	120 59.9	21.1	71 35.5	9.0	11 55.8	10.6	59.2
21	135 59.6	.. 21.2	86 03.5	9.0	11 45.2	10.6	59.2
22	150 59.3	21.3	100 31.5	9.2	11 34.6	10.7	59.1
23	165 59.0	21.4	114 59.7	9.3	S11 23.9	10.7	59.1
SD 16.3		d 0.1	SD 16.6		16.5		16.2

Twilight / Moonrise

Lat.	Twilight Naut.	Civil	Sunrise	Moonrise 14	15	16	17
°	h m	h m	h m	h m	h m	h m	h m
N 72	08 21	10 48	■	■	■	12 45	12 06	11 46
N 70	08 01	09 48	■	12 23	11 53	11 41	11 33
68	07 45	09 14	■	11 14	11 20	11 22	11 25
66	07 32	08 49	10 28	10 37	10 56	11 06	11 12
64	07 21	08 29	09 47	10 11	10 37	10 53	11 04
62	07 12	08 13	09 19	09 50	10 22	10 43	10 57
60	07 03	08 00	08 58	09 34	10 09	10 33	10 51
N 58	06 56	07 48	08 40	09 19	09 57	10 25	10 46
56	06 49	07 38	08 26	09 07	09 48	10 18	10 41
54	06 43	07 29	08 13	08 57	09 39	10 11	10 37
52	06 37	07 21	08 02	08 47	09 31	10 05	10 33
50	06 32	07 14	07 52	08 39	09 24	10 00	10 30
45	06 21	06 58	07 32	08 21	09 09	09 49	10 22
N 40	06 10	06 44	07 15	08 06	08 56	09 39	10 16
35	06 01	06 33	07 01	07 53	08 46	09 31	10 11
30	05 52	06 22	06 48	07 42	08 36	09 24	10 06
20	05 36	06 03	06 27	07 24	08 20	09 11	09 57
N 10	05 20	05 46	06 09	07 07	08 06	09 00	09 50
0	05 03	05 29	05 52	06 52	07 53	08 50	09 43
S 10	04 44	05 11	05 34	06 37	07 40	08 40	09 36
20	04 22	04 51	05 15	06 20	07 25	08 29	09 29
30	03 53	04 26	04 53	06 01	07 09	08 16	09 20
35	03 34	04 11	04 40	05 50	07 00	08 09	09 15
40	03 11	03 53	04 25	05 38	06 49	08 00	09 10
45	02 41	03 30	04 08	05 23	06 36	07 50	09 03
S 50	01 56	03 01	03 45	05 05	06 21	07 39	08 55
52	01 28	02 46	03 34	04 56	06 13	07 33	08 52
54	00 44	02 28	03 22	04 46	06 05	07 27	08 48
56	////	02 06	03 08	04 36	05 56	07 20	08 43
58	////	01 37	02 51	04 23	05 46	07 12	08 38
S 60	////	00 49	02 31	04 09	05 34	07 04	08 33

Sunset / Twilight / Moonset

Lat.	Sunset	Twilight Civil	Naut.	Moonset 14	15	16	17
°	h m	h m	h m	h m	h m	h m	h m
N 72	■	13 03	15 30	■	15 45	18 20	20 28
N 70	■	14 02	15 50	13 59	16 35	18 44	20 39
68	■	14 37	16 05	15 08	17 07	19 01	20 49
66	13 23	15 02	16 18	15 44	17 30	19 16	20 57
64	14 04	15 21	16 29	16 10	17 48	19 27	21 03
62	14 32	15 37	16 39	16 30	18 03	19 37	21 09
60	14 53	15 51	16 47	16 46	18 15	19 46	21 13
N 58	15 10	16 02	16 55	17 00	18 26	19 53	21 18
56	15 25	16 12	17 01	17 12	18 35	19 59	21 21
54	15 38	16 21	17 07	17 22	18 43	20 05	21 25
52	15 49	16 29	17 13	17 31	18 51	20 10	21 28
50	15 58	16 37	17 18	17 39	18 57	20 15	21 31
45	16 19	16 53	17 30	17 57	19 11	20 25	21 37
N 40	16 36	17 06	17 40	18 11	19 23	20 34	21 42
35	16 50	17 18	17 50	18 23	19 33	20 41	21 46
30	17 02	17 29	17 58	18 33	19 41	20 47	21 50
20	17 23	17 47	18 15	18 51	19 56	20 58	21 56
N 10	17 42	18 05	18 31	19 07	20 09	21 07	22 02
0	17 59	18 22	18 48	19 21	20 21	21 16	22 07
S 10	18 17	18 40	19 07	19 36	20 32	21 24	22 12
20	18 35	19 00	19 29	19 51	20 45	21 34	22 18
30	18 57	19 25	19 58	20 08	20 59	21 44	22 24
35	19 10	19 42	20 17	20 19	21 07	21 50	22 27
40	19 25	19 58	20 40	20 30	21 17	21 57	22 31
45	19 43	20 21	21 10	20 44	21 28	22 04	22 36
S 50	20 06	20 50	21 55	21 00	21 41	22 14	22 41
52	20 17	21 05	22 23	21 08	21 47	22 18	22 44
54	20 29	21 23	23 08	21 16	21 54	22 22	22 47
56	20 43	21 45	////	21 26	22 01	22 28	22 50
58	21 00	22 15	////	21 37	22 09	22 34	22 53
S 60	21 20	23 03	////	21 49	22 19	22 40	22 57

SUN / MOON

Day	Eqn. of Time 00h	12h	Mer. Pass.	Mer. Pass. Upper	Lower	Age	Phase
d	m s	m s	h m	h m	h m	d	%
14	05 23	05 08	11 55	13 07	00 35	01	2
15	04 54	04 39	11 55	14 07	01 37	02	7
16	04 25	04 10	11 56	15 03	02 35	03	14

UT	ARIES GHA	VENUS −3.9 GHA	VENUS Dec	MARS +1.2 GHA	MARS Dec	JUPITER −2.8 GHA	JUPITER Dec	SATURN +0.7 GHA	SATURN Dec
17 00	86 01.6	206 52.9	S19 07.3	151 02.8	S22 38.1	18 07.9	N21 07.0	229 23.5	S12 04.7
01	101 04.0	221 52.2	08.1	166 03.2	37.7	33 10.7	06.9	244 25.8	04.8
02	116 06.5	236 51.4	08.8	181 03.6	37.4	48 13.5	06.9	259 28.0	04.9
03	131 09.0	251 50.6 ..	09.5	196 04.0 ..	37.1	63 16.3 ..	06.8	274 30.2 ..	05.0
04	146 11.4	266 49.9	10.2	211 04.3	36.7	78 19.1	06.8	289 32.5	05.0
05	161 13.9	281 49.1	10.9	226 04.7	36.4	93 21.9	06.8	304 34.7	05.1
M 06	176 16.3	296 48.4	S19 11.6	241 05.1	S22 36.1	108 24.7	N21 06.7	319 36.9	S12 05.2
O 07	191 18.8	311 47.6	12.3	256 05.5	35.8	123 27.5	06.7	334 39.2	05.2
N 08	206 21.3	326 46.9	13.0	271 05.9	35.4	138 30.3	06.6	349 41.4	05.3
D 09	221 23.7	341 46.1 ..	13.8	286 06.3 ..	35.1	153 33.1 ..	06.6	4 43.6 ..	05.4
A 10	236 26.2	356 45.4	14.5	301 06.7	34.8	168 35.9	06.6	19 45.9	05.4
Y 11	251 28.7	11 44.6	15.2	316 07.0	34.4	183 38.7	06.5	34 48.1	05.5
12	266 31.1	26 43.8	S19 15.9	331 07.4	S22 34.1	198 41.5	N21 06.5	49 50.3	S12 05.6
13	281 33.6	41 43.1	16.6	346 07.8	33.8	213 44.3	06.5	64 52.6	05.6
14	296 36.1	56 42.3	17.3	1 08.2	33.4	228 47.0	06.4	79 54.8	05.7
15	311 38.5	71 41.6 ..	18.0	16 08.6 ..	33.1	243 49.8 ..	06.4	94 57.0 ..	05.8
16	326 41.0	86 40.8	18.7	31 09.0	32.8	258 52.6	06.3	109 59.3	05.9
17	341 43.5	101 40.1	19.4	46 09.4	32.4	273 55.4	06.3	125 01.5	05.9
18	356 45.9	116 39.3	S19 20.1	61 09.8	S22 32.1	288 58.2	N21 06.3	140 03.7	S12 06.0
19	11 48.4	131 38.5	20.8	76 10.1	31.8	304 01.0	06.2	155 06.0	06.1
20	26 50.8	146 37.8	21.5	91 10.5	31.4	319 03.8	06.2	170 08.2	06.1
21	41 53.3	161 37.0 ..	22.2	106 10.9 ..	31.1	334 06.6 ..	06.1	185 10.5 ..	06.2
22	56 55.8	176 36.2	22.9	121 11.3	30.8	349 09.4	06.1	200 12.7	06.3
23	71 58.2	191 35.5	23.6	136 11.7	30.4	4 12.2	06.1	215 14.9	06.3
18 00	87 00.7	206 34.7	S19 24.3	151 12.1	S22 30.1	19 15.0	N21 06.0	230 17.2	S12 06.4
01	102 03.2	221 34.0	25.0	166 12.5	29.7	34 17.8	06.0	245 19.4	06.5
02	117 05.6	236 33.2	25.7	181 12.9	29.4	49 20.6	05.9	260 21.6	06.5
03	132 08.1	251 32.4 ..	26.4	196 13.2 ..	29.1	64 23.4 ..	05.9	275 23.9 ..	06.6
04	147 10.6	266 31.7	27.1	211 13.6	28.7	79 26.2	05.9	290 26.1	06.7
05	162 13.0	281 30.9	27.8	226 14.0	28.4	94 29.0	05.8	305 28.3	06.7
T 06	177 15.5	296 30.1	S19 28.4	241 14.4	S22 28.0	109 31.8	N21 05.7	320 30.6	S12 06.8
U 07	192 18.0	311 29.4	29.1	256 14.8	27.7	124 34.6	05.7	335 32.8	06.9
E 08	207 20.4	326 28.6	29.8	271 15.2	27.4	139 37.4	05.7	350 35.0	07.0
S 09	222 22.9	341 27.8 ..	30.5	286 15.6 ..	27.0	154 40.2 ..	05.7	5 37.3 ..	07.0
D 10	237 25.3	356 27.1	31.2	301 16.0	26.7	169 42.9	05.6	20 39.5	07.1
A 11	252 27.8	11 26.3	31.9	316 16.4	26.3	184 45.7	05.6	35 41.8	07.2
Y 12	267 30.3	26 25.5	S19 32.6	331 16.7	S22 26.0	199 48.5	N21 05.5	50 44.0	S12 07.2
13	282 32.7	41 24.8	33.2	346 17.1	25.6	214 51.3	05.5	65 46.2	07.3
14	297 35.2	56 24.0	33.9	1 17.5	25.3	229 54.1	05.5	80 48.5	07.4
15	312 37.7	71 23.2 ..	34.6	16 17.9 ..	25.0	244 56.9 ..	05.4	95 50.7 ..	07.4
16	327 40.1	86 22.4	35.3	31 18.3	24.6	259 59.7	05.4	110 52.9	07.5
17	342 42.6	101 21.7	36.0	46 18.7	24.3	275 02.5	05.4	125 55.2	07.6
18	357 45.1	116 20.9	S19 36.6	61 19.1	S22 23.9	290 05.3	N21 05.3	140 57.4	S12 07.6
19	12 47.5	131 20.1	37.3	76 19.5	23.6	305 08.1	05.3	155 59.6	07.7
20	27 50.0	146 19.4	38.0	91 19.9	23.2	320 10.9	05.2	171 01.9	07.8
21	42 52.4	161 18.6 ..	38.7	106 20.3 ..	22.9	335 13.7 ..	05.2	186 04.1 ..	07.8
22	57 54.9	176 17.8	39.4	121 20.6	22.5	350 16.4	05.2	201 06.4	07.9
23	72 57.4	191 17.0	40.0	136 21.0	22.2	5 19.2	05.1	216 08.6	08.0
19 00	87 59.8	206 16.3	S19 40.7	151 21.4	S22 21.8	20 22.0	N21 05.1	231 10.8	S12 08.0
01	103 02.3	221 15.5	41.4	166 21.8	21.5	35 24.8	05.0	246 13.1	08.1
02	118 04.8	236 14.7	42.0	181 22.2	21.1	50 27.6	05.0	261 15.3	08.2
03	133 07.2	251 13.9 ..	42.7	196 22.6 ..	20.8	65 30.4 ..	05.0	276 17.5 ..	08.2
04	148 09.7	266 13.2	43.4	211 23.0	20.4	80 33.2	04.9	291 19.8	08.3
05	163 12.2	281 12.4	44.1	226 23.4	20.1	95 36.0	04.9	306 22.0	08.4
W 06	178 14.6	296 11.6	S19 44.7	241 23.8	S22 19.7	110 38.8	N21 04.8	321 24.3	S12 08.4
E 07	193 17.1	311 10.8	45.4	256 24.2	19.4	125 41.6	04.8	336 26.5	08.5
D 08	208 19.6	326 10.0	46.1	271 24.6	19.0	140 44.4	04.8	351 28.7	08.6
N 09	223 22.0	341 09.3 ..	46.7	286 24.9 ..	18.7	155 47.1 ..	04.7	6 31.0 ..	08.6
E 10	238 24.5	356 08.5	47.4	301 25.3	18.3	170 49.9	04.7	21 33.2	08.7
S 11	253 26.9	11 07.7	48.0	316 25.7	18.0	185 52.7	04.7	36 35.5	08.8
D 12	268 29.4	26 06.9	S19 48.7	331 26.1	S22 17.6	200 55.5	N21 04.6	51 37.7	S12 08.8
A 13	283 31.9	41 06.1	49.4	346 26.5	17.3	215 58.3	04.6	66 39.9	08.9
Y 14	298 34.3	56 05.4	50.0	1 26.9	16.9	231 01.1	04.5	81 42.2	09.0
15	313 36.8	71 04.6 ..	50.7	16 27.3 ..	16.6	246 03.9 ..	04.5	96 44.4 ..	09.0
16	328 39.3	86 03.8	51.3	31 27.7	16.2	261 06.7	04.5	111 46.7	09.1
17	343 41.7	101 03.0	52.0	46 28.1	15.9	276 09.4	04.4	126 48.9	09.2
18	358 44.2	116 02.2	S19 52.7	61 28.5	S22 15.5	291 12.2	N21 04.4	141 51.1	S12 09.2
19	13 46.7	131 01.4	53.3	76 28.9	15.1	306 15.0	04.3	156 53.4	09.3
20	28 49.1	146 00.7	54.0	91 29.3	14.8	321 17.8	04.3	171 55.6	09.4
21	43 51.6	160 59.9 ..	54.6	106 29.7 ..	14.4	336 20.6 ..	04.3	186 57.9 ..	09.4
22	58 54.0	175 59.1	55.3	121 30.0	14.1	351 23.4	04.2	202 00.1	09.5
23	73 56.5	190 58.3	55.9	136 30.4	13.7	6 26.2	04.2	217 02.3	09.6
Mer. Pass. 18 09.0		*v* −0.8	*d* 0.7	*v* 0.4	*d* 0.3	*v* 2.8	*d* 0.0	*v* 2.2	*d* 0.1

STARS

Name	SHA	Dec
Acamar	315 18.3	S40 15.3
Achernar	335 26.8	S57 10.5
Acrux	173 09.7	S63 10.0
Adhara	255 12.4	S28 59.5
Aldebaran	290 49.4	N16 32.0
Alioth	166 21.2	N55 53.0
Alkaid	152 59.4	N49 14.7
Al Na'ir	27 44.4	S46 54.0
Alnilam	275 46.4	S 1 11.8
Alphard	217 56.2	S 8 43.0
Alphecca	126 11.6	N26 40.2
Alpheratz	357 43.8	N29 10.0
Altair	62 08.9	N 8 54.4
Ankaa	353 16.0	S42 14.3
Antares	112 27.0	S26 27.5
Arcturus	145 56.3	N19 08.8
Atria	107 29.7	S69 02.8
Avior	234 17.6	S59 33.0
Bellatrix	278 32.0	N 6 21.6
Betelgeuse	271 01.3	N 7 24.4
Canopus	263 55.7	S52 42.3
Capella	280 34.4	N46 00.6
Deneb	49 32.0	N45 19.9
Denebola	182 34.0	N14 29.8
Diphda	348 56.1	S17 55.0
Dubhe	193 52.0	N61 40.4
Elnath	278 12.6	N28 37.0
Eltanin	90 46.8	N51 29.4
Enif	33 47.6	N 9 56.3
Fomalhaut	15 24.4	S29 33.2
Gacrux	172 01.3	S57 10.9
Gienah	175 52.7	S17 36.8
Hadar	148 48.7	S60 25.9
Hamal	328 00.9	N23 31.5
Kaus Aust.	83 44.7	S34 22.6
Kochab	137 21.0	N74 05.9
Markab	13 38.7	N15 16.7
Menkar	314 15.1	N 4 08.4
Menkent	148 08.2	S36 25.8
Miaplacidus	221 39.1	S69 46.1
Mirfak	308 40.4	N49 54.5
Nunki	75 59.1	S26 16.7
Peacock	53 20.3	S56 41.6
Pollux	243 27.8	N27 59.4
Procyon	244 59.8	N 5 11.3
Rasalhague	96 07.1	N12 33.2
Regulus	207 43.7	N11 54.0
Rigel	281 12.0	S 8 11.3
Rigil Kent.	139 52.6	S60 53.0
Sabik	102 13.3	S15 44.3
Schedar	349 40.7	N56 36.9
Shaula	96 22.8	S37 06.6
Sirius	258 33.7	S16 44.2
Spica	158 31.7	S11 13.7
Suhail	222 52.4	S43 29.1
Vega	80 39.6	N38 47.9
Zuben'ubi	137 06.0	S16 05.6

	SHA	Mer. Pass.
	° ′	h m
Venus	119 34.0	10 14
Mars	64 11.4	13 55
Jupiter	292 14.3	22 39
Saturn	143 16.5	8 38

UT	SUN GHA	SUN Dec	MOON GHA	v	MOON Dec	d	HP
d h	° ′	° ′	° ′	′	° ′	′	′
17 00	180 58.7	S23 21.5	129 28.0	9.3	S11 13.2	10.7	59.1
01	195 58.4	21.5	143 56.3	9.4	11 02.5	10.8	59.0
02	210 58.1	21.6	158 24.7	9.6	10 51.7	10.9	59.0
03	225 57.8 ..	21.7	172 53.3	9.6	10 40.8	10.9	58.9
04	240 57.4	21.8	187 21.9	9.7	10 29.9	10.9	58.9
05	255 57.1	21.9	201 50.6	9.8	10 19.0	11.0	58.9
06	270 56.8	S23 22.0	216 19.4	9.9	S10 08.0	11.1	58.8
07	285 56.5	22.0	230 48.3	9.9	9 56.9	11.0	58.8
08	300 56.2	22.1	245 17.2	10.1	9 45.9	11.1	58.7
M 09	315 55.9 ..	22.2	259 46.3	10.1	9 34.8	11.2	58.7
O 10	330 55.6	22.3	274 15.4	10.2	9 23.6	11.2	58.7
N 11	345 55.3	22.4	288 44.6	10.3	9 12.4	11.2	58.6
D 12	0 55.0	S23 22.4	303 13.9	10.4	S 9 01.2	11.2	58.6
A 13	15 54.7	22.5	317 43.3	10.5	8 50.0	11.3	58.5
Y 14	30 54.4	22.6	332 12.8	10.5	8 38.7	11.3	58.5
15	45 54.1 ..	22.7	346 42.3	10.7	8 27.4	11.3	58.5
16	60 53.8	22.7	1 12.0	10.7	8 16.1	11.4	58.4
17	75 53.5	22.8	15 41.7	10.8	8 04.7	11.4	58.4
18	90 53.1	S23 22.9	30 11.5	10.8	S 7 53.3	11.4	58.3
19	105 52.8	23.0	44 41.3	11.0	7 41.9	11.5	58.3
20	120 52.5	23.0	59 11.3	11.0	7 30.4	11.4	58.3
21	135 52.2 ..	23.1	73 41.3	11.1	7 19.0	11.5	58.2
22	150 51.9	23.2	88 11.4	11.2	7 07.5	11.5	58.2
23	165 51.6	23.3	102 41.6	11.2	6 56.0	11.5	58.1
18 00	180 51.3	S23 23.4	117 11.8	11.3	S 6 44.5	11.6	58.1
01	195 51.0	23.4	131 42.1	11.4	6 32.9	11.5	58.0
02	210 50.7	23.5	146 12.5	11.5	6 21.4	11.6	58.0
03	225 50.4 ..	23.5	160 43.0	11.5	6 09.8	11.6	58.0
04	240 50.1	23.6	175 13.5	11.6	5 58.2	11.6	57.9
05	255 49.8	23.6	189 44.1	11.6	5 46.6	11.6	57.9
06	270 49.5	S23 23.7	204 14.7	11.8	S 5 35.0	11.6	57.8
07	285 49.1	23.8	218 45.5	11.8	5 23.4	11.7	57.8
T 08	300 48.8	23.8	233 16.3	11.8	5 11.7	11.6	57.8
U 09	315 48.5 ..	23.9	247 47.1	12.0	5 00.1	11.7	57.7
E 10	330 48.2	24.0	262 18.1	12.0	4 48.4	11.6	57.7
S 11	345 47.9	24.0	276 49.1	12.0	4 36.8	11.7	57.6
D 12	0 47.6	S23 24.1	291 20.1	12.1	S 4 25.1	11.7	57.6
A 13	15 47.3	24.1	305 51.2	12.2	4 13.4	11.7	57.6
Y 14	30 47.0	24.2	320 22.4	12.2	4 01.7	11.6	57.5
15	45 46.7 ..	24.2	334 53.6	12.3	3 50.1	11.7	57.5
16	60 46.4	24.3	349 24.9	12.4	3 38.4	11.7	57.4
17	75 46.1	24.4	3 56.3	12.4	3 26.7	11.7	57.4
18	90 45.8	S23 24.4	18 27.7	12.4	S 3 15.0	11.7	57.4
19	105 45.4	24.5	32 59.1	12.6	3 03.3	11.7	57.3
20	120 45.1	24.5	47 30.7	12.5	2 51.6	11.6	57.3
21	135 44.8 ..	24.6	62 02.2	12.7	2 40.0	11.7	57.3
22	150 44.5	24.6	76 33.9	12.6	2 28.3	11.7	57.2
23	165 44.2	24.7	91 05.5	12.8	2 16.6	11.7	57.2
19 00	180 43.9	S23 24.7	105 37.3	12.7	S 2 04.9	11.6	57.1
01	195 43.6	24.8	120 09.0	12.9	1 53.3	11.7	57.1
02	210 43.3	24.8	134 40.9	12.8	1 41.6	11.6	57.1
03	225 43.0 ..	24.9	149 12.7	12.9	1 30.0	11.7	57.0
04	240 42.7	24.9	163 44.6	13.0	1 18.3	11.6	57.0
05	255 42.3	24.9	178 16.6	13.0	1 06.7	11.6	56.9
06	270 42.0	S23 25.0	192 48.6	13.1	S 0 55.1	11.6	56.9
W 07	285 41.7	25.0	207 20.7	13.1	0 43.5	11.6	56.9
E 08	300 41.4	25.1	221 52.8	13.1	0 31.9	11.6	56.8
D 09	315 41.1 ..	25.1	236 24.9	13.2	0 20.3	11.6	56.8
N 10	330 40.8	25.2	250 57.1	13.2	S 0 08.7	11.5	56.8
E 11	345 40.5	25.2	265 29.3	13.3	N 0 02.8	11.5	56.7
S 12	0 40.2	S23 25.2	280 01.6	13.3	N 0 14.3	11.6	56.7
D 13	15 39.9	25.3	294 33.9	13.3	0 25.9	11.5	56.7
A 14	30 39.6	25.3	309 06.2	13.4	0 37.4	11.5	56.6
Y 15	45 39.3 ..	25.3	323 38.6	13.4	0 48.9	11.4	56.6
16	60 38.9	25.4	338 11.0	13.5	1 00.3	11.5	56.5
17	75 38.6	25.4	352 43.5	13.4	1 11.8	11.4	56.5
18	90 38.3	S23 25.5	7 15.9	13.5	N 1 23.2	11.4	56.5
19	105 38.0	25.5	21 48.4	13.6	1 34.6	11.4	56.4
20	120 37.7	25.5	36 21.0	13.6	1 46.0	11.4	56.4
21	135 37.4 ..	25.6	50 53.6	13.5	1 57.4	11.3	56.4
22	150 37.1	25.6	65 26.2	13.6	2 08.7	11.3	56.3
23	165 36.8	25.6	79 58.8	13.7	N 2 20.0	11.3	56.3
	SD 16.3	d 0.1	SD 16.0		15.7		15.4

Lat.	Twilight Naut.	Twilight Civil	Sunrise	Moonrise 17	18	19	20
°	h m	h m	h m	h m	h m	h m	h m
N 72	08 24	10 54	■	11 46	11 32	11 19	11 06
N 70	08 04	09 52	■	11 33	11 25	11 19	11 12
68	07 48	09 17	■	11 21	11 20	11 19	11 17
66	07 35	08 52	10 32	11 12	11 16	11 19	11 22
64	07 24	08 32	09 50	11 04	11 12	11 19	11 25
62	07 14	08 16	09 22	10 57	11 09	11 19	11 28
60	07 06	08 03	09 00	10 51	11 06	11 19	11 31
N 58	06 58	07 51	08 43	10 46	11 03	11 19	11 34
56	06 51	07 41	08 28	10 41	11 01	11 19	11 36
54	06 45	07 31	08 15	10 37	10 59	11 19	11 38
52	06 40	07 23	08 04	10 33	10 57	11 19	11 40
50	06 34	07 16	07 54	10 30	10 56	11 19	11 41
45	06 22	07 00	07 34	10 22	10 52	11 19	11 45
N 40	06 12	06 46	07 17	10 16	10 49	11 19	11 48
35	06 03	06 34	07 03	10 11	10 46	11 19	11 51
30	05 54	06 24	06 50	10 06	10 44	11 19	11 53
20	05 38	06 05	06 29	09 57	10 39	11 19	11 57
N 10	05 21	05 48	06 11	09 50	10 36	11 19	12 01
0	05 04	05 31	05 53	09 43	10 32	11 19	12 04
S 10	04 45	05 12	05 35	09 36	10 29	11 19	12 08
20	04 23	04 52	05 17	09 29	10 25	11 19	12 11
30	03 54	04 27	04 54	09 20	10 21	11 19	12 16
35	03 35	04 12	04 41	09 15	10 19	11 20	12 18
40	03 12	03 54	04 26	09 10	10 16	11 20	12 21
45	02 41	03 31	04 08	09 03	10 13	11 20	12 24
S 50	01 56	03 01	03 46	08 55	10 09	11 20	12 28
52	01 28	02 46	03 35	08 52	10 07	11 20	12 30
54	00 42	02 28	03 23	08 48	10 05	11 20	12 32
56	////	02 06	03 08	08 43	10 03	11 20	12 34
58	////	01 36	02 52	08 38	10 01	11 20	12 37
S 60	////	00 46	02 31	08 33	09 58	11 20	12 40

Lat.	Sunset	Twilight Civil	Twilight Naut.	Moonset 17	18	19	20
°	h m	h m	h m	h m	h m	h m	h m
N 72	■	12 59	15 30	20 28	22 23	24 12	00 12
N 70	■	14 01	15 50	20 39	22 27	24 09	00 09
68	■	14 36	16 06	20 49	22 30	24 06	00 06
66	13 21	15 02	16 19	20 57	22 32	24 04	00 04
64	14 03	15 21	16 30	21 03	22 34	24 02	00 02
62	14 32	15 37	16 39	21 09	22 36	24 00	00 00
60	14 53	15 51	16 48	21 13	22 38	23 58	25 17
N 58	15 11	16 03	16 55	21 18	22 39	23 57	25 13
56	15 26	16 13	17 02	21 21	22 40	23 56	25 09
54	15 38	16 22	17 08	21 25	22 41	23 55	25 06
52	15 49	16 30	17 14	21 28	22 42	23 54	25 03
50	15 59	16 38	17 19	21 31	22 43	23 53	25 00
45	16 20	16 54	17 31	21 37	22 45	23 51	24 55
N 40	16 37	17 07	17 41	21 42	22 47	23 49	24 50
35	16 51	17 19	17 51	21 46	22 48	23 48	24 46
30	17 03	17 30	18 00	21 50	22 49	23 47	24 42
20	17 25	17 49	18 16	21 56	22 51	23 45	24 36
N 10	17 43	18 06	18 32	22 02	22 53	23 43	24 31
0	18 01	18 23	18 49	22 07	22 55	23 41	24 26
S 10	18 18	18 41	19 08	22 12	22 57	23 39	24 20
20	18 37	19 02	19 31	22 18	22 58	23 37	24 15
30	18 59	19 27	20 00	22 24	23 00	23 35	24 09
35	19 12	19 42	20 19	22 27	23 01	23 34	24 05
40	19 27	20 00	20 42	22 31	23 03	23 32	24 01
45	19 45	20 23	21 13	22 36	23 04	23 31	23 57
S 50	20 08	20 53	21 58	22 41	23 06	23 29	23 51
52	20 19	21 08	22 26	22 44	23 07	23 28	23 49
54	20 31	21 26	23 13	22 47	23 07	23 26	23 46
56	20 45	21 48	////	22 50	23 08	23 26	23 43
58	21 02	22 18	////	22 53	23 09	23 24	23 40
S 60	21 23	23 09	////	22 57	23 11	23 23	23 36

	SUN			MOON			
Day	Eqn. of Time 00h	Eqn. of Time 12h	Mer. Pass.	Mer. Pass. Upper	Mer. Pass. Lower	Age	Phase
d	m s	m s	h m	h m	h m	d	%
17	03 55	03 41	11 56	15 55	03 29	04	23
18	03 26	03 11	11 57	16 44	04 20	05	33
19	02 56	02 41	11 57	17 30	05 07	06	43

UT	ARIES GHA	VENUS −3.9 GHA	Dec	MARS +1.2 GHA	Dec	JUPITER −2.8 GHA	Dec	SATURN +0.6 GHA	Dec	STARS Name	SHA	Dec
d h	° ′	° ′	° ′	° ′	° ′	° ′	° ′	° ′	° ′		° ′	° ′
20 00	88 59.0	205 57.5	S19 56.6	151 30.8	S22 13.4	21 29.0	N21 04.2	232 04.6	S12 09.6	Acamar	315 18.3	S40 15.4
01	104 01.4	220 56.7	57.2	166 31.2	13.0	36 31.7	04.1	247 06.8	09.7	Achernar	335 26.8	S57 10.5
02	119 03.9	235 55.9	57.9	181 31.6	12.6	51 34.5	04.1	262 09.1	09.8	Acrux	173 09.7	S63 10.0
03	134 06.4	250 55.2	.. 58.5	196 32.0	.. 12.3	66 37.3	.. 04.0	277 11.3	.. 09.8	Adhara	255 12.4	S28 59.5
04	149 08.8	265 54.4	59.2	211 32.4	11.9	81 40.1	04.0	292 13.5	09.9	Aldebaran	290 49.4	N16 32.0
05	164 11.3	280 53.6	19 59.8	226 32.8	11.6	96 42.9	04.0	307 15.8	10.0			
06	179 13.8	295 52.8	S20 00.5	241 33.2	S22 11.2	111 45.7	N21 03.9	322 18.0	S12 10.0	Alioth	166 21.2	N55 53.0
07	194 16.2	310 52.0	01.1	256 33.6	10.8	126 48.4	03.9	337 20.3	10.1	Alkaid	152 59.4	N49 14.7
08	209 18.7	325 51.2	01.7	271 34.0	10.5	141 51.2	03.9	352 22.5	10.2	Al Na'ir	27 44.4	S46 54.0
09	224 21.2	340 50.4	.. 02.4	286 34.4	.. 10.1	156 54.0	.. 03.8	7 24.7	.. 10.2	Alnilam	275 46.4	S 1 11.8
10	239 23.6	355 49.6	03.0	301 34.8	09.7	171 56.8	03.8	22 27.0	10.3	Alphard	217 56.2	S 8 43.0
11	254 26.1	10 48.8	03.7	316 35.2	09.4	186 59.6	03.7	37 29.2	10.4			
12	269 28.5	25 48.0	S20 04.3	331 35.6	S22 09.0	202 02.4	N21 03.7	52 31.5	S12 10.4	Alphecca	126 11.6	N26 40.2
13	284 31.0	40 47.3	04.9	346 36.0	08.7	217 05.2	03.7	67 33.7	10.5	Alpheratz	357 43.8	N29 10.0
14	299 33.5	55 46.5	05.6	1 36.4	08.3	232 07.9	03.6	82 35.9	10.6	Altair	62 08.9	N 8 54.4
15	314 35.9	70 45.7	.. 06.2	16 36.7	.. 07.9	247 10.7	.. 03.6	97 38.2	.. 10.6	Ankaa	353 16.0	S42 14.3
16	329 38.4	85 44.9	06.8	31 37.1	07.6	262 13.5	03.5	112 40.4	10.7	Antares	112 27.0	S26 27.5
17	344 40.9	100 44.1	07.5	46 37.5	07.2	277 16.3	03.5	127 42.7	10.8			
18	359 43.3	115 43.3	S20 08.1	61 37.9	S22 06.8	292 19.1	N21 03.5	142 44.9	S12 10.8	Arcturus	145 56.2	N19 06.8
19	14 45.8	130 42.5	08.7	76 38.3	06.5	307 21.8	03.4	157 47.2	10.9	Atria	107 29.7	S69 02.8
20	29 48.3	145 41.7	09.4	91 38.7	06.1	322 24.6	03.4	172 49.4	11.0	Avior	234 17.6	S59 33.1
21	44 50.7	160 40.9	.. 10.0	106 39.1	.. 05.7	337 27.4	.. 03.4	187 51.6	.. 11.0	Bellatrix	278 32.0	N 6 21.6
22	59 53.2	175 40.1	10.6	121 39.5	05.4	352 30.2	03.3	202 53.9	11.1	Betelgeuse	271 01.3	N 7 24.4
23	74 55.7	190 39.3	11.3	136 39.9	05.0	7 33.0	03.3	217 56.1	11.2			
21 00	89 58.1	205 38.5	S20 11.9	151 40.3	S22 04.6	22 35.8	N21 03.2	232 58.4	S12 11.2	Canopus	263 55.7	S52 42.3
01	105 00.6	220 37.7	12.5	166 40.7	04.2	37 38.5	03.2	248 00.6	11.3	Capella	280 34.4	N46 00.6
02	120 03.0	235 36.9	13.1	181 41.1	03.9	52 41.3	03.2	263 02.9	11.4	Deneb	49 32.1	N45 19.9
03	135 05.5	250 36.1	.. 13.8	196 41.5	.. 03.5	67 44.1	.. 03.1	278 05.1	.. 11.4	Denebola	182 34.0	N14 29.8
04	150 08.0	265 35.3	14.4	211 41.9	03.1	82 46.9	03.1	293 07.3	11.5	Diphda	348 56.2	S17 55.0
05	165 10.4	280 34.5	15.0	226 42.3	02.8	97 49.7	03.1	308 09.6	11.6			
06	180 12.9	295 33.7	S20 15.6	241 42.7	S22 02.4	112 52.4	N21 03.0	323 11.8	S12 11.6	Dubhe	193 52.0	N61 40.4
07	195 15.4	310 32.9	16.2	256 43.1	02.0	127 55.2	03.0	338 14.1	11.7	Elnath	278 12.6	N28 37.0
08	210 17.8	325 32.1	16.9	271 43.5	01.6	142 58.0	02.9	353 16.3	11.7	Eltanin	90 46.8	N51 29.4
09	225 20.3	340 31.3	.. 17.5	286 43.9	.. 01.3	158 00.8	.. 02.9	8 18.6	.. 11.8	Enif	33 47.6	N 9 56.3
10	240 22.8	355 30.5	18.1	301 44.3	00.9	173 03.6	02.9	23 20.8	11.9	Fomalhaut	15 24.5	S29 33.2
11	255 25.2	10 29.7	18.7	316 44.7	00.5	188 06.3	02.8	38 23.0	11.9			
12	270 27.7	25 28.9	S20 19.3	331 45.1	S22 00.0	203 09.1	N21 02.8	53 25.3	S12 12.0	Gacrux	172 01.3	S57 10.9
13	285 30.1	40 28.1	19.9	346 45.5	21 59.8	218 11.9	02.8	68 27.5	12.1	Gienah	175 52.7	S17 36.8
14	300 32.6	55 27.3	20.6	1 45.9	59.4	233 14.7	02.7	83 29.8	12.1	Hadar	148 48.7	S60 25.9
15	315 35.1	70 26.5	.. 21.2	16 46.3	.. 59.0	248 17.5	.. 02.7	98 32.0	.. 12.2	Hamal	328 00.9	N23 31.5
16	330 37.5	85 25.7	21.8	31 46.7	58.7	263 20.2	02.6	113 34.3	12.3	Kaus Aust.	83 44.7	S34 22.6
17	345 40.0	100 24.9	22.4	46 47.1	58.3	278 23.0	02.6	128 36.5	12.3			
18	0 42.5	115 24.1	S20 23.0	61 47.5	S21 57.9	293 25.8	N21 02.5	143 38.8	S12 12.4	Kochab	137 20.9	N74 05.9
19	15 44.9	130 23.3	23.6	76 47.9	57.5	308 28.6	02.5	158 41.0	12.5	Markab	13 38.7	N15 16.7
20	30 47.4	145 22.5	24.2	91 48.3	57.1	323 31.3	02.5	173 43.2	12.5	Menkar	314 15.1	N 4 08.4
21	45 49.9	160 21.7	.. 24.8	106 48.7	.. 56.8	338 34.1	.. 02.5	188 45.5	.. 12.6	Menkent	148 08.2	S36 25.8
22	60 52.3	175 20.8	25.4	121 49.1	56.4	353 36.9	02.4	203 47.7	12.7	Miaplacidus	221 39.0	S69 46.1
23	75 54.8	190 20.0	26.0	136 49.5	56.0	8 39.7	02.4	218 50.0	12.7			
22 00	90 57.3	205 19.2	S20 26.6	151 49.9	S21 55.6	23 42.4	N21 02.3	233 52.2	S12 12.8	Mirfak	308 40.4	N49 54.5
01	105 59.7	220 18.4	27.2	166 50.3	55.2	38 45.2	02.3	248 54.5	12.8	Nunki	75 59.1	S26 16.7
02	121 02.2	235 17.6	27.8	181 50.7	54.9	53 48.0	02.3	263 56.7	12.9	Peacock	53 20.3	S56 41.6
03	136 04.6	250 16.8	.. 28.4	196 51.1	.. 54.5	68 50.8	.. 02.2	278 59.0	.. 13.0	Pollux	243 27.8	N27 59.4
04	151 07.1	265 16.0	29.0	211 51.5	54.1	83 53.5	02.2	294 01.2	13.0	Procyon	244 59.8	N 5 11.3
05	166 09.6	280 15.2	29.6	226 51.9	53.7	98 56.3	02.2	309 03.5	13.1			
06	181 12.0	295 14.4	S20 30.2	241 52.3	S21 53.3	113 59.1	N21 02.1	324 05.7	S12 13.2	Rasalhague	96 07.1	N12 33.2
07	196 14.5	310 13.6	30.8	256 52.7	53.0	129 01.9	02.1	339 07.9	13.2	Regulus	207 43.7	N11 54.0
08	211 17.0	325 12.7	31.4	271 53.1	52.6	144 04.6	02.0	354 10.2	13.3	Rigel	281 12.0	S 8 11.3
09	226 19.4	340 11.9	.. 32.0	286 53.5	.. 52.2	159 07.4	.. 02.0	9 12.4	.. 13.4	Rigil Kent.	139 52.6	S60 53.0
10	241 21.9	355 11.1	32.6	301 53.9	51.8	174 10.2	02.0	24 14.7	13.4	Sabik	102 13.3	S15 44.3
11	256 24.4	10 10.3	33.2	316 54.3	51.4	189 13.0	01.9	39 16.9	13.5			
12	271 26.8	25 09.5	S20 33.8	331 54.7	S21 51.0	204 15.7	N21 01.9	54 19.2	S12 13.6	Schedar	349 40.7	N56 36.9
13	286 29.3	40 08.7	34.4	346 55.1	50.7	219 18.5	01.9	69 21.4	13.6	Shaula	96 22.8	S37 06.6
14	301 31.8	55 07.9	35.0	1 55.5	50.3	234 21.3	01.8	84 23.7	13.7	Sirius	258 33.6	S16 44.2
15	316 34.2	70 07.0	.. 35.6	16 55.9	.. 49.9	249 24.1	.. 01.8	99 25.9	.. 13.7	Spica	158 31.7	S11 13.7
16	331 36.7	85 06.2	36.1	31 56.3	49.5	264 26.8	01.8	114 28.2	13.8	Suhail	222 52.3	S43 29.1
17	346 39.1	100 05.4	36.7	46 56.7	49.1	279 29.6	01.7	129 30.4	13.9			
18	1 41.6	115 04.6	S20 37.3	61 57.1	S21 48.7	294 32.4	N21 01.7	144 32.7	S12 13.9	Vega	80 39.6	N38 47.9
19	16 44.1	130 03.8	37.9	76 57.5	48.3	309 35.2	01.6	159 34.9	14.0	Zuben'ubi	137 06.0	S16 05.6
20	31 46.5	145 03.0	38.5	91 57.9	47.9	324 37.9	01.6	174 37.2	14.1		SHA	Mer. Pass.
21	46 49.0	160 02.1	.. 39.1	106 58.3	.. 47.6	339 40.7	.. 01.6	189 39.4	.. 14.1		° ′	h m
22	61 51.5	175 01.3	39.6	121 58.7	47.2	354 43.5	01.5	204 41.7	14.2	Venus	115 40.4	10 18
23	76 53.9	190 00.5	40.2	136 59.1	46.8	9 46.2	01.5	219 43.9	14.3	Mars	61 42.2	13 53
	h m									Jupiter	292 37.6	22 25
Mer. Pass.	17 57.2	v −0.8	d 0.6	v 0.4	d 0.4	v 2.8	d 0.0	v 2.2	d 0.1	Saturn	143 00.3	8 27

Main table

UT	SUN GHA	SUN Dec	MOON GHA	v	MOON Dec	d	HP
d h	° ′	° ′	° ′	′	° ′	′	′
20 00	180 36.5	S23 25.6	94 31.5	13.6	N 2 31.3	11.3	56.3
01	195 36.2	25.7	109 04.1	13.8	2 42.6	11.2	56.2
02	210 35.8	25.7	123 36.9	13.7	2 53.8	11.2	56.2
03	225 35.5	.. 25.7	138 09.6	13.8	3 05.0	11.2	56.2
04	240 35.2	25.7	152 42.4	13.7	3 16.2	11.2	56.1
05	255 34.9	25.8	167 15.1	13.9	3 27.4	11.1	56.1
06	270 34.6	S23 25.8	181 48.0	13.8	N 3 38.5	11.1	56.1
T 07	285 34.3	25.8	196 20.8	13.8	3 49.6	11.1	56.0
H 08	300 34.0	25.8	210 53.6	13.9	4 00.7	11.0	56.0
U 09	315 33.7	.. 25.9	225 26.5	13.9	4 11.7	11.1	56.0
R 10	330 33.4	25.9	239 59.4	13.9	4 22.8	10.9	55.9
S 11	345 33.1	25.9	254 32.3	14.0	4 33.7	11.0	55.9
D 12	0 32.7	S23 25.9	269 05.3	13.9	N 4 44.7	10.9	55.9
A 13	15 32.4	25.9	283 38.2	14.0	4 55.6	10.9	55.9
Y 14	30 32.1	26.0	298 11.2	13.9	5 06.5	10.8	55.8
15	45 31.8	.. 26.0	312 44.1	14.0	5 17.3	10.9	55.8
16	60 31.5	26.0	327 17.1	14.0	5 28.2	10.7	55.8
17	75 31.2	26.0	341 50.1	14.1	5 38.9	10.8	55.7
18	90 30.9	S23 26.0	356 23.2	14.0	N 5 49.7	10.7	55.7
19	105 30.6	26.0	10 56.2	14.0	6 00.4	10.7	55.7
20	120 30.3	26.1	25 29.2	14.1	6 11.1	10.6	55.6
21	135 30.0	.. 26.1	40 02.3	14.0	6 21.7	10.6	55.6
22	150 29.6	26.1	54 35.3	14.1	6 32.3	10.5	55.6
23	165 29.3	26.1	69 08.4	14.1	6 42.8	10.6	55.6
21 00	180 29.0	S23 26.1	83 41.5	14.1	N 6 53.4	10.4	55.5
01	195 28.7	26.1	98 14.6	14.1	7 03.8	10.5	55.5
02	210 28.4	26.1	112 47.7	14.0	7 14.3	10.4	55.5
03	225 28.1	.. 26.1	127 20.7	14.1	7 24.7	10.3	55.4
04	240 27.8	26.1	141 53.8	14.2	7 35.0	10.3	55.4
05	255 27.5	26.1	156 27.0	14.1	7 45.3	10.3	55.4
06	270 27.2	S23 26.1	171 00.1	14.1	N 7 55.6	10.2	55.4
07	285 26.9	26.1	185 33.2	14.1	8 05.8	10.1	55.3
F 08	300 26.5	26.1	200 06.3	14.1	8 16.0	10.1	55.3
R 09	315 26.2	.. 26.1	214 39.4	14.1	8 26.1	10.1	55.3
I 10	330 25.9	26.1	229 12.5	14.1	8 36.2	10.0	55.3
D 11	345 25.6	26.1	243 45.6	14.1	8 46.2	10.0	55.2
A 12	0 25.3	S23 26.1	258 18.7	14.1	N 8 56.2	10.0	55.2
Y 13	15 25.0	26.1	272 51.8	14.1	9 06.2	9.9	55.2
14	30 24.7	26.1	287 24.9	14.2	9 16.1	9.8	55.2
15	45 24.4	.. 26.1	301 58.1	14.1	9 25.9	9.9	55.1
16	60 24.0	26.1	316 31.2	14.0	9 35.8	9.7	55.1
17	75 23.7	26.1	331 04.2	14.1	9 45.5	9.7	55.1
18	90 23.4	S23 26.1	345 37.3	14.1	N 9 55.2	9.7	55.1
19	105 23.1	26.1	0 10.4	14.1	10 04.9	9.6	55.0
20	120 22.8	26.1	14 43.5	14.1	10 14.5	9.5	55.0
21	135 22.5	.. 26.1	29 16.6	14.0	10 24.0	9.5	55.0
22	150 22.2	26.1	43 49.6	14.1	10 33.5	9.5	55.0
23	165 21.9	26.1	58 22.7	14.0	10 43.0	9.4	55.0
22 00	180 21.6	S23 26.1	72 55.7	14.1	N10 52.4	9.3	54.9
01	195 21.3	26.1	87 28.8	14.0	11 01.7	9.3	54.9
02	210 20.9	26.1	102 01.8	14.0	11 11.0	9.3	54.9
03	225 20.6	.. 26.0	116 34.8	14.0	11 20.3	9.1	54.9
04	240 20.3	26.0	131 07.8	14.0	11 29.4	9.2	54.9
05	255 20.0	26.0	145 40.8	14.0	11 38.6	9.0	54.8
06	270 19.7	S23 26.0	160 13.8	14.0	N11 47.6	9.0	54.8
07	285 19.4	26.0	174 46.8	13.9	11 56.6	9.0	54.8
S 08	300 19.1	26.0	189 19.7	14.0	12 05.6	8.9	54.8
A 09	315 18.8	.. 26.0	203 52.7	13.9	12 14.5	8.8	54.8
T 10	330 18.5	25.9	218 25.6	13.9	12 23.3	8.8	54.7
U 11	345 18.1	25.9	232 58.5	13.9	12 32.1	8.7	54.7
R 12	0 17.8	S23 25.9	247 31.4	13.9	N12 40.8	8.7	54.7
D 13	15 17.5	25.9	262 04.3	13.9	12 49.5	8.6	54.7
A 14	30 17.2	25.9	276 37.2	13.8	12 58.1	8.6	54.7
Y 15	45 16.9	.. 25.8	291 10.0	13.8	13 06.7	8.4	54.6
16	60 16.6	25.8	305 42.8	13.9	13 15.1	8.5	54.6
17	75 16.3	25.8	320 15.7	13.8	13 23.6	8.3	54.6
18	90 16.0	S23 25.8	334 48.5	13.7	N13 31.9	8.3	54.6
19	105 15.7	25.7	349 21.2	13.8	13 40.2	8.2	54.6
20	120 15.4	25.7	3 54.0	13.7	13 48.4	8.2	54.5
21	135 15.0	.. 25.7	18 26.7	13.8	13 56.6	8.1	54.5
22	150 14.7	25.7	32 59.5	13.7	14 04.7	8.0	54.5
23	165 14.4	25.6	47 32.2	13.6	N14 12.7	8.0	54.5
	SD 16.3	d 0.0	SD 15.2		15.0		14.9

Twilight and Moonrise

Lat.	Twilight Naut.	Civil	Sunrise	Moonrise 20	21	22	23
°	h m	h m	h m	h m	h m	h m	h m
N 72	08 26	10 58	■	11 06	10 53	10 37	10 15
N 70	08 06	09 55	■	11 12	11 06	10 59	10 51
68	07 50	09 19	■	11 17	11 16	11 16	11 16
66	07 37	08 54	10 35	11 22	11 25	11 29	11 36
64	07 26	08 34	09 52	11 25	11 32	11 41	11 52
62	07 16	08 18	09 24	11 28	11 39	11 51	12 06
60	07 07	08 04	09 02	11 31	11 44	11 59	12 17
N 58	07 00	07 53	08 45	11 34	11 49	12 06	12 27
56	06 53	07 42	08 30	11 36	11 54	12 13	12 35
54	06 47	07 33	08 17	11 38	11 57	12 19	12 43
52	06 41	07 25	08 06	11 40	12 01	12 24	12 50
50	06 36	07 18	07 56	11 41	12 04	12 29	12 56
45	06 24	07 01	07 35	11 45	12 11	12 39	13 10
N 40	06 14	06 48	07 18	11 48	12 17	12 48	13 21
35	06 04	06 36	07 04	11 51	12 22	12 55	13 30
30	05 56	06 25	06 52	11 53	12 27	13 02	13 39
20	05 39	06 07	06 31	11 57	12 35	13 13	13 53
N 10	05 23	05 49	06 12	12 01	12 42	13 24	14 06
0	05 06	05 32	05 55	12 04	12 49	13 33	14 18
S 10	04 47	05 14	05 37	12 08	12 55	13 43	14 30
20	04 24	04 53	05 18	12 11	13 02	13 53	14 43
30	03 55	04 28	04 56	12 16	13 11	14 05	14 58
35	03 36	04 13	04 43	12 18	13 15	14 12	15 07
40	03 13	03 55	04 28	12 21	13 21	14 19	15 17
45	02 42	03 32	04 10	12 24	13 27	14 29	15 28
S 50	01 57	03 02	03 47	12 28	13 35	14 40	15 43
52	01 29	02 47	03 36	12 30	13 38	14 45	15 49
54	00 41	02 29	03 24	12 32	13 42	14 50	15 57
56	////	02 07	03 10	12 34	13 46	14 57	16 05
58	////	01 37	02 53	12 37	13 51	15 04	16 14
S 60	////	00 46	02 32	12 40	13 57	15 12	16 25

Sunset, Twilight and Moonset

Lat.	Sunset	Twilight Civil	Naut.	Moonset 20	21	22	23
°	h m	h m	h m	h m	h m	h m	h m
N 72	■	12 59	15 31	00 12	01 59	03 48	05 44
N 70	■	14 02	15 51	00 09	01 48	03 28	05 09
68	■	14 37	16 07	00 06	01 40	03 12	04 45
66	13 22	15 03	16 31	00 04	01 32	03 00	04 26
64	14 04	15 23	16 31	00 02	01 26	02 49	04 10
62	14 33	15 39	16 41	00 00	01 21	02 40	03 58
60	14 54	15 52	16 49	25 17	01 17	02 33	03 47
N 58	15 12	16 04	16 57	25 13	01 13	02 26	03 38
56	15 27	16 14	17 03	25 09	01 09	02 20	03 30
54	15 39	16 23	17 10	25 06	01 06	02 15	03 22
52	15 51	16 32	17 15	25 03	01 03	02 10	03 16
50	16 01	16 39	17 21	25 00	01 00	02 06	03 10
45	16 21	16 55	17 32	24 55	00 55	01 57	02 57
N 40	16 38	17 09	17 43	24 50	00 50	01 49	02 47
35	16 52	17 21	17 52	24 46	00 46	01 43	02 38
30	17 05	17 31	18 01	24 42	00 42	01 37	02 31
20	17 26	17 50	18 18	24 36	00 36	01 27	02 17
N 10	17 45	18 07	18 34	24 31	00 31	01 18	02 06
0	18 02	18 25	18 51	24 26	00 26	01 10	01 55
S 10	18 20	18 43	19 10	24 20	00 20	01 02	01 44
20	18 39	19 03	19 33	24 15	00 15	00 53	01 32
30	19 01	19 24	20 02	24 09	00 09	00 43	01 19
35	19 14	19 44	20 20	24 05	00 05	00 38	01 12
40	19 29	20 02	20 44	24 01	00 01	00 31	01 03
45	19 47	20 24	21 14	23 57	24 24	00 24	00 53
S 50	20 10	20 54	22 00	23 51	24 15	00 15	00 41
52	20 20	21 09	22 28	23 49	24 11	00 11	00 35
54	20 33	21 27	23 15	23 46	24 06	00 06	00 29
56	20 47	21 50	////	23 43	24 01	00 01	00 22
58	21 04	22 20	////	23 40	23 56	24 14	00 14
S 60	21 24	23 11	////	23 36	23 50	24 06	00 06

SUN / MOON

Day	Eqn. of Time 00h	12h	Mer. Pass.	Mer. Pass. Upper	Lower	Age	Phase
d	m s	m s	h m	h m	h m	d	%
20	02 26	02 12	11 58	18 15	05 53	07	53
21	01 57	01 42	11 58	18 59	06 37	08	63
22	01 27	01 12	11 59	19 44	07 22	09	72

UT	ARIES GHA	VENUS −3.9 GHA	Dec	MARS +1.2 GHA	Dec	JUPITER −2.8 GHA	Dec	SATURN +0.6 GHA	Dec	STARS Name	SHA	Dec
23 00	91 56.4	204 59.7	S20 40.8	151 59.5	S21 46.4	24 49.0	N21 01.5	234 46.1	S12 14.3	Acamar	315 18.3	S40 15.4
01	106 58.9	219 58.9	41.4	166 59.9	46.0	39 51.8	01.4	249 48.4	14.4	Achernar	335 26.8	S57 10.5
02	122 01.3	234 58.1	41.9	182 00.3	45.6	54 54.6	01.4	264 50.6	14.4	Acrux	173 09.6	S63 10.0
03	137 03.8	249 57.2	.. 42.5	197 00.7	.. 45.2	69 57.3	.. 01.4	279 52.9	.. 14.5	Adhara	255 12.4	S28 59.5
04	152 06.2	264 56.4	43.1	212 01.1	44.8	85 00.1	01.3	294 55.1	14.6	Aldebaran	290 49.4	N16 32.0
05	167 08.7	279 55.6	43.7	227 01.5	44.4	100 02.9	01.3	309 57.4	14.6			
06	182 11.2	294 54.8	S20 44.2	242 01.9	S21 44.0	115 05.6	N21 01.2	324 59.6	S12 14.7	Alioth	166 21.1	N55 53.0
07	197 13.6	309 53.9	44.8	257 02.3	43.6	130 08.4	01.2	340 01.9	14.8	Alkaid	152 59.4	N49 14.6
08	212 16.1	324 53.1	45.4	272 02.7	43.3	145 11.2	01.2	355 04.1	14.8	Al Na'ir	27 44.4	S46 54.0
S 09	227 18.6	339 52.3	.. 46.0	287 03.1	.. 42.9	160 13.9	.. 01.1	10 06.4	.. 14.9	Alnilam	275 46.4	S 1 11.8
U 10	242 21.0	354 51.5	46.5	302 03.5	42.5	175 16.7	01.1	25 08.6	14.9	Alphard	217 56.2	S 8 43.0
N 11	257 23.5	9 50.7	47.1	317 03.9	42.1	190 19.5	01.1	40 10.9	15.0			
D 12	272 26.0	24 49.8	S20 47.7	332 04.3	S21 41.7	205 22.2	N21 01.0	55 13.1	S12 15.1	Alphecca	126 11.6	N26 40.2
A 13	287 28.4	39 49.0	48.2	347 04.7	41.3	220 25.0	01.0	70 15.4	15.1	Alpheratz	357 43.8	N29 10.0
Y 14	302 30.9	54 48.2	48.8	2 05.1	40.9	235 27.8	01.0	85 17.6	15.2	Altair	62 08.9	N 8 54.3
15	317 33.4	69 47.4	.. 49.4	17 05.5	.. 40.5	250 30.5	.. 00.9	100 19.9	.. 15.3	Ankaa	353 16.0	S42 14.3
16	332 35.8	84 46.5	49.9	32 05.9	40.1	265 33.3	00.9	115 22.1	15.3	Antares	112 27.0	S26 27.5
17	347 38.3	99 45.7	50.5	47 06.3	39.7	280 36.1	00.8	130 24.4	15.4			
18	2 40.7	114 44.9	S20 51.0	62 06.7	S21 39.3	295 38.8	N21 00.8	145 26.6	S12 15.4	Arcturus	145 56.2	N19 06.8
19	17 43.2	129 44.0	51.6	77 07.2	38.9	310 41.6	00.8	160 28.9	15.5	Atria	107 29.6	S69 02.8
20	32 45.7	144 43.2	52.2	92 07.6	38.5	325 44.4	00.7	175 31.1	15.6	Avior	234 17.5	S59 33.1
21	47 48.1	159 42.4	.. 52.7	107 08.0	.. 38.1	340 47.1	.. 00.7	190 33.4	.. 15.6	Bellatrix	278 32.0	N 6 21.5
22	62 50.6	174 41.6	53.3	122 08.4	37.7	355 49.9	00.7	205 35.6	15.7	Betelgeuse	271 01.3	N 7 24.4
23	77 53.1	189 40.7	53.8	137 08.8	37.3	10 52.7	00.6	220 37.9	15.8			
24 00	92 55.5	204 39.9	S20 54.4	152 09.2	S21 36.9	25 55.4	N21 00.6	235 40.1	S12 15.8	Canopus	263 55.7	S52 42.3
01	107 58.0	219 39.1	54.9	167 09.6	36.5	40 58.2	00.6	250 42.4	15.9	Capella	280 34.4	N46 00.6
02	123 00.5	234 38.2	55.5	182 10.0	36.1	56 01.0	00.5	265 44.6	15.9	Deneb	49 32.1	N45 19.9
03	138 02.9	249 37.4	.. 56.0	197 10.4	.. 35.7	71 03.7	.. 00.5	280 46.9	.. 16.0	Denebola	182 34.0	N14 29.8
04	153 05.4	264 36.6	56.6	212 10.8	35.3	86 06.5	00.4	295 49.1	16.1	Diphda	348 56.2	S17 55.0
05	168 07.9	279 35.7	57.1	227 11.2	34.9	101 09.3	00.4	310 51.4	16.1			
06	183 10.3	294 34.9	S20 57.7	242 11.6	S21 34.5	116 12.0	N21 00.4	325 53.6	S12 16.2	Dubhe	193 51.9	N61 40.4
07	198 12.8	309 34.1	58.2	257 12.0	34.1	131 14.8	00.3	340 55.9	16.3	Elnath	278 12.6	N28 37.0
08	213 15.2	324 33.2	58.8	272 12.4	33.7	146 17.6	00.3	355 58.1	16.3	Eltanin	90 46.8	N51 29.3
M 09	228 17.7	339 32.4	.. 59.3	287 12.8	.. 33.3	161 20.3	.. 00.3	11 00.4	.. 16.4	Enif	33 47.6	N 9 56.3
O 10	243 20.2	354 31.6	20 59.9	302 13.2	32.9	176 23.1	00.2	26 02.6	16.4	Fomalhaut	15 24.5	S29 33.2
N 11	258 22.6	9 30.7	21 00.4	317 13.6	32.5	191 25.8	00.2	41 04.9	16.5			
D 12	273 25.1	24 29.9	S21 00.9	332 14.1	S21 32.1	206 28.6	N21 00.2	56 07.2	S12 16.6	Gacrux	172 01.3	S57 10.9
A 13	288 27.6	39 29.1	01.5	347 14.5	31.7	221 31.4	00.1	71 09.4	16.6	Gienah	175 52.6	S17 36.8
Y 14	303 30.0	54 28.2	02.0	2 14.9	31.3	236 34.1	00.1	86 11.7	16.7	Hadar	148 48.6	S60 25.9
15	318 32.5	69 27.4	.. 02.6	17 15.3	.. 30.9	251 36.9	.. 00.1	101 13.9	.. 16.7	Hamal	328 00.9	N23 31.5
16	333 35.0	84 26.6	03.1	32 15.7	30.5	266 39.7	00.0	116 16.2	16.8	Kaus Aust.	83 44.7	S34 22.5
17	348 37.4	99 25.7	03.6	47 16.1	30.0	281 42.4	21 00.0	131 18.4	16.9			
18	3 39.9	114 24.9	S21 04.2	62 16.5	S21 29.6	296 45.2	N20 59.9	146 20.7	S12 16.9	Kochab	137 20.9	N74 05.9
19	18 42.4	129 24.1	04.7	77 16.9	29.2	311 47.9	59.9	161 22.9	17.0	Markab	13 38.7	N15 16.7
20	33 44.8	144 23.2	05.2	92 17.3	28.8	326 50.7	59.9	176 25.2	17.1	Menkar	314 15.1	N 4 08.4
21	48 47.3	159 22.4	.. 05.8	107 17.7	.. 28.4	341 53.5	.. 59.8	191 27.4	.. 17.1	Menkent	148 08.1	S36 25.8
22	63 49.7	174 21.5	06.3	122 18.1	28.0	356 56.2	59.8	206 29.7	17.2	Miaplacidus	221 39.0	S69 46.2
23	78 52.2	189 20.7	06.8	137 18.5	27.6	11 59.0	59.8	221 31.9	17.2			
25 00	93 54.7	204 19.9	S21 07.4	152 19.0	S21 27.2	27 01.7	N20 59.7	236 34.2	S12 17.3	Mirfak	308 40.4	N49 54.5
01	108 57.1	219 19.0	07.9	167 19.4	26.8	42 04.5	59.7	251 36.4	17.4	Nunki	75 59.1	S26 16.7
02	123 59.6	234 18.2	08.4	182 19.8	26.4	57 07.3	59.7	266 38.7	17.4	Peacock	53 20.3	S56 41.6
03	139 02.1	249 17.3	.. 08.9	197 20.2	.. 25.9	72 10.0	.. 59.6	281 40.9	.. 17.5	Pollux	243 27.8	N27 59.4
04	154 04.5	264 16.5	09.5	212 20.6	25.5	87 12.8	59.6	296 43.2	17.5	Procyon	244 59.7	N 5 11.3
05	169 07.0	279 15.7	10.0	227 21.0	25.1	102 15.5	59.6	311 45.5	17.6			
06	184 09.5	294 14.8	S21 10.5	242 21.4	S21 24.7	117 18.3	N20 59.5	326 47.7	S12 17.7	Rasalhague	96 07.1	N12 33.2
07	199 11.9	309 14.0	11.0	257 21.8	24.3	132 21.1	59.5	341 50.0	17.7	Regulus	207 43.7	N11 54.0
T 08	214 14.4	324 13.1	11.5	272 22.2	23.9	147 23.8	59.5	356 52.2	17.8	Rigel	281 12.0	S 8 11.4
U 09	229 16.8	339 12.3	.. 12.1	287 22.6	.. 23.5	162 26.6	.. 59.4	11 54.5	.. 17.8	Rigil Kent.	139 52.5	S60 53.0
E 10	244 19.3	354 11.4	12.6	302 23.1	23.1	177 29.3	59.4	26 56.7	17.9	Sabik	102 13.2	S15 44.3
S 11	259 21.8	9 10.6	13.1	317 23.5	22.6	192 32.1	59.4	41 59.0	18.0			
D 12	274 24.2	24 09.8	S21 13.6	332 23.9	S21 22.2	207 34.8	N20 59.3	57 01.2	S12 18.0	Schedar	349 40.8	N56 36.9
A 13	289 26.7	39 08.9	14.1	347 24.3	21.8	222 37.6	59.3	72 03.5	18.1	Shaula	96 22.8	S37 06.6
Y 14	304 29.2	54 08.1	14.6	2 24.7	21.4	237 40.4	59.2	87 05.7	18.2	Sirius	258 33.6	S16 44.2
15	319 31.6	69 07.2	.. 15.2	17 25.1	.. 21.0	252 43.1	.. 59.2	102 08.0	.. 18.2	Spica	158 31.7	S11 13.7
16	334 34.1	84 06.4	15.7	32 25.5	20.6	267 45.9	59.2	117 10.3	18.3	Suhail	222 52.3	S43 29.1
17	349 36.6	99 05.5	16.2	47 25.9	20.1	282 48.6	59.1	132 12.5	18.3			
18	4 39.0	114 04.7	S21 16.7	62 26.3	S21 19.7	297 51.4	N20 59.1	147 14.8	S12 18.4	Vega	80 39.6	N38 47.9
19	19 41.5	129 03.8	17.2	77 26.8	19.3	312 54.1	59.1	162 17.0	18.5	Zuben'ubi	137 06.0	S16 05.6
20	34 44.0	144 03.0	17.7	92 27.2	18.9	327 56.9	59.0	177 19.3	18.5		SHA	Mer. Pass.
21	49 46.4	159 02.1	.. 18.2	107 27.6	.. 18.5	342 59.6	.. 59.0	192 21.5	.. 18.6			h m
22	64 48.9	174 01.3	18.7	122 28.0	18.1	358 02.4	59.0	207 23.8	18.6	Venus	111 44.4	10 22
23	79 51.3	189 00.4	19.2	137 28.4	17.6	13 05.2	58.9	222 26.0	18.7	Mars	59 13.6	13 51
	h m									Jupiter	292 59.9	22 12
Mer.Pass. 17 45.4		v −0.8	d 0.5	v 0.4	d 0.4	v 2.8	d 0.0	v 2.3	d 0.1	Saturn	142 44.6	8 16

SUN / MOON

UT	SUN GHA	SUN Dec	MOON GHA	v	MOON Dec	d	HP
23 00	180 14.1	S23 25.6	62 04.8	13.7	N14 20.7	7.9	54.5
01	195 13.8	25.6	76 37.5	13.6	14 28.6	7.9	54.5
02	210 13.5	25.5	91 10.1	13.6	14 36.5	7.7	54.5
03	225 13.2 ..	25.5	105 42.7	13.6	14 44.2	7.8	54.5
04	240 12.9	25.5	120 15.3	13.6	14 52.0	7.6	54.4
05	255 12.6	25.4	134 47.9	13.6	14 59.6	7.6	54.4
S 06	270 12.2	S23 25.4	149 20.5	13.5	N15 07.2	7.5	54.4
U 07	285 11.9	25.4	163 53.0	13.5	15 14.7	7.4	54.4
N 08	300 11.6	25.3	178 25.5	13.5	15 22.1	7.4	54.4
D 09	315 11.3 ..	25.3	192 58.0	13.4	15 29.5	7.3	54.4
A 10	330 11.0	25.3	207 30.4	13.5	15 36.8	7.2	54.4
Y 11	345 10.7	25.2	222 02.9	13.4	15 44.0	7.1	54.3
12	0 10.4	S23 25.2	236 35.3	13.3	N15 51.1	7.1	54.3
13	15 10.1	25.1	251 07.6	13.4	15 58.2	7.0	54.3
14	30 09.8	25.1	265 40.0	13.3	16 05.2	7.0	54.3
15	45 09.5 ..	25.1	280 12.3	13.3	16 12.2	6.8	54.3
16	60 09.1	25.0	294 44.6	13.3	16 19.0	6.8	54.3
17	75 08.8	25.0	309 16.9	13.3	16 25.8	6.8	54.3
18	90 08.5	S23 24.9	323 49.2	13.2	N16 32.6	6.6	54.3
19	105 08.2	24.9	338 21.4	13.2	16 39.2	6.6	54.2
20	120 07.9	24.8	352 53.6	13.2	16 45.8	6.5	54.2
21	135 07.6 ..	24.8	7 25.8	13.2	16 52.3	6.4	54.2
22	150 07.3	24.7	21 58.0	13.1	16 58.7	6.3	54.2
23	165 07.0	24.7	36 30.1	13.1	17 05.0	6.3	54.2
24 00	180 06.7	S23 24.6	51 02.2	13.1	N17 11.3	6.2	54.2
01	195 06.4	24.6	65 34.3	13.0	17 17.5	6.1	54.2
02	210 06.0	24.5	80 06.3	13.0	17 23.6	6.0	54.2
03	225 05.7 ..	24.5	94 38.3	13.0	17 29.6	6.0	54.2
04	240 05.4	24.4	109 10.3	13.0	17 35.6	5.8	54.2
05	255 05.1	24.4	123 42.3	13.0	17 41.4	5.8	54.2
M 06	270 04.8	S23 24.3	138 14.3	12.9	N17 47.2	5.7	54.1
O 07	285 04.5	24.3	152 46.2	12.9	17 52.9	5.7	54.1
N 08	300 04.2	24.2	167 18.1	12.8	17 58.6	5.5	54.1
D 09	315 03.9 ..	24.2	181 49.9	12.9	18 04.1	5.5	54.1
A 10	330 03.6	24.1	196 21.8	12.8	18 09.6	5.4	54.1
Y 11	345 03.3	24.0	210 53.6	12.8	18 15.0	5.3	54.1
12	0 02.9	S23 24.0	225 25.4	12.7	N18 20.3	5.2	54.1
13	15 02.6	23.9	239 57.1	12.8	18 25.5	5.2	54.1
14	30 02.3	23.9	254 28.9	12.7	18 30.7	5.0	54.1
15	45 02.0 ..	23.8	269 00.6	12.6	18 35.7	5.0	54.1
16	60 01.7	23.7	283 32.2	12.7	18 40.7	4.9	54.1
17	75 01.4	23.7	298 03.9	12.6	18 45.6	4.8	54.1
18	90 01.1	S23 23.6	312 35.5	12.6	N18 50.4	4.7	54.1
19	105 00.8	23.5	327 07.1	12.6	18 55.1	4.7	54.1
20	120 00.5	23.5	341 38.7	12.6	18 59.8	4.5	54.1
21	135 00.2 ..	23.4	356 10.3	12.5	19 04.3	4.5	54.1
22	149 59.9	23.4	10 41.8	12.5	19 08.8	4.4	54.0
23	164 59.5	23.3	25 13.3	12.5	19 13.2	4.3	54.0
25 00	179 59.2	S23 23.1	39 44.8	12.4	N19 17.5	4.2	54.0
01	194 58.9	23.1	54 16.2	12.4	19 21.7	4.1	54.0
02	209 58.6	23.0	68 47.6	12.4	19 25.8	4.0	54.0
03	224 58.3 ..	23.0	83 19.0	12.4	19 29.8	4.0	54.0
04	239 58.0	22.9	97 50.4	12.4	19 33.8	3.8	54.0
05	254 57.7	22.9	112 21.8	12.3	19 37.6	3.8	54.0
T 06	269 57.4	S23 22.8	126 53.1	12.3	N19 41.4	3.7	54.0
U 07	284 57.1	22.7	141 24.4	12.3	19 45.1	3.5	54.0
E 08	299 56.8	22.7	155 55.7	12.2	19 48.6	3.5	54.0
S 09	314 56.5 ..	22.6	170 26.9	12.3	19 52.1	3.4	54.0
D 10	329 56.1	22.5	184 58.2	12.2	19 55.5	3.4	54.0
A 11	344 55.8	22.4	199 29.4	12.2	19 58.9	3.2	54.0
Y 12	359 55.5	S23 22.3	214 00.6	12.2	N20 02.1	3.1	54.0
13	14 55.2	22.2	228 31.8	12.1	20 05.2	3.1	54.0
14	29 54.9	22.2	243 02.9	12.1	20 08.3	2.9	54.0
15	44 54.6 ..	22.1	257 34.0	12.2	20 11.2	2.9	54.0
16	59 54.3	22.0	272 05.2	12.0	20 14.1	2.7	54.0
17	74 54.0	21.9	286 36.2	12.1	20 16.8	2.7	54.0
18	89 53.7	S23 21.8	301 07.3	12.1	N20 19.5	2.6	54.0
19	104 53.4	21.8	315 38.4	12.0	20 22.1	2.5	54.0
20	119 53.1	21.7	330 09.4	12.0	20 24.6	2.4	54.0
21	134 52.8 ..	21.6	344 40.4	12.0	20 27.0	2.2	54.0
22	149 52.5	21.5	359 11.4	12.0	20 29.2	2.3	54.0
23	164 52.1	21.4	13 42.4	11.9	N20 31.5	2.1	54.0
	SD 16.3	d 0.1	SD 14.8		14.7		14.7

Twilight / Moonrise

Lat.	Naut.	Civil	Sunrise	Moonrise 23	24	25	26
N 72	08 27	10 57	▮	10 15	09 03	☐	☐
N 70	08 07	09 55	▮	10 51	09 39	10 10	☐
68	07 51	09 20	▮	11 16	10 39	11 28	11 51
66	07 38	08 55	10 35	11 36	11 47	12 06	12 38
64	07 27	08 35	09 53	11 52	12 08	12 32	13 08
62	07 17	08 19	09 25	12 06	12 25	12 53	13 31
60	07 09	08 06	09 03	12 17	12 40	13 10	13 50
N 58	07 01	07 54	08 46	12 27	12 52	13 24	14 05
56	06 54	07 44	08 31	12 35	13 03	13 36	14 18
54	06 48	07 35	08 18	12 43	13 12	13 47	14 29
52	06 43	07 26	08 07	12 50	13 20	13 56	14 39
50	06 38	07 19	07 57	12 56	13 28	14 05	14 48
45	06 26	07 03	07 37	13 10	13 44	14 23	15 07
N 40	06 15	06 49	07 20	13 21	13 57	14 38	15 23
35	06 06	06 37	07 06	13 30	14 09	14 50	15 36
30	05 57	06 27	06 53	13 39	14 18	15 01	15 47
20	05 40	06 08	06 32	13 53	14 36	15 20	16 07
N 10	05 24	05 51	06 13	14 06	14 50	15 36	16 24
0	05 07	05 33	05 56	14 18	15 04	15 52	16 40
S 10	04 48	05 15	05 38	14 30	15 19	16 07	16 56
20	04 26	04 55	05 19	14 43	15 34	16 24	17 13
30	03 57	04 30	04 57	14 58	15 51	16 43	17 33
35	03 38	04 15	04 44	15 07	16 01	16 54	17 44
40	03 15	03 56	04 29	15 17	16 13	17 07	17 57
45	02 44	03 34	04 11	15 28	16 26	17 22	18 13
S 50	01 58	03 04	03 49	15 43	16 43	17 40	18 32
52	01 31	02 49	03 38	15 49	16 51	17 49	18 41
54	00 44	02 31	03 26	15 57	17 00	17 59	18 52
56	////	02 09	03 11	16 05	17 10	18 10	19 03
58	////	01 39	02 54	16 14	17 21	18 23	19 16
S 60	////	00 48	02 34	16 25	17 34	18 38	19 32

Sunset / Twilight / Moonset

Lat.	Sunset	Civil	Naut.	Moonset 23	24	25	26
N 72	▮	13 02	15 33	05 44	08 32	☐	☐
N 70	▮	14 04	15 53	05 09	06 56	09 03	☐
68	▮	14 46	16 09	04 45	06 17	07 46	09 02
66	13 24	15 05	16 22	04 26	05 50	07 08	08 15
64	14 07	15 24	16 33	04 10	05 29	06 42	07 45
62	14 35	15 41	16 43	03 58	05 12	06 22	07 22
60	14 56	15 54	16 51	03 47	04 58	06 05	07 04
N 58	15 14	16 06	16 58	03 38	04 47	05 51	06 49
56	15 29	16 16	17 05	03 30	04 36	05 39	06 36
54	15 41	16 25	17 11	03 22	04 27	05 29	06 24
52	15 52	16 33	17 17	03 16	04 19	05 19	06 15
50	16 02	16 41	17 22	03 10	04 12	05 11	06 06
45	16 23	16 57	17 34	02 57	03 57	04 53	05 47
N 40	16 40	17 10	17 44	02 47	03 44	04 39	05 31
35	16 54	17 22	17 54	02 38	03 33	04 27	05 18
30	17 06	17 33	18 03	02 31	03 24	04 16	05 07
20	17 28	17 52	18 19	02 17	03 08	03 58	04 48
N 10	17 46	18 09	18 35	02 06	02 54	03 42	04 31
0	18 04	18 26	18 52	01 55	02 40	03 27	04 15
S 10	18 21	18 44	19 11	01 44	02 27	03 12	03 59
20	18 40	19 05	19 34	01 32	02 13	02 57	03 42
30	19 02	19 30	20 03	01 19	01 57	02 38	03 23
35	19 15	19 45	20 22	01 12	01 48	02 28	03 12
40	19 30	20 03	20 45	01 04	01 38	02 16	02 59
45	19 48	20 26	21 14	00 53	01 25	02 02	02 43
S 50	20 11	20 55	22 01	00 41	01 10	01 44	02 24
52	20 22	21 10	22 29	00 35	01 03	01 36	02 16
54	20 34	21 28	23 15	00 29	00 55	01 27	02 06
56	20 48	21 51	////	00 22	00 47	01 17	01 54
58	21 05	22 20	////	00 14	00 37	01 05	01 41
S 60	21 25	23 11	////	00 06	00 26	00 52	01 26

SUN / MOON

Day	Eqn. of Time 00h	12h	Mer. Pass.	Mer. Pass. Upper	Lower	Age	Phase %
23	00 57	00 42	11 59	20 29	08 06	10	80
24	00 27	00 12	12 00	21 16	08 52	11	87
25	00 02	00 17	12 00	22 03	09 39	12	93

UT	ARIES GHA	VENUS −3.9 GHA	Dec	MARS +1.2 GHA	Dec	JUPITER −2.8 GHA	Dec	SATURN +0.6 GHA	Dec
26 00	94 53.8	203 59.6	S21 19.7	152 28.8	S21 17.2	28 07.9	N20 58.9	237 28.3	S12 18.8
01	109 56.3	218 58.7	20.2	167 29.2	16.8	43 10.7	58.9	252 30.6	18.8
02	124 58.7	233 57.9	20.7	182 29.6	16.4	58 13.4	58.8	267 32.8	18.9
03	140 01.2	248 57.0	.. 21.2	197 30.1	.. 16.0	73 16.2	.. 58.8	282 35.1	.. 18.9
04	155 03.7	263 56.2	21.7	212 30.5	15.5	88 18.9	58.8	297 37.3	19.0
05	170 06.1	278 55.3	22.2	227 30.9	15.1	103 21.7	58.7	312 39.6	19.1
06	185 08.6	293 54.5	S21 22.7	242 31.3	S21 14.7	118 24.4	N20 58.7	327 41.8	S12 19.1
W 07	200 11.1	308 53.6	23.2	257 31.7	14.3	133 27.2	58.7	342 44.1	19.2
E 08	215 13.5	323 52.8	23.7	272 32.1	13.8	148 29.9	58.6	357 46.3	19.2
D 09	230 16.0	338 51.9	.. 24.2	287 32.5	.. 13.4	163 32.7	.. 58.6	12 48.6	.. 19.3
N 10	245 18.5	353 51.1	24.7	302 32.9	13.0	178 35.4	58.6	27 50.9	19.4
E 11	260 20.9	8 50.2	25.2	317 33.4	12.6	193 38.2	58.5	42 53.1	19.4
S 12	275 23.4	23 49.4	S21 25.7	332 33.8	S21 12.1	208 40.9	N20 58.5	57 55.4	S12 19.5
D 13	290 25.8	38 48.5	26.2	347 34.2	11.7	223 43.7	58.5	72 57.6	19.5
A 14	305 28.3	53 47.6	26.7	2 34.6	11.3	238 46.4	58.4	87 59.9	19.6
Y 15	320 30.8	68 46.8	.. 27.1	17 35.0	.. 10.9	253 49.2	.. 58.4	103 02.2	.. 19.7
16	335 33.2	83 45.9	27.6	32 35.4	10.4	268 51.9	58.4	118 04.4	19.7
17	350 35.7	98 45.1	28.1	47 35.8	10.0	283 54.7	58.3	133 06.7	19.8
18	5 38.2	113 44.2	S21 28.6	62 36.3	S21 09.6	298 57.4	N20 58.3	148 08.9	S12 19.8
19	20 40.6	128 43.4	29.1	77 36.7	09.2	314 00.2	58.3	163 11.2	19.9
20	35 43.1	143 42.5	29.6	92 37.1	08.7	329 02.9	58.2	178 13.4	19.9
21	50 45.6	158 41.6	.. 30.0	107 37.5	.. 08.3	344 05.7	.. 58.2	193 15.7	.. 20.0
22	65 48.0	173 40.8	30.5	122 37.9	07.9	359 08.4	58.2	208 18.0	20.1
23	80 50.5	188 39.9	31.0	137 38.3	07.4	14 11.2	58.1	223 20.2	20.1
27 00	95 53.0	203 39.1	S21 31.5	152 38.8	S21 07.0	29 13.9	N20 58.1	238 22.5	S12 20.2
01	110 55.4	218 38.2	32.0	167 39.2	06.6	44 16.7	58.1	253 24.7	20.2
02	125 57.9	233 37.4	32.4	182 39.6	06.1	59 19.4	58.0	268 27.0	20.3
03	141 00.3	248 36.5	.. 32.9	197 40.0	.. 05.7	74 22.2	.. 58.0	283 29.3	.. 20.4
04	156 02.8	263 35.6	33.4	212 40.4	05.3	89 24.9	58.0	298 31.5	20.4
05	171 05.3	278 34.8	33.9	227 40.8	04.9	104 27.7	57.9	313 33.8	20.5
06	186 07.7	293 33.9	S21 34.3	242 41.3	S21 04.4	119 30.4	N20 57.9	328 36.0	S12 20.5
T 07	201 10.2	308 33.0	34.8	257 41.7	04.0	134 33.2	57.9	343 38.3	20.6
H 08	216 12.7	323 32.2	35.3	272 42.1	03.6	149 35.9	57.8	358 40.6	20.7
U 09	231 15.1	338 31.3	.. 35.7	287 42.5	.. 03.1	164 38.7	.. 57.8	13 42.8	.. 20.7
R 10	246 17.6	353 30.5	36.2	302 42.9	02.7	179 41.4	57.8	28 45.1	20.8
S 11	261 20.1	8 29.6	36.7	317 43.3	02.3	194 44.1	57.7	43 47.3	20.8
D 12	276 22.5	23 28.7	S21 37.1	332 43.8	S21 01.8	209 46.9	N20 57.7	58 49.6	S12 20.9
A 13	291 25.0	38 27.9	37.6	347 44.2	01.4	224 49.6	57.7	73 51.9	20.9
Y 14	306 27.5	53 27.0	38.0	2 44.6	00.9	239 52.4	57.6	88 54.1	21.0
15	321 29.9	68 26.1	.. 38.5	17 45.0	.. 00.5	254 55.1	.. 57.6	103 56.4	.. 21.1
16	336 32.4	83 25.3	39.0	32 45.4	21 00.1	269 57.9	57.6	118 58.6	21.1
17	351 34.8	98 24.4	39.4	47 45.8	20 59.6	285 00.6	57.5	134 00.9	21.2
18	6 37.3	113 23.5	S21 39.9	62 46.3	S20 59.2	300 03.4	N20 57.5	149 03.2	S12 21.2
19	21 39.8	128 22.7	40.3	77 46.7	58.8	315 06.1	57.5	164 05.4	21.3
20	36 42.2	143 21.8	40.8	92 47.1	58.3	330 08.8	57.4	179 07.7	21.4
21	51 44.7	158 20.9	.. 41.3	107 47.5	.. 57.9	345 11.6	.. 57.4	194 09.9	.. 21.4
22	66 47.2	173 20.1	41.7	122 47.9	57.4	0 14.3	57.4	209 12.2	21.5
23	81 49.6	188 19.2	42.2	137 48.4	57.0	15 17.1	57.3	224 14.5	21.5
28 00	96 52.1	203 18.3	S21 42.6	152 48.8	S20 56.6	30 19.8	N20 57.3	239 16.7	S12 21.6
01	111 54.6	218 17.5	43.1	167 49.2	56.1	45 22.5	57.3	254 19.0	21.6
02	126 57.0	233 16.6	43.5	182 49.6	55.7	60 25.3	57.2	269 21.2	21.7
03	141 59.5	248 15.7	.. 44.0	197 50.0	.. 55.2	75 28.0	.. 57.2	284 23.5	.. 21.8
04	157 01.9	263 14.9	44.4	212 50.5	54.8	90 30.8	57.2	299 25.8	21.8
05	172 04.4	278 14.0	44.8	227 50.9	54.4	105 33.5	57.1	314 28.0	21.9
06	187 06.9	293 13.1	S21 45.3	242 51.3	S20 53.9	120 36.2	N20 57.1	329 30.3	S12 21.9
07	202 09.3	308 12.2	45.7	257 51.7	53.5	135 39.0	57.1	344 32.6	22.0
08	217 11.8	323 11.4	46.2	272 52.1	53.0	150 41.7	57.0	359 34.8	22.0
F 09	232 14.3	338 10.5	.. 46.6	287 52.6	.. 52.6	165 44.5	.. 57.0	14 37.1	.. 22.1
R 10	247 16.7	353 09.6	47.1	302 53.0	52.1	180 47.2	57.0	29 39.3	22.2
I 11	262 19.2	8 08.8	47.5	317 53.4	51.7	195 49.9	56.9	44 41.6	22.2
D 12	277 21.7	23 07.9	S21 48.0	332 53.8	S20 51.3	210 52.7	N20 56.9	59 43.9	S12 22.3
A 13	292 24.1	38 07.0	48.4	347 54.2	50.8	225 55.4	56.9	74 46.1	22.3
Y 14	307 26.6	53 06.1	48.8	2 54.6	50.4	240 58.2	56.8	89 48.4	22.4
15	322 29.1	68 05.3	.. 49.2	17 55.1	.. 49.9	256 00.9	.. 56.8	104 50.7	.. 22.4
16	337 31.5	83 04.4	49.7	32 55.5	49.5	271 03.6	56.8	119 52.9	22.5
17	352 34.0	98 03.5	50.1	47 55.9	49.0	286 06.4	56.7	134 55.2	22.6
18	7 36.4	113 02.6	S21 50.5	62 56.4	S20 48.6	301 09.1	N20 56.7	149 57.5	S12 22.6
19	22 38.9	128 01.8	51.0	77 56.8	48.1	316 11.8	56.7	164 59.7	22.7
20	37 41.4	143 00.9	51.4	92 57.2	47.7	331 14.6	56.7	180 02.0	22.7
21	52 43.8	158 00.0	.. 51.8	107 57.6	.. 47.2	346 17.3	.. 56.6	195 04.2	.. 22.8
22	67 46.3	172 59.1	52.3	122 58.0	46.8	1 20.1	56.6	210 06.5	22.8
23	82 48.8	187 58.3	52.7	137 58.5	46.3	16 22.8	56.5	225 08.8	22.9
Mer. Pass.	h m 17 33.6	v −0.9	d 0.5	v 0.4	d 0.4	v 2.7	d 0.0	v 2.3	d 0.1

STARS

Name	SHA	Dec
Acamar	315 18.3	S40 15.4
Achernar	335 26.8	S57 10.5
Acrux	173 09.6	S63 10.0
Adhara	255 12.4	S28 59.5
Aldebaran	290 49.4	N16 32.0
Alioth	166 21.1	N55 53.0
Alkaid	152 59.4	N49 14.6
Al Na'ir	27 44.4	S46 53.9
Alnilam	275 46.3	S 1 11.8
Alphard	217 56.2	S 8 43.0
Alphecca	126 11.6	N26 40.2
Alpheratz	357 43.8	N29 10.0
Altair	62 08.9	N 8 54.3
Ankaa	353 16.0	S42 14.3
Antares	112 27.0	S26 27.5
Arcturus	145 56.2	N19 06.8
Atria	107 29.6	S69 02.8
Avior	234 17.5	S59 33.1
Bellatrix	278 32.0	N 6 21.5
Betelgeuse	271 01.3	N 7 24.4
Canopus	263 55.7	S52 42.3
Capella	280 34.4	N46 00.6
Deneb	49 32.1	N45 19.9
Denebola	182 33.9	N14 29.8
Diphda	348 56.2	S17 55.0
Dubhe	193 51.9	N61 40.4
Elnath	278 12.6	N28 37.0
Eltanin	90 46.8	N51 29.3
Enif	33 47.6	N 9 56.3
Fomalhaut	15 24.5	S29 33.2
Gacrux	172 01.2	S57 10.9
Gienah	175 52.6	S17 36.8
Hadar	148 48.6	S60 25.9
Hamal	328 00.9	N23 31.5
Kaus Aust.	83 44.6	S34 22.5
Kochab	137 20.8	N74 05.9
Markab	13 38.7	N15 16.7
Menkar	314 15.1	N 4 08.4
Menkent	148 08.1	S36 25.9
Miaplacidus	221 38.4	S69 46.2
Mirfak	308 40.4	N49 54.5
Nunki	75 59.1	S26 16.7
Peacock	53 20.3	S56 41.6
Pollux	243 27.8	N27 59.4
Procyon	244 59.7	N 5 11.3
Rasalhague	96 07.1	N12 33.1
Regulus	207 43.7	N11 54.0
Rigel	281 12.0	S 8 11.4
Rigil Kent.	139 52.5	S60 53.0
Sabik	102 13.2	S15 44.3
Schedar	349 40.8	N56 36.9
Shaula	96 22.8	S37 06.6
Sirius	258 33.6	S16 44.2
Spica	158 31.7	S11 13.7
Suhail	222 52.3	S43 29.1
Vega	80 39.6	N38 47.9
Zuben'ubi	137 06.0	S16 05.6

	SHA	Mer.Pass.
		h m
Venus	107 46.1	10 26
Mars	56 45.8	13 49
Jupiter	293 21.0	21 59
Saturn	142 29.5	8 05

UT	SUN GHA	SUN Dec	MOON GHA	v	MOON Dec	d	HP
d h	° ′	° ′	° ′	′	° ′	′	′
26 00	179 51.8	S23 21.3	28 13.3	12.0	N20 33.6	2.0	54.0
01	194 51.5	21.2	42 44.3	11.9	20 35.6	1.9	54.0
02	209 51.2	21.1	57 15.2	11.9	20 37.5	1.8	54.0
03	224 50.9 ..	21.0	71 46.1	11.9	20 39.3	1.8	54.0
04	239 50.6	21.0	86 17.0	11.9	20 41.1	1.6	54.0
05	254 50.3	20.9	100 47.9	11.8	20 42.7	1.5	54.0
06	269 50.0	S23 20.8	115 18.7	11.9	N20 44.2	1.5	54.0
W 07	284 49.7	20.7	129 49.6	11.8	20 45.7	1.3	54.0
E 08	299 49.4	20.6	144 20.4	11.8	20 47.0	1.3	54.0
D 09	314 49.1 ..	20.5	158 51.2	11.8	20 48.3	1.1	54.0
N 10	329 48.8	20.4	173 22.0	11.8	20 49.4	1.1	54.0
E 11	344 48.5	20.3	187 52.8	11.8	20 50.5	0.9	54.0
S 12	359 48.1	S23 20.2	202 23.6	11.8	N20 51.4	0.9	54.0
D 13	14 47.8	20.1	216 54.4	11.7	20 52.3	0.8	54.0
A 14	29 47.5	20.0	231 25.1	11.8	20 53.1	0.6	54.0
Y 15	44 47.2 ..	19.9	245 55.9	11.7	20 53.7	0.6	54.0
16	59 46.9	19.8	260 26.6	11.8	20 54.3	0.5	54.0
17	74 46.6	19.7	274 57.4	11.7	20 54.8	0.4	54.0
18	89 46.3	S23 19.6	289 28.1	11.7	N20 55.2	0.3	54.0
19	104 46.0	19.5	303 58.8	11.7	20 55.5	0.1	54.0
20	119 45.7	19.4	318 29.5	11.7	20 55.6	0.1	54.0
21	134 45.4 ..	19.3	333 00.2	11.7	20 55.7	0.0	54.0
22	149 45.1	19.2	347 30.9	11.7	20 55.7	0.1	54.0
23	164 44.8	19.1	2 01.6	11.7	20 55.6	0.2	54.1
27 00	179 44.5	S23 19.0	16 32.3	11.7	N20 55.4	0.3	54.1
01	194 44.2	18.8	31 03.0	11.6	20 55.1	0.4	54.1
02	209 43.8	18.7	45 33.6	11.7	20 54.7	0.5	54.1
03	224 43.5 ..	18.6	60 04.3	11.7	20 54.2	0.6	54.1
04	239 43.2	18.5	74 35.0	11.6	20 53.6	0.7	54.1
05	254 42.9	18.4	89 05.6	11.7	20 52.9	0.8	54.1
06	269 42.6	S23 18.3	103 36.3	11.6	N20 52.1	0.9	54.1
T 07	284 42.3	18.2	118 06.9	11.7	20 51.2	1.0	54.1
H 08	299 42.0	18.1	132 37.6	11.7	20 50.2	1.1	54.1
U 09	314 41.7 ..	17.9	147 08.3	11.6	20 49.1	1.1	54.1
R 10	329 41.4	17.8	161 38.9	11.7	20 48.0	1.3	54.1
S 11	344 41.1	17.7	176 09.6	11.6	20 46.7	1.4	54.1
D 12	359 40.8	S23 17.6	190 40.2	11.7	N20 45.3	1.5	54.1
A 13	14 40.5	17.5	205 10.9	11.7	20 43.8	1.5	54.1
Y 14	29 40.2	17.4	219 41.6	11.6	20 42.3	1.7	54.1
15	44 39.9 ..	17.2	234 12.2	11.7	20 40.6	1.8	54.1
16	59 39.6	17.1	248 42.9	11.7	20 38.8	1.9	54.1
17	74 39.3	17.0	263 13.6	11.6	20 36.9	1.9	54.2
18	89 39.0	S23 16.9	277 44.2	11.7	N20 35.0	2.1	54.2
19	104 38.7	16.8	292 14.9	11.7	20 32.9	2.1	54.2
20	119 38.3	16.6	306 45.6	11.7	20 30.8	2.3	54.2
21	134 38.0 ..	16.5	321 16.3	11.7	20 28.5	2.3	54.2
22	149 37.7	16.4	335 47.0	11.7	20 26.2	2.5	54.2
23	164 37.4	16.3	350 17.7	11.8	20 23.7	2.5	54.2
28 00	179 37.1	S23 16.1	4 48.4	11.8	N20 21.2	2.7	54.2
01	194 36.8	16.0	19 19.2	11.7	20 18.5	2.7	54.2
02	209 36.5	15.9	33 49.9	11.7	20 15.8	2.8	54.2
03	224 36.2 ..	15.7	48 20.6	11.8	20 13.0	3.0	54.2
04	239 35.9	15.6	62 51.4	11.7	20 10.0	3.0	54.2
05	254 35.6	15.5	77 22.1	11.8	20 07.0	3.1	54.2
06	269 35.3	S23 15.3	91 52.9	11.8	N20 03.9	3.2	54.3
07	284 35.0	15.2	106 23.7	11.8	20 00.7	3.3	54.3
08	299 34.7	15.1	120 54.5	11.8	19 57.4	3.4	54.3
F 09	314 34.4 ..	14.9	135 25.3	11.8	19 54.0	3.5	54.3
R 10	329 34.1	14.8	149 56.1	11.9	19 50.5	3.6	54.3
I 11	344 33.8	14.7	164 27.0	11.8	19 46.9	3.7	54.3
D 12	359 33.5	S23 14.5	178 57.8	11.9	N19 43.2	3.8	54.3
A 13	14 33.2	14.4	193 28.7	11.8	19 39.4	3.8	54.3
Y 14	29 32.9	14.3	207 59.5	11.9	19 35.6	4.0	54.3
15	44 32.6 ..	14.1	222 30.4	11.9	19 31.6	4.0	54.3
16	59 32.3	14.0	237 01.3	11.9	19 27.6	4.2	54.3
17	74 32.0	13.8	251 32.2	12.0	19 23.4	4.2	54.4
18	89 31.7	S23 13.7	266 03.2	11.9	N19 19.2	4.3	54.4
19	104 31.4	13.6	280 34.1	12.0	19 14.9	4.5	54.4
20	119 31.1	13.4	295 05.1	12.0	19 10.4	4.5	54.4
21	134 30.8 ..	13.3	309 36.1	12.0	19 05.9	4.6	54.4
22	149 30.5	13.1	324 07.1	12.0	19 01.3	4.7	54.4
23	164 30.1	13.0	338 38.1	12.0	N18 56.6	4.7	54.4
SD 16.3	d 0.1		SD 14.7	14.7			14.8

Lat.	Twilight Naut.	Twilight Civil	Sunrise	Moonrise 26	27	28	29
°	h m	h m	h m	h m	h m	h m	h m
N 72	08 27	10 54	■	□	□	□	13 49
N 70	08 07	09 54	■	□	□	12 56	14 58
68	07 51	09 20	■	11 51	12 43	14 03	15 35
66	07 38	08 55	10 34	12 38	13 29	14 39	16 01
64	07 27	08 35	09 53	13 08	13 59	15 05	16 21
62	07 18	08 20	09 25	13 31	14 22	15 25	16 37
60	07 09	08 06	09 04	13 50	14 40	15 41	16 50
N 58	07 02	07 54	08 46	14 05	14 55	15 55	17 01
56	06 55	07 44	08 32	14 18	15 08	16 07	17 11
54	06 49	07 35	08 19	14 29	15 19	16 17	17 20
52	06 43	07 27	08 08	14 39	15 29	16 26	17 28
50	06 38	07 20	07 58	14 48	15 38	16 34	17 35
45	06 27	07 04	07 38	15 07	15 57	16 52	17 50
N 40	06 16	06 50	07 21	15 23	16 12	17 06	18 02
35	06 07	06 39	07 07	15 36	16 25	17 18	18 13
30	05 58	06 28	06 54	15 47	16 37	17 28	18 22
20	05 42	06 09	06 33	16 07	16 56	17 46	18 38
N 10	05 26	05 52	06 15	16 24	17 13	18 02	18 52
0	05 09	05 35	05 58	16 40	17 28	18 17	19 04
S 10	04 50	05 17	05 40	16 56	17 44	18 31	19 17
20	04 27	04 57	05 21	17 13	18 01	18 47	19 31
30	03 58	04 32	04 59	17 33	18 20	19 05	19 46
35	03 40	04 17	04 46	17 44	18 31	19 15	19 55
40	03 17	03 58	04 31	17 57	18 44	19 27	20 06
45	02 46	03 36	04 13	18 13	19 00	19 41	20 18
S 50	02 01	03 06	03 51	18 32	19 18	19 58	20 32
52	01 34	02 51	03 40	18 41	19 27	20 06	20 39
54	00 49	02 34	03 28	18 52	19 37	20 15	20 47
56	////	02 11	03 14	19 03	19 48	20 25	20 55
58	////	01 42	02 57	19 16	20 01	20 37	21 05
S 60	////	00 53	02 37	19 32	20 16	20 50	21 15

Lat.	Sunset	Twilight Civil	Twilight Naut.	Moonset 26	27	28	29
°	h m	h m	h m	h m	h m	h m	h m
N 72	■	13 09	15 36	□	□	□	12 07
N 70	■	14 09	15 56	□	□	11 19	10 56
68	■	14 43	16 12	09 02	09 51	10 11	10 19
66	13 29	15 08	16 25	08 15	09 04	09 35	09 52
64	14 10	15 27	16 35	07 45	08 34	09 09	09 32
62	14 38	15 43	16 45	07 22	08 12	08 49	09 15
60	14 59	15 57	16 53	07 04	07 53	08 32	09 02
N 58	15 16	16 08	17 01	06 49	07 38	08 18	08 50
56	15 31	16 18	17 07	06 36	07 25	08 06	08 39
54	15 44	16 27	17 14	06 24	07 14	07 55	08 30
52	15 55	16 35	17 19	06 15	07 04	07 46	08 22
50	16 04	16 43	17 24	06 06	06 55	07 38	08 15
45	16 23	16 59	17 36	05 47	06 36	07 20	07 59
N 40	16 42	17 12	17 46	05 31	06 20	07 05	07 46
35	16 56	17 24	17 56	05 18	06 07	06 53	07 35
30	17 08	17 35	18 04	05 07	05 56	06 42	07 25
20	17 29	17 53	18 21	04 48	05 36	06 23	07 08
N 10	17 48	18 10	18 37	04 31	05 19	06 07	06 54
0	18 05	18 28	18 54	04 15	05 03	05 52	06 40
S 10	18 23	18 46	19 13	03 59	04 47	05 37	06 26
20	18 41	19 06	19 35	03 42	04 30	05 20	06 11
30	19 03	19 31	20 04	03 23	04 11	05 01	05 54
35	19 16	19 46	20 23	03 12	03 59	04 50	05 44
40	19 31	20 04	20 46	02 59	03 46	04 38	05 33
45	19 49	20 26	21 16	02 43	03 30	04 23	05 19
S 50	20 11	20 56	22 01	02 24	03 11	04 04	05 03
52	20 22	21 11	22 28	02 16	03 02	03 56	04 55
54	20 34	21 29	23 12	02 06	02 52	03 46	04 46
56	20 49	21 51	////	01 54	02 40	03 35	04 37
58	21 05	22 20	////	01 41	02 27	03 22	04 26
S 60	21 25	23 08	////	01 26	02 11	03 07	04 13

	SUN			MOON			
Day	Eqn. of Time 00h	12h	Mer. Pass.	Mer. Pass. Upper	Lower	Age	Phase
d	m s	m s	h m	h m	h m	d	%
26	00 32	00 47	12 01	22 52	10 27	13	97
27	01 02	01 16	12 01	23 40	11 16	14	99
28	01 31	01 45	12 02	24 28	12 04	15	100

UT	ARIES GHA	VENUS −3.9 GHA	VENUS Dec	MARS +1.2 GHA	MARS Dec	JUPITER −2.7 GHA	JUPITER Dec	SATURN +0.6 GHA	SATURN Dec	Star Name	SHA	Dec
29 00	97 51.2	202 57.4	S21 53.1	152 58.9	S20 45.9	31 25.5	N20 56.5	240 11.0	S12 23.0	Acamar	315 18.3	S40 15.4
01	112 53.7	217 56.5	53.5	167 59.3	45.4	46 28.3	56.5	255 13.3	23.0	Achernar	335 26.9	S57 10.5
02	127 56.2	232 55.6	53.9	182 59.7	45.0	61 31.0	56.5	270 15.6	23.1	Acrux	173 09.5	S63 10.1
03	142 58.6	247 54.8	.. 54.4	198 00.2	.. 44.5	76 33.7	.. 56.4	285 17.8	.. 23.1	Adhara	255 12.4	S28 59.6
04	158 01.1	262 53.9	54.8	213 00.6	44.1	91 36.5	56.4	300 20.1	23.2	Aldebaran	290 49.4	N16 32.0
05	173 03.6	277 53.0	55.2	228 01.0	43.6	106 39.2	56.4	315 22.4	23.2			
06	188 06.0	292 52.1	S21 55.6	243 01.4	S20 43.2	121 41.9	N20 56.3	330 24.6	S12 23.3	Alioth	166 21.0	N55 53.0
S 07	203 08.5	307 51.2	56.0	258 01.9	42.7	136 44.7	56.3	345 26.9	23.4	Alkaid	152 59.3	N49 14.6
A 08	218 10.9	322 50.4	56.5	273 02.3	42.3	151 47.4	56.3	0 29.2	23.4	Al Na'ir	27 44.4	S46 53.9
T 09	233 13.4	337 49.5	.. 56.9	288 02.7	.. 41.8	166 50.1	.. 56.2	15 31.4	.. 23.5	Alnilam	275 46.3	S 1 11.8
U 10	248 15.9	352 48.6	57.3	303 03.1	41.4	181 52.9	56.2	30 33.7	23.5	Alphard	217 56.1	S 8 43.1
R 11	263 18.3	7 47.7	57.7	318 03.6	40.9	196 55.6	56.2	45 36.0	23.6			
D 12	278 20.8	22 46.8	S21 58.1	333 04.0	S20 40.5	211 58.3	N20 56.1	60 38.2	S12 23.6	Alphecca	126 11.5	N26 40.2
A 13	293 23.3	37 46.0	58.5	348 04.4	40.0	227 01.1	56.1	75 40.5	23.7	Alpheratz	357 43.8	N29 10.0
Y 14	308 25.7	52 45.1	58.9	3 04.8	39.6	242 03.8	56.1	90 42.8	23.7	Altair	62 08.9	N 8 54.3
15	323 28.2	67 44.2	.. 59.3	18 05.3	.. 39.1	257 06.5	.. 56.0	105 45.0	.. 23.8	Ankaa	353 16.0	S42 14.3
16	338 30.7	82 43.3	21 59.7	33 05.7	38.6	272 09.3	56.0	120 47.3	23.9	Antares	112 26.9	S26 27.5
17	353 33.1	97 42.4	22 00.1	48 06.1	38.2	287 12.0	56.0	135 49.6	23.9			
18	8 35.6	112 41.5	S22 00.5	63 06.5	S20 37.7	302 14.7	N20 55.9	150 51.8	S12 24.0	Arcturus	145 56.2	N19 06.8
19	23 38.1	127 40.7	01.0	78 07.0	37.3	317 17.4	55.9	165 54.1	24.0	Atria	107 29.6	S69 02.8
20	38 40.5	142 39.8	01.4	93 07.4	36.8	332 20.2	55.9	180 56.4	24.1	Avior	234 17.5	S59 33.1
21	53 43.0	157 38.9	.. 01.8	108 07.8	.. 36.4	347 22.9	.. 55.9	195 58.6	.. 24.1	Bellatrix	278 32.0	N 6 21.5
22	68 45.4	172 38.0	02.2	123 08.2	35.9	2 25.6	55.8	211 00.9	24.2	Betelgeuse	271 01.3	N 7 24.4
23	83 47.9	187 37.1	02.6	138 08.7	35.4	17 28.4	55.8	226 03.2	24.3			
30 00	98 50.4	202 36.2	S22 03.0	153 09.1	S20 35.0	32 31.1	N20 55.8	241 05.4	S12 24.3	Canopus	263 55.7	S52 42.3
01	113 52.8	217 35.3	03.3	168 09.5	34.5	47 33.8	55.7	256 07.7	24.4	Capella	280 34.4	N46 00.6
02	128 55.3	232 34.5	03.7	183 10.0	34.1	62 36.5	55.7	271 10.0	24.4	Deneb	49 32.1	N45 19.9
03	143 57.8	247 33.6	.. 04.1	198 10.4	.. 33.6	77 39.3	.. 55.7	286 12.2	.. 24.5	Denebola	182 33.9	N14 29.8
04	159 00.2	262 32.7	04.5	213 10.8	33.1	92 42.0	55.6	301 14.5	24.5	Diphda	348 56.2	S17 55.0
05	174 02.7	277 31.8	04.9	228 11.2	32.7	107 44.7	55.6	316 16.8	24.6			
06	189 05.2	292 30.9	S22 05.3	243 11.7	S20 32.2	122 47.5	N20 55.6	331 19.0	S12 24.6	Dubhe	193 51.8	N61 40.4
07	204 07.6	307 30.0	05.7	258 12.1	31.8	137 50.2	55.5	346 21.3	24.7	Elnath	278 12.6	N28 37.0
S 08	219 10.1	322 29.1	06.1	273 12.5	31.3	152 52.9	55.5	1 23.6	24.8	Eltanin	90 46.8	N51 29.3
U 09	234 12.6	337 28.2	.. 06.5	288 12.9	.. 30.8	167 55.6	.. 55.5	16 25.8	.. 24.8	Enif	33 47.6	N 9 56.3
N 10	249 15.0	352 27.4	06.9	303 13.4	30.4	182 58.4	55.5	31 28.1	24.9	Fomalhaut	15 24.5	S29 33.2
D 11	264 17.5	7 26.5	07.2	318 13.8	29.9	198 01.1	55.4	46 30.4	24.9			
A 12	279 19.9	22 25.6	S22 07.6	333 14.2	S20 29.4	213 03.8	N20 55.4	61 32.6	S12 25.0	Gacrux	172 01.2	S57 11.0
Y 13	294 22.4	37 24.7	08.0	348 14.7	29.0	228 06.5	55.4	76 34.9	25.0	Gienah	175 52.6	S17 36.8
14	309 24.9	52 23.8	08.4	3 15.1	28.5	243 09.3	55.3	91 37.2	25.1	Hadar	148 48.5	S60 25.9
15	324 27.3	67 22.9	.. 08.8	18 15.5	.. 28.1	258 12.0	.. 55.3	106 39.5	.. 25.1	Hamal	328 00.9	N23 31.5
16	339 29.8	82 22.0	09.2	33 16.0	27.6	273 14.7	55.3	121 41.7	25.2	Kaus Aust.	83 44.6	S34 22.5
17	354 32.3	97 21.1	09.5	48 16.4	27.1	288 17.4	55.2	136 44.0	25.2			
18	9 34.7	112 20.2	S22 09.9	63 16.8	S20 26.7	303 20.2	N20 55.2	151 46.3	S12 25.3	Kochab	137 20.8	N74 05.9
19	24 37.2	127 19.3	10.3	78 17.2	26.2	318 22.9	55.2	166 48.5	25.4	Markab	13 38.8	N15 16.7
20	39 39.7	142 18.5	10.7	93 17.7	25.7	333 25.6	55.2	181 50.8	25.4	Menkar	314 15.2	N 4 08.4
21	54 42.1	157 17.6	.. 11.0	108 18.1	.. 25.3	348 28.3	.. 55.1	196 53.1	.. 25.5	Menkent	148 08.1	S36 25.9
22	69 44.6	172 16.7	11.4	123 18.5	24.8	3 31.1	55.1	211 55.3	25.5	Miaplacidus	221 38.9	S69 46.2
23	84 47.0	187 15.8	11.8	138 19.0	24.3	18 33.8	55.1	226 57.6	25.6			
31 00	99 49.5	202 14.9	S22 12.1	153 19.4	S20 23.9	33 36.5	N20 55.0	241 59.9	S12 25.6	Mirfak	308 40.4	N49 54.5
01	114 52.0	217 14.0	12.5	168 19.8	23.4	48 39.2	55.0	257 02.2	25.7	Nunki	75 59.1	S26 16.7
02	129 54.4	232 13.1	12.9	183 20.3	22.9	63 41.9	55.0	272 04.4	25.7	Peacock	53 20.3	S56 41.6
03	144 56.9	247 12.2	.. 13.3	198 20.7	.. 22.4	78 44.7	.. 54.9	287 06.7	.. 25.8	Pollux	243 27.7	N27 59.4
04	159 59.4	262 11.3	13.6	213 21.1	22.0	93 47.4	54.9	302 09.0	25.8	Procyon	244 59.7	N 5 11.3
05	175 01.8	277 10.4	14.0	228 21.5	21.5	108 50.1	54.9	317 11.2	25.9			
06	190 04.3	292 09.5	S22 14.3	243 22.0	S20 21.0	123 52.8	N20 54.8	332 13.5	S12 26.0	Rasalhague	96 07.1	N12 33.1
07	205 06.8	307 08.6	14.7	258 22.4	20.6	138 55.5	54.8	347 15.8	26.0	Regulus	207 43.6	N11 54.0
08	220 09.2	322 07.7	15.1	273 22.8	20.1	153 58.3	54.8	2 18.1	26.1	Rigel	281 12.0	S 8 11.4
M 09	235 11.7	337 06.8	.. 15.4	288 23.3	.. 19.6	169 01.0	.. 54.8	17 20.3	.. 26.1	Rigil Kent.	139 52.4	S60 53.0
O 10	250 14.2	352 05.9	15.8	303 23.7	19.1	184 03.7	54.7	32 22.6	26.2	Sabik	102 13.2	S15 44.3
N 11	265 16.6	7 05.0	16.1	318 24.1	18.7	199 06.4	54.7	47 24.9	26.2			
D 12	280 19.1	22 04.1	S22 16.5	333 24.6	S20 18.2	214 09.1	N20 54.7	62 27.1	S12 26.3	Schedar	349 40.8	N56 36.9
A 13	295 21.5	37 03.2	16.9	348 25.0	17.7	229 11.9	54.6	77 29.4	26.3	Shaula	96 22.7	S37 06.6
Y 14	310 24.0	52 02.3	17.2	3 25.4	17.3	244 14.6	54.6	92 31.7	26.4	Sirius	258 33.6	S16 44.2
15	325 26.5	67 01.4	.. 17.6	18 25.9	.. 16.8	259 17.3	.. 54.6	107 34.0	.. 26.4	Spica	158 31.6	S11 13.7
16	340 28.9	82 00.6	17.9	33 26.3	16.3	274 20.0	54.5	122 36.2	26.5	Suhail	222 52.3	S43 29.1
17	355 31.4	96 59.7	18.3	48 26.7	15.8	289 22.7	54.5	137 38.5	26.5			
18	10 33.9	111 58.8	S22 18.6	63 27.2	S20 15.4	304 25.4	N20 54.5	152 40.8	S12 26.6	Vega	80 39.6	N38 47.9
19	25 36.3	126 57.9	19.0	78 27.6	14.9	319 28.2	54.5	167 43.0	26.7	Zuben'ubi	137 05.9	S16 05.7
20	40 38.8	141 57.0	19.3	93 28.0	14.4	334 30.9	54.4	182 45.3	26.7		SHA	Mer. Pass.
21	55 41.3	156 56.1	.. 19.7	108 28.5	.. 13.9	349 33.6	.. 54.4	197 47.6	.. 26.8		° ′	h m
22	70 43.7	171 55.2	20.0	123 28.9	13.4	4 36.3	54.4	212 49.9	26.8	Venus	103 45.9	10 30
23	85 46.2	186 54.3	20.3	138 29.3	13.0	19 39.0	54.3	227 52.1	26.9	Mars	54 18.7	13 47
	h m									Jupiter	293 40.7	21 46
Mer. Pass.	17 21.8	v −0.9	d 0.4	v 0.4	d 0.5	v 2.7	d 0.0	v 2.3	d 0.1	Saturn	142 15.1	7 54

UT	SUN GHA	SUN Dec	MOON GHA	v	Dec	d	HP
d h	° ′	° ′	° ′	′	° ′	′	′
29 00	179 29.8	S23 12.8	353 09.1	12.1	N18 51.9	4.9	54.4
01	194 29.5	12.7	7 40.2	12.0	18 47.0	5.0	54.4
02	209 29.2	12.5	22 11.2	12.1	18 42.0	5.0	54.5
03	224 28.9	.. 12.4	36 42.3	12.1	18 37.0	5.2	54.5
04	239 28.6	12.2	51 13.4	12.2	18 31.8	5.2	54.5
05	254 28.3	12.1	65 44.6	12.1	18 26.6	5.3	54.5
S 06	269 28.0	S23 11.9	80 15.7	12.2	N18 21.3	5.4	54.5
A 07	284 27.7	11.8	94 46.9	12.2	18 15.9	5.5	54.5
T 08	299 27.4	11.6	109 18.1	12.2	18 10.4	5.5	54.5
U 09	314 27.1	.. 11.5	123 49.3	12.2	18 04.9	5.7	54.5
R 10	329 26.8	11.3	138 20.5	12.3	17 59.2	5.7	54.5
D 11	344 26.5	11.2	152 51.8	12.2	17 53.5	5.9	54.6
A 12	359 26.2	S23 11.0	167 23.0	12.3	N17 47.6	5.9	54.6
Y 13	14 25.9	10.8	181 54.3	12.3	17 41.7	6.0	54.6
14	29 25.6	10.7	196 25.6	12.4	17 35.7	6.1	54.6
15	44 25.3	.. 10.5	210 57.0	12.3	17 29.6	6.1	54.6
16	59 25.0	10.4	225 28.3	12.4	17 23.5	6.3	54.6
17	74 24.7	10.2	239 59.7	12.4	17 17.2	6.3	54.6
18	89 24.4	S23 10.0	254 31.1	12.4	N17 10.9	6.4	54.6
19	104 24.1	09.9	269 02.5	12.5	17 04.5	6.5	54.7
20	119 23.8	09.7	283 34.0	12.4	16 58.0	6.6	54.7
21	134 23.5	.. 09.6	298 05.4	12.5	16 51.4	6.6	54.7
22	149 23.2	09.4	312 36.9	12.5	16 44.8	6.7	54.7
23	164 22.9	09.2	327 08.4	12.6	16 38.1	6.8	54.7
30 00	179 22.6	S23 09.1	341 40.0	12.5	N16 31.3	6.9	54.7
01	194 22.3	08.9	356 11.5	12.6	16 24.4	7.0	54.7
02	209 22.0	08.7	10 43.1	12.6	16 17.4	7.0	54.8
03	224 21.7	.. 08.6	25 14.7	12.6	16 10.4	7.2	54.8
04	239 21.4	08.4	39 46.3	12.7	16 03.2	7.2	54.8
05	254 21.1	08.2	54 18.0	12.6	15 56.0	7.2	54.8
S 06	269 20.8	S23 08.0	68 49.6	12.7	N15 48.8	7.4	54.8
U 07	284 20.5	07.9	83 21.3	12.7	15 41.4	7.4	54.8
N 08	299 20.2	07.7	97 53.0	12.8	15 34.0	7.5	54.8
D 09	314 19.9	.. 07.5	112 24.8	12.7	15 26.5	7.6	54.9
A 10	329 19.6	07.4	126 56.5	12.8	15 18.9	7.6	54.9
Y 11	344 19.3	07.2	141 28.3	12.8	15 11.3	7.7	54.9
12	359 19.0	S23 07.0	156 00.1	12.9	N15 03.6	7.8	54.9
13	14 18.7	06.8	170 32.0	12.8	14 55.8	7.9	54.9
14	29 18.4	06.7	185 03.8	12.9	14 47.9	7.9	54.9
15	44 18.1	.. 06.5	199 35.7	12.9	14 40.0	8.0	54.9
16	59 17.8	06.3	214 07.6	12.9	14 32.0	8.1	55.0
17	74 17.5	06.1	228 39.5	12.9	14 23.9	8.1	55.0
18	89 17.2	S23 05.9	243 11.4	13.0	N14 15.8	8.2	55.0
19	104 16.9	05.8	257 43.4	12.9	14 07.6	8.3	55.0
20	119 16.6	05.6	272 15.3	13.0	13 59.3	8.3	55.0
21	134 16.3	.. 05.4	286 47.3	13.1	13 51.0	8.4	55.0
22	149 16.0	05.2	301 19.4	13.0	13 42.6	8.5	55.1
23	164 15.7	05.0	315 51.4	13.1	13 34.1	8.6	55.1
31 00	179 15.4	S23 04.8	330 23.5	13.0	N13 25.5	8.6	55.1
01	194 15.1	04.7	344 55.5	13.1	13 16.9	8.6	55.1
02	209 14.9	04.5	359 27.6	13.2	13 08.3	8.8	55.1
03	224 14.6	.. 04.3	13 59.8	13.1	12 59.5	8.8	55.1
04	239 14.3	04.1	28 31.9	13.2	12 50.7	8.8	55.2
05	254 14.0	03.9	43 04.1	13.1	12 41.9	9.0	55.2
M 06	269 13.7	S23 03.7	57 36.2	13.2	N12 32.9	8.9	55.2
O 07	284 13.4	03.5	72 08.4	13.2	12 24.0	9.1	55.2
08	299 13.1	03.3	86 40.6	13.3	12 14.9	9.1	55.2
M 09	314 12.8	.. 03.1	101 12.9	13.2	12 05.8	9.2	55.2
O 10	329 12.5	02.9	115 45.1	13.3	11 56.6	9.3	55.3
N 11	344 12.2	02.7	130 17.4	13.3	11 47.4	9.3	55.3
D 12	359 11.9	S23 02.6	144 49.7	13.3	N11 38.1	9.3	55.3
A 13	14 11.6	02.4	159 22.0	13.3	11 28.8	9.4	55.3
Y 14	29 11.3	02.2	173 54.3	13.3	11 19.4	9.4	55.3
15	44 11.0	.. 02.0	188 26.6	13.3	11 10.0	9.5	55.4
16	59 10.7	01.8	202 58.9	13.4	11 00.5	9.6	55.4
17	74 10.4	01.6	217 31.3	13.4	10 50.9	9.6	55.4
18	89 10.1	S23 01.4	232 03.7	13.4	N10 41.3	9.7	55.4
19	104 09.8	01.2	246 36.1	13.3	10 31.6	9.7	55.4
20	119 09.5	01.0	261 08.4	13.5	10 21.9	9.8	55.4
21	134 09.2	.. 00.8	275 40.9	13.4	10 12.1	9.8	55.5
22	149 08.9	00.6	290 13.3	13.4	10 02.3	9.9	55.5
23	164 08.6	00.4	304 45.7	13.5	N 9 52.4	9.9	55.5
	SD 16.3	d 0.2	SD 14.9		15.0		15.1

Lat.	Twilight Naut.	Twilight Civil	Sunrise	Moonrise 29	30	31	1
°	h m	h m	h m	h m	h m	h m	h m
N 72	08 25	10 47	▬		13 49	16 15	18 12	20 02
N 70	08 06	09 52	▬		14 58	16 47	18 30	20 12
68	07 51	09 18	▬		15 35	17 10	18 44	20 19
66	07 38	08 54	10 30	16 01	17 27	18 56	20 25
64	07 27	08 35	09 51	16 21	17 42	19 05	20 30
62	07 18	08 19	09 24	16 37	17 54	19 13	20 35
60	07 10	08 06	09 03	16 50	18 04	19 20	20 39
N 58	07 02	07 55	08 46	17 01	18 13	19 27	20 42
56	06 56	07 45	08 32	17 11	18 20	19 32	20 45
54	06 50	07 36	08 19	17 20	18 27	19 37	20 48
52	06 44	07 28	08 08	17 28	18 33	19 41	20 50
50	06 39	07 20	07 59	17 35	18 39	19 45	20 53
45	06 27	07 04	07 38	17 50	18 51	19 54	20 57
N 40	06 17	06 51	07 22	18 02	19 01	20 01	21 01
35	06 08	06 40	07 08	18 13	19 09	20 07	21 05
30	05 59	06 29	06 55	18 22	19 17	20 12	21 08
20	05 43	06 11	06 34	18 38	19 30	20 21	21 13
N 10	05 27	05 53	06 16	18 52	19 41	20 29	21 18
0	05 10	05 36	05 59	19 04	19 51	20 37	21 22
S 10	04 52	05 19	05 42	19 17	20 02	20 45	21 27
20	04 29	04 58	05 23	19 31	20 13	20 53	21 31
30	04 00	04 34	05 01	19 46	20 25	21 02	21 37
35	03 42	04 19	04 48	19 55	20 32	21 07	21 40
40	03 19	04 01	04 33	20 06	20 41	21 13	21 43
45	02 49	03 38	04 16	20 18	20 50	21 20	21 47
S 50	02 05	03 09	03 53	20 32	21 02	21 28	21 52
52	01 38	02 54	03 43	20 39	21 07	21 32	21 54
54	00 56	02 37	03 31	20 47	21 13	21 36	21 56
56	////	02 15	03 17	20 55	21 20	21 41	21 59
58	////	01 47	03 00	21 05	21 27	21 46	22 02
S 60	////	01 01	02 40	21 15	21 35	21 51	22 05

Lat.	Sunset	Twilight Civil	Twilight Naut.	Moonset 29	30	31	1
°	h m	h m	h m	h m	h m	h m	h m
N 72	▬	13 19	15 41	12 07	11 18	10 57	10 42
N 70	▬	14 14	16 00	10 56	10 45	10 37	10 31
68	▬	14 47	16 15	10 19	10 21	10 22	10 21
66	13 35	15 12	16 28	09 52	10 03	10 09	10 14
64	14 15	15 31	16 39	09 32	09 48	09 59	10 07
62	14 42	15 46	16 48	09 15	09 35	09 50	10 02
60	15 03	16 00	16 56	09 02	09 24	09 42	09 57
N 58	15 20	16 11	17 03	08 50	09 15	09 35	09 52
56	15 34	16 21	17 10	08 39	09 06	09 29	09 48
54	15 46	16 30	17 16	08 30	08 59	09 23	09 45
52	15 57	16 38	17 22	08 22	08 52	09 18	09 42
50	16 07	16 45	17 27	08 15	08 46	09 14	09 39
45	16 27	17 01	17 38	07 59	08 33	09 04	09 32
N 40	16 44	17 14	17 48	07 46	08 23	08 56	09 27
35	16 58	17 26	17 58	07 35	08 13	08 49	09 22
30	17 10	17 36	18 06	07 25	08 05	08 43	09 18
20	17 31	17 55	18 22	07 08	07 51	08 32	09 11
N 10	17 49	18 12	18 38	06 54	07 39	08 22	09 05
0	18 06	18 29	18 56	06 40	07 27	08 13	08 59
S 10	18 24	18 47	19 14	06 26	07 15	08 04	08 53
20	18 42	19 07	19 36	06 11	07 03	07 55	08 46
30	19 04	19 32	20 05	05 54	06 48	07 43	08 39
35	19 17	19 47	20 23	05 44	06 40	07 37	08 35
40	19 32	20 05	20 46	05 33	06 30	07 30	08 30
45	19 50	20 27	21 16	05 19	06 19	07 21	08 24
S 50	20 12	20 56	22 00	05 03	06 05	07 10	08 17
52	20 22	21 11	22 26	04 55	05 59	07 06	08 14
54	20 34	21 28	23 08	04 46	05 52	07 00	08 11
56	20 48	21 49	////	04 37	05 44	06 54	08 07
58	21 05	22 18	////	04 26	05 35	06 48	08 02
S 60	21 24	23 03	////	04 13	05 25	06 40	07 57

	SUN			MOON			
Day	Eqn. of Time 00h	12h	Mer. Pass.	Mer. Pass. Upper	Lower	Age	Phase
d	m s	m s	h m	h m	h m	d	%
29	02 00	02 15	12 02	00 28	12 52	16	99
30	02 29	02 43	12 03	01 16	13 39	17	96
31	02 58	03 12	12 03	02 02	14 25	18	91

EXPLANATION

PRINCIPLE AND ARRANGEMENT

1. *Object.* The object of this Almanac is to provide, in a convenient form, the data required for the practice of astronomical navigation at sea.

2. *Principle.* The main contents of the Almanac consist of data from which the *Greenwich Hour Angle* (GHA) and the *Declination* (Dec) of all the bodies used for navigation can be obtained for any instant of *Universal Time* (UT), or *Greenwich Mean Time* (GMT). The *Local Hour Angle* (LHA) can then be obtained by means of the formula:

$$\text{LHA} = \text{GHA} \; {{- \text{ west}} \atop {+ \text{ east}}} \; \text{longitude}$$

The remaining data consist of: times of rising and setting of the Sun and Moon, and times of twilight; miscellaneous calendarial and planning data and auxiliary tables, including a list of Standard Times; corrections to be applied to observed altitude.

For the Sun, Moon, and planets the GHA and Dec are tabulated directly for each hour of UT throughout the year. For the stars the *Sidereal Hour Angle* (SHA) is given, and the GHA is obtained from:

$$\text{GHA Star} = \text{GHA Aries} + \text{SHA Star}$$

The SHA and Dec of the stars change slowly and may be regarded as constant over periods of several days. GHA Aries, or the Greenwich Hour Angle of the first point of Aries (the Vernal Equinox), is tabulated for each hour. Permanent tables give the appropriate increments and corrections to the tabulated hourly values of GHA and Dec for the minutes and seconds of UT.

The six-volume series of *Sight Reduction Tables for Marine Navigation* (published in U.S.A. as Pub. No. 229 and in U.K. as N.P. 401) has been designed for the solution of the navigational triangle and is intended for use with *The Nautical Almanac.*

Two alternative procedures for sight reduction are described on pages 277–318. The first requires the use of programmable calculators or computers, while the second uses a set of concise tables that is given on pages 286–317.

The tabular accuracy is $0\!\!\!.'1$ throughout. The time argument on the daily pages of this Almanac is 12^h + the Greenwich Hour Angle of the mean sun and is here denoted by UT, although it is also known as GMT. This scale may differ from the broadcast time signals (UTC) by an amount which, if ignored, will introduce an error of up to $0\!\!\!.'2$ in longitude determined from astronomical observations. (The difference arises because the time argument depends on the variable rate of rotation of the Earth while the broadcast time signals are now based on an atomic time-scale.) Step adjustments of exactly one second are made to the time signals as required (normally at 24^h on December 31 and June 30) so that the difference between the time signals and UT, as used in this Almanac, may not exceed 0^s9. Those who require to reduce observations to a precision of better than 1^s must therefore obtain the correction (DUT1) to the time signals from coding in the signal, or from other sources; the required time is given by UT1=UTC+DUT1 to a precision of 0^s1. Alternatively, the longitude, when determined from astronomical observations, may be corrected by the corresponding amount shown in the following table:

Correction to time signals	Correction to longitude
-0^s9 to -0^s7	$0\!\!\!.'2$ to east
-0^s6 to -0^s3	$0\!\!\!.'1$ to east
-0^s2 to $+0^s2$	no correction
$+0^s3$ to $+0^s6$	$0\!\!\!.'1$ to west
$+0^s7$ to $+0^s9$	$0\!\!\!.'2$ to west

3. *Lay-out.* The ephemeral data for three days are presented on an opening of two pages: the left-hand page contains the data for the planets and stars; the right-hand page contains the data for the Sun and Moon, together with times of twilight, sunrise, sunset, moonrise and moonset.

The remaining contents are arranged as follows: for ease of reference the altitude-correction tables are given on pages A2, A3, A4, xxxiv and xxxv; calendar, Moon's phases, eclipses, and planet notes (i.e. data of general interest) precede the main tabulations. The Explanation is followed by information on standard times, star charts and list of star positions, sight reduction procedures and concise sight reduction tables, tables of increments and corrections and other auxiliary tables that are frequently used.

MAIN DATA

4. *Daily pages.* The daily pages give the GHA of Aries, the GHA and Dec of the Sun, Moon, and the four navigational planets, for each hour of UT. For the Moon, values of v and d are also tabulated for each hour to facilitate the correction of GHA and Dec to intermediate times; v and d for the Sun and planets change so slowly that they are given, at the foot of the appropriate columns, once only on the page; v is zero for Aries and negligible for the Sun, and is omitted. The SHA and Dec of the 57 selected stars, arranged in alphabetical order of proper name, are also given.

5. *Stars.* The SHA and Dec of 173 stars, including the 57 selected stars, are tabulated for each month on pages 268–273; no interpolation is required and the data can be used in precisely the same way as those for the selected stars on the daily pages. The stars are arranged in order of SHA.

The list of 173 includes all stars down to magnitude 3·0, together with a few fainter ones to fill the larger gaps. The 57 selected stars have been chosen from amongst these on account of brightness and distribution in the sky; they will suffice for the majority of observations.

The 57 selected stars are known by their proper names, but they are also numbered in descending order of SHA. In the list of 173 stars, the constellation names are always given on the left-hand page; on the facing page proper names are given where well-known names exist. Numbers for the selected stars are given in both columns.

An index to the selected stars, containing lists in both alphabetical and numerical order, is given on page xxxiii and is also reprinted on the bookmark.

6. *Increments and corrections.* The tables printed on tinted paper (pages ii–xxxi) at the back of the Almanac provide the increments and corrections for minutes and seconds to be applied to the hourly values of GHA and Dec. They consist of sixty tables, one for each minute, separated into two parts: increments to GHA for Sun and planets, Aries, and Moon for every minute and second; and, for each minute, corrections to be applied to GHA and Dec corresponding to the values of v and d given on the daily pages.

The increments are based on the following adopted hourly rates of increase of the GHA: Sun and planets, 15° precisely; Aries, 15° 02′·46; Moon, 14° 19′·0. The values of v on the daily pages are the excesses of the actual hourly motions over the adopted values; they are generally positive, except for Venus. The tabulated hourly values of the Sun's GHA have been adjusted to reduce to a minimum the error caused by treating v as negligible. The values of d on the daily pages are the hourly differences of the Dec. For the Moon, the true values of v and d are given for each hour; otherwise mean values are given for the three days on the page.

7. *Method of entry.* The UT of an observation is expressed as a day and hour, followed by a number of minutes and seconds. The tabular values of GHA and Dec, and, where necessary, the corresponding values of v and d, are taken directly from the daily pages for the day and hour of UT; this hour is always *before* the time of observation. SHA and Dec of the selected stars are also taken from the daily pages.

The table of Increments and Corrections for the minute of UT is then selected. For the GHA, the increment for minutes and seconds is taken from the appropriate column opposite the seconds of UT; the v-correction is taken from the second part of the same table opposite the value of v as given on the daily pages. Both increment and v-correction are to be added to the GHA, except for Venus when v is prefixed by a minus sign and the v-correction is to be subtracted. For the Dec there is no increment, but a d-correction is applied in the same way as the v-correction; d is given without sign on the daily pages and the sign of the correction is to be supplied by inspection of the Dec column. In many cases the correction may be applied mentally.

8. *Examples.* (a) Sun and Moon. Required the GHA and Dec of the Sun and Moon on 2012 September 25 at 15^h 47^m 13^s UT.

		SUN			MOON			
		GHA	Dec	d	GHA	v	Dec	d
		° ′	° ′	′	° ′	′	° ′	′
Daily page, September 25ᵈ 15ʰ		47 07·9	S 1 10·3	1·0	279 59·5	10·4	S 13 24·8	9·5
Increments for	47ᵐ 13ˢ	11 48·3			11 16·0			
v or d corrections for	47ᵐ		+0·8		+8·2		−7·5	
Sum for September 25ᵈ 15ʰ 47ᵐ 13ˢ		58 56·2	S 1 11·1		291 23·7		S 13 17·3	

(b) Planets. Required the LHA and Dec of (i) Venus on 2012 September 25 at 10^h 07^m 03^s UT in longitude W $70°$ $25'$; (ii) Mars on 2012 September 25 at 13^h 58^m 41^s UT in longitude E $68°$ $57'$.

		VENUS				MARS			
		GHA	v	Dec	d	GHA	v	Dec	d
		° ′	′	° ′	′	° ′	′	° ′	′
Daily page, Sept. 25ᵈ	(10ʰ)	11 22·0	−0·4	N14 21·7	0·7	(13ʰ) 330 29·2	0·7	S18 59·3	0·5
Increments (planets)	(07ᵐ 03ˢ)	1 45·8				(58ᵐ 41ˢ) 14 40·3			
v or d corrections	(07ᵐ)	−0·1		−0·1		(58ᵐ) +0·7		+0·5	
Sum = GHA and Dec.		13 07·7		N14 21·6		345 10·2		S18 59·8	
Longitude	(west)	− 70 25·0				(east) + 68 57·0			
Multiples of 360°		+360				−360			
LHA planet		302 42·7				54 07·2			

(c) Stars. Required the GHA and Dec of (i) *Sirius* on 2012 September 25 at 6^h 27^m 43^s UT; (ii) *Vega* on 2012 September 25 at 19^h 55^m 23^s UT.

		Sirius			Vega	
		GHA	Dec		GHA	Dec
		° ′	° ′		° ′	° ′
Daily page (SHA and Dec)		258 34·2	S 16 43.9		80 39·3	N 38 48.2
Daily page (GHA Aries)	(6ʰ)	94 27·8		(19ʰ)	289 59·9	
Increments (Aries)	(27ᵐ 43ˢ)	6 56·9		(55ᵐ 23ˢ)	13 53·0	
Sum = GHA star		359 58·9			384 32·2	
Multiples of 360°					−360	
GHA star		359 58·9			24 32·2	

9. *Polaris (Pole Star) tables.* The tables on pages 274–276 provide means by which the latitude can be deduced from an observed altitude of *Polaris*, and they also give its azimuth; their use is explained and illustrated on those pages. They are based on the following formula:

$$\text{Latitude} - H_O = -p\cos h + \tfrac{1}{2}p\sin p\sin^2 h\tan(\text{latitude})$$

where

H_O = Apparent altitude (corrected for refraction)

p = polar distance of *Polaris* = $90°$ − Dec

h = local hour angle of *Polaris* = LHA Aries + SHA

a_0, which is a function of LHA Aries only, is the value of both terms of the above formula calculated for mean values of the SHA ($318°$ $04'$) and Dec (N $89°$ $19'.1$) of *Polaris*, for a mean latitude of $50°$, and adjusted by the addition of a constant ($58'.8$).

a_1, which is a function of LHA Aries and latitude, is the excess of the value of the second term over its mean value for latitude 50°, increased by a constant (0.6) to make it always positive. a_2, which is a function of LHA Aries and date, is the correction to the first term for the variation of *Polaris* from its adopted mean position; it is increased by a constant (0.6) to make it positive. The sum of the added constants is 1°, so that:

$$\text{Latitude} = \text{Apparent altitude (corrected for refraction)} - 1° + a_0 + a_1 + a_2$$

RISING AND SETTING PHENOMENA

10. *General.* On the right-hand daily pages are given the times of sunrise and sunset, of the beginning and end of civil and nautical twilights, and of moonrise and moonset for a range of latitudes from N 72° to S 60°. These times, which are given to the nearest minute, are strictly the UT of the phenomena on the Greenwich meridian; they are given for every day for moonrise and moonset, but only for the middle day of the three on each page for the solar phenomena.

They are approximately the Local Mean Times (LMT) of the corresponding phenomena on other meridians; they can be formally interpolated if desired. The UT of a phenomenon is obtained from the LMT by:

$$UT = LMT {+ \text{ west} \atop - \text{ east}} \text{ longitude}$$

in which the longitude must first be converted to time by the table on page i or otherwise.

Interpolation for latitude can be done mentally or with the aid of Table I on page xxxii.

The following symbols are used to indicate the conditions under which, in high latitudes, some of the phenomena do not occur:

☐ Sun or Moon remains continuously above the horizon;

■ Sun or Moon remains continuously below the horizon;

//// twilight lasts all night.

Basis of the tabulations. At sunrise and sunset 16′ is allowed for semi-diameter and 34′ for horizontal refraction, so that at the times given the Sun's upper limb is on the visible horizon; all times refer to phenomena as seen from sea level with a clear horizon.

At the times given for the beginning and end of twilight, the Sun's zenith distance is 96° for civil, and 102° for nautical twilight. The degree of illumination at the times given for civil twilight (in good conditions and in the absence of other illumination) is such that the brightest stars are visible and the horizon is clearly defined. At the times given for nautical twilight the horizon is in general not visible, and it is too dark for observation with a marine sextant.

Times corresponding to other depressions of the Sun may be obtained by interpolation or, for depressions of more than 12°, less reliably, by extrapolation; times so obtained will be subject to considerable uncertainty near extreme conditions.

At moonrise and moonset allowance is made for semi-diameter, parallax, and refraction (34′), so that at the times given the Moon's upper limb is on the visible horizon as seen from sea level.

11. *Sunrise, sunset, twilight.* The tabulated times may be regarded, without serious error, as the LMT of the phenomena on any of the three days on the page and in any longitude. Precise times may normally be obtained by interpolating the tabular values for latitude and to the correct day and longitude, the latter being expressed as a fraction of a day by dividing it by 360°, positive for west and negative for east longitudes. In the extreme conditions near ☐, ■ or //// interpolation may not be possible in one direction, but accurate times are of little value in these circumstances.

Examples. Required the UT of (a) the beginning of morning twilights and sunrise on 2012 January 13 for latitude S 48° 55′, longitude E 75° 18′; (b) sunset and the end of evening twilights on 2012 January 15 for latitude N 67° 10′, longitude W 168° 05′.

		Twilight		Sunrise		Sunset	Twilight	
	(a)	Nautical	Civil		(b)		Civil	Nautical
		d h m	d h m	d h m		d h m	d h m	d h m
From p. 19								
LMT for Lat	S 45°	13 03 08	13 03 55	13 04 31	N 66°	15 14 21	15 15 41	15 16 52
Corr. to	S 48° 55′	−30	−20	−16	N 67° 10′	−24	−12	−6
(p. xxxii, Table I)								
Long (p. i)	E 75° 18′	−5 01	−5 01	−5 01	W 168° 05′	+11 12	+11 12	+11 12
UT		12 21 37	12 22 34	12 23 14		16 01 09	16 02 41	16 03 58

The LMT are strictly for January 14 (middle date on page) and 0° longitude; for more precise times it is necessary to interpolate, but rounding errors may accumulate to about 2^m.

(a) to January $13^d - 75°/360° =$ Jan. $12^d 8$, i.e. $\frac{1}{3}(1 \cdot 2) = 0 \cdot 4$ backwards towards the data for the same latitude interpolated similarly from page 17; the corrections are -2^m to nautical twilight, -2^m to civil twilight and -2^m to sunrise.

(b) to January $15^d + 168°/360° =$ Jan. $15^d 5$, i.e. $\frac{1}{3}(1 \cdot 5) = 0 \cdot 5$ forwards towards the data for the same latitude interpolated similarly from page 21; the corrections are $+7^m$ to sunset, $+4^m$ to civil twilight, and $+4^m$ to nautical twilight.

12. *Moonrise, moonset.* Precise times of moonrise and moonset are rarely needed; a glance at the tables will generally give sufficient indication of whether the Moon is available for observation and of the hours of rising and setting. If needed, precise times may be obtained as follows. Interpolate for latitude, using Table I on page xxxii, on the day wanted and also on the preceding day in east longitudes or the following day in west longitudes; take the difference between these times and interpolate for longitude by applying to the time for the day wanted the correction from Table II on page xxxii, so that the resulting time is between the two times used. In extreme conditions near □ or ■ interpolation for latitude or longitude may be possible only in one direction; accurate times are of little value in these circumstances.

To facilitate this interpolation the times of moonrise and moonset are given for four days on each page; where no phenomenon occurs during a particular day (as happens once a month) the time of the phenomenon on the following day, increased by 24^h, is given; extra care must be taken when interpolating between two values, when one of those values exceeds 24^h. In practice it suffices to use the daily difference between the times for the nearest tabular latitude, and generally, to enter Table II with the nearest tabular arguments as in the examples below.

Examples. Required the UT of moonrise and moonset in latitude S 47° 10′, longitudes E 124° 00′ and W 78° 31′ on 2012 January 29.

	Longitude E 124° 00′		Longitude W 78° 31′	
	Moonrise	Moonset	Moonrise	Moonset
	d h m	d h m	d h m	d h m
LMT for Lat. S 45°	29 11 26	29 22 00	29 11 26	29 22 00
Lat correction (p. xxxii, Table I)	+04	−04	+04	−04
Long correction (p. xxxii, Table II)	−20	−07	+13	+07
Correct LMT	29 11 10	29 21 49	29 11 43	29 22 03
Longitude (p. i)	−8 16	−8 16	+5 14	+5 14
UT	29 02 54	29 13 33	29 16 57	30 03 17

ALTITUDE CORRECTION TABLES

13. *General.* In general two corrections are given for application to altitudes observed with a marine sextant; additional corrections are required for Venus and Mars and also for very low altitudes.

Tables of the correction for dip of the horizon, due to height of eye above sea level, are given on pages A2 and xxxiv. Strictly this correction should be applied first and subtracted from the sextant altitude to give apparent altitude, which is the correct argument for the other tables.

Separate tables are given of the second correction for the Sun, for stars and planets (on pages A2 and A3), and for the Moon (on pages xxxiv and xxxv). For the Sun, values are given for both lower and upper limbs, for two periods of the year. The star tables are used for the planets, but additional corrections for parallax (page A2) are required for Venus and Mars. The Moon tables are in two parts: the main correction is a function of apparent altitude only and is tabulated for the lower limb (30′ must be subtracted to obtain the correction for the upper limb); the other, which is given for both lower and upper limbs, depends also on the horizontal parallax, which has to be taken from the daily pages.

An additional correction, given on page A4, is required for the change in the refraction, due to variations of pressure and temperature from the adopted standard conditions; it may generally be ignored for altitudes greater than 10°, except possibly in extreme conditions. The correction tables for the Sun, stars, and planets are in two parts; only those for altitudes greater than 10° are reprinted on the bookmark.

14. *Critical tables.* Some of the altitude correction tables are arranged as critical tables. In these an interval of apparent altitude (or height of eye) corresponds to a single value of the correction; no interpolation is required. At a "critical" entry the upper of the two possible values of the correction is to be taken. For example, in the table of dip, a correction of $-4 \cdot 1$ corresponds to all values of the height of eye from $5 \cdot 3$ to $5 \cdot 5$ metres ($17 \cdot 5$ to $18 \cdot 3$ feet) inclusive.

15. *Examples.* The following examples illustrate the use of the altitude correction tables; the sextant altitudes given are assumed to be taken on 2012 February 7 with a marine sextant at height $5 \cdot 4$ metres (18 feet), temperature $-3°C$ and pressure 982 mb, the Moon sights being taken at about 10^h UT.

	SUN lower limb	SUN upper limb	MOON lower limb	MOON upper limb	VENUS	*Polaris*
	° ′	° ′	° ′	° ′	° ′	° ′
Sextant altitude	21 19·7	3 20·2	33 27·6	26 06·7	4 32·6	49 36·5
Dip, height 5·4 metres (18 feet)	−4·1	−4·1	−4·1	−4·1	−4·1	−4·1
Main correction	+13·8	−29·6	+57·4	+60·5	−10·8	−0·8
−30′ for upper limb (Moon)	—	—	—	−30·0	—	—
L, U correction for Moon	—	—	+5·5	+3·8	—	—
Additional correction for Venus	—	—	—	—	+0·1	—
Additional refraction correction	−0·1	−0·6	−0·1	−0·1	−0·5	0·0
Corrected sextant altitude	21 29·3	2 45·9	34 26·3	26 36·8	4 17·3	49 31·6

The main corrections have been taken out with apparent altitude (sextant altitude corrected for index error and dip) as argument, interpolating where possible. These refinements are rarely necessary.

16. *Composition of the Corrections.* The table for the dip of the sea horizon is based on the formula:

$$\text{Correction for dip} = -1 \cdot 76\sqrt{(\text{height of eye in metres})} = -0 \cdot 97\sqrt{(\text{height of eye in feet})}$$

The correction table for the Sun includes the effects of semi-diameter, parallax and mean refraction.

The correction tables for the stars and planets allow for the effect of mean refraction.

The phase correction for Venus has been incorporated in the tabulations for GHA and Dec, and no correction for phase is required. The additional corrections for Venus and Mars allow for parallax. Alternatively, the correction for parallax may be calculated from $p \cos H$, where p is the parallax and H is the altitude. In 2012 the values for p are:

	Jan. 1	Feb. 20	Apr. 12	May 4	May 21	June 21	July 8	July 30	Sept. 19	Dec. 31
Venus	0·1	0·2	0·3	0·4	0·5	0·4	0·3	0·2	0·1	

	Jan. 1	Jan. 8	May 5	Dec. 31
Mars	0·1	0·2	0·1	

The correction table for the Moon includes the effect of semi-diameter, parallax, augmentation and mean refraction.

Mean refraction is calculated for a temperature of 10°C (50°F), a pressure of 1010 mb (29·83 inches), humidity of 80% and wavelength 0·50169 μm.

17. *Bubble sextant observations.* When observing with a bubble sextant no correction is necessary for dip, semi-diameter, or augmentation. The altitude corrections for the stars and planets on page A2 and on the bookmark should be used for the Sun as well as for the stars and planets; for the Moon it is easiest to take the mean of the corrections for lower and upper limbs and subtract 15′ from the altitude; the correction for dip must not be applied.

AUXILIARY AND PLANNING DATA

18. *Sun and Moon.* On the daily pages are given: hourly values of the horizontal parallax of the Moon; the semi-diameters and the times of meridian passage of both Sun and Moon over the Greenwich meridian; the equation of time; the age of the Moon, the percent (%) illuminated and a symbol indicating the phase. The times of the phases of the Moon are given in UT on page 4. For the Moon, the semi-diameters for each of the three days are given at the foot of the column; for the Sun a single value is sufficient. Table II on page xxxii may be used for interpolating the time of the Moon's meridian passage for longitude. The equation of time is given daily at 00^h and 12^h UT. The sign is *positive* for unshaded values and *negative* for shaded values. To obtain apparent time add the equation of time to mean time when the sign is *positive*. Subtract the equation of time from mean time when the sign is *negative*. At 12^h UT, when the sign is *positive*, meridian passage of the Sun occurs *before* 12^h UT, otherwise it occurs *after* 12^h UT.

19. *Planets.* The magnitudes of the planets are given immediately following their names in the headings on the daily pages; also given, for the middle day of the three on the page, are their SHA at 00^h UT and their times of meridian passage.

The planet notes and diagram on pages 8 and 9 provide descriptive information as to the suitability of the planets for observation during the year, and of their positions and movements.

20. *Stars.* The time of meridian passage of the first point of Aries over the Greenwich meridian is given on the daily pages, for the middle day of the three on the page, to 0^m1. The interval between successive meridian passages is $23^h\ 56^m1$ (24^h less 3^m9) so that times for intermediate days and other meridians can readily be derived. If a precise time is required it may be obtained by finding the UT at which LHA Aries is zero.

The meridian passage of a star occurs when its LHA is zero, that is when LHA Aries + SHA = 360°. An approximate time can be obtained from the planet diagram on page 9.

The star charts on pages 266 and 267 are intended to assist identification. They show the relative positions of the stars in the sky as seen from the Earth and include all 173 stars used in the Almanac, together with a few others to complete the main constellation configurations. The local meridian at any time may be located on the chart by means of its SHA which is 360° − LHA Aries, or west longitude − GHA Aries.

21. *Star globe.* To set a star globe on which is printed a scale of LHA Aries, first set the globe for latitude and then rotate about the polar axis until the scale under the edge of the meridian circle reads LHA Aries.

To mark the positions of the Sun, Moon, and planets on the star globe, take the difference GHA Aries − GHA body and use this along the LHA Aries scale, in conjunction with the declination, to plot the position. GHA Aries − GHA body is most conveniently found by taking the difference when the GHA of the body is small (less than 15°), which happens once a day.

22. *Calendar.* On page 4 are given lists of ecclesiastical festivals, and of the principal anniversaries and holidays in the United Kingdom and the United States of America. The calendar on page 5 includes the day of the year as well as the day of the week.

Brief particulars are given, at the foot of page 5, of the solar and lunar eclipses occurring during the year; the times given are in UT. The principal features of the more important solar eclipses are shown on the maps on pages 6 and 7.

23. *Standard times.* The lists on pages 262–265 give the standard times used in most countries. In general no attempt is made to give details of the beginning and end of summer time, since they are liable to frequent changes at short notice. For the latest information consult Admiralty List of Radio Signals Volume 2 (NP 282) corrected by Section VI of the weekly edition of Admiralty Notices to Mariners.

The Date or Calendar Line is an arbitrary line, on either side of which the date differs by one day; when crossing this line on a westerly course, the date must be advanced one day; when crossing it on an easterly course, the date must be put back one day. The line is a modification of the line of the 180th meridian, and is drawn so as to include, as far as possible, islands of any one group, etc., on the same side of the line. It may be traced by starting at the South Pole and joining up to the following positions:

Lat	S	51·0	S	45·0	S	15·0	S	5·0	N	48·0	N	53·0	N	65·5
Long		180·0	W	172·5	W	172·5		180·0		180·0	E	170·0	W	169·0

thence through the middle of the Diomede Islands to Lat N 68°0, Long W 169°0, passing east of Ostrov Vrangelya (Wrangel Island) to Lat N 75°0, Long 180°0, and thence to the North Pole.

ACCURACY

24. *Main data.* The quantities tabulated in this Almanac are generally correct to the nearest 0′·1; the exception is the Sun's GHA which is deliberately adjusted by up to 0′·15 to reduce the error due to ignoring the v-correction. The GHA and Dec at intermediate times cannot be obtained to this precision, since at least two quantities must be added; moreover, the v- and d-corrections are based on mean values of v and d and are taken from tables for the whole minute only. The largest error that can occur in the GHA or Dec of any body other than the Sun or Moon is less than 0′·2; it may reach 0′·25 for the GHA of the Sun and 0′·3 for that of the Moon.

In practice it may be expected that only one third of the values of GHA and Dec taken out will have errors larger than 0′·05 and less than one tenth will have errors larger than 0′·1.

25. *Altitude corrections.* The errors in the altitude corrections are nominally of the same order as those in GHA and Dec, as they result from the addition of several quantities each correctly rounded off to 0′·1. But the actual values of the dip and of the refraction at low altitudes may, in extreme atmospheric conditions, differ considerably from the mean values used in the tables.

USE OF THIS ALMANAC IN 2013

This Almanac may be used for the Sun and stars in 2013 in the following manner.

For the Sun, take out the GHA and Dec for the same date but, for January and February, for a time 18^h 12^m 00^s *later* and, for March to December, for a time 5^h 48^m 00^s *earlier* than the UT of observation; in both cases add 87° 00′ to the GHA so obtained. The error, mainly due to planetary perturbations of the Earth, is unlikely to exceed 0′·4.

For the stars, calculate the GHA and Dec for the same date and the same time, but for January and February *add* 44′·0 and for March to December *subtract* 15′·1 from the GHA so found. The error, due to incomplete correction for precession and nutation, is unlikely to exceed 0′·4. If preferred, the same result can be obtained by using a time 18^h 12^m 00^s later for January and February, and 5^h 48^m 00^s earlier for March to December, than the UT of observation (as for the Sun) and adding 86° 59′·2 to the GHA (or adding 87° as for the Sun and subtracting 0′·8, for precession, from the SHA of the star).

The Almanac cannot be so used for the Moon or planets.

LIST I — PLACES FAST ON UTC (mainly those EAST OF GREENWICH)

The times given ⎱ *added* to UTC to give Standard Time
below should be ⎰ *subtracted* from Standard Time to give UTC.

	h	m		h	m
Admiralty Islands	10		Denmark*†	01	
Afghanistan	04	30	Djibouti	03	
Albania*	01		Egypt, Arab Republic of*	02	
Algeria	01		Equatorial Guinea, Republic of	01	
Amirante Islands	04		Eritrea	03	
Andaman Islands	05	30	Estonia*†	02	
Angola	01		Ethiopia	03	
Armenia*	04				
Australia			Fiji*	12	
Australian Capital Territory*	10		Finland*†	02	
New South Wales*[1]	10		France*†	01	
Northern Territory	09	30	Gabon	01	
Queensland	10		Georgia	04	
South Australia*	09	30	Germany*†	01	
Tasmania*	10		Gibraltar*	01	
Victoria*	10		Greece*†	02	
Western Australia	08		Guam	10	
Whitsunday Islands	10				
Austria*†	01		Hong Kong	08	
Azerbaijan*	04		Hungary*†	01	
			India	05	30
Bahrain	03		Indonesia, Republic of		
Balearic Islands*†	01		Bangka, Billiton, Java, West and		
Bangladesh	06		Central Kalimantan, Madura, Sumatra	07	
Belarus*	02		Bali, Flores, South and East		
Belgium*†	01		Kalimantan, Lombok, Sulawesi,		
Benin	01		Sumba, Sumbawa, West Timor	08	
Bosnia and Herzegovina*	01		Aru, Irian Jaya, Kai, Moluccas		
Botswana, Republic of	02		Tanimbar	09	
Brunei	08		Iran*	03	30
Bulgaria*†	02		Iraq	03	
Burma (Myanmar)	06	30	Israel*	02	
Burundi	02		Italy*†	01	
Cambodia	07		Jan Mayen Island*	01	
Cameroon Republic	01		Japan	09	
Caroline Islands[2]	10		Jordan*	02	
Central African Republic	01		Kazakhstan		
Chad	01		Western: Aktau, Uralsk, Atyrau	05	
Chagos Archipelago & Diego Garcia	06		Eastern & Central: Kzyl-Orda, Astana	06	
Chatham Islands*	12	45	Kenya	03	
China, People's Republic of	08		Kerguelen Islands	05	
Christmas Island, Indian Ocean	07		Kiribati Republic		
Cocos (Keeling) Islands	06	30	Gilbert Islands	12	
Comoro Islands (Comoros)	03		Phoenix Islands[3]	13	
Congo, Democratic Republic			Line Islands[3]	14	
West: Kinshasa, Equateur	01		Korea, North	09	
East: Orientale, Kasai, Kivu, Shaba	02		Korea, South	09	
Congo Republic	01		Kuwait	03	
Corsica*†	01		Kyrgyzstan	06	
Crete*†	02				
Croatia*	01		Laccadive Islands	05	30
Cyprus†: Ercan*, Larnaca*	02		Laos	07	
Czech Republic*†	01		Latvia*†	02	

* Daylight-saving time may be kept in these places.   † For Summer time dates see List II footnotes.
[1] Except Broken Hill Area* which keeps 09ʰ 30ᵐ.
[2] Except Pohnpei, Pingelap and Kosrae which keep 11ʰ and Palau which keeps 09ʰ.
[3] The Line and Phoenix Is. not part of the Kiribati Republic keep 10ʰ and 11ʰ, respectively, slow on UTC.

LIST I — (*continued*)

	h	m		h	m
Lebanon*	02		Irkutsk, Bratsk, Ulan-Ude	08	
Lesotho	02		Tiksi, Yakutsk, Chita	09	
Libya	02		Vladivostok, Khabarovsk, Okhotsk		
Liechtenstein*	01		Sakhalin Island	10	
Lithuania*†	02		Petropavlovsk-K., Magadan, Anadyr		
Lord Howe Island*	10	30	Kuril Islands	11	
Luxembourg*†	01		Rwanda	02	
Macau	08		Ryukyu Islands	09	
Macedonia*, former Yugoslav Republic					
Macias Nguema (Fernando Póo) ...	01		Santa Cruz Islands	11	
Madagascar, Democratic Republic of	03		Sardinia*†	01	
Malawi	02		Saudi Arabia	03	
Malaysia, Malaya, Sabah, Sarawak ...	08		Schouten Islands	09	
Maldives, Republic of The	05		Serbia*	01	
Malta*†	01		Seychelles	04	
Mariana Islands	10		Sicily*†	01	
Marshall Islands	12		Singapore	08	
Mauritius	04		Slovakia*†	01	
Moldova*	02		Slovenia*†	01	
Monaco*	01		Socotra	03	
Mongolia	08		Solomon Islands	11	
Montenegro*	01		Somalia Republic	03	
Mozambique	02		South Africa, Republic of	02	
Namibia*	01		Spain*†	01	
Nauru	12		Spanish Possessions in North Africa*	01	
Nepal	05	45	Spitsbergen (Svalbard)*	01	
Netherlands, The*†	01		Sri Lanka	05	30
New Caledonia	11		Sudan, Republic of	03	
New Zealand*	12		Swaziland	02	
Nicobar Islands	05	30	Sweden*†	01	
Niger	01		Switzerland*	01	
Nigeria, Republic of	01		Syria (Syrian Arab Republic)*	02	
Norfolk Island	11	30			
Norway*	01		Taiwan	08	
Novaya Zemlya	03		Tajikistan	05	
Okinawa	09		Tanzania	03	
Oman	04		Thailand	07	
			Timor-Leste	09	
Pagalu (Annobon Islands)	01		Tonga	13	
Pakistan	05		Tunisia	01	
Palau Islands	09		Turkey*	02	
Papua New Guinea	10		Turkmenistan	05	
Pescadores Islands	08		Tuvalu	12	
Philippine Republic	08				
Poland*†	01		Uganda	03	
			Ukraine*	02	
Qatar	03		United Arab Emirates	04	
Reunion	04		Uzbekistan	05	
Romania*†	02				
Russia [1]*			Vanuatu, Republic of	11	
Kaliningrad	02		Vietnam, Socialist Republic of	07	
Moscow, St. Petersburg, Volgograd					
Arkhangelsk, Astrakhan, Samara	03		Yemen	03	
Ekaterinburg, Ufa, Perm, Novyy Port	05				
Omsk, Novosibirsk, Tomsk	06		Zambia, Republic of	02	
Norilsk, Krasnoyarsk, Dikson	07		Zimbabwe	02	

---

* Daylight-saving time may be kept in these places.   † For Summer time dates see List II footnotes.
[1] The boundaries between the zones are irregular; listed are chief towns in each zone.

LIST II — PLACES NORMALLY KEEPING UTC

Ascension Island	Ghana	Irish Republic*†	Morocco*	Sierra Leone
Burkina-Faso	Great Britain†	Ivory Coast	Portugal*†	Togo Republic
Canary Islands*†	Guinea-Bissau	Liberia	Principe	Tristan da Cunha
Channel Islands†	Guinea Republic	Madeira*†	St. Helena	
Faeroes*, The	Iceland	Mali	São Tomé	
Gambia, The	Ireland, Northern†	Mauritania	Senegal	

* Daylight-saving time may be kept in these places.
† Summer time (daylight-saving time), one hour in advance of UTC, will be kept from 2012 March 25^d 01^h to October 28^d 01^h UTC (Ninth Summer Time Directive of the European Union). Ratification by member countries has not been verified.

LIST III — PLACES SLOW ON UTC (WEST OF GREENWICH)

The times given ⎱ subtracted from UTC to give Standard Time
below should be ⎰ added to Standard Time to give UTC.

	h m		h m
Argentina	03	Canada (continued)	
Austral (Tubuai) Islands[1]	10	Prince Edward Island*	04
Azores*†	01	Quebec, east of long. W. 63°	04
		west of long. W. 63°* ...	05
Bahamas*	05	Saskatchewan	06
Barbados	04	Yukon*	08
Belize	06	Cape Verde Islands	01
Bermuda*	04	Cayman Islands	05
Bolivia	04	Chile*	04
Brazil		Colombia	05
Fernando de Noronha I., Trindade I.,		Cook Islands	10
Oceanic Is.	02	Costa Rica	06
N and NE coastal states, Bahia,		Cuba*	05
Tocantins, Goiás*, Brasilia*,		Curaçao Island	04
Minas Gerais*, Espirito Santo*,			
S and E coastal states*	03	Dominican Republic	04
Mato Grosso do Sul*, Mato Grosso*,			
Rondônia, Amazonas, Roraima, Acre	04	Easter Island (I. de Pascua)*	06
British Antarctic Territory[2,3]	03	Ecuador	05
		El Salvador	06
Canada[3‡]			
Alberta*	07	Falkland Islands*	04
British Columbia*	08	Fernando de Noronha Island	02
Labrador*	04	French Guiana	03
Manitoba*	06		
New Brunswick*	04	Galápagos Islands	06
Newfoundland*	03 30	Greenland	
Nunavut*		Danmarkshavn, Mesters Vig	00
east of long. W. 85°	05	General*	03
long. W. 85° to W. 102°	06	Scoresby Sound*	01
west of long. W. 102°	07	Thule*, Pituffik*	04
Northwest Territories*	07	Grenada	04
Nova Scotia*	04	Guadeloupe	04
Ontario, east of long. W. 90°*	05	Guatemala	06
Ontario, west of long. W. 90°* ...	06	Guyana, Republic of	04

* Daylight-saving time may be kept in these places.   ‡ Dates for DST are given at the end of List III.
[1] This is the legal standard time, but local mean time is generally used.
[2] Stations may use UTC.
[3] Some areas may keep another time zone.

LIST III — (continued)

	h	m			h	m
Haiti	05		United States of America ‡(continued)			
Honduras	06		Idaho, southern part	07	
			northern part	08	
Jamaica	05		Illinois	06	
Johnston Island	10		Indiana ²	05	
Juan Fernandez Islands*	04		Iowa	06	
			Kansas ²	06	
Leeward Islands	04		Kentucky, eastern part	05	
			western part	06	
Marquesas Islands	09	30	Louisiana	06	
Martinique	04		Maine	05	
Mexico			Maryland	05	
General*	06		Massachusetts	05	
Sonora, Sinaloa*, Nayarit*,			Michigan ²	05	
Chihuahua*, Southern District			Minnesota	06	
of Lower California*	07		Mississippi	06	
Northern District of Lower California*	08		Missouri	06	
Midway Islands	11		Montana	07	
			Nebraska, eastern part	06	
Nicaragua	06		western part	07	
Niue	11		Nevada	08	
			New Hampshire	05	
Panama, Republic of	05		New Jersey	05	
Paraguay*	04		New Mexico	07	
Peru	05		New York	05	
Pitcairn Island	08		North Carolina	05	
Puerto Rico	04		North Dakota, eastern part	06	
			western part	07	
St. Pierre and Miquelon*	03		Ohio	05	
Samoa*	11		Oklahoma	06	
Society Islands	10		Oregon ²	08	
South Georgia	02		Pennsylvania	05	
Suriname	03		Rhode Island	05	
			South Carolina	05	
Trindade Island, South Atlantic ...	02		South Dakota, eastern part	06	
Trinidad and Tobago	04		western part	07	
Tuamotu Archipelago	10		Tennessee, eastern part	05	
Tubuai (Austral) Islands	10		western part	06	
Turks and Caicos Islands*	05		Texas ²	06	
			Utah	07	
United States of America ‡			Vermont	05	
Alabama	06		Virginia	05	
Alaska	09		Washington D.C.	05	
Aleutian Islands, east of W. 169° 30'	09		Washington	08	
Aleutian Islands, west of W. 169° 30'	10		West Virginia	05	
Arizona ¹	07		Wisconsin	06	
Arkansas	06		Wyoming	07	
California	08		Uruguay*	03	
Colorado	07				
Connecticut	05		Venezuela	04	30
Delaware	05		Virgin Islands	04	
District of Columbia	05				
Florida ²	05		Windward Islands	04	
Georgia	05				
Hawaii ¹	10				

* Daylight-saving time may be kept in these places.

‡ Daylight-saving (Summer) time, one hour fast on the time given, is kept during 2012 from March 11 (second Sunday) to November 4 (first Sunday), changing at 02ʰ 00ᵐ local clock time.

¹ Exempt from keeping daylight-saving time, except for a portion of Arizona.

² A small portion of the state is in another time zone.

NORTHERN STARS

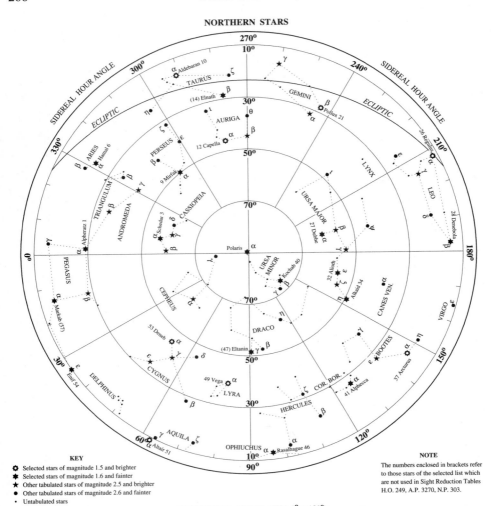

KEY

⬡ Selected stars of magnitude 1.5 and brighter
✪ Selected stars of magnitude 1.6 and fainter
★ Other tabulated stars of magnitude 2.5 and brighter
● Other tabulated stars of magnitude 2.6 and fainter
· Untabulated stars

NOTE

The numbers enclosed in brackets refer
to those stars of the selected list which
are not used in Sight Reduction Tables
H.O. 249, A.P. 3270, N.P. 303.

EQUATORIAL STARS (SHA 0° to 180°)

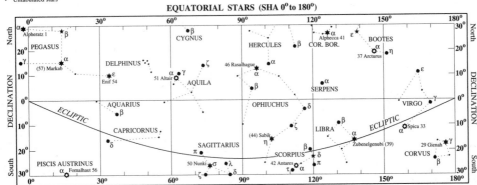

SIDEREAL HOUR ANGLE

SOUTHERN STARS

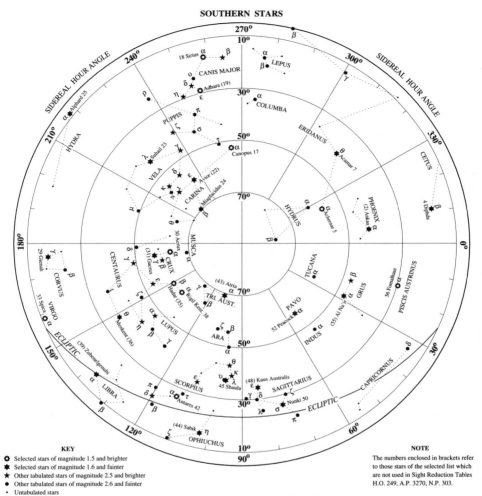

EQUATORIAL STARS (SHA 180° to 360°)

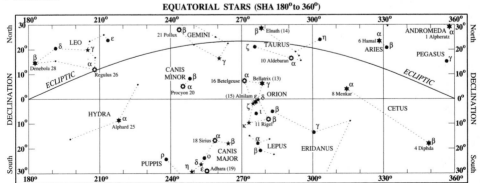

SIDEREAL HOUR ANGLE

Mag.	Name and Number		SHA						Declination						
			JAN.	FEB.	MAR.	APR.	MAY	JUNE		JAN.	FEB.	MAR.	APR.	MAY	JUNE
		°	′	′	′	′	′	′	°	′	′	′	′	′	′
3·2	γ Cephei	5	02·5	03·0	03·2	02·9	02·3	01·4	N 77	42·4	42·3	42·1	42·0	41·9	41·9
2·5	α Pegasi 57	13	39·5	39·6	39·5	39·4	39·2	39·0	N 15	16·4	16·3	16·2	16·2	16·3	16·4
2·4	β Pegasi	13	54·6	54·6	54·6	54·5	54·2	54·0	N 28	09·1	09·0	08·9	08·9	08·9	09·0
1·2	α Piscis Aust. 56	15	25·3	25·3	25·3	25·1	24·9	24·7	S 29	33·6	33·5	33·4	33·3	33·2	33·1
2·1	β Gruis	19	09·4	09·4	09·3	09·2	08·9	08·6	S 46	49·4	49·3	49·2	49·0	48·9	48·8
2·9	α Tucanæ	25	10·5	10·5	10·4	10·2	09·8	09·4	S 60	12·1	11·9	11·8	11·6	11·5	11·4
1·7	α Gruis 55	27	45·3	45·3	45·2	45·0	44·7	44·4	S 46	54·2	54·1	54·0	53·8	53·7	53·7
2·9	δ Capricorni	33	04·5	04·4	04·3	04·2	03·9	03·7	S 16	04·3	04·3	04·3	04·2	04·1	04·0
2·4	ε Pegasi 54	33	48·4	48·3	48·3	48·1	47·9	47·6	N 9	55·9	55·9	55·8	55·9	55·9	56·0
2·9	β Aquarii	36	57·1	57·1	57·0	56·8	56·6	56·4	S 5	31·0	31·0	31·0	31·0	30·9	30·8
2·4	α Cephei	40	17·5	17·5	17·3	17·0	16·6	16·2	N 62	38·4	38·3	38·1	38·1	38·1	38·2
2·5	ε Cygni	48	19·7	19·6	19·5	19·3	19·0	18·8	N 34	01·1	01·0	00·9	00·8	00·9	01·0
1·3	α Cygni 53	49	32·6	32·6	32·4	32·2	31·9	31·6	N 45	19·6	19·4	19·3	19·3	19·3	19·5
3·1	α Indi	50	24·0	23·9	23·7	23·4	23·1	22·8	S 47	14·9	14·8	14·7	14·6	14·6	14·5
1·9	α Pavonis 52	53	21·4	21·2	21·0	20·6	20·2	19·9	S 56	41·7	41·6	41·5	41·4	41·3	41·3
2·2	γ Cygni	54	20·3	20·2	20·1	19·8	19·6	19·3	N 40	17·9	17·7	17·6	17·6	17·7	17·8
0·8	α Aquilæ 51	62	09·5	09·4	09·3	09·0	08·8	08·6	N 8	54·1	54·0	54·0	54·0	54·1	54·2
2·7	γ Aquilæ	63	17·6	17·5	17·3	17·1	16·9	16·7	N 10	38·6	38·6	38·5	38·5	38·6	38·7
2·9	δ Cygni	63	40·0	39·9	39·7	39·5	39·2	39·0	N 45	09·7	09·6	09·5	09·5	09·5	09·7
3·1	β Cygni	67	12·1	12·0	11·8	11·5	11·3	11·1	N 27	59·2	59·1	59·0	59·0	59·1	59·2
2·9	π Sagittarii	72	22·9	22·7	22·5	22·3	22·0	21·9	S 21	00·2	00·2	00·1	00·1	00·1	00·0
3·0	ζ Aquilæ	73	30·7	30·5	30·3	30·1	29·9	29·7	N 13	52·9	52·9	52·8	52·8	52·9	53·0
2·6	ζ Sagittarii	74	09·4	09·3	09·0	08·8	08·5	08·3	S 29	51·7	51·6	51·6	51·6	51·5	51·5
2·0	σ Sagittarii 50	75	59·9	59·7	59·5	59·2	59·0	58·8	S 26	16·8	16·8	16·8	16·7	16·7	16·7
0·0	α Lyræ 49	80	40·0	39·9	39·7	39·4	39·2	39·0	N 38	47·7	47·6	47·5	47·5	47·6	47·8
2·8	λ Sagittarii	82	49·3	49·2	48·9	48·7	48·4	48·3	S 25	24·8	24·8	24·8	24·8	24·7	24·7
1·9	ε Sagittarii 48	83	45·5	45·3	45·0	44·8	44·5	44·3	S 34	22·6	22·6	22·5	22·5	22·5	22·5
2·7	δ Sagittarii	84	33·6	33·4	33·1	32·9	32·6	32·5	S 29	49·3	49·2	49·2	49·2	49·2	49·2
3·0	γ Sagittarii	88	21·3	21·1	20·9	20·6	20·4	20·2	S 30	25·3	25·3	25·3	25·3	25·3	25·3
2·2	γ Draconis 47	90	47·1	46·9	46·6	46·3	46·0	45·9	N 51	29·2	29·0	29·0	29·0	29·1	29·3
2·8	β Ophiuchi	93	59·0	58·9	58·6	58·4	58·2	58·1	N 4	33·8	33·7	33·7	33·7	33·7	33·8
2·4	κ Scorpii	94	10·2	10·0	09·7	09·4	09·2	09·0	S 39	02·0	02·0	02·0	02·0	02·0	02·1
1·9	θ Scorpii	95	27·3	27·0	26·7	26·4	26·2	26·0	S 43	00·2	00·1	00·1	00·1	00·2	00·2
2·1	α Ophiuchi 46	96	07·7	07·5	07·3	07·0	06·9	06·8	N 12	33·1	33·0	32·9	33·0	33·1	33·2
1·6	λ Scorpii 45	96	23·6	23·4	23·1	22·8	22·6	22·4	S 37	06·6	06·6	06·6	06·6	06·6	06·7
3·0	α Aræ	96	48·5	48·2	47·8	47·5	47·2	47·0	S 49	52·9	52·9	52·9	52·9	53·0	53·0
2·7	υ Scorpii	97	06·3	06·0	05·7	05·5	05·5	05·1	S 37	18·2	18·1	18·2	18·2	18·2	18·2
2·8	β Draconis	97	19·8	19·6	19·3	19·0	18·7	18·6	N 52	17·4	17·3	17·3	17·3	17·4	17·6
2·8	β Aræ	98	25·5	25·2	24·8	24·4	24·1	24·0	S 55	32·3	32·2	32·2	32·2	32·3	32·4
Var.‡	α Herculis	101	12·1	11·9	11·7	11·5	11·3	11·2	N 14	22·6	22·5	22·4	22·5	22·6	22·7
2·4	η Ophiuchi 44	102	14·0	13·7	13·5	13·3	13·1	13·0	S 15	44·3	44·3	44·4	44·4	44·4	44·3
3·1	ζ Aræ	105	05·7	05·4	05·0	04·6	04·3	04·2	S 56	00·3	00·3	00·3	00·3	00·4	00·5
2·3	ε Scorpii	107	15·8	15·5	15·3	15·0	14·8	14·7	S 34	18·8	18·8	18·8	18·8	18·9	18·9
1·9	α Triang. Aust. 43	107	30·9	30·4	29·8	29·2	28·8	28·6	S 69	02·7	02·6	02·7	02·7	02·8	03·0
2·8	ζ Herculis	109	34·0	33·8	33·5	33·3	33·2	33·1	N 31	34·7	34·6	34·6	34·7	34·8	34·9
2·6	ζ Ophiuchi	110	32·6	32·4	32·2	32·0	31·8	31·7	S 10	35·4	35·5	35·5	35·5	35·5	35·5
2·8	τ Scorpii	110	50·4	50·2	49·9	49·7	49·5	49·4	S 28	14·3	14·4	14·4	14·4	14·5	14·5
2·8	β Herculis	112	19·0	18·8	18·5	18·3	18·2	18·1	N 21	27·7	27·6	27·6	27·6	27·7	27·8
1·0	α Scorpii 42	112	27·7	27·5	27·2	27·0	26·8	26·7	S 26	27·4	27·4	27·5	27·5	27·5	27·6
2·7	η Draconis	113	58·1	57·8	57·4	57·1	56·9	56·9	N 61	29·0	28·9	28·9	29·0	29·1	29·3
2·7	δ Ophiuchi	116	15·3	15·1	14·8	14·6	14·5	14·5	S 3	43·5	43·6	43·6	43·6	43·6	43·5
2·6	β Scorpii	118	27·8	27·6	27·4	27·1	27·0	26·9	S 19	50·2	50·3	50·3	50·3	50·4	50·4
2·3	δ Scorpii	119	44·2	44·0	43·7	43·5	43·4	43·3	S 22	39·3	39·3	39·4	39·4	39·4	39·4
2·9	π Scorpii	120	06·2	05·9	05·7	05·5	05·3	05·3	S 26	08·8	08·9	08·9	09·0	09·0	09·0
2·8	β Trianguli Aust.	120	56·7	56·3	55·8	55·4	55·2	55·1	S 63	27·8	27·8	27·9	28·0	28·1	28·2
2·6	α Serpentis	123	47·0	46·8	46·6	46·4	46·3	46·3	N 6	23·2	23·1	23·1	23·1	23·2	23·2
2·8	γ Lupi	125	60·7	60·4	60·1	59·9	59·7	59·7	S 41	12·3	12·3	12·4	12·4	12·5	12·6
2·2	α Coronæ Bor. 41	126	12·0	11·8	11·6	11·4	11·3	11·3	N 26	40·3	40·2	40·2	40·2	40·3	40·5

‡ 2·9 — 3·6

Mag.	Name and Number		SHA							Declination					
			JULY	AUG.	SEPT.	OCT.	NOV.	DEC.		JULY	AUG.	SEPT.	OCT.	NOV.	DEC.
		° ′	′	′	′	′	′	′	° ′	′	′	′	′	′	′
3·2	γ Cephei		4	60·6	60·1	59·8	59·9	60·4	61·0	N 77	42·0	42·1	42·3	42·5	42·6	42·7
2·5	Markab 57		13	38·7	38·6	38·5	38·5	38·6	38·7	N 15	16·5	16·6	16·7	16·7	16·7	16·7
2·4	Scheat		13	53·8	53·6	53·5	53·5	53·6	53·7	N 28	09·1	09·2	09·4	09·5	09·5	09·5
1·2	Fomalhaut 56		15	24·4	24·3	24·2	24·2	24·3	24·4	S 29	33·0	33·0	33·1	33·1	33·2	33·2
2·1	β Gruis		19	08·3	08·1	08·0	08·1	08·3	08·4	S 46	48·8	48·8	48·9	49·0	49·1	49·1
2·9	α Tucanæ		25	09·1	08·8	08·8	08·9	09·2	09·4	S 60	11·4	11·5	11·6	11·8	11·8	11·8
1·7	Al Na'ir 55		27	44·1	44·0	43·9	44·0	44·2	44·4	S 46	53·7	53·7	53·8	53·9	54·0	54·0
2·9	δ Capricorni		33	03·5	03·4	03·4	03·4	03·6	03·6	S 16	04·0	03·9	03·9	04·0	04·0	04·0
2·4	Enif 54		33	47·4	47·3	47·3	47·4	47·5	47·6	N 9	56·1	56·2	56·3	56·3	56·3	56·3
2·9	β Aquarii		36	56·2	56·1	56·1	56·2	56·3	56·4	S 5	30·7	30·7	30·6	30·6	30·7	30·7
2·4	Alderamin		40	16·0	15·9	16·0	16·2	16·6	16·9	N 62	38·4	38·5	38·7	38·8	38·9	38·8
2·5	ε Cygni		48	18·6	18·6	18·6	18·8	18·9	19·0	N 34	01·2	01·3	01·4	01·5	01·5	01·5
1·3	Deneb 53		49	31·4	31·4	31·5	31·7	31·9	32·0	N 45	19·6	19·8	19·9	20·0	20·0	20·0
3·1	α Indi		50	22·6	22·5	22·6	22·7	22·9	23·0	S 47	14·6	14·6	14·7	14·8	14·8	14·8
1·9	Peacock 52		53	19·6	19·5	19·6	19·9	20·1	20·3	S 56	41·4	41·5	41·6	41·7	41·7	41·6
2·2	γ Cygni		54	19·2	19·2	19·3	19·4	19·6	19·7	N 40	18·0	18·1	18·2	18·3	18·3	18·2
0·8	Altair 51		62	08·5	08·5	08·6	08·7	08·8	08·9	N 8	54·3	54·4	54·4	54·5	54·4	54·4
2·7	γ Aquilæ		63	16·6	16·6	16·6	16·8	16·9	17·0	N 10	38·8	38·9	39·0	39·0	39·0	38·9
2·9	δ Cygni		63	38·8	38·9	39·0	39·2	39·4	39·5	N 45	09·8	10·0	10·1	10·2	10·1	10·0
3·1	Albireo		67	11·0	11·0	11·1	11·3	11·4	11·5	N 27	59·4	59·5	59·6	59·6	59·6	59·5
2·9	π Sagittarii		72	21·7	21·7	21·8	22·0	22·1	22·1	S 21	00·0	00·0	00·0	00·0	00·0	00·0
3·0	ζ Aquilæ		73	29·6	29·6	29·7	29·9	30·0	30·0	N 13	53·1	53·2	53·3	53·3	53·3	53·2
2·6	ζ Sagittarii		74	08·2	08·2	08·3	08·4	08·6	08·6	S 29	51·5	51·6	51·6	51·6	51·6	51·6
2·0	Nunki 50		75	58·7	58·7	58·8	59·0	59·1	59·1	S 26	16·7	16·7	16·7	16·7	16·7	16·7
0·0	Vega 49		80	39·0	39·0	39·2	39·4	39·5	39·6	N 38	47·9	48·1	48·1	48·1	48·1	48·0
2·8	λ Sagittarii		82	48·2	48·2	48·3	48·5	48·6	48·6	S 25	24·7	24·7	24·7	24·7	24·7	24·7
1·9	Kaus Australis 48		83	44·2	44·3	44·4	44·6	44·7	44·7	S 34	22·6	22·6	22·6	22·6	22·6	22·6
2·7	δ Sagittarii		84	32·4	32·4	32·5	32·7	32·8	32·8	S 29	49·2	49·2	49·3	49·3	49·2	49·2
3·0	γ Sagittarii		88	20·1	20·2	20·3	20·4	20·5	20·5	S 30	25·3	25·3	25·3	25·3	25·3	25·3
2·2	Eltanin 47		90	45·9	46·1	46·3	46·6	46·8	46·8	N 51	29·5	29·6	29·7	29·6	29·5	29·4
2·8	β Ophiuchi		93	58·1	58·1	58·3	58·4	58·5	58·4	N 4	33·9	34·0	34·0	34·0	33·9	33·9
2·4	κ Scorpii		94	08·9	09·0	09·1	09·3	09·4	09·4	S 39	02·1	02·1	02·2	02·1	02·1	02·0
1·9	θ Scorpii		95	25·9	26·0	26·2	26·3	26·4	26·4	S 43	00·3	00·3	00·3	00·3	00·3	00·3
2·1	Rasalhague 46		96	06·7	06·8	06·9	07·1	07·1	07·1	N 12	33·3	33·3	33·4	33·3	33·3	33·2
1·6	Shaula 45		96	22·4	22·4	22·6	22·8	22·8	22·8	S 37	06·7	06·7	06·7	06·7	06·7	06·6
3·0	α Aræ		96	47·0	47·1	47·3	47·5	47·6	47·5	S 49	53·1	53·2	53·2	53·2	53·1	53·0
2·7	υ Scorpii		97	05·0	05·1	05·3	05·4	05·5	05·5	S 37	18·3	18·3	18·3	18·3	18·2	18·2
2·8	β Draconis		97	18·7	18·8	19·1	19·4	19·6	19·6	N 52	17·8	17·9	17·9	17·9	17·8	17·6
2·8	β Aræ		98	23·9	24·0	24·2	24·5	24·6	24·6	S 55	32·5	32·5	32·6	32·5	32·4	32·3
Var.‡	α Herculis		101	11·2	11·3	11·4	11·4	11·5	11·6	N 14	22·8	22·8	22·9	22·8	22·8	22·7
2·4	Sabik 44		102	13·0	13·0	13·1	13·3	13·3	13·3	S 15	44·3	44·3	44·3	44·3	44·3	44·3
3·1	ζ Aræ		105	04·2	04·3	04·5	04·8	04·9	04·8	S 56	00·6	00·7	00·7	00·6	00·5	00·4
2·3	ε Scorpii		107	14·7	14·8	14·9	15·1	15·1	15·0	S 34	18·9	18·9	18·9	18·9	18·9	18·8
1·9	Atria 43		107	28·7	28·9	29·3	29·7	29·8	29·7	S 69	03·1	03·2	03·2	03·1	03·0	02·8
2·8	ζ Herculis		109	33·1	33·3	33·4	33·4	33·6	33·7	N 31	35·0	35·1	35·1	35·1	35·0	34·8
2·6	ζ Ophiuchi		110	31·7	31·8	31·9	32·0	32·1	32·0	S 10	35·4	35·4	35·4	35·4	35·4	35·5
2·8	τ Scorpii		110	49·4	49·5	49·7	49·8	49·8	49·7	S 28	14·5	14·5	14·5	14·4	14·4	14·4
2·8	β Herculis		112	18·2	18·3	18·4	18·5	18·6	18·5	N 21	27·9	28·0	28·0	28·0	27·9	27·8
1·0	Antares 42		112	26·7	26·8	27·0	27·1	27·1	27·0	S 26	27·6	27·6	27·5	27·5	27·5	27·5
2·7	η Draconis		113	57·0	57·3	57·7	58·0	58·2	58·2	N 61	29·4	29·5	29·5	29·4	29·3	29·1
2·7	δ Ophiuchi		116	14·5	14·5	14·7	14·8	14·8	14·7	S 3	43·5	43·5	43·4	43·4	43·5	43·5
2·6	β Scorpii		118	27·0	27·0	27·2	27·3	27·3	27·2	S 19	50·4	50·3	50·3	50·3	50·3	50·3
2·3	Dschubba		119	43·3	43·4	43·5	43·7	43·7	43·6	S 22	39·4	39·4	39·4	39·4	39·4	39·4
2·9	π Scorpii		120	05·3	05·4	05·5	05·6	05·6	05·5	S 26	09·0	09·0	09·0	08·9	08·9	08·9
2·8	β Trianguli Aust.		120	55·2	55·4	55·7	56·0	56·0	55·8	S 63	28·3	28·3	28·3	28·2	28·1	28·0
2·6	α Serpentis		123	46·3	46·4	46·5	46·6	46·6	46·5	N 6	23·3	23·3	23·3	23·3	23·3	23·2
2·8	γ Lupi		125	59·7	59·8	60·0	60·1	60·1	60·0	S 41	12·6	12·6	12·6	12·5	12·5	12·4
2·2	Alphecca 41		126	11·3	11·5	11·6	11·7	11·7	11·6	N 26	40·6	40·6	40·6	40·5	40·4	40·3

‡ 2·9 — 3·6

Mag.	Name and Number	No.	SHA °	SHA JAN	FEB	MAR	APR	MAY	JUNE	Dec.	Dec JAN	FEB	MAR	APR	MAY	JUNE
3·1	γ Ursæ Minoris		129	49·8	49·3	48·8	48·4	48·3	48·5	N 71	47·1	47·1	47·1	47·2	47·4	47·5
2·9	γ Trianguli Aust.		129	59·1	58·5	58·0	57·6	57·4	57·3	S 68	43·1	43·2	43·2	43·4	43·5	43·6
2·6	β Libræ		130	35·0	34·8	34·6	34·4	34·3	34·3	S 9	25·6	25·7	25·8	25·8	25·8	25·7
2·7	β Lupi		135	09·9	09·6	09·3	09·1	09·0	09·0	S 43	10·8	10·8	10·9	11·0	11·1	11·2
2·8	α Libræ	39	137	06·6	06·4	06·2	06·0	05·9	05·9	S 16	05·5	05·6	05·6	05·7	05·7	05·7
2·1	β Ursæ Minoris	40	137	20·3	19·7	19·2	18·8	18·8	19·1	N 74	06·0	06·0	06·0	06·2	06·3	06·5
2·4	ε Bootis		138	37·2	37·0	36·8	36·6	36·6	36·6	N 27	01·2	01·2	01·2	01·2	01·3	01·4
2·3	α Lupi		139	18·7	18·4	18·1	17·9	17·8	17·8	S 47	26·2	26·3	26·4	26·5	26·6	26·7
−0·3	α Centauri	38	139	53·3	52·8	52·5	52·2	52·1	52·2	S 60	52·8	52·9	53·0	53·1	53·3	53·4
2·3	η Centauri		140	55·6	55·3	55·1	54·9	54·8	54·8	S 42	12·5	12·6	12·6	12·8	12·8	12·9
3·0	γ Bootis		141	51·5	51·2	51·0	50·9	50·8	50·9	N 38	15·1	15·0	15·0	15·1	15·2	15·4
0·0	α Bootis	37	145	56·7	56·4	56·3	56·1	56·1	56·1	N 19	07·0	06·9	06·9	06·9	07·0	07·1
2·1	θ Centauri	36	148	08·8	08·5	08·3	08·2	08·1	08·1	S 36	25·6	25·7	25·8	25·9	26·0	26·1
0·6	β Centauri	35	148	49·4	49·0	48·7	48·4	48·4	48·5	S 60	25·6	25·7	25·8	26·0	26·1	26·2
2·6	ζ Centauri		150	55·2	54·9	54·7	54·5	54·5	54·5	S 47	20·7	20·8	20·9	21·0	21·1	21·2
2·7	η Bootis		151	10·9	10·7	10·5	10·4	10·4	10·4	N 18	20·0	20·0	20·0	20·0	20·1	20·2
1·9	η Ursæ Majoris	34	152	59·7	59·4	59·1	59·0	59·0	59·2	N 49	14·8	14·8	14·9	15·0	15·1	15·2
2·3	ε Centauri		154	49·8	49·4	49·2	49·0	49·0	49·1	S 53	31·5	31·6	31·7	31·9	32·0	32·1
1·0	α Virginis	33	158	32·3	32·1	31·9	31·8	31·8	31·8	S 11	13·5	13·6	13·7	13·7	13·7	13·7
2·3	ζ Ursæ Majoris		158	53·7	53·4	53·2	53·1	53·1	53·3	N 54	51·4	51·4	51·4	51·6	51·7	51·8
2·8	ι Centauri		159	40·5	40·2	40·0	39·9	39·9	40·0	S 36	46·5	46·6	46·7	46·8	46·9	46·9
2·8	ε Virginis		164	18·1	17·9	17·7	17·6	17·7	17·7	N 10	53·5	53·4	53·4	53·4	53·5	53·5
2·9	α Canum Venat.		165	50·9	50·6	50·5	50·4	50·5	50·6	N 38	14·9	14·8	14·9	15·0	15·1	15·2
1·8	ε Ursæ Majoris	32	166	21·4	21·1	20·9	20·8	20·9	21·1	N 55	53·3	53·3	53·4	53·5	53·6	53·7
1·3	β Crucis		167	53·0	52·6	52·4	52·3	52·4	52·5	S 59	45·1	45·2	45·4	45·6	45·7	45·8
2·9	γ Virginis		169	25·6	25·4	25·3	25·2	25·2	25·3	S 1	31·1	31·2	31·2	31·2	31·2	31·2
2·2	γ Centauri		169	26·8	26·5	26·3	26·2	26·3	26·4	S 49	01·4	01·6	01·7	01·9	02·0	02·0
2·7	α Muscæ		170	30·6	30·2	29·9	29·8	29·9	30·2	S 69	11·9	12·0	12·2	12·4	12·6	12·6
2·7	β Corvi		171	14·3	14·1	13·9	13·9	13·9	14·0	S 23	27·8	27·9	28·0	28·1	28·2	28·2
1·6	γ Crucis	31	172	01·9	01·5	01·3	01·3	01·4	01·5	S 57	10·7	10·8	11·0	11·2	11·3	11·3
1·3	α Crucis	30	173	10·2	09·8	09·6	09·6	09·7	09·9	S 63	09·8	09·9	10·1	10·3	10·4	10·5
2·6	γ Corvi	29	175	53·2	53·0	52·9	52·8	52·9	53·0	S 17	36·6	36·7	36·8	36·9	36·9	36·9
2·6	δ Centauri		177	44·7	44·4	44·3	44·2	44·3	44·5	S 50	47·3	47·4	47·6	47·7	47·8	47·9
2·4	γ Ursæ Majoris		181	22·7	22·4	22·3	22·3	22·4	22·6	N 53	37·3	37·3	37·4	37·5	37·6	37·7
2·1	β Leonis	28	182	34·5	34·3	34·2	34·2	34·3	34·4	N 14	30·0	30·0	30·0	30·0	30·1	30·1
2·6	δ Leonis		191	18·3	18·2	18·1	18·1	18·2	18·3	N 20	27·2	27·1	27·2	27·2	27·3	27·3
3·0	ψ Ursæ Majoris		192	24·4	24·2	24·1	24·2	24·3	24·5	N 44	25·6	25·6	25·7	25·8	25·9	26·0
1·8	α Ursæ Majoris	27	193	52·4	52·1	52·1	52·2	52·4	52·7	N 61	40·8	40·8	41·0	41·1	41·2	41·2
2·4	β Ursæ Majoris		194	21·0	20·7	20·7	20·7	20·9	21·2	N 56	18·7	18·7	18·8	19·0	19·1	19·1
2·7	μ Velorum		198	10·0	09·8	09·8	09·9	10·0	10·2	S 49	29·0	29·2	29·4	29·5	29·6	29·6
2·8	θ Carinæ		199	08·4	08·1	08·1	08·3	08·5	08·8	S 64	27·4	27·6	27·8	27·9	28·0	28·0
2·3	γ Leonis		204	49·9	49·8	49·8	49·8	49·9	50·0	N 19	46·6	46·5	46·5	46·6	46·6	46·7
1·4	α Leonis	26	207	44·3	44·2	44·1	44·2	44·3	44·4	N 11	54·3	54·2	54·2	54·2	54·3	54·3
3·0	ε Leonis		213	21·4	21·3	21·3	21·4	21·5	21·6	N 23	42·8	42·8	42·9	42·9	42·9	43·0
3·1	N Velorum		217	05·4	05·3	05·4	05·6	05·8	06·1	S 57	05·3	05·5	05·6	05·8	05·8	05·8
2·0	α Hydræ	25	217	56·8	56·7	56·7	56·8	56·9	57·0	S 8	42·8	42·9	43·0	43·0	43·0	43·0
2·5	κ Velorum		219	22·0	21·9	22·0	22·2	22·4	22·5	S 55	03·8	04·0	04·1	04·2	04·3	04·2
2·2	ι Carinæ		220	38·0	37·9	38·0	38·3	38·6	38·8	S 59	19·6	19·8	19·9	20·0	20·1	20·0
1·7	β Carinæ	24	221	39·0	39·0	39·2	39·6	40·0	40·4	S 69	46·0	46·2	46·4	46·5	46·5	46·5
2·2	λ Velorum	23	222	52·8	52·7	52·8	52·9	53·1	53·2	S 43	29·0	29·1	29·3	29·4	29·4	29·3
3·1	ι Ursæ Majoris		224	58·8	58·7	58·8	58·9	59·1	59·2	N 47	59·4	59·4	59·5	59·6	59·6	59·6
2·0	δ Velorum		228	43·7	43·7	43·8	44·0	44·3	44·5	S 54	45·3	45·4	45·6	45·7	45·7	45·6
1·9	ε Carinæ	22	234	17·8	17·8	18·0	18·3	18·6	18·8	S 59	33·0	33·2	33·3	33·4	33·4	33·3
1·8	γ Velorum		237	30·8	30·8	30·9	31·1	31·3	31·5	S 47	22·4	22·6	22·7	22·8	22·8	22·7
2·8	ρ Puppis		237	58·5	58·5	58·6	58·7	58·9	59·0	S 24	20·5	20·6	20·7	20·8	20·7	20·7
2·3	ζ Puppis		238	59·2	59·2	59·4	59·5	59·7	59·8	S 40	02·4	02·5	02·6	02·7	02·7	02·6
1·1	β Geminorum	21	243	28·5	28·5	28·6	28·7	28·9	28·9	N 27	59·6	59·6	59·7	59·7	59·7	59·7
0·4	α Canis Minoris	20	245	00·4	00·4	00·5	00·6	00·7	00·8	N 5	11·4	11·4	11·4	11·4	11·4	11·4

Mag.	Name and Number	No.	SHA °	JULY	AUG.	SEPT.	OCT.	NOV.	DEC.	Declination	JULY	AUG.	SEPT.	OCT.	NOV.	DEC.
3·1	γ Ursæ Minoris		129	48·9	49·4	49·9	50·3	50·5	50·4	N 71	47·6	47·7	47·6	47·5	47·3	47·1
2·9	γ Trianguli Aust.		129	57·5	57·8	58·2	58·5	58·5	58·2	S 68	43·7	43·8	43·7	43·6	43·5	43·4
2·6	β Libræ		130	34·3	34·4	34·5	34·5	34·6	34·5	S 9	25·7	25·7	25·7	25·7	25·7	25·7
2·7	β Lupi		135	09·1	09·2	09·4	09·5	09·4	09·2	S 43	11·2	11·2	11·2	11·1	11·0	11·0
2·8	Zubenelgenubi	39	137	06·0	06·1	06·2	06·3	06·2	06·1	S 16	05·7	05·6	05·6	05·6	05·6	05·6
2·1	Kochab	40	137	19·6	20·2	20·7	21·1	21·2	21·0	N 74	06·5	06·5	06·4	06·3	06·1	05·9
2·4	ε Bootis		138	36·7	36·8	36·9	37·0	37·0	36·9	N 27	01·5	01·5	01·5	01·4	01·3	01·2
2·3	α Lupi		139	17·9	18·1	18·2	18·3	18·3	18·1	S 47	26·7	26·7	26·6	26·5	26·4	26·4
−0·3	Rigil Kent.	38	139	52·4	52·6	52·9	53·0	52·9	52·6	S 60	53·4	53·4	53·4	53·2	53·1	53·0
2·3	η Centauri		140	54·9	55·0	55·2	55·2	55·2	55·0	S 42	12·9	12·9	12·9	12·8	12·7	12·7
3·0	γ Bootis		141	51·0	51·1	51·3	51·4	51·4	51·2	N 38	15·4	15·4	15·4	15·3	15·1	15·0
0·0	Arcturus	37	145	56·2	56·3	56·4	56·5	56·4	56·3	N 19	07·2	07·2	07·2	07·1	07·0	06·8
2·1	Menkent	36	148	08·2	08·4	08·5	08·5	08·4	08·2	S 36	26·1	26·0	26·0	25·9	25·8	25·8
0·6	Hadar	35	148	48·6	48·9	49·1	49·2	49·1	48·7	S 60	26·3	26·3	26·2	26·1	25·9	25·9
2·6	ζ Centauri		150	54·6	54·8	54·9	55·0	54·9	54·6	S 47	21·2	21·2	21·1	21·0	20·9	20·9
2·7	η Bootis		151	10·5	10·6	10·7	10·8	10·7	10·5	N 18	20·2	20·2	20·2	20·1	20·0	19·9
1·9	Alkaid	34	152	59·3	59·5	59·7	59·8	59·7	59·5	N 49	15·3	15·3	15·2	15·0	14·9	14·7
2·3	ε Centauri		154	49·2	49·4	49·6	49·6	49·5	49·2	S 53	32·1	32·0	31·9	31·8	31·7	31·7
1·0	Spica	33	158	31·9	32·0	32·1	32·1	32·0	31·8	S 11	13·7	13·6	13·6	13·6	13·6	13·7
2·3	Mizar		158	53·5	53·7	53·9	53·9	53·8	53·6	N 54	51·8	51·8	51·7	51·5	51·3	51·2
2·8	ι Centauri		159	40·1	40·2	40·3	40·3	40·2	39·9	S 36	46·9	46·9	46·8	46·7	46·7	46·7
2·8	ε Virginis		164	17·8	17·9	17·9	17·9	17·8	17·6	N 10	53·6	53·6	53·5	53·5	53·4	53·3
2·9	Cor Caroli		165	50·7	50·8	50·9	50·9	50·8	50·5	N 38	15·2	15·2	15·1	15·0	14·8	14·7
1·8	Alioth	32	166	21·3	21·5	21·6	21·7	21·5	21·2	N 55	53·7	53·7	53·5	53·4	53·2	53·1
1·3	Mimosa		167	52·8	53·0	53·1	53·1	52·9	52·5	S 59	45·8	45·7	45·6	45·5	45·4	45·3
2·9	γ Virginis		169	25·4	25·5	25·5	25·5	25·4	25·1	S 1	31·1	31·1	31·1	31·1	31·2	31·3
2·2	Muhlifain		169	26·5	26·7	26·8	26·7	26·5	26·2	S 49	02·0	01·9	01·8	01·7	01·7	01·7
2·7	α Muscæ		170	30·5	30·9	31·1	31·0	30·7	30·2	S 69	12·6	12·6	12·4	12·3	12·2	12·2
2·7	β Corvi		171	14·1	14·2	14·2	14·2	14·0	13·8	S 23	28·1	28·1	28·0	28·0	28·0	28·0
1·6	Gacrux	31	172	01·7	01·9	02·0	02·0	01·8	01·4	S 57	11·3	11·3	11·1	11·0	10·9	10·9
1·3	Acrux	30	173	10·1	10·4	10·5	10·5	10·2	09·8	S 63	10·5	10·4	10·3	10·1	10·0	10·0
2·6	Gienah	29	175	53·0	53·1	53·1	53·1	52·9	52·7	S 17	36·8	36·8	36·7	36·7	36·7	36·8
2·6	δ Centauri		177	44·6	44·8	44·8	44·8	44·5	44·2	S 50	47·8	47·8	47·6	47·5	47·5	47·5
2·4	Phecda		181	22·8	22·9	23·0	22·9	22·7	22·4	N 53	37·7	37·6	37·4	37·3	37·1	37·0
2·1	Denebola	28	182	34·4	34·5	34·5	34·4	34·3	34·0	N 14	30·1	30·1	30·1	30·0	29·9	29·8
2·6	δ Leonis		191	18·4	18·4	18·4	18·3	18·1	17·8	N 20	27·3	27·3	27·2	27·2	27·0	26·9
3·0	ψ Ursæ Majoris		192	24·6	24·7	24·6	24·5	24·3	24·0	N 44	25·9	25·8	25·7	25·6	25·4	25·3
1·8	Dubhe	27	193	52·9	53·0	53·0	52·8	52·5	52·1	N 61	41·1	41·0	40·9	40·7	40·5	40·4
2·4	Merak		194	21·3	21·4	21·4	21·2	20·9	20·6	N 56	19·0	18·9	18·8	18·6	18·5	18·4
2·7	μ Velorum		198	10·4	10·4	10·4	10·3	10·0	09·7	S 49	29·5	29·4	29·2	29·1	29·1	29·2
2·8	θ Carinæ		199	09·1	09·2	09·2	09·0	08·6	08·1	S 64	28·0	27·8	27·7	27·6	27·5	27·6
2·3	Algeiba		204	50·1	50·1	50·0	49·9	49·7	49·4	N 19	46·7	46·6	46·6	46·5	46·4	46·3
1·4	Regulus	26	207	44·4	44·4	44·4	44·2	44·0	43·8	N 11	54·3	54·3	54·3	54·2	54·1	54·0
3·0	ε Leonis		213	21·6	21·6	21·5	21·4	21·1	20·9	N 23	43·0	42·9	42·9	42·8	42·7	42·6
3·1	N Velorum		217	06·2	06·3	06·1	05·9	05·5	05·2	S 57	05·6	05·5	05·4	05·3	05·3	05·4
2·0	Alphard	25	217	57·0	57·0	56·9	56·7	56·5	56·2	S 8	42·9	42·9	42·8	42·8	42·9	43·0
2·5	κ Velorum		219	22·7	22·8	22·6	22·4	22·0	21·7	S 55	04·1	04·0	03·8	03·7	03·8	03·9
2·2	ι Carinæ		220	39·0	39·0	38·9	38·6	38·2	37·8	S 59	19·9	19·8	19·6	19·6	19·6	19·7
1·7	Miaplacidus	24	221	40·7	40·7	40·5	40·1	39·6	39·1	S 69	46·4	46·2	46·1	46·0	46·0	46·1
2·2	Suhail	23	222	53·3	53·3	53·2	53·0	52·7	52·4	S 43	29·2	29·1	29·0	28·9	28·9	29·1
3·1	ι Ursæ Majoris		224	59·3	59·2	59·0	58·8	58·5	58·1	N 47	59·5	59·4	59·3	59·2	59·1	59·1
2·0	δ Velorum		228	44·6	44·6	44·4	44·1	43·8	43·5	S 54	45·3	45·3	45·2	45·2	45·2	45·2
1·9	Avior	22	234	18·9	18·9	18·7	18·3	17·9	17·6	S 59	33·2	33·0	32·9	32·8	32·9	33·0
1·8	γ Velorum		237	31·5	31·4	31·3	31·0	30·7	30·4	S 47	22·6	22·4	22·3	22·3	22·3	22·5
2·8	ρ Puppis		237	59·0	58·9	58·7	58·5	58·3	58·1	S 24	20·6	20·5	20·4	20·4	20·4	20·6
2·3	ζ Puppis		238	59·8	59·8	59·6	59·4	59·1	58·9	S 40	02·5	02·3	02·2	02·2	02·3	02·4
1·1	Pollux	21	243	28·9	28·7	28·6	28·3	28·1	27·8	N 27	59·6	59·6	59·6	59·5	59·5	59·4
0·4	Procyon	20	244	60·7	60·6	60·4	60·2	60·0	59·8	N 5	11·5	11·5	11·5	11·5	11·4	11·3

Mag.	Name and Number		SHA						Declination						
			JAN.	FEB.	MAR.	APR.	MAY	JUNE		JAN.	FEB.	MAR.	APR.	MAY	JUNE
1·6	α Geminorum		246 08·8	08·8	08·9	09·0	09·2	09·2	N 31	51·5	51·5	51·6	51·6	51·6	51·6
3·3	σ Puppis		247 35·2	35·2	35·3	35·6	35·7	35·8	S 43	19·7	19·9	20·0	20·0	20·0	19·9
2·9	β Canis Minoris		248 02·3	02·3	02·4	02·5	02·6	02·7	N 8	15·7	15·7	15·7	15·7	15·7	15·7
2·4	η Canis Majoris		248 50·8	50·8	51·0	51·1	51·3	51·3	S 29	19·8	19·9	20·0	20·0	20·0	19·9
2·7	π Puppis		250 35·9	35·9	36·0	36·2	36·4	36·5	S 37	07·3	07·5	07·6	07·6	07·5	07·4
1·8	δ Canis Majoris		252 46·2	46·2	46·3	46·5	46·6	46·7	S 26	24·9	25·0	25·1	25·1	25·1	25·0
3·0	o Canis Majoris		254 06·5	06·5	06·6	06·8	06·9	07·0	S 23	51·2	51·4	51·4	51·4	51·4	51·3
1·5	ε Canis Majoris	19	255 12·9	13·0	13·1	13·3	13·4	13·4	S 28	59·5	59·6	59·7	59·7	59·6	59·5
2·9	τ Puppis		257 25·8	25·9	26·1	26·4	26·6	26·7	S 50	37·9	38·1	38·2	38·2	38·1	38·0
−1·5	α Canis Majoris	18	258 34·2	34·3	34·4	34·5	34·6	34·7	S 16	44·2	44·3	44·3	44·3	44·3	44·2
1·9	γ Geminorum		260 23·3	23·3	23·4	23·5	23·6	23·6	N 16	23·2	23·2	23·2	23·2	23·2	23·2
−0·7	α Carinæ	17	263 56·0	56·2	56·4	56·7	56·9	57·0	S 52	42·3	42·5	42·5	42·5	42·5	42·3
2·0	β Canis Majoris		264 11·0	11·0	11·1	11·3	11·4	11·4	S 17	57·9	58·0	58·0	58·0	58·0	57·9
2·6	θ Aurigæ		269 51·1	51·2	51·3	51·5	51·6	51·5	N 37	12·7	12·8	12·8	12·8	12·7	12·7
1·9	β Aurigæ		269 53·0	53·1	53·2	53·4	53·5	53·5	N 44	56·8	56·9	56·9	56·9	56·9	56·8
Var.‡	α Orionis	16	271 02·0	02·1	02·2	02·3	02·4	02·4	N 7	24·4	24·4	24·4	24·4	24·4	24·4
2·1	κ Orionis		272 54·5	54·6	54·7	54·8	54·9	54·9	S 9	40·1	40·2	40·2	40·2	40·1	40·0
1·9	ζ Orionis		274 38·9	39·0	39·1	39·2	39·3	39·3	S 1	56·3	56·4	56·4	56·4	56·4	56·3
2·6	α Columbæ		274 58·2	58·3	58·4	58·6	58·7	58·7	S 34	04·4	04·4	04·4	04·4	04·3	04·2
3·0	ζ Tauri		275 23·9	23·9	24·1	24·2	24·3	24·2	N 21	08·9	08·9	08·9	08·9	08·9	08·9
1·7	ε Orionis	15	275 47·1	47·1	47·2	47·4	47·4	47·4	S 1	11·8	11·9	11·9	11·9	11·8	11·8
2·8	ι Orionis		275 59·1	59·2	59·3	59·4	59·5	59·5	S 5	54·3	54·3	54·4	54·4	54·3	54·2
2·6	α Leporis		276 40·5	40·6	40·7	40·9	41·0	41·0	S 17	49·0	49·1	49·1	49·1	49·0	48·9
2·2	δ Orionis		276 50·1	50·2	50·3	50·4	50·5	50·5	S 0	17·6	17·6	17·6	17·6	17·6	17·5
2·8	β Leporis		277 48·0	48·1	48·3	48·4	48·5	48·5	S 20	45·2	45·3	45·3	45·3	45·2	45·1
1·7	β Tauri	14	278 13·5	13·6	13·7	13·9	13·9	13·9	N 28	37·0	37·0	37·0	37·0	37·0	36·9
1·6	γ Orionis	13	278 32·8	32·8	33·0	33·1	33·1	33·1	N 6	21·5	21·5	21·5	21·5	21·5	21·5
0·1	α Aurigæ	12	280 35·5	35·6	35·8	35·9	36·0	36·0	N 46	00·6	00·7	00·7	00·6	00·6	00·5
0·1	β Orionis	11	281 12·7	12·8	12·9	13·0	13·1	13·1	S 8	11·4	11·5	11·5	11·5	11·4	11·3
2·8	β Eridani		282 52·8	52·9	53·0	53·2	53·2	53·2	S 5	04·4	04·5	04·5	04·5	04·4	04·3
2·7	ι Aurigæ		285 32·6	32·7	32·9	33·0	33·1	33·0	N 33	11·1	11·1	11·1	11·1	11·0	11·0
0·9	α Tauri	10	290 50·2	50·3	50·5	50·6	50·6	50·5	N 16	32·0	31·9	31·9	31·9	31·9	31·9
2·9	ε Persei		300 19·4	19·5	19·7	19·8	19·8	19·7	N 40	02·8	02·8	02·8	02·8	02·7	02·6
3·0	γ Eridani		300 20·7	20·8	20·9	21·0	21·0	20·9	S 13	28·6	28·6	28·7	28·6	28·5	28·4
2·9	ζ Persei		301 16·0	16·2	16·3	16·4	16·4	16·3	N 31	55·2	55·2	55·2	55·1	55·1	55·1
2·9	η Tauri		302 56·4	56·5	56·7	56·8	56·7	56·6	N 24	08·6	08·6	08·5	08·5	08·5	08·5
1·8	α Persei	9	308 41·5	41·7	41·9	42·0	42·0	41·8	N 49	54·4	54·4	54·4	54·3	54·2	54·1
Var.§	β Persei		312 45·1	45·2	45·4	45·5	45·4	45·3	N 41	00·3	00·3	00·2	00·1	00·1	00·0
2·5	α Ceti	8	314 15·9	16·0	16·2	16·2	16·2	16·0	N 4	08·2	08·2	08·1	08·2	08·2	08·3
3·2	θ Eridani	7	315 18·9	19·1	19·2	19·3	19·3	19·2	S 40	15·6	15·6	15·6	15·5	15·3	15·2
2·0	α Ursæ Minoris		318 06·8	19·2	30·2	36·3	34·7	26·3	N 89	19·3	19·3	19·2	19·1	19·0	18·8
3·0	β Trianguli		327 25·6	25·8	25·9	25·9	25·8	25·6	N 35	02·8	02·8	02·7	02·7	02·6	02·6
2·0	α Arietis	6	328 01·8	01·9	02·0	02·0	02·0	01·8	N 23	31·3	31·2	31·2	31·2	31·1	31·2
2·3	γ Andromedæ		328 49·9	50·1	50·2	50·2	50·1	49·9	N 42	23·5	23·4	23·4	23·3	23·2	23·2
2·9	α Hydri		330 12·6	12·9	13·1	13·3	13·2	13·0	S 61	30·9	30·9	30·8	30·6	30·5	30·3
2·6	β Arietis		331 10·0	10·2	10·2	10·2	10·2	10·0	N 20	52·1	52·1	52·0	52·0	52·0	52·0
0·5	α Eridani	5	335 27·4	27·7	27·9	27·9	27·6	27·6	S 57	10·8	10·7	10·6	10·5	10·3	10·1
2·7	δ Cassiopeiæ		338 20·4	20·6	20·8	20·8	20·6	20·3	N 60	18·2	18·2	18·0	17·9	17·8	17·8
2·1	β Andromedæ		342 23·6	23·7	23·8	23·7	23·6	23·4	N 35	41·3	41·2	41·2	41·1	41·0	41·1
Var.‖	γ Cassiopeiæ		345 38·0	38·3	38·4	38·4	38·2	37·8	N 60	47·3	47·2	47·1	46·9	46·9	46·8
2·0	β Ceti	4	348 56·9	57·0	57·1	57·0	56·9	56·7	S 17	55·3	55·3	55·2	55·2	55·1	54·9
2·2	α Cassiopeiæ	3	349 41·8	42·0	42·1	42·0	41·8	41·5	N 56	36·5	36·5	36·3	36·2	36·1	36·1
2·4	α Phœnicis	2	353 16·8	16·9	16·9	16·9	16·7	16·5	S 42	14·6	14·5	14·4	14·3	14·1	14·0
2·8	β Hydri		353 24·9	25·5	25·7	25·7	25·3	24·6	S 77	11·4	11·3	11·1	10·9	10·8	10·6
2·8	γ Pegasi		356 32·0	32·0	32·1	32·0	31·8	31·6	N 15	15·2	15·1	15·1	15·1	15·1	15·2
2·3	β Cassiopeiæ		357 32·5	32·7	32·7	32·6	32·4	32·0	N 59	13·3	13·2	13·1	13·0	12·9	12·9
2·1	α Andromedæ	1	357 44·7	44·7	44·8	44·7	44·5	44·3	N 29	09·6	09·6	09·5	09·4	09·4	09·5

‡ 0·1 — 1·2   § 2·1 — 3·4   ‖ Irregular variable; 2010 mag. 2·2

Mag.	Name and Number		SHA						Declination						
			JULY	AUG.	SEPT.	OCT.	NOV.	DEC.		JULY	AUG.	SEPT.	OCT.	NOV.	DEC.
1·6	*Castor*		246	09·2	09·0	08·8	08·6	08·3	08·1	N 31	51·5	51·5	51·4	51·4	51·3	51·3
3·3	σ Puppis		247	35·8	35·7	35·5	35·3	35·0	34·8	S 43	19·7	19·6	19·5	19·5	19·5	19·7
2·9	β Canis Minoris		248	02·6	02·5	02·3	02·1	01·9	01·7	N 8	15·7	15·8	15·8	15·7	15·7	15·6
2·4	η Canis Majoris		248	51·3	51·2	51·0	50·8	50·5	50·3	S 29	19·8	19·6	19·6	19·6	19·6	19·8
2·7	π Puppis		250	36·4	36·3	36·1	35·9	35·6	35·4	S 37	07·3	07·2	07·1	07·1	07·2	07·3
1·8	*Wezen*		252	46·6	46·5	46·3	46·1	45·9	45·7	S 26	24·9	24·8	24·7	24·7	24·8	24·9
3·0	o Canis Majoris		254	06·9	06·8	06·6	06·4	06·2	06·0	S 23	51·2	51·1	51·0	51·0	51·1	51·2
1·5	*Adhara*	19	255	13·4	13·3	13·1	12·8	12·6	12·4	S 28	59·4	59·3	59·2	59·2	59·3	59·5
2·9	τ Puppis		257	26·7	26·5	26·3	26·0	25·7	25·5	S 50	37·8	37·7	37·6	37·6	37·7	37·8
−1·5	*Sirius*	18	258	34·6	34·5	34·3	34·1	33·8	33·7	S 16	44·1	44·0	43·9	43·9	44·0	44·2
1·9	*Alhena*		260	23·5	23·4	23·2	22·9	22·7	22·5	N 16	23·2	23·2	23·2	23·2	23·1	23·1
−0·7	*Canopus*	17	263	57·0	56·8	56·5	56·2	55·9	55·7	S 52	42·2	42·0	41·9	41·9	42·1	42·2
2·0	*Mirzam*		264	11·3	11·2	11·0	10·8	10·6	10·4	S 17	57·8	57·7	57·6	57·7	57·7	57·9
2·6	θ Aurigæ		269	51·4	51·2	50·9	50·7	50·4	50·2	N 37	12·6	12·6	12·6	12·6	12·6	12·6
1·9	*Menkalinan*		269	53·4	53·1	52·8	52·5	52·2	52·0	N 44	56·7	56·7	56·7	56·7	56·7	56·7
Var.‡	*Betelgeuse*	16	271	02·3	02·1	01·9	01·7	01·5	01·3	N 7	24·5	24·5	24·5	24·5	24·5	24·4
2·1	κ Orionis		272	54·8	54·6	54·4	54·2	54·0	53·9	S 9	40·0	39·9	39·8	39·9	39·9	40·0
1·9	*Alnitak*		274	39·2	39·0	38·8	38·6	38·4	38·2	S 1	56·2	56·2	56·1	56·1	56·2	56·3
2·6	*Phact*		274	58·6	58·4	58·2	58·0	57·8	57·7	S 34	04·0	03·9	03·9	03·9	04·0	04·1
3·0	ζ Tauri		275	24·1	23·9	23·7	23·4	23·2	23·1	N 21	08·9	08·9	08·9	08·9	08·9	08·9
1·7	*Alnilam*	15	275	47·3	47·1	46·9	46·7	46·5	46·4	S 1	11·7	11·6	11·6	11·6	11·7	11·7
2·8	ι Orionis		275	59·4	59·2	59·0	58·8	58·6	58·4	S 5	54·2	54·1	54·0	54·1	54·1	54·2
2·6	α Leporis		276	40·8	40·7	40·4	40·2	40·0	39·9	S 17	48·8	48·7	48·7	48·7	48·8	48·9
2·2	δ Orionis		276	50·3	50·1	49·9	49·7	49·5	49·4	S 0	17·5	17·4	17·4	17·4	17·4	17·5
2·8	β Leporis		277	48·4	48·2	48·0	47·7	47·6	47·4	S 20	45·0	44·9	44·8	44·8	44·9	45·1
1·7	*Elnath*	14	278	13·7	13·5	13·3	13·0	12·8	12·7	N 28	36·9	36·9	36·9	37·0	37·0	37·0
1·6	*Bellatrix*	13	278	33·0	32·8	32·5	32·3	32·2	32·0	N 6	21·6	21·6	21·7	21·7	21·6	21·6
0·1	*Capella*	12	280	35·8	35·5	35·2	34·9	34·6	34·4	N 46	00·4	00·4	00·4	00·4	00·5	00·5
0·1	*Rigel*	11	281	12·9	12·7	12·5	12·3	12·1	12·0	S 8	11·3	11·2	11·1	11·2	11·2	11·3
2·8	β Eridani		282	53·0	52·8	52·6	52·4	52·2	52·1	S 5	04·2	04·2	04·1	04·1	04·2	04·3
2·7	ι Aurigæ		285	32·8	32·6	32·3	32·1	31·8	31·7	N 33	11·0	11·0	11·0	11·0	11·1	11·1
0·9	*Aldebaran*	10	290	50·4	50·1	49·7	49·5	49·4	49·4	N 16	32·0	32·0	32·0	32·1	32·1	32·0
2·9	ε Persei		300	19·4	19·1	18·9	18·6	18·4	18·4	N 40	02·6	02·6	02·7	02·7	02·8	02·9
3·0	γ Eridani		300	20·8	20·5	20·3	20·2	20·0	20·0	S 13	28·3	28·2	28·2	28·2	28·3	28·4
2·9	ζ Persei		301	16·1	15·8	15·5	15·3	15·2	15·1	N 31	55·1	55·1	55·2	55·2	55·3	55·3
2·9	*Alcyone*		302	56·4	56·2	55·9	55·7	55·6	55·5	N 24	08·5	08·6	08·6	08·7	08·7	08·7
1·8	*Mirfak*	9	308	41·5	41·1	40·8	40·6	40·4	40·4	N 49	54·1	54·1	54·2	54·3	54·4	54·5
Var.§	*Algol*		312	45·0	44·7	44·4	44·2	44·1	44·1	N 41	00·0	00·1	00·2	00·3	00·4	00·4
2·5	*Menkar*	8	314	15·8	15·6	15·4	15·2	15·2	15·1	N 4	08·3	08·4	08·5	08·5	08·5	08·4
3·2	*Acamar*	7	315	19·0	18·7	18·5	18·3	18·2	18·3	S 40	15·0	15·0	15·0	15·1	15·2	15·3
2·0	*Polaris*		317	73·2	58·4	45·1	35·6	31·4	35·3	N 89	18·8	18·8	18·9	19·1	19·2	19·4
3·0	β Trianguli		327	25·3	25·1	24·8	24·7	24·6	24·6	N 35	02·7	02·8	02·9	02·9	03·0	03·1
2·0	*Hamal*	6	328	01·5	01·3	01·1	00·9	00·9	00·9	N 23	31·2	31·3	31·4	31·5	31·5	31·5
2·3	*Almak*		328	49·6	49·3	49·1	48·9	48·9	48·9	N 42	23·2	23·3	23·4	23·5	23·6	23·7
2·9	α Hydri		330	12·6	12·2	11·9	11·7	11·7	11·9	S 61	30·2	30·2	30·2	30·4	30·5	30·6
2·6	*Sheratan*		331	09·7	09·5	09·3	09·2	09·1	09·2	N 20	52·1	52·2	52·3	52·4	52·4	52·4
0·5	*Achernar*	5	335	27·3	26·9	26·7	26·5	26·6	26·7	S 57	10·0	10·0	10·1	10·2	10·4	10·5
2·7	*Ruchbah*		338	19·9	19·5	19·2	19·0	19·0	19·1	N 60	17·8	17·9	18·1	18·2	18·4	18·5
2·1	*Mirach*		342	23·1	22·8	22·6	22·6	22·5	22·6	N 35	41·1	41·2	41·4	41·5	41·6	41·6
Var.‖	γ Cassiopeiæ		345	37·4	37·0	36·7	36·6	36·7	36·8	N 60	46·9	47·0	47·2	47·3	47·5	47·6
2·0	*Diphda*	4	348	56·4	56·2	56·1	56·0	56·1	56·1	S 17	54·8	54·8	54·8	54·8	54·9	55·0
2·2	*Schedar*	3	349	41·1	40·8	40·6	40·5	40·5	40·7	N 56	36·2	36·3	36·5	36·6	36·8	36·9
2·4	*Ankaa*	2	353	16·2	15·9	15·8	15·8	15·8	16·0	S 42	13·9	13·9	14·0	14·1	14·2	14·3
2·8	β Hydri		353	23·9	23·1	22·7	22·7	23·1	23·7	S 77	10·6	10·7	10·8	10·9	11·1	11·1
2·8	*Algenib*		356	31·4	31·2	31·1	31·0	31·1	31·1	N 15	15·3	15·4	15·5	15·5	15·5	15·5
2·3	*Caph*		357	31·6	31·3	31·1	31·1	31·2	31·4	N 59	13·0	13·1	13·3	13·5	13·6	13·7
2·1	*Alpheratz*	1	357	44·0	43·8	43·7	43·6	43·7	43·8	N 29	09·6	09·7	09·8	09·9	10·0	10·0

‡ 0·1 — 1·2   § 2·1 — 3·4   ‖ Irregular variable; 2010 mag. 2·2

POLARIS (POLE STAR) TABLES, 2012
FOR DETERMINING LATITUDE FROM SEXTANT ALTITUDE AND FOR AZIMUTH

LHA ARIES	0° – 9°	10° – 19°	20° – 29°	30° – 39°	40° – 49°	50° – 59°	60° – 69°	70° – 79°	80° – 89°	90° – 99°	100° – 109°	110° – 119°
°	a_0	a_0	a_0	a_0	a_0	a_0	a_0	a_0	a_0	a_0	a_0	a_0
0	0 28·5	0 24·2	0 20·9	0 18·8	0 17·9	0 18·3	0 19·9	0 22·8	0 26·7	0 31·6	0 37·4	0 43·8
1	28·0	23·8	20·6	18·7	17·9	18·4	20·2	23·1	27·2	32·2	38·0	44·4
2	27·6	23·4	20·4	18·5	17·9	18·5	20·4	23·5	27·6	32·7	38·6	45·1
3	27·1	23·1	20·1	18·4	17·9	18·7	20·7	23·8	28·1	33·3	39·2	45·8
4	26·7	22·7	19·9	18·3	17·9	18·8	20·9	24·2	28·6	33·8	39·9	46·5
5	0 26·2	0 22·4	0 19·7	0 18·2	0 18·0	0 19·0	0 21·2	0 24·6	0 29·1	0 34·4	0 40·5	0 47·2
6	25·8	22·1	19·5	18·1	18·0	19·1	21·5	25·0	29·6	35·0	41·1	47·8
7	25·4	21·8	19·3	18·1	18·1	19·3	21·8	25·4	30·1	35·6	41·8	48·5
8	25·0	21·5	19·1	18·0	18·1	19·5	22·1	25·8	30·6	36·2	42·5	49·2
9	24·6	21·2	19·0	18·0	18·2	19·7	22·4	26·3	31·1	36·8	43·1	49·9
10	0 24·2	0 20·9	0 18·8	0 17·9	0 18·3	0 19·9	0 22·8	0 26·7	0 31·6	0 37·4	0 43·8	0 50·6

Lat.	a_1	a_1	a_1	a_1	a_1	a_1	a_1	a_1	a_1	a_1	a_1	a_1
°	,	,	,	,	,	,	,	,	,	,	,	,
0	0·5	0·5	0·6	0·6	0·6	0·6	0·6	0·5	0·5	0·4	0·4	0·3
10	·5	·5	·6	·6	·6	·6	·6	·5	·5	·4	·4	·4
20	·5	·6	·6	·6	·6	·6	·6	·5	·5	·5	·4	·4
30	·5	·6	·6	·6	·6	·6	·6	·6	·5	·5	·5	·5
40	0·6	0·6	0·6	0·6	0·6	0·6	0·6	0·6	0·6	0·5	0·5	0·5
45	·6	·6	·6	·6	·6	·6	·6	·6	·6	·6	·6	·6
50	·6	·6	·6	·6	·6	·6	·6	·6	·6	·6	·6	·6
55	·6	·6	·6	·6	·6	·6	·6	·6	·6	·6	·6	·7
60	·6	·6	·6	·6	·6	·6	·6	·6	·7	·7	·7	·7
62	0·7	0·6	0·6	0·6	0·6	0·6	0·6	0·6	0·7	0·7	0·7	0·8
64	·7	·6	·6	·6	·6	·6	·6	·7	·7	·7	·8	·8
66	·7	·7	·6	·6	·6	·6	·6	·7	·7	·8	·8	·8
68	0·7	0·7	0·6	0·6	0·6	0·6	0·6	0·7	0·7	0·8	0·8	0·9

Month	a_2	a_2	a_2	a_2	a_2	a_2	a_2	a_2	a_2	a_2	a_2	a_2
	,	,	,	,	,	,	,	,	,	,	,	,
Jan.	0·7	0·8	0·8	0·8	0·8	0·8	0·8	0·8	0·8	0·7	0·7	0·7
Feb.	·7	·7	·8	·8	·8	·9	·9	·9	·9	·9	·9	·8
Mar.	·5	·6	·7	·7	·8	·8	·9	·9	·9	·9	·9	0·9
Apr.	0·4	0·4	0·5	0·6	0·6	0·7	0·8	0·8	0·9	0·9	0·9	1·0
May	·3	·3	·4	·4	·5	·5	·6	·7	·7	·8	·9	0·9
June	·2	·2	·3	·3	·4	·4	·5	·5	·6	·7	·7	·8
July	0·3	0·3	0·3	0·3	0·3	0·3	0·4	0·4	0·4	0·5	0·6	0·6
Aug.	·4	·4	·3	·3	·3	·3	·3	·3	·3	·4	·4	·5
Sept.	·6	·5	·5	·4	·4	·4	·3	·3	·3	·3	·3	·3
Oct.	0·8	0·7	0·7	0·6	0·5	0·5	0·4	0·4	0·3	0·3	0·3	0·3
Nov.	0·9	0·9	0·8	·8	·7	·6	·6	·5	·4	·4	·3	·3
Dec.	1·0	1·0	1·0	0·9	0·9	0·8	0·7	0·7	0·6	0·5	0·4	0·4

Lat.	AZIMUTH											
°	°	°	°	°	°	°	°	°	°	°	°	°
0	0·4	0·3	0·2	0·1	0·0	359·8	359·7	359·6	359·5	359·5	359·4	359·3
20	0·4	0·3	0·2	0·1	0·0	359·8	359·7	359·6	359·5	359·4	359·4	359·3
40	0·5	0·4	0·3	0·1	0·0	359·8	359·6	359·5	359·4	359·3	359·2	359·1
50	0·6	0·5	0·3	0·1	359·9	359·8	359·6	359·4	359·3	359·1	359·0	359·0
55	0·7	0·5	0·4	0·1	359·9	359·7	359·5	359·3	359·2	359·0	358·9	358·9
60	0·8	0·6	0·4	0·2	359·9	359·7	359·5	359·2	359·1	358·9	358·8	358·7
65	1·0	0·7	0·5	0·2	359·9	359·6	359·4	359·1	358·9	358·7	358·5	358·4

Latitude = Apparent altitude (corrected for refraction) $-1° + a_0 + a_1 + a_2$

The table is entered with LHA Aries to determine the column to be used; each column refers to a range of 10°. a_0 is taken, with mental interpolation, from the upper table with the units of LHA Aries in degrees as argument; a_1, a_2 are taken, without interpolation, from the second and third tables with arguments latitude and month respectively. a_0, a_1, a_2, are always positive. The final table gives the azimuth of *Polaris*.

POLARIS (POLE STAR) TABLES, 2012

FOR DETERMINING LATITUDE FROM SEXTANT ALTITUDE AND FOR AZIMUTH

LHA ARIES	120°– 129°	130°– 139°	140°– 149°	150°– 159°	160°– 169°	170°– 179°	180°– 189°	190°– 199°	200°– 209°	210°– 219°	220°– 229°	230°– 239°
	a_0	a_0	a_0	a_0	a_0	a_0	a_0	a_0	a_0	a_0	a_0	a_0
°	° ′	° ′	° ′	° ′	° ′	° ′	° ′	° ′	° ′	° ′	° ′	° ′
0	0 50·6	0 57·7	1 04·8	1 11·7	1 18·3	1 24·2	1 29·4	1 33·6	1 36·8	1 38·8	1 39·7	1 39·3
1	51·3	58·4	05·5	12·4	18·9	24·8	29·8	34·0	37·0	39·0	39·7	39·2
2	52·0	59·1	06·2	13·1	19·5	25·3	30·3	34·3	37·3	39·1	39·7	39·1
3	52·7	59·9	06·9	13·8	20·1	25·8	30·7	34·7	37·5	39·2	39·7	39·0
4	53·4	1 00·6	07·6	14·4	20·7	26·4	31·2	35·0	37·7	39·3	39·7	38·8
5	0 54·1	1 01·3	1 08·3	1 15·1	1 21·3	1 26·9	1 31·6	1 35·3	1 38·0	1 39·4	1 39·6	1 38·7
6	54·9	02·0	09·0	15·7	21·9	27·4	32·0	35·6	38·2	39·5	39·6	38·5
7	55·6	02·7	09·7	16·4	22·5	27·9	32·4	35·9	38·3	39·6	39·5	38·3
8	56·3	03·4	10·4	17·0	23·1	28·4	32·8	36·2	38·5	39·6	39·5	38·1
9	57·0	04·1	11·1	17·6	23·6	28·9	33·2	36·5	38·7	39·6	39·4	37·9
10	0 57·7	1 04·8	1 11·7	1 18·3	1 24·2	1 29·4	1 33·6	1 36·8	1 38·8	1 39·7	1 39·3	1 37·7

Lat.	a_1	a_1	a_1	a_1	a_1	a_1	a_1	a_1	a_1	a_1	a_1	a_1
°	′	′	′	′	′	′	′	′	′	′	′	′
0	0·3	0·3	0·3	0·4	0·4	0·4	0·5	0·5	0·6	0·6	0·6	0·6
10	·4	·4	·4	·4	·4	·5	·5	·5	·6	·6	·6	·6
20	·4	·4	·4	·4	·5	·5	·5	·6	·6	·6	·6	·6
30	·5	·5	·5	·5	·5	·5	·5	·6	·6	·6	·6	·6
40	0·5	0·5	0·5	0·5	0·5	0·6	0·6	0·6	0·6	0·6	0·6	0·6
45	·6	·6	·6	·6	·6	·6	·6	·6	·6	·6	·6	·6
50	·6	·6	·6	·6	·6	·6	·6	·6	·6	·6	·6	·6
55	·7	·7	·7	·6	·6	·6	·6	·6	·6	·6	·6	·6
60	·7	·7	·7	·7	·7	·7	·6	·6	·6	·6	·6	·6
62	0·8	0·8	0·8	0·7	0·7	0·7	0·7	0·6	0·6	0·6	0·6	0·6
64	·8	·8	·8	·8	·7	·7	·7	·6	·6	·6	·6	·6
66	·9	·9	·8	·8	·8	·7	·7	·7	·6	·6	·6	·6
68	0·9	0·9	0·9	0·9	0·8	0·8	0·7	0·7	0·6	0·6	0·6	0·6

Month	a_2	a_2	a_2	a_2	a_2	a_2	a_2	a_2	a_2	a_2	a_2	a_2
	′	′	′	′	′	′	′	′	′	′	′	′
Jan.	0·7	0·6	0·6	0·6	0·5	0·5	0·5	0·4	0·4	0·4	0·4	0·4
Feb.	·8	·8	·7	·7	·6	·6	·5	·5	·4	·4	·4	·3
Mar.	0·9	0·9	0·9	·8	·8	·7	·7	·6	·5	·5	·4	·4
Apr.	1·0	1·0	1·0	0·9	0·9	0·9	0·8	0·8	0·7	0·6	0·6	0·5
May	0·9	1·0	1·0	1·0	1·0	1·0	0·9	0·9	·8	·8	·7	·7
June	·8	0·9	0·9	0·9	1·0	1·0	1·0	1·0	·9	·9	·8	·8
July	0·7	0·7	0·8	0·8	0·9	0·9	0·9	0·9	0·9	0·9	0·9	0·9
Aug.	·5	·5	·6	·7	·7	·7	·8	·8	·9	·9	·9	·9
Sept.	·4	·4	·4	·5	·5	·6	·6	·7	·7	·8	·8	·8
Oct.	0·3	0·3	0·3	0·3	0·3	0·4	0·4	0·5	0·5	0·6	0·7	0·7
Nov.	·2	·2	·2	·2	·2	·2	·3	·3	·4	·4	·5	·6
Dec.	0·3	0·2	0·2	0·2	0·2	0·1	0·2	0·2	0·2	0·3	0·3	0·4

Lat.	AZIMUTH											
°	°	°	°	°	°	°	°	°	°	°	°	°
0	359·3	359·3	359·3	359·4	359·4	359·5	359·6	359·7	359·8	359·9	0·0	0·2
20	359·3	359·3	359·3	359·3	359·4	359·5	359·6	359·7	359·8	359·9	0·0	0·2
40	359·1	359·1	359·1	359·2	359·3	359·4	359·5	359·6	359·7	359·9	0·0	0·2
50	358·9	358·9	359·0	359·0	359·1	359·2	359·4	359·5	359·7	359·9	0·1	0·2
55	358·8	358·8	358·8	358·9	359·0	359·1	359·3	359·5	359·7	359·9	0·1	0·3
60	358·6	358·6	358·7	358·8	358·9	359·0	359·2	359·4	359·6	359·8	0·1	0·3
65	358·4	358·4	358·4	358·5	358·7	358·8	359·1	359·3	359·5	359·8	0·1	0·4

ILLUSTRATION			
On 2012 April 21 at 23ʰ 18ᵐ 56ˢ UT in longitude W 37° 14′ the apparent altitude (corrected for refraction), H_O, of Polaris was 49° 31′·6	From the daily pages:	° ′	H_O 49° 31′·6
	GHA Aries (23ʰ)	195 24·9	a_0 (argument 162° 56′) 1 20·1
	Increment (18ᵐ 56ˢ)	4 44·8	a_1 (Lat 50° approx.) 0·6
	Longitude (west)	−37 14	a_2 (April) 0·9
	LHA Aries	162 56	Sum − 1° = Lat = 49° 53′·2

POLARIS (POLE STAR) TABLES, 2012
FOR DETERMINING LATITUDE FROM SEXTANT ALTITUDE AND FOR AZIMUTH

LHA ARIES	240°–249°	250°–259°	260°–269°	270°–279°	280°–289°	290°–299°	300°–309°	310°–319°	320°–329°	330°–339°	340°–349°	350°–359°
	a_0	a_0	a_0	a_0	a_0	a_0	a_0	a_0	a_0	a_0	a_0	a_0
°	° ′	° ′	° ′	° ′	° ′	° ′	° ′	° ′	° ′	° ′	° ′	° ′
0	I 37·7	I 35·0	I 31·1	I 26·3	I 20·6	I 14·3	I 07·5	I 00·5	0 53·3	0 46·4	0 39·8	0 33·8
1	37·5	34·6	30·7	25·8	20·0	13·7	06·8	0 59·8	52·6	45·7	39·2	33·2
2	37·3	34·3	30·2	25·2	19·4	13·0	06·1	59·0	51·9	45·0	38·5	32·6
3	37·0	33·9	29·8	24·7	18·8	12·3	05·4	58·3	51·2	44·4	37·9	32·1
4	36·7	33·5	29·3	24·1	18·2	11·7	04·7	57·6	50·5	43·7	37·3	31·6
5	I 36·5	I 33·2	I 28·8	I 23·6	I 17·6	I 11·0	I 04·0	0 56·9	0 49·8	0 43·0	0 36·7	0 31·0
6	36·2	32·8	28·3	23·0	16·9	10·3	03·3	56·2	49·1	42·4	36·1	30·5
7	35·9	32·4	27·8	22·4	16·3	09·6	02·6	55·5	48·4	41·7	35·5	30·0
8	35·6	32·0	27·3	21·8	15·6	08·9	01·9	54·8	47·7	41·1	34·9	29·5
9	35·3	31·5	26·8	21·2	15·0	08·2	01·2	54·1	47·1	40·4	34·3	29·0
10	I 35·0	I 31·1	I 26·3	I 20·6	I 14·3	I 07·5	I 00·5	0 53·3	0 46·4	0 39·8	0 33·8	0 28·5

Lat.	a_1	a_1	a_1	a_1	a_1	a_1	a_1	a_1	a_1	a_1	a_1	a_1
°	′	′	′	′	′	′	′	′	′	′	′	′
0	0·6	0·5	0·5	0·4	0·4	0·3	0·3	0·3	0·3	0·4	0·4	0·4
10	·6	·5	·5	·4	·4	·4	·4	·4	·4	·4	·4	·5
20	·6	·5	·5	·5	·4	·4	·4	·4	·4	·4	·5	·5
30	·6	·6	·5	·5	·5	·5	·5	·5	·5	·5	·5	·5
40	0·6	0·6	0·6	0·5	0·5	0·5	0·5	0·5	0·5	0·5	0·5	0·6
45	·6	·6	·6	·6	·6	·6	·6	·6	·6	·6	·6	·6
50	·6	·6	·6	·6	·6	·6	·6	·6	·6	·6	·6	·6
55	·6	·6	·6	·6	·6	·7	·7	·7	·7	·6	·6	·6
60	·6	·6	·7	·7	·7	·7	·7	·7	·7	·7	·7	·7
62	0·6	0·6	0·7	0·7	0·7	0·8	0·8	0·8	0·8	0·7	0·7	0·7
64	·6	·7	·7	·7	·8	·8	·8	·8	·8	·8	·7	·7
66	·6	·7	·7	·8	·8	·8	·9	·9	·8	·8	·8	·7
68	0·6	0·7	0·7	0·8	0·8	0·9	0·9	0·9	0·9	0·9	0·8	0·8

Month	a_2	a_2	a_2	a_2	a_2	a_2	a_2	a_2	a_2	a_2	a_2	a_2
	′	′	′	′	′	′	′	′	′	′	′	′
Jan.	0·4	0·4	0·4	0·5	0·5	0·5	0·5	0·6	0·6	0·6	0·7	0·7
Feb.	·3	·3	·3	·3	·3	·4	·4	·4	·5	·5	·6	·6
Mar.	·3	·3	·3	·3	·3	·3	·3	·3	·3	·4	·4	·5
Apr.	0·4	0·4	0·3	0·3	0·3	0·2	0·2	0·2	0·2	0·3	0·3	0·3
May	·6	·5	·5	·4	·3	·3	·3	·2	·2	·2	·2	·2
June	·7	·7	·6	·5	·5	·4	·4	·3	·3	·3	·2	·2
July	0·8	0·8	0·8	0·7	0·6	0·6	0·5	0·5	0·4	0·4	0·3	0·3
Aug.	·9	·9	·9	·8	·8	·7	·7	·7	·6	·5	·5	·5
Sept.	·9	·9	·9	·9	·9	·9	·8	·8	·8	·7	·7	·6
Oct.	0·8	0·8	0·9	0·9	0·9	0·9	0·9	0·9	0·9	0·9	0·9	0·8
Nov.	·6	·7	·8	·8	·9	·9	1·0	1·0	1·0	1·0	1·0	1·0
Dec.	0·5	0·5	0·6	0·7	0·8	0·8	0·9	1·0	1·0	1·0	1·0	1·1

Lat.	AZIMUTH											
°	°	°	°	°	°	°	°	°	°	°	°	°
0	0·3	0·4	0·5	0·5	0·6	0·7	0·7	0·7	0·7	0·6	0·6	0·5
20	0·3	0·4	0·5	0·6	0·6	0·7	0·7	0·7	0·7	0·7	0·6	0·5
40	0·3	0·5	0·6	0·7	0·8	0·8	0·9	0·9	0·9	0·8	0·7	0·7
50	0·4	0·6	0·7	0·8	0·9	1·0	1·1	1·1	1·0	1·0	0·9	0·8
55	0·5	0·6	0·8	0·9	1·1	1·1	1·2	1·2	1·2	1·1	1·0	0·9
60	0·5	0·7	0·9	1·1	1·2	1·3	1·3	1·4	1·3	1·3	1·2	1·0
65	0·6	0·9	1·1	1·3	1·4	1·5	1·6	1·6	1·6	1·5	1·4	1·2

Latitude = Apparent altitude (corrected for refraction) $-1° + a_0 + a_1 + a_2$

The table is entered with LHA Aries to determine the column to be used; each column refers to a range of 10°. a_0 is taken, with mental interpolation, from the upper table with the units of LHA Aries in degrees as argument; a_1, a_2 are taken, without interpolation, from the second and third tables with arguments latitude and month respectively. a_0, a_1, a_2, are always positive. The final table gives the azimuth of *Polaris*.

SIGHT REDUCTION PROCEDURES

METHODS AND FORMULAE FOR DIRECT COMPUTATION

1. *Introduction.* In this section formulae and methods are provided for *calculating* position at sea from observed altitudes taken with a marine sextant using a computer or programmable calculator.

The method uses analogous concepts and similar terminology as that used in *manual* methods of astro-navigation, where position is found by plotting position lines from their intercept and azimuth on a marine chart.

The algorithms are presented in standard algebra suitable for translating into the programming language of the user's computer. The basic ephemeris data may be taken directly from the main tabular pages of a current version of *The Nautical Almanac*. Formulae are given for calculating altitude and azimuth from the *GHA* and *Dec* of a body, and the estimated position of the observer. Formulae are also given for reducing sextant observations to observed altitudes by applying the corrections for dip, refraction, parallax and semi-diameter.

The intercept and azimuth obtained from each observation determine a position line, and the observer should lie on or close to each position line. The method of least squares is used to calculate the fix by finding the position where the sum of the squares of the distances from the position lines is a minimum. The use of least squares has other advantages. For example it is possible to improve the estimated position at the time of fix by repeating the calculation. It is also possible to include more observations in the solution and to reject doubtful ones.

2. *Notation.*

GHA = Greenwich hour angle. The range of GHA is from $0°$ to $360°$ starting at $0°$ on the Greenwich meridian increasing to the west, back to $360°$ on the Greenwich meridian.

SHA = sidereal hour angle. The range is $0°$ to $360°$.

Dec = declination. The sign convention for declination is north is positive, south is negative. The range is from $-90°$ at the south celestial pole to $+90°$ at the north celestial pole.

$Long$ = longitude. The sign convention is east is positive, west is negative. The range is $-180°$ to $+180°$.

Lat = latitude. The sign convention is north is positive, south is negative. The range is from $-90°$ to $+90°$.

LHA = $GHA + Long$ = local hour angle. The LHA increases to the west from $0°$ on the local meridian to $360°$.

H_C = calculated altitude. Above the horizon is positive, below the horizon is negative. The range is from $-90°$ in the nadir to $+90°$ in the zenith.

H_S = sextant altitude.

H = apparent altitude = sextant altitude corrected for instrumental error and dip.

H_O = observed altitude = apparent altitude corrected for refraction and, in appropriate cases, corrected for parallax and semi-diameter.

Z = Z_n = true azimuth. Z is measured from true north through east, south, west and back to north. The range is from $0°$ to $360°$.

I = sextant index error.

D = dip of horizon.

R = atmospheric refraction.

HP = horizontal parallax of the Sun, Moon, Venus or Mars.
PA = parallax in altitude of the Sun, Moon, Venus or Mars.
SD = semi-diameter of the Sun or Moon.
p = intercept = $H_O - H_C$. Towards is positive, away is negative.
T = course or track, measured as for azimuth from the north.
V = speed in knots.

3. *Entering Basic Data.*   When quantities such as *GHA* are entered, which in *The Nautical Almanac* are given in degrees and minutes, convert them to degrees and decimals of a degree by dividing the minutes by 60 and adding to the degrees; for example, if *GHA* = 123° 45′.6, enter the two numbers 123 and 45·6 into the memory and set *GHA* = 123 + 45·6/60 = 123°7600. Although four decimal places of a degree are shown in the examples, it is assumed that full precision is maintained in the calculations.

When using a computer or programmable calculator, write a subroutine to convert degrees and minutes to degrees and decimals. Scientific calculators usually have a special key for this purpose. For quantities like *Dec* which require a minus sign for southern declination, change the sign from plus to minus after the value has been converted to degrees and decimals, *e.g. Dec* = S 0° 12′.3 = S 0°.2050 = −0°.2050. Other quantities which require conversion are semi-diameter, horizontal parallax, longitude and latitude.

4. *Interpolation of GHA and Dec*   The *GHA* and *Dec* of the Sun, Moon and planets are interpolated to the time of observation by direct calculation as follows: If the universal time is $a^h \ b^m \ c^s$, form the interpolation factor $x = b/60 + c/3600$. Enter the tabular value GHA_0 for the preceding hour (a) and the tabular value GHA_1 for the following hour $(a + 1)$ then the interpolated value *GHA* is given by

$$GHA = GHA_0 + x(GHA_1 - GHA_0)$$

If the *GHA* passes through 360° between tabular values add 360° to GHA_1 before interpolation. If the interpolated value exceeds 360°, subtract 360° from *GHA*.

Similarly for declination, enter the tabular value Dec_0 for the preceding hour (a) and the tabular value Dec_1 for the following hour $(a + 1)$, then the interpolated value *Dec* is given by

$$Dec = Dec_0 + x(Dec_1 - Dec_0)$$

5. *Example.*   (a) Find the *GHA* and *Dec* of the Sun on 2012 February 1 at $15^h \ 47^m \ 13^s$ UT.

The interpolation factor $x = 47/60 + 13/3600 = 0^h.7869$
   page 31 $15^h \ GHA_0 = 41° \ 37′.3 = 41°.6217$
        $16^h \ GHA_1 = 56° \ 37′.2 = 56°.6200$
   $15^h.7869 \ GHA = 41·6217 + 0·7869(56·6200 - 41·6217) = 53°.4245$
        $15^h \ Dec_0 = S \ 17° \ 09′.0 = -17°.1500$
        $16^h \ Dec_1 = S \ 17° \ 08′.3 = -17°.1383$
   $15^h.7869 \ Dec = -17·1500 + 0·7869(-17·1383 + 17·1500) = -17°.1408$

GHA Aries is interpolated in the same way as *GHA* of a body. For a star the *SHA* and *Dec* are taken from the tabular page and do not require interpolation, then

$$GHA = GHA \ \text{Aries} + SHA$$

where *GHA* Aries is interpolated to the time of observation.

(b) Find the *GHA* and *Dec* of *Vega* on 2012 February 1 at 15^h 47^m 13^s UT.

The interpolation factor $x = 0^h7869$ as in the previous example

page 30 15^h *GHA* Aries$_0$ = 356° 14′1 = 356°2350

16^h *GHA* Aries$_1$ = 11° 16′6 = 371°2767   (360° added)

15^h7869 *GHA* Aries = $356 \cdot 2350 + 0 \cdot 7869(371 \cdot 2767 - 356 \cdot 2350) = 368°0720$

SHA = 80° 40′0 = 80°6667

GHA = *GHA* Aries + *SHA* = 88°7386   (multiple of 360° removed)

Dec = N 38° 47′6 = +38°7933

6. *The calculated altitude and azimuth.* The calculated altitude H_C and true azimuth Z are determined from the *GHA* and *Dec* interpolated to the time of observation and from the *Long* and *Lat* estimated at the time of observation as follows:

Step 1.   Calculate the local hour angle

$$LHA = GHA + Long$$

Add or subtract multiples of 360° to set *LHA* in the range 0° to 360°.

Step 2.   Calculate S, C and the altitude H_C from

$$S = \sin Dec$$
$$C = \cos Dec \cos LHA$$
$$H_C = \sin^{-1}(S \sin Lat + C \cos Lat)$$

where $\sin^{-1}$ is the inverse function of sine.

Step 3.   Calculate X and A from

$$X = (S \cos Lat - C \sin Lat)/\cos H_C$$
$$\text{If } X > +1 \quad \text{set} \quad X = +1$$
$$\text{If } X < -1 \quad \text{set} \quad X = -1$$
$$A = \cos^{-1} X$$

where $\cos^{-1}$ is the inverse function of cosine.

Step 4.   Determine the azimuth Z

$$\text{If } LHA > 180° \quad \text{then} \quad Z = A$$
$$\text{Otherwise} \quad Z = 360° - A$$

7. *Example.* Find the calculated altitude H_C and azimuth Z when

$$GHA = 53° \quad Dec = S\,15° \quad Lat = N\,32° \quad Long = W\,16°$$

For the calculation

$$GHA = 53°0000 \quad Dec = -15°0000 \quad Lat = +32°0000 \quad Long = -16°0000$$

Step 1. $LHA = 53 \cdot 0000 - 16 \cdot 0000 = 37 \cdot 0000$

Step 2. $S = -0 \cdot 2588$

$C = +0 \cdot 9659 \times 0 \cdot 7986 = 0 \cdot 7714$

$\sin H_C = -0 \cdot 2588 \times 0 \cdot 5299 + 0 \cdot 7714 \times 0 \cdot 8480 = 0 \cdot 5171$

$H_C = 31°1346$

Step 3. $X = (-0{\cdot}2588 \times 0{\cdot}8480 - 0{\cdot}7714 \times 0{\cdot}5299)/0{\cdot}8560 = -0{\cdot}7340$

$A = 137{\stackrel{\circ}{\cdot}}2239$

Step 4.   Since $LHA \leq 180°$ then $Z = 360° - A = 222{\stackrel{\circ}{\cdot}}7761$

8. *Reduction from sextant altitude to observed altitude.*   The sextant altitude H_S is corrected for both dip and index error to produce the apparent altitude. The observed altitude H_O is calculated by applying a correction for refraction. For the Sun, Moon, Venus and Mars a correction for parallax is also applied to H, and for the Sun and Moon a further correction for semi-diameter is required. The corrections are calculated as follows:

Step 1.   Calculate dip

$$D = 0{\stackrel{\circ}{\cdot}}0293\sqrt{h}$$

where h is the height of eye above the horizon in metres.

Step 2.   Calculate apparent altitude

$$H = H_S + I - D$$

where I is the sextant index error.

Step 3.   Calculate refraction (R) at a standard temperature of $10°$ Celsius (C) and pressure of 1010 millibars (mb)

$$R_0 = 0{\stackrel{\circ}{\cdot}}0167/\tan(H + 7{\cdot}32/(H + 4{\cdot}32))$$

If the temperature $T°$ C and pressure P mb are known calculate the refraction from

$$R = fR_0 \qquad \text{where} \qquad f = 0{\cdot}28P/(T + 273)$$

otherwise set $R = R_0$

Step 4.   Calculate the parallax in altitude (PA) from the horizontal parallax (HP) and the apparent altitude (H) for the Sun, Moon, Venus and Mars as follows:

$$PA = HP \cos H$$

For the Sun $HP = 0{\stackrel{\circ}{\cdot}}0024$. This correction is very small and could be ignored.

For the Moon HP is taken for the nearest hour from the main tabular page and converted to degrees.

For Venus and Mars the HP is taken from the critical table at the bottom of page 259 and converted to degrees.

For the navigational stars and the remaining planets, Jupiter and Saturn set $PA = 0$.

If an error of $0{\stackrel{\circ}{\cdot}}2$ is significant the expression for the parallax in altitude for the Moon should include a small correction OB for the oblateness of the Earth as follows:

$$PA = HP \cos H + OB$$

where $OB = -0{\stackrel{\circ}{\cdot}}0032 \sin^2 Lat \, \cos H + 0{\stackrel{\circ}{\cdot}}0032 \sin(2Lat) \cos Z \sin H$

At mid-latitudes and for altitudes of the Moon below $60°$ a simple approximation to OB is

$$OB = -0{\stackrel{\circ}{\cdot}}0017 \cos H$$

Step 5. Calculate the semi-diameter for the Sun and Moon as follows:

Sun: *SD* is taken from the main tabular page and converted to degrees.

Moon: $SD = 0°2724HP$ where HP is taken for the nearest hour from the main tabular page and converted to degrees.

Step 6. Calculate the observed altitude

$$H_O = H - R + PA \pm SD$$

where the plus sign is used if the lower limb of the Sun or Moon was observed and the minus sign if the upper limb was observed.

9. *Example.* The following example illustrates how to use a calculator to reduce the sextant altitude (H_S) to observed altitude (H_O); the sextant altitudes given are assumed to be taken on 2012 February 7 with a marine sextant, zero index error, at height 5·4 m, temperature −3° C and pressure 982 mb, the Moon sights are assumed to be taken at 10^h UT.

Body limb	Sun lower	Sun upper	Moon lower	Moon upper	Venus —	*Polaris* —
Sextant altitude: H_S	21·3283	3·3367	33·4600	26·1117	4·5433	49·6083
Step 1. Dip: $D = 0·0293\sqrt{h}$	0·0681	0·0681	0·0681	0·0681	0·0681	0·0681
Step 2. Apparent altitude: $H = H_S + I - D$	21·2602	3·2686	33·3919	26·0436	4·4752	49·5402
Step 3. Refraction: R_0 f $R = fR_0$	0·0423 1·0184 0·0431	0·2256 1·0184 0·2298	0·0251 1·0184 0·0256	0·0338 1·0184 0·0344	0·1798 1·0184 0·1831	0·0142 1·0184 0·0144
Step 4. Parallax: HP	 0·0024	 0·0024	(58′1) 0·9683	(58′1) 0·9683	(0′1) 0·0017	 —
Parallax in altitude: $PA = HP \cos H$	0·0022	0·0024	0·8085	0·8700	0·0017	—
Step 5. Semi-diameter: Sun : $SD = 16·2/60$ Moon : $SD = 0·2724HP$	0·2700 —	0·2700 —	— 0·2638	— 0·2638	— —	— —
Step 6. Observed altitude: $H_O = H - R + PA \pm SD$	21·4894	2·7712	34·4386	26·6154	4·2938	49·5258

Note that for the Moon the correction for the oblateness of the Earth of about −0°0017 cos *H*, which equals −0°0014 for the lower limb and −0°0015 for the upper limb, has been ignored in the above calculation.

10. *Position from intercept and azimuth using a chart.* An estimate is made of the position at the adopted time of fix. The position at the time of observation is then calculated by dead reckoning from the time of fix. For example if the course (track) *T* and the speed *V* (in knots) of the observer are constant then *Long* and *Lat* at the time of observation are calculated from

$$Long = L_F + t(V/60)\sin T/\cos B_F$$
$$Lat = B_F + t(V/60)\cos T$$

where L_F and B_F are the estimated longitude and latitude at the time of fix and t is the time interval in hours from the time of fix to the time of observation, t is positive if the time of observation is after the time of fix and negative if it was before.

The position line of an observation is plotted on a chart using the intercept

$$p = H_O - H_C$$

and azimuth Z with origin at the calculated position ($Long$, Lat) at the time of observation, where H_C and Z are calculated using the method in section 6, page 279. Starting from this calculated position a line is drawn on the chart along the direction of the azimuth to the body. Convert p to nautical miles by multiplying by 60. The position line is drawn at right angles to the azimuth line, distance p from ($Long$, Lat) towards the body if p is positive and distance p away from the body if p is negative. Provided there are no gross errors the navigator should be somewhere on or near the position line at the time of observation. Two or more position lines are required to determine a fix.

11. *Position from intercept and azimuth by calculation.* The position of the fix may be calculated from two or more sextant observations as follows.

If p_1, Z_1, are the intercept and azimuth of the first observation, p_2, Z_2, of the second observation and so on, form the summations

$$A = \cos^2 Z_1 + \cos^2 Z_2 + \cdots$$
$$B = \cos Z_1 \sin Z_1 + \cos Z_2 \sin Z_2 + \cdots$$
$$C = \sin^2 Z_1 + \sin^2 Z_2 + \cdots$$
$$D = p_1 \cos Z_1 + p_2 \cos Z_2 + \cdots$$
$$E = p_1 \sin Z_1 + p_2 \sin Z_2 + \cdots$$

where the number of terms in each summation is equal to the number of observations.

With $G = AC - B^2$, an improved estimate of the position at the time of fix (L_I, B_I) is given by

$$L_I = L_F + (AE - BD)/(G\cos B_F), \qquad B_I = B_F + (CD - BE)/G$$

Calculate the distance d between the initial estimated position (L_F, B_F) at the time of fix and the improved estimated position (L_I, B_I) in nautical miles from

$$d = 60\sqrt{((L_I - L_F)^2 \cos^2 B_F + (B_I - B_F)^2)}$$

If d exceeds about 20 nautical miles set $L_F = L_I$, $B_F = B_I$ and repeat the calculation until d, the distance between the position at the previous estimate and the improved estimate, is less than about 20 nautical miles.

12. *Example of direct computation.* Using the method described above, calculate the position of a ship on 2012 July 12 at $21^h\ 00^m\ 00^s$ UT from the marine sextant observations of the three stars *Regulus* (No. 26) at $20^h\ 39^m\ 23^s$ UT, *Antares* (No. 42) at $20^h\ 45^m\ 47^s$ UT and *Kochab* (No. 40) at $21^h\ 05^m\ 34^s$ UT, where the observed altitudes of the three stars corrected for the effects of refraction, dip and instrumental error, are $19°9424$, $28°9030$ and $47°2248$ respectively. The ship was travelling at a constant speed of 20 knots on a course of 325° during the period of observation, and the position of the ship at the time of fix $21^h\ 00^m\ 00^s$ UT is only known to the nearest whole degree W 15°, N 32°.

Intermediate values for the first iteration are shown in the table. *GHA* Aries was interpolated from the nearest tabular values on page 138. For the first iteration set $L_F = -15°0000$, $B_F = +32°0000$ at the time of fix at 21^h 00^m 00^s UT.

First Iteration

Body No.	Regulus 26	Antares 42	Kochab 40
time of observation	20^h 39^m 23^s	20^h 45^m 47^s	21^h 05^m 34^s
H_O	19·9424	28·9030	47·2248
interpolation factor	0·6564	0·7631	0·0928
GHA Aries	240·9882	242·5926	247·5522
SHA (page 138)	207·7400	112·4450	137·3250
GHA	88·7282	355·0376	24·8772
Dec (page 138)	+11·9050	−26·4600	+74·1083
t	−0·3436	−0·2369	+0·0928
Long	−14·9225	−14·9466	−15·0209
Lat	+31·9062	+31·9353	+32·0253
Z	271·8827	159·6831	356·0122
H_C	19·9193	28·5972	47·6249
p	+0·0231	+0·3058	−0·4001

$$A = 1·8757 \quad B = -0·4278 \quad C = 1·1243 \quad D = -0·6851 \quad E = 0·1109 \quad G = 1·9258$$
$$(A E - B D)/(G \cos B_F) = -0·0521, \qquad (C D - B E)/G = -0·3754$$

An improved estimate of the position at the time of fix is

$$L_I = L_F - 0·0521 = -15·0521 \quad \text{and} \quad B_I = B_F - 0·3754 = +31·6246$$

Since the distance between the previous estimated position and the improved estimate $d = 22·7$ nautical miles set $L_F = -15·0521$, and $B_F = +31·6246$ and repeat the calculation. The table shows the intermediate values of the calculation for the second iteration. In each iteration the quantities H_O, *GHA*, *Dec* and t do not change.

Second Iteration

Body No.	Regulus 26	Antares 42	Kochab 40
Long	−14·9749	−14·9989	−15·0729
Lat	+31·5308	+31·5599	+31·6500
Z	271·9917	159·5609	356·0610
H_C	19·9512	28·9336	47·2535
p	−0·0088	−0·0306	−0·0287

$$A = 1·8745 \quad B = -0·4305 \quad C = 1·1255 \quad D = -0·0003 \quad E = 0·0001 \quad G = 1·9244$$
$$(A E - B D)/(G \cos B_F) = +0·0000, \qquad (C D - B E)/G = -0·0002$$

An improved estimate of the position at the time of fix is

$$L_I = L_F - 0·0000 = -15·0521 \quad \text{and} \quad B_I = B_F - 0·0002 = +31·6245$$

The distance between the previous estimated position and the improved estimated position $d = 0·01$ nautical miles is so small that a third iteration would produce a negligible improvement to the estimate of the position.

USE OF CONCISE SIGHT REDUCTION TABLES

1. *Introduction.* The concise sight reduction tables given on pages 286 to 317 are intended for use when neither more extensive tables nor electronic computing aids are available. These "NAO sight reduction tables" provide for the reduction of the local hour angle and declination of a celestial object to azimuth and altitude, referred to an assumed position on the Earth, for use in the intercept method of celestial navigation which is now standard practice.

2. *Form of tables.* Entries in the reduction table are at a fixed interval of one degree for all latitudes and hour angles. A compact arrangement results from division of the navigational triangle into two right spherical triangles, so that the table has to be entered twice. Assumed latitude and local hour angle are the arguments for the first entry. The reduction table responds with the intermediate arguments A, B, and Z_1, where A is used as one of the arguments for the second entry to the table, B has to be incremented by the declination to produce the quantity F, and Z_1 is a component of the azimuth angle. The reduction table is then reentered with A and F and yields H, P, and Z_2 where H is the altitude, P is the complement of the parallactic angle, and Z_2 is the second component of the azimuth angle. It is usually necessary to adjust the tabular altitude for the fractional parts of the intermediate entering arguments to derive computed altitude, and an auxiliary table is provided for the purpose. Rules governing signs of the quantities which must be added or subtracted are given in the instructions and summarized on each tabular page. Azimuth angle is the sum of two components and is converted to true azimuth by familiar rules, repeated at the bottom of the tabular pages.

Tabular altitude and intermediate quantities are given to the nearest minute of arc, although errors of $2'$ in computed altitude may accrue during adjustment for the minutes parts of entering arguments. Components of azimuth angle are stated to $0°.1$; for derived true azimuth, only whole degrees are warranted. Since objects near the zenith are difficult to observe with a marine sextant, they should be avoided; altitudes greater than about 80° are not suited to reduction by this method.

In many circumstances the accuracy provided by these tables is sufficient. However, to maintain the full accuracy ($0'.1$) of the ephemeral data in the almanac throughout their reduction to altitude and azimuth, more extensive tables or a calculator should be used.

3. *Use of Tables.*

Step 1.   Determine the Greenwich hour angle (GHA) and Declination (Dec) of the body from the almanac. Select an assumed latitude (Lat) of integral degrees nearest to the estimated latitude. Choose an assumed longitude nearest to the estimated longitude such that the local hour angle

$$LHA = GHA \begin{matrix} - \text{ west} \\ + \text{ east} \end{matrix} \text{ longitude}$$

has integral degrees.

Step 2.   Enter the reduction table with Lat and LHA as arguments. Record the quantities A, B and Z_1. Apply the rules for the sign of B and Z_1: B is minus if $90° < LHA < 270°$: Z_1 has the same sign as B. Set $A° =$ nearest whole degree of A and $A' =$ minutes part of A. This step may be repeated for all reductions before leaving the latitude opening of the table.

Step 3.   Record the declination Dec. Apply the rules for the sign of Dec: Dec is minus if the name of Dec (i.e. N or S) is contrary to latitude. Add B and Dec algebraically to produce F. If F is negative, the object is below the horizon (in sight reduction, this can occur when the objects are close to the horizon). Regard F as positive until step 7. Set $F° =$ nearest whole degree of F and $F' =$ minutes part of F.

Step 4. Enter the reduction table a second time with $A°$ and $F°$ as arguments and record H, P, and Z_2. Set $P°$ = nearest whole degree of P and $Z_2° =$ nearest whole degree of Z_2.

Step 5. Enter the auxiliary table with F' and $P°$ as arguments to obtain $corr_1$ to H for F'. Apply the rule for the sign of $corr_1$: $corr_1$ is minus if $F < 90°$ and $F' > 29'$ or if $F > 90°$ and $F' < 30'$, otherwise $corr_1$ is plus.

Step 6. Enter the auxiliary table with A' and $Z_2°$ as arguments to obtain $corr_2$ to H for A'. Apply the rule for the sign of $corr_2$: $corr_2$ is minus if $A' < 30'$, otherwise $corr_2$ is plus.

Step 7. Calculate the computed altitude H_C as the sum of H, $corr_1$ and $corr_2$. Apply the rule for the sign of H_C: H_C is minus if F is negative.

Step 8. Apply the rule for the sign of Z_2: Z_2 is minus if $F > 90°$. If F is negative, replace Z_2 by $180° - Z_2$. Set the azimuth angle Z equal to the algebraic sum of Z_1 and Z_2 and ignore the resulting sign. Obtain the true azimuth Z_n from the rules

$$\text{For N latitude, if } LHA > 180° \quad Z_n = Z$$
$$\text{if } LHA < 180° \quad Z_n = 360° - Z$$

$$\text{For S latitude, if } LHA > 180° \quad Z_n = 180° - Z$$
$$\text{if } LHA < 180° \quad Z_n = 180° + Z$$

Observed altitude H_O is compared with H_C to obtain the altitude difference, which, with Z_n, is used to plot the position line.

4. *Example.* (a) Required the altitude and azimuth of *Schedar* on 2012 February 5 at UT 06^h 30^m from the estimated position 5° east, 53° north.

1. Assumed latitude
   From the almanac
   Assumed longitude
   Local hour angle

$$Lat = \quad 53° \text{ N}$$
$$GHA = 222° \ 02'$$
$$4° \ 58' \text{ E}$$
$$LHA = 227$$

2. Reduction table, 1st entry
   $(Lat, LHA) = (53, 227)$

3. From the almanac
   Sum = $B + Dec$

$$A = \quad 26 \quad 07 \qquad A° = 26, A' = 7$$
$$B = -27 \quad 12 \qquad Z_1 = -49.4, \qquad 90° < LHA < 270°$$
$$Dec = +56 \quad 36 \qquad \qquad \qquad \qquad Lat \text{ and } Dec \text{ same}$$
$$F = +29 \quad 24 \qquad F° = 29, F' = 24$$

4. Reduction table, 2nd entry
   $(A°, F°) = (26, 29)$

$$H = \quad 25 \quad 50 \qquad P° = 61$$
$$Z_2 = 76.3, Z_2° = 76$$

5. Auxiliary table, 1st entry
   $(F', P°) = (24, 61)$
   Sum

$$corr_1 = \quad \underline{+21} \qquad\qquad F < 90°, F' < 29'$$
$$26 \quad 11$$

6. Auxiliary table, 2nd entry
   $(A', Z_2°) = (7, 76)$

$$corr_2 = \quad \underline{-2} \qquad\qquad\qquad A' < 30'$$

7. Sum = computed altitude $\quad H_C = +26° \ 09' \qquad\qquad\qquad F > 0°$

8. Azimuth, first component
   second component
   Sum = azimuth angle

$$Z_1 = -49.4 \qquad\qquad\qquad \text{same sign as } B$$
$$Z_2 = \underline{+76.3} \qquad\qquad\qquad F < 90°, F > 0°$$
$$Z = \quad 26.9$$

True azimuth $\qquad\qquad Z_n = 027° \qquad\qquad\qquad$ N *Lat*, $LHA > 180°$

continued on page 318

SIGHT REDUCTION TABLE

B: (−) for 90° < LHA < 270°
Dec:(−) for Lat. contrary name

Z₁: same sign as B
Z₂: (−) for F > 90°

Lat./A LHA/F	/A	0° A/H	0° B/P	0° Z₁/Z₂	1° A/H	1° B/P	1° Z₁/Z₂	2° A/H	2° B/P	2° Z₁/Z₂	3° A/H	3° B/P	3° Z₁/Z₂	4° A/H	4° B/P	4° Z₁/Z₂	5° A/H	5° B/P	5° Z₁/Z₂	Lat/A	LHA
0	180	0 00	90 00	90·0	0 00	89 00	90·0	0 00	88 00	90·0	0 00	87 00	90·0	0 00	86 00	90·0	0 00	85 00	90·0	180	360
1	179	1 00	90 00	90·0	1 00	89 00	90·0	1 00	88 00	90·0	1 00	87 00	89·9	1 00	86 00	89·9	1 00	85 00	89·9	181	359
2	178	2 00	90 00	90·0	2 00	89 00	90·0	2 00	88 00	89·9	2 00	87 00	89·9	2 00	86 00	89·9	2 00	85 00	89·8	182	358
3	177	3 00	90 00	90·0	3 00	89 00	89·9	3 00	88 00	89·9	3 00	87 00	89·8	3 00	85 59	89·8	2 59	84 59	89·7	183	357
4	176	4 00	90 00	90·0	4 00	89 00	89·9	4 00	88 00	89·9	4 00	86 59	89·8	3 59	85 59	89·7	3 59	84 59	89·7	184	356
5	175	5 00	90 00	90·0	5 00	89 00	89·9	5 00	88 00	89·8	5 00	86 59	89·7	4 59	85 59	89·7	4 59	84 59	89·6	185	355
6	174	6 00	90 00	90·0	6 00	89 00	89·9	6 00	87 59	89·8	6 00	86 59	89·7	5 59	85 59	89·6	5 59	84 58	89·5	186	354
7	173	7 00	90 00	90·0	7 00	89 00	89·9	7 00	87 59	89·8	6 59	86 58	89·6	6 59	85 58	89·6	6 58	84 58	89·4	187	353
8	172	8 00	90 00	90·0	8 00	88 59	89·9	8 00	87 59	89·7	7 59	86 58	89·6	7 59	85 58	89·5	7 58	84 57	89·4	188	352
9	171	9 00	90 00	90·0	9 00	88 59	89·9	9 00	87 59	89·7	8 59	86 57	89·5	8 59	85 57	89·4	8 58	84 56	89·3	189	351
10	170	10 00	90 00	90·0	10 00	88 59	89·8	10 00	87 58	89·6	9 59	86 57	89·5	9 59	85 56	89·4	9 58	84 55	89·2	190	350
11	169	11 00	90 00	90·0	11 00	88 59	89·8	11 00	87 58	89·6	10 59	86 56	89·4	10 58	85 56	89·3	10 57	84 54	89·1	191	349
12	168	12 00	90 00	90·0	12 00	88 59	89·8	12 00	87 57	89·6	11 59	86 56	89·4	11 58	85 55	89·2	11 57	84 53	89·0	192	348
13	167	13 00	90 00	90·0	13 00	88 59	89·8	13 00	87 57	89·5	12 59	86 55	89·3	12 58	85 54	89·1	12 57	84 52	88·9	193	347
14	166	14 00	90 00	90·0	14 00	88 58	89·7	13 59	87 56	89·5	13 59	86 54	89·3	13 58	85 53	89·0	13 57	84 51	88·8	194	346
15	165	15 00	90 00	90·0	15 00	88 58	89·7	14 59	87 56	89·5	14 59	86 53	89·2	14 58	85 52	89·0	14 56	84 49	88·8	195	345
16	164	16 00	90 00	90·0	16 00	88 58	89·7	15 59	87 55	89·4	15 59	86 52	89·2	15 58	85 50	88·9	15 56	84 48	88·7	196	344
17	163	17 00	90 00	90·0	17 00	88 57	89·7	16 59	87 55	89·4	16 59	86 51	89·1	16 57	85 49	88·8	16 56	84 46	88·5	197	343
18	162	18 00	90 00	90·0	18 00	88 57	89·7	17 59	87 54	89·4	17 58	86 51	89·0	17 57	85 48	88·7	17 56	84 45	88·4	198	342
19	161	19 00	90 00	90·0	19 00	88 57	89·6	18 59	87 53	89·3	18 58	86 50	89·0	18 57	85 46	88·7	18 55	84 43	88·3	199	341
20	160	20 00	90 00	90·0	20 00	88 56	89·6	19 59	87 52	89·3	19 58	86 48	88·9	19 57	85 45	88·6	19 55	84 41	88·2	200	340
21	159	21 00	90 00	90·0	21 00	88 56	89·6	20 59	87 51	89·2	20 58	86 47	88·8	20 57	85 43	88·5	20 55	84 39	88·1	201	339
22	158	22 00	90 00	90·0	22 00	88 55	89·6	21 59	87 51	89·2	21 58	86 45	88·8	21 57	85 41	88·5	21 55	84 37	88·0	202	338
23	157	23 00	90 00	90·0	23 00	88 55	89·6	22 59	87 50	89·2	22 58	86 44	88·7	22 56	85 39	88·4	22 54	84 34	87·9	203	337
24	156	24 00	90 00	90·0	24 00	88 54	89·6	23 59	87 49	89·1	23 58	86 43	88·7	23 56	85 37	88·3	23 54	84 32	87·8	204	336
25	155	25 00	90 00	90·0	25 00	88 54	89·5	24 59	87 48	89·1	24 58	86 41	88·6	24 56	85 35	88·2	24 54	84 29	87·7	205	335
26	154	26 00	90 00	90·0	26 00	88 53	89·5	25 59	87 47	89·0	25 58	86 40	88·5	25 56	85 33	88·1	25 54	84 26	87·6	206	334
27	153	27 00	90 00	90·0	27 00	88 53	89·5	26 59	87 45	89·0	26 57	86 38	88·4	26 56	85 31	88·1	26 53	84 24	87·5	207	333
28	152	28 00	90 00	90·0	28 00	88 52	89·5	27 59	87 44	89·0	27 57	86 36	88·4	27 55	85 28	88·0	27 53	84 20	87·3	208	332
29	151	29 00	90 00	90·0	29 00	88 51	89·4	28 59	87 43	88·9	28 57	86 34	88·3	28 55	85 26	87·9	28 53	84 17	87·2	209	331
30	150	30 00	90 00	90·0	30 00	88 51	89·4	29 59	87 41	88·8	29 57	86 32	88·3	29 55	85 23	87·8	29 52	84 14	87·1	210	330
31	149	31 00	90 00	90·0	31 00	88 50	89·4	30 59	87 40	88·8	30 57	86 30	88·2	30 55	85 20	87·7	30 52	84 10	86·9	211	329
32	148	32 00	90 00	90·0	32 00	88 49	89·4	31 59	87 39	88·8	31 57	86 28	88·1	31 55	85 17	87·6	31 52	84 07	86·8	212	328
33	147	33 00	90 00	90·0	33 00	88 48	89·3	32 59	87 37	88·7	32 57	86 25	88·1	32 55	85 14	87·5	32 52	84 03	86·6	213	327
34	146	34 00	90 00	90·0	34 00	88 48	89·3	33 59	87 35	88·7	33 56	86 23	88·0	33 54	85 11	87·4	33 51	83 59	86·5	214	326
35	145	35 00	90 00	90·0	35 00	88 47	89·3	34 59	87 34	88·6	34 56	86 20	87·9	34 54	85 07	87·2	34 51	83 54	86·5	215	325
36	144	36 00	90 00	90·0	36 00	88 46	89·3	35 58	87 32	88·5	35 56	86 18	87·8	35 54	85 04	87·1	35 51	83 50	86·4	216	324
37	143	37 00	90 00	90·0	37 00	88 45	89·2	36 58	87 30	88·5	36 56	86 15	87·7	36 54	85 00	87·0	36 50	83 45	86·2	217	323
38	142	38 00	90 00	90·0	38 00	88 44	89·2	37 58	87 28	88·4	37 56	86 12	87·6	37 53	84 56	86·9	37 50	83 40	86·1	218	322
39	141	39 00	90 00	90·0	39 00	88 43	89·2	38 58	87 26	88·4	38 56	86 09	87·5	38 53	84 52	86·8	38 49	83 35	86·0	219	321
40	140	40 00	90 00	90·0	40 00	88 42	89·2	39 58	87 23	88·3	39 56	86 05	87·4	39 53	84 47	86·7	39 49	83 29	85·8	220	320
41	139	41 00	90 00	90·0	41 00	88 41	89·1	40 58	87 21	88·3	40 56	86 02	87·3	40 53	84 42	86·5	40 49	83 23	85·7	221	319
42	138	42 00	90 00	90·0	42 00	88 39	89·1	41 58	87 19	88·2	41 55	85 58	87·3	41 52	84 37	86·4	41 48	83 17	85·5	222	318
43	137	43 00	90 00	90·0	43 00	88 38	89·1	42 58	87 16	88·1	42 55	85 54	87·2	42 52	84 32	86·3	42 48	83 11	85·4	223	317
44	136	44 00	90 00	90·0	44 00	88 37	89·0	43 58	87 13	88·1	43 55	85 50	87·1	43 52	84 27	86·1	43 47	83 04	85·2	224	316
45	135	45 00	90 00	90·0	44 59	88 36	89·0	44 58	87 10	88·0	44 55	85 46	87·0	44 52	84 21	86·0	44 47	82 57	85·0	225	315

Lat./A · LHA/F	0° A/H	0° B/P	0° Z_1/Z_2	1° A/H	1° B/P	1° Z_1/Z_2	2° A/H	2° B/P	2° Z_1/Z_2	3° A/H	3° B/P	3° Z_1/Z_2	4° A/H	4° B/P	4° Z_1/Z_2	5° A/H	5° B/P	5° Z_1/Z_2	Lat./A · LHA
45 · 135	45 00	90 00	90·0	44 59	88 35	89·0	44 58	87 10	88·0	44 55	85 46	87·0	44 52	84 21	86·0	44 47	82 57	85·0	225 · 315
46 · 134	46 00	90 00	90·0	45 59	88 34	89·0	45 58	87 07	87·9	45 55	85 41	86·9	45 51	84 15	85·9	45 46	82 49	84·8	226 · 314
47 · 133	47 00	90 00	90·0	46 59	88 32	88·9	46 58	87 04	87·9	46 55	85 36	86·8	46 51	84 09	85·7	46 46	82 41	84·7	227 · 313
48 · 132	48 00	90 00	90·0	47 59	88 30	88·8	47 58	87 01	87·8	47 55	85 31	86·7	47 51	84 02	85·6	47 46	82 33	84·5	228 · 312
49 · 131	49 00	90 00	90·0	48 59	88 29	88·8	48 58	86 57	87·7	48 54	85 26	86·6	48 50	83 55	85·4	48 45	82 24	84·3	229 · 311
50 · 130	50 00	90 00	90·0	49 59	88 27	88·8	49 58	86 53	87·6	49 54	85 20	86·4	49 50	83 47	85·2	49 44	82 15	84·1	230 · 310
51 · 129	51 00	90 00	90·0	50 59	88 25	88·7	50 57	86 49	87·5	50 54	85 14	86·3	50 50	83 40	85·1	50 44	82 05	83·9	231 · 309
52 · 128	52 00	90 00	90·0	51 59	88 23	88·7	51 57	86 45	87·4	51 54	85 08	86·2	51 49	83 32	84·9	51 43	81 55	83·6	232 · 308
53 · 127	53 00	90 00	90·0	52 59	88 20	88·7	52 57	86 41	87·4	52 54	85 01	86·0	52 49	83 22	84·7	52 42	81 44	83·4	233 · 307
54 · 126	54 00	90 00	90·0	53 59	88 18	88·6	53 57	86 36	87·3	53 54	84 54	85·9	53 49	83 13	84·5	53 42	81 32	83·2	234 · 306
55 · 125	55 00	90 00	90·0	54 59	88 15	88·6	54 57	86 31	87·2	54 54	84 47	85·7	54 48	83 03	84·3	54 41	81 20	82·9	235 · 305
56 · 124	56 00	90 00	90·0	55 59	88 13	88·5	55 57	86 26	87·1	55 53	84 39	85·6	55 48	82 52	84·1	55 41	81 06	82·6	236 · 304
57 · 123	57 00	90 00	90·0	56 59	88 10	88·5	56 57	86 20	87·0	56 53	84 30	85·4	56 47	82 41	83·9	56 40	80 52	82·4	237 · 303
58 · 122	58 00	90 00	90·0	57 59	88 08	88·4	57 57	86 14	86·9	57 53	84 21	85·2	57 47	82 29	83·6	57 39	80 38	82·1	238 · 302
59 · 121	59 00	90 00	90·0	58 59	88 04	88·3	58 57	86 07	86·8	58 52	84 11	85·0	58 46	82 16	83·4	58 38	80 22	81·7	239 · 301
60 · 120	60 00	90 00	90·0	59 59	88 00	88·3	59 56	86 00	86·7	59 52	84 01	84·8	59 46	82 02	83·1	59 37	80 05	81·4	240 · 300
61 · 119	61 00	90 00	90·0	60 59	87 56	88·2	60 56	85 53	86·5	60 52	83 50	84·6	60 45	81 48	82·8	60 37	79 46	81·0	241 · 299
62 · 118	62 00	90 00	90·0	61 59	87 52	88·1	61 56	85 45	86·4	61 51	83 38	84·4	61 44	81 32	82·5	61 36	79 27	80·7	242 · 298
63 · 117	63 00	90 00	90·0	62 59	87 48	88·0	62 56	85 36	86·2	62 51	83 25	84·1	62 44	81 15	82·2	62 35	79 06	80·3	243 · 297
64 · 116	64 00	90 00	90·0	63 59	87 43	88·0	63 56	85 27	86·1	63 50	83 11	83·9	63 43	80 56	81·9	63 33	78 43	79·9	244 · 296
65 · 115	65 00	90 00	90·0	64 59	87 38	87·9	64 56	85 17	85·9	64 50	82 56	83·6	64 42	80 36	81·5	64 32	78 18	79·4	245 · 295
66 · 114	66 00	90 00	90·0	65 59	87 33	87·8	65 55	85 06	85·7	65 49	82 39	83·3	65 41	80 15	81·1	65 31	77 52	78·9	246 · 294
67 · 113	67 00	90 00	90·0	66 59	87 27	87·6	66 55	84 54	85·5	66 49	82 22	83·0	66 40	79 51	80·7	66 29	77 23	78·4	247 · 293
68 · 112	68 00	90 00	90·0	67 59	87 20	87·5	67 55	84 40	85·3	67 48	82 02	82·6	67 39	79 26	80·2	67 28	76 51	77·8	248 · 292
69 · 111	69 00	90 00	90·0	68 59	87 13	87·4	68 55	84 26	85·1	68 48	81 41	82·2	68 38	78 58	79·7	68 26	76 17	77·2	249 · 291
70 · 110	70 00	90 00	90·0	69 59	87 05	87·3	69 54	84 10	84·8	69 47	81 17	81·8	69 37	78 27	79·1	69 25	75 39	76·5	250 · 290
71 · 109	71 00	90 00	90·0	70 59	86 56	87·1	70 54	83 53	84·5	70 46	80 51	81·4	70 36	77 53	78·5	70 23	75 00	75·8	251 · 289
72 · 108	72 00	90 00	90·0	71 58	86 46	86·9	71 54	83 33	84·2	71 46	80 22	80·8	71 35	77 15	77·9	71 21	74 12	75·0	252 · 288
73 · 107	73 00	90 00	90·0	72 58	86 35	86·7	72 53	83 11	83·9	72 45	79 50	80·3	72 33	76 33	77·1	72 18	73 23	74·1	253 · 287
74 · 106	74 00	90 00	90·0	73 58	86 23	86·5	73 53	82 47	83·5	73 44	79 14	79·7	73 31	75 46	76·3	73 15	72 23	73·1	254 · 286
75 · 105	75 00	90 00	90·0	74 58	86 09	86·3	74 52	82 19	83·1	74 43	78 33	78·9	74 29	74 53	75·4	74 12	71 19	72·0	255 · 285
76 · 104	76 00	90 00	90·0	75 58	85 54	86·0	75 52	81 47	82·6	75 41	77 47	78·1	75 27	73 53	74·4	75 09	70 07	70·7	256 · 284
77 · 103	77 00	90 00	90·0	76 58	85 37	85·7	76 51	81 11	82·0	76 40	76 55	77·2	76 25	72 44	73·2	76 05	68 45	69·3	257 · 283
78 · 102	78 00	90 00	90·0	77 57	85 17	85·3	77 50	80 28	81·4	77 38	75 51	76·2	77 22	71 25	71·8	77 01	67 11	67·7	258 · 282
79 · 101	79 00	90 00	90·0	78 57	84 54	84·9	78 49	79 38	80·7	78 36	74 30	75·0	78 18	69 54	70·3	77 56	65 16	65·8	259 · 281
80 · 100	80 00	90 00	90·0	79 57	84 16	84·3	79 48	78 38	79·8	79 34	73 12	73·5	79 14	68 04	68·4	78 50	63 07	63·7	260 · 280
81 · 99	81 00	90 00	90·0	80 57	83 38	83·7	80 47	77 25	77·6	80 31	71 29	71·7	80 09	65 55	66·2	79 43	60 47	61·2	261 · 279
82 · 98	82 00	90 00	90·0	81 56	82 51	82·9	81 45	75 55	76·1	81 28	69 22	69·6	81 04	63 19	63·6	80 34	57 51	58·2	262 · 278
83 · 97	83 00	90 00	90·0	82 56	81 51	81·9	82 43	74 01	74·1	82 23	66 44	67·0	81 57	60 09	60·4	81 24	54 20	54·6	263 · 277
84 · 96	84 00	90 00	90·0	83 55	80 31	80·6	83 41	71 32	71·6	83 18	63 22	63·5	82 48	56 13	56·4	82 12	50 03	50·3	264 · 276
85 · 95	85 00	90 00	90·0	84 54	78 40	78·7	84 37	68 10	68·3	84 00	58 05	59·2	83 26	51 16	51·4	82 56	45 01	45·1	265 · 275
86 · 94	86 00	90 00	90·0	85 53	75 57	76·0	85 32	63 24	63·5	85 00	53 05	53·2	84 21	45 16	45·1	83 36	38 34	38·7	266 · 274
87 · 93	87 00	90 00	90·0	86 50	71 33	71·6	86 24	56 17	56·3	85 45	44 58	45·0	85 00	36 49	36·9	84 10	30 53	31·0	267 · 273
88 · 92	88 00	90 00	90·0	87 46	63 26	63·4	87 10	44 59	45·0	86 24	33 40	33·7	85 32	26 31	26·6	84 37	21 45	21·8	268 · 272
89 · 91	89 00	90 00	90·0	88 35	45 00	45·0	87 46	26 33	26·6	86 50	18 25	18·4	85 53	14 01	14·0	84 54	11 17	11·3	269 · 271
90 · 90	90 00	90 00	90·0	89 00	0 00	0·0	88 00	0 00	0·0	87 00	0 00	0·0	86 00	0 00	0·0	85 00	0 00	0·0	270 · 270

N. Lat: for LHA > 180° ... $Z_n = Z$
      for LHA < 180° ... $Z_n = 360° − Z$

S. Lat.: for LHA > 180° ... $Z_n = 180° − Z$
      for LHA < 180° ... $Z_n = 180° + Z$

B: (−) for 90° < LHA < 270°
Dec:(−) for Lat. contrary name

Z_1: same sign as B
Z_2: (−) for F > 90°

SIGHT REDUCTION TABLE

Lat./A LHA/F	6° A/H	6° B/P	6° Z_1/Z_2	7° A/H	7° B/P	7° Z_1/Z_2	8° A/H	8° B/P	8° Z_1/Z_2	9° A/H	9° B/P	9° Z_1/Z_2	10° A/H	10° B/P	10° Z_1/Z_2	11° A/H	11° B/P	11° Z_1/Z_2	Lat./A LHA
0 180	0 00	84 00	90·0	0 00	83 00	90·0	0 00	82 00	90·0	0 00	81 00	90·0	0 00	80 00	90·0	0 00	79 00	90·0	180
1 179	1 00	84 00	89·9	1 00	83 00	89·9	0 59	82 00	89·9	0 59	81 00	89·8	0 59	80 00	89·8	0 59	79 00	89·8	181
2 178	1 59	84 00	89·8	1 59	83 00	89·8	1 59	82 00	89·8	1 58	81 00	89·7	1 58	80 00	89·7	1 58	79 00	89·6	182
3 177	2 59	84 00	89·7	2 59	82 59	89·6	2 58	81 59	89·6	2 58	80 59	89·5	2 57	79 59	89·5	2 57	78 59	89·4	183
4 176	3 59	83 59	89·6	3 58	82 59	89·5	3 58	81 59	89·4	3 57	80 59	89·4	3 56	79 59	89·3	3 56	78 58	89·2	184
5 175	4 58	83 59	89·5	4 58	82 58	89·4	4 57	81 58	89·3	4 56	80 58	89·2	4 55	79 58	89·1	4 54	78 58	89·0	185
6 174	5 58	83 58	89·4	5 57	82 58	89·3	5 56	81 57	89·2	5 56	80 57	89·1	5 55	79 57	89·0	5 53	78 56	88·9	186
7 173	6 58	83 57	89·3	6 57	82 57	89·1	6 56	81 56	89·0	6 55	80 56	88·9	6 54	79 56	88·8	6 52	78 55	88·7	187
8 172	7 57	83 56	89·2	7 56	82 55	89·0	7 55	81 55	88·9	7 54	80 55	88·8	7 53	79 54	88·6	7 51	78 54	88·5	188
9 171	8 57	83 56	89·1	8 56	82 55	88·9	8 55	81 54	88·7	8 53	80 53	88·6	8 52	79 53	88·4	8 50	78 52	88·3	189
10 170	9 57	83 54	88·9	9 55	82 54	88·8	9 54	81 53	88·6	9 53	80 52	88·4	9 51	79 51	88·2	9 49	78 50	88·1	190
11 169	10 56	83 53	88·8	10 55	82 52	88·6	10 53	81 51	88·5	10 52	80 50	88·3	10 50	79 49	88·1	10 48	78 48	87·9	191
12 168	11 56	83 52	88·7	11 55	82 51	88·5	11 53	81 49	88·3	11 51	80 48	88·1	11 49	79 47	87·9	11 47	78 46	87·7	192
13 167	12 56	83 51	88·6	12 54	82 49	88·4	12 52	81 48	88·2	12 50	80 46	87·9	12 48	79 45	87·7	12 45	78 43	87·5	193
14 166	13 55	83 49	88·5	13 53	82 47	88·3	13 51	81 46	88·0	13 49	80 44	87·8	13 47	79 42	87·5	13 44	78 40	87·3	194
15 165	14 55	83 47	88·4	14 53	82 45	88·1	14 51	81 43	87·9	14 49	80 41	87·6	14 46	79 39	87·3	14 43	78 37	87·1	195
16 164	15 55	83 46	88·3	15 52	82 43	88·0	15 50	81 41	87·7	15 48	80 39	87·4	15 45	79 36	87·1	15 42	78 34	86·9	196
17 163	16 54	83 44	88·2	16 52	82 41	87·9	16 50	81 38	87·6	16 47	80 36	87·3	16 44	79 33	87·0	16 41	78 31	86·7	197
18 162	17 54	83 42	88·1	17 52	82 39	87·7	17 49	81 36	87·4	17 46	80 33	87·1	17 43	79 30	86·8	17 39	78 27	86·5	198
19 161	18 54	83 39	87·9	18 51	82 36	87·6	18 48	81 33	87·3	18 45	80 29	86·9	18 42	79 26	86·6	18 38	78 23	86·2	199
20 160	19 53	83 37	87·8	19 51	82 33	87·5	19 48	81 30	87·1	19 45	80 26	86·7	19 41	79 22	86·4	19 37	78 19	86·0	200
21 159	20 53	83 35	87·7	20 50	82 30	87·3	20 47	81 26	86·9	20 44	80 22	86·6	20 40	79 18	86·2	20 36	78 14	85·8	201
22 158	21 52	83 32	87·6	21 50	82 27	87·2	21 46	81 23	86·8	21 43	80 18	86·4	21 39	79 14	86·0	21 35	78 10	85·6	202
23 157	22 52	83 29	87·5	22 49	82 24	87·0	22 46	81 19	86·6	22 42	80 14	86·2	22 38	79 09	85·8	22 33	78 05	85·4	203
24 156	23 52	83 26	87·3	23 49	82 21	86·9	23 45	81 15	86·5	23 41	80 10	86·0	23 37	79 05	85·6	23 32	77 59	85·1	204
25 155	24 51	83 23	87·2	24 48	82 17	86·7	24 44	81 11	86·3	24 40	80 05	85·8	24 36	79 00	85·4	24 31	77 54	84·9	205
26 154	25 51	83 20	87·1	25 48	82 13	86·6	25 44	81 07	86·1	25 39	80 00	85·6	25 35	78 54	85·2	25 29	77 48	84·7	206
27 153	26 50	83 16	87·0	26 47	82 09	86·4	26 43	81 02	86·0	26 38	79 55	85·4	26 34	78 48	85·0	26 28	77 42	84·5	207
28 152	27 50	83 13	86·8	27 46	82 05	86·3	27 42	80 57	85·8	27 38	79 50	85·2	27 33	78 42	84·9	27 27	77 35	84·2	208
29 151	28 50	83 09	86·7	28 46	82 01	86·1	28 41	80 52	85·6	28 37	79 44	85·0	28 31	78 36	84·7	28 25	77 28	84·0	209
30 150	29 49	83 05	86·5	29 45	81 56	86·0	29 41	80 47	85·4	29 36	79 38	84·8	29 30	78 29	84·3	29 24	77 21	83·7	210
31 149	30 49	83 01	86·4	30 45	81 51	85·8	30 40	80 41	85·2	30 35	79 32	84·6	30 29	78 23	84·0	30 22	77 13	83·5	211
32 148	31 48	82 57	86·3	31 44	81 46	85·6	31 39	80 35	85·0	31 34	79 25	84·4	31 27	78 15	83·8	31 21	77 05	83·2	212
33 147	32 48	82 51	86·1	32 43	81 40	85·5	32 38	80 29	84·8	32 33	79 18	84·2	32 26	78 08	83·6	32 19	76 57	82·9	213
34 146	33 47	82 46	86·0	33 43	81 35	85·3	33 37	80 23	84·6	33 32	79 11	84·0	33 25	78 00	83·3	33 18	76 48	82·7	214
35 145	34 47	82 41	85·8	34 42	81 29	85·1	34 37	80 16	84·4	34 30	79 03	83·7	34 24	77 51	83·1	34 16	76 39	82·4	215
36 144	35 46	82 36	85·7	35 41	81 22	84·9	35 36	80 09	84·2	35 28	78 55	83·5	35 21	77 42	82·8	35 13	76 29	82·1	216
37 143	36 46	82 30	85·5	36 41	81 16	84·8	36 35	80 01	84·0	36 27	78 47	83·3	36 19	77 33	82·5	36 11	76 19	81·8	217
38 142	37 45	82 24	85·3	37 40	81 09	84·6	37 34	79 53	83·8	37 26	78 38	83·0	37 18	77 23	82·3	37 09	76 09	81·5	218
39 141	38 45	82 18	85·2	38 39	81 01	84·4	38 33	79 45	83·6	38 25	78 29	82·8	38 16	77 13	82·0	38 07	75 57	81·2	219
40 140	39 44	82 11	85·0	39 39	80 54	84·2	39 32	79 36	83·3	39 24	78 19	82·5	39 15	77 02	81·7	39 05	75 46	80·9	220
41 139	40 44	82 04	84·8	40 38	80 46	84·0	40 31	79 27	83·1	40 23	78 09	82·3	40 13	76 51	81·4	40 03	75 33	80·6	221
42 138	41 43	81 57	84·6	41 37	80 37	83·7	41 30	79 17	82·9	41 21	77 58	82·0	41 13	76 39	81·1	41 02	75 21	80·3	222
43 137	42 42	81 49	84·4	42 36	80 28	83·5	42 29	79 07	82·6	42 20	77 47	81·7	42 12	76 27	80·8	42 01	75 07	79·9	223
44 136	43 42	81 41	84·2	43 35	80 19	83·3	43 28	78 57	82·3	43 19	77 35	81·4	43 10	76 14	80·5	43 00	74 53	79·6	224
45 135	44 41	81 33	84·1	44 34	80 09	83·1	44 27	78 46	82·1	44 18	77 23	81·1	44 08	76 00	80·1	43 57	74 38	79·2	225

LHA/F	F	6° A/H	6° B/P	6° Z1/Z2	7° A/H	7° B/P	7° Z1/Z2	8° A/H	8° B/P	8° Z1/Z2	9° A/H	9° B/P	9° Z1/Z2	10° A/H	10° B/P	10° Z1/Z2	11° A/H	11° B/P	11° Z1/Z2	A	LHA
45	135	44 41	81 33	84·0	44 34	80 09	83·1	44 27	78 46	82·1	44 18	77 22	81·1	44 08	76 00	80·1	43 57	74 38	79·2	315	225
46	134	45 41	81 24	83·8	45 34	79 59	82·8	45 26	78 37	81·8	45 16	77 09	80·8	45 06	75 45	79·8	44 55	74 25	78·8	314	226
47	133	46 40	81 14	83·6	46 33	79 48	82·6	46 24	78 21	81·5	46 15	76 56	80·5	46 04	75 30	79·5	45 53	74 05	78·4	313	227
48	132	47 39	81 04	83·4	47 31	79 36	82·3	47 23	78 08	81·2	47 13	76 41	80·2	47 03	75 14	79·1	46 51	73 48	78·0	312	228
49	131	48 38	80 54	83·1	48 30	79 24	82·0	48 22	77 55	80·9	48 12	76 26	79·8	48 01	74 57	78·7	47 48	73 30	77·6	311	229
50	130	49 38	80 43	82·9	49 29	79 11	81·7	49 20	77 40	80·6	49 10	76 09	79·4	48 58	74 40	78·3	48 46	73 10	77·2	310	230
51	129	50 37	80 31	82·6	50 29	78 58	81·4	50 19	77 25	80·2	50 08	75 53	79·1	49 56	74 21	77·9	49 43	72 50	76·7	309	231
52	128	51 36	80 19	82·4	51 27	78 43	81·1	51 18	77 08	79·9	51 06	75 34	78·7	50 54	74 01	77·5	50 40	72 26	76·3	308	232
53	127	52 35	80 06	82·1	52 26	78 28	80·8	52 16	76 51	79·5	52 04	75 15	78·3	51 52	73 40	77·0	51 37	72 06	75·8	307	233
54	126	53 34	79 53	81·8	53 25	78 12	80·5	53 14	76 33	79·2	53 02	74 55	77·8	52 49	73 18	76·6	52 35	71 42	75·3	306	234
55	125	54 33	79 37	81·5	54 23	77 55	80·1	54 13	76 14	78·8	54 00	74 34	77·4	53 47	72 55	76·1	53 31	71 17	74·8	305	235
56	124	55 32	79 21	81·2	55 22	77 37	79·8	55 11	75 54	78·3	54 58	74 11	76·9	54 44	72 30	75·6	54 28	70 50	74·2	304	236
57	123	56 31	79 05	80·9	56 21	77 18	79·4	56 09	75 32	77·9	55 56	73 47	76·5	55 41	72 04	75·0	55 25	70 22	73·6	303	237
58	122	57 29	78 47	80·5	57 18	76 55	79·0	57 07	75 09	77·4	56 53	73 22	75·9	56 38	71 36	74·5	56 21	69 51	73·0	302	238
59	121	58 28	78 28	80·1	58 16	76 35	78·5	58 05	74 44	77·0	57 51	72 55	75·4	57 35	71 06	73·9	57 17	69 19	72·4	301	239
60	120	59 27	78 08	79·7	59 15	76 12	78·1	59 03	74 18	76·4	58 48	72 26	74·8	58 32	70 34	73·3	58 13	68 45	71·7	300	240
61	119	60 26	77 46	79·3	60 14	75 47	77·6	60 01	73 50	75·9	59 45	71 55	74·2	59 28	70 00	72·6	59 09	68 09	71·0	299	241
62	118	61 25	77 23	78·9	61 12	75 21	77·1	60 58	73 20	75·3	60 42	71 21	73·6	60 24	69 25	71·9	60 05	67 31	70·3	298	242
63	117	62 23	76 58	78·4	62 10	74 52	76·5	61 56	72 48	74·7	61 39	70 46	72·9	61 20	68 46	71·2	61 00	66 49	69·5	297	243
64	116	63 22	76 31	77·9	63 08	74 21	76·0	62 53	72 13	74·1	62 35	70 08	72·2	62 16	68 05	70·4	61 55	66 05	68·6	296	244
65	115	64 20	76 02	77·4	64 05	73 48	75·4	63 50	71 36	73·4	63 32	69 28	71·5	63 11	67 21	69·6	62 50	65 18	67·7	295	245
66	114	65 18	75 31	76·8	65 03	73 12	74·7	64 47	70 56	72·6	64 28	68 43	70·6	64 07	66 34	68·7	63 44	64 27	66·8	294	246
67	113	66 16	74 57	76·2	66 00	72 32	74·0	65 43	70 14	71·8	65 23	67 56	69·8	65 02	65 43	67·8	64 38	63 33	65·8	293	247
68	112	67 14	74 20	75·5	66 57	71 51	73·2	66 40	69 26	71·0	66 19	67 07	68·8	65 56	64 48	66·7	65 32	62 35	64·7	292	248
69	111	68 12	73 39	74·8	67 54	71 05	72·4	67 36	68 35	70·1	67 14	66 09	67·8	66 50	63 48	65·7	66 25	61 31	63·6	291	249
70	110	69 09	72 55	74·0	68 50	70 15	71·5	68 31	67 40	69·1	68 08	65 08	66·7	67 44	62 44	64·5	67 17	60 23	62·3	290	250
71	109	70 07	72 06	73·1	69 46	69 20	70·5	69 26	66 39	68·0	69 03	64 03	65·6	68 37	61 34	63·2	68 09	59 10	61·0	289	251
72	108	71 03	71 13	72·2	70 42	68 20	69·4	70 21	65 33	66·8	69 57	62 53	64·3	69 29	60 17	61·9	69 00	57 50	59·6	288	252
73	107	72 00	70 14	71·1	71 38	67 13	68·3	71 16	64 22	65·5	70 50	61 34	62·9	70 21	58 54	60·4	69 50	56 23	58·0	287	253
74	106	72 56	69 08	70·0	72 33	65 59	67·0	72 09	62 59	64·1	71 42	60 07	61·4	71 12	57 24	58·8	70 40	54 49	56·4	286	254
75	105	73 52	67 54	68·7	73 28	64 37	65·5	73 03	61 30	62·6	72 34	58 32	59·7	72 02	55 44	57·1	71 28	53 06	54·5	285	255
76	104	74 45	66 28	67·3	74 20	63 05	64·0	73 55	59 51	60·8	73 24	56 47	57·9	72 51	53 55	55·1	72 16	51 13	52·6	284	256
77	103	75 42	64 51	65·6	75 14	61 24	62·2	74 46	58 01	58·9	74 14	54 52	55·9	73 39	51 55	53·1	73 02	49 10	50·4	283	257
78	102	76 36	63 02	63·7	76 06	59 26	60·2	75 37	55 57	56·8	75 02	52 42	53·6	74 26	49 42	50·8	73 47	46 56	48·1	282	258
79	101	77 29	61 00	61·7	76 57	57 14	57·9	76 26	53 38	54·4	75 49	50 18	51·2	75 11	47 16	48·2	74 30	44 28	45·5	281	259
80	100	78 21	58 43	59·3	77 47	54 44	55·3	77 13	51 01	51·7	76 35	47 38	48·4	75 54	44 35	45·4	75 11	41 47	42·7	280	260
81	99	79 12	56 06	56·6	78 37	51 52	52·4	77 59	48 04	48·7	77 18	44 39	45·4	76 35	41 35	42·4	75 49	38 50	39·7	279	261
82	98	80 01	52 56	53·4	79 21	48 35	49·1	78 42	44 43	45·3	77 59	41 18	41·9	77 13	38 17	39·0	76 26	35 36	36·4	278	262
83	97	80 47	49 13	49·6	80 05	44 47	45·4	79 23	40 56	41·4	78 37	37 35	38·1	77 49	34 39	35·3	76 59	32 05	32·8	277	263
84	96	81 31	44 51	45·2	80 46	40 24	40·8	80 01	36 38	37·1	79 12	33 35	33·9	78 21	30 40	31·2	77 29	28 28	28·8	276	264
85	95	82 12	39 40	39·9	81 24	35 36	35·7	80 36	31 48	32·7	79 43	28 49	29·2	78 50	26 18	26·7	77 56	24 09	24·6	275	265
86	94	82 48	33 34	33·8	81 56	29 36	29·8	81 04	26 24	26·7	80 09	23 46	24·1	79 14	21 35	21·9	78 18	19 44	20·1	274	266
87	93	83 18	26 28	26·6	82 23	23 05	23·3	81 28	20 25	20·6	80 31	18 17	18·5	79 34	16 32	16·8	78 36	15 14	15·4	273	267
88	92	83 41	18 22	18·5	82 45	15 52	16·0	81 45	13 57	14·1	80 47	12 26	12·6	79 48	11 12	11·4	78 49	10 11	10·4	272	268
89	91	83 55	9 26	9·5	82 56	8 05	8·2	81 56	7 05	7·1	80 57	6 17	6·4	79 57	5 39	5·7	78 57	5 08	5·2	271	269
90	90	84 00	0 00	0·0	83 00	0 00	0·0	82 00	0 00	0·0	81 00	0 00	0·0	80 00	0 00	0·0	79 00	0 00	0·0	270	270

N. Lat.: for LHA > 180° .... $Z_n = Z$
for LHA < 180° .... $Z_n = 360° - Z$

S. Lat.: for LHA > 180° .... $Z_n = 180° - Z$
for LHA < 180° .... $Z_n = 180° + Z$

SIGHT REDUCTION TABLE

B: (−) for 90° < LHA < 270°
Dec:(−) for Lat. contrary name

Z₁: same sign as B
Z₂: (−) for F > 90°

Lat./A	LHA/F	12° A/H	12° B/P	12° Z_1/Z_2	13° A/H	13° B/P	13° Z_1/Z_2	14° A/H	14° B/P	14° Z_1/Z_2	15° A/H	15° B/P	15° Z_1/Z_2	16° A/H	16° B/P	16° Z_1/Z_2	17° A/H	17° B/P	17° Z_1/Z_2	Lat./A	LHA
180	0	0 00	78 00	90·0	0 00	77 00	90·0	0 00	76 00	90·0	0 00	75 00	90·0	0 00	74 00	90·0	0 00	73 00	90·0	360	180
179	1	0 59	78 00	89·8	0 58	77 00	89·8	0 58	76 00	89·8	0 58	75 00	89·8	0 58	74 00	89·7	0 57	73 00	89·7	359	181
178	2	1 57	78 00	89·6	1 57	77 00	89·6	1 56	76 00	89·5	1 56	75 00	89·5	1 55	73 59	89·4	1 55	72 59	89·4	358	182
177	3	2 56	77 59	89·4	2 55	76 59	89·4	2 55	75 59	89·3	2 54	74 59	89·2	2 53	73 59	89·2	2 52	72 59	89·1	357	183
176	4	3 55	77 58	89·2	3 54	76 58	89·1	3 53	75 58	89·1	3 52	74 58	89·0	3 51	73 58	88·9	3 49	72 58	88·8	356	184
175	5	4 53	77 57	89·0	4 52	76 57	88·9	4 51	75 57	88·8	4 50	74 57	88·7	4 48	73 57	88·6	4 47	72 56	88·5	355	185
174	6	5 52	77 56	88·7	5 51	76 56	88·6	5 49	75 56	88·6	5 48	74 55	88·5	5 46	73 55	88·3	5 44	72 55	88·2	354	186
173	7	6 51	77 55	88·5	6 49	76 54	88·4	6 47	75 54	88·4	6 46	74 54	88·2	6 44	73 53	88·1	6 42	72 53	87·9	353	187
172	8	7 49	77 53	88·3	7 48	76 53	88·2	7 46	75 52	88·1	7 44	74 52	88·0	7 41	73 51	87·8	7 39	72 51	87·6	352	188
171	9	8 48	77 51	88·1	8 46	76 51	88·0	8 44	75 50	87·9	8 41	74 49	87·7	8 39	73 48	87·5	8 36	72 48	87·3	351	189
170	10	9 47	77 49	87·9	9 44	76 48	87·7	9 42	75 48	87·6	9 39	74 47	87·4	9 37	73 46	87·2	9 34	72 45	87·0	350	190
169	11	10 45	77 47	87·7	10 43	76 46	87·5	10 40	75 45	87·3	10 37	74 44	87·1	10 34	73 43	86·9	10 31	72 42	86·7	349	191
168	12	11 44	77 44	87·5	11 41	76 43	87·3	11 38	75 42	87·1	11 35	74 41	86·9	11 32	73 40	86·6	11 28	72 39	86·4	348	192
167	13	12 43	77 42	87·3	12 40	76 40	87·0	12 36	75 39	86·8	12 33	74 37	86·6	12 29	73 36	86·3	12 25	72 35	86·1	347	193
166	14	13 41	77 39	87·0	13 38	76 37	86·8	13 35	75 35	86·5	13 31	74 34	86·3	13 27	73 32	86·1	13 23	72 31	85·8	346	194
165	15	14 40	77 36	86·8	14 36	76 33	86·6	14 33	75 32	86·3	14 29	74 30	86·0	14 24	73 28	85·8	14 20	72 26	85·5	345	195
164	16	15 38	77 32	86·6	15 35	76 30	86·3	15 31	75 28	86·0	15 26	74 25	85·8	15 22	73 23	85·5	15 17	72 21	85·2	344	196
163	17	16 37	77 28	86·4	16 33	76 26	86·1	16 29	75 23	85·8	16 24	74 21	85·5	16 19	73 18	85·2	16 14	72 16	84·9	343	197
162	18	17 36	77 24	86·1	17 31	76 21	85·8	17 27	75 19	85·5	17 22	74 16	85·2	17 17	73 13	84·9	17 11	72 11	84·6	342	198
161	19	18 34	77 20	85·9	18 30	76 17	85·6	18 25	75 14	85·2	18 20	74 11	84·9	18 14	73 08	84·6	18 08	72 05	84·3	341	199
160	20	19 33	77 15	85·7	19 28	76 12	85·3	19 23	75 08	85·0	19 17	74 05	84·7	19 12	73 02	84·3	19 05	71 59	83·9	340	200
159	21	20 31	77 10	85·4	20 26	76 07	85·1	20 21	75 03	84·7	20 15	73 59	84·3	20 09	72 55	84·0	20 03	71 52	83·6	339	201
158	22	21 29	77 05	85·2	21 24	76 01	84·8	21 19	74 57	84·4	21 13	73 53	84·0	21 06	72 49	83·6	21 00	71 45	83·3	338	202
157	23	22 28	77 00	85·0	22 23	75 55	84·5	22 17	74 51	84·1	22 10	73 46	83·7	22 04	72 42	83·3	21 57	71 38	82·9	337	203
156	24	23 27	76 54	84·7	23 21	75 49	84·3	23 15	74 44	83·9	23 08	73 39	83·4	23 01	72 34	83·0	22 53	71 30	82·6	336	204
155	25	24 25	76 48	84·5	24 19	75 43	84·0	24 13	74 37	83·6	24 06	73 32	83·1	23 58	72 27	82·7	23 50	71 22	82·2	335	205
154	26	25 23	76 42	84·2	25 17	75 36	83·7	25 10	74 30	83·3	25 03	73 24	82·8	24 55	72 18	82·4	24 47	71 13	81·9	334	206
153	27	26 22	76 35	84·0	26 15	75 28	83·5	26 08	74 22	83·0	26 01	73 16	82·5	25 52	72 10	82·0	25 44	71 04	81·5	333	207
152	28	27 20	76 28	83·7	27 13	75 21	83·2	27 06	74 14	82·7	26 58	73 07	82·2	26 50	72 00	81·6	26 41	70 54	81·2	332	208
151	29	28 18	76 20	83·4	28 11	75 13	82·9	28 04	74 05	82·4	27 55	72 58	81·8	27 47	71 51	81·3	27 37	70 44	80·8	331	209
150	30	29 17	76 13	83·2	29 09	75 04	82·6	29 01	73 56	82·0	28 53	72 48	81·5	28 44	71 40	81·0	28 34	70 33	80·4	330	210
149	31	30 15	76 04	82·9	30 07	74 56	82·3	29 59	73 47	81·7	29 50	72 38	81·2	29 41	71 30	80·6	29 30	70 22	80·0	329	211
148	32	31 13	75 56	82·6	31 05	74 46	82·0	30 57	73 37	81·4	30 47	72 28	80·8	30 37	71 19	80·2	30 27	70 11	79·6	328	212
147	33	32 10	75 47	82·3	32 03	74 37	81·7	31 54	73 27	81·1	31 44	72 17	80·5	31 34	71 07	79·9	31 23	69 58	79·2	327	213
146	34	33 08	75 37	82·0	33 01	74 26	81·4	32 52	73 16	80·7	32 41	72 05	80·1	32 31	70 55	79·5	32 19	69 45	78·8	326	214
145	35	34 06	75 27	81·7	33 59	74 16	81·0	33 49	73 04	80·4	33 38	71 53	79·7	33 28	70 42	79·1	33 16	69 32	78·4	325	215
144	36	35 06	75 17	81·4	34 56	74 04	80·7	34 46	72 52	80·0	34 36	71 40	79·4	34 24	70 29	78·7	34 12	69 18	78·0	324	216
143	37	36 04	75 06	81·1	35 54	73 53	80·4	35 44	72 40	79·7	35 33	71 27	79·0	35 21	70 15	78·3	35 08	69 03	77·6	323	217
142	38	37 02	74 54	80·8	36 52	73 40	80·0	36 41	72 27	79·3	36 30	71 13	78·6	36 17	70 00	77·8	36 04	68 48	77·1	322	218
141	39	38 00	74 42	80·4	37 49	73 27	79·7	37 38	72 13	78·9	37 26	70 59	78·2	37 13	69 45	77·4	37 00	68 32	76·7	321	219
140	40	38 57	74 30	80·1	38 47	73 14	79·3	38 35	71 58	78·5	38 23	70 43	77·7	38 10	69 29	77·0	37 56	68 15	76·2	320	220
139	41	39 55	74 16	79·8	39 44	72 59	78·9	39 32	71 43	78·1	39 19	70 27	77·3	39 06	69 12	76·5	38 51	67 57	75·7	319	221
138	42	40 53	74 02	79·4	40 41	72 45	78·5	40 29	71 27	77·7	40 16	70 10	76·9	40 02	68 54	76·1	39 47	67 38	75·3	318	222
137	43	41 51	73 48	79·0	41 39	72 29	78·2	41 26	71 11	77·3	41 12	69 53	76·4	40 58	68 36	75·6	40 42	67 19	74·7	317	223
136	44	42 48	73 34	78·6	42 36	72 12	77·7	42 23	70 53	76·9	42 09	69 34	76·0	41 54	68 16	75·1	41 38	66 58	74·2	316	224
135	45	43 46	73 16	78·3	43 33	71 55	77·3	43 19	70 35	76·4	43 05	69 15	75·5	42 49	67 56	74·6	42 33	66 37	73·7	315	225

Lat./A	12°			13°			14°			15°			16°			17°			Lat./A
LHA/F	A/H	B/P	Z₁/Z₂	A/H	B/P	Z₁/Z₂	A/H	B/P	Z₁/Z₂	A/H	B/P	Z₁/Z₂	A/H	B/P	Z₁/Z₂	A/H	B/P	Z₁/Z₂	LHA
45	43 46	73 16	78·3	43 33	71 55	77·3	43 19	70 35	76·4	43 05	69 15	75·5	42 49	67 56	74·6	42 33	66 37	73·7	315
46	44 43	72 59	77·8	44 30	71 37	76·9	44 16	70 15	75·9	44 01	68 54	75·0	43 45	67 34	74·1	43 28	66 15	73·2	314
47	45 40	72 41	77·4	45 27	71 18	76·4	45 12	69 54	75·5	44 57	68 31	74·5	44 40	67 12	73·5	44 23	65 51	72·6	313
48	46 38	72 23	77·0	46 24	70 58	76·0	46 09	69 34	75·0	45 53	68 11	74·0	45 35	66 48	73·0	45 17	65 27	72·0	312
49	47 35	72 03	76·5	47 20	70 37	75·5	47 05	69 11	74·4	46 48	67 47	73·4	46 30	66 23	72·4	46 12	65 01	71·4	311
50	48 32	71 42	76·1	48 17	70 15	75·0	48 01	68 48	73·9	47 44	67 22	72·9	47 25	65 58	71·8	47 06	64 34	70·8	310
51	49 29	71 20	75·6	49 13	69 51	74·5	48 57	68 23	73·4	48 39	66 56	72·3	48 20	65 30	71·2	48 00	64 05	70·1	309
52	50 25	70 57	75·1	50 09	69 27	73·9	49 52	67 57	72·8	49 34	66 29	71·7	49 15	65 02	70·6	48 54	63 35	69·5	308
53	51 22	70 33	74·6	51 06	69 01	73·4	50 48	67 30	72·2	50 30	66 00	71·0	50 09	64 32	69·9	49 48	63 04	68·8	307
54	52 19	70 07	74·0	52 02	68 33	72·8	51 43	67 01	71·6	51 24	65 30	70·4	51 03	64 00	69·2	50 41	62 31	68·1	306
55	53 15	69 40	73·5	52 57	68 04	72·2	52 38	66 30	70·9	52 18	64 58	69·7	51 57	63 26	68·5	51 34	61 56	67·3	305
56	54 11	69 11	72·9	53 53	67 34	71·6	53 33	65 58	70·3	53 12	64 24	69·0	52 50	62 51	67·8	52 27	61 20	66·6	304
57	55 07	68 41	72·2	54 48	67 02	70·9	54 28	65 24	69·6	54 06	63 48	68·3	53 43	62 14	67·0	53 19	60 42	65·8	303
58	56 03	68 09	71·6	55 43	66 28	70·2	55 22	64 48	68·8	55 00	63 11	67·5	54 36	61 35	66·2	54 12	60 01	64·9	302
59	56 58	67 34	70·9	56 38	65 51	69·5	56 16	64 10	68·1	55 53	62 31	66·7	55 29	60 54	65·4	55 03	59 18	64·1	301
60	57 54	66 58	70·2	57 33	65 13	68·7	57 10	63 30	67·3	56 46	61 49	65·9	56 21	60 10	64·5	55 55	58 33	63·1	300
61	58 49	66 20	69·4	58 27	64 32	67·9	58 04	62 47	66·5	57 39	61 04	65·0	57 13	59 24	63·6	56 46	57 46	62·2	299
62	59 44	65 38	68·6	59 21	63 49	67·1	58 57	62 02	65·5	58 31	60 17	64·0	58 05	58 35	62·6	57 36	56 56	61·2	298
63	60 38	64 55	67·8	60 15	63 03	66·2	59 50	61 13	64·6	59 23	59 27	63·1	58 55	57 43	61·6	58 26	56 03	60·2	297
64	61 32	64 08	66·9	61 08	62 14	65·2	60 42	60 22	63·6	60 15	58 34	62·0	59 46	56 49	60·5	59 16	55 06	59·1	296
65	62 26	63 18	66·0	62 01	61 21	64·2	61 34	59 28	62·6	61 06	57 37	61·0	60 36	55 49	59·4	60 05	54 07	57·9	295
66	63 20	62 25	65·0	62 53	60 25	63·2	62 26	58 30	61·5	61 56	56 37	59·8	61 25	54 49	58·2	60 53	53 04	56·7	294
67	64 13	61 27	63·9	63 45	59 25	62·1	63 16	57 27	60·3	62 46	55 34	58·6	62 14	53 44	57·0	61 41	51 57	55·4	293
68	65 05	60 26	62·8	64 37	58 21	61·0	64 07	56 21	59·1	63 35	54 25	57·4	63 02	52 34	55·7	62 27	50 47	54·1	292
69	65 57	59 20	61·6	65 27	57 13	59·6	64 56	55 10	57·8	64 23	53 13	56·0	63 49	51 20	54·3	63 14	49 32	52·7	291
70	66 48	58 08	60·3	66 18	55 59	58·3	65 45	53 55	56·4	65 11	51 55	54·6	64 36	50 01	52·9	64 00	48 12	51·2	290
71	67 39	56 52	58·9	67 07	54 40	56·8	66 33	52 36	54·9	65 58	50 33	53·1	65 22	48 38	51·3	64 43	46 48	49·7	289
72	68 29	55 32	57·4	67 56	53 14	55·3	67 20	51 06	53·3	66 44	49 09	51·5	66 06	47 08	49·7	65 26	45 18	48·0	288
73	69 18	54 08	55·8	68 43	51 42	53·7	68 07	49 33	51·6	67 29	47 39	49·8	66 49	45 33	48·0	66 08	43 43	46·3	287
74	70 06	52 31	54·1	69 30	50 00	51·9	68 52	47 54	49·8	68 12	46 04	47·9	67 31	43 52	46·1	66 49	42 02	44·4	286
75	70 53	50 36	52·2	70 15	48 16	50·0	69 36	46 04	47·9	68 55	44 00	46·0	68 12	42 04	44·2	67 29	40 15	42·5	285
76	71 38	48 42	50·2	70 59	46 20	47·9	70 18	44 08	45·9	69 36	42 05	43·9	68 52	40 09	42·1	68 07	38 21	40·5	284
77	72 23	46 37	48·0	71 42	44 15	45·7	70 59	42 03	43·7	70 15	40 01	41·7	69 30	38 07	39·9	68 43	36 21	38·3	283
78	73 06	44 22	45·6	72 23	42 00	43·3	71 38	39 49	41·3	70 53	37 49	39·4	70 06	35 57	37·6	69 18	34 13	36·0	282
79	73 47	41 55	43·1	73 02	39 34	40·8	72 16	37 26	38·8	71 28	35 27	36·9	70 40	33 38	35·2	69 50	31 58	33·6	281
80	74 26	39 15	40·3	73 39	36 57	38·1	72 51	34 51	36·1	72 02	32 57	34·3	71 12	31 12	32·6	70 21	29 36	31·1	280
81	75 02	36 21	37·3	74 13	34 05	35·1	73 24	32 06	33·2	72 34	30 17	31·5	71 42	28 37	29·9	70 50	27 06	28·4	279
82	75 37	33 13	34·1	74 46	31 05	32·0	73 55	29 10	30·2	73 03	27 27	28·5	72 09	25 53	27·0	71 16	24 29	25·7	278
83	76 08	29 50	30·6	75 16	27 50	28·6	74 23	26 03	26·9	73 29	24 19	25·4	72 34	23 02	24·0	71 39	21 44	22·8	277
84	76 36	26 11	26·8	75 42	24 22	25·0	74 48	22 45	23·5	73 52	21 19	22·1	72 56	20 02	20·9	72 00	18 53	19·8	276
85	77 01	22 18	22·8	76 05	20 41	21·3	75 09	19 16	19·9	74 12	18 01	18·7	73 15	16 54	17·6	72 18	15 51	16·7	275
86	77 22	18 10	18·6	76 25	16 49	17·3	75 27	15 38	16·1	74 29	14 36	15·1	73 31	13 40	14·2	72 33	12 41	13·5	274
87	77 38	13 50	14·1	76 40	12 46	13·1	75 41	11 51	12·2	74 43	11 03	11·4	73 44	10 21	10·8	72 45	9 43	10·2	273
88	77 50	9 19	9·5	76 51	8 36	8·8	75 52	7 58	8·2	74 52	7 25	7·7	73 53	6 56	7·2	72 53	6 31	6·8	272
89	77 58	4 42	4·8	76 58	4 19	4·4	75 58	4 00	4·1	74 58	3 44	3·9	73 58	3 29	3·6	72 58	3 16	3·4	271
90	78 00	0 00	0·0	77 00	0 00	0·0	76 00	0 00	0·0	75 00	0 00	0·0	74 00	0 00	0·0	73 00	0 00	0·0	270

N. Lat.: for LHA > 180° ... Z_n = Z
for LHA < 180° ... Z_n = 360° − Z

S. Lat.: for LHA > 180° ... Z_n = 180° − Z
for LHA < 180° ... Z_n = 180° + Z

SIGHT REDUCTION TABLE

B: (−) for 90° < LHA < 270°
Dec:(−) for Lat. contrary name

Z₁: same sign as B
Z₂: (−) for F > 90°

Lat./A	LHA/F	18° A/H	18° B/P	18° Z₁/Z₂	19° A/H	19° B/P	19° Z₁/Z₂	20° A/H	20° B/P	20° Z₁/Z₂	21° A/H	21° B/P	21° Z₁/Z₂	22° A/H	22° B/P	22° Z₁/Z₂	23° A/H	23° B/P	23° Z₁/Z₂	LHA	Lat./A
180	0	0 00	72 00	90.0	0 00	71 00	90.0	0 00	70 00	90.0	0 00	69 00	90.0	0 00	68 00	90.0	0 00	67 00	90.0	180	360
179	1	0 57	72 00	89.7	0 57	71 00	89.7	0 56	70 00	89.7	0 56	69 00	89.7	0 56	68 00	89.6	0 55	67 00	89.6	181	359
178	2	1 54	71 59	89.4	1 53	70 59	89.3	1 53	69 59	89.3	1 52	68 59	89.3	1 51	67 59	89.3	1 50	66 59	89.2	182	358
177	3	2 51	71 59	89.1	2 50	70 59	89.0	2 49	69 59	89.0	2 48	68 58	89.0	2 47	67 58	88.9	2 46	66 58	88.8	183	357
176	4	3 48	71 58	88.8	3 47	70 57	88.7	3 46	69 57	88.6	3 44	68 57	88.6	3 42	67 57	88.5	3 41	66 57	88.4	184	356
175	5	4 45	71 56	88.5	4 44	70 56	88.4	4 42	69 56	88.3	4 40	68 56	88.3	4 38	67 55	88.1	4 36	66 55	88.0	185	355
174	6	5 42	71 54	88.1	5 40	70 54	88.0	5 38	69 54	87.9	5 36	68 54	87.9	5 34	67 53	87.7	5 31	66 53	87.6	186	354
173	7	6 39	71 52	87.8	6 37	70 52	87.7	6 35	69 52	87.6	6 32	68 51	87.5	6 29	67 51	87.4	6 26	66 51	87.3	187	353
172	8	7 36	71 50	87.5	7 34	70 50	87.4	7 31	69 49	87.2	7 28	68 49	87.1	7 25	67 48	87.0	7 22	66 48	86.9	188	352
171	9	8 33	71 47	87.2	8 30	70 47	87.0	8 27	69 46	86.9	8 24	68 46	86.8	8 20	67 45	86.6	8 17	66 45	86.5	189	351
170	10	9 30	71 44	86.9	9 27	70 44	86.7	9 23	69 43	86.5	9 20	68 42	86.4	9 16	67 42	86.2	9 12	66 41	86.1	190	350
169	11	10 27	71 41	86.6	10 24	70 40	86.4	10 20	69 39	86.2	10 16	68 39	86.0	10 11	67 38	85.8	10 07	66 37	85.7	191	349
168	12	11 24	71 37	86.2	11 20	70 36	86.0	11 16	69 35	85.8	11 12	68 34	85.6	11 07	67 33	85.4	11 02	66 32	85.3	192	348
167	13	12 21	71 33	85.9	12 17	70 32	85.7	12 12	69 31	85.5	12 07	68 30	85.3	12 02	67 29	85.1	11 57	66 28	84.8	193	347
166	14	13 18	71 29	85.6	13 13	70 28	85.4	13 08	69 26	85.1	13 03	68 25	84.9	12 58	67 24	84.7	12 52	66 22	84.4	194	346
165	15	14 15	71 24	85.3	14 10	70 23	85.0	14 05	69 21	84.8	13 59	68 20	84.5	13 53	67 18	84.3	13 47	66 16	84.0	195	345
164	16	15 12	71 19	84.9	15 06	70 18	84.7	15 01	69 16	84.4	14 55	68 14	84.1	14 48	67 12	83.9	14 42	66 10	83.6	196	344
163	17	16 09	71 14	84.6	16 03	70 12	84.3	15 57	69 10	84.0	15 50	68 08	83.7	15 44	67 06	83.5	15 37	66 04	83.2	197	343
162	18	17 05	71 08	84.3	16 59	70 06	84.0	16 53	69 03	83.7	16 46	68 01	83.4	16 39	66 59	83.1	16 32	65 57	82.8	198	342
161	19	18 02	71 02	83.9	17 56	69 59	83.6	17 49	68 57	83.3	17 42	67 54	83.0	17 34	66 52	82.7	17 26	65 49	82.3	199	341
160	20	18 59	70 56	83.6	18 52	69 53	83.2	18 45	68 50	82.9	18 37	67 47	82.6	18 29	66 44	82.2	18 21	65 41	81.9	200	340
159	21	19 56	70 49	83.2	19 48	69 45	82.9	19 41	68 42	82.5	19 33	67 39	82.2	19 24	66 36	81.8	19 16	65 33	81.5	201	339
158	22	20 52	70 41	82.9	20 45	69 38	82.5	20 37	68 34	82.1	20 28	67 31	81.8	20 19	66 27	81.4	20 10	65 24	81.0	202	338
157	23	21 49	70 33	82.5	21 41	69 29	82.1	21 32	68 26	81.7	21 24	67 22	81.4	21 14	66 18	81.0	21 05	65 15	80.6	203	337
156	24	22 45	70 25	82.2	22 37	69 21	81.8	22 28	68 17	81.3	22 19	67 12	80.9	22 09	66 09	80.5	21 59	65 05	80.1	204	336
155	25	23 42	70 17	81.8	23 33	69 12	81.4	23 24	68 07	80.9	23 14	67 03	80.5	23 04	65 58	80.1	22 54	64 54	79.7	205	335
154	26	24 38	70 07	81.4	24 29	69 02	81.0	24 20	67 57	80.5	24 09	66 52	80.1	23 59	65 48	79.6	23 48	64 43	79.2	206	334
153	27	25 35	69 58	81.1	25 25	68 52	80.6	25 15	67 47	80.1	25 05	66 42	79.7	24 54	65 36	79.2	24 42	64 32	78.7	207	333
152	28	26 31	69 48	80.7	26 21	68 42	80.2	26 11	67 36	79.7	26 00	66 30	79.2	25 48	65 25	78.7	25 36	64 19	78.3	208	332
151	29	27 27	69 37	80.3	27 17	68 31	79.8	27 06	67 24	79.3	26 55	66 18	78.8	26 43	65 12	78.3	26 30	64 07	77.8	209	331
150	30	28 24	69 26	79.9	28 13	68 19	79.4	28 01	67 12	78.8	27 50	66 06	78.3	27 37	64 59	77.8	27 24	63 53	77.3	210	330
149	31	29 20	69 14	79.5	29 08	68 07	78.9	28 57	67 00	78.4	28 44	65 53	77.8	28 31	64 46	77.3	28 18	63 39	76.8	211	329
148	32	30 16	69 02	79.1	30 04	67 54	78.5	29 52	66 46	77.9	29 39	65 39	77.4	29 26	64 32	76.8	29 12	63 25	76.3	212	328
147	33	31 12	68 49	78.7	31 00	67 41	78.1	30 47	66 32	77.5	30 34	65 24	76.9	30 20	64 17	76.3	30 05	63 09	75.8	213	327
146	34	32 08	68 36	78.2	31 55	67 27	77.6	31 42	66 18	77.0	31 28	65 09	76.4	31 14	64 01	75.8	30 59	62 53	75.2	214	326
145	35	33 04	68 22	77.8	32 51	67 12	77.2	32 37	66 03	76.5	32 23	64 54	75.9	32 08	63 45	75.3	31 52	62 36	74.7	215	325
144	36	33 59	68 07	77.3	33 46	66 57	76.7	33 32	65 47	76.0	33 17	64 37	75.4	33 01	63 28	74.8	32 45	62 19	74.2	216	324
143	37	34 55	67 52	76.9	34 41	66 41	76.2	34 26	65 30	75.5	34 11	64 20	74.9	33 55	63 10	74.2	33 38	62 00	73.6	217	323
142	38	35 50	67 36	76.4	35 36	66 24	75.7	35 21	65 13	75.0	35 05	64 02	74.4	34 48	62 51	73.7	34 31	61 41	73.0	218	322
141	39	36 46	67 19	75.9	36 31	66 06	75.2	36 15	64 54	74.5	35 59	63 43	73.8	35 42	62 32	73.1	35 24	61 21	72.4	219	321
140	40	37 41	67 01	75.5	37 26	65 48	74.7	37 10	64 35	74.0	36 53	63 23	73.3	36 35	62 12	72.6	36 17	61 01	71.8	220	320
139	41	38 36	66 42	75.0	38 20	65 29	74.2	38 04	64 15	73.4	37 46	63 02	72.7	37 28	61 50	72.0	37 09	60 39	71.2	221	319
138	42	39 31	66 23	74.5	39 15	65 08	73.7	38 58	63 54	72.9	38 40	62 41	72.1	38 21	61 28	71.4	38 01	60 16	70.6	222	318
137	43	40 26	66 03	74.0	40 09	64 47	73.1	39 51	63 33	72.3	39 33	62 19	71.5	39 13	61 05	70.7	38 53	59 52	70.0	223	317
136	44	41 21	65 42	73.4	41 03	64 25	72.5	40 45	63 10	71.7	40 26	61 55	70.9	40 06	60 41	70.1	39 45	59 27	69.3	224	316
135	45	42 16	65 21	72.8	41 57	64 02	72.0	41 38	62 46	71.1	41 19	61 30	70.3	40 58	60 15	69.5	40 37	59 01	68.7	225	315

Lat./A LHA/F	18° A/H	18° B/P	18° Z_1/Z_2	19° A/H	19° B/P	19° Z_1/Z_2	20° A/H	20° B/P	20° Z_1/Z_2	21° A/H	21° B/P	21° Z_1/Z_2	22° A/H	22° B/P	22° Z_1/Z_2	23° A/H	23° B/P	23° Z_1/Z_2	Lat./A LHA
45	42 16	65 19	72.8	41 57	64 02	72.0	41 38	62 46	71.1	41 18	61 30	70.3	40 58	60 15	69.5	40 37	59 01	68.7	225
46	43 10	64 56	72.3	42 51	63 38	71.4	42 32	62 21	70.5	42 11	61 05	69.6	41 50	59 49	68.8	41 28	58 34	68.0	226
47	44 04	64 32	71.7	43 45	63 13	70.8	43 25	61 55	69.9	43 04	60 38	69.0	42 42	59 21	68.1	42 19	58 06	67.3	227
48	44 58	64 06	71.1	44 38	62 46	70.1	44 18	61 27	69.2	43 56	60 09	68.3	43 33	58 53	67.4	43 10	57 37	66.5	228
49	45 52	63 39	70.4	45 32	62 18	69.5	45 10	60 58	68.5	44 47	59 40	67.6	44 24	58 22	66.7	44 00	57 06	65.8	229
50	46 46	63 11	69.8	46 25	61 49	68.8	46 03	60 29	67.8	45 39	59 09	66.9	45 15	57 51	65.9	44 50	56 34	65.0	230
51	47 39	62 42	69.1	47 17	61 19	68.1	46 55	59 57	67.1	46 31	58 37	66.1	46 06	57 18	65.2	45 40	56 00	64.2	231
52	48 33	62 11	68.4	48 10	60 47	67.4	47 46	59 25	66.4	47 21	58 03	65.4	46 56	56 44	64.4	46 30	55 25	63.4	232
53	49 25	61 38	67.7	49 02	60 13	66.6	48 38	58 51	65.6	48 13	57 28	64.6	47 47	56 07	63.6	47 19	54 48	62.6	233
54	50 18	61 04	67.0	49 54	59 38	65.9	49 29	58 14	64.8	49 03	56 51	63.7	48 36	55 30	62.7	48 08	54 10	61.7	234
55	51 10	60 28	66.2	50 46	59 01	65.1	50 20	57 36	64.0	49 53	56 12	62.9	49 25	54 50	61.9	48 56	53 30	60.8	235
56	52 03	59 50	65.4	51 37	58 23	64.2	51 10	56 57	63.1	50 42	55 32	62.0	50 14	54 09	61.0	49 44	52 48	59.9	236
57	52 54	59 11	64.6	52 28	57 42	63.4	52 00	56 15	62.2	51 31	54 49	61.1	51 02	53 26	60.0	50 32	52 04	59.0	237
58	53 46	58 29	63.7	53 18	56 59	62.5	52 50	55 31	61.3	52 20	54 05	60.2	51 50	52 41	59.1	51 19	51 18	58.0	238
59	54 37	57 45	62.8	54 08	56 14	61.5	53 40	54 45	60.4	53 09	53 19	59.2	52 38	51 53	58.1	52 06	50 30	57.0	239
60	55 27	56 59	61.8	54 58	55 27	60.6	54 28	53 57	59.4	53 57	52 29	58.2	53 25	51 04	57.0	52 52	49 40	55.9	240
61	56 17	56 10	60.9	55 47	54 37	59.6	55 16	53 06	58.3	54 44	51 38	57.1	54 11	50 12	55.9	53 37	48 48	54.8	241
62	57 07	55 19	59.8	56 36	53 45	58.5	56 04	52 13	57.2	55 31	50 44	56.0	54 57	49 17	54.8	54 22	47 53	53.7	242
63	57 56	54 25	58.8	57 24	52 49	57.4	56 51	51 17	56.1	56 17	49 47	54.9	55 42	48 20	53.7	55 06	46 55	52.5	243
64	58 44	53 27	57.6	58 12	51 51	56.3	57 38	50 18	54.9	57 03	48 48	53.7	56 27	47 20	52.5	55 49	45 55	51.3	244
65	59 32	52 27	56.5	58 58	50 50	55.1	58 24	49 16	53.7	57 47	47 46	52.5	57 10	46 17	51.2	56 32	44 52	50.0	245
66	60 19	51 23	55.2	59 45	49 45	53.8	59 09	48 11	52.4	58 31	46 39	51.2	57 53	45 11	49.9	57 14	43 45	48.7	246
67	61 06	50 15	53.9	60 30	48 37	52.5	59 53	47 02	51.1	59 15	45 30	49.8	58 36	44 02	48.6	57 55	42 38	47.4	247
68	61 52	49 04	52.6	61 15	47 25	51.1	60 36	45 50	49.8	59 57	44 18	48.4	59 17	42 50	47.2	58 36	41 26	46.0	248
69	62 37	47 48	51.2	61 58	46 09	49.7	61 19	44 33	48.3	60 38	43 02	47.0	59 57	41 34	45.7	59 15	40 10	44.5	249
70	63 21	46 28	49.7	62 41	44 48	48.2	62 01	43 13	46.8	61 19	41 42	45.4	60 36	40 15	44.2	59 53	38 52	43.0	250
71	64 04	45 03	48.1	63 22	43 23	46.6	62 41	41 49	45.2	61 58	40 18	43.9	61 15	38 52	42.6	60 31	37 29	41.4	251
72	64 45	43 34	46.4	64 04	41 54	44.9	63 21	40 20	43.5	62 37	38 50	42.2	61 52	37 25	40.9	61 06	36 03	39.7	252
73	65 26	41 59	44.7	64 43	40 20	43.2	63 59	38 46	41.8	63 13	37 18	40.5	62 27	35 53	39.2	61 41	34 34	38.0	253
74	66 06	40 19	42.9	65 21	38 41	41.4	64 36	37 08	40.0	63 49	35 41	38.7	63 02	34 18	37.4	62 14	32 58	36.3	254
75	66 44	38 32	40.9	65 58	36 56	39.5	65 11	35 25	38.1	64 23	34 02	36.8	63 35	32 39	35.6	62 46	31 19	34.4	255
76	67 20	36 40	38.9	66 33	35 05	37.4	65 45	33 37	36.1	64 56	32 17	34.8	64 07	30 55	33.6	63 16	29 37	32.5	256
77	67 55	34 42	36.8	67 07	33 07	35.3	66 18	31 44	34.0	65 28	30 26	32.8	64 38	29 06	31.6	63 45	27 50	30.6	257
78	68 28	32 37	34.5	67 39	31 07	33.1	66 48	29 44	31.9	65 57	28 30	30.7	65 05	27 12	29.6	64 13	25 58	28.5	258
79	69 00	30 25	32.1	68 09	29 00	30.8	67 17	27 40	29.6	66 25	26 28	28.5	65 32	25 17	27.4	64 38	24 07	26.4	259
80	69 29	28 07	29.7	68 37	26 46	28.4	67 44	25 24	27.3	66 50	24 24	26.3	65 56	23 15	25.2	65 02	22 09	24.3	260
81	69 57	25 43	27.1	69 03	24 26	25.9	68 09	23 15	24.8	67 14	22 10	23.8	66 19	21 00	22.9	65 23	20 14	22.1	261
82	70 21	23 11	24.5	69 27	22 00	23.3	68 31	20 56	22.3	67 36	19 56	21.4	66 40	19 00	20.6	65 43	18 09	19.8	262
83	70 44	20 34	21.7	69 48	19 31	20.7	68 51	18 31	19.7	67 55	17 37	18.9	66 58	16 47	18.1	66 01	16 01	17.4	263
84	71 03	17 50	18.8	70 07	16 53	17.9	69 09	16 01	17.1	68 12	15 12	16.3	67 14	14 10	15.7	66 16	13 48	15.1	264
85	71 20	15 01	15.8	70 23	14 12	15.0	69 23	13 28	14.3	68 26	12 48	13.7	67 28	12 10	13.1	66 29	11 36	12.6	265
86	71 35	12 07	12.8	70 36	11 27	12.1	69 37	10 51	11.6	68 38	10 18	11.0	67 39	9 48	10.6	66 40	9 20	10.1	266
87	71 46	9 09	9.6	70 46	8 39	9.1	69 47	8 11	8.7	68 48	7 46	8.3	67 48	7 23	8.0	66 49	7 02	7.6	267
88	71 54	6 08	6.4	70 54	5 47	6.1	69 54	5 29	5.8	68 55	5 12	5.6	67 55	4 56	5.3	66 55	4 42	5.1	268
89	71 58	3 00	3.2	70 58	2 54	3.1	69 59	2 45	2.9	68 59	2 36	2.8	67 59	2 28	2.7	66 59	2 21	2.6	269
90	72 00	0 00	0.0	71 00	0 00	0.0	70 00	0 00	0.0	69 00	0 00	0.0	68 00	0 00	0.0	67 00	0 00	0.0	270

N. Lat: for LHA > 180° ... $Z_n = Z$
for LHA < 180° ... $Z_n = 360° - Z$

S. Lat: for LHA > 180° ... $Z_n = 180° - Z$
for LHA < 180° ... $Z_n = 180° + Z$

SIGHT REDUCTION TABLE

B: (−) for 90° < LHA < 270°
Dec:(−) for Lat. contrary name

Z₁: same sign as B
Z₂: (−) for F > 90°

Lat. / A	24°			25°			26°			27°			28°			29°			Lat. / A
LHA/F	A/H	B/P	Z₁/Z₂	A/H	B/P	Z₁/Z₂	A/H	B/P	Z₁/Z₂	A/H	B/P	Z₁/Z₂	A/H	B/P	Z₁/Z₂	A/H	B/P	Z₁/Z₂	LHA
0 180	0 00	66 00	90·0	0 00	65 00	90·0	0 00	64 00	90·0	0 00	63 00	90·0	0 00	62 00	90·0	0 00	61 00	90·0	180
1 179	0 55	66 00	89·6	0 54	65 00	89·6	0 54	64 00	89·6	0 53	63 00	89·5	0 53	62 00	89·5	0 52	61 00	89·5	181
2 178	1 50	65 59	89·2	1 49	64 59	89·2	1 48	63 59	89·1	1 47	62 59	89·1	1 46	61 58	89·1	1 45	60 59	89·0	182
3 177	2 44	65 58	88·8	2 43	64 58	88·7	2 42	63 58	88·7	2 40	62 58	88·6	2 39	61 58	88·6	2 37	60 58	88·5	183
4 176	3 39	65 57	88·4	3 37	64 57	88·3	3 36	63 57	88·2	3 34	62 57	88·2	3 32	61 57	88·1	3 30	60 56	88·1	184
5 175	4 34	65 55	88·0	4 32	64 55	87·9	4 30	63 55	87·8	4 27	62 55	87·7	4 25	61 55	87·6	4 22	60 54	87·6	185
6 174	5 29	65 53	87·6	5 26	64 53	87·5	5 23	63 53	87·4	5 21	62 52	87·3	5 18	61 52	87·2	5 15	60 52	87·1	186
7 173	6 24	65 50	87·1	6 20	64 50	87·0	6 17	63 50	86·9	6 14	62 50	86·8	6 11	61 49	86·7	6 07	60 49	86·6	187
8 172	7 18	65 47	86·7	7 15	64 47	86·6	7 11	63 47	86·5	7 07	62 46	86·3	7 04	61 46	86·2	6 59	60 46	86·1	188
9 171	8 13	65 44	86·3	8 09	64 44	86·2	8 05	63 43	86·0	8 01	62 43	85·9	7 56	61 42	85·7	7 52	60 42	85·6	189
10 170	9 08	65 40	85·9	9 03	64 40	85·7	8 59	63 39	85·6	8 54	62 39	85·4	8 49	61 38	85·3	8 44	60 38	85·1	190
11 169	10 02	65 36	85·5	9 57	64 35	85·3	9 52	63 35	85·1	9 47	62 34	85·0	9 42	61 33	84·8	9 36	60 33	84·6	191
12 168	10 57	65 32	85·1	10 52	64 31	84·9	10 46	63 30	84·7	10 41	62 29	84·5	10 35	61 28	84·3	10 29	60 28	84·1	192
13 167	11 52	65 27	84·6	11 46	64 26	84·4	11 40	63 25	84·2	11 34	62 24	84·0	11 27	61 23	83·8	11 21	60 22	83·6	193
14 166	12 46	65 21	84·2	12 40	64 20	84·0	12 34	63 19	83·8	12 27	62 18	83·5	12 20	61 17	83·3	12 13	60 16	83·1	194
15 165	13 41	65 15	83·8	13 34	64 14	83·5	13 27	63 13	83·3	13 20	62 11	83·1	13 13	61 10	82·8	13 05	60 09	82·6	195
16 164	14 35	65 09	83·3	14 28	64 07	83·1	14 21	63 06	82·8	14 13	62 04	82·6	14 05	61 03	82·3	13 57	60 02	82·1	196
17 163	15 29	65 02	82·9	15 22	64 00	82·6	15 14	62 59	82·4	15 06	61 57	82·1	14 58	60 56	81·8	14 49	59 54	81·6	197
18 162	16 24	64 55	82·5	16 16	63 53	82·2	16 08	62 51	81·9	15 59	61 49	81·6	15 50	60 47	81·3	15 41	59 46	81·0	198
19 161	17 18	64 47	82·0	17 10	63 45	81·7	17 01	62 43	81·4	16 52	61 41	81·1	16 42	60 39	80·8	16 33	59 37	80·5	199
20 160	18 12	64 39	81·6	18 03	63 36	81·3	17 54	62 34	80·9	17 44	61 32	80·6	17 35	60 30	80·3	17 24	59 28	80·0	200
21 159	19 07	64 30	81·1	18 57	63 28	80·8	18 47	62 25	80·4	18 37	61 23	80·1	18 27	60 20	79·8	18 16	59 18	79·5	201
22 158	20 01	64 21	80·7	19 51	63 18	80·3	19 41	62 15	80·0	19 30	61 13	79·6	19 19	60 10	79·3	19 08	59 08	78·9	202
23 157	20 55	64 11	80·2	20 44	63 08	79·8	20 34	62 05	79·5	20 22	61 02	79·1	20 11	59 59	78·7	19 59	58 57	78·4	203
24 156	21 49	64 01	79·7	21 38	62 58	79·3	21 27	61 54	79·0	21 15	60 51	78·6	21 03	59 48	78·2	20 50	58 45	77·8	204
25 155	22 43	63 50	79·3	22 31	62 46	78·9	22 19	61 43	78·4	22 07	60 39	78·0	21 55	59 36	77·7	21 42	58 33	77·3	205
26 154	23 36	63 39	78·8	23 25	62 35	78·4	23 12	61 31	77·9	22 59	60 27	77·5	22 46	59 24	77·1	22 33	58 20	76·7	206
27 153	24 30	63 27	78·3	24 18	62 22	77·8	24 05	61 18	77·4	23 52	60 14	77·0	23 38	59 10	76·5	23 24	58 07	76·1	207
28 152	25 24	63 14	77·8	25 11	62 10	77·3	24 57	61 05	76·9	24 43	60 01	76·4	24 29	58 57	76·0	24 15	57 53	75·5	208
29 151	26 17	63 01	77·3	26 04	61 56	76·8	25 50	60 51	76·3	25 36	59 47	75·9	25 21	58 42	75·4	25 05	57 38	75·0	209
30 150	27 11	62 48	76·8	26 57	61 42	76·3	26 42	60 37	75·8	26 27	59 32	75·3	26 12	58 27	74·8	25 56	57 23	74·4	210
31 149	28 04	62 33	76·3	27 50	61 27	75·8	27 35	60 22	75·2	27 19	59 16	74·7	27 03	58 11	74·2	26 46	57 07	73·8	211
32 148	28 57	62 18	75·7	28 42	61 12	75·2	28 27	60 06	74·7	28 10	59 00	74·2	27 54	57 55	73·7	27 37	56 50	73·1	212
33 147	29 50	62 02	75·2	29 35	60 56	74·7	29 19	59 49	74·1	29 02	58 43	73·6	28 45	57 38	73·0	28 27	56 32	72·5	213
34 146	30 43	61 46	74·7	30 28	60 39	74·1	30 10	59 32	73·5	29 53	58 26	73·0	29 35	57 20	72·4	29 17	56 14	71·9	214
35 145	31 36	61 28	74·1	31 19	60 21	73·5	31 02	59 14	72·9	30 44	58 07	72·4	30 26	57 01	71·8	30 07	55 55	71·2	215
36 144	32 29	61 10	73·5	32 11	60 02	72·9	31 53	58 55	72·3	31 35	57 48	71·7	31 16	56 41	71·2	30 56	55 34	70·6	216
37 143	33 21	60 52	73·0	33 03	59 43	72·3	32 45	58 35	71·7	32 26	57 28	71·1	32 06	56 21	70·5	31 46	55 14	69·9	217
38 142	34 13	60 32	72·4	33 55	59 23	71·7	33 36	58 15	71·1	33 16	57 07	70·5	32 56	55 59	69·9	32 35	54 53	69·3	218
39 141	35 06	60 11	71·8	34 47	59 02	71·1	34 27	57 53	70·5	34 06	56 45	69·8	33 45	55 37	69·2	33 24	54 30	68·6	219
40 140	35 58	59 50	71·2	35 38	58 40	70·5	35 17	57 31	69·8	34 56	56 22	69·1	34 34	55 14	68·5	34 12	54 07	67·9	220
41 139	36 49	59 28	70·5	36 29	58 17	69·8	36 08	57 08	69·2	35 46	55 59	68·5	35 24	54 50	67·8	35 01	53 42	67·1	221
42 138	37 41	59 04	69·9	37 20	57 54	69·2	36 58	56 43	68·5	36 36	55 34	67·8	36 13	54 25	67·1	35 49	53 17	66·4	222
43 137	38 32	58 40	69·2	38 11	57 29	68·5	37 48	56 18	67·8	37 25	55 08	67·1	37 02	53 59	66·4	36 37	52 50	65·7	223
44 136	39 23	58 15	68·6	39 01	57 03	67·8	38 38	55 52	67·1	38 14	54 41	66·3	37 50	53 32	65·6	37 25	52 23	64·9	224
45 135	40 14	57 48	67·9	39 51	56 36	67·1	39 28	55 25	66·3	39 03	54 13	65·6	38 38	53 04	64·9	38 12	51 54	64·1	225

LHA/F	F	24° A/H	24° B/P	24° Z_1/Z_2	25° A/H	25° B/P	25° Z_1/Z_2	26° A/H	26° B/P	26° Z_1/Z_2	27° A/H	27° B/P	27° Z_1/Z_2	28° A/H	28° B/P	28° Z_1/Z_2	29° A/H	29° B/P	29° Z_1/Z_2	LHA	LHA
45	135	40 14	57 48	67.9	39 51	56 36	67.1	39 28	55 24	66.3	39 03	54 13	65.6	38 38	53 04	64.9	38 12	51 54	64.1	225	315
46	134	41 05	57 21	67.2	40 41	56 10	66.4	40 17	54 56	65.6	39 52	53 44	64.8	39 26	52 34	64.1	38 59	51 25	63.3	226	314
47	133	41 55	56 52	66.4	41 31	55 38	65.6	41 05	54 25	64.8	40 41	53 14	64.0	40 13	52 04	63.3	39 46	50 54	62.5	227	313
48	132	42 45	56 22	65.7	42 20	55 08	64.9	41 54	53 55	64.0	41 28	52 43	63.2	41 00	51 32	62.5	40 32	50 22	61.7	228	312
49	131	43 35	55 50	64.9	43 09	54 36	64.1	42 42	53 22	63.2	42 15	52 10	62.4	41 47	50 59	61.6	41 18	49 48	60.9	229	311
50	130	44 25	55 17	64.1	43 58	54 02	63.3	43 31	52 49	62.4	43 03	51 36	61.6	42 34	50 24	60.8	42 04	49 14	60.0	230	310
51	129	45 14	54 43	63.3	44 47	53 28	62.4	44 18	52 13	61.6	43 49	51 00	60.7	43 20	49 48	59.9	42 49	48 38	59.1	231	309
52	128	46 03	54 08	62.5	45 35	52 52	61.6	45 06	51 37	60.7	44 36	50 23	59.8	44 05	49 11	59.0	43 34	48 00	58.2	232	308
53	127	46 51	53 30	61.6	46 22	52 14	60.7	45 53	50 59	59.8	45 21	49 45	58.9	44 51	48 32	58.1	44 18	47 21	57.2	233	307
54	126	47 39	52 51	60.8	47 09	51 34	59.8	46 39	50 19	58.9	46 07	49 05	58.0	45 35	47 52	57.1	45 02	46 41	56.3	234	306
55	125	48 27	52 11	59.8	47 56	50 54	58.9	47 25	49 38	58.0	46 53	48 23	57.0	46 19	47 10	56.2	45 46	45 59	55.3	235	305
56	124	49 14	51 28	58.9	48 43	50 11	57.9	48 10	48 54	57.0	47 37	47 40	56.1	47 03	46 27	55.2	46 29	45 15	54.3	236	304
57	123	50 01	50 44	57.9	49 28	49 26	56.9	48 55	48 09	56.0	48 21	46 54	55.0	47 46	45 41	54.1	47 11	44 30	53.3	237	303
58	122	50 47	49 58	56.9	50 14	48 39	55.9	49 40	47 22	54.9	49 05	46 07	54.0	48 29	44 54	53.1	47 53	43 43	52.2	238	302
59	121	51 33	49 09	55.9	50 58	47 50	54.9	50 24	46 33	53.9	49 48	45 18	52.9	49 11	44 05	52.0	48 34	42 54	51.1	239	301
60	120	52 18	48 19	54.8	51 43	46 59	53.8	51 07	45 43	52.8	50 30	44 28	51.8	49 53	43 14	50.9	49 14	42 03	50.0	240	300
61	119	53 02	47 26	53.7	52 26	46 07	52.7	51 49	44 50	51.7	51 12	43 35	50.7	50 33	42 21	49.7	49 54	41 10	48.8	241	299
62	118	53 46	46 31	52.6	53 09	45 12	51.5	52 31	43 54	50.5	51 52	42 39	49.5	51 13	41 27	48.6	50 32	40 16	47.6	242	298
63	117	54 29	45 33	51.4	53 51	44 14	50.3	53 13	42 57	49.3	52 33	41 42	48.3	51 52	40 30	47.3	51 13	39 19	46.4	243	297
64	116	55 12	44 30	50.2	54 33	43 14	49.1	53 53	41 57	48.1	53 13	40 40	47.1	52 31	39 30	46.1	51 49	38 20	45.2	244	296
65	115	55 53	43 30	48.9	55 14	42 11	47.8	54 34	40 55	46.8	53 51	39 40	45.8	53 10	38 28	44.8	52 26	37 16	43.9	245	295
66	114	56 34	42 25	47.6	55 53	41 06	46.5	55 12	39 50	45.4	54 29	38 36	44.4	53 46	37 25	43.5	53 02	36 16	42.6	246	294
67	113	57 14	41 16	46.2	56 32	39 58	45.1	55 51	38 42	44.1	55 06	37 29	43.1	54 22	36 19	42.1	53 37	35 11	41.2	247	293
68	112	57 53	40 05	44.8	57 10	38 47	43.7	56 27	37 32	42.7	55 42	36 19	41.7	54 57	35 10	40.7	54 11	34 03	39.8	248	292
69	111	58 32	38 50	43.3	57 47	37 33	42.2	57 03	36 18	41.2	56 17	35 07	40.2	55 31	33 59	39.3	54 44	32 53	38.4	249	291
70	110	59 09	37 32	41.8	58 24	36 16	40.7	57 38	35 02	39.7	56 51	33 52	38.7	56 04	32 45	37.8	55 16	31 41	36.9	250	290
71	109	59 46	36 11	40.2	59 00	34 55	39.2	58 12	33 43	38.1	57 24	32 33	37.2	56 36	31 28	36.3	55 47	30 28	35.4	251	289
72	108	60 19	34 46	38.6	59 32	33 32	37.6	58 44	32 21	36.5	57 56	31 14	35.6	57 06	30 10	34.7	56 16	29 08	33.8	252	288
73	107	60 53	33 18	36.9	60 05	32 05	35.9	59 16	30 56	34.9	58 26	29 51	34.0	57 36	28 48	33.1	56 46	27 49	32.2	253	287
74	106	61 25	31 46	35.2	60 36	30 35	34.2	59 46	29 28	33.2	58 56	28 25	32.3	58 05	27 24	31.4	57 13	26 26	30.6	254	286
75	105	61 56	30 10	33.4	61 06	29 02	32.4	60 15	27 57	31.4	59 24	26 55	30.5	58 31	25 57	29.7	57 39	25 00	28.9	255	285
76	104	62 26	28 31	31.5	61 34	27 25	30.5	60 42	26 23	29.6	59 50	25 23	28.8	58 57	24 28	28.0	58 01	23 35	27.2	256	284
77	103	62 55	26 48	29.6	62 01	25 45	28.6	61 08	24 46	27.8	60 15	23 49	27.0	59 21	22 56	26.2	58 27	22 05	25.5	257	283
78	102	63 24	25 02	27.6	62 26	24 01	26.7	61 32	23 05	25.9	60 38	22 12	25.1	59 44	21 21	24.4	58 49	20 34	23.7	258	282
79	101	63 44	23 12	25.5	62 50	22 15	24.7	61 55	21 21	23.9	61 00	20 32	23.2	60 05	19 44	22.5	59 09	19 00	21.8	259	281
80	100	64 07	21 18	23.4	63 12	20 25	22.6	62 16	19 36	21.9	61 20	18 49	21.2	60 24	18 05	20.6	59 28	17 24	20.0	260	280
81	99	64 28	19 22	21.3	63 32	18 33	20.5	62 35	17 47	19.9	61 39	17 04	19.2	60 42	16 24	18.6	59 45	15 46	18.1	261	279
82	98	64 47	17 22	19.1	63 50	16 37	18.4	62 53	15 56	17.8	61 56	15 17	17.2	60 58	14 40	16.7	60 01	14 06	16.2	262	278
83	97	65 05	15 18	16.8	64 06	14 38	16.2	63 08	14 02	15.6	62 10	13 27	15.1	61 12	12 55	14.7	60 14	12 25	14.2	263	277
84	96	65 18	13 13	14.5	64 20	12 38	14.0	63 22	12 06	13.5	62 23	11 36	13.0	61 25	11 07	12.6	60 26	10 41	12.2	264	276
85	95	65 31	11 05	12.1	64 32	10 35	11.7	63 33	10 08	11.3	62 35	9 42	10.9	61 36	9 19	10.6	60 37	8 56	10.2	265	275
86	94	65 41	8 54	9.8	64 42	8 30	9.4	63 43	8 08	9.1	62 44	7 48	8.8	61 44	7 28	8.5	60 45	7 10	8.2	266	274
87	93	65 49	6 42	7.3	64 50	6 24	7.1	63 50	6 07	6.8	62 51	5 55	6.6	61 51	5 37	6.4	60 52	5 24	6.2	267	273
88	92	65 55	4 29	4.9	64 56	4 17	4.7	63 56	4 06	4.6	62 56	3 56	4.4	61 56	3 45	4.3	60 56	3 36	4.1	268	272
89	91	65 59	2 15	2.5	64 59	2 09	2.4	63 59	2 03	2.3	62 59	1 58	2.2	61 59	1 53	2.1	60 59	1 48	2.1	269	271
90	90	66 00	0 00	0.0	65 00	0 00	0.0	64 00	0 00	0.0	63 00	0 00	0.0	62 00	0 00	0.0	61 00	0 00	0.0	270	270

N. Lat.: for LHA > 180° .... $Z_n = Z$
for LHA < 180° .... $Z_n = 360° - Z$

S. Lat.: for LHA > 180° .... $Z_n = 180° - Z$
for LHA < 180° .... $Z_n = 180° + Z$

SIGHT REDUCTION TABLE

B: (−) for 90° < LHA < 270°
Dec:(−) for Lat. contrary name

Z₁: same sign as B
Z₂: (−) for F > 90°

LHA/F	30° A/H	30° B/P	30° Z_1/Z_2	31° A/H	31° B/P	31° Z_1/Z_2	32° A/H	32° B/P	32° Z_1/Z_2	33° A/H	33° B/P	33° Z_1/Z_2	34° A/H	34° B/P	34° Z_1/Z_2	35° A/H	35° B/P	35° Z_1/Z_2	LHA
0	0 00	60 00	90·0	0 00	59 00	90·0	0 00	58 00	90·0	0 00	57 00	90·0	0 00	56 00	90·0	0 00	55 00	90·0	180
1	0 52	60 00	89·5	0 51	59 00	89·5	0 51	58 00	89·5	0 50	57 00	89·4	0 50	56 00	89·4	0 49	55 00	89·4	181
2	1 44	60 00	89·0	1 43	59 00	89·0	1 42	58 00	89·0	1 41	57 00	88·9	1 39	56 00	88·9	1 38	55 00	88·9	182
3	2 36	59 59	88·5	2 34	58 59	88·5	2 33	57 59	88·4	2 31	56 59	88·3	2 29	55 59	88·3	2 27	54 58	88·3	183
4	3 28	59 58	88·0	3 26	58 56	88·0	3 23	57 56	87·9	3 21	56 56	87·8	3 19	55 56	87·8	3 17	54 56	87·7	184
5	4 20	59 54	87·5	4 17	58 54	87·4	4 14	57 54	87·3	4 12	56 54	87·3	4 09	55 54	87·2	4 06	54 54	87·1	185
6	5 12	59 52	87·0	5 08	58 52	86·9	5 05	57 52	86·8	5 02	56 51	86·7	4 58	55 51	86·6	4 55	54 51	86·6	186
7	6 04	59 49	86·5	6 00	58 49	86·4	5 56	57 48	86·3	5 52	56 48	86·2	5 48	55 48	86·1	5 44	54 48	86·0	187
8	6 55	59 45	86·0	6 51	58 45	85·8	6 47	57 45	85·7	6 42	56 45	85·6	6 38	55 44	85·5	6 33	54 44	85·4	188
9	7 47	59 42	85·5	7 42	58 41	85·4	7 37	57 41	85·2	7 32	56 40	85·1	7 27	55 40	84·9	7 22	54 40	84·8	189
10	8 39	59 37	85·0	8 34	58 37	84·8	8 28	57 36	84·7	8 22	56 36	84·5	8 17	55 36	84·4	8 11	54 35	84·2	190
11	9 31	59 32	84·4	9 25	58 32	84·4	9 19	57 31	84·1	9 13	56 31	84·0	9 06	55 30	83·8	9 00	54 30	83·6	191
12	10 22	59 27	83·9	10 16	58 26	83·8	10 09	57 26	83·6	10 03	56 25	83·4	9 56	55 25	83·2	9 48	54 24	83·0	192
13	11 14	59 21	83·4	11 07	58 20	83·2	11 00	57 20	83·0	10 53	56 19	82·8	10 45	55 18	82·6	10 37	54 18	82·5	193
14	12 06	59 15	82·9	11 58	58 14	82·7	11 50	57 13	82·5	11 42	56 12	82·3	11 34	55 12	82·1	11 26	54 11	81·9	194
15	12 57	59 08	82·4	12 49	58 07	82·1	12 41	57 07	81·9	12 32	56 05	81·7	12 23	55 04	81·5	12 14	54 03	81·3	195
16	13 49	59 01	81·8	13 40	58 00	81·6	13 31	56 58	81·4	13 22	55 57	81·1	13 13	54 57	80·9	13 03	53 56	80·7	196
17	14 40	58 53	81·3	14 31	57 51	81·1	14 21	56 50	80·8	14 12	55 49	80·5	14 02	54 48	80·3	13 51	53 47	80·1	197
18	15 31	58 44	80·8	15 22	57 43	80·5	15 12	56 42	80·2	15 01	55 40	79·9	14 51	54 39	79·7	14 40	53 38	79·4	198
19	16 23	58 35	80·2	16 12	57 34	79·9	16 02	56 32	79·7	15 51	55 31	79·4	15 40	54 30	79·1	15 28	53 29	78·8	199
20	17 14	58 26	79·7	17 03	57 24	79·4	16 52	56 23	79·1	16 40	55 21	78·8	16 28	54 20	78·5	16 16	53 19	78·2	200
21	18 05	58 16	79·1	17 53	57 14	78·8	17 42	56 13	78·5	17 29	55 11	78·2	17 17	54 09	77·9	17 04	53 08	77·6	201
22	18 56	58 05	78·6	18 44	57 03	78·2	18 31	56 01	77·9	18 19	55 00	77·6	18 06	53 58	77·3	17 52	52 56	77·0	202
23	19 47	57 54	78·0	19 34	56 52	77·7	19 21	55 50	77·3	19 08	54 48	77·0	18 54	53 46	76·6	18 40	52 44	76·3	203
24	20 37	57 42	77·4	20 24	56 40	77·1	20 11	55 38	76·7	19 57	54 36	76·4	19 42	53 34	76·0	19 28	52 32	75·7	204
25	21 28	57 30	76·9	21 14	56 27	76·5	21 00	55 25	76·1	20 46	54 23	75·7	20 31	53 21	75·4	20 15	52 19	75·0	205
26	22 19	57 17	76·3	22 04	56 14	75·9	21 49	55 12	75·5	21 34	54 09	75·1	21 19	53 07	74·7	21 03	52 05	74·4	206
27	23 09	57 03	75·7	22 54	56 00	75·3	22 39	54 57	74·9	22 23	53 55	74·5	22 07	52 52	74·1	21 50	51 51	73·7	207
28	23 59	56 49	75·1	23 44	55 46	74·7	23 28	54 43	74·3	23 11	53 40	73·8	22 54	52 37	73·4	22 37	51 35	73·0	208
29	24 50	56 34	74·5	24 33	55 31	74·1	24 17	54 27	73·6	23 59	53 24	73·2	23 42	52 22	72·8	23 24	51 19	72·4	209
30	25 40	56 19	73·9	25 23	55 15	73·4	25 05	54 11	73·0	24 48	53 08	72·5	24 29	52 05	72·1	24 11	51 03	71·7	210
31	26 29	56 02	73·3	26 12	54 58	72·8	25 54	53 54	72·3	25 35	52 51	71·9	25 16	51 49	71·4	24 57	50 45	71·0	211
32	27 19	55 45	72·6	27 01	54 41	72·2	26 42	53 37	71·7	26 23	52 33	71·2	26 04	51 30	70·7	25 44	50 27	70·3	212
33	28 09	55 27	72·0	27 50	54 23	71·5	27 31	53 19	71·0	27 11	52 15	70·5	26 50	51 12	70·0	26 30	50 08	69·6	213
34	28 58	55 09	71·4	28 38	54 04	70·8	28 19	53 00	70·3	27 58	51 56	69·8	27 37	50 52	69·3	27 16	49 49	68·8	214
35	29 47	54 49	70·7	29 27	53 44	70·2	29 06	52 40	69·6	28 45	51 36	69·1	28 24	50 32	68·6	28 01	49 29	68·1	215
36	30 36	54 29	70·0	30 15	53 24	69·5	29 54	52 19	68·9	29 32	51 15	68·4	29 10	50 11	67·9	28 47	49 07	67·4	216
37	31 25	54 08	69·4	31 03	53 03	68·8	30 41	51 58	68·2	30 19	50 54	67·7	29 56	49 49	67·2	29 32	48 45	66·6	217
38	32 13	53 46	68·7	31 51	52 41	68·1	31 28	51 35	67·5	31 05	50 30	66·9	30 41	49 26	66·4	30 17	48 23	65·9	218
39	33 02	53 23	68·0	32 39	52 17	67·4	32 15	51 12	66·8	31 51	50 07	66·2	31 27	49 03	65·6	31 02	48 00	65·1	219
40	33 50	53 00	67·2	33 26	51 53	66·6	33 02	50 48	66·0	32 37	49 43	65·4	32 12	48 38	64·9	31 46	47 34	64·3	220
41	34 37	52 35	66·5	34 13	51 29	65·9	33 48	50 23	65·3	33 23	49 17	64·7	32 57	48 13	64·1	32 30	47 09	63·5	221
42	35 25	52 09	65·8	35 00	51 03	65·1	34 34	49 56	64·5	34 08	48 51	63·9	33 42	47 46	63·3	33 14	46 42	62·7	222
43	36 12	51 43	65·0	35 46	50 36	64·3	35 20	49 29	63·7	34 53	48 24	63·1	34 26	47 19	62·5	33 58	46 15	61·9	223
44	36 59	51 15	64·2	36 33	50 08	63·6	36 06	49 01	62·9	35 38	47 55	62·3	35 10	46 51	61·6	34 41	45 46	61·0	224
45	37 46	50 46	63·4	37 19	49 39	62·7	36 51	48 32	62·1	36 22	47 26	61·4	35 53	46 21	60·8	35 24	45 17	60·2	225

Lat. / A   for 90° < LHA < 270°

Lat./A	30°			31°			32°			33°			34°			35°			Lat./A	
LHA/F	A/H	B/P	Z₁/Z₂	A/H	B/P	Z₁/Z₂	A/H	B/P	Z₁/Z₂	A/H	B/P	Z₁/Z₂	A/H	B/P	Z₁/Z₂	A/H	B/P	Z₁/Z₂	LHA	A
45	37 46	50 46	63·4	37 19	49 39	62·7	36 51	48 32	62·1	36 22	47 26	61·4	35 53	46 21	60·8	35 24	45 17	60·2	225	315
46	38 32	50 16	62·6	38 04	49 08	61·9	37 36	48 02	61·2	37 06	46 56	60·6	36 37	45 51	59·9	36 06	44 46	59·3	226	314
47	39 18	49 45	61·8	38 49	48 37	61·1	38 20	47 31	60·4	37 50	46 25	59·7	37 20	45 19	59·1	36 48	44 15	58·4	227	313
48	40 04	49 13	61·0	39 34	48 05	60·2	39 04	46 58	59·5	38 33	45 51	58·8	38 02	44 46	58·2	37 30	43 42	57·5	228	312
49	40 49	48 39	60·1	40 19	47 31	59·4	39 48	46 24	58·6	39 16	45 18	57·9	38 44	44 12	57·2	38 11	43 08	56·6	229	311
50	41 34	48 04	59·2	41 03	46 56	58·5	40 31	45 49	57·7	39 59	44 42	57·0	39 26	43 37	56·3	38 52	42 33	55·6	230	310
51	42 18	47 28	58·3	41 46	46 21	57·5	41 14	45 12	56·8	40 41	44 06	56·1	40 07	43 01	55·4	39 32	41 57	54·7	231	309
52	43 02	46 50	57·4	42 29	45 42	56·6	41 56	44 34	55·9	41 22	43 28	55·1	40 47	42 23	54·4	40 12	41 19	53·7	232	308
53	43 46	46 11	56·4	43 12	45 03	55·7	42 38	43 55	54·9	42 03	42 49	54·1	41 28	41 44	53·4	40 51	40 41	52·7	233	307
54	44 29	45 31	55·5	43 54	44 23	54·7	43 19	43 15	53·9	42 44	42 09	53·1	42 07	41 04	52·4	41 30	40 01	51·7	234	306
55	45 11	44 49	54·5	44 36	43 40	53·7	44 00	42 33	52·9	43 24	41 27	52·1	42 46	40 23	51·4	42 09	39 19	50·7	235	305
56	45 53	44 05	53·5	45 17	42 57	52·6	44 41	41 50	51·8	44 03	40 44	51·1	43 25	39 40	50·3	42 46	38 37	49·6	236	304
57	46 35	43 20	52·4	45 58	42 11	51·6	45 20	41 05	50·8	44 42	39 59	50·0	44 03	38 55	49·3	43 24	37 53	48·5	237	303
58	47 16	42 33	51·3	46 38	41 25	50·5	45 59	40 18	49·7	45 20	39 13	48·9	44 40	38 09	48·2	44 00	37 07	47·5	238	302
59	47 56	41 44	50·2	47 17	40 36	49·4	46 38	39 30	48·6	45 58	38 25	47·8	45 17	37 22	47·1	44 36	36 20	46·3	239	301
60	48 35	40 54	49·1	47 56	39 46	48·3	47 16	38 40	47·5	46 35	37 35	46·7	45 53	36 33	45·9	45 11	35 32	45·2	240	300
61	49 14	40 01	47·9	48 34	38 54	47·1	47 53	37 48	46·3	47 11	36 43	45·5	46 29	35 42	44·7	45 46	34 50	44·0	241	299
62	49 53	39 07	46·8	49 11	38 00	45·9	48 29	36 55	45·1	47 47	35 52	44·3	47 03	34 50	43·6	46 19	33 50	42·8	242	298
63	50 30	38 11	45·5	49 48	37 04	44·7	49 05	36 00	43·9	48 21	34 57	43·1	47 37	33 57	42·3	46 53	32 57	41·6	243	297
64	51 07	37 13	44·3	50 23	36 07	43·4	49 40	35 03	42·6	48 55	34 01	41·8	48 10	33 01	41·1	47 25	32 03	40·4	244	296
65	51 43	36 12	43·0	50 58	35 06	42·2	50 14	34 04	41·3	49 28	33 03	40·6	48 43	32 03	39·8	47 56	31 07	39·1	245	295
66	52 18	35 10	41·7	51 33	34 02	40·8	50 47	33 04	40·0	50 00	32 02	39·3	49 14	31 05	38·5	48 26	30 09	37·8	246	294
67	52 52	34 05	40·3	52 06	32 56	39·5	51 19	32 01	38·7	50 32	30 59	37·9	49 44	30 05	37·2	48 56	29 10	36·5	247	293
68	53 25	32 59	38·9	52 38	31 49	38·1	51 50	30 57	37·3	51 02	29 53	36·6	50 14	29 03	35·8	49 25	28 09	35·2	248	292
69	53 58	31 50	37·5	53 09	30 49	36·7	52 21	29 52	35·9	51 32	28 53	35·2	50 43	27 59	34·5	49 53	27 06	33·8	249	291
70	54 28	30 39	36·1	53 39	29 39	35·2	52 50	28 42	34·5	52 00	27 41	33·8	51 11	26 53	33·1	50 20	26 02	32·4	250	290
71	54 58	29 25	34·6	54 08	28 27	33·8	53 18	27 31	33·0	52 28	26 38	32·3	51 37	25 46	31·6	50 46	24 56	31·0	251	289
72	55 27	28 09	33·0	54 37	27 13	32·2	53 45	26 18	31·5	52 54	25 27	30·8	52 03	24 37	30·2	51 10	23 48	29·5	252	288
73	55 55	26 51	31·4	55 03	25 57	30·7	54 12	25 04	30·0	53 19	24 14	29·3	52 27	23 26	28·7	51 34	22 40	28·1	253	287
74	56 21	25 31	29·8	55 29	24 39	29·1	54 36	23 48	28·4	53 43	23 00	27·8	52 50	22 14	27·1	51 57	21 29	26·6	254	286
75	56 46	24 09	28·2	55 53	23 18	27·5	55 00	22 30	26·8	54 06	21 44	26·2	53 12	21 00	25·6	52 18	20 17	25·0	255	285
76	57 10	22 44	26·5	56 16	21 56	25·8	55 23	21 10	25·2	54 28	20 26	24·6	53 33	19 44	24·0	52 38	19 04	23·5	256	284
77	57 33	21 17	24·8	56 38	20 31	24·1	55 43	19 48	23·5	54 49	19 06	23·0	53 53	18 27	22·4	52 57	17 49	21·9	257	283
78	57 54	19 48	23·0	56 59	19 05	22·4	56 02	18 24	21·9	55 08	17 45	21·3	54 11	17 08	20·8	53 15	16 32	20·3	258	282
79	58 13	18 17	21·2	57 17	17 37	20·7	56 21	16 59	20·1	55 25	16 22	19·6	54 28	15 48	19·2	53 31	15 15	18·7	259	281
80	58 32	16 44	19·4	57 35	16 07	18·9	56 38	15 32	18·4	55 41	14 58	17·9	54 44	14 26	17·5	53 47	13 56	17·1	260	280
81	58 48	15 10	17·6	57 51	14 36	17·1	56 53	14 03	16·6	55 56	13 33	16·2	54 58	13 03	15·8	54 00	12 36	15·4	261	279
82	59 03	13 33	15·7	58 05	13 02	15·3	57 07	12 33	14·9	56 09	12 06	14·5	55 11	11 40	14·1	54 13	11 14	13·8	262	278
83	59 16	11 55	13·8	58 18	11 28	13·4	57 19	11 02	13·0	56 21	10 38	12·7	55 22	10 14	12·4	54 24	9 52	12·1	263	277
84	59 28	10 15	11·9	58 29	9 52	11·5	57 30	9 30	11·2	56 31	9 09	10·9	55 32	8 49	10·6	54 34	8 29	10·4	264	276
85	59 37	8 35	9·9	58 38	8 15	9·6	57 40	7 56	9·4	56 40	7 39	9·1	55 41	7 22	8·9	54 41	7 06	8·7	265	275
86	59 46	6 53	8·0	58 46	6 37	7·7	57 47	6 22	7·5	56 47	6 08	7·3	55 48	5 54	7·1	54 48	5 41	7·0	266	274
87	59 52	5 11	6·0	58 52	4 59	5·8	57 52	4 47	5·6	56 53	4 36	5·5	55 53	4 26	5·4	54 53	4 16	5·2	267	273
88	59 56	3 28	4·0	58 55	3 19	3·9	57 57	3 12	3·8	56 56	3 05	3·7	55 56	2 58	3·6	54 57	2 51	3·5	268	272
89	59 59	1 44	2·0	58 59	1 40	1·9	57 59	1 36	1·9	56 59	1 32	1·8	55 59	1 29	1·8	54 59	1 26	1·7	269	271
90	60 00	0 00	0·0	59 00	0 00	0·0	58 00	0 00	0·0	57 00	0 00	0·0	56 00	0 00	0·0	55 00	0 00	0·0	270	270

N. Lat.: for LHA > 180° ... $Z_n = Z$
for LHA < 180° ... $Z_n = 360° - Z$

S. Lat.: for LHA > 180° ... $Z_n = 180° - Z$
for LHA < 180° ... $Z_n = 180° + Z$

SIGHT REDUCTION TABLE

B: (−) for 90° < LHA < 270°
Dec:(−) for Lat. contrary name

Z₁: same sign as B
Z₂: (−) for F > 90°

Lat./A LHA/F	A	36° A/H	36° B/P	36° Z₁/Z₂	37° A/H	37° B/P	37° Z₁/Z₂	38° A/H	38° B/P	38° Z₁/Z₂	39° A/H	39° B/P	39° Z₁/Z₂	40° A/H	40° B/P	40° Z₁/Z₂	41° A/H	41° B/P	41° Z₁/Z₂	LHA	A
0	180	0 00	54 00	90·0	0 00	53 00	90·0	0 00	52 00	90·0	0 00	51 00	90·0	0 00	50 00	90·0	0 00	49 00	90·0	180	360
1	179	0 49	54 00	89·4	0 48	53 00	89·4	0 47	52 00	89·4	0 47	51 00	89·4	0 46	50 00	89·4	0 45	49 00	89·3	181	359
2	178	1 37	53 59	88·8	1 36	52 59	88·8	1 35	51 59	88·8	1 33	50 59	88·7	1 32	49 59	88·7	1 31	48 59	88·7	182	358
3	177	2 26	53 58	88·2	2 24	52 58	88·2	2 22	51 58	88·2	2 20	50 58	88·1	2 18	49 58	88·1	2 16	48 58	88·0	183	357
4	176	3 14	53 56	87·6	3 12	52 56	87·6	3 09	51 56	87·5	3 06	50 56	87·5	3 04	49 56	87·4	3 01	48 56	87·4	184	356
5	175	4 03	53 54	87·1	3 59	52 54	87·0	3 56	51 54	86·9	3 53	50 54	86·9	3 50	49 54	86·8	3 46	48 54	86·7	185	355
6	174	4 51	53 51	86·5	4 47	52 51	86·4	4 43	51 51	86·3	4 40	50 51	86·2	4 36	49 51	86·1	4 31	48 51	86·1	186	354
7	173	5 39	53 48	85·9	5 35	52 48	85·8	5 31	51 48	85·7	5 26	50 47	85·6	5 21	49 47	85·5	5 17	48 47	85·4	187	353
8	172	6 28	53 44	85·3	6 23	52 44	85·2	6 18	51 44	85·1	6 13	50 44	84·9	6 07	49 43	84·9	6 02	48 43	84·7	188	352
9	171	7 16	53 40	84·7	7 11	52 39	84·6	7 05	51 39	84·4	6 59	50 39	84·3	6 53	49 39	84·2	6 47	48 39	84·1	189	351
10	170	8 05	53 35	84·1	7 58	52 35	83·9	7 52	51 34	83·8	7 45	50 34	83·7	7 39	49 34	83·5	7 32	48 34	83·4	190	350
11	169	8 53	53 30	83·5	8 46	52 29	83·3	8 39	51 29	83·2	8 32	50 29	83·0	8 24	49 29	82·9	8 17	48 28	82·7	191	349
12	168	9 41	53 24	82·9	9 33	52 23	82·7	9 26	51 23	82·5	9 18	50 23	82·4	9 10	49 23	82·2	9 02	48 22	82·1	192	348
13	167	10 29	53 17	82·3	10 21	52 17	82·1	10 13	51 17	81·9	10 04	50 16	81·7	9 55	49 16	81·6	9 46	48 16	81·4	193	347
14	166	11 17	53 10	81·7	11 08	52 10	81·5	10 59	51 10	81·3	10 50	50 09	81·1	10 41	49 09	80·9	10 31	48 09	80·7	194	346
15	165	12 05	53 03	81·0	11 56	52 02	80·8	11 46	51 02	80·6	11 36	50 02	80·4	11 26	49 01	80·2	11 16	48 01	80·0	195	345
16	164	12 53	52 55	80·4	12 43	51 54	80·2	12 33	50 54	80·0	12 22	49 53	79·8	12 11	48 53	79·6	12 00	47 53	79·3	196	344
17	163	13 41	52 46	79·8	13 30	51 46	79·6	13 19	50 45	79·3	13 08	49 45	79·1	12 57	48 44	78·9	12 45	47 44	78·7	197	343
18	162	14 29	52 37	79·2	14 17	51 37	78·9	14 06	50 36	78·7	13 54	49 35	78·4	13 42	48 35	78·2	13 29	47 34	78·0	198	342
19	161	15 16	52 28	78·6	15 04	51 27	78·3	14 52	50 26	78·0	14 39	49 25	77·8	14 27	48 25	77·5	14 13	47 24	77·3	199	341
20	160	16 04	52 17	78·0	15 51	51 16	77·6	15 38	50 16	77·4	15 25	49 15	77·1	15 11	48 14	76·8	14 58	47 14	76·6	200	340
21	159	16 51	52 07	77·3	16 38	51 05	77·0	16 24	50 05	76·7	16 10	49 04	76·4	15 56	48 03	76·1	15 42	47 03	75·9	201	339
22	158	17 39	51 55	76·6	17 24	50 54	76·3	17 10	49 53	76·0	16 56	48 52	75·7	16 41	47 51	75·4	16 25	46 51	75·2	202	338
23	157	18 26	51 43	76·0	18 11	50 42	75·7	17 56	49 41	75·4	17 41	48 40	75·0	17 25	47 39	74·7	17 09	46 38	74·4	203	337
24	156	19 13	51 30	75·3	18 57	50 29	75·0	18 42	49 28	74·7	18 26	48 27	74·3	18 09	47 26	74·0	17 53	46 25	73·7	204	336
25	155	20 00	51 17	74·7	19 44	50 15	74·3	19 27	49 14	74·0	19 10	48 12	73·6	18 53	47 12	73·3	18 36	46 12	73·0	205	335
26	154	20 46	51 03	74·0	20 30	50 01	73·6	20 13	49 00	73·3	19 55	47 59	72·9	19 37	46 58	72·6	19 19	45 57	72·3	206	334
27	153	21 33	50 48	73·3	21 15	49 47	73·0	20 58	48 45	72·6	20 40	47 43	72·2	20 21	46 43	71·9	20 02	45 42	71·5	207	333
28	152	22 19	50 33	72·6	22 01	49 31	72·3	21 43	48 30	71·9	21 24	47 28	71·5	21 05	46 28	71·1	20 45	45 27	70·8	208	332
29	151	23 06	50 17	72·0	22 47	49 15	71·6	22 28	48 14	71·2	22 08	47 12	70·8	21 48	46 11	70·4	21 28	45 11	70·0	209	331
30	150	23 52	50 00	71·3	23 32	48 58	70·9	23 12	47 57	70·4	22 52	46 55	70·0	22 31	45 54	69·6	22 10	44 54	69·3	210	330
31	149	24 37	49 43	70·5	24 17	48 41	70·1	23 57	47 41	69·7	23 36	46 38	69·3	23 14	45 38	68·9	22 52	44 36	68·5	211	329
32	148	25 23	49 25	69·8	25 02	48 23	69·4	24 41	47 21	69·0	24 19	46 19	68·5	23 57	45 18	68·1	23 34	44 17	67·7	212	328
33	147	26 09	49 06	69·1	25 47	48 04	68·7	25 25	47 02	68·2	25 02	46 00	67·8	24 40	44 59	67·3	24 16	43 58	66·9	213	327
34	146	26 54	48 46	68·4	26 32	47 44	67·9	26 09	46 42	67·4	25 45	45 40	67·0	25 22	44 39	66·6	24 58	43 39	66·1	214	326
35	145	27 39	48 26	67·6	27 16	47 23	67·1	26 52	46 21	66·7	26 28	45 20	66·2	26 04	44 19	65·8	25 39	43 18	65·3	215	325
36	144	28 24	48 04	66·9	28 00	47 02	66·4	27 36	46 00	65·9	27 11	44 58	65·4	26 46	43 57	65·0	26 20	42 57	64·5	216	324
37	143	29 08	47 42	66·1	28 44	46 40	65·6	28 19	45 38	65·1	27 53	44 35	64·6	27 27	43 35	64·2	27 01	42 35	63·7	217	323
38	142	29 52	47 19	65·3	29 27	46 17	64·8	29 01	45 15	64·3	28 35	44 13	63·8	28 08	43 12	63·3	27 41	42 12	62·9	218	322
39	141	30 36	46 56	64·5	30 10	45 53	64·0	29 44	44 51	63·5	29 17	43 48	63·0	28 49	42 48	62·5	28 21	41 48	62·0	219	321
40	140	31 20	46 31	63·7	30 53	45 28	63·2	30 26	44 26	62·7	29 58	43 25	62·2	29 30	42 24	61·7	29 01	41 23	61·2	220	320
41	139	32 03	46 05	62·9	31 36	45 03	62·4	31 08	44 01	61·8	30 39	42 59	61·3	30 10	41 58	60·8	29 41	40 58	60·3	221	319
42	138	32 46	45 39	62·1	32 18	44 36	61·5	31 49	43 34	61·0	31 20	42 33	60·5	30 50	41 32	60·0	30 21	40 32	59·4	222	318
43	137	33 28	45 11	61·3	33 00	44 09	60·7	32 31	43 07	60·1	32 02	42 05	59·6	31 31	41 05	59·1	30 59	40 04	58·5	223	317
44	136	34 12	44 43	60·4	33 42	43 40	59·8	33 11	42 38	59·3	32 40	41 37	58·7	32 09	40 36	58·3	31 37	39 36	57·6	224	316
45	135	34 54	44 13	59·6	34 23	43 11	59·0	33 52	42 11	58·4	33 20	41 08	57·8	32 48	40 07	57·3	32 15	39 08	56·7	225	315

LHA	F	36° A/H	36° B/P	36° Z₁/Z₂	37° A/H	37° B/P	37° Z₁/Z₂	38° A/H	38° B/P	38° Z₁/Z₂	39° A/H	39° B/P	39° Z₁/Z₂	40° A/H	40° B/P	40° Z₁/Z₂	41° A/H	41° B/P	41° Z₁/Z₂	Lat./A	LHA
45	135	34 54	44 13	59·6	34 23	43 11	59·0	33 52	42 09	58·4	33 20	41 08	57·8	32 48	40 07	57·3	32 15	39 08	56·7	225	315
46	134	35 35	43 43	58·7	35 04	42 40	58·1	34 32	41 38	57·5	33 59	40 37	56·9	33 26	39 37	56·4	32 53	38 38	55·8	226	314
47	133	36 17	43 11	57·8	35 44	42 09	57·2	35 12	41 07	56·6	34 38	40 06	56·0	34 04	39 06	55·4	33 30	38 07	54·9	227	313
48	132	36 57	42 39	56·9	36 24	41 38	56·2	35 51	40 34	55·6	35 17	39 34	55·0	34 42	38 34	54·5	34 07	37 36	53·9	228	312
49	131	37 38	42 05	55·9	37 04	41 03	55·3	36 30	40 01	54·7	35 55	39 01	54·1	35 19	38 01	53·5	34 43	37 03	53·0	229	311
50	130	38 18	41 30	55·0	37 43	40 28	54·4	37 08	39 27	53·7	36 32	38 27	53·1	35 56	37 27	52·5	35 19	36 29	52·0	230	310
51	129	38 57	40 54	54·0	38 22	39 52	53·4	37 46	38 51	52·8	37 09	37 51	52·1	36 32	36 52	51·6	35 55	35 54	51·0	231	309
52	128	39 36	40 17	53·0	39 00	39 15	52·4	38 23	38 14	51·8	37 46	37 15	51·1	37 08	36 16	50·6	36 30	35 18	50·0	232	308
53	127	40 15	39 38	52·0	39 38	38 37	51·4	39 00	37 36	50·8	38 22	36 37	50·1	37 43	35 39	49·5	37 04	34 42	49·0	233	307
54	126	40 53	38 58	51·0	40 15	37 57	50·4	39 36	36 57	49·7	38 57	35 59	49·1	38 18	35 01	48·5	37 38	34 04	47·9	234	306
55	125	41 30	38 17	50·0	40 52	37 17	49·3	40 12	36 17	48·7	39 32	35 19	48·1	38 52	34 21	47·4	38 11	33 25	46·9	235	305
56	124	42 07	37 35	48·9	41 28	36 35	48·3	40 47	35 36	47·6	40 07	34 38	47·0	39 26	33 41	46·4	38 44	32 45	45·8	236	304
57	123	42 44	36 51	47·9	42 03	35 51	47·2	41 22	34 53	46·5	40 41	33 55	45·9	39 59	32 59	45·3	39 16	32 04	44·7	237	303
58	122	43 19	36 06	46·8	42 38	35 05	46·1	41 56	34 09	45·4	41 14	33 12	44·8	40 31	32 16	44·2	39 48	31 22	43·6	238	302
59	121	43 54	35 20	45·6	43 12	34 21	45·0	42 29	33 24	44·3	41 46	32 27	43·7	41 03	31 32	43·1	40 19	30 39	42·5	239	301
60	120	44 29	34 32	44·5	43 46	33 34	43·8	43 02	32 37	43·2	42 18	31 41	42·5	41 34	30 47	41·9	40 49	29 54	41·3	240	300
61	119	45 02	33 43	43·3	44 18	32 45	42·6	43 34	31 49	42·0	42 49	30 55	41·4	42 04	30 01	40·8	41 18	29 09	40·2	241	299
62	118	45 35	32 52	42·1	44 51	31 55	41·5	44 05	31 00	40·8	43 20	30 06	40·2	42 34	29 14	39·6	41 47	28 22	39·0	242	298
63	117	46 07	32 00	40·9	45 22	31 04	40·3	44 36	30 10	39·6	43 49	29 17	39·0	43 03	28 25	38·4	42 15	27 35	37·8	243	297
64	116	46 39	31 06	39·7	45 52	30 11	39·0	45 06	29 18	38·4	44 19	28 28	37·8	43 31	27 36	37·2	42 43	26 46	36·6	244	296
65	115	47 09	30 11	38·4	46 22	29 17	37·8	45 35	28 25	37·1	44 47	27 34	36·5	43 58	26 44	36·0	43 09	25 56	35·4	245	295
66	114	47 39	29 14	37·1	46 51	28 21	36·5	46 03	27 30	35·9	45 14	26 40	35·3	44 25	25 52	34·7	43 35	25 04	34·2	246	294
67	113	48 08	28 16	35·8	47 19	27 24	35·2	46 31	26 34	34·6	45 40	25 45	34·0	44 50	24 58	33·4	44 00	24 12	32·9	247	293
68	112	48 36	27 17	34·5	47 46	26 26	33·9	46 56	25 37	33·3	46 06	24 50	32·7	45 15	24 03	32·2	44 24	23 19	31·6	248	292
69	111	49 03	26 15	33·1	48 13	25 26	32·5	47 22	24 38	31·9	46 31	23 52	31·4	45 39	23 08	30·8	44 48	22 24	30·3	249	291
70	110	49 29	25 13	31·8	48 38	24 25	31·1	47 46	23 39	30·6	46 55	22 54	30·0	46 03	22 11	29·5	45 10	21 29	29·0	250	290
71	109	49 54	24 08	30·4	49 02	23 22	29·8	48 10	22 37	29·2	47 17	21 54	28·7	46 26	21 12	28·2	45 32	20 32	27·7	251	289
72	108	50 18	23 02	28·9	49 25	22 18	28·4	48 33	21 35	27·8	47 39	20 53	27·3	46 46	20 13	26·8	45 52	19 35	26·3	252	288
73	107	50 41	21 55	27·5	49 48	21 12	26·9	48 54	20 31	26·4	48 00	19 51	25·9	47 06	19 11	25·4	46 12	18 35	25·0	253	287
74	106	51 03	20 47	26·0	50 09	20 06	25·5	49 15	19 26	25·0	48 20	18 48	24·5	47 25	18 11	24·0	46 30	17 36	23·6	254	286
75	105	51 24	19 36	24·5	50 29	18 57	24·0	49 34	18 20	23·5	48 39	17 43	23·1	47 44	17 09	22·6	46 48	16 35	22·2	255	285
76	104	51 43	18 25	23·0	50 48	17 48	22·5	49 52	17 12	22·0	48 57	16 38	21·6	48 01	16 05	21·2	47 05	15 31	20·8	256	284
77	103	52 02	17 12	21·4	51 06	16 37	21·0	50 09	16 04	20·6	49 13	15 31	20·1	48 17	15 00	19·8	47 20	14 27	19·4	257	283
78	102	52 19	15 58	19·9	51 22	15 25	19·5	50 25	14 54	19·0	49 29	14 24	18·7	48 32	13 55	18·3	47 35	13 23	18·0	258	282
79	101	52 35	14 43	18·3	51 37	14 13	17·9	50 40	13 43	17·5	49 43	13 16	17·2	48 46	12 49	16·8	47 48	12 17	16·5	259	281
80	100	52 49	13 27	16·7	51 52	12 59	16·3	50 54	12 32	16·0	49 56	12 06	15·7	48 58	11 42	15·3	48 01	11 18	15·0	260	280
81	99	53 02	12 09	15·1	52 04	11 44	14·7	51 06	11 19	14·4	50 08	10 56	14·1	49 10	10 34	13·8	48 12	10 12	13·6	261	279
82	98	53 14	10 51	13·4	52 16	10 28	13·1	51 18	10 06	12·9	50 19	9 45	12·6	49 20	9 25	12·3	48 22	9 06	12·1	262	278
83	97	53 24	9 31	11·8	52 26	9 11	11·5	51 27	8 52	11·3	50 29	8 34	11·0	49 30	8 16	10·8	48 31	7 59	10·6	263	277
84	96	53 34	8 11	10·1	52 35	7 54	9·9	51 36	7 37	9·7	50 37	7 21	9·5	49 38	7 06	9·3	48 38	6 51	9·1	264	276
85	95	53 42	6 50	8·5	52 43	6 36	8·3	51 43	6 22	8·1	50 44	6 09	7·9	49 44	5 56	7·8	48 45	5 44	7·6	265	275
86	94	53 49	5 29	6·8	52 49	5 17	6·6	51 49	5 06	6·5	50 50	4 55	6·3	49 50	4 45	6·2	48 50	4 35	6·1	266	274
87	93	53 54	4 07	5·1	52 54	3 58	5·0	51 54	3 50	4·9	50 54	3 42	4·8	49 54	3 34	4·7	48 55	3 27	4·6	267	273
88	92	53 57	2 45	3·4	52 57	2 39	3·3	51 57	2 33	3·2	50 57	2 28	3·2	49 58	2 23	3·1	48 58	2 18	3·0	268	272
89	91	53 59	1 23	1·7	52 59	1 20	1·7	51 59	1 17	1·6	50 59	1 14	1·6	49 59	1 11	1·6	48 59	1 09	1·5	269	271
90	90	54 00	0 00	0·0	53 00	0 00	0·0	52 00	0 00	0·0	51 00	0 00	0·0	50 00	0 00	0·0	49 00	0 00	0·0	270	270

N. Lat.: for LHA > 180° ... $Z_n = Z$
for LHA < 180° ... $Z_n = 360° - Z$

S. Lat.: for LHA > 180° ... $Z_n = 180° - Z$
for LHA < 180° ... $Z_n = 180° + Z$

SIGHT REDUCTION TABLE

B: (−) for 90° < LHA < 270°
Dec:(−) for Lat. contrary name

Z₁: same sign as B
Z₂: (−) for F > 90°

Lat./A (LHA/F)	42° A/H	42° B/P	42° Z_1/Z_2	43° A/H	43° B/P	43° Z_1/Z_2	44° A/H	44° B/P	44° Z_1/Z_2	45° A/H	45° B/P	45° Z_1/Z_2	46° A/H	46° B/P	46° Z_1/Z_2	47° A/H	47° B/P	47° Z_1/Z_2	Lat./A (LHA)
0 / 180	0 00	48 00	90.0	0 00	47 00	90.0	0 00	46 00	90.0	0 00	45 00	90.0	0 00	44 00	90.0	0 00	43 00	90.0	180 / 360
1 / 179	0 45	48 00	89.3	0 44	47 00	89.3	0 43	46 00	89.3	0 42	45 00	89.3	0 42	44 00	89.3	0 41	43 00	89.3	181 / 359
2 / 178	1 29	47 59	88.7	1 28	46 59	88.6	1 26	45 59	88.6	1 25	44 59	88.6	1 23	43 59	88.6	1 22	42 59	88.5	182 / 358
3 / 177	2 14	47 58	88.0	2 12	46 58	88.0	2 09	45 58	87.9	2 07	44 58	87.9	2 05	43 58	87.8	2 03	42 58	87.8	183 / 357
4 / 176	2 58	47 56	87.3	2 55	46 56	87.3	2 53	45 56	87.2	2 50	44 56	87.2	2 47	43 56	87.1	2 44	42 56	87.1	184 / 356
5 / 175	3 43	47 53	86.6	3 39	46 53	86.6	3 36	45 53	86.5	3 32	44 53	86.5	3 28	43 53	86.5	3 24	42 53	86.3	185 / 355
6 / 174	4 27	47 51	86.0	4 23	46 51	85.9	4 19	45 51	85.8	4 14	44 51	85.7	4 10	43 51	85.7	4 05	42 51	85.6	186 / 354
7 / 173	5 12	47 47	85.3	5 07	46 47	85.3	5 02	45 47	85.1	4 57	44 47	85.0	4 51	43 47	85.0	4 46	42 47	84.9	187 / 353
8 / 172	5 56	47 43	84.6	5 51	46 43	84.5	5 45	45 43	84.4	5 39	44 43	84.3	5 33	43 43	84.2	5 27	42 43	84.1	188 / 352
9 / 171	6 41	47 39	84.0	6 34	46 39	83.8	6 28	45 39	83.7	6 21	44 39	83.6	6 14	43 39	83.5	6 07	42 39	83.4	189 / 351
10 / 170	7 25	47 34	83.3	7 18	46 34	83.1	7 11	45 34	83.0	7 03	44 34	82.9	6 56	43 34	82.8	6 48	42 34	82.7	190 / 350
11 / 169	8 09	47 28	82.6	8 01	46 28	82.4	7 53	45 28	82.3	7 45	44 28	82.2	7 37	43 28	82.0	7 29	42 28	81.9	191 / 349
12 / 168	8 53	47 22	81.9	8 45	46 22	81.8	8 36	45 22	81.6	8 27	44 22	81.5	8 18	43 22	81.3	8 09	42 22	81.2	192 / 348
13 / 167	9 37	47 16	81.2	9 28	46 15	81.1	9 19	45 15	80.9	9 09	44 15	80.7	8 59	43 15	80.6	8 49	42 16	80.4	193 / 347
14 / 166	10 21	47 08	80.5	10 11	46 08	80.3	10 01	45 08	80.2	9 51	44 08	80.0	9 40	43 08	79.8	9 30	42 08	79.7	194 / 346
15 / 165	11 05	47 01	79.8	10 55	46 00	79.6	10 44	45 00	79.5	10 33	44 00	79.3	10 21	43 00	79.1	10 10	42 01	78.9	195 / 345
16 / 164	11 49	46 52	79.1	11 38	45 51	78.9	11 26	44 51	78.7	11 14	43 52	78.5	11 02	42 52	78.3	10 50	41 52	78.2	196 / 344
17 / 163	12 33	46 43	78.4	12 21	45 43	78.2	12 08	44 43	78.0	11 56	43 43	77.8	11 43	42 43	77.6	11 30	41 44	77.4	197 / 343
18 / 162	13 17	46 34	77.7	13 04	45 34	77.5	12 51	44 34	77.3	12 37	43 34	77.1	12 24	42 34	76.8	12 10	41 34	76.6	198 / 342
19 / 161	14 00	46 24	77.0	13 46	45 24	76.8	13 33	44 24	76.5	13 19	43 24	76.3	13 04	42 24	76.1	12 50	41 24	75.9	199 / 341
20 / 160	14 43	46 13	76.3	14 29	45 13	76.1	14 15	44 13	75.8	14 00	43 13	75.6	13 45	42 13	75.3	13 30	41 14	75.1	200 / 340
21 / 159	15 27	46 02	75.6	15 12	45 02	75.3	14 56	44 02	75.1	14 41	43 02	74.8	14 25	42 02	74.6	14 09	41 03	74.3	201 / 339
22 / 158	16 10	45 50	74.9	15 54	44 50	74.6	15 38	43 50	74.3	15 22	42 50	74.1	15 05	41 50	73.8	14 48	40 51	73.5	202 / 338
23 / 157	16 53	45 38	74.1	16 36	44 38	73.9	16 19	43 38	73.6	16 02	42 38	73.3	15 45	41 38	73.0	15 27	40 39	72.8	203 / 337
24 / 156	17 36	45 25	73.4	17 18	44 25	73.1	17 01	43 25	72.8	16 43	42 25	72.5	16 25	41 25	72.2	16 06	40 26	72.0	204 / 336
25 / 155	18 18	45 11	72.7	18 00	44 11	72.4	17 42	43 11	72.1	17 23	42 11	71.8	17 04	41 12	71.5	16 45	40 12	71.2	205 / 335
26 / 154	19 01	44 57	71.9	18 42	43 57	71.6	18 23	42 57	71.3	18 03	41 57	71.0	17 44	40 57	70.7	17 24	39 58	70.4	206 / 334
27 / 153	19 43	44 42	71.2	19 24	43 42	70.8	19 04	42 42	70.5	18 43	41 42	70.2	18 23	40 43	69.9	18 02	39 43	69.6	207 / 333
28 / 152	20 25	44 26	70.4	20 05	43 26	70.1	19 44	42 26	69.7	19 23	41 27	69.4	19 02	40 27	69.1	18 40	39 27	68.8	208 / 332
29 / 151	21 07	44 10	69.6	20 46	43 10	69.3	20 25	42 10	68.9	20 03	41 10	68.6	19 41	40 11	68.3	19 18	39 12	67.9	209 / 331
30 / 150	21 49	43 53	68.9	21 27	42 53	68.5	21 05	41 53	68.1	20 42	40 54	67.8	20 19	39 54	67.4	19 56	38 55	67.1	210 / 330
31 / 149	22 30	43 35	68.1	22 08	42 35	67.7	21 45	41 36	67.3	21 22	40 36	67.0	20 58	39 37	66.6	20 34	38 38	66.3	211 / 329
32 / 148	23 11	43 17	67.3	22 48	42 17	66.9	22 24	41 17	66.5	22 00	40 18	66.2	21 36	39 19	65.8	21 11	38 20	65.4	212 / 328
33 / 147	23 52	42 58	66.5	23 28	41 58	66.1	23 04	40 58	65.7	22 39	39 59	65.3	22 14	39 00	65.0	21 48	38 02	64.6	213 / 327
34 / 146	24 33	42 38	65.7	24 08	41 38	65.3	23 43	40 38	64.9	23 17	39 40	64.5	22 51	38 41	64.1	22 25	37 42	63.7	214 / 326
35 / 145	25 14	42 18	64.9	24 48	41 18	64.5	24 22	40 18	64.1	23 56	39 19	63.7	23 29	38 21	63.3	23 02	37 23	62.9	215 / 325
36 / 144	25 54	41 56	64.1	25 28	40 57	63.6	25 01	39 57	63.2	24 34	38 58	62.8	24 06	38 00	62.4	23 38	37 02	62.0	216 / 324
37 / 143	26 34	41 34	63.2	26 07	40 35	62.8	25 39	39 35	62.4	25 11	38 37	61.9	24 43	37 38	61.5	24 14	36 41	61.1	217 / 323
38 / 142	27 14	41 11	62.4	26 46	40 12	61.9	26 17	39 13	61.5	25 48	38 14	61.1	25 19	37 16	60.7	24 50	36 19	60.3	218 / 322
39 / 141	27 53	40 48	61.5	27 24	39 48	61.1	26 55	38 50	60.6	26 25	37 51	60.2	25 55	36 53	59.8	25 25	35 56	59.4	219 / 321
40 / 140	28 32	40 23	60.7	28 02	39 24	60.2	27 32	38 25	59.8	27 02	37 27	59.3	26 31	36 30	58.9	26 00	35 32	58.5	220 / 320
41 / 139	29 11	39 58	59.8	28 40	38 59	59.3	28 10	38 01	58.9	27 38	37 03	58.4	27 07	36 06	58.0	26 35	35 08	57.6	221 / 319
42 / 138	29 49	39 32	58.9	29 18	38 33	58.4	28 46	37 35	58.0	28 14	36 37	57.5	27 42	35 40	57.1	27 09	34 43	56.6	222 / 318
43 / 137	30 27	39 05	58.0	29 55	38 06	57.5	29 23	37 08	57.1	28 50	36 11	56.6	28 17	35 14	56.1	27 43	34 18	55.7	223 / 317
44 / 136	31 05	38 37	57.1	30 32	37 39	56.6	29 59	36 41	56.1	29 25	35 44	55.7	28 51	34 47	55.2	28 17	33 51	54.8	224 / 316
45 / 135	31 42	38 09	56.2	31 08	37 10	55.7	30 34	36 13	55.2	30 00	35 16	54.8	29 25	34 20	54.3	28 50	33 24	53.8	225 / 315

LHA/F	A	A/H 42°	B/P 42°	Z_1/Z_2 42°	A/H 43°	B/P 43°	Z_1/Z_2 43°	A/H 44°	B/P 44°	Z_1/Z_2 44°	A/H 45°	B/P 45°	Z_1/Z_2 45°	A/H 46°	B/P 46°	Z_1/Z_2 46°	A/H 47°	B/P 47°	Z_1/Z_2 47°	LHA	LHA
45	135	31 42	38 09	56.2	31 08	37 10	55.7	30 34	36 13	55.2	30 00	35 16	54.7	29 25	34 20	54.7	28 50	33 24	53.8	225	315
46	134	32 19	37 39	55.3	31 45	36 41	54.8	31 10	35 44	54.3	30 34	34 47	53.8	29 59	33 51	53.8	29 23	32 56	52.9	226	314
47	133	32 55	37 08	54.3	32 22	36 11	53.8	31 48	35 14	53.3	31 08	34 18	52.8	30 32	33 22	52.8	29 55	32 27	51.9	227	313
48	132	33 31	36 37	53.4	32 55	35 40	52.9	32 19	34 43	52.3	31 42	33 47	51.9	31 05	32 52	51.9	30 27	31 58	50.9	228	312
49	131	34 07	36 05	52.4	33 30	35 08	51.9	32 53	34 11	51.4	32 15	33 16	50.9	31 37	32 21	50.9	30 59	31 27	49.9	229	311
50	130	34 42	35 31	51.4	34 04	34 35	50.9	33 26	33 39	50.4	32 48	32 44	49.9	32 09	31 50	49.9	31 30	30 56	48.9	230	310
51	129	35 17	34 57	50.4	34 38	34 01	49.9	33 59	33 05	49.4	33 20	32 11	48.9	32 41	31 17	48.9	32 02	30 24	47.9	231	309
52	128	35 51	34 22	49.4	35 12	33 26	48.9	34 32	32 31	48.4	33 52	31 37	47.9	33 11	30 44	47.9	32 32	29 52	46.9	232	308
53	127	36 25	33 45	48.4	35 45	32 50	47.9	35 04	31 56	47.3	34 23	31 02	46.8	33 42	30 10	46.8	33 02	29 18	45.9	233	307
54	126	36 57	33 08	47.4	36 17	32 13	46.8	35 35	31 20	46.3	34 54	30 27	45.7	34 12	29 35	45.7	33 31	28 44	44.8	234	306
55	125	37 30	32 30	46.3	36 48	31 36	45.8	36 06	30 43	45.2	35 25	29 50	44.7	34 41	28 59	44.7	33 58	28 08	43.8	235	305
56	124	38 02	31 51	45.2	37 19	30 57	44.7	36 37	30 04	44.2	35 55	29 13	43.6	35 10	28 22	43.6	34 26	27 32	42.7	236	304
57	123	38 33	31 10	44.1	37 50	30 17	43.6	37 06	29 25	43.1	36 22	28 34	42.6	35 38	27 45	42.6	34 53	26 56	41.6	237	303
58	122	39 04	30 29	43.0	38 20	29 36	42.5	37 36	28 45	42.0	36 51	27 55	41.5	36 06	27 06	41.5	35 20	26 18	40.5	238	302
59	121	39 34	29 46	41.9	38 49	28 55	41.4	38 04	28 04	40.9	37 19	27 15	40.4	36 33	26 27	40.4	35 46	25 39	39.4	239	301
60	120	40 04	29 03	40.8	39 18	28 12	40.2	38 32	27 22	39.7	37 46	26 33	39.2	37 00	25 47	39.2	36 12	25 00	38.3	240	300
61	119	40 32	28 18	39.6	39 46	27 28	39.1	38 59	26 39	38.6	38 12	25 52	38.1	37 25	25 05	38.1	36 37	24 20	37.2	241	299
62	118	41 00	27 32	38.5	40 13	26 43	37.9	39 26	25 56	37.4	38 38	25 09	36.9	37 50	24 23	36.9	37 02	23 39	36.0	242	298
63	117	41 28	26 45	37.3	40 40	25 58	36.8	39 52	25 11	36.3	39 03	24 25	35.8	38 14	23 40	35.8	37 25	22 57	34.9	243	297
64	116	41 54	25 58	36.1	41 06	25 11	35.6	40 17	24 25	35.1	39 28	23 40	34.6	38 38	22 57	34.6	37 48	22 14	33.7	244	296
65	115	42 20	25 09	34.9	41 31	24 23	34.4	40 41	23 38	33.9	39 51	22 55	33.4	39 01	22 12	33.4	38 11	21 31	32.5	245	295
66	114	42 45	24 19	33.6	41 55	23 34	33.1	41 05	22 50	32.7	40 14	22 08	32.2	39 23	21 27	32.2	38 33	20 46	31.3	246	294
67	113	43 10	23 28	32.4	42 19	22 44	31.9	41 28	22 01	31.4	40 37	21 21	31.0	39 45	20 40	31.0	38 53	20 01	30.1	247	293
68	112	43 33	22 35	31.1	42 42	21 53	30.6	41 50	21 12	30.2	40 58	20 32	29.7	40 06	19 53	29.7	39 13	19 15	28.9	248	292
69	111	43 56	21 42	29.8	43 04	21 01	29.4	42 11	20 22	28.9	41 19	19 43	28.5	40 26	19 05	28.5	39 33	18 29	27.7	249	291
70	110	44 18	20 48	28.5	43 25	20 08	28.1	42 32	19 30	27.7	41 38	18 53	27.2	40 45	18 17	27.2	39 51	17 41	26.5	250	290
71	109	44 38	19 53	27.2	43 45	19 15	26.8	42 51	18 38	26.4	41 57	18 02	26.0	41 03	17 27	26.0	40 09	16 53	25.2	251	289
72	108	44 58	18 57	25.9	44 04	18 20	25.5	43 10	17 45	25.1	42 15	17 10	24.7	41 21	16 37	24.7	40 26	16 05	24.0	252	288
73	107	45 17	17 59	24.6	44 23	17 24	24.1	43 28	16 51	23.8	42 33	16 18	23.4	41 38	15 46	23.4	40 42	15 15	22.7	253	287
74	106	45 35	17 01	23.2	44 40	16 28	22.8	43 45	15 56	22.4	42 49	15 25	22.1	41 54	14 54	22.1	40 58	14 25	21.4	254	286
75	105	45 53	16 02	21.8	44 57	15 31	21.4	44 01	15 00	21.1	43 05	14 31	20.8	42 09	14 02	20.8	41 12	13 34	20.1	255	285
76	104	46 09	15 02	20.4	45 12	14 33	20.1	44 16	14 04	19.7	43 19	13 36	19.4	42 23	13 09	19.4	41 26	12 43	18.8	256	284
77	103	46 24	14 00	19.0	45 27	13 34	18.7	44 30	13 07	18.4	43 33	12 41	18.1	42 36	12 15	18.1	41 39	11 51	17.5	257	283
78	102	46 38	12 58	17.6	45 40	12 34	17.3	44 43	12 09	17.0	43 46	11 45	16.7	42 48	11 21	16.7	41 51	10 58	16.2	258	282
79	101	46 51	11 55	16.2	45 53	11 34	15.9	44 55	11 11	15.6	43 57	10 48	15.4	43 00	10 26	15.4	42 01	10 05	14.9	259	281
80	100	47 03	10 51	14.8	46 04	10 33	14.5	45 06	10 12	14.2	44 08	9 51	14.0	43 10	9 31	14.0	42 12	9 12	13.6	260	280
81	99	47 13	9 51	13.3	46 15	9 31	13.1	45 16	9 12	12.8	44 18	8 53	12.6	43 19	8 35	12.4	42 21	8 18	12.2	261	279
82	98	47 23	8 47	11.9	46 24	8 29	11.6	45 26	8 12	11.4	44 27	7 55	11.2	43 28	7 39	11.1	42 29	7 24	10.9	262	278
83	97	47 32	7 42	10.4	46 33	7 27	10.2	45 34	7 12	10.0	44 34	6 57	9.9	43 35	6 43	9.7	42 36	6 29	9.5	263	277
84	96	47 39	6 37	8.9	46 40	6 24	8.7	45 40	6 11	8.6	44 41	5 58	8.5	43 42	5 46	8.3	42 42	5 34	8.2	264	276
85	95	47 46	5 32	7.4	46 46	5 20	7.3	45 46	5 09	7.1	44 47	4 59	7.1	43 47	4 49	6.9	42 48	4 39	6.8	265	275
86	94	47 51	4 26	6.0	46 51	4 17	5.9	45 51	4 08	5.7	44 52	3 59	5.6	43 52	3 51	5.6	42 52	3 43	5.5	266	274
87	93	47 55	3 20	4.5	46 55	3 13	4.4	45 55	3 06	4.3	44 55	3 00	4.2	43 55	2 54	4.2	42 56	2 48	4.1	267	273
88	92	47 58	2 13	3.0	46 58	2 09	2.9	45 58	2 04	2.9	44 58	2 00	2.8	43 58	1 56	2.8	42 58	1 52	2.7	268	272
89	91	47 59	1 07	1.5	47 00	1 04	1.5	45 59	1 02	1.4	44 59	1 00	1.4	43 59	0 58	1.4	43 00	0 56	1.4	269	271
90	90	48 00	0 00	0.0	47 00	0 00	0.0	46 00	0 00	0.0	45 00	0 00	0.0	44 00	0 00	0.0	43 00	0 00	0.0	270	270

N. Lat.: for LHA > 180° ... $Z_n = Z$
for LHA < 180° ... $Z_n = 360° - Z$

S. Lat.: for LHA > 180° ... $Z_n = 180° - Z$
for LHA < 180° ... $Z_n = 180° + Z$

SIGHT REDUCTION TABLE

B: (−) for 90° < LHA < 270°
Dec:(−) for Lat. contrary name

Z₁: same sign as B
Z₂: (−) for F > 90°

Lat./A LHA/F	48° A/H	48° B/P	48° Z₁/Z₂	49° A/H	49° B/P	49° Z₁/Z₂	50° A/H	50° B/P	50° Z₁/Z₂	51° A/H	51° B/P	51° Z₁/Z₂	52° A/H	52° B/P	52° Z₁/Z₂	53° A/H	53° B/P	53° Z₁/Z₂	Lat./A LHA
0	0 00	42 00	90·0	0 00	41 00	90·0	0 00	40 00	90·0	0 00	39 00	90·0	0 00	38 00	90·0	0 00	37 00	90·0	180
1	0 40	42 00	89·3	0 39	41 00	89·2	0 39	40 00	89·2	0 38	39 00	89·2	0 37	38 00	89·2	0 36	37 00	89·2	181
2	1 20	41 59	88·5	1 19	40 59	88·5	1 17	40 00	88·5	1 16	39 00	88·4	1 14	37 59	88·4	1 12	36 59	88·4	182
3	2 00	41 58	87·8	1 58	40 58	87·7	1 56	39 58	87·7	1 53	38 58	87·7	1 51	37 58	87·6	1 48	36 58	87·6	183
4	2 41	41 56	87·0	2 37	40 56	87·0	2 34	39 56	86·9	2 31	38 56	86·9	2 28	37 56	86·8	2 24	36 56	86·8	184
5	3 21	41 53	86·3	3 17	40 53	86·2	3 13	39 54	86·2	3 09	38 54	86·1	3 05	37 54	86·1	3 00	36 54	86·0	185
6	4 01	41 51	85·5	3 56	40 51	85·5	3 51	39 51	85·4	3 46	38 51	85·3	3 41	37 51	85·3	3 36	36 51	85·2	186
7	4 41	41 47	84·8	4 35	40 47	84·7	4 30	39 47	84·6	4 24	38 47	84·5	4 18	37 48	84·5	4 12	36 48	84·4	187
8	5 21	41 43	84·0	5 14	40 43	83·9	5 08	39 43	83·9	5 01	38 44	83·8	4 55	37 44	83·7	4 48	36 44	83·6	188
9	6 01	41 39	83·3	5 53	40 39	83·2	5 46	39 39	83·1	5 39	38 39	83·0	5 32	37 39	82·9	5 24	36 40	82·8	189
10	6 40	41 34	82·5	6 32	40 34	82·4	6 25	39 34	82·3	6 16	38 34	82·2	6 08	37 35	82·1	6 00	36 35	82·0	190
11	7 20	41 28	81·8	7 11	40 28	81·7	7 03	39 29	81·5	6 54	38 29	81·4	6 45	37 29	81·3	6 36	36 29	81·2	191
12	8 00	41 22	81·0	7 50	40 22	80·9	7 41	39 23	80·8	7 31	38 23	80·6	7 21	37 23	80·5	7 11	36 24	80·4	192
13	8 39	41 16	80·3	8 29	40 16	80·1	8 19	39 16	80·0	8 08	38 16	79·8	7 58	37 17	79·7	7 47	36 17	79·6	193
14	9 19	41 09	79·5	9 08	40 09	79·3	8 57	39 09	79·2	8 45	38 09	79·0	8 34	37 10	78·9	8 22	36 10	78·7	194
15	9 58	41 01	78·8	9 47	40 01	78·6	9 35	39 02	78·4	9 22	38 02	78·2	9 10	37 02	78·1	8 58	36 03	77·9	195
16	10 38	40 53	78·0	10 25	39 53	77·8	10 12	38 53	77·6	9 59	37 54	77·4	9 46	36 54	77·3	9 33	35 55	77·1	196
17	11 17	40 44	77·2	11 04	39 44	77·0	10 50	38 45	76·8	10 36	37 45	76·6	10 22	36 44	76·5	10 08	35 47	76·3	197
18	11 56	40 34	76·4	11 42	39 35	76·2	11 27	38 35	76·0	11 13	37 35	75·8	10 58	36 37	75·6	10 43	35 38	75·5	198
19	12 35	40 25	75·6	12 20	39 25	75·4	12 05	38 26	75·2	11 49	37 26	75·0	11 34	36 27	74·8	11 18	35 28	74·6	199
20	13 13	40 14	74·9	12 58	39 15	74·6	12 42	38 15	74·4	12 26	37 15	74·2	12 09	36 17	74·0	11 53	35 18	73·8	200
21	13 52	40 03	74·1	13 36	39 04	73·8	13 19	38 04	73·6	13 02	37 05	73·4	12 45	36 06	73·2	12 27	35 08	73·0	201
22	14 31	39 51	73·3	14 14	38 52	73·0	13 56	37 53	72·8	13 38	36 54	72·6	13 20	35 55	72·3	13 02	34 56	72·1	202
23	15 09	39 39	72·5	14 51	38 40	72·2	14 33	37 41	72·0	14 14	36 42	71·7	13 55	35 43	71·5	13 36	34 45	71·3	203
24	15 48	39 26	71·7	15 29	38 27	71·4	15 10	37 28	71·2	14 50	36 30	70·9	14 30	35 31	70·7	14 10	34 33	70·4	204
25	16 26	39 13	70·9	16 06	38 14	70·6	15 46	37 15	70·3	15 25	36 17	70·1	15 05	35 18	69·8	14 44	34 20	69·6	205
26	17 03	38 59	70·1	16 43	38 00	69·8	16 22	37 01	69·5	16 01	36 03	69·2	15 39	35 05	69·0	15 18	34 07	68·7	206
27	17 41	38 44	69·3	17 20	37 46	69·0	16 58	36 47	68·7	16 36	35 48	68·4	16 14	34 51	68·1	15 51	33 53	67·9	207
28	18 19	38 29	68·4	17 56	37 30	68·1	17 34	36 32	67·8	17 11	35 34	67·5	16 48	34 36	67·3	16 25	33 38	67·0	208
29	18 56	38 13	67·6	18 33	37 15	67·3	18 09	36 16	67·0	17 46	35 18	66·7	17 22	34 21	66·4	16 58	33 23	66·1	209
30	19 33	37 57	66·8	19 09	36 58	66·5	18 45	36 00	66·1	18 21	35 03	65·8	17 56	34 05	65·5	17 31	33 08	65·2	210
31	20 10	37 40	65·9	19 45	36 41	65·6	19 20	35 44	65·3	18 55	34 46	65·0	18 29	33 49	64·7	18 03	32 52	64·4	211
32	20 46	37 22	65·1	20 21	36 24	64·8	19 55	35 28	64·4	19 29	34 29	64·1	19 02	33 32	63·8	18 36	32 35	63·5	212
33	21 22	37 03	64·2	20 57	36 06	63·9	20 30	35 08	63·6	20 03	34 11	63·2	19 35	33 14	62·9	19 08	32 18	62·6	213
34	21 58	36 44	63·4	21 31	35 47	63·0	21 04	34 49	62·7	20 36	33 53	62·3	20 08	32 56	62·0	19 40	32 00	61·7	214
35	22 34	36 25	62·5	22 06	35 27	62·1	21 38	34 30	61·8	21 10	33 33	61·4	20 41	32 37	61·1	20 12	31 41	60·8	215
36	23 10	36 04	61·6	22 41	35 07	61·2	22 12	34 10	60·9	21 43	33 14	60·5	21 13	32 18	60·2	20 43	31 22	59·9	216
37	23 45	35 43	60·8	23 15	34 46	60·3	22 45	33 49	60·0	22 15	32 53	59·6	21 45	31 58	59·3	21 14	31 02	59·0	217
38	24 20	35 21	59·9	23 49	34 25	59·4	23 19	33 28	59·1	22 48	32 31	58·7	22 16	31 37	58·4	21 45	30 42	58·0	218
39	24 54	34 59	59·0	24 23	34 02	58·5	23 52	33 07	58·2	23 19	32 11	57·8	22 48	31 16	57·5	22 15	30 21	57·1	219
40	25 28	34 36	58·1	24 57	33 40	57·6	24 24	32 44	57·3	23 52	31 49	56·9	23 19	30 54	56·5	22 45	30 00	56·2	220
41	26 02	34 12	57·1	25 30	33 16	56·7	24 57	32 21	56·3	24 23	31 26	56·0	23 49	30 32	55·6	23 15	29 38	55·2	221
42	26 36	33 47	56·2	26 02	32 52	55·8	25 28	31 57	55·4	24 54	31 02	55·0	24 20	30 08	54·6	23 45	29 15	54·3	222
43	27 09	33 22	55·3	26 35	32 27	54·8	26 00	31 32	54·5	25 25	30 38	54·1	24 50	29 45	53·6	24 14	28 52	53·3	223
44	27 42	32 56	54·3	27 07	32 01	53·9	26 31	31 07	53·5	25 55	30 13	53·1	25 19	29 20	52·7	24 43	28 28	52·4	224
45	28 14	32 30	53·4	27 38	31 35	53·0	27 02	30 41	52·5	26 25	29 48	52·1	25 48	28 55	51·8	25 11	28 03	51·4	225

Lat./A — LHA/F	48° A/H	48° B/P	48° Z₁/Z₂	49° A/H	49° B/P	49° Z₁/Z₂	50° A/H	50° B/P	50° Z₁/Z₂	51° A/H	51° B/P	51° Z₁/Z₂	52° A/H	52° B/P	52° Z₁/Z₂	53° A/H	53° B/P	53° Z₁/Z₂	Lat./A — LHA
45 / 135	28 14	32 29	53.4	27 38	31 35	53.0	27 02	30 41	52.5	26 25	29 48	52.1	25 48	28 55	51.8	25 11	28 03	51.4	225 / 315
46 / 134	28 46	32 01	52.4	28 11	31 08	52.0	27 32	30 14	51.6	26 55	29 22	51.2	26 17	28 29	50.8	25 39	27 38	50.4	226 / 314
47 / 133	29 18	31 33	51.4	28 40	30 40	51.0	28 02	29 47	50.6	27 24	28 55	50.2	26 46	28 03	49.8	26 07	27 12	49.4	227 / 313
48 / 132	29 49	31 04	50.5	29 11	30 11	50.0	28 32	29 19	49.6	27 53	28 27	49.2	27 14	27 36	48.8	26 34	26 46	48.4	228 / 312
49 / 131	30 20	30 34	49.5	29 41	29 42	49.0	29 02	28 50	48.6	28 21	27 59	48.2	27 41	27 08	47.8	27 01	26 18	47.4	229 / 311
50 / 130	30 50	30 04	48.5	30 10	29 12	48.0	29 30	28 20	47.6	28 49	27 30	47.2	28 08	26 40	46.8	27 27	25 51	46.4	230 / 310
51 / 129	31 20	29 32	47.5	30 39	28 41	47.5	29 58	27 50	46.6	29 17	27 00	46.2	28 35	26 11	45.8	27 53	25 22	45.4	231 / 309
52 / 128	31 49	29 00	46.4	31 08	28 09	46.4	30 26	27 19	45.6	29 44	26 30	45.2	29 01	25 41	44.8	28 19	24 53	44.4	232 / 308
53 / 127	32 18	28 27	45.4	31 36	27 37	45.0	30 53	26 48	44.5	30 11	25 59	44.1	29 27	25 11	43.7	28 44	24 24	43.3	233 / 307
54 / 126	32 46	27 53	44.4	32 03	27 04	43.9	31 20	26 15	43.5	30 36	25 27	43.1	29 52	24 40	42.7	29 08	23 53	42.3	234 / 306
55 / 125	33 14	27 19	43.3	32 30	26 30	42.9	31 46	25 42	42.4	31 02	24 55	42.1	30 17	24 08	41.6	29 32	23 23	41.2	235 / 305
56 / 124	33 42	26 44	42.2	32 57	25 55	41.8	32 12	25 08	41.4	31 27	24 22	41.0	30 41	23 36	40.6	29 56	22 51	40.2	236 / 304
57 / 123	34 08	26 07	41.1	33 23	25 20	40.7	32 37	24 34	40.3	31 51	23 48	39.9	31 05	23 03	39.5	30 19	22 19	39.1	237 / 303
58 / 122	34 34	25 30	40.1	33 48	24 44	39.6	33 02	23 58	39.2	32 15	23 14	38.8	31 28	22 29	38.4	30 41	21 46	38.0	238 / 302
59 / 121	35 00	24 53	39.0	34 13	24 07	38.5	33 26	23 22	38.1	32 39	22 38	37.7	31 51	21 55	37.3	31 03	21 13	37.0	239 / 301
60 / 120	35 25	24 14	37.8	34 37	23 30	37.4	33 50	22 46	37.0	33 02	22 03	36.6	32 13	21 20	36.2	31 25	20 39	35.9	240 / 300
61 / 119	35 49	23 35	36.7	35 01	22 51	36.3	34 12	22 08	35.9	33 24	21 26	35.5	32 35	20 45	35.1	31 46	20 04	34.8	241 / 299
62 / 118	36 13	22 55	35.6	35 24	22 12	35.2	34 35	21 30	34.8	33 45	20 49	34.4	32 56	20 09	34.0	32 06	19 29	33.7	242 / 298
63 / 117	36 36	22 14	34.4	35 46	21 32	34.0	34 56	20 51	33.6	34 06	20 11	33.3	33 16	19 32	32.9	32 26	18 53	32.5	243 / 297
64 / 116	36 58	21 32	33.3	36 08	20 52	32.9	35 17	20 12	32.5	34 27	19 33	32.1	33 36	18 55	31.8	32 45	18 17	31.4	244 / 296
65 / 115	37 20	20 50	32.1	36 29	20 10	31.7	35 38	19 32	31.3	34 47	18 54	31.0	33 55	18 16	30.6	33 04	17 40	30.1	245 / 295
66 / 114	37 41	20 07	30.9	36 49	19 28	30.5	35 58	18 51	30.2	35 06	18 14	29.8	34 13	17 38	29.5	33 21	17 02	29.1	246 / 294
67 / 113	38 01	19 23	29.7	37 09	18 46	29.4	36 17	18 09	29.0	35 24	17 33	28.6	34 31	16 59	28.3	33 38	16 24	28.0	247 / 293
68 / 112	38 21	18 38	28.5	37 28	18 02	28.2	36 35	17 27	27.8	35 42	16 53	27.5	34 48	16 19	27.1	33 55	15 46	26.8	248 / 292
69 / 111	38 40	17 53	27.3	37 46	17 18	27.0	36 53	16 44	26.6	35 59	16 11	26.3	35 05	15 38	26.0	34 11	15 07	25.7	249 / 291
70 / 110	38 58	17 07	26.1	38 04	16 33	25.7	37 10	16 01	25.4	36 15	15 29	25.1	35 21	14 58	24.8	34 26	14 27	24.5	250 / 290
71 / 109	39 15	16 20	24.9	38 20	15 48	24.5	37 26	15 17	24.2	36 31	14 46	23.9	35 36	14 16	23.6	34 41	13 47	23.3	251 / 289
72 / 108	39 31	15 33	23.6	38 36	15 02	23.3	37 41	14 32	23.0	36 46	14 03	22.7	35 50	13 34	22.4	34 55	13 07	22.1	252 / 288
73 / 107	39 47	14 45	22.4	38 51	14 16	22.1	37 56	13 47	21.8	37 00	13 19	21.5	36 04	12 52	21.2	35 08	12 25	20.9	253 / 287
74 / 106	40 02	13 56	21.1	39 06	13 28	20.8	38 10	13 01	20.5	37 13	12 35	20.3	36 17	12 09	20.0	35 21	11 44	19.8	254 / 286
75 / 105	40 16	13 07	19.8	39 19	12 41	19.5	38 23	12 15	19.3	37 26	11 50	19.0	36 29	11 26	18.8	35 33	11 02	18.5	255 / 285
76 / 104	40 29	12 17	18.5	39 32	11 53	18.3	38 35	11 28	18.0	37 38	11 05	17.8	36 41	10 42	17.6	35 44	10 20	17.3	256 / 284
77 / 103	40 41	11 27	17.3	39 44	11 04	17.0	38 47	10 41	16.8	37 50	10 19	16.5	36 52	9 58	16.3	35 54	9 37	16.1	257 / 283
78 / 102	40 53	10 36	16.0	39 55	10 15	15.7	38 57	9 54	15.5	38 00	9 33	15.3	37 02	9 14	15.1	36 04	8 54	14.9	258 / 282
79 / 101	41 04	9 45	14.7	40 05	9 25	14.4	39 07	9 05	14.2	38 10	8 47	14.0	37 11	8 29	13.9	36 13	8 11	13.7	259 / 281
80 / 100	41 13	8 53	13.3	40 15	8 35	13.2	39 16	8 17	13.0	38 18	8 00	12.8	37 19	7 44	12.6	36 21	7 27	12.5	260 / 280
81 / 99	41 22	8 01	12.0	40 23	7 45	11.9	39 25	7 29	11.7	38 26	7 13	11.5	37 27	6 58	11.4	36 28	6 43	11.2	261 / 279
82 / 98	41 30	7 09	10.7	40 31	6 54	10.5	39 32	6 40	10.4	38 33	6 26	10.3	37 34	6 12	10.1	36 35	5 59	10.0	262 / 278
83 / 97	41 37	6 16	9.4	40 38	6 03	9.2	39 39	5 50	9.1	38 39	5 38	9.0	37 41	5 26	8.9	36 41	5 15	8.7	263 / 277
84 / 96	41 43	5 23	8.1	40 44	5 12	7.9	39 44	5 01	7.8	38 45	4 50	7.7	37 45	4 40	7.6	36 46	4 30	7.5	264 / 276
85 / 95	41 48	4 30	6.7	40 49	4 20	6.6	39 49	4 11	6.5	38 49	4 02	6.4	37 50	3 54	6.3	36 50	3 45	6.3	265 / 275
86 / 94	41 52	3 36	5.4	40 53	3 28	5.3	39 53	3 21	5.2	38 53	3 14	5.1	37 53	3 07	5.0	36 54	3 01	5.0	266 / 274
87 / 93	41 56	2 42	4.0	40 56	2 36	4.0	39 56	2 31	3.9	38 56	2 26	3.9	37 56	2 20	3.8	36 56	2 16	3.8	267 / 273
88 / 92	41 58	1 48	2.7	40 58	1 44	2.6	39 58	1 41	2.6	38 58	1 37	2.6	37 58	1 34	2.5	36 58	1 30	2.5	268 / 272
89 / 91	42 00	0 54	1.3	41 00	0 52	1.3	40 00	0 50	1.3	39 00	0 49	1.3	38 00	0 47	1.3	37 00	0 45	1.3	269 / 271
90 / 90	42 00	0 00	0.0	41 00	0 00	0.0	40 00	0 00	0.0	39 00	0 00	0.0	38 00	0 00	0.0	37 00	0 00	0.0	270 / 270

N. Lat.: for LHA > 180° ... Zn = Z
for LHA < 180° ... Zn = 360° − Z

S. Lat.: for LHA > 180° ... Zn = 180° − Z
for LHA < 180° ... Zn = 180° + Z

B: (−) for 90° < LHA < 270°
Dec:(−) for Lat. contrary name

Z₁: same sign as B
Z₂: (−) for F > 90°

SIGHT REDUCTION TABLE

Lat. / A · LHA/F	54° A/H	54° B/P	54° Z₁/Z₂	55° A/H	55° B/P	55° Z₁/Z₂	56° A/H	56° B/P	56° Z₁/Z₂	57° A/H	57° B/P	57° Z₁/Z₂	58° A/H	58° B/P	58° Z₁/Z₂	59° A/H	59° B/P	59° Z₁/Z₂	Lat. / A · LHA
0 180	0 00	36 00	90·0	0 00	35 00	90·0	0 00	34 00	90·0	0 00	33 00	90·0	0 00	32 00	90·0	0 00	31 00	90·0	180 360
1 179	0 35	36 00	89·2	0 34	35 00	89·2	0 34	34 00	89·2	0 33	33 00	89·2	0 32	32 00	89·2	0 31	31 00	89·1	181 359
2 178	1 11	35 59	88·4	1 09	34 59	88·4	1 07	33 59	88·3	1 05	32 59	88·3	1 04	31 59	88·3	1 02	30 59	88·3	182 358
3 177	1 46	35 58	87·6	1 43	34 58	87·5	1 41	33 58	87·5	1 38	32 58	87·5	1 35	31 58	87·5	1 33	30 58	87·4	183 357
4 176	2 21	35 56	86·8	2 18	34 56	86·7	2 14	33 56	86·7	2 11	32 56	86·7	2 07	31 56	86·6	2 04	30 56	86·6	184 356
5 175	2 56	35 54	86·0	2 52	34 54	85·9	2 48	33 54	85·9	2 43	32 54	85·8	2 39	31 54	85·8	2 35	30 54	85·7	185 355
6 174	3 31	35 51	85·1	3 26	34 51	85·1	3 21	33 51	85·0	3 16	32 51	85·0	3 11	31 52	84·9	3 06	30 52	84·9	186 354
7 173	4 06	35 48	84·3	4 00	34 48	84·3	3 54	33 48	84·2	3 48	32 48	84·1	3 42	31 48	84·1	3 36	30 49	84·0	187 353
8 172	4 42	35 45	83·5	4 34	34 44	83·4	4 28	33 44	83·4	4 21	32 45	83·3	4 14	31 45	83·2	4 07	30 45	83·1	188 352
9 171	5 17	35 40	82·7	5 09	34 40	82·6	5 01	33 40	82·5	4 53	32 41	82·4	4 45	31 41	82·3	4 37	30 41	82·3	189 351
10 170	5 51	35 35	81·9	5 43	34 35	81·8	5 34	33 36	81·7	5 26	32 36	81·6	5 17	31 36	81·5	5 08	30 37	81·4	190 350
11 169	6 26	35 30	81·1	6 17	34 30	81·0	6 08	33 31	80·8	5 58	32 31	80·7	5 48	31 31	80·6	5 38	30 32	80·5	191 349
12 168	7 01	35 24	80·2	6 51	34 24	80·1	6 41	33 25	80·0	6 30	32 25	79·9	6 20	31 26	79·8	6 09	30 27	79·7	192 348
13 167	7 36	35 18	79·4	7 25	34 18	79·3	7 14	33 19	79·2	7 02	32 19	79·0	6 51	31 20	78·9	6 40	30 21	78·8	193 347
14 166	8 11	35 11	78·6	7 59	34 12	78·5	7 46	33 12	78·3	7 34	32 13	78·2	7 22	31 14	78·1	7 10	30 15	77·9	194 346
15 165	8 45	35 04	77·8	8 32	34 04	77·6	8 19	33 05	77·5	8 06	32 06	77·3	7 53	31 07	77·2	7 40	30 08	77·1	195 345
16 164	9 19	34 56	76·9	9 06	33 57	76·8	8 52	32 58	76·6	8 38	31 58	76·5	8 24	31 00	76·3	8 10	30 01	76·2	196 344
17 163	9 54	34 47	76·1	9 39	33 48	75·9	9 25	32 49	75·8	9 10	31 50	75·6	8 55	30 52	75·5	8 40	29 53	75·3	197 343
18 162	10 28	34 39	75·3	10 13	33 40	75·1	9 57	32 41	74·9	9 41	31 42	74·8	9 25	30 43	74·6	9 09	29 45	74·4	198 342
19 161	11 02	34 29	74·4	10 46	33 30	74·2	10 29	32 32	74·1	10 13	31 33	73·9	9 56	30 35	73·7	9 39	29 36	73·6	199 341
20 160	11 36	34 19	73·6	11 19	33 21	73·4	11 01	32 22	73·2	10 44	31 24	73·0	10 27	30 25	72·8	10 08	29 27	72·7	200 340
21 159	12 10	34 09	72·7	11 52	33 10	72·5	11 34	32 12	72·3	11 15	31 14	72·1	10 57	30 15	72·0	10 38	29 17	71·8	201 339
22 158	12 43	33 58	71·9	12 24	33 00	71·7	12 06	32 01	71·5	11 46	31 03	71·3	11 27	30 05	71·1	11 07	29 07	71·0	202 338
23 157	13 17	33 46	71·0	12 57	32 48	70·8	12 37	31 50	70·6	12 17	30 52	70·4	11 57	29 54	70·2	11 37	28 57	70·0	203 337
24 156	13 50	33 34	70·2	13 29	32 36	70·0	13 09	31 38	69·7	12 48	30 41	69·5	12 27	29 43	69·3	12 06	28 46	69·1	204 336
25 155	14 23	33 22	69·3	14 02	32 24	69·1	13 40	31 26	68·9	13 18	30 29	68·6	12 56	29 31	68·4	12 35	28 34	68·2	205 335
26 154	14 56	33 09	68·5	14 34	32 11	68·2	14 11	31 14	68·0	13 49	30 16	67·8	13 26	29 19	67·5	13 03	28 22	67·3	206 334
27 153	15 29	32 55	67·6	15 06	31 58	67·4	14 42	31 00	67·1	14 19	30 03	66·9	13 55	29 06	66·6	13 31	28 10	66·4	207 333
28 152	16 01	32 41	66·7	15 37	31 44	66·5	15 13	30 47	66·2	14 49	29 50	66·0	14 24	28 53	65·7	14 00	27 57	65·5	208 332
29 151	16 33	32 26	65·8	16 09	31 29	65·6	15 44	30 32	65·3	15 19	29 36	65·1	14 53	28 39	64·8	14 28	27 43	64·6	209 331
30 150	17 05	32 11	65·0	16 40	31 14	64·7	16 14	30 17	64·4	15 48	29 21	64·2	15 22	28 25	63·9	14 55	27 29	63·7	210 330
31 149	17 37	31 55	64·1	17 11	30 58	63·8	16 44	30 02	63·5	16 17	29 06	63·3	15 50	28 10	63·0	15 23	27 15	62·7	211 329
32 148	18 09	31 38	63·2	17 42	30 42	62·9	17 14	29 46	62·6	16 47	28 51	62·3	16 18	27 55	62·1	15 50	27 00	61·8	212 328
33 147	18 40	31 21	62·3	18 12	30 25	62·0	17 44	29 30	61·7	17 15	28 34	61·4	16 46	27 39	61·2	16 17	26 45	60·9	213 327
34 146	19 11	31 04	61·4	18 42	30 08	61·1	18 13	29 13	60·8	17 44	28 18	60·5	17 14	27 23	60·2	16 44	26 29	60·0	214 326
35 145	19 42	30 46	60·5	19 12	29 50	60·2	18 42	28 55	59·9	18 12	28 01	59·6	17 42	27 06	59·3	17 11	26 12	59·0	215 325
36 144	20 13	30 27	59·6	19 42	29 32	59·2	19 11	28 37	58·9	18 40	27 43	58·6	18 09	26 49	58·4	17 37	25 55	58·1	216 324
37 143	20 43	30 07	58·6	20 12	29 13	58·3	19 40	28 19	58·0	19 08	27 25	57·7	18 36	26 31	57·4	18 03	25 38	57·1	217 323
38 142	21 13	29 48	57·7	20 41	28 53	57·4	20 08	28 00	57·1	19 35	27 06	56·8	19 02	26 13	56·5	18 29	25 20	56·2	218 322
39 141	21 43	29 27	56·8	21 10	28 33	56·5	20 36	27 40	56·1	20 03	26 47	55·8	19 29	25 54	55·5	18 55	25 02	55·2	219 321
40 140	22 12	29 06	55·8	21 38	28 13	55·5	21 04	27 20	55·2	20 30	26 27	54·9	19 55	25 35	54·6	19 20	24 43	54·3	220 320
41 139	22 41	28 44	54·9	22 06	27 51	54·6	21 31	27 00	54·2	20 56	26 07	53·9	20 21	25 15	53·6	19 45	24 24	53·3	221 319
42 138	23 10	28 22	53·9	22 34	27 29	53·6	21 58	26 37	53·3	21 22	25 46	52·9	20 46	24 55	52·6	20 10	24 04	52·3	222 318
43 137	23 38	27 59	53·0	23 02	27 07	52·6	22 25	26 15	52·3	21 48	25 24	52·0	21 11	24 34	51·7	20 34	23 43	51·4	223 317
44 136	24 06	27 36	52·0	23 29	26 45	51·7	22 51	25 53	51·3	22 14	25 02	51·0	21 36	24 12	50·7	20 58	23 23	50·4	224 316
45 135	24 34	27 11	51·0	23 56	26 20	50·7	23 17	25 30	50·3	22 40	24 40	50·0	22 00	23 50	49·7	21 21	23 01	49·4	225 315

Lat./A		54°			55°			56°			57°			58°			59°			Lat./A	
A	LHA/F	A/H	B/P	Z_1/Z_2	A/H	B/P	Z_1/Z_2	A/H	B/P	Z_1/Z_2	A/H	B/P	Z_1/Z_2	A/H	B/P	Z_1/Z_2	A/H	B/P	Z_1/Z_2	A	LHA
45	135	24 34	27 11	51·0	23 56	26 20	50·7	23 17	25 30	50·3	22 39	24 40	50·0	22 00	23 50	49·7	21 21	23 01	49·4	225	315
46	134	25 01	26 47	50·0	24 22	25 56	49·7	23 43	25 06	49·4	23 04	24 17	49·0	22 24	23 28	48·7	21 45	22 39	48·4	226	314
47	133	25 28	26 22	49·1	24 48	25 32	48·7	24 08	24 42	48·4	23 29	23 53	48·0	22 48	23 05	47·7	22 08	22 17	47·4	227	313
48	132	25 54	25 56	48·1	25 14	25 06	47·7	24 33	24 17	47·4	23 53	23 29	47·0	23 11	22 41	46·7	22 32	21 54	46·4	228	312
49	131	26 20	25 29	47·1	25 39	24 40	46·7	24 58	23 52	46·4	24 16	23 05	46·0	23 34	22 17	45·7	22 52	21 31	45·4	229	311
50	130	26 46	25 02	46·0	26 04	24 14	45·7	25 22	23 26	45·3	24 40	22 39	45·0	23 57	21 53	44·7	23 16	21 07	44·4	230	310
51	129	27 11	24 34	45·0	26 28	23 47	44·7	25 45	23 00	44·3	25 02	22 14	44·0	24 19	21 28	43·7	23 36	20 43	43·4	231	309
52	128	27 36	24 06	44·0	26 52	23 19	43·6	26 09	22 33	43·3	25 25	21 48	43·0	24 41	21 03	42·7	23 57	20 18	42·3	232	308
53	127	28 00	23 37	43·0	27 16	22 51	42·6	26 32	22 05	42·3	25 47	21 21	41·9	25 02	20 37	41·6	24 17	19 53	41·3	233	307
54	126	28 24	23 07	41·9	27 39	22 22	41·6	26 54	21 38	41·2	26 09	20 54	40·9	25 23	20 10	40·6	24 37	19 27	40·3	234	306
55	125	28 47	22 37	40·9	28 01	21 53	40·5	27 16	21 09	40·2	26 30	20 26	39·9	25 44	19 43	39·5	24 57	19 01	39·2	235	305
56	124	29 10	22 07	39·8	28 24	21 23	39·5	27 37	20 40	39·1	26 50	19 57	38·8	26 04	19 16	38·5	25 17	18 34	38·2	236	304
57	123	29 32	21 35	38·8	28 45	20 52	38·4	27 58	20 10	38·1	27 11	19 28	37·8	26 24	18 48	37·4	25 35	18 07	37·1	237	303
58	122	29 54	21 03	37·7	29 06	20 21	37·3	28 19	19 40	37·0	27 31	18 59	36·7	26 42	18 19	36·4	25 53	17 40	36·1	238	302
59	121	30 15	20 31	36·6	29 27	19 50	36·3	28 38	19 10	35·9	27 50	18 30	35·6	27 01	17 50	35·3	26 10	17 12	35·0	239	301
60	120	30 36	19 58	35·5	29 47	19 18	35·2	28 58	18 38	34·9	28 09	17 59	34·5	27 19	17 21	34·2	26 27	16 43	34·0	240	300
61	119	30 56	19 24	34·4	30 07	18 45	34·1	29 17	18 06	33·8	28 27	17 29	33·5	27 37	16 51	33·2	26 44	16 14	32·9	241	299
62	118	31 16	18 50	33·3	30 26	18 12	33·0	29 35	17 34	32·7	28 45	16 57	32·4	27 54	16 21	32·1	27 01	15 45	31·8	242	298
63	117	31 35	18 15	32·2	30 44	17 38	31·9	29 53	17 02	31·6	29 02	16 26	31·3	28 10	15 50	31·0	27 19	15 15	30·7	243	297
64	116	31 53	17 40	31·1	31 02	17 04	30·8	30 10	16 28	30·5	29 19	15 53	30·2	28 27	15 19	29·9	27 35	14 45	29·6	244	296
65	115	32 11	17 04	30·0	31 19	16 29	29·7	30 27	15 55	29·4	29 35	15 20	29·1	28 42	14 48	28·8	27 50	14 15	28·5	245	295
66	114	32 29	16 28	28·8	31 36	15 54	28·5	30 43	15 20	28·2	29 50	14 48	28·0	28 57	14 16	27·7	28 04	13 44	27·4	246	294
67	113	32 45	15 51	27·7	31 52	15 18	27·4	30 59	14 46	27·1	30 05	14 14	26·8	29 12	13 43	26·6	28 18	13 13	26·3	247	293
68	112	33 01	15 14	26·5	32 08	14 42	26·3	31 14	14 11	26·0	30 20	13 40	25·7	29 26	13 10	25·5	28 31	12 41	25·2	248	292
69	111	33 17	14 36	25·4	32 23	14 05	25·1	31 28	13 35	24·8	30 34	13 06	24·6	29 39	12 37	24·4	28 44	12 09	24·1	249	291
70	110	33 32	13 57	24·2	32 37	13 27	24·0	31 42	12 59	23·7	30 47	12 31	23·5	29 52	12 04	23·2	28 58	11 36	23·0	250	290
71	109	33 46	13 18	23·1	32 51	12 51	22·8	31 55	12 23	22·6	31 00	11 56	22·3	30 04	11 30	22·1	29 09	11 04	21·9	251	289
72	108	33 59	12 39	21·9	33 04	12 13	21·6	32 08	11 46	21·4	31 12	11 21	21·2	30 15	10 56	21·0	29 20	10 31	20·8	252	288
73	107	34 12	12 00	20·7	33 16	11 34	20·5	32 20	11 09	20·2	31 23	10 45	20·0	30 27	10 21	19·8	29 30	9 58	19·6	253	287
74	106	34 24	11 19	19·5	33 28	10 55	19·3	32 31	10 32	19·1	31 34	10 09	18·9	30 37	9 46	18·7	29 41	9 24	18·5	254	286
75	105	34 36	10 39	18·3	33 39	10 16	18·1	32 42	9 54	17·9	31 44	9 32	17·7	30 47	9 11	17·5	29 50	8 50	17·4	255	285
76	104	34 46	9 58	17·1	33 49	9 37	16·9	32 52	9 16	16·7	31 54	8 56	16·6	30 57	8 36	16·4	29 59	8 16	16·2	256	284
77	103	34 56	9 17	15·9	33 59	8 57	15·7	33 01	8 38	15·6	32 03	8 19	15·4	31 05	8 00	15·2	30 07	7 42	15·1	257	283
78	102	35 06	8 35	14·7	34 08	8 17	14·5	33 10	7 59	14·4	32 13	7 41	14·2	31 13	7 24	14·1	30 15	7 07	13·9	258	282
79	101	35 14	7 54	13·5	34 16	7 37	13·3	33 18	7 20	13·2	32 19	7 04	13·0	31 21	6 48	12·9	30 22	6 32	12·8	259	281
80	100	35 22	7 11	12·3	34 24	6 56	12·1	33 25	6 41	12·0	32 26	6 26	11·9	31 27	6 12	11·7	30 29	5 57	11·6	260	280
81	99	35 29	6 29	11·1	34 30	6 15	10·9	33 32	6 01	10·8	32 33	5 48	10·7	31 34	5 35	10·6	30 35	5 22	10·5	261	279
82	98	35 36	5 46	9·9	34 37	5 34	9·7	33 37	5 22	9·6	32 38	5 10	9·5	31 41	4 58	9·4	30 40	4 47	9·3	262	278
83	97	35 41	5 04	8·6	34 42	4 53	8·5	33 43	4 42	8·4	32 43	4 32	8·3	31 44	4 21	8·2	30 45	4 11	8·2	263	277
84	96	35 46	4 21	7·4	34 47	4 11	7·3	33 47	4 02	7·2	32 48	3 54	7·1	31 48	3 44	7·1	30 49	3 36	7·0	264	276
85	95	35 51	3 37	6·2	34 51	3 30	6·1	33 51	3 22	6·0	32 52	3 14	6·0	31 52	3 07	5·9	30 52	3 00	5·8	265	275
86	94	35 54	2 54	4·9	34 54	2 48	4·9	33 54	2 42	4·8	32 55	2 36	4·8	31 55	2 30	4·7	30 55	2 24	4·7	266	274
87	93	35 57	2 11	3·7	34 57	2 06	3·7	33 57	2 01	3·6	32 57	1 57	3·6	31 57	1 52	3·5	30 57	1 48	3·5	267	273
88	92	35 58	1 27	2·5	34 59	1 24	2·4	33 59	1 21	2·4	32 59	1 18	2·4	31 59	1 15	2·4	30 59	1 12	2·3	268	272
89	91	36 00	0 44	1·2	35 00	0 42	1·2	34 00	0 40	1·2	33 00	0 39	1·2	32 00	0 37	1·2	31 00	0 36	1·2	269	271
90	90	36 00	0 00	0·0	35 00	0 00	0·0	34 00	0 00	0·0	33 00	0 00	0·0	32 00	0 00	0·0	31 00	0 00	0·0	270	270

N. Lat.: for LHA > 180° ... Z_n = Z
for LHA < 180° ... $Z_n = 360° − Z$

S. Lat.: for LHA > 180° ... $Z_n = 180° − Z$
for LHA < 180° ... $Z_n = 180° + Z$

SIGHT REDUCTION TABLE

B: (−) for 90° < LHA < 270°
Dec:(−) for Lat. contrary name

Z₁: same sign as B
Z₂: (−) for F > 90°

Lat./A	LHA/F	60° A/H	60° B/P	60° Z_1/Z_2	61° A/H	61° B/P	61° Z_1/Z_2	62° A/H	62° B/P	62° Z_1/Z_2	63° A/H	63° B/P	63° Z_1/Z_2	64° A/H	64° B/P	64° Z_1/Z_2	65° A/H	65° B/P	65° Z_1/Z_2	Lat./A	LHA
0	180	0 00	30 00	90·0	0 00	29 00	90·0	0 00	28 00	90·0	0 00	27 00	90·0	0 00	26 00	90·0	0 00	25 00	90·0	180	360
1	179	0 30	30 00	89·1	0 29	29 00	89·1	0 28	28 00	89·1	0 27	27 00	89·1	0 26	26 00	89·1	0 25	25 00	89·1	181	359
2	178	1 00	29 59	88·3	0 58	28 59	88·3	0 56	27 58	88·2	0 54	26 59	88·2	0 53	25 59	88·2	0 51	24 59	88·2	182	358
3	177	1 30	29 58	87·4	1 27	28 58	87·4	1 24	27 57	87·4	1 22	26 58	87·3	1 19	25 58	87·3	1 16	24 58	87·3	183	357
4	176	2 00	29 56	86·5	1 56	28 56	86·5	1 53	27 55	86·5	1 49	26 57	86·4	1 45	25 57	86·4	1 41	24 58	86·4	184	356
5	175	2 30	29 54	85·7	2 25	28 54	85·7	2 21	27 54	85·6	2 16	26 55	85·5	2 11	25 55	85·5	2 07	24 55	85·5	185	355
6	174	3 00	29 52	84·8	2 54	28 52	84·7	2 49	27 52	84·7	2 43	26 52	84·6	2 38	25 53	84·6	2 32	24 53	84·6	186	354
7	173	3 30	29 49	83·9	3 23	28 49	83·9	3 17	27 49	83·8	3 10	26 50	83·8	3 04	25 50	83·7	2 57	24 50	83·7	187	353
8	172	3 59	29 45	83·1	3 52	28 46	83·0	3 45	27 46	82·9	3 37	26 46	82·9	3 30	25 47	82·8	3 22	24 47	82·7	188	352
9	171	4 29	29 42	82·2	4 21	28 42	82·1	4 13	27 42	82·0	4 04	26 43	82·0	3 56	25 43	81·9	3 47	24 44	81·8	189	351
10	170	4 59	29 37	81·3	4 50	28 38	81·3	4 41	27 38	81·2	4 31	26 39	81·1	4 22	25 39	81·0	4 13	24 40	80·9	190	350
11	169	5 28	29 33	80·4	5 18	28 33	80·4	5 08	27 34	80·3	4 58	26 34	80·2	4 48	25 35	80·1	4 38	24 36	80·0	191	349
12	168	5 58	29 27	79·6	5 47	28 28	79·5	5 36	27 29	79·4	5 25	26 29	79·3	5 14	25 30	79·2	5 02	24 31	79·1	192	348
13	167	6 27	29 22	78·7	6 16	28 22	78·6	6 04	27 23	78·5	5 52	26 24	78·4	5 40	25 25	78·3	5 27	24 26	78·2	193	347
14	166	6 57	29 15	77·8	6 44	28 16	77·7	6 31	27 17	77·6	6 18	26 18	77·5	6 05	25 20	77·4	5 52	24 21	77·3	194	346
15	165	7 26	29 09	76·9	7 13	28 10	76·8	6 59	27 11	76·7	6 45	26 12	76·6	6 31	25 14	76·5	6 17	24 15	76·4	195	345
16	164	7 55	29 02	76·1	7 41	28 03	75·9	7 26	27 04	75·8	7 11	26 06	75·7	6 56	25 07	75·6	6 41	24 09	75·4	196	344
17	163	8 24	28 54	75·2	8 09	27 56	75·0	7 53	26 57	74·9	7 38	25 59	74·8	7 22	25 00	74·6	7 06	24 02	74·5	197	343
18	162	8 53	28 46	74·3	8 37	27 48	74·1	8 20	26 50	74·0	8 04	25 51	73·9	7 47	24 53	73·7	7 30	23 55	73·6	198	342
19	161	9 22	28 38	73·4	9 05	27 40	73·2	8 48	26 41	73·1	8 30	25 43	72·9	8 12	24 45	72·8	7 55	23 48	72·7	199	341
20	160	9 51	28 29	72·5	9 33	27 31	72·3	9 14	26 33	72·2	8 56	25 35	72·0	8 37	24 37	71·9	8 19	23 40	71·7	200	340
21	159	10 19	28 19	71·6	10 00	27 22	71·4	9 41	26 24	71·3	9 22	25 26	71·1	9 02	24 29	71·0	8 43	23 32	70·8	201	339
22	158	10 48	28 10	70·7	10 28	27 12	70·5	10 08	26 15	70·4	9 48	25 17	70·2	9 27	24 20	70·0	9 07	23 23	69·9	202	338
23	157	11 16	27 59	69·8	10 55	27 02	69·6	10 34	26 05	69·5	10 13	25 08	69·3	9 52	24 11	69·1	9 30	23 14	69·0	203	337
24	156	11 44	27 49	68·9	11 22	26 51	68·7	11 00	25 54	68·5	10 38	24 58	68·4	10 16	24 01	68·2	9 54	23 04	68·0	204	336
25	155	12 12	27 37	68·0	11 49	26 40	67·8	11 27	25 44	67·6	11 04	24 47	67·4	10 41	23 51	67·3	10 17	22 55	67·1	205	335
26	154	12 40	27 26	67·1	12 16	26 29	66·9	11 53	25 33	66·7	11 29	24 36	66·5	11 05	23 40	66·3	10 41	22 44	66·2	206	334
27	153	13 07	27 13	66·2	12 43	26 17	66·0	12 18	25 21	65·8	11 54	24 25	65·6	11 29	23 29	65·4	11 04	22 34	65·2	207	333
28	152	13 35	27 01	65·3	13 09	26 05	65·0	12 44	25 09	64·9	12 18	24 13	64·7	11 53	23 18	64·5	11 27	22 23	64·3	208	332
29	151	14 02	26 48	64·4	13 36	25 52	64·1	13 09	24 56	63·9	12 43	24 01	63·7	12 16	23 06	63·5	11 49	22 11	63·3	209	331
30	150	14 29	26 34	63·4	14 02	25 39	63·2	13 35	24 43	63·0	13 07	23 49	62·8	12 40	22 54	62·6	12 12	21 59	62·4	210	330
31	149	14 55	26 20	62·5	14 28	25 25	62·3	14 00	24 30	62·1	13 31	23 36	61·8	13 03	22 41	61·6	12 34	21 47	61·4	211	329
32	148	15 22	26 05	61·6	14 53	25 11	61·3	14 24	24 16	61·1	13 55	23 23	60·9	13 26	22 28	60·7	12 56	21 35	60·5	212	328
33	147	15 48	25 50	60·6	15 19	24 56	60·4	14 49	24 02	60·2	14 19	23 08	59·9	13 49	22 15	59·7	13 18	21 22	59·5	213	327
34	146	16 14	25 35	59·7	15 44	24 41	59·5	15 13	23 47	59·2	14 42	22 54	59·0	14 11	22 01	58·8	13 40	21 08	58·6	214	326
35	145	16 40	25 19	58·8	16 09	24 25	58·5	15 37	23 32	58·3	15 06	22 39	58·0	14 34	21 47	57·8	14 02	20 54	57·6	215	325
36	144	17 05	25 02	57·8	16 33	24 09	57·6	16 01	23 17	57·3	15 29	22 24	57·1	14 56	21 32	56·9	14 23	20 40	56·6	216	324
37	143	17 31	24 45	56·9	16 58	23 53	56·6	16 24	23 00	56·4	15 51	22 09	56·1	15 18	21 17	55·9	14 44	20 26	55·7	217	323
38	142	17 56	24 28	55·9	17 22	23 36	55·7	16 48	22 44	55·4	16 14	21 53	55·2	15 39	21 02	54·9	15 05	20 11	54·7	218	322
39	141	18 20	24 10	55·0	17 46	23 18	54·7	17 11	22 27	54·4	16 36	21 37	54·2	16 01	20 46	54·0	15 25	19 56	53·7	219	321
40	140	18 45	23 52	54·0	18 09	23 00	53·7	17 34	22 10	53·5	16 58	21 20	53·2	16 22	20 29	53·0	15 46	19 39	52·7	220	320
41	139	19 09	23 33	53·0	18 33	22 42	52·8	17 56	21 52	52·5	17 20	21 02	52·2	16 43	20 13	52·0	16 06	19 23	51·8	221	319
42	138	19 33	23 13	52·1	18 56	22 23	51·8	18 19	21 34	51·5	17 41	20 44	51·3	17 03	19 55	51·0	16 26	19 07	50·8	222	318
43	137	19 56	22 53	51·1	19 19	22 04	50·8	18 41	21 15	50·5	18 02	20 26	50·3	17 24	19 38	50·0	16 45	18 50	49·9	223	317
44	136	20 19	22 33	50·1	19 41	21 44	49·8	19 02	20 56	49·5	18 23	20 08	49·3	17 44	19 20	49·0	17 04	18 33	48·8	224	316
45	135	20 42	22 12	49·1	20 03	21 24	48·8	19 23	20 36	48·6	18 43	19 49	48·3	18 03	19 02	48·1	17 23	18 15	47·8	225	315

Lat. / A	LHA/F	60° A/H	60° B/P	60° Z_1/Z_2	61° A/H	61° B/P	61° Z_1/Z_2	62° A/H	62° B/P	62° Z_1/Z_2	63° A/H	63° B/P	63° Z_1/Z_2	64° A/H	64° B/P	64° Z_1/Z_2	65° A/H	65° B/P	65° Z_1/Z_2	LHA	Lat. / A
45	135	20 42	22 12	49·1	20 03	21 24	48·8	19 23	20 36	48·6	18 43	19 49	48·3	18 03	19 02	48·1	17 23	18 15	47·8	315	225
46	134	21 05	21 51	48·1	20 25	21 04	47·8	19 44	20 16	47·6	19 04	19 29	47·3	18 23	18 43	47·1	17 42	17 57	46·8	314	226
47	133	21 27	21 30	47·1	20 46	20 43	46·8	20 05	19 56	46·6	19 24	19 09	46·3	18 42	18 24	46·1	18 00	17 39	45·8	313	227
48	132	21 49	21 07	46·1	21 07	20 21	45·8	20 25	19 35	45·6	19 43	18 50	45·3	19 01	18 04	45·1	18 18	17 20	44·8	312	228
49	131	22 10	20 45	45·1	21 28	19 59	44·8	20 45	19 14	44·6	20 02	18 29	44·3	19 19	17 45	44·0	18 36	17 01	43·8	311	229
50	130	22 31	20 22	44·1	21 48	19 37	43·8	21 05	18 52	43·5	20 21	18 08	43·3	19 37	17 24	43·0	18 53	16 41	42·8	310	230
51	129	22 52	19 58	43·1	22 08	19 14	42·8	21 24	18 30	42·5	20 40	17 47	42·3	19 55	17 04	42·0	19 10	16 21	41·8	309	231
52	128	23 12	19 34	42·1	22 28	18 51	41·8	21 43	18 08	41·5	20 58	17 25	41·2	20 13	16 43	41·0	19 27	16 01	40·8	308	232
53	127	23 32	19 10	41·0	22 47	18 27	40·7	22 01	17 45	40·5	21 15	17 03	40·2	20 30	16 21	40·0	19 44	15 41	39·7	307	233
54	126	23 52	18 45	40·0	23 06	18 03	39·7	22 19	17 21	39·4	21 33	16 40	39·2	20 47	16 00	39·0	20 00	15 20	38·7	306	234
55	125	24 12	18 19	39·0	23 24	17 38	38·7	22 37	16 58	38·4	21 50	16 17	38·2	21 03	15 38	37·9	20 15	14 58	37·7	305	235
56	124	24 29	17 54	37·9	23 42	17 13	37·6	22 54	16 34	37·4	22 07	15 54	37·1	21 19	15 15	36·9	20 31	14 37	36·7	304	236
57	123	24 48	17 27	36·9	23 59	16 48	36·6	23 11	16 09	36·3	22 23	15 31	36·1	21 34	14 53	35·8	20 46	14 15	35·6	303	237
58	122	25 05	17 01	35·8	24 17	16 22	35·5	23 28	15 44	35·3	22 39	15 07	35·0	21 49	14 29	34·8	21 00	13 53	34·6	302	238
59	121	25 23	16 34	34·8	24 33	15 56	34·5	23 44	15 19	34·2	22 54	14 42	34·0	22 04	14 06	33·8	21 14	13 30	33·5	301	239
60	120	25 40	16 06	33·7	24 50	15 29	33·4	23 59	14 53	33·2	23 09	14 18	32·9	22 19	13 42	32·7	21 28	13 07	32·5	300	240
61	119	25 56	15 38	32·6	25 05	15 03	32·4	24 15	14 27	32·1	23 24	13 53	31·9	22 33	13 18	31·7	21 42	12 44	31·5	299	241
62	118	26 12	15 10	31·5	25 21	14 35	31·3	24 29	14 01	31·1	23 38	13 27	30·8	22 46	12 54	30·6	21 55	12 21	30·4	298	242
63	117	26 27	14 41	30·5	25 36	14 08	30·2	24 44	13 34	30·0	23 52	13 02	29·8	22 59	12 29	29·5	22 07	11 57	29·3	297	243
64	116	26 42	14 12	29·4	25 50	13 39	29·1	24 57	13 07	28·9	24 05	12 35	28·7	23 12	12 04	28·5	22 19	11 33	28·3	296	244
65	115	26 57	13 43	28·3	26 04	13 11	28·1	25 11	12 40	27·8	24 18	12 09	27·6	23 25	11 39	27·4	22 31	11 09	27·2	295	245
66	114	27 11	13 13	27·2	26 17	12 42	27·0	25 24	12 12	26·8	24 31	11 43	26·6	23 36	11 13	26·4	22 43	10 44	26·2	294	246
67	113	27 24	12 43	26·1	26 30	12 13	25·9	25 36	11 44	25·7	24 42	11 16	25·5	23 48	10 47	25·3	22 54	10 20	25·1	293	247
68	112	27 37	12 12	25·0	26 43	11 44	24·8	25 48	11 16	24·6	24 54	10 48	24·4	23 59	10 21	24·2	23 04	9 55	24·0	292	248
69	111	27 50	11 41	23·9	26 55	11 14	23·7	26 00	10 47	23·5	25 05	10 21	23·3	24 09	9 55	23·1	23 14	9 29	23·0	291	249
70	110	28 01	11 10	22·8	27 06	10 44	22·6	26 11	10 18	22·4	25 15	9 53	22·2	24 19	9 28	22·0	23 24	9 04	21·9	290	250
71	109	28 13	10 39	21·7	27 17	10 14	21·5	26 21	9 49	21·3	25 25	9 25	21·1	24 29	9 01	21·0	23 33	8 38	20·8	289	251
72	108	28 24	10 07	20·6	27 27	9 43	20·4	26 31	9 20	20·2	25 35	8 57	20·0	24 38	8 34	19·8	23 42	8 12	19·7	288	252
73	107	28 34	9 35	19·4	27 37	9 12	19·3	26 41	8 50	19·1	25 44	8 28	18·9	24 47	8 07	18·8	23 50	7 46	18·6	287	253
74	106	28 44	9 03	18·3	27 47	8 41	18·2	26 50	8 20	18·0	25 52	8 00	17·8	24 55	7 39	17·7	23 58	7 19	17·6	286	254
75	105	28 53	8 30	17·2	27 55	8 10	17·0	26 58	7 50	16·9	26 01	7 31	16·7	25 03	7 12	16·6	24 06	6 53	16·5	285	255
76	104	29 01	7 57	16·1	28 04	7 38	15·9	27 06	7 20	15·8	26 08	7 02	15·6	25 10	6 44	15·5	24 13	6 26	15·4	284	256
77	103	29 09	7 24	14·9	28 11	7 06	14·8	27 13	6 49	14·7	26 15	6 32	14·5	25 17	6 16	14·4	24 19	5 59	14·3	283	257
78	102	29 17	6 51	13·8	28 18	6 34	13·7	27 20	6 18	13·5	26 22	6 03	13·4	25 23	5 47	13·3	24 25	5 32	13·2	282	258
79	101	29 24	6 17	12·7	28 25	6 02	12·5	27 27	5 48	12·4	26 28	5 33	12·3	25 29	5 19	12·2	24 31	5 05	12·1	281	259
80	100	29 30	5 44	11·5	28 31	5 30	11·4	27 32	5 17	11·3	26 33	5 03	11·2	25 35	4 50	11·1	24 36	4 38	11·0	280	260
81	99	29 36	5 10	10·4	28 37	4 57	10·3	27 38	4 45	10·2	26 38	4 33	10·1	25 39	4 22	10·0	24 40	4 10	9·9	279	261
82	98	29 41	4 36	9·2	28 41	4 24	9·1	27 43	4 14	9·0	26 43	4 03	9·0	25 44	3 53	8·9	24 44	3 43	8·8	278	262
83	97	29 45	4 01	8·1	28 46	3 52	8·0	27 47	3 42	7·9	26 47	3 33	7·8	25 48	3 24	7·8	24 48	3 15	7·7	277	263
84	96	29 49	3 27	6·9	28 50	3 19	6·9	27 50	3 11	6·8	26 50	3 03	6·7	25 51	2 55	6·7	24 51	2 47	6·6	276	264
85	95	29 52	2 53	5·8	28 53	2 46	5·7	27 53	2 39	5·7	26 53	2 33	5·6	25 54	2 26	5·6	24 54	2 20	5·5	275	265
86	94	29 55	2 18	4·6	28 55	2 13	4·6	27 56	2 07	4·5	26 56	2 02	4·5	25 56	1 57	4·4	24 56	1 52	4·4	274	266
87	93	29 57	1 44	3·5	28 57	1 40	3·4	27 57	1 36	3·4	26 58	1 32	3·4	25 58	1 28	3·3	24 58	1 24	3·3	273	267
88	92	29 59	1 09	2·3	28 59	1 06	2·3	27 59	1 04	2·3	26 59	1 01	2·2	25 59	0 59	2·2	24 59	0 56	2·2	272	268
89	91	30 00	0 35	1·2	29 00	0 33	1·1	28 00	0 32	1·1	27 00	0 31	1·1	26 00	0 29	1·1	25 00	0 28	1·1	271	269
90	90	30 00	0 00	0·0	29 00	0 00	0·0	28 00	0 00	0·0	27 00	0 00	0·0	26 00	0 00	0·0	25 00	0 00	0·0	270	270

N. Lat.: for LHA > 180° ... $Z_n = Z$; for LHA < 180° ... $Z_n = 360° − Z$

S. Lat.: for LHA > 180° ... $Z_n = 180° − Z$; for LHA < 180° ... $Z_n = 180° + Z$

SIGHT REDUCTION TABLE

B: (−) for 90° < LHA < 270°
Dec:(−) for Lat. contrary name

Z₁: same sign as B
Z₂: (−) for F > 90°

Lat./A	LHA/F	66° A/H	66° B/P	66° Z₁/Z₂	67° A/H	67° B/P	67° Z₁/Z₂	68° A/H	68° B/P	68° Z₁/Z₂	69° A/H	69° B/P	69° Z₁/Z₂	70° A/H	70° B/P	70° Z₁/Z₂	71° A/H	71° B/P	71° Z₁/Z₂	Lat./A	LHA
0	180	0 00	24 00	90·0	0 00	23 00	90·0	0 00	22 00	90·0	0 00	21 00	90·0	0 00	20 00	90·0	0 00	19 00	90·0	180	360
1	179	0 24	24 00	89·1	0 23	23 00	89·1	0 22	22 00	89·1	0 22	21 00	89·1	0 21	20 00	89·1	0 20	19 00	89·1	181	359
2	178	0 49	23 59	88·2	0 47	22 59	88·2	0 45	22 00	88·1	0 43	20 59	88·1	0 41	19 59	88·1	0 39	18 59	88·1	182	358
3	177	1 13	23 58	87·3	1 10	22 58	87·3	1 07	21 58	87·2	1 04	20 58	87·2	1 02	19 58	87·2	0 59	18 59	87·2	183	357
4	176	1 38	23 57	86·3	1 34	22 57	86·3	1 30	21 57	86·3	1 26	20 57	86·3	1 22	19 57	86·2	1 18	18 58	86·2	184	356
5	175	2 02	23 55	85·4	1 57	22 55	85·4	1 52	21 55	85·4	1 47	20 56	85·3	1 42	19 56	85·3	1 38	18 56	85·3	185	355
6	174	2 26	23 53	84·5	2 20	22 53	84·5	2 15	21 53	84·5	2 09	20 54	84·4	2 03	19 54	84·3	1 57	18 54	84·3	186	354
7	173	2 50	23 50	83·6	2 44	22 51	83·6	2 37	21 51	83·6	2 30	20 51	83·5	2 23	19 52	83·4	2 16	18 52	83·4	187	353
8	172	3 15	23 48	82·7	3 07	22 48	82·7	2 59	21 48	82·6	2 52	20 49	82·6	2 44	19 49	82·5	2 36	18 50	82·4	188	352
9	171	3 39	23 44	81·8	3 30	22 45	81·8	3 22	21 45	81·7	3 13	20 46	81·6	3 04	19 46	81·6	2 55	18 47	81·5	189	351
10	170	4 03	23 41	80·8	3 53	22 41	80·8	3 44	21 42	80·8	3 34	20 42	80·7	3 24	19 43	80·6	3 14	18 44	80·5	190	350
11	169	4 27	23 36	79·9	4 17	22 37	79·9	4 06	21 38	79·8	3 55	20 39	79·7	3 45	19 40	79·6	3 34	18 41	79·6	191	349
12	168	4 51	23 32	79·0	4 40	22 32	79·0	4 28	21 34	78·9	4 16	20 35	78·8	4 05	19 36	78·7	3 53	18 37	78·6	192	348
13	167	5 15	23 27	78·1	5 03	22 28	78·1	4 50	21 29	78·0	4 37	20 30	77·8	4 25	19 32	77·8	4 12	18 33	77·7	193	347
14	166	5 39	23 21	77·2	5 25	22 23	77·2	5 12	21 24	77·1	4 58	20 26	76·9	4 45	19 27	76·8	4 31	18 28	76·7	194	346
15	165	6 03	23 16	76·2	5 48	22 17	76·1	5 34	21 19	76·1	5 19	20 21	76·0	5 05	19 22	75·9	4 50	18 24	75·8	195	345
16	164	6 26	23 10	75·3	6 11	22 12	75·2	5 56	21 13	75·2	5 40	20 15	75·0	5 25	19 17	74·9	5 09	18 19	74·8	196	344
17	163	6 50	23 04	74·4	6 34	22 06	74·3	6 17	21 08	74·3	6 01	20 09	74·1	5 44	19 11	74·0	5 28	18 14	73·9	197	343
18	162	7 13	22 57	73·5	6 56	21 59	73·3	6 39	21 01	73·3	6 21	20 03	73·1	6 04	19 06	73·0	5 46	18 08	72·9	198	342
19	161	7 37	22 50	72·5	7 19	21 52	72·5	7 00	20 54	72·4	6 42	19 57	72·2	6 24	18 59	72·1	6 05	18 02	72·0	199	341
20	160	8 00	22 42	71·6	7 41	21 45	71·5	7 22	20 47	71·5	7 02	19 50	71·2	6 43	18 53	71·1	6 24	17 56	71·0	200	340
21	159	8 23	22 34	70·7	8 03	21 37	70·7	7 43	20 40	70·5	7 23	19 43	70·3	7 02	18 46	70·2	6 42	17 49	70·1	201	339
22	158	8 46	22 26	69·7	8 25	21 29	69·6	8 04	20 32	69·6	7 43	19 35	69·3	7 22	18 39	69·2	7 00	17 42	69·1	202	338
23	157	9 09	22 17	68·8	8 47	21 21	68·7	8 25	20 24	68·7	8 03	19 28	68·4	7 41	18 31	68·3	7 19	17 35	68·1	203	337
24	156	9 31	22 08	67·9	9 09	21 12	67·7	8 46	20 16	67·7	8 23	19 19	67·4	8 00	18 24	67·3	7 37	17 28	67·2	204	336
25	155	9 54	21 58	66·9	9 30	21 03	66·8	9 07	20 07	66·8	8 43	19 11	66·5	8 19	18 15	66·3	7 55	17 20	66·2	205	335
26	154	10 16	21 49	66·0	9 52	20 53	65·8	9 27	19 57	65·8	9 02	19 02	65·5	8 37	18 07	65·4	8 12	17 12	65·2	206	334
27	153	10 38	21 38	65·0	10 13	20 43	64·9	9 48	19 48	64·9	9 22	18 53	64·6	8 56	17 58	64·4	8 30	17 03	64·3	207	333
28	152	11 00	21 28	64·1	10 34	20 33	63·9	10 08	19 38	63·9	9 41	18 43	63·6	9 14	17 49	63·5	8 48	16 55	63·3	208	332
29	151	11 22	21 17	63·1	10 55	20 22	63·0	10 28	19 28	63·0	10 00	18 34	62·6	9 33	17 39	62·5	9 05	16 46	62·3	209	331
30	150	11 44	21 05	62·2	11 16	20 11	62·0	10 48	19 17	62·0	10 19	18 23	61·7	9 51	17 30	61·5	9 22	16 36	61·4	210	330
31	149	12 06	20 54	61·2	11 37	20 00	61·1	11 07	19 06	61·1	10 38	18 13	60·7	10 09	17 20	60·5	9 39	16 27	60·4	211	329
32	148	12 27	20 41	60·3	11 57	19 48	60·1	11 27	18 55	60·1	10 57	18 02	59·7	10 27	17 09	59·6	9 56	16 17	59·4	212	328
33	147	12 48	20 29	59·3	12 17	19 36	59·1	11 46	18 43	59·1	11 15	17 51	58·8	10 45	16 58	58·6	10 12	16 06	58·4	213	327
34	146	13 09	20 16	58·4	12 37	19 23	58·2	12 06	18 31	58·2	11 34	17 39	57·8	11 02	16 47	57·6	10 29	15 56	57·5	214	326
35	145	13 29	20 02	57·4	12 57	19 10	57·2	12 24	18 19	57·2	11 52	17 27	56·8	11 19	16 36	56·7	10 46	15 45	56·5	215	325
36	144	13 50	19 49	56·4	13 17	18 57	56·2	12 43	18 06	56·2	12 10	17 15	55·9	11 36	16 25	55·7	11 02	15 34	55·5	216	324
37	143	14 10	19 34	55·5	13 36	18 44	55·3	13 02	17 53	55·3	12 28	17 03	54·9	11 53	16 12	54·7	11 18	15 23	54·5	217	323
38	142	14 30	19 20	54·5	13 55	18 30	54·3	13 20	17 40	54·3	12 45	16 50	53·9	12 09	16 00	53·7	11 34	15 11	53·5	218	322
39	141	14 49	19 05	53·5	14 14	18 16	53·3	13 38	17 26	53·3	13 02	16 37	52·9	12 25	15 48	52·7	11 49	14 59	52·6	219	321
40	140	15 09	18 50	52·5	14 33	18 01	52·3	13 56	17 12	52·3	13 19	16 23	51·9	12 42	15 35	51·7	12 05	14 47	51·6	220	320
41	139	15 29	18 34	51·5	14 51	17 46	51·3	14 14	16 57	51·3	13 36	16 09	50·9	12 58	15 22	50·8	12 20	14 34	50·6	221	319
42	138	15 48	18 18	50·6	15 09	17 30	50·3	14 31	16 43	50·3	13 52	15 55	49·9	13 14	15 08	49·8	12 35	14 21	49·6	222	318
43	137	16 06	18 02	49·6	15 27	17 15	49·4	14 48	16 28	49·4	14 08	15 41	49·0	13 29	14 54	48·8	12 50	14 08	48·6	223	317
44	136	16 25	17 46	48·6	15 45	16 59	48·4	15 05	16 12	48·4	14 25	15 26	48·0	13 45	14 40	47·8	13 04	13 55	47·6	224	316
45	135	16 43	17 29	47·6	16 02	16 42	47·4	15 22	15 57	47·4	14 41	15 11	47·0	14 00	14 26	46·8	13 19	13 41	46·6	225	315

Lat./A LHA/F		66° A/H	B/P	Z₁/Z₂	67° A/H	B/P	Z₁/Z₂	68° A/H	B/P	Z₁/Z₂	69° A/H	B/P	Z₁/Z₂	70° A/H	B/P	Z₁/Z₂	71° A/H	B/P	Z₁/Z₂	Lat./A LHA	
135	45	16 43	17 29	47·6	16 02	16 42	47·4	15 22	15 57	47·2	14 41	15 11	47·0	14 00	14 26	46·8	13 19	13 41	46·6	225	315
134	46	17 01	17 11	46·6	16 19	16 26	46·4	15 38	15 41	46·2	14 56	14 56	46·0	14 15	14 11	45·8	13 33	13 27	45·6	226	314
133	47	17 18	16 53	45·6	16 36	16 09	45·4	15 54	15 25	45·2	15 12	14 40	45·0	14 29	13 56	44·8	13 46	13 13	44·6	227	313
132	48	17 36	16 35	44·6	16 53	15 51	44·4	16 10	15 08	44·2	15 27	14 24	44·0	14 44	13 41	43·8	14 00	12 58	43·6	228	312
131	49	17 53	16 17	43·6	17 09	15 34	43·4	16 25	14 51	43·2	15 42	14 08	43·0	14 58	13 26	42·8	14 13	12 44	42·6	229	311
130	50	18 09	15 58	42·6	17 25	15 16	42·4	16 41	14 33	42·1	15 56	13 52	41·9	15 11	13 10	41·8	14 27	12 29	41·6	230	310
129	51	18 26	15 39	41·6	17 41	14 57	41·3	16 56	14 16	41·1	16 10	13 35	40·9	15 25	12 54	40·8	14 39	12 14	40·6	231	309
128	52	18 42	15 20	40·5	17 56	14 39	40·3	17 11	13 58	40·1	16 24	13 18	39·9	15 38	12 38	39·7	14 52	11 58	39·6	232	308
127	53	18 57	15 00	39·5	18 11	14 20	39·3	17 24	13 40	39·1	16 38	13 00	38·9	15 51	12 21	38·7	15 04	11 42	38·6	233	307
126	54	19 13	14 40	38·5	18 26	14 01	38·3	17 39	13 22	38·1	16 51	12 43	37·9	16 04	12 05	37·7	15 16	11 26	37·5	234	306
125	55	19 28	14 20	37·5	18 40	13 41	37·3	17 52	13 03	37·1	17 04	12 25	36·9	16 16	11 48	36·7	15 28	11 10	36·5	235	305
124	56	19 42	13 59	36·4	18 54	13 21	36·2	18 06	12 44	36·0	17 17	12 07	35·8	16 28	11 30	35·7	15 40	10 54	35·5	236	304
123	57	19 57	13 38	35·4	19 08	13 01	35·2	18 19	12 25	35·0	17 29	11 49	34·8	16 40	11 13	34·6	15 51	10 37	34·5	237	303
122	58	20 11	13 17	34·4	19 21	12 41	34·2	18 31	12 05	34·0	17 42	11 30	33·8	16 52	10 55	33·6	16 02	10 20	33·5	238	302
121	59	20 24	12 55	33·3	19 34	12 20	33·1	18 44	11 45	32·9	17 53	11 11	32·8	17 03	10 37	32·6	16 13	10 03	32·4	239	301
120	60	20 37	12 33	32·3	19 47	11 59	32·1	18 56	11 25	31·9	18 05	10 52	31·7	17 14	10 19	31·6	16 23	9 46	31·4	240	300
119	61	20 50	12 11	31·2	19 59	11 38	31·1	19 08	11 05	30·9	18 16	10 33	30·7	17 24	10 00	30·5	16 33	9 29	30·4	241	299
118	62	21 03	11 48	30·2	20 11	11 16	30·0	19 19	10 44	29·8	18 27	10 13	29·7	17 35	9 42	29·5	16 42	9 11	29·4	242	298
117	63	21 15	11 26	29·2	20 22	10 54	29·0	19 30	10 24	28·8	18 37	9 53	28·6	17 45	9 23	28·5	16 52	8 53	28·3	243	297
116	64	21 27	11 03	28·1	20 34	10 32	27·9	19 41	10 03	27·7	18 47	9 33	27·6	17 54	9 04	27·4	17 01	8 35	27·3	244	296
115	65	21 38	10 40	27·0	20 44	10 09	26·9	19 51	9 41	26·7	18 57	9 13	26·5	18 03	8 45	26·4	17 10	8 17	26·3	245	295
114	66	21 49	10 16	26·0	20 55	9 48	25·8	20 01	9 20	25·7	19 07	8 52	25·5	18 12	8 25	25·4	17 18	7 58	25·2	246	294
113	67	21 59	9 52	24·9	21 05	9 25	24·8	20 10	8 58	24·6	19 16	8 32	24·5	18 21	8 06	24·3	17 26	7 40	24·2	247	293
112	68	22 09	9 28	23·9	21 14	9 02	23·7	20 19	8 36	23·5	19 24	8 11	23·4	18 29	7 46	23·3	17 34	7 21	23·1	248	292
111	69	22 19	9 04	22·8	21 24	8 39	22·6	20 28	8 14	22·4	19 33	7 50	22·4	18 37	7 26	22·2	17 42	7 02	22·1	249	291
110	70	22 28	8 39	21·7	21 32	8 16	21·6	20 37	7 52	21·4	19 41	7 29	21·3	18 45	7 06	21·2	17 49	6 43	21·1	250	290
109	71	22 37	8 15	20·7	21 41	7 52	20·5	20 45	7 30	20·4	19 48	7 07	20·2	18 52	6 45	20·1	17 56	6 24	20·0	251	289
108	72	22 45	7 50	19·6	21 49	7 28	19·4	20 52	7 07	19·3	19 56	6 46	19·2	18 59	6 25	19·1	18 02	6 04	19·0	252	288
107	73	22 53	7 25	18·5	21 56	7 04	18·4	21 00	6 44	18·2	20 03	6 24	18·1	19 05	6 04	18·0	18 08	5 45	17·9	253	287
106	74	23 01	7 00	17·4	22 04	6 40	17·3	21 06	6 21	17·2	20 09	6 02	17·1	19 12	5 44	17·0	18 14	5 25	16·9	254	286
105	75	23 08	6 34	16·3	22 10	6 16	16·2	21 13	5 58	16·1	20 15	5 40	16·1	19 17	5 23	15·9	18 20	5 06	15·8	255	285
104	76	23 15	6 09	15·3	22 17	5 51	15·2	21 19	5 35	15·1	20 20	5 18	15·0	19 23	5 02	14·9	18 25	4 46	14·8	256	284
103	77	23 21	5 43	14·2	22 23	5 27	14·1	21 24	5 12	14·0	20 26	4 56	13·9	19 28	4 41	13·8	18 30	4 26	13·7	257	283
102	78	23 27	5 17	13·1	22 28	5 03	13·0	21 30	4 48	12·9	20 31	4 34	12·9	19 33	4 20	12·7	18 34	4 06	12·7	258	282
101	79	23 32	4 51	12·0	22 33	4 38	11·9	21 35	4 24	11·8	20 36	4 11	11·8	19 37	3 58	11·7	18 38	3 46	11·6	259	281
100	80	23 37	4 25	10·9	22 38	4 13	10·8	21 39	4 01	10·8	20 40	3 49	10·7	19 41	3 37	10·6	18 42	3 25	10·6	260	280
99	81	23 41	3 59	9·8	22 42	3 48	9·8	21 43	3 37	9·7	20 44	3 26	9·7	19 45	3 16	9·6	18 45	3 05	9·5	261	279
98	82	23 45	3 33	8·7	22 46	3 23	8·7	21 46	3 13	8·6	20 47	3 03	8·6	19 48	2 54	8·5	18 48	2 45	8·5	262	278
97	83	23 49	3 06	7·7	22 49	2 58	7·6	21 50	2 49	7·5	20 50	2 41	7·5	19 51	2 32	7·4	18 51	2 24	7·4	263	277
96	84	23 52	2 40	6·6	22 52	2 32	6·5	21 53	2 25	6·5	20 53	2 18	6·4	19 53	2 11	6·4	18 54	2 04	6·3	264	276
95	85	23 54	2 13	5·5	22 54	2 07	5·4	21 55	2 01	5·4	20 55	1 55	5·4	19 55	1 49	5·3	18 55	1 43	5·3	265	275
94	86	23 56	1 47	4·4	22 56	1 42	4·3	21 57	1 37	4·3	20 57	1 32	4·3	19 57	1 27	4·3	18 57	1 23	4·2	266	274
93	87	23 58	1 20	3·3	22 58	1 16	3·3	21 58	1 13	3·2	20 58	1 09	3·2	19 58	1 05	3·2	18 58	1 02	3·2	267	273
92	88	23 59	0 53	2·2	22 59	0 51	2·2	21 59	0 48	2·2	20 59	0 46	2·1	19 59	0 44	2·1	18 59	0 41	2·1	268	272
91	89	24 00	0 27	1·1	23 00	0 25	1·1	22 00	0 24	1·1	21 00	0 23	1·1	20 00	0 22	1·1	19 00	0 21	1·1	269	271
90	90	24 00	0 00	0·0	23 00	0 00	0·0	22 00	0 00	0·0	21 00	0 00	0·0	20 00	0 00	0·0	19 00	0 00	0·0	270	270

N. Lat.: for LHA > 180° ... $Z_n = Z$
for LHA < 180° ... $Z_n = 360° - Z$

S. Lat.: for LHA > 180° ... $Z_n = 180° - Z$
for LHA < 180° ... $Z_n = 180° + Z$

SIGHT REDUCTION TABLE

B: (−) for 90° < LHA < 270°
Dec:(−) for Lat. contrary name

Z₁: same sign as B
Z₂: (−) for F > 90°

Lat./A LHA/F	72° A/H	72° B/P	72° Z₁/Z₂	73° A/H	73° B/P	73° Z₁/Z₂	74° A/H	74° B/P	74° Z₁/Z₂	75° A/H	75° B/P	75° Z₁/Z₂	76° A/H	76° B/P	76° Z₁/Z₂	77° A/H	77° B/P	77° Z₁/Z₂	Lat./A LHA
0	0 00	18 00	90·0	0 00	17 00	90·0	0 00	16 00	90·0	0 00	15 00	90·0	0 00	14 00	90·0	0 00	13 00	90·0	180 / 360
1	0 19	18 00	89·0	0 18	17 00	89·0	0 17	16 00	89·0	0 16	15 00	89·0	0 15	14 00	89·0	0 13	13 00	89·0	181 / 359
2	0 37	17 59	88·1	0 35	16 59	88·1	0 33	15 59	88·1	0 31	14 59	88·1	0 29	14 00	88·1	0 27	13 00	88·1	182 / 358
3	0 56	17 58	87·1	0 53	16 58	87·1	0 50	15 58	87·1	0 47	14 58	87·1	0 44	13 59	87·1	0 40	12 59	87·1	183 / 357
4	1 14	17 57	86·2	1 10	16 58	86·2	1 06	15 58	86·2	1 02	14 58	86·1	0 58	13 58	86·1	0 54	12 58	86·1	184 / 356
5	1 33	17 56	85·2	1 28	16 56	85·2	1 23	15 57	85·2	1 18	14 57	85·2	1 12	13 57	85·2	1 07	12 57	85·1	185 / 355
6	1 51	17 54	84·3	1 45	16 55	84·3	1 39	15 55	84·2	1 33	14 55	84·2	1 27	13 56	84·2	1 21	12 56	84·2	186 / 354
7	2 09	17 52	83·3	2 03	16 53	83·3	1 56	15 54	83·3	1 48	14 54	83·3	1 41	13 54	83·2	1 34	12 54	83·2	187 / 353
8	2 28	17 50	82·4	2 20	16 51	82·4	2 12	15 51	82·3	2 04	14 52	82·3	1 56	13 52	82·3	1 48	12 53	82·2	188 / 352
9	2 46	17 48	81·4	2 37	16 48	81·4	2 28	15 49	81·3	2 19	14 49	81·3	2 10	13 50	81·3	2 01	12 51	81·2	189 / 351
10	3 05	17 45	80·5	2 55	16 45	80·4	2 45	15 46	80·4	2 35	14 47	80·3	2 24	13 48	80·3	2 14	12 49	80·3	190 / 350
11	3 23	17 41	79·5	3 12	16 42	79·5	3 01	15 43	79·4	2 50	14 44	79·4	2 39	13 45	79·4	2 28	12 46	79·3	191 / 349
12	3 41	17 38	78·6	3 29	16 39	78·5	3 17	15 40	78·5	3 05	14 41	78·4	2 53	13 42	78·4	2 41	12 44	78·3	192 / 348
13	3 59	17 34	77·6	3 46	16 35	77·6	3 33	15 37	77·5	3 20	14 38	77·4	3 07	13 39	77·4	2 54	12 41	77·3	193 / 347
14	4 17	17 30	76·7	4 03	16 31	76·6	3 49	15 33	76·5	3 35	14 34	76·5	3 21	13 36	76·4	3 07	12 38	76·4	194 / 346
15	4 35	17 25	75·7	4 20	16 27	75·6	4 05	15 29	75·6	3 50	14 31	75·5	3 35	13 32	75·5	3 20	12 34	75·4	195 / 345
16	4 53	17 21	74·7	4 37	16 23	74·7	4 21	15 25	74·6	4 05	14 27	74·6	3 49	13 29	74·5	3 33	12 31	74·4	196 / 344
17	5 11	17 16	73·8	4 54	16 18	73·7	4 37	15 20	73·6	4 20	14 22	73·5	4 03	13 25	73·5	3 46	12 27	73·4	197 / 343
18	5 29	17 10	72·8	5 11	16 13	72·7	4 53	15 15	72·7	4 35	14 18	72·6	4 17	13 20	72·6	3 59	12 23	72·5	198 / 342
19	5 46	17 05	71·9	5 28	16 07	71·8	5 09	15 10	71·7	4 50	14 13	71·6	4 31	13 16	71·6	4 12	12 19	71·5	199 / 341
20	6 04	16 59	70·9	5 44	16 02	70·9	5 25	15 05	70·7	5 05	14 08	70·6	4 45	13 11	70·6	4 25	12 14	70·5	200 / 340
21	6 21	16 52	70·0	6 01	15 56	69·9	5 40	14 59	69·8	5 19	14 03	69·7	4 59	13 06	69·7	4 37	12 10	69·6	201 / 339
22	6 39	16 46	69·0	6 17	15 50	68·9	5 56	14 53	68·8	5 34	13 57	68·8	5 12	13 01	68·7	4 50	12 05	68·6	202 / 338
23	6 56	16 39	68·0	6 34	15 43	67·9	6 11	14 47	67·8	5 48	13 51	67·7	5 25	12 56	67·7	5 03	12 00	67·5	203 / 337
24	7 13	16 32	67·1	6 50	15 36	66·9	6 26	14 41	66·8	6 03	13 45	66·8	5 39	12 50	66·7	5 15	11 55	66·5	204 / 336
25	7 30	16 25	66·1	7 06	15 29	66·0	6 41	14 34	65·9	6 17	13 39	65·7	5 52	12 44	65·6	5 27	11 49	65·5	205 / 335
26	7 47	16 17	65·1	7 22	15 22	65·0	6 56	14 27	64·9	6 31	13 32	64·8	6 05	12 38	64·6	5 40	11 43	64·6	206 / 334
27	8 04	16 09	64·1	7 38	15 14	64·0	7 11	14 20	63·9	6 45	13 26	63·8	6 18	12 32	63·8	5 52	11 37	63·6	207 / 333
28	8 20	16 00	63·2	7 53	15 06	63·0	7 26	14 12	62·9	6 59	13 19	62·8	6 31	12 25	62·7	6 04	11 31	62·6	208 / 332
29	8 37	15 52	62·2	8 09	14 58	62·1	7 41	14 05	61·9	7 13	13 11	61·8	6 44	12 18	61·8	6 16	11 25	61·6	209 / 331
30	8 53	15 43	61·2	8 24	14 50	61·1	7 55	13 57	61·0	7 26	13 04	60·9	6 57	12 11	60·9	6 27	11 18	60·6	210 / 330
31	9 09	15 34	60·3	8 40	14 41	60·1	8 10	13 49	60·0	7 40	12 56	59·9	7 09	12 04	59·9	6 39	11 11	59·7	211 / 329
32	9 25	15 24	59·3	8 55	14 32	59·3	8 24	13 40	59·1	7 53	12 48	58·9	7 22	11 56	58·8	6 51	11 05	58·7	212 / 328
33	9 41	15 15	58·3	9 10	14 23	58·2	8 38	13 31	58·2	8 06	12 40	57·9	7 34	11 49	57·8	7 02	10 57	57·7	213 / 327
34	9 57	15 05	57·3	9 25	14 13	57·2	8 52	13 22	57·2	8 19	12 31	56·9	7 46	11 41	56·8	7 14	10 50	56·7	214 / 326
35	10 13	14 54	56·3	9 39	14 04	56·2	9 06	13 13	56·1	8 32	12 23	55·9	7 59	11 33	55·8	7 25	10 43	55·7	215 / 325
36	10 28	14 44	55·4	9 54	13 54	55·2	9 19	13 04	55·1	8 45	12 14	54·9	8 11	11 24	54·8	7 36	10 35	54·7	216 / 324
37	10 43	14 33	54·4	10 08	13 43	54·2	9 33	12 54	54·1	8 58	12 05	53·9	8 22	11 16	53·8	7 47	10 27	53·7	217 / 323
38	10 58	14 22	53·4	10 22	13 33	53·2	9 46	12 44	53·1	9 10	11 55	53·0	8 34	11 07	52·8	7 58	10 19	52·7	218 / 322
39	11 13	14 10	52·4	10 36	13 22	52·2	9 59	12 34	52·2	9 22	11 46	51·8	8 45	10 58	51·8	8 08	10 10	51·7	219 / 321
40	11 27	13 59	51·4	10 50	13 11	51·3	10 12	12 23	51·1	9 35	11 36	51·0	8 57	10 49	50·8	8 19	10 02	50·7	220 / 320
41	11 42	13 47	50·4	11 04	13 00	50·3	10 25	12 13	50·1	9 47	11 26	50·0	9 08	10 39	49·9	8 29	9 53	49·7	221 / 319
42	11 56	13 34	49·4	11 17	12 48	49·3	10 38	12 02	49·1	9 58	11 16	49·1	9 19	10 30	49·0	8 39	9 44	48·7	222 / 318
43	12 09	13 22	48·4	11 30	12 36	48·3	10 50	11 51	48·1	10 10	11 05	48·1	9 30	10 20	47·9	8 49	9 35	47·7	223 / 317
44	12 24	13 09	47·4	11 43	12 24	47·3	11 02	11 39	47·1	10 21	10 55	47·0	9 40	10 10	46·9	8 59	9 26	46·7	224 / 316
45	12 37	12 56	46·4	11 56	12 12	46·3	11 14	11 28	46·1	10 33	10 44	46·1	9 51	10 00	45·9	9 09	9 16	45·7	225 / 315

Lat./A LHA/F	LHA	72° A/H	72° B/P	72° Z_1/Z_2	73° A/H	73° B/P	73° Z_1/Z_2	74° A/H	74° B/P	74° Z_1/Z_2	75° A/H	75° B/P	75° Z_1/Z_2	76° A/H	76° B/P	76° Z_1/Z_2	77° A/H	77° B/P	77° Z_1/Z_2	LHA	Lat./A LHA
45	135	12 37	12 56	46·4	11 56	12 12	46·3	11 14	11 28	46·1	10 33	10 44	46·0	9 51	10 00	45·9	9 09	9 16	45·7	225	315
46	134	12 51	12 43	45·4	12 08	11 59	45·3	11 26	11 16	45·1	10 44	10 32	45·0	10 01	9 50	44·9	9 19	9 07	44·7	226	314
47	133	13 04	12 30	44·4	12 21	11 47	44·3	11 38	11 04	44·1	10 55	10 21	44·0	10 11	9 39	43·9	9 28	8 57	43·7	227	313
48	132	13 17	12 16	43·4	12 33	11 34	43·3	11 49	10 52	43·1	11 05	10 10	43·0	10 21	9 28	42·9	9 37	8 47	42·7	228	312
49	131	13 29	12 02	42·4	12 45	11 21	42·3	12 00	10 39	42·1	11 16	9 58	42·0	10 31	9 17	41·9	9 46	8 37	41·7	229	311
50	130	13 42	11 48	41·4	12 57	11 07	41·3	12 11	10 27	41·1	11 26	9 46	41·0	10 41	9 06	40·9	9 55	8 26	40·7	230	310
51	129	13 54	11 33	40·4	13 08	10 53	40·3	12 22	10 14	40·1	11 36	9 34	40·0	10 50	8 55	39·8	10 04	8 16	39·7	231	309
52	128	14 06	11 19	39·4	13 19	10 40	39·2	12 33	10 01	39·1	11 46	9 22	39·0	10 59	8 44	38·8	10 13	8 05	38·7	232	308
53	127	14 17	11 04	38·4	13 30	10 26	38·2	12 43	9 47	38·1	11 56	9 09	38·0	11 08	8 32	37·8	10 21	7 55	37·7	233	307
54	126	14 29	10 49	37·4	13 41	10 11	37·2	12 53	9 34	37·1	12 05	8 57	37·0	11 17	8 20	36·8	10 29	7 44	36·7	234	306
55	125	14 40	10 33	36·4	13 51	9 57	36·2	13 03	9 20	36·1	12 14	8 44	36·0	11 26	8 08	35·8	10 37	7 33	35·7	235	305
56	124	14 51	10 18	35·3	14 02	9 42	35·2	13 13	9 07	35·1	12 23	8 31	35·0	11 34	7 56	34·8	10 45	7 21	34·7	236	304
57	123	15 01	10 02	34·3	14 12	9 27	34·2	13 21	8 53	34·0	12 32	8 18	33·9	11 42	7 44	33·8	10 52	7 10	33·7	237	303
58	122	15 12	9 46	33·3	14 21	9 12	33·1	13 31	8 38	33·0	12 41	8 05	32·9	11 50	7 32	32·8	11 00	6 58	32·7	238	302
59	121	15 22	9 30	32·3	14 31	8 57	32·1	13 40	8 24	32·0	12 49	7 51	31·9	11 58	7 19	31·8	11 07	6 47	31·7	239	301
60	120	15 31	9 14	31·3	14 40	8 41	31·1	13 49	8 10	31·0	12 57	7 38	30·9	12 06	7 06	30·8	11 14	6 35	30·6	240	300
61	119	15 41	8 57	30·2	14 49	8 26	30·1	13 57	7 55	30·0	13 05	7 24	29·8	12 13	6 54	29·7	11 21	6 23	29·6	241	299
62	118	15 50	8 40	29·2	14 58	8 10	29·1	14 05	7 40	28·9	13 13	7 10	28·8	12 20	6 41	28·7	11 27	6 11	28·6	242	298
63	117	15 59	8 23	28·2	15 06	7 54	28·0	14 13	7 25	27·9	13 20	6 56	27·8	12 27	6 27	27·7	11 34	5 59	27·6	243	297
64	116	16 08	8 06	27·2	15 14	7 38	27·0	14 21	7 10	26·9	13 27	6 42	26·8	12 34	6 14	26·7	11 40	5 47	26·6	244	296
65	115	16 16	7 49	26·1	15 22	7 22	26·0	14 28	6 55	25·9	13 34	6 28	25·8	12 40	6 01	25·7	11 46	5 34	25·6	245	295
66	114	16 24	7 32	25·1	15 29	7 05	25·0	14 35	6 39	24·9	13 41	6 13	24·7	12 46	5 47	24·6	11 52	5 22	24·6	246	294
67	113	16 32	7 14	24·1	15 37	6 49	23·9	14 42	6 24	23·8	13 47	5 59	23·7	12 52	5 34	23·6	11 57	5 09	23·5	247	293
68	112	16 39	6 56	23·0	15 44	6 32	22·9	14 48	6 08	22·8	13 53	5 44	22·7	12 58	5 20	22·6	12 02	4 57	22·5	248	292
69	111	16 46	6 38	22·0	15 50	6 15	21·9	14 55	5 52	21·8	13 59	5 29	21·7	13 03	5 06	21·6	12 07	4 44	21·5	249	291
70	110	16 53	6 20	20·9	15 57	5 58	20·8	15 01	5 36	20·7	14 05	5 14	20·6	13 08	4 52	20·6	12 12	4 31	20·5	250	290
71	109	16 59	6 02	19·9	16 03	5 41	19·8	15 06	5 20	19·7	14 10	4 59	19·6	13 13	4 38	19·5	12 17	4 18	19·5	251	289
72	108	17 05	5 44	18·9	16 09	5 24	18·8	15 12	5 04	18·7	14 15	4 44	18·6	13 18	4 24	18·5	12 21	4 05	18·4	252	288
73	107	17 11	5 26	17·8	16 14	5 06	17·7	15 17	4 48	17·6	14 20	4 29	17·6	13 23	4 10	17·5	12 25	3 52	17·4	253	287
74	106	17 17	5 07	16·8	16 19	4 49	16·7	15 22	4 31	16·6	14 24	4 13	16·5	13 27	3 56	16·5	12 29	3 38	16·4	254	286
75	105	17 22	4 48	15·7	16 24	4 31	15·7	15 26	4 15	15·6	14 29	3 58	15·5	13 31	3 42	15·4	12 33	3 25	15·4	255	285
76	104	17 27	4 30	14·7	16 29	4 14	14·6	15 31	3 58	14·5	14 33	3 43	14·5	13 35	3 27	14·4	12 36	3 12	14·4	256	284
77	103	17 31	4 11	13·6	16 33	3 56	13·6	15 35	3 41	13·5	14 36	3 27	13·4	13 38	3 13	13·4	12 40	2 58	13·3	257	283
78	102	17 36	3 52	12·6	16 37	3 38	12·5	15 38	3 25	12·5	14 40	3 11	12·4	13 41	2 58	12·4	12 43	2 45	12·3	258	282
79	101	17 39	3 33	11·5	16 41	3 20	11·5	15 42	3 08	11·4	14 43	2 56	11·4	13 44	2 43	11·3	12 45	2 31	11·3	259	281
80	100	17 43	3 14	10·5	16 44	3 02	10·4	15 45	2 51	10·4	14 46	2 40	10·3	13 47	2 29	10·3	12 48	2 18	10·3	260	280
81	99	17 46	2 55	9·5	16 47	2 44	9·4	15 48	2 34	9·4	14 49	2 24	9·3	13 49	2 14	9·3	12 50	2 04	9·2	261	279
82	98	17 49	2 35	8·4	16 50	2 26	8·4	15 50	2 17	8·3	14 51	2 08	8·3	13 52	1 59	8·2	12 52	1 50	8·2	262	278
83	97	17 52	2 16	7·4	16 52	2 08	7·3	15 52	2 00	7·3	14 53	1 52	7·2	13 54	1 44	7·2	12 54	1 37	7·2	263	277
84	96	17 54	1 57	6·3	16 54	1 50	6·3	15 55	1 43	6·2	14 55	1 36	6·2	13 55	1 30	6·2	12 56	1 23	6·2	264	276
85	95	17 56	1 37	5·3	16 56	1 32	5·2	15 56	1 26	5·2	14 56	1 20	5·1	13 57	1 15	5·2	12 57	1 09	5·1	265	275
86	94	17 57	1 18	4·2	16 57	1 13	4·2	15 58	1 09	4·2	14 58	1 04	4·1	13 58	1 00	4·1	12 58	0 55	4·1	266	274
87	93	17 58	0 58	3·2	16 59	0 55	3·1	15 59	0 52	3·1	14 59	0 48	3·1	13 59	0 45	3·1	12 59	0 42	3·1	267	273
88	92	17 59	0 39	2·1	16 59	0 37	2·1	15 59	0 34	2·1	14 59	0 32	2·1	13 59	0 30	2·1	13 00	0 28	2·1	268	272
89	91	18 00	0 19	1·1	17 00	0 18	1·0	16 00	0 17	1·0	15 00	0 16	1·0	14 00	0 15	1·0	13 00	0 14	1·0	269	271
90	90	18 00	0 00	0·0	17 00	0 00	0·0	16 00	0 00	0·0	15 00	0 00	0·0	14 00	0 00	0·0	13 00	0 00	0·0	270	270

N. Lat: for LHA > 180° ... $Z_n = Z$
for LHA < 180° ... $Z_n = 360° - Z$

S. Lat: for LHA > 180° ... $Z_n = 180° - Z$
for LHA < 180° ... $Z_n = 180° + Z$

B: (−) for 90° < LHA < 270°
Dec: (−) for Lat. contrary name

Z₁: same sign as B
Z₂: (−) for F > 90°

SIGHT REDUCTION TABLE

Lat./A LHA/F	78° A/H	78° B/P	78° Z₁/Z₂	79° A/H	79° B/P	79° Z₁/Z₂	80° A/H	80° B/P	80° Z₁/Z₂	81° A/H	81° B/P	81° Z₁/Z₂	82° A/H	82° B/P	82° Z₁/Z₂	83° A/H	83° B/P	83° Z₁/Z₂	Lat./A LHA
0 / 180	0 00	12 00	90·0	0 00	11 00	90·0	0 00	10 00	90·0	0 00	9 00	90·0	0 00	8 00	90·0	0 00	7 00	90·0	180 / 360
1 / 179	0 12	12 00	89·0	0 11	11 00	89·0	0 10	10 00	89·0	0 09	9 00	89·0	0 08	8 00	89·0	0 07	7 00	89·0	181 / 359
2 / 178	0 25	12 00	88·0	0 23	11 00	88·0	0 21	10 00	88·0	0 19	9 00	88·0	0 17	8 00	88·0	0 15	7 00	88·0	182 / 358
3 / 177	0 37	11 58	87·1	0 34	10 58	87·1	0 31	9 59	87·1	0 28	8 59	87·0	0 25	7 59	87·0	0 22	6 59	87·0	183 / 357
4 / 176	0 50	11 58	86·1	0 46	10 58	86·1	0 42	9 59	86·1	0 38	8 59	86·1	0 33	7 59	86·0	0 29	6 59	86·0	184 / 356
5 / 175	1 02	11 57	85·1	0 57	10 58	85·1	0 52	9 58	85·1	0 47	8 58	85·1	0 42	7 58	85·0	0 37	6 58	85·0	185 / 355
6 / 174	1 15	11 56	84·1	1 09	10 56	84·1	1 02	9 57	84·1	0 56	8 57	84·1	0 50	7 57	84·1	0 44	6 58	84·0	186 / 354
7 / 173	1 27	11 55	83·1	1 20	10 55	83·1	1 13	9 54	83·1	1 06	8 56	83·1	0 58	7 56	83·1	0 51	6 57	83·1	187 / 353
8 / 172	1 39	11 53	82·2	1 31	10 54	82·1	1 23	9 54	82·1	1 15	8 55	82·1	1 07	7 55	82·1	0 58	6 56	82·1	188 / 352
9 / 171	1 52	11 51	81·2	1 43	10 52	81·2	1 33	9 51	81·2	1 24	8 53	81·1	1 15	7 54	81·1	1 06	6 55	81·1	189 / 351
10 / 170	2 04	11 49	80·2	1 54	10 50	80·2	1 44	9 51	80·2	1 33	8 52	80·1	1 23	7 53	80·1	1 13	6 54	80·1	190 / 350
11 / 169	2 16	11 47	79·2	2 05	10 48	79·2	1 54	9 49	79·2	1 43	8 50	79·1	1 31	7 51	79·1	1 20	6 52	79·1	191 / 349
12 / 168	2 29	11 45	78·3	2 16	10 46	78·2	2 04	9 47	78·2	1 52	8 48	78·1	1 39	7 50	78·1	1 27	6 51	78·1	192 / 348
13 / 167	2 41	11 42	77·3	2 28	10 43	77·2	2 14	9 45	77·2	2 01	8 46	77·2	1 48	7 48	77·1	1 34	6 49	77·1	193 / 347
14 / 166	2 53	11 39	76·3	2 39	10 41	76·2	2 24	9 43	76·2	2 10	8 44	76·2	1 56	7 46	76·2	1 41	6 48	76·1	194 / 346
15 / 165	3 05	11 36	75·3	2 50	10 38	75·3	2 35	9 40	75·3	2 19	8 42	75·2	2 04	7 44	75·2	1 48	6 46	75·1	195 / 345
16 / 164	3 17	11 33	74·3	3 01	10 35	74·3	2 45	9 37	74·3	2 28	8 39	74·2	2 12	7 42	74·2	1 56	6 44	74·1	196 / 344
17 / 163	3 29	11 29	73·4	3 12	10 32	73·3	2 55	9 34	73·3	2 37	8 37	73·2	2 20	7 39	73·2	2 03	6 42	73·1	197 / 343
18 / 162	3 41	11 26	72·4	3 23	10 28	72·4	3 05	9 31	72·3	2 46	8 34	72·2	2 28	7 37	72·2	2 09	6 40	72·1	198 / 342
19 / 161	3 53	11 22	71·4	3 34	10 25	71·4	3 14	9 28	71·3	2 55	8 31	71·3	2 36	7 34	71·2	2 16	6 37	71·1	199 / 341
20 / 160	4 05	11 18	70·4	3 45	10 21	70·4	3 24	9 24	70·3	3 04	8 28	70·3	2 44	7 31	70·2	2 23	6 35	70·1	200 / 340
21 / 159	4 16	11 13	69·4	3 55	10 17	69·4	3 34	9 21	69·4	3 13	8 25	69·3	2 52	7 28	69·2	2 30	6 32	69·1	201 / 339
22 / 158	4 28	11 09	68·4	4 06	10 13	68·4	3 44	9 17	68·4	3 22	8 21	68·3	2 59	7 25	68·2	2 37	6 30	68·1	202 / 338
23 / 157	4 40	11 04	67·5	4 17	10 09	67·4	3 53	9 13	67·4	3 30	8 18	67·3	3 07	7 22	67·2	2 44	6 27	67·2	203 / 337
24 / 156	4 51	10 59	66·5	4 27	10 04	66·5	4 03	9 09	66·4	3 39	8 14	66·3	3 15	7 19	66·2	2 50	6 24	66·2	204 / 336
25 / 155	5 02	10 54	65·5	4 38	9 59	65·5	4 13	9 05	65·4	3 47	8 10	65·3	3 22	7 16	65·2	2 57	6 21	65·2	205 / 335
26 / 154	5 14	10 49	64·5	4 48	9 55	64·5	4 22	9 00	64·4	3 56	8 06	64·3	3 30	7 12	64·2	3 04	6 18	64·2	206 / 334
27 / 153	5 25	10 43	63·5	4 58	9 50	63·5	4 31	8 56	63·4	4 04	8 02	63·3	3 37	7 08	63·2	3 10	6 15	63·2	207 / 333
28 / 152	5 36	10 38	62·5	5 08	9 44	62·5	4 41	8 51	62·4	4 13	7 58	62·3	3 45	7 04	62·2	3 17	6 11	62·2	208 / 332
29 / 151	5 47	10 32	61·5	5 18	9 39	61·5	4 50	8 46	61·4	4 21	7 53	61·3	3 52	7 00	61·2	3 23	6 08	61·2	209 / 331
30 / 150	5 58	10 26	60·5	5 28	9 33	60·5	4 59	8 41	60·4	4 29	7 49	60·4	3 59	6 56	60·2	3 30	6 04	60·2	210 / 330
31 / 149	6 09	10 20	59·5	5 38	9 28	59·5	5 08	8 36	59·5	4 37	7 44	59·4	4 07	6 52	59·2	3 36	6 00	59·2	211 / 329
32 / 148	6 20	10 13	58·6	5 48	9 22	58·5	5 17	8 30	58·5	4 45	7 39	58·4	4 14	6 48	58·3	3 42	5 57	58·2	212 / 328
33 / 147	6 30	10 06	57·6	5 58	9 16	57·5	5 26	8 25	57·5	4 53	7 34	57·4	4 21	6 43	57·3	3 48	5 53	57·2	213 / 327
34 / 146	6 41	10 00	56·6	6 08	9 09	56·6	5 34	8 19	56·5	5 01	7 29	56·4	4 28	6 39	56·3	3 54	5 49	56·2	214 / 326
35 / 145	6 51	9 53	55·6	6 17	9 03	55·6	5 43	8 13	55·5	5 09	7 24	55·4	4 35	6 34	55·3	4 00	5 45	55·2	215 / 325
36 / 144	7 01	9 45	54·6	6 26	8 56	54·6	5 51	8 07	54·5	5 17	7 18	54·4	4 42	6 29	54·3	4 06	5 40	54·2	216 / 324
37 / 143	7 11	9 38	53·6	6 36	8 49	53·6	6 00	8 01	53·5	5 24	7 13	53·4	4 48	6 24	53·3	4 12	5 36	53·2	217 / 323
38 / 142	7 21	9 31	52·6	6 45	8 43	52·6	6 08	7 55	52·5	5 32	7 07	52·4	4 55	6 19	52·3	4 18	5 32	52·2	218 / 322
39 / 141	7 31	9 23	51·6	6 54	8 35	51·6	6 16	7 48	51·5	5 39	7 01	51·4	5 01	6 14	51·3	4 24	5 27	51·2	219 / 321
40 / 140	7 41	9 15	50·6	7 03	8 28	50·6	6 25	7 42	50·5	5 46	6 55	50·4	5 08	6 09	50·3	4 30	5 22	50·2	220 / 320
41 / 139	7 50	9 07	49·6	7 11	8 21	49·6	6 32	7 35	49·5	5 53	6 49	49·4	5 14	6 03	49·3	4 35	5 18	49·2	221 / 319
42 / 138	8 00	8 59	48·6	7 20	8 13	48·6	6 40	7 28	48·5	6 01	6 43	48·4	5 21	5 58	48·3	4 41	5 13	48·2	222 / 318
43 / 137	8 09	8 50	47·6	7 29	8 05	47·6	6 48	7 21	47·5	6 07	6 36	47·4	5 27	5 52	47·3	4 46	5 08	47·2	223 / 317
44 / 136	8 18	8 42	46·6	7 37	7 58	46·6	6 56	7 14	46·5	6 14	6 30	46·4	5 33	5 46	46·3	4 51	5 03	46·2	224 / 316
45 / 135	8 27	8 33	45·6	7 45	7 50	45·6	7 03	7 06	45·5	6 21	6 23	45·4	5 39	5 41	45·3	4 57	4 58	45·2	225 / 315

Lat. / A	78°			79°			80°			81°			82°			83°			Lat. / A
LHA/F	A/H	B/P	Z_1/Z_2	A/H	B/P	Z_1/Z_2	A/H	B/P	Z_1/Z_2	A/H	B/P	Z_1/Z_2	A/H	B/P	Z_1/Z_2	A/H	B/P	Z_1/Z_2	LHA
45	8 27	8 33	45·6	7 45	7 50	45·5	7 03	7 06	45·4	6 21	6 23	45·4	5 39	5 41	45·3	4 57	4 58	45·2	225
46	8 36	8 24	44·6	7 53	7 41	44·5	7 11	6 59	44·4	6 28	6 17	44·4	5 45	5 35	44·3	5 02	4 53	44·2	226
47	8 45	8 15	43·6	8 01	7 33	43·5	7 18	6 51	43·4	6 34	6 10	43·4	5 51	5 28	43·3	5 07	4 47	43·2	227
48	8 53	8 06	42·6	8 09	7 25	42·5	7 25	6 44	42·4	6 41	6 03	42·4	5 56	5 22	42·3	5 12	4 42	42·2	228
49	9 02	7 56	41·6	8 17	7 16	41·5	7 32	6 36	41·4	6 47	5 56	41·4	6 02	5 16	41·3	5 17	4 36	41·2	229
50	9 10	7 47	40·6	8 24	7 07	40·5	7 39	6 28	40·4	6 53	5 49	40·3	6 07	5 10	40·3	5 21	4 31	40·2	230
51	9 18	7 37	39·6	8 32	6 58	39·5	7 45	6 20	39·4	6 59	5 42	39·3	6 13	5 03	39·3	5 26	4 25	39·2	231
52	9 26	7 27	38·6	8 39	6 49	38·5	7 52	6 12	38·4	7 05	5 34	38·3	6 18	4 57	38·3	5 31	4 19	38·2	232
53	9 33	7 17	37·6	8 46	6 40	37·5	7 58	6 03	37·4	7 11	5 27	37·3	6 23	4 50	37·3	5 35	4 14	37·2	233
54	9 41	7 07	36·6	8 53	6 31	36·5	8 05	5 55	36·4	7 16	5 19	36·3	6 28	4 43	36·3	5 39	4 08	36·2	234
55	9 48	6 57	35·6	9 00	6 22	35·5	8 11	5 47	35·4	7 22	5 11	35·3	6 33	4 37	35·3	5 44	4 02	35·2	235
56	9 56	6 47	34·6	9 06	6 12	34·5	8 17	5 38	34·4	7 27	5 04	34·3	6 38	4 30	34·3	5 48	3 56	34·2	236
57	10 03	6 36	33·6	9 13	6 03	33·5	8 22	5 29	33·4	7 32	4 56	33·3	6 42	4 23	33·3	5 52	3 50	33·2	237
58	10 09	6 26	32·6	9 19	5 53	32·5	8 28	5 20	32·4	7 37	4 48	32·3	6 47	4 16	32·3	5 56	3 43	32·2	238
59	10 16	6 15	31·6	9 25	5 43	31·5	8 34	5 11	31·4	7 42	4 40	31·3	6 51	4 08	31·2	6 00	3 37	31·2	239
60	10 22	6 04	30·6	9 31	5 33	30·5	8 39	5 02	30·4	7 47	4 32	30·3	6 55	4 01	30·2	6 04	3 31	30·2	240
61	10 29	5 53	29·5	9 36	5 23	29·5	8 44	4 53	29·4	7 52	4 23	29·3	6 59	3 54	29·2	6 07	3 24	29·2	241
62	10 35	5 42	28·5	9 42	5 13	28·4	8 49	4 44	28·4	7 56	4 15	28·3	7 04	3 46	28·2	6 11	3 18	28·2	242
63	10 41	5 31	27·5	9 47	5 03	27·4	8 54	4 35	27·4	8 01	4 07	27·3	7 07	3 39	27·2	6 14	3 11	27·2	243
64	10 46	5 19	26·5	9 52	4 52	26·4	8 58	4 26	26·3	8 05	3 58	26·3	7 11	3 32	26·2	6 17	3 05	26·2	244
65	10 52	5 08	25·5	9 57	4 42	25·4	9 03	4 16	25·3	8 09	3 50	25·3	7 15	3 24	25·2	6 20	2 58	25·2	245
66	10 57	4 56	24·5	10 02	4 31	24·4	9 08	4 06	24·3	8 13	3 41	24·3	7 18	3 16	24·2	6 24	2 52	24·2	246
67	11 02	4 45	23·5	10 07	4 21	23·4	9 12	3 56	23·3	8 17	3 32	23·3	7 22	3 09	23·2	6 26	2 45	23·2	247
68	11 07	4 33	22·4	10 11	4 10	22·4	9 16	3 47	22·3	8 20	3 24	22·2	7 25	3 01	22·2	6 29	2 38	22·1	248
69	11 12	4 21	21·4	10 16	3 58	21·4	9 20	3 37	21·3	8 24	3 15	21·2	7 28	2 53	21·2	6 32	2 31	21·1	249
70	11 16	4 09	20·4	10 20	3 48	20·3	9 23	3 27	20·3	8 27	3 06	20·2	7 31	2 45	20·2	6 35	2 24	20·1	250
71	11 20	3 58	19·4	10 24	3 37	19·3	9 27	3 17	19·3	8 30	2 57	19·2	7 34	2 37	19·2	6 37	2 17	19·1	251
72	11 24	3 45	18·4	10 27	3 26	18·3	9 30	3 07	18·3	8 33	2 48	18·2	7 36	2 29	18·2	6 39	2 10	18·1	252
73	11 28	3 33	17·4	10 31	3 15	17·3	9 34	2 57	17·3	8 36	2 39	17·2	7 39	2 21	17·2	6 42	2 03	17·1	253
74	11 32	3 21	16·3	10 34	3 04	16·3	9 37	2 47	16·2	8 39	2 30	16·2	7 41	2 13	16·1	6 44	1 56	16·1	254
75	11 35	3 09	15·3	10 37	2 53	15·3	9 39	2 37	15·2	8 41	2 21	15·2	7 44	2 05	15·1	6 46	1 49	15·1	255
76	11 38	2 57	14·3	10 40	2 42	14·3	9 42	2 26	14·2	8 44	2 12	14·2	7 46	1 57	14·1	6 47	1 42	14·1	256
77	11 41	2 44	13·3	10 43	2 30	13·2	9 44	2 16	13·2	8 46	2 02	13·2	7 48	1 49	13·1	6 49	1 35	13·1	257
78	11 44	2 32	12·3	10 45	2 19	12·2	9 47	2 06	12·2	8 48	1 53	12·1	7 49	1 40	12·1	6 51	1 28	12·1	258
79	11 47	2 19	11·2	10 48	2 07	11·2	9 49	1 56	11·2	8 50	1 44	11·1	7 51	1 32	11·1	6 52	1 21	11·1	259
80	11 49	2 07	10·2	10 50	1 56	10·2	9 51	1 45	10·2	8 52	1 35	10·1	7 53	1 24	10·1	6 54	1 13	10·1	260
81	11 51	1 54	9·2	10 52	1 45	9·2	9 53	1 35	9·1	8 53	1 25	9·1	7 54	1 16	9·1	6 55	1 06	9·1	261
82	11 53	1 42	8·2	10 53	1 33	8·1	9 54	1 24	8·1	8 55	1 16	8·1	7 55	1 07	8·1	6 56	0 59	8·1	262
83	11 55	1 29	7·2	10 55	1 21	7·1	9 55	1 14	7·1	8 56	1 06	7·1	7 56	0 59	7·1	6 57	0 51	7·1	263
84	11 56	1 16	6·1	10 56	1 10	6·1	9 57	1 03	6·1	8 57	0 57	6·1	7 57	0 50	6·1	6 58	0 44	6·0	264
85	11 57	1 04	5·1	10 57	0 58	5·1	9 58	0 53	5·1	8 58	0 47	5·1	7 58	0 42	5·0	6 58	0 37	5·0	265
86	11 58	0 51	4·1	10 58	0 47	4·1	9 59	0 42	4·1	8 59	0 38	4·0	7 59	0 34	4·0	6 59	0 29	4·0	266
87	11 59	0 38	3·1	10 59	0 35	3·1	9 59	0 32	3·0	8 59	0 28	3·0	7 59	0 25	3·0	6 59	0 22	3·0	267
88	12 00	0 26	2·0	11 00	0 23	2·0	10 00	0 21	2·0	9 00	0 19	2·0	8 00	0 17	2·0	7 00	0 15	2·0	268
89	12 00	0 13	1·0	11 00	0 12	1·0	10 00	0 11	1·0	9 00	0 10	1·0	8 00	0 08	1·0	7 00	0 07	1·0	269
90	12 00	0 00	0·0	11 00	0 00	0·0	10 00	0 00	0·0	9 00	0 00	0·0	8 00	0 00	0·0	7 00	0 00	0·0	270

N. Lat.: for LHA > 180° ... $Z_n = Z$
for LHA < 180° ... $Z_n = 360° - Z$

S. Lat.: for LHA > 180° ... $Z_n = 180° - Z$
for LHA < 180° ... $Z_n = 180° + Z$

SIGHT REDUCTION TABLE

B: (−) for 90° < LHA < 270°
Dec:(−) for Lat. contrary name

Z_1: same sign as B
Z_2: (−) for F > 90°

LHA/F	F	84° A/H	84° B/P	84° Z_1/Z_2	85° A/H	85° B/P	85° Z_1/Z_2	86° A/H	86° B/P	86° Z_1/Z_2	87° A/H	87° B/P	87° Z_1/Z_2	88° A/H	88° B/P	88° Z_1/Z_2	89° A/H	89° B/P	89° Z_1/Z_2	LHA	LHA
0	180	0 00	6 00	90.0	0 00	5 00	90.0	0 00	4 00	90.0	0 00	3 00	90.0	0 00	2 00	90.0	0 00	1 00	90.0	180	360
1	179	0 06	6 00	89.0	0 05	5 00	89.0	0 04	4 00	89.0	0 03	3 00	89.0	0 02	2 00	89.0	0 01	1 00	89.0	181	359
2	178	0 13	6 00	88.0	0 10	5 00	88.0	0 08	4 00	88.0	0 06	3 00	88.0	0 04	2 00	88.0	0 02	1 00	88.0	182	358
3	177	0 19	6 00	87.0	0 16	5 00	87.0	0 13	4 00	87.0	0 09	3 00	87.0	0 06	2 00	87.0	0 03	1 00	87.0	183	357
4	176	0 25	5 59	86.0	0 21	4 59	86.0	0 17	3 59	86.0	0 13	2 59	86.0	0 08	2 00	86.0	0 04	1 00	86.0	184	356
5	175	0 31	5 59	85.0	0 26	4 59	85.0	0 21	3 59	85.0	0 16	2 59	85.0	0 10	1 59	85.0	0 05	1 00	85.0	185	355
6	174	0 38	5 58	84.0	0 31	4 58	84.0	0 25	3 59	84.0	0 19	2 59	84.0	0 13	1 59	84.0	0 06	1 00	84.0	186	354
7	173	0 44	5 57	83.0	0 37	4 58	83.0	0 29	3 58	83.0	0 22	2 58	83.0	0 15	1 59	83.0	0 07	1 00	83.0	187	353
8	172	0 50	5 57	82.0	0 42	4 57	82.0	0 33	3 57	82.0	0 25	2 58	82.0	0 17	1 59	82.0	0 08	0 59	82.0	188	352
9	171	0 56	5 56	81.0	0 47	4 56	81.0	0 38	3 57	81.0	0 28	2 58	81.0	0 19	1 59	81.0	0 09	0 59	81.0	189	351
10	170	1 02	5 55	80.1	0 52	4 55	80.1	0 42	3 56	80.0	0 31	2 57	80.0	0 21	1 58	80.0	0 10	0 59	80.0	190	350
11	169	1 09	5 53	79.1	0 57	4 55	79.1	0 46	3 56	79.0	0 34	2 57	79.0	0 23	1 58	79.0	0 11	0 59	79.0	191	349
12	168	1 15	5 52	78.1	1 02	4 53	78.0	0 50	3 55	78.0	0 37	2 56	78.0	0 25	1 57	78.0	0 12	0 59	78.0	192	348
13	167	1 21	5 51	77.1	1 07	4 52	77.0	0 54	3 54	77.0	0 40	2 55	77.0	0 27	1 57	77.0	0 13	0 58	77.0	193	347
14	166	1 27	5 49	76.1	1 12	4 51	76.1	0 58	3 53	76.1	0 44	2 54	76.0	0 29	1 56	76.0	0 15	0 58	76.0	194	346
15	165	1 33	5 48	75.1	1 18	4 50	75.1	1 02	3 52	75.1	0 47	2 54	75.0	0 31	1 56	75.0	0 16	0 58	75.0	195	345
16	164	1 39	5 46	74.1	1 23	4 48	74.1	1 06	3 51	74.1	0 50	2 53	74.0	0 33	1 55	74.0	0 17	0 58	74.0	196	344
17	163	1 45	5 44	73.1	1 28	4 47	73.1	1 10	3 50	73.1	0 53	2 52	73.0	0 35	1 55	73.0	0 18	0 57	73.0	197	343
18	162	1 51	5 42	72.1	1 33	4 45	72.1	1 14	3 48	72.1	0 56	2 51	72.0	0 37	1 54	72.0	0 19	0 57	72.0	198	342
19	161	1 57	5 41	71.1	1 38	4 44	71.1	1 18	3 47	71.1	0 59	2 50	71.0	0 39	1 53	71.0	0 20	0 57	71.0	199	341
20	160	2 03	5 38	70.1	1 42	4 42	70.1	1 22	3 46	70.1	1 02	2 49	70.0	0 41	1 53	70.0	0 21	0 56	70.0	200	340
21	159	2 09	5 36	69.1	1 47	4 40	69.1	1 26	3 44	69.1	1 04	2 48	69.0	0 43	1 52	69.0	0 22	0 56	69.0	201	339
22	158	2 15	5 34	68.1	1 52	4 38	68.1	1 30	3 43	68.1	1 07	2 47	68.1	0 45	1 51	68.0	0 22	0 55	68.0	202	338
23	157	2 20	5 32	67.1	1 57	4 36	67.1	1 34	3 41	67.1	1 10	2 46	67.1	0 47	1 50	67.0	0 23	0 55	67.0	203	337
24	156	2 26	5 29	66.1	2 02	4 34	66.1	1 38	3 39	66.1	1 13	2 44	66.1	0 49	1 50	66.0	0 24	0 55	66.0	204	336
25	155	2 32	5 26	65.1	2 07	4 32	65.1	1 41	3 38	65.1	1 16	2 43	65.1	0 51	1 49	65.0	0 25	0 54	65.0	205	335
26	154	2 38	5 24	64.1	2 11	4 30	64.1	1 45	3 36	64.1	1 19	2 42	64.1	0 53	1 48	64.0	0 26	0 54	64.0	206	334
27	153	2 43	5 21	63.1	2 16	4 27	63.1	1 49	3 34	63.1	1 22	2 40	63.1	0 54	1 47	63.0	0 27	0 53	63.0	207	333
28	152	2 49	5 18	62.1	2 21	4 25	62.1	1 53	3 32	62.1	1 24	2 39	62.1	0 56	1 46	62.0	0 28	0 53	62.0	208	332
29	151	2 54	5 15	61.1	2 25	4 23	61.1	1 56	3 30	61.1	1 27	2 37	61.1	0 58	1 45	61.0	0 29	0 52	61.0	209	331
30	150	3 00	5 12	60.1	2 30	4 20	60.1	2 00	3 28	60.1	1 30	2 36	60.1	1 00	1 44	60.0	0 30	0 52	60.0	210	330
31	149	3 05	5 09	59.1	2 34	4 17	59.1	2 04	3 26	59.1	1 33	2 34	59.1	1 02	1 43	59.0	0 31	0 51	59.0	211	329
32	148	3 11	5 06	58.1	2 39	4 15	58.1	2 07	3 24	58.1	1 35	2 33	58.1	1 04	1 42	58.0	0 32	0 51	58.0	212	328
33	147	3 16	5 02	57.1	2 43	4 12	57.1	2 11	3 21	57.1	1 38	2 31	57.1	1 05	1 41	57.0	0 33	0 50	57.0	213	327
34	146	3 21	4 59	56.1	2 48	4 09	56.1	2 14	3 19	56.1	1 41	2 29	56.1	1 07	1 39	56.0	0 34	0 50	56.0	214	326
35	145	3 26	4 55	55.1	2 52	4 06	55.1	2 18	3 17	55.1	1 43	2 27	55.1	1 09	1 38	55.0	0 34	0 49	55.0	215	325
36	144	3 31	4 52	54.1	2 56	4 03	54.1	2 21	3 14	54.1	1 46	2 26	54.1	1 11	1 37	54.0	0 35	0 49	54.0	216	324
37	143	3 36	4 48	53.2	3 00	4 00	53.1	2 24	3 12	53.1	1 48	2 24	53.1	1 12	1 35	53.0	0 36	0 48	53.0	217	323
38	142	3 41	4 44	52.2	3 05	3 57	52.2	2 28	3 09	52.1	1 51	2 22	52.1	1 14	1 34	52.0	0 37	0 47	52.0	218	322
39	141	3 46	4 40	51.2	3 09	3 53	51.2	2 31	3 07	51.1	1 53	2 20	51.1	1 16	1 33	51.0	0 38	0 47	51.0	219	321
40	140	3 51	4 36	50.2	3 13	3 50	50.2	2 34	3 04	50.1	1 56	2 18	50.1	1 17	1 32	50.0	0 39	0 46	50.0	220	320
41	139	3 56	4 32	49.2	3 17	3 47	49.2	2 37	3 01	49.1	1 58	2 16	49.1	1 19	1 31	49.0	0 39	0 45	49.0	221	319
42	138	4 01	4 28	48.2	3 21	3 43	48.2	2 41	2 58	48.1	2 00	2 14	48.1	1 20	1 29	48.0	0 40	0 45	48.0	222	318
43	137	4 05	4 24	47.2	3 24	3 40	47.2	2 44	2 56	47.1	2 03	2 12	47.1	1 22	1 28	47.0	0 41	0 44	47.0	223	317
44	136	4 10	4 19	46.2	3 28	3 36	46.2	2 47	2 53	46.1	2 05	2 10	46.1	1 23	1 26	46.0	0 42	0 43	46.0	224	316
45	135	4 14	4 15	45.2	3 32	3 32	45.2	2 50	2 50	45.1	2 07	2 07	45.1	1 25	1 25	45.0	0 42	0 42	45.0	225	315

S. Lat.: for LHA > 180° ... $Z_n = 180° - Z$; for LHA < 180° ... $Z_n = 180° + Z$

LHA/F	Lat/A	84° A/H	84° B/P	84° Z_1/Z_2	85° A/H	85° B/P	85° Z_1/Z_2	86° A/H	86° B/P	86° Z_1/Z_2	87° A/H	87° B/P	87° Z_1/Z_2	88° A/H	88° B/P	88° Z_1/Z_2	89° A/H	89° B/P	89° Z_1/Z_2	Lat/A	LHA
135	45	4 14	4 15	45.2	3 32	3 32	45.1	2 50	2 50	45.1	2 07	2 07	45.1	1 25	1 25	45.0	0 42	0 42	45.0	225	315
134	46	4 19	4 11	44.2	3 36	3 29	44.1	2 53	2 47	44.1	2 09	2 05	44.1	1 26	1 23	44.0	0 43	0 42	44.0	226	314
133	47	4 23	4 06	43.2	3 39	3 25	43.1	2 56	2 44	43.1	2 12	2 03	43.1	1 28	1 22	43.0	0 44	0 41	43.0	227	313
132	48	4 27	4 01	42.2	3 43	3 21	42.1	2 58	2 41	42.1	2 14	2 01	42.1	1 29	1 20	42.0	0 45	0 40	42.0	228	312
131	49	4 31	3 57	41.2	3 46	3 17	41.1	3 01	2 38	41.1	2 16	1 58	41.1	1 31	1 19	41.0	0 45	0 39	41.0	229	311
130	50	4 36	3 52	40.2	3 50	3 13	40.1	3 04	2 34	40.1	2 18	1 56	40.1	1 32	1 17	40.0	0 46	0 39	40.0	230	310
129	51	4 40	3 47	39.2	3 53	3 09	39.1	3 06	2 31	39.1	2 20	1 53	39.1	1 33	1 16	39.0	0 47	0 38	39.0	231	309
128	52	4 43	3 42	38.2	3 56	3 05	38.1	3 09	2 28	38.1	2 22	1 51	38.1	1 35	1 14	38.0	0 47	0 37	38.0	232	308
127	53	4 47	3 37	37.2	3 59	3 01	37.1	3 12	2 25	37.1	2 24	1 48	37.1	1 36	1 12	37.0	0 48	0 36	37.0	233	307
126	54	4 51	3 32	36.1	4 03	2 57	36.1	3 14	2 21	36.1	2 26	1 46	36.1	1 37	1 11	36.0	0 49	0 35	36.0	234	306
125	55	4 55	3 27	35.1	4 06	2 52	35.1	3 17	2 18	35.1	2 27	1 43	35.1	1 38	1 09	35.0	0 49	0 35	35.0	235	305
124	56	4 58	3 22	34.1	4 09	2 48	34.1	3 19	2 14	34.1	2 29	1 41	34.1	1 39	1 07	34.0	0 50	0 34	34.0	236	304
123	57	5 02	3 17	33.1	4 12	2 44	33.1	3 21	2 11	33.1	2 31	1 38	33.1	1 41	1 05	33.0	0 50	0 33	33.0	237	303
122	58	5 05	3 11	32.1	4 14	2 39	32.1	3 23	2 07	32.1	2 33	1 35	32.1	1 42	1 04	32.0	0 51	0 32	32.0	238	302
121	59	5 08	3 06	31.1	4 17	2 35	31.1	3 26	2 04	31.1	2 34	1 33	31.1	1 43	1 02	31.0	0 51	0 31	31.0	239	301
120	60	5 12	3 00	30.1	4 20	2 30	30.1	3 28	2 00	30.1	2 36	1 30	30.1	1 44	1 00	30.0	0 52	0 30	30.0	240	300
119	61	5 15	2 55	29.1	4 22	2 26	29.1	3 30	1 56	29.1	2 37	1 27	29.1	1 45	0 58	29.0	0 52	0 29	29.0	241	299
118	62	5 18	2 49	28.1	4 25	2 21	28.1	3 32	1 53	28.1	2 39	1 25	28.1	1 46	0 56	28.0	0 53	0 28	28.0	242	298
117	63	5 21	2 44	27.1	4 27	2 16	27.1	3 34	1 49	27.1	2 40	1 22	27.1	1 47	0 54	27.0	0 53	0 27	27.0	243	297
116	64	5 23	2 38	26.1	4 30	2 12	26.1	3 36	1 45	26.1	2 42	1 19	26.1	1 48	0 53	26.0	0 54	0 26	26.0	244	296
115	65	5 26	2 33	25.1	4 32	2 07	25.1	3 37	1 41	25.1	2 43	1 16	25.1	1 49	0 51	25.0	0 54	0 25	25.0	245	295
114	66	5 29	2 27	24.1	4 34	2 02	24.1	3 39	1 38	24.1	2 44	1 13	24.1	1 50	0 49	24.0	0 55	0 24	24.0	246	294
113	67	5 31	2 21	23.1	4 36	1 57	23.1	3 41	1 34	23.1	2 46	1 10	23.1	1 50	0 47	23.0	0 55	0 23	23.0	247	293
112	68	5 34	2 15	22.1	4 38	1 53	22.1	3 42	1 30	22.1	2 47	1 07	22.1	1 51	0 45	22.0	0 56	0 22	22.0	248	292
111	69	5 36	2 09	21.1	4 40	1 48	21.1	3 44	1 26	21.1	2 48	1 05	21.1	1 52	0 43	21.0	0 56	0 21	21.0	249	291
110	70	5 38	2 04	20.1	4 42	1 43	20.1	3 46	1 22	20.1	2 49	1 02	20.0	1 53	0 41	20.0	0 56	0 20	20.0	250	290
109	71	5 40	1 58	19.1	4 44	1 38	19.1	3 47	1 18	19.1	2 50	0 59	19.0	1 53	0 39	19.0	0 57	0 19	19.0	251	289
108	72	5 42	1 52	18.1	4 45	1 33	18.1	3 48	1 14	18.1	2 51	0 56	18.0	1 54	0 37	18.0	0 57	0 18	18.0	252	288
107	73	5 44	1 46	17.1	4 47	1 28	17.1	3 49	1 10	17.1	2 52	0 53	17.0	1 54	0 35	17.0	0 57	0 17	17.0	253	287
106	74	5 46	1 40	16.1	4 48	1 23	16.1	3 51	1 06	16.1	2 53	0 50	16.0	1 55	0 33	16.0	0 58	0 16	16.0	254	286
105	75	5 48	1 33	15.1	4 50	1 18	15.1	3 52	1 02	15.0	2 55	0 47	15.0	1 56	0 31	15.0	0 58	0 15	15.0	255	285
104	76	5 49	1 27	14.1	4 51	1 13	14.1	3 53	0 58	14.0	2 55	0 44	14.0	1 56	0 29	14.0	0 58	0 14	14.0	256	284
103	77	5 51	1 21	13.1	4 52	1 08	13.0	3 54	0 54	13.0	2 56	0 41	13.0	1 57	0 27	13.0	0 58	0 13	13.0	257	283
102	78	5 52	1 15	12.1	4 53	1 03	12.0	3 55	0 50	12.0	2 57	0 37	12.0	1 57	0 25	12.0	0 59	0 12	12.0	258	282
101	79	5 53	1 09	11.1	4 54	0 57	11.0	3 56	0 46	11.0	2 57	0 34	11.0	1 58	0 23	11.0	0 59	0 11	11.0	259	281
100	80	5 55	1 03	10.1	4 55	0 52	10.0	3 56	0 42	10.0	2 58	0 31	10.0	1 58	0 21	10.0	0 59	0 10	10.0	260	280
99	81	5 56	0 57	9.0	4 56	0 47	9.0	3 57	0 38	9.0	2 58	0 28	9.0	1 59	0 19	9.0	0 59	0 09	9.0	261	279
98	82	5 56	0 50	8.0	4 57	0 42	8.0	3 58	0 33	8.0	2 59	0 25	8.0	1 59	0 17	8.0	1 00	0 08	8.0	262	278
97	83	5 57	0 44	7.0	4 58	0 37	7.0	3 58	0 29	7.0	2 59	0 22	7.0	1 59	0 15	7.0	1 00	0 07	7.0	263	277
96	84	5 58	0 38	6.0	4 58	0 31	6.0	3 59	0 25	6.0	2 59	0 19	6.0	1 59	0 12	6.0	1 00	0 05	6.0	264	276
95	85	5 59	0 31	5.0	4 59	0 26	5.0	3 59	0 21	5.0	3 00	0 16	5.0	2 00	0 10	5.0	1 00	0 04	5.0	265	275
94	86	5 59	0 25	4.0	4 59	0 21	4.0	3 59	0 17	4.0	3 00	0 13	4.0	2 00	0 08	4.0	1 00	0 03	4.0	266	274
93	87	6 00	0 19	3.0	5 00	0 16	3.0	4 00	0 13	3.0	3 00	0 09	3.0	2 00	0 06	3.0	1 00	0 03	3.0	267	273
92	88	6 00	0 13	2.0	5 00	0 10	2.0	4 00	0 08	2.0	3 00	0 06	2.0	2 00	0 04	2.0	1 00	0 02	2.0	268	272
91	89	6 00	0 06	1.0	5 00	0 05	1.0	4 00	0 04	1.0	3 00	0 03	1.0	2 00	0 02	1.0	1 00	0 01	1.0	269	271
90	90	6 00	0 00	0.0	5 00	0 00	0.0	4 00	0 00	0.0	3 00	0 00	0.0	2 00	0 00	0.0	1 00	0 00	0.0	270	270

N. Lat.: for LHA > 180° ... $Z_n = Z$; for LHA < 180° ... $Z_n = 360° - Z$

AUXILIARY TABLE

Sign for corr₂ for A'. $-/+$ A'

Sign of corr₁ for F'. Reverse sign if F > 90°.

Z°₂	30	29/31	28/32	27/33	26/34	25/35	24/36	23/37	22/38	21/39	20/40	19/41	18/42	17/43	16/44	15/45	14/46	13/47	12/48	11/49	10/50	9/51	8/52	7/53	6/54	5/55	4/56	3/57	2/58	1/59	P°
89	1	1	0	0	0	0	0	0	0	0	0	0	0	0	0	0	0	0	0	0	0	0	0	0	0	0	0	0	0	0	1
88	1	1	1	1	1	1	1	1	1	1	1	1	1	1	1	1	0	0	0	0	0	0	0	0	0	0	0	0	0	0	2
87	2	2	1	1	1	1	1	1	1	1	1	1	1	1	1	1	1	1	1	1	1	0	0	0	0	0	0	0	0	0	3
86	2	2	2	2	2	2	2	2	2	1	1	1	1	1	1	1	1	1	1	1	1	1	1	0	0	0	0	0	0	0	4
85	3	3	2	2	2	2	2	2	2	2	2	2	2	1	1	1	1	1	1	1	1	1	1	1	1	0	0	0	0	0	5
84	3	3	3	3	3	3	2	2	2	2	2	2	2	2	2	2	1	1	1	1	1	1	1	1	1	1	0	0	0	0	6
83	4	4	3	3	3	3	3	3	3	3	2	2	2	2	2	2	2	2	1	1	1	1	1	1	1	1	0	0	0	0	7
82	4	4	4	4	4	3	3	3	3	3	3	3	3	2	2	2	2	2	2	2	1	1	1	1	1	1	1	0	0	0	8
81	5	5	4	4	4	4	3	4	3	3	3	3	3	3	3	2	2	2	2	2	2	1	1	1	1	1	1	0	0	0	9
80	5	5	5	5	5	4	4	4	4	4	3	3	3	3	3	3	2	2	2	2	2	2	1	1	1	1	1	1	0	0	10
79	6	6	5	5	5	5	5	4	4	4	4	4	3	3	3	3	3	2	2	2	2	2	2	1	1	1	1	1	0	0	11
78	6	6	6	6	5	5	5	5	5	4	4	4	4	4	3	3	3	3	2	2	2	2	2	2	1	1	1	1	0	0	12
77	7	7	6	6	6	6	5	5	5	5	4	4	4	4	4	3	3	3	3	2	2	2	2	2	2	1	1	1	0	0	13
76	7	7	7	7	6	6	6	6	5	5	5	5	4	4	4	4	3	3	3	3	3	2	2	2	2	2	1	1	1	0	14
75	8	8	7	7	7	6	6	6	6	5	5	5	5	4	4	4	4	3	3	3	3	2	2	2	2	2	1	1	1	0	15
74	8	8	8	7	7	7	7	6	6	6	6	5	5	5	4	4	4	4	3	3	3	2	2	2	2	2	1	1	1	1	16
73	9	8	8	8	8	7	7	7	6	6	6	6	5	5	5	4	4	4	4	3	3	3	2	2	2	2	2	1	1	1	17
72	9	9	9	8	8	8	7	7	7	6	6	6	6	5	5	5	4	4	4	4	3	3	3	2	2	2	2	1	1	1	18
71	10	9	9	9	8	8	8	7	7	7	7	6	6	6	5	5	5	4	4	4	3	3	3	2	2	2	2	1	1	1	19
70	10	10	10	9	9	9	8	8	8	7	7	6	6	6	5	5	5	4	4	4	4	3	3	3	2	2	2	1	1	1	20
69	11	10	10	10	9	9	9	8	8	8	7	7	6	6	6	5	5	5	4	4	4	3	3	3	3	2	2	1	1	1	21
68	11	11	10	10	10	9	9	9	8	8	7	7	7	6	6	6	5	5	4	4	4	3	3	3	3	2	2	2	1	1	22
67	12	11	11	11	10	10	9	9	9	8	8	7	7	7	6	6	5	5	5	4	4	4	3	3	3	2	2	2	1	1	23
66	12	12	11	11	11	10	10	9	9	9	8	8	7	7	7	6	6	5	5	5	4	4	3	3	3	3	2	2	1	1	24
65	13	12	12	11	11	11	10	10	9	9	8	8	8	7	7	6	6	5	5	5	5	4	4	3	3	3	2	2	1	1	25
64	13	13	12	12	11	11	11	10	10	9	9	8	8	7	7	7	6	6	5	5	5	4	4	3	3	3	2	2	1	1	26
63	14	13	13	12	12	11	11	10	10	10	9	9	8	8	7	7	7	6	6	5	5	4	4	4	3	3	2	2	1	1	27
62	14	14	13	13	12	12	11	11	10	10	9	9	9	8	8	7	7	6	6	5	5	4	4	4	3	3	2	2	1	1	28
61	15	14	13	13	13	12	12	11	11	10	10	9	9	8	8	7	7	6	6	6	5	4	4	4	3	3	3	2	1	1	29
60	15	14	14	13	13	12	12	11	11	10	10	9	9	8	8	7	7	6	6	6	6	5	4	4	3	3	3	2	1	1	30
59	15	15	14	14	13	13	12	12	11	11	10	10	9	9	8	8	7	7	6	6	6	5	5	4	4	3	3	2	1	1	31
58	16	15	15	14	14	13	13	12	12	11	11	10	10	9	9	8	8	7	7	6	6	5	5	4	4	3	3	2	1	1	32
57	16	16	15	15	14	14	13	12	12	11	11	11	10	9	9	8	8	7	7	6	6	5	5	4	4	3	3	2	1	1	33
56	17	16	16	15	15	14	13	13	12	12	11	11	10	10	9	8	8	7	7	7	6	5	5	4	4	3	3	2	1	1	34
55	17	17	16	15	15	14	14	13	13	12	12	11	10	10	9	9	8	7	7	7	6	5	5	4	4	3	3	2	1	1	35
54	18	17	16	16	15	15	14	13	13	12	12	11	11	10	10	9	8	8	7	7	6	5	5	4	4	3	3	2	1	1	36
53	18	17	17	16	16	15	14	14	13	13	12	12	11	10	10	9	9	8	7	7	6	6	5	4	4	3	3	2	1	1	37
52	18	18	17	17	16	15	15	14	14	13	13	12	11	11	10	9	9	8	8	7	6	6	5	4	4	3	3	2	1	1	38
51	19	18	18	17	16	16	15	14	14	13	13	12	12	11	10	9	9	8	8	7	6	6	5	4	4	3	3	2	1	1	39
50	19	19	18	17	17	16	15	15	14	13	13	12	12	11	10	10	9	8	8	7	6	6	5	4	4	3	3	2	1	1	40

F' $+/-$ P°

Top-left corner labels: **÷A′** (**+ / −**) ; left entry argument **Z₂°** ; bottom entry argument **F′ / ±** (**+ / −**) and **P°**.

For Z₂ < 10°, use 10°

For P > 80°, use 80°

The two-line column headings below are given as **(top value) / (bottom value)**. The left column shows **Z₂°** and the right-most data column the corresponding **P°**.

Z₂°	□/30	29/31	28/32	27/33	26/34	25/35	24/36	23/37	22/38	21/39	20/40	19/41	18/42	17/43	16/44	15/45	14/46	13/47	12/48	11/49	10/50	9/51	8/52	7/53	6/54	5/55	4/56	3/57	2/58	1/59	P°
49		18	18	17	17	16	15	15	14	14	13	12	12	11	10	10	9	9	8	7	7	6	5	5	4	3	3	2	1	1	41
48	20	19	18	18	17	16	16	15	14	14	13	13	12	11	11	10	9	9	8	8	7	6	5	5	4	3	3	2	1	1	42
47	20	19	19	18	17	17	16	15	15	14	14	13	12	12	11	10	10	9	8	8	7	6	5	5	4	3	3	2	1	1	43
46	21	20	19	18	18	17	16	16	15	15	14	13	13	12	11	11	10	9	8	8	7	6	5	5	4	4	3	2	1	1	44
45	21	21	20	19	18	18	17	16	16	15	14	14	13	12	12	11	10	9	9	8	7	6	6	5	4	4	3	2	1	1	45
44	22	21	20	19	19	18	17	17	16	15	15	14	13	13	12	11	10	10	9	8	7	6	6	5	4	4	3	2	1	1	46
43	22	21	21	20	19	18	18	17	16	16	15	14	13	13	12	11	11	10	9	8	7	7	6	5	4	4	3	2	1	1	47
42	23	22	21	20	20	19	18	17	17	16	15	15	14	13	12	11	11	10	9	8	8	7	6	5	5	4	3	2	1	1	48
41	23	22	21	21	20	19	18	17	17	16	15	15	14	13	12	11	11	10	9	8	8	7	6	6	5	4	3	2	2	1	49
40	23	22	21	21	20	19	18	18	17	16	16	15	14	14	13	12	11	10	9	9	8	7	6	6	5	4	3	2	2	1	50
39	23	22	22	21	20	19	19	18	17	17	16	15	14	14	13	12	11	10	9	9	8	7	6	6	5	4	3	3	2	1	51
38	24	23	22	21	21	20	19	18	18	17	16	16	15	14	13	12	12	11	10	9	8	7	6	6	5	4	4	3	2	1	52
37	24	23	22	22	21	20	19	19	18	17	16	16	15	14	13	12	12	11	10	9	8	7	7	6	5	4	4	3	2	1	53
36	24	23	23	22	21	20	19	19	18	17	17	16	15	14	13	12	12	11	10	9	8	7	7	6	5	4	4	3	2	1	54
35	25	24	23	22	21	20	20	19	18	17	17	16	15	15	14	13	12	11	10	9	9	8	7	6	5	4	4	3	2	2	55
34	25	24	23	22	22	21	20	19	18	18	17	16	15	15	14	13	12	11	10	10	9	8	7	6	5	4	4	3	2	2	56
33	25	25	24	23	22	21	20	20	19	18	17	17	16	15	14	13	13	12	10	10	9	8	7	6	5	5	4	3	2	2	57
32	25	25	24	23	22	21	21	20	19	18	17	17	16	15	14	13	13	12	11	10	9	8	7	6	5	5	4	3	2	2	58
31	26	25	24	23	22	21	21	20	19	18	18	17	16	15	14	13	13	12	11	10	9	8	7	6	6	5	4	3	2	2	59
30	26	25	24	23	23	22	21	20	19	18	18	17	16	16	14	13	13	12	11	10	9	8	7	6	6	5	4	3	2	2	60
29	26	25	24	24	23	22	21	20	19	19	18	17	16	16	15	13	13	12	11	10	9	8	7	6	6	5	4	3	2	2	61
28	27	26	25	24	23	22	21	20	20	19	18	18	16	16	15	14	13	12	11	10	9	8	7	6	6	5	4	3	2	2	62
27	27	26	25	24	23	22	22	21	20	19	18	18	17	16	15	14	13	12	11	10	10	8	7	7	6	5	4	3	2	2	63
26	27	26	25	24	23	23	22	21	20	19	18	18	17	16	15	14	13	12	11	10	10	8	7	7	6	5	4	3	2	2	64
25	27	26	25	24	24	23	22	21	20	19	19	18	17	16	15	14	14	12	11	11	10	8	8	7	6	5	5	3	2	2	65
24	28	26	26	25	24	23	22	21	20	19	19	18	17	16	15	14	14	13	12	11	10	9	8	7	6	5	5	3	2	2	66
23	28	27	26	25	24	23	22	22	20	20	19	18	17	17	15	14	14	13	12	11	10	9	8	7	6	5	5	3	2	2	67
22	28	27	26	25	24	23	23	22	21	20	19	18	17	17	16	14	14	13	12	11	10	9	8	7	6	5	5	3	2	2	68
21	28	27	26	25	24	24	23	22	21	20	19	18	17	17	16	14	14	13	12	11	10	9	8	7	6	5	5	3	2	2	69
20	29	27	26	25	24	24	23	22	21	20	19	18	17	17	16	14	14	13	12	11	10	9	8	7	6	5	5	3	2	2	70
19	29	28	26	25	25	24	23	22	21	20	19	18	18	17	16	14	14	13	12	11	10	9	8	7	6	5	5	3	2	2	71
18	29	28	27	26	25	24	23	22	21	20	20	19	18	17	16	15	14	13	12	11	10	9	8	7	6	5	5	3	2	2	72
17	29	28	27	26	25	24	23	22	21	20	20	19	18	17	16	15	14	13	12	11	10	9	8	7	6	5	5	3	2	2	73
16	29	28	27	26	25	24	23	23	21	20	20	19	18	17	16	15	14	13	12	11	10	9	8	7	6	5	5	3	2	2	74
15	29	28	27	26	25	24	23	23	21	21	20	19	18	17	16	15	14	13	12	11	10	9	8	7	6	5	5	3	2	2	75
14	30	28	27	26	25	24	23	23	22	21	20	19	18	17	16	15	14	13	12	11	10	9	8	7	6	5	5	3	2	2	76
13	30	28	27	26	25	25	24	23	22	21	20	19	18	18	16	15	15	13	12	11	10	9	8	7	6	5	5	3	2	2	77
12	30	29	28	27	26	25	24	23	22	21	20	19	18	18	16	15	15	13	12	11	10	9	8	7	6	5	5	3	2	2	78
11	30	29	28	27	26	25	24	23	22	21	20	19	18	18	17	15	15	13	12	11	10	9	8	7	6	5	5	3	2	2	79
10	30	29	28	27	26	25	24	23	22	21	20	19	18	18	17	15	15	13	12	11	10	9	8	7	6	5	5	3	2	2	80

USE OF CONCISE SIGHT REDUCTION TABLES (continued)

4. *Example.* (b) Required the altitude and azimuth of *Vega* on 2012 July 29 at UT 04^h 47^m from the estimated position 152° west, 15° south.

1. Assumed latitude $Lat =$ 15° S
   From the almanac $GHA =$ 99° 39′
   Assumed longitude   151° 39′ W
   Local hour angle $LHA =$ 308

2. Reduction table, 1st entry
   $(Lat, LHA) = (15, 308)$ $A =$ 49   34 $A° = 50, A' = 34$
                          $B = +66$ 29 $Z_1 = +71·7,$ $LHA > 270°$
3. From the almanac $Dec = -38$ 48   *Lat* and *Dec* contrary
   Sum $= B + Dec$ $F = +27$ 41 $F° = 28, F' = 41$

4. Reduction table, 2nd entry
   $(A°, F°) = (50, 28)$ $H =$ 17   34 $P° = 37$
                                            $Z_2 = 67·8, Z_2° = 68$
5. Auxiliary table, 1st entry
   $(F', P°) = (41, 37)$ $corr_1 =$ -11 $F < 90°, F' > 29'$
   Sum   17   23
6. Auxiliary table, 2nd entry
   $(A', Z_2°) = (34, 68)$ $corr_2 =$ $+10$ $A' > 30'$
7. Sum = computed altitude $H_c = +17° $ 33′ $F > 0°$

8. Azimuth,   first component $Z_1 = +71·7$ same sign as B
          second component $Z_2 = +67·8$ $F < 90°, F > 0°$
   Sum = azimuth angle $Z =$ 139·5

   True azimuth $Z_n =$ 040°   S *Lat*, $LHA > 180°$

5. *Form for use with the Concise Sight Reduction Tables.* The form on the following page lays out the procedure explained on pages 284-285. Each step is shown, with notes and rules to ensure accuracy, rather than speed, throughout the calculation. The form is mainly intended for the calculation of star positions. It therefore includes the formation of the Greenwich hour of Aries (*GHA* Aries), and thus the Greenwich hour angle of the star (*GHA*) from its tabular sidereal hour angle (*SHA*). These calculations, included in step 1 of the form, can easily be replaced by the interpolation of *GHA* and *Dec* for the Sun, Moon or planets.

The form may be freely copied, however, acknowledgement of the source is requested.

Date & UT of observation			Body	Estimated Latitude & Longitude	
	h	m s		° ′	° ′

Step	Calculate Altitude & Azimuth			Summary of Rules & Notes
Assumed latitude	$Lat =$	°		Nearest estimated latitude, integral number of degrees.
Assumed longitude	$Long =$	° ′		Choose $Long$ so that LHA has integral number of degrees.
1. From the almanac:	$Dec =$	° ′		Record the Dec for use in Step 3.
GHA Aries ʰ	$=$	° !		Needed if using SHA. Tabular value.
Increment ᵐ ˢ	$=$	° !		for minutes and seconds of time.
SHA	$SHA =$	° !		
$GHA = GHA\ Aries + SHA$	$GHA =$	° ′		Remove multiples of 360°.
Assumed longitude	$Long =$	° ′		West longitudes are negative.
$LHA = GHA + Long$	$LHA =$	°		Remove multiples of 360°.
2. Reduction table, 1ˢᵗ entry				
$(Lat, LHA) = ($ °, °$)$	$A =$	° ′	$A° =$ °	nearest whole degree of A.
record A, B and Z_1.			$A' =$ ′	minutes part of A.
	$B =$	° ′		B is minus if $90° < LHA < 270°$.
			$Z_1 =$ °	Z_1 has the same sign as B.
3. From step 1	$Dec =$	° ′		Dec is minus if contrary to Lat.
$F = B + Dec$	$F =$	° ′		Regard F as positive until step 7.
			$F° =$ °	nearest whole degree of F.
			$F' =$ ′	minutes part of F.
4. Reduction table, 2ⁿᵈ entry				
$(A°, F°) = ($ °, °$)$	$H =$	° ′	$P° =$ °	nearest whole degree of P.
record H, P and Z_2.			$Z_2 =$ °	
5. Auxiliary table, 1ˢᵗ entry				
$(F', P°) = ($ ′, °$)$	$corr_1 =$	′		$corr_1$ is minus if $F < 90°$ & $F' > 29'$,
record $corr_1$				or if $F > 90°$ & $F' < 30'$.
6. Auxiliary table, 2ⁿᵈ entry				$Z_2°$ nearest whole degree of Z_2.
$(A', Z_2°) = ($ ′, °$)$	$corr_2 =$	′		$corr_2$ is minus if $A' < 30'$.
record $corr_2$				
7. Calculated altitude =	$Hc =$	° ′		Hc is minus if F is negative, and
$Hc = H + corr_1 + corr_2$				object is below the horizon.
8. Azimuth, 1ˢᵗ component	$Z_1 =$	°		Z_1 has the same sign as B.
2ⁿᵈ component	$Z_2 =$	°		Z_2 is minus if $F > 90°$.
				If F is negative, $Z_2 = 180° - Z_2$
$Z = Z_1 + Z_2$	$Z =$	°		Ignore the sign of Z.
				N Lat: If $LHA > 180°$, $Z_n = Z$, or if $LHA < 180°$, $Z_n = 360° - Z$,
				S Lat: If $LHA > 180°$, $Z_n = 180° - Z$, or
True azimuth	$Z_n =$	°		if $LHA < 180°$, $Z_n = 180° + Z$.

©HMNAO

For use with *The Nautical Almanac's* Concise Sight Reduction Tables pages 284-318.

CONVERSION OF ARC TO TIME

0°–59°	h m	60°–119°	h m	120°–179°	h m	180°–239°	h m	240°–299°	h m	300°–359°	h m	′	0′.00 m s	0′.25 m s	0′.50 m s	0′.75 m s
0	0 00	60	4 00	120	8 00	180	12 00	240	16 00	300	20 00	0	0 00	0 01	0 02	0 03
1	0 04	61	4 04	121	8 04	181	12 04	241	16 04	301	20 04	1	0 04	0 05	0 06	0 07
2	0 08	62	4 08	122	8 08	182	12 08	242	16 08	302	20 08	2	0 08	0 09	0 10	0 11
3	0 12	63	4 12	123	8 12	183	12 12	243	16 12	303	20 12	3	0 12	0 13	0 14	0 15
4	0 16	64	4 16	124	8 16	184	12 16	244	16 16	304	20 16	4	0 16	0 17	0 18	0 19
5	0 20	65	4 20	125	8 20	185	12 20	245	16 20	305	20 20	5	0 20	0 21	0 22	0 23
6	0 24	66	4 24	126	8 24	186	12 24	246	16 24	306	20 24	6	0 24	0 25	0 26	0 27
7	0 28	67	4 28	127	8 28	187	12 28	247	16 28	307	20 28	7	0 28	0 29	0 30	0 31
8	0 32	68	4 32	128	8 32	188	12 32	248	16 32	308	20 32	8	0 32	0 33	0 34	0 35
9	0 36	69	4 36	129	8 36	189	12 36	249	16 36	309	20 36	9	0 36	0 37	0 38	0 39
10	0 40	70	4 40	130	8 40	190	12 40	250	16 40	310	20 40	10	0 40	0 41	0 42	0 43
11	0 44	71	4 44	131	8 44	191	12 44	251	16 44	311	20 44	11	0 44	0 45	0 46	0 47
12	0 48	72	4 48	132	8 48	192	12 48	252	16 48	312	20 48	12	0 48	0 49	0 50	0 51
13	0 52	73	4 52	133	8 52	193	12 52	253	16 52	313	20 52	13	0 52	0 53	0 54	0 55
14	0 56	74	4 56	134	8 56	194	12 56	254	16 56	314	20 56	14	0 56	0 57	0 58	0 59
15	1 00	75	5 00	135	9 00	195	13 00	255	17 00	315	21 00	15	1 00	1 01	1 02	1 03
16	1 04	76	5 04	136	9 04	196	13 04	256	17 04	316	21 04	16	1 04	1 05	1 06	1 07
17	1 08	77	5 08	137	9 08	197	13 08	257	17 08	317	21 08	17	1 08	1 09	1 10	1 11
18	1 12	78	5 12	138	9 12	198	13 12	258	17 12	318	21 12	18	1 12	1 13	1 14	1 15
19	1 16	79	5 16	139	9 16	199	13 16	259	17 16	319	21 16	19	1 16	1 17	1 18	1 19
20	1 20	80	5 20	140	9 20	200	13 20	260	17 20	320	21 20	20	1 20	1 21	1 22	1 23
21	1 24	81	5 24	141	9 24	201	13 24	261	17 24	321	21 24	21	1 24	1 25	1 26	1 27
22	1 28	82	5 28	142	9 28	202	13 28	262	17 28	322	21 28	22	1 28	1 29	1 30	1 31
23	1 32	83	5 32	143	9 32	203	13 32	263	17 32	323	21 32	23	1 32	1 33	1 34	1 35
24	1 36	84	5 36	144	9 36	204	13 36	264	17 36	324	21 36	24	1 36	1 37	1 38	1 39
25	1 40	85	5 40	145	9 40	205	13 40	265	17 40	325	21 40	25	1 40	1 41	1 42	1 43
26	1 44	86	5 44	146	9 44	206	13 44	266	17 44	326	21 44	26	1 44	1 45	1 46	1 47
27	1 48	87	5 48	147	9 48	207	13 48	267	17 48	327	21 48	27	1 48	1 49	1 50	1 51
28	1 52	88	5 52	148	9 52	208	13 52	268	17 52	328	21 52	28	1 52	1 53	1 54	1 55
29	1 56	89	5 56	149	9 56	209	13 56	269	17 56	329	21 56	29	1 56	1 57	1 58	1 59
30	2 00	90	6 00	150	10 00	210	14 00	270	18 00	330	22 00	30	2 00	2 01	2 02	2 03
31	2 04	91	6 04	151	10 04	211	14 04	271	18 04	331	22 04	31	2 04	2 05	2 06	2 07
32	2 08	92	6 08	152	10 08	212	14 08	272	18 08	332	22 08	32	2 08	2 09	2 10	2 11
33	2 12	93	6 12	153	10 12	213	14 12	273	18 12	333	22 12	33	2 12	2 13	2 14	2 15
34	2 16	94	6 16	154	10 16	214	14 16	274	18 16	334	22 16	34	2 16	2 17	2 18	2 19
35	2 20	95	6 20	155	10 20	215	14 20	275	18 20	335	22 20	35	2 20	2 21	2 22	2 23
36	2 24	96	6 24	156	10 24	216	14 24	276	18 24	336	22 24	36	2 24	2 25	2 26	2 27
37	2 28	97	6 28	157	10 28	217	14 28	277	18 28	337	22 28	37	2 28	2 29	2 30	2 31
38	2 32	98	6 32	158	10 32	218	14 32	278	18 32	338	22 32	38	2 32	2 33	2 34	2 35
39	2 36	99	6 36	159	10 36	219	14 36	279	18 36	339	22 36	39	2 36	2 37	2 38	2 39
40	2 40	100	6 40	160	10 40	220	14 40	280	18 40	340	22 40	40	2 40	2 41	2 42	2 43
41	2 44	101	6 44	161	10 44	221	14 44	281	18 44	341	22 44	41	2 44	2 45	2 46	2 47
42	2 48	102	6 48	162	10 48	222	14 48	282	18 48	342	22 48	42	2 48	2 49	2 50	2 51
43	2 52	103	6 52	163	10 52	223	14 52	283	18 52	343	22 52	43	2 52	2 53	2 54	2 55
44	2 56	104	6 56	164	10 56	224	14 56	284	18 56	344	22 56	44	2 56	2 57	2 58	2 59
45	3 00	105	7 00	165	11 00	225	15 00	285	19 00	345	23 00	45	3 00	3 01	3 02	3 03
46	3 04	106	7 04	166	11 04	226	15 04	286	19 04	346	23 04	46	3 04	3 05	3 06	3 07
47	3 08	107	7 08	167	11 08	227	15 08	287	19 08	347	23 08	47	3 08	3 09	3 10	3 11
48	3 12	108	7 12	168	11 12	228	15 12	288	19 12	348	23 12	48	3 12	3 13	3 14	3 15
49	3 16	109	7 16	169	11 16	229	15 16	289	19 16	349	23 16	49	3 16	3 17	3 18	3 19
50	3 20	110	7 20	170	11 20	230	15 20	290	19 20	350	23 20	50	3 20	3 21	3 22	3 23
51	3 24	111	7 24	171	11 24	231	15 24	291	19 24	351	23 24	51	3 24	3 25	3 26	3 27
52	3 28	112	7 28	172	11 28	232	15 28	292	19 28	352	23 28	52	3 28	3 29	3 30	3 31
53	3 32	113	7 32	173	11 32	233	15 32	293	19 32	353	23 32	53	3 32	3 33	3 34	3 35
54	3 36	114	7 36	174	11 36	234	15 36	294	19 36	354	23 36	54	3 36	3 37	3 38	3 39
55	3 40	115	7 40	175	11 40	235	15 40	295	19 40	355	23 40	55	3 40	3 41	3 42	3 43
56	3 44	116	7 44	176	11 44	236	15 44	296	19 44	356	23 44	56	3 44	3 45	3 46	3 47
57	3 48	117	7 48	177	11 48	237	15 48	297	19 48	357	23 48	57	3 48	3 49	3 50	3 51
58	3 52	118	7 52	178	11 52	238	15 52	298	19 52	358	23 52	58	3 52	3 53	3 54	3 55
59	3 56	119	7 56	179	11 56	239	15 56	299	19 56	359	23 56	59	3 56	3 57	3 58	3 59

The above table is for converting expressions in arc to their equivalent in time; its main use in this Almanac is for the conversion of longitude for application to LMT (added if *west*, subtracted if *east*) to give UT or vice versa, particularly in the case of sunrise, sunset, etc.

i

0	SUN PLANETS	ARIES	MOON	v or d Corrⁿ	v or d Corrⁿ	v or d Corrⁿ	1	SUN PLANETS	ARIES	MOON	v or d Corrⁿ	v or d Corrⁿ	v or d Corrⁿ
s	° ′	° ′	° ′	′ ′	′ ′	′ ′	s	° ′	° ′	° ′	′ ′	′ ′	′ ′
00	0 00·0	0 00·0	0 00·0	0·0 0·0	6·0 0·1	12·0 0·1	00	0 15·0	0 15·0	0 14·3	0·0 0·0	6·0 0·2	12·0 0·3
01	0 00·3	0 00·3	0 00·2	0·1 0·0	6·1 0·1	12·1 0·1	01	0 15·3	0 15·3	0 14·6	0·1 0·0	6·1 0·2	12·1 0·3
02	0 00·5	0 00·5	0 00·5	0·2 0·0	6·2 0·1	12·2 0·1	02	0 15·5	0 15·5	0 14·8	0·2 0·0	6·2 0·2	12·2 0·3
03	0 00·8	0 00·8	0 00·7	0·3 0·0	6·3 0·1	12·3 0·1	03	0 15·8	0 15·8	0 15·0	0·3 0·0	6·3 0·2	12·3 0·3
04	0 01·0	0 01·0	0 01·0	0·4 0·0	6·4 0·1	12·4 0·1	04	0 16·0	0 16·0	0 15·3	0·4 0·0	6·4 0·2	12·4 0·3
05	0 01·3	0 01·3	0 01·2	0·5 0·0	6·5 0·1	12·5 0·1	05	0 16·3	0 16·3	0 15·5	0·5 0·0	6·5 0·2	12·5 0·3
06	0 01·5	0 01·5	0 01·4	0·6 0·0	6·6 0·1	12·6 0·1	06	0 16·5	0 16·5	0 15·7	0·6 0·0	6·6 0·2	12·6 0·3
07	0 01·8	0 01·8	0 01·7	0·7 0·0	6·7 0·1	12·7 0·1	07	0 16·8	0 16·8	0 16·0	0·7 0·0	6·7 0·2	12·7 0·3
08	0 02·0	0 02·0	0 01·9	0·8 0·0	6·8 0·1	12·8 0·1	08	0 17·0	0 17·0	0 16·2	0·8 0·0	6·8 0·2	12·8 0·3
09	0 02·3	0 02·3	0 02·1	0·9 0·0	6·9 0·1	12·9 0·1	09	0 17·3	0 17·3	0 16·5	0·9 0·0	6·9 0·2	12·9 0·3
10	0 02·5	0 02·5	0 02·4	1·0 0·0	7·0 0·1	13·0 0·1	10	0 17·5	0 17·5	0 16·7	1·0 0·0	7·0 0·2	13·0 0·3
11	0 02·8	0 02·8	0 02·6	1·1 0·0	7·1 0·1	13·1 0·1	11	0 17·8	0 17·8	0 16·9	1·1 0·0	7·1 0·2	13·1 0·3
12	0 03·0	0 03·0	0 02·9	1·2 0·0	7·2 0·1	13·2 0·1	12	0 18·0	0 18·0	0 17·2	1·2 0·0	7·2 0·2	13·2 0·3
13	0 03·3	0 03·3	0 03·1	1·3 0·0	7·3 0·1	13·3 0·1	13	0 18·3	0 18·3	0 17·4	1·3 0·0	7·3 0·2	13·3 0·3
14	0 03·5	0 03·5	0 03·3	1·4 0·0	7·4 0·1	13·4 0·1	14	0 18·5	0 18·6	0 17·7	1·4 0·0	7·4 0·2	13·4 0·3
15	0 03·8	0 03·8	0 03·6	1·5 0·0	7·5 0·1	13·5 0·1	15	0 18·8	0 18·8	0 17·9	1·5 0·0	7·5 0·2	13·5 0·3
16	0 04·0	0 04·0	0 03·8	1·6 0·0	7·6 0·1	13·6 0·1	16	0 19·0	0 19·1	0 18·1	1·6 0·0	7·6 0·2	13·6 0·3
17	0 04·3	0 04·3	0 04·1	1·7 0·0	7·7 0·1	13·7 0·1	17	0 19·3	0 19·3	0 18·4	1·7 0·0	7·7 0·2	13·7 0·3
18	0 04·5	0 04·5	0 04·3	1·8 0·0	7·8 0·1	13·8 0·1	18	0 19·5	0 19·6	0 18·6	1·8 0·0	7·8 0·2	13·8 0·3
19	0 04·8	0 04·8	0 04·5	1·9 0·0	7·9 0·1	13·9 0·1	19	0 19·8	0 19·8	0 18·9	1·9 0·0	7·9 0·2	13·9 0·3
20	0 05·0	0 05·0	0 04·8	2·0 0·0	8·0 0·1	14·0 0·1	20	0 20·0	0 20·1	0 19·1	2·0 0·1	8·0 0·2	14·0 0·4
21	0 05·3	0 05·3	0 05·0	2·1 0·0	8·1 0·1	14·1 0·1	21	0 20·3	0 20·3	0 19·3	2·1 0·1	8·1 0·2	14·1 0·4
22	0 05·5	0 05·5	0 05·2	2·2 0·0	8·2 0·1	14·2 0·1	22	0 20·5	0 20·6	0 19·6	2·2 0·1	8·2 0·2	14·2 0·4
23	0 05·8	0 05·8	0 05·5	2·3 0·0	8·3 0·1	14·3 0·1	23	0 20·8	0 20·8	0 19·8	2·3 0·1	8·3 0·2	14·3 0·4
24	0 06·0	0 06·0	0 05·7	2·4 0·0	8·4 0·1	14·4 0·1	24	0 21·0	0 21·1	0 20·0	2·4 0·1	8·4 0·2	14·4 0·4
25	0 06·3	0 06·3	0 06·0	2·5 0·0	8·5 0·1	14·5 0·1	25	0 21·3	0 21·3	0 20·3	2·5 0·1	8·5 0·2	14·5 0·4
26	0 06·5	0 06·5	0 06·2	2·6 0·0	8·6 0·1	14·6 0·1	26	0 21·5	0 21·6	0 20·5	2·6 0·1	8·6 0·2	14·6 0·4
27	0 06·8	0 06·8	0 06·4	2·7 0·0	8·7 0·1	14·7 0·1	27	0 21·8	0 21·8	0 20·8	2·7 0·1	8·7 0·2	14·7 0·4
28	0 07·0	0 07·0	0 06·7	2·8 0·0	8·8 0·1	14·8 0·1	28	0 22·0	0 22·1	0 21·0	2·8 0·1	8·8 0·2	14·8 0·4
29	0 07·3	0 07·3	0 06·9	2·9 0·0	8·9 0·1	14·9 0·1	29	0 22·3	0 22·3	0 21·2	2·9 0·1	8·9 0·2	14·9 0·4
30	0 07·5	0 07·5	0 07·2	3·0 0·0	9·0 0·1	15·0 0·1	30	0 22·5	0 22·6	0 21·5	3·0 0·1	9·0 0·2	15·0 0·4
31	0 07·8	0 07·8	0 07·4	3·1 0·0	9·1 0·1	15·1 0·1	31	0 22·8	0 22·8	0 21·7	3·1 0·1	9·1 0·2	15·1 0·4
32	0 08·0	0 08·0	0 07·6	3·2 0·0	9·2 0·1	15·2 0·1	32	0 23·0	0 23·1	0 22·0	3·2 0·1	9·2 0·2	15·2 0·4
33	0 08·3	0 08·3	0 07·9	3·3 0·0	9·3 0·1	15·3 0·1	33	0 23·3	0 23·3	0 22·2	3·3 0·1	9·3 0·2	15·3 0·4
34	0 08·5	0 08·5	0 08·1	3·4 0·0	9·4 0·1	15·4 0·1	34	0 23·5	0 23·6	0 22·4	3·4 0·1	9·4 0·2	15·4 0·4
35	0 08·8	0 08·8	0 08·4	3·5 0·0	9·5 0·1	15·5 0·1	35	0 23·8	0 23·8	0 22·7	3·5 0·1	9·5 0·2	15·5 0·4
36	0 09·0	0 09·0	0 08·6	3·6 0·0	9·6 0·1	15·6 0·1	36	0 24·0	0 24·1	0 22·9	3·6 0·1	9·6 0·2	15·6 0·4
37	0 09·3	0 09·3	0 08·8	3·7 0·0	9·7 0·1	15·7 0·1	37	0 24·3	0 24·3	0 23·1	3·7 0·1	9·7 0·2	15·7 0·4
38	0 09·5	0 09·5	0 09·1	3·8 0·0	9·8 0·1	15·8 0·1	38	0 24·5	0 24·6	0 23·4	3·8 0·1	9·8 0·2	15·8 0·4
39	0 09·8	0 09·8	0 09·3	3·9 0·0	9·9 0·1	15·9 0·1	39	0 24·8	0 24·8	0 23·6	3·9 0·1	9·9 0·2	15·9 0·4
40	0 10·0	0 10·0	0 09·5	4·0 0·0	10·0 0·1	16·0 0·1	40	0 25·0	0 25·1	0 23·9	4·0 0·1	10·0 0·3	16·0 0·4
41	0 10·3	0 10·3	0 09·8	4·1 0·0	10·1 0·1	16·1 0·1	41	0 25·3	0 25·3	0 24·1	4·1 0·1	10·1 0·3	16·1 0·4
42	0 10·5	0 10·5	0 10·0	4·2 0·0	10·2 0·1	16·2 0·1	42	0 25·5	0 25·6	0 24·3	4·2 0·1	10·2 0·3	16·2 0·4
43	0 10·8	0 10·8	0 10·3	4·3 0·0	10·3 0·1	16·3 0·1	43	0 25·8	0 25·8	0 24·6	4·3 0·1	10·3 0·3	16·3 0·4
44	0 11·0	0 11·0	0 10·5	4·4 0·0	10·4 0·1	16·4 0·1	44	0 26·0	0 26·1	0 24·8	4·4 0·1	10·4 0·3	16·4 0·4
45	0 11·3	0 11·3	0 10·7	4·5 0·0	10·5 0·1	16·5 0·1	45	0 26·3	0 26·3	0 25·1	4·5 0·1	10·5 0·3	16·5 0·4
46	0 11·5	0 11·5	0 11·0	4·6 0·0	10·6 0·1	16·6 0·1	46	0 26·5	0 26·6	0 25·3	4·6 0·1	10·6 0·3	16·6 0·4
47	0 11·8	0 11·8	0 11·2	4·7 0·0	10·7 0·1	16·7 0·1	47	0 26·8	0 26·8	0 25·5	4·7 0·1	10·7 0·3	16·7 0·4
48	0 12·0	0 12·0	0 11·5	4·8 0·0	10·8 0·1	16·8 0·1	48	0 27·0	0 27·1	0 25·8	4·8 0·1	10·8 0·3	16·8 0·4
49	0 12·3	0 12·3	0 11·7	4·9 0·0	10·9 0·1	16·9 0·1	49	0 27·3	0 27·3	0 26·0	4·9 0·1	10·9 0·3	16·9 0·4
50	0 12·5	0 12·5	0 11·9	5·0 0·0	11·0 0·1	17·0 0·1	50	0 27·5	0 27·6	0 26·2	5·0 0·1	11·0 0·3	17·0 0·4
51	0 12·8	0 12·8	0 12·2	5·1 0·0	11·1 0·1	17·1 0·1	51	0 27·8	0 27·8	0 26·5	5·1 0·1	11·1 0·3	17·1 0·4
52	0 13·0	0 13·0	0 12·4	5·2 0·0	11·2 0·1	17·2 0·1	52	0 28·0	0 28·1	0 26·7	5·2 0·1	11·2 0·3	17·2 0·4
53	0 13·3	0 13·3	0 12·6	5·3 0·0	11·3 0·1	17·3 0·1	53	0 28·3	0 28·3	0 27·0	5·3 0·1	11·3 0·3	17·3 0·4
54	0 13·5	0 13·5	0 12·9	5·4 0·0	11·4 0·1	17·4 0·1	54	0 28·5	0 28·6	0 27·2	5·4 0·1	11·4 0·3	17·4 0·4
55	0 13·8	0 13·8	0 13·1	5·5 0·0	11·5 0·1	17·5 0·1	55	0 28·8	0 28·8	0 27·4	5·5 0·1	11·5 0·3	17·5 0·4
56	0 14·0	0 14·0	0 13·4	5·6 0·0	11·6 0·1	17·6 0·1	56	0 29·0	0 29·1	0 27·7	5·6 0·1	11·6 0·3	17·6 0·4
57	0 14·3	0 14·3	0 13·6	5·7 0·0	11·7 0·1	17·7 0·1	57	0 29·3	0 29·3	0 27·9	5·7 0·1	11·7 0·3	17·7 0·4
58	0 14·5	0 14·5	0 13·8	5·8 0·0	11·8 0·1	17·8 0·1	58	0 29·5	0 29·6	0 28·2	5·8 0·1	11·8 0·3	17·8 0·4
59	0 14·8	0 14·8	0 14·1	5·9 0·0	11·9 0·1	17·9 0·1	59	0 29·8	0 29·8	0 28·4	5·9 0·1	11·9 0·3	17·9 0·4
60	0 15·0	0 15·0	0 14·3	6·0 0·1	12·0 0·1	18·0 0·2	60	0 30·0	0 30·1	0 28·6	6·0 0·2	12·0 0·3	18·0 0·5

2ᵐ

m 2	SUN PLANETS	ARIES	MOON	v or d / Corrⁿ	v or d / Corrⁿ	v or d / Corrⁿ
s	° ′	° ′	° ′	′ ′	′ ′	′ ′
00	0 30·0	0 30·1	0 28·6	0·0 0·0	6·0 0·3	12·0 0·5
01	0 30·3	0 30·3	0 28·9	0·1 0·0	6·1 0·3	12·1 0·5
02	0 30·5	0 30·6	0 29·1	0·2 0·0	6·2 0·3	12·2 0·5
03	0 30·8	0 30·8	0 29·3	0·3 0·0	6·3 0·3	12·3 0·5
04	0 31·0	0 31·1	0 29·6	0·4 0·0	6·4 0·3	12·4 0·5
05	0 31·3	0 31·3	0 29·8	0·5 0·0	6·5 0·3	12·5 0·5
06	0 31·5	0 31·6	0 30·1	0·6 0·0	6·6 0·3	12·6 0·5
07	0 31·8	0 31·8	0 30·3	0·7 0·0	6·7 0·3	12·7 0·5
08	0 32·0	0 32·1	0 30·5	0·8 0·0	6·8 0·3	12·8 0·5
09	0 32·3	0 32·3	0 30·8	0·9 0·0	6·9 0·3	12·9 0·5
10	0 32·5	0 32·6	0 31·0	1·0 0·0	7·0 0·3	13·0 0·5
11	0 32·8	0 32·8	0 31·3	1·1 0·0	7·1 0·3	13·1 0·5
12	0 33·0	0 33·1	0 31·5	1·2 0·1	7·2 0·3	13·2 0·6
13	0 33·3	0 33·3	0 31·7	1·3 0·1	7·3 0·3	13·3 0·6
14	0 33·5	0 33·6	0 32·0	1·4 0·1	7·4 0·3	13·4 0·6
15	0 33·8	0 33·8	0 32·2	1·5 0·1	7·5 0·3	13·5 0·6
16	0 34·0	0 34·1	0 32·5	1·6 0·1	7·6 0·3	13·6 0·6
17	0 34·3	0 34·3	0 32·7	1·7 0·1	7·7 0·3	13·7 0·6
18	0 34·5	0 34·6	0 32·9	1·8 0·1	7·8 0·3	13·8 0·6
19	0 34·8	0 34·8	0 33·2	1·9 0·1	7·9 0·3	13·9 0·6
20	0 35·0	0 35·1	0 33·4	2·0 0·1	8·0 0·3	14·0 0·6
21	0 35·3	0 35·3	0 33·6	2·1 0·1	8·1 0·3	14·1 0·6
22	0 35·5	0 35·6	0 33·9	2·2 0·1	8·2 0·3	14·2 0·6
23	0 35·8	0 35·8	0 34·1	2·3 0·1	8·3 0·3	14·3 0·6
24	0 36·0	0 36·1	0 34·4	2·4 0·1	8·4 0·4	14·4 0·6
25	0 36·3	0 36·3	0 34·6	2·5 0·1	8·5 0·4	14·5 0·6
26	0 36·5	0 36·6	0 34·8	2·6 0·1	8·6 0·4	14·6 0·6
27	0 36·8	0 36·9	0 35·1	2·7 0·1	8·7 0·4	14·7 0·6
28	0 37·0	0 37·1	0 35·3	2·8 0·1	8·8 0·4	14·8 0·6
29	0 37·3	0 37·4	0 35·6	2·9 0·1	8·9 0·4	14·9 0·6
30	0 37·5	0 37·6	0 35·8	3·0 0·1	9·0 0·4	15·0 0·6
31	0 37·8	0 37·9	0 36·0	3·1 0·1	9·1 0·4	15·1 0·6
32	0 38·0	0 38·1	0 36·3	3·2 0·1	9·2 0·4	15·2 0·6
33	0 38·3	0 38·4	0 36·5	3·3 0·1	9·3 0·4	15·3 0·6
34	0 38·5	0 38·6	0 36·7	3·4 0·1	9·4 0·4	15·4 0·6
35	0 38·8	0 38·9	0 37·0	3·5 0·1	9·5 0·4	15·5 0·6
36	0 39·0	0 39·1	0 37·2	3·6 0·2	9·6 0·4	15·6 0·7
37	0 39·3	0 39·4	0 37·5	3·7 0·2	9·7 0·4	15·7 0·7
38	0 39·5	0 39·6	0 37·7	3·8 0·2	9·8 0·4	15·8 0·7
39	0 39·8	0 39·9	0 37·9	3·9 0·2	9·9 0·4	15·9 0·7
40	0 40·0	0 40·1	0 38·2	4·0 0·2	10·0 0·4	16·0 0·7
41	0 40·3	0 40·4	0 38·4	4·1 0·2	10·1 0·4	16·1 0·7
42	0 40·5	0 40·6	0 38·7	4·2 0·2	10·2 0·4	16·2 0·7
43	0 40·8	0 40·9	0 38·9	4·3 0·2	10·3 0·4	16·3 0·7
44	0 41·0	0 41·1	0 39·1	4·4 0·2	10·4 0·4	16·4 0·7
45	0 41·3	0 41·4	0 39·4	4·5 0·2	10·5 0·4	16·5 0·7
46	0 41·5	0 41·6	0 39·6	4·6 0·2	10·6 0·4	16·6 0·7
47	0 41·8	0 41·9	0 39·8	4·7 0·2	10·7 0·4	16·7 0·7
48	0 42·0	0 42·1	0 40·1	4·8 0·2	10·8 0·5	16·8 0·7
49	0 42·3	0 42·4	0 40·3	4·9 0·2	10·9 0·5	16·9 0·7
50	0 42·5	0 42·6	0 40·6	5·0 0·2	11·0 0·5	17·0 0·7
51	0 42·8	0 42·9	0 40·8	5·1 0·2	11·1 0·5	17·1 0·7
52	0 43·0	0 43·1	0 41·0	5·2 0·2	11·2 0·5	17·2 0·7
53	0 43·3	0 43·4	0 41·3	5·3 0·2	11·3 0·5	17·3 0·7
54	0 43·5	0 43·6	0 41·5	5·4 0·2	11·4 0·5	17·4 0·7
55	0 43·8	0 43·9	0 41·8	5·5 0·2	11·5 0·5	17·5 0·7
56	0 44·0	0 44·1	0 42·0	5·6 0·2	11·6 0·5	17·6 0·7
57	0 44·3	0 44·4	0 42·2	5·7 0·2	11·7 0·5	17·7 0·7
58	0 44·5	0 44·6	0 42·5	5·8 0·2	11·8 0·5	17·8 0·7
59	0 44·8	0 44·9	0 42·7	5·9 0·2	11·9 0·5	17·9 0·7
60	0 45·0	0 45·1	0 43·0	6·0 0·3	12·0 0·5	18·0 0·8

3ᵐ

m 3	SUN PLANETS	ARIES	MOON	v or d / Corrⁿ	v or d / Corrⁿ	v or d / Corrⁿ
s	° ′	° ′	° ′	′ ′	′ ′	′ ′
00	0 45·0	0 45·1	0 43·0	0·0 0·0	6·0 0·4	12·0 0·7
01	0 45·3	0 45·4	0 43·2	0·1 0·0	6·1 0·4	12·1 0·7
02	0 45·5	0 45·6	0 43·4	0·2 0·0	6·2 0·4	12·2 0·7
03	0 45·8	0 45·9	0 43·7	0·3 0·0	6·3 0·4	12·3 0·7
04	0 46·0	0 46·1	0 43·9	0·4 0·0	6·4 0·4	12·4 0·7
05	0 46·3	0 46·4	0 44·1	0·5 0·0	6·5 0·4	12·5 0·7
06	0 46·5	0 46·6	0 44·4	0·6 0·0	6·6 0·4	12·6 0·7
07	0 46·8	0 46·9	0 44·6	0·7 0·0	6·7 0·4	12·7 0·7
08	0 47·0	0 47·1	0 44·9	0·8 0·0	6·8 0·4	12·8 0·7
09	0 47·3	0 47·4	0 45·1	0·9 0·1	6·9 0·4	12·9 0·8
10	0 47·5	0 47·6	0 45·3	1·0 0·1	7·0 0·4	13·0 0·8
11	0 47·8	0 47·9	0 45·6	1·1 0·1	7·1 0·4	13·1 0·8
12	0 48·0	0 48·1	0 45·8	1·2 0·1	7·2 0·4	13·2 0·8
13	0 48·3	0 48·4	0 46·1	1·3 0·1	7·3 0·4	13·3 0·8
14	0 48·5	0 48·6	0 46·3	1·4 0·1	7·4 0·4	13·4 0·8
15	0 48·8	0 48·9	0 46·5	1·5 0·1	7·5 0·4	13·5 0·8
16	0 49·0	0 49·1	0 46·8	1·6 0·1	7·6 0·4	13·6 0·8
17	0 49·3	0 49·4	0 47·0	1·7 0·1	7·7 0·4	13·7 0·8
18	0 49·5	0 49·6	0 47·2	1·8 0·1	7·8 0·5	13·8 0·8
19	0 49·8	0 49·9	0 47·5	1·9 0·1	7·9 0·5	13·9 0·8
20	0 50·0	0 50·1	0 47·7	2·0 0·1	8·0 0·5	14·0 0·8
21	0 50·3	0 50·4	0 48·0	2·1 0·1	8·1 0·5	14·1 0·8
22	0 50·5	0 50·6	0 48·2	2·2 0·1	8·2 0·5	14·2 0·8
23	0 50·8	0 50·9	0 48·4	2·3 0·1	8·3 0·5	14·3 0·8
24	0 51·0	0 51·1	0 48·7	2·4 0·1	8·4 0·5	14·4 0·8
25	0 51·3	0 51·4	0 48·9	2·5 0·1	8·5 0·5	14·5 0·8
26	0 51·5	0 51·6	0 49·2	2·6 0·2	8·6 0·5	14·6 0·9
27	0 51·8	0 51·9	0 49·4	2·7 0·2	8·7 0·5	14·7 0·9
28	0 52·0	0 52·1	0 49·6	2·8 0·2	8·8 0·5	14·8 0·9
29	0 52·3	0 52·4	0 49·9	2·9 0·2	8·9 0·5	14·9 0·9
30	0 52·5	0 52·6	0 50·1	3·0 0·2	9·0 0·5	15·0 0·9
31	0 52·8	0 52·9	0 50·3	3·1 0·2	9·1 0·5	15·1 0·9
32	0 53·0	0 53·1	0 50·6	3·2 0·2	9·2 0·5	15·2 0·9
33	0 53·3	0 53·4	0 50·8	3·3 0·2	9·3 0·5	15·3 0·9
34	0 53·5	0 53·6	0 51·1	3·4 0·2	9·4 0·5	15·4 0·9
35	0 53·8	0 53·9	0 51·3	3·5 0·2	9·5 0·6	15·5 0·9
36	0 54·0	0 54·1	0 51·5	3·6 0·2	9·6 0·6	15·6 0·9
37	0 54·3	0 54·4	0 51·8	3·7 0·2	9·7 0·6	15·7 0·9
38	0 54·5	0 54·6	0 52·0	3·8 0·2	9·8 0·6	15·8 0·9
39	0 54·8	0 54·9	0 52·3	3·9 0·2	9·9 0·6	15·9 0·9
40	0 55·0	0 55·2	0 52·5	4·0 0·2	10·0 0·6	16·0 0·9
41	0 55·3	0 55·4	0 52·7	4·1 0·2	10·1 0·6	16·1 0·9
42	0 55·5	0 55·7	0 53·0	4·2 0·2	10·2 0·6	16·2 0·9
43	0 55·8	0 55·9	0 53·2	4·3 0·3	10·3 0·6	16·3 1·0
44	0 56·0	0 56·2	0 53·4	4·4 0·3	10·4 0·6	16·4 1·0
45	0 56·3	0 56·4	0 53·7	4·5 0·3	10·5 0·6	16·5 1·0
46	0 56·5	0 56·7	0 53·9	4·6 0·3	10·6 0·6	16·6 1·0
47	0 56·8	0 56·9	0 54·2	4·7 0·3	10·7 0·6	16·7 1·0
48	0 57·0	0 57·2	0 54·4	4·8 0·3	10·8 0·6	16·8 1·0
49	0 57·3	0 57·4	0 54·6	4·9 0·3	10·9 0·6	16·9 1·0
50	0 57·5	0 57·7	0 54·9	5·0 0·3	11·0 0·6	17·0 1·0
51	0 57·8	0 57·9	0 55·1	5·1 0·3	11·1 0·6	17·1 1·0
52	0 58·0	0 58·2	0 55·4	5·2 0·3	11·2 0·7	17·2 1·0
53	0 58·3	0 58·4	0 55·6	5·3 0·3	11·3 0·7	17·3 1·0
54	0 58·5	0 58·7	0 55·8	5·4 0·3	11·4 0·7	17·4 1·0
55	0 58·8	0 58·9	0 56·1	5·5 0·3	11·5 0·7	17·5 1·0
56	0 59·0	0 59·2	0 56·3	5·6 0·3	11·6 0·7	17·6 1·0
57	0 59·3	0 59·4	0 56·6	5·7 0·3	11·7 0·7	17·7 1·0
58	0 59·5	0 59·7	0 56·8	5·8 0·3	11·8 0·7	17·8 1·0
59	0 59·8	0 59·9	0 57·0	5·9 0·3	11·9 0·7	17·9 1·0
60	1 00·0	1 00·2	0 57·3	6·0 0·4	12·0 0·7	18·0 1·1

4ᵐ INCREMENTS AND CORRECTIONS 5ᵐ

m 4	SUN PLANETS	ARIES	MOON	v or d	Corrⁿ	v or d	Corrⁿ	v or d	Corrⁿ
s	° ′	° ′	° ′	′	′	′	′	′	′
00	1 00·0	1 00·2	0 57·3	0·0	0·0	6·0	0·5	12·0	0·9
01	1 00·3	1 00·4	0 57·5	0·1	0·0	6·1	0·5	12·1	0·9
02	1 00·5	1 00·7	0 57·7	0·2	0·0	6·2	0·5	12·2	0·9
03	1 00·8	1 00·9	0 58·0	0·3	0·0	6·3	0·5	12·3	0·9
04	1 01·0	1 01·2	0 58·2	0·4	0·0	6·4	0·5	12·4	0·9
05	1 01·3	1 01·4	0 58·5	0·5	0·0	6·5	0·5	12·5	0·9
06	1 01·5	1 01·7	0 58·7	0·6	0·0	6·6	0·5	12·6	0·9
07	1 01·8	1 01·9	0 58·9	0·7	0·1	6·7	0·5	12·7	1·0
08	1 02·0	1 02·2	0 59·2	0·8	0·1	6·8	0·5	12·8	1·0
09	1 02·3	1 02·4	0 59·4	0·9	0·1	6·9	0·5	12·9	1·0
10	1 02·5	1 02·7	0 59·7	1·0	0·1	7·0	0·5	13·0	1·0
11	1 02·8	1 02·9	0 59·9	1·1	0·1	7·1	0·5	13·1	1·0
12	1 03·0	1 03·2	1 00·1	1·2	0·1	7·2	0·5	13·2	1·0
13	1 03·3	1 03·4	1 00·4	1·3	0·1	7·3	0·5	13·3	1·0
14	1 03·5	1 03·7	1 00·6	1·4	0·1	7·4	0·6	13·4	1·0
15	1 03·8	1 03·9	1 00·8	1·5	0·1	7·5	0·6	13·5	1·0
16	1 04·0	1 04·2	1 01·1	1·6	0·1	7·6	0·6	13·6	1·0
17	1 04·3	1 04·4	1 01·3	1·7	0·1	7·7	0·6	13·7	1·0
18	1 04·5	1 04·7	1 01·6	1·8	0·1	7·8	0·6	13·8	1·0
19	1 04·8	1 04·9	1 01·8	1·9	0·1	7·9	0·6	13·9	1·0
20	1 05·0	1 05·2	1 02·0	2·0	0·2	8·0	0·6	14·0	1·1
21	1 05·3	1 05·4	1 02·3	2·1	0·2	8·1	0·6	14·1	1·1
22	1 05·5	1 05·7	1 02·5	2·2	0·2	8·2	0·6	14·2	1·1
23	1 05·8	1 05·9	1 02·8	2·3	0·2	8·3	0·6	14·3	1·1
24	1 06·0	1 06·2	1 03·0	2·4	0·2	8·4	0·6	14·4	1·1
25	1 06·3	1 06·4	1 03·2	2·5	0·2	8·5	0·6	14·5	1·1
26	1 06·5	1 06·7	1 03·5	2·6	0·2	8·6	0·6	14·6	1·1
27	1 06·8	1 06·9	1 03·7	2·7	0·2	8·7	0·7	14·7	1·1
28	1 07·0	1 07·2	1 03·9	2·8	0·2	8·8	0·7	14·8	1·1
29	1 07·3	1 07·4	1 04·2	2·9	0·2	8·9	0·7	14·9	1·1
30	1 07·5	1 07·7	1 04·4	3·0	0·2	9·0	0·7	15·0	1·1
31	1 07·8	1 07·9	1 04·7	3·1	0·2	9·1	0·7	15·1	1·1
32	1 08·0	1 08·2	1 04·9	3·2	0·2	9·2	0·7	15·2	1·1
33	1 08·3	1 08·4	1 05·1	3·3	0·2	9·3	0·7	15·3	1·1
34	1 08·5	1 08·7	1 05·4	3·4	0·3	9·4	0·7	15·4	1·2
35	1 08·8	1 08·9	1 05·6	3·5	0·3	9·5	0·7	15·5	1·2
36	1 09·0	1 09·2	1 05·9	3·6	0·3	9·6	0·7	15·6	1·2
37	1 09·3	1 09·4	1 06·1	3·7	0·3	9·7	0·7	15·7	1·2
38	1 09·5	1 09·7	1 06·3	3·8	0·3	9·8	0·7	15·8	1·2
39	1 09·8	1 09·9	1 06·6	3·9	0·3	9·9	0·7	15·9	1·2
40	1 10·0	1 10·2	1 06·8	4·0	0·3	10·0	0·8	16·0	1·2
41	1 10·3	1 10·4	1 07·0	4·1	0·3	10·1	0·8	16·1	1·2
42	1 10·5	1 10·7	1 07·3	4·2	0·3	10·2	0·8	16·2	1·2
43	1 10·8	1 10·9	1 07·5	4·3	0·3	10·3	0·8	16·3	1·2
44	1 11·0	1 11·2	1 07·8	4·4	0·3	10·4	0·8	16·4	1·2
45	1 11·3	1 11·4	1 08·0	4·5	0·3	10·5	0·8	16·5	1·2
46	1 11·5	1 11·7	1 08·2	4·6	0·3	10·6	0·8	16·6	1·2
47	1 11·8	1 11·9	1 08·5	4·7	0·4	10·7	0·8	16·7	1·3
48	1 12·0	1 12·2	1 08·7	4·8	0·4	10·8	0·8	16·8	1·3
49	1 12·3	1 12·4	1 09·0	4·9	0·4	10·9	0·8	16·9	1·3
50	1 12·5	1 12·7	1 09·2	5·0	0·4	11·0	0·8	17·0	1·3
51	1 12·8	1 12·9	1 09·4	5·1	0·4	11·1	0·8	17·1	1·3
52	1 13·0	1 13·2	1 09·7	5·2	0·4	11·2	0·8	17·2	1·3
53	1 13·3	1 13·5	1 09·9	5·3	0·4	11·3	0·8	17·3	1·3
54	1 13·5	1 13·7	1 10·2	5·4	0·4	11·4	0·9	17·4	1·3
55	1 13·8	1 14·0	1 10·4	5·5	0·4	11·5	0·9	17·5	1·3
56	1 14·0	1 14·2	1 10·6	5·6	0·4	11·6	0·9	17·6	1·3
57	1 14·3	1 14·5	1 10·9	5·7	0·4	11·7	0·9	17·7	1·3
58	1 14·5	1 14·7	1 11·1	5·8	0·4	11·8	0·9	17·8	1·3
59	1 14·8	1 15·0	1 11·3	5·9	0·4	11·9	0·9	17·9	1·3
60	1 15·0	1 15·2	1 11·6	6·0	0·5	12·0	0·9	18·0	1·4

m 5	SUN PLANETS	ARIES	MOON	v or d	Corrⁿ	v or d	Corrⁿ	v or d	Corrⁿ
s	° ′	° ′	° ′	′	′	′	′	′	′
00	1 15·0	1 15·2	1 11·6	0·0	0·0	6·0	0·6	12·0	1·1
01	1 15·3	1 15·5	1 11·8	0·1	0·0	6·1	0·6	12·1	1·1
02	1 15·5	1 15·7	1 12·1	0·2	0·0	6·2	0·6	12·2	1·1
03	1 15·8	1 16·0	1 12·3	0·3	0·0	6·3	0·6	12·3	1·1
04	1 16·0	1 16·2	1 12·5	0·4	0·0	6·4	0·6	12·4	1·1
05	1 16·3	1 16·5	1 12·8	0·5	0·0	6·5	0·6	12·5	1·1
06	1 16·5	1 16·7	1 13·0	0·6	0·1	6·6	0·6	12·6	1·2
07	1 16·8	1 17·0	1 13·3	0·7	0·1	6·7	0·6	12·7	1·2
08	1 17·0	1 17·2	1 13·5	0·8	0·1	6·8	0·6	12·8	1·2
09	1 17·3	1 17·5	1 13·7	0·9	0·1	6·9	0·6	12·9	1·2
10	1 17·5	1 17·7	1 14·0	1·0	0·1	7·0	0·6	13·0	1·2
11	1 17·8	1 18·0	1 14·2	1·1	0·1	7·1	0·7	13·1	1·2
12	1 18·0	1 18·2	1 14·4	1·2	0·1	7·2	0·7	13·2	1·2
13	1 18·3	1 18·5	1 14·7	1·3	0·1	7·3	0·7	13·3	1·2
14	1 18·5	1 18·7	1 14·9	1·4	0·1	7·4	0·7	13·4	1·2
15	1 18·8	1 19·0	1 15·2	1·5	0·1	7·5	0·7	13·5	1·2
16	1 19·0	1 19·2	1 15·4	1·6	0·1	7·6	0·7	13·6	1·2
17	1 19·3	1 19·5	1 15·6	1·7	0·2	7·7	0·7	13·7	1·3
18	1 19·5	1 19·7	1 15·9	1·8	0·2	7·8	0·7	13·8	1·3
19	1 19·8	1 20·0	1 16·1	1·9	0·2	7·9	0·7	13·9	1·3
20	1 20·0	1 20·2	1 16·4	2·0	0·2	8·0	0·7	14·0	1·3
21	1 20·3	1 20·5	1 16·6	2·1	0·2	8·1	0·7	14·1	1·3
22	1 20·5	1 20·7	1 16·8	2·2	0·2	8·2	0·8	14·2	1·3
23	1 20·8	1 21·0	1 17·1	2·3	0·2	8·3	0·8	14·3	1·3
24	1 21·0	1 21·2	1 17·3	2·4	0·2	8·4	0·8	14·4	1·3
25	1 21·3	1 21·5	1 17·5	2·5	0·2	8·5	0·8	14·5	1·3
26	1 21·5	1 21·7	1 17·8	2·6	0·2	8·6	0·8	14·6	1·3
27	1 21·8	1 22·0	1 18·0	2·7	0·2	8·7	0·8	14·7	1·3
28	1 22·0	1 22·2	1 18·3	2·8	0·3	8·8	0·8	14·8	1·4
29	1 22·3	1 22·5	1 18·5	2·9	0·3	8·9	0·8	14·9	1·4
30	1 22·5	1 22·7	1 18·7	3·0	0·3	9·0	0·8	15·0	1·4
31	1 22·8	1 23·0	1 19·0	3·1	0·3	9·1	0·8	15·1	1·4
32	1 23·0	1 23·2	1 19·2	3·2	0·3	9·2	0·8	15·2	1·4
33	1 23·3	1 23·5	1 19·5	3·3	0·3	9·3	0·9	15·3	1·4
34	1 23·5	1 23·7	1 19·7	3·4	0·3	9·4	0·9	15·4	1·4
35	1 23·8	1 24·0	1 19·9	3·5	0·3	9·5	0·9	15·5	1·4
36	1 24·0	1 24·2	1 20·2	3·6	0·3	9·6	0·9	15·6	1·4
37	1 24·3	1 24·5	1 20·4	3·7	0·3	9·7	0·9	15·7	1·4
38	1 24·5	1 24·7	1 20·7	3·8	0·3	9·8	0·9	15·8	1·4
39	1 24·8	1 25·0	1 20·9	3·9	0·4	9·9	0·9	15·9	1·5
40	1 25·0	1 25·2	1 21·1	4·0	0·4	10·0	0·9	16·0	1·5
41	1 25·3	1 25·5	1 21·4	4·1	0·4	10·1	0·9	16·1	1·5
42	1 25·5	1 25·7	1 21·6	4·2	0·4	10·2	0·9	16·2	1·5
43	1 25·8	1 26·0	1 21·8	4·3	0·4	10·3	0·9	16·3	1·5
44	1 26·0	1 26·2	1 22·1	4·4	0·4	10·4	1·0	16·4	1·5
45	1 26·3	1 26·5	1 22·3	4·5	0·4	10·5	1·0	16·5	1·5
46	1 26·5	1 26·7	1 22·6	4·6	0·4	10·6	1·0	16·6	1·5
47	1 26·8	1 27·0	1 22·8	4·7	0·4	10·7	1·0	16·7	1·5
48	1 27·0	1 27·2	1 23·0	4·8	0·4	10·8	1·0	16·8	1·5
49	1 27·3	1 27·5	1 23·3	4·9	0·4	10·9	1·0	16·9	1·5
50	1 27·5	1 27·7	1 23·5	5·0	0·5	11·0	1·0	17·0	1·6
51	1 27·8	1 28·0	1 23·8	5·1	0·5	11·1	1·0	17·1	1·6
52	1 28·0	1 28·2	1 24·0	5·2	0·5	11·2	1·0	17·2	1·6
53	1 28·3	1 28·5	1 24·2	5·3	0·5	11·3	1·0	17·3	1·6
54	1 28·5	1 28·7	1 24·5	5·4	0·5	11·4	1·0	17·4	1·6
55	1 28·8	1 29·0	1 24·7	5·5	0·5	11·5	1·1	17·5	1·6
56	1 29·0	1 29·2	1 24·9	5·6	0·5	11·6	1·1	17·6	1·6
57	1 29·3	1 29·5	1 25·2	5·7	0·5	11·7	1·1	17·7	1·6
58	1 29·5	1 29·7	1 25·4	5·8	0·5	11·8	1·1	17·8	1·6
59	1 29·8	1 30·0	1 25·7	5·9	0·5	11·9	1·1	17·9	1·6
60	1 30·0	1 30·2	1 25·9	6·0	0·6	12·0	1·1	18·0	1·7

6 m s	SUN PLANETS	ARIES	MOON	v or d	Corrⁿ	v or d	Corrⁿ	v or d	Corrⁿ
	° ′	° ′	° ′	′	′	′	′	′	′
00	1 30·0	1 30·2	1 25·9	0·0	0·0	6·0	0·7	12·0	1·3
01	1 30·3	1 30·5	1 26·1	0·1	0·0	6·1	0·7	12·1	1·3
02	1 30·5	1 30·7	1 26·4	0·2	0·0	6·2	0·7	12·2	1·3
03	1 30·8	1 31·0	1 26·6	0·3	0·0	6·3	0·7	12·3	1·3
04	1 31·0	1 31·2	1 26·9	0·4	0·0	6·4	0·7	12·4	1·3
05	1 31·3	1 31·5	1 27·1	0·5	0·1	6·5	0·7	12·5	1·4
06	1 31·5	1 31·8	1 27·3	0·6	0·1	6·6	0·7	12·6	1·4
07	1 31·8	1 32·0	1 27·6	0·7	0·1	6·7	0·7	12·7	1·4
08	1 32·0	1 32·3	1 27·8	0·8	0·1	6·8	0·7	12·8	1·4
09	1 32·3	1 32·5	1 28·0	0·9	0·1	6·9	0·7	12·9	1·4
10	1 32·5	1 32·8	1 28·3	1·0	0·1	7·0	0·8	13·0	1·4
11	1 32·8	1 33·0	1 28·5	1·1	0·1	7·1	0·8	13·1	1·4
12	1 33·0	1 33·3	1 28·8	1·2	0·1	7·2	0·8	13·2	1·4
13	1 33·3	1 33·5	1 29·0	1·3	0·1	7·3	0·8	13·3	1·4
14	1 33·5	1 33·8	1 29·2	1·4	0·2	7·4	0·8	13·4	1·5
15	1 33·8	1 34·0	1 29·5	1·5	0·2	7·5	0·8	13·5	1·5
16	1 34·0	1 34·3	1 29·7	1·6	0·2	7·6	0·8	13·6	1·5
17	1 34·3	1 34·5	1 30·0	1·7	0·2	7·7	0·8	13·7	1·5
18	1 34·5	1 34·8	1 30·2	1·8	0·2	7·8	0·8	13·8	1·5
19	1 34·8	1 35·0	1 30·4	1·9	0·2	7·9	0·9	13·9	1·5
20	1 35·0	1 35·3	1 30·7	2·0	0·2	8·0	0·9	14·0	1·5
21	1 35·3	1 35·5	1 30·9	2·1	0·2	8·1	0·9	14·1	1·5
22	1 35·5	1 35·8	1 31·1	2·2	0·2	8·2	0·9	14·2	1·5
23	1 35·8	1 36·0	1 31·4	2·3	0·2	8·3	0·9	14·3	1·5
24	1 36·0	1 36·3	1 31·6	2·4	0·3	8·4	0·9	14·4	1·6
25	1 36·3	1 36·5	1 31·9	2·5	0·3	8·5	0·9	14·5	1·6
26	1 36·5	1 36·8	1 32·1	2·6	0·3	8·6	0·9	14·6	1·6
27	1 36·8	1 37·0	1 32·3	2·7	0·3	8·7	0·9	14·7	1·6
28	1 37·0	1 37·3	1 32·6	2·8	0·3	8·8	1·0	14·8	1·6
29	1 37·3	1 37·5	1 32·8	2·9	0·3	8·9	1·0	14·9	1·6
30	1 37·5	1 37·8	1 33·1	3·0	0·3	9·0	1·0	15·0	1·6
31	1 37·8	1 38·0	1 33·3	3·1	0·3	9·1	1·0	15·1	1·6
32	1 38·0	1 38·3	1 33·5	3·2	0·3	9·2	1·0	15·2	1·6
33	1 38·3	1 38·5	1 33·8	3·3	0·4	9·3	1·0	15·3	1·7
34	1 38·5	1 38·8	1 34·0	3·4	0·4	9·4	1·0	15·4	1·7
35	1 38·8	1 39·0	1 34·3	3·5	0·4	9·5	1·0	15·5	1·7
36	1 39·0	1 39·3	1 34·5	3·6	0·4	9·6	1·0	15·6	1·7
37	1 39·3	1 39·5	1 34·7	3·7	0·4	9·7	1·1	15·7	1·7
38	1 39·5	1 39·8	1 35·0	3·8	0·4	9·8	1·1	15·8	1·7
39	1 39·8	1 40·0	1 35·2	3·9	0·4	9·9	1·1	15·9	1·7
40	1 40·0	1 40·3	1 35·4	4·0	0·4	10·0	1·1	16·0	1·7
41	1 40·3	1 40·5	1 35·7	4·1	0·4	10·1	1·1	16·1	1·7
42	1 40·5	1 40·8	1 35·9	4·2	0·5	10·2	1·1	16·2	1·8
43	1 40·8	1 41·0	1 36·2	4·3	0·5	10·3	1·1	16·3	1·8
44	1 41·0	1 41·3	1 36·4	4·4	0·5	10·4	1·1	16·4	1·8
45	1 41·3	1 41·5	1 36·6	4·5	0·5	10·5	1·1	16·5	1·8
46	1 41·5	1 41·8	1 36·9	4·6	0·5	10·6	1·1	16·6	1·8
47	1 41·8	1 42·0	1 37·1	4·7	0·5	10·7	1·2	16·7	1·8
48	1 42·0	1 42·3	1 37·4	4·8	0·5	10·8	1·2	16·8	1·8
49	1 42·3	1 42·5	1 37·6	4·9	0·5	10·9	1·2	16·9	1·8
50	1 42·5	1 42·8	1 37·8	5·0	0·5	11·0	1·2	17·0	1·8
51	1 42·8	1 43·0	1 38·1	5·1	0·6	11·1	1·2	17·1	1·9
52	1 43·0	1 43·3	1 38·3	5·2	0·6	11·2	1·2	17·2	1·9
53	1 43·3	1 43·5	1 38·5	5·3	0·6	11·3	1·2	17·3	1·9
54	1 43·5	1 43·8	1 38·8	5·4	0·6	11·4	1·2	17·4	1·9
55	1 43·8	1 44·0	1 39·0	5·5	0·6	11·5	1·2	17·5	1·9
56	1 44·0	1 44·3	1 39·3	5·6	0·6	11·6	1·3	17·6	1·9
57	1 44·3	1 44·5	1 39·5	5·7	0·6	11·7	1·3	17·7	1·9
58	1 44·5	1 44·8	1 39·7	5·8	0·6	11·8	1·3	17·8	1·9
59	1 44·8	1 45·0	1 40·0	5·9	0·6	11·9	1·3	17·9	1·9
60	1 45·0	1 45·3	1 40·2	6·0	0·7	12·0	1·3	18·0	2·0

7 m s	SUN PLANETS	ARIES	MOON	v or d	Corrⁿ	v or d	Corrⁿ	v or d	Corrⁿ
	° ′	° ′	° ′	′	′	′	′	′	′
00	1 45·0	1 45·3	1 40·2	0·0	0·0	6·0	0·8	12·0	1·5
01	1 45·3	1 45·5	1 40·5	0·1	0·0	6·1	0·8	12·1	1·5
02	1 45·5	1 45·8	1 40·7	0·2	0·0	6·2	0·8	12·2	1·5
03	1 45·8	1 46·0	1 40·9	0·3	0·0	6·3	0·8	12·3	1·5
04	1 46·0	1 46·3	1 41·2	0·4	0·1	6·4	0·8	12·4	1·6
05	1 46·3	1 46·5	1 41·4	0·5	0·1	6·5	0·8	12·5	1·6
06	1 46·5	1 46·8	1 41·6	0·6	0·1	6·6	0·8	12·6	1·6
07	1 46·8	1 47·0	1 41·9	0·7	0·1	6·7	0·8	12·7	1·6
08	1 47·0	1 47·3	1 42·1	0·8	0·1	6·8	0·9	12·8	1·6
09	1 47·3	1 47·5	1 42·4	0·9	0·1	6·9	0·9	12·9	1·6
10	1 47·5	1 47·8	1 42·6	1·0	0·1	7·0	0·9	13·0	1·6
11	1 47·8	1 48·0	1 42·8	1·1	0·1	7·1	0·9	13·1	1·6
12	1 48·0	1 48·3	1 43·1	1·2	0·2	7·2	0·9	13·2	1·7
13	1 48·3	1 48·5	1 43·3	1·3	0·2	7·3	0·9	13·3	1·7
14	1 48·5	1 48·8	1 43·6	1·4	0·2	7·4	0·9	13·4	1·7
15	1 48·8	1 49·0	1 43·8	1·5	0·2	7·5	0·9	13·5	1·7
16	1 49·0	1 49·3	1 44·0	1·6	0·2	7·6	1·0	13·6	1·7
17	1 49·3	1 49·5	1 44·3	1·7	0·2	7·7	1·0	13·7	1·7
18	1 49·5	1 49·8	1 44·5	1·8	0·2	7·8	1·0	13·8	1·7
19	1 49·8	1 50·1	1 44·8	1·9	0·2	7·9	1·0	13·9	1·7
20	1 50·0	1 50·3	1 45·0	2·0	0·3	8·0	1·0	14·0	1·8
21	1 50·3	1 50·6	1 45·2	2·1	0·3	8·1	1·0	14·1	1·8
22	1 50·5	1 50·8	1 45·5	2·2	0·3	8·2	1·0	14·2	1·8
23	1 50·8	1 51·1	1 45·7	2·3	0·3	8·3	1·0	14·3	1·8
24	1 51·0	1 51·3	1 45·9	2·4	0·3	8·4	1·1	14·4	1·8
25	1 51·3	1 51·6	1 46·2	2·5	0·3	8·5	1·1	14·5	1·8
26	1 51·5	1 51·8	1 46·4	2·6	0·3	8·6	1·1	14·6	1·8
27	1 51·8	1 52·1	1 46·7	2·7	0·3	8·7	1·1	14·7	1·8
28	1 52·0	1 52·3	1 46·9	2·8	0·4	8·8	1·1	14·8	1·9
29	1 52·3	1 52·6	1 47·1	2·9	0·4	8·9	1·1	14·9	1·9
30	1 52·5	1 52·8	1 47·4	3·0	0·4	9·0	1·1	15·0	1·9
31	1 52·8	1 53·1	1 47·6	3·1	0·4	9·1	1·1	15·1	1·9
32	1 53·0	1 53·3	1 47·9	3·2	0·4	9·2	1·2	15·2	1·9
33	1 53·3	1 53·6	1 48·1	3·3	0·4	9·3	1·2	15·3	1·9
34	1 53·5	1 53·8	1 48·3	3·4	0·4	9·4	1·2	15·4	1·9
35	1 53·8	1 54·1	1 48·6	3·5	0·4	9·5	1·2	15·5	1·9
36	1 54·0	1 54·3	1 48·8	3·6	0·5	9·6	1·2	15·6	2·0
37	1 54·3	1 54·6	1 49·0	3·7	0·5	9·7	1·2	15·7	2·0
38	1 54·5	1 54·8	1 49·3	3·8	0·5	9·8	1·2	15·8	2·0
39	1 54·8	1 55·1	1 49·5	3·9	0·5	9·9	1·2	15·9	2·0
40	1 55·0	1 55·3	1 49·8	4·0	0·5	10·0	1·3	16·0	2·0
41	1 55·3	1 55·6	1 50·0	4·1	0·5	10·1	1·3	16·1	2·0
42	1 55·5	1 55·8	1 50·2	4·2	0·5	10·2	1·3	16·2	2·0
43	1 55·8	1 56·1	1 50·5	4·3	0·5	10·3	1·3	16·3	2·0
44	1 56·0	1 56·3	1 50·7	4·4	0·6	10·4	1·3	16·4	2·1
45	1 56·3	1 56·6	1 51·0	4·5	0·6	10·5	1·3	16·5	2·1
46	1 56·5	1 56·8	1 51·2	4·6	0·6	10·6	1·3	16·6	2·1
47	1 56·8	1 57·1	1 51·4	4·7	0·6	10·7	1·3	16·7	2·1
48	1 57·0	1 57·3	1 51·7	4·8	0·6	10·8	1·4	16·8	2·1
49	1 57·3	1 57·6	1 51·9	4·9	0·6	10·9	1·4	16·9	2·1
50	1 57·5	1 57·8	1 52·1	5·0	0·6	11·0	1·4	17·0	2·1
51	1 57·8	1 58·1	1 52·4	5·1	0·6	11·1	1·4	17·1	2·1
52	1 58·0	1 58·3	1 52·6	5·2	0·7	11·2	1·4	17·2	2·2
53	1 58·3	1 58·6	1 52·9	5·3	0·7	11·3	1·4	17·3	2·2
54	1 58·5	1 58·8	1 53·1	5·4	0·7	11·4	1·4	17·4	2·2
55	1 58·8	1 59·1	1 53·3	5·5	0·7	11·5	1·4	17·5	2·2
56	1 59·0	1 59·3	1 53·6	5·6	0·7	11·6	1·5	17·6	2·2
57	1 59·3	1 59·6	1 53·8	5·7	0·7	11·7	1·5	17·7	2·2
58	1 59·5	1 59·8	1 54·1	5·8	0·7	11·8	1·5	17·8	2·2
59	1 59·8	2 00·1	1 54·3	5·9	0·7	11·9	1·5	17·9	2·2
60	2 00·0	2 00·3	1 54·5	6·0	0·8	12·0	1·5	18·0	2·3

8	SUN PLANETS	ARIES	MOON	v or Corrⁿ d	v or Corrⁿ d	v or Corrⁿ d
s	° ′	° ′	° ′	′ ′	′ ′	′ ′
00	2 00·0	2 00·3	1 54·5	0·0 0·0	6·0 0·9	12·0 1·7
01	2 00·3	2 00·6	1 54·8	0·1 0·0	6·1 0·9	12·1 1·7
02	2 00·5	2 00·8	1 55·0	0·2 0·0	6·2 0·9	12·2 1·7
03	2 00·8	2 01·1	1 55·2	0·3 0·0	6·3 0·9	12·3 1·7
04	2 01·0	2 01·3	1 55·5	0·4 0·1	6·4 0·9	12·4 1·8
05	2 01·3	2 01·6	1 55·7	0·5 0·1	6·5 0·9	12·5 1·8
06	2 01·5	2 01·8	1 56·0	0·6 0·1	6·6 0·9	12·6 1·8
07	2 01·8	2 02·1	1 56·2	0·7 0·1	6·7 0·9	12·7 1·8
08	2 02·0	2 02·3	1 56·4	0·8 0·1	6·8 1·0	12·8 1·8
09	2 02·3	2 02·6	1 56·7	0·9 0·1	6·9 1·0	12·9 1·8
10	2 02·5	2 02·8	1 56·9	1·0 0·1	7·0 1·0	13·0 1·8
11	2 02·8	2 03·1	1 57·2	1·1 0·2	7·1 1·0	13·1 1·9
12	2 03·0	2 03·3	1 57·4	1·2 0·2	7·2 1·0	13·2 1·9
13	2 03·3	2 03·6	1 57·6	1·3 0·2	7·3 1·0	13·3 1·9
14	2 03·5	2 03·8	1 57·9	1·4 0·2	7·4 1·0	13·4 1·9
15	2 03·8	2 04·1	1 58·1	1·5 0·2	7·5 1·1	13·5 1·9
16	2 04·0	2 04·3	1 58·4	1·6 0·2	7·6 1·1	13·6 1·9
17	2 04·3	2 04·6	1 58·6	1·7 0·2	7·7 1·1	13·7 1·9
18	2 04·5	2 04·8	1 58·8	1·8 0·3	7·8 1·1	13·8 2·0
19	2 04·8	2 05·1	1 59·1	1·9 0·3	7·9 1·1	13·9 2·0
20	2 05·0	2 05·3	1 59·3	2·0 0·3	8·0 1·1	14·0 2·0
21	2 05·3	2 05·6	1 59·5	2·1 0·3	8·1 1·1	14·1 2·0
22	2 05·5	2 05·8	1 59·8	2·2 0·3	8·2 1·2	14·2 2·0
23	2 05·8	2 06·1	2 00·0	2·3 0·3	8·3 1·2	14·3 2·0
24	2 06·0	2 06·3	2 00·3	2·4 0·3	8·4 1·2	14·4 2·0
25	2 06·3	2 06·6	2 00·5	2·5 0·4	8·5 1·2	14·5 2·1
26	2 06·5	2 06·8	2 00·7	2·6 0·4	8·6 1·2	14·6 2·1
27	2 06·8	2 07·1	2 01·0	2·7 0·4	8·7 1·2	14·7 2·1
28	2 07·0	2 07·3	2 01·2	2·8 0·4	8·8 1·2	14·8 2·1
29	2 07·3	2 07·6	2 01·5	2·9 0·4	8·9 1·3	14·9 2·1
30	2 07·5	2 07·8	2 01·7	3·0 0·4	9·0 1·3	15·0 2·1
31	2 07·8	2 08·1	2 01·9	3·1 0·4	9·1 1·3	15·1 2·1
32	2 08·0	2 08·4	2 02·2	3·2 0·5	9·2 1·3	15·2 2·2
33	2 08·3	2 08·6	2 02·4	3·3 0·5	9·3 1·3	15·3 2·2
34	2 08·5	2 08·9	2 02·6	3·4 0·5	9·4 1·3	15·4 2·2
35	2 08·8	2 09·1	2 02·9	3·5 0·5	9·5 1·3	15·5 2·2
36	2 09·0	2 09·4	2 03·1	3·6 0·5	9·6 1·4	15·6 2·2
37	2 09·3	2 09·6	2 03·4	3·7 0·5	9·7 1·4	15·7 2·2
38	2 09·5	2 09·9	2 03·6	3·8 0·5	9·8 1·4	15·8 2·2
39	2 09·8	2 10·1	2 03·8	3·9 0·6	9·9 1·4	15·9 2·3
40	2 10·0	2 10·4	2 04·1	4·0 0·6	10·0 1·4	16·0 2·3
41	2 10·3	2 10·6	2 04·3	4·1 0·6	10·1 1·4	16·1 2·3
42	2 10·5	2 10·9	2 04·6	4·2 0·6	10·2 1·4	16·2 2·3
43	2 10·8	2 11·1	2 04·8	4·3 0·6	10·3 1·5	16·3 2·3
44	2 11·0	2 11·4	2 05·0	4·4 0·6	10·4 1·5	16·4 2·3
45	2 11·3	2 11·6	2 05·3	4·5 0·6	10·5 1·5	16·5 2·3
46	2 11·5	2 11·9	2 05·5	4·6 0·7	10·6 1·5	16·6 2·4
47	2 11·8	2 12·1	2 05·7	4·7 0·7	10·7 1·5	16·7 2·4
48	2 12·0	2 12·4	2 06·0	4·8 0·7	10·8 1·5	16·8 2·4
49	2 12·3	2 12·6	2 06·2	4·9 0·7	10·9 1·5	16·9 2·4
50	2 12·5	2 12·9	2 06·5	5·0 0·7	11·0 1·6	17·0 2·4
51	2 12·8	2 13·1	2 06·7	5·1 0·7	11·1 1·6	17·1 2·4
52	2 13·0	2 13·4	2 06·9	5·2 0·7	11·2 1·6	17·2 2·4
53	2 13·3	2 13·6	2 07·2	5·3 0·8	11·3 1·6	17·3 2·5
54	2 13·5	2 13·9	2 07·4	5·4 0·8	11·4 1·6	17·4 2·5
55	2 13·8	2 14·1	2 07·7	5·5 0·8	11·5 1·6	17·5 2·5
56	2 14·0	2 14·4	2 07·9	5·6 0·8	11·6 1·6	17·6 2·5
57	2 14·3	2 14·6	2 08·1	5·7 0·8	11·7 1·7	17·7 2·5
58	2 14·5	2 14·9	2 08·4	5·8 0·8	11·8 1·7	17·8 2·5
59	2 14·8	2 15·1	2 08·6	5·9 0·8	11·9 1·7	17·9 2·5
60	2 15·0	2 15·4	2 08·9	6·0 0·9	12·0 1·7	18·0 2·6

9	SUN PLANETS	ARIES	MOON	v or Corrⁿ d	v or Corrⁿ d	v or Corrⁿ d
s	° ′	° ′	° ′	′ ′	′ ′	′ ′
00	2 15·0	2 15·4	2 08·9	0·0 0·0	6·0 1·0	12·0 1·9
01	2 15·3	2 15·6	2 09·1	0·1 0·0	6·1 1·0	12·1 1·9
02	2 15·5	2 15·9	2 09·3	0·2 0·0	6·2 1·0	12·2 1·9
03	2 15·8	2 16·1	2 09·6	0·3 0·0	6·3 1·0	12·3 1·9
04	2 16·0	2 16·4	2 09·8	0·4 0·1	6·4 1·0	12·4 2·0
05	2 16·3	2 16·6	2 10·0	0·5 0·1	6·5 1·0	12·5 2·0
06	2 16·5	2 16·9	2 10·3	0·6 0·1	6·6 1·0	12·6 2·0
07	2 16·8	2 17·1	2 10·5	0·7 0·1	6·7 1·1	12·7 2·0
08	2 17·0	2 17·4	2 10·8	0·8 0·1	6·8 1·1	12·8 2·0
09	2 17·3	2 17·6	2 11·0	0·9 0·1	6·9 1·1	12·9 2·0
10	2 17·5	2 17·9	2 11·2	1·0 0·2	7·0 1·1	13·0 2·1
11	2 17·8	2 18·1	2 11·5	1·1 0·2	7·1 1·1	13·1 2·1
12	2 18·0	2 18·4	2 11·7	1·2 0·2	7·2 1·1	13·2 2·1
13	2 18·3	2 18·6	2 12·0	1·3 0·2	7·3 1·2	13·3 2·1
14	2 18·5	2 18·9	2 12·2	1·4 0·2	7·4 1·2	13·4 2·1
15	2 18·8	2 19·1	2 12·4	1·5 0·2	7·5 1·2	13·5 2·1
16	2 19·0	2 19·4	2 12·7	1·6 0·3	7·6 1·2	13·6 2·2
17	2 19·3	2 19·6	2 12·9	1·7 0·3	7·7 1·2	13·7 2·2
18	2 19·5	2 19·9	2 13·1	1·8 0·3	7·8 1·2	13·8 2·2
19	2 19·8	2 20·1	2 13·4	1·9 0·3	7·9 1·3	13·9 2·2
20	2 20·0	2 20·4	2 13·6	2·0 0·3	8·0 1·3	14·0 2·2
21	2 20·3	2 20·6	2 13·9	2·1 0·3	8·1 1·3	14·1 2·2
22	2 20·5	2 20·9	2 14·1	2·2 0·3	8·2 1·3	14·2 2·2
23	2 20·8	2 21·1	2 14·3	2·3 0·4	8·3 1·3	14·3 2·3
24	2 21·0	2 21·4	2 14·6	2·4 0·4	8·4 1·3	14·4 2·3
25	2 21·3	2 21·6	2 14·8	2·5 0·4	8·5 1·3	14·5 2·3
26	2 21·5	2 21·9	2 15·1	2·6 0·4	8·6 1·4	14·6 2·3
27	2 21·8	2 22·1	2 15·3	2·7 0·4	8·7 1·4	14·7 2·3
28	2 22·0	2 22·4	2 15·5	2·8 0·4	8·8 1·4	14·8 2·3
29	2 22·3	2 22·6	2 15·8	2·9 0·5	8·9 1·4	14·9 2·4
30	2 22·5	2 22·9	2 16·0	3·0 0·5	9·0 1·4	15·0 2·4
31	2 22·8	2 23·1	2 16·2	3·1 0·5	9·1 1·4	15·1 2·4
32	2 23·0	2 23·4	2 16·5	3·2 0·5	9·2 1·5	15·2 2·4
33	2 23·3	2 23·6	2 16·7	3·3 0·5	9·3 1·5	15·3 2·4
34	2 23·5	2 23·9	2 17·0	3·4 0·5	9·4 1·5	15·4 2·4
35	2 23·8	2 24·1	2 17·2	3·5 0·6	9·5 1·5	15·5 2·5
36	2 24·0	2 24·4	2 17·4	3·6 0·6	9·6 1·5	15·6 2·5
37	2 24·3	2 24·6	2 17·7	3·7 0·6	9·7 1·5	15·7 2·5
38	2 24·5	2 24·9	2 17·9	3·8 0·6	9·8 1·6	15·8 2·5
39	2 24·8	2 25·1	2 18·2	3·9 0·6	9·9 1·6	15·9 2·5
40	2 25·0	2 25·4	2 18·4	4·0 0·6	10·0 1·6	16·0 2·5
41	2 25·3	2 25·6	2 18·6	4·1 0·6	10·1 1·6	16·1 2·5
42	2 25·5	2 25·9	2 18·9	4·2 0·7	10·2 1·6	16·2 2·6
43	2 25·8	2 26·1	2 19·1	4·3 0·7	10·3 1·6	16·3 2·6
44	2 26·0	2 26·4	2 19·3	4·4 0·7	10·4 1·6	16·4 2·6
45	2 26·3	2 26·7	2 19·6	4·5 0·7	10·5 1·7	16·5 2·6
46	2 26·5	2 26·9	2 19·8	4·6 0·7	10·6 1·7	16·6 2·6
47	2 26·8	2 27·2	2 20·1	4·7 0·7	10·7 1·7	16·7 2·6
48	2 27·0	2 27·4	2 20·3	4·8 0·8	10·8 1·7	16·8 2·7
49	2 27·3	2 27·7	2 20·5	4·9 0·8	10·9 1·7	16·9 2·7
50	2 27·5	2 27·9	2 20·8	5·0 0·8	11·0 1·7	17·0 2·7
51	2 27·8	2 28·2	2 21·0	5·1 0·8	11·1 1·8	17·1 2·7
52	2 28·0	2 28·4	2 21·3	5·2 0·8	11·2 1·8	17·2 2·7
53	2 28·3	2 28·7	2 21·5	5·3 0·8	11·3 1·8	17·3 2·7
54	2 28·5	2 28·9	2 21·7	5·4 0·9	11·4 1·8	17·4 2·8
55	2 28·8	2 29·2	2 22·0	5·5 0·9	11·5 1·8	17·5 2·8
56	2 29·0	2 29·4	2 22·2	5·6 0·9	11·6 1·8	17·6 2·8
57	2 29·3	2 29·7	2 22·5	5·7 0·9	11·7 1·9	17·7 2·8
58	2 29·5	2 29·9	2 22·7	5·8 0·9	11·8 1·9	17·8 2·8
59	2 29·8	2 30·2	2 22·9	5·9 0·9	11·9 1·9	17·9 2·8
60	2 30·0	2 30·4	2 23·2	6·0 1·0	12·0 1·9	18·0 2·9

10ᵐ

10	SUN PLANETS	ARIES	MOON	v or Corrⁿ d	v or Corrⁿ d	v or Corrⁿ d
s	° ′	° ′	° ′	′ ′	′ ′	′ ′
00	2 30·0	2 30·4	2 23·2	0·0 0·0	6·0 1·1	12·0 2·1
01	2 30·3	2 30·7	2 23·4	0·1 0·0	6·1 1·1	12·1 2·1
02	2 30·5	2 30·9	2 23·6	0·2 0·0	6·2 1·1	12·2 2·1
03	2 30·8	2 31·2	2 23·9	0·3 0·1	6·3 1·1	12·3 2·2
04	2 31·0	2 31·4	2 24·1	0·4 0·1	6·4 1·1	12·4 2·2
05	2 31·3	2 31·7	2 24·4	0·5 0·1	6·5 1·1	12·5 2·2
06	2 31·5	2 31·9	2 24·6	0·6 0·1	6·6 1·2	12·6 2·2
07	2 31·8	2 32·2	2 24·8	0·7 0·1	6·7 1·2	12·7 2·2
08	2 32·0	2 32·4	2 25·1	0·8 0·1	6·8 1·2	12·8 2·2
09	2 32·3	2 32·7	2 25·3	0·9 0·2	6·9 1·2	12·9 2·3
10	2 32·5	2 32·9	2 25·6	1·0 0·2	7·0 1·2	13·0 2·3
11	2 32·8	2 33·2	2 25·8	1·1 0·2	7·1 1·2	13·1 2·3
12	2 33·0	2 33·4	2 26·0	1·2 0·2	7·2 1·3	13·2 2·3
13	2 33·3	2 33·7	2 26·3	1·3 0·2	7·3 1·3	13·3 2·3
14	2 33·5	2 33·9	2 26·5	1·4 0·2	7·4 1·3	13·4 2·3
15	2 33·8	2 34·2	2 26·7	1·5 0·3	7·5 1·3	13·5 2·4
16	2 34·0	2 34·4	2 27·0	1·6 0·3	7·6 1·3	13·6 2·4
17	2 34·3	2 34·7	2 27·2	1·7 0·3	7·7 1·3	13·7 2·4
18	2 34·5	2 34·9	2 27·5	1·8 0·3	7·8 1·4	13·8 2·4
19	2 34·8	2 35·2	2 27·7	1·9 0·3	7·9 1·4	13·9 2·4
20	2 35·0	2 35·4	2 27·9	2·0 0·4	8·0 1·4	14·0 2·5
21	2 35·3	2 35·7	2 28·2	2·1 0·4	8·1 1·4	14·1 2·5
22	2 35·5	2 35·9	2 28·4	2·2 0·4	8·2 1·4	14·2 2·5
23	2 35·8	2 36·2	2 28·7	2·3 0·4	8·3 1·5	14·3 2·5
24	2 36·0	2 36·4	2 28·9	2·4 0·4	8·4 1·5	14·4 2·5
25	2 36·3	2 36·7	2 29·1	2·5 0·4	8·5 1·5	14·5 2·5
26	2 36·5	2 36·9	2 29·4	2·6 0·5	8·6 1·5	14·6 2·6
27	2 36·8	2 37·2	2 29·6	2·7 0·5	8·7 1·5	14·7 2·6
28	2 37·0	2 37·4	2 29·8	2·8 0·5	8·8 1·5	14·8 2·6
29	2 37·3	2 37·7	2 30·1	2·9 0·5	8·9 1·6	14·9 2·6
30	2 37·5	2 37·9	2 30·3	3·0 0·5	9·0 1·6	15·0 2·6
31	2 37·8	2 38·2	2 30·6	3·1 0·5	9·1 1·6	15·1 2·6
32	2 38·0	2 38·4	2 30·8	3·2 0·6	9·2 1·6	15·2 2·7
33	2 38·3	2 38·7	2 31·0	3·3 0·6	9·3 1·6	15·3 2·7
34	2 38·5	2 38·9	2 31·3	3·4 0·6	9·4 1·6	15·4 2·7
35	2 38·8	2 39·2	2 31·5	3·5 0·6	9·5 1·7	15·5 2·7
36	2 39·0	2 39·4	2 31·8	3·6 0·6	9·6 1·7	15·6 2·7
37	2 39·3	2 39·7	2 32·0	3·7 0·6	9·7 1·7	15·7 2·7
38	2 39·5	2 39·9	2 32·2	3·8 0·7	9·8 1·7	15·8 2·8
39	2 39·8	2 40·2	2 32·5	3·9 0·7	9·9 1·7	15·9 2·8
40	2 40·0	2 40·4	2 32·7	4·0 0·7	10·0 1·8	16·0 2·8
41	2 40·3	2 40·7	2 32·9	4·1 0·7	10·1 1·8	16·1 2·8
42	2 40·5	2 40·9	2 33·2	4·2 0·7	10·2 1·8	16·2 2·8
43	2 40·8	2 41·2	2 33·4	4·3 0·8	10·3 1·8	16·3 2·9
44	2 41·0	2 41·4	2 33·7	4·4 0·8	10·4 1·8	16·4 2·9
45	2 41·3	2 41·7	2 33·9	4·5 0·8	10·5 1·8	16·5 2·9
46	2 41·5	2 41·9	2 34·1	4·6 0·8	10·6 1·9	16·6 2·9
47	2 41·8	2 42·2	2 34·4	4·7 0·8	10·7 1·9	16·7 2·9
48	2 42·0	2 42·4	2 34·6	4·8 0·8	10·8 1·9	16·8 2·9
49	2 42·3	2 42·7	2 34·9	4·9 0·9	10·9 1·9	16·9 3·0
50	2 42·5	2 42·9	2 35·1	5·0 0·9	11·0 1·9	17·0 3·0
51	2 42·8	2 43·2	2 35·3	5·1 0·9	11·1 1·9	17·1 3·0
52	2 43·0	2 43·4	2 35·6	5·2 0·9	11·2 2·0	17·2 3·0
53	2 43·3	2 43·7	2 35·8	5·3 0·9	11·3 2·0	17·3 3·0
54	2 43·5	2 43·9	2 36·1	5·4 0·9	11·4 2·0	17·4 3·0
55	2 43·8	2 44·2	2 36·3	5·5 1·0	11·5 2·0	17·5 3·1
56	2 44·0	2 44·4	2 36·5	5·6 1·0	11·6 2·0	17·6 3·1
57	2 44·3	2 44·7	2 36·8	5·7 1·0	11·7 2·0	17·7 3·1
58	2 44·5	2 45·0	2 37·0	5·8 1·0	11·8 2·1	17·8 3·1
59	2 44·8	2 45·2	2 37·2	5·9 1·0	11·9 2·1	17·9 3·1
60	2 45·0	2 45·5	2 37·5	6·0 1·1	12·0 2·1	18·0 3·2

11ᵐ

11	SUN PLANETS	ARIES	MOON	v or Corrⁿ d	v or Corrⁿ d	v or Corrⁿ d
s	° ′	° ′	° ′	′ ′	′ ′	′ ′
00	2 45·0	2 45·5	2 37·5	0·0 0·0	6·0 1·2	12·0 2·3
01	2 45·3	2 45·7	2 37·7	0·1 0·0	6·1 1·2	12·1 2·3
02	2 45·5	2 46·0	2 38·0	0·2 0·0	6·2 1·2	12·2 2·3
03	2 45·8	2 46·2	2 38·2	0·3 0·1	6·3 1·2	12·3 2·4
04	2 46·0	2 46·5	2 38·4	0·4 0·1	6·4 1·2	12·4 2·4
05	2 46·3	2 46·7	2 38·7	0·5 0·1	6·5 1·2	12·5 2·4
06	2 46·5	2 47·0	2 38·9	0·6 0·1	6·6 1·3	12·6 2·4
07	2 46·8	2 47·2	2 39·2	0·7 0·1	6·7 1·3	12·7 2·4
08	2 47·0	2 47·5	2 39·4	0·8 0·2	6·8 1·3	12·8 2·5
09	2 47·3	2 47·7	2 39·6	0·9 0·2	6·9 1·3	12·9 2·5
10	2 47·5	2 48·0	2 39·9	1·0 0·2	7·0 1·3	13·0 2·5
11	2 47·8	2 48·2	2 40·1	1·1 0·2	7·1 1·4	13·1 2·5
12	2 48·0	2 48·5	2 40·3	1·2 0·2	7·2 1·4	13·2 2·5
13	2 48·3	2 48·7	2 40·6	1·3 0·2	7·3 1·4	13·3 2·5
14	2 48·5	2 49·0	2 40·8	1·4 0·3	7·4 1·4	13·4 2·6
15	2 48·8	2 49·2	2 41·1	1·5 0·3	7·5 1·4	13·5 2·6
16	2 49·0	2 49·5	2 41·3	1·6 0·3	7·6 1·5	13·6 2·6
17	2 49·3	2 49·7	2 41·5	1·7 0·3	7·7 1·5	13·7 2·6
18	2 49·5	2 50·0	2 41·8	1·8 0·3	7·8 1·5	13·8 2·6
19	2 49·8	2 50·2	2 42·0	1·9 0·4	7·9 1·5	13·9 2·7
20	2 50·0	2 50·5	2 42·3	2·0 0·4	8·0 1·5	14·0 2·7
21	2 50·3	2 50·7	2 42·5	2·1 0·4	8·1 1·6	14·1 2·7
22	2 50·5	2 51·0	2 42·7	2·2 0·4	8·2 1·6	14·2 2·7
23	2 50·8	2 51·2	2 43·0	2·3 0·4	8·3 1·6	14·3 2·7
24	2 51·0	2 51·5	2 43·2	2·4 0·5	8·4 1·6	14·4 2·8
25	2 51·3	2 51·7	2 43·4	2·5 0·5	8·5 1·6	14·5 2·8
26	2 51·5	2 52·0	2 43·7	2·6 0·5	8·6 1·6	14·6 2·8
27	2 51·8	2 52·2	2 43·9	2·7 0·5	8·7 1·7	14·7 2·8
28	2 52·0	2 52·5	2 44·2	2·8 0·5	8·8 1·7	14·8 2·8
29	2 52·3	2 52·7	2 44·4	2·9 0·6	8·9 1·7	14·9 2·9
30	2 52·5	2 53·0	2 44·6	3·0 0·6	9·0 1·7	15·0 2·9
31	2 52·8	2 53·2	2 44·9	3·1 0·6	9·1 1·7	15·1 2·9
32	2 53·0	2 53·5	2 45·1	3·2 0·6	9·2 1·8	15·2 2·9
33	2 53·3	2 53·7	2 45·4	3·3 0·6	9·3 1·8	15·3 2·9
34	2 53·5	2 54·0	2 45·6	3·4 0·7	9·4 1·8	15·4 3·0
35	2 53·8	2 54·2	2 45·8	3·5 0·7	9·5 1·8	15·5 3·0
36	2 54·0	2 54·5	2 46·1	3·6 0·7	9·6 1·8	15·6 3·0
37	2 54·3	2 54·7	2 46·3	3·7 0·7	9·7 1·9	15·7 3·0
38	2 54·5	2 55·0	2 46·6	3·8 0·7	9·8 1·9	15·8 3·0
39	2 54·8	2 55·2	2 46·8	3·9 0·7	9·9 1·9	15·9 3·0
40	2 55·0	2 55·5	2 47·0	4·0 0·8	10·0 1·9	16·0 3·1
41	2 55·3	2 55·7	2 47·3	4·1 0·8	10·1 1·9	16·1 3·1
42	2 55·5	2 56·0	2 47·5	4·2 0·8	10·2 2·0	16·2 3·1
43	2 55·8	2 56·2	2 47·7	4·3 0·8	10·3 2·0	16·3 3·1
44	2 56·0	2 56·5	2 48·0	4·4 0·8	10·4 2·0	16·4 3·1
45	2 56·3	2 56·7	2 48·2	4·5 0·9	10·5 2·0	16·5 3·2
46	2 56·5	2 57·0	2 48·5	4·6 0·9	10·6 2·0	16·6 3·2
47	2 56·8	2 57·2	2 48·7	4·7 0·9	10·7 2·1	16·7 3·2
48	2 57·0	2 57·5	2 48·9	4·8 0·9	10·8 2·1	16·8 3·2
49	2 57·3	2 57·7	2 49·2	4·9 0·9	10·9 2·1	16·9 3·2
50	2 57·5	2 58·0	2 49·4	5·0 1·0	11·0 2·1	17·0 3·3
51	2 57·8	2 58·2	2 49·7	5·1 1·0	11·1 2·1	17·1 3·3
52	2 58·0	2 58·5	2 49·9	5·2 1·0	11·2 2·1	17·2 3·3
53	2 58·3	2 58·7	2 50·1	5·3 1·0	11·3 2·2	17·3 3·3
54	2 58·5	2 59·0	2 50·4	5·4 1·0	11·4 2·2	17·4 3·3
55	2 58·8	2 59·2	2 50·6	5·5 1·1	11·5 2·2	17·5 3·4
56	2 59·0	2 59·5	2 50·8	5·6 1·1	11·6 2·2	17·6 3·4
57	2 59·3	2 59·7	2 51·1	5·7 1·1	11·7 2·2	17·7 3·4
58	2 59·5	3 00·0	2 51·3	5·8 1·1	11·8 2·3	17·8 3·4
59	2 59·8	3 00·2	2 51·6	5·9 1·1	11·9 2·3	17·9 3·4
60	3 00·0	3 00·5	2 51·8	6·0 1·2	12·0 2·3	18·0 3·5

12ᵐ

12 (s)	SUN PLANETS	ARIES	MOON	v or Corrⁿ d	v or Corrⁿ d	v or Corrⁿ d
	° ′	° ′	° ′	′ ′	′ ′	′ ′
00	3 00·0	3 00·5	2 51·8	0·0 0·0	6·0 1·3	12·0 2·5
01	3 00·3	3 00·7	2 52·0	0·1 0·0	6·1 1·3	12·1 2·5
02	3 00·5	3 01·0	2 52·3	0·2 0·0	6·2 1·3	12·2 2·5
03	3 00·8	3 01·2	2 52·5	0·3 0·1	6·3 1·3	12·3 2·6
04	3 01·0	3 01·5	2 52·8	0·4 0·1	6·4 1·3	12·4 2·6
05	3 01·3	3 01·7	2 53·0	0·5 0·1	6·5 1·4	12·5 2·6
06	3 01·5	3 02·0	2 53·2	0·6 0·1	6·6 1·4	12·6 2·6
07	3 01·8	3 02·2	2 53·5	0·7 0·1	6·7 1·4	12·7 2·6
08	3 02·0	3 02·5	2 53·7	0·8 0·2	6·8 1·4	12·8 2·7
09	3 02·3	3 02·7	2 53·9	0·9 0·2	6·9 1·4	12·9 2·7
10	3 02·5	3 03·0	2 54·2	1·0 0·2	7·0 1·5	13·0 2·7
11	3 02·8	3 03·3	2 54·4	1·1 0·2	7·1 1·5	13·1 2·7
12	3 03·0	3 03·5	2 54·7	1·2 0·3	7·2 1·5	13·2 2·8
13	3 03·3	3 03·8	2 54·9	1·3 0·3	7·3 1·5	13·3 2·8
14	3 03·5	3 04·0	2 55·1	1·4 0·3	7·4 1·5	13·4 2·8
15	3 03·8	3 04·3	2 55·4	1·5 0·3	7·5 1·6	13·5 2·8
16	3 04·0	3 04·5	2 55·6	1·6 0·3	7·6 1·6	13·6 2·8
17	3 04·3	3 04·8	2 55·9	1·7 0·4	7·7 1·6	13·7 2·9
18	3 04·5	3 05·0	2 56·1	1·8 0·4	7·8 1·6	13·8 2·9
19	3 04·8	3 05·3	2 56·3	1·9 0·4	7·9 1·6	13·9 2·9
20	3 05·0	3 05·5	2 56·6	2·0 0·4	8·0 1·7	14·0 2·9
21	3 05·3	3 05·8	2 56·8	2·1 0·4	8·1 1·7	14·1 2·9
22	3 05·5	3 06·0	2 57·0	2·2 0·5	8·2 1·7	14·2 3·0
23	3 05·8	3 06·3	2 57·3	2·3 0·5	8·3 1·7	14·3 3·0
24	3 06·0	3 06·5	2 57·5	2·4 0·5	8·4 1·8	14·4 3·0
25	3 06·3	3 06·8	2 57·8	2·5 0·5	8·5 1·8	14·5 3·0
26	3 06·5	3 07·0	2 58·0	2·6 0·5	8·6 1·8	14·6 3·0
27	3 06·8	3 07·3	2 58·2	2·7 0·6	8·7 1·8	14·7 3·1
28	3 07·0	3 07·5	2 58·5	2·8 0·6	8·8 1·8	14·8 3·1
29	3 07·3	3 07·8	2 58·7	2·9 0·6	8·9 1·9	14·9 3·1
30	3 07·5	3 08·0	2 59·0	3·0 0·6	9·0 1·9	15·0 3·1
31	3 07·8	3 08·3	2 59·2	3·1 0·6	9·1 1·9	15·1 3·1
32	3 08·0	3 08·5	2 59·4	3·2 0·7	9·2 1·9	15·2 3·2
33	3 08·3	3 08·8	2 59·7	3·3 0·7	9·3 1·9	15·3 3·2
34	3 08·5	3 09·0	2 59·9	3·4 0·7	9·4 2·0	15·4 3·2
35	3 08·8	3 09·3	3 00·2	3·5 0·7	9·5 2·0	15·5 3·2
36	3 09·0	3 09·5	3 00·4	3·6 0·8	9·6 2·0	15·6 3·3
37	3 09·3	3 09·8	3 00·6	3·7 0·8	9·7 2·0	15·7 3·3
38	3 09·5	3 10·0	3 00·9	3·8 0·8	9·8 2·0	15·8 3·3
39	3 09·8	3 10·3	3 01·1	3·9 0·8	9·9 2·1	15·9 3·3
40	3 10·0	3 10·5	3 01·3	4·0 0·8	10·0 2·1	16·0 3·3
41	3 10·3	3 10·8	3 01·6	4·1 0·9	10·1 2·1	16·1 3·4
42	3 10·5	3 11·0	3 01·8	4·2 0·9	10·2 2·1	16·2 3·4
43	3 10·8	3 11·3	3 02·1	4·3 0·9	10·3 2·1	16·3 3·4
44	3 11·0	3 11·5	3 02·3	4·4 0·9	10·4 2·2	16·4 3·4
45	3 11·3	3 11·8	3 02·5	4·5 0·9	10·5 2·2	16·5 3·4
46	3 11·5	3 12·0	3 02·8	4·6 1·0	10·6 2·2	16·6 3·5
47	3 11·8	3 12·3	3 03·0	4·7 1·0	10·7 2·2	16·7 3·5
48	3 12·0	3 12·5	3 03·3	4·8 1·0	10·8 2·3	16·8 3·5
49	3 12·3	3 12·8	3 03·5	4·9 1·0	10·9 2·3	16·9 3·5
50	3 12·5	3 13·0	3 03·7	5·0 1·0	11·0 2·3	17·0 3·5
51	3 12·8	3 13·3	3 04·0	5·1 1·1	11·1 2·3	17·1 3·6
52	3 13·0	3 13·5	3 04·2	5·2 1·1	11·2 2·3	17·2 3·6
53	3 13·3	3 13·8	3 04·4	5·3 1·1	11·3 2·4	17·3 3·6
54	3 13·5	3 14·0	3 04·7	5·4 1·1	11·4 2·4	17·4 3·6
55	3 13·8	3 14·3	3 04·9	5·5 1·1	11·5 2·4	17·5 3·6
56	3 14·0	3 14·5	3 05·2	5·6 1·2	11·6 2·4	17·6 3·7
57	3 14·3	3 14·8	3 05·4	5·7 1·2	11·7 2·4	17·7 3·7
58	3 14·5	3 15·0	3 05·6	5·8 1·2	11·8 2·5	17·8 3·7
59	3 14·8	3 15·3	3 05·9	5·9 1·2	11·9 2·5	17·9 3·7
60	3 15·0	3 15·5	3 06·1	6·0 1·3	12·0 2·5	18·0 3·8

13ᵐ

13 (s)	SUN PLANETS	ARIES	MOON	v or Corrⁿ d	v or Corrⁿ d	v or Corrⁿ d
	° ′	° ′	° ′	′ ′	′ ′	′ ′
00	3 15·0	3 15·5	3 06·1	0·0 0·0	6·0 1·4	12·0 2·7
01	3 15·3	3 15·8	3 06·4	0·1 0·0	6·1 1·4	12·1 2·7
02	3 15·5	3 16·0	3 06·6	0·2 0·0	6·2 1·4	12·2 2·7
03	3 15·8	3 16·3	3 06·8	0·3 0·1	6·3 1·4	12·3 2·8
04	3 16·0	3 16·5	3 07·1	0·4 0·1	6·4 1·4	12·4 2·8
05	3 16·3	3 16·8	3 07·3	0·5 0·1	6·5 1·5	12·5 2·8
06	3 16·5	3 17·0	3 07·5	0·6 0·1	6·6 1·5	12·6 2·8
07	3 16·8	3 17·3	3 07·8	0·7 0·2	6·7 1·5	12·7 2·9
08	3 17·0	3 17·5	3 08·0	0·8 0·2	6·8 1·5	12·8 2·9
09	3 17·3	3 17·8	3 08·3	0·9 0·2	6·9 1·6	12·9 2·9
10	3 17·5	3 18·0	3 08·5	1·0 0·2	7·0 1·6	13·0 2·9
11	3 17·8	3 18·3	3 08·7	1·1 0·2	7·1 1·6	13·1 3·0
12	3 18·0	3 18·5	3 09·0	1·2 0·3	7·2 1·6	13·2 3·0
13	3 18·3	3 18·8	3 09·2	1·3 0·3	7·3 1·6	13·3 3·0
14	3 18·5	3 19·0	3 09·5	1·4 0·3	7·4 1·7	13·4 3·0
15	3 18·8	3 19·3	3 09·7	1·5 0·3	7·5 1·7	13·5 3·0
16	3 19·0	3 19·5	3 09·9	1·6 0·4	7·6 1·7	13·6 3·1
17	3 19·3	3 19·8	3 10·2	1·7 0·4	7·7 1·7	13·7 3·1
18	3 19·5	3 20·0	3 10·4	1·8 0·4	7·8 1·8	13·8 3·1
19	3 19·8	3 20·3	3 10·7	1·9 0·4	7·9 1·8	13·9 3·1
20	3 20·0	3 20·5	3 10·9	2·0 0·5	8·0 1·8	14·0 3·2
21	3 20·3	3 20·8	3 11·1	2·1 0·5	8·1 1·8	14·1 3·2
22	3 20·5	3 21·0	3 11·4	2·2 0·5	8·2 1·8	14·2 3·2
23	3 20·8	3 21·3	3 11·6	2·3 0·5	8·3 1·9	14·3 3·2
24	3 21·0	3 21·6	3 11·8	2·4 0·5	8·4 1·9	14·4 3·2
25	3 21·3	3 21·8	3 12·1	2·5 0·6	8·5 1·9	14·5 3·3
26	3 21·5	3 22·1	3 12·3	2·6 0·6	8·6 1·9	14·6 3·3
27	3 21·8	3 22·3	3 12·6	2·7 0·6	8·7 2·0	14·7 3·3
28	3 22·0	3 22·6	3 12·8	2·8 0·6	8·8 2·0	14·8 3·3
29	3 22·3	3 22·8	3 13·0	2·9 0·7	8·9 2·0	14·9 3·4
30	3 22·5	3 23·1	3 13·3	3·0 0·7	9·0 2·0	15·0 3·4
31	3 22·8	3 23·3	3 13·5	3·1 0·7	9·1 2·0	15·1 3·4
32	3 23·0	3 23·6	3 13·8	3·2 0·7	9·2 2·1	15·2 3·4
33	3 23·3	3 23·8	3 14·0	3·3 0·7	9·3 2·1	15·3 3·4
34	3 23·5	3 24·1	3 14·2	3·4 0·8	9·4 2·1	15·4 3·5
35	3 23·8	3 24·3	3 14·5	3·5 0·8	9·5 2·1	15·5 3·5
36	3 24·0	3 24·6	3 14·7	3·6 0·8	9·6 2·2	15·6 3·5
37	3 24·3	3 24·8	3 14·9	3·7 0·8	9·7 2·2	15·7 3·5
38	3 24·5	3 25·1	3 15·2	3·8 0·9	9·8 2·2	15·8 3·6
39	3 24·8	3 25·3	3 15·4	3·9 0·9	9·9 2·2	15·9 3·6
40	3 25·0	3 25·6	3 15·7	4·0 0·9	10·0 2·3	16·0 3·6
41	3 25·3	3 25·8	3 15·9	4·1 0·9	10·1 2·3	16·1 3·6
42	3 25·5	3 26·1	3 16·1	4·2 0·9	10·2 2·3	16·2 3·6
43	3 25·8	3 26·3	3 16·4	4·3 1·0	10·3 2·3	16·3 3·7
44	3 26·0	3 26·6	3 16·6	4·4 1·0	10·4 2·3	16·4 3·7
45	3 26·3	3 26·8	3 16·9	4·5 1·0	10·5 2·4	16·5 3·7
46	3 26·5	3 27·1	3 17·1	4·6 1·0	10·6 2·4	16·6 3·7
47	3 26·8	3 27·3	3 17·3	4·7 1·1	10·7 2·4	16·7 3·8
48	3 27·0	3 27·6	3 17·6	4·8 1·1	10·8 2·4	16·8 3·8
49	3 27·3	3 27·8	3 17·8	4·9 1·1	10·9 2·5	16·9 3·8
50	3 27·5	3 28·1	3 18·0	5·0 1·1	11·0 2·5	17·0 3·8
51	3 27·8	3 28·3	3 18·3	5·1 1·1	11·1 2·5	17·1 3·8
52	3 28·0	3 28·6	3 18·5	5·2 1·2	11·2 2·5	17·2 3·9
53	3 28·3	3 28·8	3 18·8	5·3 1·2	11·3 2·5	17·3 3·9
54	3 28·5	3 29·1	3 19·0	5·4 1·2	11·4 2·6	17·4 3·9
55	3 28·8	3 29·3	3 19·2	5·5 1·2	11·5 2·6	17·5 3·9
56	3 29·0	3 29·6	3 19·5	5·6 1·3	11·6 2·6	17·6 4·0
57	3 29·3	3 29·8	3 19·7	5·7 1·3	11·7 2·6	17·7 4·0
58	3 29·5	3 30·1	3 20·0	5·8 1·3	11·8 2·7	17·8 4·0
59	3 29·8	3 30·3	3 20·2	5·9 1·3	11·9 2·7	17·9 4·0
60	3 30·0	3 30·6	3 20·4	6·0 1·4	12·0 2·7	18·0 4·1

14	SUN PLANETS	ARIES	MOON	v or d Corrⁿ	v or d Corrⁿ	v or d Corrⁿ		15	SUN PLANETS	ARIES	MOON	v or d Corrⁿ	v or d Corrⁿ	v or d Corrⁿ
s	° ′	° ′	° ′	′ ′	′ ′	′ ′		s	° ′	° ′	° ′	′ ′	′ ′	′ ′
00	3 30·0	3 30·6	3 20·4	0·0 0·0	6·0 1·5	12·0 2·9		00	3 45·0	3 45·6	3 34·8	0·0 0·0	6·0 1·6	12·0 3·1
01	3 30·3	3 30·8	3 20·7	0·1 0·0	6·1 1·5	12·1 2·9		01	3 45·3	3 45·9	3 35·0	0·1 0·0	6·1 1·6	12·1 3·1
02	3 30·5	3 31·1	3 20·9	0·2 0·0	6·2 1·5	12·2 2·9		02	3 45·5	3 46·1	3 35·2	0·2 0·1	6·2 1·6	12·2 3·2
03	3 30·8	3 31·3	3 21·1	0·3 0·1	6·3 1·5	12·3 3·0		03	3 45·8	3 46·4	3 35·5	0·3 0·1	6·3 1·6	12·3 3·2
04	3 31·0	3 31·6	3 21·4	0·4 0·1	6·4 1·5	12·4 3·0		04	3 46·0	3 46·6	3 35·7	0·4 0·1	6·4 1·7	12·4 3·2
05	3 31·3	3 31·8	3 21·6	0·5 0·1	6·5 1·6	12·5 3·0		05	3 46·3	3 46·9	3 35·9	0·5 0·1	6·5 1·7	12·5 3·2
06	3 31·5	3 32·1	3 21·9	0·6 0·1	6·6 1·6	12·6 3·0		06	3 46·5	3 47·1	3 36·2	0·6 0·2	6·6 1·7	12·6 3·3
07	3 31·8	3 32·3	3 22·1	0·7 0·2	6·7 1·6	12·7 3·1		07	3 46·8	3 47·4	3 36·4	0·7 0·2	6·7 1·7	12·7 3·3
08	3 32·0	3 32·6	3 22·3	0·8 0·2	6·8 1·6	12·8 3·1		08	3 47·0	3 47·6	3 36·7	0·8 0·2	6·8 1·8	12·8 3·3
09	3 32·3	3 32·8	3 22·6	0·9 0·2	6·9 1·7	12·9 3·1		09	3 47·3	3 47·9	3 36·9	0·9 0·2	6·9 1·8	12·9 3·3
10	3 32·5	3 33·1	3 22·8	1·0 0·2	7·0 1·7	13·0 3·1		10	3 47·5	3 48·1	3 37·1	1·0 0·3	7·0 1·8	13·0 3·4
11	3 32·8	3 33·3	3 23·1	1·1 0·3	7·1 1·7	13·1 3·2		11	3 47·8	3 48·4	3 37·4	1·1 0·3	7·1 1·8	13·1 3·4
12	3 33·0	3 33·6	3 23·3	1·2 0·3	7·2 1·7	13·2 3·2		12	3 48·0	3 48·6	3 37·6	1·2 0·3	7·2 1·9	13·2 3·4
13	3 33·3	3 33·8	3 23·5	1·3 0·3	7·3 1·8	13·3 3·2		13	3 48·3	3 48·9	3 37·9	1·3 0·3	7·3 1·9	13·3 3·4
14	3 33·5	3 34·1	3 23·8	1·4 0·3	7·4 1·8	13·4 3·2		14	3 48·5	3 49·1	3 38·1	1·4 0·4	7·4 1·9	13·4 3·5
15	3 33·8	3 34·3	3 24·0	1·5 0·4	7·5 1·8	13·5 3·3		15	3 48·8	3 49·4	3 38·3	1·5 0·4	7·5 1·9	13·5 3·5
16	3 34·0	3 34·6	3 24·3	1·6 0·4	7·6 1·8	13·6 3·3		16	3 49·0	3 49·6	3 38·6	1·6 0·4	7·6 2·0	13·6 3·5
17	3 34·3	3 34·8	3 24·5	1·7 0·4	7·7 1·9	13·7 3·3		17	3 49·3	3 49·9	3 38·8	1·7 0·4	7·7 2·0	13·7 3·5
18	3 34·5	3 35·1	3 24·7	1·8 0·4	7·8 1·9	13·8 3·3		18	3 49·5	3 50·1	3 39·0	1·8 0·5	7·8 2·0	13·8 3·6
19	3 34·8	3 35·3	3 25·0	1·9 0·5	7·9 1·9	13·9 3·4		19	3 49·8	3 50·4	3 39·3	1·9 0·5	7·9 2·0	13·9 3·6
20	3 35·0	3 35·6	3 25·2	2·0 0·5	8·0 1·9	14·0 3·4		20	3 50·0	3 50·6	3 39·5	2·0 0·5	8·0 2·1	14·0 3·6
21	3 35·3	3 35·8	3 25·4	2·1 0·5	8·1 2·0	14·1 3·4		21	3 50·3	3 50·9	3 39·8	2·1 0·5	8·1 2·1	14·1 3·6
22	3 35·5	3 36·1	3 25·7	2·2 0·5	8·2 2·0	14·2 3·4		22	3 50·5	3 51·1	3 40·0	2·2 0·6	8·2 2·1	14·2 3·7
23	3 35·8	3 36·3	3 25·9	2·3 0·6	8·3 2·0	14·3 3·5		23	3 50·8	3 51·4	3 40·2	2·3 0·6	8·3 2·1	14·3 3·7
24	3 36·0	3 36·6	3 26·2	2·4 0·6	8·4 2·0	14·4 3·5		24	3 51·0	3 51·6	3 40·5	2·4 0·6	8·4 2·2	14·4 3·7
25	3 36·3	3 36·8	3 26·4	2·5 0·6	8·5 2·1	14·5 3·5		25	3 51·3	3 51·9	3 40·7	2·5 0·6	8·5 2·2	14·5 3·7
26	3 36·5	3 37·1	3 26·6	2·6 0·6	8·6 2·1	14·6 3·5		26	3 51·5	3 52·1	3 41·0	2·6 0·7	8·6 2·2	14·6 3·8
27	3 36·8	3 37·3	3 26·9	2·7 0·7	8·7 2·1	14·7 3·6		27	3 51·8	3 52·4	3 41·2	2·7 0·7	8·7 2·2	14·7 3·8
28	3 37·0	3 37·6	3 27·1	2·8 0·7	8·8 2·1	14·8 3·6		28	3 52·0	3 52·6	3 41·4	2·8 0·7	8·8 2·3	14·8 3·8
29	3 37·3	3 37·8	3 27·4	2·9 0·7	8·9 2·2	14·9 3·6		29	3 52·3	3 52·9	3 41·7	2·9 0·7	8·9 2·3	14·9 3·8
30	3 37·5	3 38·1	3 27·6	3·0 0·7	9·0 2·2	15·0 3·6		30	3 52·5	3 53·1	3 41·9	3·0 0·8	9·0 2·3	15·0 3·9
31	3 37·8	3 38·3	3 27·8	3·1 0·7	9·1 2·2	15·1 3·6		31	3 52·8	3 53·4	3 42·1	3·1 0·8	9·1 2·4	15·1 3·9
32	3 38·0	3 38·6	3 28·1	3·2 0·8	9·2 2·2	15·2 3·7		32	3 53·0	3 53·6	3 42·4	3·2 0·8	9·2 2·4	15·2 3·9
33	3 38·3	3 38·8	3 28·3	3·3 0·8	9·3 2·2	15·3 3·7		33	3 53·3	3 53·9	3 42·6	3·3 0·9	9·3 2·4	15·3 4·0
34	3 38·5	3 39·1	3 28·5	3·4 0·8	9·4 2·3	15·4 3·7		34	3 53·5	3 54·1	3 42·9	3·4 0·9	9·4 2·4	15·4 4·0
35	3 38·8	3 39·3	3 28·8	3·5 0·8	9·5 2·3	15·5 3·7		35	3 53·8	3 54·4	3 43·1	3·5 0·9	9·5 2·5	15·5 4·0
36	3 39·0	3 39·6	3 29·0	3·6 0·9	9·6 2·3	15·6 3·8		36	3 54·0	3 54·6	3 43·3	3·6 0·9	9·6 2·5	15·6 4·0
37	3 39·3	3 39·9	3 29·3	3·7 0·9	9·7 2·3	15·7 3·8		37	3 54·3	3 54·9	3 43·6	3·7 1·0	9·7 2·5	15·7 4·1
38	3 39·5	3 40·1	3 29·5	3·8 0·9	9·8 2·4	15·8 3·8		38	3 54·5	3 55·1	3 43·8	3·8 1·0	9·8 2·5	15·8 4·1
39	3 39·8	3 40·4	3 29·7	3·9 0·9	9·9 2·4	15·9 3·8		39	3 54·8	3 55·4	3 44·1	3·9 1·0	9·9 2·6	15·9 4·1
40	3 40·0	3 40·6	3 30·0	4·0 1·0	10·0 2·4	16·0 3·9		40	3 55·0	3 55·6	3 44·3	4·0 1·0	10·0 2·6	16·0 4·1
41	3 40·3	3 40·9	3 30·2	4·1 1·0	10·1 2·4	16·1 3·9		41	3 55·3	3 55·9	3 44·5	4·1 1·1	10·1 2·6	16·1 4·2
42	3 40·5	3 41·1	3 30·5	4·2 1·0	10·2 2·5	16·2 3·9		42	3 55·5	3 56·1	3 44·8	4·2 1·1	10·2 2·6	16·2 4·2
43	3 40·8	3 41·4	3 30·7	4·3 1·0	10·3 2·5	16·3 3·9		43	3 55·8	3 56·4	3 45·0	4·3 1·1	10·3 2·7	16·3 4·2
44	3 41·0	3 41·6	3 30·9	4·4 1·1	10·4 2·5	16·4 4·0		44	3 56·0	3 56·6	3 45·2	4·4 1·1	10·4 2·7	16·4 4·2
45	3 41·3	3 41·9	3 31·2	4·5 1·1	10·5 2·5	16·5 4·0		45	3 56·3	3 56·9	3 45·5	4·5 1·2	10·5 2·7	16·5 4·3
46	3 41·5	3 42·1	3 31·4	4·6 1·1	10·6 2·6	16·6 4·0		46	3 56·5	3 57·1	3 45·7	4·6 1·2	10·6 2·7	16·6 4·3
47	3 41·8	3 42·4	3 31·6	4·7 1·1	10·7 2·6	16·7 4·0		47	3 56·8	3 57·4	3 46·0	4·7 1·2	10·7 2·8	16·7 4·3
48	3 42·0	3 42·6	3 31·9	4·8 1·2	10·8 2·6	16·8 4·1		48	3 57·0	3 57·6	3 46·2	4·8 1·2	10·8 2·8	16·8 4·3
49	3 42·3	3 42·9	3 32·1	4·9 1·2	10·9 2·6	16·9 4·1		49	3 57·3	3 57·9	3 46·4	4·9 1·3	10·9 2·8	16·9 4·4
50	3 42·5	3 43·1	3 32·4	5·0 1·2	11·0 2·7	17·0 4·1		50	3 57·5	3 58·2	3 46·7	5·0 1·3	11·0 2·8	17·0 4·4
51	3 42·8	3 43·4	3 32·6	5·1 1·2	11·1 2·7	17·1 4·1		51	3 57·8	3 58·4	3 46·9	5·1 1·3	11·1 2·9	17·1 4·4
52	3 43·0	3 43·6	3 32·8	5·2 1·3	11·2 2·7	17·2 4·2		52	3 58·0	3 58·7	3 47·2	5·2 1·3	11·2 2·9	17·2 4·4
53	3 43·3	3 43·9	3 33·1	5·3 1·3	11·3 2·7	17·3 4·2		53	3 58·3	3 58·9	3 47·4	5·3 1·4	11·3 2·9	17·3 4·5
54	3 43·5	3 44·1	3 33·3	5·4 1·3	11·4 2·8	17·4 4·2		54	3 58·5	3 59·2	3 47·6	5·4 1·4	11·4 2·9	17·4 4·5
55	3 43·8	3 44·4	3 33·6	5·5 1·3	11·5 2·8	17·5 4·2		55	3 58·8	3 59·4	3 47·9	5·5 1·4	11·5 3·0	17·5 4·5
56	3 44·0	3 44·6	3 33·8	5·6 1·4	11·6 2·8	17·6 4·3		56	3 59·0	3 59·7	3 48·1	5·6 1·4	11·6 3·0	17·6 4·5
57	3 44·3	3 44·9	3 34·0	5·7 1·4	11·7 2·8	17·7 4·3		57	3 59·3	3 59·9	3 48·4	5·7 1·5	11·7 3·0	17·7 4·6
58	3 44·5	3 45·1	3 34·3	5·8 1·4	11·8 2·9	17·8 4·3		58	3 59·5	4 00·2	3 48·6	5·8 1·5	11·8 3·0	17·8 4·6
59	3 44·8	3 45·4	3 34·5	5·9 1·4	11·9 2·9	17·9 4·3		59	3 59·8	4 00·4	3 48·8	5·9 1·5	11·9 3·1	17·9 4·6
60	3 45·0	3 45·6	3 34·8	6·0 1·5	12·0 2·9	18·0 4·4		60	4 00·0	4 00·7	3 49·1	6·0 1·6	12·0 3·1	18·0 4·7

16ᵐ

m 16 s	SUN PLANETS ° ′	ARIES ° ′	MOON ° ′	v or d ′	Corrⁿ ′	v or d ′	Corrⁿ ′	v or d ′	Corrⁿ ′
00	4 00·0	4 00·7	3 49·1	0·0	0·0	6·0	1·7	12·0	3·3
01	4 00·3	4 00·9	3 49·3	0·1	0·0	6·1	1·7	12·1	3·3
02	4 00·5	4 01·2	3 49·5	0·2	0·1	6·2	1·7	12·2	3·4
03	4 00·8	4 01·4	3 49·8	0·3	0·1	6·3	1·7	12·3	3·4
04	4 01·0	4 01·7	3 50·0	0·4	0·1	6·4	1·8	12·4	3·4
05	4 01·3	4 01·9	3 50·3	0·5	0·1	6·5	1·8	12·5	3·4
06	4 01·5	4 02·2	3 50·5	0·6	0·2	6·6	1·8	12·6	3·5
07	4 01·8	4 02·4	3 50·7	0·7	0·2	6·7	1·8	12·7	3·5
08	4 02·0	4 02·7	3 51·0	0·8	0·2	6·8	1·9	12·8	3·5
09	4 02·3	4 02·9	3 51·2	0·9	0·2	6·9	1·9	12·9	3·5
10	4 02·5	4 03·2	3 51·5	1·0	0·3	7·0	1·9	13·0	3·6
11	4 02·8	4 03·4	3 51·7	1·1	0·3	7·1	2·0	13·1	3·6
12	4 03·0	4 03·7	3 51·9	1·2	0·3	7·2	2·0	13·2	3·6
13	4 03·3	4 03·9	3 52·2	1·3	0·4	7·3	2·0	13·3	3·7
14	4 03·5	4 04·2	3 52·4	1·4	0·4	7·4	2·0	13·4	3·7
15	4 03·8	4 04·4	3 52·6	1·5	0·4	7·5	2·1	13·5	3·7
16	4 04·0	4 04·7	3 52·9	1·6	0·4	7·6	2·1	13·6	3·7
17	4 04·3	4 04·9	3 53·1	1·7	0·5	7·7	2·1	13·7	3·8
18	4 04·5	4 05·2	3 53·4	1·8	0·5	7·8	2·1	13·8	3·8
19	4 04·8	4 05·4	3 53·6	1·9	0·5	7·9	2·2	13·9	3·8
20	4 05·0	4 05·7	3 53·8	2·0	0·6	8·0	2·2	14·0	3·9
21	4 05·3	4 05·9	3 54·1	2·1	0·6	8·1	2·2	14·1	3·9
22	4 05·5	4 06·2	3 54·3	2·2	0·6	8·2	2·3	14·2	3·9
23	4 05·8	4 06·4	3 54·6	2·3	0·6	8·3	2·3	14·3	3·9
24	4 06·0	4 06·7	3 54·8	2·4	0·7	8·4	2·3	14·4	4·0
25	4 06·3	4 06·9	3 55·0	2·5	0·7	8·5	2·3	14·5	4·0
26	4 06·5	4 07·2	3 55·3	2·6	0·7	8·6	2·4	14·6	4·0
27	4 06·8	4 07·4	3 55·5	2·7	0·7	8·7	2·4	14·7	4·0
28	4 07·0	4 07·7	3 55·7	2·8	0·8	8·8	2·4	14·8	4·1
29	4 07·3	4 07·9	3 56·0	2·9	0·8	8·9	2·4	14·9	4·1
30	4 07·5	4 08·2	3 56·2	3·0	0·8	9·0	2·5	15·0	4·1
31	4 07·8	4 08·4	3 56·5	3·1	0·9	9·1	2·5	15·1	4·2
32	4 08·0	4 08·7	3 56·7	3·2	0·9	9·2	2·5	15·2	4·2
33	4 08·3	4 08·9	3 56·9	3·3	0·9	9·3	2·6	15·3	4·2
34	4 08·5	4 09·2	3 57·2	3·4	0·9	9·4	2·6	15·4	4·2
35	4 08·8	4 09·4	3 57·4	3·5	1·0	9·5	2·6	15·5	4·3
36	4 09·0	4 09·7	3 57·7	3·6	1·0	9·6	2·6	15·6	4·3
37	4 09·3	4 09·9	3 57·9	3·7	1·0	9·7	2·7	15·7	4·3
38	4 09·5	4 10·2	3 58·1	3·8	1·0	9·8	2·7	15·8	4·3
39	4 09·8	4 10·4	3 58·4	3·9	1·1	9·9	2·7	15·9	4·4
40	4 10·0	4 10·7	3 58·6	4·0	1·1	10·0	2·8	16·0	4·4
41	4 10·3	4 10·9	3 58·8	4·1	1·1	10·1	2·8	16·1	4·4
42	4 10·5	4 11·2	3 59·1	4·2	1·2	10·2	2·8	16·2	4·5
43	4 10·8	4 11·4	3 59·3	4·3	1·2	10·3	2·8	16·3	4·5
44	4 11·0	4 11·7	3 59·6	4·4	1·2	10·4	2·9	16·4	4·5
45	4 11·3	4 11·9	3 59·8	4·5	1·2	10·5	2·9	16·5	4·5
46	4 11·5	4 12·2	4 00·0	4·6	1·3	10·6	2·9	16·6	4·6
47	4 11·8	4 12·4	4 00·3	4·7	1·3	10·7	2·9	16·7	4·6
48	4 12·0	4 12·7	4 00·5	4·8	1·3	10·8	3·0	16·8	4·6
49	4 12·3	4 12·9	4 00·8	4·9	1·3	10·9	3·0	16·9	4·6
50	4 12·5	4 13·2	4 01·0	5·0	1·4	11·0	3·0	17·0	4·7
51	4 12·8	4 13·4	4 01·2	5·1	1·4	11·1	3·1	17·1	4·7
52	4 13·0	4 13·7	4 01·5	5·2	1·4	11·2	3·1	17·2	4·7
53	4 13·3	4 13·9	4 01·7	5·3	1·5	11·3	3·1	17·3	4·8
54	4 13·5	4 14·2	4 02·0	5·4	1·5	11·4	3·1	17·4	4·8
55	4 13·8	4 14·4	4 02·2	5·5	1·5	11·5	3·2	17·5	4·8
56	4 14·0	4 14·7	4 02·4	5·6	1·5	11·6	3·2	17·6	4·8
57	4 14·3	4 14·9	4 02·7	5·7	1·6	11·7	3·2	17·7	4·9
58	4 14·5	4 15·2	4 02·9	5·8	1·6	11·8	3·2	17·8	4·9
59	4 14·8	4 15·4	4 03·1	5·9	1·6	11·9	3·3	17·9	4·9
60	4 15·0	4 15·7	4 03·4	6·0	1·7	12·0	3·3	18·0	5·0

17ᵐ

m 17 s	SUN PLANETS ° ′	ARIES ° ′	MOON ° ′	v or d ′	Corrⁿ ′	v or d ′	Corrⁿ ′	v or d ′	Corrⁿ ′
00	4 15·0	4 15·7	4 03·4	0·0	0·0	6·0	1·8	12·0	3·5
01	4 15·3	4 15·9	4 03·6	0·1	0·0	6·1	1·8	12·1	3·5
02	4 15·5	4 16·2	4 03·9	0·2	0·1	6·2	1·8	12·2	3·6
03	4 15·8	4 16·5	4 04·1	0·3	0·1	6·3	1·8	12·3	3·6
04	4 16·0	4 16·7	4 04·3	0·4	0·1	6·4	1·9	12·4	3·6
05	4 16·3	4 17·0	4 04·6	0·5	0·1	6·5	1·9	12·5	3·6
06	4 16·5	4 17·2	4 04·8	0·6	0·2	6·6	1·9	12·6	3·7
07	4 16·8	4 17·5	4 05·1	0·7	0·2	6·7	2·0	12·7	3·7
08	4 17·0	4 17·7	4 05·3	0·8	0·2	6·8	2·0	12·8	3·7
09	4 17·3	4 18·0	4 05·5	0·9	0·3	6·9	2·0	12·9	3·8
10	4 17·5	4 18·2	4 05·8	1·0	0·3	7·0	2·0	13·0	3·8
11	4 17·8	4 18·5	4 06·0	1·1	0·3	7·1	2·1	13·1	3·8
12	4 18·0	4 18·7	4 06·2	1·2	0·4	7·2	2·1	13·2	3·9
13	4 18·3	4 19·0	4 06·5	1·3	0·4	7·3	2·1	13·3	3·9
14	4 18·5	4 19·2	4 06·7	1·4	0·4	7·4	2·2	13·4	3·9
15	4 18·8	4 19·5	4 07·0	1·5	0·4	7·5	2·2	13·5	3·9
16	4 19·0	4 19·7	4 07·2	1·6	0·5	7·6	2·2	13·6	4·0
17	4 19·3	4 20·0	4 07·4	1·7	0·5	7·7	2·2	13·7	4·0
18	4 19·5	4 20·2	4 07·7	1·8	0·5	7·8	2·3	13·8	4·0
19	4 19·8	4 20·5	4 07·9	1·9	0·6	7·9	2·3	13·9	4·1
20	4 20·0	4 20·7	4 08·2	2·0	0·6	8·0	2·3	14·0	4·1
21	4 20·3	4 21·0	4 08·4	2·1	0·6	8·1	2·4	14·1	4·1
22	4 20·5	4 21·2	4 08·6	2·2	0·6	8·2	2·4	14·2	4·1
23	4 20·8	4 21·5	4 08·9	2·3	0·7	8·3	2·4	14·3	4·2
24	4 21·0	4 21·7	4 09·1	2·4	0·7	8·4	2·5	14·4	4·2
25	4 21·3	4 22·0	4 09·3	2·5	0·7	8·5	2·5	14·5	4·2
26	4 21·5	4 22·2	4 09·6	2·6	0·8	8·6	2·5	14·6	4·3
27	4 21·8	4 22·5	4 09·8	2·7	0·8	8·7	2·5	14·7	4·3
28	4 22·0	4 22·7	4 10·1	2·8	0·8	8·8	2·6	14·8	4·3
29	4 22·3	4 23·0	4 10·3	2·9	0·8	8·9	2·6	14·9	4·3
30	4 22·5	4 23·2	4 10·5	3·0	0·9	9·0	2·6	15·0	4·4
31	4 22·8	4 23·5	4 10·8	3·1	0·9	9·1	2·7	15·1	4·4
32	4 23·0	4 23·7	4 11·0	3·2	0·9	9·2	2·7	15·2	4·4
33	4 23·3	4 24·0	4 11·3	3·3	1·0	9·3	2·7	15·3	4·5
34	4 23·5	4 24·2	4 11·5	3·4	1·0	9·4	2·7	15·4	4·5
35	4 23·8	4 24·5	4 11·7	3·5	1·0	9·5	2·8	15·5	4·5
36	4 24·0	4 24·7	4 12·0	3·6	1·1	9·6	2·8	15·6	4·6
37	4 24·3	4 25·0	4 12·2	3·7	1·1	9·7	2·8	15·7	4·6
38	4 24·5	4 25·2	4 12·5	3·8	1·1	9·8	2·9	15·8	4·6
39	4 24·8	4 25·5	4 12·7	3·9	1·1	9·9	2·9	15·9	4·6
40	4 25·0	4 25·7	4 12·9	4·0	1·2	10·0	2·9	16·0	4·7
41	4 25·3	4 26·0	4 13·2	4·1	1·2	10·1	2·9	16·1	4·7
42	4 25·5	4 26·2	4 13·4	4·2	1·2	10·2	3·0	16·2	4·7
43	4 25·8	4 26·5	4 13·6	4·3	1·3	10·3	3·0	16·3	4·8
44	4 26·0	4 26·7	4 13·9	4·4	1·3	10·4	3·0	16·4	4·8
45	4 26·3	4 27·0	4 14·1	4·5	1·3	10·5	3·1	16·5	4·8
46	4 26·5	4 27·2	4 14·4	4·6	1·3	10·6	3·1	16·6	4·8
47	4 26·8	4 27·5	4 14·6	4·7	1·4	10·7	3·1	16·7	4·9
48	4 27·0	4 27·7	4 14·8	4·8	1·4	10·8	3·2	16·8	4·9
49	4 27·3	4 28·0	4 15·1	4·9	1·4	10·9	3·2	16·9	4·9
50	4 27·5	4 28·2	4 15·3	5·0	1·5	11·0	3·2	17·0	5·0
51	4 27·8	4 28·5	4 15·6	5·1	1·5	11·1	3·2	17·1	5·0
52	4 28·0	4 28·7	4 15·8	5·2	1·5	11·2	3·3	17·2	5·0
53	4 28·3	4 29·0	4 16·0	5·3	1·5	11·3	3·3	17·3	5·0
54	4 28·5	4 29·2	4 16·3	5·4	1·6	11·4	3·3	17·4	5·1
55	4 28·8	4 29·5	4 16·5	5·5	1·6	11·5	3·4	17·5	5·1
56	4 29·0	4 29·7	4 16·7	5·6	1·6	11·6	3·4	17·6	5·1
57	4 29·3	4 30·0	4 17·0	5·7	1·7	11·7	3·4	17·7	5·2
58	4 29·5	4 30·2	4 17·2	5·8	1·7	11·8	3·4	17·8	5·2
59	4 29·8	4 30·5	4 17·5	5·9	1·7	11·9	3·5	17·9	5·2
60	4 30·0	4 30·7	4 17·7	6·0	1·8	12·0	3·5	18·0	5·3

18	SUN PLANETS	ARIES	MOON	v or d Corrⁿ	v or d Corrⁿ	v or d Corrⁿ	19	SUN PLANETS	ARIES	MOON	v or d Corrⁿ	v or d Corrⁿ	v or d Corrⁿ
s	° ′	° ′	° ′	′ ′	′ ′	′ ′	s	° ′	° ′	° ′	′ ′	′ ′	′ ′
00	4 30·0	4 30·7	4 17·7	0·0 0·0	6·0 1·9	12·0 3·7	00	4 45·0	4 45·8	4 32·0	0·0 0·0	6·0 2·0	12·0 3·9
01	4 30·3	4 31·0	4 17·9	0·1 0·0	6·1 1·9	12·1 3·7	01	4 45·3	4 46·0	4 32·3	0·1 0·0	6·1 2·0	12·1 3·9
02	4 30·5	4 31·2	4 18·2	0·2 0·1	6·2 1·9	12·2 3·8	02	4 45·5	4 46·3	4 32·5	0·2 0·1	6·2 2·0	12·2 4·0
03	4 30·8	4 31·5	4 18·4	0·3 0·1	6·3 1·9	12·3 3·8	03	4 45·8	4 46·5	4 32·7	0·3 0·1	6·3 2·0	12·3 4·0
04	4 31·0	4 31·7	4 18·7	0·4 0·1	6·4 2·0	12·4 3·8	04	4 46·0	4 46·8	4 33·0	0·4 0·1	6·4 2·1	12·4 4·0
05	4 31·3	4 32·0	4 18·9	0·5 0·2	6·5 2·0	12·5 3·9	05	4 46·3	4 47·0	4 33·2	0·5 0·2	6·5 2·1	12·5 4·1
06	4 31·5	4 32·2	4 19·1	0·6 0·2	6·6 2·0	12·6 3·9	06	4 46·5	4 47·3	4 33·4	0·6 0·2	6·6 2·1	12·6 4·1
07	4 31·8	4 32·5	4 19·4	0·7 0·2	6·7 2·1	12·7 3·9	07	4 46·8	4 47·5	4 33·7	0·7 0·2	6·7 2·2	12·7 4·1
08	4 32·0	4 32·7	4 19·6	0·8 0·2	6·8 2·1	12·8 3·9	08	4 47·0	4 47·8	4 33·9	0·8 0·3	6·8 2·2	12·8 4·2
09	4 32·3	4 33·0	4 19·8	0·9 0·3	6·9 2·1	12·9 4·0	09	4 47·3	4 48·0	4 34·2	0·9 0·3	6·9 2·2	12·9 4·2
10	4 32·5	4 33·2	4 20·1	1·0 0·3	7·0 2·2	13·0 4·0	10	4 47·5	4 48·3	4 34·4	1·0 0·3	7·0 2·3	13·0 4·2
11	4 32·8	4 33·5	4 20·3	1·1 0·3	7·1 2·2	13·1 4·0	11	4 47·8	4 48·5	4 34·6	1·1 0·4	7·1 2·3	13·1 4·3
12	4 33·0	4 33·7	4 20·6	1·2 0·4	7·2 2·2	13·2 4·1	12	4 48·0	4 48·8	4 34·9	1·2 0·4	7·2 2·3	13·2 4·3
13	4 33·3	4 34·0	4 20·8	1·3 0·4	7·3 2·3	13·3 4·1	13	4 48·3	4 49·0	4 35·1	1·3 0·4	7·3 2·4	13·3 4·3
14	4 33·5	4 34·2	4 21·0	1·4 0·4	7·4 2·3	13·4 4·1	14	4 48·5	4 49·3	4 35·4	1·4 0·5	7·4 2·4	13·4 4·4
15	4 33·8	4 34·5	4 21·3	1·5 0·5	7·5 2·3	13·5 4·2	15	4 48·8	4 49·5	4 35·6	1·5 0·5	7·5 2·4	13·5 4·4
16	4 34·0	4 34·8	4 21·5	1·6 0·5	7·6 2·3	13·6 4·2	16	4 49·0	4 49·8	4 35·8	1·6 0·5	7·6 2·5	13·6 4·4
17	4 34·3	4 35·0	4 21·8	1·7 0·5	7·7 2·4	13·7 4·2	17	4 49·3	4 50·0	4 36·1	1·7 0·6	7·7 2·5	13·7 4·5
18	4 34·5	4 35·3	4 22·0	1·8 0·6	7·8 2·4	13·8 4·3	18	4 49·5	4 50·3	4 36·3	1·8 0·6	7·8 2·5	13·8 4·5
19	4 34·8	4 35·5	4 22·2	1·9 0·6	7·9 2·4	13·9 4·3	19	4 49·8	4 50·5	4 36·6	1·9 0·6	7·9 2·6	13·9 4·5
20	4 35·0	4 35·8	4 22·5	2·0 0·6	8·0 2·5	14·0 4·3	20	4 50·0	4 50·8	4 36·8	2·0 0·7	8·0 2·6	14·0 4·6
21	4 35·3	4 36·0	4 22·7	2·1 0·6	8·1 2·5	14·1 4·3	21	4 50·3	4 51·0	4 37·0	2·1 0·7	8·1 2·6	14·1 4·6
22	4 35·5	4 36·3	4 22·9	2·2 0·7	8·2 2·5	14·2 4·4	22	4 50·5	4 51·3	4 37·3	2·2 0·7	8·2 2·7	14·2 4·6
23	4 35·8	4 36·5	4 23·2	2·3 0·7	8·3 2·6	14·3 4·4	23	4 50·8	4 51·5	4 37·5	2·3 0·7	8·3 2·7	14·3 4·6
24	4 36·0	4 36·8	4 23·4	2·4 0·7	8·4 2·6	14·4 4·4	24	4 51·0	4 51·8	4 37·7	2·4 0·8	8·4 2·7	14·4 4·7
25	4 36·3	4 37·0	4 23·7	2·5 0·8	8·5 2·6	14·5 4·5	25	4 51·3	4 52·0	4 38·0	2·5 0·8	8·5 2·8	14·5 4·7
26	4 36·5	4 37·3	4 23·9	2·6 0·8	8·6 2·7	14·6 4·5	26	4 51·5	4 52·3	4 38·2	2·6 0·8	8·6 2·8	14·6 4·7
27	4 36·8	4 37·5	4 24·1	2·7 0·8	8·7 2·7	14·7 4·5	27	4 51·8	4 52·5	4 38·5	2·7 0·9	8·7 2·8	14·7 4·8
28	4 37·0	4 37·8	4 24·4	2·8 0·9	8·8 2·7	14·8 4·6	28	4 52·0	4 52·8	4 38·7	2·8 0·9	8·8 2·9	14·8 4·8
29	4 37·3	4 38·0	4 24·6	2·9 0·9	8·9 2·7	14·9 4·6	29	4 52·3	4 53·1	4 38·9	2·9 0·9	8·9 2·9	14·9 4·8
30	4 37·5	4 38·3	4 24·9	3·0 0·9	9·0 2·8	15·0 4·6	30	4 52·5	4 53·3	4 39·2	3·0 1·0	9·0 2·9	15·0 4·9
31	4 37·8	4 38·5	4 25·1	3·1 1·0	9·1 2·8	15·1 4·7	31	4 52·8	4 53·6	4 39·4	3·1 1·0	9·1 3·0	15·1 4·9
32	4 38·0	4 38·8	4 25·3	3·2 1·0	9·2 2·8	15·2 4·7	32	4 53·0	4 53·8	4 39·7	3·2 1·0	9·2 3·0	15·2 4·9
33	4 38·3	4 39·0	4 25·6	3·3 1·0	9·3 2·9	15·3 4·7	33	4 53·3	4 54·1	4 39·9	3·3 1·1	9·3 3·0	15·3 5·0
34	4 38·5	4 39·3	4 25·8	3·4 1·0	9·4 2·9	15·4 4·7	34	4 53·5	4 54·3	4 40·1	3·4 1·1	9·4 3·1	15·4 5·0
35	4 38·8	4 39·5	4 26·1	3·5 1·1	9·5 2·9	15·5 4·8	35	4 53·8	4 54·6	4 40·4	3·5 1·1	9·5 3·1	15·5 5·0
36	4 39·0	4 39·8	4 26·3	3·6 1·1	9·6 3·0	15·6 4·8	36	4 54·0	4 54·8	4 40·6	3·6 1·2	9·6 3·1	15·6 5·1
37	4 39·3	4 40·0	4 26·5	3·7 1·1	9·7 3·0	15·7 4·8	37	4 54·3	4 55·1	4 40·8	3·7 1·2	9·7 3·2	15·7 5·1
38	4 39·5	4 40·3	4 26·8	3·8 1·2	9·8 3·0	15·8 4·9	38	4 54·5	4 55·3	4 41·1	3·8 1·2	9·8 3·2	15·8 5·1
39	4 39·8	4 40·5	4 27·0	3·9 1·2	9·9 3·1	15·9 4·9	39	4 54·8	4 55·6	4 41·3	3·9 1·3	9·9 3·2	15·9 5·2
40	4 40·0	4 40·8	4 27·2	4·0 1·2	10·0 3·1	16·0 4·9	40	4 55·0	4 55·8	4 41·6	4·0 1·3	10·0 3·3	16·0 5·2
41	4 40·3	4 41·0	4 27·5	4·1 1·3	10·1 3·1	16·1 5·0	41	4 55·3	4 56·1	4 41·8	4·1 1·3	10·1 3·3	16·1 5·2
42	4 40·5	4 41·3	4 27·7	4·2 1·3	10·2 3·1	16·2 5·0	42	4 55·5	4 56·3	4 42·0	4·2 1·4	10·2 3·3	16·2 5·3
43	4 40·8	4 41·5	4 28·0	4·3 1·3	10·3 3·2	16·3 5·0	43	4 55·8	4 56·6	4 42·3	4·3 1·4	10·3 3·3	16·3 5·3
44	4 41·0	4 41·8	4 28·2	4·4 1·4	10·4 3·2	16·4 5·1	44	4 56·0	4 56·8	4 42·5	4·4 1·4	10·4 3·4	16·4 5·3
45	4 41·3	4 42·0	4 28·4	4·5 1·4	10·5 3·2	16·5 5·1	45	4 56·3	4 57·1	4 42·8	4·5 1·5	10·5 3·4	16·5 5·4
46	4 41·5	4 42·3	4 28·7	4·6 1·4	10·6 3·3	16·6 5·1	46	4 56·5	4 57·3	4 43·0	4·6 1·5	10·6 3·4	16·6 5·4
47	4 41·8	4 42·5	4 28·9	4·7 1·4	10·7 3·3	16·7 5·1	47	4 56·8	4 57·6	4 43·2	4·7 1·5	10·7 3·5	16·7 5·4
48	4 42·0	4 42·8	4 29·2	4·8 1·5	10·8 3·3	16·8 5·2	48	4 57·0	4 57·8	4 43·5	4·8 1·6	10·8 3·5	16·8 5·5
49	4 42·3	4 43·0	4 29·4	4·9 1·5	10·9 3·4	16·9 5·2	49	4 57·3	4 58·1	4 43·7	4·9 1·6	10·9 3·5	16·9 5·5
50	4 42·5	4 43·3	4 29·6	5·0 1·5	11·0 3·4	17·0 5·2	50	4 57·5	4 58·3	4 43·9	5·0 1·6	11·0 3·6	17·0 5·5
51	4 42·8	4 43·5	4 29·9	5·1 1·6	11·1 3·4	17·1 5·3	51	4 57·8	4 58·6	4 44·2	5·1 1·7	11·1 3·6	17·1 5·6
52	4 43·0	4 43·8	4 30·1	5·2 1·6	11·2 3·5	17·2 5·3	52	4 58·0	4 58·8	4 44·4	5·2 1·7	11·2 3·6	17·2 5·6
53	4 43·3	4 44·0	4 30·3	5·3 1·6	11·3 3·5	17·3 5·3	53	4 58·3	4 59·1	4 44·7	5·3 1·7	11·3 3·7	17·3 5·6
54	4 43·5	4 44·3	4 30·6	5·4 1·7	11·4 3·5	17·4 5·4	54	4 58·5	4 59·3	4 44·9	5·4 1·8	11·4 3·7	17·4 5·7
55	4 43·8	4 44·5	4 30·8	5·5 1·7	11·5 3·5	17·5 5·4	55	4 58·8	4 59·6	4 45·1	5·5 1·8	11·5 3·7	17·5 5·7
56	4 44·0	4 44·8	4 31·1	5·6 1·7	11·6 3·6	17·6 5·4	56	4 59·0	4 59·8	4 45·4	5·6 1·8	11·6 3·8	17·6 5·7
57	4 44·3	4 45·0	4 31·3	5·7 1·8	11·7 3·6	17·7 5·5	57	4 59·3	5 00·1	4 45·6	5·7 1·9	11·7 3·8	17·7 5·8
58	4 44·5	4 45·3	4 31·5	5·8 1·8	11·8 3·6	17·8 5·5	58	4 59·5	5 00·3	4 45·9	5·8 1·9	11·8 3·8	17·8 5·8
59	4 44·8	4 45·5	4 31·8	5·9 1·8	11·9 3·7	17·9 5·5	59	4 59·8	5 00·6	4 46·1	5·9 1·9	11·9 3·9	17·9 5·8
60	4 45·0	4 45·8	4 32·0	6·0 1·9	12·0 3·7	18·0 5·6	60	5 00·0	5 00·8	4 46·3	6·0 2·0	12·0 3·9	18·0 5·9

20ᵐ

20 s	SUN PLANETS	ARIES	MOON	v or d Corrⁿ	v or d Corrⁿ	v or d Corrⁿ
00	5 00·0	5 00·8	4 46·3	0·0 0·0	6·0 2·1	12·0 4·1
01	5 00·3	5 01·1	4 46·6	0·1 0·0	6·1 2·1	12·1 4·1
02	5 00·5	5 01·3	4 46·8	0·2 0·1	6·2 2·1	12·2 4·2
03	5 00·8	5 01·6	4 47·0	0·3 0·1	6·3 2·2	12·3 4·2
04	5 01·0	5 01·8	4 47·3	0·4 0·1	6·4 2·2	12·4 4·2
05	5 01·3	5 02·1	4 47·5	0·5 0·2	6·5 2·2	12·5 4·3
06	5 01·5	5 02·3	4 47·8	0·6 0·2	6·6 2·3	12·6 4·3
07	5 01·8	5 02·6	4 48·0	0·7 0·2	6·7 2·3	12·7 4·3
08	5 02·0	5 02·8	4 48·2	0·8 0·3	6·8 2·3	12·8 4·4
09	5 02·3	5 03·1	4 48·5	0·9 0·3	6·9 2·4	12·9 4·4
10	5 02·5	5 03·3	4 48·7	1·0 0·3	7·0 2·4	13·0 4·4
11	5 02·8	5 03·6	4 49·0	1·1 0·4	7·1 2·4	13·1 4·5
12	5 03·0	5 03·8	4 49·2	1·2 0·4	7·2 2·5	13·2 4·5
13	5 03·3	5 04·1	4 49·4	1·3 0·4	7·3 2·5	13·3 4·5
14	5 03·5	5 04·3	4 49·7	1·4 0·5	7·4 2·5	13·4 4·6
15	5 03·8	5 04·6	4 49·9	1·5 0·5	7·5 2·6	13·5 4·6
16	5 04·0	5 04·8	4 50·2	1·6 0·5	7·6 2·6	13·6 4·6
17	5 04·3	5 05·1	4 50·4	1·7 0·6	7·7 2·6	13·7 4·7
18	5 04·5	5 05·3	4 50·6	1·8 0·6	7·8 2·7	13·8 4·7
19	5 04·8	5 05·6	4 50·9	1·9 0·6	7·9 2·7	13·9 4·7
20	5 05·0	5 05·8	4 51·1	2·0 0·7	8·0 2·7	14·0 4·8
21	5 05·3	5 06·1	4 51·3	2·1 0·7	8·1 2·8	14·1 4·8
22	5 05·5	5 06·3	4 51·6	2·2 0·8	8·2 2·8	14·2 4·9
23	5 05·8	5 06·6	4 51·8	2·3 0·8	8·3 2·8	14·3 4·9
24	5 06·0	5 06·8	4 52·1	2·4 0·8	8·4 2·9	14·4 4·9
25	5 06·3	5 07·1	4 52·3	2·5 0·9	8·5 2·9	14·5 5·0
26	5 06·5	5 07·3	4 52·5	2·6 0·9	8·6 2·9	14·6 5·0
27	5 06·8	5 07·6	4 52·8	2·7 0·9	8·7 3·0	14·7 5·0
28	5 07·0	5 07·8	4 53·0	2·8 1·0	8·8 3·0	14·8 5·1
29	5 07·3	5 08·1	4 53·3	2·9 1·0	8·9 3·0	14·9 5·1
30	5 07·5	5 08·3	4 53·5	3·0 1·0	9·0 3·1	15·0 5·1
31	5 07·8	5 08·6	4 53·7	3·1 1·1	9·1 3·1	15·1 5·2
32	5 08·0	5 08·8	4 54·0	3·2 1·1	9·2 3·1	15·2 5·2
33	5 08·3	5 09·1	4 54·2	3·3 1·1	9·3 3·2	15·3 5·2
34	5 08·5	5 09·3	4 54·4	3·4 1·2	9·4 3·2	15·4 5·3
35	5 08·8	5 09·6	4 54·7	3·5 1·2	9·5 3·2	15·5 5·3
36	5 09·0	5 09·8	4 54·9	3·6 1·2	9·6 3·3	15·6 5·3
37	5 09·3	5 10·1	4 55·2	3·7 1·3	9·7 3·3	15·7 5·4
38	5 09·5	5 10·3	4 55·4	3·8 1·3	9·8 3·3	15·8 5·4
39	5 09·8	5 10·6	4 55·6	3·9 1·3	9·9 3·4	15·9 5·4
40	5 10·0	5 10·8	4 55·9	4·0 1·4	10·0 3·4	16·0 5·5
41	5 10·3	5 11·1	4 56·1	4·1 1·4	10·1 3·5	16·1 5·5
42	5 10·5	5 11·4	4 56·4	4·2 1·4	10·2 3·5	16·2 5·5
43	5 10·8	5 11·6	4 56·6	4·3 1·5	10·3 3·5	16·3 5·6
44	5 11·0	5 11·9	4 56·8	4·4 1·5	10·4 3·6	16·4 5·6
45	5 11·3	5 12·1	4 57·1	4·5 1·5	10·5 3·6	16·5 5·6
46	5 11·5	5 12·4	4 57·3	4·6 1·6	10·6 3·6	16·6 5·7
47	5 11·8	5 12·6	4 57·5	4·7 1·6	10·7 3·7	16·7 5·7
48	5 12·0	5 12·9	4 57·8	4·8 1·6	10·8 3·7	16·8 5·7
49	5 12·3	5 13·1	4 58·0	4·9 1·7	10·9 3·7	16·9 5·8
50	5 12·5	5 13·4	4 58·3	5·0 1·7	11·0 3·8	17·0 5·8
51	5 12·8	5 13·6	4 58·5	5·1 1·7	11·1 3·8	17·1 5·8
52	5 13·0	5 13·9	4 58·7	5·2 1·8	11·2 3·8	17·2 5·9
53	5 13·3	5 14·1	4 59·0	5·3 1·8	11·3 3·9	17·3 5·9
54	5 13·5	5 14·4	4 59·2	5·4 1·8	11·4 3·9	17·4 5·9
55	5 13·8	5 14·6	4 59·5	5·5 1·9	11·5 3·9	17·5 6·0
56	5 14·0	5 14·9	4 59·7	5·6 1·9	11·6 4·0	17·6 6·0
57	5 14·3	5 15·1	4 59·9	5·7 1·9	11·7 4·0	17·7 6·1
58	5 14·5	5 15·4	5 00·2	5·8 2·0	11·8 4·0	17·8 6·1
59	5 14·8	5 15·6	5 00·4	5·9 2·0	11·9 4·1	17·9 6·1
60	5 15·0	5 15·9	5 00·7	6·0 2·1	12·0 4·1	18·0 6·2

21ᵐ

21 s	SUN PLANETS	ARIES	MOON	v or d Corrⁿ	v or d Corrⁿ	v or d Corrⁿ
00	5 15·0	5 15·9	5 00·7	0·0 0·0	6·0 2·2	12·0 4·3
01	5 15·3	5 16·1	5 00·9	0·1 0·0	6·1 2·2	12·1 4·3
02	5 15·5	5 16·4	5 01·1	0·2 0·1	6·2 2·2	12·2 4·4
03	5 15·8	5 16·6	5 01·4	0·3 0·1	6·3 2·3	12·3 4·4
04	5 16·0	5 16·9	5 01·6	0·4 0·1	6·4 2·3	12·4 4·4
05	5 16·3	5 17·1	5 01·8	0·5 0·2	6·5 2·3	12·5 4·5
06	5 16·5	5 17·4	5 02·1	0·6 0·2	6·6 2·4	12·6 4·5
07	5 16·8	5 17·6	5 02·3	0·7 0·3	6·7 2·4	12·7 4·6
08	5 17·0	5 17·9	5 02·6	0·8 0·3	6·8 2·4	12·8 4·6
09	5 17·3	5 18·1	5 02·8	0·9 0·3	6·9 2·5	12·9 4·6
10	5 17·5	5 18·4	5 03·0	1·0 0·4	7·0 2·5	13·0 4·7
11	5 17·8	5 18·6	5 03·3	1·1 0·4	7·1 2·5	13·1 4·7
12	5 18·0	5 18·9	5 03·5	1·2 0·4	7·2 2·6	13·2 4·7
13	5 18·3	5 19·1	5 03·8	1·3 0·5	7·3 2·6	13·3 4·8
14	5 18·5	5 19·4	5 04·0	1·4 0·5	7·4 2·7	13·4 4·8
15	5 18·8	5 19·6	5 04·2	1·5 0·5	7·5 2·7	13·5 4·8
16	5 19·0	5 19·9	5 04·5	1·6 0·6	7·6 2·7	13·6 4·9
17	5 19·3	5 20·1	5 04·7	1·7 0·6	7·7 2·8	13·7 4·9
18	5 19·5	5 20·4	5 04·9	1·8 0·6	7·8 2·8	13·8 4·9
19	5 19·8	5 20·6	5 05·2	1·9 0·7	7·9 2·8	13·9 5·0
20	5 20·0	5 20·9	5 05·4	2·0 0·7	8·0 2·9	14·0 5·0
21	5 20·3	5 21·1	5 05·7	2·1 0·8	8·1 2·9	14·1 5·1
22	5 20·5	5 21·4	5 05·9	2·2 0·8	8·2 2·9	14·2 5·1
23	5 20·8	5 21·6	5 06·1	2·3 0·8	8·3 3·0	14·3 5·1
24	5 21·0	5 21·9	5 06·4	2·4 0·9	8·4 3·0	14·4 5·2
25	5 21·3	5 22·1	5 06·6	2·5 0·9	8·5 3·0	14·5 5·2
26	5 21·5	5 22·4	5 06·9	2·6 0·9	8·6 3·1	14·6 5·2
27	5 21·8	5 22·6	5 07·1	2·7 1·0	8·7 3·1	14·7 5·3
28	5 22·0	5 22·9	5 07·3	2·8 1·0	8·8 3·2	14·8 5·3
29	5 22·3	5 23·1	5 07·6	2·9 1·0	8·9 3·2	14·9 5·3
30	5 22·5	5 23·4	5 07·8	3·0 1·1	9·0 3·2	15·0 5·4
31	5 22·8	5 23·6	5 08·0	3·1 1·1	9·1 3·3	15·1 5·4
32	5 23·0	5 23·9	5 08·3	3·2 1·1	9·2 3·3	15·2 5·4
33	5 23·3	5 24·1	5 08·5	3·3 1·2	9·3 3·3	15·3 5·5
34	5 23·5	5 24·4	5 08·8	3·4 1·2	9·4 3·4	15·4 5·5
35	5 23·8	5 24·6	5 09·0	3·5 1·3	9·5 3·4	15·5 5·6
36	5 24·0	5 24·9	5 09·2	3·6 1·3	9·6 3·4	15·6 5·6
37	5 24·3	5 25·1	5 09·5	3·7 1·3	9·7 3·5	15·7 5·6
38	5 24·5	5 25·4	5 09·7	3·8 1·4	9·8 3·5	15·8 5·7
39	5 24·8	5 25·6	5 10·0	3·9 1·4	9·9 3·5	15·9 5·7
40	5 25·0	5 25·9	5 10·2	4·0 1·4	10·0 3·6	16·0 5·7
41	5 25·3	5 26·1	5 10·4	4·1 1·5	10·1 3·6	16·1 5·8
42	5 25·5	5 26·4	5 10·7	4·2 1·5	10·2 3·7	16·2 5·8
43	5 25·8	5 26·6	5 10·9	4·3 1·5	10·3 3·7	16·3 5·8
44	5 26·0	5 26·9	5 11·1	4·4 1·6	10·4 3·7	16·4 5·9
45	5 26·3	5 27·1	5 11·4	4·5 1·6	10·5 3·8	16·5 5·9
46	5 26·5	5 27·4	5 11·6	4·6 1·6	10·6 3·8	16·6 5·9
47	5 26·8	5 27·6	5 11·9	4·7 1·7	10·7 3·8	16·7 6·0
48	5 27·0	5 27·9	5 12·1	4·8 1·7	10·8 3·9	16·8 6·0
49	5 27·3	5 28·1	5 12·3	4·9 1·8	10·9 3·9	16·9 6·1
50	5 27·5	5 28·4	5 12·6	5·0 1·8	11·0 3·9	17·0 6·1
51	5 27·8	5 28·6	5 12·8	5·1 1·8	11·1 4·0	17·1 6·1
52	5 28·0	5 28·9	5 13·1	5·2 1·9	11·2 4·0	17·2 6·2
53	5 28·3	5 29·1	5 13·3	5·3 1·9	11·3 4·0	17·3 6·2
54	5 28·5	5 29·4	5 13·5	5·4 1·9	11·4 4·1	17·4 6·2
55	5 28·8	5 29·7	5 13·8	5·5 2·0	11·5 4·1	17·5 6·3
56	5 29·0	5 29·9	5 14·0	5·6 2·0	11·6 4·2	17·6 6·3
57	5 29·3	5 30·2	5 14·3	5·7 2·0	11·7 4·2	17·7 6·3
58	5 29·5	5 30·4	5 14·5	5·8 2·1	11·8 4·2	17·8 6·4
59	5 29·8	5 30·7	5 14·7	5·9 2·1	11·9 4·3	17·9 6·4
60	5 30·0	5 30·9	5 15·0	6·0 2·2	12·0 4·3	18·0 6·5

22ᵐ

22 s	SUN PLANETS	ARIES	MOON	v or Corrⁿ d	v or Corrⁿ d	v or Corrⁿ d
	° ′	° ′	° ′	′ ′	′ ′	′ ′
00	5 30.0	5 30.9	5 15.0	0.0 0.0	6.0 2.3	12.0 4.5
01	5 30.3	5 31.2	5 15.2	0.1 0.0	6.1 2.3	12.1 4.5
02	5 30.5	5 31.4	5 15.4	0.2 0.1	6.2 2.3	12.2 4.6
03	5 30.8	5 31.7	5 15.7	0.3 0.1	6.3 2.4	12.3 4.6
04	5 31.0	5 31.9	5 15.9	0.4 0.2	6.4 2.4	12.4 4.7
05	5 31.3	5 32.2	5 16.2	0.5 0.2	6.5 2.4	12.5 4.7
06	5 31.5	5 32.4	5 16.4	0.6 0.2	6.6 2.5	12.6 4.7
07	5 31.8	5 32.7	5 16.6	0.7 0.3	6.7 2.5	12.7 4.8
08	5 32.0	5 32.9	5 16.9	0.8 0.3	6.8 2.6	12.8 4.8
09	5 32.3	5 33.2	5 17.1	0.9 0.3	6.9 2.6	12.9 4.8
10	5 32.5	5 33.4	5 17.4	1.0 0.4	7.0 2.6	13.0 4.9
11	5 32.8	5 33.7	5 17.6	1.1 0.4	7.1 2.7	13.1 4.9
12	5 33.0	5 33.9	5 17.8	1.2 0.5	7.2 2.7	13.2 5.0
13	5 33.3	5 34.2	5 18.1	1.3 0.5	7.3 2.7	13.3 5.0
14	5 33.5	5 34.4	5 18.3	1.4 0.5	7.4 2.8	13.4 5.0
15	5 33.8	5 34.7	5 18.5	1.5 0.6	7.5 2.8	13.5 5.1
16	5 34.0	5 34.9	5 18.8	1.6 0.6	7.6 2.9	13.6 5.1
17	5 34.3	5 35.2	5 19.0	1.7 0.6	7.7 2.9	13.7 5.1
18	5 34.5	5 35.4	5 19.3	1.8 0.7	7.8 2.9	13.8 5.2
19	5 34.8	5 35.7	5 19.5	1.9 0.7	7.9 3.0	13.9 5.2
20	5 35.0	5 35.9	5 19.7	2.0 0.8	8.0 3.0	14.0 5.3
21	5 35.3	5 36.2	5 20.0	2.1 0.8	8.1 3.0	14.1 5.3
22	5 35.5	5 36.4	5 20.2	2.2 0.8	8.2 3.1	14.2 5.3
23	5 35.8	5 36.7	5 20.5	2.3 0.9	8.3 3.1	14.3 5.4
24	5 36.0	5 36.9	5 20.7	2.4 0.9	8.4 3.2	14.4 5.4
25	5 36.3	5 37.2	5 20.9	2.5 0.9	8.5 3.2	14.5 5.4
26	5 36.5	5 37.4	5 21.2	2.6 1.0	8.6 3.2	14.6 5.5
27	5 36.8	5 37.7	5 21.4	2.7 1.0	8.7 3.3	14.7 5.5
28	5 37.0	5 37.9	5 21.6	2.8 1.0	8.8 3.3	14.8 5.6
29	5 37.3	5 38.2	5 21.9	2.9 1.1	8.9 3.3	14.9 5.6
30	5 37.5	5 38.4	5 22.1	3.0 1.1	9.0 3.4	15.0 5.6
31	5 37.8	5 38.7	5 22.4	3.1 1.2	9.1 3.4	15.1 5.7
32	5 38.0	5 38.9	5 22.6	3.2 1.2	9.2 3.5	15.2 5.7
33	5 38.3	5 39.2	5 22.8	3.3 1.2	9.3 3.5	15.3 5.7
34	5 38.5	5 39.4	5 23.1	3.4 1.3	9.4 3.5	15.4 5.8
35	5 38.8	5 39.7	5 23.3	3.5 1.3	9.5 3.6	15.5 5.8
36	5 39.0	5 39.9	5 23.6	3.6 1.4	9.6 3.6	15.6 5.9
37	5 39.3	5 40.2	5 23.8	3.7 1.4	9.7 3.6	15.7 5.9
38	5 39.5	5 40.4	5 24.0	3.8 1.4	9.8 3.7	15.8 5.9
39	5 39.8	5 40.7	5 24.3	3.9 1.5	9.9 3.7	15.9 6.0
40	5 40.0	5 40.9	5 24.5	4.0 1.5	10.0 3.8	16.0 6.0
41	5 40.3	5 41.2	5 24.7	4.1 1.5	10.1 3.8	16.1 6.0
42	5 40.5	5 41.4	5 25.0	4.2 1.6	10.2 3.8	16.2 6.1
43	5 40.8	5 41.7	5 25.2	4.3 1.6	10.3 3.9	16.3 6.1
44	5 41.0	5 41.9	5 25.5	4.4 1.7	10.4 3.9	16.4 6.1
45	5 41.3	5 42.2	5 25.7	4.5 1.7	10.5 3.9	16.5 6.2
46	5 41.5	5 42.4	5 25.9	4.6 1.7	10.6 4.0	16.6 6.2
47	5 41.8	5 42.7	5 26.2	4.7 1.8	10.7 4.0	16.7 6.3
48	5 42.0	5 42.9	5 26.4	4.8 1.8	10.8 4.1	16.8 6.3
49	5 42.3	5 43.2	5 26.7	4.9 1.8	10.9 4.1	16.9 6.3
50	5 42.5	5 43.4	5 26.9	5.0 1.9	11.0 4.1	17.0 6.4
51	5 42.8	5 43.7	5 27.1	5.1 1.9	11.1 4.2	17.1 6.4
52	5 43.0	5 43.9	5 27.4	5.2 2.0	11.2 4.2	17.2 6.5
53	5 43.3	5 44.2	5 27.6	5.3 2.0	11.3 4.2	17.3 6.5
54	5 43.5	5 44.4	5 27.9	5.4 2.0	11.4 4.3	17.4 6.5
55	5 43.8	5 44.7	5 28.1	5.5 2.1	11.5 4.3	17.5 6.6
56	5 44.0	5 44.9	5 28.3	5.6 2.1	11.6 4.4	17.6 6.6
57	5 44.3	5 45.2	5 28.6	5.7 2.1	11.7 4.4	17.7 6.6
58	5 44.5	5 45.4	5 28.8	5.8 2.2	11.8 4.4	17.8 6.7
59	5 44.8	5 45.7	5 29.0	5.9 2.2	11.9 4.5	17.9 6.7
60	5 45.0	5 45.9	5 29.3	6.0 2.3	12.0 4.5	18.0 6.8

23ᵐ

23 s	SUN PLANETS	ARIES	MOON	v or Corrⁿ d	v or Corrⁿ d	v or Corrⁿ d
	° ′	° ′	° ′	′ ′	′ ′	′ ′
00	5 45.0	5 45.9	5 29.3	0.0 0.0	6.0 2.4	12.0 4.7
01	5 45.3	5 46.2	5 29.5	0.1 0.0	6.1 2.4	12.1 4.7
02	5 45.5	5 46.4	5 29.8	0.2 0.1	6.2 2.4	12.2 4.8
03	5 45.8	5 46.7	5 30.0	0.3 0.1	6.3 2.5	12.3 4.8
04	5 46.0	5 46.9	5 30.2	0.4 0.2	6.4 2.5	12.4 4.9
05	5 46.3	5 47.2	5 30.5	0.5 0.2	6.5 2.5	12.5 4.9
06	5 46.5	5 47.4	5 30.7	0.6 0.2	6.6 2.6	12.6 4.9
07	5 46.8	5 47.7	5 31.0	0.7 0.3	6.7 2.6	12.7 5.0
08	5 47.0	5 48.0	5 31.2	0.8 0.3	6.8 2.7	12.8 5.0
09	5 47.3	5 48.2	5 31.4	0.9 0.4	6.9 2.7	12.9 5.1
10	5 47.5	5 48.5	5 31.7	1.0 0.4	7.0 2.7	13.0 5.1
11	5 47.8	5 48.7	5 31.9	1.1 0.4	7.1 2.8	13.1 5.1
12	5 48.0	5 49.0	5 32.1	1.2 0.5	7.2 2.8	13.2 5.2
13	5 48.3	5 49.2	5 32.4	1.3 0.5	7.3 2.9	13.3 5.2
14	5 48.5	5 49.5	5 32.6	1.4 0.5	7.4 2.9	13.4 5.2
15	5 48.8	5 49.7	5 32.9	1.5 0.6	7.5 2.9	13.5 5.3
16	5 49.0	5 50.0	5 33.1	1.6 0.6	7.6 3.0	13.6 5.3
17	5 49.3	5 50.2	5 33.3	1.7 0.7	7.7 3.0	13.7 5.4
18	5 49.5	5 50.5	5 33.6	1.8 0.7	7.8 3.1	13.8 5.4
19	5 49.8	5 50.7	5 33.8	1.9 0.7	7.9 3.1	13.9 5.4
20	5 50.0	5 51.0	5 34.1	2.0 0.8	8.0 3.1	14.0 5.5
21	5 50.3	5 51.2	5 34.3	2.1 0.8	8.1 3.2	14.1 5.5
22	5 50.5	5 51.5	5 34.5	2.2 0.9	8.2 3.2	14.2 5.6
23	5 50.8	5 51.7	5 34.8	2.3 0.9	8.3 3.3	14.3 5.6
24	5 51.0	5 52.0	5 35.0	2.4 0.9	8.4 3.3	14.4 5.6
25	5 51.3	5 52.2	5 35.2	2.5 1.0	8.5 3.3	14.5 5.7
26	5 51.5	5 52.5	5 35.5	2.6 1.0	8.6 3.4	14.6 5.7
27	5 51.8	5 52.7	5 35.7	2.7 1.1	8.7 3.4	14.7 5.8
28	5 52.0	5 53.0	5 36.0	2.8 1.1	8.8 3.4	14.8 5.8
29	5 52.3	5 53.2	5 36.2	2.9 1.1	8.9 3.5	14.9 5.8
30	5 52.5	5 53.5	5 36.4	3.0 1.2	9.0 3.5	15.0 5.9
31	5 52.8	5 53.7	5 36.7	3.1 1.2	9.1 3.6	15.1 5.9
32	5 53.0	5 54.0	5 36.9	3.2 1.3	9.2 3.6	15.2 6.0
33	5 53.3	5 54.2	5 37.2	3.3 1.3	9.3 3.6	15.3 6.0
34	5 53.5	5 54.5	5 37.4	3.4 1.3	9.4 3.7	15.4 6.0
35	5 53.8	5 54.7	5 37.6	3.5 1.4	9.5 3.7	15.5 6.1
36	5 54.0	5 55.0	5 37.9	3.6 1.4	9.6 3.8	15.6 6.1
37	5 54.3	5 55.2	5 38.1	3.7 1.4	9.7 3.8	15.7 6.1
38	5 54.5	5 55.5	5 38.4	3.8 1.5	9.8 3.8	15.8 6.2
39	5 54.8	5 55.7	5 38.6	3.9 1.5	9.9 3.9	15.9 6.2
40	5 55.0	5 56.0	5 38.8	4.0 1.6	10.0 3.9	16.0 6.3
41	5 55.3	5 56.2	5 39.1	4.1 1.6	10.1 4.0	16.1 6.3
42	5 55.5	5 56.5	5 39.3	4.2 1.6	10.2 4.0	16.2 6.3
43	5 55.8	5 56.7	5 39.5	4.3 1.7	10.3 4.0	16.3 6.4
44	5 56.0	5 57.0	5 39.8	4.4 1.7	10.4 4.1	16.4 6.4
45	5 56.3	5 57.2	5 40.0	4.5 1.8	10.5 4.1	16.5 6.5
46	5 56.5	5 57.5	5 40.3	4.6 1.8	10.6 4.2	16.6 6.5
47	5 56.8	5 57.7	5 40.5	4.7 1.8	10.7 4.2	16.7 6.5
48	5 57.0	5 58.0	5 40.7	4.8 1.9	10.8 4.2	16.8 6.6
49	5 57.3	5 58.2	5 41.0	4.9 1.9	10.9 4.3	16.9 6.6
50	5 57.5	5 58.5	5 41.2	5.0 2.0	11.0 4.3	17.0 6.7
51	5 57.8	5 58.7	5 41.5	5.1 2.0	11.1 4.3	17.1 6.7
52	5 58.0	5 59.0	5 41.7	5.2 2.0	11.2 4.4	17.2 6.7
53	5 58.3	5 59.2	5 41.9	5.3 2.1	11.3 4.4	17.3 6.8
54	5 58.5	5 59.5	5 42.2	5.4 2.1	11.4 4.5	17.4 6.8
55	5 58.8	5 59.7	5 42.4	5.5 2.2	11.5 4.5	17.5 6.9
56	5 59.0	6 00.0	5 42.6	5.6 2.2	11.6 4.5	17.6 6.9
57	5 59.3	6 00.2	5 42.9	5.7 2.2	11.7 4.6	17.7 6.9
58	5 59.5	6 00.5	5 43.1	5.8 2.3	11.8 4.6	17.8 7.0
59	5 59.8	6 00.7	5 43.4	5.9 2.3	11.9 4.7	17.9 7.0
60	6 00.0	6 01.0	5 43.6	6.0 2.4	12.0 4.7	18.0 7.1

^{m}24	SUN PLANETS	ARIES	MOON	v or Corr^n d		v or Corr^n d		v or Corr^n d	
s	° ′	° ′	° ′	′	′	′	′	′	′
00	6 00·0	6 01·0	5 43·6	0·0	0·0	6·0	2·5	12·0	4·9
01	6 00·3	6 01·2	5 43·8	0·1	0·0	6·1	2·5	12·1	4·9
02	6 00·5	6 01·5	5 44·1	0·2	0·1	6·2	2·5	12·2	5·0
03	6 00·8	6 01·7	5 44·3	0·3	0·1	6·3	2·6	12·3	5·0
04	6 01·0	6 02·0	5 44·6	0·4	0·2	6·4	2·6	12·4	5·1
05	6 01·3	6 02·2	5 44·8	0·5	0·2	6·5	2·7	12·5	5·1
06	6 01·5	6 02·5	5 45·0	0·6	0·2	6·6	2·7	12·6	5·1
07	6 01·8	6 02·7	5 45·3	0·7	0·3	6·7	2·7	12·7	5·2
08	6 02·0	6 03·0	5 45·5	0·8	0·3	6·8	2·8	12·8	5·2
09	6 02·3	6 03·2	5 45·7	0·9	0·4	6·9	2·8	12·9	5·3
10	6 02·5	6 03·5	5 46·0	1·0	0·4	7·0	2·9	13·0	5·3
11	6 02·8	6 03·7	5 46·2	1·1	0·4	7·1	2·9	13·1	5·3
12	6 03·0	6 04·0	5 46·5	1·2	0·5	7·2	2·9	13·2	5·4
13	6 03·3	6 04·2	5 46·7	1·3	0·5	7·3	3·0	13·3	5·4
14	6 03·5	6 04·5	5 46·9	1·4	0·6	7·4	3·0	13·4	5·5
15	6 03·8	6 04·7	5 47·2	1·5	0·6	7·5	3·1	13·5	5·5
16	6 04·0	6 05·0	5 47·4	1·6	0·7	7·6	3·1	13·6	5·6
17	6 04·3	6 05·2	5 47·7	1·7	0·7	7·7	3·1	13·7	5·6
18	6 04·5	6 05·5	5 47·9	1·8	0·7	7·8	3·2	13·8	5·6
19	6 04·8	6 05·7	5 48·1	1·9	0·8	7·9	3·2	13·9	5·7
20	6 05·0	6 06·0	5 48·4	2·0	0·8	8·0	3·3	14·0	5·7
21	6 05·3	6 06·3	5 48·6	2·1	0·9	8·1	3·3	14·1	5·8
22	6 05·5	6 06·5	5 48·8	2·2	0·9	8·2	3·3	14·2	5·8
23	6 05·8	6 06·8	5 49·1	2·3	0·9	8·3	3·4	14·3	5·8
24	6 06·0	6 07·0	5 49·3	2·4	1·0	8·4	3·4	14·4	5·9
25	6 06·3	6 07·3	5 49·6	2·5	1·0	8·5	3·5	14·5	5·9
26	6 06·5	6 07·5	5 49·8	2·6	1·1	8·6	3·5	14·6	6·0
27	6 06·8	6 07·8	5 50·0	2·7	1·1	8·7	3·6	14·7	6·0
28	6 07·0	6 08·0	5 50·3	2·8	1·1	8·8	3·6	14·8	6·0
29	6 07·3	6 08·3	5 50·5	2·9	1·2	8·9	3·6	14·9	6·1
30	6 07·5	6 08·5	5 50·8	3·0	1·2	9·0	3·7	15·0	6·1
31	6 07·8	6 08·8	5 51·0	3·1	1·3	9·1	3·7	15·1	6·2
32	6 08·0	6 09·0	5 51·2	3·2	1·3	9·2	3·8	15·2	6·2
33	6 08·3	6 09·3	5 51·5	3·3	1·3	9·3	3·8	15·3	6·2
34	6 08·5	6 09·5	5 51·7	3·4	1·4	9·4	3·8	15·4	6·3
35	6 08·8	6 09·8	5 52·0	3·5	1·4	9·5	3·9	15·5	6·3
36	6 09·0	6 10·0	5 52·2	3·6	1·5	9·6	3·9	15·6	6·4
37	6 09·3	6 10·3	5 52·4	3·7	1·5	9·7	4·0	15·7	6·4
38	6 09·5	6 10·5	5 52·7	3·8	1·6	9·8	4·0	15·8	6·5
39	6 09·8	6 10·8	5 52·9	3·9	1·6	9·9	4·0	15·9	6·5
40	6 10·0	6 11·0	5 53·1	4·0	1·6	10·0	4·1	16·0	6·5
41	6 10·3	6 11·3	5 53·4	4·1	1·7	10·1	4·1	16·1	6·6
42	6 10·5	6 11·5	5 53·6	4·2	1·7	10·2	4·2	16·2	6·6
43	6 10·8	6 11·8	5 53·9	4·3	1·8	10·3	4·2	16·3	6·7
44	6 11·0	6 12·0	5 54·1	4·4	1·8	10·4	4·2	16·4	6·7
45	6 11·3	6 12·3	5 54·3	4·5	1·8	10·5	4·3	16·5	6·7
46	6 11·5	6 12·5	5 54·6	4·6	1·9	10·6	4·3	16·6	6·8
47	6 11·8	6 12·8	5 54·8	4·7	1·9	10·7	4·4	16·7	6·8
48	6 12·0	6 13·0	5 55·1	4·8	2·0	10·8	4·4	16·8	6·9
49	6 12·3	6 13·3	5 55·3	4·9	2·0	10·9	4·5	16·9	6·9
50	6 12·5	6 13·5	5 55·5	5·0	2·0	11·0	4·5	17·0	6·9
51	6 12·8	6 13·8	5 55·8	5·1	2·1	11·1	4·5	17·1	7·0
52	6 13·0	6 14·0	5 56·0	5·2	2·1	11·2	4·6	17·2	7·0
53	6 13·3	6 14·3	5 56·2	5·3	2·2	11·3	4·6	17·3	7·1
54	6 13·5	6 14·5	5 56·5	5·4	2·2	11·4	4·7	17·4	7·1
55	6 13·8	6 14·8	5 56·7	5·5	2·2	11·5	4·7	17·5	7·1
56	6 14·0	6 15·0	5 57·0	5·6	2·3	11·6	4·7	17·6	7·2
57	6 14·3	6 15·3	5 57·2	5·7	2·3	11·7	4·8	17·7	7·2
58	6 14·5	6 15·5	5 57·4	5·8	2·4	11·8	4·8	17·8	7·3
59	6 14·8	6 15·8	5 57·7	5·9	2·4	11·9	4·9	17·9	7·3
60	6 15·0	6 16·0	5 57·9	6·0	2·5	12·0	4·9	18·0	7·4

^{m}25	SUN PLANETS	ARIES	MOON	v or Corr^n d		v or Corr^n d		v or Corr^n d	
s	° ′	° ′	° ′	′	′	′	′	′	′
00	6 15·0	6 16·0	5 57·9	0·0	0·0	6·0	2·6	12·0	5·1
01	6 15·3	6 16·3	5 58·2	0·1	0·0	6·1	2·6	12·1	5·1
02	6 15·5	6 16·5	5 58·4	0·2	0·1	6·2	2·6	12·2	5·2
03	6 15·8	6 16·8	5 58·6	0·3	0·1	6·3	2·7	12·3	5·2
04	6 16·0	6 17·0	5 58·9	0·4	0·2	6·4	2·7	12·4	5·3
05	6 16·3	6 17·3	5 59·1	0·5	0·2	6·5	2·8	12·5	5·3
06	6 16·5	6 17·5	5 59·3	0·6	0·3	6·6	2·8	12·6	5·4
07	6 16·8	6 17·8	5 59·6	0·7	0·3	6·7	2·8	12·7	5·4
08	6 17·0	6 18·0	5 59·8	0·8	0·3	6·8	2·9	12·8	5·4
09	6 17·3	6 18·3	6 00·1	0·9	0·4	6·9	2·9	12·9	5·5
10	6 17·5	6 18·5	6 00·3	1·0	0·4	7·0	3·0	13·0	5·5
11	6 17·8	6 18·8	6 00·5	1·1	0·5	7·1	3·0	13·1	5·6
12	6 18·0	6 19·0	6 00·8	1·2	0·5	7·2	3·1	13·2	5·6
13	6 18·3	6 19·3	6 01·0	1·3	0·6	7·3	3·1	13·3	5·7
14	6 18·5	6 19·5	6 01·3	1·4	0·6	7·4	3·1	13·4	5·7
15	6 18·8	6 19·8	6 01·5	1·5	0·6	7·5	3·2	13·5	5·7
16	6 19·0	6 20·0	6 01·7	1·6	0·7	7·6	3·2	13·6	5·8
17	6 19·3	6 20·3	6 02·0	1·7	0·7	7·7	3·3	13·7	5·8
18	6 19·5	6 20·5	6 02·2	1·8	0·8	7·8	3·3	13·8	5·9
19	6 19·8	6 20·8	6 02·5	1·9	0·8	7·9	3·4	13·9	5·9
20	6 20·0	6 21·0	6 02·7	2·0	0·9	8·0	3·4	14·0	6·0
21	6 20·3	6 21·3	6 02·9	2·1	0·9	8·1	3·4	14·1	6·0
22	6 20·5	6 21·5	6 03·2	2·2	0·9	8·2	3·5	14·2	6·0
23	6 20·8	6 21·8	6 03·4	2·3	1·0	8·3	3·5	14·3	6·1
24	6 21·0	6 22·0	6 03·6	2·4	1·0	8·4	3·6	14·4	6·1
25	6 21·3	6 22·3	6 03·9	2·5	1·1	8·5	3·6	14·5	6·2
26	6 21·5	6 22·5	6 04·1	2·6	1·1	8·6	3·7	14·6	6·2
27	6 21·8	6 22·8	6 04·4	2·7	1·1	8·7	3·7	14·7	6·2
28	6 22·0	6 23·0	6 04·6	2·8	1·2	8·8	3·7	14·8	6·3
29	6 22·3	6 23·3	6 04·8	2·9	1·2	8·9	3·8	14·9	6·3
30	6 22·5	6 23·5	6 05·1	3·0	1·3	9·0	3·8	15·0	6·4
31	6 22·8	6 23·8	6 05·3	3·1	1·3	9·1	3·9	15·1	6·4
32	6 23·0	6 24·0	6 05·6	3·2	1·4	9·2	3·9	15·2	6·5
33	6 23·3	6 24·3	6 05·8	3·3	1·4	9·3	4·0	15·3	6·5
34	6 23·5	6 24·5	6 06·0	3·4	1·4	9·4	4·0	15·4	6·5
35	6 23·8	6 24·8	6 06·3	3·5	1·5	9·5	4·0	15·5	6·6
36	6 24·0	6 25·1	6 06·5	3·6	1·5	9·6	4·1	15·6	6·6
37	6 24·3	6 25·3	6 06·7	3·7	1·6	9·7	4·1	15·7	6·7
38	6 24·5	6 25·6	6 07·0	3·8	1·6	9·8	4·2	15·8	6·7
39	6 24·8	6 25·8	6 07·2	3·9	1·7	9·9	4·2	15·9	6·8
40	6 25·0	6 26·1	6 07·5	4·0	1·7	10·0	4·3	16·0	6·8
41	6 25·3	6 26·3	6 07·7	4·1	1·7	10·1	4·3	16·1	6·8
42	6 25·5	6 26·6	6 07·9	4·2	1·8	10·2	4·3	16·2	6·9
43	6 25·8	6 26·8	6 08·2	4·3	1·8	10·3	4·4	16·3	6·9
44	6 26·0	6 27·1	6 08·4	4·4	1·9	10·4	4·4	16·4	7·0
45	6 26·3	6 27·3	6 08·7	4·5	1·9	10·5	4·5	16·5	7·0
46	6 26·5	6 27·6	6 08·9	4·6	2·0	10·6	4·5	16·6	7·1
47	6 26·8	6 27·8	6 09·1	4·7	2·0	10·7	4·5	16·7	7·1
48	6 27·0	6 28·1	6 09·4	4·8	2·0	10·8	4·6	16·8	7·1
49	6 27·3	6 28·3	6 09·6	4·9	2·1	10·9	4·6	16·9	7·2
50	6 27·5	6 28·6	6 09·8	5·0	2·1	11·0	4·7	17·0	7·2
51	6 27·8	6 28·8	6 10·1	5·1	2·2	11·1	4·7	17·1	7·3
52	6 28·0	6 29·1	6 10·3	5·2	2·2	11·2	4·8	17·2	7·3
53	6 28·3	6 29·3	6 10·6	5·3	2·3	11·3	4·8	17·3	7·4
54	6 28·5	6 29·6	6 10·8	5·4	2·3	11·4	4·8	17·4	7·4
55	6 28·8	6 29·8	6 11·0	5·5	2·3	11·5	4·9	17·5	7·4
56	6 29·0	6 30·1	6 11·3	5·6	2·4	11·6	4·9	17·6	7·5
57	6 29·3	6 30·3	6 11·5	5·7	2·4	11·7	5·0	17·7	7·5
58	6 29·5	6 30·6	6 11·8	5·8	2·5	11·8	5·0	17·8	7·6
59	6 29·8	6 30·8	6 12·0	5·9	2·5	11·9	5·1	17·9	7·6
60	6 30·0	6 31·1	6 12·2	6·0	2·6	12·0	5·1	18·0	7·7

26ᵐ

26ᵐ s	SUN PLANETS	ARIES	MOON	v or d Corrⁿ	v or d Corrⁿ	v or d Corrⁿ
00	6 30·0	6 31·1	6 12·2	0·0 0·0	6·0 2·7	12·0 5·3
01	6 30·3	6 31·3	6 12·5	0·1 0·0	6·1 2·7	12·1 5·3
02	6 30·5	6 31·6	6 12·7	0·2 0·1	6·2 2·7	12·2 5·4
03	6 30·8	6 31·8	6 12·9	0·3 0·1	6·3 2·8	12·3 5·4
04	6 31·0	6 32·1	6 13·2	0·4 0·2	6·4 2·8	12·4 5·5
05	6 31·3	6 32·3	6 13·4	0·5 0·2	6·5 2·9	12·5 5·5
06	6 31·5	6 32·6	6 13·7	0·6 0·3	6·6 2·9	12·6 5·6
07	6 31·8	6 32·8	6 13·9	0·7 0·3	6·7 3·0	12·7 5·6
08	6 32·0	6 33·1	6 14·1	0·8 0·4	6·8 3·0	12·8 5·7
09	6 32·3	6 33·3	6 14·4	0·9 0·4	6·9 3·0	12·9 5·7
10	6 32·5	6 33·6	6 14·6	1·0 0·4	7·0 3·1	13·0 5·7
11	6 32·8	6 33·8	6 14·9	1·1 0·5	7·1 3·1	13·1 5·8
12	6 33·0	6 34·1	6 15·1	1·2 0·5	7·2 3·2	13·2 5·8
13	6 33·3	6 34·3	6 15·3	1·3 0·6	7·3 3·2	13·3 5·9
14	6 33·5	6 34·6	6 15·6	1·4 0·6	7·4 3·3	13·4 5·9
15	6 33·8	6 34·8	6 15·8	1·5 0·7	7·5 3·3	13·5 6·0
16	6 34·0	6 35·1	6 16·1	1·6 0·7	7·6 3·4	13·6 6·0
17	6 34·3	6 35·3	6 16·3	1·7 0·8	7·7 3·4	13·7 6·1
18	6 34·5	6 35·6	6 16·5	1·8 0·8	7·8 3·4	13·8 6·1
19	6 34·8	6 35·8	6 16·8	1·9 0·8	7·9 3·5	13·9 6·1
20	6 35·0	6 36·1	6 17·0	2·0 0·9	8·0 3·5	14·0 6·2
21	6 35·3	6 36·3	6 17·2	2·1 0·9	8·1 3·6	14·1 6·2
22	6 35·5	6 36·6	6 17·5	2·2 1·0	8·2 3·6	14·2 6·3
23	6 35·8	6 36·8	6 17·7	2·3 1·0	8·3 3·7	14·3 6·3
24	6 36·0	6 37·1	6 18·0	2·4 1·1	8·4 3·7	14·4 6·4
25	6 36·3	6 37·3	6 18·2	2·5 1·1	8·5 3·8	14·5 6·4
26	6 36·5	6 37·6	6 18·4	2·6 1·1	8·6 3·8	14·6 6·4
27	6 36·8	6 37·8	6 18·7	2·7 1·2	8·7 3·8	14·7 6·5
28	6 37·0	6 38·1	6 18·9	2·8 1·2	8·8 3·9	14·8 6·5
29	6 37·3	6 38·3	6 19·2	2·9 1·3	8·9 3·9	14·9 6·6
30	6 37·5	6 38·6	6 19·4	3·0 1·3	9·0 4·0	15·0 6·6
31	6 37·8	6 38·8	6 19·6	3·1 1·4	9·1 4·0	15·1 6·7
32	6 38·0	6 39·1	6 19·9	3·2 1·4	9·2 4·1	15·2 6·7
33	6 38·3	6 39·3	6 20·1	3·3 1·5	9·3 4·1	15·3 6·8
34	6 38·5	6 39·6	6 20·3	3·4 1·5	9·4 4·2	15·4 6·8
35	6 38·8	6 39·8	6 20·6	3·5 1·5	9·5 4·2	15·5 6·8
36	6 39·0	6 40·1	6 20·8	3·6 1·6	9·6 4·2	15·6 6·9
37	6 39·3	6 40·3	6 21·1	3·7 1·6	9·7 4·3	15·7 6·9
38	6 39·5	6 40·6	6 21·3	3·8 1·7	9·8 4·3	15·8 7·0
39	6 39·8	6 40·8	6 21·5	3·9 1·7	9·9 4·4	15·9 7·0
40	6 40·0	6 41·1	6 21·8	4·0 1·8	10·0 4·4	16·0 7·1
41	6 40·3	6 41·3	6 22·0	4·1 1·8	10·1 4·5	16·1 7·1
42	6 40·5	6 41·6	6 22·3	4·2 1·9	10·2 4·5	16·2 7·2
43	6 40·8	6 41·8	6 22·5	4·3 1·9	10·3 4·5	16·3 7·2
44	6 41·0	6 42·1	6 22·7	4·4 1·9	10·4 4·6	16·4 7·2
45	6 41·3	6 42·3	6 23·0	4·5 2·0	10·5 4·6	16·5 7·3
46	6 41·5	6 42·6	6 23·2	4·6 2·0	10·6 4·7	16·6 7·3
47	6 41·8	6 42·8	6 23·4	4·7 2·1	10·7 4·7	16·7 7·4
48	6 42·0	6 43·1	6 23·7	4·8 2·1	10·8 4·8	16·8 7·4
49	6 42·3	6 43·4	6 23·9	4·9 2·2	10·9 4·8	16·9 7·5
50	6 42·5	6 43·6	6 24·2	5·0 2·2	11·0 4·9	17·0 7·5
51	6 42·8	6 43·9	6 24·4	5·1 2·3	11·1 4·9	17·1 7·6
52	6 43·0	6 44·1	6 24·6	5·2 2·3	11·2 4·9	17·2 7·6
53	6 43·3	6 44·4	6 24·9	5·3 2·3	11·3 5·0	17·3 7·6
54	6 43·5	6 44·6	6 25·1	5·4 2·4	11·4 5·0	17·4 7·7
55	6 43·8	6 44·9	6 25·4	5·5 2·4	11·5 5·1	17·5 7·7
56	6 44·0	6 45·1	6 25·6	5·6 2·5	11·6 5·1	17·6 7·8
57	6 44·3	6 45·4	6 25·8	5·7 2·5	11·7 5·2	17·7 7·8
58	6 44·5	6 45·6	6 26·1	5·8 2·6	11·8 5·2	17·8 7·9
59	6 44·8	6 45·9	6 26·3	5·9 2·6	11·9 5·3	17·9 7·9
60	6 45·0	6 46·1	6 26·6	6·0 2·7	12·0 5·3	18·0 8·0

27ᵐ

27ᵐ s	SUN PLANETS	ARIES	MOON	v or d Corrⁿ	v or d Corrⁿ	v or d Corrⁿ
00	6 45·0	6 46·1	6 26·6	0·0 0·0	6·0 2·8	12·0 5·5
01	6 45·3	6 46·4	6 26·8	0·1 0·0	6·1 2·8	12·1 5·5
02	6 45·5	6 46·6	6 27·0	0·2 0·1	6·2 2·8	12·2 5·6
03	6 45·8	6 46·9	6 27·3	0·3 0·1	6·3 2·9	12·3 5·6
04	6 46·0	6 47·1	6 27·5	0·4 0·2	6·4 2·9	12·4 5·7
05	6 46·3	6 47·4	6 27·7	0·5 0·2	6·5 3·0	12·5 5·7
06	6 46·5	6 47·6	6 28·0	0·6 0·3	6·6 3·0	12·6 5·8
07	6 46·8	6 47·9	6 28·2	0·7 0·3	6·7 3·1	12·7 5·8
08	6 47·0	6 48·1	6 28·5	0·8 0·4	6·8 3·1	12·8 5·9
09	6 47·3	6 48·4	6 28·7	0·9 0·4	6·9 3·2	12·9 5·9
10	6 47·5	6 48·6	6 28·9	1·0 0·5	7·0 3·2	13·0 6·0
11	6 47·8	6 48·9	6 29·2	1·1 0·5	7·1 3·3	13·1 6·0
12	6 48·0	6 49·1	6 29·4	1·2 0·6	7·2 3·3	13·2 6·1
13	6 48·3	6 49·4	6 29·7	1·3 0·6	7·3 3·3	13·3 6·1
14	6 48·5	6 49·6	6 29·9	1·4 0·6	7·4 3·4	13·4 6·1
15	6 48·8	6 49·9	6 30·1	1·5 0·7	7·5 3·4	13·5 6·2
16	6 49·0	6 50·1	6 30·4	1·6 0·7	7·6 3·5	13·6 6·2
17	6 49·3	6 50·4	6 30·6	1·7 0·8	7·7 3·5	13·7 6·3
18	6 49·5	6 50·6	6 30·8	1·8 0·8	7·8 3·6	13·8 6·3
19	6 49·8	6 50·9	6 31·1	1·9 0·9	7·9 3·6	13·9 6·4
20	6 50·0	6 51·1	6 31·3	2·0 0·9	8·0 3·7	14·0 6·4
21	6 50·3	6 51·4	6 31·6	2·1 1·0	8·1 3·7	14·1 6·5
22	6 50·5	6 51·6	6 31·8	2·2 1·0	8·2 3·8	14·2 6·5
23	6 50·8	6 51·9	6 32·0	2·3 1·1	8·3 3·8	14·3 6·6
24	6 51·0	6 52·1	6 32·3	2·4 1·1	8·4 3·9	14·4 6·6
25	6 51·3	6 52·4	6 32·5	2·5 1·1	8·5 3·9	14·5 6·6
26	6 51·5	6 52·6	6 32·8	2·6 1·2	8·6 3·9	14·6 6·7
27	6 51·8	6 52·9	6 33·0	2·7 1·2	8·7 4·0	14·7 6·7
28	6 52·0	6 53·1	6 33·2	2·8 1·3	8·8 4·0	14·8 6·8
29	6 52·3	6 53·4	6 33·5	2·9 1·3	8·9 4·1	14·9 6·8
30	6 52·5	6 53·6	6 33·7	3·0 1·4	9·0 4·1	15·0 6·9
31	6 52·8	6 53·9	6 33·9	3·1 1·4	9·1 4·2	15·1 6·9
32	6 53·0	6 54·1	6 34·2	3·2 1·5	9·2 4·2	15·2 7·0
33	6 53·3	6 54·4	6 34·4	3·3 1·5	9·3 4·3	15·3 7·0
34	6 53·5	6 54·6	6 34·7	3·4 1·5	9·4 4·3	15·4 7·1
35	6 53·8	6 54·9	6 34·9	3·5 1·6	9·5 4·4	15·5 7·1
36	6 54·0	6 55·1	6 35·1	3·6 1·7	9·6 4·4	15·6 7·2
37	6 54·3	6 55·4	6 35·4	3·7 1·6	9·7 4·3	15·7 7·2
38	6 54·5	6 55·6	6 35·6	3·8 1·7	9·8 4·5	15·8 7·2
39	6 54·8	6 55·9	6 35·9	3·9 1·8	9·9 4·5	15·9 7·3
40	6 55·0	6 56·1	6 36·1	4·0 1·8	10·0 4·6	16·0 7·3
41	6 55·3	6 56·4	6 36·3	4·1 1·9	10·1 4·6	16·1 7·4
42	6 55·5	6 56·6	6 36·6	4·2 1·9	10·2 4·7	16·2 7·4
43	6 55·8	6 56·9	6 36·8	4·3 2·0	10·3 4·7	16·3 7·5
44	6 56·0	6 57·1	6 37·0	4·4 2·0	10·4 4·8	16·4 7·5
45	6 56·3	6 57·4	6 37·3	4·5 2·1	10·5 4·8	16·5 7·6
46	6 56·5	6 57·6	6 37·5	4·6 2·1	10·6 4·9	16·6 7·6
47	6 56·8	6 57·9	6 37·8	4·7 2·2	10·7 4·9	16·7 7·7
48	6 57·0	6 58·1	6 38·0	4·8 2·2	10·8 5·0	16·8 7·7
49	6 57·3	6 58·4	6 38·2	4·9 2·2	10·9 5·0	16·9 7·7
50	6 57·5	6 58·6	6 38·5	5·0 2·3	11·0 5·0	17·0 7·8
51	6 57·8	6 58·9	6 38·7	5·1 2·3	11·1 5·1	17·1 7·8
52	6 58·0	6 59·1	6 39·0	5·2 2·4	11·2 5·1	17·2 7·9
53	6 58·3	6 59·4	6 39·2	5·3 2·4	11·3 5·2	17·3 7·9
54	6 58·5	6 59·6	6 39·4	5·4 2·5	11·4 5·2	17·4 8·0
55	6 58·8	6 59·9	6 39·7	5·5 2·5	11·5 5·3	17·5 8·0
56	6 59·0	7 00·1	6 39·9	5·6 2·6	11·6 5·3	17·6 8·1
57	6 59·3	7 00·4	6 40·2	5·7 2·6	11·7 5·4	17·7 8·1
58	6 59·5	7 00·6	6 40·4	5·8 2·7	11·8 5·4	17·8 8·2
59	6 59·8	7 00·9	6 40·6	5·9 2·7	11·9 5·5	17·9 8·2
60	7 00·0	7 01·1	6 40·9	6·0 2·8	12·0 5·5	18·0 8·3

28 m	SUN PLANETS	ARIES	MOON	v or d Corrn	v or d Corrn	v or d Corrn	29 m	SUN PLANETS	ARIES	MOON	v or d Corrn	v or d Corrn	v or d Corrn
s	° '	° '	° '	' '	' '	' '	s	° '	° '	° '	' '	' '	' '
00	7 00·0	7 01·1	6 40·9	0·0 0·0	6·0 2·9	12·0 5·7	00	7 15·0	7 16·2	6 55·2	0·0 0·0	6·0 3·0	12·0 5·9
01	7 00·3	7 01·4	6 41·1	0·1 0·0	6·1 2·9	12·1 5·7	01	7 15·3	7 16·4	6 55·4	0·1 0·0	6·1 3·0	12·1 5·9
02	7 00·5	7 01·7	6 41·3	0·2 0·1	6·2 2·9	12·2 5·8	02	7 15·5	7 16·7	6 55·7	0·2 0·1	6·2 3·0	12·2 6·0
03	7 00·8	7 01·9	6 41·6	0·3 0·1	6·3 3·0	12·3 5·8	03	7 15·8	7 16·9	6 55·9	0·3 0·1	6·3 3·1	12·3 6·0
04	7 01·0	7 02·2	6 41·8	0·4 0·2	6·4 3·0	12·4 5·9	04	7 16·0	7 17·2	6 56·1	0·4 0·2	6·4 3·1	12·4 6·1
05	7 01·3	7 02·4	6 42·1	0·5 0·2	6·5 3·1	12·5 5·9	05	7 16·3	7 17·4	6 56·4	0·5 0·2	6·5 3·2	12·5 6·1
06	7 01·5	7 02·7	6 42·3	0·6 0·3	6·6 3·1	12·6 6·0	06	7 16·5	7 17·7	6 56·6	0·6 0·3	6·6 3·2	12·6 6·2
07	7 01·8	7 02·9	6 42·5	0·7 0·3	6·7 3·2	12·7 6·0	07	7 16·8	7 17·9	6 56·9	0·7 0·3	6·7 3·3	12·7 6·2
08	7 02·0	7 03·2	6 42·8	0·8 0·4	6·8 3·2	12·8 6·1	08	7 17·0	7 18·2	6 57·1	0·8 0·4	6·8 3·3	12·8 6·3
09	7 02·3	7 03·4	6 43·0	0·9 0·4	6·9 3·3	12·9 6·1	09	7 17·3	7 18·4	6 57·3	0·9 0·4	6·9 3·4	12·9 6·3
10	7 02·5	7 03·7	6 43·3	1·0 0·5	7·0 3·3	13·0 6·2	10	7 17·5	7 18·7	6 57·6	1·0 0·5	7·0 3·4	13·0 6·4
11	7 02·8	7 03·9	6 43·5	1·1 0·5	7·1 3·4	13·1 6·2	11	7 17·8	7 18·9	6 57·8	1·1 0·5	7·1 3·5	13·1 6·4
12	7 03·0	7 04·2	6 43·7	1·2 0·6	7·2 3·4	13·2 6·3	12	7 18·0	7 19·2	6 58·0	1·2 0·6	7·2 3·5	13·2 6·5
13	7 03·3	7 04·4	6 44·0	1·3 0·6	7·3 3·5	13·3 6·3	13	7 18·3	7 19·4	6 58·3	1·3 0·6	7·3 3·6	13·3 6·5
14	7 03·5	7 04·7	6 44·2	1·4 0·7	7·4 3·5	13·4 6·4	14	7 18·5	7 19·7	6 58·5	1·4 0·7	7·4 3·6	13·4 6·6
15	7 03·8	7 04·9	6 44·4	1·5 0·7	7·5 3·6	13·5 6·4	15	7 18·8	7 20·0	6 58·8	1·5 0·7	7·5 3·7	13·5 6·6
16	7 04·0	7 05·2	6 44·7	1·6 0·8	7·6 3·6	13·6 6·5	16	7 19·0	7 20·2	6 59·0	1·6 0·8	7·6 3·7	13·6 6·7
17	7 04·3	7 05·4	6 44·9	1·7 0·8	7·7 3·7	13·7 6·5	17	7 19·3	7 20·5	6 59·2	1·7 0·8	7·7 3·8	13·7 6·7
18	7 04·5	7 05·7	6 45·2	1·8 0·9	7·8 3·7	13·8 6·6	18	7 19·5	7 20·7	6 59·5	1·8 0·9	7·8 3·8	13·8 6·8
19	7 04·8	7 05·9	6 45·4	1·9 0·9	7·9 3·8	13·9 6·6	19	7 19·8	7 21·0	6 59·7	1·9 0·9	7·9 3·9	13·9 6·8
20	7 05·0	7 06·2	6 45·6	2·0 1·0	8·0 3·8	14·0 6·7	20	7 20·0	7 21·2	7 00·0	2·0 1·0	8·0 3·9	14·0 6·9
21	7 05·3	7 06·4	6 45·9	2·1 1·0	8·1 3·8	14·1 6·7	21	7 20·3	7 21·5	7 00·2	2·1 1·0	8·1 4·0	14·1 6·9
22	7 05·5	7 06·7	6 46·1	2·2 1·0	8·2 3·9	14·2 6·7	22	7 20·5	7 21·7	7 00·4	2·2 1·1	8·2 4·0	14·2 7·0
23	7 05·8	7 06·9	6 46·4	2·3 1·1	8·3 3·9	14·3 6·8	23	7 20·8	7 22·0	7 00·7	2·3 1·1	8·3 4·1	14·3 7·0
24	7 06·0	7 07·2	6 46·6	2·4 1·1	8·4 4·0	14·4 6·8	24	7 21·0	7 22·2	7 00·9	2·4 1·2	8·4 4·1	14·4 7·1
25	7 06·3	7 07·4	6 46·8	2·5 1·2	8·5 4·0	14·5 6·9	25	7 21·3	7 22·5	7 01·1	2·5 1·2	8·5 4·2	14·5 7·1
26	7 06·5	7 07·7	6 47·1	2·6 1·2	8·6 4·1	14·6 6·9	26	7 21·5	7 22·7	7 01·4	2·6 1·3	8·6 4·2	14·6 7·2
27	7 06·8	7 07·9	6 47·3	2·7 1·3	8·7 4·1	14·7 7·0	27	7 21·8	7 23·0	7 01·6	2·7 1·3	8·7 4·3	14·7 7·2
28	7 07·0	7 08·2	6 47·5	2·8 1·3	8·8 4·2	14·8 7·0	28	7 22·0	7 23·2	7 01·9	2·8 1·4	8·8 4·3	14·8 7·3
29	7 07·3	7 08·4	6 47·8	2·9 1·4	8·9 4·2	14·9 7·1	29	7 22·3	7 23·5	7 02·1	2·9 1·4	8·9 4·4	14·9 7·3
30	7 07·5	7 08·7	6 48·0	3·0 1·4	9·0 4·3	15·0 7·1	30	7 22·5	7 23·7	7 02·3	3·0 1·5	9·0 4·4	15·0 7·4
31	7 07·8	7 08·9	6 48·3	3·1 1·5	9·1 4·3	15·1 7·2	31	7 22·8	7 24·0	7 02·6	3·1 1·5	9·1 4·5	15·1 7·4
32	7 08·0	7 09·2	6 48·5	3·2 1·5	9·2 4·4	15·2 7·2	32	7 23·0	7 24·2	7 02·8	3·2 1·6	9·2 4·5	15·2 7·5
33	7 08·3	7 09·4	6 48·7	3·3 1·6	9·3 4·4	15·3 7·3	33	7 23·3	7 24·5	7 03·1	3·3 1·6	9·3 4·6	15·3 7·5
34	7 08·5	7 09·7	6 49·0	3·4 1·6	9·4 4·5	15·4 7·3	34	7 23·5	7 24·7	7 03·3	3·4 1·7	9·4 4·6	15·4 7·6
35	7 08·8	7 09·9	6 49·2	3·5 1·7	9·5 4·5	15·5 7·4	35	7 23·8	7 25·0	7 03·5	3·5 1·7	9·5 4·7	15·5 7·6
36	7 09·0	7 10·2	6 49·5	3·6 1·7	9·6 4·6	15·6 7·4	36	7 24·0	7 25·2	7 03·8	3·6 1·8	9·6 4·7	15·6 7·7
37	7 09·3	7 10·4	6 49·7	3·7 1·8	9·7 4·6	15·7 7·5	37	7 24·3	7 25·5	7 04·0	3·7 1·8	9·7 4·8	15·7 7·7
38	7 09·5	7 10·7	6 49·9	3·8 1·8	9·8 4·7	15·8 7·5	38	7 24·5	7 25·7	7 04·3	3·8 1·9	9·8 4·8	15·8 7·8
39	7 09·8	7 10·9	6 50·2	3·9 1·9	9·9 4·7	15·9 7·6	39	7 24·8	7 26·0	7 04·5	3·9 1·9	9·9 4·9	15·9 7·8
40	7 10·0	7 11·2	6 50·4	4·0 1·9	10·0 4·8	16·0 7·6	40	7 25·0	7 26·2	7 04·7	4·0 2·0	10·0 4·9	16·0 7·9
41	7 10·3	7 11·4	6 50·6	4·1 1·9	10·1 4·8	16·1 7·6	41	7 25·3	7 26·5	7 05·0	4·1 2·0	10·1 5·0	16·1 7·9
42	7 10·5	7 11·7	6 50·9	4·2 2·0	10·2 4·8	16·2 7·7	42	7 25·5	7 26·7	7 05·2	4·2 2·1	10·2 5·0	16·2 8·0
43	7 10·8	7 11·9	6 51·1	4·3 2·0	10·3 4·9	16·3 7·7	43	7 25·8	7 27·0	7 05·4	4·3 2·1	10·3 5·1	16·3 8·0
44	7 11·0	7 12·2	6 51·4	4·4 2·1	10·4 4·9	16·4 7·8	44	7 26·0	7 27·2	7 05·7	4·4 2·2	10·4 5·1	16·4 8·1
45	7 11·3	7 12·4	6 51·6	4·5 2·1	10·5 5·0	16·5 7·8	45	7 26·3	7 27·5	7 05·9	4·5 2·2	10·5 5·2	16·5 8·1
46	7 11·5	7 12·7	6 51·8	4·6 2·2	10·6 5·0	16·6 7·9	46	7 26·5	7 27·7	7 06·2	4·6 2·3	10·6 5·2	16·6 8·2
47	7 11·8	7 12·9	6 52·1	4·7 2·2	10·7 5·1	16·7 7·9	47	7 26·8	7 28·0	7 06·4	4·7 2·3	10·7 5·3	16·7 8·2
48	7 12·0	7 13·2	6 52·3	4·8 2·3	10·8 5·1	16·8 8·0	48	7 27·0	7 28·2	7 06·6	4·8 2·4	10·8 5·3	16·8 8·3
49	7 12·3	7 13·4	6 52·6	4·9 2·3	10·9 5·2	16·9 8·0	49	7 27·3	7 28·5	7 06·9	4·9 2·4	10·9 5·4	16·9 8·3
50	7 12·5	7 13·7	6 52·8	5·0 2·4	11·0 5·2	17·0 8·1	50	7 27·5	7 28·7	7 07·1	5·0 2·5	11·0 5·4	17·0 8·4
51	7 12·8	7 13·9	6 53·0	5·1 2·4	11·1 5·3	17·1 8·1	51	7 27·8	7 29·0	7 07·4	5·1 2·5	11·1 5·5	17·1 8·4
52	7 13·0	7 14·2	6 53·3	5·2 2·5	11·2 5·3	17·2 8·2	52	7 28·0	7 29·2	7 07·6	5·2 2·6	11·2 5·5	17·2 8·5
53	7 13·3	7 14·4	6 53·5	5·3 2·5	11·3 5·4	17·3 8·2	53	7 28·3	7 29·5	7 07·8	5·3 2·6	11·3 5·6	17·3 8·5
54	7 13·5	7 14·7	6 53·8	5·4 2·6	11·4 5·4	17·4 8·3	54	7 28·5	7 29·7	7 08·1	5·4 2·7	11·4 5·6	17·4 8·6
55	7 13·8	7 14·9	6 54·0	5·5 2·6	11·5 5·5	17·5 8·3	55	7 28·8	7 30·0	7 08·3	5·5 2·7	11·5 5·7	17·5 8·6
56	7 14·0	7 15·2	6 54·2	5·6 2·7	11·6 5·5	17·6 8·4	56	7 29·0	7 30·2	7 08·5	5·6 2·8	11·6 5·7	17·6 8·7
57	7 14·3	7 15·4	6 54·5	5·7 2·7	11·7 5·6	17·7 8·4	57	7 29·3	7 30·5	7 08·8	5·7 2·8	11·7 5·8	17·7 8·7
58	7 14·5	7 15·7	6 54·7	5·8 2·8	11·8 5·6	17·8 8·5	58	7 29·5	7 30·7	7 09·0	5·8 2·9	11·8 5·8	17·8 8·8
59	7 14·8	7 15·9	6 54·9	5·9 2·8	11·9 5·7	17·9 8·5	59	7 29·8	7 31·0	7 09·3	5·9 2·9	11·9 5·9	17·9 8·8
60	7 15·0	7 16·2	6 55·2	6·0 2·9	12·0 5·7	18·0 8·6	60	7 30·0	7 31·2	7 09·5	6·0 3·0	12·0 5·9	18·0 8·9

30ᵐ

s	SUN PLANETS	ARIES	MOON	v or d	Corrⁿ	v or d	Corrⁿ	v or d	Corrⁿ
00	7 30.0	7 31.2	7 09.5	0.0	0.0	6.0	3.1	12.0	6.1
01	7 30.3	7 31.5	7 09.7	0.1	0.1	6.1	3.1	12.1	6.2
02	7 30.5	7 31.7	7 10.0	0.2	0.1	6.2	3.2	12.2	6.2
03	7 30.8	7 32.0	7 10.2	0.3	0.2	6.3	3.2	12.3	6.3
04	7 31.0	7 32.2	7 10.5	0.4	0.2	6.4	3.3	12.4	6.3
05	7 31.3	7 32.5	7 10.7	0.5	0.3	6.5	3.3	12.5	6.4
06	7 31.5	7 32.7	7 10.9	0.6	0.3	6.6	3.4	12.6	6.4
07	7 31.8	7 33.0	7 11.2	0.7	0.4	6.7	3.4	12.7	6.5
08	7 32.0	7 33.2	7 11.4	0.8	0.4	6.8	3.5	12.8	6.5
09	7 32.3	7 33.5	7 11.6	0.9	0.5	6.9	3.5	12.9	6.6
10	7 32.5	7 33.7	7 11.9	1.0	0.5	7.0	3.6	13.0	6.6
11	7 32.8	7 34.0	7 12.1	1.1	0.6	7.1	3.6	13.1	6.7
12	7 33.0	7 34.2	7 12.4	1.2	0.6	7.2	3.7	13.2	6.7
13	7 33.3	7 34.5	7 12.6	1.3	0.7	7.3	3.7	13.3	6.8
14	7 33.5	7 34.7	7 12.8	1.4	0.7	7.4	3.8	13.4	6.8
15	7 33.8	7 35.0	7 13.1	1.5	0.8	7.5	3.8	13.5	6.9
16	7 34.0	7 35.2	7 13.3	1.6	0.8	7.6	3.9	13.6	6.9
17	7 34.3	7 35.5	7 13.6	1.7	0.9	7.7	3.9	13.7	7.0
18	7 34.5	7 35.7	7 13.8	1.8	0.9	7.8	4.0	13.8	7.0
19	7 34.8	7 36.0	7 14.0	1.9	1.0	7.9	4.0	13.9	7.1
20	7 35.0	7 36.2	7 14.3	2.0	1.0	8.0	4.1	14.0	7.1
21	7 35.3	7 36.5	7 14.5	2.1	1.1	8.1	4.1	14.1	7.2
22	7 35.5	7 36.7	7 14.7	2.2	1.1	8.2	4.2	14.2	7.2
23	7 35.8	7 37.0	7 15.0	2.3	1.2	8.3	4.2	14.3	7.3
24	7 36.0	7 37.2	7 15.2	2.4	1.2	8.4	4.3	14.4	7.3
25	7 36.3	7 37.5	7 15.5	2.5	1.3	8.5	4.3	14.5	7.4
26	7 36.5	7 37.7	7 15.7	2.6	1.3	8.6	4.4	14.6	7.4
27	7 36.8	7 38.0	7 15.9	2.7	1.4	8.7	4.4	14.7	7.5
28	7 37.0	7 38.3	7 16.2	2.8	1.4	8.8	4.5	14.8	7.5
29	7 37.3	7 38.5	7 16.4	2.9	1.5	8.9	4.5	14.9	7.6
30	7 37.5	7 38.8	7 16.7	3.0	1.5	9.0	4.6	15.0	7.6
31	7 37.8	7 39.0	7 16.9	3.1	1.6	9.1	4.6	15.1	7.7
32	7 38.0	7 39.3	7 17.1	3.2	1.6	9.2	4.7	15.2	7.7
33	7 38.3	7 39.5	7 17.4	3.3	1.7	9.3	4.7	15.3	7.8
34	7 38.5	7 39.8	7 17.6	3.4	1.7	9.4	4.8	15.4	7.8
35	7 38.8	7 40.0	7 17.9	3.5	1.8	9.5	4.8	15.5	7.9
36	7 39.0	7 40.3	7 18.1	3.6	1.8	9.6	4.9	15.6	7.9
37	7 39.3	7 40.5	7 18.3	3.7	1.9	9.7	4.9	15.7	8.0
38	7 39.5	7 40.8	7 18.6	3.8	1.9	9.8	5.0	15.8	8.0
39	7 39.8	7 41.0	7 18.8	3.9	2.0	9.9	5.0	15.9	8.1
40	7 40.0	7 41.3	7 19.0	4.0	2.0	10.0	5.1	16.0	8.1
41	7 40.3	7 41.5	7 19.3	4.1	2.1	10.1	5.1	16.1	8.2
42	7 40.5	7 41.8	7 19.5	4.2	2.1	10.2	5.2	16.2	8.2
43	7 40.8	7 42.0	7 19.8	4.3	2.2	10.3	5.2	16.3	8.3
44	7 41.0	7 42.3	7 20.0	4.4	2.2	10.4	5.3	16.4	8.3
45	7 41.3	7 42.5	7 20.2	4.5	2.3	10.5	5.3	16.5	8.4
46	7 41.5	7 42.8	7 20.5	4.6	2.3	10.6	5.4	16.6	8.4
47	7 41.8	7 43.0	7 20.7	4.7	2.4	10.7	5.4	16.7	8.5
48	7 42.0	7 43.3	7 21.0	4.8	2.4	10.8	5.5	16.8	8.5
49	7 42.3	7 43.5	7 21.2	4.9	2.5	10.9	5.5	16.9	8.6
50	7 42.5	7 43.8	7 21.4	5.0	2.5	11.0	5.6	17.0	8.6
51	7 42.8	7 44.0	7 21.7	5.1	2.6	11.1	5.6	17.1	8.7
52	7 43.0	7 44.3	7 21.9	5.2	2.6	11.2	5.7	17.2	8.7
53	7 43.3	7 44.5	7 22.1	5.3	2.7	11.3	5.7	17.3	8.8
54	7 43.5	7 44.8	7 22.4	5.4	2.7	11.4	5.8	17.4	8.8
55	7 43.8	7 45.0	7 22.6	5.5	2.8	11.5	5.8	17.5	8.9
56	7 44.0	7 45.3	7 22.9	5.6	2.8	11.6	5.9	17.6	8.9
57	7 44.3	7 45.5	7 23.1	5.7	2.9	11.7	5.9	17.7	9.0
58	7 44.5	7 45.8	7 23.3	5.8	2.9	11.8	6.0	17.8	9.0
59	7 44.8	7 46.0	7 23.6	5.9	3.0	11.9	6.0	17.9	9.1
60	7 45.0	7 46.3	7 23.8	6.0	3.1	12.0	6.1	18.0	9.2

31ᵐ

s	SUN PLANETS	ARIES	MOON	v or d	Corrⁿ	v or d	Corrⁿ	v or d	Corrⁿ
00	7 45.0	7 46.3	7 23.8	0.0	0.0	6.0	3.2	12.0	6.3
01	7 45.3	7 46.5	7 24.1	0.1	0.1	6.1	3.2	12.1	6.4
02	7 45.5	7 46.8	7 24.3	0.2	0.1	6.2	3.3	12.2	6.4
03	7 45.8	7 47.0	7 24.5	0.3	0.2	6.3	3.3	12.3	6.5
04	7 46.0	7 47.3	7 24.8	0.4	0.2	6.4	3.4	12.4	6.5
05	7 46.3	7 47.5	7 25.0	0.5	0.3	6.5	3.4	12.5	6.6
06	7 46.5	7 47.8	7 25.2	0.6	0.3	6.6	3.5	12.6	6.6
07	7 46.8	7 48.0	7 25.5	0.7	0.4	6.7	3.5	12.7	6.7
08	7 47.0	7 48.3	7 25.7	0.8	0.4	6.8	3.6	12.8	6.7
09	7 47.3	7 48.5	7 26.0	0.9	0.5	6.9	3.6	12.9	6.8
10	7 47.5	7 48.8	7 26.2	1.0	0.5	7.0	3.7	13.0	6.8
11	7 47.8	7 49.0	7 26.4	1.1	0.6	7.1	3.7	13.1	6.9
12	7 48.0	7 49.3	7 26.7	1.2	0.6	7.2	3.8	13.2	6.9
13	7 48.3	7 49.5	7 26.9	1.3	0.7	7.3	3.8	13.3	7.0
14	7 48.5	7 49.8	7 27.2	1.4	0.7	7.4	3.9	13.4	7.0
15	7 48.8	7 50.0	7 27.4	1.5	0.8	7.5	3.9	13.5	7.1
16	7 49.0	7 50.3	7 27.6	1.6	0.8	7.6	4.0	13.6	7.1
17	7 49.3	7 50.5	7 27.9	1.7	0.9	7.7	4.0	13.7	7.2
18	7 49.5	7 50.8	7 28.1	1.8	0.9	7.8	4.1	13.8	7.2
19	7 49.8	7 51.0	7 28.4	1.9	1.0	7.9	4.1	13.9	7.3
20	7 50.0	7 51.3	7 28.6	2.0	1.1	8.0	4.2	14.0	7.4
21	7 50.3	7 51.5	7 28.8	2.1	1.1	8.1	4.3	14.1	7.4
22	7 50.5	7 51.8	7 29.1	2.2	1.2	8.2	4.3	14.2	7.5
23	7 50.8	7 52.0	7 29.3	2.3	1.2	8.3	4.4	14.3	7.5
24	7 51.0	7 52.3	7 29.5	2.4	1.3	8.4	4.4	14.4	7.6
25	7 51.3	7 52.5	7 29.8	2.5	1.3	8.5	4.5	14.5	7.6
26	7 51.5	7 52.8	7 30.0	2.6	1.4	8.6	4.5	14.6	7.7
27	7 51.8	7 53.0	7 30.3	2.7	1.4	8.7	4.6	14.7	7.7
28	7 52.0	7 53.3	7 30.5	2.8	1.5	8.8	4.6	14.8	7.8
29	7 52.3	7 53.5	7 30.7	2.9	1.5	8.9	4.7	14.9	7.8
30	7 52.5	7 53.8	7 31.0	3.0	1.6	9.0	4.7	15.0	7.9
31	7 52.8	7 54.0	7 31.2	3.1	1.6	9.1	4.8	15.1	7.9
32	7 53.0	7 54.3	7 31.5	3.2	1.7	9.2	4.8	15.2	8.0
33	7 53.3	7 54.5	7 31.7	3.3	1.7	9.3	4.9	15.3	8.0
34	7 53.5	7 54.8	7 31.9	3.4	1.8	9.4	4.9	15.4	8.1
35	7 53.8	7 55.0	7 32.2	3.5	1.8	9.5	5.0	15.5	8.1
36	7 54.0	7 55.3	7 32.4	3.6	1.9	9.6	5.0	15.6	8.2
37	7 54.3	7 55.5	7 32.6	3.7	1.9	9.7	5.1	15.7	8.2
38	7 54.5	7 55.8	7 32.9	3.8	2.0	9.8	5.1	15.8	8.3
39	7 54.8	7 56.0	7 33.1	3.9	2.0	9.9	5.2	15.9	8.3
40	7 55.0	7 56.3	7 33.4	4.0	2.1	10.0	5.3	16.0	8.4
41	7 55.3	7 56.6	7 33.6	4.1	2.2	10.1	5.3	16.1	8.5
42	7 55.5	7 56.8	7 33.8	4.2	2.2	10.2	5.4	16.2	8.5
43	7 55.8	7 57.1	7 34.1	4.3	2.3	10.3	5.4	16.3	8.6
44	7 56.0	7 57.3	7 34.3	4.4	2.3	10.4	5.5	16.4	8.6
45	7 56.3	7 57.6	7 34.6	4.5	2.4	10.5	5.5	16.5	8.7
46	7 56.5	7 57.8	7 34.8	4.6	2.4	10.6	5.6	16.6	8.7
47	7 56.8	7 58.1	7 35.0	4.7	2.5	10.7	5.6	16.7	8.8
48	7 57.0	7 58.3	7 35.3	4.8	2.5	10.8	5.7	16.8	8.8
49	7 57.3	7 58.6	7 35.5	4.9	2.6	10.9	5.7	16.9	8.9
50	7 57.5	7 58.8	7 35.7	5.0	2.6	11.0	5.8	17.0	8.9
51	7 57.8	7 59.1	7 36.0	5.1	2.7	11.1	5.8	17.1	9.0
52	7 58.0	7 59.3	7 36.2	5.2	2.7	11.2	5.9	17.2	9.0
53	7 58.3	7 59.6	7 36.5	5.3	2.8	11.3	5.9	17.3	9.1
54	7 58.5	7 59.8	7 36.7	5.4	2.8	11.4	6.0	17.4	9.1
55	7 58.8	8 00.1	7 36.9	5.5	2.9	11.5	6.0	17.5	9.2
56	7 59.0	8 00.3	7 37.2	5.6	2.9	11.6	6.1	17.6	9.2
57	7 59.3	8 00.6	7 37.4	5.7	3.0	11.7	6.1	17.7	9.3
58	7 59.5	8 00.8	7 37.7	5.8	3.0	11.8	6.2	17.8	9.3
59	7 59.8	8 01.1	7 37.9	5.9	3.1	11.9	6.2	17.9	9.4
60	8 00.0	8 01.3	7 38.1	6.0	3.2	12.0	6.3	18.0	9.5

32ᵐ

32 m	SUN PLANETS	ARIES	MOON	v or d Corrⁿ	v or d Corrⁿ	v or d Corrⁿ
s	° ′	° ′	° ′	′ ′	′ ′	′ ′
00	8 00·0	8 01·3	7 38·1	0·0 0·0	6·0 3·3	12·0 6·5
01	8 00·3	8 01·6	7 38·4	0·1 0·1	6·1 3·3	12·1 6·6
02	8 00·5	8 01·8	7 38·6	0·2 0·1	6·2 3·4	12·2 6·6
03	8 00·8	8 02·1	7 38·8	0·3 0·2	6·3 3·4	12·3 6·7
04	8 01·0	8 02·3	7 39·1	0·4 0·2	6·4 3·5	12·4 6·7
05	8 01·3	8 02·6	7 39·3	0·5 0·3	6·5 3·5	12·5 6·8
06	8 01·5	8 02·8	7 39·6	0·6 0·3	6·6 3·6	12·6 6·8
07	8 01·8	8 03·1	7 39·8	0·7 0·4	6·7 3·6	12·7 6·9
08	8 02·0	8 03·3	7 40·0	0·8 0·4	6·8 3·7	12·8 6·9
09	8 02·3	8 03·6	7 40·3	0·9 0·5	6·9 3·7	12·9 7·0
10	8 02·5	8 03·8	7 40·5	1·0 0·5	7·0 3·8	13·0 7·0
11	8 02·8	8 04·1	7 40·8	1·1 0·6	7·1 3·8	13·1 7·1
12	8 03·0	8 04·3	7 41·0	1·2 0·7	7·2 3·9	13·2 7·2
13	8 03·3	8 04·6	7 41·2	1·3 0·7	7·3 4·0	13·3 7·2
14	8 03·5	8 04·8	7 41·5	1·4 0·8	7·4 4·0	13·4 7·3
15	8 03·8	8 05·1	7 41·7	1·5 0·8	7·5 4·1	13·5 7·3
16	8 04·0	8 05·3	7 42·0	1·6 0·9	7·6 4·1	13·6 7·4
17	8 04·3	8 05·6	7 42·2	1·7 0·9	7·7 4·2	13·7 7·4
18	8 04·5	8 05·8	7 42·4	1·8 1·0	7·8 4·2	13·8 7·5
19	8 04·8	8 06·1	7 42·7	1·9 1·0	7·9 4·3	13·9 7·5
20	8 05·0	8 06·3	7 42·9	2·0 1·1	8·0 4·3	14·0 7·6
21	8 05·3	8 06·6	7 43·1	2·1 1·1	8·1 4·4	14·1 7·6
22	8 05·5	8 06·8	7 43·4	2·2 1·2	8·2 4·4	14·2 7·7
23	8 05·8	8 07·1	7 43·6	2·3 1·2	8·3 4·5	14·3 7·7
24	8 06·0	8 07·3	7 43·9	2·4 1·3	8·4 4·6	14·4 7·8
25	8 06·3	8 07·6	7 44·1	2·5 1·4	8·5 4·6	14·5 7·9
26	8 06·5	8 07·8	7 44·3	2·6 1·4	8·6 4·7	14·6 7·9
27	8 06·8	8 08·1	7 44·6	2·7 1·5	8·7 4·7	14·7 8·0
28	8 07·0	8 08·3	7 44·8	2·8 1·5	8·8 4·8	14·8 8·0
29	8 07·3	8 08·6	7 45·1	2·9 1·6	8·9 4·8	14·9 8·1
30	8 07·5	8 08·8	7 45·3	3·0 1·6	9·0 4·9	15·0 8·1
31	8 07·8	8 09·1	7 45·5	3·1 1·7	9·1 4·9	15·1 8·2
32	8 08·0	8 09·3	7 45·8	3·2 1·7	9·2 5·0	15·2 8·2
33	8 08·3	8 09·6	7 46·0	3·3 1·8	9·3 5·0	15·3 8·3
34	8 08·5	8 09·8	7 46·2	3·4 1·8	9·4 5·1	15·4 8·3
35	8 08·8	8 10·1	7 46·5	3·5 1·9	9·5 5·1	15·5 8·4
36	8 09·0	8 10·3	7 46·7	3·6 2·0	9·6 5·2	15·6 8·5
37	8 09·3	8 10·6	7 47·0	3·7 2·0	9·7 5·3	15·7 8·5
38	8 09·5	8 10·8	7 47·2	3·8 2·1	9·8 5·3	15·8 8·6
39	8 09·8	8 11·1	7 47·4	3·9 2·1	9·9 5·4	15·9 8·6
40	8 10·0	8 11·3	7 47·7	4·0 2·2	10·0 5·4	16·0 8·7
41	8 10·3	8 11·6	7 47·9	4·1 2·2	10·1 5·5	16·1 8·7
42	8 10·5	8 11·8	7 48·2	4·2 2·3	10·2 5·5	16·2 8·8
43	8 10·8	8 12·1	7 48·4	4·3 2·3	10·3 5·6	16·3 8·8
44	8 11·0	8 12·3	7 48·6	4·4 2·4	10·4 5·6	16·4 8·9
45	8 11·3	8 12·6	7 48·9	4·5 2·4	10·5 5·7	16·5 8·9
46	8 11·5	8 12·8	7 49·1	4·6 2·5	10·6 5·7	16·6 9·0
47	8 11·8	8 13·1	7 49·3	4·7 2·5	10·7 5·8	16·7 9·0
48	8 12·0	8 13·3	7 49·6	4·8 2·6	10·8 5·8	16·8 9·1
49	8 12·3	8 13·6	7 49·8	4·9 2·7	10·9 5·9	16·9 9·2
50	8 12·5	8 13·8	7 50·1	5·0 2·7	11·0 6·0	17·0 9·2
51	8 12·8	8 14·1	7 50·3	5·1 2·8	11·1 6·0	17·1 9·3
52	8 13·0	8 14·3	7 50·5	5·2 2·8	11·2 6·1	17·2 9·3
53	8 13·3	8 14·6	7 50·8	5·3 2·9	11·3 6·1	17·3 9·4
54	8 13·5	8 14·9	7 51·0	5·4 2·9	11·4 6·2	17·4 9·4
55	8 13·8	8 15·1	7 51·3	5·5 3·0	11·5 6·2	17·5 9·5
56	8 14·0	8 15·4	7 51·5	5·6 3·0	11·6 6·3	17·6 9·5
57	8 14·3	8 15·6	7 51·7	5·7 3·1	11·7 6·3	17·7 9·6
58	8 14·5	8 15·9	7 52·0	5·8 3·1	11·8 6·4	17·8 9·6
59	8 14·8	8 16·1	7 52·2	5·9 3·2	11·9 6·4	17·9 9·7
60	8 15·0	8 16·4	7 52·5	6·0 3·3	12·0 6·5	18·0 9·8

33ᵐ

33 m	SUN PLANETS	ARIES	MOON	v or d Corrⁿ	v or d Corrⁿ	v or d Corrⁿ
s	° ′	° ′	° ′	′ ′	′ ′	′ ′
00	8 15·0	8 16·4	7 52·5	0·0 0·0	6·0 3·4	12·0 6·7
01	8 15·3	8 16·6	7 52·7	0·1 0·1	6·1 3·4	12·1 6·8
02	8 15·5	8 16·9	7 52·9	0·2 0·1	6·2 3·5	12·2 6·8
03	8 15·8	8 17·1	7 53·2	0·3 0·2	6·3 3·5	12·3 6·9
04	8 16·0	8 17·4	7 53·4	0·4 0·2	6·4 3·6	12·4 6·9
05	8 16·3	8 17·6	7 53·6	0·5 0·3	6·5 3·6	12·5 7·0
06	8 16·5	8 17·9	7 53·9	0·6 0·3	6·6 3·7	12·6 7·0
07	8 16·8	8 18·1	7 54·1	0·7 0·4	6·7 3·7	12·7 7·1
08	8 17·0	8 18·4	7 54·4	0·8 0·4	6·8 3·8	12·8 7·1
09	8 17·3	8 18·6	7 54·6	0·9 0·5	6·9 3·9	12·9 7·2
10	8 17·5	8 18·9	7 54·8	1·0 0·6	7·0 3·9	13·0 7·3
11	8 17·8	8 19·1	7 55·1	1·1 0·6	7·1 4·0	13·1 7·3
12	8 18·0	8 19·4	7 55·3	1·2 0·7	7·2 4·0	13·2 7·4
13	8 18·3	8 19·6	7 55·6	1·3 0·7	7·3 4·1	13·3 7·4
14	8 18·5	8 19·9	7 55·8	1·4 0·8	7·4 4·1	13·4 7·5
15	8 18·8	8 20·1	7 56·0	1·5 0·8	7·5 4·2	13·5 7·5
16	8 19·0	8 20·4	7 56·3	1·6 0·9	7·6 4·2	13·6 7·6
17	8 19·3	8 20·6	7 56·5	1·7 0·9	7·7 4·3	13·7 7·6
18	8 19·5	8 20·9	7 56·7	1·8 1·0	7·8 4·4	13·8 7·7
19	8 19·8	8 21·1	7 57·0	1·9 1·1	7·9 4·4	13·9 7·8
20	8 20·0	8 21·4	7 57·2	2·0 1·1	8·0 4·5	14·0 7·8
21	8 20·3	8 21·6	7 57·5	2·1 1·2	8·1 4·5	14·1 7·9
22	8 20·5	8 21·9	7 57·7	2·2 1·2	8·2 4·6	14·2 7·9
23	8 20·8	8 22·1	7 57·9	2·3 1·3	8·3 4·6	14·3 8·0
24	8 21·0	8 22·4	7 58·2	2·4 1·3	8·4 4·7	14·4 8·0
25	8 21·3	8 22·6	7 58·4	2·5 1·4	8·5 4·7	14·5 8·1
26	8 21·5	8 22·9	7 58·7	2·6 1·5	8·6 4·8	14·6 8·2
27	8 21·8	8 23·1	7 58·9	2·7 1·5	8·7 4·9	14·7 8·2
28	8 22·0	8 23·4	7 59·1	2·8 1·6	8·8 4·9	14·8 8·3
29	8 22·3	8 23·6	7 59·4	2·9 1·6	8·9 5·0	14·9 8·3
30	8 22·5	8 23·9	7 59·6	3·0 1·7	9·0 5·0	15·0 8·4
31	8 22·8	8 24·1	7 59·8	3·1 1·7	9·1 5·1	15·1 8·4
32	8 23·0	8 24·4	8 00·1	3·2 1·8	9·2 5·1	15·2 8·5
33	8 23·3	8 24·6	8 00·3	3·3 1·8	9·3 5·2	15·3 8·5
34	8 23·5	8 24·9	8 00·6	3·4 1·9	9·4 5·2	15·4 8·6
35	8 23·8	8 25·1	8 00·8	3·5 2·0	9·5 5·3	15·5 8·7
36	8 24·0	8 25·4	8 01·0	3·6 2·0	9·6 5·4	15·6 8·7
37	8 24·3	8 25·6	8 01·3	3·7 2·1	9·7 5·4	15·7 8·8
38	8 24·5	8 25·9	8 01·5	3·8 2·1	9·8 5·5	15·8 8·8
39	8 24·8	8 26·1	8 01·8	3·9 2·2	9·9 5·5	15·9 8·9
40	8 25·0	8 26·4	8 02·0	4·0 2·2	10·0 5·6	16·0 8·9
41	8 25·3	8 26·6	8 02·2	4·1 2·3	10·1 5·6	16·1 9·0
42	8 25·5	8 26·9	8 02·5	4·2 2·3	10·2 5·7	16·2 9·0
43	8 25·8	8 27·1	8 02·7	4·3 2·4	10·3 5·8	16·3 9·1
44	8 26·0	8 27·4	8 02·9	4·4 2·5	10·4 5·8	16·4 9·2
45	8 26·3	8 27·6	8 03·2	4·5 2·5	10·5 5·9	16·5 9·2
46	8 26·5	8 27·9	8 03·4	4·6 2·6	10·6 5·9	16·6 9·3
47	8 26·8	8 28·1	8 03·7	4·7 2·6	10·7 6·0	16·7 9·3
48	8 27·0	8 28·4	8 03·9	4·8 2·7	10·8 6·0	16·8 9·4
49	8 27·3	8 28·6	8 04·1	4·9 2·7	10·9 6·1	16·9 9·4
50	8 27·5	8 28·9	8 04·4	5·0 2·8	11·0 6·1	17·0 9·5
51	8 27·8	8 29·1	8 04·6	5·1 2·8	11·1 6·2	17·1 9·5
52	8 28·0	8 29·4	8 04·9	5·2 2·9	11·2 6·3	17·2 9·6
53	8 28·3	8 29·6	8 05·1	5·3 3·0	11·3 6·3	17·3 9·7
54	8 28·5	8 29·9	8 05·3	5·4 3·0	11·4 6·4	17·4 9·7
55	8 28·8	8 30·1	8 05·6	5·5 3·1	11·5 6·4	17·5 9·8
56	8 29·0	8 30·4	8 05·8	5·6 3·1	11·6 6·5	17·6 9·8
57	8 29·3	8 30·6	8 06·1	5·7 3·2	11·7 6·5	17·7 9·9
58	8 29·5	8 30·9	8 06·3	5·8 3·2	11·8 6·6	17·8 9·9
59	8 29·8	8 31·1	8 06·5	5·9 3·3	11·9 6·6	17·9 10·0
60	8 30·0	8 31·4	8 06·8	6·0 3·4	12·0 6·7	18·0 10·1

34	SUN PLANETS	ARIES	MOON	v or Corrⁿ d	v or Corrⁿ d	v or Corrⁿ d
s	° ′	° ′	° ′	′ ′	′ ′	′ ′
00	8 30·0	8 31·4	8 06·8	0·0 0·0	6·0 3·5	12·0 6·9
01	8 30·3	8 31·6	8 07·0	0·1 0·1	6·1 3·5	12·1 7·0
02	8 30·5	8 31·9	8 07·2	0·2 0·1	6·2 3·6	12·2 7·0
03	8 30·8	8 32·1	8 07·5	0·3 0·2	6·3 3·6	12·3 7·1
04	8 31·0	8 32·4	8 07·7	0·4 0·2	6·4 3·7	12·4 7·1
05	8 31·3	8 32·6	8 08·0	0·5 0·3	6·5 3·7	12·5 7·2
06	8 31·5	8 32·9	8 08·2	0·6 0·3	6·6 3·8	12·6 7·2
07	8 31·8	8 33·2	8 08·4	0·7 0·4	6·7 3·9	12·7 7·3
08	8 32·0	8 33·4	8 08·7	0·8 0·5	6·8 3·9	12·8 7·4
09	8 32·3	8 33·7	8 08·9	0·9 0·5	6·9 4·0	12·9 7·4
10	8 32·5	8 33·9	8 09·2	1·0 0·6	7·0 4·0	13·0 7·5
11	8 32·8	8 34·2	8 09·4	1·1 0·6	7·1 4·1	13·1 7·5
12	8 33·0	8 34·4	8 09·6	1·2 0·7	7·2 4·1	13·2 7·6
13	8 33·3	8 34·7	8 09·9	1·3 0·7	7·3 4·2	13·3 7·6
14	8 33·5	8 34·9	8 10·1	1·4 0·8	7·4 4·3	13·4 7·7
15	8 33·8	8 35·2	8 10·3	1·5 0·9	7·5 4·3	13·5 7·8
16	8 34·0	8 35·4	8 10·6	1·6 0·9	7·6 4·4	13·6 7·8
17	8 34·3	8 35·7	8 10·8	1·7 1·0	7·7 4·4	13·7 7·9
18	8 34·5	8 35·9	8 11·1	1·8 1·0	7·8 4·5	13·8 7·9
19	8 34·8	8 36·2	8 11·3	1·9 1·1	7·9 4·5	13·9 8·0
20	8 35·0	8 36·4	8 11·5	2·0 1·2	8·0 4·6	14·0 8·1
21	8 35·3	8 36·7	8 11·8	2·1 1·2	8·1 4·7	14·1 8·1
22	8 35·5	8 36·9	8 12·0	2·2 1·3	8·2 4·7	14·2 8·2
23	8 35·8	8 37·2	8 12·3	2·3 1·3	8·3 4·8	14·3 8·2
24	8 36·0	8 37·4	8 12·5	2·4 1·4	8·4 4·8	14·4 8·3
25	8 36·3	8 37·7	8 12·7	2·5 1·4	8·5 4·9	14·5 8·3
26	8 36·5	8 37·9	8 13·0	2·6 1·5	8·6 4·9	14·6 8·4
27	8 36·8	8 38·2	8 13·2	2·7 1·6	8·7 5·0	14·7 8·5
28	8 37·0	8 38·4	8 13·4	2·8 1·6	8·8 5·1	14·8 8·5
29	8 37·3	8 38·7	8 13·7	2·9 1·7	8·9 5·1	14·9 8·6
30	8 37·5	8 38·9	8 13·9	3·0 1·7	9·0 5·2	15·0 8·6
31	8 37·8	8 39·2	8 14·2	3·1 1·8	9·1 5·2	15·1 8·7
32	8 38·0	8 39·4	8 14·4	3·2 1·8	9·2 5·3	15·2 8·7
33	8 38·3	8 39·7	8 14·6	3·3 1·9	9·3 5·3	15·3 8·8
34	8 38·5	8 39·9	8 14·9	3·4 2·0	9·4 5·4	15·4 8·9
35	8 38·8	8 40·2	8 15·1	3·5 2·0	9·5 5·5	15·5 8·9
36	8 39·0	8 40·4	8 15·4	3·6 2·1	9·6 5·5	15·6 9·0
37	8 39·3	8 40·7	8 15·6	3·7 2·1	9·7 5·6	15·7 9·0
38	8 39·5	8 40·9	8 15·8	3·8 2·2	9·8 5·6	15·8 9·1
39	8 39·8	8 41·2	8 16·1	3·9 2·2	9·9 5·7	15·9 9·1
40	8 40·0	8 41·4	8 16·3	4·0 2·3	10·0 5·8	16·0 9·2
41	8 40·3	8 41·7	8 16·5	4·1 2·4	10·1 5·8	16·1 9·3
42	8 40·5	8 41·9	8 16·8	4·2 2·4	10·2 5·9	16·2 9·3
43	8 40·8	8 42·2	8 17·0	4·3 2·5	10·3 5·9	16·3 9·4
44	8 41·0	8 42·4	8 17·3	4·4 2·5	10·4 6·0	16·4 9·4
45	8 41·3	8 42·7	8 17·5	4·5 2·6	10·5 6·0	16·5 9·5
46	8 41·5	8 42·9	8 17·7	4·6 2·6	10·6 6·1	16·6 9·5
47	8 41·8	8 43·2	8 18·0	4·7 2·7	10·7 6·2	16·7 9·6
48	8 42·0	8 43·4	8 18·2	4·8 2·8	10·8 6·2	16·8 9·7
49	8 42·3	8 43·7	8 18·5	4·9 2·8	10·9 6·3	16·9 9·7
50	8 42·5	8 43·9	8 18·7	5·0 2·9	11·0 6·3	17·0 9·8
51	8 42·8	8 44·2	8 18·9	5·1 2·9	11·1 6·4	17·1 9·8
52	8 43·0	8 44·4	8 19·2	5·2 3·0	11·2 6·4	17·2 9·9
53	8 43·3	8 44·7	8 19·4	5·3 3·0	11·3 6·5	17·3 9·9
54	8 43·5	8 44·9	8 19·7	5·4 3·1	11·4 6·6	17·4 10·0
55	8 43·8	8 45·2	8 19·9	5·5 3·2	11·5 6·6	17·5 10·1
56	8 44·0	8 45·4	8 20·1	5·6 3·2	11·6 6·7	17·6 10·1
57	8 44·3	8 45·7	8 20·4	5·7 3·3	11·7 6·7	17·7 10·2
58	8 44·5	8 45·9	8 20·6	5·8 3·3	11·8 6·8	17·8 10·2
59	8 44·8	8 46·2	8 20·8	5·9 3·4	11·9 6·8	17·9 10·3
60	8 45·0	8 46·4	8 21·1	6·0 3·5	12·0 6·9	18·0 10·4

35	SUN PLANETS	ARIES	MOON	v or Corrⁿ d	v or Corrⁿ d	v or Corrⁿ d
s	° ′	° ′	° ′	′ ′	′ ′	′ ′
00	8 45·0	8 46·4	8 21·1	0·0 0·0	6·0 3·6	12·0 7·1
01	8 45·3	8 46·7	8 21·3	0·1 0·1	6·1 3·6	12·1 7·2
02	8 45·5	8 46·9	8 21·6	0·2 0·1	6·2 3·7	12·2 7·2
03	8 45·8	8 47·2	8 21·8	0·3 0·2	6·3 3·7	12·3 7·3
04	8 46·0	8 47·4	8 22·0	0·4 0·2	6·4 3·8	12·4 7·3
05	8 46·3	8 47·7	8 22·3	0·5 0·3	6·5 3·8	12·5 7·4
06	8 46·5	8 47·9	8 22·5	0·6 0·4	6·6 3·9	12·6 7·5
07	8 46·8	8 48·2	8 22·8	0·7 0·4	6·7 4·0	12·7 7·5
08	8 47·0	8 48·4	8 23·0	0·8 0·5	6·8 4·0	12·8 7·6
09	8 47·3	8 48·7	8 23·2	0·9 0·5	6·9 4·1	12·9 7·6
10	8 47·5	8 48·9	8 23·5	1·0 0·6	7·0 4·1	13·0 7·7
11	8 47·8	8 49·2	8 23·7	1·1 0·7	7·1 4·2	13·1 7·7
12	8 48·0	8 49·4	8 23·9	1·2 0·7	7·2 4·3	13·2 7·8
13	8 48·3	8 49·7	8 24·2	1·3 0·8	7·3 4·3	13·3 7·8
14	8 48·5	8 49·9	8 24·4	1·4 0·8	7·4 4·4	13·4 7·9
15	8 48·8	8 50·2	8 24·7	1·5 0·9	7·5 4·4	13·5 8·0
16	8 49·0	8 50·4	8 24·9	1·6 0·9	7·6 4·5	13·6 8·0
17	8 49·3	8 50·7	8 25·1	1·7 1·0	7·7 4·6	13·7 8·1
18	8 49·5	8 50·9	8 25·4	1·8 1·1	7·8 4·6	13·8 8·2
19	8 49·8	8 51·2	8 25·6	1·9 1·1	7·9 4·7	13·9 8·2
20	8 50·0	8 51·5	8 25·9	2·0 1·2	8·0 4·7	14·0 8·3
21	8 50·3	8 51·7	8 26·1	2·1 1·2	8·1 4·8	14·1 8·3
22	8 50·5	8 52·0	8 26·3	2·2 1·3	8·2 4·9	14·2 8·4
23	8 50·8	8 52·2	8 26·6	2·3 1·4	8·3 4·9	14·3 8·5
24	8 51·0	8 52·5	8 26·8	2·4 1·4	8·4 5·0	14·4 8·5
25	8 51·3	8 52·7	8 27·0	2·5 1·5	8·5 5·0	14·5 8·6
26	8 51·5	8 53·0	8 27·3	2·6 1·5	8·6 5·1	14·6 8·6
27	8 51·8	8 53·2	8 27·5	2·7 1·6	8·7 5·1	14·7 8·7
28	8 52·0	8 53·5	8 27·8	2·8 1·7	8·8 5·2	14·8 8·8
29	8 52·3	8 53·7	8 28·0	2·9 1·7	8·9 5·3	14·9 8·8
30	8 52·5	8 54·0	8 28·2	3·0 1·8	9·0 5·3	15·0 8·9
31	8 52·8	8 54·2	8 28·5	3·1 1·8	9·1 5·4	15·1 8·9
32	8 53·0	8 54·5	8 28·7	3·2 1·9	9·2 5·4	15·2 9·0
33	8 53·3	8 54·7	8 29·0	3·3 2·0	9·3 5·5	15·3 9·1
34	8 53·5	8 55·0	8 29·2	3·4 2·0	9·4 5·6	15·4 9·1
35	8 53·8	8 55·2	8 29·4	3·5 2·1	9·5 5·6	15·5 9·2
36	8 54·0	8 55·5	8 29·7	3·6 2·1	9·6 5·7	15·6 9·2
37	8 54·3	8 55·7	8 29·9	3·7 2·2	9·7 5·7	15·7 9·3
38	8 54·5	8 56·0	8 30·2	3·8 2·2	9·8 5·8	15·8 9·3
39	8 54·8	8 56·2	8 30·4	3·9 2·3	9·9 5·9	15·9 9·4
40	8 55·0	8 56·5	8 30·6	4·0 2·4	10·0 5·9	16·0 9·5
41	8 55·3	8 56·7	8 30·9	4·1 2·4	10·1 6·0	16·1 9·5
42	8 55·5	8 57·0	8 31·1	4·2 2·5	10·2 6·0	16·2 9·6
43	8 55·8	8 57·2	8 31·3	4·3 2·5	10·3 6·1	16·3 9·6
44	8 56·0	8 57·5	8 31·6	4·4 2·6	10·4 6·2	16·4 9·7
45	8 56·3	8 57·7	8 31·8	4·5 2·7	10·5 6·2	16·5 9·8
46	8 56·5	8 58·0	8 32·1	4·6 2·7	10·6 6·3	16·6 9·8
47	8 56·8	8 58·2	8 32·3	4·7 2·8	10·7 6·3	16·7 9·9
48	8 57·0	8 58·5	8 32·5	4·8 2·8	10·8 6·4	16·8 9·9
49	8 57·3	8 58·7	8 32·8	4·9 2·9	10·9 6·4	16·9 10·0
50	8 57·5	8 59·0	8 33·0	5·0 3·0	11·0 6·5	17·0 10·1
51	8 57·8	8 59·2	8 33·3	5·1 3·0	11·1 6·6	17·1 10·1
52	8 58·0	8 59·5	8 33·5	5·2 3·1	11·2 6·6	17·2 10·2
53	8 58·3	8 59·7	8 33·7	5·3 3·1	11·3 6·7	17·3 10·2
54	8 58·5	9 00·0	8 34·0	5·4 3·2	11·4 6·7	17·4 10·3
55	8 58·8	9 00·2	8 34·2	5·5 3·3	11·5 6·8	17·5 10·4
56	8 59·0	9 00·5	8 34·4	5·6 3·3	11·6 6·9	17·6 10·4
57	8 59·3	9 00·7	8 34·7	5·7 3·4	11·7 6·9	17·7 10·5
58	8 59·5	9 01·0	8 34·9	5·8 3·4	11·8 7·0	17·8 10·5
59	8 59·8	9 01·2	8 35·2	5·9 3·5	11·9 7·0	17·9 10·6
60	9 00·0	9 01·5	8 35·4	6·0 3·6	12·0 7·1	18·0 10·7

36ᵐ

36	SUN PLANETS	ARIES	MOON	v or Corrⁿ d	v or Corrⁿ d	v or Corrⁿ d
s	° ′	° ′	° ′	′ ′	′ ′	′ ′
00	9 00.0	9 01.5	8 35.4	0.0 0.0	6.0 3.7	12.0 7.3
01	9 00.3	9 01.7	8 35.6	0.1 0.1	6.1 3.7	12.1 7.4
02	9 00.5	9 02.0	8 35.9	0.2 0.1	6.2 3.8	12.2 7.4
03	9 00.8	9 02.2	8 36.1	0.3 0.2	6.3 3.8	12.3 7.5
04	9 01.0	9 02.5	8 36.4	0.4 0.2	6.4 3.9	12.4 7.5
05	9 01.3	9 02.7	8 36.6	0.5 0.3	6.5 4.0	12.5 7.6
06	9 01.5	9 03.0	8 36.8	0.6 0.4	6.6 4.0	12.6 7.7
07	9 01.8	9 03.2	8 37.1	0.7 0.4	6.7 4.1	12.7 7.7
08	9 02.0	9 03.5	8 37.3	0.8 0.5	6.8 4.1	12.8 7.8
09	9 02.3	9 03.7	8 37.5	0.9 0.5	6.9 4.2	12.9 7.8
10	9 02.5	9 04.0	8 37.8	1.0 0.6	7.0 4.3	13.0 7.9
11	9 02.8	9 04.2	8 38.0	1.1 0.7	7.1 4.3	13.1 8.0
12	9 03.0	9 04.5	8 38.3	1.2 0.7	7.2 4.4	13.2 8.0
13	9 03.3	9 04.7	8 38.5	1.3 0.8	7.3 4.4	13.3 8.1
14	9 03.5	9 05.0	8 38.7	1.4 0.9	7.4 4.5	13.4 8.2
15	9 03.8	9 05.2	8 39.0	1.5 0.9	7.5 4.6	13.5 8.2
16	9 04.0	9 05.5	8 39.2	1.6 1.0	7.6 4.6	13.6 8.3
17	9 04.3	9 05.7	8 39.5	1.7 1.0	7.7 4.7	13.7 8.3
18	9 04.5	9 06.0	8 39.7	1.8 1.1	7.8 4.7	13.8 8.4
19	9 04.8	9 06.2	8 39.9	1.9 1.2	7.9 4.8	13.9 8.5
20	9 05.0	9 06.5	8 40.2	2.0 1.2	8.0 4.9	14.0 8.5
21	9 05.3	9 06.7	8 40.4	2.1 1.3	8.1 4.9	14.1 8.6
22	9 05.5	9 07.0	8 40.6	2.2 1.3	8.2 5.0	14.2 8.6
23	9 05.8	9 07.2	8 40.9	2.3 1.4	8.3 5.0	14.3 8.7
24	9 06.0	9 07.5	8 41.1	2.4 1.5	8.4 5.1	14.4 8.8
25	9 06.3	9 07.7	8 41.4	2.5 1.5	8.5 5.2	14.5 8.8
26	9 06.5	9 08.0	8 41.6	2.6 1.6	8.6 5.2	14.6 8.9
27	9 06.8	9 08.2	8 41.8	2.7 1.6	8.7 5.3	14.7 8.9
28	9 07.0	9 08.5	8 42.1	2.8 1.7	8.8 5.4	14.8 9.0
29	9 07.3	9 08.7	8 42.3	2.9 1.8	8.9 5.4	14.9 9.1
30	9 07.5	9 09.0	8 42.6	3.0 1.8	9.0 5.5	15.0 9.1
31	9 07.8	9 09.2	8 42.8	3.1 1.9	9.1 5.5	15.1 9.2
32	9 08.0	9 09.5	8 43.0	3.2 1.9	9.2 5.6	15.2 9.2
33	9 08.3	9 09.8	8 43.3	3.3 2.0	9.3 5.7	15.3 9.3
34	9 08.5	9 10.0	8 43.5	3.4 2.1	9.4 5.7	15.4 9.4
35	9 08.8	9 10.3	8 43.8	3.5 2.1	9.5 5.8	15.5 9.4
36	9 09.0	9 10.5	8 44.0	3.6 2.2	9.6 5.8	15.6 9.5
37	9 09.3	9 10.8	8 44.2	3.7 2.3	9.7 5.9	15.7 9.6
38	9 09.5	9 11.0	8 44.5	3.8 2.3	9.8 6.0	15.8 9.6
39	9 09.8	9 11.3	8 44.7	3.9 2.4	9.9 6.0	15.9 9.7
40	9 10.0	9 11.5	8 44.9	4.0 2.4	10.0 6.1	16.0 9.7
41	9 10.3	9 11.8	8 45.2	4.1 2.5	10.1 6.1	16.1 9.8
42	9 10.5	9 12.0	8 45.4	4.2 2.6	10.2 6.2	16.2 9.9
43	9 10.8	9 12.3	8 45.7	4.3 2.6	10.3 6.3	16.3 9.9
44	9 11.0	9 12.5	8 45.9	4.4 2.7	10.4 6.3	16.4 10.0
45	9 11.3	9 12.8	8 46.1	4.5 2.7	10.5 6.4	16.5 10.0
46	9 11.5	9 13.0	8 46.4	4.6 2.8	10.6 6.4	16.6 10.1
47	9 11.8	9 13.3	8 46.6	4.7 2.9	10.7 6.5	16.7 10.2
48	9 12.0	9 13.5	8 46.9	4.8 2.9	10.8 6.6	16.8 10.2
49	9 12.3	9 13.8	8 47.1	4.9 3.0	10.9 6.6	16.9 10.3
50	9 12.5	9 14.0	8 47.3	5.0 3.0	11.0 6.7	17.0 10.3
51	9 12.8	9 14.3	8 47.6	5.1 3.1	11.1 6.8	17.1 10.4
52	9 13.0	9 14.5	8 47.8	5.2 3.2	11.2 6.8	17.2 10.5
53	9 13.3	9 14.8	8 48.0	5.3 3.2	11.3 6.9	17.3 10.5
54	9 13.5	9 15.0	8 48.3	5.4 3.3	11.4 6.9	17.4 10.6
55	9 13.8	9 15.3	8 48.5	5.5 3.3	11.5 7.0	17.5 10.6
56	9 14.0	9 15.5	8 48.8	5.6 3.4	11.6 7.1	17.6 10.7
57	9 14.3	9 15.8	8 49.0	5.7 3.5	11.7 7.1	17.7 10.8
58	9 14.5	9 16.0	8 49.2	5.8 3.5	11.8 7.2	17.8 10.8
59	9 14.8	9 16.3	8 49.5	5.9 3.6	11.9 7.2	17.9 10.9
60	9 15.0	9 16.5	8 49.7	6.0 3.7	12.0 7.3	18.0 11.0

37ᵐ

37	SUN PLANETS	ARIES	MOON	v or Corrⁿ d	v or Corrⁿ d	v or Corrⁿ d
s	° ′	° ′	° ′	′ ′	′ ′	′ ′
00	9 15.0	9 16.5	8 49.7	0.0 0.0	6.0 3.8	12.0 7.5
01	9 15.3	9 16.8	8 50.0	0.1 0.1	6.1 3.8	12.1 7.6
02	9 15.5	9 17.0	8 50.2	0.2 0.1	6.2 3.9	12.2 7.6
03	9 15.8	9 17.3	8 50.4	0.3 0.2	6.3 3.9	12.3 7.7
04	9 16.0	9 17.5	8 50.7	0.4 0.3	6.4 4.0	12.4 7.8
05	9 16.3	9 17.8	8 50.9	0.5 0.3	6.5 4.1	12.5 7.8
06	9 16.5	9 18.0	8 51.1	0.6 0.4	6.6 4.1	12.6 7.9
07	9 16.8	9 18.3	8 51.4	0.7 0.4	6.7 4.2	12.7 7.9
08	9 17.0	9 18.5	8 51.6	0.8 0.5	6.8 4.3	12.8 8.0
09	9 17.3	9 18.8	8 51.9	0.9 0.6	6.9 4.3	12.9 8.1
10	9 17.5	9 19.0	8 52.1	1.0 0.6	7.0 4.4	13.0 8.1
11	9 17.8	9 19.3	8 52.3	1.1 0.7	7.1 4.4	13.1 8.2
12	9 18.0	9 19.5	8 52.6	1.2 0.8	7.2 4.5	13.2 8.3
13	9 18.3	9 19.8	8 52.8	1.3 0.8	7.3 4.6	13.3 8.3
14	9 18.5	9 20.0	8 53.1	1.4 0.9	7.4 4.6	13.4 8.4
15	9 18.8	9 20.3	8 53.3	1.5 0.9	7.5 4.7	13.5 8.4
16	9 19.0	9 20.5	8 53.5	1.6 1.0	7.6 4.8	13.6 8.5
17	9 19.3	9 20.8	8 53.8	1.7 1.1	7.7 4.8	13.7 8.6
18	9 19.5	9 21.0	8 54.0	1.8 1.1	7.8 4.9	13.8 8.6
19	9 19.8	9 21.3	8 54.3	1.9 1.2	7.9 4.9	13.9 8.7
20	9 20.0	9 21.5	8 54.5	2.0 1.3	8.0 5.0	14.0 8.8
21	9 20.3	9 21.8	8 54.7	2.1 1.3	8.1 5.1	14.1 8.8
22	9 20.5	9 22.0	8 55.0	2.2 1.4	8.2 5.1	14.2 8.9
23	9 20.8	9 22.3	8 55.2	2.3 1.4	8.3 5.2	14.3 8.9
24	9 21.0	9 22.5	8 55.4	2.4 1.5	8.4 5.3	14.4 9.0
25	9 21.3	9 22.8	8 55.7	2.5 1.6	8.5 5.3	14.5 9.1
26	9 21.5	9 23.0	8 55.9	2.6 1.6	8.6 5.4	14.6 9.1
27	9 21.8	9 23.3	8 56.2	2.7 1.7	8.7 5.4	14.7 9.2
28	9 22.0	9 23.5	8 56.4	2.8 1.8	8.8 5.5	14.8 9.3
29	9 22.3	9 23.8	8 56.6	2.9 1.8	8.9 5.6	14.9 9.3
30	9 22.5	9 24.0	8 56.9	3.0 1.9	9.0 5.6	15.0 9.4
31	9 22.8	9 24.3	8 57.1	3.1 1.9	9.1 5.7	15.1 9.4
32	9 23.0	9 24.5	8 57.4	3.2 2.0	9.2 5.8	15.2 9.5
33	9 23.3	9 24.8	8 57.6	3.3 2.1	9.3 5.8	15.3 9.6
34	9 23.5	9 25.0	8 57.8	3.4 2.1	9.4 5.9	15.4 9.6
35	9 23.8	9 25.3	8 58.1	3.5 2.2	9.5 5.9	15.5 9.7
36	9 24.0	9 25.5	8 58.3	3.6 2.3	9.6 6.0	15.6 9.8
37	9 24.3	9 25.8	8 58.5	3.7 2.3	9.7 6.1	15.7 9.8
38	9 24.5	9 26.0	8 58.8	3.8 2.4	9.8 6.1	15.8 9.9
39	9 24.8	9 26.3	8 59.0	3.9 2.4	9.9 6.2	15.9 9.9
40	9 25.0	9 26.5	8 59.3	4.0 2.5	10.0 6.3	16.0 10.0
41	9 25.3	9 26.8	8 59.5	4.1 2.6	10.1 6.3	16.1 10.1
42	9 25.5	9 27.0	8 59.7	4.2 2.6	10.2 6.4	16.2 10.1
43	9 25.8	9 27.3	9 00.0	4.3 2.7	10.3 6.4	16.3 10.2
44	9 26.0	9 27.5	9 00.2	4.4 2.8	10.4 6.5	16.4 10.3
45	9 26.3	9 27.8	9 00.4	4.5 2.8	10.5 6.6	16.5 10.3
46	9 26.5	9 28.1	9 00.7	4.6 2.9	10.6 6.6	16.6 10.4
47	9 26.8	9 28.3	9 00.9	4.7 2.9	10.7 6.7	16.7 10.4
48	9 27.0	9 28.6	9 01.2	4.8 3.0	10.8 6.8	16.8 10.5
49	9 27.3	9 28.8	9 01.4	4.9 3.1	10.9 6.8	16.9 10.6
50	9 27.5	9 29.1	9 01.6	5.0 3.1	11.0 6.9	17.0 10.6
51	9 27.8	9 29.3	9 01.9	5.1 3.2	11.1 6.9	17.1 10.7
52	9 28.0	9 29.6	9 02.1	5.2 3.3	11.2 7.0	17.2 10.8
53	9 28.3	9 29.8	9 02.4	5.3 3.3	11.3 7.1	17.3 10.8
54	9 28.5	9 30.1	9 02.6	5.4 3.4	11.4 7.1	17.4 10.9
55	9 28.8	9 30.3	9 02.8	5.5 3.4	11.5 7.2	17.5 10.9
56	9 29.0	9 30.6	9 03.1	5.6 3.5	11.6 7.3	17.6 11.0
57	9 29.3	9 30.8	9 03.3	5.7 3.6	11.7 7.3	17.7 11.1
58	9 29.5	9 31.1	9 03.6	5.8 3.6	11.8 7.4	17.8 11.1
59	9 29.8	9 31.3	9 03.8	5.9 3.7	11.9 7.4	17.9 11.2
60	9 30.0	9 31.6	9 04.0	6.0 3.8	12.0 7.5	18.0 11.3

38ᵐ

38 s	SUN PLANETS	ARIES	MOON	v or d	Corrⁿ	v or d	Corrⁿ	v or d	Corrⁿ
00	9 30.0	9 31.6	9 04.0	0.0	0.0	6.0	3.9	12.0	7.7
01	9 30.3	9 31.8	9 04.3	0.1	0.1	6.1	3.9	12.1	7.8
02	9 30.5	9 32.1	9 04.5	0.2	0.1	6.2	4.0	12.2	7.8
03	9 30.8	9 32.3	9 04.7	0.3	0.2	6.3	4.0	12.3	7.9
04	9 31.0	9 32.6	9 05.0	0.4	0.3	6.4	4.1	12.4	8.0
05	9 31.3	9 32.8	9 05.2	0.5	0.3	6.5	4.2	12.5	8.0
06	9 31.5	9 33.1	9 05.5	0.6	0.4	6.6	4.2	12.6	8.1
07	9 31.8	9 33.3	9 05.7	0.7	0.4	6.7	4.3	12.7	8.1
08	9 32.0	9 33.6	9 05.9	0.8	0.5	6.8	4.4	12.8	8.2
09	9 32.3	9 33.8	9 06.2	0.9	0.6	6.9	4.4	12.9	8.3
10	9 32.5	9 34.1	9 06.4	1.0	0.6	7.0	4.5	13.0	8.3
11	9 32.8	9 34.3	9 06.7	1.1	0.7	7.1	4.6	13.1	8.4
12	9 33.0	9 34.6	9 06.9	1.2	0.8	7.2	4.6	13.2	8.5
13	9 33.3	9 34.8	9 07.1	1.3	0.8	7.3	4.7	13.3	8.5
14	9 33.5	9 35.1	9 07.4	1.4	0.9	7.4	4.7	13.4	8.6
15	9 33.8	9 35.3	9 07.6	1.5	1.0	7.5	4.8	13.5	8.7
16	9 34.0	9 35.6	9 07.9	1.6	1.0	7.6	4.9	13.6	8.7
17	9 34.3	9 35.8	9 08.1	1.7	1.1	7.7	4.9	13.7	8.8
18	9 34.5	9 36.1	9 08.3	1.8	1.2	7.8	5.0	13.8	8.9
19	9 34.8	9 36.3	9 08.6	1.9	1.2	7.9	5.1	13.9	8.9
20	9 35.0	9 36.6	9 08.8	2.0	1.3	8.0	5.1	14.0	9.0
21	9 35.3	9 36.8	9 09.0	2.1	1.3	8.1	5.2	14.1	9.0
22	9 35.5	9 37.1	9 09.3	2.2	1.4	8.2	5.3	14.2	9.1
23	9 35.8	9 37.3	9 09.5	2.3	1.5	8.3	5.3	14.3	9.2
24	9 36.0	9 37.6	9 09.8	2.4	1.5	8.4	5.4	14.4	9.2
25	9 36.3	9 37.8	9 10.0	2.5	1.6	8.5	5.5	14.5	9.3
26	9 36.5	9 38.1	9 10.2	2.6	1.7	8.6	5.5	14.6	9.4
27	9 36.8	9 38.3	9 10.5	2.7	1.7	8.7	5.6	14.7	9.4
28	9 37.0	9 38.6	9 10.7	2.8	1.8	8.8	5.6	14.8	9.5
29	9 37.3	9 38.8	9 11.0	2.9	1.9	8.9	5.7	14.9	9.6
30	9 37.5	9 39.1	9 11.2	3.0	1.9	9.0	5.8	15.0	9.6
31	9 37.8	9 39.3	9 11.4	3.1	2.0	9.1	5.8	15.1	9.7
32	9 38.0	9 39.6	9 11.7	3.2	2.1	9.2	5.9	15.2	9.8
33	9 38.3	9 39.8	9 11.9	3.3	2.1	9.3	6.0	15.3	9.8
34	9 38.5	9 40.1	9 12.1	3.4	2.2	9.4	6.0	15.4	9.9
35	9 38.8	9 40.3	9 12.4	3.5	2.2	9.5	6.1	15.5	9.9
36	9 39.0	9 40.6	9 12.6	3.6	2.3	9.6	6.2	15.6	10.0
37	9 39.3	9 40.8	9 12.9	3.7	2.4	9.7	6.2	15.7	10.1
38	9 39.5	9 41.1	9 13.1	3.8	2.4	9.8	6.3	15.8	10.1
39	9 39.8	9 41.3	9 13.3	3.9	2.5	9.9	6.4	15.9	10.2
40	9 40.0	9 41.6	9 13.6	4.0	2.6	10.0	6.4	16.0	10.3
41	9 40.3	9 41.8	9 13.8	4.1	2.6	10.1	6.5	16.1	10.3
42	9 40.5	9 42.1	9 14.1	4.2	2.7	10.2	6.5	16.2	10.4
43	9 40.8	9 42.3	9 14.3	4.3	2.8	10.3	6.6	16.3	10.5
44	9 41.0	9 42.6	9 14.5	4.4	2.8	10.4	6.7	16.4	10.5
45	9 41.3	9 42.8	9 14.8	4.5	2.9	10.5	6.7	16.5	10.6
46	9 41.5	9 43.1	9 15.0	4.6	3.0	10.6	6.8	16.6	10.7
47	9 41.8	9 43.3	9 15.2	4.7	3.0	10.7	6.9	16.7	10.7
48	9 42.0	9 43.6	9 15.5	4.8	3.1	10.8	6.9	16.8	10.8
49	9 42.3	9 43.8	9 15.7	4.9	3.1	10.9	7.0	16.9	10.8
50	9 42.5	9 44.1	9 16.0	5.0	3.2	11.0	7.1	17.0	10.9
51	9 42.8	9 44.3	9 16.2	5.1	3.3	11.1	7.1	17.1	11.0
52	9 43.0	9 44.6	9 16.4	5.2	3.3	11.2	7.2	17.2	11.0
53	9 43.3	9 44.8	9 16.7	5.3	3.4	11.3	7.3	17.3	11.1
54	9 43.5	9 45.1	9 16.9	5.4	3.5	11.4	7.3	17.4	11.2
55	9 43.8	9 45.3	9 17.2	5.5	3.5	11.5	7.4	17.5	11.2
56	9 44.0	9 45.6	9 17.4	5.6	3.6	11.6	7.4	17.6	11.3
57	9 44.3	9 45.8	9 17.6	5.7	3.7	11.7	7.5	17.7	11.4
58	9 44.5	9 46.1	9 17.9	5.8	3.7	11.8	7.6	17.8	11.4
59	9 44.8	9 46.4	9 18.1	5.9	3.8	11.9	7.6	17.9	11.5
60	9 45.0	9 46.6	9 18.4	6.0	3.9	12.0	7.7	18.0	11.6

39ᵐ

39 s	SUN PLANETS	ARIES	MOON	v or d	Corrⁿ	v or d	Corrⁿ	v or d	Corrⁿ
00	9 45.0	9 46.6	9 18.4	0.0	0.0	6.0	4.0	12.0	7.9
01	9 45.3	9 46.9	9 18.6	0.1	0.1	6.1	4.0	12.1	8.0
02	9 45.5	9 47.1	9 18.8	0.2	0.1	6.2	4.1	12.2	8.0
03	9 45.8	9 47.4	9 19.1	0.3	0.2	6.3	4.1	12.3	8.1
04	9 46.0	9 47.6	9 19.3	0.4	0.3	6.4	4.2	12.4	8.2
05	9 46.3	9 47.9	9 19.5	0.5	0.3	6.5	4.3	12.5	8.2
06	9 46.5	9 48.1	9 19.8	0.6	0.4	6.6	4.3	12.6	8.3
07	9 46.8	9 48.4	9 20.0	0.7	0.5	6.7	4.4	12.7	8.3
08	9 47.0	9 48.6	9 20.3	0.8	0.5	6.8	4.5	12.8	8.4
09	9 47.3	9 48.9	9 20.5	0.9	0.6	6.9	4.5	12.9	8.5
10	9 47.5	9 49.1	9 20.7	1.0	0.7	7.0	4.6	13.0	8.6
11	9 47.8	9 49.4	9 21.0	1.1	0.7	7.1	4.7	13.1	8.6
12	9 48.0	9 49.6	9 21.2	1.2	0.8	7.2	4.7	13.2	8.7
13	9 48.3	9 49.9	9 21.5	1.3	0.9	7.3	4.8	13.3	8.8
14	9 48.5	9 50.1	9 21.7	1.4	0.9	7.4	4.9	13.4	8.8
15	9 48.8	9 50.4	9 21.9	1.5	1.0	7.5	4.9	13.5	8.9
16	9 49.0	9 50.6	9 22.2	1.6	1.1	7.6	5.0	13.6	9.0
17	9 49.3	9 50.9	9 22.4	1.7	1.1	7.7	5.1	13.7	9.0
18	9 49.5	9 51.1	9 22.6	1.8	1.2	7.8	5.1	13.8	9.1
19	9 49.8	9 51.4	9 22.9	1.9	1.3	7.9	5.2	13.9	9.2
20	9 50.0	9 51.6	9 23.1	2.0	1.3	8.0	5.3	14.0	9.2
21	9 50.3	9 51.9	9 23.4	2.1	1.4	8.1	5.3	14.1	9.3
22	9 50.5	9 52.1	9 23.6	2.2	1.4	8.2	5.4	14.2	9.3
23	9 50.8	9 52.4	9 23.8	2.3	1.5	8.3	5.5	14.3	9.4
24	9 51.0	9 52.6	9 24.1	2.4	1.6	8.4	5.5	14.4	9.5
25	9 51.3	9 52.9	9 24.3	2.5	1.6	8.5	5.6	14.5	9.5
26	9 51.5	9 53.1	9 24.6	2.6	1.7	8.6	5.7	14.6	9.6
27	9 51.8	9 53.4	9 24.8	2.7	1.8	8.7	5.7	14.7	9.7
28	9 52.0	9 53.6	9 25.0	2.8	1.8	8.8	5.8	14.8	9.7
29	9 52.3	9 53.9	9 25.3	2.9	1.9	8.9	5.9	14.9	9.8
30	9 52.5	9 54.1	9 25.5	3.0	2.0	9.0	5.9	15.0	9.9
31	9 52.8	9 54.4	9 25.7	3.1	2.0	9.1	6.0	15.1	9.9
32	9 53.0	9 54.6	9 26.0	3.2	2.1	9.2	6.1	15.2	10.0
33	9 53.3	9 54.9	9 26.2	3.3	2.2	9.3	6.1	15.3	10.1
34	9 53.5	9 55.1	9 26.5	3.4	2.2	9.4	6.2	15.4	10.1
35	9 53.8	9 55.4	9 26.7	3.5	2.3	9.5	6.3	15.5	10.2
36	9 54.0	9 55.6	9 26.9	3.6	2.4	9.6	6.3	15.6	10.3
37	9 54.3	9 55.9	9 27.2	3.7	2.4	9.7	6.4	15.7	10.3
38	9 54.5	9 56.1	9 27.4	3.8	2.5	9.8	6.5	15.8	10.4
39	9 54.8	9 56.4	9 27.7	3.9	2.6	9.9	6.5	15.9	10.5
40	9 55.0	9 56.6	9 27.9	4.0	2.6	10.0	6.6	16.0	10.5
41	9 55.3	9 56.9	9 28.1	4.1	2.7	10.1	6.7	16.1	10.6
42	9 55.5	9 57.1	9 28.4	4.2	2.8	10.2	6.7	16.2	10.7
43	9 55.8	9 57.4	9 28.6	4.3	2.8	10.3	6.8	16.3	10.7
44	9 56.0	9 57.6	9 28.8	4.4	2.9	10.4	6.9	16.4	10.8
45	9 56.3	9 57.9	9 29.1	4.5	3.0	10.5	6.9	16.5	10.9
46	9 56.5	9 58.1	9 29.3	4.6	3.0	10.6	7.0	16.6	10.9
47	9 56.8	9 58.4	9 29.6	4.7	3.1	10.7	7.0	16.7	11.0
48	9 57.0	9 58.6	9 29.8	4.8	3.2	10.8	7.1	16.8	11.1
49	9 57.3	9 58.9	9 30.0	4.9	3.2	10.9	7.2	16.9	11.1
50	9 57.5	9 59.1	9 30.3	5.0	3.3	11.0	7.2	17.0	11.2
51	9 57.8	9 59.4	9 30.5	5.1	3.3	11.1	7.3	17.1	11.3
52	9 58.0	9 59.6	9 30.8	5.2	3.4	11.2	7.4	17.2	11.3
53	9 58.3	9 59.9	9 31.0	5.3	3.5	11.3	7.4	17.3	11.4
54	9 58.5	10 00.1	9 31.2	5.4	3.6	11.4	7.5	17.4	11.5
55	9 58.8	10 00.4	9 31.5	5.5	3.6	11.5	7.6	17.5	11.5
56	9 59.0	10 00.6	9 31.7	5.6	3.7	11.6	7.6	17.6	11.6
57	9 59.3	10 00.9	9 32.0	5.7	3.8	11.7	7.7	17.7	11.7
58	9 59.5	10 01.1	9 32.2	5.8	3.8	11.8	7.8	17.8	11.7
59	9 59.8	10 01.4	9 32.4	5.9	3.9	11.9	7.8	17.9	11.8
60	10 00.0	10 01.6	9 32.7	6.0	4.0	12.0	7.9	18.0	11.9

40ᵐ

40	SUN PLANETS	ARIES	MOON	v or d Corrⁿ	v or d Corrⁿ	v or d Corrⁿ
s	° ′	° ′	° ′	′ ′	′ ′	′ ′
00	10 00·0	10 01·6	9 32·7	0·0 0·0	6·0 4·1	12·0 8·1
01	10 00·3	10 01·9	9 32·9	0·1 0·1	6·1 4·1	12·1 8·2
02	10 00·5	10 02·1	9 33·1	0·2 0·1	6·2 4·2	12·2 8·2
03	10 00·8	10 02·4	9 33·4	0·3 0·2	6·3 4·3	12·3 8·3
04	10 01·0	10 02·6	9 33·6	0·4 0·3	6·4 4·3	12·4 8·4
05	10 01·3	10 02·9	9 33·9	0·5 0·3	6·5 4·4	12·5 8·4
06	10 01·5	10 03·1	9 34·1	0·6 0·4	6·6 4·5	12·6 8·5
07	10 01·8	10 03·4	9 34·3	0·7 0·5	6·7 4·5	12·7 8·6
08	10 02·0	10 03·6	9 34·6	0·8 0·5	6·8 4·6	12·8 8·6
09	10 02·3	10 03·9	9 34·8	0·9 0·6	6·9 4·7	12·9 8·7
10	10 02·5	10 04·1	9 35·1	1·0 0·7	7·0 4·7	13·0 8·8
11	10 02·8	10 04·4	9 35·3	1·1 0·7	7·1 4·8	13·1 8·8
12	10 03·0	10 04·7	9 35·5	1·2 0·8	7·2 4·9	13·2 8·9
13	10 03·3	10 04·9	9 35·8	1·3 0·9	7·3 4·9	13·3 9·0
14	10 03·5	10 05·2	9 36·0	1·4 0·9	7·4 5·0	13·4 9·0
15	10 03·8	10 05·4	9 36·2	1·5 1·0	7·5 5·1	13·5 9·1
16	10 04·0	10 05·7	9 36·5	1·6 1·1	7·6 5·1	13·6 9·2
17	10 04·3	10 05·9	9 36·7	1·7 1·1	7·7 5·2	13·7 9·2
18	10 04·5	10 06·2	9 37·0	1·8 1·2	7·8 5·3	13·8 9·3
19	10 04·8	10 06·4	9 37·2	1·9 1·3	7·9 5·3	13·9 9·4
20	10 05·0	10 06·7	9 37·4	2·0 1·4	8·0 5·4	14·0 9·5
21	10 05·3	10 06·9	9 37·7	2·1 1·4	8·1 5·5	14·1 9·5
22	10 05·5	10 07·2	9 37·9	2·2 1·5	8·2 5·5	14·2 9·6
23	10 05·8	10 07·4	9 38·2	2·3 1·6	8·3 5·6	14·3 9·7
24	10 06·0	10 07·7	9 38·4	2·4 1·6	8·4 5·7	14·4 9·7
25	10 06·3	10 07·9	9 38·6	2·5 1·7	8·5 5·7	14·5 9·8
26	10 06·5	10 08·2	9 38·9	2·6 1·8	8·6 5·8	14·6 9·9
27	10 06·8	10 08·4	9 39·1	2·7 1·8	8·7 5·9	14·7 9·9
28	10 07·0	10 08·7	9 39·3	2·8 1·9	8·8 5·9	14·8 10·0
29	10 07·3	10 08·9	9 39·6	2·9 2·0	8·9 6·0	14·9 10·1
30	10 07·5	10 09·2	9 39·8	3·0 2·0	9·0 6·1	15·0 10·1
31	10 07·8	10 09·4	9 40·1	3·1 2·1	9·1 6·1	15·1 10·2
32	10 08·0	10 09·7	9 40·3	3·2 2·2	9·2 6·2	15·2 10·3
33	10 08·3	10 09·9	9 40·5	3·3 2·2	9·3 6·3	15·3 10·3
34	10 08·5	10 10·2	9 40·8	3·4 2·3	9·4 6·3	15·4 10·4
35	10 08·8	10 10·4	9 41·0	3·5 2·4	9·5 6·4	15·5 10·5
36	10 09·0	10 10·7	9 41·3	3·6 2·4	9·6 6·5	15·6 10·5
37	10 09·3	10 10·9	9 41·5	3·7 2·5	9·7 6·5	15·7 10·6
38	10 09·5	10 11·2	9 41·7	3·8 2·6	9·8 6·6	15·8 10·7
39	10 09·8	10 11·4	9 42·0	3·9 2·6	9·9 6·7	15·9 10·7
40	10 10·0	10 11·7	9 42·2	4·0 2·7	10·0 6·8	16·0 10·8
41	10 10·3	10 11·9	9 42·4	4·1 2·8	10·1 6·8	16·1 10·9
42	10 10·5	10 12·2	9 42·7	4·2 2·8	10·2 6·9	16·2 10·9
43	10 10·8	10 12·4	9 42·9	4·3 2·9	10·3 7·0	16·3 11·0
44	10 11·0	10 12·7	9 43·2	4·4 3·0	10·4 7·0	16·4 11·1
45	10 11·3	10 12·9	9 43·4	4·5 3·0	10·5 7·1	16·5 11·1
46	10 11·5	10 13·2	9 43·6	4·6 3·1	10·6 7·2	16·6 11·2
47	10 11·8	10 13·4	9 43·9	4·7 3·2	10·7 7·2	16·7 11·3
48	10 12·0	10 13·7	9 44·1	4·8 3·2	10·8 7·3	16·8 11·3
49	10 12·3	10 13·9	9 44·4	4·9 3·3	10·9 7·4	16·9 11·4
50	10 12·5	10 14·2	9 44·6	5·0 3·4	11·0 7·4	17·0 11·5
51	10 12·8	10 14·4	9 44·8	5·1 3·4	11·1 7·5	17·1 11·5
52	10 13·0	10 14·7	9 45·1	5·2 3·5	11·2 7·6	17·2 11·6
53	10 13·3	10 14·9	9 45·3	5·3 3·6	11·3 7·6	17·3 11·7
54	10 13·5	10 15·2	9 45·6	5·4 3·6	11·4 7·7	17·4 11·7
55	10 13·8	10 15·4	9 45·8	5·5 3·7	11·5 7·8	17·5 11·8
56	10 14·0	10 15·7	9 46·0	5·6 3·8	11·6 7·8	17·6 11·9
57	10 14·3	10 15·9	9 46·3	5·7 3·8	11·7 7·9	17·7 11·9
58	10 14·5	10 16·2	9 46·5	5·8 3·9	11·8 8·0	17·8 12·0
59	10 14·8	10 16·4	9 46·7	5·9 3·9	11·9 8·0	17·9 12·1
60	10 15·0	10 16·7	9 47·0	6·0 4·1	12·0 8·1	18·0 12·2

41ᵐ

41	SUN PLANETS	ARIES	MOON	v or d Corrⁿ	v or d Corrⁿ	v or d Corrⁿ
s	° ′	° ′	° ′	′ ′	′ ′	′ ′
00	10 15·0	10 16·7	9 47·0	0·0 0·0	6·0 4·2	12·0 8·3
01	10 15·3	10 16·9	9 47·2	0·1 0·1	6·1 4·2	12·1 8·4
02	10 15·5	10 17·2	9 47·5	0·2 0·1	6·2 4·3	12·2 8·4
03	10 15·8	10 17·4	9 47·7	0·3 0·2	6·3 4·4	12·3 8·5
04	10 16·0	10 17·7	9 47·9	0·4 0·3	6·4 4·4	12·4 8·6
05	10 16·3	10 17·9	9 48·2	0·5 0·3	6·5 4·5	12·5 8·6
06	10 16·5	10 18·2	9 48·4	0·6 0·4	6·6 4·6	12·6 8·7
07	10 16·8	10 18·4	9 48·7	0·7 0·5	6·7 4·6	12·7 8·8
08	10 17·0	10 18·7	9 48·9	0·8 0·6	6·8 4·7	12·8 8·9
09	10 17·3	10 18·9	9 49·1	0·9 0·6	6·9 4·8	12·9 8·9
10	10 17·5	10 19·2	9 49·4	1·0 0·7	7·0 4·8	13·0 9·0
11	10 17·8	10 19·4	9 49·6	1·1 0·8	7·1 4·9	13·1 9·1
12	10 18·0	10 19·7	9 49·8	1·2 0·8	7·2 5·0	13·2 9·1
13	10 18·3	10 19·9	9 50·1	1·3 0·9	7·3 5·0	13·3 9·2
14	10 18·5	10 20·2	9 50·3	1·4 1·0	7·4 5·1	13·4 9·3
15	10 18·8	10 20·4	9 50·6	1·5 1·0	7·5 5·2	13·5 9·3
16	10 19·0	10 20·7	9 50·8	1·6 1·1	7·6 5·3	13·6 9·4
17	10 19·3	10 20·9	9 51·0	1·7 1·2	7·7 5·3	13·7 9·5
18	10 19·5	10 21·2	9 51·3	1·8 1·2	7·8 5·4	13·8 9·5
19	10 19·8	10 21·4	9 51·5	1·9 1·3	7·9 5·5	13·9 9·6
20	10 20·0	10 21·7	9 51·8	2·0 1·4	8·0 5·5	14·0 9·7
21	10 20·3	10 21·9	9 52·0	2·1 1·5	8·1 5·6	14·1 9·8
22	10 20·5	10 22·2	9 52·2	2·2 1·5	8·2 5·7	14·2 9·8
23	10 20·8	10 22·4	9 52·5	2·3 1·6	8·3 5·7	14·3 9·9
24	10 21·0	10 22·7	9 52·7	2·4 1·7	8·4 5·8	14·4 10·0
25	10 21·3	10 23·0	9 52·9	2·5 1·7	8·5 5·9	14·5 10·0
26	10 21·5	10 23·2	9 53·2	2·6 1·8	8·6 5·9	14·6 10·1
27	10 21·8	10 23·5	9 53·4	2·7 1·9	8·7 6·0	14·7 10·2
28	10 22·0	10 23·7	9 53·7	2·8 1·9	8·8 6·1	14·8 10·2
29	10 22·3	10 24·0	9 53·9	2·9 2·0	8·9 6·2	14·9 10·3
30	10 22·5	10 24·2	9 54·1	3·0 2·1	9·0 6·2	15·0 10·4
31	10 22·8	10 24·5	9 54·4	3·1 2·1	9·1 6·3	15·1 10·4
32	10 23·0	10 24·7	9 54·6	3·2 2·2	9·2 6·4	15·2 10·5
33	10 23·3	10 25·0	9 54·9	3·3 2·3	9·3 6·4	15·3 10·6
34	10 23·5	10 25·2	9 55·1	3·4 2·4	9·4 6·5	15·4 10·7
35	10 23·8	10 25·5	9 55·3	3·5 2·4	9·5 6·6	15·5 10·7
36	10 24·0	10 25·7	9 55·6	3·6 2·5	9·6 6·6	15·6 10·8
37	10 24·3	10 26·0	9 55·8	3·7 2·6	9·7 6·7	15·7 10·9
38	10 24·5	10 26·2	9 56·1	3·8 2·6	9·8 6·8	15·8 10·9
39	10 24·8	10 26·5	9 56·3	3·9 2·7	9·9 6·8	15·9 11·0
40	10 25·0	10 26·7	9 56·5	4·0 2·8	10·0 6·9	16·0 11·1
41	10 25·3	10 27·0	9 56·8	4·1 2·8	10·1 7·0	16·1 11·1
42	10 25·5	10 27·2	9 57·0	4·2 2·9	10·2 7·1	16·2 11·2
43	10 25·8	10 27·5	9 57·2	4·3 3·0	10·3 7·1	16·3 11·3
44	10 26·0	10 27·7	9 57·5	4·4 3·0	10·4 7·2	16·4 11·3
45	10 26·3	10 28·0	9 57·7	4·5 3·1	10·5 7·3	16·5 11·4
46	10 26·5	10 28·2	9 58·0	4·6 3·2	10·6 7·3	16·6 11·5
47	10 26·8	10 28·5	9 58·2	4·7 3·3	10·7 7·4	16·7 11·6
48	10 27·0	10 28·7	9 58·4	4·8 3·3	10·8 7·5	16·8 11·6
49	10 27·3	10 29·0	9 58·7	4·9 3·4	10·9 7·5	16·9 11·7
50	10 27·5	10 29·2	9 58·9	5·0 3·5	11·0 7·6	17·0 11·8
51	10 27·8	10 29·5	9 59·2	5·1 3·5	11·1 7·7	17·1 11·8
52	10 28·0	10 29·7	9 59·4	5·2 3·6	11·2 7·7	17·2 11·9
53	10 28·3	10 30·0	9 59·6	5·3 3·7	11·3 7·8	17·3 12·0
54	10 28·5	10 30·2	9 59·9	5·4 3·7	11·4 7·9	17·4 12·0
55	10 28·8	10 30·5	10 00·1	5·5 3·8	11·5 8·0	17·5 12·1
56	10 29·0	10 30·7	10 00·3	5·6 3·9	11·6 8·0	17·6 12·2
57	10 29·3	10 31·0	10 00·6	5·7 3·9	11·7 8·1	17·7 12·2
58	10 29·5	10 31·2	10 00·8	5·8 4·0	11·8 8·2	17·8 12·3
59	10 29·8	10 31·5	10 01·1	5·9 4·1	11·9 8·2	17·9 12·4
60	10 30·0	10 31·7	10 01·3	6·0 4·2	12·0 8·3	18·0 12·5

42 m	SUN PLANETS	ARIES	MOON	v or Corrⁿ d	v or Corrⁿ d	v or Corrⁿ d
s	° ′	° ′	° ′	′ ′	′ ′	′ ′
00	10 30·0	10 31·7	10 01·3	0·0 0·0	6·0 4·3	12·0 8·5
01	10 30·3	10 32·0	10 01·5	0·1 0·1	6·1 4·3	12·1 8·6
02	10 30·5	10 32·2	10 01·8	0·2 0·1	6·2 4·4	12·2 8·6
03	10 30·8	10 32·5	10 02·0	0·3 0·2	6·3 4·5	12·3 8·7
04	10 31·0	10 32·7	10 02·3	0·4 0·3	6·4 4·5	12·4 8·8
05	10 31·3	10 33·0	10 02·5	0·5 0·4	6·5 4·6	12·5 8·9
06	10 31·5	10 33·2	10 02·7	0·6 0·4	6·6 4·7	12·6 8·9
07	10 31·8	10 33·5	10 03·0	0·7 0·5	6·7 4·7	12·7 9·0
08	10 32·0	10 33·7	10 03·2	0·8 0·6	6·8 4·8	12·8 9·1
09	10 32·3	10 34·0	10 03·4	0·9 0·6	6·9 4·9	12·9 9·1
10	10 32·5	10 34·2	10 03·7	1·0 0·7	7·0 5·0	13·0 9·2
11	10 32·8	10 34·5	10 03·9	1·1 0·8	7·1 5·0	13·1 9·3
12	10 33·0	10 34·7	10 04·2	1·2 0·9	7·2 5·1	13·2 9·4
13	10 33·3	10 35·0	10 04·4	1·3 0·9	7·3 5·2	13·3 9·4
14	10 33·5	10 35·2	10 04·6	1·4 1·0	7·4 5·2	13·4 9·5
15	10 33·8	10 35·5	10 04·9	1·5 1·1	7·5 5·3	13·5 9·6
16	10 34·0	10 35·7	10 05·1	1·6 1·1	7·6 5·4	13·6 9·6
17	10 34·3	10 36·0	10 05·4	1·7 1·2	7·7 5·5	13·7 9·7
18	10 34·5	10 36·2	10 05·6	1·8 1·3	7·8 5·5	13·8 9·8
19	10 34·8	10 36·5	10 05·8	1·9 1·3	7·9 5·6	13·9 9·8
20	10 35·0	10 36·7	10 06·1	2·0 1·4	8·0 5·7	14·0 9·9
21	10 35·3	10 37·0	10 06·3	2·1 1·5	8·1 5·7	14·1 10·0
22	10 35·5	10 37·2	10 06·5	2·2 1·6	8·2 5·8	14·2 10·1
23	10 35·8	10 37·5	10 06·8	2·3 1·6	8·3 5·9	14·3 10·1
24	10 36·0	10 37·7	10 07·0	2·4 1·7	8·4 6·0	14·4 10·2
25	10 36·3	10 38·0	10 07·3	2·5 1·8	8·5 6·0	14·5 10·3
26	10 36·5	10 38·2	10 07·5	2·6 1·8	8·6 6·1	14·6 10·3
27	10 36·8	10 38·5	10 07·7	2·7 1·9	8·7 6·2	14·7 10·4
28	10 37·0	10 38·7	10 08·0	2·8 2·0	8·8 6·2	14·8 10·5
29	10 37·3	10 39·0	10 08·2	2·9 2·1	8·9 6·3	14·9 10·6
30	10 37·5	10 39·2	10 08·5	3·0 2·1	9·0 6·4	15·0 10·6
31	10 37·8	10 39·5	10 08·7	3·1 2·2	9·1 6·4	15·1 10·7
32	10 38·0	10 39·7	10 08·9	3·2 2·3	9·2 6·5	15·2 10·8
33	10 38·3	10 40·0	10 09·2	3·3 2·3	9·3 6·6	15·3 10·8
34	10 38·5	10 40·2	10 09·4	3·4 2·4	9·4 6·7	15·4 10·9
35	10 38·8	10 40·5	10 09·7	3·5 2·5	9·5 6·7	15·5 11·0
36	10 39·0	10 40·7	10 09·9	3·6 2·6	9·6 6·8	15·6 11·1
37	10 39·3	10 41·0	10 10·1	3·7 2·6	9·7 6·9	15·7 11·1
38	10 39·5	10 41·3	10 10·4	3·8 2·7	9·8 6·9	15·8 11·2
39	10 39·8	10 41·5	10 10·6	3·9 2·8	9·9 7·0	15·9 11·3
40	10 40·0	10 41·8	10 10·8	4·0 2·8	10·0 7·1	16·0 11·3
41	10 40·3	10 42·0	10 11·1	4·1 2·9	10·1 7·2	16·1 11·4
42	10 40·5	10 42·3	10 11·3	4·2 3·0	10·2 7·2	16·2 11·5
43	10 40·8	10 42·5	10 11·6	4·3 3·0	10·3 7·3	16·3 11·5
44	10 41·0	10 42·8	10 11·8	4·4 3·1	10·4 7·4	16·4 11·6
45	10 41·3	10 43·0	10 12·0	4·5 3·2	10·5 7·4	16·5 11·7
46	10 41·5	10 43·3	10 12·3	4·6 3·3	10·6 7·5	16·6 11·8
47	10 41·8	10 43·5	10 12·5	4·7 3·3	10·7 7·6	16·7 11·8
48	10 42·0	10 43·8	10 12·8	4·8 3·4	10·8 7·7	16·8 11·9
49	10 42·3	10 44·0	10 13·0	4·9 3·5	10·9 7·7	16·9 12·0
50	10 42·5	10 44·3	10 13·2	5·0 3·5	11·0 7·8	17·0 12·0
51	10 42·8	10 44·5	10 13·5	5·1 3·6	11·1 7·9	17·1 12·1
52	10 43·0	10 44·8	10 13·7	5·2 3·7	11·2 7·9	17·2 12·2
53	10 43·3	10 45·0	10 13·9	5·3 3·8	11·3 8·0	17·3 12·3
54	10 43·5	10 45·3	10 14·2	5·4 3·8	11·4 8·1	17·4 12·3
55	10 43·8	10 45·5	10 14·4	5·5 3·9	11·5 8·1	17·5 12·4
56	10 44·0	10 45·8	10 14·7	5·6 4·0	11·6 8·2	17·6 12·5
57	10 44·3	10 46·0	10 14·9	5·7 4·0	11·7 8·3	17·7 12·5
58	10 44·5	10 46·3	10 15·1	5·8 4·1	11·8 8·4	17·8 12·6
59	10 44·8	10 46·5	10 15·4	5·9 4·2	11·9 8·4	17·9 12·7
60	10 45·0	10 46·8	10 15·6	6·0 4·3	12·0 8·5	18·0 12·8

43 m	SUN PLANETS	ARIES	MOON	v or Corrⁿ d	v or Corrⁿ d	v or Corrⁿ d
s	° ′	° ′	° ′	′ ′	′ ′	′ ′
00	10 45·0	10 46·8	10 15·6	0·0 0·0	6·0 4·4	12·0 8·7
01	10 45·3	10 47·0	10 15·9	0·1 0·1	6·1 4·4	12·1 8·8
02	10 45·5	10 47·3	10 16·1	0·2 0·1	6·2 4·5	12·2 8·8
03	10 45·8	10 47·5	10 16·3	0·3 0·2	6·3 4·6	12·3 8·9
04	10 46·0	10 47·8	10 16·6	0·4 0·3	6·4 4·6	12·4 9·0
05	10 46·3	10 48·0	10 16·8	0·5 0·4	6·5 4·7	12·5 9·1
06	10 46·5	10 48·3	10 17·0	0·6 0·4	6·6 4·8	12·6 9·1
07	10 46·8	10 48·5	10 17·3	0·7 0·5	6·7 4·9	12·7 9·2
08	10 47·0	10 48·8	10 17·5	0·8 0·6	6·8 4·9	12·8 9·3
09	10 47·3	10 49·0	10 17·8	0·9 0·7	6·9 5·0	12·9 9·4
10	10 47·5	10 49·3	10 18·0	1·0 0·7	7·0 5·1	13·0 9·4
11	10 47·8	10 49·5	10 18·2	1·1 0·8	7·1 5·1	13·1 9·5
12	10 48·0	10 49·8	10 18·5	1·2 0·9	7·2 5·2	13·2 9·6
13	10 48·3	10 50·0	10 18·7	1·3 0·9	7·3 5·3	13·3 9·6
14	10 48·5	10 50·3	10 19·0	1·4 1·0	7·4 5·4	13·4 9·7
15	10 48·8	10 50·5	10 19·2	1·5 1·1	7·5 5·4	13·5 9·8
16	10 49·0	10 50·8	10 19·4	1·6 1·2	7·6 5·5	13·6 9·9
17	10 49·3	10 51·0	10 19·7	1·7 1·2	7·7 5·6	13·7 9·9
18	10 49·5	10 51·3	10 19·9	1·8 1·3	7·8 5·7	13·8 10·0
19	10 49·8	10 51·5	10 20·2	1·9 1·4	7·9 5·7	13·9 10·1
20	10 50·0	10 51·8	10 20·4	2·0 1·5	8·0 5·8	14·0 10·2
21	10 50·3	10 52·0	10 20·6	2·1 1·5	8·1 5·9	14·1 10·2
22	10 50·5	10 52·3	10 20·9	2·2 1·6	8·2 5·9	14·2 10·3
23	10 50·8	10 52·5	10 21·1	2·3 1·7	8·3 6·0	14·3 10·4
24	10 51·0	10 52·8	10 21·3	2·4 1·7	8·4 6·1	14·4 10·4
25	10 51·3	10 53·0	10 21·6	2·5 1·8	8·5 6·2	14·5 10·5
26	10 51·5	10 53·3	10 21·8	2·6 1·9	8·6 6·2	14·6 10·6
27	10 51·8	10 53·5	10 22·1	2·7 2·0	8·7 6·3	14·7 10·7
28	10 52·0	10 53·8	10 22·3	2·8 2·0	8·8 6·4	14·8 10·7
29	10 52·3	10 54·0	10 22·5	2·9 2·1	8·9 6·5	14·9 10·8
30	10 52·5	10 54·3	10 22·8	3·0 2·2	9·0 6·5	15·0 10·9
31	10 52·8	10 54·5	10 23·0	3·1 2·2	9·1 6·6	15·1 10·9
32	10 53·0	10 54·8	10 23·3	3·2 2·3	9·2 6·7	15·2 11·0
33	10 53·3	10 55·0	10 23·5	3·3 2·4	9·3 6·7	15·3 11·1
34	10 53·5	10 55·3	10 23·7	3·4 2·4	9·4 6·8	15·4 11·2
35	10 53·8	10 55·5	10 24·0	3·5 2·5	9·5 6·9	15·5 11·2
36	10 54·0	10 55·8	10 24·2	3·6 2·6	9·6 7·0	15·6 11·3
37	10 54·3	10 56·0	10 24·4	3·7 2·7	9·7 7·0	15·7 11·4
38	10 54·5	10 56·3	10 24·7	3·8 2·8	9·8 7·1	15·8 11·5
39	10 54·8	10 56·5	10 24·9	3·9 2·8	9·9 7·2	15·9 11·5
40	10 55·0	10 56·8	10 25·2	4·0 2·9	10·0 7·3	16·0 11·6
41	10 55·3	10 57·0	10 25·4	4·1 3·0	10·1 7·3	16·1 11·7
42	10 55·5	10 57·3	10 25·6	4·2 3·0	10·2 7·4	16·2 11·7
43	10 55·8	10 57·5	10 25·9	4·3 3·1	10·3 7·5	16·3 11·8
44	10 56·0	10 57·8	10 26·1	4·4 3·2	10·4 7·5	16·4 11·9
45	10 56·3	10 58·0	10 26·4	4·5 3·3	10·5 7·6	16·5 12·0
46	10 56·5	10 58·3	10 26·6	4·6 3·3	10·6 7·7	16·6 12·0
47	10 56·8	10 58·5	10 26·8	4·7 3·4	10·7 7·8	16·7 12·1
48	10 57·0	10 58·8	10 27·1	4·8 3·5	10·8 7·8	16·8 12·2
49	10 57·3	10 59·0	10 27·3	4·9 3·6	10·9 7·9	16·9 12·3
50	10 57·5	10 59·3	10 27·5	5·0 3·6	11·0 8·0	17·0 12·3
51	10 57·8	10 59·6	10 27·8	5·1 3·7	11·1 8·0	17·1 12·4
52	10 58·0	10 59·8	10 28·0	5·2 3·8	11·2 8·1	17·2 12·5
53	10 58·3	11 00·1	10 28·3	5·3 3·8	11·3 8·2	17·3 12·5
54	10 58·5	11 00·3	10 28·5	5·4 3·9	11·4 8·3	17·4 12·6
55	10 58·8	11 00·6	10 28·7	5·5 4·0	11·5 8·3	17·5 12·7
56	10 59·0	11 00·8	10 29·0	5·6 4·1	11·6 8·4	17·6 12·8
57	10 59·3	11 01·1	10 29·2	5·7 4·1	11·7 8·5	17·7 12·8
58	10 59·5	11 01·3	10 29·5	5·8 4·2	11·8 8·6	17·8 12·9
59	10 59·8	11 01·6	10 29·7	5·9 4·3	11·9 8·6	17·9 13·0
60	11 00·0	11 01·8	10 29·9	6·0 4·4	12·0 8·7	18·0 13·1

44 s	SUN PLANETS	ARIES	MOON	v or d Corrⁿ	v or d Corrⁿ	v or d Corrⁿ
	° ′	° ′	° ′	′ ′	′ ′	′ ′
00	11 00·0	11 01·8	10 29·9	0·0 0·0	6·0 4·5	12·0 8·9
01	11 00·3	11 02·1	10 30·2	0·1 0·1	6·1 4·5	12·1 9·0
02	11 00·5	11 02·3	10 30·4	0·2 0·1	6·2 4·6	12·2 9·0
03	11 00·8	11 02·6	10 30·6	0·3 0·2	6·3 4·7	12·3 9·1
04	11 01·0	11 02·8	10 30·9	0·4 0·3	6·4 4·7	12·4 9·2
05	11 01·3	11 03·1	10 31·1	0·5 0·4	6·5 4·8	12·5 9·3
06	11 01·5	11 03·3	10 31·4	0·6 0·4	6·6 4·9	12·6 9·3
07	11 01·8	11 03·6	10 31·6	0·7 0·5	6·7 5·0	12·7 9·4
08	11 02·0	11 03·8	10 31·8	0·8 0·6	6·8 5·0	12·8 9·5
09	11 02·3	11 04·1	10 32·1	0·9 0·7	6·9 5·1	12·9 9·6
10	11 02·5	11 04·3	10 32·3	1·0 0·7	7·0 5·2	13·0 9·6
11	11 02·8	11 04·6	10 32·6	1·1 0·8	7·1 5·3	13·1 9·7
12	11 03·0	11 04·8	10 32·8	1·2 0·9	7·2 5·3	13·2 9·8
13	11 03·3	11 05·1	10 33·0	1·3 1·0	7·3 5·4	13·3 9·9
14	11 03·5	11 05·3	10 33·3	1·4 1·0	7·4 5·5	13·4 9·9
15	11 03·8	11 05·6	10 33·5	1·5 1·1	7·5 5·6	13·5 10·0
16	11 04·0	11 05·8	10 33·8	1·6 1·2	7·6 5·6	13·6 10·1
17	11 04·3	11 06·1	10 34·0	1·7 1·3	7·7 5·7	13·7 10·2
18	11 04·5	11 06·3	10 34·2	1·8 1·3	7·8 5·8	13·8 10·2
19	11 04·8	11 06·6	10 34·5	1·9 1·4	7·9 5·9	13·9 10·3
20	11 05·0	11 06·8	10 34·7	2·0 1·5	8·0 5·9	14·0 10·4
21	11 05·3	11 07·1	10 34·9	2·1 1·6	8·1 6·0	14·1 10·5
22	11 05·5	11 07·3	10 35·2	2·2 1·6	8·2 6·1	14·2 10·5
23	11 05·8	11 07·6	10 35·4	2·3 1·7	8·3 6·2	14·3 10·6
24	11 06·0	11 07·8	10 35·7	2·4 1·8	8·4 6·2	14·4 10·7
25	11 06·3	11 08·1	10 35·9	2·5 1·9	8·5 6·3	14·5 10·8
26	11 06·5	11 08·3	10 36·1	2·6 1·9	8·6 6·4	14·6 10·8
27	11 06·8	11 08·6	10 36·4	2·7 2·0	8·7 6·5	14·7 10·9
28	11 07·0	11 08·8	10 36·6	2·8 2·1	8·8 6·5	14·8 11·0
29	11 07·3	11 09·1	10 36·9	2·9 2·2	8·9 6·6	14·9 11·1
30	11 07·5	11 09·3	10 37·1	3·0 2·2	9·0 6·7	15·0 11·1
31	11 07·8	11 09·6	10 37·3	3·1 2·3	9·1 6·7	15·1 11·2
32	11 08·0	11 09·8	10 37·6	3·2 2·4	9·2 6·8	15·2 11·3
33	11 08·3	11 10·1	10 37·8	3·3 2·4	9·3 6·9	15·3 11·3
34	11 08·5	11 10·3	10 38·0	3·4 2·5	9·4 7·0	15·4 11·4
35	11 08·8	11 10·6	10 38·3	3·5 2·6	9·5 7·0	15·5 11·5
36	11 09·0	11 10·8	10 38·5	3·6 2·7	9·6 7·1	15·6 11·6
37	11 09·3	11 11·1	10 38·8	3·7 2·7	9·7 7·2	15·7 11·6
38	11 09·5	11 11·3	10 39·0	3·8 2·8	9·8 7·3	15·8 11·7
39	11 09·8	11 11·6	10 39·2	3·9 2·9	9·9 7·3	15·9 11·8
40	11 10·0	11 11·8	10 39·5	4·0 3·0	10·0 7·4	16·0 11·9
41	11 10·3	11 12·1	10 39·7	4·1 3·0	10·1 7·5	16·1 11·9
42	11 10·5	11 12·3	10 40·0	4·2 3·1	10·2 7·6	16·2 12·0
43	11 10·8	11 12·6	10 40·2	4·3 3·2	10·3 7·6	16·3 12·1
44	11 11·0	11 12·8	10 40·4	4·4 3·3	10·4 7·7	16·4 12·2
45	11 11·3	11 13·1	10 40·7	4·5 3·3	10·5 7·8	16·5 12·2
46	11 11·5	11 13·3	10 40·9	4·6 3·4	10·6 7·9	16·6 12·3
47	11 11·8	11 13·6	10 41·1	4·7 3·5	10·7 7·9	16·7 12·4
48	11 12·0	11 13·8	10 41·4	4·8 3·6	10·8 8·0	16·8 12·5
49	11 12·3	11 14·1	10 41·6	4·9 3·6	10·9 8·1	16·9 12·5
50	11 12·5	11 14·3	10 41·9	5·0 3·7	11·0 8·2	17·0 12·6
51	11 12·8	11 14·6	10 42·1	5·1 3·8	11·1 8·2	17·1 12·7
52	11 13·0	11 14·8	10 42·3	5·2 3·9	11·2 8·3	17·2 12·8
53	11 13·3	11 15·1	10 42·6	5·3 3·9	11·3 8·4	17·3 12·8
54	11 13·5	11 15·3	10 42·8	5·4 4·0	11·4 8·5	17·4 12·9
55	11 13·8	11 15·6	10 43·1	5·5 4·1	11·5 8·5	17·5 13·0
56	11 14·0	11 15·8	10 43·3	5·6 4·2	11·6 8·6	17·6 13·1
57	11 14·3	11 16·1	10 43·5	5·7 4·2	11·7 8·7	17·7 13·1
58	11 14·5	11 16·3	10 43·8	5·8 4·3	11·8 8·8	17·8 13·2
59	11 14·8	11 16·6	10 44·0	5·9 4·4	11·9 8·8	17·9 13·3
60	11 15·0	11 16·8	10 44·3	6·0 4·5	12·0 8·9	18·0 13·4

45 s	SUN PLANETS	ARIES	MOON	v or d Corrⁿ	v or d Corrⁿ	v or d Corrⁿ
	° ′	° ′	° ′	′ ′	′ ′	′ ′
00	11 15·0	11 16·8	10 44·3	0·0 0·0	6·0 4·6	12·0 9·1
01	11 15·3	11 17·1	10 44·5	0·1 0·1	6·1 4·6	12·1 9·2
02	11 15·5	11 17·3	10 44·7	0·2 0·2	6·2 4·7	12·2 9·3
03	11 15·8	11 17·6	10 45·0	0·3 0·2	6·3 4·8	12·3 9·3
04	11 16·0	11 17·9	10 45·2	0·4 0·3	6·4 4·9	12·4 9·4
05	11 16·3	11 18·1	10 45·4	0·5 0·4	6·5 4·9	12·5 9·5
06	11 16·5	11 18·4	10 45·7	0·6 0·5	6·6 5·0	12·6 9·6
07	11 16·8	11 18·6	10 45·9	0·7 0·5	6·7 5·1	12·7 9·6
08	11 17·0	11 18·9	10 46·2	0·8 0·6	6·8 5·2	12·8 9·7
09	11 17·3	11 19·1	10 46·4	0·9 0·7	6·9 5·2	12·9 9·8
10	11 17·5	11 19·4	10 46·6	1·0 0·8	7·0 5·3	13·0 9·9
11	11 17·8	11 19·6	10 46·9	1·1 0·8	7·1 5·4	13·1 9·9
12	11 18·0	11 19·9	10 47·1	1·2 0·9	7·2 5·5	13·2 10·0
13	11 18·3	11 20·1	10 47·4	1·3 1·0	7·3 5·5	13·3 10·1
14	11 18·5	11 20·4	10 47·6	1·4 1·1	7·4 5·6	13·4 10·2
15	11 18·8	11 20·6	10 47·8	1·5 1·1	7·5 5·7	13·5 10·2
16	11 19·0	11 20·9	10 48·1	1·6 1·2	7·6 5·8	13·6 10·3
17	11 19·3	11 21·1	10 48·3	1·7 1·3	7·7 5·8	13·7 10·4
18	11 19·5	11 21·4	10 48·5	1·8 1·4	7·8 5·9	13·8 10·5
19	11 19·8	11 21·6	10 48·8	1·9 1·4	7·9 6·0	13·9 10·5
20	11 20·0	11 21·9	10 49·0	2·0 1·5	8·0 6·1	14·0 10·6
21	11 20·3	11 22·1	10 49·3	2·1 1·6	8·1 6·1	14·1 10·7
22	11 20·5	11 22·4	10 49·5	2·2 1·7	8·2 6·2	14·2 10·8
23	11 20·8	11 22·6	10 49·7	2·3 1·7	8·3 6·3	14·3 10·8
24	11 21·0	11 22·9	10 50·0	2·4 1·8	8·4 6·4	14·4 10·9
25	11 21·3	11 23·1	10 50·2	2·5 1·9	8·5 6·4	14·5 11·0
26	11 21·5	11 23·4	10 50·5	2·6 2·0	8·6 6·5	14·6 11·1
27	11 21·8	11 23·6	10 50·7	2·7 2·0	8·7 6·6	14·7 11·1
28	11 22·0	11 23·9	10 50·9	2·8 2·1	8·8 6·7	14·8 11·2
29	11 22·3	11 24·1	10 51·2	2·9 2·2	8·9 6·7	14·9 11·3
30	11 22·5	11 24·4	10 51·4	3·0 2·3	9·0 6·8	15·0 11·4
31	11 22·8	11 24·6	10 51·6	3·1 2·4	9·1 6·9	15·1 11·5
32	11 23·0	11 24·9	10 51·9	3·2 2·4	9·2 7·0	15·2 11·5
33	11 23·3	11 25·1	10 52·1	3·3 2·5	9·3 7·1	15·3 11·6
34	11 23·5	11 25·4	10 52·4	3·4 2·6	9·4 7·1	15·4 11·7
35	11 23·8	11 25·6	10 52·6	3·5 2·7	9·5 7·2	15·5 11·8
36	11 24·0	11 25·9	10 52·8	3·6 2·7	9·6 7·3	15·6 11·8
37	11 24·3	11 26·1	10 53·1	3·7 2·8	9·7 7·4	15·7 11·9
38	11 24·5	11 26·4	10 53·3	3·8 2·9	9·8 7·4	15·8 12·0
39	11 24·8	11 26·6	10 53·6	3·9 3·0	9·9 7·5	15·9 12·1
40	11 25·0	11 26·9	10 53·8	4·0 3·0	10·0 7·6	16·0 12·1
41	11 25·3	11 27·1	10 54·0	4·1 3·1	10·1 7·7	16·1 12·2
42	11 25·5	11 27·4	10 54·3	4·2 3·2	10·2 7·7	16·2 12·3
43	11 25·8	11 27·6	10 54·5	4·3 3·3	10·3 7·8	16·3 12·4
44	11 26·0	11 27·9	10 54·7	4·4 3·3	10·4 7·9	16·4 12·4
45	11 26·3	11 28·1	10 55·0	4·5 3·4	10·5 8·0	16·5 12·5
46	11 26·5	11 28·4	10 55·2	4·6 3·5	10·6 8·0	16·6 12·6
47	11 26·8	11 28·6	10 55·5	4·7 3·6	10·7 8·1	16·7 12·7
48	11 27·0	11 28·9	10 55·7	4·8 3·6	10·8 8·2	16·8 12·7
49	11 27·3	11 29·1	10 55·9	4·9 3·7	10·9 8·3	16·9 12·8
50	11 27·5	11 29·4	10 56·2	5·0 3·8	11·0 8·3	17·0 12·9
51	11 27·8	11 29·6	10 56·4	5·1 3·9	11·1 8·4	17·1 13·0
52	11 28·0	11 29·9	10 56·7	5·2 3·9	11·2 8·5	17·2 13·0
53	11 28·3	11 30·1	10 56·9	5·3 4·0	11·3 8·6	17·3 13·1
54	11 28·5	11 30·4	10 57·1	5·4 4·1	11·4 8·6	17·4 13·2
55	11 28·8	11 30·6	10 57·4	5·5 4·2	11·5 8·7	17·5 13·3
56	11 29·0	11 30·9	10 57·6	5·6 4·2	11·6 8·8	17·6 13·3
57	11 29·3	11 31·1	10 57·9	5·7 4·3	11·7 8·9	17·7 13·4
58	11 29·5	11 31·4	10 58·1	5·8 4·4	11·8 8·9	17·8 13·5
59	11 29·8	11 31·6	10 58·3	5·9 4·5	11·9 9·0	17·9 13·6
60	11 30·0	11 31·9	10 58·6	6·0 4·6	12·0 9·1	18·0 13·7

46ᵐ

46	SUN PLANETS	ARIES	MOON	v or d Corrn	v or d Corrn	v or d Corrn
s	° ′	° ′	° ′	′ ′	′ ′	′ ′
00	11 30·0	11 31·9	10 58·6	0·0 0·0	6·0 4·7	12·0 9·3
01	11 30·3	11 32·1	10 58·8	0·1 0·1	6·1 4·7	12·1 9·4
02	11 30·5	11 32·4	10 59·0	0·2 0·2	6·2 4·8	12·2 9·5
03	11 30·8	11 32·6	10 59·3	0·3 0·2	6·3 4·9	12·3 9·5
04	11 31·0	11 32·9	10 59·5	0·4 0·3	6·4 5·0	12·4 9·6
05	11 31·3	11 33·1	10 59·8	0·5 0·4	6·5 5·0	12·5 9·7
06	11 31·5	11 33·4	11 00·0	0·6 0·5	6·6 5·1	12·6 9·8
07	11 31·8	11 33·6	11 00·2	0·7 0·5	6·7 5·2	12·7 9·8
08	11 32·0	11 33·9	11 00·5	0·8 0·6	6·8 5·3	12·8 9·9
09	11 32·3	11 34·1	11 00·7	0·9 0·7	6·9 5·3	12·9 10·0
10	11 32·5	11 34·4	11 01·0	1·0 0·8	7·0 5·4	13·0 10·1
11	11 32·8	11 34·6	11 01·2	1·1 0·9	7·1 5·5	13·1 10·2
12	11 33·0	11 34·9	11 01·4	1·2 0·9	7·2 5·6	13·2 10·2
13	11 33·3	11 35·1	11 01·7	1·3 1·0	7·3 5·7	13·3 10·3
14	11 33·5	11 35·4	11 01·9	1·4 1·1	7·4 5·7	13·4 10·4
15	11 33·8	11 35·6	11 02·1	1·5 1·2	7·5 5·8	13·5 10·5
16	11 34·0	11 35·9	11 02·4	1·6 1·2	7·6 5·9	13·6 10·5
17	11 34·3	11 36·2	11 02·6	1·7 1·3	7·7 6·0	13·7 10·6
18	11 34·5	11 36·4	11 02·9	1·8 1·4	7·8 6·0	13·8 10·7
19	11 34·8	11 36·7	11 03·1	1·9 1·5	7·9 6·1	13·9 10·8
20	11 35·0	11 36·9	11 03·3	2·0 1·6	8·0 6·2	14·0 10·9
21	11 35·3	11 37·2	11 03·6	2·1 1·6	8·1 6·3	14·1 10·9
22	11 35·5	11 37·4	11 03·8	2·2 1·7	8·2 6·4	14·2 11·0
23	11 35·8	11 37·7	11 04·1	2·3 1·8	8·3 6·4	14·3 11·1
24	11 36·0	11 37·9	11 04·3	2·4 1·9	8·4 6·5	14·4 11·2
25	11 36·3	11 38·2	11 04·5	2·5 1·9	8·5 6·6	14·5 11·2
26	11 36·5	11 38·4	11 04·8	2·6 2·0	8·6 6·7	14·6 11·3
27	11 36·8	11 38·7	11 05·0	2·7 2·1	8·7 6·7	14·7 11·4
28	11 37·0	11 38·9	11 05·2	2·8 2·2	8·8 6·8	14·8 11·5
29	11 37·3	11 39·2	11 05·5	2·9 2·2	8·9 6·9	14·9 11·5
30	11 37·5	11 39·4	11 05·7	3·0 2·3	9·0 7·0	15·0 11·6
31	11 37·8	11 39·7	11 06·0	3·1 2·4	9·1 7·1	15·1 11·7
32	11 38·0	11 39·9	11 06·2	3·2 2·5	9·2 7·1	15·2 11·8
33	11 38·3	11 40·2	11 06·4	3·3 2·6	9·3 7·2	15·3 11·9
34	11 38·5	11 40·4	11 06·7	3·4 2·6	9·4 7·3	15·4 11·9
35	11 38·8	11 40·7	11 06·9	3·5 2·7	9·5 7·4	15·5 12·0
36	11 39·0	11 40·9	11 07·2	3·6 2·8	9·6 7·4	15·6 12·1
37	11 39·3	11 41·2	11 07·4	3·7 2·9	9·7 7·5	15·7 12·2
38	11 39·5	11 41·4	11 07·6	3·8 2·9	9·8 7·6	15·8 12·2
39	11 39·8	11 41·7	11 07·9	3·9 3·0	9·9 7·7	15·9 12·3
40	11 40·0	11 41·9	11 08·1	4·0 3·1	10·0 7·8	16·0 12·4
41	11 40·3	11 42·2	11 08·3	4·1 3·2	10·1 7·8	16·1 12·5
42	11 40·5	11 42·4	11 08·6	4·2 3·3	10·2 7·9	16·2 12·6
43	11 40·8	11 42·7	11 08·8	4·3 3·3	10·3 8·0	16·3 12·6
44	11 41·0	11 42·9	11 09·1	4·4 3·4	10·4 8·1	16·4 12·7
45	11 41·3	11 43·2	11 09·3	4·5 3·5	10·5 8·1	16·5 12·8
46	11 41·5	11 43·4	11 09·5	4·6 3·6	10·6 8·2	16·6 12·9
47	11 41·8	11 43·7	11 09·8	4·7 3·6	10·7 8·3	16·7 12·9
48	11 42·0	11 43·9	11 10·0	4·8 3·7	10·8 8·4	16·8 13·0
49	11 42·3	11 44·2	11 10·3	4·9 3·8	10·9 8·4	16·9 13·1
50	11 42·5	11 44·4	11 10·5	5·0 3·9	11·0 8·5	17·0 13·2
51	11 42·8	11 44·7	11 10·7	5·1 4·0	11·1 8·6	17·1 13·3
52	11 43·0	11 44·9	11 11·0	5·2 4·0	11·2 8·7	17·2 13·3
53	11 43·3	11 45·2	11 11·2	5·3 4·1	11·3 8·8	17·3 13·4
54	11 43·5	11 45·4	11 11·5	5·4 4·2	11·4 8·8	17·4 13·5
55	11 43·8	11 45·7	11 11·7	5·5 4·3	11·5 8·9	17·5 13·6
56	11 44·0	11 45·9	11 11·9	5·6 4·3	11·6 9·0	17·6 13·6
57	11 44·3	11 46·2	11 12·2	5·7 4·4	11·7 9·1	17·7 13·7
58	11 44·5	11 46·4	11 12·4	5·8 4·5	11·8 9·1	17·8 13·8
59	11 44·8	11 46·7	11 12·6	5·9 4·6	11·9 9·2	17·9 13·9
60	11 45·0	11 46·9	11 12·9	6·0 4·7	12·0 9·3	18·0 14·0

47ᵐ

47	SUN PLANETS	ARIES	MOON	v or d Corrn	v or d Corrn	v or d Corrn
s	° ′	° ′	° ′	′ ′	′ ′	′ ′
00	11 45·0	11 46·9	11 12·9	0·0 0·0	6·0 4·8	12·0 9·5
01	11 45·3	11 47·2	11 13·1	0·1 0·1	6·1 4·8	12·1 9·6
02	11 45·5	11 47·4	11 13·4	0·2 0·2	6·2 4·9	12·2 9·7
03	11 45·8	11 47·7	11 13·6	0·3 0·2	6·3 5·0	12·3 9·7
04	11 46·0	11 47·9	11 13·8	0·4 0·3	6·4 5·1	12·4 9·8
05	11 46·3	11 48·2	11 14·1	0·5 0·4	6·5 5·1	12·5 9·9
06	11 46·5	11 48·4	11 14·3	0·6 0·5	6·6 5·2	12·6 10·0
07	11 46·8	11 48·7	11 14·6	0·7 0·6	6·7 5·3	12·7 10·1
08	11 47·0	11 48·9	11 14·8	0·8 0·6	6·8 5·4	12·8 10·1
09	11 47·3	11 49·2	11 15·0	0·9 0·7	6·9 5·5	12·9 10·2
10	11 47·5	11 49·4	11 15·3	1·0 0·8	7·0 5·5	13·0 10·3
11	11 47·8	11 49·7	11 15·5	1·1 0·9	7·1 5·6	13·1 10·4
12	11 48·0	11 49·9	11 15·7	1·2 1·0	7·2 5·7	13·2 10·5
13	11 48·3	11 50·2	11 16·0	1·3 1·0	7·3 5·8	13·3 10·5
14	11 48·5	11 50·4	11 16·2	1·4 1·1	7·4 5·9	13·4 10·6
15	11 48·8	11 50·7	11 16·5	1·5 1·2	7·5 5·9	13·5 10·7
16	11 49·0	11 50·9	11 16·7	1·6 1·3	7·6 6·0	13·6 10·8
17	11 49·3	11 51·2	11 16·9	1·7 1·3	7·7 6·1	13·7 10·8
18	11 49·5	11 51·4	11 17·2	1·8 1·4	7·8 6·2	13·8 10·9
19	11 49·8	11 51·7	11 17·4	1·9 1·5	7·9 6·3	13·9 11·0
20	11 50·0	11 51·9	11 17·7	2·0 1·6	8·0 6·3	14·0 11·1
21	11 50·3	11 52·2	11 17·9	2·1 1·7	8·1 6·4	14·1 11·2
22	11 50·5	11 52·4	11 18·1	2·2 1·7	8·2 6·5	14·2 11·2
23	11 50·8	11 52·7	11 18·4	2·3 1·8	8·3 6·6	14·3 11·3
24	11 51·0	11 52·9	11 18·6	2·4 1·9	8·4 6·7	14·4 11·4
25	11 51·3	11 53·2	11 18·8	2·5 2·0	8·5 6·7	14·5 11·5
26	11 51·5	11 53·4	11 19·1	2·6 2·1	8·6 6·8	14·6 11·6
27	11 51·8	11 53·7	11 19·3	2·7 2·1	8·7 6·9	14·7 11·6
28	11 52·0	11 53·9	11 19·6	2·8 2·2	8·8 7·0	14·8 11·7
29	11 52·3	11 54·2	11 19·8	2·9 2·3	8·9 7·0	14·9 11·8
30	11 52·5	11 54·5	11 20·0	3·0 2·4	9·0 7·1	15·0 11·9
31	11 52·8	11 54·7	11 20·3	3·1 2·5	9·1 7·2	15·1 12·0
32	11 53·0	11 55·0	11 20·5	3·2 2·5	9·2 7·3	15·2 12·0
33	11 53·3	11 55·2	11 20·8	3·3 2·6	9·3 7·4	15·3 12·1
34	11 53·5	11 55·5	11 21·0	3·4 2·7	9·4 7·4	15·4 12·2
35	11 53·8	11 55·7	11 21·2	3·5 2·8	9·5 7·5	15·5 12·3
36	11 54·0	11 56·0	11 21·5	3·6 2·9	9·6 7·6	15·6 12·4
37	11 54·3	11 56·2	11 21·7	3·7 2·9	9·7 7·7	15·7 12·4
38	11 54·5	11 56·5	11 22·0	3·8 3·0	9·8 7·8	15·8 12·5
39	11 54·8	11 56·7	11 22·2	3·9 3·1	9·9 7·8	15·9 12·6
40	11 55·0	11 57·0	11 22·4	4·0 3·2	10·0 7·9	16·0 12·7
41	11 55·3	11 57·2	11 22·7	4·1 3·2	10·1 8·0	16·1 12·7
42	11 55·5	11 57·5	11 22·9	4·2 3·3	10·2 8·1	16·2 12·8
43	11 55·8	11 57·7	11 23·1	4·3 3·4	10·3 8·2	16·3 12·9
44	11 56·0	11 58·0	11 23·4	4·4 3·5	10·4 8·2	16·4 13·0
45	11 56·3	11 58·2	11 23·6	4·5 3·6	10·5 8·3	16·5 13·1
46	11 56·5	11 58·5	11 23·9	4·6 3·6	10·6 8·4	16·6 13·1
47	11 56·8	11 58·7	11 24·1	4·7 3·7	10·7 8·5	16·7 13·2
48	11 57·0	11 59·0	11 24·3	4·8 3·8	10·8 8·6	16·8 13·3
49	11 57·3	11 59·2	11 24·6	4·9 3·9	10·9 8·6	16·9 13·4
50	11 57·5	11 59·5	11 24·8	5·0 4·0	11·0 8·7	17·0 13·5
51	11 57·8	11 59·7	11 25·1	5·1 4·0	11·1 8·8	17·1 13·5
52	11 58·0	12 00·0	11 25·3	5·2 4·1	11·2 8·9	17·2 13·6
53	11 58·3	12 00·2	11 25·5	5·3 4·2	11·3 8·9	17·3 13·7
54	11 58·5	12 00·5	11 25·8	5·4 4·3	11·4 9·0	17·4 13·8
55	11 58·8	12 00·7	11 26·0	5·5 4·4	11·5 9·1	17·5 13·9
56	11 59·0	12 01·0	11 26·2	5·6 4·4	11·6 9·2	17·6 13·9
57	11 59·3	12 01·2	11 26·5	5·7 4·5	11·7 9·3	17·7 14·0
58	11 59·5	12 01·5	11 26·7	5·8 4·6	11·8 9·3	17·8 14·1
59	11 59·8	12 01·7	11 27·0	5·9 4·7	11·9 9·4	17·9 14·2
60	12 00·0	12 02·0	11 27·2	6·0 4·8	12·0 9·5	18·0 14·3

48ᵐ	SUN PLANETS	ARIES	MOON	v or d	Corrⁿ	v or d	Corrⁿ	v or d	Corrⁿ
s	° ′	° ′	° ′	′	′	′	′	′	′
00	12 00·0	12 02·0	11 27·2	0·0	0·0	6·0	4·9	12·0	9·7
01	12 00·3	12 02·2	11 27·4	0·1	0·1	6·1	4·9	12·1	9·8
02	12 00·5	12 02·5	11 27·7	0·2	0·2	6·2	5·0	12·2	9·9
03	12 00·8	12 02·7	11 27·9	0·3	0·2	6·3	5·1	12·3	9·9
04	12 01·0	12 03·0	11 28·2	0·4	0·3	6·4	5·2	12·4	10·0
05	12 01·3	12 03·2	11 28·4	0·5	0·4	6·5	5·3	12·5	10·1
06	12 01·5	12 03·5	11 28·6	0·6	0·5	6·6	5·3	12·6	10·2
07	12 01·8	12 03·7	11 28·9	0·7	0·6	6·7	5·4	12·7	10·3
08	12 02·0	12 04·0	11 29·1	0·8	0·6	6·8	5·5	12·8	10·3
09	12 02·3	12 04·2	11 29·3	0·9	0·7	6·9	5·6	12·9	10·4
10	12 02·5	12 04·5	11 29·6	1·0	0·8	7·0	5·7	13·0	10·5
11	12 02·8	12 04·7	11 29·8	1·1	0·9	7·1	5·7	13·1	10·6
12	12 03·0	12 05·0	11 30·1	1·2	1·0	7·2	5·8	13·2	10·7
13	12 03·3	12 05·2	11 30·3	1·3	1·1	7·3	5·9	13·3	10·8
14	12 03·5	12 05·5	11 30·5	1·4	1·1	7·4	6·0	13·4	10·8
15	12 03·8	12 05·7	11 30·8	1·5	1·2	7·5	6·1	13·5	10·9
16	12 04·0	12 06·0	11 31·0	1·6	1·3	7·6	6·1	13·6	11·0
17	12 04·3	12 06·2	11 31·3	1·7	1·4	7·7	6·2	13·7	11·1
18	12 04·5	12 06·5	11 31·5	1·8	1·5	7·8	6·3	13·8	11·2
19	12 04·8	12 06·7	11 31·7	1·9	1·5	7·9	6·4	13·9	11·2
20	12 05·0	12 07·0	11 32·0	2·0	1·6	8·0	6·5	14·0	11·3
21	12 05·3	12 07·2	11 32·2	2·1	1·7	8·1	6·5	14·1	11·4
22	12 05·5	12 07·5	11 32·4	2·2	1·8	8·2	6·6	14·2	11·5
23	12 05·8	12 07·7	11 32·7	2·3	1·9	8·3	6·7	14·3	11·6
24	12 06·0	12 08·0	11 32·9	2·4	1·9	8·4	6·8	14·4	11·6
25	12 06·3	12 08·2	11 33·2	2·5	2·0	8·5	6·9	14·5	11·7
26	12 06·5	12 08·5	11 33·4	2·6	2·1	8·6	7·0	14·6	11·8
27	12 06·8	12 08·7	11 33·6	2·7	2·2	8·7	7·0	14·7	11·9
28	12 07·0	12 09·0	11 33·9	2·8	2·3	8·8	7·1	14·8	12·0
29	12 07·3	12 09·2	11 34·1	2·9	2·3	8·9	7·2	14·9	12·0
30	12 07·5	12 09·5	11 34·4	3·0	2·4	9·0	7·3	15·0	12·1
31	12 07·8	12 09·7	11 34·6	3·1	2·5	9·1	7·4	15·1	12·2
32	12 08·0	12 10·0	11 34·8	3·2	2·6	9·2	7·4	15·2	12·3
33	12 08·3	12 10·2	11 35·1	3·3	2·7	9·3	7·5	15·3	12·4
34	12 08·5	12 10·5	11 35·3	3·4	2·7	9·4	7·6	15·4	12·4
35	12 08·8	12 10·7	11 35·6	3·5	2·8	9·5	7·7	15·5	12·5
36	12 09·0	12 11·0	11 35·8	3·6	2·9	9·6	7·8	15·6	12·6
37	12 09·3	12 11·2	11 36·0	3·7	3·0	9·7	7·8	15·7	12·7
38	12 09·5	12 11·5	11 36·3	3·8	3·1	9·8	7·9	15·8	12·8
39	12 09·8	12 11·7	11 36·5	3·9	3·2	9·9	8·0	15·9	12·9
40	12 10·0	12 12·0	11 36·7	4·0	3·2	10·0	8·1	16·0	12·9
41	12 10·3	12 12·2	11 37·0	4·1	3·3	10·1	8·2	16·1	13·0
42	12 10·5	12 12·5	11 37·2	4·2	3·4	10·2	8·2	16·2	13·1
43	12 10·8	12 12·8	11 37·5	4·3	3·5	10·3	8·3	16·3	13·2
44	12 11·0	12 13·0	11 37·7	4·4	3·6	10·4	8·4	16·4	13·3
45	12 11·3	12 13·3	11 37·9	4·5	3·6	10·5	8·5	16·5	13·3
46	12 11·5	12 13·5	11 38·2	4·6	3·7	10·6	8·6	16·6	13·4
47	12 11·8	12 13·8	11 38·4	4·7	3·8	10·7	8·6	16·7	13·5
48	12 12·0	12 14·0	11 38·7	4·8	3·9	10·8	8·7	16·8	13·6
49	12 12·3	12 14·3	11 38·9	4·9	4·0	10·9	8·8	16·9	13·7
50	12 12·5	12 14·5	11 39·1	5·0	4·0	11·0	8·9	17·0	13·7
51	12 12·8	12 14·8	11 39·4	5·1	4·1	11·1	9·0	17·1	13·8
52	12 13·0	12 15·0	11 39·6	5·2	4·2	11·2	9·1	17·2	13·9
53	12 13·3	12 15·3	11 39·8	5·3	4·3	11·3	9·1	17·3	14·0
54	12 13·5	12 15·5	11 40·1	5·4	4·4	11·4	9·2	17·4	14·1
55	12 13·8	12 15·8	11 40·3	5·5	4·4	11·5	9·3	17·5	14·1
56	12 14·0	12 16·0	11 40·6	5·6	4·5	11·6	9·4	17·6	14·2
57	12 14·3	12 16·3	11 40·8	5·7	4·6	11·7	9·5	17·7	14·3
58	12 14·5	12 16·5	11 41·0	5·8	4·7	11·8	9·5	17·8	14·4
59	12 14·8	12 16·8	11 41·3	5·9	4·8	11·9	9·6	17·9	14·5
60	12 15·0	12 17·0	11 41·5	6·0	4·9	12·0	9·7	18·0	14·6

49ᵐ	SUN PLANETS	ARIES	MOON	v or d	Corrⁿ	v or d	Corrⁿ	v or d	Corrⁿ
s	° ′	° ′	° ′	′	′	′	′	′	′
00	12 15·0	12 17·0	11 41·5	0·0	0·0	6·0	5·0	12·0	9·9
01	12 15·3	12 17·3	11 41·8	0·1	0·1	6·1	5·0	12·1	10·0
02	12 15·5	12 17·5	11 42·0	0·2	0·2	6·2	5·1	12·2	10·1
03	12 15·8	12 17·8	11 42·2	0·3	0·2	6·3	5·2	12·3	10·1
04	12 16·0	12 18·0	11 42·5	0·4	0·3	6·4	5·3	12·4	10·2
05	12 16·3	12 18·3	11 42·7	0·5	0·4	6·5	5·4	12·5	10·3
06	12 16·5	12 18·5	11 42·9	0·6	0·5	6·6	5·4	12·6	10·4
07	12 16·8	12 18·8	11 43·2	0·7	0·6	6·7	5·5	12·7	10·5
08	12 17·0	12 19·0	11 43·4	0·8	0·7	6·8	5·6	12·8	10·6
09	12 17·3	12 19·3	11 43·7	0·9	0·7	6·9	5·7	12·9	10·6
10	12 17·5	12 19·5	11 43·9	1·0	0·8	7·0	5·8	13·0	10·7
11	12 17·8	12 19·8	11 44·1	1·1	0·9	7·1	5·9	13·1	10·8
12	12 18·0	12 20·0	11 44·4	1·2	1·0	7·2	5·9	13·2	10·9
13	12 18·3	12 20·3	11 44·6	1·3	1·1	7·3	6·0	13·3	11·0
14	12 18·5	12 20·5	11 44·9	1·4	1·2	7·4	6·1	13·4	11·1
15	12 18·8	12 20·8	11 45·1	1·5	1·2	7·5	6·2	13·5	11·1
16	12 19·0	12 21·0	11 45·3	1·6	1·3	7·6	6·3	13·6	11·2
17	12 19·3	12 21·3	11 45·6	1·7	1·4	7·7	6·4	13·7	11·3
18	12 19·5	12 21·5	11 45·8	1·8	1·5	7·8	6·4	13·8	11·4
19	12 19·8	12 21·8	11 46·1	1·9	1·6	7·9	6·5	13·9	11·5
20	12 20·0	12 22·0	11 46·3	2·0	1·7	8·0	6·6	14·0	11·6
21	12 20·3	12 22·3	11 46·5	2·1	1·7	8·1	6·7	14·1	11·6
22	12 20·5	12 22·5	11 46·8	2·2	1·8	8·2	6·8	14·2	11·7
23	12 20·8	12 22·8	11 47·0	2·3	1·9	8·3	6·8	14·3	11·8
24	12 21·0	12 23·0	11 47·2	2·4	2·0	8·4	6·9	14·4	11·9
25	12 21·3	12 23·3	11 47·5	2·5	2·1	8·5	7·0	14·5	12·0
26	12 21·5	12 23·5	11 47·7	2·6	2·1	8·6	7·1	14·6	12·0
27	12 21·8	12 23·8	11 48·0	2·7	2·2	8·7	7·2	14·7	12·1
28	12 22·0	12 24·0	11 48·2	2·8	2·3	8·8	7·3	14·8	12·2
29	12 22·3	12 24·3	11 48·4	2·9	2·4	8·9	7·3	14·9	12·3
30	12 22·5	12 24·5	11 48·7	3·0	2·5	9·0	7·4	15·0	12·4
31	12 22·8	12 24·8	11 48·9	3·1	2·6	9·1	7·5	15·1	12·5
32	12 23·0	12 25·0	11 49·2	3·2	2·6	9·2	7·6	15·2	12·5
33	12 23·3	12 25·3	11 49·4	3·3	2·7	9·3	7·7	15·3	12·6
34	12 23·5	12 25·5	11 49·6	3·4	2·8	9·4	7·8	15·4	12·7
35	12 23·8	12 25·8	11 49·9	3·5	2·9	9·5	7·8	15·5	12·8
36	12 24·0	12 26·0	11 50·1	3·6	3·0	9·6	7·9	15·6	12·9
37	12 24·3	12 26·3	11 50·3	3·7	3·1	9·7	8·0	15·7	13·0
38	12 24·5	12 26·5	11 50·6	3·8	3·1	9·8	8·1	15·8	13·0
39	12 24·8	12 26·8	11 50·8	3·9	3·2	9·9	8·2	15·9	13·1
40	12 25·0	12 27·0	11 51·1	4·0	3·3	10·0	8·3	16·0	13·2
41	12 25·3	12 27·3	11 51·3	4·1	3·4	10·1	8·3	16·1	13·3
42	12 25·5	12 27·5	11 51·5	4·2	3·5	10·2	8·4	16·2	13·4
43	12 25·8	12 27·8	11 51·8	4·3	3·5	10·3	8·5	16·3	13·4
44	12 26·0	12 28·0	11 52·0	4·4	3·6	10·4	8·6	16·4	13·5
45	12 26·3	12 28·3	11 52·3	4·5	3·7	10·5	8·7	16·5	13·6
46	12 26·5	12 28·5	11 52·5	4·6	3·8	10·6	8·7	16·6	13·7
47	12 26·8	12 28·8	11 52·7	4·7	3·9	10·7	8·8	16·7	13·8
48	12 27·0	12 29·0	11 53·0	4·8	4·0	10·8	8·9	16·8	13·9
49	12 27·3	12 29·3	11 53·2	4·9	4·0	10·9	9·0	16·9	13·9
50	12 27·5	12 29·5	11 53·4	5·0	4·1	11·0	9·1	17·0	14·0
51	12 27·8	12 29·8	11 53·7	5·1	4·2	11·1	9·2	17·1	14·1
52	12 28·0	12 30·0	11 53·9	5·2	4·3	11·2	9·2	17·2	14·2
53	12 28·3	12 30·3	11 54·2	5·3	4·4	11·3	9·3	17·3	14·3
54	12 28·5	12 30·5	11 54·4	5·4	4·5	11·4	9·4	17·4	14·4
55	12 28·8	12 30·8	11 54·6	5·5	4·5	11·5	9·5	17·5	14·4
56	12 29·0	12 31·1	11 54·9	5·6	4·6	11·6	9·6	17·6	14·5
57	12 29·3	12 31·3	11 55·1	5·7	4·7	11·7	9·7	17·7	14·6
58	12 29·5	12 31·6	11 55·4	5·8	4·8	11·8	9·7	17·8	14·7
59	12 29·8	12 31·8	11 55·6	5·9	4·9	11·9	9·8	17·9	14·8
60	12 30·0	12 32·1	11 55·8	6·0	5·0	12·0	9·9	18·0	14·9

50ᵐ

s	SUN PLANETS	ARIES	MOON	v or d / Corrⁿ	v or d / Corrⁿ	v or d / Corrⁿ
00	12 30.0	12 32.1	11 55.8	0.0 0.0	6.0 5.1	12.0 10.1
01	12 30.3	12 32.3	11 56.1	0.1 0.1	6.1 5.1	12.1 10.2
02	12 30.5	12 32.6	11 56.3	0.2 0.2	6.2 5.2	12.2 10.3
03	12 30.8	12 32.8	11 56.5	0.3 0.3	6.3 5.3	12.3 10.4
04	12 31.0	12 33.1	11 56.8	0.4 0.3	6.4 5.4	12.4 10.4
05	12 31.3	12 33.3	11 57.0	0.5 0.4	6.5 5.5	12.5 10.5
06	12 31.5	12 33.6	11 57.3	0.6 0.5	6.6 5.6	12.6 10.6
07	12 31.8	12 33.8	11 57.5	0.7 0.6	6.7 5.6	12.7 10.7
08	12 32.0	12 34.1	11 57.7	0.8 0.7	6.8 5.7	12.8 10.8
09	12 32.3	12 34.3	11 58.0	0.9 0.8	6.9 5.8	12.9 10.9
10	12 32.5	12 34.6	11 58.2	1.0 0.8	7.0 5.9	13.0 10.9
11	12 32.8	12 34.8	11 58.5	1.1 0.9	7.1 6.0	13.1 11.0
12	12 33.0	12 35.1	11 58.7	1.2 1.0	7.2 6.1	13.2 11.1
13	12 33.3	12 35.3	11 58.9	1.3 1.1	7.3 6.1	13.3 11.2
14	12 33.5	12 35.6	11 59.2	1.4 1.2	7.4 6.2	13.4 11.3
15	12 33.8	12 35.8	11 59.4	1.5 1.3	7.5 6.3	13.5 11.4
16	12 34.0	12 36.1	11 59.7	1.6 1.3	7.6 6.4	13.6 11.4
17	12 34.3	12 36.3	11 59.9	1.7 1.4	7.7 6.5	13.7 11.5
18	12 34.5	12 36.6	12 00.1	1.8 1.5	7.8 6.6	13.8 11.6
19	12 34.8	12 36.8	12 00.4	1.9 1.6	7.9 6.6	13.9 11.7
20	12 35.0	12 37.1	12 00.6	2.0 1.7	8.0 6.7	14.0 11.8
21	12 35.3	12 37.3	12 00.8	2.1 1.8	8.1 6.8	14.1 11.9
22	12 35.5	12 37.6	12 01.1	2.2 1.9	8.2 6.9	14.2 12.0
23	12 35.8	12 37.8	12 01.3	2.3 1.9	8.3 7.0	14.3 12.0
24	12 36.0	12 38.1	12 01.6	2.4 2.0	8.4 7.1	14.4 12.1
25	12 36.3	12 38.3	12 01.8	2.5 2.1	8.5 7.2	14.5 12.2
26	12 36.5	12 38.6	12 02.0	2.6 2.2	8.6 7.2	14.6 12.3
27	12 36.8	12 38.8	12 02.3	2.7 2.3	8.7 7.3	14.7 12.4
28	12 37.0	12 39.1	12 02.5	2.8 2.4	8.8 7.4	14.8 12.5
29	12 37.3	12 39.3	12 02.8	2.9 2.4	8.9 7.5	14.9 12.5
30	12 37.5	12 39.6	12 03.0	3.0 2.5	9.0 7.6	15.0 12.6
31	12 37.8	12 39.8	12 03.2	3.1 2.6	9.1 7.7	15.1 12.7
32	12 38.0	12 40.1	12 03.5	3.2 2.7	9.2 7.7	15.2 12.8
33	12 38.3	12 40.3	12 03.7	3.3 2.8	9.3 7.8	15.3 12.9
34	12 38.5	12 40.6	12 03.9	3.4 2.9	9.4 7.9	15.4 13.0
35	12 38.8	12 40.8	12 04.2	3.5 2.9	9.5 8.0	15.5 13.0
36	12 39.0	12 41.1	12 04.4	3.6 3.0	9.6 8.1	15.6 13.1
37	12 39.3	12 41.3	12 04.7	3.7 3.1	9.7 8.2	15.7 13.2
38	12 39.5	12 41.6	12 04.9	3.8 3.2	9.8 8.2	15.8 13.3
39	12 39.8	12 41.8	12 05.1	3.9 3.3	9.9 8.3	15.9 13.4
40	12 40.0	12 42.1	12 05.4	4.0 3.4	10.0 8.4	16.0 13.5
41	12 40.3	12 42.3	12 05.6	4.1 3.5	10.1 8.5	16.1 13.6
42	12 40.5	12 42.6	12 05.9	4.2 3.5	10.2 8.6	16.2 13.6
43	12 40.8	12 42.8	12 06.1	4.3 3.6	10.3 8.7	16.3 13.7
44	12 41.0	12 43.1	12 06.3	4.4 3.7	10.4 8.8	16.4 13.8
45	12 41.3	12 43.3	12 06.6	4.5 3.8	10.5 8.8	16.5 13.9
46	12 41.5	12 43.6	12 06.8	4.6 3.9	10.6 8.9	16.6 14.0
47	12 41.8	12 43.8	12 07.0	4.7 4.0	10.7 9.0	16.7 14.1
48	12 42.0	12 44.1	12 07.3	4.8 4.0	10.8 9.1	16.8 14.1
49	12 42.3	12 44.3	12 07.5	4.9 4.1	10.9 9.2	16.9 14.2
50	12 42.5	12 44.6	12 07.8	5.0 4.2	11.0 9.3	17.0 14.3
51	12 42.8	12 44.8	12 08.0	5.1 4.3	11.1 9.3	17.1 14.4
52	12 43.0	12 45.1	12 08.2	5.2 4.4	11.2 9.4	17.2 14.5
53	12 43.3	12 45.3	12 08.5	5.3 4.5	11.3 9.5	17.3 14.6
54	12 43.5	12 45.6	12 08.7	5.4 4.5	11.4 9.6	17.4 14.6
55	12 43.8	12 45.8	12 09.0	5.5 4.6	11.5 9.7	17.5 14.7
56	12 44.0	12 46.1	12 09.2	5.6 4.7	11.6 9.8	17.6 14.8
57	12 44.3	12 46.3	12 09.4	5.7 4.8	11.7 9.8	17.7 14.9
58	12 44.5	12 46.6	12 09.7	5.8 4.9	11.8 9.9	17.8 15.0
59	12 44.8	12 46.8	12 09.9	5.9 5.0	11.9 10.0	17.9 15.1
60	12 45.0	12 47.1	12 10.2	6.0 5.1	12.0 10.1	18.0 15.2

51ᵐ

s	SUN PLANETS	ARIES	MOON	v or d / Corrⁿ	v or d / Corrⁿ	v or d / Corrⁿ
00	12 45.0	12 47.1	12 10.2	0.0 0.0	6.0 5.2	12.0 10.3
01	12 45.3	12 47.3	12 10.4	0.1 0.1	6.1 5.2	12.1 10.4
02	12 45.5	12 47.6	12 10.6	0.2 0.2	6.2 5.3	12.2 10.5
03	12 45.8	12 47.8	12 10.9	0.3 0.3	6.3 5.4	12.3 10.6
04	12 46.0	12 48.1	12 11.1	0.4 0.3	6.4 5.5	12.4 10.6
05	12 46.3	12 48.3	12 11.3	0.5 0.4	6.5 5.6	12.5 10.7
06	12 46.5	12 48.6	12 11.6	0.6 0.5	6.6 5.7	12.6 10.8
07	12 46.8	12 48.8	12 11.8	0.7 0.6	6.7 5.8	12.7 10.9
08	12 47.0	12 49.1	12 12.1	0.8 0.7	6.8 5.8	12.8 11.0
09	12 47.3	12 49.4	12 12.3	0.9 0.8	6.9 5.9	12.9 11.1
10	12 47.5	12 49.6	12 12.5	1.0 0.9	7.0 6.0	13.0 11.2
11	12 47.8	12 49.9	12 12.8	1.1 0.9	7.1 6.1	13.1 11.2
12	12 48.0	12 50.1	12 13.0	1.2 1.0	7.2 6.2	13.2 11.3
13	12 48.3	12 50.4	12 13.3	1.3 1.1	7.3 6.3	13.3 11.4
14	12 48.5	12 50.6	12 13.5	1.4 1.2	7.4 6.4	13.4 11.5
15	12 48.8	12 50.9	12 13.7	1.5 1.3	7.5 6.4	13.5 11.6
16	12 49.0	12 51.1	12 14.0	1.6 1.4	7.6 6.5	13.6 11.7
17	12 49.3	12 51.4	12 14.2	1.7 1.5	7.7 6.6	13.7 11.8
18	12 49.5	12 51.6	12 14.4	1.8 1.5	7.8 6.7	13.8 11.8
19	12 49.8	12 51.9	12 14.7	1.9 1.6	7.9 6.8	13.9 11.9
20	12 50.0	12 52.1	12 14.9	2.0 1.7	8.0 6.9	14.0 12.0
21	12 50.3	12 52.4	12 15.2	2.1 1.8	8.1 7.0	14.1 12.1
22	12 50.5	12 52.6	12 15.4	2.2 1.9	8.2 7.0	14.2 12.2
23	12 50.8	12 52.9	12 15.6	2.3 2.0	8.3 7.1	14.3 12.3
24	12 51.0	12 53.1	12 15.9	2.4 2.1	8.4 7.2	14.4 12.4
25	12 51.3	12 53.4	12 16.1	2.5 2.1	8.5 7.3	14.5 12.4
26	12 51.5	12 53.6	12 16.4	2.6 2.2	8.6 7.4	14.6 12.5
27	12 51.8	12 53.9	12 16.6	2.7 2.3	8.7 7.5	14.7 12.6
28	12 52.0	12 54.1	12 16.8	2.8 2.4	8.8 7.6	14.8 12.7
29	12 52.3	12 54.4	12 17.1	2.9 2.5	8.9 7.6	14.9 12.8
30	12 52.5	12 54.6	12 17.3	3.0 2.6	9.0 7.7	15.0 12.9
31	12 52.8	12 54.9	12 17.5	3.1 2.7	9.1 7.8	15.1 13.0
32	12 53.0	12 55.1	12 17.8	3.2 2.7	9.2 7.9	15.2 13.0
33	12 53.3	12 55.4	12 18.0	3.3 2.8	9.3 8.0	15.3 13.1
34	12 53.5	12 55.6	12 18.3	3.4 2.9	9.4 8.1	15.4 13.2
35	12 53.8	12 55.9	12 18.5	3.5 3.0	9.5 8.2	15.5 13.3
36	12 54.0	12 56.1	12 18.7	3.6 3.1	9.6 8.2	15.6 13.4
37	12 54.3	12 56.4	12 19.0	3.7 3.2	9.7 8.3	15.7 13.5
38	12 54.5	12 56.6	12 19.2	3.8 3.3	9.8 8.4	15.8 13.6
39	12 54.8	12 56.9	12 19.5	3.9 3.3	9.9 8.5	15.9 13.6
40	12 55.0	12 57.1	12 19.7	4.0 3.4	10.0 8.6	16.0 13.7
41	12 55.3	12 57.4	12 19.9	4.1 3.5	10.1 8.7	16.1 13.8
42	12 55.5	12 57.6	12 20.2	4.2 3.6	10.2 8.8	16.2 13.9
43	12 55.8	12 57.9	12 20.4	4.3 3.7	10.3 8.8	16.3 14.0
44	12 56.0	12 58.1	12 20.6	4.4 3.8	10.4 8.9	16.4 14.1
45	12 56.3	12 58.4	12 20.9	4.5 3.9	10.5 9.0	16.5 14.2
46	12 56.5	12 58.6	12 21.1	4.6 3.9	10.6 9.1	16.6 14.2
47	12 56.8	12 58.9	12 21.4	4.7 4.0	10.7 9.2	16.7 14.3
48	12 57.0	12 59.1	12 21.6	4.8 4.1	10.8 9.3	16.8 14.4
49	12 57.3	12 59.4	12 21.8	4.9 4.2	10.9 9.4	16.9 14.5
50	12 57.5	12 59.6	12 22.1	5.0 4.3	11.0 9.4	17.0 14.6
51	12 57.8	12 59.9	12 22.3	5.1 4.4	11.1 9.5	17.1 14.7
52	12 58.0	13 00.1	12 22.6	5.2 4.5	11.2 9.6	17.2 14.8
53	12 58.3	13 00.4	12 22.8	5.3 4.5	11.3 9.7	17.3 14.8
54	12 58.5	13 00.6	12 23.0	5.4 4.6	11.4 9.8	17.4 14.9
55	12 58.8	13 00.9	12 23.3	5.5 4.7	11.5 9.9	17.5 15.0
56	12 59.0	13 01.1	12 23.5	5.6 4.8	11.6 10.0	17.6 15.1
57	12 59.3	13 01.4	12 23.8	5.7 4.9	11.7 10.0	17.7 15.2
58	12 59.5	13 01.6	12 24.0	5.8 5.0	11.8 10.1	17.8 15.3
59	12 59.8	13 01.9	12 24.2	5.9 5.1	11.9 10.2	17.9 15.4
60	13 00.0	13 02.1	12 24.5	6.0 5.2	12.0 10.3	18.0 15.5

52	SUN PLANETS	ARIES	MOON	v or d	Corrⁿ	v or d	Corrⁿ	v or d	Corrⁿ
s	° ′	° ′	° ′	′	′	′	′	′	′
00	13 00·0	13 02·1	12 24·5	0·0	0·0	6·0	5·3	12·0	10·5
01	13 00·3	13 02·4	12 24·7	0·1	0·1	6·1	5·3	12·1	10·6
02	13 00·5	13 02·6	12 24·9	0·2	0·2	6·2	5·4	12·2	10·7
03	13 00·8	13 02·9	12 25·2	0·3	0·3	6·3	5·5	12·3	10·8
04	13 01·0	13 03·1	12 25·4	0·4	0·4	6·4	5·6	12·4	10·9
05	13 01·3	13 03·4	12 25·7	0·5	0·4	6·5	5·7	12·5	10·9
06	13 01·5	13 03·6	12 25·9	0·6	0·5	6·6	5·8	12·6	11·0
07	13 01·8	13 03·9	12 26·1	0·7	0·6	6·7	5·9	12·7	11·1
08	13 02·0	13 04·1	12 26·4	0·8	0·7	6·8	6·0	12·8	11·2
09	13 02·3	13 04·4	12 26·6	0·9	0·8	6·9	6·0	12·9	11·3
10	13 02·5	13 04·6	12 26·9	1·0	0·9	7·0	6·1	13·0	11·4
11	13 02·8	13 04·9	12 27·1	1·1	1·0	7·1	6·2	13·1	11·5
12	13 03·0	13 05·1	12 27·3	1·2	1·1	7·2	6·3	13·2	11·6
13	13 03·3	13 05·4	12 27·6	1·3	1·1	7·3	6·4	13·3	11·6
14	13 03·5	13 05·6	12 27·8	1·4	1·2	7·4	6·5	13·4	11·7
15	13 03·8	13 05·9	12 28·0	1·5	1·3	7·5	6·6	13·5	11·8
16	13 04·0	13 06·1	12 28·3	1·6	1·4	7·6	6·7	13·6	11·9
17	13 04·3	13 06·4	12 28·5	1·7	1·5	7·7	6·7	13·7	12·0
18	13 04·5	13 06·6	12 28·8	1·8	1·6	7·8	6·8	13·8	12·1
19	13 04·8	13 06·9	12 29·0	1·9	1·7	7·9	6·9	13·9	12·2
20	13 05·0	13 07·1	12 29·2	2·0	1·8	8·0	7·0	14·0	12·3
21	13 05·3	13 07·4	12 29·5	2·1	1·8	8·1	7·1	14·1	12·4
22	13 05·5	13 07·7	12 29·7	2·2	1·9	8·2	7·2	14·2	12·4
23	13 05·8	13 07·9	12 30·0	2·3	2·0	8·3	7·3	14·3	12·5
24	13 06·0	13 08·2	12 30·2	2·4	2·1	8·4	7·4	14·4	12·6
25	13 06·3	13 08·4	12 30·4	2·5	2·2	8·5	7·4	14·5	12·7
26	13 06·5	13 08·7	12 30·7	2·6	2·3	8·6	7·5	14·6	12·8
27	13 06·8	13 08·9	12 30·9	2·7	2·4	8·7	7·6	14·7	12·9
28	13 07·0	13 09·2	12 31·1	2·8	2·5	8·8	7·7	14·8	13·0
29	13 07·3	13 09·4	12 31·4	2·9	2·5	8·9	7·8	14·9	13·0
30	13 07·5	13 09·7	12 31·6	3·0	2·6	9·0	7·9	15·0	13·1
31	13 07·8	13 09·9	12 31·9	3·1	2·7	9·1	8·0	15·1	13·2
32	13 08·0	13 10·2	12 32·1	3·2	2·8	9·2	8·0	15·2	13·3
33	13 08·3	13 10·4	12 32·3	3·3	2·9	9·3	8·1	15·3	13·4
34	13 08·5	13 10·7	12 32·6	3·4	3·0	9·4	8·2	15·4	13·5
35	13 08·8	13 11·2	12 32·8	3·5	3·1	9·5	8·3	15·5	13·6
36	13 09·0	13 11·2	12 33·1	3·6	3·2	9·6	8·4	15·6	13·7
37	13 09·3	13 11·4	12 33·3	3·7	3·2	9·7	8·5	15·7	13·7
38	13 09·5	13 11·7	12 33·5	3·8	3·3	9·8	8·6	15·8	13·8
39	13 09·8	13 11·9	12 33·8	3·9	3·4	9·9	8·7	15·9	13·9
40	13 10·0	13 12·2	12 34·0	4·0	3·5	10·0	8·8	16·0	14·0
41	13 10·3	13 12·4	12 34·2	4·1	3·6	10·1	8·8	16·1	14·1
42	13 10·5	13 12·7	12 34·5	4·2	3·7	10·2	8·9	16·2	14·2
43	13 10·8	13 12·9	12 34·7	4·3	3·8	10·3	9·0	16·3	14·3
44	13 11·0	13 13·2	12 35·0	4·4	3·9	10·4	9·1	16·4	14·3
45	13 11·3	13 13·4	12 35·2	4·5	3·9	10·5	9·2	16·5	14·4
46	13 11·5	13 13·7	12 35·4	4·6	4·0	10·6	9·3	16·6	14·5
47	13 11·8	13 13·9	12 35·7	4·7	4·1	10·7	9·4	16·7	14·6
48	13 12·0	13 14·2	12 35·9	4·8	4·2	10·8	9·5	16·8	14·7
49	13 12·3	13 14·4	12 36·2	4·9	4·3	10·9	9·5	16·9	14·8
50	13 12·5	13 14·7	12 36·4	5·0	4·4	11·0	9·6	17·0	14·9
51	13 12·8	13 14·9	12 36·6	5·1	4·5	11·1	9·7	17·1	15·0
52	13 13·0	13 15·2	12 36·9	5·2	4·6	11·2	9·8	17·2	15·1
53	13 13·3	13 15·4	12 37·1	5·3	4·6	11·3	9·9	17·3	15·1
54	13 13·5	13 15·7	12 37·4	5·4	4·7	11·4	10·0	17·4	15·2
55	13 13·8	13 15·9	12 37·6	5·5	4·8	11·5	10·1	17·5	15·3
56	13 14·0	13 16·2	12 37·8	5·6	4·9	11·6	10·2	17·6	15·4
57	13 14·3	13 16·4	12 38·1	5·7	5·0	11·7	10·2	17·7	15·5
58	13 14·5	13 16·7	12 38·3	5·8	5·1	11·8	10·3	17·8	15·6
59	13 14·8	13 16·9	12 38·5	5·9	5·2	11·9	10·4	17·9	15·7
60	13 15·0	13 17·2	12 38·8	6·0	5·3	12·0	10·5	18·0	15·8

53	SUN PLANETS	ARIES	MOON	v or d	Corrⁿ	v or d	Corrⁿ	v or d	Corrⁿ
s	° ′	° ′	° ′	′	′	′	′	′	′
00	13 15·0	13 17·2	12 38·8	0·0	0·0	6·0	5·4	12·0	10·7
01	13 15·3	13 17·4	12 39·0	0·1	0·1	6·1	5·4	12·1	10·8
02	13 15·5	13 17·7	12 39·3	0·2	0·2	6·2	5·5	12·2	10·9
03	13 15·8	13 17·9	12 39·5	0·3	0·3	6·3	5·6	12·3	11·0
04	13 16·0	13 18·2	12 39·7	0·4	0·4	6·4	5·7	12·4	11·1
05	13 16·3	13 18·4	12 40·0	0·5	0·4	6·5	5·8	12·5	11·1
06	13 16·5	13 18·7	12 40·2	0·6	0·5	6·6	5·9	12·6	11·2
07	13 16·8	13 18·9	12 40·5	0·7	0·6	6·7	6·0	12·7	11·3
08	13 17·0	13 19·2	12 40·7	0·8	0·7	6·8	6·1	12·8	11·4
09	13 17·3	13 19·4	12 40·9	0·9	0·8	6·9	6·2	12·9	11·5
10	13 17·5	13 19·7	12 41·2	1·0	0·9	7·0	6·2	13·0	11·6
11	13 17·8	13 19·9	12 41·4	1·1	1·0	7·1	6·3	13·1	11·7
12	13 18·0	13 20·2	12 41·6	1·2	1·1	7·2	6·4	13·2	11·8
13	13 18·3	13 20·4	12 41·9	1·3	1·2	7·3	6·5	13·3	11·9
14	13 18·5	13 20·7	12 42·1	1·4	1·2	7·4	6·6	13·4	11·9
15	13 18·8	13 20·9	12 42·4	1·5	1·3	7·5	6·7	13·5	12·0
16	13 19·0	13 21·2	12 42·6	1·6	1·4	7·6	6·8	13·6	12·1
17	13 19·3	13 21·4	12 42·8	1·7	1·5	7·7	6·9	13·7	12·2
18	13 19·5	13 21·7	12 43·1	1·8	1·6	7·8	7·0	13·8	12·3
19	13 19·8	13 21·9	12 43·3	1·9	1·7	7·9	7·0	13·9	12·4
20	13 20·0	13 22·2	12 43·6	2·0	1·8	8·0	7·1	14·0	12·5
21	13 20·3	13 22·4	12 43·8	2·1	1·9	8·1	7·2	14·1	12·6
22	13 20·5	13 22·7	12 44·0	2·2	2·0	8·2	7·3	14·2	12·7
23	13 20·8	13 22·9	12 44·3	2·3	2·1	8·3	7·4	14·3	12·8
24	13 21·0	13 23·2	12 44·5	2·4	2·1	8·4	7·5	14·4	12·8
25	13 21·3	13 23·4	12 44·7	2·5	2·2	8·5	7·6	14·5	12·9
26	13 21·5	13 23·7	12 45·0	2·6	2·3	8·6	7·7	14·6	13·0
27	13 21·8	13 23·9	12 45·2	2·7	2·4	8·7	7·8	14·7	13·1
28	13 22·0	13 24·2	12 45·5	2·8	2·5	8·8	7·8	14·8	13·2
29	13 22·3	13 24·4	12 45·7	2·9	2·6	8·9	7·9	14·9	13·3
30	13 22·5	13 24·7	12 45·9	3·0	2·7	9·0	8·0	15·0	13·4
31	13 22·8	13 24·9	12 46·2	3·1	2·8	9·1	8·1	15·1	13·5
32	13 23·0	13 25·2	12 46·4	3·2	2·9	9·2	8·2	15·2	13·6
33	13 23·3	13 25·4	12 46·7	3·3	2·9	9·3	8·3	15·3	13·6
34	13 23·5	13 25·7	12 46·9	3·4	3·0	9·4	8·4	15·4	13·7
35	13 23·8	13 26·0	12 47·1	3·5	3·1	9·5	8·5	15·5	13·8
36	13 24·0	13 26·2	12 47·4	3·6	3·2	9·6	8·6	15·6	13·9
37	13 24·3	13 26·5	12 47·6	3·7	3·3	9·7	8·6	15·7	14·0
38	13 24·5	13 26·7	12 47·9	3·8	3·4	9·8	8·7	15·8	14·1
39	13 24·8	13 27·0	12 48·1	3·9	3·5	9·9	8·8	15·9	14·2
40	13 25·0	13 27·2	12 48·3	4·0	3·6	10·0	8·9	16·0	14·3
41	13 25·3	13 27·5	12 48·6	4·1	3·7	10·1	9·0	16·1	14·4
42	13 25·5	13 27·7	12 48·8	4·2	3·7	10·2	9·1	16·2	14·4
43	13 25·8	13 28·0	12 49·0	4·3	3·8	10·3	9·2	16·3	14·5
44	13 26·0	13 28·2	12 49·3	4·4	3·9	10·4	9·3	16·4	14·6
45	13 26·3	13 28·5	12 49·5	4·5	4·0	10·5	9·4	16·5	14·7
46	13 26·5	13 28·7	12 49·8	4·6	4·1	10·6	9·5	16·6	14·8
47	13 26·8	13 29·0	12 50·0	4·7	4·2	10·7	9·5	16·7	14·9
48	13 27·0	13 29·2	12 50·2	4·8	4·3	10·8	9·6	16·8	15·0
49	13 27·3	13 29·5	12 50·5	4·9	4·4	10·9	9·7	16·9	15·1
50	13 27·5	13 29·7	12 50·7	5·0	4·5	11·0	9·8	17·0	15·2
51	13 27·8	13 30·0	12 51·0	5·1	4·5	11·1	9·9	17·1	15·2
52	13 28·0	13 30·2	12 51·2	5·2	4·6	11·2	10·0	17·2	15·3
53	13 28·3	13 30·5	12 51·4	5·3	4·7	11·3	10·1	17·3	15·4
54	13 28·5	13 30·7	12 51·7	5·4	4·8	11·4	10·2	17·4	15·5
55	13 28·8	13 31·0	12 51·9	5·5	4·9	11·5	10·3	17·5	15·6
56	13 29·0	13 31·2	12 52·1	5·6	5·0	11·6	10·3	17·6	15·7
57	13 29·3	13 31·5	12 52·4	5·7	5·1	11·7	10·4	17·7	15·8
58	13 29·5	13 31·7	12 52·6	5·8	5·2	11·8	10·5	17·8	15·9
59	13 29·8	13 32·0	12 52·9	5·9	5·3	11·9	10·6	17·9	16·0
60	13 30·0	13 32·2	12 53·1	6·0	5·4	12·0	10·7	18·0	16·1

54^m	SUN PLANETS	ARIES	MOON	v or Corrⁿ d		v or Corrⁿ d		v or Corrⁿ d	
s	° ′	° ′	° ′	′	′	′	′	′	′
00	13 30·0	13 32·2	12 53·1	0·0	0·0	6·0	5·5	12·0	10·9
01	13 30·3	13 32·5	12 53·3	0·1	0·1	6·1	5·5	12·1	11·0
02	13 30·5	13 32·7	12 53·6	0·2	0·2	6·2	5·6	12·2	11·1
03	13 30·8	13 33·0	12 53·8	0·3	0·3	6·3	5·7	12·3	11·2
04	13 31·0	13 33·2	12 54·1	0·4	0·4	6·4	5·8	12·4	11·3
05	13 31·3	13 33·5	12 54·3	0·5	0·5	6·5	5·9	12·5	11·4
06	13 31·5	13 33·7	12 54·5	0·6	0·5	6·6	6·0	12·6	11·4
07	13 31·8	13 34·0	12 54·8	0·7	0·6	6·7	6·1	12·7	11·5
08	13 32·0	13 34·2	12 55·0	0·8	0·7	6·8	6·2	12·8	11·6
09	13 32·3	13 34·5	12 55·2	0·9	0·8	6·9	6·3	12·9	11·7
10	13 32·5	13 34·7	12 55·5	1·0	0·9	7·0	6·4	13·0	11·8
11	13 32·8	13 35·0	12 55·7	1·1	1·0	7·1	6·4	13·1	11·9
12	13 33·0	13 35·2	12 56·0	1·2	1·1	7·2	6·5	13·2	12·0
13	13 33·3	13 35·5	12 56·2	1·3	1·2	7·3	6·6	13·3	12·1
14	13 33·5	13 35·7	12 56·4	1·4	1·3	7·4	6·7	13·4	12·2
15	13 33·8	13 36·0	12 56·7	1·5	1·4	7·5	6·8	13·5	12·3
16	13 34·0	13 36·2	12 56·9	1·6	1·5	7·6	6·9	13·6	12·4
17	13 34·3	13 36·5	12 57·2	1·7	1·5	7·7	7·0	13·7	12·4
18	13 34·5	13 36·7	12 57·4	1·8	1·6	7·8	7·1	13·8	12·5
19	13 34·8	13 37·0	12 57·6	1·9	1·7	7·9	7·2	13·9	12·6
20	13 35·0	13 37·2	12 57·9	2·0	1·8	8·0	7·3	14·0	12·7
21	13 35·3	13 37·5	12 58·1	2·1	1·9	8·1	7·4	14·1	12·8
22	13 35·5	13 37·7	12 58·3	2·2	2·0	8·2	7·4	14·2	12·9
23	13 35·8	13 38·0	12 58·6	2·3	2·1	8·3	7·5	14·3	13·0
24	13 36·0	13 38·2	12 58·8	2·4	2·2	8·4	7·6	14·4	13·1
25	13 36·3	13 38·5	12 59·1	2·5	2·3	8·5	7·7	14·5	13·2
26	13 36·5	13 38·7	12 59·3	2·6	2·4	8·6	7·8	14·6	13·3
27	13 36·8	13 39·0	12 59·5	2·7	2·5	8·7	7·9	14·7	13·4
28	13 37·0	13 39·2	12 59·8	2·8	2·5	8·8	8·0	14·8	13·4
29	13 37·3	13 39·5	13 00·0	2·9	2·6	8·9	8·1	14·9	13·5
30	13 37·5	13 39·7	13 00·3	3·0	2·7	9·0	8·2	15·0	13·6
31	13 37·8	13 40·0	13 00·5	3·1	2·8	9·1	8·3	15·1	13·7
32	13 38·0	13 40·2	13 00·7	3·2	2·9	9·2	8·4	15·2	13·8
33	13 38·3	13 40·5	13 01·0	3·3	3·0	9·3	8·4	15·3	13·9
34	13 38·5	13 40·7	13 01·2	3·4	3·1	9·4	8·5	15·4	14·0
35	13 38·8	13 41·0	13 01·5	3·5	3·2	9·5	8·6	15·5	14·1
36	13 39·0	13 41·2	13 01·7	3·6	3·3	9·6	8·7	15·6	14·2
37	13 39·3	13 41·5	13 01·9	3·7	3·4	9·7	8·8	15·7	14·3
38	13 39·5	13 41·7	13 02·2	3·8	3·5	9·8	8·9	15·8	14·4
39	13 39·8	13 42·0	13 02·4	3·9	3·5	9·9	9·0	15·9	14·4
40	13 40·0	13 42·2	13 02·6	4·0	3·6	10·0	9·1	16·0	14·5
41	13 40·3	13 42·5	13 02·9	4·1	3·7	10·1	9·2	16·1	14·6
42	13 40·5	13 42·7	13 03·1	4·2	3·8	10·2	9·3	16·2	14·7
43	13 40·8	13 43·0	13 03·4	4·3	3·9	10·3	9·4	16·3	14·8
44	13 41·0	13 43·2	13 03·6	4·4	4·0	10·4	9·4	16·4	14·9
45	13 41·3	13 43·5	13 03·8	4·5	4·1	10·5	9·5	16·5	15·0
46	13 41·5	13 43·7	13 04·1	4·6	4·2	10·6	9·6	16·6	15·1
47	13 41·8	13 44·0	13 04·3	4·7	4·3	10·7	9·7	16·7	15·2
48	13 42·0	13 44·3	13 04·6	4·8	4·4	10·8	9·8	16·8	15·3
49	13 42·3	13 44·5	13 04·8	4·9	4·5	10·9	9·9	16·9	15·4
50	13 42·5	13 44·8	13 05·0	5·0	4·5	11·0	10·0	17·0	15·4
51	13 42·8	13 45·0	13 05·3	5·1	4·6	11·1	10·1	17·1	15·5
52	13 43·0	13 45·3	13 05·5	5·2	4·7	11·2	10·2	17·2	15·6
53	13 43·3	13 45·5	13 05·7	5·3	4·8	11·3	10·3	17·3	15·7
54	13 43·5	13 45·8	13 06·0	5·4	4·9	11·4	10·4	17·4	15·8
55	13 43·8	13 46·0	13 06·2	5·5	5·0	11·5	10·4	17·5	15·9
56	13 44·0	13 46·3	13 06·5	5·6	5·1	11·6	10·5	17·6	16·0
57	13 44·3	13 46·5	13 06·7	5·7	5·2	11·7	10·6	17·7	16·1
58	13 44·5	13 46·8	13 06·9	5·8	5·3	11·8	10·7	17·8	16·2
59	13 44·8	13 47·0	13 07·2	5·9	5·4	11·9	10·8	17·9	16·3
60	13 45·0	13 47·3	13 07·4	6·0	5·5	12·0	10·9	18·0	16·4

55^m	SUN PLANETS	ARIES	MOON	v or Corrⁿ d		v or Corrⁿ d		v or Corrⁿ d	
s	° ′	° ′	° ′	′	′	′	′	′	′
00	13 45·0	13 47·3	13 07·4	0·0	0·0	6·0	5·6	12·0	11·1
01	13 45·3	13 47·5	13 07·7	0·1	0·1	6·1	5·6	12·1	11·2
02	13 45·5	13 47·8	13 07·9	0·2	0·2	6·2	5·7	12·2	11·3
03	13 45·8	13 48·0	13 08·1	0·3	0·3	6·3	5·8	12·3	11·4
04	13 46·0	13 48·3	13 08·4	0·4	0·4	6·4	5·9	12·4	11·5
05	13 46·3	13 48·5	13 08·6	0·5	0·5	6·5	6·0	12·5	11·6
06	13 46·5	13 48·8	13 08·8	0·6	0·6	6·6	6·1	12·6	11·7
07	13 46·8	13 49·0	13 09·1	0·7	0·6	6·7	6·2	12·7	11·7
08	13 47·0	13 49·3	13 09·3	0·8	0·7	6·8	6·3	12·8	11·8
09	13 47·3	13 49·5	13 09·6	0·9	0·8	6·9	6·4	12·9	11·9
10	13 47·5	13 49·8	13 09·8	1·0	0·9	7·0	6·5	13·0	12·0
11	13 47·8	13 50·0	13 10·0	1·1	1·0	7·1	6·6	13·1	12·1
12	13 48·0	13 50·3	13 10·3	1·2	1·1	7·2	6·7	13·2	12·2
13	13 48·3	13 50·5	13 10·5	1·3	1·2	7·3	6·8	13·3	12·3
14	13 48·5	13 50·8	13 10·8	1·4	1·3	7·4	6·8	13·4	12·4
15	13 48·8	13 51·0	13 11·0	1·5	1·4	7·5	6·9	13·5	12·5
16	13 49·0	13 51·3	13 11·2	1·6	1·5	7·6	7·0	13·6	12·6
17	13 49·3	13 51·5	13 11·5	1·7	1·6	7·7	7·1	13·7	12·7
18	13 49·5	13 51·8	13 11·7	1·8	1·7	7·8	7·2	13·8	12·8
19	13 49·8	13 52·0	13 12·0	1·9	1·8	7·9	7·3	13·9	12·9
20	13 50·0	13 52·3	13 12·2	2·0	1·9	8·0	7·4	14·0	13·0
21	13 50·3	13 52·5	13 12·4	2·1	1·9	8·1	7·5	14·1	13·0
22	13 50·5	13 52·8	13 12·7	2·2	2·0	8·2	7·6	14·2	13·1
23	13 50·8	13 53·0	13 12·9	2·3	2·1	8·3	7·7	14·3	13·2
24	13 51·0	13 53·3	13 13·1	2·4	2·2	8·4	7·8	14·4	13·3
25	13 51·3	13 53·5	13 13·4	2·5	2·3	8·5	7·9	14·5	13·4
26	13 51·5	13 53·8	13 13·6	2·6	2·4	8·6	8·0	14·6	13·5
27	13 51·8	13 54·0	13 13·9	2·7	2·5	8·7	8·0	14·7	13·6
28	13 52·0	13 54·3	13 14·1	2·8	2·6	8·8	8·1	14·8	13·7
29	13 52·3	13 54·5	13 14·3	2·9	2·7	8·9	8·2	14·9	13·8
30	13 52·5	13 54·8	13 14·6	3·0	2·8	9·0	8·3	15·0	13·9
31	13 52·8	13 55·0	13 14·8	3·1	2·9	9·1	8·4	15·1	14·0
32	13 53·0	13 55·3	13 15·1	3·2	3·0	9·2	8·5	15·2	14·1
33	13 53·3	13 55·5	13 15·3	3·3	3·1	9·3	8·6	15·3	14·2
34	13 53·5	13 55·8	13 15·5	3·4	3·1	9·4	8·7	15·4	14·2
35	13 53·8	13 56·0	13 15·8	3·5	3·2	9·5	8·8	15·5	14·3
36	13 54·0	13 56·3	13 16·0	3·6	3·3	9·6	8·9	15·6	14·4
37	13 54·3	13 56·5	13 16·2	3·7	3·4	9·7	9·0	15·7	14·5
38	13 54·5	13 56·8	13 16·5	3·8	3·5	9·8	9·1	15·8	14·6
39	13 54·8	13 57·0	13 16·7	3·9	3·6	9·9	9·2	15·9	14·7
40	13 55·0	13 57·3	13 17·0	4·0	3·7	10·0	9·3	16·0	14·8
41	13 55·3	13 57·5	13 17·2	4·1	3·8	10·1	9·3	16·1	14·9
42	13 55·5	13 57·8	13 17·4	4·2	3·9	10·2	9·4	16·2	15·0
43	13 55·8	13 58·0	13 17·7	4·3	4·0	10·3	9·5	16·3	15·1
44	13 56·0	13 58·3	13 17·9	4·4	4·1	10·4	9·6	16·4	15·2
45	13 56·3	13 58·5	13 18·2	4·5	4·2	10·5	9·7	16·5	15·3
46	13 56·5	13 58·8	13 18·4	4·6	4·3	10·6	9·8	16·6	15·4
47	13 56·8	13 59·0	13 18·6	4·7	4·3	10·7	9·9	16·7	15·4
48	13 57·0	13 59·3	13 18·9	4·8	4·4	10·8	10·0	16·8	15·5
49	13 57·3	13 59·5	13 19·1	4·9	4·5	10·9	10·1	16·9	15·6
50	13 57·5	13 59·8	13 19·3	5·0	4·6	11·0	10·2	17·0	15·7
51	13 57·8	14 00·0	13 19·6	5·1	4·7	11·1	10·3	17·1	15·8
52	13 58·0	14 00·3	13 19·8	5·2	4·8	11·2	10·4	17·2	15·9
53	13 58·3	14 00·5	13 20·1	5·3	4·9	11·3	10·5	17·3	16·0
54	13 58·5	14 00·8	13 20·3	5·4	5·0	11·4	10·5	17·4	16·1
55	13 58·8	14 01·0	13 20·5	5·5	5·1	11·5	10·6	17·5	16·2
56	13 59·0	14 01·3	13 20·8	5·6	5·2	11·6	10·7	17·6	16·3
57	13 59·3	14 01·5	13 21·0	5·7	5·3	11·7	10·8	17·7	16·4
58	13 59·5	14 01·8	13 21·3	5·8	5·4	11·8	10·9	17·8	16·5
59	13 59·8	14 02·0	13 21·5	5·9	5·5	11·9	11·0	17·9	16·6
60	14 00·0	14 02·3	13 21·7	6·0	5·6	12·0	11·1	18·0	16·7

56ᵐ s	SUN PLANETS	ARIES	MOON	v or d Corrn	v or d Corrn	v or d Corrn
00	14 00·0	14 02·3	13 21·7	0·0 0·0	6·0 5·7	12·0 11·3
01	14 00·3	14 02·6	13 22·0	0·1 0·1	6·1 5·7	12·1 11·4
02	14 00·5	14 02·8	13 22·2	0·2 0·2	6·2 5·8	12·2 11·5
03	14 00·8	14 03·1	13 22·4	0·3 0·3	6·3 5·9	12·3 11·6
04	14 01·0	14 03·3	13 22·7	0·4 0·4	6·4 6·0	12·4 11·7
05	14 01·3	14 03·6	13 22·9	0·5 0·5	6·5 6·1	12·5 11·8
06	14 01·5	14 03·8	13 23·2	0·6 0·6	6·6 6·2	12·6 11·9
07	14 01·8	14 04·1	13 23·4	0·7 0·7	6·7 6·3	12·7 12·0
08	14 02·0	14 04·3	13 23·6	0·8 0·8	6·8 6·4	12·8 12·1
09	14 02·3	14 04·6	13 23·9	0·9 0·8	6·9 6·5	12·9 12·1
10	14 02·5	14 04·8	13 24·1	1·0 0·9	7·0 6·6	13·0 12·2
11	14 02·8	14 05·1	13 24·4	1·1 1·0	7·1 6·7	13·1 12·3
12	14 03·0	14 05·3	13 24·6	1·2 1·1	7·2 6·8	13·2 12·4
13	14 03·3	14 05·6	13 24·8	1·3 1·2	7·3 6·9	13·3 12·5
14	14 03·5	14 05·8	13 25·1	1·4 1·3	7·4 7·0	13·4 12·6
15	14 03·8	14 06·1	13 25·3	1·5 1·4	7·5 7·1	13·5 12·7
16	14 04·0	14 06·3	13 25·6	1·6 1·5	7·6 7·2	13·6 12·8
17	14 04·3	14 06·6	13 25·8	1·7 1·6	7·7 7·3	13·7 12·9
18	14 04·5	14 06·8	13 26·0	1·8 1·7	7·8 7·3	13·8 13·0
19	14 04·8	14 07·1	13 26·3	1·9 1·8	7·9 7·4	13·9 13·1
20	14 05·0	14 07·3	13 26·5	2·0 1·9	8·0 7·5	14·0 13·2
21	14 05·3	14 07·6	13 26·7	2·1 2·0	8·1 7·6	14·1 13·3
22	14 05·5	14 07·8	13 27·0	2·2 2·1	8·2 7·7	14·2 13·4
23	14 05·8	14 08·1	13 27·2	2·3 2·2	8·3 7·8	14·3 13·5
24	14 06·0	14 08·3	13 27·5	2·4 2·3	8·4 7·9	14·4 13·6
25	14 06·3	14 08·6	13 27·7	2·5 2·4	8·5 8·0	14·5 13·7
26	14 06·5	14 08·8	13 27·9	2·6 2·4	8·6 8·1	14·6 13·7
27	14 06·8	14 09·1	13 28·2	2·7 2·5	8·7 8·2	14·7 13·8
28	14 07·0	14 09·3	13 28·4	2·8 2·6	8·8 8·3	14·8 13·9
29	14 07·3	14 09·6	13 28·7	2·9 2·7	8·9 8·4	14·9 14·0
30	14 07·5	14 09·8	13 28·9	3·0 2·8	9·0 8·5	15·0 14·1
31	14 07·8	14 10·1	13 29·1	3·1 2·9	9·1 8·6	15·1 14·2
32	14 08·0	14 10·3	13 29·4	3·2 3·0	9·2 8·7	15·2 14·3
33	14 08·3	14 10·6	13 29·6	3·3 3·1	9·3 8·8	15·3 14·4
34	14 08·5	14 10·8	13 29·8	3·4 3·2	9·4 8·9	15·4 14·5
35	14 08·8	14 11·1	13 30·1	3·5 3·3	9·5 8·9	15·5 14·6
36	14 09·0	14 11·3	13 30·3	3·6 3·4	9·6 9·0	15·6 14·7
37	14 09·3	14 11·6	13 30·6	3·7 3·5	9·7 9·1	15·7 14·8
38	14 09·5	14 11·8	13 30·8	3·8 3·6	9·8 9·2	15·8 14·9
39	14 09·8	14 12·1	13 31·0	3·9 3·7	9·9 9·3	15·9 15·0
40	14 10·0	14 12·3	13 31·3	4·0 3·8	10·0 9·4	16·0 15·1
41	14 10·3	14 12·6	13 31·5	4·1 3·9	10·1 9·5	16·1 15·2
42	14 10·5	14 12·8	13 31·8	4·2 4·0	10·2 9·6	16·2 15·3
43	14 10·8	14 13·1	13 32·0	4·3 4·0	10·3 9·7	16·3 15·3
44	14 11·0	14 13·3	13 32·2	4·4 4·1	10·4 9·8	16·4 15·4
45	14 11·3	14 13·6	13 32·5	4·5 4·2	10·5 9·9	16·5 15·5
46	14 11·5	14 13·8	13 32·7	4·6 4·3	10·6 10·0	16·6 15·6
47	14 11·8	14 14·1	13 32·9	4·7 4·4	10·7 10·1	16·7 15·7
48	14 12·0	14 14·3	13 33·2	4·8 4·5	10·8 10·2	16·8 15·8
49	14 12·3	14 14·6	13 33·4	4·9 4·6	10·9 10·3	16·9 15·9
50	14 12·5	14 14·8	13 33·7	5·0 4·7	11·0 10·4	17·0 16·0
51	14 12·8	14 15·1	13 33·9	5·1 4·8	11·1 10·5	17·1 16·1
52	14 13·0	14 15·3	13 34·1	5·2 4·9	11·2 10·5	17·2 16·2
53	14 13·3	14 15·6	13 34·4	5·3 5·0	11·3 10·6	17·3 16·3
54	14 13·5	14 15·8	13 34·6	5·4 5·1	11·4 10·7	17·4 16·4
55	14 13·8	14 16·1	13 34·9	5·5 5·2	11·5 10·8	17·5 16·5
56	14 14·0	14 16·3	13 35·1	5·6 5·3	11·6 10·9	17·6 16·6
57	14 14·3	14 16·6	13 35·3	5·7 5·4	11·7 11·0	17·7 16·7
58	14 14·5	14 16·8	13 35·6	5·8 5·5	11·8 11·1	17·8 16·8
59	14 14·8	14 17·1	13 35·8	5·9 5·6	11·9 11·2	17·9 16·9
60	14 15·0	14 17·3	13 36·1	6·0 5·7	12·0 11·3	18·0 17·0

57ᵐ s	SUN PLANETS	ARIES	MOON	v or d Corrn	v or d Corrn	v or d Corrn
00	14 15·0	14 17·3	13 36·1	0·0 0·0	6·0 5·8	12·0 11·5
01	14 15·3	14 17·6	13 36·3	0·1 0·1	6·1 5·8	12·1 11·6
02	14 15·5	14 17·8	13 36·5	0·2 0·2	6·2 5·9	12·2 11·7
03	14 15·8	14 18·1	13 36·8	0·3 0·3	6·3 6·0	12·3 11·8
04	14 16·0	14 18·3	13 37·0	0·4 0·4	6·4 6·1	12·4 11·9
05	14 16·3	14 18·6	13 37·2	0·5 0·5	6·5 6·2	12·5 12·0
06	14 16·5	14 18·8	13 37·5	0·6 0·6	6·6 6·3	12·6 12·1
07	14 16·8	14 19·1	13 37·7	0·7 0·7	6·7 6·4	12·7 12·2
08	14 17·0	14 19·3	13 38·0	0·8 0·8	6·8 6·5	12·8 12·3
09	14 17·3	14 19·6	13 38·2	0·9 0·9	6·9 6·6	12·9 12·4
10	14 17·5	14 19·8	13 38·4	1·0 1·0	7·0 6·7	13·0 12·5
11	14 17·8	14 20·1	13 38·7	1·1 1·1	7·1 6·8	13·1 12·6
12	14 18·0	14 20·3	13 38·9	1·2 1·2	7·2 6·9	13·2 12·7
13	14 18·3	14 20·6	13 39·2	1·3 1·2	7·3 7·0	13·3 12·7
14	14 18·5	14 20·9	13 39·4	1·4 1·3	7·4 7·1	13·4 12·8
15	14 18·8	14 21·1	13 39·6	1·5 1·4	7·5 7·2	13·5 12·9
16	14 19·0	14 21·4	13 39·9	1·6 1·5	7·6 7·3	13·6 13·0
17	14 19·3	14 21·6	13 40·1	1·7 1·6	7·7 7·4	13·7 13·1
18	14 19·5	14 21·9	13 40·3	1·8 1·7	7·8 7·5	13·8 13·2
19	14 19·8	14 22·1	13 40·6	1·9 1·8	7·9 7·6	13·9 13·3
20	14 20·0	14 22·4	13 40·8	2·0 1·9	8·0 7·7	14·0 13·4
21	14 20·3	14 22·6	13 41·1	2·1 2·0	8·1 7·8	14·1 13·5
22	14 20·5	14 22·9	13 41·3	2·2 2·1	8·2 7·9	14·2 13·6
23	14 20·8	14 23·1	13 41·5	2·3 2·2	8·3 8·0	14·3 13·7
24	14 21·0	14 23·4	13 41·8	2·4 2·3	8·4 8·1	14·4 13·8
25	14 21·3	14 23·6	13 42·0	2·5 2·4	8·5 8·1	14·5 13·9
26	14 21·5	14 23·9	13 42·3	2·6 2·5	8·6 8·2	14·6 14·0
27	14 21·8	14 24·1	13 42·5	2·7 2·6	8·7 8·3	14·7 14·1
28	14 22·0	14 24·4	13 42·7	2·8 2·7	8·8 8·4	14·8 14·2
29	14 22·3	14 24·6	13 43·0	2·9 2·8	8·9 8·5	14·9 14·3
30	14 22·5	14 24·9	13 43·2	3·0 2·9	9·0 8·6	15·0 14·4
31	14 22·8	14 25·1	13 43·4	3·1 3·0	9·1 8·7	15·1 14·5
32	14 23·0	14 25·4	13 43·7	3·2 3·1	9·2 8·8	15·2 14·6
33	14 23·3	14 25·6	13 43·9	3·3 3·2	9·3 8·9	15·3 14·7
34	14 23·5	14 25·9	13 44·2	3·4 3·3	9·4 9·0	15·4 14·8
35	14 23·8	14 26·1	13 44·4	3·5 3·4	9·5 9·1	15·5 14·9
36	14 24·0	14 26·4	13 44·6	3·6 3·5	9·6 9·2	15·6 15·0
37	14 24·3	14 26·6	13 44·9	3·7 3·5	9·7 9·3	15·7 15·0
38	14 24·5	14 26·9	13 45·1	3·8 3·6	9·8 9·4	15·8 15·1
39	14 24·8	14 27·1	13 45·4	3·9 3·7	9·9 9·5	15·9 15·2
40	14 25·0	14 27·4	13 45·6	4·0 3·8	10·0 9·6	16·0 15·3
41	14 25·3	14 27·6	13 45·8	4·1 3·9	10·1 9·7	16·1 15·4
42	14 25·5	14 27·9	13 46·1	4·2 4·0	10·2 9·8	16·2 15·5
43	14 25·8	14 28·1	13 46·3	4·3 4·1	10·3 9·9	16·3 15·6
44	14 26·0	14 28·4	13 46·5	4·4 4·2	10·4 10·0	16·4 15·7
45	14 26·3	14 28·6	13 46·8	4·5 4·3	10·5 10·1	16·5 15·8
46	14 26·5	14 28·9	13 47·0	4·6 4·4	10·6 10·2	16·6 15·9
47	14 26·8	14 29·1	13 47·3	4·7 4·5	10·7 10·3	16·7 16·0
48	14 27·0	14 29·4	13 47·5	4·8 4·6	10·8 10·4	16·8 16·1
49	14 27·3	14 29·6	13 47·7	4·9 4·7	10·9 10·4	16·9 16·2
50	14 27·5	14 29·9	13 48·0	5·0 4·8	11·0 10·5	17·0 16·3
51	14 27·8	14 30·1	13 48·2	5·1 4·9	11·1 10·6	17·1 16·4
52	14 28·0	14 30·4	13 48·5	5·2 5·0	11·2 10·7	17·2 16·5
53	14 28·3	14 30·6	13 48·7	5·3 5·1	11·3 10·8	17·3 16·6
54	14 28·5	14 30·9	13 48·9	5·4 5·2	11·4 10·9	17·4 16·7
55	14 28·8	14 31·1	13 49·2	5·5 5·3	11·5 11·0	17·5 16·8
56	14 29·0	14 31·4	13 49·4	5·6 5·4	11·6 11·1	17·6 16·9
57	14 29·3	14 31·6	13 49·7	5·7 5·5	11·7 11·2	17·7 17·0
58	14 29·5	14 31·9	13 49·9	5·8 5·6	11·8 11·3	17·8 17·1
59	14 29·8	14 32·1	13 50·1	5·9 5·7	11·9 11·4	17·9 17·2
60	14 30·0	14 32·4	13 50·4	6·0 5·8	12·0 11·5	18·0 17·3

58ᵐ

58	SUN PLANETS	ARIES	MOON	v or d Corrⁿ	v or d Corrⁿ	v or d Corrⁿ
s	° ′	° ′	° ′	′ ′	′ ′	′ ′
00	14 30·0	14 32·4	13 50·4	0·0 0·0	6·0 5·9	12·0 11·7
01	14 30·3	14 32·6	13 50·6	0·1 0·1	6·1 5·9	12·1 11·8
02	14 30·5	14 32·9	13 50·8	0·2 0·2	6·2 6·0	12·2 11·9
03	14 30·8	14 33·1	13 51·1	0·3 0·3	6·3 6·1	12·3 12·0
04	14 31·0	14 33·4	13 51·3	0·4 0·4	6·4 6·2	12·4 12·1
05	14 31·3	14 33·6	13 51·6	0·5 0·5	6·5 6·3	12·5 12·2
06	14 31·5	14 33·9	13 51·8	0·6 0·6	6·6 6·4	12·6 12·3
07	14 31·8	14 34·1	13 52·0	0·7 0·7	6·7 6·5	12·7 12·4
08	14 32·0	14 34·4	13 52·3	0·8 0·8	6·8 6·6	12·8 12·5
09	14 32·3	14 34·6	13 52·5	0·9 0·9	6·9 6·7	12·9 12·6
10	14 32·5	14 34·9	13 52·8	1·0 1·0	7·0 6·8	13·0 12·7
11	14 32·8	14 35·1	13 53·0	1·1 1·1	7·1 6·9	13·1 12·8
12	14 33·0	14 35·4	13 53·2	1·2 1·2	7·2 7·0	13·2 12·9
13	14 33·3	14 35·6	13 53·5	1·3 1·3	7·3 7·1	13·3 13·0
14	14 33·5	14 35·9	13 53·7	1·4 1·4	7·4 7·2	13·4 13·1
15	14 33·8	14 36·1	13 53·9	1·5 1·5	7·5 7·3	13·5 13·2
16	14 34·0	14 36·4	13 54·2	1·6 1·6	7·6 7·4	13·6 13·3
17	14 34·3	14 36·6	13 54·4	1·7 1·7	7·7 7·5	13·7 13·4
18	14 34·5	14 36·9	13 54·7	1·8 1·8	7·8 7·6	13·8 13·5
19	14 34·8	14 37·1	13 54·9	1·9 1·9	7·9 7·7	13·9 13·6
20	14 35·0	14 37·4	13 55·1	2·0 2·0	8·0 7·8	14·0 13·7
21	14 35·3	14 37·6	13 55·4	2·1 2·0	8·1 7·9	14·1 13·7
22	14 35·5	14 37·9	13 55·6	2·2 2·1	8·2 8·0	14·2 13·8
23	14 35·8	14 38·1	13 55·9	2·3 2·2	8·3 8·1	14·3 13·9
24	14 36·0	14 38·4	13 56·1	2·4 2·3	8·4 8·2	14·4 14·0
25	14 36·3	14 38·6	13 56·3	2·5 2·4	8·5 8·3	14·5 14·1
26	14 36·5	14 38·9	13 56·6	2·6 2·5	8·6 8·4	14·6 14·2
27	14 36·8	14 39·2	13 56·8	2·7 2·6	8·7 8·5	14·7 14·3
28	14 37·0	14 39·4	13 57·0	2·8 2·7	8·8 8·6	14·8 14·4
29	14 37·3	14 39·7	13 57·3	2·9 2·8	8·9 8·7	14·9 14·5
30	14 37·5	14 39·9	13 57·5	3·0 2·9	9·0 8·8	15·0 14·6
31	14 37·8	14 40·2	13 57·8	3·1 3·0	9·1 8·9	15·1 14·7
32	14 38·0	14 40·4	13 58·0	3·2 3·1	9·2 9·0	15·2 14·8
33	14 38·3	14 40·7	13 58·2	3·3 3·2	9·3 9·1	15·3 14·9
34	14 38·5	14 40·9	13 58·5	3·4 3·3	9·4 9·2	15·4 15·0
35	14 38·8	14 41·2	13 58·7	3·5 3·4	9·5 9·3	15·5 15·1
36	14 39·0	14 41·4	13 59·0	3·6 3·5	9·6 9·4	15·6 15·2
37	14 39·3	14 41·7	13 59·2	3·7 3·6	9·7 9·5	15·7 15·3
38	14 39·5	14 41·9	13 59·4	3·8 3·7	9·8 9·6	15·8 15·4
39	14 39·8	14 42·2	13 59·7	3·9 3·8	9·9 9·7	15·9 15·5
40	14 40·0	14 42·4	13 59·9	4·0 3·9	10·0 9·8	16·0 15·6
41	14 40·3	14 42·7	14 00·1	4·1 4·0	10·1 9·8	16·1 15·7
42	14 40·5	14 42·9	14 00·4	4·2 4·1	10·2 9·9	16·2 15·8
43	14 40·8	14 43·2	14 00·6	4·3 4·2	10·3 10·0	16·3 15·9
44	14 41·0	14 43·4	14 00·9	4·4 4·3	10·4 10·1	16·4 16·0
45	14 41·3	14 43·7	14 01·1	4·5 4·4	10·5 10·2	16·5 16·1
46	14 41·5	14 43·9	14 01·3	4·6 4·5	10·6 10·3	16·6 16·2
47	14 41·8	14 44·2	14 01·6	4·7 4·6	10·7 10·4	16·7 16·3
48	14 42·0	14 44·4	14 01·8	4·8 4·7	10·8 10·5	16·8 16·4
49	14 42·3	14 44·7	14 02·1	4·9 4·8	10·9 10·6	16·9 16·5
50	14 42·5	14 44·9	14 02·3	5·0 4·9	11·0 10·7	17·0 16·6
51	14 42·8	14 45·2	14 02·5	5·1 5·0	11·1 10·8	17·1 16·7
52	14 43·0	14 45·4	14 02·8	5·2 5·1	11·2 10·9	17·2 16·8
53	14 43·3	14 45·7	14 03·0	5·3 5·2	11·3 11·0	17·3 16·9
54	14 43·5	14 45·9	14 03·3	5·4 5·3	11·4 11·1	17·4 17·0
55	14 43·8	14 46·2	14 03·5	5·5 5·4	11·5 11·2	17·5 17·1
56	14 44·0	14 46·4	14 03·7	5·6 5·5	11·6 11·3	17·6 17·2
57	14 44·3	14 46·7	14 04·0	5·7 5·6	11·7 11·4	17·7 17·3
58	14 44·5	14 46·9	14 04·2	5·8 5·7	11·8 11·5	17·8 17·4
59	14 44·8	14 47·2	14 04·4	5·9 5·8	11·9 11·6	17·9 17·5
60	14 45·0	14 47·4	14 04·7	6·0 5·9	12·0 11·7	18·0 17·6

59ᵐ

59	SUN PLANETS	ARIES	MOON	v or d Corrⁿ	v or d Corrⁿ	v or d Corrⁿ
s	° ′	° ′	° ′	′ ′	′ ′	′ ′
00	14 45·0	14 47·4	14 04·7	0·0 0·0	6·0 6·0	12·0 11·9
01	14 45·3	14 47·7	14 04·9	0·1 0·1	6·1 6·0	12·1 12·0
02	14 45·5	14 47·9	14 05·2	0·2 0·2	6·2 6·1	12·2 12·1
03	14 45·8	14 48·2	14 05·4	0·3 0·3	6·3 6·2	12·3 12·2
04	14 46·0	14 48·4	14 05·6	0·4 0·4	6·4 6·3	12·4 12·3
05	14 46·3	14 48·7	14 05·9	0·5 0·5	6·5 6·4	12·5 12·4
06	14 46·5	14 48·9	14 06·1	0·6 0·6	6·6 6·5	12·6 12·5
07	14 46·8	14 49·2	14 06·4	0·7 0·7	6·7 6·6	12·7 12·6
08	14 47·0	14 49·4	14 06·6	0·8 0·8	6·8 6·7	12·8 12·7
09	14 47·3	14 49·7	14 06·8	0·9 0·9	6·9 6·8	12·9 12·8
10	14 47·5	14 49·9	14 07·1	1·0 1·0	7·0 6·9	13·0 12·9
11	14 47·8	14 50·2	14 07·3	1·1 1·1	7·1 7·0	13·1 13·0
12	14 48·0	14 50·4	14 07·5	1·2 1·2	7·2 7·1	13·2 13·1
13	14 48·3	14 50·7	14 07·8	1·3 1·3	7·3 7·2	13·3 13·2
14	14 48·5	14 50·9	14 08·0	1·4 1·4	7·4 7·3	13·4 13·3
15	14 48·8	14 51·2	14 08·3	1·5 1·5	7·5 7·4	13·5 13·4
16	14 49·0	14 51·4	14 08·5	1·6 1·6	7·6 7·5	13·6 13·5
17	14 49·3	14 51·7	14 08·7	1·7 1·7	7·7 7·6	13·7 13·6
18	14 49·5	14 51·9	14 09·0	1·8 1·8	7·8 7·7	13·8 13·7
19	14 49·8	14 52·2	14 09·2	1·9 1·9	7·9 7·8	13·9 13·8
20	14 50·0	14 52·4	14 09·5	2·0 2·0	8·0 7·9	14·0 13·9
21	14 50·3	14 52·7	14 09·7	2·1 2·1	8·1 8·0	14·1 14·0
22	14 50·5	14 52·9	14 09·9	2·2 2·2	8·2 8·1	14·2 14·1
23	14 50·8	14 53·2	14 10·2	2·3 2·3	8·3 8·2	14·3 14·2
24	14 51·0	14 53·4	14 10·4	2·4 2·4	8·4 8·3	14·4 14·3
25	14 51·3	14 53·7	14 10·6	2·5 2·5	8·5 8·4	14·5 14·4
26	14 51·5	14 53·9	14 10·9	2·6 2·6	8·6 8·5	14·6 14·5
27	14 51·8	14 54·2	14 11·1	2·7 2·7	8·7 8·6	14·7 14·6
28	14 52·0	14 54·4	14 11·4	2·8 2·8	8·8 8·7	14·8 14·7
29	14 52·3	14 54·7	14 11·6	2·9 2·9	8·9 8·8	14·9 14·8
30	14 52·5	14 54·9	14 11·8	3·0 3·0	9·0 8·9	15·0 14·9
31	14 52·8	14 55·2	14 12·1	3·1 3·1	9·1 9·0	15·1 15·0
32	14 53·0	14 55·4	14 12·3	3·2 3·2	9·2 9·1	15·2 15·1
33	14 53·3	14 55·7	14 12·6	3·3 3·3	9·3 9·2	15·3 15·2
34	14 53·5	14 55·9	14 12·8	3·4 3·4	9·4 9·3	15·4 15·3
35	14 53·8	14 56·2	14 13·0	3·5 3·5	9·5 9·4	15·5 15·4
36	14 54·0	14 56·4	14 13·3	3·6 3·6	9·6 9·5	15·6 15·5
37	14 54·3	14 56·7	14 13·5	3·7 3·7	9·7 9·6	15·7 15·6
38	14 54·5	14 56·9	14 13·8	3·8 3·8	9·8 9·7	15·8 15·7
39	14 54·8	14 57·2	14 14·0	3·9 3·9	9·9 9·8	15·9 15·8
40	14 55·0	14 57·5	14 14·2	4·0 4·0	10·0 9·9	16·0 15·9
41	14 55·3	14 57·7	14 14·5	4·1 4·1	10·1 10·0	16·1 16·0
42	14 55·5	14 58·0	14 14·7	4·2 4·2	10·2 10·1	16·2 16·1
43	14 55·8	14 58·2	14 14·9	4·3 4·3	10·3 10·2	16·3 16·2
44	14 56·0	14 58·5	14 15·2	4·4 4·4	10·4 10·3	16·4 16·3
45	14 56·3	14 58·7	14 15·4	4·5 4·5	10·5 10·4	16·5 16·4
46	14 56·5	14 59·0	14 15·7	4·6 4·6	10·6 10·5	16·6 16·5
47	14 56·8	14 59·2	14 15·9	4·7 4·7	10·7 10·6	16·7 16·6
48	14 57·0	14 59·5	14 16·1	4·8 4·8	10·8 10·7	16·8 16·7
49	14 57·3	14 59·7	14 16·4	4·9 4·9	10·9 10·8	16·9 16·8
50	14 57·5	15 00·0	14 16·6	5·0 5·0	11·0 10·9	17·0 16·9
51	14 57·8	15 00·2	14 16·9	5·1 5·1	11·1 11·0	17·1 17·0
52	14 58·0	15 00·5	14 17·1	5·2 5·2	11·2 11·1	17·2 17·1
53	14 58·3	15 00·7	14 17·3	5·3 5·3	11·3 11·2	17·3 17·2
54	14 58·5	15 01·0	14 17·6	5·4 5·4	11·4 11·3	17·4 17·3
55	14 58·8	15 01·2	14 17·8	5·5 5·5	11·5 11·4	17·5 17·4
56	14 59·0	15 01·5	14 18·0	5·6 5·6	11·6 11·5	17·6 17·5
57	14 59·3	15 01·7	14 18·3	5·7 5·7	11·7 11·6	17·7 17·6
58	14 59·5	15 02·0	14 18·5	5·8 5·8	11·8 11·7	17·8 17·7
59	14 59·8	15 02·2	14 18·8	5·9 5·9	11·9 11·8	17·9 17·8
60	15 00·0	15 02·5	14 19·0	6·0 6·0	12·0 11·9	18·0 17·9

TABLES FOR INTERPOLATING SUNRISE, MOONRISE, ETC.

TABLE I—FOR LATITUDE

Tabular Interval			Difference between the times for consecutive latitudes															
$10°$	$5°$	$2°$	5^m	10^m	15^m	20^m	25^m	30^m	35^m	40^m	45^m	50^m	55^m	60^m	1^h05^m	1^h10^m	1^h15^m	1^h20^m
° ′	° ′	° ′	m	m	m	m	m	m	m	m	m	m	m	m	h m	h m	h m	h m
0 30	0 15	0 06	0	0	1	1	1	1	1	2	2	2	2	2	0 02	0 02	0 02	0 02
1 00	0 30	0 12	0	1	1	2	2	3	3	3	4	4	4	5	05	05	05	05
1 30	0 45	0 18	1	1	2	3	3	4	4	5	5	6	7	7	07	07	07	07
2 00	1 00	0 24	1	2	3	4	5	5	6	7	7	8	9	10	10	10	10	10
2 30	1 15	0 30	1	2	4	5	6	7	8	9	9	10	11	12	12	13	13	13
3 00	1 30	0 36	1	3	4	6	7	8	9	10	11	12	13	14	0 15	0 15	0 16	0 16
3 30	1 45	0 42	2	3	5	7	8	10	11	12	13	14	16	17	18	18	19	19
4 00	2 00	0 48	2	4	6	8	9	11	13	14	15	16	18	19	20	21	22	22
4 30	2 15	0 54	2	4	7	9	11	13	15	16	18	19	21	22	23	24	25	26
5 00	2 30	1 00	2	5	7	10	12	14	16	18	20	22	23	25	26	27	28	29
5 30	2 45	1 06	3	5	8	11	13	16	18	20	22	24	26	28	0 29	0 30	0 31	0 32
6 00	3 00	1 12	3	6	9	12	14	17	20	22	24	26	29	31	32	33	34	36
6 30	3 15	1 18	3	6	10	13	16	19	22	24	26	29	31	34	36	37	38	40
7 00	3 30	1 24	3	7	10	14	17	20	23	26	29	31	34	37	39	41	42	44
7 30	3 45	1 30	4	7	11	15	18	22	25	28	31	34	37	40	43	44	46	48
8 00	4 00	1 36	4	8	12	16	20	23	27	30	34	37	41	44	0 47	0 48	0 51	0 53
8 30	4 15	1 42	4	8	13	17	21	25	29	33	36	40	44	48	0 51	0 53	0 56	0 58
9 00	4 30	1 48	4	9	13	18	22	27	31	35	39	43	47	52	0 55	0 58	1 01	1 04
9 30	4 45	1 54	5	9	14	19	24	28	33	38	42	47	51	56	1 00	1 04	1 08	1 12
10 00	5 00	2 00	5	10	15	20	25	30	35	40	45	50	55	60	1 05	1 10	1 15	1 20

Table I is for interpolating the LMT of sunrise, twilight, moonrise, etc., for latitude. It is to be entered, in the appropriate column on the left, with the difference between true latitude and the nearest tabular latitude which is *less* than the true latitude; and with the argument at the top which is the nearest value of the difference between the times for the tabular latitude and the next higher one; the correction so obtained is applied to the time for the tabular latitude; the sign of the correction can be seen by inspection. It is to be noted that the interpolation is not linear, so that when using this table it is essential to take out the tabular phenomenon for the latitude *less* than the true latitude.

TABLE II—FOR LONGITUDE

Long. East or West	Difference between the times for given date and preceding date (for east longitude) or for given date and following date (for west longitude)																		
	10^m	20^m	30^m	40^m	50^m	60^m	1^h+10^m	20^m	30^m	1^h+40^m	50^m	60^m	2^h10^m	2^h20^m	2^h30^m	2^h40^m	2^h50^m	3^h00^m
°	m	m	m	m	m	m	m	m	m	m	m	m	h m	h m	h m	h m	h m	h m
0	0	0	0	0	0	0	0	0	0	0	0	0	0 00	0 00	0 00	0 00	0 00	0 00
10	0	1	1	1	1	2	2	2	2	3	3	3	04	04	04	04	05	05
20	1	1	2	2	3	3	4	4	5	6	6	7	07	08	08	09	09	10
30	1	2	2	3	4	5	6	7	7	8	9	10	11	12	12	13	14	15
40	1	2	3	4	6	7	8	9	10	11	12	13	14	16	17	18	19	20
50	1	3	4	6	7	8	10	11	12	14	15	17	0 18	0 19	0 21	0 22	0 24	0 25
60	2	3	5	7	8	10	12	13	15	17	18	20	22	23	25	27	28	30
70	2	4	6	8	10	12	14	16	17	19	21	23	25	27	29	31	33	35
80	2	4	7	9	11	13	16	18	20	22	24	27	29	31	33	36	38	40
90	2	5	7	10	12	15	17	20	22	25	27	30	32	35	37	40	42	45
100	3	6	8	11	14	17	19	22	25	28	31	33	0 36	0 39	0 42	0 44	0 47	0 50
110	3	6	9	12	15	18	21	24	27	31	34	37	40	43	46	49	0 52	0 55
120	3	7	10	13	17	20	23	27	30	33	37	40	43	47	50	53	0 57	1 00
130	4	7	11	14	18	22	25	29	32	36	40	43	47	51	54	0 58	1 01	1 05
140	4	8	12	16	19	23	27	31	35	39	43	47	51	54	0 58	1 02	1 06	1 10
150	4	8	13	17	21	25	29	33	38	42	46	50	0 54	0 58	1 03	1 07	1 11	1 15
160	4	9	13	18	22	27	31	36	40	44	49	53	0 58	1 02	1 07	1 11	1 16	1 20
170	5	9	14	19	24	28	33	38	42	47	52	57	1 01	1 06	1 11	1 16	1 20	1 25
180	5	10	15	20	25	30	35	40	45	50	55	60	1 05	1 10	1 15	1 20	1 25	1 30

Table II is for interpolating the LMT of moonrise, moonset and the Moon's meridian passage for longitude. It is entered with longitude and with the difference between the times for the given date and for the preceding date (in east longitudes) or following date (in west longitudes). The correction is normally *added* for west longitudes and *subtracted* for east longitudes, but if, as occasionally happens, the times become earlier each day instead of later, the signs of the corrections must be reversed.

INDEX TO SELECTED STARS, 2012

Name	No	Mag	SHA	Dec
			°	°
Acamar	7	3·2	315	S 40
Achernar	5	0·5	335	S 57
Acrux	30	1·3	173	S 63
Adhara	19	1·5	255	S 29
Aldebaran	10	0·9	291	N 17
Alioth	32	1·8	166	N 56
Alkaid	34	1·9	153	N 49
Al Na'ir	55	1·7	28	S 47
Alnilam	15	1·7	276	S 1
Alphard	25	2·0	218	S 9
Alphecca	41	2·2	126	N 27
Alpheratz	1	2·1	358	N 29
Altair	51	0·8	62	N 9
Ankaa	2	2·4	353	S 42
Antares	42	1·0	112	S 26
Arcturus	37	0·0	146	N 19
Atria	43	1·9	107	S 69
Avior	22	1·9	234	S 60
Bellatrix	13	1·6	279	N 6
Betelgeuse	16	Var.*	271	N 7
Canopus	17	−0·7	264	S 53
Capella	12	0·1	281	N 46
Deneb	53	1·3	50	N 45
Denebola	28	2·1	183	N 15
Diphda	4	2·0	349	S 18
Dubhe	27	1·8	194	N 62
Elnath	14	1·7	278	N 29
Eltanin	47	2·2	91	N 51
Enif	54	2·4	34	N 10
Fomalhaut	56	1·2	15	S 30
Gacrux	31	1·6	172	S 57
Gienah	29	2·6	176	S 18
Hadar	35	0·6	149	S 60
Hamal	6	2·0	328	N 24
Kaus Australis	48	1·9	84	S 34
Kochab	40	2·1	137	N 74
Markab	57	2·5	14	N 15
Menkar	8	2·5	314	N 4
Menkent	36	2·1	148	S 36
Miaplacidus	24	1·7	222	S 70
Mirfak	9	1·8	309	N 50
Nunki	50	2·0	76	S 26
Peacock	52	1·9	53	S 57
Pollux	21	1·1	243	N 28
Procyon	20	0·4	245	N 5
Rasalhague	46	2·1	96	N 13
Regulus	26	1·4	208	N 12
Rigel	11	0·1	281	S 8
Rigil Kentaurus	38	−0·3	140	S 61
Sabik	44	2·4	102	S 16
Schedar	3	2·2	350	N 57
Shaula	45	1·6	96	S 37
Sirius	18	−1·5	259	S 17
Spica	33	1·0	159	S 11
Suhail	23	2·2	223	S 43
Vega	49	0·0	81	N 39
Zubenelgenubi	39	2·8	137	S 16

No	Name	Mag	SHA	Dec
			°	°
1	Alpheratz	2·1	358	N 29
2	Ankaa	2·4	353	S 42
3	Schedar	2·2	350	N 57
4	Diphda	2·0	349	S 18
5	Achernar	0·5	335	S 57
6	Hamal	2·0	328	N 24
7	Acamar	3·2	315	S 40
8	Menkar	2·5	314	N 4
9	Mirfak	1·8	309	N 50
10	Aldebaran	0·9	291	N 17
11	Rigel	0·1	281	S 8
12	Capella	0·1	281	N 46
13	Bellatrix	1·6	279	N 6
14	Elnath	1·7	278	N 29
15	Alnilam	1·7	276	S 1
16	Betelgeuse	Var.*	271	N 7
17	Canopus	−0·7	264	S 53
18	Sirius	−1·5	259	S 17
19	Adhara	1·5	255	S 29
20	Procyon	0·4	245	N 5
21	Pollux	1·1	243	N 28
22	Avior	1·9	234	S 60
23	Suhail	2·2	223	S 43
24	Miaplacidus	1·7	222	S 70
25	Alphard	2·0	218	S 9
26	Regulus	1·4	208	N 12
27	Dubhe	1·8	194	N 62
28	Denebola	2·1	183	N 15
29	Gienah	2·6	176	S 18
30	Acrux	1·3	173	S 63
31	Gacrux	1·6	172	S 57
32	Alioth	1·8	166	N 56
33	Spica	1·0	159	S 11
34	Alkaid	1·9	153	N 49
35	Hadar	0·6	149	S 60
36	Menkent	2·1	148	S 36
37	Arcturus	0·0	146	N 19
38	Rigil Kentaurus	−0·3	140	S 61
39	Zubenelgenubi	2·8	137	S 16
40	Kochab	2·1	137	N 74
41	Alphecca	2·2	126	N 27
42	Antares	1·0	112	S 26
43	Atria	1·9	107	S 69
44	Sabik	2·4	102	S 16
45	Shaula	1·6	96	S 37
46	Rasalhague	2·1	96	N 13
47	Eltanin	2·2	91	N 51
48	Kaus Australis	1·9	84	S 34
49	Vega	0·0	81	N 39
50	Nunki	2·0	76	S 26
51	Altair	0·8	62	N 9
52	Peacock	1·9	53	S 57
53	Deneb	1·3	50	N 45
54	Enif	2·4	34	N 10
55	Al Na'ir	1·7	28	S 47
56	Fomalhaut	1·2	15	S 30
57	Markab	2·5	14	N 15

*0·1 — 1·2

xxxiii

ALTITUDE CORRECTION TABLES 0°–35°— MOON

App. Alt.	0°–4° Corrⁿ	5°–9° Corrⁿ	10°–14° Corrⁿ	15°–19° Corrⁿ	20°–24° Corrⁿ	25°–29° Corrⁿ	30°–34° Corrⁿ	App. Alt.
00	0° 34.5	5° 58.2	10° 62.1	15° 62.8	20° 62.2	25° 60.8	30° 58.9	00
10	36.5	58.5	62.2	62.8	62.2	60.8	58.8	10
20	38.3	58.7	62.2	62.8	62.1	60.7	58.8	20
30	40.0	58.9	62.3	62.8	62.1	60.7	58.7	30
40	41.5	59.1	62.3	62.8	62.0	60.6	58.6	40
50	42.9	59.3	62.4	62.7	62.0	60.6	58.5	50
00	1° 44.2	6° 59.5	11° 62.4	16° 62.7	21° 62.0	26° 60.5	31° 58.5	00
10	45.4	59.7	62.4	62.7	61.9	60.4	58.4	10
20	46.5	59.9	62.5	62.7	61.9	60.4	58.3	20
30	47.5	60.0	62.5	62.7	61.9	60.3	58.2	30
40	48.4	60.2	62.5	62.7	61.8	60.3	58.2	40
50	49.3	60.3	62.6	62.7	61.8	60.2	58.1	50
00	2° 50.1	7° 60.5	12° 62.6	17° 62.7	22° 61.7	27° 60.1	32° 58.0	00
10	50.8	60.6	62.6	62.6	61.7	60.1	57.9	10
20	51.5	60.7	62.6	62.6	61.6	60.0	57.8	20
30	52.2	60.9	62.7	62.6	61.6	59.9	57.8	30
40	52.8	61.0	62.7	62.6	61.6	59.9	57.7	40
50	53.4	61.1	62.7	62.6	61.5	59.8	57.6	50
00	3° 53.9	8° 61.2	13° 62.7	18° 62.5	23° 61.5	28° 59.7	33° 57.5	00
10	54.4	61.3	62.7	62.5	61.4	59.7	57.4	10
20	54.9	61.4	62.7	62.5	61.4	59.6	57.4	20
30	55.3	61.5	62.8	62.5	61.3	59.5	57.3	30
40	55.7	61.6	62.8	62.4	61.3	59.5	57.2	40
50	56.1	61.6	62.8	62.4	61.2	59.4	57.1	50
00	4° 56.4	9° 61.7	14° 62.8	19° 62.4	24° 61.2	29° 59.3	34° 57.0	00
10	56.8	61.8	62.8	62.4	61.1	59.3	56.9	10
20	57.1	61.9	62.8	62.3	61.1	59.2	56.9	20
30	57.4	61.9	62.8	62.3	61.0	59.1	56.8	30
40	57.7	62.0	62.8	62.3	61.0	59.1	56.7	40
50	58.0	62.1	62.8	62.2	60.9	59.0	56.6	50

HP	L	U	L	U	L	U	L	U	L	U	L	U	L	U	HP
54.0	0.3	0.9	0.3	0.9	0.4	1.0	0.5	1.1	0.6	1.2	0.7	1.3	0.9	1.5	54.0
54.3	0.7	1.1	0.7	1.2	0.8	1.2	0.8	1.3	0.9	1.4	1.1	1.5	1.2	1.7	54.3
54.6	1.1	1.4	1.1	1.4	1.1	1.4	1.2	1.5	1.3	1.6	1.4	1.7	1.5	1.8	54.6
54.9	1.4	1.6	1.5	1.6	1.5	1.6	1.6	1.7	1.6	1.8	1.8	1.9	1.9	2.0	54.9
55.2	1.8	1.8	1.8	1.8	1.9	1.8	1.9	1.9	2.0	2.0	2.1	2.1	2.2	2.2	55.2
55.5	2.2	2.0	2.2	2.0	2.3	2.1	2.3	2.1	2.4	2.2	2.4	2.3	2.5	2.4	55.5
55.8	2.6	2.2	2.6	2.2	2.6	2.3	2.7	2.3	2.7	2.4	2.8	2.4	2.9	2.5	55.8
56.1	3.0	2.4	3.0	2.5	3.0	2.5	3.0	2.5	3.1	2.6	3.1	2.6	3.2	2.7	56.1
56.4	3.3	2.7	3.4	2.7	3.4	2.7	3.4	2.7	3.4	2.8	3.5	2.8	3.5	2.9	56.4
56.7	3.7	2.9	3.7	2.9	3.8	2.9	3.8	2.9	3.8	3.0	3.8	3.0	3.9	3.0	56.7
57.0	4.1	3.1	4.1	3.1	4.1	3.1	4.1	3.1	4.2	3.2	4.2	3.2	4.2	3.2	57.0
57.3	4.5	3.3	4.5	3.3	4.5	3.3	4.5	3.3	4.5	3.3	4.5	3.4	4.6	3.4	57.3
57.6	4.9	3.5	4.9	3.5	4.9	3.5	4.9	3.5	4.9	3.5	4.9	3.5	4.9	3.6	57.6
57.9	5.3	3.8	5.3	3.8	5.2	3.8	5.2	3.7	5.2	3.7	5.2	3.7	5.2	3.7	57.9
58.2	5.6	4.0	5.6	4.0	5.6	4.0	5.6	4.0	5.6	3.9	5.6	3.9	5.6	3.9	58.2
58.5	6.0	4.2	6.0	4.2	6.0	4.2	6.0	4.2	6.0	4.1	5.9	4.1	5.9	4.1	58.5
58.8	6.4	4.4	6.4	4.4	6.4	4.4	6.3	4.4	6.3	4.3	6.3	4.3	6.2	4.2	58.8
59.1	6.8	4.6	6.8	4.6	6.7	4.6	6.7	4.6	6.7	4.5	6.6	4.5	6.6	4.4	59.1
59.4	7.2	4.8	7.1	4.8	7.1	4.8	7.1	4.8	7.0	4.7	7.0	4.7	6.9	4.6	59.4
59.7	7.5	5.1	7.5	5.0	7.5	5.0	7.5	5.0	7.4	4.9	7.3	4.8	7.2	4.8	59.7
60.0	7.9	5.3	7.9	5.3	7.9	5.2	7.8	5.2	7.8	5.1	7.7	5.0	7.6	4.9	60.0
60.3	8.3	5.5	8.3	5.5	8.2	5.4	8.2	5.4	8.1	5.3	8.0	5.2	7.9	5.1	60.3
60.6	8.7	5.7	8.7	5.7	8.6	5.7	8.6	5.6	8.5	5.5	8.4	5.4	8.2	5.3	60.6
60.9	9.1	5.9	9.0	5.9	9.0	5.9	8.9	5.8	8.8	5.7	8.7	5.6	8.6	5.4	60.9
61.2	9.5	6.2	9.4	6.1	9.4	6.1	9.3	6.0	9.2	5.9	9.1	5.8	8.9	5.6	61.2
61.5	9.8	6.4	9.8	6.3	9.7	6.3	9.7	6.2	9.5	6.1	9.4	5.9	9.2	5.8	61.5

DIP

Ht. of Eye	Corrⁿ	Ht. of Eye	Ht. of Eye	Corrⁿ	Ht. of Eye
m		ft.	m		ft.
2.4	−2.8	8.0	9.5	−5.5	31.5
2.6	−2.9	8.6	9.9	−5.6	32.7
2.8	−3.0	9.2	10.3	−5.7	33.9
3.0	−3.1	9.8	10.6	−5.8	35.1
3.2	−3.2	10.5	11.0	−5.9	36.3
3.4	−3.3	11.2	11.4	−6.0	37.6
3.6	−3.4	11.9	11.8	−6.1	38.9
3.8	−3.5	12.6	12.2	−6.2	40.1
4.0	−3.6	13.3	12.6	−6.3	41.5
4.3	−3.7	14.1	13.0	−6.4	42.8
4.5	−3.8	14.9	13.4	−6.5	44.2
4.7	−3.9	15.7	13.8	−6.6	45.5
5.0	−4.0	16.5	14.2	−6.7	46.9
5.2	−4.1	17.4	14.7	−6.8	48.4
5.5	−4.2	18.3	15.1	−6.9	49.8
5.8	−4.3	19.1	15.5	−7.0	51.3
6.1	−4.4	20.1	16.0	−7.1	52.8
6.3	−4.5	21.0	16.5	−7.2	54.3
6.6	−4.6	22.0	16.9	−7.3	55.8
6.9	−4.7	22.9	17.4	−7.4	57.4
7.2	−4.8	23.9	17.9	−7.5	58.9
7.5	−4.9	24.9	18.4	−7.6	60.5
7.9	−5.0	26.0	18.8	−7.7	62.1
8.2	−5.1	27.1	19.3	−7.8	63.8
8.5	−5.2	28.1	19.8	−7.9	65.4
8.8	−5.3	29.2	20.4	−8.0	67.1
9.2	−5.4	30.4	20.9	−8.1	68.8
9.5		31.5	21.4		70.5

MOON CORRECTION TABLE

The correction is in two parts; the first correction is taken from the upper part of the table with argument apparent altitude, and the second from the lower part, with argument HP, in the same column as that from which the first correction was taken. Separate corrections are given in the lower part for lower (L) and upper (U) limbs. All corrections are to be **added** to apparent altitude, *but 30′ is to be subtracted from the altitude of the upper limb.*

For corrections for pressure and temperature see page A4.

For bubble sextant observations ignore dip, take the mean of upper and lower limb corrections and subtract 15′ from the altitude.

App. Alt. = Apparent altitude = Sextant altitude corrected for index error and dip.

ALTITUDE CORRECTION TABLES 35°–90°— MOON

App. Alt.	35°–39° Corrⁿ	40°–44° Corrⁿ	45°–49° Corrⁿ	50°–54° Corrⁿ	55°–59° Corrⁿ	60°–64° Corrⁿ	65°–69° Corrⁿ	70°–74° Corrⁿ	75°–79° Corrⁿ	80°–84° Corrⁿ	85°–89° Corrⁿ	App. Alt.
00	35 56·5	40 53·7	45 50·5	50 46·9	55 43·1	60 38·9	65 34·6	70 30·0	75 25·3	80 20·5	85 15·6	00
10	56·4	53·6	50·4	46·8	42·9	38·8	34·4	29·9	25·2	20·4	15·5	10
20	56·3	53·5	50·2	46·7	42·8	38·7	34·3	29·7	25·0	20·2	15·3	20
30	56·2	53·4	50·1	46·5	42·7	38·5	34·1	29·6	24·9	20·0	15·1	30
40	56·2	53·3	50·0	46·4	42·5	38·4	34·0	29·4	24·7	19·9	15·0	40
50	56·1	53·2	49·9	46·3	42·4	38·2	33·8	29·3	24·5	19·7	14·8	50
00	36 56·0	41 53·1	46 49·8	51 46·2	56 42·3	61 38·1	66 33·7	71 29·1	76 24·4	81 19·6	86 14·6	00
10	55·9	53·0	49·7	46·0	42·1	37·9	33·5	29·0	24·2	19·4	14·5	10
20	55·8	52·9	49·5	45·9	42·0	37·8	33·4	28·8	24·1	19·2	14·3	20
30	55·7	52·8	49·4	45·8	41·9	37·7	33·2	28·7	23·9	19·1	14·2	30
40	55·6	52·6	49·3	45·7	41·7	37·5	33·1	28·5	23·8	18·9	14·0	40
50	55·5	52·5	49·2	45·5	41·6	37·4	32·9	28·3	23·6	18·7	13·8	50
00	37 55·4	42 52·4	47 49·1	52 45·4	57 41·4	62 37·2	67 32·8	72 28·2	77 23·4	82 18·6	87 13·7	00
10	55·3	52·3	49·0	45·3	41·3	37·1	32·6	28·0	23·3	18·4	13·5	10
20	55·2	52·2	48·8	45·2	41·2	36·9	32·5	27·9	23·1	18·2	13·3	20
30	55·1	52·1	48·7	45·0	41·0	36·8	32·3	27·7	22·9	18·1	13·2	30
40	55·0	52·0	48·6	44·9	40·9	36·6	32·2	27·6	22·8	17·9	13·0	40
50	55·0	51·9	48·5	44·8	40·8	36·5	32·0	27·4	22·6	17·8	12·8	50
00	38 54·9	43 51·8	48 48·4	53 44·6	58 40·6	63 36·4	68 31·9	73 27·2	78 22·5	83 17·6	88 12·7	00
10	54·8	51·7	48·3	44·5	40·5	36·2	31·7	27·1	22·3	17·4	12·5	10
20	54·7	51·6	48·1	44·4	40·3	36·1	31·6	26·9	22·1	17·3	12·3	20
30	54·6	51·5	48·0	44·2	40·2	35·9	31·4	26·8	22·0	17·1	12·2	30
40	54·5	51·4	47·9	44·1	40·1	35·8	31·3	26·6	21·8	16·9	12·0	40
50	54·4	51·2	47·8	44·0	39·9	35·6	31·1	26·5	21·7	16·8	11·8	50
00	39 54·3	44 51·1	49 47·7	54 43·9	59 39·8	64 35·5	69 31·0	74 26·3	79 21·5	84 16·6	89 11·7	00
10	54·2	51·0	47·5	43·7	39·6	35·3	30·8	26·1	21·3	16·4	11·5	10
20	54·1	50·9	47·4	43·6	39·5	35·2	30·7	26·0	21·2	16·3	11·4	20
30	54·0	50·8	47·3	43·5	39·4	35·0	30·5	25·8	21·0	16·1	11·2	30
40	53·9	50·7	47·2	43·3	39·2	34·9	30·4	25·7	20·9	16·0	11·0	40
50	53·8	50·6	47·0	43·2	39·1	34·7	30·2	25·5	20·7	15·8	10·9	50

HP	L U	L U	L U	L U	L U	L U	L U	L U	L U	L U	L U	HP
54·0	1·1 1·7	1·3 1·9	1·5 2·1	1·7 2·4	2·0 2·6	2·3 2·9	2·6 3·2	2·9 3·5	3·2 3·8	3·5 4·1	3·8 4·5	54·0
54·3	1·4 1·8	1·6 2·0	1·8 2·2	2·0 2·5	2·2 2·7	2·5 3·0	2·8 3·2	3·1 3·5	3·3 3·8	3·6 4·1	3·9 4·4	54·3
54·6	1·7 2·0	1·9 2·2	2·1 2·4	2·3 2·6	2·5 2·8	2·7 3·0	3·0 3·3	3·2 3·5	3·5 3·8	3·8 4·0	4·0 4·3	54·6
54·9	2·0 2·2	2·2 2·3	2·3 2·5	2·5 2·7	2·7 2·9	2·9 3·1	3·2 3·3	3·4 3·5	3·6 3·8	3·9 4·0	4·1 4·3	54·9
55·2	2·3 2·3	2·5 2·4	2·6 2·6	2·8 2·8	3·0 2·9	3·2 3·1	3·4 3·3	3·6 3·5	3·8 3·7	4·0 4·0	4·2 4·2	55·2
55·5	2·7 2·5	2·8 2·6	2·9 2·7	3·1 2·9	3·2 3·0	3·4 3·2	3·6 3·4	3·7 3·5	3·9 3·7	4·1 3·9	4·3 4·1	55·5
55·8	3·0 2·6	3·1 2·7	3·2 2·8	3·3 3·0	3·5 3·1	3·6 3·3	3·8 3·4	3·9 3·6	4·1 3·7	4·2 3·9	4·4 4·0	55·8
56·1	3·3 2·8	3·4 2·9	3·5 3·0	3·6 3·1	3·7 3·2	3·8 3·3	4·0 3·4	4·1 3·6	4·2 3·7	4·4 3·8	4·5 4·0	56·1
56·4	3·6 2·9	3·7 3·0	3·8 3·1	3·9 3·2	3·9 3·3	4·0 3·4	4·1 3·5	4·3 3·6	4·4 3·7	4·5 3·8	4·6 3·9	56·4
56·7	3·9 3·1	4·0 3·1	4·1 3·2	4·1 3·3	4·2 3·3	4·3 3·4	4·3 3·5	4·4 3·6	4·5 3·7	4·6 3·8	4·7 3·8	56·7
57·0	4·3 3·2	4·3 3·3	4·3 3·3	4·4 3·4	4·4 3·4	4·5 3·5	4·5 3·5	4·6 3·6	4·7 3·6	4·7 3·7	4·8 3·8	57·0
57·3	4·6 3·4	4·6 3·4	4·6 3·4	4·6 3·5	4·7 3·5	4·7 3·5	4·7 3·6	4·8 3·6	4·8 3·6	4·8 3·7	4·9 3·7	57·3
57·6	4·9 3·6	4·9 3·6	4·9 3·6	4·9 3·6	4·9 3·6	4·9 3·6	4·9 3·6	4·9 3·6	5·0 3·6	5·0 3·6	5·0 3·6	57·6
57·9	5·2 3·7	5·2 3·7	5·2 3·7	5·2 3·7	5·2 3·7	5·1 3·6	5·1 3·6	5·1 3·6	5·1 3·6	5·1 3·6	5·1 3·6	57·9
58·2	5·5 3·9	5·5 3·8	5·5 3·8	5·4 3·8	5·4 3·7	5·4 3·7	5·3 3·7	5·3 3·6	5·2 3·6	5·2 3·5	5·2 3·5	58·2
58·5	5·9 4·0	5·8 4·0	5·8 3·9	5·7 3·9	5·6 3·8	5·6 3·8	5·5 3·7	5·5 3·6	5·4 3·5	5·3 3·5	5·3 3·4	58·5
58·8	6·2 4·2	6·1 4·1	6·0 4·1	6·0 4·0	5·9 3·9	5·8 3·8	5·7 3·7	5·6 3·6	5·5 3·5	5·4 3·5	5·3 3·4	58·8
59·1	6·5 4·3	6·4 4·3	6·3 4·2	6·2 4·1	6·1 4·0	6·0 3·9	5·9 3·8	5·8 3·6	5·7 3·5	5·6 3·4	5·4 3·3	59·1
59·4	6·8 4·5	6·7 4·4	6·6 4·3	6·5 4·2	6·4 4·1	6·2 3·9	6·1 3·8	6·0 3·7	5·8 3·5	5·7 3·4	5·5 3·2	59·4
59·7	7·1 4·7	7·0 4·5	6·9 4·4	6·8 4·3	6·6 4·1	6·5 4·0	6·3 3·8	6·1 3·7	6·0 3·5	5·8 3·3	5·6 3·2	59·7
60·0	7·5 4·8	7·3 4·7	7·2 4·5	7·0 4·4	6·9 4·2	6·7 4·0	6·5 3·9	6·3 3·7	6·1 3·5	5·9 3·3	5·7 3·1	60·0
60·3	7·8 5·0	7·6 4·8	7·5 4·7	7·3 4·5	7·1 4·3	6·9 4·1	6·7 3·9	6·5 3·7	6·3 3·5	6·0 3·2	5·8 3·0	60·3
60·6	8·1 5·1	7·9 5·0	7·7 4·8	7·6 4·6	7·3 4·4	7·1 4·2	6·9 3·9	6·7 3·7	6·4 3·4	6·2 3·2	5·9 2·9	60·6
60·9	8·4 5·3	8·2 5·1	8·0 4·9	7·8 4·7	7·6 4·5	7·3 4·2	7·1 4·0	6·8 3·7	6·6 3·4	6·3 3·2	6·0 2·9	60·9
61·2	8·7 5·4	8·5 5·2	8·3 5·0	8·1 4·8	7·8 4·5	7·6 4·3	7·3 4·0	7·0 3·7	6·7 3·4	6·4 3·1	6·1 2·8	61·2
61·5	9·1 5·6	8·8 5·4	8·6 5·1	8·3 4·9	8·1 4·6	7·8 4·3	7·5 4·0	7·2 3·7	6·9 3·4	6·5 3·1	6·2 2·7	61·5